Beyond Our Borders

Landmark in the Law

Business Law Today
TEXT & SUMMARIZED CASES
E-Commerce, Legal, Ethical, and Global Environment

NINTH EDITION

Roger LeRoy Miller
Institute for University Studies
Arlington, Texas

Gaylord A. Jentz
Herbert D. Kelleher
Emeritus Professor in Business Law
MSIS Department
University of Texas at Austin

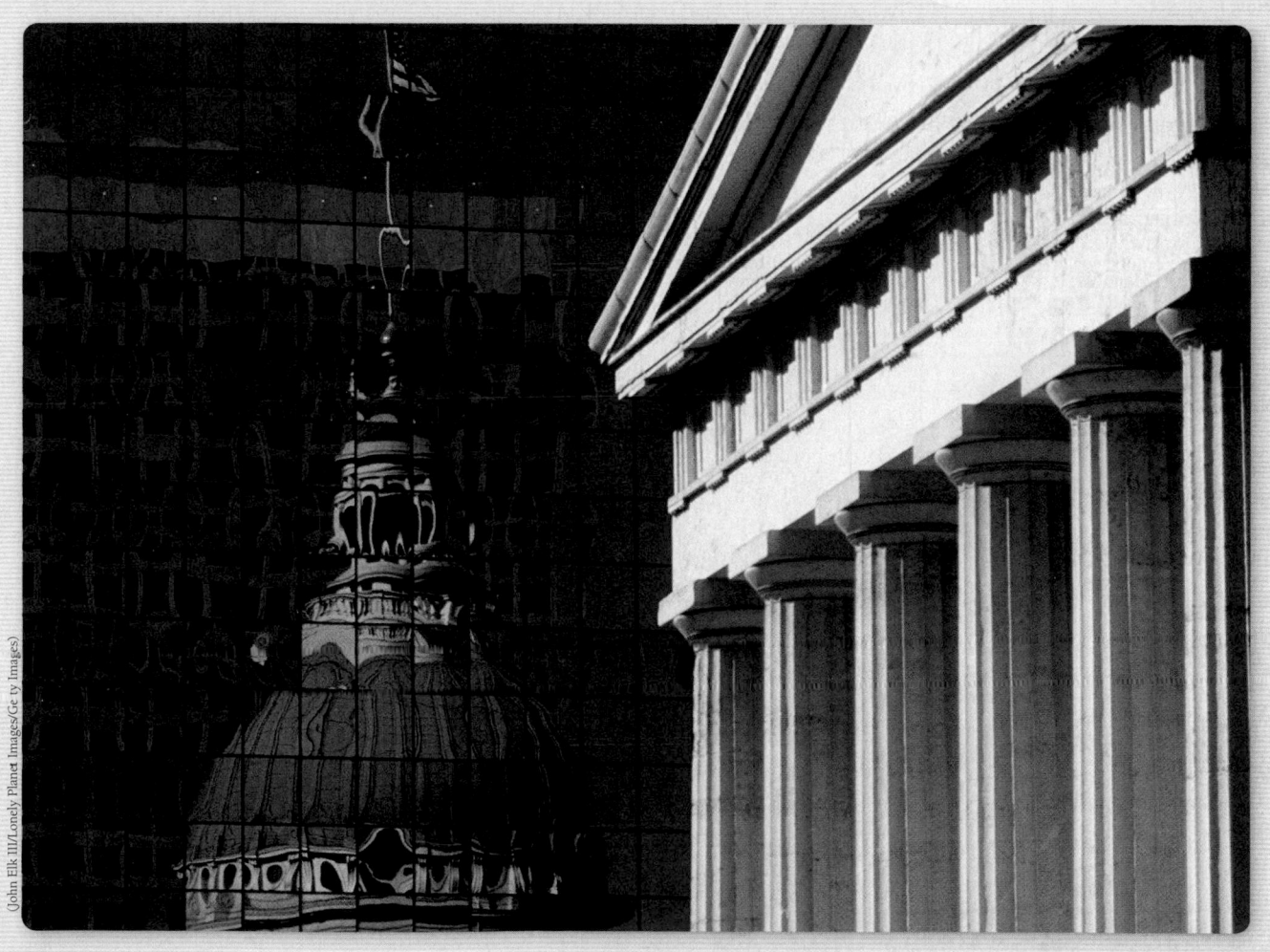

(John Elk III/Lonely Planet Images/Getty Images)

SOUTH-WESTERN
CENGAGE Learning

Australia • Brazil • Japan • Korea • Mexico • Singapore • Spain • United Kingdom • United States

SOUTH-WESTERN
CENGAGE Learning™

Business Law Today
Standard Edition
TEXT & SUMMARIZED CASES
E-Commerce, Legal, Ethical,
and Global Environment
NINTH EDITION

Vice President and Editorial Director:
Jack Calhoun

Editor-in-Chief:
Rob Dewey

Senior Acquisitions Editor:
Vicky True

Senior Developmental Editor:
Jan Lamar

Executive Marketing Manager:
Lisa L. Lysne

Marketing Manager:
Jennifer Garamy

Marketing Coordinator:
Heather Mooney

**Associate Marketing Communications
Manager:**
Suzanne Istvan

Production Manager:
Bill Stryker

Technology Project Manager:
Kristen Meere

Manufacturing Buyer:
Kevin Kluck

Editorial Assistant:
Nicole Parsons

Compositor:
Parkwood Composition Service

Senior Art Director:
Michelle Kunkler

Internal Designer:
Bill Stryker

Cover Designer:
Larry Hanes/Design Phase

Cover Images:
© Sarah Skiba/iStockphoto
© Marcela Barsse/iStockphoto
© Andrey Prokhorov/iStockphoto

For product information and technology assistance, contact us at
Cengage Learning Academic Resource Center, 1-800-423-0563

For permission to use material from this text or product, submit all requests online at **www.cengage.com/permissions**.
Further permissions questions can be emailed to
permissionrequest@cengage.com.

ExamView® and ExamView Pro® are registered trademarks of FSCreations, Inc. Windows is a registered trademark of the Microsoft Corporation used herein under license. Macintosh and Power Macintosh are registered trademarks of Apple Computer, Inc. used herein under license.

© 2011, 2008 Cengage Learning. All Rights Reserved.
Cengage Learning WebTutor™ is a trademark of Cengage Learning.

Library of Congress Control Number: 2009937993

Student Edition ISBN-13: 978-0-324-78652-1
Student Edition ISBN-10: 0-324-78652-2

Instructor's Edition ISBN-13: 978-0-324-78682-8
Instructor's Edition ISBN-10: 0-324-78682-4

South-Western Cengage Learning
5191 Natorp Blvd.
Mason, OH 45040
USA

Cengage Learning products are represented in Canada by Nelson Education, Ltd.

For your course and learning solutions, visit **www.cengage.com**.

Purchase any of our products at your local college store or at our preferred online store **www.ichapters.com**.

Printed in the United States
2 3 4 5 6 7 13 12 11

Contents in Brief

Contents *

*Consult the inside front and back covers of this book for
easy reference to the many special features in this textbook.

▶ *Unit Two*

Contracts 217

Unit Four

Agency and Employment Law 579

Unit Five

Business Organizations 667

▶ Unit Six

Government Regulation 811

Unit Seven

Property and Its Protection 883

Appendices

Business law and the legal environment should be an exciting, contemporary, and interesting course. *Business Law Today,* Ninth Edition, imparts this excitement to your students. We have spent a great deal of effort in giving this book a visual appeal that will encourage students to learn the law. By incorporating the latest research results, *Business Law Today* continues its established tradition of being the most up-to-date text on the market. The law presented in the Ninth Edition of *Business Law Today* includes new statutes, regulations, and cases, as well as the most recent developments in cyberlaw.

You will find that coverage of traditional business law has not been sacrificed in the process of creating this text. Additionally, *Business Law Today* explicitly addresses the American Assembly of Collegiate Schools of Business's (AACSB's) broad array of curriculum requirements. For example, many of the features and special pedagogical devices in this text focus on the global, political, ethical, social, environmental, technological, and cultural contexts of business law. In addition, critical-thinking skills are reinforced throughout.

A New Chapter on Cyber Crime

Cyber crime has become an increasingly critical problem for businesses today. We believe that this problem has become important enough to warrant a separate chapter, which is new to this edition. In it, we examine such cyber crimes as hacking, identity theft, phishing, spamming, and online credit-card fraud. We also discuss the difficulties in prosecuting cyber criminals, many of whom reside in other countries.

▶ Practical and Effective Learning Tools

Instructors have come to rely on the coverage, accuracy, and applicability of *Business Law Today.* For this edition, we have included a number of features to make the text more applicable to today's business environment and to promote critical-thinking skills. We have also significantly streamlined and reorganized the materials, and have focused on making the text more cohesive and understandable.

We have added a new *Linking the Law* feature (discussed next) to encourage interdisciplinary learning and have added many new highlighted and numbered *Case Examples* to help students understand how courts decide real-world disputes. As in the last edition, we continue to provide a variety of assessment tools, including the new *ExamPrep* section, plus sample questions and *Reviewing* features. The subsections that follow outline the new and retained special features of this text.

New Feature Links the Law to Other Business School Disciplines

For the Ninth Edition of *Business Law Today,* we have added a **special new feature entitled** *Linking the Law to* **[Accounting, Economics, Finance, Management, Marketing, Taxation].** These special features appear in selected chapters to underscore how the law relates to various other disciplines in the typical business school curriculum. They not only enable instructors to meet AACSB teaching requirements but also provide vital and practical information to students on how the subjects they study are interconnected. In addition, each of these features concludes with a *For Critical Analysis* question designed to encourage students to engage in critical thinking and to consider the implications of the topic under discussion. Some of the new *Linking the Law* features include:

- *Linking the Law to Managerial Accounting:* Managing a Company's Reputation (Chapter 8).
- *Linking the Law to Economics:* Banking in the Period of Crisis (Chapter 19).
- *Linking the Law to Marketing:* Going Global (Chapter 22).
- *Linking the Law to Taxation:* The Consequences of Your Business Organization Choice (Chapter 26).

New Highlighted and Numbered *Case Examples*

One of the most appreciated features of *Business Law Today* has always been the highlighted numbered examples that appear throughout the book to illustrate the legal principles under discussion. For this edition, rather than presenting more summarized cases in each chapter, we have expanded the in-text numbered examples to include **Case Examples.** These *Case Examples* are integrated appropriately throughout the text and present the facts, issues, and rulings from actual court cases. Students can quickly read through the example to see how courts apply the legal principles under discussion.

Business Applications

Every chapter in the Ninth Edition concludes with either a *Linking the Law* feature (previously discussed) or a **Business Application** feature. The *Business Applications* focus on practical considerations related to the chapter's contents and conclude with a **checklist** of tips for the businessperson. For example, some of the topics include:

- Determining How Much Force You Can Use to Prevent Crimes on Business Premises (Chapter 6).
- How to Develop an Employee Internet Policy (Chapter 24).
- How Do You Choose between LLCs and LLPs? (Chapter 28).

Preventing Legal Disputes

For the Ninth Edition of *Business Law Today,* we continue our emphasis on providing practical information in every chapter through a special feature entitled **Preventing Legal Disputes.** These brief, integrated sections offer sensible guidance on steps that businesspersons can take in their daily transactions to avoid legal disputes and litigation in a particular area.

Adapting the Law to the Online Environment

The Ninth Edition contains many new **Adapting the Law to the Online Environment** features, which examine cutting-edge cyberlaw issues coming before today's courts. Here are some examples of these features:

- The Supreme Court Upholds a Law That Prohibits Pandering Virtual Child Pornography (Chapter 2).
- Should CDA Immunity Extend to Negligence Claims against MySpace? (Chapter 4).
- Should the Law Continue to Allow Business Process Patents? (Chapter 7).
- The Debt That Never Goes Away—It's Discharged in Bankruptcy but Still on the Debtor's Credit Report (Chapter 21).
- Corporate Blogs and Tweets Must Comply with the Securities and Exchange Act (Chapter 31).

Each feature concludes with a *For Critical Analysis* section that asks the student to think critically about some facet of the issues discussed in the feature. **Suggested answers to these questions are included in both the *Instructor's Manual* and the *Answers Manual* that accompany this text.**

Critical-Thinking and Legal Reasoning Elements

Because today's business leaders are often required to think "outside the box" when making business decisions, we offer many **critical-thinking elements** that challenge students' understanding of the materials beyond simple retention. Your students' critical-thinking and legal reasoning skills will be increased as they work through the numerous pedagogical devices throughout the text. Nearly every feature and every case presented in the text conclude with some type of critical-thinking question. These questions include *For Critical Analysis, What If the Facts Were Different?* and *Why Is This Case Important?*

In addition, in the chapter-ending materials, we include a separate section of questions that focus on critical thinking and writing.

- Nearly every chapter includes a *Critical Legal Thinking* question that requires students to think critically about some aspect of the law discussed in the chapter.
- Selected chapters include a *Critical Thinking and Writing Assignment for Business* question that focuses on critical thinking and writing in a business-oriented context.
- For selected chapters, *Case Analysis Questions* are included to improve the students' ability to analyze cases and perform legal reasoning. Students are asked to read through a case excerpt that is provided in Appendix F, brief the case, and then answer a series of questions relating to the case.

Additionally, for the Ninth Edition, we have completely revised and updated the *Handbook on Critical Thinking in Business Law and the Legal Environment.* This important revised resource will enhance your students' ability to think critically about issues in business law and the legal environment. It is available on request as a bundle with the main text. Ask your South-Western/Cengage Learning sales representative about this impressive package.

Reviewing Features and *ExamPrep* Sections

At the end of each chapter in this text, we include a *Reviewing* feature that helps solidify students' understanding of the chapter materials. Each of these features presents a hypothetical scenario and then asks a series of questions that require students to identify the issues and apply the legal concepts discussed in the chapter. They are intended to help students review the chapter materials in a simple and interesting way. An instructor can use these features as the basis for a lively in-class discussion or encourage students to use them for self-study and assessment before completing homework assignments.

Also in every chapter, following the *Chapter Summary,* appears a new *ExamPrep* section that includes two *Issue Spotters* related to the chapter's topics. These *Issue Spotters* facilitate student learning and review of the chapter materials. In addition, the section refers students to the text's Web site for the answers to the *Issue Spotters* and for additional study tools, such as *Flashcards* and *Interactive Quizzes* correlated to the chapter.

Beyond Our Borders

These features give students an awareness of the global legal environment by indicating how international laws or the laws of other nations deal with specific legal concepts or topics being discussed in the chapter. Each of these features concludes with a *For Critical Analysis* question. **Suggested answers to these questions are included in both the *Instructor's Manual* and the *Answers Manual* that accompany this text.**

Landmark in the Law

This feature discusses a landmark case, statute, or other legal development that has had a significant effect on business law. Each of these features has a section titled *Application to Today's World,* which indicates how the law discussed in the feature affects the legal landscape of today's world. In addition, a **Relevant Web Sites** section directs students to the book's Companion Web site for links to additional information available online.

Two Questions with Sample Answers in Each Chapter

For those instructors who would like students to have sample answers available for some of the chapter-ending questions, we have included two such questions in every chapter. Each chapter includes a **Hypothetical Question with Sample Answer** that is answered in Appendix E of the text and a **Case Problem with Sample Answer** that is based on an actual case and answered on the text's Web site. Students can compare their own answers to the answers provided to determine whether they have applied the law correctly and to learn what needs to be included when answering the end-of-chapter questions and case problems. The sample answers to both types of questions are posted on the text's Web site (located at www.cengage.com/blaw/blt) for your convenience.

Ethical Issues

In addition to a chapter on ethics, chapter-ending ethical questions, and the **Ethical Considerations** in many of the *For Critical Analysis* questions in cases presented in this text, we have included special features called **Ethical Issues.** These features, which are closely integrated with the text, open with a question addressing an ethical dimension of the topic being discussed. They are intended to make sure students understand that ethics is an integral part of a business law course.

Business Law Today on the Web

For this edition of *Business Law Today*, we have redesigned and streamlined the text's Web site so that users can easily locate the resources they seek. When you visit our Web site at www.cengage.com/blaw/blt, you will find a broad array of teaching/learning resources, including the following:

- **Relevant Web sites** for all of the *Landmark in the Law* features and the *Classic Cases* that are presented in this text.
- **Sample Answers** to the *Case Problems with Sample Answers* and the *Hypothetical Questions with Sample Answers* that appear at the end of every chapter.
- **Answers to the Issue Spotters** referenced in the *ExamPrep* section of every chapter.
- **Answers to the even-numbered For Review questions** that appear at the end of every chapter.
- **Videos** referenced in the *Video Questions* that appear at the ends of selected chapters of *Business Law Today,* Ninth Edition (available only with a passcode).
- **Practical Internet Exercises** for every chapter in the text (at least two per chapter) that provide students with practical information on topics covered in the text and acquaint students with the legal resources that are available online.
- **Interactive quizzes** for every chapter in this text that include a number of questions related to each chapter's contents.
- **Key terms** for every chapter in the text.
- **Flashcards** that provide students with an optional study tool to review the key terms in every chapter.
- **Appendix A: How to Brief Cases and Analyze Case Problems** This useful appendix for the book is also posted on the Web site.
- **PowerPoint slides** revised for this edition.
- **Legal reference materials** that offer links to selected statutes referenced in the text, a Spanish glossary, and other important legal resources.

- *Online Legal Research Guide: 2010–2011 Edition* that includes hyperlinks to various Web sites and tips for evaluating the information provided.
- *Court case updates* that present summaries of new cases from around the country that specifically relate to the topics covered in the chapters of this text.

Business Law Digital Video Library

Business Law Today includes *Video Questions* at the end of selected chapters that can be used as homework assignments, discussion starters, or classroom demonstrations. Each of these questions directs students to the text's Web site (at www.cengage.com/blaw/blt) to view a video relevant to a topic covered in the chapter. This instruction is followed by a series of questions based on the video. The questions are repeated on the Web site, when the student accesses the video. **Suggested answers for all of the *Video Questions* are given in both the *Instructor's Manual* and the *Answers Manual* that accompany this text.**

The videos are part of *Business Law Digital Video Library,* a compendium of more than sixty-five video scenarios and explanations. An access code for the videos can be packaged with each new copy of this textbook for no additional charge. If *Business Law Digital Video Library* access did not come packaged with the textbook, it can be purchased online at www.cengage.com/blaw/dvl.

 Case Presentation and Special Pedagogy

In addition to the components of the *Business Law Today* teaching/learning package described above, the Ninth Edition offers an effective case presentation and a number of special pedagogical devices, including those described here.

Case Presentation and Format

For this edition, we have carefully selected recent cases for each chapter that not only provide on-point illustrations of the legal principles discussed in the chapter but also are of high interest to students. The cases are numbered sequentially for easy referencing in class discussions, homework assignments, and examinations. The vast majority of cases in this text are new to the Ninth Edition.

Each case is presented in a special format, which begins with the case title and citation (including parallel citations). Whenever possible, we also include a URL, just below the case citation, that can be used to access the case online (a footnote to the URL explains how to find the specific case at that Web site). We then briefly outline the facts of the dispute, the legal issue presented, and the court's decision. To enhance student understanding, we paraphrase the reason for the court's decision.

Each case concludes with one of the following:

- *For Critical Analysis* These questions require students to think about the court's holding from a variety of different perspectives. For instance, a student might be asked to consider the economic or social ramifications of a particular ruling. **Suggested answers to these questions are included in both the *Instructor's Manual* and the *Answers Manual* that accompany this text.**
- *What If the Facts Were Different?* These questions ask the student to decide whether a specified change in the facts of the case would alter the outcome of the case and how. **Suggested answers to these questions are included in both the *Instructor's Manual* and the *Answers Manual* that accompany this text.**
- *Why Is This Case Important?* These questions, which are answered in the text, clearly set forth the importance of the court's decision in the specific case in the legal environment.

Some of these questions focus specifically on why businesspersons today should heed the court's ruling in a particular case.

- *Impact of This Case on Today's Law* For *Classic Cases,* we include these sections to clarify the relevance of the case to modern law. We also have a section titled *Relevant Web Sites* at the conclusion of each *Classic Case* that directs students to the Web site for additional online resources.

Other Pedagogical Devices within Each Chapter

- *Learning Objectives* (a series of brief questions at the beginning of each chapter provide a framework for the student as he or she reads through the chapter).
- *Chapter Outline* (an outline of the chapter's first-level headings).
- *Margin definitions.*
- **Margin** *On the Web features* directing students to relevant Web sites where they will find online articles, statutes, or other legal or information sources concerning a topic being discussed in the text.
- *Highlighted and numbered examples illustrating legal principles.*
- *Highlighted and numbered Case Examples* that are new to this edition and provide illustrations of legal principles in actual court cases.
- *URLs for cases*—Whenever possible, we have included URLs, just below the case citation, that can be used to access the cases presented in the text.
- *Quotations*—Many of the quotations are new to this edition.
- *Exhibits and forms.*
- *Concept Summaries*—Whenever key areas of law need additional emphasis, we provide a concept summary to add clarity.
- *Photographs (with critical-thinking questions) and cartoons.*

Chapter-Ending Pedagogy

- *Key Terms* (with appropriate page references).
- *Chapter Summary* (in graphic format with page references).
- *ExamPrep* (including two new *Issue Spotters* for each chapter).
- *For Review* (the questions set forth in the chapter-opening *Learning Objectives* section are presented again to aid the student in reviewing the chapter. Answers to the even-numbered questions for each chapter are provided on the text's Web site).
- *Hypothetical Questions and Case Problems* (which include a *Hypothetical Question with Sample Answer,* a *Case Problem with Sample Answer,* and *A Question of Ethics* in every chapter).
- *Critical Thinking and Writing Assignments for Business* (including *Critical Legal Thinking* and *Video Questions* in selected chapters).
- *Case Problem with Sample Answer* (as discussed earlier, each chapter contains one of these case problems, for which the answer has been provided on the text's Web site at www.cengage.com/blaw/blt).
- *Practical Internet Exercises* for each chapter.

Unit-Ending Pedagogy—*Cumulative Business Hypotheticals*

Each unit in *Business Law Today,* Ninth Edition, concludes with a section titled **Cumulative Business Hypothetical.** The section introduces a hypothetical business firm and then asks a series of questions about how the law applies to various actions taken by the firm. To answer the questions, the student must apply the laws discussed throughout the unit. **Suggested answers to the unit-ending cumulative questions are included in both the *Instructor's Manual* and the *Answers Manual* that accompany this text.**

Unit-Ending Pedagogy—*Extended Case Studies*

At the end of each unit is a two-page feature entitled *Extended Case Study*. This feature focuses on a recent court case relating to a topic covered in the unit. Each feature opens with an introductory section, which discusses the background and significance of the case being presented. Then we present excerpts from the court's **majority opinion** and from a **dissenting opinion** in the case. The feature concludes with *Questions for Analysis*—a series of questions that prompt the student to think critically about the legal, ethical, economic, global, or general business implications of the case. **Suggested answers to these questions are included in both the *Instructor's Manual* and the *Answers Manual* that accompany this text.**

 Supplemental Teaching Materials

This edition of *Business Law Today* is accompanied by an expansive number of teaching and learning supplements. Individually and in conjunction with a number of our colleagues, we have developed supplementary teaching materials that we believe are the best available today. Each component of the supplements package is listed below.

Printed Supplements

- *Instructor's Manual* (includes at least one **additional case on point** per chapter, answers to all *For Critical Analysis* questions, *Reviewing* features, *Video Questions, Cumulative Business Hypotheticals,* and *Extended Case Studies.* The *Instructor's Manual* is also available on the *Instructor's Resource CD-ROM,* or IRCD, described below).
- *Study Guide.*
- A comprehensive *Test Bank* (also available on the IRCD).
- *Answers Manual* (includes answers to the *Hypothetical Questions and Case Problems, For Critical Analysis* questions, and *Video Questions* in the text. Also available on the IRCD.)
- *Handbook on Critical Thinking in Business Law and the Legal Environment* (an important resource that has been completely revised and updated for this edition).

Software, Video, and Multimedia Supplements

- *Instructor's Resource CD-ROM (IRCD)*—The IRCD includes the following supplements: *Instructor's Manual, Answers Manual, Test Bank,* Case-Problem Cases, Case Printouts, ExamView, PowerPoint slides, Lecture Outline System, transparency masters, *Instructor's Manual* for the *Drama of the Law* video series, *Handbook of Landmark Cases and Statutes in Business Law and the Legal Environment, Handbook on Critical Thinking in Business Law and the Legal Environment,* and *A Guide to Personal Law.*
- *Business Law Digital Video Library*—Provides access to more than sixty-five videos that spark class discussion and clarify core legal concepts. Access is available as an optional package with each new text at no additional cost. If *Business Law Digital Video Library* access did not come packaged with the textbook, it can be purchased online at www.cengage.com/blaw/dvl.
- *CengageNOW* for *Business Law Today* (at an additional cost)—Arguably the most comprehensive online learning and assessment tool for business law and the legal environment on the market today. For more information, contact your South-Western/Cengage Learning Sales Representative. For a demo of this complete online learning system, go to www.cengage.com/tlc.

- *Global Economic Watch*—An online portal that addresses issues raised by the most recent global economic crisis and includes a global issues database, an overview and timeline of events, and links to the latest news. For more information on how you can access this new resource, please visit www.cengage.com/thewatch.

 For Users of the Eighth Edition

We thought that those of you who have been using *Business Law Today* would like to know some of the major changes that have been made for the Ninth Edition. In addition to the changes noted below, you will find that most of the cases in this text are new to this edition. Nearly every chapter has two new cases, and some chapters have three new cases. Each chapter also has one, two, or even three new case problems.

New Features and Special Pedagogy

We have added the following entirely new elements for the Ninth Edition:

- *Linking the Law* features that relate legal principles to other business disciplines.
- *Case Examples* that are highlighted and numbered consecutively with the other in-text examples to illustrate legal principles, but are based on the facts and decisions of actual courts.
- *ExamPrep* sections in every chapter that include two *Issue Spotters* as well as references to the Interactive Quizzes and Flashcards available on the text's Web site.

Significantly Revised Chapters

Every chapter of the Ninth Edition has been revised as necessary to incorporate new developments in the law or to streamline the presentations. We have reorganized the chapters for the Ninth Edition to facilitate testing. Other major changes and additions made for this edition include the following:

- Chapter 5 (Intellectual Property and Internet Law)—The materials on intellectual property rights in the online environment have been thoroughly revised and updated. A new subsection addresses the problem of counterfeit goods, and the discussion of domain names and cybersquatting has been updated. Several recent Supreme Court cases are discussed in the text and in the feature dealing with business process patents.
- Chapter 7 (Cyber Crime)—This chapter is entirely new to this edition and deals with the growing problem of cyber crime, including many types of Internet fraud, identity theft, phishing, cyberstalking, credit-card crime, hackers, piracy, spam, and online gambling. The chapter also covers some of the difficulties involved in prosecuting cyber crime.
- Chapter 8 (Ethics and Business Decision Making)—This chapter has been substantially revised and refocused to be more pragmatic. The chapter now includes a step-by-step approach to making ethical business decisions, as well as several new features discussing how companies and management can deal with attacks on a company's reputation.
- Chapters 9 through 14 (the Contracts unit)—We have merged our discussion of online contracting and electronic signatures with our coverage of traditional contracts. We have added more examples, case examples, updates throughout, and streamlined coverage.
- Chapters 15 through 22 (Commercial Transactions)—We have streamlined and reorganized our materials so that we have an entire unit that deals with commercial transactions and aspects of the Uniform Commercial Code. This new unit includes several chapters on sales and lease law, as well as chapters on negotiable instruments, banking and security interests, creditors' rights and bankruptcy, and international law in the

global economy. We have focused on making these materials more comprehensible and readable, particularly in the areas of negotiable instruments and secured transactions.

- Chapter 24 (Employment, Immigration, and Labor Law) and Chapter 25 (Employment Discrimination)—These two chapters covering employment law have been thoroughly revised and updated to include discussions of legal issues facing employers today. Chapter 24 includes an entirely new section on immigration law, a topic of increasing importance to employers. It also includes the 2009 changes to the Family and Medical Leave Act and an updated discussion of electronic monitoring of employees. Chapter 25 includes the latest developments and United States Supreme Court decisions on constructive discharge, retaliation, religious discrimination, and age discrimination. It also includes the 2009 equal pay legislation, the 2008 amendments to the Americans with Disabilities Act, and a new subsection covering association discrimination.

- Chapter 29 (Corporate Formation, Merger, and Termination)—This chapter provides an updated and streamlined presentation of issues surrounding corporation formation and termination. The chapter was revamped to include more on taxation, holding companies, venture capital, and private equity capital. We have updated the materials on mergers, consolidations, and share exchanges, and include recent examples throughout.

- Chapter 30 (Corporate Directors, Officers, and Shareholders)—This chapter now includes a new exhibit on directors' duties, a new classic case on the duty of loyalty, a discussion of directors' committees, and up-to-date information on e-proxy rules.

- Chapter 31 (Investor Protection, Insider Trading, and Corporate Governance)—We have revamped this chapter to discuss the simplified registration process for "well-known seasoned issuers" and provide recent examples of insider trading and online securities fraud. Several new features discuss the disclosure of financial information on corporate blogs and tweets, and the tax consequences of deleveraging during an economic crisis.

- Chapter 32 (Promoting Competition)—We have reworked the materials on relevant market somewhat and added more discussion of the Robinson-Patman Act and the Herfindahl-Hirschman Index (HHI). The chapter includes updated interlocking directorate figures and an updated discussion of global antitrust law.

- Chapter 33 (Consumer and Environmental Law)—The chapter has been thoroughly updated to include more detail on the national permit system under the Clean Water Act and an updated discussion of credit protection that includes the 2009 changes to federal credit-card rules.

- Chapter 34 (Liability of Accountants and Other Professionals)—This chapter, which was added in the Eighth Edition, has been updated to discuss how the Securities and Exchange Commission has recently adopted global accounting rules. It also includes a new feature on statistical sampling when conducting audits.

▶ Acknowledgments

Numerous careful and conscientious users of *Business Law Today* were kind enough to help us revise this book. In addition, the staff at South-Western/Cengage Learning went out of their way to make sure that this edition came out early and in accurate form. In particular, we wish to thank Rob Dewey and Vicky True for their countless new ideas, many of which have been incorporated into the Ninth Edition. We also extend special thanks to Jan Lamar, our longtime developmental editor, for her many useful suggestions and for her efforts in coordinating reviews and ensuring the timely and accurate publication of all supplemental materials. We are particularly indebted to Jennifer Garamy for her support and excellent marketing advice.

Our production manager and designer, Bill Stryker, made sure that we came out with an error-free, visually attractive edition. We will always be in his debt. We thank our photo researcher, Anne Sheroff, for providing us with an amazingly varied number of choices of photographs for this edition. We are also indebted to the staff at Parkwood Composition, our compositor. Their ability to generate the pages for this text quickly and accurately made it possible for us to meet our ambitious printing schedule.

We must especially thank Katherine Marie Silsbee for her management of the project, as well as for the application of her superb research and editorial skills. We also wish to thank William Eric Hollowell, coauthor of the *Instructor's Manual, Study Guide, Test Bank,* and *Online Legal Research Guide,* for his excellent research efforts. The copyediting services of Pat Lewis were invaluable, and the proofreading by Kristi Wiswell and Jeni Henrickson will not go unnoticed. We also thank Vickie Reierson and Roxanna Lee for their proof-reading, project management, and other assistance, which helped to ensure an error-free text. Finally, our appreciation goes to Suzanne Jasin for her many special efforts on the projects.

Acknowledgments for Previous Editions

John J. Balek
Morton College, Illinois

Jay Ballantine
University of Colorado, Boulder

Lorraine K. Bannai
Western Washington University

Marlene E. Barken
Ithaca College, New York

Daryl Barton
Eastern Michigan University

Merlin Bauer
Mid State Technical College, Wisconsin

Donna E. Becker
Frederick Community College, Maryland

Richard J. Bennet
Three Rivers Community College, Connecticut

Brad Botz
Garden City Community College, Kansas

Teresa Brady
Holy Family College, Philadelphia

Lee B. Burgunder
*California Polytechnic University—
San Luis Obispo*

Bradley D. Childs
Belmont University, Tennessee

Dale Clark
Corning Community College, New York

Stanley J. Dabrowski
Hudson County Community College, New Jersey

Sandra J. Defebaugh
Eastern Michigan University

Patricia L. DeFrain
Glendale College, California

Julia G. Derrick
Brevard Community College, Florida

Joe D. Dillsaver
Northeastern State University, Oklahoma

Claude W. Dotson
Northwest College, Wyoming

Larry R. Edwards
*Tarrant County Junior College, South
Campus, Texas*

Jacolin Eichelberger
Hillsborough Community College, Florida

George E. Eigsti
Kansas City, Kansas, Community College

Florence E. Elliott-Howard
Stephen F. Austin State University, Texas

Tony Enerva
Lakeland Community College, Ohio

Benjamin C. Fassberg
*Prince George's Community College,
Maryland*

Jerry Furniss
University of Montana

Elizabeth J. Guerriero
Northeast Louisiana University

Phil Harmeson
University of South Dakota

Nancy L. Hart
Midland College, Texas

Janine S. Hiller
*Virginia Polytechnic Institute & State
University*

Karen A. Holmes
Hudson Valley Community College, New York

Fred Ittner
College of Alameda, California

Susan S. Jarvis
University of Texas, Pan American, Texas

Jack E. Karns
East Carolina University, North Carolina

Sarah Weiner Keidan
Oakland Community College, Michigan

Richard N. Kleeberg
Solano Community College, California

Bradley T. Lutz
Hillsborough Community College, Florida

Darlene Mallick
Anne Arundel Community College, Maryland

John D. Mallonee
Manatee Community College, Florida

Joseph D. Marcus
Prince George's Community College, Maryland

Woodrow J. Maxwell
Hudson Valley Community College, New York

Beverly McCormick
Morehead State University, Kentucky

William J. McDevitt
Saint Joseph's University, Pennsylvania

John W. McGee
Aims Community College, Colorado

James K. Miersma
Milwaukee Area Technical Institute, Wisconsin

Susan J. Mitchell
Des Moines Area Community College, Iowa

Jim Lee Morgan
West Los Angeles College, California

Jack K. Morton
University of Montana

Solange North
Fox Valley Technical Institute, Wisconsin

Jamie L. O'Brien
South Dakota State University

Robert H. Orr
Florida Community College at Jacksonville

George Otto
Truman College, Illinois

Thomas L. Palmer
Northern Arizona University

David W. Pan
University of Tulsa, Oklahoma

Donald L. Petote
Genessee Community College, New York

Francis D. Polk
Ocean County College, New Jersey

Gregory Rabb
Jamestown Community College, New York

Brad Reid
Abilene Christian University, Texas

Donald A. Roark
University of West Florida

Hugh Rode
Utah Valley State College

William M. Rutledge
Macomb Community College, Michigan

Martha Wright Sartoris
North Hennepin Community College, Minnesota

Anne W. Schacherl
Madison Area Technical College, Wisconsin

Edward F. Shafer
Rochester Community College, Minnesota

Lou Ann Simpson
Drake University, Iowa

Denise Smith
Missouri Western State College

Hugh M. Spall
Central Washington University

Maurice Tonissi
Quinsigamond Community College, Massachusetts

James D. Van Tassel
Mission College, California

Frederick J. Walsh
Franklin Pierce College, New Hampshire

James E. Walsh, Jr.
Tidewater Community College, Virginia

Randy Waterman
Richland College, Texas

Jerry Wegman
University of Idaho, Idaho

Edward L. Welsh, Jr.
Phoenix College, Arizona

Clark W. Wheeler
Santa Fe Community College, Florida

Lori Whisenant
University of Houston, Texas

Kay O. Wilburn
The University of Alabama at Birmingham

James L. Wittenbach
University of Notre Dame, Indiana

Joseph Zavaglia, Jr.
Brookdale Community College, New Jersey

Acknowledgments for the Ninth Edition

John Ballantine
University of Colorado, Boulder

Victor C. Parker, Jr.
North Georgia College and State University

Denise A. Bartles, J.D.
Missouri Western State University

Anne Montgomery Ricketts
University of Findlay, Ohio

Dr. Anne Berre
Schreiner University, Texas

Dr. William J. Russell
Northwest Nazarene University, Idaho

Peter Clapp
St. Mary's College, Moraga, California

Lance Shoemaker, J.D., M.C.P., M.A.
West Valley College, California

Tammy W. Cowart
University of Texas, Tyler

Catherine A. Stevens
College of Southern Maryland

Thomas M. Hughes
University of South Carolina

Russell A. Waldon
College of the Canyons, California

Ruth R. O'Keefe
Jacksonville University, Florida

John G. Williams, J.D.
Northwestern State University, Louisiana

We know that we are not perfect. If you or your students find something you don't like or want us to change, let us know. Use the "Contact Us" button in the blue bar that runs across the Web site for this text. In the alternative, pass along your thoughts to your South-Western/Cengage Learning sales representative. Your comments will help us make *Business Law Today* an even better book in the future.

Roger LeRoy Miller
Gaylord A. Jentz

Dedication

To Kim, Jay, Sidney, and Johnny,
who are the world's best house guests.
You are always welcome.

                                    R.L.M.

To my wife, JoAnn; my children, Kathy,
Gary, Lori, and Rory; and my grandchildren,
Erin, Megan, Eric, Emily, Michelle, Javier,
Carmen, and Steve.

                                    G.A.J.

The Legal Environment of Business

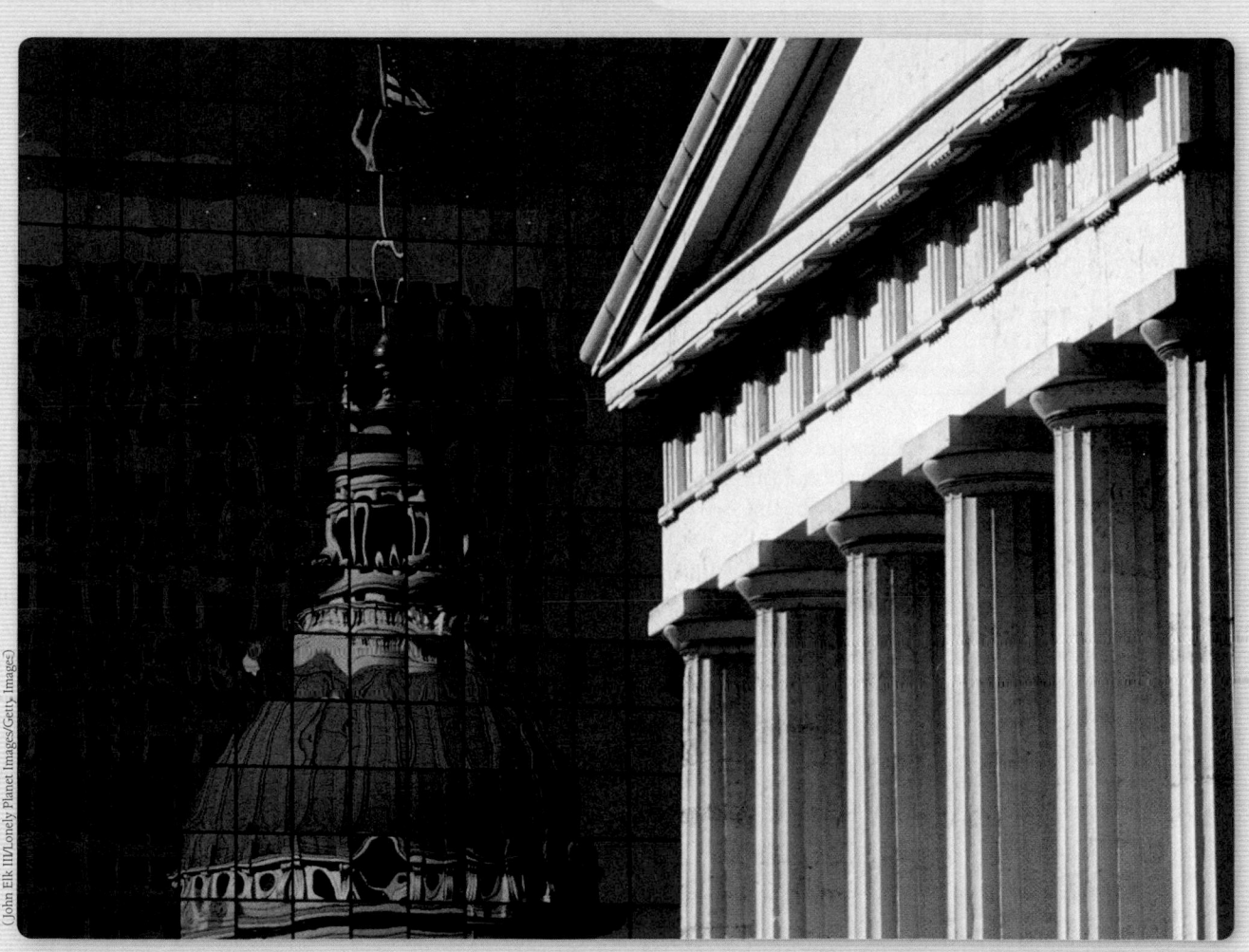

(John Elk III/Lonely Planet Images/Getty Images)

Chapter 1

The Legal Environment

> "Laws should be like clothes. They should be made to fit the people they are meant to serve."
>
> —Clarence Darrow, 1857–1938
> (American lawyer)

(Pink Fish 13/Creative Commons)

Learning Objectives

After reading this chapter, you should be able to answer the following questions:

1. What are four primary sources of law in the United States?

2. What is the common law tradition?

3. What is a precedent? When might a court depart from precedent?

4. What is the difference between remedies at law and remedies in equity?

5. What are some important differences between civil law and criminal law?

Clarence Darrow's assertion in the chapter-opening quotation is that laws should be created to serve the public. As part of the public, the law is of interest to you. Those entering the world of business will find themselves subject to numerous laws and government regulations. A basic knowledge of these laws and regulations is beneficial—if not essential—to anyone contemplating a successful career in today's business environment.

Although the law has various definitions, they all are based on the general observation that **law** consists of *enforceable rules governing relationships among individuals and between individuals and their society.* In some societies, these enforceable rules consist of unwritten principles of behavior, while in other societies they are set forth in ancient or contemporary law codes. In the United States, our rules consist of written laws and court decisions created by modern legislative and judicial bodies. Regardless of how such rules are created, they all have one feature in common: *they establish rights, duties, and privileges that are consistent with the values and beliefs of a society or its ruling group.*

In this introductory chapter, we first look at an important question for any student reading this text: How does the legal environment affect business decision making? We next describe the basic sources of American law, the common law tradition, and some basic schools of legal thought. We conclude the chapter with a discussion of some general classifications of law.

Law A body of enforceable rules governing relationships among individuals and between individuals and their society.

Business Activities and the Legal Environment

As those entering the business world will learn, laws and government regulations affect all business activities—hiring and firing decisions, workplace safety, the manufacturing and marketing of products, and business financing, to name just a few. To make good business decisions, a basic knowledge of the laws and regulations governing these activities is essential. Moreover, in today's setting, simply being aware of what conduct can lead to legal liability is not enough. Businesspersons are also under increasing pressure to make ethical decisions and to consider the consequences of their decisions for stockholders and employees (as will be discussed in Chapter 8).

Many Different Laws May Affect a Single Business Transaction

As you will note, each chapter in this text covers a specific area of the law and shows how the legal rules in that area affect business activities. Although compartmentalizing the law in this fashion facilitates learning, it does not indicate the extent to which many different laws may apply to just one transaction. **EXAMPLE 1.1** Suppose that you are the president of NetSys, Inc., a company that creates and maintains computer network systems for other business firms. NetSys also markets software for internal computer networks. One day, Janet Hernandez, an operations officer for Southwest Distribution Corporation (SDC), contacts you by e-mail about a possible contract involving SDC's computer network. In deciding whether to enter into a contract with SDC, you need to consider, among other things, the legal requirements for an enforceable contract. Are the requirements different for a contract for services and a contract for products? What are your options if SDC **breaches** (breaks, or fails to perform) the contract? The answers to these questions are part of contract law and sales law.

Breach The failure to perform a legal obligation.

Other questions might concern payment under the contract. How can you guarantee that NetSys will be paid? For example, if SDC pays with a check that is returned for insufficient funds, what are your options? Answers to these questions can be found in the laws that relate to negotiable instruments (such as checks) and creditors' rights. Also, a dispute may arise over the rights to NetSys's software, or there may be a question of liability if the software is defective. There may even be an issue as to whether you and Hernandez had the authority to make the deal in the first place. Resolutions of these questions may be found in the laws that relate to intellectual property, e-commerce, torts, product liability, agency, business organizations, or professional liability. ●

Finally, if any dispute cannot be resolved amicably, then the laws and the rules concerning courts and court procedures spell out the steps of a lawsuit. Exhibit 1–1 on the following page illustrates the various areas of the law that may influence business decision making.

Preventing Legal Disputes

To prevent potential legal disputes, be aware of the many different laws that may apply to a single business transaction. It is equally important to understand enough about the law to know when to turn to an expert for advice. It is impossible for nonexperts to keep up with the myriad rules and regulations that govern the conduct of business in the United States. When you need to choose an attorney, try to obtain recommendations from friends, relatives, or business associates who have had long-standing relationships with their attorneys. If that fails, contact your local or state bar association, or check FindLaw's online directory (at lawyers.findlaw.com).

Linking the Law to Other Business School Disciplines

In all likelihood, you are taking a business law or legal environment course because you intend to enter the business world, though some of you may also plan to become full-time practicing attorneys. Many of you are taking other business school courses—business

• *Exhibit* **1-1 Areas of the Law That May Affect Business Decision Making**

communications, business statistics, economics, finance, management, marketing, and taxation, to name just a few possibilities. Most of you will take a course in accounting as well. One of our goals in this text is to show how legal concepts can be useful for managers and businesspersons, whether their activities focus on finance, marketing, or some other business discipline. To that end, fifteen chapters conclude with a special feature called "*Linking the Law to* [a specific business course]." The link between the law and accounting is so significant that it is treated in an entire chapter (Chapter 34).

The Role of the Law in a Small Business

Some of you may end up working in a small business or even owning and running one yourselves. The small-business owner/operator is the most general of managers. When you seek additional financing, you become a finance manager. When you "go over the books" with your bookkeeper, you become an accountant. When you decide on a new advertising campaign, you are suddenly the marketing manager. When you consider the impact that a new tax provision will have on your business, you now are a tax practitioner. When you hire employees and determine their salaries and benefits, you become a human resources manager. Finally, when you try to predict market trends, interest rates, and other macroeconomic phenomena, you take on the role of a managerial economist.

Just as the various business school disciplines are linked to the law, so too are all of these different managerial roles that a small-business owner/operator must perform. Exhibit 1–2 shows some of the legal issues that may arise as part of the management of a small business. Large businesses face many of these issues, too.

Primary Source of Law   A document that establishes the law on a particular issue, such as a constitution, a statute, an administrative rule, or a court decision.

 Sources of American Law

There are numerous sources of American law. **Primary sources of law,** or sources that establish the law, include the following:

• *Exhibit* **1–2 Linking the Law to the Management of a Small Business**

Business Organization
What is the most appropriate business organizational form, and what type of personal liability does it entail?

↓

Taxation
How will the small business be taxed, and are there ways to reduce those taxes?

↓

Intellectual Property
Does the small business have any patents or other intellectual property that needs to be protected, and if so, what steps should be taken?

↓

Administrative Law
What types of government regulations apply to the business, and what must the firm do to comply with them?

↓

Employment
Does the business need an employment manual, and does management have to explicitly inform employees of their rights?

↓

Contracts, Sales, and Leases
Will the firm be regularly entering into contracts with others, and if so, should it hire an attorney to review those contracts?

↓

Accounting
Do the financial statements created by an accountant need to be verified for accuracy?

↓

Finance
What are appropriate and legal ways to raise additional capital so that the business can grow?

• The U.S. Constitution and the constitutions of the various states.
• Statutes, or laws, passed by Congress and by state legislatures.
• Regulations created by administrative agencies, such as the federal Food and Drug Administration.
• Case law (court decisions).

We describe each of these important primary sources of law in the following pages. (See the appendix at the end of this chapter for a discussion of how to find statutes, regulations, and case law.)

Secondary Source of Law   A publication that summarizes or interprets the law, such as a legal encyclopedia, a legal treatise, or an article in a law review.

Secondary sources of law are books and articles that summarize and clarify the primary sources of law. Legal encyclopedias, compilations (such as *Restatements of the Law*, which summarize court decisions on a particular topic), official comments to statutes, treatises, articles in law reviews published by law schools, and articles in other legal journals are examples of secondary sources of law. Courts often refer to secondary sources of law for guidance in interpreting and applying the primary sources of law discussed here.

Constitutional Law

Constitutional Law   The body of law derived from the U.S. Constitution and the constitutions of the various states.

The federal government and the states have separate written constitutions that set forth the general organization, powers, and limits of their respective governments. **Constitutional law** is the law as expressed in these constitutions.

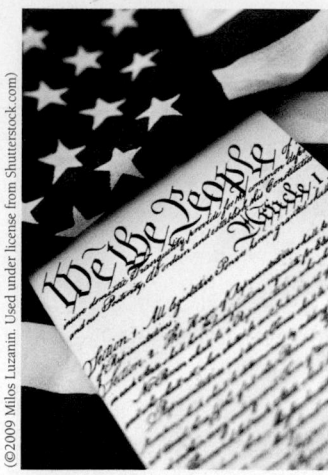

Statutory Law   The body of law enacted by legislative bodies (as opposed to constitutional law, administrative law, or case law).

Citation   A reference to a publication in which a legal authority–such as a statute or a court decision–or other source can be found.

Ordinance   A regulation enacted by a city or county legislative body that becomes part of that state's statutory law.

ON THE WEB   To find state compilations (codes) of statutory laws, go to **findlaw.com/casecode/state.html**.

Uniform Law   A model law created by the National Conference of Commissioners on Uniform State Laws and/or the American Law Institute for the states to consider adopting. Each state has the option of adopting or rejecting all or part of a uniform law. If a state adopts the law, it becomes statutory law in that state.

ON THE WEB   You can find links to most uniform laws at the Web site of the National Conference of Commissioners on Uniform State Laws. Go to **www.nccusl.org**.

The U.S. Constitution is the supreme law of the land. As such, it is the basis of all law in the United States. A law in violation of the Constitution, if challenged, will be declared unconstitutional and will not be enforced no matter what its source. Because of its paramount importance in the American legal system, we discuss the U.S. Constitution at length in Chapter 2 and present the complete text of the Constitution in Appendix B.

The Tenth Amendment to the U.S. Constitution reserves to the states all powers not granted to the federal government. Each state in the union has its own constitution. Unless it conflicts with the U.S. Constitution or a federal law, a state constitution is supreme within the state's borders.

Statutory Law

Laws enacted by legislative bodies at any level of government, such as the statutes passed by Congress or by state legislatures, make up the body of law generally referred to as **statutory law.** When a legislature passes a statute, that statute ultimately is included in the federal code of laws or the relevant state code of laws. Whenever a particular statute is mentioned in this text, we usually provide a footnote showing its **citation** (a reference to a publication in which a legal authority—such as a statute or a court decision—or other source can be found). In the appendix following this chapter, we explain how you can use these citations to find statutory law.

Statutory law also includes local **ordinances**—statutes (laws, rules, or orders) passed by municipal or county governing units to govern matters not covered by federal or state law. Ordinances commonly have to do with city or county land use (zoning ordinances), building and safety codes, and other matters affecting only the local governing unit.

A federal statute, of course, applies to all states. A state statute, in contrast, applies only within the state's borders. State laws thus may vary from state to state. No federal statute may violate the U.S. Constitution, and no state statute or local ordinance may violate the U.S. Constitution or the relevant state constitution.

UNIFORM LAWS   During the 1800s, the differences among state laws frequently created difficulties for businesspersons conducting trade and commerce among the states. To counter these problems, a group of legal scholars and lawyers formed the National Conference of Commissioners on Uniform State Laws (NCCUSL) in 1892 to draft **uniform laws** ("model statutes") for the states to consider adopting. The NCCUSL still exists today and continues to issue uniform laws: it has issued more than two hundred uniform acts since its inception.

Each state has the option of adopting or rejecting a uniform law. *Only if a state legislature adopts a uniform law does that law become part of the statutory law of that state.* Note that a state legislature may adopt all or part of a uniform law as it is written, or the legislature may rewrite the law however the legislature wishes. Hence, even though many states may have adopted a uniform law, those states' laws may not be entirely "uniform."

THE UNIFORM COMMERCIAL CODE (UCC)   One of the most important uniform acts is the Uniform Commercial Code (UCC), which was created through the joint efforts of the NCCUSL and the American Law Institute.[1] The UCC was first issued in 1952 and has been adopted in all fifty states,[2] the District of Columbia, and the Virgin Islands. The UCC facilitates commerce among the states by providing a uniform, yet flexible, set of rules governing commercial transactions. Because of its importance in the area of commercial law, we cite the UCC frequently in this text. We also present excerpts of the UCC in Appendix C. (For a discussion of the creation of the UCC, see the *Landmark in the Law* feature in Chapter 15.)

---

1. This institute was formed in the 1920s and consists of practicing attorneys, legal scholars, and judges.
2. Louisiana has adopted only Articles 1, 3, 4, 5, 7, 8, and 9.

Administrative Law

Another important source of American law is **administrative law,** which consists of the rules, orders, and decisions of administrative agencies. An **administrative agency** is a federal, state, or local government agency established to perform a specific function. Rules issued by various administrative agencies now affect almost every aspect of a business's operations, including the firm's capital structure and financing, its hiring and firing procedures, its relations with employees and unions, and the way it manufactures and markets its products. (See the *Linking the Law* feature on pages 17 and 18.)

Administrative Law The body of law created by administrative agencies (in the form of rules, regulations, orders, and decisions) in order to carry out their duties and responsibilities.

Administrative Agency A federal or state government agency established to perform a specific function. Administrative agencies are authorized by legislative acts to make and enforce rules in order to administer and enforce the acts.

FEDERAL AGENCIES At the national level, numerous *executive agencies* exist within the cabinet departments of the executive branch. For example, the Food and Drug Administration is within the U.S. Department of Health and Human Services. Executive agencies are subject to the authority of the president, who has the power to appoint and remove officers of federal agencies. There are also major *independent regulatory agencies* at the federal level, including the Federal Trade Commission, the Securities and Exchange Commission, and the Federal Communications Commission. The president's power is less pronounced in regard to independent agencies, whose officers serve for fixed terms and cannot be removed without just cause.

STATE AND LOCAL AGENCIES There are administrative agencies at the state and local levels as well. Commonly, a state agency (such as a state pollution-control agency) is created as a parallel to a federal agency (such as the Environmental Protection Agency). Just as federal statutes take precedence over conflicting state statutes, so do federal agency regulations take precedence over conflicting state regulations. Because the rules of state and local agencies vary widely, we focus here exclusively on federal administrative law.

AGENCY CREATION Because Congress cannot possibly oversee the actual implementation of all the laws it enacts, it must delegate such tasks to others, especially when the legislation involves highly technical matters, such as air and water pollution. Congress creates an administrative agency by enacting **enabling legislation,** which specifies the name, composition, purpose, and powers of the agency being created.

Enabling Legislation A statute enacted by Congress that authorizes the creation of an administrative agency and specifies the name, composition, purpose, and powers of the agency being created.

EXAMPLE 1.2 The Federal Trade Commission (FTC) was created in 1914 by the Federal Trade Commission Act.[3] This act prohibits unfair and deceptive trade practices. It also describes the procedures the agency must follow to charge persons or organizations with violations of the act, and it provides for judicial review (review by the courts) of agency orders. Other portions of the act grant the agency powers to "make rules and regulations for the purpose of carrying out the Act," conduct investigations of business practices, obtain reports from interstate corporations concerning their business practices, investigate possible violations of the act, publish findings of its investigations, and recommend new legislation. The act also empowers the FTC to hold trial-like hearings and to **adjudicate** (resolve judicially) certain kinds of disputes that involve FTC regulations. ●

Adjudicate To render a judicial decision. In the administrative process, adjudication is the trial-like proceeding in which an administrative law judge hears and decides issues that arise when an administrative agency charges a person or a firm with violating a law or regulation enforced by the agency.

Note that the powers granted to the FTC incorporate functions associated with the legislative branch of government (rulemaking), the executive branch (investigation and enforcement), and the judicial branch (adjudication). Taken together, these functions constitute **administrative process,** which is the administration of law by administrative agencies.

Administrative Process The procedure used by administrative agencies in administering the law.

RULEMAKING A major function of an administrative agency is **rulemaking**—formulating new regulations. In an agency's enabling legislation, Congress confers the agency's power to make **legislative rules,** or substantive rules, which are legally binding on all

Rulemaking The process undertaken by an administrative agency when formally adopting a new regulation or amending an old one. Rulemaking involves notifying the public of a proposed rule or change and receiving and considering the public's comments.

Legislative Rule An administrative agency rule that carries the same weight as a congressionally enacted statute.

---

3. 15 U.S.C. Sections 45–58.

businesses. The Administrative Procedure Act of 1946 (APA)[4] imposes strict procedural requirements that agencies must follow in legislative rulemaking and other functions. **EXAMPLE 1.3** The Occupational Safety and Health Act of 1970 authorized the Occupational Safety and Health Administration (OSHA) to develop and issue rules governing safety in the workplace. When OSHA wants to formulate rules regarding safety in the steel industry, it has to follow specific procedures outlined by the APA. ●

Legislative rulemaking commonly involves three steps. First, the agency must give public notice of the proposed rulemaking proceedings, where and when the proceedings will be held, the agency's legal authority for the proceedings, and the terms or subject matter of the proposed rule. The notice must be published in the *Federal Register,* a daily publication of the U.S. government. Second, following this notice, the agency must allow ample time for interested parties to comment in writing on the proposed rule. The agency takes these comments into consideration when drafting the final version of the regulation. The third and last step is the drafting of the final rule and its publication in the *Federal Register*. (See the appendix at the end of this chapter for an explanation of how to find agency regulations.)

Note that in addition to making legislative rules, which are subject to the procedural requirements of the APA, agencies also issue **interpretive rules**—rules that specify how the agency will interpret and apply its regulations. The APA does not apply to interpretive rulemaking. Interpretive rules are not legally binding on all businesses but simply indicate how an agency plans to interpret and enforce its statutory authority. **EXAMPLE 1.4** The Equal Employment Opportunity Commission periodically issues interpretive rules indicating how it plans to interpret the provisions of certain statutes, such as the Americans with Disabilities Act. These informal rules provide enforcement guidelines for agency officials. ●

INVESTIGATION AND ENFORCEMENT   Agencies have both investigatory and prosecutorial powers. An agency can request that individuals or organizations hand over specified books, papers, electronic records, or other documents. In addition, agencies may conduct on-site inspections, although a search warrant is normally required for such inspections. Sometimes, a search of a home, an office, or a factory is the only means of obtaining evidence needed to prove a regulatory violation. Agencies investigate a wide range of activities, including coal mining, automobile manufacturing, and the industrial discharge of pollutants into the environment.

After investigating a suspected rule violation, an agency may decide to take action against an individual or a business. Most administrative actions are resolved through negotiated settlement at their initial stages without the need for formal adjudication. If a settlement cannot be reached, though, the agency may issue a formal complaint and proceed to adjudication.

ADJUDICATION   Agency adjudication involves a trial-like hearing before an **administrative law judge (ALJ)**. Hearing procedures vary widely from agency to agency. After the hearing, the ALJ renders a decision in the case. The ALJ can compel the charged party to pay a fine or can prohibit the party from carrying on some specified activity. Either side may appeal the ALJ's decision to the commission or board that governs the agency. If the party fails to get relief there, appeal can be made to a federal court. If no party appeals the case, the ALJ's decision becomes final.

Margin notes:

ON THE WEB You can find proposed and final rules issued by administrative agencies by accessing the *Federal Register* online at **www.gpoaccess.gov/fr/index.html**.

Interpretive Rule An administrative agency rule that is simply a statement or opinion issued by the agency explaining how it interprets and intends to apply the statutes it enforces. Such rules are not binding on private individuals or organizations.

Administrative Law Judge (ALJ) One who presides over an administrative agency hearing and has the power to administer oaths, take testimony, rule on questions of evidence, and make determinations of fact.

---

4. 5 U.S.C. Sections 551–706.

Ethical Issue

Do administrative agencies exercise too much authority? Administrative agencies, such as the Federal Trade Commission, combine in a single governmental entity functions normally divided among the three branches of government. They create rules, conduct investigations, and prosecute and pass judgment on violators. Yet administrative agencies' powers often go unchecked by the other branches, causing some businesspersons to suggest that it is unethical to allow agencies—which were not even mentioned in the U.S. Constitution—to wield so many powers.

Although agency rulemaking must comply with the requirements of the Administrative Procedure Act (APA), the act applies only to legislative, not interpretive, rulemaking. In addition, the APA is largely procedural and aimed at preventing arbitrariness: it does little to ensure that the rules passed by agencies are fair or correct. Even on those rare occasions when an agency's ruling is challenged and later reviewed by a court, the court cannot reverse the agency's decision unless the agency exceeded its authority or acted arbitrarily. Courts typically are reluctant to second-guess an agency's rules, interpretations, and decisions.[5] Moreover, once an agency has final regulations in place, it is difficult to revoke or alter them. President Barack Obama discovered this in 2009 when he tried to change some of the rules that his predecessor, President George W. Bush, had put into place in the last few months of his administration.

Case Law and Common Law Doctrines

The rules of law announced in court decisions constitute another basic source of American law. These rules of law include interpretations of constitutional provisions, of statutes enacted by legislatures, and of regulations created by administrative agencies. Today, this body of judge-made law is referred to as **case law.** Case law—the doctrines and principles announced in cases—governs all areas not covered by statutory law or administrative law and is part of our common law tradition. We look at the origins and characteristics of the common law tradition in some detail in the pages that follow.

Case Law The rules of law announced in court decisions. Case law includes the aggregate of reported cases that interpret judicial precedents, statutes, regulations, and constitutional provisions.

▶ The Common Law Tradition

Because of our colonial heritage, much of American law is based on the English legal system. A knowledge of this tradition is crucial to understanding our legal system today because judges in the United States still apply common law principles when deciding cases.

Early English Courts

After the Normans conquered England in 1066, William the Conqueror and his successors began the process of unifying the country under their rule. One of the means they used to do this was the establishment of the king's courts, or *curiae regis*. Before the Norman Conquest, disputes had been settled according to the local legal customs and traditions in various regions of the country. The king's courts sought to establish a uniform set of rules for the country as a whole. What evolved in these courts was the beginning of the **common law**—a body of general rules that applied throughout the entire English realm. Eventually, the common law tradition became part of the heritage of all nations that were once British colonies, including the United States.

Common Law The body of law developed from custom or judicial decisions in English and U.S. courts, not attributable to a legislature.

Courts developed the common law rules from the principles underlying judges' decisions in actual legal controversies. Judges attempted to be consistent, and whenever possible, they based their decisions on the principles suggested by earlier cases. They sought to decide similar cases in a similar way and considered new cases with care, because they knew that their decisions would make new law. Each interpretation became part of the law

---

5. See, for example, *Citizens' Committee to Save Our Canyons v. Krueger,* 513 F.3d 1169 (10th Cir. 2008).

Precedent   A court decision that furnishes an example or authority for deciding subsequent cases involving identical or similar facts.

on the subject and served as a legal **precedent**—that is, a court decision that furnished an example or authority for deciding subsequent cases involving identical or similar legal principles or facts.

In the early years of the common law, there was no single place or publication where court opinions, or written decisions, could be found. Beginning in the late thirteenth and early fourteenth centuries, however, portions of significant decisions from each year were gathered together and recorded in *Year Books*. The *Year Books* were useful references for lawyers and judges. In the sixteenth century, the *Year Books* were discontinued, and other reports of cases became available. (See the appendix to this chapter for a discussion of how cases are reported, or published, in the United States today.)

Stare Decisis

Stare Decisis   A common law doctrine under which judges are obligated to follow the precedents established in prior decisions.

The practice of deciding new cases with reference to former decisions, or precedents, eventually became a cornerstone of the English and U.S. judicial systems. The practice forms a doctrine called *stare decisis*[6] ("to stand on decided cases").

THE IMPORTANCE OF PRECEDENTS IN JUDICIAL DECISION MAKING   Under the doctrine of *stare decisis,* once a court has set forth a principle of law as being applicable to a certain set of facts, that court and courts of lower rank must adhere to that principle and apply it in future cases involving similar fact patterns. *Stare decisis* has two aspects: first, decisions made by a higher court are binding on lower courts; and second, a court should not overturn its own precedents unless there is a strong reason to do so.

Binding Authority   Any source of law that a court must follow when deciding a case. Binding authorities include constitutions, statutes, and regulations that govern the issue being decided, as well as court decisions that are controlling precedents within the jurisdiction.

Controlling precedents in a *jurisdiction* (an area in which a court or courts have the power to apply the law—see Chapter 3) are referred to as binding authorities. A **binding authority** is any source of law that a court must follow when deciding a case. Binding authorities include constitutions, statutes, and regulations that govern the issue being decided, as well as court decisions that are controlling precedents within the jurisdiction. United States Supreme Court case decisions, no matter how old, remain controlling until they are overruled by a subsequent decision of the Supreme Court, by a constitutional amendment, or by congressional legislation.

STARE DECISIS AND LEGAL STABILITY   The doctrine of *stare decisis* helps the courts to be more efficient because if other courts have carefully reasoned through a similar case, their legal reasoning and opinions can serve as guides. *Stare decisis* also makes the law more stable and predictable. If the law on a given subject is well settled, someone bringing a case to court can usually rely on the court to make a decision based on what the law has been.

DEPARTURES FROM PRECEDENT   Although courts are obligated to follow precedents, sometimes a court will depart from the rule of precedent if it decides that a given precedent should no longer be followed. If a court decides that a precedent is simply incorrect or that technological or social changes have rendered the precedent inapplicable, the court might rule contrary to the precedent. Cases that overturn precedent often receive a great deal of publicity.

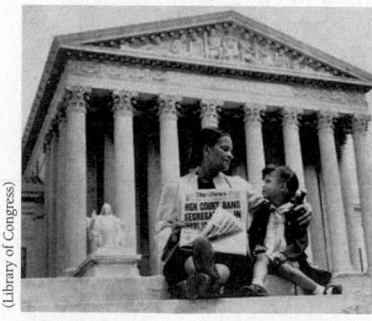

(Library of Congress)

In a 1954 photo, Nettie Hunt sits on the steps of the United States Supreme Court building with her daughter after the court's landmark ruling in Brown v. Board of Education of Topeka.

CASE EXAMPLE 1.5   In *Brown v. Board of Education of Topeka,*[7] the United States Supreme Court expressly overturned precedent when it concluded that separate educational facilities for whites and blacks, which had been upheld as constitutional in numerous previous cases,[8] were inherently unequal. The Supreme Court's departure from precedent in the

---

6. Pronounced *stahr*-ee dih-*si*-sis.

7. 347 U.S. 483, 74 S.Ct. 686, 98 L.Ed. 873 (1954). See the appendix at the end of this chapter for an explanation of how to read legal citations.

8. See *Plessy v. Ferguson,* 163 U.S. 537, 16 S.Ct. 1138, 41 L.Ed. 256 (1896).

ON THE WEB To learn how the
Supreme Court justified its departure
from precedent in the 1954 *Brown* decision, you can access the Court's opinion
online by going to
findlaw.com/casecode/supreme.html,
entering "347" and "483" in the boxes
below the "Citation Search" heading,
and clicking on "get it."

Persuasive Authority   Any legal authority
or source of law that a court may look to
for guidance but on which it need not rely
in making its decision. Persuasive authorities include cases from other jurisdictions
and secondary sources of law.

Remedy   The relief given to an innocent
party to enforce a right or compensate
for the violation of a right.

Plaintiff   One who initiates a lawsuit.

Defendant   One against whom a lawsuit is
brought; the accused person in a criminal
proceeding.

*"Laws and institutions, like
clocks, must occasionally be
cleaned, wound up, and set
to true time."*

Henry Ward Beecher, 1813–1887
(American politician)

Brown decision received a tremendous amount of publicity as people began to realize the ramifications of this change in the law. ●

WHEN THERE IS NO PRECEDENT   At times, cases arise for which there are no precedents within the jurisdiction. When hearing such cases, called "cases of first impression," courts often look at precedents established in other jurisdictions for guidance. Precedents from other jurisdictions, because they are not binding on the court, are referred to as **persuasive authorities.** A court may also consider various other factors, including legal principles and policies underlying previous court decisions or existing statutes, fairness, social values and customs, public policy, and data and concepts drawn from the social sciences.

Can a court consider unpublished decisions as persuasive precedent? See this chapter's *Adapting the Law to the Online Environment* feature on the following page for a discussion of this issue.

Equitable Remedies and Courts of Equity

A **remedy** is the means given to a party to enforce a right or to compensate for the violation of a right. **EXAMPLE 1.6**   Shem is injured because of Rowan's wrongdoing. If Shem files a lawsuit and is successful, a court can order Rowan to compensate Shem for the harm by paying Shem a certain amount. The compensation is Shem's remedy. ●

The kinds of remedies available in the early king's courts of England were severely restricted. If one person wronged another, the king's courts could award as compensation either money or property, including land. These courts became known as *courts of law,* and the remedies were called *remedies at law.* Even though this system introduced uniformity in the settling of disputes, when plaintiffs wanted a remedy other than economic compensation, the courts of law could do nothing, so "no remedy, no right."

REMEDIES IN EQUITY   *Equity* is a branch of law, founded on what might be described as notions of justice and fair dealing, that seeks to supply a remedy when no adequate remedy at law is available. When individuals could not obtain an adequate remedy in a court of law, they petitioned the king for relief. Most of these petitions were decided by an adviser to the king, called a *chancellor,* who had the power to grant new and unique remedies. Eventually, formal chancery courts, or *courts of equity,* were established. Thus, two distinct court systems were created, each having its own set of judges and its own set of remedies. The remedies granted by these courts were called *remedies in equity.*

Plaintiffs (those bringing lawsuits) had to specify whether they were bringing an "action at law" or an "action in equity," and they chose their courts accordingly. **EXAMPLE 1.7**   A plaintiff might ask a court of equity to order the **defendant** (the person against whom a lawsuit is brought) to perform within the terms of a contract. A court of law could not issue such an order because its remedies were limited to payment of money or property as compensation for damages. A court of equity, however, could issue a decree for *specific performance*—an order to perform what was promised. A court of equity could also issue an *injunction,* directing a party to do or refrain from doing a particular act. In certain cases, a court of equity could allow for the *rescission* (cancellation) of the contract, thereby returning the parties to the positions that they held prior to the contract's formation. ● Equitable remedies will be discussed in greater detail in Chapter 14.

THE MERGING OF LAW AND EQUITY   Today, in most states, the courts of law and equity have merged, and thus the distinction between the two courts has largely disappeared. A plaintiff may now request both legal and equitable remedies in the same action, and the trial court judge may grant either form—or both forms—of relief. The distinction

Adapting the Law to the Online Environment

How the Internet Is Expanding Precedent

The notion that courts should rely on precedents to decide the outcome of similar cases has long been a cornerstone of U.S. law. Nevertheless, the availability of "unpublished opinions" over the Internet is changing what the law considers to be precedent. An *unpublished opinion* is a decision issued by an appellate (reviewing) court that is not intended for publication in a reporter (the bound books that contain court opinions).[a] Courts traditionally have not considered unpublished opinions to be "precedents," binding or persuasive, and often have not allowed attorneys to refer to (cite) these decisions in their arguments.

Increased Online Availability

The number of court decisions not published in printed books has risen dramatically in recent years. Nearly 80 percent of the decisions of the federal appellate courts are unpublished, and the number is equally high in some state court systems. Even though certain decisions are not intended for publication, they are posted ("published") almost immediately in online legal databases, such as Westlaw and Lexis. With the proliferation of free legal databases and court Web sites, the general public also has almost instant access to the unpublished decisions of most courts. This situation has caused many to question why these opinions have no precedential effect.

Should Unpublished Decisions Establish Precedent?

Prior to the Internet, not considering unpublished decisions as precedent might have been justified on the grounds of fairness. How could lawyers

know about decisions if they were not printed in the case reporters? Now that opinions are so readily available on the Web, however, this justification is no longer valid. Moreover, it now seems unfair *not* to consider these decisions as precedent because they are so publicly accessible. Some claim that unpublished decisions could make bad precedents because these decisions frequently are written by staff attorneys and law clerks, rather than by judges, so the reasoning may be inferior. If the decision is considered merely as persuasive precedent, however, then judges who disagree with the reasoning are free to reject the conclusion.

The United States Supreme Court Changed the Federal Rules on Unpublished Opinions

The United States Supreme Court made history in 2006 when it announced that it would allow lawyers to cite unpublished decisions in all federal courts. Rule 32.1 of the Federal Rules of Appellate Procedure states that federal courts may not prohibit or restrict the citation of federal judicial opinions that have been designated as "not for publication," "nonprecedential," or "not precedent." The rule applies only to federal courts and only to unpublished opinions issued after January 1, 2007. It does not specify what weight a court must give to its own unpublished opinions or to those from another court. Basically, Rule 32.1 establishes a uniform rule for all of the federal courts that allows attorneys to cite—and judges to consider as persuasive precedent—unpublished decisions. The rule is a clear example of how technology—the availability of unpublished opinions over the Internet—has affected the law.

FOR CRITICAL ANALYSIS

Now that federal courts allow unpublished decisions to be used as persuasive precedent, should state courts follow? Why or why not?

a. Recently decided cases that are not yet published are also sometimes called *unpublished opinions,* but because these decisions will eventually be printed in reporters, we do not include them here.

REMEMBER   Even though courts of law and equity have merged, the principles of equity still apply, and courts will not grant an equitable remedy unless the remedy at law is inadequate.

Equitable Principles and Maxims
General propositions or principles of law that have to do with fairness (equity).

between remedies at law and equity remains significant, however, because a court normally will grant an equitable remedy only when the remedy at law (monetary damages) is inadequate. To request the proper remedy, a businessperson (or her or his attorney) must know what remedies are available for the specific kinds of harms suffered. Exhibit 1–3 summarizes the procedural differences (applicable in most states) between an action at law and an action in equity.

EQUITABLE PRINCIPLES AND MAXIMS   Over time, the courts have developed a number of **equitable principles and maxims** that provide guidance in deciding whether plaintiffs should be granted equitable relief. Because of their importance, both historically and in our judicial system today, these principles and maxims are set forth in this chapter's *Landmark in the Law* feature.

• *Exhibit* 1–3 **Procedural Differences between an Action at Law and an Action in Equity**

PROCEDURE	ACTION AT LAW	ACTION IN EQUITY
Initiation of lawsuit	By filing a complaint.	By filing a petition.
Decision	By jury or judge.	By judge (no jury).
Result	Judgment.	Decree.
Remedy	Monetary damages.	Injunction, specific performance, or rescission.

Jurisprudence   The science or philosophy of law.

Natural Law   The belief that government and the legal system should reflect universal moral and ethical principles that are inherent in human nature. The natural law school is the oldest and one of the most significant schools of legal thought.

Statute of Limitations   A federal or state statute setting the maximum time period during which a certain action can be brought or certain rights enforced.

Schools of Legal Thought

How judges apply the law to specific cases, including disputes relating to the business world, depends in part on their philosophical approaches to law. Part of the study of law, often referred to as **jurisprudence,** involves learning about different schools of legal thought and discovering how each school's approach to law can affect judicial decision making.

THE NATURAL LAW SCHOOL   Those who adhere to the **natural law** theory believe that a higher or universal law exists that applies to all human beings and that written laws should imitate these inherent principles. If a written law is unjust, then it is not a true (natural) law and need not be obeyed.

 Landmark in the Law   **Equitable Principles and Maxims**

In medieval England, courts of equity were expected to use discretion in supplementing the common law. Even today, when the same court can award both legal and equitable remedies, it must exercise discretion. Students of business law should know that courts often invoke equitable principles and maxims when making their decisions. Here are some of the most significant equitable principles and maxims:

1. *Whoever seeks equity must do equity.* (Anyone who wishes to be treated fairly must treat others fairly.)
2. *Where there is equal equity, the law must prevail.* (The law will determine the outcome of a controversy in which the merits of both sides are equal.)
3. *One seeking the aid of an equity court must come to the court with clean hands.* (Plaintiffs must have acted fairly and honestly.)
4. *Equity will not suffer a wrong to be without a remedy.* (Equitable relief will be awarded when there is a right to relief and there is no adequate remedy at law.)
5. *Equity regards substance rather than form.* (Equity is more concerned with fairness and justice than with legal technicalities.)
6. *Equity aids the vigilant, not those who rest on their rights.* (Equity will not help those who neglect their rights for an unreasonable period of time.)

   The last maxim has come to be known as the *equitable doctrine of laches.* The doctrine arose to encourage people to bring lawsuits while the evidence was fresh; if they failed to do so, they would not be allowed to bring a lawsuit. What constitutes a reasonable time, of course, varies according to the circumstances of the case. Time periods for different types of cases are now usually fixed by **statutes of limitations**. After the time allowed under a statute of limitations has expired, no action can be brought, no matter how strong the case was originally.

• **Application to Today's World**   *The equitable maxims listed above underlie many of the legal rules and principles that are commonly applied by the courts today—and that you will read about in this book. For example, in Chapter 10 you will read about the* doctrine of promissory estoppel. *Under this doctrine, a person who has reasonably and substantially relied on the promise of another may be able to obtain some measure of recovery, even though no enforceable contract, or agreement, exists. The court will* estop *(bar, or impede) the one making the promise from asserting the lack of a valid contract as a defense. The rationale underlying the doctrine of promissory estoppel is similar to that expressed in the fourth and fifth maxims on the left.*

• **Relevant Web Sites**   To locate information on the Web concerning equitable principles and maxims, go to this text's Web site at www.cengage.com/blaw/blt, select "Chapter 1," and click on "URLs for Landmarks."

The natural law tradition is one of the oldest and most significant schools of jurisprudence. It dates back to the days of the Greek philosopher Aristotle (384–322 B.C.E.), who distinguished between natural law and the laws governing a particular nation. According to Aristotle, natural law applies universally to all humankind.

The notion that people have "natural rights" stems from the natural law tradition. Those who claim that a specific foreign government is depriving certain citizens of their human rights are implicitly appealing to a higher law that has universal applicability. The question of the universality of basic human rights also comes into play in the context of international business operations. For example, U.S. companies that have operations abroad often hire foreign workers as employees. Should the same laws that protect U.S. employees apply to these foreign employees? This question is rooted implicitly in a concept of universal rights that has its origins in the natural law tradition.

Legal Positivism   A school of legal thought centered on the assumption that there is no law higher than the laws created by a national government. Laws must be obeyed, even if they are unjust, to prevent anarchy.

LEGAL POSITIVISM   In contrast, *positive,* or national, law (the written law of a given society at a particular point in time) applies only to the citizens of that nation or society. Those who adhere to **legal positivism** believe that there can be no higher law than a nation's positive law. According to the positivist school, there is no such thing as "natural rights." Rather, human rights exist solely because of laws. If the laws are not enforced, anarchy will result. Thus, whether a law is "bad" or "good" is irrelevant. The law is the law and must be obeyed until it is changed—in an orderly manner through a legitimate lawmaking process. A judge with positivist leanings probably would be more inclined to defer to an existing law than would a judge who adheres to the natural law tradition.

Historical School   A school of legal thought that emphasizes the evolutionary process of law and looks to the past to discover what the principles of contemporary law should be.

THE HISTORICAL SCHOOL   The **historical school** of legal thought emphasizes the evolutionary process of law by concentrating on the origin and history of the legal system. This school looks to the past to discover what the principles of contemporary law should be. The legal doctrines that have withstood the passage of time—those that have worked in the past—are deemed best suited for shaping present laws. Hence, law derives its legitimacy and authority from adhering to the standards that historical development has shown to be workable. Followers of the historical school are more likely than those of other schools to adhere strictly to decisions made in past cases.

Legal Realism   A school of legal thought of the 1920s and 1930s that generally advocated a less abstract and more realistic approach to the law, an approach that takes into account customary practices and the circumstances in which transactions take place. This school left a lasting imprint on American jurisprudence.

Sociological School   A school of legal thought that views the law as a tool for promoting justice in society.

LEGAL REALISM   In the 1920s and 1930s, a number of jurists and scholars, known as *legal realists,* rebelled against the historical approach to law. **Legal realism** is based on the idea that law is just one of many institutions in society and that it is shaped by social forces and needs. This school holds that because the law is a human enterprise, judges should take social and economic realities into account when deciding cases. Legal realists also believe that the law can never be applied with total uniformity. Given that judges are human beings with unique personalities, value systems, and intellects, different judges will obviously bring different reasoning processes to the same case.

Legal realism strongly influenced the growth of what is sometimes called the **sociological school** of jurisprudence. This school views law as a tool for promoting justice in society. In the 1960s, for example, the justices of the United States Supreme Court played a leading role in the civil rights movement by upholding long-neglected laws calling for equal treatment for all Americans, including African Americans and other minorities. Generally, jurists who adhere to the sociological school are more likely to depart from past decisions than are those jurists who adhere to the other schools of legal thought.

Substantive Law   Law that defines, describes, regulates, and creates legal rights and obligations.

Procedural Law   Law that establishes the methods of enforcing the rights established by substantive law.

▶ Classifications of Law

The law may be broken down according to several classification systems. For example, one classification system divides law into **substantive law** (all laws that define, describe, regulate, and create legal rights and obligations) and **procedural law** (all laws that establish the methods of enforcing the rights established by substantive law). **EXAMPLE 1.8** A state law that provides employees with the right to workers' compensation benefits for any on-the-job injuries they sustain is a substantive law because it creates legal rights (workers' compensation laws will be discussed in Chapter 24). Procedural laws, in contrast, establish the method by which an employee must notify the employer about an on-the-job injury, prove the injury, and periodically submit additional proof to continue receiving workers' compensation benefits. Note that a law regarding workers' compensation may contain both substantive and procedural provisions. ●

Other classification systems divide law into federal law and state law or private law (dealing with relationships between persons) and public law (addressing the relationship between persons and their governments). Frequently, people use the term **cyberlaw** to refer to the emerging body of law that governs transactions conducted via the Internet. Cyberlaw is not really a classification of law, nor is it a new *type* of law. Rather, it is an informal term used to describe traditional legal principles that have been modified and adapted to fit situations that are unique to the online world. Of course, in some areas new statutes have been enacted, at both the federal and state levels, to cover specific types of problems stemming from online communications. Throughout this book, you will read about how the law is evolving to govern specific legal issues that arise in the online context.

Civil Law and Criminal Law

Civil law spells out the rights and duties that exist between persons and between persons and their governments, and the relief available when a person's rights are violated. Typically, in a civil case, a private party sues another private party (although the government can also sue a party for a civil law violation) to make that other party comply with a duty or pay for the damage caused by the failure to comply with a duty. **EXAMPLE 1.9** If a seller fails to perform a contract with a buyer, the buyer may bring a lawsuit against the seller. The purpose of the lawsuit will be either to compel the seller to perform as promised or, more commonly, to obtain monetary damages for the seller's failure to perform. ●

Much of the law that we discuss in this text is civil law. Contract law, for example, which we will discuss in Chapters 9 through 14, is civil law. The whole body of tort law (see Chapter 4) is civil law. Note that *civil law* is not the same as a *civil law system*. As you will read shortly, a **civil law system** is a legal system based on a written code of laws.

Criminal law has to do with wrongs committed against society for which society demands redress. Criminal acts are proscribed by local, state, or federal government statutes (see Chapters 6 and 7). Thus, criminal defendants are prosecuted by public officials, such as a district attorney (D.A.), on behalf of the state, not by their victims or other private parties. Whereas in a civil case the object is to obtain a remedy (such as monetary damages) to compensate the injured party, in a criminal case the object is to punish the wrongdoer in an attempt to deter others from similar actions. Penalties for violations of criminal statutes consist of fines and/or imprisonment—and, in some cases, death. We will discuss the differences between civil and criminal law in greater detail in Chapter 6.

National and International Law

Although the focus of this book is U.S. business law, increasingly businesspersons in this country engage in transactions that extend beyond our national borders. In these situations, the laws of other nations or the laws governing relationships among nations may come into play. For this reason, those who pursue a career in business today should have an understanding of the global legal environment.

Cyberlaw An informal term used to refer to all laws governing electronic communications and transactions, particularly those conducted via the Internet.

Civil Law The branch of law dealing with the definition and enforcement of all private or public rights, as opposed to criminal matters.

Civil Law System A system of law derived from that of the Roman Empire and based on a code rather than case law; the predominant system of law in the nations of continental Europe and the nations that were once their colonies. In the United States, Louisiana, because of its historical ties to France, has, in part, a civil law system.

Criminal Law Law that defines and governs actions that constitute crimes. Generally, criminal law has to do with wrongful actions committed against society for which society demands redress.

Trials in criminal courts often concern charges of robbery and assault, as is the case here in the Clark County Regional Justice Center in Las Vegas, Nevada, presided over by Judge Joe Bonaventure, Jr.

(Gary Thompson-Pool/Getty Images)

National Law   Law that pertains to a particular nation (as opposed to international law).

ON THE WEB The Library of Congress offers extensive information on national and international law at **www.loc.gov.**

NATIONAL LAW   The law of a particular nation, such as the United States or Sweden, is **national law.** National law, of course, varies from country to country because each country's law reflects the interests, customs, activities, and values that are unique to that nation's culture. Even though the laws and legal systems of various countries differ substantially, broad similarities do exist, as discussed in this chapter's *Beyond Our Borders* feature.

Beyond Our Borders   National Law Systems

Despite their varying cultures and customs, almost all countries have laws governing torts, contracts, employment, and other areas, just as the United States does. In part, this is because two types of legal systems predominate around the globe today. One is the common law system of England and the United States, which we have discussed elsewhere. The other system is based on Roman civil law, or "code law." The term *civil law,* as used here, refers not to civil as opposed to criminal law but to codified law—an ordered grouping of legal principles enacted into law by a legislature or governing body. In a *civil law system,* the primary source of law is a statutory code, and case precedents are not judicially binding, as they normally are in a common law system. Although judges in a civil law system commonly refer to previous decisions as sources of legal guidance, they are not bound by precedent; in other words, the doctrine of *stare decisis* does not apply.

A third, less prevalent, legal system is common in Islamic countries, where the law is

often influenced by *sharia,* the religious law of Islam. *Sharia* is a comprehensive code of principles that governs both the public and private lives of Islamic persons, directing many aspects of day-to-day life, including politics, economics, banking, business law, contract law, and social issues. Although *sharia* affects the legal codes of many Muslim countries, the extent of its impact and its interpretation vary widely. In some Middle Eastern nations, aspects of *sharia* have been codified in modern legal codes and are enforced by national judicial systems.

The accompanying exhibit lists some countries that today follow either the common law system or the civil law system. Generally, those countries that were once colonies of Great Britain retained their English common law heritage after they achieved independence. Similarly, the civil law system, which is followed in most continental European nations, was retained in the Latin American, African, and Asian countries that were once colonies of those nations. Japan and South Africa also

have civil law systems. In the United States, the state of Louisiana, because of its historical ties to France, has, in part, a civil law system. The legal systems of Puerto Rico, Québec, and Scotland similarly include elements of the civil law system.

Realize that although national law systems share many commonalities, they also have distinct differences. Even when the basic principles are fundamentally similar (as they are in contract law, for example), significant variations exist in the practical application and effect of these laws across countries. Therefore, anyone who plans to do business in another nation would be wise to become familiar with its laws.

• For Critical Analysis
Does the civil law system offer any advantages over the common law system, or vice versa? Explain.

The Legal Systems of Selected Nations

CIVIL LAW		COMMON LAW	
Argentina	Indonesia	Australia	Nigeria
Austria	Iran	Bangladesh	Singapore
Brazil	Italy	Canada	United Kingdom
Chile	Japan	Ghana	United States
China	Mexico	India	Zambia
Egypt	Poland	Israel	
Finland	South Korea	Jamaica	
France	Sweden	Kenya	
Germany	Tunisia	Malaysia	
Greece	Venezuela	New Zealand	

International Law   The law that governs relations among nations. National laws, customs, treaties, and international conferences and organizations are generally considered to be the most important sources of international law.

INTERNATIONAL LAW   In contrast to national law, international law applies to more than one nation. **International law** can be defined as a body of written and unwritten laws observed by independent nations and governing the acts of individuals as well as governments. International law is an intermingling of rules and constraints derived from a variety of sources, including the laws of individual nations, the customs that have evolved among nations in their relations with one another, and treaties and international organizations. In essence, international law is the result of centuries-old attempts to reconcile the traditional need of each nation to be the final authority over its own affairs with the desire of nations to benefit economically from trade and harmonious relations with one another.

The key difference between national law and international law is that government authorities can enforce national law. If a nation violates an international law, however, the most that other countries or international organizations can do (if persuasive tactics fail) is to take coercive actions against the violating nation. Coercive actions range from the severance of diplomatic relations and boycotts to, as a last resort, war. We will examine the laws governing international business transactions in later chapters (including parts of Chapters 15 through 17, which cover contracts for the sale and lease of goods, and all of Chapter 22).

 ## Reviewing . . . The Legal Environment

Suppose that the California legislature passes a law that severely restricts carbon dioxide emissions from automobiles in that state. A group of automobile manufacturers files a suit against the state of California to prevent the enforcement of the law. The automakers claim that a federal law already sets fuel economy standards nationwide and that these standards are essentially the same as carbon dioxide emission standards. According to the automobile manufacturers, it is unfair to allow California to impose more stringent regulations than those set by the federal law. Using the information presented in the chapter, answer the following questions.

1. Who are the parties (the plaintiffs and the defendant) in this lawsuit?
2. Are the plaintiffs seeking a legal remedy or an equitable remedy? Why?
3. What is the primary source of the law that is at issue here?
4. Read through the appendix that follows this chapter, and then answer the following question: Where would you look to find the relevant California and federal laws?

 # Linking the Law *to Management*
Dealing with Administrative Law

Whether you end up owning your own small business or working for a large corporation, you will be dealing with multiple aspects of administrative law. Recall from page 7 that administrative law involves all of the rules, orders, and decisions of administrative agencies. At the federal level, these include the Food and Drug Administration, the Equal Employment Opportunity Commission, the National Labor Relations Board, and the Occupational Safety and Health Administration. All federal, state, and local government administrative agencies create rules that have the force of law. As a manager, you probably will have to pay more attention to administrative rules and regulations than to laws passed by local, state, and federal legislatures.

Federal versus State and Local Agency Regulations

The three levels of government create three levels of rules and regulations though their respective administrative agencies. Typically, at least at the state level, there are agencies that govern business activities in a manner similar to federal agencies. You may face situations in which a state agency regulation and a federal agency regulation conflict. In general, federal agency regulations preempt, or take precedence over, conflicting state (or local) regulations.

As a manager, you will have to learn about agency regulations that pertain to your business activities. It will be up to you, as a manager or

Continued

small-business owner, to ferret out those regulations that are most important and could potentially create the most liability if you violate them.

When Should You Participate in the Rulemaking Process?

All federal agencies and many state agencies invite public comments on proposed rules. For example, suppose that you manage a large construction company and your state occupational safety agency proposes a new rule requiring every employee on a construction site to wear hearing protection. You believe that the rule will lead to a *less* safe environment because your employees will not be able to communicate easily with one another.

Should you spend time offering comments to the agency? As an efficient manager, you make a trade-off calculation: First, you determine the value of the time that you would spend in attempting to prevent or at least alter the proposed rule. Then you compare this implicit cost with your estimate of the potential benefits your company would receive if the rule were *not* put into place.

Be Prepared for Investigations

All administrative agencies have investigatory powers. Agencies' investigators usually have the power to search business premises, although normally they first have to obtain a search warrant. As a manager, you often have the choice of cooperating with agency investigators or providing just the minimum amount of assistance. If you receive investigators on a routine basis, you will often opt for cooperation. In contrast, if your business is rarely investigated, you may decide that the on-site proposed inspection is overreaching. Then you must contact your company's attorney for advice on how to proceed.

If an administrative agency cites you for a regulatory violation, you will probably negotiate a settlement with the agency rather than take your case before an administrative law judge. Again, as a manager, you have to weigh the cost of the negotiated settlement with the potential cost of fighting the enforcement action.

Management Involves Flexibility

Throughout your business career, you will face hundreds of administrative rules and regulations, investigations, and perhaps enforcement proceedings for rule violations. You may sometimes be frustrated by seemingly meaningless regulations. You must accept that these are part of the legal environment in which you will work. The rational manager looks at administrative law as just another parameter that he or she cannot easily alter.

FOR CRITICAL ANALYSIS

Why are owner/operators of small businesses at a disadvantage relative to large corporations when they attempt to decipher complex regulations that apply to their businesses?

 Key Terms

adjudicate 7	defendant 11	plaintiff 11
administrative agency 7	enabling legislation 7	precedent 10
administrative law 7	equitable principles and maxims 12	primary source of law 4
administrative law judge (ALJ) 8	historical school 14	procedural law 14
administrative process 7	international law 17	remedy 11
binding authority 10	interpretive rule 8	rulemaking 7
breach 3	jurisprudence 13	secondary source of law 5
case law 9	law 2	sociological school 14
citation 6	legal positivism 14	*stare decisis* 10
civil law 15	legal realism 14	statute of limitations 13
civil law system 15	legislative rule 7	statutory law 6
common law 9	national law 16	substantive law 14
constitutional law 5	natural law 13	uniform law 6
criminal law 15	ordinance 6	
cyberlaw 15	persuasive authority 11	

Chapter Summary: The Legal Environment

Sources of American Law (See pages 4–9.)	1. *Constitutional law*—The law as expressed in the U.S. Constitution and the various state constitutions. The U.S. Constitution is the supreme law of the land. State constitutions are supreme within state borders to the extent that they do not violate the U.S. Constitution or a federal law. 2. *Statutory law*—Laws or ordinances created by federal, state, and local legislatures and governing bodies. None of these laws can violate the U.S. Constitution or the relevant state constitutions. Uniform laws, when adopted by a state legislature, become statutory law in that state. 3. *Administrative law*—The rules, orders, and decisions of federal or state government administrative agencies. Federal administrative agencies are created by enabling legislation enacted by the U.S. Congress. Agency functions include rulemaking, investigation and enforcement, and adjudication. 4. *Case law and common law doctrines*—Judge-made law, including interpretations of constitutional provisions, of statutes enacted by legislatures, and of regulations created by administrative agencies. The common law—the doctrines and principles embodied in case law—governs all areas not covered by statutory law (or agency regulations issued to implement various statutes).

The Common Law Tradition (See pages 9–14.)	1. *Common law*—Law that originated in medieval England with the creation of the king's courts, or *curiae regis,* and the development of a body of rules that were common to (or applied throughout) the land.
	2. *Stare decisis*—A doctrine under which judges "stand on decided cases"—or follow the rule of precedent—in deciding cases. *Stare decisis* is the cornerstone of the common law tradition.
	3. *Remedies*—A remedy is the means by which a court enforces a right or compensates for a violation of a right. Courts typically grant legal remedies (monetary damages) but may also grant equitable remedies (specific performance, injunction, or rescission) when the legal remedy is inadequate or unavailable.
	4. *Schools of legal thought*—Judges' decision making is influenced by their philosophy of law. Four important schools of legal thought, or legal philosophies, are the following:
	  a. *Natural law tradition*—One of the oldest and most significant schools of legal thought. Those who believe in natural law hold that there is a universal law applicable to all human beings and that this law is of a higher order than positive, or conventional, law.
	  b. *Legal positivism*—A school of legal thought centered on the assumption that there is no law higher than the laws created by the government. Laws must be obeyed, even if they are unjust, to prevent anarchy.
	  c. *Historical school*—A school of legal thought that stresses the evolutionary nature of law and looks to doctrines that have withstood the passage of time for guidance in shaping present laws.
	  d. *Legal realism*—A school of legal thought that generally advocates a less abstract and more realistic approach to the law that takes into account customary practices and the circumstances in which transactions take place.

Classifications of Law (See pages 14–18.)	The law may be broken down according to several classification systems, such as substantive or procedural law, federal or state law, and private or public law. Two broad classifications are civil and criminal law, and national and international law. Cyberlaw is not really a classification of law but a term that is used for the growing body of case law and statutory law that applies to Internet transactions.

 ExamPrep

ISSUE SPOTTERS

1 The First Amendment to the U.S. Constitution provides protection for the free exercise of religion. A state legislature enacts a law that outlaws all religions that do not derive from the Judeo-Christian tradition. Is this law valid within that state? Why or why not?

2 Apples & Oranges Corporation learns that a federal administrative agency is considering a rule that will have a negative impact on the firm's ability to do business. Does the firm have any opportunity to express its opinion about the pending rule? Explain.

BEFORE THE TEST

Check your answers to the Issue Spotters, and at the same time, take the interactive quiz for this chapter. Go to **www.cengage.com/blaw/blt** and click on "Chapter 1." First, click on "Answers to Issue Spotters" to check your answers. Next, click on "Interactive Quiz" to assess your mastery of the concepts in this chapter. Then click on "Flashcards" to review this chapter's Key Term definitions.

 For Review

Answers for the even-numbered questions in this For Review *section can be found on this text's accompanying Web site at* **www.cengage.com/blaw/blt**. *Select "Chapter 1" and click on "For Review."*

1 What are four primary sources of law in the United States?
2 What is the common law tradition?
3 What is a precedent? When might a court depart from precedent?
4 What is the difference between remedies at law and remedies in equity?
5 What are some important differences between civil law and criminal law?

 Hypothetical Scenarios and Case Problems

1–1 Binding versus Persuasive Authority. A county court in Illinois is deciding a case involving an issue that has never been addressed before in that state's courts. The Iowa Supreme Court, however, recently decided a case involving a very similar fact pattern. Is the Illinois court obligated to follow the Iowa Supreme Court's decision on the issue? If the United States Supreme Court had decided a similar case, would that decision be binding on the Illinois court? Explain.

1–2 Remedies. Arthur Rabe is suing Xavier Sanchez for breaching a contract in which Sanchez promised to sell Rabe a Van Gogh painting for $150,000.
  1 In this lawsuit, who is the plaintiff, and who is the defendant?
  2 If Rabe wants Sanchez to perform the contract as promised, what remedy should Rabe seek?
  3 Suppose that Rabe wants to cancel the contract because Sanchez fraudulently misrepresented the painting as an original Van Gogh when in fact it is a copy. In this situation, what remedy should Rabe seek?
  4 Will the remedy Rabe seeks in either situation be a remedy at law or a remedy in equity?
  5 Suppose that the court finds in Rabe's favor and grants one of these remedies. Sanchez then appeals the decision to a higher court. Read through the subsection entitled "Appellants and Appellees" in the appendix following this chapter. On appeal, which party in the Rabe-Sanchez case will be the appellant (or petitioner), and which party will be the appellee (or respondent)?

1–3 Legal Systems. What are the key differences between a common law system and a civil law system? Why do some countries have common law systems and others have civil law systems?

1–4 [?] **Hypothetical Question with Sample Answer** This chapter discussed a number of sources of American law.

Which source of law takes priority in each of the following situations, and why?
  1 A federal statute conflicts with the U.S. Constitution.
  2 A federal statute conflicts with a state constitution.
  3 A state statute conflicts with the common law of that state.
  4 A state constitutional amendment conflicts with the U.S. Constitution.
  5 A federal administrative regulation conflicts with a state constitution.

—For a sample answer to Question 1–4, go to Appendix E at the end of this text.

1–5 Philosophy of Law. After World War II ended in 1945, an international tribunal of judges convened at Nuremberg, Germany. The judges convicted several Nazi war criminals of "crimes against humanity." Assuming that the Nazis who were convicted had not disobeyed any law of their country and had merely been following their government's (Hitler's) orders, what law had they violated? Explain.

1–6 Reading Citations. Assume that you want to read the court's entire opinion in the case of *Citizens' Committee to Save Our Canyons v. Krueger,* 513 F.3d 1169 (10th Cir. 2008). (Note that this case is mentioned in footnote 5 of this chapter.) Read the section entitled "Finding Case Law" in the appendix that follows this chapter, and then explain specifically where you would find the court's opinion.

1–7 Stare Decisis. In the text of this chapter, we stated that the doctrine of *stare decisis* "became a cornerstone of the English and U.S. judicial systems." What does *stare decisis* mean, and why has this doctrine been so fundamental in the development of our legal tradition?

1–8 Court Opinions. Read through the subsection entitled "Case Titles and Terminology" in the appendix following this chapter. What is the difference between a concurring opinion and a majority opinion? Between a concurring opinion and a dissenting opinion? Why do judges and justices write concurring and dissenting opinions, given that these opinions will not affect the outcome of the case at hand, which has already been decided by majority vote?

1–9   **A Question of Ethics** *On July 5, 1884, Dudley, Stephens, and Brooks—"all able-bodied English seamen"—and a teenage English boy were cast adrift in a lifeboat following a storm at sea. They had no water with them in the boat, and all they had for sustenance were two one-pound tins of turnips. On July 24, Dudley proposed that one of the four in the lifeboat be sacrificed to save the others. Stephens agreed with Dudley, but Brooks refused to consent—and the boy was never asked for his opinion. On July 25, Dudley killed the boy, and the three men then fed on the boy's body*

and blood. Four days later, the men were rescued by a passing vessel. They were taken to England and tried for the murder of the boy. If the men had not fed on the boy's body, they would probably have died of starvation within the four-day period. The boy, who was in a much weaker condition, would likely have died before the rest. [Regina v. Dudley and Stephens, *14 Q.B.D. (Queen's Bench Division, England) 273 (1884)]*

1 The basic question in this case is whether the survivors should be subject to penalties under English criminal law, given the men's unusual circumstances. You be the judge and decide the issue. Give the reasons for your decision.

2 Should judges ever have the power to look beyond the written "letter of the law" in making their decisions? Why or why not?

 ## Critical Thinking and Writing Assignments

1–10 Critical Legal Thinking. Courts can overturn precedents and thus change the common law. Should judges have the same authority to overrule statutory law? Should they be able to overturn administrative rules? Explain your answers.

1–11 Critical Thinking and Writing Assignment for Business. John's company is involved in a lawsuit with a customer, Beth. John

argues that for fifty years, in cases involving circumstances similar to this case, judges have ruled in a way that indicates that this case should be decided in favor of John's company. Is this a valid argument? If so, must the judge in this case rule as those other judges did? What argument could Beth use to counter John's reasoning?

 ## Practical Internet Exercises

Go to this text's Web site at **www.cengage.com/blaw/blt**, select "Chapter 1," and click on "Practical Internet Exercises." There you will find the following Internet research exercises that you can perform to learn more about the topics covered in this chapter.

Practical Internet Exercise 1–1: LEGAL PERSPECTIVE—Internet Sources of Law

Practical Internet Exercise 1–2: MANAGEMENT PERSPECTIVE—Online Assistance from Government Agencies

The statutes, agency regulations, and case law referred to in this text establish the rights and duties of businesspersons engaged in various types of activities. The cases presented in the following chapters provide you with concise, real-life illustrations of how the courts interpret and apply these laws. Because of the importance of knowing how to find statutory, administrative, and case law, this appendix offers a brief introduction to how these laws are published and to the legal "shorthand" employed in referencing these legal sources.

▶ Finding Statutory and Administrative Law

When Congress passes laws, they are collected in a publication titled *United States Statutes at Large*. When state legislatures pass laws, they are collected in similar state publications. Most frequently, however, laws are referred to in their codified form—that is, the form in which they appear in the federal and state codes. In these codes, laws are compiled by subject.

United States Code

ON THE WEB You can search the *United States Code* online at **www.law.cornell.edu/uscode**.

The *United States Code* (U.S.C.) arranges all existing federal laws of a public and permanent nature by subject. Each of the fifty subjects into which the U.S.C. arranges the laws is given a title and a title number. For example, laws relating to commerce and trade are collected in "Title 15, Commerce and Trade." Titles are subdivided by sections. A citation to the U.S.C. includes title and section numbers. Thus, a reference to "15 U.S.C. Section 1" means that the statute can be found in Section 1 of Title 15. ("Section" may also be designated by the symbol §, and "Sections" by §§.) In addition to the print publication of the U.S.C., the federal government also provides a searchable online database of the *United States Code* at **www.gpoaccess.gov/uscode/index.html**.

Commercial publications of these laws and regulations are available and are widely used. For example, West Group publishes the *United States Code Annotated* (U.S.C.A.). The U.S.C.A. contains the complete text of laws included in the U.S.C., notes of court decisions that interpret and apply specific sections of the statutes, and the text of presidential proclamations and executive orders. The U.S.C.A. also includes research aids, such as cross-references to related statutes, historical notes, and library references. A citation to the U.S.C.A. is similar to a citation to the U.S.C.: "15 U.S.C.A. Section 1."

State Codes

State codes follow the U.S.C. pattern of arranging law by subject. The state codes may be called codes, revisions, compilations, consolidations, general statutes, or statutes, depending on the preferences of the state. In some codes, subjects are designated by number. In others, they are designated by name. For example, "13 Pennsylvania Consolidated Statutes Section 1101" means that the statute can be found in Title 13, Section 1101, of the Pennsylvania code. "California Commercial Code Section 1101" means the statute can be found in Section 1101 under the subject heading "Commercial Code" of the California code. Abbreviations may be used. For example, "13 Pennsylvania Consolidated Statutes Section 1101" may be abbreviated "13 Pa. C.S. § 1101," and "California Commercial Code Section 1101" may be abbreviated "Cal. Com. Code § 1101."

Administrative Rules

Rules and regulations adopted by federal administrative agencies are compiled in the *Code of Federal Regulations* (C.F.R.). Like the U.S.C., the C.F.R. is divided into fifty titles. Rules within each title are assigned section numbers. A full citation to the C.F.R. includes title and section numbers. For example, a reference to "17 C.F.R. Section 230.504" means that the rule can be found in Section 230.504 of Title 17.

 Finding Case Law

Before discussing the case reporting system, we need to look briefly at the court system (which will be discussed in detail in Chapter 3). There are two types of courts in the United States: federal courts and state courts. Both the federal and state court systems consist of several levels, or tiers, of courts. *Trial courts,* in which evidence is presented and testimony is given, are on the bottom tier (which also includes lower courts handling specialized issues). Decisions from a trial court can be appealed to a higher court, which commonly would be an intermediate *court of appeals,* or an *appellate court.* Decisions from these intermediate courts of appeals may be appealed to an even higher court, such as a state supreme court or the United States Supreme Court.

State Court Decisions

Most state trial court decisions are not published. Except in New York and a few other states that publish selected opinions of their trial courts, decisions from state trial courts are merely filed in the office of the clerk of the court, where the decisions are available for public inspection. (Increasingly, they can be found online as well.) Written decisions of the appellate, or reviewing, courts, however, are published and distributed. As you will note, most of the state court cases presented in this book are from state appellate courts. The reported appellate decisions are published in volumes called *reports* or *reporters,* which are numbered consecutively. State appellate court decisions are found in the state reporters of that particular state.

Additionally, state court opinions appear in regional units of the *National Reporter System,* published by West Group. Most lawyers and libraries have the West reporters because they report cases more quickly and are distributed more widely than the state-published reports. In fact, many states have eliminated their own reporters in favor of West's National Reporter System. The National Reporter System divides the states into the following geographic areas: *Atlantic* (A. or A.2d), *North Eastern* (N.E. or N.E.2d), *North Western* (N.W. or N.W.2d), *Pacific* (P., P.2d, or P.3d), *South Eastern* (S.E. or S.E.2d), *South Western* (S.W., S.W.2d, or S.W.3d), and *Southern* (So. or So.2d). (The *2d* and *3d* in the abbreviations refer to *Second Series* and *Third Series,* respectively.) The states included in each of these regional divisions are indicated in Exhibit 1A–1 on the following page, which illustrates West's National Reporter System.

After appellate decisions have been published, they are normally referred to (cited) by the name of the case; the volume, name, and page number of the state's official reporter (if different from West's National Reporter System); the volume, name, and page number of the *National Reporter;* and the volume, name, and page number of any other selected reporter. This information is included in the *citation.* (Citing a reporter by volume number, name, and page number, in that order, is common to all citations.) When more than one reporter is cited for the same case, each reference is called a *parallel citation.* Note that some states have adopted a "public domain citation system" that uses a somewhat different format for the citation. For example, in Wisconsin, a Wisconsin Supreme Court decision might be designated "2010 WI 40," meaning that the decision was the fortieth issued by the Wisconsin Supreme Court in the year 2010. Parallel citations to

• *Exhibit* **1A–1** West's National Reporter System—Regional/Federal

Regional Reporters	Coverage Beginning	Coverage
Atlantic Reporter (A. or A.2d)	1885	Connecticut, Delaware, District of Columbia, Maine, Maryland, New Hampshire, New Jersey, Pennsylvania, Rhode Island, and Vermont.
North Eastern Reporter (N.E. or N.E.2d)	1885	Illinois, Indiana, Massachusetts, New York, and Ohio.
North Western Reporter (N.W. or N.W.2d)	1879	Iowa, Michigan, Minnesota, Nebraska, North Dakota, South Dakota, and Wisconsin.
Pacific Reporter (P., P.2d, or P.3d)	1883	Alaska, Arizona, California, Colorado, Hawaii, Idaho, Kansas, Montana, Nevada, New Mexico, Oklahoma, Oregon, Utah, Washington, and Wyoming.
South Eastern Reporter (S.E. or S.E.2d)	1887	Georgia, North Carolina, South Carolina, Virginia, and West Virginia.
South Western Reporter (S.W., S.W.2d, or S.W.3d)	1886	Arkansas, Kentucky, Missouri, Tennessee, and Texas.
Southern Reporter (So. or So.2d)	1887	Alabama, Florida, Louisiana, and Mississippi.
Federal Reporters		
Federal Reporter (F., F.2d, or F.3d)	1880	U.S. Circuit Courts from 1880 to 1912; U.S. Commerce Court from 1911 to 1913; U.S. District Courts from 1880 to 1932; U.S. Court of Claims (now called U.S. Court of Federal Claims) from 1929 to 1932 and since 1960; U.S. Courts of Appeals since 1891; U.S. Court of Customs and Patent Appeals since 1929; U.S. Emergency Court of Appeals since 1943.
Federal Supplement (F.Supp. or F.Supp.2d)	1932	U.S. Court of Claims from 1932 to 1960; U.S. District Courts since 1932; U.S. Customs Court since 1956.
Federal Rules Decisions (F.R.D.)	1939	U.S. District Courts involving the Federal Rules of Civil Procedure since 1939 and Federal Rules of Criminal Procedure since 1946.
Supreme Court Reporter (S.Ct.)	1882	United States Supreme Court since the October term of 1882.
Bankruptcy Reporter (Bankr.)	1980	Bankruptcy decisions of U.S. Bankruptcy Courts, U.S. District Courts, U.S. Courts of Appeals, and the United States Supreme Court.
Military Justice Reporter (M.J.)	1978	U.S. Court of Military Appeals and Courts of Military Review for the Army, Navy, Air Force, and Coast Guard.

NATIONAL REPORTER SYSTEM MAP

the *Wisconsin Reports* and West's *North Western Reporter* are still included after the public domain citation.

Consider the following case: *State v. Faison,* 112 Conn.App. 373, 962 A.2d 860 (2009). We see that the opinion in this case can be found in Volume 112 of the official *Connecticut Appellate Reports,* which reports only the decisions of the intermediate appellate courts in Connecticut, on page 373. The parallel citation is to Volume 962 of the *Atlantic Reporter, Second Series,* page 860. When we present opinions in this text (starting in Chapter 2), we give the name of the court hearing the case and the year of the court's decision in addition to the reporter. A few states—including those with intermediate appellate courts, such as California, Illinois, and New York—have more than one reporter for opinions issued by their courts. Sample citations from these courts, as well as others, are listed and explained in Exhibit 1A–2 starting on the following page.

Federal Court Decisions

Federal district (trial) court decisions are published unofficially in West's *Federal Supplement* (F. Supp. or F.Supp.2d), and opinions from the circuit courts of appeals (federal reviewing courts) are reported unofficially in West's *Federal Reporter* (F., F.2d, or F.3d). Cases concerning federal bankruptcy law are published unofficially in West's *Bankruptcy Reporter* (Bankr.). The official edition of United States Supreme Court decisions is the *United States Reports* (U.S.), which is published by the federal government. Unofficial editions of Supreme Court cases include West's *Supreme Court Reporter* (S.Ct.) and the *Lawyers' Edition of the Supreme Court Reports* (L.Ed. or L.Ed.2d). Sample citations for federal court decisions are also listed and explained in Exhibit 1A–2.

ON THE WEB To find links to Supreme Court opinions and opinions issued by the federal appellate courts, a good starting point is FindLaw's guide at findlaw.com/10fedgov/judicial.

Unpublished Opinions and Old Cases

Many court opinions that are not yet published or that are not intended for formal publication can be accessed through Westlaw® (abbreviated in citations as "WL"), an online legal database maintained by West Group. When no citation to a published reporter is available for cases cited in this text, we give the WL citation (see Exhibit 1A–2 on page 28 for an example). Sometimes, both in this text and in other legal sources, you will see blanks left in a citation. This occurs when the decision will be published, but the particular volume number or page number is not yet available.

On a few occasions, this text cites opinions from old, classic cases dating to the nineteenth century or earlier; some of these are from the English courts. The citations to these cases may not conform to the descriptions given above because the reporters in which they were published have since been replaced.

▶ Reading and Understanding Case Law

The cases in this text have been condensed from the full text of the courts' opinions and paraphrased by the authors. For those wishing to review court cases for future research projects or to gain additional legal information, the following sections will provide useful insights into how to read and understand case law.

Case Titles and Terminology

The title of a case, such as *Adams v. Jones,* indicates the names of the parties to the lawsuit. The *v.* in the case title stands for *versus,* which means "against." In the trial court, Adams was the plaintiff—the person who filed the suit. Jones was the defendant. If the case is appealed, however, the appellate court will sometimes place the name of the party appealing the decision first, so the case may be called *Jones v. Adams.* Because some reviewing

● *Exhibit* 1A–2 **How to Read Citations**

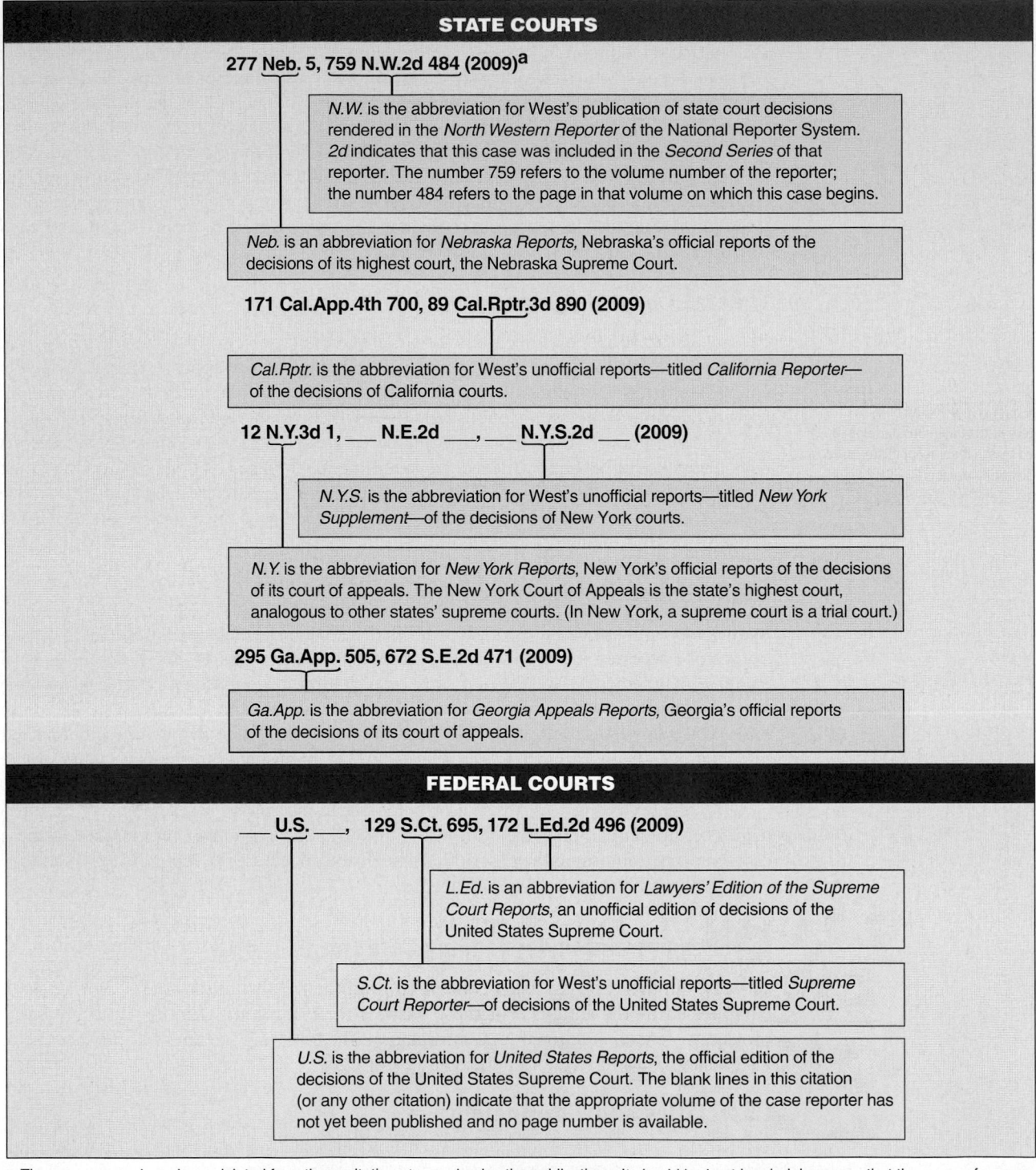

STATE COURTS

277 Neb. 5, 759 N.W.2d 484 (2009)ᵃ

> *N.W.* is the abbreviation for West's publication of state court decisions rendered in the *North Western Reporter* of the National Reporter System. *2d* indicates that this case was included in the *Second Series* of that reporter. The number 759 refers to the volume number of the reporter; the number 484 refers to the page in that volume on which this case begins.

> *Neb.* is an abbreviation for *Nebraska Reports,* Nebraska's official reports of the decisions of its highest court, the Nebraska Supreme Court.

171 Cal.App.4th 700, 89 Cal.Rptr.3d 890 (2009)

> *Cal.Rptr.* is the abbreviation for West's unofficial reports—titled *California Reporter*—of the decisions of California courts.

12 N.Y.3d 1, ___ N.E.2d ___, ___ N.Y.S.2d ___ (2009)

> *N.Y.S.* is the abbreviation for West's unofficial reports—titled *New York Supplement*—of the decisions of New York courts.

> *N.Y.* is the abbreviation for *New York Reports*, New York's official reports of the decisions of its court of appeals. The New York Court of Appeals is the state's highest court, analogous to other states' supreme courts. (In New York, a supreme court is a trial court.)

295 Ga.App. 505, 672 S.E.2d 471 (2009)

> *Ga.App.* is the abbreviation for *Georgia Appeals Reports,* Georgia's official reports of the decisions of its court of appeals.

FEDERAL COURTS

___ U.S. ___, 129 S.Ct. 695, 172 L.Ed.2d 496 (2009)

> *L.Ed.* is an abbreviation for *Lawyers' Edition of the Supreme Court Reports*, an unofficial edition of decisions of the United States Supreme Court.

> *S.Ct.* is the abbreviation for West's unofficial reports—titled *Supreme Court Reporter*—of decisions of the United States Supreme Court.

> *U.S.* is the abbreviation for *United States Reports*, the official edition of the decisions of the United States Supreme Court. The blank lines in this citation (or any other citation) indicate that the appropriate volume of the case reporter has not yet been published and no page number is available.

a. The case names have been deleted from these citations to emphasize the publications. It should be kept in mind, however, that the name of a case is as important as the specific page numbers in the volumes in which it is found. If a citation is incorrect, the correct citation may be found in a publication's index of case names. In addition to providing a check on errors in citations, the date of a case is important because the value of a recent case as an authority is likely to be greater than that of older cases from the same court.

● *Exhibit* 1A–2 **How to Read Citations–Continued**

FEDERAL COURTS (Continued)

551 F.3d 1099 (9th Cir. 2009)

9th Cir. is an abbreviation denoting that this case was decided in the U.S. Court of Appeals for the Ninth Circuit.

597 F.Supp.2d 470 (M.D.Pa. 2009)

M.D.Pa. is an abbreviation indicating that the U.S. District Court for the Middle District of Pennsylvania decided this case.

ENGLISH COURTS

9 Exch. 341, 156 Eng.Rep. 145 (1854)

Eng.Rep. is an abbreviation for *English Reports, Full Reprint,* a series of reports containing selected decisions made in English courts between 1378 and 1865.

Exch. is an abbreviation for *English Exchequer Reports*, which includes the original reports of cases decided in England's Court of Exchequer.

STATUTORY AND OTHER CITATIONS

18 U.S.C. Section 1961(1)(A)

U.S.C. denotes *United States Code*, the codification of *United States Statutes at Large.* The number 18 refers to the statute's U.S.C. title number and 1961 to its section number within that title. The number 1 in parentheses refers to a subsection within the section, and the letter A in parentheses to a subdivision within the subsection.

UCC 2–206(1)(b)

UCC is an abbreviation for *Uniform Commercial Code*. The first number 2 is a reference to an article of the UCC, and 206 to a section within that article. The number 1 in parentheses refers to a subsection within the section, and the letter b in parentheses to a subdivision within the subsection.

Restatement (Third) of Torts, Section 6

Restatement (Third) of Torts refers to the third edition of the American Law Institute's *Restatement of the Law of Torts.* The number 6 refers to a specific section.

17 C.F.R. Section 230.505

C.F.R. is an abbreviation for *Code of Federal Regulations*, a compilation of federal administrative regulations. The number 17 designates the regulation's title number, and 230.505 designates a specific section within that title.

Continued

● *Exhibit* 1A–2 How to Read Citations–Continued

WESTLAW® CITATIONS[b]

2009 WL 649691

WL is an abbreviation for Westlaw. The number 2009 is the year of the document that can be found with this citation in the Westlaw database. The number 649691 is a number assigned to a specific document. A higher number indicates that a document was added to the Westlaw database later in the year.

UNIFORM RESOURCE LOCATORS (URLs)

http://www.westlaw.com[c]

The suffix *com* is the top level domain (TLD) for this Web site. The TLD *com* is an abbreviation for "commercial," which usually means that a for-profit entity hosts (maintains or supports) this Web site.

westlaw is the host name—the part of the domain name selected by the organization that registered the name. In this case, West Group registered the name. This Internet site is the Westlaw database on the Web.

www is an abbreviation for "World Wide Web." The Web is a system of Internet servers that support documents formatted in *HTML* (hypertext markup language) and other formats as well.

http://www.uscourts.gov

This is "The Federal Judiciary Home Page." The host is the Administrative Office of the U.S. Courts. The TLD *gov* is an abbreviation for "government." This Web site includes information and links from, and about, the federal courts.

http://www.law.cornell.edu/index.html

This part of a URL points to a Web page or file at a specific location within the host's domain. This page is a menu with links to documents within the domain and to other Internet resources.

This is the host name for a Web site that contains the Internet publications of the Legal Information Institute (LII), which is a part of Cornell Law School. The LII site includes a variety of legal materials and links to other legal resources on the Internet. The TLD *edu* is an abbreviation for "educational institution" (a school or a university).

http://www.ipl.org/div/news

This part of the Web site points to a static *news* page at this Web site, which provides links to online newspapers from around the world.

div is an abbreviation for "division," which is the way that the Internet Public Library tags the content on its Web site as relating to a specific topic.

ipl is an abbreviation for "Internet Public Library," which is an online service that provides reference resources and links to other information services on the Web. The IPL is supported chiefly by the School of Information at the University of Michigan. The TLD *org* is an abbreviation for "organization" (normally nonprofit).

b. Many court decisions that are not yet published or that are not intended for publication can be accessed through Westlaw, an online legal database.

c. The basic form for a URL is "service://hostname/path." The Internet service for all of the URLs in this text is *http* (hypertext transfer protocol). Because most Web browsers add this prefix automatically when a user enters a host name or a hostname/path, we have generally omitted the *http://* from the URLs listed in this text.

courts retain the trial court order of names, it is often impossible to distinguish the plaintiff from the defendant in the title of a reported appellate court decision. You must carefully read the facts of each case to identify the parties.

The following terms and phrases are frequently encountered in court opinions and legal publications. Because it is important to understand what these terms and phrases mean, we define and discuss them here.

PLAINTIFFS AND DEFENDANTS As mentioned in Chapter 1, the plaintiff in a lawsuit is the party that initiates the action. The defendant is the party against which a lawsuit is brought. Lawsuits frequently involve more than one plaintiff and/or defendant.

APPELLANTS AND APPELLEES The *appellant* is the party that appeals a case to another court or jurisdiction from the court or jurisdiction in which the case was originally brought. Sometimes, an appellant is referred to as the *petitioner*. The *appellee* is the party against which the appeal is taken. Sometimes, the appellee is referred to as the *respondent*.

JUDGES AND JUSTICES The terms *judge* and *justice* are usually synonymous and represent two designations given to judges in various courts. All members of the United States Supreme Court, for example, are referred to as justices. And justice is the formal title usually given to judges of appellate courts, although this is not always the case. In New York, a justice is a judge of the trial court (which is called the Supreme Court), and a member of the Court of Appeals (the state's highest court) is called a judge. The term *justice* is commonly abbreviated to J., and *justices* to JJ. A Supreme Court case might refer to Justice Thomas as Thomas, J., or to Chief Justice Roberts as Roberts, C.J.

DECISIONS AND OPINIONS Most decisions reached by reviewing, or appellate, courts are explained in written *opinions*. The opinion contains the court's reasons for its decision, the rules of law that apply, and the judgment. When all judges or justices unanimously agree on an opinion, the opinion is written for the entire court and can be deemed a *unanimous opinion*. When there is not unanimous agreement, a *majority opinion* is written, outlining the views of the majority of the judges or justices deciding the case.

Often, a judge or justice who feels strongly about making or emphasizing a point that was not made or emphasized in the unanimous or majority opinion will write a *concurring opinion*. That means the judge or justice agrees (concurs) with the judgment given in the unanimous or majority opinion but for different reasons. When there is not a unanimous opinion, a *dissenting opinion* is usually written by a judge or justice who does not agree with the majority. (See the *Extended Case Study* following Chapter 8 for an example of a dissenting opinion.) The dissenting opinion is important because it may form the basis of the arguments used years later in overruling the precedential majority opinion. Occasionally, a court issues a *per curiam* (Latin for "of the court") opinion, which does not indicate which judge or justice authored the opinion.

A Sample Court Case

Knowing how to read and analyze a court opinion is an essential step in undertaking accurate legal research. A further step involves "briefing" the case. Legal researchers routinely brief cases by summarizing and reducing the texts of the opinions to their essential elements. (For instructions on how to brief a case, go to Appendix A at the end of this text.) The cases contained within the chapters of this text have already been analyzed and briefed by the authors, and the essential aspects of each case are presented in a convenient format consisting of four basic sections: *Facts, Issue, Decision,* and *Reason,* as shown in

Exhibit 1A–3, which has also been annotated to illustrate the kind of information that is contained in each section.

Throughout this text, in addition to this basic format, we sometimes include a special introductory section entitled *Historical and Social [Economic, Technological, Political,* or *other] Setting.* In some instances, a *Company Profile* is included in place of the introductory setting. These profiles provide background on one of the parties to the lawsuit. Each case is followed by either a brief *For Critical Analysis* section, which, as in Exhibit 1A–3, presents a question regarding some issue raised by the case; a *Why Is This Case Important?* section, which explains the significance of the case; or a *What If the Facts Were Different?* question, which alters the facts slightly and asks you to consider how this would change the outcome. A section entitled *Impact of This Case on Today's Law* concludes each of the *Classic Cases* that appear throughout the text to indicate the significance of the case for today's legal landscape.

● *Exhibit* **1A–3 A Sample Court Case**

1

Sample Case ▶ **Doe 1 v. AOL, LLC**

United States Court of Appeals, Ninth Circuit, ├**2**
552 F.3d 1077 (2009).
www.ca9.uscourts.gov[a] **3**

4 **FACTS**   On July 31, 2006, AOL, LLC, made public the Internet search records of more than 650,000 of its members. The records contained identifying data, as well as information about "struggles with various highly personal issues, including sexuality, mental illness, recovery from alcoholism, and victimization" from abuse. AOL admitted it made a mistake and took the data down, but other Web sites reproduced them in searchable form. The AOL members—including "Doe 1," who proceeded anonymously because of the nature of the disclosed information—filed a class-action suit in a federal district court against AOL, alleging, in part, violations of California law. AOL filed a motion to dismiss the action on the basis of a "forum selection" and "choice of law" clause in its member agreement that designates Virginia courts and law to govern all member disputes. The court granted the motion. The plaintiffs appealed to the U.S. Court of Appeals for the Ninth Circuit.

5 **ISSUE**   Is the clause in AOL's member agreement unenforceable as a violation of California public policy?

---

a. In the left-hand column, in the "Decisions" pull-down menu, click on "Opinions." On that page, click on "Advanced Search" in the "by Case No.:" box, type "07-15323," and click on "Search." In the result, click on the appropriate link to access the opinion. The U.S. Court of Appeals for the Ninth Circuit maintains this Web site.

6 **DECISION**   Yes. The federal appellate court reversed the judgment and remanded the case. The forum selection clause was unenforceable against the subclass of plaintiffs who are California residents.

7 **REASON**   Under a previous decision of the United States Supreme Court, a forum selection clause is unenforceable "if enforcement would contravene a strong public policy of the forum in which suit is brought." California has declared in other cases that the AOL clause at issue here contravenes a strong public policy as applied to California residents. In one case, for example, a court held that the clause violated California public policy that strongly favors consumer class actions, because the actions are not available in Virginia courts, and that the clause violated the California Consumer Legal Remedies Act (CLRA). The CLRA states, "Any waiver by a consumer of the provisions of this [act] is contrary to public policy and shall be unenforceable." The AOL clause is a waiver of remedies provided by the CLRA. The clause also violates California's public policy to protect consumers against unfair and deceptive business practices.

8 **FOR CRITICAL ANALYSIS—Economic Consideration**
Should mere residency at the time of filing a complaint be sufficient to invoke California public policy, or should there be an additional requirement? Explain.

Review of Sample Court Case

1. The name of the case is *Doe 1 v. AOL, LLC*. An anonymous party whose personal information was allegedly revealed in the incident that instigated this case is the plaintiff; the Internet service provider that made that information available is the named defendant.

2. The court deciding this case is the United States Court of Appeals for the Ninth Circuit.

3. The case citation includes a citation to the official *Federal Reporter, Third Series*. The case can be found in Volume 552 of the *Federal Reporter, Third Series*, on page 1,077. There is also an address for a Web site at which the opinion can be accessed.

4. The *Facts* section identifies the plaintiff and the defendants; describes the events leading up to this suit; and tells what the plaintiff sought to obtain by bringing this action. Because this is a case before an appellate court, the ruling of the lower court is also included here.

5. The *Issue* section presents the central issue (or issues) to be decided by the court. In this case, the court is to determine the enforceability of a clause in the parties' contract. Most cases concern more than one issue, but the authors of this textbook have edited each case to focus on just one issue.

6. The *Decision* section, as the term indicates, contains the court's decision on the issue or issues. The decision reflects the opinion of the judge, or the majority of the judges or justices, hearing the case. In this particular case, the court reversed the lower court's judgment. Decisions by appellate courts are frequently phrased in reference to the lower court's decision—that is, the appellate court may "affirm" the lower court's ruling or "reverse" it. In either situation, the appellate court may remand, or send back, the case for further proceedings.

7. The *Reason* section indicates what relevant laws and judicial principles were applied in forming the particular conclusion arrived at in the case at bar ("before the court"). In this case, the principle that was applied concerned the enforceability of a contract clause that arguably contravened the public policy of the plaintiff's state of residence. The court determined that the clause is not enforceable in those circumstances.

8. The *For Critical Analysis—Economic Consideration* section raises a question to be considered in relation to the case just presented. Here, the question involves an "economic" consideration. In other cases presented in this text, the "consideration" may involve an environmental, ethical, global, legal, political, social, or technological consideration.

Constitutional Law

> "The United States Constitution has proved itself the most marvelously elastic compilation of rules of government ever written."
>
> —Franklin D. Roosevelt, 1882–1945
> (Thirty-second president of the United States, 1933–1945)

Chapter Outline

- The Constitutional Powers of Government
- Business and the Bill of Rights
- Due Process and Equal Protection
- Privacy Rights

Learning Objectives

After reading this chapter, you should be able to answer the following questions:

1. What is the basic structure of the U.S. government?

2. What constitutional clause gives the federal government the power to regulate commercial activities among the various states?

3. What constitutional clause allows laws enacted by the federal government to take priority over conflicting state laws?

4. What is the Bill of Rights? What freedoms does the First Amendment guarantee?

5. Where in the Constitution can the due process clause be found?

The U.S. Constitution is brief.[1] It consists of only about seven thousand words, which is less than one-third of the number of words in the average state constitution. Perhaps its brevity explains why it has proved to be so "marvelously elastic," as Franklin Roosevelt pointed out in the chapter-opening quotation, and why it has survived for more than two hundred years—longer than any other written constitution in the world.

Laws that govern business have their origin in the lawmaking authority granted by this document, which is the supreme law in this country. As mentioned in Chapter 1, neither Congress nor any state can enact a law that is in conflict with the Constitution. In this chapter, we first look at some basic constitutional concepts and clauses and their significance for business. Then we examine how certain fundamental freedoms guaranteed by the Constitution affect businesspersons and the workplace.

 ## The Constitutional Powers of Government

Following the Revolutionary War, the states created a *confederal* form of government in which the states had the authority to govern themselves and the national government could exercise only limited powers. When problems arose because the nation was facing an economic crisis and state laws interfered with the free flow of commerce, a national convention

ON THE WEB You can find a copy of the U.S. Constitution online, as well as information about the document, including its history, at **www.constitutioncenter.org**.

---

1. See Appendix B for the full text of the U.S. Constitution.

was called, and the delegates drafted the U.S. Constitution. This document, after its ratification by the states in 1789, became the basis for an entirely new form of government.

A Federal Form of Government

The new government created by the Constitution reflected a series of compromises made by the convention delegates on various issues. Some delegates wanted sovereign power to remain with the states; others wanted the national government alone to exercise sovereign power. The end result was a compromise—a **federal form of government** in which the national government and the states *share* sovereign power.

The Constitution sets forth specific powers that can be exercised by the national government and provides that the national government has the implied power to undertake actions necessary to carry out its expressly designated powers. All other powers are "reserved" to the states. The broad language of the Constitution, though, has left much room for debate over the specific nature and scope of these powers. Generally, it has been the task of the courts to determine where the boundary line between state and national powers should lie—and that line changes over time. In the past, for example, the national government met little resistance from the courts when extending its regulatory authority over broad areas of social and economic life. Today, in contrast, the courts, and particularly the United States Supreme Court, are sometimes more willing to interpret the Constitution in such a way as to curb the national government's regulatory powers.

The Separation of Powers

To make it difficult for the national government to use its power arbitrarily, the Constitution divided the national government's powers among the three branches of government. The legislative branch makes the laws, the executive branch enforces the laws, and the judicial branch interprets the laws. Each branch performs a separate function, and no branch may exercise the authority of another branch.

Additionally, a system of **checks and balances** allows each branch to limit the actions of the other two branches, thus preventing any one branch from exercising too much power. The following are examples of these checks and balances:

1. The legislative branch (Congress) can enact a law, but the executive branch (the president) has the constitutional authority to veto that law.
2. The executive branch is responsible for foreign affairs, but treaties with foreign governments require the advice and consent of the Senate.
3. Congress determines the jurisdiction of the federal courts, and the president appoints federal judges, with the advice and consent of the Senate, but the judicial branch has the power to hold actions of the other two branches unconstitutional.[2]

The Commerce Clause

To prevent states from establishing laws and regulations that would interfere with trade and commerce among the states, the Constitution expressly delegated to the national government the power to regulate interstate commerce. Article I, Section 8, of the U.S. Constitution expressly permits Congress "[t]o regulate Commerce with foreign Nations, and among the several States, and with the Indian Tribes." This clause, referred to as the **commerce clause**, has had a greater impact on business than any other provision in the Constitution.

Initially, the commerce power was interpreted as being limited to *interstate* commerce (commerce among the states) and not applicable to *intrastate* commerce (commerce within

---

Federal Form of Government A system of government in which the states form a union and the sovereign power is divided between the central government and the member states.

ON THE WEB The *Federalist Papers,* which are a series of essays by the founders explaining their views on federalism, are available online at **www.law.emory.edu/FEDERAL/federalist**.

Checks and Balances The principle under which the powers of the national government are divided among three separate branches—the executive, legislative, and judicial branches—each of which exercises a check on the actions of the others.

Commerce Clause The provision in Article I, Section 8, of the U.S. Constitution that gives Congress the power to regulate interstate commerce.

After the president signs legislation into law, what responsibilities remain with the executive branch?

(AP Photo / Ron Edmonds)

---

2. See the *Landmark in the Law* feature in Chapter 3 on *Marbury v. Madison,* 5 U.S. (1 Cranch) 137, 2 L.Ed. 60 (1803), a case in which the doctrine of judicial review was clearly enunciated by Chief Justice John Marshall.

Landmark in the Law   Gibbons v. Ogden (1824)

The commerce clause of the U.S. Constitution gives Congress the power "[t]o regulate Commerce with foreign Nations, and among the several States, and with the Indian Tribes." Prior to the commerce clause, state policies tended to restrict commerce within and beyond their borders, which hampered trade by making market exchanges inefficient and costly. The goal of the clause was to unify the states' commerce policies and improve the efficiency of exchanges. The problem was that although the commerce clause gave Congress some authority to regulate trade among the states, the extent of that power was unclear. What exactly does "to regulate commerce" mean? What does "commerce" entail? These questions came before the United States Supreme Court in 1824 in the case of *Gibbons v. Ogden*.[a]

Background   In 1803, Robert Fulton, the inventor of the steamboat, and Robert Livingston, who was the ambassador to France, secured a monopoly on steam navigation on the waters in the state of New York from the New York legislature. Their monopoly extended to interstate waterways—those areas of water that stretch between states. Fulton and Livingston licensed Aaron Ogden, a former governor of New Jersey and a U.S. senator, to operate steam-powered ferryboats between New York and New Jersey.

Thomas Gibbons operated a ferry service between New Jersey and New York, which had been licensed by Congress under a 1793 act regulating the coasting trade. Although the federal government had licensed Gibbons to operate boats in interstate waters, he did not have the state of New York's permission to compete with Ogden in that area. Ogden sued Gibbons. The New York state courts granted Ogden's request for an injunction—an order prohibiting Gibbons from operating in New York waters. Gibbons appealed the decision to the United States Supreme Court.

Marshall's Decision   The issue before the Court was whether the law regulated commerce that was "among the several states." Sitting as chief justice on the Supreme Court was John Marshall, an advocate of a strong national government. In his decision, Marshall defined the word *commerce* as used in the commerce clause to mean all commercial intercourse—that is, all business dealings that affect more than one state. This broader definition includes navigation. The Court ruled against Ogden's monopoly, reversing the injunction against Gibbons. Marshall used this opportunity not only to expand the definition of commerce but also to validate and increase the power of the national legislature to regulate commerce. Said Marshall, "What is this power? It is the power . . . to prescribe the rule by which commerce is to be governed." Marshall held that the power to regulate interstate commerce is an exclusive power of the national government and that this power includes the power to regulate any intrastate commerce that substantially affects interstate commerce.

• **Application to Today's World**   *Marshall's broad definition of the commerce power established the foundation for the expansion of national powers in the years to come. Today, the national government continues to rely on the commerce clause for its constitutional authority to regulate business activities. Marshall's conclusion that the power to regulate interstate commerce was an exclusive power of the national government has also had significant consequences. By implication, this means that a state* cannot *regulate activities that extend beyond its borders, such as out-of-state online gambling operations that affect the welfare of in-state citizens. It also means that state regulations over in-state activities normally will be invalidated if the regulations substantially burden interstate commerce.*

• **Relevant Web Sites**   To locate information on the Web concerning the *Gibbons v. Ogden* decision, go to this text's Web site at www.cengage.com/blaw/blt, select "Chapter 2," and click on "URLs for Landmarks."

---

a. 22 U.S. (9 Wheat.) 1, 6 L.Ed. 23 (1824).

a state). In 1824, however, in *Gibbons v. Ogden* (see the chapter's *Landmark in the Law* feature above), the United States Supreme Court held that commerce within a state could also be regulated by the national government as long as the commerce *substantially affected* commerce involving more than one state.

THE COMMERCE CLAUSE AND THE EXPANSION OF NATIONAL POWERS   In *Gibbons v. Ogden*, the commerce clause was expanded to regulate activities that "substantially affect interstate commerce." As the nation grew and faced new kinds of problems, the commerce clause became a vehicle for the additional expansion of the national government's regulatory powers. Even activities that seemed purely local came under the regulatory reach of the national government if those activities were deemed to substantially affect interstate commerce. **CASE EXAMPLE 2.1** In 1942, in *Wickard v. Filburn*,[3] the Supreme Court held that wheat production by an individual farmer intended wholly for consumption on his own farm was subject to federal regulation. The Court reasoned that the home consumption of wheat reduced the market demand for wheat and thus could have a substantial effect on interstate commerce. •

The following classic case involved a challenge to the scope of the national government's constitutional authority to regulate local activities.

3. 317 U.S. 111, 63 S.Ct. 82, 87 L.Ed. 122 (1942).

Classic Case 2.1 Heart of Atlanta Motel v. United States

Supreme Court of the United States, 379 U.S. 241, 85 S.Ct. 348, 13 L.Ed.2d 258 (1964).
www.law.cornell.edu/supct/cases/name.htm[a]

HISTORICAL AND SOCIAL SETTING *In the first half of the twentieth century, state governments sanctioned segregation on the basis of race. In 1954, the United States Supreme Court held that racially segregated school systems violated the Constitution. In the following decade, the Court ordered an end to racial segregation imposed by the states in other public facilities, such as beaches, golf courses, buses, parks, auditoriums, and courtroom seating. Privately owned facilities that excluded or segregated African Americans and others on the basis of race were not subject to the same constitutional restrictions, however. Congress passed the Civil Rights Act of 1964 to prohibit racial discrimination in "establishments affecting interstate commerce." These facilities included "places of public accommodation."*

Morton Rolleston stands in front of his Heart of Atlanta Motel, where he refused to rent rooms to African Americans. He sought to have the Civil Rights Act declared unconstitutional. Ultimately, the United States Supreme Court ruled against him.

FACTS The owner of the Heart of Atlanta Motel, in violation of the Civil Rights Act of 1964, refused to rent rooms to African Americans. The motel owner brought an action in a federal district court to have the Civil Rights Act declared unconstitutional, alleging that Congress had exceeded its constitutional authority to regulate commerce by enacting the act. The owner argued that his motel was not engaged in interstate commerce but was "of a purely local character." The motel, however, was accessible to state and interstate highways. The owner advertised nationally, maintained billboards throughout the state, and accepted convention trade from outside the state (75 percent of the guests were residents of other states). The court ruled that the act did not

violate the Constitution and enjoined (prohibited) the owner from discriminating on the basis of race. The owner appealed. The case ultimately went to the United States Supreme Court.

ISSUE Did Congress exceed its constitutional power to regulate interstate commerce by enacting the Civil Rights Act of 1964?

DECISION No. The United States Supreme Court upheld the constitutionality of the act.

REASON The Court noted that the act was passed to correct "the deprivation of personal dignity" accompanying the denial of equal access to "public establishments." Testimony before Congress leading to the passage of the act indicated that African Americans in particular experienced substantial discrimination in attempting to secure lodging while traveling. This discrimination impeded interstate travel and thus impeded interstate commerce. As for the owner's argument that his motel was "of a purely local character," the Court said that even if this was true, the motel affected interstate commerce. According to the Court, "if it is interstate commerce that feels the pinch, it does not matter how local the operation that applies the squeeze." Therefore, under the commerce clause, "the power of Congress to promote interstate commerce also includes the power to regulate the local incidents thereof, including local activities."

IMPACT OF THIS CASE ON TODAY'S LAW *If the United States Supreme Court had invalidated the Civil Rights Act of 1964, the legal landscape of the United States would be much different today. The act prohibits discrimination based on race, color, national origin, religion, or gender in all "public accommodations," including hotels and restaurants. The act also prohibits discrimination in employment based on these criteria. Although state laws now prohibit many of these forms of discrimination as well, the protections available vary from state to state—and it is not certain when (and if) such laws would have been passed had the 1964 federal Civil Rights Act been deemed unconstitutional.*

RELEVANT WEB SITES *To locate information on the Web concerning the Heart of Atlanta Motel case, go to this text's Web site at www.cengage.com/blaw/blt. Select "Chapter 2" and click on "Classic Cases."*

a. This is the "Historic Supreme Court Decisions–by Party Name" page within the "Supreme Court" collection that is available at the Web site of the Legal Information Institute. Click on the "H" link, or scroll down the list of cases to the entry for the *Heart of Atlanta* case. Click on the case name, and select the format in which you would like to view the case.

THE COMMERCE POWER TODAY   Today, at least theoretically, the power over commerce authorizes the national government to regulate every commercial enterprise in the United States. Federal (national) legislation governs almost every major activity conducted by businesses—from hiring and firing decisions to workplace safety, competitive practices, and financing. Since 1995, however, the United States Supreme Court has imposed some curbs on the national government's regulatory authority under the commerce clause. In that year, the Court held—for the first time in sixty years—that Congress had exceeded its regulatory authority under the commerce clause. The Court struck down an act that banned the possession of guns within one thousand feet of any school because the act attempted to regulate an area that had "nothing to do with commerce."[4] Subsequently, the Court invalidated key portions of two other federal acts on the ground that they exceeded Congress's commerce clause authority.[5]

In one notable case, however, the Supreme Court did allow the federal government to regulate noncommercial activities taking place wholly within a state's borders. **CASE EXAMPLE 2.2**   Eleven states, including California, have adopted "medical marijuana" laws that legalize marijuana for medical purposes. Marijuana possession, however, is illegal under the federal Controlled Substances Act (CSA).[6] After the federal government seized the marijuana that two seriously ill California women were using on the advice of their physicians, the women filed a lawsuit. They argued that it was unconstitutional for the federal statute to prohibit them from using marijuana for medical purposes that were legal within the state. In 2005, however, the Supreme Court held that Congress has the authority to prohibit the *intra*state possession and noncommercial cultivation of marijuana as part of a larger regulatory scheme (the CSA).[7] In other words, state medical marijuana laws do not insulate the users from federal prosecution. ●

THE REGULATORY POWERS OF THE STATES   As part of their inherent sovereignty, state governments have the authority to regulate affairs within their borders. This authority stems in part from the Tenth Amendment to the Constitution, which reserves to the states all powers not delegated to the national government. State regulatory powers are often referred to as **police powers.** The term encompasses not only the enforcement of criminal law but also the right of state governments to regulate private activities in order to protect or promote the public order, health, safety, morals, and general welfare. Fire and building codes, antidiscrimination laws, parking regulations, zoning restrictions, licensing requirements, and thousands of other state statutes have been enacted pursuant to a state's police powers. Local governments, including cities, also exercise police powers.[8] Generally, state laws enacted pursuant to a state's police powers carry a strong presumption of validity.

Police Powers   Powers possessed by the states as part of their inherent sovereignty. These powers may be exercised to protect or promote the public order, health, safety, morals, and general welfare.

This store in Los Angeles advertises the sale of medical marijuana, which is legal under California state law. Does federal law also apply? Why or why not?

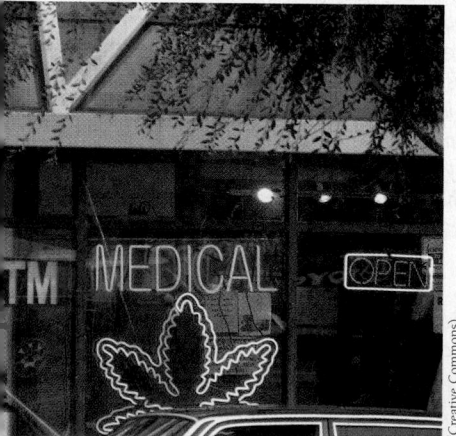

THE "DORMANT" COMMERCE CLAUSE   The United States Supreme Court has interpreted the commerce clause to mean that the national government has the exclusive authority to regulate commerce that substantially affects trade and commerce among the states. This express grant of authority to the national government, which is often referred to as the "positive" aspect of the commerce clause, implies a negative aspect—that the states do not have the authority to regulate interstate commerce. This negative aspect of the commerce clause is often referred to as the "dormant" (implied) commerce clause.

---

4. The United States Supreme Court held the Gun-Free School Zones Act of 1990 to be unconstitutional in *United States v. Lopez,* 514 U.S. 549, 115 S.Ct. 1624, 131 L.Ed.2d 626 (1995).
5. See *Printz v. United States,* 521 U.S. 898, 117 S.Ct. 2365, 138 L.Ed.2d 914 (1997), involving the Brady Handgun Violence Prevention Act of 1993; and *United States v. Morrison,* 529 U.S. 598, 120 S.Ct. 1740, 146 L.Ed.2d 658 (2000), concerning the federal Violence Against Women Act of 1994.
6. 21 U.S.C. Sections 801 *et seq.*
7. *Gonzales v. Raich,* 545 U.S. 1, 125 S.Ct. 2195, 162 L.Ed.2d 1 (2005).
8. Local governments derive their authority to regulate their communities from the state because they are creatures of the state. In other words, they cannot come into existence unless authorized by the state to do so.

California legislation that went into effect in 2009 requires chain restaurants to disclose calorie information on standard menu items. How might restaurant chains use the dormant commerce clause to sue California in an attempt to rescind this legislation?

Supremacy Clause The requirement in Article VI of the U.S. Constitution that provides that the Constitution, laws, and treaties of the United States are "the supreme Law of the Land." Under this clause, state and local laws that directly conflict with federal law will be rendered invalid.

Preemption A doctrine under which certain federal laws preempt, or take precedence over, conflicting state or local laws.

Bill of Rights The first ten amendments to the U.S. Constitution.

The dormant commerce clause comes into play when state regulations affect interstate commerce. In this situation, the courts normally weigh the state's interest in regulating a certain matter against the burden that the state's regulation places on interstate commerce. Because courts balance the interests involved, predicting the outcome in a particular case can be extremely difficult.

CASE EXAMPLE 2.3 A small town in the Florida Keys, Islamorada, attempted to preserve its "unique and natural" character by enacting an ordinance banning some retail chains and restaurants. Two business owners who were prevented from selling their properties to Starbucks and Walgreens filed a lawsuit against the town. Ultimately, a federal appellate court ruled that the ordinance violated the dormant commerce clause because the city had shown no legitimate local purpose to justify the ordinance's discriminatory effect on interstate commerce.[9] •

The Supremacy Clause

Article VI of the Constitution provides that the Constitution, laws, and treaties of the United States are "the supreme Law of the Land." This article, commonly referred to as the **supremacy clause,** is important in the ordering of state and federal relationships. When there is a direct conflict between a federal law and a state law, the state law is rendered invalid. Because some powers are *concurrent* (shared by the federal government and the states), however, it is necessary to determine which law governs in a particular circumstance.

Preemption occurs when Congress chooses to act exclusively in a concurrent area. In this circumstance, a valid federal statute or regulation will take precedence over a conflicting state or local law or regulation on the same general subject. Often, it is not clear whether Congress, in passing a law, intended to preempt an entire subject area against state regulation. In these situations, it is left to the courts to determine whether Congress intended to exercise exclusive power over a given area. No single factor is decisive as to whether a court will find preemption. Generally, congressional intent to preempt will be found if a federal law regulating an activity is so pervasive, comprehensive, or detailed that the states have little or no room to regulate in that area. Also, when a federal statute creates an agency—such as the National Labor Relations Board—to enforce the law, matters that may come within the agency's jurisdiction will likely preempt state laws.

CASE EXAMPLE 2.4 In 2008, the United States Supreme Court heard a case involving a man who alleged that he had been injured by a faulty medical device (a balloon catheter that had been inserted into his artery following a heart attack). The Court found that the Medical Device Amendments of 1976 had included a preemption provision and that the device had passed the U.S. Food and Drug Administration's rigorous premarket approval process. Therefore, the Court ruled that the federal regulation of medical devices preempted the injured party's state common law claims for negligence, strict liability, and implied warranty (see Chapters 4 and 17).[10] •

▶ Business and the Bill of Rights

The importance of having a written declaration of the rights of individuals eventually caused the first Congress of the United States to enact twelve amendments to the Constitution and submit them to the states for approval. The first ten of these amendments, commonly known as the **Bill of Rights,** were adopted in 1791 and embody a series of protections for the individual against various types of interference by the federal government.[11] Some constitutional

---

9. *Island Silver and Spice, Inc. v. Islamorada,* 542 F.3d 844 (11th Cir. 2008). See also *Granholm v. Heald,* 544 U.S. 460, 125 S.Ct. 1885, 161 L.Ed.2d 796 (2005).

10. *Riegel v. Medtronic, Inc.,* ___ U.S. ___, 128 S.Ct. 999, 169 L.Ed.2d 892 (2008).

11. One of the proposed amendments was ratified more than two hundred years later (in 1992) and became the Twenty-seventh Amendment to the Constitution. See Appendix B.

protections apply to business entities as well. For example, corporations exist as separate legal entities, or legal persons, and enjoy many of the same rights and privileges as natural persons do. Summarized here are the protections guaranteed by these ten amendments (see the Constitution in Appendix B for the complete text of each amendment):

1. The First Amendment guarantees the freedoms of religion, speech, and the press and the rights to assemble peaceably and to petition the government.
2. The Second Amendment guarantees the right to keep and bear arms.
3. The Third Amendment prohibits, in peacetime, the lodging of soldiers in any house without the owner's consent.
4. The Fourth Amendment prohibits unreasonable searches and seizures of persons or property.
5. The Fifth Amendment guarantees the rights to *indictment* (formal accusation) by grand jury, to due process of law, and to fair payment when private property is taken for public use. The Fifth Amendment also prohibits compulsory self-incrimination and double jeopardy (trial for the same crime twice).
6. The Sixth Amendment guarantees the accused in a criminal case the right to a speedy and public trial by an impartial jury and with counsel. The accused has the right to cross-examine witnesses against him or her and to solicit testimony from witnesses in his or her favor.
7. The Seventh Amendment guarantees the right to a trial by jury in a civil (noncriminal) case involving at least twenty dollars.[12]
8. The Eighth Amendment prohibits excessive bail and fines, as well as cruel and unusual punishment.
9. The Ninth Amendment establishes that the people have rights in addition to those specified in the Constitution.
10. The Tenth Amendment establishes that those powers neither delegated to the federal government nor denied to the states are reserved for the states.

We will look closely at several of these amendments in Chapter 6, in the context of criminal law and procedures. In this chapter, we examine two important guarantees of the First Amendment—freedom of speech and freedom of religion.

Limits on Both Federal and State Governmental Actions

As originally intended, the Bill of Rights limited only the powers of the national government. Over time, however, the United States Supreme Court "incorporated" most of these rights into the protections against state actions afforded by the Fourteenth Amendment to the Constitution. That amendment, passed in 1868 after the Civil War, provides, in part, that "[n]o State shall . . . deprive any person of life, liberty, or property, without due process of law." Starting in 1925, the Supreme Court began to define various rights and liberties guaranteed in the national Constitution as constituting "due process of law," which was required of state governments under the Fourteenth Amendment. Today, most of the rights and liberties set forth in the Bill of Rights apply to state governments as well as to the national government.

The rights secured by the Bill of Rights are not absolute. Many of the rights guaranteed by the first ten amendments are described in very general terms. For example, the Second Amendment states that people have a right to keep and bear arms, but it does not explain the extent of this right. As the Supreme Court noted in 2008, this does not mean that people can "keep and carry any weapon whatsoever in any manner whatsoever and for whatever purpose."[13] Legislatures can prohibit the carrying of concealed weapons or certain types of

"The way I see it, the Constitution cuts both ways. The First Amendment gives you the right to say what you want, but the Second Amendment gives me the right to shoot you for it."

BE CAREFUL   Although most of these rights apply to actions of the states, some of them apply only to actions of the federal government.

---

12. Twenty dollars was forty days' pay for the average person when the Bill of Rights was written.
13. *District of Columbia v. Heller*, ___ U.S. ___, 128 S.Ct. 2783, 171 L.Ed.2d 637 (2008).

weapons, such as machine guns. Ultimately, it is the Supreme Court, as the final interpreter of the Constitution, that gives meaning to these rights and determines their boundaries. (For a discussion of how the Supreme Court may consider other nations' laws when determining the appropriate balance of individual rights, see this chapter's *Beyond Our Borders* feature.)

The First Amendment—Freedom of Speech

A democratic form of government cannot survive unless people can freely voice their political opinions and criticize government actions or policies. Freedom of speech, particularly political speech, is thus a prized right, and traditionally the courts have protected this right to the fullest extent possible.

Symbolic speech—gestures, movements, articles of clothing, and other forms of expressive conduct—is also given substantial protection by the courts. The Supreme Court

REMEMBER The First Amendment guarantee of freedom of speech applies only to *government* restrictions on speech.

Symbolic Speech Nonverbal expressions of beliefs. Symbolic speech, which includes gestures, movements, and articles of clothing, is given substantial protection by the courts.

Beyond Our Borders · The Impact of Foreign Law on the United States Supreme Court

As noted in the text, the United States Supreme Court interprets and gives meaning to the rights provided in the U.S. Constitution. Determining the appropriate balance of rights and protections stemming from the Constitution is not an easy task, especially because society's perceptions and needs change over time. The justices on the Supreme Court are noticeably influenced by the opinions and beliefs of U.S. citizens. This is particularly true when the Court is faced with issues of freedom of speech or religion, obscenity, or privacy. Changing views on controversial topics, such as privacy in an era of terrorist

(Richard Carson/Reuters)

These demonstrators show their appreciation for the United States Supreme Court's decision in Lawrence v. Texas *in 2003. It was the first Supreme Court case that referenced foreign law in its published majority decision. Do all Supreme Court justices agree that it is appropriate to use foreign law in U.S. judicial decisions? Why or why not?*

threats or the rights of gay men and lesbians, may affect the way the Supreme Court decides a case. But should the Court also consider other nations' laws and world opinion when balancing individual rights in the United States?

Over the past ten years, justices on the Supreme Court have increasingly considered foreign law when deciding issues of national importance. For example, in 2003—for the first time ever—foreign law was cited in a majority opinion of the Supreme Court (references to foreign law had appeared in footnotes and dissents on a few occasions in the past). The case was a controversial one in which the Court struck down laws that prohibit oral and anal sex between consenting adults of the same sex. In the majority opinion (an opinion that the majority of justices have signed), Justice Anthony Kennedy mentioned that the European Court of Human Rights and other foreign courts have consistently acknowledged that homosexuals have a right "to engage in intimate, consensual conduct."[a] In 2005, the Court again looked at foreign law when deciding whether the death penalty was an

appropriate punishment for juveniles.[b] Then, in 2008, a majority of the Supreme Court justices concluded that the U.S. Constitution applied to foreign nationals who were apprehended by U.S. authorities as enemy combatants and detained at Guantánamo Bay, Cuba.[c] Although the Bush administration contended that noncitizens held abroad had no constitutional rights, the Court found that these detainees had the same constitutional rights to contest their detention as citizens did.

The practice of looking at foreign law has many critics, including Justice Antonin Scalia, who believes that foreign views are irrelevant to rulings on U.S. law. Other Supreme Court justices, however, including Justice Stephen Breyer, believe that in our increasingly global community we should not ignore the court opinions of the rest of the world.

• For Critical Analysis
Should U.S. courts, and particularly the United States Supreme Court, look to other nations' laws for guidance when deciding important issues—including those involving rights granted by the Constitution? If so, what impact might this have on their decisions? Explain.

---

a. *Lawrence v. Texas,* 539 U.S. 558, 123 S.Ct. 2472, 156 L.Ed.2d 508 (2003). Other cases in which the Court has referenced foreign law include *Grutter v. Bollinger,* 539 U.S. 306, 123 S.Ct. 2325, 156 L.Ed.2d 304 (2003), in the dissent; and *Atkins v. Virginia,* 536 U.S. 304, 122 S.Ct. 2242, 153 L.Ed.2d 335 (2002), in footnote 21 to the majority opinion.

b. *Roper v. Simmons,* 543 U.S. 551, 125 S.Ct. 1183, 161 L.Ed.2d 1 (2005).

c. *Boumediene v. Bush,* __ U.S. __, 128 S.Ct. 2229, 171 L.Ed.2d 41 (2008).

held that the burning of the American flag to protest government policies is a constitutionally protected form of expression.[14] Similarly, wearing a T-shirt with a photo of a presidential candidate would be a constitutionally protected form of expression. The test is whether a reasonable person would interpret the conduct as conveying some sort of message. **EXAMPLE 2.5** As a form of expression, Bryan has gang signs tattooed on his torso, arms, neck, and legs. If a reasonable person would interpret this conduct as conveying a message, then it might be a protected form of symbolic speech. •

REASONABLE RESTRICTIONS Expression—oral, written, or symbolized by conduct—is subject to reasonable restrictions. A balance must be struck between a government's obligation to protect its citizens and those citizens' exercise of their rights. Reasonableness is analyzed on a case-by-case basis. If a restriction imposed by the government is content neutral, then a court may allow it. To be content neutral, the restriction must be aimed at combating some secondary societal problem, such as crime, and not be aimed at suppressing the expressive conduct or its message. **CASE EXAMPLE 2.6** Courts have often protected nude dancing as a form of symbolic expression. Nevertheless, the courts typically allow content-neutral laws that ban all public nudity. In 2008, a man was charged with dancing nude at an annual "anti-Christmas" protest in Harvard Square, Cambridge, Massachusetts. The man argued that the statute was overbroad and unconstitutional, and a trial court agreed. On appeal, a state appellate court reversed. The court found that the statute was constitutional because it banned public displays of open and gross lewdness in situations in which there was an unsuspecting or unwilling audience.[15] •

The United States Supreme Court has also held that schools may restrict students' free speech right at school events. **CASE EXAMPLE 2.7** In 2007, the Court heard a case involving a high school student who had held up a banner saying "Bong Hits 4 Jesus" at an off-campus but school-sanctioned event. In a split decision, the majority of the Court ruled that school officials did not violate the students' free speech rights when they confiscated the banner and suspended the student for ten days. Because the banner could reasonably be interpreted as promoting drugs, the Court concluded that the school's actions were justified. Several justices disagreed, however, noting that the majority's holding creates a special exception that will allow schools to censor any student speech that mentions drugs.[16] •

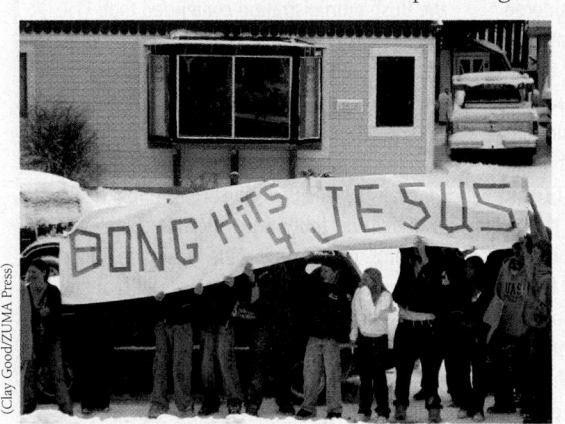

These students at Juneau-Douglas High School in Alaska unfurled this banner during an off-campus, school-sanctioned event. Why did the United States Supreme Court rule that the school could suspend the students responsible for this action?

CORPORATE POLITICAL SPEECH Political speech by corporations also falls within the protection of the First Amendment. **CASE EXAMPLE 2.8** Many years ago the United States Supreme Court reviewed a Massachusetts statute that prohibited corporations from making political contributions or expenditures that individuals were permitted to make. The Court ruled that the Massachusetts law was unconstitutional because it violated the right of corporations to freedom of speech.[17] • The Court has also held that a law prohibiting a corporation from using bill inserts to express its views on controversial issues violated the First Amendment.[18]

Although the Supreme Court has reversed this trend somewhat,[19] corporate political speech continues to be given significant protection under the First Amendment. For instance, in 2003 and again in 2007, the Supreme Court struck down portions of bipar-

---

14. See *Texas v. Johnson,* 491 U.S. 397, 109 S.Ct. 2533, 105 L.Ed.2d 342 (1989).
15. *Commonwealth v. Ora,* 451 Mass. 125, 883 N.E.2d 1217 (2008).
16. *Morse v. Frederick,* 551 U.S. 393, 127 S.Ct. 2618, 168 L.Ed.2d 290 (2007).
17. *First National Bank of Boston v. Bellotti,* 435 U.S. 765, 98 S.Ct. 1407, 55 L.Ed.2d 707 (1978).
18. *Consolidated Edison Co. v. Public Service Commission,* 447 U.S. 530, 100 S.Ct. 2326, 65 L.Ed.2d 319 (1980).
19. See *Austin v. Michigan Chamber of Commerce,* 494 U.S. 652, 110 S.Ct. 1391, 108 L.Ed.2d 652 (1990), in which the Court upheld a state law prohibiting corporations from using general corporate funds for independent expenditures in state political campaigns.

tisan campaign-finance reform laws as unconstitutional restraints on corporate political speech.[20]

ON THE WEB You can find extensive information relating to advertising law at **www.advertisinglaw.com**.

COMMERCIAL SPEECH   The courts also give substantial protection to *commercial speech*, which consists of communications—primarily advertising and marketing—made by business firms that involve only their commercial interests. The protection given to commercial speech under the First Amendment is not as extensive as that afforded to noncommercial speech, however. A state may restrict certain kinds of advertising, for instance, in the interest of protecting consumers from being misled by the advertising practices. States also have a legitimate interest in the beautification of roadsides, and this interest allows states to place restraints on billboard advertising. **CASE EXAMPLE 2.9** Café Erotica, a nude dancing establishment, sued the state after being denied a permit to erect a billboard along an interstate highway in Florida. The state appellate court decided that because the law directly advanced a substantial government interest in highway beautification and safety, it was not an unconstitutional restraint on commercial speech.[21] ●

Generally, a restriction on commercial speech will be considered valid as long as it (1) seeks to implement a substantial government interest, (2) directly advances that interest, and (3) goes no further than necessary to accomplish its objective. At issue in the following case was whether a government agency had unconstitutionally restricted commercial speech when it prohibited the inclusion of a certain illustration on beer labels.

---

20. See *McConnell v. Federal Election Commission*, 540 U.S. 93, 124 S.Ct. 619, 157 L.Ed.2d 491 (2003); and *Federal Election Commission v. Wisconsin Right to Life, Inc.*, 551 U.S. 449, 127 S.Ct. 2652, 168 L.Ed.2d 329 (2007).

21. *Café Erotica v. Florida Department of Transportation*, 830 So.2d 181 (Fla.App. 1 Dist. 2002); review denied, *Café Erotica/We Dare to Bare v. Florida Department of Transportation*, 845 So.2d 888 (Fla. 2003).

Case 2.2   **Bad Frog Brewery, Inc. v. New York State Liquor Authority**

United States Court of Appeals, Second Circuit, 134 F.3d 87 (1998).
www.findlaw.com/casecode/index.html[a]

(Courtesy of Bad Frog Beer)

FACTS   Bad Frog Brewery, Inc., makes and sells alcoholic beverages. Some of the beverages feature labels with a drawing of a frog making the gesture generally known as "giving the finger." Bad Frog's authorized New York distributor, Renaissance Beer Company, applied to the New York State Liquor Authority (NYSLA) for brand label approval, as required by state law before the beer could be sold in New York. The NYSLA denied the application, in part, because "the label could appear in grocery and convenience stores, with obvious exposure on the shelf to children of tender age." Bad Frog filed a suit in a federal district court against the NYSLA, asking for, among other things, an injunction against the denial of the application. The court granted summary judgment in favor of the NYSLA. Bad Frog appealed to the U.S. Court of Appeals for the Second Circuit.

ISSUE   Was the NYSLA's ban of Bad Frog's beer labels a reasonable restriction on commercial speech?

DECISION   No. The U.S. Court of Appeals for the Second Circuit reversed the judgment of the district court and remanded the case for judgment to be entered in favor of Bad Frog.

REASON   The appellate court held that the NYSLA's denial of Bad Frog's application violated the First Amendment. The ban on the use of the labels lacked a "reasonable fit" with the state's interest in shielding minors from vulgarity, and the NYSLA did not adequately consider alternatives to the ban. The court acknowledged that the NYSLA's interest "in protecting children from vulgar and profane advertising" was "substantial." The question was whether banning Bad Frog's labels "directly advanced" that interest. "In view of the wide currency of vulgar displays throughout contemporary society, including comic books targeted directly at children, barring such displays from labels for alcoholic beverages cannot realistically be expected to reduce children's exposure to such displays to any significant degree." The court concluded that a commercial speech limitation must be "part of a substantial effort to advance a valid state interest, not merely the

---

a. Under the heading "US Court of Appeals," click on "2nd." Enter "Bad Frog Brewery" in the "Party Name Search" box, and click on "search." On the resulting page, click on the case name to access the opinion.

Case 2.2–Continues next page ➡

Case 2.2–Continued

removal of a few grains of offensive sand from a beach of vulgarity." Finally, as to whether the ban on the labels was more extensive than necessary to serve this interest, the court pointed out that there were "numerous less intrusive alternatives." For example, the NYSLA could have placed restrictions on the permissible locations where the appellant's products could be displayed in stores.

WHAT IF THE FACTS WERE DIFFERENT?   *If Bad Frog had sought to use the label to market toys instead of beer, would the court's ruling likely have been the same? Explain your answer.*

UNPROTECTED SPEECH   The United States Supreme Court has made it clear that certain types of speech will not be given any protection under the First Amendment. Speech that harms the good reputation of another, or defamatory speech (see Chapter 4), will not be protected. Speech that violates criminal laws (such as threatening speech) is not constitutionally protected. Other unprotected speech includes "fighting words," or words that are likely to incite others to respond violently.

The First Amendment, as interpreted by the Supreme Court, also does not protect obscene speech. Establishing an objective definition of obscene speech has proved difficult, however, and the Court has grappled with this problem from time to time. In a 1973 case, *Miller v. California,*[22] the Supreme Court created a test for legal obscenity, which involved a set of requirements that must be met for material to be legally obscene. Under this test, material is obscene if (1) the average person finds that it violates contemporary community standards; (2) the work taken as a whole appeals to a prurient (arousing or obsessive) interest in sex; (3) the work shows patently offensive sexual conduct; and (4) the work lacks serious redeeming literary, artistic, political, or scientific merit.

Because community standards vary widely, the *Miller* test has had inconsistent application, and obscenity remains a constitutionally unsettled issue. Numerous state and federal statutes make it a crime to disseminate and possess obscene materials, including child pornography.

ON THE WEB   To learn about issues involving free speech and cyberspace, go to the Web site of the American Civil Liberties Union (ACLU) at **www.aclu.org**. Click on one of the issues listed on the right side of the screen for links to ACLU articles on that issue.

Filtering Software   A computer program that is designed to block access to certain Web sites, based on their content. The software blocks the retrieval of a site whose URL or key words are on a list within the program.

Meta Tag   A key word in a document that can serve as an index reference to the document. On the Web, search engines return results based, in part, on these tags in Web documents.

ONLINE OBSCENITY   Congress's first two attempts at protecting minors from pornographic materials on the Internet—the Communications Decency Act (CDA) of 1996[23] and the Child Online Protection Act (COPA) of 1998[24]—failed. Ultimately, the United States Supreme Court struck down both the CDA and COPA as unconstitutional restraints on speech, largely because the wording of these acts was overbroad and would restrict nonpornographic materials.[25]

In 2000, Congress enacted the Children's Internet Protection Act (CIPA),[26] which requires public schools and libraries to block adult content from access by children by installing **filtering software.** Such software is designed to prevent persons from viewing certain Web sites by responding to a site's Internet address or its **meta tags,** or key words. CIPA was also challenged on constitutional grounds, but in 2003 the Supreme Court held that the act did not violate the First Amendment. The Court concluded that because libraries can disable the filters for any patrons who ask, the system is reasonably flexible and does not burden free speech to an unconstitutional extent.[27]

Because of the difficulties of policing the Internet, as well as the constitutional complexities of prohibiting online obscenity through legislation, it remains a continuing problem worldwide. In 2005, the Federal Bureau of Investigation established an Anti-Porn Squad to target and prosecute companies that distribute child pornography in cyberspace. The Fed-

---

22. 413 U.S. 15, 93 S.Ct. 2607, 37 L.Ed.2d 419 (1973).
23. 47 U.S.C. Section 223(a)(1)(B)(ii).
24. 47 U.S.C. Section 231.
25. See *Reno v. American Civil Liberties Union,* 521 U.S. 844, 117 S.Ct. 2329, 138 L.Ed.2d 874 (1997); *Ashcroft v. American Civil Liberties Union,* 535 U.S. 564, 122 S.Ct. 1700, 152 L.Ed.2d 771 (2002); and *American Civil Liberties Union v. Ashcroft,* 322 F.3d 240 (3d Cir. 2003).
26. 17 U.S.C. Sections 1701–1741.
27. *United States v. American Library Association,* 539 U.S. 194, 123 S.Ct. 2297, 156 L.Ed.2d 221 (2003).

Adapting the Law to the Online Environment

The Supreme Court Upholds a Law That Prohibits Pandering Virtual Child Pornography

Millions of pornographic images of children are available on the Internet. Some of these images are of actual children engaged in sexual activity. Others are virtual (computer-generated) pornography—that is, images made to look like children engaged in sexual acts. Whereas child pornography is illegal, the United States Supreme Court has ruled that virtual pornography is legally protected under the First Amendment because it does not involve the exploitation of real children.[a] In its ruling, the Supreme Court struck down as overly broad, and therefore unconstitutional, provisions of the Child Pornography Prevention Act of 1996 (CPPA), which, among other things, prohibited any visual depiction including a "computer-generated image" that "is, or appears to be, of a minor engaging in sexually explicit conduct."

This ruling and the difficulty in distinguishing between real and virtual pornography have created problems for prosecutors, however. Before they can convict someone of disseminating child pornography on the Internet, they must prove that the images depict real children. To help remedy this problem, Congress enacted the Protect Act of 2003 (here, *Protect* stands for "Prosecutorial Remedies and Other Tools to end the Exploitation of Children Today").[b]

The Protect Act's Pandering Provisions

One of the Protect Act's many provisions prohibits misrepresenting virtual child pornography as actual child pornography. The act makes it a crime to knowingly advertise, present, distribute, or solicit "any material or purported material in a manner that reflects the belief, or that is intended to cause another to believe, that the material or purported material" is illegal child pornography.[c] Thus, it is a crime to intentionally distribute virtual child pornography.

The Protect Act's "pandering" provision was challenged in a 2008 case, *United States v. Williams.*[d] The defendant, Michael Williams, sent a message to an Internet chat room that read "Dad of Toddler has 'good' pics of her an [sic] me for swap of your toddler pics." A law enforcement agent responded by sending a private message to Williams that contained photos of a college-aged female, which were computer altered to look like a ten-year-old girl. Williams requested explicit photos of the girl, but the agent did not respond. After that, Williams sent another public message that accused the agent of being a cop and included a hyperlink containing seven pictures of minors engaging in sexually explicit conduct.

Williams was arrested and charged with possession of child pornography and pandering material that appears to be child pornography. He claimed that the Protect Act's pandering provision was—like its predecessor (the CPPA)—unconstitutionally overbroad and vague. (He later pleaded guilty to the charges but preserved the issue of constitutionality for appeal.)

Is the Protect Act Constitutional?

On appeal, the federal appellate court held that the pandering provision of the Protect Act was unconstitutional because it criminalized speech regarding child pornography. The court reasoned that, under the act, a person who distributes innocent pictures via the Internet (such as sending an e-mail labeled "good pictures of the kids in bed") could be penalized for offering child pornography.

The United States Supreme Court reversed that decision, ruling that the Protect Act was neither unconstitutionally overbroad nor impermissibly vague. The Court held that the statute was valid because it does not prohibit a substantial amount of protected speech. Rather, the act generally prohibits offers to provide and requests to obtain child pornography—both of which are unprotected speech. Thus, the act's pandering provisions remedied the constitutional defects of the CPPA, which had made it illegal to possess virtual child pornography.

FOR CRITICAL ANALYSIS

Why should it be illegal to "pander" virtual child pornography when it is not illegal to possess it?

---

a. *Ashcroft v. Free Speech Coalition,* 535 U.S. 234, 122 S.Ct. 1389, 152 L.Ed.2d 403 (2002).
b. 18 U.S.C. Section 2252A(a)(5)(B).
c. 18 U.S.C. Section 2252A(a)(3)(B).
d. 553 U.S. ___, 128 S.Ct. 1830, 170 L.Ed.2d 650 (2008).

---

eral Communications Commission has also passed new obscenity regulations for television networks. For a discussion of how the law is evolving, see this chapter's *Adapting the Law to the Online Environment* feature.

The First Amendment—Freedom of Religion

The First Amendment states that the government may neither establish any religion nor prohibit the free exercise of religious practices. The first part of this constitutional provision is referred to as the **establishment clause**, and the second part is known as the **free exercise clause.** Government action, both federal and state, must be consistent with this constitutional mandate.

THE ESTABLISHMENT CLAUSE   The establishment clause prohibits the government from establishing a state-sponsored religion, as well as from passing laws that promote (aid or endorse) religion or show a preference for one religion over another. Although the

Establishment Clause   The provision in the First Amendment to the U.S. Constitution that prohibits the government from establishing any state-sponsored religion or enacting any law that promotes religion or favors one religion over another.

Free Exercise Clause   The provision in the First Amendment to the U.S. Constitution that prohibits the government from interfering with people's religious practices or forms of worship.

establishment clause involves the separation of church and state, it does not require a complete separation. Rather, it requires the government to accommodate religions. Federal or state laws that do not promote or place a significant burden on religion are constitutional even if they have some impact on religion. For a government law or policy to be constitutional, it must not have the primary effect of promoting or inhibiting religion.

Establishment clause cases often involve such issues as the legality of allowing or requiring school prayers, using state-issued vouchers to pay tuition at religious schools, and teaching creation theories versus evolution. In 2007, for instance, several taxpayers challenged the Bush administration's faith-based initiative expenditures as violating the establishment clause. President George W. Bush had issued executive orders creating a White House office within federal agencies to ensure that faith-based community groups were eligible to compete for federal financial support. Ultimately, however, the United States Supreme Court dismissed the action because the taxpayers did not have a sufficient stake in the controversy (called *standing*—see Chapter 3) to bring a lawsuit challenging executive orders.[28] (Taxpayers do have standing to challenge legislation in court.) The high court never ruled on the establishment clause issue.

Religious displays on public property have often been challenged as violating the establishment clause, and the United States Supreme Court has ruled on several such cases. Generally, the Court has focused on the proximity of the religious display to nonreligious symbols, such as reindeer and candy canes, or to symbols from different religions, such as a menorah (a nine-branched candelabrum used in celebrating Hanukkah). **CASE EXAMPLE 2.10** In 2005, the Supreme Court took a slightly different approach. The dispute involved a six-foot-tall monument of the Ten Commandments on the Texas state capitol grounds. The Court held that the monument did not violate the establishment clause because the Ten Commandments had historical as well as religious significance.[29] ●

Can a secular court resolve an internal church dispute over property ownership without becoming impermissibly entangled with questions of religion? The court in the following case faced that question.

---

28. *Hein v. Freedom from Religion Foundation, Inc.*, 551 U.S. 587, 127 S.Ct. 2553, 168 L.Ed.2d 424 (2007). *Standing* is a basic requirement for any plaintiff to file or maintain a cause of action.
29. *Van Orden v. Perry*, 545 U.S. 677, 125 S.Ct. 2854, 162 L.Ed.2d 607 (2005).

Case 2.3   **In re Episcopal Church Cases**

California Supreme Court, 45 Cal.4th 467, 198 P.3d 66, 87 Cal.Rptr.3d 275 (2009).

HISTORICAL AND POLITICAL SETTING   *The Protestant Episcopal Church in the United States of America organized in 1789 after seceding from the Church of England during the Revolutionary War. The Episcopal Church is divided into dioceses, and each diocese is divided into missions and parishes, which are individual churches where members meet to worship. The Los Angeles Diocese in California included St. James Parish. In 1950, the Episcopal bishop in Los Angeles, who governs the diocese, deeded to St. James Parish the property on which its church building stands. In 1979, the Episcopal Church added to its "general convention" (its governing document) a canon to provide that "all real and personal property held by or for the benefit of any Parish * * * is held in trust for this Church."*

FACTS   In 2003, the Episcopal Church in New Hampshire ordained an openly gay man as a bishop. Some members of St. James Parish did not agree with this ordination. St. James's vestry (a board of elected laypersons that, with a rector, governs an Episcopal parish) voted to

end its affiliation with the Episcopal Church and to affiliate with the Anglican Church of Uganda. After the disaffiliation, a dispute arose as to who owned the church building that the parish used for worship and the property on which the building stands. To resolve this dispute, the Episcopal Church and others filed a suit in a California state court against St. James and others, with both sides claiming ownership. The court ruled that the parish owned the building and the property, but a state intermediate appellate court reversed this judgment. St. James appealed to the California Supreme Court, arguing, in part, that the parish's name was on the deed to the property.

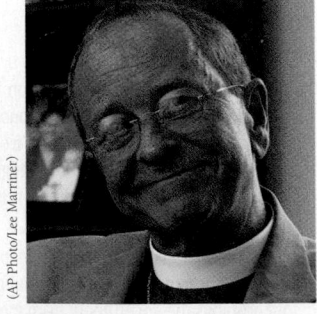

V. Gene Robinson, the Episcopal church's first openly gay bishop.

Case 2.3–Continued

ISSUE Can a secular court resolve a church property dispute without "establishing" a church in violation of the First Amendment?

DECISION Yes. The California Supreme Court affirmed the appellate court's judgment. The state supreme court applied "neutral principles of law" and concluded that the Episcopal Church, not St. James Parish, owned the property in question.

REASON The court acknowledged that the First Amendment prohibits state courts from deciding questions of religious doctrine. On those points, a court should defer to the highest ecclesiastical authority. But to the extent that a secular court can resolve a property dispute without referring to church doctrine, it should apply what the United States Supreme Court has called "neutral principles of law." The court should consider the deeds to the property; the local church's governing documents; the general church's constitution, canons, and rules; and other relevant sources, including state statutes. Although the deeds to the property in this case had long been in the name of the parish, the local church had agreed from the beginning of its existence to be part of the greater church and to be bound by its governing documents. Those documents clearly state that church property is held in trust for the general church and may be controlled by the local church only as long as it remains a part of the general church. When St. James disaffiliated from the Episcopal Church, it did not have the right to take church property with it.

FOR CRITICAL ANALYSIS—Political Consideration
Should the court have considered whether the Episcopal Church had abandoned or departed from the tenets of faith and practice that it had held at the time of St. James's affiliation? Why or why not?

BEWARE The free exercise clause applies only to the actions of the state and federal governments. Nevertheless, under federal employment laws (see Chapter 25), employers may be required to accommodate their employees' religious beliefs, at least to a reasonable extent.

Why did the United States Supreme Court determine that this monument with the Ten Commandments located outside the Texas State Capitol did not violate the establishment clause of the First Amendment to the U.S. Constitution?

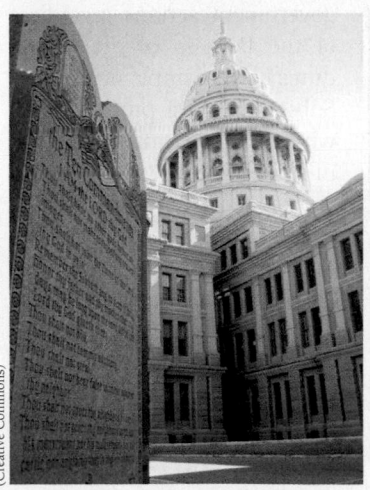

(Creative Commons)

THE FREE EXERCISE CLAUSE The free exercise clause guarantees that a person can hold any religious belief that she or he wants; or a person can have no religious belief. The constitutional guarantee of personal religious freedom restricts only the actions of the government and not those of individuals or private businesses.

When religious *practices* work against public policy and the public welfare, however, the government can act. For instance, the government can require a child to receive certain types of vaccinations or medical treatment when a child's life is in danger—regardless of the child's or parent's religious beliefs. When public safety is an issue, an individual's religious beliefs often have to give way to the government's interests in protecting the public. **EXAMPLE 2.11** According to the Muslim faith, it is a religious violation for a woman to appear in public without a scarf, known as a *hijab*, over her head. Due to public safety concerns, many courts today do not allow the wearing of any headgear (hats or scarves) in courtrooms. In 2008, a Muslim woman was prevented from entering a courthouse with her husband in Douglasville, Georgia, because she refused to remove her scarf. As she left, she uttered an expletive at the court official and was arrested and brought before the judge, who ordered her to serve ten days in jail. Similar incidents have occurred in other states. ●

According to the United States Supreme Court, the free exercise clause protects the use of a controlled substance in the practice of a sincerely held religious belief. **CASE EXAMPLE 2.12** A religious sect in New Mexico follows the practices of a Brazil-based church. Its members ingest hoasca tea as part of a ritual to connect with and better understand God. Hoasca tea, which is brewed from plants native to the Amazon rain forest, contains an illegal hallucinogenic drug, dimethyltryptamine (DMT), that is regulated by the federal Controlled Substances Act. When federal drug agents confiscated the church's shipment of hoasca tea as it entered the country, the church members filed a lawsuit claiming that the confiscation violated their right to freely exercise their religion. Ultimately, the Supreme Court agreed, ruling that the government had failed to demonstrate a sufficiently compelling interest in barring the sect's sacramental use of hoasca. In short, the Supreme Court will allow the use of illegal hallucinogenic drugs as a religious practice but will not sanction the use of marijuana for medical purposes.[30] ●

---

30. *Gonzales v. O Centro Espirita Beneficente Uniao Do Vegetal,* 546 U.S. 418, 126 S.Ct. 1211, 163 L.Ed.2d 1017 (2006).

Due Process and Equal Protection

Two other constitutional guarantees of great significance to Americans are mandated by the due process clauses of the Fifth and Fourteenth Amendments and the equal protection clause of the Fourteenth Amendment.

Due Process

Both the Fifth and the Fourteenth Amendments provide that no person shall be deprived "of life, liberty, or property, without due process of law." The **due process clause** of each of these constitutional amendments has two aspects—procedural and substantive. Note that the due process clause applies to "legal persons," such as corporations, as well as to individuals.

Due Process Clause The provisions in the Fifth and Fourteenth Amendments to the U.S. Constitution that guarantee that no person shall be deprived of life, liberty, or property without due process of law. Similar clauses are found in most state constitutions.

PROCEDURAL DUE PROCESS Procedural due process requires that any government decision to take life, liberty, or property must be made fairly; that is, the government must give a person proper notice and an opportunity to be heard. Fair procedures must be used in determining whether a person will be subjected to punishment or have some burden imposed on him or her. Fair procedure has been interpreted as requiring that the person have at least an opportunity to object to a proposed action before a fair, neutral decision maker (who need not be a judge). **EXAMPLE 2.13** In most states, a driver's license is construed as a property interest. Therefore, the state must provide some sort of opportunity for the driver to object before suspending or terminating the person's license. ●

Preventing Legal Disputes

Many of the constitutional protections discussed in this chapter have become part of our culture in the United States. Due process, especially procedural due process, has become synonymous with what Americans consider "fair." For this reason, if you wish to avoid legal disputes, you should consider giving due process to anyone who might object to some of your business decisions or actions, whether that person is an employee, a partner, an affiliate, or a customer. For instance, giving ample notice of new policies to all affected persons is a prudent move, as is giving them at least an opportunity to express their opinions on the matter. Providing an opportunity to be heard is often the ideal way to make people feel that they are being treated fairly. People are less likely to sue a businessperson or firm that they believe is fair and listens to both sides of an issue.

SUBSTANTIVE DUE PROCESS Substantive due process protects an individual's life, liberty, or property against certain government actions regardless of the fairness of the procedures used to implement them. Substantive due process limits what the government may do in its legislative and executive capacities. Legislation must be fair and reasonable in content and must further a legitimate governmental objective. Only when state conduct is arbitrary or shocks the conscience, however, will it rise to the level of violating substantive due process.

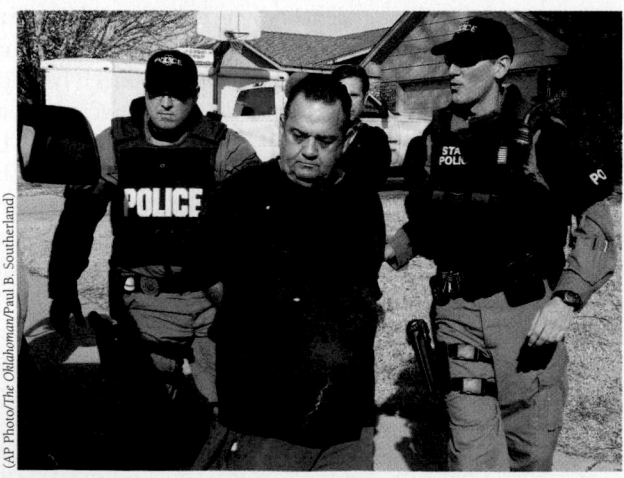

These Oklahoma police officers arrest a suspect on drug-related charges. If this person wants to challenge his arrest and incarceration on substantive due process grounds, how might he proceed? Why might he have a better chance of prevailing if he challenges his arrest on procedural due process grounds instead?

(AP Photo/*The Oklahoman*/Paul B. Southerland)

"Our Constitution protects aliens, drunks, and U.S. senators."

Will Rogers, 1879–1935
(American humorist)

Equal Protection Clause The provision in the Fourteenth Amendment to the U.S. Constitution that guarantees that no state will "deny to any person within its jurisdiction the equal protection of the laws." This clause mandates that the state governments must treat similarly situated individuals in a similar manner.

The city of Portland, Oregon, passed an anti-camping ordinance to rid itself of homeless camps like the one under this city bridge. Could the homeless argue that the city ordinance violated their substantial due process rights, including the right to shelter?

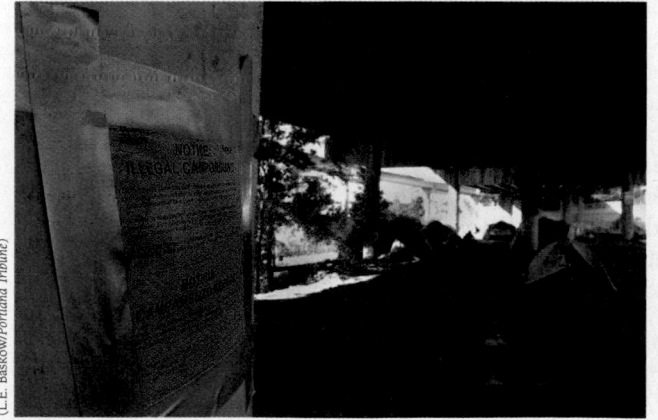

(L.E. Baskow/Portland Tribune)

If a law or other governmental action limits a fundamental right, it will be held to violate substantive due process unless it promotes a compelling or overriding state interest. Fundamental rights include interstate travel, privacy, voting, marriage and family, and all First Amendment rights. Thus, a state must have a substantial reason for taking any action that infringes on a person's free speech rights. In situations not involving fundamental rights, a law or action does not violate substantive due process if it rationally relates to any legitimate governmental end. It is almost impossible for a law or action to fail the "rationality" test. Under this test, almost any government regulation of business will be upheld as reasonable.

Equal Protection

Under the Fourteenth Amendment, a state may not "deny to any person within its jurisdiction the equal protection of the laws." The United States Supreme Court has used the due process clause of the Fifth Amendment to make the **equal protection clause** applicable to the federal government as well. Equal protection means that the government must treat similarly situated individuals in a similar manner.

Both substantive due process and equal protection require review of the substance of the law or other governmental action rather than review of the procedures used. When a law or action limits the liberty of all persons to do something, it may violate substantive due process; when a law or action limits the liberty of some persons but not others, it may violate the equal protection clause. **EXAMPLE 2.14** If a law prohibits all advertising on the sides of trucks, it raises a substantive due process question; if it makes an exception to allow truck owners to advertise their own businesses, it raises an equal protection issue. •

In an equal protection inquiry, when a law or action distinguishes between or among individuals, the basis for the distinction—that is, the classification—is examined. Depending on the classification, the courts apply different levels of scrutiny, or "tests," to determine whether the law or action violates the equal protection clause. The courts use one of three standards: strict scrutiny, intermediate scrutiny, or the "rational basis" test.

STRICT SCRUTINY If a law or action prohibits or inhibits some persons from exercising a fundamental right, the law or action will be subject to "strict scrutiny" by the courts. Under this standard, the classification must be necessary to promote a *compelling state interest.* Also, if the classification is based on a *suspect trait*—such as race, national origin, or citizenship status—it must be necessary to promote a compelling government interest. Compelling state interests include remedying past unconstitutional or illegal discrimination, but do not include correcting the general effects of "society's discrimination." **EXAMPLE 2.15** For a city to give preference to minority applicants in awarding construction contracts, it normally must identify past unconstitutional or illegal discrimination against minority construction firms. Because the policy is based on suspect traits (race and national origin), it will violate the equal protection clause *unless* it is necessary to promote a compelling state interest. • Generally, few laws or actions survive strict-scrutiny analysis by the courts.

INTERMEDIATE SCRUTINY Another standard, that of "intermediate scrutiny," is applied in cases involving discrimination based on gender or legitimacy. Laws using these classifications must be *substantially related to important government objectives.* **EXAMPLE 2.16** An important government objective is preventing illegitimate teenage pregnancies. Because males and females are not similarly situated in this regard—only females can become pregnant—a law that punishes men but not women for statutory rape will be upheld even though it treats men and women unequally. ●

The state also has an important objective in establishing time limits (called *statutes of limitation*) for how long after an event a particular type of action can be brought. Nevertheless, the limitation period must be substantially related to the important objective of preventing fraudulent or outdated claims. **EXAMPLE 2.17** A state law requires illegitimate children to bring paternity suits within six years of their births in order to seek support from their fathers. A court will strike down this law if legitimate children are allowed to seek support from their parents at any time because distinguishing between support claims on the basis of legitimacy is not related to the important government objective of preventing fraudulent or outdated claims. ●

THE "RATIONAL BASIS" TEST   In matters of economic and social welfare, a classification will be considered valid if there is any conceivable "rational basis" on which the classification might relate to a *legitimate government interest.* It is almost impossible for a law or action to fail the rational basis test. **EXAMPLE 2.18** A city ordinance that in effect prohibits all pushcart vendors, except a specific few, from operating in a particular area of the city will be upheld if the city offers a rational basis—such as reducing traffic in that area—for the ordinance. In contrast, a law that provides unemployment benefits only to people over six feet tall would clearly fail the rational basis test because it could not further any legitimate government interest. ●

▶ Privacy Rights

In the past, privacy issues typically related to personal information that government agencies, including the Federal Bureau of Investigation, might obtain and keep about an individual. Later, concerns about what banks and insurance companies might know and transmit to others about individuals became an issue. Since the 1990s, one of the major concerns of individuals has been how to protect privacy rights in cyberspace and how to safeguard private information that may be revealed online (including credit-card numbers and financial information). The increasing value of personal information for online marketers—who are willing to pay a high price for such information to those who collect it—has exacerbated the situation. (See the *Business Application* feature at the end of this chapter for further discussion of the collection of personal information by businesses.)

Today, individuals face additional concerns about government intrusions into their privacy. The USA Patriot Act was passed by Congress in the wake of the terrorist attacks of September 11, 2001, and then reauthorized in 2006.[31] The Patriot Act has given increased authority to government officials to monitor Internet activities (such as e-mail and Web site visits) and to gain access to personal financial data and student information. Using technology, law enforcement officials can track the telephone and e-mail conversations of one party to find out the identity of the other party or parties. The government must certify that the information likely to be obtained is relevant to an ongoing criminal investigation, but it does not have to provide proof of any wrongdoing to gain access to this information. Privacy advocates argue that this law has adversely affected the constitutional rights of all Americans, and it has been widely criticized in the media.

In this section, we look at the protection of privacy rights under the U.S. Constitution and various federal statutes. Note that state constitutions and statutes also protect individuals' pri-

ON THE WEB The Patriot Reauthorization Act required the U.S. Department of Justice to periodically provide special reports to Congress on the implementation of the USA Patriot Act and the number of complaints the department has received. You can read these reports at www.usdoj.gov/oig/special/index.htm.

"There was, of course, no way of knowing whether you were being watched at any given moment."

George Orwell, 1903–1950
(Author, from his famous novel *1984*)

---

31. The Uniting and Strengthening America by Providing Appropriate Tools Required to Intercept and Obstruct Terrorism Act of 2001, also known as the USA Patriot Act, was enacted as Pub. L. No. 107-56 (2001) and reauthorized by Pub. L. No. 109-173 (2006).

vacy rights, often to a significant degree. Privacy rights are also protected to an extent under tort law (see Chapter 4), consumer law (see Chapter 33), and employment law (see Chapter 24).

Ethical Issue ⚖

> **Does the threat of terrorism justify the U.S. government's invasion of its citizens' privacy?**
> Since the USA Patriot Act was enacted, the National Security Agency (NSA) has engaged in domestic surveillance and monitoring activities that have been highly controversial. Critics claim that these activities endanger numerous constitutionally protected freedoms, such as the right to privacy and the right to be free from unreasonable searches (under the Fourth Amendment). In December 2005, government sources leaked that President George W. Bush had authorized the NSA to secretly intercept phone calls between U.S. citizens and suspected terrorists abroad—without first obtaining a warrant as would be required even under the Patriot Act. Although eavesdropping on phone calls and monitoring e-mails are certainly powerful tools for tracking down terrorists, they are also the kind of activities that the framers of the Constitution sought to curtail.
>
> Some claim that the government's intrusion into our private communications is warranted because the government is looking only for those "bad" people who interact with terrorists. If the government can monitor what any person views or searches for on the Internet, however, are anyone's Internet activities really private? To illustrate, consider what happened in August 2006, when America Online (AOL) released randomly selected user search log data from 658,000 subscribers. AOL's intention was to benefit researchers at universities and small businesses that normally would not have access to this type of data. To protect subscribers' privacy, the data identified users by numbers rather than by names. As it turned out, though, an individual's identity could be tracked down using various bits of information. All search engines compile this type of user data, which can be valuable for marketing purposes. Such data can also be invaluable to government law enforcement. For example, searches for "how to make homemade bombs" or "biological weapons" *might* indicate a propensity for terrorist activities. But what happens if government monitors find that a person has searched for "underground kiddy porn pictures" or "how to make meth"? Should law enforcement officials ignore information found online about illegal activities unrelated to terrorism?

Constitutional Protection of Privacy Rights

The U.S. Constitution does not explicitly mention a general right to privacy. In a 1928 Supreme Court case, *Olmstead v. United States*,[32] Justice Louis Brandeis stated in his dissent that the right to privacy is "the most comprehensive of rights and the right most valued by civilized men." At that time, the majority of the justices did not agree, and it was not until the 1960s that a majority on the Supreme Court endorsed the view that the Constitution protects individual privacy rights.

In a landmark 1965 case, *Griswold v. Connecticut*,[33] the Supreme Court invalidated a Connecticut law that effectively prohibited the use of contraceptives. The Court held that the law violated the right to privacy. Justice William O. Douglas formulated a unique way of reading this right into the Bill of Rights. He claimed that "emanations" from the rights guaranteed by the First, Third, Fourth, Fifth, and Ninth Amendments formed and gave "life and substance" to "penumbras" (partial shadows) around these guaranteed rights. These penumbras included an implied constitutional right to privacy.

When we read these amendments, we can see the foundation for Justice Douglas's reasoning. Consider the Fourth Amendment. By prohibiting unreasonable searches and seizures, the amendment effectively protects individuals' privacy. Consider also the words of the Ninth Amendment: "The enumeration in the Constitution of certain rights, shall

> *"There is nothing new in the realization that the Constitution sometimes insulates the criminality of a few in order to protect the privacy of us all."*
>
> Antonin Scalia, 1936–present
> (United States Supreme Court justice, 1986–present)

---

32. 277 U.S. 438, 48 S.Ct. 564, 72 L.Ed. 944 (1928).
33. 381 U.S. 479, 85 S.Ct. 1678, 14 L.Ed.2d 510 (1965).

> *"The things most people want to know about are usually none of their business."*
>
> George Bernard Shaw, 1856–1950
> (Irish dramatist and socialist)

not be construed to deny or disparage others retained by the people." In other words, just because the Constitution, including its amendments, does not specifically mention the right to privacy does not mean that this right is denied to the people. Indeed, many people today consider privacy one of the most important rights guaranteed by the U.S. Constitution.

Federal Statutes Protecting Privacy Rights

In the last several decades, Congress has enacted a number of statutes that protect the privacy of individuals in various areas of concern. In the 1960s, Americans were sufficiently alarmed by the accumulation of personal information in government files that they pressured Congress to pass laws permitting individuals to access their files. Congress responded in 1966 with the Freedom of Information Act, which allows any person to request copies of any information on her or him contained in federal government files. In 1974, Congress passed the Privacy Act, which also gives persons the right to access such information. These and other major federal laws protecting privacy rights are listed and described in Exhibit 2–1.

Responding to the growing need to protect the privacy of individuals' health records—particularly computerized records—Congress passed the Health Insurance Portability and

● *Exhibit* **2–1** Federal Legislation Relating to Privacy

TITLE	PROVISIONS CONCERNING PRIVACY
Freedom of Information Act (1966)	Provides that individuals have a right to obtain access to information about them collected in government files.
Family and Educational Rights and Privacy Act (1974)	Limits access to computer-stored records of education-related evaluations and grades in private and public colleges and universities.
Privacy Act (1974)	Protects the privacy of individuals about whom the federal government has information. Under this act, agencies that use or disclose personal information must make sure that the information is reliable and guard against its misuse. Individuals must be able to find out what data concerning them the agency is compiling and how the data will be used. In addition, the agency must give individuals a means to correct inaccurate data and must obtain their consent before using the data for any other purpose.
Tax Reform Act (1976)	Preserves the privacy of personal financial information.
Right to Financial Privacy Act (1978)	Prohibits financial institutions from providing the federal government with access to a customer's records unless the customer authorizes the disclosure.
Electronic Communications Privacy Act (1986)	Prohibits the interception of information communicated by electronic means.
Driver's Privacy Protection Act (1994)	Prevents states from disclosing or selling a driver's personal information without the driver's consent.
Health Insurance Portability and Accountability Act (1996)	Prohibits the use of a consumer's medical information for any purpose other than that for which such information was provided, unless the consumer expressly consents to the use.
Financial Services Modernization Act (Gramm-Leach-Bliley Act) (1999)	Prohibits the disclosure of nonpublic personal information about a consumer to an unaffiliated third party unless strict disclosure and opt-out requirements are met.

The Health Insurance Portability and Accountability Act (HIPAA) requires that medical records be kept private under most circumstances. This physician's office created higher countertops to prevent others from viewing private records. Under HIPAA, the federal government can levy fines of up to $250,000 for violations of the act.

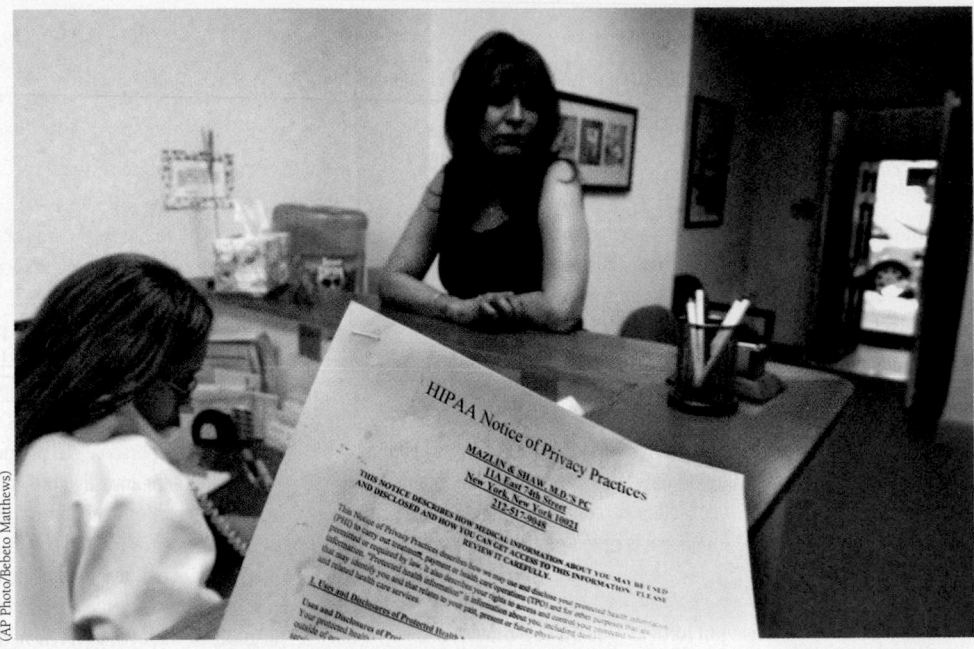

(AP Photo/Bebeto Matthews)

Accountability Act (HIPAA) of 1996.[34] This act defines and limits the circumstances in which an individual's "protected health information" may be used or disclosed.

HIPAA requires health-care providers and health-care plans, including certain employers who sponsor health plans, to inform patients of their privacy rights and of how their personal medical information may be used. The act also generally states that a person's medical records may not be used for purposes unrelated to health care—such as marketing—or disclosed to others without the individual's permission. In 2009, Congress expanded HIPAA provisions to apply to *vendors* (who maintain personal health records for health-care providers) and to electronic records shared by multiple medical providers. Congress also authorized the Federal Trade Commission to enforce HIPAA and pursue violators.[35]

---

34. HIPAA was enacted as Pub. L. No. 104-191 (1996) and is codified in 29 U.S.C.A. Sections 1181 *et seq.*
35. These provisions were part of the American Recovery and Reinvestment Act (ARRA) of 2009, popularly known as the stimulus law. See 45 C.F.R. Sections 164.510 and 164.512(f)(2).

 Reviewing . . . Constitutional Law

A state legislature enacted a statute that required any motorcycle operator or passenger on the state's highways to wear a protective helmet. Jim Alderman, a licensed motorcycle operator, sued the state to block enforcement of the law. Alderman asserted that the statute violated the equal protection clause because it placed requirements on motorcyclists that were not imposed on other motorists. Using the information presented in the chapter, answer the following questions.

1. Why does this statute raise equal protection issues instead of substantive due process concerns?
2. What are the three levels of scrutiny that the courts use in determining whether a law violates the equal protection clause?
3. Which standard, or test, of scrutiny would apply to this situation? Why?
4. Applying this standard, or test, is the helmet statute constitutional? Why or why not?

Business Application

Is "Pretexting" Illegal?*

Almost all businesses, institutions, and organizations gather information from and about their customers, constituents, or members. Many businesses also want information about potential customers. In all probability, these individuals are already on the mailing list of some business or other organization. Unless the owner of the list has a privacy policy that prohibits the sharing of certain information without the person's consent, a business may purchase the list and proceed to offer its product or service to all the people on it. Locating potential customers in this manner may be completely legal, depending on how the information was obtained in the first place. One method of collecting personal information that skirts the boundary between legal and illegal is called pretexting.

What Is "Pretexting"?

A *pretext* is a false motive put forth to hide the real motive, and *pretexting* is the process of obtaining information by false means. The term *pretexting* was first used in the 1990s to describe a scam in which pretexters obtained Social Security numbers by claiming that they were from the Social Security Administration and that their computer had broken down. Today, pretexters may try to obtain personal data by claiming that they are taking a survey for a research firm, a political party, or even a charity. Then they proceed to ask for information such as the person's insurance or telephone company, where he or she banks, and perhaps the name of his or her broker. They may even ask the names of household pets because these are often used as passwords for online financial accounts.

Once they obtain the information, the pretexters sell it to a data broker. The data broker in turn sells the information to someone else, who may be a legitimate businessperson looking for information on potential customers, an investigator working for a client in a divorce case, or an individual intent on identity theft.

Is Pretexting Illegal?

In 1999, Congress passed the Gramm-Leach-Bliley Act, which made pretexting to obtain financial information illegal. Initially, it was not clear whether that law prohibited lying to obtain *nonfinancial* information for purposes other than identity theft. After the media reported that a blogger

paid $89.95 to obtain records of cell phone calls made by retired general Wesley Clark and that phone records were for sale on the Internet, Congress held hearings.

Also fueling the debate over pretexting was a scandal involving Hewlett-Packard's board of directors. To find out who had leaked confidential company information to the press, Hewlett-Packard chair, Patricia C. Dunn, hired private investigators who used false pretenses to gain access to individuals' personal cell phone records. Dunn claimed that she was not aware of the investigators' methods and had assumed that they had obtained the information from public records. Although she was indicted in 2006 for her role in the pretexting, the criminal charges were later dropped. Several civil lawsuits followed. In 2007, the company paid $14.5 million in fines to settle a lawsuit filed by the California attorney general. In 2008, Hewlett-Packard reached a settlement with the New York Times Company and three *BusinessWeek* magazine journalists in connection with the scandal.

To clarify the law on pretexting to gain access to phone records, Congress enacted the Telephone Records and Privacy Protection Act. This act makes it a federal crime to pretend to be someone else or to make false representations for the purpose of obtaining another person's confidential phone records. The act also prohibits the buying, selling, transferring, or receiving of such phone records without the phone owner's permission. The Federal Trade Commission investigates and prosecutes violators, who can be fined and sentenced to up to ten years in prison.

CHECKLIST FOR PROVIDING OR SECURING CUSTOMER INFORMATION

1. **Make sure that your company has a privacy policy. If it does not, one should be created.**
2. **Never provide a third party with information unless your company's privacy policy specifically allows you to do so.**
3. **If you wish to acquire personal information on potential customers from a third party, make sure the data broker is legitimate, and find out how the information was acquired.**
4. **Treat all pretexting as illegal.**

*This *Business Application* is not meant to substitute for the services of an attorney who is licensed to practice law in your state.

 Key Terms

Bill of Rights 37
checks and balances 33
commerce clause 33
due process clause 46
equal protection clause 47

establishment clause 43
federal form of government 33
filtering software 42
free exercise clause 43
meta tag 42

police powers 36
preemption 37
supremacy clause 37
symbolic speech 39

Chapter Summary: Constitutional Law

The Constitutional Powers of Government (See pages 32–33.)	The U.S. Constitution established a federal form of government, in which government powers are shared by the national government and the state governments. At the national level, government powers are divided among the legislative, executive, and judicial branches.
The Commerce Clause (See pages 33–37.)	1. *The expansion of national powers*—The commerce clause expressly permits Congress to regulate commerce. Over time, courts expansively interpreted this clause, thereby enabling the national government to wield extensive powers over the economic life of the nation. 2. *The commerce power today*—Today, the commerce power authorizes the national government, at least theoretically, to regulate every commercial enterprise in the United States. In recent years, the Supreme Court has reined in somewhat the national government's regulatory powers under the commerce clause. 3. *The regulatory powers of the states*—The Tenth Amendment reserves to the states all powers not expressly delegated to the national government. Under their police powers, state governments may regulate private activities in order to protect or promote the public order, health, safety, morals, and general welfare. 4. *The "dormant" commerce clause*—If state regulations substantially interfere with interstate commerce, they will be held to violate the "dormant" commerce clause of the U.S. Constitution. The positive aspect of the commerce clause, which gives the national government the exclusive authority to regulate interstate commerce, implies a "dormant" aspect—that the states do *not* have this power.
The Supremacy Clause (See page 37.)	The U.S. Constitution provides that the Constitution, laws, and treaties of the United States are "the supreme Law of the Land." Whenever a state law directly conflicts with a federal law, the state law is rendered invalid.
Business and the Bill of Rights (See pages 37–45.)	The Bill of Rights, which consists of the first ten amendments to the U.S. Constitution, was adopted in 1791 and embodies a series of protections for individuals—and, in some instances, business entities—against various types of interference by the federal government. Today, most of the protections apply against state governments as well. Freedoms guaranteed by the First Amendment that affect businesses include the following: 1. *Freedom of speech*—Speech, including symbolic speech, is given the fullest possible protection by the courts. Corporate political speech and commercial speech also receive substantial protection under the First Amendment. Certain types of speech, such as defamatory speech and lewd or obscene speech, are not protected under the First Amendment. Government attempts to regulate unprotected forms of speech in the online environment have, to date, met with numerous challenges. 2. *Freedom of religion*—Under the First Amendment, the government may neither establish any religion (the establishment clause) nor prohibit the free exercise of religion (the free exercise clause).
Due Process and Equal Protection (See pages 46–48.)	1. *Due process*—Both the Fifth and the Fourteenth Amendments provide that no person shall be deprived of "life, liberty, or property, without due process of law." Procedural due process requires that any government decision to take life, liberty, or property must be made fairly, using fair procedures. Substantive due process focuses on the content of legislation. Generally, a law that limits a fundamental right violates substantive due process unless the law promotes a compelling state interest, such as public safety. 2. *Equal protection*—Under the Fourteenth Amendment, a law or action that limits the liberty of some persons but not others may violate the equal protection clause. Such a law may be deemed valid, however, if there is a rational basis for the discriminatory treatment of a given group or if the law substantially relates to an important government objective.
Privacy Rights (See pages 48–51.)	Americans are increasingly becoming concerned about privacy issues raised by Internet-related technology. The Constitution does not contain a specific guarantee of a right to privacy, but such a right has been derived from guarantees found in several constitutional amendments. A number of federal statutes protect privacy rights. Privacy rights are also protected by many state constitutions and statutes, as well as under tort law.

ExamPrep

ISSUE SPOTTERS

1 Can a state, in the interest of energy conservation, ban all advertising by power utilities if conservation could be accomplished by less restrictive means? Why or why not?

2 Would it be a violation of equal protection for a state to impose a higher tax on out-of-state companies doing business in the state than it imposes on in-state companies if the only reason for the tax is to protect the local firms from out-of-state competition? Explain.

BEFORE THE TEST

Check your answers to the Issue Spotters, and at the same time, take the interactive quiz for this chapter. Go to **www.cengage.com/blaw/blt** and click on "Chapter 2." First, click on "Answers to Issue Spotters" to check your answers. Next, click on "Interactive Quiz" to assess your mastery of the concepts in this chapter. Then click on "Flashcards" to review this chapter's Key Term definitions.

 For Review

Answers for the even-numbered questions in this **For Review** *section can be found on this text's accompanying Web site at* **www.cengage.com/blaw/blt**. *Select "Chapter 2" and click on "For Review."*

1 What is the basic structure of the U.S. government?

2 What constitutional clause gives the federal government the power to regulate commercial activities among the various states?

3 What constitutional clause allows laws enacted by the federal government to take priority over conflicting state laws?

4 What is the Bill of Rights? What freedoms does the First Amendment guarantee?

5 Where in the Constitution can the due process clause be found?

 Hypothetical Scenarios and Case Problems

2–1 Commercial Speech. A mayoral election is about to be held in a large U.S. city. One of the candidates is Luis Delgado, and his campaign supporters wish to post campaign signs on lampposts and utility poles throughout the city. A city ordinance, however, prohibits the posting of any signs on public property. Delgado's supporters contend that the city ordinance is unconstitutional because it violates their rights to free speech. What factors might a court consider in determining the constitutionality of this ordinance?

2–2 **Hypothetical Question with Sample Answer** Thomas worked in the nonmilitary operations of a large firm that produced both military and nonmilitary goods. When the company discontinued the production of nonmilitary goods, Thomas was transferred to the plant producing military equipment. Thomas left his job, claiming that it violated his religious principles to participate in the manufacture of goods to be used in destroying life. In effect, he argued, the transfer to the military equipment plant forced him to quit his job. He was denied unemployment compensation by the state because he had not been effectively "discharged" by the employer but had voluntarily terminated his employment. Did the state's denial of unemployment benefits to Thomas violate the free exercise clause of the First Amendment? Explain.

—**For a sample answer to Question 2–2, go to Appendix E at the end of this text.**

2–3 Commerce Clause. Suppose that Georgia enacts a law requiring the use of contoured rear-fender mudguards on trucks and trailers operating within its state lines. The statute further makes it illegal for trucks and trailers to use straight mudguards. In thirty-five other states, straight mudguards are legal. Moreover, in the neighboring state of Florida, straight mudguards are explicitly required by law. There is some evidence suggesting that contoured mudguards might be a little safer than straight mudguards. Discuss whether this Georgia statute would violate the commerce clause of the U.S. Constitution.

2–4 Freedom of Religion. A business has a backlog of orders, and to meet its deadlines, management decides to run the firm seven days a week, eight hours a day. One of the employees, Marjorie Tollens, refuses to work on Saturday on religious grounds. Her refusal to work means that the firm may not meet its production deadlines and may therefore suffer a loss of future business. The firm fires Tollens and replaces her with an employee who is willing to work seven days a week. Tollens claims that in terminating her employment, her employer violated her constitutional right to the free exercise of her religion. Do you agree? Why or why not?

2–5 Equal Protection. With the objectives of preventing crime, maintaining property values, and preserving the quality of urban life, New York City enacted an ordinance to regulate the locations of commercial establishments that featured adult entertainment. The ordinance expressly applied to female, but not male, topless entertainment. Adele Buzzetti owned the Cozy Cabin, a New York City cabaret that featured female topless dancers. Buzzetti and an anonymous dancer filed a suit in a federal district court against the city, asking the court to block the enforcement of the ordinance. The plaintiffs argued, in part, that the ordinance violated the equal protection clause. Under the equal protection clause, what standard applies to the court's consideration of this ordinance? Under this test, how should the court rule? Why?

2–6 Case Problem with Sample Answer To protect the privacy of individuals identified in information systems maintained by federal agencies, the Privacy Act of 1974 regulates the use of the information. The statute provides for a minimum award of $1,000 to the "person entitled to recovery" for "actual damages sustained" caused by "intentional or willful actions." Buck Doe filed for certain disability benefits with an office of the U.S. Department of Labor (DOL). The application form asked for Doe's Social Security number, which the DOL used to identify his claim on documents sent to groups of claimants, their employers, and the lawyers involved in their cases. This disclosed Doe's Social Security number beyond the limits set by the Privacy Act. Doe filed a suit in a federal district court against the DOL, alleging that he was "torn * * * all to pieces" and "greatly concerned and worried" because of the disclosure of his Social Security number and its potentially "devastating" consequences. He did not offer any proof of actual injury, however. Should damages be awarded in such circumstances solely on the basis of the agency's conduct, or should proof of some actual injury be required? Why? [*Doe v. Chao,* 540 U.S. 614, 124 S.Ct. 1204, 157 L.Ed.2d 1122 (2004)]

—**After you have answered Problem 2–6, compare your answer with the sample answer given on the Web site that accompanies this text. Go to www.cengage.com/blaw/ blt, select "Chapter 2," and click on "Case Problem with Sample Answer."**

2–7 Supremacy Clause. The Federal Communications Act of 1934 grants the right to govern all *interstate* telecommunications to the Federal Communications Commission (FCC) and the right to regulate all *intrastate* telecommunications to the states. The federal Telephone Consumer Protection Act of 1991, the Junk Fax Protection Act of 2005, and FCC rules permit a party to send unsolicited fax ads to recipients with whom they have an "established business relationship" if those ads include an "opt-out" alternative. Section 17538.43 of California's Business and Professions Code (known as "SB 833") was enacted in 2005 to provide the citizens of California with greater protection than that afforded under federal law. SB 833 omits the "established business relationship" exception and requires a sender to obtain a recipient's express consent (or "opt-in") before faxing an ad to that party. The rule applies whether the sender is located in California or outside that state. The Chamber of Commerce of the United States filed a suit against Bill Lockyer, California's state attorney general, seeking to block the enforcement of SB 833. What principles support the plaintiff's position? How should the court resolve the issue? Explain. [*Chamber of Commerce of the United States. v. Lockyer,* 463 F.3d 1076 (9th Cir. 2006)]

2–8 Freedom of Speech. For decades, New York City has had to deal with the vandalism and defacement of public property caused by unauthorized graffiti. Among other attempts to stop the damage, in December 2005 the city banned the sale of aerosol spray-paint cans and broad-tipped indelible markers to persons under twenty-one years of age and prohibited them from possessing such items on property other than their own. By May 1, 2006, five people—all under age twenty-one—had been cited for violations of these regulations, while 871 individuals had been arrested for actually making graffiti. Artists who wished to create graffiti on legal surfaces, such as canvas, wood, and clothing, included college student Lindsey Vincenty, who was studying visual arts. Unable to buy her supplies in the city or to carry them in the city if she bought them elsewhere, Vincenty and others filed a suit in a federal district court on behalf of themselves and other young artists against Michael Bloomberg, the city's mayor, and others. The plaintiffs claimed that, among other things, the new rules violated their right to freedom of speech. They asked the court to enjoin the rules' enforcement. Should the court grant this request? Why or why not? [*Vincenty v. Bloomberg,* 476 F.3d 74 (2d Cir. 2007)]

2–9 Due Process. In 2006, the Russ College of Engineering and Technology of Ohio University announced that an investigation had found "rampant and flagrant plagiarism" in the theses of mechanical engineering graduate students. Faculty singled out for "ignoring their ethical responsibilities and contributing to an atmosphere of negligence toward issues of academic misconduct" included Jay Gunasekera, professor of mechanical engineering and chair of the department. These findings were publicized in a press conference. The university then prohibited Gunasekera from advising graduate students. He filed a suit in a federal district court against Dennis Irwin, the dean of Russ College, and others, for violating his "due-process rights when they publicized accusations about his role in plagiarism by his graduate student advisees without providing him with a meaningful opportunity to clear his name" in public. Irwin asked the court to dismiss the suit. What does due process require in these circumstances? Why? [*Gunasekera v. Irwin,* 551 F.3d 461 (6th Cir. 2009)]

2–10 A Question of Ethics *Aric Toll owns and manages the Balboa Island Village Inn, a restaurant and bar in Newport Beach, California. Anne Lemen owns the "Island Cottage," a residence across an alley from the inn. Lemen often complained to the authorities about excessive noise and the behavior of the inn's customers, whom she called "drunks" and "whores." Lemen referred to Theresa Toll, Aric's wife, as "Madam Whore." Lemen told the inn's bartender Ewa Cook that Cook "worked for Satan," was "Satan's wife," and was "going to have Satan's children." She told the inn's neighbors that it was "a whorehouse" with "prostitution going on inside" and that it sold illegal drugs, sold alcohol to minors, made* *"sex videos," was involved in child pornography, had "Mafia connections," encouraged "lesbian activity," and stayed open until 6:00 A.M. Lemen also voiced her complaints to potential customers, and the inn's sales dropped more than 20 percent. The inn filed a suit in a California state court against Lemen, asserting defamation and other claims. [Balboa Island Village Inn, Inc. v. Lemen, 40 Cal.4th 1141, 156 P.3d 339 (2007)]*

1 Are Lemen's statements about the inn's owners, customers, and activities protected by the U.S. Constitution? Should such statements be protected? In whose favor should the court rule? Why?

2 Did Lemen behave unethically in the circumstances of this case? Explain.

 ## Critical Thinking and Writing Assignments

2–11 Critical Legal Thinking. Do you think that the threat of terrorism in the United States justifies the imposition of limits on the right to privacy? Generally, in the wake of the September 11, 2001, terrorist attacks, should Americans allow the federal government to listen to their phone calls and monitor their e-mails and Internet activity?

2–12 Critical Thinking and Writing Assignment for Business. The commerce clause, as originally interpreted by the United States Supreme Court, was thought to allow the federal government to regulate interstate commerce. Over time, however, the Supreme Court has made it clear that the commerce clause applies not only to interstate commerce, but also to commerce that is purely intrastate. Today, the federal government has the power to regulate every commercial enterprise in the United States. What does this mean for commercial businesses that operate only within the borders of one state? Does it promote or discourage intrastate commerce?

Practical Internet Exercises

Go to this text's Web site at **www.cengage.com/blaw/blt**, select "Chapter 2," and click on "Practical Internet Exercises." There you will find the following Internet research exercises that you can perform to learn more about the topics covered in this chapter.

Practical Internet Exercise 2–1: LEGAL PERSPECTIVE—Commercial Speech
Practical Internet Exercise 2–2: MANAGEMENT PERSPECTIVE—Privacy Rights in Cyberspace

Chapter 3

Courts and Alternative Dispute Resolution

"An eye for an eye will make the whole world blind."

—Mahatma Gandhi, 1869–1948
(Indian political and spiritual leader)

(© Moodboard Micro/Corbis)

Learning Objectives

After reading this chapter, you should be able to answer the following questions:

1. What is judicial review? How and when was the power of judicial review established?

2. Before a court can hear a case, it must have jurisdiction. Over what must it have jurisdiction? How are the courts applying traditional jurisdictional concepts to cases involving Internet transactions?

3. What is the difference between a trial court and an apellate court?

4. What is discovery, and how does electronic discovery differ from traditional discovery?

5. What are three alternative methods of resolving disputes?

Every society needs to have an established method for resolving disputes. Without one, as Mahatma Gandhi implied in the chapter-opening quotation, the biblical "eye for an eye" would lead to anarchy. This is particularly true in the business world—nearly every businessperson will face a lawsuit at some time in his or her career. For this reason, anyone involved in business needs to have an understanding of court systems in the United States, as well as the various methods of dispute resolution that can be pursued outside the courts.

In this chapter, after examining the judiciary's overall role in the American governmental scheme, we discuss some basic requirements that must be met before a party may bring a lawsuit before a particular court. We then look at the court systems of the United States in some detail and, to clarify judicial procedures, follow a hypothetical case through a state court system. Throughout this chapter, we indicate how court doctrines and procedures are being adapted to the needs of a cyber age. The chapter concludes with an overview of some alternative methods of settling disputes, including online dispute resolution.

▶ The Judiciary's Role in American Government

As you learned in Chapter 1, the body of American law includes the federal and state constitutions, statutes passed by legislative bodies, administrative law, and the case decisions and legal principles that form the common law. These laws would be meaningless, however,

(AP Photo/Nati Harnik)

The head of Nebraska's highest court delivers his State of the Judiciary address to that state's lawmakers. What is the main duty of the judiciary in the American governmental system?

Judicial Review   The process by which a court decides on the constitutionality of legislative enactments and actions of the executive branch.

Jurisdiction   The authority of a court to hear and decide a specific case.

without the courts to interpret and apply them. This is the essential role of the judiciary—the courts—in the American governmental system: to interpret and apply the law.

Judicial Review

As the branch of government entrusted with interpreting the laws, the judiciary can decide, among other things, whether the laws or actions of the other two branches are constitutional. The process for making such a determination is known as **judicial review**. The power of judicial review enables the judicial branch to act as a check on the other two branches of government, in line with the checks-and-balances system established by the U.S. Constitution. (Today, nearly all nations with constitutional democracies, including Canada, France, and Germany, have some form of judicial review.)

The Origins of Judicial Review in the United States

The power of judicial review was not mentioned in the Constitution, but the concept was not new at the time the nation was founded. Indeed, before 1789 state courts had already overturned state legislative acts that conflicted with state constitutions. Additionally, many of the founders expected the United States Supreme Court to assume a similar role with respect to the federal Constitution. Alexander Hamilton and James Madison both emphasized the importance of judicial review in their essays urging the adoption of the new Constitution. When was the doctrine of judicial review established? See this chapter's *Landmark in the Law* feature for the answer.

▶ **Basic Judicial Requirements**

Before a court can hear a lawsuit, certain requirements must first be met. These requirements relate to jurisdiction, venue, and standing to sue. We examine each of these important concepts here.

Jurisdiction

In Latin, *juris* means "law," and *diction* means "to speak." Thus, "the power to speak the law" is the literal meaning of the term **jurisdiction**. Before any court can hear a case, it must have jurisdiction over the person (or company) against whom the suit is brought (the defendant) or over the property involved in the suit. The court must also have jurisdiction over the subject matter of the dispute.

JURISDICTION OVER PERSONS OR PROPERTY   Generally, a court can exercise personal jurisdiction (*in personam* jurisdiction) over any person or business that resides in a certain geographic area. A state trial court, for example, normally has jurisdictional authority over residents (including businesses) in a particular area of the state, such as a county or district. A state's highest court (often called the state supreme court)[1] has jurisdiction over all residents of that state.

A court can also exercise jurisdiction over property that is located within its boundaries. This kind of jurisdiction is known as *in rem* jurisdiction, or "jurisdiction over the thing." **EXAMPLE 3.1**   A dispute arises over the ownership of a boat in dry dock in Fort Lauderdale, Florida. The boat is owned by an Ohio resident, over whom a Florida court normally cannot exercise personal jurisdiction. The other party to the dispute is a resident of Nebraska.

---

1. As will be discussed shortly, a state's highest court is frequently referred to as the state supreme court, but there are exceptions. For example, in New York, the supreme court is a trial court.

Landmark in the Law   *Marbury v. Madison* (1803)

The *Marbury v. Madison*[a] decision is widely viewed as a cornerstone of constitutional law. When Thomas Jefferson defeated the incumbent president, John Adams, in the presidential election of 1800, Adams feared the Jeffersonians' antipathy toward business and toward a strong national government. Adams thus rushed to "pack" the judiciary with loyal Federalists (those who believed in a strong national government) by appointing what came to be called "midnight judges" just before he left office. All of the fifty-nine judicial appointment letters had to be certified and delivered, but Adams's secretary of state (John Marshall) was able to deliver only forty-two of them by the time Jefferson took over as president. Jefferson refused to order his secretary of state, James Madison, to deliver the remaining commissions.

Marshall's Dilemma   William Marbury and three others to whom the commissions had not been delivered sought a writ of *mandamus* (an order directing a government official to fulfill a duty) from the United States Supreme Court, as authorized by the Judiciary Act of 1789. As fate would have it, John Marshall had just been appointed as chief justice of the Supreme Court. Marshall faced a dilemma: If he ordered the commissions delivered, the new secretary of state (Madison) could simply refuse to deliver them—and the Court had no way to compel him to act. At the same time, if Marshall simply allowed the new administration to do as it wished, the Court's power would be severely eroded.

Marshall's Decision   Marshall masterfully fashioned his decision to enlarge the power of the Supreme Court by affirming the Court's power

of judicial review. He stated, "It is emphatically the province and duty of the Judicial Department to say what the law is. . . . If two laws conflict with each other, the courts must decide on the operation of each. . . . So if the law be in opposition to the Constitution . . . [t]he Court must determine which of these conflicting rules governs the case."

Marshall's decision did not require anyone to do anything. He concluded that the highest court did not have the power to issue a writ of *mandamus* in this particular case. Although the Judiciary Act of 1789 specified that the Supreme Court could issue writs of *mandamus* as part of its original jurisdiction, Article III of the Constitution, which spelled out the Court's original jurisdiction, did not mention writs of *mandamus*. Because Congress did not have the right to expand the Supreme Court's jurisdiction, this section of the Judiciary Act of 1789 was unconstitutional—and thus void. The *Marbury* decision continues to this day to stand as a judicial and political masterpiece.

• Application to Today's World   *Since the* Marbury v. Madison *decision, the power of judicial review has remained unchallenged and today is exercised by both federal and state courts. If the courts did not have the power of judicial review, the constitutionality of Congress's acts could not be challenged in court—a congressional statute would remain law unless changed by Congress. The courts of other countries that have adopted a constitutional democracy often cite this decision as a justification for judicial review.*

• Relevant Web Sites   To locate information on the Web concerning the *Marbury v. Madison* decision, go to this text's Web site at www.cengage.com/blaw/blt, select "Chapter 3," and click on "URLs for Landmarks."

a. 5 U.S. (1 Cranch) 137, 2 L.Ed. 60 (1803).

In this situation, a lawsuit concerning the boat could be brought in a Florida state court on the basis of the court's *in rem* jurisdiction. •

Long Arm Statute   A state statute that permits a state to obtain personal jurisdiction over nonresident defendants. A defendant must have certain "minimum contacts" with that state for the statute to apply.

Long Arm Statutes.   Under the authority of a state **long arm statute,** a court can exercise personal jurisdiction over certain out-of-state defendants based on activities that took place within the state. Before exercising long arm jurisdiction over a nonresident, however, the court must be convinced that the defendant had sufficient contacts, or *minimum contacts,* with the state to justify the jurisdiction.[2] Generally, this means that the defendant must have enough of a connection to the state for the judge to conclude that it is fair for the state to exercise power over the defendant. If an out-of-state defendant caused an automobile accident or sold defective goods within the state, for instance, a court will usually find that minimum contacts exist to exercise jurisdiction over that defendant.

CASE EXAMPLE 3.2   After an Xbox game system caught fire in Bonnie Broquet's home in Texas and caused substantial personal injuries, Broquet filed a lawsuit in a Texas court against Ji-Haw Industrial Company, a nonresident company that made the Xbox components. Broquet alleged that Ji-Haw's components were defective and had caused the fire.

2. The minimum-contacts standard was established in *International Shoe Co. v. State of Washington,* 326 U.S. 310, 66 S.Ct. 154, 90 L.Ed. 95 (1945).

(Creative Commons)

This XBox is made from numerous components, many of which are manufactured in different countries. If a defect in one of those foreign-manufactured components causes injury, can the user sue in her or his state of residence nonetheless? Why or why not?

Ji-Haw argued that the Texas court lacked jurisdiction over it, but in 2008, a state appellate court held that the Texas long arm statute authorized the exercise of jurisdiction over the out-of-state defendant.[3] ●

Similarly, a state may exercise personal jurisdiction over a nonresident defendant who is sued for breaching a contract that was formed within the state, even when that contract was negotiated over the phone or through correspondence. **EXAMPLE 3.3** Sharon Mills, a California resident, forms a corporation to distribute a documentary film on global climate change. Brad Cole, an environmentalist who lives in Ohio, loans the corporation funds that he borrows from an Ohio bank. A year later, the film is still not completed. Mills agrees to repay Cole's loan in a contract arranged through phone calls and correspondence between California and Ohio. When Mills does not repay the loan, Cole files a lawsuit in an Ohio court. In this situation, the Ohio court can likely exercise jurisdiction over Mills because her phone calls and letters have established sufficient contacts with the state of Ohio. ●

Corporate Contacts. Because corporations are considered legal persons, courts use the same principles to determine whether it is fair to exercise jurisdiction over a corporation.[4] A corporation normally is subject to personal jurisdiction in the state in which it is incorporated, has its principal office, and is doing business. Courts apply the minimum-contacts test to determine if they can exercise jurisdiction over out-of-state corporations.

The minimum-contacts requirement is usually met if the corporation advertises or sells its products within the state, or places its goods into the "stream of commerce" with the intent that the goods be sold in the state. **EXAMPLE 3.4** .A business is incorporated under the laws of Maine but has a branch office and manufacturing plant in Georgia. The corporation also advertises and sells its products in Georgia. These activities would likely constitute sufficient contacts with the state of Georgia to allow a Georgia court to exercise jurisdiction over the corporation. ●

JURISDICTION OVER SUBJECT MATTER Jurisdiction over subject matter is a limitation on the types of cases a court can hear. In both the federal and state court systems, there are courts of *general* (unlimited) *jurisdiction* and courts of *limited jurisdiction*. An example of a court of general jurisdiction is a state trial court or a federal district court. An example of a state court of limited jurisdiction is a probate court. **Probate courts** are state courts that handle only matters relating to the transfer of a person's assets and obligations after that person's death, including matters relating to the custody and guardianship of children. An example of a federal court of limited subject-matter jurisdiction is a bankruptcy court. **Bankruptcy courts** handle only bankruptcy proceedings, which are governed by federal bankruptcy law (will be discussed in Chapter 21).

A court's jurisdiction over subject matter is usually defined in the statute or constitution creating the court. In both the federal and state court systems, a court's subject-matter jurisdiction can be limited not only by the subject of the lawsuit but also by the amount in controversy, by whether a case is a felony (a more serious type of crime) or a misdemeanor (a less serious type of crime), or by whether the proceeding is a trial or an appeal.

ORIGINAL AND APPELLATE JURISDICTION The distinction between courts of original jurisdiction and courts of appellate jurisdiction normally lies in whether the case is being heard for the first time. Courts having original jurisdiction are courts of the first instance, or trial courts—that is, courts in which lawsuits begin, trials take place, and evidence is presented. In the federal court system, the *district courts* are trial courts. In the various

Probate Court A state court of limited jurisdiction that conducts proceedings relating to the settlement of a deceased person's estate.

Bankruptcy Court A federal court of limited jurisdiction that handles only bankruptcy proceedings, which are governed by federal bankruptcy law.

---

3. *Ji-Haw Industrial Co. v. Broquet,* 2008 WL 441822 (Tex.App.—San Antonio 2008).
4. In the eyes of the law, corporations are "legal persons"—entities that can sue and be sued. See Chapter 29.

state court systems, the trial courts are known by various names, as will be discussed shortly.

The key point here is that any court having original jurisdiction is normally known as a trial court. Courts having appellate jurisdiction act as reviewing courts, or appellate courts. In general, cases can be brought before appellate courts only on appeal from an order or a judgment of a trial court or other lower court.

JURISDICTION OF THE FEDERAL COURTS   Because the federal government is a government of limited powers, the jurisdiction of the federal courts is limited. Federal courts have subject-matter jurisdiction in two situations.

Federal Questions.   Article III of the U.S. Constitution establishes the boundaries of federal judicial power. Section 2 of Article III states that "[t]he judicial Power shall extend to all Cases, in Law and Equity, arising under this Constitution, the Laws of the United States, and Treaties made, or which shall be made, under their Authority." This clause means that whenever a plaintiff's cause of action is based, at least in part, on the U.S. Constitution, a treaty, or a federal law, then a **federal question** arises, and the case comes under the judicial power of the federal courts. Any lawsuit involving a federal question, such as a person's rights under the U.S. Constitution, can originate in a federal court. Note that in a case based on a federal question, a federal court will apply federal law.

> **Federal Question**   A question that pertains to the U.S. Constitution, acts of Congress, or treaties. A federal question provides a basis for federal jurisdiction.

Diversity of Citizenship.   Federal district courts can also exercise original jurisdiction over cases involving **diversity of citizenship.** The most common type of diversity jurisdiction has two requirements:[5] (1) the plaintiff and defendant must be residents of different states, and (2) the dollar amount in controversy must exceed $75,000. For purposes of diversity jurisdiction, a corporation is a citizen of both the state in which it is incorporated and the state in which its principal place of business is located. A case involving diversity of citizenship can be filed in the appropriate federal district court. If the case starts in a state court, it can sometimes be transferred, or "removed," to a federal court. A large percentage of the cases filed in federal courts each year are based on diversity of citizenship.

As noted, a federal court will apply federal law in cases involving federal questions. In a case based on diversity of citizenship, in contrast, a federal court will apply the relevant state law (which is often the law of the state in which the court sits).

> **Diversity of Citizenship**   Under Article III, Section 2, of the U.S. Constitution, a basis for federal district court jurisdiction over a lawsuit between (1) citizens of different states, (2) a foreign country and citizens of a state or of different states, or (3) citizens of a state and citizens or subjects of a foreign country. The amount in controversy must be more than $75,000 before a federal district court can take jurisdiction in such cases.

EXCLUSIVE VERSUS CONCURRENT JURISDICTION   When both federal and state courts have the power to hear a case, as is true in lawsuits involving diversity of citizenship, **concurrent jurisdiction** exists. When cases can be tried only in federal courts or only in state courts, **exclusive jurisdiction** exists. Federal courts have exclusive jurisdiction in cases involving federal crimes, bankruptcy, patents, and copyrights; in suits against the United States; and in some areas of admiralty law (law governing transportation on the seas and ocean waters). State courts also have exclusive jurisdiction over certain subject matter—for example, divorce and adoption. When concurrent jurisdiction exists, a party may choose to bring a suit in either a federal court or a state court. The concepts of exclusive and concurrent jurisdiction are illustrated in Exhibit 3–1 on the following page.

> **Concurrent Jurisdiction**   Jurisdiction that exists when two different courts have the power to hear a case. For example, some cases can be heard in a federal or a state court.

> **Exclusive Jurisdiction**   Jurisdiction that exists when a case can be heard only in a particular court or type of court.

Jurisdiction in Cyberspace

The Internet's capacity to bypass political and geographic boundaries undercuts the traditional basis on which courts assert personal jurisdiction. As already discussed, for a court

---

5. Diversity jurisdiction also exists in cases between (1) a foreign country and citizens of a state or of different states and (2) citizens of a state and citizens or subjects of a foreign country. These bases for diversity jurisdiction are less commonly used.

● *Exhibit* **3–1** **Exclusive and Concurrent Jurisdiction**

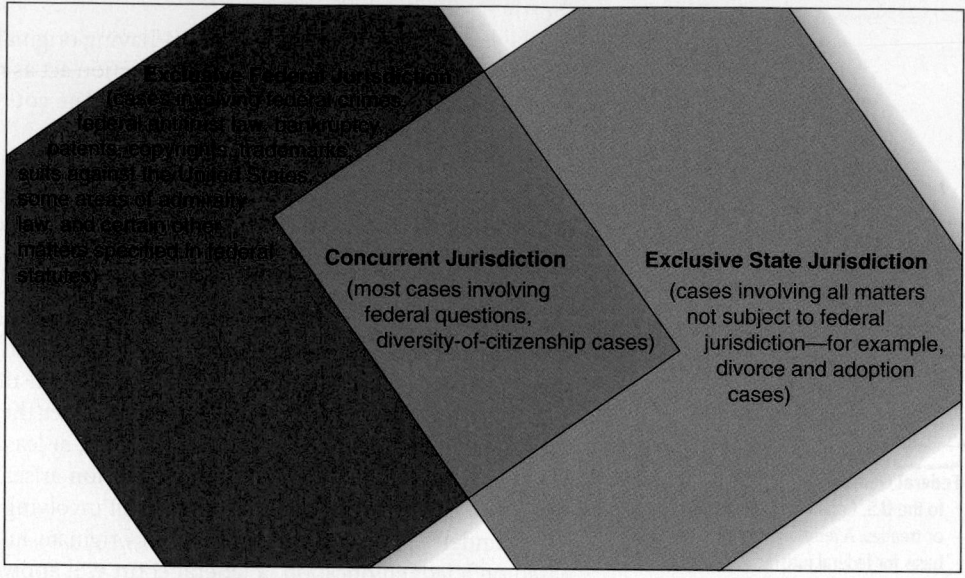

Exclusive Federal Jurisdiction
(cases involving federal crimes,
federal antitrust law, bankruptcy,
patents, copyrights, trademarks,
suits against the United States,
some areas of admiralty
law, and certain other
matters specified in federal
statutes)

Concurrent Jurisdiction
(most cases involving
federal questions,
diversity-of-citizenship cases)

Exclusive State Jurisdiction
(cases involving all matters
not subject to federal
jurisdiction—for example,
divorce and adoption
cases)

to compel a defendant to come before it, there must be at least minimum contacts—the presence of a salesperson within the state, for example. Are there sufficient minimum contacts if the defendant's only connection to a jurisdiction is an ad on a Web site originating from a remote location?

THE "SLIDING-SCALE" STANDARD   The courts have developed a standard—called a "sliding-scale" standard—for determining when the exercise of jurisdiction over an out-of-state defendant is proper. In developing this standard, the courts have identified three types of Internet business contacts: (1) substantial business conducted over the Internet (with contracts and sales, for example); (2) some interactivity through a Web site; and (3) passive advertising. Jurisdiction is proper for the first category, improper for the third, and may or may not be appropriate for the second.[6] An Internet communication is typically considered passive if people have to voluntarily access it to read the message, and active if it is sent to specific individuals.

In certain situations, even a single contact can satisfy the minimum-contacts requirement. **CASE EXAMPLE 3.5** A Louisiana resident, Daniel Crummey, purchased a used recreational vehicle (RV) from sellers in Texas after viewing numerous photos of it on eBay. The sellers' statements on eBay claimed that "everything works great on this RV and will provide comfort and dependability for years to come. This RV will go to Alaska and back without problems!" Crummey picked up the RV in Texas, but on the drive back to Louisiana, the RV quit working. He filed a suit in Louisiana against the sellers alleging that the vehicle was defective, but the sellers claimed that the Louisiana court lacked jurisdiction. Because the sellers had used eBay to market and sell the RV to a Louisiana buyer—and had regularly used eBay to sell vehicles to remote parties in the past—the court found that jurisdiction was proper.[7] ●

---

6. For a leading case on this issue, see *Zippo Manufacturing Co. v. Zippo Dot Com, Inc.*, 952 F.Supp. 1119 (W.D.Pa. 1997).

7. *Crummey v. Morgan*, 965 So.2d 497 (La.App.1 Cir. 2007). But note that a single sale on eBay does not necessarily confer jurisdiction. Jurisdiction depends on whether the seller regularly uses eBay as a means for doing business with remote buyers. See *Boschetto v. Hansing*, 539 F.3d 1011 (9th Cir. 2008).

Preventing Legal Disputes

Those of you with an entrepreneurial spirit may be eager to establish Web sites to promote products and solicit orders. Be aware, however, that you can be sued in states in which you have never been physically present if you have had sufficient contacts with residents of those states over the Internet. Before you create a Web site that is the least bit interactive, you need to consult an attorney to find out whether you will be subjecting yourself to jurisdiction in every state. Becoming informed about the extent of your potential exposure to lawsuits in various locations is an important part of preventing litigation.

INTERNATIONAL JURISDICTIONAL ISSUES   Because the Internet is global in scope, it obviously raises international jurisdictional issues. The world's courts seem to be developing a standard that echoes the "minimum-contacts" requirement applied by U.S. courts. Most courts are indicating that minimum contacts—doing business within the jurisdiction, for example—are enough to compel a defendant to appear and that a physical presence is not necessary. The effect of this standard is that a business firm has to comply with the laws in any jurisdiction in which it targets customers for its products. This situation is complicated by the fact that many countries' laws on particular issues—free speech, for example—are very different from U.S. laws.

CASE EXAMPLE 3.6   Yahoo operated an online auction site on which Nazi memorabilia were offered for sale. In France, the display of any symbols of Nazi ideology subjects the person or entity displaying them to both criminal and civil liability. The International League against Racism and Anti-Semitism filed a lawsuit in Paris against Yahoo for displaying Nazi memorabilia and offering them for sale via its Web site.

The French court asserted jurisdiction over Yahoo on the ground that the materials on the company's U.S.-based servers could be viewed on a Web site accessible in France. The French court ordered Yahoo to eliminate all Internet access in France to the Nazi memorabilia offered for sale through its online auctions. Yahoo then took the case to a federal district court in the United States, claiming that the French court's order violated the First Amendment. Although the federal district court ruled in favor of Yahoo, the U.S. Court of Appeals for the Ninth Circuit reversed. According to the appellate court, U.S. courts lacked personal jurisdiction over the French groups involved. The ruling leaves open the possibility that Yahoo, and anyone else who posts anything on the Internet, could be held answerable to the laws of any country in which the message might be received.[8] ●

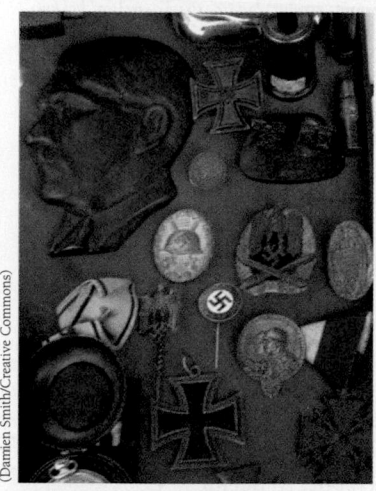

World War II Nazi memorabilia cannot legally be advertised or sold in many countries. Why is this an issue in the United States, where there are no such restrictions?

(Damien Smith/Creative Commons)

Venue

Venue   The geographic district in which a legal action is tried and from which the jury is selected.

Jurisdiction has to do with whether a court has authority to hear a case involving specific persons, property, or subject matter. **Venue**[9] is concerned with the most appropriate physical location for a trial. Two state courts (or two federal courts) may have the authority to exercise jurisdiction over a case, but it may be more appropriate or convenient to hear the case in one court than in the other.

Basically, the concept of venue reflects the policy that a court trying a suit should be in the geographic neighborhood (usually the county) where the incident leading to the lawsuit occurred or where the parties involved in the lawsuit reside. Venue in a civil case typically is where the defendant resides, whereas venue in a criminal case normally is where the crime occurred. Pretrial publicity or other factors, though, may require a change of venue to another community, especially in criminal cases when the defendant's right to a fair and impartial jury has been impaired. **EXAMPLE 3.7**   In 2008, police raided a compound of Mormon polygamists in Texas and removed 468 children (mostly girls) from the ranch. Authorities suspected that some of the girls were being sexually and physically abused

---

8. *Yahoo!, Inc. v. La Ligue Contre le Racisme et l'Antisémitisme,* 379 F.3d 1120 (9th Cir. 2004); on rehearing, *Yahoo!, Inc. v. La Ligue Contre le Racisme et l'Antisémitisme,* 433 F.3d 1199 (9th Cir. 2006); *cert.* denied, 547 U.S. 1163, 126 S.Ct. 2332, 164 L.Ed.2d 848 (2006).

9. Pronounced ven-yoo.

after a sixteen-year-old girl called to report that her fifty-year-old husband had beaten and raped her. The raid received a lot of media attention, and the people living in the nearby towns would likely have been influenced by this publicity. In that situation, if the government filed criminal charges against a member of the religious sect, that individual might request—and would probably receive—a change of venue to another location. ●

Standing to Sue

Standing to Sue   The requirement that an individual must have a sufficient stake in a controversy before he or she can bring a lawsuit. The plaintiff must demonstrate that he or she has been either injured or threatened with injury.

Justiciable Controversy   A controversy that is not hypothetical or academic but real and substantial; a requirement that must be satisfied before a court will hear a case.

Before a person can bring a lawsuit before a court, the party must have **standing to sue,** or a sufficient "stake" in the matter to justify seeking relief through the court system. In other words, to have standing, a party must have a legally protected and tangible interest at stake in the litigation. The party bringing the lawsuit must have suffered a harm, or have been threatened by a harm, as a result of the action about which she or he has complained. Standing to sue also requires that the controversy at issue be a **justiciable**[10] **controversy**—a controversy that is real and substantial, as opposed to hypothetical or academic. As United States Supreme Court chief justice John Roberts recently noted, a lack of standing is like Bob Dylan's line in the song "Like a Rolling Stone": "When you got nothing, you got nothing to lose."[11]

CASE EXAMPLE 3.8   James Bush visited the Federal Bureau of Investigation's (FBI's) office in San Jose, California, on two occasions in December 2007. He filled out complaint forms indicating that he was seeking records under the Freedom of Information Act (FOIA— see Chapter 33) regarding a police brutality claim and the FBI's failure to investigate it. In August 2008, Bush filed a suit against the U.S. Department of Justice in an attempt to compel the FBI to provide the requested records. The court dismissed the lawsuit on the ground that no justiciable controversy existed. Bush had failed to comply with the requirements of the FOIA when he filled out the forms, so the FBI was not obligated to provide any records. Thus, there was no actual controversy for the court to decide.[12] ●

Note that in some situations a person may have standing to sue on behalf of another person, such as a minor or a mentally incompetent person. **EXAMPLE 3.9**   Three-year-old Emma suffers serious injuries as a result of a defectively manufactured toy. Because Emma is a minor, her parent or legal guardian can bring a lawsuit on her behalf. ●

In the following case, involving a suit between a state and an agency of the federal government, the court was asked to determine whether the state's allegations rose to the level of a "concrete, particularized, actual or imminent" injury against the state independent from any harm to private parties.

"Although it's nothing serious, let's keep an eye on it to make sure it doesn't turn into a major lawsuit."

---

10. Pronounced jus-*tish*-uh-bul.

11. The chief justice stated, "The absence of any substantive recovery means that respondents cannot benefit from the judgment they seek and thus lack Article III standing." He then quoted Bob Dylan's lyrics from "Like a Rolling Stone," on *Highway 61 Revisited* (Columbia Records 1965). This was the first time that a member of the Supreme Court cited rock lyrics in an opinion. See *Sprint Communications Co. v. APCC Services, Inc.,* ____ U.S. ____, 128 S.Ct. 2531, 171 L.Ed.2d 424 (2008).

12. *Bush v. Department of Justice,* 2008 WL 5245046 (N.D.Cal. 2008).

Case 3.1   Oregon v. Legal Services Corp.

United States Court of Appeals, Ninth Circuit, 552 F.3d 965 (2009).
www.ca9.uscourts.gov [a]

FACTS   The federal government established the Legal Services Corporation (LSC) to provide federal funds to local legal assistance programs

for individuals who cannot afford legal assistance. LSC restricts the use of the funds for some purposes, including participating in class-action lawsuits. The recipients must maintain legal, physical, and

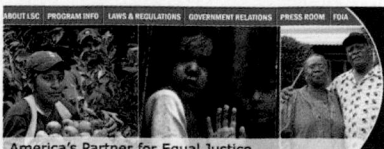

The home page banner from Legal Services Corporation's Web site.

---

a. In the left-hand column, in the "Decisions" pull-down menu, click on "Opinions." On that page, click on "Advanced Search." In the "by Case No.:" box, type "06-36012" and click on "Search." In the result, click on the appropriate link to access the opinion. The U.S. Court of Appeals for the Ninth Circuit maintains this Web site.

Case 3.1–Continued

financial separation from organizations that engage in these activities. In 2005, in the interest of cutting costs, Oregon directed legal assistance programs in the state to consolidate in situations in which separate organizations provided services in the same geographic area. LSC did not approve of the integration of programs that received its funds with programs that were engaged in restricted activities. Oregon filed a suit in a federal district court against LSC, alleging that the state's ability to provide legal services to its citizens was frustrated. The court dismissed the suit "on the merits." Oregon appealed to the U.S. Court of Appeals for the Ninth Circuit.

ISSUE   Does Oregon have standing to bring this claim?

DECISION   No. The court agreed that the complaint should be dismissed, but vacated the judgment and remanded the case for an entry of dismissal based on the plaintiff's lack of standing.

REASON   In this case, there is no injury to Oregon. The state has not accepted LSC funds and is not bound by the restrictions. The state does not

have the authority to accept or refuse the funds on behalf of its legal services programs, which are all private organizations. Nor does the state have the right to control the conditions for any grant of federal funds to private organizations. Thus, LSC's decision to fund some legal assistance programs and not others, subject to certain restrictions, does not injure Oregon, and the state cannot claim that it does simply because those restrictions do not complement the state's policy to consolidate the programs. "Oregon may continue to regulate its legal service programs as it desires, but it cannot depend on * * * financial support from LSC to [any] legal services provider within the state if it makes choices that conflict with the LSC * * * regulations."

FOR CRITICAL ANALYSIS—Legal Consideration   *Under what circumstances might a state suffer an injury that would give it the standing to sue to block the enforcement of restrictions on the use of federal funds? (Hint: Would it be ethical for a state to change its policies to follow LSC's restrictions and continue the funding?)*

 ## The State and Federal Court Systems

As mentioned earlier in this chapter, each state has its own court system. Additionally, there is a system of federal courts. Even though there are fifty-two court systems—one for each of the fifty states, one for the District of Columbia, plus a federal system—similarities abound. Exhibit 3–2 illustrates the basic organizational structure characteristic of the court systems in many states. The exhibit also shows how the federal court system is structured. Keep in mind that the federal courts are not superior to the state courts; they are simply an independent system of courts, which derives its authority from Article III, Sections 1 and 2, of the U.S. Constitution. We turn now to an examination of these court systems, beginning with the state courts.

● *Exhibit* **3–2 State and Federal Court Systems**

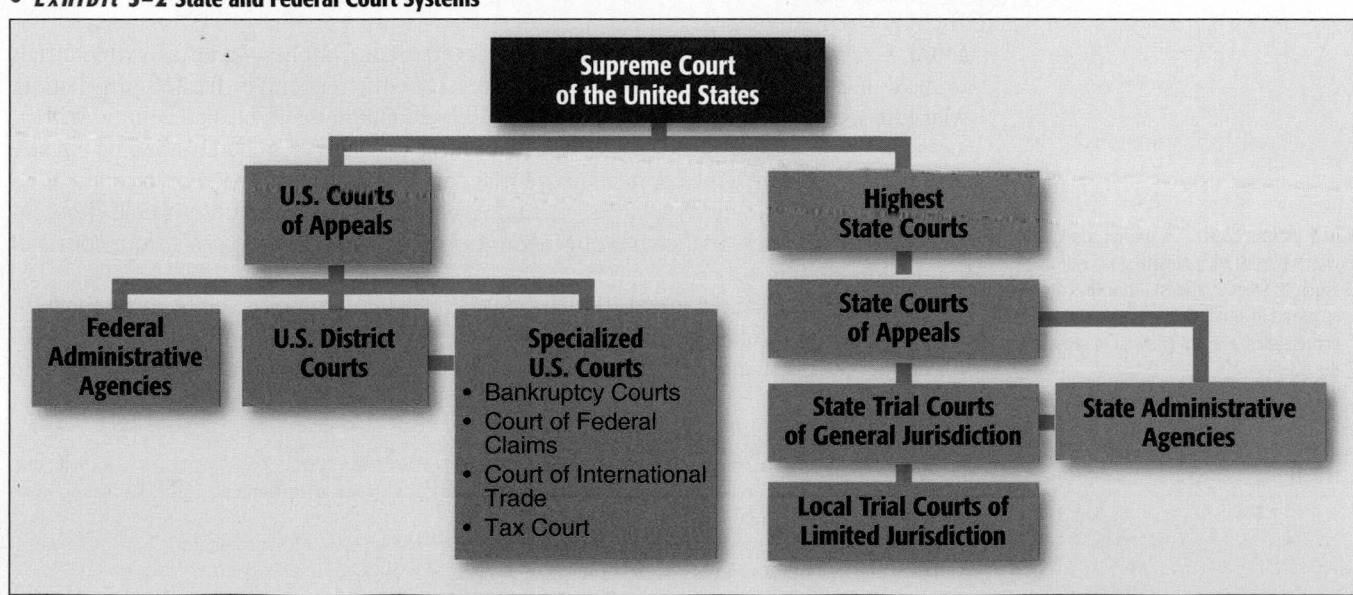

The State Court Systems

ON THE WEB If you want to find information on state court systems, the National Center for State Courts (NCSC) offers links to the Web pages of all state courts at **www.ncsconline.org**.

Typically, a state court system will include several levels, or tiers, of courts. As indicated in Exhibit 3–2 on the previous page, state courts may include (1) trial courts of limited jurisdiction, (2) trial courts of general jurisdiction, (3) appellate courts, and (4) the state's highest court (often called the state supreme court). Generally, any person who is a party to a lawsuit has the opportunity to plead the case before a trial court and then, if he or she loses, before at least one level of appellate court. Only if the case involves a federal statute or a federal constitutional issue, may the decision of a state supreme court on that issue be further appealed to the United States Supreme Court.

The states use various methods to select judges for their courts: in most states, judges are elected, but in some states, they are appointed. Usually, states specify the number of years that a judge will serve. In contrast, as you will read shortly, judges in the federal court system are appointed by the president of the United States and, if they are confirmed by the Senate, hold office for life—unless they engage in blatantly illegal conduct.

Ethical Issue ⚖️

Does the use of private judges threaten our system of justice? The use of private judges has gained popularity in some states. In California, for example, a number of celebrity divorces—such as that of Brad Pitt and Jennifer Aniston—have taken place in private forums out of the public eye. Unlike a divorce mediator, a private judge (usually a retired judge who charges the parties a hefty fee) has the power to conduct trials and grant legal resolutions, such as divorce decrees. Private judges increasingly are being used to resolve commercial disputes, as well as divorces and custody battles. One reason is that a private judge usually can hear a case sooner than it would be heard in a regular court. Another reason is that proceedings before a private judge can be kept secret. But is it ethical to allow parties to pay extra for a private judge and secret proceedings?

In Ohio, for example, a state statute allows the parties to any civil action to have their dispute tried by a retired judge of their choosing who will make a decision in the matter.[13] A few years ago, private judging came under criticism in that state because private judges were conducting jury trials and using county courtrooms at the expense of taxpayers. Also, a public judge refused to give up jurisdiction over one case on the ground that private judges are not authorized to conduct jury trials. The Ohio Supreme Court agreed, noting that private judging raises significant public-policy issues that the legislature needs to consider.[14] Similarly, the Supreme Court of Rhode Island is considering whether to allow private judging based on a state statute that was enacted in 1984 but has never been used.[15] The state's highest court decided to hold public hearings to review the statute after a family court judge who was retiring expressed an interest in continuing on as a private judge.

TRIAL COURTS   Trial courts are exactly what their name implies—courts in which trials are held and testimony taken. State trial courts have either general or limited jurisdiction. Trial courts that have general jurisdiction as to subject matter may be called county, district, superior, or circuit courts.[16] The jurisdiction of these courts is often determined by the size of the county in which the court sits. State trial courts of general jurisdiction have jurisdiction over a wide variety of subjects, including both civil disputes and criminal prosecutions. (In some states, trial courts of general jurisdiction may hear appeals from courts of limited jurisdiction.)

Small Claims Court A special court in which parties may litigate small claims (such as $5,000 or less). Attorneys are not required in small claims courts and, in some states, are not allowed to represent the parties.

Some courts of limited jurisdiction are called special inferior trial courts or minor judiciary courts. **Small claims courts** are inferior trial courts that hear only civil cases involving claims of less than a certain amount, such as $5,000 (the amount varies from state to

---

13. See Ohio Revised Code Section 2701.10.

14. *State ex rel. Russo v. McDonnell,* 110 Ohio St.3d 144, 852 N.E.2d 145 (2006). (*Ex rel.* is Latin for *ex relatione.* The phrase refers to an action brought on behalf of the state, by the attorney general, at the instigation of an individual who has a private interest in the matter.)

15. Retired Justice Trial Act, Section 8-17-1 of the General Laws of the State of Rhode Island.

16. The name in Ohio is court of common pleas; the name in New York is supreme court.

state). Suits brought in small claims courts are generally conducted informally, and lawyers are not required (in a few states, lawyers are not even allowed). Another example of an inferior trial court is a local municipal court that hears mainly traffic cases. Decisions of small claims courts and municipal courts may sometimes be appealed to a state trial court of general jurisdiction. Other courts of limited jurisdiction as to subject matter include domestic relations or family courts, which handle primarily divorce actions and child-custody disputes, and probate courts, as mentioned earlier. A few states have even established Islamic law courts, which are courts of limited jurisdiction that serve the American Muslim community. (See this chapter's *Beyond Our Borders* feature below for a discussion of the rise of Islamic law courts.)

APPELLATE, OR REVIEWING, COURTS   Every state has at least one court of appeals (appellate court, or reviewing court), which may be an intermediate appellate court or the state's highest court. About three-fourths of the states have intermediate appellate courts. Generally, courts of appeals do not conduct new trials, in which evidence is submitted to the court and witnesses are examined. Rather, an appellate court panel of three or more

 Beyond Our Borders   **Islamic Law Courts Abroad and at Home**

As discussed in Chapter 1, Islamic law is one of the world's three most common legal systems, along with civil law and common law. In most Islamic countries, the law is based on *sharia,* a system of law derived from the Qur'an as well as the sayings and doings of Muhammad and his companions. *Sharia* means "way" and provides the legal framework for many aspects of Muslim life, including politics, banking, business, family, economics, and social issues.

Islamic Law in Britain and Canada

In 2008, the archbishop of Canterbury—the leader of the Church of England—argued that it was time for Britain to consider "crafting a just and constructive relationship between Islamic law and the statutory law of the United Kingdom." Even before the archbishop made his proposal, *sharia* was already being applied in Britain via councils that rule on Islamic civil justice through a number of mosques in that country. These councils arbitrate disputes between British Muslims involving child custody, property, employment, and housing. Of course, the councils do not deal with criminal law or with any civil issues that would put *sharia* in direct conflict with British statutory law. Most Islamic law cases involve marriage or divorce.

In late 2008, Britain officially sanctioned the authority of *sharia* judges to rule on divorce and financial disputes between couples. Britain

now has five officially recognized *sharia* courts that have the full power of their equivalent courts within the traditional British judicial system.

As early as 2003 in Ontario, Canada, a group of Canadian Muslims established a judicial tribunal using *sharia.* To date, this tribunal has resolved only marital disagreements and some other civil disputes. Initially, there was some heated debate about whether Canada should or even legally could allow *sharia* law to be applied to any aspect of Canadian life or business. Under Ontario law, however, the regular judicial system must uphold such agreements as long as they are voluntary and negotiated through an arbitrator. Any agreements that violate Canada's Charter of Rights and Freedoms are not upheld in the traditional judicial system. Canadian Muslims have also created the Islamic Institute of Civil Justice to oversee *sharia* tribunals that arbitrate family disputes among Muslims.

Islamic Law Courts in the United States

About the time that Britain was formally recognizing Islamic law courts, a controversy about the same issue erupted in Detroit, Michigan, where there is a large American Muslim community. In reality, courts in Texas and Minnesota had already ruled on the legality of arbitration clauses that require recourse

to Islamic law courts. In the Texas case, an American Muslim couple was married and was issued a "Society of Arlington Islamic Marriage Certificate." A number of years later, a dispute arose over marital property and the nonpayment of a "dowry for the bride." The parties involved had signed an arbitration agreement in which all claims and disputes were to be submitted to arbitration in front of the Texas Islamic Court in Richardson, Texas. A Texas appeals court ruled that the arbitration agreement was valid and enforceable.[a]

The case in Minnesota involved an Islamic arbitration committee decision that was contested by one of the parties who had agreed to arbitrate any differences before the committee. Again, the appeals court affirmed the arbitration award.[b]

• For Critical Analysis
One of the arguments against allowing sharia courts in the United States is that we would no longer have a common legal framework within our society. Do you agree or disagree? Why?

---
a. *Jabri v. Qaddura,* 108 S.W.3d 404 (Tex.App.–Fort Worth 2003).
b. *Abd Alla v. Mourssi,* 680 N.W.2d 569 (Minn.App. 2004).

Question of Fact In a lawsuit, an issue that involves only disputed facts, and not what the law is on a given point. Questions of fact are decided by the jury in a jury trial (by the judge if there is no jury).

Question of Law In a lawsuit, an issue involving the application or interpretation of a law. Only a judge, not a jury, can rule on questions of law.

BE CAREFUL The decisions of a state's highest court are final on questions of state law.

ON THE WEB To find information about the federal court system and links to all federal courts, go to the home page of the federal judiciary at www.uscourts.gov.

judges reviews the record of the case on appeal, which includes a transcript of the trial proceedings, and determines whether the trial court committed an error.

Usually, appellate courts focus on questions of law, not questions of fact. A **question of fact** deals with what really happened in regard to the dispute being tried—such as whether a party actually burned a flag. A **question of law** concerns the application or interpretation of the law—such as whether flag-burning is a form of speech protected by the First Amendment to the U.S. Constitution. Only a judge, not a jury, can rule on questions of law. Appellate courts normally defer (or give weight) to a trial court's findings on questions of fact because the trial court judge and jury were in a better position to evaluate testimony by directly observing witnesses' gestures, demeanor, and nonverbal behavior during the trial. At the appellate level, the judges review the written transcript of the trial, which does not include these nonverbal elements.

An appellate court will challenge a trial court's finding of fact only when the finding is clearly erroneous (that is, when it is contrary to the evidence presented at trial) or when there is no evidence to support the finding. **EXAMPLE 3.10** A jury concludes that a manufacturer's product harmed the plaintiff, but no evidence was submitted to the court to support that conclusion. In this situation, the appellate court will hold that the trial court's decision was erroneous. • The options exercised by appellate courts will be discussed further later in this chapter.

HIGHEST STATE COURTS The highest appellate court in a state is usually called the supreme court but may be called by some other name. For example, in both New York and Maryland, the highest state court is called the court of appeals. The decisions of each state's highest court are final on all questions of state law. Only when issues of federal law are involved can a decision made by a state's highest court be overruled by the United States Supreme Court.

The Federal Court System

The federal court system is basically a three-tiered model consisting of (1) U.S. district courts (trial courts of general jurisdiction) and various courts of limited jurisdiction, (2) U.S. courts of appeals (intermediate courts of appeals), and (3) the United States Supreme Court. Unlike state court judges, who are usually elected, federal court judges—including the justices of the Supreme Court—are appointed by the president of the United States and confirmed by the U.S. Senate. All federal judges receive lifetime appointments (because under Article III they "hold their offices during Good Behavior"), but they do not receive regular salary increases. In fact, in 2009 Chief Justice Roberts of the United States Supreme Court complained that Congress had given its members a 2.8 percent cost-of-living increase, but refused to give an identical pay increase to federal judges.

U.S. DISTRICT COURTS At the federal level, the equivalent of a state trial court of general jurisdiction is the district court. There is at least one federal district court in every state. The number of judicial districts can vary over time, primarily owing to population changes and corresponding caseloads. There are ninety-four federal judicial districts. U.S. district courts have original jurisdiction in federal matters. Federal cases typically originate in district courts. There are other courts with original, but special (or limited), jurisdiction, such as the federal bankruptcy courts and others shown in Exhibit 3–2 on page 65.

U.S. COURTS OF APPEALS In the federal court system, there are thirteen U.S. courts of appeals—also referred to as U.S. circuit courts of appeals. The federal courts of appeals for twelve of the circuits, including the U.S. Court of Appeals for the District of Columbia Circuit, hear appeals from the federal district courts located within their respective judicial circuits. The Court of Appeals for the Thirteenth Circuit, called the Federal Circuit, has

• *Exhibit* **3–3** **Boundaries of the U.S. Courts of Appeals and U.S. District Courts**

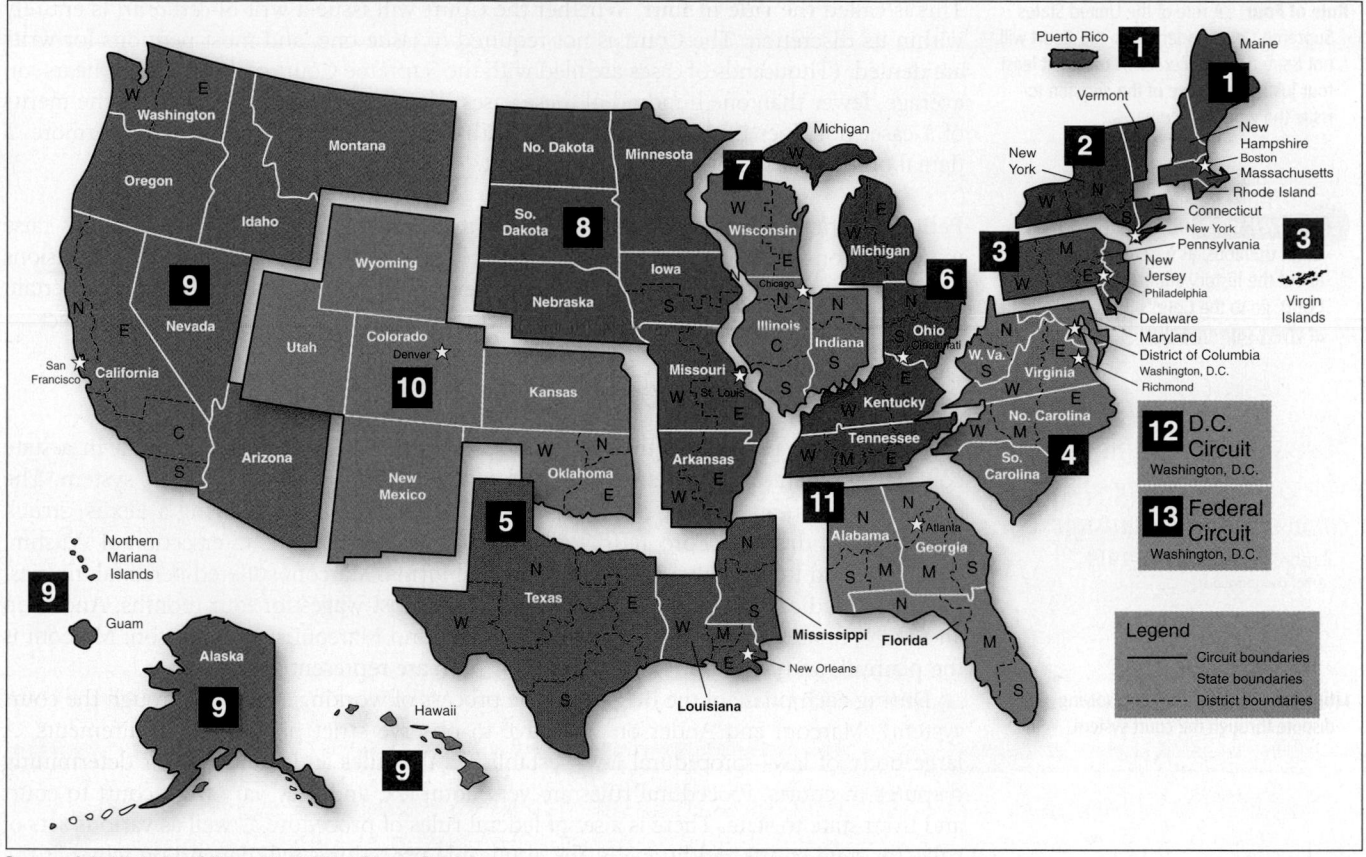

Source: Administrative Office of the United States Courts.

national appellate jurisdiction over certain types of cases, such as cases involving patent law and cases in which the U.S. government is a defendant.

The decisions of the circuit courts of appeals are final in most cases, but appeal to the United States Supreme Court is possible. Exhibit 3–3 shows the geographic boundaries of the U.S. circuit courts of appeals and the boundaries of the U.S. district courts within each circuit.

THE UNITED STATES SUPREME COURT   The highest level of the three-tiered model of the federal court system is the United States Supreme Court. According to the language of Article III of the U.S. Constitution, there is only one national Supreme Court. All other courts in the federal system are considered "inferior." Congress is empowered to create other inferior courts as it deems necessary. The inferior courts that Congress has created include the second tier in our model—the U.S. courts of appeals—as well as the district courts and any other courts of limited, or specialized, jurisdiction.

The United States Supreme Court consists of nine justices. Although the Supreme Court has original, or trial, jurisdiction in rare instances (set forth in Article III, Section 2), most of its work is as an appeals court. The Supreme Court can review any case decided by any of the federal courts of appeals, and it also has appellate authority over some cases decided in the state courts.

Appeals to the Supreme Court.   To bring a case before the Supreme Court, a party requests that the Court issue a writ of *certiorari*. A **writ of *certiorari***[17] is an order issued by the Supreme Court to a lower court requiring the latter to send it the record of the case for

---

ON THE WEB   The decisions of all of the U.S. courts of appeals, as well as those of the United States Supreme Court, are now published online shortly after the decisions are rendered. You can find these decisions and obtain information about the federal court system by accessing the Federal Court Locator at **www.law.vill. edu/library/researchandstudyguides/ federalcourtlocator.asp**.

Writ of *Certiorari*   A writ from a higher court asking a lower court for the record of a case.

---

17. Pronounced sur-shee-uh-*rah*-ree.

Rule of Four   A rule of the United States Supreme Court under which the Court will not issue a writ of *certiorari* unless at least four justices approve of the decision to issue the writ.

ON THE WEB   To access Supreme Court opinions, as well as information about the history and function of the Court, go to the Court's official Web site at www.supremecourtus.gov.

"Lawsuit: A machine which you go into as a pig and come out of as a sausage."
Ambrose Bierce, 1842–1914
(American journalist)

Litigation   The process of resolving a dispute through the court system.

Pleadings   Statements made by the plaintiff and the defendant in a lawsuit that detail the facts, charges, and defenses involved in the litigation. The complaint and answer are part of the pleadings.

Complaint   The pleading made by a plaintiff alleging wrongdoing on the part of the defendant; the document that, when filed with a court, initiates a lawsuit.

review. The Court will not issue a writ unless at least four of the nine justices approve of it. This is called the **rule of four.** Whether the Court will issue a writ of *certiorari* is entirely within its discretion. The Court is not required to issue one, and most petitions for writs are denied. (Thousands of cases are filed with the Supreme Court each year; yet it hears, on average, fewer than one hundred of these cases.)[18] A denial is not a decision on the merits of a case, nor does it indicate agreement with the lower court's opinion. Furthermore, a denial of the writ has no value as a precedent.

Petitions Granted by the Court.   Typically, the Court grants petitions when cases raise important constitutional questions or when the lower courts are issuing conflicting decisions on a significant issue. The justices, however, never explain their reasons for hearing certain cases and not others, so it is difficult to predict which type of case the Court might select.

Following a State Court Case

To illustrate the procedures that would be followed in a civil lawsuit brought in a state court, we present a hypothetical case and follow it through the state court system. The case involves an automobile accident in which Kevin Anderson, driving a Lexus, struck Lisa Marconi, driving a Ford Taurus. The accident occurred at the intersection of Wilshire Boulevard and Rodeo Drive in Beverly Hills, California. Marconi suffered personal injuries, incurring medical and hospital expenses as well as lost wages for four months. Anderson and Marconi are unable to agree on a settlement, and Marconi sues Anderson. Marconi is the plaintiff, and Anderson is the defendant. Both are represented by lawyers.

During each phase of the **litigation** (the process of working a lawsuit through the court system), Marconi and Anderson will have to observe strict procedural requirements. A large body of law—procedural law—establishes the rules and standards for determining disputes in courts. Procedural rules are very complex, and they vary from court to court and from state to state. There is a set of federal rules of procedure as well as various sets of rules for state courts. Additionally, the applicable procedures will depend on whether the case is a civil or criminal proceeding. Generally, the Marconi-Anderson civil lawsuit will involve the procedures discussed in the following subsections. Keep in mind that attempts to settle the case may be ongoing throughout the trial.

The Pleadings

The complaint and answer (and the counterclaim and reply)—all of which are discussed below—taken together are called the **pleadings.** The pleadings inform each party of the other's claims and specify the issues (disputed questions) involved in the case. The style and form of the pleadings may be quite different in different states.

THE PLAINTIFF'S COMPLAINT   Marconi's suit against Anderson commences when her lawyer files a **complaint** with the appropriate court. The complaint contains a statement alleging (1) the facts necessary for the court to take jurisdiction, (2) a brief summary of the facts necessary to show that the plaintiff is entitled to a remedy,[19] and (3) a statement of the remedy the plaintiff is seeking. Complaints may be lengthy or brief, depending on the complexity of the case and the rules of the jurisdiction.

---

18. From the mid-1950s through the early 1990s, the United States Supreme Court reviewed more cases per year than it has in the last few years. In the Court's 1982–1983 term, for example, the Court issued opinions in 151 cases. In contrast, in its 2008–2009 term, the Court issued opinions in only 83 cases.

19. The factual allegations in a complaint must be enough to raise a right to relief above the speculative level; they must plausibly suggest that the plaintiff is entitled to a remedy. *Bell Atlantic Corp. v. Twombly,* 550 U.S. 544, 127 S.Ct. 1955, 167 L.Ed.2d 929 (2007).

Summons A document informing a defendant that a legal action has been commenced against her or him and that the defendant must appear in court on a certain date to answer the plaintiff's complaint.

Default Judgment A judgment entered by a court against a defendant who has failed to appear in court to answer or defend against the plaintiff's claim.

Answer Procedurally, a defendant's response to the plaintiff's complaint.

Counterclaim A claim made by a defendant in a civil lawsuit against the plaintiff. In effect, the defendant is suing the plaintiff.

Reply Procedurally, a plaintiff's response to a defendant's answer.

Motion to Dismiss A pleading in which a defendant asserts that the plaintiff's claim fails to state a cause of action (that is, has no basis in law) or that there are other grounds on which the suit should be dismissed. Although the defendant normally is the party requesting a dismissal, either the plaintiff or the court can also make a motion to dismiss the case.

Motion for Judgment on the Pleadings A motion by either party to a lawsuit at the close of the pleadings requesting the court to decide the issue solely on the pleadings without proceeding to trial. The motion will be granted only if no facts are in dispute.

Motion for Summary Judgment A motion requesting the court to enter a judgment without proceeding to trial. The motion can be based on evidence outside the pleadings and will be granted only if no facts are in dispute.

After the complaint has been filed, the sheriff, a deputy of the county, or another *process server* (one who delivers a complaint and summons) serves a **summons** and a copy of the complaint on defendant Anderson. The summons notifies Anderson that he must file an answer to the complaint with both the court and the plaintiff's attorney within a specified time period (usually twenty to thirty days). The summons also informs Anderson that failure to answer may result in a **default judgment** for the plaintiff, meaning the plaintiff could be awarded the damages alleged in her complaint. Service of process is essential in our legal system. No case can proceed to a trial unless the plaintiff can prove that he or she has properly served the defendant.

THE DEFENDANT'S ANSWER The defendant's **answer** either admits the statements or allegations set forth in the complaint or denies them and outlines any defenses that the defendant may have. If Anderson admits to all of Marconi's allegations in his answer, the court will enter a judgment for Marconi. If Anderson denies any of Marconi's allegations, the litigation will go forward.

Anderson can deny Marconi's allegations and set forth his own claim that Marconi was in fact negligent and therefore owes him compensation for the damage to his Lexus. This is appropriately called a **counterclaim.** If Anderson files a counterclaim, Marconi will have to answer it with a pleading, normally called a **reply,** which has the same characteristics as an answer.

Anderson can also admit the truth of Marconi's complaint but raise new facts that may result in dismissal of the action. This is called raising an *affirmative defense.* For example, Anderson could assert the expiration of the time period under the relevant *statute of limitations* (a state or federal statute that sets the maximum time period during which a certain action can be brought or rights enforced) as an affirmative defense.

MOTION TO DISMISS A **motion to dismiss** requests the court to dismiss the case for stated reasons. Grounds for dismissal of a case include improper delivery of the complaint and summons, improper venue, and the plaintiff's failure to state a claim for which a court could grant relief (a remedy). For instance, if Marconi had suffered no injuries or losses as a result of Anderson's negligence, Anderson could move to have the case dismissed because Marconi would not have stated a claim for which relief could be granted.

If the judge grants the motion to dismiss, the plaintiff generally is given time to file an amended complaint. If the judge denies the motion, the suit will go forward, and the defendant must then file an answer. Note that if Marconi wishes to discontinue the suit because, for example, an out-of-court settlement has been reached, she can likewise move for dismissal. The court can also dismiss the case on its own motion.

Pretrial Motions

Either party may attempt to get the case dismissed before trial through the use of various pretrial motions. We have already mentioned the motion to dismiss. Two other important pretrial motions are the motion for judgment on the pleadings and the motion for summary judgment.

At the close of the pleadings, either party may make a **motion for judgment on the pleadings,** or on the merits of the case. The judge will grant the motion only when there is no dispute over the facts of the case and the sole issue to be resolved is a question of law. In deciding on the motion, the judge may consider only the evidence contained in the pleadings.

In contrast, in a **motion for summary judgment,** the court may consider evidence outside the pleadings, such as sworn statements (affidavits) by parties or witnesses, or other documents relating to the case. Either party can make a motion for summary judgment. As with the motion for judgment on the pleadings, a motion for summary judgment will be granted only if there are no genuine questions of fact and the sole question is a question of law.

Discovery

Discovery A phase in the litigation process during which the opposing parties may obtain information from each other and from third parties prior to trial.

Before a trial begins, each party can use a number of procedural devices to obtain information and gather evidence about the case from the other party or from third parties. The process of obtaining such information is known as **discovery**. Discovery includes gaining access to witnesses, documents, records, and other types of evidence.

The Federal Rules of Civil Procedure and similar rules in the states set forth the guidelines for discovery activity. Generally, discovery is allowed regarding any matter that is not privileged and is relevant to the claim or defense of any party. Discovery rules also attempt to protect witnesses and parties from undue harassment and to safeguard privileged or confidential material from being disclosed. If a discovery request involves privileged or confidential business information, a court can deny the request and can limit the scope of discovery in a number of ways. For instance, a court can require the party to submit the materials to the judge in a sealed envelope so that the judge can decide if they should be disclosed to the opposing party.

Discovery prevents surprises at trial by giving parties access to evidence that might otherwise be hidden. This allows both parties to learn as much as they can about what to expect at a trial before they reach the courtroom. It also serves to narrow the issues so that trial time is spent on the main questions in the case.

Deposition The testimony of a party to a lawsuit or a witness taken under oath before a trial.

DEPOSITIONS AND INTERROGATORIES Discovery can involve the use of depositions or interrogatories, or both. A **deposition** is sworn testimony by a party to the lawsuit or any witness. The person being deposed (the deponent) answers questions asked by the attorneys, and the questions and answers are recorded by an authorized court official and sworn to and signed by the deponent. (Occasionally, written depositions are taken when witnesses are unable to appear in person.) The answers given to depositions will, of course, help the attorneys prepare their cases. They can also be used in court to impeach (challenge the credibility of) a party or a witness who changes her or his testimony at the trial. In addition, the answers given in a deposition can be used as testimony if the witness is not available at trial.

Interrogatories A series of written questions for which written answers are prepared by a party to a lawsuit, usually with the assistance of the party's attorney, and then signed under oath.

Interrogatories are written questions for which written answers are prepared and then signed under oath. The main difference between interrogatories and written depositions is that interrogatories are directed to a party to the lawsuit (the plaintiff or the defendant), not to a witness, and the party can prepare answers with the aid of an attorney. The scope of interrogatories is broader because parties are obligated to answer the questions, even if that means disclosing information from their records and files.

REQUESTS FOR OTHER INFORMATION A party can serve a written request on the other party for an admission of the truth on matters relating to the trial. Any matter admitted under such a request is conclusively established for the trial. For example, Marconi can ask Anderson to admit that he was driving at a speed of forty-five miles an hour. A request for admission saves time at trial because the parties will not have to spend time proving facts on which they already agree.

A party can also gain access to documents and other items not in her or his possession in order to inspect and examine them. Likewise, a party can gain "entry upon land" to inspect the premises. Anderson's attorney, for example, normally can gain permission to inspect and photocopy Marconi's car repair bills.

When the physical or mental condition of one party is in question, the opposing party can ask the court to order a physical or mental examination. If the court issues the order, which it will do only if the need for the information outweighs the right to privacy of the person to be examined, the opposing party can obtain the results of the examination.

ELECTRONIC DISCOVERY   Any relevant material, including information stored electronically, can be the object of a discovery request. The federal rules and most state rules now specifically allow all parties to obtain electronic "data compilations." Electronic evidence, or **e-evidence,** includes all types of computer-generated or electronically recorded information, such as e-mail, voice mail, spreadsheets, word-processing documents, and other data. E-evidence can reveal significant facts that are not discoverable by other means. For example, computers automatically record certain information about files—such as who created the file and when, and who accessed, modified, or transmitted it—on their hard drives. This information can be obtained only from the file in its electronic format—not from printed-out versions.

E-Discovery Procedures.   Amendments to the Federal Rules of Civil Procedure that took effect in 2006 deal specifically with the preservation, retrieval, and production of electronic data. Although traditional means, such as interrogatories and depositions, are still used to find out about the e-evidence, a party must usually hire an expert to retrieve evidence in its electronic format. The expert uses software to reconstruct e-mail exchanges and establish who knew what and when they knew it. The expert can even recover files that the user thought had been deleted from a computer.

Advantages and Disadvantages.   Electronic discovery has significant advantages over paper discovery. Back-up copies of documents and e-mail can provide useful—and often quite damaging—information about how a particular matter progressed over several weeks or months. E-discovery can uncover the proverbial smoking gun that leads to litigation success, but it is also time consuming and expensive, especially when lawsuits involve large firms with multiple offices. Also, many firms are finding it difficult to fulfill their duty to preserve electronic evidence from a vast number of sources. For a discussion of some of the problems associated with preserving electronic evidence for discovery, see this chapter's *Adapting the Law to the Online Environment* feature on the next page.

Pretrial Conference

Either party or the court can request a pretrial conference, or hearing. Usually, the hearing consists of an informal discussion between the judge and the opposing attorneys after discovery has taken place. The purpose of the hearing is to explore the possibility of a settlement without trial and, if this is not possible, to identify the matters that are in dispute and to plan the course of the trial.

Jury Selection

A trial can be held with or without a jury. The Seventh Amendment to the U.S. Constitution guarantees the right to a jury trial for cases in *federal* courts when the amount in controversy exceeds $20, but this guarantee does not apply to state courts. Most states have similar guarantees in their own constitutions (although the threshold dollar amount is higher than $20). The right to a trial by jury does not have to be exercised, and many cases are tried without a jury. In most states and in federal courts, one of the parties must request a jury in a civil case, or the judge presumes the parties waive the right.

Before a jury trial commences, a jury must be selected. The jury selection process is known as **voir dire.**[20] During *voir dire* in most jurisdictions, attorneys for the plaintiff and the defendant ask prospective jurors oral questions to determine whether a potential jury member is biased or has any connection with a party to the action or with a prospective

---

E-Evidence Evidence that consists of computer-generated or electronically recorded information, including e-mail, voice mail, spreadsheets, word-processing documents, and other data.

"The judicial system is the most expensive machine ever invented for finding out what happened and what to do about it."

Irving R. Kaufman, 1910–1992
(American jurist)

ON THE WEB Picking the "right" jury is often an important aspect of litigation strategy, and a number of firms now specialize in jury consulting services. You can learn more about these services by going to the Web site of the Jury Research Institute at **www.jri-inc.com.**

Voir Dire An Old French phrase meaning "to speak the truth." In legal language, the process in which the attorneys question prospective jurors to learn about their backgrounds, attitudes, biases, and other characteristics that may affect their ability to serve as impartial jurors.

---

20. Pronounced vwahr *deehr.*

Adapting the Law to the Online Environment

The Duty to Preserve Electronic Evidence for Discovery

Today, less than 0.5 percent of new information is created on paper. Instead of sending letters and memos, people send e-mails and text messages, creating a massive amount of electronically stored information (ESI). The law requires parties to preserve ESI whenever there is a "reasonable anticipation of litigation."

Why Companies Fail to Preserve E-Evidence

Preserving e-evidence can be a challenge, though, particularly for large corporations that have electronic data scattered across multiple networks, servers, desktops, laptops, handheld devices, and even home computers. While many companies have policies regarding back-up of office e-mail and computer systems, these may cover only a fraction of the e-evidence requested in a lawsuit.

Technological advances further complicate the situation. Users of BlackBerrys, for example, can configure them so that messages are transmitted with limited or no archiving rather than going through a company's servers and being recorded. How can a company preserve e-evidence that is never on its servers? In one case, the court held that a company had a duty to preserve transitory "server log data," which exist only temporarily on a computer's memory.[a]

Potential Sanctions and Malpractice Claims

A court may impose sanctions (such as fines) on a party that fails to preserve electronic evidence or to comply with e-discovery requests. A firm may be sanctioned if it provides e-mails without the attachments, does not produce all of the e-evidence requested, or fails to suspend its automatic e-mail deletion procedures.[b] Nearly 25 percent of the reported opinions on e-discovery from 2008 involved sanctions for failure to

preserve e-evidence.[c] Attorneys who fail to properly advise their clients concerning the duty to preserve e-evidence also often face sanctions and malpractice claims.[d]

Lessons from Intel

A party that fails to preserve e-evidence may even find itself at such a disadvantage that it will settle a dispute rather than continue litigation. For example, Advanced Micro Devices, Inc. (AMD), sued Intel Corporation, one of the world's largest microprocessor suppliers, for violating antitrust laws. Immediately after the lawsuit was filed, Intel began collecting and preserving the ESI on its servers. Although the company instructed its employees to retain documents and e-mails related to competition with AMD, many employees saved only copies of the e-mails that they had received and not e-mails that they had sent. In addition, Intel did not stop its automatic e-mail deletion system, causing other information to be lost. In the end, although Intel produced data that were equivalent to "somewhere in the neighborhood of a pile 137 miles high" in paper, its failure to preserve e-evidence led it to settle the dispute in 2008.[e]

FOR CRITICAL ANALYSIS

How might a large company protect itself from allegations that it intentionally failed to preserve electronic data?

---

a. See *Columbia Pictures v. Brunnell,* 2007 WL 2080419 (C.D.Cal. 2007).
b. See, for example, *John B. v. Goetz,* 531 F.3d 448 (6th Cir. 2008); and *Wingnut Films, Ltd. v. Katija Motion Pictures,* 2007 WL 2758571 (C.D.Cal. 2007).

c. Sheri Qualters, "25% of Reported E-discovery Opinions in 2008 Involved Sanction Issues," *National Law Journal,* December 12, 2008.
d. See, for example, *Qualcomm, Inc. v. Broadcom Corp.,* 539 F.Supp.2d 1214 (S.D.Cal. 2007).
e. See *In re Intel Corp. Microprocessor Antitrust Litigation,* 2008 WL 2310288 (D.Del. 2008). See also *Adams v. Gateway, Inc.,* 2006 WL 2563418 (D. Utah 2006).

TAKE NOTE A prospective juror cannot be excluded solely on the basis of his or her race or gender.

witness. In some jurisdictions, the judge may do all or part of the questioning based on written questions submitted by counsel for the parties.

During *voir dire,* a party may challenge a prospective juror *peremptorily*—that is, ask that an individual not be sworn in as a juror without providing any reason. Alternatively, a party may challenge a prospective juror *for cause*—that is, provide a reason why an individual should not be sworn in as a juror. If the judge grants the challenge, the individual is asked to step down. A prospective juror may not be excluded from the jury by the use of discriminatory challenges, however, such as those based on racial criteria or gender.

At the Trial

At the beginning of the trial, the attorneys present their opening arguments, setting forth the facts that they expect to prove during the trial. Then the plaintiff's case is presented. In our hypothetical case, Marconi's lawyer would introduce evidence (relevant documents, exhibits, and the testimony of witnesses) to support Marconi's position. The defendant has the opportunity to challenge any evidence introduced and to cross-examine any of the plaintiff's witnesses.

Motion for a Directed Verdict In a jury trial, a motion for the judge to take the decision out of the hands of the jury and to direct a verdict for the party who filed the motion on the ground that the other party has not produced sufficient evidence to support her or his claim.

At the end of the plaintiff's case, the defendant's attorney has the opportunity to ask the judge to direct a verdict for the defendant on the ground that the plaintiff has presented no evidence that would justify the granting of the plaintiff's remedy. This is called a **motion for a directed verdict** (known in federal courts as a *motion for judgment as a matter of law*). If the motion is not granted (it seldom is granted), the defendant's attorney then presents the evidence and witnesses for the defendant's case. At the conclusion of the defendant's case, the defendant's attorney has another opportunity to make a motion for a directed verdict. The plaintiff's attorney can challenge any evidence introduced and cross-examine the defendant's witnesses.

After the defense concludes its presentation, the attorneys present their closing arguments, each urging a verdict in favor of her or his client. The judge instructs the jury in the law that applies to the case (these instructions are often called *charges*), and the jury retires to the jury room to deliberate a verdict. In the Marconi-Anderson case, the jury will not only decide for the plaintiff or for the defendant but, if it finds for the plaintiff, will also decide on the amount of the **award** (the compensation to be paid to her).

Award In litigation, the amount of monetary compensation awarded to a plaintiff in a civil lawsuit as damages. In the context of alternative dispute resolution, the decision rendered by an arbitrator.

Posttrial Motions

After the jury has rendered its verdict, either party may make a posttrial motion. If Marconi wins and Anderson's attorney has previously moved for a directed verdict, Anderson's attorney may make a **motion for judgment n.o.v.** (from the Latin *non obstante veredicto*, which means "notwithstanding the verdict"—called a *motion for judgment as a matter of law* in the federal courts). Such a motion will be granted only if the jury's verdict was unreasonable and erroneous. If the judge grants the motion, the jury's verdict will be set aside, and a judgment will be entered in favor of the opposite party (Anderson).

Motion for Judgment N.O.V. A motion requesting the court to grant judgment in favor of the party making the motion on the ground that the jury's verdict against him or her was unreasonable and erroneous.

Motion for a New Trial A motion asserting that the trial was so fundamentally flawed (because of error, newly discovered evidence, prejudice, or another reason) that a new trial is necessary to prevent a miscarriage of justice.

Alternatively, Anderson could make a **motion for a new trial**, asking the judge to set aside the adverse verdict and to hold a new trial. The motion will be granted if, after looking at all the evidence, the judge is convinced that the jury was in error but does not feel that it is appropriate to grant judgment for the other side. A judge can also grant a new trial on the basis of newly discovered evidence, misconduct by the participants or the jury during the trial, or error by the judge.

The Appeal

Assume here that any posttrial motion is denied and that Anderson appeals the case. (If Marconi wins but receives a smaller monetary award than she sought, she can appeal also.) Keep in mind, though, that a party cannot appeal a trial court's decision simply because he or she is dissatisfied with the outcome of the trial. A party must have legitimate grounds to file an appeal; that is, he or she must be able to claim that the lower court committed an error. If Anderson has grounds to appeal the case, a notice of appeal must be filed with the clerk of the trial court within a prescribed time. Anderson now becomes the appellant, or petitioner, and Marconi becomes the appellee, or respondent.

Brief A formal legal document prepared by a party's attorney for the appellant or the appellee (in answer to the appellant's brief) and submitted to an appellate court when a case is appealed. The appellant's brief outlines the facts and issues of the case, the judge's rulings or jury's findings that should be reversed or modified, the applicable law, and the arguments on the client's behalf.

FILING THE APPEAL Anderson's attorney files the record on appeal with the appellate court. The record includes the pleadings, the trial transcript, the judge's rulings on motions made by the parties, and other trial-related documents. Anderson's attorney will also provide the reviewing court with a condensation of the record, known as an *abstract*, and a brief. The **brief** is a formal legal document outlining the facts and issues of the case, the judge's rulings or jury's findings that should be reversed or modified, the applicable law, and arguments on Anderson's behalf (citing applicable statutes and relevant cases as precedents).

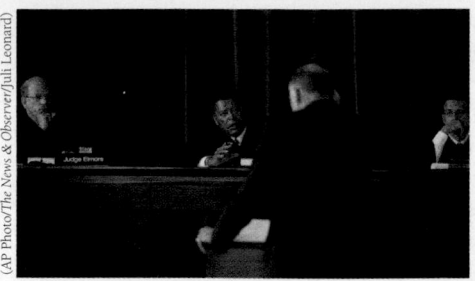

Most appellate decisions are made by three-judge panels. Do such court proceedings usually involve new evidence? Why or why not?

Marconi's attorney will file an answering brief. Anderson's attorney can file a reply to Marconi's brief, although it is not required. The reviewing court then considers the case.

APPELLATE REVIEW   As mentioned earlier, a court of appeals does not hear evidence. Rather, it reviews the record for errors of law. Its decision concerning a case is based on the record on appeal, the abstracts, and the attorneys' briefs. The attorneys can present oral arguments, after which the case is taken under advisement. In general, appellate courts do not reverse findings of fact unless the findings are unsupported or contradicted by the evidence.

An appellate court has the following options after reviewing a case:

1. The court can *affirm* the trial court's decision.
2. The court can *reverse* the trial court's judgment if it concludes that the trial court erred or that the jury did not receive proper instructions.
3. The appellate court can *remand* (send back) the case to the trial court for further proceedings consistent with its opinion on the matter.
4. The court might also affirm or reverse a decision *in part*. For example, the court might affirm the jury's finding that Anderson was negligent but remand the case for further proceedings on another issue (such as the extent of Marconi's damages).
5. An appellate court can also *modify* a lower court's decision. If the appellate court decides that the jury awarded an excessive amount in damages, for example, the court might reduce the award to a more appropriate, or fairer, amount.

Appellate courts apply different standards of review depending on the type of issue involved and the lower court's rulings. Generally, these standards require the reviewing court to give a certain amount of deference, or weight, to the findings of lower courts on specific issues. The following case illustrates the importance of standards of review as a means of exercising judicial restraint.

Case 3.2   **Evans v. Eaton Corp.**

United States Court of Appeals, Fourth Circuit, 514 F.3d 315 (2008).

FACTS   Eaton Corporation is a multinational manufacturing company that funds and administers a long-term disability benefits plan for its employees. Brenda Evans was an employee at Eaton. In 1998, due to severe rheumatoid arthritis, Evans quit her job at Eaton and filed for disability benefits. Eaton paid disability benefits to Evans without controversy prior to 2003,

but that year, Evans's disability status became questionable. Her physician had prescribed a new medication that had dramatically improved Evans's arthritis. In addition, Evans had injured her spine in a car accident in 2002 and was claiming to be disabled by continuing back problems as well as arthritis. But diagnostic exams indicated that the injuries to Evans's back were not severe, and she could cook, shop, do laundry, wash dishes, and drive about seven miles a day. By 2004, medical opinion on Evans's condition was mixed. Some physicians who had examined Evans concluded that she was still disabled, but several other physicians had determined that Evans was no longer totally disabled and could work. On that basis, Eaton terminated her disability benefits. Evans filed a complaint in the U.S. District Court for South Carolina alleging violations of the Employee Retirement Income Security Act

of 1974 (ERISA, a federal law regulating pension plans that will be discussed in Chapter 24). The district court examined the evidence in great detail and concluded that Eaton had abused its discretion in failing to find Evans's examining physicians' opinions more credible. Eaton appealed.

ISSUE   When applying the abuse of discretion standard, should a reviewing court reverse a decision simply because it would have arrived at a different conclusion based on its perception of the witnesses' credibility?

DECISION   No. The U.S. Court of Appeals for the Fourth Circuit reversed the district court's award of benefits to Evans and remanded the case with instructions to the district court to enter a judgment in favor of Eaton. The district court incorrectly applied the abuse of discretion standard when reviewing Eaton's termination of Evans's benefits.

REASON   When reviewing a decision for abuse of discretion, a court must give deference, or weight, to the findings of fact made by the trial court—or in this case, the ERISA plan administrator. The court found that the ERISA plan's language was unambiguous and gave Eaton "discretion-

Case 3.2–Continued

ary authority to determine eligibility for benefits." It also gave the plan administrator "the power and discretion to determine all questions of fact * * * arising in connection with the administration, interpretation and application of the Plan." The court reasoned that "the abuse of discretion standard requires a reviewing court to show enough deference to a primary decision-maker's judgment that the court does not reverse merely because it would have come to a different result." Moreover, under this standard, a reviewing court must give weight to the administrator's decision "even if another, and arguably a better, decision-maker might have come to a different, and arguably a better, result."

FOR CRITICAL ANALYSIS—Ethical Consideration   *The appellate court noted in this case that the district court's decision—which granted benefits to Evans—might arguably have been a better decision under the facts. If the court believed that the district court's conclusion was arguably better, then why did it reverse the decision? What does this tell you about the standards for review that appellate judges use?*

APPEAL TO A HIGHER APPELLATE COURT   If the reviewing court is an intermediate appellate court, the losing party may decide to appeal to the state supreme court (the highest state court). Such a petition corresponds to a petition for a writ of *certiorari* from the United States Supreme Court. Although the losing party has a right to ask (petition) a higher court to review the case, the party does not have a right to have the case heard by the higher appellate court.

Appellate courts normally have discretionary power and can accept or reject an appeal. Like the United States Supreme Court, in general state supreme courts deny most appeals. If the appeal is granted, new briefs must be filed before the state supreme court, and the attorneys may be allowed or requested to present oral arguments. Like the intermediate appellate court, the supreme court may reverse or affirm the appellate court's decision or remand the case. At this point, the case typically has reached its end (unless a federal question is at issue and one of the parties has legitimate grounds to seek review by a federal appellate court).

Enforcing the Judgment

The uncertainties of the litigation process are compounded by the lack of guarantees that any judgment will be enforceable. Even if a plaintiff wins an award of damages in court, the defendant may not have sufficient assets or insurance to cover that amount. Usually, one of the factors considered before a lawsuit is initiated is whether the defendant has sufficient assets to cover the amount of damages sought, should the plaintiff win the case. What other factors should be considered when deciding whether to initiate a lawsuit? See the *Business Application* feature at the end of this chapter for answers to this question.

▶ The Courts Adapt to the Online World

We have already mentioned that the courts have attempted to adapt traditional jurisdictional concepts to the online world. Not surprisingly, the Internet has also brought about changes in court procedures and practices, including new methods for filing pleadings and other documents and issuing decisions and opinions. Some jurisdictions are exploring the possibility of cyber courts, in which legal proceedings could be conducted totally online.

Electronic Filing

ON THE WEB For a list of the federal courts that accept electronic filing, go to the following page at a Web site maintained by the Administrative Office of the U.S. Courts: **www.uscourts.gov/cmecf/ cmecf_court.html**.

The federal court system has now implemented its electronic filing system, Case Management/Electronic Case Files (CM/ECF), in nearly all of the federal courts. The system is available in federal district, appellate, and bankruptcy courts, as well as the Court of International Trade and the Court of Federal Claims. More than 33 million cases are on the CM/ECF system. Users can create a document using conventional word-processing software, save it as a PDF file, then log on to a court's Web site, and submit the PDF to the court via the Internet. Access to the electronic documents filed on CM/ECF is available through a system called PACER (Public Access to Court Electronic Records), which is a service of the U.S. Judiciary.

More than 60 percent of the states have some form of electronic filing. Some states, including Arizona, California, Colorado, Delaware, Mississippi, New Jersey, New York, and Nevada, offer statewide e-filing systems. Generally, when electronic filing is made available, it is optional. Nonetheless, some state courts have now made e-filing mandatory in certain types of disputes, such as complex civil litigation.

Courts Online

Most courts today have sites on the Web. Of course, each court decides what to make available at its site. Some courts display only the names of court personnel and office phone numbers. Others add court rules and forms. Many appellate court sites include judicial decisions, although the decisions may remain online for only a limited time. In addition, in some states, such as California and Florida, court clerks offer **docket** (the court's schedule of cases to be heard) information and other searchable databases online.

Appellate court decisions are often posted online immediately after they are rendered. Recent decisions of the U.S. courts of appeals, for example, are available online at their Web sites. The United States Supreme Court also has an official Web site and publishes its opinions there immediately after they are announced to the public. (These Web sites are listed elsewhere in this chapter in the *On the Web* features.) In fact, even decisions that are designated as unpublished opinions by the appellate courts are often published online (as discussed in the *Adapting the Law to the Online Environment* feature in Chapter 1 on page 12).

Cyber Courts and Proceedings

Someday, litigants may be able to use cyber courts, in which judicial proceedings take place only on the Internet. The parties to a case could meet online to make their arguments and present their evidence. This might be done with e-mail submissions, through video cameras, in designated chat rooms, at closed sites, or through the use of other Internet facilities. These courtrooms could be efficient and economical. We might also see the use of virtual lawyers, judges, and juries—and possibly the replacement of court personnel with computer software.

Already the state of Michigan has passed legislation creating cyber courts that will hear cases involving technology issues and high-tech businesses. In 2008, the state of Wisconsin enacted a rule authorizing the use of videoconferencing in both civil and criminal trials, at the discretion of the trial court.[21] In some situations, a Wisconsin judge can allow videoconferencing even over the objection of the parties, provided certain operational criteria are met.

The courts may also use the Internet in other ways. In a groundbreaking decision in early 2001, for instance, a Florida county court granted "virtual" visitation rights in a couple's divorce proceeding. Each parent was ordered to set up a computerized videoconferencing system so that his or her child could visit with the parent who did not have custody via the Internet at any time.

 ## Alternative Dispute Resolution

Litigation is expensive. It is also time consuming. Because of the backlog of cases pending in many courts, several years may pass before a case is actually tried. For these and other reasons, more and more businesspersons are turning to **alternative dispute resolution (ADR)** as a means of settling their disputes.

---

21. Wisconsin Statute Section 751.12.

ON THE WEB For links to state court rules addressing electronic filing, go to the following site, which is provided by the National Center for State Courts: **www.ncsconline.org/wc/courtopics/topiclisting.asp**.

Docket The list of cases entered on a court's calendar and thus scheduled to be heard by the court.

Alternative Dispute Resolution (ADR) The resolution of disputes in ways other than those involved in the traditional judicial process. Negotiation, mediation, and arbitration are forms of ADR.

The great advantage of ADR is its flexibility. Methods of ADR range from the parties sitting down together and attempting to work out their differences to multinational corporations agreeing to resolve a dispute through a formal hearing before a panel of experts. Normally, the parties themselves can control how the dispute will be settled, what procedures will be used, whether a neutral third party will be present or make a decision, and whether that decision will be legally binding or nonbinding.

Today, more than 90 percent of cases are settled before trial through some form of ADR. Indeed, most states either require or encourage parties to undertake ADR prior to trial. Many federal courts have instituted ADR programs as well. In the following pages, we examine the basic forms of ADR. Keep in mind, though, that new methods of ADR—and new combinations of existing methods—are constantly being devised and employed.

Negotiation

Negotiation A process in which parties attempt to settle their dispute informally, with or without attorneys to represent them.

The simplest form of ADR is **negotiation,** a process in which the parties attempt to settle their dispute informally, with or without attorneys to represent them. Attorneys frequently advise their clients to negotiate a settlement voluntarily before they proceed to trial. Parties may even try to negotiate a settlement during a trial, or after the trial but before an appeal. Negotiation traditionally involves just the parties themselves and (typically) their attorneys. The attorneys, though, are advocates—they are obligated to put their clients' interests first.

Mediation

Mediation A method of settling disputes outside the courts by using the services of a neutral third party, who acts as a communicating agent between the parties and assists them in negotiating a settlement.

In **mediation,** a neutral third party acts as a mediator and works with both sides in the dispute to facilitate a resolution. The mediator talks with the parties separately as well as jointly and emphasizes their points of agreement in an attempt to help the parties evaluate their options. Although the mediator may propose a solution (called a *mediator's proposal*), he or she does not make a decision resolving the matter. States that require parties to undergo ADR before trial often offer mediation as one of the ADR options or (as in Florida) the only option.

One of the biggest advantages of mediation is that it is not as adversarial as litigation. In trials, the parties "do battle" with each other in the courtroom, trying to prove one another wrong, while the judge is usually a passive observer. In mediation, the mediator takes an active role and attempts to bring the parties together so that they can come to a mutually satisfactory resolution. The mediation process tends to reduce the hostility between the disputants, allowing them to resume their former relationship without bad feelings. For this reason, mediation is often the preferred form of ADR for disputes involving business partners, employers and employees, or other parties involved in long-term relationships.

EXAMPLE 3.11 Two business partners, Mark Shalen and Charles Rowe, have a dispute over how the profits of their firm should be distributed. If the dispute is litigated, the parties will be adversaries, and their respective attorneys will emphasize how the parties' positions differ, not what they have in common. In contrast, when the dispute is mediated, the mediator emphasizes the common ground shared by Shalen and Rowe and helps them work toward agreement. The two men can work out the distribution of profits without damaging their continuing relationship as partners. ●

Arbitration

Arbitration The settling of a dispute by submitting it to a disinterested third party (other than a court), who renders a decision that is (most often) legally binding.

A more formal method of ADR is **arbitration,** in which an arbitrator (a neutral third party or a panel of experts) hears a dispute and imposes a resolution on the parties. Arbitration is unlike other forms of ADR because the third party hearing the dispute makes a decision for the parties. Exhibit 3–4 on the next page outlines the basic differences among the three traditional forms of ADR. Usually, the parties in arbitration agree that the third party's decision

• *Exhibit* 3–4 Basic Differences in the Traditional Forms of Alternative Dispute Resolution

TYPE OF ADR	DESCRIPTION	NEUTRAL THIRD PARTY PRESENT	WHO DECIDES THE RESOLUTION
Negotiation	The parties meet informally with or without their attorneys and attempt to agree on a resolution.	No	The parties themselves reach a resolution.
Mediation	A neutral third party meets with the parties and emphasizes points of agreement to help them resolve their dispute.	Yes	The parties, but the mediator may suggest or propose a resolution.
Arbitration	The parties present their arguments and evidence before an arbitrator at a hearing, and the arbitrator renders a decision resolving the parties' dispute.	Yes	The arbitrator imposes a resolution on the parties that may be either binding or nonbinding.

ON THE WEB For a collection of information and links related to alternative dispute resolution, mediation, and arbitration, go to the Web site of Hieros Gamos at www.hg.org/adr.html.

Arbitration Clause   A clause in a contract that provides that, in the event of a dispute, the parties will submit the dispute to arbitration rather than litigate the dispute in court.

Supporters of a union that represents firefighters stage a protest during a contract dispute with Philadelphia. An arbitration panel ruled in favor of the union and ordered a wage increase, and the city appealed. On what grounds can a court, on appeal, set aside the decision of an arbitration panel?

(Courtesy of the Philadelphia Fire Fighters' Union)

will be *legally binding*, although the parties can also agree to *nonbinding* arbitration. (Arbitration that is mandated by the courts often is nonbinding.) In nonbinding arbitration, the parties can go forward with a lawsuit if they do not agree with the arbitrator's decision.

In some respects, formal arbitration resembles a trial, although usually the procedural rules are much less restrictive than those governing litigation. In the typical arbitration, the parties present opening arguments and ask for specific remedies. Evidence is then presented, and witnesses may be called and examined by both sides. The arbitrator then renders a decision, which is called an *award*.

An arbitrator's award is usually the final word on the matter. Although the parties may appeal an arbitrator's decision, a court's review of the decision will be much more restricted in scope than an appellate court's review of a trial court's decision. The general view is that because the parties were free to frame the issues and set the powers of the arbitrator at the outset, they cannot complain about the results. The award will be set aside only if the arbitrator's conduct or "bad faith" substantially prejudiced the rights of one of the parties, if the award violates an established public policy, or if the arbitrator exceeded her or his powers (arbitrated issues that the parties did not agree to submit to arbitration).

ARBITRATION CLAUSES AND STATUTES   Just about any commercial matter can be submitted to arbitration. Frequently, parties include an **arbitration clause** in a contract (a written agreement—see Chapter 9); the clause provides that any dispute that arises under the contract will be resolved through arbitration rather than through the court system. Parties can also agree to arbitrate a dispute after a dispute arises.

Most states have statutes (often based in part on the Uniform Arbitration Act of 1955) under which arbitration clauses will be enforced, and some state statutes compel arbitration of certain types of disputes, such as those involving public employees. At the federal level, the Federal Arbitration Act (FAA), enacted in 1925, enforces arbitration clauses in contracts involving maritime activity and interstate commerce (though its applicability to employment contracts has been controversial, as discussed in a later subsection). Because of the breadth of the commerce clause (see Chapter 2), arbitration agreements involving transactions only slightly connected to the flow of interstate commerce may fall under the FAA.

CASE EXAMPLE 3.12   Buckeye Check Cashing, Inc., cashes personal checks for consumers in Florida. Buckeye would agree to delay submitting a consumer's check for payment if the consumer paid a "finance charge." For each transaction, the consumer signed an agreement that included an arbitration clause. A group of consumers filed a lawsuit claiming that Buckeye was charging an illegally high rate of interest in violation of state law. Buckeye filed a motion to compel arbitration, which the trial court denied, and the case was appealed. The plaintiffs argued that the entire contract—including the arbitration clause—was illegal and therefore arbitration was not required. The United States Supreme Court found that the arbitration provision was *severable,* or capable of being separated, from the rest of the contract. The Court held that when the challenge is to the validity of a contract as a whole, and not specifically to an arbitration clause within the contract, an arbitrator must resolve the dispute. This is true even if the contract later proves to be unenforceable, because the FAA established a national policy favoring arbitration and that policy extends to both federal and state courts.[22] ●

KEEP IN MIND Litigation—even of a dispute over whether a particular matter should be submitted to arbitration—can be time consuming and expensive.

THE ISSUE OF ARBITRABILITY Notice that in the preceding case example, the issue before the United States Supreme Court was *not* the basic controversy (whether the interest rate charged was illegally high) but rather the issue of arbitrability—that is, whether the matter was one that had to be resolved by arbitration under the arbitration clause. Such actions, in which one party files a motion to compel arbitration, often occur when a dispute arises over an agreement that contains an arbitration clause. If the court finds that the subject matter in controversy is covered by the agreement to arbitrate—even when the claim involves the violation of a statute, such as an employment statute—then a party may be compelled to arbitrate the dispute. Usually, a court will allow the claim to be arbitrated if the court, in interpreting the statute, can find no legislative intent to the contrary.

No party, however, will be ordered to submit a particular dispute to arbitration unless the court is convinced that the party consented to do so.[23] Additionally, the courts will not compel arbitration if it is clear that the prescribed arbitration rules and procedures are inherently unfair to one of the parties.

The terms of an arbitration agreement can limit the types of disputes that the parties agree to arbitrate. When the parties do not specify limits, however, disputes can arise as to whether a particular matter is covered by the arbitration agreement; then it is up to the court to resolve the issue of arbitrability. In the following case, the parties had previously agreed to arbitrate disputes involving their contract to develop software, but the dispute involved claims of copyright infringement (see Chapter 5). The question was whether the copyright infringement claims were beyond the scope of the arbitration clause.

---

22. *Buckeye Check Cashing, Inc. v. Cardegna,* 546 U.S. 440, 126 S.Ct. 1204, 163 L.Ed.2d 1038 (2006).
23. See, for example, *Wright v. Universal Maritime Service Corp.,* 525 U.S. 70, 119 S.Ct. 391, 142 L.Ed.2d 361 (1998).

Case 3.3 NCR Corp. v. Korala Associates, Ltd.

United States Court of Appeals, Sixth Circuit, 512 F.3d 807 (2008).
www.ca6.uscourts.gov[a]

COMPANY PROFILE In 1884, John H. Patterson founded the National Cash Register Company (NCR), maker of the first mechanical cash registers. In 1906, NCR created a cash register run by an electric motor. By 1914, the company had developed one of the first automated credit systems. By the 1950s, NCR had branched out into transistorized business computers and later into liquid crystal displays and data warehousing. Today, NCR is a worldwide provider of automated teller machines (ATMs), integrated hardware and software systems, and related maintenance and support services. More than 300,000 NCR ATMs are installed throughout the world.

FACTS To upgrade the security of its ATMs, NCR developed a software solution to install in all of its machines. At the same time, Korala Associates, Ltd. (KAL), claimed to have developed a similar security upgrade for NCR's ATMs. Indeed, KAL had entered into a contract with NCR in 1998 (the "1998 Agreement") to develop such software. To enable KAL to do so, NCR loaned to KAL a proprietary ATM that contained copyrighted

(Wikipedia Image)

A vintage NCR cash register on display in a museum.

a. Click on "Opinions Search" and then on "Short Title," and type "NCR." Click on "Submit Query." Next, click on the opinion link in the first column of the row corresponding to the name of this case.

Case 3.3—Continues next page ➡

Case 3.3—Continued

software called "APTRA XFS." NCR alleged that KAL "obtained access to, made unauthorized use of, and engaged in unauthorized copying of the APTRA XFS software." By so doing, KAL developed its own version of a security upgrade for NCR's ATMs. When NCR brought suit against KAL, the latter moved to compel arbitration under the terms of the 1998 Agreement. At trial, KAL prevailed. NCR appealed the order compelling arbitration.

ISSUE   Did the arbitration clause in the parties' agreement regarding software development require the arbitration of a later dispute involving copyright infringement?

DECISION   Yes. The U.S. Court of Appeals for the Sixth Circuit affirmed the part of the district court's decision compelling arbitration as to NCR's claims relating to direct copyright infringement of the APTRA XFS software.

REASON   The court pointed out that the 1998 Agreement clearly provided for arbitration. As to the issue of whether NCR's claims fell within the substantive scope of the agreement, the court observed that "as a matter of Federal law, any doubts concerning the scope of arbitrable issues should be resolved in favor of arbitration." Because the arbitration clause in the 1998 Agreement was so broad, the appellate court reasoned that a trial court should follow the "presumption of arbitration and resolve doubts in favor of arbitration." Consequently, the court found that NCR's copyright infringement claims fell within the scope of the arbitration agreement.

FOR CRITICAL ANALYSIS—Social Consideration   *Why do you think that NCR did not want its claims decided by arbitration?*

MANDATORY ARBITRATION IN THE EMPLOYMENT CONTEXT   A significant question in the last several years has concerned mandatory arbitration clauses in employment contracts. Many claim that employees' rights are not sufficiently protected when workers are forced, as a condition of being hired, to agree to arbitrate all disputes and thus waive their rights under statutes specifically designed to protect employees. The United States Supreme Court, however, has generally held that mandatory arbitration clauses in employment contracts are enforceable.

CASE EXAMPLE 3.13   In a landmark decision, *Gilmer v. Interstate/Johnson Lane Corp.*,[24] the Supreme Court held that a claim brought under a federal statute prohibiting age discrimination (see Chapter 25) could be subject to arbitration. The Court concluded that the employee had waived his right to sue when he agreed, as part of a required registration application to be a securities representative with the New York Stock Exchange, to arbitrate "any dispute, claim, or controversy" relating to his employment. ●

Since the *Gilmer* decision, some courts have refused to enforce one-sided arbitration clauses on the ground that they are unconscionable (see Chapter 11).[25] Thus, businesspersons considering using arbitration clauses in employment contracts should be careful that they are not too one sided—especially provisions on how the parties will split the costs of the arbitration procedure. Also, note that Congress is considering legislation (the Arbitration Fairness Act) that, if enacted, would effectively ban arbitration clauses in employment, consumer, and franchise contracts.

Other Types of ADR

The three forms of ADR just discussed are the oldest and traditionally the most commonly used. In recent years, a variety of new types of ADR have emerged. Some parties today are using *assisted negotiation*, in which a third party participates in the negotiation process. The third party may be an expert in the subject matter of the dispute. In *early neutral case evaluation*, the parties explain the situation to the expert, and the expert assesses the strengths and weaknesses of each party's claims. Another form of assisted negotiation is the *mini-trial*, in which the parties present arguments before the third party (usually an expert), who renders an advisory opinion on how a court would likely decide the issue. This proceed-

---

24. 500 U.S. 20, 111 S.Ct. 1647, 114 L.Ed.2d 26 (1991).
25. See, for example, *Davis v. O'Melveny & Myers, LLC*, 485 F.3d 1066 (9th Cir. 2007); and *Nagrampa v. MailCoups, Inc.*, 469 F.3d 1257 (9th Cir. 2006).

ing is designed to assist the parties in determining whether they should settle or take the dispute to court.

Other types of ADR combine characteristics of mediation with those of arbitration. In *binding mediation,* for example, the parties agree that if they cannot resolve the dispute, the mediator may make a legally binding decision on the issue. In *mediation-arbitration,* or "med-arb," the parties agree to attempt to settle their dispute through mediation. If no settlement is reached, the dispute will be arbitrated.

Today's courts are also experimenting with a variety of ADR alternatives to speed up (and reduce the cost of) justice. Numerous federal courts now hold **summary jury trials (SJTs),** in which the parties present their arguments and evidence and the jury renders a verdict. The jury's verdict is not binding, but it does act as a guide to both sides in reaching an agreement during the mandatory negotiations that immediately follow the trial. Other alternatives being employed by the courts include summary procedures for commercial litigation and the appointment of special masters to assist judges in deciding complex issues.

Providers of ADR Services

ADR services are provided by both government agencies and private organizations. A major provider of ADR services is the American Arbitration Association (AAA), which was founded in 1926 and now handles more than 200,000 claims a year in its numerous offices worldwide. Most of the largest U.S. law firms are members of this nonprofit association. Cases brought before the AAA are heard by an expert or a panel of experts in the area relating to the dispute and are usually settled quickly. The AAA has a special team devoted to resolving large, complex disputes across a wide range of industries.

Hundreds of for-profit firms around the country also provide various forms of dispute-resolution services. Typically, these firms hire retired judges to conduct arbitration hearings or otherwise assist parties in settling their disputes. The judges follow procedures similar to those of the federal courts and use similar rules. Usually, each party to the dispute pays a filing fee and a designated fee for a hearing session or conference.

Online Dispute Resolution

An increasing number of companies and organizations offer dispute-resolution services using the Internet. The settlement of disputes in these online forums is known as **online dispute resolution (ODR).** The disputes have most commonly involved disagreements over the rights to domain names (Web site addresses—see Chapter 5) or over the quality of goods sold via the Internet, including goods sold through Internet auction sites.

ODR may be best suited for resolving small- to medium-sized business liability claims, which may not be worth the expense of litigation or traditional ADR. Rules being developed in online forums, however, may ultimately become a code of conduct for everyone who does business in cyberspace. Most online forums do not automatically apply the law of any specific jurisdiction. Instead, results are often based on general, universal legal principles. As with most offline methods of dispute resolution, any party may appeal to a court at any time.

Interestingly, some cities are using ODR as a means of resolving claims against them. **EXAMPLE 3.14** New York City has been using Cybersettle (**www.cybersettle.com**) to resolve auto accident, sidewalk, and other personal-injury claims made against the city. In 2007, Cybersettle signed a three-year contract with the city to provide services for negotiating settlements over the Internet. Using this system, parties with complaints submit their claims, and the city submits its offers confidentially via the Internet. Whenever an offer exceeds the claim, a settlement is reached, and the plaintiff gets to keep half of the difference between his or her claim and the city's offer as a bonus. ●

Summary Jury Trial (SJT)   A method of settling disputes, used in many federal courts, in which a trial is held, but the jury's verdict is not binding. The verdict acts only as a guide to both sides in reaching an agreement during the mandatory negotiations that immediately follow the summary jury trial.

ON THE WEB To obtain information on the services offered by the American Arbitration Association (AAA), as well as forms that are used to submit a case for arbitration, go to the AAA's Web site at **www.adr.org**.

Online Dispute Resolution (ODR)   The resolution of disputes with the assistance of organizations that offer dispute-resolution services via the Internet.

Reviewing . . . Courts and Alternative Dispute Resolution

Stan Garner resides in Illinois and promotes boxing matches for SuperSports, Inc., an Illinois corporation. Garner created the promotional concept of the "Ages" fights—a series of three boxing matches pitting an older fighter (George Foreman) against a younger fighter. The concept included titles for each of the three fights ("Challenge of the Ages," "Battle of the Ages," and "Fight of the Ages"), as well as promotional epithets to characterize the two fighters ("the Foreman Factor"). Garner contacted George Foreman and his manager, who both reside in Texas, to sell the idea, and they arranged a meeting at Caesar's Palace in Las Vegas, Nevada. At some point in the negotiations, Foreman's manager signed a nondisclosure agreement prohibiting him from disclosing Garner's promotional concepts unless they signed a contract. Nevertheless, after negotiations fell through, Foreman used Garner's "Battle of the Ages" concept to promote a subsequent fight. Garner filed a lawsuit against Foreman and his manager in a federal district court in Illinois, alleging breach of contract. Using the information presented in the chapter, answer the following questions.

1. On what basis might the federal district court in Illinois exercise jurisdiction in this case?
2. Does the federal district court have original or appellate jurisdiction?
3. Suppose that Garner had filed his action in an Illinois state court. Could an Illinois state court exercise personal jurisdiction over Foreman or his manager? Why or why not?
4. Assume that Garner had filed his action in a Nevada state court. Would that court have personal jurisdiction over Foreman or his manager? Explain.

Business Application
To Sue or Not to Sue?*

Inadvertently or intentionally, wrongs are committed every day in the United States. Sometimes, businesspersons believe that wrongs have been committed against them by other businesspersons, by consumers, or by the government. If you are deciding whether to sue for a wrong committed against you or your business, you must consider many issues.

The Question of Cost

Competent legal advice is expensive. Commercial business law attorneys charge $100 to $600 an hour, plus expenses. It is almost always worthwhile to make an initial visit to an attorney who has skills in the area in which you are going to sue to get an estimate of the expected costs of pursuing redress for your grievance. Note that less than 10 percent of all corporate lawsuits go to trial—the rest are settled beforehand. You may end up settling for far less than you think you are "owed" simply because of the length of time it will take and the cost of going to court. And then you might not win, anyway! Basically, you must do a cost-benefit analysis to determine whether you should sue. An attorney can give you an estimate of the costs involved in litigation. Realize, though, that litigation also involves nondollar costs such as time away from your business, stress, and publicity. You can "guesstimate" the benefits by multiplying the probable size of the award by the probability of obtaining that award.

The Alternatives before You

Negotiation, mediation, arbitration, and other alternative dispute resolution (ADR) forms are becoming increasingly attractive alternatives

to court litigation because they usually yield quick results at a comparatively low cost. Most disputes relating to business can be mediated or arbitrated through the American Arbitration Association (AAA).

There are numerous other ADR providers as well. You can obtain information on ADR from the AAA, courthouses, chambers of commerce, law firms, state bar associations, or the American Bar Association. The Yellow Pages in large metropolitan areas usually list agencies and firms that can help you settle your dispute out of court. You can also locate providers on the Web by using a general search engine and searching for arbitration providers in a specific city.

CHECKLIST FOR DECIDING WHETHER TO SUE

1. **Are you prepared to pay for going to court? Make this decision only after you have consulted an attorney to get an estimate of the costs of litigating the dispute.**
2. **Do you have the patience to follow a court case through the judicial system, even if it takes several years?**
3. **Is there a way for you to settle your grievance without going to court? Even if the settlement is less than you think you are owed, you may be better off settling now for the smaller figure.**
4. **Can you use some form of ADR? Investigate these alternatives— they are usually cheaper and quicker to use than the courts.**

*This *Business Application* is not meant to substitute for the services of an attorney who is licensed to practice law in your state.

Key Terms

alternative dispute resolution (ADR) 78	exclusive jurisdiction 61	online dispute resolution (ODR) 83
answer 71	federal question 61	pleadings 70
arbitration 79	interrogatories 72	probate court 60
arbitration clause 80	judicial review 58	question of fact 68
award 75	jurisdiction 58	question of law 68
bankruptcy court 60	justiciable controversy 64	reply 71
brief 75	litigation 70	rule of four 70
complaint 70	long arm statute 59	small claims court 66
concurrent jurisdiction 61	mediation 79	standing to sue 64
counterclaim 71	motion for a directed verdict 75	summary jury trial (SJT) 83
default judgment 71	motion for a new trial 75	summons 71
deposition 72	motion for judgment *n.o.v.* 75	venue 63
discovery 72	motion for judgment on the pleadings 71	*voir dire* 73
diversity of citizenship 61	motion for summary judgment 71	writ of *certiorari* 69
docket 78	motion to dismiss 71	
e-evidence 73	negotiation 79	

Chapter Summary: Courts and Alternative Dispute Resolution

The Judiciary's Role in American Government (See pages 57–58.)	The role of the judiciary—the courts—in the American governmental system is to interpret and apply the law. Through the process of judicial review—determining the constitutionality of laws—the judicial branch acts as a check on the executive and legislative branches of government.

Basic Judicial Requirements (See pages 58–65.)	1. *Jurisdiction*—Before a court can hear a case, it must have jurisdiction over the person against whom the suit is brought or the property involved in the suit, as well as jurisdiction over the subject matter.
	   a. Limited versus general jurisdiction—Limited jurisdiction exists when a court is limited to a specific subject matter, such as probate or divorce. General jurisdiction exists when a court can hear any kind of case.
	   b. Original versus appellate jurisdiction—Original jurisdiction exists when courts have authority to hear a case for the first time (trial courts). Appellate jurisdiction exists with courts of appeals, or reviewing courts; generally, appellate courts do not have original jurisdiction.
	   c. Federal jurisdiction—Arises (1) when a federal question is involved (when the plaintiff's cause of action is based, at least in part, on the U.S. Constitution, a treaty, or a federal law) or (2) when a case involves diversity of citizenship (citizens of different states, for example) and the amount in controversy exceeds $75,000.
	   d. Concurrent versus exclusive jurisdiction—Concurrent jurisdiction exists when two different courts have authority to hear the same case. Exclusive jurisdiction exists when only state courts or only federal courts have authority to hear a case.
	2. *Jurisdiction in cyberspace*—Because the Internet does not have physical boundaries, traditional jurisdictional concepts have been difficult to apply in cases involving activities conducted via the Web. Gradually, the courts are developing standards to use in determining when jurisdiction over a Web site owner or operator located in another state is proper.
	3. *Venue*—Venue has to do with the most appropriate location for a trial.
	4. *Standing to sue*—A requirement that a party must have a legally protected and tangible interest at stake sufficient to justify seeking relief through the court system. The controversy at issue must also be a justiciable controversy—one that is real and substantial, as opposed to hypothetical or academic.

Continued

Chapter Summary: Courts and Alternative Dispute Resolution—Continued

The State and Federal Court Systems (See pages 65–70.)	1. *Trial courts*—Courts of original jurisdiction, in which legal actions are initiated. 　a. State—Courts of general jurisdiction can hear any case; courts of limited jurisdiction include domestic relations courts, probate courts, traffic courts, and small claims courts. 　b. Federal—The federal district court is the equivalent of the state trial court. Federal courts of limited jurisdiction include the U.S. Tax Court, the U.S. Bankruptcy Court, and the U.S. Court of Federal Claims. 2. *Intermediate appellate courts*—Courts of appeals, or reviewing courts; generally without original jurisdiction. Many states have an intermediate appellate court; in the federal court system, the U.S. circuit courts of appeals are the intermediate appellate courts. 3. *Supreme (highest) courts*—Each state has a supreme court, although it may be called by some other name; appeal from the state supreme court to the United States Supreme Court is possible only if the case involves a federal question. The United States Supreme Court is the highest court in the federal court system.
Following a State Court Case (See pages 70–77.)	Rules of procedure prescribe the way in which disputes are handled in the courts. Rules differ from court to court, and separate sets of rules exist for federal and state courts, as well as for criminal and civil cases. A civil court case in a state court would involve the following procedures: 1. *The pleadings—* 　a. Complaint—Filed by the plaintiff with the court to initiate the lawsuit; served with a summons on the defendant. 　b. Answer—A response to the complaint in which the defendant admits or denies the allegations made by the plaintiff; may assert a counterclaim or an affirmative defense. 　c. Motion to dismiss—A request to the court to dismiss the case for stated reasons, such as the plaintiff's failure to state a claim for which relief can be granted. 2. *Pretrial motions (in addition to the motion to dismiss)—* 　a. Motion for judgment on the pleadings—May be made by either party; will be granted if the parties agree on the facts and the only question is how the law applies to the facts. The judge bases the decision solely on the pleadings. 　b. Motion for summary judgment—May be made by either party; will be granted if the parties agree on the facts. The judge applies the law in rendering a judgment. The judge can consider evidence outside the pleadings when evaluating the motion. 3. *Discovery*—The process of gathering evidence concerning the case. Discovery involves depositions, interrogatories, and various requests for information. Discovery may also involve electronically recorded information, such as e-mail, voice mail, word-processing documents, and other data compilations. Although electronic discovery has significant advantages over paper discovery, it is also more time consuming and expensive and often requires the parties to hire experts. 4. *Pretrial conference*—Either party or the court can request a pretrial conference to identify the matters in dispute after discovery has taken place and to plan the course of the trial. 5. *Trial*—Following jury selection (*voir dire*), the trial begins with opening statements from both parties' attorneys. The following events then occur: 　a. The plaintiff's introduction of evidence (including the testimony of witnesses) supporting the plaintiff's position. The defendant's attorney can challenge evidence and cross-examine witnesses. 　b. The defendant's introduction of evidence (including the testimony of witnesses) supporting the defendant's position. The plaintiff's attorney can challenge evidence and cross-examine witnesses. 　c. Closing arguments by the attorneys in favor of their respective clients, the judge's instructions to the jury, and the jury's verdict. 6. *Posttrial motions—* 　a. Motion for judgment *n.o.v.* ("notwithstanding the verdict")—Will be granted if the judge is convinced that the jury was in error. 　b. Motion for a new trial—Will be granted if the judge is convinced that the jury was in error; can also be granted on the grounds of newly discovered evidence, misconduct by the participants during the trial, or error by the judge. 7. *Appeal*—Either party can appeal the trial court's judgment to an appropriate court of appeals. After reviewing the record on appeal, the appellate court holds a hearing and renders its opinion.

Chapter Summary: Courts and Alternative Dispute Resolution–Continued

The Courts Adapt to the Online World (See pages 77–78.)	A number of state and federal courts now allow parties to file litigation-related documents with the courts via the Internet. Nearly all of the federal appellate courts and bankruptcy courts and a majority of the federal district courts have implemented electronic filing systems.
Alternative Dispute Resolution (See pages 78–83.)	1. *Negotiation*–The parties come together, with or without attorneys to represent them, and try to reach a settlement without the involvement of a third party. 2. *Mediation*–The parties themselves reach an agreement with the help of a neutral third party, called a mediator. The mediator may propose a solution but does not make a decision resolving the matter. 3. *Arbitration*–A more formal method of ADR in which the parties submit their dispute to a neutral third party, the arbitrator, who renders a decision. The decision may or may not be legally binding. 4. *Other types of ADR*–These include early neutral case evaluation, mini-trials, and summary jury trials (SJTs); generally, these are forms of "assisted negotiation." 5. *Providers of ADR services*–The leading nonprofit provider of ADR services is the American Arbitration Association. Hundreds of for-profit firms also provide ADR services. 6. *Online dispute resolution*–A number of organizations now offer negotiation, mediation, and arbitration services through online forums.

ExamPrep

ISSUE SPOTTERS

1 Sue contracts with Tom to deliver a quantity of computers to Sue's Computer Store. They disagree over the amount, the delivery date, the price, and the quality. Sue files a suit against Tom in a state court. Their state requires that their dispute be submitted to mediation or nonbinding arbitration. If the dispute is not resolved, or if either party disagrees with the decision of the mediator or arbitrator, will a court hear the case? Explain.

2 At the trial, after Sue calls her witnesses, offers her evidence, and otherwise presents her side of the case, Tom has at least two choices between courses of action. Tom can call his first witness. What else might he do?

BEFORE THE TEST

Check your answers to the Issue Spotters, and at the same time, take the interactive quiz for this chapter. Go to **www.cengage.com/blaw/blt** and click on "Chapter 3." First, click on "Answers to Issue Spotters" to check your answers. Next, click on "Interactive Quiz" to assess your mastery of the concepts in this chapter. Then click on "Flashcards" to review this chapter's Key Term definitions.

For Review

Answers for the even-numbered questions in this For Review *section can be found on this text's accompanying Web site at* **www.cengage.com/blaw/blt**. *Select "Chapter 3" and click on "For Review."*

1 What is judicial review? How and when was the power of judicial review established?

2 Before a court can hear a case, it must have jurisdiction. Over what must it have jurisdiction? How are the courts applying traditional jurisdictional concepts to cases involving Internet transactions?

3 What is the difference between a trial court and an appellate court?

4 What is discovery, and how does electronic discovery differ from traditional discovery?

5 What are three alternative methods of resolving disputes?

Hypothetical Scenarios and Case Problems

3–1 **Standing.** Jack and Maggie Turton bought a house in Jefferson County, Idaho, located directly across the street from a gravel pit. A few years later, the county converted the pit to a land-fill. The landfill accepted many kinds of trash that cause harm to the environment, including major appliances, animal car-casses, containers with hazardous content warnings, leaking car batteries, and waste oil. The Turtons complained to the county, but the county did nothing. The Turtons then filed a lawsuit against the county alleging violations of federal environmental laws pertaining to groundwater contamination and other pollution. Do the Turtons have standing to sue? Why or why not?

3–2 **Hypothetical Question with Sample Answer** Marya Callais, a citizen of Florida, was walking along a busy street in Tallahassee when a large crate flew off a passing truck and hit her, causing numerous injuries to Callais. She incurred a great deal of pain and suffering plus significant medical expenses, and she could not work for six months. She wishes to sue the trucking firm for $300,000 in damages. The firm's headquarters are in Georgia, although the company does business in Florida. In what court may Callais bring suit—a Florida state court, a Georgia state court, or a federal court? What factors might influence her decision?

—For a sample answer to Question 3–2, go to Appendix E at the end of this text.

3–3 **Discovery.** Advance Technology Consultants, Inc. (ATC), contracted with RoadTrac, LLC, to provide software and client software systems for the products of global positioning satellite (GPS) technology being developed by RoadTrac. Road-Trac agreed to provide ATC with hardware with which ATC's software would interface. Problems soon arose, however, and RoadTrac filed a lawsuit against ATC alleging breach of contract. During discovery, RoadTrac requested ATC's customer lists and marketing procedures. ATC objected to providing this information because RoadTrac and ATC had become competitors in the GPS industry. Should a party to a lawsuit have to hand over its confidential business secrets as part of a discovery request? Why or why not? What limitations might a court consider imposing before requiring ATC to produce this material?

3–4 **Appellate Review.** BSH Home Appliances Corp. makes appliances under the Bosch, Siemens, Thermador, and Gaggenau brands. To make and market the "Pro 27 Stainless Steel Range," a restaurant-quality range for home use, BSH gave specifications for its burner to Detroit Radiant Products Co. and requested a price for 30,000 units. Detroit quoted a price of $28.25 per unit and offered to absorb all tooling and research and development costs. In 2001 and 2003, BSH sent Detroit two purchase orders, for 15,000 and 16,000 units, respectively. In 2004, after Detroit had shipped 12,886 units, BSH stopped scheduling deliveries. Detroit filed a suit against BSH, alleging breach of contract. BSH argued, in part, that the second purchase order had replaced the first, rather than adding to it. After a trial, a federal district court issued its "Findings of Fact and Conclusions of Law." The court found that the two purchase orders "required BSH to purchase 31,000 units of the burner at $28.25 per unit." The court ruled that Detroit was entitled to $418,261 for 18,114 unsold burners. BSH appealed to the U.S. Court of Appeals for the Sixth Circuit. Can an appellate court set aside a trial court's findings of fact? Can an appellate court come to its own conclusions of law? What should the

court rule in this case? Explain. [*Detroit Radiant Products Co. v. BSH Home Appliances Corp.*, 473 F.3d 623 (6th Cir. 2007)]

3–5 **Case Problem with Sample Answer** Kathleen Lowden sued cellular phone company T-Mobile USA, Inc., contending that its service agreements were not enforceable under Washington state law. Lowden moved to create a class-action lawsuit, in which her claims would extend to similarly affected customers. She contended that T-Mobile had improperly charged her fees beyond the advertised price of service and charged her for roaming calls that should not have been classified as roaming. T-Mobile moved to force arbitration in accordance with provisions that were clearly set forth in the service agreement. The agreement also specified that no class-action lawsuit could be brought, so T-Mobile asked the court to dismiss the class-action request. Was T-Mobile correct that Lowden's only course of action would be to file arbitration personally? [*Lowden v. T-Mobile USA, Inc.*, 512 F.3d 1213 (9th Cir. 2008)]

—After you have answered Problem 3–5, compare your answer with the sample answer given on the Web site that accompanies this text. Go to **www.cengage.com/blaw/blt**, select "Chapter 3," and click on "Case Problem with Sample Answer."

3–6 **Arbitration.** Thomas Baker and others who had bought new homes from Osborne Development Corp. brought a lawsuit, claiming multiple defects in the houses they had purchased. When Osborne sold the homes, it paid for them to be in a new home warranty program administered by Home Buyers Warranty (HBW). When the company enrolled a home with HBW, it paid a fee and filled out a form that stated the following: "By signing below, you acknowledge that you . . . CONSENT TO THE TERMS OF THESE DOCUMENTS INCLUDING THE BINDING ARBITRATION PROVISION contained therein." HBW then issued warranty booklets to the new homeowners that stated, "Any and all claims, disputes and controversies by or between the Homeowner, the Builder, the Warranty Insurer and/or HBW . . . shall be submitted to arbitration." Are the new homeowners bound by the arbitration agreement, or can they sue the builder, Osborne, in court? [*Baker v. Osborne Development Corp.*, 159 Cal.App.4th 884, 71 Cal.Rptr.3d 854 (Cal. App. 2008)]

3–7 **Discovery.** Rita Peatie filed a suit in a Connecticut state court in October 2004 against Wal-Mart Stores, Inc., to recover for injuries to her head, neck, and shoulder. Peatie claimed that she had been struck two years earlier by a metal cylinder falling from a store ceiling. The parties agreed to nonbinding arbitration. Ten days before the hearing in January 2006, the plaintiff asked for, and was granted, four more months to conduct discovery. On the morning of the rescheduled hearing, she asked for more time, but the court denied this request. The hearing was held, and the arbitrator ruled in Wal-Mart's favor. Peatie filed a motion for a new trial, which was granted. Five months later, she sought through discovery to acquire any photos, records, and reports held by Wal-Mart regarding her alleged injury. The court issued a "protective order" against the request, stating that the time for discovery had long been over. On the day of the trial—four years after the alleged injury—the plaintiff asked the court to lift the order. Should the court do it? Why or why not? [*Peatie v. Wal-Mart Stores, Inc.*, 112 Conn. App. 8, 961 A.2d 1016 (2009)]

3–8   **A Question of Ethics** *Nellie Lumpkin, who suffered from various illnesses, including dementia, was admitted to the Picayune Convalescent Center, a nursing home. Because of Lumpkin's mental condition, her daughter, Beverly McDaniel, filled out the admissions paperwork and signed the admissions agreement. It included a clause requiring the parties to submit to arbitration any disputes that arose. After Lumpkin left the center two years later, she sued, through her husband, for negligent treatment and*

malpractice during her stay. The center moved to force the matter to arbitration. The trial court held that the arbitration agreement was not enforceable. The center appealed. [Covenant Health & Rehabilitation of Picayune, LP v. Lumpkin, ___ So.2d ___ (Miss.App. 2008)]

1 Should a dispute involving medical malpractice be forced into arbitration? This is a claim of negligent care, not a breach of a commercial contract. Is it ethical for medical facilities to impose such a requirement? Is there really any bargaining over such terms?

2 Should a person with limited mental capacity be held to the arbitration clause agreed to by her next of kin who signed on her behalf?

 ## Critical Thinking and Writing Assignments

3–9   Critical Legal Thinking. Suppose that a state statute requires that all civil lawsuits involving damages of less than $50,000 be arbitrated and allows such a case to be tried in court only if a party is dissatisfied with the arbitrator's decision. Suppose further that the statute also provides that if a trial does not result in an improvement of more than 10 percent in the position of the party who demanded the trial, that party must pay the entire costs of the arbitration proceeding. Would such a statute violate litigants' rights of access to the courts and to trial by jury? Would it matter if the statute was part of a pilot program and affected only a few judicial districts in the state?

3–10   **Video Question** Go to this text's Web site at **www. cengage.com/blaw/blt** and select "Chapter 3." Click on "Video Questions" and view the video titled *Jurisdiction in Cyberspace*. Then answer the following questions.

1 What standard would a court apply to determine whether it has jurisdiction over the out-of-state computer firm in the video?

2 What factors is a court likely to consider in assessing whether sufficient contacts exist when the only connection to the jurisdiction is through a Web site?

3 How do you think a court would resolve the issue in this case?

Practical Internet Exercises

Go to this text's Web site at **www.cengage.com/blaw/blt**, select "Chapter 3," and click on "Practical Internet Exercises." There you will find the following Internet research exercises that you can perform to learn more about the topics covered in this chapter.

Practical Internet Exercise 3–1: LEGAL PERSPECTIVE—The Judiciary's Role in American Government
Practical Internet Exercise 3–2: MANAGEMENT PERSPECTIVE—Alternative Dispute Resolution
Practical Internet Exercise 3–3: SOCIAL PERSPECTIVE—Resolve a Dispute Online

Torts and Cyber Torts

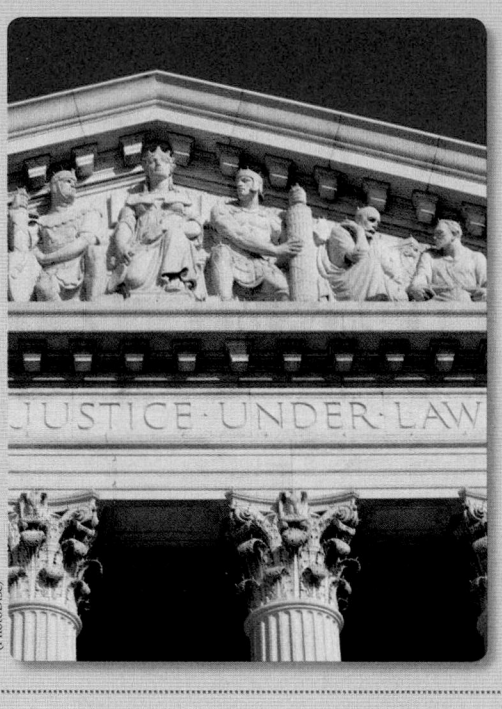

(PhotoDisc)

JUSTICE·UNDER·LAW

Learning Objectives

After reading this chapter, you should be able to answer the following questions:

1. What is a tort?

2. What is the purpose of tort law? What are two basic categories of torts?

3. What are the four elements of negligence?

4. What is meant by strict liability? In what circumstances is strict liability applied?

5. What is a cyber tort, and how are tort theories being applied in cyberspace?

Tort A civil wrong not arising from a breach of contract; a breach of a legal duty that proximately causes harm or injury to another.

Torts are wrongful actions.[1] Most of us agree with the chapter-opening quotation—two wrongs do not make a right. Tort law is our nation's attempt to right a wrong. Through tort law, society tries to ensure that those who have suffered injuries as a result of the wrongful conduct of others receive compensation from the wrongdoers. Although some torts, such as assault and trespass, originated in the English common law, the field of tort law continues to expand. As new ways to commit wrongs are discovered, such as the use of the Internet to commit wrongful acts, the courts are extending tort law to cover these wrongs.

As you will see in later chapters of this book, many of the lawsuits brought by or against business firms are based on the tort theories discussed in this chapter. Some of the torts examined here can occur in any context, including the business environment. Others, traditionally referred to as **business torts**, involve wrongful interference with the business rights of others. Business torts include such vague concepts as *unfair competition* and *wrongfully interfering with the business relations of another.*

Business Tort Wrongful interference with another's business rights.

Cyber Tort A tort committed in cyberspace.

Torts committed via the Internet are sometimes referred to as **cyber torts**. We look at how the courts have applied traditional tort law to wrongful actions in the online environment in the concluding pages of this chapter.

---

1. The word *tort* is French for "wrong."

The Basis of Tort Law

Two notions serve as the basis of all torts: wrongs and compensation. Tort law is designed to compensate those who have suffered a loss or injury due to another person's wrongful act. In a tort action, one person or group brings a personal suit against another person or group to obtain compensation (monetary **damages**) or other relief for the harm suffered.

Damages Money sought as a remedy for a breach of contract or a tortious action.

The Purpose of Tort Law

Generally, the purpose of tort law is to provide remedies for the invasion of various *protected interests.* Society recognizes an interest in personal physical safety, and tort law provides remedies for acts that cause physical injury or interfere with physical security and freedom of movement. Society recognizes an interest in protecting real and personal property, and tort law provides remedies for acts that cause destruction or damage to property. Society also recognizes an interest in protecting certain intangible interests, such as personal privacy, family relations, reputation, and dignity, and tort law provides remedies for invasion of these protected interests.

Damages Available in Tort Actions

Because the purpose of tort law is to compensate the injured party for the damage suffered, it is important to have a basic understanding of the types of damages that plaintiffs seek in tort actions.

Compensatory Damages A monetary award equivalent to the actual value of injuries or damage sustained by the aggrieved party.

COMPENSATORY DAMAGES **Compensatory damages** are intended to compensate or reimburse a plaintiff for actual losses—to make the plaintiff whole and put her or him in the same position that she or he would have been in had the tort not occurred. Compensatory damages awards are often broken down into special damages and general damages. *Special damages* compensate the plaintiff for quantifiable monetary losses, such as medical expenses, lost wages and benefits (now and in the future), extra costs, the loss of irreplaceable items, and the costs of repairing or replacing damaged property. *General damages* compensate individuals (not companies) for the nonmonetary aspects of the harm suffered, such as pain and suffering. A court might award general damages for physical or emotional pain and suffering, loss of companionship, loss of consortium (losing the emotional and physical benefits of a spousal relationship), disfigurement, loss of reputation, or loss or impairment of mental or physical capacity.

Punitive Damages Monetary damages that may be awarded to a plaintiff to punish the defendant and deter similar conduct in the future.

PUNITIVE DAMAGES Occasionally, **punitive damages** may also be awarded in tort cases to punish the wrongdoer and deter others from similar wrongdoing. Punitive damages are appropriate only when the defendant's conduct was particularly egregious (bad) or reprehensible (unacceptable). Usually, this means that punitive damages are available mainly in intentional tort actions and only rarely in negligence lawsuits (*intentional torts* and *negligence* will be explained later in the chapter). They may be awarded, however, in suits involving *gross negligence,* which can be defined as an intentional failure to perform a manifest duty in reckless disregard of the consequences of such a failure for the life or property of another.

Great judicial restraint is exercised in granting punitive damages to plaintiffs in tort actions, because punitive damages are subject to the limitations imposed by the due process clause of the U.S. Constitution (discussed in Chapter 2). The United States Supreme Court has held that a punitive damages award that is grossly excessive furthers no legitimate purpose and violates due process requirements.[2] The Court's holding applies equally

---

2. *State Farm Mutual Automobile Insurance Co. v. Campbell,* 538 U.S. 408, 123 S.Ct. 1513, 155 L.Ed.2d 585 (2003).

to punitive damages awards in gross negligence cases (discussed later in this chapter) and product liability cases (see Chapter 17). Consequently, an appellate court will sometimes reduce the amount of punitive damages awarded to a plaintiff because the amount was excessive and thereby violates the due process clause.[3]

Tort Reform

> **ON THE WEB** You can find cases and articles on torts in the tort law library at the Internet Law Library's Web site. Go to www.lawguru.com/ilawlib.

Critics of the current tort law system contend that it encourages trivial and unfounded lawsuits, which clog the courts, and is unnecessarily costly. In particular, they say, damages awards are often excessive and bear little relationship to the actual damage suffered. Such large awards encourage plaintiffs and their lawyers to bring frivolous suits. The result, in the critics' view, is a system that disproportionately rewards a few plaintiffs while imposing a "tort tax" on business and society as a whole. Furthermore, the tax manifests itself in other ways. Because physicians, hospitals, and pharmaceutical companies are worried about medical malpractice suits, they have changed their behavior. Physicians, for example, order more tests than necessary, adding to the nation's health-care costs.

TORT REFORM GOALS   Critics wish to reduce both the number of tort cases brought each year and the amount of damages awarded. They advocate (1) limiting the amount of both punitive damages and general damages that can be awarded; (2) capping the amount that attorneys can collect in contingency fees (attorneys' fees that are based on a percentage of the damages awarded to the client); and (3) requiring the losing party to pay both the plaintiff's and the defendant's expenses to discourage the filing of meritless suits.

TORT REFORM LEGISLATION   The federal government and a number of states have begun to take some steps toward tort reform. At the federal level, the Class Action Fairness Act (CAFA) of 2005[4] shifted jurisdiction over large interstate tort and product liability class-action lawsuits (lawsuits filed by a large number of plaintiffs) from the state courts to the federal courts. The intent was to prevent plaintiffs' attorneys from *forum shopping*— shopping around for a state court known to be sympathetic to their clients' cause and predisposed to award large damages in class-action suits.

At the state level, more than twenty states have placed caps ranging from $250,000 to $750,000 on general damages, especially in medical malpractice suits. More than thirty states have limited punitive damages, with some imposing outright bans.

Classifications of Torts

There are two broad classifications of torts: *intentional torts* and *unintentional torts* (torts involving negligence). The classification of a particular tort depends largely on how the tort occurs (intentionally or negligently) and the surrounding circumstances. In the following pages, you will read about these two classifications of torts.

 Intentional Torts against Persons

Intentional Tort   A wrongful act knowingly committed.

Tortfeasor   One who commits a tort.

An **intentional tort,** as the term implies, requires *intent*. The **tortfeasor** (the one committing the tort) must intend to commit an act, the consequences of which interfere with the personal or business interests of another in a way not permitted by law. An evil or harmful motive is not required—in fact, the actor may even have a beneficial motive for committing what turns out to be a tortious act. In tort law, intent means only that the actor intended the consequences of his or her act or knew with substantial certainty that certain consequences would result from the act. The law generally assumes that individuals intend the *normal*

---

3. See, for example, *Buell-Wilson v. Ford Motor Co.,* 160 Cal.App.4th 1107, 73 Cal.Rptr.3d 277 (2008).
4. 28 U.S.C. Sections 1453, 1711–1715.

consequences of their actions. Thus, forcefully pushing another—even if done in jest and without any evil motive—is an intentional tort if injury results, because the object of a strong push can ordinarily be expected to fall down.

This section discusses intentional torts against persons, which include assault and battery, false imprisonment, infliction of emotional distress, defamation, invasion of the right to privacy, appropriation, misrepresentation, abusive or frivolous litigation, and wrongful interference.

Assault and Battery

Assault Any word or action intended to make another person fearful of immediate physical harm; a reasonably believable threat.

An **assault** is any intentional and unexcused threat of immediate harmful or offensive contact, including words or acts that create in another person a reasonable apprehension of harmful contact. An assault can be completed even if there is no actual contact with the plaintiff, provided the defendant's conduct creates a reasonable apprehension of imminent harm in the plaintiff. Tort law aims to protect individuals from having to expect harmful or offensive contact.

Battery The unexcused, harmful or offensive, intentional touching of another.

The *completion* of the act that caused the apprehension, if it results in harm to the plaintiff, is a **battery,** which is defined as an unexcused and harmful or offensive physical contact *intentionally* performed. **EXAMPLE 4.1** Ivan threatens Jean with a gun and then shoots her. The pointing of the gun at Jean is an assault; the firing of the gun (if the bullet hits Jean) is a battery. ● The contact can be harmful, or it can be merely offensive (such as an unwelcome kiss). Physical injury need not occur. The contact can involve any part of the body or anything attached to it—for example, a hat, a purse, or a chair in which one is sitting. Whether the contact is offensive or not is determined by the *reasonable person standard.*[5] The contact can be made by the defendant or by some force the defendant sets in motion—for example, a rock thrown, food poisoned, or a stick swung.

COMPENSATION   If the plaintiff shows that there was contact, and the jury (or judge, if there is no jury) agrees that the contact was offensive, the plaintiff has a right to compensation. There is no need to show that the defendant acted out of malice; the person could have just been joking or playing around. The underlying motive does not matter, only the intent to bring about the harmful or offensive contact to the plaintiff. In fact, proving a motive is never necessary (but is sometimes relevant). A plaintiff may be compensated for the emotional harm or loss of reputation resulting from a battery, as well as for physical harm.

Defense A reason offered and alleged by a defendant in an action or lawsuit as to why the plaintiff should not recover or establish what she or he seeks.

DEFENSES TO ASSAULT AND BATTERY   A defendant who is sued for assault, battery, or both can raise any of the following legally recognized **defenses** (reasons why plaintiffs should not obtain what they are seeking):

1. *Consent.* When a person consents to the act that is allegedly tortious, this may be a complete or partial defense to liability (legal responsibility).
2. *Self-defense.* An individual who is defending her or his life or physical well-being can claim self-defense. In situations of both *real* and *apparent* danger, a person may use whatever force is *reasonably* necessary to prevent harmful contact.
3. *Defense of others.* An individual can act in a reasonable manner to protect others who are in real or apparent danger.
4. *Defense of property.* Reasonable force may be used in attempting to remove intruders from one's home, although force that is likely to cause death or great bodily injury can never be used just to protect property.

BE AWARE Defendants who are sued for other torts can sometimes raise these same four defenses.

---

5. The reasonable person standard is an objective test of how a reasonable person would have acted under the same circumstances. See "The Duty of Care and Its Breach" later in this chapter.

False Imprisonment

False imprisonment is the intentional confinement or restraint of another person's activities without justification. False imprisonment interferes with the freedom to move without restraint. The confinement can be accomplished through the use of physical barriers, physical restraint, or threats of physical force. Moral pressure or threats of future harm do not constitute false imprisonment. It is essential that the person under restraint does not wish to be restrained.

Businesspersons are often confronted with suits for false imprisonment after they have attempted to confine a suspected shoplifter for questioning. Under the "privilege to detain" granted to merchants in most states, a merchant can use *reasonable force* to detain or delay a person suspected of shoplifting the merchant's property. Although laws pertaining to the privilege to detain vary from state to state, generally they require that any detention be conducted in a *reasonable* manner and for only a *reasonable* length of time. Undue force or unreasonable detention can lead to liability for the business.

Intentional Infliction of Emotional Distress

The tort of *intentional infliction of emotional distress* can be defined as an intentional act that amounts to extreme and outrageous conduct resulting in severe emotional distress to another. **EXAMPLE 4.2** A prankster telephones a pregnant woman and says that her husband and son have been in a horrible accident. As a result, the woman suffers intense mental anguish and a miscarriage. In this situation, the woman can sue for intentional infliction of emotional distress. ●

Courts in most jurisdictions are wary of emotional distress claims and confine them to truly outrageous behavior. Generally, repeated annoyances (such as those experienced by a person who is being stalked), coupled with threats, are sufficient to support a claim. Acts that cause indignity or annoyance alone usually are not enough.

Note that when the outrageous conduct consists of speech about a public figure, the First Amendment's guarantee of freedom of speech also limits emotional distress claims. **CASE EXAMPLE 4.3** *Hustler* magazine once printed a fake advertisement that showed a picture of the Reverend Jerry Falwell and described him as having lost his virginity to his mother in an outhouse while he was drunk. Falwell sued the magazine for intentional infliction of emotional distress and won, but the United States Supreme Court overturned the decision. The Court held that creators of parodies of public figures are protected under the First Amendment from intentional infliction of emotional distress claims. (The Court applied the same standards that apply to public figures in defamation lawsuits, discussed next).[6] ●

Defamation

As discussed in Chapter 2, the freedom of speech guaranteed by the First Amendment to the U.S. Constitution is not absolute. In interpreting the First Amendment, the courts must balance free speech rights against other strong social interests, including society's interest in preventing and redressing attacks on reputation. (Nations with fewer free speech protections have seen an increase in defamation lawsuits targeting U.S. journalists as defendants. See this chapter's *Beyond Our Borders* feature for a discussion of this trend.)

Defamation **Defamation** of character involves wrongfully hurting a person's good reputation. The law has imposed a general duty on all persons to refrain from making *false*, defamatory *statements of fact* about others. Breaching this duty in writing or other permanent form

Defamation Anything published or publicly spoken that causes injury to another's good name, reputation, or character.

---

6. *Hustler Magazine, Inc. v. Falwell*, 485 U.S. 46, 108 S.Ct. 876, 99 L.Ed.2d 41 (1988). For another example of how the courts protect parody, see *Busch v. Viacom International, Inc.*, 477 F.Supp.2d 764 (N.D.Tex. 2007), involving a fake endorsement of televangelist Pat Robertson's diet shake.

Beyond Our Borders — "Libel Tourism"

As mentioned earlier, U.S. plaintiffs sometimes engage in forum shopping by trying to have their complaints heard by a particular state's court that is likely to be sympathetic to their claims. *Libel tourism* is essentially forum shopping on an international scale. Rather than filing a defamation lawsuit in the United States where the freedoms of speech and press are strongly protected, a plaintiff files it in a foreign jurisdiction where there is a greater chance of winning.

Libel tourism has increased in recent years, particularly in England and Wales, where it is easier for plaintiffs to win libel cases—even sham claims. In England, the law of defamation assumes that the offending speech is false (libelous), and the writer or author (the defendant) must prove that it is true in order to prevail. In contrast, U.S. law presumes that the speech is true (not libelous), and the plaintiff has the burden of proving that the statements were false.

The Threat of Libel Tourism

Libel tourism can have a chilling effect on the speech of U.S. journalists and authors because the fear of liability in other nations may prevent them from freely discussing topics of profound public importance. Libel tourism could even increase the threat to our nation's security if it discourages authors from writing about the persons supporting or financing terrorism or other dangerous activities.

The threat of libel tourism captured media attention when Khalid bin Mahfouz, a Saudi Arabian businessman, sued U.S. resident Dr. Rachel Ehrenfeld. In her book, *Funding Evil: How Terrorism Is Financed—and How to Stop It*, Ehrenfeld claimed that Mahfouz finances Islamic terrorist groups. Mahfouz filed the lawsuit in a court in London, England, which took jurisdiction because twenty-three copies of the book had been sold online to residents of the United Kingdom. Ehrenfeld did not go to the English court to defend herself, and a judgment of $225,000 was entered against her. She then countersued Mahfouz in a U.S. court in an attempt to show that she was protected under the First Amendment and had not committed libel, but that case was dismissed for lack of jurisdiction.[a]

---

a. *Ehrenfeld v. Mahfouz*, 518 F.3d 102 (2d Cir. 2008).

The U.S. Response

In response to the *Ehrenfeld* case, the New York state legislature enacted the Libel Terrorism Reform Act in 2008.[b] The act enables New York courts to assert jurisdiction over anyone who obtains a foreign libel judgment against a writer or publisher living in New York State. It also prevents courts from enforcing foreign libel judgments unless the foreign country provides equal or greater free speech protection than is available in the United States and New York. In 2008, the federal government proposed similar legislation, the Libel Terrorism Protection Act, but it has not yet become law.

• For Critical Analysis

Why do we need special legislation designed to control foreign libel claims against U.S. citizens? Explain.

---

b. McKinney's Consolidated Laws of New York Sections 302 and 5304.

Libel Defamation in writing or other form having the quality of permanence (such as a digital recording).

Slander Defamation in oral form.

Actionable Capable of serving as the basis of a lawsuit. An actionable claim can be pursued in a lawsuit or other court action.

(such as a digital recording) involves the tort of **libel.** Breaching this duty orally involves the tort of **slander.** As you will read later in this chapter, the tort of defamation can also arise when a false statement of fact is made about a person's product, business, or legal ownership rights to property.

Often at issue in defamation lawsuits (including online defamation, discussed later in this chapter) is whether the defendant made a statement of fact or a *statement of opinion.*[7] Statements of opinion normally are not **actionable** (capable of serving as the basis of a lawsuit) because they are protected under the First Amendment. In other words, making a negative statement about another person is not defamation unless the statement is false and represents something as a fact (for example, "Lane cheats on his taxes") rather than a personal opinion (for example, "Lane is a jerk").

THE PUBLICATION REQUIREMENT   The basis of the tort of defamation is the publication of a statement or statements that hold an individual up to contempt, ridicule, or hatred. *Publication* here means that the defamatory statements are communicated to persons other than the defamed party. **EXAMPLE 4.4**   If Thompson writes Andrews a private letter accusing him of embezzling funds, the action does not constitute libel. If Peters falsely states that Gordon is dishonest and incompetent when no one else is around, the action does not constitute slander. In neither instance was the message communicated to a third party. •

---

7.   See, for example, *Lott v. Levitt,* 469 F.Supp.2d 575 (N.D.Ill. 2007).

The courts have generally held that even dictating a letter to a secretary constitutes publication, although the publication may be privileged (privileged communications will be discussed shortly). Moreover, if a third party overhears defamatory statements by chance, the courts usually hold that this also constitutes publication. Defamatory statements made via the Internet are also actionable, as you will read later in this chapter. Note further that any individual who republishes or repeats defamatory statements is liable even if that person reveals the source of such statements.

DAMAGES FOR LIBEL   Once a defendant's liability for libel is established, general damages are presumed as a matter of law. As mentioned earlier, general damages are designed to compensate the plaintiff for nonspecific harms such as disgrace or dishonor in the eyes of the community, humiliation, injured reputation, and emotional distress—harms that are difficult to measure. In other words, to recover damages in a libel case, the plaintiff need not prove that she or he was actually injured in any way as a result of the libelous statement.

DAMAGES FOR SLANDER   In contrast to cases alleging libel, in a case alleging slander, the plaintiff must prove *special damages* to establish the defendant's liability. In other words, the plaintiff must show that the slanderous statement caused the plaintiff to suffer actual economic or monetary losses. Unless this initial hurdle of proving special damages is overcome, a plaintiff alleging slander normally cannot go forward with the suit and recover any damages. This requirement is imposed in cases involving slander because slanderous statements have a temporary quality. In contrast, a libelous (written) statement has the quality of permanence, can be circulated widely, and usually results from some degree of deliberation on the part of the author.

Exceptions to the burden of proving special damages in cases alleging slander are made for certain types of slanderous statements. If a false statement constitutes "slander *per se*," no proof of special damages is required for it to be actionable. The following four types of utterances are considered to be slander *per se*:

1. A statement that another has a loathsome disease (historically, leprosy and sexually transmitted diseases, but now also including allegations of mental illness).
2. A statement that another has committed improprieties while engaging in a business, profession, or trade.
3. A statement that another has committed or has been imprisoned for a serious crime.
4. A statement that a person (usually only unmarried persons and sometimes only women) is unchaste or has engaged in serious sexual misconduct.

DEFENSES AGAINST DEFAMATION   Truth is normally an absolute defense against a defamation charge. In other words, if the defendant in a defamation suit can prove that his or her allegedly defamatory statements were true, normally no tort has been committed. Other defenses to defamation may exist if the statement is privileged or concerns a public figure. Note that the majority of defamation actions in the United States are filed in state courts, and the states may differ both in how they define defamation and in the particular defenses they allow, such as privilege (discussed next).

Privilege   A legal right, exemption, or immunity granted to a person or a class of persons. In the context of defamation, an absolute privilege immunizes the person making the statements from a lawsuit, regardless of whether the statements were malicious.

Privileged Communications.   In some circumstances, a person will not be liable for defamatory statements because she or he enjoys a **privilege**, or immunity. Privileged communications are of two types: absolute and qualified.[8] Only in judicial proceedings and certain government proceedings is an *absolute* privilege granted. Thus, statements made in a courtroom by attorneys and judges during a trial are absolutely privileged, as are statements made by government officials during legislative debate.

---

8. Note that the term *privileged communication* in this context is not the same as privileged communication between a professional, such as an attorney, and his or her client. The latter type of privilege will be discussed in Chapter 34, in the context of the liability of professionals.

In other situations, a person will not be liable for defamatory statements because he or she has a *qualified,* or conditional, privilege. An employer's statements in written evaluations of employees are an example of a qualified privilege. Generally, if the statements are made in good faith and the publication is limited to those who have a legitimate interest in the communication, the statements fall within the area of qualified privilege. **EXAMPLE 4.5** Jorge applies for membership at the local country club. After the country club's board rejects his application, Jorge sues the club's office manager for making allegedly defamatory statements to the board concerning a conversation she had with Jorge. Assuming that the office manager had simply relayed what she thought was her duty to convey to the club's board, her statements would likely be protected by qualified privilege.[9] ●

The concept of conditional privilege rests on the assumption that in some situations, the right to know or speak is paramount to the right not to be defamed. Only if the privilege is abused or the statement is knowingly false or malicious will the person be liable for damages.

Public Figures.   Public officials who exercise substantial governmental power and any persons in the public limelight are considered *public figures.* In general, public figures are considered fair game, and false and defamatory statements about them that appear in the media will not constitute defamation unless the statements are made with **actual malice.**[10] To be made with actual malice, a statement must be made *with either knowledge of falsity or a reckless disregard of the truth.* Statements made about public figures, especially when the statements are made via a public medium, are usually related to matters of general interest; they are made about people who substantially affect all of us. Furthermore, public figures generally have some access to a public medium for answering disparaging (belittling, discrediting) falsehoods about themselves; private individuals do not. For these reasons, public figures have a greater burden of proof in defamation cases (they must prove actual malice) than do private individuals.

Invasion of the Right to Privacy

A person has a right to solitude and freedom from prying public eyes—in other words, to privacy. As discussed in Chapter 2, the Supreme Court has held that a fundamental right to privacy is implied by various amendments to the U.S. Constitution. Some state constitutions also explicitly provide for privacy rights. In addition, a number of federal and state statutes have been enacted to protect individual rights in specific areas. Tort law also safeguards these rights through the tort of *invasion of privacy.* Four acts qualify as an invasion of privacy:

1. *Appropriation of identity.* Under the common law, using a person's name, picture, or other likeness for commercial purposes without permission is a tortious invasion of privacy. Most states today have also enacted statutes prohibiting appropriation (discussed further in the next subsection).
2. *Intrusion into an individual's affairs or seclusion.* For example, invading someone's home or illegally searching someone's briefcase is an invasion of privacy. The tort has been held to extend to eavesdropping by wiretap, the unauthorized scanning of a bank account, compulsory blood testing, and window peeping.
3. *False light.* Publication of information that places a person in a false light is another category of invasion of privacy. This could be a story attributing to the person ideas not held or actions not taken by the person. (Publishing such a story could involve the tort of defamation as well.)
4. *Public disclosure of private facts.* This type of invasion of privacy occurs when a person publicly discloses private facts about an individual that an ordinary person would

Actual Malice The deliberate intent to cause harm, which exists when a person makes a statement either knowing that it is false or showing a reckless disregard for whether it is true. In a defamation suit, a statement made about a public figure normally must be made with actual malice for the plaintiff to recover damages.

ON THE WEB You can find information and cases relating to employee privacy rights with respect to electronic monitoring at the Web site of the American Civil Liberties Union (ACLU). Go to **www.aclu.org/privacy/workplace/ index.html**.

---

9. For a case involving a qualified privilege, see *Hickson Corp. v. Northern Crossarm Co.,* 357 F.3d 1256 (11th Cir. 2004).
10. *New York Times Co. v. Sullivan,* 376 U.S. 254, 84 S.Ct. 710, 11 L.Ed.2d 686 (1964).

find objectionable or embarrassing. A newspaper account of a private citizen's sex life or financial affairs could be an actionable invasion of privacy, even if the information revealed is true, because it is not of public concern.

Appropriation

Appropriation In tort law, the use by one person of another person's name, likeness, or other identifying characteristic, without permission and for the benefit of the user.

The use by one person of another person's name, likeness, or other identifying characteristic, without permission and for the benefit of the user, constitutes the tort of **appropriation.** Under the law, an individual's right to privacy normally includes the right to the exclusive use of her or his identity.

CASE EXAMPLE 4.6 Vanna White, the hostess of the popular television game show *Wheel of Fortune,* brought a case against Samsung Electronics America, Inc. Without White's permission, Samsung included in one of its advertisements a depiction of a robot dressed in a wig, gown, and jewelry, posed in a scene that resembled the *Wheel of Fortune* set, in a stance for which White is famous. The court held in White's favor, holding that the tort of appropriation does not require the use of a celebrity's name or likeness. The court stated that Samsung's robot ad left "little doubt" as to the identity of the celebrity whom the ad was meant to depict.[11] ●

DEGREE OF LIKENESS In recent cases, courts have reached different conclusions as to the degree of likeness that is required to impose liability for the tort of appropriation. **CASE EXAMPLE 4.7** Anthony "Tony" Twist, a former professional hockey player who had a reputation for fighting, sued the publishers of the comic book *Spawn,* which included an evil character named Anthony Tony Twist Twistelli. The Missouri Supreme Court held that the use of Tony Twist's name alone was sufficient proof of likeness to support a misappropriation claim.[12] Ultimately, the hockey player was awarded $15 million in damages.[13] ●

In contrast, some courts have held that even when an animated character in a video or a video game is made to look like an actual person, there are not enough similarities to constitute appropriation. **CASE EXAMPLE 4.8** The Naked Cowboy, Robert Burck, has been a street entertainer in New York City's Times Square for more than ten years. He performs for tourists wearing only a white cowboy hat, white cowboy boots, and white underwear and carrying a guitar strategically placed to give the illusion of nudity. Burck has become a well-known persona, appearing in television shows, movies, and video games, and has licensed his name and likeness to certain companies, including Chevrolet. When Mars, Inc., the maker of M&Ms candy, began using a video on billboards in Times Square that depicted a blue M&M dressed up exactly like The Naked Cowboy, Burck sued for appropriation. In 2008, a federal district court held that Mars's creation of a cartoon character dressed in The Naked Cowboy's signature costume did not amount to appropriation by use of Burck's "portrait or picture." (Burck was allowed to continue his lawsuit against Mars for allegedly violating trademark law—to be discussed in Chapter 5.)[14] ●

Robert Burck bills himself as The Naked Cowboy and performs regularly in New York City's Times Square. He has licensed his name and likeness to Chevrolet and to other companies. Given his fame, was he able to prevent M&M Candies from appropriating his likeness for an animated billboard commercial?

(AP Photo/Diane Bondareff)

RIGHT OF PUBLICITY AS A PROPERTY RIGHT In some states, the common law tort of appropriation has become known as the right of publicity.[15] Rather than being aimed at protecting a person's right to be left alone (privacy), this right protects an individual's pecuniary (financial) interest in the commercial exploitation of his or her identity. In other

---

11. *White v. Samsung Electronics America, Inc.,* 971 F.2d 1395 (9th Cir. 1992).
12. *Doe v. TCI Cablevision,* 110 S.W.3d 363 (Mo. 2003).
13. The amount of damages was subsequently affirmed on appeal. See *Doe v. McFarlane,* 207 S.W.3d 52 (Mo. App. 2006).
14. *Burck v. Mars, Inc.,* 571 F.Supp.2d 446 (S.D.N.Y. 2008). See also *Kirby v. Sega of America, Inc.,* 144 Cal.App.4th 47, 50 Cal.Rptr.3d 607 (2006).
15. See, for example, California Civil Code Sections 3344 and 3344.1.

words, it gives public figures, celebrities, and entertainers a right to sue anyone who uses their images for commercial benefit without their permission.

Cases involving the right of publicity generally turn on whether the use was commercial. For instance, if a television news program reports on a celebrity and shows an image of the person, the use likely would not be classified as commercial; in contrast, featuring the celebrity's image on a poster without his or her permission would be a commercial use.

Fraudulent Misrepresentation

A misrepresentation leads another to believe in a condition that is different from the condition that actually exists. This is often accomplished through a false or incorrect statement. Although persons sometimes make misrepresentations accidentally because they are unaware of the existing facts, the tort of **fraudulent misrepresentation,** or fraud, involves *intentional* deceit for personal gain. The tort includes several elements:

1. The misrepresentation of facts or conditions with knowledge that they are false or with reckless disregard for the truth.
2. An intent to induce another to rely on the misrepresentation.
3. Justifiable reliance by the deceived party.
4. Damages suffered as a result of the reliance.
5. A causal connection between the misrepresentation and the injury suffered.

For fraud to occur, more than mere **puffery,** or *seller's talk,* must be involved. Fraud exists only when a person represents as a fact something she or he knows is untrue. For example, it is fraud to claim that a roof does not leak when one knows it does. Facts are objectively ascertainable, whereas seller's talk is not. "I am the best accountant in town" is seller's talk. The speaker is not trying to represent something as fact because the term *best* is a subjective, not an objective, term.[16]

STATEMENT OF FACT VERSUS OPINION   Normally, the tort of misrepresentation or fraud occurs only when there is reliance on a *statement of fact.* Sometimes, however, reliance on a *statement of opinion* may involve the tort of misrepresentation if the individual making the statement of opinion has a superior knowledge of the subject matter. For instance, when a lawyer makes a statement of opinion about the law in a state in which the lawyer is licensed to practice, a court would construe reliance on such a statement to be equivalent to reliance on a statement of fact. We will examine fraudulent misrepresentation in further detail in Chapter 12, in the context of contract law.

NEGLIGENT MISREPRESENTATION   Sometimes, a tort action can arise from misrepresentations that are made negligently rather than intentionally. The key difference between intentional and negligent misrepresentation is whether the person making the misrepresentation had actual knowledge of its falsity. Negligent misrepresentation only requires that the person making the statement or omission did not have a reasonable basis for believing its truthfulness. Liability for negligent misrepresentation usually arises when the defendant who made the misrepresentation owed a duty of care to the particular plaintiff to supply correct information. Statements or omissions made by attorneys and accountants to their clients, for example, can lead to liability for negligent misrepresentation.

In the following case, a commercial tenant claimed that the landlord made negligent misrepresentations about the size of a leased space.

Fraudulent Misrepresentation Any misrepresentation, either by misstatement or by omission of a material fact, knowingly made with the intention of deceiving another and on which a reasonable person would and does rely to his or her detriment.

Puffery A salesperson's often exaggerated claims concerning the quality of property offered for sale. Such claims involve opinions rather than facts and are not considered to be legally binding promises or warranties.

ON THE WEB The 'Lectric Law Library's Legal Lexicon includes a useful discussion of the elements of fraud, as well as different types of fraud. To access this page, go to **www.lectlaw.com/def/f079.htm**.

---

16. In contracts for the sale of goods, Article 2 of the Uniform Commercial Code distinguishes, for warranty purposes, between statements of opinion (puffery) and statements of fact. See Chapter 17 for a further discussion of this issue.

Case 4.1   McClain v. Octagon Plaza, LLC

Court of Appeal of California, Second District, 159 Cal.App.4th 784, 71 Cal.Rptr.3d 885 (2008).

FACTS   Kelly McClain operates a business known as "A+ Teaching Supplies." Ted and Wanda Charanian, who are married, are the principals of Octagon, LLC, which owns and manages a shopping center in Valencia, California. On February 28, 2003, McClain agreed to lease commercial space within the shopping center. The lease described the size of the unit leased by McClain as "approximately 2,624 square feet," and attached to the lease was a diagram of the shopping center that represented the size of the unit as 2,624 square feet. Because the base rent in the shopping center was $1.45 per square foot, McClain's total base rent would be $3,804 per month. Moreover, because the unit supposedly occupied 23 percent of the shopping center, McClain would be responsible for this share of the common expenses. McClain claimed that the Charanians knew that the representations were materially inaccurate.

(www.octagonplaza.com)

Octagon Plaza shopping center in Valencia, California.

As a result of Octagon's misrepresentations, McClain was induced to enter into a lease that obliged her to pay excess rent. At trial, the Charanians prevailed. McClain appealed.

ISSUE   Did the Charanians negligently misrepresent the size of the rental property?

DECISION   Yes. The state intermediate appellate court reversed the trial court's judgment on misrepresentation.

REASON   The court reasoned that McClain had justifiably relied on the representations of the landlords concerning the size of the rental unit. The Charanians had exaggerated the size of the unit McClain was leasing by 186 square feet, or 7.6 percent of its actual size. Although the Charanians may not have intentionally misrepresented the size, the discrepancy "operated to increase the rental payments incurred by McClain's retail business by more than $90,000 over the term of the lease."

FOR CRITICAL ANALYSIS—Ethical Consideration   *At what point do misrepresentations about the size of leased space become unethical—at 1 percent, 2 percent, or more? Explain your answer.*

Abusive or Frivolous Litigation

Persons or businesses generally have a right to sue when they have been injured. In recent years, however, an increasing number of meritless lawsuits are being filed—simply to harass the defendant. Defending oneself in legal proceedings can be costly, time consuming, and emotionally draining. Tort law recognizes that people have a right not to be sued without a legally just and proper reason, and therefore it protects individuals from the misuse of litigation. Torts related to abusive litigation include malicious prosecution and abuse of process.

If a party initiates a lawsuit out of malice and without probable cause (a legitimate legal reason), and ends up losing the suit, that party can be sued for *malicious prosecution*. In some states, the plaintiff (who was the defendant in the first proceeding) must also prove injury other than the normal costs of litigation, such as lost profits. *Abuse of process* can apply to any person using a legal process against another in an improper manner or to accomplish a purpose for which it was not designed. The key difference between the torts of abuse of process and malicious prosecution is the level of proof required to succeed. Abuse of process does not require the plaintiff to prove malice or show that the defendant (who was previously the plaintiff) lost in a prior legal proceeding.[17] In addition, an abuse of process claim is not limited to prior litigation. It can be based on the wrongful use of subpoenas, court orders to attach or seize real property, or other types of formal legal process.

---

17. See *Bernhard-Thomas Building Systems, LLC v. Dunican*, 918 A.2d 889 (Conn.App. 2007); and *Hewitt v. Rice*, 154 P.3d 408 (Colo. 2007).

Wrongful Interference

Business torts involving wrongful interference are generally divided into two categories: wrongful interference with a contractual relationship and wrongful interference with a business relationship.

WRONGFUL INTERFERENCE WITH A CONTRACTUAL RELATIONSHIP   The body of tort law relating to *intentional interference with a contractual relationship* has expanded greatly in recent years. **CASE EXAMPLE 4.9**   A landmark case involved an opera singer, Joanna Wagner, who was under contract to sing for a man named Lumley for a specified period of years. A man named Gye, who knew of this contract, nonetheless "enticed" Wagner to refuse to carry out the agreement, and Wagner began to sing for Gye. Gye's action constituted a tort because it wrongfully interfered with the contractual relationship between Wagner and Lumley.[18] (Of course, Wagner's refusal to carry out the agreement also entitled Lumley to sue Wagner for breach of contract.) ●

Three elements are necessary for wrongful interference with a contractual relationship to occur:

1. A valid, enforceable contract must exist between two parties.
2. A third party must know that this contract exists.
3. The third party must *intentionally* induce a party to breach the contract.

In principle, any lawful contract can be the basis for an action of this type. The contract could be between a firm and its employees or a firm and its customers. Sometimes, a competitor draws away one of a firm's key employees. To recover damages from the competitor, the original employer must show that the competitor knew of the contract's existence and intentionally induced the breach.

EXAMPLE 4.10   Sutter is under contract to do gardening work on Carlin's estate every week for fifty-two weeks at a specified price per week. Mellon, who needs gardening services and knows nothing about the Sutter-Carlin contract, contacts Sutter and offers to pay a wage substantially higher than that offered by Carlin. Sutter breaches his contract with Carlin so that he can work for Mellon. Carlin cannot sue Mellon because Mellon knew nothing of the Sutter-Carlin contract and was totally unaware that the higher wage he offered induced Sutter to breach that contract. ●

WRONGFUL INTERFERENCE WITH A BUSINESS RELATIONSHIP   Businesspersons devise countless schemes to attract customers, but they are prohibited from unreasonably interfering with another's business in their attempts to gain a share of the market. There is a difference between *competitive methods* and *predatory behavior*—actions undertaken with the intention of unlawfully driving competitors completely out of the market.

Attempting to attract customers in general is a legitimate business practice, whereas specifically targeting the customers of a competitor is more likely to be predatory. **EXAMPLE 4.11** A shopping mall contains two athletic shoe stores: Joe's and SneakerSprint. Joe's cannot station an employee at the entrance of SneakerSprint to divert customers by telling them that Joe's will beat SneakerSprint's prices. This type of activity constitutes the tort of wrongful interference with a business relationship, which is commonly considered to be an unfair trade practice. If this type of activity were permitted, Joe's would reap the benefits of SneakerSprint's advertising. ●

DEFENSES TO WRONGFUL INTERFERENCE   A person can avoid liability for the tort of wrongful interference with a contractual or business relationship by showing that the

> **REMEMBER**   It is the intent to do an act that is important in tort law, not the motive behind the intent.

---

18. *Lumley v. Gye,* 118 Eng.Rep. 749 (1853).

interference was justified, or permissible. Bona fide competitive behavior is a permissible interference even if it results in the breaking of a contract. **EXAMPLE 4.12** If Antonio's Meats advertises so effectively that it induces Sam's Restaurant to break its contract with Burke's Meat Company, Burke's Meat Company will be unable to recover against Antonio's Meats on a wrongful interference theory. After all, the public policy that favors free competition in advertising outweighs any possible instability that such competitive activity might cause in contractual relations. ● Although luring customers away from a competitor through aggressive marketing and advertising strategies obviously interferes with the competitor's relationship with its customers, courts typically allow such activities in the spirit of competition.

 ## Intentional Torts against Property

Intentional torts against property include trespass to land, trespass to personal property, conversion, and disparagement of property. These torts are wrongful actions that interfere with individuals' legally recognized rights with regard to their land or personal property. The law distinguishes real property from personal property (see Chapters 35 and 36). *Real property* is land and things "permanently" attached to the land. *Personal property* consists of all other items, which are basically movable. Thus, a house and lot are real property, whereas the furniture inside a house is personal property. Cash and stocks and bonds are also personal property.

Trespass to Land

A **trespass to land** occurs anytime a person, without permission, enters onto, above, or below the surface of land that is owned by another; causes anything to enter onto the land; or remains on the land or permits anything to remain on it. Actual harm to the land is not an essential element of this tort because the tort is designed to protect the right of an owner to exclusive possession of her or his property. Common types of trespass to land include walking or driving on someone else's land, shooting a gun over the land, throwing rocks at a building that belongs to someone else, building a dam across a river and thereby causing water to back up on someone else's land, and constructing a building so that part of it is on an adjoining landowner's property.

TRESPASS CRITERIA, RIGHTS, AND DUTIES   Before a person can be a trespasser, the real property owner (or other person in actual and exclusive possession of the property) must establish that person as a trespasser. For example, "posted" trespass signs expressly establish as a trespasser a person who ignores these signs and enters onto the property. A guest in your home is not a trespasser—unless she or he has been asked to leave but refuses. Any person who enters onto your property to commit an illegal act (such as a thief entering a lumberyard at night to steal lumber) is established impliedly as a trespasser, without posted signs.

At common law, a trespasser is liable for damages caused to the property and generally cannot hold the owner liable for injuries sustained on the premises. This common law rule is being abandoned in many jurisdictions in favor of a *reasonable duty of care* rule that varies depending on the status of the parties. For instance, a landowner may have a duty to post a notice that guard dogs patrol the property. Also, under the *attractive nuisance* doctrine, children do not assume the risks of the premises if they are attracted to the property by some object, such as a swimming pool, an abandoned building, or a sand pile. Trespassers normally can be removed from the premises through the use of reasonable force without the owner's being liable for assault, battery, or false imprisonment.

DEFENSES AGAINST TRESPASS TO LAND   One defense to a claim of trespass to land is to show that the trespass was warranted—for example, that the trespasser entered the property to assist someone in danger. Another defense is for the trespasser to show that he or she had a license to come onto the land. A *licensee* is one who is invited (or allowed to enter) onto the property of another for the licensee's benefit. A person who enters another's property to read an electric meter, for example, is a licensee. When you purchase a ticket to attend a movie or sporting event, you are licensed to go onto the property of another to view that movie or event. Note that licenses to enter are *revocable* by the property owner. If a property owner asks a meter reader to leave and the meter reader refuses to do so, the meter reader at that point becomes a trespasser.

Trespass to Personal Property

Trespass to Personal Property The unlawful taking or harming of another's personal property; interference with another's right to the exclusive possession of his or her personal property.

Whenever an individual wrongfully takes or harms the personal property of another or otherwise interferes with the lawful owner's possession of personal property, **trespass to personal property** occurs (also called *trespass to chattels* or *trespass to personalty*[19]). In this context, harm means not only destruction of the property, but also anything that diminishes its value, condition, or quality. Trespass to personal property involves intentional meddling with a possessory interest, including barring an owner's access to personal property. **EXAMPLE 4.13** Kelly takes Ryan's business law book as a practical joke and hides it so that Ryan is unable to find it for several days before the final examination. Here, Kelly has engaged in a trespass to personal property. (Kelly has also committed the tort of *conversion*—to be discussed next.) •

A complete defense to a claim of trespass to personal property is to show that the trespass was warranted. Most states, for example, allow automobile repair shops to hold a customer's car (under what is called an *artisan's lien,* which will be discussed in Chapter 21) when the customer refuses to pay for repairs already completed.

Conversion

Conversion Wrongfully taking or retaining possession of an individual's personal property and placing it in the service of another.

Whenever a person wrongfully possesses or uses the personal property of another without permission, the tort of **conversion** occurs. Any act that deprives an owner of personal property or the use of that property without that owner's permission and without just cause can be conversion. Even the taking of electronic records and data can be a form of conversion.[20]

Often, when conversion occurs, a trespass to personal property also occurs because the original taking of the personal property from the owner was a trespass, and wrongfully retaining it is conversion. Conversion is the civil side of crimes related to theft, but it is not limited to theft. Even if the rightful owner consented to the initial taking of the property, so there was no theft or trespass, a failure to return the personal property may still be conversion. **EXAMPLE 4.14** Chen borrows Mark's iPod to use while traveling home from school for the holidays. When Chen returns to school, Mark asks for his iPod back. Chen tells Mark that she gave it to her little brother for Christmas. In this situation, Mark can sue Chen for conversion, and Chen will have to either return the iPod or pay damages equal to its value. •

KEEP IN MIND   In tort law, the underlying motive for an act does not matter. What matters is the intent to do the act that results in the tort.

Even if a person mistakenly believed that she or he was entitled to the goods, the tort of conversion may occur. In other words, good intentions are not a defense against conversion; in fact, conversion can be an entirely innocent act. Someone who buys stolen goods, for example, can be liable for conversion even if he or she did not know that the goods were stolen. If the true owner brings a tort action against the buyer, the buyer must either return the property to the owner or pay the owner the full value of the property, despite having already paid the purchase price to the thief. A successful defense against the charge of conversion is that the purported owner does not, in fact, own the property or does not have a right to possess it that is superior to the right of the holder.

The issue in the following case involved a university's conversion of the fruits of a professor's life's work—that is, property created and accumulated over decades. The focus was on how to make a fair estimate of its value.

---

19. Pronounced *per*-sun-ul-tee.
20. See, for example, *Thyroff v. Nationwide Mutual Insurance Co.,* 8 N.Y.3d 283, 864 N.E.2d 1272, 832 N.Y.S.2d 873 (2007).

Case 4.2   Trustees of University of District of Columbia v. Vossoughi

District of Columbia Court of Appeals, 963 A.2d 1162 (2009).

The University of the District of Columbia was chartered in 1974 and is the only public higher education institution in Washington, D.C. It offers more than 175 undergraduate and graduate academic degree programs.

FACTS Jafar Vossoughi is an expert in applied mechanics and experimental biomechanics, which encompasses the testing of mechanical theories and the creation and use of experimental devices for biomechanical research. In the 1990s, while teaching at the University of the District of Columbia (UDC), Vossoughi set up a laboratory to conduct research. When his employment contract expired, he remained on campus and continued his research. In 2000, without Vossoughi's knowledge, UDC cleaned out the laboratory and trashed most of its contents. Vossoughi filed a suit in a District of Columbia court against UDC, seeking damages for the loss of his course materials, unpublished research data, unique scientific instruments, and other items. He personally testified as to the "replacement cost." A jury found UDC liable for conversion (the wrongful taking of someone's personal property) and awarded Vossoughi $1.65 million. UDC appealed.

ISSUE Is "replacement cost" an appropriate measure of the damages for conversion of property?

DECISION Yes. The District of Columbia Court of Appeals affirmed the award. Vossoughi's evidence was "not speculative and unreliable."

REASON The usual measure of damages for conversion of property is its "fair market value" at the time of the conversion. But fair market value can be inadequate. A "person tortiously deprived of property is entitled to damages based upon its special value to him if that is greater than its market value." And, when property "is replaceable, it is appropriate to measure damages for its loss by the cost of replacement." Vossoughi's course materials, research data, and scientific instruments had great value to him but no comparable, if any, market value. He based his estimates of the value of the property on the time it would take him to duplicate it. He was qualified to make these estimates because he knew the materials' quality and condition. Two experts in his field who were familiar with his work corroborated his figures.

FOR CRITICAL ANALYSIS—Economic Consideration
Should plaintiffs be required to prove the amount of their damages with certainty and exactitude? Why or why not?

Disparagement of Property

Disparagement of Property An economically injurious falsehood made about another's product or property; a general term for torts that are more specifically referred to as *slander of quality* or *slander of title*.

Slander of Quality (Trade Libel) The publication of false information about another's product, alleging that it is not what its seller claims.

Slander of Title The publication of a statement that denies or casts doubt on another's legal ownership of any property, causing financial loss to that property's owner.

Disparagement of property occurs when economically injurious falsehoods are made about another's product or property, not about another's reputation. Disparagement of property is a general term for torts specifically referred to as *slander of quality* or *slander of title*. Publication of false information about another's product, alleging that it is not what its seller claims, constitutes the tort of **slander of quality**, or **trade libel**. To establish trade libel, the plaintiff must prove that the improper publication caused a third party to refrain from dealing with the plaintiff and that the plaintiff sustained economic damages (such as lost profits) as a result.

An improper publication may be both a slander of quality and defamation of character. For example, a statement that disparages the quality of a product may also, by implication, disparage the character of the person who would sell such a product.

When a publication denies or casts doubt on another's legal ownership of any property, and this results in financial loss to that property's owner, the tort of **slander of title** may exist. Usually, this is an intentional tort in which someone knowingly publishes an untrue statement about property with the intent of discouraging a third party from dealing with the person slandered. For instance, a car dealer would have difficulty attracting customers after competitors published a notice that the dealer's stock consisted of stolen automobiles.

▶ Unintentional Torts (Negligence)

The tort of **negligence** occurs when someone suffers injury because of another's failure to live up to a required *duty of care.* In contrast to intentional torts, in torts involving negligence, the tortfeasor neither wishes to bring about the consequences of the act nor believes that they will occur. The actor's conduct merely creates a *risk* of such consequences. If no risk is created, there is no negligence. Moreover, the risk must be foreseeable—that is, it must be such that a reasonable person engaging in the same activity would anticipate the risk and guard against it. In determining what is reasonable conduct, courts consider the nature of the possible harm.

Many of the actions discussed earlier in the chapter in the section on intentional torts constitute negligence if the element of intent is missing. **EXAMPLE 4.15** Juan walks up to Maya and intentionally shoves her. Maya falls and breaks an arm as a result. In this situation, Juan has committed an intentional tort (assault and battery).If Juan carelessly bumps into Maya, however, and she falls and breaks an arm as a result, Juan's action will constitute negligence. In either situation, Juan has committed a tort. ●

To succeed in a negligence action, the plaintiff must prove each of the following:

1. That the defendant owed a duty of care to the plaintiff.
2. That the defendant breached that duty.
3. That the plaintiff suffered a legally recognizable injury.
4. That the defendant's breach caused the plaintiff's injury.

We discuss each of these four elements of negligence next.

The Duty of Care and Its Breach

Central to the tort of negligence is the concept of a **duty of care.** The basic principle underlying the duty of care is that people in society are free to act as they please so long as their actions do not infringe on the interests of others.

When someone fails to comply with the duty to exercise reasonable care, a potentially tortious act may have been committed. Failure to live up to a standard of care may be an act (setting fire to a building) or an omission (neglecting to put out a campfire). It may be a careless act or a carefully performed but nevertheless dangerous act that results in injury. Courts consider the nature of the act (whether it is outrageous or commonplace), the manner in which the act was performed (cautiously versus heedlessly), and the nature of the injury (whether it is serious or slight).

THE REASONABLE PERSON STANDARD Tort law measures duty by the **reasonable person standard.** In determining whether a duty of care has been breached, the courts ask how a reasonable person would have acted in the same circumstances. The reasonable person standard is said to be (though in an absolute sense it cannot be) objective. It is not necessarily how a particular person would act. It is society's judgment on how people *should* act. If the so-called reasonable person existed, he or she would be careful, conscientious, even tempered, and honest. The courts frequently use this hypothetical reasonable person in decisions relating to other areas of law as well. That individuals are required to exercise a reasonable standard of care in their activities is a pervasive concept in business law, and many of the issues discussed in subsequent chapters of this text have to do with this duty.

In negligence cases, the degree of care to be exercised varies, depending on the defendant's occupation or profession, her or his relationship with the plaintiff, and other factors. Generally, whether an action constitutes a breach of the duty of care is determined on a case-by-case basis. The outcome depends on how the judge (or jury, if it is a jury trial)

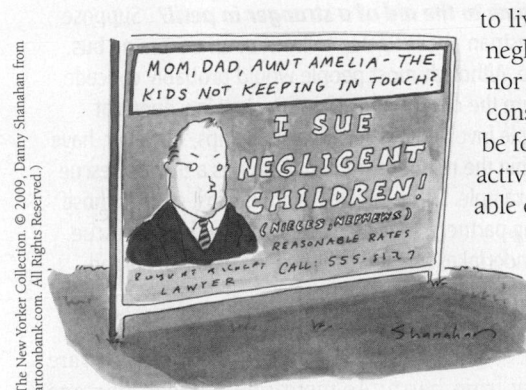

MOM, DAD, AUNT AMELIA - THE KIDS NOT KEEPING IN TOUCH?

I SUE NEGLIGENT CHILDREN! (NIECES, NEPHEWS) REASONABLE RATES

AUGUST RICKERT CALL: 555-8127 LAWYER

Negligence The failure to exercise the standard of care that a reasonable person would exercise in similar circumstances.

Duty of Care The duty of all persons, as established by tort law, to exercise a reasonable amount of care in their dealings with others. Failure to exercise due care, which is normally determined by the reasonable person standard, constitutes the tort of negligence.

Reasonable Person Standard The standard of behavior expected of a hypothetical "reasonable person"; the standard against which negligence is measured and that must be observed to avoid liability for negligence.

decides a reasonable person in the position of the defendant would act in the particular circumstances of the case.

Does a person's duty of care include a duty to come to the aid of a stranger in peril? Suppose that you are walking down the street and see a pedestrian about to step in front of an oncoming bus. Do you have a legal duty to warn that individual? No. Although most people would probably concede that the observer has an *ethical* or moral duty to warn the other in this situation, tort law does not impose a general duty to rescue others in peril. People involved in special relationships, however, have been held to have a duty to rescue other parties within the relationship. A person has a duty to rescue his or her child or spouse if either is in danger, for example. Other special relationships, such as those between teachers and students or hiking and hunting partners, may also give rise to a duty to rescue. In addition, if a person who has no duty to rescue undertakes a rescue, then the rescuer is charged with a duty to follow through with due care in the rescue attempt.

THE DUTY OF LANDOWNERS   Landowners are expected to exercise reasonable care to protect persons coming onto their property from harm. As mentioned earlier, in some jurisdictions, landowners are held to owe a duty to protect even trespassers against certain risks. Landowners who rent or lease premises to tenants (see Chapter 36) are expected to exercise reasonable care to ensure that the tenants and their guests are not harmed in common areas, such as stairways, entryways, and laundry rooms.

Duty to Warn Business Invitees of Risks.   Retailers and other firms that explicitly or implicitly invite persons to come onto their premises are usually charged with a duty to exercise reasonable care to protect those persons, who are considered **business invitees**. **EXAMPLE 4.16** Liz enters a supermarket, slips on a wet floor, and sustains injuries as a result. The owner of the supermarket would be liable for damages if, when Liz slipped, there was no sign warning that the floor was wet. A court would hold that the business owner was negligent because the owner failed to exercise a reasonable degree of care in protecting the store's customers against foreseeable risks about which the owner knew or *should have known*. That a patron might slip on the wet floor and be injured was a foreseeable risk, and the owner should have taken care to avoid this risk or to warn the customer of it (by posting a sign or setting out orange cones, for example). ●

The landowner also has a duty to discover and remove any hidden dangers that might injure a customer or other invitee. Store owners have a duty to protect customers from potentially slipping and injuring themselves on merchandise that has fallen off the shelves.

Business Invitee   A person, such as a customer or a client, who is invited onto business premises by the owner of those premises for business purposes.

Obvious Risks Provide an Exception.   Some risks, of course, are so obvious that the owner need not warn of them. For instance, a business owner does not need to warn customers to open a door before attempting to walk through it. Other risks, however, may seem obvious to a business owner but may not be so in the eyes of another, such as a child. In addition, even if a risk is obvious, that does not necessarily excuse a business owner from the duty to protect its customers from foreseeable harm. **CASE EXAMPLE 4.17** Giorgio's Grill in Hollywood, Florida, is a restaurant that becomes a nightclub after hours. At those times, traditionally, as the manager of Giorgio's knew, the staff and customers threw paper napkins into the air as the music played. The napkins landed on the floor, but no one picked them up. One night, Jane Izquierdo went to Giorgio's. Although she had been to the club on other occasions and knew about the napkin-throwing tradition, she slipped and fell, breaking her leg. She sued Giorgio's for negligence but lost at trial because a jury found that the risk of slipping on the napkins was obvious. A state appellate court reversed, however, holding that the obviousness of a risk does not discharge a business owner's duty to its invitees to maintain the premises in a safe condition.[21] ●

"A little neglect may breed great mischief."
Benjamin Franklin, 1706–1790
(American politician and inventor)

---

21. *Izquierdo v. Gyroscope, Inc.*, 946 So.2d 115 (Fla.App. 2007).

It can be difficult to determine whether a risk is obvious. Because you can be held liable if you fail to discover hidden dangers on business premises that could cause injuries to customers, you should post warnings of any conceivable risks on the property. Be vigilant and frequently reassess potential hazards. Train your employees to be on the lookout for possibly dangerous conditions at all times and to notify a superior immediately if they notice something. Remember that a finding of liability in a single lawsuit can leave a small enterprise close to bankruptcy. To prevent potential negligence liability, make sure that your business premises are as safe as possible for all persons who might be there, including children, the elderly, and individuals with disabilities.

ON THE WEB You can locate the professional standards for various organizations at www.lib.uwaterloo.ca/society/standards.html.

Malpractice Professional misconduct or the lack of the requisite degree of skill as a professional. Negligence—the failure to exercise due care—on the part of a professional, such as a physician, is commonly referred to as malpractice.

Causation in Fact An act or omission without which an event would not have occurred.

Stella Liebeck was awarded several million dollars by a jury after she accidentally spilled a cup of hot McDonald's coffee on her lap. McDonald's appealed and the award was reduced. Does such an award constitute compensatory damages?

(AP Photo/Joe Marquette)

THE DUTY OF PROFESSIONALS   If an individual has knowledge, skill, or intelligence superior to that of an ordinary person, the individual's conduct must be consistent with that status. Because professionals—including physicians, dentists, architects, engineers, accountants, lawyers, and others—are required to have a certain level of knowledge and training, a higher standard of care applies. In determining whether professionals have exercised reasonable care, the law takes their training and expertise into account. Thus, an accountant's conduct is judged not by the reasonable person standard, but by the reasonable accountant standard.

If a professional violates her or his duty of care toward a client, the professional may be sued for **malpractice,** which is essentially professional negligence. For example, a patient might sue a physician for *medical malpractice*. A client might sue an attorney for *legal malpractice*. We will discuss the liability of accountants and attorneys in more detail in Chapter 34.

The Injury Requirement and Damages

For a tort to have been committed, the plaintiff must have suffered a *legally recognizable* injury. To recover damages (receive compensation), the plaintiff must have suffered some loss, harm, wrong, or invasion of a protected interest. Essentially, the purpose of tort law is to compensate for legally recognized injuries resulting from wrongful acts. If no harm or injury results from a given negligent action, there is nothing to compensate—and no tort exists. **EXAMPLE 4.18** If you carelessly bump into a passerby, who stumbles and falls as a result, you may be liable in tort if the passerby is injured in the fall. If the person is unharmed, however, there normally cannot be a suit for damages because no injury was suffered. ●

Compensatory damages are the norm in negligence cases. As noted earlier, a court will award punitive damages only if the defendant's conduct was grossly negligent, reflecting an intentional failure to perform a duty with reckless disregard of the consequences to others.

Causation

Another element necessary to a negligence action is *causation*. If a person fails in a duty of care and someone suffers an injury, the wrongful activity must have caused the harm for the activity to be considered a tort. In deciding whether there is causation, the court must address two questions:

1. *Is there causation in fact?* Did the injury occur because of the defendant's act, or would it have occurred anyway? If an injury would not have occurred without the defendant's act, then there is causation in fact. **Causation in fact** can usually be determined by the use of the *but for* test: "but for" the wrongful act, the injury would not have occurred. Theoretically, causation in fact is limitless. One could claim, for example, that "but for" the creation of the world, a particular injury would not have occurred. Thus, as a practical matter, the law has to establish limits, and it does so through the concept of proximate cause.

Proximate Cause   Legal cause; exists when the connection between an act and an injury is strong enough to justify imposing liability.

NOTE   Proximate cause can be thought of as a question of social policy. Should the defendant be made to bear the loss instead of the plaintiff?

2. *Was the act the proximate cause of the injury?* **Proximate cause,** or legal cause, exists when the connection between an act and an injury is strong enough to justify imposing liability. Proximate cause is used by judges to limit the scope of the defendant's liability to a subset of the total number of potential plaintiffs that might have been harmed by the defendant's actions. **EXAMPLE 4.19** Ackerman carelessly leaves a campfire burning. The fire not only burns down the forest but also sets off an explosion in a nearby chemical plant that spills chemicals into a river, killing all the fish for a hundred miles downstream and ruining the economy of a tourist resort. Should Ackerman be liable to the resort owners? To the tourists whose vacations were ruined? These are questions of proximate cause that a court must decide. ●

Both of these numbered questions must be answered in the affirmative for liability in tort to arise. If a defendant's action constitutes causation in fact but a court decides that the action was not the proximate cause of the plaintiff's injury, the causation requirement has not been met—and the defendant normally will not be liable to the plaintiff.

Questions of proximate cause are linked to the concept of foreseeability because it would be unfair to impose liability on a defendant unless the defendant's actions created a foreseeable risk of injury. Probably the most cited case on proximate cause is the *Palsgraf* case, which is discussed in this chapter's *Landmark in the Law* feature. In determining the issue of proximate cause, the court addressed the following question: Does a defendant's duty of care extend only to those who may be injured as a result of a foreseeable risk, or does it extend also to a person whose injury could not reasonably be foreseen?

Defenses to Negligence

Defendants often defend against negligence claims by asserting that the plaintiffs failed to prove the existence of one or more of the required elements for negligence. Additionally, there are three basic *affirmative* defenses in negligence cases (defenses that a defendant can use to avoid liability even if the facts are as the plaintiff state): (1) assumption of risk, (2) superseding cause, and (3) contributory and comparative negligence.

Assumption of Risk   A doctrine under which a plaintiff may not recover for injuries or damage suffered from risks he or she knows of and has voluntarily assumed.

ASSUMPTION OF RISK   A plaintiff who voluntarily enters into a risky situation, knowing the risk involved, will not be allowed to recover. This is the defense of **assumption of risk.** The requirements of this defense are (1) knowledge of the risk and (2) voluntary assumption of the risk. This defense is frequently asserted when the plaintiff is injured during recreational activities that involve known risk, such as skiing and skydiving. Note that assumption of risk can apply not only to participants in sporting events, but also to spectators and bystanders who are injured while attending those events.

The risk can be assumed by express agreement, or the assumption of risk can be implied by the plaintiff's knowledge of the risk and subsequent conduct. **EXAMPLE 4.20** A race car driver, Bryan Stewart, knows that there is a risk of being injured or killed in a crash whenever he enters a race. Therefore, a court will deem that Stewart has assumed the risk of racing. Of course, a person does not assume a risk different from or greater than the risk normally carried by the activity. Thus, Stewart would not assume the risk that the banking in the curves of the racetrack will give way during the race because of a construction defect. ●

Courts do not apply the assumption of risk doctrine in emergency situations. Nor does it apply when a statute protects a class of people from harm and a member of the class is injured by the harm. For instance, because federal and state statutes protect employees from harmful working conditions, employees do not assume the risks associated with the workplace. An employee who is injured generally will be compensated regardless of fault under state workers' compensation statutes (see Chapter 24).

Landmark in the Law   *Palsgraf v. Long Island Railroad Co.* (1928)

In 1928, the New York Court of Appeals (that state's highest court) issued its decision in *Palsgraf v. Long Island Railroad Co.,*[a] a case that has become a landmark in negligence law and proximate cause.

The Facts of the Case   The plaintiff, Palsgraf, was waiting for a train on a station platform. A man carrying a small package wrapped in newspaper was rushing to catch a train that had begun to move away from the platform. As the man attempted to jump aboard the moving train, he seemed unsteady and about to fall. A railroad guard on the train car reached forward to grab him, and another guard on the platform pushed him from behind to help him board the train. In the process, the man's package fell on the railroad tracks and exploded, because it contained fireworks. The repercussions of the explosion caused scales at the other end of the train platform to fall on Palsgraf, who was injured as a result. She sued the railroad company for damages in a New York state court.

The Question of Proximate Cause   At the trial, the jury found that the railroad guards were negligent in their conduct. On appeal, the question before the New York Court of Appeals was whether the conduct of the railroad guards was the proximate cause of Palsgraf's injuries. In other words, did the guards' duty of care extend to Palsgraf, who was outside the zone of danger and whose injury could not reasonably have been foreseen?

_____

a. 248 N.Y. 339, 162 N.E. 99 (1928).

The court stated that the question of whether the guards were negligent *with respect to Palsgraf* depended on whether her injury was *reasonably foreseeable* to the railroad guards. Although the guards may have acted negligently with respect to the man boarding the train, this had no bearing on the question of their negligence with respect to Palsgraf. This was not a situation in which a person commited an act so potentially harmful (for example, firing a gun at a building) that he or she would be held responsible for any harm that resulted. The court stated that here "there was nothing in the situation to suggest to the most cautious mind that the parcel wrapped in newspaper would spread wreckage through the station." The court thus concluded that the railroad guards were not negligent with respect to Palsgraf because her injury was not reasonably foreseeable.

• **Application to Today's World**   *The* Palsgraf *case established foreseeability as the test for proximate cause. Today, the courts continue to apply this test in determining proximate cause—and thus tort liability for injuries. Generally, if the victim of a harm or the consequences of a harm done are unforeseeable, there is no proximate cause. Note, though, that in the online environment, distinctions based on physical proximity, such as the "zone of danger" cited by the court in this case, are largely inapplicable.*

• **Relevant Web Sites**   To locate information on the Web concerning the *Palsgraf* decision, go to this text's Web site at www.cengage.com/blaw/blt, select "Chapter 4," and click on "URLs for Landmarks."

SUPERSEDING CAUSE   An unforeseeable intervening event may break the connection between a wrongful act and an injury to another. If so, the event acts as a *superseding cause*—that is, it relieves a defendant of liability for injuries caused by the intervening event. **EXAMPLE 4.21**   Derrick, while riding his bicycle, negligently hits Julie, who is walking on the sidewalk. As a result of the impact, Julie falls and fractures her hip. While she is waiting for help to arrive, a small aircraft crashes nearby and explodes, and some of the fiery debris hits her, causing her to sustain severe burns. Derrick will be liable for Julie's fractured hip because the risk of hitting her with his bicycle was foreseeable. Normally, Derrick will not be liable for the burns caused by the plane crash—because the risk of a plane's crashing nearby and injuring Julie was not foreseeable. •

CONTRIBUTORY AND COMPARATIVE NEGLIGENCE   All individuals are expected to exercise a reasonable degree of care in looking out for themselves. In the past, under the common law doctrine of **contributory negligence,** a plaintiff who was also negligent (failed to exercise a reasonable degree of care) could not recover anything from the defendant. Under this rule, no matter how insignificant the plaintiff's negligence was relative to the defendant's negligence, the plaintiff was precluded from recovering any damages. Today, only a few jurisdictions still hold to this doctrine.

In the majority of states, the doctrine of contributory negligence has been replaced by a **comparative negligence** standard. Under this standard, both the plaintiff's and the

Contributory Negligence   A rule in tort law that completely bars the plaintiff from recovering any damages if the damage suffered is partly the plaintiff's own fault; used in a minority of states.

Comparative Negligence   A rule in tort law that reduces the plaintiff's recovery in proportion to the plaintiff's degree of fault, rather than barring recovery completely; used in the majority of states.

defendant's negligence are computed, and the liability for damages is distributed accordingly. Some jurisdictions have adopted a "pure" form of comparative negligence that allows the plaintiff to recover, even if the extent of his or her fault is greater than that of the defendant. For example, if the plaintiff was 80 percent at fault and the defendant 20 percent at fault, the plaintiff may recover 20 percent of his or her damages. Many states' comparative negligence statutes, however, contain a "50 percent" rule under which the plaintiff recovers nothing if she or he was more than 50 percent at fault. Following this rule, a plaintiff who is 35 percent at fault could recover 65 percent of his or her damages, but a plaintiff who is 65 percent (more than 50 percent) at fault could recover nothing.

Special Negligence Doctrines and Statutes

There are a number of special doctrines and statutes relating to negligence. We examine a few of them here.

Res Ipsa Loquitur   *A doctrine under which negligence may be inferred simply because an event occurred, if it is the type of event that would not occur in the absence of negligence. Literally, the term means "the facts speak for themselves."*

RES IPSA LOQUITUR   Generally, in lawsuits involving negligence, the plaintiff has the burden of proving that the defendant was negligent. In certain situations, however, under the doctrine of *res ipsa loquitur*[22] (meaning "the facts speak for themselves"), the courts may infer that negligence has occurred. Then the burden of proof rests on the defendant—to prove she or he was *not* negligent. This doctrine is applied only when the event creating the damage or injury is one that ordinarily would occur only as a result of negligence.

CASE EXAMPLE 4.22   Mary Gubbins undergoes abdominal surgery and following the surgery has nerve damage in her spine near the area of the operation. She is unable to walk or stand for months, and even after regaining some use of her legs through physical therapy, her mobility is impaired and she experiences pain. In her subsequent negligence lawsuit, Gubbins can assert *res ipsa loquitur,* because the injury would never have occurred in the absence of the surgeon's negligence.[23] ●

Negligence *Per Se*   *An action or failure to act in violation of a statutory requirement.*

NEGLIGENCE *PER SE*   Certain conduct, whether it consists of an action or a failure to act, may be treated as **negligence *per se*** (*per se* means "in or of itself"). Negligence *per se* may occur if an individual violates a statute or ordinance and thereby causes the kind of harm that the statute was intended to prevent. The statute must clearly set out what standard of conduct is expected, when and where it is expected, and of whom it is expected. The standard of conduct required by the statute is the duty that the defendant owes to the plaintiff, and a violation of the statute is the breach of that duty.

CASE EXAMPLE 4.23   A Delaware statute states that anyone "who operates a motor vehicle and who fails to give full time and attention to the operation of the vehicle" is guilty of inattentive driving. Michael Moore was cited for inattentive driving after he collided with Debra Wright's car when he backed a truck out of a parking space. Moore paid the ticket, which meant that he pleaded guilty to violating the statute. The day after the accident, Wright began having back pain, which eventually required surgery. She sued Moore for damages, alleging negligence *per se.* The Delaware Supreme Court ruled that the inattentive driving statute set forth a sufficiently specific standard of conduct to warrant application of negligence *per se.*[24] ●

"DANGER INVITES RESCUE" DOCTRINE   Sometimes, a person who is trying to avoid harm—such as an individual who swerves to avoid a head-on collision with a drunk driver—ends up causing harm to another (such as a cyclist riding in the bike lane) as a result. In those situations, the original wrongdoer (the drunk driver in this scenario) is liable to anyone who is injured, even if the injury actually resulted from another person's

---

22. Pronounced *rehz ihp*-suh *low*-kwuh-tuhr.
23. *Gubbins v. Hurson,* 885 A.2d 269 (D.C. 2005).
24. *Wright v. Moore,* 931 A.2d 405 (Del.Supr. 2007).

attempt to escape harm. The "danger invites rescue" doctrine extends the same protection to a person who is trying to rescue another from harm—the original wrongdoer is liable for injuries to an individual attempting a rescue. The idea is that the rescuer should not be held liable for any damages because he or she did not cause the danger and because danger invites rescue.

EXAMPLE 4.24   Ludley, while driving down a street, fails to see a stop sign because he is trying to stop a squabble between his two young children in the car's back seat. Salter, on the curb near the stop sign, realizes that Ludley is about to hit a pedestrian and runs into the street to push the pedestrian out of the way. If Ludley's vehicle hits Salter instead, Ludley will be liable for Salter's injury, as well as for any injuries the other pedestrian sustained. ● Rescuers may injure themselves, or the person rescued, or even a stranger, but the original wrongdoer will still be liable.

SPECIAL NEGLIGENCE STATUTES   A number of states have enacted statutes prescribing duties and responsibilities in certain circumstances. For example, most states now have what are called **Good Samaritan statutes.**[25] Under these statutes, someone who is aided voluntarily by another cannot turn around and sue the "Good Samaritan" for negligence. These laws were passed largely to protect physicians and medical personnel who voluntarily render medical services in emergency situations to those in need, such as individuals hurt in car accidents. Indeed, the California Supreme Court has interpreted the state's Good Samaritan statute to mean that a person who renders nonmedical aid is not immune from liability.[26] Thus, only medical personnel and persons rendering medical aid in emergencies are protected in California.

Many states have also passed **dram shop acts,**[27] under which a tavern owner or bartender may be held liable for injuries caused by a person who became intoxicated while drinking at the bar or who was already intoxicated when served by the bartender. Some states' statutes also impose liability on *social hosts* (persons hosting parties) for injuries caused by guests who became intoxicated at the hosts' homes. Under these statutes, it is unnecessary to prove that the tavern owner, bartender, or social host was negligent.

▶ Strict Liability

Another category of torts is called **strict liability,** or *liability without fault.* Intentional torts and torts of negligence involve acts that depart from a reasonable standard of care and cause injuries. Under the doctrine of strict liability, liability for injury is imposed for reasons other than fault. Strict liability for damages proximately caused by an abnormally dangerous or exceptional activity is one application of this doctrine. Courts apply the doctrine of strict liability in such cases because of the extreme risk of the activity. Even if blasting with dynamite is performed with all reasonable care, there is still a risk of injury. Balancing that risk against the potential for harm, it seems reasonable to ask the person engaged in the activity to pay for injuries caused by that activity. Although there is no fault, there is still responsibility because of the dangerous nature of the undertaking.

There are other applications of the strict liability principle. Persons who keep dangerous animals, for example, are strictly liable for any harm inflicted by the animals. A significant application of strict liability is in the area of *product liability*—liability of manufacturers and sellers for harmful or defective products. Liability here is a matter of social policy and is based on two factors: (1) the manufacturer or seller can better bear the cost of injury because it can spread the

Good Samaritan Statute   A state statute stipulating that persons who provide emergency services to, or rescue, someone in peril cannot be sued for negligence, unless they act recklessly, thereby causing further harm.

Dram Shop Act   A state statute that imposes liability on the owners of bars and taverns, as well as those who serve alcoholic drinks to the public, for injuries resulting from accidents caused by intoxicated persons when the sellers or servers of alcoholic drinks contributed to the intoxication.

Strict Liability   Liability regardless of fault. In tort law, strict liability is imposed on those engaged in abnormally dangerous activities, on persons who keep dangerous animals, and on manufacturers or sellers that introduce into commerce goods that are unreasonably dangerous when in a defective condition.

---

25. These laws derive their name from the Good Samaritan story in the Bible. In the story, a traveler who had been robbed and beaten lay along the roadside, ignored by those passing by. Eventually, a man from the country of Samaria (the "Good Samaritan") stopped to render assistance to the injured person.
26. *Van Horn v. Watson,* 45 Cal.4th 322, 197 P.3d 164, 86 Cal.Rptr.3d 350 (2008).
27. Historically, a *dram* was a small unit of liquid, and spirits were sold in drams. Thus, a dram shop was a place where liquor was sold in drams.

cost throughout society by increasing prices of goods and services, and (2) the manufacturer or seller is making a profit from its activities and therefore should bear the cost of injury as an operating expense. We will discuss product liability in greater detail in Chapter 17.

 Cyber Torts—Online Defamation

Torts can also be committed in the online environment. To date, most *cyber torts* have involved defamation, so this discussion will focus on how the traditional tort law concerning defamation is being adapted to apply to online defamation.

Identifying the Author of Online Defamation

An initial issue raised by online defamation was simply discovering who was committing it. In the real world, identifying the author of a defamatory remark generally is an easy matter, but suppose that a business firm has discovered that defamatory statements about its policies and products are being posted in an online forum. Such forums allow anyone—customers, employees, or crackpots—to complain about a firm that they dislike while remaining anonymous.

Therefore, a threshold barrier to anyone who seeks to bring an action for online defamation is discovering the identity of the person who posted the defamatory message. An Internet service provider (ISP)—a company that provides connections to the Internet—can disclose personal information about its customers only when ordered to do so by a court. Consequently, businesses and individuals are increasingly bringing lawsuits against "John Does" (John Doe, Jane Doe, and the like are fictitious names used in lawsuits when the identity of a party is not known or when a party wishes to conceal his or her name for privacy reasons). Then, using the authority of the courts, the plaintiffs can obtain from the ISPs the identity of the persons responsible for the defamatory messages.

Liability of Internet Service Providers

Recall from the discussion of defamation earlier in this chapter that those who repeat or otherwise disseminate defamatory statements made by others can be held liable for defamation. Thus, newspapers, magazines, and radio and television stations can be subject to liability for defamatory content that they publish or broadcast, even though the content was prepared or created by others. Applying this rule to cyberspace, however, raises an important issue: Should ISPs be regarded as publishers and therefore be held liable for defamatory messages that are posted by their users in online forums or other arenas?

Before 1996, the courts grappled with this question. Then Congress passed the Communications Decency Act (CDA), which states that "[n]o provider or user of an interactive computer service shall be treated as the publisher or speaker of any information provided by another information content provider."[28] Thus, under the CDA, ISPs generally are treated differently from publishers in other media and are not liable for publishing defamatory statements that come from a third party.[29] (For a discussion of whether CDA immunity should extend to claims of negligence against MySpace, see this chapter's *Adapting the Law to the Online Environment*.)

Although the courts generally have construed the CDA as providing a broad shield to protect ISPs from liability for third-party content, recently some courts have started establishing some limits to CDA immunity.[30] In the following case, the court considered the scope of immunity that could be accorded to an online roommate-matching service under the CDA.

(AP Photo/Manu Fernandez)

U.S. film director Woody Allen sued a clothing company, known for its racy ads featuring scantily clad models, for using his image on the Internet. Can the Internet service provider through which the offending ads were directed be held liable?

---

28. 47 U.S.C. Section 230.

29. For a leading case on this issue, see *Zeran v. America Online, Inc.,* 129 F.3d 327 (4th Cir. 1997); *cert.* denied, 524 U.S. 937, 118 S.Ct. 2341, 141 L.Ed.2d 712 (1998). See also *Noah v. AOL Time Warner, Inc.,* 261 F.Supp.2d 532 (E.D.Va. 2003); and *Doe v. Bates,* 2006 WL 3813758 (E.D.Tex. 2006).

30. See, for example, *Chicago Lawyers' Committee for Civil Rights Under Law, Inc. v. Craigslist, Inc.,* 519 F.3d 666 (7th Cir. 2008); *Anthony v. Yahoo, Inc.,* 421 F.Supp.2d 1257 (N.D.Cal. 2006); and *Almeida v. Amazon.com, Inc.,* 456 F.3d 1316 (11th Cir. 2006).

Case 4.3   **Fair Housing Council of San Fernando Valley v. Roommate.com, LLC**

United States Court of Appeals, Ninth Circuit, 521 F.3d 1157 (2008).

FACTS   Roommate.com, LLC (Roommate), operates a roommate-matching Web site that helps individuals find roommates based on their descriptions and roommate preferences. To become members, users answer online questions that ask about the users and their roommate preferences, including age, gender, and other characteristics. Users choose answers in drop-down and select-a-box menus. Members can create personal profiles and search lists, and send "roommail" messages to other members. Roommate also e-mails newsletters to members listing compatible members who have places to rent. The Fair Housing Council of San Fernando Valley filed a suit in a federal district court against Roommate, claiming that it had violated the Fair Housing Act (FHA) by requiring members to answer questions that could enable other members to discriminate for or against them. The court held that the Communications Decency Act (CDA) barred this claim and dismissed it. The council appealed.

Can an Internet service offering to match roommates allow those using the service to specify desired characteristics, such as sexual orientation, gender, age, and race?

ISSUE   Is an online roommate-matching service that asks users to answer questions and then posts the answers to those questions on its Web site immune from liability for the content under the CDA?

DECISION   No. The U.S. Court of Appeals for the Ninth Circuit concluded that the CDA does not provide immunity to Roommate for all of the content on its Web site and in its e-mail newsletters. The appellate court reversed the lower court's summary judgment and remanded the case for "a determination of whether [Roommate's] non-immune publication and distribution of information violates the FHA."

REASON   The appellate court reasoned that when an Internet service provider (ISP) becomes an information-content provider, the immunity from liability for content under the CDA no longer applies. Roommate is responsible for the questionnaires that it requires users to fill out to register with the service because it created the forms and the answer choices. Consequently, Roommate must be considered a content provider of these questionnaires. Roommate's search mechanism and e-mail notifications "mean that it is neither a passive pass-through of information provided by others nor merely a facilitator of expression by individuals. By categorizing, channeling, and limiting the distribution of users' profiles, Roommate provides an additional layer of information that it is responsible at least in part for creating or developing."

WHY IS THIS CASE IMPORTANT?   *This case sent an important message to ISPs that immunity under the CDA is not absolute. When an ISP creates a Web site based on users' responses to questionnaires, the ISP becomes an information-content provider and CDA immunity no longer applies. Today, Web-based businesses may potentially incur liability for Internet sites that are interactive and post information that the company is partly responsible for creating.*

Adapting the Law to the Online Environment

Should CDA Immunity Extend to Negligence Claims against MySpace?

At the age of thirteen, Julie Doe established a MySpace page. To circumvent the security procedures that MySpace has set up to protect minors, she lied and said that she was eighteen years old. Peter Solis, a nineteen-year-old male, initiated online contact with Julie, and the two eventually agreed to meet. When they met, Solis sexually assaulted Julie. Julie's mother then filed a negligence lawsuit against MySpace, which claimed that it was immune from liability under the Communications Decency Act (CDA). Two courts concluded that MySpace was immune from negligence liability under the CDA, but the case has been appealed to the United States Supreme Court.[a]

The CDA generally protects ISPs from liability for publishing third parties' defamatory statements. This case raises a new issue: Should the CDA also preclude negligence claims? After all, many MySpace users are minors, and the company touts its ability to protect them from sexual predators. Sexual assaults on minors contacted through online social networking sites are increasing. One of Congress's goals in enacting the CDA was to encourage ISPs to take steps to protect children from harms that they might encounter on the Internet.

FOR CRITICAL ANALYSIS

If providers of social networking sites are failing to protect their minor users, why should they be immune from negligence claims?

a. *Doe v. MySpace, Inc.,* 528 F.3d 413 (5th Cir. 2008). The plaintiff has petitioned the United States Supreme Court to review the case, 2008 WL 4263552.

Reviewing . . . Torts and Cyber Torts

Two sisters, Darla and Irene, are partners in an import business located in a small town in Rhode Island. Irene is also campaigning to be the mayor of their town. Both sisters travel to other countries to purchase the goods they sell at their retail store. Irene buys Indonesian goods, and Darla buys goods from Africa. After a tsunami (tidal wave) destroys many of the cities in Indonesia to which Irene usually travels, she phones one of her contacts there and asks him to procure some items and ship them to her. He informs her that it will be impossible to buy these items now because the townspeople are being evacuated due to a water shortage. Irene is angry and tells the man that if he cannot purchase the goods, he should just take them without paying for them after the town has been evacuated. Darla overhears her sister's instructions and is outraged. They have a falling-out, and Darla decides that she no longer wishes to be in business with her sister. Using the information presented in the chapter, answer the following questions.

1. Suppose that Darla tells several of her friends about Irene's instructing the man to take goods without paying for them after the tsunami. If Irene files a tort action against Darla alleging slander, will her suit be successful? Why or why not?

2. Now suppose that Irene wins the election and becomes the city's mayor. Darla then writes a letter to the editor of the local newspaper disclosing Irene's misconduct. If Irene accuses Darla of committing libel, what defenses could Darla assert?

3. If Irene accepts goods shipped from Indonesia that were wrongfully obtained, has she committed an intentional tort against property? Explain.

4. Suppose now that Darla was in the store one day with an elderly customer, Betty Green, who was looking for a graduation gift for her granddaughter. When Darla went to the counter to answer the phone, Green continued to wander around the store and eventually went through an open door into the stockroom area, where she fell over some boxes on the floor and fractured her hip. Green files a negligence action against the store. Did Darla breach her duty of care? Why or why not?

Business Application
How Important Is Tort Liability to Business?*

Although there are more claims for breach of contract than any other category of lawsuits, the dollar amount of damages awarded in tort actions is typically much higher than the awards in contract claims. Tort claims are also commonplace for businesses.

Because of the potential for large damages awards for intentional and unintentional acts, businesspersons should take preventive measures to avoid tort liability as much as possible. Remember that injured persons can bring most tort actions against a business as well as against another person. In fact, if given a choice, plaintiffs often sue a business rather than an individual because the business is more likely to have "deep pockets" (the ability to pay large damages awards). Moreover, sometimes businesses can be held liable for torts that individuals cannot.

The Extent of Business Negligence Liability

A business can be exposed to negligence liability in a wide variety of instances. Liability to business invitees is a clear example. A business that fails to warn invitees that its floor is slippery after a rainstorm, or that its parking lot is icy after snow, may be liable to an injured customer. Indeed, business owners can be liable for nearly any fall or other injury that occurs on business premises.

Even the hiring of employees can lead to negligence liability. For example, a business can be liable if it fails to do a criminal background check before hiring a person to supervise a child-care center when an investigation would have revealed that the person had previously been convicted of sexual assault. Failing to properly supervise or instruct employees can also lead to liability for a business.

Professionals such as physicians, lawyers, engineers, and accountants have a duty to their clients to exercise the skills, knowledge, and intelligence they profess to have or the standards expected of their profession. Providing anything less to the client or patient is a special type of negligence called malpractice.

Liability for Torts of Employees and Agents

A business can also be held liable for the negligence or intentional torts of its employees and agents. As you will learn in Chapters 23, 24, and 25, a business is liable for the torts committed by an employee who is acting within the scope of his or her employment or an agent who is acting with the authority of the business. Therefore, if a sales agent commits fraud while acting within the scope of her or his employment, the business will be held liable.

*This *Business Application* is not meant to substitute for the services of an attorney who is licensed to practice law in your state.

CHECKLIST FOR MINIMIZING BUSINESS TORT LIABILITY

1. Constantly inspect the premises and look for areas where customers or employees might trip, slide, or fall. Take corrective action whenever you find a problem.

2. Train employees on the importance of periodic safety inspections and the procedures for reporting unsafe conditions.

3. Routinely maintain all business equipment (including vehicles).

4. Check with your liability insurance company for suggestions on improving the safety of your premises and operations.

5. Make sure that your general liability policy will adequately cover the potential exposure of the business, and reassess your coverage annually.

6. Review the background and qualifications of individuals you are considering hiring as employees or agents.

7. Investigate and review all negligence claims promptly. Most claims can be settled at low cost without a filed lawsuit.

 Key Terms

actionable 95	damages 91	proximate cause 108
actual malice 97	defamation 94	puffery 99
appropriation 98	defense 93	punitive damages 91
assault 93	disparagement of property 104	reasonable person standard 105
assumption of risk 108	dram shop act 111	*res ipsa loquitur* 110
battery 93	duty of care 105	slander 95
business invitee 106	fraudulent misrepresentation 99	slander of quality (trade libel) 104
business tort 90	Good Samaritan statute 111	slander of title 104
causation in fact 107	intentional tort 92	strict liability 111
comparative negligence 109	libel 95	tort 90
compensatory damages 91	malpractice 107	tortfeasor 92
contributory negligence 109	negligence 105	trespass to land 102
conversion 103	negligence *per se* 110	trespass to personal property 103
cyber tort 90	privilege 96	

 Chapter Summary: Torts and Cyber Torts

Intentional Torts against Persons (See pages 92–102.)	1. *Assault and battery*—An assault is an unexcused and intentional act that causes another person to be apprehensive of immediate harm. A battery is an assault that results in physical contact.
	2. *False imprisonment*—The intentional confinement or restraint of another person's movement without justification.
	3. *Intentional infliction of emotional distress*—An intentional act that amounts to extreme and outrageous conduct resulting in severe emotional distress to another.
	4. *Defamation (libel or slander)*—A false statement of fact, not made under privilege, that is communicated to a third person and that causes damage to a person's reputation. For public figures, the plaintiff must also prove actual malice.
	5. *Invasion of the right to privacy*—The use of a person's name or likeness for commercial purposes without permission, wrongful intrusion into a person's private activities, publication of information that places a person in a false light, or disclosure of private facts that an ordinary person would find objectionable.
	6. *Appropriation*—The use of another person's name, likeness, or other identifying characteristic, without permission and for the benefit of the user. Courts disagree on the degree of likeness required.
	7. *Misrepresentation (fraud)*—A false representation made by one party, through misstatement of facts or through conduct, with the intention of deceiving another and on which the other reasonably relies to his or her detriment. Negligent misrepresentation occurs when a person supplies information without having a reasonable basis for believing its truthfulness.

Continued

Chapter Summary: Torts and Cyber Torts—Continued

Intentional Torts against Persons—Continued	8. *Abusive or frivolous litigation*—If a party initiates a lawsuit out of malice and without probable cause (a legitimate legal reason), and ends up losing the suit, that party can be sued for the tort of *malicious prosecution*. When a person uses a legal process against another in an improper manner or to accomplish a purpose for which it was not designed, that person can be sued for *abuse of process*. 9. *Wrongful interference*—The knowing, intentional interference by a third party with an enforceable contractual relationship or an established business relationship between other parties for the purpose of advancing the economic interests of the third party.
Intentional Torts against Property (See pages 102–104.)	1. *Trespass to land*—The invasion of another's real property without consent or privilege. 2. *Trespass to personal property*—Unlawfully damaging or interfering with the owner's right to use, possess, or enjoy her or his personal property. 3. *Conversion*—Wrongfully taking personal property from its rightful owner or possessor and placing it in the service of another. 4. *Disparagement of property*—Any economically injurious falsehood that is made about another's product or property; an inclusive term for the torts of slander of quality and slander of title.

Unintentional Torts (Negligence) (See pages 105–111.)	1. *Negligence*—The careless performance of a legally required duty or the failure to perform a legally required act. Elements that must be proved are that a legal duty of care exists, that the defendant breached that duty, and that the breach caused damage or injury to another.
	2. *Defenses to negligence*—The basic affirmative defenses in negligence cases are assumption of risk, superseding cause, and contributory or comparative negligence.
	3. *Special negligence doctrines and statutes*—
	   a. *Res ipsa loquitur*—A doctrine under which a plaintiff need not prove negligence on the part of the defendant because "the facts speak for themselves."
	   b. Negligence *per se*—A type of negligence that may occur if a person violates a statute or an ordinance and the violation causes another to suffer the kind of injury that the statute or ordinance was intended to prevent.
	   c. Special negligence statutes—State statutes that prescribe duties and responsibilities in certain circumstances, the violation of which will impose civil liability. Dram shop acts and Good Samaritan statutes are examples of special negligence statutes.

Strict Liability (See pages 111–112.)	Under the doctrine of strict liability, a person may be held liable, regardless of the degree of care exercised, for damages or injuries caused by her or his product or activity. Strict liability includes liability for harms caused by abnormally dangerous activities, by dangerous animals, and by defective products (product liability).
Cyber Torts— Online Defamation (See pages 112–114.)	General tort principles are being extended to cover cyber torts, or torts that occur in cyberspace, such as online defamation. Federal and state statutes may also apply to certain forms of cyber torts. For example, under the federal Communications Decency Act of 1996, Internet service providers (ISPs) are not liable for defamatory messages posted by their subscribers.

 ExamPrep

ISSUE SPOTTERS

1 Jana leaves her truck's motor running while she enters a Kwik-Pik Store. The truck's transmission engages and the vehicle crashes into a gas pump, starting a fire that spreads to a warehouse on the next block. The warehouse collapses, causing its billboard to fall and injure Lou, a bystander. Can Lou recover from Jana? Why or why not?

2 A water pipe bursts, flooding a Metal Fabrication Company utility room and tripping the circuit breakers on a panel in the room. Metal Fabrication contacts Nouri, a licensed electrician with five years' experience, to check the damage and turn the breakers back on. Without testing for short circuits, which Nouri knows that he should do, he tries to switch on a breaker. He is electrocuted, and his wife sues Metal Fabrication for damages, alleging negligence. What might the firm successfully claim in defense?

BEFORE THE TEST

Check your answers to the Issue Spotters, and at the same time, take the interactive quiz for this chapter. Go to **www.cengage.com/blaw/blt** and click on "Chapter 4." First, click on "Answers to Issue Spotters" to check your answers. Next, click on "Interactive Quiz" to assess your mastery of the concepts in this chapter. Then click on "Flashcards" to review this chapter's Key Term definitions.

▶ For Review

Answers for the even-numbered questions in this For Review *section can be found on this text's accompanying Web site at* **www.cengage.com/blaw/blt**. *Select "Chapter 4" and click on "For Review."*

1 What is a tort?

2 What is the purpose of tort law? What are two basic categories of torts?

3 What are the four elements of negligence?

4 What is meant by strict liability? In what circumstances is strict liability applied?

5 What is a cyber tort, and how are tort theories being applied in cyberspace?

▶ Hypothetical Scenarios and Case Problems

4–1 Defenses to Negligence. Corinna was riding her bike on a city street. While she was riding, she frequently looked back to verify that the books that she had fastened to the rear part of her bike were still attached. On one occasion while she was looking behind her, she failed to notice a car that was entering an intersection just as she was crossing it. The car hit her, causing her to sustain numerous injuries. Three eyewitnesses stated that the driver of the car had failed to stop at the stop sign before entering the intersection. Corinna sued the driver of the car for negligence. What defenses might the defendant driver raise in this lawsuit? Discuss fully.

4–2 **Hypothetical Question with Sample Answer** Lothar owns a bakery. He has been trying to obtain a long-term contract with the owner of Martha's Tea Salons for some time. Lothar starts an intensive advertising campaign on radio and television and in the local newspaper. The advertising is so persuasive that Martha decides to break her contract with Harley's Bakery so that she can patronize Lothar's bakery. Is Lothar liable to Harley's Bakery for the tort of wrongful interference with a contractual relationship? Is Martha liable for this tort?

—**For a sample answer to Question 4–2, go to Appendix E at the end of this text.**

4–3 Negligence. Shannon's physician gives her some pain medication and tells her not to drive after taking it because the medication induces drowsiness. In spite of the doctor's warning, Shannon decides to drive to the store while on the medication. Owing to her lack of alertness, she fails to stop at a traffic light and crashes into another vehicle, causing a passenger in that vehicle to be injured. Is Shannon liable for the tort of negligence?

4–4 Liability to Business Invitees. Kim went to Ling's Market to pick up a few items for dinner. It was a stormy day, and the wind had blown water through the market's door each time it opened. As Kim entered through the door, she slipped and fell in the rainwater that had accumulated on the floor. The manager knew of the weather conditions but had not posted any sign to warn customers of the water hazard. Kim injured her back as a result of the fall and sued Ling's for damages. Can Ling's be held liable for negligence? Discuss.

4–5 **Case Problem with Sample Answer** Neal Peterson's entire family skied, and Peterson started skiing at the age of two. In 2000, at the age of eleven, Peterson was in his fourth year as a member of a ski race team. After a race one morning in February, Peterson continued to practice his skills through the afternoon. Coming down a slope very fast, at a point when his skis were not touching the ground, Peterson collided with David Donahue. Donahue, a forty-three-year-old advanced skier, was skating (skiing slowly) across the slope toward the parking lot. Peterson and Donahue knew that falls or collisions and accidents and injuries were possible with skiing. Donahue saw Peterson "split seconds" before the impact, which knocked Donahue out of his skis and down the slope ten or twelve feet. When Donahue saw Peterson lying motionless nearby, he immediately sought help. To recover for his injuries, Peterson filed a suit in a Minnesota state court against Donahue, alleging negligence. Based on these facts, which defense to a claim of negligence is Donahue most likely to assert? How is the court likely to apply that defense and rule on Peterson's claim? Why? [*Peterson ex rel. Peterson v. Donahue,* 733 N.W.2d 790 (Minn.App. 2007)]

—**After you have answered Problem 4–5, compare your answer with the sample answer given on the Web site that accompanies this text. Go to www.cengage.com/blaw/blt, select "Chapter 4," and click on "Case Problem with Sample Answer."**

4–6 Negligence. Mitsubishi Motors North America, Inc., operates an auto plant in Normal, Illinois. In 2003, TNT Logistics Corp. coordinated deliveries of auto parts to the plant and DeKeyser

Express, Inc., transported the parts. On January 21, TNT told DeKeyser to transport three pallets of parts from Trelleborg YSH, Inc., to the plant. DeKeyser dispatched its driver Lola Camp. At Trelleborg's loading dock, Camp noticed that the pallets would fit inside the trailer only if they were stacked. Camp was concerned that the load might shift during transport. DeKeyser dispatcher, Ken Kasprzak, and TNT supervisor, Alan Marten, told her that she would not be liable for any damage. Trelleborg loaded the pallets. Camp drove to TNT's dock in Normal. When she opened the trailer door, the top pallet slipped. Trying to close the door to prevent its fall, Camp injured her shoulder and arm. She filed a suit against TNT and Trelleborg, claiming negligence. What is their defense? Discuss. [*Camp v. TNT Logistics Corp.*, 553 F.3d 502 (7th Cir. 2009)]

4–7   **A Question of Ethics** *White Plains Coat & Apron Co. is a New York–based linen rental business. Cintas Corp. is a nationwide business that rents similar products. White Plains had five-year exclusive contracts with some of its customers. As a result of Cintas's soliciting of business, dozens of White Plains'* customers breached their contracts and entered into rental agreements with Cintas. White Plains demanded that Cintas stop soliciting White Plains' customers. Cintas refused. White Plains filed a suit in a federal district court against Cintas, alleging wrongful interference with existing contracts. Cintas argued that it had no knowledge of any contracts with White Plains and had not induced any breach. The court dismissed the suit, ruling that Cintas had a legitimate interest as a competitor in soliciting business and making a profit. White Plains appealed to the U.S. Court of Appeals for the Second Circuit. [White Plains Coat & Apron Co. v. Cintas Corp., 8 N.Y.3d 422, 867 N.E.2d 381 (2007)]*

1 What two important policy interests are at odds in wrongful interference cases? When there is an existing contract, which of these interests should be accorded priority?

2 The U.S Court of Appeals for the Second Circuit asked the New York Court of Appeals to answer a question: Is a general interest in soliciting business for profit a sufficient defense to a claim of wrongful interference with a contractual relationship? What do you think? Why?

Critical Thinking and Writing Assignments

4–8 Critical Legal Thinking. What general principle underlies the common law doctrine that business owners have a duty of care toward their customers? Does the duty of care unfairly burden business owners? Why or why not?

4–9 Video Question Go to this text's Web site at **www.cengage.com/blaw/blt** and select "Chapter 4." Click on "Video Questions" and view the video titled *Jaws*. Then answer the following questions.

1 In the video, the mayor (Murray Hamilton) and a few other men try to persuade Chief Brody (Roy Scheider) not to close the town's beaches. If Chief Brody keeps the beaches open and a swimmer is injured or killed because he failed to warn swimmers about the potential shark danger, has he committed a tort? If so, what kind of tort (intentional tort against persons, intentional tort against property, or negligence)? Explain your answer.

2 Can Chief Brody be held liable for any injuries or deaths to swimmers under the doctrine of strict liability? Why or why not?

3 Suppose that Chief Brody goes against the mayor's instructions and warns people to stay out of the water. Nevertheless, several swimmers do not heed his warning and are injured as a result. What defense or defenses could Chief Brody raise under these circumstances if he is sued for negligence?

4–10 Case Analysis Question Go to Appendix F at the end of this text and examine Case No. 1 [*Lott v. Levitt*, 469 F.Supp.2d 575 (N.D.Ill. 2007)]. This case has been excerpted there in great detail. Review and then brief the case, making sure that your brief answers the following questions.

1 Issue: At the center of the dispute in this case was a distinction between what types of speech?

2 Rule of Law: What difference does it make what type of speech a particular statement is?

3 Applying the Rule of Law: How does a court determine which type of speech a certain statement comprises?

4 Conclusion: In this case, how was the speech at issue classified, and why? What effect did that decision have on the parties' suit?

Practical Internet Exercises

Go to this text's Web site at **www.cengage.com/blaw/blt**, select "Chapter 4," and click on "Practical Internet Exercises." There you will find the following Internet research exercises that you can perform to learn more about the topics covered in this chapter.

Practical Internet Exercise 4–1: LEGAL PERSPECTIVE—Online Defamation
Practical Internet Exercise 4–2: MANAGEMENT PERSPECTIVE—The Duty to Warn

Chapter 5

Intellectual Property and Internet Law

(Cytech/Creative Commons)

Chapter Outline

- Trademarks and Related Property
- Cyber Marks
- Patents
- Copyrights
- Trade Secrets
- International Protection for Intellectual Property

> "The Internet is just a world passing around notes in a classroom."
>
> —Jon Stewart, 1962–present
> (American comedian and host of *The Daily Show*)

Learning Objectives

After reading this chapter, you should be able to answer the following questions:

1. What is intellectual property?

2. Why does the law protect trademarks and patents?

3. What laws protect authors' rights in the works they generate?

4. What are trade secrets, and what laws offer protection for this form of intellectual property?

5. What steps have been taken to protect intellectual property rights in today's digital age?

Intellectual Property Property resulting from intellectual, creative processes.

Of significant concern to businesspersons today is the need to protect their rights in intellectual property, which may exceed the value of their physical property, such as machines and buildings. **Intellectual property** is any property resulting from intellectual, creative processes—the products of an individual's mind. Although it is an abstract term for an abstract concept, intellectual property is nonetheless familiar to almost everyone. The information contained in books and computer files is intellectual property. The software you use, the movies you see, and the music you listen to are all forms of intellectual property.

The need to protect creative works was recognized by the framers of the U.S. Constitution more than two hundred years ago: Article I, Section 8, of the Constitution authorized Congress "[t]o promote the Progress of Science and useful Arts, by securing for limited Times to Authors and Inventors the exclusive Right to their respective Writings and Discoveries." Laws protecting patents, trademarks, and copyrights are explicitly designed to protect and reward inventive and artistic creativity.

In today's global economy, however, protecting intellectual property in one country is no longer sufficient, and the United States is participating in various international agreements to secure ownership rights in intellectual property in other countries. Because the Internet allows the world to "pass around notes" so quickly, as Jon Stewart joked in the chapter-opening quotation, protecting these rights in today's online environment has proved particularly challenging.

▶ Trademarks and Related Property

Trademark A distinctive mark, motto, device, or emblem that a manufacturer stamps, prints, or otherwise affixes to the goods it produces so that they may be identified on the market and their origins made known. Once a trademark is established (under the common law or through registration), the owner is entitled to its exclusive use.

A **trademark** is a distinctive mark, motto, device, or emblem that a manufacturer stamps, prints, or otherwise affixes to the goods it produces so that they may be identified on the market and their origins made known. At common law, the person who used a symbol or mark to identify a business or product was protected in the use of that trademark. Clearly, by using another's trademark, a business could lead consumers to believe that its goods were made by the other business. The law seeks to avoid this kind of confusion. (For information on how companies use trademarks and service marks, see this chapter's *Linking the Law to Marketing* feature on page 140.)

In the following classic case concerning Coca-Cola, the defendants argued that the Coca-Cola trademark was entitled to no protection under the law because the term did not accurately represent the product.

Classic Case 5.1   The Coca-Cola Co. v. Koke Co. of America

Supreme Court of the United States, 254 U.S. 143, 41 S.Ct. 113, 65 L.Ed. 189 (1920).
www.findlaw.com/casecode/supreme.html[a]

(Wikimedia Commons and The Library of Congress)

An 1890s advertisement showing model Hilda Clark in formal 19th century attire. The ad is entitled, "Drink Coca-Cola 5¢."

COMPANY PROFILE *John Pemberton, an Atlanta pharmacist, invented a caramel-colored, carbonated soft drink in 1886. His bookkeeper, Frank Robinson, named the beverage Coca-Cola after two of the ingredients, coca leaves and kola nuts. Asa Candler bought the Coca-Cola Company in 1891 and, within seven years, had made the soft drink available in all of the United States, as well as in parts of Canada and Mexico. Candler continued to sell Coke aggressively and to open up new markets, reaching Europe before 1910. In doing so, however, he attracted numerous competitors, some of whom tried to capitalize directly on the Coke name.*

FACTS The Coca-Cola Company brought an action in a federal district court to enjoin other beverage companies from using the words *Koke* and *Dope* for the defendants' products. The defendants contended that the Coca-Cola trademark was a fraudulent representation and that Coca-Cola was therefore not entitled to any help from the courts. By use of the Coca-Cola name, the defendants alleged, the Coca-Cola Company represented

that the beverage contained cocaine (from coca leaves). The district court granted the injunction, but the federal appellate court reversed. The Coca-Cola Company appealed to the United States Supreme Court.

ISSUE Did the marketing of products called Koke and Dope by the Koke Company of America and other firms constitute an infringement on Coca-Cola's trademark?

DECISION Yes for Koke, but no for Dope. The United States Supreme Court enjoined the competing beverage companies from calling their products Koke but did not prevent them from calling their products Dope.

REASON The Court noted that, to be sure, before 1900 the Coca-Cola beverage had contained a small amount of cocaine. This ingredient had been deleted from the formula by 1906 at the latest, however, and the Coca-Cola Company had advertised to the public that no cocaine was present in its drink. Coca-Cola was a widely popular drink "to be had at almost any soda fountain." Because of the public's widespread familiarity with Coca-Cola, the retention of the name (referring to coca leaves and kola nuts) was not misleading: "Coca-Cola probably means to most persons the plaintiff's familiar product to be had everywhere rather than a compound of particular substances." The name *Coke* was found to be so common a term for the trademarked product Coca-Cola that the defendants' use of the similar-sounding *Koke* as a name for their beverages was disallowed. The Court could find no reason to restrain the defendants from using the name *Dope,* however.

WHAT IF THE FACTS WERE DIFFERENT? *Suppose that Coca-Cola had been trying to make the public believe that its product contained cocaine. Would the result in the case likely have been different? Explain your answer.*

IMPACT OF THIS CASE ON TODAY'S LAW *In this early case, the United States Supreme Court made it clear that trademarks*

---

a. This is the "U.S. Supreme Court Opinions" page within the Web site of the "Find-Law Internet Legal Resources" database. This page provides several options for accessing an opinion. Because you know the citation for this case, you can go to the "Citation Search" box, type in the appropriate volume and page numbers for the *United States Reports* ("254" and "143," respectively, for the *Coca-Cola* case), and click on "Get It."

Case 5.1—Continued

and trade names (and nicknames for those marks and names, such as the nickname "Coke" for "Coca-Cola") that are in common use receive protection under the common law. This holding is significant historically because it is the predecessor to the federal statute later passed to protect trademark rights (the Lanham Act of 1946, to be discussed shortly).

RELEVANT WEB SITES *To locate information on the Web concerning the Coca-Cola decision, go to this text's Web site at* www.cengage.com/blaw/blt. *Select "Chapter 5" and click on "Classic Cases."*

Statutory Protection of Trademarks

ON THE WEB You can find answers to frequently asked questions (FAQs) about trademark and patent law, as well as a host of other information, at the Web site of the U.S. Patent and Trademark Office. Go to www.uspto.gov.

Statutory protection of trademarks and related property is provided at the federal level by the Lanham Act of 1946.[1] The Lanham Act was enacted in part to protect manufacturers from losing business to rival companies that used confusingly similar trademarks. The act incorporates the common law of trademarks and provides remedies for owners of trademarks who wish to enforce their claims in federal court. Many states also have trademark statutes.

TRADEMARK DILUTION Before 1995, federal trademark law prohibited only the unauthorized use of the same mark on competing—or on noncompeting but "related"—goods or services. Protection was given only when the unauthorized use would likely confuse consumers as to the origin of those goods and services. In 1995, Congress amended the Lanham Act by passing the Federal Trademark Dilution Act,[2] which allowed trademark owners to bring a suit in federal court for trademark *dilution*. Trademark dilution laws protect "distinctive" or "famous" trademarks (such as Jergens, McDonald's, Dell, and Apple) from certain unauthorized uses even when the use is on noncompeting goods or is unlikely to confuse. More than half of the states have also enacted trademark dilution laws.

USE OF A SIMILAR MARK MAY CONSTITUTE TRADEMARK DILUTION A famous mark may be diluted not only by the use of an *identical* mark but also by the use of a *similar* mark, provided that it reduces the value of the famous mark.[3] **CASE EXAMPLE 5.1** A woman opened a coffee shop under the name "Sambuck's Coffeehouse" in Astoria, Oregon, even though she knew that "Starbucks" was one of the largest coffee chains in the nation. When Starbucks Corporation filed a dilution lawsuit, the federal court ruled that use of the "Sambuck's" mark constituted trademark dilution because it created confusion for consumers. Not only was there a "high degree" of similarity between the marks, but also both companies provided coffee-related services through "stand-alone" retail stores. Therefore, the use of the similar mark (Sambuck's) reduced the value of the famous mark (Starbucks).[4] ●

This coffee shop in Astoria, Oregon, used to be named "Sambuck's Coffeehouse" before Starbucks successfully sued for trademark dilution. Why would Starbucks spend the resources necessary to sue a single coffee shop in a small town?

(AP Photo/The Daily Astorian/Kara Hansen)

Trademark Registration

Trademarks may be registered with the state or with the federal government. To register for protection under federal trademark law, a person must file an application with the U.S. Patent and Trademark Office in Washington, D.C. A mark can be registered (1) if it is currently in commerce or (2) if the applicant intends to put the mark into commerce within six months.

---

1. 15 U.S.C. Sections 1051–1128.
2. 15 U.S.C. Section 1125.
3. See *Moseley v. V Secret Catalogue, Inc.*, 537 U.S. 418, 123 S.Ct. 1115, 155 L.Ed.2d 1 (2003).
4. *Starbucks Corp. v. Lundberg*, 2005 WL 3183858 (D.Or. 2005).

ON THE WEB To access the federal database of registered trademarks, go to **www.uspto.gov/main/trademarks.htm**.

In special circumstances, the six-month period can be extended by thirty months, giving the applicant a total of three years from the date of notice of trademark approval to make use of the mark and file the required use statement. Registration is postponed until the mark is actually used. Nonetheless, during this waiting period, the applicant's trademark is protected against a third party who has neither used the mark previously nor filed an application for it. Registration is renewable between the fifth and sixth years after the initial registration and every ten years thereafter (every twenty years for trademarks registered before 1990).

Trademark Infringement

Registration of a trademark with the U.S. Patent and Trademark Office gives notice on a nationwide basis that the trademark belongs exclusively to the registrant. The registrant is also allowed to use the symbol ® to indicate that the mark has been registered. Whenever someone else uses that trademark in its entirety or copies it to a substantial degree, intentionally or unintentionally, the trademark has been *infringed* (used without authorization).

When a trademark has been infringed, the owner has a cause of action against the infringer. To succeed in a trademark infringement action, the owner must show that the defendant's use of the mark created a likelihood of confusion about the origin of the defendant's goods or services. The owner need not prove that the infringer acted intentionally or that the trademark was registered (although registration does provide proof of the date of inception of the trademark's use).

The most commonly granted remedy for trademark infringement is an *injunction* to prevent further infringement. Under the Lanham Act, a trademark owner that successfully proves infringement can recover actual damages, plus the profits that the infringer wrongfully received from the unauthorized use of the mark. A court can also order the destruction of any goods bearing the unauthorized trademark. In some situations, the trademark owner may also be able to recover attorneys' fees.

Distinctiveness of the Mark

A central objective of the Lanham Act is to reduce the likelihood that consumers will be confused by similar marks. For that reason, only those trademarks that are deemed sufficiently distinctive from all competing trademarks will be protected.

STRONG MARKS   Fanciful, arbitrary, or suggestive trademarks are generally considered to be the most distinctive (strongest) trademarks because they are normally taken from outside the context of the particular product and thus provide the best means of distinguishing one product from another. Fanciful trademarks include invented words, such as "Xerox" for one manufacturer's copiers and "Kodak" for another company's photographic products. Arbitrary trademarks use common words in a fictitious or arbitrary manner to create a distinctive mark that identifies the source of the product, such as "Dutch Boy" as a name on a can of paint.

A single letter used in a particular style can be an arbitrary trademark. **CASE EXAMPLE 5.2** Sports entertainment company ESPN sued Quiksilver, Inc., a maker of surfer clothing, alleging trademark infringement. ESPN claimed that Quiksilver had used the stylized "X" mark on its clothing that ESPN uses in connection with the "X Games," a competition focusing on extreme action sports such as skateboarding and snowboarding. Quiksilver filed counterclaims for trademark infringement and dilution, arguing that it has a long history of using the stylized X on its products. ESPN created the X Games in the mid-1990s, and Quiksilver has been using the X mark since 1994. ESPN, which has trademark applications pending for the stylized X, asked the court to dismiss Quiksilver's counterclaims. In 2008, a federal district court held that the X on Quiksilver's clothing is clearly an arbitrary mark. Noting that "the two Xs are similar enough that a consumer might well confuse them," the court refused to dismiss Quiksilver's claims and allowed the dispute to go to trial.[5] •

---

5. *ESPN, Inc. v. Quiksilver, Inc.*, 586 F.Supp.2d 219 (S.D.N.Y. 2008).

Suggestive trademarks bring to mind something about a product without describing the product directly. For instance, "Dairy Queen" suggests an association between its products and milk, but it does not directly describe ice cream.

SECONDARY MEANING   Descriptive terms, geographic terms, and personal names are not inherently distinctive and do not receive protection under the law *until* they acquire a secondary meaning. **CASE EXAMPLE 5.3**   Frosty Treats, Inc., sells frozen desserts out of ice cream trucks. The video game series Twisted Metal depicted an ice cream truck with a clown character on it that was similar to the clowns on Frosty Treats' trucks. In the last game of the series, the truck bears the label "Frosty Treats." Frosty Treats sued for trademark infringement, but the court held that "Frosty Treats" is a descriptive term that is not protected by trademark law unless it has acquired a secondary meaning. To establish secondary meaning, Frosty Treats would have to show that the public recognizes its trademark and associates it with a single source. Because Frosty Treats failed to do so, the court entered a judgment in favor of the video game producer.[6] ●

A secondary meaning arises when customers begin to associate a specific term or phrase, such as "London Fog," with specific trademarked items (coats with "London Fog" labels) made by a particular company. Whether a secondary meaning becomes attached to a term or name usually depends on how extensively the product is advertised, the market for the product, the number of sales, and other factors. Once a secondary meaning is attached to a term or name, a trademark is considered distinctive and is protected. Even a color can qualify for trademark protection, such as the color schemes used by four state university sports teams, including Ohio State University and Louisiana State University.[7]

GENERIC TERMS   Generic terms are terms that refer to an entire class of products, such as *bicycle* and *computer*. Generic terms receive no protection, even if they acquire secondary meanings. A particularly thorny problem for a business arises when its trademark acquires generic use. For instance, *aspirin* and *thermos* were originally trademarked products, but today the words are used generically. Other trademarks that have acquired generic use include *escalator, trampoline, raisin bran, dry ice, lanolin, linoleum, nylon,* and *cornflakes.*[8]

Service, Certification, and Collective Marks

A **service mark** is essentially a trademark that is used to distinguish the *services* (rather than the products) of one person or company from those of another. For instance, each airline has a particular mark or symbol associated with its name. Titles and character names used in radio and television are frequently registered as service marks.

Other marks protected by law include certification marks and collective marks. A **certification mark** is used by one or more persons, other than the owner, to certify the region, materials, mode of manufacture, quality, or other characteristic of specific goods or services. Certification marks include such marks as "Good Housekeeping Seal of Approval" and "UL Tested." When used by members of a cooperative, association, union, or other organization, a certification mark is referred to as a **collective mark.** **EXAMPLE 5.4** Collective marks appear at the ends of movie credits to indicate the various associations and organizations that participated in making the movie. The union marks found on the tags of certain products are also collective marks. ●

Service Mark   A mark used in the sale or advertising of services to distinguish the services of one person from those of others. Titles, character names, and other distinctive features of radio and television programs may be registered as service marks.

Certification Mark   A mark used by one or more persons, other than the owner, to certify the region, materials, mode of manufacture, quality, or other characteristic of specific goods or services.

Collective Mark   A mark used by members of a cooperative, association, union, or other organization to certify the region, materials, mode of manufacture, quality, or other characteristic of specific goods or services.

---

6. *Frosty Treats, Inc., v. Sony Computer Entertainment America, Inc.,* 426 F.3d 1001 (8th Cir. 2005).

7. *Board of Supervisors of LA State University v. Smack Apparel Co.,* 438 F.Supp.2d 653 (2006); see also *Qualitex Co. v. Jacobson Products Co.,* 514 U.S. 159, 115 S.Ct. 1300, 131 L.Ed.2d 248 (1995).

8. See, for example, *Boston Duck Tours, LP v. Super Duck Tours, LLC,* 531 F.3d 1 (1st Cir. 2008).

Trade Dress

Trade Dress The image and overall appearance of a product–for example, the distinctive decor, menu, layout, and style of service of a particular restaurant. Basically, trade dress is subject to the same protection as trademarks.

The term **trade dress** refers to the image and overall appearance of a product. Trade dress is a broad concept and can include all or part of the total image or overall impression created by a product or its packaging. **EXAMPLE 5.5** The distinctive decor, menu, and style of service of a particular restaurant may be regarded as the restaurant's trade dress. Similarly, trade dress can include the layout and appearance of a mail-order catalogue, the use of a lighthouse as part of a golf hole's design, the fish shape of a cracker, or the G-shaped design of a Gucci watch. ●

Basically, trade dress is subject to the same protection as trademarks. In cases involving trade dress infringement, as in trademark infringement cases, a major consideration is whether consumers are likely to be confused by the allegedly infringing use.

Counterfeit Goods

Counterfeit goods copy or otherwise imitate trademarked goods but are not genuine. The importation of goods bearing counterfeit (fake) trademarks poses a growing problem for U.S. businesses, consumers, and law enforcement. In addition to having negative financial effects on legitimate businesses, sales of certain counterfeit goods, such as pharmaceuticals and nutritional supplements, can present serious public health risks. It is estimated that nearly 7 percent of the goods imported into the United States are counterfeit.

STOP COUNTERFEITING IN MANUFACTURED GOODS ACT   Congress enacted the Stop Counterfeiting in Manufactured Goods Act[9] (SCMGA) to combat counterfeit goods. The act made it a crime to intentionally traffic in, or attempt to traffic in, counterfeit goods or services, or to knowingly use a counterfeit mark on or in connection with goods or services. Before this act, the law did not prohibit the creation or shipment of counterfeit labels that were not attached to a product.[10] Therefore, counterfeiters would make labels and packaging bearing a fake trademark, ship the labels to another location, and then affix them to inferior products to deceive buyers. The SCMGA closed this loophole by making it a crime to traffic in counterfeit labels, stickers, packaging, and the like, whether or not they are attached to goods.

Trade Name A term that is used to indicate part or all of a business's name and that is directly related to the business's reputation and goodwill. Trade names are protected under the common law (and under trademark law, if the name is the same as the firm's trademarked product).

PENALTIES FOR COUNTERFEITING   Persons found guilty of violating the SCMGA may be fined up to $2 million or imprisoned for up to ten years (or more if they are repeat offenders). If a court finds that the statute was violated, it must order the defendant to forfeit the counterfeit products (which are then destroyed), as well as any property used in the commission of the crime. The defendant must also pay restitution to the trademark holder or victim in an amount equal to the victim's actual loss. **CASE EXAMPLE 5.6** A defendant pleaded guilty to conspiring to import cigarette-rolling papers from Mexico that were falsely marked as "Zig-Zags" and sell them in the United States. The defendant was sentenced to prison and ordered to pay $566,267 in restitution. On appeal, the court affirmed the prison sentence but ordered the trial court to reduce the amount of restitution because it exceeded the actual loss suffered by the legitimate sellers of Zig-Zag rolling papers.[11] ●

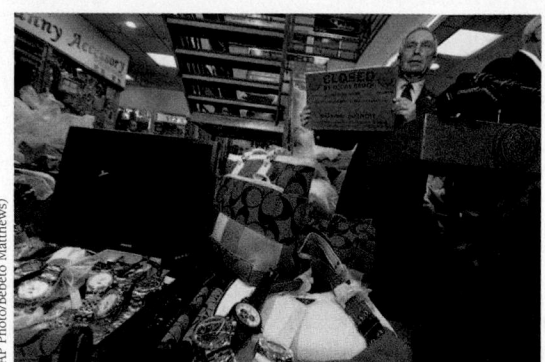

(AP Photo/Bebeto Matthews)

New York City mayor Michael Bloomberg stands amidst seized counterfeit goods in Chinatown's New Land Shopping Center. These included counterfeit Coach, Fendi, Prada, and Rolex goods. What sanctions can be imposed on those found guilty under current law?

Trade Names

Trademarks apply to *products*. The term **trade name** is used to indicate part or all of a business's name, whether the business is a sole proprietorship, a partnership, or a corporation. Generally, a trade name is directly

---

9. Pub. L. No. 109-181 (2006), which amended 18 U.S.C. Sections 2318–2320.
10. See, for example, *Commonwealth v. Crespo,* 884 A.2d 960 (Pa. 2005).
11. *United States v. Beydoun,* 469 F.3d 102 (5th Cir. 2006).

related to a business and its goodwill. Trade names may be protected as trademarks if the trade name is the same as the company's trademarked product—for example, Coca-Cola. Unless it is also used as a trademark or service mark, a trade name cannot be registered with the federal government. Trade names are protected under the common law, however. As with trademarks, words must be unusual or fancifully used if they are to be protected as trade names. For instance, the courts held that the word *Safeway* was sufficiently fanciful to obtain protection as a trade name for a grocery chain.

▶ Cyber Marks

Cyber Mark   A trademark in cyberspace.

In cyberspace, trademarks are sometimes referred to as **cyber marks.** We turn now to a discussion of how new laws and the courts are addressing trademark-related issues in cyberspace.

Domain Names

Domain Name   The last part of an Internet address, such as "westlaw.com." The top level (the part of the name to the right of the period) indicates the type of entity that operates the site (*com* is an abbreviation for "commercial"). The second level (the part of the name to the left of the period) is chosen by the entity.

As e-commerce expanded worldwide, one issue that emerged involved the rights of a trademark owner to use the mark as part of a domain name. A **domain name** is part of an Internet address, such as "westlaw.com." Every domain name ends with a top level domain (TLD), which is the part to the right of the period that indicates the type of entity that operates the site (for example, *com* is an abbreviation for "commercial").

The second level domain (SLD)—the part of the name to the left of the period—is chosen by the business entity or individual registering the domain name. Competition for SLDs among firms with similar names and products has led to numerous disputes. By using the same, or a similar, domain name, parties have attempted to profit from a competitor's goodwill, sell pornography, offer for sale another party's domain name, or otherwise infringe on others' trademarks.

The Internet Corporation for Assigned Names and Numbers (ICANN), a nonprofit corporation, oversees the distribution of domain names and operates an online arbitration system. Due to numerous complaints, ICANN completely overhauled the domain name distribution system and started selling domain names under a new system in 2009. One of the goals of the new system is to alleviate the problem of *cybersquatting.* **Cybersquatting** occurs when a person registers a domain name that is the same as, or confusingly similar to, the trademark of another and then offers to sell the domain name back to the trademark owner.

Cybersquatting   The act of registering a domain name that is the same as, or confusingly similar to, the trademark of another and then offering to sell that domain name back to the trademark owner.

Anticybersquatting Legislation

During the 1990s, cybersquatting led to so much litigation that Congress passed the Anticybersquatting Consumer Protection Act of 1999 (ACPA), which amended the Lanham Act—the federal law protecting trademarks discussed earlier. The ACPA makes it illegal to "register, traffic in, or use" a domain name (1) if the name is identical or confusingly similar to the trademark of another and (2) if the person registering, trafficking in, or using the domain name has a "bad faith intent" to profit from that trademark.

THE ONGOING PROBLEM OF CYBERSQUATTING   Despite the ACPA, cybersquatting continues to present a problem for businesses, largely because more TLDs are now available and many more companies are registering domain names. Indeed, domain name registrars have proliferated. These companies charge a fee to businesses and individuals to register new names and to renew annual registrations (often through automated software). Many of these companies also buy and sell expired domain names. Although all registrars are supposed to relay information about these transactions to ICANN and the other companies that keep a master list of domain names, this does not always occur. The speed at which domain names change hands and the difficulty in tracking mass automated registrations have created an environment in which cybersquatting can flourish.

Cybersquatters have also developed new tactics, such as *typosquatting* (registering a name that is a misspelling of a popular brand, for example, hotmial.com or myspac. com). Because many Internet users are not perfect typists, Web pages using these misspelled names can generate significant traffic. More traffic generally means increased profits (advertisers often pay Web sites based on the number of unique visits, or hits), which in turn provides incentive for more cybersquatters. Also, if the misspelling is significant, the trademark owner may have difficulty proving that the name is identical or confusingly similar to the owner's mark, as required by the ACPA.

Cybersquatting is costly for businesses, which must attempt to register all variations of a name to protect their domain name rights from would-be cybersquatters. Large corporations may have to register thousands of domain names across the globe just to protect their basic brands and trademarks.

APPLICABILITY OF THE ACPA AND SANCTIONS UNDER THE ACT   The ACPA applies to all domain name registrations of trademarks. Successful plaintiffs in suits brought under the act can collect actual damages and profits or elect to receive statutory damages that range from $1,000 to $100,000.

Although some companies have been successful suing under the ACPA, there are roadblocks to pursuing such lawsuits. Some domain name registrars offer privacy services that hide the true owners of Web sites, making it difficult for trademark owners to identify cybersquatters. Thus, before a trademark owner can bring a suit, he or she has to ask the court for a subpoena to discover the identity of the owner of the infringing Web site. Because of the high costs of court proceedings, discovery, and even arbitration, many disputes over cybersquatting are settled out of court.

Meta Tags

Search engines compile their results by looking through a Web site's key-word field. *Meta tags,* or key words (see Chapter 2), may be inserted into this field to increase the likelihood that a site will be included in search engine results, even though the site may have nothing to do with the inserted words. Using this same technique, one site may appropriate the key words of other sites with more frequent hits so that the appropriating site appears in the same search engine results as the more popular sites. Using another's trademark in a meta tag without the owner's permission, however, normally constitutes trademark infringement.

Some uses of another's trademark as a meta tag may be permissible if the use is reasonably necessary and does not suggest that the owner authorized or sponsored the use. **CASE EXAMPLE 5.7**   Terri Welles, a former model who had been "Playmate of the Year" in *Playboy* magazine, established a Web site that used the terms *Playboy* and *Playmate* as meta tags. Playboy Enterprises, Inc., which publishes *Playboy,* filed a suit seeking to prevent Welles from using these meta tags. The court determined that Welles's use of Playboy's meta tags to direct users to her Web site was permissible because it did not suggest sponsorship and there were no descriptive substitutes for the terms *Playboy* and *Playmate.*[12] ●

Dilution in the Online World

As discussed earlier, trademark *dilution* occurs when a trademark is used, without authorization, in a way that diminishes the distinctive quality of the mark. Unlike trademark infringement, a claim of dilution does not require proof that consumers are likely to be confused by a connection between the unauthorized use and the mark. For this reason, the products involved do not have to be similar. **CASE EXAMPLE 5.8**   In the first case alleging dilution on the Web, a court precluded the use of "candyland.com" as the URL for an adult site. The suit was brought by the maker of the Candyland children's game and owner of

---

12. *Playboy Enterprises, Inc. v. Welles,* 279 F.3d 796 (9th Cir. 2002). See also *Canfield v. Health Communications, Inc.,* 2008 WL 961318 (C.D.Cal. 2008).

the Candyland mark. Although consumers were not likely to connect candyland.com with the children's game, the court reasoned that the sexually explicit adult site would dilute the value of the Candyland mark.[13] ●

Licensing

License In the context of intellectual property law, an agreement permitting the use of a trademark, copyright, patent, or trade secret for certain limited purposes.

One way to make use of another's trademark or other form of intellectual property, while avoiding litigation, is to obtain a license to do so. A **license** in this context is an agreement permitting the use of a trademark, copyright, patent, or trade secret for certain limited purposes. The party that owns the intellectual property rights and issues the license is the *licensor*, and the party obtaining the license is the *licensee*.

A license grants only the rights expressly described in the license agreement. A licensor might, for example, allow the licensee to use the trademark as part of its company name, or as part of its domain name, but not otherwise use the mark on any products or services. Disputes frequently arise over licensing agreements, particularly when the license involves Internet uses.

Typically, license agreements are very detailed and should be carefully drafted. **CASE EXAMPLE 5.9** Perry Ellis International, Inc. (PEI), owns a family of registered trademarks, including "Perry Ellis America" (the PEA trademark). The PEA trademark is distinctive and is known worldwide as a mark of quality apparel. In 2006, PEI granted URI Corporation an exclusive license to manufacture and distribute footwear using the PEA trademark in Mexico. The agreement required URI to comply with numerous conditions regarding the manufacturing and distribution of the licensed footwear and to sell the shoes only in certain (listed) high-quality stores. URI was not permitted to authorize any other party to use the PEA trademark. Despite this explicit licensing agreement, PEI discovered that footwear bearing its PEA trademark was being sold in discount stores in Mexico. PEI terminated the agreement and filed a lawsuit in a federal district court against URI. PEI was awarded more than $1 million in damages.[14] ●

In the following case, a licensee continued to use a trademark after its owner withdrew permission. The court had to decide whether this constituted infringing conduct.

---

13. *Hasbro, Inc. v. Internet Entertainment Group, Ltd.,* 1996 WL 84858 (W.D.Wash. 1996).
14. *Perry Ellis International, Inc. v. URI Corporation,* 2007 WL 3047143 (S.D.Fla. 2007).

Case 5.2 **George V Restauration S.A. v. Little Rest Twelve, Inc.**

New York Supreme Court, Appellate Division, 58 A.D.3d 428, 871 N.Y.S.2d 65 (2009).
www.courts.state.ny.us/decisions/index.shtml[a]

The Buddha Bar NYC.

(Niche Media/WireImage)

FACTS George V Restauration S.A. and others owned and operated the Buddha Bar Paris, a restaurant with an Asian theme in Paris, France. In 2005, one of the owners allowed Little Rest Twelve, Inc., to use the Buddha Bar trademark and its associated concept in New York City under the name *Buddha Bar NYC.* Little Rest paid royal-ties for its use of the Buddha Bar mark and advertised Buddha Bar NYC's affiliation with Buddha Bar Paris, a connection also noted on its Web site and in the media. When a dispute arose, the owners of Buddha Bar Paris withdrew their permission for Buddha Bar NYC's use of their mark, but Little Rest continued to use it. The owners of the mark filed a suit in a New York state court against Little Rest, alleging trademark infringement. The court denied the plaintiffs' motion for a preliminary injunction. They appealed.

ISSUE Is a licensee entitled to continue using a mark after its owner terminates the license?

DECISION No. The state intermediate appellate court reversed the lower court's order, granted the plaintiffs' motion, and remanded the case.

---

a. In the left-hand column, in the "Appellate Divisions" list, click on "1st Dept." At the bottom of the page under "Archives," select "2009" and "January." On that page, scroll to "Cases Decided January 6, 2009" and click on the name of the case to access the opinion. The New York State Law Reporting Bureau maintains this Web site.

Case 5.2–Continues next page ➡

Case 5.2–Continued

REASON In a trademark infringement action, a showing of a likeli-hood of confusion establishes that the owners of the mark are likely to succeed in their cause and that they will suffer "irreparable harm" if a pre-liminary injunction were not issued. Irreparable harm occurs when a for-mer licensee's use of a mark creates "an increased danger that consumers will be confused and believe that the former licensee is still an authorized representative of the trademark holder." In this case, likely confusion was shown by the strength of the Buddha Bar mark and the plaintiffs' ability to license it to others, the media's references to the mark, Little Rest's use of the identical mark, Buddha Bar NYC's previous association with Buddha Bar Paris in ad campaigns and on its Web site, and Little Rest's use of the mark in the same manner as the plaintiffs.

FOR CRITICAL ANALYSIS—Technological Consider-ation *Could Little Rest prevent confusion between the Buddha Bars in New York City and Paris by posting a disclaimer on Buddha Bar NYC's Web site? Would such a disclaimer be effective? Explain your answer.*

Preventing Legal Disputes

To avoid litigation, consult with an attorney before signing any licensing contract to make sure that the wording of the contract is very clear as to what rights are or are not being conveyed. Moreover, to prevent misunderstandings over the scope of the rights being acquired, determine whether any other parties hold licenses to use that particular intellectual property and the extent of those rights.

▶ Patents

Patent A government grant that gives an inventor the exclusive right or privilege to make, use, or sell his or her invention for a limited time period.

A **patent** is a grant from the government that gives an inventor the exclusive right to make, use, and sell an invention for a period of twenty years. Patents for designs, as opposed to inventions, are given for a fourteen-year period. For either a regular patent or a design patent, the applicant must demonstrate to the satisfaction of the U.S. Patent and Trademark Office that the invention, discovery, process, or design is *novel, useful,* and *not obvious* in light of current technology.

In contrast to patent law in many other countries, in the United States the first person to invent a product or process gets the patent rights rather than the first person to file for a patent on that product or process. Because it is difficult to prove who invented an item first, however, the first person to file an application is often deemed the first to invent (unless the inventor has detailed research notes or other evidence). An inventor can publish the invention or offer it for sale before filing a patent application but must apply for a patent within one year of doing so or forfeit the patent rights.

"To invent, you need a good imagination and a pile of junk."

Thomas Edison, 1847–1931
(American inventor)

The period of patent protection begins on the date when the patent application is filed, rather than when the patent is issued, which can sometimes be years later. After the patent period ends (either fourteen or twenty years later), the product or process enters the public domain, and anyone can make, sell, or use the invention without paying the patent holder.

Searchable Patent Databases

A significant development relating to patents is the availability online of the world's pat-ent databases. The Web site of the U.S. Patent and Trademark Office provides searchable databases covering U.S. patents granted since 1976. The Web site of the European Patent Office provides online access to 50 million patent documents in more than seventy nations through a searchable network of databases. Businesses use these searchable databases in many ways. Because patents are valuable assets, businesses may need to perform patent searches to list or inventory their assets.

ON THE WEB You can access the European Patent Office's Web site at **www.epo.org**.

What Is Patentable?

Under federal law, "[w]hoever invents or discovers any new and useful process, machine, manufacture, or composition of matter, or any new and useful improvement thereof, may obtain a patent therefor, subject to the conditions and requirements of

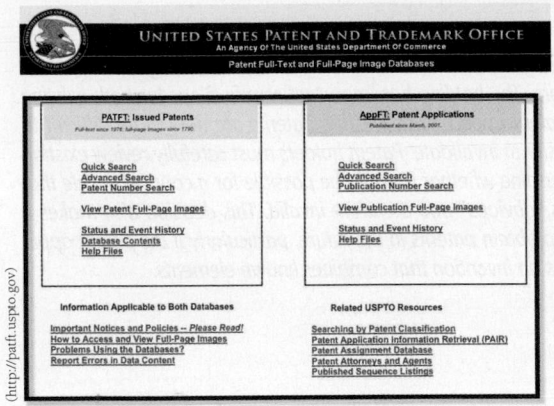

This is the home page of the U.S. Patent and Trademark Office.

this title."[15] Thus, to be patentable, the item must be novel and not obvious.

Almost anything is patentable, except the laws of nature,[16] natural phenomena, and abstract ideas (including algorithms[17]). (See this chapter's *Adapting the Law to the Online Environment* feature on page 131 for a discussion of an emerging debate over whether business processes should be patentable.) Even artistic methods, certain works of art, and the structures of storylines are patentable, provided that they are novel and not obvious.

Plants that are reproduced asexually (by means other than from seed), such as hybrid or genetically engineered plants, are patentable in the United States, as are genetically engineered (or cloned) microorganisms and animals. **CASE EXAMPLE 5.10** Monsanto, Inc., has been selling its patented genetically modified (GM) seeds to farmers as a way to achieve higher yields from crops using fewer pesticides. Monsanto requires farmers who buy GM seeds to sign licensing agreements promising to plant the seeds for only one crop and to pay a technology fee for each acre planted. To ensure compliance, Monsanto has assigned seventy-five employees to investigate and prosecute farmers who use the GM seeds illegally. Monsanto has filed more than ninety lawsuits against nearly 150 farmers in the United States and has been awarded more than $15 million in damages (not including out-of-court settlement amounts).[18] ●

In the following case, the focus was on the application of the test for determining whether a patent claim is "obvious."

---

15. 35 U.S.C. 101.

16. Several justices of the United States Supreme Court indicated that they believed a process to diagnose vitamin deficiencies should not be patentable because allowing a patent would improperly give a monopoly over a scientific relationship, or law of nature. Nevertheless, the majority of the Court allowed the patent to stand. *Laboratory Corporation of America Holdings v. Metabolite Laboratories, Inc.,* 548 U.S. 124, 126 S.Ct. 2921, 165 L.Ed.2d 399 (2006).

17. An *algorithm* is a step-by-step procedure, formula, or set of instructions for accomplishing a specific task—such as the set of rules used by a search engine to rank the listings contained within its index in response to a particular query.

18. See, for example, *Monsanto Co. v. Scruggs,* 459 F.3d 1328 (2006); *Monsanto Co. v. McFarling,* __ F.Supp.2d __ (E.D.Mo. 2005); and *Sample v. Monsanto Co.,* 283 F.Supp.2d 1088 (2003).

Case 5.3 **KSR International Co. v. Teleflex, Inc.**

Supreme Court of the United States, 550 U.S. 398, 127 S.Ct. 1727, 167 L.Ed.2d 705 (2007).

FACTS Teleflex, Inc., sued KSR International Company for patent infringement. Teleflex holds the exclusive license to a patent for a device developed by Steven J. Engelgau. The patent issued is entitled "Adjustable Pedal with Electronic Throttle Control." In brief, the Engelgau patent combines an electronic sensor with an adjustable automobile pedal so that the pedal's position can be transmitted to a computer that controls the throttle in the vehicle's engine. KSR contended that the patent could not create a claim because the subject matter was obvious. The district court concluded that the Engelgau patent was invalid because it was obvious—several existing patents already covered all of the important aspects of electronic pedal sensors for computer-controlled throttles. On appeal, the U.S. Court of Appeals for the Federal Circuit reversed the district court's ruling. KSR appealed to the United States Supreme Court.

ISSUE Was Teleflex's patent invalid because several existing patents already covered the important aspects of the adjustable automobile pedal with electronic throttle control, making its invention obvious?

DECISION Yes. The United States Supreme Court reversed the judgment of the court of appeals and remanded the case.

REASON The Court pointed out that in many previous decisions it had held "that a patent for a combination which only unites old elements with no change in their respective functions * * * obviously withdraws what is already known into the field of its monopoly and diminishes the resources available to skillful [persons]. * * * If a technique has been used to improve one device, and a person of ordinary skill in the art would recognize that

Case 5.3—Continues next page ➡

Case 5.3—Continued

it would improve similar devices in the same way, using the technique is obvious unless its actual application is beyond his or her skill." In sum, the Court reasoned that there was little difference between what existed in the "teachings" of previously filed patents and the adjustable electronic pedal disclosed in the Engelgau patent.

WHY IS THIS CASE IMPORTANT? *The decision in this case dramatically changed the standard of obviousness that is applied in patent*

law. This case has been widely acknowledged as the most significant patent decision in years. The holding has important ramifications for both existing patents and patent applications. Existing patents are now more difficult to defend and easier to invalidate. Patent holders must carefully review existing patents to determine whether it would be possible for a court to decide that the patent was "obvious" and therefore invalid. This decision also makes it more difficult to obtain patents in the future, particularly if the patent application concerns an invention that combines known elements.

Patent Infringement

If a firm makes, uses, or sells another's patented design, product, or process without the patent owner's permission, it commits the tort of patent infringement. Patent infringement may occur even though the patent owner has not put the patented product in commerce. Patent infringement may also occur even though not all features or parts of an invention are copied. (With respect to a patented process, however, all steps or their equivalent must be copied for infringement to exist.)

Remedies for Patent Infringement

If a patent is infringed, the patent holder may sue for relief in federal court. The patent holder can seek an injunction against the infringer and can also request damages for royalties and lost profits. In some cases, the court may grant the winning party reimbursement for attorneys' fees and costs. If the court determines that the infringement was willful, the court can triple the amount of damages awarded (treble damages).

In the past, permanent injunctions were routinely granted to prevent future infringement. In 2006, however, the United States Supreme Court ruled that patent holders are not automatically entitled to a permanent injunction against future infringing activities. According to the Supreme Court, a patent holder must prove that it has suffered irreparable injury and that the public interest would not be disserved by a permanent injunction.[19] This decision gives courts discretion to decide what is equitable in the circumstances and allows them to consider what is in the public interest rather than just the interests of the parties. In one case, for example, a court determined that a patent holder was not entitled to an injunction against Microsoft because the public might suffer negative effects from changes in Microsoft's Office Suite.[20]

Wal-Mart creates and markets private brands in its stores. This is a photo of a running shoe that it has created and sold. Nike has marketed a similarly constructed shoe for several years. Nike sued Wal-Mart for patent infringement because of the springlike device in the heel of the Wal-Mart version. What type of out-of-court settlement might the companies agree to?

(AP Photo/Paul Sakuma)

▶ Copyrights

Copyright The exclusive right of an author or originator of a literary or artistic production to publish, print, or sell that production for a statutory period of time. A copyright has the same monopolistic nature as a patent or trademark, but it differs in that it applies exclusively to works of art, literature, and other works of authorship (including computer programs).

A **copyright** is an intangible property right granted by federal statute to the author or originator of certain literary or artistic productions. The Copyright Act of 1976,[21] as amended, governs copyrights. Works created after January 1, 1978, are automatically given statutory copyright protection for the life of the author plus 70 years. For copyrights owned by publishing houses, the copyright expires 95 years from the date of publication or 120 years

---

19. *eBay, Inc. v. MercExchange, LLC,* 547 U.S. 388, 126 S.Ct. 1837, 164 L.Ed.2d 641 (2006).
20. See *Z4 Technologies, Inc. v. Microsoft Corp.,* 434 F.Supp.2d 437 (2006).
21. 17 U.S.C. Sections 101 *et seq.*

Adapting the Law to the Online Environment

Should the Law Continue to Allow Business Process Patents?

At one time, it was difficult for developers and manufacturers of software to obtain patent protection because many software products simply automate procedures that can be performed manually. In other words, it was thought that computer programs did not meet the "novel" and "not obvious" requirements for patents. This changed in 1981 when the United States Supreme Court held that a patent could be obtained for a *process* that incorporates a computer program.[a] Then, in a landmark 1998 case, *State Street Bank & Trust Co. v. Signature Financial Group, Inc.,*[b] a federal appellate court ruled that business processes are patentable.

Skyrocketing Demand

Since the *State Street* case, numerous firms have applied for and received patents on business processes or methods. Walker Digital holds a business process patent for its "Dutch auction" system, which allows Priceline.com users to name their own price for airline tickets and hotels. Amazon.com has patented its "one-click" online payment system.

The U.S. Patent and Trademark Office (USPTO) has issued thousands of business process patents, and many more applications are clogging its system. These applications frequently involve ideas about a business process, blurring the distinction between ideas (which are not patentable) and processes (which are). In addition, because business process patents often involve fields that provide services, such as accounting and finance, determining when a process originated or who first developed it can be difficult. Consequently, business process patents are more likely to lead to litigation than patents on tangible inventions, such as machines.

A 2008 Case Significantly Limited Business Process Patents

In 2008, the U.S. Court of Appeals for the Federal Circuit—the same court that decided the *State Street* case—reversed its earlier decision and invalidated "pure" business process patents.[c] In the *Bilski* case, two men had applied for a patent for a process that uses transactions to hedge the risk in commodity trading. The USPTO denied their application because it was not limited to a particular machine and did not describe any methods for working out which transactions to perform. The men appealed.

After soliciting input from numerous interest groups, the appellate court established a new test for business process patents. A business process patent is valid only if the process (1) is carried out by a particular machine or apparatus or (2) transforms a particular article into a different state or object. Because the men's process did not meet the machine-or-transformation test, the court affirmed the USPTO's decision.

One of the dissenting judges in the *Bilski* case, Judge Haldane Robert Mayer, would have done away with them altogether. Judge Mayer lamented that "the patent system is intended to protect and promote advances in science and technology, not ideas about how to structure commercial transactions." In Mayer's view, these patents "do not promote 'useful arts' because they are not directed to any technological or scientific innovation." Although they may use technology, such as computers, the creative part of business methods is in the thought process rather than the technology.

FOR CRITICAL ANALYSIS

Some patent experts think that the Bilski *decision, and sentiments such as those expressed by Judge Mayer, may signal an end to all business process patents in the near future. Should business process patents be severely limited or eliminated? Why or why not?*

---

a. *Diamond v. Diehr,* 450 U.S. 175, 101 S.Ct. 1048, 67 L.Ed.2d 155 (1981).
b. 149 F.3d 1368 (Fed.Cir. 1998).

c. *In re Bilski,* 545 F.3d 943 (Fed.Cir. 2008).

ON THE WEB For information on copyrights, go to the U.S. Copyright Office at www.copyright.gov.

from the date of creation, whichever is first. For works by more than one author, the copyright expires 70 years after the death of the last surviving author.[22]

Copyrights can be registered with the U.S. Copyright Office in Washington, D.C. A copyright owner no longer needs to place a © or *Copr.* or *Copyright* on the work, however, to have the work protected against infringement. Chances are that if somebody created it, somebody owns it.

---

22. These time periods reflect the extensions of the length of copyright protection enacted by Congress in the Copyright Term Extension Act of 1998. 17 U.S.C.A. Section 302. The United States Supreme Court upheld the constitutionality of the act in 2003. See *Eldred v. Ashcroft,* 537 U.S. 186, 123 S.Ct. 769, 154 L.Ed.2d 683 (2003).

(AP Photo/Manny Garcia/Shepard Fairey)

Artist Shepard Fairey created a poster (right) of Barack Obama during the 2008 presidential campaign. Clearly, this poster was based on an Associated Press file photo of Obama taken by Manny Garcia (left). Did Fairey violate copyright law? Why or why not?

What Is Protected Expression?

Works that are copyrightable include books, records, films, artworks, architectural plans, menus, music videos, product packaging, and computer software. To be protected, a work must be "fixed in a durable medium" from which it can be perceived, reproduced, or communicated. Protection is automatic. Registration is not required.

To obtain protection under the Copyright Act, a work must be original and fall into one of the following categories:

1. Literary works (including newspaper and magazine articles, computer and training manuals, catalogues, brochures, and print advertisements).
2. Musical works and accompanying words (including advertising jingles).
3. Dramatic works and accompanying music.
4. Pantomimes and choreographic works (including ballets and other forms of dance).
5. Pictorial, graphic, and sculptural works (including cartoons, maps, posters, statues, and even stuffed animals).
6. Motion pictures and other audiovisual works (including multimedia works).
7. Sound recordings.
8. Architectural works.

SECTION 102 EXCLUSIONS   It is not possible to copyright an *idea*. Section 102 of the Copyright Act specifically excludes copyright protection for any "idea, procedure, process, system, method of operation, concept, principle, or discovery, regardless of the form in which it is described, explained, illustrated, or embodied." Thus, others can freely use the underlying ideas or principles embodied in a work. What is copyrightable is the particular way in which an idea is *expressed*. Whenever an idea and an expression are inseparable, the expression cannot be copyrighted. Generally, anything that is not an original expression will not qualify for copyright protection. Facts widely known to the public are not copyrightable. Page numbers are not copyrightable because they follow a sequence known to everyone. Mathematical calculations are not copyrightable.

BE CAREFUL   If a creative work does not fall into a certain category, it might not be copyrighted, but it may be protected by other intellectual property law.

Ethical Issue ⚖

Should the federal Copyright Act preempt plaintiffs from bringing "idea-submission" claims under state law? In the past, federal courts generally held that the Copyright Act preempted (or superseded—see Chapter 2) claims in state courts alleging the theft of ideas. In 2004, however, the U.S. Court of Appeals for the Ninth Circuit's decision in the case *Grosso v. Miramax Film Corp.*,[23] opened the door to such claims. The plaintiff, Jeff Grosso, had submitted a screenplay called *The Shell Game* to Miramax. He claimed that the film company stole the ideas and themes of his work (poker settings, characters, and jargon) when it made the movie *Rounders.* The court held that the Copyright Act did not preempt Grosso's state contract law claim (alleging the existence of an implied contract—see Chapter 9).

Since 2005, numerous cases have been filed in state courts alleging that an idea that was pitched to a television network or movie producer was "stolen" and that the person whose idea it was should be compensated.[24] In California, plaintiffs have filed idea-submission lawsuits over television series, such as *Lost* and *Project Runway,* and motion pictures, including *The Last Samurai* and *The Wedding Crashers.* These plaintiffs were unable to maintain a copyright claim in federal court because the law does not protect ideas (only expressions of ideas). Should they be allowed to sue over the ideas in state courts?

---

23. 383 F.3d 965 (9th Cir. 2004); *cert.* denied, 546 U.S. 824, 126 S.Ct. 361, 163 L.Ed.2d 68 (2005).
24. See, for example, *A Slice of Pie Productions, LLC, v. Wayans Brothers Entertainment,* 487 F.Supp.2d 41 (D.Conn. 2007).

> *"Don't worry about people stealing an idea. If it's original and it's any good, you'll have to ram it down their throats."*
>
> Howard Aiken, 1900–1973
> (Engineer and pioneer in computing)

COMPILATIONS OF FACTS   Unlike ideas, *compilations* of facts are copyrightable. Under Section 103 of the Copyright Act, a compilation is a work formed by the collection and assembling of preexisting materials or of data that are selected, coordinated, or arranged in such a way that the resulting work as a whole constitutes an original work of authorship. The key requirement for the copyrightability of a compilation is originality. **EXAMPLE 5.11** The White Pages of a telephone directory do not qualify for copyright protection because they simply list alphabetically names and telephone numbers. The Yellow Pages of a directory can be copyrightable, provided that the information is selected, coordinated, or arranged in an original way. Similarly, a compilation of information about yachts listed for sale may qualify for copyright protection.[25] ●

Copyright Infringement

Whenever the form or expression of an idea is copied, an infringement of copyright occurs. The reproduction does not have to be exactly the same as the original, nor does it have to reproduce the original in its entirety. If a substantial part of the original is reproduced, copyright infringement has occurred.

DAMAGES FOR COPYRIGHT INFRINGEMENT   Those who infringe copyrights may be liable for damages or criminal penalties. These range from actual damages or statutory damages, imposed at the court's discretion, to criminal proceedings for willful violations. Actual damages are based on the harm caused to the copyright holder by the infringement, while statutory damages, not to exceed $150,000, are provided for under the Copyright Act. In addition, criminal proceedings may result in fines and/or imprisonment.

THE "FAIR USE" EXCEPTION   An exception to liability for copyright infringement is made under the "fair use" doctrine. In certain circumstances, a person or organization can reproduce copyrighted material without paying royalties (fees paid to the copyright holder for the privilege of reproducing the copyrighted material). Section 107 of the Copyright Act provides as follows:

> [T]he fair use of a copyrighted work, including such use by reproduction in copies or phonorecords or by any other means specified by [Section 106 of the Copyright Act], for purposes such as criticism, comment, news reporting, teaching (including multiple copies for classroom use), scholarship, or research, is not an infringement of copyright. In determining whether the use made of a work in any particular case is a fair use the factors to be considered shall include—
> (1) the purpose and character of the use, including whether such use is of a commercial nature or is for nonprofit educational purposes;
> (2) the nature of the copyrighted work;
> (3) the amount and substantiality of the portion used in relation to the copyrighted work as a whole; and
> (4) the effect of the use upon the potential market for or value of the copyrighted work.

Because these guidelines are very broad, the courts determine whether a particular use is fair on a case-by-case basis. Thus, anyone reproducing copyrighted material may be committing a violation. In determining whether a use is fair, courts have often considered the fourth factor to be the most important.

ON THE WEB You can find a host of information on copyright law, including the Copyright Act and significant United States Supreme Court cases in the area of copyright law, at **topics.law.cornell.edu/wex/copyright**.

---

25. *BUC International Corp. v. International Yacht Council, Ltd.,* 489 F.3d 1129 (11th Cir. 2007).

Copyright Protection for Software

In 1980, Congress passed the Computer Software Copyright Act, which amended the Copyright Act of 1976 to include computer programs in the list of creative works protected by federal copyright law. Not all aspects of software may be protected, however. Generally, the courts have extended copyright protection not only to those parts of a computer program that can be read by humans, such as the high-level language of a source code, but also to the binary-language object code of a computer program, which is readable only by the computer. Additionally, such elements as the overall structure, sequence, and organization of a program have been deemed copyrightable. For the most part, though, courts have not extended copyright protection to the "look and feel"—the general appearance, command structure, video images, menus, windows, and other screen displays—of computer programs.

Copyrights in Digital Information

Copyright law is probably the most important form of intellectual property protection on the Internet, largely because much of the material on the Web (including software, for example) is copyrighted and in order to be transferred online, it must be "copied." Generally, anytime a party downloads software or music into a computer's random access memory, or RAM, without authorization, a copyright is infringed. Technology has vastly increased the potential for copyright infringement. **CASE EXAMPLE 5.12**   In one case, a rap song that was included in the sound track of a movie had used only a few seconds from the guitar solo of another's copyrighted sound recording without permission. Nevertheless, a federal appellate court held that digitally sampling a copyrighted sound recording of any length constitutes copyright infringement.[26] ●

Initially, criminal penalties for copyright violations could be imposed only if unauthorized copies were exchanged for financial gain. Yet much piracy of copyrighted materials was "altruistic" in nature; unauthorized copies were made simply to be shared with others. Then, Congress passed the No Electronic Theft (NET) Act of 1997. This act extended criminal liability for the piracy of copyrighted materials to persons who exchange unauthorized copies of copyrighted works without realizing a profit. The act also altered the traditional "fair use" doctrine by imposing penalties on those who make unauthorized electronic copies of books, magazines, movies, or music for *personal* use. The criminal penalties for violating the act include fines as high as $250,000 and incarceration for up to five years.

In 1998, Congress passed further legislation to protect copyright holders—the Digital Millennium Copyright Act. Because of its significance in protecting against the piracy of copyrighted materials in the online environment, this act is presented as this chapter's *Landmark in the Law* feature.

ON THE WEB For information and tips on how to avoid copyright law violations with digital media, go to **uits.iu.edu/page/ahmf**.

MP3 and File-Sharing Technology

Soon after the Internet became popular, a few enterprising programmers created software to compress large data files, particularly those associated with music, so that they could more easily be transmitted online. The best-known compression and decompression system is MP3, which enables music fans to download songs or entire CDs onto their computers or onto a portable listening device, such as an iPod. The MP3 system also made it possible for music fans to access other fans' files by engaging in file-sharing via the Internet.

File-sharing is accomplished through **peer-to-peer (P2P) networking.** The concept is simple. Rather than going through a central Web server, P2P involves numerous personal computers (PCs) that are connected to the Internet. Individuals on the same network can

Peer-to-Peer (P2P) Networking The sharing of resources (such as files, hard drives, and processing styles) among multiple computers without necessarily requiring a central network server.

---

26. *Bridgeport Music, Inc. v. Dimension Films,* 410 F.3d 792 (6th Cir. 2005).

Landmark in the Law The Digital Millennium Copyright Act of 1998

The United States leads the world in the production of creative products, including books, films, videos, recordings, and software. In fact, as indicated earlier, the creative industries are more important to the U.S. economy than the traditional product industries are. Exports of U.S. creative products, for example, surpass those of every other U.S. industry in value.

Given the importance of intellectual property to the U.S. economy, the United States has actively supported international efforts to protect ownership rights in intellectual property, including copyrights. In 1996, to curb unauthorized copying of copyrighted materials, the World Intellectual Property Organization (WIPO) enacted a treaty to upgrade global standards of copyright protection, particularly for the Internet.

Implementing the WIPO Treaty Congress implemented the provisions of the WIPO treaty by updating U.S. copyright law. The law—the Digital Millennium Copyright Act of 1998—is a landmark step in the protection of copyright owners and, because of the leading position of the United States in the creative industries, serves as a model for other nations. Among other things, the act established civil and criminal penalties for anyone who circumvents (bypasses) encryption software or other technological antipiracy protection. Also prohibited are the manufacture, import, sale, and distribution of devices or services for circumvention.

The act provides for exceptions to fit the needs of libraries, scientists, universities, and others. In general, the law does not restrict the "fair use" of circumvention methods for educational and other noncommercial purposes. For example, circumvention is allowed to test computer secu-

rity, conduct encryption research, protect personal privacy, and enable parents to monitor their children's use of the Internet. The exceptions are to be reconsidered every three years.

Limiting the Liability of Internet Service Providers The 1998 act also limited the liability of Internet service providers (ISPs). Under the act, an ISP is not liable for any copyright infringement by its customer *unless* the ISP is aware of the subscriber's violation. An ISP may be held liable only if it fails to take action to shut the subscriber down after learning of the violation. A copyright holder has to act promptly, however, by pursuing a claim in court, or the subscriber has the right to be restored to online access.

• **Application to Today's World** *Without the Digital Millennium Copyright Act of 1998, copyright owners would have a more difficult time obtaining legal redress against those who, without authorization, decrypt and/or copy copyrighted materials. Nevertheless, problems remain, particularly because of the global nature of the Internet. From a practical standpoint, the degree of protection afforded to copyright holders depends on the extent to which other nations that have signed the WIPO treaty actually implement its provisions and agree on the interpretation of terms, such as what constitutes an electronic copy.*

• **Relevant Web Sites** To locate information on the Web concerning the Digital Millennium Copyright Act of 1998, go to this text's Web site at www.cengage.com/blaw/blt, select "Chapter 5," and click on "URLs for Landmarks."

Distributed Network A network that can be used by persons located (distributed) around the country or the globe to share computer files.

Cloud Computing A subscription-based or pay-per-use service that, in real time over the Internet, extends a computer's software or storage capabilities. By using the services of large companies with excess storage and computing capacity, a company can increase its information technology capabilities without investing in new infrastructure, training new personnel, or licensing new software.

access files stored on a single PC through a **distributed network,** which has parts dispersed in many locations. Persons scattered throughout the country or the world can work together on the same project by using file-sharing programs.

A newer method of sharing files via the Internet is **cloud computing,** which is essentially a subscription-based or pay-per-use service that extends a computer's software or storage capabilities. Cloud computing can deliver a single application through a browser to multiple users, or it may be a utility program to pool resources and provide data storage and virtual servers that can be accessed on demand. Amazon, Facebook, Google, IBM, and Sun Microsystems are using and developing more cloud computing services.

SHARING STORED MUSIC FILES When file-sharing is used to download others' stored music files, copyright issues arise. Recording artists and their labels stand to lose large amounts of royalties and revenues if relatively few CDs are purchased and then made available on distributed networks, from which everyone can get them for free. **CASE EXAMPLE 5.13** The issue of file-sharing infringement has been the subject of an ongoing debate since the highly publicized case of *A&M Records, Inc. v. Napster, Inc.*[27] Napster, Inc., operated a Web

27. 239 F.3d 1004 (9th Cir. 2001).

site with free software that enabled users to copy and transfer MP3 files via the Internet. When firms in the recording industry sued Napster, the court held that Napster was liable for contributory and vicarious[28] (indirect) copyright infringement because it had assisted others in obtaining unauthorized copies of copyrighted music. ●

THE EVOLUTION OF FILE-SHARING TECHNOLOGIES   After the *Napster* decision, the recording industry filed and won numerous lawsuits against companies that distribute online file-sharing software. Other companies then developed technologies that allow P2P network users to share stored music files, without paying a fee, more quickly and efficiently than ever. Software such as Morpheus, KaZaA, and LimeWire, for example, provides users with an interface that is similar to a Web browser.[29] When a user performs a search, the software locates a list of peers that have the file available for downloading. Because of the automated procedures, the companies do not maintain a central index and are unable to supervise whether users are exchanging copyrighted files.

In 2005, the United States Supreme Court clarified that companies that distribute file-sharing software intending that it be used to violate copyright laws can be liable for users' copyright infringement. **CASE EXAMPLE 5.14**   In *Metro-Goldwyn-Mayer Studios, Inc. v. Grokster, Ltd.,*[30] music and film industry organizations sued Grokster, Ltd., and StreamCast Networks, Inc. for contributory and vicarious copyright infringement. The Supreme Court held that anyone who distributes file-sharing software "with the object of promoting its use to infringe the copyright, as shown by clear expression or other affirmative steps taken to foster infringement, is liable for the resulting acts of infringement by third parties." ● Although the music and film industries won the *Grokster* case, they have not been able to prevent new technology from enabling copyright infringement, as will be discussed in Chapter 7.

 Trade Secrets

The law of trade secrets protects some business processes and information that are not or cannot be patented, copyrighted, or trademarked against appropriation by a competitor. A **trade secret** is basically information of commercial value. This may include customer lists, plans, research and development, pricing information, marketing techniques, and production methods—anything that makes an individual company unique and that would have value to a competitor.

Unlike copyright and trademark protection, protection of trade secrets extends both to ideas and to their expression. (For this reason, and because there are no registration or filing requirements for trade secrets, trade secret protection may be well suited for software.) Of course, the secret formula, method, or other information must be disclosed to some persons, particularly to key employees. Businesses generally attempt to protect their trade secrets by having all employees who use the process or information agree in their contracts, or in confidentiality agreements, never to divulge it.[31]

Trade Secret   Information or process that gives a business an advantage over competitors that do not know the information or process.

---

28. *Vicarious (indirect) liability* exists when one person is subject to liability for another's actions. A common example occurs in the employment context, when an employer is held vicariously liable by third parties for torts committed by employees in the course of their employment.

29. Note that in 2005, KaZaA entered into a settlement agreement with four major music companies that had alleged copyright infringement. KaZaA agreed to offer only legitimate, fee-based music downloads in the future.

30. 545 U.S. 913, 125 S.Ct. 2764, 162 L.Ed.2d 781 (2005). Grokster, Ltd., later settled this dispute out of court and stopped distributing its software.

31. See, for example, *Verigy US, Inc. v. Mayder,* 2008 WL 564634 (N.D.Cal. 2008); and *Gleeson v. Preferred Sourcing, LLC,* 883 N.E.2d 164 (Ind.App. 2008).

State and Federal Law on Trade Secrets

Under Section 757 of the *Restatement of Torts,* those who disclose or use another's trade secret, without authorization, are liable to that other party if (1) they discovered the secret by improper means or (2) their disclosure or use constitutes a breach of a duty owed to the other party. The theft of confidential business data by industrial espionage, as when a business taps into a competitor's computer, is a theft of trade secrets without any contractual violation and is actionable in itself.

Although trade secrets have long been protected under the common law, today most states' laws are based on the Uniform Trade Secrets Act, which has been adopted in forty-seven states. Additionally, in 1996 Congress passed the Economic Espionage Act, which made the theft of trade secrets a federal crime. We will examine the provisions and significance of this act in Chapter 6, in the context of crimes related to business.

Trade Secrets in Cyberspace

Today's computer technology undercuts a business firm's ability to protect its confidential information, including trade secrets. For instance, a dishonest employee could e-mail trade secrets in a company's computer to a competitor or a future employer. If e-mail is not an option, the employee might walk out with the information on a flash pen drive.

For a comprehensive summary of trade secrets and other forms of intellectual property, see Exhibit 5–1 on the following page.

▶ International Protection for Intellectual Property

For many years, the United States has been a party to various international agreements relating to intellectual property rights. For example, the Paris Convention of 1883, to which about 172 countries are signatory, allows parties in one country to file for patent and trademark protection in any of the other member countries. Other international agreements include the Berne Convention, the Trade-Related Aspects of Intellectual Property Rights, or, more simply, TRIPS agreement, and the Madrid Protocol. To learn about a new international treaty being negotiated that will affect international property rights, see this chapter's *Beyond Our Borders* feature on page 139.

The Berne Convention

Under the Berne Convention of 1886, an international copyright agreement, if a U.S. citizen writes a book, every country that has signed the convention must recognize the U.S. author's copyright in the book. Also, if a citizen of a country that has not signed the convention first publishes a book in one of the 163 countries that have signed, all other countries that have signed the convention must recognize that author's copyright. Copyright notice is not needed to gain protection under the Berne Convention for works published after March 1, 1989.

This convention and other international agreements have given some protection to intellectual property on a worldwide level. None of them, however, has been as significant and far reaching in scope as the agreement discussed next.

The TRIPS Agreement

Representatives from more than one hundred nations signed the TRIPS agreement in 1994. The agreement established, for the first time, standards for the international protection of intellectual property rights, including patents, trademarks, and copyrights for movies, computer programs, books, and music. The TRIPS agreement provides that

ON THE WEB The Web site of the American Society of International Law provides the texts of the Berne Convention and other international treaties, as well as other information and resources on international intellectual property law, at www.asil.org/electronic-resources.cfm.

• *Exhibit* 5–1 Forms of Intellectual Property

	DEFINITION	HOW ACQUIRED	DURATION	REMEDY FOR INFRINGEMENT
Patent	A grant from the government that gives an inventor exclusive rights to an invention.	By filing a patent application with the U.S. Patent and Trademark Office and receiving its approval.	Twenty years from the date of the application; for design patents, fourteen years.	Monetary damages, including royalties and lost profits, *plus* attorneys' fees. Damages may be tripled for intentional infringements.
Copyright	The right of an author or originator of a literary or artistic work, or other production that falls within a specified category, to have the exclusive use of that work for a given period of time.	Automatic (once the work or creation is put in tangible form). Only the *expression* of an idea (and not the idea itself) can be protected by copyright.	For authors: the life of the author, plus 70 years. For publishers: 95 years after the date of publication or 120 years after creation.	Actual damages plus profits received by the party who infringed *or* statutory damages under the Copyright Act, *plus* costs and attorneys' fees in either situation.
Trademark (service mark and trade dress)	Any distinctive word, name, symbol, or device (image or appearance), or combination thereof, that an entity uses to distinguish its goods or services from those of others. The owner has the exclusive right to use that mark or trade dress.	1. At common law, ownership created by use of the mark. 2. Registration with the appropriate federal or state office gives notice and is permitted if the mark is currently in use or will be within the next six months.	Unlimited, as long as it is in use. To continue notice by registration, the owner must renew by filing between the fifth and sixth years, and thereafter, every ten years.	1. Injunction prohibiting the future use of the mark. 2. Actual damages plus profits received by the party who infringed (can be increased under the Lanham Act). 3. Destruction of articles that infringed. 4. *Plus* costs and attorneys' fees.
Trade Secret	Any information that a business possesses and that gives the business an advantage over competitors (including formulas, lists, patterns, plans, processes, and programs).	Through the originality and development of the information and processes that constitute the business secret and are unknown to others.	Unlimited, so long as not revealed to others. Once revealed to others, it is no longer a trade secret.	Monetary damages for misappropriation (the Uniform Trade Secrets Act also permits punitive damages if willful), *plus* costs and attorneys' fees.

each member country must include in its domestic laws broad intellectual property rights and effective remedies (including civil and criminal penalties) for violations of those rights.

Generally, the TRIPS agreement forbids member nations from discriminating against foreign owners of intellectual property rights (in the administration, regulation, or adjudication of such rights). In other words, a member nation cannot give its own nationals (citizens) favorable treatment without offering the same treatment to nationals of all member countries. **EXAMPLE 5.15** A U.S. software manufacturer brings a suit for the infringement of intellectual property rights under Germany's national laws. Because Germany is a member nation, the U.S. manufacturer is entitled to receive the same treatment as a German manufacturer. • Each member nation must also ensure that legal procedures are available for parties who wish to bring actions for infringement of intellectual property rights. Additionally, a related document established a mechanism for settling disputes among member nations.

Beyond Our Borders **The Anti-Counterfeiting Trade Agreement**

In 2008, the United States began negotiating a new international treaty with the European Union, Japan, and Switzerland. By 2009, Australia, Canada, Jordan, Mexico, Morocco, New Zealand, South Korea, and the United Arab Emirates had joined the negotiations. The treaty, called the Anti-Counterfeiting Trade Agreement (ACTA), will establish its own governing body that is separate and distinct from existing organizations, such as the World Trade Organization and the World Intellectual Property Organization.

The treaty will apply not only to counterfeit physical goods, such as medications, but also to pirated copyrighted works being distributed via the Internet and other information technology. The goal is to create a new standard of enforcement for intellectual property rights that goes beyond the TRIPS agreement and encourages international cooperation and information sharing among signatory countries.

The specific terms of the treaty have not been released to the public, but there is considerable speculation about what it may contain. According to some media reports, one provision may authorize random border searches of electronic devices, such as laptops and iPods, for infringing content. Another provision supposedly would require Internet service providers to provide information about suspected copyright infringers without a warrant. Remember, though, that at this point the actual terms of the treaty are unknown, and the final provisions may differ considerably from the preliminary reports. The global financial crisis may also have an effect on the negotiations.

• For Critical Analysis
Why would the parties to the ACTA negotiations be reluctant to disclose the details of the provisions under consideration?

The Madrid Protocol

In the past, one of the difficulties in protecting U.S. trademarks internationally was that it was time consuming and expensive to apply for trademark registration in foreign countries. The filing fees and procedures for trademark registration vary significantly among individual countries. The Madrid Protocol, however, which was signed into law in 2003, may help to resolve these problems. The Madrid Protocol is an international treaty that has been signed by seventy-three countries. Under its provisions, a U.S. company wishing to register its trademark abroad can submit a single application and designate other member countries in which it would like to register the mark. The treaty was designed to reduce the costs of obtaining international trademark protection by more than 60 percent.

Although the Madrid Protocol may simplify and reduce the cost of trademark registration in foreign nations, it remains to be seen whether it will provide significant benefits to trademark owners. Even with an easier registration process, the issue of whether member countries will enforce the law and protect the mark still remains.

Reviewing . . . Intellectual Property and Internet Law

Two computer science majors, Trent and Xavier, have an idea for a new video game, which they propose to call "Hallowed." They form a business and begin developing their idea. Several months later, Trent and Xavier run into a problem with their design and consult with a friend, Brad, who is an expert in creating computer source codes. After the software is completed but before Hallowed is marketed, a video game called Halo 2 is released for both the Xbox and Playstation 3 systems. Halo 2 uses source codes similar to those of Hallowed and imitates Hallowed's overall look and feel, although not all the features are alike. Using the information presented in the chapter, answer the following questions.

1. Would the name *Hallowed* receive protection as a trademark or as trade dress?
2. If Trent and Xavier had obtained a business process patent on Hallowed, would the release of Halo 2 infringe on their patent? Why or why not?
3. Based only on the facts described above, could Trent and Xavier sue the makers of Halo 2 for copyright infringement? Why or why not?
4. Suppose that Trent and Xavier discover that Brad took the idea of Hallowed and sold it to the company that produced Halo 2. Which type of intellectual property issue does this raise?

Linking the Law *to Marketing*
Trademarks and Service Marks

In your marketing course, you have learned or will learn about the importance of trademarks. As a marketing manager, you will be involved with creating trademarks or service marks for your firm, protecting the firm's existing marks, and ensuring that you do not infringe on anyone else's marks.

The Broad Range of Trademarks and Service Marks

The courts have held that trademarks and service marks consist of much more than well-known brand names, such as Sony or Microsoft. As a marketing manager, you will need to be aware that parts of a brand or other product identification often qualify for trademark protection.

- **Catchy phrases**—Certain brands have established phrases that are associated with them, such as Nike's "Just Do It!" As a marketing manager for a competing product, you will have to avoid such catchy phrases in your own marketing program. Note, though, that not all phrases can become part of a trademark or service mark. When a phrase is extremely common, the courts normally will not grant trademark or service mark protection to it. America Online, Inc., was unable to protect its phrases "You have mail" and "You've got mail" that were associated with its e-mail notification system.

- **Abbreviations**—The public sometimes abbreviates a well-known trademark. For example, Budweiser beer became known as Bud and Coca-Cola as Coke. As a marketing manager, you should avoid using any name for a product or service that closely resembles a well-known abbreviation, such as Koke for a cola drink.

- **Shapes**—The shape of a brand name, a service mark, or a container can take on exclusivity if the shape clearly aids in product or service identification. For example, just about everyone throughout the world recognizes the shape of a Coca-Cola bottle. As a marketing manager, you would do well to avoid using a similar shape for a new carbonated drink.

- **Ornamental colors**—Sometimes, color combinations can become part of a service mark or trademark. For example, Federal Express

Corporation (now FedEx) established its unique identity with the use of bright orange and purple. The courts have protected this color combination. The same holds for the black-and-copper color combination of Duracell batteries.

- **Ornamental designs**—Symbols and designs associated with a particular mark normally are protected. Marketing managers should not attempt to copy them. Levi's places a small tag on the left side of the rear pocket of its jeans. Cross uses a cutoff black cone on the top of its pens.

- **Sounds**—Sounds can also be protected. For example, the familiar roar of the Metro-Goldwyn-Mayer lion is protected.

When to Protect Your Trademarks and Service Marks

Once your company has established a trademark or a service mark, as a manager, you will have to decide how aggressively you wish to protect those marks. If you fail to protect them, your company faces the possibility that they will become generic. Remember that *aspirin, cellophane, thermos, dry ice, shredded wheat,* and many other familiar terms were once legally protected trademarks.

Protecting exclusive rights to a mark can be expensive, however, so you will have to determine how much it is worth to your company to protect your rights. Coca-Cola and Rolls-Royce run newspaper and magazine ads stating that their names are protected trademarks and cannot be used as generic terms. Occasionally, such ads threaten lawsuits against any competitors that infringe the trademarks. If you work in a small company, making such major expenditures to protect your trademarks and service marks will not be cost-effective.

FOR CRITICAL ANALYSIS

The U.S. Patent and Trademark Office requires that a registered trademark or service mark be put into commercial use within three years after the application has been approved. Why do you think the federal government put this requirement into place?

 Key Terms

certification mark 123	distributed network 135	service mark 123
cloud computing 135	domain name 125	trade dress 124
collective mark 123	intellectual property 119	trade name 124
copyright 130	license 127	trade secret 136
cyber mark 125	patent 128	trademark 120
cybersquatting 125	peer-to-peer (P2P) networking 134	

Chapter Summary: Intellectual Property and Internet Law

Trademarks and Related Property (See pages 120–125.)	1. A *trademark* is a distinctive mark, motto, device, or emblem that a manufacturer stamps, prints, or otherwise affixes to the goods it produces so that they may be identified on the market and their origin vouched for. 2. The major federal statutes protecting trademarks and related property are the Lanham Act of 1946 and the Federal Trademark Dilution Act of 1995. Generally, to be protected, a trademark must be sufficiently distinctive from all competing trademarks. 3. *Trademark infringement* occurs when one uses a mark that is the same as, or confusingly similar to, the protected trademark, service mark, trade name, or trade dress of another without permission when marketing goods or services.
Cyber Marks (See pages 125–128.)	A *cyber mark* is a trademark in cyberspace. Trademark infringement in cyberspace occurs when one person uses, in a domain name or in meta tags, a name that is the same as, or confusingly similar to, the protected mark of another.
Patents (See pages 128–130.)	1. A *patent* is a grant from the government that gives an inventor the exclusive right to make, use, and sell an invention for a period of twenty years (fourteen years for a design patent) from the date when the application for a patent is filed. To be patentable, an invention (or a discovery, process, or design) must be genuine, novel, useful, and not obvious in light of current technology. Computer software may be patented. 2. Almost anything is patentable, except the laws of nature, natural phenomena, and abstract ideas (including algorithms). Even business processes or methods are patentable if they relate to a machine or transformation. 3. *Patent infringement* occurs when one uses or sells another's patented design, product, or process without the patent owner's permission. The patent holder can sue the infringer in federal court and request an injunction, but must prove irreparable injury to obtain a permanent injunction against the infringer. The patent holder can also request damages and attorneys' fees; if the infringement was willful, the court can grant treble damages.
Copyrights (See pages 130–136.)	1. A *copyright* is an intangible property right granted by federal statute to the author or originator of certain literary or artistic productions. The Copyright Act of 1976, as amended, governs copyrights. Computer software may be copyrighted. 2. *Copyright infringement* occurs whenever the form or expression of an idea is copied without the permission of the copyright holder. An exception applies if the copying is deemed a "fair use." 3. To protect copyrights in digital information, Congress passed the No Electronic Theft Act of 1997 and the Digital Millennium Copyright Act of 1998. 4. Technology that allows users to share files via the Internet on distributed networks often raises copyright infringement issues. 5. The United States Supreme Court has ruled that companies that provide file-sharing software to users can be held liable for contributory and vicarious copyright liability if they take affirmative steps to promote copyright infringement.
Trade Secrets (See pages 136–137.)	*Trade secrets* include customer lists, plans, research and development, and pricing information, for example. Trade secrets are protected under the common law and, in some states, under statutory law against misappropriation by competitors. The Economic Espionage Act of 1996 made the theft of trade secrets a federal crime (see Chapter 6).
International Protection for Intellectual Property (See pages 137–139.)	Various international agreements provide international protection for intellectual property. A landmark agreement is the 1994 agreement on Trade-Related Aspects of Intellectual Property Rights (TRIPS), which provides for enforcement procedures in all countries signatory to the agreement.

ExamPrep

ISSUE SPOTTERS

1 Global Products develops, patents, and markets software. World Copies, Inc., sells Global's software without the maker's permission. Is this patent infringement? If so, how might Global save the cost of suing World for infringement and at the same time profit from World's sales?

2 Eagle Corporation began marketing software in 2000 under the mark "Eagle." In 2009, Eagle.com, Inc., a different company selling different products, begins to use "eagle" as part of its URL and registers it as a domain name. Can Eagle Corporation stop this use of "eagle"? If so, what must the company show?

BEFORE THE TEST

Check your answers to the Issue Spotters, and at the same time, take the interactive quiz for this chapter. Go to **www.cengage.com/blaw/blt** and click on "Chapter 5." First, click on "Answers to Issue Spotters" to check your answers. Next, click on "Interactive Quiz" to assess your mastery of the concepts in this chapter. Then click on "Flashcards" to review this chapter's Key Term definitions.

 For Review

Answers for the even-numbered questions in this For Review *section can be found on this text's accompanying Web site at* **www.cengage.com/blaw/blt**. *Select "Chapter 5" and click on "For Review."*

1 What is intellectual property?

2 Why does the law protect trademarks and patents?

3 What laws protect authors' rights in the works they generate?

4 What are trade secrets, and what laws offer protection for this form of intellectual property?

5 What steps have been taken to protect intellectual property rights in today's digital age?

 Hypothetical Scenarios and Case Problems

5–1 Patent Infringement. John and Andrew Doney invented a hard-bearing device for balancing rotors. Although they registered their invention with the U.S. Patent and Trademark Office, it was never used as an automobile wheel balancer. Some time later, Exetron Corp. produced an automobile wheel balancer that used a hard-bearing device with a support plate similar to that of the Doneys' device. Given that the Doneys had not used their device for automobile wheel balancing, does Exetron's use of a similar device infringe on the Doneys' patent?

5–2 **[?] Hypothetical Question with Sample Answer** In which of the following situations would a court likely hold Maruta liable for copyright infringement?

1 At the library, Maruta photocopies ten pages from a scholarly journal relating to a topic on which she is writing a term paper.

2 Maruta makes leather handbags and sells them in her small shop. She advertises her handbags as "Vutton handbags," hoping that customers might mistakenly assume that they were made by Vuitton, the well-known maker of high-quality luggage and handbags.

3 Maruta owns a video store. She purchases one copy of several popular movie DVDs from various distributors. Then, using blank DVDs, she burns copies of the movies to rent or sell to her customers.

4 Maruta teaches Latin American history at a small university. She has a digital video recorder and frequently records television programs relating to Latin America and puts them on DVDs. She then takes the DVDs to her classroom so that her students can watch them.

—For a sample answer to Question 5–2, go to Appendix E at the end of this text.

5–3 Copyright Infringement. Professor Littrell is teaching a summer seminar in business torts at State University. Several times during the course, he makes copies of relevant sections from business law texts and distributes them to his students. Littrell does not realize that the daughter of one of the textbook authors is a member of his seminar. She tells her father about Littrell's copying activities, which have taken place without her father's or his publisher's permission. Her father sues Littrell for copyright infringement. Littrell claims protection under the fair use doctrine. Who will prevail? Explain.

5–4 Trade Secrets. Briefing.com offers Internet-based analyses of investment opportunities to investors. Richard Green is the company's president. One of Briefing.com's competitors is StreetAccount, LLC (limited liability company), whose owners include Gregory Jones and Cynthia Dietzmann. Jones worked for Briefing.com for six years until he quit in March 2003, and he was a member of its board of directors until April 2003.

Dietzmann worked for Briefing.com for seven years until she quit in March 2003. As Briefing.com employees, Jones and Dietzmann had access to confidential business data. For instance, Dietzmann developed a list of contacts through which Briefing.com obtained market information to display online. When Dietzmann quit, however, she did not return all of the contact information to the company. Briefing.com and Green filed a suit in a federal district court against Jones, Dietzmann, and StreetAccount, alleging that they appropriated these data and other "trade secrets" to form a competing business. What are trade secrets? Why are they protected? Under what circumstances is a party liable at common law for their appropriation? How should these principles apply in this case? [*Briefing.com v. Jones*, 2006 WY 16, 126 P.3d 928 (2006)]

5–5 **Case Problem with Sample Answer** In 1969, Jack Masquelier, a professor of pharmacology, discovered a chemical antioxidant made from the bark of a French pine tree. The substance supposedly assists in nutritional distribution and blood circulation. Horphag Research, Ltd., began to sell the product under the name Pycnogenol, which Horphag registered as a trademark in 1993. Pycnogenol became one of the fifteen best-selling herbal supplements in the United States. In 1999, through the Web site **healthierlife.com**, Larry Garcia began to sell Masquelier's Original OPCs, a supplement derived from grape pits. Claiming that this product was the "true Pycnogenol," Garcia used the mark as a meta tag and a generic term, attributing the results of research on Horphag's product to Masquelier's and altering quotations from scientific literature to substitute the name of Masquelier's product for Horphag's. Some customers who had bought Garcia's product learned that it was not Horphag's product only after they contacted Horphag. Others called Horphag to ask whether Garcia "was selling . . . real Pycnogenol." Horphag filed a suit in a federal district court against Garcia, alleging, in part, that he was diluting Horphag's mark. What is trademark dilution? Did it occur here? Explain. [*Horphag Research, Ltd. v. Garcia*, 475 F.3d 1029 (9th Cir. 2007)]

—After you have answered Problem 5–5, compare your answer with the sample answer given on the Web site that accompanies this text. Go to **www.cengage.com/blaw/blt**, select "Chapter 5," and click on "Case Problem with Sample Answer."

5–6 **Copyright.** Redwin Wilchcombe is a musician and music producer. In 2002, Wilchcombe met Jonathan Smith, known as

Lil Jon, a member of Lil Jon & The East Side Boyz (LJESB). Lil Jon and LJESB are under contract to give TeeVee Toons, Inc. (TVT), all rights to LJESB's recordings and Lil Jon's songs. At Lil Jon's request, based on his idea, and with his suggestions, Wilchcombe composed, performed, and recorded a song titled "Tha Weedman" for LJESB's album *Kings of Crunk*. They did not discuss payment and Wilchcombe was not paid, but he was given credit on the album as a producer. By 2005, the album had sold 2 million copies. Wilchcombe filed a suit in a federal district court against TVT and the others, alleging copyright infringement. The defendants asserted that they had a license to use the song. Wilchcombe argued that he never granted a license to anyone. Do these facts indicate that the defendants had a license to use Wilchcombe's song? If so, what does that mean for Wilchcombe's cause? Explain. [*Wilchcombe v. TeeVee Toons, Inc.*, 555 F.3d 949 (11th Cir. 2009)]

5–7 **A Question of Ethics** *Custom Copies, Inc., in Gainesville, Florida, is a copy shop, reproducing and distributing, for profit, on request, material published and owned by others. One of the copy shop's primary activities is the preparation and sale of coursepacks, which contain compilations of readings for college courses. For a particular coursepack, a teacher selects the readings and delivers a syllabus to the copy shop, which obtains the materials from a library, copies them, and then binds and sells the copies. Blackwell Publishing, Inc., in Malden, Massachusetts, publishes books and journals in medicine and other fields and owns the copyrights to these publications. Blackwell and others filed a suit in a federal district court against Custom Copies, alleging copyright infringement for its "routine and systematic reproduction of materials from plaintiffs' publications, without seeking permission," to compile coursepacks for classes at the University of Florida. The plaintiffs asked the court to issue an injunction and award them damages, as well as the profit from the infringement. The defendant filed a motion to dismiss the complaint. [Blackwell Publishing, Inc. v. Custom Copies, Inc., __ F.Supp.2d __ (N.D.Fla. 2007)]*

1 Custom Copies argued, in part, that it did not "distribute" the coursepacks. Does a copy shop violate copyright law if it only copies materials for coursepacks? Does the copying fall under the "fair use" exception? Should the court grant the defendants' motion? Why or why not?

2 What is the potential impact if copies of a book or journal are created and sold without the permission of, and the payment of royalties or a fee to, the copyright owner? Explain.

▶ Critical Thinking and Writing Assignments

5–8 **Critical Legal Thinking.** In the United States, patent protection is granted to the first person to invent a given product or process, even though another person may be the first to file for a patent on the same product or process. What are the advantages of this patenting procedure? Can you think of any disadvantages? Explain.

5–9 **Critical Thinking and Writing Assignment for Business.** Sync Computers, Inc., makes computer-related products under the brand name "Sync," which the company registers as a trademark. Without Sync's permission, E-Product Corp. embeds the Sync mark in E-Product's Web site, in black type on a blue background. This tag causes the E-Product site to be returned at the top of the list of results on a search engine query for "Sync." Does E-Product's use of the Sync mark as a meta tag without Sync's permission constitute trademark infringement? Explain.

 Practical Internet Exercises

Go to this text's Web site at **www.cengage.com/blaw/blt**, select "Chapter 5," and click on "Practical Internet Exercises." There you will find the following Internet research exercises that you can perform to learn more about the topics covered in this chapter.

Practical Internet Exercise 5–1: LEGAL PERSPECTIVE—**Unwarranted Legal Threats**
Practical Internet Exercise 5–2: TECHNOLOGICAL PERSPECTIVE—**File-Sharing**
Practical Internet Exercise 5–3: MANAGEMENT PERSPECTIVE—**Protecting Intellectual Property across Borders**

Chapter 6

Criminal Law

(AP Photo/Douglas C. Pizac)

> "The crime problem is getting really serious. The other day, the Statue of Liberty had both hands up."
>
> —Jay Leno, 1950–present
> (American comedian and television host)

Chapter Outline

- Civil Law and Criminal Law
- Criminal Liability
- Types of Crimes
- Defenses to Criminal Liability
- Constitutional Safeguards and Criminal Procedures
- Criminal Process

Learning Objectives

After reading this chapter, you should be able to answer the following questions:

1. What two elements must exist before a person can be held liable for a crime? Can a corporation commit crimes?

2. What are five broad categories of crimes? What is white-collar crime?

3. What defenses might be raised by criminal defendants to avoid liability for criminal acts?

4. What constitutional safeguards exist to protect persons accused of crimes?

5. What are the basic steps in the criminal process?

Criminal law is an important part of the legal environment of business. Various sanctions are used to bring about a society in which individuals engaging in business can compete and flourish. These sanctions include damages for various types of tortious conduct (as discussed in Chapter 4), damages for breach of contract (to be discussed in Chapter 14), and the equitable remedies (as discussed in Chapter 1). Additional sanctions are imposed under criminal law. Many statutes regulating business provide for criminal as well as civil sanctions. As noted in the chapter-opening quotation, crime is a serious problem in the United States, and some fear that the nation's economic crisis will result in even higher crime rates.

In this chapter, following a brief summary of the major differences between criminal and civil law, we look at how crimes are classified and what elements must be present for criminal liability to exist. We then examine various categories of crimes (with the exception of crimes committed in cyberspace, which will be discussed in Chapter 7), the defenses that can be raised to avoid liability for criminal actions, and criminal procedural law.

▶ Civil Law and Criminal Law

Remember from Chapter 1 that *civil law* spells out the duties that exist between persons or between persons and their governments, excluding the duty not to commit crimes. Contract law, for example, is part of civil law. The whole body of tort law, which deals with the

Crime A wrong against society proclaimed in a statute and, if committed, punishable by society through fines and/or imprisonment—and, in some cases, death.

infringement by one person on the legally recognized rights of another, is also an area of civil law.

Criminal law, in contrast, has to do with crime. A **crime** can be defined as a wrong against society proclaimed in a statute and, if committed, punishable by society through fines and/ or imprisonment—and, in some cases, death. (Although crimes in our nation are defined by statute, this is not necessarily true in other societies. For a discussion of how some residents of Afghanistan and Pakistan base their criminal law on a tribal code, see this chapter's *Beyond Our Borders* feature.) As mentioned in Chapter 1, because crimes are *offenses against society as a whole,* criminals are prosecuted by a public official, such as a district attorney (D.A.), rather than by the crime victims. Victims often report the crime to the police, but ultimately it is the D.A.'s office that decides whether to file criminal charges and to what extent to pursue the prosecution or carry out additional investigation.

Key Differences between Civil Law and Criminal Law

Because the state has extensive resources at its disposal when prosecuting criminal cases, there are numerous procedural safeguards to protect the rights of defendants. We look here at one of these safeguards—the higher burden of proof that applies in a criminal case—as well as the harsher sanctions for criminal acts as compared to civil wrongs. Exhibit 6–1 summarizes these and other key differences between civil law and criminal law.

Beyond a Reasonable Doubt The standard of proof used in criminal cases. If there is any reasonable doubt that a criminal defendant committed the crime with which she or he has been charged, then the verdict must be "not guilty."

BURDEN OF PROOF   In a civil case, the plaintiff usually must prove his or her case by a *preponderance of the evidence.* Under this standard, the plaintiff must convince the court that, based on the evidence presented by both parties, it is more likely than not that the plaintiff's allegation is true.

In a criminal case, in contrast, the state must prove its case **beyond a reasonable doubt.** If the jury views the evidence in the case as reasonably permitting either a guilty or a not guilty verdict, then the jury's verdict must be *not* guilty. In other words, the government (prosecutor) must prove beyond a reasonable doubt that the defendant has committed every essential element of the offense with which she or he is charged. If the jurors are not convinced of the defendant's guilt beyond a reasonable doubt, they must find the defendant not guilty. Note also that in a criminal case, the jury's verdict normally must be unanimous—agreed to by all members of the jury—to convict the defendant.[1] (In a civil trial by jury, in contrast, typically only three-fourths of the jurors need to agree.)

---

1. Note that there are exceptions—a few states allow jury verdicts that are not unanimous. Arizona, for example, allows six of eight jurors to reach a verdict in criminal cases. Louisiana and Oregon have also relaxed the requirement of unanimous jury verdicts.

● *Exhibit* 6–1 Key Differences between Civil Law and Criminal Law

ISSUE	CIVIL LAW	CRIMINAL LAW
Party who brings suit	The person who suffered harm.	The state.
Wrongful act	Causing harm to a person or to a person's property.	Violating a statute that prohibits some type of activity.
Burden of proof	Preponderance of the evidence.	Beyond a reasonable doubt.
Verdict	Three-fourths majority (typically).	Unanimous (almost always).
Remedy	Damages to compensate for the harm or a decree to achieve an equitable result.	Punishment (fine, imprisonment, or death).

Beyond Our Borders — An Absence of Codified Criminal Law: The Pushtun Way

The mountainous area spanning the border between southwestern Afghanistan and north-western Pakistan is one of the most remote regions in the world. It is the home of about 28 million Pushtuns. With a well-below-average literacy rate and a population spread thinly over vast mountain ranges and steppes, the Pushtuns have shown little interest in written, codified criminal law. Instead, for millennia they have relied on a tribal code of ethics known as *Pushtunwali* to regulate behavior in their society.

The fundamental value of *Pushtunwali* is *nang,* or honor. A person who loses *nang* is effectively rejected by the community. A Pushtun's *nang* is closely related to his property—that is, his money, his land, and his women. If any of these are dishonored, the Pushtun is required by the code to take revenge. In one recent example, a Pushtun

businessman's daughter eloped against his wishes, fleeing to the Afghan capital of Kabul with her boyfriend. The businessman sold his land, tracked the couple to Kabul, and killed his daughter's lover. He promised to do the

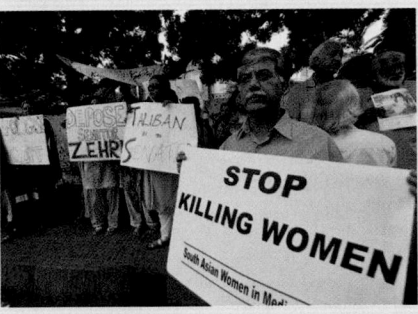

Pakistani human rights activists held a protest over "honor" killings. Every year, mainly in rural areas in Pakistan, more than 4,000 people are killed in the name of family honor.

same to his daughter, who sought refuge with a Western human rights organization.

Under the rules of *Pushtunwali,* tribal councils called *jirga* are convened on a semiregular basis to moderate disputes. *Jirga* are composed of *spingeeri* ("white beards"), who make their decisions based on history, custom, and their own experience. At a recent *jirga,* after a Pushtun named Khan admitted to killing every male member of a rival family, the *spingeeri* decided that his punishment would be the destruction of two of his homes and a fine of 500,000 rupees (about $8,500).

• For Critical Analysis
Should foreign governments pressure the Pushtuns to modify their criminal laws so that they are more in keeping with "modern" values? Why or why not?

CRIMINAL SANCTIONS The sanctions imposed on criminal wrongdoers are also harsher than those that are applied in civil cases. Remember from Chapter 4 that the purpose of tort law is to allow persons harmed by the wrongful acts of others to obtain compensation from the wrongdoer rather than to punish the wrongdoer. In contrast, criminal sanctions are designed to punish those who commit crimes and to deter others from committing similar acts in the future. Criminal sanctions include fines as well as the much harsher penalty of the loss of one's liberty by incarceration in a jail or prison. The harshest criminal sanction is, of course, the death penalty.

Civil Liability for Criminal Acts

Some torts, such as assault and battery, provide a basis for a criminal prosecution as well as a tort action. **EXAMPLE 6.1** Joe is walking down the street, minding his own business, when suddenly a person attacks him. In the ensuing struggle, the attacker stabs Joe several times, seriously injuring him. A police officer restrains and arrests the wrongdoer. In this situation, the attacker may be subject both to criminal prosecution by the state and to a tort lawsuit brought by Joe. • Exhibit 6–2 on the following page illustrates how the same act can result in both a tort action and a criminal action against the wrongdoer.

 Criminal Liability

Two elements must exist simultaneously for a person to be convicted of a crime: (1) the performance of a prohibited act and (2) a specified state of mind or intent on the part of the actor. Additionally, to establish criminal liability, there must be a *concurrence* between the act and the intent. In other words, these two elements must occur together.

• *Exhibit* 6-2 Tort Lawsuit and Criminal Prosecution for the Same Act

The Criminal Act

Every criminal statute prohibits certain behavior. Most crimes require an act of *commission;* that is, a person must *do* something in order to be accused of a crime. In criminal law, a prohibited act is referred to as the **actus reus**,[2] or guilty act. In some situations, an act of *omission* can be a crime, but only when a person has a legal duty to perform the omitted act, such as failing to file a tax return. For instance, in 2008 Michael Rosenthal, a prominent tax attorney in Honolulu, pleaded guilty to failing to file a federal tax return in 2000.

The *guilty act* requirement is based on one of the premises of criminal law—that a person is punished for harm done to society. For a crime to exist, the guilty act must cause some harm to a person or to property. Thinking about killing someone or about stealing a car may be wrong, but the thoughts do no harm until they are translated into action. Of course, a person can be punished for attempting murder or robbery, but normally only if he or she took substantial steps toward the criminal objective.

State of Mind

A wrongful mental state (**mens rea**)[3] is generally required to establish criminal liability. What constitutes such a mental state varies according to the wrongful action. For murder, the act is the taking of a life, and the mental state is the intent to take life. For theft, the

Actus Reus   A guilty (prohibited) act. The commission of a prohibited act is one of the two essential elements required for criminal liability, the other element being the intent to commit a crime.

Mens Rea   Mental state, or intent. Normally, a wrongful mental state is as necessary as a wrongful act to establish criminal liability. What constitutes such a mental state varies according to the wrongful action. Thus, for murder, the *mens rea* is the intent to take a life.

---

2. Pronounced *ak*-tuhs *ray*-uhs.
3. Pronounced *mehns ray*-uh.

guilty act is the taking of another person's property, and the mental state involves both the knowledge that the property belongs to another and the intent to deprive the owner of it.

A guilty mental state can be attributed to acts of negligence or recklessness as well. *Criminal negligence* involves the mental state in which the defendant takes an unjustified, substantial, and foreseeable risk that results in harm. Under the Model Penal Code, a defendant is negligent even if she or he was not actually aware of the risk but *should have been aware* of it.[4] A defendant is criminally reckless if he or she consciously disregards a substantial and unjustifiable risk.

Corporate Criminal Liability

ON THE WEB Many state criminal codes are now online. To find your state's code, go to www.findlaw.com/casecode.

As will be discussed in Chapter 29, a *corporation* is a legal entity created under the laws of a state. At one time, it was thought that a corporation could not incur criminal liability because, although a corporation is a legal person, it can act only through its agents (corporate directors, officers, and employees). Therefore, the corporate entity itself could not "intend" to commit a crime. Over time, this view has changed. Obviously, corporations cannot be imprisoned, but they can be fined or denied certain legal privileges (such as necessary licenses).

LIABILITY OF THE CORPORATE ENTITY   Today, corporations are normally liable for the crimes committed by their agents and employees within the course and scope of their employment.[5] For such criminal liability to be imposed, the prosecutor typically must show that the corporation could have prevented the act or that a supervisor within the corporation authorized or had knowledge of the act. In addition, corporations can be criminally liable for failing to perform specific duties imposed by law (such as duties under environmental laws or securities laws).

CASE EXAMPLE 6.2   A prostitution ring, the Gold Club, was operating out of Economy Inn and Scottish Inn motels in West Virginia. A motel corporate officer and manager gave discounted rates to Gold Club prostitutes, and they paid him in cash. The corporation received a portion of the funds generated by the Gold Club's illegal operations. (Although the motel's registration forms showed that it received only $700 over six months, the prosecution alleged that the total was several times that amount because most rentals to prostitutes took place without forms.) At trial, a jury found that the corporation was criminally liable because a supervisor within the corporation—the motel manager—had knowledge of the prostitution and the corporation had allowed it to continue.[6] •

LIABILITY OF CORPORATE OFFICERS AND DIRECTORS   Corporate directors and officers are personally liable for the crimes they commit, regardless of whether the crimes were committed for their personal benefit or on the corporation's behalf. Additionally, corporate directors and officers may be held liable for the actions of employees under their supervision. Under what has become known as the *responsible corporate officer doctrine*, a court may impose criminal liability on a corporate officer regardless of whether she or he participated in, directed, or even knew about a given criminal violation.[7]

CASE EXAMPLE 6.3   The Customer Company owned and operated an underground storage tank that leaked more than 3,000 gallons of gasoline into the ground in California.

---

4. Model Penal Code Section 2.02(2)(d).
5. See Model Penal Code Section 2.07.
6. As a result of the convictions, the motel manager was sentenced to fifteen months in prison, and the corporation was ordered to forfeit the Scottish Inn property. *United States v. Singh,* 518 F.3d 236 (4th Cir. 2008).
7. For a landmark case in this area, see *United States v. Park,* 421 U.S. 658, 95 S.Ct. 1903, 44 L.Ed.2d 489 (1975).

The company was a corporation owned by the Roscoe family. After the leak occurred, an employee, John Johnson, notified the state environmental agency, and the Roscoes hired an environmental services firm to clean up the spill. The clean-up did not occur immediately, however, and the state sent many notices to John Roscoe, a corporate officer, warning him that the company was violating federal and state environmental laws. Roscoe gave the letters to Johnson, who passed them on to the environmental services firm, but nothing was cleaned up. The state eventually filed criminal charges against the corporation and the Roscoes individually, and they were convicted. On appeal, the court affirmed the Roscoes' convictions under the responsible corporate officer doctrine. The Roscoes were in positions of responsibility, they had influence over the corporation's actions, and their failure to act caused a violation of environmental laws.[8] ●

Preventing Legal Disputes

If you become a corporate officer or director at some point in your career, you need to be aware that you can be held liable for the crimes of your subordinates. You should always be familiar with any criminal statutes relevant to the corporation's particular industry or trade. Also, make sure that corporate employees are trained in how to comply with the multitude of applicable laws, particularly environmental laws and health and safety regulations, which frequently involve criminal sanctions.

▶ Types of Crimes

Federal, state, and local laws provide for the classification and punishment of hundreds of thousands of different criminal acts. Traditionally, though, crimes have been grouped into five broad categories, or types: violent crime (crimes against persons), property crime, public order crime, white-collar crime, and organized crime. Within each of these categories, crimes may also be separated into more than one classification. *Cyber crime*—which refers to crimes committed in cyberspace with the use of computers—is less a category of crime than a new way to commit crime. We will examine cyber crime in detail in Chapter 7.

Robbery The act of forcefully and unlawfully taking personal property of any value from another. Force or intimidation is usually necessary for an act of theft to be considered a robbery.

Violent Crime

Crimes against persons, because they cause others to suffer harm or death, are referred to as *violent crimes*. Murder is a violent crime. So, too, is sexual assault, or rape. **Robbery**—defined as the taking of cash, personal property, or any other article of value from a person by means of force or fear—is another violent crime. Typically, states have more severe penalties for *aggravated robbery*—robbery with the use of a deadly weapon.

Assault and battery, which were discussed in Chapter 4 in the context of tort law, are also classified as violent crimes. Remember that assault can involve an object or force put into motion by a person. **EXAMPLE 6.4** In 2009, on the anniversary of the landmark abortion rights decision in *Roe v. Wade*, a man drove his sport utility vehicle into an abortion clinic in Saint Paul, Minnesota. The police arrested him for aggravated assault even though no one was injured by his act. ●

Each of these violent crimes is further classified by degree, depending on the circumstances surrounding the criminal act. These circumstances include the intent of the person committing the crime, whether a weapon was used, and (in cases other than murder) the level of pain and suffering experienced by the victim.

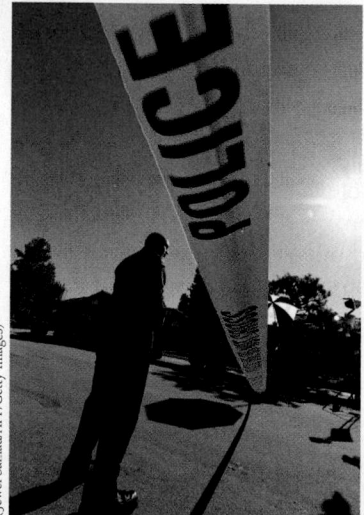

Police have cordoned off a crime scene after a shooting incident in Covina, California. What are the other categories of crimes besides violent crime?

(Jewel Samad/AFP/Getty Images)

---

8. The Roscoes and the corporation were sentenced to pay penalties of $2,493,250. *People v. Roscoe,* 169 Cal.App.4th 829, 87 Cal.Rptr.3d 187 (3 Dist. 2008).

Property Crime

The most common type of criminal activity is property crime—crimes in which the goal of the offender is some form of economic gain or the damaging of property. Robbery is a form of property crime, as well as a violent crime, because the offender seeks to gain the property of another. We look here at a number of other crimes that fall within the general category of property crime.

Burglary The unlawful entry or breaking into a building with the intent to commit a felony. (Some state statutes expand this to include the intent to commit any crime.)

Larceny The wrongful taking and carrying away of another person's personal property with the intent to permanently deprive the owner of the property. Some states classify larceny as either grand or petit, depending on the property's value.

BURGLARY   Traditionally, **burglary** was defined under the common law as breaking and entering the dwelling of another at night with the intent to commit a felony. Originally, the definition was aimed at protecting an individual's home and its occupants. Most state statutes have eliminated some of the requirements found in the common law definition. The time of day at which the breaking and entering occurs, for example, is usually immaterial. State statutes frequently omit the element of breaking, and some states do not require that the building be a dwelling. When a deadly weapon is used in a burglary, the person can be charged with *aggravated burglary* and punished more severely.

LARCENY   Under the common law, the crime of **larceny** involved the unlawful taking and carrying away of someone else's personal property with the intent to permanently deprive the owner of possession. Put simply, larceny is stealing or theft. Whereas robbery involves force or fear, larceny does not. Therefore, picking pockets is larceny, not robbery. Similarly, taking company products and supplies home for personal use, if one is not authorized to do so, is larceny. (Note that a person who commits larceny generally can also be sued under tort law because the act of taking possession of another's property involves a trespass to personal property.)

Most states have expanded the definition of property that is subject to larceny statutes. Stealing computer programs or computer time may constitute larceny even though the "property" consists of magnetic impulses (see the discussion of computer crime in Chapter 7). So, too, can the theft of natural gas or Internet and television cable service.

The common law distinguished between grand and petit larceny depending on the value of the property taken. Many states have abolished this distinction, but in those that have not, grand larceny (or theft) is a felony, and petit larceny (or theft) is a misdemeanor.

A home damaged by Hurricane Katrina in 2005 and subsequently looted. The sign facetiously thanks the perpetrator for "robbing" the property. Given the circumstances, was the crime committed here robbery, burglary, or some other property crime?

OBTAINING GOODS BY FALSE PRETENSES   It is a criminal act to obtain goods by means of false pretenses, such as buying groceries with a check knowing that you have insufficient funds to cover it or offering to sell someone a digital camera knowing that you do not actually own the camera. Statutes dealing with such illegal activities vary widely from state to state.

RECEIVING STOLEN GOODS   It is a crime to receive stolen goods. The recipient of such goods need not know the true identity of the owner or the thief. All that is necessary is that the recipient knows or should have known that the goods are stolen, which implies an intent to deprive the owner of those goods.

Arson The intentional burning of another's building. Some statutes have expanded this to include any real property regardless of ownership and the destruction of property by other means—for example, by explosion.

ARSON   The willful and malicious burning of a building (and, in some states, personal property) owned by another is the crime of **arson**. At common law, arson traditionally applied only to burning down another person's house. The law was designed to protect human life. Today, arson statutes have been extended to cover the destruction of any building, regardless of ownership, by fire or explosion.

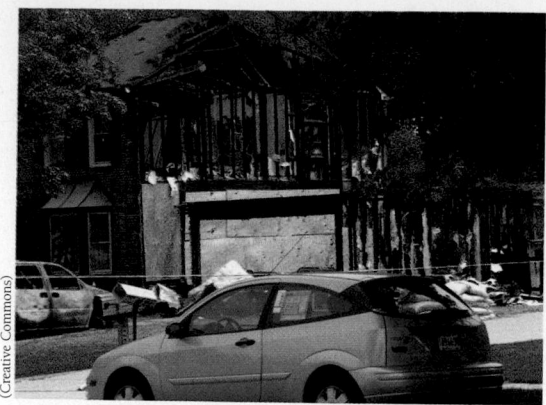

(Creative Commons)

This California home was damaged by arson. If the owner of the home hired someone else to burn it down, what crimes has the owner committed?

Every state has a special statute that covers the act of burning a building for the purpose of collecting insurance. **EXAMPLE 6.5** Benton owns an insured apartment building that is falling apart. If he sets fire to it himself or pays someone else to do so, he is guilty not only of arson but also of defrauding the insurer, which is attempted larceny. ● Of course, the insurer need not pay the claim when insurance fraud is proved.

FORGERY   The fraudulent making or altering of any writing (including electronic records) in a way that changes the legal rights and liabilities of another is **forgery**. **EXAMPLE 6.6** Without authorization, Severson signs Bennett's name to the back of a check made out to Bennett and attempts to cash it. Severson has committed the crime of forgery. ● Forgery also includes changing trademarks, falsifying public records, counterfeiting, and altering a legal document.

Public Order Crime

Historically, societies have always outlawed activities that are considered to be contrary to public values and morals. Today, the most common public order crimes include public drunkenness, prostitution, gambling, and illegal drug use. These crimes are sometimes referred to as victimless crimes because they normally harm only the offender. From a broader perspective, however, they are deemed detrimental to society as a whole because they may create an environment that gives rise to property and violent crimes. **CASE EXAMPLE 6.7** A New Yorker who was traveling from Texas to California on a Continental Airlines flight became angry and yelled obscenities at a flight attendant after a beverage cart struck his knee. The pilot diverted the plane to another airport and landed, and Arthur David Proskin was removed and arrested. Proskin later pleaded guilty to interfering with a flight crew, admitting that he was trying to get the airline to offer him a free ticket. In 2009, a federal court in Texas sentenced him to serve two and a half years in prison for his crime.[9] ●

White-Collar Crime

Crimes that typically occur only in the business context are popularly referred to as **white-collar crimes.** Although there is no official definition of white-collar crime, the term is commonly used to mean an illegal act or series of acts committed by an individual or business entity using some nonviolent means. Usually, this kind of crime is committed in the course of a legitimate occupation. Corporate crimes fall into this category. In addition, certain property crimes, such as larceny and forgery, may also be white-collar crimes if they occur within the business context.

EMBEZZLEMENT   When a person who is entrusted with another person's funds or property fraudulently appropriates it, **embezzlement** occurs. Typically, embezzlement is carried out by an employee who steals funds. Banks are particularly prone to this problem, but embezzlement can occur in any firm. In a number of businesses, corporate officers or accountants have fraudulently converted funds for their own benefit and then "fixed" the books to cover up their crime. Embezzlement is not larceny, because the wrongdoer does not physically take the property from the possession of another, and it is not robbery, because force or fear is not used.

Embezzlement occurs whether the embezzler takes the funds directly from the victim or from a third person. If the financial officer of a large corporation pockets checks from

Forgery   The fraudulent making or altering of any writing in a way that changes the legal rights and liabilities of another.

White-Collar Crime   Nonviolent crime committed by individuals or corporations to obtain a personal or business advantage.

Embezzlement   The fraudulent appropriation of funds or other property by a person to whom the funds or property has been entrusted.

---

9. "Prison for NY Man over Ruckus on Continental Jet," *San Francisco Chronicle,* January 23, 2009.

> "It was beautiful and simple as all truly great swindles are."
>
> O. Henry, 1862–1910
> (American writer)

third parties that were given to her to deposit into the corporate account, she is embezzling. Frequently, an embezzler takes a relatively small amount at one time but does so repeatedly over a long period. This might be done by underreporting income or deposits and embezzling the remaining amount, for example, or by creating fictitious persons or accounts and writing checks to them from the corporate account. Even an employer's failure to remit state withholding taxes that were collected from employee wages can constitute embezzlement.

Practically speaking, an embezzler who returns what has been taken may not be prosecuted because the owner is unwilling to take the time to make a complaint, cooperate with the state's investigative efforts, and appear in court. Also, the owner may not want the crime to become public knowledge. Nevertheless, the intent to return the embezzled property is not a defense to the crime of embezzlement.

MAIL AND WIRE FRAUD   One of the most potent weapons against white-collar criminals is the Mail Fraud Act of 1990.[10] Under this act, it is a federal crime (mail fraud) to use the mails to defraud the public. Illegal use of the mails must involve (1) mailing or causing someone else to mail a writing—something written, printed, or photocopied—for the purpose of executing a scheme to defraud and (2) a contemplated or an organized scheme to defraud by false pretenses. **CASE EXAMPLE 6.8**   A federal grand jury indicted Joseph Bruno, the former New York Senate majority leader, on charges of mail fraud. Prosecutors alleged that Bruno engaged in a scheme to defraud the public when he accepted $3.2 million from labor unions and business firms in exchange for using his position to steer contracts and grants to them.[11] ●

Federal law also makes it a crime to use wire (for example, the telephone), radio, or television transmissions to defraud.[12] Violators may be fined up to $1,000, imprisoned for up to five years, or both. If the violation affects a financial institution, the violator may be fined up to $1 million, imprisoned for up to thirty years, or both.

BRIBERY   The crime of bribery involves offering to give something of value to someone in an attempt to influence that person, who is usually, but not always, a public official, to act in a way that serves a private interest. Three types of bribery are considered crimes: bribery of public officials, commercial bribery, and bribery of foreign officials. As an element of the crime of bribery, intent must be present and proved. The bribe itself can be anything the recipient considers to be valuable. Realize that the *crime of bribery occurs when the bribe is offered*—it is not required that the bribe be accepted. *Accepting a bribe* is a separate crime.

Commercial bribery involves corrupt dealings between private persons or businesses. Typically, people make commercial bribes to obtain proprietary information, cover up an inferior product, or secure new business. Industrial espionage sometimes involves commercial bribes. **EXAMPLE 6.9**   Kent works at the firm of Jacoby & Meyers. He offers to pay Laurel, an employee in a competing firm, in exchange for that firm's trade secrets and pricing schedules. Kent has committed commercial bribery. ● So-called kickbacks, or payoffs for special favors or services, are a form of commercial bribery in some situations.

Bribing foreign officials to obtain favorable business contracts is a crime. The Foreign Corrupt Practices Act of 1977, which will be discussed in Chapter 8, was passed to curb the use of bribery by U.S. businesspersons in securing foreign contracts.

Bernard Madoff (center) leaves a U.S. district court in New York. Over a thirty-year period, he engaged in the largest Ponzi scheme ever, bilking his clients and others out of $65 billion. Why were his criminal actions not a type of larceny?

(AP Photo/Kathy Willens)

---

10. 18 U.S.C. Sections 1341–1342.
11. "Former NY Senate Majority Leader Indicted," *Findlaw Legal News*, January 23, 2009.
12. 18 U.S.C. Section 1343.

BANKRUPTCY FRAUD   Federal bankruptcy law (see Chapter 21) allows individuals and businesses to be relieved of oppressive debt through bankruptcy proceedings. Numerous white-collar crimes may be committed during the many phases of a bankruptcy proceeding. A creditor, for example, may file a false claim against the debtor. Also, a debtor may attempt to protect assets from creditors by fraudulently transferring property to favored parties. For instance, a company-owned automobile may be "sold" at a bargain price to a trusted friend or relative. Closely related to the crime of fraudulent transfer of property is the crime of fraudulent concealment of property, such as hiding gold coins.

THE THEFT OF TRADE SECRETS   As discussed in Chapter 5, trade secrets constitute a form of intellectual property that can be extremely valuable for many businesses. The Economic Espionage Act of 1996[13] made the theft of trade secrets a federal crime. The act also made it a federal crime to buy or possess trade secrets of another person, knowing that the trade secrets were stolen or otherwise acquired without the owner's authorization.

Violations of the act can result in steep penalties. An individual who violates the act can be imprisoned for up to ten years and fined up to $500,000. If a corporation or other organization violates the act, it can be fined up to $5 million. Additionally, the law provides that any property acquired as a result of the violation, such as airplanes and automobiles, and any property used in the commission of the violation, such as computers and other electronic devices, are subject to criminal *forfeiture*—meaning that the government can take the property. A theft of trade secrets conducted via the Internet, for example, could result in the forfeiture of every computer or other device used to commit or facilitate the crime.

INSIDER TRADING   An individual who obtains "inside information" about the plans of a publicly listed corporation can often make stock-trading profits by purchasing or selling corporate securities based on the information. **Insider trading** is a violation of securities law and will be considered more fully in Chapter 31. Generally, the rule is that a person who possesses inside information and has a duty not to disclose it to outsiders may not profit from the purchase or sale of securities based on that information until the information is made available to the public.

Organized Crime

As mentioned, white-collar crime takes place within the confines of the legitimate business world. *Organized crime,* in contrast, operates *illegitimately* by, among other things, providing illegal goods and services. For organized crime, the traditional preferred markets are gambling, prostitution, illegal narcotics, and loan sharking (lending at higher than legal interest rates), along with counterfeiting and credit-card scams.

MONEY LAUNDERING   The profits from organized crime and illegal activities amount to billions of dollars a year, particularly the profits from illegal drug transactions and, to a lesser extent, from racketeering, prostitution, and gambling. Under federal law, banks, savings and loan associations, and other financial institutions are required to report currency transactions involving more than $10,000. Consequently, those who engage in illegal activities face difficulties in depositing their cash profits from illegal transactions.

As an alternative to simply storing cash from illegal transactions in a safe-deposit box, wrongdoers and racketeers have invented ways to launder "dirty" money to make it "clean" through legitimate business. **Money laundering** is engaging in financial transactions to conceal the identity, source, or destination of illegally gained funds.

---

13. 18 U.S.C. Sections 1831–1839.

Insider Trading   The purchase or sale of securities on the basis of *inside information* (information that has not been made available to the public).

ON THE WEB   You can find a wealth of information on famous criminal trials at a Web site maintained by the University of Missouri–Kansas City law school. Go to **www.law.umkc.edu/faculty/projects/ ftrials/ftrials.html**.

Money Laundering   Engaging in financial transactions to conceal the identity, source, or destination of illegally gained funds.

EXAMPLE 6.10 Harris, a successful drug dealer, becomes a partner with a restaurateur. Little by little, the restaurant shows increasing profits. As a partner in the restaurant, Harris is able to report the "profits" of the restaurant as legitimate income on which he pays federal and state taxes. He can then spend those funds without worrying that his lifestyle may exceed the level possible with his reported income. •

THE RACKETEER INFLUENCED AND CORRUPT ORGANIZATIONS ACT

In 1970, in an effort to curb the apparently increasing entry of organized crime into the legitimate business world, Congress passed the Racketeer Influenced and Corrupt Organizations Act (RICO).[14] The statute, which was enacted as part of the Organized Crime Control Act, makes it a federal crime to (1) use income obtained from racketeering activity to purchase any interest in an enterprise, (2) acquire or maintain an interest in an enterprise through racketeering activity, (3) conduct or participate in the affairs of an enterprise through racketeering activity, or (4) conspire to do any of the preceding activities.

The broad language of RICO has allowed it to be applied in cases that have little or nothing to do with organized crime. In fact, today the statute is used more often to attack white-collar crimes rather than organized crime. In addition, RICO creates civil as well as criminal liability.

Criminal Provisions. RICO incorporates by reference twenty-six separate types of federal crimes and nine types of state felonies[15] and declares that if a person commits two of these offenses, he or she is guilty of "racketeering activity." Under the criminal provisions of RICO, any individual found guilty is subject to a fine of up to $25,000 per violation, imprisonment for up to twenty years, or both. Additionally, the statute provides that those who violate RICO may be required to forfeit (give up) any assets, in the form of property or cash, that were acquired as a result of the illegal activity or that were "involved in" or an "instrumentality of" the activity.

Civil Liability. In the event of a RICO violation, the government can seek civil penalties, including the divestiture of a defendant's interest in a business (called forfeiture) or the dissolution of the business. Moreover, in some cases, the statute allows private individuals to sue violators and potentially recover three times their actual losses (treble damages), plus attorneys' fees, for business injuries caused by a violation of the statute. This is perhaps the most controversial aspect of RICO and one that continues to cause debate in the nation's federal courts.

The prospect of receiving treble damages in civil RICO lawsuits has given plaintiffs a financial incentive to pursue businesses and employers for violations. **CASE EXAMPLE 6.11** Mohawk Industries, Inc., one of the largest carpeting manufacturers in the United States, was sued by a group of its employees for RICO violations. The employees claimed that Mohawk conspired with recruiting agencies to hire and harbor illegal immigrants in an effort to keep labor costs low. The employees argued that Mohawk's pattern of illegal hiring expanded Mohawk's hourly workforce and resulted in lower wages for the plaintiffs. Mohawk filed a motion to dismiss, arguing that its conduct had not violated RICO. A federal appellate court remanded the case, however. The court ruled that the plaintiffs had presented sufficient evidence of racketeering activity for the case to go to trial.[16] •

Joseph "Joey the Clown" Lombardo is a reputed mob boss in Chicago. The federal government successfully prosecuted him as a leader of that city's major organized crime family and for the murder of a government witness in a union pension fraud case. How do members of organized crime entities typically obtain revenues for their organization?

(AP Photo/U.S. Attorney's Office, Northern District of Illinois)

---

14. 18 U.S.C. Sections 1961–1968.

15. See 18 U.S.C. Section 1961(1)(A).

16. *Williams v. Mohawk Industries, Inc.,* 465 F.3d 1277 (11th Cir. 2006); *cert.* granted, 546 U.S. 1075, 126 S.Ct. 830, 163 L.Ed.2d 705 (2005); and *cert.* dismissed, 547 U.S. 516, 126 S.Ct. 2016, 164 L.Ed.2d 776 (2006). The holding in this case conflicts with a decision in another federal circuit; see *Baker v. IBP, Inc.,* 357 F.3d 685 (7th Cir. 2004).

Felony A crime—such as arson, murder, rape, or robbery—that carries the most severe sanctions, ranging from one year in a state or federal prison to the death penalty.

Misdemeanor A lesser crime than a felony, punishable by a fine or incarceration in jail for up to one year.

Petty Offense In criminal law, the least serious kind of criminal offense, such as a traffic or building-code violation.

Classification of Crimes

Depending on their degree of seriousness, crimes typically are classified as felonies or misdemeanors. **Felonies** are serious crimes punishable by death or by imprisonment for more than a year. Many states also define different degrees of felony offenses and vary the punishment according to the degree. **Misdemeanors** are less serious crimes, punishable by a fine or by confinement for up to a year. In most jurisdictions, **petty offenses** are considered to be a subset of misdemeanors. Petty offenses are minor violations, such as jaywalking or violations of building codes. Even for petty offenses, however, a guilty party can be put in jail for a few days, fined, or both, depending on state or local law.

 Defenses to Criminal Liability

Persons charged with crimes may be relieved of criminal liability if they can show that their criminal actions were justified under the circumstances. In certain circumstances, the law may also allow a person to be excused from criminal liability because she or he lacks the required mental state. We look at several of the defenses to criminal liability here.

Note that procedural violations, such as obtaining evidence without a valid search warrant, may also operate as defenses. As you will read later in this chapter, evidence obtained in violation of a defendant's constitutional rights normally may not be admitted in court. If the evidence is suppressed, then there may be no basis for prosecuting the defendant.

Justifiable Use of Force

Self-Defense The legally recognized privilege to protect oneself or one's property against injury by another. The privilege of self-defense usually applies only to acts that are reasonably necessary to protect oneself, one's property, or another person.

Probably the best-known defense to criminal liability is **self-defense.** Other situations, however, also justify the use of force: the defense of one's dwelling, the defense of other property, and the prevention of a crime. In all of these situations, it is important to distinguish between deadly and nondeadly force. *Deadly force* is likely to result in death or serious bodily harm. *Nondeadly force* is force that reasonably appears necessary to prevent the imminent use of criminal force.

Generally speaking, people can use the amount of nondeadly force that seems necessary to protect themselves, their dwellings, or other property or to prevent the commission of a crime. Deadly force can be used in self-defense if the defender *reasonably believes* that imminent death or grievous bodily harm will otherwise result, if the attacker is using unlawful force (an example of lawful force is that exerted by a police officer), and if the defender has not initiated or provoked the attack. Deadly force normally can be used to defend a dwelling only if the unlawful entry is violent and the person believes deadly force is necessary to prevent imminent death or great bodily harm. In some jurisdictions, however, deadly force can also be used if the person believes it is necessary to prevent the commission of a felony in the dwelling. Many states are expanding the situations in which the use of deadly force can be justified (see the *Business Application* feature at the end of this chapter for further discussion).

ON THE WEB You can gain insights into criminal law and criminal procedures, including a number of the defenses that can be raised to avoid criminal liability, by looking at some of the famous criminal law cases included on truTV's (formerly Court TV) Web site. Go to **www.trutv.com/index.html**.

Necessity

Sometimes, criminal defendants can be relieved of liability by showing that a criminal act was necessary to prevent an even greater harm. **EXAMPLE 6.12** Trevor is a convicted felon and, as such, is legally prohibited from possessing a firearm. While he and his wife are in a convenience store, a man draws a gun, points it at the cashier, and asks for all the cash. Afraid that the man will start shooting, Trevor grabs the gun and holds onto it until police arrive. In this situation, if Trevor is charged with possession of a firearm, he can assert the defense of necessity. •

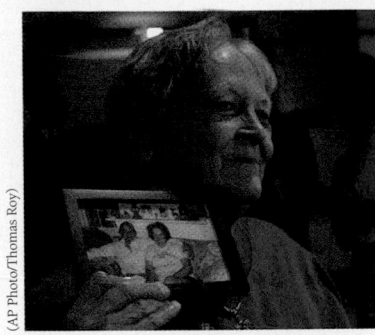

Donna Boston is the mother of Michael Delodge, shown in this photo with her. Her son was the boyfriend of Sheila LaBarre, who murdered him because LaBarre said she was "an angel sent from God" to punish pedophiles. The jury rejected her insanity defense. What are some of the tests for sanity?

Insanity

A person who suffers from a mental illness may be incapable of the state of mind required to commit a crime. Thus, insanity can be a defense to a criminal charge. Note that an insanity defense does not allow a person to avoid prison. It simply means that if the defendant successfully proves insanity, she or he will be placed in a mental institution.

The courts have had difficulty deciding what the test for legal insanity should be, however, and psychiatrists as well as lawyers are critical of the tests used. Almost all federal courts and some states use the relatively liberal substantial capacity test set forth in the Model Penal Code:

> A person is not responsible for criminal conduct if at the time of such conduct as a result of mental disease or defect he or she lacks substantial capacity either to appreciate the wrongfulness of his [or her] conduct or to conform his [or her] conduct to the requirements of the law.

Some states use the *M'Naghten* test,[17] under which a criminal defendant is not responsible if, at the time of the offense, he or she did not know the nature and quality of the act or did not know that the act was wrong. Other states use the irresistible-impulse test. A person operating under an irresistible impulse may know an act is wrong but cannot refrain from doing it. Under any of these tests, proving insanity is extremely difficult. For this reason, the insanity defense is rarely used and usually is not successful.

Mistake

COMPARE "Ignorance" is a lack of information. "Mistake" is a confusion of information.

Everyone has heard the saying "Ignorance of the law is no excuse." Ordinarily, ignorance of the law or a mistaken idea about what the law requires is not a valid defense. A *mistake of fact,* as opposed to a *mistake of law,* can excuse criminal responsibility if it negates the mental state necessary to commit a crime. **EXAMPLE 6.13** If Oliver Wheaton mistakenly walks off with Julie Tyson's briefcase because he thinks it is his, there is no crime. Theft requires knowledge that the property belongs to another. (If Wheaton's act causes Tyson to incur damages, however, she may sue him in a civil action for trespass to personal property or conversion—torts that were discussed in Chapter 4.) ●

Duress

Duress Unlawful pressure brought to bear on a person, causing the person to perform an act that she or he would not otherwise perform.

Duress exists when the *wrongful threat* of one person induces another person to perform an act that she or he would not otherwise perform. In such a situation, duress is said to negate the mental state necessary to commit a crime because the defendant was forced or compelled to commit the act. Duress can be used as a defense to most crimes except murder. The states vary in how duress is defined and what types of crimes it can excuse, however. Generally, to successfully assert duress as a defense, the defendant must reasonably believe in the immediate danger, and the jury (or judge) must conclude that the defendant's belief was reasonable.

Entrapment

Entrapment In criminal law, a defense in which the defendant claims that he or she was induced by a public official—usually an undercover agent or police officer—to commit a crime that he or she would otherwise not have committed.

Entrapment is a defense designed to prevent police officers or other government agents from enticing persons to commit crimes in order to later prosecute them for criminal acts. In the typical entrapment case, an undercover agent *suggests* that a crime be committed and somehow pressures or induces an individual to commit it. The agent then arrests the individual for the crime.

---

17. A rule derived from *M'Naghten's* Case, 8 Eng.Rep. 718 (1843).

For entrapment to succeed as a defense, both the suggestion and the inducement must take place. The defense is intended not to prevent law enforcement agents from setting a trap for an unwary criminal but rather to prevent them from pushing the individual into it. The crucial issue is whether the person who committed a crime was predisposed to commit the illegal act or did so because the agent induced it.

Statute of Limitations

With some exceptions, such as for the crime of murder, statutes of limitations apply to crimes just as they do to civil wrongs. In other words, the state must initiate criminal prosecution within a certain number of years. If a criminal action is brought after the statutory time period has expired, the accused person can raise the statute of limitations as a defense.

Immunity

Self-Incrimination The giving of testimony that may subject the testifier to criminal prosecution. The Fifth Amendment to the U.S. Constitution protects against self-incrimination by providing that no person "shall be compelled in any criminal case to be a witness against himself."

At times, the government may wish to obtain information from a person accused of a crime. Accused persons are understandably reluctant to give information if it will be used to prosecute them, and they cannot be forced to do so. The privilege against **self-incrimination** is granted by the Fifth Amendment to the U.S. Constitution, which reads, in part, "nor shall [any person] be compelled in any criminal case to be a witness against himself." When the state wishes to obtain information from a person accused of a crime, the state can grant *immunity* from prosecution or agree to prosecute for a less serious offense in exchange for the information. Once immunity is given, the person can no longer refuse to testify on Fifth Amendment grounds because he or she now has an absolute privilege against self-incrimination.

Plea Bargaining The process by which a criminal defendant and the prosecutor in a criminal case work out a mutually satisfactory disposition of the case, subject to court approval; usually involves the defendant's pleading guilty to a lesser offense in return for a lighter sentence.

Often, a grant of immunity from prosecution for a serious crime is part of the **plea bargaining** between the defendant and the prosecuting attorney. The defendant may be convicted of a lesser offense, while the state uses the defendant's testimony to prosecute accomplices for serious crimes carrying heavy penalties.

Search Warrant An order granted by a public authority, such as a judge, that authorizes law enforcement personnel to search particular premises or property.

▶ Constitutional Safeguards and Criminal Procedures

Criminal law brings the power of the state, with all its resources, to bear against the individual. Criminal procedures are designed to protect the constitutional rights of individuals and to prevent the arbitrary use of power on the part of the government.

This Madison, Wisconsin, police officer pats down a homeless person. What document provides the most safeguards for this man?

The U.S. Constitution provides specific safeguards for those accused of crimes, as mentioned in Chapter 2. Most of these safeguards protect individuals against state government actions, as well as federal government actions, by virtue of the due process clause of the Fourteenth Amendment. These protections are set forth in the Fourth, Fifth, Sixth, and Eighth Amendments.

(Charles Osgood/Chicago Tribune/MCT/Landov)

Fourth Amendment Protections

The Fourth Amendment protects the "right of the people to be secure in their persons, houses, papers, and effects." Before searching or seizing private property, law enforcement officers must obtain a **search warrant**—an order from a judge or other public official authorizing the search or seizure.

SEARCH WARRANTS AND PROBABLE CAUSE To obtain a search warrant, law enforcement officers must convince a judge that they

Probable Cause Reasonable grounds for believing that a person should be arrested or searched.

have reasonable grounds, or **probable cause,** to believe a search will reveal a specific illegality. Probable cause requires the officers to have trustworthy evidence that would convince a reasonable person that the proposed search or seizure is more likely justified than not. Furthermore, the Fourth Amendment prohibits general warrants. It requires a particular description of what is to be searched or seized. General searches through a person's belongings are impermissible. The search cannot extend beyond what is described in the warrant. Although search warrants require specificity, if a search warrant is issued for a person's residence, items that are in that residence may be searched even if they do not belong to that individual.

CASE EXAMPLE 6.14 Paycom Billing Services, Inc., an online payment service, stores vast amounts of customer credit-card information. Christopher Adjani, a former employee, threatened to sell Paycom's confidential client information if the company did not pay him $3 million. Pursuant to an investigation, the Federal Bureau of Investigation (FBI) obtained a search warrant to search Adjani's person, automobile, and residence, including computer equipment. When the FBI agents served the warrant, they discovered evidence of the criminal scheme in the e-mail communications on a computer in Adjani's residence. The computer belonged to Adjani's live-in girlfriend. Adjani filed a motion to suppress this evidence, claiming that because he did not own the computer, it was beyond the scope of the warrant. The trial court granted the defendant's motion and suppressed the incriminating e-mails, but a federal appellate court reversed. The court held that the search of the computer was proper, given the alleged involvement of computers in the crime.[18] ●

ON THE WEB You can learn about some of the constitutional questions raised by various criminal laws and procedures by going to the Web site of the American Civil Liberties Union at **www.aclu.org**.

SEARCHES AND SEIZURES IN THE BUSINESS CONTEXT Because of the strong governmental interest in protecting the public, a warrant normally is not required for the seizure of spoiled or contaminated food. Nor are warrants required for searches of businesses in such highly regulated industries as liquor, guns, and strip mining.

The standard used for highly regulated industries is sometimes applied in other contexts as well. **CASE EXAMPLE 6.15** Christian Hartwell was attempting to board a flight from Philadelphia to Phoenix, Arizona. When he walked through the security checkpoint, he set off the alarm. Airport security took him aside and eventually discovered that he had two packages of crack cocaine in his pocket. Hartwell appealed his conviction for possession of drugs, claiming that the airport search was suspicionless and violated his Fourth Amendment rights. A federal appellate court held that airports can be treated as highly regulated industries and that suspicionless checkpoint screening of airline passengers is constitutional.[19] ●

Generally, however, government inspectors do not have the right to search business premises without a warrant, although the standard of probable cause is not the same as that required in nonbusiness contexts. The existence of a general and neutral plan of enforcement will justify the issuance of a warrant. Lawyers and accountants frequently possess the business records of their clients, and inspecting these documents while they are out of the hands of their true owners also requires a warrant.

In the following case, after receiving a report of suspected health-care fraud, state officials entered and searched the office of a licensed physician without obtaining a warrant. The physician claimed that the search was unreasonable and improper.

---

18. *United States v. Adjani,* 452 F.3d 1140 (9th Cir. 2006).
19. *United States v. Hartwell,* 436 F.3d 174 (3d Cir. 2006).

Case 6.1   United States v. Moon

United States Court of Appeals, Sixth Circuit, 513 F.3d 208 (2008).
www.ca6.uscourts.gov[a]

Dr. Young Moon, a Tennessee oncologist, administered partial doses of chemotherapy to her patients but charged insurance companies for full doses, pocketing the difference for herself. Was the search that uncovered the scam legal, however?

FACTS Young Moon, a licensed physician specializing in oncology and hematology, operated a medical practice in Crossville, Tennessee. As part of her practice, Moon contracted with the state of Tennessee to provide medical treatment to patients pursuant to a state and federally funded health benefit program for the uninsured known as "TennCare." Moon routinely utilized chemotherapy medications in her treatment of cancer patients insured under the program. In March 2001, the Tennessee Bureau of Investigation (TBI) received a complaint from one of Moon's employees alleging that she administered partial doses of chemotherapy medication while billing the insurance program for full doses. On January 9, 2002, investigating agents conducted an on-site review at Moon's office. The agents identified themselves, informed Moon of a general complaint against her, and requested permission to "scan" particular patient records. Moon agreed. She also provided the agents with a location where they could scan the requested files. Subsequently, the federal district court convicted Moon of health-care fraud. She appealed her conviction, arguing that the evidence against her should have been suppressed because it was obtained without a search warrant.

ISSUE Can state officials scan a physician's business records without a warrant if the physician agreed to allow the search?

DECISION Yes. The U.S. Court of Appeals for the Sixth Circuit affirmed the district court's decision.

REASON The appellate court acknowledged that the Fourth Amendment prohibits the government from conducting unreasonable searches and seizures, but found that in this case an exception applied. "The well-delineated exception at issue here is consent. If an officer obtains consent to search, a warrantless search does not offend the Constitution." Further, "consent is voluntary when it is unequivocal, specific, and intelligently given, uncontaminated by duress or coercion." Moon clearly stated that it would be acceptable for the agents to access the requested files and that they could "scan whatever they needed to." Because Moon voluntarily allowed the agents to examine her files and to scan them, the resulting evidence did not have to be suppressed. A search warrant was not necessary.

WHAT IF THE FACTS WERE DIFFERENT? *Suppose that Dr. Moon had proved that using partial doses of the chemotherapy drugs did not affect the "cure" rate for her cancer patients. Would the court have ruled differently? Why or why not?*

---

a. Click on "Opinions Search" and in the "Short Title contains" box, type in "Moon." Click on "Submit Query." Under "Published Opinions," select the link to "08a0031p.06" to access the opinion.

....

Fifth Amendment Protections

The Fifth Amendment offers significant protections for accused persons. One is the guarantee that no one can be deprived of "life, liberty, or property without due process of law." Two other important Fifth Amendment provisions protect persons against double jeopardy and self-incrimination.

DUE PROCESS OF LAW Remember from Chapter 2 that *due process of law* has both procedural and substantive aspects. Procedural due process requirements underlie criminal procedures. Basically, the law must be carried out in a fair and orderly way. In criminal cases, due process means that defendants should have an opportunity to object to the charges against them before a fair, neutral decision maker, such as a judge. Defendants must also be given the opportunity to confront and cross-examine witnesses and accusers and to present their own witnesses.

Double Jeopardy A situation occurring when a person is tried twice for the same criminal offense; prohibited by the Fifth Amendment to the U.S. Constitution.

DOUBLE JEOPARDY The Fifth Amendment also protects persons from **double jeopardy** (being tried twice for the same criminal offense). The prohibition against double jeopardy means that once a criminal defendant is acquitted (found "not guilty") of a particular crime, the government may not retry him or her for the same crime.

The prohibition against double jeopardy does not preclude the crime victim from bringing a civil suit against that same person to recover damages, however. In other words, a person found "not guilty" of assault and battery in a state criminal case can be sued for damages by the victim in a civil tort case.

Additionally, a state's prosecution of a crime will not prevent a separate federal prosecution relating to the same activity (and vice versa), provided the activity can be classified as a different crime. Therefore, a person who is found not guilty of police brutality in a state court can still be prosecuted in a federal court for civil rights violations resulting from the same action.

SELF-INCRIMINATION   As explained earlier, the Fifth Amendment grants a privilege against self-incrimination. Thus, in any criminal proceeding, an accused person cannot be compelled to give testimony that might subject her or him to any criminal prosecution.

BE AWARE The Fifth Amendment protection against self-incrimination does not cover partnerships or corporations.

The Fifth Amendment's guarantee against self-incrimination extends only to natural persons. Because a corporation is a legal entity and not a natural person, the privilege against self-incrimination does not apply to it. Similarly, the business records of a partnership do not receive Fifth Amendment protection. When a partnership is required to produce these records, it must do so even if the information incriminates the persons who constitute the business entity. Sole proprietors and sole practitioners (those who fully own their businesses) who have not incorporated normally cannot be compelled to produce their business records. These individuals have full protection against self-incrimination because they function in only one capacity; there is no separate business entity (see Chapter 26).

Protections under the Sixth and Eighth Amendments

The Sixth Amendment guarantees several important rights for criminal defendants: the right to a speedy trial, the right to a jury trial, the right to a public trial, the right to confront witnesses, and the right to counsel. The Sixth Amendment right to counsel is one of the rights of which a suspect must be advised when he or she is arrested. In many cases, a statement that a criminal suspect makes in the absence of counsel is not admissible at trial unless the suspect has knowingly and voluntarily waived this right.

The Eighth Amendment prohibits excessive bail and fines, as well as cruel and unusual punishment. Under this amendment, prison officials are required to provide humane conditions of confinement, including adequate food, clothing, shelter, and medical care. If a prisoner has a serious medical problem, for instance, and a correction officer is deliberately indifferent to it, a court could find that the prisoner's Eighth Amendment rights were violated. Critics of the death penalty claim that it constitutes cruel and unusual punishment.[20]

The Exclusionary Rule and the *Miranda* Rule

Two other procedural protections for criminal defendants are the exclusionary rule and the *Miranda* rule.

Exclusionary Rule In criminal procedure, a rule under which any evidence that is obtained in violation of the accused's constitutional rights guaranteed by the Fourth, Fifth, and Sixth Amendments to the U.S. Constitution, as well as any evidence derived from illegally obtained evidence, will not be admissible in court.

THE EXCLUSIONARY RULE   Under what is known as the **exclusionary rule**, all evidence obtained in violation of the constitutional rights spelled out in the Fourth, Fifth, and Sixth Amendments, as well as all evidence derived from illegally obtained evidence, normally must be excluded from the trial. Evidence derived from illegally obtained evidence is known as the "fruit of the poisonous tree." For example, if a confession is obtained after an illegal arrest, the arrest is "the poisonous tree," and the confession, if "tainted" by the arrest, is the "fruit."

---

20. For an example of a case challenging the constitutionality of the death penalty, see *Baze v. Rees*, ___ U.S. ___, 128 S.Ct. 1520, 170 L.Ed.2d 420 (2008).

The purpose of the exclusionary rule is to deter police from conducting warrantless searches and engaging in other misconduct. The rule is sometimes criticized because it can lead to injustice. Many a defendant has "gotten off on a technicality" because law enforcement personnel failed to observe procedural requirements. Even though a defendant may be obviously guilty, if the evidence of that guilt was obtained improperly (without a valid search warrant, for example), it normally cannot be used against the defendant in court.

If a suspect is arrested on the basis of a police officer's mistaken belief that there is an outstanding arrest warrant for that individual, should evidence found during a search incident to the arrest be excluded from the trial? This question arose in the following case.

Case 6.2   Herring v. United States

Supreme Court of the United States, __ U.S. __, 129 S.Ct. 695, 172 L.Ed.2d 496 (2009).
www.findlaw.com/casecode/supreme.html[a]

Bennie Herring.
(Coffee County Sheriff's Office)

FACTS   The Dale County, Alabama, sheriff's office maintains copies of arrest warrants in a computer database. When a warrant is recalled, Sharon Morgan, the warrant clerk, enters this information in the database and also throws out the physical copy. In July 2004, Sandy Pope, the warrant clerk in the sheriff's department in neighboring Coffee County, asked Morgan if there were any outstanding warrants for the arrest of Bennie Herring. Morgan checked her database and told Pope that there was a warrant. Coffee County officers arrested Herring. A search revealed methamphetamine in his pocket and an illegal gun in his truck. Meanwhile, Morgan learned that a mistake had been made: the warrant had been recalled. Herring was charged in a federal district court with illegal possession of a gun and drugs. He filed a motion to exclude the evidence on the ground that his arrest had been illegal. The court denied the motion, the U.S. Court of Appeals for the Eleventh Circuit affirmed the denial, and Herring appealed.

ISSUE   Is evidence found during a search incident to an arrest that was based on a mistake admissible in the prosecution of the arrested individual?

DECISION   Yes. The United States Supreme Court affirmed the lower court's judgment.

REASON   The abuses that gave rise to the exclusionary rule involved intentional conduct that was clearly unconstitutional—for example, entering homes or businesses, sometimes forcibly, without search warrants or probable cause. The exclusionary rule applies in such cases because its deterrent effect on police misconduct outweighs the substantial social cost of "letting guilty and possibly dangerous defendants go free." But when a police mistake leading to an unlawful search is the result of an isolated instance of negligence—not "systemic error or reckless disregard of constitutional requirements"—the exclusionary rule does not apply. Thus, a police officer's reasonable reliance on mistaken information in a sheriff's computer database that an arrest warrant is outstanding does not require the exclusion of subsequently acquired evidence if there is "no basis for believing that application of the exclusionary rule in those circumstances would have any significant effect in deterring the errors."

WHY IS THIS CASE IMPORTANT?   *This was the first time that the United States Supreme Court found that an exception existed to bar application of the exclusionary rule when a police officer honestly and reasonably relied in good faith on a warrant that later proved to be a mistake. The Court decided that the police clerk's negligence in mistakenly identifying an arrest warrant for the defendant did not justify application of the exclusionary rule. Because the officer's error was not "deliberate" and the officers involved were not "culpable" (at fault), the evidence discovered after the defendant's subsequent arrest was admissible at trial. Courts in the future will apply the "deliberate and culpable" test to determine whether to admit evidence obtained as a result of a police error or unconstitutional search.*

---

a. In the "Browse Supreme Court Opinions" section, click on "2009." On that page, scroll to the name of the case and click on it to access the opinion. FindLaw maintains this Web site.

REMEMBER   Once a suspect has been informed of his or her rights, anything that person says can be used as evidence in a trial.

THE *MIRANDA* RULE   In *Miranda v. Arizona,* a case decided in 1966, the United States Supreme Court established the rule that individuals who are arrested must be informed of certain constitutional rights, including their Fifth Amendment right to remain silent and their Sixth Amendment right to counsel. If the arresting officers fail to inform a criminal suspect of these constitutional rights, any statements the suspect makes normally will not be admissible in court. Although the Supreme Court's *Miranda* decision was controversial, it has survived attempts by Congress to overrule the decision.[21] Because of its importance in criminal procedure, the *Miranda* case is presented as this chapter's *Landmark in the Law* feature.

EXCEPTIONS TO THE *MIRANDA* RULE   Over time, as part of a continuing attempt to balance the rights of accused persons against the rights of society, the United States Supreme Court has carved out numerous exceptions to the *Miranda* rule. For example, the Court has recognized a "public safety" exception, holding that certain statements—such as statements concerning the location of a weapon—are admissible even if the defendant was not given *Miranda* warnings. Additionally, a suspect must unequivocally and assertively request to exercise his or her right to counsel in order to stop police questioning. Saying "Maybe I should talk to a lawyer" during an interrogation after being taken into custody is not enough. Police officers are not required to decipher the suspect's intentions in such situations.

ON THE WEB If you are interested in reading the Supreme Court's opinion in *Miranda v. Arizona*, go to **www.supct. law.cornell.edu/supct/cases/name.htm**. Select "M" from the menu at the top of the page, and scroll down the page that opens to the *Miranda v. Arizona* case.

---

21. *Dickerson v. United States*, 530 U.S. 428, 120 S.Ct. 2326, 147 L.Ed.2d 405 (2000).

Landmark in the Law   *Miranda v. Arizona* (1966)

The United States Supreme Court's decision in *Miranda v. Arizona*[a] has been cited in more court decisions than any other case in the history of American law. Through television shows and other media, the case has also become familiar to most of the adult population in the United States.

The case arose after Ernesto Miranda was arrested in his home, on March 13, 1963, for the kidnapping and rape of an eighteen-year-old woman. Miranda was taken to a police station in Phoenix, Arizona, and questioned by two police officers. Two hours later, the officers emerged from the interrogation room with a written confession signed by Miranda.

Rulings by the Lower Courts   The confession was admitted into evidence at the trial, and Miranda was convicted and sentenced to prison for twenty to thirty years. Miranda appealed his conviction, claiming that he had not been informed of his constitutional rights. He did not assert that he was innocent of the crime or that his confession was false or made under duress. He claimed only that he would not have confessed if he had been advised of his right to remain silent and to have an attorney. The Supreme Court of Arizona held that Miranda's constitutional rights had not been violated and affirmed his conviction. In its decision, the court emphasized that Miranda had not specifically requested an attorney.

The Supreme Court's Decision   The *Miranda* case was subsequently consolidated with three other cases involving similar issues and reviewed

by the United States Supreme Court. In its decision, the Court stated that whenever an individual is taken into custody, "the following measures are required: He must be warned prior to any questioning that he has the right to remain silent, that anything he says can be used against him in a court of law, that he has the right to the presence of an attorney, and that if he cannot afford an attorney one will be appointed for him prior to any questioning if he so desires." If the accused waives his or her rights to remain silent and to have counsel present, the government must be able to demonstrate that the waiver was made knowingly, intelligently, and voluntarily.

• Application to Today's World   *Today, both on television and in the real world, police officers routinely advise suspects of their "Miranda rights" on arrest. When Ernesto Miranda himself was later murdered, the suspected murderer was "read his Miranda rights." Interestingly, this decision has also had ramifications for criminal procedure in Great Britain. British police officers are required, when making arrests, to inform suspects, "You do not have to say anything. But if you do not mention now something which you later use in your defense, the court may decide that your failure to mention it now strengthens the case against you. A record will be made of everything you say, and it may be given in evidence if you are brought to trial."*

• Relevant Web Sites   To locate information on the Web concerning the *Miranda* decision, go to this text's Web site at **www.cengage.com/ blaw/blt**, select "Chapter 6," and click on "URLs for Landmarks."

---

a. 384 U.S. 436, 86 S.Ct. 1602, 16 L.Ed.2d 694 (1966).

ON THE WEB To learn more about criminal procedures, access the following site and select "Anatomy of a Murder: A Trip through Our Nation's Legal Justice System": **library.thinkquest.org/2760/ home.htm**.

Indictment   A charge by a grand jury that a named person has committed a crime.

Grand Jury   A group of citizens called to decide, after hearing the state's evidence, whether a reasonable basis (probable cause) exists for believing that a crime has been committed and that a trial ought to be held.

Information   A formal accusation or complaint (without an indictment) issued in certain types of actions (usually criminal actions involving lesser crimes) by a government prosecutor.

"In school, every period ends with a bell. Every sentence ends with a period. Every crime ends with a sentence."

Steven Wright, 1955–present
(American comedian)

Criminal Process

As mentioned, a criminal prosecution differs significantly from a civil case in several respects. These differences reflect the desire to safeguard the rights of the individual against the state. Exhibit 6–3 summarizes the major procedural steps in processing a criminal case. Here we discuss three phases of the criminal process—arrest, indictment or information, and trial—in more detail.

Arrest

Before a warrant for arrest can be issued, there must be probable cause to believe that the individual in question has committed a crime. As discussed earlier, *probable cause* can be defined as a substantial likelihood that the person has committed or is about to commit a crime. Note that probable cause involves a likelihood, not just a possibility. Arrests can be made without a warrant if there is no time to get one, but the action of the arresting officer is still judged by the standard of probable cause.

Indictment or Information

Individuals must be formally charged with having committed specific crimes before they can be brought to trial. If issued by a grand jury, this charge is called an **indictment**.[22] A **grand jury** usually consists of more jurors than the ordinary trial jury. A grand jury does not determine the guilt or innocence of an accused party; rather, its function is to hear the state's evidence and to determine whether a reasonable basis (probable cause) exists for believing that a crime has been committed and that a trial ought to be held.

Usually, grand juries are used in cases involving serious crimes, such as murder. For lesser crimes, an individual may be formally charged with a crime by what is called an **information**, or criminal complaint. An information will be issued by a government prosecutor if the prosecutor determines that there is sufficient evidence to justify bringing the individual to trial.

Trial

At a criminal trial, the accused person does not have to prove anything; the entire burden of proof is on the prosecutor (the state). As mentioned earlier, the prosecution must show that, based on all the evidence presented, the defendant's guilt is established *beyond a reasonable doubt.* If there is a reasonable doubt as to whether a criminal defendant committed the crime with which she or he has been charged, then the verdict must be "not guilty." Note that giving a verdict of "not guilty" is not the same as stating that the defendant is innocent; it merely means that not enough evidence was properly presented to the court to prove guilt beyond a reasonable doubt.

Courts have complex rules about what types of evidence may be presented and how the evidence may be brought out in criminal cases. These rules are designed to ensure that evidence in trials is relevant, reliable, and not prejudicial toward the defendant.

Sentencing Guidelines

In 1984, Congress passed the Sentencing Reform Act. This act created the U.S. Sentencing Commission, which was charged with the task of standardizing sentences for federal crimes. The commission's guidelines, which became effective in 1987, established a range of possible penalties for each federal crime and required the judge to select a sentence

---

22. Pronounced in-*dyte*-ment.

• *Exhibit* 6–3 Major Procedural Steps in a Criminal Case

ARREST
Police officer takes suspect into custody. Most arrests are made without a warrant. After the arrest, the officer searches the suspect, who is then taken to the police station.

BOOKING
At the police station, the suspect is searched again, photographed, fingerprinted, and allowed at least one telephone call. After the booking, charges are reviewed, and if they are not dropped, a complaint is filed and a magistrate (judge) reviews the case for probable cause.

INITIAL APPEARANCE
The defendant appears before the judge, who informs the defendant of the charges and of his or her rights. If the defendant requests a lawyer and cannot afford one, a lawyer is appointed. The judge sets bail (conditions under which a suspect can obtain release pending disposition of the case).

GRAND JURY
A grand jury determines if there is probable cause to believe that the defendant committed the crime. The federal government and about half of the states require grand jury indictments for at least some felonies.

PRELIMINARY HEARING
In a court proceeding, a prosecutor presents evidence, and the judge determines if there is probable cause to hold the defendant over for trial.

INDICTMENT
An *indictment* is a written document issued by the grand jury to formally charge the defendant with a crime.

INFORMATION
An *information* is a formal criminal charge made by the prosecutor.

ARRAIGNMENT
The defendant is brought before the court, informed of the charges, and asked to enter a plea.

PLEA BARGAIN
A plea bargain is a prosecutor's promise to make concessions (or promise to seek concessions) in return for a defendant's guilty plea. Concessions may include a reduced charge or a lesser sentence.

GUILTY PLEA
In many jurisdictions, most cases that reach the arraignment stage do not go to trial but are resolved by a guilty plea, often as a result of a plea bargain. The judge sets the case for sentencing.

TRIAL
Trials can be either jury trials or bench trials. (In a bench trial, there is no jury, and the judge decides questions of fact as well as questions of law.) If the verdict is "guilty," the judge sets a date for the sentencing. Everyone convicted of a crime has the right to an appeal.

from within that range. In other words, the guidelines originally established a mandatory system because judges were not allowed to deviate from the specified sentencing range. Some federal judges felt uneasy about imposing long prison sentences on certain criminal defendants, particularly first-time offenders, and in illegal substances cases involving small quantities of drugs.[23]

In 2005, the Supreme Court held that certain provisions of the federal sentencing guidelines were unconstitutional.[24] **CASE EXAMPLE 6.16** Freddie Booker was arrested with 92.5 grams of crack cocaine in his possession. Booker admitted to police that he had sold an additional 566 grams of crack cocaine, but he was never charged with, or tried for, possessing this additional quantity. Nevertheless, under the federal sentencing guidelines the judge was required to sentence Booker to twenty-two years in prison. The Supreme Court ruled that this sentence was unconstitutional because a jury did not find beyond a reasonable doubt that Booker had possessed the additional 566 grams of crack. ●

Essentially, the Supreme Court's ruling changed the federal sentencing guidelines from mandatory to advisory. Depending on the circumstances of the case, a federal trial judge may now depart from the guidelines if he or she believes that it is reasonable to do so. Sentencing guidelines still exist and provide for enhanced punishment for certain types of crimes, including white-collar crimes, violations of the Sarbanes-Oxley Act (will be discussed in Chapter 8), and violations of securities laws.[25] In 2009, the Supreme Court considered the sentencing guidelines again and held that a sentencing judge cannot presume that a sentence within the applicable guidelines is reasonable.[26] The judge must take into account the various sentencing factors that apply to an individual defendant before concluding that a particular sentence is reasonable.

ON THE WEB The U.S. Sentencing Guidelines can be found online at www.ussc.gov.

---

23. See, for example, *United States v. Angelos,* 345 F.Supp.2d 1227 (D. Utah 2004).

24. *United States v. Booker,* 543 U.S. 220, 125 S.Ct. 738, 160 L.Ed.2d 621 (2005).

25. The sentencing guidelines were amended in 2003, as required under the Sarbanes-Oxley Act of 2002, to impose stiffer penalties for corporate securities fraud—see Chapter 31.

26. *Nelson v. United States,* ___ U.S. ___, 129 S.Ct. 890, 172 L.Ed.2d 719 (2009).

Reviewing . . . Criminal Law

Edward Hanousek worked for Pacific & Arctic Railway and Navigation Company (P&A) as a roadmaster of the White Pass & Yukon Railroad in Alaska. As an officer of the corporation, Hanousek was responsible "for every detail of the safe and efficient maintenance and construction of track, structures, and marine facilities of the entire railroad," including special projects. One project was a rock quarry, known as "6-mile," above the Skagway River. Next to the quarry, and just beneath the surface, ran a high-pressure oil pipeline owned by Pacific & Arctic Pipeline, Inc., P&A's sister company. When the quarry's backhoe operator punctured the pipeline, an estimated 1,000 to 5,000 gallons of oil were discharged into the river. Hanousek was charged with negligently discharging a harmful quantity of oil into a navigable water of the United States in violation of the criminal provisions of the Clean Water Act (CWA). Using the information presented in the chapter, answer the following questions.

1. Did Hanousek have the required mental state (*mens rea*) to be convicted of a crime? Why or why not?

2. Which theory discussed in the chapter would enable a court to hold Hanousek criminally liable for violating the statute regardless of whether he participated in, directed, or even knew about the specific violation?

3. Could the quarry's backhoe operator who punctured the pipeline also be charged with a crime in this situation? Explain.

4. Suppose that at trial, Hanousek argued that he could not be convicted because he was not aware of the requirements of the CWA. Would this defense be successful? Why or why not?

Business Application

Determining How Much Force You Can Use to Prevent Crimes on Business Premises*

Traditionally, the justifiable use of force, or self-defense, doctrine required prosecutors to distinguish between deadly and nondeadly force. In general, state laws have allowed individuals to use the amount of *nondeadly force* that is reasonably necessary to protect themselves, their dwellings, businesses, or other property. Most states have allowed a person to use *deadly force* only when the person reasonably believed that imminent death or bodily harm would otherwise result. Additionally, the attacker had to be using unlawful force, and the defender had to have no other possible response or alternative way out of the life-threatening situation.

"Duty-to-Retreat" versus "Stand-Your-Ground" Laws

Today, many states still have "duty-to-retreat" laws. Under these laws, when a person's home or business is invaded or an assailant approaches, the person is required to retreat (and cannot use deadly force) unless her or his life is in danger. Other states, in contrast, are taking a very different approach and expanding the occasions when deadly force can be used in self-defense. Because such laws allow or even encourage the defender to stay and use force, they are known as "stand-your-ground" laws.

Florida, for example, allows the use of deadly force to prevent the commission of a "forcible felony," including robbery, carjacking, and sexual battery. Similar legislation eliminating the duty to retreat has been passed in at least seventeen other states, including Alaska, Arizona, Georgia, Idaho, Indiana, Kansas, Kentucky, Louisiana, Michigan, Mississippi, Missouri, Ohio, Oklahoma, South Carolina, South Dakota, Tennessee, and Texas. In some states, such as Louisiana, a person may use deadly force to prevent someone from breaking into his or her home, car, or place of business. Courts in Connecticut allow the use of deadly force not only to prevent a person from unlawful entry, but also when reasonably necessary to prevent arson or some other violent crime from being committed on the premises.

CHECKLIST FOR THE BUSINESS OWNER

1. **Find out if state law authorizes the use of deadly force to prevent a criminal attack in places of business, as well as homes and vehicles, and any conditions of use, such as whether there is a duty to retreat.**
2. **If you have employees who will be on the premises, provide training in the defensive measures they may take in various situations.**
3. **Note that even in states that impose a duty to retreat, there is no duty to retreat if doing so would increase, rather than avoid, the danger.**
4. **Contact your business liability insurance provider for ways to reduce the likelihood of crime on the premises. Insurance coverage often costs less in states *without* a duty to retreat because many statutes provide that the business owner is not liable in a civil action for injuries to the attacker.**

*This *Business Application* is not meant to substitute for the services of an attorney who is licensed to practice law in your state.

 Key Terms

actus reus 148	felony 156	petty offense 156
arson 151	forgery 152	plea bargaining 150
beyond a reasonable doubt 146	grand jury 164	probable cause 159
burglary 151	indictment 164	robbery 150
crime 146	information 164	search warrant 158
double jeopardy 160	insider trading 154	self-defense 156
duress 157	larceny 151	self-incrimination 158
embezzlement 152	*mens rea* 148	white-collar crime 152
entrapment 157	misdemeanor 156	
exclusionary rule 161	money laundering 154	

Chapter Summary: Criminal Law

Civil Law and Criminal Law (See pages 145–147.)	1. *Civil law*—Spells out the duties that exist between persons or between citizens and their governments, excluding the duty not to commit crimes. 2. *Criminal law*—Has to do with crimes, which are defined as wrongs against society proclaimed in statutes and, if committed, punishable by society through fines and/or imprisonment—and, in some cases, death. Because crimes are *offenses against society as a whole,* they are prosecuted by a public official, not by victims. 3. *Key differences*—An important difference between civil and criminal law is that the standard of proof is higher in criminal cases (see Exhibit 6–1 on page 146 for other differences between civil and criminal law). 4. *Civil liability for criminal acts*—A criminal act may give rise to both criminal liability and tort liability (see Exhibit 6–2 on page 148 for an example of criminal and tort liability for the same act).
Criminal Liability (See pages 147–150.)	1. *Guilty act*—In general, some form of harmful act must be committed for a crime to exist. 2. *Intent*—An intent to commit a crime, or a wrongful mental state, is generally required for a crime to exist. 3. *Liability of corporations*—Corporations normally are liable for the crimes committed by their agents and employees within the course and scope of their employment. Corporations cannot be imprisoned, but they can be fined or denied certain legal privileges. 4. *Liability of corporate officers and directors*—Corporate directors and officers are personally liable for the crimes they commit and may be held liable for the actions of employees under their supervision.

Types of Crimes (See pages 150–156.)	1. Crimes fall into five general categories: violent crime, property crime, public order crime, white-collar crime, and organized crime.
	  a. Violent crimes are those that cause others to suffer harm or death, including murder, assault and battery, sexual assault (rape), and robbery.
	  b. Property crimes are the most common form of crime. The offender's goal is to obtain some economic gain or to damage property. This category includes burglary, larceny, obtaining goods by false pretenses, receiving stolen property, arson, and forgery.
	  c. Public order crimes are acts, such as public drunkenness, prostitution, gambling, and illegal drug use, that a statute has established are contrary to public values and morals.
	  d. White-collar crimes are illegal acts committed by a person or business using nonviolent means to obtain a personal or business advantage. Usually, such crimes are committed in the course of a legitimate occupation. Embezzlement, mail and wire fraud, bribery, bankruptcy fraud, the theft of trade secrets, and insider trading are examples of this category of crime.
	  e. Organized crime is a form of crime conducted by groups operating illegitimately to satisfy the public's demand for illegal goods and services (such as gambling or illegal narcotics). This category of crime also includes money laundering and racketeering (RICO) violations.
	2. Each type of crime may also be classified according to its degree of seriousness. Felonies are serious crimes punishable by death or by imprisonment for more than one year. Misdemeanors are less serious crimes punishable by fines or by confinement for up to one year.

Defenses to Criminal Liability (See pages 156–158.)	Defenses to criminal liability include justifiable use of force, necessity, insanity, mistake, duress, entrapment, and the statute of limitations. Also, in some cases defendants may be relieved of criminal liability, at least in part, if they are given immunity.
Constitutional Safeguards and Criminal Procedures (See pages 158–163.)	1. *Fourth Amendment*—Provides protection against unreasonable searches and seizures and requires that probable cause exist before a warrant for a search or an arrest can be issued. 2. *Fifth Amendment*—Requires due process of law, prohibits double jeopardy, and protects against self-incrimination. 3. *Sixth Amendment*—Provides guarantees of a speedy trial, a trial by jury, a public trial, the right to confront witnesses, and the right to counsel. 4. *Eighth Amendment*—Prohibits excessive bail and fines, and cruel and unusual punishment. 5. *Exclusionary rule*—A criminal procedural rule that prohibits the introduction at trial of all evidence obtained in violation of constitutional rights, as well as any evidence derived from the illegally obtained evidence. 6. *Miranda rule*—A rule set forth by the Supreme Court in *Miranda v. Arizona* holding that individuals who are arrested must be informed of certain constitutional rights, including their right to counsel.

Chapter Summary: Criminal Law—Continued

Criminal Process (See pages 164–166.)	1. *Arrest, indictment, and trial*—Procedures governing arrest, indictment, and trial for a crime are designed to safeguard the rights of the individual against the state. See Exhibit 6–3 on page 165 for a summary of the procedural steps involved in prosecuting a criminal case. 2. *Sentencing guidelines*—The federal government has established sentencing laws or guidelines, which are no longer mandatory but provide a range of penalties for each federal crime.

 ExamPrep

ISSUE SPOTTERS

1 Ethan drives off in Floyd's car mistakenly believing that it is his. Is this theft? Why or why not?

2 Daisy takes her roommate's credit card, intending to charge expenses that she incurs on a vacation. Her first stop is a gas station, where she uses the card to pay for gas. With respect to the gas station, has she committed a crime? If so, what is it?

BEFORE THE TEST

Check your answers to the Issue Spotters, and at the same time, take the interactive quiz for this chapter. Go to **www.cengage.com/blaw/blt** and click on "Chapter 6." First, click on "Answers to Issue Spotters" to check your answers. Next, click on "Interactive Quiz" to assess your mastery of the concepts in this chapter. Then click on "Flashcards" to review this chapter's Key Term definitions.

 For Review

Answers for the even-numbered questions in this For Review *section can be found on this text's accompanying Web site at* **www.cengage.com/blaw/blt**. *Select "Chapter 6" and click on "For Review."*

1 What two elements must exist before a person can be held liable for a crime? Can a corporation commit crimes?

2 What are five broad categories of crimes? What is white-collar crime?

3 What defenses might be raised by criminal defendants to avoid liability for criminal acts?

4 What constitutional safeguards exist to protect persons accused of crimes?

5 What are the basic steps in the criminal process?

 Hypothetical Scenarios and Case Problems

6–1 Double Jeopardy. Armington, while robbing a drugstore, shot and seriously injured Jennings, a drugstore clerk. Armington was subsequently convicted of armed robbery and assault and battery in a criminal trial. Jennings later brought a civil tort suit against Armington for damages. Armington contended that he could not be tried again for the same crime, as that would constitute double jeopardy, which is prohibited by the Fifth Amendment to the U.S. Constitution. Is Armington correct? Explain.

6–2 **Hypothetical Question with Sample Answer** The following situations are similar (all involve the theft of Makoto's laptop computer), yet they represent three different crimes. Identify the three crimes, noting the differences among them.

1 While passing Makoto's house one night, Sarah sees a laptop computer left unattended on Makoto's porch. Sarah takes the computer, carries it home, and tells everyone she owns it.

2 While passing Makoto's house one night, Sarah sees Makoto outside with a laptop computer. Holding Makoto at gunpoint, Sarah forces him to give up the computer. Then Sarah runs away with it.

3 While passing Makoto's house one night, Sarah sees a laptop computer on a desk near a window. Sarah breaks the lock on the front door, enters, and leaves with the computer.

—**For a sample answer to Question 6–2, go to Appendix E at the end of this text.**

6–3 Right to Counsel. In 2007, Braden Loeser, a twenty-one-year-old college student, was arrested in Springfield, Oregon, for driving under the influence of alcohol (DUI). Loeser was informed of his right to apply for court-appointed counsel and waived it. At his arraignment, he pleaded guilty. Six weeks later, he appeared for sentencing, again waived his right to counsel, and was sentenced to two days in jail. In 2008, Loeser was convicted of DUI again, and in 2009, he was charged with DUI for a third time. Under Oregon law, a third DUI offense is a felony. Loeser argued that the court should not use his first DUI conviction to enhance the third DUI charge. He claimed that his 2007 waiver of counsel was not "intelligent" because the court had not made him aware of "the dangers and disadvantages of self-representation." What determines whether a person's choice in any situation is "intelligent"? What should determine whether a defendant's waiver of counsel is "intelligent" at critical stages of a criminal proceeding?

6–4   Trial. Robert Michels met Allison Formal through an online dating Web site in 2002. Michels represented himself as the retired chief executive officer of a large company that he had sold for millions of dollars. In January 2003, Michels proposed that he and Formal create a limited liability company (a special form of business organization that will be discussed in Chapter 28)—Formal Properties Trust, LLC—to "channel their investments in real estate." Formal agreed to contribute $100,000 to the company and wrote two $50,000 checks to "Michels and Associates, LLC." Six months later, Michels told Formal that their LLC had been formed in Delaware. Later, Formal asked Michels about her investments. He responded evasively, and she demanded that an independent accountant review the firm's records. Michels refused. Formal contacted the police. Michels was charged in a Virginia state court with obtaining money by false pretenses. The Delaware secretary of state verified, in two certified documents, that "Formal Properties Trust, LLC" and "Michels and Associates, LLC" did not exist in Delaware. Did the admission of the Delaware secretary of state's certified documents at Michels's trial violate his rights under the Sixth Amendment? Why or why not? [*Michels v. Commonwealth of Virginia,* 47 Va.App. 461, 624 S.E.2d 675 (2006)]

6–5   Case Problem with Sample Answer Helm Instruction Co. in Maumee, Ohio, makes custom electrical control systems. In September 1998, Helm hired Patrick Walsh to work as comptroller. Walsh soon developed a close relationship with Richard Wilhelm, Helm's president, who granted Walsh's request to hire Shari Price as Walsh's assistant. Wilhelm was not aware that Walsh and Price were engaged in an extramarital affair. Over the next five years, Walsh and Price spent more than $200,000 of Helm's funds on themselves. Among other things, Walsh drew unauthorized checks on Helm's accounts to pay his personal credit-card bills and issued to Price and himself unauthorized salary increases, overtime payments, and tuition reimbursement payments, altering Helm's records to hide the payments. After an investigation, Helm officials confronted Walsh. He denied the affair with Price, claimed that his unauthorized use of Helm's funds was an "interest-free loan," and argued that it was less of a burden on the company

to pay his credit-card bills than to give him the salary increases to which he felt he was entitled. Did Walsh commit a crime? If so, what crime did he commit? Discuss. [*State v. Walsh,* 113 Ohio App.3d 1515, 866 N.E.2d 513 (6 Dist. 2007)]

—**After you have answered Problem 6–5, compare your answer with the sample answer given on the Web site that accompanies this text. Go to www.cengage.com/blaw/blt, select "Chapter 6," and click on "Case Problem with Sample Answer."**

6–6   Fourth Amendment. Three police officers, including Maria Trevizo, were on patrol in Tucson, Arizona, near a neighborhood associated with the Crips gang, when they pulled over a car with a suspended registration. Each officer talked to one of the three occupants. Trevizo spoke with Lemon Johnson, who was wearing clothing consistent with Crips membership. Visible in his jacket pocket was a police scanner, and he said that he had served time in prison for burglary. Trevizo asked him to get out of the car and patted him down "for officer safety." She found a gun. Johnson was charged in an Arizona state court with illegal possession of a weapon. What standard should apply to an officer's patdown of a passenger during a traffic stop? Should a search warrant be required? Could a search proceed solely on the basis of probable cause? Would a reasonable suspicion short of probable cause be sufficient? Why? Discuss. [*Arizona v. Johnson,* __ U.S. __, 129 S.Ct. 781, 172 L.Ed.2d 694 (2009)]

6–7   A Question of Ethics *A troublesome issue concerning the constitutional privilege against self-incrimination has to do with the extent to which trickery by law enforcement officers during an interrogation may overwhelm a suspect's will to avoid self-incrimination. For example, in one case two officers questioned Charles McFarland, who was incarcerated in a state prison, about his connection to a handgun that had been used to shoot two other officers. McFarland was advised of his rights but was not asked whether he was willing to waive those rights. Instead, to induce McFarland to speak, the officers deceived him into believing that "[n]obody is going to give you charges," and he made incriminating admissions. He was indicted for possessing a handgun as a convicted felon. [United States v. McFarland, 424 F.Supp.2d 427 (N.D.N.Y. 2006)]*

1 Review the discussion of *Miranda v. Arizona* in this chapter's *Landmark in the Law* feature on page 163. Should McFarland's statements be suppressed—that is, not be admissible at trial—because he was not asked whether he was willing to waive his rights before he made his self-incriminating statements? Does the *Miranda* rule apply to McFarland's situation?

2 Do you think that it is fair for the police to resort to trickery and deception to bring those who may have committed crimes to justice? Why or why not? What rights or public policies must be balanced in deciding this issue?

Critical Thinking and Writing Assignments

6–8 **For Critical Analysis.** Do you think that criminal procedure in this country is weighted too heavily in favor of accused persons? Can you think of a fairer way to balance the constitutional rights of accused persons against the right of society to be protected against criminal behavior? Should different criminal procedures be used when terrorism is involved? Explain.

6–9 **Critical Legal Thinking.** Ray steals a purse from an unattended car at a gas station. Because the purse contains money and a handgun, Ray is convicted of grand theft of property (cash) and grand theft of a firearm. On appeal, Ray claims that he is not guilty of grand theft of a firearm because he did not know that the purse contained a gun. Can Ray be convicted of grand theft of a firearm even though he did not know that the gun was in the purse?

 ## Practical Internet Exercises

Go to this text's Web site at **www.cengage.com/blaw/blt**, select "Chapter 6," and click on "Practical Internet Exercises." There you will find the following Internet research exercises that you can perform to learn more about the topics covered in this chapter.

Practical Internet Exercise 6–1: LEGAL PERSPECTIVE—Revisiting *Miranda*

Practical Internet Exercise 6–2: MANAGEMENT PERSPECTIVE—Corporate Criminal Liability

Chapter 7

Cyber Crime

(AP Photo/Adele Starr)

> "In cyberspace, the First Amendment is a local ordinance."
>
> —John Perry Barlow, 1947–present
> (American lyricist and essayist)

Chapter Outline

- Computer Crime and the Internet
- Cyber Crimes against Persons and Property
- Cyber Crimes in the Business World
- The Spread of Spam
- Cyber Crimes against the Community—Gambling in Cyberspace
- Fighting Cyber Crime

Learning Objectives

After reading this chapter, you should be able to answer the following questions:

1. What distinguishes cyber crime from "traditional" crime?

2. How has the Internet expanded opportunities for identity theft?

3. What are three reasons that cyberstalking may be more commonplace than physical stalking?

4. What are three major reasons that the Internet is conducive to juvenile cyber crime?

5. How do encryption programs protect digital data from unauthorized access?

One day, fashion retailer Forever 21 announced that someone had stolen account details of nearly 100,000 credit and debit cards via the Internet. Another day, the Best Western Hotel Group admitted that the payment details of 8 million guests had also been stolen via the Internet. On any given day, if you connect an unprotected computer to the Internet, within four minutes, that computer will be taken over by a remote network and turned into a "zombie," just like tens of millions of other computers around the globe. The Internet provides enormous benefits by linking people and businesses around the world, but as these examples suggest, the Internet can also be a dangerous place. Certainly, one of the reasons that crime has flourished on the Internet is the difficulty in regulating something that has a global presence but no physical place. As the chapter-opening quotation reminds us, in cyberspace the First Amendment—and U.S. law in general—is only "a local ordinance."

Computer Crime and the Internet

Computer Crime Any wrongful act that is directed against computers and computer parts or that involves the wrongful use or abuse of computers or software.

The U.S. Department of Justice broadly defines **computer crime** as "any violation of criminal law that involves knowledge of computer technology for [its] perpetration, investigation, or prosecution."[1] More specifically, computer crimes can be divided into three categories, according to the computer's role in the particular criminal act:

---

1. National Institute of Justice, *Computer Crime: Criminal Justice Resource Manual* (Washington, D.C.: U.S. Department of Justice, 1989), p. 2.

1. The computer is the *object* of a crime, such as when the computer itself or its software is stolen.
2. The computer is the *subject* of a crime, just as a house is the subject of a burglary. This type of computer crime occurs, for example, when someone "breaks into" a computer to steal personal information such as a credit-card number.
3. The computer is the *instrument* of a crime, as when someone uses a computer to con a gullible person out of a great deal of funds.

A number of the white-collar crimes discussed in Chapter 6, such as fraud, embezzlement, and the theft of intellectual property, are now committed with the aid of computers and are thus considered computer crimes.

Cyber Crime A crime that occurs online, in the virtual community of the Internet, as opposed to in the physical world.

In this chapter, we will be using a broader term, **cyber crime,** to describe any criminal activity occurring via a computer in the virtual community of the Internet. Most cyber crimes are not "new" crimes. Rather, they are existing crimes in which the Internet is the instrument of wrongdoing. **CASE EXAMPLE 7.1** When Dr. Anna Maria Santi of Queens, New York, was arrested for the illegal sale of steroids and other performance-enhancing drugs over the Internet, she was charged with criminal sale of a controlled substance. The charge would have been the same if she had sold the drugs through the mail or face to face on a street corner.[2] •

It is very difficult, if not impossible, to tell how much cyber crime actually takes place. Often, people never know that they have been the victims of this type of criminal activity. Furthermore, businesses sometimes fail to report such crimes for fear of losing customer confidence. Nonetheless, by June 2007 the Internet Crime Complaint Center, operated as a partnership between the Federal Bureau of Investigation (FBI) and the National White Collar Crime Center, had received its one-millionth complaint after only seven years of operation.[3] Furthermore, the United States appears to have gained the unwanted distinction of being the world's leader in cyber crime, with more than one-third of all global computer attacks originating in this country.[4]

Cyber Crimes against Persons and Property

Perpetrators of cyber crimes are often aided by certain aspects of the Internet, such as its ability to cloak the user's identity and its effectiveness as a conduit for transferring—or stealing—large amounts of information very quickly. The challenge for the courts is to apply traditional laws, which were designed to protect persons from physical harm or to safeguard their physical property, to crimes committed in cyberspace. Here, we look at several types of activity that constitute "updated" crimes against persons and property—cyber consumer fraud, cyber theft, and cyberstalking.

Cyber Consumer Fraud

Cyber Fraud Any misrepresentation knowingly made over the Internet with the intention of deceiving another and on which a reasonable person would and does rely to his or her detriment.

The expanding world of e-commerce has created many benefits for consumers. It has also led to some challenging problems, including fraud conducted via the Internet. As discussed in Chapter 4, fraud is any misrepresentation knowingly made with the intention of deceiving another and on which a reasonable person would and does rely to her or his detriment. **Cyber fraud,** then, is fraud committed over the Internet.

---

2. *People v. Santi,* 3 N.Y.3d 234, 818 N.E.2d 1146, 785 N.Y.S.2d 405 (2004). In 2008, Dr. Santi was sentenced to serve three to six years in prison as a result of her conviction.
3. Internet Crime Complaint Center, "The Internet Crime Complaint Center Hits 1 Million!" *IC3.gov,* at **www.ic3.gov/media/2007/070613.htm**.
4. *Symantec Internet Security Threat Report: Trends for July–December 08, Executive Summary* (Cupertino, Calif.: Symantec Corporation, March 2009), p. 3.

Frauds that were once conducted solely by mail or phone can now be found online, and new technology has led to increasingly creative ways to commit fraud. Some perpetrators of fraud even look for victims on social networks and dating sites. They persuade their victims to wire funds to their putative love interests to pay for travel for meetings (which never occur)—a type of fraud that is rarely reported to the FBI. **EXAMPLE 7.2** Recently, online advertisements featuring adorable photos of "free" English bulldog puppies began appearing on the Internet. A number of respondents paid close to $1,000 in "shipping fees" (from West Africa), "customs costs," "health insurance," and other bogus charges before realizing that no puppy would be forthcoming. •

Sometimes, Internet fraud is just an electronic version of frauds that used to be perpetrated by sending letters. **EXAMPLE 7.3** Perhaps the longest-running Internet fraud is the "Nigerian letter fraud scam." In this swindle, individuals are sent e-mails promising them a percentage if they will send funds to help fictitious officials from the African country transfer millions of nonexistent dollars to Western banks. The scam was recently updated to reflect current events, with con artists sending out e-mails asking for financial help in retrieving the fortune of a loved one or associate who had perished as a result of the conflicts in Iraq and Afghanistan. •

No one knows the full extent of cyber fraud, but indications are that it is a very common form of cyber crime. In 2009, the Internet Crime Complaint Center received more than 200,000 complaints of online crime involving losses of hundreds of millions of dollars.[5] Fraud Web sites increased from fewer than one hundred at the beginning of 2006 to more than ten thousand by 2009. As you can see from Exhibit 7–1, the two most widely reported forms of cyber crime are auction fraud and retail fraud.

ONLINE AUCTION FRAUD   In its most basic form, online auction fraud is a simple process. A person puts up an expensive item for auction, on either a legitimate or a fake auction site, and then refuses to send the product after receiving payment. Or, as a variation, the wrongdoer may provide the purchaser with an item that is worth less than the one offered in the auction. The larger online auction sites such as eBay try to protect consumers against such schemes by providing warnings about deceptive sellers or offering various forms of insurance. The nature of the Internet, however, makes it nearly impossible to block completely fraudulent auction activity. Because users can assume multiple identities, it is very difficult to pinpoint a fraudulent seller—he or she will simply change his or her screen name with each auction.

ONLINE RETAIL FRAUD   Somewhat similar to online auction fraud is online retail fraud, in which consumers pay directly (without bidding) for items that are never delivered. Because most online consumers will purchase items only from reputable, well-known sites such as Amazon.com, criminals have had to take advantage of some of the complexities of cyberspace to lure in unsuspecting customers. Again, though determining the actual extent of online sales fraud is difficult, anecdotal evidence suggests that it is a substantial problem. **CASE EXAMPLE 7.4** Jeremy Jaynes grossed more than $750,000 per week selling nonexistent or worthless products, such as "penny stock pickers" and Internet history erasers. By the time he was arrested in 2003, he had amassed an estimated $24 million from his various fraudulent schemes.[6] •

• *Exhibit 7–1* **Online Criminal Activities**
The Internet Crime Complaint Center receives about 200,000 complaints of online criminal behavior each year. As the graph shows, many of these complaints involve auction fraud.

Source: National White Collar Crime Center and Federal Bureau of Investigation, *Internet Crime Report, 2006* (Washington, D.C.: Internet Crime Complaint Center, 2007), p. 7.

5. National White Collar Crime Center and Federal Bureau of Investigation, *Internet Crime Report: January 1, 2007–December 31, 2009* (Washington, D.C.: Internet Crime Complaint Center, 2009), p. 4.
6. *Jaynes v. Commonwealth of Virginia*, 276 Va. 443 (2008).

Cyber Theft

In cyberspace, thieves are not subject to the physical limitations of the "real" world. A thief can steal data stored in a networked computer with network access from anywhere on the globe. Only the speed of the connection and the thief's computer equipment limit the quantity of data that can be stolen.

IDENTITY THEFT Not surprisingly, there has been an increase in **identity theft,** which occurs when the wrongdoer steals a form of identification—such as a name, date of birth, or Social Security number—and uses the information to access the victim's financial resources. This crime existed to a certain extent before widespread use of the Internet. For instance, thieves would "steal" calling-card numbers by watching people using public telephones, or they would rifle through garbage to find bank account or credit-card numbers. The identity thief would then use the calling-card or credit-card number or withdraw funds from the victim's account until the theft was discovered.

The Internet has provided even easier access to private data. Frequent Web surfers surrender a wealth of information about themselves without knowing it. Many Web sites use "cookies" to collect data on those who visit their sites. The data can include the areas of the site the user visits and the links on which the user clicks. Furthermore, Web browsers often store information such as the consumer's name and e-mail address. Finally, every time a purchase is made online, the item is linked to the purchaser's name, allowing Web retailers to amass a database of who is buying what.

Identity theft criminals have devised even more ingenious methods. **EXAMPLE 7.5** Recently, many corporate executives received fake subpoenas from a nonexistent federal district court in San Diego, commanding them to appear before a grand jury. The e-mail contained a link that could be clicked to view the entire subpoena. When the executive clicked on the link, however, malicious software was downloaded. It recorded all keystrokes on the computer and sent the data to the cyber crooks. ●

THE LOW COST OF BLACK MARKET DATA As many consumers are discovering, any information that can be collected can be stolen. About 3 percent of all American households—3.6 million in total—report that at least one member has been the victim of a recent identity theft.[7] In reality, the cyber criminals who steal people's identities normally do not use them. Instead, they sell the information on the Internet. Several hundred Web sites sell black market private data, most of them hosted on Russian servers and out of reach of U.S. authorities. For more on the Russian connection, see this chapter's *Beyond Our Borders* feature on the following page.

---

7. Bureau of Justice Statistics, *Identity Theft, 2007* (Washington, D.C.: U.S. Department of Justice, April 2008), p. 1.

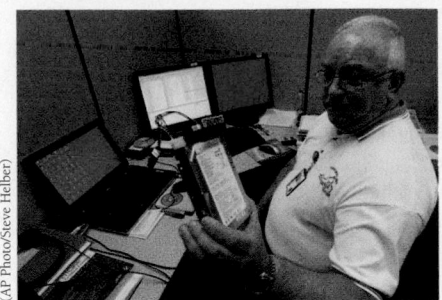
(AP Photo/Steve Helber)

This member of the State Police Computer Evidence Recovery Unit in Richmond, Virginia, works on extracting criminal evidence from a hard drive. Increasingly, cities are establishing cyber crime investigation centers.

Identity Theft The theft of identity information, such as a person's name, driver's license number, or Social Security number. The information is then usually used to access the victim's financial resources.

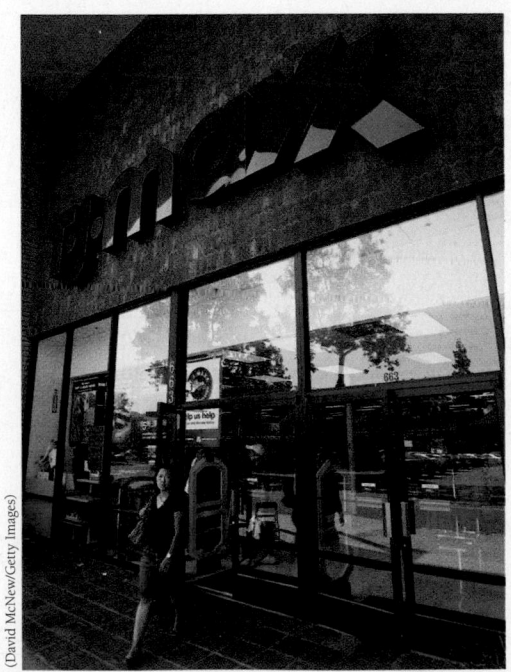
(David McNew/Getty Images)

T.J. Maxx has retail stores throughout the United States. Actually, T.J. Maxx is part of TJX Companies, Inc., which includes Marshalls, HomeGoods, and A.J. Wright. TJX is one of the largest companies in the so-called "off-price retailing industry." As a large retailer, TJX has credit and debit card information for tens of millions of former and current customers. Recently, 40 million credit and debit card numbers were stolen from that company's computers. The information was then sold to individuals who used it to steal tens of thousands of dollars at a time through automated teller machines in the United States and Europe. This cyber crime represents one of the biggest identity theft cases on record. Ultimately, eleven individuals were apprehended and charged with computer fraud and other crimes. Many of the accused were residents of Belarus, China, Estonia, and Ukraine.

Beyond Our Borders   Russian Hackers to the Fore

In the world of identity theft, the Russians are out in front. The best-known young Russian techie uses the name A-Z. He created the program ZeuS. This program helps cyber criminals around the world steal identities and carry out other scams on a massive scale.

The $6 Million Run

A few years ago, German criminals joined forces with A-Z. Using ZeuS, they sent blasts of e-mails with links to news stories, e-greeting cards, and celebrity videos. Any recipient who clicked on the links had ZeuS automatically installed on his or her computer. Then ZeuS collected data from online banking pages and other filled-out forms. After several months of recording such data, the German cyber

criminals sent e-mails to the targets asking them to "click here" to reset their banking security codes. Using the actual security codes, the criminals extracted $6 million from thousands of banks in Britain, Italy, Spain, and the United States.

Enter the Coreflood Gang

For several years, another group of cyber criminals in southern Russia has used a program called Coreflood to penetrate company, university, and government computer networks. Coreflood is actually a **Trojan horse**, a program that masquerades as legitimate but in fact allows someone to gain unauthorized access to a computer. When a computer user visited certain Web sites and downloaded

legitimate-appearing software, she or he obtained Coreflood as well. Once installed in one computer, Coreflood can spread through a computer network where it collects passwords and personal banking information. The Coreflood gang collects the information and stores it on rented servers. The pilfered data are then used to make cash withdrawals. An enormous number of infected computers are feeding private data to these criminals. Researchers from the cyberspace security firm F-Secure discovered more than 31,000 infected computers in just one U.S. school district.

• For Critical Analysis

Why will cyber crime always be a worldwide problem? Explain.

Trojan Horse   A computer program that appears to perform a legitimate function but in fact performs a malicious function that allows the sender to gain unauthorized access to the user's computer; named after the wooden horse that enabled the Greek forces to gain access to the city of Troy in the ancient story.

Phishing   The attempt to acquire financial data, passwords, or other personal information from consumers by sending e-mail messages that purport to be from a legitimate business, such as a bank or a credit-card company.

> *"I don't need to worry about identity theft because no one wants to be me."*
>
> Jay London, 1966–present
> (American comedian)

Competition among those who traffic in the tools of identity theft has become so fierce that the price of the private information has plummeted. Among identity thieves, stolen credit-card numbers are sold for as little as $1 each, while a complete identity, including date of birth, bank account, and government-issued identification numbers, can be purchased for less than $15.[8] (See this chapter's *Business Application* on page 188 for information on how businesses can avoid being the targets of identity theft.)

Many online criminals are turning to *synthetic identity theft*.[9] Rather than pilfering a "true" identity, they use a fabricated identity to gain access to online funds.[10]

PHISHING   A distinct form of identity theft known as **phishing** has added a different wrinkle to the practice. In a phishing attack, the perpetrators "fish" for financial data and passwords from consumers by posing as a legitimate business such as a bank or credit-card company. The "phisher" sends an e-mail asking the recipient to "update" or "confirm" vital information, often with the threat that an account or some other service will be discontinued if the information is not provided. Once the unsuspecting individual enters the information, the phisher can use it to masquerade as that person or to drain his or her bank or credit account. **EXAMPLE 7.6** Customers of Wachovia bank (bought by Wells Fargo) received official-looking e-mails telling them to type in personal information on a Web form to complete a mandatory installation of a new Internet security certificate. Of course, the Web site was bogus. People who filled out the forms had their computers infected with a Trojan horse that funneled their data to a computer server; the cyber criminals then sold the data. In another scheme, e-mails purportedly from the Internal Revenue Service were sent to a number of small-business owners, among others. These e-mails requested bank account information for direct deposit of federal tax refunds, which of course never came. •

---

8. *Symantec Internet Security Threat Report: Trends for July–December 08, Executive Summary* (Cupertino, Calif.: Symantec Corporation, March 2009), p. 3.

9. "ID Analytics Announces New Data Analysis Findings," *IDAnalytics.com*, February 9, 2005, at <u>www.idanalytics.com/news_and_events/2005209.html</u>.

10. Mary T. Monahan, *2007 Identity Fraud Survey* (Pleasanton, Calif.: Javelin Strategy & Research, February 2007), p. 1.

This screen shot of the Japanese version of Yahoo's home page looks exactly like the real version. Japanese police arrested a man who created this fake Web site so that he could engage in phishing. The man used personal information that he was able to steal through this Web site to defraud many Japanese of a considerable amount of wealth. Why is phishing so difficult to stop?

Vishing   A variation of phishing that involves some form of voice communication. The consumer receives either an e-mail or a phone call from someone claiming to be from a legitimate business and asking for personal information; instead of being asked to respond by e-mail as in phishing, the consumer is asked to call a phone number.

Cyberstalking   The crime of stalking committed in cyberspace though the use of the Internet, e-mail, or another form of electronic communication. Generally, stalking involves harassing a person and putting that person in reasonable fear for his or her safety or the safety of the person's immediate family.

VISHING   When phishing involves some form of voice communication, the scam is known as **vishing.** In one variation, the consumer receives an e-mail saying there is a problem with an account and that she or he should call a certain telephone number to resolve the problem. Sometimes, the e-mail even says that a telephone call is being requested so that the recipient will know that this is not a phishing attempt. Of course, the goal is to get the consumer to divulge passwords and account information during the call. In one scheme, e-mails seemingly from the Federal Bureau of Investigation asked recipients to call a special telephone number and provide account information. Vishing scams use Voice over Internet Protocol (VoIP) service, which enables telephone calls to be made over the Internet. Such calls are inexpensive and enable scammers to easily hide their identity.

EMPLOYMENT FRAUD   Cyber criminals also look for victims at online job-posting sites. Claiming to be an employment officer in a well-known company, the criminal sends bogus e-mail messages to job seekers. The message asks the unsuspecting job seeker to reveal enough information to allow for identity theft. **CASE EXAMPLE 7.7**   The job site Monster.com had to ask all of its users to change their passwords because cyber thieves had broken into its databases to steal user identities, passwords, and other data. The theft of 4.5 million users' personal information from Monster.com was one of Britain's largest cyber theft cases.[11] ● As the recession dragged on into 2010 and the unemployment rate continued to rise, opportunities for employment fraud were also on the increase.

Cyberstalking

California passed the first antistalking law in 1990, in response to the murders by stalkers of six women—including Rebecca Shaeffer, a television star. The law made it a crime to harass or follow a person while making a "credible threat" that puts the person in reasonable fear for her or his safety or the safety of the person's immediate family.[12] Almost every state and the federal government followed with their own antistalking legislation.

By the mid-1990s, it had become clear that these laws, most of which required a "physical act," such as following the victim, were insufficient. They could not protect persons against **cyberstalking,** in which the perpetrator uses the Internet, e-mail, or some other form of electronic communication to carry out the harassment. In 1998, California, once again leading the way, amended its stalking statute to include threats made through an electronic communication device.[13] Today, forty-five states and the federal government have their own legislation that makes cyberstalking a crime.

THE THREAT OF CYBERSTALKING   The only limitations on a cyberstalker's methods are computer savvy and imagination. He or she may send threatening e-mail messages directly to the victim or menace the victim in a live chat room. Some cyberstalkers deceive other Internet users into harassing or threatening their victim

PLEASE REMAIN ON HOLD WHILE WE COMPLETE THE FINAL DETAILS OF THE THEFT OF YOUR IDENTITY.

A COURTESY CALL

---

11. John Bingham, "Monster.com Hacking Follows Tradition of Cyber Theft," *Telegraph.co.uk,* January 28, 2009.

12. California Penal Code Sections 646.9(g) and (h).

13. *Ibid.*

by impersonating that victim while making provocative comments online. **CASE EXAMPLE 7.8** Jason Russell of Gladstone, Missouri, took advantage of spyware technology to essentially hijack his ex-wife's computer. He sent her an anonymous e-mail that contained a forged e-greeting card. When his ex-wife downloaded the card, she unwittingly transferred and activated Lover-Spy software onto her computer. This software allowed Russell to monitor her online activities from his own home computer. Eventually, a federal court judge sentenced Russell to three years on probation, including four months of home detention.[14] •

AN EASIER ALTERNATIVE

Although no trustworthy statistics exist, most experts assume that cyberstalking is more commonplace than physical stalking.[15] While it takes a great deal of effort to physically stalk someone, it is relatively easy to harass a victim with electronic messages. Furthermore, the possibility of personal confrontation may discourage a physical stalker from closely pursuing the victim. This disincentive is irrelevant in cyberspace. Finally, physical stalking requires that the stalker and the victim be in the same geographic location. A cyberstalker can carry on the harassment from anywhere on the planet, as long as he or she has access to a computer.

CYBERSTALKING ON SOCIAL NETWORKS

Malevolent individuals have discovered that they can cyber harass—cyberbully—individuals by establising phony accounts in social networks, such as Facebook and MySpace. The cyberbully creates a fictitious persona, who then communicates with the target, often a teenager. **CASE EXAMPLE 7.9** Lori Drew created phony MySpace accounts to help her daughter, Sarah, intimidate a thirteen-year-old classmate, Megan Meier. Mother and daughter "constructed" a teenaged boy named Josh Evans, who started communicating with Megan. One day when Megan was feeling depressed, "Josh" said via "his" MySpace account that "the world would be a better place without you." Megan hanged herself that same day. A jury convicted Drew of computer fraud because she used false information to register with MySpace, but a judge later overturned this conviction, finding that the law was not intended to criminalize her conduct.[16] •

In many cases that involve cyberstalking and other cyber crimes, a key issue is venue—the appropriate location for the trial. That was the question in the following case.

---

14. Jim Middlemiss, "Gone Phishing," *Wall Street & Technology*, August 2004, p. 38.
15. Kimberly Wingteung Seto, "How Should Legislation Deal with Children as the Victims and Perpetrators of Cyberstalking?" *Cardozo Women's Law Journal*, Vol. 9, 2002, p. 67.
16. "'MySpace Mom' Lori Drew's conviction thrown out," arstechnica.com, July 2, 2009.

Case 7.1   State v. Cline

Court of Appeals of Ohio, Second District, ___ N.E.2d ___ (2008).

FACTS   In 1999 and 2000, James Cline met Robin Rabook, Betty Smith, and Sonja Risner in Internet chat rooms. Cline had several dates with each woman, but they declined further contact. He then used his knowledge of computers, the Internet, and the women's personal information to harass them via e-mail and in other ways. He locked the women out of their Internet accounts, scheduled dates for them without their knowledge, used their names to send vulgar messages to others, and sent crude messages about the women to others. He directed still more harassment at Risner, who lived in Champaign County, Ohio, in an attempt to "emotionally destroy" her. Cline was convicted in an Ohio state court of unauthorized use of a computer and other crimes. He appealed, claiming, among other things, that venue was improper because his computer was in another county and he did not directly access the women's computers in Champaign County. Instead, he accessed their Internet service accounts, which were based in California.

ISSUE   Was venue proper?

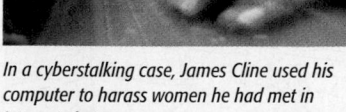

In a cyberstalking case, James Cline used his computer to harass women he had met in Internet chat rooms.

(Creative Commons)

Case 7.1–Continued

DECISION Yes. A state intermediate appellate court affirmed the judgment of the trial court.

REASON Under an Ohio state statute, when a "course of criminal conduct" involves a computer, "the offender may be tried * * * in any jurisdiction from which or into which, as part of the offense, any writing, data, or image is disseminated or transmitted by means of a computer." Cline's misuse of Rabook's, Smith's, and Risner's Internet accounts was part of a course of criminal conduct involving the same means and methods, and victims from the same group—women who had been intimately involved with Cline but had terminated their relationships with him. His criminal conduct toward each of the women had the same purpose: harassment and intimidation. The criminal conduct involved computers and included the dissemination of information through those computers to Risner, a Champaign County resident. For these reasons, Champaign County was a proper venue.

FOR CRITICAL ANALYSIS—Technological Consideration *The victims' Internet accounts were provided by Yahoo!, Inc., which is based in California. Cline's computer was in Montgomery County, Ohio. Would venue have been proper in either of these locations? Why or why not?*

Cyber Crimes in the Business World

Just as cyberspace can be a dangerous place for consumers, it presents a number of hazards for businesses that wish to offer their services on the Internet. The same circumstances that enable companies to reach a wide number of consumers also leave them vulnerable to cyber crime. The Federal Bureau of Investigation (FBI) estimates that all types of computer crime do about $400 billion in damage to U.S. businesses each year.[17]

Credit-Card Crime on the Web

In the previous section, credit-card theft was mentioned in connection with identity theft. An important point to note, however, is that stolen credit cards are much more likely to hurt merchants and credit-card issuers (such as banks) than the consumer from whom the card or card number has been appropriated. In most situations, the legitimate holders of credit cards are not held responsible for the costs of purchases made with a stolen number. That means the financial burden must be borne either by the merchant or by the credit-card company. Most credit-card issuers require merchants to cover the costs—especially if the address to which the goods are sent does not match the billing address of the credit card.

Companies take further risks by storing their customers' credit-card numbers. In doing so, companies provide quicker service; the consumer can make a purchase by providing a code or clicking on a particular icon without entering the lengthy card number. These electronic warehouses are, however, quite tempting to cyber thieves. **CASE EXAMPLE 7.10** Several years ago, an unknown person was able to gain access to computerized records at Card-Systems Solutions, a company in Tucson, Arizona, that processes credit-card transactions for small Internet businesses. The breach exposed 40 million credit-card numbers.[18] ●

Hackers

Hacker A person who uses one computer to break into another.

Botnet A network of computers that have been appropriated without the knowledge of their owners and used to spread harmful programs via the Internet; short for *robot network*.

The person who "broke into" CardSystems' database to steal the credit-card numbers was a hacker. A **hacker** is someone who uses one computer to break into another. The danger posed by hackers has increased significantly because of **botnets,** or networks of computers that have been appropriated by hackers without the knowledge of their owners. A hacker will secretly install a program on thousands, if not millions, of personal computer "robots," or "bots," that allows him or her to forward transmissions to an even larger number of

---

17. "Cybercrime Is Getting Organized," *Wired*, September 15, 2006, at **www.wired.com/techbiz/media/news/2006/09/71793**.

18. According to the Federal Trade Commission, the case was later settled. See **www.ftc.gov/opa/2006/02/cardsystems_r.shtm**.

Malware Any program that is harmful to a computer or a computer user; for example, worms and viruses.

Worm A computer program that can automatically replicate itself over a network such as the Internet and interfere with the normal use of a computer. A worm does not need to be attached to an existing file to move from one network to another.

Virus A computer program that can replicate itself over a network, such as the Internet, and interfere with the normal use of a computer. A virus cannot exist as a separate entity and must attach itself to another program to move through a network.

systems. **CASE EXAMPLE 7.11** Christoper Maxwell was sentenced to three years in prison after pleading guilty to using a botnet. Maxwell spread unwanted advertising to tens of thousands of computers, including those belonging to a Seattle hospital and to the U.S. Department of Defense.[19] •

Botnets are one of the latest forms of **malware,** a term that refers to any program that is harmful to a computer or, by extension, a computer user. A **worm,** for example, is a software program that is capable of reproducing itself as it spreads from one computer to the next. **EXAMPLE 7.12** In 2009, a computer worm called "Conflicker" spread to more than a million computers around the world in a three-week period. It was transmitted to some computers through the use of Facebook and Twitter. This worm also infected servers and any device plugged into an infected computer via a USB port, such as iPods and pen drives. Security advisers at F-Secure determined that any person or group controlling Conflicker could engage in a variety of criminal activities on an unprecedented scale. Microsoft developed a clean-up removal tool for infected computers and servers. The only problem is that Conflicker blocks Internet traffic attempting to access the tool. •

A **virus,** another form of malware, is also able to reproduce itself, but must be attached to an "infected" host file to travel from one computer network to another. **EXAMPLE 7.13** Hackers are now capable of corrupting banner ads that use Adobe's Flash Player. When an Internet user clicks on the banner ad, a virus is installed. • Worms and viruses can be programmed to perform a number of functions, such as prompting host computers to continually "crash" and reboot, or otherwise infect the system.

THE SCOPE OF THE PROBLEM Though the hackers and other "techies" who create worms and viruses are often romanticized as youthful rebels, they cause significant damage. A destructive virus can overload a company's computer system, making e-mail and many other functions impossible until it is cleaned out of the system. This cleansing process can cost between $100,000 and $5 million per day, depending on the size of the computer system affected. Experts estimate that about ten thousand viruses and worms are spreading through the Internet at any given time, with five hundred new ones being created every month.[20]

The Computer Crime and Security Survey polled more than six hundred U.S. companies and large government institutions and found that 52 percent had suffered security breaches through computer-based means.[21]

JUVENILE CYBER CRIME In the early 2000s, a series of "hack attacks" were launched against some of the largest Internet companies, including Amazon.com and eBay. The sites either froze or significantly slowed down, causing nearly $2 billion in damage for the parent companies. While the FBI was searching for the hacker, one of its investigation chiefs joked that the companies' computer systems were so vulnerable that any fifteen-year-old with technological expertise could break into them.

As it turned out, the FBI agent was only a year off. The culprit was a sixteen-year-old Canadian high school dropout who was employed as a kitchen worker in Montreal when he was arrested. The teenager, who went by the moniker of Mafiaboy, had uploaded software programs on Web sites in Europe and South Korea, from which he bombarded the American companies with e-mails. According to Assistant U.S. Attorney Joseph V. DeMarco, it should come as no surprise that Mafiaboy could cause so much damage. DeMarco believes

"Mafiaboy" (on right) walks with his attorney during his trial in 2001. When he was sixteen years old, this Canadian high school dropout uploaded software programs on Web sites in Europe and South Korea, from which he sent a very large number of e-mails to Internet companies, such as Amazon.com and eBay. Those two companies lost nearly $2 billion as a result.

(Phil Carpenter/AFP/Getty Images)

---

19. See **www.usdoj.gov/criminal/cybercrime/maxwellPlea.htm** and **www.usdoj.gov/usao/waw/press/2006/aug/maxwell.html**.

20. "Multimedia Available: One Step Ahead of the Hackers," *Business Wire,* December 13, 2005.

21. Lawrence A. Gordon, Martin P. Loeb, William Lucyshyn, and Robert Richardson, *2006 CSI/FBI Computer Crime and Security Survey* (San Francisco: Computer Security Institute, 2006), p. 12.

that there are three main reasons why cyber crime is clearly suited to the habits and limitations of juveniles:

1. *The enormous technological capacities of personal computers.* Most juvenile delinquents will never commit crimes more serious than shoplifting and other forms of petty theft. Advanced computer equipment and software, however, give these youths the ability to carry out complex criminal fraud and hacking schemes without leaving their bedrooms. Thus, computer technology has given juveniles the ability to "commit offenses that are disproportionate to their age." In addition, about 87 percent of all children have access to the Internet at home, at school, or through a library.[22]
2. *The anonymity of the Internet.* The physical world denies juveniles the ability to commit many crimes. It would be very difficult, for example, for a teenager to run a fraudulent auction in person. The Internet allows young people to depict themselves as adults, thereby opening up a number of criminal possibilities that would otherwise be denied to them. The lack of a driver's license or the wealth necessary to travel does not limit a cyber juvenile delinquent's ability to commit far-reaching offenses.
3. *The acceptance of hacking in youth culture.* A poll of nearly 50,000 elementary and middle school students conducted by Scholastic, Inc., found that nearly half of them did not consider hacking to be a crime. Thus, DeMarco believes, there is an "ethical deficit" when it comes to youth and computer crimes: juveniles who would never consider robbery or burglary are not troubled by the prospect of committing cyber crimes.[23]

New Service-Based Hacking Available at Low Cost

The business computer application trend is toward "software as a service" (SAAS). Instead of buying software to install on your computer, you connect to Web-based software. You can write e-mails, edit spreadsheets, and the like using your Web browser. Cyber criminals have adapted this method and now offer "crimeware as a service" (CAAS).

A would-be thief no longer has to be a computer hacker to create a botnet or steal banking information and credit-card numbers. He or she can rent the online services of cyber criminals to do the work on such sites as NeoSploit. The thief can even target individual groups, such as U.S. physicians or British attorneys. The cost of renting a Web site to do the work is only a few cents per target computer.

Hacking and Cyberterrorism

Hackers who break into computers without authorization often commit cyber theft. Sometimes, though, their principal aim is to prove how smart they are by gaining access to others' password-protected computers and causing problems.

Cyberterrorist A person who uses the Internet to attack or sabotage businesses and government agencies with the purpose of disrupting infrastructure systems.

Cyberterrorists are hackers who, rather than trying to gain attention, strive to remain undetected so that they can exploit computers for a serious impact. Just as "real" terrorists destroyed the World Trade Center towers and a portion of the Pentagon in September 2001, cyberterrorists might explode "logic bombs" to shut down central computers. Such activities can pose a danger to national security. **EXAMPLE 7.14** In 2009, Chinese and Russian cyber spies reportedly hacked into our nation's electrical power grid and left behind software that could be used to disrupt the system during a war or crisis. U.S. intelligence officials were concerned that the hackers might try to hijack electrical facilities or a nuclear power plant via the Internet. •

Cyberterrorists as well as hackers may target businesses. The goals of a hacking operation might include a wholesale theft of data, such as a merchant's customer files, or the

---

22. Amanda Lenhart, Mary Madden, and Paul Hitlin, *Teens and Technology* (Washington, D.C.: Pew Internet and American Life Project, July 2008), p. ii.
23. Joseph V. DeMarco, *It's Not Just Fun and "War Games"—Juveniles and Computer Crimes* (Washington, D.C.: U.S. Department of Justice, 2007).

monitoring of a computer to discover a business firm's plans and transactions. A cyberterrorist might also want to insert false codes or data. For example, the processing control system of a food manufacturer could be changed to alter the levels of ingredients so that consumers of the food would become ill.

A cyberterrorist attack on a major financial institution such as the New York Stock Exchange or a large bank could leave securities or money markets in flux and seriously affect the daily lives of millions of citizens. Similarly, any prolonged disruption of computer, cable, satellite, or telecommunications systems due to the actions of expert hackers would have serious repercussions on business operations—and national security—on a global level. Computer viruses are another tool that can be used by cyberterrorists to cripple communications networks.

Pirating Intellectual Property Online

In Chapter 5, we examined *intellectual property*, which consists of goods and services that result from intellectual, creative processes. As we pointed out, the government provides various forms of protection for intellectual property such as copyrights and patents. These protections ensure that a person who writes a book or a song or creates a software program is financially rewarded if that product is sold in the marketplace.

Intellectual property such as books, films, music, and software is vulnerable to "piracy"— the unauthorized copying and use of the property. In the past, copying intellectual products was time consuming, and the quality of the pirated copies was clearly inferior. In today's online world, however, things have changed. Simply clicking a mouse can now reproduce millions of unauthorized copies, and pirated duplicates of copyrighted works obtained via the Internet are the same as the original, or close to it.

The Business Software Alliance estimates that 35 percent of all business software is pirated, costing software makers more than $5 billion per year.[24] The International Federation of the Phonographic Industry believes that 37 percent of purchased CDs have been pirated.[25] In the United States, digital pirates can be prosecuted under the No Electronic Theft Act[26] and the Digital Millennium Copyright Act.[27] In 2005, the entertainment industry celebrated the United States Supreme Court's decision in *Metro-Goldwyn-Mayer Studios, Inc. v. Grokster, Ltd.*[28] As discussed in Chapter 5, the ruling provided film and music companies with the ability to file piracy lawsuits against Internet file-sharing Web sites that market software used primarily to illegally download intellectual property. By 2009, the recording industry announced that it would no longer file lawsuits against most individuals who pirate music online. The music industry continues to look for a business model that will allow it to make profits in spite of widespread pirating.

 The Spread of Spam

Spam Bulk e-mails, particularly of commercial advertising, sent in large quantities without the consent of the recipient.

Businesses and individuals alike are targets of **spam**, or unsolicited "junk e-mails" that flood virtual mailboxes with advertisements, solicitations, and other messages. Considered relatively harmless in the early days of the Internet's popularity, by 2009 spam accounted for more than 73 percent of all e-mails.[29] Far from being harmless, the unwanted files can wreak havoc on business operations.

---

24. *Fourth Annual BSA and IDC Global Software Piracy Study* (Washington, D.C.: Business Software Alliance, 2007), p. 2.

25. *The Recording Industry 2006 Commercial Piracy Report* (London: International Federation of the Phonographic Industry, July 2006), p. 4.

26. 17 U.S.C. Section 23199(c).

27. 17 U.S.C. Sections 2301 *et seq.*

28. 545 U.S. 913, 125 S.Ct. 2764, 162 L.Ed.2d 781 (2005).

29. "Increased Spam Levels Fueled through Aggressive Botnet Activities," *Business Wire,* November 2, 2008.

ON THE WEB The Center for Democracy and Technology conducted a study on spam. The report and the center's recommendations on how to avoid receiving spam are available online at **www.cdt.org/speech/ spam/030319spamreport.shtml**.

State Regulation of Spam

In an attempt to combat spam, thirty-six states have enacted laws that prohibit or regulate its use. Many state laws that regulate spam require the senders of e-mail ads to instruct the recipients on how they can "opt out" of further e-mail ads from the same sources. For instance, in some states an unsolicited e-mail ad must include a toll-free phone number or return e-mail address through which the recipient can contact the sender to request that no more ads be e-mailed. Responding to complaints from overwhelmed constituents, a number of jurisdictions have started to pass antispamming laws.

The Federal CAN-SPAM Act

In 2003, Congress enacted the Controlling the Assault of Non-Solicited Pornography and Marketing (CAN-SPAM) Act, which took effect on January 1, 2004. The legislation applies to any "commercial electronic mail messages" that are sent to promote a commercial product or service. Significantly, the statute preempts state antispam laws except for those provisions in state laws that prohibit false and deceptive e-mailing practices.

Generally, the act permits the use of unsolicited commercial e-mail but prohibits certain types of spamming activities, including the use of a false return address and the use of false, misleading, or deceptive information when sending e-mail. The statute also prohibits the use of "dictionary attacks"—sending messages to randomly generated e-mail addresses—and the "harvesting" of e-mail addresses from Web sites with specialized software.

CASE EXAMPLE 7.15 In 2007, federal officials arrested Robert Alan Soloway, considered one of the world's most prolific spammers. Because Soloway had been using botnets (described earlier) to send out hundreds of millions of unwanted e-mails, he was charged under antiidentity theft laws for the appropriation of other people's domain names, among other crimes. In 2008, Soloway, known as the "Spam King," pleaded guilty to mail fraud and failure to pay taxes.[30] • Arresting prolific spammers, however, has done little to curb spam, which continues to flow at a rate of 70 billion messages per day.[31]

The U.S. Safe Web Act

After the CAN-SPAM Act of 2003 prohibited false and deceptive e-mails originating in the United States, spamming from servers located in other nations increased. These crossborder spammers generally were able to escape detection and legal sanctions because the Federal Trade Commission (FTC) lacked the authority to investigate foreign spamming.

Congress sought to rectify the situation by enacting the U.S. Safe Web Act of 2006 (also known as the Undertaking Spam, Spyware, and Fraud Enforcement with Enforcers Beyond Borders Act). The act allows the FTC to cooperate and share information with foreign agencies in investigating and prosecuting those involved in Internet fraud and deception, including spamming, spyware, and various Internet frauds. It also provides Internet service providers (ISPs) with a "safe harbor" (immunity from liability) for supplying information to the FTC concerning possible unfair or deceptive conduct in foreign jurisdictions.

▶ Cyber Crimes against the Community–Gambling in Cyberspace

One of the greatest challenges in cyberspace is how to enforce laws governing activities that are prohibited under certain circumstances but are not always illegal. Such laws generally reflect the will of the community, which recognizes behavior as acceptable under some circumstances and unacceptable under others. **EXAMPLE 7.16** While it is legal in many areas

---

30. See **www.usdoj.gov/usao/waw/press/2008/mar/soloway.html**.
31. Anick Jesdanun, "Output Unaffected by Spammer's Arrest," *Charleston* (West Virginia) *Gazette*, June 1, 2007, p. 5A.

to sell a pornographic video to a fifty-year-old, it is never legal to sell the same item to a fifteen-year-old. Similarly, placing a bet on a football game with a bookmaker in Las Vegas, Nevada, is legal, but doing the same thing with a bookmaker in Cleveland, Ohio, is not. Of course, in cyberspace it is often impossible to know whether the customer buying porn is aged fifty or fifteen, or if the person placing the bet is from Las Vegas or Cleveland. ● In the following paragraphs, we will examine some of the challenges involved in regulating online gambling.

These two youths are engaged in online gambling. Why is it difficult to prevent young people from illegally participating in this activity?

(Orin Optiglot/Creative Commons)

Legal Confusion over Online Gambling

In general, gambling is illegal. All states have statutes that regulate gambling—defined as any scheme that involves the distribution of property by chance among persons who have paid valuable consideration for the opportunity to receive the property. In some states, certain forms of gambling, such as casino gambling or horseracing, are legal. Many states also have legalized state-operated lotteries, as well as lotteries, such as bingo, conducted for charitable purposes. A number of states also allow gambling on Native American reservations.

In the past, this "mixed bag" of gambling laws has presented a legal quandary: Can citizens in a state that does not allow gambling place bets to a Web site located in a state that does? After all, states have no constitutional authority over activities that take place in other states. Complicating the problem was the fact that many Internet gambling sites are located outside the United States in countries where Internet gambling is legal, and no state government has authority over activities that take place in other countries.

Property, including funds, involved in illegal gambling can be seized under federal law through a civil forfeiture action. A defendant may assert a defense to reclaim the property, but should a criminal fugitive—a person who is evading custody in a criminal proceeding—be entitled to file such a claim? That was the question in the following case.

| Case 7.2 | United States v. $6,976,934.65, Plus Interest Deposited into Royal Bank of Scotland International |

United States Court of Appeals, District of Columbia Circuit, 554 F.3d 123 (2009).
www.cadc.uscourts.gov/internet/home.nsf[a]

A typical online gambling game.

(Creative Commons)

FACTS William Scott operated World Wide Tele-Sports, an Internet sports-betting service based on a Caribbean island. In 1998, the United States charged Scott with soliciting and accepting wagers from U.S. residents through illegal offshore Web sites. Unable to arrest Scott, who lived abroad, the government followed some of the proceeds from the enterprise to an account at the Royal Bank of Scotland International (RBSI) held by Soulbury Limited, a British corporation of which Scott was the majority shareholder. The United States filed a civil action in a federal district court, seeking the forfeiture of $6,976,934.65, plus interest, from RBSI's account with a U.S. bank. Soulbury denied that the funds were linked to Scott and filed a claim for the funds. Meanwhile, in 2005, Scott was indicted on money-laundering charges related to the gambling violations. Under the Civil Asset Forfeiture Reform Act, also known as the *fugitive disentitlement statute,* a court can dismiss a claim in a civil forfeiture case based on a defendant's evasion of a separate criminal proceeding. The government filed a motion to dismiss Soulbury's claim under the fugitive disentitlement statute. The court issued a summary judgment in the government's favor. Soulbury appealed.

---

a. In the middle of the page, click on the "Opinions" box. On that page, in the "Month:" menu select "January," in the "Year:" menu select "2009," and click on "Go!" Scroll to the name of the case and click on its number to access the opinion. The U.S. Court of Appeals for the District of Columbia Circuit maintains this Web site.

Case 7.2–Continued

ISSUE   Were the indictments against Scott sufficiently "related" to the civil forfeiture action to apply the fugitive disentitlement statute?

DECISION   Yes. But the U.S. Court of Appeals for the District of Columbia Circuit found that other fact issues still had to be decided. The appellate court reversed the judgment and remanded the case.

REASON   One of the requirements of the fugitive disentitlement statute is that a civil action be related to the criminal prosecution being evaded. The U.S. Court of Appeals for the District of Columbia Circuit reasoned that the natural reading of the word *related* in this statute means that the same facts underlie both proceedings. The government must seek through the forfeiture action to recover property that is involved in, derived from, traceable to, obtained by, or used to facilitate a crime for which the defendant is evading prosecution. In this case, the illegal gambling and money-laundering prosecutions were both related to the forfeiture action. Each prosecution involved charges based on Scott's operation of World Wide Tele-Sports.

FOR CRITICAL ANALYSIS—Global Consideration
Is the global reach of the Internet a reason in support of a court's assertion of authority over activities that occur in another jurisdiction? Discuss.

Congress Takes Action

In 2006, Congress, concerned about money laundering stemming from online gambling, the problem of addiction, and underage gambling, passed legislation that greatly strengthened efforts to reduce online gaming. The Unlawful Internet Gambling Enforcement Act of 2006 cut off the money flow to Internet gambling sites by barring the use of electronic payments, such as credit-card transactions, at those sites.[32]

The reaction by the online gambling industry was swift and dramatic: after the passage of this bill, many of the foreign-based companies suspended the use of real money on the Web sites serving the United States. Without the incentive of playing for cash, the sites have lost their appeal for most clients. In 2005, approximately 12 million Americans wagered $6 billion online,[33] but as soon as the law was enacted, those numbers plummeted.

 Fighting Cyber Crime

Passing a law does not guarantee that the law will be effectively enforced. For example, although the Unlawful Internet Gambling Enforcement Act reduced visible Internet gambling, few believe that it will stop the practice altogether. "Prohibitions don't work," says Michael Bolcerek, president of the Poker Player's Alliance. "This [legislation] won't stop anything. It will just drive people underground."[34]

Prosecuting Cyber Crimes

The "location" of cyber crime (cyberspace) has raised new issues in the investigation of crimes and the prosecution of offenders. A threshold issue is, of course, jurisdiction. A person who commits an act against a business in California, where the act is a cyber crime, might never have set foot in California but might instead reside in New York, or even in Canada, where the act may not be a crime. If the crime was committed via e-mail, the question arises as to whether the e-mail would constitute sufficient "minimum contacts" for the victim's state to exercise jurisdiction over the perpetrator.

Identifying the wrongdoer can also be difficult. Cyber criminals do not leave physical traces, such as fingerprints or DNA samples, as evidence of their crimes. Even electronic

---

32. 31 U.S.C. Sections 5361 *et seq.*
33. George Will, "Prohibition II: Good Grief," *Newsweek,* October 23, 2006, p. 78.
34. Quoted in Michael McCarthy, "Feds Go After Offshore Online Betting Industry," *USA Today,* July 19, 2006, p. 6C.

"footprints" can be hard to find and follow. For instance, e-mail may be sent through a *remailer*—an online service that guarantees that a message cannot be traced to its source.

For these reasons, laws written to protect physical property are difficult to apply in cyberspace. Nonetheless, governments at both the state and federal levels have taken significant steps toward controlling cyber crime, both by applying existing criminal statutes and by enacting new laws that specifically address wrongs committed in cyberspace.

The Computer Fraud and Abuse Act

Perhaps the most significant federal statute specifically addressing cyber crime is the Counterfeit Access Device and Computer Fraud and Abuse Act of 1984 (commonly known as the Computer Fraud and Abuse Act, or CFAA). This act, as amended by the National Information Infrastructure Protection Act of 1996, provides, among other things, that a person who accesses a computer online, without authority, to obtain classified, restricted, or protected data, or attempts to do so, is subject to criminal prosecution.[35] Such data could include financial and credit records, medical records, legal files, military and national security files, and other confidential information in government or private computers. The crime has two elements: accessing a computer without authority and taking the data.

This theft is a felony if it is committed for a commercial purpose or for private financial gain, or if the value of the stolen data (or computer time) exceeds $5,000. Penalties include fines and imprisonment for up to twenty years. A victim of computer theft can also bring a civil suit against the violator to obtain damages, an injunction, and other relief.

(For a discussion of one case involving students who were accused of violating the Computer Fraud and Abuse Act, see this chapter's *Adapting the Law to the Online Environment* feature.)

Private Efforts to Combat Cyber Crime

Whatever laws are passed, the federal government has limited regulatory oversight over the Internet. Hence, it has little choice but to rely on the voluntary efforts of private companies to secure their computer infrastructures. Although many federal officials do not believe private companies are being sufficiently diligent in this area, the fear of being "hacked" has spurred a multibillion-dollar industry that helps clients—either individuals or businesses—protect the integrity of their computer systems.

Every computer hooked up to the Internet is a potential security breach; experts must help devise elaborate and ever-changing password systems to ensure that only authorized users access data. They also install protective programs, such as firewalls and antivirus software, which can limit outside access to a computer or network. Because cyber criminals are constantly updating their technology, cyberspace security firms help their clients do the same with their defensive systems.

Perhaps the most successful way to protect computer information is to encrypt it. Through **encryption,** a message (plaintext) is transformed into something (ciphertext) that only the sender and receiver can understand. Unless a third party is able to "break the code," the information will stay secure. Encryption is particularly useful in protecting the content of e-mails. The main drawback of this technology is the rate at which it becomes obsolete. As a rule, computing power doubles every eighteen months, which means that programs to break the "latest" encryption code are always imminent. Consequently, those who use encryption must ensure that they update their systems at the same rate as those who would abuse it.

Encryption The process by which a message is transmitted into a form or code that the sender and receiver intend not to be understandable by third parties.

---

35. 18 U.S.C. Section 1030.

Adapting the Law to the Online Environment

Can Students Who Gain Unauthorized Access to an Online Antiplagiarism Service Be Subject to the Computer Fraud and Abuse Act?

The Computer Fraud and Abuse Act is primarily a criminal statute in that its main purpose is to deter computer hackers. Nevertheless, in certain circumstances, private parties may bring a civil suit alleging a violation of the act. One recent case arose when four high school students were required to submit written assignments to an online antiplagiarism service, which then archived the students' work.

Fighting Student Plagiarism

Instructors in high schools, colleges, and universities worldwide face a plagiarism problem of epic proportions. Any student can access various online sources from which work can be plagiarized. As a result, several companies, including iParadigms, LLC, have created software and other services to help instructors detect plagiarism. One of iParadigms' products is Turnitin Plagiarism Detection Service. Instructors can require their students to submit written assignments to Turnitin, which then compares the students' work to more than 10 billion Web pages; 70 million student papers; 10,000 newspapers, magazines, and scholarly journals; plus thousands of books. Students who submit their work to Turnitin must agree to allow iParadigms to archive their papers in the Turnitin master file.

Does Gaining Unauthorized Access to an Online Service Violate the Computer Fraud and Abuse Act?

Four high school students who were required to submit their assignments to Turnitin filed a suit in a federal district court, claiming that the archiving of their papers infringed their copyright interests. The court found that the archiving of the papers qualified as a "fair use" and thus did not infringe the students' copyright interests. Hence, the court granted summary judgment for iParadigms, LLC, a decision that was upheld on appeal by the U.S. Court of Appeals for the Fourth Circuit.[a]

Meanwhile, iParadigms had counterclaimed, alleging that one of the high school students had gained unauthorized access to the company's online services in violation of the Computer Fraud and Abuse Act. Using a password and login ID obtained via the Internet, the student had registered and submitted papers to Turnitin, misrepresenting himself as a student of a university in which he was not enrolled and had never attended.

Was this a violation of the Computer Fraud and Abuse Act? The federal district court did not believe so. On appeal, though, the decision was reversed and remanded. The appellate court observed that iParadigms had to spend costly resources to determine whether there was a glitch in its online registration program. These expenses fell under the economic damages part of the act, which defines "loss" as:

> any reasonable cost to any victim, including the cost of responding to an offense, conducting a damage assessment, and restoring . . . the system . . . to its condition prior to the offense, and any revenue lost, cost incurred, or other consequential damages incurred because of interruption to service.[b]

The federal appeals court also ruled in iParadigms' favor on a separate counterclaim, finding that the defendant had violated the Virginia Computer Crimes Act.[c] The consequential damages presented by iParadigms fit within the "any damages" language of the Virginia law.

FOR CRITICAL ANALYSIS

What might have motivated the four high school students to bring this lawsuit?

a. *A.V. ex rel. Vanderhye v. iParadigms, LLC,* 562 F.3d 630 (4th Cir. 2009).

b. 18 U.S.C. Section 1030(a)(11).
c. Virginia Code Annotated Sections 18.2-152.3 and 18.2-152.6.

 ## Reviewing . . . Cyber Crime

One day, Kendra Donahue received an e-mail advertisement offering a free sample bottle of a "superfood" nutritional supplement made from acai berries, which are supposed to boost energy and aid weight loss. She clicked on the link to place an order and filled out an online form with her name, address, and credit-card number to pay for the shipping charges. Although Donahue read the terms displayed, nothing on the page indicated that she was signing up for a monthly shipment. Shortly before the bottle of pills arrived, Donahue received a phone call from her credit-card company asking if she had authorized a charge on her credit card at a grocery store in Israel. She told the company representative that she had not. When Donahue received her credit-card statement, she found a number of other unauthorized charges. A month later, she received a second bottle of the supplement in the mail and then discovered that her credit card had been charged $85 for this shipment. She called the 800 number on the invoice, but no one answered, so she contacted the seller via the Internet. An online agent at the seller's Web site indicated that she would cancel future monthly shipments to Donahue (but claimed that the terms were posted at the Web site). In order to obtain a refund, however, Donahue would have to pay to ship the bottle back to a post office box in Florida. If the bottle arrived within fifteen days, the company would refund the charges. When asked about the unauthorized charges on Donahue's card, the seller's agent claimed that the company did not sell her credit-card information to any third party or have any contacts with Israel. Using the information presented in the chapter, answer the following questions.

1. What is the term for the type of e-mail that Donahue received offering a sample of the nutritional supplement?
2. Assuming that the information contained in the e-mail was not false or misleading, did it violate any federal law? Why or why not?
3. Is it clear that the company that sold the acai berry supplement to Donahue was engaged in a crime relating to her credit card? Why or why not?
4. Suppose that when Donahue clicked on the link in the e-mail, malicious software was downloaded onto her computer. Whenever Donahue subsequently typed in her personal information online, that program then recorded the keystrokes and sent the data to cyber crooks. What crime has been committed, and why might it be difficult to prosecute?

Business Application

How Can You Protect against Identity Theft?*

Victims of identity theft spend, on average, about six hundred hours resolving the situation after someone has fraudulently used their names to purchase goods or services, open accounts, or make unauthorized charges to their accounts. Moreover, businesses typically are unable to recoup the costs of these unauthorized purchases because they usually can hold only the thief responsible.

Sources of Information That Might Be Used

The rise in identity theft has been fueled by the vast amount of personal information stored in databases. Educational institutions, governments, and businesses all store vast quantities of information about their students, clients, and customers. As a number of recent incidents demonstrate, unless measures are taken to secure these databases, they are vulnerable to thieves.

For example, personal information was stolen from numerous universities (including Georgetown University, Ohio University, the University of Texas, and Vermont State College). Even more disturbing is the number of U.S. government databases that have been breached. For example, a laptop computer containing confidential information for about 26.5 million veterans was stolen from an employee at the U.S. Department of Veterans Affairs.

Cities, counties, Internet sources (such as Hotels.com and Neinet), insurance companies (such as Aetna), manufacturing firms (such as Honeywell), nonprofit organizations, and even newspapers (such as the *Boston Globe*) have lost copious amounts of personal information in the last few years. Thus, every business should take steps to secure its data.

CHECKLIST FOR THE BUSINESS OWNER

1. **Review what personal information is kept in your computer databases. Wherever possible, eliminate Social Security numbers and other personal information and code all account numbers to limit access to just you.**
2. **Review employee access to databases containing personal account information. Some employees should have no access, some limited access, and some full access. Instruct your employees in how computers and personal information are to be used and not used.**
3. **Establish policies on what types of information may be stored on portable sources, such as laptop computers. Monitoring is important. Also maintain accurate records of where confidential data are kept and who has access to the data.**
4. **Consider using passwords and digital signatures to protect your computer system and data against unauthorized use.**
5. **Shred paper documents as much as possible—remember that thieves may attempt to rummage through your trash.**
6. **Be prepared for possible identity theft when your wallet, purse, credit card, checks, or mail is stolen—report the loss immediately to credit-card companies, banks, and credit bureaus. Do not keep passwords or personal identification numbers in your wallet.**
7. **Avoid giving any personal information over the telephone and always verify the identity of the caller.**

*This *Business Application* is not meant to substitute for the services of an attorney who is licensed to practice law in your state.

Key Terms

botnet 179	encryption 186	Trojan horse 176
computer crime 172	hacker 179	virus 180
cyber crime 173	identity theft 175	vishing 177
cyber fraud 173	malware 180	worm 180
cyberstalking 177	phishing 176	
cyberterrorist 181	spam 182	

Chapter Summary: Cyber Crime

Computer Crime and the Internet (See pages 172–173.)	Most cyber crimes are not "new" types of crimes. Rather, they are traditional crimes committed in cyberspace.
Cyber Crimes against Persons and Property (See pages 173–179.)	1. *Cyber consumer fraud*—When misrepresentations are knowingly made over the Internet to deceive another, it is cyber fraud. The two most widely reported forms of cyber crime are online auction fraud and online retail fraud. 2. *Cyber theft*—In cyberspace, thieves can steal data from anywhere in the world. Their task is made easier by the fact that many e-businesses store information such as the consumer's name, e-mail address, and credit-card numbers. Phishing, vishing, and employment fraud are variations of identity theft. 3. *Cyberstalking*—Cyberstalking is pervasive because harassing someone with electronic messages takes less effort than physically stalking; there is no possibility of physical confrontation; and a cyberstalker can reach the victim from anywhere.
Cyber Crimes in the Business World (See pages 179–182.)	1. *Credit-card crime*—The financial burden of stolen credit-card numbers falls on merchants and credit-card issuers more than consumers. 2. *Hackers*—A hacker is a person who uses one computer to break into another. The danger posed by hackers is significantly greater when they appropriate networks of computers, called botnets. 3. *Malware*—Malware is any program that is harmful to a computer or, by extension, a computer user. Worms, viruses, and botnets are examples. 4. *Juvenile cyber crime*—The Internet makes juvenile cyber crime easier for three reasons: (a) Juveniles can commit crimes without leaving their homes; (b) the anonymity of cyberspace allows young people to commit crimes that would otherwise be almost impossible, given their limitations of size, funds, and experience; and (c) hacking and other cyber crimes are often not recognized as unethical in youth culture. 5. *Hacking and cyberterrorism*—Some hackers simply want to prove how smart they are, but others have more malicious purposes. Cyberterrorists aim to cause serious problems for computer systems. They may target businesses to find out a firm's plans or transactions, or insert false codes or data to damage a firm's product. A cyberterrorist attack on a major U.S. financial institution or telecommunications system could have serious repercussions, including jeopardizing national security. 6. *Pirating of intellectual property*—On the Internet, millions of unauthorized high-quality copies of intellectual property can be reproduced at the click of a mouse. In addition to music CDs, a great deal of business software is pirated, and this poses significant problems for today's businesspersons.
The Spread of Spam (See pages 182–183.)	Unsolicited junk e-mail accounts for nearly three-quarters of all e-mails. Laws to combat spam have been enacted by thirty-six states and the federal government, but the flow of spam continues. In 2006, Congress enacted the U.S. Safe Web Act to address the problems with spam that originates from other nations and allow the federal government to investigate cross-border spammers.

Continued

Chapter Summary: Cyber Crime—Continued

Cyber Crimes against the Community— Gambling in Cyberspace (See pages 183–185.)	One of the biggest challenges in cyberspace is how to enforce laws that make it a crime to engage in certain activities, such as gambling, in some situations but not in others. All states have laws regulating gambling, but it has been difficult to enforce laws prohibiting gambling on the Internet. In 2006, Congress passed the Unlawful Internet Gambling Enforcement Act, which barred the use of electronic payments at Internet gambling sites.
Fighting Cyber Crime (See pages 185–187.)	Prosecuting cyber crime is more difficult than traditional crime. Identifying the wrongdoer through electronic fingerprints left on the Internet is complicated, and there are sometimes jurisdictional issues when the suspect lives in another jurisdiction or nation. A significant federal statute is the Computer Fraud and Abuse Act of 1984, as amended by the National Information Infrastructure Protection Act of 1996. The most successful way of fighting cyber crime, however, may be the use of encryption by private businesses to protect data.

 ExamPrep

ISSUE SPOTTERS

1 Ben downloads consumer credit files from a computer of Consumer Credit Agency, without permission. He then sells the data to Dawn. Has Ben committed a crime? If so, what is it?

2 Pete is a college student who is addicted to gambling. Stacey operates a gambling Web site from his residence in Gibraltar. Stacey allows Pete to place bets via the Internet using his credit card for payment. Has Stacey violated any criminal laws in the United States? If so, what law has he violated?

BEFORE THE TEST

Check your answers to the Issue Spotters, and at the same time, take the interactive quiz for this chapter. Go to **www.cengage.com/blaw/blt** and click on "Chapter 7." First, click on "Answers to Issue Spotters" to check your answers. Next, click on "Interactive Quiz" to assess your mastery of the concepts in this chapter. Then click on "Flashcards" to review this chapter's Key Term definitions.

 For Review

Answers for the even-numbered questions in this **For Review** *section can be found on this text's accompanying Web site at* **www.cengage.com/blaw/blt**. *Select "Chapter 7" and click on "For Review."*

1 What distinguishes cyber crime from "traditional" crime?

2 How has the Internet expanded opportunities for identity theft?

3 What are three reasons that cyberstalking may be more commonplace than physical stalking?

4 What are three major reasons that the Internet is conducive to juvenile cyber crime?

5 How do encryption programs protect digital data from unauthorized access?

 Hypothetical Scenarios and Case Problems

7–1 Cyber Scam. Kayla, a student at Learnwell University, owes $20,000 in unpaid tuition. If Kayla does not pay the tuition, Learnwell will not allow her to graduate. To obtain the funds to pay the debt, she sends e-mail letters to persons that she does not know asking them for financial help to send her child, who has a disability, to a special school. In reality, Kayla has no children. Is this a crime? If so, which one?

7–2 Types of Crimes. The following situations are similar, but each represents a variation of a particular crime. Identify the crime and point out the differences in the variations.

1 Chen, posing fraudulently as Diamond Credit Card Co., e-mails Emily, stating that the company has observed "suspicious" activity in her account and has frozen the account. The e-mail asks her to "re-register" her credit-card number and password to reopen the account.

2 Claiming falsely to be Big Buy Retail Finance Co., Conner e-mails Dino, asking him to "confirm or update" his "personal security information" to prevent his Big Buy account from being discontinued.

3 Felicia posts her résumé on GotWork.com, an online job- and résumé-posting site, seeking a position in business and managerial finance and accounting. Hayden, who misrepresents himself as an employment officer with International Bank & Commerce Corp., sends her an e-mail asking for more personal information.

7–3 **Hypothetical Question with Sample Answer** Simon's credit-card limit has been reached. He owes more than $10,000. Titan Credit Corp., the creditor, refuses to extend the time for payment. Using his extensive knowledge of software code, Simon appropriates from his home computer other computers to "break" into Titan's network and alter figures in its database to indicate that his debt has been paid. Simon intends to "fix" the figures when he can actually pay the debt. What is the term for what Simon has done? Is this a crime? If so, which one?

—For a sample answer to Question 7–3, go to Appendix E at the end of this text.

7–4 **Information Protection.** Oliver uses his knowledge of computers and software to enter into, without authority, the databases of government agencies and private companies, which often never realize that their systems have been breached. One evening, Oliver breaches a data bank of Peppy Energy Drinks, Inc., discovering confidential marketing plans. Oliver copies the plans, which he then offers for sale to Quito Beverage Co., Peppy's competitor. If Oliver does not otherwise disturb Peppy's data, has he committed a crime? If so, what are the penalties? What might Peppy do to prevent similar breaches in the future?

7–5 **Case Problem with Sample Answer** Oleksiy Sharapka ordered merchandise online using stolen credit cards. He had the items sent to outlets of Mail Boxes, Etc., and then arranged for someone to deliver the items to his house. He subsequently shipped the goods overseas, primarily to Russia. Sharapka was indicted in a federal district court. At the time of his arrest, government agents found in his possession, among other things, more than three hundred stolen credit-card numbers, including numbers issued by American Express. There was evidence that he had used more than ten of the American Express numbers to buy goods worth between $400,000 and $1 million from at least fourteen vendors. Did Sharapka commit any crimes? If so, who were his victims? Explain. [*United States v. Sharapka,* 526 F.3d 58 (1st Cir. 2008)]

—After you have answered Problem 7–5, compare your answer with the sample answer given on the Web site that accompanies this text. Go to **www.cengage.com/blaw/blt**, select "Chapter 7," and click on "Case Problem with Sample Answer."

7–6 **Online Gambling.** Internet Community & Entertainment Corp. operated Betcha.com, an online person-to-person betting platform. For a small fee, a user who registered and funded an account could offer bets to, and accept bets from, other users. A user had to agree that bets were "nonbinding"; bettors were not required to pay if they lost. When a user listed a bet, the site deducted a fee from the user's account. When a bettor accepted the bet, the site deducted a matching fee from the bettor's account. Wagered funds were placed in escrow until the bet was settled. The Washington State Gambling Commission executed a search warrant against the site's offices and seized its computers. Betcha.com filed a suit against the state. Does wagering on Betcha.com meet the definition of *gambling*? Explain. [*Internet Community & Entertainment Corp. v. State,* 148 Wash.App. 795, 201 P.3d 1045 (Div. 2 2009)]

7–7 **Intellectual Property.** Jiri Klimecek was a member of a group that overrode copyright protection in movies, video games, and software and then made them available for download online. Klimecek bought and installed hardware and software to set up a computer server and paid half of the monthly service charges to connect the server to the Internet. He knew that users around the world could access the server to upload and download copyrighted works. He obtained access to Czech movies and music to make them available. Klimecek was indicted in a federal district court for copyright infringement. He claimed that he did not understand the full scope of the operation. Did Klimecek commit a crime? If so, was he a "minor participant" entitled to a reduced sentence? Explain. [*United States v. Klimecek,* __ F.3d __ (7th Cir. 2009)]

7–8 **A Question of Ethics** *Davis Omole had good grades in high school, where he played on the football and chess teams, and went on to college. Twenty-year-old Omole was also one of the chief architects of a scheme through which more than one hundred individuals were defrauded. Omole worked at a cell phone store where he stole customers' personal information. He and others used the stolen identities to create a hundred different accounts on eBay, through which they held more than three hundred auctions listing for sale items (such as cell phones, plasma televisions, stereos, and more) that they did not own and did not intend to sell. From these auctions, they collected $90,000. To avoid getting caught, they continuously closed and opened the eBay accounts, activated and deactivated cell phone and e-mail accounts, and changed mailing addresses and post office boxes. Omole, who had previously been convicted in a state court for Internet fraud, was convicted in a federal district court of identity theft and wire fraud.* [*United States v. Omole,* 523 F.3d 691 (7th Cir. 2008)]

1 Before Omole's trial, he sent e-mail messages to his victims ridiculing them and calling them stupid for having been cheated. During his trial, he displayed contempt for the court. What does this behavior suggest about Omole's ethics?

2 Under federal sentencing guidelines, Omole could have been imprisoned for more than eight years, but he received only three years, two of which comprised the mandatory sentence for identity theft. Was this sentence too lenient? Explain.

 ## Critical Thinking and Writing Assignments

7–9 **For Critical Analysis.** Cyber crime costs consumers millions of dollars per year, and it costs businesses, including banks and other credit-card issuers, even more. Nonetheless, when cyber criminals are caught and convicted, they are rarely ordered to pay restitution or sentenced to long prison terms. Do you think that stiffer sentences would reduce the amount of cyber crime? Why or why not?

 ## Practical Internet Exercises

Go to this text's Web site at **www.cengage.com/blaw/blt**, select "Chapter 7," and click on "Practical Internet Exercises." There you will find the following Internet research exercises that you can perform to learn more about the topics covered in this chapter.

Practical Internet Exercise 7–1: MANAGEMENT PERSPECTIVE—Hackers
Practical Internet Exercise 7–2: SOCIAL PERSPECTIVE—Legal and Illegal Uses of Spam
Practical Internet Exercise 7–3: INTERNATIONAL PERSPECTIVE—Fighting Cyber Crime Worldwide

Chapter 8

Ethics and Business Decision Making

(©Scott Waldron, 2009. Used under license from Shutterstock.com)

"New occasions teach new duties."

—James Russell Lowell, 1819–1891
(American editor, poet, and diplomat)

Chapter Outline

- Business Ethics
- Ethical Transgressions by Financial Institutions
- Approaches to Ethical Reasoning
- Making Ethical Business Decisions
- Practical Solutions to Corporate Ethics Questions
- Business Ethics on a Global Level

Learning Objectives

After reading this chapter, you should be able to answer the following questions:

1. What is business ethics, and why is it important?

2. How can business leaders encourage their companies to act ethically?

3. How do duty-based ethical standards differ from outcome-based ethical standards?

4. What are six guidelines that an employee can use to evaluate whether his or her actions are ethical?

5. What types of ethical issues might arise in the context of international business transactions?

In the early 2000s, ethics scandals erupted throughout corporate America. Heads of major corporations (some of which no longer exist) were tried for fraud, conspiracy, conspiracy to commit securities fraud, grand larceny, and obstruction of justice. Former multimillionaires (and even billionaires) who once ran multinational corporations are now serving sentences in federal penitentiaries. The giant energy company Enron in particular dominated headlines. Its investors lost around $60 billion when the company ceased to exist.

Fast-forward to the end of the 2000s. One man, Bernard Madoff, reportedly bilked investors out of more than $65 billion through a Ponzi[1] scheme that he had perpetrated for decades. Madoff's victims included not just naïve retirees but also some of the world's largest and best-known financial institutions such as the Royal Bank of Scotland, France's BNP Paribas, Spain's Banco Santander, and Japan's Nomura. But ethical lapses were not limited to Madoff. Ethical problems in many financial institutions contributed to the onset of the deepest recession since the Great Depression of the 1930s. Not only did some $9 trillion in investment capital evaporate, but millions of workers lost their jobs. The point is clear: the scope and scale of corporate unethical behavior, especially in the financial sector, skyrocketed in the first decade of the twenty-first century—with enormous repercussions for everyone, not just in the United States, but around the world.

---

1. A Ponzi scheme is a type of illegal pyramid scheme named after Charles Ponzi, who duped thousands of New England residents into investing in a postage-stamp speculation scheme in the 1920s.

As the chapter-opening quotation states, "New occasions teach new duties." Indeed, the ethics scandals of the last fifteen years have taught businesspersons all over the world that business ethics cannot be taken lightly. Acting ethically in a business context can mean billions of dollars—made or lost—for corporations, shareholders, and employees, and can have far-reaching effects on society and the global economy.

▶ Business Ethics

Ethics   Moral principles and values applied to social behavior.

As you might imagine, business ethics is derived from the concept of ethics. **Ethics** can be defined as the study of what constitutes right or wrong behavior. It is the branch of philosophy that focuses on morality and the way in which moral principles are derived and applied to one's conduct in daily life. Ethics has to do with questions relating to the fairness, justness, rightness, or wrongness of an action.

Business Ethics   Ethics in a business context; a consensus as to what constitutes right or wrong behavior in the world of business and the application of moral principles to situations that arise in a business setting.

Business ethics focuses on what constitutes right or wrong behavior in the business world and on how businesspersons apply moral and ethical principles to situations that arise in the workplace. Because business decision makers often address more complex ethical dilemmas than they face in their personal lives, business ethics is more complicated than personal ethics.

Why Is Business Ethics Important?

To see why business ethics is so important, reread the first paragraph of this chapter. All of the corporate executives who are sitting behind bars could have avoided these outcomes had they engaged in ethical decision making during their careers. As a result of their crimes, all of their companies suffered losses, and some, such as Enron, were forced to enter bankruptcy, causing thousands of workers to lose their jobs. If the executives had acted ethically, the corporations, shareholders, and employees of those companies would not have paid such a high price. Thus, an in-depth understanding of business ethics is important to the long-run viability of a corporation. It is also important to the well-being of individual officers and directors and to the firm's employees. Finally, unethical corporate decision making can negatively affect suppliers, consumers, the community, and society as a whole.

> "You never get a second chance to make a good first impression."
>
> Will Rogers, 1879–1935
> (American humorist)

The Moral Minimum

Moral Minimum   The minimum degree of ethical behavior expected of a business firm, which is usually defined as compliance with the law.

The minimum acceptable standard for ethical business behavior—known as the **moral minimum**—normally is considered to be compliance with the law. In many corporate scandals, had most of the businesspersons involved simply followed the law, they would not have gotten into trouble. Note, though, that in the interest of preserving personal freedom, as well as for practical reasons, the law does not—and cannot—codify all ethical requirements.

As they make business decisions, businesspersons must remember that just because an action is legal does not necessarily make it ethical. For instance, no law specifies the salaries that public corporations can pay their officers. Nevertheless, if a corporation pays its officers an excessive amount relative to other employees, or to what officers at other corporations are paid, the executives' compensation might be challenged as unethical. (Executive bonuses can also present ethical problems—see the discussion later in this chapter.)

"Gray Areas" in the Law

In many situations, business firms can predict with a fair amount of certainty whether a given action would be legal. For instance, firing an employee solely because of that person's race or gender would clearly violate federal laws prohibiting employment discrimination. In some situations, though, the legality of a particular action may be less clear. In part, this is because there are so many laws regulating business that it is increasingly possible to violate one of them without realizing it. The law also contains numerous "gray areas," making it difficult to predict with certainty how a court will apply a given law to a particular action.

"But in the business world, failure is rewarded with big bailouts."

In addition, many rules of law require a court to determine what is "foreseeable" or "reasonable" in a particular situation. Because a business has no way of predicting how a specific court will decide these issues, decision makers need to proceed with caution and evaluate an action and its consequences from an ethical perspective. The same problem often occurs in cases involving the Internet because it is often unclear how a court will apply existing laws in the context of cyberspace. Generally, if a company can demonstrate that it acted in good faith and responsibly in the circumstances, it has a better chance of successfully defending its action in court or before an administrative law judge.

Short-Run Profit Maximization

Some people argue that a corporation's only goal should be profit maximization, which will be reflected in a higher market value. When all firms strictly adhere to the goal of profit maximization, resources tend to flow to where they are most highly valued by society. Thus, in theory, profit maximization ultimately leads to the most efficient allocation of scarce resources.

Corporate executives and employees have to distinguish, however, between *short-run* and *long-run* profit maximization. In the short run, a company may increase its profits by continuing to sell a product, even though it knows that the product is defective. In the long run, though, because of lawsuits, large settlements, and bad publicity, such unethical conduct will cause profits to suffer. Thus, business ethics is consistent only with long-run profit maximization. An overemphasis on short-term profit maximization is the most common reason that ethical problems occur in business.

CASE EXAMPLE 8.1 When the powerful narcotic painkiller OxyContin was first marketed, its manufacturer, Purdue Pharma, claimed that it was unlikely to lead to drug addiction or abuse. Internal company documents later showed, however, that the company's executives knew that OxyContin could be addictive, but they kept this risk a secret to boost sales and maximize short-term profits. In 2007, Purdue Pharma and three former executives pleaded guilty to criminal charges that they misled regulators, patients, and physicians about OxyContin's risks of addiction. Purdue Pharma agreed to pay $600 million in fines and other payments. The three former executives agreed to pay $34.5 million in fines and were barred from federal health programs for a period of fifteen years—a ruling that was upheld by an administrative law judge in 2009. Thus, the company's focus on maximizing profits in the short run led to unethical conduct that hurt profits in the long run.[2] ●

The following case provides an example of unethical—and illegal—conduct designed to enhance a company's short-term outlook that in the end killed the firm.

> "*It's easy to make a buck. It's a lot tougher to make a difference.*"
> Tom Brokaw, 1940–present
> (American television journalist)

---

2. *United States v. Purdue Frederick Co., Inc.*, 495 F. Supp.2d 569 (W.D.Va. 2007); see also **www.oig.hhs.gov/ publications/docs/press/2009/hhs_oig_press_01232009.pdf**.

Case 8.1 — United States v. Skilling

United States Court of Appeals, Fifth Circuit, 554 F.3d 529 (2009).
www.ca5.uscourts.gov[a]

COMPANY PROFILE *In the 1990s, Enron Corporation was an international, multibillion-dollar enterprise consisting of four businesses that bought and sold energy, owned energy networks, and bought and sold bandwidth capacity. "Wholesale," the division that bought and sold energy wholesale, was the most profitable and accounted for 90 percent of Enron's revenues. Jeffrey Skilling–Enron's president and chief operating officer, and a member of its board of directors–boasted at a conference with financial analysts in January 2001 that Enron's retail energy and bandwidth sales divisions had "sustainable high earnings power." Skilling*

---

a. In the left-hand column, in the "Opinions" column, click on "Opinions Page." On that page, in the "and/or Docket number is:" box, type "06-20885" and click on "Search." In the result, click on the docket number to access the opinion. The U.S. Court of Appeals for the Fifth Circuit maintains this Web site.

Case 8.1–Continues next page ➡

Case 8.1–Continued

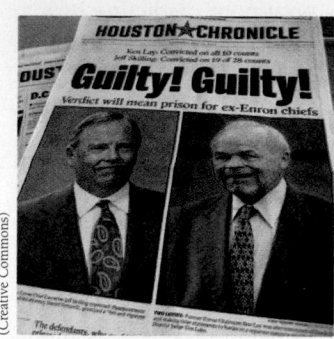

Jeffrey Skilling (left) and Enron's former chief executive officer, Kenneth Lay (right). Of what were they guilty?

became Enron's chief executive officer (CEO) in February 2001.

FACTS In August 2001, Jeffrey Skilling resigned his position as Enron's CEO. Four months later, Enron filed for bankruptcy. An investigation uncovered a conspiracy to deceive investors about Enron's finances to ensure that its stock price remained high. Among other things, Skilling had shifted more than $2 billion in losses from Enron's struggling divisions to Wholesale. He had overstated Enron's profits in calls to investors and in press releases. To hide more losses, he had arranged deals between Enron's executives and third parties, which he falsely portrayed to Enron's accountants and to the Securities and Exchange Commission as producing income. Skilling was convicted in a federal district court of various crimes, including conspiring to commit fraud to deprive Enron and its shareholders of the "honest services" of its employees. He was sentenced to 292 months' imprisonment and three years' supervised release, and ordered to pay $45 million in restitution. Skilling appealed.

ISSUE Is openly committing fraud in the corporate interest subject to penalties under federal law?

DECISION Yes. The U.S Court of Appeals for the Fifth Circuit affirmed the conviction but vacated the sentence on the ground that the lower court had enhanced it incorrectly. The case was remanded for resentencing.

REASON Skilling argued that because he did not act secretly in pursuit of Enron's goal of achieving a higher stock price, his conduct fell under an exception to honest-services fraud. Under this exception, "when an employer (1) creates a particular goal, (2) aligns the employees' interests with the employer's interest in achieving that goal, and (3) has higher-level management sanction improper conduct to reach the goal, then lower-level employees following their boss's direction are not liable for honest-services fraud." The court disagreed with Skilling's contention. Keeping the stock price high might have been in Enron's and Skilling's mutual interest, but "no one at Enron sanctioned Skilling's improper conduct." Neither the board of directors nor "any other decision maker specifically directed the improper means that he undertook to achieve his goals."

WHY IS THIS CASE IMPORTANT? *Nearly ten years after Enron's demise—at that time, one of the largest bankruptcies in U.S. history—Jeffrey Skilling still remains a symbol of corporate greed and deceit. By upholding his fraud convictions, the federal appellate court sent a clear message to the corporate world that unethical business practices have serious consequences.*

The Importance of Ethical Leadership

Talking about ethical business decision making is meaningless if management does not set standards. Furthermore, managers must apply the same standards to themselves as they do to the employees of the company.

> "What you do speaks so loudly that I cannot hear what you say."
> Ralph Waldo Emerson, 1803–1882
> (American essayist and poet)

ATTITUDE OF TOP MANAGEMENT One of the most important ways to create and maintain an ethical workplace is for top management to demonstrate its commitment to ethical decision making. A manager who is not totally committed to an ethical workplace rarely succeeds in creating one. Management's behavior, more than anything else, sets the ethical tone of a firm. Employees take their cues from management. **EXAMPLE 8.2** Devon, a SureTek employee, observes his manager cheating on her expense account. Devon quickly understands that such behavior is acceptable. Later, when Devon is promoted to a managerial position, he "pads" his expense account as well, knowing that he is unlikely to face sanctions for doing so. ●

Managers who set unrealistic production or sales goals increase the probability that employees will act unethically. If a sales quota can be met only through high-pressure, unethical sales tactics, employees will try to act "in the best interest of the company" and will continue to behave unethically.

A manager who looks the other way when she or he knows about an employee's unethical behavior also sets an example—one indicating that ethical transgressions will be accepted. Managers have found that discharging even one employee for ethical reasons has a tremendous impact as a deterrent to unethical behavior in the workplace.

BEHAVIOR OF OWNERS AND MANAGERS   Business owners and managers sometimes take more active roles in fostering unethical and illegal conduct. This may indicate to their co-owners, co-managers, employees, and others that unethical business behavior will be tolerated.

PERIODIC EVALUATION   Some companies require their managers to meet individually with employees and grade them on their ethical (or unethical) behavior. **EXAMPLE 8.3** Brighton Company asks its employees to fill out ethical checklists each month and return them to their supervisors. This practice serves two purposes: it demonstrates to employees that ethics matters, and it gives employees an opportunity to reflect on how well they have measured up in terms of ethical performance. ●

Creating Ethical Codes of Conduct

One of the most effective ways of setting a tone of ethical behavior within an organization is to create an ethical code of conduct. A well-written code of ethics explicitly states a company's ethical priorities and demonstrates the company's commitment to ethical behavior.

This chapter concludes with a foldout exhibit showing the code of ethics of Costco Wholesale Corporation as an example. This code of conduct indicates Costco's commitment to legal compliance, as well as to the welfare of its members (those who purchase its goods), its employees, and its suppliers. The code also details some specific ways in which the interests and welfare of these different groups will be protected. You will also see that Costco acknowledges that by protecting these groups' interests, it will realize its "ultimate goal"—rewarding its shareholders with maximum shareholder value.

PROVIDING ETHICS TRAINING TO EMPLOYEES   For an ethical code to be effective, its provisions must be clearly communicated to employees. Most large companies have implemented ethics training programs, in which managers discuss with employees on a face-to-face basis the firm's policies and the importance of ethical conduct. Some firms hold periodic ethics seminars during which employees can openly discuss any ethical problems that they may be experiencing and learn how the firm's ethical policies apply to those specific problems. Smaller firms should also offer some form of ethics training to employees because if a firm is accused of an ethics violation, the court will consider the presence or absence of such training in evaluating the firm's conduct.

Preventing Legal Disputes ⚖

To avoid disputes over ethical violations, you should first create a written ethical code that is expressed in clear and understandable language. The code should establish specific procedures that employees can follow if they have questions or complaints. It should assure employees that their jobs will be secure and that they will not face reprisals if they do file a complaint. A well-written code might also include examples to clarify what the company considers to be acceptable and unacceptable conduct. You should also hold periodic training meetings so that you can explain to employees face to face why ethics is important to the company.

ON THE WEB For an example of a company that provides online ethics and compliance training to companies nationwide, go to the Web site of Integrity Interactive Corporation at www.integrity-interactive.com/welcome.htm.

THE SARBANES-OXLEY ACT AND WEB-BASED REPORTING SYSTEMS   The Sarbanes-Oxley Act of 2002[3] requires companies to set up confidential systems so that employees and others can "raise red flags" about suspected illegal or unethical auditing and accounting practices. (The Sarbanes-Oxley Act will be discussed in more detail in Chapters 31 and 34, and excerpts and explanatory comments on this important law appear in Appendix D of this text.)

---

3. 15 U.S.C. Sections 7201 *et seq.*

Some companies have implemented online reporting systems to accomplish this goal. In one such system, employees can click on an icon on their computers that anonymously links them with EthicsPoint, an organization based in Portland, Oregon. Through EthicsPoint, employees can report suspicious accounting practices, sexual harassment, and other possibly unethical behavior. EthicsPoint, in turn, alerts management personnel or the audit committee at the designated company to the possible problem. Those who have used the system say that it is less inhibiting than calling a company's toll-free number.

▶ Ethical Transgressions by Financial Institutions

One of the best ways to learn the ethical responsibilities inherent in operating a business is to look at the mistakes made by other companies. In the following subsections, we describe some of the most egregious ethical failures of financial institutions during the late 2000s. Many of these ethical wrongdoings received wide publicity and raised public awareness of the need for ethical leadership throughout all businesses.

Corporate Stock Buybacks

By now, you are probably aware that many of the greatest financial companies in the United States have either gone bankrupt, been taken over by the federal government, or been bailed out by U.S. taxpayers. What most people do not know is that those same corporations were using their own cash funds to prop up the value of their stock in the years just before the economic crisis that started in 2008.

Stock Buyback   The purchase of shares of a company's own stock by that company on the open market.

The theory behind a **stock buyback** is simple—the management of a corporation believes that the market price of its shares is "below their fair value." Therefore, instead of issuing dividends to shareholders or reinvesting profits, management uses the company's funds to buy its shares in the open market, thereby boosting the price of the stock. From 2005 to 2007, stock buybacks for the top five hundred U.S. corporations added up to $1.4 *trillion*.

Stock Option   An agreement that grants the owner the option to buy a given number of shares of stock, usually within a set time period.

Who benefits from stock buybacks? The main individual beneficiaries are corporate executives who have been given **stock options,** which enable them to buy shares of the corporation's stock at a set price. When the market price rises above that level, the executives can profit by selling their shares. Although stock buybacks are legal and can serve legitimate purposes, they can easily be abused if managers use them just to increase the stock price in the short term so that they can profit from their options without considering the long-term needs of the company.

Lehman Brothers was an investment banking firm that had been in business for more than 150 years. When the U.S. Treasury refused to bail out the firm in 2008, it went bankrupt. Were its stock buybacks earlier that same year unethical? Why or why not?

In the investment banking business, which almost disappeared entirely in the latter half of 2008, stock buybacks were particularly egregious. In the first half of 2008, Lehman Brothers Holdings was buying back its own stock—yet in September of that year, it filed for bankruptcy. According to financial writer Liam Denning, Lehman's buybacks were "akin to giving away the fire extinguisher even as your house begins to fill with smoke." Goldman Sachs, another investment bank, bought back $15 billion of its stock in 2007. By the end of 2008, U.S. taxpayers had provided $10 billion in bailout funds to that same company.

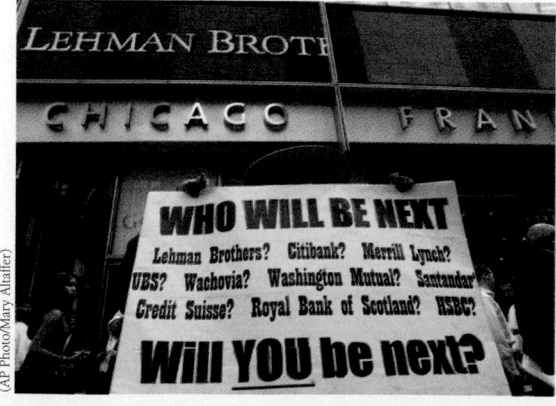

(AP Photo/Mary Altaffer)

Startling Executive Decisions at American International Group

For years, American International Group (AIG) was a respected, conservative worldwide insurance company based in New York. Then, during the early 2000s, it decided to enter an area in which it had little expertise—

the issuance of insurance contracts guaranteeing certain types of complicated financial contracts. When many of those insured contracts failed, AIG experienced multibillion-dollar losses. Finally, the company sought a federal bailout that eventually amounted to almost $200 billion of U.S. taxpayers' funds.

While some company executives were testifying before Congress after receiving the funds, other AIG executives spent almost $400,000 on a retreat at a resort in California. In essence, U.S. taxpayers were footing the bill. To most observers, such hubris was as incomprehensible as it was unethical.

Executive Bonuses

Until the economic crisis began in the late 2000s, the bonuses paid in the financial industry did not make headlines. After all, times were good, and why shouldn't those responsible for record company earnings be rewarded? When investment banks and commercial banks began to fail, however, or had to be bailed out or taken over by the federal government, executive bonuses became an issue of paramount importance.

Certainly, the system of rewards in banking became perverse during the 2000s. Executives and others in the industry were paid a percentage of their firm's profits, no matter how risky their investment actions had been. In other words, commissions and bonuses were based on sales of risky assets to investors. These included securities based on subprime mortgages, collateralized debt obligations, and other mortgages. When the subprime mortgage crisis started in 2007, the worldwide house of cards came tumbling down, but those who had created and sold those risky assets suffered no liability—and even received bonuses.

BONUSES AND SALARIES BEFORE THE CRISIS   Consider Lehman Brothers before its bankruptcy. Its chief executive officer, Richard Fuld, Jr., earned almost $500 million between 2000 and the firm's demise in 2008. Even after Lehman Brothers entered bankruptcy, its new owners, Barclays and Nomura, legally owed $3.5 billion in bonuses to employees still on the payroll. In 2006, Goldman Sachs awarded its employees a total of $16.5 billion in bonuses, or an average of almost $750,000 for each employee.

Overall, in 2007 profits on Wall Street had already begun to drop—sometimes dramatically. Citigroup's profits, for example, were down 83 percent compared to the previous year. Bonuses, in contrast, declined by less than 5 percent. The bonus payout in 2007 for all Wall Street firms combined was $33.2 billion.

SOME BONUSES WERE PAID EARLY   Another flagrant example of what could be deemed inappropriate compensation involved executives at Merrill Lynch. In 2008, the company suffered huge losses, many of which were not fully disclosed when Bank of America bought Merrill Lynch at the end of that year. Nevertheless, executives at Merrill Lynch passed out $5 billion in bonuses in December—before the takeover and earlier than management had allowed in previous years. One month later, Bank of America had to ask the federal government—that is, U.S. taxpayers—for an additional bailout of $20 billion.

CONGRESS ACTS TO LIMIT BONUSES   In response to mounting public outrage about the bonuses paid by firms receiving taxpayer funds, Congress included a provision in the American Recovery and Reinvestment Tax Act of 2009 that appeared likely to change the compensation system in the financial industry dramatically. The provision did not cap executive salaries but

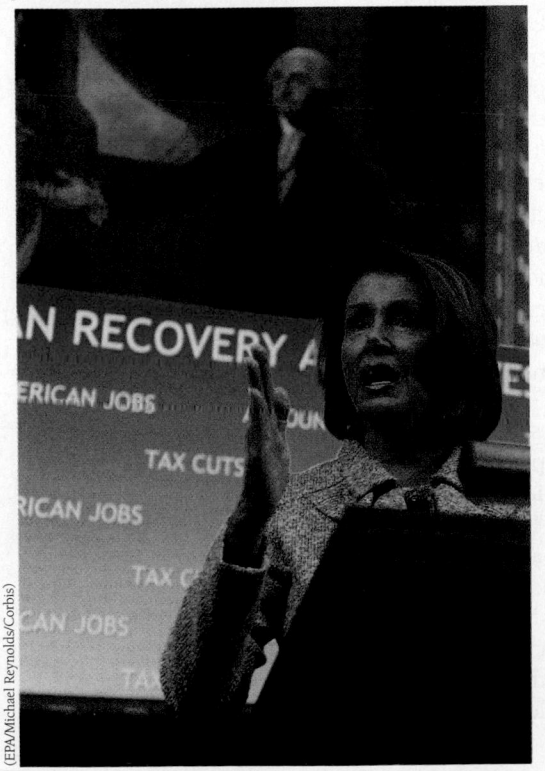

Speaker of the House Nancy Pelosi presents the American Recovery and Reinvestment Act (the economic stimulus bill) before it was passed by Congress and signed into law by President Barack Obama. One provision in that act restricted bonuses that can be paid by companies receiving bailout funds from the U.S. government. Why did the government seek to restrict bonus payments in the financial industry?

(EPA/Michael Reynolds/Corbis)

instead severely restricted the bonuses that can be paid by firms that receive bailout funds under the Troubled Asset Relief Program (TARP).[4]

The act prohibits such a firm from paying any cash bonuses to its five most senior officers and its twenty highest-paid executives. Any bonuses that are paid must be in the form of restricted stock that cannot be sold until the firm has paid back all of the TARP funds that it has received. Furthermore, even these bonuses cannot exceed one-third of an executive's annual salary. Although some observers pointed out that the new rules would likely make it difficult for firms to keep valued employees, others saw the restrictions as an appropriate response to an industry that appeared to have lost its ethical bearings.

▶ Approaches to Ethical Reasoning

Ethical Reasoning A reasoning process in which an individual links his or her moral convictions or ethical standards to the particular situation at hand.

Each individual, when faced with a particular ethical dilemma, engages in **ethical reasoning**—that is, a reasoning process in which the individual examines the situation at hand in light of his or her moral convictions or ethical standards. Businesspersons do likewise when making decisions with ethical implications.

How do business decision makers decide whether a given action is the "right" one for their firms? What ethical standards should be applied? Broadly speaking, ethical reasoning relating to business traditionally has been characterized by two fundamental approaches. One approach defines ethical behavior in terms of duty, which also implies certain rights. The other approach determines what is ethical in terms of the consequences, or outcome, of any given action. We examine each of these approaches here.

In addition to the two basic ethical approaches, several theories have been developed that specifically address the social responsibility of corporations. Because these theories also influence today's business decision makers, we conclude this section with a short discussion of the different views of corporate social responsibility.

Duty-Based Ethics

Duty-based ethical standards often are derived from revealed truths, such as religious precepts. They can also be derived through philosophical reasoning.

RELIGIOUS ETHICAL STANDARDS   In the Judeo-Christian tradition, which is the dominant religious tradition in the United States, the Ten Commandments of the Old Testament establish fundamental rules for moral action. Other religions have their own sources of revealed truth. Religious rules generally are absolute with respect to the behavior of their adherents. **EXAMPLE 8.4**   The commandment "Thou shalt not steal" is an absolute mandate for a person who believes that the Ten Commandments reflect revealed truth. Even a benevolent motive for stealing (such as Robin Hood's) cannot justify the act because the act itself is inherently immoral and thus wrong. ●

"When I do good, I feel good. When I do bad, I feel bad. And that's my religion."

Abraham Lincoln, 1809–1865
(Sixteenth president of the United States, 1861–1865)

KANTIAN ETHICS   Duty-based ethical standards may also be derived solely from philosophical reasoning. The German philosopher Immanuel Kant (1724–1804), for example, identified some general guiding principles for moral behavior based on what he believed to be the fundamental nature of human beings. Kant believed that human beings are qualitatively different from other physical objects and are endowed with moral integrity and the capacity to reason and conduct their affairs rationally. Therefore, a person's thoughts and actions should be respected. When human beings are treated merely as a means to an end, they are being treated as the equivalent of objects and are being denied their basic humanity.

A central theme in Kantian ethics is that individuals should evaluate their actions in light of the consequences that would follow if *everyone* in society acted in the same way.

---

4. 12 U.S.C. Section 5211.

Categorical Imperative A concept developed by the philosopher Immanuel Kant as an ethical guideline for behavior. In deciding whether an action is right or wrong, or desirable or undesirable, a person should evaluate the action in terms of what would happen if everybody else in the same situation, or category, acted the same way.

This **categorical imperative** can be applied to any action. **EXAMPLE 8.5** Suppose that you are deciding whether to cheat on an examination. If you have adopted Kant's categorical imperative, you will decide *not* to cheat because if everyone cheated, the examination (and the entire education system) would be meaningless. ●

THE PRINCIPLE OF RIGHTS   Because a duty cannot exist without a corresponding right, duty-based ethical standards imply that human beings have basic rights. The principle that human beings have certain fundamental rights (to life, liberty, and the pursuit of happiness, for example) is deeply embedded in Western culture. As discussed in Chapter 1, the natural law tradition embraces the concept that certain actions (such as killing another person) are morally wrong because they are contrary to nature (the natural desire to continue living). Those who adhere to this **principle of rights**, or "rights theory," believe that a key factor in determining whether a business decision is ethical is how that decision affects the rights of others. These others include the firm's owners, its employees, the consumers of its products or services, its suppliers, the community in which it does business, and society as a whole.

Principle of Rights The principle that human beings have certain fundamental rights (to life, liberty, and the pursuit of happiness, for example). Those who adhere to this "rights theory" believe that a key factor in determining whether a business decision is ethical is how that decision affects the rights of various groups. These groups include the firm's owners, its employees, the consumers of its products or services, its suppliers, the community in which it does business, and society as a whole.

A potential dilemma for those who support rights theory, however, is that there are often conflicting rights and people may disagree on which rights are most important. When considering all those affected by a business decision, for example, how much weight should be given to employees relative to shareholders, customers relative to the community, or employees relative to society as a whole?

In general, rights theorists believe that whichever right is stronger in a particular circumstance takes precedence. **EXAMPLE 8.6** A firm can either keep a manufacturing plant open, saving the jobs of twelve workers, or shut the plant down and avoid contaminating a river with pollutants that would endanger the health of tens of thousands of people. In this situation, a rights theorist can easily choose which group to favor. (Not all choices are so clear-cut, however.) ●

Outcome-Based Ethics: Utilitarianism

"The greatest good for the greatest number" is a paraphrase of the major premise of the utilitarian approach to ethics. **Utilitarianism** is a philosophical theory developed by Jeremy Bentham (1748–1832) and modified by John Stuart Mill (1806–1873)—both British philosophers. In contrast to duty-based ethics, utilitarianism is outcome oriented. It focuses on the consequences of an action, not on the nature of the action itself or on any set of preestablished moral values or religious beliefs.

Utilitarianism An approach to ethical reasoning that evaluates behavior in light of the consequences of that behavior for those who will be affected by it, rather than on the basis of any absolute ethical or moral values. In utilitarian reasoning, a "good" decision is one that results in the greatest good for the greatest number of people affected by the decision.

Under a utilitarian model of ethics, an action is morally correct, or "right," when, among the people it affects, it produces the greatest amount of good for the greatest number. When an action affects the majority adversely, it is morally wrong. Applying the utilitarian theory thus requires (1) a determination of which individuals will be affected by the action in question; (2) a **cost-benefit analysis**, which involves an assessment of the negative and positive effects of alternative actions on these individuals; and (3) a choice among alternative actions that will produce maximum societal utility (the greatest positive net benefits for the greatest number of individuals).

Cost-Benefit Analysis A decision-making technique that involves weighing the costs of a given action against the benefits of that action.

Corporate Social Responsibility

For many years, groups concerned with civil rights, employee safety and welfare, consumer protection, environmental preservation, and other causes have pressured corporate America to behave in a responsible manner with respect to these causes. Thus was born the concept of **corporate social responsibility**—the idea that those who run corporations can and should act ethically and be accountable to society for their actions. Just what constitutes corporate social responsibility has been debated for some time, however, and there are a number of different theories today.

Corporate Social Responsibility The idea that corporations can and should act ethically and be accountable to society for their actions.

STAKEHOLDER APPROACH   One view of corporate social responsibility stresses that corporations have a duty not just to shareholders, but also to other groups affected by corporate decisions ("stakeholders"). Under this approach, a corporation would consider the impact of its decision on the firm's employees, customers, creditors, suppliers, and the community in which the corporation operates. The reasoning behind this "stakeholder view" is that in some circumstances, one or more of these other groups may have a greater stake in company decisions than the shareholders do. Although this may be true, as mentioned earlier in this chapter, it is often difficult to decide which group's interests should receive greater weight if the interests conflict.

EXAMPLE 8.7   During our worst recession in decades in the late 2000s, layoffs numbered in the millions. Nonetheless, some corporations succeeded in reducing labor costs without layoffs. To avoid slashing their workforces, these employers turned to alternatives such as (1) four-day work weeks, (2) unpaid vacations and voluntary furloughs, (3) wage freezes, (4) pension cuts, and (5) flexible work schedules. Some companies asked for and received from their workers 1 percent wage cuts to prevent layoffs. Examples of companies finding alternatives to layoffs included the computermaker Dell (extended unpaid holidays), network router company Cisco Systems (four-day end-of-year shutdowns), Motorola (salary cuts), and Honda (voluntary unpaid vacation time). Professor Jennifer Chatman remarked, "Organizations are trying to cut costs in the name of avoiding layoffs. It's not just that organizations are saying 'we're cutting costs,' they're saying: 'we're doing this to keep from losing people.'"[5] ●

Bill Gates, founder and former chairman of Microsoft, Inc., with his wife, Melinda, at a press conference concerning their charity foundation. Bill Gates indicated that he would launch a campaign to encourage the wealthiest Chinese to sign up for philanthropic endeavors. They also announced a $34 million grant to the Global Network for Neglected Tropical Diseases. How do their charitable actions reflect on the business community at large?

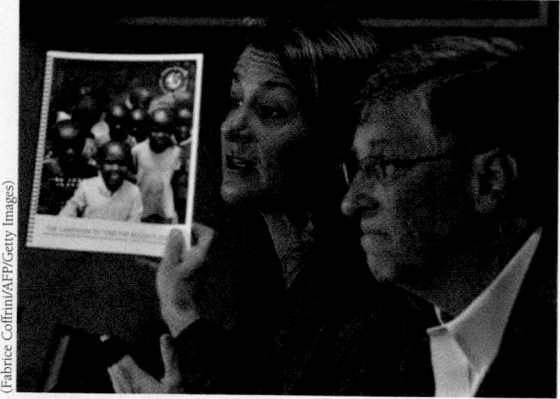

(Fabrice Coffrini/AFP/Getty Images)

CORPORATE CITIZENSHIP   Another theory of social responsibility argues that corporations should behave as good citizens by promoting goals that society deems worthwhile and taking positive steps toward solving social problems. The idea is that because business controls so much of the wealth and power of this country, business, in turn, has a responsibility to society to use that wealth and power in socially beneficial ways. Under a corporate citizenship view, companies are judged on how much they donate to social causes, as well as how they conduct their operations with respect to employment discrimination, human rights, environmental concerns, and similar issues.

In the following case, a corporation's board of directors focused solely on the shareholders' profits and failed to check the actions of the firm's chief executive officer (CEO). If the board had applied a different set of priorities, the shareholders might have been in a better financial position, however.

5. Jennifer Chatman is a professor at the Hass School of Business at the University of California–Berkeley. This quotation is from Matt Richtel, "Some Firms Use Scalpel, Not Ax, to Cut Costs," *The New York Times,* December 28, 2008.

Case 8.2   **Fog Cutter Capital Group, Inc. v. Securities and Exchange Commission**

United States Court of Appeals, District of Columbia, 474 F.3d 822 (2007).

FACTS   The National Association of Securities Dealers (NASD) operates the Nasdaq, an electronic securities exchange, on which Fog Cutter Capital Group was listed.[a] Andrew Wiederhorn founded Fog Cutter in 1997 to manage a restaurant chain and make other investments. With family

a. Securities (stocks and bonds) can be bought and sold through national exchanges. Whether a security is listed on an exchange is subject to the discretion of the organization that operates it. The Securities and Exchange Commission oversees the securities exchanges (see Chapter 31).

members, Wiederhorn controlled more than 50 percent of Fog Cutter's stock. The firm agreed that if Wiederhorn was terminated "for cause," he was entitled only to his salary through the date of termination. If terminated "without cause," he would be owed three times his $350,000 annual salary, three times his largest annual bonus from the previous three years, and any unpaid salary and bonus. "Cause" included the conviction of a felony. In 2001, Wiederhorn became the target of an investigation into the collapse of Capital Consultants, LLC. Fog Cutter then redefined "cause" in his termination agreement to cover only a felony involving Fog Cutter. In June 2004,

Case 8.2–Continued

Andrew Wiederhorn just prior to his lengthy federal prison term. While in prison, he continued to receive salary payments from Fog Cutter Capital Group.

Wiederhorn agreed to plead guilty to two felonies, serve eighteen months in prison, pay a $25,000 fine, and pay $2 million to Capital Consultants. The day before he entered his plea, Fog Cutter agreed that while he was in prison, he would keep his title, responsibilities, salary, bonuses, and other benefits. It also agreed to a $2 million "leave of absence payment." In July, the NASD delisted Fog Cutter from the Nasdaq. Fog Cutter appealed this decision to the Securities and Exchange Commission (SEC), which dismissed the appeal. Fog Cutter petitioned the U.S. Court of Appeals for the District of Columbia Circuit for review.

ISSUE Was the SEC's action justified?

DECISION Yes. The U.S. Court of Appeals for the District of Columbia Circuit denied the firm's petition for review. The SEC's dismissal was not "arbitrary, capricious, or an abuse of discretion."

REASON Fog Cutter's deals with Wiederhorn indicated that, as the SEC found, he had "thorough control" over the firm. As further evidence in support of the SEC's decision, the court noted that Fog Cutter had done nothing to check Wiederhorn's conduct. In fact, the board's actions only "aggravated the concerns Wiederhorn's conviction and imprisonment raised." In its petition for review of the SEC's dismissal, Fog Cutter claimed that the NASD's decision was unfair. The court pointed out, however, that the decision was in accord with the NASD's rules, which gave it "broad discretion to determine whether the public interest requires delisting securities in light of events at a company." In this case, "Fog Cutter made a deal with Wiederhorn that cost the company $4.75 million in a year in which it reported a $3.93 million net loss. We know as well that Fog Cutter handed Wiederhorn a $2 million bonus right before he went off to prison, a bonus stemming directly from the consequences of Wiederhorn's criminal activity." Fog Cutter knew that Wiederhorn would use this "bonus" to pay Capital Consultants. In its appeal, Fog Cutter also claimed that if it fired Wiederhorn in light of his guilty plea, it would have to pay him $6 million under his termination agreement. But, the court responded, Fog Cutter amended this agreement during the investigation of Wiederhorn "knowing full well" that it would "dramatically" increase the cost of firing him.

FOR CRITICAL ANALYSIS—Ethical Consideration *Should more consideration have been given to the fact that Fog Cutter was not convicted of a violation of the law? Why or why not?*

A Way of Doing Business. A survey of U.S. executives undertaken by the Boston College Center for Corporate Citizenship found that more than 70 percent of those polled agreed that corporate citizenship must be treated as a priority. More than 60 percent said that good corporate citizenship added to their companies' profits. Strategist Michelle Bernhart has argued that corporate social responsibility cannot attain its maximum effectiveness unless it is treated as a way of doing business rather than as a special program.

Not all socially responsible activities can benefit a corporation, however. Corporate responsibility is most successful when a company undertakes activities that are relevant and significant to its stakeholders and related to its business operations. **EXAMPLE 8.8** The Brazilian firm Companhia Vale do Rio Doce is one of the world's largest diversified metals and mining companies. In 2008, it invested more than $150 million in social projects, including healthcare, infrastructure, and education. At the same time, it invested more than $300 million in environmental protection. One of its projects involves the rehabilitation of native species in the Amazon valley. To that end, it is planting almost 200 million trees in an attempt to restore 1,150 square miles of land where cattle breeding and farming have caused deforestation. •

The Employee Recruiting and Retention Advantage. One key corporate stakeholder is of course a company's workforce, which may include potential employees—job seekers. Surveys of college students about to enter the job market confirm that young people are looking for socially responsible employers. Younger workers generally are altruistic. They want to work for a company that allows them to participate in community projects. Corporations that engage in meaningful social activities find that they retain workers longer, particularly younger ones. **EXAMPLE 8.9** At the accounting firm PKF Texas, employees support a variety of business, educational, and philanthropic organizations. As a result, this company is able to recruit and retain a younger workforce. Its average turnover rate is half the industry average. •

▶ Making Ethical Business Decisions

As Dean Krehmeyer, executive director of the Business Roundtable's Institute for Corporate Ethics, once said, "Evidence strongly suggests being ethical—doing the right thing—pays." Instilling ethical business decision making into the fabric of a business organization is no small task, even if ethics "pays." The job is to encourage people to understand that they have to think more broadly about how their decisions will affect employees, shareholders, customers, and even the community. Great companies, such as Enron and the worldwide accounting firm Arthur Andersen, were brought down by the unethical behavior of a few. A two-hundred-year-old British investment bank, Barings Bank, was destroyed by the actions of one employee and a few of his friends. Clearly, ensuring that all employees get on the ethical business decision-making "bandwagon" is crucial in today's fast-paced world.

The George S. May International Company has provided six basic guidelines to help corporate employees judge their actions. Each employee—no matter what her or his level in the organization—should evaluate her or his actions using the following six guidelines:

1. *The law.* Is the action you are considering legal? If you do not know the laws governing the action, then find out. Ignorance of the law is no excuse.
2. *Rules and procedures.* Are you following the internal rules and procedures that have already been laid out by your company? They have been developed to avoid problems. Is what you are planning to do consistent with your company's policies and procedures? If not, stop.
3. *Values.* Laws and internal company policies reinforce society's values. You might wish to ask yourself whether you are attempting to find a loophole in the law or in your company's policies. Next, you have to ask yourself whether you are following the "spirit" of the law as well as the letter of the law or the internal policy.
4. *Conscience.* If you feel any guilt, let your conscience be your guide. Alternatively, ask yourself whether you would be happy to be interviewed by the national news media about the actions you are going to take.
5. *Promises.* Every business organization is based on trust. Your customers believe that your company will do what it is supposed to do. The same is true for your suppliers and employees. Will your actions live up to the commitments you have made to others, both inside the business and outside?
6. *Heroes.* We all have heroes who are role models for us. Is what you are planning on doing an action that your "hero" would take? If not, how would your hero act? That is how you should be acting.

> "Never let your sense of morals prevent you from doing what is right."
>
> Isaac Asimov, 1920–1992
> (Russian-born writer and scientist)

▶ Practical Solutions to Corporate Ethics Questions

Corporate ethics officers and ethics committees require a practical method to investigate and solve specific ethics problems. Ethics consultant Leonard H. Bucklin of Corporate-Ethics.US has devised a procedure that he calls Business Process Pragmatism.[6] It involves the following five steps:

1. *Inquiry.* Of course, an understanding of the facts must be the initial action. The parties involved might include the mass media, the public, employees, or customers. At this stage of the process, the ethical problem or problems are specified. A list of relevant ethical principles is created.
2. *Discussion.* Here, a list of action options is developed. Each option carries with it certain ethical principles. Finally, resolution goals should also be listed.

---

6. Corporate-Ethics and Business Process Pragmatism are registered trademarks.

3. *Decision.* Working together, those participating in the process craft a consensus decision, or a consensus plan of action for the corporation.
4. *Justification.* Does the consensus solution withstand moral scrutiny? At this point in the process, reasons should be attached to each proposed action or series of actions. Will the stakeholders involved accept these reasons?
5. *Evaluation.* Do the solutions to the corporate ethics issue satisfy corporate values, community values, and individual values? Ultimately, can the consensus resolution to the corporate ethics problem withstand the moral scrutiny of the decisions taken and the process used to reach those decisions?

▶ Business Ethics on a Global Level

> "Next to doing the right thing, the most important thing is to let people know you are doing the right thing."
>
> John D. Rockefeller, 1839–1897
> (American industrialist and philanthropist)

Given the various cultures and religions throughout the world, it is not surprising that conflicts in ethics frequently arise between foreign and U.S. businesspersons. **EXAMPLE 8.10** In certain countries, the consumption of alcohol and specific foods is forbidden for religious reasons. Under such circumstances, it would be thoughtless and imprudent for a U.S. businessperson to invite a local business contact out for a drink. ●

The role played by women in other countries may also present some difficult ethical problems for firms doing business internationally. Equal employment opportunity is a fundamental public policy in the United States, and Title VII of the Civil Rights Act of 1964 prohibits discrimination against women in the employment context (see Chapter 25). Some other countries, however, offer little protection for women against gender discrimination in the workplace, including sexual harassment.

We look here at how laws governing workers in other countries, particularly developing countries, have created some especially difficult ethical problems for U.S. sellers of goods manufactured in foreign countries. We also examine some of the ethical ramifications of laws prohibiting U.S. businesspersons from bribing foreign officials to obtain favorable business contracts.

ON THE WEB Global Exchange offers information on global business activities, including some of the ethical issues stemming from those activities, at www.globalexchange.org

Monitoring the Employment Practices of Foreign Suppliers

Many U.S. businesses now contract with companies in developing nations to produce goods, such as shoes and clothing, because the wage rates in those nations are significantly lower than wages in the United States. Yet what if a foreign company exploits its workers—by hiring women and children at below-minimum-wage rates, for example, or by requiring its employees to work long hours in a workplace full of health hazards? What if the company's supervisors routinely engage in workplace conduct that is offensive to women?

Given today's global communications network, few companies can assume that their actions in other nations will go unnoticed by "corporate watch" groups that discover and publicize unethical corporate behavior. (For a discussion of how the Internet has increased the ability of critics to publicize a corporation's misdeeds, see this chapter's *Adapting the Law to the Online Environment* feature on the following page.) As a result, U.S. businesses today usually take steps to avoid such adverse publicity—either by refusing to deal with certain suppliers or by arranging to monitor their suppliers' workplaces to make sure that the employees are not being mistreated.

The Foreign Corrupt Practices Act

Another ethical problem in international business dealings has to do with the legitimacy of certain "side" payments to government officials. In the United States, the majority of contracts are formed within the private sector. In many foreign countries, however, government officials make the decisions on most major construction and manufacturing contracts because of extensive government regulation and control over trade and industry.

Adapting the Law to the Online Environment

Corporate Reputations under Attack

In the pre-Internet days, disgruntled employees and customers wrote letters of complaint to corporate management or to the editors of local newspapers. Occasionally, an investigative reporter would write an exposé of alleged corporate misdeeds. Today, those unhappy employees and customers have gone online. To locate them, just type in the name of any major corporation. You will find electronic links to blogs, wikis, message boards, and online communities—many of which post unadorned criticisms of corporate giants. Some disgruntled employees and consumers have even created rogue Web sites that mimic the look of the target corporation's official Web site, except that the rogue sites feature chat rooms and postings of "horror stories" about the corporation.

Damage to Corporate Reputations

Clearly, by providing a forum for complaints, the Internet has increased the potential for damage to the reputation of any major (or minor) corporation. Now a relatively small number of unhappy employees, for example, may make the entire world aware of a single incident that is not at all representative of how the corporation ordinarily operates.

Special Interest Groups Go on the Attack

Special interest groups are also using the Internet to attack corporations they do not like. Rather than writing letters or giving speeches to a limited audience, a special interest group can now go online and mercilessly "expose" what it considers to be a corporation's "bad practices." Wal-Mart and Nike in particular have been frequent targets for advocacy groups that believe that those corporations exploit their workers.

Online Attacks: Often Inaccurate, but Probably Legal

Corporations often point out that many of the complaints and charges leveled against them are unfounded or exaggerated. Sometimes, management has tried to argue that the online attacks are libelous. The courts, however, disagree. To date, most courts have regarded online attacks as simply the expression of opinion and therefore a form of speech protected by the First Amendment.

In contrast, if employees breach company rules against the disclosure of internal financial information or trade secrets, the courts have been willing to side with the employers. Note, also, that a strong basis for successful lawsuits against inappropriate employee online disclosures always includes a clear set of written guidelines about what employees can do when they blog or generate other online content.

FOR CRITICAL ANALYSIS

How might online attacks actually help corporations in the long run? (Hint: Some online criticisms might be accurate.)

> *"Never doubt that a small group of committed citizens can change the world; indeed, it is the only thing that ever has."*
>
> Margaret Mead, 1901–1978
> (American anthropologist)

Side payments to government officials in exchange for favorable business contracts are not unusual in such countries, where they are not considered to be unethical. In the past, U.S. corporations doing business in these countries largely followed the dictum "When in Rome, do as the Romans do."

In the 1970s, however, the U.S. press, and government officials as well, uncovered a number of business scandals involving large side payments by U.S. corporations to foreign representatives for the purpose of securing advantageous international trade contracts. In response to this unethical behavior, in 1977 Congress passed the Foreign Corrupt Practices Act[7] (FCPA), which prohibits U.S. businesspersons from bribing foreign officials to secure advantageous contracts.

PROHIBITION AGAINST THE BRIBERY OF FOREIGN OFFICIALS   The first part of the FCPA applies to all U.S. companies and their directors, officers, shareholders, employees, and agents. This part prohibits the bribery of officials of foreign governments if the purpose of the payment is to get the officials to act in their official capacity to provide business opportunities. (To read about how the FCPA is being used to prosecute foreign companies involved in bribery outside the United States, see this chapter's *Beyond Our Borders* feature.)

---

7. 15 U.S.C. Sections 78dd-1 *et seq.*

Beyond Our Borders   The United States Looks into International Bribery

Until a few years ago, the application of the Foreign Corrupt Practices Act (FCPA) was confined to U.S. companies that allegedly bribed foreign officials. More recently, that act has become an instrument for prosecuting foreign companies suspected of bribing officials outside the United States. The U.S. Department of Justice estimates that more than fifty such cases are under investigation or prosecution within this country. Today, the Federal Bureau of Investigation has a five-member team to examine possible violations of U.S. laws by foreign corporations in their attempts to secure additional business.

The Ongoing BAE Systems Investigation
The British military manufacturer BAE Systems has been embroiled in a bribery scandal for years. Allegedly, BAE clandestinely paid billions of dollars to members of the Saudi Arabian royal family to secure an $80 billion contract

for advanced fighter jets. When the British government refused to pursue this case, U.S. officials picked up the slack. They looked at BAE bank accounts in various places, including the Caribbean, Central Europe, Romania, Sweden, and Switzerland. According to the U.S. government, this investigation was justified under the FCPA. The U.S. Justice Department discovered, for example, that BAE deposited $2 billion into Saudi Prince Bandar bin Sultan's bank account in Washington, D.C.

The Rest of the World Is Watching
The outcome of the Justice Department's investigation of BAE and its payments to the Saudi royal family is being watched by large multinationals throughout the globe. BAE and the Saudis have acknowledged the payments but have denied any wrongdoing. They say that the British and Saudi governments knew of these payments.

If the Justice Department determines that the payments were bribes and decides to prosecute, however, some BAE executives potentially could go to prison. BAE might also be barred from doing business with the U.S. government. Many other large companies have taken notice. In the wake of this ongoing investigation, an oil services company, Baker Hughes, admitted that it had bribed officials in Angola, Russia, and elsewhere. It paid a $44 million fine. Another oil services company, Halliburton, is under investigation for similar bribes in Nigeria.

• For Critical Analysis
Why do you think bribery investigations always seem to center on companies involved in selling military goods or oil production services as opposed to, say, companies selling leather goods, luxury perfumes, or high-quality silverware?

The FCPA does not prohibit payment of substantial sums to minor officials whose duties are ministerial. These payments are often referred to as "grease," or facilitating payments. They are meant to accelerate the performance of administrative services that might otherwise be carried out at a slow pace. Thus, for example, if a firm makes a payment to a minor official to speed up an import licensing process, the firm has not violated the FCPA.

Generally, the act, as amended, permits payments to foreign officials if such payments are lawful within the foreign country. The act also does not prohibit payments to private foreign companies or other third parties unless the U.S. firm knows that the payments will be passed on to a foreign government in violation of the FCPA. Business firms that violate the FCPA may be fined up to $2 million. Individual officers or directors who violate the act may be fined up to $100,000 (the fine cannot be paid by the company) and may be imprisoned for up to five years.

ACCOUNTING REQUIREMENTS   In the past, bribes were often concealed in corporate financial records. Thus, the second part of the FCPA is directed toward accountants. All companies must keep detailed records that "accurately and fairly" reflect the company's financial activities. In addition, all companies must have an accounting system that provides "reasonable assurance" that all transactions entered into by the company are accounted for and legal. These requirements assist in detecting illegal bribes. The FCPA further prohibits any person from making false statements to accountants or false entries in any record or account.

Reviewing . . . Ethics and Business Decision Making

Isabel Arnett was promoted to CEO of Tamik, Inc., a pharmaceutical company that manufactures a vaccine called Kafluk, which supposedly provides some defense against bird flu. The company began marketing Kafluk throughout Asia. After numerous media reports that bird flu might soon become a worldwide epidemic, the demand for Kafluk increased, sales soared, and Tamik earned record profits. Tamik's CEO, Arnett, then began receiving disturbing reports from Southeast Asia that in some patients, Kafluk had caused psychiatric disturbances, including severe hallucinations, and heart and lung problems. Arnett was informed that six children in Japan had committed suicide by jumping out of windows after receiving the vaccine. To cover up the story and prevent negative publicity, Arnett instructed Tamik's partners in Asia to offer cash to the Japanese families whose children had died in exchange for their silence. Arnett also refused to authorize additional research within the company to study the potential side effects of Kafluk. Using the information presented in the chapter, answer the following questions.

1. This scenario illustrates one of the main reasons why ethical problems occur in business. What is that reason?
2. Would a person who adheres to the principle of rights consider it ethical for Arnett not to disclose potential safety concerns and to refuse to perform additional research on Kafluk? Why or why not?
3. If Kafluk prevented fifty Asian people who were exposed to bird flu from dying, would Arnett's conduct in this situation be ethical under a utilitarian cost-benefit analysis? Why or why not?
4. Did Tamik or Arnett violate the Foreign Corrupt Practices Act in this scenario? Why or why not?

Linking the Law *to Managerial Accounting*
Managing a Company's Reputation

While in business school, all of you must take basic accounting courses. Accounting generally is associated with developing balance sheets and profit-and-loss statements, but it can also be used as a support system to provide information that can help managers do their jobs correctly. Enter managerial accounting, which is defined as the provision of accounting information for a company's internal use. Managerial accounting is used within a company for planning, controlling, and decision making.

Increasingly, managerial accounting is also being used to *manage corporate reputations.* To this end, more than 2,500 multinationals now release to the public large quantities of managerial accounting information.

Internal Reports Designed for External Scrutiny

Some large companies refer to the managerial accounting information that they release to the public as their corporate sustainability reports. Dow Chemical Company, for example, issues its Global Reporting Initiative Sustainability Report annually. So does Waste Management, Inc., which calls its report "The Color of Our World."

Other corporations call their published documents social responsibility reports. The antivirus software company Symantec Corporation issued its first corporate responsibility report in 2008. The report demonstrated the company's focus on critical environmental, social, and governance issues. Among other things, Symantec pointed out that it had adopted the Calvert Women's Principles, the first global code of corporate conduct designed to empower, advance, and invest in women worldwide.

A smaller number of multinationals provide what they call citizenship reports. For example, in 2009 General Electric (GE) released its Fifth Annual Citizenship Report, which it calls "Investing and Delivering in

Citizenship." GE's emphasis is on energy and climate change, demographics, growth markets, and financial markets. It even has a Web site that provides detailed performance metrics (**www.ge.com/citizenship**).

The Hitachi Group releases an Annual Corporate Social Responsibility Report, which outlines its environmental strategy, including its attempts to reduce carbon dioxide emissions (so-called greenhouse gases). It typically discusses human rights policy and its commitment to human rights awareness.

Why Use Managerial Accounting to Manage Reputations?

We live in an age of information. The advent of 24/7 cable news networks, Internet bloggers, and online newspapers guarantees that any news, whether positive or negative, about a corporation will be known throughout the world almost immediately. Consequently, corporations want to manage their reputations by preparing and releasing the news that the public, their shareholders, and government officials will receive. In a world in which corporations are often blamed for anything bad that happens, corporations are finding that managerial accounting information can provide a useful counterweight. To this end, some corporations have combined their social responsibility reports with their traditional financial accounting information. When a corporation's reputation is on the line, the future is at stake.

FOR CRITICAL ANALYSIS

Valuable company resources are used to create and publish corporate social responsibility reports. Under what circumstances can a corporation justify such expenditures?

Key Terms

business ethics 194	ethical reasoning 200	stock buyback 198
categorical imperative 201	ethics 194	stock option 198
corporate social responsibility 201	moral minimum 194	utilitarianism 201
cost-benefit analysis 201	principle of rights 201	

 Chapter Summary: Ethics and Business Decision Making

Business Ethics **(See pages 194–198.)**	1. *Ethics*—Business ethics focuses on how moral and ethical principles are applied in the business context. 2. *The moral minimum*—Lawful behavior is the moral minimum. The law has its limits, though, and some actions may be legal but not ethical. 3. *Legal uncertainties*—It may be difficult to predict with certainty whether particular actions are legal, given the numerous and frequent changes in the laws regulating business and the "gray areas" in the law. 4. *Short-term profit maximization*—One of the most pervasive reasons why ethical breaches occur is the focus on short-term profit maximization. Executives should distinguish between short-run and long-run profit goals and focus on maximizing profits over the long run because only long-run profit maximization is consistent with business ethics. 5. *The importance of ethical leadership*—Management's commitment and behavior are essential in creating an ethical workplace. Management's behavior, more than anything else, sets the ethical tone of a firm and influences the behavior of employees. 6. *Ethical codes*—Most large firms have ethical codes or policies and training programs to help employees determine whether certain actions are ethical. In addition, the Sarbanes-Oxley Act requires firms to set up confidential systems so that employees and others can report suspected illegal or unethical auditing or accounting practices.
Ethical Transgressions **by Financial Institutions** **(See pages 198–200.)**	During the late 2000s, corporate wrongdoing in the U.S. financial markets escalated. A number of investment banking firms, such as Lehman Brothers Holdings and Goldman Sachs, were nearly bankrupted by their abusive use of stock buybacks and stock options. AIG, an insurance giant, was also on the brink of bankruptcy when the government stepped in with federal bailout funds. Exorbitant bonuses paid to Wall Street executives added to the financial industries' problems and fueled public outrage. U.S. taxpayers paid the price through the federal bailouts and a deepening nationwide recession.
Approaches to **Ethical Reasoning** **(See pages 200–203.)**	1. *Duty-based ethics*—Ethics based on religious beliefs; philosophical reasoning, such as that of Immanuel Kant; and the basic rights of human beings (the principle of rights). A potential problem for those who support this approach is deciding which rights are more important in a given situation. Management constantly faces ethical conflicts and trade-offs when considering all those affected by a business decision. 2. *Outcome-based ethics (utilitarianism)*—Ethics based on philosophical reasoning, such as that of John Stuart Mill. Applying this theory requires a cost-benefit analysis, weighing the negative effects against the positive and deciding which course of action produces the best outcome. 3. *Corporate social responsibility*—A number of theories based on the idea that corporations can and should act ethically and be accountable to society for their actions. These include the stakeholder approach and corporate citizenship.
Making Ethical **Business Decisions** **(See page 204.)**	Making ethical business decisions is crucial in today's legal environment. Doing the right thing pays off in the long run, both in terms of increasing profits and avoiding negative publicity and the potential for bankruptcy. We provide six guidelines for making ethical business decisions on page 204.
Practical Solutions **to Corporate Ethics** **Questions** **(See pages 204–205.)**	Corporate ethics officers and ethics committees require a practical method to investigate and solve specific ethics problems. For a five-step pragmatic procedure to solve ethical problems recommended by one expert, see pages 204 and 205.

Continued

Chapter Summary: Ethics and Business Decision Making—Continued

Business Ethics on a Global Level (See pages 205–207.)	Businesses must take account of the many cultural, religious, and legal differences among nations. Notable differences relate to the role of women in society, employment laws governing workplace conditions, and the practice of giving side payments to foreign officials to secure favorable contracts.

ExamPrep

ISSUE SPOTTERS

1 Delta Tools, Inc., markets a product that under some circumstances is capable of seriously injuring consumers. Does Delta owe an ethical duty to remove this product from the market, even if the injuries result only from misuse? Why or why not?

2 Acme Corporation decides to respond to what it sees as a moral obligation to correct for past discrimination by adjusting pay differences among its employees. Does this raise an ethical conflict among Acme's employees? Between Acme and its employees? Between Acme and its shareholders? Explain your answers.

BEFORE THE TEST

Check your answers to the Issue Spotters, and at the same time, take the interactive quiz for this chapter. Go to **www.cengage.com/blaw/blt** and click on "Chapter 8." First, click on "Answers to Issue Spotters" to check your answers. Next, click on "Interactive Quiz" to assess your mastery of the concepts in this chapter. Then click on "Flashcards" to review this chapter's Key Term definitions.

For Review

Answers for the even-numbered questions in this **For Review** *section can be found on this text's accompanying Web site at* **www.cengage.com/blaw/blt**. *Select "Chapter 8" and click on "For Review."*

1 What is business ethics, and why is it important?
2 How can business leaders encourage their companies to act ethically?
3 How do duty-based ethical standards differ from outcome-based ethical standards?
4 What are six guidelines that an employee can use to evaluate whether his or her actions are ethical?
5 What types of ethical issues might arise in the context of international business transactions?

Hypothetical Scenarios and Case Problems

8–1   Business Ethics. Jason Trevor owns a commercial bakery in Blakely, Georgia, that produces a variety of goods sold in grocery stores. Trevor is required by law to perform internal tests on food produced at his plant to check for contamination. Three times in 2008, the tests of food products that contained peanut butter were positive for salmonella contamination. Trevor was not required to report the results to U.S. Food and Drug Administration officials, however, so he did not. Instead, Trevor instructed his employees to simply repeat the tests until the outcome was negative. Therefore, the products that had originally tested positive for salmonella were eventually shipped out to retailers. Five people who ate Trevor's baked goods in 2008 became seriously ill, and one person died from salmonella. Even though Trevor's conduct was legal, was it unethical for him to sell goods that had once tested positive for salmonella? If Trevor had followed the six basic guidelines for making ethical business decisions, would he still have sold the contaminated goods? Why or why not?

8–2   Hypothetical Question with Sample Answer Shokun Steel Co. owns many steel plants. One of its plants is much older than the others. Equipment at that plant is outdated and inefficient, and the costs of production at that plant are now two times higher than at any of Shokun's other plants. The company cannot raise the price of steel because of competition, both domestic and international. The plant employs more than a thousand workers and is located in Twin Firs, Pennsylvania, which has a population of about 45,000. Shokun is contemplating whether to close the plant. What factors should the firm consider in making its decision? Will the firm violate any ethical duties if it closes the plant? Analyze these questions from the two basic perspectives on ethical reasoning discussed in this chapter.

—For a sample answer to Question 8–2, go to Appendix E at the end of this text.

8-3 Ethical Conduct. Unable to pay more than $1.2 billion in debt, Big Mountain Metals, Inc., filed a petition to declare bankruptcy in a federal bankruptcy court in July 2009. Big Mountain's creditors included Bank of New London and Suzuki Bank, among others. The court appointed Morgan Crawford to work as a "disinterested" (neutral) party with Big Mountain and the creditors to resolve their disputes; the court set an hourly fee as Crawford's compensation. Crawford told the banks that he wanted them to pay him an additional percentage fee based on the "success" he attained in finding "new value" to pay Big Mountain's debts. He said that without such a deal, he would not perform his mediation duties. Suzuki Bank agreed; the other banks disputed the deal, but no one told the court. In October 2010, Crawford asked the court for nearly $2.5 million in compensation, including the hourly fees, which totaled about $531,000, and the percentage fees. Big Mountain and others asked the court to deny Crawford any fees on the basis that he had improperly negotiated "secret side agreements." How did Crawford violate his duties as a "disinterested" party? Should he be denied compensation? Why or why not?

8-4 **Case Problem with Sample Answer** In 1999, Andrew Fastow, chief financial officer of Enron Corp., asked Merrill Lynch, an investment firm, to participate in a bogus sale of three barges so that Enron could record earnings of $12.5 million from the sale. Through a third entity, Fastow bought the barges back within six months and paid Merrill for its participation. Five Merrill employees were convicted of conspiracy to commit wire fraud, in part, on an "honest services" theory. Under this theory, employees deprive their employer of "honest services" when the employees promote their own interests, rather than the interests of the employer. Four of the employees appealed to the U.S. Court of Appeals for the Fifth Circuit, arguing that this charge did not apply to the conduct in which they engaged. The court agreed, reasoning that the barge deal was conducted to benefit Enron, not to enrich the Merrill employees at Enron's expense. Meanwhile, Kevin Howard, chief financial officer of Enron Broadband Services (EBS), engaged in "Project Braveheart," which enabled EBS to show earnings of $111 million in 2000 and 2001. Braveheart involved the sale of an interest in the future revenue of a video-on-demand venture to nCube, a small technology firm, which was paid for its help when EBS bought the interest back. Howard was convicted of wire fraud, in part, on the "honest services" theory. He filed a motion to vacate this conviction on the same basis that the Merrill employees had argued. Did Howard act unethically? Explain. Should the court grant his motion? Discuss. [*United States v. Howard*, 471 F. Supp.2d 772 (S.D.Tex. 2007)]

—After you have answered Problem 8–4, compare your answer with the sample answer given on the Web site that accompanies this text. Go to **www.cengage.com/blaw/blt**, select "Chapter 8," and click on "Case Problem with Sample Answer."

8-5 Corporate Social Responsibility. Methamphetamine (meth) is an addictive, synthetic drug made chiefly in small toxic labs (STLs) in homes, tents, barns, or hotel rooms. The manufacturing process is dangerous, often resulting in explosions, burns, and toxic fumes. The government has spent considerable resources to find and eradicate STLs, imprison meth dealers and users, treat addicts, and provide services for families affected by these activities. Meth cannot be made without ephedrine or pseudoephedrine, which are ingredients in cold and allergy medications. Arkansas has one of the highest numbers of STLs in the United States. In an effort to recoup the costs of dealing with the meth epidemic, twenty counties in Arkansas filed a suit in a federal district court against Pfizer, Inc., and other companies that make or distribute cold and allergy medications. What is the defendants' ethical responsibility in this case, and to whom do they owe it? Why? [*Ashley County, Arkansas v. Pfizer, Inc.*, 552 F.3d 659 (8th Cir. 2009)]

8-6 Business Ethics on a Global Scale. In the 1990s, Pfizer, Inc., developed a new antibiotic called Trovan (trovafloxacin mesylate). Tests showed that in animals Trovan had life-threatening side effects, including joint disease, abnormal cartilage growth, liver damage, and a degenerative bone condition. In 1996, an epidemic of bacterial meningitis swept across Nigeria. Pfizer sent three U.S. physicians to test Trovan on children who were patients in Nigeria's Infectious Disease Hospital. Pfizer did not obtain the patients' consent, alert them to the risks, or tell them that Médecins Sans Frontières (Doctors without Borders) was providing an effective conventional treatment at the same site. Eleven children died in the experiment, and others were left blind, deaf, paralyzed, or brain damaged. Rabi Abdullahi and other Nigerian children filed a suit in a U.S. federal district court against Pfizer, alleging a violation of a customary international law norm prohibiting involuntary medical experimentation on humans. Did Pfizer violate any ethical standards? What might Pfizer have done to avert the consequences? Explain. [*Abdullahi v. Pfizer, Inc.*, 562 F.3d 163 (2d Cir. 2009)]

8-7 **A Question of Ethics** *Steven Soderbergh is the Academy Award–winning director of* Erin Brockovich, Traffic, *and many other films. CleanFlicks, LLC, filed a suit in a federal district court against Soderbergh, fifteen other directors, and the Directors Guild of America. The plaintiff asked the court to rule that it had the right to sell DVDs of the defendants' films altered without the defendants' consent to delete scenes of "sex, nudity, profanity and gory violence." CleanFlicks sold or rented the edited DVDs under the slogan "It's About Choice" to consumers, sometimes indirectly through retailers. It would not sell to retailers that made unauthorized copies of the edited films. The defendants, with DreamWorks LLC and seven other movie studios that own the copyrights to the films, filed a counterclaim against CleanFlicks and* *others engaged in the same business, alleging copyright infringement. Those filing the counterclaim asked the court to enjoin (prevent) CleanFlicks and the others from making and marketing altered versions of the films. [CleanFlicks of Colorado, LLC v. Soderbergh, 433 F.Supp.2d 1236 (D.Colo. 2006)]*

1 Movie studios often edit their films to conform to content and other standards and sell the edited versions to network television and other commercial buyers. In this case, however, the studios objected when CleanFlicks edited the films and sold the altered versions directly to consumers. Similarly, CleanFlicks made unauthorized copies of the studios' DVDs to edit the films, but objected to others' making unauthorized copies of the altered versions. Is there any-

thing unethical about these apparently contradictory positions? Why or why not?

2 CleanFlicks and its competitors asserted, in part, that they were making "fair use" of the studios' copyrighted works. They argued that by their actions "they are criticizing the objectionable content commonly found in current movies and that they are providing more socially acceptable alternatives to enable families to view the films together, without exposing children to the presumed harmful effects emanating from the objectionable content." If you were the judge, how would you view this argument? Is a court the appropriate forum for making determinations of public or social policy? Explain.

 Critical Thinking and Writing Assignments

8–8 Critical Legal Thinking. Human rights groups, environmental activists, and other interest groups concerned with unethical business practices have often conducted publicity campaigns against various corporations that those groups feel have engaged in unethical practices. Can a small group of well-organized activists dictate how a major corporation conducts its affairs? Discuss fully.

8–9 Critical Thinking and Writing Assignment for Business. Assume that you are a high-level manager for a shoe manufacturer. You know that your firm could increase its profit margin by producing shoes in Indonesia, where you could hire women for $100 a month to assemble them. You also know that human rights advocates recently accused a competing shoe manufacturer of engaging in exploitative labor practices because the manufacturer sold shoes made by Indonesian women for similarly low wages. You personally do not believe that paying $100 a month to Indonesian women is unethical because you know that in their country, $100 a month is a better-than-average wage rate. Assuming that the decision is yours to make, should you have the shoes manufactured in Indonesia and make higher profits

for your company? Should you instead avoid the risk of negative publicity and the consequences of that publicity for the firm's reputation and subsequent profits? Are there other alternatives? Discuss fully.

8–10 [VIDEO] **Video Question** Go to this text's Web site at **www.cengage.com/blaw/blt** and select "Chapter 8." Click on "Video Questions" and view the video titled *Ethics: Business Ethics an Oxymoron?* Then answer the following questions.

1 According to the instructor in the video, what is the primary reason that businesses act ethically?

2 Which of the two approaches to ethical reasoning that were discussed in the chapter seems to have had more influence on the instructor in the discussion of how business activities are related to societies? Explain your answer.

3 The instructor asserts that "[i]n the end, it is the unethical behavior that becomes costly, and conversely ethical behavior creates its own competitive advantage." Do you agree with this statement? Why or why not?

 Practical Internet Exercises

Go to this text's Web site at **www.cengage.com/blaw/blt**, select "Chapter 8," and click on "Practical Internet Exercises." There you will find the following Internet research exercises that you can perform to learn more about the topics covered in this chapter.

Practical Internet Exercise 8–1: LEGAL PERSPECTIVE—Ethics in Business
Practical Internet Exercise 8–2: MANAGEMENT PERSPECTIVE—Environmental Self-Audits

Unit One | Cumulative Business Hypothetical

CompTac, Inc., which is headquartered in San Francisco, California, is one of the leading software manufacturers in the United States. The company invests millions of dollars in researching and developing new software applications and computer games that are sold worldwide. It also has a large service department and has taken great pains to offer its customers excellent support services.

1. CompTac routinely purchases some of the materials necessary to produce its computer games from a New York firm, Electrotex, Inc. A dispute arises between the two firms, and CompTac wants to sue Electrotex for breach of contract. Can CompTac bring the suit in a California state court? Can CompTac bring the suit in a federal court? Explain.

2. A customer at one of CompTac's retail stores stumbles over a crate in the parking lot and breaks her leg. The crate had just moments before fallen off a CompTac truck that was delivering goods from a CompTac warehouse to the store. The customer sues CompTac, alleging negligence. Will she succeed in her suit? Why or why not?

3. Roban Electronics, a software manufacturer and one of CompTac's major competitors, has been trying to convince one of CompTac's key employees, Jim Baxter, to come to work for Roban. Roban knows that Baxter has a written employment contract with CompTac, which Baxter would breach if he left CompTac before the contract expired. Baxter goes to work for Roban, and the departure of its key employee causes CompTac to suffer substantial losses due to delays in completing new software. Can CompTac sue Roban to recoup some of these losses? If so, on what ground?

4. One of CompTac's employees in its accounting division, Alan Green, has a gambling problem. To repay a gambling debt of $10,000, Green decides to "borrow" some cash from CompTac to cover the debt. Using his "hacking" skills and his knowledge of CompTac account numbers, Green electronically transfers CompTac funds into his personal checking account. A week later, he is luckier at gambling and uses the same electronic procedures to transfer funds from his personal checking account to the relevant CompTac account. Has Green committed any crimes? If so, what are they?

5. One of CompTac's best-selling products is a computer game that includes some extremely violent actions. Groups of parents, educators, and consumer activists have bombarded CompTac with letters and e-mail messages calling on the company to stop selling the product. CompTac executives are concerned about the public outcry, but at the same time, they realize that the game is CompTac's major source of profits. If it ceased marketing the game, the company could go bankrupt. If you were a CompTac decision maker, what would your decision be in this situation? How would you justify your decision from an ethical perspective?

Unit One | Extended Case Study: *Paduano v. American Honda Motor Co.*

The effect and importance of the U.S. Constitution's supremacy clause were discussed in Chapter 2. When there is a direct conflict between a federal law and a state law, the state law is rendered invalid. If Congress has chosen to act exclusively in an area, the federal statute will take precedence over a conflicting state law on the same subject under the doctrine of preemption.

There is a strong presumption against preemption, however, because the states are independent "sovereigns" in our federal system. In areas in which the states have traditionally exercised their police power, on a subject such as consumer protection, for example, this presumption applies with particular force.

In this Extended Case Study, we review Paduano v. American Honda Motor Co.,[1] a case in which a new car buyer complained about the vehicle's inability to achieve the fuel economy advertised in the automaker's brochure. The defendant contended that federal law preempted the plaintiff's claims, which were founded on state law.

---

1. 169 Cal.App.4th 1453, 88 Cal.Rptr.3d 90 (4 Dist. 2009).

Continued

CASE BACKGROUND

Gaetano Paduano bought a new Honda Civic Hybrid in California in June 2004. The Environmental Protection Agency's (EPA's) fuel economy estimate stated on the federally mandated new car label was 47 miles per gallon (mpg) for city driving and 48 mpg for highway driving. Honda's sales brochure repeated the fuel economy estimate and added, "Just drive the Hybrid like you would a conventional car and save on fuel bills."

Paduano drove the vehicle for about a year but was frustrated with its fuel economy performance, which was less than half of the EPA estimate. A service employee at a Honda dealership told him that to achieve the estimate he would have to drive differently. The employee said, "It is very difficult to get MPG on [the] highway and to drive with traffic in a safe manner." The required "special" manner "would create a driving hazard." Paduano asked American Honda Motor Company to repurchase the vehicle. Honda refused.

Paduano filed a suit in a California state court against the automaker, alleging, among other things, deceptive advertising in violation of the state's Consumer Legal Remedies Act and Unfair Competition Law. Honda argued that the federal Energy Policy and Conservation Act (EPCA), which prescribed the EPA fuel economy estimate, preempted Paduano's claims. The court issued a summary judgment in Honda's favor. Paduano appealed to a state intermediate appellate court.

MAJORITY OPINION

AARON, J.

* * * *

The basic rules of preemption are not in dispute: *Under the supremacy clause of the United States Constitution, Congress has the power to preempt state law concerning matters that lie within the authority of Congress.* In determining whether federal law preempts state law, a court's task is to discern congressional intent. Congress's express intent in this regard will be found when Congress explicitly states that it is preempting state authority. [Emphasis added.]

* * * *

Honda * * * argues that [the EPCA] prevents Paduano from pursuing his * * * claims. That provision states in pertinent part,

> When a requirement under [the EPCA] is in effect, a State or a political subdivision of a State may adopt or enforce a law or regulation on disclosure of fuel economy or fuel operating costs for an automobile covered by [the EPCA] only if the law or regulation is identical to that requirement.

* * * Honda goes on to assert that "Paduano's deceptive advertising and misrepresentation claims would impose *non* identical disclosure requirements."

Contrary to Honda's characterization * * *, Paduano's claims are based on statements Honda made in its advertising brochure to the effect that one may drive a Civic Hybrid in the same manner as one would a conventional car, and need not do anything "special," in order to achieve the beneficial fuel economy of the EPA estimates. * * * Paduano is challenging * * * Honda's * * * commentary in which it alludes to those estimates in a manner that may give consumers the misimpression that they will be able to achieve mileage close to the EPA estimates while driving a Honda hybrid in the same manner as they would a conventional vehicle. Paduano does not seek to require Honda to provide "additional alleged facts" regarding the Civic Hybrid's fuel economy, as Honda suggests, but rather, seeks to prevent Honda from making misleading claims about how easy it is to

achieve better fuel economy. Contrary to Honda's assertions, if Paduano were to prevail on his claims, Honda would not have to do anything differently with regard to its disclosure of the EPA mileage estimates.

* * * *

* * * [The EPCA's] express preemption provisions do not purport to take away states' power to regulate the advertising of new vehicles, even when that advertising includes the EPA mileage estimates. *As long as a state's regulation does not require a manufacturer to provide a fuel estimate different from the EPA fuel economy estimate, or to make claims that go beyond, or are contrary to, what the federal scheme requires, the EPCA does not preempt such regulation.* * * * Allowing states to regulate false advertising and unfair business practices may further the goals of the EPCA, and we reject Honda's claim. [Emphasis added.]

* * * *

* * * We * * * conclude that federal law does not preempt Paduano's claims concerning Honda's advertising.

* * * *

The summary judgment is reversed. * * * The matter is remanded to the trial court for further proceedings.

DISSENTING OPINION

O'ROURKE, J., * * * dissenting * * *.

* * * In my view, Paduano's false advertising claims under the Consumer Legal Remedies Act (CLRA) and Unfair Competition Law (UCL) are * * * preempted by the Energy Policy and Conservation Act of 1975 (EPCA) because those claims are necessarily predicated on Honda's representations about fuel economy and the Honda Civic Hybrid's asserted failure to meet the federal Environmental Protection Agency's (EPA) estimates as to fuel economy. * * * Paduano seeks to impose a legal duty on Honda to change its disclosures concerning fuel economy to something different from the EPA estimate. In such a case, the EPCA expressly preempts enforcement of his UCL and CLRA causes of action. * * * Accordingly, I respectfully dissent from * * * the majority opinion.

Extended Case Study: *Paduano v. American Honda Motor Co.*—Continued

* * * *

Because Paduano's sought-after relief would require that Honda change its advertising to either eliminate or reduce the EPA mileage estimate, or include additional disclosures relating to the EPA mileage estimate and his car's fuel economy, his state law false advertising claims fail under express preemption principles as imposing a legal obligation related to fuel economy standards or they fail because they would impose disclosure requirements concerning fuel economy that are not identical to the EPCA.

This conclusion as to preemption is not impacted by the fact that Paduano's claims are made under consumer protection laws. A presumption against preemption is characteristically applied where the field is one that the states have traditionally occupied and regulated, but such a presumption is not triggered when the state regulates in an area where there has been a history of significant federal presence. In my view, the EPCA and its corresponding federal regulations reflect a significant federal presence with respect to the measurement and disclosure of automobile fuel economy estimates and standards, as well as the advertising concerning a new vehicle's fuel economy.

QUESTIONS FOR ANALYSIS

1. **Law.** What was the majority's decision on the principal issue before the court in this case? What were the reasons for this decision?
2. **Law.** How would the dissent apply the law to the facts differently than the majority did? What were the dissent's reasons?
3. **Ethics.** Suppose that the defendant automaker opposed this action solely to avoid paying for a car that had proved to be a "lemon." Would this have been unethical? Explain.
4. **Economic Dimensions.** Is either the majority's ruling or the dissent's position more favorable for the auto market? Why or why not?
5. **Implications for the Businessperson.** What does the interpretation of the law in this case suggest to businesspersons who sell products labeled with statements mandated by federal or state law?

Contracts

(AP Photo/Carlos Osorio)

Chapter 9

Nature and Classification

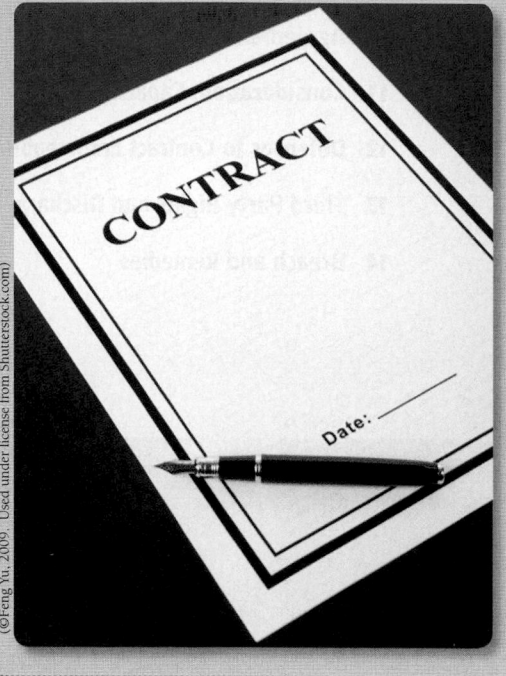

(©Feng Yu, 2009. Used under license from Shutterstock.com)

> "All sensible people are selfish, and nature is tugging at every contract to make the terms of it fair."
>
> —Ralph Waldo Emerson, 1803–1882
> (American essayist and poet)

Chapter Outline

- An Overview of Contract Law
- Elements of a Contract
- Types of Contracts
- Quasi Contracts
- Interpretation of Contracts

Learning Objectives

After reading this chapter, you should be able to answer the following questions:

1. What is a contract? What is the objective theory of contracts?

2. What are the four basic elements necessary to the formation of a valid contract?

3. What is the difference between an implied-in-fact contract and an implied-in-law contract (quasi contract)?

4. How does a void contract differ from a voidable contract? What is an unenforceable contract?

5. What rules guide the courts in interpreting contracts?

Promise An assertion that something either will or will not happen in the future.

As Ralph Waldo Emerson observed in the chapter-opening quotation, people act in their own self-interest by nature, and this influences the terms they seek in their contracts. Contract law must therefore provide rules to determine which contract terms will be enforced and which promises must be kept. A **promise** is an assertion that something either will or will not happen in the future.

Like other types of law, contract law reflects our social values, interests, and expectations at a given point in time. It shows, for example, what kinds of promises our society thinks should be legally binding. It distinguishes between promises that create only *moral* obligations (such as a promise to take a friend to lunch) and promises that are legally binding (such as a promise to pay for merchandise purchased).

Contract law also demonstrates what excuses our society accepts for breaking certain types of promises. In addition, it shows what promises are considered to be contrary to public policy—against the interests of society as a whole—and therefore legally invalid. When the person making a promise is a child or is mentally incompetent, for example, a question will arise as to whether the promise should be enforced. Resolving such questions is the essence of contract law.

An Overview of Contract Law

Before we look at the numerous rules that courts use to determine whether a particular promise will be enforced, it is necessary to understand some fundamental concepts of contract law. In this section, we describe the sources and general function of contract law and introduce the objective theory of contracts.

Sources of Contract Law

The common law governs all contracts except when it has been modified or replaced by statutory law, such as the Uniform Commercial Code (UCC),[1] or by administrative agency regulations. Contracts relating to services, real estate, employment, and insurance, for example, generally are governed by the common law of contracts.

Contracts for the sale and lease of goods, however, are governed by the UCC—to the extent that the UCC has modified general contract law. The relationship between general contract law and the law governing sales and leases of goods will be explored in detail in Chapter 15. In this unit covering the common law of contracts (Chapters 9 through 14), we indicate briefly in footnotes the areas in which the UCC has significantly altered common law contract principles.

The Function of Contracts

No aspect of modern life is entirely free of contractual relationships. You acquire rights and obligations, for example, when you borrow funds, buy or lease a house, obtain insurance, form a business, and purchase goods or services. Contract law is designed to provide stability and predictability both for buyers and sellers in the marketplace.

Contract law assures the parties to private agreements that the promises they make will be enforceable. Clearly, many promises are kept because the parties involved feel a moral obligation to do so or because keeping a promise is in their mutual self-interest. The **promisor** (the person making the promise) and the **promisee** (the person to whom the promise is made) may decide to honor their agreement for other reasons. Nevertheless, the rules of contract law are often followed in business agreements to avoid potential problems.

By supplying procedures for enforcing private agreements, contract law provides an essential condition for the existence of a market economy. Without a legal framework of reasonably assured expectations within which to plan and venture, businesspersons would be able to rely only on the good faith of others. Duty and good faith are usually sufficient, but when dramatic price changes or adverse economic conditions make it costly to comply with a promise, these elements may not be enough. Contract law is necessary to ensure compliance with a promise or to entitle the innocent party to some form of relief.

Definition of a Contract

A **contract** is an agreement that can be enforced in court. It is formed by two or more parties who agree to perform or to refrain from performing some act now or in the future. Generally, contract disputes arise when there is a promise of future performance. If the contractual promise is not fulfilled, the party who made it is subject to the sanctions of a court (see Chapter 14). That party may be required to pay monetary damages for failing to perform the contractual promise; in limited instances, the party may be required to perform the promised act.

Promisor A person who makes a promise.

Promisee A person to whom a promise is made.

ON THE WEB An extensive definition of the term *contract* is offered by the 'Lectric Law Library at **www.lectlaw.com/def/c123.htm**.

Contract An agreement that can be enforced in court; formed by two or more competent parties who agree, for consideration, to perform or to refrain from performing some legal act now or in the future.

---

1. See Chapter 1 and Chapter 15 for further discussions of the significance and coverage of the Uniform Commercial Code (UCC). Excerpts from the UCC are presented in Appendix C at the end of this book.

The Objective Theory of Contracts

Objective Theory of Contracts A theory under which the intent to form a contract will be judged by outward, objective facts (what the party said when entering into the contract, how the party acted or appeared, and the circumstances surrounding the transaction) as interpreted by a reasonable person, rather than by the party's own secret, subjective intentions.

In determining whether a contract has been formed, the element of intent is of prime importance. In contract law, intent is determined by what is referred to as the **objective theory of contracts,** not by the personal or subjective intent, or belief, of a party. The theory is that a party's intention to enter into a contract is judged by outward, objective facts as interpreted by a *reasonable person,* rather than by the party's own secret, subjective intentions. Objective facts include (1) what the party said when entering into the contract, (2) how the party acted or appeared, and (3) the circumstances surrounding the transaction. As will be discussed later in this chapter, in the section on express versus implied contracts, intent to form a contract may be manifested by conduct, as well as by words, oral or written.

Freedom of Contract and Freedom from Contract

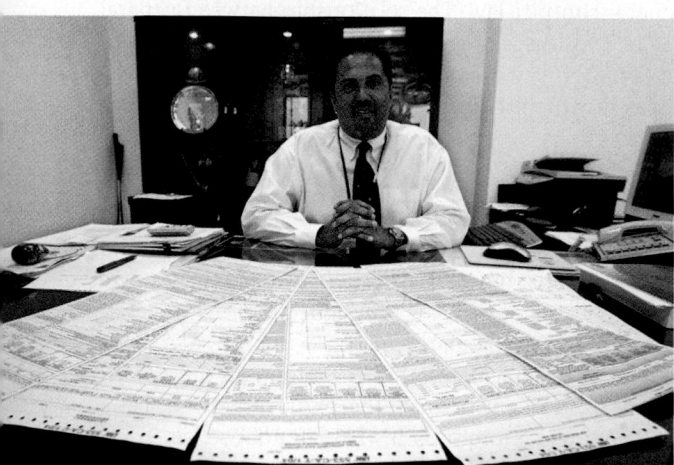

The manager of a Toyota dealership in Glendora, California, displays the same contract written in four different Asian languages (Chinese, Korean, Vietnamese, and Tagalog). A consumer protection law in California requires that certain businesses, such as car dealers and apartment owners, that have employees who orally negotiate contracts in these languages to provide written contracts in that same language. Why might it be important to the enforceability of a written contract that the consumer can actually read its provisions?

As a general rule, the law recognizes everyone's ability to enter freely into contractual arrangements. This recognition is called *freedom of contract,* a freedom protected by the U.S. Constitution in Article I, Section 10. Because freedom of contract is a fundamental public policy of the United States, courts rarely interfere with contracts that have been voluntarily made.

Of course, as in other areas of the law, there are many exceptions to the general rule that contracts voluntarily negotiated will be enforced. For example, illegal bargains, agreements that unreasonably restrain trade, and certain unfair contracts made between one party with a great amount of bargaining power and another with little power are generally not enforced. In addition, as you will read in Chapter 11, certain contracts and clauses may not be enforceable if they are contrary to public policy, fairness, and justice. These exceptions provide *freedom from contract* for persons who may have been forced into making contracts unfavorable to themselves.

▶ Elements of a Contract

The many topics that will be discussed in the following chapters on contract law require an understanding of the basic elements of a valid contract and the way in which a contract is created. You will also need an understanding of the types of circumstances in which even legally valid contracts will not be enforced.

Requirements of a Valid Contract

The following list briefly describes the four requirements that must be met for a valid contract to exist. If any of these elements is lacking, no contract will have been formed. (Each item will be explained more fully in subsequent chapters.)

1. *Agreement.* An agreement to form a contract includes an *offer* and an *acceptance.* One party must offer to enter into a legal agreement, and another party must accept the terms of the offer (see Chapter 10).
2. *Consideration.* Any promises made by the parties must be supported by legally sufficient and bargained-for consideration (something of value received or promised to convince a person to make a deal) (see Chapter 11).
3. *Contractual capacity.* Both parties entering into the contract must have the contractual capacity to do so; the law must recognize them as possessing characteristics that qualify them as competent parties (see Chapter 11).

4. *Legality.* The contract's purpose must be to accomplish some goal that is legal and not against public policy (see Chapter 11).

Defenses to the Enforceability of a Contract

Even if all of the elements of a valid contract are present, a contract may be unenforceable if the following requirements are not met.

1. *Genuineness of assent.* The apparent consent of both parties must be genuine. For example, if a contract was formed as a result of fraud, mistake, or duress, the contract may not be enforceable.
2. *Form.* The contract must be in whatever form the law requires; for example, some contracts must be in writing to be enforceable.

The failure to fulfill either requirement may be raised as a *defense* to the enforceability of an otherwise valid contract. Both requirements will be explained in more detail in Chapter 12.

 Types of Contracts

There are numerous types of contracts. They are categorized based on legal distinctions as to their formation, performance, and enforceability. Exhibit 9–1 illustrates three classifications, or categories, of contracts based on their mode of formation.

ON THE WEB For an excellent overview of the basic principles of contract law, go to library.findlaw.com/1999/Jan/1/241463.html.

Contract Formation

As you can see in Exhibit 9–1, three classifications of contracts are based on how and when a contract is formed. The best way to explain each type of contract is to compare one type with another, as we do in the following pages.

BILATERAL VERSUS UNILATERAL CONTRACTS Every contract involves at least two parties. The **offeror** is the party making the offer. The **offeree** is the party to whom the offer is made. The offeror always promises to do or not to do something and thus is also a promisor. Whether the contract is classified as *bilateral* or *unilateral* depends on what the offeree must do to accept the offer and bind the offeror to a contract.

Offeror A person who makes an offer.

Offeree A person to whom an offer is made.

Bilateral Contracts.   If the offeree can accept simply by promising to perform, the contract is a **bilateral contract.** Hence, a bilateral contract is a "promise for a promise." An example of a bilateral contract is a contract in which one person agrees to buy another person's automobile for a specified price. No performance, such as the payment of funds or

Bilateral Contract A type of contract that arises when a promise is given in exchange for a return promise.

• *Exhibit* **9–1 Classifications Based on Contract Formation**

delivery of goods, need take place for a bilateral contract to be formed. The contract comes into existence at the moment the promises are exchanged.

EXAMPLE 9.1   Javier offers to buy Ann's digital camera for $200. Javier tells Ann that he will give her the cash for the camera on the following Friday, when he gets paid. Ann accepts Javier's offer and promises to give him the camera when he pays her on Friday. Javier and Ann have formed a bilateral contract. ●

Unilateral Contracts.   If the offer is phrased so that the offeree can accept only by completing the contract performance, the contract is a **unilateral contract.** Hence, a unilateral contract is a "promise for an act." In other words, the contract is formed not at the moment when promises are exchanged but rather when the contract is *performed.* **EXAMPLE 9.2**   Reese says to Celia, "If you drive my car from New York to Los Angeles, I'll give you $1,000." Only on Celia's completion of the act—bringing the car to Los Angeles—does she fully accept Reese's offer to pay $1,000. If she chooses not to accept the offer to drive the car to Los Angeles, there are no legal consequences. ●

Contests, lotteries, and other competitions offering prizes are also examples of offers for unilateral contracts. If a person complies with the rules of the contest—such as by submitting the right lottery number at the right place and time—a unilateral contract is formed, binding the organization offering the prize to a contract to perform as promised in the offer.

Unilateral Contract A contract that results when an offer can be accepted only by the offeree's performance.

Ethical Issue ⚖️ ......

Can a company that sponsors a contest change the prize from what it originally advertised?
Courts have historically treated contests as unilateral contracts. Unilateral contracts typically cannot be modified by the offeror after the offeree has begun to perform. But this same principle may not apply to contest terms if the company sponsoring the contest reserves the right to cancel the contest or change its terms. For example, Donna Englert entered the "Quarter Million Dollar Challenge" contest sponsored by Nutritional Sciences, LLC. A panel of judges picked the winners of certain categories based on the contestant's body transformation after using Nutritional Sciences' products and training plans for thirteen weeks. When Englert was chosen as female runner-up in her age group, she thought she would receive the advertised prize of $1,500 cash and $500 worth of Nutritional Sciences' products. Instead, the company sent her a "challenge winner agreement" for $250 cash and $250 worth of products. Englert refused to sign the agreement and filed a lawsuit alleging breach of contract. The state trial court dismissed her claim, and she appealed.

The state appellate court noted that the contestant's compliance with the rules of a contest is necessary to form a binding unilateral contract. Here, the contest rules stipulated that "all winners must agree to the regulations outlined specifically for winners before claiming championship or money." Next to this statement was an asterisk corresponding to a note reserving the right of Nutritional Sciences to cancel the contest or alter its terms at any time. Because of this provision, the court ruled that Nutritional Sciences did not breach the contract when it subsequently changed the cash prize from $1,500 to $250.[2]

Revocation of Offers for Unilateral Contracts.   A problem arises in unilateral contracts when the promisor attempts to *revoke* (cancel) the offer after the promisee has begun performance but before the act has been completed. **EXAMPLE 9.3**   Roberta offers to buy Ed's sailboat, moored in San Francisco, on delivery of the boat to Roberta's dock in Newport Beach, three hundred miles south of San Francisco. Ed rigs the boat and sets sail. Shortly before his arrival at Newport Beach, Ed receives a radio message from Roberta withdrawing her offer. Roberta's offer is to form a unilateral contract, and only Ed's delivery of the sailboat at her dock is an acceptance. ●

ON THE WEB For easy-to-understand definitions of legal terms and concepts, including terms and concepts relating to contract law, go to **dictionary.law.com** and key in a term, such as *contract* or *consideration.*

---

2. *Englert v. Nutritional Sciences, LLC,* 2008 WL 4416597 (Ohio App. 2008).

In contract law, offers are normally *revocable* (capable of being taken back, or canceled) until accepted. Under the traditional view of unilateral contracts, Roberta's revocation would terminate the offer. Because of the harsh effect on the offeree of the revocation of an offer to form a unilateral contract, the modern-day view is that once performance has been *substantially* undertaken, the offeror cannot revoke the offer. Thus, in our example, even though Ed has not yet accepted the offer by complete performance, Roberta is prohibited from revoking it. Ed can deliver the boat and bind Roberta to the contract.

FORMAL VERSUS INFORMAL CONTRACTS   Another classification system divides contracts into formal contracts and informal contracts. **Formal contracts** are contracts that require a special form or method of creation (formation) to be enforceable.[3] For example, *negotiable instruments,* which include checks, drafts, promissory notes, and certificates of deposit (as will be discussed in Chapter 18), are formal contracts because, under the Uniform Commercial Code, a special form and language are required to create them. Letters of credit, which are frequently used in international sales contracts (see Chapter 22), are another type of formal contract.

Informal contracts (also called *simple contracts*) include all other contracts. No special form is required (except for certain types of contracts that must be in writing), as the contracts are usually based on their substance rather than their form. Typically, businesspersons put their contracts in writing to ensure that there is some proof of a contract's existence should problems arise.

EXPRESS VERSUS IMPLIED CONTRACTS   Contracts may also be formed and categorized as express or implied by the conduct of the parties. In an **express contract,** the terms of the agreement are fully and explicitly stated in words, oral or written. A signed lease for an apartment or a house is an express written contract. If a classmate accepts your offer to sell your textbooks from last semester for $75, an express oral contract has been made.

A contract that is implied from the conduct of the parties is called an **implied-in-fact contract,** or an implied contract. This type of contract differs from an express contract in that the *conduct* of the parties, rather than their words, creates and defines at least some of the terms of the contract. For an implied-in-fact contract to arise, certain requirements must be met. Normally, if the following conditions exist, a court will hold that an implied contract was formed:

1. The plaintiff furnished some service or property.
2. The plaintiff expected to be paid for that service or property, and the defendant knew or should have known that payment was expected (by using the objective-theory-of-contracts test discussed on page 220).
3. The defendant had a chance to reject the services or property and did not.

EXAMPLE 9.4   You need an accountant to fill out your tax return this year, so you search the Web and find an accounting firm located in your neighborhood. You drop by the firm's office, talk to an accountant, and learn what fees will be charged. The next day you return and give the receptionist all of the necessary information and documents, such as canceled checks and W-2 forms. Then you walk out the door without saying anything expressly to the accountant. In this situation, you have entered into an implied-in-fact contract to pay the accountant the usual and reasonable fees for her accounting services. The contract is implied by your conduct and by hers. She expects to be paid for completing your tax

Formal Contract   A contract that by law requires a specific form, such as being executed under seal, for its validity.

Informal Contract   A contract that does not require a specified form or formality to be valid.

Express Contract   A contract in which the terms of the agreement are stated in words, oral or written.

Implied-in-Fact Contract   A contract formed in whole or in part from the conduct of the parties (as opposed to an express contract).

KEEP IN MIND   Not every contract is a document with "Contract" printed in block letters at the top. A contract can be expressed in a letter, a memo, or another document.

---

3. See *Restatement (Second) of Contracts,* Section 6, which explains that formal contracts include (1) contracts under seal, (2) recognizances, (3) negotiable instruments, and (4) letters of credit. As mentioned in Chapter 1, *Restatements of the Law* are books that summarize court decisions on a particular topic and that courts often refer to for guidance.

return. By bringing in the records she will need to do the work, you have implied an intent to pay for her services. ● (For an example of how an implied-in-fact contract can arise from employment manuals, see the *Business Application* feature at the end of this chapter.)

Note that a contract can be a mixture of an express contract and an implied-in-fact contract. In other words, a contract may contain some express terms, while others are implied. During the construction of a home, the homeowner often asks the builder to make changes in the original specifications. When do these changes form part of an implied-in-fact contract that makes the homeowner liable to the builder for any extra expenses? That was the issue in the following case.

Case 9.1   Uhrhahn Construction & Design, Inc. v. Hopkins

Court of Appeals of Utah, 179 P.3d 808 (2008).

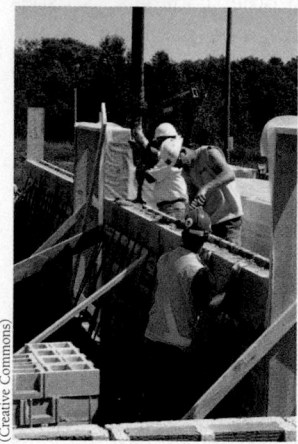

A wall using Durisol blocks, which are made from various recycled materials and require more labor to complete than cinder blocks. Can a contractor ask a higher price for using Durisol blocks?

FACTS   Uhrhahn Construction was hired by Lamar Hopkins and his wife for several projects in the building of their home. Each project was based on a cost estimate and specifications. Each of the proposals accepted by Hopkins said that any changes in the signed contracts would be made only "upon written orders." When work was in progress, Hopkins made several requests for changes. There was no written record of these changes, but Uhrhahn performed the work and Hopkins paid for it. A dispute arose after Hopkins requested that Uhrhahn use Durisol blocks rather than cinder blocks in some construction. The original proposal specified cinder blocks, but Hopkins told Uhrhahn that the change should be made because Durisol was "easier to install than traditional cinder block and would take half the time." Hopkins said the total cost would be the same. Uhrhahn orally agreed to the change, but demanded extra payment when it discovered that Durisol blocks were more complicated to use than cinder blocks. Hopkins refused to pay, claiming that the cost should be the same. Uhrhahn sued. The trial court held for Uhrhahn, finding that the Durisol blocks were more costly to install. The homeowners appealed.

ISSUE   Did the homeowners and the builder have an implied-in-fact contract regarding the substitution of Durisol blocks for the cinder blocks specified in the contract?

DECISION   Yes. The Utah appeals court affirmed the decision of the trial court, finding that there was a valid contract between the parties and that both parties had agreed to oral changes in the contract. The changes created an implied-in-fact contract by which the builder agreed to provide extra work in exchange for additional compensation from the homeowners.

REASON   The court found that the elements of a contract were present—offer and acceptance, competent parties, and consideration. The terms were clearly specified in the proposals accepted by Hopkins. Uhrhahn promised to perform work in exchange for payment. Although the contract stated that any changes would be in writing, both parties waived that term in the contract when they orally agreed on some changes in the work performed. As often happens in construction, changes were requested that were outside the contract. The builder did the work, and the buyer accepted the work. Such oral modification of the original contract creates an enforceable contract, and payment is due for the extra work. This is an implied-in-fact contract. Hopkins asked Uhrhahn to perform certain work. Uhrhahn expected to be compensated for the work, and Hopkins knew or should have known that Uhrhahn would expect to be paid for work that was outside the specifications of the original contract.

FOR CRITICAL ANALYSIS—Technological Consideration   *Would the outcome of this case have been different if the parties had communicated by e-mail for all details regarding changes in the work performed? Why or why not?*

Contract Performance

Executed Contract   A contract that has been completely performed by both parties.

Executory Contract   A contract that has not as yet been fully performed.

Contracts are also classified according to their state of performance. A contract that has been fully performed on both sides is called an **executed contract.** A contract that has not been fully performed on either side is called an **executory contract.** If one party has fully performed but the other has not, the contract is said to be executed on the one side and executory on the other, but the contract is still classified as executory.

Thirteen-year-old classical singing star Faryl Smith (center) was a finalist on the television show Britain's Got Talent. *Her debut CD was a hit in the United Kingdom and in the United States. Here, she is signing a recording contract with Universal Classics and Jazz label. What requirements are there to make this contract valid?*

Valid Contract A contract that results when the elements necessary for contract formation (agreement, consideration, legal purpose, and contractual capacity) are present.

Voidable Contract A contract that may be legally avoided (canceled, or annulled) at the option of one or both of the parties.

Unenforceable Contract A valid contract rendered unenforceable by some statute or law.

Void Contract A contract having no legal force or binding effect.

Quasi Contract A fictional contract imposed on the parties by a court in the interests of fairness and justice; usually imposed to avoid the unjust enrichment of one party at the expense of another.

EXAMPLE 9.5 You agreed to buy ten tons of coal from Western Coal Company. Western has delivered the coal to your steel mill, where it is now being burned. At this point, the contract is an executory contract—it is executed on the part of Western and executory on your part. After you pay Western for the coal, the contract will be executed on both sides. ●

Contract Enforceability

A **valid contract** has the four elements necessary for contract formation: (1) an agreement (offer and acceptance) (2) supported by legally sufficient consideration (3) for a legal purpose and (4) made by parties who have the legal capacity to enter into the contract. As mentioned, we will discuss each of these elements in the following chapters. As you can see in Exhibit 9–2 on the following page, valid contracts may be enforceable, voidable, or unenforceable. Additionally, a contract may be referred to as a *void contract.* We look next at the meaning of the terms *voidable, unenforceable,* and *void* in relation to contract enforceability.

VOIDABLE CONTRACTS A **voidable contract** is a *valid* contract but one that can be avoided at the option of one or both of the parties. The party having the option can elect either to avoid any duty to perform or to *ratify* (make valid) the contract. If the contract is avoided, both parties are released from it. If it is ratified, both parties must fully perform their respective legal obligations.

As a general rule, for example, contracts made by minors are voidable at the option of the minor (as will be discussed in Chapter 11). Additionally, contracts entered into under fraudulent conditions are voidable at the option of the defrauded party. Contracts entered into under legally defined duress or undue influence are also voidable (see Chapter 12).

UNENFORCEABLE CONTRACTS An **unenforceable contract** is one that cannot be enforced because of certain legal defenses against it. It is not unenforceable because a party failed to satisfy a legal requirement of the contract; rather, it is a valid contract rendered unenforceable by some statute or law. For example, some contracts must be in writing (see Chapter 12), and if they are not, they will not be enforceable except in certain exceptional circumstances.

VOID CONTRACTS A **void contract** is no contract at all. The terms *void* and *contract* are contradictory. None of the parties has any legal obligations if a contract is void. A contract can be void because, for example, one of the parties was previously determined by a court to be legally insane (and thus lacked the legal capacity to enter into a contract) or because the purpose of the contract was illegal.

▶ Quasi Contracts

Quasi contracts, or contracts *implied in law,* are wholly different from actual contracts. Express contracts and implied-in-fact contracts are actual or true contracts formed by the words or actions of the parties. The word *quasi* is Latin for "as if" or "analogous to." Quasi contracts are not true contracts because they do not arise from any agreement, express or implied, between the parties themselves. Rather, quasi contracts are fictional contracts that courts can impose on the parties "as if" the parties had entered into an actual contract. They are equitable rather than legal contracts. Usually, quasi contracts are imposed to avoid the *unjust enrichment* of one party at the expense of another. The doctrine of unjust enrichment is based on the theory that individuals should not be allowed to profit or enrich themselves inequitably at the expense of others.

● *Exhibit* 9-2 Enforceable, Voidable, Unenforceable, and Void Contracts

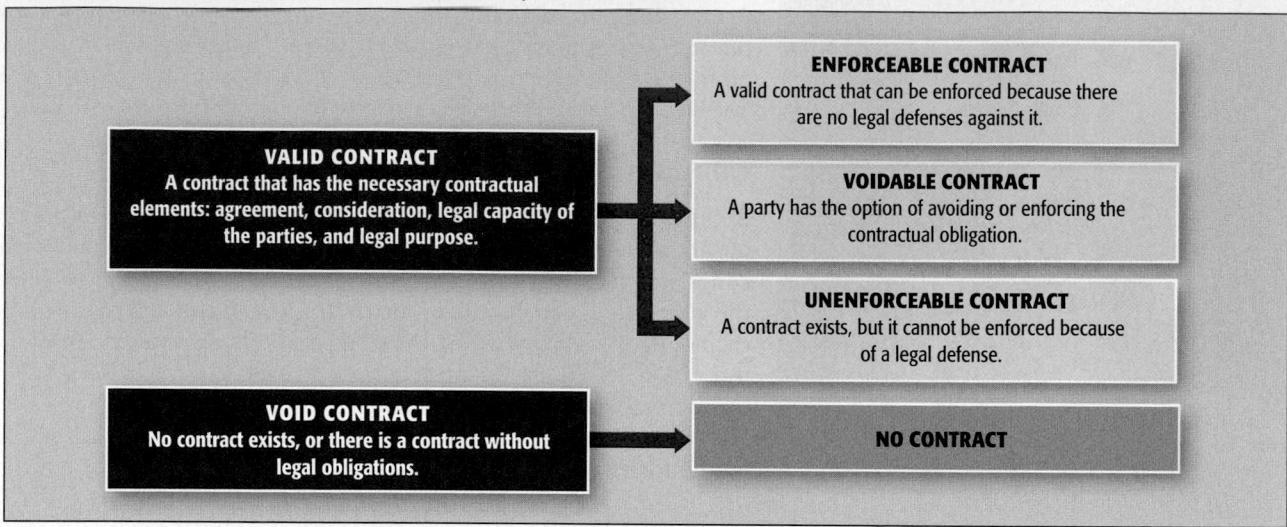

EXAMPLE 9.6   A vacationing physician is driving down the highway and finds Emerson lying unconscious on the side of the road. The physician renders medical aid that saves Emerson's life. Although the injured, unconscious Emerson did not solicit the medical aid and was not aware that the aid had been rendered, Emerson received a valuable benefit, and the requirements for a quasi contract were fulfilled. In such a situation, the law normally will impose a quasi contract, and Emerson will have to pay the physician for the reasonable value of the medical services provided. ●

Limitations on Quasi-Contractual Recovery

Although quasi contracts exist to prevent unjust enrichment, the party who obtains a benefit is not liable for the fair value in some situations. Basically, a party who has conferred a benefit on someone else unnecessarily or as a result of misconduct or negligence cannot invoke the doctrine of quasi contract. The enrichment in those situations will not be considered "unjust." **CASE EXAMPLE 9.7**   Qwest Wireless, LLC, provides wireless phone services in Arizona and thirteen other states. Qwest marketed and sold handset insurance to its wireless customers, although it did not have a license to sell insurance in Arizona or in any other state. Patrick and Vicki Van Zanen sued Qwest in a federal court for unjust enrichment based on its receipt of sales commissions for the insurance. The court agreed that Qwest had violated the insurance-licensing statute, but found that the sales commissions did not constitute unjust enrichment because the customers had, in fact, received the insurance. Qwest had not retained a benefit (the commissions) without paying for it (providing insurance); thus, the Van Zanens and other customers did not suffer unfair detriment.[4] ●

When an Actual Contract Exists

The doctrine of quasi contract generally cannot be used when an actual contract covers the area in controversy. This is because a remedy already exists if a party is unjustly enriched as a result of a breach of contract: the nonbreaching party can sue the breaching party for breach of contract. **EXAMPLE 9.8**   Fung contracts with Cameron to deliver a furnace to a

---

4. *Van Zanen v. Qwest Wireless, LLC,* 522 F.3d 1127 (10th Cir. 2008).

building owned by Bateman. Fung delivers the furnace, but Cameron never pays Fung. Bateman has been unjustly enriched in this situation, to be sure. Nevertheless, Fung cannot recover from Bateman in quasi contract because Fung had an actual contract with Cameron. Fung already has a remedy—he can sue for breach of contract to recover the price of the furnace from Cameron. In this situation, the court does not need to impose a quasi contract to achieve justice. ●

▶ Interpretation of Contracts

Sometimes, parties agree that a contract has been formed but disagree on its meaning or legal effect. One reason that this may happen is that one of the parties is not familiar with the legal terminology used in the contract. To an extent, *plain language laws* have helped to avoid this difficulty. Sometimes, though, a dispute may still arise over the meaning of a contract simply because the rights or obligations under the contract are not expressed clearly—no matter how "plain" the language used.

In this section, we look at some common law rules of contract interpretation. These rules, including the *plain meaning rule* and various other rules that have evolved over time, provide the courts with guidelines for deciding disputes over how contract terms or provisions should be interpreted. Exhibit 9–3 provides a brief graphic summary of how these rules are applied.

Preventing Legal Disputes 🖊

To avoid disputes over contract interpretation, make sure your intentions are clearly expressed in your contracts. Careful drafting of contracts not only helps prevent potential disputes over the meaning of certain terms but may also be crucial if the firm brings a lawsuit or needs to defend against a lawsuit for breach of contract. By using simple, clear language and avoiding legalese, you have taken a major step toward avoiding contract disputes.

Plain Language Laws

The federal government and a majority of the states have enacted plain language laws to regulate legal writing and eliminate "legalese." All federal agencies are required to use plain language in most of their forms and written communications. Plain language requirements have been extended to agency rulemaking as well. States frequently have plain language

● *Exhibit* **9–3** Rules of Contract Interpretation

WRITTEN CONTRACT

PLAIN MEANING RULE
If a court determines that the terms of the contract are clear from the written document alone, the plain meaning rule will apply, and the contract will be enforced according to what it clearly states.

OTHER RULES OF INTERPRETATION
If a court finds that there is a need to determine the parties' intentions from the terms of the contract, the court will apply a number of well-established rules of interpretation. For example, one rule of interpretation states that specific wording will be given greater weight than general wording.

laws that apply to consumer contracts, which are those made primarily for personal, family, or household purposes. The legal profession has also moved toward plain English, and court rules in many jurisdictions require attorneys to use plain language in court documents.

The Plain Meaning Rule

NOTE   No one can avoid contractual obligations by claiming that she or he did not read the contract. A contract normally is interpreted as if each party read every word carefully.

When a contract's writing is clear and unequivocal, a court will enforce it according to its obvious terms. The meaning of the terms must be determined from *the face of the instrument*—from the written document alone. This is sometimes referred to as the *plain meaning rule*.

Under this rule, if a contract's words appear to be clear and unambiguous, a court cannot consider *extrinsic evidence*, which is any evidence not contained in the document itself. Admissibility of extrinsic evidence can significantly affect how a court interprets ambiguous contractual provisions and thus can affect the outcome of litigation. The following case illustrates these points.

Case 9.2   Wagner v. Columbia Pictures Industries, Inc.

California Court of Appeal, Second District, 146 Cal.App.4th 586, 52 Cal.Rptr.3d 898 (2007).

Lucy Liu (left), Drew Barrymore (right), and Cameron Diaz starred in the Charlie's Angels *movies.*

FACTS   Actor Robert Wagner entered into an agreement with Spelling-Goldberg Productions (SGP) "relating to *Charlie's Angels* (herein called the 'series')." The contract entitled Wagner to 50 percent of the net profits that SGP received "for the right to exhibit photoplays of the series and from the exploitation of all ancillary, music and subsidiary rights in connection therewith." SGP hired Ivan Goff and Ben Roberts to write the series, under a contract subject to the Writers Guild of America Minimum Basic Agreement (MBA).[a] The MBA stipulates that the writer of a television show retains the right to make and market films based on the material, subject to the producer's right to buy this right if the writer decides to sell it within five years. The first *Charlie's Angels* episode aired in 1976. In 1982, SGP sold its rights to the series to Columbia Pictures Industries, Inc. Thirteen years later, Columbia bought the movie rights to the material from Goff's and Roberts's heirs. In 2000 and 2003, Columbia produced and distributed two *Charlie's Angels* films. Wagner filed a suit in a California state court against Columbia, claiming a share of the profits from the films. The court granted Columbia's motion for summary judgment. Wagner appealed to a state intermediate appellate court.

ISSUE   Does the language of the Wagner contract with SGP entitle Columbia to all of the profits from the two *Charlie's Angels* films?

DECISION   Yes. The state intermediate appellate court affirmed the lower court's judgment. The contract "unambiguously" stated the conditions under which the parties were to share the films' profits, and those conditions had not occurred.

REASON   Wagner offered evidence to show that a previous contract with SGP involving a property titled *Love Song* had been intended to give him half of the net profits that SGP received from the property from all sources without limitation as to source or time. Wagner argued that because the profits provision in the *Charlie's Angels* agreement used identical language, the provision should be interpreted to give him the same share. The court stated that an "agreement is the writing itself." Extrinsic evidence is not admissible "to show intention independent of an unambiguous written instrument." In this case, even if the parties intended Wagner to share in the profits from all sources, "they did not say so in their contract." Under the language of the contract, Wagner was entitled to share in the profits from the exercise of the movie rights to *Charlie's Angels* if those rights were exploited as "ancillary" or "subsidiary" to the primary "right to exhibit photoplays of the series," but not if those rights were acquired separately. SGP's contract with Goff and Roberts was subject to the MBA, under which the writers kept the movie rights, which the producer could buy if the writers opted to sell them within five years. SGP did not acquire the movie rights to *Charlie's Angels* by exercising this right within the five-year period. Columbia obtained those rights independently more than five years later.

FOR CRITICAL ANALYSIS—Legal Consideration   *How might the result in this case have been different if the court had allowed Wagner's extrinsic evidence of a prior contract regarding "Love Song" to be used as evidence in this dispute?*

---

a.   The Writers Guild of America is an association of screen and television writers that negotiates industrywide agreements with motion picture and television producers to cover the rights of its members.

(AP Photo/Ann Johansson)

Other Rules of Interpretation

Generally, a court will interpret the language to give effect to the parties' intent *as expressed in their contract*. This is the primary purpose of the rules of interpretation—to determine the parties' intent from the language used in their agreement and to give effect to that intent. A court normally will not make or remake a contract, nor will it normally interpret the language according to what the parties *claim* their intent was when they made the contract.[5] The courts use the following rules in interpreting contractual terms:

1. Insofar as possible, a reasonable, lawful, and effective meaning will be given to all of a contract's terms.
2. A contract will be interpreted as a whole; individual, specific clauses will be considered subordinate to the contract's general intent. All writings that are a part of the same transaction will be interpreted together.
3. Terms that were the subject of separate negotiation will be given greater consideration than standardized terms and terms that were not negotiated separately.
4. A word will be given its ordinary, commonly accepted meaning, and a technical word or term will be given its technical meaning, unless the parties clearly intended something else.
5. Specific and exact wording will be given greater consideration than general language.
6. Written or typewritten terms prevail over preprinted terms.
7. Because a contract should be drafted in clear and unambiguous language, a party that uses ambiguous expressions is held to be responsible for the ambiguities. Thus, when the language has more than one meaning, it will be interpreted *against* the party that drafted the contract.
8. Evidence of trade usage, prior dealing, and course of performance may be admitted to clarify the meaning of an ambiguously worded contract. (We will define and discuss these terms in Chapter 15.) What each of the parties does pursuant to the contract will be interpreted as consistent with what the other does and with any relevant usage of trade and course of dealing or performance. Express terms (terms expressly stated in the contract) are given the greatest weight, followed by course of performance, course of dealing, and custom and usage of trade—in that order. When considering custom and usage, a court will look at the trade customs and usage common to the particular business or industry and to the locale in which the contract was made or is to be performed.

In the following case, the court was asked to interpret the phrase "increase of hazard" as it appeared in an insurance policy.

> *"The difference between the right word and the almost right word is the difference between lightning and a lightning bug."*
>
> Mark Twain, 1835–1910
> (American author and humorist)

---

5. Nevertheless, if a court finds that, even after applying the rules of interpretation, the terms are susceptible to more than one meaning, the court may permit extrinsic evidence to prove what the parties intended. See, for example, *Langdon v. United Restaurants, Inc.*, 105 S.W.3d 882 (Mo.Ct.App. 2003).

Case 9.3 U.S. Bank, N.A. v. Tennessee Farmers Mutual Insurance Co.

Tennessee Supreme Court, 277 S.W.3d 381 (2009).
www.tsc.state.tn.us[a]

FACTS Jessica Robbins bought a house in Humboldt, Tennessee. U.S. Bank, N.A.,[b] financed the purchase. Tennessee Farmers Mutual Insurance Company issued the homeowner's insurance policy. The policy included a "standard mortgage clause" that promised payment to the bank unless the house was lost due to an "increase in hazard" that the bank knew about but did not tell the insurer. When Robbins fell behind on her mortgage payments, the bank started foreclosure proceedings. No one told the insurer. Robbins filed for bankruptcy, which postponed foreclosure. Meanwhile, the house "blew up," in Robbins's words, and was destroyed in a fire caused by

---

a. In the left-hand column, in the "Court & Ethics Opinions" pull-down menu, select "Supreme Court 1st Quarter 2009." On that page, scroll to the summary of the case and click on "View" to access the opinion. The Tennessee Court System maintains this Web site.

b. The abbreviation *N.A.* stands for *National Association,* which means the bank was chartered by the federal government under the National Bank Act.

Case 9.3—Continues next page ➡

Case 9.3–Continued

(trixieskips/Creative Commons)

Chemicals and materials used to make methamphetamine destroyed a residence and started a legal dispute between the mortgage lender and the mortgage insurer.

chemicals used to make methamphetamine. The bank filed a claim under the policy, but the insurer refused to pay. The bank then filed a suit in a Tennessee state court against the insurer on the ground of breach of contract. The insurer argued that it had not been told by the bank of an "increase in hazard"–the foreclosure. The court ruled in favor of the bank, an appellate court reversed in favor of the insurer, and the bank appealed.

ISSUE   Does the phrase "increase of hazard," by its ordinary meaning, include the commencement of foreclosure proceedings?

DECISION   No. The Tennessee Supreme Court reversed the judgment of the appellate court and remanded the case to the trial court. The failure to notify the insurer of the foreclosure did not breach the terms of the policy.

REASON   An insurance policy is subject to the same rules of construction as any other contract and should be interpreted and enforced as written. Its terms should be given their plain, ordinary meaning because "the primary rule of contract interpretation is to ascertain and give effect to the intent of the parties." In cases involving standard mortgage clauses that require notice of an "increase of hazard," other courts have found that the plain meaning of the words refers to physical conditions on the property that pose a risk, not to events such as foreclosure. Thus, the bank was not required to notify the insurer under the terms of the policy, and the lack of notice did not invalidate the coverage. Besides, the house "burned not because of an impending foreclosure sale, but rather due to a mishap during an occupant's production of an illegal substance." And because of the homeowner's bankruptcy, "at the time of the fire, there was no ongoing foreclosure proceeding."

WHY IS THIS CASE IMPORTANT?   *This case underscores the importance of insurance to businesses that lend money or otherwise extend credit secured by the property of a borrower who retains its possession. Those businesses should be certain that their interests are protected by the applicable policy. The court's interpretation of the policy at issue here–and the reasoning that determined the outcome–emphasize the significance of the words used in an insurance contract.*

 Reviewing . . . Nature and Classification

Mitsui Bank hired Ross Duncan as a branch manager in one of its Southern California locations. At that time, Duncan received an employee handbook informing him that Mitsui would review his performance and salary level annually. In 2008, Mitsui decided to create a new lending program to help financially troubled businesses stay afloat. It hired Duncan as the credit development officer (CDO) and gave him a written compensation plan. Duncan's compensation was to be based on the new program's success and involved a bonus and commissions based on new loans and sales volume. The written plan also stated, "This compensation plan will be reviewed and potentially amended after one year and will be subject to such review and amendment annually thereafter." Duncan's efforts as CDO were successful, and the business-lending program he developed grew to represent 25 percent of Mitsui's business in 2009 and 40 percent by 2010. Nevertheless, Mitsui not only refused to give Duncan a raise in 2009 but also amended his compensation plan to significantly reduce his compensation and to change his performance evaluation schedule to every six months. When he had still not received a raise by 2010, Duncan retired as CDO and filed a lawsuit claiming breach of contract. Using the information presented in the chapter, answer the following questions.

1. What are the four requirements of a valid contract?
2. Did Duncan have a valid contract with Mitsui for employment as credit development officer? If so, was it a bilateral or a unilateral contract?
3. What are the requirements of an implied-in-fact contract?
4. Can Duncan establish an implied-in-fact contract based on the employment manual or the written compensation plan? Why or why not?

Business Application

How Can You Avoid Unintended Employment Contracts?*

Employers have learned many lessons from court decisions. In recent years, for example, the message has been clear that employers should be cautious about what they say in their employment manuals.

Employment Manuals and Implied-in-Fact Contracts

Promises made in an employment manual may create an implied-in-fact employment contract. If an employment handbook states that employees will be fired only for specific causes, the employer may be held to that "promise." This is true even if, by state law, employment is "at will"—that is, the employer is allowed to hire and fire employees at will, with or without cause. The at-will doctrine will not apply if the terms of employment are subject to an implied contract between the employer and the employee. If a court holds that an implied employment contract exists—on the basis of promises made in an employment manual—the employment is no longer at will. The employer will be bound by the contract and liable for damages for breaching the contract.

Taking Precautions

Employers who wish to avoid potential liability for breaching unintended employment contracts should therefore make it clear to employees that the policies expressed in an employment manual are not to be interpreted as contractual promises. An effective way to do this is to inform employees, when initially giving them the handbook or discussing its contents with them, that the handbook is not intended as a contract and to include a disclaimer to that effect in the employment manual. The disclaimer might read as follows: "This policy manual describes the basic personnel policies

and practices of our Company. You should understand that the manual does not modify our Company's 'at-will' employment doctrine or provide employees with any kind of contractual rights."

The employer should make the disclaimer clear and prominent so that the applicant cannot later claim that it was the employer's fault that the employee did not see the disclaimer. A disclaimer will be clear and prominent if it is set off from the surrounding text by the use of larger type, a different color, all capital letters, or some other device that calls the reader's attention to it.

The employer should also avoid including in the handbook any definite promises such as that employees will be fired only for cause or that after they have worked for a specific length of time, they will not be fired except for certain reasons.

CHECKLIST FOR THE EMPLOYER

1. **Inform new employees that statements in an employment handbook are not intended as contractual terms.**
2. **Include clear and prominent disclaimers to this effect in employment applications and in the employment handbook.**
3. **Ask employees to sign a statement that they have read the disclaimer and understand that the employment handbook is not a contract and does not create any legally binding obligations.**
4. **Avoid including in the handbook any definite promises relating to job security, and include a clear and prominent disclaimer of contractual liability for any statements made within the handbook.**

*This *Business Application* is not meant to substitute for the services of an attorney who is licensed to practice law in your state.

 Key Terms

bilateral contract 221	informal contract 223	quasi contract 225
contract 219	objective theory of contracts 220	unenforceable contract 225
executed contract 224	offeree 221	unilateral contract 222
executory contract 224	offeror 221	valid contract 225
express contract 223	promise 218	void contract 225
formal contract 223	promisee 219	voidable contract 225
implied-in-fact contract 223	promisor 219	

Chapter Summary: Nature and Classification

An Overview of Contract Law (See pages 219–220.)	1. *Sources of contract law*–The common law governs all contracts except when it has been modified or replaced by statutory law, such as the Uniform Commercial Code (UCC), or by administrative agency regulations. The UCC governs contracts for the sale or lease of goods (see Chapter 15). 2. *The function of contracts*–Contract law establishes what kinds of promises will be legally binding and supplies procedures for enforcing legally binding promises, or agreements. 3. *The definition of a contract*–A contract is an agreement that can be enforced in court. It is formed by two or more competent parties who agree to perform or to refrain from performing some act now or in the future. 4. *Objective theory of contracts*–In contract law, intent is determined by objective facts, not by the personal or subjective intent, or belief, of a party.
Elements of a Contract (See pages 220–221.)	1. *Requirements of a valid contract*–The four requirements of a valid contract are agreement, consideration, contractual capacity, and legality. 2. *Defenses to the enforceability of a contract*–Even if the four requirements of a valid contract are met, a contract may be unenforceable if it lacks genuineness of assent or is not in the required form.
Types of Contracts (See pages 221–225.)	1. *Bilateral*–A promise for a promise. 2. *Unilateral*–A promise for an act (acceptance is the completed–or substantial–performance of the contract by the offeree). 3. *Formal*–Requires a special form for contract formation. 4. *Informal*–Requires no special form for contract formation. 5. *Express*–Formed by words (oral, written, or a combination). 6. *Implied in fact*–Formed at least in part by the conduct of the parties. 7. *Executed*–A fully performed contract. 8. *Executory*–A contract not yet fully performed. 9. *Valid*–A contract that has the necessary contractual elements of offer and acceptance, consideration, parties with legal capacity, and a legal purpose. 10. *Voidable*–A contract in which a party has the option of avoiding or enforcing the contractual obligation. 11. *Unenforceable*–A valid contract that cannot be enforced because of a legal defense. 12. *Void*–No contract exists, or there is a contract without legal obligations.
Quasi Contracts (See pages 225–227.)	A quasi contract, or a contract implied in law, is a contract that is imposed by law to prevent unjust enrichment.
Interpretation of Contracts (See pages 227–229.)	Increasingly, plain language laws require private contracts to be written in plain language so that the terms are clear and understandable to the parties. Under the plain meaning rule, a court will enforce the contract according to its plain terms, the meaning of which must be determined from the written document alone. Other rules applied by the courts when interpreting contracts are set out on page 229.

 ExamPrep

ISSUE SPOTTERS

1 Joli signs and returns a letter from Kerin, referring to a book and its price. When Kerin delivers the book, Joli sends it back, claiming that they have no contract. Kerin claims they do. What standard determines whether these parties have a contract?

2 Dyna tells Ed that she will pay Ed $1,000 to set fire to Dyna's store, so that she can collect funds under a fire insurance policy. Ed sets fire to the store, but Dyna refuses to pay. Can Ed recover? Why or why not?

BEFORE THE TEST

Check your answers to the Issue Spotters, and at the same time, take the interactive quiz for this chapter. Go to **www.cengage.com/blaw/blt** and click on "Chapter 9." First, click on "Answers to Issue Spotters" to check your answers.

Next, click on "Interactive Quiz" to assess your mastery of the concepts in this chapter. Then click on "Flashcards" to review this chapter's Key Term definitions.

For Review

Answers for the even-numbered questions in this For Review *section can be found on this text's accompanying Web site at* **www.cengage.com/blaw/blt**. *Select "Chapter 9" and click on "For Review."*

1 What is a contract? What is the objective theory of contracts?

2 What are the four basic elements necessary to the formation of a valid contract?

3 What is the difference between an implied-in-fact contract and an implied-in-law contract (quasi contract)?

4 How does a void contract differ from a voidable contract? What is an unenforceable contract?

5 What rules guide the courts in interpreting contracts?

Hypothetical Scenarios and Case Problems

9–1 Express versus Implied Contracts. Suppose that a local businessperson, McDougal, is a good friend of Krunch, the owner of a local candy store. Every day on his lunch hour, McDougal goes into Krunch's candy store and spends about five minutes looking at the candy. After examining Krunch's candy and talking with Krunch, McDougal usually buys one or two candy bars. One afternoon, McDougal goes into Krunch's candy shop, looks at the candy, and picks up a $1 candy bar. Seeing that Krunch is very busy, he catches Krunch's eye, waves the candy bar at Krunch without saying a word, and walks out. Is there a contract? If so, classify it within the categories presented in this chapter.

9–2 Hypothetical Question with Sample Answer Janine was hospitalized with severe abdominal pain and placed in an intensive care unit. Her doctor told the hospital personnel to order around-the-clock nursing care for Janine. At the hospital's request, a nursing services firm, Nursing Services Unlimited, provided two weeks of in-hospital care and, after Janine was sent home, an additional two weeks of at-home care. During the at-home period of care, Janine was fully aware that she was receiving the benefit of the nursing services. Nursing Services later billed Janine $4,000 for the nursing care, but Janine refused to pay on the ground that she had never contracted for the services, either orally or in writing. In view of the fact that no express contract was ever formed, can Nursing Services recover the $4,000 from Janine? If so, under what legal theory? Discuss.

—For a sample answer to Question 9–2, go to Appendix E at the end of this text.

9–3 Contract Classification. Jay's Flying Advertising, LLC, contracted with Big Bob's Burger restaurant to fly an advertisement above the Connecticut beaches. The advertisement offered $5,000 to any person who could swim from the Connecticut beaches to Long Island across the Long Island Sound in less than a day. Frank Dimitri saw the streamer and accepted the challenge. He started his marathon swim that same day at 10 A.M. After he had been swimming for four hours and was about halfway across the sound, Dimitri saw another plane pulling a streamer that read, "Big Bob's Burger revokes." Is there a contract between Dimitri and Big Bob's? If there is a contract, what type(s) of contract is (are) formed?

9–4 Implied Contract. Thomas Rinks and Joseph Shields developed Psycho Chihuahua, a caricature of a Chihuahua dog with a "do-not-back-down" attitude. They promoted and marketed the character through their company, Wrench, L.L.C. Ed Alfaro and Rudy Pollak, representatives of Taco Bell Corp., learned of Psycho Chihuahua and met with Rinks and Shields to talk about using the character as a Taco Bell "icon." Wrench sent artwork, merchandise, and marketing ideas to Alfaro, who promoted the character within Taco Bell. Alfaro asked Wrench to propose terms for Taco Bell's use of Psycho Chihuahua. Taco Bell did not accept Wrench's terms, but Alfaro continued to promote the character within the company. Meanwhile, Taco Bell hired a new advertising agency, which proposed an advertising campaign involving a Chihuahua. When Alfaro learned of this proposal, he sent the Psycho Chihuahua materials to the agency. Taco Bell made a Chihuahua the focus of its marketing but paid nothing to Wrench. Wrench filed a suit against Taco Bell in a federal district court, claiming, in part, that it had an implied contract with Taco Bell, which the latter breached. Do these facts satisfy the requirements for an implied contract? Why or why not? [*Wrench, L.L.C. v. Taco Bell Corp.*, 256 F.3d 446 (6th Cir. 2001), *cert.* denied, 534 U.S. 1114, 122 S.Ct. 921 151 L.Ed.2d 805 (2002)]

9–5 Case Problem with Sample Answer In December 2000, Nextel South Corp., a communications firm, contacted R. A. Clark Consulting, Ltd., an executive search firm, about finding an employment manager for Nextel's call center in Atlanta, Georgia. Over the next six months, Clark screened, evaluated, and interviewed more than three hundred candidates. Clark provided Nextel with more than fifteen candidate summaries, including one for Dan Sax. Nextel hired Sax for the position at an annual salary of $75,000. Sax started work on June 25, 2001, took two weeks' vacation, and quit on July 31

in the middle of a project. Clark spent the next six weeks looking for a replacement, until Nextel asked Clark to stop. Clark billed Nextel for its service, but Nextel refused to pay, asserting, in part, that the parties had not signed an agreement. Nextel's typical agreement specified payment to an employment agency of 20 percent of an employee's salary. Clark filed a suit in a Georgia state court against Nextel to recover the reasonable value of its services. What is a quasi contract? What would Clark have to show to recover on this basis? Should the court rule in Clark's favor? Explain. [*Nextel South Corp. v. R. A. Clark Consulting, Ltd.,* 266 Ga.App. 85, 596 S.E.2d 416 (2004)]
—**After you have answered Problem 9–5, compare your answer with the sample answer given on the Web site that accompanies this text. Go to www.cengage.com/blaw/blt, select "Chapter 9," and click on "Case Problem with Sample Answer."**

9–6 Contract Enforceability. California's Subdivision Map Act (SMA) prohibits the sale of real property until a map of its subdivision is filed with, and approved by, the appropriate state agency. In November 2004, Black Hills Investments, Inc., entered into two contracts with Albertson's, Inc., to buy two parcels of property in a shopping center development. Each contract required that "all governmental approvals relating to any lot split [or] subdivision" be obtained before the sale but permitted Albertson's to waive this condition. Black Hills made a $133,000 deposit on the purchase. A few weeks later, before the sales were complete, Albertson's filed with a local state agency a map that subdivided the shopping center into four parcels, including the two that Black Hills had agreed to buy. In January 2005, Black Hills objected to concessions that Albertson's had made to a buyer of one of the other parcels, told Albertson's that it was terminating its deal, and asked for a return of its deposit. Albertson's refused. Black Hills filed a suit in a California state court against Albertson's, arguing that the contracts were void. Are these contracts valid, voidable, unenforceable, or void? Explain. [*Black Hills Investments, Inc. v. Albertson's, Inc.,* 146 Cal.App.4th 883, 53 Cal.Rptr.3d 263 (4 Dist. 2007)]

9–7 Interpretation of Contracts. Lisa and Darrell Miller married in 1983 and had two children, Landon and Spencer. The Millers divorced in 2003 and entered into a "Joint Custody Implementation Plan" (JCIP). Under the JCIP, Darrell agreed to "begin setting funds aside for the minor children to attend post-secondary education necessary to pay tuition, books, supplies, and room and board not to exceed four (4) years."

After Landon's eighteenth birthday, Darrell filed a petition in a Louisiana state court to reduce the amount of the child support that he was paying to Lisa. In response, she asked the court to order Darrell to pay the boys' college expenses but offered no evidence to support the request. Darrell contended that the JCIP was not clear on this point. Do the rules of contract interpretation, applied to the phrasing of the Millers' JCIP, support Lisa's request or Darrell's contention? Explain. [*Miller v. Miller,* 1 So.3d 815 (La.App. 2009)]

9–8 ⚖ **A Question of Ethics** *International Business Machines Corp.* (IBM) *hired Niels Jensen in 2000 as a software sales representative. In 2001, IBM presented a new "Software Sales Incentive Plan" (SIP) at a conference for its sales employees. A brochure given to the attendees stated, "[T]here are no caps to your earnings; the more you sell, * * * the more earnings for you." The brochure outlined how the plan worked and referred the employees to the "Sales Incentives" section of IBM's corporate intranet for more details. Jensen was given a "quota letter" that said he would be paid $75,000 as a base salary and, if he attained his quota, an additional $75,000 as incentive pay. In September, Jensen closed a deal with the U.S. Department of the Treasury's Internal Revenue Service worth more than $24 million to IBM. Relying on the SIP brochure, Jensen estimated his commission to be $2.6 million. IBM paid him less than $500,000, however. Jensen filed a suit in a federal district court against IBM, contending that the SIP brochure and quota letter constituted a unilateral offer that became a binding contract when Jensen closed the sale. In view of these facts, consider the following questions.* [*Jensen v. International Business Machines Corp.,* 454 F.3d 382 (4th Cir. 2006)]

1 Would it be fair to the employer in this case to hold that the SIP brochure and the quota letter created a unilateral contract if IBM did not *intend* to create such a contract? Would it be fair to the employee to hold that *no* contract was created? Explain.

2 The "Sales Incentives" section of IBM's intranet included a clause providing that "[m]anagement will decide if an adjustment to the payment is appropriate" when an employee closes a large transaction. Jensen's quota letter stated, "[The SIP] program does not constitute a promise by IBM to make any distributions under it. IBM reserves the right to adjust the program terms or to cancel or otherwise modify the program at any time." How do these statements affect your answers to the above questions? From an ethical perspective, would it be fair to hold that a contract exists despite these statements?

▶ **Critical Thinking and Writing Assignments**

9–9 Critical Legal Thinking. Review the basic requirements for a valid contract listed at the beginning of this chapter. In view of those requirements, analyze the relationship entered into when

a student enrolls in a college or university. Has a contract been formed? If so, is it a bilateral contract or a unilateral contract? Discuss.

Practical Internet Exercises

Go to this text's Web site at **www.cengage.com/blaw/blt**, select "Chapter 9," and click on "Practical Internet Exercises." There you will find the following Internet research exercises that you can perform to learn more about the topics covered in this chapter.

Practical Internet Exercise 9–1: LEGAL PERSPECTIVE—Contracts and Contract Provisions
Practical Internet Exercise 9–2: MANAGEMENT PERSPECTIVE—Implied Employment Contracts
Practical Internet Exercise 9–3: HISTORICAL PERSPECTIVE—Contracts in Ancient Mesopotamia

Chapter 10

Agreement in Traditional and E-Contracts

> "It is necessity that makes laws."
> —Voltaire, 1649–1778
> (French philosopher and writer)

Chapter Outline

- Agreement
- Agreement in E-Contracts
- The Uniform Electronic Transactions Act

(©Jamaka, 2009. Used under license from Shutterstock.com)

posit or any other account(s) in my/our name(s) den
onditions set out below. In consideration of Nation
es to me/us, I/we agree to be bound by the terms and c
ereafter opened or continued in the same name(s) by the

TERMS AND CONDITIONS

person "I", "me", or "my" shall
conditions shall bind each one
collectively and all agreements,
mers are joint and several

costs and expenses
therewith at such rates
in its absolute discretio
the manner and, at such
discretion

Learning Objectives

After reading this chapter, you should be able to answer the following questions:

1. What elements are necessary for an effective offer? What are some examples of nonoffers?

2. In what circumstances will an offer be irrevocable?

3. What are the elements that are necessary for an effective acceptance?

4. How do shrink-wrap and click-on agreements differ from other contracts? How have traditional laws been applied to these agreements?

5. What is the Uniform Electronic Transactions Act? What are some of the major provisions of this act?

Voltaire's statement that it is "necessity that makes laws" is certainly true in regard to contracts. In Chapter 9, we pointed out that promises and agreements, and the knowledge that some of those promises and agreements will be legally enforced, are essential to civilized society. The homes we live in, the food we eat, the clothes we wear, the cars we drive, the books we read, the videos and recordings we watch and listen to—all of these have been purchased through contractual agreements. Contract law developed over time, through the common law tradition, to meet society's need to know with certainty what kinds of promises, or contracts, will be enforced and the point at which a valid and binding contract is formed.

For a contract to be valid and enforceable, the requirements listed in Chapter 9 must be met. In this chapter, we look closely at the first of these requirements, *agreement*. Agreement is required to form a contract, regardless of whether it is formed in the traditional way by exchanging paper documents or online by exchanging electronic messages or documents. In today's world, many contracts are formed via the Internet. We discuss online offers and acceptances and examine some laws that have been created to apply to electronic contracts, or **e-contracts,** in the latter part of this chapter.

E-Contract A contract that is formed electronically.

Agreement A meeting of two or more minds in regard to the terms of a contract; usually broken down into two events—an offer by one party to form a contract and an acceptance of the offer by the person to whom the offer is made.

▶ Agreement

An essential element for contract formation is **agreement**—the parties must agree on the terms of the contract. Ordinarily, agreement is evidenced by two events: an *offer* and an *acceptance*. One party offers a certain bargain to another party, who then accepts that bargain.

Because words often fail to convey the precise meaning intended, the law of contracts generally adheres to the *objective theory of contracts*, as discussed in Chapter 9. Under this theory, a party's words and conduct are held to mean whatever a reasonable person in the offeree's position would think they meant.

Requirements of the Offer

Offer A promise or commitment to perform or refrain from performing some specified act in the future.

An **offer** is a promise or commitment to perform or refrain from performing some specified act in the future. As discussed in Chapter 9, the party making an offer is called the *offeror*, and the party to whom the offer is made is called the *offeree*.

Three elements are necessary for an offer to be effective:

1. There must be a serious, objective intention by the offeror.
2. The terms of the offer must be reasonably certain, or definite, so that the parties and the court can ascertain the terms of the contract.
3. The offer must be communicated to the offeree.

Once an effective offer has been made, the offeree's acceptance of that offer creates a legally binding contract (providing the other essential elements for a valid and enforceable contract are present).

INTENTION The first requirement for an effective offer is a serious, objective intention on the part of the offeror. Intent is not determined by the *subjective* intentions, beliefs, or assumptions of the offeror. Rather, it is determined by what a reasonable person in the offeree's position would conclude the offeror's words and actions meant. Offers made in obvious anger, jest, or undue excitement do not meet the serious-and-objective-intent test. Because these offers are not effective, an offeree's acceptance does not create an agreement.

EXAMPLE 10.1 You and three classmates ride to school each day in Julio's new automobile, which has a market value of $20,000. One cold morning, the four of you get into the car, but it will not start. Julio yells in anger, "I'll sell this car to anyone for $500!" You drop $500 in his lap. A reasonable person, taking into consideration Julio's frustration and the obvious difference in value between the car's market price and the purchase price, would declare that Julio's offer was not made with serious and objective intent and that you do not have an agreement. •

The concept of intention can be further clarified through an examination of the types of statements that are *not* offers. We look at these expressions and statements in the subsections that follow. In the classic case presented next, the court considered whether an offer made "after a few drinks" met the serious-intent requirement.

Classic Case 10.1 **Lucy v. Zehmer**

Supreme Court of Appeals of Virginia, 196 Va. 493, 84 S.E.2d 516 (1954).

FACTS W. O. Lucy and A. H. Zehmer had known each other for fifteen to twenty years. For some time, Lucy had been wanting to buy Zehmer's farm. Zehmer had always told Lucy that he was not interested in selling. One night, Lucy stopped in to visit with the Zehmers at a restaurant they operated. Lucy said to Zehmer, "I bet you wouldn't take $50,000 for that place." Zehmer replied, "Yes, I would, too; you wouldn't give fifty." Throughout the evening, the conversation returned to the sale of the farm. At the same time, the parties were drinking whiskey. Eventually, Zehmer wrote up an agreement, on the back of a restaurant check, for the sale

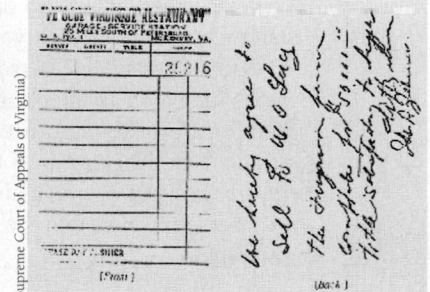

(Supreme Court of Appeals of Virginia)

The receipt from Ye Olde Virginnie Restaurant on which is written: "We hereby agree to sell to W. O. Lucy the Ferguson Farm complete for $50,000.00, title satisfactory to buyer," and signed by the defendants, A. H. and Ida Zehmer.

Case 10.1–Continues next page ➡

Case 10.1–Continued

of the farm, and he asked his wife, Ida, to sign it–which she did. When Lucy brought an action in a Virginia state court to enforce the agreement, Zehmer argued that he had been "high as a Georgia pine" at the time and that the offer had been made in jest: "two doggoned drunks bluffing to see who could talk the biggest and say the most." Lucy claimed that he had not been intoxicated and did not think Zehmer had been, either, given the way Zehmer handled the transaction. The trial court ruled in favor of the Zehmers, and Lucy appealed.

ISSUE   Can the agreement be avoided on the basis of intoxication?

DECISION   No. The agreement to sell the farm was binding.

REASON   The court held that the evidence given about the nature of the conversation, the appearance and completeness of the agreement, and the signing all tended to show that a serious business transaction, not a casual jest, was intended. The court had to look into the objective meaning of the words and acts of the Zehmers: "An agreement or mutual assent is of course essential to a valid contract, but the law imputes to a person an intention corresponding to the reasonable meaning of his words and acts. If his words and acts, judged by a reasonable standard, manifest an inten-

tion to agree, it is immaterial what may be the real but unexpressed state of mind."

WHAT IF THE FACTS WERE DIFFERENT?   *Suppose that the day after Lucy signed the agreement, he decided that he did not want the farm after all, and Zehmer sued Lucy to perform the contract. Would this change in the facts alter the court's decision that Lucy and Zehmer had created an enforceable contract? Why or why not?*

IMPACT OF THIS CASE ON TODAY'S LAW   *This is a classic case in contract law because it so clearly illustrates the objective theory of contracts with respect to determining whether an offer was intended. Today, the objective theory of contracts continues to be applied by the courts, and the* Lucy v. Zehmer *decision is routinely cited as a significant precedent in this area.*

RELEVANT WEB SITES   *To locate information on the Web concerning the* Lucy v. Zehmer *decision, go to this text's Web site at* www.cengage.com/blaw/blt. *Select "Chapter 10" and click on "Classic Cases."*

BE CAREFUL   An opinion is not an offer and not a contract term. Goods or services can be "perfect" in one party's opinion and "poor" in another's.

Expressions of Opinion.   An expression of opinion is not an offer. It does not demonstrate an intention to enter into a binding agreement. **CASE EXAMPLE 10.2**   Hawkins took his son to McGee, a physician, and asked McGee to operate on the son's hand. McGee said that the boy would be in the hospital three or four days and that the hand would *probably* heal a few days later. The son's hand did not heal for a month, but nonetheless the father did not win a suit for breach of contract. The court held that McGee did not make an offer to heal the son's hand in three or four days. He merely expressed an opinion as to when the hand would heal.[1] ●

Statements of Future Intent.   A statement of an *intention* to do something in the future is not an offer. **EXAMPLE 10.3**   If Samir says, "I *plan* to sell my stock in Novation, Inc., for $150 per share," a contract is not created if John "accepts" and tenders $150 per share for the stock. Samir has merely expressed his intention to enter into a future contract for the sale of the stock. If John accepts and tenders the $150 per share, no contract is formed, because a reasonable person would conclude that Samir was only *thinking about* selling his stock, not *promising* to sell it. ●

Preliminary Negotiations.   A request or invitation to negotiate is not an offer; it only expresses a willingness to discuss the possibility of entering into a contract. Examples are statements such as "Will you sell Forest Acres?" and "I wouldn't sell my car for less than $8,000." A reasonable person in the offeree's position would not conclude that such statements indicated an intention to enter into binding obligations. Likewise, when the government and private firms need to have construction work done, they invite contractors to submit bids. The *invitation* to submit bids is not an offer, and a contractor does not bind the government or private firm by submitting a bid. (The bids that the contractors submit are offers, however, and the government or private firm can bind the contractor by accepting the bid.)

---

1. *Hawkins v. McGee*, 84 N.H. 114, 146 A. 641 (1929).

(Paul Friel/Creative Commons)

A $27 million Harrier fighter jet that was offered as a prize in PepsiCo's "Drink Pepsi—Get Stuff" ad campaign. Although the jet was a fanciful jest by PepsiCo, one consumer took the offer seriously and attempted to fulfill the terms for the prize. Is PepsiCo's "offer" of the jet enforceable?

KEEP IN MIND Advertisements are not binding, but they cannot be deceptive.

Advertisements, Catalogues, and Circulars. In general, advertisements, mail-order catalogues, price lists, and circular letters (meant for the general public) are treated as invitations to negotiate, not as offers to form a contract.[2]

CASE EXAMPLE 10.4 An advertisement on the *Science*NOW Web site asked readers to submit "news tips," which the organization would then investigate for possible inclusion in its magazine or on the Web site. Erik Trell, a professor and physician, submitted a manuscript in which he claimed to have solved a famous mathematical problem. When *Science*NOW did not publish the information, Trell filed a lawsuit for breach of contract. He claimed that the *Science*NOW ad was an offer, which he had accepted by submitting his manuscript. The court dismissed Trell's suit, holding that the ad was not an offer, but merely an invitation.[3] ●

Price lists are another form of invitation to negotiate or trade. A seller's price list is not an offer to sell at that price; it merely invites the buyer to offer to buy at that price. In fact, the seller usually puts "prices subject to change" on the price list. Only in rare circumstances will a price quotation be construed as an offer.

Although most advertisements and the like are treated as invitations to negotiate, this does not mean that an advertisement can never be an offer. On some occasions, courts have construed advertisements to be offers because the ads contained definite terms that invited acceptance (such as an ad offering a reward for the return of a lost dog).

Auctions. In an auction, a seller "offers" goods for sale through an auctioneer, but this is not an offer to form a contract. Rather, it is an invitation asking bidders to submit offers. In the context of an auction, a bidder is the offeror, and the auctioneer is the offeree. The offer is accepted when the auctioneer strikes the hammer. Before the fall of the hammer, a bidder may revoke (take back) her or his bid, or the auctioneer may reject that bid or all bids. Typically, an auctioneer will reject a bid that is below the price the seller is willing to accept.

When the auctioneer accepts a higher bid, he or she rejects all previous bids. Because rejection terminates an offer (as will be discussed later), those bids represent offers that have been terminated. Thus, if the highest bidder withdraws his or her bid before the hammer falls, none of the previous bids is reinstated. If the bid is not withdrawn or rejected, the contract is formed when the auctioneer announces, "Going once, going twice, sold!" (or something similar) and lets the hammer fall.

Traditionally, auctions have been either "with reserve" or "without reserve." In an auction with reserve, the seller

---

2. *Restatement (Second) of Contracts*, Section 26, Comment b.

3. *Trell v. American Association for the Advancement of Science*, __ F.Supp.2d __ (W.D.N.Y. 2007).

(Stephen Hilger/Bloomberg News/Landov)

Sotheby's is one of the best-known art auction firms. Here, the auctioneer is accepting bids on Francis Bacon's 1902 painting entitled Study from Innocent X. *This six-and-a-half-foot study of the couching Pope Innocent X ultimately sold for $52.7 million to a telephone bidder. If this were an auction with reserve, could the painting's owner withdraw the painting from the bidding process at any time? Who is the offeror? Who is the offeree?*

(through the auctioneer) may withdraw the goods at any time before the auctioneer closes the sale by announcement or by the fall of the hammer. All auctions are assumed to be auctions with reserve unless the terms of the auction are explicitly stated to be *without reserve*. In an auction without reserve, the goods cannot be withdrawn by the seller and must be sold to the highest bidder. In auctions with reserve, the seller may reserve the right to confirm or reject the sale even after "the hammer has fallen." In this situation, the seller is obligated to notify those attending the auction that sales of goods made during the auction are not final until confirmed by the seller.[4]

Agreements to Agree.   Traditionally, agreements to agree—that is, agreements to agree to the material terms of a contract at some future date—were not considered to be binding contracts. The modern view, however, is that agreements to agree may be enforceable agreements (contracts) if it is clear that the parties intend to be bound by the agreements. In other words, under the modern view the emphasis is on the parties' intent rather than on form.

CASE EXAMPLE 10.5   After a customer was injured and nearly drowned on a water ride at one of its amusement parks, Six Flags, Inc., filed a lawsuit against the manufacturer that had designed the ride. The defendant manufacturer claimed that there was no binding contract between the parties, only preliminary negotiations that were never formalized into a contract to construct the ride. The court, however, held that a faxed document specifying the details of the water ride, along with the parties' subsequent actions (beginning construction and handwriting notes on the fax), was sufficient to show an intent to be bound. Because of the court's finding, the manufacturer was required to provide insurance for the water ride at Six Flags, and its insurer was required to defend Six Flags in the personal-injury lawsuit that arose out of the incident.[5] ●

Increasingly, the courts are holding that a preliminary agreement constitutes a binding contract if the parties have agreed on all essential terms and no disputed issues remain to be resolved.[6] In contrast, if the parties agree on certain major terms but leave other terms open for further negotiation, a preliminary agreement is binding only in the sense that the parties have committed themselves to negotiate the undecided terms in good faith in an effort to reach a final agreement.[7]

In the following case, the dispute was over an agreement to settle a case during the trial. One party claimed that the agreement formed via e-mail was binding, and the other party claimed that it was merely an agreement to agree or to work out the terms of a settlement in the future. Can an exchange of e-mails create a complete and unambiguous agreement?

4. These rules apply under both the common law of contracts and the Uniform Commercial Code, or UCC. See UCC 2–328.

5. *Six Flags, Inc. v. Steadfast Insurance Co.,* 474 F.Supp.2d 201 (D.Mass. 2007).

6. See, for example, *Tractebel Energy Marketing, Inc. v. AEP Power Marketing, Inc.,* 487 F.3d 89 (2d Cir. 2007); and *Florine On Call, Ltd. v. Fluorogas Limited,* No. 01-CV-186 (W.D.Tex. 2002), contract issue affirmed on appeal at 380 F.3d 849 (5th Cir. 2004).

7. See, for example, *MBH, Inc. v. John Otte Oil & Propane, Inc.,* 727 N.W.2d 238 (Neb.App. 2007); and *Barrand v. Whataburger, Inc.,* 214 S.W.3d 122 (Tex.App.—Corpus Christi 2006).

> ### "I fear explanations explanatory of things explained."
>
> Abraham Lincoln, 1809–1865
> (Sixteenth president of the United States, 1861–1865)

Case 10.2 Basis Technology Corp. v. Amazon.com, Inc.

Appeals Court of Massachusetts, 71 Mass.App.Ct. 29, 878 N.E.2d 952 (2008).
www.malawyersweekly.com/macoa.cfm[a]

a. In the search box on the right, enter "71 Mass.App.Ct. 29," and click on "Search." On the resulting page, click on the case name.

FACTS   Basis Technology Corporation created software and provided technical services for a Japanese-language Web site operated by Amazon.com, Inc. The agreement between the two companies allowed for

Case 10.2–Continued

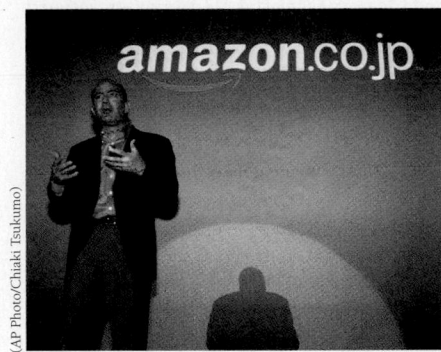

(AP Photo/Chiaki Tsukumo)

Amazon.com founder and chief executive Jeff Bezos speaks during a news conference announcing the online retailer's launch of its Japanese-language Internet site.

separately negotiated contracts for additional services that Basis might provide to Amazon. At the end of 1999, Basis and Amazon entered into stock-purchase agreements. Later, Amazon objected to certain actions related to the securities that Basis sold. Basis sued Amazon for various claims involving these securities and for failing to pay for services performed by Basis that were not included in the original agreement. During the trial, the two parties appeared to reach an agreement to settle out of court via a series of e-mail exchanges outlining the settlement. When Amazon reneged, Basis served a motion to enforce the proposed settlement. The trial judge entered a judgment against Amazon, which appealed.

ISSUE Did the agreement that the two parties entered into via e-mail constitute a binding settlement contract?

DECISION Yes. The Appeals Court of Massachusetts affirmed the trial court's finding that Amazon intended to be bound by the terms of the e-mail exchanges.

REASON The court examined the evidence consisting of e-mails between the two parties. It pointed out that in open court and on the record, counsel "reported the result of the settlement without specification of the terms." Amazon claimed that the e-mail terms were incomplete and were not definite enough to form an agreement. The court noted, nonetheless, that "provisions are not ambiguous simply because the parties have developed different interpretations of them." In the exchange of e-mails, the essential business terms were indeed resolved. Afterwards, the parties were simply proceeding to record the settlement terms, not to create them. The e-mails constituted a complete and unambiguous statement of the parties' desire to be bound by the settlement terms.

WHAT IF THE FACTS WERE DIFFERENT? *Assume that, instead of exchanging e-mails, the attorneys for both sides had a phone conversation that included all of the terms to which they actually agreed in their e-mail exchanges. Would the court have ruled differently? Why or why not?*

Preventing Legal Disputes

To avoid potential legal disputes, be cautious when drafting a memorandum that outlines a preliminary agreement or understanding with another party. If all the major terms are included, a court might hold that the agreement is binding even though you intended it to be only a tentative agreement. One way to avoid being bound is to include in the writing the points of disagreement, as well as those points on which you and the other party agree. Alternatively, you could add a disclaimer to the memorandum stating that, although you anticipate entering a contract in the future, neither party intends to be legally bound to the terms that were discussed. That way, the other party cannot claim that you have already reached an agreement on all essential terms.

DEFINITENESS The second requirement for an effective offer involves the definiteness of its terms. An offer must have reasonably definite terms so that a court can determine if a breach has occurred and give an appropriate remedy.[8]

An offer may invite an acceptance to be worded in such specific terms that the contract is made definite. **EXAMPLE 10.6** Marcus Business Machines contacts your corporation and offers to sell "from one to ten MacCool copying machines for $1,600 each; state number desired in acceptance." Your corporation agrees to buy two copiers. Because the quantity is specified in the acceptance, the terms are definite, and the contract is enforceable. ●

COMMUNICATION A third requirement for an effective offer is communication—the offer must be communicated to the offeree. **EXAMPLE 10.7** Tolson advertises a reward for

---

8. *Restatement (Second) of Contracts*, Section 33. The UCC has relaxed the requirements regarding the definiteness of terms in contracts for the sale of goods. See UCC 2–204(3).

the return of her lost cat. Dirk, not knowing of the reward, finds the cat and returns it to Tolson. Ordinarily, Dirk cannot recover the reward because an essential element of a reward contract is that the one who claims the reward must have known it was offered. A few states would allow recovery of the reward, but not on contract principles—Dirk would be allowed to recover on the basis that it would be unfair to deny him the reward just because he did not know about it. ●

Termination of the Offer

The communication of an effective offer to an offeree gives the offeree the power to transform the offer into a binding, legal obligation (a contract) by an acceptance. This power of acceptance does not continue forever, though. It can be terminated by either the *action of the parties* or by *operation of law.*

TERMINATION BY ACTION OF THE PARTIES   An offer can be terminated by the action of the parties in any of three ways: by revocation, by rejection, or by counteroffer.

Revocation   In contract law, the withdrawal of an offer by an offeror. Unless the offer is irrevocable, it can be revoked at any time prior to acceptance without liability.

Revocation of the Offer.   The offeror's act of withdrawing an offer is referred to as **revocation.** Unless an offer is irrevocable, the offeror usually can revoke the offer (even if he or she has promised to keep the offer open), as long as the revocation is communicated to the offeree before the offeree accepts. Revocation may be accomplished by an express repudiation of the offer (for example, with a statement such as "I withdraw my previous offer of October 17") or by the performance of acts that are inconsistent with the existence of the offer and that are made known to the offeree.

EXAMPLE 10.8   Michelle offers to sell some land to Gary. A month passes, and Gary, who has not accepted the offer, learns that Michelle has sold the property to Liam. Because Michelle's sale of the land to Liam is inconsistent with the continued existence of the offer to Gary, the offer to Gary is effectively revoked. ●

The general rule followed by most states is that a revocation becomes effective when the offeree or the offeree's agent (a person who acts on behalf of another) actually receives it. Therefore, a letter of revocation mailed on April 1 and delivered at the offeree's residence or place of business on April 3 becomes effective on April 3.

An offer made to the general public can be revoked in the same manner in which the offer was originally communicated. **EXAMPLE 10.9**   An electronic goods store offers a $10,000 reward to anyone providing information leading to the apprehension of the persons who burglarized its downtown store. The offer is published in three local papers and in four papers in neighboring communities. To revoke the offer, the store must publish the revocation in all seven papers for the same number of days it published the offer. The revocation is then accessible to the general public, and the offer is revoked even if some particular offeree does not know about the revocation. ●

Option Contract   A contract under which the offeror cannot revoke the offer for a stipulated time period. During this period, the offeree can accept or reject the offer without fear that the offer will be made to another person. The offeree must give consideration for the option (the irrevocable offer) to be enforceable.

Irrevocable Offers.   Although most offers are revocable, some can be made irrevocable. Increasingly, courts refuse to allow an offeror to revoke an offer when the offeree has changed position because of justifiable reliance on the offer (under the doctrine of *detrimental reliance,* or *promissory estoppel,* which will be discussed in Chapter 11). In some circumstances, "firm offers" made by merchants may also be considered irrevocable. We will discuss these offers in Chapter 15.

Another form of irrevocable offer is an option contract. An **option contract** is created when an offeror promises to hold an offer open for a specified period of time in return for a payment (consideration) given by the offeree. An option contract takes away the offeror's power to revoke an offer for the period of time specified in the option. If no time is specified, then a reasonable period of time is implied.

Option contracts are frequently used in conjunction with the sale of real estate. **EXAMPLE 10.10** Tyrell agrees to lease a house from Jackson, the property owner. The lease contract includes a clause stating that Tyrell will pay $15,000 for an option to purchase the property within a specified period of time. If Tyrell decides not to purchase the house after the specified period has lapsed, he loses the $15,000, and Jackson is free to sell the property to another buyer. ●

An option to be notified of "any bona fide offer" to buy certain real estate so that the party with the option could exercise it first was at the center of the dispute in the following case.

Case 10.3 T. W. Nickerson, Inc. v. Fleet National Bank

Appeals Court of Massachusetts, 73 Mass.App.Ct. 434, 898 N.E.2d 868 (2009).

T. W. Nickerson, Inc., in Chatham, Massachusetts, processes wood waste and other debris.

(Space Boy/Creative Commons)

COMPANY PROFILE *T. W. Nickerson, Inc., in Chatham, Massachusetts, processes wood waste and other debris from developers and sells it as loam, gravel, mulch, and other landscaping materials, including pavers and driveway stones. Nickerson also rents bobcats, excavators, loaders, and other equipment. Qualified operators are available for hire with the equipment for excavation and construction projects. To deliver its products, the company maintains a fleet of heavy-duty trucks.*

FACTS In 1993, Steven Clark bought T. W. Nickerson, Inc., from Theodore Nickerson and entered into a lease for the land on which the company was operated. The lease gave the lessee "the right of first refusal to purchase the entire leasehold premises at a price equal to any bona fide offer" and required notice of any offer in writing. The lessor was Fleet National Bank, which held the land in trust for Theodore and later for his spouse, Lillian, and their children. In April 2002, the parties were negotiating a possible sale of the land to Clark for as much as $300,000, when Lillian died. Fleet ended the trust and distributed its assets to the Nickerson children, who, without notifying Clark, made a deal to sell the land to Anthony Bridgewater for $400,000. Bridgewater told Clark about the deal. Clark's company filed a suit in a Massachusetts state court against Fleet and the others for violating the lease's "implied covenant of good faith and fair dealing." The court dismissed the claims. The plaintiff appealed.

ISSUE Is an option contract that requires notice of "any bona fide offer" breached if the party holding the option is not notified of all the terms?

DECISION Yes. A state intermediate appellate court reversed the judgment of the lower court and remanded the case for an assessment of damages.

REASON Bridgewater's oral comment about his purchase of the land did not satisfy the lease's requirement of notice to Clark, the party with the option. The failure to notify Clark in writing of the terms of Bridgewater's deal was a violation of the lease. In the context of a right of first refusal to buy real estate, with a requirement of notice of any offer in writing, the party with the option must be provided with all the terms of the offer for the notice to be sufficient. On written notice of "any bona fide offer" to buy, the right of first refusal becomes an option to buy the property at the price, and on the terms, stated in the offer. The owner of the property is obligated under such a right of first refusal to provide "seasonable disclosure" of the terms of an offer to the party with the option. "Because the holder of the right must meet the terms and conditions of the third-party offer, it cannot be called upon to exercise or lose that right unless the *entire* offer is communicated to him in such a form as to enable him to evaluate it and make a decision."

FOR CRITICAL ANALYSIS—Environmental Consideration *Other than price, why might the Nickerson children have wanted to quickly sell the land on which Clark operated his firm? Discuss. (Hint: Consider the possible negative environmental aspects of the business being sold.)*

Rejection of the Offer by the Offeree. If the offeree rejects the offer—by words or by conduct—the offer is terminated. Any subsequent attempt by the offeree to accept will be construed as a new offer, giving the original offeror (now the offeree) the power of acceptance.

Like a revocation, a rejection of an offer is effective only when it is actually received by the offeror or the offeror's agent. **EXAMPLE 10.11** Goldfinch Farms offers to sell specialty Maitake mushrooms to a Japanese buyer, Kinoko Foods. If Kinoko rejects the offer by sending a letter via U.S. mail, the rejection will not be effective (and the offer will not be terminated) until Goldfinch receives the letter. ●

Merely inquiring about an offer does not constitute rejection. **EXAMPLE 10.12** A friend offers to buy your Wii gaming system with additional accessories for $300. You respond, "Is this your best offer?" or "Will you pay me $375 for it?" A reasonable person would conclude that you did not reject the offer but merely made an inquiry for further consideration of the offer. You can still accept and bind your friend to the $300 purchase price. When the offeree merely inquires as to the firmness of the offer, there is no reason to presume that she or he intends to reject it. ●

Counteroffer An offeree's response to an offer in which the offeree rejects the original offer and at the same time makes a new offer.

Counteroffer by the Offeree. A **counteroffer** is a rejection of the original offer and the simultaneous making of a new offer. **EXAMPLE 10.13** Burke offers to sell his home to Lang for $270,000. Lang responds, "Your price is too high. I'll offer to purchase your house for $250,000." Lang's response is called a counteroffer because it rejects Burke's offer to sell at $270,000 and creates a new offer by Lang to purchase the home at a price of $250,000. ●

Mirror Image Rule A common law rule that requires that the terms of the offeree's acceptance adhere exactly to the terms of the offeror's offer for a valid contract to be formed.

At common law, the **mirror image rule** requires that the offeree's acceptance match the offeror's offer exactly. In other words, the terms of the acceptance must "mirror" those of the offer. If the acceptance materially changes or adds to the terms of the original offer, it will be considered not an acceptance but a counteroffer—which, of course, need not be accepted. The original offeror can, however, accept the terms of the counteroffer and create a valid contract.[9]

TERMINATION BY OPERATION OF LAW The power of the offeree to transform the offer into a binding, legal obligation can be terminated by operation of law through the occurrence of any of the following events:

1. Lapse of time.
2. Destruction of the specific subject matter of the offer.
3. Death or incompetence of the offeror or the offeree.
4. Supervening illegality of the proposed contract.

Lapse of Time. An offer terminates automatically by law when the period of time *specified in the offer* has passed. If the offer states that it will be left open until a particular date, then the offer will terminate at midnight on that day. If the offer states that it will be left open for a number of days, such as ten days, this time period normally begins to run when the offer is actually received by the offeree, not when it is formed or sent. When the offer is delayed (through the misdelivery of mail, for example), the period begins to run from the date the offeree would have received the offer, but only if the offeree knows or should know that the offer is delayed.[10]

EXAMPLE 10.14 Suppose that Beth offers to sell her boat to Jonah, stating that the offer will remain open until May 20. Unless Jonah accepts the offer by midnight on May 20, the offer will lapse (terminate). Now suppose that Beth writes a letter to Jonah, offering to sell him her boat if Jonah accepts the offer within twenty days of the letter's date, which is May 1. Jonah must accept within twenty days after May 1, or the offer will terminate. Suppose

---

9. The mirror image rule has been greatly modified in regard to sales contracts. Section 2–207 of the UCC provides that a contract is formed if the offeree makes a definite expression of acceptance (such as signing the form in the appropriate location), even though the terms of the acceptance modify or add to the terms of the original offer (see Chapter 15).

10. *Restatement (Second) of Contracts*, Section 49.

that instead of including the date May 1 in her letter, Beth had simply written to Jonah offering to sell him her boat if Jonah accepted within twenty days. In this instance, Jonah must accept within twenty days of receiving the letter. The same rule would apply if Beth used insufficient postage and Jonah received the letter ten days late without knowing that it had been delayed. If, however, Jonah knew that the letter was delayed, the offer would lapse twenty days after the day he ordinarily would have received the offer had Beth used sufficient postage. ●

If the offer does not specify a time for acceptance, the offer terminates at the end of a *reasonable* period of time. A reasonable period of time is determined by the subject matter of the contract, business and market conditions, and other relevant circumstances. An offer to sell farm produce, for example, will terminate sooner than an offer to sell farm equipment because farm produce is perishable and subject to greater fluctuations in market value.

ON THE WEB You can find answers to some common questions about contract law at the following Web site: **law.freeadvice.com/general_practice/ contract_law/84**.

Destruction of the Subject Matter.   An offer is automatically terminated if the specific subject matter of the offer is destroyed before the offer is accepted. **EXAMPLE 10.15** Bekins offers to sell his prize cow to Yates. If the cow becomes ill and dies before Yates accepts, the offer is automatically terminated. (Note that if Yates had accepted the offer before the cow died, a contract would have been formed. Nonetheless, because the cow was dead, a court would likely excuse Bekins's obligation to perform the contract on the basis of impossibility of performance—see Chapter 12.) ●

Death or Incompetence of the Offeror or Offeree.   An offeree's power of acceptance is terminated when the offeror or offeree dies or is deprived of legal capacity to enter into the proposed contract, *unless the offer is irrevocable.* A revocable offer is personal to both parties and normally cannot pass to a decedent's heirs or estate or to the guardian of a mentally incompetent person. This rule applies whether or not one party had notice of the death or incompetence of the other party. **EXAMPLE 10.16** Kapola, who is quite ill, writes to her friend Amanda, offering to sell Amanda her grand piano for only $400. That night, Kapola dies. The next day, Amanda, not knowing of Kapola's death, writes a letter to Kapola, accepting the offer and enclosing a check for $400. Is there a contract? No. There is no contract because the offer automatically terminated on Kapola's death. ●

Supervening Illegality of the Proposed Contract.   A statute or court decision that makes an offer illegal automatically terminates the offer. **EXAMPLE 10.17** Acme Finance Corporation offers to lend Carlos $20,000 at 15 percent interest annually, but before Carlos can accept, the state legislature enacts a statute prohibiting loans at interest rates greater than 12 percent. In this situation, the offer is automatically terminated. (If the statute is enacted after Carlos accepts the offer, a valid contract is formed, but the contract may still be unenforceable—see Chapter 11.) ●

Acceptance

Acceptance A voluntary act by the offeree that shows assent, or agreement, to the terms of an offer; may consist of words or conduct.

An **acceptance** is a voluntary act by the offeree that shows assent, or agreement, to the terms of an offer. The offeree's act may consist of words or conduct. The acceptance must be unequivocal and must be communicated to the offeror.

WHO CAN ACCEPT?   Generally, a third person cannot substitute for the offeree and effectively accept the offer. After all, the identity of the offeree is as much a condition of a bargaining offer as any other term contained therein. Thus, except in special circumstances, only the person to whom the offer is made or that person's agent can accept the offer and create a binding contract. For instance, Lottie makes an offer to Paul. Paul is not interested, but his friend José accepts the offer. No contract is formed.

UNEQUIVOCAL ACCEPTANCE   To exercise the power of acceptance effectively, the offeree must accept unequivocally. This is the *mirror image rule* previously discussed. If the acceptance is subject to new conditions or if the terms of the acceptance materially change the original offer, the acceptance may be deemed a counteroffer that implicitly rejects the original offer.

Certain terms, when included in an acceptance, will not change the offer sufficiently to constitute rejection.   **EXAMPLE 10.18**   In response to an art dealer's offer to sell a painting, the offeree, Ashton Gibbs, replies, "I accept; please send a written contract." Gibbs is requesting a written contract but is not making it a condition for acceptance. Therefore, the acceptance is effective without the written contract. In contrast, if Gibbs replies, "I accept *if* you send a written contract," the acceptance is expressly conditioned on the request for a writing, and the statement is not an acceptance but a counteroffer. (Notice how important each word is!)[11] ●

SILENCE AS ACCEPTANCE   Ordinarily, silence cannot constitute acceptance, even if the offeror states, "By your silence and inaction, you will be deemed to have accepted this offer." This general rule applies because an offeree should not be put under a burden of liability to act affirmatively in order to reject an offer. No consideration—that is, nothing of value—has passed to the offeree to impose such a liability.

In some instances, however, the offeree does have a duty to speak; if so, his or her silence or inaction will operate as an acceptance. Silence may be an acceptance when an offeree takes the benefit of offered services even though he or she had an opportunity to reject them and knew that they were offered with the expectation of compensation.   **EXAMPLE 10.19**   John is a student who earns extra income by washing store windows. John taps on the window of a store, catches the attention of the store's manager, and points to the window and raises his cleaner, signaling that he will be washing the window. The manager does nothing to stop him. Here, the store manager's silence constitutes an acceptance, and an implied-in-fact contract is created. The store is bound to pay a reasonable value for John's work. ●

Silence can also operate as an acceptance when the offeree has had prior dealings with the offeror. If a merchant, for example, routinely receives shipments from a supplier and in the past has always notified the supplier when defective goods are rejected, then silence constitutes acceptance. Also, if a buyer solicits an offer specifying that certain terms and conditions are acceptable, and the seller makes the offer in response to the solicitation, the buyer has a duty to reject—that is, a duty to tell the seller that the offer is not acceptable. Failure to reject (silence) will operate as an acceptance.

COMMUNICATION OF ACCEPTANCE   In a bilateral contract, communication of acceptance is necessary because acceptance is in the form of a promise (not performance), and the contract is formed when the promise is made (rather than when the act is performed). Communication of acceptance is not necessary if the offer dispenses with the requirement, however, or if the offer can be accepted by silence.[12]

Because a unilateral contract calls for the full performance of some act, acceptance is usually evident, and notification is unnecessary. Nevertheless, exceptions do exist, such as when the offeror requests notice of acceptance or has no way of determining whether the requested act has been performed.

---

11. As noted in footnote 9, in regard to sales contracts, the UCC provides that an acceptance may still be effective even if some terms are added. The new terms are simply treated as proposals for additions to the contract, unless both parties are merchants. If the parties are merchants, the additional terms (with some exceptions) become part of the contract [UCC 2–207(2)].

12. Under UCC 2–206(1)(b), an order or other offer to buy goods that are to be promptly shipped may be treated as either a bilateral or a unilateral offer and can be accepted by a promise to ship or by actual shipment.

MODE AND TIMELINESS OF ACCEPTANCE   Acceptance in bilateral contracts must be timely. The general rule is that acceptance in a bilateral contract is timely if it is made before the offer is terminated. Problems may arise, though, when the parties involved are not dealing face to face. In such situations, the offeree should use an authorized mode of communication.

The Mailbox Rule.   Acceptance takes effect, thus completing formation of the contract, at the time the offeree sends or delivers the communication via the mode expressly or impliedly authorized by the offeror. This is the so-called **mailbox rule,** also called the *deposited acceptance rule,* which the majority of courts follow. Under this rule, if the authorized mode of communication is the mail, then an acceptance becomes valid when it is dispatched (placed in the control of the U.S. Postal Service)—*not* when it is received by the offeror.

The mailbox rule does not apply to instantaneous forms of communication, such as when the parties are dealing face to face, by telephone, or by fax. There is still some uncertainty in the courts as to whether e-mail should be considered an instantaneous form of communication to which the mailbox rule does not apply. If the parties have agreed to conduct transactions electronically and if the Uniform Electronic Transactions Act (UETA—to be discussed later in this chapter) applies, then e-mail is considered sent when it either leaves the sender's control or is received by the recipient. This rule, which takes the place of the mailbox rule when the UETA applies, essentially allows an e-mail acceptance to become effective when sent (as it would if sent by U.S. mail).

Authorized Means of Communication.   A means of communicating acceptance can be expressly authorized by the offeror or impliedly authorized by the facts and circumstances surrounding the situation. An acceptance sent by means not expressly or impliedly authorized normally is not effective until it is received by the offeror.

When an offeror specifies how acceptance should be made (for example, by overnight delivery), express authorization is said to exist, and the contract is not formed unless the offeree uses that specified mode of acceptance. Moreover, both offeror and offeree are bound in contract the moment this means of acceptance is employed. **EXAMPLE 10.20** Shaylee & Perkins, a Massachusetts firm, offers to sell a container of antique furniture to Leaham's Antiques in Colorado. The offer states that Leaham's must accept the offer via FedEx overnight delivery. The acceptance is effective (and a binding contract is formed) the moment that Leaham's gives the overnight envelope containing the acceptance to the FedEx driver. ●

If the offeror does not expressly authorize a certain mode of acceptance, then acceptance can be made by any reasonable means.[13] Courts look at the prevailing business usages and the surrounding circumstances to determine whether the mode of acceptance used was reasonable. Usually, the offeror's choice of a particular means in making the offer implies that the offeree can use the *same or a faster* means for acceptance. Thus, if the offer is made via priority mail, it would be reasonable to accept the offer via priority mail or by a faster method, such as by fax or FedEx.

Substitute Method of Acceptance.   If the offeror authorizes a particular method of acceptance, but the offeree accepts by a different means, the acceptance may still be effective if the substituted method serves the same purpose as the authorized means. The use of a substitute method of acceptance is not effective on dispatch, though, and no contract will be formed until the acceptance is received by the offeror. Thus, if an offer specifies FedEx

Mailbox Rule   A rule providing that an acceptance of an offer becomes effective on dispatch (on being placed in an official mailbox), if mail is, expressly or impliedly, an authorized means of communication of acceptance to the offeror.

---

13. Note that UCC 2–206(1)(a) states specifically that an acceptance of an offer for the sale of goods can be made by any medium that is *reasonable* under the circumstances.

overnight delivery but the offeree accepts by overnight delivery from another carrier, such as UPS, the acceptance will still be effective, but not until the offeror receives it.

 Agreement in E-Contracts

Numerous contracts are formed online. Electronic contracts, or e-contracts, must meet the same basic requirements (agreement, consideration, contractual capacity, and legality) as paper contracts. Disputes concerning e-contracts, however, tend to center on contract terms and whether the parties voluntarily agreed to those terms.

Online contracts may be formed not only for the sale of goods and services but also for *licensing.* The "sale" of software generally involves a license, or a right to use the software, rather than the passage of title (ownership rights) from the seller to the buyer. **EXAMPLE 10.21** Galynn wants to obtain software that will allow her to work on spreadsheets on her Black-Berry. She goes online and purchases GridMagic. During the transaction, she has to click on several on-screen "I agree" boxes to indicate that she understands that she is purchasing only the right to use the software and will not obtain any ownership rights. After she agrees to these terms (the licensing agreement), she can download the software. ●

As you read through the following subsections, keep in mind that although we typically refer to the offeror and the offeree as a *seller* and a *buyer,* in many online transactions these parties would be more accurately described as a *licensor* and a *licensee.*

Online Offers

Sellers doing business via the Internet can protect themselves against contract disputes and legal liability by creating offers that clearly spell out the terms that will govern their transactions if the offers are accepted. All important terms should be conspicuous and easy to view.

DISPLAYING THE OFFER   The seller's Web site should include a hypertext link to a page containing the full contract so that potential buyers are made aware of the terms to which they are assenting. The contract generally must be displayed online in a readable format such as a twelve-point typeface. All provisions should be reasonably clear. **EXAMPLE 10.22** Netquip sells a variety of heavy equipment, such as trucks and trailers, online at its Web site. Because Netquip's pricing schedule is very complex, the schedule must be fully provided and explained on the Web site. In addition, the terms of the sale (such as any warranties and the refund policy) must be fully disclosed. ●

PROVISIONS TO INCLUDE   An important rule to keep in mind is that the offeror controls the offer and thus the resulting contract. The seller should therefore anticipate the terms she or he wants to include in a contract and provide for them in the offer. In some instances, a standardized contract form may suffice. At a minimum, an online offer should include the following provisions:

1. A clause that clearly indicates what constitutes the buyer's agreement to the terms of the offer, such as a box containing the words "I accept" that the buyer can click on to indicate acceptance. (Mechanisms for accepting online offers will be discussed in detail later in this chapter.)
2. A provision specifying how payment for the goods (including any applicable taxes) must be made.
3. A statement of the seller's refund and return policies.
4. Disclaimers of liability for certain uses of the goods. For example, an online seller of business forms may add a disclaimer that the seller does not accept responsibility for the buyer's reliance on the forms rather than on an attorney's advice.

"If two men agree on everything, you can be sure one of them is doing the thinking."

Lyndon Baines Johnson, 1908–1973
(Thirty-sixth president of the United States, 1963–1969)

5. A provision specifying the remedies available to the buyer if the goods are found to be defective or if the contract is otherwise breached. Any limitation of remedies should be clearly spelled out.

6. A statement indicating how the seller will use the information gathered about the buyer.

7. Provisions relating to dispute settlement, such as an arbitration clause or a *forum-selection clause* (discussed next).

Forum-Selection Clause A provision in a contract designating the court, jurisdiction, or tribunal that will decide any disputes arising under the contract.

DISPUTE-SETTLEMENT PROVISIONS Online offers frequently include provisions relating to dispute settlement. For example, the offer might include an arbitration clause specifying that any dispute arising under the contract will be arbitrated in a designated forum.

Many online contracts also contain a **forum-selection clause** indicating the forum, or location (such as a court or jurisdiction), for the resolution of any dispute arising under the contract. As discussed in Chapter 3, significant jurisdictional issues may occur when parties are at a great distance, as they often are when they form contracts via the Internet. A forum-selection clause will help to avert future jurisdictional problems and also help to ensure that the seller will not be required to appear in court in a distant state.

Online Acceptances

The *Restatement (Second) of Contracts*—a compilation of common law contract principles—states that parties may agree to a contract "by written or spoken words or by other action or by failure to act."[14] The Uniform Commercial Code (UCC), which governs sales contracts, has a similar provision. Section 2–204 of the UCC states that any contract for the sale of goods "may be made in any manner sufficient to show agreement, including conduct by both parties which recognizes the existence of such a contract."

Click-On Agreement An agreement that arises when a buyer, engaging in a transaction on a computer, indicates assent to be bound by the terms of an offer by clicking on a button that says, for example, "I agree"; sometimes referred to as a *click-on license* or a *click-wrap agreement.*

CLICK-ON AGREEMENTS The courts have used these provisions to conclude that a binding contract can be created by conduct, including the act of clicking on a box indicating "I accept" or "I agree" to accept an online offer. The agreement resulting from such an acceptance is often called a **click-on agreement** (sometimes it is referred to as a *click-on license* or *click-wrap agreement*). Exhibit 10–1 shows a portion of a typical click-on agreement that accompanies a software package.

Generally, the law does not require that the parties have read all of the terms in a contract for it to be effective. Therefore, clicking on a box that states "I agree" to certain terms can be enough. The terms may be contained on a Web site through which the buyer is obtaining goods or services, or they may appear on a computer screen when software is loaded from a CD-ROM or DVD or downloaded from the Internet.

CASE EXAMPLE 10.23 DocMagic, Inc., a California firm, created a software program for Mortgage Plus, Inc., a mortgage lender in Kansas. Before the software could be installed, a window displayed a "Software License and User Agreement" on the screen. The agreement asked, "Do you accept all terms of the preceding License Agreement? If you choose No, Setup will close." A click on a "Yes" button was needed to continue. The agreement also included a clause designating California as the forum for

• *Exhibit* 10–1 A Click-On Agreement Sample

This exhibit illustrates an online offer to form a contract. To accept the offer, the user simply scrolls down the page and clicks on the "I Accept" button.

Type the characters you see in the picture

Picture: **XUXMagON**

The picture contains 8 characters.

Characters:

Review and accept the agreements

- Microsoft service agreement
- Microsoft online privacy statement

To accept the terms of service, click **I accept**. Clicking "I accept" means that you agree to the terms of the Microsoft service agreement and privacy statement. You understand that you are creating credentials that you can use on other Windows Live ID sites and services, you agree to receive required notices from Microsoft electronically, and you agree to receive targeted advertisements and periodic member e-mails. If you do not agree to these terms, click Cancel.

(I Accept) (Cancel)

---

14. *Restatement (Second) of Contracts,* Section 19.

the resolution of any disputes. Mortgage Plus installed the software and used it to prepare loan documents. People who had obtained loans from Mortgage Plus subsequently filed claims against the firm, charging it with mistakes, which cost $150,000 to resolve. Mortgage Plus filed a lawsuit against DocMagic in a federal court in Kansas alleging a defect in the software. DocMagic claimed that the dispute had to be resolved in California because of the forum-selection clause in the click-on software licensing agreement. The court agreed and transferred the case. Because a user had to agree to the terms before the software could be installed and used, the forum-selection clause was valid and enforceable.[15] ●

Shrink-Wrap Agreement An agreement whose terms are expressed in a document located inside a box in which goods (usually software) are packaged; sometimes called a *shrink-wrap license.*

SHRINK-WRAP AGREEMENTS   A **shrink-wrap agreement** (or *shrink-wrap license*) is an agreement whose terms are expressed inside a box in which the goods are packaged. (The term *shrink-wrap* refers to the plastic that covers the box.) Usually, the party who opens the box is told that she or he agrees to the terms by keeping whatever is in the box. Similarly, when the purchaser opens a software package, he or she agrees to abide by the terms of the limited license agreement.

EXAMPLE 10.24 John orders a new computer from a national company, which ships the computer to him. Along with the computer, the box contains an agreement setting forth the terms of the sale, including what remedies are available. The document also states that John's retention of the computer for longer than thirty days will be construed as an acceptance of the terms. ●

In most instances, a shrink-wrap agreement is not between a retailer and a buyer, but between the manufacturer of the hardware or software and the ultimate buyer-user of the product. The terms generally concern warranties, remedies, and other issues associated with the use of the product.

Shrink-Wrap Agreements and Enforceable Contract Terms.   In some cases, the courts have enforced the terms of shrink-wrap agreements in the same way as the terms of other contracts. These courts have reasoned that by including the terms with the product, the seller proposed a contract that the buyer could accept by using the product after having an opportunity to read the terms. Thus, a buyer's failure to object to terms contained within a shrink-wrapped software package may constitute an acceptance of the terms by conduct. Also, it seems practical from a business's point of view to enclose a full statement of the legal terms of a sale with the product rather than to read the statement over the phone, for example, when a buyer calls to order the product.

Shrink-Wrap Terms That May Not Be Enforced.   Nevertheless, the courts have sometimes refused to enforce certain terms included in shrink-wrap agreements because the buyer did not expressly consent. One factor that courts consider important is whether the parties form their contract before or after the seller communicates the terms of the shrink-wrap agreement to the buyer. If a buyer orders a product over the telephone, for instance, and is not informed of an arbitration clause or forum-selection clause at that time, the buyer clearly has not expressly agreed to these terms. If the buyer discovers the clauses in the shrink-wrap terms *after* the parties entered into a contract, a court may conclude that those terms were proposals for additional terms and were not part of the contract.

Ethical Issue ⚖

Is it fair to enforce shrink-wrap and click-wrap terms that buyers were not aware of at the time they agreed to a purchase? Most people realize that if they sign a written contract without reading it, they can be held to its terms. But are most people aware that they can be legally bound by a whole host of conditions included in the packaging of electronics or software, not to mention the music, movies, and software they download from the Web? Simply by buying and keeping the latest

---

15. *Mortgage Plus, Inc. v. DocMagic, Inc.,* 2004 WL 2331918 (D.Kan. 2004).

electronic gadgets, we enter into binding contracts with the manufacturers that include rather one-sided terms. The terms may be unfair, but the law says we are bound. For instance, just by installing or downloading certain software today, users routinely agree to allow the companies to install tracking software on their computers. Moreover, many software programs—including some that are designed to combat *malware* (see Chapter 7)—automatically delete files from the users' hard drives. Consumers and businesspersons are often unaware of these consequences, and yet by buying and installing the software, they have agreed that they will not hold the manufacturer liable.

Browse-Wrap Term A term or condition of use that is presented to an Internet user at the time certain products, such as software, are being downloaded but that need not be agreed to (by clicking "I agree," for example) before the user is able to install or use the product.

BROWSE-WRAP TERMS Like the terms of a click-on agreement, **browse-wrap terms** can occur in a transaction conducted over the Internet. Unlike a click-on agreement, however, browse-wrap terms do not require an Internet user to assent to the terms before, say, downloading or using certain software. In other words, a person can install the software without clicking "I agree" to the terms of a license. Browse-wrap terms are often unenforceable because they do not satisfy the agreement requirement of contract formation.[16]

E-Signature Technologies

E-Signature As defined by the Uniform Electronic Transactions Act, "an electronic sound, symbol, or process attached to or logically associated with a record and executed or adopted by a person with the intent to sign the record."

Today, numerous technologies allow electronic documents to be signed. An **e-signature** has been defined as "an electronic sound, symbol, or process attached to or logically associated with a record and executed or adopted by a person with the intent to sign the record."[17] Thus, e-signatures include encrypted digital signatures, names (intended as signatures) at the ends of e-mail messages, and "clicks" on a Web page if the click includes the identification of the person. The technologies for creating e-signatures generally fall into one of two categories, *digitized handwritten signatures* and *digital signatures based on a public-key infrastructure*. A digitized signature is a graphical image of a handwritten signature that is often created using a digital pen and pad, such as an ePad, and special software. For security reasons, the strokes of a person's signature can be measured by software to authenticate the person signing (this is referred to as signature dynamics).

In a public-key infrastructure (such as an asymmetric cryptosystem), two mathematically linked but different keys are generated—a private signing key and a public validation key. A digital signature is created when the signer uses the private key to create a unique mark on an electronic document. The appropriate software enables the recipient of the document to use the public key to verify the identity of the signer. A **cybernotary,** or legally recognized certification authority, issues the key pair, identifies the owner of the keys, and certifies the validity of the public key. The cybernotary also serves as a repository for public keys.

Cybernotary A legally recognized authority that can certify the validity of digital signatures.

An e-signature.

State Laws Governing E-Signatures

Most states have laws governing e-signatures. The problem is that state e-signature laws are not uniform. Some states—California is a notable example—prohibit many types of documents from being signed with e-signatures, whereas other states are more permissive. Additionally, some states recognize only digital signatures as valid, while others permit other types of e-signatures.

In an attempt to create more uniformity among the states, in 1999 the National Conference of Commissioners on Uniform State Laws and the American Law Institute promulgated the Uniform Electronic Transactions

---

16. See, for example, *Jesmer v. Retail Magic, Inc.*, 863 N.Y.S.2d 737 (2008).

17. This definition is from the Uniform Electronic Transactions Act, which will be discussed later in this chapter.

Act (UETA). To date, the UETA has been adopted, at least in part, by forty-eight states. Among other things, the UETA declares that a signature may not be denied legal effect or enforceability solely because it is in electronic form. (The provisions of the UETA will be discussed in more detail shortly.)

Federal Law on E-Signatures and E-Documents

In 2000, Congress enacted the Electronic Signatures in Global and National Commerce Act (E-SIGN Act),[18] which provides that no contract, record, or signature may be "denied legal effect" solely because it is in electronic form. In other words, under this law, an electronic signature is as valid as a signature on paper, and an e-document can be as enforceable as a paper one.

For an e-signature to be enforceable, the contracting parties must have agreed to use electronic signatures. For an electronic document to be valid, it must be in a form that can be retained and accurately reproduced.

The E-SIGN Act does not apply to all types of documents, however. Contracts and documents that are exempt include court papers, divorce decrees, evictions, foreclosures, health-insurance terminations, prenuptial agreements, and wills. Also, the only agreements governed by the UCC that fall under this law are those covered by Articles 2 and 2A and UCC 1–107 and 1–206. Despite these limitations, the E-SIGN Act significantly expanded the possibilities for contracting online. For a discussion of global laws on e-signatures and e-commerce, see this chapter's *Beyond Our Borders* feature.

Partnering Agreements

Partnering Agreement An agreement between a seller and a buyer who frequently do business with each other concerning the terms and conditions that will apply to all subsequently formed electronic contracts.

One way that online sellers and buyers can prevent disputes over signatures in their e-contracts, as well as disputes over the terms and conditions of those contracts, is to form partnering agreements. In a **partnering agreement,** a seller and a buyer who frequently do business with each other agree in advance on the terms and conditions that will apply to all transactions subsequently conducted electronically. The partnering agreement can also establish special access and identification codes to be used by the parties when transacting business electronically.

A partnering agreement reduces the likelihood that disputes will arise under the contract because the buyer and the seller have agreed in advance to the terms and conditions that will accompany each sale. Furthermore, if a dispute does arise, a court or arbitration forum will be able to refer to the partnering agreement when determining the parties' intent.

▶ The Uniform Electronic Transactions Act

As noted earlier, the Uniform Electronic Transactions Act (UETA) was set forth in 1999. It represents one of the first comprehensive efforts to create uniform laws pertaining to e-commerce.

Record According to the Uniform Electronic Transactions Act, information that is either inscribed on a tangible medium or stored in an electronic or other medium and is retrievable.

The primary purpose of the UETA is to remove barriers to e-commerce by giving the same legal effect to electronic records and signatures as is currently given to paper documents and signatures. As mentioned earlier, the UETA broadly defines an *e-signature* as "an electronic sound, symbol, or process attached to or logically associated with a record and executed or adopted by a person with the intent to sign the record."[19] A **record** is "information that is inscribed on a tangible medium or that is stored in an electronic or other medium and is retrievable in perceivable [visual] form."[20]

---

18. 15 U.S.C. Sections 7001 *et seq.*
19. UETA 102(8).
20. UETA 102(15).

Beyond Our Borders   International Use and Regulation of the Internet

Today, much of the e-commerce conducted on a worldwide basis involves buyers and sellers from the United States. The preeminence of U.S. law in this area is likely to be challenged in the future, however, as Internet use continues to expand worldwide. Already, several international organizations have created their own regulations for global Internet transactions.

For example, in 2005 the United Nations Convention on the Use of Electronic Communications in International Contracts was completed. A major goal of the treaty is to improve commercial certainty by determining an Internet user's location for legal purposes. The treaty also establishes standards for creating functional equivalence between electronic communications and paper documents. In addition, the treaty provides that e-signatures

be treated as the equivalent of signatures on paper documents.

Another treaty that will help to foster international trade is the 2005 Convention on the Choice of Court Agreements. Although this treaty does not specifically address e-commerce and applies only to business-to-business transactions, not business-to-consumer transactions, it will provide more certainty regarding jurisdiction and recognition of judgments by other nations' courts. Such matters are important both to offline and online transactions, so the convention should enhance e-commerce as well. Steps are being taken to combat cyber crime (see Chapter 7) on an international basis. The Council of Europe recently created the Cyber-Crime Convention, which has been signed by forty-three nations,

including the United States. This treaty provides mechanisms for international cooperation in the battle against Internet-related crime. It prohibits unauthorized access to an Internet computer system, unauthorized interception of Internet data, Internet fraud and forgery, and copyright infringement via the Internet.

• For Critical Analysis
There are about two hundred sovereign nations in the world today, but only eighteen have signed the Electronic Communications Convention, and forty-three have signed the Cyber-Crime Convention. Why do you think so many nations' governments are reluctant to be bound by international conventions?

The Scope and Applicability of the UETA

The UETA does not create new rules for electronic contracts but rather establishes that records, signatures, and contracts may not be denied enforceability solely due to their electronic form. The UETA does not apply to all writings and signatures. It covers only electronic records and electronic signatures *relating to a transaction*. A *transaction* is defined as an interaction between two or more people relating to business, commercial, or governmental activities.[21]

The act specifically does not apply to wills or testamentary trusts or to transactions governed by the UCC (other than those covered by Articles 2 and 2A).[22] In addition, the provisions of the UETA allow the states to exclude its application to other areas of law.

As described earlier, Congress passed the E-SIGN Act in 2000, a year after the UETA was presented to the states for adoption. Thus, a significant issue was to what extent the federal E-SIGN Act preempted the UETA as adopted by the states.

The Federal E-SIGN Act and the UETA

The E-SIGN Act[23] refers explicitly to the UETA and provides that if a state has enacted the uniform version of the UETA, it is not preempted by the E-SIGN Act. In other words, if the state has enacted the UETA without modification, state law will govern. The problem is that many states have enacted nonuniform (modified) versions of the UETA, largely for the purpose of excluding other areas of state law from the UETA's terms. The E-SIGN Act specifies that those exclusions will be preempted to the extent that they are inconsistent with the E-SIGN Act's provisions.

---

21. UETA 2(12) and 3.
22. UETA 3(b).
23. 15 U.S.C. Section 7002(2)(A)(i).

The E-SIGN Act, however, explicitly allows the states to enact alternative requirements for the use of electronic records or electronic signatures. Generally, however, the requirements must be consistent with the provisions of the E-SIGN Act, and the state must not give greater legal status or effect to one specific type of technology. Additionally, if a state enacts alternative requirements *after* the E-SIGN Act was adopted, the state law must specifically refer to the E-SIGN Act. The relationship between the UETA and the E-SIGN Act is illustrated in Exhibit 10–2.

Highlights of the UETA

We look next at selected provisions of the UETA. Our discussion is, of course, based on the act's uniform provisions. Keep in mind that the states that have enacted the UETA may have adopted slightly different versions.

THE PARTIES MUST AGREE TO CONDUCT TRANSACTIONS ELECTRONICALLY   The UETA will not apply to a transaction unless each of the parties has previously agreed to conduct transactions by electronic means. The agreement need not be explicit, however, and it may be implied by the conduct of the parties and the surrounding circumstances.[24] In the comments that accompany the UETA, the drafters stated that it may be reasonable to infer that a person who gives out a business card with an e-mail address on it has consented to transact business electronically.[25] The party's agreement may also be inferred from a letter or other writing, as well as from some verbal communication. Nothing in the UETA requires that the agreement to conduct transactions electronically be made electronically.

Note, however, that some courts have required that the parties' agreement to conduct transactions electronically be clear and unequivocal. For example, in one Louisiana case, the fact that the parties had *negotiated* the terms of previous contracts via e-mail was not sufficient evidence by itself to show that the parties had *agreed* to transact business electronically.[26]

---

24. UETA 5(b).
25. UETA 5, Comment 4B.
26. *EPCO Carbondioxide Products, Inc. v. St. Paul Travelers Insurance Co.*, 2007 WL 1347785 (W.D.La. 2007).

● ***Exhibit* 10–2** The E-SIGN Act and the UETA

A person who has previously agreed to an electronic transaction can also withdraw his or her consent and refuse to conduct further business electronically. Additionally, the act expressly gives parties the power to vary the UETA's provisions by contract. In other words, *parties can opt out of all or some of the terms of the UETA*. If the parties do not opt out of the terms of the UETA, however, the UETA will govern their electronic transactions.

ATTRIBUTION   In the context of electronic transactions, the term *attribution* refers to the procedures that may be used to ensure that the person sending an electronic record is the same person whose e-signature accompanies the record. Under the UETA, if an electronic record or signature is the act of a particular person, the record or signature may be attributed to that person. If a person types her or his name at the bottom of an e-mail purchase order, that name will qualify as a "signature" and be attributed to the person whose name appears. Just as in paper contracts, one may use any relevant evidence to prove that the record or signature is or is not the act of the person.[27]

Note that even if an individual's name does not appear on a record, the UETA states that the effect of the record is to be determined from the context and surrounding circumstances. In other words, a record may have legal effect even if no one has signed it. **EXAMPLE 10.25** J. P. Darby sends a fax to Corina Scott. The fax contains a letterhead identifying Darby as the sender, but Darby's signature does not appear on the faxed document. Depending on the circumstances, the fax may be attributed to Darby. ●

The UETA does not contain any express provisions about what constitutes fraud or whether an *agent* (a person who acts on behalf of another—see Chapter 23) is authorized to enter a contract. Under the UETA, other state laws control if any issues relating to agency, authority, forgery, or contract formation arise.

NOTARIZATION   If existing state law requires a document to be notarized, the UETA provides that this requirement is satisfied by the electronic signature of a notary public or other person authorized to verify signatures. **EXAMPLE 10.26** Joel receives an offer to purchase real estate and wants to send his acceptance via e-mail. The state in which Joel resides requires his acceptance to be notarized. Under the UETA, the requirement is satisfied if a notary public is present to verify Joel's identity and affix an e-signature to his e-mail acceptance. ●

THE EFFECT OF ERRORS   The UETA encourages, but does not require, the use of security procedures (such as encryption) to verify changes to electronic documents and to correct errors. Section 10 of the UETA provides that if the parties have agreed to a security procedure and one party does not detect an error because he or she did not follow the procedure, the conforming party can legally avoid the effect of the change or error. If the parties have not agreed to use a security procedure, then other state laws (including contract law governing mistakes—see Chapter 12) will determine the effect of the error on the parties' agreement. To avoid the effect of errors, a party must promptly notify the other party of the error and of her or his intent not to be bound by the error. In addition, the party must take reasonable steps to return any benefit received: parties cannot avoid a transaction if they have benefited.

TIMING   Section 15 of the UETA sets forth provisions relating to the sending and receiving of electronic records. These provisions apply unless the parties agree to different terms. Under Section 15, an electronic record is considered *sent* when it is properly directed to the intended recipient in a form readable by the recipient's computer system. Once the electronic record leaves the control of the sender or comes under the control of the recipient, the UETA deems it to have been sent. An electronic record is considered *received* when

ON THE WEB At the Web site of the Consumers Union, you can read an article discussing some concerns that consumer groups have had about many of the provisions in the UETA. Go to www.consumersunion.org/finance/899nclcwc.htm.

---

27. UETA 9.

it enters the recipient's processing system in a readable form—*even if no individual is aware of its receipt.*

Additionally, the UETA provides that, unless otherwise agreed, an electronic record is to be sent from or received at the party's principal place of business. If a party has no place of business, the provision then authorizes the place of sending or receipt to be the party's residence. If a party has multiple places of business, the record should be sent from or received at the location that has the closest relationship to the underlying transaction.

 ## Reviewing . . . Agreement in Traditional and E-Contracts

Ted and Betty Hyatt live in California, a state that has extensive statutory protection for consumers. The Hyatts decided to buy a computer so that they could use e-mail to stay in touch with their grandchildren, who live in another state. Over the phone, they ordered a computer from CompuEdge, Inc. When the box arrived, it was sealed with a brightly colored sticker warning that the terms enclosed within the box would govern the sale unless the customer returned the computer within thirty days. Among those terms was a clause that required any disputes to be resolved in Tennessee state courts. The Hyatts then signed up for Internet service through CyberTool, an Internet service provider. They downloaded CyberTool's software and clicked on the "quick install" box that allowed them to bypass CyberTool's "Terms of Service" page. It was possible to read this page by scrolling to the next screen, but the Hyatts did not realize this. The terms included a clause that stated all disputes were to be submitted to a Virginia state court. As soon as the Hyatts attempted to e-mail their grandchildren, they experienced problems using CyberTool's e-mail service, which continually stated that the network was busy. They also were unable to receive the photos sent by their grandchildren. Using the information presented in the chapter, answer the following questions.

1. Did the Hyatts accept the list of contract terms included in the computer box? Why or why not? What is the name used for this type of e-contract?
2. What type of agreement did the Hyatts form with CyberTool?
3. Suppose that the Hyatts experienced trouble with the computer's components after they had used the computer for two months. What factors will a court consider in deciding whether to enforce the forum-selection clause? Would a court be likely to enforce the clause in this contract? Why or why not?
4. Are the Hyatts bound by the contract terms specified on CyberTool's "Terms of Service" page that they did not read? Which of the required elements for contract formation might the Hyatts claim were lacking? How might a court rule on this issue?

 # Linking the Law *to Marketing*
Customer Relationship Management

As you learned in this chapter, increasingly the contracting process is moving online. Online offers for millions of goods and services populate large and small e-commerce Web sites. The vast amount of data collected from online shoppers has pushed *customer relationship management* (CRM) to the fore. CRM is a marketing strategy that allows companies to acquire information about customers' wants, needs, and behaviors. The companies can then use that information to build customer relationships and loyalty. The focus of CRM is understanding customers as individuals rather than simply as a group of consumers. As Exhibit 10–3 shows, CRM is a closed system that uses feedback from customers to build relationships with those customers.

Two Examples—Netflix and Amazon

If you are a customer of Netflix.com, you choose DVDs that are sent to you by mail (or streamed online) based on your individual tastes and preferences. Netflix asks you to rate movies you have rented (or even seen in theaters) on a scale of one to five stars. Using a computer algorithm, Netflix then creates an individualized rating system that predicts how you will rate thousands of different movies. As you rate more movies, the predictive reliability becomes more accurate. By applying your individual rating system to movies you have not seen, Netflix is able to suggest movies that you might like.

• *Exhibit* **10-3 A Customer Relationship Management Cycle**

Amazon.com uses similar technology to recommend books and music that you might wish to buy. Amazon sends out numerous "person-alized" e-mails to its customers with suggestions based on those customers' individualized-buying habits.

For both Netflix and Amazon, CRM allows for a focused marketing effort, rather than the typical shotgun approach used by spam advertising on the Internet.

CRM in Online versus Traditional Companies

For online companies such as Amazon and Netflix, all customer information has some value because the cost of obtaining it, analyzing it, and utilizing it is so small. In contrast, for traditional companies obtaining data to be used for CRM requires a different process that is much more costly. An automobile company, for example, obtains customer information from a variety of sources, including dealers, customer surveys, online inquiries, and the like. Integrating, storing, and managing such information makes CRM much more expensive for traditional companies than for online companies.

FOR CRITICAL ANALYSIS

Online companies not only target individual customers, they also utilize each customer's buying habits to create generalized marketing campaigns. Might any privacy issues arise as an online company creates a database to be used for generalized marketing campaigns? Explain your answer.

 Key Terms

acceptance 245	e-contract 236	option contract 242
agreement 236	e-signature 251	partnering agreement 252
browse-wrap term 251	forum-selection clause 249	record 252
click-on agreement 249	mailbox rule 247	revocation 242
counteroffer 244	mirror image rule 244	shrink-wrap agreement 250
cybernotary 251	offer 237	

 Chapter Summary: Agreement in Traditional and E-Contracts

Requirements of the Offer (See pages 237–242.)	1. *Intent*—There must be a serious, objective intention by the offeror to become bound by the offer. Nonoffer situations include (a) expressions of opinion; (b) statements of intention; (c) preliminary negotiations; (d) generally, advertisements, catalogues, price lists, and circulars; (e) solicitations for bids made by an auctioneer; and (f) traditionally, agreements to agree in the future. 2. *Definiteness*—The terms of the offer must be sufficiently definite to be ascertainable by the parties or by a court. 3. *Communication*—The offer must be communicated to the offeree.

Continued

Chapter Summary: Agreement in Traditional and E-Contracts—Continued

Termination of the Offer
(See pages 242–245.)
	1. *By action of the parties*—
	  a. Revocation—Unless the offer is irrevocable, it can be revoked at any time before acceptance without liability. Revocation is not effective until received by the offeree or the offeree's agent. Some offers, such as a merchant's firm offer and option contracts, are irrevocable.
	  b. Rejection—Accomplished by words or actions that demonstrate a clear intent not to accept the offer; not effective until received by the offeror or the offeror's agent.
	  c. Counteroffer—A rejection of the original offer and the making of a new offer.
	2. *By operation of law*—
	  a. Lapse of time—The offer terminates (1) at the end of the time period specified in the offer or (2) if no time period is stated in the offer, at the end of a reasonable time period.
	  b. Destruction of the specific subject matter of the offer—Automatically terminates the offer.
	  c. Death or incompetence of the offeror or offeree—Terminates the offer unless the offer is irrevocable.
	  d. Illegality—Supervening illegality terminates the offer.

Acceptance (See pages 245–248.)	1. Can be made only by the offeree or the offeree's agent. 2. Must be unequivocal. Under the common law (mirror image rule), if new terms or conditions are added to the acceptance, it will be considered a counteroffer. 3. Acceptance of a unilateral offer is effective on full performance of the requested act. Generally, no communication is necessary. 4. Acceptance of a bilateral offer can be communicated by the offeree by any authorized mode of communication and is effective on dispatch. If the offeror does not specify the mode of communication, acceptance can be made by any reasonable means. Usually, the same means used by the offeror or a faster means can be used.
Online Offers (See pages 248–249.)	The terms of contract offers presented via the Internet should be as inclusive as the terms in an offer made in a written (paper) document. The offer should be displayed in an easily readable format and should include some mechanism, such as an "I agree" or "I accept" box, by which the customer may accept the offer. Because jurisdictional issues frequently arise with online transactions, the offer should include dispute-settlement provisions, as well as a forum-selection clause.

Online Acceptances
(See pages 249–251.)
	1. *Click-on agreement*—
	  a. Definition—An agreement created when a buyer, completing a transaction on a computer, is required to indicate her or his assent to be bound by the terms of an offer by clicking on a box that says, for example, "I agree." The terms of the agreement may appear on the Web site through which the buyer is obtaining goods or services, or they may appear on a computer screen when software is downloaded.
	  b. Enforceability—The courts have enforced click-on agreements, holding that by clicking on "I agree," the offeree has indicated acceptance by conduct. Browse-wrap terms (terms in a license that an Internet user does not have to read prior to downloading the product, such as software), however, may not be enforced on the ground that the user is not made aware that he or she is entering into a contract.
	2. *Shrink-wrap agreement*—
	  a. Definition—An agreement whose terms are expressed inside a box in which the goods are packaged. The party who opens the box is informed that, by keeping the goods that are in the box, he or she agrees to the terms of the shrink-wrap agreement.
	  b. Enforceability—The courts have often enforced shrink-wrap agreements, even if the purchaser-user of the goods did not read the terms of the agreement. A court may deem a shrink-wrap agreement unenforceable, however, if the buyer learns of the shrink-wrap terms after the parties entered into the agreement.

E-Signatures (See pages 251–252.)	The Uniform Electronic Transactions Act (UETA) defines an e-signature as "an electronic sound, symbol, or process attached to or logically associated with a record and executed or adopted by a person with the intent to sign the record."

Chapter Summary: Agreement in Traditional and E-Contracts—Continued

E-Signatures—Continued	1. *E-signature technologies*—The two main categories are digitized handwritten signatures and digital signatures based on a public-key infrastructure. 2. *State laws governing e-signatures*—Although most states have laws governing e-signatures, these laws are not uniform. The UETA provides for the validity of e-signatures and may ultimately create more uniformity among the states in this respect. 3. *Federal law on e-signatures and e-documents*—The Electronic Signatures in Global and National Commerce Act (E-SIGN Act) of 2000 gave validity to e-signatures by providing that no contract, record, or signature may be "denied legal effect" solely because it is in an electronic form. 4. *Partnering agreements*—To reduce the likelihood that disputes will arise under their e-contracts, parties who frequently do business with each other online may form a partnering agreement, setting out the terms and conditions that will apply to all their subsequent electronic transactions.
The Uniform Electronic Transactions Act (UETA) (See pages 252–256.)	This uniform act has been adopted, at least in part, by most states, to create rules to support the enforcement of e-contracts. Under the UETA, contracts entered into online, as well as other documents, are presumed to be valid. The UETA does not apply to certain transactions governed by the UCC or to wills or testamentary trusts.

 ExamPrep

ISSUE SPOTTERS

1 Joe advertises in the *New York Times* that he will pay $5,000 to anyone giving him information as to the whereabouts of Elaine. Max sees a copy of the ad in a Tokyo newspaper, in Japanese, and sends Joe the requested information. Does Max get the reward? Why or why not?

2 Applied Products, Inc., does business with Beltway Distributors, Inc., online. Under the Uniform Electronic Transactions Act, what determines the effect of the electronic documents evidencing the parties' deal? Is a party's "signature" necessary? Explain.

BEFORE THE TEST

Check your answers to the Issue Spotters, and at the same time, take the interactive quiz for this chapter. Go to **www.cengage.com/blaw/blt** and click on "Chapter 10." First, click on "Answers to Issue Spotters" to check your answers. Next, click on "Interactive Quiz" to assess your mastery of the concepts in this chapter. Then click on "Flashcards" to review this chapter's Key Term definitions.

 For Review

Answers for the even-numbered questions in this **For Review** *section can be found on this text's accompanying Web site at* **www.cengage.com/blaw/blt**. *Select "Chapter 10" and click on "For Review."*

1 What elements are necessary for an effective offer? What are some examples of nonoffers?
2 In what circumstances will an offer be irrevocable?
3 What are the elements that are necessary for an effective acceptance?
4 How do shrink-wrap and click-on agreements differ from other contracts? How have traditional laws been applied to these agreements?
5 What is the Uniform Electronic Transactions Act? What are some of the major provisions of this act?

 Hypothetical Scenarios and Case Problems

10–1 Agreement. Ball writes to Sullivan and inquires how much Sullivan is asking for a specific forty-acre tract of land Sullivan owns. In a letter received by Ball, Sullivan states, "I will not take less than $60,000 for the forty-acre tract as specified." Ball immediately sends Sullivan a fax stating, "I accept your offer for $60,000 for the forty-acre tract as specified."

Discuss whether Ball can hold Sullivan to a contract for sale of the land.

10–2 Online Acceptance. Anne is a reporter for *Daily Business Journal,* a print publication consulted by investors and other businesspersons. She often uses the Internet to perform research for the articles that she writes for the publication. While visiting the Web site of Cyberspace Investments Corp., Anne reads a pop-up window that states, "Our business newsletter, *E-Commerce Weekly,* is available at a one-year subscription rate of $5 per issue. To subscribe, enter your e-mail address below and click 'SUBSCRIBE.' By subscribing, you agree to the terms of the subscriber's agreement. To read this agreement, click 'AGREE-MENT.'" Anne enters her e-mail address but does not click on "AGREEMENT" to read the terms. Has Anne entered into an enforceable contract to pay for *E-Commerce Weekly?* Explain.

10–3 **Hypothetical Question with Sample Answer** Chernek, the sole owner of a small business, has a large piece of used farm equipment for sale. He offers to sell the equipment to Bollow for $10,000. Discuss the legal effects of the following events on the offer:

1 Chernek dies prior to Bollow's acceptance, and at the time she accepts, Bollow is unaware of Chernek's death.

2 The night before Bollow accepts, a fire destroys the equipment.

3 Bollow pays $100 for a thirty-day option to purchase the equipment. During this period, Chernek dies, and Bollow accepts the offer, knowing of Chernek's death.

4 Bollow pays $100 for a thirty-day option to purchase the equipment. During this period, Bollow dies, and Bollow's estate accepts Chernek's offer within the stipulated time period.

—For a sample answer to Question 10–3, go to Appendix E at the end of this text.

10–4 Offer and Acceptance. Carrie offered to sell a set of legal encyclopedias to Antonio for $300. Antonio said that he would think about her offer and let her know his decision the next day. Norvel, who had overheard the conversation between Carrie and Antonio, said to Carrie, "I accept your offer" and gave her $300. Carrie gave Norvel the books. The next day, Antonio, who had no idea that Carrie had already sold the books to Norvel, told Carrie that he accepted her offer. Has Carrie breached a valid contract with Antonio? Explain.

10–5 E-Signatures. Stewart Lamle invented "Farook," a board game similar to "Tic Tac Toe." In May 1996, Lamle began negotiating with Mattel, Inc., to license Farook for distribution outside the United States. On June 11, 1997, the parties met and agreed on many terms, including a three-year duration, the geographic scope of the agreement, a schedule for payment, and a royalty percentage. On June 26, Mike Bucher, a Mattel employee, sent Lamle an e-mail titled "Farook Deal" that repeated these terms and added that they "ha[ve] been agreed [to] . . . by . . . Mattel subject to contract. . . . Best regards Mike Bucher." Lamle faxed Mattel a more formal draft of the terms, but Mattel did not sign it. Mattel displayed Farook at its Pre-Toy Fair in August. After the fair, Mattel sent Lamle a fax saying that it no longer wished to license his game. Lamle filed a suit in a federal district court against Mattel, asserting,

in part, breach of contract. One of the issues was whether the parties had entered into a contract. Could Bucher's name on the June 26 e-mail be considered a valid signature under the Uniform Electronic Transactions Act (UETA)? Could it be considered a valid signature outside the UETA? Why or why not? [*Lamle v. Mattel, Inc.,* 394 F.3d 1355 (Fed.Cir. 2005)]

10–6 **Case Problem with Sample Answer** In August 2000, in California, Terry Reigelsperger sought treatment for pain in his lower back from chiropractor James Siller. Reigelsperger felt better after the treatment and did not intend to return for more, although he did not mention this to Siller. Before leaving the office, Reigelsperger signed an "informed consent" form that read, in part, "I intend this consent form to cover the entire course of treatment for my present condition and for any future condition(s) for which I seek treatment." He also signed an agreement that required the parties to submit to arbitration "any dispute as to medical malpractice. . . . This agreement is intended to bind the patient and the health care provider . . . who now or in the future treat[s] the patient." Two years later, Reigelsperger sought treatment from Siller for a different condition relating to his cervical spine and shoulder. Claiming malpractice with respect to the second treatment, Reigelsperger filed a suit in a California state court against Siller. Siller asked the court to order that the dispute be submitted to arbitration. Did Reigelsperger's lack of intent to return to Siller after his first treatment affect the enforceability of the arbitration agreement and consent form? Why or why not? [*Reigelsperger v. Siller,* 40 Cal.4th 574, 53 Cal.Rptr.3d 887, 150 P.3d 764 (2007)]

—After you have answered Problem 10–6, go to this book's Web site at **www.cengage.com/blaw/blt**, select "Chapter 10," and click on "Case Problem with Sample Answer."

10–7 Online Acceptances. Internet Archive (IA) is devoted to preserving a record of resources on the Internet for future generations. IA uses the "Wayback Machine" to automatically browse Web sites and reproduce their contents in an archive. IA does not ask the owners' permission before copying their material but will remove it on request. Suzanne Shell, a resident of Colorado, owns **www.profane-justice.org**, which is dedicated to providing information to individuals accused of child abuse or neglect. The site warns, "IF YOU COPY OR DISTRIBUTE ANYTHING ON THIS SITE YOU ARE ENTERING INTO A CONTRACT." The terms, which can be accessed only by clicking on a link, include, among other charges, a fee of $5,000 for each page copied "in advance of printing." Neither the warning nor the terms require a user to indicate assent. When Shell discovered that the Wayback Machine had copied the contents of her site—approximately eighty-seven times between May 1999 and October 2004—she asked IA to remove the copies from its archive and pay her $100,000. IA removed the copies and filed a suit in a federal district court against Shell, who responded, in part, with a counterclaim for breach of contract. IA filed a motion to dismiss this claim. Did IA contract with Shell? Explain. [*Internet Archive v. Shell,* __ F.Supp.2d __ (D.Colo. 2007)]

10–8 Acceptance. Evelyn Kowalchuk, an eighty-eight-year-old widow, and her son, Peter, put their savings into accounts managed by Matthew Stroup. Later, they initiated an arbitration proceeding before the National Association of Securities Dealers (NASD), asserting that Stroup fraudulently or negligently handled their accounts. They asked for an award of $832,000. After the hearing, but before a decision was rendered, Stroup offered to pay the Kowalchuks $285,000, and they e-mailed their acceptance. Stroup signed a settlement agreement and faxed it to the Kowalchuks for their signatures. Meanwhile, the NASD issued an award in the Kowalchuks' favor for $88,788. Stroup immediately told them that he was withdrawing his settlement "offer." When Stroup did not pay according to its terms, the Kowalchuks filed a suit in a New York state court against him for breach of contract. Did these parties have a contract? Why or why not? [*Kowalchuk v. Stroup,* 873 N.Y.S.2d 43 (N.Y.A.D. 1 Dept. 2009)]

10–9 **A Question of Ethics** *In 2000 and 2001, Dewayne Hubbert, Elden Craft, Chris Grout, and Rhonda Byington bought computers from Dell Corp. through its Web site. Before buying, Hubbert and the others configured their own computers. To make a purchase, each buyer completed forms on five Web pages. On each page, Dell's "Terms and Conditions of Sale" were accessible by clicking on a blue hyperlink. A statement on three of the pages reads, "All sales are subject to Dell's Term[s] and Conditions of Sale," but a buyer was not required to click an assent to the terms to* complete a purchase. *The terms were also printed on the backs of the invoices and on separate documents contained in the shipping boxes with the computers. Among those terms was a "Binding Arbitration" clause. The computers contained Pentium 4 microprocessors, which Dell advertised as the fastest, most powerful Intel Pentium processor available. In 2002, Hubbert and the others filed a suit in an Illinois state court against Dell, alleging that this marketing was false, misleading, and deceptive. The plaintiffs claimed that the Pentium 4 microprocessor was slower and less powerful, and provided less performance, than either a Pentium III or an AMD Athlon, and at a greater cost. Dell asked the court to compel arbitration. [Hubbert v. Dell Corp., 359 Ill.App.3d 976, 835 N.E.2d 113, 296 Ill.Dec. 258 (5 Dist. 2005)]*

1 Should the court enforce the arbitration clause in this case? If you were the judge, how would you rule on this issue?

2 In your opinion, do shrink-wrap, click-on, and browse-wrap terms impose too great a burden on purchasers? Why or why not?

3 An ongoing complaint about shrink-wrap, click-on, and browse-wrap terms is that sellers (often large corporations) draft them and buyers (typically individual consumers) do not read them. Should purchasers be bound in contract by terms that they have not even read? Why or why not?

Critical Thinking and Writing Assignments

10–10 **Case Analysis Question** Go to Appendix F at the end of this text and examine Case No. 2 [*Feldman v. Google, Inc.,* 513 F.Supp.2d 229 (E.D.Pa. 2007)]. This case has been excerpted there in great detail. Review and then brief the case, making sure that your brief answers the following questions.

1 **Issue:** The dispute between the parties to this case centered on what agreement and asked which question?

2 **Rule of Law:** What rule concerning the existence of a contract did the court apply in this case?

3 **Applying the Rule of Law:** How did the language in the parties' agreement and its context affect the application of the rule of law?

4 **Conclusion:** In whose favor did the court rule? Why?

10–11 **Video Question** Go to this text's Web site at **www.cengage.com/blaw/blt** and select "Chapter 10." Click on "Video Questions" and view the video titled *E-Contracts: Agreeing Online.* Then answer the following questions.

1 According to the instructor in the video, what is the key factor in determining whether a particular term in an online agreement is enforceable?

2 Suppose that you click on "I accept" in order to download software from the Internet. You do not read the terms of the agreement before accepting it, even though you know that such agreements often contain forum-selection and arbitration clauses. The software later causes irreparable harm to your computer system, and you want to sue. When you go to the Web site and view the agreement, however, you discover that a choice-of-law clause in the contract specified that the law of Nigeria controls. Is this term enforceable? Is it a term that should reasonably be expected in an online contract?

3 Does it matter what the term actually says if it is a type of term that one could reasonably expect to be in the contract? What arguments can be made for and against enforcing a choice-of-law clause in an online contract?

Practical Internet Exercises

Go to this text's Web site at **www.cengage.com/blaw/blt**, select "Chapter 10," and click on "Practical Internet Exercises." There you will find the following Internet research exercises that you can perform to learn more about the topics covered in this chapter.

Practical Internet Exercise 10–1: LEGAL PERSPECTIVE—Contract Terms
Practical Internet Exercise 10–2: ETHICAL PERSPECTIVE—Offers and Advertisements

Chapter 11

Consideration, Capacity, and Legality

(©Dmitriy Shironosov, 2009. Used under license from Shutterstock.com)

Chapter Outline

- Consideration
- Promissory Estoppel
- Contractual Capacity
- Legality
- The Effect of Illegality

> "Liberty of contract is not an absolute concept. It is relative to many conditions of time and place and circumstance."
>
> —Benjamin Cardozo, 1870–1938
> (Associate justice of the United States Supreme Court, 1932–1938)

Learning Objectives

After reading this chapter, you should be able to answer the following questions:

1. What is consideration? What is required for consideration to be legally sufficient?

2. In what circumstances might a promise be enforced despite a lack of consideration?

3. Does a minor have the capacity to enter into an enforceable contract? What does it mean to disaffirm a contract?

4. Under what circumstances will a covenant not to compete be enforceable? When will such covenants not be enforced?

5. What is an exculpatory clause? In what circumstances might exculpatory clauses be enforced? When will they not be enforced?

Courts generally want contracts to be enforceable, and much of the law is devoted to aiding the enforceability of contracts. Before a court will enforce a contractual promise, however, it must be convinced that there was some exchange of consideration underlying the bargain. Furthermore, as indicated in the chapter-opening quotation, "liberty of contract" is not absolute. In other words, not all people can make legally binding contracts at all times. Contracts entered into by persons lacking the capacity to do so may be voidable. Similarly, contracts calling for the performance of an illegal act are illegal and thus void—they are not contracts at all. In this chapter, we first examine the requirement of consideration and then look at contractual capacity and legality.

▶ Consideration

In every legal system, some promises will be enforced, and other promises will not be enforced. The simple fact that a party has made a promise, then, does not mean that the promise is enforceable. Under the common law, a primary basis for the enforcement of promises is consideration. **Consideration** usually is defined as the value given in return for a promise.

Consideration Generally, the value given in return for a promise; involves two elements—the giving of something of legally sufficient value and a bargained-for exchange. The consideration must result in a detriment to the promisee or a benefit to the promisor.

262

Often, consideration is broken down into two parts: (1) something of *legally sufficient value* must be given in exchange for the promise, and (2) there must be a *bargained-for exchange*.

Legal Value

The "something of legally sufficient value" may consist of (1) a promise to do something that one has no prior legal duty to do (to pay on receipt of certain goods, for example), (2) the performance of an action that one is otherwise not obligated to undertake (such as providing accounting services), or (3) the refraining from an action that one has a legal right to undertake (called a **forbearance**).

Consideration in bilateral contracts normally consists of a promise in return for a promise, as explained in Chapter 9. **EXAMPLE 11.1** In a contract for the sale of goods, the seller promises to ship specific goods to the buyer, and the buyer promises to pay for those goods when they are received. Each of these promises constitutes consideration for the contract. ●

In contrast, unilateral contracts involve a promise in return for a performance. **EXAMPLE 11.2** Anita says to her neighbor, "If you paint my garage, I will pay you $800." Anita's neighbor paints the garage. The act of painting the garage is the consideration that creates Anita's contractual obligation to pay her neighbor $800. ●

What if, in return for a promise to pay, a person refrains from pursuing harmful habits, such as the use of tobacco and alcohol? Does such forbearance create consideration for the contract? This was the issue in *Hamer v. Sidway,* a classic case concerning consideration that we present as this chapter's *Landmark in the Law* feature on the following page.

Bargained-for Exchange

The second element of consideration is that it must provide the basis for the bargain struck between the contracting parties. The promise given by the promisor must induce the promisee to incur a legal detriment either now or in the future, and the detriment incurred must induce the promisor to make the promise. This element of bargained-for exchange distinguishes contracts from gifts.

EXAMPLE 11.3 Roberto says to his son, "In consideration of the fact that you are not as wealthy as your brothers, I will pay you $5,000." The fact that the word *consideration* is used does not, by itself, mean that consideration has been given. Indeed, Roberto's promise is not enforceable because the son need not do anything to receive the $5,000 promised. Because the son does not need to give Roberto something of legal value in return for his promise, there is no bargained-for exchange. Rather, Roberto has simply stated his motive for giving his son a gift. ●

Legal Sufficiency and Adequacy of Consideration

Legal sufficiency of consideration involves the requirement that consideration be something of value in the eyes of the law. Adequacy of consideration involves "how much" consideration is given. Essentially, adequacy of consideration concerns the fairness of the bargain. On the surface, fairness would appear to be an issue when the items exchanged are of unequal value. In general, however, a court will not question the adequacy of consideration if the consideration is legally sufficient. Under the doctrine of freedom of contract, parties are usually free to bargain as they wish. If people could sue merely because they had entered into an unwise contract, the courts would be overloaded with frivolous suits.

The determination of whether consideration exists does not depend on the comparative value of the things exchanged. In many situations, the exchange of promises and potential benefits is deemed sufficient as consideration.

an action that one has a legal right to undertake.

> "*Understanding does not necessarily mean agreement.*"
> Howard Vernon, 1914–1996
> (Swiss actor)

Landmark in the Law   *Hamer v. Sidway* (1891)

In *Hamer v. Sidway,*[a] the issue before the court arose from a contract created in 1869 between William Story, Sr., and his nephew, William Story, II. The uncle promised his nephew that if the nephew refrained from drinking alcohol, using tobacco, and playing billiards and cards for money until he reached the age of twenty-one, the uncle would pay him $5,000 (about $75,000 in today's dollars). The nephew, who indulged occasionally in all of these "vices," agreed to refrain from them and did so for the next six years. Following his twenty-first birthday in 1875, the nephew wrote to his uncle that he had performed his part of the bargain and was thus entitled to the promised $5,000 (plus interest). A few days later, the uncle wrote the nephew a letter stating, "[Y]ou shall have the five thousand dollars, as I promised you." The uncle said that the money was in the bank and that the nephew could "consider this money on interest."

The Issue of Consideration   The nephew left the money in the care of his uncle, who held it for the next twelve years. When the uncle died in 1887, however, the executor of the uncle's estate refused to pay the $5,000 (plus interest) claim brought by Hamer, a third party to whom the promise had been *assigned.* (The law allows parties to assign, or transfer, rights in contracts to third parties; see Chapter 13.) The executor, Sidway, contended that the contract was invalid because there was insufficient consideration to support it. The uncle had received nothing, and the

nephew had actually benefited by fulfilling the uncle's wishes. Therefore, no contract existed.

The Court's Conclusion   Although a lower court upheld Sidway's position, the New York Court of Appeals reversed and ruled in favor of the plaintiff, Hamer. "The promisee used tobacco, occasionally drank liquor, and he had a legal right to do so," the court stated. "That right he abandoned for a period of years upon the strength of the promise of the testator [one who makes a will] that for such forbearance he would give him $5,000. We need not speculate on the effort which may have been required to give up the use of those stimulants. It is sufficient that he restricted his lawful freedom of action within certain prescribed limits upon the faith of his uncle's agreement."

• **Application to Today's World**   *Although this case was decided more than a century ago, the principles enunciated by the court remain applicable to contracts formed today, including online contracts. For a contract to be valid and binding, consideration must be given, and that consideration must be something of legally sufficient value.*

• **Relevant Web Sites**   To locate information on the Web concerning the *Hamer v. Sidway* decision, go to this text's Web site at www.cengage.com/blaw/blt, select "Chapter 11," and click on "URLs for Landmarks."

---

a. 124 N.Y. 538, 27 N.E. 256 (1891).

BE AWARE   A consumer's signature on a contract does not always guarantee that the contract will be enforced. The contract must also comply with state and federal consumer protection laws.

When there is a large disparity in the amount or value of the consideration exchanged, it may raise a red flag for a court to look more closely at the bargain. Shockingly inadequate consideration can indicate that fraud, duress, or undue influence was involved or that the element of bargained-for exchange was lacking. (Defenses to enforceability will be discussed in Chapter 12.) It may also cause a judge to question whether the contract is so one sided that it is unconscionable,[1] a concept that will be discussed later in this chapter.

Judges are uneasy about enforcing unequal bargains, and it is their task to make certain that there was not some defect in the contract's formation that negated voluntary consent. **EXAMPLE 11.4**   An elderly person, Elizabeth Crain, sells her Mercedes-Benz convertible to her neighbor for $5,000 even though it is worth more than $50,000. Because the disparity in value might indicate that the sale involved undue influence or fraud, a judge would want to make sure that Crain voluntarily entered into this agreement. •

Contracts That Lack Consideration

ON THE WEB   To learn more about how the courts decide such issues as whether consideration was lacking for a particular contract, look at relevant case law, which can be accessed through the Web site of Cornell University's School of Law at topics.law.cornell.edu/wex/ Contracts.

Sometimes, one or both of the parties to a contract may think that they have exchanged consideration when in fact they have not. Here we look at some situations in which the parties' promises or actions do not qualify as contractual consideration.

PREEXISTING DUTY   Under most circumstances, a promise to do what one already has a legal duty to do does not constitute legally sufficient consideration. A sheriff, for example,

---

1. Pronounced un-*kon*-shun-uh-bul.

Large construction jobs are often awarded to the lowest bidder. What if the contractor, while in the course of completing a job, encounters extraordinary difficulties that were unforeseen when the bid was made? Does the contractor have to absorb all of the additional costs? Why or why not?

Rescission A remedy whereby a contract is canceled and the parties are returned to the positions they occupied before the contract was made; may be effected through the mutual consent of the parties, by the parties' conduct, or by court decree.

Past Consideration An act that takes place before the contract is made and that ordinarily, by itself, cannot be consideration for a later promise to pay for the act.

cannot collect a reward for information leading to the capture of a criminal if the sheriff already has a legal duty to capture the criminal.

Likewise, if a party is already bound by contract to perform a certain duty, that duty cannot serve as consideration for a second contract. **EXAMPLE 11.5** Bauman-Bache, Inc., begins construction on a seven-story office building and after three months demands an extra $75,000 on its contract. If the extra $75,000 is not paid, the firm will stop working. The owner of the land, having no one else to complete construction, agrees to pay the extra $75,000. The agreement is not enforceable because it is not supported by legally sufficient consideration; Bauman-Bache had a preexisting contractual duty to complete the building. ●

Unforeseen Difficulties.   The rule regarding preexisting duty is meant to prevent extortion and the so-called holdup game. What happens, though, when an honest contractor, who has contracted with a landowner to build a house, runs into extraordinary difficulties that were totally unforeseen at the time the contract was formed? In the interests of fairness and equity, the courts sometimes allow exceptions to the preexisting duty rule. Therefore, if a landowner agrees to pay extra compensation to a contractor for overcoming unforeseen difficulties (such as having to use special equipment to remove an unforeseen obstacle), a court may decide not to apply the preexisting duty rule. When the unforeseen difficulties that give rise to a contract modification are the types of risks ordinarily assumed in business, however, the courts will usually assert the preexisting duty rule.[2]

Rescission and New Contract.   The law recognizes that two parties can mutually agree to rescind, or cancel, their contract, at least to the extent that it is executory (still to be carried out). **Rescission**[3] is the unmaking of a contract so as to return the parties to the positions they occupied before the contract was made. Sometimes, parties rescind a contract and make a new contract at the same time. When this occurs, it is often difficult to determine whether there was consideration for the new contract or whether the parties had a preexisting duty under the previous contract. If a court finds there was a preexisting duty, then the new contract will be invalid because there was no consideration.

PAST CONSIDERATION   Promises made in return for actions or events that have already taken place are unenforceable. These promises lack consideration in that the element of bargained-for exchange is missing. In short, you can bargain for something to take place now or in the future but not for something that has already taken place. Therefore, **past consideration** is no consideration.

CASE EXAMPLE 11.6 Blackmon became friends with Iverson when Iverson was a high school student who showed tremendous promise as an athlete. One evening, Blackmon suggested that Iverson use "The Answer" as a nickname in the summer league basketball tournaments. Blackmon said that Iverson would be "The Answer" to all of the National Basketball Association's woes. Later that night, Iverson said that he would give Blackmon 25 percent of any proceeds from the merchandising of products that used "The Answer" as a logo or a slogan. Because Iverson's promise was made in return for past consideration (Blackmon's earlier suggestion), it was unenforceable; in effect, Iverson stated his intention to give Blackmon a gift.[4] ●

As you will read later in this chapter, an employer will often ask an employee to sign a *noncompete agreement,* also called a *covenant not to compete.* Under such an agreement, the

---

2. Note that under the Uniform Commercial Code (UCC), any agreement modifying a contract within Article 2 on sales needs no consideration to be binding. See UCC 2–209(1).

3. Pronounced reh-*sih*-zhen.

4. *Blackmon v. Iverson,* 324 F.Supp.2d 602 (E.D.Pa. 2003).

employee agrees not to work for competitors of the employer for a certain period of time after the employment relationship ends. In the following case, the court had to decide if continued employment constituted valid consideration for a noncompete agreement or if it was past consideration.

Case 11.1   Access Organics, Inc. v. Hernandez

Supreme Court of Montana, 341 Mont. 73, 175 P.3d 899 (2008).

(Anna Duncan Art/Creative Commons)

Organic products have become staple items in most markets. Under what circumstances can an employer enforce a noncompete agreement with its organic foods manager?

FACTS   Bonnie Poux hired Andy Hernandez to sell organic produce for her sole proprietorship, Access Organics, Inc. Four months later, he was promoted to sales manager. Soon after, he signed a noncompete agreement in which he agreed "not to directly or indirectly compete with the business . . . for a period of two years following termination of employment." Later, the business encountered financial difficulties. Hernandez left and went into business with another former employee to compete with Access Organics in the sale of produce in the same part of Montana. Poux then sued to enforce the noncompete agreement. The trial court found that Hernandez had violated the noncompete agreement and ordered him not to compete directly with Access Organics for the two-year period called for in the agreement. The court held that the agreement was valid because it was supported by consideration, which was continued employment at Access Organics at the time the agreement was signed. Hernandez appealed.

ISSUE   Is continued employment valid consideration to support a noncompete agreement that an employee signed shortly after being hired?

DECISION   No. Montana's highest court held that the noncompete agreement was invalid because it was not supported by consideration. Because no contract had been formed, the court reversed the trial court's order enforcing the agreement.

REASON   The court noted that although covenants not to compete are restraints of trade and therefore disfavored, they are upheld in some circumstances if they are supported by consideration. Consideration exists if the employee enters into the noncompete agreement at the time of hiring because then the agreement is part of a bargained-for exchange. In this case, however, Hernandez signed the agreement more than four months after accepting his initial employment. Hernandez was simply told to sign the agreement when he was already working for Access Organics. His prior employment was not consideration because past consideration is insufficient to support a promise. This was an "afterthought agreement" that could have been valid if it had been supported by a pay increase or some other new benefit, but it was not. Because the agreement was unsupported by consideration, it did not create an enforceable contract.

FOR CRITICAL ANALYSIS—Ethical Consideration   *How could Access Organics have obtained a noncompete agreement from Hernandez that would have been enforced?*

ILLUSORY PROMISES   If the terms of the contract express such uncertainty of performance that the promisor has not definitely promised to do anything, the promise is said to be *illusory*—without consideration and unenforceable. **EXAMPLE 11.7**   The president of Tuscan Corporation says to his employees, "All of you have worked hard, and if profits remain high, a 10 percent bonus at the end of the year will be given—if management thinks it is warranted." This is an *illusory promise,* or no promise at all, because performance depends solely on the discretion of the president (the management). There is no bargained-for consideration. The statement declares merely that management may or may not do something in the future. ●

Option-to-cancel clauses in contracts for specified time periods sometimes present problems in regard to consideration. **EXAMPLE 11.8**   Abe contracts to hire Chris for one year at $5,000 per month, reserving the right to cancel the contract at any time. On close examination of these words, you can see that Abe has not actually agreed to hire Chris, as

Abe can cancel without liability before Chris starts performance. Abe has not given up the opportunity of hiring someone else. This contract is therefore illusory. Now suppose that Abe contracts to hire Chris for a one-year period at $5,000 per month, reserving the right to cancel the contract at any time after Chris has begun performance by giving Chris thirty days' notice. Abe, by saying that he will give Chris thirty days' notice, is relinquishing the opportunity (legal right) to hire someone else instead of Chris for a thirty-day period. If Chris works for one month, at the end of which Abe gives him thirty days' notice, Chris has a valid and enforceable contractual claim for $10,000 for two months' salary. ●

Settlement of Claims

Businesspersons and others often enter into contracts to settle legal claims. It is important to understand the nature of the consideration given in these settlement agreements, or contracts. Claims are commonly settled through an *accord and satisfaction,* in which a debtor offers to pay a lesser amount than the creditor says is owed. Claims may also be settled by the signing of a *release* or a *covenant not to sue.*

REMEMBER Businesspersons should consider settling potential legal disputes to save both their own time and resources and those of the courts.

Accord and Satisfaction A common means of settling a disputed claim, whereby a debtor offers to pay a lesser amount than the creditor purports to be owed. The creditor's acceptance of the offer creates an accord (agreement), and when the accord is executed, satisfaction occurs.

Liquidated Debt A debt for which the amount has been ascertained, fixed, agreed on, settled, or exactly determined. If the amount of the debt is in dispute, the debt is considered unliquidated.

ACCORD AND SATISFACTION In an **accord and satisfaction,** a debtor offers to pay, and a creditor accepts, a lesser amount than the creditor originally claimed was owed. The *accord* is the agreement under which one of the parties promises to give or perform, and the other to accept, in satisfaction of a claim, something other than that on which the parties originally agreed. *Satisfaction* is the performance (usually payment), which takes place after the accord is executed. A basic rule is that there can be no satisfaction unless there is first an accord. For accord and satisfaction to occur, the amount of the debt *must be in dispute.*

If a debt is *liquidated,* accord and satisfaction cannot take place. A **liquidated debt** is one whose amount has been ascertained, fixed, agreed on, settled, or exactly determined. **EXAMPLE 11.9** Barbara Kwan signs an installment loan contract with her banker. In the contract, Kwan agrees to pay a specified rate of interest on a specified amount of borrowed funds at monthly intervals for two years. Because both parties know the precise amount of the total obligation, it is a liquidated debt. ● In the majority of states, acceptance of (an accord for) a lesser sum than the entire amount of a liquidated debt is not satisfaction, and the balance of the debt is still legally owed. The reason for this rule is that the debtor has given no consideration to satisfy the obligation of paying the balance to the creditor— because the debtor has a preexisting legal obligation to pay the entire debt.

An *unliquidated debt* is the opposite of a liquidated debt. The amount of the debt is *not* settled, fixed, agreed on, ascertained, or determined, and reasonable persons may differ over the amount owed. In these circumstances, acceptance of payment of the lesser sum operates as a satisfaction, or discharge, of the debt because there is valid consideration— the parties give up a legal right to contest the amount in dispute.

Release A contract in which one party forfeits the right to pursue a legal claim against the other party.

ON THE WEB To read an article on FindLaw about when it is appropriate for businesses to use release forms, go to **smallbusiness.findlaw.com/ business-operations/insurance/ liability-release-forms.html**.

RELEASE A **release** is a contract in which one party forfeits the right to pursue a legal claim against the other party. It bars any further recovery beyond the terms stated in the release. Releases will generally be binding if they are (1) given in good faith, (2) stated in a signed writing (required by many states), and (3) accompanied by consideration.[5] Clearly, parties are better off if they know the extent of their injuries or damages before signing releases.

EXAMPLE 11.10 Your car is damaged in an accident caused by Raoul's negligence. Raoul offers to give you $3,000 if you will release him from further liability resulting from the accident. You believe that this amount will cover your repairs, so you agree and sign the release. Later, you discover that the repairs to your car will cost $4,200. Can you collect

---

5. Under the UCC, a written, signed waiver or renunciation by an aggrieved party discharges any further liability for a breach, even without consideration [UCC 1–107].

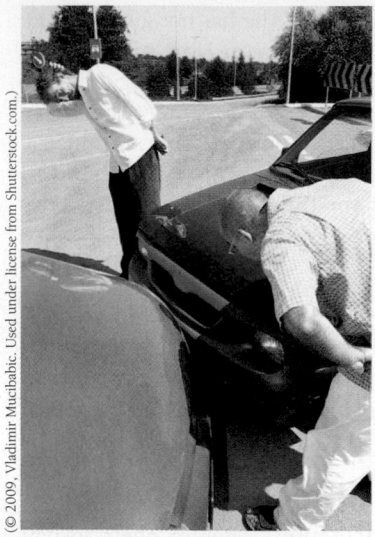

The negligent party in this accident negotiated a release that the non-negligent party signed. If the cash settlement turned out to be insufficient, can the non-negligent party sue to recover the additional loss? Why or why not?

Covenant Not to Sue An agreement to substitute a contractual obligation for some other type of legal action based on a valid claim.

Promissory Estoppel A doctrine that applies when a promisor makes a clear and definite promise on which the promisee justifiably relies. Such a promise is binding if justice will be better served by the enforcement of the promise.

Estopped Barred, impeded, or precluded.

the balance from Raoul? Normally, the answer is no; you are limited to the $3,000 in the release. Why? The reason is that a valid contract existed. You and Raoul both voluntarily consented to the terms (hence, agreement existed), and sufficient consideration was present. The consideration was the legal detriment you suffered (you forfeited your right to sue to recover damages, should they be more than $3,000) in exchange for Raoul's promise to give you $3,000. ●

COVENANT NOT TO SUE   Unlike a release, a **covenant not to sue** does not always bar further recovery. The parties simply substitute a contractual obligation for some other type of legal action based on a valid claim. Suppose (in the preceding example) that you agree with Raoul not to sue for damages in a tort action if he will pay for the damage to your car. If Raoul fails to pay, you can bring an action for breach of contract.

▶ Promissory Estoppel

Sometimes, individuals rely on promises, and their reliance may form a basis for a court to infer contract rights and duties. Under the doctrine of **promissory estoppel** (also called *detrimental reliance*), a person who has reasonably and substantially relied on the promise of another can obtain some measure of recovery. Promissory estoppel is applied in a variety of contexts and allows a party to recover on a promise even though it was made *without consideration*. Under this doctrine, a court may enforce an otherwise unenforceable promise to avoid the injustice that would otherwise result.

Requirements to Establish Promissory Estoppel

For the doctrine to be applied, the following elements are required:

1. There must be a clear and definite promise.
2. The promisor should have expected that the promisee would rely on the promise.
3. The promisee reasonably relied on the promise by acting or refraining from some act.
4. The promisee's reliance was definite and resulted in substantial detriment.
5. Enforcement of the promise is necessary to avoid injustice.

If these requirements are met, a promise may be enforced even though it is not supported by consideration. In essence, the promisor (the offeror) will be **estopped** (barred or prevented) from asserting lack of consideration as a defense.

Application of Promissory Estoppel

Promissory estoppel was originally applied to situations involving gifts (I promise to pay you $1,000 a week so that you will not have to work) and donations to charities (I promise to contribute $50,000 a year to the All Saints orphanage). Later, courts began to apply the doctrine to avoid inequity or hardship in other situations, including business transactions. **EXAMPLE 11.11** An employer, Jay Bailey, orally promises to pay each of his five employees $2,000 a month for the remainder of their lives after they retire. When Sal Hernandez retires, he receives the monthly amount for two years, but then Bailey stops paying. Under the doctrine of promissory estoppel, Hernandez can sue Bailey in an attempt to enforce his promise. ●

Promissory estoppel is similar in some ways to the doctrine of quasi contract that was discussed in Chapter 9. In both situations, a court is acting in the interests of equity and imposes contract obligations on the parties to prevent unfairness even though no actual contract exists. In quasi contracts, however, no promise at all was made, whereas with promissory estoppel, a promise was made and relied on, but it was unenforceable.

▶ Contractual Capacity

Contractual Capacity   The threshold mental capacity required by law for a party who enters into a contract to be bound by that contract.

Contractual capacity is the legal ability to enter into a contractual relationship. Courts generally presume the existence of contractual capacity, but in some situations, capacity is lacking or may be questionable. A person who has been determined by a court to be mentally incompetent, for example, cannot form a legally binding contract with another party. In other situations, a party may have the capacity to enter into a valid contract but may also have the right to avoid liability under it. For example, minors—or *infants,* as they are commonly referred to in the law—usually are not legally bound by contracts. In this section, we look at the effect of youth, intoxication, and mental incompetence on contractual capacity.

Minors

ON THE WEB The Legal Information Institute at Cornell Law School provides a table with links to state statutes governing the emancipation of minors. Go to **topics.law.cornell.edu/wex/ table_emancipation.**

Today, in almost all states, the *age of majority* (when a person is no longer a minor) for contractual purposes is eighteen years—the so-called coming of age.[6] In addition, some states provide for the termination of minority on marriage. Minority status may also be terminated by a minor's **emancipation,** which occurs when a child's parent or legal guardian relinquishes the legal right to exercise control over the child. Normally, minors who leave home to support themselves are considered emancipated. Several jurisdictions permit minors to petition a court for emancipation. For business purposes, a minor may petition a court to be treated as an adult.

Emancipation   In regard to minors, the act of being freed from parental control; occurs when a child's parent or legal guardian relinquishes the legal right to exercise control over the child. Normally, a minor who leaves home to support himself or herself is considered emancipated.

The general rule is that a minor can enter into any contract an adult can, provided that the contract is not one prohibited by law for minors (for example, the sale of alcoholic beverages or tobacco). A contract entered into by a minor, however, is voidable at the option of that minor, subject to certain exceptions (to be discussed shortly). To exercise the option to avoid a contract, a minor need only manifest an intention not to be bound by it. The minor "avoids" the contract by disaffirming it.

Disaffirmance   The legal avoidance, or setting aside, of a contractual obligation.

DISAFFIRMANCE   The legal avoidance, or setting aside, of a contractual obligation is referred to as **disaffirmance.** To disaffirm, a minor must express through words or conduct, his or her intent not to be bound to the contract. The minor must disaffirm the entire contract, not merely a portion of it. For instance, a minor cannot decide to keep part of the goods purchased under a contract and return the remaining goods. When a minor disaffirms a contract, the minor can recover any property that she or he transferred to the adult as consideration for the contract, even if it is then in the possession of a third party.[7]

A contract can ordinarily be disaffirmed at any time during minority[8] or for a reasonable time after the minor comes of age. What constitutes a "reasonable" time may vary. Two months would probably be considered reasonable, but except in unusual circumstances, a court may not find it reasonable to wait a year or more after coming of age to disaffirm. If an individual fails to disaffirm an executed contract within a reasonable time after reaching the age of majority, a court will likely hold that the contract has been ratified (*ratification* will be discussed shortly).

Note that an adult who enters into a contract with a minor cannot avoid his or her contractual duties on the ground that the minor can do so. Unless the minor exercises the option to disaffirm the contract, the adult party normally is bound by it.

---

6. The age of majority may still be twenty-one for other purposes, such as the purchase and consumption of alcohol.

7. Section 2–403(1) of the UCC allows an exception if the third party is a "good faith purchaser for value." See Chapter 16.

8. In some states, however, a minor who enters into a contract for the sale of land cannot disaffirm the contract until she or he reaches the age of majority.

A Minor's Obligations on Disaffirmance   Although all states' laws permit minors to disaffirm contracts (with certain exceptions), including executed contracts, state laws differ on the extent of a minor's obligations on disaffirmance. Courts in most states hold that the minor need only return the goods (or other consideration) subject to the contract, provided the goods are in the minor's possession or control. Even if the minor returns damaged goods, the minor often is entitled to disaffirm the contract and obtain a refund of the purchase price.

A growing number of states place an additional duty on the minor to restore the adult party to the position she or he held before the contract was made. These courts may hold a minor responsible for damage, ordinary wear and tear, and depreciation of goods that the minor used prior to disaffirmance. **CASE EXAMPLE 11.12** Sixteen-year-old Joseph Dodson bought a truck for $4,900 from a used-car dealer. Although the truck developed mechanical problems nine months later, Dodson continued to drive it until the engine blew up and it stopped running. Dodson then disaffirmed the contract and attempted to return the truck to the dealer for a refund of the full purchase price. The dealer refused to accept the truck or to provide a refund. Dodson filed a suit. Ultimately, the Tennessee Supreme Court allowed Dodson to disaffirm the contract but required him to compensate the seller for the depreciated value—not the purchase price—of the truck.[9] ●

Exceptions to a Minor's Right to Disaffirm   State courts and legislatures have carved out several exceptions to the minor's right to disaffirm. Some contracts, such as marriage contracts and contracts to enlist in the armed services, cannot be avoided on the ground of public policy. Other contracts may not be disaffirmed for different reasons.

Although ordinarily minors can disaffirm contracts even when they have misrepresented their age, a growing number of states have enacted laws to prohibit disaffirmance in such situations. Some state laws also prohibit minors from disaffirming contracts entered into by a minor who is engaged in business as an adult.

In addition, a minor who enters into a contract for necessaries may disaffirm the contract but remains liable for the reasonable value of the goods used. **Necessaries** are basic needs, such as food, clothing, shelter, and medical services, at a level of value required to maintain the minor's standard of living or financial and social status. Thus, what will be considered a necessary for one person may be a luxury for another.

Ratification   In contract law, **ratification** is the act of accepting and giving legal force to an obligation that previously was not enforceable. A minor who has reached the age of majority can ratify a contract expressly or impliedly. *Express* ratification occurs when the individual, on reaching the age of majority, states orally or in writing that she or he intends to be bound by the contract. *Implied* ratification takes place when the minor, on reaching the age of majority, indicates an intent to abide by the contract.

EXAMPLE 11.13   Lin enters into a contract to sell her laptop to Andrew, a minor. Andrew does not disaffirm the contract. If, on reaching the age of majority, he writes a letter to Lin stating that he still agrees to buy the laptop, he has expressly ratified the contract. If, instead, Andrew takes possession of the laptop as a minor and continues to use it well after reaching the age of majority, he has impliedly ratified the contract. ●

If a minor fails to disaffirm a contract within a reasonable time after reaching the age of majority, then a court must determine whether the conduct constitutes implied ratification or disaffirmance. Generally, courts presume that a contract that is *executed* (fully performed by both sides) was ratified. A contract that is still *executory* (not yet performed by both parties) is normally considered to be disaffirmed.

Necessaries   Necessities required for life, such as food, shelter, clothing, and medical attention; may include whatever is believed to be necessary to maintain a person's standard of living or financial and social status.

Ratification   The act of accepting and giving legal force to an obligation that previously was not enforceable.

BE AWARE   A minor's station in life (including financial and social status and lifestyle) is important in determining whether an item is a necessary or a luxury. For example, clothing is a necessary, but if a minor from a low-income family contracts for the purchase of a $2,000 leather coat, a court may deem the coat a luxury. In this situation, the contract would not be for "necessaries."

---

9. *Dodson v. Shrader,* 824 S.W.2d 545 (Tenn. 1992).

PARENTS' LIABILITY   As a general rule, parents are not liable for the contracts made by minor children acting on their own, except contracts for necessaries, which the parents are legally required to provide. This is why businesses ordinarily require parents to cosign any contract made with a minor. The parents then become personally obligated to perform the conditions of the contract, even if their child avoids liability. (Parents can sometimes be held liable for a minor's torts, however, depending on state law.)

Intoxicated Persons

Intoxication is a condition in which a person's normal capacity to act or think is inhibited by alcohol or some other drug. A contract entered into by an intoxicated person can be either voidable or valid (and thus enforceable). If the person was sufficiently intoxicated to lack mental capacity, then the transaction may be voidable at the option of the intoxicated person even if the intoxication was purely voluntary. If, despite intoxication, the person understood the legal consequences of the agreement, the contract is enforceable. Courts look at objective indications of the situation to determine if the intoxicated person possessed or lacked the required capacity.

For the contract to be voidable, the person must prove that the intoxication impaired her or his reason and judgment so severely that she or he did not comprehend the legal consequences of entering into the contract. In addition, the person claiming intoxication must be able to return all consideration received. As a practical matter, courts rarely permit contracts to be avoided on the ground of intoxication, because it is difficult to determine whether a party was sufficiently intoxicated to avoid legal duties.

Mentally Incompetent Persons

Contracts made by mentally incompetent persons can be void, voidable, or valid. We look here at the circumstances that determine when these classifications apply.

WHEN THE CONTRACT WILL BE VOID   If a court has previously determined that a person is mentally incompetent and has appointed a guardian to represent the person, any contract made by that mentally incompetent person is *void*—no contract exists. Only the guardian can enter into a binding contract on behalf of the mentally incompetent person.

WHEN THE CONTRACT WILL BE VOIDABLE   If a court has not previously judged a person to be mentally incompetent but in fact the person was incompetent at the time, the contract may be *voidable*. A contract is voidable if the person did not know he or she was entering into the contract or lacked the mental capacity to comprehend its nature, purpose, and consequences. In such situations, the contract is voidable at the option of the mentally incompetent person but not the other party. The contract may then be disaffirmed or ratified (if the person regains mental competence). Like intoxicated persons, mentally incompetent persons must return any consideration and pay for the reasonable value of any necessaries they receive.

EXAMPLE 11.14   Milo, a mentally incompetent man who had not been previously declared incompetent by a judge, agrees to sell twenty lots in a prime residential neighborhood to Pierce. At the time of entering into the contract, Milo is confused over which lots he is selling and how much they are worth. As a result, he contracts to sell the properties for substantially less than their market value. If the court finds that Milo was unable to understand the nature and consequences of the contract, the contract is voidable. Milo can avoid the sale, provided that he returns any consideration that he received. •

WHEN THE CONTRACT WILL BE VALID   A contract entered into by a mentally incompetent person (whom a court has not previously declared incompetent) may also be *valid* if the person had capacity *at the time the contract was formed*. An otherwise incompetent person who understands the nature, purpose, and consequences at the time of entering into a contract is bound by it. Some people who are incompetent due to age or illness have *lucid intervals*—temporary periods of sufficient intelligence, judgment, and will—during which they will be considered to have legal capacity to enter into contracts.

 Legality

For a contract to be valid and enforceable, it must be formed for a legal purpose. Legality is the fourth requirement for a valid contract to exist. A contract to do something that is prohibited by federal or state statutory law is illegal and, as such, is void from the outset and thus unenforceable. Additionally, a contract to commit a tortious act (see Chapter 4) or to commit an action that is contrary to public policy is illegal and unenforceable.

Contracts Contrary to Statute

Statutes often set forth rules specifying which terms and clauses may be included in contracts and which are prohibited. We examine here several ways in which contracts may be contrary to a statute and thus illegal.

CONTRACTS TO COMMIT A CRIME   Any contract to commit a crime is a contract in violation of a statute. Thus, a contract to sell illegal drugs in violation of criminal laws is unenforceable, as is a contract to cover up a corporation's violation of the Sarbanes-Oxley Act (see Chapter 31). Similarly, a contract to smuggle undocumented workers from another country into the United States for an employer is illegal (see Chapter 24), as is a contract to dump hazardous waste in violation of environmental laws (see Chapter 33). If the object or performance of a contract is rendered illegal by statute *after* the contract has been formed, the contract is considered to be discharged by law. (See the discussion in Chapter 13 on pages 327–329.)

Usury Charging an illegal rate of interest.

USURY   Almost every state has a statute that sets the maximum rate of interest that can be charged for different types of transactions, including ordinary loans. (For a discussion of a new federal law that limits certain interest rates, see the *Linking the Law to Economics* feature on page 281.) A lender who makes a loan at an interest rate above the lawful maximum commits **usury.** Although usurious contracts are illegal, most states simply limit the interest that the lender may collect on the contract to the lawful maximum interest rate in that state. In a few states, the lender can recover the principal amount of the loan but no interest.

Although usury statutes place a ceiling on allowable rates of interest, exceptions are made to facilitate business transactions. For example, many states exempt corporate loans from the usury laws. In addition, almost all states have special statutes allowing much higher interest rates on small loans to help those borrowers who need funds and could not otherwise obtain loans.

GAMBLING   Gambling is the creation of risk for the purpose of assuming it. Any scheme that involves the distribution of property by chance among persons who have paid valuable consideration for the opportunity (chance) to receive the property is gambling. Traditionally, the states have deemed gambling contracts illegal and thus void. It is sometimes difficult, however, to distinguish a gambling contract from the risk sharing inherent in almost all contracts. (See Chapter 7 for a discussion of how criminal laws are being applied to online gambling and fantasy sports leagues.)

All states have statutes that regulate gambling, and many states allow certain forms of gambling, such as horse racing, poker machines, and charity-sponsored bingo. In addition, nearly all states allow state-operated lotteries and gambling on Indian reservations.

Nevertheless, even in states that permit certain types of gambling, courts often find that gambling contracts are illegal.

CASE EXAMPLE 11.15 Casino gambling is legal in Louisiana, as are video poker machines. Nevertheless, Louisiana courts still refused to enforce a contract between a gaming company and a restaurant relating to the installation of video poker machines. Gaming Venture, Inc. (GVI), had entered into two contracts with Tastee Restaurant Corporation. One was a licensing agreement, and the other was a gaming device placement agreement that authorized GVI to install poker machines in various Tastee locations. When several Tastee restaurants refused to install the machines, GVI brought a suit for breach of contract. The state appellate court held that the two agreements were illegal and void. For them to have been enforceable, GVI would have needed prior approval of the two contracts from the state video gaming commission. Without that, the contracts were illegal gambling contracts.[10] ●

LICENSING STATUTES All states require members of certain professions—including physicians, lawyers, real estate brokers, accountants, architects, electricians, and stockbrokers—to have licenses. Some licenses are obtained only after extensive schooling and examinations, which indicate to the public that a special skill has been acquired. Others require only that the particular person be of good moral character and pay a fee.

Whether a contract with an unlicensed person is legal and enforceable depends on the purpose of the licensing statute. If the statute's purpose is to protect the public from unauthorized practitioners, then a contract involving an unlicensed practitioner generally is illegal and unenforceable. If the purpose is merely to raise government revenues, however, a contract with an unlicensed person may be enforced (and the unlicensed practitioner fined).

EXAMPLE 11.16 A state requires a stockbroker to be licensed and to file a bond with the state to protect the public from fraudulent transactions in stocks. Because the purpose of the statute is to protect the public, a court will deem a contract with an unlicensed stockbroker in that state to be illegal and unenforceable. ●

Ethical Issue ⚖️

Is a contract between Fox Television's Judge Alex and his unlicensed talent agent enforceable? Normally, refusing to enforce a contract with an unlicensed practitioner leads to a just result—the person without a license is not rewarded for conducting business illegally. Occasionally, though, the rule can have the opposite result and unfairly deny payment to someone who has provided competent services. Consider a case involving a former Florida state court judge, Alex Ferrer, who gave up working as a real judge to become a judge on national television. (TV trials are actually arbitration proceedings.) Ferrer, a licensed attorney, signed a contract with a California attorney, Arnold Preston. In the contract, Preston agreed to promote Ferrer's career as a TV judge, and in exchange, Ferrer promised to pay Preston 12 percent of his income. Preston helped Ferrer get a job as the judge on *Judge Alex,* a Fox Television series modeled after the popular *Judge Judy.* After he became a celebrity, Judge Alex claimed that he did not have to pay because the contract was illegal—Preston was not a registered talent agent under California's Talent Agencies Act (TAA).

Because the contract contained an arbitration clause, Preston filed a petition to arbitrate the dispute under the Federal Arbitration Act (FAA—see Chapter 3), arguing that he was entitled to payment as Ferrer's manager under the contract. Ferrer sought to avoid arbitration and argued that the TAA gave California's labor commissioner exclusive jurisdiction over claims involving unlicensed talent agents. In 2008, the dispute reached the United States Supreme Court, but only on the issue of arbitration—the Court did not rule on the legality of the contract. The Court held that the FAA supersedes the state's TAA and therefore arbitration was required.[11] The Court left it to the arbitrator to decide whether a lawyer (Ferrer) can legally refuse to pay another lawyer (Preston) for his services because he was not licensed as a talent agent.

---

10. *Gaming Venture, Inc. v. Tastee Restaurant Corp.,* 996 So.2d 515 (La.App. 5 Cir. 2008).
11. *Preston v. Ferrer,* ___ U.S. ___, 128 S.Ct. 978, 169 L.Ed.2d 917 (2008).

Contracts Contrary to Public Policy

Although contracts involve private parties, some are not enforceable because of the negative impact they would have on society. These contracts are said to be *contrary to public policy*. Examples include a contract to commit an immoral act, such as selling a child, and a contract that prohibits marriage. **EXAMPLE 11.17** Everett offers a young man $10,000 if he refrains from marrying Everett's daughter. If the young man accepts, no contract is formed (the contract is void) because it is contrary to public policy. Thus, if the man marries Everett's daughter, Everett cannot sue him for breach of contract. ● Business contracts that may be contrary to public policy include contracts in restraint of trade and unconscionable contracts or clauses.

CONTRACTS IN RESTRAINT OF TRADE The United States has a strong public policy favoring competition in the economy. Thus, contracts that restrain trade, or anticompetitive agreements, are generally unenforceable because they are contrary to public policy. Typically, anticompetitive agreements also violate one or more federal or state antitrust laws (these laws will be discussed in Chapter 32). An exception is recognized when the restraint is reasonable and is an ancillary (secondary, or subordinate) part of the contract. Such restraints often are included in contracts for the sale of an ongoing business and employment contracts.

Covenant Not to Compete A contractual promise of one party to refrain from conducting business similar to that of another party for a certain period of time and within a specified geographic area. Courts commonly enforce such covenants if they are reasonable in terms of time and geographic area and are part of, or supplemental to, a contract for the sale of a business or an employment contract.

Covenants Not to Compete and the Sale of an Ongoing Business. Many contracts involve a type of restraint called a **covenant not to compete,** or a restrictive covenant (promise). A covenant not to compete may be created when a seller agrees not to open a new store in a certain geographic area surrounding the old store. Such an agreement enables the seller to sell, and the purchaser to buy, the goodwill and reputation of an ongoing business without having to worry that the seller will open a competing business a block away. Provided the restrictive covenant is reasonable and is an ancillary part of the sale of an ongoing business, it is enforceable.

Employment Contract A contract between an employer and an employee in which the terms and conditions of employment are stated.

Covenants Not to Compete in Employment Contracts. Agreements not to compete can also be included in **employment contracts** (contracts stating the terms and conditions of employment). People in middle-level and upper-level management positions commonly agree not to work for competitors or not to start a competing business for a specified period of time after terminating employment. Such agreements generally are legal in most states so long as the specified period of time (of restraint) is not excessive in duration and the geographic restriction is reasonable. What constitutes a reasonable time period may be shorter in the online environment than in conventional employment contracts because the restrictions would apply worldwide.

To be reasonable, a restriction on competition must protect a legitimate business interest and must not be any greater than necessary to protect that interest.[12] **CASE EXAMPLE 11.18** Safety and Compliance Management, Inc. (S & C), provides drug- and alcohol-testing services. S & C hired Angela Burgess primarily to retrieve specimens from clients and transport them to the lab. She signed a covenant not to compete "in any area of business" conducted by S & C for a period of two years from the date of termination. When Burgess quit her job at S & C and went to work at a nearby hospital as a medical assistant, S & C filed a lawsuit claiming that she was breaching the noncompete agreement. The hospital also offered drug-testing services, and Burgess sometimes collected specimens from patients. The court, however, found that because S & C's noncompete agreement failed to specify with par-

---

12. See, for example, *Gould & Lamb, LLC v. D'Alusio*, 949 So.2d 1212 (Fla.App. 2007); and *Freeman v. Brown Hiller, Inc.*, 102 Ark.App. 76, 281 S.W.3d 749 (2008).

ticularity the activities that Burgess was prohibited from performing, it was too broad and indefinite to be enforceable. The noncompete agreement imposed a greater limitation on Burgess than was necessary for the protection of S & C, and was thus unreasonable.[13] ●

The contract in the following case provided an exclusive license to open and operate comedy clubs under a certain famous trademark. It also included a covenant not to compete. The question was whether the restraint was reasonable.

Case 11.2 Comedy Club, Inc. v. Improv West Associates

United States Court of Appeals, Ninth Circuit, 553 F.3d 1277 (2009).
www.ca9.uscourts.gov[a]

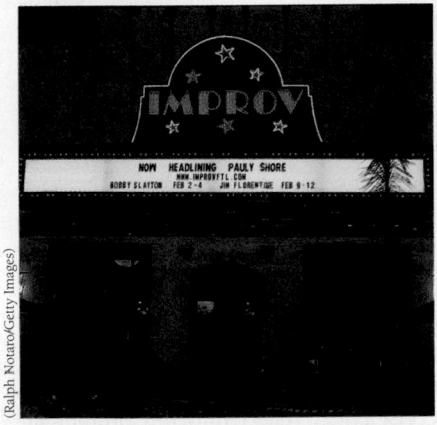

This well-known comedy club, The Improv, is located in Florida. The owner of the "Improv" trademark is Improv West Associates. How can Improv West protect its trademark?

FACTS Improv West Associates is the founder of the Improv Comedy Club and owner of the "Improv" trademark. Comedy Club, Inc. (CCI), owns and operates restaurants and comedy clubs. Improv West granted CCI an exclusive license to open four Improv clubs per year in 2001, 2002, and 2003. Their agreement prohibited CCI from opening any non-Improv comedy clubs "in the contiguous United States" until 2019. When CCI failed to open eight clubs by the end of 2002, Improv West commenced arbitration. The arbitrator's award in 2005 stated that CCI had forfeited its right to open Improv clubs, but that the parties' agreement had not terminated and the covenant not to compete was enforceable—CCI could not open any new comedy clubs for its duration. A federal district court confirmed the award, and CCI appealed.

ISSUE Is a covenant not to compete in the comedy club business for fourteen years in forty-eight states too broad to be enforced?

DECISION Yes. The U.S. Court of Appeals for the Ninth Circuit reversed part of the lower court's confirmation of the award and remanded the case.

REASON The court said that terminating CCI's exclusive right to open Improv clubs due to its inadequate performance of the parties' contract "makes sense" and that Improv West should be protected from "improper" competition. But the covenant not to compete in this case has "dramatic geographic and temporal [relating to time] scope. * * * For more than fourteen years the entire contiguous United States comedy club market, except for CCI's current Improv clubs, is off limits to CCI." The effect would be to foreclose competition in a substantial share of the comedy club business. This restraint is "too broad to be countenanced." The covenant should be tailored to cover only the areas in which CCI is operating Improv clubs under the parties' agreement. It should allow CCI to open non-Improv clubs in "all those counties" where it does not operate an Improv club.

WHY IS THIS CASE IMPORTANT? *Competition is a paramount principle of our capitalist economic system. But business competitiveness requires the support of our laws if it is to be more than a statement of belief. This case shows the multifaceted role that the law can play to encourage competition by removing unfair restraints and by enforcing proper limits.*

a. In the left-hand column, in the "Decisions" pull-down menu, click on "Opinions." On that page, click on "Advanced Search." Then, in the "by Case No.:" box, type "05-55739" and click on "Search." In the result, click on the "01/29/2009" link to access the opinion.

Enforcement Problems. The laws governing the enforceability of covenants not to compete vary significantly from state to state. In some states, such as Texas, such a covenant will not be enforced unless the employee has received some benefit in return for signing the noncompete agreement. This is true even if the covenant is reasonable as to time and area. If the employee receives no benefit, the covenant will be deemed void (see, for example,

---

13. *Stultz v. Safety and Compliance Management, Inc.,* 285 Ga.App. 799, 648 S.E.2d 129 (2007).

Case 11.1 earlier in this chapter on page 266). California prohibits the enforcement of covenants not to compete altogether.

Occasionally, depending on the jurisdiction, courts will *reform* covenants not to compete. If a covenant is found to be unreasonable in time or geographic area, the court may convert the terms into reasonable ones and then enforce the reformed covenant. This presents a problem, however, in that the judge has implicitly become a party to the contract. Consequently, courts usually resort to contract **reformation** only when necessary to prevent undue burdens or hardships.

Reformation A court-ordered correction of a written contract so that it reflects the true intentions of the parties.

Preventing Legal Disputes

A business clearly has a legitimate interest in having employees sign covenants not to compete and in preventing them from using the valuable skills and training provided by the business for the benefit of a competitor. The problem is that these covenants frequently lead to litigation. Moreover, it is difficult to predict what a court will consider reasonable in a given situation. Therefore, you need to be aware of the difficulties in enforcing noncompete agreements. Seek the advice of counsel in the relevant jurisdiction when drafting covenants not to compete. Avoid overreaching in terms of time and geographic restrictions, particularly if you are the manager of a high-tech or Web-based company. Consider using noncompete clauses only for key employees and, if necessary, offer some compensation (consideration) for signing the agreement. If an employee signed a noncompete clause when he or she was hired, be sure to discuss the meaning of that clause and your expectations with the employee at the time of termination.

UNCONSCIONABLE CONTRACTS OR CLAUSES   Ordinarily, a court does not look at the fairness or equity of a contract, or, as discussed earlier, inquire into the adequacy of consideration. Persons are assumed to be reasonably intelligent, and the courts will not come to their aid just because they have made unwise or foolish bargains. In certain circumstances, however, bargains are so oppressive that the courts relieve innocent parties of part or all of their duties. Such bargains are deemed **unconscionable** because they are so unscrupulous or grossly unfair as to be "void of conscience." The Uniform Commercial Code (UCC) incorporates the concept of unconscionability in its provisions with regard to the sale and lease of goods.[14] A contract can be unconscionable on either procedural or substantive grounds, as discussed in the following subsections and illustrated graphically in Exhibit 11–1.

Unconscionable (Contract or Clause) A contract or clause that is void on the basis of public policy because one party, as a result of disproportionate bargaining power, is forced to accept terms that are unfairly burdensome and that unfairly benefit the dominating party.

"Better a friendly refusal than an unwilling consent."

Spanish Proverb

Procedural Unconscionability.   Procedural unconscionability often involves inconspicuous print, unintelligible language ("legalese"), or the lack of an opportunity to read the contract or ask questions about its meaning. This type of unconscionability typically arises when a party's lack of knowledge or understanding of the contract terms deprived him or her of any meaningful choice.

Procedural unconscionability can also occur when there is such a disparity in bargaining power between the two parties that the weaker party's consent is not voluntary. This type of situation often involves an **adhesion contract,** which is a standard-form contract written exclusively by one party (the dominant party, usually the seller or creditor) and presented to the other (the adhering party, usually the buyer or borrower) on a take-it-or-leave-it basis. In other words, the adhering party has no opportunity to negotiate the terms of the contract. Not all adhesion contracts are unconscionable, only those that unreasonably favor the drafter.[15]

Adhesion Contract A "standard-form" contract, such as that between a large retailer and a consumer, in which the stronger party dictates the terms.

Substantive Unconscionability.   Substantive unconscionability occurs when contracts, or portions of contracts, are oppressive or overly harsh. Courts generally focus on provisions

---

14. See UCC 2–302 and 2–719.
15. See, for example, *Thibodeau v. Comcast Corp.,* 2006 PA Super. 346, 912 A.2d 874 (2006).

• *Exhibit* **11–1 Unconscionability**

that deprive one party of the benefits of the agreement or leave that party without remedy for nonperformance by the other. **CASE EXAMPLE 11.19** A person with little income and only a fourth-grade education agrees to purchase a refrigerator for $4,500 and signs a two-year installment contract. The same type of refrigerator usually sells for $900 on the market. Despite the general rule that the courts will not inquire into the adequacy of the consideration, some courts have held that this type of contract is unconscionable because the contract terms are so oppressive as to "shock the conscience" of the court.[16] •

Substantive unconscionability can arise in a wide variety of business contexts. For example, a contract clause that gives the business entity unrestricted access to the courts but requires the other party to arbitrate any dispute with the firm may be unconscionable.[17] Similarly, an arbitration clause in a credit-card agreement that prevents credit-card holders from obtaining relief for abusive debt-collection practices under consumer law may be unconscionable.[18] Contracts drafted by insurance companies and cell phone providers have been struck down as substantively unconscionable when they included provisions that were overly harsh or one sided.[19]

EXCULPATORY CLAUSES Often closely related to the concept of unconscionability are **exculpatory clauses,** which release a party from liability in the event of monetary or physical injury, *no matter who is at fault.* Indeed, courts sometimes refuse to enforce such clauses because they deem them to be unconscionable. Exculpatory clauses found in rental

REMEMBER Nearly everyone is liable for her or his own torts, and this responsibility cannot be contracted away.

Exculpatory Clause A clause that releases a contractual party from liability in the event of monetary or physical injury, no matter who is at fault.

---

16. See, for example, *Jones v. Star Credit Corp.,* 59 Misc.2d 189, 298 N.Y.S.2d 264 (1969). This case will be presented in Chapter 15 as Case 15.3.
17. See, for example, *Wisconsin Auto Loans, Inc. v. Jones,* 290 Wis.2d 514, 714 N.W.2d 155 (2006).
18. See, for example, *Coady v. Cross County Bank,* 2007 WI App 26, 729 N.W.2d 732 (Wis.App. 2007).
19. See, for example, *Gatton v. T-Mobile USA, Inc.,* 152 Cal.App.4th 571, 61 Cal.Rptr.3d 344 (2007); *Kinkel v. Cingular Wireless, LLC,* 223 Ill.2d 1, 857 N.E.2d 250, 306 Ill.Dec. 157 (2006); and *Aul v. Golden Rule Insurance Co.,* 2007 WL 1695243 (Wis.App. 2007).

(AP Photo/The Canadian Press/Peter McCabe)

Under what circumstances might an injured skier successfully sue a ski resort?

agreements for commercial property are frequently held to be contrary to public policy, and such clauses are almost always unenforceable in residential property leases. Exculpatory clauses in the employment context may be deemed unconscionable when they attempt to remove the employer's potential liability for injuries to employees.

Although courts view exculpatory clauses with disfavor, they do enforce such clauses when they do not contravene public policy, are not ambiguous, and do not claim to protect parties from liability for intentional misconduct. Businesses such as health clubs, racetracks, amusement parks, skiing facilities, horse-rental operations, golf-cart concessions, and skydiving organizations frequently use exculpatory clauses to limit their liability for patrons' injuries. Because these services are not essential, the firms offering them are sometimes considered to have no relative advantage in bargaining strength, and anyone contracting for their services is considered to do so voluntarily.

Sometimes, a company includes an indemnification provision in its contracts with *independent contractors* (see Chapter 23). Such a provision, or clause, removes any responsibility on the company's part for accidents that happen to the independent contractor while working for the company. When is such a provision against public policy? This was the main question in the following case.

Case 11.3   Speedway SuperAmerica, LLC v. Erwin

Court of Appeals of Kentucky, 250 S.W.3d 339 (2008).

(Bill Stryker)

Speedway SuperAmerica, LLC, has about 1,600 stores similar to this one. Speedway is a wholly-owned subsidiary of Marathon Oil Corporation.

FACTS Speedway SuperAmerica, LLC, hired Sebert Erwin to provide "General Contracting" for five years, but reserved the right to end the contract at any time. The contract contained an *indemnification* clause. Under that clause, Erwin promised to "hold harmless" Speedway for anything that happened to him while working for the company. One day, Erwin was told to report to a Speedway gas station in another city and help remove a walk-in freezer. When he was helping load it on a truck, he fell and was injured. Erwin sued Speedway for damages resulting from the injury he had suffered. Speedway counterclaimed, seeking enforcement of the contract's indemnification clause. Erwin moved to dismiss the counterclaim on the ground that the indemnification clause

was invalid because it was against public policy. The trial court held for Erwin. Speedway appealed.

ISSUE Was the indemnification (exculpatory) clause that Erwin signed agreeing not to hold Speedway liable for any injuries he might receive while working for it contrary to public policy?

DECISION Yes. The Kentucky appellate court affirmed the trial court's ruling, holding that the indemnification clause was contrary to public policy and could not be enforced.

REASON The court noted, "The predominant fact of this case is the disparity in bargaining power existing between these two parties." The contract was one sided because it was between a chain of convenience stores and a single worker. Although such contracts are not always against public policy, they are when there is no bargaining between parties of similar strength. Here, the contract involved one worker with an eighth-grade education and a large company; the bargaining powers were clearly unequal. Erwin was called an independent contractor even though he did not have control over his work. The contract stated that he agreed to defend the owner and hold

Case 11.3—Continued

it harmless in the event of any negligence. As an independent contractor rather than as an employee, Erwin had no right to workers' compensation or other benefits that normally would be due to an employee. The court reasoned that the contract was the equivalent of an exculpatory clause, releasing the employer from any liability regardless of fault.

WHAT IF THE FACTS WERE DIFFERENT?   *Suppose that Erwin worked for another company as a mover and his employer had sent him to help Speedway move the freezer. Suppose further that the indemnification clause was in a contract signed between Speedway and Erwin's employer. Would that clause be valid? Explain your answer.*

▶ The Effect of Illegality

In general, an illegal contract is void: the contract is deemed never to have existed, and the courts will not aid either party. In most illegal contracts, both parties are considered to be equally at fault—*in pari delicto.* If the contract is executory (not yet fulfilled), neither party can enforce it. If it has been executed, neither party can recover damages.

The courts usually are not concerned if one wrongdoer in an illegal contract is unjustly enriched at the expense of the other—except under certain circumstances (to be discussed shortly). The main reason for this hands-off attitude is a belief that a plaintiff who has broken the law by entering into an illegal bargain should not be allowed to obtain help from the courts. Another justification is the hoped-for deterrent effect: a plaintiff who suffers a loss because of an illegal bargain will presumably be deterred from entering into similar illegal bargains in the future.

There are exceptions to the general rule that neither party to an illegal bargain can sue for breach and neither party can recover for performance rendered. We look at these exceptions here.

Justifiable Ignorance of the Facts

When one of the parties to a contract is relatively innocent (has no reason to know that the contract is illegal), that party can often recover any benefits conferred in a partially executed contract. In this situation, the courts will not enforce the contract but will allow the parties to return to their original positions.

A court may sometimes permit an innocent party who has fully performed under a contract to enforce the contract against the guilty party. **EXAMPLE 11.20** A trucking company contracts with Gillespie to carry crated goods to a specific destination for a normal fee of $5,000. The trucker delivers the crates and later finds out that they contained illegal goods. Although the shipment, use, and sale of the goods are illegal under the law, the trucker, being an innocent party, can normally still legally collect the $5,000 from Gillespie. ●

Members of Protected Classes

When a statute protects a certain class of people, a member of that class can enforce an illegal contract even though the other party cannot. **EXAMPLE 11.21** Statutes prohibit certain employees (such as flight attendants) from working more than a specified number of hours per month. These employees thus constitute a class protected by statute. An employee who is required to work more than the maximum can recover for those extra hours of service. ●

Blue Sky Laws   State laws that regulate the offering and sale of securities for the protection of the public.

Other examples of statutes designed to protect a particular class of people are **blue sky laws**—state laws that regulate the offering and sale of securities for the protection of the public (see Chapter 31)—and state statutes regulating the sale of insurance. If an insurance company violates a statute when selling insurance, the purchaser can nevertheless enforce the policy and recover from the insurer.

Withdrawal from an Illegal Agreement

If the illegal part of a bargain has not yet been performed, the party rendering performance can withdraw from the contract and recover the performance or its value. **EXAMPLE 11.22** Marta and Ande decide to wager (illegally) on the outcome of a boxing match. Each deposits money with a stakeholder, who agrees to pay the winner of the bet. At this point, each party has performed part of the agreement, but the illegal part of the agreement will not occur until the money is paid to the winner. Before such payment occurs, either party is entitled to withdraw from the agreement by giving notice to the stakeholder of his or her withdrawal. ●

Severable, or Divisible, Contracts

A contract that is *severable,* or divisible, consists of distinct parts that can be performed separately, with separate consideration provided for each part. With an *indivisible* contract, in contrast, the parties intended that complete performance by each party would be essential, even if the contract contains a number of seemingly separate provisions.

　　If a contract is divisible into legal and illegal portions, a court may enforce the legal portion but not the illegal one, so long as the illegal portion does not affect the essence of the bargain. This approach is consistent with the basic policy of enforcing the legal intentions of the contracting parties whenever possible. **EXAMPLE 11.23** Cole signs an employment contract that includes an overly broad and thus illegal covenant not to compete. In that situation, a court might allow the employment contract to be enforceable but reform the unreasonably broad covenant by converting its terms into reasonable ones. Alternatively, the court could declare the covenant illegal (and thus void) and enforce the remaining employment terms. ●

Contracts Illegal through Fraud, Duress, or Undue Influence

Often, one party to an illegal contract is more at fault than the other. When a party has been induced to enter into an illegal bargain through fraud, duress, or undue influence on the part of the other party to the agreement, the first party will be allowed to recover for the performance or its value.

 Reviewing . . . Consideration, Capacity, and Legality

Renee Beaver started racing go-karts competitively in 2006, when she was fourteen. Many of the races required her to sign an exculpatory clause to participate, which she or her parents regularly signed. In 2009, right before her birthday, she participated in the annual Elkhart Grand Prix, a series of races in Elkhart, Indiana. During the event in which she drove, a piece of foam padding used as a course barrier was torn from its base and ended up on the track. A portion of the padding struck Beaver in the head, and another portion was thrown into oncoming traffic, causing a multikart collision during which she sustained severe injuries. Beaver filed an action against the race organizers for negligence. The organizers could not locate the exculpatory clause that Beaver was supposed to have signed. Race organizers argued that she must have signed one to enter the race, but even if she had not signed one, her actions showed her intent to be bound by its terms. Using the information presented in the chapter, answer the following questions.

1. Did Beaver have the contractual capacity to enter a contract with an exculpatory clause? Why or why not?
2. Assuming that Beaver did, in fact, sign the exculpatory clause, did she later disaffirm or ratify the contract? Explain.
3. Now assume that Beaver had stated that she was eighteen years old at the time that she signed the exculpatory clause. How might this affect Beaver's ability to disaffirm or ratify the contract?
4. Now suppose that Beaver can prove that she did not actually sign an exculpatory clause and this convinces race organizers to pursue a settlement. They offer to pay Beaver one-half of the amount that she is claiming in damages if she now signs a release of all claims. Because Beaver is young and the full effects of her injuries may not be clear at this time, what other type of settlement agreement might she prefer? What is the consideration to support any settlement agreement that Beaver enters into with the race organizers?

Linking the Law *to Economics*

Usury Laws Become Federal

As you learned in this chapter, usury laws set maximum interest rates that lenders can charge. Until the financial meltdown of 2008–2010, state legislators originated usury laws. Federal legislation, in contrast, concerned itself with regulating disclosure of credit policies. (As a result, credit agreements today average twenty-one pages in length compared to only three pages in the 1980s.)

In reaction to the financial hardships that Americans were facing in the latest recession, the Federal Reserve System instituted wide-ranging restrictions on the way banks and other credit-card issuers can price their products and adjust those prices to changing credit conditions. Many of the Federal Reserve restrictions became part of The Credit Cardholder's Bill of Rights Act of 2009. This new law places even more constraints on what credit-card issuers can do, especially with respect to those who continue to make late payments. In addition, there are severe limits on fees accessed on over-the-limit credit charges. In effect, we now have a federal usury law.

Your Economics Courses Can Help with the Analysis

At some point in your business school curriculum, you have taken, or will take, basic economics. At the heart of microeconomic analysis are the laws of supply and demand. You can apply supply-and-demand analysis to the federal usury law environment.

The new Federal Reserve regulations on credit-card issuers constitute a system of *price controls* on one aspect of the credit market. Here, the price controls are the upper limits on prices—that is, on interest rates and fees on credit cards. These controls will keep credit-card interest rates below the competitive levels that would be determined by supply and demand.

You may have already learned in your economics courses that on the demand side of any market (here, credit), a legal maximum price below the equilibrium price will cause consumers to demand more—in this instance, they will try to borrow more via credit cards. On the supply side, in contrast, credit-card issuers will reduce the amount of credit they offer because their profits will have been reduced because of the price controls. The result is an excess quantity demanded of credit-card credit.

Less Credit Available and at a Higher Cost

The Federal Reserve's implicit price controls reduce the amount of credit available to consumers. Almost immediately after the new rules went into effect, credit-card issuers reduced the number of credit cards they offered. Additionally, thousands of customers had their existing credit cards canceled. Finally, credit-card companies denied, and continue to deny, a large number of consumer applications for credit cards. Why? The reason is that credit-card issuers are no longer able to cover the expected costs of servicing the cards of higher-risk customers.

Credit-card credit has become more expensive in several ways. Some of the higher costs have come in the form of longer, more time-consuming application procedures. Another aspect is that those denied normal credit cards have had to turn to consumer finance companies. The latter charge interest rates of 30 to 40 percent per year, compared to the 15 to 25 percent routinely charged on credit-card balances.

Some Individuals Do Benefit

The negative aspects of price controls (usury laws) on credit-card credit do not apply to everyone. In particular, affluent customers with excellent credit ratings have essentially been untouched. The fees and interest charges most affected by the new regulations are those that apply to customers with the poorest ratings—generally low-income individuals. As a result, lower-income individuals are actually hurt the most by usury laws. They are the ones whose applications for credit cards are being denied. They are the ones who turn to consumer finance companies as an alternative.

FOR CRITICAL ANALYSIS

Is there also another cost to society of implementing the Federal Reserve System's restrictions on credit-card interest rates and fees? (Hint: Someone has to oversee the implementation.)

 Key Terms

accord and satisfaction 267	emancipation 269	promissory estoppel 268
adhesion contract 276	employment contract 274	ratification 270
blue sky laws 279	estopped 268	reformation 276
consideration 262	exculpatory clause 277	release 267
contractual capacity 269	forbearance 263	rescission 265
covenant not to compete 274	liquidated debt 267	unconscionable 276
covenant not to sue 268	necessaries 270	usury 272
disaffirmance 269	past consideration 265	

Chapter Summary: Consideration, Capacity, and Legality

Consideration
(See pages 262–268.)
	1. *Elements of consideration—*
	  a. Something of *legally sufficient value* must be given in exchange for a promise.
	  b. There must be a *bargained-for exchange.*
	2. *Legal sufficiency and adequacy of consideration—*Legal sufficiency means that something of legal value must be given in exchange for a promise. Adequacy relates to "how much" consideration is given and whether a fair bargain was reached. Courts will inquire into the adequacy of consideration only when fraud, undue influence, duress, or unconscionability may be involved.
	3. *Contracts that lack consideration—*Consideration is lacking in the following situations:
	  a. *Preexisting duty—*A promise to do what one already has a legal duty to do is not legally sufficient consideration for a new contract.
	  b. *Past consideration—*Actions or events that have already taken place do not constitute legally sufficient consideration.
	  c. *Illusory promises—*When the nature or extent of performance is too uncertain, the promise is rendered illusory (without consideration and unenforceable).
	4. *Settlement of claims—*Disputes may be settled by the following, which are enforceable provided there is consideration:
	  a. *Accord and satisfaction—*An *accord* is an agreement in which a debtor offers to pay a lesser amount than the creditor claims is owed. *Satisfaction* takes place when the accord is executed.
	  b. *Release—*An agreement in which, for consideration, a party forfeits the right to seek further recovery beyond the terms specified in the release.
	  c. *Covenant not to sue—*An agreement not to sue on a present, valid claim.

Promissory Estoppel (See page 268.)	The equitable doctrine of promissory estoppel applies when a promisor should have expected a promise to induce definite and substantial action or forbearance by the promisee, and the promisee does act in reliance on the promise. Such a promise is binding, even though there is no consideration, if injustice can be avoided only by enforcement of the promise. Also known as the doctrine of *detrimental reliance.*
CONTRACTUAL CAPACITY	

Minors
(See pages 269–271.)
	1. *General rule—*Contracts with minors are voidable at the option of the minor.
	2. *Disaffirmance—*The legal avoidance of a contractual obligation.
	  a. Disaffirmance can take place (in most states) at any time during minority and within a reasonable time after the minor has reached the age of majority.
	  b. The minor must disaffirm the entire contract, not just part of it.
	  c. When disaffirming executed contracts, the minor has a duty to return the received goods if they are still in the minor's control or (in some states) to pay their reasonable value.
	  d. A minor who has committed an act of fraud (such as misrepresenting her or his age) will be denied the right to disaffirm by some courts.
	  e. A minor may disaffirm a contract for necessaries but remains liable for the reasonable value of the goods.
	3. *Ratification—*The acceptance, or affirmation, of a legal obligation; may be express or implied.
	  a. *Express ratification—*Occurs when the minor, in writing or orally, explicitly assumes the obligations imposed by the contract.
	  b. *Implied ratification—*Occurs when the conduct of the minor is inconsistent with disaffirmance or when the minor fails to disaffirm an executed contract within a reasonable time after reaching the age of majority.
	4. *Parents' liability—*Generally, except for contracts for necessaries, parents are not liable for the contracts made by minor children acting on their own. Parents may be liable for minors' torts in certain circumstances, however.
	5. *Emancipation—*Occurs when a child's parent or legal guardian relinquishes the legal right to exercise control over the child. Normally, minors who leave home to support themselves are considered emancipated. In some jurisdictions, minors are permitted to petition a court for emancipation for limited purposes.

Intoxicated Persons (See page 271.)	1. A contract entered into by an intoxicated person is voidable at the option of the intoxicated person if the person was sufficiently intoxicated to lack mental capacity, even if the intoxication was voluntary. 2. A contract with an intoxicated person is enforceable if, despite being intoxicated, the person understood the legal consequences of entering into the contract.

Chapter Summary: Consideration, Capacity, and Legality—Continued

Mentally Incompetent Persons (See pages 271–272.)	1. A contract made by a person previously judged by a court to be mentally incompetent is void. 2. A contract made by a person who is mentally incompetent, but has not been previously declared incompetent by a court, is voidable at the option of that person.
LEGALITY	
Contracts Contrary to Statute (See pages 272–273.)	1. *Usury*—Usury occurs when a lender makes a loan at an interest rate above the lawful maximum. The maximum rate of interest varies from state to state. 2. *Gambling*—Gambling contracts that contravene (go against) state statutes are deemed illegal and thus void. 3. *Licensing statutes*—Contracts entered into by persons who do not have a license, when one is required by statute, will not be enforceable *unless* the underlying purpose of the statute is to raise government revenues (and not to protect the public from unauthorized practitioners).
Contracts Contrary to Public Policy (See pages 274–279.)	1. *Contracts in restraint of trade*—Contracts to reduce or restrain free competition are illegal and prohibited by statutes. An exception is a *covenant not to compete.* Such covenants usually are enforced by the courts if the terms are secondary to a contract (such as a contract for the sale of a business or an employment contract) and are reasonable as to time and area of restraint. Courts tend to scrutinize covenants not to compete closely and, at times, may reform them if they are overbroad rather than declaring the entire covenant unenforceable. 2. *Unconscionable contracts and clauses*—When a contract or contract clause is so unfair that it is oppressive to one party, it may be deemed unconscionable; as such, it is illegal and cannot be enforced. 3. *Exculpatory clauses*—An exculpatory clause is a clause that releases a party from liability in the event of monetary or physical injury, no matter who is at fault. In certain situations, exculpatory clauses may be contrary to public policy and thus unenforceable.
EFFECT OF ILLEGALITY	
General Rule (See page 279.)	In general, an illegal contract is void, and the courts will not aid either party when both parties are considered to be equally at fault *(in pari delicto)*. If the contract is executory, neither party can enforce it. If the contract is executed, neither party can recover damages.
Exceptions (See pages 279–280.)	Several exceptions exist to the general rule that neither party to an illegal bargain will be able to recover. In the following situations, the court may grant recovery: 1. *Justifiable ignorance of the facts*—When one party to the contract is relatively innocent. 2. *Members of protected classes*—When one party to the contract is a member of a group of persons protected by statute, such as employees. 3. *Withdrawal from an illegal agreement*—When either party seeks to recover consideration given for an illegal contract before the illegal act is performed. 4. *Severable, or divisible, contracts*—When the court can divide the contract into illegal and legal portions and the illegal portion is not essential to the bargain. 5. *Fraud, duress, or undue influence*—When one party was induced to enter into an illegal bargain through fraud, duress, or undue influence.

 ExamPrep

ISSUE SPOTTERS

1 In September, Sharyn agrees to work for Totem Productions, Inc., at $500 a week for a year beginning January 1. In October, Sharyn is offered the same work at $600 a week by Umber Shows, Ltd. When Sharyn tells Totem about the other offer, they tear up their contract and agree that Sharyn will be paid $575. Is the new contract binding? Explain.

2 Sun Airlines, Inc., prints on its tickets that it is not liable for any injury to a passenger caused by the airline's negligence. If the cause of an accident is found to be the airline's negligence, can it use the clause as a defense to liability? Why or why not?

BEFORE THE TEST

Check your answers to the Issue Spotters, and at the same time, take the interactive quiz for this chapter. Go to **www.cengage.com/blaw/blt** and click on "Chapter 11." First, click on "Answers to Issue Spotters" to check your answers.

Next, click on "Interactive Quiz" to assess your mastery of the concepts in this chapter. Then click on "Flashcards" to review this chapter's Key Term definitions.

 For Review

Answers for the even-numbered questions in this For Review *section can be found on this text's accompanying Web site at* **www.cengage.com/blaw/blt**. *Select "Chapter 11" and click on "For Review."*

1 What is consideration? What is required for consideration to be legally sufficient?

2 In what circumstances might a promise be enforced despite a lack of consideration?

3 Does a minor have the capacity to enter into an enforceable contract? What does it mean to disaffirm a contract?

4 Under what circumstances will a covenant not to compete be enforceable? When will such covenants not be enforced?

5 What is an exculpatory clause? In what circumstances might exculpatory clauses be enforced? When will they not be enforced?

 Hypothetical Scenarios and Case Problems

11–1 **Contracts by Minors.** Kalen is a seventeen-year-old minor who has just graduated from high school. He is attending a university two hundred miles from home and has contracted to rent an apartment near the university for one year at $500 per month. He is working at a convenience store to earn enough income to be self-supporting. After living in the apartment and paying monthly rent for four months, he becomes involved in a dispute with his landlord. Kalen, still a minor, moves out and returns the key to the landlord. The landlord wants to hold Kalen liable for the balance of the payments due under the lease. Discuss fully Kalen's liability in this situation.

11–2 **Consideration.** Daniel, a recent college graduate, is on his way home for the Christmas holidays from his new job. He gets caught in a snowstorm and is taken in by an elderly couple, who provide him with food and shelter. After the snowplows have cleared the road, Daniel proceeds home. Daniel's father, Fred, is most appreciative of the elderly couple's action and in a letter promises to pay them $500. The elderly couple, in need of funds, accept Fred's offer. Then, because of a dispute with Daniel, Fred refuses to pay the elderly couple the $500. Discuss whether the couple can hold Fred liable in contract for the services rendered to Daniel.

11–3 **Hypothetical Question with Sample Answer** A famous New York City hotel, Hotel Lux, is noted for its food as well as its luxury accommodations. Hotel Lux contracts with a famous chef, Chef Perlee, to become its head chef at $6,000 per month. The contract states that should Perlee leave the employment of Hotel Lux for any reason, he will not work as a chef for any hotel or restaurant in New York, New Jersey, or Pennsylvania for a period of one year. During the first six months of the contract, Hotel Lux extensively advertises Perlee as its head chef, and business at the hotel is excellent. Then a dispute arises between the hotel management and Perlee, and Perlee terminates his employment. One month later, he is hired by a famous New Jersey restaurant just across the New York state line. Hotel Lux learns of Perlee's employment through a large advertisement in a New York City newspaper. It seeks to enjoin (prevent) Perlee from working in that restaurant as a chef for one year. Discuss how successful Hotel Lux will be in its action.

—**For a sample answer to Question 11–3, go to Appendix E at the end of this text.**

11–4 **Mental Incompetence.** Joanne is a seventy-five-year-old widow who survives on her husband's small pension. Joanne has become increasingly forgetful, and her family worries that she may have Alzheimer's disease (a brain disorder that seriously affects a person's ability to carry out daily activities). No physician has diagnosed her, however, and no court has ruled on Joanne's legal competence. One day while out shopping, Joanne stops by a store that is having a sale on pianos and enters into a fifteen-year installment contract to buy a grand piano. When the piano arrives the next day, Joanne seems confused and repeatedly asks the deliveryperson why a piano is being delivered. Joanne claims that she does not recall buying a piano. Explain whether this contract is void, voidable, or valid. Can Joanne avoid her contractual obligation to buy the piano? If so, how?

11–5 **Adequacy of Consideration.** As a child, Martha Carr once visited her mother's 108-acre tract of unimproved land in Richland County, South Carolina. In 1968, Betty and Raymond Campbell leased the land. Carr, a resident of New York, was diagnosed as having schizophrenia and depression in 1986, was hospitalized five or six times, and takes prescription drugs for the illnesses. In 1996, Carr inherited the Richland property and, two years later, contacted the Campbells about selling the land. Carr asked Betty about the value of the land, and Betty said that the county tax assessor had determined that the land's *agricultural value* was $54,000. The Campbells knew at the time that the county had assessed the total property value at $103,700 for tax purposes. On August 6, Carr signed a contract to sell the land to the Campbells for $54,000. Believing the price to be unfair, however, Carr did not deliver the deed. The Campbells filed a suit in a South Carolina state court against Carr, seeking specific performance of the contract. At trial, an expert real estate appraiser testified that the *real market value* of the property was $162,000 at the time of the contract. Under what circumstances will a court examine the adequacy of consideration? Are those circumstances present in this case? Should the court enforce the contract between Carr and the Campbells? Explain. [*Campbell v. Carr,* 361 S.C. 258, 603 S.E.2d 625 (2004)]

11–6 Misrepresentation of Age. Millennium Club, Inc., operates a tavern in South Bend, Indiana. In January 2003, Pamela Avila and other minors gained admission by misrepresenting that they were at least twenty-one years old. According to Millennium's representatives, the minors used false driver's licenses, "fraudulent transfer of a stamp used to gain admission by another patron or other means of false identification." To gain access, the minors also signed affidavits falsely attesting to the fact that they were twenty-one or older. When the state filed criminal charges against the Millennium Club, Millennium filed a suit in an Indiana state court against Avila and more than two hundred others, seeking damages of $3,000 each for misrepresenting their ages. The minors filed a motion to dismiss the complaint. Should the court grant the motion? What are the competing policy interests in this case? If the Millennium Club was not careful in checking the minors' identification, should it be allowed to recover? If the Millennium Club reasonably relied on the minors' representations, should the minors be allowed to avoid liability? Discuss. [*Millennium Club, Inc. v. Avila,* 809 N.E.2d 906 (Ind.App. 2004)]

11–7 Case Problem with Sample Answer Under California law, a contract to manage a professional boxer must be in writing, and the manager must be licensed by the state athletic commission. Marco Antonio Barrera is a professional boxer and two-time world champion. In May 2003, José Castillo, who was not licensed by the state, orally agreed to assume Barrera's management. He "understood" that he would be paid in accord with the "practice in the professional boxing industry, but in no case less than ten percent (10%) of the gross revenue" that Barrera generated as a boxer and through endorsements. Among other accomplishments, Castillo negotiated an exclusive promotion contract for Barrera with Golden Boy Promotions, Inc., which is owned and operated by Oscar De La Hoya. Castillo also helped Barrera settle three lawsuits and resolve unrelated tax problems so that Barrera could continue boxing. Castillo did not train Barrera, pick his opponents, or arrange his fights, however. When Barrera abruptly stopped communicating with Castillo, the latter filed a suit in a California state court against Barrera and others, alleging breach of contract. Under what circumstances is a contract with an unlicensed practitioner enforceable? Is the alleged contract in this

case enforceable? Why or why not? [*Castillo v. Barrera,* 146 Cal. App.4th 1317, 53 Cal.Rptr.3d 494 (2 Dist. 2007)]

—After you have answered Problem 11–7, compare your answer with the sample answer given on the Web site that accompanies this text. Go to **www.cengage.com/blaw/blt**, select "Chapter 11," and click on "Case Problem with Sample Answer."

11–8 Unconscionable Contracts or Clauses. Roberto Basulto and Raquel Gonzalez, who did not speak English, responded to an ad on Spanish-language television sponsored by Hialeah Automotive, LLC, which does business as Potamkin Dodge. Potamkin's staff understood that Basulto and Gonzalez did not speak or read English and conducted the entire transaction in Spanish. They explained the English-language contract, but did not explain an accompanying arbitration agreement. This agreement limited the amount of damages that the buyers could seek in court to less than $5,000, but did not limit Potamkin's right to pursue greater damages. Basulto and Gonzalez bought a Dodge Caravan and signed the contract in blank. Potamkin later filled in a lower trade-in allowance than agreed and refused to change it. The buyers returned the van—having driven it a total of seven miles—and asked for a return of their trade-in vehicle, but it had been sold. The buyers filed a suit in a Florida state court against Potamkin. The dealer sought arbitration. Was the arbitration agreement unconscionable? Why or why not? [*Hialeah Automotive, LLC v. Basulto,* __ So.2d __, 2009 WL 187584 (Fla.App. 3 Dist. 2009)]

11–9 A Question of Ethics *Dow AgroSciences, LLC (DAS), makes and sells agricultural seed products. In 2000, Timothy Glenn, a DAS sales manager, signed a covenant not to compete. He agreed that for two years from the date of his termination, he would not "engage in or contribute my knowledge to any work or activity involving an area of technology or business that is then competitive with a technology or business with respect to which I had access to Confidential Information during the five years immediately prior to such termination." Working with DAS business, operations, and research and development personnel, and being a member of high-level teams, Glenn had access to confidential DAS information, including agreements with DAS's business partners, marketing plans, litigation details, product secrets, new product development, future plans, and pricing strategies. In 2006, Glenn resigned to work for Pioneer Hi-Bred International, Inc., a DAS competitor. DAS filed a suit in an Indiana state court against Glenn, asking that he be enjoined from accepting any "position that would call on him to use confidential DAS information." [*Glenn v. Dow AgroSciences, LLC, 861 N.E.2d 1 (Ind.App. 2007)]*

1 Generally, what interests are served by enforcing covenants not to compete? What interests are served by refusing to enforce them?

2 What argument could be made in support of reforming (and then enforcing) illegal covenants not to compete? What argument could be made against this practice?

3 How should the court rule in this case? Why?

Critical Thinking and Writing Assignments

11–10 Critical Legal Thinking. Under what circumstances should courts examine the adequacy of consideration?

11–11 For Critical Analysis. Are legalized forms of gambling, such as state-operated lotteries, consistent with a continuing public policy against the enforcement of gambling contracts? Why or why not?

 Practical Internet Exercises

Go to this text's Web site at **www.cengage.com/blaw/blt**, select "Chapter 11," and click on "Practical Internet Exercises." There you will find the following Internet research exercises that you can perform to learn more about the topics covered in this chapter.

Practical Internet Exercise 11–1: MANAGEMENT PERSPECTIVE—**Minors and the Law**
Practical Internet Exercise 11–2: SOCIAL PERSPECTIVE—**Promissory Estoppel**
Practical Internet Exercise 11–3: LEGAL PERSPECTIVE—**Covenants Not to Compete**

Chapter 12

Defenses to Contract Enforceability

(©Denisenko, 2009. Used under license from Shutterstock.com)

Chapter Outline

- Voluntary Consent
- The Statute of Frauds–Writing Requirement
- The Statute of Frauds–Sufficiency of the Writing
- The Parol Evidence Rule

Learning Objectives

After reading this chapter, you should be able to answer the following questions:

1. In what types of situations might voluntary consent to a contract's terms be lacking?

2. What is the difference between a mistake of value or quality and a mistake of fact?

3. What are the elements of fraudulent misrepresentation?

4. What contracts must be in writing to be enforceable?

5. What is parol evidence? When is it admissible to clarify the terms of a written contract?

An otherwise valid contract may still be unenforceable if the parties have not genuinely agreed to its terms. As mentioned in Chapter 9, lack of genuine assent, or voluntary consent, is a *defense* to the enforcement of a contract. As Eleanor Roosevelt stated in the chapter-opening quotation, "Understanding is a two-way street." If one party does not voluntarily consent to the terms of a contract, then there is no genuine "meeting of the minds," and the law will not enforce the contract, as we discuss in the first part of this chapter.

A contract that is otherwise valid may also be unenforceable if it is not in the proper form. For example, if a contract is required by law to be in writing and there is no written evidence of the contract, it may not be enforceable. In the second part of this chapter, we examine the kinds of contracts that require a writing under what is called the *Statute of Frauds*. The chapter concludes with a discussion of the parol evidence rule, under which courts determine the admissibility at trial of evidence extraneous (external) to written contracts.

▶ Voluntary Consent

Voluntary consent (assent) may be lacking because of mistake, fraudulent misrepresentation, undue influence, or duress. Generally, a party who demonstrates that he or she did not genuinely agree to the terms of a contract can choose either to carry out the contract or to rescind (cancel) it and thus avoid the entire transaction.

Mistakes

We all make mistakes, so it is not surprising that mistakes are made when contracts are created. In certain circumstances, contract law allows a contract to be avoided on the basis of mistake. It is important to distinguish between *mistakes of fact* and *mistakes of value or quality*. Only a mistake of fact may allow a contract to be avoided.

EXAMPLE 12.1   Paco buys a violin from Beverly for $250. Although the violin is very old, neither party believes that it is valuable. Later, however, an antiques dealer informs the parties that the violin is rare and worth thousands of dollars. Here, both parties were mistaken, but the mistake is a mistake of *value* rather than a mistake of *fact* that warrants contract rescission. Therefore, Beverly cannot rescind the contract. •

Mistakes of fact occur in two forms—*unilateral* and *bilateral (mutual)*. A unilateral mistake is made by only one of the contracting parties; a mutual mistake is made by both. We look next at these two types of mistakes and illustrate them graphically in Exhibit 12–1.

UNILATERAL MISTAKES   A unilateral mistake occurs when only one party is mistaken as to a *material fact*—that is, a fact important to the subject matter of the contract. Generally, a unilateral mistake does not give the mistaken party any right to relief from the contract. In other words, the contract normally is enforceable against the mistaken party. **EXAMPLE 12.2** Elena intends to sell her motor home for $17,500. When she learns that Chin is interested in buying a used motor home, she faxes a letter offering to sell the vehicle to him. When typing the fax, however, she mistakenly keys in the price of $15,700. Chin immediately sends Elena a fax accepting her offer. Even though Elena intended to sell her motor home for $17,500, she has made a unilateral mistake and is bound by the contract to sell the vehicle to Chin for $15,700. •

There are at least two exceptions to this rule.[1] First, if the *other* party to the contract knows or should have known that a mistake of fact was made, the contract may not be enforceable. **EXAMPLE 12.3**   In the above example, if Chin knew that Elena intended to sell her motor home for $17,500, then Elena's unilateral mistake (stating $15,700 in her offer) may render the resulting contract unenforceable. •   The second exception arises when a unilateral mistake of fact was due to a mathematical mistake in addition, subtraction, division, or multiplication and was made inadvertently and without gross (extreme) negli-

BE CAREFUL   What a party to a contract knows or should know can determine whether the contract is enforceable.

---

1. The *Restatement (Second) of Contracts,* Section 153, liberalizes the general rule to take into account the modern trend of allowing avoidance in some circumstances even though only one party has been mistaken.

• *Exhibit* **12–1 Mistakes of Fact**

gence. If a contractor's bid was significantly low because he or she made a mistake in addition when totaling the estimated costs, any contract resulting from the bid normally may be rescinded. Of course, in both situations, the mistake must still involve some *material fact*.

BILATERAL (MUTUAL) MISTAKES

When both parties are mistaken about the same material fact, the contract can be rescinded by either party. It is a "mutual misunderstanding concerning a basic assumption on which the contract was made."[2] Note that, as with unilateral mistakes, the mistake must be about a *material fact* (one that is important and central to the contract). When a bilateral mistake occurs, normally the contract is voidable by the adversely affected party and can be rescinded, or canceled. **EXAMPLE 12.4** Gilbert contracts to sell Magellan three tracts of undeveloped land for $6 million on the basis of a surveyor's report showing the layout and acreage. After agreeing to the price, the parties discover that the surveyor made an error and that the tracts actually contain 10 percent more acreage than reported. In this situation, Gilbert can seek rescission (cancellation) of the contract based on mutual mistake. The same result—rescission—would occur if both parties had mistakenly believed that the tracts of land were adjoining but they were not.[3] ●

A word or term in a contract may be subject to more than one reasonable interpretation. If the parties to the contract attach materially different meanings to the term, their mutual misunderstanding may allow the contract to be rescinded. **CASE EXAMPLE 12.5** In a classic case, *Raffles v. Wichelhaus*,[4] Wichelhaus purchased a shipment of cotton from Raffles to arrive on a ship called the *Peerless* from Bombay, India. Wichelhaus meant a ship called *Peerless* sailing from Bombay in October; Raffles meant a different ship called *Peerless* sailing from Bombay in December. When the goods arrived on the December *Peerless* and Raffles tried to deliver them, Wichelhaus refused to accept them. The British court held for Wichelhaus, concluding that a mutual mistake had been made because the parties had attached materially different meanings to an essential term of the contract (which ship *Peerless* was to transport the goods). ●

In the following case, the court had to grapple with the question of whether a mutual mistake of fact had occurred.

---

2. *Restatement (Second) of Contracts*, Section 152.
3. See, for example, *Rawson v. UMLIC VP, L.L.C.*, 933 So.2d 1206 (Fla.App. 2006).
4. 159 Eng.Rep. 375 (1864).

Case 12.1 Inkel v. Pride Chevrolet-Pontiac, Inc.

Supreme Court of Vermont, 945 A.2d 855 (2008).

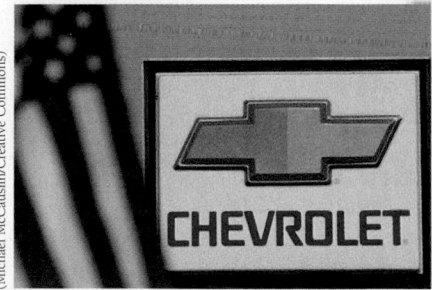

Was there a mutual mistake in a lease contract or was a Chevrolet dealer engaged in consumer fraud?

FACTS The Inkels, who live in Vermont, called Pride Chevrolet-Pontiac, Inc., in Boston about buying a new Chevy Tahoe. They said that they would trade in a high-mileage vehicle they had leased. The sales representative told them that the high-mileage penalty would probably not apply as the lease was from a bank, not a dealership. When the Inkels took delivery of the new Tahoe and left their old vehicle at Pride, the price on the contract was $41,200. In small print on the back of the agreement was a provision that the buyer was responsible for any problems with the trade-in vehicle. A month after the sale, Pride told the Inkels they owed another $16,435 because there was a misunderstanding with the leasing company about the high-mileage charge. The Inkels refused to pay. Pride demanded that they return the Tahoe and wanted to cancel the deal; the Inkels refused. The Inkels then sued Pride for breach of contract and other claims. A Vermont trial court held that a mutual mistake had been made in the contract and that the Inkels should have agreed to undo the deal. The court granted summary judgment for Pride and ordered the Inkels to pay damages. They appealed.

Case 12.1–Continues next page ➡

Case 12.1–Continued

ISSUE   Was the parties' misunderstanding about whether a high-mileage penalty would be assessed on the trade-in vehicle a mutual mistake of fact?

DECISION   The Supreme Court of Vermont reversed the lower court's summary judgment in favor of Pride and remanded the case back to the trial court for further proceedings. It was unclear whether there had been a mutual mistake, and the court was concerned that Pride might have engaged in consumer fraud.

REASON   For a court to find that a mutual mistake occurred, evidence would have to be produced at trial to show that both parties had been mistaken about the same material fact. Pride knew about the terms of its

contract, and the Inkels knew their vehicle was high mileage. It appears that either Pride was hiding the truth about what would happen due to the high mileage on the trade-in car, or the Inkels were trying to take advantage of Pride's ignorance about the extra payoff needed to their bank for their high-mileage vehicle. Even if there was a mutual mistake, which should be determined at trial, it was not clear that Pride offered to rescind the contract when it said the Inkels could return the vehicle. The terms of a return were never clarified.

FOR CRITICAL ANALYSIS—Ethical Consideration   *If a Pride sales representative led the Inkels to believe that the dealership did not care about the excessive miles on the trade-in vehicle, should Pride be willing to incur the loss? Why or why not?*

Fraudulent Misrepresentation

Although fraud is a tort (see Chapter 4), the presence of fraud also affects the authenticity of the innocent party's consent to a contract. When an innocent party is fraudulently induced to enter into a contract, the contract usually can be avoided because she or he has not *voluntarily* consented to the terms.[5] Normally, the innocent party can either rescind (cancel) the contract and be restored to her or his original position or enforce the contract and seek damages for injuries resulting from the fraud.

Generally, fraudulent misrepresentation refers only to misrepresentation that is consciously false and is intended to mislead another. Typically, fraud involves three elements:

KEEP IN MIND   To collect damages in almost any lawsuit, there must be some sort of injury.

1. A misrepresentation of a material fact must occur.
2. There must be an intent to deceive.
3. The innocent party must justifiably rely on the misrepresentation.

Additionally, to collect damages, a party must have been injured as a result of the misrepresentation.

Fraudulent misrepresentation can also occur in the online environment. For a case involving allegations that Yahoo fraudulently posted online personal ads, see this chapter's *Adapting the Law to the Online Environment* feature. Because curbing Internet fraud is a major challenge in today's world, we also will explore the topic further in Chapter 33, in the context of consumer law.

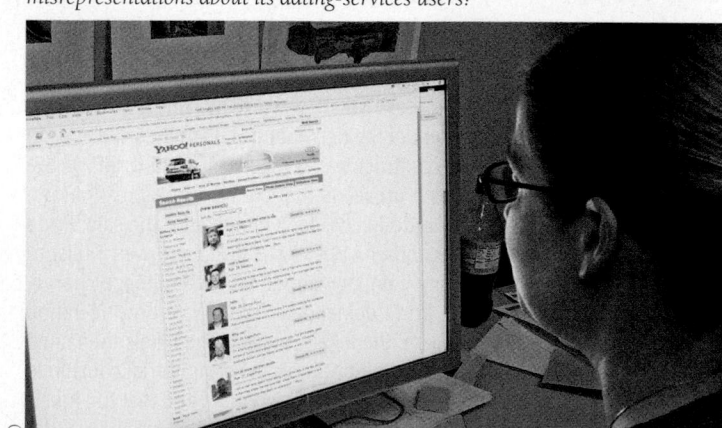

A woman browses through some online personal ads. Individuals who post their profiles on an Internet dating site may tend to exaggerate their attractive traits and may even make statements about themselves that they know to be false. But what happens when Yahoo or Google makes fraudulent misrepresentations about its dating-services users?

(Bill Stryker)

MISREPRESENTATION HAS OCCURRED   The first element of proving fraud is to show that misrepresentation of a material fact has occurred. This misrepresentation can occur by words or actions. For instance, an art gallery owner's statement "This painting is a Picasso" is a misrepresentation of fact if the painting was done by another artist. Similarly, if a customer asks to see only Paul Wright paintings and the owner immediately leads the customer over to paintings that were not done by Wright, the owner's actions can be a misrepresentation.

---

5. *Restatement (Second) of Contracts*, Sections 163 and 164.

Adapting the Law to the Online Environment

Online Personals–Fraud and Misrepresentation Issues

Keying the words *online personals* into the Google search engine will return more than 35 million hits, including Match.com, Chanceforlove.com, Widowsorwidowers.com, Makefriendsonline.com, and Yahoo! Personals. Yahoo! Personals, which calls itself the "top online dating site," offers two options. One, aimed at people looking for casual dates, allows users to create their own profiles, browse member profiles, and exchange e-mail or instant messages. The second option, called Yahoo! Personals Primer, is for people who want serious relationships. Users must take a relationship test. Then they can use Yahoo's computerized matching system to "zero in on marriage material." With this service, users can chat on the phone as well as exchange e-mail.

The Thorny Problem of Misrepresentation

When singles (and others) create their profiles for online dating services, they tend to exaggerate their more appealing features and downplay or omit their less attractive attributes. All users of such services are aware that the profiles may not correspond exactly with reality, but they do assume that the profiles are not complete misrepresentations. In 2006, nonetheless, Robert Anthony, individually and on behalf of others, brought a suit against Yahoo in federal district court, alleging fraud and negligent misrepresentation, among other things.

In his complaint, Anthony claimed that Yahoo was not just posting fictitious or exaggerated profiles submitted by users but was deliberately and intentionally originating, creating, and perpetuating false and/or nonexistent profiles. According to Anthony, many profiles used the exact same phrases "with such unique dictation and vernacular [language] that such a random occurrence would not be possible." Anthony also argued that some photo images had multiple identities—that is, the same photo appeared in several different profiles. He also alleged that Yahoo continued to circulate profiles of "actual, legitimate former subscribers whose subscriptions had expired." Finally, Anthony claimed that when a subscription neared its end date, Yahoo would send the subscriber a fake profile, heralding it as a "potential 'new match.'"

Did Yahoo Have Immunity?

Yahoo asked the court to dismiss the complaint on the grounds that the lawsuit was barred by the Communications Decency Act (CDA) of 1996.[a] As discussed in Chapter 4, the CDA shields Internet service providers (ISPs) from liability for any information submitted by another information content provider. In other words, an interactive computer service cannot be held liable under state law as a publisher of information that originates from a third party information content provider. The CDA defines an information content provider as "any person or entity that is responsible, in whole or in part, for the creation or development of information provided through the Internet or any other interactive computer service."[b]

The court rejected Yahoo's claim that it had immunity under the CDA and held that Yahoo had become an information content provider itself when it created bogus user profiles. The court observed that there is no case precedent for immunizing a defendant from liability if *it* creates tortious content. Thus, the court denied Yahoo's motion to dismiss and allowed Anthony's claims of fraud and negligent misrepresentation to proceed to trial.[c]

FOR CRITICAL ANALYSIS

Assume that Anthony had contacted various users of Yahoo's online dating service only to discover that each user's profile exaggerated the user's physical appearance, intelligence, and occupation. Would Anthony prevail if he brought a lawsuit for fraudulent misrepresentation against Yahoo in that situation? Why or why not?

---

a. 47 U.S.C. Section 230.
b. 47 U.S.C. Section 230(f)(3).
c. *Anthony v. Yahoo!, Inc.,* 421 F.Supp.2d 1257 (N.D.Cal. 2006). See also *Doe v. SexSearch.com,* 502 F.Supp.2d 719 (N.D. Ohio 2007); and *Fair Housing Council of San Fernando Valley v. Roommate.com, LLC,* 521 F.3d 1157 (9th Cir. 2008), presented in Chapter 4 as Case 4.3 on page 113.

Statements of Opinion Do Not Qualify. Statements of opinion and representations of future facts (predictions) are generally not subject to claims of fraud. Every person is expected to exercise care and judgment when entering into contracts, and the law will not come to the aid of one who simply makes an unwise bargain. Statements such as "This land will be worth twice as much next year" and "This car will last for years and years" are statements of opinion, not fact. Contracting parties should recognize them as opinions and not rely on them. A fact is objective and verifiable; an opinion is usually subject to debate. Therefore, a seller is allowed to use *puffery* to sell her or his goods without being liable for fraud.

Opinions from Experts Can Qualify. Nevertheless, in certain situations, such as when a naïve purchaser relies on an opinion from an expert, the innocent party may be entitled to rescission or reformation. (*Reformation* is an equitable remedy by which a court alters the terms of a contract to reflect the true intentions of the parties.)

CASE EXAMPLE 12.6 A classic case involved Audrey E. Vokes, a widow without family, who attended a dance party at an Arthur Murray dance school in 1961. The dance instructor praised Vokes's grace, poise, and potential as an excellent dancer, and convinced her that she could become an accomplished dancer. Over a period of sixteen months, the instructor sold her 2,302 hours of dancing lessons for a total amount of $31,090.45 (equivalent to $140,000 in 2010). When it became clear to Vokes that she did not, in fact, have the potential to be an excellent dancer, she filed a suit against the school, alleging fraudulent misrepresentation. The court held that because the dance school had superior knowledge about a person's dance potential, the instructor's statements could be considered statements of fact rather than opinion.[6] ●

Misrepresentation by Conduct. Misrepresentation also occurs when a party takes specific action to conceal a fact that is material to the contract.[7] For example, if a seller, by her or his actions, prevents a buyer from learning of some fact that is material to the contract, such behavior constitutes misrepresentation by conduct. **EXAMPLE 12.7** Cummings contracts to purchase a racehorse from Garner. The horse is blind in one eye, but when Garner shows the horse, he skillfully conceals this fact by keeping the horse's head turned so that Cummings does not see the defect. The concealment constitutes fraud. ● Another example of misrepresentation by conduct is the untruthful denial of knowledge or information concerning facts that are material to the contract when such knowledge or information is requested.

Misrepresentation of Law. Misrepresentation of law *ordinarily* does not entitle a party to be relieved of a contract. **EXAMPLE 12.8** Debbie has a parcel of property that she is trying to sell to Barry. Debbie knows that a local ordinance prohibits building anything higher than three stories on the property. Nonetheless, she tells Barry, "You can build a condominium fifty stories high if you want to." Barry buys the land and later discovers that Debbie's statement is false. Normally, Barry cannot avoid the contract because under the common law, people are assumed to know state and local laws. ● Exceptions to this rule occur, however, when the misrepresenting party is in a profession known to require greater knowledge of the law than the average citizen possesses, such as real estate brokers or lawyers.

Misrepresentation by Silence. Ordinarily, neither party to a contract has a duty to come forward and disclose facts, and a contract normally will not be set aside because certain pertinent information has not been volunteered. **EXAMPLE 12.9** Suppose that you are selling a car that has been in an accident and has been repaired. You do not need to volunteer this information to a potential buyer. If, however, the purchaser asks you if the car has had extensive bodywork and you lie, you have committed a fraudulent misrepresentation. ●

Generally, if the seller knows of a serious defect or a serious potential problem that the buyer cannot reasonably be expected to discover, the seller may have a duty to speak. Normally, the seller must disclose only "latent" defects—that is, defects that could not readily be ascertained. Thus, termites in a house may

> "If a man smiles all the time, he's probably selling something that doesn't work."
>
> George Carlin, 1937–2008
> (American comedian)

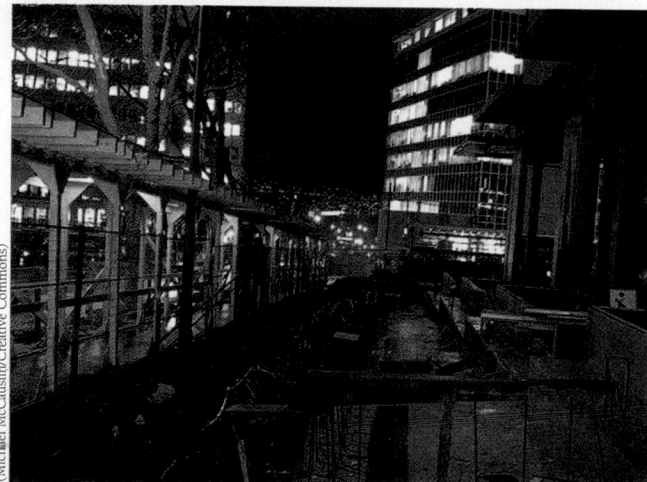

Suppose that a city solicited bids from contractors to expand its public transportation system on this strip of land without disclosing the existence of a subsoil condition that would greatly increase the project's cost. Assuming that the city was aware of the situation, would it have had a duty to disclose the condition to bidders? What effect would the city's silence have on the resulting contract?

(Michael McCauslin/Creative Commons)

---

6. *Vokes v. Arthur Murray, Inc.,* 212 So.2d 906 (Fla.App. 1968).
7. *Restatement (Second) of Contracts,* Section 160.

not be a latent defect because a buyer could normally discover their presence through a termite inspection. Also, when the parties are in a *fiduciary relationship* (one of trust, such as partners, physician and patient, or attorney and client), there is a duty to disclose material facts; failure to do so may constitute fraud.

In the following case, a student sought to rescind a pair of mortgages on a New York condominium apartment on the ground that it had been a gift and she had been defrauded into signing the loan documents.

Case 12.2 Rosenzweig v. Givens

New York Supreme Court, Appellate Division, 62 A.D.3d 1, 879 N.Y.S.2d 387 (2009).
www.courts.state.ny.us/decisions/index.shtml[a]

HISTORICAL AND ECONOMIC SETTING *For some students at postsecondary institutions in the early 2000s, tuition rose at an unprecedented rate. At the same time, the prices of homes began to rise. Lenders to these markets sometimes bundled and sold the loans—and their risk—to third party investors, making more capital available for the extension of still more credit. Unscrupulous persons took advantage of gullible parties on all sides of these transactions. When the bubble burst toward the end of the first decade of the 2000s, it affected many people in different ways.*

The Chelsea neighborhood in New York City where Radiah Givens lives in an apartment that she claimed was given to her by Joseph Rosenzweig under what the court described as "highly unusual circumstances."

FACTS Radiah Givens, a student, was involved in a romantic relationship with Joseph Rosenzweig, an attorney nineteen years her senior. In 2002, she moved into an apartment on which he made the down payment and acted as the lender for two mortgages totaling $285,300. His attorney had her sign the mortgage documents, but Rosenzweig made the payments and paid the household expenses. In 2004, Givens and Rosenz-

weig married in Jamaica. A year later, he forged her signature to obtain a bank loan for $150,000. She soon learned of the forgery and discovered that from the beginning of their relationship he had been married to someone else, with whom he had children. The Givens-Rosenzweig marriage was annulled. He then filed a suit in a New York state court against her to collect on the mortgages. The court issued a summary judgment in Rosenzweig's favor. Givens appealed, claiming that the apartment had been a gift.

ISSUE Could Rosenzweig have committed fraud against Givens?

DECISION Yes. A state intermediate appellate court reversed the lower court's judgment and remanded the case for discovery and trial.

REASON Agreements between spouses involve a fiduciary relationship requiring the utmost good faith. Givens and Rosenzweig were not married on the day she signed the mortgage documents, but a similar fiduciary relationship may have existed between these parties, considering their romantic involvement, their age difference, and his professional status. Their later marriage may have been "a sham one because plaintiff was a bigamist," but Givens believed that they were husband and wife. His attorney's role in the deal also raised questions. In these "highly unusual circumstances," Givens had "raised an issue of fact about whether plaintiff tricked her into signing the mortgage documents by claiming they were merely a formality to effectuate his gift." Indications that the apartment was a gift included the lack of a demand for payment until their relationship disintegrated.

FOR CRITICAL ANALYSIS—Ethical Consideration *Could Rosenzweig be characterized as a scoundrel? If so, should this influence the decision in this case? Discuss.*

a. In the left-hand column, in the "Appellate Divisions" list, click on "1st Dept." On that page, in the "Archives" section, in the "2009" pull-down menu, select "January." In the result, scroll to "Cases Decided January 8, 2009" and click on the name of the case to access the opinion.

Scienter Knowledge by the misrepresenting party that material facts have been falsely represented or omitted with an intent to deceive.

INTENT TO DECEIVE The second element of fraud is knowledge on the part of the misrepresenting party that facts have been misrepresented. This element, usually called *scienter*,[8] or "guilty knowledge," generally signifies that there was an intent to deceive. *Scienter* clearly exists if a party knows that a fact is not as stated. *Scienter* also exists if a party makes a statement that he or she believes not to be true or makes a statement recklessly,

---

8. Pronounced sy-*en*-ter.

without regard to whether it is true or false. Finally, this element is met if a party says or implies that a statement is made on some basis, such as personal knowledge or personal investigation, when it is not.

CASE EXAMPLE 12.10 A convicted felon, Robert Sarvis, applied for a position as an adjunct professor two weeks after his release from prison. On his résumé, he lied about his past work history by representing that he had been the president of a corporation for fourteen years and had taught business law at another college. At his interview, Sarvis stated that he was "well equipped to teach" business law and ethics and that he had "a great interest and knowledge of business law." After he was hired and began working, Sarvis's probation officer alerted the school to his criminal history. The school immediately fired Sarvis, and he brought a lawsuit against the school for breaching his employment contract. The school claimed that it was not liable for the breach because Sarvis had fraudulently misrepresented his background during the hiring process. The court agreed. Sarvis had not fully disclosed his personal history, he clearly had an intent to deceive, and the school had justifiably relied on his misrepresentations. Therefore, the school could rescind Sarvis's employment contract.[9] •

RELIANCE ON THE MISREPRESENTATION

The third element of fraud is *justifiable reliance* on the misrepresentation of fact. The deceived party must have a justifiable reason for relying on the misrepresentation, and the misrepresentation must be an important factor (but not necessarily the sole factor) in inducing the party to enter into the contract.

Reliance is not justified if the innocent party knows the true facts or relies on obviously extravagant statements. **EXAMPLE 12.11** If a used-car dealer tells you, "This old Cadillac will get over sixty miles to the gallon," you normally would not be justified in relying on this statement. Suppose, however, that Merkel, a bank director, induces O'Connell, a co-director, to sign a statement that the bank has sufficient assets to meet its liabilities by telling O'Connell, "We have plenty of assets to satisfy our creditors." This statement is false. If O'Connell knows the true facts or, as a bank director, should know the true facts, he is not justified in relying on Merkel's statement. If O'Connell does not know the true facts, however, *and has no way of finding them out*, he may be justified in relying on the statement. •

> **REMEMBER** An opinion is neither a contract offer, nor a contract term, nor fraud.

Ethical Issue

> *How much information must employers disclose to prospective employees?* One of the problems employers face is that it is not always clear what information they should disclose to prospective employees. To lure qualified workers, employers are often tempted to "promise the moon" and paint their companies' prospects as bright. Employers must be careful, though, to avoid any conduct that could be interpreted by a court as intentionally deceptive. In particular, they must avoid making any statements about their companies' future prospects or financial health that they know to be false. If they do make a false statement on which a prospective employee relies to her or his detriment, they may be sued for fraudulent misrepresentation.
>
> In one case, for example, an employee accepted a job with a brokerage firm because he relied on assurances that the firm was not about to be sold. In fact, negotiations to sell the firm were under way at the time he was hired. The employee filed a fraud claim against the firm and won, and the trial court awarded him more than $6 million in damages.[10] In another case, Kevin Helmer filed a fraud lawsuit against his former employer and supervisor, Bingham Toyota Isuzu and Bob Clark. Helmer claimed that he was fraudulently induced to leave a prior job with another Toyota dealership due to false promises made to him by Clark concerning the amount of compensation that he would receive. A jury found in Helmer's favor, awarding him $450,913 in compensatory damages and $1.5 million in punitive damages. (Later, the court reduced the punitive damages award to $675,000.)[11]

---

9. *Sarvis v. Vermont State Colleges,* 172 Vt. 76, 772 A.2d 494 (2001).

10. *McConkey v. AON Corp.,* 354 N.J.Super. 25, 804 A.2d 572 (A.D. 2002).

11. *Helmer v. Bingham Toyota Isuzu,* 129 Cal.App.4th 1121, 29 Cal.Rptr.3d 136 (2005).

INJURY TO THE INNOCENT PARTY Most courts do not require a showing of injury when the action is to rescind (cancel) the contract. These courts hold that because rescission returns the parties to the positions they held before the contract was made, a showing of injury to the innocent party is unnecessary.

To recover damages caused by fraud, however, proof of an injury is universally required. The measure of damages is ordinarily equal to the property's value had it been delivered as represented, less the actual price paid for the property. In actions based on fraud, courts often award *punitive,* or *exemplary, damages,* which are granted to a plaintiff over and above the compensation for the actual loss. As pointed out in Chapter 4, punitive damages are based on the public-policy consideration of punishing the defendant or setting an example to deter similar wrongdoing by others.

Preventing Legal Disputes

To avoid making comments that might later be construed as a misrepresentation of material fact, be careful what you say to clients and customers. If you are selling products or services, assume that all customers are naïve and are relying on your representations. Instruct employees to phrase their comments so that customers understand that any statements that are not factual are the employee's opinion. If someone asks a question that is beyond the employee's knowledge, it is better to say that he or she does not know than to guess and have the customer rely on a representation that turns out to be false. This can be particularly important when the questions concern topics such as compatibility or speed of electronic and digital goods, software, or related services.

In addition, be careful about what you say when interviewing potential employees. Do not speculate on the financial health of the firm or exaggerate the company's future prospects—especially in today's economic climate. Exercising caution in the statements you make to others in a business context is the best way to avoid potential lawsuits for fraudulent misrepresentation.

Undue Influence

Undue influence arises from relationships in which one party can greatly influence another party, thus overcoming that party's free will. A contract entered into under excessive or undue influence lacks voluntary assent and is therefore voidable.[12]

There are various types of relationships in which one party may dominate another party, thus unfairly influencing him or her. Minors and elderly people, for example, are often under the influence of guardians (persons legally responsible for others). If a guardian induces a young or elderly ward (a person whom the guardian looks after) to enter into a contract that benefits the guardian, the guardian may have exerted undue influence. Undue influence can arise from a number of confidential or fiduciary relationships, including attorney-client, physician-patient, guardian-ward, parent-child, husband-wife, and trustee-beneficiary.

The essential feature of undue influence is that the party being taken advantage of does not, in reality, exercise free will in entering into a contract. It is not enough that a person is elderly or suffers from some mental or physical impairment. There must be clear and convincing evidence that the person did not act out of her or his free will.

ON THE WEB To read more about contesting contracts on the grounds of fraud and duress, go to **consumer-law.lawyers.com/ Contesting-Contracts.html**.

Duress

Consent to the terms of a contract is not genuine if one of the parties is forced into the agreement. Forcing a party to enter into a contract because of the fear created by threats is referred to as *duress.*[13] In addition, blackmail or extortion to induce consent to a contract

---

12. *Restatement (Second) of Contracts,* Section 177.
13. *Restatement (Second) of Contracts,* Sections 174 and 175.

constitutes duress. Generally, for duress to occur, the threatened act must be wrongful or illegal. Threatening to exercise a legal right, such as the right to sue someone, ordinarily is not illegal and usually does not constitute duress.

Duress is both a defense to the enforcement of a contract and a ground for rescission of a contract. Therefore, a party who signs a contract under duress can choose to carry out the contract or to avoid the entire transaction. (The wronged party usually has this choice in cases in which assent is not real or genuine.)

Economic need is generally not sufficient to constitute duress, even when one party exacts a very high price for an item the other party needs. If the party exacting the price also creates the need, however, economic duress may be found. **EXAMPLE 12.12** The Internal Revenue Service (IRS) assessed a large tax and penalty against Weller. Weller retained Eyman to contest the assessment. Two days before the deadline for filing a reply with the IRS, Eyman declined to represent Weller unless he agreed to pay a very high fee for Eyman's services. In this situation, a court might find that the agreement was unenforceable because of economic duress. Although Eyman had threatened only to withdraw his services, something that he was legally entitled to do, he was responsible for delaying his withdrawal until just before the deadline. Weller was thus forced into either signing the contract or losing his right to challenge the IRS assessment. •

▶ The Statute of Frauds—Writing Requirement

Every state has a statute that stipulates what types of contracts must be in writing or be evidenced by a record. In this text, we refer to such a statute as the **Statute of Frauds.** The primary purpose of the statute is to ensure that, for certain types of contracts, there is reliable evidence of the contracts and their terms. These types of contracts are those historically deemed to be important or complex. Although the statutes vary slightly from state to state, the following types of contracts are normally required to be in writing or evidenced by a written memorandum:

1. Contracts involving interests in land.
2. Contracts that cannot by their terms be performed within one year from the date of formation.
3. Collateral contracts, such as promises to answer for the debt or duty of another.
4. Promises made in consideration of marriage.
5. Under the Uniform Commercial Code (UCC—see Chapter 15), contracts for the sale of goods priced at $500 or more.

> *"A verbal contract isn't worth the paper it's written on."*
>
> Samuel Goldwyn, 1879–1974
> (Hollywood motion picture producer)

Agreements or promises that fit into one or more of these categories are said to "fall under" or "fall within" the Statute of Frauds. (Certain exceptions are made to the Statute of Frauds, however, as you will read later in this section.)

The actual name of the Statute of Frauds is misleading because it does not apply to fraud. Rather, the statute denies enforceability to certain contracts that do not comply with its requirements. The name derives from an English act passed in 1677, which is presented as this chapter's *Landmark in the Law* feature.

Contracts Involving Interests in Land

Land is a form of *real property,* or real estate, which includes not only land but all physical objects that are permanently attached to the soil, such as buildings, plants, trees, and the soil itself. Under the Statute of Frauds, a contract involving an interest in land must be evidenced by a writing to be enforceable.[14] **EXAMPLE 12.13** If Carol contracts orally to sell Seaside

---

14. In some states, the contract will be enforced if each party admits to the existence of the oral contract in court or admits to its existence during discovery before trial (see Chapter 3).

Landmark in the Law   The Statute of Frauds

On April 12, 1677, the English Parliament passed "An Act for the Prevention of Frauds and Perjuries." Four days later, the act was signed by King Charles II and became the law of the land. The act contained twenty-five sections and stipulated that certain types of contracts would henceforth have to be in writing or evidenced by a written memorandum if they were to be enforceable by the courts.[a]

Enforcement of Oral Promises   The English act was enacted specifically to prevent the many frauds that were being perpetrated through the perjured testimony of witnesses in cases involving breached oral agreements, for which no written evidence existed. During the early history of the common law in England, the courts generally did not enforce oral contracts, but in the fourteenth century, they began to be enforced in certain *assumpsit* actions.[b] These actions, to which the origins of modern contract law are traced, allowed a party to sue and obtain relief when a promise or contract had been breached. During the next two centuries, the king's courts commonly enforced oral promises in actions in *assumpsit*.

---

a. These contracts are discussed in the text of this chapter.
b. *Assumpsit* is Latin for "he or she undertook" or "he or she promised." The emergence of remedies for breached promises and duties dates to these actions. One of the earliest cases occurred in 1370, when the court allowed an individual to sue a person who, in trying to cure the plaintiff's horse, had acted so negligently that the horse died. Another such action was permitted in 1375, when a plaintiff obtained relief for having been maimed by a surgeon hired to cure him.

Problems with Oral Contracts   Because the courts enforced oral contracts on the strength of oral testimony by witnesses, it was not too difficult to evade justice by alleging that a contract had been breached and then procuring "convincing" witnesses to support the claim. The possibility of fraud in such actions was enhanced by the fact that seventeenth-century English courts did not allow oral testimony to be given by the parties to a lawsuit—or by any parties with an interest in the litigation, such as husbands or wives. Defenses against actions for breach of contract were thus limited to written evidence and the testimony given by third parties. The Statute of Frauds was enacted to minimize the possibility of fraud in oral contracts relating to certain types of transactions.

• **Application to Today's World**   *Essentially, the Statute of Frauds offers a defense against contracts that fall under the statute. Indeed, some have criticized the statute because, although it was created to protect the innocent, it can also be used as a technical defense by a party who has breached a genuine, mutually agreed-on oral contract—if the contract falls within the Statute of Frauds. For this reason, some legal scholars believe the act has caused more fraud than it has prevented. Nonetheless, U.S. courts continue to apply the Statute of Frauds to disputes involving oral contracts. The definitions of such terms as* writing *and* signature, *however, have changed to accommodate electronic documents—as you read in the discussion of e-contracts in Chapter 10.*

• **Relevant Web Sites**   *To locate information on the Web concerning the Statute of Frauds, go to this text's Web site at* www.cengage.com/blaw/blt, *select "Chapter 12," and click on "URLs for Landmarks."*

Shelter to Axel but later decides not to sell, Axel cannot enforce the contract. Similarly, if Axel refuses to close the deal, Carol cannot force Axel to pay for the land by bringing a lawsuit. The Statute of Frauds is a *defense* to the enforcement of this type of oral contract. •

A contract for the sale of land ordinarily involves the entire interest in the real property, including buildings, growing crops, vegetation, minerals, timber, and anything else affixed to the land. Therefore, a *fixture* (personal property so affixed or so used as to become a part of the realty—see Chapter 36) is treated as real property.

The Statute of Frauds requires written contracts not just for the sale of land but also for the transfer of other interests in land, such as mortgages, easements, and leases. We describe these other interests in Chapter 36.

The One-Year Rule

ON THE WEB For an interesting discussion of the history and current applicability of the Statute of Frauds, both internationally and in the United States, go to en.Wikipedia.org/wiki/Statute_of_frauds.

Contracts that cannot, *by their own terms,* be performed within one year *from the day after* the contract is formed must be in writing to be enforceable. Because disputes over such contracts are unlikely to occur until some time after the contracts are made, resolution of these disputes is difficult unless the contract terms have been put in writing. The one-year period begins to run *the day after the contract is made.*

EXAMPLE 12.14 Superior University forms a contract with Kimi San stating that San will teach three courses in history during the coming academic year (September 15 through June 15). If the contract is formed in March, it must be in writing to be enforceable—because it cannot be performed within one year. If the contract is not formed until July, however, it will not have to be in writing to be enforceable—because it can be performed within one year. ● Exhibit 12–2 graphically illustrates the one-year rule.

Normally, the test for determining whether an oral contract is enforceable under the one-year rule of the Statute of Frauds is whether performance is *possible* within one year from the day after the date of contract formation—not whether the agreement is *likely* to be performed within one year. When performance of a contract is objectively impossible during the one-year period, the oral contract will be unenforceable.

EXAMPLE 12.15 Bankers Life orally contracts to lend $40,000 to Janet Lawrence "as long as Lawrence and Associates operates its financial consulting firm in Omaha, Nebraska." The contract does not fall within the Statute of Frauds—no writing is required—because Lawrence and Associates could go out of business in one year or less. In this event, the contract would be fully performed within one year. Similarly, an oral contract for lifetime employment does not fall within the Statute of Frauds. Because an employee who is hired "for life" can die within a year, the courts reason that the contract can be performed within one year.[15] ●

Collateral Promises

A **collateral promise,** or secondary promise, is one that is ancillary (subsidiary) to a principal transaction or primary contractual relationship. In other words, a collateral promise is one made by a third party to assume the debts or obligations of a primary party to a contract if that party does not perform. Any collateral promise of this nature falls under the Statute of Frauds and therefore must be in writing to be enforceable. To understand this concept, it is important to distinguish between primary and secondary promises and obligations.

Collateral Promise A secondary promise that is ancillary (subsidiary) to a principal transaction or primary contractual relationship, such as a promise made by one person to pay the debts of another if the latter fails to perform. A collateral promise normally must be in writing to be enforceable.

---

15. See, for example, *Gavengno v. TLT Construction Corp.*, 67 Mass.App.Ct. 1102, 851 N.E.2d 1133 (2006).

● *Exhibit* **12–2 The One-Year Rule**
Under the Statute of Frauds, contracts that by their terms are impossible to perform within one year from the day after the date of contract formation must be in writing to be enforceable. Put another way, if it is at all possible to perform an oral contract within one year from the day after the contract is made, the contract will fall outside the Statute of Frauds and be enforceable.

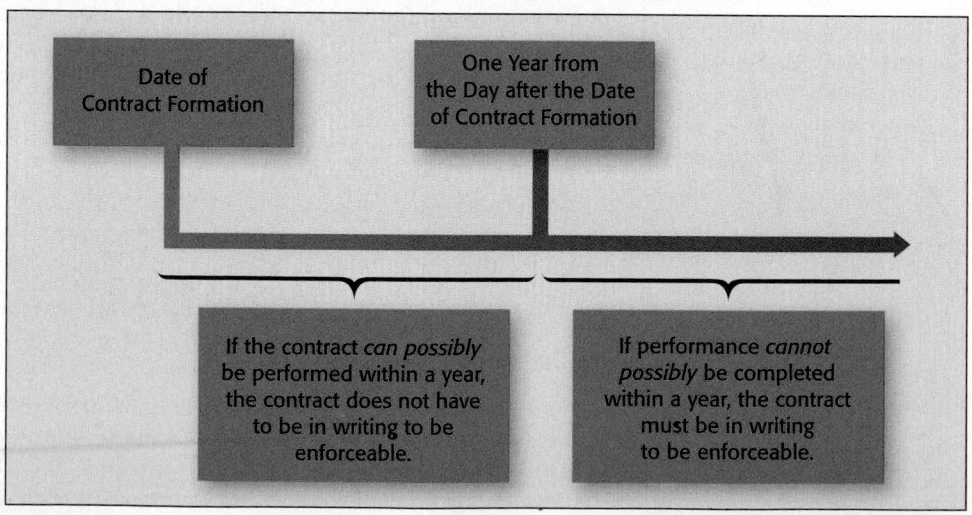

PRIMARY VERSUS SECONDARY OBLIGATIONS   A contract in which a party assumes a primary obligation normally does not need to be in writing to be enforceable. **EXAMPLE 12.16** Kenneth orally contracts with Joanne's Floral Boutique to send his mother a dozen roses for Mother's Day. Kenneth promises to pay the boutique when he receives the bill for the flowers. Kenneth is a direct party to this contract and has incurred a *primary* obligation under the contract. Because he is a party to the contract and has a primary obligation to Joanne's Floral Boutique, this contract does not fall under the Statute of Frauds and does not have to be in writing to be enforceable. If Kenneth fails to pay and the florist sues him for payment, Kenneth cannot raise the Statute of Frauds as a defense. He cannot claim that the contract is unenforceable because it was not in writing. ●

In contrast, a contract in which a party assumes a secondary obligation does have to be in writing to be enforceable. **EXAMPLE 12.17**   Kenneth's mother borrows $10,000 from the Medford Trust Company on a promissory note payable in six months. Kenneth promises the bank officer handling the loan that he will pay the $10,000 *if his mother does not pay the loan on time.* Kenneth, in this situation, becomes what is known as a *guarantor* on the loan. He is guaranteeing to the bank (the creditor) that he will pay the loan if his mother fails to do so. This kind of collateral promise, in which the guarantor states that he or she will become responsible only if the primary party does not perform, must be in writing to be enforceable. ●   We will return to the concept of guaranty and the distinction between primary and secondary obligations in Chapter 21, in the context of creditors' rights.

AN EXCEPTION—THE "MAIN PURPOSE" RULE   An oral promise to answer for the debt of another is covered by the Statute of Frauds *unless* the guarantor's purpose in accepting secondary liability is to secure a personal benefit. Under the "main purpose" rule, this type of contract need not be in writing.[16] The assumption is that a court can infer from the circumstances of a case whether a "leading objective" of the promisor was to secure a personal benefit.

EXAMPLE 12.18   Carrie Braswell contracts with Custom Manufacturing Company to have some machines custom made for her factory. She promises Newform Supply, Custom's supplier, that if Newform continues to deliver the materials to Custom for the production of the custom-made machines, she will guarantee payment. This promise need not be in writing, even though the effect may be to pay the debt of another, because Braswell's main purpose is to secure a benefit for herself. ●

Another typical application of the main purpose doctrine occurs when one creditor guarantees the debtor's debt to another creditor to forestall litigation. This allows the debtor to remain in business long enough to generate profits sufficient to pay *both* creditors. In this situation, the guaranty does not need to be in writing to be enforceable.

Promises Made in Consideration of Marriage

A unilateral promise to make a monetary payment or to give property in consideration of marriage must be in writing. **EXAMPLE 12.19**   Baumann promises to pay Joe Villard $10,000 if Villard marries Baumann's daughter. Because the promise is in consideration of marriage, it must be in writing to be enforceable. ●   The same rule applies to **prenuptial agreements**—agreements made before marriage (also called *antenuptial agreements*) that define each partner's ownership rights in the other partner's property. A prospective wife or husband may wish to limit the amount the prospective spouse can obtain if the marriage ends in divorce. Prenuptial agreements made in consideration of marriage must be in writing to be enforceable.

Prenuptial Agreement   An agreement made before marriage that defines each partner's ownership rights in the other partner's property. Prenuptial agreements must be in writing to be enforceable.

"Now, according to this agreement, his problems will be your problems, and your problems will be your problems."

---

16. *Restatement (Second) of Contracts,* Section 116.

Generally, courts tend to give more credence to prenuptial agreements that are accompanied by consideration. **EXAMPLE 12.20** Maureen, who is not wealthy, marries Kaiser, who has a net worth of $300 million. Kaiser has several children, and he wants them to receive most of his wealth on his death. Prior to their marriage, Maureen and Kaiser draft and sign a prenuptial agreement in which Kaiser promises to give Maureen $100,000 per year for the rest of her life if they divorce. As consideration for consenting to this amount, Kaiser offers Maureen $1 million. If Maureen consents to the agreement and accepts the $1 million, very likely a court would hold that this prenuptial agreement is valid, should it ever be contested. •

Contracts for the Sale of Goods

The Uniform Commercial Code (UCC—see Chapter 15) includes Statute of Frauds provisions that require written evidence or an electronic record of a contract. Section 2–201 requires a writing or memorandum for the sale of goods priced at $500 or more under the UCC (this low threshold amount may be increased in the future). A writing that will satisfy the UCC requirement need only state the quantity term; other terms agreed on need not be stated "accurately" in the writing, as long as they adequately reflect both parties' intentions.

The contract will not be enforceable, however, for any quantity greater than that set forth in the writing. In addition, the writing must have been signed by the person to be charged—that is, by the person who refuses to perform or the one being sued. Beyond these two requirements, the writing need not designate the buyer or the seller, the terms of payment, or the price. (See this chapter's *Beyond Our Borders* feature on page 302 to learn whether other countries have requirements similar to those in the Statute of Frauds.)

Exceptions to the Statute of Frauds

Exceptions to the applicability of the Statute of Frauds are made in certain situations. We describe those situations here.

PARTIAL PERFORMANCE   In cases involving oral contracts for the transfer of interests in land, if the purchaser has paid part of the price, taken possession, and made valuable improvements to the property, and if the parties cannot be returned to their positions prior to the contract, a court may grant *specific performance* (performance of the contract according to its precise terms). Whether a court will enforce an oral contract for an interest in land when partial performance has taken place is usually determined by the degree of injury that would be suffered if the court chose *not* to enforce the oral contract. In some states, mere reliance on certain types of oral contracts is enough to remove them from the Statute of Frauds. Under the UCC, an oral contract for goods priced at $500 or more is enforceable to the extent that a seller accepts payment or a buyer accepts delivery of the goods.[17]

The existence and extent of a contract to supply computer kiosks for use in school cafeterias were in dispute in the following case.

17. UCC 2–201(3)(c). See Chapter 15.

ON THE WEB The online version of UCC Section 2–201 on the Statute of Frauds includes links to definitions of certain terms used in the section. To access this text, go to **www.law.cornell. edu/ucc/2/2-201.html**.

Case 12.3   **School-Link Technologies, Inc. v. Applied Resources, Inc.**

United States District Court, District of Kansas, 471 F.Supp.2d 1101 (2007).

FACTS   Applied Resources, Inc. (ARI), makes computer hardware for point-of-sale systems: kiosks consisting of computers encased in chassis on which card readers or other payment devices are mounted. School-Link Technologies, Inc. (SLT), sells food-service technology to schools. In August 2003, the New York City Department of Education (NYCDOE) asked SLT to propose a cafeteria payment system that included kiosks. SLT asked ARI to participate in a pilot project, orally promising ARI that it would be the exclusive supplier of as many as 1,500 kiosks if the NYCDOE awarded the contract to SLT. ARI agreed. SLT intended to cut ARI out of the deal, however, and told the NYCDOE that SLT would be making its own kiosks. Meanwhile,

Case 12.3—Continued

(Baerbel Schmidt/Stone/Getty Images)

A plan to upgrade New York City schools' cafeterias point-of-sale terminals brought two companies to a legal dispute.

SLT paid ARI in advance for a certain number of goods, but insisted on onerous terms for a written contract to which ARI would not agree. ARI suspended production of the prepaid items and refused to refund more than $55,000 of SLT's funds. SLT filed a suit in a federal district court against ARI. ARI responded, in part, with a counterclaim for breach of contract, asserting that SLT failed to use ARI as an exclusive supplier as promised. ARI sought the expenses it incurred for the pilot project and the amount of profit that it would have realized on the entire deal. SLT filed a motion for summary judgment on this claim.

ISSUE Was the oral agreement for the kiosks enforceable to the extent to which it had been performed?

DECISION Yes. The court denied SLT's motion for summary judgment on ARI's counterclaim for breach of contract "with respect to goods which SLT already received and accepted, i.e., the goods for the pilot program with the NYCDOE."

REASON The court acknowledged that, according to the Uniform Commercial Code, a contract for a sale of goods for a price of $500 or more generally must be in writing and must be signed by the party against whom enforcement is sought. The court reasoned that "[b]ecause the NYCDOE contract undisputedly involved the sale of goods in excess of $500, the parties' oral contract that ARI would be the exclusive supplier of kiosks for the project is not enforceable in the absence of an applicable exception to this general rule." Under the partial performance exception to the rule, an oral contract for a sale of goods priced at $500 or more that would otherwise be unenforceable for the lack of a writing is enforceable to the extent that the seller delivers the goods and the buyer accepts them. In that situation, the performance serves as a substitute for the required writing. Thus, in this case, the court concluded that the alleged oral contract between SLT and ARI, to the effect that ARI would be the exclusive supplier of kiosks for SLT's contract with the NYCDOE, was enforceable to the extent that ARI had delivered the kiosks for the pilot project and SLT had accepted them. The court added, however, that "the remaining aspect of that claim is barred by the [S]tatute of [F]rauds."

FOR CRITICAL ANALYSIS—Social Consideration *Could ARI successfully assert a claim against SLT based on fraudulent misrepresentation? Explain.*

ADMISSIONS In some states, if a party against whom enforcement of an oral contract is sought admits in pleadings, testimony, or otherwise in court proceedings that a contract for sale was made, the contract will be enforceable.[18] A contract subject to the UCC will be enforceable, but only to the extent of the quantity admitted.[19] **EXAMPLE 12.21** The president of Ashley Corporation admits under oath that an oral agreement was made with Com Best to pay $10,000 for certain business equipment. In this situation, a court will enforce the agreement only to the extent admitted (the $10,000), even if Com Best claims that the agreement involved $20,000 of equipment. ●

PROMISSORY ESTOPPEL In some states, an oral contract that would otherwise be unenforceable under the Statute of Frauds may be enforced under the doctrine of promissory estoppel, or detrimental reliance, discussed in Chapter 11. Section 139 of the *Restatement (Second) of Contracts* provides that an oral promise can be enforceable, notwithstanding the Statute of Frauds, if the promisee has justifiably relied on it to her or his detriment. For the contract to be enforceable, the reliance must have been foreseeable to the person making the promise, and enforcing the promise must be the only way to avoid injustice.

SPECIAL EXCEPTIONS UNDER THE UCC Special exceptions to the applicability of the Statute of Frauds exist for sales contracts. Oral contracts for customized goods may be enforced in certain circumstances. Another exception has to do with oral contracts *between merchants* that have been confirmed in writing. We will examine these exceptions in more detail in Chapter 15. Exhibit 12–3 on page 303 graphically summarizes the types of contracts that fall under the Statute of Frauds and the various exceptions that apply.

ON THE WEB For information on the *Restatements of the Law,* including the *Restatement (Second) of Contracts,* go to the American Law Institute's Web site at www.ali.org.

---

18. *Restatement (Second) of Contracts,* Section 133.
19. UCC 2–201(3)(b). See Chapter 15.

Beyond Our Borders   The Statute of Frauds and International Sales Contracts

As you will read in Chapter 15, the Convention on Contracts for the International Sale of Goods (CISG) provides rules that govern international sales contracts between citizens of countries that have ratified the convention (agreement). Article 11 of the CISG does not incorporate any Statute of Frauds provisions. Rather, it states that a "contract for sale need not be concluded in or evidenced by writing and is not subject to any other requirements as to form."

Article 11 accords with the legal customs of most nations, which no longer require contracts to meet certain formal or writing requirements to be enforceable. Ironically, even England, the nation that enacted the original Statute of Frauds in 1677, has repealed all of it except the provisions relating to collateral promises and to transfers of interests in land. Many other countries that once had such statutes have also repealed all or parts of them. Civil law countries, such as France, have never

required certain types of contracts to be in writing. Obviously, without a writing requirement, contracts can take on any form.

• **For Critical Analysis**
If a country does not have a Statute of Frauds and a dispute arises concerning an oral agreement, how can the parties substantiate their respective positions?

 ## The Statute of Frauds—Sufficiency of the Writing

A written contract will satisfy the writing requirement of the Statute of Frauds. A *written memorandum* (written or electronic evidence of the oral contract) signed by the party against whom enforcement is sought will also satisfy the writing requirement. The signature need not be placed at the end of the document but can be anywhere in the writing; it can even be initials rather than the full name. As discussed in Chapter 10, in today's business world there are many ways to create signatures electronically, and electronic signatures generally satisfy the Statute of Frauds.

What Constitutes a Writing?

> *"The pen is mightier than the sword, and considerably easier to write with."*
>
> Marty Feldman, 1934–1982
> (English actor and comedian)

A writing can consist of any confirmation, invoice, sales slip, check, fax, or e-mail—or such items in combination. The written contract need not consist of a single document to constitute an enforceable contract. One document may incorporate another document by expressly referring to it. Several documents may form a single contract if they are physically attached—such as by staple, paper clip, or glue—or even if they are only placed in the same envelope. (See the *Linking the Law to Business Communication* feature on pages 306 and 307.)

EXAMPLE 12.22 Simpson orally agrees to sell some land next to a shopping mall to Terro Properties. Simpson gives Terro an unsigned memo that contains a legal description of the property, and Terro gives Simpson an unsigned first draft of their contract. Simpson sends Terro a signed letter that refers to the memo and to the first and final drafts of the contract. Terro sends Simpson an unsigned copy of the final draft of the contract with a signed check stapled to it. Together, the documents can constitute a writing sufficient to satisfy the Statute of Frauds and bind both parties to the terms of the contract as evidenced by the writings. •

What Must Be Contained in the Writing?

A memorandum or note evidencing the oral contract need only contain the essential terms of the contract, not every term. There must, of course, also be some indication that the parties voluntarily agreed to the terms. A faxed memo of the terms of an agreement could be sufficient if it shows that there was a meeting of the minds and that the faxed terms were not just part of the preliminary negotiations.[20] Under the UCC, in regard to the sale

---

20. See, for example, *Coca-Cola Co. v. Babyback's International, Inc.*, 841 N.E.2d 557 (Ind.App. 2006).

• *Exhibit* 12-3 Contracts Subject to the Statute of Frauds

a. Some states follow Section 133 (on admissions) and Section 139 (on promissory estoppel) of the *Restatement (Second) of Contracts.*

of goods, the writing need only state the quantity and be signed by the party against whom enforcement is sought.

Because only the party against whom enforcement is sought must have signed the writing, a contract may be enforceable by one of its parties but not by the other. **EXAMPLE 12.23** Rock orally agrees to buy Betty Devlin's lake house and lot for $350,000. Devlin writes Rock a letter confirming the sale by identifying the parties and the essential terms of the sales contract—price, method of payment, and legal address—and signs the letter. Devlin has made a written memorandum of the oral land contract. Because she signed the letter, she normally can be held to the oral contract by Rock. Devlin cannot enforce the agreement against Rock, however. Because he has not signed or entered into a written contract or memorandum, Rock can plead the Statute of Frauds as a defense. •

▶ The Parol Evidence Rule

Sometimes, a written contract does not include—or contradicts—an oral understanding reached by the parties before or at the time of contracting. For instance, a landlord might tell a person who agrees to rent an apartment that she or he can have a cat, whereas the lease contract clearly states that no pets are allowed. In determining the outcome of such disputes, the courts look to a common law rule governing the admissibility in court of oral evidence, or *parol evidence.*

Parol Evidence Rule A substantive rule of contracts, as well as a procedural rule of evidence, under which a court will not receive into evidence the parties' prior negotiations, prior agreements, or contemporaneous oral agreements if that evidence contradicts or varies the terms of the parties' written contract.

Under the **parol evidence rule,** if a court finds that a written contract represents the complete and final statement of the parties' agreement, then it will not allow either party to present parol evidence (testimony or other evidence of communications between the parties that are not contained in the contract itself). In other words, a party cannot introduce in court evidence of the parties' prior negotiations, prior agreements, or contemporaneous oral agreements if that evidence contradicts or varies the terms of the parties' written contract.[21]

CASE EXAMPLE 12.24 Pittsburgh Steelers Sports, Inc., sent Ronald Yocca a brochure that advertised a new stadium to be built for the Pittsburgh Steelers football team. The brochure publicly offered to sell stadium builder licenses (SBLs), which granted the right to buy annual season tickets to the games. Prices varied, depending on the seats' locations, which

---

21. *Restatement (Second) of Contracts,* Section 213.

were indicated by small diagrams. Yocca applied for an SBL, listing his seating preferences. The Steelers sent him a letter notifying him of the section in which his seat was located and a diagram that showed different seating sections than were shown in the brochure. The Steelers also sent Yocca documents setting forth the terms of the SBL agreement, which included a clause that read, "This Agreement contains the entire agreement of the parties." Yocca's signature was required, and he signed the documents. When Yocca went to the stadium, he discovered that his seat was not where he expected it to be. He filed a lawsuit claiming breach of contract because the seat assignments differed from those advertised in the brochure. The court, however, concluded that the brochure was not part of the parties' contract and dismissed the suit. The SBL documents that Yocca had signed constituted the parties' entire contract and, under the parol evidence rule, could not be supplemented by previous negotiations or agreements.[22] ●

Exceptions to the Parol Evidence Rule

Because of the rigidity of the parol evidence rule, courts make several exceptions. These exceptions include the following:

NOTE The parol evidence rule and its exceptions relate to the rules concerning the *interpretation* of contracts.

1. *Contracts subsequently modified.* Evidence of a *subsequent modification* of a written contract can be introduced in court. Keep in mind that the oral modifications may not be enforceable if they come under the Statute of Frauds—for example, if they increase the price of the goods for sale to $500 or more or increase the term for performance to more than one year. Also, oral modifications will not be enforceable if the original contract provides that any modification must be in writing.[23]
2. *Voidable or void contracts.* Oral evidence can be introduced in all cases to show that the contract was voidable or void (for example, induced by mistake, fraud, or misrepresentation). In this situation, if deception led one of the parties to agree to the terms of a written contract, oral evidence indicating fraud should not be excluded. Courts frown on bad faith and are quick to allow the introduction at trial of parol evidence when it establishes fraud.
3. *Contracts containing ambiguous terms.* When the terms of a written contract are ambiguous, evidence is admissible to show the meaning of the terms.
4. *Incomplete contracts.* Evidence is admissible when the written contract is incomplete in that it lacks one or more of the essential terms. The courts allow evidence to "fill in the gaps" in the contract.
5. *Prior dealing, course of performance, or usage of trade.* Under the UCC, evidence can be introduced to explain or supplement a written contract by showing a prior dealing, course of performance, or usage of trade.[24] This is because when buyers and sellers deal with each other over extended periods of time, certain customary practices develop. These practices are often overlooked in the writing of the contract, so courts allow the introduction of evidence to show how the parties have acted in the past. Usage of trade—practices and customs generally followed in a particular industry—can also shed light on the meaning of certain contract provisions, and thus evidence of trade usage may be admissible. We will discuss these terms in further detail in Chapter 15, in the context of sales contracts.
6. *Contracts subject to an orally agreed-on condition precedent.* As you will read in Chapter 13, sometimes the parties agree that a condition must be fulfilled before a party is required to perform the contract. This is called a *condition precedent.* If the parties have orally agreed on a condition precedent and the condition does not conflict with the terms of a written agreement, then a court may allow parol evidence to prove the oral condition. The parol evidence rule does not apply here because the existence of the entire written

---

22. *Yocca v. Pittsburgh Steelers Sports, Inc.,* 578 Pa. 479, 854 A.2d 425 (2004).
23. UCC 2–209(2), (3). See Chapter 15.
24. UCC 1–205, 2–202. See Chapter 15.

contract is subject to an orally agreed-on condition. Proof of the condition does not alter or modify the written terms but affects the *enforceability* of the written contract.

EXAMPLE 12.25 A city leases property for an airport from a well-established helicopter business. The lease is renewable every five years. During the second five-year lease, a dispute arises, and the parties go to mediation. They enter into a settlement memorandum under which they agree to amend the lease agreement subject to the approval of the city council. The city amends the lease, but the helicopter business refuses to sign it, contending that the council has not given its approval. In this situation, the council's approval is a condition precedent to the formation of the settlement memorandum contract. Therefore, the parol evidence rule does not apply, and oral evidence is admissible to show that no agreement exists as to the terms of the settlement. •

7. *Contracts with an obvious or gross clerical (or typographic) error.* When an *obvious* or *gross* clerical (or typographic) error exists that clearly would not represent the agreement of the parties, parol evidence is admissible to correct the error. **EXAMPLE 12.26** Davis agrees to lease 1,000 square feet of office space from Stone Enterprises at the current monthly rate of $3 per square foot. The signed written lease provides for a monthly lease payment of $300 rather than the $3,000 agreed to by the parties. Because the error is obvious, Stone Enterprises would be allowed to admit parol evidence to correct the mistake. •

Integrated Contracts

The determination of whether evidence will be allowed basically depends on whether the written contract is intended to be a complete and final statement of the terms of the agreement. If it is so intended, it is referred to as an **integrated contract,** and extraneous evidence (evidence from outside the contract) is excluded.

An integrated contract can be either completely or partially integrated. If it contains all of the terms of the parties' agreement, then it is completely integrated. If it contains only some of the terms that the parties agreed on and not others, it is partially integrated. If the contract is only partially integrated, evidence of consistent additional terms is admissible to supplement the written agreement.[25] Note that for both completely and partially integrated contracts, courts exclude any evidence that *contradicts* the writing and allow parol evidence only to add to the terms of a partially integrated contract. Exhibit 12–4 illustrates the relationship between integrated contracts and the parol evidence rule.

> **Integrated Contract** A written contract that constitutes the final expression of the parties' agreement. If a contract is integrated, evidence extraneous to the contract that contradicts or alters the meaning of the contract in any way is inadmissible.

---

25. *Restatement (Second) of Contracts,* Section 216.

• *Exhibit* **12–4 Parol Evidence Rule**

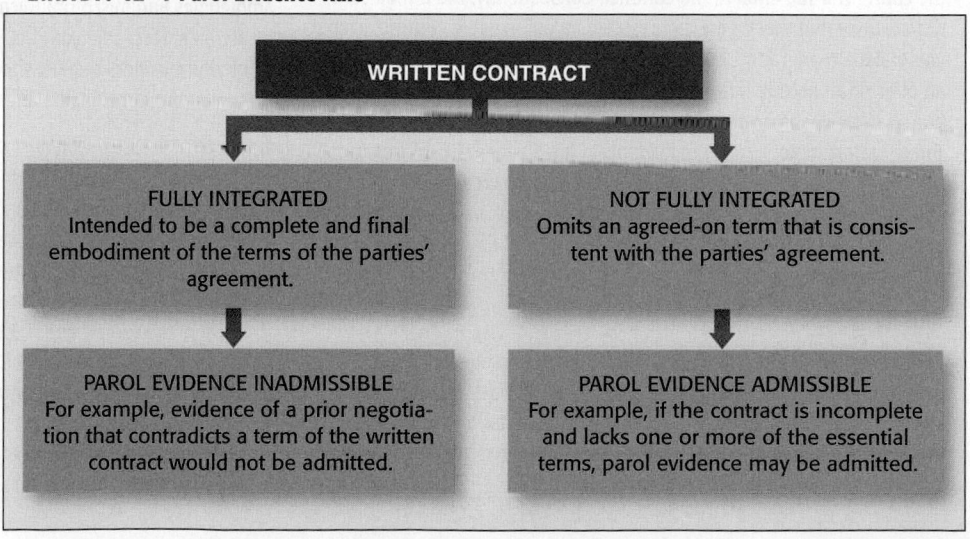

WRITTEN CONTRACT	
FULLY INTEGRATED Intended to be a complete and final embodiment of the terms of the parties' agreement.	**NOT FULLY INTEGRATED** Omits an agreed-on term that is consistent with the parties' agreement.
PAROL EVIDENCE INADMISSIBLE For example, evidence of a prior negotiation that contradicts a term of the written contract would not be admitted.	**PAROL EVIDENCE ADMISSIBLE** For example, if the contract is incomplete and lacks one or more of the essential terms, parol evidence may be admitted.

Reviewing . . . Defenses to Contract Enforceability

Charter Golf, Inc., manufactures and sells golf apparel and supplies. Ken Odin had worked as a Charter sales representative for six months when he was offered a position with a competing firm. Charter's president, Jerry Montieth, offered Odin a 10 percent commission "for the rest of his life" if Ken would turn down the offer and stay on with Charter. He also promised that Odin would not be fired unless he was dishonest. Odin turned down the competitor's offer and stayed with Charter. Three years later, Charter fired Odin for no reason. Odin sued, alleging breach of contract. Using the information presented in the chapter, answer the following questions.

1. Would a court likely decide that Montieth's employment contract with Odin falls within the Statute of Frauds? Why or why not?
2. Assume that the court does find that the contract falls within the Statute of Frauds and that the state in which the court sits recognizes every exception to the Statute of Frauds discussed in the chapter. What exception provides Odin with the best chance of enforcing the oral contract in this situation?
3. Now suppose that Montieth had taken out a pencil, written "10 percent for life" on the back of a register receipt, and handed it to Odin. Would this satisfy the Statute of Frauds? Why or why not?
4. Assume that Odin had signed a written employment contract at the time he was hired by Charter, but it was not completely integrated. Would a court allow Odin to present parol evidence of Montieth's subsequent promises?

Linking the Law *to Business Communication*
When E-Mails Become Enforceable Contracts

Most business students must take a course in business communication. These courses cover the planning and preparation of oral and written communications, including electronic messages. Indeed, e-mails have become so pervasive that an increasing number of contracts are created via e-mail.

Voluntary Consent and Mistakes

One possible defense to contract enforceability is a lack of voluntary consent, sometimes due to mistakes. Often, when a mistake is unilateral, the courts will still enforce the contract. Consequently, the e-mail communications that you create can result in an enforceable contract even if you make a typographic error in, say, a dollar amount. If you are making an offer or an acceptance via e-mail, you have to treat that communication as carefully as if you were writing or typing it on a sheet of paper. Today, unfortunately, many individuals in the business world treat e-mails somewhat casually. When you realize that you are creating an enforceable contract if you make an offer or an acceptance via e-mail, then you know that you have to reread your e-mails several times before you hit the send button.

The Sufficiency of the Writing

In this chapter, you learned about the Statute of Frauds. The legal definitions of written memoranda and signatures have changed in our electronic age. Today, an e-mail definitely constitutes a writing. A writing can also be a series of e-mail exchanges between two parties. In other words, five e-mail exchanges taken together may form a single contract. (In the past, before e-mails and faxes, this applied to written communications on pieces of paper that were stapled or clipped together.) If one or more e-mails name the parties, identify the subject matter, and lay out the consideration, a court normally will accept those e-mails as constituting a writing sufficient to satisfy the Statute of Frauds.

The Importance of Clear, Precise E-Mail Language

In addition to typographic errors, casually written e-mails may contain ambiguities and miscommunications. Nevertheless, those e-mails may create an enforceable contract, whether you intend it or not. Therefore, all of your business e-mails should be carefully written. At a minimum, when you are e-mailing business contacts, you should:

1. *Create a precise and informative subject line.* Rather than saying "we should discuss" or "important information," be specific in the subject line of the e-mail, such as "change delivery date for portable generators."
2. *Repeat the subject within the body of the e-mail message.* In the actual e-mail message, avoid phrases with indefinite antecedents such as "This is . . . ." Good business e-mail communication involves a repetition of most of the subject line. That way, if your recipient skips the subject line, the message will still be clear.
3. *Focus on a limited number of subjects, usually one.* Do not ramble and discuss a variety of topics in your e-mail. If necessary, send several e-mails on several different topics.

4. *Create e-mails that are just as attractive as if you were having them written on letterhead.* Obviously, e-mails that have no particular format, no paragraphs, bad grammar, misspellings, and incorrect punctuation create a negative impression. More important, if your language is not precise, you may find that you have created an enforceable contract when you did not intend to do so. At a minimum, use the spelling and grammar checker in your word-processing program.

5. *Proof your work.* This aspect of e-mail communications is so important that it is worth repeating. Proofing your e-mails before you hit the send

button is the most important step that you can take to avoid contract misinterpretations.

FOR CRITICAL ANALYSIS
Sometimes, in contract disputes, one party can produce a copy of an e-mail that supposedly was sent, but the other party contends that it was never received. How can the sender avoid this problem?

 Key Terms

collateral promise 298	parol evidence rule 303	*scienter* 293
integrated contract 305	prenuptial agreement 299	Statute of Frauds 296

 Chapter Summary: Defenses to Contract Enforceability

VOLUNTARY CONSENT	
Mistakes (See pages 288–290.)	1. *Unilateral*—Generally, the mistaken party is bound by the contract *unless* (a) the other party knows or should have known of the mistake or (b) the mistake is an inadvertent mathematical error—such as an error in addition or subtraction—committed without gross negligence. 2. *Bilateral (mutual)*—When both parties are mistaken about the same material fact, such as identity, either party can avoid the contract.
Fraudulent Misrepresentation (See pages 290–295.)	When fraud occurs, usually the innocent party can enforce or avoid the contract. The following elements are necessary to establish fraud: 1. A misrepresentation of a material fact must occur. 2. There must be an intent to deceive. 3. The innocent party must justifiably rely on the misrepresentation.
Undue Influence (See page 295.)	Undue influence arises from special relationships, such as fiduciary or confidential relationships, in which one party's free will has been overcome by the undue influence exerted by the other party. Usually, the contract is voidable.
Duress (See pages 295–296.)	Duress is the tactic of forcing a party to enter a contract under the fear of a threat—for example, the threat of violence or serious economic loss. The party forced to enter the contract can rescind the contract.
FORM	

The Statute of Frauds— Writing Requirement (See pages 296–302.)	1. *Applicability*—The following types of contracts fall under the Statute of Frauds and must be in writing to be enforceable:
	  a. Contracts involving interests in land—The statute applies to any contract for an interest in realty, such as a sale, a lease, or a mortgage.
	  b. Contracts that cannot by their terms be performed within one year—The statute applies only to contracts that are objectively impossible to perform fully within one year from (the day after) the contract's formation.
	  c. Collateral promises—The statute applies only to express contracts made between the guarantor and the creditor whose terms make the guarantor secondarily liable. *Exception:* the "main purpose" rule.

Continued

Chapter Summary: Defenses to Contract Enforceability—Continued

The Statute of Frauds–Writing Requirement–Continued	d. Promises made in consideration of marriage–The statute applies to promises to make a monetary payment or give property in consideration of a promise to marry and to prenuptial agreements made in consideration of marriage. e. Contracts for the sale of goods priced at $500 or more–Under the Statute of Frauds provision in Section 2–201 of the Uniform Commercial Code. 2. *Exceptions*–Partial performance, admissions, and promissory estoppel.
The Statute of Frauds–Sufficiency of the Writing (See pages 302–303.)	To constitute an enforceable contract under the Statute of Frauds, a writing must be signed by the party against whom enforcement is sought, name the parties, identify the subject matter, and state with reasonable certainty the essential terms of the contract. Under the UCC, a contract for a sale of goods is not enforceable beyond the quantity of goods shown in the contract.
The Parol Evidence Rule (See pages 303–305.)	The parol evidence rule prohibits the introduction at trial of evidence of the parties' prior negotiations, prior agreements, or contemporaneous oral agreements that contradicts or varies the terms of the parties' written contract. The written contract is assumed to be the complete embodiment of the parties' agreement. Exceptions are made in the circumstances listed on pages 304–305.

 ExamPrep

ISSUE SPOTTERS

1 Elle, an accountant, certifies several audit reports to Flite Corporation, Elle's client, knowing that Flite intends to use the reports to obtain loans from Good Credit Company (GCC). Elle believes that the reports are true and does not intend to deceive GCC, but does not check the reports before certifying them. Can Elle be held liable to GCC? Why or why not?

2 My-T Quality Goods, Inc., and Nu! Sales Corporation orally agree to a deal. My-T writes up the essential terms on company letterhead stationery and files the memo in My-T's office. If Nu! Sales later refuses to complete the transaction, is this memo a sufficient writing to enforce the contract against it? Explain your answer.

BEFORE THE TEST

Check your answers to the Issue Spotters, and at the same time, take the interactive quiz for this chapter. Go to **www.cengage.com/blaw/blt** and click on "Chapter 12." First, click on "Answers to Issue Spotters" to check your answers. Next, click on "Interactive Quiz" to assess your mastery of the concepts in this chapter. Then click on "Flashcards" to review this chapter's Key Term definitions.

 For Review

Answers for the even-numbered questions in this For Review *section can be found on this text's accompanying Web site at* **www.cengage.com/blaw/blt**. *Select "Chapter 12" and click on "For Review."*

1 In what types of situations might voluntary consent to a contract's terms be lacking?
2 What is the difference between a mistake of value or quality and a mistake of fact?
3 What are the elements of fraudulent misrepresentation?
4 What contracts must be in writing to be enforceable?
5 What is parol evidence? When is it admissible to clarify the terms of a written contract?

 Hypothetical Scenarios and Case Problems

12–1 Voluntary Consent. Jerome is an elderly man who lives with his nephew, Philip. Jerome is totally dependent on Philip's support. Philip tells Jerome that unless Jerome transfers a tract of land he owns to Philip for a price 30 percent below market value, Philip will no longer support and take care of him.

Jerome enters into the contract. Discuss fully whether Jerome can set aside this contract.

12–2 **Hypothetical Question with Sample Answer** Gemma promises a local hardware store that she will pay for a lawn mower that her brother is purchasing on credit if the brother fails to pay the debt. Must this promise be in writing to be enforceable? Why or why not?

—For a sample answer to Question 12–2, go to Appendix E at the end of this text.

12–3 Fraudulent Misrepresentation. Larry offered to sell Stanley his car and told Stanley that the car had been driven only 25,000 miles and had never been in an accident. Stanley hired Cohen, a mechanic, to appraise the condition of the car, and Cohen said that the car probably had at least 50,000 miles on it and probably had been in an accident. In spite of this information, Stanley still thought the car would be a good buy for the price, so he purchased it. Later, when the car developed numerous mechanical problems, Stanley sought to rescind the contract on the basis of Larry's fraudulent misrepresentation of the auto's condition. Will Stanley be able to rescind his contract? Discuss.

12–4 Oral Contracts. Jason Novell, doing business as Novell Associates, hired Barbara Meade as an independent contractor in March 2007. The parties orally agreed on the terms of employment, including payment to Meade of a share of the company's income, but they did not put anything in writing. In March 2009, Meade quit. Novell then told Meade that she was entitled to $9,602.17—25 percent of the difference between the accounts receivable and the accounts payable as of Meade's last day. Meade disagreed and demanded more than $63,500—25 percent of the revenue from all invoices, less the cost of materials and outside processing, for each of the years that she worked for Novell. Novell refused. Meade filed a lawsuit in a state court against Novell, alleging breach of contract. In Novell's response and at the trial, he testified that the parties had an oral contract under which Meade was entitled to 25 percent of the difference between accounts receivable and payable as of the date of Meade's termination. Did the parties have an enforceable contract? How should the court rule, and why?

12–5 The Parol Evidence Rule. Carlin Krieg owned a dairy farm in St. Joe, Indiana, that was appraised at $154,000 in December 1997. In August 1999, Krieg told Donald Hieber that he intended to sell the farm for $106,000. Hieber offered to buy it. Krieg also told Hieber that he wanted to retain a "right of residency" for life in the farm. In October, Krieg and Hieber executed a "Purchase Agreement" that provided that Krieg "shall transfer full and complete possession" of the farm "subject to [his] right of residency." The agreement also contained an integration clause stating that "there are no conditions, representations, warranties, or agreements not stated in this instrument." In November 2000, the house was burned in a fire, rendering it unlivable. Hieber filed an insurance claim for the damage and received the proceeds, but he did not fix the house. Krieg filed a suit in an Indiana state court against Hieber, alleging breach of contract. Is there any basis on which the court can consider evidence regarding the parties' negotiations prior to their agreement for the sale of the farm? Explain. [*Krieg v. Hieber,* 802 N.E.2d 938 (Ind.App. 2004)]

12–6 Contract for a Sale of Goods. Milton Blankenship agreed in writing to buy 15 acres of Ella Mae Henry's junkyard property for $15,000 per acre with a ten-year option to buy the remaining 28.32 acres. Blankenship orally agreed to (1) begin operating a car skeleton processing plant within six to fifteen months;

(2) buy as many car skeletons generated by the yard as Clifford Henry wanted to sell him, at a certain premium over the market price; and (3) allow all junk vehicles on the property to remain until they were processed at the new plant. Blankenship never operated such a plant, never bought any vehicles from the yard, and demanded that all vehicles be removed from the property. To obtain the remaining 28.32 acres, Blankenship filed a suit in a Georgia state court against Henry, who responded with a counterclaim for breach of contract. Under oath during discovery, Henry testified that their oral agreement allowed him to sell "as many of the car skeletons generated by the Henry junkyard" as he wished, and Blankenship testified that he had agreed to buy as many skeletons as Henry was willing to sell. Does the Statute of Frauds undercut or support Henry's counterclaim? Explain. [*Henry v. Blankenship,* 284 Ga.App. 578, 644 S.E.2d 419 (2007)]

12–7 Case Problem with Sample Answer According to the student handbook at Cleveland Chiropractic College (CCC) in Missouri, *academic misconduct* includes "selling . . . any copy of any material intended to be used as an instrument of academic evaluation in advance of its initial administration." Leonard Verni was enrolled at CCC in Dr. Aleksandr Makarov's dermatology class. Before the first examination, Verni was reported to be selling copies of the test. CCC investigated and concluded that Verni had committed academic misconduct. Verni was dismissed from CCC, which informed him of his right to an appeal. According to the handbook, at the hearing on appeal a student could have an attorney or other adviser, present witnesses' testimony and other evidence, and "question any testimony . . . against him/her." At his hearing, however, Verni did not bring his attorney, present evidence on his behalf, or question any adverse witnesses. When the dismissal was upheld, Verni filed a suit in a Missouri state court against CCC and others, claiming, in part, fraudulent misrepresentation. Verni argued that because he "relied" on the handbook's "representation" that CCC would follow its appeal procedure, he was unable to properly refute the charges against him. Can Verni succeed with this argument? Explain. [*Verni v. Cleveland Chiropractic College,* 212 S.W.3d 150 (Mo. 2007)]

—After you have answered Problem 12–7, compare your answer with the sample answer given on the Web site that accompanies this text. Go to **www.cengage.com/blaw/blt**, select "Chapter 12," and click on "Case Problem with Sample Answer."

12–8 Fraudulent Misrepresentation. Peggy Williams helped eighty-seven-year-old Melvin Kaufman care for his wife and Williams's great aunt, Elsie, for several years before Elsie's death. Melvin then asked Williams to "take care of him the rest of his life." He conveyed his house to her for "Ten and No/100 Dollars ($10.00), and other good and valuable consideration," according to the deed, and executed a power of attorney in her favor. When he returned from a trip to visit his brother, however, Williams had locked him out of the house. He filed a suit in a Texas state court, alleging fraud. He claimed that he had deeded the house to her in exchange for her promise of care, but that she had not taken care of him and had not paid him the ten dollars. Williams admitted that she had not paid the ten dollars, but argued that she had made no such promise, that Melvin had given her the house when he had been unable to sell it, and that his trip had been intended as a move. Do these facts show fraud? Why or why not? [*Williams v. Kaufman,* 275 S.W.3d 637 (Tex.App.—Beaumont 2009)]

12–9 **A Question of Ethics** *On behalf of BRJM, LLC, Nicolas Kepple offered Howard Engelsen $210,000 for a parcel of land known as lot five on the north side of Barnes Road in Stonington, Connecticut. Engelsen's company, Output Systems, Inc., owned the land. Engelsen had the lot surveyed and obtained an appraisal. The appraiser valued the property at $277,000, after determining that it was three acres and thus could not be subdivided because it did not meet the town's minimum legal requirement of 3.7 acres for subdivision. Engelsen responded to Kepple's offer with a counteroffer of $230,000, which Kepple accepted. On May 3, 2002, the parties signed a contract. When Engelsen refused to go through with the deal, BRJM filed a suit in a Connecticut state court against*

Output, seeking specific performance and other relief. The defendant asserted the defense of mutual mistake on at least two grounds. [BRJM, LLC v. Output Systems, Inc., 100 Conn.App. 143, 917 A.2d 605 (2007)]

1 In the counteroffer, Engelsen asked Kepple to remove from their contract a clause requiring written confirmation of the availability of a "free split," which meant that the property could be subdivided without the town's prior approval. Kepple agreed. After signing the contract, Kepple learned that the property was *not* entitled to a free split. Would this circumstance qualify as a mistake on which the *defendant* could avoid the contract? Why or why not?

2 After signing the contract, Engelsen obtained a second appraisal that established the size of lot five as 3.71 acres, which meant that it could be subdivided, and valued the property at $490,000. Can the defendant avoid the contract on the basis of a mistake in the first appraisal? Explain.

▶ Critical Thinking and Writing Assignments

12–10 Critical Legal Thinking. Describe the types of individuals who might be capable of exerting undue influence on others.

12–11 **Video Question** Go to this text's Web site at **www.cengage.com/blaw/blt** and select "Chapter 12." Click on "Video Questions" and view the video titled *Mistake.* Then answer the following questions.

1 What kind of mistake is involved in the dispute shown in the video (bilateral or unilateral, mistake of fact or mistake of value)?

2 According to the chapter, in what two situations would the supermarket be able to rescind a contract to sell peppers to Melnick at the incorrectly advertised price?

3 Does it matter if the price that was advertised was a reasonable price for the peppers? Why or why not?

▶ Practical Internet Exercises

Go to this text's Web site at **www.cengage.com/blaw/blt**, select "Chapter 12," and click on "Practical Internet Exercises." There you will find the following Internet research exercises that you can perform to learn more about the topics covered in this chapter.

Practical Internet Exercise 12–1: LEGAL PERSPECTIVE—Promissory Estoppel and the Statute of Frauds
Practical Internet Exercise 12–2: MANAGEMENT PERSPECTIVE—Fraudulent Misrepresentation
Practical Internet Exercise 12–3: ECONOMIC PERSPECTIVE—Economic Duress

Third Party Rights and Discharge

> "The laws of a state change with the changing times."
>
> —Aeschylus, 525–456 B.C.E.
> (Greek dramatist)

Chapter Outline

- Assignments
- Delegations
- Third Party Beneficiaries
- Contract Discharge

Learning Objectives

After reading this chapter, you should be able to answer the following questions:

1. What is the difference between an assignment and a delegation?

2. What rights can be assigned despite a contract clause expressly prohibiting assignment?

3. What factors indicate that a third party beneficiary is an intended beneficiary?

4. How are most contracts discharged?

5. What is a contractual condition, and how might a condition affect contractual obligations?

Privity of Contract The relationship that exists between the promisor and the promisee of a contract.

Because a contract is a private agreement between the parties who have entered into that contract, it is fitting that these parties alone should have rights and liabilities under the contract. This concept is referred to as **privity of contract,** and it establishes the basic principle that third parties have no rights in contracts to which they are not parties.

You may be convinced by now that for every rule of contract law, there is an exception. As times change, so must the laws, as indicated in the chapter-opening quotation. When justice cannot be served by adherence to a rule of law, exceptions to the rule must be made. In this chapter, we look at some exceptions to the rule of privity of contract. These exceptions include *assignments* and *delegations,* as well as *third party beneficiary contracts.* We also examine how contractual obligations can be *discharged.* Normally, contract discharge is accomplished by both parties performing the acts promised in the contract. In the latter part of this chapter, we look at the degree of performance required to discharge a contractual obligation, as well as at some other ways in which contract discharge can occur.

Assignments

In a bilateral contract, the two parties have corresponding rights and duties. One party has a *right* to require the other to perform some task, and the other has a *duty* to perform it. Sometimes, though, a party will transfer her or his rights under the contract to someone

Assignment   The act of transferring to another all or part of one's rights arising under a contract.

else. The transfer of contract *rights* to a third person is known as an **assignment**. (The transfer of contract duties is a *delegation,* as will be discussed later in this chapter.)

Assignments are important because they are often used in business financing. Lending institutions, such as banks, frequently assign the rights to receive payments under their loan contracts to other firms, which pay for those rights. If you obtain a loan from your local bank to purchase a car, you may later receive a notice stating that your bank has transferred (assigned) its rights to receive payments on the loan to another firm and that you should make your payments to that other firm.

Lenders that make *mortgage loans* (loans to allow prospective home buyers to purchase land or a home) often assign their rights to collect the mortgage payments to a third party, such as Chase Home Mortgage Company. Following an assignment, the home buyer is notified that future payments must be made to the third party, rather than to the original lender. Billions of dollars change hands daily in the business world in the form of assignments of rights in contracts.

Effect of an Assignment

Assignor   A party who transfers (assigns) his or her rights under a contract to another party (called the *assignee*).

Assignee   A party to whom the rights under a contract are transferred, or assigned.

Obligee   One to whom an obligation is owed.

Obligor   One who owes an obligation to another.

In an assignment, the party assigning the rights to a third party is known as the **assignor**,[1] and the party receiving the rights is the **assignee**.[2] Other terms traditionally used to describe the parties in assignment relationships are the **obligee** (the person to whom a duty, or obligation, is owed) and the **obligor** (the person who is obligated to perform the duty).

When rights under a contract are assigned unconditionally, the rights of the *assignor* (the party making the assignment) are extinguished.[3] The third party (the *assignee,* or the party receiving the assignment) has a right to demand performance from the other original party to the contract (the *obligor,* the person who is obligated to perform). **EXAMPLE 13.1**   Brent (the obligor) owes Alex $1,000, and Alex, the obligee, assigns to Carmen the right to receive the $1,000 (thus, Alex is now the assignor). Here, a valid assignment of a debt exists. Carmen, the assignee, can enforce the contract against Brent, the obligor, if Brent fails to perform (pay the $1,000). ● Exhibit 13–1 illustrates assignment relationships.

The assignee obtains only those rights that the assignor originally had. Also, the assignee's rights are subject to the defenses that the obligor has against the assignor. **EXAMPLE 13.2**   Brent owes Alex $1,000 under a contract in which Brent agreed to buy Alex's MacBook Pro laptop. Alex assigns his right to receive the $1,000 to Carmen. Brent, in deciding to purchase the laptop, relied on Alex's fraudulent misrepresentation that the computer had 4 megabytes of memory. When Brent discovers that the computer has only 2 megabytes of memory, he tells Alex that he is going to return the laptop and cancel the contract. Even though Alex has assigned his "right" to receive the $1,000 to Carmen, Brent need not pay Carmen the $1,000—Brent can raise the defense of Alex's fraudulent misrepresentation to avoid payment. ●

Rights That Cannot Be Assigned

As a general rule, all rights can be assigned. Exceptions are made, however, in the following special circumstances.

ON THE WEB   You can find a number of forms that can be used in the assignment of different types of contracts, at **www.ilrg.com/forms/#transfers**. This site is maintained by the Internet Legal Research Group.

WHEN A STATUTE EXPRESSLY PROHIBITS ASSIGNMENT   If a statute expressly prohibits assignment, the particular right in question cannot be assigned. **EXAMPLE 13.3**   Marn is a new employee of CompuFuture, Inc. CompuFuture is an employer governed by workers'

---

1. Pronounced uh-*sye*-nore.
2. Pronounced uh-*sye*-nee.
3. *Restatement (Second) of Contracts,* Section 317.

• *Exhibit* 13–1 Assignment Relationships

In the assignment relationship illustrated here, Alex assigns his *rights* under a contract that he made with Brent to a third party, Carmen. Alex thus becomes the *assignor* and Carmen the *assignee* of the contractual rights. Brent, the *obligor* (the party owing performance under the contract), now owes performance to Carmen instead of to Alex. Alex's original contract rights are extinguished after the assignment.

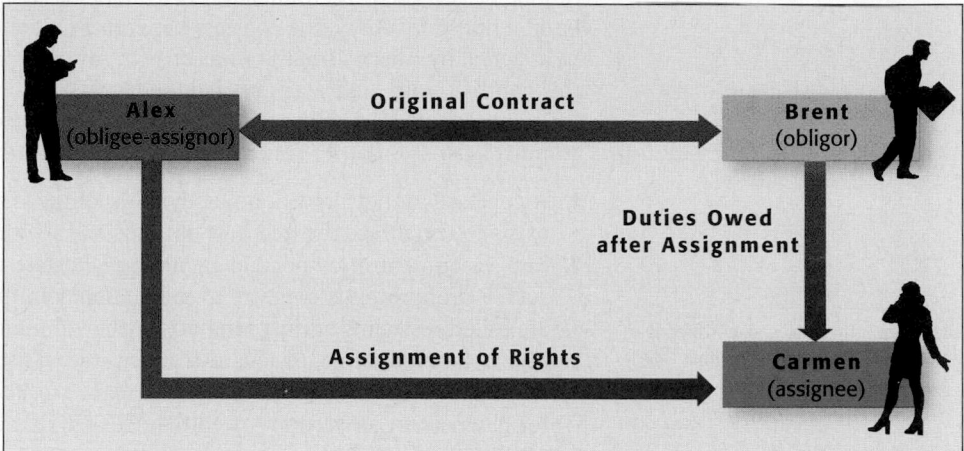

compensation statutes (see Chapter 24) in this state, so Marn is a covered employee. Marn has a relatively high-risk job. In need of a loan, she borrows from Stark, assigning to Stark all workers' compensation benefits due her should she be injured on the job. A state statute prohibits the assignment of *future* workers' compensation benefits, and thus such rights cannot be assigned. •

A music teacher instructs his pupil. Assuming that the boy's mother, Katherine, contracted with the teacher for his services, can Katherine assign the right to receive music lessons to another party? Why or why not?

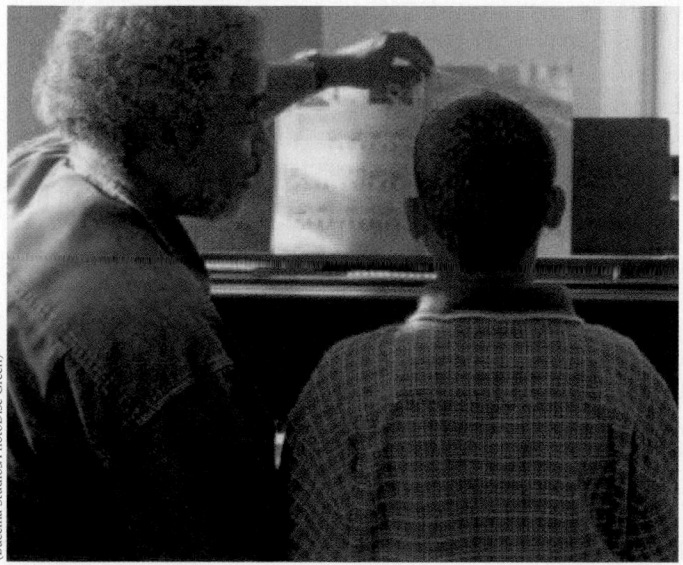

(Buccina Studios/PhotoDisc Green)

WHEN A CONTRACT IS PERSONAL IN NATURE   When a contract is for personal services, the rights under the contract normally cannot be assigned unless all that remains is a monetary payment.[4] **EXAMPLE 13.4**   Brent signs a contract to be a tutor for Alex's children. Alex then attempts to assign to Carmen his right to Brent's services. Carmen cannot enforce the contract against Brent. Brent may not like Carmen's children or for some other reason may not want to tutor them. Because personal services are unique to the person rendering them, rights to receive personal services cannot be assigned. •

WHEN AN ASSIGNMENT WILL SIGNIFICANTLY CHANGE THE RISK OR DUTIES OF THE OBLIGOR   A right cannot be assigned if assignment will significantly increase or alter the risks or the duties of the obligor (the party owing performance under the contract).[5] **EXAMPLE 13.5**   Alex has a hotel, and to insure it, he takes out a policy with Northwest Insurance Company. The policy insures against fire, theft, floods, and vandalism. Alex attempts to assign the insurance policy to Carmen, who also owns a hotel. The assignment is ineffective because it may substantially alter the insurance

---

4. *Restatement (Second) of Contracts,* Sections 317 and 318.
5. See Section 2–210(2) of the Uniform Commercial Code (UCC).

CHAPTER 13   Third-Party Rights and Discharge

> "Man, an animal that makes bargains."
>
> Adam Smith, 1723–1790
> (Scottish economist and philosopher)

company's duty of performance and the risk that the company undertakes. An insurance company evaluates the particular risk of a certain party and tailors its policy to fit that risk. If the policy is assigned to a third party, the insurance risk is materially altered. ●

WHEN THE CONTRACT PROHIBITS ASSIGNMENT   If a contract stipulates that the right cannot be assigned, then *ordinarily* it cannot be assigned. **EXAMPLE 13.6** Brent agrees to build a house for Alex. The contract between Brent and Alex states, "This contract cannot be assigned by Alex without Brent's consent. Any assignment without such consent renders this contract void, and all rights hereunder will thereupon terminate." Alex then assigns his rights to Carmen, without first obtaining Brent's consent. Carmen cannot enforce the contract against Brent. ● This rule has several exceptions:

1. A contract cannot prevent an assignment of the right to receive funds. This exception exists to encourage the free flow of funds and credit in modern business settings.
2. The assignment of ownership rights in real estate often cannot be prohibited because such a prohibition is contrary to public policy in most states. Prohibitions of this kind are called restraints against **alienation** (the voluntary transfer of land ownership).
3. The assignment of negotiable instruments (see Chapter 18) cannot be prohibited.
4. In a contract for the sale of goods, the right to receive damages for breach of contract or for payment of an account owed may be assigned even though the sales contract prohibits such an assignment.[6]

Alienation The process of transferring land out of one's possession (thus "alienating" the land from oneself).

Notice of Assignment

Once a valid assignment of rights has been made to a third party, the third party should notify the obligor of the assignment (for example, in Exhibit 13–1 on the previous page, Carmen should notify Brent). Giving notice is not legally necessary to establish the validity of the assignment because an assignment is effective immediately, whether or not notice is given. Two major problems arise, however, when notice of the assignment is *not* given to the obligor:

1. If the assignor assigns the same right to two different persons, the question arises as to which one has priority—that is, which one has the right to the performance by the obligor. Although the rule most often observed in the United States is that the first assignment in time is the first in right, some states follow the English rule, which basically gives priority to the first assignee who gives notice. **EXAMPLE 13.7** Brent owes Alex $5,000 on a contractual obligation. On May 1, Alex assigns this monetary claim to Carmen, but she does not give notice of the assignment to Brent. On June 1, for services Dorman has rendered to Alex, Alex assigns the same monetary claim (to collect $5,000 from Brent) to Dorman. Dorman immediately notifies Brent of the assignment. In the majority of states, Carmen would have priority because the assignment to her was first in time. In some states, however, Dorman would have priority because he gave first notice. ●
2. Until the obligor has notice of an assignment, the obligor can discharge his or her obligation by performance to the assignor, and this performance constitutes a discharge to the assignee. Once the obligor receives proper notice, only performance to the assignee can discharge the obligor's obligations. **EXAMPLE 13.8** Suppose that Alex, in the above example, assigns to Carmen his right to collect $5,000 from Brent, and Carmen does not give notice to Brent. Brent subsequently pays Alex the $5,000. Although the assignment was valid, Brent's payment to Alex is a discharge of the debt, and Carmen's failure to notify Brent of the assignment causes her to lose the right to collect the $5,000 from

---

6. UCC 2–210(2).

Brent. (Note that Carmen still has a claim against Alex for the $5,000.) If Carmen had given Brent notice of the assignment, however, Brent's payment to Alex would not have discharged the debt. •

Preventing Legal Disputes

Providing notice of assignment, though not legally required, is one of the best ways to avoid potential legal disputes over assignments. Whether you are the assignee or the assignor, you should inform the obligor of the assignment. An assignee who does not give notice may lose the right to performance, but failure to notify the obligor may have repercussions for the assignor as well. If no notice is given and the obligor performs the duty for the assignor, the assignee, to whom the right to receive performance was assigned, can sue the assignor for breach of contract. Litigation may also ensue if the assignor has assigned a right to two different parties, as may happen when rights that overlap (such as rights to receive various profits from a given enterprise) are assigned.

▶ Delegations

Delegation of Duties   The act of transferring to another all or part of one's duties arising under a contract.

Delegator   A party who transfers (delegates) her or his obligations under a contract to another party (called the *delegatee*).

Delegatee   A party to whom contractual obligations are transferred, or delegated.

Just as a party can transfer rights to a third party through an assignment, a party can also transfer duties. Duties are not assigned, however; they are *delegated*. Normally, a **delegation of duties** does not relieve the party making the delegation (the **delegator**) of the obligation to perform in the event that the party to whom the duty has been delegated (the **delegatee**) fails to perform. No special form is required to create a valid delegation of duties. As long as the delegator expresses an intention to make the delegation, it is effective; the delegator need not even use the word *delegate*. Exhibit 13–2 graphically illustrates delegation relationships.

Duties That Cannot Be Delegated

As a general rule, any duty can be delegated. This rule has some exceptions, however. Delegation is prohibited in the following circumstances:

1. When performance depends on the personal skill or talents of the obligor.
2. When special trust has been placed in the obligor.

• *Exhibit* 13–2 Delegation Relationships

In the delegation relationship illustrated here, Brent delegates his *duties* under a contract that he made with Alex to a third party, Carmen. Brent thus becomes the *delegator* and Carmen the *delegatee* of the contractual duties. Carmen now owes performance of the contractual duties to Alex. Note that a delegation of duties normally does not relieve the delegator (Brent) of liability if the delegatee (Carmen) fails to perform the contractual duties.

3. When performance by a third party will vary materially from that expected by the obligee (the one to whom performance is owed) under the contract.

4. When the contract expressly prohibits delegation.

The following examples will help to clarify the kinds of duties that can and cannot be delegated:

1. Brent contracts with Alex to tutor Alex about financial underwriting and investment banking. Brent, a businessperson known for his expertise in finance, delegates his duties to a third party, Carmen. This delegation is ineffective because Brent contracted to render a service that is founded on his *expertise* and Alex placed *special trust* in Brent's teaching ability. The delegation materially changes the performance that Alex expected under the contract.

2. Brent, a famous musician, contracts with Alex to *personally* perform at a concert. Then Brent receives a better offer elsewhere and delegates his duty to perform to another musician, Miles. Regardless of Miles's musical talents, the delegation is not effective without Alex's consent because the contract was for *personal* performance.

3. Brent, an accountant, contracts to perform annual audits of Alex's business records for the next five years. The contract states that Brent must provide the services himself and cannot delegate these duties to another. Two years later, Brent is busy on other projects and delegates his obligations to perform Alex's audit to Arianna, who is a certified public accountant at the same firm. This delegation is not effective because the contract *expressly prohibited* delegation.

4. Alex is a wealthy philanthropist who recently created a charitable foundation. Alex has known Brent for twenty years and knows that Brent shares his beliefs on many humanitarian issues. He contracts with Brent to be in charge of allocating funds among various charitable causes. Six months later, Brent is experiencing health problems and delegates his duties to Drew. Alex does not approve of Drew as a replacement. In this situation, Alex can claim the delegation was not effective because it *materially altered his expectations* under the contract. Alex had reasonable expectations about the types of charities to which Brent would give the foundation's funds, and substituting Drew's performance materially changes those expectations.

5. Brent contracts with Alex to pick up and deliver heavy construction machinery to Alex's property. Brent delegates this duty to Carmen, who is in the business of delivering heavy machinery. This delegation is effective. The performance required is of a routine and non-personal nature, and the delegation does not change Alex's expectations under the contract.

Effect of a Delegation

If a delegation of duties is enforceable, the *obligee* (the one to whom performance is owed) must accept performance from the delegatee (the one to whom the duties are delegated). **EXAMPLE 13.9** In the fifth example in the above list, Brent delegates his duty (to pick up and deliver heavy construction machinery to Alex's property) to Carmen. In that situation, Alex (the obligee) must accept performance from Carmen (the delegatee) because the delegation was effective. The obligee can legally refuse performance from the delegatee only if the duty is one that cannot be delegated. •

A valid delegation of duties does not relieve the delegator of obligations under the contract.[7] **EXAMPLE 13.10** In the preceding example, if Carmen (the delegatee) fails to perform, Brent (the delegator) is still liable to Alex (the obligee). The obligee can also hold the delegatee liable if the delegatee made a promise of performance that will directly benefit the

COMPARE In an assignment, the assignor's original contract rights are extinguished after the assignment. In a delegation, the delegator remains liable for performance under the contract if the delegatee fails to perform.

---

7. For a classic case on this issue, see *Crane Ice Cream Co. v. Terminal Freezing & Heating Co.*, 147 Md. 588, 128 A. 280 (1925).

obligee. In this situation, there is an "assumption of duty" on the part of the delegatee, and breach of this duty makes the delegatee liable to the obligee. For example, if Carmen (the delegatee) promises Brent (the delegator), in a contract, to pick up and deliver the construction equipment to Alex's property but fails to do so, Alex (the obligee) can sue Brent, Carmen, or both. ● Although there are many exceptions, the general rule today is that the obligee can sue both the delegatee and the delegator.

The *Concept Summary* below summarizes the basic principles of the laws governing assignments and delegations.

"Assignment of All Rights"

Sometimes, a contract provides for an "assignment of all rights." The traditional view was that under this type of assignment, the assignee did not assume any duties. This view was based on the theory that the assignee's agreement to accept the benefits of the contract was not sufficient to imply a promise to assume the duties of the contract.

Modern authorities, however, take the view that the probable intent in using such general words is to create both an assignment of rights and an assumption of duties.[8] Therefore, when general words are used (for example, "I assign the contract" or "all my rights under the contract"), the contract is construed as implying both an assignment of rights and an assumption of duties. (See the *Business Application* feature at the end of this chapter for factors that should be considered when dealing with assignments and delegations.)

 Third Party Beneficiaries

As mentioned earlier in this chapter, to have contractual rights, a person normally must be a party to the contract. In other words, privity of contract must exist. An exception to the doctrine of privity exists when the original parties to the contract intend, *at the time of contracting,* that the contract performance directly benefit a third person. In this situation,

---

8. See UCC 2–210(1), (4); and *Restatement (Second) of Contracts*, Section 328.

Concept Summary Assignments and Delegations		
Which rights can be assigned, and which duties can be delegated?	**All rights can be assigned *unless:*** 1. A statute expressly prohibits assignment. 2. The contract is for personal services. 3. The assignment will materially alter the obligor's risk or duties. 4. The contract prohibits assignment.	**All duties can be delegated *unless:*** 1. Performance depends on the obligor's personal skills or talents. 2. Special trust has been placed in the obligor. 3. Performance by a third party will vary materially from that expected by the obligee. 4. The contract prohibits delegation.
What if the contract prohibits assignment or delegation?	**No rights can be assigned *except:*** 1. Rights to receive funds. 2. Ownership rights in real estate. 3. Rights to negotiable instruments. 4. Rights to payments under a sales contract or damages for breach of a sales contract.	**No duties can be delegated.**
What is the effect on the original party's rights?	On a valid assignment, effective immediately, the original party (assignor) no longer has any rights under the contract.	On a valid delegation, if the delegatee fails to perform, the original party (delegator) is liable to the obligee (who may also hold the delegatee liable).

Third Party Beneficiary   One for whose benefit a promise is made in a contract but who is not a party to the contract.

Intended Beneficiary   A third party for whose benefit a contract is formed. An intended beneficiary can sue the promisor if such a contract is breached.

the third person becomes a **third party beneficiary** of the contract. As an **intended beneficiary** of the contract, the third party has legal rights and can sue the promisor directly for breach of the contract.

Who, though, is the promisor? In bilateral contracts, both parties to the contract are promisors because they both make promises that can be enforced. In third party beneficiary contracts, courts determine the identity of the promisor by asking which party made the promise that benefits the third party—that person is the promisor. Allowing the third party to sue the promisor directly in effect circumvents the "middle person" (the promisee) and thus reduces the burden on the courts. Otherwise, the third party would sue the promisee, who would then sue the promisor.

A classic case in the area of third party beneficiary contracts is *Lawrence v. Fox*—a case decided in 1859. In the *Lawrence* case, which is presented as this chapter's *Landmark in the Law* feature, the court set aside the traditional requirement of privity and allowed a third party to bring a suit directly against the promisor.

Types of Intended Beneficiaries

The law distinguishes between *intended* beneficiaries and *incidental* beneficiaries. Only intended beneficiaries acquire legal rights in a contract. One type of intended beneficiary is a *creditor beneficiary*. Like the plaintiff in *Lawrence v. Fox,* a creditor beneficiary benefits from a contract in which one party (the promisor) promises another party (the promisee) to pay a debt that the promisee owes to a third party (the creditor beneficiary). As an intended beneficiary, the creditor beneficiary can sue the promisor directly to enforce the contract.

Another type of intended beneficiary is a *donee* beneficiary. When a contract is made for the express purpose of giving a *gift* to a third party, the third party (the donee beneficiary) can sue the promisor directly to enforce the promise.[9] The most common donee beneficiary contract is a life insurance contract. **EXAMPLE 13.11** Akins (the promisee) pays premiums to Standard Life, a life insurance company, and Standard Life (the promisor) promises to pay a certain amount on Akins's death to anyone Akins designates as a beneficiary. The designated beneficiary is a donee beneficiary under the life insurance policy and can enforce the promise made by the insurance company to pay her or him on Akins's death. ●

As the law concerning third party beneficiaries evolved, numerous cases arose in which the third party beneficiary did not fit readily into either the creditor beneficiary or the donee beneficiary category. Thus, the modern view, and the one adopted by the *Restatement (Second) of Contracts*, does not draw such clear lines and distinguishes only between intended beneficiaries (who can sue to enforce contracts made for their benefit) and incidental beneficiaries (who cannot sue, as will be discussed shortly).

When the Rights of an Intended Beneficiary Vest

An intended third party beneficiary cannot enforce a contract against the original parties until the rights of the third party have *vested,* meaning that the rights have taken effect and cannot be taken away. Until these rights have vested, the original parties to the contract—the promisor and the promisee—can modify or rescind the contract without the consent of the third party. When do the rights of third parties vest? Generally, the rights vest when one of the following occurs:

1. When the third party demonstrates express consent to the agreement, such as by sending a letter or note acknowledging awareness of, and consent to, a contract formed for her or his benefit.

---

9. This principle was first enunciated in *Seaver v. Ransom,* 224 N.Y. 233, 120 N.E. 639 (1918).

Landmark in the Law   *Lawrence v. Fox* (1859)

In 1859, the New York Court of Appeals (that state's highest court) decided a case, *Lawrence v. Fox*,[a] in which the court departed from the doctrine of privity of contract and allowed a third party to sue the promisor directly. Prior to that time, contractual liability had always been limited to the parties to the contract.

Case Background   The case involved three parties—Holly, Lawrence, and Fox. Holly had borrowed $300 from Lawrence. Shortly thereafter, Holly loaned $300 to Fox, who in return promised Holly that he would pay Holly's debt to Lawrence on the following day. When Lawrence failed in his attempts to obtain the $300 from Fox, he sued Fox to recover the funds.

Why didn't Lawrence sue Holly directly, rather than pursue the unusual route of suing Fox, which meant that his chances at recovery were much slimmer? According to one scholar, the answer to this question is that the "Holly" in this case was probably Merwin Spencer Hawley. Both Hawley and the defendant, Arthur Wellesley Fox, were prominent members of the business community in Buffalo, New York. Evidence at trial suggested that the debt Hawley owed Lawrence was a gambling debt. Because gambling was illegal under New York law, Lawrence could not recover directly from Hawley in court, as the contract would have been deemed illegal.[b]

The Issue before the Court and the Court's Ruling   In any event, the issue before the court was whether Lawrence, who was not a party to the Holly-Fox contract, could sue Fox directly to recover the $300. The court held that Lawrence could do so. It was manifestly "just," declared the court, to allow Lawrence to recover the funds from Fox. The court enunciated the principle of law that "[in the case of] a promise made for the benefit of another, he for whose benefit it is made may bring an action for its breach."

• **Application to Today's World**   *At the time this decision was rendered, allowing a third party to sue a promisor directly was a novel idea and represented a radical departure from contract law. Although privity of contract remained the guiding principle until after the turn of the century, in two leading cases decided in 1916[c] and 1918,[d] the New York Court of Appeals cited* Lawrence v. Fox *in justifying its departure from the principle of privity of contract. Since then, the third party beneficiary rule has been continuously expanded in scope.*

• **Relevant Web Sites**   To locate information on the Web concerning the *Lawrence v. Fox* decision, go to this text's Web site at www.cengage.com/blaw/blt, select "Chapter 13," and click on "URLs for Landmarks."

---

a. 20 N.Y. 268 (1859).
b. See Antony Jon Waters, "The Property in the Promise: A Study of the Third Party Beneficiary Rule," 98 *Harvard Law Review* 1109, 1168 (1985).

c. *MacPherson v. Buick Motor Co.,* 217 N.Y. 382, 111 N.E. 1050 (1916). This case will be discussed in Chapter 17 in the *Landmark in the Law* feature.
d. *Seaver v. Ransom,* 224 N.Y. 233, 120 N.E. 639 (1918).

---

2. When the third party materially alters his or her position in detrimental reliance on the contract, such as when a donee beneficiary contracts to have a home built in reliance on the receipt of funds promised to him or her in a donee beneficiary contract.

3. When the conditions for vesting are satisfied. For example, the rights of a beneficiary under a life insurance policy vest when the insured person dies.

If the contract expressly reserves to the contracting parties the right to cancel, rescind, or modify the contract, the rights of the third party beneficiary are subject to any changes that result. In such a situation, the vesting of the third party's rights does not terminate the power of the original contracting parties to alter their legal relationships.[10]

Intended versus Incidental Beneficiaries

Incidental Beneficiary   A third party who incidentally benefits from a contract but whose benefit was not the reason the contract was formed. An incidental beneficiary has no rights in a contract and cannot sue to have the contract enforced.

The benefit that an **incidental beneficiary** receives from a contract between two parties is unintentional. Because the benefit is *unintentional*, an incidental beneficiary cannot sue to enforce the contract. Exhibit 13–3 on the following page graphically illustrates the distinction between intended and incidental beneficiaries.

---

10. Defenses raised against third party beneficiaries are given in the *Restatement (Second) of Contracts,* Section 309.

• *Exhibit* **13–3** **Third Party Beneficiaries**

In determining whether a party is an intended or an incidental beneficiary, the courts focus on the parties' intent, as expressed in the contract language and implied by the surrounding circumstances. Any beneficiary who is not deemed an intended beneficiary is considered incidental. Although no single test can embrace all possible situations, courts often apply the *reasonable person* test: Would a reasonable person in the position of the beneficiary believe that the promisee intended to confer on the beneficiary the right to enforce the contract? In addition, the presence of one or more of the following factors strongly indicates that the third party is an intended beneficiary to the contract:

1. Performance is rendered directly to the third party.
2. The third party has the right to control the details of performance.
3. The third party is expressly designated as a beneficiary in the contract.

In the following case, a national beauty pageant organization and one of its state affiliates agreed that the national organization would accept the winner of the state contest as a competitor in the national pageant. When the state winner was asked to resign her title, she filed a suit to enforce the agreement to have herself declared a contestant in the national pageant. The national organization argued that she was an incidental, not an intended, beneficiary of the agreement.

Case 13.1   **Revels v. Miss America Organization**

Court of Appeals of North Carolina, 182 N.C.App. 334, 641 S.E.2d 721 (2007).
www.nccourts.org[a]

FACTS   The Miss North Carolina Pageant Organization, Inc. (MNCPO), is a franchisee of the Miss America Organization (MAO). Under the "Miss America Organization Official Franchise Agreement," the MNCPO conducts a public contest (the State Finals) to select Miss North Carolina and to prepare her for participation in the Miss America pageant (the National Finals).[b] In return, the MAO "accept[s] the winner of the State Finals . . . as a contestant in the National Finals." On June 22, 2002, the MNCPO designated

---

a. From the home page, click on "Court Opinions." In the result, under "Court of Appeals" heading, click on "2007." Then scroll down to the "20 March 2007" section and click on the name of the case to access the opinion. The North Carolina Administrative Office of the Courts maintains this Web site.

b. A *franchise* is an arrangement by which the owner of a trademark, or other intellectual property, licenses the use of the mark to another party under specific conditions (see Chapter 26).

Case 13.1–Continued

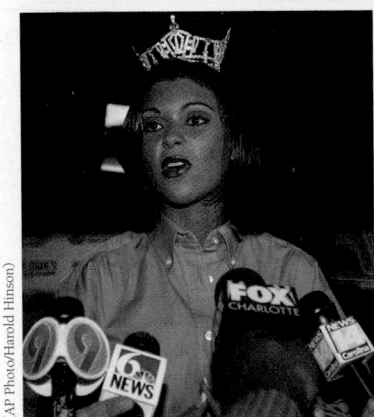

Rebekah Revels talks to reporters in Concord, North Carolina. Was she an intended beneficiary of the contract with the beauty pageant organizations?

Rebekah Revels "Miss North Carolina 2002." On July 19, the MAO received an anonymous e-mail (which was later determined to have been sent by Revels's ex-boyfriend), implying that she had formerly cohabited with a "male non-relative" and that nude photos of her existed. Revels confirmed the existence of the photos. On July 22, the MAO and the MNCPO asked Revels to resign as Miss North Carolina and told her that if she refused, she would be excluded from competing in the National Finals. On July 23, she resigned. She then filed a suit in a North Carolina state court against the MAO, the MNCPO, and others, asserting, among other things, breach of contract. The court issued a summary judgment in the MAO's favor. Revels appealed this judgment to a state intermediate appellate court.

ISSUE   Was Revels an intended beneficiary of the contract between the MAO and the MNCPO?

DECISION   No. The state appellate court affirmed the lower court's judgment in favor of the MAO. Revels was an incidental rather than an intended beneficiary.

REASON   The reviewing court held that "in order to establish a claim as a third-party beneficiary, plaintiff must show (1) that a contract exists between two persons or entities; (2) that the contract is valid and enforceable; and (3) that the contract was executed for the direct, and not incidental, benefit of the third party." The court pointed out that under that test, Revels was an incidental beneficiary of the agreement between the MAO and the MNCPO. Although the agreement provided that the MAO would accept the winner of the State Finals as a contestant in the National Finals, this did not establish that the two organizations intended to make the winner a direct beneficiary of the agreement. Thus, Revels was an incidental beneficiary and could not maintain an action against the MAO based on the agreement.

FOR CRITICAL ANALYSIS—Technological Consideration   *How might Revels's third party status with respect to the agreement between the MAO and the MNCPO have been affected if the contracting parties had conducted their business online? Explain.*

▶ Contract Discharge

Discharge   The termination of an obligation. In contract law, discharge occurs when the parties have fully performed their contractual obligations or when events, conduct of the parties, or operation of law releases the parties from performance.

Performance   In contract law, the fulfillment of one's duties arising under a contract with another; the normal way of discharging one's contractual obligations.

Condition   A qualification, provision, or clause in a contractual agreement, the occurrence or nonoccurrence of which creates, suspends, or terminates the obligations of the contracting parties.

The most common way to **discharge,** or terminate, one's contractual duties is by the **performance** of those duties. The duty to perform under a contract may be *conditioned* on the occurrence or nonoccurrence of a certain event, or the duty may be *absolute*. As shown in Exhibit 13–4 on the next page, in addition to performance, a contract can be discharged in numerous other ways, including discharge by agreement of the parties and discharge by operation of law.

Conditions of Performance

In most contracts, promises of performance are not expressly conditioned or qualified. Instead, they are *absolute promises*. They must be performed, or the party promising the act will be in breach of contract. **EXAMPLE 13.12** JoAnne contracts to sell Alfonso a painting for $10,000. The parties' promises are unconditional: JoAnne's transfer of the painting to Alfonso and Alfonso's payment of $10,000 to JoAnne. The payment does not have to be made if the painting is not transferred. ●

In some situations, however, contractual promises are conditioned. A **condition** is a possible future event, the occurrence or nonoccurrence of which will trigger the performance of a legal obligation or terminate an existing obligation under a contract. If the condition is not satisfied, the obligations of the parties are discharged. **EXAMPLE 13.13** Alfonso, in the above example, offers to purchase JoAnne's painting only if an independent appraisal indicates that it is worth at least $10,000. JoAnne accepts Alfonso's offer. Their obligations (promises) are conditioned on the outcome of the appraisal. Should this condition not be

• *Exhibit* **13–4 Contract Discharge**

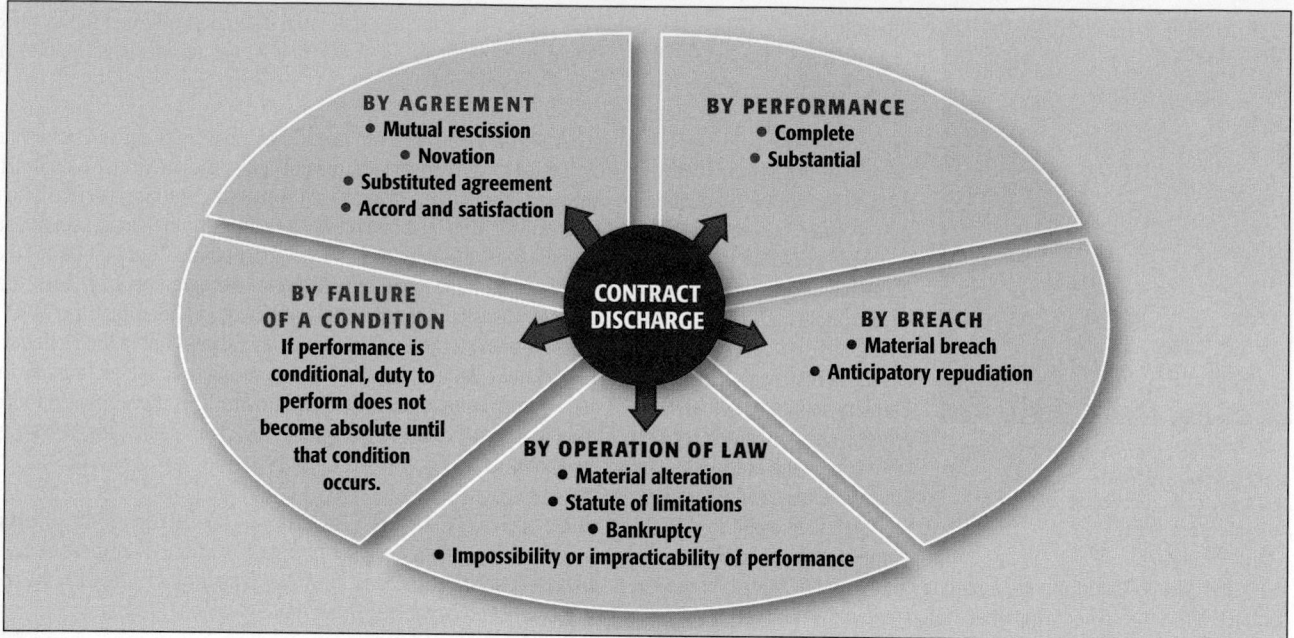

satisfied (for example, if the appraiser deems the value of the painting to be only $5,000), their obligations to each other are discharged and cannot be enforced. •

We look next at three types of conditions that can be present in any given contract: *conditions precedent, conditions subsequent,* and *concurrent conditions.*

CONDITIONS PRECEDENT   A condition that must be fulfilled before a party's promise becomes absolute is called a **condition precedent.** The condition precedes the absolute duty to perform, as in the JoAnne-Alfonso example just given. Real estate contracts frequently are conditioned on the buyer's ability to obtain financing. **EXAMPLE 13.14** Fisher promises to buy Calvin's house if Salvation Bank approves Fisher's mortgage application. The Fisher-Calvin contract is therefore subject to a condition precedent—the bank's approval of Fisher's mortgage application. If the bank does not approve the application, the contract will fail because the condition precedent was not met. • Insurance contracts frequently specify that certain conditions, such as passing a physical examination, must be met before the insurance company will be obligated to perform under the contract.

Condition Precedent   In a contractual agreement, a condition that must be met before a party's promise becomes absolute.

Condition Subsequent   A condition in a contract that, if it occurs, operates to terminate a party's absolute promise to perform.

CONDITIONS SUBSEQUENT   When a condition operates to terminate a party's absolute promise to perform, it is called a **condition subsequent.** The condition follows, or is subsequent to, the absolute duty to perform. If the condition occurs, the party need not perform any further. **EXAMPLE 13.15** A law firm hires Julia Darby, a recent law school graduate and a newly licensed attorney. Their contract provides that the firm's obligation to continue employing Darby is discharged if she fails to maintain her license to practice law. This is a condition subsequent because a failure to maintain the license will discharge a duty that has already arisen. •

Generally, conditions precedent are common, and conditions subsequent are rare. The *Restatement (Second) of Contracts* deletes the terms *condition subsequent* and *condition precedent* and refers to both simply as "conditions."[11]

---

11. *Restatement (Second) of Contracts,* Section 224. Note that the difference between conditions precedent and conditions subsequent can be important procedurally, because a plaintiff must prove a condition precedent whereas the defendant normally proves a condition subsequent.

Concurrent Conditions Conditions that must occur or be performed at the same time; they are mutually dependent. No obligations arise until these conditions are simultaneously performed.

Tender An unconditional offer to perform an obligation by a person who is ready, willing, and able to do so.

(Brian Teutsch/Creative Commons)

A woman shakes hands with a salesperson after agreeing to purchase a car. Suppose that the agreement is conditioned on the dealer's installing certain optional equipment. When the woman returns to the dealership the following day, she discovers that the optional features that were agreed on have not been added to the car. Is she still obligated to buy the car? Why or why not? What type of condition is this?

CONCURRENT CONDITIONS When each party's absolute duty to perform is conditioned on the other party's absolute duty to perform, **concurrent conditions** are present. These conditions exist only when the parties expressly or impliedly are to perform their respective duties *simultaneously*. **EXAMPLE 13.16** If a buyer promises to pay for goods when they are delivered by the seller, each party's absolute duty to perform is conditioned on the other party's absolute duty to perform. The buyer's duty to pay for the goods does not become absolute until the seller either delivers or attempts to deliver the goods. Likewise, the seller's duty to deliver the goods does not become absolute until the buyer pays or attempts to pay for the goods. Therefore, neither can recover from the other for breach without first tendering performance. ●

Discharge by Performance

The contract comes to an end when both parties fulfill their respective duties by performing the acts they have promised. Performance can also be accomplished by tender. **Tender** is an unconditional offer to perform by a person who is ready, willing, and able to do so. Therefore, a seller who places goods at the disposal of a buyer has tendered delivery and can demand payment according to the terms of the agreement. A buyer who offers to pay for goods has tendered payment and can demand delivery of the goods.

Once performance has been tendered, the party making the tender has done everything possible to carry out the terms of the contract. If the other party then refuses to perform, the party making the tender can consider the duty discharged and sue for breach of contract.

COMPLETE PERFORMANCE When a party performs exactly as agreed, there is no question as to whether the contract has been performed. When a party's performance is perfect, it is said to be complete.

Normally, conditions expressly stated in the contract must fully occur in all aspects for complete performance (strict performance) of the contract to take place. Any deviation breaches the contract and discharges the other party's obligations to perform. For example, most construction contracts require the builder to meet certain specifications. If the specifications are conditions, complete performance is required to avoid material breach. (*Material breach* will be discussed shortly.) If the conditions are met, the other party to the contract must then fulfill her or his obligation to pay the builder. If the specifications are not conditions and if the builder, without the other party's permission, fails to meet the specifications, performance is not complete. What effect does such a failure have on the other party's obligation to pay? The answer is part of the doctrine of *substantial performance*.

SUBSTANTIAL PERFORMANCE A party who in good faith performs substantially all of the terms of a contract can enforce the contract against the other party under the doctrine of substantial performance. Note that good faith is required. Intentionally failing to comply with the terms is a breach of the contract.

To qualify as *substantial performance,* the performance must not vary greatly from the performance promised in the contract, and it must create substantially the same benefits as those promised in the contract. If the omission, variance, or defect in performance is unimportant and can easily be compensated for by awarding damages, a court is likely to hold that the contract has been substantially performed. Courts decide whether the performance was substantial on a case-by-case basis, examining all of the facts of the particular situation. If performance is substantial, the other party's duty to perform remains absolute (except that the party can sue for damages due to the minor deviations).

EXAMPLE 13.17 A couple contracts with a construction company to build a house. The contract specifies that Brand X plasterboard be used for the walls. The builder cannot obtain Brand X plasterboard, and the buyers are on holiday in the mountains of Peru and are unreachable. The builder decides to install Brand Y instead, which he knows is identical in quality and durability to Brand X plasterboard. All other aspects of construction conform to the contract. In this situation, a court will likely hold that the builder substantially performed his end of the bargain, and therefore the couple will be obligated to pay the builder. Although the court might award the couple damages for the use of a different brand of plasterboard, the couple would still have to pay the contractor the contract price, less the amount of damages. ●

When a contract requires one party to meet the other party's demand, what percentage of compliance constitutes substantial performance? Does the duty of good faith require that this demand be put ahead of other customers' needs? Those were the questions in the following case.

Case 13.2　Wisconsin Electric Power Co. v. Union Pacific Railroad Co.

United States Court of Appeals, Seventh Circuit, 557 F.3d 504 (2009).
www.ca7.uscourts.gov[a]

HISTORICAL AND ENVIRONMENTAL SETTING *Japan attacked Pearl Harbor in Hawaii on December 7, 1941. Thrust suddenly into World War II, the United States began to ramp up the manufacture of war matériel. Fear of an invasion of the West Coast led some companies to move their facilities inland. Geneva Steel Company built a steel mill in Utah. Half a century later, Union Pacific Railroad Company was transporting iron ore from mines in Minnesota to the mill. On the return trips, the cars could be loaded with coal or other resources for delivery in the Upper Midwest. In 2001, Geneva Steel declared bankruptcy. Three years later, the mill stopped buying iron ore and closed.*

A Union Pacific freight train.

FACTS In 1999, Wisconsin Electric Power Company (WEPCO) contracted with Union Pacific to transport coal to WEPCO from mines in Colorado. The contract required WEPCO to notify Union Pacific monthly of how many tons of coal (within a certain maximum) it wanted shipped the next month. Union Pacific was to make "good faith reasonable efforts" to meet the schedule. The contract also required WEPCO to supply the railcars. When WEPCO did not supply the railcars, however, Union Pacific used its own railcars to deliver 84 percent of the requested coal. Claiming that the minimum percentage should have exceeded 90 percent and that Union Pacific was shipping less because other customers paid higher rates, WEPCO filed a suit in a federal district court against the railroad for breach of contract. The court issued a summary judgment in the defendant's favor. WEPCO appealed.

ISSUE Does "84 percent" constitute substantial performance of this contract?

DECISION Yes. The U.S. Court of Appeals for the Seventh Circuit affirmed the lower court's judgment. Union Pacific did not breach its duty of good faith performance.

REASON The contract did not require Union Pacific to comply strictly with WEPCO's schedule—Union Pacific merely had to make "good faith reasonable efforts." Also, the contract required Union Pacific to transport tonnages that WEPCO specified only if WEPCO supplied the railcars for the shipment. But WEPCO had failed to provide the railcars for the deliveries that it cited in charging Union Pacific with breach. As for the allegation that Union Pacific was putting other, higher-paying customers' requests ahead of WEPCO's demands, good faith does not require a contracting party to put one customer ahead of others "even if the others are paying you more." A party is entitled to protect its own economic interest. WEPCO was asking for "an unmanageable judicial task—that of working out an equitable allocation of Union Pacific's railcars among its various customers."

FOR CRITICAL ANALYSIS—Economic Consideration
Why would a different customer have paid a higher rate than WEPCO to Union Pacific for the transport of resources or other products?

a. In the left-hand column, click on "Opinions." On that page, in the "Case Number:" box, type "08-2693" and click on "List Case(s)." In the result, click on the appropriate link to access the opinion. The U.S. Court of Appeals for the Seventh Circuit maintains this Web site.

PERFORMANCE TO THE SATISFACTION OF ANOTHER Contracts often state that completed work must personally satisfy one of the parties or a third person. The question is whether this satisfaction becomes a condition precedent, requiring actual personal satisfaction or approval for discharge, or whether the test of satisfaction is performance that would satisfy a *reasonable person* (substantial performance).

(AGRR 4059/Creative Commons)

ON THE WEB For a summary of
how contracts may be discharged and
other principles of contract law, go to
contracts.lawyers.com, and click on the
"Terminating a Contract" link.

When the subject matter of the contract is *personal,* a contract to be performed to the
satisfaction of one of the parties is conditioned, and performance must actually satisfy that
party. For example, contracts for portraits, works of art, and tailoring are considered personal. Therefore, only the personal satisfaction of the party fulfills the condition—unless a
court finds that the party is expressing dissatisfaction only to avoid payment or otherwise
is not acting in good faith.

Most other contracts need to be performed only to the satisfaction of a reasonable person unless they *expressly state otherwise.* When such contracts require performance to the
satisfaction of a third party (for example, "to the satisfaction of Robert Ames, the supervising engineer"), the courts are divided. A majority of courts require the work to be satisfactory to a reasonable person, but some courts hold that the personal satisfaction of the third
party designated in the contract (Robert Ames, in this example) must be met. Again, the
personal judgment must be made honestly, or the condition will be excused.

Breach of Contract The failure, without
legal excuse, of a promisor to perform the
obligations of a contract.

MATERIAL BREACH OF CONTRACT   A **breach of contract** is the nonperformance of
a contractual duty. A breach is *material* when performance is not at least substantial.[12] If
there is a material breach, the nonbreaching party is excused from the performance of
contractual duties and can sue for damages caused by the breach. If the breach is *minor*
(not material), the nonbreaching party's duty to perform may
sometimes be suspended until the breach is remedied, but the
duty is not entirely excused. Once the minor breach is cured, the
nonbreaching party must resume performance of the contractual
obligations.

Any breach entitles the nonbreaching party to sue for damages, but only a material breach discharges the nonbreaching
party from the contract. The policy underlying these rules is that
contracts should go forward when only minor problems occur,
but contracts should be terminated if major problems arise.[13]

CASE EXAMPLE 13.18 Su Yong Kim sold an apartment building in
Portland, Oregon. At the time of the sale, the building's plumbing
violated the city's housing code. The contract therefore included
a clause stating that the seller (Kim) agreed to correct the violations within eight months after the contract was signed. A year
later, Kim still had not made the necessary repairs, and the new
owners were being fined by the city for continuing code violations. The buyers stopped making payments under the contract,
and the dispute ended up in court. The court found that the
seller's failure to make the required repairs was a material breach
of the contract because it defeated the purpose of the contract.

(Brendan McDermid/Reuters/Corbis Collection: Reuters)

*Radio personality Howard Stern holds a news conference during
which he says that he will sue his former employer, CBS, for allegedly
breaching his contract. What would constitute a true breach of his
contract? How could he be compensated?*

The buyers had purchased the building to lease it out to tenants, but instead they were
losing tenants and paying fines to the city due to the substandard plumbing. Because Kim's
breach was material, the buyers were not obligated to continue to perform their obligation
to make payments under the contract.[14] ●

Anticipatory Repudiation An assertion
or action by a party indicating that he or
she will not perform an obligation that the
party is contractually obligated to perform
at a future time.

ANTICIPATORY REPUDIATION OF A CONTRACT   Before either party to a contract has
a duty to perform, one of the parties may refuse to perform her or his contractual obligations. This is called **anticipatory repudiation.**[15] When anticipatory repudiation occurs, it
is treated as a material breach of contract, and the nonbreaching party is permitted to bring

---

12. *Restatement (Second) of Contracts,* Section 241.
13. See UCC 2–612, which deals with installment contracts for the sale of goods.
14. *Kim v. Park,* 192 Or.App. 365, 86 P.3d 63 (2004).
15. *Restatement (Second) of Contracts,* Section 253; and UCC 2–610.

an action for damages immediately, even though the scheduled time for performance under the contract may still be in the future.[16] Until the nonbreaching party treats this early repudiation as a breach, however, the breaching party can retract the anticipatory repudiation by proper notice and restore the parties to their original obligations.[17]

An anticipatory repudiation is treated as a present, material breach for two reasons. First, the nonbreaching party should not be required to remain ready and willing to perform when the other party has already repudiated the contract. Second, the nonbreaching party should have the opportunity to seek a similar contract elsewhere and may have the duty to do so to minimize his or her loss.

Quite often, an anticipatory repudiation occurs when a sharp fluctuation in market prices creates a situation in which performance of the contract would be extremely unfavorable to one of the parties. **EXAMPLE 13.19** Shasta Corporation contracts to manufacture and sell 100,000 personal computers to New Age, Inc., a retailer of computer equipment. Delivery is to be made two months from the date of the contract. One month later, three suppliers of computer parts raise their prices to Shasta. Because of these higher prices, Shasta stands to lose $500,000 if it sells the computers to New Age at the contract price. Shasta writes to New Age, stating that it cannot deliver the 100,000 computers at the contract price. Even though you may sympathize with Shasta, its letter is an anticipatory repudiation of the contract. New Age can treat the repudiation as a material breach and immediately pursue remedies, even though the contract delivery date is still a month away. •

Discharge by Agreement

Any contract can be discharged by agreement of the parties. The agreement can be contained in the original contract, or the parties can form a new contract for the express purpose of discharging the original contract.

DISCHARGE BY RESCISSION   As mentioned in previous chapters, rescission is the process in which the parties cancel the contract and are returned to the positions they occupied prior to the contract's formation. For *mutual rescission* to take place, the parties must make another agreement that also satisfies the legal requirements for a contract—there must be an *offer,* an *acceptance,* and *consideration.* Ordinarily, if the parties agree to rescind the original contract, their promises not to perform those acts promised in the original contract will be legal consideration for the second contract. Agreements to rescind executory contracts (in which neither party has performed) are enforceable even if they are made orally and the original agreement was in writing. Under the Uniform Commercial Code, however, an agreement rescinding a contract for the sale of goods, regardless of price, must be in writing when the contract requires a written rescission. Also, agreements to rescind contracts involving transfers of realty must be evidenced by a writing.

When one party has fully performed, an agreement to rescind the original contract usually is not enforceable unless additional consideration or restitution is made. Because the performing party has received no consideration for the promise to call off the original bargain, additional consideration is necessary.

DISCHARGE BY NOVATION   The process of **novation** substitutes a third party for one of the original parties. Essentially, the parties to the original contract and one or more new

REMEMBER The risks that prices will fluctuate and values will change are ordinary business risks for which the law does not provide relief.

Novation The substitution, by agreement, of a new contract for an old one, with the rights under the old one being terminated. Typically, novation involves the substitution of a new person who is responsible for the contract and the removal of the original party's rights and duties under the contract.

---

16. The doctrine of anticipatory repudiation first arose in the landmark case of *Hochster v. De La Tour,* 2 Ellis and Blackburn Reports 678 (1853), when an English court recognized the delay and expense inherent in a rule requiring a nonbreaching party to wait until the time of performance before suing for an anticipatory repudiation.

17. See UCC 2–611.

parties all get together and agree to the substitution. The requirements of a novation are as follows:

1. The existence of a previous, valid obligation.
2. Agreement by all of the parties to a new contract.
3. The extinguishing of the old obligation (discharge of the prior party).
4. A new, valid contract.

EXAMPLE 13.20   Union Corporation contracts to sell its pharmaceutical division to British Pharmaceuticals, Ltd. Before the transfer is completed, Union, British Pharmaceuticals, and a third company, Otis Chemicals, execute a new agreement to transfer all of British Pharmaceuticals' rights and duties in the transaction to Otis Chemicals. As long as the new contract is supported by consideration, the novation will discharge the original contract (between Union and British Pharmaceuticals) and replace it with the new contract (between Union and Otis Chemicals). ●

A novation expressly or impliedly revokes and discharges a prior contract. The parties involved may expressly state in the new contract that the old contract is now discharged. If the parties do not expressly discharge the old contract, it will be impliedly discharged if the new contract's terms are inconsistent with the old contract's terms.

DISCHARGE BY ACCORD AND SATISFACTION   As Chapter 11 explained, in an *accord* and *satisfaction,* the parties agree to accept performance different from the performance originally promised. An *accord* is an executory contract (one that has not yet been performed) to perform some act to satisfy an existing contractual duty that is not yet discharged.[18] A *satisfaction* is the performance of the accord agreement. An *accord* and its *satisfaction* discharge the original contractual obligation.

Once the accord has been made, the original obligation is merely suspended until the accord agreement is fully performed. If it is not performed, the party to whom performance is owed can bring an action on the original obligation or for breach of the accord. **EXAMPLE 13.21**   Shep obtains a judgment against Marla for $8,000. Later, both parties agree that the judgment can be satisfied by Marla's transfer of her automobile to Shep. This agreement to accept the auto in lieu of $8,000 in cash is the accord. If Marla transfers her automobile to Shep, the accord agreement is fully performed, and the $8,000 debt is discharged. If Marla refuses to transfer her car, the accord is breached. Because the original obligation is merely suspended, Shep can sue to enforce the judgment for $8,000 in cash or bring an action for breach of the accord. ●

Discharge by Operation of Law

Under some circumstances, contractual duties may be discharged by operation of law. These circumstances include material alteration of the contract, the running of the relevant statute of limitations, bankruptcy, and impossibility of performance.

CONTRACT ALTERATION   To discourage parties from altering written contracts, the law allows an innocent party to be discharged when one party has materially altered a written contract without the knowledge or consent of the other party. For example, if a party alters a material term of the contract—such as the quantity term or the price term—without the knowledge or consent of the other party, the party who was unaware of the alteration can treat the contract as discharged or terminated.

STATUTES OF LIMITATIONS   As mentioned earlier in this text, statutes of limitations limit the period during which a party can sue on a particular cause of action. After the applicable

"Law is a practical matter."
Roscoe Pound, 1870–1964
(American jurist)

---

18. *Restatement (Second) of Contracts,* Section 281.

limitations period has passed, a suit can no longer be brought. For example, the limitations period for bringing lawsuits for breach of oral contracts is usually two to three years; for written contracts, four to five years; and for recovery of amounts awarded in judgment, ten to twenty years, depending on state law. Lawsuits for breach of a contract for the sale of goods must be brought within four years after the cause of action has accrued. By original agreement, the parties can agree to reduce this four-year period to not less than a one-year period. They cannot, however, agree to extend it beyond the four-year limitations period.

BANKRUPTCY   A proceeding in bankruptcy attempts to allocate the debtor's assets to the creditors in a fair and equitable fashion. Once the assets have been allocated, the debtor receives a *discharge in bankruptcy* (see Chapter 21). A discharge in bankruptcy ordinarily bars the creditors from enforcing most of the debtor's contracts.

WHEN PERFORMANCE IS IMPOSSIBLE   After a contract has been made, performance may become impossible in an objective sense. This is known as **impossibility of performance** and may discharge the contract.[19] Performance may also become so difficult or costly due to some unforeseen event that a court will consider it commercially unfeasible, or impracticable, as will be discussed later in the chapter.

> **Impossibility of Performance**   A doctrine under which a party to a contract is relieved of his or her duty to perform when performance becomes objectively impossible or totally impracticable (through no fault of either party).

Objective Impossibility.   *Objective impossibility* ("It can't be done") must be distinguished from subjective impossibility ("I'm sorry, I simply can't do it"). An example of subjective impossibility occurs when a party cannot deliver goods on time because of freight car shortages or cannot make payment on time because the bank is closed. In effect, the nonperforming party is saying, "It is impossible for *me* to perform," rather than "It is impossible for *anyone* to perform." Accordingly, such excuses do not discharge a contract, and the nonperforming party is normally held in breach of contract. Three basic types of situations will generally qualify as grounds for the discharge of contractual obligations based on impossibility of performance:[20]

1. *When a party whose personal performance is essential to the completion of the contract dies or becomes incapacitated prior to performance.* **EXAMPLE 13.22** Fred, a famous dancer, contracts with Ethereal Dancing Guild to play a leading role in its new ballet. Before the ballet can be performed, Fred becomes ill and dies. His personal performance was essential to the completion of the contract. Thus, his death discharges the contract and his estate's liability for his nonperformance. •

2. *When the specific subject matter of the contract is destroyed.* **EXAMPLE 13.23** A-1 Farm Equipment agrees to sell Gudgel the green tractor on its lot and promises to have the tractor ready for Gudgel to pick up on Saturday. On Friday night, however, a truck veers off the nearby highway and smashes into the tractor, destroying it beyond repair. Because the contract was for this specific tractor, A-1's performance is rendered impossible owing to the accident. •

(Matt Biddulph/Creative Commons)

If a fire incapacitated a commercial bakery's oven, would the bakery be excused from performing its contracts until the oven was fixed? If the bakery had a contract for a special holiday order and the oven could not be fixed until after the holiday, would that contract be discharged? Why or why not?

---

19. *Restatement (Second) of Contracts*, Section 261.
20. *Restatement (Second) of Contracts*, Sections 262–266; and UCC 2–615.

3. *When a change in the law renders performance illegal.* **EXAMPLE 13.24** A contract to build an apartment building becomes impossible to perform when the zoning laws are changed to prohibit the construction of residential rental property at the planned location. A contract to paint a bridge using lead paint becomes impossible when the government passes new regulations forbidding the use of lead paint on bridges.[21] •

Temporary Impossibility.   An occurrence or event that makes performance temporarily impossible operates to suspend performance until the impossibility ceases. Then, ordinarily, the parties must perform the contract as originally planned. If, however, the lapse of time and the change in circumstances surrounding the contract make it substantially more burdensome for the parties to perform the promised acts, the contract is discharged.[22]

CASE EXAMPLE 13.25   On August 22, 2005, Keefe Hurwitz contracted to sell his home in Madisonville, Louisiana, to Wesley and Gwendolyn Payne for a price of $241,500. On August 26—just four days after the parties signed the contract—Hurricane Katrina made landfall and caused extensive damage to the house. The cost of repairs was estimated at $60,000, and Hurwitz would have to make the repairs before the closing date (see Chapter 36). Hurwitz did not have the funds and refused to pay $60,000 for the repairs only to sell the property to the Paynes for the previously agreed-on price of $241,500. The Paynes filed a lawsuit to enforce the contract. Hurwitz claimed that Hurricane Katrina had made it impossible for him to perform and had discharged his duties under the contract. The court, however, ruled that Hurricane Katrina had caused only a temporary impossibility. Hurwitz was required to pay for the necessary repairs and to perform the contract as written. In other words, he could not obtain a higher purchase price to offset the cost of the repairs.[23] •

Ethical Issue ⚖

Should the courts allow the defense of impossibility of performance to be used more often? The doctrine of impossibility of performance is applied only when the parties could not have reasonably foreseen, at the time the contract was formed, the event or events that rendered performance impossible. In some cases, the courts may seem to go too far in holding that the parties should have foreseen certain events or conditions, thus precluding the parties from avoiding contractual obligations under the doctrine of impossibility of performance. Actually, courts today are more likely to allow parties to raise this defense than were courts in the past, which rarely excused parties from performance under this doctrine. Indeed, until the latter part of the nineteenth century, courts were reluctant to discharge a contract even when performance appeared to be impossible. Generally, the courts must balance the freedom of parties to contract (and assume the risks involved) against the injustice that may result when certain contractual obligations are enforced. If the courts allowed parties to raise impossibility of performance as a defense to contractual obligations more often, freedom of contract would suffer.

Commercial Impracticability   A doctrine under which a seller may be excused from performing a contract when (1) a contingency occurs, (2) the contingency's occurrence makes performance impracticable, and (3) the nonoccurrence of the contingency was a basic assumption on which the contract was made. Although UCC Section 2–615 expressly frees only sellers under this doctrine, courts have not distinguished between buyers and sellers in applying it.

COMMERCIAL IMPRACTICABILITY   Courts may excuse parties from their performance obligations when the performance becomes much more difficult or expensive than the parties originally contemplated at the time the contract was formed. For someone to invoke the doctrine of **commercial impracticability** successfully, however, the anticipated performance must become *extremely* difficult or costly.[24]

---

21. *M. J. Paquet, Inc. v. New Jersey Department of Transportation,* 171 N.J. 378, 794 A.2d 141 (2002).

22. For a leading case, see *Autry v. Republic Productions,* 30 Cal.2d 144, 180 P.2d 888 (1947). The case involved an actor, Gene Autry, who was temporarily unable to perform a contract because he was drafted to serve in World War II. After the war, the value of the dollar had declined so much that performance of the contract would have been substantially burdensome to him. Hence, Autry's contract was discharged.

23. *Payne v. Hurwitz,* 978 So.2d 1000 (La.App. 1st Cir. 2008).

24. *Restatement (Second) of Contracts,* Section 264.

NOTE The doctrine of commercial impracticability does not provide relief from such events as ordinary price increases or easily predictable changes in the weather.

The added burden of performing not only must be extreme but also *must not have been known by the parties when the contract was made.* For instance, in one classic case, a court held that a contract could be discharged because a party would have to pay ten times more than the original estimate to excavate a certain amount of gravel.[25] In another case, the court allowed a party to rescind a contract for the sale of land because of a potential problem with contaminated groundwater under the land. The court found that "the potential for substantial and unbargained-for" liability made contract performance economically impracticable. Interestingly, the court in that case also noted that the possibility of "environmental degradation with consequences extending well beyond the parties' land sale" was just as important to its decision as the economic considerations.[26] (See this chapter's *Beyond Our Borders* feature for a discussion of Germany's approach to impracticability and impossibility of performance.)

The contract dispute in the following case arose out of the cancellation of a wedding reception due to a power failure. Is a power failure sufficient to invoke the doctrine of commercial impracticability?

25. *Mineral Park Land Co. v. Howard*, 172 Cal. 289, 156 P. 458 (1916).
26. *Cape-France Enterprises v. Estate of Peed*, 305 Mont. 513, 29 P.3d 1011 (2001).

Case 13.3   Facto v. Pantagis

Superior Court of New Jersey, Appellate Division, 390 N.J.Super. 227, 915 A.2d 59 (2007).
lawlibrary.rutgers.edu/search.shtml[a]

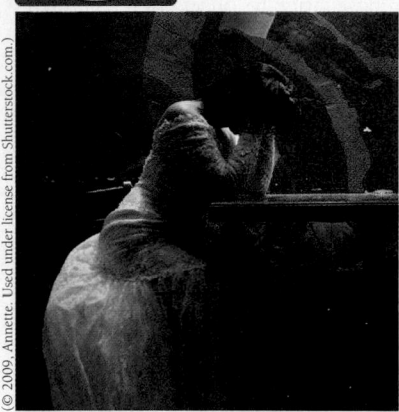

Did a power failure that left a wedding party in the dim light of an emergency generator, without air-conditioning or music, also constitute an "act of God," thus relieving the caterer of the duty to perform a contract?

FACTS Leo and Elizabeth Facto contracted with Snuffy Pantagis Enterprise, Inc., for the use of Pantagis Renaissance, a banquet hall in Scotch Plains, New Jersey, for a wedding reception in August 2002. The Factos paid the $10,578 price in advance. The contract excused Pantagis from performance "if it is prevented from doing so by an act of God (e.g., flood, power failure, etc.), or other unforeseen events or circumstances." Soon after the reception began, there was a power failure. The lights and the air-conditioning shut off. The band hired for the reception refused to play without electricity to power their instruments, and the lack of lighting prevented the photographer and videographer from taking pictures. The temperature was in the 90s, the humidity was high, and the guests quickly became uncomfortable. Three hours later, after a fight between a guest and a Pantagis employee, the emergency lights began to fade, and the police evacuated the hall. The Factos filed a suit in a New Jersey state court against Pantagis, alleging breach of contract, among other things. The Factos sought to recover their prepayment, plus amounts paid to the band, the photographer, and the videographer. The court concluded that Pantagis did not breach the contract and dismissed the complaint. The Factos appealed to a state intermediate appellate court.

ISSUE Can a power failure constitute the kind of unexpected occurrence that relieves a party of the duty to perform a contract?

DECISION Yes. The state intermediate appellate court agreed that the power failure relieved Pantagis of its contractual obligation, but held that Pantagis's inability to perform also relieved the Factos of their obligation. The court reversed the dismissal and remanded the case for an award to the Factos of the amount of their prepayment less the value of the services they received.

REASON The appellate court did not attribute any significance to the contract's reference to a power failure as "an act of God." The court reasoned that "even if a power failure caused by circumstances other than a natural event [was] not considered to be 'an act of God,' it still would constitute an unforeseen event or circumstance that would excuse performance." Of course, a power failure is not absolutely unforeseeable during hot summer months. But "absolute unforeseeability of a condition is not a prerequisite to the defense of impracticability." It is "the destruction or * * * deterioration of a specific thing necessary for the performance of the contract [that] makes performance impracticable." In this case, the power failure was area-wide and beyond the control of Pantagis, which was prevented from performing its contract. Because Pantagis was not in breach, however, did not mean that the Factos could not recover the amount they prepaid for the reception. When "one party to a contract is excused from

a. In the "Search for Cases by Party Name" section, select the "Appellate Division," type "Pantagis" in the "First Name:" box, and click on "Submit Form." In the result, click on the "click here to get this case" link to access the opinion. The Rutgers University School of Law in Camden, New Jersey, maintains this Web site.

Case 13.3–Continued

performance as a result of an unforeseen event that makes performance impracticable, the other party is also generally excused from performance." Therefore, the power failure that relieved Pantagis of its obligation to the Factos also relieved the Factos of their obligation to Pantagis.

FOR CRITICAL ANALYSIS—Social Consideration
If Pantagis offered to reschedule the reception, should it be absolved of the obligation to refund the Factos' prepayment? Explain.

Frustration of Purpose A court-created doctrine under which a party to a contract will be relieved of her or his duty to perform when the objective purpose for performance no longer exists (due to reasons beyond that party's control).

FRUSTRATION OF PURPOSE   Closely allied with the doctrine of commercial impracticability is the doctrine of **frustration of purpose.** In principle, a contract will be discharged if supervening circumstances make it impossible to attain the purpose both parties had in mind when making the contract. As with commercial impracticability, the supervening event must not have been foreseeable at the time of the contracting.[27]

27. See, for example, *East Capitol View Community Development Corp. v. Robinson,* 941 A.2d 1036 (D.C.App. 2008).

Beyond Our Borders   Impossibility or Impracticability of Performance in Germany

In the United States, when a party alleges that contract performance is impossible or impracticable because of circumstances unforeseen at the time the contract was formed, a court will either discharge the party's contractual obligations or hold the party to the contract. In other words, if a court agrees that the contract is impossible or impracticable to perform, the remedy is to rescind (cancel) the contract. Under German law, however, a court may adjust the terms of (reform) a contract in light of economic developments. If an unforeseen event affects the foundation of the agreement, the court can alter the contract's terms in view of the disruption in expectations, thus making the contract fair to the parties.

• **For Critical Analysis**
When a contract becomes impossible or impracticable to perform, which remedy would a businessperson prefer—rescission or reformation? Explain your answer.

Reviewing . . . Third Party Rights and Discharge

Val's Foods signs a contract to buy 1,500 pounds of basil from Sun Farms, a small organic herb grower, as long as an independent organization inspects and certifies that the crop contains no pesticide or herbicide residue. Val's has a contract with several restaurant chains to supply pesto and intends to use Sun Farms' basil in the pesto to fulfill these contracts. When Sun Farms is preparing to harvest the basil, an unexpected hailstorm destroys half the crop. Sun Farms attempts to purchase additional basil from other farms, but it is late in the season and the price is twice the normal market price. Sun Farms is too small to absorb this cost and immediately notifies Val's that it will not fulfill the contract. Using the information presented in the chapter, answer the following questions.

1. Suppose that Sun Farms supplies the basil that survived the storm but the basil does not pass the chemical-residue inspection. Which concept discussed in the chapter might allow Val's to refuse to perform the contract in this situation?
2. Under which legal theory or theories might Sun Farms claim that its obligation under the contract has been discharged by operation of law? Discuss fully.
3. Suppose that Sun Farms contacts every basil grower in the country and buys the last remaining chemical-free basil anywhere. Nevertheless, Sun Farms is able to ship only 1,475 pounds to Val's. Would this fulfill Sun Farms' obligations to Val's? Why or why not?
4. Now suppose that Sun Farms sells its operations to Happy Valley Farms. As a part of the sale, all three parties agree that Happy Valley will provide the basil as stated under the original contract. What is this type of agreement called?

Business Application

Dealing with Third Party Rights*

Assignments of contractual rights and delegations of duties are common in the business world. As you discovered in this chapter, third party rights and duties stem from the law on assignments, delegations, and third party beneficiaries. A third party may even be unaware that he or she has rights in a contract, as can happen when a person is the beneficiary of a life insurance policy. In certain situations, businesses may wish to attempt to prohibit a third party from acquiring such rights.

The general rule, though, is that any contractual right or duty can be assigned or delegated unless the assignment or delegation is prohibited by (1) the contract, (2) a statute, or (3) other limitations.

For example, a tenant under a long-term lease contract may assign the lease to another party. To avoid such assignments, property owners often prohibit the assignment of the balance of a lease term unless the property owner's consent is obtained.

When a contract calls for the manufacture and sale of goods, the manufacturers may assign or delegate the production of such goods to a third party unless prohibited by the contract. Consequently, most purchase orders (contracts) have a clause that prohibits such assignments or delegations without the buyer's consent.

CHECKLIST FOR THE BUSINESSPERSON

1. **Determine whether you can assign or delegate your rights or duties under a contract to a third party.**
2. **If you can assign or delegate your contract rights or performance, attempt to determine your benefits and obligations, such as notice to customers, if you do make the assignment or delegation.**
3. **If you do not want your contract rights or duties to be assigned or delegated, insert a contract clause that prohibits assignment or delegation without your consent.**
4. **Whenever you might be a third party beneficiary to a contract, such as a creditor beneficiary, take steps to determine your rights.**

* This *Business Application* is not meant to substitute for the services of an attorney who is licensed to practice law in your state.

 Key Terms

alienation 314	condition precedent 322	intended beneficiary 318
anticipatory repudiation 325	condition subsequent 322	novation 326
assignee 312	delegatee 315	obligee 312
assignment 312	delegation of duties 315	obligor 312
assignor 312	delegator 315	performance 321
breach of contract 325	discharge 321	privity of contract 311
commercial impracticability 329	frustration of purpose 331	tender 323
concurrent conditions 323	impossibility of performance 328	third party beneficiary 318
condition 321	incidental beneficiary 319	

 Chapter Summary: Third Party Rights and Discharge

THIRD PARTY RIGHTS	
Assignments **(See pages 311–315.)**	1. An assignment is the transfer of rights under a contract to a third party. The person assigning the rights is the *assignor*, and the party to whom the rights are assigned is the *assignee*. The assignee has a right to demand performance from the other original party to the contract. 2. Generally, all rights can be assigned. For exceptions, see the *Concept Summary* on page 317.

Chapter Summary: Third Party Rights and Discharge—Continued

Assignments—Continued	3. The assignee should notify the obligor of the assignment. Although not legally required, notification avoids two potential problems:
	   a. If the assignor assigns the same right to two different persons, generally the first assignment in time is the first in right, but in some states the first assignee to give notice takes priority.
	   b. Until the obligor is notified of the assignment, the obligor can tender performance to the assignor. If the assignor accepts the performance, the obligor's duties under the contract are discharged without benefit to the assignee.

Delegations (See pages 315–317.)	1. A delegation is the transfer of duties under a contract to a third party (the *delegatee*), who then assumes the obligation of performing the contractual duties previously held by the one making the delegation (the *delegator*). 2. As a general rule, any duty can be delegated, except in the circumstances listed in the *Concept Summary* on page 317. 3. A valid delegation of duties does not relieve the delegator of obligations under the contract. If the delegatee fails to perform, the delegator is still liable to the obligee. 4. An "assignment of all rights" or an "assignment of the contract" is often construed to mean that both the rights and the duties arising under the contract are transferred to a third party.
Third Party Beneficiaries (See pages 317–321.)	A third party beneficiary contract is one made for the purpose of benefiting a third party. 1. *Intended beneficiary*—One for whose benefit a contract is created. When the promisor (the one making the contractual promise that benefits a third party) fails to perform as promised, the third party can sue the promisor directly. Examples of third party beneficiaries are creditor and donee beneficiaries. 2. *Incidental beneficiary*—A third party who indirectly (incidentally) benefits from a contract but for whose benefit the contract was not specifically intended. Incidental beneficiaries have no rights to the benefits received and cannot sue to have the contract enforced.
CONTRACT DISCHARGE	
Conditions of Performance (See pages 321–323.)	Contract obligations may be subject to the following types of conditions: 1. *Condition precedent*—A condition that must be fulfilled before a party's promise becomes absolute. 2. *Condition subsequent*—A condition that operates to terminate a party's absolute promise to perform. 3. *Concurrent conditions*—Conditions that must be performed simultaneously. Each party's absolute duty to perform is conditioned on the other party's absolute duty to perform.
Discharge by Performance (See pages 323–326.)	A contract may be discharged by complete (strict) performance or by substantial performance. In some instances, performance must be to the satisfaction of another. Totally inadequate performance constitutes a material breach of the contract. An anticipatory repudiation of a contract allows the other party to sue immediately for breach of contract.
Discharge by Agreement (See pages 326–327.)	Parties may agree to discharge their contractual obligations in several ways: 1. *By rescission*—The parties mutually agree to rescind (cancel) the contract. 2. *By novation*—A new party is substituted for one of the primary parties to a contract. 3. *By accord and satisfaction*—The parties agree to render and accept performance different from that on which they originally agreed.
Discharge by Operation of Law (See pages 327–331.)	Parties' obligations under contracts may be discharged by operation of law owing to one of the following: 1. Contract alteration. 2. Statutes of limitations. 3. Bankruptcy. 4. Impossibility of performance. 5. Impracticability of performance. 6. Frustration of purpose.

ExamPrep

ISSUE SPOTTERS

1 Eagle Company contracts to build a house for Frank. The contract states that "any assignment of this contract renders the contract void." After Eagle builds the house, but before Frank pays, Eagle assigns its right to payment to Good Credit Company. Can Good Credit enforce the contract against Frank? Why or why not?

2 Ready Foods contracts to buy from Speedy Distributors two hundred carloads of frozen pizzas. Before Ready or Speedy starts performing, can they call off the deal? What if Speedy has already shipped the pizzas? Explain your answers.

BEFORE THE TEST

Check your answers to the Issue Spotters, and at the same time, take the interactive quiz for this chapter. Go to **www.cengage.com/blaw/blt** and click on "Chapter 13." First, click on "Answers to Issue Spotters" to check your answers. Next, click on "Interactive Quiz" to assess your mastery of the concepts in this chapter. Then click on "Flashcards" to review this chapter's Key Term definitions.

For Review

Answers for the even-numbered questions in this For Review *section can be found on this text's accompanying Web site at* **www.cengage.com/blaw/blt**. *Select "Chapter 13" and click on "For Review."*

1 What is the difference between an assignment and a delegation?
2 What rights can be assigned despite a contract clause expressly prohibiting assignment?
3 What factors indicate that a third party beneficiary is an intended beneficiary?
4 How are most contracts discharged?
5 What is a contractual condition, and how might a condition affect contractual obligations?

Hypothetical Scenarios and Case Problems

13–1 Third Party Beneficiaries. Wilken owes Rivera $2,000. Howie promises Wilken that he will pay Rivera the $2,000 in return for Wilken's promise to give Howie's children guitar lessons. Is Rivera an intended beneficiary of the Howie-Wilken contract? Explain.

13–2 Anticipatory Repudiation. ABC Clothiers, Inc., has a contract with Taylor & Sons, a retailer, to deliver one thousand summer suits to Taylor's place of business on or before May 1. On April 1, Taylor senior receives a letter from ABC informing him that ABC will not be able to make the delivery as scheduled. Taylor is very upset, as he had planned a big ad campaign. He wants to file a suit against ABC immediately (April 2). Taylor's son, Tom, tells his father that filing a lawsuit is not proper until ABC actually fails to deliver the suits on May 1. Discuss fully who is correct, Taylor senior or Tom.

13–3 **Hypothetical Question with Sample Answer** Aron, a college student, signs a one-year lease agreement that runs from September 1 to August 31. The lease agreement specifies that the lease cannot be assigned without the land-

lord's consent. In late May, Aron decides not to go to summer school and assigns the balance of the lease (three months) to a close friend, Erica. The landlord objects to the assignment and denies Erica access to the apartment. Aron claims that Erica is financially sound and should be allowed the full rights and privileges of an assignee. Discuss fully whether the landlord or Aron is correct.

—For a sample answer to Question 13–3, go to Appendix E at the end of this text.

13–4 Impossibility of Performance. Millie contracted to sell Frank 1,000 bushels of corn to be grown on her farm. Owing to a drought during the growing season, Millie's yield was much less than anticipated, and she could deliver only 250 bushels to Frank. Frank accepted the lesser amount but sued Millie for breach of contract. Can Millie defend successfully on the basis of objective impossibility of performance? Explain.

13–5 Material Breach. Kermit Johnson formed FB&I Building Products, Inc., in Watertown, South Dakota, to sell building materials. In December 1998, FB&I contracted with Superior Truss

& Components in Minneota, Minnesota, "to exclusively sell Superior's open-faced wall panels, floor panels, roof trusses and other miscellaneous products." In March 2000, FB&I agreed to exclusively sell Component Manufacturing Co.'s building products in Colorado. Two months later, Superior learned of FB&I's deal with Component and terminated its contract with FB&I. That contract provided that on cancellation, "FB&I will be entitled to retain the customers that they continue to sell and service with Superior products." Superior refused to honor this provision. Between the cancellation of FB&I's contract and 2004, Superior made $2,327,528 in sales to FB&I customers without paying a commission. FB&I filed a suit in a South Dakota state court against Superior, alleging, in part, breach of contract and seeking the unpaid commissions. Superior insisted that FB&I had materially breached their contract, excusing Superior from performing. In whose favor should the court rule and why? [*FB&I Building Products, Inc. v. Superior Truss & Components, a Division of Banks Lumber, Inc.*, 727 N.W.2d 474 (S.D. 2007)]

13–6 **Case Problem with Sample Answer** National Association for Stock Car Auto Racing, Inc. (NASCAR), sanctions stock car races. NASCAR and Sprint Nextel Corp. agreed that Sprint would become the Official Series Sponsor of the NASCAR NEXTEL Cup Series in 2004. The agreement granted sponsorship exclusivity to Sprint and contained a list of "Competitors" who were barred from sponsoring Series's events. Excepted were existing sponsorships: in "Driver and Car Owner Agreements" between NASCAR and the cars' owners, NASCAR promised to "preserve and protect" those sponsorships, which could continue and be renewed despite Sprint's exclusivity. RCR Team #31, LLC, owns the #31 Car in the Series. Cingular Wireless, LLC, a Sprint competitor, had been #31 Car's primary sponsor since 2001. In 2007, Cingular changed its name to AT&T Mobility, LLC, and proposed a new paint scheme for the #31 Car that called for the Cingular logo to remain on the hood while the AT&T logo would be added on the rear quarter panel. NASCAR rejected the proposal. AT&T filed a suit in a federal district court against NASCAR, claiming, in part, that NASCAR was in breach of its "Driver and Car Owner Agreement" with RCR. Can AT&T maintain an action against NASCAR based on this agreement? Explain. [*AT&T Mobility, LLC v. National Association for Stock Car Auto Racing, Inc.*, 487 F.Supp.2d 1370 (N.D.Ga. 2007)]
—After you have answered Problem 13–6, compare your answer with the sample answer given on the Web site that accompanies this text. Go to **www.cengage.com/blaw/blt**, select "Chapter 13," and click on "Case Problem with Sample Answer."

13–7 **Breach of Contract.** Roger Bannister was the director of technical and product development for Bemis Co. He signed a covenant not to compete that prohibited him from working for a "conflicting organization" for eighteen months following his termination, but required Bemis to pay his salary if he was unable to find a job "consistent with his abilities and education." Bemis terminated Bannister. Mondi Packaging, a Bemis competitor, told him that it would like to offer him a job but could not do so because of the noncompete agreement. Bemis released Bannister from the agreement with respect to "all other companies than Mondi" and refused to pay his salary. Nine months later, Bannister accepted a position with Bancroft Bag, Inc., another Bemis competitor. He filed a suit in a federal district court against his former employer. Do these facts show a material breach of contract? If so, what is the appropriate remedy? Explain. [*Bannister v. Bemis Co.*, 556 F.3d 882 (8th Cir. 2009)]

13–8 **A Question of Ethics** *King County, Washington, hired Frank Coluccio Construction Co. (FCCC) to act as general contractor for a public works project involving the construction of a small utility tunnel under the Duwamish Waterway. FCCC hired Donald B. Murphy Contractors, Inc. (DBM), as a subcontractor. DBM was responsible for constructing an access shaft at the eastern end of the tunnel. Problems arose during construction, including a "blow-in" of the access shaft when it filled with water, soil, and debris. FCCC and DBM incurred substantial expenses from the repairs and delays. Under the project contract, King County was supposed to buy an insurance policy to "insure against physical loss or damage by perils included under an 'All Risk' Builder's Risk policy." Any claim under this policy was to be filed through the insured. King County, which had general property damage insurance, did not obtain an all-risk builder's risk policy. For the losses attributable to the blow-in, FCCC and DBM submitted builder's risk claims, which the county denied. FCCC filed a suit in a Washington state court against King County, alleging, among other claims, breach of contract. [Frank Coluccio Construction Co. v. King County, 136 Wash.App. 751, 150 P.3d 1147 (Div. 1 2007)]*

1 At the county's request, King County's property damage policy specifically excluded coverage of tunnels. The county drafted its contract with FCCC to require the all-risk builder's risk policy and authorize itself to "sponsor" claims. When FCCC and DBM filed their claims, the county secretly colluded with its property damage insurer to deny payment. What do these facts indicate about the county's ethics and legal liability in this situation?

2 Could DBM, as a third party to the contract between King County and FCCC, maintain an action on the contract against King County? Discuss.

3 All-risk insurance is a promise to pay on the "fortuitous" happening of a loss or damage from any cause except those that are specifically excluded. Payment usually is not made on a loss that, at the time the insurance was obtained, the claimant subjectively knew would occur. If a loss results from faulty workmanship on the part of a contractor, should the obligation to pay under an all-risk policy be discharged? Explain.

Critical Thinking and Writing Assignments

13–9 Critical Legal Thinking. The concept of substantial performance permits a party to be discharged from a contract even though the party has not fully performed her or his obligations according to the contract's terms. Is this fair? What policy interests are at issue here?

13–10 **Video Question** Go to this text's Web site at **www.cengage.com/blaw/blt** and select "Chapter 13." Click on "Video Questions" and view the video titled *Third Party Beneficiaries.* Then answer the following questions.

1 Discuss whether a valid contract was formed when Oscar and Vinny bet on the outcome of a football game. Would Vinny be able to enforce the contract in court?

2 Is the Fresh Air Fund an incidental or an intended beneficiary? Why?

3 Can Maria sue to enforce Vinny's promise to donate Oscar's winnings to the Fresh Air Fund?

Practical Internet Exercises

Go to this text's Web site at **www.cengage.com/blaw/blt**, select "Chapter 13," and click on "Practical Internet Exercises." There you will find the following Internet research exercises that you can perform to learn more about the topics covered in this chapter.

Practical Internet Exercise 13–1: LEGAL PERSPECTIVE—Anticipatory Repudiation

Practical Internet Exercise 13–2: MANAGEMENT PERSPECTIVE—Commercial Impracticability

Chapter 14

Breach and Remedies

(©Juriah Mosin, 2009. Used under license from Shutterstock.com)

Chapter Outline

- Damages
- Equitable Remedies
- Recovery Based on Quasi Contract
- Contract Provisions Limiting Remedies

Learning Objectives

After reading this chapter, you should be able to answer the following questions:

1. What is the difference between compensatory damages and consequential damages? What are nominal damages, and when do courts award nominal damages?

2. What is the standard measure of compensatory damages when a contract is breached? How are damages computed differently in construction contracts?

3. Under what circumstances is the remedy of rescission and restitution available?

4. When do courts grant specific performance as a remedy?

5. What is a limitation-of-liability clause, and when will courts enforce it?

Normally, people enter into contracts to secure some advantage. When it is no longer advantageous for a party to fulfill her or his contractual obligations, that party may *breach,* or fail to perform, the contract.[1] Once one party breaches the contract, the other party—the nonbreaching party—can choose one or more of several remedies. A *remedy* is the relief provided to an innocent party when the other party has breached the contract. It is the means employed to enforce a right or to redress an injury. While there may not be a remedy for "everything," as indicated in the chapter-opening quotation, there is a remedy available for nearly every contract breach.

The most common remedies available to a nonbreaching party under contract law include damages, rescission and restitution, specific performance, and reformation. As discussed in Chapter 1, courts distinguish between *remedies at law* and *remedies in equity.* Today, the remedy at law is normally monetary damages. We discuss this remedy in the first part of this chapter. Equitable remedies include rescission and restitution, specific

---

1. A *breach of contract* occurs when one party fails to perform part or all of the required duties under a contract. *Restatement (Second) of Contracts,* Section 235(2).

performance, and reformation, all of which we examine later in the chapter. Usually, a court will not award an equitable remedy unless the remedy at law is inadequate. In the final pages of this chapter, we look at some special legal doctrines and concepts relating to remedies.

Damages

A breach of contract entitles the nonbreaching party to sue for monetary damages. As you read in Chapter 4, tort law damages are designed to compensate a party for harm suffered as a result of another's wrongful act. In the context of contract law, damages are designed to compensate the nonbreaching party for the loss of the bargain. Often, courts say that innocent parties are to be placed in the position they would have occupied had the contract been fully performed.[2]

Types of Damages

There are basically four broad categories of damages:

1. Compensatory (to cover direct losses and costs).
2. Consequential (to cover indirect and foreseeable losses).
3. Punitive (to punish and deter wrongdoing).
4. Nominal (to recognize wrongdoing when no monetary loss is shown).

Compensatory and punitive damages were discussed in Chapter 4 in the context of tort law. Here, we look at these types of damages, as well as consequential and nominal damages, in the context of contract law.

COMPENSATORY DAMAGES   Damages that compensate the nonbreaching party for the *loss of the bargain* are known as *compensatory damages*. These damages compensate the injured party only for damages actually sustained and proved to have arisen directly from the loss of the bargain caused by the breach of contract. They simply replace what was lost because of the wrong or damage.

   The standard measure of compensatory damages is the difference between the value of the breaching party's promised performance under the contract and the value of her or his actual performance. This amount is reduced by any loss that the injured party has avoided.
   EXAMPLE 14.1   You contract with Marinot Industries to perform certain personal services exclusively for Marinot during August for a payment of $4,000. Marinot cancels the contract and is in breach. You are able to find another job during August but can earn only $3,000. You normally can sue Marinot for breach and recover $1,000 as compensatory damages. You may also recover from Marinot the amount that you spent to find the other job. ● Expenses that are directly incurred because of a breach of contract—such as those incurred to obtain performance from another source—are called **incidental damages**.

   The measurement of compensatory damages varies by type of contract. Certain types of contracts deserve special mention—contracts for the sale of goods, contracts for the sale of land, and construction contracts.

Sale of Goods.   In a contract for the sale of goods, the usual measure of compensatory damages is the difference between the contract price and the market price.[3] **EXAMPLE 14.2** Medik Laboratories contracts to buy ten model UTS 400 network servers from Cal Indus-

---

2. *Restatement (Second) of Contracts,* Section 347.

3. This is the difference between the contract price and the market price at the time and place at which the goods were to be delivered or tendered. [See UCC 2–708, 2–713, and 2–715(1).]

tries for $4,000 each. Cal Industries, however, fails to deliver the ten servers to Medik. The market price of the servers at the time Medik learns of the breach is $4,500. Therefore, Medik's measure of damages is $5,000 (10 × $500), plus any incidental damages (expenses) caused by the breach. ● When the buyer breaches and the seller has not yet produced the goods, compensatory damages normally equal the seller's lost profits on the sale, rather than the difference between the contract price and the market price.

ON THE WEB For a summary of how contracts may be breached and other information on contract law, go to **consumer-law.lawyers.com/ Contract-Termination.html**.

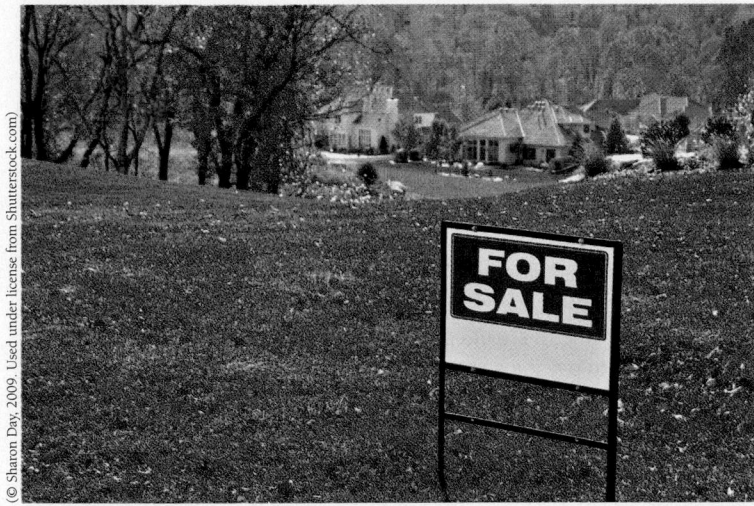

In principle, each parcel of land is unique. Therefore, a breach of the sales contract may lead to the remedy of specific performance. What happens if the property is already sold?

Sale of Land. Ordinarily, because each parcel of land is unique, the remedy for a seller's breach of a contract for a sale of real estate is specific performance—that is, the buyer is awarded the parcel of property for which he or she bargained (*specific performance* will be discussed more fully later in this chapter). When this remedy is unavailable (because the property has been sold, for example) or when the buyer is the party in breach, the measure of damages is typically the difference between the contract price and the market price of the land. The majority of states follow this rule.

Construction Contracts. The measure of damages in a building or construction contract varies depending on which party breaches and when the breach occurs. If the owner breaches *before performance has begun,* the contractor can recover only the profits that would have been made on the contract (that is, the total contract price less the cost of materials and labor). If the owner breaches *during performance,* the contractor can recover the profits plus the costs incurred in partially constructing the building. If the owner breaches *after the construction has been completed,* the contractor can recover the entire contract price plus interest.

When the contractor breaches the construction contract—either by failing to begin construction or by stopping work partway through the project—the measure of damages is the cost of completion, which includes reasonable compensation for any delay in performance. If the contractor finishes late, the measure of damages is the loss of use. Exhibit 14–1 summarizes the rules concerning the measurement of damages in breached construction contracts. (The *Business Application* feature at the end of this chapter offers some suggestions on what to do if you cannot perform.)

Consequential Damages Special damages that compensate for a loss that does not directly or immediately result from the breach (for example, lost profits). For the plaintiff to collect consequential damages, they must have been reasonably foreseeable at the time the breach or injury occurred.

CONSEQUENTIAL DAMAGES Foreseeable damages that result from a party's breach of contract are called **consequential damages**, or *special damages*. They differ from

● *Exhibit* 14–1 Measurement of Damages—Breach of Construction Contracts

PARTY IN BREACH	TIME OF BREACH	MEASUREMENT OF DAMAGES
Owner	Before construction has begun.	Profits (contract price less cost of materials and labor).
Owner	During construction.	Profits plus costs incurred up to time of breach.
Owner	After construction is completed.	Full contract price plus interest.
Contractor	Before construction has begun.	Cost in excess of contract price to complete work.
Contractor	Before construction is completed.	Generally, all costs incurred by owner to complete.

"A long dispute means that both parties are wrong."

Voltaire, 1694–1778
(French philosopher)

NOTE To avoid the risk of consequential damages, a seller can limit the buyer's remedies via contract.

Preventing Legal Disputes

compensatory damages in that they are caused by special circumstances beyond the contract itself and flow from the consequences, or results, of a breach.

When a seller fails to deliver goods, knowing that the buyer is planning to use or resell those goods immediately, a court may award consequential damages (in addition to compensatory damages) for the loss of profits from the planned resale. **EXAMPLE 14.3** Gilmore contracts to have a specific item shipped to her—one that she desperately needs to repair her printing press. In her contract with the shipper, Gilmore states that she must receive the item by Monday, or she will not be able to print her paper and will lose $3,000. If the shipper is late, Gilmore normally can recover the consequential damages caused by the delay (that is, the $3,000 in losses). •

To recover consequential damages, the breaching party must know (or have reason to know) that special circumstances will cause the nonbreaching party to suffer an additional loss.[4] See this chapter's *Landmark in the Law* feature for a discussion of *Hadley v. Baxendale*, a case decided in England in 1854.

It is sometimes impossible to prevent contract disputes. You should realize at the outset, though, that collecting damages through a court judgment requires litigation, which can be expensive and time consuming. Also, keep in mind that court judgments are often difficult to enforce, particularly if the breaching party does not have sufficient assets to pay the damages awarded.[5] For these reasons, most parties choose to settle their contract disputes before trial rather than litigate in hopes of being awarded—and being able to collect—damages (or other remedies). Another alternative you should consider is mediation, which can help reduce the cost of resolving a dispute and may allow for the possibility of future business transactions between the parties.

PUNITIVE DAMAGES Punitive, or exemplary, damages, generally are not awarded in an action for breach of contract. Such damages have no legitimate place in contract law because they are, in essence, penalties, and a breach of contract is not unlawful in a criminal sense. A contract is simply a civil relationship between the parties. The law may compensate one party for the loss of the bargain—no more and no less.

In a few situations, when a person's actions cause both a breach of contract and a tort, punitive damages may be available. Overall, though, punitive damages are almost never available in contract disputes.

Nominal Damages A small monetary award (often one dollar) granted to a plaintiff when no actual damage was suffered.

NOMINAL DAMAGES When no actual damage or financial loss results from a breach of contract and only a technical injury is involved, the court may award **nominal damages** to the innocent party. Nominal damages awards are often small, such as one dollar, but they do establish that the defendant acted wrongfully. Most lawsuits for nominal damages are brought as a matter of principle under the theory that a breach has occurred and some damages must be imposed regardless of actual loss.

EXAMPLE 14.4 Hernandez contracts to buy potatoes at fifty cents a pound from Stanley. Stanley breaches the contract and does not deliver the potatoes. Meanwhile, the price of potatoes falls. Hernandez is able to buy them in the open market at half the price he agreed to pay Stanley. Hernandez is clearly better off because of Stanley's breach. Thus, because Hernandez sustained only a technical injury and suffered no monetary loss, if he sues for breach of contract and wins, the court will likely award only nominal damages. •

---

4. UCC 2–715(2). See Chapter 16.

5. The party who is ordered to pay a judgment may be insolvent (unable to pay his or her bills when they come due) or have insufficient funds, or the party's assets may be protected under exemption laws (see Chapter 21).

Landmark in the Law   *Hadley v. Baxendale* (1854)

The rule that notice of special ("consequential") circumstances must be given if consequential damages are to be recovered was first enunciated in *Hadley v. Baxendale*,[a] a landmark case decided in 1854.

Case Background   This case involved a broken crankshaft used in a flour mill run by the Hadley family in Gloucester, England. The crankshaft attached to the steam engine in the mill broke, and the shaft had to be sent to a foundry located in Greenwich so that a new shaft could be made to fit the other parts of the engine.

The Hadleys hired Baxendale, a common carrier, to transport the shaft from Gloucester to Greenwich. Baxendale received payment in advance and promised to deliver the shaft the following day. It was not delivered for several days, however. As a consequence, the mill was closed during those days because the Hadleys had no extra crankshaft on hand to use. The Hadleys sued Baxendale to recover the profits they lost during that time. Baxendale contended that the loss of profits was "too remote."

In the mid-1800s, it was common knowledge that large mills, such as that run by the Hadleys, normally had more than one crankshaft in case the main one broke and had to be repaired, as happened in this situation. It is against this background that the parties argued their respective positions on whether the damages resulting from loss of profits while the crankshaft was out for repair were "too remote" to be recoverable.

The Issue before the Court and the Court's Ruling   The crucial issue before the court was whether the Hadleys had informed the carrier, Baxendale, of the special circumstances surrounding the crankshaft's

---

a. 9 Exch. 341, 156 Eng.Rep. 145 (1854).

repair. Specifically, did Baxendale know at the time of the contract that the mill would have to shut down while the crankshaft was being repaired?

In the court's opinion, however, the only circumstances communicated by the Hadleys to Baxendale at the time the contract was made were that the item to be transported was a broken crankshaft of a mill and that the Hadleys were the owners and operators of that mill. The court concluded that these circumstances did not reasonably indicate that the mill would have to stop operations if the delivery of the crankshaft was delayed.

• Application to Today's World   *Today, the rule enunciated by the court in this case still applies. When damages are awarded, compensation is given only for those injuries that the defendant could reasonably have foreseen as a probable result of the usual course of events following a breach. If the injury complained of is outside the usual and foreseeable course of events, the plaintiff must show specifically that the defendant had reason to know the facts and foresee the injury. This rule applies to contracts in the online environment as well. For example, suppose that a Web merchant loses business (and profits) due to a computer system's failure. If the failure was caused by malfunctioning software, the merchant normally may recover the lost profits from the software maker if these consequential damages were foreseeable.*

• Relevant Web Sites   To locate information on the Web concerning the *Hadley v. Baxendale* decision, go to this text's Web site at www.cengage.com/blaw/blt, select "Chapter 14," and click on "URLs for Landmarks."

Mitigation of Damages

Mitigation of Damages A rule requiring a plaintiff to do whatever is reasonable to minimize the damages caused by the defendant.

In most situations, when a breach of contract occurs, the injured party is held to a duty to mitigate, or reduce, the damages that he or she suffers. Under this doctrine of **mitigation of damages,** the required action depends on the nature of the situation.

In the majority of states, a person whose employment has been wrongfully terminated has a duty to mitigate damages incurred because of the employer's breach of the employment contract. In other words, wrongfully terminated employees have a duty to take similar jobs if they are available. If the employees fail to do this, the damages they receive will be equivalent to their salaries less the incomes they would have received in similar jobs obtained by reasonable means. Normally, the employee is under no duty to take a job that is not of the same type and rank.

CASE EXAMPLE 14.5 Harry De La Concha was employed by Fordham University. De La Concha claimed that he was injured in an altercation with Fordham's director of human resources and filed for workers' compensation benefits. (These benefits are available for on-the-job injuries regardless of fault, as you will read in Chapter 24.) Fordham then fired De La Concha, who sought to be reinstated by arguing that he had been terminated in retaliation for filing a workers' compensation claim. The New York state workers' compensation board held that De La Concha had failed to mitigate his damages because he had not even looked for another job, and a state court affirmed the decision. Because De La Concha had failed to mitigate his damages, any compensation he received would be reduced by the amount he could have obtained from other employment.[6] ●

Some states require a landlord to use reasonable means to find a new tenant if a tenant abandons the premises and fails to pay rent. If an acceptable tenant becomes available, the landlord is required to lease the premises to this tenant to mitigate the damages recoverable from the former tenant. The former tenant is still liable for the difference between the amount of the rent under the original lease and the rent received from the new tenant. If the landlord has not taken reasonable steps to find a new tenant, a court will likely reduce any award by the amount of rent the landlord could have received had he or she done so. Whether a tenant farmer acceptably attempted to mitigate his damages on his landlord's breach of their lease was at issue in the following case.

6. *De La Concha v. Fordham University*, 814 N.Y.S.2d 320, 28 A.3d 963 (2006).

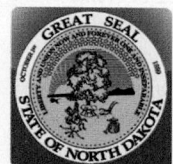

Case 14.1 Hanson v. Boeder

Supreme Court of North Dakota, 2007 ND 20, 727 N.W.2d 280 (2007).
www.ndcourts.com/court/opinions.htm[a]

Part of the five-year farming lease in this case included the use of grain bins such as these in North Dakota.

FACTS In 1998, Paul Hanson signed a five-year lease to farm 1,350 acres of Donald Boeder's land in Steele County, North Dakota, for $50 per acre beginning with the 1999 crop year. Under the lease, Hanson could use grain bins with a capacity of 93,000 bushels and two machine sheds on the property. The rent was $67,515 per year, with half due on April 1 and the balance due on November 1. In 2003, Boeder and Hanson renewed the lease for a second five-year period. During both terms, Boeder and Hanson disagreed about Hanson's farming practices, but during the second term, their disagreement escalated. In August 2005, Boeder told Hanson that their lease was over. Boeder also told Hanson not to till the land in the fall because it had been leased to a new tenant who wanted to do it himself. Hanson continued to work Boeder's land, however, while running ads in the local newspapers for other farmland to rent. Unable to find other land, Hanson filed a suit in a North Dakota state court against Boeder for breach of contract, asking the court to assess damages. The court awarded Hanson $315,194.26 to cover his lost profits, the lost use of the bins and sheds, and the value of the fall tillage. Boeder appealed to the North Dakota Supreme Court, arguing, among other things, that Hanson failed to mitigate his damages.

ISSUE Did Hanson take appropriate steps to mitigate his damages?

DECISION Yes. The Supreme Court of North Dakota affirmed the lower court's award of damages to Hanson.

REASON The state supreme court explained that normally "for the breach of an obligation arising from contract, the measure of damages * * * is the amount which will compensate the party aggrieved for all the detriment proximately caused thereby or which in the ordinary course of things would be likely to result therefrom." The court recognized that "a person injured by the wrongful acts of another has a duty to mitigate or minimize the damages and must protect himself if he can do so with reasonable exertion or at trifling expense, and can recover from the delinquent party only such damages as he could not, with reasonable effort, have avoided." In this case, Hanson had not been aware of any farmland available for lease, and he had run ads in the local newspapers seeking other farmland to rent. That Hanson was unsuccessful affected the amount of his recovery, but it did not point to a failure to mitigate his damages.

FOR CRITICAL ANALYSIS—Social Consideration *During the trial, Boeder tried to retract his repudiation of the lease to allow Hanson to continue farming for the rest of the lease term. Should the court have considered this an acceptable substitute to mitigate Hanson's damages? Why or why not?*

---

a. Click on the "By ND citation" link. In the result, click on "2007" and then on the name of the case to access the opinion. The North Dakota Supreme Court maintains this Web site.

Liquidated Damages versus Penalties

Liquidated Damages An amount, stipulated in a contract, that the parties to the contract believe to be a reasonable estimation of the damages that will occur in the event of a breach.

Penalty A contractual clause that states that a certain amount of monetary damages will be paid in the event of a future default or breach of contract. The damages are a punishment for a default and not an accurate measure of compensation for the contract's breach. The agreement as to the penalty amount will not be enforced, and recovery will be limited to actual damages.

A **liquidated damages** provision in a contract specifies that a certain dollar amount is to be paid in the event of a future default or breach of contract. (*Liquidated* means determined, settled, or fixed.) Liquidated damages differ from penalties. A **penalty** specifies a certain amount to be paid in the event of a default or breach of contract and is designed to penalize the breaching party. Liquidated damages provisions normally are enforceable. In contrast, if a court finds that a provision calls for a penalty, the agreement as to the amount will not be enforced, and recovery will be limited to actual damages.[7]

To determine whether a particular provision is for liquidated damages or for a penalty, the court must answer two questions:

1. At the time the contract was formed, was it apparent that damages would be difficult to estimate in the event of a breach?
2. Was the amount set as damages a reasonable estimate and not excessive?[8]

If the answers to both questions are yes, the provision normally will be enforced. If either answer is no, the provision normally will not be enforced. Liquidated damages provisions are frequently used in construction contracts because it is difficult to estimate the amount of damages that would be caused by a delay in completing the work. **EXAMPLE 14.6** Ray Curl is a construction contractor. He enters into a contract with a developer to build a home in a new subdivision. The contract includes a clause that requires Curl to pay $300 for every day he is late in completing the project. This is a liquidated damages provision because it specifies a reasonable amount that Curl must pay to the developer if his performance is late. ●

The *Concept Summary* below summarizes the rules on the availability of the different types of damages.

---

7. This is also the rule under the UCC. See UCC 2–718(1).
8. *Restatement (Second) of Contracts*, Section 356(1).

Concept Summary   **Damages**

REMEDY	AVAILABILITY	RESULT
Compensatory Damages	A party sustains and proves an injury arising directly from the loss of the bargain.	The injured party is compensated for the loss of the bargain.
Consequential Damages	Special circumstances, of which the breaching party is aware or should be aware, cause the injured party additional loss.	The injured party is given the entire benefit of the bargain, such as forgone profits.
Punitive Damages	Damages that normally are available only when a tort is also involved.	The wrongdoer is punished, and others are deterred from committing similar acts.
Nominal Damages	There is no financial loss.	Wrongdoing is established without actual damages being suffered. The plaintiff is awarded a nominal amount (such as $1) in damages.
Liquidated Damages	A contract provides a specific amount to be paid as damages in the event that the contract is later breached.	The nonbreaching party is paid the amount stipulated in the contract for the breach, unless the amount is construed as a penalty.

▶ Equitable Remedies

Sometimes, damages are an inadequate remedy for a breach of contract. In these situations, the nonbreaching party may ask the court for an equitable remedy. Equitable remedies include rescission and restitution, specific performance, and reformation.

Rescission and Restitution

CONTRAST   Restitution offers several advantages over traditional damages. First, restitution may be available in situations when damages cannot be proved or are difficult to prove. Second, restitution can be used to recover specific property. Third, restitution sometimes results in a greater overall award.

As discussed in Chapter 13, *rescission* is essentially an action to undo, or cancel, a contract—to return nonbreaching parties to the positions that they occupied prior to the transaction.[9] When fraud, mistake, duress, undue influence, lack of capacity, or failure of consideration is present, rescission is available. Rescission may also be available by statute.[10] The failure of one party to perform under a contract entitles the other party to rescind the contract. The rescinding party must give prompt notice to the breaching party.

Restitution   An equitable remedy under which a person is restored to his or her original position prior to loss or injury, or placed in the position he or she would have been in had the breach not occurred.

RESTITUTION   To rescind a contract, both parties generally must make **restitution** to each other by returning goods, property, or funds previously conveyed.[11] If the property or goods can be returned, they must be. If the property or goods have been consumed, restitution must be made in an equivalent dollar amount.

Essentially, restitution involves the recapture of a benefit conferred on the defendant that has unjustly enriched her or him. **EXAMPLE 14.7**   Andrea pays $32,000 to Miles in return for his promise to design a house for her. The next day, Miles calls Andrea and tells her that he has taken a position with a large architectural firm in another state and cannot design the house. Andrea decides to hire another architect that afternoon. Andrea can require restitution of $32,000 because Miles has received an unjust benefit of $32,000. ●

Former professional U.S. cyclist Tyler Hamilton (below) won a gold medal at the 2004 Olympics, where he failed a test for blood doping (receiving blood transfusions to boost performance). Because the antidoping laboratory could not confirm the doping allegation with the second blood sample, Hamilton retained his gold medal. Nonetheless, his professional cycling team, Phonak, terminated his contract after he was given a two-year suspension. Could Phonak sue Hamilton for restitution of payments already made to him on their contract?

(Richard Masoner/Creative Commons)

RESTITUTION IS NOT LIMITED TO RESCISSION CASES   Restitution may be required when a contract is rescinded, but the right to restitution is not limited to rescission cases. Because an award of restitution basically gives back or returns something to its rightful owner, a party can seek restitution in actions for breach of contract, tort actions, and other types of actions. For instance, restitution can be obtained when funds or property has been transferred by mistake or because of fraud or incapacity. Similarly, restitution might be available when there has been misconduct by a party with a special relationship with the other party. Even in criminal cases a court can order restitution of funds or property obtained through embezzlement, conversion, theft, or copyright infringement.

---

9. The rescission discussed here refers to *unilateral* rescission, in which only one party wants to undo the contract. In *mutual* rescission, which we discussed in Chapter 13, both parties agree to undo the contract. Mutual rescission discharges the contract; unilateral rescission is generally available as a remedy for breach of contract.

10. Many states have laws that allow persons who enter into "home solicitation contracts" to rescind these contracts within three business days for any reason. See, for example, California Civil Code Section 1689.5.

11. *Restatement (Second) of Contracts,* Section 370.

Specific Performance

Specific Performance An equitable remedy requiring exactly the performance that was specified in a contract; usually granted only when monetary damages would be an inadequate remedy and the subject matter of the contract is unique (for example, real property).

Suppose that a seller contracts to sell some valuable coins to a buyer. If the seller breaches the contract, would specific performance be an appropriate remedy for the buyer to seek? Why or why not?

The equitable remedy of **specific performance** calls for the performance of the act promised in the contract. This remedy is attractive to a nonbreaching party because it provides the exact bargain promised in the contract. It also avoids some of the problems inherent in a suit for monetary damages, such as collecting a judgment and arranging another contract. Moreover, the actual performance may be more valuable than the monetary damages.

(PhotoDisc/Getty Images)

Normally, however, specific performance will not be granted unless the party's legal remedy (monetary damages) is inadequate.[12] For this reason, contracts for the sale of goods rarely qualify for specific performance. Monetary damages ordinarily are adequate in sales contracts because substantially identical goods can be bought or sold in the market. Only if the goods are unique will a court grant specific performance. For instance, paintings, sculptures, and rare books and coins are often unique, and monetary damages will not enable a buyer to obtain substantially identical substitutes in the market.

Ethical Issue ⚖️

Should specific performance be granted to compel performance of a $15.4 billion merger contract? In July 2008, Dow Chemical Company entered into an agreement to buy Rohm & Haas Company, another large chemical corporation, for $15.4 billion. In the contract, Dow agreed to pay a premium over Rohm & Haas's stock price at that time. Dow was counting on financing the merger, in part, with funds obtained from another billion-dollar deal in Kuwait. Unfortunately, due to the global financial crisis, the Kuwait deal fell through in December 2008, and Dow had difficulty arranging alternative financing. When the deal did not close as it was supposed to on January 27, 2009, Rohm & Haas filed a breach of contract lawsuit.[13] Rohm & Haas sought specific performance of the contract. Dow claimed that its performance should be excused because the global economic crisis had made the contract commercially impracticable (discussed in Chapter 12).

On the day that the trial was to begin, Dow and Rohm & Haas reached a settlement, in which Dow agreed to go through with the deal at the agreed-on price (although by this time, the stock prices of other chemical companies had fallen substantially as the economy declined). Nevertheless, the dispute raised interesting questions about the proper remedy for breaching a merger contract. Is the legal remedy of damages adequate to compensate a firm that contracted to be acquired? Or should the law consider every business "unique" so that a contract to buy another company qualifies for specific performance? Clearly, specific performance of the merger contract was more valuable to Rohm & Haas and its shareholders because they received a higher price for their stock than its then-current market value. But specific performance is an equitable remedy, so a court might also have considered the fairness (and burden) of enforcing the bargain on Dow, its shareholders, and its employees, a number of whom were likely to be laid off as a result of the merger.

SALE OF LAND A court will grant specific performance to a buyer in an action for a breach of contract involving the sale of land. In this situation, the legal remedy of monetary damages will not compensate the buyer adequately because every parcel of land is unique,

---

12. *Restatement (Second) of Contracts,* Section 359.
13. *Rohm & Haas Co. v. Dow Chemical Co.,* 2009 WL 445612 (Del.Ch. 2009).

as was discussed on page 339. The same land in the same location obviously cannot be obtained elsewhere. Only when specific performance is unavailable (for example, when the seller has sold the property to someone else) will damages be awarded instead.

Is specific performance warranted when one of the parties has substantially—but not *fully*—performed under the contract? That was the question in the following case.

Case 14.2   Stainbrook v. Low

Court of Appeals of Indiana, 842 N.E.2d 386 (2006).

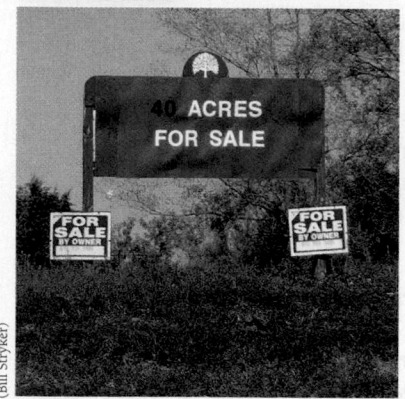

Three days before closing a real estate transaction to buy forty acres of land, the seller dies. Can the executor of the estate back out of the deal?

FACTS   In April 2004, Howard Stainbrook agreed to sell to Trent Low forty acres of land in Jennings County, Indiana, for $45,000. Thirty-two of the acres were wooded and eight were tillable. Under the agreement, Low was to pay for a survey of the property and other costs, including a tax payment due in November. Low gave Stainbrook a check for $1,000 to show his intent to fulfill the contract. They agreed to close the deal on May 11, and Low made financial arrangements to meet his obligations. On May 8, a tractor rolled over on Stainbrook, and he died. Stainbrook's son, David, became the executor of his father's estate. David asked Low to withdraw his offer to buy the forty acres. Low refused and filed a suit in an Indiana state court against David, seeking to enforce the contract. The court ordered specific performance. David appealed to a state intermediate appellate court, arguing, among other things, that his father's contract with Low was "ambiguous and inequitable."

ISSUE   Is complete performance of a contract required for the party to be entitled to the remedy of specific performance?

DECISION   No. A party who has substantially performed or offered to perform his or her obligations under a contract is entitled to pursue specific performance as a remedy. The state intermediate appellate court held that specific performance was an appropriate remedy in this case and affirmed the lower court's order.

REASON   The appellate court explained that a contracting party's substantial performance is sufficient to support a court's order for specific performance. Here, "Low both offered to perform and substantially performed his contractual obligations." The appellate court found that Low had offered to make the tax payment that was due, but Stainbrook's estate refused the offer. Also, Low had obtained financing before the closing date, and there was nothing to indicate that he was not prepared to meet his financial obligations and go forward with the sale. Moreover, although the survey had not yet been arranged, there was no evidence that Low would not have paid for the survey of the land as required by the contract. Because Low had substantially performed under the terms of the contract, the court held that Low was entitled to the remedy of specific performance.

WHY IS THIS CASE IMPORTANT?   *The court reaffirmed the principle that "specific performance is a matter of course when it involves contracts to purchase real estate." The court also emphasized that "a party seeking specific performance of a real estate contract must prove that he has substantially performed his contract obligations or offered to do so." The court's reasoning underscores the importance of focusing on the elements of a principle to resolve a case fairly.*

CONTRACTS FOR PERSONAL SERVICES   Personal-service contracts require one party to work personally for another party. Courts normally refuse to grant specific performance of contracts for personal services. This is because ordering a party to perform personal services against his or her will amounts to a type of involuntary servitude, which is contrary to the public policy expressed in the Thirteenth Amendment to the U.S. Constitution. Moreover, the courts do not want to monitor contracts for personal services, which usually require the exercise of personal judgment or talent.

EXAMPLE 14.8   If you contract with a surgeon to perform brain surgery on you and she refuses to perform, the court will not compel (nor would you want) the surgeon to perform under these circumstances. There is no way the court can assure meaningful performance

• *Exhibit* 14–2 Remedies for Breach of Contract

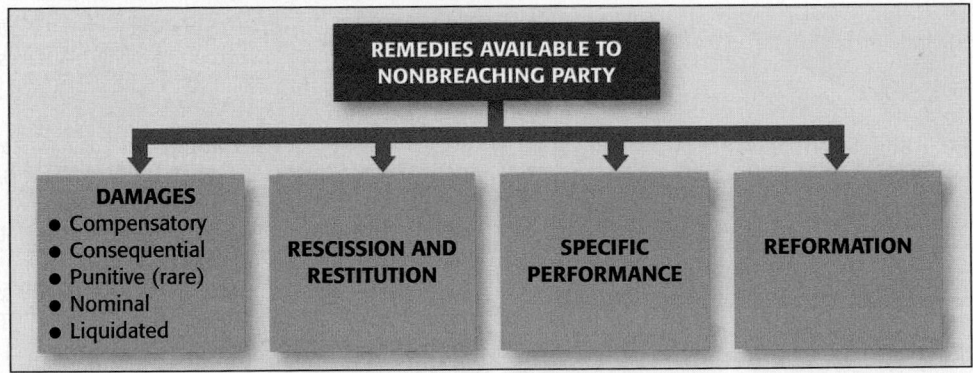

in such a situation.[14] • If a contract is not deemed personal, the remedy at law of monetary damages may be adequate if substantially identical service (for example, lawn mowing) is available from other persons.

Reformation

Reformation is an equitable remedy used when the parties have *imperfectly* expressed their agreement in writing. Reformation allows a court to rewrite the contract to reflect the parties' true intentions. Courts order reformation most often when fraud or mutual mistake is present. **EXAMPLE 14.9** If Carson contracts to buy a forklift from Shelley but the written contract refers to a crane, a mutual mistake has occurred. Accordingly, a court could reform the contract so that the writing conforms to the parties' original intention as to which piece of equipment is being sold. • Exhibit 14–2 graphically presents the remedies, including reformation, that are available to the nonbreaching party.

Courts frequently reform contracts in two other situations. The first occurs when two parties who have made a binding oral contract agree to put the oral contract in writing but, in doing so, they make an error in stating the terms. Usually, the courts allow into evidence the correct terms of the oral contract, thereby reforming the written contract. The second situation occurs when the parties have executed a written covenant not to compete (see Chapter 11). If the covenant not to compete is for a valid and legitimate purpose (such as the sale of a business) but the area or time restraints are unreasonable, some courts will reform the restraints by making them reasonable and will enforce the entire contract as reformed. Other courts, however, will throw out the entire restrictive covenant as illegal.

In the following case, a court was asked to reform a deed eight months after the transaction in which the deed played a principal part.

> *"Controversy equalizes fools and wise men—and the fools know it."*
>
> Oliver Wendell Holmes, 1809–1894
> (American author)

---

14. Similarly, courts often refuse to order specific performance of construction contracts because courts are not set up to operate as construction supervisors or engineers.

Case 14.3 **Drake v. Hance**

Court of Appeals of North Carolina, 673 S.E.2d 411 (2009).
www.nccourts.org[a]

a. In the "Favorites" column, click on "Court Opinions." On that page, in the "Court of Appeals Opinions" section, click on "2009." In the result, scroll to "3 March 2009" and click on the name of the case to access the opinion. The North Carolina Administrative Office of the Courts maintains this Web site.

FACTS In June 2005, Eric and Debra Hance agreed to buy Garry and Wanda Drake's home in Monroe, North Carolina. The contract described

Case 14.3–Continues next page ➡

Case 14.3–Continued

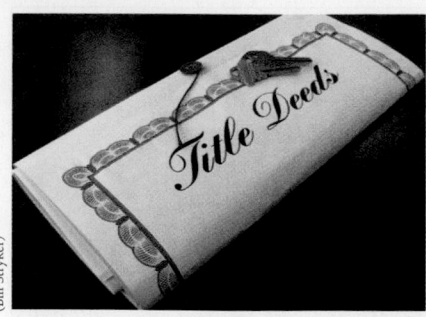

(Bill Stryker)

Property not intended to be included in a sale is listed in the buyer's deed. Can the deed be reformed to remove the unintended additional property?

the property as "#15 Legacy Lake." The deed, however, listed "lot 15, Legacy Lake" *and* "lot 11, Legacy Lake." Lot 15 is the property on which the home sits. Lot 11 is a vacant lot across the street. After the sale, the deed was filed with the appropriate state office. Eight months later, when the Drakes tried to sell lot 11 to a third party, they learned that it had been listed on the Hances' deed. The Drakes told the Hances, who denied that any mistake had been made. The Drakes filed a suit in a North Carolina state court against the Hances, alleging an intent to sell only lot 15. The attorney who closed the sale testified that the deed was drafted improperly. The court reformed it. The Hances appealed.

ISSUE   Can a legal document be reformed based on the testimony of the party who drafted it?

DECISION   Yes. A state intermediate appellate court affirmed the lower court's action. The Drakes had intended for the deed to include only one lot.

REASON   A deed is a written document that conveys an interest in real property. In most circumstances, parties cannot offer evidence to contradict it. But if a party can show that a mutual mistake was made in the deed's execution, evidence can be introduced to show the parties' true intentions. If the evidence is "strong, cogent, and convincing," the deed can be reformed. In this case, there was an "ambiguity" between the descriptions in the contract and the deed. The trial court could admit parol evidence to explain the discrepancy and determine the parties' intent. The closing attorney testified to a mistake in drafting the deed to include both lots. The court found this testimony "exceptionally persuasive." The court did not err in reforming the deed based on this evidence.

WHY IS THIS CASE IMPORTANT?   *The significance of honesty, good faith, and credibility in a contractual transaction could not be clearer than it is in the facts and outcome of this case. From the negotiation of a deal, through the draft of its conditions and the performance of its duties, to admitting its terms, the parties should act with integrity. One party's attempt to take unfair advantage of the other is likely to result in a gain of no advantage at all.*

 Recovery Based on Quasi Contract

BEWARE   The function of a quasi contract is to impose a legal obligation on a party who made no actual promise.

In some situations, when no actual contract exists, a court may step in to prevent one party from being unjustly enriched at the expense of another party. As discussed in Chapter 9, *quasi contract* is a legal theory under which an obligation is imposed in the absence of an agreement. A quasi contract is not a true contract but rather a fictional contract that is imposed on the parties to prevent unjust enrichment.

When Quasi Contracts Are Used

Quasi contracts allow the courts to act as if a contract exists when there is no actual contract or agreement between the parties. The courts can also use this theory when the parties entered into a contract, but it is unenforceable for some reason.

Quasi-contractual recovery is often granted when one party has partially performed under a contract that is unenforceable. It provides an alternative to suing for damages and allows the party to recover the reasonable value of the partial performance. **EXAMPLE 14.10** Ericson contracts to build two oil derricks for Petro Industries. The derricks are to be built over a period of three years, but the parties do not create a written contract. Therefore, the Statute of Frauds will bar the enforcement of the contract.[15] After Ericson completes one

---

15. Contracts that by their terms cannot be performed within one year from the day after the date of contract formation must be in writing to be enforceable (see Chapter 12).

derrick, Petro Industries informs him that it will not pay for the derrick. Ericson can sue Petro Industries under the theory of quasi contract. ●

The Requirements of Quasi Contract

To recover on a quasi contract theory, the party seeking recovery must show the following:

1. The party conferred a benefit on the other party.
2. The party conferred the benefit with the reasonable expectation of being paid.
3. The party did not act as a volunteer in conferring the benefit.
4. The party receiving the benefit would be unjustly enriched if allowed to retain the benefit without paying for it.

Applying these requirements to Example 14.10 above, Ericson can sue in quasi contract because all of the conditions for quasi-contractual recovery have been fulfilled. Ericson conferred a benefit on Petro Industries by building the oil derrick. Ericson build the derrick with the reasonable expectation of being paid. He did not intend to act as a volunteer. Petro Industries would be unjustly enriched if it was allowed to keep the derrick without paying Ericson for the work. Therefore, Ericson should be able to recover the reasonable value of the oil derrick that was built (under the theory of *quantum meruit*[16]—"as much as he or she deserves"). The reasonable value is ordinarily equal to the fair market value.

 Contract Provisions Limiting Remedies

A contract may include provisions stating that no damages can be recovered for certain types of breaches or that damages will be limited to a maximum amount. The contract may also provide that the only remedy for breach is replacement, repair, or refund of the purchase price. Provisions stating that no damages can be recovered are called *exculpatory clauses* (see Chapter 11). Provisions that affect the availability of certain remedies are called *limitation-of-liability clauses.*

RECALL Exculpatory clauses may be held unconscionable, depending on the relative bargaining positions of the parties and the importance to the public interest of the business seeking to enforce the clause.

The UCC Allows Sales Contracts to Limit Remedies

The Uniform Commercial Code (UCC) provides that in a contract for the sale of goods, remedies can be limited. We will examine the UCC provisions on limitation-of-liability clauses in Chapter 16, in the context of the remedies available on the breach of a contract for the sale or lease of goods.[17]

Enforceability of Limitation-of-Liability Clauses

Whether a limitation of liability clause in a contract will be enforced depends on the type of breach that is excused by the provision. Generally, a provision excluding liability for fraudulent or intentional injury will not be enforced. Likewise, a clause excluding liability for illegal acts or violations of law will not be enforced.

A clause excluding liability for negligence may be enforced in certain situations, however. When an exculpatory clause for negligence is contained in a contract made between parties who have roughly equal bargaining positions, the clause usually will be enforced. If the clause is contained in a contract between persons with unequal bargaining power, then it may not be enforced.

---

16. Pronounced *kwahn*-tuhm *mehr*-oo-wuht.
17. UCC 2–719.

CASE EXAMPLE 14.11   Eric Lucier and his girlfriend contracted to buy their first home. They hired Cambridge Associates, Limited (CAL), to perform a home inspection for $385 and report any problems. The home-inspection contract limited CAL's liability to "$500, or 50% of fees actually paid to CAL by Client, whichever sum is smaller. Such causes include, but are not limited to, CAL's negligence, errors, omissions, . . . [or] breach of contract." The home passed the inspection, the sale was completed, and the couple moved in. Shortly after that, Lucier and his girlfriend noticed leaks, which required roof repairs estimated to cost $8,000 to $10,000. They filed a lawsuit against CAL seeking damages. CAL argued that under the limitation-of-liability clause in its contract, its liability was limited to one-half of the contract price, or $192.50. A New Jersey state appellate court held that the limitation-of-liability clause was unenforceable because it was in an adhesion contract that was forced on inexperienced buyers with little or no bargaining power. The court also found that limiting liability in home-inspection contracts was contrary to the state's public policy of requiring "reliable evaluation of a home's fitness for purchase and holding professionals to certain industry standards."[18] ●

18. *Lucier v. Williams,* 366 N.J.Super. 485, 841 A.2d 907 (2004).

Reviewing . . . Breach and Remedies

Kyle Bruno enters into a contract with X Entertainment to be a stuntman in a movie being produced. Bruno is widely known as the best motorcycle stuntman in the business, and the movie to be produced, *Xtreme Riders,* has numerous scenes involving high-speed freestyle street-bike stunts. Filming is set to begin August 1 and end by December 1 so that the film can be released the following summer. Both parties to the contract have stipulated that the filming must end on time in order to capture the profits from the summer movie market. The contract states that Bruno will be paid 10 percent of the net proceeds from the movie for his stunts. The contract also includes a liquidated damages provision, which specifies that if Bruno breaches the contract, he will owe X Entertainment $1 million. In addition, the contract includes a limitation-of-liability clause stating that if Bruno is injured during filming, X Entertainment's liability is limited to nominal damages. Using the information presented in the chapter, answer the following questions.

1. One day, while Bruno is preparing for a difficult stunt, he gets into an argument with the director and refuses to perform any stunts. Can X Entertainment seek specific performance of the contract? Why or why not?
2. Suppose that while performing a high-speed wheelie on a motorcycle, Bruno is injured by an intentionally reckless act of an X Entertainment employee. Will a court be likely to enforce the limitation-of-liability clause? Why or why not?
3. What factors would a court consider to determine if the $1 million liquidated damages clause is valid or is a penalty?
4. Suppose that there was no liquidated damages clause (or the court refused to enforce it) and X Entertainment breached the contract. The breach caused the release of the film to be delayed until after summer. Could Bruno seek consequential (special) damages for lost profits from the summer movie market in that situation? Explain.

Business Application

What Do You Do When You Cannot Perform?*

Not every contract can be performed. If you are a contractor, you may take on a job that, for one reason or another, you cannot or do not wish to perform. Simply walking away from the job and hoping for the best normally is not the most effective way to avoid litigation—which can be costly, time consuming, and emotionally draining. Instead, you should consider various options that may reduce the likelihood of litigation.

* This *Business Application* is not meant to substitute for the services of an attorney who is licensed to practice law in your state.

For example, suppose that you are a building contractor and you sign a contract to build a home for the Andersons according to a set of plans that they provided. Performance is to begin on June 15. On June 1, Central Enterprises offers you a position that will pay you two and a half times as much net income as you could earn as an independent builder. To take the job, you have to start on June 15. You cannot be in two places at the same time, so to accept the new position, you must breach the contract with the Andersons.

Consider Your Options

What can you do in this situation? One option is to subcontract the work to another builder and oversee the work yourself to make sure it conforms to the contract. Another option is to negotiate with the Andersons for a release. You can offer to find another qualified builder who will build a house of the same quality at the same price. Alternatively, you can offer to pay any additional costs if another builder takes the job and is more expensive. In any event, this additional cost would be one measure of damages that a court would impose on you if the Andersons prevailed in a suit for breach of contract (in addition to any costs the Andersons suffer as a result of the breach, such as costs due to the delay in construction). Thus, by making the offer, you might be able to avoid the expense of litigation—if the Andersons accept your offer.

Settlement Offers

Often, parties are reluctant to propose compromise settlements because they fear that what they say will be used against them in court if litigation ensues. Generally, however, offers for settlement will not be admitted in court to prove that you are liable for a breach of contract (though they are at times admissible to prove a party breached the duty of good faith).

CHECKLIST FOR IF YOU CANNOT PERFORM

1. **Consider a compromise.**
2. **Subcontract out the work and oversee it.**
3. **Offer to find an alternative contractor to fulfill your obligation.**
4. **Make a cash offer to "buy" a release from your contract. Work with an attorney in making the offer unless the amount involved is insignificant.**

 ## Key Terms

consequential damages 339	mitigation of damages 341	restitution 344
incidental damages 338	nominal damages 340	specific performance 345
liquidated damages 343	penalty 343	

 ## Chapter Summary: Breach and Remedies

COMMON REMEDIES AVAILABLE TO NONBREACHING PARTY	

Damages
(See pages 338–343.)
	The legal remedy designed to compensate the nonbreaching party for the loss of the bargain. By awarding monetary damages, the court tries to place the parties in the positions that they would have occupied had the contract been fully performed. The nonbreaching party frequently has a duty to *mitigate* (lessen or reduce) the damages incurred as a result of the contract's breach. There are five broad categories of damages:
	1. *Compensatory damages*—Damages that compensate the nonbreaching party for injuries actually sustained and proved to have arisen directly from the loss of the bargain resulting from the breach of contract.
	  a. In breached contracts for the sale of goods, the usual measure of compensatory damages is the difference between the contract price and the market price.
	  b. In breached contracts for the sale of land, the measure of damages is ordinarily the same as in contracts for the sale of goods.
	  c. In breached construction contracts, the measure of damages depends on which party breaches and at what stage of construction the breach occurs.

Continued

Chapter Summary: Breach and Remedies—Continued

Damages—Continued	2. *Consequential damages*—Damages resulting from special circumstances beyond the contract itself; the damages flow only from the consequences of a breach. For a party to recover consequential damages, the damages must be the foreseeable result of a breach of contract, and the breaching party must have known at the time the contract was formed that special circumstances existed that would cause the nonbreaching party to incur additional loss on breach of the contract. Also called *special damages*. 3. *Punitive damages*—Damages awarded to punish the breaching party. Usually not awarded in an action for breach of contract unless a tort is involved. 4. *Nominal damages*—Damages small in amount (such as one dollar) that are awarded when a breach has occurred but no actual injury has been suffered. Awarded only to establish that the defendant acted wrongfully. 5. *Liquidated damages*—Damages that may be specified in a contract as the amount to be paid to the nonbreaching party in the event the contract is breached in the future. Clauses providing for liquidated damages are enforced if the damages were difficult to estimate at the time the contract was formed and if the amount stipulated is reasonable. If the amount is construed to be a penalty, the clause will not be enforced.
Rescission and Restitution (See page 344.)	1. *Rescission*—A remedy whereby a contract is canceled and the parties are restored to the original positions that they occupied prior to the transaction. Available when fraud, a mistake, duress, or failure of consideration is present. The rescinding party must give prompt notice of the rescission to the breaching party. 2. *Restitution*—When a contract is rescinded, both parties must make restitution to each other by returning the goods, property, or funds previously conveyed. Restitution prevents the unjust enrichment of the parties.
Specific Performance (See pages 345–347.)	An equitable remedy calling for the performance of the act promised in the contract. This remedy is available only in special situations—such as those involving contracts for the sale of unique goods or land—and when monetary damages would be an inadequate remedy. Specific performance is not available as a remedy for breached contracts for personal services.
Reformation (See pages 347–348.)	An equitable remedy allowing a contract to be "reformed," or rewritten, to reflect the parties' true intentions. Available when an agreement is imperfectly expressed in writing.
Recovery Based on Quasi Contract (See pages 348–349.)	An equitable theory imposed by the courts to obtain justice and prevent unjust enrichment in a situation in which no enforceable contract exists. The party seeking recovery must show the following: 1. A benefit was conferred on the other party. 2. The party conferring the benefit did so with the expectation of being paid. 3. The benefit was not volunteered. 4. The party receiving the benefit would be unjustly enriched if allowed to retain the benefit without paying for it.
CONTRACT DOCTRINES RELATING TO REMEDIES	
Contract Provisions Limiting Remedies (See pages 349–350.)	A contract may provide that no damages (or only a limited amount of damages) can be recovered in the event the contract is breached. Under the Uniform Commercial Code (UCC), remedies may be limited in contracts for the sale of goods. Clauses excluding liability for fraudulent or intentional injury or for illegal acts cannot be enforced. Clauses excluding liability for negligence may be enforced if both parties hold roughly equal bargaining power.

 ExamPrep

ISSUE SPOTTERS

1 Greg contracts to build a storage shed for Haney, who pays Greg in advance, but Greg completes only half the work. Haney pays Ipswich $500 to finish the shed. If Haney sues Greg, what would be the measure of recovery?

2 Lyle contracts to sell his ranch to Marley, who is to take possession on June 1. Lyle delays the transfer until August 1. Marley incurs expenses in providing for livestock that he bought for the ranch. When they made the contract, Lyle had no reason to know of the livestock. Is Lyle liable for Marley's expenses in providing for the cattle? Why or why not?

BEFORE THE TEST

Check your answers to the Issue Spotters, and at the same time, take the interactive quiz for this chapter. Go to **www.cengage.com/blaw/blt** and click on "Chapter 14." First, click on "Answers to Issue Spotters" to check your answers. Next, click on "Interactive Quiz" to assess your mastery of the concepts in this chapter. Then click on "Flashcards" to review this chapter's Key Term definitions.

 For Review

Answers for the even-numbered questions in this For Review *section can be found on this text's accompanying Web site at* **www.cengage.com/blaw/blt**. *Select "Chapter 14" and click on "For Review."*

1 What is the difference between compensatory damages and consequential damages? What are nominal damages, and when do courts award nominal damages?
2 What is the standard measure of compensatory damages when a contract is breached? How are damages computed differently in construction contracts?
3 Under what circumstances is the remedy of rescission and restitution available?
4 When do courts grant specific performance as a remedy?
5 What is a limitation-of-liability clause, and when will courts enforce it?

 Hypothetical Scenarios and Case Problems

14–1 Liquidated Damages. Carnack contracts to sell his house and lot to Willard for $100,000. The terms of the contract call for Willard to make a deposit of 10 percent of the purchase price as a down payment. The terms further stipulate that should the buyer breach the contract, Carnack will retain the deposit as liquidated damages. Willard makes the deposit, but because her expected financing of the $90,000 balance falls through, she breaches the contract. Two weeks later, Carnack sells the house and lot to Balkova for $105,000. Willard demands her $10,000 back, but Carnack refuses, claiming that Willard's breach and the contract terms entitle him to keep the deposit. Discuss who is correct.

14–2 Hypothetical Question with Sample Answer In which of the following situations might a court grant specific performance as a remedy for the breach of the contract?
1 Tarrington contracts to sell her house and lot to Rainier. Then, on finding another buyer willing to pay a higher purchase price, she refuses to deed the property to Rainier.
2 Marita contracts to sing and dance in Horace's nightclub for one month, beginning June 1. She then refuses to perform.
3 Juan contracts to purchase a rare coin from Edmund, who is breaking up his coin collection. At the last minute, Edmund decides to keep his coin collection intact and refuses to deliver the coin to Juan.
4 Astro Computer Corp. has three shareholders: Coase, who owns 48 percent of the stock; De Valle, who owns 48 percent; and Cary, who owns 4 percent. Cary contracts to sell his 4 percent to De Valle but later refuses to transfer the shares to him.

—For a sample answer to Question 14–2, go to Appendix E at the end of this text.

14–3 Measure of Damages. Johnson contracted to lease a house to Fox for $700 a month, beginning October 1. Fox stipulated in the contract that before he moved in, the interior of the house had to be completely repainted. On September 9, Johnson hired Keever to do the required painting for $1,000. He told Keever that the painting had to be finished by October 1 but did not explain why. On September 28, Keever quit for no reason, having completed approximately 80 percent of the work. Johnson then paid Sam $300 to finish the painting, but Sam did not finish until October 4. When Fox found that the painting had not been completed as stipulated in his contract with Johnson, he leased another home. Johnson found another tenant who would lease the property at $700 a month, beginning October 15. Johnson then sued Keever for breach of contract, claiming damages of $650. This amount included the $300 Johnson paid Sam to finish the painting and $350 for rent for the first half of October, which Johnson had lost as a result of Keever's breach. Johnson had not yet paid Keever anything for Keever's work. Can Johnson collect the $650 from Keever? Explain.

14–4 Mitigation of Damages. Lauren Barton, a single mother with three children, lived in Portland, Oregon. Cynthia VanHorn also lived in Oregon until she moved to New York City to open and operate an art gallery. VanHorn asked Barton to manage the gallery under a one-year contract for an annual salary of $72,000. To begin work, Barton relocated to New York. As part of the move, Barton transferred custody of her children to her husband, who lived in London, England. In accepting the job, Barton also forfeited her husband's alimony and child-support payments, including unpaid amounts of nearly $30,000. Before Barton started work, VanHorn repudiated the contract. Unable to find employment for more than an annual salary of $25,000, Barton moved to London to be near her children. Barton filed a suit in an Oregon state court against VanHorn, seeking damages for breach of contract. Should the court hold, as VanHorn argued, that Barton did not take reasonable steps to mitigate her damages? Why or why not?

14–5 Liquidated Damages versus Penalties. Every homeowner in the Putnam County, Indiana, subdivision of Stardust Hills must be a member of the Stardust Hills Owners Association, Inc., and must pay annual dues of $200 for the maintenance of common areas and other community services. Under the association's rules, dues paid more than ten days late "shall bear a delinquent fee at a rate of $2.00 per day." Phyllis Gaddis failed to pay the dues on a Stardust Hills lot that she owned. Late fees began to accrue. Nearly two months later, the association filed a suit in an Indiana state court to collect the unpaid dues and the late fees. Gaddis argued in response that the delinquent fee was an unenforceable penalty. What questions should be considered in determining the status of this fee? Should the association's rule regarding assessment of the fee be enforced? Explain. [*Gaddis v. Stardust Hills Owners Association, Inc.,* 804 N.E.2d 231 (Ind.App. 2004)]

14–6   **Case Problem with Sample Answer** Tyna Ek met Russell Peterson in Seattle, Washington. Peterson persuaded Ek to buy a boat that he had once owned, the *O'Hana Kai,* which was in Juneau, Alaska. Ek paid the boat's current owner $43,000 for the boat, and in January 2000, she and Peterson entered into a contract, under which Peterson agreed to make the vessel seaworthy so that within one month it could be transported to Seattle, where he would pay its moorage costs. He would renovate the boat at his own expense in return for a portion of the profit on its resale in 2001. On the sale, Ek would recover her costs, and then Peterson would be reimbursed for his. Ek loaned Peterson her cell phone so that they could communicate while he prepared the vessel for the trip to Seattle. In March, Peterson, who was still in Alaska, borrowed $4,000 from Ek. Two months later, Ek began to receive unanticipated, unauthorized bills for vessel parts and moorage, the use of her phone, and charges on her credit card. She went to Juneau to take possession of the boat. Peterson moved it to Petersburg, Alaska, where he registered it under a false name, and then to Taku Harbor, where the police seized it. Ek filed a suit in an Alaska state court against Peterson, alleging breach of contract and seeking damages. If the court finds in Ek's favor, what should her damages include? Discuss. [*Peterson v. Ek,* 93 P.3d 458 (Alaska 2004)]

—**After you have answered Problem 14–6, compare your answer with the sample answer given on the Web site that accompanies this text. Go to www.cengage.com/blaw/blt, select "Chapter 14," and click on "Case Problem with Sample Answer."**

14–7 Remedies. On July 7, 2000, Frances Morelli agreed to sell to Judith Bucklin a house at 126 Lakedell Drive in Warwick, Rhode Island, for $77,000. Bucklin made a deposit on the house. The closing at which the parties would exchange the deed for the price was scheduled for September 1. The agreement did not state that "time is of the essence," but it did provide, in "Paragraph 10" that "[i]f Seller is unable to [convey good, clear, insurable, and marketable title], Buyer shall have the option to: (a) accept such title as Seller is able to convey without abatement or reduction of the Purchase Price, or (b) cancel this Agreement and receive a return of all Deposits." An examination of the public records revealed that the house did not have marketable title. Wishing to be flexible, Bucklin offered Morelli time to resolve the problem, and the closing did not occur as scheduled. Morelli decided "the deal is over" and offered to return the deposit. Bucklin refused and, in mid-October, decided to exercise her option under Paragraph 10(a). She notified Morelli, who did not respond. Bucklin filed a suit in a Rhode Island state court against Morelli. In whose favor should the court rule? Should damages be awarded? If not, what is the appropriate remedy? Why? [*Bucklin v. Morelli,* 912 A.2d 931 (R.I. 2007)]

14–8 Quasi Contract. Middleton Motors, Inc., a struggling Ford dealership in Madison, Wisconsin, sought managerial and financial assistance from Lindquist Ford, Inc., a successful Ford dealership in Bettendorf, Iowa. While the two dealerships negotiated the terms for the services and a cash infusion, Lindquist sent Craig Miller, its general manager, to assume control of Middleton. After about a year, the parties had not agreed on the terms, Lindquist had not invested any funds, Middleton had not made a profit, and Miller was fired without being paid. Lindquist and Miller filed a suit in a federal district court against Middleton based on quasi contract, seeking to recover Miller's pay for his time. What are the requirements to recover on a quasi-contract theory? Which of these requirements is most likely to be disputed in this case? Why? [*Lindquist Ford, Inc. v. Middleton Motors, Inc.,* 557 F.3d 469 (7th Cir. 2009)]

14–9   **A Question of Ethics** *In 2004, Tamara Cohen, a real estate broker, began showing property in Manhattan to Steven Galistinos, who represented comedian Jerry Seinfeld and his wife, Jessica. According to Cohen, she told Galistinos that her commission would be 5 or 6 percent, and he agreed. According to Galistinos, there was no such agreement. Cohen spoke with Maximillan Sanchez, another broker, about a townhouse owned by Ray and Harriet Mayeri. According to Cohen, Sanchez said that the commission would be 6 percent, which they agreed to split equally. Sanchez later acknowledged that they agreed to split the fee, but claimed that they did not discuss a specific amount. On a Friday in February 2005, Cohen showed the townhouse to Jessica. According to Cohen, she told Jessica that the commission would be 6 percent, with the Seinfelds paying half, and Jessica agreed. According to Jessica, there was no such conversation. Later that day, Galistinos asked Cohen to arrange for the Seinfelds to see the premises again. Cohen told Galistinos that her religious beliefs prevented her from showing property on Friday evenings or Saturdays before sundown. She suggested the following Monday or Tuesday, but Galistinos said that Jerry would not be available and asked her to contact Carolyn Liebling, Jerry's business manager. Cohen left Liebling a message. Over the weekend, the Seinfelds toured the building on their own and agreed to buy the property for $3.95 million. Despite repeated attempts, they were unable to contact Cohen. [*Cohen v. Seinfeld,* 15 Misc.3d 1118(A), 839 N.Y.S.2d 432 (Sup. 2007)]*

1 The contract between the Seinfelds and the Mayeris stated that the sellers would pay Sanchez's fee and the "buyers will pay buyer's real estate broker's fees." The Mayeris paid Sanchez $118,500, which is 3 percent of $3.95 million. The Seinfelds refused to pay Cohen. She filed a suit in a New York state court against them, asserting, among other things, breach of contract. Should the court order the Seinfelds to

pay Cohen? If so, is she entitled to a full commission even though she was not available to show the townhouse when the Seinfelds wanted to see it? Explain.

2 What obligation do parties involved in business deals owe to each other with respect to their religious beliefs? How might the situation in this case have been avoided?

Critical Thinking and Writing Assignments

14–10 Critical Legal Thinking. Review the discussion of the doctrine of mitigation of damages in this chapter. What are some of the advantages and disadvantages of this doctrine?

14–11 **Video Question** Go to this text's Web site at **www.cengage.com/blaw/blt** and select "Chapter 14." Click on "Video Questions" and view the video titled *Midnight Run.* **Then answer the following questions.**

1 In the video, Eddie (Joe Pantoliano) and Jack (Robert De Niro) negotiate a contract for Jack to find "the Duke," a mob accountant who embezzled funds, and bring him back for

trial. Assume that the contract is valid. If Jack breaches the contract by failing to bring in the Duke, what kinds of remedies, if any, can Eddie seek? Explain your answer.

2 Would the equitable remedy of specific performance be available to either Jack or Eddie in the event of a breach? Why or why not?

3 Now assume that the contract between Eddie and Jack is unenforceable. Nevertheless, Jack performs his side of the bargain by bringing in the Duke. Does Jack have any legal recourse in this situation? Explain.

Practical Internet Exercises

Go to this text's Web site at **www.cengage.com/blaw/blt**, select "Chapter 14," and click on "Practical Internet Exercises." There you will find the following Internet research exercises that you can perform to learn more about the topics covered in this chapter.

Practical Internet Exercise 14–1: Legal Perspective—**Contract Damages and Contract Theory**
Practical Internet Exercise 14–2: Management Perspective—**The Duty to Mitigate**

Cumulative Business Hypothetical

Alberto Corelli offers to pay $2,500 to purchase a painting titled Moonrise *from Tara Shelley, an artist whose works have been causing a stir in the art world. Shelley accepts Corelli's offer. Assuming that the contract has met all of the requirements for a valid contract, answer the following questions.*

1. Corelli was a minor when he purchased the painting. Is the contract void? Is it voidable? What is the difference between these two concepts? A month after his eighteenth birthday, Corelli decides that he would rather have the $2,500 than the painting. He informs Shelley that he is disaffirming the contract and requests that Shelley return the $2,500 to him. When Shelley refuses to do so, Corelli brings a court action to recover the $2,500. What will the court likely decide in this situation? Why?

2. Both parties are adults, the contract is oral, and the painting is still in progress. Corelli pays Shelley the $2,500 in return for her promise to deliver the painting to his home when it is finished. A week or so later, after Shelley finishes the painting, a visitor to her gallery offers her $3,500 for it. Shelley sells the painting to the visitor and sends Corelli a signed letter explaining that she is "canceling" their contract for the *Moonrise* painting. Corelli sues Shelley to enforce the contract. Is the contract enforceable? Explain.

3. Both parties are adults, and the contract, which is in writing, states that Corelli will pay Shelley the $2,500 the following day. In the meantime, Shelley allows Corelli to take the painting home with him. The next day, Corelli's son returns the painting to Shelley, stating that he is canceling the contract. He explains that his father has been behaving strangely lately, that he seems to be mentally incompetent at times, and that he clearly was not acting rationally when he bought the painting, which he could not afford. Is the contract enforceable? Discuss fully.

4. Both parties are adults, and the contract is in writing. The contract calls for Shelley to deliver the painting to Corelli's

gallery in two weeks. Corelli has already arranged to sell the painting to a third party for $4,000, for a $1,500 profit, but it must be available for the third party in two weeks or the sale will not go through. Shelley knows this but does not deliver the painting at the time promised. Corelli sues Shelley for $1,500 in damages. Shelley claims that performance was impossible because her mother fell seriously ill and required Shelley's care. Who will win this lawsuit, and why?

5. Both parties are adults, and Shelley, on her Web site, offers to sell the painting for $2,500. Corelli accepts the offer by clicking on an "I accept" box on the computer screen displaying the offer. Among other terms, the online offer includes a forum-selection clause stating that any disputes under the contract are to be resolved by a court in California, the state in which Shelley lives. After Corelli receives the painting, he notices a smear of paint across the lower corner of the painting that was not visible in the digitized image that appeared on Shelley's Web site. Corelli calls Shelley, tells her about the smear, and says that he wants to cancel the contract and return the painting. When Shelley refuses to cooperate, Corelli sues her in a Texas state court, seeking to rescind the contract. Shelley claims that any suit against her must be filed in a California court in accordance with the forum-selection clause. Corelli maintains that the forum-selection clause is unconscionable and should not be enforced. What factors will the court consider in deciding this case? What will the court likely decide? Would it matter whether Corelli read the terms of the online offer before clicking on "I accept"?

Extended Case Study: *Braddock v. Braddock*

Fraudulent misrepresentation, as discussed in Chapter 12, is one of the events that may cause a contract to lack voluntary consent. To be fraudulent, there must be a misrepresentation of a present, material fact. A representation, or prediction, of a future fact does not qualify. The misrepresentation must be consciously false and intended to mislead an innocent party, who must justifiably rely on it. When an innocent party is fraudulently induced to enter into a contract, the party can rescind the contract and be restored to her or his original position or enforce the contract and seek damages for injuries resulting from the fraud.

In this Extended Case Study, we set out Braddock v. Braddock,[1] *a case in which an individual sacrificed his career and relocated his home and family based on his cousin's representations about a newly formed entrepreneurial venture. What was presented to the individual about his place in the new enterprise did not occur. Were the cousin's statements fraudulent? Or were they simply expressions of expectation–predictions of future possibilities–subject to contingencies that neither party could control?*

1. 60 A.D.3d 84, 871 N.Y.S.2d 68 (1 Dept. 2009). This opinion can be read online at **www.courts.state.ny.us/decisions/index.shtml**. In the left-hand column, in the "Appellate Divisions" list, click on "1st Dept." On that page, in the "Archives" section, in the "2009" pull-down menu, select "January." In the result, scroll to "Cases Decided January 6, 2009" and click on the name of the case to access the opinion.

CASE BACKGROUND

David Braddock wanted to form Broad Oak Energy, Inc. (BOE), to tap oil and gas reserves in Louisiana and Texas. He asked his cousin John, an investment banker in New York, to find an investor to provide BOE with $75 to $150 million. David assured John that he would be BOE's chief financial officer (CFO) and land manager and that he would receive half as much stock in the company as would be issued to David, who would serve as the company's chief executive officer. John quit his job, agreed to accept a significantly reduced fee to find an investor for BOE, and moved his family to Texas. As a result of John's efforts, Warburg Pincus, LLC, agreed to provide $150 million in start-up capital.

A couple of weeks later, David told John that Warburg Pincus insisted John not be made CFO or land manager. David offered him the position of landman, a substantially reduced position with lesser salary, benefits, and terms. Surprised, John nevertheless cooperated. He signed "engagement agreements" to accept the lesser position as an "employee at will," subject to discharge for any reason at any time. Stress soon began to take a toll on his health, and he was granted a conditional medical leave of absence. The next month, BOE terminated his employment.

John filed a suit in a New York state court against David, asserting that these circumstances constituted fraud. The court dismissed the complaint. John appealed to a state intermediate appellate court.

MAJORITY OPINION

SAXE, J.

* * * *

To plead a claim for [fraud], a plaintiff must assert the *misrepresentation of a material fact, which was known by the defendant to be false and intended to be relied on when made, and that there was justifiable reliance and resulting injury. The complaint here sufficiently sets forth these elements.* [Emphasis added.]

* * * *

[John's] allegations satisfy the particularity requirement for a fraud claim.

* * * *

* * * Since David and John are cousins, John's reliance on David's good faith may be found to be reasonable even where it might not be reasonable in the context of an arm's length transaction with a stranger. Family members stand in a fiduciary relationship [one of trust] toward one another in a co-owned business venture. * * * Under the circumstances alleged here, John had reason to believe that David would treat him, in their interaction, with good faith and integrity.

* * * *

The situation presented here should be distinguished from cases in which a plaintiff who was involved in a business deal claims that, in the original discussions of the deal, misrepresentations were made as to its terms but the falsity of those representations was revealed by the time the deal was executed. In such cases, the ultimate terms of the deal, if agreed upon, are all that the plaintiff is entitled to, and he will not be permitted to seek damages based upon the original misrepresentations, because he did not rely on them in electing to go through with the deal. Here, in contrast, John's subsequent execution of documents that fundamentally altered the originally promised terms of his position with the company was not merely an election to enter into the deal anyway. First of all, even before he executed * * * the agreements * * * , the deal was essentially under way, at least on his part, in that he had already sacrificed his former life and undertaken tasks to forward the venture, and he was no longer in a position to reject the offered terms or even to negotiate effectively. Indeed, when the allegations are understood in the context of an ongoing attempt by John to salvage something from his dashed expectations, the fact that he subsequently acceded to new and lesser terms should not justify holding * * * that he did not reasonably rely on his cousin's alleged misrepresentations and false assurances, to his own severe detriment.

If all these interactions had been between strangers conducting an arm's length business transaction, strict reliance on the signed written documents, to the exclusion of the parties' words and conduct, would be appropriate. But the expectation of the good faith of a family member in circumstances such as these may justify some reliance on assurances that are not incorporated into written documents drafted and executed later.

* * * *

Here, * * * the issues of material misrepresentation and reasonable reliance are not subject to summary disposition

Continued

[settlement], and the fiduciary relationship between the parties, with its concomitant [associated] mutual obligation to act in good faith, makes John's reliance on David's assurances all the more reasonable.

* * * *

* * * Defendants' motion to dismiss the complaint for failure to state a cause of action * * * [is] denied * * * so as to reinstate the [plaintiff's fraud] cause of action.

DISSENTING OPINION

LIPPMAN, P.J., (dissenting).

* * * *

* * * It is, in essence, alleged that John's entire course of conduct in providing investment banking services for a discounted fee, giving up his lucrative New York employment as an investment banker and advisor, moving to Texas and agreeing to take the non-executive position with BOE from which he was eventually dismissed * * * was induced by David's * * * assurances.

* * * *

* * * At the time of David's nominal assurances, BOE was but an unfunded shell requiring for its viability an enormous infusion of capital. And, while John was confident of procuring financing for the venture, there had been, at the time, neither a commitment of funds nor even the emergence of a leading candidate to provide such a commitment. Moreover, John, in addition to being an experienced investment banker and financial consultant, was, by reason of his own prior professional involvement in oil and gas ventures and his extensive familial connections to the industry, particularly well aware of the risks such ventures entailed. * * * In these circumstances, * * * no promise of high executive-level employment in the company * * * could reasonably have been viewed as an "assurance" or a "guarantee." * * * What he now terms "assurances" and "guarantees" could have been reasonably understood as only expressions of expectation or intent, the realization of which would depend upon contingencies not within the power of the parties to foreseeably accommodate to their stated objectives.

* * * While he may have had a moral claim to rely upon his cousin even when objective circumstances counseled otherwise, there is no legal right to recovery in fraud that may be vindicated upon such a predicate.

Accordingly, I would affirm the dismissal of plaintiffs' fraud cause of action.

QUESTIONS FOR ANALYSIS

1. **Law.** What did the majority conclude on the issue before the court in this case? What reasoning supported this conclusion?
2. **Law.** On what important point did the dissent disagree with the majority, and why?
3. **Ethics.** How do you view David's statements and John's actions? Did David take unethical advantage of his cousin, luring him in bad faith? Was John too willing to rely on assurances that he should have known from experience would not occur? Discuss.
4. **Economic Dimensions.** What does this case indicate about employment and employment contracts?
5. **Implications for the Investor.** Why would an investor like Warburg Pincus not want someone like John in an executive role in an enterprise for which the investor was providing significant capital?

Commercial Transactions

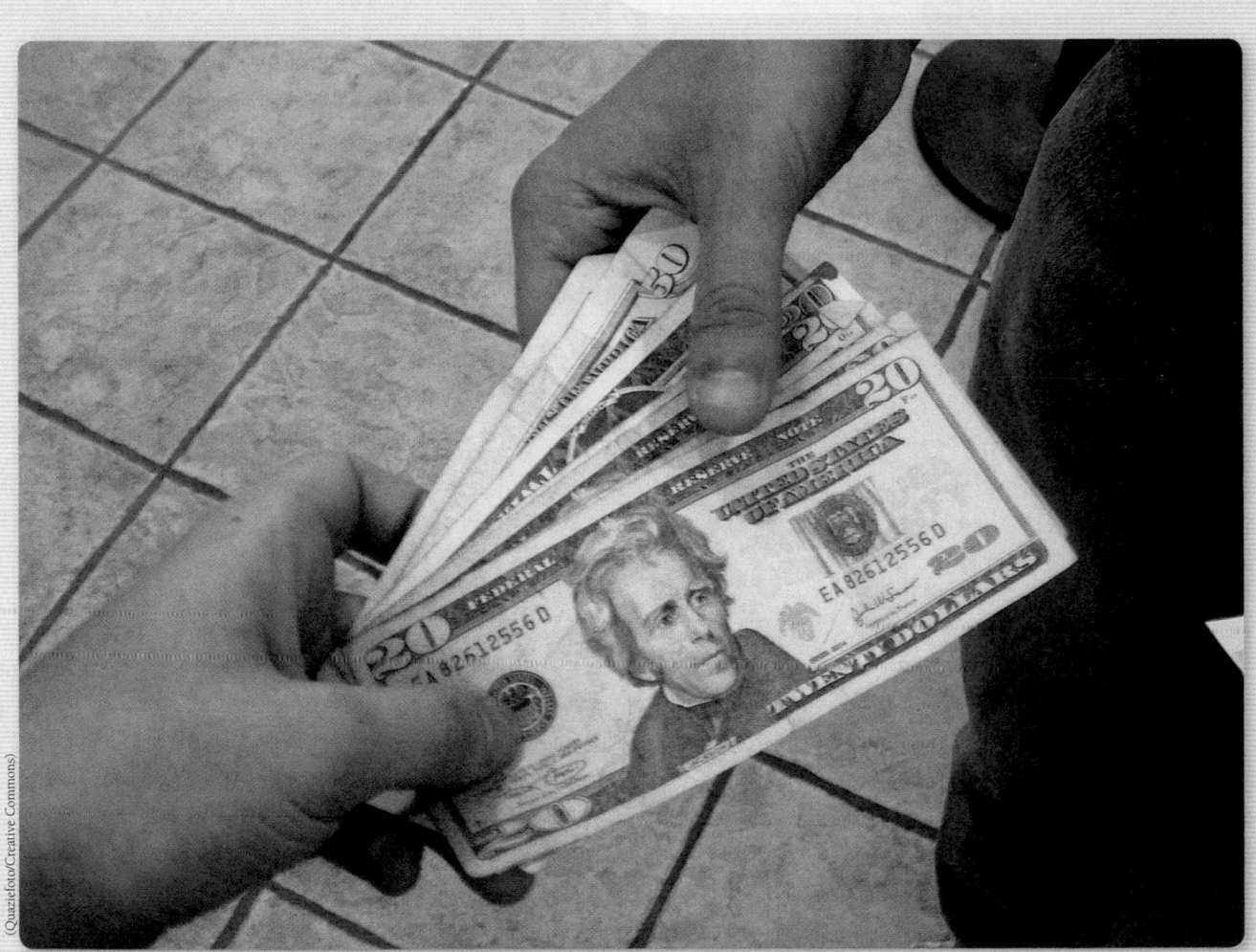

(QuazieFoto/Creative Commons)

The Formation of Sales and Lease Contracts

Chapter Outline

- The Scope of the UCC and Articles 2 (Sales) and 2A (Leases)
- The Formation of Sales and Lease Contracts
- Title and Risk of Loss
- Contracts for the International Sale of Goods

(TheTruthAbout/Creative Commons)

Learning Objectives

After reading this chapter, you should be able to answer the following questions:

1. How do Article 2 and Article 2A of the UCC differ? What types of transactions does each article cover?

2. In a sales contract, if an offeree includes additional or different terms in an acceptance, will a contract result? If so, what happens to these terms?

3. What exceptions to the writing requirements of the Statute of Frauds are provided in Article 2 and Article 2A of the UCC?

4. Risk of loss does not necessarily pass with title. If the parties to a contract do not expressly agree when risk passes and the goods are to be delivered without movement by the seller, when does risk pass?

5. What law governs contracts for the international sale of goods?

The chapter-opening quotation echoes a sentiment that most Americans believe—free commerce will benefit our nation. This is particularly true with respect to the Uniform Commercial Code (UCC). The UCC facilitates commercial transactions by making the laws governing sales and lease contracts uniform, clearer, simpler, and more readily applicable to the numerous difficulties that can arise during such transactions. Recall from Chapter 1 that the UCC is one of many uniform (model) acts drafted by the National Conference of Commissioners on Uniform State Laws and submitted to the states for adoption. Once a state legislature has adopted a uniform act, the act becomes statutory law in that state. Thus, when we turn to sales and lease contracts, we move away from common law principles and into the area of statutory law.

We open this chapter with a discussion of the general coverage of the UCC and its significance as a legal landmark. We then look at the scope of the UCC's Article 2 (on sales) and Article 2A (on leases) as a background to the formation of contracts for the sale and lease of goods. We next examine how the UCC deals with the transfer of ownership rights in (title to) goods in sales contracts using the concepts of identification, risk of loss, and insurable interest. Because international sales transactions are increasingly commonplace in the business world, we conclude this chapter with an examination of the United Nations Convention on Contracts for the International Sale of Goods (CISG), which governs international sales contracts.

The Scope of the UCC and Articles 2 (Sales) and 2A (Leases)

The UCC attempts to provide a consistent and integrated framework of rules to deal with all phases ordinarily arising in a commercial sales or lease transaction from start to finish. For example, consider the following events, all of which may occur during a single transaction:

ON THE WEB To view the text of the UCC—and keep up to date on its various revisions—go to the Web site of the National Conference of Commissioners on Uniform State Laws (NCCUSL) at www.nccusl.org.

1. *A contract for the sale or lease of goods is formed and executed.* Article 2 and Article 2A of the UCC provide rules governing all aspects of this transaction.
2. *The transaction may involve a payment—by check, electronic fund transfer, or other means.* Article 3 (on negotiable instruments), Article 4 (on bank deposits and collections), Article 4A (on fund transfers), and Article 5 (on letters of credit) cover this part of the transaction.
3. *The transaction may involve a bill of lading or a warehouse receipt that covers goods when they are shipped or stored.* Article 7 (on documents of title) deals with this subject.
4. *The transaction may involve a demand by the seller or lender for some form of security for the remaining balance owed.* Article 9 (on secured transactions) covers this part of the transaction.

The UCC has been adopted in whole or in part by all of the states.[1] Because of its importance in the area of commercial transactions, we present the UCC as this chapter's *Landmark in the Law* feature.

1. Louisiana has not adopted Articles 2 and 2A, however.

Landmark in the Law   The Uniform Commercial Code

Of all the attempts to produce a uniform body of laws relating to commercial transactions in the United States, none has been as comprehensive or successful as the Uniform Commercial Code (UCC).

The Origins of the UCC The UCC was the brainchild of William A. Schnader, president of the National Conference of Commissioners on Uniform State Laws (NCCUSL). The drafting of the UCC began in 1945. The most significant individual involved in the project was its chief editor, Karl N. Llewellyn of the Columbia University Law School. Llewellyn's intellect, continuous efforts, and ability to compromise made the first version of the UCC—completed in 1949—a legal landmark. Over the next several years, the UCC was substantially accepted by almost every state in the nation.

Periodic Changes and Updates Various articles and sections of the UCC are periodically changed or supplemented to clarify certain rules or to establish new rules when changes in business customs render the existing UCC provisions inapplicable. For example, because of the increasing importance of leases of goods in the commercial context, Article 2A

governing leases was added to the UCC. To clarify the rights of parties to commercial fund transfers, particularly electronic fund transfers, Article 4A was issued. Articles 3 and 4, on negotiable instruments and banking relationships, underwent significant revision in the 1990s. Because of other changes in business and in the law, the NCCUSL has recommended the repeal of Article 6 (on bulk transfers), offering a revised Article 6 to those states that prefer not to repeal it. The NCCUSL has also revised Article 9, covering secured transactions. The revised Article 9, which has been adopted by all of the states, will be discussed at length in Chapter 20.

• **Application to Today's World** *By periodically revising the UCC's articles, the NCCUSL has been able to adapt its provisions to changing business customs and practices. UCC provisions governing sales and lease contracts have also been extended to contracts formed in the online environment.*

• **Relevant Web Sites** To locate information on the Web concerning the Uniform Commercial Code, go to this text's Web site at www.cengage.com/blaw/blt, select "Chapter 15," and click on "URLs for Landmarks."

Article 2—Sales

Sales Contract   A contract for the sale of goods under which the ownership of goods is transferred from a seller to a buyer for a price.

Article 2 of the UCC governs **sales contracts,** or contracts for the sale of goods. To facilitate commercial transactions, Article 2 modifies some of the common law contract requirements that were discussed in Chapters 9 through 14. To the extent that it has not been modified by the UCC, however, the common law of contracts also applies to sales contracts. In general, the rule is that when a UCC provision addresses a certain issue, the UCC governs; when the UCC is silent, the common law governs. The relationship between general contract law and the law governing sales of goods is illustrated in Exhibit 15–1. (For a discussion of some problems surrounding state taxation of sales that take place over the Internet, see this chapter's *Adapting the Law to the Online Environment* feature.)

Keep in mind that Article 2 deals with the sale of *goods;* it does not deal with real property (real estate), services, or intangible property such as stocks and bonds. Thus, if a dispute involves real estate or services, the common law applies. Also note that in some situations, the rules under the UCC can vary quite a bit, depending on whether the buyer or the seller is a merchant. We look now at how the UCC defines three important terms: *sale, goods,* and *merchant status.*

Sale   The passing of title to property from the seller to the buyer for a price.

Tangible Property   Property that has physical existence and can be distinguished by the senses of touch and sight. A car is tangible property; a patent right is intangible property.

Intangible Property   Property that cannot be seen or touched but exists only conceptually, such as corporate stocks and bonds, patents and copyrights, and ordinary contract rights. Article 2 of the UCC does not govern intangible property.

WHAT IS A SALE?   The UCC defines a **sale** as "the passing of title [evidence of ownership] from the seller to the buyer for a price" [UCC 2–106(1)]. The price may be payable in cash (or its equivalent), or in other goods or services.

WHAT ARE GOODS?   To be characterized as a *good,* the item of property must be *tangible,* and it must be *movable.* **Tangible property** has physical existence—it can be touched or seen. **Intangible property**—such as corporate stocks and bonds, patents and

● *Exhibit* **15–1 The Law Governing Contracts**
This exhibit graphically illustrates the relationship between general contract law and statutory law (UCC Articles 2 and 2A) governing contracts for the sale and lease of goods. Sales contracts are not governed exclusively by Article 2 of the UCC but are also governed by general contract law whenever it is relevant and has not been modified by the UCC.

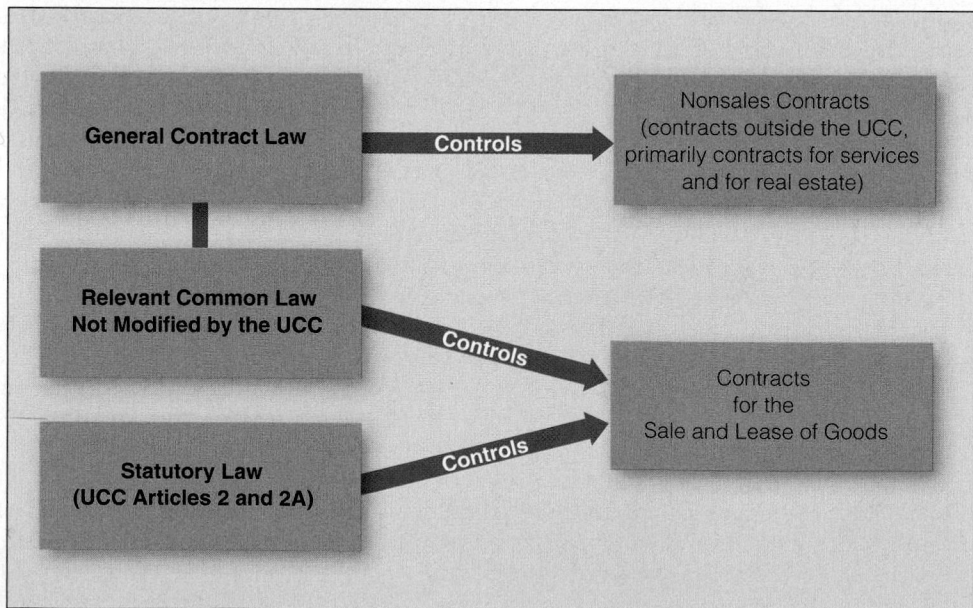

Adapting the Law to the Online Environment

The Thorny Issue of Taxing Internet Sales

From the very beginning of e-commerce, cities and states have complained that they are losing millions, if not billions, of dollars of potential tax revenues because nearly all e-commerce companies do not collect state and local sales taxes. Although most states have laws requiring their residents to report purchases from other states and to pay taxes on those purchases (so-called use taxes), few (if any) U.S. consumers ever comply with these laws. Certainly, the possibility of avoiding sales taxes has likely contributed to the growth of e-commerce. Not surprisingly, retailers with investment in physical sales outlets have complained to local, state, and federal governments about this "sales tax inequity."

Local Governments Are Suing Online Travel Companies

One recent trend in the effort to collect taxes from e-commerce has focused on online travel companies, including Travelocity, Priceline.com, Hotels.com, and Orbitz.com. By 2010, at least a dozen cities, including Atlanta, Charleston, Philadelphia, and San Antonio, had filed suits claiming that the online travel companies owed taxes on hotel reservations that they had booked. All of the cities involved in the suits impose hotel occupancy taxes. In Atlanta, for example, the local statute authorizes the city to devise "a rate of taxation, the manner of imposition, payment, and collection of the tax, and all other procedures related to the tax."[a]

At issue in the lawsuits is not whether the online travel companies owe hotel occupancy tax, but rather the amount of tax that they owe and the procedure that should be used to collect it. Online travel companies, such as Hotels.com, typically purchase blocks of hotel rooms at a wholesale rate and subsequently resell the rooms to customers at a marked-up retail rate, keeping the difference as profit. The company forwards to the hotel an amount intended to cover the hotel occupancy tax on the wholesale price of the rooms sold. The hotel then remits to the city taxing authority the tax on the rooms sold by the online travel agency. Thus, the online travel companies do not remit taxes directly to any city authorities.

In calculating the amount of tax owed, the online travel companies assess the occupancy tax rates on the wholesale prices of the rooms, rather than the retail prices that they charge. The cities claim that the online travel companies should be assessing the hotel occupancy tax on the retail prices of the rooms. The cities also want the online companies to register with the local jurisdictions and to collect and remit the required taxes directly.

What the Courts Have Been Deciding

More than a dozen cases have been brought against online travel agencies, but so far the courts have been divided. Many of these cases have been brought in federal district courts, and those courts have often ruled in favor of the cities.[b] Some state courts have also upheld the cities' claims. In one case, for example, the Supreme Court of Georgia reversed the lower court's dismissal and remanded the case for trial on Atlanta's claim concerning the city's hotel tax ordinance.[c] Given that most cities and counties have found themselves in dire financial straits during the latest recession, we can expect to see more such suits around the country.

FOR CRITICAL ANALYSIS

Why do you think that cities and states have not brought similar lawsuits against e-commerce retailers such as Amazon.com?

---

a. OCGA Section 48-13-53, which is the Enabling Statutes for the city of Atlanta.

b. See, for example, *City of Goodlettsville v. Priceline.com, Inc.,* 605 F.Supp.2d 982 (M.D.Tenn. 2009) and *City of Findlay v. Hotels.com,* **561 F.Supp.2d 917 (N.D. Ohio 2008).**

c. *City of Atlanta v. Hotels.com, L.P.,* 285 Ga. 231, 674 S.E.2d 898 (2009).

---

copyrights, and ordinary contract rights—has only conceptual existence and thus does not come under Article 2. A movable item can be carried from place to place. Hence, real estate is excluded from Article 2.

Two issues often give rise to disputes in determining whether the object of a contract is goods and thus whether Article 2 is applicable. One problem has to do with *goods associated with real estate,* such as crops or timber, and the other concerns contracts involving a combination of *goods and services.*

Goods Associated with Real Estate.   Goods associated with real estate often fall within the scope of Article 2. Section 2–107 provides the following rules:

1. A contract for the sale of minerals or the like (including oil and gas) or a structure (such as a building) is a contract for the sale of goods if *severance, or separation, is to be made by the seller.* If the *buyer* is to sever (separate) the minerals or structure from the land,

the contract is considered to be a sale of real estate governed by the principles of real property law, not the UCC.

2. A sale of growing crops (such as potatoes, carrots, and wheat) or timber to be cut is considered to be a contract for the sale of goods *regardless of who severs them.*

3. Other "things attached" to realty but capable of severance without material harm to the land are considered goods *regardless of who severs them.* Examples of "things attached" that are severable without harm to realty include a window air conditioner in a house and stools in a restaurant. Thus, the removal and sale of these items would be considered a sale of goods. The test is whether removal will cause substantial harm to the real property to which the item is attached.

Goods and Services Combined.   In cases involving contracts in which goods and services are combined, courts have reached different results. For instance, is providing blood to a patient during an operation a "sale of goods" or the "performance of a medical service"? Some courts say it is a good; others say it is a service. Because the UCC does not provide the answers to such questions, the courts generally use the **predominant-factor test** to determine whether a contract is primarily for the sale of goods or for the sale of services.[2] This determination is important because the UCC will apply to services provided under a mixed contract that is predominantly for goods, even though the majority of courts treat services as being excluded by the UCC.

In other words, if a court decides that a mixed contract is primarily a goods contract, *any* dispute, even a dispute over the services portion, will be decided under the UCC. Likewise, any disagreement over a predominantly services contract will not be decided using the UCC, even if the dispute involves the goods portion of the contract. If the transaction is not covered by the UCC, then UCC provisions, including those relating to implied warranties, will not apply. **EXAMPLE 15.1** An accounting firm contracts to purchase customized software from Micro Systems. The contract states that half of the purchase price is for Micro's professional services and the other half is for the goods (the software). If a court determines that the contract is predominantly for the software, rather than the services to customize the software, the court will hold that the transaction falls under Article 2. Conversely, if the court finds that the services are predominant, it will hold that the transaction is not governed by the UCC. ●

If an entire business, including a truck and its equipment, is sold, but the contract does not specify what portion of the sale price relates to the goods, does Article 2 of the UCC still apply to the transaction? That was the main issue in the following case.

Predominant-Factor Test A test courts use to determine whether a contract is primarily for the sale of goods or for the sale of services.

Is providing blood to a patient during an operation a "sale of goods" or the "performance of a medical service"?

---

2. UCC 2–314(1) does stipulate that serving food or drinks is a "sale of goods" for purposes of the implied warranty of merchantability, as will be discussed in Chapter 17. The UCC also specifies that selling unborn animals and rare coins qualifies as a "sale of goods."

Case 15.1 **Jannusch v. Naffziger**

Appellate Court of Illinois, Fourth District, 379 Ill.App.3d 381, 883 N.E.2d 711 (2008).

FACTS   Gene and Martha Jannusch ran Festival Foods, which provided concessions at events around Illinois and Indiana. They owned a truck, a trailer, freezers, roasters, chairs, tables, a fountain service, signs, and lighting. Lindsey and Louann Naffziger were interested in buying the conces-

Case 15.1–Continued

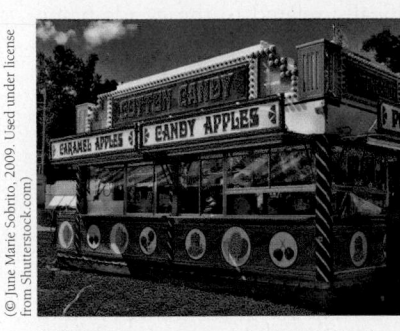

With $10,000 down, on a price of $150,000, the defendant bought a concession business and took possession of the equipment. Later, the defendant wanted out of the deal.

sions business. They met with the Jannusches and orally agreed to a price of $150,000. The Naffzigers paid $10,000 down with the balance to come from a bank loan. They took possession of the equipment and began to use it immediately in Festival Foods operations at various events, even though Gene Jannusch kept the titles to the truck and trailer in his name. Gene Jannusch was paid to attend two events with the Naffzigers to provide advice about running the operation. After six events, and at the end of the outdoor season, the Naffzigers returned the truck and all the equipment to its storage location and wanted out of the deal. They said the business did not generate as much income as they expected. The Jannusches sued the Naffzigers for the balance due on the purchase price. The trial court held that the Uniform Commercial Code (UCC) governed the case but that there was not enough evidence to show that the parties had a sufficient meeting of the minds to form a contract. The Jannusches appealed.

ISSUE   Were the goods the predominant factor in the sale of this business?

DECISION   Yes. The appeals court reversed the decision of the trial court, finding that a contract had been formed under the UCC and that the Naffzigers had breached it.

REASON   The oral agreement for the sale of the business was predominantly one for the sale of goods and therefore was within Article 2 of the UCC. The oral agreement was sufficiently definite to form a sales contract, even though it did not specify the price of each item being sold or distinguish between the value of the equipment and the value of the goodwill of the business. The Naffzigers made a payment, took possession of the business, and operated it as their own. Although some terms of the contract were missing, it was definite enough to be enforced. The fact that a specific promise was not in writing does not preclude its enforcement.

WHY IS THIS CASE IMPORTANT?   *This case illustrates how important it is to anticipate the factors that courts consider in determining whether Article 2 of the UCC applies. The facts of each situation are carefully considered. For example, even though the purchase of software may appear to be a purchase of goods, if the contract also provides for installing and modifying the software, a court might construe the contract as predominantly for services. For the buyer, this would mean that the UCC does not apply, which may be a very important consideration in some transactions.*

ON THE WEB   Cornell University's Legal Information Institute offers online access to the UCC as enacted in several of the states at **www.law.cornell.edu/statutes.html#state**.

WHO IS A MERCHANT?   Article 2 governs the sale of goods in general. It applies to sales transactions between all buyers and sellers. In a limited number of instances, however, the UCC presumes that certain special business standards ought to be imposed on merchants because they possess a relatively high degree of commercial expertise.[3] Such standards do not apply to the casual or inexperienced seller or buyer (a "consumer"). Section 2–104 sets out three ways in which merchant status can arise:

1. A merchant is a person who *deals in goods of the kind* involved in the sales contract. Thus, a retailer, a wholesaler, or a manufacturer is a merchant of those goods sold in the business. A merchant for one type of goods is not necessarily a merchant for another type. For instance, a sporting equipment retailer is a merchant when selling tennis rackets but not when selling a used computer.

2. A merchant is a person who, by occupation, *holds himself or herself out as having special knowledge and skill* related to the practices or goods involved in the transaction. Note that this broad definition may include banks or universities as merchants.

3. A person who *employs a merchant as a broker, agent, or other intermediary* has the status of merchant in that transaction. Hence, if an art collector hires a broker to purchase or sell art for her, the collector is considered a merchant in the transaction.

---

3. The provisions that apply only to merchants deal principally with the Statute of Frauds, firm offers, confirmatory memorandums, warranties, and contract modifications. These special rules reflect expedient business practices commonly known to merchants in the commercial setting. They will be discussed later in this chapter.

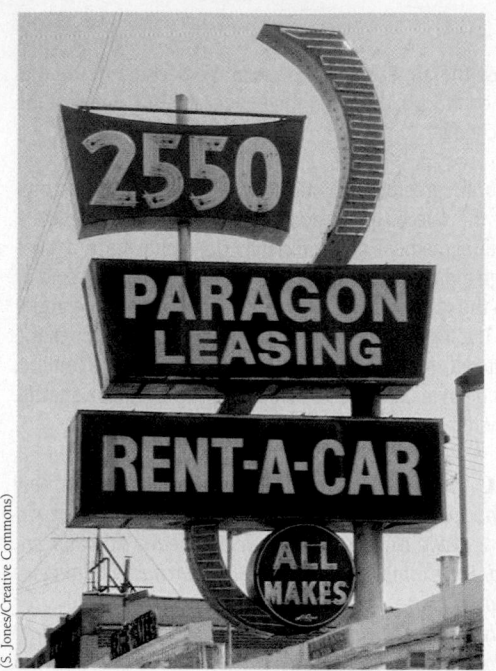

(S. Jones/Creative Commons)

A company offering leases for automobiles. All such leases are governed by Article 2 of the UCC. What leases are not governed by the UCC?

Merchant   A person who is engaged in the purchase and sale of goods. Under the UCC, a person who deals in goods of the kind involved in the sales contract or who holds herself or himself out as having skill or knowledge peculiar to the practices or goods being purchased or sold [UCC 2–104].

Lease   Under Article 2A of the UCC, a transfer of the right to possess and use goods for a period of time in exchange for payment.

Lease Agreement   In regard to the lease of goods, an agreement in which one person (the lessor) agrees to transfer the right to the possession and use of property to another person (the lessee) in exchange for rental payments.

Lessor   A person who transfers the right to the possession and use of goods to another in exchange for rental payments.

Lessee   A person who acquires the right to the possession and use of another's goods in exchange for rental payments.

In summary, a person is a **merchant** when she or he, acting in a mercantile capacity, possesses or uses an expertise specifically related to the goods being sold. This basic distinction is not always clear-cut. For instance, state courts appear to be split on whether farmers should be considered merchants. In some states, farmers are considered merchants because they sell products or livestock on a regular basis. In other states, courts have held that the drafters of the UCC did not intend to include farmers as merchants.

The Scope of Article 2A—Leases

Leases of personal property (goods) have become increasingly common. In this context, a **lease** is a transfer of the right to possess and use goods for a period of time in exchange for payment. Article 2A of the UCC was created to fill the need for uniform guidelines in this area. Article 2A covers any transaction that creates a lease of goods, as well as subleases of goods [UCC 2A–102, 2A–103(1)(k)]. Except that it applies to leases, rather than sales, of goods, Article 2A is essentially a repetition of Article 2 and varies only to reflect differences between sales and lease transactions. (Note that Article 2A is not concerned with leases of real property, such as land or buildings. The laws governing leases of real property will be discussed in Chapter 36.)

DEFINITION OF A LEASE AGREEMENT   Article 2A defines a **lease agreement** as a lessor and lessee's bargain with respect to the lease of goods, as found in their language and as implied by other circumstances, including course of dealing and usage of trade or course of performance [UCC 2A–103(1)(k)]. A **lessor** is one who transfers the right to the possession and use of goods under a lease [UCC 2A–103(1)(p)]. A **lessee** is one who acquires the right to the temporary possession and use of goods under a lease [UCC 2A–103(1)(o)]. In other words, the lessee is the party who is leasing the goods from the lessor. Article 2A applies to all types of leases of goods, including commercial leases and consumer leases. Special rules apply to certain types of leases, however, including consumer leases.

CONSUMER LEASES   A *consumer lease* involves three elements: (1) a lessor who regularly engages in the business of leasing or selling; (2) a lessee (except an organization) who leases the goods "primarily for a personal, family, or household purpose"; and (3) total lease payments that are less than a dollar amount set by state statute [UCC 2A–103(1)(e)]. To ensure special protection for consumers, certain provisions of Article 2A apply only to consumer leases. For instance, one provision states that a consumer may recover attorneys' fees if a court finds that a term in a consumer lease contract is unconscionable [UCC 2A–108(4)(a)].

▶ The Formation of Sales and Lease Contracts

In regard to the formation of sales and lease contracts, Article 2 and Article 2A of the UCC modify common law contract rules in several ways. Remember, though, that parties to sales contracts are free to basically establish whatever terms they wish. The UCC comes into play only when the parties have failed to provide in their contract for a contingency that later gives rise to a dispute. The UCC makes this clear time and again by using such phrases as "unless the parties otherwise agree" or "absent a contrary agreement by the parties."

Offer

In general contract law, the moment a definite offer is met by an unqualified acceptance, a binding contract is formed. In commercial sales transactions, the verbal exchanges, cor-

NOTE Under the UCC, it is the actions of the parties that determine whether they intended to form a contract.

respondence, and actions of the parties may not reveal exactly when a binding contractual obligation arises. The UCC states that an agreement sufficient to constitute a contract can exist even if the moment of its making is undetermined [UCC 2–204(2), 2A–204(2)].

OPEN TERMS Remember from Chapter 10 that under the common law of contracts, an offer must be definite enough for the parties (and the courts) to ascertain its essential terms when it is accepted. In contrast, the UCC states that a sales or lease contract will not fail for indefiniteness even if one or more terms are left open as long as (1) the parties intended to make a contract and (2) there is a reasonably certain basis for the court to grant an appropriate remedy [UCC 2–204(3), 2A–204(3)].

EXAMPLE 15.2 Mike agrees to lease a highly specialized computer work station from Office Mart. Mike and one of Office Mart's sales representatives sign a lease agreement that leaves some of the details blank, to be "worked out" the following week, when the leasing manager will be back from her vacation. In the meantime, Office Mart obtains the necessary equipment from one of its suppliers and spends several days modifying the equipment to suit Mike's needs. When the leasing manager returns, she calls Mike and tells him that his work station is ready. Mike says he is no longer interested in the work station, as he has arranged to lease the same type of equipment for a lower price from another firm. Office Mart sues Mike to recover its costs in obtaining and modifying the equipment, and one of the issues before the court is whether the parties had an enforceable contract. The court will likely hold that they did, based on their intent and conduct, despite the "blanks" in their written agreement. •

Open Price Term. If the parties have not agreed on a price, the court will determine a "reasonable price at the time for delivery" [UCC 2–305(1)]. If either the buyer or the seller is to determine the price, the price is to be fixed (set) in good faith [UCC 2–305(2)]. Under the UCC, *good faith* means honesty in fact and the observance of reasonable commercial standards of fair dealing in the trade [UCC 2–103(1)(b)]. The concepts of *good faith* and *commercial reasonableness* permeate the UCC.

Sometimes, the price fails to be fixed through the fault of one of the parties. In that situation, the other party can treat the contract as canceled or fix a reasonable price. **EXAMPLE 15.3** Perez and Merrick enter into a contract for the sale of unfinished doors and agree that Perez will determine the price. Perez refuses to specify the price. Merrick can either treat the contract as canceled or set a reasonable price [UCC 2–305(3)]. •

Open Payment Term. When parties do not specify payment terms, payment is due at the time and place at which the buyer is to receive the goods [UCC 2–310(a)]. The buyer can tender payment using any commercially normal or acceptable means, such as a check or credit card. If the seller demands payment in cash, however, the buyer must be given a reasonable time to obtain it [UCC 2–511(2)].

CASE EXAMPLE 15.4 Max Alexander agreed to purchase hay from Wagner's farm. Alexander left his truck and trailer at the farm for the seller to load the hay. Nothing was said about when payment was due, and the parties were unaware of the UCC's rules. When Alexander came back to get the hay, a dispute broke out. Alexander claimed that he had been given less hay than he had ordered and argued that he did not have to pay at that time. Wagner refused to release the hay (or the vehicles on which the hay was loaded) until Alexander paid for it. Eventually, Alexander jumped into his truck and drove off without paying for the hay—for which he was later prosecuted for the crime of theft (see Chapter 6). Because the parties had failed to specify when payment was due, UCC 2–310(a) controlled, and payment was due at the time Alexander picked up the hay.[4] •

> *"Business, more than any other occupation, is a continual dealing with the future; it is a continual calculation, an instinctive exercise in foresight."*
> Henry R. Luce, 1898–1967
> (U.S. editor and publisher who founded *Time, Fortune, Life,* and *Sports Illustrated*)

CONTRAST The common law requires that the parties make their terms definite before they have a contract. The UCC applies general commercial standards to make the terms of a contract definite.

---

4. *State v. Alexander,* 186 Or.App. 600, 64 P.3d 1148 (2003).

Open Delivery Term.   When no delivery terms are specified, the buyer normally takes delivery at the seller's place of business [UCC 2–308(a)]. If the seller has no place of business, the seller's residence is used. When goods are located in some other place and both parties know it, delivery is made there. If the time for shipment or delivery is not clearly specified in the sales contract, the court will infer a "reasonable" time for performance [UCC 2–309(1)].

Duration of an Ongoing Contract.   A single contract might specify successive performances but not indicate how long the parties are required to deal with each other. In this situation, either party may terminate the ongoing contractual relationship. Principles of good faith and sound commercial practice call for reasonable notification before termination, however, to give the other party time to make substitute arrangements [UCC 2–309(2), (3)].

Options and Cooperation Regarding Performance.   When the contract contemplates shipment of the goods but does not specify the shipping arrangements, the *seller* has the right to make these arrangements in good faith, using commercial reasonableness in the situation [UCC 2–311].

When a sales contract omits terms relating to the assortment of goods, the *buyer* can specify the assortment. **EXAMPLE 15.5** Petry Drugs, Inc., agrees to purchase one thousand toothbrushes from Marconi's Dental Supply. The toothbrushes come in a variety of colors, but the contract does not specify color. Petry, the buyer, has the right to take six hundred blue toothbrushes and four hundred green ones if it wishes. Petry, however, must exercise good faith and commercial reasonableness in making its selection [UCC 2–311]. ●

Open Quantity Term.   Normally, if the parties do not specify a quantity, a court will have no basis for determining a remedy. This is because there is almost no way to determine objectively what is a reasonable quantity of goods for someone to buy (whereas a court can objectively determine a reasonable price for particular goods by looking at the market). Nevertheless, the UCC recognizes two exceptions involving requirements and output contracts [UCC 2–306(1)].

In a **requirements contract,** the buyer agrees to purchase and the seller agrees to sell all or up to a stated amount of what the buyer *needs* or *requires*. **EXAMPLE 15.6** Umpqua Cannery forms a contract with Al Garcia. The cannery agrees to purchase from Garcia, and Garcia agrees to sell to the cannery, all of the green beans that the cannery needs or requires during the following summer. ● There is implicit consideration in a requirements contract because the buyer (the cannery, in this situation) gives up the right to buy green beans from any other seller, and this forfeited right creates a legal detriment (that is, consideration). Requirements contracts are common in the business world and normally are enforceable. In contrast, if the buyer promises to purchase only if the buyer *wishes* to do so, or if the buyer reserves the right to buy the goods from someone other than the seller, the promise is illusory (without consideration) and unenforceable by either party.

In an **output contract,** the seller agrees to sell and the buyer agrees to buy all or up to a stated amount of what the seller *produces*. **EXAMPLE 15.7** Al Garcia forms a contract with Umpqua Cannery. Garcia agrees to sell to the cannery, and the cannery agrees to purchase from Garcia, all of the beans that Garcia produces on his farm during the following summer. ● Again, because the seller essentially forfeits the right to sell goods to another buyer, there is implicit consideration in an output contract.

The UCC imposes a *good faith limitation* on requirements and output contracts. The quantity under such contracts is the amount of requirements or the amount of output that occurs during a *normal* production year. The actual quantity purchased or sold cannot be unreasonably disproportionate to normal or comparable prior requirements or output [UCC 2–306(1)].

Requirements Contract   An agreement in which a buyer agrees to purchase and the seller agrees to sell all or up to a stated amount of what the buyer needs or requires.

Output Contract   An agreement in which a seller agrees to sell and a buyer agrees to buy all or up to a stated amount of what the seller produces.

Preventing Legal Disputes ⚖

If you leave certain terms of a sales or lease contract open, the UCC allows a court to supply the missing terms. Although this can sometimes be advantageous (to establish that a contract existed, for instance), it can also be a major disadvantage. If you fail to state a price in your contract offer, for example, a court will impose a reasonable price by looking at the market price of similar goods *at the time of delivery.* Thus, instead of receiving the usual price you charge for the goods, you will receive what a court considers a reasonable price when the goods are delivered. Therefore, when drafting contracts for the sale or lease of goods, make sure that the contract clearly states any terms that are essential to the bargain, particularly price. It is generally better to establish the terms of your own contracts rather than to leave it up to a court to determine what terms are reasonable after a dispute has arisen.

MERCHANT'S FIRM OFFER   Under regular contract principles, an offer can be revoked at any time before acceptance. The major common law exception is an *option contract* (discussed in Chapter 10), in which the offeree pays consideration for the offeror's irrevocable promise to keep the offer open for a stated period. The UCC creates a second exception for firm offers made by a merchant to sell, buy, or lease goods.

A **firm offer** arises when a merchant-offeror gives *assurances* in a *signed writing* that the offer will remain open. The merchant's firm offer is irrevocable without the necessity of consideration[5] for the stated period or, if no definite period is stated, a reasonable period (neither period to exceed three months) [UCC 2–205, 2A–205]. **EXAMPLE 15.8** Osaka, a used-car dealer, writes a letter to Saucedo on January 1 stating, "I have a 2009 Suzuki SX4 on the lot that I'll sell you for $22,500 any time between now and January 31." This writing creates a firm offer, and Osaka will be liable for breach if he sells that Suzuki SX4 to someone other than Saucedo before January 31. ●

It is necessary that the offer be both *written* and *signed* by the offeror.[6] When a firm offer is contained in a form contract prepared by the offeree, the offeror must also sign a separate assurance of the firm offer. This requirement ensures that the offeror is aware of the offer. For instance, an offeree might respond to an initial offer by sending its own form contract containing a clause stating that the offer will remain open for three months. If the firm offer is buried amid copious language in one of the pages of the offeree's form contract, the offeror may inadvertently sign the contract without realizing that it contains a firm offer, thus defeating the purpose of the rule—which is to give effect to a merchant's deliberate intent to be bound to a firm offer.

Acceptance

Acceptance of an offer to buy, sell, or lease goods generally may be made in any reasonable manner and by any reasonable means. The UCC permits acceptance of an offer to buy goods "either by a prompt *promise* to ship or by the prompt or current shipment of conforming or nonconforming goods" [UCC 2–206(1)(b)]. *Conforming goods* accord with the contract's terms; *nonconforming goods* do not.

The prompt shipment of nonconforming goods constitutes both an acceptance, which creates a contract, and a breach of that contract. This rule does not apply if the seller **seasonably** (within a reasonable amount of time) notifies the buyer that the nonconforming shipment is offered only as an *accommodation,* or as a favor. The notice of accommodation must clearly indicate to the buyer that the shipment does not constitute an acceptance and that, therefore, no contract has been formed.

Firm Offer   An offer (by a merchant) that is irrevocable without the necessity of consideration for a stated period of time or, if no definite period is stated, for a reasonable time (neither period to exceed three months). A firm offer by a merchant must be in writing and must be signed by the offeror.

BE AWARE   The UCC provides that acceptance can be made by any means of communication that is reasonable under the circumstances.

Seasonably   Within a specified time period or, if no period is specified, within a reasonable time.

---

5. If the offeree pays consideration, then an option contract (not a merchant's firm offer) is formed.

6. *Signed* includes any symbol executed or adopted by a party with a present intention to authenticate a writing [UCC 1–201(39)]. A complete signature is not required. Therefore, initials, a thumbprint, a trade name, or any mark used in lieu of a written signature will suffice, regardless of its location on the document.

EXAMPLE 15.9 McFarrell Pharmacy orders five cases of Johnson & Johnson 3-by-5-inch gauze pads from H.T. Medical Supply, Inc. If H.T. ships five cases of Xeroform 3-by-5-inch gauze pads instead, the shipment acts as both an acceptance of McFarrell's offer and a *breach* of the resulting contract. McFarrell may sue H.T. for any appropriate damages. If, however, H.T. notifies McFarrell that the Xeroform gauze pads are being shipped *as an accommodation*—because H.T. has only Xeroform pads in stock—the shipment will constitute a counteroffer, not an acceptance. A contract will be formed only if McFarrell accepts the Xeroform gauze pads. ●

COMMUNICATION OF ACCEPTANCE   Under the common law, because a unilateral offer invites acceptance by a performance, the offeree need not notify the offeror of performance unless the offeror would not otherwise know about it. In other words, a unilateral offer can be accepted by beginning performance. The UCC is more stringent than the common law in this regard because it requires notification. Under the UCC, if the offeror is not notified within a reasonable time that the offeree has accepted the contract by beginning performance, then the offeror can treat the offer as having lapsed before acceptance [UCC 2–206(2), 2A–206(2)].

ADDITIONAL TERMS   Recall from Chapter 10 that under the common law, the *mirror image rule* requires that the terms of the acceptance exactly match those of the offer. Thus, if Alderman makes an offer to Beale, and Beale in turn accepts but in the acceptance makes some slight modification to the terms of the offer, there is no contract. The UCC dispenses with the mirror image rule. Generally, the UCC takes the position that if the offeree's response indicates a *definite* acceptance of the offer, a contract is formed even if the acceptance includes additional or different terms from those contained in the offer [UCC 2–207(1)]. Whether the additional terms become part of the contract depends, in part, on whether the parties are nonmerchants or merchants.

Rules When One Party or Both Parties Are Nonmerchants.   If one (or both) of the parties is a *nonmerchant,* the contract is formed according to the terms of the original offer submitted by the original offeror and not according to the additional terms of the acceptance [UCC 2–207(2)]. **EXAMPLE 15.10** Tolsen offers in writing to sell his laptop computer and printer to Valdez for $1,500. Valdez faxes a reply to Tolsen stating, "I accept your offer to purchase your laptop and printer for $1,500. I *would like* a box of laser printer paper and two extra toner cartridges to be included in the purchase price." Valdez has given Tolsen a definite expression of acceptance (creating a contract), even though the acceptance also *suggests* an added term for the offer. Because Tolsen is not a merchant, the additional term is merely a proposal (suggestion), and Tolsen is not legally obligated to comply with that term. ●

Rules When Both Parties Are Merchants.   The drafters of the UCC created a special rule for merchants to avoid the "battle of the forms," which occurs when two merchants exchange separate standard forms containing different contract terms. Under UCC 2–207(2), in contracts *between merchants*, the additional terms *automatically* become part of the contract unless one of the following conditions exists:

1. The original offer expressly limited acceptance to its terms.
2. The new or changed terms materially alter the contract.
3. The offeror objects to the new or changed terms within a reasonable period of time.

Generally, if the modification does not involve an unreasonable element of surprise or hardship for the offeror, the court will hold that the modification did not materially alter the contract. Courts also consider the parties' prior dealings and course of performance when determining whether the alteration is material.

Conditioned on Offeror's Assent. Regardless of merchant status, the UCC provides that the offeree's expression cannot be construed as an acceptance if it contains additional or different terms that are explicitly conditioned on the offeror's assent to those terms [UCC 2–207(1)]. **EXAMPLE 15.11** Philips offers to sell Hundert 650 pounds of turkey thighs at a specified price and with specified delivery terms. Hundert responds, "I accept your offer for 650 pounds of turkey thighs *on the condition that you give me ninety days to pay for them*." Hundert's response will be construed not as an acceptance but as a counteroffer, which Philips may or may not accept. •

Additional Terms May Be Stricken. The UCC provides yet another option for dealing with conflicting terms in the parties' writings. Section 2–207(3) states that conduct by both parties that recognizes the existence of a contract is sufficient to establish a contract for the sale of goods even though the writings of the parties do not otherwise establish a contract. In this situation, "the terms of the particular contract will consist of those terms on which the writings of the parties agree, together with any supplementary terms incorporated under any other provisions of this Act." In a dispute over contract terms, this provision allows a court simply to strike from the contract those terms on which the parties do not agree.

EXAMPLE 15.12 SMT Marketing orders goods over the phone from Brigg Sales, Inc., which ships the goods with an acknowledgment form (confirming the order) to SMT. SMT accepts and pays for the goods. The parties' writings do not establish a contract, but there is no question that a contract exists. If a dispute arises over the terms, such as the extent of any warranties, UCC 2–207(3) provides the governing rule. •

Consideration

The common law rule that a contract requires consideration also applies to sales and lease contracts. Unlike the common law, however, the UCC does not require a contract modification to be supported by new consideration. An agreement modifying a contract for the sale or lease of goods "needs no consideration to be binding" [UCC 2–209(1), 2A–208(1)].

MODIFICATIONS MUST BE MADE IN GOOD FAITH Of course, a contract modification must be sought in good faith [UCC 1–304]. **EXAMPLE 15.13** Allied, Inc., agrees to lease a new recreational vehicle (RV) to Diane Lee for a stated monthly payment. Subsequently, a sudden shift in the market makes it difficult for Allied to lease the new RV to Lee at the contract price without suffering a loss. Allied tells Lee of the situation, and she agrees to pay an additional sum for the lease of the RV. Later, Lee reconsiders and refuses to pay more than the original price. Under the UCC, Lee's promise to modify the contract needs no consideration to be binding. Hence, she is bound by the modified contract. •

In this example, a shift in the market is a *good faith* reason for contract modification. What if there really was no shift in the market, however, and Allied knew that Lee needed to lease the new RV immediately but refused to deliver it unless she agreed to pay a higher price? This attempt at extortion through modification without a legitimate commercial reason would be ineffective because it would violate the duty of good faith. Allied would not be permitted to enforce the higher price.

WHEN MODIFICATION WITHOUT CONSIDERATION REQUIRES A WRITING In some situations, an agreement to modify a sales or lease contract without consideration must be in writing to be enforceable. If the contract itself prohibits any changes to the contract unless they are in a signed writing, for instance, then only those changes agreed to in a signed writing are enforceable. If a consumer (nonmerchant buyer) is dealing with a merchant and the merchant supplies the form that contains a prohibition against oral modification, the consumer must sign a separate acknowledgment of such a clause [UCC 2–209(2), 2A–208(2)].

Also, any modification that brings a sales contract under Article 2's Statute of Frauds provision usually must be in writing to be enforceable. Thus, if an oral contract for the sale of goods priced at $400 is modified so that the contract goods are priced at $600, the modification must be in writing to be enforceable [UCC 2–209(3)]. (This is because the UCC's Statute of Frauds provision, as you will read shortly, requires a written record of sales contracts for goods priced at $500 or more.) If, however, the buyer accepts delivery of the goods after the modification, he or she is bound to the $600 price [UCC 2–201(3)(c)]. (Unlike Article 2, Article 2A does not say whether a lease as modified needs to satisfy the Statute of Frauds.)

The Statute of Frauds

BE AWARE   It has been proposed that the UCC be revised to eliminate the Statute of Frauds.

The UCC contains Statute of Frauds provisions covering sales and lease contracts. Under these provisions, sales contracts for goods priced at $500 or more and lease contracts requiring payments of $1,000 or more must be in writing to be enforceable [UCC 2–201(1), 2A–201(1)]. (These low threshold amounts may eventually be raised.)

SUFFICIENCY OF THE WRITING   The UCC has greatly relaxed the requirements for the sufficiency of a writing to satisfy the Statute of Frauds. A writing or a memorandum will be sufficient as long as it indicates that the parties intended to form a contract and as long as it is signed by the party (or agent of the party—see Chapter 23) against whom enforcement is sought. The contract normally will not be enforceable beyond the quantity of goods shown in the writing, however. All other terms can be proved in court by oral testimony. For leases, the writing must reasonably identify and describe the goods leased and the lease term.

SPECIAL RULES FOR CONTRACTS BETWEEN MERCHANTS   Once again, the UCC provides a special rule for merchants in sales transactions (there is no corresponding rule that applies to leases under Article 2A). Merchants can satisfy the Statute of Frauds if, after the parties have agreed orally, one of the merchants sends a signed written confirmation to the other merchant within a reasonable time. The communication must indicate the terms of the agreement, and the merchant receiving the confirmation must have reason to know of its contents. Unless the merchant who receives the confirmation gives written notice of objection to its contents within ten days after receipt, the writing is sufficient against the receiving merchant, even though she or he has not signed anything [UCC 2–201(2)]. Generally, courts even hold that it is sufficient if a merchant sends an e-mail confirmation of the agreement.[7]

EXAMPLE 15.14   Alfonso is a merchant-buyer in Cleveland. He contracts over the telephone to purchase $4,000 worth of spare aircraft parts from Goldstein, a merchant-seller in New York City. Two days later, Goldstein sends a written and signed confirmation detailing the terms of the oral contract, and Alfonso subsequently receives it. If Alfonso does not notify Goldstein in writing of his objection to the contents of the confirmation within ten days of receipt, Alfonso cannot raise the Statute of Frauds as a defense against the enforcement of the oral contract. ●

EXCEPTIONS   In addition to the special rules for merchants, the UCC defines three exceptions to the writing requirements of the Statute of Frauds. An oral contract for the

---

7. See, for example, *Bazak International Corp. v. Tarrant Apparel Group*, 378 F.Supp.2d 377 (S.D.N.Y. 2005); and *Great White Bear, LLC v. Mervyns, LLC*, 2007 WL 1295747 (S.D.N.Y. 2007).

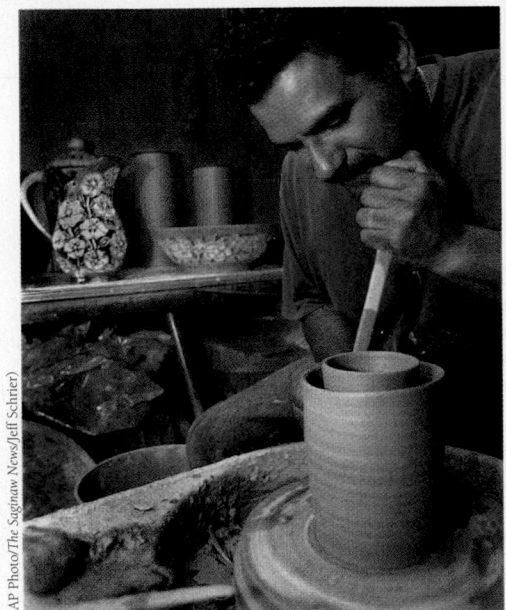

(AP Photo/The Saginaw News/Jeff Schrier)

An artisan creates a specially designed "bowl within a bowl" out of one piece of clay. If a restaurant orally contracted with the artisan to create twenty of the specially designed bowls for use in its business at a price of $800, would the contract have to be in writing to be enforceable? Why or why not?

sale of goods priced at $500 or more or the lease of goods involving total payments of $1,000 or more will be enforceable despite the absence of a writing in the circumstances discussed in the following subsections [UCC 2–201(3), 2A–201(4)]. These exceptions and other ways in which sales law differs from general contract law are summarized in the *Concept Summary* below.

Specially Manufactured Goods.   An oral contract is enforceable if (1) it is for goods that are specially manufactured for a particular buyer or specially manufactured or obtained for a particular lessee, (2) these goods are not suitable for resale or lease to others in the ordinary course of the seller's or lessor's business, and (3) the seller or lessor has substantially started to manufacture the goods or has made commitments for their manufacture or procurement. In this situation, once the seller or lessor has taken action, the buyer or lessee cannot repudiate the agreement claiming the Statute of Frauds as a defense.

EXAMPLE 15.15 Womach orders custom-made draperies for her new boutique. The price is $6,000, and the contract is oral. When the merchant-seller manufactures the draperies and tenders delivery to Womach, she refuses to pay for them even though the job has been completed on time. Womach claims that she is not liable because the contract was oral. Clearly, if the unique style and color of the draperies make it improbable that the seller can find another buyer, Womach is liable to the seller. Note that the seller must have made a substantial beginning in manufacturing the specialized item prior to the buyer's repudiation. (Here, the manufacture was completed.) Of course, the court must still be convinced by evidence of the terms of the oral contract. ●

Admissions.   An oral contract for the sale or lease of goods is enforceable if the party against whom enforcement of the contract is sought admits in pleadings, testimony, or other court proceedings that a contract for sale was made. In this situation, the contract will be enforceable even though it was oral, but enforceability will be limited to the quantity of goods admitted.

Concept Summary   **Major Differences between Contract Law and Sales Law**

	CONTRACT LAW	**SALES LAW**
Contract Terms	Contract must contain all material terms.	Open terms are acceptable, if parties intended to form a contract, but the contract is not enforceable beyond quantity term.
Acceptance	Mirror image rule applies. If additional terms are added in acceptance, counteroffer is created.	Additional terms will not negate acceptance unless acceptance is made expressly conditional on assent to the additional terms.
Contract Modification	Modification requires consideration.	Modification does not require consideration.
Irrevocable Offers	Option contracts (with consideration).	Merchants' firm offers (without consideration).
Statute of Frauds Requirements	All material terms must be included in the writing.	Writing is required only for the sale of goods of $500 or more, but contract is not enforceable beyond quantity specified. Merchants can satisfy the requirement by a confirmatory memorandum evidencing their agreement. *Exceptions:* 1. Specially manufactured goods. 2. Admissions by party against whom enforcement is sought. 3. Partial performance.

Is it possible to admit to a contract in court and also assert the Statute of Frauds as a defense? That was the position of one of the parties in the following case.

Case 15.2   Glacial Plains Cooperative v. Lindgren

Court of Appeals of Minnesota, 759 N.W.2d 661 (2009).
www.lawlibrary.state.mn.us/archive[a]

COMPANY PROFILE *Glacial Plains Cooperative is a locally owned agricultural cooperative based in west central Minnesota. Glacial Plains employs fifty to one hundred workers, who supply grain marketing, seed, energy, feed, and agronomy products and services. Recent annual sales have averaged between $50 million and $100 million. The cooperative also offers short-term, low-interest loans and other financial products to its members. Glacial Plains' motto is "Solid Performance and Returning Cash to Member Owners."*

Does the admissions exception to the Statute of Frauds apply because the written agreement to sell grain was unsigned?

FACTS Gerald Lindgren, a farmer, agreed by phone to sell grain to Glacial Plains Cooperative. They reached four agreements: two for the delivery of 9,000 and 10,000 bushels of soybeans in the fall of 2006, one for the delivery of 65,000 bushels of corn in the same season, and one for the sale of 30,000 bushels of corn in the fall of 2007. Glacial Plains sent Lindgren four written—but unsigned—contracts. Lindgren made the soybean deliveries and part of the first corn delivery, but sold the rest of his corn to another dealer. Glacial Plains bought corn elsewhere, paying a higher price, and filed a suit in a Minnesota state

court against Lindgren for breach of contract. During a deposition and in papers filed with the court, Lindgren acknowledged his oral agreements with Glacial Plains and admitted that he did not fully perform. He argued, nonetheless, that the agreements were unenforceable because they were not signed. The court denied Lindgren's defense. He appealed.

ISSUE Does the admissions exception to the Statute of Frauds apply in these circumstances?

DECISION Yes. A state intermediate appellate court affirmed the lower court's decision and remanded the case for a determination of the contracts' terms.

REASON Under UCC 2–207, a contract for a sale of goods for the price of $500 or more is not enforceable "unless there is some writing sufficient to indicate that a contract for sale has been made between the parties and signed by the party against whom enforcement is sought." The contract may be enforceable even when there is no signed writing "if the party against whom enforcement is sought admits in pleading, testimony or otherwise in court that a contract for sale was made" [UCC 2–201(3)(b)]. In this case, Lindgren made such admissions during his deposition and in documents filed with the court. The court applied the admissions exception to conclude that the agreements were enforceable.

FOR CRITICAL ANALYSIS—Ethical Consideration *Suppose that Lindgren had admitted to a lesser quantity than he had orally promised to Glacial Plains but that other proof of the true orally agreed-to terms was available. What might have been the result? Explain your answer.*

a. In the "Court of Appeals Opinions" box, click on "Index by Release Date." On that page, in the "Published" column, in the "2009" section, select "January–March." In the result, scroll to "January 27, 2009" and click on the docket number of the case to access the opinion. The Minnesota State Law Library maintains this Web site.

Partial Performance. An oral contract for the sale or lease of goods is enforceable if payment has been made and accepted or goods have been received and accepted. This is the "partial performance" exception. The oral contract will be enforced at least to the extent that performance *actually* took place.

EXAMPLE 15.16 Allan orally contracts to lease to Opus Enterprises a thousand chairs at $2 each to be used during a one-day concert. Before delivery, Opus sends Allan a check for $1,000, which Allan cashes. Later, when Allan attempts to deliver the chairs, Opus refuses delivery, claiming the Statute of Frauds as a defense, and demands the return of its $1,000. Under the UCC's partial performance rule, Allan can enforce the oral contract by tender of delivery of five hundred chairs for the $1,000 accepted. Similarly, if Opus had made no payment but had accepted the delivery of five hundred chairs from Allan, the oral contract would have been enforceable against Opus for $1,000, the lease payment due for the five hundred chairs delivered. ●

Parol Evidence

> *"Whatever is not nailed down is mine. Whatever I can pry loose is not nailed down."*
>
> Collis P. Huntington, 1821–1900
> (U.S. railroad magnate)

Recall from Chapter 12 that *parol evidence* is testimony or other evidence of the parties' prior negotiations, prior agreements, or contemporaneous oral agreements. When the parties to a sales contract set forth its terms in a confirmatory memorandum or in other writing that is intended as a complete and final statement of their agreement, it is considered *fully integrated* and the *parol evidence rule* applies. The terms of a fully integrated contract cannot be contradicted by evidence of any prior agreements or contemporaneous oral agreements. If, however, the writing contains some of the terms the parties agreed on but not others, then the contract is not fully integrated.

When a court finds that the terms of the sales contract are *not fully integrated,* then the court may allow evidence of *consistent additional terms* to explain or supplement the terms stated in the contract. The court may also allow the parties to submit evidence of *course of dealing, usage of trade,* or *course of performance* [UCC 2–202, 2A–202].

Course of Dealing Prior conduct between the parties to a contract that establishes a common basis for their understanding.

COURSE OF DEALING AND USAGE OF TRADE   Under the UCC, the meaning of any agreement, evidenced by the language of the parties and by their actions, must be interpreted in light of commercial practices and other surrounding circumstances. In interpreting a commercial agreement, the court will assume that the course of prior dealing between the parties and the usage of trade were taken into account when the agreement was phrased.

A **course of dealing** is a sequence of previous actions and communications between the parties to a particular transaction that establishes a common basis for their understanding [UCC 1–303(b)]. A course of dealing is restricted to the sequence of actions and communications between the parties that occurred prior to the agreement in question. Under the UCC, a course of performance (discussed below) or course of dealing between the parties—or one that the parties are (or should be) aware of because it is widely used in the particular trade or industry—is relevant in ascertaining the meaning of the parties' agreement, may give particular meaning to specific terms of the agreement, and may supplement or qualify the terms of the agreement [UCC 1–303(d)].

Usage of Trade Any practice or method of dealing having such regularity of observance in a place, vocation, or trade as to justify an expectation that it will be observed with respect to the transaction in question.

Usage of trade is any practice or method of dealing having such regularity of observance in a place, vocation, or trade as to justify an expectation that it will be observed with respect to the transaction in question [UCC 1–303(c)]. Further, the express terms of an agreement and an applicable course of dealing or usage of trade will be construed to be consistent with each other whenever reasonable. When such a construction is *unreasonable,* however, the express terms in the agreement will prevail [UCC 1–303(e)].

Course of Performance The conduct that occurs under the terms of a particular agreement. Such conduct indicates what the parties to an agreement intended it to mean.

COURSE OF PERFORMANCE   A **course of performance** is the conduct that occurs under the terms of a particular agreement [UCC 1–303(a)]. Presumably, the parties themselves know best what they meant by their words, and the course of performance actually undertaken under their agreement is the best indication of what they meant [UCC 2–208(1), 2A–207(1)].

EXAMPLE 15.17 Janson's Lumber Company contracts with Barrymore to sell Barrymore a specified number of "two-by-fours." The lumber in fact does not measure 2 inches by 4 inches but rather $1^{7}/8$ inches by $3^{3}/4$ inches. Janson's agrees to deliver the lumber in five deliveries, and Barrymore, without objection, accepts the lumber in the first three deliveries. On the fourth delivery, however, Barrymore objects that the two-by-fours do not measure 2 inches by 4 inches. The course of performance in this transaction—that is, the fact that Barrymore accepted three deliveries without objection under the agreement—is relevant in determining that here the term *two-by-four* actually means "$1^{7}/8$ by $3^{3}/4$." Janson's can also prove that two-by-fours need not be exactly 2 inches by 4 inches by applying usage of trade, course of prior dealing, or both. Janson's can, for example, show that in previous transactions, Barrymore took $1^{7}/8$-by-$3^{3}/4$-inch lumber without objection. In addition, Janson's can show that in the lumber trade, two-by-fours are commonly $1^{7}/8$ inches by $3^{3}/4$ inches. •

RULES OF CONSTRUCTION   The UCC provides *rules of construction* for interpreting contracts. Express terms, course of performance, course of dealing, and usage of trade are to be construed together when they do not contradict one another. When such a construction is unreasonable, however, the following order of priority controls: (1) express terms, (2) course of performance, (3) course of dealing, and (4) usage of trade [UCC 1–303(e), 2–208(2), 2A–207(2)].

Unconscionability

As discussed in Chapter 11, an unconscionable contract is one that is so unfair and one sided that it would be unreasonable to enforce it. The UCC allows the court to evaluate a contract or any clause in a contract, and if the court deems it to have been unconscionable at the time it was made, the court can (1) refuse to enforce the contract, (2) enforce the remainder of the contract without the unconscionable clause, or (3) limit the application of any unconscionable clauses to avoid an unconscionable result [UCC 2–302, 2A–108]. The following classic case illustrates an early application of the UCC's unconscionability provisions.

Classic Case 15.3   Jones v. Star Credit Corp.

Supreme Court of New York, Nassau County, 59 Misc.2d 189, 298 N.Y.S.2d 264 (1969).

HISTORICAL AND ECONOMIC SETTING   *In the sixth century, Roman civil law allowed the courts to rescind a contract if the market value of the goods that were the subject of the contract equaled less than half the contract price. This same ratio has appeared over the last forty years in many cases in which courts have found contract clauses to be unconscionable under UCC 2–302 on the ground that the price was excessive. Most of the litigants who have used UCC 2–302 successfully have been consumers who were poor or otherwise at a disadvantage. In a Connecticut case, for example, the court held that a contract requiring a person who was poor to make payments totaling $1,248 for a television set that retailed for $499 was unconscionable.*[a] *The seller had not told the buyer the full purchase price. In a New York case, the court held that a contract requiring a Spanish-speaking consumer to make payments totaling nearly $1,150 for a freezer that wholesaled for less than $350 was unconscionable.*[b] *The contract was in English, and the salesperson did not translate or explain it.*

It has long been established by courts that contracts for goods with a purchase price significantly higher than the true market value are unconscionable and therefore unenforceable.

FACTS   The Joneses, the plaintiffs, agreed to purchase a freezer for $900 as the result of a salesperson's visit to their home. Tax and financing charges raised the total price to $1,234.80. At trial, the freezer was found to have a maximum retail value of approximately $300. The plaintiffs, who had made payments totaling $619.88, brought a suit in a New York state court to have the purchase contract declared unconscionable under the UCC.

ISSUE   Can this contract be denied enforcement on the ground of unconscionability?

DECISION   Yes. The court held that the contract was not enforceable as it stood, and the contract was reformed so that no further payments were required.

REASON   The court relied on UCC 2–302(1), which states that if "the court as a matter of law finds the contract or any clause of the contract to have been unconscionable at the time it was made, the court may * * * so limit the application of any unconscionable clause as to avoid any unconscionable result." The court then examined the disparity between the $900 purchase price and the $300 retail value, as well as the fact that the credit charges alone exceeded the retail value. These excessive charges were exacted despite the seller's knowledge of the plaintiffs' limited resources. The court reformed the contract so that the plaintiffs' payments, amounting to more than $600, were regarded as payment in full.

IMPACT OF THIS CASE ON TODAY'S LAW   *This early case illustrates the approach that many courts today take when deciding whether a sales contract is unconscionable—an approach that focuses on "excessive" price and unequal bargaining power.*

RELEVANT WEB SITES   *To locate information on the Web concerning the* Jones v. Star Credit Corp. *decision, go to this text's Web site at* www.cengage.com/blaw/blt. *Select "Chapter 15" and click on "Classic Cases."*

---

a. *Murphy v. McNamara,* 36 Conn.Supp. 183, 416 A.2d 170 (1979).
b. *Frostifresh Corp. v. Reynoso,* 52 Misc.2d 26, 274 N.Y.S.2d 757 (1966), reversed on issue of damages, 54 Misc.2d 119, 281 N.Y.S.2d 946 (1967).

▶ Title and Risk of Loss

Before the creation of the UCC, *title*—the right of ownership—was the central concept in sales law, controlling all issues of rights and remedies of the parties to a sales contract. In some situations, title is still relevant under the UCC, and the UCC has special rules for determining who has title. (These rules do not apply to leased goods, obviously, because title remains with the lessor, or owner, of the goods.) In most situations, however, the UCC has replaced the concept of title with three other concepts: (1) identification, (2) risk of loss, and (3) insurable interest.

Identification

> **"To win, you have to risk loss."**
>
> Jean-Claude Killy, 1943–present
> (French alpine skier)

Identification   In a sale of goods, the express designation of the goods provided for in the contract.

Before any interest in specific goods can pass from the seller or lessor to the buyer or lessee, the goods must exist and be identified as the specific goods designated in the contract. **Identification** takes place when specific goods are designated as the subject matter of a sales or lease contract. Title and risk of loss cannot pass from seller to buyer unless the goods are identified to the contract. (As mentioned, title to leased goods does not pass to the lessee.) Identification is significant because it gives the buyer or lessee the right to insure the goods and the right to recover from third parties who damage the goods.

The parties can agree in their contract on when identification will take place (although it will not effectively pass title and risk of loss to the buyer on future goods, such as unborn cattle). If the parties do not so specify, however, the UCC provisions discussed here determine when identification takes place [UCC 2–501(1), 2A–217].

EXISTING GOODS   If the contract calls for the sale or lease of specific goods that are already in existence, identification takes place at the time the contract is made. **EXAMPLE 15.18** You contract to purchase or lease a fleet of five cars designated by their vehicle identification numbers (VINs). Because the cars are identified by their VINs, identification has taken place, and you acquire an insurable interest in them at the time of contracting. ●

FUTURE GOODS   If a sale involves unborn animals to be born within twelve months after contracting, identification takes place when the animals are conceived. If a lease involves any unborn animals, identification occurs when the animals are conceived. If a sale involves crops that are to be harvested within twelve months (or the next harvest season occurring after contracting, whichever is longer), identification takes place when the crops are planted; otherwise, identification takes place when they begin to grow. In a sale or lease of any other future goods, identification occurs when the goods are shipped, marked, or otherwise designated by the seller or lessor as the goods to which the contract refers.

Fungible Goods   Goods that are alike by physical nature, by agreement, or by trade usage (for example, wheat, oil, and wine that are identical in type and quality). When owners hold fungible goods as tenants in common, title and risk can pass without actually separating the goods being sold from the larger mass.

GOODS THAT ARE PART OF A LARGER MASS   As a general rule, goods that are part of a larger mass are identified when the goods are marked, shipped, or somehow designated by the seller or lessor as the particular goods that are the subject of the contract. **EXAMPLE 15.19** A buyer orders 1,000 cases of beans from a 10,000-case lot. Until the seller separates the 1,000 cases of beans from the 10,000-case lot, title and risk of loss remain with the seller. ●

A common exception to this rule involves fungible goods. **Fungible goods** are goods that are alike by physical nature, by agreement, or by trade usage, such as specific grades or types of wheat, oil, and wine, that are usually stored in large containers. If more than one person owns an interest in the fungible goods as *tenants in common* (see Chapter 36), a seller-owner can pass title and risk of loss to the buyer without an actual separation. The buyer replaces the seller as an owner in common [UCC 2–105(4)].

Passage of Title

Once goods exist and are identified, the provisions of UCC 2–401 apply to the passage of title. In nearly all subsections of UCC 2–401, the words "unless otherwise explicitly agreed" appear, meaning that any explicit understanding between the buyer and the seller determines when title passes. Without an explicit agreement to the contrary, *title passes to the buyer at the time and the place the seller performs by delivering the goods* [UCC 2–401(2)]. For instance, if a person buys cattle at a livestock auction, title will pass to the buyer when the cattle are physically delivered to him or her (unless, of course, the parties agree otherwise).

Shipment Contract A contract for the sale of goods in which the seller is required or authorized to ship the goods by carrier. The seller assumes liability for any losses or damage to the goods until they are delivered to the carrier.

SHIPMENT AND DESTINATION CONTRACTS   Unless otherwise agreed, delivery arrangements can determine when title passes from the seller to the buyer. In a **shipment contract,** the seller is required or authorized to ship goods by carrier, such as a trucking company. Under a shipment contract, the seller is required only to deliver conforming goods into the hands of a carrier, and title passes to the buyer at the time and place of shipment [UCC 2–401(2)(a)]. Generally, *all contracts are assumed to be shipment contracts if nothing to the contrary is stated in the contract.*

Destination Contract A contract for the sale of goods in which the seller is required or authorized to ship the goods by carrier and tender delivery of the goods at a particular destination. The seller assumes liability for any losses or damage to the goods until they are tendered at the destination specified in the contract.

In a **destination contract,** the seller is required to deliver the goods to a particular destination, usually directly to the buyer, but sometimes to another party designated by the buyer. Title passes to the buyer when the goods are *tendered* at that destination [UCC 2–401(2)(b)]. As you will read in Chapter 16, *tender of delivery* occurs when the seller places or holds conforming goods at the buyer's disposal (with any necessary notice), enabling the buyer to take possession [UCC 2–503(1)].

Document of Title A paper exchanged in the regular course of business that evidences the right to possession of goods (for example, a bill of lading or a warehouse receipt).

DELIVERY WITHOUT MOVEMENT OF THE GOODS   When the sales contract does not call for the seller to ship or deliver the goods (when the buyer is to pick up the goods), the passage of title depends on whether the seller must deliver a **document of title,** such as a bill of lading or a warehouse receipt, to the buyer. A *bill of lading* is a receipt for goods that is signed by a carrier and serves as a contract for the transport of the goods. A *warehouse receipt* is a receipt issued by a warehouser for goods stored in a warehouse.

When a document of title is required, title passes to the buyer *when and where the document is delivered.* Thus, if the goods are stored in a warehouse, title passes to the buyer when the appropriate documents are delivered to the buyer. The goods never move. In fact, the buyer can choose to leave the goods at the same warehouse for a period of time, and the buyer's title to those goods will be unaffected.

When no documents of title are required and delivery is made without moving the goods, title passes at the time and place the sales contract is made, if the goods have already been identified. If the goods have not been identified, title does not pass until identification occurs [UCC 2–401(3)]. **EXAMPLE 15.20** Juarez sells lumber to Bodan. They agree that Bodan will pick up the lumber at the lumberyard. If the lumber has been identified (segregated, marked, or in any other way distinguished from all other lumber), title passes to Bodan when the contract is signed. If the lumber is still in large storage bins at the lumberyard, title does not pass to Bodan until the particular pieces of lumber to be sold under this contract are identified. •

SALES OR LEASES BY NONOWNERS   Problems occur when persons who acquire goods with *imperfect* titles attempt to sell or lease them. Sections 2–402 and 2–403 of the UCC deal with the rights of two parties who lay claim to the same goods, sold with imperfect titles. Generally, a buyer acquires at least whatever title the seller has to the goods sold.

Void Title.   A buyer may unknowingly purchase goods from a seller who is not the owner of the goods. If the seller is a thief, the seller's title is *void*—legally, no title exists. Thus, the buyer acquires no title, and the real owner can reclaim the goods from the buyer. If the goods were only leased, the same result would occur because the lessor has no leasehold interest to transfer.

EXAMPLE 15.21 If Saki steals diamonds owned by Maren, Saki has a *void title* to those diamonds. If Saki sells the diamonds to Shannon, Maren can reclaim them from Shannon even though Shannon acted in good faith and honestly was not aware that the goods were stolen. • (Article 2A contains similar provisions for leases.)

Voidable Title. A seller has *voidable title* if the goods that she or he is selling were obtained by fraud, paid for with a check that is later dishonored, purchased from a minor, or purchased on credit when the seller was insolvent. (Under the UCC, a person is **insolvent** when that person ceases to pay his [or her] debts in the ordinary course of business, cannot pay his [or her] debts as they become due, or is insolvent within the meaning of federal bankruptcy law [UCC 1–201(23)].)

In contrast to a seller with *void title,* a seller with *voidable title* has the power to transfer good title to a good faith purchaser for value. A **good faith purchaser** is one who buys without knowledge of circumstances that would make a person of ordinary prudence inquire about the validity of the seller's title to the goods. One who purchases *for value* gives legally sufficient consideration (value) for the goods purchased. The real, or original, owner cannot recover goods from a good faith purchaser for value [UCC 2–403(1)].[8] If the buyer of the goods is not a good faith purchaser for value, then the actual owner of the goods can reclaim them from the buyer (or from the seller, if the goods are still in the seller's possession).

The Entrustment Rule. According to Section 2–403(2), entrusting goods to a merchant *who deals in goods of that kind* gives the merchant the power to transfer all rights to a *buyer in the ordinary course of business.* Entrusting includes both turning over the goods to the merchant and leaving purchased goods with the merchant for later delivery or pickup [UCC 2–403(3)]. Article 2A provides a similar rule for leased goods [UCC 2A–305(2)].

A buyer in the ordinary course of business is a person who, in good faith and without knowledge that the sale violates the ownership rights or security interest of a third party, buys in ordinary course from a person (other than a pawnbroker) in the business of selling goods of that kind [UCC 1–201(9)]. (A *security interest* is any interest in personal property that secures the payment of or the performance of an obligation—see Chapter 20.)

EXAMPLE 15.22 Jan leaves her watch with a jeweler to be repaired. The jeweler sells new and used watches. The jeweler sells Jan's watch to Kim, a customer, who does not know that the jeweler has no right to sell it. Kim, as a good faith buyer, gets good title against Jan's claim of ownership.[9] Kim, however, obtains only those rights held by the person entrusting the goods (here, Jan). Suppose that in fact Jan had stolen the watch from Greg and then left it with the jeweler to be repaired. The jeweler then sells it to Kim. In this situation, Kim gets good title against Jan, who entrusted the watch to the jeweler, but not against Greg (the real owner), who neither entrusted the watch to Jan nor authorized Jan to entrust it. •

Insolvent Under the UCC, a term describing a person who ceases to pay "his [or her] debts in the ordinary course of business or cannot pay his [or her] debts as they become due or is insolvent within the meaning of federal bankruptcy law" [UCC 1–201(23)].

Good Faith Purchaser A purchaser who buys without notice of any circumstance that would cause a person of ordinary prudence to inquire as to whether the seller has valid title to the goods being sold.

BE AWARE The purpose of holding most goods in inventory is to turn those goods into cash by selling them. That is one of the reasons for the entrustment rule.

Ethical Issue ⚖️

Why should a buyer in the ordinary course of business prevail over an original owner of goods? Cases involving the entrustment rule often pit one innocent party (the original owner of goods) against another innocent party (a purchaser of the goods who qualifies as "a buyer in the ordinary course of business"). For example, suppose that Kristina Wang takes her vacuum cleaner for repairs to a dishonest merchant who is also in the business of selling new and used vacuum cleaners. If the

---

8. The real owner could, of course, sue the person who initially obtained voidable title to the goods.
9. Jan, of course, can sue the jeweler for the tort of trespass to personalty or conversion (see Chapter 4) for the equivalent cash value of the watch.

merchant sells Wang's vacuum cleaner to a buyer in the ordinary course of business, the buyer takes good title to the vacuum cleaner. Even though both Wang and the buyer have been equally victimized by the dishonest merchant, the buyer's claim to the cleaner will take priority. Why is this? Why didn't the drafters of the UCC give the original owners of the property (goods) priority in these situations? The answer is that the underlying policy of the UCC is to promote commerce and a free marketplace, and protecting Wang's property rights instead of the rights of the buyer in the ordinary course of business would not further this goal.

Risk of Loss

Under the UCC, risk of loss does not necessarily pass with title. When risk of loss passes from a seller or lessor to a buyer or lessee is generally determined by the contract between the parties. Sometimes, the contract states expressly when the risk of loss passes. At other times, it does not, and a court must interpret the performance and delivery terms of the contract to determine whether the risk has passed.

DELIVERY WITH MOVEMENT OF THE GOODS—CARRIER CASES   When the contract involves movement of the goods through a common carrier but does not specify when risk of loss passes, the courts first look for specific delivery terms in the contract. The terms that have traditionally been used in contracts within the United States are listed and defined in Exhibit 15–2. These terms determine which party will pay the costs of delivering the goods and who bears the risk of loss. If the contract does not include these terms, then the courts must decide whether the contract is a shipment or a destination contract.

Shipment Contracts.   In a shipment contract, the seller or lessor is required or authorized to ship goods by carrier, but is not required to deliver them to a particular final destination. The risk of loss in a shipment contract passes to the buyer or lessee when the goods are delivered to the carrier [UCC 2–319(1)(a), 2–509(1)(a), 2A–219(2)(a)].

EXAMPLE 15.23   A seller in Texas sells five hundred cases of grapefruit to a buyer in New York, F.O.B. Houston (free on board in Houston—that is, the buyer pays the transportation charges from Houston). The contract authorizes shipment by carrier; it does not require that the seller tender the grapefruit in New York. Risk passes to the buyer when conforming goods are properly placed in the possession of the carrier. If the goods are damaged in transit, the loss is the buyer's. (Actually, buyers have recourse against carriers, subject to

● *Exhibit* **15–2 Contract Terms–Definitions**
The contract terms listed and defined in this exhibit help to determine which party will bear the costs of delivery and when risk of loss will pass from the seller to the buyer.

F.O.B. (free on board)—Indicates that the selling price of goods includes transportation costs to the specific F.O.B. place named in the contract. The seller pays the expenses and carries the risk of loss to the F.O.B. place named [UCC 2–319(1)]. If the named place is the place from which the goods are shipped (for example, the seller's city or place of business), the contract is a shipment contract. If the named place is the place to which the goods are to be shipped (for example, the buyer's city or place of business), the contract is a destination contract.

F.A.S. (free alongside)—Requires that the seller, at his or her own expense and risk, deliver the goods alongside the carrier before risk passes to the buyer [UCC 2–319(2)].

C.I.F. or **C.&F.** (cost, insurance, and freight or just cost and freight)—Requires, among other things, that the seller "put the goods in the possession of a carrier" before risk passes to the buyer [UCC 2–320(2)]. (These are basically pricing terms, and the contracts remain shipment contracts, not destination contracts.)

Delivery ex-ship (delivery from the carrying vessel)—Means that risk of loss does not pass to the buyer until the goods are properly unloaded from the ship or other carrier [UCC 2–322].

Sample Sales Contract for Purchase of Green Coffee by Starbucks Coffee Company

Starbucks Coffee Company was founded in 1971, when it opened its first store in Seattle's Pike Place Market. Today, Starbucks is the leading roaster and retailer of specialty coffee in the world. As of mid-2009, the company had more than 16,000 stores in forty-eight countries. Starbucks's chairman and chief global strategist, Howard Schultz, has been instrumental in the company's expansion.

Schultz joined the company in 1982, when Starbucks was still only a small, but highly respected, roaster and retailer of whole-bean and ground coffee. A business trip to Italy opened Schultz's eyes to the rich tradition and popularity of the espresso bar. Espresso drinks became the foundation of his vision for the company, and when Schultz purchased Starbucks in 1987, Starbucks started brewing. In a few years, the company had expanded to numerous locations in the United States and was available in restaurants, hotels, and airports, as well as by mail-order catalogue. In 1992, Starbucks began to sell shares of the company's stock to the public.

"In the early days, there were only a few members of the financial community who believed in our viability and staying power," says Schultz. No one dreamed that Starbucks would grow from a company that was worth approximately $270 million in 1992 into a company that is worth nearly $8.15 billion today. With the forward-thinking Schultz at the helm, however, Starbucks blossomed into one of the world's most admired brands. Since opening its first international location in 1996, Starbucks has expanded to nearly 3,000 international locations throughout North America and Europe, as well as in the Middle East and Pacific Rim. Starbucks coffee is now available in supermarkets and online.

The company has also given back to the communities in which it operates—sponsoring cultural events, such as jazz and film festivals, and donating money to charities, especially those that benefit children. Starbucks provides funding for education and literacy programs, college scholarship programs, and international relief organizations. Starbucks is also strongly committed to promoting environmentally sound methods of growing coffee.

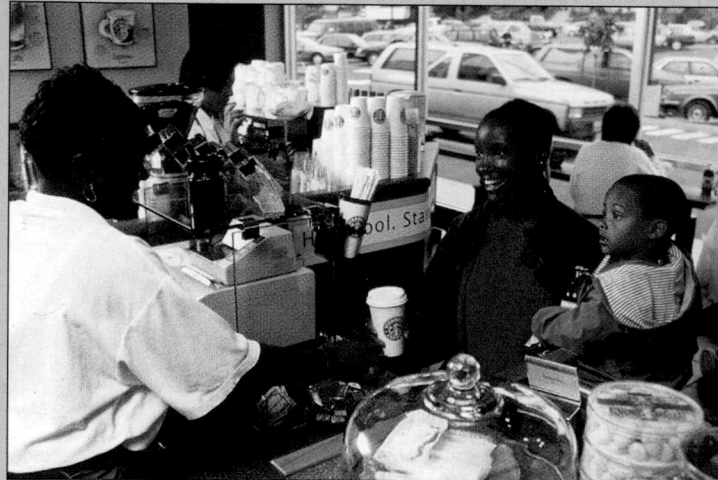

(Jill Doran for Starbucks Coffee)

❶ This is a contract for a sale of coffee to be *imported*. If the parties' principal places of business are located in different countries, the contract may be subject to the United Nations Convention on Contracts for the International Sale of Goods (CISG). See Chapter 15. If the parties' principal places of business are located in the United States, the contract may be subject to the Uniform Commercial Code (UCC).

❷ Quantity is one of the most important terms to include in a contract. Without it, a court may not be able to enforce the contract. See Chapter 15.

❸ Weight per unit (bag) can be exactly stated or approximately stated. If it is not so stated, usage of trade in international contracts determines standards of weight.

❹ Packaging requirements can be conditions for acceptance and payment. Bulk shipments are not permitted without the consent of the buyer. See Chapter 12 for an explanation of the different types of conditions.

❺ A description of the coffee and the "Markings" constitute express warranties. Warranties in contracts for domestic sales of goods are discussed in Chapter 17. International contracts rely more heavily on descriptions and models or samples.

❻ Under the UCC, parties can enter into a valid contract even though the price is not set. See Chapter 15. Under the CISG, a contract must provide for an exact determination of the price.

❼ The terms of payment can take one of two forms: credit or cash. Credit terms can be complicated. A cash term can be simple, and payment can be made by any means acceptable in the ordinary course of business (for example, a personal check or a letter of credit). If the seller insists on actual cash, the buyer must be given a reasonable time to get it. See Chapter 16.

❽ *Tender* means the seller places goods that conform to the contract at the buyer's disposition. What constitutes a valid tender is explained in Chapter 16. This contract requires that the coffee meet all import regulations and that it be ready for pickup by the buyer at a "Bonded Public Warehouse." (A *bonded warehouse* is a place in which goods can be stored without paying taxes until the goods are removed.) For a discussion of the responsibilities of the parties when goods are in a warehouse, see Chapter 35.

❾ The delivery date is significant because, if it is not met, the buyer can hold the seller in breach of the contract. Under this contract, the seller can be given a "period" within which to deliver the goods, instead of being required to deliver on a specific day, which could present problems. The seller is also given some time to rectify goods that do not pass inspection (see the "Guarantee" clause on page two). For a discussion of the remedies of the buyer and seller, see Chapter 16.

❿ As part of a proper tender, the seller (or its agent) must inform the buyer (or its agent) when the goods have arrived at their destination. The responsibilities of agents are set out in Chapter 23.

⓫ In some contracts, delivered and shipped weights can be important. During shipping, some loss can be attributed to the type of goods (spoilage of fresh produce, for example) or to the transportation itself. A seller and buyer can agree on the extent to which either of them will bear such losses.

⓬ Documents are often incorporated in a contract by reference, because including them word for word can make a contract difficult to read. If the document is later revised, the whole contract might have to be reworked. Documents that are typically incorporated by reference include detailed payment and delivery terms, special provisions, and sets of rules, codes, and standards.

⓭ In international sales transactions, and for domestic deals involving certain products, brokers are used to form the contracts. When so used, the brokers are entitled to a commission. See Chapter 23.

OVERLAND COFFEE IMPORT CONTRACT
OF THE
GREEN COFFEE ASSOCIATION
OF
NEW YORK CITY, INC.*

Contract Seller's No.: **504617**
Buyer's No.: **P9264**
Date: **9/11/10**

SOLD BY: **XYZ Co.**
TO: **Starbucks**

QUANTITY: **Five Hundred** (**500**) Bags Tons of **Mexican** coffee weighing about **152.117 lbs.** per bag.

PACKAGING: Coffee must be packed in clean sound bags of uniform size made of sisal, henequen, jute, burlap, or similar woven material, without inner lining or outer covering of any material properly sewn by hand and/or machine.
Bulk shipments are allowed if agreed by mutual consent of Buyer and Seller.

DESCRIPTION: **High grown Mexican Altura**

PRICE: At **Ten/$10.00 dollars** U.S. Currency, per **lb.** net, (U.S. Funds) Upon delivery in Bonded Public Warehouse at **Laredo, TX**
(City and State)

PAYMENT: **Cash against warehouse receipts**

Bill and tender to DATE when all import requirements and governmental regulations have been satisfied, and coffee delivered or discharged (as per contract terms). Seller is obliged to give the Buyer two (2) calendar days free time in Bonded Public Warehouse following but not including date of tender.

ARRIVAL: During **December** via **truck**
(Period) (Method of Transportation)
from **Mexico** for arrival at **Laredo, TX, USA**
(Country of Exportation) (Country of Importation)
Partial shipments permitted.

ADVICE OF ARRIVAL: Advice of arrival with warehouse name and location, together with the quantity, description, marks and place of entry, must be transmitted directly, or through Seller's Agent/Broker, to the Buyer or his Agent/Broker. Advice will be given as soon as known but not later than the fifth business day following arrival at the named warehouse. Such advice may be given verbally with written confirmation to be sent the same day.

WEIGHTS: (1) DELIVERED WEIGHTS: Coffee covered by this contract is to be weighed at location named in tender. Actual tare to be allowed.
(2) SHIPPING WEIGHTS: Coffee covered by this contract is sold on shipping weights. Any loss in weight exceeding **1/2** percent at location named in tender is for account of Seller at contract price.
(3) Coffee is to be weighed within fifteen (15) calendar days after tender. Weighing expenses, if any, for account of **seller** (Seller or Buyer)

MARKINGS: Bags to be branded in English with the name of Country of Origin and otherwise to comply with laws and regulations of the Country of Importation, in effect at the time of entry, governing marking of import merchandise. Any expense incurred by failure to comply with these regulations to be borne by Exporter/Seller.

RULINGS: The "Rulings on Coffee Contracts" of the Green Coffee Association of New York City, Inc., in effect on the date this contract is made, is incorporated for all purposes as a part of this agreement, and together herewith, constitute the entire contract. No variation or addition hereto shall be valid unless signed by the parties to the contract.
Seller guarantees that the terms printed on the reverse hereof, which by reference are made a part hereof, are identical with the terms as printed in By-Laws and Rules of the Green Coffee Association of New York City, Inc., heretofore adopted.
Exceptions to this guarantee are:

ACCEPTED: **XYZ Co.**   COMMISSION TO BE PAID BY: **seller**

BY_____ Seller
Starbucks Agent

BY_____ Buyer   **ABC Brokerage**
Agent   Broker(s)

When this contract is executed by a person acting for another, such person hereby represents that he is fully authorized to commit his principal.

certain limitations, and buyers usually insure the goods from the time the goods leave the seller.) ●

Destination Contracts.   In a destination contract, the risk of loss passes to the buyer or lessee when the goods are tendered to the buyer or lessee at the specified destination [UCC 2–319(1)(b), 2–509(1)(b), 2A–219(2)(b)]. In Example 15.23, if the contract had been F.O.B. New York, the risk of loss during transit to New York would have been the seller's.

DELIVERY WITHOUT MOVEMENT OF THE GOODS   The UCC also addresses situations in which the contract does not require the goods to be shipped or moved. Frequently, the buyer or lessee is to pick up the goods from the seller or lessor, or the goods are held by a bailee. Under the UCC, a **bailee** is a party who, by a bill of lading, warehouse receipt, or other document of title, acknowledges possession of goods and/or contracts to deliver them. A warehousing company, for example, or a trucking company that normally issues documents of title for the goods it receives is a bailee.[10]

> **Bailee** Under the UCC, a party who, by a bill of lading, warehouse receipt, or other document of title, acknowledges possession of goods and/or contracts to deliver them.

Goods Held by the Seller.   When the seller keeps the goods for pick up, a document of title usually is not used. If the seller is a merchant, risk of loss to goods held by the seller passes to the buyer when the buyer *actually takes physical possession of the goods* [UCC 2–509(3)]. In other words, the merchant bears the risk of loss between the time the contract is formed and the time the buyer picks up the goods.

If the seller is not a merchant, the risk of loss to goods held by the seller passes to the buyer on *tender of delivery* [UCC 2–509(3)]. This means that the seller bears the risk of loss until he or she makes the goods available to the buyer and notifies the buyer that the goods are ready to be picked up. With respect to leases, the risk of loss passes to the lessee on the lessee's receipt of the goods if the lessor is a merchant. Otherwise, the risk passes to the lessee on tender of delivery [UCC 2A–219(2)(c)].

Goods Held by the Bailee.   When a bailee is holding goods for a person who has contracted to sell them and the goods are to be delivered without being moved, the goods are usually represented by a document of title, such as a bill of lading or a warehouse receipt. Risk of loss passes to the buyer when (1) the buyer receives a negotiable document of title for the goods, (2) the bailee acknowledges the buyer's right to possess the goods, or (3) the buyer receives a nonnegotiable document of title or a writing (record) directing the bailee to deliver the goods *and* has had a *reasonable* time to present the document to the bailee and demand the goods. Obviously, if the bailee refuses to honor the document, the risk of loss remains with the seller [UCC 2–503(4)(b), 2–509(2)].

With respect to leases, if goods held by a bailee are to be delivered without being moved, the risk of loss passes to the lessee on acknowledgment by the bailee of the lessee's right to possession of the goods [UCC 2A–219(2)(b)].

RISK OF LOSS WHEN THE CONTRACT IS BREACHED   When a sales or lease contract is breached, the transfer of risk operates differently depending on which party breaches. Generally, the party in breach bears the risk of loss.

> **Cure** The right of a party who tenders nonconforming performance to correct that performance within the contract period [UCC 2–508(1)].

When the Seller or Lessor Breaches.   If the goods are so nonconforming that the buyer has the right to reject them, the risk of loss does not pass to the buyer until (1) the defects are **cured** (that is, until the goods are repaired, replaced, or discounted in price by the seller); or (2) the buyer accepts the goods in spite of their defects (thus waiving the right to

---

10. Bailments will be discussed in Chapter 35.

reject). **EXAMPLE 15.24** A buyer orders ten white refrigerators from a seller, F.O.B. the seller's plant. The seller ships amber refrigerators instead. The amber refrigerators (nonconforming goods) are damaged in transit. The risk of loss falls on the seller. Had the seller shipped white refrigerators (conforming goods) instead, the risk would have fallen on the buyer [UCC 2–510(1)]. ●

If a buyer accepts a shipment of goods and later discovers a defect, acceptance can be revoked. Revocation allows the buyer to pass the risk of loss back to the seller, at least to the extent that the buyer's insurance does not cover the loss [UCC 2–510(2)].

When the Buyer or Lessee Breaches. The general rule is that when a buyer or lessee breaches a contract, the risk of loss immediately shifts to the buyer or lessee. This rule has three important limitations:

1. The seller or lessor must already have identified the contract goods.
2. The buyer or lessee bears the risk for only a commercially reasonable time after the seller or lessor has learned of the breach.
3. The buyer or lessee is liable only to the extent of any deficiency in the seller's insurance coverage [UCC 2–510(3), 2A–220(2)].

Insurable Interest

Parties to sales and lease contracts often obtain insurance coverage to protect against damage, loss, or destruction of goods. Any party purchasing insurance, however, must have a sufficient interest in the insured item to obtain a valid policy. Insurance laws—not the UCC—determine sufficiency (see Chapter 37). The UCC is helpful, however, because it contains certain rules regarding insurable interests in goods.

Insurable Interest In regard to the sale or lease of goods, a property interest in the goods that is sufficiently substantial to permit a party to insure against damage to the goods.

INSURABLE INTEREST OF THE BUYER OR LESSEE A buyer or lessee has an **insurable interest** in identified goods. The moment the contract goods are identified by the seller or lessor, the buyer or lessee has a special property interest that allows the buyer or lessee to obtain necessary insurance coverage for those goods even before the risk of loss has passed [UCC 2–501(1), 2A–218(1)]. Buyers obtain an insurable interest in crops at the time of identification. **EXAMPLE 15.25** In March, a farmer sells a cotton crop that he hopes to harvest in October. When the crop is planted, the buyer acquires an insurable interest in it because those goods (the cotton crop) are identified to the sales contract between the seller and the buyer. ●

INSURABLE INTEREST OF THE SELLER OR LESSOR A seller has an insurable interest in goods if she or he retains title to the goods. Even after title passes to the buyer, a seller who has a security interest in the goods (a right to secure payment—see Chapter 20) still has an insurable interest and can insure the goods [UCC 2–501(2)]. Hence, both a buyer and a seller can have an insurable interest in identical goods at the same time. Of course, the buyer or seller must sustain an actual loss to have the right to recover from an insurance company. In regard to leases, the lessor retains an insurable interest in leased goods until the lessee exercises an option to buy and the risk of loss has passed to the lessee [UCC 2A–218(3)]. (See the *Business Application* feature at the end of this chapter for a discussion of insurance coverage and other measures that buyers and sellers can take to protect against losses.)

▶ Contracts for the International Sale of Goods

International sales contracts between firms or individuals located in different countries are governed by the 1980 United Nations Convention on Contracts for the International Sale of Goods (CISG). The CISG governs international contracts only if the countries of the parties to the contract have ratified the CISG and if the parties have not agreed that some other law will govern their contract. As of 2010, the CISG had been adopted by seventy countries, including the United States, Canada, Mexico, some Central and South American countries, and most European nations.

Applicability of the CISG

Essentially, the CISG is to international sales contracts what Article 2 of the UCC is to domestic sales contracts. As discussed in this chapter, in domestic transactions the UCC applies when the parties to a contract for a sale of goods have failed to specify in writing some important term concerning price, delivery, or the like. Similarly, whenever the parties subject to the CISG have failed to specify in writing the precise terms of a contract for the international sale of goods, the CISG will be applied. Unlike the UCC, *the CISG does not apply to consumer sales,* and neither the UCC nor the CISG applies to contracts for services.

Businesspersons must take special care when drafting international sales contracts to avoid problems caused by distance, including language differences and varying national laws. The fold-out exhibit for this chapter, which shows an actual international sales contract used by Starbucks Coffee Company, illustrates many of the special terms and clauses that are typically contained in international contracts for the sale of goods. Annotations in the exhibit explain the meaning and significance of specific clauses in the contract. (See Chapter 22 for a discussion of other laws that frame global business transactions.)

A Comparison of CISG and UCC Provisions

The provisions of the CISG, although similar for the most part to those of the UCC, differ from them in certain respects. We have already mentioned some of these differences. In the *Beyond Our Borders* feature in Chapter 12 on page 302, for example, we pointed out that the CISG does not include any Statute of Frauds provisions. Under Article 11 of the CISG, an international sales contract does not need to be evidenced by a writing or to be in any particular form.

We look here at some differences between the UCC and the CISG with respect to contract formation. In the following chapters, we will continue to point out differences between the CISG and the UCC as they relate to the topics covered. These topics include risk of loss, performance, remedies, and warranties.

OFFERS   Some differences between the UCC and the CISG have to do with offers. For instance, the UCC provides that a merchant's firm offer is irrevocable, even without consideration, if the merchant gives assurances in a signed writing. In contrast, under the CISG, an offer can become irrevocable without a signed writing. Article 16(2) of the CISG provides that an offer will be irrevocable if the merchant-offeror simply states orally that the offer is irrevocable or if the offeree reasonably relies on the offer as being irrevocable. In both of these situations, the offer will be irrevocable even without a writing and without consideration.

Another difference is that, under the UCC, if the price term is left open, the court will determine "a reasonable price at the time for delivery" [UCC 2–305(1)]. Under the CISG, however, the price term must be specified, or at least provisions for its specification must be included in the agreement; otherwise, normally no contract will exist.

ACCEPTANCES   Like UCC 2–207, the CISG provides that a contract can be formed even though the acceptance contains additional terms, unless the additional terms materially alter the contract. Under the CISG, however, the definition of a "material alteration" includes virtually any change in the terms. If an additional term relates to payment, quality, quantity, price, time and place of delivery, extent of one party's liability to the other, or the

ON THE WEB The full text of the CISG is available online at the Pace University School of Law's Institute of International Commercial Law. Go to **cisgw3.law.pace.edu**.

ON THE WEB To read an in-depth article comparing the provisions of the CISG and the UCC, go to **www.cisg.law. pace.edu/cisg/thesis/Oberman.html**.

settlement of disputes, the CISG considers the added term a "material alteration." In effect, then, the CISG requires that the terms of the acceptance mirror those of the offer.

Additionally, under the UCC, an acceptance is effective on dispatch. Under the CISG, however, a contract is not created until the offeror receives the acceptance. (The offer becomes irrevocable, however, when the acceptance is sent.) Also, in contrast to the UCC, the CISG provides that acceptance by performance does not require that the offeror be notified of the performance.

 ## Reviewing . . . The Formation of Sales and Lease Contracts

Guy Holcomb owns and operates Oasis Goodtime Emporium, an adult entertainment establishment. Holcomb wanted to create an adult Internet system for Oasis that would offer customers adult theme videos and "live" chat room programs using performers at the club. On May 10, Holcomb signed a work order authorizing Crossroads Consulting Group (CCG) "to deliver a working prototype of a customer chat system, demonstrating the integration of live video and chatting in a Web browser." In exchange for creating the prototype, Holcomb agreed to pay CCG $64,697. On May 20, Holcomb signed an additional work order in the amount of $12,943 for CCG to install a customized firewall system. The work orders stated that Holcomb would make monthly installment payments to CCG, and both parties expected the work would be finished by September. Due to unforeseen problems largely attributable to system configuration and software incompatibility, the project required more time than anticipated. By the end of the summer, the Web site was still not ready, and Holcomb had fallen behind in the payments to CCG. CCG was threatening to cease work and file suit for breach of contract unless the bill was paid. Rather than make further payments, Holcomb wanted to abandon the Web site project. Using the information presented in the chapter, answer the following questions.

1. Would a court be likely to decide that the transaction between Holcomb and CCG was covered by the Uniform Commercial Code (UCC)? Why or why not?
2. Would a court be likely to consider Holcomb a merchant under the UCC? Why or why not?
3. Did the parties have a valid contract under the UCC? Explain.
4. Suppose that Holcomb and CCG meet in October in an attempt to resolve their problems. At that time, the parties reach an oral agreement that CCG will continue to work without demanding full payment of the past-due amounts and Holcomb will pay CCG $5,000 per week. Assuming that the contract falls under the UCC, is the oral agreement enforceable? Why or why not?

Business Application
Who Bears the Risk of Loss—the Seller or the Buyer?*

The shipment of goods is a major aspect of commercial transactions. Many issues arise when an unforeseen event, such as fire or theft, causes damage to goods in transit. At the time of contract negotiation, both the seller and the buyer should determine the importance of the risk of loss. In some circumstances, risk is relatively unimportant (such as when ten boxes of copier paper are being sold), and the delivery terms should simply reflect costs and price. In other circumstances, risk is extremely important (such as when a fragile piece of pharmaceutical testing equipment is being sold), and the parties will need an express agreement as to the moment risk is to pass so that they can insure the goods accordingly. The point is that risk should be considered before a loss occurs, not after.

A major consideration relating to risk is when to insure goods against possible losses. Buyers and sellers should determine the point at which they have an insurable interest in the goods and obtain insurance coverage to protect them against loss from that point.

CHECKLIST TO DETERMINE RISK OF LOSS
The UCC uses a three-part checklist to determine risk of loss:

1. **If the contract includes terms allocating the risk of loss, those terms are binding and must be applied.**
2. **If the contract is silent as to risk, and either party breaches the contract, the breaching party is liable for the risk of loss.**
3. **When the contract makes no reference to risk and the goods are to be shipped or delivered, if neither party breaches, then the risk of loss is borne by the party having control over the goods (delivery terms).**

* This *Business Application* is not meant to substitute for the services of an attorney who is licensed to practice law in your state.

If You Are the Seller

If you are a seller of goods to be shipped, realize that as long as you have control over the goods, you are liable for any loss unless the buyer is in breach or the contract contains an explicit agreement to the contrary. When there is no explicit agreement, the delivery terms in your contract can serve as a basis for determining control. Thus, "F.O.B. buyer's business" is a destination-delivery term, and risk of loss for goods shipped under these terms does not pass to the buyer until there is a tender of delivery at the point of destination. Any loss or damage in transit falls on the seller because the seller has control until proper tender has been made.

If You Are the Buyer

From the buyer's point of view, it is important to remember that most sellers prefer "F.O.B. seller's business" as a delivery term. Under these terms, once the goods are delivered to the carrier, the buyer bears the risk of loss. Thus, if conforming goods are completely destroyed or lost in transit, the buyer not only suffers the loss but is obligated to pay the seller the contract price.

CHECKLIST FOR THE SELLER OR THE BUYER

1. **Prior to entering into a contract, determine the importance of the risk of loss for a given sale.**
2. **If risk is extremely important, the contract should expressly state the moment the risk of loss will pass from the seller to the buyer. This clause could even provide that risk will not pass until the goods are "delivered, installed, inspected, and tested (or in running order for a period of time)."**
3. **If an express clause is not agreed on, delivery terms determine the passage of risk of loss.**
4. **When appropriate, either party or both parties should consider procuring insurance.**

 ## Key Terms

bailee 381	identification 377	output contract 368
course of dealing 375	insolvent 379	predominant-factor test 364
course of performance 375	insurable interest 382	requirements contract 368
cure 381	intangible property 362	sale 362
destination contract 378	lease 366	sales contract 362
document of title 378	lease agreement 366	seasonably 369
firm offer 369	lessee 366	shipment contract 378
fungible goods 377	lessor 366	tangible property 362
good faith purchaser 379	merchant 366	usage of trade 375

 ## Chapter Summary: The Formation of Sales and Lease Contracts

The Scope of the UCC and Articles 2 (Sales) and 2A (Leases) (See pages 361–366.)	1. *The UCC*—The UCC attempts to provide a consistent, uniform, and integrated framework of rules to deal with all phases *ordinarily arising* in a commercial sales or lease transaction, including contract formation, passage of title and risk of loss, performance, remedies, payment for goods, warehoused goods, and secured transactions. 2. *Article 2 (sales)*—Article 2 governs contracts for the sale of goods (tangible, movable personal property). The common law of contracts also applies to sales contracts to the extent that the common law has not been modified by the UCC. If there is a conflict between a common law rule and the UCC, the UCC controls. 3. *Article 2A (leases)*—Article 2A governs contracts for the lease of goods. Except that it applies to leases, instead of sales, of goods, Article 2A is essentially a repetition of Article 2 and varies only to reflect differences between sales and lease transactions.
The Formation of Sales and Lease Contracts (See pages 366–376.)	1. *Offer*— a. Not all terms have to be included for a contract to be formed (only the subject matter and quantity term must be specified). b. The price does not have to be included for a contract to be formed.

Continued

Chapter Summary: The Formation of Sales and Lease Contracts—Continued

The Formation of Sales and Lease Contracts—Continued	c. Particulars of performance can be left open.
	  d. A written and signed offer by a *merchant,* covering a period of three months or less, is irrevocable without payment of consideration.
	2. *Acceptance—*
	  a. Acceptance may be made by any reasonable means of communication; it is effective when dispatched.
	  b. An offer can be accepted by a promise to ship or by prompt shipment of conforming goods, or by prompt shipment of nonconforming goods if not accompanied by a notice of accommodation.
	  c. Acceptance by performance requires notice within a reasonable time; otherwise, the offer can be treated as lapsed.
	  d. A definite expression of acceptance creates a contract even if the terms of the acceptance vary from those of the offer, unless the varied terms in the acceptance are expressly conditioned on the offeror's assent to those terms.
	3. *Consideration*—A modification of a contract for the sale of goods does not require consideration.
	4. *The Statute of Frauds—*
	  a. All contracts for the sale of goods priced at $500 or more must be in writing. A writing is sufficient as long as it indicates a contract between the parties and is signed by the party against whom enforcement is sought. A contract is not enforceable beyond the quantity shown in the writing.
	  b. When written confirmation of an oral contract *between merchants* is not objected to in writing by the receiver within ten days, the contract is enforceable.
	  c. For exceptions to the Statute of Frauds, see the *Concept Summary* on page 373.
	5. *Parol evidence rule—*
	  a. The terms of a clearly and completely worded written contract cannot be contradicted by evidence of prior agreements or contemporaneous oral agreements.
	  b. Evidence is admissible to clarify the terms of a writing if the contract terms are ambiguous or if evidence of course of dealing, usage of trade, or course of performance is necessary to learn or to clarify the parties' intentions.
	6. *Unconscionability*—An unconscionable contract is one that is so unfair and one sided that it would be unreasonable to enforce it. If the court deems a sales contract to have been unconscionable at the time it was made, the court can (a) refuse to enforce the contract, (b) refuse to enforce the unconscionable clause, or (c) limit the application of any unconscionable clauses to avoid an unconscionable result.

Title and Risk of Loss
(See pages 377–382.)
	1. *Shipment contract*—In the absence of an agreement, title and risk pass on the seller's or lessor's delivery of conforming goods to the carrier [UCC 2–319(1)(a), 2–401(2)(a), 2–509(1)(a), 2A–219(2)(a)].
	2. *Destination contract*—In the absence of an agreement, title and risk pass on the seller's or lessor's *tender* of delivery of conforming goods to the buyer or lessee at the point of destination [UCC 2–319(1)(b), 2–401(2)(b), 2–509(1)(b), 2A–219(2)(b)].
	3. *Delivery without movement of the goods*—In the absence of an agreement, if the goods are not represented by a document of title, title passes on the formation of the contract, and risk passes on the buyer's or lessee's receipt of the goods if the seller or lessor is a merchant or on the tender of delivery if the seller or lessor is a nonmerchant.
	4. *Sales and leases by nonowners*—Between the owner and a good faith purchaser or between the lessee and a sublessee:
	  a. Void title—Owner prevails [UCC 2–403(1)].
	  b. Voidable title—Buyer prevails [UCC 2–403(1)].
	  c. Entrusting to a merchant—Buyer or sublessee prevails [UCC 2–403(2), (3); 2A–305(2)].
	5. *Risk of loss when the contract is breached—*
	  a. If the seller or lessor breaches by tendering nonconforming goods that are rejected by the buyer or lessee, the risk of loss does not pass to the buyer or lessee until the defects are cured (unless the buyer or lessee accepts the goods in spite of their defects, thus waiving the right to reject) [UCC 2–510(1), 2A–220(1)].
	  b. If the buyer or lessee breaches the contract, the risk of loss immediately shifts to the buyer or lessee for goods that are identified to the contract. The buyer or lessee bears the risk for only a commercially reasonable time after the seller or lessor has learned of the breach [UCC 2–510(3), 2A–220(2)].

Chapter Summary: The Formation of Sales and Lease Contracts—Continued

Contracts for the International Sale of Goods (See pages 382–384.)	International sales contracts are governed by the United Nations Convention on Contracts for the International Sale of Goods (CISG)—if the countries of the parties to the contract have ratified the CISG (and if the parties have not agreed that some other law will govern their contract). Essentially, the CISG is to international sales contracts what Article 2 of the UCC is to domestic sales contracts. Whenever parties who are subject to the CISG have failed to specify in writing the precise terms of a contract for the international sale of goods, the CISG will be applied.

 ExamPrep

ISSUE SPOTTERS

1   E-Design, Inc., orders 150 computer desks. Fav-O-Rite Supplies, Inc., ships 150 printer stands. Is this an acceptance of the offer or a counteroffer? If it is an acceptance, is it a breach of the contract? What if Fav-O-Rite told E-Design it was sending the printer stands as "an accommodation"?

2   Truck Parts, Inc. (TPI), often sells supplies to United Fix-It Company (UFC), which services trucks. Over the phone, they negotiate for the sale of eighty-four sets of tires. TPI sends a letter to UFC detailing the terms and two weeks later ships the tires. Is there an enforceable contract between them? Why or why not?

BEFORE THE TEST

Check your answers to the Issue Spotters, and at the same time, take the interactive quiz for this chapter. Go to **www.cengage.com/blaw/blt** and click on "Chapter 15." First, click on "Answers to Issue Spotters" to check your answers. Next, click on "Interactive Quiz" to assess your mastery of the concepts in this chapter. Then click on "Flashcards" to review this chapter's Key Term definitions.

 For Review

Answers for the even-numbered questions in this For Review section can be found on this text's accompanying Web site at **www.cengage.com/blaw/blt**. *Select "Chapter 15" and click on "For Review."*

1   How do Article 2 and Article 2A of the UCC differ? What types of transactions does each article cover?

2   In a sales contract, if an offeree includes additional or different terms in an acceptance, will a contract result? If so, what happens to these terms?

3   What exceptions to the writing requirements of the Statute of Frauds are provided in Article 2 and Article 2A of the UCC?

4   Risk of loss does not necessarily pass with title. If the parties to a contract do not expressly agree when risk passes and the goods are to be delivered without movement by the seller, when does risk pass?

5   What law governs contracts for the international sale of goods?

 Hypothetical Scenarios and Case Problems

15–1 Statute of Frauds. Fresher Foods, Inc., orally agreed to purchase one thousand bushels of corn for $1.25 per bushel from Dale Vernon, a farmer. Fresher Foods paid $125 down and agreed to pay the remainder of the purchase price on delivery, which was scheduled for one week later. When Fresher Foods tendered the balance of $1,125 on the scheduled day of delivery and requested the corn, Vernon refused to deliver it. Fresher Foods sued Vernon for damages, claiming that Vernon had breached their oral contract. Can Fresher Foods recover? If so, to what extent?

15–2 Merchant's Firm Offer. On September 1, Jennings, a used-car dealer, wrote a letter to Wheeler, stating, "I have a 1955 Thunderbird convertible in mint condition that I will sell you for $13,500 at any time before October 9. [signed] Peter Jennings." By September 15, having heard nothing from Wheeler, Jennings sold the Thunderbird to another party. On September 29, Wheeler accepted Jennings's offer and tendered the $13,500. When Jennings told Wheeler he had sold the car to another party, Wheeler claimed Jennings had breached their contract. Is Jennings in breach? Explain.

15–3 **Hypothetical Question with Sample Answer** When will risk of loss pass from the seller to the buyer under each of the following contracts, assuming the parties have not expressly agreed on when risk of loss would pass?

1 A New York seller contracts with a San Francisco buyer to ship goods to the buyer F.O.B. San Francisco.

2 A New York seller contracts with a San Francisco buyer to ship goods to the buyer in San Francisco. There is no indication as to whether the shipment will be F.O.B. New York or F.O.B. San Francisco.

3 A seller contracts with a buyer to sell goods located on the seller's premises. The buyer pays for the goods and arranges to pick them up the next week at the seller's place of business.

4 A seller contracts with a buyer to sell goods located in a warehouse.

—**For a sample answer to Question 15–3, go to Appendix E at the end of this text.**

15–4 **Offer.** In 1998, Johnson Controls, Inc. (JCI), began buying auto parts from Q. C. Onics Ventures, LP. For each part, JCI would inform Onics of its need and ask the price. Onics would analyze the specifications, contact its suppliers, and respond with a formal quotation. A quote listed a part's number and description, the price per unit, and an estimate of units available for a given year. A quote did not state payment terms, an acceptance date, the time of performance, warranties, or quantities. JCI would select a supplier and issue a purchase order for a part. The purchase order required the seller to supply all of JCI's requirements for the part but gave the buyer the right to end the deal at any time. Using this procedure, JCI issued hundreds of purchase orders. In July 2001, JCI terminated its relationship with Onics and began buying parts through another supplier. Onics filed a suit in a federal district court against JCI, alleging breach of contract. Which documents—the price quotations or the purchase orders—constituted offers? Which were acceptances? What effect would the answers to these questions have on the result in this case? Explain. [*Q. C. Onics Ventures, LP v. Johnson Controls, Inc.,* __ F.Supp.2d __ (N.D.Ind. 2006)]

15–5 **Case Problem with Sample Answer** Clear Lakes Trout Co. operates a fish hatchery in Idaho. Rodney and Carla Griffith are trout growers. Clear Lakes agreed to sell "small trout" to the Griffiths, who agreed to sell the trout back when they had grown to "market size." At the time, in the trade "market size" referred to fish approximating one-pound live weight. The parties did business without a written agreement until September 1998, when they executed a contract with a six-year duration. The contract did not define "market size." All went well until September 2001, after which there was a demand for larger fish. Clear Lakes began taking deliveries later and in smaller loads, leaving the Griffiths with overcrowded ponds and other problems. In 2003, the Griffiths refused to accept more fish and filed a suit in an Idaho state court against Clear Lakes, alleging breach of contract. Clear Lakes argued that there was no contract because the parties

had different interpretations of "market size." Clear Lakes claimed that "market size" varied according to whatever its customers demanded. The Griffiths asserted that the term referred to fish of about one-pound live weight. Is outside evidence admissible to explain the terms of a contract? Are there any exceptions that could apply in this case? If so, what is the likely result? Explain. [*Griffith v. Clear Lakes Trout Co.,* 143 Idaho 733, 152 P.3d 604 (2007)]

—**After you have answered Problem 15–5, compare your answer with the sample answer given on the Web site that accompanies this text. Go to www.cengage.com/blaw/blt, select "Chapter 15," and click on "Case Problem with Sample Answer."**

15–6 **Shipment and Destination Contracts.** In 2003, Karen Pearson and Steve and Tara Carlson agreed to buy a 2004 Dynasty recreational vehicle (RV) from DeMartini's RV Sales in Grass Valley, California. On September 29, Pearson, the Carlsons, and DeMartini's signed a contract providing that "seller agrees to deliver the vehicle to you on the date this contract is signed." The buyers made a payment of $145,000 on the total price of $356,416 the next day, when they also signed a form acknowledging that the RV had been inspected and accepted. They agreed to return later to have the RV transported out of state for delivery (to avoid paying state sales tax on the purchase). On October 7, Steve Carlson returned to DeMartini's to ride with the seller's driver to Nevada to consummate the out-of-state delivery. When the RV developed problems, Pearson and the Carlsons filed a suit in a federal district court against the RV's manufacturer, Monaco Coach Corp., alleging breach of warranty under state law. The applicable statute is expressly limited to goods sold in California. Monaco argued that this RV had been sold in Nevada. How does the UCC define a sale? What does the UCC provide with respect to the passage of title? How do these provisions apply here? Discuss. [*Carlson v. Monaco Coach Corp.,* 486 F.Supp.2d 1127 (E.D.Cal. 2007)]

15–7 **Offer and Acceptance.** Continental Insurance Co. issued a policy to cover shipments by Oakley Fertilizer, Inc. Oakley agreed to ship three thousand tons of fertilizer by barge to Ameropa North America in Caruthersville, Missouri, from New Orleans, Louisiana. Oakley sent Ameropa a contract form that set out these terms and stated that title and risk would pass to the buyer after the seller was paid for the goods. Ameropa e-mailed a different form that set out the same essential terms but stated, "F.O.B. BARGE EX NEW ORLEANS." The cargo was loaded onto barges but had not yet been delivered when it was damaged by Hurricane Katrina. Oakley filed a claim for the loss with Continental but was denied coverage. Oakley filed a suit in a Missouri state court against the insurer. Continental argued that title and risk passed to Ameropa before the damage as per the buyer's form under Section 2–207(3) of the UCC because the parties did not have a valid contract under UCC 2–207(1). Apply UCC 2–207 to these facts. Is Continental correct? Explain. [*Oakley Fertilizer, Inc. v. Continental Insurance Co.,* 276 S.W.3d 342 (Mo.App.E.D. 2009)]

15–8 **A Question of Ethics** *Daniel Fox owned Fox & Lamberth Enterprises, Inc., a kitchen and bath remodeling business, in Dayton, Ohio. Fox leased a building from Carl and Bellulah Hussong. Craftsmen Home Improvement, Inc., also remodeled baths and kitchens. When Fox planned to close his business, Craftsmen expressed an interest in buying his showroom assets. Fox set a price of $50,000. Craftsmen's owners agreed and gave Fox a list of the desired items and "A Bill of Sale" that set the terms for payment. The parties did not discuss Fox's arrangement with the Hussongs, but Craftsmen expected to negotiate a new lease and extensively modified the premises, including removing some of the displays to its own showroom. When the Hussongs and Craftsmen could not agree on new terms, Craftsmen told Fox that the deal was off.* [*Fox & Lamberth Enterprises, Inc. v. Craftsmen Home Improvement, Inc., __ N.E.2d __ (2 Dist. 2006)*]

1 In Fox's suit in an Ohio state court for breach of contract, Craftsmen raised the Statute of Frauds as a defense. What are the requirements of the Statute of Frauds? Did the deal between Fox and Craftsmen meet these requirements? Did it fall under one of the exceptions? Explain.

2 Craftsmen also claimed that the "predominant factor" of its agreement with Fox was a lease for the Hussongs' building. What is the predominant-factor test? Does it apply here? In any event, is it fair to hold a party to a contract to buy a business's assets when the buyer is unable to negotiate a favorable lease of the premises on which the assets are located? Discuss.

▶ Critical Thinking and Writing Assignments

15–9 **Case Analysis Question** Go to Appendix F at the end of this text and examine Case No. 3 [*Spray-Tek, Inc. v. Robbins Motor Transportation, Inc.*, 426 F.Supp.2d 875 (W.D.Wis. 2006)]. This case has been excerpted there in great detail. Review and then brief the case, making sure that your brief answers the following questions.

1 **Issue:** What contract provision was at the heart of the dispute between the parties to this case, and why?

2 **Rule of Law:** What rule of law did the court apply to interpret this provision?

3 **Applying the Rule of Law:** How did the court apply this rule to interpret the provision at the center of this case?

4 **Conclusion:** Did the court resolve the dispute between these parties with respect to determining who suffered the loss and how much that loss was? Explain.

15–10 **Video Question** Go to this text's Web site at **www.cengage.com/blaw/blt** and select "Chapter 15." Click on "Video Questions" and view the video titled *Sales and Lease Contracts: Price as a Term*. Then answer the following questions.

1 Is Anna correct in assuming that a contract can exist even though the sales price for the computer equipment was not specified? Explain.

2 According to the Uniform Commercial Code (UCC), what conditions must be satisfied in order for a contract to be formed when certain terms are left open? What terms (in addition to price) can be left open?

3 Are the e-mail messages that Anna refers to sufficient proof of the contract?

4 Would parol evidence be admissible?

▶ Practical Internet Exercises

Go to this text's Web site at **www.cengage.com/blaw/blt**, select "Chapter 15," and click on "Practical Internet Exercises." There you will find the following Internet research exercises that you can perform to learn more about the topics covered in this chapter.

Practical Internet Exercise 15–1: LEGAL PERSPECTIVE—Is It a Contract?

Practical Internet Exercise 15–2: MANAGEMENT PERSPECTIVE—A Checklist for Sales Contracts

Practical Internet Exercise 15–3: SOCIAL PERSPECTIVE—The Entrustment Rule

Chapter 16

Performance and Breach of Sales and Lease Contracts

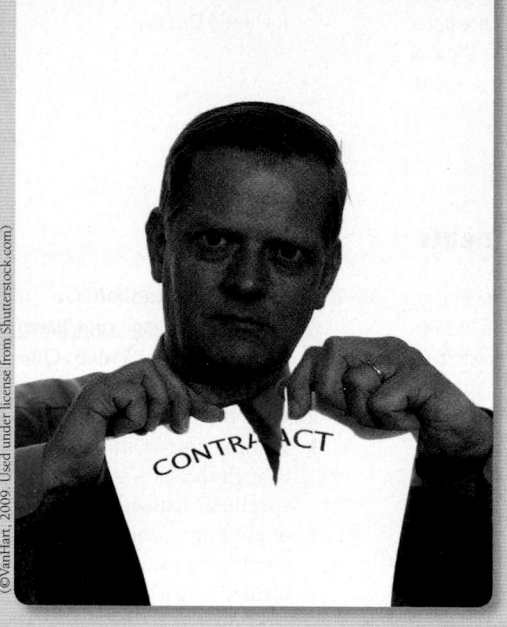

(©VanHart, 2009. Used under license from Shutterstock.com)

Chapter Outline

- Performance Obligations
- Obligations of the Seller or Lessor
- Obligations of the Buyer or Lessee
- Anticipatory Repudiation
- Remedies of the Seller or Lessor
- Remedies of the Buyer or Lessee
- Limitation of Remedies

Learning Objectives

After reading this chapter, you should be able to answer the following questions:

1. What are the respective obligations of the parties under a contract for the sale or lease of goods?

2. What is the perfect tender rule? What are some important exceptions to this rule that apply to sales and lease contracts?

3. What options are available to the nonbreaching party when the other party to a sales or lease contract repudiates the contract prior to the time for performance?

4. What remedies are available to a seller or lessor when the buyer or lessee breaches the contract? What remedies are available to a buyer or lessee if the seller or lessor breaches the contract?

5. In contracts subject to the UCC, are parties free to limit the remedies available to the nonbreaching party on a breach of contract? If so, in what ways?

The performance required of the parties under a sales or lease contract consists of the duties and obligations each party has under the terms of the contract. Keep in mind that a party's "duties and obligations" include those specified by the agreement, by custom, and by the Uniform Commercial Code (UCC). Because, as the chapter-opening quotation says, good faith "holds commerce together," the UCC also imposes a duty of good faith on the parties involved in commercial contracts. This duty basically requires honesty and fair dealing. In this chapter, we examine the performance obligations of the parties under a sales or lease contract.

Sometimes, circumstances make it difficult for a person to carry out the promised performance, and the contract is breached. When breach occurs, the aggrieved party looks for remedies—which we discuss in the second half of this chapter.

▶ Performance Obligations

As discussed in previous chapters and noted in this chapter's introduction, the standards of good faith and commercial reasonableness are read into every contract. These standards provide a framework for the entire agreement. If a sales contract leaves open some particulars of performance, for instance, the parties must exercise good faith and commercial reasonableness when later specifying the details.

In the performance of a sales or lease contract, the basic obligation of the seller or lessor is to *transfer and deliver conforming goods*. The basic obligation of the buyer or lessee is to *accept and pay for conforming goods* in accordance with the contract [UCC 2–301, 2A–516(1)]. Overall performance of a sales or lease contract is controlled by the agreement between the parties. When the contract is unclear and disputes arise, the courts look to the UCC and impose standards of good faith and commercial reasonableness.

▶ Obligations of the Seller or Lessor

Conforming Goods Goods that conform to contract specifications.

Tender of Delivery Under the Uniform Commercial Code, a seller's or lessor's act of placing conforming goods at the disposal of the buyer or lessee and giving the buyer or lessee whatever notification is reasonably necessary to enable the buyer or lessee to take delivery.

The major obligation of the seller or lessor under a sales or lease contract is to tender conforming goods to the buyer or lessee. Goods that conform to the contract description in every way are called **conforming goods.** To fulfill the contract, the seller or lessor must either deliver or tender delivery of conforming goods to the buyer or lessee. **Tender of delivery** occurs when the seller or lessor makes conforming goods available to the buyer or lessee and gives the buyer or lessee whatever notification is reasonably necessary to enable the buyer or lessee to take delivery [UCC 2–503(1), 2A–508(1)].

Tender must occur at a *reasonable hour* and in a *reasonable manner*. In other words, a seller cannot call the buyer at 2:00 A.M. and say, "The goods are ready. I'll give you twenty minutes to get them." Unless the parties have agreed otherwise, the goods must be tendered for delivery at a reasonable hour and kept available for a reasonable period of time to enable the buyer to take possession of them [UCC 2–503(1)(a)].

Normally, all goods called for by a contract must be tendered in a single delivery—unless the parties have agreed that the goods may be delivered in several lots or *installments* [UCC 2–307, 2–612, 2A–510]. Hence, an order for 1,000 shirts cannot be delivered 2 shirts at a time. If, however, the parties agree that the shirts will be delivered in four lots of 250 each as they are produced (for summer, fall, winter, and spring stock), then delivery may occur in this manner.

Place of Delivery

The UCC provides for the place of delivery pursuant to a contract only if the contract does not. The buyer and seller (or lessor and lessee) may agree that the goods will be delivered to a particular destination where the buyer or lessee will take possession. If the contract does not designate the place of delivery, then the goods must be made available to the buyer at the *seller's place of business* or, if the seller has none, at the seller's residence [UCC 2–308(a)]. If, at the time of contracting, the parties know that the goods identified to the contract are located somewhere other than the seller's business, then *the location of the goods* is the place for their delivery [UCC 2–308(b)].

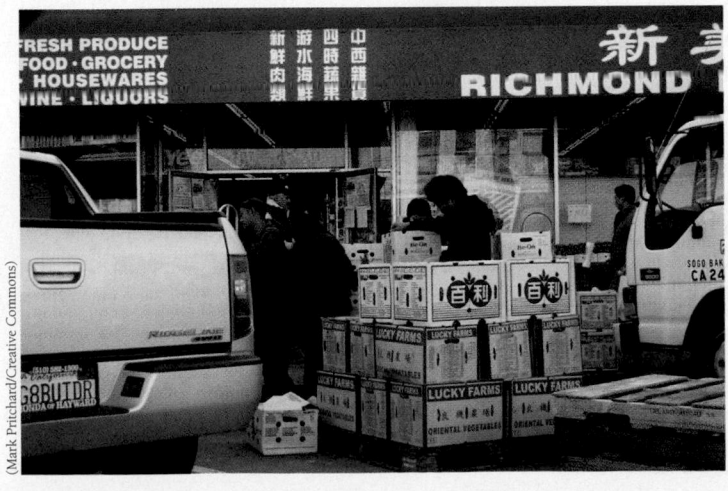

(Mark Pritchard/Creative Commons)

EXAMPLE 16.1 Li Wan and Jo Boyd both live in San Francisco. In San Francisco, Wan contracts to sell Boyd five used trucks, which both parties know are located in a Chicago warehouse. If nothing more is specified in the contract, the place of delivery for the trucks is Chicago. Wan may tender delivery either by giving Boyd a negotiable or

A vendor transfers boxes of produce into a store on San Francisco's Clement Street. Tender of delivery requires that the seller or lessor delivers all goods called for in the contract at a reasonable hour and keeps them available for a reasonable period of time to enable the buyer to take possession of them. Under what circumstances can the goods be delivered in more than one delivery?

nonnegotiable document of title or by obtaining the bailee's (warehouser's) acknowledgment that the buyer is entitled to possession.[1] ●

Delivery via Carrier

In many instances, it is clear from surrounding circumstances or delivery terms in the contract (such as F.O.B. or F.A.S. terms, shown in Exhibit 15–2 on page 380) that the parties intended the goods to be moved by a carrier. In carrier contracts, the seller fulfills the obligation to deliver the goods through either a shipment contract or a destination contract.

SHIPMENT CONTRACTS   Recall from Chapter 15 that a *shipment contract* requires or authorizes the seller to ship goods by a carrier, rather than to deliver them at a particular destination [UCC 2–319, 2–509(1)(a)]. Under a shipment contract, unless otherwise agreed, the seller must do the following:

1. Put the goods into the hands of the carrier.
2. Make a contract for their transportation that is reasonable according to the nature of the goods and their value. (For example, certain types of goods need refrigeration in transit.)
3. Obtain and promptly deliver or tender to the buyer any documents necessary to enable the buyer to obtain possession of the goods from the carrier.
4. Promptly notify the buyer that shipment has been made [UCC 2–504].

If the seller fails to notify the buyer that shipment has been made or fails to make a proper contract for transportation, the buyer can treat the contract as breached and reject the goods, but only if a *material loss* of the goods or a significant *delay* results. Of course, the parties can agree that a lesser amount of loss or that any delay will be grounds for rejection.

DESTINATION CONTRACTS   In a *destination contract,* the seller agrees to deliver conforming goods to the buyer at a particular destination. The seller must provide the buyer with any documents of title necessary to enable the buyer to obtain delivery from the carrier [UCC 2–503].

The Perfect Tender Rule

As previously noted, the seller or lessor has an obligation to ship or tender *conforming goods,* and the buyer or lessee is required to accept and pay for the goods according to the terms of the contract. Under the common law, the seller was obligated to deliver goods in conformity with the terms of the contract in every detail. This was called the *perfect tender* doctrine. The UCC preserves the perfect tender doctrine by stating that if goods or tender of delivery fails *in any respect* to conform to the contract, the buyer or lessee has the right to accept the goods, reject the entire shipment, or accept part and reject part [UCC 2–601, 2A–509].

EXAMPLE 16.2   A lessor contracts to lease fifty NEC monitors to be delivered at the lessee's place of business on or before October 1. On September 28, the lessor discovers that it has only thirty NEC monitors in inventory, but that it will have another forty NEC monitors within the next two weeks. The lessor tenders delivery of the thirty NEC monitors on October 1, with the promise that the other monitors will be delivered within two weeks. Because the lessor failed to make a perfect tender of fifty NEC monitors, the lessee has the right to reject the entire shipment and hold the lessor in breach. ●

---

1. If the seller delivers a nonnegotiable document of title or merely instructs the bailee in a writing (or electronic record) to release the goods to the buyer without the bailee's *acknowledgment* of the buyer's rights, this is also a sufficient tender, unless the buyer objects [UCC 2–503(4)]. Risk of loss, however, does not pass until the buyer has a reasonable amount of time in which to present the document or to give the bailee instructions for delivery, as discussed in Chapter 15.

Exceptions to the Perfect Tender Rule

Because of the rigidity of the perfect tender rule, several exceptions to the rule have been created, some of which are discussed here.

AGREEMENT OF THE PARTIES Exceptions to the perfect tender rule may be established by agreement. If the parties have agreed, for example, that defective goods or parts will not be rejected if the seller or lessor is able to repair or replace them within a reasonable period of time, the perfect tender rule does not apply.

CURE The UCC does not specifically define the term *cure,* but it refers to the right of the seller or lessor to repair, adjust, or replace defective or nonconforming goods [UCC 2–508, 2A–513]. When any tender of delivery is rejected because of nonconforming goods and the time for performance has not yet expired, the seller or lessor can notify the buyer or lessee promptly of the intention to cure and can then do so *within the contract time for performance* [UCC 2–508(1), 2A–513(1)]. Once the time for performance has expired, the seller or lessor still has a reasonable time in which to cure if, at the time of delivery, he or she had *reasonable grounds to believe that the nonconforming goods would be acceptable to the buyer or lessee* [UCC 2–508(2), 2A–513(2)].

EXAMPLE 16.3 In the past, EZ Office Supply frequently accepted blue pens when the seller, Baxter's Wholesale, did not have black pens in stock. In this context, Baxter's has reasonable grounds to believe that EZ will again accept such a substitute. Even if EZ rejects the substituted goods on a particular occasion, because Baxter's had reasonable grounds to believe that the substitution would be acceptable, it will have a reasonable time to cure by tendering black pens. ● A seller or lessor may sometimes tender nonconforming goods with a price allowance (discount), which can also serve as "reasonable grounds" to believe the buyer or lessee will accept the nonconforming tender.

The right to cure means that, to reject goods, the buyer or lessee must inform the seller or lessor of a particular defect. For instance, if a lessee refuses a tender of goods as nonconforming but does not disclose the nature of the defect to the lessor, the lessee cannot later assert the defect as a defense if the defect is one that the lessor could have cured. Generally, buyers and lessees must act in good faith and state specific reasons for refusing to accept goods [UCC 2–605, 2A–514].

SUBSTITUTION OF CARRIERS When an agreed-on manner of delivery (such as the carrier to be used to transport the goods) becomes impracticable or unavailable through no fault of either party, but a commercially reasonable substitute is available, the seller must use this substitute performance, which is sufficient tender to the buyer [UCC 2–614(1)].

EXAMPLE 16.4 A sales contract calls for a large generator to be delivered via Roadway Trucking Corporation on or before June 1. The contract terms clearly state the importance of the delivery date. The employees of Roadway Trucking go on strike. The seller is required to make a reasonable substitute tender, perhaps by rail if that is available. Note that the seller normally will be responsible for any additional shipping costs, unless other arrangements have been made in the sales contract. ●

INSTALLMENT CONTRACTS An **installment contract** is a single contract that requires or authorizes delivery in two or more separate lots to be accepted and paid for separately. With an installment contract, a buyer or lessee can reject an installment *only if the nonconformity substantially impairs the value* of the installment and cannot be cured [UCC 2–307, 2–612(2), 2A–510(1)]. If the buyer or lessee subsequently accepts a nonconforming installment and fails to notify the seller or lessor of cancellation, however, the contract is reinstated [UCC 2–612(3), 2A–510(2)].

A seller or lessor may sometimes tender nonconforming goods, say blue pens for black pens. What options does the buyer or lessee have when confronted with a tender of nonconforming goods?

(©Marko Poplasen, 2009. Used under license from Shutterstock.com)

"Resolve to perform what you ought; perform without fail what you resolve."

Benjamin Franklin, 1706–1790
(American politician and inventor)

Installment Contract Under the UCC, a contract that requires or authorizes delivery in two or more separate lots to be accepted and paid for separately.

Unless the contract provides otherwise, the entire installment contract is breached only when one or more nonconforming installments *substantially* impair the value of the *whole contract.* **EXAMPLE 16.5** A contract calls for the parts of a machine to be delivered in installments. The first part is necessary for the operation of the machine, but when it is delivered, it is irreparably defective. The failure of this first installment will be a breach of the whole contract because the machine will not operate without the first part. The situation would likely be different, however, if the contract had called for twenty carloads of plywood and only 6 percent of one carload had deviated from the thickness specifications in the contract. It is unlikely that a court would find that a defect in 6 percent of one installment substantially impaired the value of the whole contract. ●

The point to remember is that the UCC significantly alters the right of the buyer or lessee to reject the entire contract if the contract requires delivery to be made in several installments. The UCC strictly limits rejection to cases of *substantial* nonconformity.

COMMERCIAL IMPRACTICABILITY   As mentioned in Chapter 13, occurrences unforeseen by either party when a contract was made may make performance commercially impracticable. When this occurs, the rule of perfect tender no longer holds. According to UCC 2–615(a) and 2A–405(a), a delay in delivery or nondelivery in whole or in part is not a breach when performance has been made impracticable "by the occurrence of a contingency the nonoccurrence of which was a basic assumption on which the contract was made." The seller or lessor must, however, notify the buyer or lessee as soon as practicable that there will be a delay or nondelivery.

Foreseeable versus Unforeseeable Contingencies.   The doctrine of commercial impracticability extends only to problems that could not have been foreseen. **EXAMPLE 16.6** A major oil company that receives its supplies from the Middle East has a contract to supply a buyer with 100,000 gallons of oil. Because of an oil embargo by the Organization of Petroleum Exporting Countries, the seller is unable to secure oil supplies to meet the terms of the contract. Because of the same embargo, the seller cannot secure oil from any other source. This situation comes fully under the commercial impracticability exception to the perfect tender doctrine. ●

Can unanticipated increases in a seller's costs, which make performance "impracticable," constitute a valid defense to performance on the basis of commercial impracticability? The court dealt with this question in the following classic case.

> *"Obstacles are those frightful things you see when you take your eyes off your goal."*
>
> Henry Ford, 1863–1947
> (Founder of Ford Motor Company)

Classic Case 16.1   **Maple Farms, Inc. v. City School District of Elmira**

Supreme Court of New York, 76 Misc.2d 1080, 352 N.Y.S.2d 784 (1974).

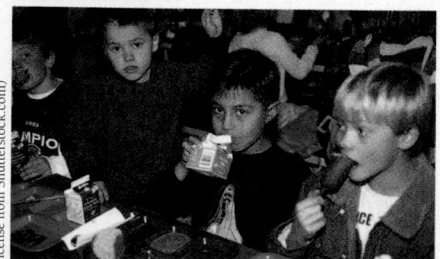

A requirement contract set the price of milk for a New York school district. An unanticipated 23 percent spike in the market price of raw milk brought a lawsuit seeking a cancellation of the agreement.

FACTS On June 15, 1973, Maple Farms, Inc., formed an agreement with the city school district of Elmira, New York, to supply the school district with milk for the 1973–1974 school year. The agreement was in the form of a requirements contract, under which Maple Farms would sell to the school district all the milk the district required at a fixed price—which was the June market price of milk. By December 1973, the price of raw milk had increased by 23 percent over the price specified in the contract. This meant that if the terms of the contract were fulfilled, Maple Farms would lose $7,350. Because it had similar contracts with other school districts, Maple Farms stood to lose a great deal if it was held to the price stated in the contracts. When the school district would not agree to release Maple Farms from its contract, Maple Farms brought an action in a New York state court for a declaratory judgment (a determination of the parties' rights under a contract). Maple Farms contended that the substantial increase in the price of raw milk was an event not contemplated by the parties when the contract was formed and that, given the increased price, performance of the contract was commercially impracticable.

Case 16.1–Continued

ISSUE Can Maple Farms be released from the contract on the ground of commercial impracticability?

DECISION No. The court ruled that performance in this case was not impracticable.

REASON The court reasoned that commercial impracticability arises when an event occurs that is totally unexpected and unforeseeable by the parties. The increased price of raw milk was not totally unexpected, given that in the previous year the price of milk had risen 10 percent and that the price of milk had traditionally varied. Additionally, the general inflation of prices in the United States should have been anticipated. Maple Farms had reason to know these facts and could have included a clause in its contract with the school district to protect itself from its present situation. The court also noted that, for the school district, the primary purpose of the contract was to protect itself (for budgeting purposes) against price fluctuations.

WHAT IF THE FACTS WERE DIFFERENT? *Suppose that the court had ruled in the plaintiff's favor. How might that ruling have affected the plaintiff's contracts with other parties?*

IMPACT OF THIS CASE ON TODAY'S LAW *This case is a classic illustration of the UCC's commercial impracticability doctrine. Under this doctrine, parties who freely enter into contracts normally will not be excused from their contractual obligations simply because changed circumstances make performance difficult or unprofitable. Rather, to be excused from performance, a party must show that the changed circumstances were unforeseeable at the time the contract was formed. This principle continues to be applied today.*

RELEVANT WEB SITES *To locate information on the Web concerning the* Maple Farms, Inc. v. City School District of Elmira *decision, go to this text's Web site at* www.cengage.com/blaw/blt. *Select "Chapter 16" and click on "Classic Cases."*

Partial Performance. Sometimes, an unforeseen event only *partially* affects the capacity of the seller or lessor to perform, and the seller or lessor is thus able to fulfill the contract *partially* but cannot tender total performance. In this event, the seller or lessor is required to allocate in a fair and reasonable manner any remaining production and deliveries among those to whom it is contractually obligated to deliver the goods, and this allocation may take into account its regular customers [UCC 2–615(b), 2A–405(b)]. The buyer or lessee must receive notice of the allocation and has the right to accept or reject it [UCC 2–615(c), 2A–405(c)].

EXAMPLE 16.7 A Florida orange grower, Best Citrus, Inc., contracts to sell this season's crop to a number of customers, including Martin's grocery chain. Martin's contracts to purchase two thousand crates of oranges. Best Citrus has sprayed some of its orange groves with a chemical called Karmoxin. The Department of Agriculture discovers that persons who eat products sprayed with Karmoxin may develop cancer. The department issues an order prohibiting the sale of these products. Best Citrus picks only those oranges not sprayed with Karmoxin, but there are not enough to meet all the contracted-for deliveries. In this situation, Best Citrus is required to allocate its production. It notifies Martin's that it cannot deliver the full quantity specified in the contract and indicates the amount it will be able to deliver. Martin's can either accept or reject the allocation, but Best Citrus has no further contractual liability. ●

Ethical Issue ⚖

Should parties be able to use the global financial crisis as a reason to escape their contractual obligations? The global financial crisis has made everyone's life more difficult, but when economic conditions make it difficult for parties to sales or lease contracts to perform, should courts void the deals as commercially impracticable? After all, most people did not foresee that 2008 and 2009 would bring what has been called an "unprecedented" economic crisis. Even Alan Greenspan, the former chair of the Federal Reserve Board, in his testimony before Congress on October 23, 2008, called it "a once-in-a-century credit tsunami."[2]

Since Greenspan's comment, several companies have argued that this economic crisis is the equivalent of a natural disaster that has made it commercially impracticable for them to fulfill their contracts. Dow

---

2. "The Financial Crisis Excuse," *Business Week*, February 23, 2009.

Chemical, for instance, attempted to claim that it could not procure financing to go through with its merger contract with Rohm & Haas, as discussed in Chapter 14's *Ethical Issue* on page 345.

Hoosier Energy Rural Electric Cooperative, which owns and operates an electricity-generating plant in Indiana, also claimed commercial impracticability as a reason to escape from a contract. Hoosier had entered into a complicated "sale in–lease out" arrangement with John Hancock Life Insurance Company, under which Hoosier was to make lease payments to John Hancock for sixty-three years. The lease payments were guaranteed by Ambac Assurance Corporation. But when the credit crisis began, Ambac's credit rating was downgraded. Under the terms of the contract, this meant that Hoosier would have to pay $120 million to John Hancock or find another guarantor within a very short time. Hoosier went to court, claiming, among other things, that the obstacles it faced in finding another guarantor "were the product of the credit crisis. . . . Those effects were not anticipated and could not have been guarded against." The court agreed and issued an injunction that prevented John Hancock from obtaining the $120 million payment, even though Hoosier had agreed to the payment when it entered into the contract.[3]

A fire destroys a building holding warehoused goods in Bloomington, Illinois. Suppose that there were goods inside that had been identified to a sales contract but for which the risk of loss had not yet passed to the buyer. If the buyer sues the seller for breaching the contract by not delivering the goods, will the seller be held liable? Why or why not?

("Syslfrog"/Creative Commons)

DESTRUCTION OF IDENTIFIED GOODS   Sometimes, an unexpected event, such as a fire, totally destroys goods through no fault of either party and before risk passes to the buyer or lessee. In such a situation, *if the goods were identified at the time the contract was formed*, the parties are excused from performance [UCC 2–613, 2A–221]. If the goods are only partially destroyed, however, the buyer or lessee can inspect them and either treat the contract as void or accept the goods with a reduction of the contract price.

EXAMPLE 16.8   Atlas Sporting Equipment agrees to lease to River Bicycles sixty bicycles of a particular model that has been discontinued. No other bicycles of that model are available. River specifies that it needs the bicycles to rent to tourists. Before Atlas can deliver the bicycles, they are destroyed by a fire. In this situation, Atlas is not liable to River for failing to deliver the bicycles. The goods were destroyed through no fault of either party, before the risk of loss passed to the lessee. The loss was total, so the contract is avoided. Clearly, Atlas has no obligation to tender the bicycles, and River has no obligation to pay for them. •

ASSURANCE AND COOPERATION   Two other exceptions to the perfect tender doctrine apply equally to parties to sales and lease contracts: the right of assurance and the duty of cooperation.

The Right of Assurance.   The UCC provides that if one party to a contract has "reasonable grounds" to believe that the other party will not perform as contracted, he or she may *in writing* "demand adequate assurance of due performance" from the other party. Until such assurance is received, he or she may "suspend" further performance (such as payments due under the contract) without liability. What constitutes "reasonable grounds" is determined by commercial standards. If such assurances are not forthcoming within a reasonable time (not to exceed thirty days), the failure to respond may be treated as a *repudiation* of the contract [UCC 2–609, 2A–401].

---

3. *Hoosier Energy Rural Electric Cooperative, Inc. v. John Hancock Life Insurance Co.*, 588 F.Supp.2d 919 (S.D.Ind. 2008).

CASE EXAMPLE 16.9   Two companies that make road-surfacing materials, Koch Materials Company and Shore Slurry Seal, Inc., enter into a contract. Koch obtains a license to use Novachip, a special material made by Shore, and Shore agrees to buy all of its asphalt from Koch for the next seven years. A few years into the contract term, Shore notifies Koch that it is planning to sell its assets to Asphalt Paving Systems, Inc. Koch demands assurances that Asphalt Paving will continue the deal, but Shore refuses to provide assurances. In this situation, Koch can treat Shore's failure to give assurances as a repudiation and file a suit against Shore for breach of contract.[4] ●

Preventing Legal Disputes

Whenever you have doubts about the other party's ability or willingness to perform a sales contract, you should demand adequate assurances. Rather than having to "wait and see" (and possibly incur significant losses as a result), the UCC allows a party with reasonable suspicions to seek adequate assurance of performance from the other party. If the other party fails to give assurance, you can treat it as an *anticipatory repudiation* (a breach, as will be discussed shortly) and pursue damages. Perhaps more importantly, the other party's failure to give assurance allows you to suspend further performance, which can save your business from sustaining substantial losses that could be recovered only through litigation. Ultimately, it may be better simply to withdraw from a deal when the other party will not provide assurances of performance than to continue performing a contract that is likely to be breached anyway.

The Duty of Cooperation.   Sometimes, the performance of one party depends on the cooperation of the other. The UCC provides that when such cooperation is not forthcoming, the other party can suspend her or his own performance without liability and hold the uncooperative party in breach or proceed to perform the contract in any reasonable manner [UCC 2–311(3)].

EXAMPLE 16.10   Aman is required by contract to deliver 1,200 model HE washing machines to various locations in California. Deliveries are to be made on or before October 1, and the locations are to be specified later by Farrell. Aman has repeatedly requested the delivery locations, but Farrell has not responded. On October 1, the washing machines are ready to be shipped, but Farrell still refuses to give Aman the delivery locations. Aman does not ship on October 1. Can Aman be held liable? The answer is no. Aman is excused for any resulting delay of performance because of Farrell's failure to cooperate. ●

▶ Obligations of the Buyer or Lessee

The main obligation of the buyer or lessee under a sales or lease contract is to pay for the goods tendered in accordance with the contract. Once the seller or lessor has adequately tendered delivery, the buyer or lessee is obligated to accept the goods and pay for them according to the terms of the contract.

Payment

In the absence of any specific agreements, the buyer or lessee must make payment at the time and place the goods are *received* [UCC 2–310(a), 2A–516(1)]. When a sale is made on credit, the buyer is obliged to pay according to the specified credit terms (for example, 60, 90, or 120 days), not when the goods are received. The credit period usually begins on the *date of shipment* [UCC 2–310(d)]. Under a lease contract, a lessee must pay the lease payment that was specified in the contract [UCC 2A–516(1)].

> "**Death, they say, acquits us of all obligations.**"
> Michel de Montaigne, 1533–1592
> (French writer and philosopher)

---

4. *Koch Materials Co. v. Shore Slurry Seal, Inc.*, 205 F.Supp.2d 324 (D.N.J. 2002).

Payment can be made by any means agreed on by the parties—cash or any other method generally acceptable in the commercial world. If the seller demands cash when the buyer offers a check, credit card, or the like, the seller must permit the buyer reasonable time to obtain legal tender [UCC 2–511].

Right of Inspection

Unless the parties otherwise agree, or for C.O.D. (collect on delivery) transactions, the buyer or lessee has an absolute right to inspect the goods before making payment. This right allows the buyer or lessee to verify, before making payment, that the goods tendered or delivered are what were contracted for or ordered. If the goods are not what were ordered, the buyer or lessee has no duty to pay. *An opportunity for inspection is therefore a condition precedent to the right of the seller or lessor to enforce payment* [UCC 2–513(1), 2A–515(1)].

Inspection can take place at any reasonable place and time and in any reasonable manner. Generally, what is reasonable is determined by custom of the trade, past practices of the parties, and the like. The buyer bears the costs of inspecting the goods (unless otherwise agreed), but if the goods are rejected because they are not conforming, the buyer can recover the costs of inspection from the seller [UCC 2–513(2)].

Acceptance

A buyer or lessee demonstrates acceptance of the delivered goods by doing any of the following:

1. If, after having had a reasonable opportunity to inspect the goods, the buyer or lessee signifies to the seller or lessor that the goods either are conforming or are acceptable in spite of their nonconformity [UCC 2–606(1)(a), 2A–515(1)(a)].
2. If the buyer or lessee has had a reasonable opportunity to inspect the goods and has *failed to reject* them within a reasonable period of time, then acceptance is presumed [UCC 2–602(1), 2–606(1)(b), 2A–515(1)(b)].
3. In sales contracts, if the buyer *performs any act inconsistent with the seller's ownership,* then the buyer will be deemed to have accepted the goods. For example, any use or resale of the goods—except for the limited purpose of testing or inspecting the goods—generally constitutes an acceptance [UCC 2–606(1)(c)].

Partial Acceptance

If some of the goods delivered do not conform to the contract and the seller or lessor has failed to cure, the buyer or lessee can make a *partial* acceptance [UCC 2–601(c), 2A–509(1)]. The same is true if the nonconformity was not reasonably discoverable before acceptance. (In the latter situation, the buyer or lessee may be able to revoke the acceptance, as will be discussed later in this chapter.)

A buyer or lessee cannot accept less than a single commercial unit, however. The UCC defines a *commercial unit* as a unit of goods that, by commercial usage, is viewed as a "single whole" for purposes of sale, and its division would materially impair the character of the unit, its market value, or its use [UCC 2–105(6), 2A–103(1)(c)]. A commercial unit can be a single article (such as a machine), a set of articles (such as a suite of furniture or an assortment of sizes), a quantity (such as a bale, a gross, or a carload), or any other unit treated in the trade as a single whole.

 Anticipatory Repudiation

What if, before the time for contract performance, one party clearly communicates to the other the intention not to perform? As discussed in Chapter 13, such an action is a breach of the contract by anticipatory repudiation.

Suspension of Performance Obligations

When anticipatory repudiation occurs, the nonbreaching party has a choice of two responses: (1) treat the repudiation as a final breach by pursuing a remedy or (2) wait to see if the repudiating party will decide to honor the contract despite the avowed intention to renege [UCC 2–610, 2A–402]. In either situation, the nonbreaching party may suspend performance.

A Repudiation May Be Retracted

The UCC permits the breaching party to "retract" his or her repudiation (subject to some limitations). This can be done by any method that clearly indicates the party's intent to perform. Once retraction is made, the rights of the repudiating party under the contract are reinstated. There can be no retraction, however, if since the time of the repudiation the other party has canceled or materially changed position or otherwise indicated that the repudiation is final [UCC 2–611, 2A–403].

EXAMPLE 16.11 Cora, who owns a small inn, purchases a suite of furniture from Horton's Furniture Warehouse on April 1. The contract states, "Delivery must be made on or before May 1." On April 10, Horton informs Cora that he cannot make delivery until May 10 and asks her to consent to the modified delivery date. In this situation, Cora has the option of either treating Horton's notice of late delivery as a final breach of contract and pursuing a remedy or agreeing to the changed delivery date. Suppose that Cora does neither for two weeks. On April 24, Horton informs Cora that he will be able to deliver the furniture by May 1 after all. In effect, Horton has retracted his repudiation, reinstating the rights and obligations of the parties under the original contract. Note that if Cora had indicated after Horton's repudiation that she was canceling the contract, Horton would not have been able to retract his repudiation. ●

 Remedies of the Seller or Lessor

When the buyer or lessee is in breach, the seller or lessor has numerous remedies available under the UCC. Generally, the remedies available to the seller or lessor depend on the circumstances at the time of the breach, such as which party has possession of the goods, whether the goods are in transit, and whether the buyer or lessee has rejected or accepted the goods.

When the Goods Are in the Possession of the Seller or Lessor

Under the UCC, if the buyer or lessee breaches the contract before the goods have been delivered to her or him, the seller or lessor has the right to pursue the following remedies:

NOTE A buyer or lessee breaches a contract by wrongfully rejecting the goods, wrongfully revoking acceptance, refusing to pay, or repudiating the contract.

1. Cancel (rescind) the contract.
2. Resell the goods and sue to recover damages.
3. Sue to recover the purchase price or lease payments due.
4. Sue to recover damages for the buyer's nonacceptance.

THE RIGHT TO CANCEL THE CONTRACT If the buyer or lessee breaches the contract, the seller or lessor can choose to cancel (rescind) the contract [UCC 2–703(f), 2A–523(1) (a)]. The seller must notify the buyer or lessee of the cancellation, and at that point all remaining obligations of the seller or lessor are discharged. The buyer or lessee is not discharged from all remaining obligations, however; he or she is in breach, and the seller or lessor can pursue remedies available under the UCC for breach.

THE RIGHT TO WITHHOLD DELIVERY In general, sellers and lessors can withhold or discontinue performance of their obligations under sales or lease contracts when the buyers or lessees are in breach. This is true whether a buyer or lessee has wrongfully rejected or revoked acceptance of contract goods (rejection and revocation of acceptance will be discussed later), failed to make a payment, or repudiated the contract [UCC 2–703(a), 2A–523(1)(c)]. The seller or lessor can also refuse to deliver the goods to a buyer or lessee who is insolvent (unable to pay debts as they become due), unless the buyer or lessee pays in cash [UCC 2–702(1), 2A–525(1)].

THE RIGHT TO RESELL OR DISPOSE OF THE GOODS   When a buyer or lessee breaches or repudiates a sales contract while the seller or lessor is still in possession of the goods, the seller or lessor can resell or dispose of the goods. The seller can retain any profits made as a result of the sale and can hold the buyer or lessee liable for any loss [UCC 2–703(d), 2–706(1), 2A–523(1)(e), 2A–527(1)]. The seller must give the original buyer reasonable notice of the resale, unless the goods are perishable or will rapidly decline in value [UCC 2–706(2), (3)].

When the goods contracted for are unfinished at the time of breach, the seller or lessor can either (1) cease manufacturing the goods and resell them for scrap or salvage value or (2) complete the manufacture and resell or dispose of them, holding the buyer or lessee liable for any deficiency. In choosing between these two alternatives, the seller or lessor must exercise reasonable commercial judgment to mitigate the loss and obtain maximum value from the unfinished goods [UCC 2–704(2), 2A–524(2)]. Any resale of the goods must be made in good faith and in a commercially reasonable manner.

In sales transactions, the seller can recover any deficiency between the resale price and the contract price, along with **incidental damages,** defined as the costs resulting from the breach [UCC 2–706(1), 2–710]. In lease transactions, the lessor may lease the goods to another party and recover from the original lessee, as damages, any unpaid lease payments up to the beginning date of the lease term under the new lease. The lessor can also recover any deficiency between the lease payments due under the original lease contract and those due under the new lease contract, along with incidental damages [UCC 2A–527(2)].

THE RIGHT TO RECOVER THE PURCHASE PRICE OR THE LEASE PAYMENTS DUE
Under the UCC, an unpaid seller or lessor can bring an action to recover the purchase price or payments due under the lease contract, plus incidental damages [UCC 2–709(1), 2A–529(1)]. If a seller or lessor is unable to resell or dispose of goods and sues for the contract price or lease payments due, the goods must be held for the buyer or lessee. The seller or lessor can resell or dispose of the goods at any time prior to collection (of the judgment) from the buyer or lessee, but must credit the net proceeds from the sale to the buyer or lessee.

EXAMPLE 16.12   Southern Realty contracts to purchase one thousand pens with its name inscribed on them from Gem Point. When Gem Point tenders delivery of the pens, Southern Realty wrongfully refuses to accept them. In this situation, Gem Point can bring an action for the purchase price because it delivered conforming goods, and Southern Realty refused to accept or pay for the goods. Gem Point obviously cannot resell the pens inscribed with the buyer's business name, so this situation falls under UCC 2–709. Gem Point is required to make the pens available for Southern Realty, but can resell them (in the event that it can find a buyer) at any time before collecting the judgment from Southern Realty. •

THE RIGHT TO RECOVER DAMAGES   If a buyer or lessee repudiates a contract or wrongfully refuses to accept the goods, a seller or lessor can maintain an action to recover the damages that were sustained. Ordinarily, the amount of damages equals the difference between the contract price or lease payments and the market price or lease payments at the time and place of tender of the goods, plus incidental damages [UCC 2–708(1), 2A–528(1)]. When the ordinary measure of damages is inadequate to put the seller or lessor in as good a position as the buyer's or lessee's performance would have, the UCC

Incidental Damages   All costs resulting from a breach of contract, including all reasonable expenses incurred because of the breach.

provides an alternative. In that situation, the proper measure of damages is the lost profits of the seller or lessor, including a reasonable allowance for overhead and other expenses [UCC 2–708(2), 2A–528(2)].

When the Goods Are in Transit

If the seller or lessor has delivered the goods to a carrier or a bailee but the buyer or lessee has not yet received them, the goods are said to be *in transit*. If, while the goods are in transit, the seller or lessor learns that the buyer or lessee is insolvent, the seller or lessor can stop the carrier or bailee from delivering the goods, regardless of the quantity of goods shipped. If the buyer or lessee is in breach but is not insolvent, the seller or lessor can stop the goods in transit only if the quantity shipped is at least a carload, a truckload, a planeload, or a larger shipment [UCC 2–705(1), 2A–526(1)].

EXAMPLE 16.13 Arturo Ortega orders a truckload of lumber from Timber Products, Inc., to be shipped to Ortega six weeks later. Ortega, who owes Timber Products for a past shipment, promises to pay the debt immediately and to pay for the current shipment as soon as it is received. After the lumber has been shipped, a bankruptcy court judge notifies Timber Products that Ortega has filed a petition in bankruptcy and listed Timber Products as one of his creditors (see Chapter 21). If the goods are still in transit, Timber Products can stop the carrier from delivering the lumber to Ortega. •

REQUIREMENTS FOR STOPPING DELIVERY To stop delivery, the seller or lessor must *timely notify* the carrier or other bailee that the goods are to be returned or held for the seller or lessor. If the carrier has sufficient time to stop delivery, it must hold and deliver the goods according to the instructions of the seller or lessor, who is liable to the carrier for any additional costs incurred [UCC 2–705(3), 2A–526(3)].

The sellor or lessor has the right to stop delivery of the goods under UCC 2–705(2) and 2A–526(2) until the time when:

1. The buyer or lessee obtains possession of the goods.
2. The carrier or the bailee acknowledges the rights of the buyer or lessee in the goods (by reshipping or holding the goods for the buyer or lessee, for example).
3. A negotiable document of title covering the goods has been properly transferred to the buyer (in sales transactions only), giving the buyer ownership rights in the goods [UCC 2–702].

REMEDIES ONCE THE GOODS ARE RECLAIMED Once the seller or lessor reclaims the goods in transit, she or he can pursue the remedies allowed to sellers and lessors when the goods are in their possession.

When the Goods Are in the Possession of the Buyer or Lessee

When the buyer or lessee breaches a sales or lease contract and the goods are in the buyer's or lessee's possession, the seller or lessor can sue to recover the purchase price of the goods or the lease payments due, plus incidental damages [UCC 2–709(1), 2A–529(1)].

In some situations, a seller may also have a right to reclaim the goods from the buyer. For instance, in a sales contract, if the buyer has received the goods on credit and the seller discovers that the buyer is insolvent, the seller can demand return of the goods [UCC 2–702(2)]. Ordinarily, the demand must be made within ten days of the buyer's receipt of the goods.[5] The seller's right to reclaim the goods is subject to the rights of a good faith

RECALL Incidental damages include all reasonable expenses incurred because of a breach of contract.

---

5. The seller can demand and reclaim the goods at any time, though, if the buyer misrepresented his or her solvency in writing within three months prior to the delivery of the goods.

purchaser or other subsequent buyer in the ordinary course of business who purchases the goods from the buyer before the seller reclaims them.

In regard to lease contracts, if the lessee is in default (fails to make payments that are due, for example) the lessor may reclaim the leased goods that are in the lessee's possession [UCC 2A–525(2)].

▶ Remedies of the Buyer or Lessee

When the seller or lessor breaches the contract, the buyer or lessee has numerous remedies available under the UCC. Like the remedies available to sellers and lessors, the remedies of buyers and lessees depend on the circumstances existing at the time of the breach. (See the *Business Application* feature at the end of this chapter for some suggestions on what to do when a contract is breached.)

NOTE A seller or lessor breaches a contract by wrongfully failing to deliver the goods, delivering nonconforming goods, making an improper tender of the goods, or repudiating the contract.

When the Seller or Lessor Refuses to Deliver the Goods

If the seller or lessor refuses to deliver the goods or the buyer or lessee has rejected the goods, the remedies available to the buyer or lessee include the right to:

1. Cancel (rescind) the contract.
2. Obtain goods that have been paid for if the seller or lessor is insolvent.
3. Sue to obtain specific performance if the goods are unique or damages are an inadequate remedy.
4. Buy other goods (obtain cover) and obtain damages from the seller.
5. Sue to obtain identified goods held by a third party (replevy goods).
6. Sue to obtain damages.

THE RIGHT TO CANCEL THE CONTRACT   When a seller or lessor fails to make proper delivery or repudiates the contract, the buyer or lessee can cancel, or rescind, the contract. On notice of cancellation, the buyer or lessee is relieved of any further obligations under the contract but retains all rights to other remedies against the seller [UCC 2–711(1), 2A–508(1)(a)]. (The right to cancel the contract is also available to a buyer or lessee who has rightfully rejected goods or revoked acceptance, as will be discussed shortly.)

THE RIGHT TO OBTAIN THE GOODS ON INSOLVENCY   If a buyer or lessee has made a partial or full payment for goods that are in the possession of a seller or lessor who is or becomes insolvent, the buyer or lessee has a right to obtain the goods. To exercise this right, the goods must be identified to the contract and the buyer or lessee must pay any remaining balance of the price to the seller or lessor [UCC 2–502, 2A–522].

THE RIGHT TO OBTAIN SPECIFIC PERFORMANCE   A buyer or lessee can obtain specific performance when the goods are unique and the remedy at law is inadequate [UCC 2–716(1), 2A–521(1)]. Ordinarily, a successful suit for monetary damages is sufficient to place a buyer or lessee in the position he or she would have occupied if the seller or lessor had fully performed. When the contract is for the purchase of a particular work of art or a similarly unique item, however, monetary damages may not be sufficient. Under these circumstances, equity will require that the seller or lessor perform exactly by delivering the particular goods identified to the contract (a remedy of specific performance).

Animals are items of property and can be quantified as "goods." An animal such as a pet may seem unique to its owner. But can a pet possess the quality of "uniqueness" necessary for an award of specific performance? That was the question in the following case.

Case 16.2 Houseman v. Dare

Superior Court of New Jersey, Appellate Division, 405 N.J.Super. 538, 966 A.2d 24 (2009).
www.lawlibrary.rutgers.edu/search.shtml[a]

Are there any circumstances under which ownership of a pet can involve specific performance?

FACTS Doreen Houseman and Eric Dare were together for thirteen years. They bought a house and were engaged to marry. They also bought a pedigree dog for $1,500, which they registered with the American Kennel Club as joint owners. When Dare decided to end the relationship, they agreed that he could pay Houseman for her interest in the house and she would move out. They also agreed that she could take the dog. She asked him to memorialize the agreement about the dog in writing, but he told her that she could trust him. She allowed him to take the dog for visits. After one such visit, Dare kept the dog. Houseman filed a suit in a New Jersey state court against Dare. In a summary judgment, the court concluded that specific performance is not available as a remedy for the breach of an oral agreement about the possession of a dog and awarded Houseman $1,500. She appealed.

ISSUE Can a dog have the unique value essential to an award of specific performance?

DECISION Yes. A state intermediate appellate court reversed the lower court's decision and remanded the case for trial.

REASON The trial court committed an error when it issued its summary judgment without considering the parties' oral agreement. Agreements about property jointly owned by persons who live together are "material in actions concerning its division." Specific performance can be awarded for the breach of an agreement for the possession of goods or property when damages are not adequate to protect the interest of the injured party. For example, specific performance is an appropriate remedy when an agreement concerns "heirlooms, family treasures and works of art that induce a strong sentimental attachment." This sentiment includes the "special subjective benefits" that a party derives from possession. Pets have special "subjective value" to their owners. In this case, the special value of the dog to Houseman was shown by her prompt effort to enforce her right of possession when Dare did not return the dog.

WHY IS THIS CASE IMPORTANT? *To some people, a dog is just a dog. To others, a dog is more valuable than the worthiest of other possessions. This may be true for any item of property to which its owner has developed a strong emotional attachment. This case shows the extent to which the subjective value of a piece of property can determine its uniqueness to the parties involved. In a dispute over the ownership of property, courts can consider this subjective value as support for imposing specific performance.*

---

a. In the "Search for Cases by Party Name" section, in the box, in the left column, check "Appellate Division." In the right column, in the "First Name:" box, type "Houseman" and click on "Submit Form." In the result, click on "click here to get this document" to access the opinion. The Rutgers University School of Law in Camden, New Jersey, maintains this Web site.

Cover Under the UCC, a remedy that allows the buyer or lessee, on the seller's or lessor's breach, to purchase the goods, in good faith and within a reasonable time, from another seller or lessor and substitute them for the goods due under the contract. If the cost of cover exceeds the cost of the contract goods, the breaching seller or lessor will be liable to the buyer or lessee for the difference, plus incidental and consequential damages.

THE RIGHT OF COVER In certain situations, buyers and lessees can protect themselves by obtaining **cover**—that is, by purchasing or leasing other goods to substitute for those due under the contract. This option is available when the seller or lessor repudiates the contract or fails to deliver the goods, or when a buyer or lessee has rightfully rejected goods or revoked acceptance.

In obtaining cover, the buyer or lessee must act in good faith and without unreasonable delay [UCC 2–712, 2A–518]. After purchasing or leasing substitute goods, the buyer or lessee can recover damages from the seller or lessor. The measure of damages is the difference between the cost of cover and the contract price (or lease payments), plus incidental and consequential damages, less the expenses (such as delivery costs) that were saved as a result of the breach [UCC 2–712, 2–715, 2A–518]. Consequential damages are any losses suffered by the buyer or lessee that the seller or lessor could have foreseen (had reason to know about) at the time of contract formation and any injury to the buyer's or lessee's person or property proximately resulting from the contract's breach [UCC 2–715(2), 2A–520(2)].

Buyers and lessees are not required to cover, and failure to do so will not bar them from using any other remedies available under the UCC. A buyer or lessee who fails to cover, however, may *not* be able to collect consequential damages that could have been avoided by purchasing or leasing substitute goods.

THE RIGHT TO REPLEVY GOODS

Buyers and lessees also have the right to replevy goods. Replevin[6] is an action to recover specific goods in the hands of a party who is wrongfully withholding them from the other party. Outside the UCC, the term *replevin* refers to a *prejudgment process* (a proceeding that takes place prior to a court's judgment) that permits the seizure of specific personal property in which a party claims a right or an interest. Under the UCC, the buyer or lessee can replevy goods subject to the contract if the seller or lessor has repudiated or breached the contract. To maintain an action to replevy goods, usually buyers and lessees must show that they are unable to cover for the goods after a reasonable effort [UCC 2–716(3), 2A–521(3)].

Replevin An action to recover identified goods in the hands of a party who is wrongfully withholding them from the other party. Under the UCC, this remedy is usually available only if the buyer or lessee is unable to cover.

THE RIGHT TO RECOVER DAMAGES

If a seller or lessor repudiates the sales contract or fails to deliver the goods, the buyer or lessee can sue for damages. The measure of recovery is the difference between the contract price (or lease payments) and the market price of (or lease payments that could be obtained for) the goods at the time the buyer (or lessee) *learned* of the breach. The market price or market lease payments are determined at the place where the seller or lessor was supposed to deliver the goods. The buyer or lessee can also recover incidental and consequential damages, less the expenses that were saved as a result of the breach [UCC 2–713, 2A–519].

RECALL Consequential damages compensate for a loss (such as lost profits) that is not direct but was reasonably foreseeable at the time of the breach.

EXAMPLE 16.14 Schilling orders ten thousand bushels of wheat from Valdone for $5 a bushel, with delivery due on June 14 and payment due on June 20. Valdone does not deliver on June 14. On June 14, the market price of wheat is $5.50 per bushel. Schilling chooses to do without the wheat. He sues Valdone for damages for nondelivery. Schilling can recover $0.50 × 10,000, or $5,000, plus any expenses the breach may have caused him. The measure of damages is the market price less the contract price on the day Schilling was to have received delivery. Any expenses Schilling saved by the breach would be deducted from the damages. •

When the Seller or Lessor Delivers Nonconforming Goods

When the seller or lessor delivers nonconforming goods, the buyer or lessee has several remedies available under the UCC.

THE RIGHT TO REJECT THE GOODS

If either the goods or the tender of the goods by the seller or lessor fails to conform to the contract *in any respect,* the buyer or lessee can reject the goods in whole or in part [UCC 2–601, 2A–509]. If the buyer or lessee rejects the goods, she or he may then obtain cover, cancel the contract, or sue for damages for breach of contract, just as if the seller or lessor had refused to deliver the goods (see the earlier discussion of these remedies).

CASE EXAMPLE 16.15 Jorge Jauregui contracted to buy a Kawai RX5 piano from Bobb's Piano Sales. Bobb's represented that the piano was in new condition and qualified for the manufacturer's warranty. Jauregui paid the contract price, but the piano was delivered with "unacceptable damage," according to Jauregui, who videotaped its condition. Jauregui rejected the piano and filed a lawsuit for breach of contract. The court ruled that Bobb's had breached the contract by delivering nonconforming goods. Jauregui was entitled to damages equal to the contract price with interest, plus the sales tax, delivery charge, and attorneys' fees.[7] •

---

6. Pronounced ruh-*pleh*-vun.
7. *Jauregui v. Bobb's Piano Sales & Service, Inc.,* 922 So.2d 303 (Fla.App. 2006).

Timeliness and Reason for Rejection Required. The buyer or lessee must reject the goods within a reasonable amount of time after delivery and must *seasonably* (timely) notify the seller or lessor [UCC 2–602(1), 2A–509(2)]. If the buyer or lessee fails to reject the goods within a reasonable amount of time, acceptance will be presumed.

When rejecting goods, the buyer or lessee must also designate defects that would have been apparent to the seller or lessor on reasonable inspection. Failure to do so precludes the buyer or lessee from using such defects to justify rejection or to establish breach when the seller could have cured the defects if they had been disclosed in a timely fashion [UCC 2–605, 2A–514].

An employee at a retail establishment sorts through boxes of nonconforming goods that will be returned to the manufacturers. If the merchant buyer is following the seller's instructions for rejecting the goods, who should bear the cost of having employees perform this task?

(Photo Courtesy of KBToys.com and eToys.com)

Duties of Merchant Buyers and Lessees When Goods Are Rejected. What happens if a *merchant buyer* or *lessee* rightfully rejects goods and the seller or lessor has no agent or business at the place of rejection? In that situation, the merchant buyer or lessee has a good faith obligation to follow any reasonable instructions received from the seller or lessor with respect to the goods [UCC 2–603, 2A–511]. The buyer or lessee is entitled to be reimbursed for the care and cost entailed in following the instructions. The same requirements hold if the buyer or lessee rightfully revokes his or her acceptance of the goods at some later time [UCC 2–608(3), 2A–517(5)]. (Revocation of acceptance will be discussed shortly.)

If no instructions are forthcoming and the goods are perishable or threaten to decline in value quickly, the buyer can resell the goods in good faith, taking the appropriate reimbursement from the proceeds and a selling commission (not to exceed 10 percent of the gross proceeds) [UCC 2–603(1), (2); 2A–511(1), (2)]. If the goods are not perishable, the buyer or lessee may store them for the seller or lessor or reship them to the seller or lessor [UCC 2–604, 2A–512].

REVOCATION OF ACCEPTANCE Acceptance of the goods precludes the buyer or lessee from exercising the right of rejection, but it does not necessarily prevent the buyer or lessee from pursuing other remedies. In certain circumstances, a buyer or lessee is permitted to *revoke* her or his acceptance of the goods. Acceptance of a lot or a commercial unit can be revoked if the nonconformity *substantially* impairs the value of the lot or unit and if one of the following factors is present:

1. Acceptance was predicated on the reasonable assumption that the nonconformity would be cured, and it has not been cured within a reasonable time [UCC 2–608(1)(a), 2A–517(1)(a)].
2. The buyer or lessee did not discover the nonconformity before acceptance, either because it was difficult to discover before acceptance or because assurances made by the seller or lessor that the goods were conforming kept the buyer or lessee from inspecting the goods [UCC 2–608(1)(b), 2A–517(1)(b)].

Revocation of acceptance is not effective until the seller or lessor is notified, which must occur within a reasonable time after the buyer or lessee either discovers or *should have discovered* the grounds for revocation. Additionally, revocation must occur before the goods have undergone any substantial change (such as spoilage) not caused by their own defects [UCC 2–608(2), 2A–517(4)]. Once acceptance is revoked, the buyer or lessee can pursue remedies, just as if the goods had been rejected. (See this chapter's *Beyond Our Borders* feature on page 407 for a glimpse at how international sales law deals with revocation of acceptance.)

THE RIGHT TO RECOVER DAMAGES FOR ACCEPTED GOODS   A buyer or lessee who has accepted nonconforming goods may also keep the goods and recover damages caused by the breach. To do so, the buyer or lessee must notify the seller or lessor of the breach within a reasonable time after the defect was or should have been discovered. Failure to give notice of the defects (breach) to the seller or lessor bars the buyer or lessee from pursuing any remedy [UCC 2–607(3), 2A–516(3)]. In addition, the parties to a sales or lease contract can insert a provision requiring the buyer or lessee to give notice of any defects in the goods within a set period.

When the goods delivered are not as promised, the measure of damages equals the difference between the value of the goods as accepted and their value if they had been delivered as warranted [UCC 2–714(2), 2A–519(4)]. The buyer or lessee is also entitled to incidental and consequential damages when appropriate [UCC 2–714(3), 2A–519(3)]. The UCC also permits the buyer or lessee, with proper notice to the seller or lessor, to deduct all or any part of the damages from the price or lease payments still due under the contract [UCC 2–717, 2A–516(1)].

Is two years after a sale of goods a reasonable time period in which to discover a defect in those goods and notify the seller of a breach? That was the question in the following case.

Case 16.3   Fitl v. Strek

Supreme Court of Nebraska, 269 Neb. 51, 690 N.W.2d 605 (2005).
www.findlaw.com/11stategov/ne/neca.html[a]

A 1952 Mickey Mantle Topps baseball card.

FACTS   Over the Labor Day weekend in 1995, James Fitl attended a sports-card show in San Francisco, California, where he met Mark Strek, doing business as Star Cards of San Francisco, an exhibitor at the show. Later, on Strek's representation that a certain 1952 Mickey Mantle Topps baseball card was in near-mint condition, Fitl bought the card from Strek for $17,750. Strek delivered it to Fitl in Omaha, Nebraska, and Fitl placed it in a safe-deposit box. In May 1997, Fitl sent the card to Professional Sports Authenticators (PSA), a sports-card grading service. PSA told Fitl that the card was ungradable because it had been discolored and doctored. Fitl complained to Strek, who replied that Fitl should have initiated a return of the card within "a typical grace period for the unconditional return of a card, . . . 7 days to 1 month" of its receipt. In August, Fitl sent the card to ASA Accugrade, Inc. (ASA), another grading service, for a second opinion of the value. ASA also concluded that the card had been refinished and trimmed. Fitl filed a suit in a Nebraska state court against Strek, seeking damages. The court awarded Fitl $17,750, plus his court costs. Strek appealed to the Nebraska Supreme Court.

ISSUE   Is two years after a sale of goods a reasonable time to discover a defect in those goods and notify the seller of a breach?

DECISION   Yes. The state supreme court affirmed the decision of the lower court.

REASON   Section 2–607(3)(a) of the UCC states, "Where a tender has been accepted * * * the buyer must within a reasonable time after he discovers or should have discovered any breach notify the seller of breach or be barred from any remedy." "What is a reasonable time for taking any action depends on the nature, purpose and circumstances of such action" [UCC1–205(a)]. The state supreme court concluded that the buyer (Fitl) had reasonably relied on the seller's (Strek's) representation that the goods were "authentic," which they were not, and when their defects were discovered, Fitl had given a timely notice. The court reasoned that "the policies behind the notice requirement, to allow the seller to correct a defect, to prepare for negotiation and litigation, and to protect against stale claims at a time beyond which an investigation can be completed, were not unfairly prejudiced by the lack of an earlier notice to Strek. Any problem Strek may have had with the party from whom he obtained the baseball card was a separate matter from his transaction with Fitl, and an investigation into the source of the altered card would not have minimized Fitl's damages."

WHAT IF THE FACTS WERE DIFFERENT?   *Suppose that Fitl and Strek had included in their deal a written clause requiring Fitl to give notice of any defect in the card within "7 days to 1 month" of its receipt. Would the result have been different? Why or why not?*

---

a. In the "Supreme Court Opinions" section, in the "2005" row, click on "January." In the result, click on the appropriate link next to the name of the case to access the opinion.

(Terren in Virginia/Creative Commons)

Beyond Our Borders | The CISG's Approach to Revocation of Acceptance

Under the UCC, a buyer or lessee who has accepted goods may be able to revoke acceptance under the circumstances mentioned on pages 404 and 405. The United Nations Convention on Contracts for the International Sale of Goods (CISG) also allows buyers to rescind their contracts after they have accepted the goods.

The CISG, however, takes a somewhat different—and more direct—approach to the problem than the UCC does. In the same circumstances that permit a buyer to revoke acceptance under the UCC, under the CISG the buyer can simply declare that the seller has *fundamentally* breached the contract and proceed to sue the seller for the breach. Article 25 of the CISG states that a "breach of contract committed by one of the parties is fundamental if it results in such detriment to the other party as substantially to deprive him [or her] of what he [or she] is entitled to expect under the contract." For example, to revoke acceptance of a shipment under the CISG, a buyer need not prove that the nonconformity of one shipment substantially impaired the value of the whole lot. The buyer can simply file a lawsuit alleging the seller is in breach.

• For Critical Analysis
What is the essential difference between revoking acceptance and bringing a suit for breach of contract?

▶ Limitation of Remedies

The parties to a sales or lease contract can vary their respective rights and obligations by contractual agreement. For example, a seller and buyer can expressly provide for remedies in addition to those provided in the UCC. They can also provide remedies in lieu of those provided in the UCC, or they can change the measure of damages. The seller can provide that the buyer's only remedy on breach of warranty will be repair or replacement of the item, or the seller can limit the buyer's remedy to return of the goods and refund of the purchase price. In sales and lease contracts, an agreed-on remedy is in addition to those provided in the UCC unless the parties expressly agree that the remedy is exclusive of all others [UCC 2–719(1), 2A–503(1), (2)].

Exclusive Remedies

If the parties state that a remedy is exclusive, then it is the sole remedy. **EXAMPLE 16.16** Standard Tool Company agrees to sell a pipe-cutting machine to United Pipe & Tubing Corporation. The contract limits United's remedy exclusively to repair or replacement of any defective parts. Thus, repair or replacement of defective parts is the buyer's exclusive remedy under this contract. ●

When circumstances cause an exclusive remedy to fail in its essential purpose, however, it is no longer exclusive, and the buyer or lessee may pursue other remedies available under the UCC [UCC 2–719(2), 2A–503(2)]. **EXAMPLE 16.17** In the example just given, suppose that Standard Tool Company is unable to repair a defective part, and no replacement parts are available. In this situation, because the exclusive remedy failed in its essential purpose, the buyer normally will be entitled to seek other remedies provided to a buyer by the UCC. ●

How can a computer manufacturer limit its liability when it contracts with a merchant buyer?

Limitations on Consequential Damages

As discussed in Chapter 14, *consequential damages* are special damages that compensate for indirect losses (such as lost profits) resulting from a breach of contract that were reasonably foreseeable. Under the UCC, parties to a contract can limit or exclude consequential damages, provided the limitation is not unconscionable. When the buyer or lessee is a consumer, any limitation of consequential damages for personal injuries resulting from consumer goods is *prima facie* (presumptively—on its face) unconscionable. The limitation of consequential damages is not necessarily unconscionable when the loss is commercial in nature—for example, lost profits and property damage [UCC 2–719(3), 2A–503(3)].

Statute of Limitations

An action for breach of contract under the UCC must be commenced *within four years after the cause of action accrues*—that is, within four years after the breach occurs [UCC 2-725(1)]. In addition to filing suit within the four-year period, a buyer or lessee who has accepted nonconforming goods usually must notify the breaching party of the breach within a reasonable time, or the aggrieved party is barred from pursuing any remedy [UCC 2–607(3)(a), 2A–516(3)]. The parties can agree in their contract to reduce this period to not less than one year, but cannot extend it beyond four years [UCC 2–725(1), 2A–506(1)]. A cause of action accrues for breach of warranty when the seller or lessor tenders delivery. This is the rule even if the aggrieved party is unaware that the cause of action has accrued [UCC 2–725(2), 2A–506(2)].

 Reviewing . . . Performance and Breach of Sales and Lease Contracts

GFI, Inc., a Hong Kong company, makes audio decoder chips, one of the essential components used in the manufacture of MP3 players. Egan Electronics contracts with GFI to buy 10,000 chips on an installment contract, with 2,500 chips to be shipped every three months, F.O.B. Hong Kong via Air Express. At the time for the first delivery, GFI delivers only 2,400 chips but explains to Egan that while the shipment is less than 5 percent short, the chips are of a higher quality than those specified in the contract and are worth 5 percent more than the contract price. Egan accepts the shipment and pays GFI the contract price. At the time for the second shipment, GFI makes a shipment identical to the first. Egan again accepts and pays for the chips. At the time for the third shipment, GFI ships 2,400 of the same chips, but this time GFI sends them via Hong Kong Air instead of Air Express. While in transit, the chips are destroyed. When it is time for the fourth shipment, GFI again sends 2,400 chips, but this time Egan rejects the chips without explanation. Using the information presented in the chapter, answer the following questions.

1. Did GFI have a legitimate reason to expect that Egan would accept the fourth shipment? Why or why not?
2. Does the substitution of carriers in the third shipment constitute a breach of the contract by GFI? Explain.
3. Suppose that the silicon used for the chips becomes unavailable for a period of time and that GFI cannot manufacture enough chips to fulfill the contract, but does ship as many as it can to Egan. Under what doctrine might a court release GFI from further performance of the contract?
4. Under the UCC, does Egan have a right to reject the fourth shipment? Why or why not?

Business Application

What Can You Do When a Contract Is Breached?*

A contract for the sale of goods has been breached. Can the dispute be settled without a trip to court? The answer depends on the willingness of the parties to agree on an appropriate remedy.

Contractual Clauses on Applicable Remedies

Often, the parties to sales and lease contracts agree in advance, in their contracts, on what remedies will be applicable in the event of a breach. This may take the form of a contract provision restricting or expanding remedies available under the Uniform Commercial Code [UCC 2–719]. Such clauses help to reduce uncertainty and the necessity for costly litigation.

When the Contract Is Silent on Applicable Remedies

If your agreement does not cover a breach and you are the nonbreaching party, the UCC gives you a variety of alternatives. You

* This *Business Application* is not meant to substitute for the services of an attorney who is licensed to practice law in your state.

need to determine the available remedies, analyze these remedies and put them in order of priority, and then predict how successful you might be in pursuing each remedy if you decide to go to court. Next, look at the position of the breaching party to determine the basis for negotiating a settlement.

For example, when defective goods are delivered and accepted, usually it is preferable for the buyer and seller to reach an agreement on a reduced purchase price. Practically speaking, though, the buyer may be unable to obtain a partial refund from the seller. In this situation, UCC 2–717 allows the buyer to give notice of the intention to deduct the damages from any part of the purchase price not yet paid. If you are a buyer who has accepted defective goods and has not yet paid in full, you may wish to exercise your rights under UCC 2–717 and deduct appropriate

damages from your final payment. Remember that most breaches of contract do not end up in court–they are settled beforehand.

CHECKLIST FOR THE NONBREACHING PARTY TO A CONTRACT

1. **Ascertain if a remedy is explicitly written into your contract. Use that remedy, if possible, to avoid litigation.**
2. **If no specific remedy is available, look to the UCC.**
3. **Assess how successful you might be in pursuing a remedy if you go to court.**
4. **Analyze the position of the breaching party.**
5. **Determine whether a negotiated settlement is preferable to a lawsuit, which is best done by consulting your attorney.**

 Key Terms

conforming goods 391
cover 403

incidental damages 400
installment contract 393

replevin 404
tender of delivery 391

 Chapter Summary: Performance and Breach of Sales and Lease Contracts

REQUIREMENTS OF PERFORMANCE	
Obligations of the Seller or Lessor (See pages 391–397.)	1. The seller or lessor must tender *conforming* goods to the buyer or lessee. Tender must take place at a *reasonable hour* and in a *reasonable manner.* Under the perfect tender doctrine, the seller or lessor must tender goods that conform exactly to the terms of the contract [UCC 2–503(1), 2A–508(1)]. 2. If the seller or lessor tenders nonconforming goods prior to the performance date and the buyer or lessee rejects them, the seller or lessor may *cure* (repair or replace the goods) within the contract time for performance [UCC 2–508(1), 2A–513(1)]. If the seller or lessor had reasonable grounds to believe that the buyer or lessee would accept the tendered goods, on the buyer's or lessee's rejection the seller or lessor has a reasonable time to substitute conforming goods without liability [UCC 2–508(2), 2A–513(2)]. 3. If the agreed-on means of delivery becomes impracticable or unavailable, the seller must substitute an alternative means (such as a different carrier) if one is available [UCC 2–614(1)]. 4. If a seller or lessor tenders nonconforming goods in any one installment under an installment contract, the buyer or lessee may reject the installment only if its value is substantially impaired and cannot be cured. The entire installment contract is breached only when one or more nonconforming installments *substantially* impair the value of the *whole* contract [UCC 2–612, 2A–510]. 5. When performance becomes commercially impracticable owing to circumstances that were not foreseeable when the contract was formed, the perfect tender rule no longer holds [UCC 2–615, 2A–405].
Obligations of the Buyer or Lessee (See pages 397–398.)	1. On tender of delivery by the seller or lessor, the buyer or lessee must pay for the goods at the time and place the goods are *received,* unless the sale is made on credit. Payment may be made by any method generally acceptable in the commercial world unless the seller demands cash [UCC 2–310, 2–511]. In lease contracts, the lessee must make lease payments in accordance with the contract [UCC 2A–516(1)]. 2. Unless otherwise agreed, the buyer or lessee has an absolute right to inspect the goods before acceptance [UCC 2–513(1), 2A–515(1)]. 3. The buyer or lessee can manifest acceptance of delivered goods expressly in words or by conduct or by failing to reject the goods after a reasonable period of time following inspection or after having had a reasonable opportunity to inspect them [UCC 2–606(1), 2A–515(1)]. A buyer will be deemed to have accepted goods if he or she performs any act inconsistent with the seller's ownership [UCC 2–606(1)(c)].

Continued

Chapter Summary: Performance and Breach of Sales and Lease Contracts—Continued

Obligations of the Buyer or Lessee—Continued	4. The buyer or lessee can make a partial acceptance if some of the goods do not conform to the contract and the seller or lessor failed to cure [2–601(c), 2A–509(1)].
Anticipatory Repudiation (See pages 398–399.)	If, before the time for performance, one party clearly indicates to the other an intention not to perform, under UCC 2–610 and 2A–402, the aggrieved party may do the following: 1. Await performance by the repudiating party for a commercially reasonable time. 2. Resort to any remedy for breach. 3. In either situation, suspend performance.
	REMEDIES FOR BREACH OF CONTRACT
Remedies of the Seller or Lessor (See pages 399–402.)	1. *When the goods are in the possession of the seller or lessor*—The seller or lessor may do the following: a. Cancel the contract [UCC 2–703(f), 2A–523(1)(a)]. b. Withhold delivery [UCC 2–703(a), 2A–523(1)(c)]. c. Resell or dispose of the goods [UCC 2–703(d), 2–706(1), 2A–523(1)(e), 2A–527(1)]. d. Sue to recover the purchase price or lease payments due [UCC 2–709(1), 2A–529(1)]. e. Sue to recover damages [UCC 2–708, 2A–528]. 2. *When the goods are in transit*—The seller or lessor may stop the carrier or bailee from delivering the goods [UCC 2–705, 2A–526]. 3. *When the goods are in the possession of the buyer or lessee*—The seller or lessor may do the following: a. Sue to recover the purchase price or lease payments due [UCC 2–709(1), 2A–529(1)]. b. Reclaim the goods. A seller may reclaim goods received by an insolvent buyer if the demand is made within ten days of receipt (reclaiming goods excludes all other remedies) [UCC 2–702(2)]; a lessor may repossess goods if the lessee is in default [UCC 2A 525(2)].
Remedies of the Buyer or Lessee (See pages 402–407.)	1. *When the seller or lessor refuses to deliver the goods*—The buyer or lessee may do the following: a. Cancel the contract [UCC 2–711(1), 2A–508(1)(a)]. b. Recover the goods if the seller or lessor becomes insolvent within ten days after receiving the first payment and the goods are identified to the contract [UCC 2–502, 2A–522]. c. Obtain specific performance (when the goods are unique and when the remedy at law is inadequate) [UCC 2–716(1), 2A–521(1)]. d. Obtain cover [UCC 2–712, 2A–518]. e. Replevy the goods (if cover is unavailable) [UCC 2–716(3), 2A–521(3)]. f. Sue to recover damages [UCC 2–713, 2A–519]. 2. *When the seller or lessor delivers or tenders delivery of nonconforming goods*—The buyer or lessee may do the following: a. Reject the goods [UCC 2–601, 2A–509]. b. Revoke acceptance if the nonconformity *substantially* impairs the value of the unit or lot and if one of the following factors is present: (1) Acceptance was predicated on the reasonable assumption that the nonconformity would be cured and it was not cured within a reasonable time [UCC 2–608(1)(a), 2A–517(1)(a)]. (2) The buyer or lessee did not discover the nonconformity before acceptance, either because it was difficult to discover before acceptance or because the seller's or lessor's assurance that the goods were conforming kept the buyer or lessee from inspecting the goods [UCC 2–608(1)(b), 2A–517(1)(b)]. c. Accept the goods and recover damages [UCC 2–607, 2–714, 2–717, 2A–519].
Limitation of Remedies (See pages 407–408.)	1. Remedies may be limited in sales or lease contracts by agreement of the parties. If the contract states that a remedy is exclusive, then that is the sole remedy unless the remedy fails in its essential purpose. Sellers and lessors can also limit the rights of buyers and lessees to consequential damages unless the limitation is unconscionable [UCC 2–719, 2A–503]. 2. The UCC has a four-year statute of limitations for actions involving breach of contract. By agreement, the parties to a sales or lease contract can reduce this period to not less than one year, but they cannot extend it beyond four years [UCC 2–725(1), 2A–506(1)].

ExamPrep

ISSUE SPOTTERS

1 Country Fruit Stand orders eighty cases of peaches from Down Home Farms. Without stating a reason, Down Home untimely delivers thirty cases instead of eighty. Does Country have the right to reject the shipment? Explain.

2 Brite Images, Inc. (BI), agrees to sell Catalog Corporation (CC) five thousand posters of celebrities, to be delivered on May 1. On April 1, BI repudiates the contract. CC informs BI that it expects delivery. Can CC sue BI without waiting until May 1? Why or why not?

BEFORE THE TEST

Check your answers to the Issue Spotters, and at the same time, take the interactive quiz for this chapter. Go to **www.cengage.com/blaw/blt** and click on "Chapter 16." First, click on "Answers to Issue Spotters" to check your answers. Next, click on "Interactive Quiz" to assess your mastery of the concepts in this chapter. Then click on "Flashcards" to review this chapter's Key Term definitions.

 For Review

Answers for the even-numbered questions in this **For Review** *section can be found on this text's accompanying Web site at* **www.cengage.com/blaw/blt**. *Select "Chapter 16" and click on "For Review."*

1 What are the respective obligations of the parties under a contract for the sale or lease of goods?

2 What is the perfect tender rule? What are some important exceptions to this rule that apply to sales and lease contracts?

3 What options are available to the nonbreaching party when the other party to a sales or lease contract repudiates the contract prior to the time for performance?

4 What remedies are available to a seller or lessor when the buyer or lessee breaches the contract? What remedies are available to a buyer or lessee if the seller or lessor breaches the contract?

5 In contracts subject to the UCC, are parties free to limit the remedies available to the nonbreaching party on a breach of contract? If so, in what ways?

 Hypothetical Scenarios and Case Problems

16–1 Remedies. Genix, Inc., has contracted to sell Larson five hundred washing machines of a certain model at list price. Genix is to ship the goods on or before December 1. Genix produces one thousand washing machines of this model but has not yet prepared Larson's shipment. On November 1, Larson repudiates the contract. Discuss the remedies available to Genix in this situation.

16–2 Hypothetical Question with Sample Answer Cummings ordered two model X Super Fidelity speakers from Jamestown Wholesale Electronics, Inc. Jamestown shipped the speakers via United Parcel Service, C.O.D. (collect on delivery), although Cummings had not requested or agreed to a C.O.D. shipment of the goods. When the speakers were delivered, Cummings refused to accept them because he would not be able to inspect them before payment. Jamestown claimed that it had shipped conforming goods and that Cummings had breached their contract. Had Cummings breached the contract? Explain.

—**For a sample answer to Question 16–2, go to Appendix E at the end of this text.**

16–3 Anticipatory Repudiation. Moore contracted in writing to sell her 2002 Ford Taurus to Hammer for $8,500. Moore agreed to deliver the car on Wednesday, and Hammer promised to pay the $8,500 on the following Friday. On Tuesday, Hammer informed Moore that he would not be buying the car after all. By Friday, Hammer had changed his mind again and tendered $8,500 to Moore. Moore, although she had not sold the car to another party, refused the tender and refused to deliver. Hammer claimed that Moore had breached their contract. Moore contended that Hammer's repudiation released her from her duty to perform under the contract. Who is correct, and why?

16–4 Acceptance. In April 2007, Stark, Ltd., applied for credit and opened an account with Quality Distributors, Inc., to obtain snack foods and other items for Stark's convenience stores. For three months, Quality delivered the goods and Stark paid the invoices. In July, Quality was dissolved, and its assets were distributed to J. F. Hughes Co. Hughes continued to deliver the goods to Stark, which continued to pay the invoices until November, when the firm began to experience financial difficulties. By January 2008, Stark owed Hughes $54,241.77.

Hughes then dealt with Stark only on a collect-on-delivery basis until Stark's stores closed in 2009. Hughes filed a lawsuit in a state court against Stark and its owner to recover amounts due on unpaid invoices. To successfully plead its case, Hughes had to show that there was a contract between the parties. One question was whether Stark had manifested acceptance of the goods delivered by Hughes. How does a buyer manifest acceptance? Was there an acceptance in this case?

16–5   **Case Problem with Sample Answer** Eaton Corp. bought four air-conditioning units from Trane Co., an operating division of American Standard, Inc., in 1998. The contract stated in part, "NEITHER PARTY SHALL BE LIABLE FOR . . . CONSEQUENTIAL DAMAGES." Trane was responsible for servicing the units. During the last ten days of March 2003, Trane's employees serviced and inspected the units, changed the filters and belts, and made a material list for repairs. On April 3, a fire occurred at Eaton's facility, extensively damaging the units and the facility, although no one was hurt. Alleging that the fire started in the electric motor of one of the units, and that Trane's faulty servicing of the units caused the fire, Eaton filed a suit in a federal district court against Trane. Eaton asserted breach of contract, among other claims, and asked for consequential damages. Trane filed a motion for summary judgment, based on the limitation-of-remedies clause. What are consequential damages? Can these be limited in some circumstances? Is the clause valid in this case? Explain. [*Eaton Corp. v. Trane Carolina Plains*, 350 F.Supp.2d 699 (D.S.C. 2004)]

—After you have answered Problem 16–5, compare your answer with the sample answer given on the Web site that accompanies this text. Go to **www.cengage.com/blaw/blt**, select "Chapter 16," and click on "Case Problem with Sample Answer."

16–6 **Remedies of the Buyer.** L.V.R.V., Inc., sells recreational vehicles (RVs) in Las Vegas, Nevada, as Wheeler's Las Vegas RV. In September 1997, Wheeler's sold a Santara RV made by Coachmen Recreational Vehicle Co. to Arthur and Roswitha Waddell. The Waddells hoped to spend two or three years driving around the country, but almost immediately—and repeatedly—they experienced problems with the RV. Its entry door popped open. Its cooling and heating systems did not work properly. Its batteries did not maintain a charge. Most significantly, its engine overheated when ascending a moderate grade. The Waddells brought it to Wheeler's service department for repairs. Over the next year and a half, the RV spent more than seven months at Wheeler's. In March 1999, the Waddells filed a complaint in

a Nevada state court against the dealer to revoke their acceptance of the RV. What are the requirements for a buyer's revocation of acceptance? Were the requirements met in this case? In whose favor should the court rule? Why? [*Waddell v. L.V.R.V., Inc.*, 122 Nev. 125, 125 P.3d 1160 (2006)]

16–7 **Obligations of the Seller.** Flint Hills Resources, LP, a crude oil refiner, agreed to buy "approximately 1,000 barrels per day" of Mexican natural gas condensate from JAG Energy Inc., an oil broker. Four months into the contract, Pemex, the only authorized seller of freshly extracted Mexican condensate, warned Flint Hills that some companies might be selling stolen Mexican condensate. Fearing potential criminal liability, Flint Hills refused to accept more deliveries from JAG without proof of the title to its product. JAG promised to forward documents showing its chain of title. When, after several weeks, JAG did not produce the documents, Flint Hills canceled their agreement. JAG filed a suit in a federal district court against Flint Hills, alleging breach. Did Flint Hills have a right to demand assurance of JAG's title to its product? If so, did the buyer act reasonably in exercising that right? Explain. [*Flint Hills Resources, LP v. Jag Energy, Inc.*, 559 F.3d 373 (5th Cir. 2009)]

16–8 **A Question of Ethics** *Scotwood Industries, Inc., sells calcium chloride flake for use in ice melt products. Between July and September 2004, Scotwood delivered thirty-seven shipments of flake to Frank Miller & Sons, Inc. After each delivery, Scotwood billed Miller, which paid thirty-five of the invoices and processed 30 to 50 percent of the flake. In August, Miller began complaining about the quality. Scotwood assured Miller that it would remedy the situation. Finally, in October, Miller told Scotwood, "[T]his is totally unacceptable. We are willing to discuss Scotwood picking up the material." Miller claimed that the flake was substantially defective because it was chunked. Calcium chloride maintains its purity for up to five years, but if it is exposed to and absorbs moisture, it chunks, making it unusable. In response to Scotwood's suit to collect payment on the unpaid invoices, Miller filed a counterclaim in a federal district court for breach of contract, seeking to recover based on revocation of acceptance, among other things.* [*Scotwood Industries, Inc. v. Frank Miller & Sons, Inc.*, 435 F.Supp.2d 1160 (D.Kan. 2006)]

1 What is revocation of acceptance? How does a buyer effectively exercise this option? Do the facts in this case support this theory as a ground for Miller to recover damages? Why or why not?

2 Is there an ethical basis for allowing a buyer to revoke acceptance of goods and recover damages? If so, is there an ethical limit to this right? Discuss.

▶ Critical Thinking and Writing Assignments

16–9 **Critical Legal Thinking.** Under what circumstances should courts not allow fully informed contracting parties to agree to limit remedies?

16–10 **Critical Thinking and Writing Assignment for Business.** Suppose that you are a collector of antique cars and you need to purchase spare parts for a 1938 engine. These parts are not made anymore and are scarce. You discover that Beem has the spare parts that you need. To get the contract with Beem, you agree to pay 50 percent of the purchase price in advance. You send the payment on May 1, and Beem receives it on May 2. On May 3, Beem, having found another buyer willing to pay substantially more for the parts, informs you that he will not deliver as contracted. That same day, you learn that Beem is insolvent. Discuss fully any possible remedies that would enable you to take possession of these parts.

 Practical Internet Exercises

Go to this text's Web site at **www.cengage.com/blaw/blt**, select "Chapter 16," and click on "Practical Internet Exercises." There you will find the following Internet research exercises that you can perform to learn more about the topics covered in this chapter.

Practical Internet Exercise 16–1: MANAGEMENT PERSPECTIVE—The Right to Reject Goods
Practical Internet Exercise 16–2: LEGAL PERSPECTIVE—International Performance Requirements

Warranties and Product Liability

(Digital Sextant/Creative Commons)

> **"I'll warrant him heart-whole."**
>
> —William Shakespeare, 1564–1616
> (English dramatist and poet)

Learning Objectives

After reading this chapter, you should be able to answer the following questions:

1. What factors determine whether a seller's or lessor's statement constitutes an express warranty or mere puffery?

2. What implied warranties arise under the UCC?

3. Can a manufacturer be held liable to any person who suffers an injury proximately caused by the manufacturer's negligently made product?

4. What are the elements of a cause of action in strict product liability?

5. What defenses to liability can be raised in a product liability lawsuit?

Warranty is an age-old concept. In sales and lease law, a warranty is an assurance by one party of the existence of a fact on which the other party can rely. In the chapter-opening quotation, a character in William Shakespeare's play *As You Like It* warranted his friend "heart-whole." In commercial law, sellers and lessors warrant to those who purchase or lease their goods that the goods are as represented or will be as promised.

The Uniform Commercial Code (UCC) has numerous rules governing product warranties as they occur in sales and lease contracts. Those rules are the subject matter of the first part of this chapter. A natural addition to the discussion is *product liability:* Who is liable to consumers, users, and bystanders for physical harm and property damage caused by a particular good or its use? Product liability encompasses the contract theory of warranty, as well as the tort theories of negligence and strict liability (discussed in Chapter 4). Warranty law is also part of the broad body of consumer protection law that will be discussed in Chapter 33.

▶ Warranties

Most goods are covered by some type of warranty designed to protect consumers. Article 2 (on sales) and Article 2A (on leases) of the UCC designate several types of warranties that can arise in a sales or lease contract, including warranties of title, express warranties, and implied warranties. We discuss these types of warranties in the following subsections, as well as a federal statute that is designed to prevent deception and make warranties more understandable.

Warranties of Title

Under the UCC, three types of title warranties—*good title, no liens,* and *no infringements*—can automatically arise in sales and lease contracts. In most sales, sellers warrant that they have good and valid title to the goods sold and that transfer of the title is rightful [UCC 2–312(1)(a)]. If the buyer subsequently learns that the seller did not have good title to goods that were purchased, the buyer can sue the seller for breach of this warranty. (There is no warranty of good title in lease contracts because title to the goods does not pass to the lessee, as discussed in Chapter 15.)

An additional warranty of title shields buyers and lessees who are *unaware* of any encumbrances, or **liens** (claims, charges, or liabilities—see Chapter 21), against goods at the time the contract is made [UCC 2–312(1)(b), 2A–211(1)]. This warranty protects buyers who, for example, unknowingly purchase goods that are subject to a creditor's security interest (an interest in the goods that secures payment or performance, to be discussed in Chapter 20). If a creditor legally repossesses the goods from a buyer *who had no actual knowledge of the security interest,* the buyer can recover from the seller for breach of warranty.

Finally, when the seller or lessor is a merchant, he or she automatically warrants that the buyer or lessee takes the goods *free of infringements.* In other words, a merchant promises that the goods delivered are free from any copyright, trademark, or patent claims of a third person [UCC 2–312(3), 2A–211(2)].

Express Warranties

A seller or lessor can create an **express warranty** by making representations concerning the quality, condition, description, or performance potential of the goods. Under UCC 2–313 and 2A–210, express warranties arise when a seller or lessor indicates any of the following:

1. That the goods conform to any *affirmation* (declaration that something is true) or *promise* of fact that the seller or lessor makes to the buyer or lessee about the goods. Such affirmations or promises are usually made during the bargaining process. Statements such as "these drill bits will penetrate stainless steel—and without dulling" are express warranties.

2. That the goods conform to any *description* of them. For example, a label that reads "Crate contains one 150-horsepower diesel engine" or a contract that calls for the delivery of a "camel's-hair coat" creates an express warranty.

3. That the goods conform to any *sample or model* of the goods shown to the buyer or lessee.

BASIS OF THE BARGAIN To create an express warranty, a seller or lessor does not have to use formal words such as *warrant* or *guarantee* [UCC 2–313(2), 2A–210(2)]. It is only necessary that a reasonable buyer or lessee would regard the representation of fact as part of the basis of the bargain [UCC 2–313(1), 2A–210(1)]. Just what constitutes the basis of the bargain is hard to say. The UCC does not define the concept, and it is a question of fact in each case whether a representation was made at such a time and in such a way that it induced the buyer or lessee to enter into the contract.

STATEMENTS OF OPINION AND VALUE Only statements of fact create express warranties. If the seller or lessor makes a statement that relates to the supposed value or worth of the goods, or makes a statement of opinion or recommendation about the goods, the seller or lessor is not creating an express warranty [UCC 2–313(2), 2A–210(2)].

Lien An encumbrance on a property to satisfy a debt or protect a claim for payment of a debt.

Express Warranty A seller's or lessor's oral or written promise or affirmation of fact ancillary (secondary) to an underlying sales or lease agreement, as to the quality, condition, description, or performance of the goods being sold or leased.

(©Sonia.eps, 2009. Used under license from Shutterstock.com.)

This label constitutes an express warranty that the goods to which it is affixed are made with 100 percent natural materials. Does the buyer have to request any further expression of this express warranty for it to be valid?

(Ladyphoenixx/Creative Commons)

Marlboro cigarettes sit on a shelf in a retail store. Suppose that the store clerk tells a customer that these cigarettes "are the best," and the customer buys three cartons. The customer later develops lung cancer from smoking and sues the seller. In this situation, would the seller's statements be enough to create an express warranty? Why or why not?

EXAMPLE 17.1 A seller claims that "this is the best used car to come along in years; it has four new tires and a 250-horsepower engine just rebuilt this year." The seller has made several *affirmations of fact* that can create a warranty: the automobile has an engine; it has a 250-horsepower engine; it was rebuilt this year; there are four tires on the automobile; and the tires are new. The seller's *opinion* that the vehicle is "the best used car to come along in years," however, is known as "puffery" and creates no warranty. (*Puffery* is the expression of opinion by a seller or lessor that is not made as a representation of fact.) ●

A statement relating to the value of the goods, such as "this is worth a fortune" or "anywhere else you'd pay $10,000 for it," usually does not create a warranty. If the seller or lessor is an expert and gives an opinion as an expert to a layperson, though, then a warranty may be created.

It is not always easy to determine whether a statement constitutes an express warranty or puffing. The reasonableness of the buyer's or lessee's reliance appears to be the controlling criterion in many cases. For instance, a salesperson's statements that a ladder "will never break" and will "last a lifetime" are so clearly improbable that no reasonable buyer should rely on them. Courts also look at the context in which a statement is made to determine the reasonableness of the buyer's or lessee's reliance. For instance, a reasonable person is more likely to rely on a written statement made in an advertisement than on a statement made orally by a salesperson.

Preventing Legal Disputes

If you are in the business of selling or leasing goods, be careful about the words you use with customers, in writing and orally. If you do not intend to make an express warranty, do not make a promise or an affirmation of fact concerning the performance or quality of a product that you sell. Examine your firm's advertisements, brochures, and promotional materials, as well as any standard order forms and contracts, for statements that could be considered an express warranty. To avoid unintended warranties, instruct all employees on how the promises they make to buyers during a sale can create warranties.

Implied Warranties

Implied Warranty A warranty that arises by law because of the circumstances of a sale rather than by the seller's express promise.

An **implied warranty** is one that *the law derives* by implication or inference because of the circumstances of a sale, rather than by the seller's express promise. In an action based on breach of implied warranty, it is necessary to show that an implied warranty existed and that the breach of the warranty proximately caused[1] the damage sustained. We look here at some of the implied warranties that arise under the UCC.

Implied Warranty of Merchantability A warranty that goods being sold or leased are reasonably fit for the general purpose for which they are sold or leased, are properly packaged and labeled, and are of proper quality. The warranty automatically arises in every sale or lease of goods made by a merchant who deals in goods of the kind sold or leased.

IMPLIED WARRANTY OF MERCHANTABILITY Every sale or lease of goods made *by a merchant who deals in goods of the kind sold or leased* automatically gives rise to an **implied warranty of merchantability** [UCC 2–314, 2A–212]. **EXAMPLE 17.2** A merchant who is in the business of selling ski equipment makes an implied warranty of merchantability every time she sells a pair of skis. A neighbor selling his skis at a garage sale does not (because he is not in the business of selling goods of this type). ●

Merchantable Goods.   Goods that are *merchantable* are "reasonably fit for the ordinary purposes for which such goods are used." They must be of at least average, fair, or medium-grade quality. The quality must be comparable to a level that will pass without objection

---

1. Proximate, or legal, cause exists when the connection between an act and an injury is strong enough to justify imposing liability—see Chapter 4.

in the trade or market for goods of the same description. To be merchantable, the goods must also be adequately packaged and labeled as provided, and they must conform to the promises or affirmations of fact made on the container or label, if any.

The warranty of merchantability may be breached even though the merchant did not know or could not have discovered that a product was defective (not merchantable). Of course, merchants are not absolute insurers against all accidents occurring in connection with their goods. For instance, a bar of soap is not unmerchantable merely because a user could slip and fall by stepping on it.

If the buyer of a product that requires a significant number of repairs sells the item before filing a complaint against its manufacturer, is the sale evidence of the product's merchantability? That was the question in the following case.

Case 17.1   Shoop v. DaimlerChrysler Corp.

Appellate Court of Illinois, First District, 371 Ill.App.3d 1058, 864 N.E.2d 785 (2007).

COMPANY PROFILE   *In 1920, Walter Chrysler, the head of manufacturing operations for General Motors Corporation (GMC), became dissatisfied with its management and quit. He took over Maxwell Motor Company and renamed it Chrysler Corporation. For most of its history, Chrysler ranked third in vehicle sales among the "Big Three" U.S. automakers—GMC, Ford Motor Company, and Chrysler. In 1998, Germany's Daimler-Benz AG, the maker of Mercedes-Benz automobiles, bought Chrysler and created DaimlerChrysler AG. The new entity proved less successful than its investors had hoped, and in 2007 Chrysler was sold to Cerberus Capital Management, which renamed it Chrysler, LLC (www.chrysler.com). Its vehicles are sold under the Chrysler, Dodge, Jeep, and Mopar brands. In 2009, Chrysler and Fiat merged as part of a government-forced reorganization.*

(Mike Mariano/Creative Commons)

Did DaimlerChrysler breach the implied warranty of merchantability on a particular Dodge Dakota truck with a troublesome history of repairs?

FACTS   In April 2002, Darrell Shoop bought a 2002 Dodge Dakota truck for $28,000 from Dempsey Dodge in Chicago, Illinois. DaimlerChrysler Corporation had manufactured the Dakota. Problems with the truck arose almost immediately. Defects in the engine, suspension, steering, transmission, and other components required repairs twelve times within the first eighteen months, including at least five times for the same defect, which remained uncorrected. In May 2005, after having driven the Dakota 39,000 miles, Shoop accepted $16,500 for the trade-in

value of the truck as part of a purchase of a new vehicle. At the time, a comparable vehicle in average condition would have had an average trade-in value of $14,425 and an average retail value of $17,225. Shoop filed a suit in an Illinois state court against DaimlerChrysler, alleging, among other things, a breach of the implied warranty of merchantability. DaimlerChrysler countered, in part, that Shoop's sale of the Dakota was evidence of its merchantability. The court issued a summary judgment in DaimlerChrysler's favor. Shoop appealed to a state intermediate appellate court.

ISSUE   Was there sufficient evidence that DaimlerChrysler breached the implied warranty of merchantability to send the issue to trial?

DECISION   Yes. The state appellate court reversed the lower court's summary judgment and remanded the case for trial.

REASON   For automobiles, fitness for the ordinary purpose of driving implies that the vehicle should be in safe condition and free from defects. The reviewing court stated that, in addition, "breach of an implied warranty of merchantability may also occur when the warrantor has unsuccessfully attempted to repair or replace defective parts. Whether an implied warranty has been breached is a question of fact." The facts in this case were clear: the plaintiff was required to take the truck to the Chrysler dealership twelve times within eighteen months. The dealership was unable to cure the defects after a reasonable number of attempts. The state appellate court concluded that "a genuine issue of material fact existed as to whether Chrysler breached the implied warranty of merchantability."

FOR CRITICAL ANALYSIS—Legal Consideration   *If Shoop is allowed to recover damages for breach of warranty, what should be the measure of those damages?*

Merchantable Food.   The UCC recognizes the serving of food or drink to be consumed on or off the premises as a sale of goods subject to the implied warranty of merchantability [UCC 2–314(1)]. "Merchantable" food means food that is fit to eat. Courts generally determine whether food is fit to eat on the basis of consumer expectations. The courts assume that consumers should reasonably expect on occasion to find bones in fish fillets, cherry pits in cherry pie, or a nutshell in a package of shelled nuts, for example—because such substances are natural incidents of the food. In contrast, consumers would not reasonably expect to find an inchworm in a can of peas or a piece of glass in a soft drink—because these substances are not natural to the food product.[2] In the following classic case, the court had to determine whether a fish bone was a substance that one should reasonably expect to find in fish chowder.

---

2. See, for example, *Ruvolo v. Homovich*, 149 Ohio App.3d 701, 778 N.E.2d 661 (2002).

Classic Case 17.2 Webster v. Blue Ship Tea Room, Inc.

Supreme Judicial Court of Massachusetts, 347 Mass. 421, 198 N.E.2d 309 (1964).

HISTORICAL AND CULTURAL SETTING *Chowder, a soup or stew made with fresh fish, possibly originated in the fishing villages of Brittany (a French province to the west of Paris) and was probably carried to Canada and New England by Breton immigrants. In the nineteenth century and earlier, recipes for chowder did not call for the removal of the fish bones. Chowder recipes in the first half of the twentieth century were the same as in previous centuries, sometimes specifying that the fish head, tail, and backbone were to be broken in pieces and boiled, with the "liquor thus produced . . . added to the balance of the chowder."[a] By the middle of the twentieth century, there was a considerable body of case law concerning implied warranties and foreign and natural substances in food. It was perhaps inevitable that sooner or later, a consumer injured by a fish bone in chowder would challenge the merchantability of chowder containing fish bones.*

(Harry Chamberlain/StockFood Creative/Getty Images)

Does serving fish chowder with a bone constitute a breach of an implied warranty of merchantability?

FACTS Blue Ship Tea Room, Inc., was located in Boston in an old building overlooking the ocean. Priscilla Webster, who had been born and raised in New England, went to the restaurant and ordered fish chowder. The chowder was milky in color. After three or four spoonfuls, she felt something lodged in her throat. As a result, she underwent two esophagoscopies; in the second esophagoscopy, a fish bone was found and removed. Webster filed a lawsuit against the restaurant in a Massachusetts state court for breach of the implied warranty of

merchantability. The jury rendered a verdict for Webster, and the restaurant appealed to the state's highest court.

ISSUE Does serving fish chowder that contains a bone constitute a breach of an implied warranty of merchantability by the restaurant?

DECISION No. The Supreme Judicial Court of Massachusetts held that Webster could not recover against Blue Ship Tea Room because no breach of warranty had occurred.

REASON The court, citing UCC Section 2–314, stated that "a warranty that goods shall be merchantable is implied in a contract for their sale if the seller is a merchant with respect to goods of that kind. Under this section the serving for value of food or drink to be consumed either on the premises or elsewhere is a sale. * * * Goods to be merchantable must at least be * * * fit for the ordinary purposes for which such goods are used." The question here was whether a fish bone made the chowder unfit for eating. In the judge's opinion, "the joys of life in New England include the ready availability of fresh fish chowder. We should be prepared to cope with the hazards of fish bones, the occasional presence of which in chowders is, it seems to us, to be anticipated, and which, in the light of a hallowed tradition, do not impair their fitness or merchantability."

IMPACT OF THIS CASE ON TODAY'S LAW *This classic case, phrased in memorable language, was an early application of the UCC's implied warranty of merchantability to food products. The case established the rule that consumers should expect to find, on occasion, elements of food products that are natural to the product (such as fish bones in fish chowder). Courts today still apply this rule.*

RELEVANT WEB SITES *To locate information on the Web concerning the* Webster v. Blue Ship Tea Room, Inc., *decision, go to this text's Web site at* www.cengage.com/blaw/blt. *Select "Chapter 17" and click on "Classic Cases."*

---

a. Fannie Farmer, *The Boston Cooking School Cook Book* (Boston: Little, Brown, 1937), p. 166.

Implied Warranty of Fitness for a Particular Purpose A warranty that goods sold or leased are fit for a particular purpose. The warranty arises when any seller or lessor knows the particular purpose for which a buyer or lessee will use the goods and knows that the buyer or lessee is relying on the skill and judgment of the seller or lessor to select suitable goods.

IMPLIED WARRANTY OF FITNESS FOR A PARTICULAR PURPOSE The **implied warranty of fitness for a particular purpose** arises when any seller or lessor (merchant or nonmerchant) knows the particular purpose for which a buyer or lessee will use the goods *and* knows that the buyer or lessee is relying on the skill and judgment of the seller or lessor to select suitable goods [UCC 2–315, 2A–213].

Particular versus Ordinary Purpose. A "particular purpose" of the buyer or lessee differs from the "ordinary purpose for which goods are used" (merchantability). Goods can be merchantable but unfit for a particular purpose. **EXAMPLE 17.3** You need a gallon of paint to match the color of your living room walls—a light shade somewhere between coral and peach. You take a sample to your local hardware store and request a gallon of paint of that color. Instead, you are given a gallon of bright blue paint. Here, the salesperson has not breached any warranty of implied merchantability—the bright blue paint is of high quality and suitable for interior walls—but he or she has breached an implied warranty of fitness for a particular purpose. •

Knowledge and Reliance Requirements. A seller or lessor is not required to have actual knowledge of the buyer's or lessee's particular purpose, so long as the seller or lessor "has reason to know" the purpose. For an implied warranty to be created, however, the buyer or lessee must have *relied* on the skill or judgment of the seller or lessor in selecting or furnishing suitable goods. **EXAMPLE 17.4** Bloomberg leases a computer from Future Tech, a lessor of technical business equipment. Bloomberg tells the clerk that she wants a computer that will run a complicated new engineering graphics program at a realistic speed. Future Tech leases Bloomberg an Architex One computer with a CPU speed of only 2.4 gigahertz, even though a speed of at least 3.8 gigahertz would be required to run Bloomberg's graphics program at a "realistic speed." Bloomberg, after discovering that it takes forever to run her program, demands a full refund. Here, because Future Tech has breached the implied warranty of fitness for a particular purpose, Bloomberg normally will be able to recover. The clerk knew specifically that Bloomberg wanted a computer with enough speed to run certain software. Furthermore, Bloomberg relied on the clerk to furnish a computer that would fulfill this purpose. Because Future Tech did not do so, the warranty was breached. •

WARRANTIES IMPLIED FROM PRIOR DEALINGS OR TRADE CUSTOM Implied warranties can also arise (or be excluded or modified) as a result of course of dealing or usage of trade [UCC 2–314(3), 2A–212(3)]. In the absence of evidence to the contrary, when both parties to a sales or lease contract have knowledge of a well-recognized trade custom, the courts will infer that both parties intended for that trade custom to apply to their contract. **EXAMPLE 17.5** Suppose that it is an industry-wide custom to lubricate new cars before they are delivered to buyers. Latoya buys a new car from Bender Chevrolet. After the purchase, Latoya discovers that Bender failed to lubricate the car before delivering it to her. In this situation, Latoya can hold the dealer liable for damages resulting from the breach of an implied warranty. (This, of course, would also be negligence on the part of the dealer.) •

Overlapping Warranties

Sometimes, two or more warranties are made in a single transaction. An implied warranty of merchantability, an implied warranty of fitness for a particular purpose, or both can exist in addition to an express warranty. For instance, when a sales contract for a new car states that "this car engine is warranted to be free from defects for 36,000 miles or thirty-six months, whichever occurs first," there is an express warranty against all defects and an implied warranty that the car will be fit for normal use.

BE AWARE Express and implied warranties do not necessarily displace each other. More than one warranty can cover the same goods in the same transaction.

The rule under the UCC is that express and implied warranties are construed as *cumulative* if they are consistent with one another [UCC 2–317, 2A–215]. In other words, courts interpret two or more warranties as being in agreement with each other unless this construction is unreasonable. If it is unreasonable, then a court will hold that the warranties are inconsistent and apply the following rules to interpret which warranty is most important:

1. *Express* warranties displace inconsistent *implied* warranties, except for implied warranties of fitness for a particular purpose.
2. Samples take precedence over inconsistent general descriptions.
3. Exact or technical specifications displace inconsistent samples or general descriptions.

EXAMPLE 17.6 Suppose that when Bloomberg leases the computer from Future Tech in Example 17.4, the contract contains an express warranty concerning the speed of the CPU and the application programs that the computer is capable of running. Bloomberg does not realize that the speed expressly warranted in the contract is insufficient for her needs. Bloomberg later claims that Future Tech has breached the implied warranty of fitness for a particular purpose because she made it clear that she was leasing the computer to perform certain tasks. In this situation, Bloomberg has a good claim for the breach of implied warranty of fitness for a particular purpose, because she had discussed with Future Tech the specific tasks that she needed the computer to perform. Although the express warranty on CPU speed takes precedence over the implied warranty of merchantability, it normally does not take precedence over an implied warranty of fitness for a particular purpose. Bloomberg normally will prevail. ●

Warranty Disclaimers

The UCC generally permits warranties to be disclaimed or limited by specific and unambiguous language, provided that the buyer or lessee is protected from surprise. The manner in which a seller or lessor can disclaim warranties varies depending on the type of warranty.

EXPRESS WARRANTIES   A seller or lessor can disclaim all oral express warranties by including in the contract a written (or an electronic record) disclaimer in language that is clear and conspicuous, and called to a buyer's or lessee's attention [UCC 2–316(1), 2A–214(1)]. This allows the seller or lessor to avoid false allegations that oral warranties were made, and it ensures that only representations made by properly authorized individuals are included in the bargain.

Note, however, that a buyer or lessee must be made aware of any warranty disclaimers or modifications *at the time the contract is formed.* In other words, any oral or written warranties—or disclaimers—made during the bargaining process as part of a contract's formation cannot be modified at a later time by the seller or lessor.

REMEMBER   If a seller or lessor carefully refrains from making any promise or affirmation of fact relating to the goods, describing the goods, or using a model or sample, no express warranty is created.

IMPLIED WARRANTIES   Generally, unless circumstances indicate otherwise, the implied warranties of merchantability and fitness are disclaimed by the expressions "as is," "with all faults," and other similar phrases that in common understanding call the buyer's or lessee's attention to the fact that there are no implied warranties [UCC 2–316(3)(a), 2A–214(3)(a)]. (Note, however, that some states have laws that forbid "as is" sales. Other states do not allow disclaimers of warranties of merchantability for consumer goods.)

ON THE WEB   For an example of a warranty disclaimer, go to www.bizguardian.com/terms.php.

CASE EXAMPLE 17.7   Sue Hallett saw an advertisement offering a "lovely, eleven-year-old mare" with extensive jumping ability for sale. After visiting Mandy Morningstar's ranch and examining the horse twice, Hallett contracted to buy the mare for $2,950. The contract she signed described the horse as an eleven-year-old mare, but indicated that the horse was being sold "as is." Shortly after the purchase, a veterinarian determined that the horse was actually sixteen years old and in no condition for jumping. Hallett immediately notified her bank and stopped payment on the check she had written to pay for the horse. Hallett also tried to return the horse and cancel the contract with Morningstar, but Morningstar refused and filed a suit against Hallett, claiming breach of contract. The trial court found in favor of Morningstar because Hallett had examined the horse and was satisfied with its condition at the time she signed the "as is" sales contract. The appellate court reversed, however, finding that the statement in the contract describing the horse as eleven years old constituted an express warranty, which Morningstar had breached. The appellate court reasoned that although the "as is" clause effectively disclaimed any implied warranties (of merchantability and fitness for a particular purpose, such as jumping), it did not disclaim the express warranty concerning the horse's age.[3] ●

WATCH OUT Courts generally view warranty disclaimers unfavorably, especially when consumers are involved.

Disclaimer of the Implied Warranty of Merchantability. To specifically disclaim an implied warranty of merchantability, a seller or lessor must mention the word *merchantability* [UCC 2–316(2), 2A–214(2)]. The disclaimer need not be written, but if it is, the writing (or record) must be conspicuous [UCC 2–316(2), 2A–214(4)]. Under the UCC, a term or clause is conspicuous when it is written or displayed in such a way that a reasonable person would notice it. Conspicuous terms include words set in capital letters, in a larger font size, or in a different color so as to be set off from the surrounding text.

Disclaimer of the Implied Warranty of Fitness. To specifically disclaim an implied warranty of fitness for a particular purpose, the disclaimer *must* be in a writing (or record) and must be conspicuous. The word *fitness* does not have to be mentioned; it is sufficient if, for example, the disclaimer states, "THERE ARE NO WARRANTIES THAT EXTEND BEYOND THE DESCRIPTION ON THE FACE HEREOF."

BUYER'S OR LESSEE'S EXAMINATION OR REFUSAL TO INSPECT If a buyer or lessee actually examines the goods (or a sample or model) as fully as desired before entering into a contract, or if the buyer or lessee refuses to examine the goods on the seller's or lessor's request that he or she do so, *there is no implied warranty with respect to defects that a reasonable examination would reveal or defects that are actually found* [UCC 2–316(3)(b), 2A–214(2)(b)].

EXAMPLE 17.8 Joplin buys a lamp at Gershwin's Store. No express warranties are made. Gershwin asks Joplin to inspect the lamp before buying it, but she refuses. Had Joplin inspected the lamp, she would have noticed that the base was obviously cracked and the electrical cord was pulled loose. If the lamp later cracks or starts a fire in Joplin's home and she is injured, she normally will not be able to hold Gershwin's liable for breach of the warranty of merchantability. Because Joplin refused to examine the lamp when asked by Gershwin, Joplin will be deemed to have assumed the risk that it was defective. ●

WARRANTY DISCLAIMERS AND UNCONSCIONABILITY The UCC sections dealing with warranty disclaimers do not refer specifically to unconscionability as a factor. Ultimately, however, the courts will test warranty disclaimers with reference to the UCC's unconscionability standards [UCC 2–302, 2A–108]. Such factors as lack of bargaining position, take-it-or-leave-it choices, and a buyer's or lessee's failure to understand or know of a warranty disclaimer will become relevant to the issue of unconscionability.

Magnuson-Moss Warranty Act

The Magnuson-Moss Warranty Act of 1975[4] was designed to prevent deception in warranties by making them easier to understand. The act modifies UCC warranty rules to some extent when *consumer* transactions are involved. The UCC, however, remains the primary codification of warranty rules for commercial transactions.

---

3. *Morningstar v. Hallett,* 858 A.2d 125 (Pa.Super.Ct. 2004).
4. 15 U.S.C. Sections 2301–2312.

Under the Magnuson-Moss Act, no seller or lessor is required to give an express written warranty for consumer goods sold. If a seller or lessor chooses to make an express written warranty, however, and the goods are priced at more than $25, the warranty must be labeled as "full" or "limited." A *full warranty* requires free repair or replacement of any defective part. If the product cannot be repaired within a reasonable time, the consumer has the choice of a refund or a replacement without charge. A full warranty can be for an unlimited or limited time period, such as a "full twelve-month warranty." A *limited warranty* is one in which the buyer's recourse is limited in some fashion, such as to replacement of an item. The fact that only a limited warranty is being given must be conspicuously stated.

The Magnuson-Moss Act further requires the warrantor to make certain disclosures fully and conspicuously in a single document in "readily understood language." It must state the names and addresses of the warrantor(s), specifically what is warranted, and the procedures for enforcing the warranty. It must also clarify that the buyer has legal rights and explain any limitations on warranty relief.

> "Every state has a lemon law—for better or for worse."
>
> Vince Megna, 1944–present
> (U.S. lawyer)

Lemon Laws

Some purchasers of defective automobiles—called "lemons"—found that the remedies provided by the UCC were inadequate due to limitations imposed by the seller. In response to the frustrations of these buyers, all of the states have enacted *lemon laws*.

A woman considering purchasing a new car meets a salesman. If the woman buys the car and it turns out to be defective, what rights does she have under most lemon laws? Can she immediately file a lawsuit in court against the manufacturer? Why or why not?

(Brian Teutsch/Creative Commons)

Coverage of Lemon Laws

Basically, state lemon laws provide remedies to consumers who buy automobiles that repeatedly fail to meet standards of quality and performance because they are "lemons." Although lemon laws vary by state, typically they apply to automobiles under warranty that are defective in a way that significantly affects the vehicle's value or use. Lemon laws do not necessarily cover used-car purchases (unless the car is covered by a manufacturer's extended warranty) or vehicles that are leased.[5]

Generally, the seller or manufacturer is given a number of opportunities to remedy the defect (usually four). If the seller fails to cure the problem despite a reasonable number of attempts (as specified by state law), the buyer is entitled to a new car, replacement of defective parts, or return of all consideration paid. Buyers who prevail in a lemon law dispute may also be entitled to reimbursement for their attorneys' fees.

Arbitration Is Typical Procedure

In most states, lemon laws require an aggrieved new-car owner to give the dealer or manufacturer an opportunity to solve the problem. If the problem persists, the owner must then submit complaints to the arbitration program specified in the manufacturer's warranty before taking the case to court. Decisions by arbitration panels are binding on the manufacturer—that is, cannot be appealed by the manufacturer to the courts—but usually are not binding on the purchaser.

Most major automobile companies operate their own arbitration panels, but some use independent arbitration services, such as those provided by the Better Business Bureau. Because industry-sponsored arbitration boards have been criticized for not being truly impartial, some states have established mandatory, government-sponsored arbitration programs for lemon-law disputes.

---

5. Note that in some states, such as California, these laws may extend beyond automobile purchases and apply to other consumer goods.

Product Liability

Those who make, sell, or lease goods can be held liable for physical harm or property damage caused by those goods to a consumer, user, or bystander. This is called **product liability.** Product liability claims may be based on the warranty theories just discussed, as well as on the theories of negligence, misrepresentation, and strict liability. We look here at product liability based on negligence and misrepresentation.

Product Liability The legal liability of manufacturers, sellers, and lessors of goods to consumers, users, and bystanders for injuries or damage that are caused by the goods.

Negligence

Chapter 4 defined *negligence* as the failure to exercise the degree of care that a reasonable, prudent person would have exercised under the circumstances. If a manufacturer fails to exercise "due care" to make a product safe, a person who is injured by the product may sue the manufacturer for negligence.

RECALL The elements of negligence include a duty of care, a breach of the duty, and an injury to the plaintiff proximately caused by the breach.

DUE CARE MUST BE EXERCISED   The manufacturer must exercise due care in designing the product, selecting the materials, using the appropriate production process, assembling the product, and placing adequate warnings on the label informing the user of dangers of which an ordinary person might not be aware. The duty of care also extends to the inspection and testing of any purchased products that are used in the final product sold by the manufacturer.

PRIVITY OF CONTRACT NOT REQUIRED   A product liability action based on negligence does not require *privity of contract* between the injured plaintiff and the defendant manufacturer. As discussed in Chapter 13, *privity of contract* refers to the relationship that exists between the promisor and the promisee of a contract; privity is the reason that only the parties to a contract normally can enforce that contract. In the context of product liability law, privity is not required. This means that a person who was injured by a product need not be the one who actually purchased the product—that is, need not be in privity—to maintain a negligence suit against the manufacturer or seller of a defective product. A manufacturer is liable for its failure to exercise due care to *any person* who sustains an injury proximately caused by a negligently made (defective) product.

Relative to the long history of the common law, this exception to the privity requirement is a fairly recent development, dating to the early part of the twentieth century. A leading case in this respect is *MacPherson v. Buick Motor Co.*, which is presented as this chapter's *Landmark in the Law* feature on the next page.

Misrepresentation

When a user or consumer is injured as a result of a manufacturer's or seller's fraudulent misrepresentation, the basis of liability may be the tort of fraud. The intentional mislabeling of packaged cosmetics, for instance, or the intentional concealment of a product's defects would constitute fraudulent misrepresentation. The misrepresentation must be of a material fact, and the seller must have intended to induce the buyer's reliance on the misrepresentation. Misrepresentation on a label or advertisement is enough to show an intent to induce the reliance of anyone who may use the product. In addition, the buyer must have relied on the misrepresentation.

 Strict Product Liability

Under the doctrine of strict liability (discussed in Chapter 4), people may be liable for the results of their acts regardless of their intentions or their exercise of reasonable care. In addition, liability does not depend on privity of contract. The injured party does not have

Landmark in the Law   *MacPherson v. Buick Motor Co.* (1916)

In the landmark case of *MacPherson v. Buick Motor Co.*,[a] the New York Court of Appeals—New York's highest court—considered the liability of a manufacturer that failed to exercise reasonable care in manufacturing a finished product.

Case Background   Donald MacPherson suffered injuries while riding in a Buick automobile that suddenly collapsed because one of the wheels was made of defective wood. The spokes crumbled into fragments, throwing MacPherson out of the vehicle and injuring him.

MacPherson had purchased the car from a Buick dealer, but he brought a lawsuit against the manufacturer, Buick Motor Company. Buick itself had not made the wheel but had bought it from another manufacturer. There was evidence, though, that the defects could have been discovered by a reasonable inspection by Buick and that no such inspection had taken place. MacPherson charged Buick with negligence for putting a human life in imminent danger.

The Issue before the Court and the Court's Ruling   The primary issue was whether Buick owed a duty of care to anyone except the immediate purchaser of the car—that is, the Buick dealer. In deciding the issue, Justice Benjamin Cardozo stated that "if the nature of a thing is such

that it is reasonably certain to place life and limb in peril when negligently made, it is then a thing of danger. . . . If to the element of danger there is added knowledge that the thing will be used by persons other than the purchaser, and used without new tests, then, irrespective of contract, the manufacturer of this thing of danger is under a duty to make it carefully."

The court concluded that "beyond all question, the nature of an automobile gives warning of probable danger if its construction is defective. This automobile was designed to go 50 miles an hour. Unless its wheels were sound and strong, injury was almost certain." Although Buick itself had not manufactured the wheel, the court held that Buick had a duty to inspect the wheels and that Buick "was responsible for the finished product." Therefore, Buick was liable to MacPherson for the injuries he sustained when he was thrown from the car.

• **Application to Today's World**   *This landmark decision was a significant step in creating the legal environment of the modern world. As often happens, technological developments necessitated changes in the law. Today, automobile manufacturers are commonly held liable when their negligence causes product users to be injured.*

• **Relevant Web Sites**   To locate information on the Web concerning the *MacPherson* decision, go to this text's Web site at www.cengage.com/blaw/blt, select "Chapter 17," and click on "URLs for Landmarks."

---

a. 217 N.Y. 382, 111 N.E. 1050 (1916).

---

to be the buyer or a third party beneficiary, as required under contract warranty theory. In the 1960s, courts applied the doctrine of strict liability in several landmark cases involving manufactured goods, and it has since become a common method of holding manufacturers liable.

Strict Product Liability and Public Policy

The law imposes strict product liability as a matter of public policy. This public policy rests on the threefold assumption that (1) consumers should be protected against unsafe products; (2) manufacturers and distributors should not escape liability for faulty products simply because they are not in privity of contract with the ultimate user of those products; and (3) manufacturers, sellers, and lessors of products are generally in a better position than consumers to bear the costs associated with injuries caused by their products—costs that they can ultimately pass on to all consumers in the form of higher prices.

California was the first state to impose strict product liability in tort on manufacturers. In a landmark decision, *Greenman v. Yuba Power Products, Inc.*,[6] the California Supreme Court set out the reason for applying tort law rather than contract law in cases involving consumers injured by defective products. According to the court, the "purpose of such liability is to [e]nsure that the costs of injuries resulting from defective products are borne by the manufacturers . . . rather than by the injured persons who are powerless to protect themselves."

ON THE WEB For an overview of product liability, go to FindLaw for Small Business at smallbusiness.findlaw.com/business-operations/insurance/liability-product-overview.html.

---

6. 59 Cal.2d 57, 377 P.2d 897, 27 Cal.Rptr. 697 (1963).

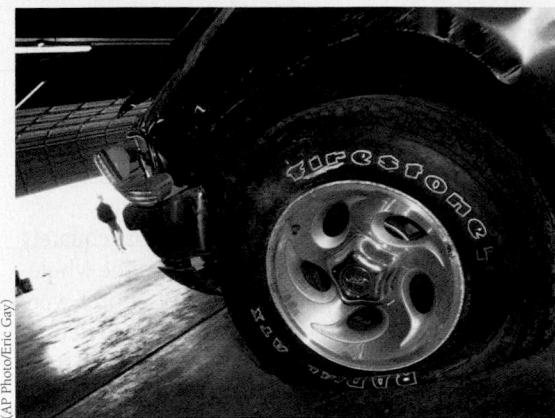

Suppose that Ford Motor Company installs Firestone tires on all new Ford Explorers. The tires are defective and cause numerous accidents involving people driving new Explorers. Who should bear the costs of the resulting injuries (Ford, Firestone, or the drivers' insurance companies) and why?

Unreasonably Dangerous Product In product liability law, a product that is defective to the point of threatening a consumer's health and safety. A product will be considered unreasonably dangerous if it is dangerous beyond the expectation of the ordinary consumer or if a less dangerous alternative was economically feasible for the manufacturer, but the manufacturer failed to produce it.

Requirements for Strict Liability

After the *Restatement (Second) of Torts* was issued in 1964, Section 402A became a widely accepted statement of how the doctrine of strict liability should be applied to sellers of goods (including manufacturers, processors, assemblers, packagers, bottlers, wholesalers, distributors, retailers, and lessors). The bases for an action in strict liability that are set forth in Section 402A of the *Restatement* can be summarized as the following series of six requirements. Depending on the jurisdiction, if these requirements are met, a manufacturer's liability to an injured party can be almost unlimited.

1. The product must be in a *defective condition* when the defendant sells it.
2. The defendant must normally be engaged in the *business of selling* (or otherwise distributing) that product.
3. The product must be *unreasonably dangerous* to the user or consumer because of its defective condition (in most states).
4. The plaintiff must incur *physical harm* to self or property by use or consumption of the product.
5. The defective condition must be the *proximate cause* of the injury or damage.
6. The *goods must not have been substantially changed* from the time the product was sold to the time the injury was sustained.

PROVING A DEFECTIVE CONDITION Under these requirements, in any action against a manufacturer, seller, or lessor, the plaintiff does not have to show why or in what manner the product became defective. The plaintiff does, however, have to prove that the product was defective at the time it left the hands of the seller or lessor and that this defective condition made it "unreasonably dangerous" to the user or consumer. Unless evidence can be presented that will support the conclusion that the product was defective when it was sold or leased, the plaintiff normally will not succeed. If the product was delivered in a safe condition and subsequent mishandling made it harmful to the user, the seller or lessor usually is not strictly liable.

UNREASONABLY DANGEROUS PRODUCTS The *Restatement* recognizes that many products cannot possibly be made entirely safe for all consumption, and thus holds sellers or lessors liable only for products that are *unreasonably* dangerous. A court may consider a product so defective as to be an **unreasonably dangerous product** in either of the following situations.

1. The product is dangerous beyond the expectation of the ordinary consumer.
2. A less dangerous alternative was economically feasible for the manufacturer, but the manufacturer failed to produce it.

As will be discussed next, a product may be unreasonably dangerous due to a flaw in the manufacturing process, a design defect, or an inadequate warning.

Product Defects—*Restatement (Third) of Torts*

Because Section 402A of the *Restatement (Second) of Torts* did not clearly define such terms as "defective" and "unreasonably dangerous," they were interpreted differently by different courts. In 1997, to address these concerns, the American Law Institute issued the *Restatement (Third) of Torts: Products Liability*. This *Restatement* defines the three types of product defects that have traditionally been recognized in product liability law—manufacturing defects, design defects, and inadequate warnings.

Sony manufactured defective lithiumion cell batteries, some of which caught on fire. Dell and other computer companies bought these Sony batteries for use in their laptop computers. To what extent is Sony liable? To what extent are Dell and other laptop makers who purchased these batteries liable?

MANUFACTURING DEFECTS   According to Section 2(a) of the *Restatement (Third) of Torts: Products Liability,* a product "contains a manufacturing defect when the product departs from its intended design even though all possible care was exercised in the preparation and marketing of the product." Basically, a manufacturing defect is a departure from a product unit's design specifications, which results in products that are physically flawed, damaged, or incorrectly assembled. A glass bottle that is made too thin and explodes in a consumer's face is an example of a manufacturing defect.

Usually, such defects occur when a manufacturer fails to assemble, test, or adequately check the quality of a product. Liability is imposed on the manufacturer (and on the wholesaler and retailer) regardless of whether the manufacturer's quality control efforts were "reasonable." The idea behind holding defendants strictly liable for manufacturing defects is to encourage greater investment in product safety and stringent quality control standards. (For more information on how effective quality control procedures can help businesses reduce their potential legal liability for breached warranties and defective products, see the *Linking the Law to Management* feature at the end of this chapter.)

CASE EXAMPLE 17.9   Kevin Schmude purchased an eight-foot stepladder and used it to install radio-frequency shielding in a hospital room. While Schmude was standing on the ladder, it collapsed, and he was seriously injured. He filed a lawsuit against the ladder's maker, Tricam Industries, Inc., based on a manufacturing defect. Experts testified that when the ladder was assembled, the preexisting holes in the top cap did not properly line up with the holes in the rear right rail and backing plate. As a result of the misalignment, the rivet at the rear legs of the ladder was more likely to fail. A jury concluded that this manufacturing defect made the ladder unreasonably dangerous and awarded Schmude more than $677,000 in damages.[7] ●

DESIGN DEFECTS   Unlike a product with a manufacturing defect, a product with a design defect is made in conformity with the manufacturer's design specifications, but nevertheless results in injury to the user because the design itself is flawed. The product's design creates an unreasonable risk to the user. A product "is defective in design when the foreseeable risks of harm posed by the product could have been reduced or avoided by the adoption of a reasonable alternative design by the seller or other distributor, or a predecessor in the commercial chain of distribution, and the omission of the alternative design renders the product not reasonably safe."[8]

Test for Design Defects.   To successfully assert a design defect, a plaintiff has to show that a reasonable alternative design was available and that the defendant's failure to adopt the alternative design rendered the product unreasonably dangerous. In other words, a manufacturer or other defendant is liable only when the harm was reasonably preventable. **CASE EXAMPLE 17.10**   Gillespie, who cut off several of his fingers while operating a table saw, filed a lawsuit against the maker of the table saw. Gillespie alleged that the blade guards on the saw were defectively designed. At trial, however, an expert testified that the alternative design for blade guards used for table saws could not have been used for the particular cut that Gillespie was performing at the time he was injured. The court found that Gillespie's claim about defective blade guards must fail because there was no proof that the "better" design of guard would have prevented his injury.[9] ●

Factors to Be Considered.   According to the Official Comments accompanying the *Restatement (Third) of Torts,* a court can consider a broad range of factors in deciding claims

---

7. *Schmude v. Tricam Industries, Inc.,* 550 F.Supp.2d 846 (E.D.Wis. 2008).

8. *Restatement (Third) of Torts: Products Liability,* Section 2(b).

9. *Gillespie v. Sears, Roebuck & Co.,* 386 F.3d 21 (1st Cir. 2004).

of design defects. These factors include the magnitude and probability of the foreseeable risks, as well as the relative advantages and disadvantages of the product as designed and as it alternatively could have been designed.

EXAMPLE 17.11   A nine-year-old child finds rat poison in a cupboard at the local boys' club and eats it, thinking that it is candy. The child dies, and his parents file a suit against the manufacturer, alleging that the rat poison was defectively designed because it looked like candy and was supposed to be placed in cupboards. In this situation, a court would probably consider factors such as the foreseeability that a child would think the rat poison was candy, the gravity of the potential harm from consumption, the availability of an alternative design, and the usefulness of the product. If the parents could offer sufficient evidence for a reasonable person to conclude that the harm was plausibly preventable, then the manufacturer could be held liable. ●

INADEQUATE WARNINGS   A product may also be deemed defective because of inadequate instructions or warnings. A product will be considered defective "when the foreseeable risks of harm posed by the product could have been reduced or avoided by the provision of reasonable instructions or warnings by the seller or other distributor, or a predecessor in the commercial chain of distribution, and the omission of the instructions or warnings renders the product not reasonably safe."[10] Generally, a seller must also warn consumers of the harm that can result from the *foreseeable misuse* of its product.

Important factors for a court to consider include the risks of a product, the "content and comprehensibility" and "intensity of expression" of warnings and instructions, and the "characteristics of expected user groups."[11] Courts apply a "reasonableness" test to determine if the warnings adequately alert consumers to the product's risks. For example, children will likely respond more readily to bright, bold, simple warning labels, while educated adults might need more detailed information.

There is no duty to warn about risks that are obvious or commonly known. Warnings about such risks do not add to the safety of a product and could even detract from it by making other warnings seem less significant. The obviousness of a risk and a user's decision to proceed in the face of that risk may be a defense in a product liability suit based on a warning defect. (This defense and other defenses in product liability suits will be discussed later in this chapter.)

An action alleging that a product is defective due to an inadequate label can be based on state law. (For a discussion of a case involving a state law that required warning labels on violent video games, see this chapter's *Adapting the Law to the Online Environment* feature on page 429.) Can a state claim be asserted if a federal agency approved the label? That was the question in the following case.

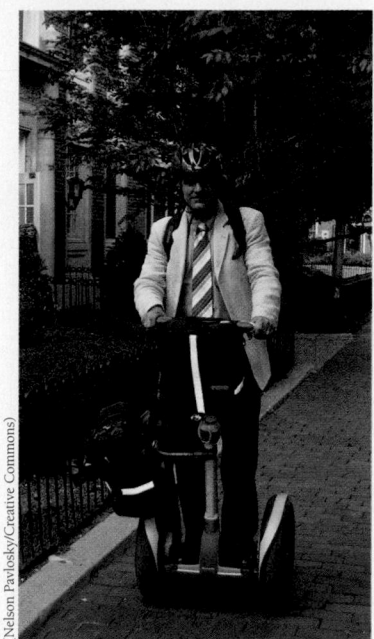

Segway, Inc., manufacturer of the Segway® Personal Transporter, voluntarily recalled all of its transporters to fix a software problem that could lead to users falling and injuring themselves. If a person was injured by such a malfunction of the software in the machine, what would the victim have to prove to establish that the device had a design defect?

(Nelson Pavlosky/Creative Commons)

---

10. *Restatement (Third) of Torts: Products Liability,* Section 2(c).
11. *Restatement (Third) of Torts: Products Liability,* Section 2, Comment h.

Case 17.3   **Wyeth v. Levine**

Supreme Court of the United States, __ U.S. __, 129 S.Ct. 1187, 173 L.Ed.2d 51 (2009).
www.findlaw.com/casecode/supreme.html[a]

HISTORICAL AND POLITICAL SETTING   *Today, more than eleven thousand drugs are available in the U.S. health-care market. The federal Food and Drug Administration (FDA) has the administrative power to monitor and regulate these drugs and their sales, but has limited resources with which to exercise this authority. Before Congress enacted the first significant federal public health law—the Federal Food and Drugs Act—in 1906, consumers injured by unsafe and ineffective drugs or their inadequate warnings could bring claims under state law. Aware of this situation, Congress did not attempt to change it.*

---

a. In the "Browse Supreme Court Opinions" section, click on "2009." On that page, scroll to the name of the case and click on it to access the opinion.

Case 17.3—Continues next page ➡

Case 17.3–Continued

A drug injected into a patient, using a push-syringe method, caused serious complications for that patient. Are there grounds for a state-law product liability lawsuit when the purportedly inadequate label had already been approved by the U.S. Food and Drug Administration?

FACTS Diane Levine, a professional guitar player and pianist, visited Plainfield Health Center in Vermont for treatment of a migraine headache. A physician's assistant gave her Phenergan (an antihistamine used to treat nausea) with a syringe (the IV-push method). The drug's label, which the FDA had approved, did not warn that this method was more risky than the IV-drip method.

Phenergan entered Levine's artery and, because the drug is corrosive, led to gangrene and the amputation of her forearm. She filed a suit in a Vermont state court against Wyeth, the drug's manufacturer, alleging that the label's warning was inadequate. Levine was awarded damages of $7.4 million. The Vermont Supreme Court affirmed the result. Wyeth appealed.

ISSUE Can an injured party bring a *state-law* action for product liability based on an inadequate warning if a *federal* agency approved the label?

DECISION Yes. The United States Supreme Court affirmed the lower court's decision. The FDA's approval of Phenergan's label did not preempt Levine's claim against the drug's manufacturer.

REASON Wyeth argued that it would not be possible to change Phenergan's label to comply with the state-law duty underlying Levine's claim without violating the company's federal labeling duties. But an FDA regulation allows a drug maker to change a label to strengthen a warning *before* obtaining the agency's approval. Wyeth also contended that enhancing the label would have violated the purposes of federal drug labeling laws. The Court found that "all evidence of Congress' purposes is to the contrary." Congress enacted the Food, Drug and Cosmetic Act in 1938 to "bolster consumer protection against harmful products" and has not added a preemption provision for drugs. Congress is certainly aware of state tort litigation in this field. These circumstances are "powerful evidence that Congress did not intend FDA oversight to be the exclusive means of ensuring drug safety and effectiveness."

FOR CRITICAL ANALYSIS—Political Consideration *In a 2006 preamble to a regulation, for the first time the FDA expressed the opinion that state-law actions "threaten FDA's statutorily prescribed role as the expert Federal agency responsible for evaluating and regulating drugs." What might have motivated this dramatic change in the agency's traditional position?*

Market-Share Liability

Market-Share Liability A theory under which liability is shared among all firms that manufactured and distributed a particular product during a certain period of time. This form of liability sharing is used only when the true source of the harmful product is unidentifiable; it is not recognized in many jurisdictions.

Generally, in all cases involving product liability, a plaintiff must prove that the defective product that caused her or his injury was the product of a specific defendant. In a few situations, however, courts have dropped this requirement when a plaintiff cannot prove which of many distributors of a harmful product supplied the particular product that caused the injuries. Under a theory of **market-share liability**, all firms that manufactured and distributed the product during the period in question are held liable for the plaintiff's injuries in proportion to the firms' respective shares of the market for that product during that period.

CASE EXAMPLE 17.12 A man with hemophilia (a blood-clotting disorder) received injections of a blood protein known as antihemophiliac factor (AHF) concentrate. When he later tested positive for the AIDS (acquired immune deficiency syndrome) virus, he sued. Because it was not known which manufacturer was responsible for the particular AHF received by the plaintiff, the court held that all of the manufacturers of AHF could be held liable under a market-share theory of liability.[12] ●

Courts in many jurisdictions do not recognize this theory of liability, believing that it deviates too significantly from traditional legal principles.[13] In jurisdictions that do recog-

---

12. *Smith v. Cutter Biological, Inc.*, 72 Haw. 416, 823 P.2d 717 (1991). See also *Sutowski v. Eli Lilly & Co.*, 92 Ohio St.3d 347, 696 N.E.2d 187 (1998); and *In re Methyl Tertiary Butyl Ether (MTBE) Products Liability Litigation*, 447 F.Supp.2d 289 (S.D.N.Y. 2006).

13. For the Illinois Supreme Court's position on market-share liability, see *Smith v. Eli Lilly Co.*, 137 Ill.2d 252, 560 N.E.2d 324, 148 Ill.Dec. 22 (1990). Pennsylvania law also does not recognize market-share liability. See *Bortell v. Eli Lilly & Co.*, 406 F.Supp.2d 1 (D.D.C. 2005).

Adapting the Law to the Online Environment

Should Video Games Be Required to Have Warning Labels?

Just about any product that you purchase in the physical world has one or more warning labels. Indeed, some critics argue that these labels have become so long and so ubiquitous that consumers now ignore them. In other words, putting warnings on just about everything defeats their original purpose. In the online environment, warning labels are not so extensive—at least not yet.

So far, video games have largely escaped mandated warning labels, although the video game industry has instituted a voluntary rating system to provide consumers and retailers with information about a video game's content. The Entertainment Software Rating Board assigns each video game one of six age-specific ratings, ranging from "Early Childhood" to "Adults Only."

Should video games, whether they are downloaded from the manufacturer's site or bought on a CD-ROM or DVD, have additional warnings that would advise potential users (or their parents) that the games might be overly violent? When the California legislature enacted a new law imposing restrictions and a labeling requirement on the sale or rental of "violent video games" to minors, this issue became paramount.[a]

Video Software Dealers Sue the State

Immediately after the labeling requirement was enacted, the Video Software Dealers Association, along with the Entertainment Software Association, brought a suit in federal district court seeking to invalidate the law. The court granted summary judgment in favor of the plaintiffs and also denied California's cross motion for summary judgment in its favor.

The act defined a violent video game as one in which "the range of options available to a player includes killing, maiming, dismembering, or sexually assaulting an image of a human being." While agreeing that some video games are unquestionably violent by everyday standards, the trial court pointed out, as did the federal court that heard the appeal, that

many video games are based on popular novels or motion pictures and have extensive plot lines. Accordingly, the court found that the definition of a violent video game was unconstitutionally vague and thus violated the First Amendment's guarantee of freedom of speech. The court also noted the existence of the voluntary rating system.

Constitutional Issues Prevail

The state appealed, but the U.S. Court of Appeals for the Ninth Circuit also found that the definition of a violent video game in the statute was unconstitutionally broad.[b] The appeals court noted that other federal circuit courts had already ruled against extending restrictions on sex-based content to restrictions on violence in video games.[c]

The legislation required all violent video games to be labeled on the front with a four-square-inch warning in the form of the number "18." The court, however, held that the labeling requirement failed the rational relationship test, which requires a label to be reasonably related to the state's interest in preventing deception of the customers.[d] Despite the court's decision, some legislators in California and other states have vowed to pursue new legislation that will require violent video games to carry warning labels.

FOR CRITICAL ANALYSIS

Why do you think that some legislators believe that the six-part voluntary labeling system for video games is not sufficient to protect minors?

a. California Civil Code Sections 1746–1746.5.

b. *Video Software Dealers Association v. Schwarzenegger,* 556 F.3d 950 (9th Cir. 2009).

c. See, for example, *International Digital Software Association v. St. Louis County,* 329 F.3d 954 (8th Cir. 2003).

d. See *Zauderer v. Office of Disciplinary Counsel,* 471 U.S. 626, 105 S.Ct. 2265, 85 L.Ed.2d 652 (1985).

nize market-share liability, it is usually applied in cases involving drugs or chemicals, when it is difficult or impossible to determine which company made a particular product.

Other Applications of Strict Liability

Almost all courts extend the strict liability of manufacturers and other sellers to injured bystanders. **EXAMPLE 17.13** A forklift that Trent is operating will not go into reverse, and as a result, it runs into a bystander. In this situation, the bystander can sue the manufacturer of the defective forklift under strict liability (and possibly bring a negligence action against the forklift operator as well). •

Strict liability also applies to suppliers of component parts. **EXAMPLE 17.14** Toyota buys brake pads from a subcontractor and puts them in Corollas without changing their composition. If those pads are defective, both the supplier of the brake pads and Toyota will be held strictly liable for the injuries caused by the defects. •

▶ Defenses to Product Liability

Defendants in product liability suits can raise a number of defenses. One defense, of course, is to show that there is no basis for the plaintiff's claim. For example, in a product liability case based on negligence, if a defendant can show that the plaintiff has *not* met the requirements (such as causation) for an action in negligence, generally the defendant will not be liable. Similarly, in a case involving strict product liability, a defendant can claim that the plaintiff failed to meet one of the requirements. If the defendant, for instance, establishes that the goods were altered after they were sold, the defendant normally will not be held liable.[14] A defendant may also assert that the *statute of limitations* (see Chapter 1) for a product liability claim has lapsed.[15] Several other defenses may also be available to defendants, as discussed next. Today, some defendants are raising the defense of preemption—that government regulations preempt claims for product liability.

Ethical Issue ⚖

Should companies be able to escape liability for defective products that were the subject of government regulation? The federal government has instituted numerous regulations that attempt to ensure the safety of products distributed to the public. (Consumer protection legislation will be discussed in Chapter 33.) Before 2008, a person who was injured by a product could assert a product liability claim regardless of whether the product was subject to government regulations. Under the United States Supreme Court's decision in *Riegel v. Medtronic, Inc.,*[16] however, the injured party may not be able to sue the manufacturer of defective products that are subject to federal regulatory schemes.

In the *Medtronic* case, the Court observed that the Medical Device Amendments of 1976 (MDA) created a comprehensive scheme of federal safety oversight for medical devices. The MDA requires the U.S. Food and Drug Administration to review the design, labeling, and manufacturing of these devices before they are marketed to make sure that they are safe and effective. The Court reasoned that because premarket approval is a "rigorous process," it preempts all common law claims challenging the safety or effectiveness of a medical device that has been approved. Therefore, a man who was injured by an approved medical device (in this case, a balloon catheter) could not sue its maker for negligence or strict product liability, or claim that the device was defectively designed.

The *Medtronic* decision has been controversial and caused somewhat of a split in the lower courts. Some courts have extended the preemption defense to other product liability actions, but other courts have been unwilling to deny an injured party relief simply because the federal government was supposed to ensure the product's safety.[17] Even the United States Supreme Court refused to extend the preemption defense to preclude a drug maker's liability in *Wyeth v. Levine,* the case presented as Case 17.3 in this chapter.

ON THE WEB For information on the product liability litigation against tobacco companies, including defenses raised by tobacco manufacturers in trial-related documents, go to the following page of the University of California, San Francisco's Web site at **www.library.ucsf.edu/tobacco/litigation**.

Assumption of Risk

Assumption of risk can sometimes be used as a defense in a product liability action. To establish such a defense, the defendant must show that (1) the plaintiff knew and appreciated the risk created by the product defect and (2) the plaintiff voluntarily assumed the risk, even though it was unreasonable to do so. (See Chapter 4 for a more detailed discussion of assumption of risk.)

---

14. See, for example, *Edmondson v. Macclesfield L-P Gas Co.,* 642 S.E.2d 265 (N.C.App. 2007); and *Pichardo v. C. S. Brown Co.,* 35 A.D.3d 303, 827 N.Y.S.2d 131 (N.Y.App. 2006).

15. Similar state statutes, called *statutes of repose,* place outer time limits on product liability actions.

16. ___ U.S. ___, 128 S.Ct. 999, 169 L.Ed.2d 892 (2008); this case was mentioned in Case Example 2.4 in Chapter 2 on page 37.

17. See, for example, *Paduano v. American Honda Motor Co.,* 169 Cal.App.4th 1453, 88 Cal.Rptr.3d 90 (2009); this case was presented as the *Extended Case Study* for Unit 1 on page 213; and *McDarby v. Merck & Co.,* 402 N.J.Super. 10, 949 A.2d 223 (2008).

Product Misuse

Similar to the defense of voluntary assumption of risk is that of product misuse, which occurs when a product is used for a purpose for which it was not intended. The courts have severely limited this defense, however, and it is now recognized as a defense only when the particular use was not reasonably foreseeable. If the misuse is foreseeable, the seller must take measures to guard against it.

Comparative Negligence (Fault)

Developments in the area of comparative negligence, or fault (discussed in Chapter 4), have also affected the doctrine of strict liability. In the past, the plaintiff's conduct was not a defense to liability for a defective product. Today, courts in many jurisdictions consider the negligent or intentional actions of both the plaintiff and the defendant when apportioning liability and awarding damages.[18] This means that a defendant may be able to limit at least some of its liability for injuries caused by its defective product if it can show that the plaintiff's misuse of the product contributed to the injuries. When proved, comparative negligence differs from other defenses in that it does not completely absolve the defendant of liability, but it can reduce the amount of damages that will be awarded to the plaintiff.

CASE EXAMPLE 17.15 Dan Smith, a mechanic in Alaska, was not wearing a hard hat at work when he was asked to start a diesel engine of an air compressor. Because the compressor was an older model, he had to prop open a door to start it. When Smith got the engine started, the door fell from its position and hit his head. The injury caused him to suffer from seizures and epilepsy. Smith sued the manufacturer, claiming that the engine was defectively designed. The manufacturer argued that Smith had been negligent by failing to wear his hard hat and by propping the door open in an unsafe manner. Smith's attorney claimed that the plaintiff's ordinary negligence could not be used as a defense in product liability cases, but the Alaska Supreme Court disagreed. Alaska, like many other states, allows comparative negligence to be raised as a defense in product liability lawsuits.[19] ●

Commonly Known Dangers

The dangers associated with certain products (such as sharp knives and guns) are so commonly known that manufacturers need not warn users of those dangers. If a defendant succeeds in convincing the court that a plaintiff's injury resulted from a commonly known danger, the defendant normally will not be liable.

CASE EXAMPLE 17.16 A classic case on this issue involved a plaintiff who was injured when an elastic exercise rope that she had purchased slipped off her foot and struck her in the eye, causing a detachment of the retina. The plaintiff claimed that the manufacturer should be liable because it had failed to warn users that the exercise rope might slip off a foot in such a manner. The court stated that to hold the manufacturer liable in these circumstances "would go beyond the reasonable dictates of justice in fixing the liabilities of manufacturers." After all, stated the court, "[a]lmost every physical object can be inherently dangerous or potentially dangerous in a sense. . . . A manufacturer cannot manufacture a knife that will not cut or a hammer that will not mash a thumb or a stove that will not burn a finger. The law does not require [manufacturers] to warn of such common dangers."[20] ●

---

18. See, for example, *State Farm Insurance Companies v. Premier Manufactured Systems, Inc.,* 213 Ariz. 419, 142 P.3d 1232 (2006); and *Ready v. United/Goedecke Services, Inc.,* 367 Ill.App.3d 272, 854 N.E.2d 758 (2006).
19. *Smith v. Ingersoll-Rand Co.,* 14 P.3d 990 (Alaska 2000). See also *Winschel v. Brown,* 171 P.3d 142 (Alaska 2007).
20. *Jamieson v. Woodward & Lothrop,* 247 F.2d 23, 101 D.C.App. 32 (1957).

Knowledgeable User

A related defense is the *knowledgeable user* defense. If a particular danger (such as electrical shock) is or should be commonly known by particular users of the product (such as electricians), the manufacturer of electrical equipment need not warn these users of the danger. **CASE EXAMPLE 17.17**   The parents of a group of teenagers who had become overweight and developed health problems filed a product liability lawsuit against McDonald's. The teenagers claimed that the well-known fast-food chain should be held liable for failing to warn customers of the adverse health effects of eating its food products. The court rejected this claim, however, based on the knowledgeable user defense. The court found that it is well known that the food at McDonald's contains high levels of cholesterol, fat, salt, and sugar and is therefore unhealthful. The court's opinion, which thwarted numerous future lawsuits against fast-food restaurants, stated: "If consumers know (or reasonably should know) the potential ill health effects of eating at McDonald's, they cannot blame McDonald's if they, nonetheless, choose to satiate [satisfy] their appetite with a surfeit [excess] of super-sized McDonald's products."[21] ●

---

21. *Pelman v. McDonald's Corp.*, 237 F.Supp.2d 512 (S.D.N.Y. 2003).

 Reviewing . . . Warranties and Product Liability

Shalene Kolchek bought a Great Lakes Spa from Val Porter, a dealer who was selling spas at the state fair. Porter told Kolchek that Great Lakes spas are "top of the line" and "the Cadillac of spas" and indicated that the spa she was buying was "fully warranted for three years." Kolchek signed an installment sale contract; then Porter handed her the manufacturer's paperwork and arranged for the spa to be delivered and installed for her. Three months later, Kolchek noticed that one corner of the spa was leaking onto her new deck and causing damage. She complained to Porter, but he did nothing about the problem. Kolchek's family continued to use the spa. Using the information presented in the chapter, answer the following questions.

1. Did Porter's statement that the spa was "top of the line" and "the Cadillac of spas" create any type of warranty? Why or why not?
2. Did Porter breach the implied warranty of merchantability? Why or why not?
3. One night, Kolchek's six-year-old daughter, Litisha, was in the spa with her mother. Litisha's hair became entangled in the spa's drain, and she was sucked down and held under water for a prolonged period, causing her to suffer brain damage. Under which theory or theories of product liability can Kolchek sue Porter to recover for Litisha's injuries?
4. If Kolchek had negligently left Litisha alone in the spa before the incident described in the previous question, what defense to liability might Porter assert?

Linking the Law *to Management*
Quality Control

In this chapter, you learned that breaches of warranties and manufacturing and design defects can give rise to liability. Although it is possible to minimize liability through warranty disclaimers and various defenses to product liability claims, all businesspersons know that such disclaimers and defenses do not necessarily fend off expensive lawsuits.

The legal issues surrounding product liability and warranties relate directly to quality control. As all of your management courses will emphasize, quality control is a major issue facing every manager in all

organizations. Companies that have cost-effective quality control systems produce products with fewer manufacturing and design defects. As a result, these companies incur fewer potential and actual warranty and product liability lawsuits.

Three Types of Quality Control

Most management systems involve three types of quality control— preventive, concurrent, and feedback. They apply at different stages of the process: preventive quality control occurs before the process begins, concurrent control takes place during the process, and feedback control occurs after it is finished.

In a typical manufacturing process, for example, preventive quality control might involve inspecting raw materials before they are put into the production process. Once the process begins, measuring and monitoring devices constantly assess quality standards as part of a concurrent quality control system. When the standards are not being met, employees correct the problem.

Once the manufacturing is completed, the products undergo a final quality inspection as part of the feedback quality control system. Of course, there are economic limits to how complete the final inspection will be. A refrigerator can be tested for an hour, a day, or a year. Management faces a trade-off. The less the refrigerator is tested, the sooner it gets to market and the faster the company receives its payment. The shorter the testing period, however, the higher the probability of a defect that will cost the manufacturer because of its expressed or implied warranties.

Total Quality Management (TQM)

Some managers attempt to reduce warranty and product liability costs by relying on a concurrent quality control system known as total quality management (TQM). This is an organization-wide effort to infuse quality into every activity in a company through continuous improvement.

Quality circles are a popular TQM technique. These are groups of six to twelve employees who volunteer to meet regularly to discuss problems and how to solve them. In a continuous stream manufacturing process, for example, a quality circle might consist of workers from different phases in the production process. Quality circles force changes in the production process that affect workers who are actually on the production line.

Benchmarking is another technique used in TQM. In benchmarking, a company continuously measures its products against those of its toughest competitors or the industry leaders in order to identify areas for improvement. In the automobile industry, benchmarking enabled several Japanese firms to overtake U.S. automakers in terms of quality. Some argue that Toyota gained worldwide market share by effectively using this type of quality control management system.

Another TQM system is called *Six Sigma*. Motorola introduced the quality principles in this system in the late 1980s, but Six Sigma has now become a generic term for a quality control approach that takes nothing for granted. It is based on a five-step methodology: define, measure, analyze, improve, and control. Six Sigma controls emphasize discipline and a relentless attempt to achieve higher quality (and lower costs). A possible impediment to a company's instituting a Six Sigma program is that it requires a major commitment from top management because it may involve widespread changes throughout the entire organization.

FOR CRITICAL ANALYSIS

Quality control leads to fewer defective products and fewer lawsuits. Consequently, managers know that quality control is important to their company's long-term financial health. At the same time, the more quality control that managers impose on their organization, the higher the average cost per unit of whatever is produced and sold. How does a manager decide how much quality control to undertake?

 ## Key Terms

express warranty 415	implied warranty	product liability 423
implied warranty 416	of merchantability 416	unreasonably dangerous product 425
implied warranty of fitness	lien 415	
for a particular purpose 419	market-share liability 428	

 ## Chapter Summary: Warranties and Product Liability

WARRANTIES	
Warranties of Title **(See pages 414–415.)**	In most sales, sellers warrant that they have good and valid title to the goods sold and that transfer of the title is rightful [UCC 2–312(1)(a)]. A second warranty of title shields buyers and lessees who are *unaware* of any encumbrances, or liens, against goods at the time the contract is made [UCC 2–312(1)(b), 2A–211(1)]. Third, when the seller or lessor is a merchant, he or she automatically warrants that the buyer or lessee takes the goods *free of infringements* [UCC 2–312(3), 2A–211(2)].

Continued

Chapter Summary: Warranties and Product Liability—Continued

Express Warranties (See pages 415–416.)	1. *Under the UCC*—An express warranty arises under the UCC when a seller or lessor indicates, as part of the basis of the bargain, any of the following [UCC 2–313, 2A–210]:
	  a. An affirmation or promise of fact.
	  b. A description of the goods.
	  c. A sample shown as conforming to the contract goods.
	2. *Under the Magnuson-Moss Warranty Act*—Express written warranties covering consumer goods priced at more than $25, *if made,* must be labeled as one of the following:
	  a. Full warranty—Free repair or replacement of defective parts; refund or replacement for goods if they cannot be repaired in a reasonable time.
	  b. Limited warranty—When less than a full warranty is being offered.

Implied Warranty of Merchantability (See pages 416–418.)	When a seller or lessor is a merchant who deals in goods of the kind sold or leased, the seller or lessor warrants that the goods sold or leased are properly packaged and labeled, are of proper quality, and are reasonably fit for the ordinary purposes for which such goods are used [UCC 2–314, 2A–212].
Implied Warranty of Fitness for a Particular Purpose (See page 419.)	Arises when the buyer's or lessee's purpose or use is expressly or impliedly known by the seller or lessor, and the buyer or lessee purchases or leases the goods in reliance on the seller's or lessor's selection [UCC 2–315, 2A–213]. Other implied warranties can arise as a result of course of dealing or usage of trade [UCC 2–314(3), 2A–212(3)].
Overlapping Warranties (See pages 419–420.)	The UCC construes warranties as cumulative if they are consistent with each other. If warranties are inconsistent, then express warranties take precedence over implied warranties, except for the implied warranty of fitness for a particular purpose. Also, samples take precedence over general descriptions, and exact or technical specifications displace inconsistent samples or general descriptions.
Warranty Disclaimers (See pages 420–421.)	Express warranties can be disclaimed in language that is clear and conspicuous and called to the buyer's or lessee's attention at the time the contract is formed. A disclaimer of the implied warranty of merchantability must specifically mention the word *merchantability.* The disclaimer need not be in writing, but if it is written, it must be conspicuous. A disclaimer of the implied warranty of fitness *must* be in writing and be conspicuous, though it need not mention the word *fitness.*
	PRODUCT LIABILITY
Liability Based on Negligence (See page 423.)	1. The manufacturer must use due care in designing the product, selecting materials, using the appropriate production process, assembling and testing the product, and placing adequate warnings on the label or product. 2. Privity of contract is not required. A manufacturer is liable for failure to exercise due care to any person who sustains an injury proximately caused by a negligently made (defective) product. 3. Fraudulent misrepresentation of a product may result in product liability based on the tort of fraud.
Strict Liability— Requirements (See page 425.)	1. The defendant must sell the product in a defective condition. 2. The defendant must normally be engaged in the business of selling that product. 3. The product must be unreasonably dangerous to the user or consumer because of its defective condition (in most states). 4. The plaintiff must incur physical harm to self or property by use or consumption of the product. 5. The defective condition must be the proximate cause of the injury or damage. 6. The goods must not have been substantially changed from the time the product was sold to the time the injury was sustained.
Strict Liability— Product Defects (See pages 425–428.)	A product may be defective in three basic ways: 1. In its manufacture. 2. In its design. 3. In the instructions or warnings that come with it.
Market-Share Liability (See pages 428–429.)	When plaintiffs cannot prove which of many distributors of a defective product supplied the particular product that caused the plaintiffs' injuries, some courts apply market-share liability. All firms that manufactured and distributed the harmful product during the period in question are then held liable for the plaintiffs' injuries in proportion to the firms' respective shares of the market, as directed by the court.

Chapter Summary: Warranties and Product Liability–Continued

Other Applications of Strict Liability (See pages 429–430.)	1. Manufacturers and other sellers are liable for harms suffered by bystanders as a result of defective products. 2. Suppliers of component parts are strictly liable for defective parts that, when incorporated into a product, cause injuries to users.
Defense to Product Liability (See pages 430–432.)	1. *Assumption of risk*—The user or consumer knew of the risk of harm and voluntarily assumed it. 2. *Product misuse*—The user or consumer misused the product in a way unforeseeable by the manufacturer. 3. *Comparative negligence*—Liability may be distributed between the plaintiff and the defendant under the doctrine of comparative negligence if the plaintiff's misuse of the product contributed to the risk of injury. 4. *Commonly known dangers*—If a defendant succeeds in convincing the court that a plaintiff's injury resulted from a commonly known danger, such as the danger associated with using a sharp knife, the defendant will not be liable. 5. *Knowledgeable user*—If a particular danger is or should be commonly known by particular users of the product, the manufacturer of the product need not warn these users of the danger.

 ## ExamPrep

ISSUE SPOTTERS

1 Rim Corporation makes tire rims, which it sells to Superior Vehicles, Inc., who installs them onto cars. One set of rims is defective, which an inspection would reveal. Superior does not inspect the rims. The car with the defective rims is sold to Town Auto Sales, which sells the car to Uri. Soon, the car is in an accident caused by the defective rims, and Uri is injured. Is Superior Vehicles liable? Explain your answer.

2 Real Chocolate Company makes a box of candy, which it sells to Sweet Things, Inc., a distributor. Sweet sells the box to a Tasty Candy store, where Jill buys it. Jill gives it to Ken, who breaks a tooth on a stone the same size and color as a piece of the candy. If Real, Sweet, and Tasty were not negligent, can they be liable for the injury? Why or why not?

BEFORE THE TEST

Check your answers to the Issue Spotters, and at the same time, take the interactive quiz for this chapter. Go to **www.cengage.com/blaw/blt** and click on "Chapter 17." First, click on "Answers to Issue Spotters" to check your answers. Next, click on "Interactive Quiz" to assess your mastery of the concepts in this chapter. Then click on "Flashcards" to review this chapter's Key Term definitions.

 ## For Review

Answers for the even-numbered questions in this For Review *section can be found on this text's accompanying Web site at* **www.cengage.com/blaw/blt**. *Select "Chapter 17" and click on "For Review."*

1 What factors determine whether a seller's or lessor's statement constitutes an express warranty or mere puffery?
2 What implied warranties arise under the UCC?
3 Can a manufacturer be held liable to any person who suffers an injury proximately caused by the manufacturer's negligently made product?
4 What are the elements of a cause of action in strict product liability?
5 What defenses to liability can be raised in a product liability lawsuit?

Hypothetical Scenarios and Case Problems

17–1 Product Liability. Carmen buys a television set manufactured by AKI Electronics. She is going on vacation, so she takes the set to her mother's house for her mother to use. Because the set is defective, it explodes, causing considerable damage to her mother's house. Carmen's mother sues AKI for the damage to her house. Discuss the theories under which Carmen's mother can recover from AKI.

17–2 **Hypothetical Question with Sample Answer** Tandy purchased a washing machine from Marshall Appliances. The sales contract included a provision explicitly disclaiming all express or implied warranties, including the implied warranty of merchantability. The disclaimer was printed in the same size and color as the rest of the contract. The machine turned out to be a "lemon" and never functioned properly. Tandy sought a refund of the purchase price, claiming that Marshall had breached the implied warranty of merchantability. Can Tandy recover her money, notwithstanding the warranty disclaimer in the contract? Explain.

—**For a sample answer to Question 17–2, go to Appendix E at the end of this text.**

17–3 Product Liability. Jason Clark, an experienced hunter, bought a paintball gun. Clark practiced with the gun and knew how to screw in the carbon dioxide cartridge, pump the gun, and use its safety and trigger. Although Clark was aware that he could purchase protective eyewear, he chose not to buy it. Clark had taken gun safety courses and understood that it was "common sense" not to shoot anyone in the face. Clark's friend, Chris Wright, also owned a paintball gun and was similarly familiar with the gun's use and its risks. Clark, Wright, and their friends played a game that involved shooting paintballs at cars whose occupants also had the guns. One night, while Clark and Wright were cruising with their guns, Wright shot at Clark's car, but hit Clark in the eye. Clark filed a product liability lawsuit against the manufacturer of Wright's paintball gun to recover for the injury. Clark claimed that the gun was defectively designed. During the trial, Wright testified that his gun "never malfunctioned." In whose favor should the court rule? Why?

17–4 Express Warranties. Videotape is recorded magnetically. The magnetic particles that constitute the recorded image are bound to the tape's polyester base. The binder that holds the particles to the base breaks down over time. This breakdown, which is called sticky shed syndrome, causes the image to deteriorate. The Walt Disney Co. made many of its movies available on tape. Buena Vista Home Entertainment, Inc., sold the tapes, which it described as part of a "Gold Collection" or "Masterpiece Collection." The advertising included such statements as "Give Your Children The Memories Of A Lifetime—Collect Each Timeless Masterpiece!" and "Available For A Limited Time Only!" Charmaine Schreib and others who bought the tapes filed a suit in an Illinois state court against Disney and Buena Vista, alleging, among other things, breach of warranty. The plaintiffs claimed that the defendants' marketing promised

the tapes would last for generations. In reality, the tapes were as subject to sticky shed syndrome as other tapes. Did the ads create an express warranty? In whose favor should the court rule on this issue? Explain. [*Schreib v. The Walt Disney Co.,* ___ N.E.2d ___ (Ill.App. 1 Dist. 2006)]

17–5 **Case Problem with Sample Answer** Bret D'Auguste was an experienced skier when he rented equipment to ski at Hunter Mountain Ski Bowl, Inc., owned by Shanty Hollow Corp., in New York. The adjustable retention/release value for the bindings on the rented equipment was set at a level that, according to skiing industry standards, was too low—meaning that the skis would be released too easily—given D'Auguste's height, weight, and ability. When D'Auguste entered a "double black diamond," or extremely difficult, trail, he noticed immediately that the surface consisted of ice and virtually no snow. He tried to exit the steeply declining trail by making a sharp right turn, but in the attempt, his left ski snapped off. D'Auguste lost his balance, fell, and slid down the mountain, striking his face and head against a fence along the trail. According to a report by a rental shop employee, one of the bindings on D'Auguste's skis had a "cracked heel housing." D'Auguste filed a suit in a New York state court against Shanty Hollow and others, including the bindings' manufacturer, on a theory of strict product liability. The manufacturer filed a motion for summary judgment. On what basis might the court *grant* the motion? On what basis might the court *deny* the motion? How should the court rule? Explain. [*D'Auguste v. Shanty Hollow Corp.,* 26 A.D.3d 403, 809 N.Y.S.2d 555 (2 Dept. 2006)]

—**After you have answered Problem 17–5, compare your answer with the sample answer given on the Web site that accompanies this text. Go to www.cengage.com/blaw/blt, select "Chapter 17," and click on "Case Problem with Sample Answer."**

17–6 Implied Warranties. Peter and Tanya Rothing operate Diamond R Stables near Belgrade, Montana, where they bred, trained, and sold horses. Arnold Kallestad owns a ranch in Gallatin County, Montana, where he grows hay and grain, and raises Red Angus cattle. For more than twenty years, Kallestad has sold between 300 and 1,000 tons of hay annually, sometimes advertising it for sale in the *Bozeman Daily Chronicle*. In 2001, the Rothings bought hay from Kallestad for $90 a ton. They received delivery on April 23. In less than two weeks, at least nine of the Rothings' horses exhibited symptoms of poisoning that was diagnosed as botulism. Before the outbreak was over, nineteen animals died. Robert Whitlock, associate professor of medicine and the director of the Botulism Laboratory at the University of Pennsylvania, concluded that Kallestad's hay was the source. The Rothings filed a suit in a Montana state court against Kallestad, claiming, in part, breach of the implied warranty of merchantability. Kallestad asked the court to dismiss this claim on the ground that, if botulism had been present, it had been in no way foreseeable. Should the court grant this request? Why or why not? [*Rothing v. Kallestad,* 337 Mont. 193, 159 P.3d 222 (2007)]

17–7 Defenses to Product Liability. Terry Kunkle and VanBuren High hosted a Christmas party in Berkeley County, South Carolina. Guests had drinks and hors d'oeuvres at a residence and adjourned to dinner in a barn across a public road. Brandon Stroud ferried the guests to the barn in a golf car made by Textron, Inc. The golf car was not equipped with lights, and Textron did not warn against its use on public roads at night. South Carolina does not require golf cars to be equipped with lights, but does ban their operation on public roads at night. As Stroud attempted to cross the road at 8:30 P.M., his golf car was struck by a vehicle driven by Joseph Thornley. Stroud was killed. His estate filed a suit in a South Carolina state court against Textron, alleging strict product liability and product liability based on negligence. The estate claimed that the golf car was defective and unreasonably dangerous. What might Textron assert in its defense? Explain. [*Moore v. Barony House Restaurant, LLC,* 382 S.C. 35, 674 S.E.2d 500 (S.C.App. 2009)]

17–8 **A Question of Ethics** *Susan Calles lived with her four daughters, Amanda, age 11, Victoria, age 5, and Jenna and Jillian, age 3. In March 1998, Calles bought an Aim N Flame utility lighter, which she stored on the top shelf of her kitchen cabinet. A trigger can ignite the Aim N Flame after an "ON/OFF" switch is slid to the "on" position. On the night of March 31, Calles and Victoria left to get videos. Jenna and Jillian were in bed, and Amanda was watching television. Calles returned to find fire trucks and emergency vehicles* around her home. *Robert Finn, a fire investigator, determined that Jenna had started a fire using the lighter. Jillian suffered smoke inhalation, was hospitalized, and died on April 21. Calles filed a suit in an Illinois state court against Scripto-Tokai Corp., which distributed the Aim N Flame, and others. In her suit, which was grounded in part in strict liability claims, Calles alleged that the lighter was an "unreasonably dangerous product." Scripto filed a motion for summary judgment.* [*Calles v. Scripto-Tokai Corp.,* 224 Ill.2d 247, 864 N.E.2d 249, 309 Ill.Dec. 383 (2007)]

1 A product is "unreasonably dangerous" when it is dangerous beyond the expectation of the ordinary consumer. Whose expectation—Calles's or Jenna's—applies here? Why? Does the lighter pass this test? Explain.

2 A product is also "unreasonably dangerous" when a less dangerous alternative was economically feasible for its maker, who failed to produce it. Scripto contended that because its product was "simple" and the danger was "obvious," it should not be liable under this test. Do you agree? Why or why not?

3 Calles presented evidence as to the likelihood and seriousness of injury from lighters that do not have child-safety devices. Scripto argued that the Aim N Flame is a useful, inexpensive, alternative source of fire and is safer than a match. Calles admitted that she was aware of the dangers presented by lighters in the hands of children. Scripto admitted that it had been a defendant in at least twenty-five suits for injuries that occurred under similar circumstances. With these factors in mind, how should the court rule? Why?

Critical Thinking and Writing Assignments

17–9 Critical Legal Thinking. The United States has the strictest product liability laws in the world today. Why do you think many other countries, particularly developing countries, are more lax with respect to holding manufacturers liable for product defects?

17–10 Video Question Go to this text's Web site at **www.cengage.com/blaw/blt** and select "Chapter 17." Click on "Video Questions" and view the video titled *Warranties.* Then answer the following questions.

1 Discuss whether the grocery store's label of a "Party Platter for Twenty" creates an express warranty under the Uniform Commercial Code that the platter will actually serve twenty people.

2 List and describe any implied warranties discussed in the chapter that apply to this scenario.

3 How would a court determine whether Oscar had breached any express or implied warranties concerning the quantity of food on the platter?

Practical Internet Exercises

Go to this text's Web site at **www.cengage.com/blaw/blt**, select "Chapter 17," and click on "Practical Internet Exercises." There you will find the following Internet research exercises that you can perform to learn more about the topics covered in this chapter.

Practical Internet Exercise 17–1: LEGAL PERSPECTIVE—Product Liability Litigation
Practical Internet Exercise 17–2: MANAGEMENT PERSPECTIVE—Warranties
Practical Internet Exercise 17–3: SOCIAL PERSPECTIVE—Lemon Laws

Chapter 18

Negotiable Instruments: Transferability and Liability

Chapter Outline

- Types of Instruments
- Requirements for Negotiability
- Transfer of Instruments
- Holder in Due Course (HDC)
- Signature and Warranty Liability
- Defenses, Limitations, and Discharge

(© Yellowj, 2009. Used under license from Shutterstock.com)

Learning Objectives

After reading this chapter, you should be able to answer the following questions:

1. What requirements must an instrument meet to be negotiable?

2. What are the requirements for attaining the status of a holder in due course (HDC)?

3. What is the difference between signature liability and warranty liability?

4. Certain defenses are valid against all holders, including HDCs. What are these defenses called? Name four defenses that fall within this category.

5. Certain defenses can be used against an ordinary holder but are not effective against an HDC. What are these defenses called? Name four defenses that fall within this category.

Negotiable Instrument A signed writing (record) that contains an unconditional promise or order to pay an exact sum on demand or at an exact future time to a specific person or order, or to bearer.

Most commercial transactions would be inconceivable without negotiable instruments. A **negotiable instrument** is a signed writing (record) that contains an unconditional promise or order to pay an exact sum on demand or at a specified future time to a specific person or order, or to bearer. Most negotiable instruments are paper documents, which is why they are sometimes referred to as *commercial paper.* The checks you write are negotiable instruments.

A negotiable instrument can function as a substitute for cash or as an extension of credit. As indicated in the chapter-opening quotation, "many generations" passed before paper became an acceptable substitute for gold or silver in commerce. For a negotiable instrument to operate *practically* as either a substitute for cash or a credit device, or both, it is essential that the instrument be *easily transferable without danger of being uncollectible.* Each rule described in the following pages can be examined in light of this essential function of negotiable instruments.

Negotiable instruments must meet special requirements relating to form and content that are imposed by Article 3 of the Uniform Commercial Code (UCC) and discussed throughout this chapter. Article 3 also governs the process of *negotiation* (transferring an instrument from one party to another), as will be discussed. Article 4 of the UCC, which governs bank deposits and collections, will be discussed in Chapter 19. Excerpts from the revised Articles 3 and 4 are included in Appendix C.

 Types of Instruments

UCC 3–104(b) defines *instrument* as a "negotiable instrument."[1] For that reason, whenever the term *instrument* is used in this book, it refers to a negotiable instrument. The UCC specifies four types of negotiable instruments: *drafts, checks, promissory notes,* and *certificates of deposit* (CDs). These instruments, which are summarized briefly in Exhibit 18–1, are frequently divided into the two classifications that we will discuss in the following subsections: *orders to pay* (drafts and checks) and *promises to pay* (promissory notes and CDs).

Negotiable instruments may also be classified as either demand instruments or time instruments. A *demand instrument* is payable on demand; that is, it is payable immediately after it is issued and thereafter for a reasonable period of time. All checks are demand instruments because, by definition, they must be payable on demand. A *time instrument* is payable at a future date.

Drafts and Checks (Orders to Pay)

A **draft** is an unconditional written order to pay rather than a promise to pay. Drafts involve three parties. The party creating the draft (the **drawer**) orders another party (the **drawee**) to pay funds, usually to a third party (the **payee**). The most common type of draft is a check, but drafts other than checks may be used in commercial transactions.

---

1. Note that all of the references to Article 3 of the UCC in this chapter are to the 1990 version of Article 3, which has been adopted by nearly every state.

On The Web To find Article 3 of the UCC as adopted by a particular state, go to the Web site of Cornell University's Law School at www.law.cornell.edu/ucc/ucc.table.html.

Draft Any instrument drawn on a drawee that orders the drawee to pay a certain sum of money, usually to a third party (the payee), on demand or at a definite future time.

Drawer The party that initiates a draft (such as a check), thereby ordering the drawee to pay.

Drawee The party that is ordered to pay a draft or check. With a check, a bank or a financial institution is always the drawee.

Payee A person to whom an instrument is made payable.

• *Exhibit* **18–1 Basic Types of Negotiable Instruments**

INSTRUMENTS	CHARACTERISTICS	PARTIES
ORDERS TO PAY **Draft**	An order by one person to another person or to bearer [UCC 3–104(e)].	Drawer—The person who signs or makes the order to pay [UCC 3–103(a)(3)].
Check	A draft drawn on a bank and payable on demand [UCC 3–104(f)].[a] (With certain types of checks, such as cashier's checks, the bank is both the drawer and the drawee—see Chapter 19 for details.)	Drawee—The person to whom the order to pay is made [UCC 3–103(a)(2)]. Payee—The person to whom payment is ordered.
PROMISES TO PAY **Promissory note**	A promise by one party to pay funds to another party or to bearer [UCC 3–104(e)].	Maker—The person who promises to pay [UCC 3–103(a)(5)]. Payee—The person to whom the promise is made.
Certificate of deposit	A note issued by a bank acknowledging a deposit of funds made payable to the holder of the note [UCC 3–104(j)].	

a. Under UCC 4–105(1), banks include savings banks, savings and loan associations, credit unions, and trust companies. (Trust companies are organizations that perform the fiduciary functions of trusts and agencies.)

Time Drafts and Sight Drafts

A *time draft* is payable at a definite future time. A *sight draft* (or demand draft) is payable on sight—that is, when it is presented to the drawee (usually a bank or financial institution) for payment. A sight draft may be payable on acceptance. **Acceptance** is the drawee's written promise to pay the draft when it comes due. Usually, an instrument is accepted by writing the word *accepted* across its face, followed by the date of acceptance and the signature of the drawee. A draft can be both a time and a sight draft; such a draft is payable at a stated time after sight (a draft that states it is payable ninety days after sight, for instance).

Exhibit 18–2 shows a typical time draft. For the drawee to be obligated to honor the order, the drawee must be obligated to the drawer either by agreement or through a debtor-creditor relationship. **EXAMPLE 18.1** On January 16, Ourtown Real Estate orders $1,000 worth of office supplies from Eastman Supply Company, with payment due in ninety days. Also on January 16, Ourtown sends Eastman a draft drawn on its account with the First National Bank of Whiteacre as payment. In this scenario, the drawer is Ourtown, the drawee is Ourtown's bank (First National Bank of Whiteacre), and the payee is Eastman Supply Company. ●

Trade Acceptances

A *trade acceptance* is a type of draft that is commonly used in the sale of goods. In this draft, the seller is both the drawer and the payee. The buyer to whom credit is extended is the drawee. **EXAMPLE 18.2** Jackson Street Bistro buys its restaurant supplies from Osaka Industries. When Jackson requests supplies, Osaka creates a draft ordering Jackson to pay Osaka for the supplies within ninety days. Jackson accepts the draft by signing its face and is then obligated to make the payment. This is a trade acceptance and can be sold to a third party if Osaka is in need of cash before the payment is due. ● (If the draft orders the buyer's bank to pay, it is called a *banker's acceptance*.)

Checks

As mentioned, the most commonly used type of draft is a **check**. The writer of the check is the drawer, the bank on which the check is drawn is the drawee, and the person to whom the check is payable is the payee. Checks are demand instruments because they are payable on demand.

Acceptance In negotiable instruments law, the drawee's signed agreement to pay a draft when it is presented.

> *"The two most beautiful words in the English language are 'check enclosed.'"*
>
> Dorothy Parker, 1893–1967
> (American author and poet)

Check A draft drawn by a drawer ordering the drawee bank or financial institution to pay a certain amount of money to the holder on demand.

● *Exhibit* 18–2 A Typical Time Draft

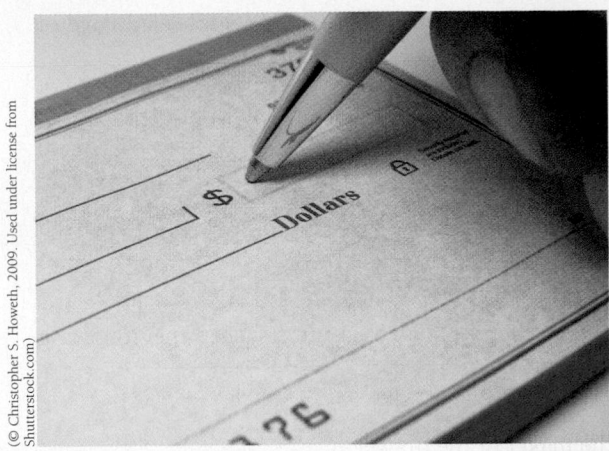

A check is the most commonly used type of draft. The person writing the check is the drawer; the bank on which it is written is the drawee; the person to whom it is payable is the payee. Why are checks called demand instruments?

Promissory Note A written promise made by one person (the maker) to pay a fixed amount of money to another person (the payee or a subsequent holder) on demand or on a specified date.

Maker One who promises to pay a fixed amount of money to the holder of a promissory note or a certificate of deposit (CD).

Certificate of Deposit (CD) A note issued by a bank in which the bank acknowledges the receipt of funds from a party and promises to repay that amount, with interest, to the party on a certain date.

Checks will be discussed more fully in Chapter 19, but it should be noted here that with certain types of checks, such as *cashier's checks,* the bank is both the drawer and the drawee. The bank customer purchases a cashier's check from the bank—that is, pays the bank the amount of the check—and indicates to whom the check should be made payable. The bank, not the customer, is the drawer of the check, as well as the drawee. A cashier's check functions the same as cash because the bank has committed itself to paying the stated amount on demand.

Promissory Notes

A **promissory note** is a written promise made by one person (the **maker** of the promise to pay) to another (usually a payee). A promissory note, which is often referred to simply as a *note,* can be made payable at a definite time or on demand. It can name a specific payee or merely be payable to bearer (bearer instruments will be discussed later in this chapter). **EXAMPLE 18.3** On April 30, Laurence and Margaret Roberts sign a writing unconditionally promising to pay "to the order of" the First National Bank of Whiteacre $3,000 (with 8 percent interest) on or before June 29. This writing is a promissory note. • A typical promissory note is shown in Exhibit 18–3.

Certificates of Deposit

A **certificate of deposit (CD)** is a type of note. A CD is issued when a party deposits funds with a bank that the bank promises to repay, with interest, on a certain date [UCC 3–104(j)]. The bank is the maker of the note, and the depositor is the payee. **EXAMPLE 18.4** On February 15, Sara Levin deposits $5,000 with the First National Bank of Whiteacre. The bank issues a CD, in which it promises to repay the $5,000, plus 3.25 percent annual interest, on August 15. •

Certificates of deposit in small denominations (for amounts up to $100,000) are often sold by savings and loan associations, savings banks, commercial banks, and credit unions.

• *Exhibit* **18–3** **A Typical Promissory Note**

(George Frey/Bloomberg News/Landov)

This bank advertises eight-month certificates of deposit (CDs) at an interest rate of 4.25 percent. What types of restrictions are there on the ability of a CD's purchaser to withdraw funds?

Certificates of deposit for amounts over $100,000 are called large or jumbo CDs. Exhibit 18–4 shows a typical small CD.

Because CDs are time deposits, the purchaser-payee typically is not allowed to withdraw the funds before the date of maturity (except in limited circumstances, such as disability or death). If a payee wants to access the funds prior to the maturity date, he or she can sell (negotiate) the CD to a third party.

▶ Requirements for Negotiability

For an instrument to be negotiable, it must meet the following requirements:

1. Be in writing.
2. Be signed by the maker or the drawer.
3. Be an unconditional promise or order to pay.
4. State a fixed amount of money.
5. Be payable on demand or at a definite time.
6. Be payable to order or to bearer, unless it is a check.

Written Form

Negotiable instruments must be in written form [UCC 3–103(a)(6), (9)]. This is because negotiable instruments must possess the quality of certainty that only formal, written expression can give. The writing must have the following qualities:

1. The writing must be on material that lends itself to *permanence*. Instruments carved in blocks of ice or recorded on other impermanent surfaces would not qualify as negotiable instruments. **EXAMPLE 18.5** Suzanne writes in the sand, "I promise to pay $500 to the order of Jack." This cannot be a negotiable instrument because, although it is in writing, it lacks permanence. ●

2. The writing must also have *portability*. Although the UCC does not explicitly state this requirement, if an instrument is not movable, it obviously cannot meet the requirement that it be freely transferable. **EXAMPLE 18.6** Charles writes on the side of a cow, "I promise

● *Exhibit* **18–4 A Typical Small Certificate of Deposit**

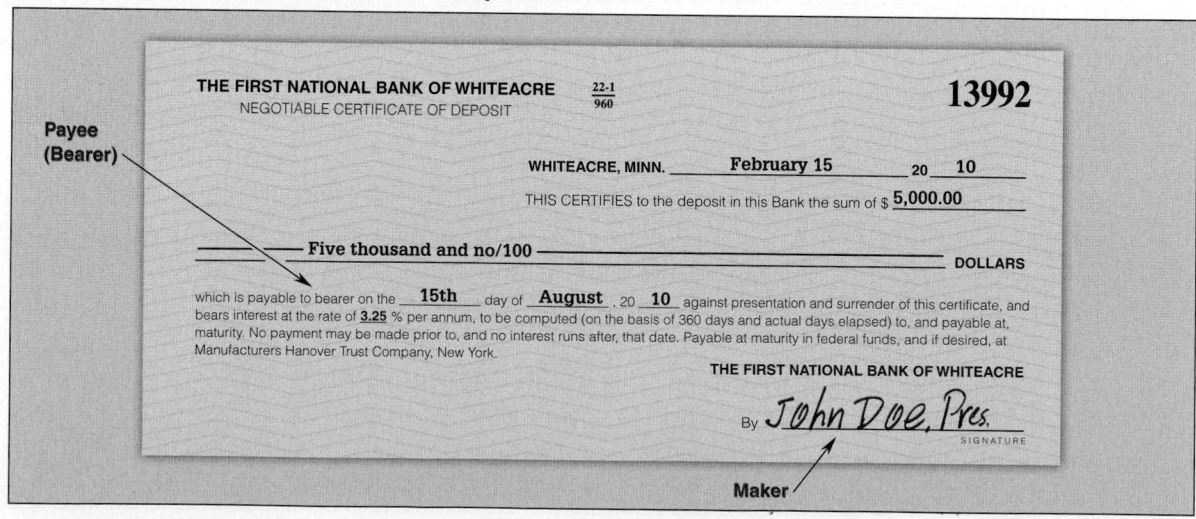

to pay $500 to the order of Jason." Technically, this would meet the requirements of a negotiable instrument—except for portability. A cow cannot easily be transferred in the ordinary course of business. Thus, the "instrument" is nonnegotiable. ●

The UCC nevertheless gives considerable leeway as to what can be a negotiable instrument. Courts have found checks and notes written on napkins, menus, tablecloths, shirts, and a variety of other materials to be negotiable instruments.

Signatures

For an instrument to be negotiable, it must be signed by (1) the maker, if it is a note or a certificate of deposit, or (2) the drawer, if it is a draft or a check [UCC 3–103(a)(3)]. If a person signs an instrument as an authorized agent of the maker or drawer, the maker or drawer has effectively signed the instrument. (Agents' signatures will be discussed in Chapter 23.)

The UCC is quite lenient with regard to what constitutes a signature. Nearly any symbol executed or adopted by a person with the intent to authenticate a written or electronic document can be a signature. A signature can be made manually or by some device, such as a rubber stamp or thumbprint, and can consist of any name, including a trade or assumed name, or a word, mark, or symbol [UCC 3–401(b)]. If necessary, *parol evidence* (see Chapter 12) is admissible to identify the signer. When the signer is identified, the signature becomes effective.

The location of the signature on the document is unimportant, although the usual place is the lower right-hand corner. A *handwritten* statement on the body of the instrument, such as "I, Jerome Garcia, promise to pay Elena Greer," is sufficient to act as a signature.

Preventing Legal Disputes

Although there are almost no limitations on the manner in which a signature can be made, be careful about receiving an instrument that has been signed in an unusual way. Oddities on a negotiable instrument can open the door to disputes and lead to litigation. Furthermore, an unusual signature clearly decreases the *marketability* of an instrument because it creates uncertainty.

Unconditional Promise or Order to Pay

REMEMBER Negotiable instruments are classified as promises to pay or orders to pay.

The terms of the promise or order must be included in the writing on the face of a negotiable instrument. The terms must also be *unconditional*—that is, they cannot be conditioned on the occurrence or nonoccurrence of some other event or agreement [UCC 3–104(a)].

> *"I'm a writer. I write checks. They're not very good."*
>
> Wendy Liebman, 1961–present
> (American comedian)

PROMISE OR ORDER For an instrument to be negotiable, it must contain an express order or promise to pay. If a buyer executes a promissory note using the words "I promise to pay Jonas $1,000 on demand for the purchase of these goods," then this requirement for a negotiable instrument is satisfied. A mere acknowledgment of the debt, such as an I.O.U. ("I owe you"), might logically *imply* a promise, but it is not sufficient under the UCC because the promise must be an affirmative (express) undertaking [UCC 3–103(a)(9)]. If such words as "to be paid on demand" or "due on demand" are added to an I.O.U., however, the need for an express promise to pay is satisfied.[2]

An *order* is associated with three-party instruments, such as checks, drafts, and trade acceptances. An order directs a third party to pay the instrument as drawn. In the typical

---

2. A certificate of deposit (CD) is an exception in this respect. A CD does not have to contain an express promise because the bank's acknowledgment of the deposit and the other terms of the instrument clearly indicate a promise by the bank to repay the funds [UCC 3–104(j)].

check, for example, the word *pay* (to the order of a payee) is a command to the drawee bank to pay the check when presented; thus, it is an order. A command, such as "pay," is mandatory even if it is accompanied by courteous words as in "Please pay" or "Kindly pay." Stating "I wish you would pay" does not fulfill this requirement. An order may be addressed to one party or to more than one party, either jointly ("to A *and* B") or alternatively ("to A *or* B") [UCC 3–103(a)(6)].

UNCONDITIONALITY OF PROMISE OR ORDER   Only unconditional promises or orders can be negotiable. A promise or order is conditional (and therefore *not* negotiable) if it states (1) an express condition to payment, (2) that the promise or order is subject to or governed by another writing, or (3) that the rights or obligations with respect to the promise or order are stated in another writing.

A mere reference to another writing, however, does not make the promise or order conditional [UCC 3–106(a)]. For example, the words "As per contract" or "This debt arises from the sale of goods X and Y" do not render an instrument nonnegotiable. Similarly, a statement in the instrument that payment can be made only out of a particular fund or source will not render the instrument nonnegotiable [UCC 3–106(b)(ii)]. **EXAMPLE 18.7** The terms of Biggs's note state that payment will be made out of the proceeds of next year's cotton crop. This does not make the note nonnegotiable—although the payee of such a note may find the note commercially unacceptable and refuse to take it. ●

(AP Photo/Mark Lennihan)

Because of intense competition among financial institutions, most of them widely advertise whatever interest rates they are offering on various certificates of deposit, as well as on other investment instruments and accounts. What limits the amount of interest that financial institutions are willing to pay to receive deposits?

BE AWARE   Interest payable on an instrument normally cannot exceed the maximum limit on interest under a state's usury statute.

Acceptor   A drawee that is legally obligated to pay an instrument when it is presented later for payment.

A Fixed Amount of Money

Negotiable instruments must state with certainty a fixed amount of money to be paid at any time the instrument is payable [UCC 3–104(a)]. The term *fixed amount* means an amount that is ascertainable from the face of the instrument. A demand note payable with 8 percent interest meets the requirement of a fixed amount because its amount can be determined at the time it is payable or at any time thereafter [UCC 3–104(a)].

The rate of interest may also be determined with reference to information that is not contained in the instrument if that information is readily ascertainable by reference to a formula or a source described in the instrument [UCC 3–112(b)]. For instance, an instrument that is payable at the *legal rate of interest* (a rate of interest fixed by statute) is negotiable. Mortgage notes tied to a variable rate of interest (a rate that fluctuates as a result of market conditions) are also negotiable.

UCC 3–104(a) provides that a fixed amount is to be *payable in money*. The UCC defines money as "a medium of exchange authorized or adopted by a domestic or foreign government as a part of its currency" [UCC 1–201(24)]. Thus, a note that promises "to pay on demand $1,000 in gold" is not negotiable because gold is not a medium of exchange adopted by the U.S. government. An instrument payable in the United States with a face amount stated in a foreign currency is negotiable, however, and can be paid in the foreign currency or in the equivalent of U.S. dollars [UCC 3–107].

Payable on Demand or at a Definite Time

To determine the value of a negotiable instrument, it is necessary to know when the maker, drawee, or acceptor (an **acceptor** is a drawee that promises to pay an instrument when it is presented later for payment) is required to pay the instrument. A negotiable instrument must therefore "be payable on demand or at a definite time" [UCC 3–104(a)(2)].

Presentment The act of presenting an instrument to the party liable on the instrument in order to collect payment. Presentment also occurs when a person presents an instrument to a drawee for a required acceptance.

PAYABLE ON DEMAND   Instruments that are payable on demand include those that contain the words "Payable at sight" or "Payable upon presentment." **Presentment** means a demand made by or on behalf of a person entitled to enforce an instrument to either pay or accept the instrument [UCC 3–501]. Thus, presentment occurs when a person brings the instrument to the appropriate party for payment or acceptance.

The very nature of the instrument may indicate that it is payable on demand. For example, a check, by definition, is payable on demand [UCC 3–104(f)]. If no time for payment is specified and the person responsible for payment must pay on the instrument's presentment, the instrument is payable on demand [UCC 3–108(a)].

CASE EXAMPLE 18.8   Patrick Gowin was an employee of a granite countertop business owned by John Stathis. In November 2000, Gowin signed a promissory note agreeing to pay $12,500 in order to become a co-owner of the business. The note was dated January 15, 2000 (ten months before it was signed), and required him to make installment payments starting in February 2000. Stathis told Gowin not to worry about the note and never requested any payments. Gowin continued working at the business until 2002 and then quit. Stathis claimed that Gowin did not own any interest in the business because he had never paid in the $12,500. When Gowin brought a lawsuit, the court reasoned that because compliance with the stated dates was impossible, the note effectively did not state a date for its payment and therefore was a demand note under UCC 3–108(a). The court also concluded that because no demand for payment had been made, Gowin's obligation to make it had not arisen and the termination of his ownership interest in the granite business was improper.[3] ●

PAYABLE AT A DEFINITE TIME   If an instrument is not payable on demand, to be negotiable it must be payable at a definite time. An instrument is payable at a definite time if it states that it is payable (1) on a specified date, (2) within a definite period of time (such as thirty days) after being presented for payment, or (3) on a date or time readily ascertainable at the time the promise or order is issued [UCC 3–108(b)]. The maker or drawee in a time draft, for example, is under no obligation to pay until the specified time.

When an instrument is payable by the maker or drawer on or before a stated date, it is clearly payable at a definite time. The maker or drawer has the *option* of paying before the stated maturity date, but the holder can still rely on payment being made by the maturity date. The option to pay early does not violate the definite-time requirement.

In contrast, an instrument that is undated and made payable "one month after date" is clearly nonnegotiable. There is no way to determine the maturity date from the face of the instrument.

Acceleration Clause A clause that allows a payee or other holder of a time instrument to demand payment of the entire amount due, with interest, if a certain event occurs, such as a default in the payment of an installment when due.

Holder Any person in possession of an instrument drawn, issued, or indorsed to him or her, to his or her order, to bearer, or in blank.

ACCELERATION CLAUSE   An **acceleration clause** allows a payee or other holder of a time instrument to demand payment of the entire amount due, with interest, if a certain event occurs, such as a default in the payment of an installment when due. (A **holder** is any person in possession of an instrument drawn, issued, or indorsed to him or her, to his or her order, to bearer, or in blank [UCC 1–201(20)].)

Under the UCC, instruments that include acceleration clauses are negotiable because (1) the exact value of the instrument can be ascertained and (2) the instrument will be payable on a specified date if the event allowing acceleration does not occur [UCC 3–108(b)(ii)]. Thus, the specified date is the outside limit used to determine the value and negotiability of the instrument.

In the following case, a promissory note that was to be paid in installments contained an acceleration clause. The question was whether the party entitled to payment waived its right to accelerate the note when it accepted late payments from the maker.

---

3. *Gowin v. Granite Depot, LLC*, 272 Va. 246, 634 S.E.2d 714 (2006).

Case 18.1 — Foundation Property Investments, LLC v. CTP, LLC

Court of Appeals of Kansas, 37 Kan.App.2d 890, 159 P.3d 1042 (2007).
www.kscourts.org/Cases-and-Opinions/opinions[a]

Do late payments on a loan to purchase a truck stop, once tolerated for a period of time, invalidate an acceleration clause for full payment in the original promissory note?

FACTS In April 2004, CTP, LLC, bought a truck stop in South Hutchinson, Kansas. As part of the deal, CTP borrowed $96,000 from Foundation Property Investments, LLC. The loan was evidenced by a promissory note, which provided that CTP was to make monthly payments of $673.54 between June 1, 2004, and June 1, 2009. The note stated that on default in any payment, "the whole amount then unpaid shall become immediately due and payable at the option of the holder without notice." CTP paid the first four installments on or before the due dates, but beginning in October 2004, CTP paid the next ten installments late. In July 2005, citing the late payments, Foundation demanded full payment of the note by the end of the month. CTP responded that the parties' course of dealing permitted payments to be made beyond their due dates. Foundation filed a suit in a Kansas state court against CTP to collect the note's full amount. CTP asserted that Foundation had waived its right to accelerate the note by its acceptance of late payments. The court determined that Foundation was entitled to payment of the note in full, plus interest and attorneys' fees and costs, for a total of $110,975.58, and issued a summary judgment in Foundation's favor. CTP appealed to a state intermediate appellate court.

ISSUE Does a party that repeatedly accepts late payments on a promissory note waive the right to enforce the note's acceleration clause for failure to make timely payments?

DECISION Yes. The state intermediate appellate court reversed the lower court's ruling and remanded the case with instructions to enter a judgment in CTP's favor.

REASON The court looked at the plaintiff's actions to determine whether it had relinquished its right to accelerate. *Course of dealing* is defined as "a sequence of previous conduct between the parties to a particular transaction which is fairly to be regarded as establishing a common basis of understanding for interpreting their expressions and other conduct." The reviewing court pointed out that Foundation never objected to CTP's late payments during the nine-month period. The action of accepting late payments "was inconsistent with [Foundation's] claim or right to receive prompt payments. Accordingly, the trial court incorrectly determined that Foundation's conduct did not constitute a waiver of its right of acceleration." The acceptance of late payments did constitute a waiver. CTP was not required to pay the note in full, plus interest and attorneys' fees and costs.

FOR CRITICAL ANALYSIS—Global Consideration *Suppose that Foundation was an entity based outside the United States. Could it have successfully claimed, in attempting to enforce the acceleration clause, that it had not given CTP notice because it had not been aware of Kansas law? Discuss.*

---

a. In the menu at the left, click on "Search by Docket Number." In the result, in the right-hand column, click on "96000–96999." On the next page, scroll to "96697" and click on the number to access the opinion. The Kansas courts, Washburn University School of Law Library, and University of Kansas School of Law Library maintain this Web site.

Extension Clause A clause in a time instrument that allows the instrument's date of maturity to be extended into the future.

EXTENSION CLAUSE The reverse of an acceleration clause is an **extension clause,** which allows the date of maturity to be extended into the future [UCC 3–108(b)(iii), (iv)]. To keep the instrument negotiable, the interval of the extension must be specified if the right to extend the time of payment is given to the maker or drawer of the instrument. If, however, the holder of the instrument can extend the time of payment, the extended maturity date does not have to be specified.

Payable to Order or to Bearer

Order Instrument A negotiable instrument that is payable "to the order of an identified person" or "to an identified person or order."

An **order instrument** is an instrument that is payable (1) "to the order of an identified person" or (2) "to an identified person or order" [UCC 3–109(b)]. An identified person is the person "to whom the instrument is initially payable" as determined by the intent of the maker or drawer [UCC 3–110(a)]. The identified person, in turn, may transfer the instrument to whomever he or she wishes. Thus, the maker or drawer is agreeing to pay either the person specified on the instrument or whomever that person might designate. In this way, the instrument retains its transferability.

Note that in order instruments, the person specified must be identified with *certainty* because the transfer of an order instrument requires the *indorsement,* or signature, of the payee (*indorsements* will be discussed at length later in this chapter). An order instrument made "Payable to the order of my nicest cousin," for instance, is not negotiable because it does not clearly specify the payee.

Bearer Instrument Any instrument that is not payable to a specific person, including instruments payable to the bearer or to "cash."

Bearer A person in possession of an instrument payable to bearer or indorsed in blank.

NOTE An instrument that purports to be payable both to order and to bearer is a contradiction in terms. Such an instrument is a bearer instrument.

A **bearer instrument** is an instrument that does not designate a specific payee [UCC 3–109(a)]. The term **bearer** refers to a person in possession of an instrument that is payable to bearer or indorsed in blank (with a signature only, as will be discussed shortly) [UCC 1–201(5), 3–109(a), 3–109(c)]. This means that the maker or drawer agrees to pay anyone who presents the instrument for payment.

Any instrument containing terms such as "Payable to Kathy Esposito or bearer" or "Pay to the order of cash" is a bearer instrument. In addition, an instrument that "indicates that it is not payable to an identified person" is a bearer instrument [UCC 3–109(a)(3)]. Thus, an instrument "payable to X" or "payable to Batman" can be negotiated as a bearer instrument, just as though it were payable to cash. An instrument made payable to a *nonexistent organization* or company is not a negotiable bearer instrument, however [UCC 3–109, Comment 2].

Factors That Do Not Affect Negotiability

Certain ambiguities or omissions will not affect the negotiability of an instrument. The UCC provides the following rules for clearing up ambiguous terms:

1. Unless the date of an instrument is necessary to determine a definite time for payment, the fact that an instrument is *undated* does not affect its negotiability. A typical example is an undated check, which is still negotiable. If a check is not dated, its date is the date of its issue, meaning the date the maker first delivers the check to another person to give that person rights in the check [UCC 3–113(b)].

2. Antedating or postdating an instrument does not affect the instrument's negotiability [UCC 3–113(a)]. *Antedating* occurs when a party puts a date on the instrument that is before the actual date; *postdating* occurs when a party puts a date on an instrument that is after the actual date. **EXAMPLE 18.9** On May 1, Avery draws a check on her account with First State Bank made payable to Consumer Credit Corporation. Avery postdates the check "May 15." Consumer Credit can negotiate the check, and, unless Avery tells First State otherwise, the bank can charge the amount of the check to Avery's account before May 15 [UCC 4–401(c)]. ●

3. Handwritten terms outweigh typewritten and printed terms (preprinted terms on forms, for example), and typewritten terms outweigh printed terms [UCC 3–114]. **EXAMPLE 18.10** Like most checks, your check is printed "Pay to the order of" with a blank next to it. In handwriting, you insert in the blank, "Anita Delgado or bearer." The handwritten terms will outweigh the printed form (an order instrument), and the check will be a bearer instrument. ●

4. Words outweigh figures unless the words are ambiguous [UCC 3–114]. This rule is important when the numerical amount and the written amount on a check differ. **EXAMPLE 18.11** Rob issues a check payable to Standard Appliance Company. For the amount, he fills in the numbers "$100" and writes in the words "One thousand and 00/100" dollars. The check is payable in the amount of $1,000. ●

5. When an instrument does not specify a particular interest rate but simply states "with interest," the interest rate is the *judgment rate of interest* (a rate of interest fixed by statute that is applied to a monetary judgment awarded by a court until the judgment is paid or terminated) [UCC 3–112(b)].

6. A check is negotiable even if there is a notation on it stating that it is "nonnegotiable" or "not governed by Article 3." Any other instrument, in contrast, can be made nonnegotiable

by the maker's or drawer's conspicuously noting on it that it is "nonnegotiable" or "not governed by Article 3" [UCC 3–104(d)].

 Transfer of Instruments

Once issued, a negotiable instrument can be transferred by *assignment* or by *negotiation*. Only a transfer by negotiation can result in the party obtaining the instrument receiving the rights of a holder.

Transfer by Assignment

Recall from Chapter 13 that an assignment is a transfer of rights under a contract. Under general contract principles, a transfer by assignment to an assignee gives the assignee only those rights that the assignor possessed. Any defenses that can be raised against an assignor can normally be raised against the assignee. This same principle applies when a negotiable instrument, such as a promissory note, is transferred by assignment. The transferee is then an *assignee* rather than a *holder.* Sometimes, a transfer fails to qualify as a negotiation because it fails to meet one or more of the requirements of a negotiable instrument, discussed above. When this occurs, the transfer becomes an assignment.

Transfer by Negotiation

> **Negotiation** The transfer of an instrument in such form that the transferee (the person to whom the instrument is transferred) becomes a holder.

Negotiation is the transfer of an instrument in such form that the transferee (the person to whom the instrument is transferred) becomes a holder [UCC 3–201(a)]. Under UCC principles, a transfer by negotiation creates a holder who, at the very least, receives the rights of the previous possessor [UCC 3–203(b)]. Unlike an assignment, a transfer by negotiation can make it possible for a holder to receive more rights in the instrument than the prior possessor had [UCC 3–202(b), 3–305, 3–306]. A holder who receives greater rights is known as a *holder in due course,* a concept we will discuss later in this chapter.

There are two methods of negotiating an instrument so that the receiver becomes a holder. The method used depends on whether the instrument is order paper or bearer paper.

NEGOTIATING ORDER INSTRUMENTS   An order instrument contains the name of a payee capable of indorsing it, as in "Pay to the order of Lloyd Sorenson." If the instrument is an order instrument, it is negotiated by delivery with any necessary indorsements.

EXAMPLE 18.12 National Express Corporation issues a payroll check "to the order of Lloyd Sorenson." Sorenson takes the check to the bank, signs his name on the back (an indorsement), gives it to the teller (a delivery), and receives cash. Sorenson has *negotiated* the check to the bank [UCC 3–201(b)]. •

Negotiating order instruments requires both delivery and indorsement (indorsements will be discussed shortly). If Sorenson had taken the check to the bank and delivered it to the teller without signing it, the transfer would not qualify as a negotiation. In that situation, the transfer would be treated as an assignment, and the bank would become an assignee rather than a holder.

NEGOTIATING BEARER INSTRUMENTS   If an instrument is payable to bearer, it is negotiated by delivery—that is, by transfer into another person's possession. Indorsement is not necessary [UCC 3–201(b)]. The use of bearer instruments thus involves more risk through loss or theft than the use of order instruments.

EXAMPLE 18.13 Richard Kray writes a check "payable to cash" and hands it to Jessie Arnold (a delivery). Kray has issued the check (a bearer instrument) to Arnold. Arnold

> *"Money has little value to its possessor unless it also has value to others."*
>
> Leland Stanford, 1824–1893
> (U.S. senator and founder of Stanford University)

places the check in her wallet, which is subsequently stolen. The thief has possession of the check. At this point, the thief has no rights to the check. If the thief "delivers" the check to an innocent third person, however, negotiation will be complete. All rights to the check will be passed absolutely to that third person, and Arnold will lose all rights to recover the proceeds of the check from that person [UCC 3–306]. Of course, Arnold could attempt to recover the amount from the thief if the thief can be found. •

Indorsements

Indorsement A signature placed on an instrument for the purpose of transferring one's ownership rights in the instrument.

Indorsements are required whenever the instrument being negotiated is classified as an order instrument. An **indorsement** is a signature with or without additional words or statements. It is most often written on the back of the instrument itself. If there is no room on the instrument, the indorsement can be on a separate piece of paper that is firmly affixed to the instrument, such as with staples [UCC 3–204(a)]. A person who transfers an instrument by signing (indorsing) it and delivering it to another person is an *indorser*. The person to whom the check is indorsed and delivered is the *indorsee*.

We examine here the four categories of indorsements: blank, special, qualified, and restrictive. Note that a single indorsement may have characteristics of more than one category. In other words, these categories are not mutually exclusive.

Blank Indorsement An indorsement that specifies no particular indorsee and can consist of a mere signature. An order instrument that is indorsed in blank becomes a bearer instrument.

BLANK INDORSEMENTS A **blank indorsement** does not specify a particular indorsee and can consist of a mere signature [UCC 3–205(b)]. Hence, a check payable "to the order of Alan Luberda" is indorsed in blank if Luberda simply writes his signature on the back of the check—as shown in Exhibit 18–5. An order instrument indorsed in blank becomes a bearer instrument and can be negotiated by delivery alone, as already discussed. In other words, a blank indorsement converts an order instrument to a bearer instrument, which anybody can cash.

• *Exhibit* **18–5 A Blank Indorsement**

Alan Luberda

Special Indorsement An indorsement on an instrument that indicates the specific person to whom the indorser intends to make the instrument payable; that is, it names the indorsee.

SPECIAL INDORSEMENTS A **special indorsement** contains the signature of the indorser and identifies the person to whom the instrument is made payable; that is, it names the indorsee [UCC 3–205(a)]. For instance, words such as "Pay to the order of Clay" or "Pay to Clay," followed by the signature of the indorser, create a special indorsement. When an instrument is indorsed in this way, it is an order instrument.

To avoid the risk of loss from theft, a holder may convert a blank indorsement to a special indorsement by writing, above the signature of the indorser, words identifying the indorsee [UCC 3–205(c)]. This changes the bearer instrument back to an order instrument.

EXAMPLE 18.14 A check is made payable to Peter Rabe. He indorses the check in blank by simply signing his name on the back and delivers the check to Anthony Bartomo. Anthony is unable to cash the check immediately and wants to avoid any risk should he lose the check. He therefore prints "Pay to Anthony Bartomo" above Peter's blank indorsement (see Exhibit 18–6). In this manner, Anthony has converted Peter's blank indorsement into a special indorsement. Further negotiation now requires Anthony Bartomo's indorsement plus delivery. •

• *Exhibit* **18–6 A Special Indorsement**

Pay to Anthony Bartomo
Peter Rabe

QUALIFIED INDORSEMENTS Generally, an indorser, *merely by indorsing*, impliedly promises to pay the holder or any subsequent indorser, the amount of the instrument in the event that the drawer or maker defaults on the payment [UCC 3–415(a)]. Usually, then,

Qualified Indorsement An indorsement on a negotiable instrument in which the indorser disclaims any contract liability on the instrument. The notation "without recourse" is commonly used to create a qualified indorsement.

indorsements are *unqualified indorsements;* that is, the indorser is guaranteeing payment of the instrument in addition to transferring title to it. An indorser who does not wish to be liable on an instrument can use a **qualified indorsement** to disclaim this liability [UCC 3–415(b)]. The notation "without recourse" is commonly used to create a qualified indorsement, such as the one shown in Exhibit 18–7.

Qualified indorsements are often used by persons (agents) acting in a representative capacity, such as insurance agents that receive checks payable to them that are really intended as payment to the insurance company. The "without recourse" indorsement relieves the agent from any liability on a check. If the instrument is dishonored, the holder cannot obtain recovery from the agent who indorsed "without recourse" unless the indorser has breached one of the transfer warranties (relating to title, signature, and material alteration) that will be discussed later in this chapter.

• *Exhibit* 18–7 A Qualified Indorsement

Pay to Elvie Ling, without recourse.
Bridgett Cage

Restrictive Indorsement Any indorsement on a negotiable instrument that requires the indorsee to comply with certain instructions regarding the funds involved. A restrictive indorsement does not prohibit the further negotiation of the instrument.

RESTRICTIVE INDORSEMENTS A **restrictive indorsement** requires the indorsee to comply with certain instructions regarding the funds involved, but it does not prohibit the further negotiation of an instrument [UCC 3–206(a)]. Although most indorsements are nonrestrictive because there are no instructions or conditions attached to the payment of funds, many forms of restrictive indorsements do exist, including those discussed here.

Conditional Indorsements. When payment depends on the occurrence of some event specified in the indorsement, the instrument has a conditional indorsement. **EXAMPLE 18.15** Ken Barton indorses a check, "Pay to Lars Johansen if he completes the renovation of my kitchen by June 1, 2011. [Signed] Ken Barton." Barton has created a conditional indorsement. • A conditional indorsement (on the back of the instrument) does not prevent further negotiation of the instrument.

Indorsements for Deposit or Collection. A common type of restrictive indorsement is one that makes the indorsee (almost always a bank) a collecting agent of the indorser [UCC 3–206(c)]. **EXAMPLE 18.16** Stephanie Mallak has received a check and wants to deposit it into her checking account at the bank. She can indorse the check "For deposit [or collection] only. [Signed] Stephanie Mallak" (see Exhibit 18–8). She may also wish to write her bank account number on the check. A "For Deposit" or "For Collection" indorsement locks the instrument into the bank-collection process and thus prohibits further negotiation except by the bank. Following this indorsement, only the bank can acquire the rights of a holder. •

• *Exhibit* 18–8 "For Deposit" and "For Collection" Indorsements

For deposit only
Stephanie Mallak

or

For Collection only
Stephanie Mallak

Trust Indorsement An indorsement for the benefit of the indorser or a third person; also known as an agency indorsement. The indorsement results in legal title vesting in the original indorsee.

Trust (Agency) Indorsements. An indorsement to a person who is to hold or use the funds for the benefit of the indorser or a third party is called a **trust indorsement** (also known as an *agency indorsement*) [UCC 3–206(d), (e)]. **EXAMPLE 18.17** Robert Emerson asks his accountant, Ada Johnson, to pay some bills for his invalid wife, Sarah, while he is out of the country. He indorses a check as follows: "Pay to Ada Johnson as Agent for Sarah Emerson." This agency indorsement obligates Johnson to use the funds only for the benefit of Sarah Emerson. • Exhibit 18–9 shows sample trust (agency) indorsements.

• *Exhibit* 18-9 Trust (Agency) Indorsements

Pay to Ada Johnson in trust for Sarah Emerson *Robert Emerson*	**or** Pay to Ada Johnson as Agent for Sarah Emerson *Robert Emerson*

Ethical Issue ⚖

Why should fiduciary restrictions on an instrument apply only to the original indorsee? Article 3 of the UCC gives the force of law to the ethical duties of an indorsee on a trust instrument to use the funds in accordance with the wishes of the indorser. Yet what if the original indorsee disregards the fiduciary restrictions on the trust instrument and then transfers it to another person? In this situation, according to Article 3, the subsequent purchaser has no obligation to verify that the original indorsee fulfilled the fiduciary requirements. Although this may seem unfair, consider the alternative. If all subsequent holders were obligated to verify that the terms of the trust indorsement were fulfilled, the ease with which instruments could be transferred would be impaired—and so would their function as substitutes for cash. By holding only the original indorsee to the fiduciary restrictions on an instrument with a trust indorsement, the UCC furthers one of its basic goals—to encourage the free flow of commerce by making the laws practical and reasonable. Article 3's provisions relating to trust indorsements are just one example of the many ways in which the UCC balances this goal against other ethical principles.

MISSPELLED NAMES An indorsement should be identical to the name that appears on the instrument. A payee or indorsee whose name is misspelled can indorse with the misspelled name, the correct name, or both [UCC 3–204(d)]. For example, if Sheryl Kruger receives a check payable to the order of Sherrill Krooger, she can indorse the check either "Sheryl Kruger" or "Sherrill Krooger," or both. The usual practice is to indorse with the name as it appears on the instrument, followed by the correct name. (See the *Business Application* feature at the end of the chapter for suggestions to help businesspersons avoid problems with indorsements.)

ALTERNATIVE OR JOINT PAYEES An instrument payable to two or more persons *in the alternative* (for example, "Pay to the order of Tuan or Johnson") requires the indorsement of only one of the payees. In contrast, if an instrument is made payable to two or more persons *jointly* (for example, "Pay to the order of Sharrie and Bob Covington"), all of the payees' indorsements are necessary for negotiation.

If an instrument payable to two or more persons does not clearly indicate whether it is payable in the alternative or jointly (for example, "Pay to the order of John and/or Sara Fitzgerald"), then the instrument is payable to the persons alternatively [UCC 3–110(d)]. The same principles apply to special indorsements that indicate more than one identified person to whom the indorser intends to make the instrument payable [UCC 3–205(a)].

CASE EXAMPLE 18.18 Hyatt Corporation hired Skyscraper Building Maintenance, LLC, to perform maintenance services at some of its Florida hotels. Under an agreement with Skyscraper, J & D Financial Corporation asked Hyatt to make checks for the services payable to Skyscraper and J & D. Hyatt issued many checks to the two payees, but two of the checks that a bank negotiated were indorsed only by Skyscraper and were made payable to "J & D Financial Corp. Skyscraper Building Maint." Parties listed in this manner—without including an "and" or "or" between them—are referred to as *stacked payees.* J & D and Hyatt filed a lawsuit and claimed that the checks were payable *jointly,* requiring indorsement by both payees. The bank argued that the checks were payable to J & D and Skyscraper *alternatively.* A state court found that the bank was not liable because a check payable to stacked payees is ambiguous (unclear) and thus payable alternatively under UCC 3–110(d). Consequently, the bank could negotiate the check when it was indorsed by only one of the two payees.[4] •

---

4. *Hyatt Corp. v. Palm Beach National Bank,* 840 So.2d 300 (Fla.App. 2003).

Holder in Due Course (HDC)

Holder in Due Course (HDC) A holder who acquires a negotiable instrument for value; in good faith; and without notice that the instrument is overdue, that it has been dishonored, that any person has a defense against it or a claim to it, or that the instrument contains unauthorized signatures, has been altered, or is so irregular or incomplete as to call into question its authenticity.

Often, whether a holder is entitled to obtain payment will depend on whether the holder is a *holder in due course*. An ordinary holder obtains only those rights that the transferor had in the instrument, as mentioned previously. In this respect, a holder has the same status as an assignee (see Chapter 13). Like an assignee, a holder normally is subject to the same defenses that could be asserted against the transferor.

In contrast, a **holder in due course** is a holder who, by meeting certain acquisition requirements (to be discussed shortly), takes an instrument *free* of most of the defenses and claims that could be asserted against the transferor. **EXAMPLE 18.19** Marcia Cambry signs a $1,000 note payable to Alex Jerrod in payment for some ancient Roman coins. Jerrod negotiates the note to Alicia Larson, who promises to pay Jerrod for it in thirty days. During the next month, Larson learns that Jerrod has breached his contract with Cambry by delivering coins that were not from the Roman era, as promised, and that for this reason Cambry will not honor the $1,000 note. Whether Larson can hold Cambry liable on the note depends on whether Larson has met the requirements for HDC status. If Larson has met these requirements and thus has HDC status, Larson is entitled to payment on the note. If Larson has not met these requirements, she has the status of an ordinary holder, and Cambry's defense of breach of contract against payment to Jerrod will also be effective against Larson. •

Requirements for HDC Status

The basic requirements for attaining HDC status are set forth in UCC 3–302. A holder of a negotiable instrument is an HDC if she or he takes the instrument (1) for value; (2) in good faith; and (3) without notice that it is defective (such as when the instrument is overdue, dishonored, irregular, or incomplete). We now examine each of these requirements.

TAKING FOR VALUE An HDC must have given *value* for the instrument [UCC 3–302(a)(2)(i)]. A person who receives an instrument as a gift or inherits it has not met the requirement of value. In these situations, the person becomes an ordinary holder and does not possess the rights of an HDC.

Under UCC 3–303(a), a holder takes an instrument for value if the holder has done any of the following:

1. Performed the promise for which the instrument was issued or transferred.
2. Acquired a security interest or other lien in the instrument, excluding a lien obtained by a judicial proceeding (see Chapters 20 and 21).
3. Taken the instrument in payment of, or as security for, a preexisting claim. **EXAMPLE 18.20** Zon owes Dwyer $2,000 on a past-due account. If Zon negotiates a $2,000 note signed by Gordon to Dwyer and Dwyer accepts it to discharge the overdue account balance, Dwyer has given value for the instrument. •
4. Given a negotiable instrument as payment for the instrument. **EXAMPLE 18.21** Justin issued a $500 negotiable promissory note to Paulene. The note is due six months from the date issued. Paulene needs cash and does not want to wait for the maturity date to collect. She negotiates the note to her friend Kristen, who pays her $200 in cash and writes her a check—a negotiable instrument—for the balance of $300. Kristen has given full value for the note by paying $200 in cash and issuing Paulene the check for $300. •
5. Given an irrevocable commitment (such as a letter of credit) as payment for the instrument.

If a person promises to perform or give value in the future, that person is not an HDC. A holder takes an instrument for value *only to the extent that the promise has been performed* [UCC 3–303(a)(1)]. Therefore, in the Larson-Cambry scenario, which was presented ear-

• Exhibit 18–10 Taking for Value

By exchanging defective goods for the note, Jerrod breached his contract with Cambry. Cambry could assert this defense if Jerrod presented the note to her for payment. Jerrod exchanged the note for Larson's promise to pay in thirty days, however. Because Larson did not take the note for value, she is not a holder in due course. Thus, Cambry can assert against Larson the defense of Jerrod's breach when Larson submits the note to Cambry for payment. In contrast, if Larson had taken the note for value, Cambry could not assert that defense and would be liable to pay the note.

lier as Example 18.19 on the facing page, Larson is not an HDC because she did not take the instrument (Cambry's note) for value—she has not yet paid Jerrod for the note. Thus, Cambry's defense of breach of contract is valid against Larson as well as Jerrod. Exhibit 18–10 illustrates these concepts.

TAKING IN GOOD FAITH To qualify as an HDC, a holder must take the instrument in *good faith* [UCC 3–302(a)(2)(ii)]. This means that the holder must have acted honestly in the process of acquiring the instrument. UCC 3–103(a)(4) defines *good faith* as "honesty in fact and the observance of reasonable commercial standards of fair dealing."

The good faith requirement applies only to the *holder*. It is immaterial whether the transferor acted in good faith. Thus, even a person who takes a negotiable instrument from a thief may become an HDC if the person acquired the instrument in good faith and had no reason to be suspicious of the transaction.

Because of the good faith requirement, one must ask whether the purchaser, when acquiring the instrument, honestly believed that the instrument was not defective. Courts examine the facts of each case to decide whether good faith existed. In the following case, the court had to deal with the meaning of accepting a check in good faith.

> *"Carpe per diem—seize the check."*
>
> Robin Williams, 1952–present
> (Comedian and actor)

Case 18.2 **Georg v. Metro Fixtures Contractors, Inc.**

Supreme Court of Colorado, 178 P.3d 1209 (2008).

Cassandra Demery.

FACTS Clinton Georg employed Cassandra Demery as a bookkeeper at his business, Freestyle, until he discovered that she had embezzled more than $200,000 and had failed to pay $240,000 in state and federal taxes owed by Freestyle. Georg fired Demery and said that if she did not repay the embezzled funds, he would notify the authorities. Demery went to work as a bookkeeper for Metro Fixtures, a company owned by her parents. She wrote a check to Freestyle for $189,000 out of Metro's account and deposited it into Freestyle's checking account. She told Georg that the check was a loan from her family to enable her to repay him. Georg used the funds to pay his back taxes. Two years later, Metro discovered Demery's theft and sued Georg and Freestyle for *conversion* (see Chapter 4), as Demery had no authority to take the funds. The trial court held that Freestyle was a holder in due course (HDC) and granted summary judgment. Metro appealed. The appeals court reversed, holding that because Demery deposited the check directly into Freestyle's account, Freestyle could not have been an HDC as it never had actual possession of the check. Georg and Freestyle appealed.

Case 18.2–Continues next page ➡

Case 18.2—Continued

ISSUE   Did Freestyle take the check that Demery wrote from Metro's account in good faith and therefore become an HDC?

DECISION   Yes. The Colorado Supreme Court reversed the ruling of the appellate court and found that the payee, Freestyle, was an HDC based on its constructive possession of the check.

REASON   The court reasoned that Demery was the wrongdoer in this case and that either Metro or Freestyle would have to absorb the loss. Even though Metro did not authorize Demery to issue the check for $189,000, she had the authority to issue checks for Metro. Georg had no reason to

know that Demery had lied when she said her parents, who owned the company, had loaned her the funds. Because Demery deposited the check into Freestyle's account, Freestyle clearly had constructive possession of it, and this was sufficient under the circumstances. Therefore, Freestyle took the check in good faith. The UCC intends to protect the party least able to protect itself. Metro gave Demery authority to write checks on its account, so it should bear the loss.

WHAT IF THE FACTS WERE DIFFERENT?   *Suppose that Demery had gone to work for a company not owned or managed by a family member and had stolen funds from it to pay Georg. Would Georg then be the more innocent party? Why or why not?*

TAKING WITHOUT NOTICE   The final requirement for HDC status involves *notice* [UCC 3–302]. A person will not qualify for HDC protection if he or she is *on notice* (knows or has reason to know) that the instrument being acquired is defective in any one of the following ways [UCC 3–302(a)]:

1. It is overdue.
2. It has been dishonored.
3. It is part of a series of which at least one instrument has an uncured (uncorrected) default.
4. It contains an unauthorized signature or has been altered.
5. There is a defense against the instrument or a claim to the instrument.
6. The instrument is so irregular or incomplete as to call into question its authenticity.

A holder will be deemed to have notice if she or he (1) has actual knowledge of the defect; (2) has received written notice (such as a letter listing the serial numbers of stolen bearer instruments); or (3) has reason to know that a defect exists, given all the facts and circumstances known at the time in question [UCC 1–201(25)]. The holder must also have received the notice "at a time and in a manner that gives a reasonable opportunity to act on it" [UCC 3–302(f)]. A purchaser's knowledge of certain facts, such as insolvency proceedings against the instrument's maker or drawer, does not constitute notice that the instrument is defective [UCC 3–302(b)].

What steps should a bank take to determine that there are no defenses against the payment of a check? In the following case, a bank phoned the issuer of a cashier's check to confirm that it was "good" and the court had to determine whether this was sufficient.

Case 18.3   **South Central Bank of Daviess County v. Lynnville National Bank**

Indiana Court of Appeals, 901 N.E.2d 576 (2009).

COMPANY PROFILE   *South Central Bank of Kentucky (www. southcentralbank.com) can trace its beginning to 1889, when Deposit Bank of Monroe County was chartered. In 1972, James Bale bought Deposit Bank with the goal of more fully providing banking services to rural Kentucky. Over the next thirty-five years, South Central grew from a single branch with $10 million in assets to a bank holding company composed of five individually chartered banks with more than twenty-six offices across the*

state and assets of more than $800 million. The organization's motto— "Hometown banking . . . there is a difference"—epitomizes the banks' focus on the needs of the people in the communities they serve.

FACTS   Lynnville National Bank in Lynnville, Indiana, issued a cashier's check for $31,917.55 payable to Landmark Housing Center, Inc. The check represented a loan to Bryan and Lisa Fisher to buy a manufactured home.

Case 18.3—Continued

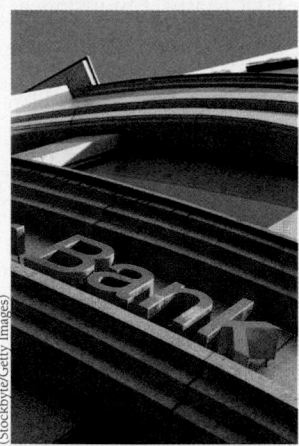

(Stockbyte/Getty Images)

Can a bank properly pay a cashier's check on its issuer's confirmation of the check's date, amount, and payee?

The same day, Landmark deposited the check into its account with South Central Bank of Daviess County in Owensboro, Kentucky. South Central phoned Lynnville and, on confirmation of the date, amount, and payee of the check, paid its entire amount. Two days later, Lynnville learned that Landmark was unable to fulfill its contract with the Fishers. Lynnville then told South Central that payment on the cashier's check would be refused. South Central filed a suit in an Indiana state court against Lynnville, seeking to recover the amount of the check, plus interest and fees. The court entered a summary judgment in the defendant's favor. South Central appealed.

ISSUE   Can a bank properly pay a cashier's check on its issuer's confirmation of the check's date, amount, and payee?

DECISION   Yes. The state intermediate appellate court reversed the lower court's judgment and remanded the case for entry of a judgment in

South Central's favor for the amount of the check, plus expenses and interest, and for a determination of consequential damages.

REASON   South Central took the check for value and in good faith, and then asked Lynnville for confirmation. This was not required and "certainly means that South Central was without notice of any problems with the instrument. Indeed, at that time, Lynnville was without notice of any problems." South Central accepted the check and became a holder in due course (HDC) under Indiana Code Section 26-1-3.1-302 (Indiana's version of UCC 3–302). None of the defenses available to an issuer against an HDC under Indiana Code Section 26-1-3.1-305 (UCC 3–305) were available to Lynnville. An issuer of a cashier's check may refuse payment in specific circumstances, set out in Indiana Code Section 26-1-3.1-411 (UCC 3–411), none of which applied in this case. Lynnville argued that it refused to pay as an accommodation to the Fishers on the ground of fraud. But Lynnville can assert only its own defenses, and it had no claim against Landmark for fraud because the bank was not a victim of the fraud.

FOR CRITICAL ANALYSIS—Economic Consideration
What effect would a decision in favor of Lynnville have had on the status of a cashier's check as a substitute for cash?

REMEMBER Demand instruments are payable immediately. Time instruments are payable at a future date.

Overdue Instruments.   What constitutes notice that an instrument is overdue depends on whether it is a demand instrument (payable on demand) or a time instrument (payable at a definite time). A purchaser has notice that a *demand instrument* is overdue if she or he either takes the instrument knowing that demand has been made or takes the instrument an unreasonable length of time after its issue. For a check, a "reasonable time" is ninety days after the date of the check. For all other demand instruments, what will be considered a reasonable time depends on the circumstances [UCC 3–304(a)].

Normally, a *time instrument* is overdue the day after its due date; hence, anyone who takes a time instrument after the due date is on notice that it is overdue [UCC 3–304(b) (2)]. Thus, if a promissory note due on May 15 is purchased on May 16, the purchaser will be an ordinary holder, not an HDC. If an instrument states that it is "Payable in thirty days," counting begins the day after the instrument is dated. Thus, a note dated December 1 that is payable in thirty days is due by midnight on December 31. If the payment date falls on a Sunday or holiday, the instrument is payable on the next business day.

Dishonor To refuse to pay or accept a negotiable instrument, whichever is required, even though the instrument is presented in a timely and proper manner.

Dishonored Instruments.   An instrument is **dishonored** when it is presented in a timely manner for payment or acceptance, whichever is required, and payment or acceptance is refused. The holder is on notice if he or she (1) has actual knowledge of the dishonor or (2) has knowledge of facts that would lead him or her to suspect that an instrument has been dishonored [UCC 3–302(a)(2)]. Conversely, if a person purchasing an instrument does not know and has no reason to know that it has been dishonored, the person is *not* put on notice and therefore can become an HDC.

Notice of Claims or Defenses.   A holder cannot become an HDC if she or he has notice of any claim to the instrument or any defense against it [UCC 3–302(a)(2)]. Any obvious

Shelter Principle   The principle that the holder of a negotiable instrument who cannot qualify as a holder in due course (HDC), but who derives his or her title through an HDC, acquires the rights of an HDC.

"Most men are admirers of justice—when justice happens to be on their side."
Richard Whately, 1787–1863
(English theologian and logician)

irregularity on the face of an instrument that calls into question its validity or terms of ownership, or that creates an ambiguity as to the party to pay, will bar HDC status. For instance, if an instrument is so incomplete on its face that an element of negotiability is lacking (for example, the amount is not filled in), the purchaser cannot become an HDC. A good forgery of a signature or the careful alteration of an instrument, however, can go undetected by reasonable examination. In that situation, the purchaser can qualify as an HDC.

Holder through an HDC

A person who does not qualify as an HDC but who derives his or her title through an HDC can acquire the rights and privileges of an HDC. This rule, which is sometimes called the **shelter principle,** is set out in UCC 3–203(b). The shelter principle extends the benefits of HDC status and is designed to aid the HDC in readily disposing of the instrument. Under this rule, anyone—no matter how far removed from an HDC—who can ultimately trace his or her title back to an HDC may acquire the rights of an HDC. By extending the benefits of HDC status, the shelter principle promotes the marketability and free transferability of negotiable instruments.

There are some limitations on the shelter principle, though. Certain persons who formerly held instruments cannot improve their positions by later reacquiring the instruments from HDCs [UCC 3–203(b)]. If a holder participated in fraud or illegality affecting the instrument, or had notice of a claim or defense against an instrument, that holder is not allowed to improve her or his status by repurchasing the instrument from a later HDC.

▶ Signature and Warranty Liability

Liability on negotiable instruments can arise either from a person's signature or from the warranties that are implied when the person presents the instrument for negotiation. Signature liability requires the transferor's signature whereas no signature is required to impose warranty liability. We discuss signature liability (both primary and secondary) and warranty liability in the subsections that follow.

Signature Liability

The general rule is that every party, except a qualified indorser,[5] who signs a negotiable instrument is either primarily or secondarily liable for payment of that instrument when it comes due. Signature liability is contractual liability—no person will be held contractually liable for an instrument that he or she has not signed.

PRIMARY LIABILITY   A person who is primarily liable on a negotiable instrument is absolutely required to pay the instrument—unless, of course, he or she has a valid defense to payment [UCC 3–305]. Only *makers* and *acceptors* of instruments are primarily liable.

The maker of a promissory note unconditionally promises to pay the note. It is the maker's promise to pay that makes the note a negotiable instrument. If the instrument was incomplete when the maker signed it, the maker is obligated to pay it according to its stated terms or according to terms that were agreed on and later filled in to complete the instrument [UCC 3–115, 3–407(a), 3–412]. **EXAMPLE 18.22** Tristan executes a preprinted promissory note to Sharon, without filling in the blank for a due date. If Sharon does not complete the form by adding the date, the note will be payable on demand. If Sharon subsequently fills in a due date that Tristan authorized, the note is payable on the stated due date. In either situation, Tristan (the maker) is obligated to pay the note. ●

---

5. A qualified indorser—one who indorses "without recourse"—undertakes no contractual obligation to pay. A qualified indorser merely assumes warranty liability, which will be discussed later in this chapter.

As mentioned earlier, an *acceptor* is a drawee that promises to pay an instrument, such as a *trade acceptance* or a *certified check* (to be discussed in Chapter 19), when it is presented for payment. Once a drawee indicates acceptance by signing the draft, the drawee becomes an acceptor and is obligated to pay the draft when it is presented for payment [UCC 3–409(a)]. Failure to pay an accepted draft when presented leads to primary signature liability.

SECONDARY LIABILITY   *Drawers* and *indorsers* are secondarily liable. On a negotiable instrument, secondary liability is similar to the liability of a guarantor in a simple contract in the sense that it is *contingent liability*. In other words, a drawer or an indorser will be liable only if the party that is responsible for paying the instrument refuses to do so (dishonors the instrument). The drawer's secondary liability on drafts and checks does not arise until the drawee fails to pay or to accept the instrument, whichever is required [UCC 3–412, 3–415].

Dishonor of an instrument thus triggers the liability of parties who are secondarily liable on the instrument—that is, the drawer and *unqualified* indorsers. **EXAMPLE 18.23** Nina Lee writes a check on her account at Universal Bank payable to the order of Stephen Miller. Universal Bank refuses to pay the check when Miller presents it for payment, thus dishonoring the check. In this situation, Lee will be liable to Miller on the basis of her secondary liability. ● Drawers are secondarily liable on drafts unless they disclaim their liability by drawing the instruments "without recourse" (if the draft is a check, however, a drawer cannot disclaim liability) [UCC 3–414(e)].

Parties are secondarily liable on a negotiable instrument only if the following events occur:[6]

1. The instrument is properly and timely presented.
2. The instrument is dishonored.
3. Timely notice of dishonor is given to the secondarily liable party.

Proper Presentment.   As previously explained, *presentment* occurs when a person presents an instrument either to the party liable on the instrument for payment or to a drawee for acceptance. The UCC requires that a holder present the instrument to the appropriate party, in a timely fashion, and give reasonable identification if requested [UCC 3–414(f), 3–415(e), 3–501]. The party to whom the instrument must be presented depends on the type of instrument involved. A note or CD must be presented to the maker for payment. A draft is presented to the drawee for acceptance, payment, or both. A check is presented to the drawee for payment [UCC 3–501(a), 3–502(b)].

Presentment can be made by any commercially reasonable means, including oral, written, or electronic communication [UCC 3–501(b)]. It is ordinarily effective when the demand for payment or acceptance is received (unless presentment takes place after an established cutoff hour, in which case it may be treated as occurring the next business day).

Timely Presentment.   Timeliness is important for proper presentment [UCC 3–414(f), 3–415(e), 3–501(b)(4)]. Failure to present an instrument on time is the most common reason for improper presentment and leads to unqualified indorsers being discharged from secondary liability. The holder of a domestic check must present that check for payment or collection within thirty days of its *date* to hold the drawer secondarily liable, and within thirty days after its indorsement to hold the indorser secondarily liable. The time for proper presentment for different types of instruments is shown in Exhibit 18–11 on the next page.

---

6. These requirements are necessary for a secondarily liable party to have signature liability on a negotiable instrument, but they are not necessary for a secondarily liable party to have warranty liability (to be discussed later in the chapter).

• *Exhibit* 18–11 Time for Proper Presentment

TYPE OF INSTRUMENT	FOR ACCEPTANCE	FOR PAYMENT
Time	On or before due date.	On due date.
Demand	Within a reasonable time (after date of issue or after secondary party becomes liable on the instrument).	Within a reasonable time.
Check	Not applicable.	Within thirty days of its date, to hold drawer secondarily liable. Within thirty days of indorsement, to hold indorser secondarily liable.

Dishonor.   As mentioned previously, an instrument is dishonored when the required acceptance or payment is refused or cannot be obtained within the prescribed time. An instrument is also dishonored when the required presentment is excused (as it would be, for example, if the maker had died) and the instrument is not properly accepted or paid [UCC 3–502(e), 3–504].

In certain situations, a postponement of payment or a refusal to pay an instrument will *not* dishonor the instrument. When presentment is made after an established cutoff hour (not earlier than 2:00 P.M.), for instance, a bank can postpone payment until the following business day without dishonoring the instrument. In addition, when the holder refuses to exhibit the instrument, to give reasonable identification (sometimes even a thumbprint), or to sign a receipt for the payment on the instrument, a bank's refusal to pay does not dishonor the instrument.

Proper Notice.   Once an instrument has been dishonored, proper notice must be given to secondary parties (drawers and indorsers) for them to be held contractually liable. Notice may be given in any reasonable manner, including an oral, written, or electronic communication, as well as notice written or stamped on the instrument itself. The bank must give any necessary notice before its midnight deadline (midnight of the next banking day after receipt). Notice by any party other than a bank must be given within thirty days following the day of dishonor or the day on which the person who is secondarily liable receives notice of dishonor [UCC 3–503].

The movie Catch Me If You Can, *starring Tom Hanks and Leonardo DiCaprio, depicted the exploits of Frank Abagnale, Jr. (below). One of the easiest illegal activities that Abagnale engaged in was forging and cashing checks for large sums. In general, who is liable for forged checks?*

(AP Photo/Tyler Morning Telegraph/D.J. Peters)

UNAUTHORIZED SIGNATURES   Unauthorized signatures arise in two situations—when a person forges another person's name on a negotiable instrument and when an *agent* (see Chapter 23) who lacks authority signs an instrument on behalf of a principal. The general rule is that an unauthorized signature is wholly inoperative and will not bind the person whose name is signed or forged.

EXAMPLE 18.24 Parker finds Dolby's checkbook lying in the street, writes out a check to himself, and forges Dolby's signature. Banks normally have a duty to determine whether a person's signature on a check is forged. If a bank fails to determine that Dolby's signature is not genuine and cashes the check for Parker, the bank will generally be liable to Dolby for the amount. • (The liability of banks for paying checks with forged signatures will be discussed further in Chapter 19.) Similarly, if an agent lacks the authority to sign the principal's name or has exceeded the authority given by the principal, the signature does not bind the principal but will bind the "unauthorized signer" [UCC 3–403(a)].

There are two exceptions to the general rule that an unauthorized signature will not bind the person whose name is signed:

1. When the person whose name is signed ratifies (affirms) the signature, he or she will be bound [UCC 3–403(a)].
2. When the negligence of the person whose name was forged substantially contributed to the forgery, a court may not allow the person to deny the effectiveness of an unauthorized signature [UCC 3–115, 3–406, 4–401(d)(2)].

SPECIAL RULES FOR UNAUTHORIZED INDORSEMENTS   Generally, when an indorsement is forged or unauthorized, the burden of loss falls on the first party to take the instrument with the forged or unauthorized indorsement. The reason for this general rule is that the first party to take an instrument is in the best position to prevent the loss. **EXAMPLE 18.25** Jen Nilson steals a check that is payable to Inga Leed and drawn on Universal Bank. Nilson indorses the check "Inga Leed" and presents the check to Universal Bank for payment. The bank, without asking Nilson for identification, pays the check, and Nilson disappears. In this situation, Leed will not be liable on the check because her indorsement was forged. The bank will bear the loss, which it might have avoided if it had requested identification from Nilson. ●

There are two important exceptions to this general rule, which cause the loss to fall on the maker or drawer. These exceptions arise when an indorsement is made by an imposter or by a fictitious payee.

Imposter   One who, by use of the mails, Internet, telephone, or personal appearance, induces a maker or drawer to issue an instrument in the name of an impersonated payee. Indorsements by imposters are treated as authorized indorsements under Article 3 of the UCC.

Imposter Rule.   An **imposter** is one who, by her or his personal appearance or use of the mails, Internet, telephone, or other communication, induces a maker or drawer to issue an instrument in the name of an impersonated payee. If the maker or drawer believes the imposter to be the named payee at the time of issue, the indorsement by the imposter is not treated as unauthorized when the instrument is transferred to an innocent party. This is because the maker or drawer *intended* the imposter to receive the instrument. In this situation, under the UCC's *imposter rule,* the imposter's indorsement will be effective—that is, not considered a forgery—insofar as the drawer or maker is concerned [UCC 3–404(a)]. **EXAMPLE 18.26** Carol impersonates Donna and induces Edward to write a check payable to the order of Donna. Carol, continuing to impersonate Donna, negotiates the check to First National Bank as payment on her loan there. As the drawer of the check, Edward is liable for its amount to First National. ●

Fictitious Payee   A payee on a negotiable instrument whom the maker or drawer does not intend to have an interest in the instrument. Indorsements by fictitious payees are treated as authorized indorsements under Article 3 of the UCC.

Fictitious Payee Rule.   When a person causes an instrument to be issued to a payee who will have *no interest* in the instrument, the payee is referred to as a **fictitious payee.** A fictitious payee can be a person or firm that does not truly exist, or it may be an identifiable party that will not acquire any interest in the instrument. Under the UCC's *fictitious payee rule,* the payee's indorsement is not treated as a forgery, and an innocent holder can hold the maker or drawer liable on the instrument [UCC 3–404(b), 3–405].

Situations involving fictitious payees most often arise when (1) a dishonest employee deceives the employer into signing an instrument payable to a party with no right to receive payment on the instrument or (2) a dishonest employee or agent has the authority to issue an instrument on behalf of the employer. Regardless of whether a dishonest employee actually signs the check or merely supplies his or her employer with names of fictitious creditors (or with true names of creditors having fictitious debts), the result is the same under the UCC.

Warranty Liability

In addition to the signature liability, transferors make certain implied warranties regarding the instruments that they are negotiating. Warranty liability arises even when a transferor does not indorse (sign) the instrument [UCC 3–416, 3–417]. Warranty liability is

"Life is unfair."
Milton Friedman, 1912–2006
(American economist)

particularly important when a holder cannot hold a party liable on her or his signature, such as when a person delivers a bearer instrument. Unlike secondary signature liability, warranty liability is not subject to the conditions of proper presentment, dishonor, or notice of dishonor.

Warranties fall into two categories: those that arise on the *transfer* of a negotiable instrument and those that arise on *presentment*. Both transfer and presentment warranties attempt to shift liability back to a wrongdoer or to the person who dealt face to face with the wrongdoer and thus was in the best position to prevent the wrongdoing.

TRANSFER WARRANTIES   The UCC describes five **transfer warranties** [UCC 3–416].[7] For transfer warranties to arise, an instrument *must be transferred for consideration.* One who transfers an instrument for consideration makes the following warranties to all subsequent transferees and holders who take the instrument in good faith (with some exceptions, as will be noted shortly):

Transfer Warranties Implied warranties, made by any person who transfers an instrument for consideration to subsequent transferees and holders who take the instrument in good faith, that (1) the transferor is entitled to enforce the instrument; (2) all signatures are authentic and authorized; (3) the instrument has not been altered; (4) the instrument is not subject to a defense or claim of any party that can be asserted against the transferor; and (5) the transferor has no knowledge of any insolvency proceedings against the maker, the acceptor, or the drawer of the instrument.

1. The transferor is entitled to enforce the instrument.
2. All signatures are authentic and authorized.
3. The instrument has not been altered.
4. The instrument is not subject to a defense or claim of any party that can be asserted against the transferor.
5. The transferor has no knowledge of any insolvency (bankruptcy) proceedings against the maker, the acceptor, or the drawer of the instrument.

Parties to Whom Warranty Liability Extends.   Transfer of order paper, for consideration, by indorsement and delivery extends warranty liability to any subsequent holder who takes the instrument in good faith. The warranties of a person who transfers *without indorsement* (by the delivery of a bearer instrument), however, will extend the transferor's warranties only to the immediate transferee [UCC 3–416(a)].

Recovery for Breach of Warranty.   A transferee or holder who takes an instrument in good faith can sue on the basis of a breach of warranty as soon as he or she has reason to know of the breach [UCC 3–416(d)]. Notice of a claim for breach of warranty must be given to the warrantor within thirty days after the transferee or holder has reason to know of the breach and the identity of the warrantor, or the warrantor is not liable for any loss caused by a delay [UCC 3–416(c)]. The transferee or holder can recover damages for the breach in an amount equal to the loss suffered (but not more than the amount of the instrument), plus expenses and any loss of interest caused by the breach [UCC 3–416(b)]. These warranties can be disclaimed with respect to any instrument except a check [UCC 3–416(c)].

Presentment Warranties Implied warranties, made by any person who presents an instrument for payment or acceptance, that (1) the person obtaining payment or acceptance is entitled to enforce the instrument or is authorized to obtain payment or acceptance on behalf of a person who is entitled to enforce the instrument, (2) the instrument has not been altered, and (3) the person obtaining payment or acceptance has no knowledge that the signature of the drawer of the instrument is unauthorized.

PRESENTMENT WARRANTIES   Any person who presents an instrument for payment or acceptance makes the following **presentment warranties** to any other person who in good faith pays or accepts the instrument [UCC 3–417(a), 3–417(d)]:

1. The person obtaining payment or acceptance is entitled to enforce the instrument or is authorized to obtain payment or acceptance on behalf of a person who is entitled to

---

7. A 2002 amendment to UCC 3–416(a) adds a sixth warranty: "with respect to a remotely created consumer item, that the person on whose account the item is drawn authorized the issuance of the item in the amount for which the item is drawn." UCC 3–103(16) defines a "remotely created consumer item" as an item, such as a check, drawn on a consumer account, which is not created by the payor bank and does not contain the drawer's handwritten signature. For example, a telemarketer submits an instrument to a bank for payment, claiming that the consumer on whose account the instrument purports to be drawn authorized it over the phone. Under this amendment, a bank that accepts and pays the instrument warrants to the next bank in the collection chain that the consumer authorized the item in that amount.

enforce the instrument. (This is, in effect, a warranty that there are no missing or unauthorized indorsements.)

2. The instrument has not been altered.

3. The person obtaining payment or acceptance has no knowledge that the signature of the issuer of the instrument is unauthorized.[8]

These warranties are referred to as presentment warranties because they protect the person to whom the instrument is presented. They often have the effect of shifting liability back to the party that was in the best position to prevent the wrongdoing. The second and third warranties do not apply to makers, acceptors, and drawers. It is assumed that a drawer or a maker will recognize his or her own signature and that a maker or an acceptor will recognize whether an instrument has been materially altered.

▶ Defenses, Limitations, and Discharge

Persons who would otherwise be liable on negotiable instruments may be able to avoid liability by raising certain defenses. There are two general categories of defenses—*universal defenses* and *personal defenses*, which are discussed below.

Universal Defenses

Universal Defense A defense that is valid against all holders of a negotiable instrument, including holders in due course (HDCs) and holders with the rights of HDCs.

Universal defenses (also called *real defenses*) are valid against *all* holders, including HDCs and holders who take through an HDC. Universal defenses include those described here.

FORGERY   Forgery of a maker's or drawer's signature cannot bind the person whose name is used unless that person ratifies (approves or validates) the signature or is barred from denying it (because the forgery was made possible by the maker's or drawer's negligence, for example) [UCC 3–403(a)]. Thus, when a person forges an instrument, the person whose name is forged normally has no liability to pay any holder or any HDC the value of the forged instrument.

FRAUD IN THE EXECUTION   If a person is deceived into signing a negotiable instrument, believing that she or he is signing something other than a negotiable instrument (such as a receipt), *fraud in the execution,* or fraud in the inception, is committed against the signer [UCC 3–305(a)(1)]. Fraud in the execution is a universal defense.

The defense of fraud in the execution cannot be raised, however, if a reasonable inquiry would have revealed the nature and terms of the instrument. Thus, the signer's age, experience, and intelligence are relevant because they frequently determine whether the signer should have known the nature of the transaction before signing.

RECALL Words outweigh figures on a negotiable instrument if the written amount and the amount given in figures are different.

MATERIAL ALTERATION   An alteration is material if it changes the obligations of the parties in the instrument *in any way.* Examples include any unauthorized addition of words or numbers or other changes to complete an incomplete instrument that affect the obligation of a party to the instrument [UCC 3–407(a)]. Making any change in the amount, the date, or the rate of interest—even if the change is only one penny, one day, or 1 percent—is material. It is not a material alteration, however, to correct the maker's address or to change the figures on a check so that they agree with the written amount. If the alteration is not material, any holder is entitled to enforce the instrument according to its terms.

Material alteration is a *complete defense* against an ordinary holder, but only a partial defense against an HDC. An ordinary holder can recover nothing on an instrument if it has

---

8. As discussed in footnote 7, the 2002 amendments to Article 3 of the UCC provide additional protection for "remotely created" consumer items in the context of presentment also [see Amended UCC 3–417(a)(4)].

been materially altered [UCC 3–407(b)]. In contrast, when the holder is an HDC and an original term, such as the monetary amount payable, has been *altered,* the HDC can enforce the instrument against the maker or drawer according to the *original* terms but not for the altered amount.

If the instrument was originally incomplete and was later completed in an unauthorized manner, however, alteration no longer can be claimed as a defense against an HDC, and the HDC can enforce the instrument as completed [UCC 3–407(b)].

DISCHARGE IN BANKRUPTCY
Discharge in bankruptcy (see Chapter 21) is an absolute defense on any instrument, regardless of the status of the holder, because the purpose of bankruptcy is to settle finally all of the insolvent party's debts [UCC 3–305(a)(1)].

MINORITY
Minority, or infancy, is a universal defense only to the extent that state law recognizes it as a defense to a simple contract (see Chapter 11). Because state laws on minority vary, so do determinations of whether minority is a universal defense against an HDC [UCC 3–305(a)(1)(i)].

ILLEGALITY
Certain types of illegality constitute universal defenses. Other types constitute personal defenses—that is, defenses that are effective against ordinary holders but not against HDCs. If a statute provides that an illegal transaction is void, then the defense is universal—that is, absolute against both an ordinary holder and an HDC. If the law merely makes the instrument voidable, then the illegality is still a personal defense against an ordinary holder but not against an HDC [UCC 3–305(a)(1)(ii)].

MENTAL INCAPACITY
If a person has been declared by a court to be mentally incompetent, then any instrument issued thereafter by that person is void. The instrument is void *ab initio* (from the beginning) and unenforceable by any holder or HDC [UCC 3–305(a)(1)(ii)]. Mental incapacity in these circumstances is thus a universal defense. If a court has not declared the person to be mentally incompetent, however, then mental incapacity operates as a defense against an ordinary holder but not against an HDC.

EXTREME DURESS
When a person signs and issues a negotiable instrument under such extreme duress as an immediate threat of force or violence (for example, at gunpoint), the instrument is void and unenforceable by any holder or HDC [UCC 3–305(a)(1)(ii)]. (Ordinary duress is a defense against ordinary holders but not against HDCs.)

Personal Defenses

Personal defenses (sometimes called *limited defenses*), such as those described here, can be used to avoid payment to an ordinary holder of a negotiable instrument, but not to an HDC or a holder with the rights of an HDC.

BREACH OF CONTRACT OR BREACH OF WARRANTY
When there is a breach of the underlying contract for which the negotiable instrument was issued, the maker of a note can refuse to pay it, or the drawer of a check can order his or her bank to stop payment on the check. Breach of warranty can also be claimed as a defense to liability on the instrument.

LACK OR FAILURE OF CONSIDERATION
The absence of consideration (value) may be a successful personal defense in some instances [UCC 3–303(b), 3–305(a)(2)]. **EXAMPLE 18.27** Tara gives Clem, as a gift, a note that states, "I promise to pay you $100,000." Clem accepts the note. Because there is no consideration for Tara's promise, a court will not enforce the promise. ●

BE AWARE Minority, illegality, mental incapacity, and duress can be universal defenses or personal defenses, depending in some circumstances on state law rather than the UCC.

Personal Defense A defense that can be used to avoid payment to an ordinary holder of a negotiable instrument but not a holder in due course (HDC) or a holder with the rights of an HDC.

FRAUD IN THE INDUCEMENT (ORDINARY FRAUD) A person who issues a negotiable instrument based on false statements by the other party will be able to avoid payment on that instrument, unless the holder is an HDC.

ILLEGALITY As mentioned, if a statute provides that an illegal transaction is voidable, the defense is personal.

MENTAL INCAPACITY As mentioned, if a maker or drawer issues a negotiable instrument while mentally incompetent but has not been declared incompetent by a court, the instrument is voidable [UCC 3–305(a)(1)(ii)]. In this situation, mental incapacity can serve only as a personal defense.

Federal Limitations on the Rights of HDCs

Under the HDC doctrine, a consumer who purchased a defective product (such as a defective automobile) would continue to be liable to HDCs even if the consumer returned the defective product to the retailer. To protect consumers, in 1976 the Federal Trade Commission (FTC) issued a rule that effectively abolished the HDC doctrine in consumer transactions. How does this rule curb the rights of HDCs? See this chapter's *Landmark in the Law* feature.

Discharge from Liability

Discharge from liability on an instrument can occur in several ways. The liability of all parties to an instrument is discharged when the party primarily liable on it pays to the holder

---

 Landmark in the Law   **Federal Trade Commission Rule 433**

In 1976, the Federal Trade Commission (FTC) issued Rule 433,[a] which severely limited the rights of HDCs that purchase instruments arising out of *consumer credit* transactions. The rule, entitled "Preservation of Consumers' Claims and Defenses," applies to any seller or lessor of goods or services who takes or receives a consumer credit contract. The rule also applies to a seller or lessor who accepts as full or partial payment for a sale or lease the proceeds of any purchase-money loan[b] made in connection with any consumer credit contract. Under the rule, these parties must include the following provision in the consumer credit contract:

NOTICE
ANY HOLDER OF THIS CONSUMER CREDIT CONTRACT IS SUBJECT TO ALL CLAIMS AND DEFENSES WHICH THE DEBTOR COULD ASSERT AGAINST THE SELLER OF GOODS OR SERVICES OBTAINED PURSUANT HERETO OR WITH THE PROCEEDS HEREOF. RECOVERY HEREUNDER BY THE DEBTOR SHALL NOT EXCEED AMOUNTS PAID BY THE DEBTOR HEREUNDER.

Thus, a consumer who is a party to a consumer credit transaction can bring any defense she or he has against the seller of a product against a subsequent holder as well. In essence, the FTC rule places an HDC of the negotiable instrument in the position of a contract assignee. The rule makes the buyer's duty to pay conditional on the seller's full performance of the contract. Finally, the rule clearly reduces the degree of transferability of negotiable instruments resulting from consumer credit contracts.

What if the seller does not include the notice in a promissory note and then sells the note to a third party, such as a bank? In this situation, the seller has violated the rule, but the bank has not. Because the FTC rule does not prohibit third parties from purchasing notes or credit contracts that do *not* contain the required provision, the third party does not become subject to the buyer's defenses against the seller. Thus, a few consumers remain unprotected by the FTC rule.

• **Application to Today's World** *The FTC rule has been invoked in many cases involving automobiles that turned out to be "lemons," even when the consumer credit contract did not contain the FTC notice. In these and other actions to collect on notes issued to finance purchases, when the notice was not included in the accompanying documents, the courts have generally implied its existence as a contract term.*

• **Relevant Web Sites** To locate information on the Web concerning FTC Rule 433, go to this text's Web site at www.cengage. com/blaw/blt, select "Chapter 18," and click on "URLs for Landmarks."

a. 16 C.F.R. Section 433.2. The rule was enacted pursuant to the FTC's authority under the Federal Trade Commission Act, 15 U.S.C. Sections 41–58.
b. In a *purchase-money loan,* a seller or lessor advances funds to a buyer or lessee, through a credit contract, for the purchase or lease of goods.

the full amount due [UCC 3–602, 3–603]. Payment by any other party discharges only the liability of that party and subsequent parties.

Intentional cancellation of an instrument discharges the liability of all parties [UCC 3–604]. Intentionally writing "Paid" across the face of an instrument cancels it, as does intentionally tearing it up. If a holder intentionally crosses out a party's signature, that party's liability and the liability of subsequent indorsers who have already indorsed the instrument are discharged. Materially altering an instrument may discharge the liability of any party affected by the alteration, as previously discussed [UCC 3–407(b)]. (An HDC may be able to enforce a materially altered instrument against its maker or drawer according to the instrument's original terms, however.)

Discharge of liability can also occur when a holder impairs another party's right of recourse (right to seek reimbursement) on the instrument [UCC 3–605]. This occurs when, for example, the holder releases, or agrees not to sue, a party against whom the indorser has a right of recourse.

 Reviewing . . . Negotiable Instruments: Transferability and Liability

Robert Durbin, a student, borrowed funds from a bank for his education and signed a promissory note for their repayment. The bank lent the funds under a federal program designed to assist students at postsecondary institutions. Under this program, repayment ordinarily begins nine to twelve months after the student borrower fails to carry at least one-half of the normal full-time course load at his or her school. The federal government guarantees that the note will be fully paid. If the student defaults on the payments, the lender presents the current balance—principal, interest, and costs—to the government. When the government pays the balance, it becomes the lender, and the borrower owes the government directly. After Durbin defaulted on his note, the government paid the lender the balance due and took possession of the note. Durbin then refused to pay the government, claiming that the government was not the holder of the note. The government filed a suit in a federal district court against Durbin to collect the amount due. Using the information presented in the chapter, answer the following questions.

1. Using the categories discussed in the chapter, what type of negotiable instrument was the note that Durbin signed (an order to pay or a promise to pay)? Explain.
2. Suppose that the note did not state a specific interest rate but instead referred to a statute that established the maximum interest rate for government-guaranteed student loans. Would the note fail to meet the requirements for negotiability in that situation? Why or why not?
3. How does a party who is not named by a negotiable instrument (in this situation, the government) obtain a right to enforce the instrument?
4. Suppose that in court, Durbin argues that because the school closed down before he could finish his education, there was a failure of consideration: he did not get something of value in exchange for his promise to pay. Assuming that the government is a holder of the promissory note, would this argument likely be successful against it? Why or why not?

Business Application
Pitfalls When Writing and Indorsing Checks*

As a businessperson (and as a consumer), you will certainly be writing and receiving checks. Both activities can involve pitfalls.

Checks Drawn in Blank

The danger in signing a blank check is clear. Anyone can write in an unauthorized amount and cash the check. Although you may be able to

assert lack of authorization against the person who filled in the check, subsequent holders of the properly indorsed check may be able to enforce the check as completed. While you are haggling with the person who inserted the unauthorized amount and who may not be able to repay it, you will also have to honor the check for the unauthorized amount to a subsequent holder in due course.

* This *Business Application* is not meant to substitute for the services of an attorney who is licensed to practice law in your state.

Checks Payable to "Cash"

It is equally dangerous to write out and sign a check payable to "cash" until you are actually at the bank. Remember that checks payable to "cash" are bearer instruments. This means that if you lose or misplace the check, anybody who finds it can present it (with proper identification) to the bank for payment.

Checks Indorsed in Blank

A negotiable instrument with a blank indorsement also has dangers; as a bearer instrument, it may be as easily transferred as cash. When you make a bank deposit, therefore, you should sign (indorse) the back of the check in blank only in the presence of a teller. If you choose to sign it ahead of time, always insert the words "For deposit only" before you sign your name. As a precaution, you should consider obtaining an indorsement stamp from your bank. Then, when you receive a check payable to your business, you can indorse it immediately. The stamped indorsement will indicate that the check is for deposit only to your business account specified by the number.

CHECKLIST FOR THE USE OF NEGOTIABLE INSTRUMENTS

1. **A good rule of thumb is never to sign a blank check.**
2. **Another good rule of thumb is never to write and sign a check payable to "cash" until you are actually at the bank. If you must write the check ahead of time, consider making the check payable to the bank rather than to "cash."**
3. **Be wary of indorsing a check in blank unless a bank teller is simultaneously giving you a receipt for your deposit.**
4. **Consider obtaining an indorsement stamp from your bank so that when you receive checks, you can immediately indorse them "for deposit only" to your account.**

 ## Key Terms

acceleration clause 445
acceptance 440
acceptor 444
bearer 447
bearer instrument 447
blank indorsement 449
certificate of deposit (CD) 441
check 440
dishonor 455
draft 439
drawee 439
drawer 439

extension clause 446
fictitious payee 459
holder 445
holder in due course (HDC) 452
imposter 459
indorsement 449
maker 441
negotiable instrument 438
negotiation 448
order instrument 446
payee 439
personal defense 462

presentment 445
presentment warranties 460
promissory note 441
qualified indorsement 450
restrictive indorsement 450
shelter principle 456
special indorsement 449
transfer warranties 460
trust indorsement 450
universal defense 461

 ## Chapter Summary: Negotiable Instruments: Transferability and Liability

Types of Instruments **(See pages 439–442.)**	The UCC specifies four types of negotiable instruments: drafts, checks, promissory notes, and certificates of deposit (CDs). These instruments fall into two basic classifications: 1. *Demand instruments versus time instruments*–A demand instrument is payable on demand (when the holder presents it to the maker or drawer). A time instrument is payable at a future date. 2. *Orders to pay versus promises to pay*–Checks and drafts are *orders* to pay. Promissory notes and CDs are *promises* to pay.
Requirements **for Negotiability** **(See pages 442–447.)**	To be negotiable, an instrument must meet the requirements stated below. 1. *Be in writing*–A writing can be on anything that is readily transferable and has a degree of permanence [UCC 3–103(a)(6), (9)].

Continued

Chapter Summary: Negotiable Instruments: Transferability and Liability—Continued

Requirements for Negotiability—Continued	2. *Be signed by the maker or drawer*—The signature can be anyplace on the face of the instrument, can be in any form (including a rubber stamp), and can be made in a representative capacity [UCC 3–103(a)(3), 3–401(b)].
	3. *Be an unconditional promise or order to pay*—
	  a. A promise must be more than a mere acknowledgment of a debt [UCC 3–103(a)(6), (9)].
	  b. The words "I/We promise" or "Pay" meet this criterion.
	  c. Payment cannot be expressly conditioned on the occurrence of an event and cannot be made subject to or governed by another contract [UCC 3–106].
	4. *State a fixed amount of money*—
	  a. An amount is considered a fixed sum if it is ascertainable from the face of the instrument or (for the interest rate) readily determinable by a formula described in the instrument [UCC 3–104(a), 3–112(b)].
	  b. Any medium of exchange recognized as the currency of a government is money [UCC 1–201(24)].
	5. *Be payable on demand or at a definite time*—
	  a. Any instrument that is payable on sight, presentation, or issue, or that does not state any time for payment, is a demand instrument [UCC 3–104(a)(2)].
	  b. An instrument is still payable at a definite time, even if it is payable on or before a stated date or within a fixed period after sight or if the drawer or maker has an option to extend the time for a definite period [UCC 3–108(a), (b), (c)].
	  c. Acceleration clauses do not affect the negotiability of the instrument.
	6. *Be payable to order or bearer*—
	  a. An order instrument must identify the payee with certainty.
	  b. An instrument that indicates it is not payable to an identified person is payable to bearer [UCC 3–109(a)(3)].

Factors That Do Not Affect Negotiability (See pages 447–448.)	Certain ambiguities or omissions will not affect an instrument's negotiability. See pages 447–448 for a list of these factors.

Transfer of Instruments (See pages 448–451.)	1. *Transfer by assignment*—A transfer by assignment to an assignee gives the assignee only those rights that the assignor possessed. Any defenses against payment that can be raised against an assignor normally can be raised against the assignee.
	2. *Transfer by negotiation*—An order instrument is negotiated by indorsement and delivery; a bearer instrument is negotiated by delivery only.
	3. *Indorsements*—
	  a. Blank indorsements do not specify a particular indorsee and can consist of a mere signature (see Exhibit 18–5 on page 449).
	  b. Special indorsements contain the signature of the indorser and identify the indorsee (see Exhibit 18–6 on page 449).
	  c. Qualified indorsements contain language, such as the notation "without recourse," that indicates the indorser is not guaranteeing payment of the instrument (see Exhibit 18–7 on page 450).
	  d. Restrictive indorsements, such as "For deposit only," require the indorsee to comply with certain instructions regarding the funds involved, but do not prohibit further negotiation of an instrument.

Holder in Due Course (HDC) (See pages 452–456.)	1. *Holder*—A person in the possession of an instrument drawn, issued, or indorsed to him or her, to his or her order, to bearer, or in blank. A holder obtains only those rights that the transferor had in the instrument.
	2. *Holder in due course (HDC)*—A holder who, by meeting certain acquisition requirements (summarized next), takes an instrument free of most defenses and claims to which the transferor was subject.
	3. *Requirements for HDC status*—To be an HDC, a holder must take the instrument:
	  a. For value—A holder must give value to become an HDC and can take an instrument for value in any of the five ways listed on page 452 [UCC 3–303].
	  b. In good faith—Good faith is defined as "honesty in fact and the observance of reasonable commercial standards of fair dealing" [UCC 3–103(a)(4)].

Chapter Summary: Negotiable Instruments: Transferability and Liability—Continued

Holder in Due Course (HDC)—Continued	c. Without notice—To be an HDC, a holder must not be on notice that the instrument is defective because it is overdue, has been dishonored, is part of a series of which at least one instrument has a uncured defect, contains an unauthorized signature or has been altered, or is so irregular or incomplete as to call its authenticity into question. 4. *Shelter principle*—A holder who cannot qualify as an HDC has the *rights* of an HDC if he or she derives title through an HDC, unless the holder engaged in fraud or illegality affecting the instrument [UCC 3–203(b)].

Signature and Warranty Liability (See pages 456–461.)	Liability on negotiable instruments can arise either from a person's signature or from the (transfer and presentment) warranties that are implied when a person presents the instrument for negotiation.
	1. *Signature liability*—Every party (except a qualified indorser) who signs a negotiable instrument is either primarily or secondarily liable for payment of the instrument when it comes due.
	  a. Primary liability—Makers and acceptors are primarily liable (an *acceptor* is a drawee that promises in writing to pay an instrument when it is presented for payment at a later time) [UCC 3–115, 3–407, 3–409, 3–412].
	  b. Secondary liability—Drawers and indorsers are secondarily liable [UCC 3–412, 3–414, 3–415, 3–501, 3–502, 3–503]. Parties are secondarily liable on an instrument only if (1) presentment is proper and timely, (2) the instrument is dishonored, and (3) they received timely notice of dishonor.
	2. *Transfer warranties*—Any person who transfers an instrument for consideration makes the following warranties to subsequent transferees and holders [UCC 3–416]:
	  a. The transferor is entitled to enforce the instrument.
	  b. All signatures are authentic and authorized.
	  c. The instrument has not been altered.
	  d. The instrument is not subject to a defense or claim of any party that can be asserted against the transferor.
	  e. The transferor has no knowledge of any insolvency proceedings against the maker, the acceptor, or the drawer of the instrument.
	3. *Presentment warranties*—Any person who presents an instrument for payment or acceptance makes the following warranties to any other person who in good faith pays or accepts the instrument [UCC 3–417(a), 3–417(d)]:
	  a. The person obtaining payment or acceptance is entitled to enforce the instrument or is authorized to obtain payment or acceptance on behalf of a person who is entitled to enforce the instrument. (This is, in effect, a warranty that there are no missing or unauthorized indorsements.)
	  b. The instrument has not been altered.
	  c. The person obtaining payment or acceptance has no knowledge that the signature of the drawer of the instrument is unauthorized.

Defenses, Limitations, and Discharge (See pages 461–463.)	1. *Universal (real) defenses*—The following defenses are valid against all holders, including HDCs and holders with the rights of HDCs [UCC 3–305, 3–403, 3–407]:
	  a. Forgery.
	  b. Fraud in the execution.
	  c. Material alteration.
	  d. Discharge in bankruptcy.
	  e. Minority—if the contract is voidable under state law.
	  f. Illegality, mental incapacity, or extreme duress—if the contract is void under state law.
	2. *Personal (limited) defenses*—The following defenses are valid against ordinary holders but not against HDCs or holders with the rights of HDCs [UCC 3–303, 3–305]:
	  a Breach of contract or breach of warranty.
	  b. Lack or failure of consideration (value).
	  c. Fraud in the inducement.
	  d. Illegality and mental incapacity—if the contract is voidable.
	  e. Ordinary duress or undue influence that renders the contract voidable.

Continued

Chapter Summary: Negotiable Instruments: Transferability and Liability–Continued

Defenses, Limitations, and Discharge–Continued	3. *Federal limitations on the rights of HDCs*–Rule 433 of the Federal Trade Commission, issued in 1976, limits the rights of HDCs who purchase instruments arising out of consumer credit transactions. The rule allows a consumer who is a party to a consumer credit transaction to bring any defense he or she has against the seller against a subsequent holder as well, even if the subsequent holder is an HDC. 4. *Discharge from liability*–All parties to a negotiable instrument will be discharged when the party primarily liable on it pays to the holder the full amount due. Discharge can also occur in other circumstances (if the instrument has been canceled or materially altered, for example) [UCC 3–602 through 3–605].

 ExamPrep

ISSUE SPOTTERS

1 Sabrina owes $600 to Yale, who asks Sabrina to sign an instrument for the debt. If included on that instrument, which of the following would prevent its negotiability—"I.O.U. $600," "I promise to pay $600," or an instruction to Sabrina's bank stating, "I wish you would pay $600 to Yale"?

2 Rye signs corporate checks for Suchin Corporation. Rye writes a check payable to U-All Company, to which Suchin owes no money. Rye signs the check, forges U-All's indorsement, and cashes the check at Viceroy Bank, the drawee. Does Suchin have any recourse against the bank for the payment? Why or why not?

BEFORE THE TEST

Check your answers to the Issue Spotters, and at the same time, take the interactive quiz for this chapter. Go to **www.cengage.com/blaw/blt** and click on "Chapter 18." First, click on "Answers to Issue Spotters" to check your answers. Next, click on "Interactive Quiz" to assess your mastery of the concepts in this chapter. Then click on "Flashcards" to review this chapter's Key Term definitions.

 For Review

Answers for the even-numbered questions in this For Review *section can be found on this text's accompanying Web site at* **www.cengage.com/blaw/blt**. *Select "Chapter 18" and click on "For Review."*

1 What requirements must an instrument meet to be negotiable?
2 What are the requirements for attaining the status of a holder in due course (HDC)?
3 What is the difference between signature liability and warranty liability?
4 Certain defenses are valid against all holders, including HDCs. What are these defenses called? Name four defenses that fall within this category.
5 Certain defenses can be used against an ordinary holder but are not effective against an HDC. What are these defenses called? Name four defenses that fall within this category.

 Hypothetical Scenarios and Case Problems

18–1 Indorsements. A check drawn by David for $500 is made payable to the order of Matthew and issued to Matthew. Matthew owes his landlord $500 in rent and transfers the check to his landlord with the following indorsement: "For rent paid. [Signed] Matthew." Matthew's landlord has contracted to have Lambert do some landscaping on the property. When Lambert insists on immediate payment, the landlord transfers the check to Lambert without indorsement. Later, to pay for some palm trees purchased from Green's Nursery, Lambert transfers the check with the following indorsement: "Pay to Green's Nursery,

without recourse. [Signed] Lambert." Green's Nursery sends the check to its bank indorsed "For deposit only. [Signed] Green's Nursery."
1 Classify each of these indorsements.
2 Was the transfer from Matthew's landlord to Lambert, without indorsement, an assignment or a negotiation? Explain.

18–2 **Hypothetical Question with Sample Answer** Muriel Evans writes the following note on the back of an envelope: "I, Muriel Evans, promise to pay Karen Marvin or bearer $100 on demand." Is this a negotiable instrument? Discuss fully.

—For a sample answer to Question 18–2, go to Appendix E at the end of this text.

18–3 Signature Liability. Marion makes a promissory note payable to the order of Perry. Perry indorses the note by writing "without recourse, Perry" and transfers the note for value to Steven. Steven, in need of cash, negotiates the note to Harriet by indorsing it with the words "Pay to Harriet, [signed] Steven." On the due date, Harriet presents the note to Marion for payment, only to learn that Marion has filed for bankruptcy and will have all debts (including the note) discharged in bankruptcy. Discuss fully whether Harriet can hold Marion, Perry, or Steven liable on the note.

18–4 Negotiability. In September 2001, Cory Babcock and Honest Air Conditioning & Heating, Inc., bought a new 2001 Chevrolet Corvette from Cox Chevrolet in Sarasota, Florida. Their retail installment sales contract (RISC) required monthly payments until $52,516.20 was paid. The RISC imposed many other conditions on the buyers and seller with respect to the payment for, and handling of, the Corvette. Cox assigned the RISC to General Motors Acceptance Corp. (GMAC). In August 2002, the buyers sold the car to Florida Auto Brokers, which agreed to pay the balance due on the RISC. The check to GMAC for this amount was dishonored for insufficient funds, however, after the vehicle's title had been forwarded. GMAC filed a suit in a Florida state court against Honest Air and Babcock, seeking $35,815.26 as damages for breach of contract. The defendants argued that the RISC was a negotiable instrument. A ruling in their favor on this point would reduce any damages due GMAC to less than the Corvette's current value. What are the requirements for an instrument to be negotiable? Does the RISC qualify? Explain. [*General Motors Acceptance Corp. v. Honest Air Conditioning & Heating, Inc.,* 933 So.2d 34 (Fla.App. 2 Dist. 2006)]

18–5 Holder in Due Course. Robert Triffin bought a number of dishonored checks from McCall's Liquor Corp., Community Check Cashing II, LLC (CCC), and other licensed check-cashing businesses in New Jersey. Seventeen of the checks had been dishonored as counterfeit. In an attempt to recover on the items, Triffin met with the drawer, Automatic Data Processing, Inc. (ADP). At the meeting, Triffin said that he knew the checks were counterfeit. When ADP refused to pay, Triffin filed suits in New Jersey state courts to collect, asserting claims totaling $11,021.33. With each complaint were copies of assignment agreements corresponding to each check. Each agreement stated, among other things, that the seller was a holder in due course (HDC) and had assigned its rights in the check to Triffin. ADP had not previously seen these agreements. A private investigator determined that the forms attached to the McCall's and CCC checks had not been signed by their sellers but that Triffin had scanned the signatures into his computer and pasted them onto the agreements. ADP claimed fraud. Does Triffin qualify as an HDC? If not, did he acquire the rights of an HDC under the shelter principle? As for the fraud claim, which element of fraud would ADP be least likely to prove? [*Triffin v. Automatic Data Processing, Inc.,* 394 N.J.Super. 237, 926 A.2d 362 (App.Div. 2007)]

18–6 Case Problem with Sample Answer American International Group, Inc. (AIG), an insurance company, issued a check to Jermielem Merriwether in connection with a personal-injury matter. Merriwether presented the check to A-1 Check Cashing Emporium (A-1) for payment. A-1's clerk forgot to have Merriwether sign the check. When he could not reach Merriwether and ask him to come back to A-1 to sign the check, the clerk printed Merriwether's name on the back and deposited it for collection. When the check was not paid, A-1 sold it to Robert Triffin, who is in the business of buying dishonored checks. When Triffin could not get the check honored, he sued AIG, contending that he, through A-1, had the right to collect on the check as a holder in due course (HDC). The trial court rejected that claim. Triffin appealed. On what basis could he claim HDC status? [*Triffin v. American International Group, Inc.,* __ A.2d __ (N.J.Super. 2008)]

—After you have answered Problem 18–6, compare your answer with the sample answer given on the Web site that accompanies this text. Go to **www.cengage.com/blaw/blt**, select "Chapter 18," and click on "Case Problem with Sample Answer."

18–7 Unauthorized Indorsements. Stephen Schor, an accountant in New York City, advised his client, Andre Romanelli, Inc., to open an account at J. P. Morgan Chase Bank, N.A., to obtain a favorable interest rate on a line of credit. Romanelli's representative signed a signature card, which he gave to Schor. When the accountant later told Romanelli that the rate was not favorable, the firm told him not to open the account. Schor signed a blank line on the signature card, changed the mailing address to his office, and opened the account in Romanelli's name. In a purported attempt to obtain credit for the firm elsewhere, Schor had its principals write checks payable to themselves for more than $4.5 million, ostensibly to pay taxes. He indorsed and deposited the checks in the Chase account and eventually withdrew and spent the funds. Romanelli filed a suit in a New York state court against the bank, alleging that a drawer is not liable on an unauthorized indorsement. Is this the rule? What are its exceptions? Which principle applies to these facts, and why? [*Andre Romanelli, Inc. v. Citibank, N.A.,* 60 A.D.3d 428, 875 N.Y.S.2d 14 (1 Dept. 2009)]

18–8 A Question of Ethics *Clarence Morgan, Jr., owned Easy Way Automotive, a car dealership in D'Lo, Mississippi. Easy Way sold a truck to Loyd Barnard, who signed a note for the amount of the price payable to Trustmark National Bank in six months. Before the note came due, Barnard returned the truck to Easy Way, which sold it to another buyer. Using some of the proceeds from the second sale, Easy Way sent a check to Trustmark to pay Barnard's note. Meanwhile, Barnard obtained another truck from Easy Way financed through another six-month note payable to Trustmark. After eight of these deals, some of which involved more than one truck, an Easy Way check to Trustmark was dishonored. In a suit in a Mississippi state court, Trustmark sought to recover the amounts of two of the notes from Barnard. Trustmark had not secured titles to two of the trucks covered by the notes, however, and this complicated Barnard's efforts to reclaim the vehicles from the later buyers.*

[Trustmark National Bank v. Barnard, *930 So.2d 1281* (Miss. App. 2006)]

1 On what basis might Barnard be liable on the Trustmark notes? Would he be primarily or secondarily liable? Could this liability be discharged on the theory that Barnard's right of recourse had been impaired when Trustmark did not secure titles to the trucks covered by the notes? Explain.

2 Easy Way's account had been subject to other recent overdrafts, and a week after the check to Trustmark was returned for insufficient funds, Morgan committed suicide. At the same time, Barnard was unable to obtain a mortgage because the unpaid notes affected his credit rating. How do the circumstances of this case underscore the importance of practicing business ethics?

 ## Critical Thinking and Writing Assignments

18–9 **Critical Thinking and Writing Assignment for Business.** Karen Thorpe is a purchasing agent for GymNast, Inc., a manufacturer of sports equipment. Karen has authority to sign checks in payment for purchases made by GymNast. Karen makes out three checks to suppliers and signs each one differently, as follows:

1 GymNast, Inc., by Karen Thorpe, purchasing agent.

2 Karen Thorpe, purchasing agent.

3 Karen Thorpe.

Discuss whether Karen is personally liable on each signature and whether the principal, GymNast, Inc., can be held liable.

18–10 **Video Question** Go to this text's Web site at **www.cengage.com/blaw/blt** and select "Chapter 18." Click on "Video Questions" and view the video titled *Negotiable Instruments.* **Then answer the following questions.**

1 Who is the maker of the promissory note discussed in the video?

2 Is the note in the video payable on demand or at a definite time?

3 Does the note contain an unconditional promise or order to pay?

4 If the note does not meet the requirements of negotiability, can Onyx assign the note (assignment was discussed in Chapter 13) to the bank in exchange for cash?

 ## Practical Internet Exercises

Go to this text's Web site at **www.cengage.com/blaw/blt**, select "Chapter 18," and click on "Practical Internet Exercises." There you will find the following Internet research exercises that you can perform to learn more about the topics covered in this chapter.

Practical Internet Exercise 18–1: LEGAL PERSPECTIVE—Overview of Negotiable Instruments

Practical Internet Exercise 18–2: LEGAL PERSPECTIVE—Fictitious Payees

Practical Internet Exercise 18–3: MANAGEMENT PERSPECTIVE—Holder in Due Course

Chapter 19

Checks and Banking in the Digital Age

©Robert Pernell, 2009. Used under license from Shutterstock.com)

> "Money is just what we use to keep tally."
>
> —Henry Ford, 1863–1947
> (American automobile manufacturer)

Learning Objectives

After reading this chapter, you should be able to answer the following questions:

1. What type of check does a bank agree in advance to accept when the check is presented for payment?

2. When may a bank properly dishonor a customer's check without the bank being liable to the customer?

3. What duties does the Uniform Commercial Code impose on a bank's customers with regard to forged and altered checks? What are the consequences if a customer is negligent in performing those duties?

4. What are the four most common types of electronic fund transfers?

5. What laws apply to e-money transactions and online banking services?

Checks are the most common type of negotiable instruments regulated by the Uniform Commercial Code (UCC). Checks are convenient to use because they serve as a substitute for cash. Thus, as Henry Ford said in the chapter-opening quotation, checks help us to "keep tally." To be sure, most students today tend to use debit cards rather than checks for many retail transactions. Debit cards now account for more retail payments than checks. Nonetheless, commercial checks remain an integral part of the U.S. economic system.

Articles 3 and 4 of the UCC govern issues relating to checks. Article 4 of the UCC governs bank deposits and collections as well as bank-customer relationships. Article 4 also regulates the relationships of banks with one another as they process checks for payment, and it establishes a framework for deposit and checking agreements between a bank and its customers. A check therefore may fall within the scope of Article 3 and yet be subject to the provisions of Article 4 while in the course of collection. If a conflict between Article 3 and Article 4 arises, Article 4 controls [UCC 4–102(a)].

▶ Checks

Check A draft drawn by a drawer ordering the drawee bank or financial institution to pay a fixed amount of money to the holder on demand.

A **check** is a special type of draft that is drawn on a bank, ordering the bank to pay a fixed amount of money on demand [UCC 3–104(f)]. Article 4 defines a bank as "a person engaged in the business of banking, including a savings bank, savings and loan association, credit union or trust company" [UCC 4–105(1)]. If any other institution (such as a brokerage firm) handles a check for payment or for collection, the check is not covered by Article 4.

Recall from the preceding chapter that a person who writes a check is called the *drawer*. The drawer is a depositor in the bank on which the check is drawn. The person to whom the check is payable is the *payee*. The bank or financial institution on which the check is drawn is the *drawee*. When Anita Cruzak writes a check from her checking account to pay her college tuition, she is the drawer, her bank is the drawee, and her college is the payee. We now look at some special types of checks.

Cashier's Checks

Cashier's Check A check drawn by a bank on itself.

Checks usually are three-party instruments, but on certain types of checks, the bank can serve as both the drawer and the drawee. For example, when a bank draws a check on itself, the check is called a **cashier's check** and is a negotiable instrument on issue (see Exhibit 19–1) [UCC 3–104(g)]. Normally, a cashier's check indicates a specific payee. In effect, with a cashier's check, the bank assumes responsibility for paying the check, thus making the check more readily acceptable as a substitute for cash.

EXAMPLE 19.1 Kramer needs to pay a moving company $8,000 for moving his household goods to a new home in another state. The moving company requests payment in the form of a cashier's check. Kramer goes to a bank (he does not need to have an account at the bank) and purchases a cashier's check, payable to the moving company, in the amount of $8,000. Kramer has to pay the bank the $8,000 for the check, plus a small service fee. He then gives the check to the moving company. ●

Cashier's checks are sometimes used in the business community as nearly the equivalent of cash. Except in very limited circumstances, the issuing bank must honor its cashier's checks when they are presented for payment. If a bank wrongfully dishonors a cashier's check, a holder can recover from the bank all expenses incurred, interest, and consequential damages [UCC 3–411]. This same rule applies if a bank wrongfully dishonors a certified check (to be discussed shortly) or a teller's check. (A *teller's check* is a check drawn by a bank on another bank or, when drawn on a nonbank, payable at or through a bank [UCC

● *Exhibit* **19–1** A Cashier's Check

*The abbreviation *NT&SA* stands for National Trust and Savings Association. The Bank of America NT&SA is a subsidiary of Bank of America Corporation, which is engaged in financial services, insurance, investment management, and other businesses.

3–104(h)]. For instance, when a credit union issues a check to withdraw funds from its account at another financial institution, and the teller at the credit union signs the check, it is a teller's check.)

Rather than being treated as the equivalent of cash, should a cashier's check be treated as a note with all of the applicable defenses? That was the question in the following case.

Case 19.1 MidAmerica Bank, FSB v. Charter One Bank

Illinois Supreme Court, 232 Ill.2d 560, 905 N.E.2d 839 (2009).

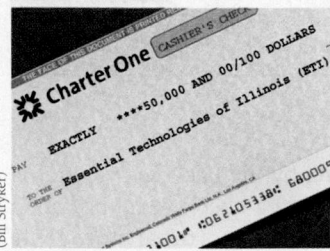

(Bill Stryker)

Can a bank obtain payment on a $50,000 cashier's check after the drawee's bank issues a stop-payment order four days after the check was issued?

FACTS Mary Christelle was the mother of David Hernandez, president of Essential Technologies of Illinois (ETI). Christelle bought a $50,000 cashier's check from Charter One Bank payable to ETI. ETI deposited the check into its account with MidAmerica Bank, FSB. Four days later, Christelle asked Charter One to *stop payment* (see the discussion on pages 476 and 477). Charter One agreed and refused to honor the check. MidAmerica returned the check to ETI. Within two weeks, ETI's account had a negative balance of $52,000. MidAmerica closed the account and filed a suit in an Illinois state court against Charter One, alleging that the defendant wrongfully dishonored the cashier's check. Charter One argued that a cashier's check should be treated as a note subject to the defense of fraud. The court ruled in MidAmerica's favor, but a state intermediate appellate court reversed the ruling. MidAmerica appealed.

ISSUE Can a bank obtain payment on a cashier's check over the drawee bank's stop-payment order?

DECISION Yes. The Illinois Supreme Court reversed the lower court's decision, awarded MidAmerica the amount of the check, and remanded the case for a determination of interest and fees.

REASON A bank's refusal to pay a cashier's check based on its customer's request to stop payment is wrongful under UCC 3–411 because a customer has no right to stop payment on a cashier's check under UCC 4–403, which permits payment to be stopped only on items drawn "on the customer's account." A cashier's check is drawn on the issuing bank, not on the customer's account. Thus, Christelle had no right to stop payment after she gave the check to ETI. As for Charter One's argument that the check should be treated as a note, the court agreed that the drawer of a cashier's check has the same liability as the maker of a note "because a bank issuing a cashier's check is both the drawer and drawee of the check." But "the UCC provides that cashier's checks are drafts, not notes." Besides, the bank cannot assert fraud as a defense because it did not know of any fraud when it dishonored the check.

WHY IS THIS CASE IMPORTANT? *As noted earlier in the text, the UCC has been amended periodically since it was first issued in 1949. In particular, Article 3 was significantly revised in 1990 when many sections were rewritten and renumbered. The reasoning in this case underscores that through all of the changes, the treatment of cashier's checks as "cash equivalents" in the world of commerce has never varied, and none of the amendments to Article 3 have been intended to alter that status.*

Traveler's Checks

Traveler's Check A check that is payable on demand, drawn on or payable through a financial institution (bank), and designated as a traveler's check.

A **traveler's check** is an instrument that is payable on demand, drawn on or payable at or through a financial institution (such as a bank), and designated as a traveler's check. The issuing institution is directly obligated to accept and pay its traveler's check according to the check's terms. Traveler's checks are designed as a safe substitute for cash when a person is on vacation or traveling and are issued for a fixed amount, such as $20, $50, or $100. The purchaser is required to sign the check at the time it is bought and again at the time it is used [UCC 3–104(i)]. Most major banks today do not issue traveler's checks; rather, they purchase and issue American Express traveler's checks for their customers (see Exhibit 19–2 on the following page).

• *Exhibit* **19-2** A Traveler's Check

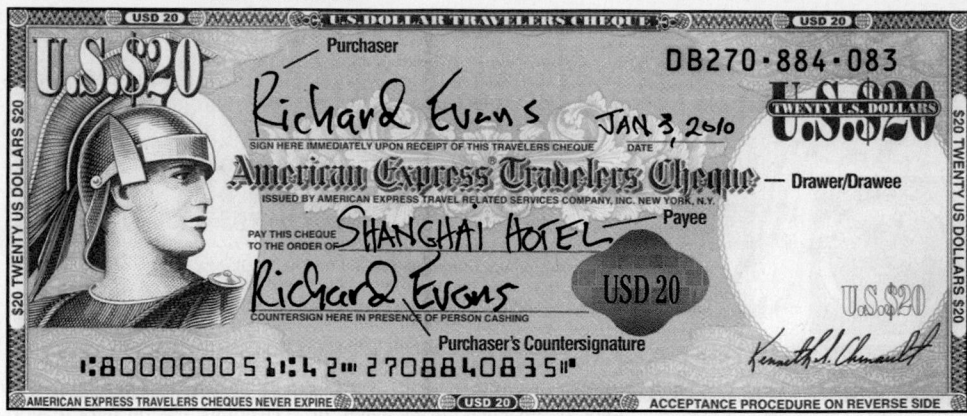

Certified Checks

Certified Check   A check that has been accepted in writing by the bank on which it is drawn. Essentially, the bank, by certifying (accepting) the check, promises to pay the check at the time the check is presented.

A **certified check** is a check that has been *accepted* in writing by the bank on which it is drawn [UCC 3–409(d)]. When a drawee bank *certifies* (accepts) a check, it immediately charges the drawer's account with the amount of the check and transfers those funds to its own certified check account. In effect, the bank is agreeing in advance to accept that check when it is presented for payment and to make payment from those funds reserved in the certified check account. Essentially, certification prevents the bank from denying liability. It is a promise that sufficient funds are on deposit *and have been set aside* to cover the check.

To certify a check, the bank writes or stamps the word *certified* on the face of the check and typically writes the amount that it will pay.[1] Either the drawer or the holder (payee) of a check can request certification, but the drawee bank is not required to certify a check. (Note, though, that a bank's refusal to certify a check is not a dishonor of the check [UCC 3–409(d)].) Once a check is certified, the drawer and any prior indorsers are completely discharged from liability on the check [UCC 3–414(c), 3–415(d)]. Only the certifying bank is required to pay the instrument.

▶ The Bank-Customer Relationship

The bank-customer relationship begins when the customer opens a checking account and deposits funds that the bank will use to pay for checks written by the customer. Essentially, three types of relationships come into being, as discussed next.

Creditor-Debtor Relationship

A creditor-debtor relationship is created between a customer and a bank when, for example, the customer makes cash deposits into a checking account. When a customer makes a deposit, the customer becomes a creditor, and the bank a debtor, for the amount deposited.

Agency Relationship

An agency relationship also arises between the customer and the bank when the customer writes a check on his or her account. In effect, the customer is ordering the bank to pay

ON THE WEB Cornell University's Legal Information Institute provides an overview of banking, as well as a "menu of sources" of federal and state statutes and court decisions relating to banking transactions. To access this information, go to **topics.law.cornell.edu/wex/ Banking**.

---

1. If the certification does not state an amount, and the amount is later increased and the instrument negotiated to a holder in due course (HDC), the obligation of the certifying bank is the amount of the instrument when it was taken by the HDC [UCC 3–413(b)].

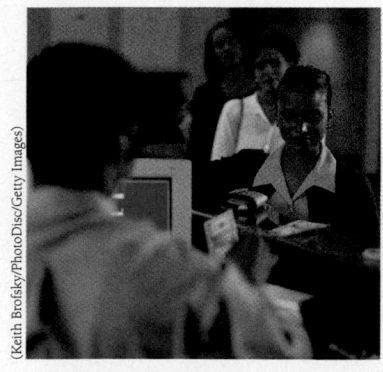

When this customer deposits cash into her regular checking account, what three types of relationships are created?

the amount specified on the check to the holder when the holder presents the check to the bank for payment. In this situation, the bank becomes the customer's agent and is obligated to honor the customer's request. Similarly, if the customer deposits a check into her or his account, the bank, as the customer's agent, is obligated to collect payment on the check from the bank on which the check was drawn. To transfer checkbook funds among different banks, each bank acts as the agent of collection for its customer [UCC 4–201(a)].

Contractual Relationship

Whenever a bank-customer relationship is established, certain contractual rights and duties arise. The specific rights and duties of the bank and its customer depend on the nature of the transaction. The respective rights and duties of banks and their customers are discussed in detail in the following pages. Another aspect of the bank-customer relationship—deposit insurance—is examined in the *Linking the Law to Economics* feature at the end of this chapter.

▶ Bank's Duty to Honor Checks

When a banking institution provides checking services, it agrees to honor the checks written by its customers, with the usual stipulation that the account must have sufficient funds available to pay each check [UCC 4–401(a)]. When a drawee bank *wrongfully* fails to honor a check, it is liable to its customer for damages resulting from its refusal to pay [UCC 4–402(b)]. The customer does not have to prove that the bank breached its contractual commitment or was negligent.

The customer's agreement with the bank includes a general obligation to keep sufficient funds on deposit to cover all checks written. The customer is liable to the payee or to the holder of a check in a civil suit if a check is dishonored for insufficient funds. If intent to defraud can be proved, the customer can also be subject to criminal prosecution for writing a bad check.

When the bank properly dishonors a check for insufficient funds, it has no liability to the customer. The bank may rightfully refuse payment on a customer's check in other circumstances as well. We look here at the rights and duties of both the bank and its customers in relation to specific situations.

Overdrafts

Overdraft A check that is paid by the bank when the checking account on which the check is written contains insufficient funds to cover the check.

When the bank receives an item properly payable from its customer's checking account but the account contains insufficient funds to cover the amount of the check, the bank has two options. It can either (1) dishonor the item or (2) pay the item and charge the customer's account, thus creating an **overdraft,** providing that the customer has authorized the payment and the payment does not violate any bank-customer agreement [UCC 4–401(a)].[2] The bank can subtract the difference (plus a service charge) from the customer's next deposit or other customer funds because the check carries with it an enforceable implied promise to reimburse the bank.

A bank can expressly agree with a customer to accept overdrafts through what is sometimes called an "overdraft protection agreement." If such an agreement is formed, any failure of the bank to honor a check because it would create an overdraft breaches this agreement and is treated as a wrongful dishonor [UCC 4–402(a)].

_____

2. With a joint account, the bank cannot hold the nonsigning customer liable for payment of an overdraft unless that person benefited from its proceeds [UCC 4–401(b)].

Postdated Checks

A bank may also charge a postdated check against a customer's account, unless the customer notifies the bank, in a timely manner, not to pay the check until the stated date. The notice of postdating must be given in time to allow the bank to act on the notice before committing itself to pay on the check. The UCC states that the bank should treat a notice of postdating the same as a stop-payment order—to be discussed shortly. If the bank fails to act on the customer's notice and charges the customer's account before the date on the postdated check, the bank may be liable for any damages incurred by the customer [UCC 4–401(c)].[3]

Stale Checks

Stale Check   A check, other than a certified check, that is presented for payment more than six months after its date.

Commercial banking practice regards a check that is presented for payment more than six months from its date as a **stale check.** A bank is not obligated to pay an uncertified check presented more than six months from its date [UCC 4–404]. When receiving a stale check for payment, the bank has the option of paying or not paying the check. The bank may consult the customer before paying the check. If a bank pays a stale check in good faith without consulting the customer, however, the bank has the right to charge the customer's account for the amount of the check.

Stop-Payment Orders

Stop-Payment Order   An order by a bank customer to his or her bank not to pay or certify a certain check.

A **stop-payment order** is an order by a customer to his or her bank not to pay or certify a certain check. Only a customer or a person authorized to draw on the account can order the bank not to pay the check when it is presented for payment [UCC 4–403(a)].[4] A customer has no right to stop payment on a check that has been certified or accepted by a bank, however. The customer must issue the stop-payment order within a reasonable time and in a reasonable manner to permit the bank to act on it [UCC 4–403(a)]. Although a stop-payment order can be given orally, usually by phone, it is binding on the bank for only fourteen calendar days unless confirmed in writing.[5] A written stop-payment order (the bank typically provides a preprinted form for the customer) or an oral order confirmed in writing is effective for six months, at which time it must be renewed in writing [UCC 4–403(b)].

BANK'S LIABILITY FOR WRONGFUL PAYMENT   If the bank pays the check in spite of a stop-payment order, the bank will be obligated to recredit the customer's account. In addition, if the bank's payment over a stop-payment order causes subsequent checks written on the drawer's account to "bounce," the bank will be liable for the resultant costs the drawer incurs.

The bank is liable only for the amount of the actual damages suffered by the drawer, however [UCC 4–403(c)]. **EXAMPLE 19.2**   Mako Murano orders six bamboo palms from a local nursery at $50 each and gives the nursery a check for $300. Later that day, the nursery tells Murano that it will not deliver the palms as arranged. Murano immediately calls his bank and stops payment on the check. If the bank nonetheless honors the check, the bank will be liable to Murano for the full $300. The result would be different, however, if the

---

3. As noted in Chapter 18, postdating does not affect the negotiability of a check. Under the automated check-collection system now in use, a check is usually paid without respect to its date. Thus, today banks typically ignore the dates on checks (and treat them as demand instruments) unless they have received notice from a customer that a check was postdated.

4. For a deceased customer, any person claiming a legitimate interest in the account may issue a stop-payment order [UCC 4–405].

5. Some states do not recognize oral stop-payment orders; they must be in writing.

nursery had delivered five palms. In that situation, Murano would owe the nursery $250 for the delivered palms, and his actual losses would be only $50. Consequently, the bank would be liable to Murano for only $50. ●

CUSTOMER'S LIABILITY FOR WRONGFUL STOP-PAYMENT ORDER   A stop-payment order has its risks for a customer. The customer-drawer must have a *valid legal ground* for issuing such an order; otherwise, the holder can sue the drawer for payment. Moreover, defenses sufficient to refuse payment against a payee may not be valid grounds to prevent payment against a subsequent holder in due course [UCC 3–305, 3–306]. A person who wrongfully stops payment on a check is liable to the payee for the amount of the check and can also be liable for consequential damages incurred by the payee.

Death or Incompetence of a Customer

Neither the death nor the incompetence of a customer revokes a bank's authority to pay an item until the bank is informed of the situation and has had a reasonable amount of time to act on the notice. Thus, if a bank is unaware that the customer who wrote a check has been declared incompetent or has died, the bank can pay the item without incurring liability [UCC 4–405]. Even when a bank knows of the death of its customer, for ten days after the *date of death,* it can pay or certify checks drawn on or before the date of death. An exception to this rule is made if a person claiming an interest in that account, such as an heir, orders the bank to stop payment. Without this provision, banks would constantly be required to verify the continued life and competence of their drawers.

Checks Bearing Forged Drawers' Signatures

When a bank pays a check on which the drawer's signature is forged, generally the bank is liable. A bank may be able to recover at least some of the loss from the customer, however, if the customer's negligence contributed to the making of the forgery. A bank may also obtain partial recovery from the forger of the check (if he or she can be found) or from the holder who presented the check for payment (if the holder knew that the signature was forged).

THE GENERAL RULE   A forged signature on a check has no legal effect as the signature of a drawer [UCC 3–403(a)]. For this reason, banks require a signature card from each customer who opens a checking account. Signature cards allow the bank to verify whether the signatures on its customers' checks are genuine. The general rule is that the bank must recredit the customer's account when it pays a check with a forged signature. (Note that banks today normally verify signatures only on checks that exceed a certain threshold, such as $2,500 or some higher amount. Even though a bank sometimes incurs liability costs when it has paid forged checks, the costs involved in verifying every check's signature would be much higher.)

Note that a bank may contractually shift to the customer the risk of forged checks created by the use of facsimile or other nonmanual signatures. For instance, the contract might stipulate that the customer is solely responsible for maintaining security over any device affixing a signature.

CUSTOMER NEGLIGENCE   When the customer's negligence substantially contributes to the forgery, the bank normally will not be obligated to recredit the customer's account for the amount of the check [UCC 3–406]. The customer's liability may be reduced, however, by the amount of loss caused by negligence on the part of the bank (or other "person") paying

In general, a bank is liable when it pays a check on which the drawer's (account holder's) signature is forged. In contrast, under certain circumstances, the customer is liable. What are those circumstances?

(Leland Bobbe/Stone/Getty Images)

the instrument or taking it for value if the negligence substantially contributed to the loss [UCC 3–406(b)].

EXAMPLE 19.3   Gemco Corporation uses special check-writing equipment to write its payroll and business checks. Gemco discovers that one of its employees used the equipment to write himself a check for $10,000 and that the bank subsequently honored it. Gemco asks the bank to recredit $10,000 to its account for improperly paying the forged check. If the bank can show that Gemco failed to take reasonable care in controlling access to the check-writing equipment, the bank will not be required to recredit Gemco's account for the amount of the forged check. If Gemco can show that negligence on the part of the bank contributed substantially to the loss, however, then Gemco's liability may be reduced proportionately. ●

In the following case, an employee opened a bogus bank account and fraudulently deposited his employer's checks in it for years. The court had to determine if the bank should have requested written authorization from the company before opening the account.

Case 19.2   Auto-Owners Insurance Co. v. Bank One

Supreme Court of Indiana, 879 N.E.2d 1086 (2008).

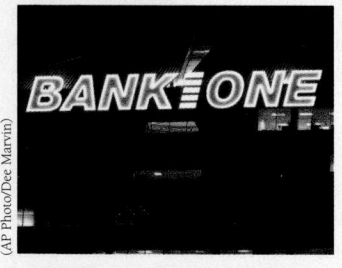

(AP Photo/Dee Marvin)

Did Bank One's failure to request proof from a customer that he was authorized to deposit checks, which were in fact embezzled from his employer, substantially contribute to the employer's loss?

FACTS   Kenneth Wulf worked in the claims department of Auto-Owners Insurance Company for ten years. When the department received checks, a staff member would note them in the file and send them on to headquarters. Wulf opened a checking account at Bank One in the name of "Auto-Owners, Kenneth B. Wulf." Over a period of eight years, he deposited $546,000 worth of checks that he had stolen from Auto-Owners and endorsed with a stamp that read "Auto-Owners Insurance Deposit Only." When the scam was finally discovered, Auto-Owners sued Bank One, contending that it had failed to exercise ordinary care in opening the account because it had not asked for documentation to show that Wulf was authorized to open an account in the name of Auto-Owners. The lower courts rejected that argument and granted summary judgment for Bank One. Auto-Owners appealed.

ISSUE   Did the bank's failure to request proof from Wulf that he was authorized to deposit checks made payable to Auto-Owners substantially contribute to the loss?

DECISION   No. The state supreme court affirmed the decision of the lower courts, finding that Bank One's conduct did not "substantially contribute" to the losses suffered by Auto-Owners.

REASON   The court reasoned that UCC 3–405(b) makes no mention of a bank's responsibilities when opening an account for a new customer. Rather, subsection (b) requires ordinary care from a bank in the "paying" or "taking" of an instrument. Therefore, the bank did not breach any duty to the insurance company by opening Wulf's checking account. In such cases, the courts consider all of the facts surrounding the transactions that occurred. Here, the major reasons for the losses suffered by Auto-Owners were its weak internal monitoring of its own files and the lack of controls in the handling of company checks. The bank did not worsen the situation by allowing Wulf to have a checking account.

FOR CRITICAL ANALYSIS—Management Consideration
What reasonable steps could Auto-Owners have taken to prevent such internal fraud?

"Canceled checks will be to future historians and cultural anthropologists what the Dead Sea Scrolls and hieroglyphics are to us."

Brent Staples, 1951–present
(American journalist)

Timely Examination of Bank Statements Required.   Banks typically send or make available (such as with online statements) to their customers monthly statements detailing activity in their checking accounts. In the past, banks routinely included the canceled checks themselves (or photocopies of the canceled checks), with the statement sent to the customer. Today, most banks simply provide the customer with information (check number, amount, and date of payment) on the statement that will allow the customer to reasonably identify the checks that the bank has paid [UCC 4–406(a), (b)]. If the bank retains the

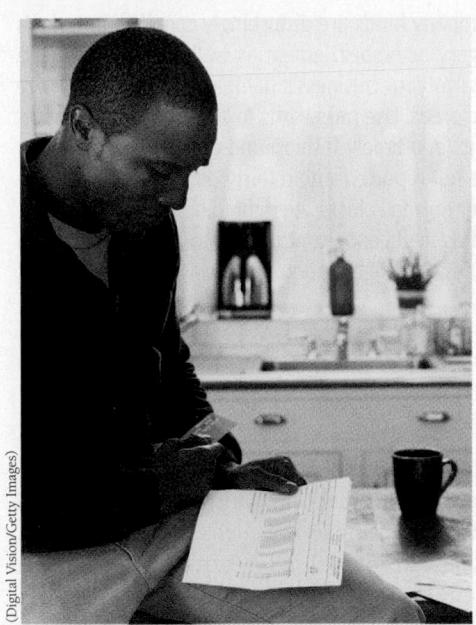

(Digital Vision/Getty Images)

Most banks issue a recapitulation of all transactions that each customer engaged in. These so-called bank statements are issued monthly. Why should bank customers examine them carefully?

KEEP IN MIND If a bank is forced to recredit a customer's account, the bank may recover from the forger or from the party that cashed the check (usually a different customer or a collecting bank).

canceled checks, it must keep the checks—or legible copies of the checks—for seven years [UCC 4–406(b)]. The customer can obtain a copy of a canceled check during this period of time.

The customer has a duty to promptly examine bank statements (and canceled checks or photocopies, if they are included) with reasonable care and to report any alterations or forged signatures [UCC 4–406(c)]. This includes forged signatures of indorsers, if discovered (to be discussed shortly). If the customer fails to fulfill this duty and the bank suffers a loss as a result, the customer will be liable for the loss [UCC 4–406(d)].

Consequences of Failing to Detect Forgeries.   Sometimes, the same wrongdoer has forged the customer's signature on a series of checks. In that situation, the customer, to recover for all the forged items, must discover and report the *first* forged check to the bank within thirty calendar days of the receipt of the bank statement [UCC 4–406(d)(2)]. Failure to notify the bank within this period of time discharges the bank's liability for *all* of the forged checks that it pays prior to notification.

CASE EXAMPLE 19.4 Joseph Montanez, an employee and bookkeeper for Espresso Roma Corporation, used stolen computer software and blank checks to generate company checks on his home computer. The series of forged checks spanned a period of more than two years and totaled more than $330,000. When the bank statements containing the forged checks arrived in the mail, Montanez sorted through the statements and removed the checks so that the forgeries would go undetected. Eventually, Espresso Roma discovered the forgeries and asked the bank to recredit its account. The bank refused and litigation ensued. The court held that the bank was not liable for the forged checks because Espresso Roma failed to report the first forgeries within the UCC's time period of thirty days.[6] ●

WHEN THE BANK IS ALSO NEGLIGENT   In one situation, a bank customer can escape liability, at least in part, for failing to notify the bank of forged or altered checks promptly or within the required thirty-day period. That situation occurs when the customer can prove that the bank was also negligent—that is, the bank failed to exercise ordinary care. Then the bank will also be liable, and the loss will be allocated between the bank and the customer on the basis of comparative negligence [UCC 4–406(e)]. In other words, even though a customer may have been negligent, the bank may still have to recredit the customer's account for a portion of the loss if the bank failed to exercise ordinary care.

The UCC defines *ordinary care* as the "observance of reasonable commercial standards, prevailing in the area in which [a] person is located, with respect to the business in which that person is engaged" [UCC 3–103]. As mentioned earlier, it is customary in the banking industry to manually examine signatures only on checks over a certain amount (such as $2,500 or some higher amount). Thus, if a bank, in accordance with prevailing banking standards, fails to examine a signature on a particular check, the bank has not necessarily breached its duty to exercise ordinary care.

Regardless of the degree of care exercised by the customer or the bank, the UCC places an absolute time limit on the liability of a bank for paying a check with a forged customer signature. A customer who fails to report a forged signature within one year from the date that the statement was made available for inspection loses the legal right to have the bank recredit his or her account [UCC 4–406(f)].

---

6. *Espresso Roma Corp. v. Bank of America, N.A.,* 100 Cal.App.4th 525, 124 Cal.Rptr.2d 549 (2002).

Checks forged by employees and embezzlement of company funds are disturbingly common in today's business world. To avoid significant losses due to forgery or embezzlement as well as litigation, keep a watchful eye on business bank accounts. Limit access to your business's bank accounts. Never leave company checkbooks or signature stamps in unsecured areas. Use passwords to limit access to computerized check-writing software. Examine bank statements in a timely fashion and be on the lookout for suspicious transactions. Remember that if forgeries are not reported within thirty days of the first statement in which a forged item appears, the account holder normally loses the right to hold the bank liable. Be careful not to do anything that could be construed as negligence contributing to a forgery (or to a subsequent alteration of a check, to be discussed shortly). Be diligent about reviewing bank statements and reporting discrepancies to the bank.

Checks Bearing Forged Indorsements

A bank that pays a customer's check bearing a forged indorsement must recredit the customer's account or be liable to the customer-drawer for breach of contract. **EXAMPLE 19.5** Simon issues a $500 check "to the order of Antonio." Juan steals the check, forges Antonio's indorsement, and cashes the check. When the check reaches Simon's bank, the bank pays it and debits Simon's account. The bank must recredit the $500 to Simon's account because it failed to carry out Simon's order to pay "to the order of Antonio" [UCC 4–401(a)]. Of course, Simon's bank can in turn recover—for breach of warranty (see Chapter 18)—from the bank that cashed the check when Juan presented it [UCC 4–207(a)(2)]. ●

Eventually, the loss usually falls on the first party to take the instrument bearing the forged indorsement because, as discussed in Chapter 18, a forged indorsement does not transfer title. Thus, whoever takes an instrument with a forged indorsement cannot become a holder.

In any event, the customer has a duty to report forged indorsements, whether discovered or not, promptly. Failure to report forged indorsements within a three-year period after the forged items have been made available to the customer relieves the bank of liability [UCC 4–111].

Altered Checks

The customer's instruction to the bank is to pay the exact amount on the face of the check to the holder. The bank has a duty to examine each check before making final payment. If it fails to detect an alteration, it is liable to its customer for the loss because it did not pay as the customer ordered. The loss is the difference between the original amount of the check and the amount actually paid [UCC 4–401(d)(1)]. **EXAMPLE 19.6** A check written for $11 is raised to $111. The customer's account will be charged $11 (the amount the customer ordered the bank to pay). The bank normally will be responsible for the $100. ●

CUSTOMER NEGLIGENCE As in a situation involving a forged drawer's signature, a customer's negligence can shift the loss when payment is made on an altered check (unless the bank was also negligent). For example, a person may carelessly write a check leaving large gaps around the numbers and words where additional numbers and words can be inserted (see Exhibit 19–3).

(Keith Brofsky/PhotoDisc/Getty Images)

Banks are increasingly demanding that thumbprints accompany check indorsements in order to reduce forgeries.

● *Exhibit* **19–3** **A Poorly Filled-Out Check**

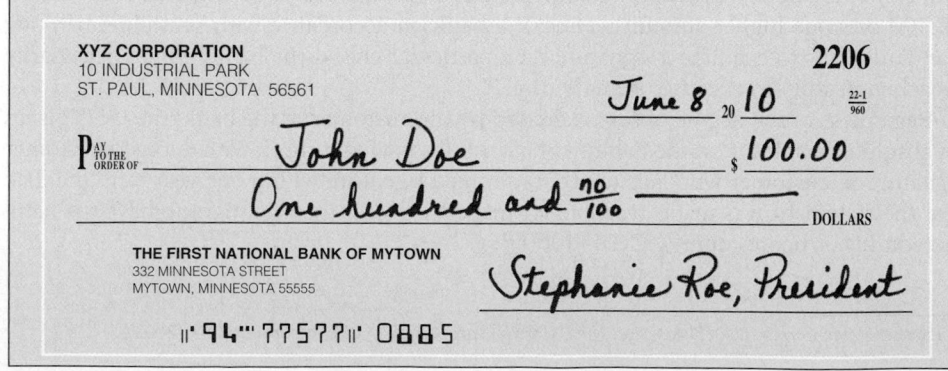

XYZ CORPORATION
10 INDUSTRIAL PARK
ST. PAUL, MINNESOTA 56561

2206

June 8 20 10   22-1/960

PAY TO THE ORDER OF ___ *John Doe* ___ $ *100.00*

One hundred and 70/100 ___ DOLLARS

THE FIRST NATIONAL BANK OF MYTOWN
332 MINNESOTA STREET
MYTOWN, MINNESOTA 55555

Stephanie Roe, President

⑆94⑈77577⑈ 0885

Similarly, a person who signs a check and leaves the dollar amount for someone else to fill in is barred from protesting when the bank unknowingly and in good faith pays whatever amount is shown [UCC 4–401(d)(2)]. Finally, if the bank can trace its loss on successive altered checks to the customer's failure to discover the initial alteration, then the bank can reduce its liability for reimbursing the customer's account [UCC 4–406].

In every situation involving a forged drawer's signature or an alteration, a bank must observe reasonable commercial standards of care in paying on a customer's checks [UCC 4–406(e)]. The customer's negligence can be used as a defense only if the bank has exercised ordinary care.

OTHER PARTIES FROM WHOM THE BANK MAY RECOVER The bank is entitled to recover the amount of loss from the transferor who, by presenting the check for payment, warrants that the check has not been materially altered (warranty liability was discussed in Chapter 18). This rule has two exceptions, though. If the bank is the drawer (as it is on a cashier's check and a teller's check), it cannot recover from the presenting party if the party is a holder in due course (HDC) acting in good faith [UCC 3–417(a)(2), 4–208(a)(2)]. The reason is that an instrument's drawer is in a better position than an HDC to know whether the instrument has been altered.

Similarly, an HDC who presents a certified check for payment in good faith will not be held liable under warranty principles if the check was altered before the HDC acquired it [UCC 3–417(a)(2), 4–207(a)(2)]. **EXAMPLE 19.7** Jordan draws a check for $500 payable to David. David alters the amount to $5,000. The drawee bank, First National, certifies the check for $5,000. David negotiates the check to Ethan, an HDC. The drawee bank pays Ethan $5,000. On discovering the mistake, the bank cannot recover from Ethan the $4,500 paid by mistake, even though the bank was not in a superior position to detect the alteration. This is in accord with the purpose of certification, which is to obtain the definite obligation of a bank to honor a definite instrument. ●

The *Concept Summary* on the next page summarizes the rights and liabilities of a bank and its customers in regard to checks.

▶ Bank's Duty to Accept Deposits

A bank has a duty to its customer to accept the customer's deposits of cash and checks. When checks are deposited, the bank must make the funds represented by those checks available within certain time frames. A bank also has a duty to collect payment on any checks payable or indorsed to its customers and deposited by them into their accounts. Cash deposits made in U.S. currency are received into customers' accounts without being subject to further collection procedures.

Availability Schedule for Deposited Checks

The Expedited Funds Availability Act of 1987[7] and Regulation CC,[8] which was issued by the Federal Reserve Board of Governors (the *Federal Reserve System* will be discussed shortly) to implement the act, require that any local check deposited must be available for withdrawal by check or as cash within one business day from the date of deposit. A check is classified as a local check if the first bank to receive the check for payment and the bank on which the check is drawn are located in the same check-processing region (check-processing regions are designated by the Federal Reserve Board of Governors). For nonlocal checks, the funds must be available for withdrawal within not more than five business days. Note that under the Check Clearing in the 21st Century Act (Check 21),[9] a bank will

A woman stands at the Vcom kiosk in a 7-Eleven convenience store. These machines can provide a number of services, including ATM transactions, check cashing, money orders, wire transfers, and even bill paying in some locations. How many days after a deposit do funds normally become available for withdrawal from this type of machine?

(AP Photo/Jon Freilich)

---

7. 12 U.S.C. Sections 4001–4010.
8. 12 C.F.R. Sections 229.1–229.42.
9. 12 U.S.C. Sections 5001–5018.

Concept Summary   Bank's Duty to Honor Checks

SITUATION	BASIC RULES
Wrongful Dishonor [UCC 4–402]	The bank is liable to its customer for actual damages proved if it wrongfully dishonors a check due to mistake. When the bank properly dishonors a check (for insufficient funds or because of a stop-payment order, for example), it has no liability to the customer.
Overdraft [UCC 4–401]	The bank has a right to charge a customer's account for any item properly payable, even if the charge results in an overdraft.
Postdated Check [UCC 4–401]	The bank may charge a postdated check against a customer's account, unless the customer notifies the bank of the postdating in time to allow the bank to act on the customer's notice before committing itself to pay on the check.
Stale Check [UCC 4–404]	The bank is not obligated to pay an uncertified check presented more than six months after its date, but the bank may do so in good faith without liability.
Stop-Payment Order [UCC 4–403]	The customer (or a "person authorized to draw on the account") must make a stop-payment order in time for the bank to have a reasonable opportunity to act. Oral orders are binding for only fourteen days unless they are confirmed in writing. Written orders are effective for only six months unless renewed in writing. The bank is liable for wrongful payment over a timely stop-payment order to the extent that the customer suffers a loss. A customer has no right to stop payment on a check that has been certified or accepted by a bank, however. A person who stops payment on a check without a valid legal ground can be held liable for actual and consequential damages incurred by the payee.
Death or Incompetence of a Customer [UCC 4–405]	So long as the bank does not know of the death or incompetence of a customer, the bank can pay an item without liability. Even with knowledge of a customer's death, a bank can honor or certify checks (in the absence of a stop-payment order) for ten days after the date of the customer's death.
Forged Signature or Alteration [UCC 4–406]	The customer has a duty to examine account statements with reasonable care on receipt and to notify the bank promptly of any forged signatures or alterations. On a series of forged signatures or alterations by the same wrongdoer, examination and report must be made within thirty calendar days of receipt of the first statement containing a forged or altered item. The customer's failure to comply with these rules releases the bank from liability unless the bank failed to exercise reasonable care, in which case liability may be apportioned according to a comparative negligence standard. Regardless of care or lack of care, the customer is barred from holding the bank liable after one year for forged customer signatures or alterations and after three years for forged indorsements.

have to credit a customer's account as soon as the bank receives the funds (Check 21 will be discussed in this chapter's *Landmark in the Law* feature on page 484). In addition, the Expedited Funds Availability Act requires the following:

1. That funds be available on the next business day for cash deposits and wire transfers, government checks, the first $100 of a day's check deposits, cashier's checks, certified checks, and checks for which the depositary and payor banks are branches of the same institution (*depositary* and *payor banks* will be discussed shortly).

2. That the first $100 of any deposit be available for cash withdrawal on the opening of the next business day after deposit. If a local check is deposited, the next $400 is to be available for withdrawal by no later than 5:00 P.M. the next business day. If, for example, you deposit a local check for $500 on Monday, you can withdraw $100 in cash at the opening of the business day on Tuesday, and an additional $400 must be available for withdrawal by no later than 5:00 P.M. on Wednesday.

A different availability schedule applies to deposits made at *nonproprietary* automated teller machines (ATMs). These are ATMs that are not owned or operated by the bank receiving the deposits. Basically, a five-day hold is permitted on all deposits, including cash deposits, made at nonproprietary ATMs. Other exceptions also exist. A depository institution has eight days to make funds available in new accounts (those open less than thirty days) and has an extra four days on deposits that exceed $5,000 (except deposits of government and cashier's checks).

Ethical Issue ⚖️

Has the Expedited Funds Availability Act (EFAA) encouraged fraud? Since the EFAA was enacted in 1987, millions of people have fallen prey to a variety of check-fraud scams. The fraudsters contact a person—via e-mail, telephone, or letter—and say that they will send the person a check for a certain amount if the person agrees to wire some of the funds back to them, typically to cover "fees and taxes." The victim receives a check, deposits it into his or her account, and waits to see if the check "clears." A day or so later, when the law says that the funds must be made available, the victim confirms that the funds are in his or her bank account and wires the requested amount back to the fraudsters.

Unfortunately, by the time the bank discovers that the check is a fake and notifies the customer that it has "bounced," the customer has already sent thousands of dollars to the fraudsters. Because the check was counterfeit, the bank has no liability on it, and the loss falls on the customer. The incidence of these scams is increasing, largely because the fraudsters know that the law requires U.S. banks to make the funds available immediately on deposited checks, even if those checks later prove to be counterfeit. Moreover, technology has improved the fraudsters' ability to create checks that look real. Although the EFAA was intended to protect bank customers, it now appears to be having the opposite effect—making them a target for fraud.

The Traditional Collection Process

Usually, deposited checks involve parties that do business at different banks, but sometimes checks are written between customers of the same bank. Either situation brings into play the bank collection process as it operates within the statutory framework of Article 4 of the UCC. Note that the check-collection process described in the following subsections will continue to be modified as the banking industry implements Check 21.

Depositary Bank The first bank to receive a check for payment.

Payor Bank The bank on which a check is drawn (the drawee bank).

Collecting Bank Any bank handling an item for collection, except the payor bank.

Intermediary Bank Any bank to which an item is transferred in the course of collection, except the depositary or payor bank.

DESIGNATIONS OF BANKS INVOLVED IN THE COLLECTION PROCESS   The first bank to receive a check for payment is the **depositary bank**.[10] For example, when a person deposits an IRS tax-refund check into a personal checking account at the local bank, that bank is the depositary bank. The bank on which a check is drawn (the drawee bank) is called the **payor bank**. Any bank except the payor bank that handles a check during some phase of the collection process is a **collecting bank**. Any bank except the payor bank or the depositary bank to which an item is transferred in the course of this collection process is called an **intermediary bank**.

During the collection process, any bank can take on one or more of the various roles of depositary, payor, collecting, and intermediary bank. **EXAMPLE 19.8** A buyer in New York writes a check on her New York bank and sends it to a seller in San Francisco. The seller deposits the check in her San Francisco bank account. The seller's bank is both a *depositary bank* and a *collecting bank*. The buyer's bank in New York is the *payor bank*. As the check travels from San Francisco to New York, any collecting bank handling the item in the collection process (other than the depositary bank and the payor bank) is also called an *intermediary bank*. Exhibit 19–4 on page 485 illustrates how various banks function in the collection process in the context of this example. ●

CHECK COLLECTION BETWEEN CUSTOMERS OF THE SAME BANK   An item that is payable by the depositary bank (also the payor bank) that receives it is called an "on-us item." If

---

10. All definitions in this section are found in UCC 4–105. The terms *depositary* and *depository* have different meanings in the banking context. A depository bank refers to a *physical place* (a bank or other institution) in which deposits or funds are held or stored.

Landmark in the Law   Check Clearing in the 21st Century Act (Check 21)

In the traditional collection process, paper checks had to be physically transported before they could be cleared. To streamline this costly and time-consuming process and improve the overall efficiency of the nation's payment system, Congress passed the Check Clearing in the 21st Century Act (Check 21).

Purpose of Check 21   Before the implementation of Check 21, banks had to present the original paper check for payment in the absence of an agreement for presentment in some other form. Although the Uniform Commercial Code authorizes banks to use other means of presentment, such as electronic presentment, a broad-based system of electronic presentment failed to develop because it required agreements among individual banks.[a] Check 21 has changed this situation by creating a new negotiable instrument called a *substitute check.* Although the act does not require banks to change their current check-collection practices, the creation of substitute checks certainly facilitates the use of electronic check processing.

Substitute Checks   A substitute check is a paper reproduction of the front and back of an original check that contains all of the same information required on checks for automated processing. Banks create a substitute check from a digital image of an original check. In essence, those financial institutions that exchange digital images of checks do not have to send the original paper checks. They can simply transmit the information electronically and replace the original checks with the substitute checks. Banks that do not exchange checks electronically are required to accept substitute checks in the same way that they accept original checks.

By eliminating the original check after a substitute check is created, the financial system can prevent the check from being paid twice and reduce the expense of paper storage and retrieval. Nevertheless, at least for quite a while, not all checks will be converted to substitute checks. Thus, if a bank returns canceled checks to deposit holders at the end of each month, some of those returned checks may be substitute checks, and some may be original canceled paper checks.

The New System Means Reduced "Float" Time   Sometimes, individuals and businesses write checks even though they have insufficient funds in their accounts to cover those checks. Such check writers are relying on "float," or the time between when a check is written and when the amount is actually deducted from the account. When all checks had to be physically transported, the float time could be several days, but as Check 21 has been implemented, the time required to process checks (the float time) has been substantially reduced. Consequently, account holders who plan to cover their checks after writing them have experienced unexpected overdrafts.

Faster Access to Funds   The Expedited Funds Availability Act required that the Federal Reserve Board revise the availability schedule for funds from deposited checks to correspond to reductions in check-processing time.[b] Therefore, as the speed of check processing increases under Check 21, the Federal Reserve Board will reduce the maximum time that a bank can hold funds from deposited checks before making them available to the depositor. Thus, account holders will have faster access to their deposited funds.

• **Application to Today's World**   *As more financial institutions make agreements to transfer digital images of checks, the check-processing system will become more efficient and therefore less costly, affecting banking fees everywhere. Customers increasingly will be unable to rely on banking float when they are low on funds, so they should make sure that funds are available to cover checks when they are written. No customers can opt out of Check 21 and demand that their original canceled checks be returned with their monthly statements, nor can they refuse to accept a substitute check as proof of payment.*

• **Relevant Web Sites**   To locate information on the Web concerning Check 21, go to this text's Web site at www.cengage.com/blaw/blt, select "Chapter 19," and click on "URLs for Landmarks."

---

a. UCC 3–501(b)(2) and 4–110.

b. 12 U.S.C. Sections 4001–4010.

the bank does not dishonor the check by the opening of the second banking day following its receipt, the check is considered paid [UCC 4–215(e)(2)].

CHECK COLLECTION BETWEEN CUSTOMERS OF DIFFERENT BANKS   Once a depositary bank receives a check, it must arrange to present it either directly or through intermediary banks to the appropriate payor bank. Each bank in the collection chain must pass the check on before midnight of the next banking day following its receipt [UCC 4–202(b)].[11] A "banking day" is any part of a day that the bank is open to carry on substantially all

---

11. A bank may take a "reasonably longer time" in certain circumstances, such as when the bank's computer system is down due to a power failure, but the bank must show that its action is still timely [UCC 4–202(b)].

• *Exhibit* 19–4 The Check-Collection Process

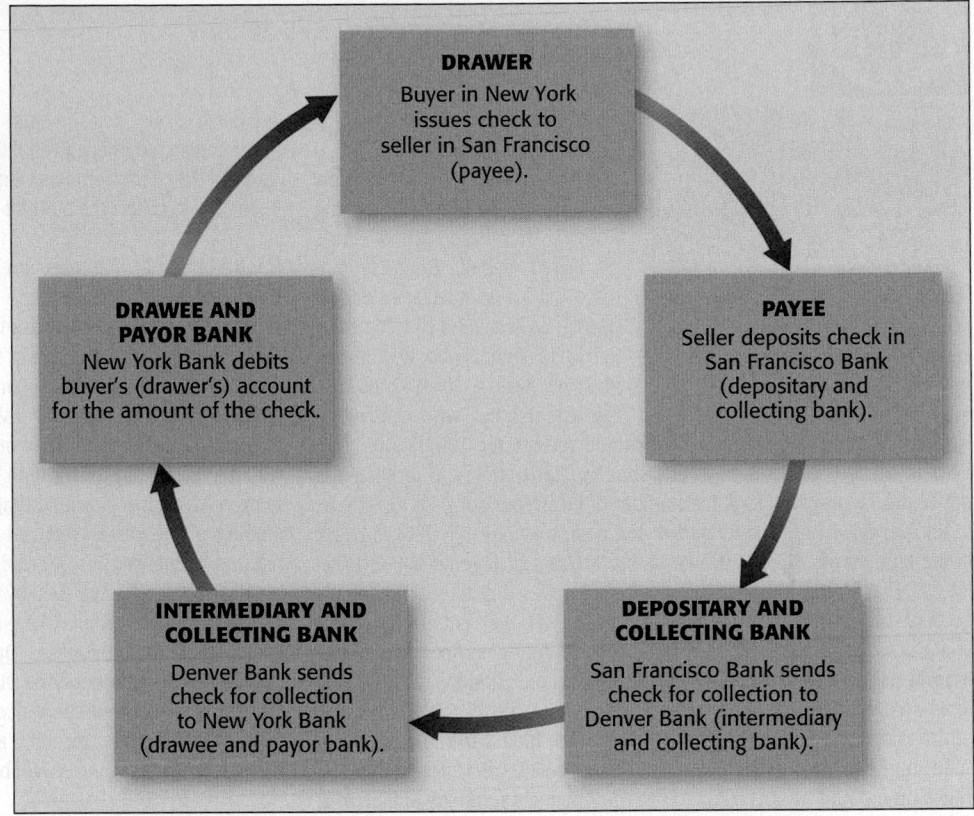

DRAWER
Buyer in New York
issues check to
seller in San Francisco
(payee).

PAYEE
Seller deposits check in
San Francisco Bank
(depositary and
collecting bank).

**DEPOSITARY AND
COLLECTING BANK**
San Francisco Bank sends
check for collection to
Denver Bank (intermediary
and collecting bank).

**INTERMEDIARY AND
COLLECTING BANK**
Denver Bank sends
check for collection
to New York Bank
(drawee and payor bank).

**DRAWEE AND
PAYOR BANK**
New York Bank debits
buyer's (drawer's) account
for the amount of the check.

of its banking functions. Thus, if only a bank's drive-through facilities are open, a check deposited on Saturday would not trigger the bank's midnight deadline until the following Monday. When the check reaches the payor bank, that bank is liable for the face amount of the check, unless the payor bank dishonors the check or returns it by midnight on the next banking day following receipt [UCC 4–302].[12]

Because of this deadline and because banks need to maintain an even work flow in the many items they handle daily, the UCC permits what is called *deferred posting*. According to UCC 4–108, "a bank may fix an afternoon hour of 2:00 P.M. or later as a cutoff hour for the handling of money and items and the making of entries on its books." Any checks received after that hour "may be treated as being received at the opening of the next banking day." Thus, if a bank's "cutoff hour" is 3:00 P.M., a check received by a payor bank at 4:00 P.M. on Monday would be deferred for posting until Tuesday. In this situation, the payor bank's deadline would be midnight Wednesday.

Does a delay of more than one month in a bank's notice to its customer that a check deposited in his account is counterfeit reduce the customer's liability for overdrafts in his account? That was the customer's contention in the following case.

---

12. Most checks are cleared by a computerized process, and communication and computer facilities may fail because of electrical outages, equipment malfunction, or other conditions. A bank may be "excused" from liability for failing to meet its midnight deadline if such conditions arise and the bank has exercised "such diligence as the circumstances require" [UCC 4–109(d)].

Case 19.3   Bank One, N.A. v. Dunn

Court of Appeal of Louisiana, Second Circuit, 927 So.2d 645 (2006).

Is a bank liable to its customer for a delay in determining the counterfeit nature of a check?

FACTS   Floyd Dunn, a U.S. citizen, was hired to lobby in the United States for Zaire (now the Democratic Republic of the Congo). After three years of efforts on Zaire's behalf, Dunn submitted a bill for $500,000. Instead of paying, Zaire agreed to trade computers to Dunn, who was to sell them to Nigeria for $32,100,000. "Senator Frank," who claimed to be from Nigeria, told Dunn that he would receive the $32,100,000 after he paid alleged "back taxes" to that country. Frank offered to facilitate the payments. Dunn gave Frank the number of his account at Bank One, N.A., in Shreveport, Louisiana. As part of the deal, on August 1, 2001, a check in the amount of $315,000 drawn on the account of Argenbright Security, Inc., at First Union National Bank of Georgia was deposited into Dunn's account—which had never held more than $5,000—and sent out for collection. Because the check contained an incorrect routing number, its processing was delayed. Meanwhile, on Frank's instructions, Dunn wired $277,000 to an account at a Virginia bank. On September 24, the $315,000 check was returned to Bank One as counterfeit. Bank One filed a suit in a Louisiana state court against Dunn, alleging that he owed $281,019.11, the amount by which his account was overdrawn. The court issued a summary judgment in Bank One's favor. Dunn appealed to a state intermediate appellate court.

ISSUE   Is a bank liable to its customer for a delay in determining the counterfeit nature of a check?

DECISION   No. The state intermediate appellate court affirmed the lower court's judgment. Even if Dunn had received notice of the counterfeit status of the check from Bank One before September 24, he would not have been able to collect the amount of the check from Argenbright Security.

REASON   In the collection process, a bank is required to pass on a check before midnight of the next banking day following the check's receipt. The appellate court acknowledged that under UCC 4–202, the bank must "exercise ordinary care in sending a notice of dishonor after learning that the item has not been paid or accepted." The court explained that "[n]otifying the customer of dishonor after the bank's midnight deadline may constitute the exercise of ordinary care if the bank took proper action within a reasonably longer time." Of course, the bank is liable for its failure to exercise ordinary care. In that situation, the measure of damages is the amount of the check "reduced by an amount that could not have been realized by the exercise of ordinary care." In other words, if a check could not have been collected even by the use of ordinary care, the recovery for a failure to exercise ordinary care is reduced by the amount of the uncollectible check. Thus, in this case, "Dunn's liability is not diminished because of Bank One's delay in notifying Dunn that the check was counterfeit. Even if Dunn had received earlier notice from Bank One that the check was counterfeit, he still had no recourse against Argenbright Security. The $315,000 was uncollectible against Argenbright Security."

FOR CRITICAL ANALYSIS—Ethical Consideration
Does a bank have a duty to protect its customers from their own naïveté, as exemplified in this case by Dunn's giving his bank account information to someone he did not know? Why or why not?

Federal Reserve System   A network of twelve district banks and related branches located around the country and headed by the Federal Reserve Board of Governors. Most banks in the United States have Federal Reserve accounts.

Clearinghouse   A system or place where banks exchange checks and drafts drawn on each other and settle daily balances.

ON THE WEB   You can obtain extensive information about the Federal Reserve System by accessing "the Fed's" home page at www.federalreserve.gov.

HOW THE FEDERAL RESERVE SYSTEM CLEARS CHECKS   The **Federal Reserve System** is a network of twelve district banks, which are located around the country and headed by the Federal Reserve Board of Governors. Most banks in the United States have Federal Reserve accounts. The Federal Reserve System has greatly simplified the check-collection process by acting as a **clearinghouse**—a system or a place where banks exchange checks and drafts drawn on each other and settle daily balances.

EXAMPLE 19.9   Pamela Moy of Philadelphia writes a check to Jeanne Sutton in San Francisco. When Sutton receives the check in the mail, she deposits it in her bank. Her bank then deposits the check in the Federal Reserve Bank of San Francisco, which transfers it to the Federal Reserve Bank of Philadelphia. That Federal Reserve bank then sends the check to Moy's bank, which deducts the amount of the check from Moy's account. ●

ELECTRONIC CHECK PRESENTMENT   In the past, most checks were processed manually—the employees of each bank in the collection chain would physically handle each check that passed through the bank for collection or payment. Today, most checks are processed electronically, which has been facilitated by Check 21, as described in the *Landmark in the Law* feature on page 484. Whereas manual check processing can take days, *electronic* *check presentment* can be done on the day of deposit. Items are encoded with information (such as the amount of the check) that is read and processed by other banks' computers. In some situations, a check may be retained at its place of deposit, and only its image or description is presented for payment under an electronic presentment agreement [UCC 4–110].[13]

A bank that encodes information on an item warrants to any subsequent bank or payor that the encoded information is correct [UCC 4–209]. This is also true for a bank that retains an item while transmitting its image or information describing it as presentation for payment.

Regulation CC provides that a returned check must be encoded with the routing number of the depositary bank, the amount of the check, and other information and adds that this "does not affect a paying bank's responsibility to return a check within the deadlines required by the U.C.C." Under UCC 4–301(d)(2), an item is returned "when it is sent or delivered to the bank's customer or transferor or pursuant to his [or her] instructions."

▶ Electronic Fund Transfers

Electronic Fund Transfer (EFT) A transfer of funds through the use of an electronic terminal, a telephone, a computer, or magnetic tape.

The application of computer technology to banking, in the form of electronic fund transfer systems, has helped to relieve banking institutions of the burden of having to move mountains of paperwork to process fund transfers. An **electronic fund transfer (EFT)** is a transfer of funds through the use of an electronic terminal, a telephone, a computer, or magnetic tape. The law governing EFTs depends on the type of transfer involved. Consumer fund transfers are governed by the Electronic Fund Transfer Act (EFTA) of 1978.[14] Commercial fund transfers are governed by Article 4A of the UCC.

Although electronic banking offers numerous benefits, it also poses difficulties on occasion. It is difficult to issue stop-payment orders with electronic banking. Also, fewer records are available to prove or disprove that a transaction took place. The possibilities for tampering with a person's private banking information have also increased.

Types of EFT Systems

"*I saw a bank that said '24-Hour Banking,' but I don't have that much time.*"
Steven Wright, 1955–present
(American comedian)

Most banks today offer EFT services to their customers. The following are the most common types of EFT systems used by bank customers:

1. *Automated teller machines* (ATMs)—The machines are connected online to the bank's computers. A customer inserts a plastic card (called an *ATM* or *debit card*) issued by the bank and keys in a *personal identification number* (PIN) to access her or his accounts and conduct banking transactions.
2. *Point-of-sale systems*—Online terminals allow consumers to transfer funds to merchants to pay for purchases using a debit card.
3. *Direct deposits and withdrawals*—Customers can authorize the bank to allow another party—such as the government or an employer—to make direct deposits into their accounts. Similarly, customers can request the bank to make automatic payments to a third party at regular, recurrent intervals from the customer's funds (insurance premiums or loan payments, for example).
4. *Internet payment systems*—Many financial institutions permit their customers to access the institution's computer system via the Internet and direct a transfer of funds between accounts or pay a particular bill, such as a utility bill, for example.

---

13. This section of the UCC assumes that no bank will participate in an electronic presentment program without an express agreement (which is no longer true since Check 21 went into effect). See Comment 2 to UCC 4–110.
14. 15 U.S.C. Sections 1693–1693r. The EFTA amended Title IX of the Consumer Credit Protection Act.

Regulation E A set of rules issued by the Federal Reserve System's Board of Governors to protect users of electronic fund transfer systems.

Consumer Fund Transfers

The Electronic Fund Transfer Act (EFTA) provides a basic framework for the rights, liabilities, and responsibilities of users of EFT systems. Additionally, the act gave the Federal Reserve Board authority to issue rules and regulations to help implement the act's provisions. The Federal Reserve Board's implemental regulation is called **Regulation E.**

The EFTA governs financial institutions that offer electronic fund transfers involving consumer accounts. The types of accounts covered include checking accounts, savings accounts, and any other asset accounts established for personal, family, or household purposes. Telephone transfers are covered by the EFTA only if they are made in accordance with a prearranged plan under which periodic or recurring transfers are contemplated.

DISCLOSURE REQUIREMENTS   The EFTA is essentially a disclosure law benefiting consumers. The act requires financial institutions to inform consumers of their rights and responsibilities, including those listed here, with respect to EFT systems.

1. If a customer's debit card is lost or stolen and used without his or her permission, the customer may be required to pay no more than $50. The customer, however, must notify the bank of the loss or theft within two days of learning about it. Otherwise, the liability increases to $500. The customer may be liable for more than $500 if he or she does not report the unauthorized use within sixty days after it appears on the customer's statement. (If a customer voluntarily gives her or his debit card to another, who then uses it improperly, the protections just mentioned do not apply.)
2. The customer must discover any error on the monthly statement within sixty days and must notify the bank. The bank then has ten days to investigate and must report its conclusions to the customer in writing. If the bank takes longer than ten days, it must return the disputed amount to the customer's account until it finds the error. If there is no error, the customer has to return the disputed funds to the bank.
3. The bank must furnish receipts for transactions made through computer terminals, but it is not obligated to do so for telephone transfers.
4. The bank must provide a monthly statement for every month in which there is an electronic transfer of funds. Otherwise, the bank must provide statements every quarter. The statement must show the amount and date of the transfer, the names of the retailers or other third parties involved, the location or identification of the terminal, and the fees. Additionally, the statement must give an address and a phone number for inquiries and error notices.
5. Any preauthorized payment for utility bills and insurance premiums can be stopped three days before the scheduled transfer if the customer notifies the financial institution orally or in writing. (The institution may require the customer to provide written confirmation within fourteen days of an oral notification.)

BE CAREFUL The EFTA does not provide for the reversal of an electronic transfer of funds once it has occurred.

UNAUTHORIZED ELECTRONIC FUND TRANSFERS   Because of the vulnerability of EFT systems to fraudulent activities, the EFTA clearly defined what constitutes an unauthorized transfer. Under the act, a transfer is unauthorized if (1) it is initiated by a person other than the consumer who has no actual authority to initiate the transfer; (2) the consumer receives no benefit from it; and (3) the consumer did not furnish the person "with the card, code, or other means of access" to her or his account. Unauthorized access to an EFT system constitutes a federal felony, and those convicted may be fined up to $10,000 and sentenced to as long as ten years in prison.

VIOLATIONS AND DAMAGES   Banks must strictly comply with the terms of the EFTA and are liable for any failure to adhere to its provisions. For a bank's violation of the EFTA, a consumer may recover both actual damages (including attorneys' fees and costs) and punitive damages of not less than $100 and not more than $1,000. (Unlike actual damages, *punitive damages* are assessed to punish a defendant or to deter similar wrongdoers.) Failure to investigate an error in good faith makes the bank liable for treble damages (three times the amount of damages). Even when a customer has sustained no actual damage, the bank may be liable for legal costs and punitive damages if it fails to follow the proper procedures outlined by the EFTA in regard to error resolution.

Commercial Transfers

Funds are also transferred electronically "by wire" between commercial parties. In fact, the dollar volume of payments by wire transfer is more than $1 trillion a day—an amount that far exceeds the dollar volume of payments made by other means. The two major wire payment systems are the Federal Reserve's wire transfer network (Fedwire) and the New York Clearing House Interbank Payments Systems (CHIPS).

Commercial wire transfers are governed by Article 4A of the UCC, which has been adopted by most states (and is included in Appendix C). **EXAMPLE 19.10** Jellux, Inc., owes $5 million to Perot Corporation. Instead of sending Perot a check or some other instrument that would enable Perot to obtain payment, Jellux instructs its bank, East Bank, to credit $5 million to Perot's account in West Bank. East Bank debits Jellux's East Bank account and wires $5 million to Perot's West Bank account. In more complex transactions, additional banks would be involved. •

 E-Money and Online Banking

New forms of electronic payments (e-payments) have the potential to replace *physical* cash—coins and paper currency—with *virtual* cash in the form of electronic impulses. This is the unique promise of **digital cash,** which consists of funds stored on microchips and on other computer devices. Online banking has also become commonplace in today's world. In a few minutes, anybody with the proper software can access his or her account, transfer funds, write "checks," pay bills, monitor investments, and often even buy and sell stocks.

Various forms of electronic money, or **e-money,** are emerging. The simplest kind of e-money system uses **stored-value cards.** These are plastic cards embossed with magnetic strips containing magnetically encoded data. In some applications, a stored-value card can be used only to purchase specific goods and services offered by the card issuer. **Smart cards** are plastic cards containing computer microchips that can hold more information than a magnetic strip. A smart card carries and processes security programming. This capability gives smart cards a technical advantage over stored-value cards. The microprocessors on smart cards can also authenticate the validity of transactions. Retailers can program electronic cash registers to confirm the authenticity of a smart card by examining a unique digital signature stored on its microchip. (Digital signatures were discussed in Chapter 10.)

Online Banking Services

Most customers use three kinds of online banking services: bill consolidation and payment, transferring funds among accounts, and applying for loans. Customers typically have to appear in person to finalize the terms of a loan, however.

Two important banking activities generally are not yet available online: depositing and withdrawing funds. With smart cards, people could transfer funds on the Internet, thereby effectively transforming their personal computers into ATMs. Many observers believe that online banking is the way to introduce people to e-money and smart cards.

Since the late 1990s, several banks have operated exclusively on the Internet. These "virtual banks" have no physical branch offices. Because few people are equipped to send

---

NOTE If any part of an electronic fund transfer is covered by the EFTA, the entire transfer is excluded from UCC Article 4A.

Digital Cash Funds contained on computer software, in the form of secure programs stored on microchips and on other computer devices.

E-Money Prepaid funds recorded on a computer or a card (such as a smart card or a stored-value card).

Stored-Value Card A card bearing a magnetic strip that holds magnetically encoded data, providing access to stored funds.

Smart Card A card containing a microprocessor that permits storage of funds via security programming, can communicate with other computers, and does not require online authorization for fund transfers.

ON THE WEB For tips on how to bank over the Internet safely, read the information provided by the Federal Deposit Insurance Corporation (FDIC) at **www.fdic.gov/bank/individual/online/safe.html**.

funds to virtual banks via smart-card technology, the virtual banks have accepted deposits through physical delivery systems, such as the U.S. Postal Service or FedEx.

Privacy Protection

At the present time, it is not clear which, if any, laws apply to the security of e-money payment information and e-money issuers' financial records. The Federal Reserve has decided not to impose Regulation E, which governs certain electronic fund transfers, on e-money transactions. Federal laws prohibiting unauthorized access to electronic communications might apply, however. For instance, the Electronic Communications Privacy Act of 1986[15] prohibits any person from knowingly divulging to any other person the contents of an electronic communication while that communication is in transmission or in electronic storage.

E-MONEY ISSUERS' FINANCIAL RECORDS   Under the Right to Financial Privacy Act of 1978,[16] before a financial institution may give financial information about you to a federal agency, you must explicitly consent. If you do not, a federal agency wishing to access your financial records must obtain a warrant. A digital cash issuer may be subject to this act if that issuer is deemed to be (1) a bank by virtue of its holding customer funds or (2) any entity that issues a physical card similar to a credit or debit card.

CONSUMER FINANCIAL DATA   In 1999, Congress passed the Financial Services Modernization Act,[17] also known as the Gramm-Leach-Bliley Act, in an attempt to delineate how financial institutions can treat customer data. In general, the act and its rules[18] place restrictions and obligations on financial institutions to protect consumer data and privacy. Every financial institution must provide its customers with information on its privacy policies and practices. No financial institution can disclose nonpublic personal information about a consumer to an unaffiliated third party unless the act's disclosure and opt-out requirements are met.

---

15. 18 U.S.C. Sections 2510–2521.
16. 12 U.S.C. Sections 3401 *et seq.*
17. 12 U.S.C. Sections 24a, 248b, 1820a, 1828b, 1831v–1831y, 1848a, 2908, 4809; 15 U.S.C. Sections 80b-10a, 6701, 6711–6717, 6731–6735, 6751–6766, 6781, 6801–6809, 6821–6827, 6901–6910; and others.
18. 12 C.F.R. Part 40.

 Reviewing . . . Checks and Banking in the Digital Age

RPM Pizza, Inc., issued a check for $96,000 to Systems Marketing for an advertising campaign. A few days later, RPM decided not to go through with the deal and placed a written stop-payment order on the check. RPM and Systems had no further contact for many months. Three weeks after the stop-payment order expired, however, Toby Rierson, an employee at Systems, cashed the check. Bank One Cambridge, RPM's bank, paid the check with funds from RPM's account. Because the check was more than six months old, it was stale, and thus, according to standard banking procedures as well as Bank One's own policies, the signature on the check should have been specially verified, but it was not. RPM filed a suit in a federal district court against Bank One to recover the amount of the check. Using the information presented in the chapter, answer the following questions.

1. How long is a written stop-payment order effective? What could RPM have done to further prevent this check from being cashed?
2. What would happen if it turned out that RPM did not have a legitimate reason for stopping payment on the check?
3. What are a bank's obligations with respect to stale checks?
4. Would a court be likely to hold the bank liable for the amount of the check because it failed to verify the signature on the check? Why or why not?

Linking the Law *to Economics*

Banking in a Period of Crisis

In this chapter, you learned about the bank-customer relationship as well as a bank's duty to honor checks and accept deposits. In the macroeconomics courses that your business school offers, the focus on the banking sector is quite different. At a minimum, the courses examine banking panics and what they did to the economy. During the recession that started in December 2007, the federal government wanted to make sure that no banking panics would occur.

Preventing Bank Runs

A *bank run* occurs when depositors simultaneously rush to convert their bank deposits into currency. Bank runs take place when depositors believe that the assets of their bank are not sufficient to cover its liabilities—the customers' deposits. The largest number of bank runs in modern history occurred during the Great Depression in the 1930s when nine thousand banks failed. In 1933, the federal government set up a system of deposit insurance to prevent bank runs.

Enter Deposit Insurance

The Federal Deposit Insurance Corporation (FDIC) and the Federal Savings and Loan Insurance Corporation (FSLIC) were created in the 1930s to insure deposits and prevent bank runs. In 1971, the National Credit Union Shares Insurance Fund (NCUSIF) was added to insure credit union deposits. Although the names and form of some of these organizations have changed over the years, the principle remains the same: to insure all accounts in banks, savings and loan associations, and credit unions against losses up to a specified limit. In 1933, each account was insured up to $2,500. In 2008, the insurance limit reached $250,000. Although federal insurance for bank deposits may seem like a good idea, there are problems associated with it.

Adverse Selection:
An Unintended Consequence of Deposit Insurance

Since the creation of deposit insurance, few, if any, depositors ever examine the financial condition or lending activities of the depository institutions in which they have checking and savings accounts. Depositors no longer have any substantial incentive to investigate the track record of the owners and managers of banks. Consequently, since 1933 the marketplace does little to monitor or punish past performances of owners or managers of depository institutions. As a result, we tend to see *adverse selection*—

instead of banks being owned and operated by individuals who are prudent and make careful decisions on behalf of depositors, many banks are being run by managers who have a high tolerance for taking big risks with other people's money and are good at selling those risks to them.

Moral Hazard:
Another Unintended Consequence of Deposit Insurance

In your finance courses in business school, you learn that the riskier the loan, the higher the interest rate that a lending institution can charge the borrower. Bank managers must weigh the trade-off between risk and return when deciding which loan applicants should receive funds. Poor credit risks offer high profits, assuming that they actually pay off their debts. Good credit risks are more likely to pay their debts, but can obtain loans at lower rates.

Particularly since the fall of 2008 when the federal deposit insurance limit was increased to $250,000 per account, depository institution managers have had a greater incentive to make risky loans. Why? The reason is that by doing so, in the short run the banks make higher profits, and the managers receive higher salaries and bonuses. If some of these risky loans are not repaid, what is the likely outcome? The banks' losses are limited because the federal government—you, the taxpayer—will cover any shortfall between the banks' assets and their liabilities. Consequently, federal deposit insurance means that banks get to enjoy all of the profits of risk taking without bearing all of the consequences of that risk taking.

Thus, another unintended consequence of federal deposit insurance is to encourage *moral hazard.* Bank managers have an incentive to take more risks in their lending policies than they otherwise would. After deposit insurance limits were increased to $250,000 during the latest economic crisis, confidence in banks was renewed, and depositors were encouraged to keep more funds in banks. The bad news will be forthcoming in the long run—these higher deposit insurance limits will encourage both adverse selection (more risk-favoring bank managers) and moral hazard (more risk taking by bank managers).

FOR CRITICAL ANALYSIS

Imagine the United States without federal deposit insurance. What are some of the mechanisms that would arise to "punish" bank managers who acted irresponsibly?

 Key Terms

cashier's check 472
certified check 474

check 471
clearinghouse 486

collecting bank 483
depositary bank 483

digital cash 489
electronic fund transfer (EFT) 487
e-money 489
Federal Reserve System 486
intermediary bank 483

overdraft 475
payor bank 483
Regulation E 488
smart card 489
stale check 476

stop-payment order 476
stored-value card 489
traveler's check 473

 ## Chapter Summary: Checks and Banking in the Digital Age

Checks (See pages 471–474.)	1. *Cashier's check*—A check drawn by a bank on itself (the bank is both the drawer and the drawee) and purchased by a customer. In effect, the bank assumes responsibility for paying the check, thus making the check nearly the equivalent of cash. 2. *Traveler's check*—An instrument on which a financial institution is both the drawer and the drawee. The purchaser must provide his or her signature as a countersignature for a traveler's check to become a negotiable instrument. 3. *Certified check*—A check for which the drawee bank certifies in writing that it has set aside funds from the drawer's account to ensure payment of the check on presentation. On certification, the drawer and all prior indorsers are completely discharged from liability on the check.
The Bank-Customer Relationship (See pages 474–475.)	1. *Creditor-debtor relationship*—The bank and its customer have a creditor-debtor relationship (the bank is the debtor because it holds the customer's funds on deposit). 2. *Agency relationship*—Because a bank must act in accordance with the customer's orders in regard to the customer's deposited money, an agency relationship also arises—the bank is the agent for the customer, who is the principal. 3. *Contractual relationship*—The bank's relationship with its customer is also contractual; both the bank and the customer assume certain contractual duties when a customer opens a bank account.
Bank's Duty to Honor Checks (See pages 475–481.)	Generally, a bank has a duty to honor its customers' checks, provided that the customers have sufficient funds on deposit to cover the checks [UCC 4–401(a)]. The bank is liable to its customers for actual damages proved to be due to wrongful dishonor. The bank's duty to honor its customers' checks is not absolute. See the *Concept Summary* on page 482 for a detailed list of the rights and liabilities of the bank and the customer in various situations, such as overdrafts and forged signatures.

Bank's Duty to Accept Deposits
(See pages 481–487.)
	A bank has a duty to accept deposits made by its customers into their accounts. Funds represented by checks deposited must be made available to customers according to a schedule mandated by the Expedited Funds Availability Act of 1987 and Regulation CC. A bank also has a duty to collect payment on any checks deposited by its customers. When checks deposited by customers are drawn on other banks, the check-collection process comes into play.
	1. *Definitions of banks*—UCC 4–105 provides the following definitions of banks involved in the collection process:
	   a. Depositary bank—The first bank to accept a check for payment.
	   b. Payor bank—The bank on which a check is drawn.
	   c. Collecting bank—Any bank except the payor bank that handles a check during the collection process.
	   d. Intermediary bank—Any bank except the payor bank or the depositary bank to which an item is transferred in the course of the collection process.
	2. *Check collection between customers of the same bank*—A check payable by the depositary bank that receives it is an "on-us item"; if the bank does not dishonor the check by the opening of the second banking day following its receipt, the check is considered paid [UCC 4–215(e)(2)].
	3. *Check collection between customers of different banks*—Each bank in the collection process must pass the check on to the next appropriate bank before midnight of the next banking day following its receipt [UCC 4–108, 4–202(b), 4–302].
	4. *How the Federal Reserve System clears checks*—The Federal Reserve System facilitates the check-clearing process by serving as a clearinghouse for checks.

Chapter Summary: Checks and Banking in the Digital Age–Continued

Bank's Duty to Accept Deposits–Continued	5. *Electronic check presentment*–When checks are presented electronically, items are encoded with information (such as the amount of the check) that is read and processed by other banks' computers. In some situations, a check may be retained at its place of deposit, and only its image or information describing it is presented for payment under a Federal Reserve agreement, clearinghouse rule, or other agreement [UCC 4–110].

Electronic Fund Transfers (See pages 487–489.)	1. *Types of EFT systems*–
	    a. Automated teller machines (ATMs).
	    b. Point-of-sale systems.
	    c. Direct deposits and withdrawals.
	    d. Internet payment systems.
	2. *Consumer fund transfers*–Consumer fund transfers are governed by the Electronic Fund Transfer Act (EFTA) of 1978. The EFTA is basically a disclosure law that sets forth the rights and duties of the bank and the customer with respect to EFT systems. Banks must comply strictly with EFTA requirements.
	3. *Commercial transfers*–Article 4A of the UCC, which has been adopted by almost all of the states, governs fund transfers not subject to the EFTA or other federal or state statutes.

E-Money and Online Banking (See pages 489–490.)	1. *New forms of e-payments*–These include stored-value cards and smart cards.
	2. *Current online banking services*–
	    a. Bill consolidation and payment.
	    b. Transferring funds among accounts.
	    c. Applying for loans.
	3. *Privacy protection*–It is not clear which laws apply to the security of e-money payment information and e-money issuers' financial records. The Financial Services Modernization Act (the Gramm-Leach-Bliley Act) outlines how financial institutions can treat consumer data in general. The Right to Financial Privacy Act may also apply.

 ExamPrep

ISSUE SPOTTERS

1 Lyn writes a check for $900 to Mac, who indorses the check in blank and transfers it to Nan. She presents the check to Omega Bank, the drawee bank, for payment. Omega does not honor the check. Is Lyn liable to Nan? Could Lyn be subject to criminal prosecution? Why or why not?

2 Roni writes a check for $700 to Sela. Sela indorses the check in blank and transfers it to Titus, who alters the check to read $7,000 and presents it to Union Bank, the drawee, for payment. The bank cashes it. Roni discovers the alteration and sues the bank. How much, if anything, can Roni recover? From whom can the bank recover this amount?

BEFORE THE TEST

Check your answers to the Issue Spotters, and at the same time, take the interactive quiz for this chapter. Go to **www.cengage.com/blaw/blt** and click on "Chapter 19." First, click on "Answers to Issue Spotters" to check your answers. Next, click on "Interactive Quiz" to assess your mastery of the concepts in this chapter. Then click on "Flashcards" to review this chapter's Key Term definitions.

 For Review

Answers for the even-numbered questions in this For Review section can be found on this text's accompanying Web site at **www.cengage.com/blaw/blt**. *Select "Chapter 19" and click on "For Review."*

1 What type of check does a bank agree in advance to accept when the check is presented for payment?

2 When may a bank properly dishonor a customer's check without the bank being liable to the customer?

3 What duties does the Uniform Commercial Code impose on a bank's customers with regard to forged and altered checks? What are the consequences if a customer is negligent in performing those duties?

4 What are the four most common types of electronic fund transfers?

5 What laws apply to e-money transactions and online banking services?

▶ Hypothetical Scenarios and Case Problems

19–1 Forged Checks. Roy Supply, Inc., and R. M. R. Drywall, Inc., had checking accounts at Wells Fargo Bank. Both accounts required all checks to carry two signatures—that of Edward Roy and that of Twila June Moore, both of whom were executive officers of both companies. Between January 2006 and March 2008, the bank honored hundreds of checks on which Roy's signature was forged by Moore. On January 31, 2009, Roy and the two corporations notified the bank of the forgeries and then filed a suit in a California state court against the bank, alleging negligence. Who is liable for the amounts of the forged checks? Why?

19–2 **Hypothetical Question with Sample Answer** iBank operates exclusively on the Web with no physical branch offices. Although some of iBank's business is transacted with smart-card technology, most of its business with its customers is conducted through the mail. iBank offers free checking, no-fee money market accounts, mortgage refinancing, and other services. With what regulation covering banks might iBank find it difficult to comply, and what is the difficulty?

—**For a sample answer to Question 19–2, go to Appendix E at the end of this text.**

19–3 Bank's Duty to Honor Checks. On January 5, Brian drafts a check for $3,000 drawn on Southern Marine Bank and payable to his assistant, Shanta. Brian puts last year's date on the check by mistake. On January 7, before Shanta has had a chance to go to the bank, Brian is killed in an automobile accident. Southern Marine Bank is aware of Brian's death. On January 10, Shanta presents the check to the bank, and the bank honors the check by payment to Shanta. Later, Brian's widow, Joyce, claims that because the bank knew of Brian's death and also because the check was by date over one year old, the bank acted wrongfully when it paid Shanta. Joyce, as executor of Brian's estate and sole heir by his will, demands that Southern Marine Bank recredit Brian's estate for the check paid to Shanta. Discuss fully Southern Marine's liability in light of Joyce's demand.

19–4 Forged Signatures. Cynthia Stafford worked as an administrative professional at Gerber & Gerber, P.C. (professional corporation), a law firm, for more than two years. During that time, she stole ten checks payable to Gerber & Gerber (G&G), which she indorsed in blank by forging one of the attorney's signatures. She then indorsed the forged checks in her name and deposited them in her account at Regions Bank. Over the same period, G&G deposited in its accounts at Regions Bank thousands of checks amounting to $300 million to $400 million.

Each G&G check was indorsed with a rubber stamp for deposit into the G&G account. The thefts were made possible in part because G&G kept unindorsed checks in an open file accessible to all employees and Stafford was sometimes the person assigned to stamp the checks. When the thefts were discovered, G&G filed a suit in a Georgia state court against Regions Bank to recover the stolen funds, alleging, among other things, negligence. Regions Bank filed a motion for summary judgment. What principles apply to attribute liability between these parties? How should the court rule on the bank's motion? Explain. [*Gerber & Gerber, P.C. v. Regions Bank,* 596 S.E.2d 174 (Ga.App. 2004)]

19–5 **Case Problem with Sample Answer** In December 1999, Jenny Triplett applied for a bookkeeping position with Spacemakers of America, Inc., in Atlanta, Georgia. Spacemakers hired Triplett and delegated to her all responsibility for maintaining the company checkbook and reconciling it with the monthly statements from SunTrust Bank. Triplett also handled invoices from vendors. Spacemakers' president, Dennis Rose, reviewed the invoices and signed the checks to pay them, but no other employee checked Triplett's work. By the end of her first full month of employment, Triplett had forged six checks totaling more than $22,000, all payable to Triple M Entertainment, which was not a Spacemakers vendor. By October 2000, Triplett had forged fifty-nine more checks, totaling more than $475,000. A SunTrust employee became suspicious of an item that required sight inspection under the bank's fraud detection standards, which exceeded those of other banks in the area. Triplett was arrested. Spacemakers filed a suit in a Georgia state court against SunTrust. The bank filed a motion for summary judgment. On what basis could the bank avoid liability? In whose favor should the court rule, and why? [*Spacemakers of America, Inc. v. SunTrust Bank,* 271 Ga.App. 335, 609 S.E.2d 683 (2005)]

—**After you have answered Problem 19–5, compare your answer with the sample answer given on the Web site that accompanies this text. Go to www.cengage.com/blaw/blt, select "Chapter 19," and click on "Case Problem with Sample Answer."**

19–6 Forged Indorsements. In 1994, Brian and Penny Grieme bought a house in Mandan, North Dakota. They borrowed for the purchase through a loan program financed by the North Dakota Housing Finance Agency (NDHFA). The Griemes obtained insurance for the house from Center Mutual Insurance Co. When a hailstorm damaged the house in 2001, Center Mutual determined that the loss was $4,378 and issued a check for that amount, drawn on Bremer Bank, N.A. The check's payees included Brian Grieme and the NDHFA. Grieme presented the check for payment to Wells Fargo Bank of Tempe, Arizona. The back of the check bore his signature and in hand-printed block letters the words "ND Housing Finance." The check was processed for collection and paid, and the canceled check was returned to Center Mutual. By the time the insurer learned that NDHFA's indorsement had been forged, the Griemes had canceled their policy, defaulted on their loan, and filed for bankruptcy. The NDHFA filed a suit in a North Dakota state court against Center Mutual for the amount of the check. Who is most likely to suffer the loss in this case? Why? [*State ex rel. North Dakota Housing Finance Agency v. Center Mutual Insurance Co.*, 720 N.W.2d 425 (N.Dak. 2006)]

19–7 Bank's Duty to Honor Checks. Sheila Bartell was arrested and subject to various charges related to burglary, the possession for sale of methamphetamine, and other crimes. She pleaded guilty in a California state court to some charges in exchange for the dismissal of others and an agreement to reimburse the victims. The victims included "Rita E.," who reported that her checkbook had been stolen and her signature forged on three checks totaling $590. Wells Fargo Bank had "covered" the checks and credited her account, however, so the court ordered Bartell to pay the bank. Bartell appealed, arguing that the bank was not entitled to restitution. What principles apply when a person forges a drawer's signature on a check? Is the bank entitled to recover from the defendant? Explain. [*People v. Bartell*, 170 Cal. App.4th 1258, 88 Cal.Rptr.3d 844 (3 Dist. 2009)]

19–8 **A Question of Ethics** *From the 1960s, James Johnson served as Bradley Union's personal caretaker and assistant, and was authorized by Union to handle his banking transactions. Louise Johnson, James's wife, wrote checks on Union's checking account to pay his bills, normally signing the checks "Brad Union." Branch Banking & Trust Co. (BB&T) managed Union's account. In December 2000, on the basis of Union's deteriorating mental and physical condition, a North Carolina state court declared him incompetent. Douglas Maxwell was appointed as Union's guardian. Maxwell "froze" Union's checking account and asked BB&T for copies of the canceled checks, which were provided by July 2001. Maxwell believed that Union's signature on the checks had been forged. In August 2002, Maxwell contacted BB&T, which refused to recredit Union's account. Maxwell filed a suit on Union's behalf in a North Carolina state court against BB&T.* [*Union v. Branch Banking & Trust Co.*, 176 N.C.App. 711, 627 S.E.2d 276 (2006)]

1 Before Maxwell's appointment, BB&T sent monthly statements and canceled checks to Union, and Johnson reviewed them, but no unauthorized signatures were ever reported. On whom can liability be imposed in the case of a forged drawer's signature on a check? What are the limits set by Section 4–406(f) of the Uniform Commercial Code? Should Johnson's position, Union's incompetence, or Maxwell's appointment affect the application of these principles? Explain.

2 Why was this suit brought against BB&T? Is BB&T liable? If not, who is? Why? Regardless of any violations of the law, did anyone act unethically in this case? If so, who and why?

 Critical Thinking and Writing Assignments

19–9 Critical Legal Thinking. Since the 1990 revision of Article 4, a bank is no longer required to include the customer's canceled checks when it sends monthly statements to the customer. A bank may simply itemize the checks (by number, date, and amount); it may provide photocopies of the checks as well but is not required to do so. What implications do the revised rules have for bank customers in terms of liability for unauthorized signatures and indorsements?

19–10 **Case Analysis Question** Go to Appendix F at the end of this text and examine Case No. 4 [*NBT Bank, N.A. v. First National Community Bank*, 393 F.3d 404 (3d Cir. 2004)]. This case has been excerpted there in great detail.

Review and then brief the case, making sure that your brief answers the following questions.

1 **Issue:** The main issue in this case concerned the effect of an item on the face of a check and a specific time period. What was the item, what was the time period, and what was the question?

2 **Rule of Law:** Liability was assessed in this case according to what rule of law?

3 **Applying the Rule of Law:** What was most significant to the court's determination of the measure of damages?

4 **Conclusion:** How did the court resolve the dispute among the parties in this case?

 Practical Internet Exercises

Go to this text's Web site at **www.cengage.com/blaw/blt**, select "Chapter 19," and click on "Practical Internet Exercises." There you will find the following Internet research exercises that you can perform to learn more about the topics covered in this chapter.

Practical Internet Exercise 19–1: Management Perspective—**Check Fraud**
Practical Internet Exercise 19–2: Legal Perspective—**Smart Cards**

Security Interests in Personal Property

"I will pay you some, and, as most debtors do, promise you infinitely."

—William Shakespeare, 1564–1616
(English dramatist and poet)

Chapter Outline

- The Terminology of Secured Transactions
- Creating a Security Interest
- Perfecting a Security Interest
- The Scope of a Security Interest
- Priorities
- Rights and Duties of Debtors and Creditors
- Default

(AP Photo/Toby Talbot)

Learning Objectives

After reading this chapter, you should be able to answer the following questions:

1. What is a security interest? Who is a secured party? What is a security agreement? What is a financing statement?

2. What three requirements must be met to create an enforceable security interest?

3. What is the most common method of perfecting a security interest under Article 9?

4. If two secured parties have perfected security interests in the collateral of the debtor, which party has priority to the collateral on the debtor's default?

5. What rights does a secured creditor have on the debtor's default?

Secured Transaction Any transaction in which the payment of a debt is guaranteed, or secured, by personal property owned by the debtor or in which the debtor has a legal interest.

ON THE WEB To find Article 9 of the UCC as adopted by a particular state, go to the Web site of Cornell University's Law School at www.law.cornell.edu/ucc/ucc.table.html.

Whenever the payment of a debt is guaranteed, or *secured,* by personal property owned by the debtor or in which the debtor has a legal interest, the transaction becomes known as a **secured transaction.** The concept of the secured transaction is as basic to modern business practice as the concept of credit. When buying or leasing goods, debtors frequently pay some portion of the price now and promise to pay the remainder in the future, as William Shakespeare observed in the chapter-opening quotation. Logically, sellers and lenders do not want to risk nonpayment, so they usually will not sell goods or lend funds unless the payment is somehow guaranteed. Indeed, business as we know it could not exist without laws permitting and governing secured transactions.

Article 9 of the Uniform Commercial Code (UCC) governs secured transactions in personal property. Personal property includes accounts, agricultural liens, *chattel paper* (any writing evidencing a debt secured by personal property), *fixtures* (certain property that is attached to land—see Chapter 36), instruments, and other types of intangible property, such as patents. Article 9 does not cover other creditor devices, such as liens and real estate mortgages, which will be discussed in Chapter 21. In this chapter, we first look at the terminology of secured transactions. We then discuss how the rights and duties of creditors and debtors are created and enforced under Article 9. As will become evident, the law of secured transactions tends to favor the rights of creditors, but it also offers debtors some protections, though to a lesser extent.

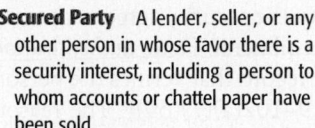 **The Terminology of Secured Transactions**

The UCC's terminology is now uniformly adopted in all documents used in situations involving secured transactions. A brief summary of the UCC's definitions of terms relating to secured transactions follows.

1. A **secured party** is any creditor who has a *security interest* in the *debtor's collateral*. This creditor can be a seller, a lender, a cosigner, or even a buyer of accounts or chattel paper [UCC 9–102(a)(72)].
2. A **debtor** is the "person" who *owes payment* or other performance of a secured obligation [UCC 9–102(a)(28)].
3. A **security interest** is the *interest* in the collateral (such as personal property or fixtures) that *secures payment or performance of an obligation* [UCC 1–201(37)].
4. A **security agreement** is an *agreement* that *creates* or provides for a *security interest* [UCC 9–102(a)(73)].
5. **Collateral** is the *subject* of the *security interest* [UCC 9–102(a)(12)].
6. A **financing statement**—referred to as the UCC-1 form—is the *instrument normally filed* to give *public notice* to *third parties* of the *secured party's security interest* [UCC 9–102(a)(39)].

These basic definitions form the concept under which a debtor-creditor relationship becomes a secured transaction relationship (see Exhibit 20–1).

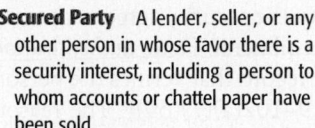 **Creating a Security Interest**

A creditor has two main concerns if the debtor **defaults** (fails to pay the debt as promised): (1) Can the debt be satisfied through the possession and (usually) sale of the collateral? (2) Will the creditor have priority over any other creditors or buyers who may have rights in the same collateral? These two concerns are met through the creation and perfection of a security interest. We begin by examining how a security interest is created.

To become a secured party, the creditor must obtain a security interest in the collateral of the debtor. Three requirements must be met for a creditor to have an enforceable security interest:

1. Unless the creditor has possession of the collateral, there must be a written or authenticated security agreement that clearly describes the collateral subject to the security interest and is signed or authenticated by the debtor.
2. The secured party must give something of value to the debtor.
3. The debtor must have "rights" in the collateral.

Secured Party   A lender, seller, or any other person in whose favor there is a security interest, including a person to whom accounts or chattel paper have been sold.

Debtor   Under Article 9 of the UCC, any party who owes payment or performance of a secured obligation, whether or not the party actually owns or has rights in the collateral.

Security Interest   Any interest in personal property or fixtures that secures payment or performance of an obligation.

Security Agreement   An agreement that creates or provides for a security interest between the debtor and a secured party.

Collateral   Under Article 9 of the UCC, the property subject to a security interest, including accounts and chattel paper that have been sold.

Financing Statement   A document prepared by a secured creditor, and filed with the appropriate state or local official, to give notice to the public that the creditor has a security interest in collateral belonging to the debtor named in the statement. The financing statement must contain the names and addresses of both the debtor and the secured party and must describe the collateral by type or item.

Default   Failure to observe a promise or discharge an obligation; commonly used to refer to failure to pay a debt when it is due.

● *Exhibit* **20–1** Secured Transactions–Concept and Terminology

In a security agreement, a debtor and a creditor agree that the creditor will have a security interest in collateral in which the debtor has rights. In essence, the collateral secures the loan and ensures the creditor of payment should the debtor default.

Attachment   In a secured transaction, the process by which a secured creditor's interest "attaches" to the property of another (collateral) and the creditor's security interest becomes enforceable.

Once these requirements have been met, the creditor's rights are said to attach to the collateral. **Attachment** gives the creditor an enforceable security interest in the collateral [UCC 9–203].[1]

Written or Authenticated Security Agreement

When the collateral is *not* in the possession of the secured party, the security agreement must be either written or authenticated, and it must describe the collateral. Here, *authentication* means to sign, execute, or adopt any symbol on an electronic record that verifies the person signing has the intent to adopt or accept the record [UCC 9–102(a)(7)(69)]. The reason authentication is acceptable is to provide for electronic filing (the filing process will be discussed later).

A security agreement must contain a description of the collateral that reasonably identifies it. Generally, such phrases as "all the debtor's personal property" or "all the debtor's assets" would *not* constitute a sufficient description [UCC 9–108(c)].

Secured Party Must Give Value

The secured party must give something of value to the debtor. Some examples of value include a binding commitment to extend credit or consideration to support a simple contract [UCC 1–204]. Normally, the value given by a secured party is in the form of a direct loan or a commitment to sell goods on credit.

Debtor Must Have Rights in the Collateral

The debtor must have rights in the collateral; that is, the debtor must have a current or a future ownership interest in or right to obtain possession of that collateral. For instance, a retail seller-debtor can give a secured party a security interest not only in existing inventory owned by the retailer but also in *future* inventory to be acquired by the retailer.

One common misconception about having rights in the collateral is that the debtor must have title. This is not a requirement. A beneficial interest in a trust (*trusts* will be discussed in Chapter 37), when the trustee holds title to the trust property, can be the subject of a security interest for a loan that a creditor makes to the beneficiary.

(©Adam Borkowski, 2009. Used under license from Shutterstock.com)

A retail clothing store may borrow funds using its existing and future inventory as collateral when agreeing to a security interest by the lender.

▶ Perfecting a Security Interest

Perfection   The legal process by which secured parties protect themselves against the claims of third parties who may wish to have their debts satisfied out of the same collateral; usually accomplished by filing a financing statement with the appropriate government official.

Perfection is the legal process by which secured parties protect themselves against the claims of third parties who may wish to have their debts satisfied out of the same collateral. Whether a secured party's security interest is perfected or unperfected can have serious consequences for the secured party if, for example, the debtor defaults on the debt or files for bankruptcy. What if the debtor has borrowed from two different creditors, using the same property as collateral for both loans? If the debtor defaults on both loans, which of the two creditors has first rights to the collateral? In this situation, the creditor with a perfected security interest will prevail.

---

1. Note that in the context of judicial liens, to be discussed in Chapter 21, the term *attachment* has a different meaning. In that context, it refers to a court-ordered seizure and taking into custody of property prior to the securing of a court judgment for a past-due debt.

Assume that this tractor is collateral for a bank loan. How would this collateral be classified—tangible or intangible?

Usually, perfection is accomplished by filing a financing statement with the office of the appropriate government official. In some circumstances, however, a security interest becomes perfected without the filing of a financing statement. Where or how a security interest is perfected sometimes depends on the type of collateral. Collateral is generally divided into two classifications: *tangible collateral* (collateral that can be seen, felt, and touched) and *intangible collateral* (collateral that consists of or generates rights). (See the *Business Application* feature at the end of this chapter for additional information on perfecting a security interest.)

Exhibit 20–2 on the next page summarizes the various classifications of collateral and the methods of perfecting a security interest in collateral falling within each of these classifications.[2]

Perfection by Filing

The most common means of perfection is by filing a *financing statement*—a document that gives public notice to third parties of the secured party's security interest—with the office of the appropriate government official. The security agreement itself can also be filed to perfect the security interest. The financing statement must provide the names of the debtor and the secured party, and must indicate the collateral covered by the financing statement. A uniform financing statement form is now used in all states [see UCC 9–521].

Communication of the financing statement to the appropriate filing office, together with the correct filing fee, or the acceptance of the financing statement by the filing officer constitutes a filing [UCC 9–516(a)]. The word *communication* means that the filing can be accomplished electronically [UCC 9–102(a)(18)]. Once completed, filings are indexed in the name of the debtor so that they can be located by subsequent searchers. A financing statement may be filed even before a security agreement is made or a security interest attaches [UCC 9–502(d)].

THE DEBTOR'S NAME The UCC requires that a financing statement be filed under the name of the debtor [UCC 9–502(a)(1)]. Slight variations in names normally will not be considered misleading if a search of the filing office's records, using a standard computer search engine routinely used by that office, would disclose the filings [UCC 9–506(c)].[3] If the debtor is identified by the correct name at the time of the filing of a financing statement, the secured party's interest retains its priority even if the debtor later changes his or her name. Because most states use electronic filing systems, UCC 9–503 sets out some detailed rules for determining when the debtor's name as it appears on a financing statement is sufficient.

Specific Types of Debtors. For corporations, which are organizations that have registered with the state, the debtor's name on the financing statement must be "the name of the debtor indicated on the public record of the debtor's jurisdiction of organization" [UCC 9–503(a)(1)]. If the debtor is a trust or a trustee with respect to property held in trust, the filed financing statement must disclose this information and must provide the trust's name

---

2. There are additional classifications, such as agricultural liens, investment property, and commercial tort claims. For definitions of these types of collateral, see UCC 9–102(a)(5), (a)(13), and (a)(49).

3. If the name listed in the financing statement is so inaccurate that a search using the standard search engine will not disclose the debtor's name, then the financing statement is deemed seriously misleading under UCC 9–506. See also UCC 9–507, which governs the effectiveness of financing statements found to be seriously misleading.

● *Exhibit* **20-2** Selected Types of Collateral and Their Methods of Perfection

TANGIBLE COLLATERAL All things that are movable at the time the security interest attaches (such as livestock) or that are attached to the land, including timber to be cut and growing crops.		METHOD OF PERFECTION
Consumer Goods [UCC 9-301, 9-303, 9-309(1), 9-310(a), 9-313(a)]	Goods used or bought primarily for personal, family, or household purposes—for example, household furniture [UCC 9-102(a)(23)].	For purchase-money security interest, attachment (that is, the creation of a security interest) is sufficient; for boats, motor vehicles, and trailers, filing or compliance with a certificate-of-title statute is required; for other consumer goods, general rules of filing or possession apply.
Equipment [UCC 9-301, 9-310(a), 9-313(a)]	Goods bought for or used primarily in business (and not part of inventory or farm products)—for example, a delivery truck [UCC 9-102(a)(33)].	Filing or (rarely) possession by secured party.
Inventory [UCC 9-301, 9-310(a), 9-313(a)]	Goods held by a person for sale or under a contract of service or lease; raw materials held for production and work in progress [UCC 9-102(a)(48)].	Filing or (rarely) possession by secured party.
INTANGIBLE COLLATERAL Nonphysical property that exists only in connection with something else.		METHOD OF PERFECTION
Chattel Paper [UCC 9-301, 9-310(a), 9-312(a), 9-313(a), 9-314(a)]	A writing or electronic record that evidences both a monetary obligation and a security interest in goods and software used in goods—for example, a security agreement or a security agreement and promissory note.	Filing or possession or control by secured party.
Instruments [UCC 9-301, 9-309(4), 9-310(a), 9-312(a) and (e), 9-313(a)]	A negotiable instrument, such as a check, note, certificate of deposit, or draft, or other writing that evidences a right to the payment of money and is not a security agreement or lease but rather a type that can ordinarily be transferred (after indorsement, if necessary) by delivery [UCC 9-102(a)(47)].	Except for temporary perfected status, filing or possession. For the sale of promissory notes, perfection can be by attachment (automatically on the creation of the security interest).
Accounts [UCC 9-301, 9-309(2) and (5), 9-310(a)]	Any right to receive payment for property (real or personal), including intellectual licensed property, services, insurance policies, and certain other receivables.	Filing required except for certain assignments that can be perfected by attachment (automatically on the creation of the security interest).
Deposit Accounts [UCC 9-104, 9-304, 9-312(b), 9-314(a)]	Any demand, time, savings, passbook, or similar account maintained with a bank [UCC 9-102(a)(29)].	Perfection by control, such as when the secured party is the bank in which the account is maintained or when the parties have agreed that the secured party can direct the disposition of funds in a particular account.

as specified in its official documents [UCC 9–503(a)(3)]. For all others, the filed financing statement must disclose "the individual or organizational name of the debtor" [UCC 9–503(a)(4)(A)]. As used here, the word *organization* includes unincorporated associations, such as clubs and some churches, as well as joint ventures and general partnerships. If an organizational debtor does not have a group name, the names of the individuals in the group must be listed.

Trade Names.   Providing only the debtor's trade name (or a fictitious name) in a financing statement is *not* sufficient for perfection [UCC 9–503(c)]. **EXAMPLE 20.1** A loan is being made to a sole proprietorship owned by Peter Jones. The trade, or fictitious, name is Pete's Plumbing. A financing statement filed in the trade name Pete's Plumbing would not be sufficient because it does not identify Peter Jones as the actual debtor. As will be discussed in Chapter 26, a sole proprietorship (such as Pete's Plumbing) is not a legal entity distinct from the person who owns it. ● The reason for this rule is to ensure that the debtor's name on a financing statement is one that prospective lenders can locate and recognize in future searches.

Preventing Legal Disputes 🔍

In today's business climate, debtors frequently change their trade names. This can make it difficult to find out whether the debtor's collateral is subject to a prior perfected security interest. You should keep this in mind when making loans or extending credit. When searching the records, find out if the business has used any other names in the past and include those former names in your search. Remember that the key to determining if a security interest has been perfected is whether the financing statement adequately notifies other potential creditors that a security interest exists. If a search of the records using the debtor's correct name would disclose the interest, the filing is generally sufficient. To prevent legal problems, make sure that no other creditor has a prior interest in the property being used as collateral, and file the financing statement under the correct name.

"Leave your coats on the bed for collateral."

DESCRIPTION OF THE COLLATERAL Both the security agreement and the financing statement must describe the collateral in which the secured party has a security interest. The security agreement must describe the collateral because no security interest in goods can exist unless the parties agree on which goods are subject to the security interest. The financing statement must also describe the collateral because the purpose of filing the statement is to give public notice of the fact that certain goods of the debtor are subject to a security interest. For land-related security interests, a legal description of the realty is also required [UCC 9–502(b)].

Sometimes, the descriptions in the two documents vary, with the description in the security agreement being more precise than the description in the financing statement, which is allowed to be more general. **EXAMPLE 20.2** A security agreement for a commercial loan to a manufacturer may list all of the manufacturer's equipment subject to the loan by serial number. The financing statement for the equipment may simply state "all equipment owned or hereafter acquired." ●

The UCC permits broad, general descriptions in the financing statement, such as "all assets" or "all personal property." Generally, whenever the description in a financing statement accurately describes the agreement between the secured party and the debtor, the description is sufficient [UCC 9–504].

A financing statement must disclose the individual or organizational name of the debtor. The word organization *includes some churches.*

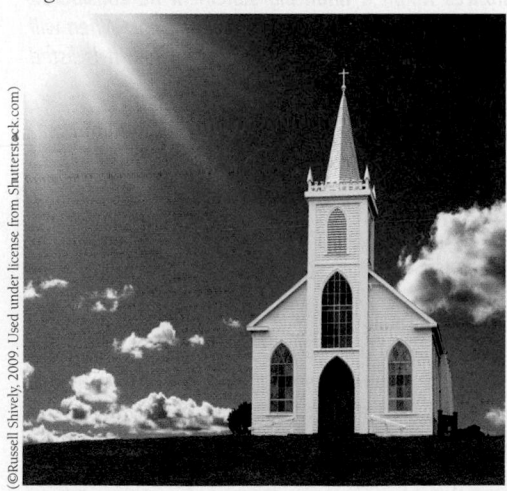

WHERE TO FILE In most states, a financing statement must be filed centrally in the appropriate state office, such as the office of the secretary of state, in the state where the debtor is located. Filing in the county where the collateral is located is required only when the collateral consists of timber to be cut, fixtures, or items to be extracted—such as oil, coal, gas, and minerals [UCC 9–301(3) and (4), 9–502(b)].

The state office in which a financing statement should be filed depends on the *debtor's location,* not the location of the collateral [UCC 9–301]. The debtor's location is determined as follows [UCC 9–307]:

1. For *individual debtors,* it is the state of the debtor's principal residence.
2. For an organization that is registered with the state, such as a corporation or limited liability company, it is the state in which the organization is registered. Thus, if a debtor is incorporated in Maryland and has its chief executive office in New York, a secured party would file the financing statement in Maryland—the state of the debtor's organizational formation.

3. For all other entities, it is the state in which the business is located or, if the debtor has more than one office, the place from which the debtor manages its business operations and affairs.

CONSEQUENCES OF AN IMPROPER FILING   Any improper filing renders the security interest unperfected and reduces the secured party's claim in bankruptcy to that of an unsecured creditor. For instance, if the debtor's name on the financing statement is seriously misleading or if the collateral is not sufficiently described in the financing statement, the filing may not be effective. The following case provides an illustration.

Case 20.1   Corona Fruits & Veggies, Inc. v. Frozsun Foods, Inc.

Court of Appeal of California, Second District, 143 Cal.App.4th 319, 48 Cal.Rptr.3d 868 (2006).

How do the proceeds of the sale of strawberries get distributed to creditors when one creditor's financing paperwork has an error?

FACTS   In July 2001, Corona Fruits & Veggies, Inc., and Corona Marketing Company sublet farmland in Santa Barbara County, California, to Armando Munoz Juarez, a strawberry farmer. The Corona companies also loaned funds to Juarez for payroll and production expenses. The sublease and other documents involved in the transaction set out Juarez's full name, but Juarez generally went by the name "Munoz" and signed the sublease "Armando Munoz." The Coronas filed UCC-1 financing statements that identified the debtor as "Armando Munoz." In December, Juarez contracted to sell strawberries to Frozsun Foods, Inc., which advanced funds secured by a financing statement that identified the debtor as "Armando Juarez." By the next July, Juarez owed the Coronas $230,482.52 and Frozsun $19,648.52. When Juarez did not repay the Coronas, they took possession of the farmland, harvested and sold the strawberries, and kept the proceeds. The Coronas and Frozsun filed a suit in a California state court against Juarez to collect the rest of his debt. The court ruled that Frozsun's interest took priority because only its financing statement was recorded properly. The Coronas appealed to a state intermediate appellate court.

ISSUE   Does a creditor fail to perfect a security interest if the financing statement lists the debtor's name incorrectly?

DECISION   Yes. The state intermediate appellate court affirmed the lower court's ruling. "Shakespeare asked, 'What's in a name?' We supply an answer * * * : Everything when the last name is true and nothing when the last name is false."

REASON   The appellate court recognized that "minor errors in a UCC financing statement do not affect the effectiveness of the financing statement." It is only when "errors render the document seriously misleading to other creditors" that the effectiveness of a statement is undercut. "When a creditor files a UCC-1 financing statement, the debtor's true last name is crucial because the financing statements are indexed by last names. A subsequent creditor who loans [funds] to a debtor with the same name is put on notice that its lien is secondary." In this case, Juarez's identification cards and tax returns stated his true, full name, and the Coronas identified him by this name in their contracts, business records, and checks, and even in their pleadings filed with the court. The Coronas could have used this name in their financing statements, too, to protect the priority of their security interests, but they did not. Frozsun searched the UCC records under the name "Juarez" and did not find the Coronas' statements. For these reasons, Frozsun's interest was superior.

FOR CRITICAL ANALYSIS—Technological Consideration
Under what circumstances might a financing statement be considered effective even if it does not identify the debtor correctly? (Hint: When will a computer's search engine find a debtor's name even when it is listed incorrectly?)

Perfection without Filing

In two types of situations, security interests can be perfected without filing a financing statement. The first occurs when the collateral is transferred into the possession of the secured party. The second occurs when the security interest is one of a limited number under the UCC that can be perfected on attachment (without a filing and without having to possess the goods) [UCC 9–309]. The phrase *perfected on attachment* means that these security interests are automatically perfected at the time of their creation. Two of the more common security interests that are perfected on attachment are a *purchase-money security interest* in consumer goods (defined and explained shortly) and an assignment of a beneficial interest in a decedent's estate [UCC 9–309(1), (13)].

Pledge A common law security device (retained in Article 9 of the UCC) in which personal property is transferred into the possession of the creditor as security for the payment of a debt and retained by the creditor until the debt is paid.

PERFECTION BY POSSESSION

In the past, one of the most common means of obtaining financing was to **pledge** certain collateral as security for the debt and transfer the collateral into the creditor's possession. When the debt was paid, the collateral was returned to the debtor. Although the debtor usually entered into a written security agreement, an oral security agreement was also enforceable as long as the secured party possessed the collateral.

Article 9 of the UCC retained the common law pledge and the principle that the security agreement need not be in writing to be enforceable if the collateral is transferred to the secured party [UCC 9–310, 9–312(b), 9–313]. **EXAMPLE 20.3** Sheila needs cash to pay for a medical procedure. She gets a loan for $4,000 from Trent; as security on the loan, she gives him a promissory note on which she is the payee. Even though the agreement to hold the note as collateral was oral, Trent has a perfected security interest and does not need to file a financing statement. No other creditor of Sheila's can attempt to recover the promissory note from Trent in payment for other debts. •

For most collateral, possession by the secured party is impractical because it denies the debtor the right to use or derive income from the property to pay off the debt. **EXAMPLE 20.4** Jed, a farmer, takes out a loan to finance the purchase of a large corn harvester and uses the equipment as collateral. Clearly, the purpose of the purchase would be defeated if Jed transferred the collateral into the creditor's possession, because he would not be able to use the equipment to harvest his corn. • Certain items, however, such as stocks, bonds, negotiable instruments, and jewelry, are commonly transferred into the creditor's possession when they are used as collateral for loans.

> *"People may live as much retired from the world as they like, but sooner or later, they find themselves debtor or creditor to someone."*
>
> Johann Wolfgang von Goethe,
> 1749–1832
> (German writer)

PERFECTION BY ATTACHMENT—THE PURCHASE-MONEY SECURITY INTEREST IN CONSUMER GOODS

Under the UCC, fourteen types of security interests are perfected automatically at the time they are created [UCC 9–309]. The most common of these is the **purchase-money security interest (PMSI)** in *consumer goods* (items bought primarily for personal, family, or household purposes). A PMSI in consumer goods is created when a person buys goods and the seller or lender agrees to extend credit for part or all of the purchase price of the goods. The entity that extends the credit and obtains the PMSI can be either the seller (a store, for example) or a financial institution that lends the buyer the funds with which to purchase the goods [UCC 9–102(a)(2)].

Purchase-Money Security Interest (PMSI) A security interest that arises when a seller or lender extends credit for part or all of the purchase price of goods purchased by a buyer.

Automatic Perfection. A PMSI in consumer goods is perfected automatically at the time of a credit sale—that is, at the time the PMSI is created. The seller in this situation does not need to do anything more to perfect her or his interest. **EXAMPLE 20.5** Jamie wants to purchase a new high-definition television from ABC Television, Inc. The purchase price is $2,500. Not being able to pay the entire amount in cash, Jamie signs a purchase agreement to pay $1,000 down and $100 per month until the balance plus interest is fully paid. ABC is to retain a security interest in the television until full payment has been made. Because the security interest was created as part of the purchase agreement, it is a PMSI in consumer goods. ABC does not need to do anything else to perfect its security interest. •

If a couple purchases a large flat-screen TV on an installment plan, what kind of security interest is created?

(AP Photo/Mark Lennihan)

Exceptions to the Rule of Automatic Perfection. There are exceptions to the rule of automatic perfection. First, certain types of security interests that are subject to other federal or state laws may require additional steps to be perfected [UCC 9–311]. For instance, most states have certificate-of-title statutes that establish perfection requirements for specific goods, such as automobiles, trailers, boats, mobile homes, and farm tractors. If a consumer in these jurisdictions purchases a boat, for example, the secured party will need to file a certificate of title with the appropriate state official to perfect the PMSI. A second exception involves PMSIs in nonconsumer goods, such as livestock or a business's inventory, which are not automatically perfected (these types of PMSIs are discussed later in this chapter in the context of priorities).

Effective Time Duration of Perfection

Continuation Statement A statement that, if filed within six months prior to the expiration date of the original financing statement, continues the perfection of the original security interest for another five years. The perfection of a security interest can be continued in the same manner indefinitely.

A financing statement is effective for five years from the date of filing [UCC 9–515]. If a **continuation statement** is filed within six months *prior to* the expiration date, the effectiveness of the original statement is continued for another five years, starting with the expiration date of the first five-year period [UCC 9–515(d), (e)]. The effectiveness of the statement can be continued in the same manner indefinitely. Any attempt to file a continuation statement outside the six-month window will render the continuation ineffective, and the perfection will lapse at the end of the five-year period.

If a financing statement lapses, the security interest that had been perfected by the filing now becomes unperfected. A purchaser for value can acquire the collateral as if the security interest had never been perfected [UCC 9–515(c)].

▶ The Scope of a Security Interest

As previously stated, a security interest can cover property that the debtor has ownership or possessory rights in now or in the future. Therefore, security agreements can cover the proceeds from the sale of collateral, after-acquired property, and future advances, as discussed next.

Proceeds

Proceeds Under Article 9 of the UCC, whatever is received when collateral is sold or otherwise disposed of, such as by exchange.

Proceeds are whatever cash or property is received when collateral is sold or disposed of in some other way [UCC 9–102(a)(64)]. A security interest in the collateral gives the secured party a security interest in the proceeds acquired from the sale of that collateral. **EXAMPLE 20.6** People's Bank has a perfected security interest in the inventory of a retail seller of heavy farm machinery. The retailer sells a tractor out of this inventory to Jacob Dunn, a farmer, who is by definition a *buyer in the ordinary course of business* (this term will be discussed later in the chapter). Dunn agrees, in a security agreement, to make monthly payments to the retailer for a period of twenty-four months. If the retailer goes into default on the loan from the bank, the bank is entitled to the remaining payments Dunn owes to the retailer as proceeds. ●

A security interest in proceeds perfects automatically on the *perfection* of the secured party's security interest in the original collateral and remains perfected for twenty days after the debtor receives the proceeds. One way to extend the twenty-day automatic perfection period is to provide for extended coverage in the original security agreement [UCC 9–315(c), (d)]. This is typically done when the collateral is the type that is likely to be sold, such as a retailer's inventory—for example, of computers or cell phones. The UCC also permits a security interest in identifiable cash proceeds to remain perfected after twenty days [UCC 9–315(d)(2)].

After-Acquired Property

After-Acquired Property Property that is acquired by the debtor after the execution of a security agreement.

After-acquired property is property that the debtor acquired after the execution of the security agreement. The security agreement may provide for a security interest in after-acquired property, such as a debtor's inventory [UCC 9–204(1)]. Generally, the debtor will purchase new inventory to replace the inventory sold. The secured party wants this newly acquired inventory to be subject to the original security interest. Thus, the after-acquired property clause continues the secured party's claim to any inventory acquired thereafter. (This is not to say that the original security interest will take priority over the rights of all other creditors with regard to this after-acquired inventory, as will be discussed later.)

EXAMPLE 20.7 Amato buys factory equipment from Bronson on credit, giving as security an interest in all of her equipment—both what she is buying and what she already owns. The security interest with Bronson contains an after-acquired property clause. Six months later, Amato pays cash to another seller of factory equipment for more equipment. Six months after that, Amato goes out of business before she has paid off her debt to Bronson. Bronson has a security interest in all of Amato's equipment, even the equipment bought from the other seller. •

Future Advances

Often, a debtor will arrange with a bank to have a *continuing line of credit* under which the debtor can borrow funds intermittently. Advances against lines of credit can be subject to a properly perfected security interest in certain collateral. The security agreement may provide that any future advances made against that line of credit are also subject to the security interest in the same collateral [UCC 9–204(c)]. Future advances do not have to be of the same type or otherwise related to the original advance to benefit from this type of **cross-collateralization**.[4] Cross-collateralization occurs when an asset that is not the subject of a loan is used to secure that loan.

EXAMPLE 20.8 Stroh is the owner of a small manufacturing plant with equipment valued at $1 million. He has an immediate need for $50,000 of working capital, so he obtains a loan from Midwestern Bank and signs a security agreement, putting up all of his equipment as security. The bank properly perfects its security interest. The security agreement provides that Stroh can borrow up to $500,000 in the future, using the same equipment as collateral for any future advances. In this situation, Midwestern Bank does not have to execute a new security agreement and perfect a security interest in the collateral each time an advance is made, up to a cumulative total of $500,000. For priority purposes, each advance is perfected as of the date of the *original* perfection. •

The Floating-Lien Concept

A security agreement that provides for a security interest in proceeds, in after-acquired property, or in collateral subject to future advances by the secured party (or in all three) is often characterized as a **floating lien.** This type of security interest continues in the collateral or proceeds even if the collateral is sold, exchanged, or disposed of in some other way.

A FLOATING LIEN IN INVENTORY Floating liens commonly arise in the financing of inventories. A creditor is not interested in specific pieces of inventory, which are constantly changing, so the lien "floats" from one item to another, as the inventory changes.

EXAMPLE 20.9 Cascade Sports, Inc., is an Oregon corporation that operates as a cross-country ski dealer and has a line of credit with Portland First Bank to finance its inventory of cross-country skis. Cascade and Portland First enter into a security agreement that provides for coverage of proceeds, after-acquired inventory, present inventory, and future advances. Portland First perfects its security interest in the inventory by filing centrally with the office of the secretary of state in Oregon. One day, Cascade sells a new pair of the latest cross-country skis and receives a used pair in trade. That same day, Cascade

Cross-Collateralization The use of an asset that is not the subject of a loan to collateralize that loan.

Floating lien A security interest in proceeds, after-acquired property, or collateral subject to future advances by the secured party (or all three); a security interest in collateral that is retained even when the collateral changes in character, classification, or location.

---

4. See official Comment 5 to UCC 9–204.

purchases two new pairs of cross-country skis from a local manufacturer for cash. Later that day, to meet its payroll, Cascade borrows $8,000 from Portland First Bank under the security agreement.

Portland First gets a perfected security interest in the used pair of skis under the proceeds clause, has a perfected security interest in the two new pairs of skis purchased from the local manufacturer under the after-acquired property clause, and has the new amount of funds advanced to Cascade secured on all of the above collateral by the future-advances clause. All of this is accomplished under the original perfected security interest. The various items in the inventory have changed, but Portland First still has a perfected security interest in Cascade's inventory. Hence, it has a floating lien in the inventory. •

A Floating Lien in a Shifting Stock of Goods   The concept of the floating lien can also apply to a shifting stock of goods. The lien can start with raw materials; follow them as they become finished goods and inventories; and continue as the goods are sold and are turned into accounts receivable, chattel paper, or cash.

▶ Priorities

When more than one party claims an interest in the same collateral, which has priority? The UCC sets out detailed rules to answer this question. Although in many situations the party who has a perfected security interest will have priority, there are exceptions.

General Rules of Priority

The basic rule is that when more than one security interest has been perfected in the same collateral, the first security interest to be perfected (or filed) has priority over any security interests that are perfected later. If only one of the conflicting security interests has been perfected, then that security interest has priority. If none of the security interests have been perfected, then the first security interest that attaches has priority. The UCC's rules of priority can be summarized as follows:

1. *A perfected security interest has priority over unsecured creditors and unperfected security interests.* When two or more parties have claims to the same collateral, a perfected secured party's interest has priority over the interests of most other parties [UCC 9–322(a)(2)]. This includes priority to the proceeds from a sale of collateral resulting from a bankruptcy (giving the perfected secured party rights superior to that of the bankruptcy trustee, which will be discussed in Chapter 21).
2. *Conflicting perfected security interests.* When two or more secured parties have perfected security interests in the same collateral, the first to perfect (by filing or taking possession of the collateral) generally has priority [UCC 9–322(a)(1)].
3. *Conflicting unperfected security interests.* When two conflicting security interests are unperfected, the first to attach (be created) has priority [UCC 9–322(a)(3)]. This is sometimes called the "first-in-time" rule.

Exceptions to the General Rule

Under some circumstances, on the debtor's default, the perfection of a security interest will not protect a secured party against certain other third parties having claims to the collateral. For example, the UCC provides that in some instances a PMSI, properly perfected,[5] will prevail over another security interest in after-acquired collateral, even though the other

This woman owns a store that sells antique clocks and other used objects. As a creditor, why would you want a floating lien in a debtor's inventory?

(BobPhoto/Creative Commons)

KEEP IN MIND Secured creditors—perfected or not–have priority over unsecured creditors.

---

5. Recall that, with some exceptions (such as motor vehicles), a PMSI in *consumer goods* is automatically perfected—no filing is necessary. A PMSI that is not in consumer goods must still be perfected, however.

was perfected first. We discuss several significant exceptions to the general rules of priority in the following subsections.

BUYERS IN THE ORDINARY COURSE OF BUSINESS   Under the UCC, a person who buys "in the ordinary course of business" takes the goods free from any security interest created by the seller *even if the security interest is perfected and the buyer knows of its existence* [UCC 9–320(a)]. In other words, a buyer in the ordinary course will have priority even if a previously perfected security interest exists as to the goods. The rationale for this rule is obvious: if buyers could not obtain the goods free and clear of any security interest the merchant had created—for example, in inventory—the free flow of goods in the marketplace would be hindered.

A *buyer in the ordinary course of business* is a person who in good faith, and without knowledge that the sale violates the rights of another in the goods, buys goods in the ordinary course from a person in the business of selling goods of that kind [UCC 1–201(9)]. Note that the buyer can know about the existence of a perfected security interest, so long as he or she does not know that buying the goods violates the rights of any third party. **CASE EXAMPLE 20.10**   Dublin Auto Sales is an auto dealer in Ohio. Dublin Auto granted a security interest in its inventory to Heartland Bank for a $300,000 line of credit. Heartland perfected its security interest by filing financing statements with the appropriate state offices. Dublin Auto used $9,000 of its credit to buy a 1997 Ford F-150 and $13,000 to buy a 1999 Jeep Cherokee and delivered the certificates of title, which designated Dublin Auto as the owner, to Heartland. In March 2002, Dublin Auto sold the F-150 for $15,386.63 to Joe and Michael Murphy, and the Jeep for $14,045 to Michael Laxton. National City Bank financed both purchases. New certificates of title designated the buyers as the owners and Heartland as the "first lienholder." Heartland received none of the funds from the sales and consequently filed a suit in an Ohio state court against National City and others, seeking a declaration that its security interest in the vehicles took priority. The court, however, ruled in National City's favor. Because both the Murphys and Laxton were buyers in the ordinary course of business, Heartland's security interest in the motor vehicles at issue was extinguished on the sale of the vehicles to the Murphys and Laxton.[6] •

PMSI IN GOODS OTHER THAN INVENTORY AND LIVESTOCK   An important exception to the first-in-time rule involves certain types of collateral, such as equipment, that is *not* inventory (or livestock) and in which one of the secured parties has a perfected PMSI [UCC 9–324(a)]. **EXAMPLE 20.11**   Sandoval borrows funds from West Bank, signing a security agreement in which she puts up all of her present and after-acquired equipment as security. On May 1, West Bank perfects this security interest (which is not a PMSI). On July 1, Sandoval purchases a new piece of equipment from Zylex Company on credit, signing a security agreement. The delivery date for the new equipment is August 1.

Zylex thus has a PMSI in the new equipment (that is not part of its inventory), but the PMSI is not in consumer goods and thus is not automatically perfected. If Sandoval defaults on her payments to both West Bank and Zylex, which of them has priority with regard to the new piece of equipment? Generally, West Bank would have priority because its interest perfected first in time. In this situation, however, Zylex has a PMSI, and provided that Zylex perfected its interest in the equipment within twenty days after Sandoval took possession on August 1, Zylex has priority. •

PMSI IN INVENTORY   Another important exception to the first-in-time rule has to do with security interests in inventory [UCC 9–324(b)]. **CASE EXAMPLE 20.12**   Rebel Rents, Inc., was a California firm that offered a variety of equipment for sale or lease. In September

---

6. *Heartland Bank v. National City Bank,* 171 Ohio App.3d 132, 869 N.E.2d 746 (2007).

2000, Rebel bought certain equipment from Snorkel International, Inc., to use as inventory. Textron Financial Corporation agreed to finance the purchase, for which Rebel granted Textron a security interest in the equipment and its proceeds. In December 2000, General Electric Capital Corporation (GECC) agreed to loan Rebel up to $25 million, for which Rebel granted GECC a security interest in substantially all of Rebel's assets, including its inventory and proceeds.

On January 5, 2001, GECC filed a financing statement with the California secretary of state to perfect its interest. Textron filed its financing statement on January 16. Rebel filed a bankruptcy petition with a federal bankruptcy court in September 2002. Between that date and September 2003, Rebel obtained $430,661 from leasing the Snorkel equipment. Pursuant to an order of the court, Rebel surrendered the Snorkel equipment to Textron. Textron asserted that because of its security interest, it was also owed the income from the recent leases. The court, however, ruled that GECC's security interest had priority over Textron's interest in Rebel's income because of the date of perfection. Textron's security interest attached on September 14, 2000, but was not perfected until January 16, 2001. GECC's financing statement was filed on January 5—eleven days before Textron's financing statement was filed.[7] ●

BUYERS OF THE COLLATERAL   The UCC recognizes that there are certain types of buyers whose interest in purchased goods could conflict with those of a perfected secured party on the debtor's default. These include buyers in the ordinary course of business (as discussed), as well as buyers of farm products, instruments, documents, or securities. The UCC sets down special rules of priority for these types of buyers. See Exhibit 20–3 for a review of the rules on the priority of claims to a debtor's collateral.

 Rights and Duties of Debtors and Creditors

> *"A man who pays his bills on time is soon forgotten."*
> Oscar Wilde, 1854–1900
> (Irish author and poet)

The security agreement itself determines most of the rights and duties of the debtor and the secured party. The UCC, however, imposes some rights and duties that are applicable in the absence of a valid security agreement that states the contrary.

Information Requests

At the time of filing, a secured party has the option of furnishing a *copy* of the financing statement being filed to the filing officer and requesting that the filing officer make a note of the file number, the date, and the hour of the original filing on the copy [UCC 9–523(a)]. The filing officer must send this copy to the person designated by the secured party or to the debtor, if the debtor makes the request. Under UCC 9–523(c) and (d), a filing officer must also give information to a person who is contemplating obtaining a security interest from a prospective debtor. The filing officer must issue a certificate that provides information on possible perfected financing statements with respect to the named debtor.

Release, Assignment, and Amendment

A secured party can release all or part of any collateral described in the financing statement, thereby terminating its security interest in that collateral. The release is recorded by filing a uniform amendment form [UCC 9–512, 9–521(b)]. A secured party can also assign all or part of the security interest to a third party (the assignee). The assignee becomes the secured party of record if the assignment is filed by use of a uniform amendment form [UCC 9–514, 9–521(a)].

---

7. *In re Rebel Rents, Inc.,* 307 Bankr. 171 (C.D.Cal. 2004).

● *Exhibit* **20–3** **Priority of Claims to a Debtor's Collateral**

PARTIES	PRIORITY
Perfected Secured Party versus **Unsecured Parties and Creditors**	A perfected secured party's interest has priority over the interests of most other parties, including unsecured creditors, unperfected secured parties, subsequent lien creditors, trustees in bankruptcy, and buyers who do not purchase the collateral in the ordinary course of business.
Perfected Secured Party versus **Perfected Secured Party**	Between two perfected secured parties in the same collateral, the general rule is that the first in time of perfection is the first in right to the collateral [UCC 9–322(a)(1)].
Perfected Secured Party versus **Perfected PMSI**	A PMSI, even if second in time of perfection, has priority providing that the following conditions are met: 1. *Other collateral*—A PMSI has priority, providing it is perfected within twenty days after the debtor takes possession [UCC 9–324(a)]. 2. *Inventory*—A PMSI has priority if it is perfected and proper written or authenticated notice is given to the other security-interest holder *on* or *before* the time the debtor takes possession [UCC 9–324(b)]. 3. *Software*—Applies to a PMSI in software only if used in goods subject to a PMSI. If the goods are inventory, priority is determined the same as for inventory; if they are not, priority is determined as for goods other than inventory [UCC 9–103(c), 9–324(f)].
Perfected Secured Party versus **Purchaser of Debtor's Collateral**	1. *Buyer of goods in the ordinary course of the seller's business*—Buyer prevails over a secured party's security interest, even if perfected and even if the buyer knows of the security interest [UCC 9–320(a)]. 2. *Buyer of consumer goods purchased outside the ordinary course of business*—Buyer prevails over a secured party's interest, even if perfected by attachment, providing the buyer purchased as follows: a. For value. b. Without actual knowledge of the security interest. c. For use as a consumer good. d. Prior to the secured party's perfection by *filing* [UCC 9–320(b)]. 3. *Buyer of chattel paper*—Buyer prevails if the buyer: a. Gave new value in making the purchase. b. Took possession in the ordinary course of the buyer's business. c. Took without knowledge of the security interest [UCC 9–330]. 4. *Buyer of instruments, documents, or securities*—Buyer who is a holder in due course, a holder to whom negotiable documents have been duly negotiated, or a bona fide purchaser of securities has priority over a previously perfected security interest [UCC 9–330(d), 9–331(a)]. 5. *Buyer of farm products*—Buyer from a farmer takes free and clear of perfected security interests unless, where permitted, a secured party files centrally an effective financing statement (EFS) or the buyer receives proper notice of the security interest before the sale.
Unperfected Secured Party versus **Unsecured Creditor**	An unperfected secured party prevails over unsecured creditors and creditors who have obtained judgments against the debtor but who have not begun the legal process to collect on those judgments [UCC 9–201(a)].

If the debtor and the secured party agree, they can amend the financing statement—to add new collateral, for instance—by filing a uniform amendment form that indicates the file number of the initial financing statement [UCC 9–512(a)]. The amendment does not extend the time period of perfection, but if collateral is added, the perfection date (for priority purposes) for the new collateral begins on the date the amendment is filed [UCC 9–512(b), (c)].

Confirmation or Accounting Request by Debtor

The debtor may believe that the amount of the unpaid debt or the listing of the collateral subject to the security interest is inaccurate. The debtor has the right to request a confirmation of the unpaid debt or listing of collateral [UCC 9–210]. The debtor is entitled to one request without charge every six months.

The secured party must comply with the debtor's confirmation request by authenticating and sending to the debtor an accounting within fourteen days after the request is received. Otherwise, the secured party will be held liable for any loss suffered by the debtor, plus $500 [UCC 9–210, 9–625(f)].

Termination Statement

When the debtor has fully paid the debt, if the secured party perfected the security interest by filing, the debtor is entitled to have a termination statement filed. Such a statement demonstrates to the public that the filed perfected security interest has been terminated [UCC 9–513].

Whenever consumer goods are involved, the secured party *must* file a termination statement (or, alternatively, a release) within one month of the final payment or within twenty days of receiving the debtor's authenticated demand, whichever is earlier [UCC 9–513(b)].

When the collateral is other than consumer goods, on an authenticated demand by the debtor, the secured party must either send a termination statement to the debtor or file such a statement within twenty days [UCC 9–513(c)]. Otherwise, the secured party is not required to file or send a termination statement. Whenever a secured party fails to file or send the termination statement as requested, the debtor can recover $500 plus any additional loss suffered [UCC 9–625(e)(4), (f)].

 Default

Article 9 defines the rights, duties, and remedies of the secured party and of the debtor on the debtor's default. Should the secured party fail to comply with her or his duties, the debtor is afforded particular rights and remedies.

The topic of default is one of great concern to secured lenders and to the lawyers who draft security agreements. What constitutes default is not always clear. In fact, Article 9 does not define the term. Consequently, parties are encouraged in practice—and by the UCC—to include in their security agreements certain standards to be applied in determining when default has actually occurred. In so doing, the parties can stipulate the conditions that will constitute a default [UCC 9–601, 9–603]. Often, these critical terms are shaped by the creditor in an attempt to provide the maximum protection possible. The ultimate terms, however, may not go beyond the limitations imposed by the good faith requirement and the unconscionability provisions of the UCC.

Any breach of the terms of the security agreement can constitute default. Nevertheless, default occurs most commonly when the debtor fails to meet the scheduled payments that the parties have agreed on or when the debtor becomes bankrupt.

Basic Remedies

The rights and remedies set out in UCC 9–601(a) and (b) are *cumulative* [UCC 9–601(c)]. Therefore, if a creditor is unsuccessful in enforcing rights by one method, he or she can pursue another method. Generally, a secured party's remedies can be divided into the two basic categories discussed next.

REPOSSESSION OF THE COLLATERAL—THE SELF-HELP REMEDY

On the debtor's default, a secured party can take peaceful possession of the collateral without the use of judicial process [UCC 9–609(b)]. This provision is often referred to as the "self-help" provision of Article 9. The

> *"If you think nobody cares if you're alive, try missing a couple of car payments."*
>
> Earl Wilson, 1907–1987
> (American journalist)

When a consumer is unable to make payments on a loan, she or he is in default.

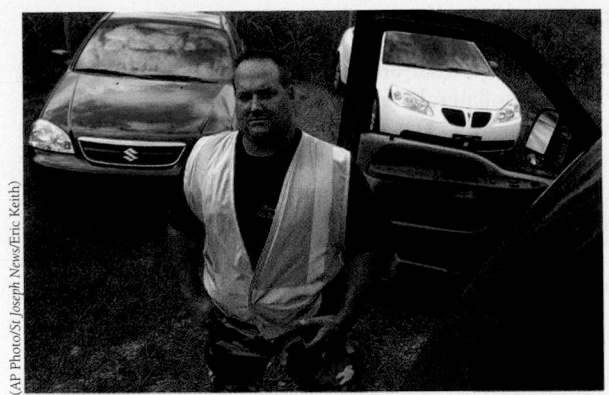

A secured party can take "peaceful possession" of cars that were used as collateral for consumer loans. What constitutes peaceful possession?

Execution An action to carry into effect the directions in a court decree or judgment.

Levy The obtaining of funds by legal process through the seizure and sale of nonexempt property, usually done after a writ of execution has been issued.

UCC does not define *peaceful possession,* however. The general rule is that the collateral has been taken peacefully if the secured party can take possession without committing (1) trespass onto land, (2) assault and/or battery, or (3) breaking and entering. On taking possession, the secured party may either retain the collateral for satisfaction of the debt [UCC 9–620] or resell the goods and apply the proceeds toward the debt [UCC 9–610].

JUDICIAL REMEDIES Alternatively, a secured party can relinquish the security interest and use any judicial remedy available, such as obtaining a judgment on the underlying debt, followed by execution and levy. (**Execution** is the implementation of a court's decree or judgment. **Levy** is the obtaining of funds by legal process through the seizure and sale of nonexempt property, usually done after a writ of execution has been issued.) Execution and levy are rarely undertaken unless the collateral is no longer in existence or has declined so much in value that it is worth substantially less than the amount of the debt and the debtor has other assets available that may be legally seized to satisfy the debt [UCC 9–601(a)].[8]

If a customer finances a purchase through a bank loan, returns the item, and refuses to make the loan payments, what are the rights of the secured party (the bank)? That was one of the issues in the following case.

---

8. Some assets are exempt from creditors' claims—see Chapter 21.

Case 20.2 **First National Bank of Litchfield v. Miller**

Supreme Court of Connecticut, 285 Conn. 294, 939 A.2d 572 (2008).

Can someone be released from loan payments for a boat they returned to the seller?

FACTS The Millers wanted to buy a boat from Norwest Marine, so they made a deposit and signed a form contract. Title and ownership would pass when the Millers made full payment, although delivery would occur earlier. The agreement stated that the Millers had inspected and accepted the boat and that the document constituted the entire agreement between the parties. The Millers needed financing and contacted First National Bank of Litchfield to begin the loan process. The Millers signed a loan agreement with the bank, which sent Norwest full payment for the boat. When the Millers took delivery of the boat, it did not run properly, so they returned it to Norwest for repairs. After the repairs were completed, the Millers refused to accept the boat, claiming that it was not satisfactory. They told the bank that they did not want the boat, and they stopped making loan payments. The bank sued, contending that the Millers had breached the retail contract by refusing to make monthly payments. The Millers filed claims against the bank and Norwest asserting that they had committed fraud. The trial court held for the bank, awarding it the full amount owed under the loan contract, plus attorneys' fees. The Millers

appealed, and the appellate court reversed and remanded. The case was certified to the state's highest court for review.

ISSUE Were the Millers released from making loan payments on the boat they had purchased because they had returned it to the seller?

DECISION No. The state supreme court reinstated the verdict of the trial court, holding that the Millers had accepted delivery of the boat under the UCC and were required to pay under the financing agreement.

REASON The court noted that the Millers had signed a purchase agreement stating that they had inspected the boat and were satisfied with it. Additionally, they had signed a retail installment contract with the bank stating that they had already accepted delivery of the boat, and it was registered in their names. Norwest acted in good faith by performing warranty repair work that solved the boat's mechanical problem. Norwest also installed some equipment specifically requested by the Millers. The Millers could not claim that they had never taken delivery of the boat, and they were therefore responsible for the loan they had accepted.

FOR CRITICAL ANALYSIS—Legal Consideration *How could Norwest and the bank have avoided the problem that arose in this case?*

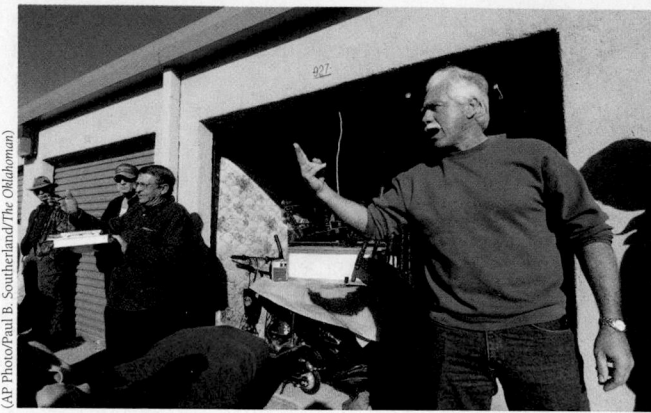

(AP Photo/Paul B. Southerland/The Oklahoman)

An auctioneer stands in front of a self-storage unit where personal belongings are being sold. The rental fees for the space had not been paid for months, so the business owner wishes to recoup those fees from the proceeds of the auction. Is such a private auction in accordance with the disposition of collateral procedures sanctioned by Article 9 of the Uniform Commercial Code? Why or why not?

Disposition of Collateral

Once default has occurred and the secured party has obtained possession of the collateral, the secured party has several options. The secured party can (1) retain the collateral in full or partial satisfaction of the debt, or (2) sell, lease, license, or otherwise dispose of the collateral in any commercially reasonable manner and apply the proceeds toward satisfaction of the debt [UCC 9–602(7), 9–603, 9–610(a), 9–613, 9–620]. Any sale is always subject to procedures established by state law.

RETENTION OF COLLATERAL BY THE SECURED PARTY   The UCC acknowledges that parties are sometimes better off if they do not sell the collateral. Therefore, a secured party may retain the collateral unless it consists of consumer goods and the debtor has paid 60 percent or more of the purchase price in a PMSI or debt in a non-PMSI—as will be discussed shortly [UCC 9–620(e)].

This general right, however, is subject to several conditions. The secured party must notify the debtor of its proposal to retain the collateral. Notice is required unless the debtor has signed a statement renouncing or modifying her or his rights *after default* [UCC 9–620(a), 9–621]. If the collateral is consumer goods, the secured party does not need to give any other notice. In all other situations, the secured party must send notice to any other secured party from whom the secured party has received written or authenticated notice of a claim of interest in the collateral. The secured party must also send notice to any other **junior lienholder** (one holding a lien that is subordinate to one or more other liens on the same property) who has filed a statutory lien (such as a *mechanic's lien*—see Chapter 21) or a security interest in the collateral ten days before the debtor consented to the retention [UCC 9–621].

If, within twenty days after the notice is sent, the secured party receives an objection sent by a person entitled to receive notification, the secured party must sell or otherwise dispose of the collateral (disposition procedures will be discussed shortly). If no written objection is received, the secured party may retain the collateral in full or partial satisfaction of the debtor's obligation [UCC 9–620(a), 9–621].

Junior Lienholder   A party that holds a lien that is subordinate to one or more other liens on the same property.

CONSUMER GOODS   When the collateral is consumer goods and the debtor has paid 60 percent or more of the purchase price or loan amount, the secured party must sell or otherwise dispose of the repossessed collateral within ninety days [UCC 9–620(e), (f)]. Failure to comply opens the secured party to an action for conversion or other liability under UCC 9–625(b) and (c) unless the consumer-debtor signed a written statement *after default* renouncing or modifying the right to demand the sale of the goods [UCC 9–624].

REMEMBER   Conversion is a tort that involves depriving an owner of personal property without the owner's permission.

DISPOSITION PROCEDURES   A secured party who does not choose to retain the collateral or who is required to sell it must resort to the disposition procedures prescribed in the UCC. The UCC allows substantial flexibility with regard to disposition. A secured party may sell, lease, license, or otherwise dispose of any or all of the collateral in its present condition or following any commercially reasonable preparation or processing [UCC 9–610(a)].

The collateral can be disposed of at public or private proceedings, but every aspect of the disposition's method, manner, time, and place must be commercially reasonable [UCC 9–610(b)]. The secured party must notify the debtor and other specified parties in writing ahead of time about the sale or disposition of the collateral. Notification is not required if the collateral is perishable, will decline rapidly in value, or is a type customarily sold on a recognized market [UCC 9–611(b), (c)]. The debtor may waive the right to receive this notice, but only after default [UCC 9–624(a)].

The secured party may purchase the collateral at a public sale, but not at a private sale—unless the collateral is of a kind customarily sold on a recognized market or is the subject of widely distributed standard price quotations [UCC 9–610(c)]. If the secured party does not dispose of the collateral in a commercially reasonable manner and the price paid for the collateral is affected, a court can reduce the amount of any deficiency that the debtor owes to the secured party [UCC 9–626(a)(3)].

Under the UCC, the secured party must meet a high standard when disposing of collateral. Although obtaining a satisfactory price is the purpose of requiring the secured party to resell collateral in a commercially reasonable way, price is only one aspect, as the following case makes clear.

Case 20.3   **Hicklin v. Onyx Acceptance Corp.**

Delaware Supreme Court, 970 A.2d 244 (2009).
www.courts.state.de.us/Courts[a]

HISTORICAL AND TECHNOLOGICAL SETTING   *The first organized auctions were held during the Roman Empire to sell locally produced goods. During the 1700s, auctions were used in America primarily to sell property to satisfy debts. Today, auctions serve many purposes, including the sale of repossessed collateral. In a public auction, which is open to the general public, the price is determined after competitive bidding. An advertisement or other public notice must precede the sale. The most convenient way to publicize a sale is online where announcement boards and other sites list current and future auctions. A private auction, which is open only to a select group of bidders, does not need to be publicized, although if repossessed collateral is sold at a private auction, the debtor must be notified.*

(Hoyt E. Carrier II/
GrandRapids Press/Landov)

Was the price obtained on the sale of a car at auction commercially reasonable?

FACTS   Shannon Hicklin bought a 1993 Ford Explorer under an installment sales contract. When she fell three payments behind–still owing $5,741.65–Onyx Acceptance Corporation repossessed the car. The car was sold for $1,500 at a private auction held by ABC Washington-Dulles, LLC. After deducting the costs of repossession and sale, there was a deficiency under the contract of $5,018.88. Onyx filed a suit in a Delaware state court to collect this amount from Hicklin. To establish that the sale was commercially reasonable, Onyx

offered proof only of the price. The court found that the fair market value of the car at the time of the sale was $2,335 and held that the sale was commercially reasonable solely because the auction price was more than 50 percent of this estimated market value at the time of the auction. The court granted Onyx a deficiency judgment, which a state intermediate appellate court affirmed. Hicklin appealed.

ISSUE   Does the price obtained on a sale of collateral prove, without more evidence, that the sale was commercially reasonable?

DECISION   No. The Delaware Supreme Court reversed the lower court's judgment and remanded the case.

REASON   Under UCC 9–610(a), Onyx could prove that its sale was commercially reasonable in one of two ways. It could show that every aspect of the sale was conducted in a commercially reasonable manner or, under UCC 9–627(b)(3), that the sale conformed with the reasonable commercial practices among dealers in the type of property that was the subject of the disposition. Onyx did not meet either of these standards. Because every aspect of a sale must be commercially reasonable, Onyx's showing only that the private auction sale grossed more than 50 percent of the value of the collateral was not enough. Onyx did not provide any proof of the details of the auction–its procedure, publicity, attendance, or convenience of location. Nor did Onyx offer any proof that the sale conformed to the accepted practices in its trade.

FOR CRITICAL ANALYSIS—Ethical Consideration   *Why does UCC 9–627(b)(3) require that a sale be conducted in conformity with the reasonable commercial practices among dealers in the type of property that was the subject of the disposition?*

---

a. In the left-hand column, click on "Supreme Court." On that page, in the "Opinions" pull-down menu, select "Supreme." In the result, in the "Year" pull-down menu, select "2009." Scroll to the name of the case and click on it to access the opinion. The Delaware Judicial Information Center maintains this Web site.

PROCEEDS FROM THE DISPOSITION   Proceeds from the disposition of collateral after default on the underlying debt are distributed in the following order:

1. Reasonable expenses incurred by the secured party in repossessing, storing, and reselling the collateral.
2. Balance of the debt owed to the secured party.
3. Junior lienholders who have made written or authenticated demands.
4. Unless the collateral consists of accounts, payment intangibles, promissory notes, or chattel paper, any surplus goes to the debtor [UCC 9–608(a); 9–615(a), (e)].

NONCASH PROCEEDS   Whenever the secured party receives noncash proceeds from the disposition of collateral after default, the secured party must make a value determination and apply this value in a commercially reasonable manner [UCC 9–608(a)(3), 9–615(c)].

DEFICIENCY JUDGMENT   Often, after proper disposition of the collateral, the secured party has not collected all that the debtor still owes. Unless otherwise agreed, the debtor is liable for any deficiency, and the creditor can obtain a **deficiency judgment** from a court to collect the deficiency.[9] Note, however, that if the underlying transaction was, for example, a sale of accounts or of chattel paper, the debtor is entitled to any surplus or is liable for any deficiency only if the security agreement so provides [UCC 9–615(d), (e)].

> **Deficiency Judgment**   A judgment against a debtor for the amount of a debt remaining unpaid after the collateral has been repossessed and sold.

> **How long should a secured party have to seek a deficiency judgment?** Because of depreciation, the amount received from the sale of collateral is frequently less than the amount the debtor owes the secured party. As noted, the secured party can file a suit against the debtor in an attempt to collect the balance due. Practically speaking, however, debtors who have defaulted on a loan rarely have the cash to pay any deficiency. Article 9 does not contain a statute of limitations provision, so it is not clear how long secured parties have after default to file a deficiency suit against debtors. If a secured party waits until the debtor becomes solvent again, the court may not allow the suit. Is this fair?
>
> Consider, for instance, a case that came before the Vermont Supreme Court.[10] Duane Ouimette had bought a car with an extended warranty from a dealership under a retail installment sales contract. The contract was assigned to DaimlerChrysler. When Ouimette failed to make the payments, DaimlerChrysler repossessed the car and sold it at an auction. After the car was sold, Ouimette still owed more than $10,000 on the loan. Five and a half years later, DaimlerChrysler sued to collect the deficiency judgment, arguing that the company should have six years to file a deficiency action. The court noted that Vermont had never addressed the issue of what limitation period should apply to deficiency suits. Because the contract involved the sale of a car, however, the court held that the four-year limitation period stated in Article 2 applied. (Indeed, most courts that have considered this issue have come to this same conclusion when the security interest involved the sale of a motor vehicle.[11]) Thus, the creditor's suit was too late.

REDEMPTION RIGHTS   At any time before the secured party disposes of the collateral or enters into a contract for its disposition, or before the debtor's obligation has been discharged through the secured party's retention of the collateral, the debtor or any other secured party can exercise the right of *redemption* of the collateral. The debtor or other

---

9. As noted previously, the amount of the deficiency judgment may be reduced if the secured party failed to act in a commercially reasonable manner in disposing of the collateral.
10. *DaimlerChrysler Services North America, LLC v. Ouimette*, 175 Vt. 316, 830 A.2d 38 (2003). See also *Thomas v. Branch Banking and Trust Co.*, 443 F.Supp.2d 806 (N.D.W.Va. 2006).
11. See *Credit Acceptance Corp. v. Coates*, 75 Va.Cir. 267, 2008 WL 3889424 (2008), in which the court observed that nine of the eleven states that have addressed the issue consider installment contracts for the sale of a motor vehicle to be governed by the limitations period of Article 2.

secured party can do this by tendering performance of all obligations secured by the collateral and by paying the expenses reasonably incurred by the secured party in retaking and maintaining the collateral [UCC 9–623].

 ## Reviewing . . . Security Interests in Personal Property

Paul Barton owned a small property-management company, doing business as Brighton Homes. In October, Barton went on a spending spree. First, he bought a Bose surround-sound system for his home from KDM Electronics. The next day, he purchased a Wilderness Systems kayak from Outdoor Outfitters, and the day after that he bought a new Toyota 4-Runner financed through Bridgeport Auto. Two weeks later, Barton purchased six new iMac computers for his office, also from KDM Electronics. Barton bought all of these items under installment sales contracts. Six months later, Barton's property-management business was failing, and he could not make the payments due on any of these purchases and thus defaulted on the loans. Using the information presented in the chapter, answer the following questions.

1. For which of Barton's purchases (the surround-sound system, the kayak, the 4-Runner, and the six iMacs) would the creditor need to file a financing statement to perfect its security interest?
2. Suppose that Barton's contract for the office computers mentioned only the name *Brighton Homes*. What would be the consequences if KDM Electronics filed a financing statement that listed only Brighton Homes as the debtor's name?
3. Which of these purchases would qualify as a PMSI in consumer goods?
4. Suppose that after KDM Electronics repossesses the surround-sound system, it decides to keep the system rather than sell it. Can KDM do this under Article 9? Why or why not?

Business Application
How Do You Perfect a Security Interest?*

Perfecting your security interest as a creditor is crucial, particularly when the debt is large and you wish to protect the priority of your security interest over others who have an interest in the debtor's collateral. Failure to perfect or to perfect properly may result in your becoming the equivalent of an unsecured creditor.

Perfection by Filing

Perfection is most commonly accomplished by filing a financing statement in the appropriate location. Generally, the moment the filing takes place, your priority is established over the other creditors—as well as over some purchasers of the collateral and a subsequent trustee in bankruptcy.

When you create a security agreement, describe the collateral in terms that are specific enough to put third parties on notice of your security interest in that collateral. Although the UCC permits broad general descriptions (such as "all assets") in the financing statement (as opposed to the security agreement), if your description is insufficient or misleading, your security interest will not be perfected.

Priority between Two Perfected Secured Parties

Sometimes, two secured parties have a security interest in the same debtor's collateral. On the debtor's default, the question arises as to which perfected secured party prevails. The answer is important for

businesspersons because the loser most often ends up with the same status as an unsecured creditor.

The general rule is that the first creditor to perfect will have priority. An exception to the first-in-time rule applies, however, if the first perfection does not involve a purchase-money security interest (PMSI) and the second is a PMSI. This exception can be extremely important if the collateral is inventory or other goods, such as equipment, and the security agreement for the first-in-time non-PMSI contains an after-acquired property clause. This clause and the "timely" perfection of the PMSI (with proper notice for inventory) will come into conflict. In this situation, the perfected PMSI holder has priority to the debtor's newly acquired inventory or equipment.

CHECKLIST FOR PERFECTING YOUR SECURITY INTEREST

1. **File a financing statement promptly.**
2. **Describe the collateral sufficiently—sometimes, it is better to err by giving too much detail than by giving too little.**
3. **If you are a holder of a PMSI, be sure that it is properly perfected (give proper notice if it involves inventory) so that you have priority over a previously perfected non-PMSI in the same collateral.**

* This *Business Application* is not meant to substitute for the services of an attorney who is licensed to practice law in your state.

Key Terms

after-acquired property 504
attachment 498
collateral 497
continuation statement 504
cross-collateralization 505
debtor 497
default 497

deficiency judgment 514
execution 511
financing statement 497
floating lien 505
junior lienholder 512
levy 511
perfection 498

pledge 503
proceeds 504
purchase-money security interest (PMSI) 503
secured party 497
secured transaction 496
security agreement 497
security interest 497

 Chapter Summary: Security Interests in Personal Property

Creating a Security Interest (See pages 497–498.)	1. Unless the creditor has possession of the collateral, there must be a written or authenticated security agreement that is signed or authenticated by the debtor and describes the collateral subject to the security interest. 2. The secured party must give value to the debtor. 3. The debtor must have rights in the collateral—some ownership interest in or right to obtain possession of the specified collateral.

Perfecting a Security Interest (See pages 498–504.)	1. *Perfection by filing*—The most common method of perfection is by filing a financing statement containing the names of the secured party and the debtor and indicating the collateral covered by the financing statement.
	  a. Communication of the financing statement to the appropriate filing office, together with the correct filing fee, constitutes a filing.
	  b. The financing statement must be filed under the name of the debtor; fictitious (trade) names normally are not sufficient.
	  c. The classification of collateral determines whether filing is necessary and, if it is, where to file (see Exhibit 20–2 on page 500).
	2. *Perfection without filing*—
	  a. By transfer of collateral—The debtor can transfer possession of the collateral to the secured party. A *pledge* is an example of this type of transfer.
	  b. By attachment, such as the attachment of a purchase-money security interest (PMSI) in consumer goods—If the secured party has a PMSI in consumer goods (goods bought or used by the debtor for personal, family, or household purposes), the secured party's security interest is perfected automatically. In all, fourteen types of security interests can be perfected by attachment.

The Scope of a Security Interest (See pages 504–506.)	A security agreement can cover the following types of property: 1. *Collateral in the present possession or control of the debtor.* 2. *Proceeds from a sale, exchange, or disposition of secured collateral.* 3. *After-acquired property*—A security agreement may provide that property acquired after the execution of the security agreement will also be secured by the agreement. This provision is often included in security agreements covering a debtor's inventory. 4. *Future advances*—A security agreement may provide that any future advances made against a line of credit will be subject to the initial security interest in the same collateral.
Priorities (See pages 506–508.)	See Exhibit 20–3 on page 509.
Rights and Duties of Debtors and Creditors (See pages 508–510.)	1. *Information request*—On request by any person, the filing officer must send a statement listing the file number, the date, and the hour of the filing of financing statements and other documents covering collateral of a particular debtor.

Chapter Summary: Security Interests in Personal Property—Continued

Rights and Duties of Debtors and Creditors—Continued	2. *Release, assignment, and amendment*—A secured party may (a) release part or all of the collateral described in a filed financing statement, thus ending the creditor's security interest; (b) assign part or all of the security interest to another party; and (c) amend a filed financing statement. 3. *Confirmation or accounting request by debtor*—The debtor has the right to request a confirmation of his or her view of the unpaid debt or listing of collateral. The secured party must authenticate and send to the debtor an accounting within fourteen days after the request is received. 4. *Termination statement*—When a debt is paid, the secured party generally must send a *termination statement* to the debtor or file such a statement with the filing officer to whom the original financing statement was given. If the financing statement covers consumer goods, the termination statement must be filed by the secured party within one month after the debt is paid.

Default
(See pages 510–515.)
	On the debtor's default, the secured party may do either of the following:
	1. Take possession (peacefully or by court order) of the collateral covered by the security agreement and then pursue one of two alternatives:
	  a. Retain the collateral (unless the secured party has a PMSI in consumer goods and the debtor has paid 60 percent or more of the selling price or loan). The secured party may be required to give notice to the debtor and to other secured parties or lienholders with an interest in the collateral. If any of the notified parties objects within twenty days, the creditor must dispose of the collateral.
	  b. Dispose of the collateral in accordance with the requirements of UCC 9–602(7), 9–603, 9–610(a), and 9–613. The disposition must be carried out in a commercially reasonable manner. Unless the collateral is perishable or will rapidly decline in value, notice of the disposition must be given to the debtor and other specified parties. The proceeds are applied as follows:
	    (1) Reasonable expenses incurred by the secured party in repossessing, storing, and reselling the collateral.
	    (2) The balance of the debt owed to the secured party.
	    (3) Junior lienholders who have made written or authenticated demands.
	    (4) Surplus to the debtor (unless the collateral consists of accounts, payment intangibles, promissory notes, or chattel paper).
	2. Relinquish the security interest and use any judicial remedy available, such as proceeding to judgment on the underlying debt, followed by execution and levy on the nonexempt assets of the debtor.

 ExamPrep

ISSUE SPOTTERS

1 Nero needs $500 to buy textbooks and other supplies. Olivia agrees to loan Nero $500, accepting as collateral Nero's computer. They put their agreement in writing. How can Olivia let other creditors know of her interest in the computer?
2 Liberty Bank loans $5,000 to Michelle to buy a car, which is used as collateral to secure the loan. Michelle has paid less than 50 percent of the loan, when she defaults. Liberty could repossess and keep the car, but the bank does not want it. What are the alternatives?

BEFORE THE TEST

Check your answers to the Issue Spotters, and at the same time, take the interactive quiz for this chapter. Go to **www.cengage.com/blaw/blt** and click on "Chapter 20." First, click on "Answers to Issue Spotters" to check your answers. Next, click on "Interactive Quiz" to assess your mastery of the concepts in this chapter. Then click on "Flashcards" to review this chapter's Key Term definitions.

 For Review

Answers for the even-numbered questions in this For Review *section can be found on this text's accompanying Web site at* **www.cengage.com/blaw/blt**. *Select "Chapter 20" and click on "For Review."*

1 What is a security interest? Who is a secured party? What is a security agreement? What is a financing statement?

2 What three requirements must be met to create an enforceable security interest?

3 What is the most common method of perfecting a security interest under Article 9?

4 If two secured parties have perfected security interests in the collateral of the debtor, which party has priority to the collateral on the debtor's default?

5 What rights does a secured creditor have on the debtor's default?

▶ Hypothetical Scenarios and Case Problems

20–1 Priority Disputes. Redford is a seller of electric generators. He purchases a large quantity of generators from a manufacturer, Mallon Corp., by making a down payment and signing an agreement to pay the balance over a period of time. The agreement gives Mallon Corp. a security interest in the generators and the proceeds. Mallon Corp. properly files a financing statement on its security interest. Redford receives the generators and immediately sells one of them to Garfield on an installment contract with payment to be made in twelve equal installments. At the time of the sale, Garfield knows of Mallon's security interest. Two months later, Redford goes into default on his payments to Mallon. Discuss Mallon's rights against purchaser Garfield in this situation.

20–2 **Hypothetical Question with Sample Answer** Marsh has a prize horse named Arabian Knight. Marsh is in need of working capital. She borrows $5,000 from Mendez, who takes possession of Arabian Knight as security for the loan. No written agreement is signed. Discuss whether, in the absence of a written agreement, Mendez has a security interest in Arabian Knight. If Mendez does have a security interest, is it a perfected security interest? Explain.

—For a sample answer to Question 20–2, go to Appendix E at the end of this text.

20–3 The Scope of a Security Interest. Edward owned a retail sporting goods shop. A new ski resort was being constructed in his area, and to take advantage of the potential business, Edward decided to expand his operations. He borrowed a large sum from his bank, which took a security interest in his present inventory and any after-acquired inventory as collateral for the loan. The bank properly perfected the security interest by filing a financing statement. Edward's business was profitable, so he doubled his inventory. A year later, just a few months after the ski resort had opened, an avalanche destroyed the ski slope and lodge. Edward's business consequently took a turn for the worse, and he defaulted on his debt to the bank. The bank then sought possession of his entire inventory, even though the inventory was now twice as large as it had been when the loan was made. Edward claimed that the bank had rights to only half of his inventory. Is Edward correct? Explain.

20–4 Priorities. EX Services, Inc., was an excavating business. Union Bank made loans to EX, subject to a perfected security interest in its equipment and other assets, including "after-acquired property." In late 2006, EX leased heavy construction equipment from Mac's Machinery. The lease agreements required monthly payments, which EX often made late or missed. After

eighteen months, Mac's demanded that EX either return the equipment or buy it. While attempting to obtain financing for the purchase, EX continued to make monthly payments. In November 2009, Mac's, which had not filed a financing statement to cover the transaction, demanded full payment of the amount due. Before paying the price, EX went out of business and surrendered its assets to Union, which prepared to sell them. Mac's objected and filed a lawsuit against Union to recover the equipment, claiming that the bank's security interest had not attached to the equipment because EX had not paid for it. Who has priority to the equipment, and why?

20–5 Security Interest. In St. Louis, Missouri, in August 2000, Richard Miller orally agreed to loan Jeff Miller $35,000 in exchange for a security interest in a 1999 Kodiak dump truck. The Millers did not put anything in writing concerning the loan, its repayment terms, or Richard's security interest or rights in the truck. Jeff used the amount of the loan to buy the truck, which he kept in his possession. In June 2004, Jeff filed a petition to obtain a discharge of his debts in bankruptcy. Richard claimed that he had a security interest in the truck and thus was entitled to any proceeds from its sale. What are a creditor's main concerns on a debtor's default? How does a creditor satisfy these concerns? What are the requirements for a creditor to have an enforceable security interest? Are these requirements met in this case? Considering these points, what is the court likely to rule with respect to Richard's claim? [*In re Miller,* 320 Bankr. 911 (E.D.Mo. 2005)]

20–6 **Case Problem with Sample Answer** In 2002, Michael Sabol, doing business in the recording industry as Sound Farm Productions, applied to Morton Community Bank in Bloomington, Illinois, for a $58,000 loan to expand his business. Besides the loan application, Sabol signed a promissory note that referred to the bank's rights in "any collateral." Sabol also signed a letter that stated, "the undersigned does hereby authorize Morton Community Bank to execute, file and record all financing statements, amendments, termination statements and all other statements authorized by Article 9 of the Illinois Uniform Commercial Code, as to any security interest." Sabol did not sign any other documents, including the financing statement, which did, however, contain a description of the collateral. Less than three years later, without having repaid the loan, Sabol filed a petition in a federal bankruptcy court to declare bankruptcy. The bank claimed a security interest in Sabol's sound equipment. What are the elements of an enforceable security interest? What are the requirements of each of those elements? Does the bank have a valid security interest in this case? Explain. [*In re Sabol,* 337 Bankr. 195 (C.D.Ill. 2006)]

—After you have answered Problem 20–6, compare your answer with the sample answer given on the Web site that accompanies this text. Go to **www.cengage.com/blaw/blt**, select "Chapter 20," and click on "Case Problem with Sample Answer."

20–7 Default. Primesouth Bank issued a loan to Okefenokee Aircraft, Inc. (OAI), to buy a plane. OAI executed a note in favor of Primesouth in the amount of $161,306.25, plus interest. The plane secured the note. When OAI defaulted, Primesouth repossessed the plane. Instead of disposing of the collateral and seeking a deficiency judgment, however, the bank retained possession of the plane and filed a suit in a Georgia state court against OAI to enforce the note. OAI did not deny defaulting on the note or dispute the amount due. Instead, OAI argued that Primesouth Bank was not acting in a commercially reasonable manner. According to OAI, the creditor must sell the collateral and apply the proceeds against the debt. What is a secured creditor's obligation in these circumstances? Can the creditor retain the collateral and seek a judgment for the amount of the underlying debt, or is a sale required? Discuss. [*Okefenokee Aircraft, Inc. v. Primesouth Bank,* 296 Ga.App. 872, 676 S.E.2d 394 (2009)]

20–8 **A Question of Ethics** *In 1995, Mark Denton cosigned a $101,250 loan that the First Interstate Bank (FIB) in Missoula, Montana, issued to Denton's friend Eric Anderson.*

Denton's business assets—a mini-warehouse operation—secured the loan. On his own, Anderson obtained a $260,000 U.S. Small Business Administration (SBA) loan from FIB at the same time. The purpose of both loans was to buy logging equipment with which Anderson could start a business. In 1997, the business failed. As a consequence, FIB repossessed and sold the equipment and applied the proceeds to the SBA loan. FIB then asked Denton to pay the other loan's outstanding balance ($98,460) plus interest. When Denton refused, FIB initiated proceedings to obtain his business assets. Denton filed a suit in a Montana state court against FIB, claiming, in part, that Anderson's equipment was the collateral for the loan that FIB was attempting to collect from Denton. [Denton v. First Interstate Bank of Commerce, 2006 MT 193, 333 Mont. 169, 142 P.3d 797 (2006)]

1 Denton's assets served as the security for Anderson's loan because Anderson had nothing to offer. When the loan was obtained, Dean Gillmore, FIB's loan officer, explained to them that if Anderson defaulted, the proceeds from the sale of the logging equipment would be applied to the SBA loan first. Under these circumstances, is it fair to hold Denton liable for the unpaid balance of Anderson's loan? Why or why not?

2 Denton argued that the loan contract was unconscionable and constituted a "contract of adhesion." What makes a contract unconscionable? Did the transaction between the parties in this case qualify? What is a "contract of adhesion"? Was this deal unenforceable on that basis? Explain.

▶ Critical Thinking and Writing Assignments

20–9 Critical Legal Thinking. Review the three requirements for an enforceable security interest. Why is each of these requirements necessary?

20–10 **Video Question** Go to this text's Web site at **www.cengage.com/blaw/blt** and select "Chapter 20." Click on "Video Questions" and view the video titled *Secured Transactions.* Then answer the following questions.

1 This chapter lists three requirements for creating a security interest. In the video, which requirement does Laura assert has not been met?

2 What, if anything, must the bank have done to perfect its interest in the editing equipment?

3 If the bank exercises its self-help remedy to repossess Onyx's editing equipment, does Laura have any chance of getting it back? Explain.

4 Assume that the bank had a perfected security interest and repossessed the editing equipment. Also assume that the purchase price (and the loan amount) for the equipment was $100,000, of which Onyx has paid $65,000. Discuss the rights and duties of the bank with regard to the collateral in this situation.

▶ Practical Internet Exercises

Go to this text's Web site at **www.cengage.com/blaw/blt**, select "Chapter 20," and click on "Practical Internet Exercises." There you will find the following Internet research exercises that you can perform to learn more about the topics covered in this chapter.

Practical Internet Exercise 20–1: LEGAL PERSPECTIVE—**Repossession**
Practical Internet Exercise 20–2: MANAGEMENT PERSPECTIVE—**Filing Financial Statements**

Creditors' Rights and Bankruptcy

Chapter Outline

- Laws Assisting Creditors
- Laws Assisting Debtors
- Bankruptcy Proceedings
- Chapter 7–Liquidation
- Chapter 11–Reorganization
- Bankruptcy Relief under Chapter 13 and Chapter 12

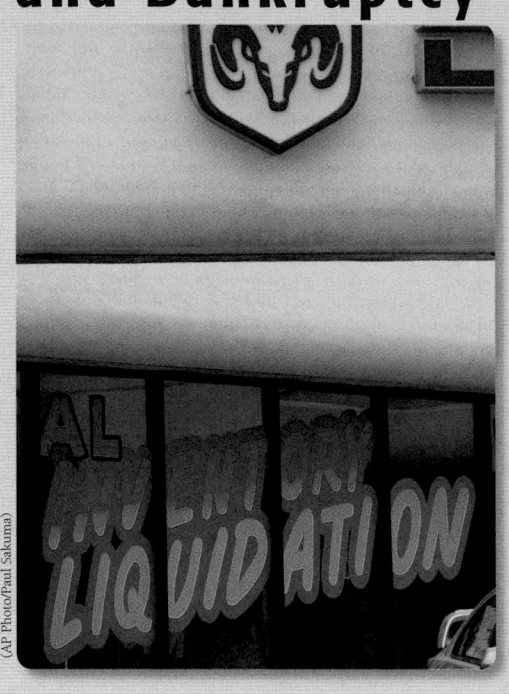

(AP Photo/Paul Sakuma)

Learning Objectives

After reading this chapter, you should be able to answer the following questions:

1. What is a prejudgment attachment? What is a writ of execution? How does a creditor use these remedies?

2. What is garnishment? When might a creditor undertake a garnishment proceeding?

3. In a bankruptcy proceeding, what constitutes the debtor's estate in property? What property is exempt from the estate under federal bankruptcy law?

4. What is the difference between an exception to discharge and an objection to discharge?

5. In a Chapter 11 reorganization, what is the role of the debtor in possession?

In the chapter-opening quotation, America's font of practical wisdom, Benjamin Franklin, observed a truth known to all debtors—that creditors do observe "set days and times" and will expect to recover their loaned funds by the agreed-on dates. Historically, debtors and their families were subjected to punishment, including involuntary servitude and imprisonment, when they were unable to pay debts. The modern legal system, however, has moved away from a punishment philosophy in dealing with debtors. In fact, until a new bankruptcy law was enacted in 2005, many observers argued that it had moved too far in the other direction, to the detriment of creditors.

Normally, creditors have no problem collecting the debts owed to them. When disputes arise over the amount owed, however, or when the debtor simply cannot or will not pay, what happens? What remedies are available to creditors when debtors default? We have already discussed, in Chapter 20, the remedies available to secured creditors under Article 9 of the Uniform Commercial Code (UCC). In the first part of this chapter, we focus on some basic laws that assist the debtor and creditor in resolving their dispute. We then examine the process of bankruptcy as a last resort in resolving debtor-creditor problems. We specifically include changes resulting from the 2005 Bankruptcy Reform Act.

Laws Assisting Creditors

Both the common law and statutory laws other than Article 9 of the UCC create various rights and remedies for creditors. Here we discuss some of these rights and remedies.

Liens

As explained in Chapter 18, a *lien* is an encumbrance on (claim against) property to satisfy a debt or protect a claim for the payment of a debt. Creditors' liens may arise under the common law or under statutory law. Statutory liens include *mechanic's liens*. Liens created at common law include *artisan's liens*. *Judicial liens* include those that represent a creditor's efforts to collect on a debt before or after a judgment is entered by a court.

Generally, a lien creditor has priority over an unperfected secured party but not over a perfected secured party. In other words, if a person becomes a lien creditor *before* another party perfects a security interest in the same property, the lienholder has priority. If a lien is obtained *after* another's security interest in the property is perfected, the lienholder does not have priority. This is true for all liens except mechanic's and artisan's liens, which normally have priority over perfected security interests—unless a statute provides otherwise.

MECHANIC'S LIEN   When a person contracts for labor, services, or materials to be furnished for the purpose of making improvements on real property (land and things attached to the land, such as buildings and trees—see Chapter 36) but does not immediately pay for the improvements, the creditor can file a **mechanic's lien** on the property. This creates a special type of debtor-creditor relationship in which the real estate itself becomes security for the debt.

EXAMPLE 21.1   A painter agrees to paint a house for a homeowner for an agreed-on price to cover labor and materials. If the homeowner refuses to pay for the work or pays only a portion of the charges, a mechanic's lien against the property can be created. The painter is the lienholder, and the real property is encumbered (burdened) with a mechanic's lien for the amount owed. If the homeowner does not pay the lien, the property can be sold to satisfy the debt. Notice of the foreclosure (the process by which the creditor deprives the debtor of his or her property) and sale must be given to the debtor in advance, however. ●

Note that state law governs the procedures that must be followed to create a mechanic's lien. Generally, the lienholder must file a written notice of lien against the particular property involved. The notice of lien must be filed within a specific time period, normally measured from the last date on which materials or labor were provided (usually within 60 to 120 days). If the property owner fails to pay the debt, the lienholder is entitled to foreclose on the real estate on which the work or materials were provided and to sell it to satisfy the amount of the debt.

ARTISAN'S LIEN   An **artisan's lien** is a security device created at common law through which a creditor can recover payment from a debtor for labor and materials furnished for the repair or improvement of personal property. In contrast to a mechanic's lien, an artisan's lien is *possessory*. The lienholder ordinarily must have retained possession of the property and have expressly or impliedly agreed to provide the services on a cash, not a credit, basis. The lien remains in existence as long as the lienholder maintains possession, and the lien is

Mechanic's Lien   A statutory lien on the real property of another to ensure payment for work performed and materials furnished in the repair or improvement of real property, such as a building.

Artisan's Lien   A possessory lien given to a person who has made improvements and added value to another person's personal property as security for payment for services performed.

Sometimes, homeowners contract for significant improvements to their structures. When the homeowners fail to pay those individuals or companies that provided labor and materials for the renovations, a mechanic's lien is automatically created. Why do mechanic's liens have priority over perfected security interests?

(AP Photo/Columbus Ledger-Enquirer/Joe Paul)

terminated once possession is voluntarily surrendered—unless the surrender is only temporary.

EXAMPLE 21.2   Tenetia leaves her diamond ring at the jeweler's to be repaired and to have her initials engraved on the band. In the absence of an agreement, the jeweler can keep the ring until Tenetia pays for the services. Should Tenetia fail to pay, the jeweler has a lien on Tenetia's ring for the amount of the bill and normally can sell the ring in satisfaction of the lien. ●

Modern statutes permit the holder of an artisan's lien to foreclose and sell the property subject to the lien to satisfy payment of the debt. As with a mechanic's lien, the holder of an artisan's lien is required to give notice to the owner of the property prior to foreclosure and sale. The sale proceeds are used to pay the debt and the costs of the legal proceedings, and the surplus, if any, is paid to the former owner.

JUDICIAL LIENS   When a debt is past due, a creditor can bring a legal action against the debtor to collect the debt. If the creditor is successful in the action, the court awards the creditor a judgment against the debtor (usually for the amount of the debt plus any interest and legal costs incurred in obtaining the judgment). Frequently, however, the creditor is unable to collect the awarded amount.

To ensure that a judgment in the creditor's favor will be collectible, the creditor is permitted to request that certain nonexempt property of the debtor be seized to satisfy the debt. (As will be discussed later in this chapter, under state or federal statutes, certain property is exempt from attachment by creditors.) A court's order to seize the debtor's property is known as a *writ of attachment* if it is issued prior to a judgment in the creditor's favor; if the order is issued after a judgment, it is referred to as a *writ of execution.*

Writ of Attachment.   Recall from Chapter 20 that *attachment,* in the context of secured transactions, refers to the process through which a security interest in a debtor's collateral becomes enforceable. In the context of judicial liens, this word has another meaning: **attachment** is a court-ordered seizure and taking into custody of property prior to the securing of a judgment for a past-due debt. Attachment rights are created by state statutes. Normally, attachment is a *prejudgment* remedy occurring either at the time a lawsuit is filed or immediately afterwards. To attach before judgment, a creditor must comply with the specific state's statutory restrictions and requirements. The due process clause of the Fourteenth Amendment to the U.S. Constitution also applies and requires that the debtor be given notice and an opportunity to be heard (see Chapter 2).

The creditor must have an enforceable right to payment of the debt under law and must follow certain procedures. Otherwise, the creditor can be liable for damages for wrongful attachment. She or he must file with the court an *affidavit* (a written or printed statement, made under oath or sworn to) stating that the debtor is in default and indicating the statutory grounds under which attachment is sought. The creditor must also post a bond to cover at least the court costs, the value of the loss of use of the good suffered by the debtor, and the value of the property attached. When the court is satisfied that all the requirements have been met, it issues a **writ of attachment,** which directs the sheriff or other public officer to seize nonexempt property. If the creditor prevails at trial, the seized property can be sold to satisfy the judgment.

Writ of Execution.   If the creditor wins at trial and the debtor will not or cannot pay the judgment, the creditor is entitled to go back to the court and request a **writ of execution.** This writ is a court order directing the

Attachment   In the context of judicial liens, a court-ordered seizure and taking into custody of property prior to the securing of a judgment for a past-due debt.

Writ of Attachment   A court's order, issued prior to a trial to collect a debt, directing the sheriff or other public officer to seize nonexempt property of the debtor. If the creditor prevails at trial, the seized property can be sold to satisfy the judgment.

Writ of Execution   A court's order, issued after a judgment has been entered against a debtor, directing the sheriff to seize and sell any of the debtor's nonexempt real or personal property.

The bank that loaned funds for purchase of this boat can bring legal action to collect the debt. Once a judgment against the debtor is rendered, what happens next?

sheriff to seize (levy) and sell any of the debtor's nonexempt real or personal property that is within the court's geographic jurisdiction (usually the county in which the courthouse is located). The proceeds of the sale are used to pay off the judgment, accrued interest, and the costs of the sale. Any excess is paid to the debtor. The debtor can pay the judgment and redeem the nonexempt property any time before the sale takes place. (Because of exemption laws and bankruptcy laws, however, many judgments are uncollectible.)

Garnishment

Garnishment A legal process used by a creditor to collect a debt by seizing property of the debtor (such as wages) that is being held by a third party (such as the debtor's employer).

An order for **garnishment** permits a creditor to collect a debt by seizing property of the debtor that is being held by a third party. In a garnishment proceeding, the third party—the person or entity that the court is ordering to garnish an individual's property—is called the *garnishee*. Frequently, a garnishee is the debtor's employer. A creditor may seek a garnishment judgment against the debtor's employer so that part of the debtor's usual paycheck will be paid to the creditor. In some situations, however, the garnishee is a third party that holds funds belonging to the debtor (such as a bank) or has possession of, or exercises control over, other types of property belonging to the debtor. A creditor can garnish almost all types of property—including tax refunds, pensions, and trust funds—as long as the property is not exempt from garnishment and is in the possession of a third party.

GARNISHMENT PROCEEDINGS   The legal proceeding for a garnishment action is governed by state law, and garnishment operates differently from state to state. As a result of a garnishment proceeding, as noted, the court orders a third party (such as the debtor's employer) to turn over property owned by the debtor (such as wages) to pay the debt. Garnishment can be a prejudgment remedy, requiring a hearing before a court, but it is most often a postjudgment remedy. According to the laws in some states, the creditor needs to obtain only one order of garnishment, which will then apply continuously to the debtor's wages until the entire debt is paid. In other states, the judgment creditor must go back to court for a separate order of garnishment for each pay period.

LAWS LIMITING THE AMOUNT OF WAGES SUBJECT TO GARNISHMENT   Both federal and state laws limit the amount that can be taken from a debtor's weekly take-home pay through garnishment proceedings.[1] Federal law provides a framework to protect debtors from suffering unduly when paying judgment debts.[2] State laws also provide dollar exemptions, and these amounts are often larger than those provided by federal law. Under federal law, an employer cannot dismiss an employee because his or her wages are being garnished.

Creditors' Composition Agreements

Creditors' Composition Agreement An agreement formed between a debtor and his or her creditors in which the creditors agree to accept a lesser sum than that owed by the debtor in full satisfaction of the debt.

Creditors may contract with the debtor for discharge of the debtor's liquidated debts (debts that are definite, or fixed, in amount) on payment of a sum less than that owed. These agreements are called **creditors' composition agreements,** or simply *composition agreements,* and usually are held to be enforceable.

Mortgage Foreclosure

Mortgage A written instrument giving a creditor an interest in (lien on) the debtor's real property as security for payment of a debt.

A **mortgage** is a written instrument giving a creditor an interest in (lien on) the debtor's real property as security for the payment of a debt. Financial institutions grant mortgage loans

---

1. Some states (for example, Texas) do not permit garnishment of wages by private parties except under a child-support order.
2. For example, the federal Consumer Credit Protection Act of 1968, 15 U.S.C. Sections 1601–1693r, provides that a debtor can retain either 75 percent of disposable earnings per week or a sum equivalent to thirty hours of work paid at federal minimum-wage rates, whichever is greater.

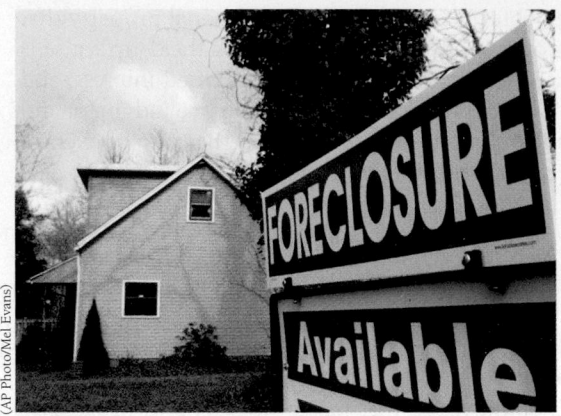

(AP Photo/Mel Evans)

Since the beginning of the economic crisis in the United States, many homes have been foreclosed, like this one in Egg Harbor Township, New Jersey. Foreclosure occurs after the mortgagor fails to make timely payments. The methods of foreclosure are state-specific. What happens when, upon the sale of the foreclosed property, the funds obtained by the creditor are less than the funds loaned?

for the purchase of property—usually a dwelling and the land on which it sits (*real property* will be discussed in Chapter 36). Given the relatively large sums that many individuals borrow to purchase a home, defaults are not uncommon, especially during periods of weak economic conditions such as the recession that began in late 2007.

On the debtor's default, the entire debt is due and payable, allowing the mortgage holder to foreclose on the mortgaged property. The usual method of foreclosure is by judicial sale of the property, although the statutory methods of foreclosure vary from state to state. If the proceeds of the foreclosure sale are sufficient to cover both the costs of the foreclosure and the mortgaged debt, the debtor receives any surplus. If the sale proceeds are insufficient to cover the costs and the debt, however, the **mortgagee** (the creditor-lender) can seek to recover the difference from other property owned by the **mortgagor** (the debtor) by obtaining a deficiency judgment representing the difference between the mortgaged debt and the amount actually received from the proceeds of the foreclosure sale. The mortgagee obtains a deficiency judgment in a separate legal action pursued subsequent to the foreclosure action.

Mortgagee   Under a mortgage agreement, the creditor who takes a security interest in the debtor's property.

Mortgagor   Under a mortgage agreement, the debtor who gives the creditor a security interest in the debtor's property in return for a mortgage loan.

Ethical Issue ⚖️

"Mortgage: a house with a guilty conscience."

Anonymous

Should debtors who took out disadvantageous mortgages be rescued from foreclosure by the federal government? Mortgage lenders usually extend credit to high-risk borrowers through mortgages at higher-than-normal interest rates (called subprime mortgages) or through adjustable-rate mortgages (ARMs). The recent widespread use of subprime mortgages and ARMs resulted in many borrowers being overextended and unable to make their loan payments on time. In addition, as housing prices dropped, some borrowers could not sell their homes for the amount that they owed on their mortgages. In fact, by the end of 2008, in certain areas, such as California, more than 30 percent of the homes were worth less than the homeowners owed on their mortgages. Consequently, the number of home foreclosures increased dramatically in 2008 and 2009. Some commentators claimed that the mortgage lenders were responsible for the problem because they sometimes encouraged people to borrow more than they could "afford." Others argued that it is ultimately the borrowers' responsibility to understand the terms and decide if they are able to repay their mortgage loans. After all, freedom of contract means that people are free to enter into bad bargains.

In 2008, Congress enacted legislation designed to help some troubled borrowers refinance their mortgage loans.[3] The law raised the national debt ceiling to $10 trillion (an increase of $800 billion) to fund the bailout of two government-sponsored mortgage industry giants (Fannie Mae and Freddie Mac—federalized in September 2008) and expanded the Federal Housing Administration's loan guarantee program. If an existing mortgage lender agreed to write down the loan balance to 90 percent of the home's current value, the government would guarantee a new fixed-rate loan. Although this legislation was expected to help only about 400,000 homeowners,[4] in 2009 the Obama administration substantially expanded the program in an effort to provide assistance to the 3 to 4 million homeowners believed to be at risk of foreclosure.

---

3. House Resolution 3221, a bill to provide needed housing reform and for other purposes; also known as the Foreclosure Prevention Act of 2008.

4. Ron Sherer, "Big Housing Bill: No Rescue Soon," *The Christian Science Monitor,* August 1, 2008; and David M. Herszenhorn, "Bush Signs Sweeping Housing Bill," *The New York Times,* July 31, 2008.

Suretyship and Guaranty

When a third person promises to pay a debt owed by another in the event the debtor does not pay, either a *suretyship* or a *guaranty* relationship is created. Suretyship and guaranty provide creditors with the right to seek payment from the third party if the primary debtor defaults on her or his obligations. Exhibit 21–1 illustrates the relationship between a suretyship or guaranty party and the creditor. At common law, there were significant differences in the liability of a surety and a guarantor, as discussed in the following subsections. Today, however, the distinctions outlined here have been abolished in some states.

Suretyship An express contract in which a third party to a debtor-creditor relationship (the surety) promises to be primarily responsible for the debtor's obligation.

Surety A person, such as a cosigner on a note, who agrees to be primarily responsible for the debt of another.

SURETY   A contract of strict **suretyship** is a promise made by a third person to be responsible for the debtor's obligation. It is an express contract between the **surety** (the third party) and the creditor. The surety in the strictest sense is primarily liable for the debt of the principal. The creditor need not exhaust all legal remedies against the principal debtor before holding the surety responsible for payment. The creditor can demand payment from the surety from the moment the debt is due.

EXAMPLE 21.3 Roberto Delmar wants to borrow from the bank to buy a used car. Because Roberto is still in college, the bank will not lend him the funds unless his father, José Delmar, who has dealt with the bank before, will cosign the note (add his signature to the note, thereby becoming a surety and thus jointly liable for payment of the debt). When José Delmar cosigns the note, he becomes primarily liable to the bank. On the note's due date, the bank can seek payment from either Roberto or José Delmar, or both jointly. •

Guarantor A person who agrees to satisfy the debt of another (the debtor) only after the principal debtor defaults. Thus, a guarantor's liability is secondary.

GUARANTY   With a suretyship arrangement, the surety is *primarily* liable for the debtor's obligation. With a guaranty arrangement, the **guarantor**—the third person making the guaranty—is *secondarily* liable. The guarantor can be required to pay the obligation *only after the principal debtor defaults,* and default usually takes place only after the creditor has made an attempt to collect from the debtor.

EXAMPLE 21.4 BX Enterprises, a small corporation, needs to borrow funds to meet its payroll. The bank is skeptical about the creditworthiness of BX and requires Dawson, its president, who is a wealthy businessperson and the owner of 70 percent of BX Enterprises,

• *Exhibit* 21–1 Suretyship and Guaranty Parties

In a suretyship or guaranty arrangement, a third party promises to be responsible for a debtor's obligations. A third party who agrees to be responsible for the debt even if the primary debtor does not default is known as a surety; a third party who agrees to be *secondarily* responsible for the debt—that is, responsible only if the primary debtor defaults—is known as a guarantor. A promise of guaranty (a collateral, or secondary, promise) normally must be in writing to be enforceable.

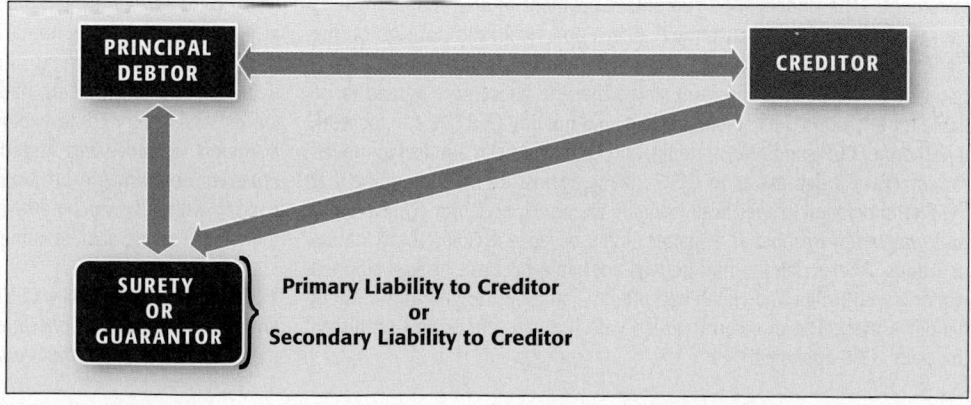

to sign an agreement making himself personally liable for payment if BX does not pay off the loan. As a guarantor of the loan, Dawson cannot be held liable until BX Enterprises is in default. ●

Under the Statute of Frauds, a guaranty contract between the guarantor and the creditor must be in writing to be enforceable unless the *main purpose rule* applies (see Chapter 12 on page 299).[5] A suretyship agreement, by contrast, need not be in writing to be enforceable. In other words, surety agreements can be oral, whereas guaranty contracts must be written.

In the following case, the issue was whether a guaranty form for a partnership's debt was actually made out in the guarantors' names and whether the guarantors signed this form.

---

5. Briefly, the main purpose rule, or exception, provides that if the main purpose of the guaranty agreement is to benefit the guarantor, then the contract need not be in writing to be enforceable.

Case 21.1   Capital Color Printing, Inc. v. Ahern

Court of Appeals of Georgia, 291 Ga.App. 101, 661 S.E.2d 578 (2008).

A printing company was not paid $76,000 for work that it had completed. The buyers of this printing work used a standard credit form. Can the Statute of Frauds be used to avoid payment?

FACTS Quality Printing is a printing broker that sells printing services to customers but subcontracts the printing work to third parties. It contacted Capital Color Printing, Inc. (CCP), about doing some work. The credit manager at CCP said that Jason Ahern and Todd Heflin, the owners of Quality, would have to execute personal guaranties before CCP would do any work. Quality sent CCP a credit application that contained a guaranty. The names "Ahern" and "Heflin" appeared on the "Your Name" line. Quality's name, address, tax number, and other information were provided in the "Customer" box on the form. Ahern and Heflin stated that they were partners who owned Quality. Below the signature line was the following statement: "The undersigned guarantees payment of any and all invoices for services rendered to customer." Ahern and Heflin did not sign on the signature line, but their names were signed where printed names were requested. The back of the form stated that the guarantors agreed to be liable for any unpaid bills. When Quality did not pay CCP $76,000 for work it had done, CCP sued Ahern, Heflin, and Quality. Ahern and Heflin moved for summary judgment as to CCP's claims against them, contending that the guaranty failed to specifically identify the principal debtor (Quality) and thus was unenforceable as a matter of law because it violated the Statute of Frauds. Ahern claimed that he was not liable because he had stopped working with Heflin and Heflin had put his name on the guaranty without his permission. The trial court agreed with the defendants and dismissed the claim. CCP appealed.

ISSUE Does the preprinted credit form that identified Quality Printing as the "customer" and included a guaranty and what appeared to be the signatures of Ahern and Heflin satisfy the requirements of the Statute of Frauds?

DECISION Yes. The appeals court reversed the lower court, holding that CCP was entitled to summary judgment against Heflin as guarantor of payment for services performed for Quality. The court remanded the case for a trial to determine if Ahern was liable on the debt or if Heflin had forged his name on the guaranty.

REASON The owners (Ahern and Heflin) claimed that the Statute of Frauds was violated because the guaranty did not specify the name of the principal debtor, Quality. That would be true if the document failed to identify Quality at all, but the form identified Quality as the customer, and that would, taken as a whole, sufficiently identify Quality as the principal debtor. The law does not require a specific format for such forms, only the ability to identify the roles of the parties named in the document. While the signature lines on the form were left blank, the evidence indicated that Heflin filled in both his and Ahern's name as guarantors, even though the signatures were in the wrong place on the form. Ahern claimed that his signature was a forgery and that he had ended his business dealings with Heflin. On remand, a jury could explore the details of the business relationship. If Ahern's signature was forged, only Heflin might be liable. If Heflin had *apparent authority* (to be discussed in Chapter 23) to bind Ahern to the contract with CCP, which performed $76,000 in printing services for Quality, then Ahern would also be liable on the guaranty.

FOR CRITICAL ANALYSIS—Global Consideration *If a firm was attempting to obtain a guaranty from third parties to a contract with a company in another country, what steps might be taken?*

ACTIONS THAT RELEASE THE SURETY AND GUARANTOR

The actions that will release the surety from an obligation are basically the same as those that will discharge the guarantor. Making any material modification in the terms of the original contract between the principal debtor and the creditor—without the consent of the surety or guarantor—will discharge the surety or guarantor's obligation. (The extent to which the surety or guarantor is discharged depends on whether he or she was compensated and to what extent he or she suffered a loss from the modification.) Similarly, if a creditor surrenders the collateral to the debtor or impairs the collateral without the consent of the surety or guarantor, this can reduce the obligation of the surety or guarantor.

Naturally, any payment of the principal obligation by the debtor or by another person on the debtor's behalf will discharge the surety or guarantor from the obligation. Even if the creditor refused to accept payment of the principal debt when it was tendered, the obligation of the surety or guarantor can be discharged.

DEFENSES OF THE SURETY AND THE GUARANTOR

Generally, the surety or guarantor can also assert any of the defenses available to a principal debtor to avoid liability on the obligation to the creditor. A few exceptions do exist, however. The surety or guarantor cannot assert the principal debtor's incapacity or bankruptcy as a defense, nor can the surety assert the statute of limitations as a defense.

Obviously, a surety or guarantor may also have her or his own defenses—for example, her or his own incapacity or bankruptcy. If the creditor fraudulently induced the surety to guarantee the debt of the debtor, the surety can assert fraud as a defense. In most states, the creditor has a legal duty to inform the surety, before the formation of the suretyship contract, of material facts known by the creditor that would substantially increase the surety's risk. Failure to so inform may constitute fraud and makes the suretyship obligation voidable.

RIGHTS OF THE SURETY AND THE GUARANTOR

Usually, when the surety or guarantor pays the debt owed to the creditor, the surety or guarantor is entitled to certain rights. Because the rights of the surety and guarantor are basically the same, the following discussion applies to both.

Right of Subrogation The right of a person to stand in the place of (be substituted for) another, giving the substituted party the same legal rights that the original party had.

The Right of Subrogation. The surety has the legal **right of subrogation.** Simply stated, this means that any right the creditor had against the debtor now becomes the right of the surety. Included are creditor rights in bankruptcy, rights to collateral possessed by the creditor, and rights to judgments secured by the creditor. In short, the surety now stands in the shoes of the creditor and may pursue any remedies that were available to the creditor against the debtor.

Right of Reimbursement The legal right of a person to be restored, repaid, or indemnified for costs, expenses, or losses incurred or expended on behalf of another.

The Right of Reimbursement. The surety has a **right of reimbursement** from the debtor. Basically, the surety is entitled to receive from the debtor all outlays made on behalf of the suretyship arrangement. Such outlays can include expenses incurred as well as the actual amount of the debt paid to the creditor.

Co-Surety A joint surety; a person who assumes liability jointly with another surety for the payment of an obligation.

Right of Contribution The right of a co-surety who pays more than her or his proportionate share on a debtor's default to recover the excess paid from other co-sureties.

The Right of Contribution. In a situation involving **co-sureties** (two or more sureties on the same obligation owed by the debtor), a surety who pays more than her or his proportionate share on a debtor's default is entitled to recover from the co-sureties the amount paid above the surety's obligation. This is the **right of contribution.** Generally, a co-surety's liability either is determined by agreement between the co-sureties or, in the absence of an agreement, is specified in the suretyship contract itself.

EXAMPLE 21.5 Two co-sureties are obligated under a suretyship contract to guarantee the debt of a debtor. Together, the sureties' maximum liability is $25,000. As specified in the suretyship contract, Surety A's maximum liability is $15,000, and surety B's is $10,000. The debtor owes $10,000 and is in default. Surety A pays the creditor the entire $10,000. In the absence of any agreement between the two co-sureties, Surety A can recover $4,000 from Surety B ($10,000/$25,000 × $10,000 = $4,000). ●

Preventing Legal Disputes

> Be careful when signing guaranty contracts and explicitly indicate if you are signing on behalf of a company rather than personally. If you are a corporate officer or director and you sign your name on a guaranty without indicating that you are signing as a representative of the corporation, you might be held personally liable. Although a guaranty contract may be preferable to a suretyship contract in some states because it creates secondary rather than primary liability, a guaranty still involves substantial risk. Depending on the wording used in a guaranty contract, the extent of the guarantor's liability may be unlimited or may continue over a series of transactions. Be absolutely clear about the potential liability before agreeing to serve as a guarantor, and contact an attorney for guidance.

▶ Laws Assisting Debtors

Homestead Exemption A law permitting a debtor to retain the family home, either in its entirety or up to a specified dollar amount, free from the claims of unsecured creditors or trustees in bankruptcy.

Under most state laws, certain personal property is exempt from satisfaction of judgment debts. Commonly, clothing is exempt. Under what circumstances might clothing not be exempt?

©Shannon West, 2009. Used under license from Shutterstock.com)

The law protects debtors as well as creditors. Certain property of the debtor, for example, is exempt from creditors' actions. Probably the most familiar exemption is the **homestead exemption.** Each state permits the debtor to retain the family home, either in its entirety or up to a specified dollar amount, free from the claims of unsecured creditors or trustees in bankruptcy (discussed later in this chapter). The purpose of the homestead exemption is to ensure that the debtor will retain some form of shelter. (Note that federal bankruptcy law now places a cap on the amount that debtors can claim under a state's homestead exemption, as will be discussed later in this chapter.)

EXAMPLE 21.6   Van Cleave owes Acosta $40,000. The debt is the subject of a lawsuit, and the court awards Acosta a judgment of $40,000 against Van Cleave. Van Cleave's home is valued at $50,000, and the state exemption on homesteads is $25,000. There are no outstanding mortgages or other liens. To satisfy the judgment debt, Van Cleave's family home is sold at public auction for $45,000. The proceeds of the sale are distributed as follows:

1. Van Cleave is given $25,000 as his homestead exemption.
2. Acosta is paid $20,000 toward the judgment debt, leaving a $20,000 deficiency judgment that can be satisfied from any other nonexempt property (personal or real) that Van Cleave may have, if allowed by state law. ●

Various types of personal property may also be exempt from satisfaction of judgment debts. Personal property that is most often exempt under state law includes the following:

1. Household furniture up to a specified dollar amount.
2. Clothing and certain personal possessions, such as family pictures or a religious text.
3. A vehicle (or vehicles) for transportation (at least up to a specified dollar amount).
4. Certain classified animals, usually livestock but including pets.
5. Equipment that the debtor uses in a business or trade, such as tools or professional instruments, up to a specified dollar amount.

▶ Bankruptcy Proceedings

Bankruptcy law in the United States has two goals—to protect a debtor by giving him or her a fresh start, free from creditors' claims, and to ensure equitable treatment to creditors who are competing for a debtor's assets. Bankruptcy law is federal law, but state laws on secured transactions, liens, judgments, and exemptions also play a role in federal bankruptcy proceedings.

Bankruptcy law prior to 2005 was based on the Bankruptcy Reform Act of 1978, as amended (called the Bankruptcy Code). In 2005, Congress enacted bankruptcy reform legislation that significantly overhauled certain provisions of the Bankruptcy Code for the first time in twenty-five years.[6] Because of its significance for creditors and debtors alike, we present the Bankruptcy Reform Act of 2005 as this chapter's *Landmark in the Law* feature on the following page.

Bankruptcy Courts

Bankruptcy proceedings are held in federal bankruptcy courts, which are under the authority of U.S. district courts, and rulings by bankruptcy courts can be appealed to the district courts. The bankruptcy court holds proceedings dealing with the procedures required to administer the debtor's estate in bankruptcy (the debtor's assets, as will be discussed shortly). A bankruptcy court can conduct a jury trial if the appropriate district court has authorized it and if the parties to the bankruptcy consent to a jury trial.

Types of Bankruptcy Relief

The Bankruptcy Code is contained in Title 11 of the *United States Code* (U.S.C.) and has eight "chapters." Chapters 1, 3, and 5 of the Code include general definitional provisions and provisions governing case administration and procedures, creditors, the debtor, and the estate. These three chapters of the Code normally apply to all types of bankruptcies. There are five other chapters that set forth the different types of relief that debtors may seek. Chapter 7 provides for **liquidation** proceedings (the selling of all nonexempt assets and the distribution of the proceeds to the debtor's creditors). Chapter 9 governs the adjustment of the debts of municipalities. Chapter 11 governs reorganizations. Chapter 12 (for family farmers and family fishermen) and Chapter 13 (for individuals) provide for adjustment of the debts of parties with regular income.[7] A debtor (except for a municipality) need not be insolvent[8] to file for bankruptcy relief under the Bankruptcy Code. Anyone obligated to a creditor can declare bankruptcy.

Special Treatment of Consumer-Debtors

To fully inform a consumer-debtor of the various types of relief available, the Code requires that the clerk of the court provide certain information to all consumer-debtors before the commencement of a bankruptcy filing. A **consumer-debtor** is a debtor whose debts result primarily from the purchase of goods for personal, family, or household use. First, the clerk must give consumer-debtors written notice of the general purpose, benefits, and costs of each chapter of bankruptcy under which they may proceed. Second, the clerk must provide consumer-debtors with informational materials on the types of services available from credit counseling agencies.

---

6. The full title of the act is the Bankruptcy Abuse Prevention and Consumer Protection Act of 2005, Pub. L. No. 109-8, 119 Stat. 23 (April 20, 2005).

7. There are no Chapters 2, 4, 6, 8, or 10 in Title 11. Such "gaps" are not uncommon in the *United States Code*. They occur because, when a statute is enacted, chapter numbers (or other subdivisional unit numbers) are sometimes reserved for future use. (A gap may also appear if a law has been repealed.)

8. The inability to pay debts as they come due is known as *equitable* insolvency. A *balance-sheet* insolvency, which exists when a debtor's liabilities exceed assets, is not the test. Thus, it is possible for debtors to petition voluntarily for bankruptcy even though their assets far exceed their liabilities. This situation may occur when a debtor's cash-flow problems become severe.

RECALL Congress regulates the jurisdiction of the federal courts, within the limits set by the U.S. Constitution. Congress can expand or reduce the number of federal courts at any time.

Liquidation The sale of all of the nonexempt assets of a debtor and the distribution of the proceeds to the debtor's creditors. Chapter 7 of the Bankruptcy Code provides for liquidation bankruptcy proceedings.

Consumer-Debtor An individual whose debts are primarily consumer debts (debts for purchases made primarily for personal, family, or household use).

In 2009, singer Courtney Love owed $350,000 to American Express. If American Express succeeds in obtaining a judgment, what types of personal property would Love be allowed to keep?

Landmark in the Law   The Bankruptcy Reform Act of 2005

When Congress enacted the Bankruptcy Reform Act of 1978, many claimed that the new act made it too easy for debtors to file for bankruptcy protection. The Bankruptcy Reform Act of 2005 was passed, in part, in response to businesses' concerns about the rise in personal bankruptcy filings. From 1978 to 2005, personal bankruptcy filings increased dramatically. Well before 2005, various business groups—including credit-card companies and banks—were claiming that the bankruptcy process was being abused and that reform was necessary. As Mallory Duncan of the National Retail Federation put it, bankruptcy had gone from being a "stigma" to being a "financial planning tool" for many debtors.[a]

More Repayment Plans, Fewer Liquidation Bankruptcies   One of the major goals of the Bankruptcy Reform Act of 2005 is to require consumers to pay as many of their debts as they possibly can instead of having those debts fully discharged in bankruptcy. Before the reforms, the vast majority of bankruptcies were filed under Chapter 7 of the Bankruptcy Code, which permits debtors, with some exceptions, to have *all* of their debts discharged in bankruptcy. Only about 20 percent of personal bankruptcies were filed under Chapter 13 of the Bankruptcy Code. As you will read later in this chapter, this part of the Bankruptcy Code requires the debtor to establish a repayment plan and pay off as many of his or her debts as possible over a maximum period of five years. Under the 2005 legislation, more debtors have to file for bankruptcy under Chapter 13.

Other Significant Provisions of the Act   Another important provision of the Bankruptcy Reform Act of 2005 involves the homestead

a. As quoted in Nedra Pickler, "Bush Signs Big Rewrite of Bankruptcy Law," *The Los Angeles Times,* April 20, 2005.

exemption. Before the passage of the act, some states allowed debtors petitioning for bankruptcy to exempt all of the *equity* (the market value minus the outstanding mortgage owed) in their homes during bankruptcy proceedings. The 2005 act leaves these exemptions in place but puts some limits on their use. The 2005 act also included a number of other changes. For example, one provision gave child-support obligations priority over other debts and allows enforcement agencies to continue efforts to collect child-support payments.

• **Application to Today's World**   *The Bankruptcy Reform Act of 2005 subjected a large class of individuals to increased financial risk. Supporters of the law hoped that it would curb abuse by deterring financially troubled debtors from viewing bankruptcy as a mere "planning tool" instead of as a last resort. Certainly, fewer debtors are allowed to have their debts discharged in Chapter 7 liquidation proceedings. At the same time, the act made it more difficult for debtors to obtain a "fresh start" financially—one of the major goals of bankruptcy law in the United States. Since the 2005 act, more debtors are forced to file under Chapter 13. Additionally, the bankruptcy process has become more time consuming and costly because it requires more extensive documentation and certification. These changes in the law, in conjunction with the global financial crisis that began in 2007, have left many Americans unable to obtain relief from their debts.*

• **Relevant Web Sites**   To locate information on the Web concerning the 2005 bankruptcy reform legislation, go to this text's Web site at www.cengage.com/blaw/blt, select "Chapter 21," and click on "URLs for Landmarks."

In the following pages, we deal first with liquidation proceedings under Chapter 7 of the Code. We then examine the procedures required for Chapter 11 reorganizations and for Chapter 12 and Chapter 13 plans.

 ## Chapter 7–Liquidation

Liquidation is the most familiar type of bankruptcy proceeding and is often referred to as an *ordinary,* or *straight, bankruptcy.* Put simply, a debtor in a liquidation bankruptcy turns all assets over to a trustee. The trustee sells the nonexempt assets and distributes the proceeds to creditors. With certain exceptions, the remaining debts are then **discharged** (extinguished), and the debtor is relieved of the obligation to pay the debts.

Any "person"—defined as including individuals, partnerships, and corporations[9]—may be a debtor under Chapter 7. Railroads, insurance companies, banks, savings and loan

Discharge   In bankruptcy proceedings, the extinction of the debtor's dischargeable debts, thereby relieving the debtor of the obligation to pay the debts.

---

9. The definition of *corporation* includes unincorporated companies and associations. It also covers labor unions.

(AP Photo/Paul Sakuma)

This Chrysler/Dodge/Jeep dealership in Colma, California, voluntarily entered into liquidation. U.S. automobile dealers were hard hit during the economic crisis. Chrysler and General Motors went into bankruptcy. During the process, many individual dealers were forced to close down.

Petition in Bankruptcy   The document that is filed with a bankruptcy court to initiate bankruptcy proceedings. The official forms required for a petition in bankruptcy must be completed accurately, sworn to under oath, and signed by the debtor.

U.S. Trustee   A government official who performs certain administrative tasks that a bankruptcy judge would otherwise have to perform.

associations, investment companies licensed by the U.S. Small Business Administration, and credit unions *cannot* be Chapter 7 debtors, however. Other chapters of the Code or other federal or state statutes apply to them. A husband and wife may file jointly for bankruptcy under a single petition.

A straight bankruptcy may be commenced by the filing of either a voluntary or an involuntary **petition in bankruptcy**— the document that is filed with a bankruptcy court to initiate bankruptcy proceedings. If a debtor files the petition, then it is a *voluntary bankruptcy*. If one or more creditors file a petition to force the debtor into bankruptcy, then it is called an *involuntary bankruptcy*. We discuss both voluntary and involuntary bankruptcy proceedings under Chapter 7 in the following subsections.

Voluntary Bankruptcy

To bring a voluntary petition in bankruptcy, the debtor files official forms designated for that purpose in the bankruptcy court. The Bankruptcy Reform Act of 2005 specifies that *before* debtors can file a petition, they must receive credit counseling from an approved nonprofit agency within the 180-day period preceding the date of filing. The act required the **U.S. trustee** (a government official who performs appointment and other administrative tasks that a bankruptcy judge would otherwise have to perform) to approve nonprofit budget and counseling agencies and make a list of approved agencies publicly available. A debtor filing a Chapter 7 petition must include a certificate proving that he or she attended an individual or group briefing from an approved counseling agency within the last 180 days (roughly six months).

A consumer-debtor who is filing a liquidation bankruptcy must confirm the accuracy of the petition's contents. The debtor must also state in the petition, at the time of filing, that he or she understands the relief available under other chapters of the Code and has chosen to proceed under Chapter 7. If an attorney is representing the consumer-debtor, the attorney must file an affidavit stating that she or he has informed the debtor of the relief available under each chapter of bankruptcy. In addition, the attorney must reasonably attempt to verify the accuracy of the consumer-debtor's petition and schedules (described below). Failure to do so is considered perjury.

CHAPTER 7 SCHEDULES   The voluntary petition contains the following schedules:

1. A list of both secured and unsecured creditors, their addresses, and the amount of debt owed to each.
2. A statement of the financial affairs of the debtor.
3. A list of all property owned by the debtor, including property claimed by the debtor to be exempt.
4. A list of current income and expenses.
5. A certificate of credit counseling (as discussed previously).
6. Proof of payments received from employers within sixty days prior to the filing of the petition.
7. A statement of the amount of monthly income, itemized to show how the amount is calculated.
8. A copy of the debtor's federal income tax return for the most recent year ending immediately before the filing of the petition.

As previously noted, the official forms must be completed accurately, sworn to under oath, and signed by the debtor. To conceal assets or knowingly supply false information on these schedules is a crime under the bankruptcy laws.

ADDITIONAL INFORMATION MAY BE REQUIRED   At the request of the court, the U.S. trustee, or any party of interest, the debtor must file tax returns at the end of each tax year while the case is pending and provide copies to the court. This requirement also applies to Chapter 11 and 13 bankruptcies (will be discussed later in this chapter). In addition, if requested by the U.S. trustee or bankruptcy trustee, the debtor must provide a photo document establishing his or her identity (such as a driver's license or passport) or other such personal identifying information.

With the exception of tax returns, failure to file the required schedules within forty-five days after the filing of the petition (unless an extension up to forty-five days is granted) will result in an automatic dismissal of the petition. The debtor has up to seven days before the date of the first creditors' meeting to provide a copy of the most current tax returns to the trustee.

WHEN SUBSTANTIAL ABUSE WILL BE PRESUMED   The Bankruptcy Reform Act of 2005 established a new system of "means testing"—based on the debtor's income—to determine whether a debtor's petition is presumed to be a "substantial abuse" of Chapter 7. If the debtor's family income is greater than the median family income in the state in which the petition is filed, the trustee or any party in interest (such as a creditor) can bring a motion to dismiss the Chapter 7 petition. State median incomes vary from state to state and are calculated and reported by the U.S. Bureau of the Census.

The debtor's current monthly income is calculated using the last six months' average income, less certain "allowed expenses" reflecting the basic needs of the debtor. The monthly amount is then multiplied by twelve. If the resulting income exceeds the state median income by $6,000 or more,[10] abuse is presumed, and the trustee or any creditor can file a motion to dismiss the petition. A debtor can rebut (refute) the presumption of abuse "by demonstrating special circumstances that justify additional expenses or adjustments of current monthly income for which there is no reasonable alternative." (An example might be anticipated medical costs not covered by health insurance.) These additional expenses or adjustments must be itemized and their accuracy attested to under oath by the debtor.

WHEN SUBSTANTIAL ABUSE WILL NOT BE PRESUMED   If the debtor's income is below the state median (or if the debtor has successfully refuted the means-test presumption), abuse will not be presumed. In these situations, the court may still find substantial abuse, but the creditors will not have standing (see Chapter 3) to file a motion to dismiss. Basically, this leaves intact the prior law on substantial abuse, allowing the court to consider such factors as the debtor's bad faith or circumstances indicating substantial abuse.

CASE EXAMPLE 21.7   At thirty-three years old, Lisa Hebbring owned a single-family home in Reno, Nevada, valued at $160,000, on which she owed $154,103. She also owned a Volkswagen Beetle valued at $14,000, on which she owed $18,839, and other personal property valued at $1,775. Hebbring was earning $49,000 per year as a customer service representative for SBC Nevada when she filed a Chapter 7 bankruptcy petition, seeking relief from $11,124 in credit-card debt. Her petition listed monthly net income of $2,813 and expenditures of $2,897, for a deficit of $84. In calculating her income, Hebbring excluded a $232 monthly pretax deduction for a contribution to a retirement plan maintained by her employer and an $81 monthly after-tax deduction for a contribution to her

"Capitalism without bankruptcy is like Christianity without hell."

Frank Borman, 1928–present
(U.S. astronaut and businessman)

---

10. This amount ($6,000) is the equivalent of $100 per month for five years, indicating that the debtor could pay at least $100 per month under a Chapter 13 five-year repayment plan.

own retirement savings. The U.S. trustee filed a motion to dismiss Hebbring's petition for substantial abuse, claiming that the retirement savings contributions should be disallowed. The court agreed and dismissed the Chapter 7 petition. Because Hebbring's retirement contributions were not reasonably necessary based on her age and financial circumstances, the bankruptcy court (and a federal appellate court on appeal) found that she was capable of paying her unsecured debts.[11] ●

ADDITIONAL GROUNDS FOR DISMISSAL   As noted, a debtor's voluntary petition for Chapter 7 relief may be dismissed for substantial abuse or for failing to provide the necessary documents (such as schedules and tax returns) within the specified time. In addition, a motion to dismiss a Chapter 7 filing may be granted in two other situations under the Bankruptcy Reform Act of 2005. First, if the debtor has been convicted of a violent crime or a drug-trafficking offense, the victim can file a motion to dismiss the voluntary petition.[12] Second, if the debtor fails to pay postpetition domestic-support obligations (which include child and spousal support), the court may dismiss the debtor's Chapter 7 petition.

ORDER FOR RELIEF   If the voluntary petition for bankruptcy is found to be proper, the filing of the petition will itself constitute an order for relief. (An **order for relief** is the court's grant of assistance to a debtor.) Once a consumer-debtor's voluntary petition has been filed, the clerk of the court (or other appointee) must give the trustee and creditors notice of the order for relief by mail not more than twenty days after the entry of the order.

Involuntary Bankruptcy

An involuntary bankruptcy occurs when the debtor's creditors force the debtor into bankruptcy proceedings. An involuntary case cannot be filed against a farmer[13] or a charitable institution. For an involuntary action to be filed against other debtors, the following requirements must be met: If the debtor has twelve or more creditors, three or more of those creditors having unsecured claims totaling at least $13,475 must join in the petition. If a debtor has fewer than twelve creditors, one or more creditors having a claim of $13,475 or more may file.

If the debtor challenges the involuntary petition, a hearing will be held, and the debtor's challenge will fail if the bankruptcy court finds either of the following:

1. That the debtor generally is not paying debts as they become due.
2. That a general receiver, custodian, or assignee took possession of, or was appointed to take charge of, substantially all of the debtor's property within 120 days before the filing of the involuntary petition.

If the court allows the bankruptcy to proceed, the debtor will be required to supply the same information in the bankruptcy schedules as in a voluntary bankruptcy.

An involuntary petition should not be used as an everyday debt-collection device, and the Code provides penalties for the filing of frivolous (unjustified) petitions against debtors. If the court dismisses an involuntary petition, the petitioning creditors may be required to pay the costs and attorneys' fees incurred by the debtor in defending against the petition. If the petition was filed in bad faith, damages can be awarded for injury to the debtor's reputation. Punitive damages may also be awarded.

Order for Relief   A court's grant of assistance to a complainant. In bankruptcy proceedings, the order relieves the debtor of the immediate obligation to pay the debts listed in the bankruptcy petition.

"I hope that after I die, people will say of me: 'That guy sure owed me a lot of money.'"

Jack Handey, 1949–present
(American humorist)

---

11. *Hebbring v. U.S. Trustee,* 463 F.3d 902 (9th Cir. 2006).
12. Note that the court may not dismiss a case on this ground if the debtor's bankruptcy is necessary to satisfy a claim for a domestic-support obligation.
13. The definition of *farmer* includes persons who receive more than 50 percent of their gross income from farming operations, such as tilling the soil; dairy farming; ranching; or the production or raising of crops, poultry, or livestock. Corporations and partnerships, as well as individuals, can be farmers.

Automatic Stay

Automatic Stay In bankruptcy proceedings, the suspension of almost all litigation and other action by creditors against the debtor or the debtor's property. The stay is effective the moment the debtor files a petition in bankruptcy.

The moment a petition, either voluntary or involuntary, is filed, an **automatic stay**, or suspension, of almost all actions by creditors against the debtor or the debtor's property normally goes into effect. In other words, once a petition has been filed, creditors cannot contact the debtor by phone or mail or start any legal proceedings to recover debts or to repossess property. If a creditor knowingly violates the automatic stay (a willful violation), any injured party, including the debtor, is entitled to recover actual damages, costs, and attorneys' fees and may be entitled to punitive damages as well.

Until the bankruptcy proceeding is closed or dismissed, the automatic stay prohibits a creditor from taking any act to collect, assess, or recover a claim against the debtor that arose before the filing of the petition. Did a university's refusal to provide a transcript unless a debt was paid constitute an act to collect a debt in violation of the automatic stay? That was the issue in the following case.

Case 21.2   In re Kuehn

United States Court of Appeals, Seventh Circuit, 563 F.3d 289 (2009).
www.ca7.uscourts.gov[a]

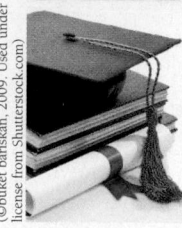

(©buket barıskan, 2009. Used under license from Shutterstock.com)

Is a student entitled to a copy of her transcript if she owes the university $6,000 in tuition?

FACTS   Stefanie Kuehn, an art teacher, obtained a master's degree at Cardinal Stritch University in Wisconsin. But when Kuehn asked for a transcript—which was required to receive an increase in salary from her school district—the university refused because she owed more than $6,000 in tuition. Kuehn offered to pay the nominal transcript fee but not the tuition. She then filed a petition in a federal bankruptcy court, listing the university as her only creditor. While the case was pending, she again asked for a transcript. The university once more refused unless she paid the tuition. Kuehn complained to the court, which ordered the university to provide a transcript. A federal district court affirmed the order. The university appealed.

ISSUE   Does a university violate the automatic stay by refusing to provide a transcript because a debt remains unpaid?

DECISION   Yes. The U.S. Court of Appeals for the Seventh Circuit affirmed the lower court's order. Kuehn had a right to a copy of her tran-

script, and the university's refusal to honor that right until she paid her tuition was an act to collect a debt in violation of the automatic stay.

REASON   The court observed that property interests are created and defined by the law. Nothing in the Bankruptcy Code or other federal law creates or affects property rights in grades or the right to a transcript. No Wisconsin statute applies either, but under the state's common law, property rights may arise from custom. In Wisconsin, universities have consistently provided certified transcripts at or around cost. This indicates that providing a transcript is an implied part of the "educational contract," covered by tuition and other fees. Because a transcript is part of the package of goods and services that a college offers in exchange for tuition, a student has a property right to a certified copy. In this case, Kuehn was willing to pay the cost. The university's only reason for refusing to provide the transcript was to induce Kuehn to pay her unpaid tuition. But the automatic stay prohibits a creditor from acting to collect a claim against a debtor that arose before the filing of a bankruptcy petition.

WHY IS THIS CASE IMPORTANT?   *This is the first case in which a federal appellate court concluded that a student has a property right to receive a certified transcript. The court confirmed that a student and his or her college might be joint owners of the data reflecting grades because that is how the "educational contract" normally is understood, but the student's right is not limited to his or her "intangible" grades. The grades would be worthless without the proof that a transcript provides.*

---

a. In the left-hand column, click on "Opinions." On that page, in the "Case Number:" box, type "07-3954" and click on "List Case(s)." In the result, click on the appropriate link to access the opinion.

EXCEPTIONS TO THE AUTOMATIC STAY   There are several exceptions to the automatic stay. Collection efforts can continue for domestic-support obligations, which include any debt owed to or recoverable by a spouse, former spouse, child of the debtor, a child's parent or guardian, or a governmental unit. In addition, proceedings against the debtor related to divorce, child custody or visitation, domestic violence, and support enforcement are not stayed. Also excepted are investigations by a securities regulatory agency (see Chapter 31) and certain statutory liens for property taxes.

LIMITATIONS ON THE AUTOMATIC STAY   A secured creditor or other party in interest can petition the bankruptcy court for relief from the automatic stay. If a creditor or other party requests relief from the stay, the stay will automatically terminate sixty days after the request, unless the court grants an extension[14] or the parties agree otherwise. Also, the automatic stay on secured debts normally will terminate thirty days after the petition is filed if the debtor had filed a bankruptcy petition that was dismissed within the prior year.

If the debtor had two or more bankruptcy petitions dismissed during the prior year, the Code presumes bad faith, and the automatic stay does not go into effect until the court determines that the petition was filed in good faith. In addition, the automatic stay on secured property terminates forty-five days after the creditors' meeting (explained below) unless the debtor redeems or reaffirms certain debts (*reaffirmation* will be discussed later in this chapter). In other words, the debtor cannot keep the secured property (such as a financed automobile), even if she or he continues to make payments on it, without reinstating the rights of the secured party to collect on the debt.

Property of the Estate

On the commencement of a liquidation proceeding under Chapter 7, an **estate in property** is created. The estate consists of all the debtor's interests in property currently held, wherever located, together with *community property* (property jointly owned by a husband and wife in certain states—see Chapter 36), property transferred in a transaction voidable by the trustee, proceeds and profits from the property of the estate, and certain after-acquired property. Interests in certain property—such as gifts, inheritances, property settlements (from divorce), and life insurance death proceeds—to which the debtor becomes entitled *within 180 days after filing* may also become part of the estate. Withholdings for employee benefit plan contributions are excluded from the estate. Generally, though, the filing of a bankruptcy petition fixes a dividing line: property acquired prior to the filing of the petition becomes property of the estate, and property acquired after the filing of the petition, except as just noted, remains the debtor's.

> **Estate in Property** In bankruptcy proceedings, all of the debtor's interests in property currently held, wherever located, together with certain jointly owned property, property transferred in transactions voidable by the trustee, proceeds and profits from the property of the estate, and certain property interests to which the debtor becomes entitled within 180 days after filing for bankruptcy.

Creditors' Meeting and Claims

Within a reasonable time after the order of relief has been granted (not more than forty days), the trustee must call a meeting of the creditors listed in the schedules filed by the debtor. The bankruptcy judge does not attend this meeting, but the debtor must attend and submit to an examination under oath. At the meeting, the trustee ensures that the debtor is aware of the potential consequences of bankruptcy and of his or her ability to file under a different chapter of the Bankruptcy Code.

To be entitled to receive a portion of the debtor's estate, each creditor normally files a *proof of claim* with the bankruptcy court clerk within ninety days of the creditors' meeting.[15] The proof of claim lists the creditor's name and address, as well as the amount that the creditor asserts is owed to the creditor by the debtor. A proof of claim is necessary if there is any dispute concerning the claim. If a creditor fails to file a proof of claim, the bankruptcy court or trustee may file the proof of claim on the creditor's behalf but is not obligated to do so.

---

14. The court might grant an extension, for example, on a motion by the trustee that the property is of value to the estate.

15. This ninety-day rule applies in Chapter 12 and Chapter 13 bankruptcies as well.

Exemptions

The trustee takes control over the debtor's property, but an individual debtor is entitled to exempt certain property from the bankruptcy. The Bankruptcy Code exempts the following property:[16]

1. Up to $20,200 in equity in the debtor's residence and burial plot (the homestead exemption).
2. Interest in a motor vehicle up to $3,225.
3. Interest, up to $525 for a particular item, in household goods and furnishings, wearing apparel, appliances, books, animals, crops, and musical instruments (the aggregate total of all items is limited to $10,775).
4. Interest in jewelry up to $1,350.
5. Interest in any other property up to $1,075, plus any unused part of the $20,200 homestead exemption up to $10,125.
6. Interest in any tools of the debtor's trade up to $2,025.
7. Any unmatured life insurance contracts owned by the debtor.
8. Certain interests in accrued dividends and interest under life insurance contracts owned by the debtor, not to exceed $10,775.
9. Professionally prescribed health aids.
10. The right to receive Social Security and certain welfare benefits, alimony and support, certain retirement funds and pensions, and education savings accounts held for specific periods of time.
11. The right to receive certain personal-injury and other awards up to $20,200.

(Rex Features)

Seen here is the interior of a private jet that was once owned by Bernard Madoff, who is serving 150 years in prison for the largest financial fraud in U.S. history. If Madoff had been involved in a simple bankruptcy proceeding, would he have been allowed to keep his jet?

Individual states have the power to pass legislation precluding debtors from using the federal exemptions within the state; a majority of the states have done this, as mentioned earlier in this chapter. In those states, debtors may use only state, not federal, exemptions. In the rest of the states, an individual debtor (or a husband and wife filing jointly) may choose either the exemptions provided under state law or the federal exemptions.

The Homestead Exemption

As previously mentioned, the 2005 reforms significantly changed the law for those debtors seeking to use state homestead exemption statutes. In six states, including Florida and Texas, homestead exemptions allow debtors petitioning for bankruptcy to shield *unlimited* amounts of equity in their homes from creditors. The Code now places limits on the amount that can be claimed as exempt in bankruptcy. In addition, the debtor must have lived in the state for two years before filing the petition to be able to use the state homestead exemption (prior law required only six months).

In addition, if the homestead was acquired within three and one-half years preceding the date of filing, the maximum equity exempted is $136,875 even if the state law would permit a higher amount. Also, if the debtor owes a debt arising from a violation of securities law or if the debtor committed certain criminal or tortious acts in the previous five years that indicate the filing was substantial abuse, the debtor may not exempt any amount of equity.

---

16. The dollar amounts stated in the Bankruptcy Code are adjusted automatically every three years on April 1 based on changes in the Consumer Price Index. The adjusted amounts are rounded to the nearest $25. The amounts stated in this chapter are in accordance with those computed on April 1, 2007.

The Trustee

Promptly after the order for relief has been entered, a trustee is appointed. The basic duty of the trustee is to collect the debtor's available estate and reduce it to cash for distribution, preserving the interests of both the debtor and the unsecured creditors. This requires that the trustee be accountable for administering the debtor's estate. To enable the trustee to accomplish this duty, the Code gives the trustee certain powers, stated in both general and specific terms. These powers must be exercised within two years of the order for relief.

The trustee is required to promptly review all materials filed by the debtor to determine if there is substantial abuse. Within ten days after the first meeting of the creditors, the trustee must file a statement as to whether the case is presumed to be an abuse under the means test. The trustee must provide all creditors with a copy of this statement. When there is a presumption of abuse, the trustee must either file a motion to dismiss the petition (or convert it to a Chapter 13 case) or file a statement setting forth the reasons why the motion would not be appropriate. If the debtor owes a domestic-support obligation (such as child support), the trustee must provide written notice of the bankruptcy to the claim holder (a former spouse, for example).

ON THE WEB For an overview of bankruptcy law and procedures with links to relevant Bankruptcy Code sections and cases, go to **www.law.cornell. edu/wex/index.php/bankruptcy**.

TRUSTEE'S POWERS   The trustee occupies a position *equivalent* in rights to that of certain other parties. For example, the trustee has the same rights as a creditor who could have obtained a judicial lien or levied execution on the debtor's property. This means that a trustee has priority over an unperfected secured party (see Chapter 20) to the debtor's property. This right of a trustee, equivalent to that of a lien creditor, is known as the *strong-arm power*. A trustee also has power equivalent to that of a *bona fide purchaser* of real property from the debtor.

The trustee has the power to require persons holding the debtor's property at the time the petition is filed to deliver the property to the trustee. Usually, a trustee does not take actual physical possession of a debtor's property but instead takes constructive possession by exercising control over the property. **EXAMPLE 21.8**   A trustee needs to obtain possession of a debtor's business inventory. To effectively take (constructive) possession, the trustee could notify the debtor, change the locks on the business's doors, and hire a security guard—without actually moving the inventory. ●

AVOIDANCE POWERS   The trustee also has specific powers of *avoidance*—that is, the trustee can set aside a sale or other transfer of the debtor's property, taking it back as a part of the debtor's estate. These powers include any voidable rights available to the debtor, preferences, certain statutory liens, and fraudulent transfers by the debtor, as will be discussed next.

Note that the debtor shares most of the trustee's avoidance powers. Thus, if the trustee does not take action to enforce any of these rights, the debtor in a liquidation bankruptcy can enforce it.[17]

VOIDABLE RIGHTS   A trustee steps into the shoes of the debtor. Thus, any reason that a debtor can use to obtain the return of his or her property can be used by the trustee as well. The grounds for recovery include fraud, duress, incapacity, and mutual mistake.

EXAMPLE 21.9   Blane sells his boat to Inga. Inga gives Blane a check, knowing that she has insufficient funds in her bank account to cover the check. Inga has committed fraud. Blane has the right to avoid that transfer and recover the boat from Inga. If Blane files for

---

17. Under a Chapter 11 bankruptcy (to be discussed later), for which no trustee other than the debtor generally exists, the debtor has the same avoidance powers as a trustee under Chapter 7. Under Chapters 12 and 13 (also to be discussed later), a trustee must be appointed.

bankruptcy, the trustee can exercise the same right to recover the boat from Inga, and the boat becomes part of the debtor's estate. •

PREFERENCES   A debtor is not permitted to make a property transfer or a payment that favors—or gives a **preference** to—one creditor over others. The trustee is allowed to recover payments made both voluntarily and involuntarily to one creditor in preference over another. If a **preferred creditor** (one who has received a preferential transfer from the debtor) has sold the property to an innocent third party, the trustee cannot recover the property from the innocent party. The preferred creditor, however, generally *can* be held accountable for the value of the property.

To have made a preferential payment that can be recovered, an *insolvent* debtor generally must have transferred property, for a *preexisting* debt, during the *ninety days* prior to the filing of the petition in bankruptcy. The transfer must have given the creditor more than the creditor would have received as a result of the bankruptcy proceedings. The trustee does not have to prove insolvency, as the Code provides that the debtor is presumed to be insolvent during this ninety-day period.

Preferences to Insiders.   Sometimes, the creditor receiving the preference is an *insider*—an individual, a partner, a partnership, or an officer or a director of a corporation (or a relative of one of these) who has a close relationship with the debtor. In this situation, the avoidance power of the trustee is extended to transfers made within *one year* before filing; the *presumption* of insolvency is still confined to the ninety-day period, though. Therefore, the trustee must prove that the debtor was insolvent at the time of an earlier transfer.

Transfers That Do Not Constitute Preferences.   Not all transfers are preferences. To be a preference, the transfer must be made in exchange for something other than current consideration. Therefore, most courts do not consider a debtor's payment for services rendered within fifteen days prior to the payment to be a preference. If a creditor receives payment in the ordinary course of business, such as payment of last month's telephone bill, the trustee in bankruptcy cannot recover the payment. To be recoverable, a preference must be a transfer for an antecedent (preexisting) debt, such as a year-old printing bill.

In addition, the Code permits a consumer-debtor to transfer any property to a creditor up to a total value of $5,475, without the transfer's constituting a preference. Payments of domestic-support debts do not constitute a preference. Also, transfers that were made as part of an alternative repayment schedule negotiated by an approved credit counseling agency are not preferences.

LIENS ON THE DEBTOR'S PROPERTY   The trustee has the power to avoid certain statutory liens against the debtor's property, such as a landlord's lien for unpaid rent. The trustee can avoid statutory liens that first became effective at the time the bankruptcy petition was filed or when the debtor became insolvent. The trustee can also avoid any lien against a good faith purchaser that was not perfected or enforceable on the date of the bankruptcy filing.

FRAUDULENT TRANSFERS   The trustee may avoid fraudulent transfers or obligations if they (1) were made within two years of the filing of the petition or (2) were made with actual intent to hinder, delay, or defraud a creditor. Transfers made for less than reasonably equivalent consideration are also vulnerable if the debtor thereby became insolvent, was left engaged in business with an unreasonably small amount of capital, or intended to incur debts that would be beyond her or his ability to pay. When a fraudulent transfer is made outside the Code's two-year limit, creditors may seek alternative relief under state laws. Some state laws allow creditors to recover for transfers made up to three years before the filing of a petition.

Preference   In bankruptcy proceedings, property transfers or payments made by the debtor that favor (give preference to) one creditor over others. The bankruptcy trustee is allowed to recover payments made both voluntarily and involuntarily to one creditor in preference over another.

Preferred Creditor   In the context of bankruptcy, a creditor who has received a preferential transfer from a debtor.

NOTE   Usually, when property is recovered as a preference, the trustee sells it and distributes the proceeds to the debtor's creditors.

Distribution of Property

ON THE WEB To read a brief primer on the distribution of property in a Chapter 7 bankruptcy, go to **www.lawdog.com/bkrcy/lib2a8.htm**.

The Code provides specific rules for the distribution of the debtor's property to secured and unsecured creditors (discussed next). If any amount remains after the priority classes of creditors have been satisfied, it is turned over to the debtor. Exhibit 21–2 illustrates graphically the collection and distribution of property in most voluntary bankruptcies.

In a bankruptcy case in which the debtor has no assets,[18] creditors are notified of the debtor's petition for bankruptcy but are instructed not to file a claim. In such a case, the unsecured creditors will receive no payment, and most, if not all, of these debts will be discharged.

DISTRIBUTION TO SECURED CREDITORS The rights of perfected secured creditors were discussed in Chapter 20. The Code provides that a consumer-debtor, either within thirty days of filing a liquidation petition or before the date of the first meeting of the creditors (whichever is first), must file with the clerk a statement of intention with respect to the secured collateral. The statement must indicate whether the debtor will redeem the collateral (make a single payment equal to the current value of the property), reaffirm the debt (continue making payments on the debt), or surrender the property to the secured party.[19] The trustee is obligated to enforce the debtor's statement within forty-five days after the meeting of the creditors. As noted previously, failure of the debtor to redeem or reaffirm within forty-five days terminates the automatic stay.

DISTRIBUTION TO UNSECURED CREDITORS Bankruptcy law establishes an order of priority for classes of debts owed to *unsecured* creditors, and they are paid in the order of their priority. Each class must be fully paid before the next class is entitled to any of the remaining proceeds. If there are insufficient proceeds to pay fully all the creditors in a class, the proceeds are distributed *proportionately* to the creditors in that class, and classes lower

---

18. This type of bankruptcy is called a "no-asset" case.
19. Also, if applicable, the debtor must specify whether the collateral will be claimed as exempt property.

● *Exhibit* **21–2 Collection and Distribution of Property in Most Voluntary Bankruptcies**
This exhibit illustrates the property that might be collected in a debtor's voluntary bankruptcy and how it might be distributed to creditors. Involuntary bankruptcies and some voluntary bankruptcies could include additional types of property and other creditors.

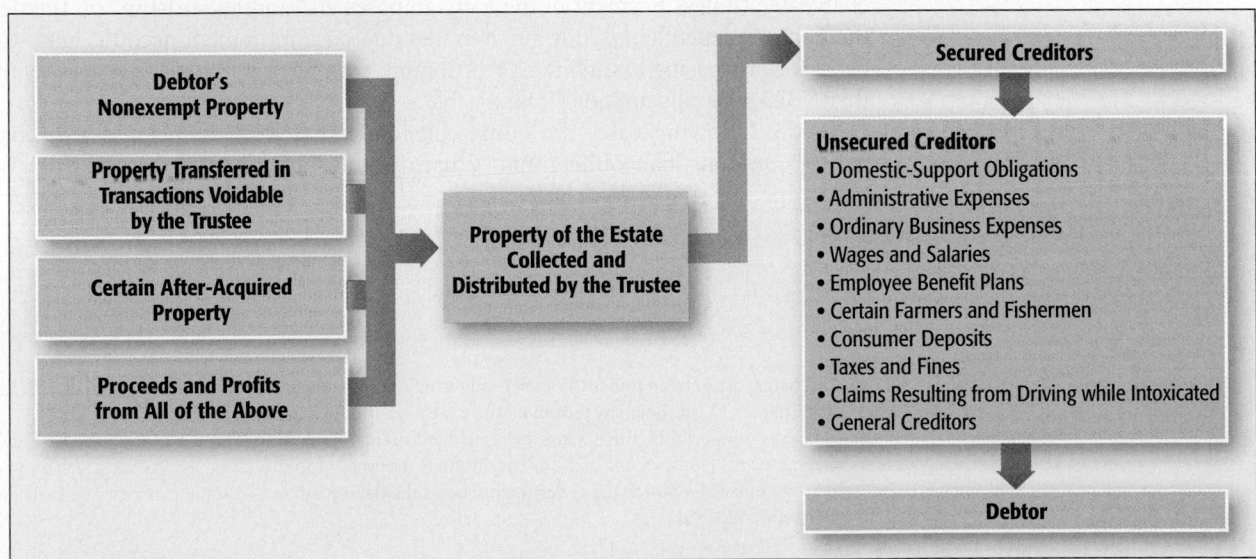

in priority receive nothing. If there is any balance remaining after all the creditors are paid, it is returned to the debtor.

Note that the reform act elevated domestic-support (mainly child-support) obligations to the highest priority of unsecured claims—so these are the first debts to be paid. After that, administrative expenses related to the bankruptcy (such as court costs, trustee fees, and attorneys' fees) are paid; next come any expenses that a debtor in an involuntary bankruptcy incurs in the ordinary course of business. Unpaid wages, salaries, and commissions earned within ninety days prior to the petition are paid next, followed by certain claims for contributions to employee benefit plans, claims by some farmers and fishermen, consumer deposits, and certain taxes. Claims of general creditors rank last in the order of priority, which is why these unsecured creditors often receive little, if anything, in a Chapter 7 bankruptcy.

Discharge

From the debtor's point of view, the purpose of a liquidation proceeding is to obtain a fresh start through the discharge of debts.[20] As mentioned earlier, once the debtor's assets have been distributed to creditors as permitted by the Code, the debtor's remaining debts are then discharged, meaning that the debtor is not obligated to pay them. Certain debts, however, are not dischargeable in bankruptcy. Also, certain debtors may not qualify to have all debts discharged in bankruptcy. These situations are discussed below.

BE AWARE Often, a discharge in bankruptcy—even under Chapter 7—does not free a debtor of *all* of her or his debts.

EXCEPTIONS TO DISCHARGE   Discharge of a debt may be denied because of the nature of the claim or the conduct of the debtor. A court will not discharge claims that are based on a debtor's willful or malicious conduct or fraud, or claims related to property or funds that the debtor obtained by false pretenses, embezzlement, or larceny. Any monetary judgment against the debtor for driving while intoxicated cannot be discharged in bankruptcy. When a debtor fails to list a creditor on the bankruptcy schedules, that creditor's claims are not dischargeable because the creditor was not notified of the bankruptcy.

Claims that are not dischargeable in a liquidation bankruptcy include amounts due to the government for taxes, fines, or penalties, and any amounts borrowed to pay these debts.[21] Domestic-support obligations and property settlements arising from a divorce or separation cannot be discharged. Certain student loans or educational debts are not dischargeable (unless payment of the loans imposes an "undue hardship" on the debtor and the debtor's dependents), nor are amounts due on a retirement account loan. Consumer debts for purchasing luxury items worth more than $550 and cash advances totaling more than $825 generally are not dischargeable.

In the following case, the court considered whether to order the discharge of a debtor's student loan obligations. What does a debtor have to prove to show undue hardship?

---

20. Discharges are granted under Chapter 7 only to *individuals,* not to corporations or partnerships. The latter may use Chapter 11, or they may terminate their existence under state law.

21. Taxes accruing within three years prior to bankruptcy are nondischargeable, including federal and state income taxes, employment taxes, taxes on gross receipts, property taxes, excise taxes, customs duties, and any other taxes for which the government claims the debtor is liable in some capacity. See 11 U.S.C. Sections 507(a)(8), 523(a)(1).

Case 21.3 In re Mosley

United States Court of Appeals, Eleventh Circuit, 494 F.3d 1320 (2007).

Do injuries sustained in a tank accident during military training lead to debt relief of student loans?

FACTS Keldric Mosley incurred student loans while attending Alcorn State University between 1989 and 1994. At Alcorn, Mosley joined the U.S. Army Reserve Officers' Training Corps. During training, Mosley was injured after a fall from a tank. Medical problems from his injuries led him to resign his commission. From 1994 to 1999, he worked briefly for several employers, but depressed and physically limited by his injuries, he was unable to keep any of the jobs. He tried to return to school but could not obtain financial aid because of the debt he had incurred at Alcorn. In 1999, a federal bankruptcy court granted him a discharge under Chapter 7, but it did not include the student loans. In 2000, after a week at a Georgia mental-health facility, Mosley was prescribed medication for depression and other problems through the U.S. Department of Veterans Affairs (VA). By 2004, his monthly income consisted primarily of $210 in disability benefits from the VA. Homeless and in debt for $45,000 to Educational Credit Management Corporation (ECMC), Mosley asked the bankruptcy court to reopen his case. The court granted him a discharge of his student loans on the basis of undue hardship. ECMC appealed.

ISSUE Was Mosley's testimony regarding his physical and emotional problems enough to prove undue hardship, thus releasing him from his student loan obligations?

DECISION Yes. The U.S. Court of Appeals for the Eleventh Circuit affirmed the lower court's discharge of Mosley's student loans based on undue hardship. The court found that Mosley's detailed testimony about his depression provided sufficient evidence of undue hardship.

REASON To establish undue hardship, the debtor must show (1) that he or she "cannot maintain, based on current income and expenses, a 'minimal' standard of living * * * if forced to repay the loans; (2) that additional circumstances exist indicating that this state of affairs is likely to persist for a significant portion of the repayment period of the student loans; and (3) that the debtor has made good faith efforts to repay the loans." The plaintiff, ECMC, claimed that the bankruptcy court was too lax in accepting the debtor's testimony as evidence showing that he would remain in the same financial situation for a long period of time. ECMC contended that Mosley needed to present the opinion of a medical expert on the subject of his future recovery. The court, however, reasoned that Mosley's testimony did not purport to give a medical prognosis, but rather related from personal knowledge his struggles with depression and other medical problems. The court concluded that Mosley's medical problems, lack of skills, and dire living conditions made it unlikely that he would be able to hold a job and repay the loans. Mosley had made good faith efforts to repay his student loans and "would suffer undue hardship if they were excepted from [bankruptcy] discharge."

WHAT IF THE FACTS WERE DIFFERENT? *Suppose that Mosley relocated to a country with a lower cost of living than the United States. Should his change in circumstances be a ground for revoking the discharge of his student loans? Explain your answer.*

OBJECTIONS TO DISCHARGE In addition to the exceptions to discharge previously listed, a bankruptcy court may also deny the discharge of the *debtor* (as opposed to the debt). Grounds for the denial of discharge of the debtor include the following:

1. The debtor's concealment or destruction of property with the intent to hinder, delay, or defraud a creditor.
2. The debtor's fraudulent concealment or destruction of financial records.
3. The granting of a discharge to the debtor within eight years prior to the filing of the petition.
4. The debtor's failure to complete the required consumer education course (unless such a course was not available).
5. Proceedings in which the debtor could be found guilty of a felony. (Basically, a court may not discharge any debt until the completion of the felony proceedings against the debtor.)

The purpose of denying a discharge on these or other grounds is to prevent a debtor from avoiding, through bankruptcy, the consequences of his or her wrongful conduct.

When a discharge is denied under these circumstances, the debtor's assets are still distributed to the creditors, but the debtor remains liable for the unpaid portions of all claims.

REVOCATION OF DISCHARGE   On petition by the trustee or a creditor, the bankruptcy court may, within one year, revoke the discharge decree if it is discovered that the debtor was fraudulent or dishonest during the bankruptcy proceedings. The revocation renders the discharge void, allowing creditors not satisfied by the distribution of the debtor's estate to proceed with their claims against the debtor.

REAFFIRMATION OF DEBT   An agreement to pay a debt dischargeable in bankruptcy is called a **reaffirmation agreement.** A debtor may wish to pay a debt—for example, a debt owed to a family member, physician, bank, or some other creditor—even though the debt could be discharged in bankruptcy. Also, as noted previously, a debtor cannot retain secured property while continuing to pay without entering into a reaffirmation agreement.

> **Reaffirmation Agreement** An agreement between a debtor and a creditor in which the debtor voluntarily agrees to pay, or reaffirm, a debt dischargeable in bankruptcy. To be enforceable, the agreement must be made before the debtor is granted a discharge.

To be enforceable, reaffirmation agreements must be made before the debtor is granted a discharge. The agreement must be signed and filed with the court (along with the original disclosure documents, as you will read shortly). Court approval is required unless the debtor is represented by an attorney during the negotiation of the reaffirmation and submits the proper documents and certifications. Even when the debtor is represented by an attorney, court approval may be required if it appears that the reaffirmation will result in undue hardship to the debtor. When court approval is required, a separate hearing will take place. The court will approve the reaffirmation only if it finds that the agreement will not result in undue hardship to the debtor and that the reaffirmation is consistent with the debtor's best interests.

NEW REAFFIRMATION DISCLOSURES   To discourage creditors from engaging in abusive reaffirmation practices, the Code provides the specific language for several pages of disclosures that must be given to debtors entering reaffirmation agreements. Among other things, these disclosures explain that the debtor is not required to reaffirm any debt, but that liens on secured property, such as mortgages and cars, will remain in effect even if the debt is not reaffirmed.

The reaffirmation agreement must disclose the amount of the debt reaffirmed, the rate of interest, the date payments begin, and the right to rescind. The disclosures also caution the debtor: "Only agree to reaffirm a debt if it is in your best interest. Be sure you can afford the payments you agree to make." The original disclosure documents must be signed by the debtor, certified by the debtor's attorney, and filed with the court at the same time as the reaffirmation agreement. A reaffirmation agreement that is not accompanied by the original signed disclosures will not be effective. (Sometimes, creditors and credit-reporting agencies have engaged in another form of abuse—failing to remove discharged debts from consumers' credit reports. See this chapter's *Adapting the Law to the Online Environment* feature for a discussion of this issue.)

▶ Chapter 11–Reorganization

The type of bankruptcy proceeding used most commonly by corporate debtors is the Chapter 11 *reorganization.* In a reorganization, the creditors and the debtor formulate a plan under which the debtor pays a portion of its debts and the rest of the debts are discharged. The debtor is allowed to continue in business. Although this type of bankruptcy is generally a corporate reorganization, any debtors (including individuals but excluding stockbrokers and commodities brokers) who are eligible for Chapter 7 relief are eligible for relief under Chapter 11.

Adapting the Law to the Online Environment

The Debt That Never Goes Away—It's Discharged in Bankruptcy but Still on the Debtor's Credit Report

Bankruptcy, especially under Chapter 7, allows a judge to discharge certain debts. When these debts are discharged, they are no longer supposed to appear on the debtor's online credit report.

For Dan Rathavongsa, a factory worker in Raleigh, North Carolina, however, the discharged debt did not go away. A bankruptcy judge discharged a $9,523 debt that he owed to Capital One Financial. Nonetheless, Capital One continued to report Rathavongsa's debt to the various credit bureaus as a "live" balance. When Rathavongsa tried to obtain a mortgage for a new house a year after the debt had been discharged, the would-be lender told him that he would have to either pay the Capital One debt or prove that the debt had been discharged. When Capital One refused to revise his credit report, Rathavongsa gave in and paid Capital One for a debt he no longer legally owed.

Discharged Debts Attract Buyers

Capital One is not alone. Many credit-card companies and other creditors have been keeping debts active even after they have been discharged by a bankruptcy court. Consequently, some aggressive entrepreneurs have founded companies with names such as Max Recovery and eCast Settlement that purchase discharged debt obligations at pennies on the dollar. Then, they pursue the debtors and pressure them to pay the debts, even though the debts have already been discharged in bankruptcy. Some of these companies have been successful enough to become publicly traded on a stock exchange.

The billions of dollars' worth of debts that have been discharged in bankruptcy should have a zero-dollar value, yet the fact that there are buyers for these debts indicates that some consumers have been paying them. Indeed, as the number of bankruptcies rose during the recession that began in late 2007, the price of discharged Chapter 7 debt actually increased—to about seven cents on the dollar. Certainly, one reason why consumers have paid debts that they did not owe is because they found

themselves in the same situation as Rathavongsa—their credit reports still listed the debt as active.

A Federal Judge Issues an Order That Changes the Reporting of Discharged Debt

That situation may be changing, thanks to an order issued by a federal district judge in 2008. A class-action lawsuit was brought against the three major credit-reporting agencies—Equifax, Experian, and TransUnion—all of which have a major online presence. The plaintiffs included consumers from across the country. They claimed that the agencies violated the federal Fair Credit Reporting Act by failing to follow reasonable procedures to ensure the accurate reporting of debts discharged in Chapter 7 bankruptcies. The court agreed and ordered the agencies to revise their procedures by October 1, 2008.[a]

Previously, the credit bureaus would remove debts incurred before bankruptcy only if the creditors updated their accounts—which often was not done. Today, the credit agencies are required to automatically report all prebankruptcy debt as "discharged," unless the debt is nondischargeable. Although the purchasers of discharged debt may still attempt to pressure consumers into paying debts that they do not owe, the change in the credit bureaus' procedures gives consumers help in their efforts to rebuild their lives after bankruptcy.

FOR CRITICAL ANALYSIS

About five years ago, one could buy debt that had been discharged in bankruptcy for less than five cents on the dollar. Why do you think the price increased to seven cents on the dollar?

---

a. *White v. Experian Information Solutions,* No. 05-CV-1-70 DOC (C.D.Cal. 2008).

BE AWARE Chapter 11 proceedings are typically prolonged and costly. Whether a firm survives largely depends on its size and its ability to attract investors despite its Chapter 11 status.

In 1994, Congress established a "fast-track" Chapter 11 procedure for small-business debtors whose liabilities do not exceed $2.19 million and who do not own or manage real estate. The fast track enables a debtor to avoid the appointment of a creditors' committee and also shortens the filing periods and relaxes certain other requirements. Because the process is shorter and simpler, it is less costly.

The same principles that govern the filing of a liquidation (Chapter 7) petition apply to reorganization (Chapter 11) proceedings. The case may be brought either voluntarily or involuntarily. The same guidelines govern the entry of the order for relief. The automatic-stay provision and its exceptions apply in reorganizations as well, as do the provisions regarding substantial abuse and additional grounds for dismissal (or conversion) of bankruptcy petitions. Also, the 2005 act provided specific rules and limitations for *individual* debtors who file a Chapter 11 petition, such as requiring that an individual debtor's post-petition acquisitions and earnings become the property of the bankruptcy estate.

Focus Is on the Best Interests of the Creditors

Under Section 305(a) of the Bankruptcy Code, a court, after notice and a hearing, may dismiss or suspend all proceedings in a case at any time if dismissal or suspension would better serve the interests of the creditors. Section 1112 also allows a court, after notice and a hearing, to dismiss a case under reorganization "for cause." Cause includes the absence of a reasonable likelihood of rehabilitation, the inability to effect a plan, and an unreasonable delay by the debtor that is prejudicial to (may harm the interests of) creditors.[22]

In some instances, creditors may prefer private, negotiated adjustments of creditor-debtor relations, also known as **workouts,** to bankruptcy proceedings. Often, these out-of-court workouts are much more flexible and thus more conducive to a speedy settlement. Speed is critical because delay is one of the most costly elements in any bankruptcy proceeding. Another advantage of workouts is that they avoid the various administrative costs of bankruptcy proceedings.

> **Workout**   An out-of-court agreement between a debtor and creditors in which the parties work out a payment plan or schedule under which the debtor's debts can be discharged.

Debtor in Possession

On entry of the order for relief, the debtor in Chapter 11 generally continues to operate the business as a **debtor in possession (DIP).** The court, however, may appoint a trustee (often referred to as a *receiver*) to operate the debtor's business if gross mismanagement of the business is shown or if appointing a trustee is in the best interests of the estate.

The DIP's role is similar to that of a trustee in a liquidation. The DIP is entitled to avoid preferential payments made to creditors and fraudulent transfers of assets. The DIP has the power to decide whether to cancel or assume prepetition executory contracts (those that are not yet performed) or unexpired leases. Cancellation of executory contracts or unexpired leases can be a substantial benefit to a Chapter 11 debtor. **EXAMPLE 21.10** Five years ago, before the recession, APT Corporation leased an office building for a twenty-year term. Now, APT can no longer afford to pay the rent due under the lease and has filed for Chapter 11 reorganization. In this situation, the debtor in possession could cancel the lease of the office building so that APT will not be required to continue paying the substantial rent on it for fifteen more years. •

> **Debtor in Possession (DIP)**   In Chapter 11 bankruptcy proceedings, a debtor who is allowed to continue in possession of the estate in property (the business) and to continue business operations.

Creditors' Committees

As soon as practicable after the entry of the order for relief, a committee of unsecured creditors is appointed. If the debtor has filed a plan accepted by the creditors, however, the trustee may decide not to call a meeting of the creditors. The committee may consult with the trustee or the DIP concerning the administration of the case or the formulation of the plan. Additional creditors' committees may be appointed to represent special interest creditors, and a court may order the trustee to change a committee's membership as needed to ensure adequate representation of the creditors.

Orders affecting the estate generally will be entered only with the consent of the committee or after a hearing in which the judge is informed of the position of the committee. As mentioned earlier, businesses with debts of less than $2.19 million that do not own or manage real estate can avoid creditors' committees through fast-track proceedings. In these cases, orders can be entered without a committee's consent.

The Reorganization Plan

A reorganization plan is established to conserve and administer the debtor's assets in the hope of an eventual return to successful operation and solvency.

---

22. See 11 U.S.C. Section 1112(b). Debtors are not prohibited from filing successive petitions, however. A debtor whose petition is dismissed, for example, can file a new Chapter 11 petition (which may be granted unless it is filed in bad faith).

FILING THE PLAN   Only the debtor may file a plan within the first 120 days after the date of the order for relief. The 120-day period may be extended, but not beyond 18 months from the date of the order for relief. If the debtor does not meet the 120-day deadline or obtain an extension, and if the debtor fails to obtain the required creditor consent (discussed below) within 180 days, any party may propose a plan up to 20 months from the date of the order for relief. (In other words, the 180-day period cannot be extended beyond 20 months past the date of the order for relief.) For a small-business debtor, the time for the debtor's filing is 180 days. The plan must be fair and equitable and must do the following:

1. Designate classes of claims and interests.
2. Specify the treatment to be afforded the classes. (The plan must provide the same treatment for all claims in a particular class.)
3. Provide an adequate means for execution. (Individual debtors must utilize postpetition assets as necessary to execute the plan.)
4. Provide for payment of tax claims over a five-year period.

ACCEPTANCE AND CONFIRMATION OF THE PLAN   Once the plan has been developed, it is submitted to each class of creditors for acceptance. Each class must accept the plan unless the class is not adversely affected by it. A class has accepted the plan when a majority of the creditors, representing two-thirds of the amount of the total claim, vote to approve it. Confirmation is conditioned on the debtor's certifying that all postpetition domestic-support obligations have been paid in full. For small-business debtors, if the plan meets the listed requirements, the court must confirm the plan within forty-five days (unless this period is extended).

Even when all classes of creditors accept the plan, the court may refuse to confirm it if it is not "in the best interests of the creditors."[23] A former spouse or child of the debtor can block the plan if it does not provide for payment of her or his claims in cash. If an unsecured creditor objects to the plan, specific rules apply to the value of property to be distributed under the plan. The plan can also be modified upon the request of the debtor, trustee, U.S. trustee, or holder of the unsecured claim. Tax claims must be paid over a five-year period.

Cram-Down Provision   A provision of the Bankruptcy Code that allows a court to confirm a debtor's Chapter 11 reorganization plan even though only one class of creditors has accepted it.

Even if only one class of creditors has accepted the plan, the court may still confirm the plan under the Code's so-called **cram-down provision.** In other words, the court may confirm the plan over the objections of a class of creditors. Before the court can exercise this right of cram-down confirmation, it must be demonstrated that the plan is fair and equitable, and does not discriminate unfairly against any creditors.

DISCHARGE   The plan is binding on confirmation. Individual debtors must complete the plan prior to discharge, unless the court orders otherwise. For all other debtors, the court may order discharge at any time after the plan is confirmed. The debtor is given a reorganization discharge from all claims not protected under the plan. This discharge does not apply to any claims that would be denied discharge under liquidation.

▶ Bankruptcy Relief under Chapter 13 and Chapter 12

In addition to bankruptcy relief through liquidation (Chapter 7) and reorganization (Chapter 11), the Code also provides for individuals' repayment plans (Chapter 13) and family-farmer and family-fisherman debt adjustments (Chapter 12), as discussed next.

---

23. The plan need not provide for full repayment to unsecured creditors. Instead, creditors receive a percentage of each dollar owed to them by the debtor.

Individuals' Repayment Plan—Chapter 13

Chapter 13 of the Bankruptcy Code provides for the "Adjustment of Debts of an Individual with Regular Income." Individuals (not partnerships or corporations) with regular income who owe fixed unsecured debts of less than $336,900 or fixed secured debts of less than $1,010,650 may take advantage of bankruptcy repayment plans. Among those eligible are salaried employees; sole proprietors; and individuals who live on welfare, Social Security, fixed pensions, or investment income. Many small-business debtors have a choice of filing under either Chapter 11 or Chapter 13. Repayment plans offer some advantages because they are typically less expensive and less complicated than reorganization or liquidation proceedings.

FILING THE PETITION   A Chapter 13 repayment plan case can be initiated only by the filing of a voluntary petition by the debtor or by the conversion of a Chapter 7 petition (because of a finding of substantial abuse under the means test, for example). Certain liquidation and reorganization cases may be converted to Chapter 13 with the consent of the debtor.[24] A trustee, who will make payments under the plan, must be appointed. On the filing of a repayment plan petition, the automatic stay previously discussed takes effect. Although the stay applies to all or part of the debtor's consumer debt, it does not apply to any business debt incurred by the debtor or to any domestic-support obligations.

GOOD FAITH REQUIREMENT   The Bankruptcy Code imposes the requirement of good faith on a debtor at both the time of the filing of the petition and the time of the filing of the plan. The Code does not define good faith, but if the circumstances as a whole indicate bad faith, a court can dismiss a debtor's Chapter 13 petition.

CASE EXAMPLE 21.11   Roger and Pauline Buis bought an air show business, including a helicopter, a trailer, and props, from Robert and Annette Hosking. The Buises formed Otto Airshows and decorated the helicopter as "Otto the Clown." They performed in air shows and took passengers on flights for a fee. Several years later, the Buises accused a competitor of safety lapses, and the competitor filed and won a defamation lawsuit against the Buises and Otto Airshows. The Buises then stopped doing business as Otto Airshows and formed a new firm, Prop and Rotor Aviation, Inc., to which they leased the Otto equipment. Within a month, they filed a bankruptcy petition under Chapter 13. The plan and the schedules did not mention the lawsuit, the equipment lease, and several other items. The court therefore dismissed the Buises' petition due to bad faith. The debtors had not included all of their assets and liabilities on their initial petition, and they had timed its filing to avoid payment on the defamation judgment.[25] ●

THE REPAYMENT PLAN   A plan of rehabilitation by repayment must provide for the following:

1. The turning over to the trustee of such future earnings or income of the debtor as is necessary for execution of the plan.
2. Full payment through deferred cash payments of all claims entitled to priority, such as taxes.[26]
3. Identical treatment of all claims within a particular class. (The Code permits the debtor to list co-debtors, such as guarantors or sureties, as a separate class.)

---

24. A Chapter 13 repayment plan may be converted to a Chapter 7 liquidation either at the request of the debtor or, under certain circumstances, "for cause" by a creditor. A Chapter 13 case may be converted to a Chapter 11 case after a hearing.
25. *In re Buis,* 337 Bankr. 243 (N.D.Fla. 2006).
26. As with a Chapter 11 reorganization plan, full repayment of all claims is not always required.

Filing the Plan. Only the debtor may file for a repayment plan. This plan may provide either for payment of all obligations in full or for payment of a lesser amount. The length of the payment plan can be three or five years, depending on the debtor's family income. If the debtor's family income is greater than the state median family income under the means test (previously discussed), the proposed plan must be for five years. The term may not exceed five years, however.

The debtor must begin making payments under the proposed plan within thirty days after the plan has been *filed* and must continue to make "timely" payments from her or his disposable income. Failure of the debtor to make timely payments or to commence payments within the thirty-day period will allow the court to convert the case to a liquidation bankruptcy or to dismiss the petition.

Confirmation of the Plan. After the plan is filed, the court holds a confirmation hearing, at which interested parties (such as creditors) may object to the plan. The hearing must be held at least twenty days, but no more than forty-five days, after the meeting of the creditors. The debtor must have filed all prepetition tax returns and paid all postpetition domestic-support obligations before a court will confirm any plan. The court will confirm a plan with respect to each claim of a secured creditor under any of the following circumstances:

1. If the secured creditors have accepted the plan.
2. If the plan provides that secured creditors retain their liens until there is payment in full or until the debtor receives a discharge.
3. If the debtor surrenders the property securing the claims to the creditors.

DISCHARGE After the completion of all payments, the court grants a discharge of all debts provided for by the repayment plan. Except for allowed claims not provided for by the plan, certain long-term debts provided for by the plan, certain tax claims, payments on retirement accounts, and claims for domestic-support obligations, all other debts are dischargeable. Under prior law, a discharge of debts under a Chapter 13 repayment plan was sometimes referred to as a "superdischarge" because it allowed the discharge of fraudulently incurred debt and claims resulting from malicious or willful injury. The 2005 reforms, however, deleted most of the "superdischarge" provisions, especially for debts based on fraud or taxes. Today, even debts related to injury or property damage caused while driving under the influence of alcohol or drugs are nondischargeable.

BE CAREFUL Courts, trustees, and creditors carefully monitor Chapter 13 debtors. If payments are not made, a court can require that the debtor explain why and may allow a creditor to take back her or his property.

CASE EXAMPLE 21.12 James Ellett owed $18,000 in personal income taxes to the state of California at the time he petitioned for Chapter 13 bankruptcy. Ellett listed the debt in his petition but misstated the last digit of his Social Security number (SSN). Because of this error, the California Franchise Tax Board (FTB) did not receive any notice of Ellett's bankruptcy and never filed a proof of claim or received any distribution through his repayment plan. After Ellett completed the repayment plan and received a discharge, the FTB attempted to collect the tax debt. Ellett filed a lawsuit seeking a court declaration that the debt to the FTB was discharged. The court ruled against him, and he appealed. A federal appellate court concluded that because of Ellett's negligence in listing an erroneous SSN on his bankruptcy petition, the FTB was never notified of his bankruptcy; thus, the tax debt was not discharged.[27] •

Family Farmers and Fishermen—Chapter 12

In 1986, to help relieve economic pressure on small farmers, Congress created Chapter 12 of the Bankruptcy Code. In 2005, Congress extended this protection to family fishermen,

---

27. *Ellett v. Stanislaus,* 506 F.3d 774 (9th Cir. 2007). Stanislaus was the name of the director of the Franchise Tax Board.

modified its provisions somewhat, and made it a permanent chapter in the Bankruptcy Code (previously, it had to be periodically renewed by Congress).

For purposes of Chapter 12, a *family farmer* is one whose gross income is at least 50 percent farm dependent and whose debts are at least 50 percent farm related.[28] The total debt must not exceed $3,544,525. A partnership or a closely held corporation (see Chapter 29) that is at least 50 percent owned by the farm family can also qualify as a family farmer.[29]

A *family fisherman* is one whose gross income is at least 50 percent dependent on commercial fishing operations and whose debts are at least 80 percent related to commercial fishing. The total debt for a family fisherman must not exceed $1,642,500. As with family farmers, a partnership or closely held corporation can also qualify.

FILING THE PETITION The procedure for filing a family-farmer or family-fisherman bankruptcy plan is very similar to the procedure for filing a repayment plan under Chapter 13. The debtor must file a plan not later than ninety days after the order for relief. The filing of the petition acts as an automatic stay against creditors' and co-obligors' actions against the estate.

A farmer or fisherman who has already filed a reorganization or repayment plan may convert the plan to a Chapter 12 plan. The debtor may also convert a Chapter 12 plan to a liquidation plan.

CONTENT AND CONFIRMATION OF THE PLAN The content of a plan under Chapter 12 is basically the same as that of a Chapter 13 repayment plan. The plan can be modified by the debtor but, except for cause, must be confirmed or denied within forty-five days of the filing of the plan.

Court confirmation of the plan is the same as for a repayment plan. In summary, the plan must provide for payment of secured debts at the value of the collateral. If the secured debt exceeds the value of the collateral, the remaining debt is unsecured. For unsecured debtors, the plan must be confirmed if either the value of the property to be distributed under the plan equals the amount of the claim or the plan provides that all of the debtor's disposable income to be received in a three-year period (or longer, by court approval) will be applied to making payments. Completion of payments under the plan discharges all debts provided for by the plan.

---

28. Note that the Bankruptcy Code defines a *family farmer* and a *farmer* differently. To be a farmer, a person or business must receive 50 percent of gross income from a farming operation that the person or business owns or operates—see footnote 13.

29. Note that for a corporation or partnership to qualify under Chapter 12, at least 80 percent of the value of the firm's assets must consist of assets related to the farming operation.

 Reviewing . . . Creditors' Rights and Bankruptcy

Three months ago, Janet Hart's husband of twenty years died of cancer. Although he had medical insurance, he left Janet with outstanding medical bills of more than $50,000. Janet has worked at the local library for the past ten years, earning $1,500 per month. Since her husband's death, Janet also has received $1,500 in Social Security benefits and $1,100 in life insurance proceeds every month, giving her a monthly income of $4,300. After she pays the mortgage payment of $1,500 and the amounts due on other debts each month, Janet barely has enough left over to buy groceries for her family (she has two teenage daughters at home). She decides to file for Chapter 7 bankruptcy, hoping for a fresh start. Using the information provided in the chapter, answer the following questions.

1. Under the Bankruptcy Code after the reform act, what must Janet do before filing a petition for relief under Chapter 7?
2. How much time does Janet have after filing the bankruptcy petition to submit the required schedules? What happens if Janet does not meet the deadline?

3. Assume that Janet files a petition under Chapter 7. Further assume that the median family income in the state in which Janet lives is $49,300. What steps would a court take to determine whether Janet's petition is presumed to be "substantial abuse" under the means test?

4. Suppose that the court determines that no presumption of substantial abuse applies in Janet's case. Nevertheless, the court finds that Janet does have the ability to pay at least a portion of the medical bills out of her disposable income. What would the court likely order in that situation?

Linking the Law *to Economics*

The Effects of Bankruptcy Law on Consumers and Businesses

The economic crisis that started in late 2007 led to a significant increase in bankruptcy filings by U.S. consumers and businesses. In 2008, bankruptcy filings by consumers were up by more than 30 percent. In the same year, 136 publicly traded U.S. companies filed for bankruptcy, an increase of 74 percent from a year earlier. In a typical month in 2009, about 100,000 consumers filed for bankruptcy protection.

Bankruptcy in the United States is permitted under Article I, Section 8 of the U.S. Constitution, which authorizes Congress to enact "uniform Laws on the subject of Bankruptcies throughout the United States." In your business law or legal environment course, you learn about the types of bankruptcy and their procedures. In contrast, in your economics courses, you learn about how bankruptcy law affects the behavior of individuals and businesses.

Bankruptcy Laws Can Change the Incentives Facing Consumers

Before the framing of the U.S. Constitution, there were debtors' prisons in the United States, and debtors who could not pay their debts were sometimes sent to prison. The threat of going to prison certainly caused consumers to borrow less and to make a great effort to repay what they owed. Today, of course, we no longer have debtors' prisons, so consumers who are unable to pay their debts know that although they may be ruined financially if they have to file for bankruptcy, they will not go to prison.

It goes without saying that the easier and less costly it is for consumers to declare bankruptcy and effectively "start over with a clean slate,"

the more debt they will demand and the less they will worry about repaying their creditors. Indeed, one of the reasons that the bankruptcy reform law was enacted in 2005 was to prevent abuse of the bankruptcy process. According to some, it had become too easy for consumers to avoid paying their debts in full.

Bankruptcy Law Also Affects the Incentives of Businesses That Lend

Consumers typically obtain credit from banks, credit-card companies, auto loan companies, finance companies, and major retailers. These lending entities end up charging a competitive interest rate because the market for consumer credit is highly competitive. That competitive interest rate includes a risk premium to cover the consumer debt that is never repaid. Consequently, the easier it is for consumers to file for bankruptcy and wipe out their debts, the higher the risk to the lenders. In other words, the more forgiving the bankruptcy laws are, the more the lending entities will charge consumers for credit. As you learn in your economics courses, all government actions that change incentives lead to other changes in the economy. In this situation, laws that are more favorable to borrowers are by definition less favorable to lenders. The result is higher market interest rates for loans.

FOR CRITICAL ANALYSIS
In what ways do bankruptcy laws benefit the economy as a whole?

 Key Terms

artisan's lien 521	estate in property 535	order for relief 533
attachment 522	garnishment 523	petition in bankruptcy 531
automatic stay 534	guarantor 525	preference 538
consumer-debtor 529	homestead exemption 528	preferred creditor 538
co-surety 527	liquidation 529	reaffirmation agreement 542
cram-down provision 545	mechanic's lien 521	right of contribution 527
creditors' composition agreement 523	mortgage 523	right of reimbursement 527
debtor in possession (DIP) 544	mortgagee 524	right of subrogation 527
discharge 530	mortgagor 524	surety 525

Chapter Summary: Creditors' Rights and Bankruptcy

LAWS ASSISTING CREDITORS	

Liens
(See pages 521–523.)
	1. *Mechanic's lien*—A nonpossessory, filed lien on an owner's real estate for labor, services, or materials furnished to or made on the realty.
	2. *Artisan's lien*—A possessory lien on an owner's personal property for labor performed or value added.
	3. *Judicial liens*—
	   a. Writ of attachment—A court-ordered seizure of property prior to a court's final determination of the creditor's rights to the property. Attachment is available only on the creditor's posting of a bond and strict compliance with the applicable state statutes.
	   b. Writ of execution—A court order directing the sheriff to seize (levy) and sell a debtor's nonexempt real or personal property to satisfy a court's judgment in the creditor's favor.

Garnishment (See page 523.)	A collection remedy that allows the creditor to attach a debtor's funds (such as wages owed or bank accounts) and property that are held by a third person.
Creditors' Composition Agreements (See page 523.)	A contract between a debtor and his or her creditors by which the debtor's debts are discharged by payment of a sum less than the amount that is actually owed.
Mortgage Foreclosure (See pages 523–524.)	On the debtor's default, the entire mortgage debt is due and payable, allowing the creditor to foreclose on the realty by selling it to satisfy the debt.
Suretyship and Guaranty (See pages 525–528.)	Under contract, a third person agrees to be primarily or secondarily liable for the debt owed by the principal debtor. A creditor can turn to this third person for satisfaction of the debt.
LAWS ASSISTING DEBTORS	
Exemptions (See page 528.)	Certain property of a debtor is exempt from creditors' actions under state laws. Each state permits a debtor to retain the family home, either in its entirety or up to a specified dollar amount, free from the claims of unsecured creditors or trustees in bankruptcy (homestead exemption).

BANKRUPTCY—A COMPARISON OF CHAPTERS 7, 11, 12, AND 13			
Issue	**Chapter 7**	**Chapter 11**	**Chapters 12 and 13**
Purpose	Liquidation.	Reorganization.	Adjustment.
Who Can Petition	Debtor (voluntary) or creditors (involuntary).	Debtor (voluntary) or creditors (involuntary).	Debtor (voluntary) only.
Who Can Be a Debtor	Any "person" (including partnerships and corporations) except railroads, insurance companies, banks, savings and loan institutions, investment companies licensed by the U.S. Small Business Administration, and credit unions. Farmers and charitable institutions cannot be involuntarily petitioned.	Any debtor eligible for Chapter 7 relief; railroads are also eligible.	*Chapter 12*—Any family farmer (one whose gross income is at least 50 percent farm dependent and whose debts are at least 50 percent farm related) or family fisherman (one whose gross income is at least 50 percent dependent on and whose debts are at least 80 percent related to commercial fishing) or any partnership or closely held corporation at least 50 percent owned by a family farmer or fisherman, when total debt does not exceed $3,544,525 for a family farmer and $1,642,500 for a family fisherman.

Chapter Summary: Creditors' Rights and Bankruptcy—Continued

Who Can Be a Debtor—Continued			*Chapter 13*—Any individual (not partnerships or corporations) with regular income who owes fixed (liquidated) unsecured debts of less than $336,900 or fixed secured debts of less than $1,010,650.
Procedure Leading to Discharge	Nonexempt property is sold with proceeds to be distributed (in order) to priority groups. Dischargeable debts are terminated.	Plan is submitted; if it is approved and followed, debts are discharged.	Plan is submitted and must be approved if the value of the property to be distributed equals the amount of the claims or if the debtor turns over disposable income for a three-year or five-year period; if the plan is followed, debts are discharged.
Advantages	On liquidation and distribution, most debts are discharged, and the debtor has an opportunity for a fresh start.	Debtor continues in business. Creditors can either accept the plan, or it can be "crammed down" on them. The plan allows for the reorganization and liquidation of debts over the plan period.	Debtor continues in business or possession of assets. If the plan is approved, most debts are discharged after a three-year period.

 ## ExamPrep

ISSUE SPOTTERS

1 Joe contracts with Larry of Midwest Roofing to fix Joe's roof. Joe pays half of the contract price in advance. Larry and Midwest complete the job, but Joe refuses to pay the rest of the price. What can Larry and Midwest do?
2 Ogden is a vice president of Plumbing Service, Inc. (PSI). On May 1, Ogden loans PSI $10,000. On June 1, the firm repays the loan. On July 1, PSI files for bankruptcy. Quentin is appointed trustee. Can Quentin recover the $10,000 paid to Ogden on June 1?

BEFORE THE TEST

Check your answers to the Issue Spotters, and at the same time, take the interactive quiz for this chapter. Go to **www.cengage.com/blaw/blt** and click on "Chapter 21." First, click on "Answers to Issue Spotters" to check your answers. Next, click on "Interactive Quiz" to assess your mastery of the concepts in this chapter. Then click on "Flashcards" to review this chapter's Key Term definitions.

 ## For Review

Answers for the even-numbered questions in this For Review *section can be found on this text's accompanying Web site at* **www.cengage.com/blaw/blt**. *Select "Chapter 21" and click on "For Review."*

1 What is a prejudgment attachment? What is a writ of execution? How does a creditor use these remedies?
2 What is garnishment? When might a creditor undertake a garnishment proceeding?
3 In a bankruptcy proceeding, what constitutes the debtor's estate in property? What property is exempt from the estate under federal bankruptcy law?
4 What is the difference between an exception to discharge and an objection to discharge?
5 In a Chapter 11 reorganization, what is the role of the debtor in possession?

Hypothetical Scenarios and Case Problems

21-1 Artisan's Lien. Air Ruidoso, Ltd., operated a commuter airline and air charter service between Ruidoso, New Mexico, and airports in Albuquerque and El Paso. Executive Aviation Center, Inc., provided services for airlines at the Albuquerque International Airport. When Air Ruidoso failed to pay more than $10,000 that it owed for fuel, oil, and oxygen, Executive Aviation took possession of Air Ruidoso's plane. Executive Aviation claimed that it had a lien on the plane and filed a suit in a New Mexico state court to foreclose. Do supplies such as fuel, oil, and oxygen qualify as "materials" for the purpose of creating an artisan's lien? Why or why not?

21-2 **Hypothetical Question with Sample Answer** Runyan voluntarily petitions for bankruptcy. He has three major claims against his estate. One is by Calvin, a friend who holds Runyan's negotiable promissory note for $2,500; one is by Kohak, an employee who is owed three months' back wages of $4,500; and one is by the First Bank of Sunny Acres on an unsecured loan of $5,000. In addition, Martinez, an accountant retained by the trustee, is owed $500, and property taxes of $1,000 are owed to Micanopa County. Runyan's nonexempt property has been liquidated, and the proceeds total $5,000. Discuss fully what amount each party will receive, and why.

—For a sample answer to Question 21-2, go to Appendix E at the end of this text.

21-3 Rights of the Surety. Meredith, a farmer, borrowed $5,000 from Farmer's Bank and gave the bank $4,000 in bearer bonds to hold as collateral for the loan. Meredith's neighbor, Peterson, who had known Meredith for years, signed as a surety on the note. Because of a drought, Meredith's harvest that year was only a fraction of what it normally was, and he was forced to default on his payments to Farmer's Bank. The bank did not immediately sell the bonds but instead requested $5,000 from Peterson. Peterson paid the $5,000 and then demanded that the bank give him the $4,000 in securities. Can Peterson enforce this demand? Explain.

21-4 Liens. Karen and Gerald Baldwin owned property in Rapid City, South Dakota, which they leased to Wyoming Alaska Corp. (WACO) for use as a gas station and convenience store. The lease obligated the Baldwins to make repairs, but WACO was authorized to make necessary repairs. After seventeen years, the property was in such poor repair that customers were tripping over chunks of concrete in the parking lot and an underground gasoline storage tank was leaking. The store's manager hired Duffield Construction, Inc., to install a new tank and make other repairs. The Baldwins saw the new tank sitting on the property before the work began. When WACO paid only a small portion of the cost, Duffield filed a mechanic's lien and asked a South Dakota state court to foreclose on the property. The Baldwins disputed the lien, arguing that they did not request the work. What is the purpose of a mechanic's lien? Should property owners who do not contract for improvements be liable for the cost under such a lien? How might owners protect themselves against a lien for work that

they do not request? Explain. [*Duffield Construction, Inc. v. Baldwin*, 679 N.W.2d 477 (S.Dak. 2004)]

21-5 Exceptions to Discharge. Between 1988 and 1992, Lorna Nys took out thirteen student loans, totaling about $30,000, to finance an associate of arts degree in drafting from the College of the Redwoods and a bachelor of arts degree from Humboldt State University (HSU) in California. In 1996, Nys began working at HSU as a drafting technician. As a "Drafter II," the highest-paying drafting position at HSU, Nys's gross income in 2002 was $40,244. She was fifty-one years old, her net monthly income was $2,299.33, and she had $2,295.05 in monthly expenses, including saving $140 for her retirement, which she planned for age sixty-five. When Educational Credit Management Corp. (ECMC) began to collect payments on Nys's student loans, she filed a Chapter 7 petition in a federal bankruptcy court, seeking a discharge of the loans. ECMC argued that Nys did not show any "additional circumstances" that would impede her ability to repay. What is the standard for the discharge of student loans under Chapter 7? Does Nys meet that standard? Why or why not? [*In re Nys*, 446 F.3d 938 (9th Cir. 2006)]

21-6 **Case Problem with Sample Answer** James Stout, a professor of economics and business at Cornell College in Mount Vernon, Iowa, filed a petition in bankruptcy under Chapter 7, seeking to discharge about $95,000 in credit-card debts. At the time, Stout had been divorced for ten years and had custody of his children: Z. S., who attended college, and G. S., who was twelve years old. Stout's ex-wife did not contribute child support. According to Stout, G. S. was an "elite" ice-skater who practiced twenty hours a week and had placed between first and third at more than forty competitive events. He had decided to home school G. S., whose achievements were average for her grade level despite her frequent absences from public school. His petition showed monthly income of $4,227 and expenses of $4,806. The expenses included annual home school costs of $8,400 and annual skating expenses of $6,000. They did not include Z. S.'s college costs, such as airfare for his upcoming studies in Europe, and other items. The trustee allowed monthly expenses of $3,227—with nothing for skating—and asked the court to dismiss the petition. Can the court grant this request? Should it? If so, what might it encourage Stout to do? Explain. [*In re Stout*, 336 Bankr. 138 (N.D. Iowa 2006)]

—After you have answered Problem 21-6, compare your answer with the sample answer given on the Web site that accompanies this text. Go to www.cengage.com/blaw/blt, select "Chapter 21," and click on "Case Problem with Sample Answer."

21-7 Discharge in Bankruptcy. Rhonda Schroeder married Gennady Shvartsshteyn (Gene) in 1997. Gene worked at Royal Courier and Air Domestic Connect in Illinois, where Melissa Winyard also worked in 1999 and 2000. During this time, Gene and Winyard had an affair. A year after leaving Royal, Winyard filed a petition in a federal bankruptcy court under Chapter 7 and was granted a discharge of her debts. Sometime later, in a letter to Schroeder who had learned of the affair, Winyard wrote, "I never intentionally wanted any of this to happen. I never wanted to disrupt your marriage." Schroeder obtained a divorce and, in 2005, filed a suit in an Illinois state court against Winyard, alleging "alienation of affection." Schroeder claimed that there had been "mutual love and affection" in her marriage until Winyard engaged in conduct intended to alienate her husband's affection. Schroeder charged that Winyard "caused him to have sexual intercourse with her," resulting in "the destruction of the marital relationship." Winyard filed a motion for summary judgment on the ground that any liability on her part had been discharged in her bankruptcy. Is there an exception to discharge for "willful and malicious conduct"? If so, does Schroeder's claim qualify? Discuss. [*Schroeder v. Winyard*, 375 Ill.App.3d 358, 873 N.E.2d 35, 313 Ill.Dec. 740 (2 Dist. 2007)]

21–8 Discharge in Bankruptcy. Cathy Coleman took out loans to complete her college education. After graduation, Coleman was irregularly employed as a teacher before filing a petition in a federal bankruptcy court under Chapter 13. The court confirmed a five-year plan under which Coleman was required to commit all of her disposable income to paying the student loans. Less than a year later, she was laid off. Still owing more than $100,000 to Educational Credit Management Corp., Coleman asked the court to discharge the debt on the ground that it would be undue hardship for her to pay it. Under Chapter 13, when is a debtor normally entitled to a discharge? Are student loans dischargeable? If not, is "undue hardship" a legitimate ground for an exception? With respect to a debtor, what is the goal of bankruptcy? With these facts and principles in mind, what argument could be made in support of Coleman's request? [*In re Coleman*, 560 F.3d 1000 (9th Cir. 2009)]

21–9 **A Question of Ethics** *In January 2003, Gary Ryder and Washington Mutual Bank, F.A., executed a note in which Ryder promised to pay $2,450,000, plus interest at a rate that could vary from month to month. The amount of the first payment was $10,933. The note was to be paid in full by February 1, 2033. A mortgage on Ryder's real property at 345 Round Hill Road in Greenwich, Connecticut, in favor of the bank secured his obligations under the note. The note and mortgage required that he pay the taxes on the property, which he did not do in 2004 and 2005. The bank notified him that he was in default and, when he failed to act, paid $50,095.92 in taxes, penalties, interest, and fees. Other disputes arose between the parties, and Ryder filed a suit in a federal district court against the bank, alleging, in part, breach of contract. He charged, among other things, that some of his timely payments were not processed and were subjected to incorrect late fees, forcing him to make excessive payments and ultimately resulting in "non-payment by Ryder." [Ryder v. Washington Mutual Bank, F.A., 501 F.Supp.2d 311 (D.Conn. 2007)]*

1 The bank filed a counterclaim, seeking to foreclose on the mortgage. What should a creditor be required to prove to foreclose on mortgaged property? What would be a debtor's most effective defense? Which party in this case is likely to prevail on the bank's counterclaim? Why?

2 The parties agreed to a settlement that released the bank from Ryder's claims and required him to pay the note by January 31, 2007. The court dismissed the suit, but when Ryder did not make the payment, the bank asked the court to reopen the case. The bank then asked for a judgment in its favor on Ryder's complaint, arguing that the settlement had "immediately" released the bank from his claims. Does this seem fair? Why or why not?

▶ Critical Thinking and Writing Assignments

21–10 Critical Legal Thinking. Do you think that the law favors debtors at the expense of creditors, or vice versa? Does the 2005 act adequately balance the interests of creditors and debtors?

21–11 Critical Thinking and Writing Assignment for Business. In what circumstances would a creditor resort to each of the following remedies when trying to collect on debt?

1 Mechanic's lien
2 Artisan's lien
3 Writ of attachment
4 Writ of execution
5 Garnishment

▶ Practical Internet Exercises

Go to this text's Web site at **www.cengage.com/blaw/blt**, select "Chapter 21," and click on "Practical Internet Exercises." There you will find the following Internet research exercises that you can perform to learn more about the topics covered in this chapter.

Practical Internet Exercise 21–1: LEGAL PERSPECTIVE—Debtor-Creditor Relations
Practical Internet Exercise 21–2: MANAGEMENT PERSPECTIVE—Bankruptcy Alternatives

International Law in a Global Economy

"The merchant has no country."

—Thomas Jefferson, 1743–1826
(Third president of the United States, 1801–1809)

Chapter Outline

- International Law— Sources and Principles
- Doing Business Internationally
- Regulation of Specific Business Activities
- Commercial Contracts in an International Setting
- Payment Methods for International Transactions
- U.S. Laws in a Global Context

Learning Objectives

After reading this chapter, you should be able to answer the following questions:

1. What is the principle of comity, and why do courts deciding disputes involving a foreign law or judicial decree apply this principle?

2. What is the act of state doctrine? In what circumstances is this doctrine applied?

3. Under the Foreign Sovereign Immunities Act of 1976, on what bases might a foreign state be considered subject to the jurisdiction of U.S. courts?

4. In what circumstances will U.S. antitrust laws be applied extraterritorially?

5. Do U.S. laws prohibiting employment discrimination apply in all circumstances to U.S. employees working for U.S. employers abroad?

International business transactions are not unique to the modern world. Indeed, commerce has always crossed national borders, as President Thomas Jefferson noted in the chapter-opening quotation. What is new in our day is the dramatic growth in world trade and the emergence of a global business community. Because exchanges of goods, services, and ideas on a global level are now routine, students of business law and the legal environment should be familiar with the laws pertaining to international business transactions.

Laws affecting the international legal environment of business include both international law and national law. **International law** can be defined as a body of law—formed as a result of international customs, treaties, and organizations—that governs relations among or between nations. International law may be public, creating standards for the nations themselves; or it may be private, establishing international standards for private transactions that cross national borders. *National law,* as pointed out in Chapter 1, is the law of a particular nation, such as Brazil, Germany, Japan, or the United States.

In this chapter, we examine how both international law and national law frame business operations in the global context. We also look at some selected areas relating to business activities in a global context, including international sales contracts, civil dispute resolution, letters of credit, and investment protection. We conclude the chapter with a discussion of the application of certain U.S. laws in a transnational setting.

International Law The law that governs relations among nations. International customs, treaties, and organizations are important sources of international law.

International Law—Sources and Principles

The major difference between international law and national law is that government authorities can enforce national law. What government, however, can enforce international law? By definition, a *nation* is a sovereign entity—meaning that there is no higher authority to which that nation must submit. If a nation violates an international law and persuasive tactics fail, other countries or international organizations have no recourse except to take coercive actions—from severance of diplomatic relations and boycotts to, as a last resort, war—against the violating nation.

In essence, international law attempts to reconcile the need of each country to be the final authority over its own affairs with the desire of nations to benefit economically from trade and harmonious relations with one another. Sovereign nations can, and do, voluntarily agree to be governed in certain respects by international law for the purpose of facilitating international trade and commerce, as well as civilized discourse. As a result, a body of international law has evolved.

Sources of International Law

Basically, there are three sources of international law: international customs, treaties and international agreements, and international organizations and conferences. We look at each of these sources here.

INTERNATIONAL CUSTOMS   One important source of international law consists of the international customs that have evolved among nations in their relations with one another. Article 38(1) of the Statute of the International Court of Justice refers to an international custom as "evidence of a general practice accepted as law." The legal principles and doctrines that you will read about shortly are rooted in international customs and traditions that have evolved over time in the international arena.

TREATIES AND INTERNATIONAL AGREEMENTS   Treaties and other explicit agreements between or among foreign nations provide another important source of international law. A **treaty** is an agreement or contract between two or more nations that must be authorized and ratified by the supreme power of each nation. Under Article II, Section 2, of the U.S. Constitution, the president has the power "by and with the Advice and Consent of the Senate, to make Treaties, provided two-thirds of the Senators present concur."

A *bilateral* agreement, as the term implies, is an agreement formed by two nations to govern their commercial exchanges or other relations with one another. A *multilateral* agreement is formed by several nations. For example, regional trade associations such as the Andean Common Market (ANCOM), the Association of Southeast Asian Nations (ASEAN), and the European Union (EU) are the result of multilateral trade agreements.

INTERNATIONAL ORGANIZATIONS   In international law, the term **international organization** generally refers to an organization that is composed mainly of officials of member nations and usually established by treaty. The United States is a member of more than one hundred multilateral and bilateral organizations, including at least twenty through the United Nations. These organizations adopt resolutions, declarations, and other types of standards that often require nations to behave in a particular manner. The General Assembly of the United Nations, for example, has adopted numerous nonbinding resolutions and declarations that embody principles of international law. Disputes involving these resolutions and declarations may be brought before the International Court of Justice. That court,

ON THE WEB FindLaw's Web site includes an extensive array of links to international doctrines, treaties, and other nations' laws. Go to **library.findlaw.com** and select "International Law."

Treaty   In international law, a formal written agreement negotiated between two nations or among several nations. In the United States, all treaties must be approved by the Senate.

International Organization   Any membership group that operates across national borders. These organizations can be governmental organizations, such as the United Nations, or nongovernmental organizations, such as the Red Cross.

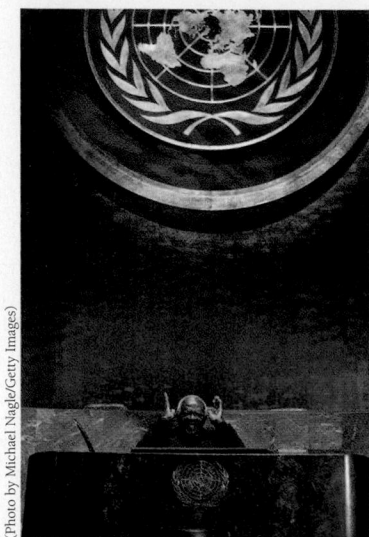

Archbishop Desmond Tutu speaks at the United Nations. How is the United Nations a source of international law?

Comity   The principle by which one nation defers to and gives effect to the laws and judicial decrees of another nation. This recognition is based primarily on respect.

Act of State Doctrine   A doctrine providing that the judicial branch of one country will not examine the validity of public acts committed by a recognized foreign government within its own territory.

Expropriation   The seizure by a government of a privately owned business or personal property for a proper public purpose and with just compensation.

Confiscation   A government's taking of a privately owned business or personal property without a proper public purpose or an award of just compensation.

however, normally has authority to settle legal disputes only when nations voluntarily submit to its jurisdiction.

The United Nations Commission on International Trade Law has made considerable progress in establishing uniformity in international law as it relates to trade and commerce. One of the commission's most significant creations to date is the 1980 Convention on Contracts for the International Sale of Goods (CISG). As discussed in Chapter 15, the CISG is similar to Article 2 of the Uniform Commercial Code. It is designed to settle disputes between parties to sales contracts if the parties have not agreed otherwise in their contracts. The CISG governs only sales contracts between trading partners in nations that have ratified the CISG, however.

International Principles and Doctrines

Over time, a number of legal principles and doctrines have evolved and have been employed by the courts of various nations to resolve or reduce conflicts that involve a foreign element. The three important legal principles discussed next are based primarily on courtesy and respect, and are applied in the interests of maintaining harmonious relations among nations.

THE PRINCIPLE OF COMITY   Under the principle of **comity**, one nation will defer to and give effect to the laws and judicial decrees of another country, as long as they are consistent with the law and public policy of the accommodating nation.

EXAMPLE 22.1   A Swedish seller and a U.S. buyer have formed a contract, which the buyer breaches. The seller sues the buyer in a Swedish court, which awards damages. The buyer's assets, however, are in the United States and cannot be reached unless the judgment is enforced by a U.S. court of law. In this situation, if a U.S. court determines that the procedures and laws applied in the Swedish court were consistent with U.S. national law and policy, that court will likely defer to (and enforce) the foreign court's judgment. ●

One way to understand the principle of comity (and the *act of state doctrine*, which will be discussed shortly) is to consider the relationships among the states in our federal form of government. Each state honors (gives "full faith and credit" to) the contracts, property deeds, wills, and other legal obligations formed in other states, as well as judicial decisions with respect to such obligations. On a worldwide basis, nations similarly attempt to honor judgments rendered in other countries when it is feasible to do so. Of course, in the United States the states are constitutionally required to honor other states' actions, whereas internationally, nations are not *required* to honor the actions of other nations.

THE ACT OF STATE DOCTRINE   The **act of state doctrine** provides that the judicial branch of one country will not examine the validity of public acts committed by a recognized foreign government within its own territory. The act of state doctrine can have important consequences for individuals and firms doing business with, and investing in, other countries. This doctrine is frequently employed in situations involving expropriation or confiscation. **Expropriation** occurs when a government seizes a privately owned business or privately owned goods for a proper public purpose and awards just compensation. When a government seizes private property for an illegal purpose or without just compensation, the taking is referred to as a **confiscation**. The line between these two forms of taking is sometimes blurred because of differing interpretations of what is illegal and what constitutes just compensation.

EXAMPLE 22.2   Flaherty, Inc., a U.S. company, owns a mine in Brazil. The government of Brazil seizes the mine for public use and claims that the profits that Flaherty realized from the mine in preceding years constitute just compensation. Flaherty disagrees, but the act of state doctrine may prevent the company's recovery in a U.S. court. ● Note that in a case

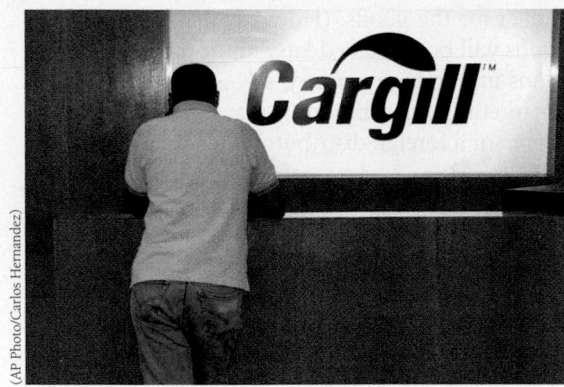

(AP Photo/Carlos Hernandez)

In 2009, President Hugo Chavez of Venezuela ordered the expropriation of a rice-processing plant owned by the American food company Cargill, Inc. What would determine if this was an expropriation or a confiscation?

Sovereign Immunity A doctrine that immunizes foreign nations from the jurisdiction of U.S. courts when certain conditions are satisfied.

Export The sale of goods and services by domestic firms to buyers located in other countries.

"Commerce is the great civilizer. We exchange ideas when we exchange fabrics."

Robert G. Ingersoll, 1833–1899
(American politician and orator)

alleging that a foreign government has wrongfully taken the plaintiff's property, the defendant government has the burden of proving that the taking was an expropriation, not a confiscation.

When applicable, both the act of state doctrine and the doctrine of *sovereign immunity* (to be discussed next) tend to immunize (protect) foreign governments from the jurisdiction of U.S. courts. This means that firms or individuals who own property overseas often have diminished legal protection against government actions in the countries in which they operate.

THE DOCTRINE OF SOVEREIGN IMMUNITY When certain conditions are satisfied, the doctrine of **sovereign immunity** immunizes foreign nations from the jurisdiction of U.S. courts. In 1976, Congress codified this rule in the Foreign Sovereign Immunities Act (FSIA).[1] The FSIA exclusively governs the circumstances in which an action may be brought in the United States against a foreign nation, including attempts to attach a foreign nation's property. Because the law is jurisdictional in nature, a plaintiff has the burden of showing that a defendant is not entitled to sovereign immunity.

Section 1605 of the FSIA sets forth the major exceptions to the jurisdictional immunity of a foreign state. A foreign state is not immune from the jurisdiction of U.S. courts in the following situations:

1. When the foreign state has waived its immunity either explicitly or by implication.
2. When the foreign state has engaged in commercial activity within the United States or in commercial activity outside the United States that has "a direct effect in the United States."[2]
3. When the foreign state has committed a tort in the United States or has violated certain international laws.

In applying the FSIA, questions frequently arise as to whether an entity is a "foreign state" and what constitutes a "commercial activity." Under Section 1603 of the FSIA, a *foreign state* includes both a political subdivision of a foreign state and an instrumentality of a foreign state. Section 1603 broadly defines a *commercial activity* as a commercial activity that is carried out by a foreign state within the United States, but it does not describe the particulars of what constitutes a commercial activity. Thus, the courts are left to decide whether a particular activity is governmental or commercial in nature.

▶ Doing Business Internationally

A U.S. domestic firm can engage in international business transactions in a number of ways. The simplest way is for U.S. firms to **export** their goods and services to markets abroad. Alternatively, a U.S. firm can establish foreign production facilities so as to be closer to the foreign market or markets in which its products are sold. The advantages may include lower labor costs, fewer government regulations, and lower taxes and trade barriers. A domestic firm can also obtain revenues by licensing its technology to an existing foreign company or by selling franchises to overseas entities.

Exporting

Exporting can take two forms: direct exporting and indirect exporting. In *direct exporting*, a U.S. company signs a sales contract with a foreign purchaser that provides for the conditions

---

1. 28 U.S.C. Sections 1602–1611.
2. See, for example, *O'Bryan v. Holy See*, 556 F.3d 361 (6th Cir. 2009).

A worker is helping to manufacture a Ford S-MAX at the Chongqing Changan factory in China. Manufacturing abroad is an alternative to direct or indirect exporting. What are some of the reasons why U.S. companies choose to create manufacturing sites in other countries?

Distribution Agreement   A contract between a seller and a distributor of the seller's products setting out the terms and conditions of the distributorship.

Coca-Cola Bottling Company licenses firms throughout the world to produce its soft drinks. All such firms must keep Coca-Cola's syrup formula a secret. Why would foreign companies choose to pay for a license with Coca-Cola rather than create their own competitive soft drinks?

of shipment and payment for the goods. (How payments are made in international transactions will be discussed later in this chapter.) If sufficient business develops in a foreign country, a U.S. corporation may set up a specialized marketing organization in that foreign market by appointing a foreign agent or a foreign distributor. This is called *indirect exporting*.

When a U.S. firm desires to limit its involvement in an international market, it will typically establish an *agency relationship* with a foreign firm. (*Agency* will be discussed in Chapter 23.) The foreign firm then acts as the U.S. firm's agent and can enter into contracts in the foreign location on behalf of the principal (the U.S. company).

When a foreign country represents a substantial market, a U.S. firm may wish to appoint a distributor located in that country. The U.S. firm and the distributor enter into a **distribution agreement**, which is a contract between the seller and the distributor setting out the terms and conditions of the distributorship. These terms and conditions—for example, price, currency of payment, availability of supplies, and method of payment—primarily involve contract law. Disputes concerning distribution agreements may involve jurisdictional or other issues, as well as contract law, which will be discussed later in this chapter.

Manufacturing Abroad

An alternative to direct or indirect exporting is the establishment of foreign manufacturing facilities. Typically, U.S. firms establish manufacturing plants abroad if they believe that doing so will reduce their costs—particularly for labor, shipping, and raw materials—and enable them to compete more effectively in foreign markets. Foreign firms have done the same in the United States. Sony, Nissan, and other Japanese manufacturers have established U.S. plants to avoid import duties that the U.S. Congress may impose on Japanese products entering this country.

A U.S. firm may license a foreign manufacturing company to use its copyrighted, patented, or trademarked intellectual property or trade secrets. Like any other licensing agreement (see Chapters 5 and 10), a licensing agreement with a foreign-based firm calls for a payment of royalties on some basis—such as so many cents per unit produced or a certain percentage of profits from units sold in a particular geographic territory. As will be discussed in Chapter 26, franchising is a well-known form of licensing. **EXAMPLE 22.3** The Coca-Cola Bottling Company licenses firms worldwide to use (and keep confidential) its secret formula for the syrup used in its soft drink. In return, the foreign firms licensed to make the syrup pay Coca-Cola a percentage of the income earned from the sale of the soft drink. ● Once a firm's trademark is known worldwide, the firm may experience increased demand for other products it manufactures or sells—obviously an important consideration.

Another way to expand into a foreign market is to establish a wholly owned subsidiary firm in a foreign country. When a wholly owned subsidiary is established, the parent company, which remains in the United States, retains complete ownership of all the facilities in the foreign country, as well as complete authority and control over all phases of the operation. A U.S. firm can also expand into international markets through a joint venture. In a joint venture, the U.S. company owns only part of the operation; the rest is owned either by local owners in the foreign country or by another foreign entity. All of the firms involved in a joint venture share responsibilities, as well as profits and liabilities. (Joint ventures will be discussed in Chapter 28.)

 Regulation of Specific Business Activities

Doing business abroad can affect the economies, foreign policies, domestic policies, and other national interests of the countries involved. For this reason, nations impose laws to restrict or facilitate international business. Controls may also be imposed by international agreements. Here, we discuss how different types of international activities are regulated.

Investing

Firms that invest in foreign nations face the risk that the foreign government may take possession of the investment property. Expropriation, as already mentioned, occurs when property is taken and the owner is paid just compensation for what is taken. Expropriation does not violate generally observed principles of international law. Such principles are normally violated, however, when a government confiscates property without compensation (or without adequate compensation). Few remedies are available for confiscation of property by a foreign government. Claims are often resolved by lump-sum settlements after negotiations between the United States and the taking nation.

To counter the deterrent effect that the possibility of confiscation may have on potential investors, many countries guarantee that foreign investors will be compensated if their property is taken. A guaranty can take the form of statutory laws or provisions in international treaties. As further protection for foreign investments, some countries provide insurance for their citizens' investments abroad.

Export Controls

The U.S. Constitution provides in Article I, Section 9, that "No Tax or Duty shall be laid on Articles exported from any State." Thus, Congress cannot impose any export taxes. Congress can, however, use a variety of other devices to control exports. Congress may set export quotas on various items, such as grain being sold abroad. Under the Export Administration Act of 1979,[3] the flow of technologically advanced products and technical data can be restricted.

While restricting certain exports, the United States (and other nations) also uses devices such as export incentives and subsidies to stimulate other exports and thereby aid domestic businesses. Under the Export Trading Company Act of 1982,[4] U.S. banks are encouraged to invest in export trading companies, which are formed when exporting firms join together to export a line of goods. The Export-Import Bank of the United States provides financial assistance, consisting primarily of credit guaranties given to commercial banks that in turn lend funds to U.S. exporting companies.

Import Controls

All nations have restrictions on imports, and the United States is no exception. Restrictions include strict prohibitions, quotas, and tariffs. Under the Trading with the Enemy Act of 1917,[5] for instance, no goods may be imported from nations that have been designated enemies of the United States. Other laws prohibit the importation of illegal drugs, books

---

3. 50 U.S.C. Sections 2401–2420.
4. 15 U.S.C. Sections 4001, 4003.
5. 12 U.S.C. Section 95a.

ON THE WEB For information on the legal requirements of doing business abroad, a good source is the Internet Law Library's collection of laws of other nations. Go to **www.lawguru.com/ilawlib**.

NOTE Most countries restrict exports for the same reasons: to protect national security, to further foreign policy objectives, and to prevent the spread of nuclear weapons.

"The notion dies hard that in some sort of way exports are patriotic but imports are immoral."

Lord Harlech, 1918–1985
(English writer)

that urge insurrection against the United States, and agricultural products that pose dangers to domestic crops or animals.

The import of goods that infringe U.S. patents is also prohibited. The International Trade Commission investigates allegations that imported goods infringe U.S. patents and imposes penalties if necessary. In the following case, a party fined more than $13.5 million for importing certain disposable cameras appealed to the U.S. Court of Appeals for the Federal Circuit.

Case 22.1 Fuji Photo Film Co. v. International Trade Commission

United States Court of Appeals, Federal Circuit, 474 F.3d 1281 (2007).

Did a recycler of disposable cameras violate a cease-and-desist order by continuing to import the cameras during litigation?

(Reuters/Yuriko Nakao)

FACTS Fuji Photo Film Company owns fifteen U.S. patents for "lens-fitted film packages" (LFFPs), popularly known as disposable cameras. An LFFP consists of a plastic shell preloaded with film. To develop the film, a consumer gives the LFFP to a film processor and receives back the negatives and prints, but not the shell. Fuji makes and sells LFFPs. Jazz Photo Corporation collected used LFFP shells in the United States, shipped them abroad to have new film inserted, and then imported them back into the United States for sale. The International Trade Commission (ITC) determined that Jazz's resale of shells originally sold outside the United States infringed Fuji's patents. In 1999, the ITC issued a cease-and-desist order to stop the imports. While the order was being disputed at the ITC and in the courts, between August 2001 and December 2003 Jazz imported and sold 27 million refurbished LFFPs. Fuji complained to the ITC, which fined Jazz more than $13.5 million. Jack Benun, Jazz's chief operating officer, appealed to the U.S. Court of Appeals for the Federal Circuit.

ISSUE Did Jazz violate the cease-and-desist order?

DECISION Yes. The U.S. Court of Appeals for the Federal Circuit affirmed this part of the ITC's decision. The court held, among other things,

that "substantial evidence supports the finding that the majority of the cameras were first sold abroad."

REASON The court explained that to determine whether Jazz had violated Fuji's patents, the ITC used identifying numbers printed on Fuji's LFFPs and Fuji's production and shipping databases to pinpoint where Jazz's refurbished LFFPs were first sold. Against this evidence, Benun asserted that Jazz utilized its own "informed compliance program" to track the LFFP shells from their collection to their sale. Benun argued that this tracking system ensured that only shells collected from the United States were refurbished for sale here. The court reasoned, however, that this tracking program would ensure "at most" only that Jazz refurbished LFFPs collected from the United States, not that Jazz refurbished LFFPs first sold here. Besides, Jazz's tracking program was "too incomplete and disorganized to be credible." Because "there was no suggestion that the incomplete and disorganized nature of the program was due to Fuji's actions, this ground alone was sufficient to justify a conclusion that Benun" did not prove the refurbished LFFPs had been sold first in the United States.

FOR CRITICAL ANALYSIS—Ethical Consideration *Suppose that, after this decision, Jazz fully compensated Fuji for the infringing sales of LFFPs. Would Jazz have acquired the right to refurbish those LFFPs in the future? Explain.*

Quota A set limit on the amount of goods that can be imported.

Tariff A tax on imported goods.

QUOTAS AND TARIFFS Limits on the amounts of goods that can be imported are known as **quotas.** At one time, the United States had legal quotas on the number of automobiles that could be imported from Japan. Today, Japan "voluntarily" restricts the number of automobiles exported to the United States. **Tariffs** are taxes on imports. A tariff usually is a percentage of the value of the import, but it can be a flat rate per unit (for example, per barrel of oil). Tariffs raise the prices of goods, causing some consumers to purchase more domestically manufactured goods and fewer imported goods. (For a discussion of tariffs and other considerations for businesses going global, see this chapter's *Linking the Law to Marketing* feature on page 570.)

Sometimes, countries impose tariffs on goods from a particular nation in retaliation for political acts. **EXAMPLE 22.4** In 2009, Mexico imposed tariffs of 10 to 20 percent on ninety products exported from the United States in retaliation for the Obama administration's can-

> *"Tariff: a scale of taxes on imports, designed to protect the domestic producer against the greed of his consumer."*
>
> Ambrose Bierce, 1842–1914
> (American journalist)

cellation of a cross-border trucking program. The program had been instituted to comply with a provision in the North American Free Trade Agreement (discussed shortly) intended to eventually grant Mexican trucks full access to U.S. highways. U.S truck drivers opposed the program, however, and consumer protection groups claimed that the Mexican trucks posed safety issues. President Barack Obama signed legislation that cut off funding for the program, but he asked his trade representative to look into creating a new program for cross-border transportation. •

In the following case, an importer provided invoices that understated the value of its imports and resulted in lower tariffs than would have been paid on the full value of the goods. Was this fraud or negligence?

Case 22.2 United States v. Inn Foods, Inc.

United States Court of Appeals, Federal Circuit, 560 F.3d 1338 (2009).
www.cafc.uscourts.gov[a]

COMPANY PROFILE *Inn Foods, Inc. (www.innfoods.com), was established in 1976 as a subsidiary of the VPS Companies, Inc. Inn Foods imports frozen fruits and vegetables into the United States from sources worldwide. At its plants in California and Texas, the company blends, custom packages, co-packs, flavors, and seasons vegetables, pasta, potatoes, rice, fruits, and other food products. Each year, Inn Foods sells more than 157 million pounds of food. Its customers include buyers in the food service industry, industrial food markets, and retail food markets at locations around the globe.*

A company importing frozen produce uses a double-invoicing system to undervalue its purchases and reduce its tariff payments. Is it fraud?

FACTS Between 1987 and 1990, Inn Foods imported frozen produce from six Mexican growers who agreed to issue invoices that understated the value of the produce. For each understated invoice, Inn Foods sent an order confirmation that estimated the produce's actual market value. Inn Foods later remitted the difference to the growers. Through this double-invoicing system, Inn Foods undervalued its purchases by approximately $3.5 million and paid lower tariff taxes as a result. During an investigation by U.S. Customs and Border Protection, Inn Foods' accounting supervisor denied the existence of the double invoices. The federal government filed an action in the U.S. Court of International Trade against Inn Foods. The court held the defendant liable for

fraud and assessed the amount of the unpaid taxes—$624,602.55—plus an additional penalty of $7.5 million. Inn Foods appealed, claiming that it had acted negligently, not fraudulently.

ISSUE Does an importer's use of a double-invoicing system constitute proof of an intent to defraud the government of import duties?

DECISION Yes. The U.S. Court of Appeals for the Federal Circuit affirmed the lower court's judgment.

REASON The evidence showed that Inn Foods "knowingly entered goods by means of a material false statement." Each grower sent Inn Foods a copy of an undervalued invoice. The company knew that these invoices were "grossly undervalued and false"—the growers set out the details of the specific undervaluation in correspondence to Inn Foods. On receipt, Inn Foods adjusted the prices to reflect their true estimated value. The company entered the higher amount into its accounting system, sent a confirmation to the grower with the higher price, and paid the grower based on the confirmed price. But Inn Foods knew the false invoices would be used to import goods into the United States. The company used the undervalued invoices to declare the value of the produce to U.S. Customs and Border Protection for import. Moreover, Inn Foods concealed the existence of the double invoices during the government's investigation.

FOR CRITICAL ANALYSIS—Ethical Consideration *After Inn Foods learned of the investigation, the company included a disclaimer on some shipments stating that the declared value "is strictly for customs clearance" while the company determines the "true transaction value." Does this disclaimer legally or ethically absolve the importer of intent to defraud?*

---

a. In the links at the top of the page, click on "Opinions & orders." On that page, click on "2009." In the result, scroll to the name of the case and click on it to access the opinion. The U.S. Court of Appeals for the Federal Circuit maintains this Web site.

Dumping The selling of goods in a foreign country at a price below the price charged for the same goods in the domestic market.

ANTIDUMPING DUTIES The United States has specific laws directed at what it sees as unfair international trade practices. **Dumping**, for example, is the sale of imported goods at "less than fair value." "Fair value" is usually determined by the price of those goods in the exporting country. Foreign firms that engage in dumping in the United States hope to undersell U.S. businesses to obtain a larger share of the U.S. market. To prevent this, an extra tariff—known as an *antidumping duty*—may be assessed on the imports.

Minimizing Trade Barriers

Restrictions on imports are also known as *trade barriers*. The elimination of trade barriers is sometimes seen as essential to the world's economic well-being. Most of the world's leading trading nations are members of the World Trade Organization (WTO), which was established in 1995. To minimize trade barriers among nations, each member country of the WTO is required to grant **normal trade relations (NTR) status** (formerly known as most-favored-nation status) to other member countries. This means each member is obligated to treat other members at least as well as it treats the country that receives its most favorable treatment with regard to imports or exports. Various regional trade agreements and associations also help to minimize trade barriers between nations.

Normal Trade Relations (NTR) Status
A status granted by each member country of the World Trade Organization to other member countries. Each member is required to treat other members at least as well as it treats the country that receives its most favorable treatment with respect to trade.

THE EUROPEAN UNION (EU)   The European Union (EU) arose out the 1957 Treaty of Rome, which created the Common Market, a free trade zone comprising the nations of Belgium, France, Italy, Luxembourg, the Netherlands, and West Germany. Today, the EU is a single integrated trading unit made up of twenty-seven European nations.

The EU has gone a long way toward creating a new body of law to govern all of the member nations—although some of its efforts to create uniform laws have been confounded by nationalism. The council and the commission issue regulations, or directives, that define EU law in various areas, such as environmental law, product liability, anticompetitive practices, and corporations. The directives normally are binding on all member countries.

THE NORTH AMERICAN FREE TRADE AGREEMENT (NAFTA)   The North American Free Trade Agreement (NAFTA) created a regional trading unit consisting of Canada, Mexico, and the United States. The goal of NAFTA is to eliminate tariffs among these three countries on substantially all goods by reducing the tariffs incrementally over a period of time. NAFTA gives the three countries a competitive advantage by retaining tariffs on goods imported from countries outside the NAFTA trading unit. Additionally, NAFTA provides for the elimination of barriers that traditionally have prevented the cross-border movement of services, such as financial and transportation services. NAFTA also attempts to eliminate citizenship requirements for the licensing of accountants, attorneys, physicians, and other professionals.

THE CENTRAL AMERICA–DOMINICAN REPUBLIC–UNITED STATES FREE TRADE AGREEMENT (CAFTA-DR)   The Central America–Dominican Republic–United States Free Trade Agreement (CAFTA-DR) was formed by Costa Rica, the Dominican Republic, El Salvador, Guatemala, Honduras, Nicaragua, and the United States. Its purpose is to reduce tariffs and improve market access among all of the signatory nations, including the United States. As of 2010, legislatures from all seven countries had approved the CAFTA-DR, despite significant opposition in certain nations.

Bribing Foreign Officials

Giving cash or in-kind benefits to foreign government officials to obtain business contracts and other favors is often considered normal practice. To reduce such bribery by representatives of U.S. corporations, Congress enacted the Foreign Corrupt Practices Act in 1977.[6] This act and its implications for American businesspersons engaged in international business transactions were discussed in Chapter 6.

(Wikimedia Commons)

The European Union (EU) is a single-integrated trading block comprised of twenty-seven European nations. Shown above is the seat of the European Parliament in Strasbourg, France. The EU issues regulations that relate to product liability, anticompetitive practices, consumer health and safety, and environmental issues. Are these regulations binding on all EU members?

---

6. 15 U.S.C. Sections 78m–78ff.

▶ Commercial Contracts in an International Setting

Like all commercial contracts, an international contract should be in writing. For an example of an actual international sales contract from Starbucks Coffee Company, refer back to the foldout exhibit at the end of Chapter 15.

Contract Clauses

Language and legal differences among nations can create special problems for parties to international contracts when disputes arise. To avoid these problems, parties should include special provisions in the contract that designate the language of the contract, where any disputes will be resolved, and the substantive law that will be applied in settling any disputes. Parties to international contracts should also indicate in their contracts what acts or events will excuse the parties from performance under the contract and whether disputes under the contract will be arbitrated or litigated.

In 1992, the heads of Canada, Mexico, and the United States, along with their chief negotiators, signed a draft of the North American Free Trade Agreement, which eventually took effect two years later. Who benefits from such an agreement?

(George Bush Presidential Library and Museum)

CHOICE OF LANGUAGE A deal struck between a U.S. company and a company in another country normally involves two languages. Typically, many phrases in one language are not readily translatable into another. Consequently, the complex contractual terms involved may not be understood by one party in the other party's language. To make sure that no disputes arise out of this language problem, an international sales contract should have a **choice-of-language clause** designating the official language by which the contract will be interpreted in the event of disagreement.

Choice-of-Language Clause A clause in a contract designating the official language by which the contract will be interpreted in the event of a future disagreement over the contract's terms.

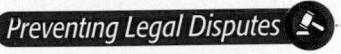

Preventing Legal Disputes

When entering into international contracts, always determine whether the foreign nation has any applicable language requirements. Some nations have mandatory language requirements. In France, for instance, certain legal documents, such as the prospectuses used in securities offerings (see Chapter 29), must be written in French. In addition, contracts with any state or local authority in France, instruction manuals, and warranties for goods and services offered for sale in France must also be written in French. To avoid disputes, know the law of the jurisdiction before you enter into any agreements in that nation. The language requirements in a nation may influence your decision whether to enter into a contract in that location and will definitely affect your decision whether to include a choice-of-law clause (to be discussed shortly).

Forum-Selection Clause A provision in a contract designating the court, jurisdiction, or tribunal that will decide any disputes arising under the contract.

CHOICE OF FORUM When a dispute arises, litigation may be pursued in courts of different nations. There are no universally accepted rules as to which court has jurisdiction over a particular subject matter or parties to a dispute. Consequently, parties to an international transaction should always include in the contract a **forum-selection clause** indicating what court, jurisdiction, or tribunal will decide any disputes arising under the contract. It is especially important to indicate the specific court that will have jurisdiction. The forum does not necessarily have to be within the geographic boundaries of the home nation of either party.

CASE EXAMPLE 22.5 Garware Polyester, Ltd., based in Mumbai, India, developed and made plastics and high-tech polyester film. Intermax Trading Corporation, based in New York, acted as Garware's North American sales agent and sold its products on a commission basis. Garware and Intermax had executed a series of agency agreements under which the courts of Mumbai, India, would have exclusive jurisdiction over any disputes relating to their agreement. When Intermax fell behind in its payments to Garware, Garware filed a lawsuit in a U.S. court to collect the balance due, claiming that the forum-selection clause did not apply to sales of warehoused goods. The court, however, sided with Intermax. Because the forum-selection clause was valid and enforceable, Garware had to bring its complaints against Intermax in a court in India.[7] ●

CHOICE OF LAW　A contractual provision designating the applicable law—such as the law of Germany or the United Kingdom or California—is called a **choice-of-law clause**. Every international contract typically includes a choice-of-law clause. At common law (and in European civil law systems), parties are allowed to choose the law that will govern their contractual relationship, provided that the law chosen is the law of a jurisdiction that has a substantial relationship to the parties and to the international business transaction.

> **Choice-of-Law Clause**　A clause in a contract designating the law (such as the law of a particular state or nation) that will govern the contract.

Under Section 1–105 of the Uniform Commercial Code, parties may choose the law that will govern the contract as long as the choice is "reasonable." Article 6 of the United Nations Convention on Contracts for the International Sale of Goods (discussed in Chapter 15 on pages 382–384), however, imposes no limitation on the parties' choice of what law will govern the contract. The 1986 Hague Convention on the Law Applicable to Contracts for the International Sale of Goods—often referred to as the Choice-of-Law Convention—allows unlimited autonomy in the choice of law. The Hague Convention indicates that whenever a contract does not specify a choice of law, the governing law is that of the country in which the *seller's* place of business is located.

FORCE MAJEURE CLAUSE　Every contract, particularly those involving international transactions, should have a *force majeure* **clause**. *Force majeure* is a French term meaning "impossible or irresistible force"—sometimes loosely identified as "an act of God." In international business contracts, *force majeure* clauses commonly stipulate that in addition to acts of God, a number of other eventualities (such as government orders or embargoes, for example) may excuse a party from liability for nonperformance.

> **Force Majeure Clause**　A provision in a contract stipulating that certain unforeseen events—such as war, political upheavals, or acts of God—will excuse a party from liability for nonperformance of contractual obligations.

Civil Dispute Resolution

International contracts frequently include arbitration clauses. By means of such clauses, the parties agree in advance to be bound by the decision of a specified third party in the event of a dispute, as discussed in Chapter 3. (For an example of an arbitration clause in an international contract, refer to the foldout exhibit at the end of Chapter 15.) The United Nations Convention on the Recognition and Enforcement of Foreign Arbitral Awards (often referred to as the New York Convention) assists in the enforcement of arbitration clauses, as do provisions in specific treaties among nations. The New York Convention has been implemented in nearly one hundred countries, including the United States.

If a sales contract does not include an arbitration clause, litigation may occur. If the contract contains forum-selection and choice-of-law clauses, the lawsuit will be heard by a court in the specified forum and decided according to that forum's law. If no forum and choice of law have been specified, however, legal proceedings will be more complex and attended by much more uncertainty. For instance, litigation may take place in two or more countries, with each country applying its own choice-of-law rules to determine the substantive law that will be applied to the particular transactions. Even if a plaintiff wins a favorable judgment in a lawsuit litigated in the plaintiff's country, there is no way to predict whether courts in the defendant's country will enforce the judgment. (For a further discussion of this issue, see this chapter's *Beyond Our Borders* feature.)

---

7. *Garware Polyester, Ltd. v. Intermax Trading Corp.,* ___ F.Supp.2d ___ (S.D.N.Y. 2001); see also *Laasko v. Xerox Corp.,* 566 F.Supp.2d 1018 (C.D.Cal. 2008).

Beyond Our Borders   Arbitration versus Litigation

One of the reasons many businesspersons find it advantageous to include arbitration clauses in their international contracts is that arbitration awards are usually easier to enforce than court judgments. As mentioned, the New York Convention provides for the enforcement of arbitration awards in those countries that have signed the convention. In contrast, the enforcement of court judgments normally depends on the principle of comity and bilateral agreements providing for such enforcement.

How the principle of comity is applied varies from one nation to another, though, and many countries have not signed bilateral agreements agreeing to enforce judgments rendered in U.S. courts. Furthermore, a U.S. court may not enforce a foreign court's judgment if it conflicts with U.S. laws or policies, especially if the case involves important constitutional rights such as freedom of the press or freedom of religion. For example, a U.S. federal appellate

court refused to enforce the judgment of a British court in a libel (defamation) case. The court pointed out that the judgment was contrary to the public policy of the United States, which generally favors a much broader and more protective freedom of the press than has ever been provided by English law.[a]

Similarly, a U.S. court refused to enforce a French default judgment against Viewfinder, Inc., a U.S. firm that operated a Web site. The firm's Web site posted photographs from fashion shows and information about the fashion industry. Several French clothing designers filed an action in a French court alleging that the Web site showed photos of

their clothing designs. Because Viewfinder defaulted and did not appear in the French court to contest the allegations, the French court awarded the designers the equivalent of more than $175,000. When the designers came to the United States to enforce the judgment, Viewfinder asserted a number of arguments as to why the U.S. court should not enforce the French judgment. Ultimately, Viewfinder convinced the U.S. court that its conduct on the Web site was protected expression under the First Amendment.[b]

• For Critical Analysis
What might be some other advantages of arbitrating disputes involving international transactions? Are there any disadvantages?

a. *Matusevitch v. Telnikoff,* 159 F.3d 636 (D.C.Cir. 1998). Note that a U.S. court may be less likely to have public-policy concerns when enforcing a foreign judgment based on a contract. See, for example, *Society of Lloyd's v. Siemon-Netto,* 457 F.3d 94 (C.A.D.C. 2006).

b. *Sarl Louis Feraud International v. Viewfinder, Inc.,* 489 F.3d 474 (2d Cir. 2007).

▶ Payment Methods for International Transactions

Currency differences between nations and the geographic distance between parties to international sales contracts add a degree of complexity to international sales that does not exist in the domestic market. Because international contracts involve greater financial risks, special care should be taken in drafting these contracts to specify both the currency in which payment is to be made and the method of payment.

Monetary Systems

Although our national currency, the U.S. dollar, is one of the primary forms of international currency, any U.S. firm undertaking business transactions abroad must be prepared to deal with one or more other currencies. After all, a Japanese firm may want to be paid in Japanese yen for goods and services sold outside Japan. Both firms therefore must rely on the convertibility of currencies.

Currencies are convertible when they can be freely exchanged one for the other at some specified market rate in a **foreign exchange market.** Foreign exchange markets make up a worldwide system for the buying and selling of foreign currencies. The foreign exchange rate is simply the price of a unit of one country's currency in terms of another country's currency. For example, if today's exchange rate is one hundred Japanese yen for one dollar, that means that anybody with one hundred yen can obtain one dollar, and vice versa. Like other prices, the exchange rate is set by the forces of supply and demand.

Frequently, a U.S. company can rely on its domestic bank to take care of all international transfers of funds. Commercial banks often transfer funds internationally through their **correspondent banks** in other countries. **EXAMPLE 22.6** A customer of Citibank wishes to pay

Foreign Exchange Market A worldwide system in which foreign currencies are bought and sold.

Correspondent Bank A bank in which another bank has an account (and vice versa) for the purpose of facilitating fund transfers.

(Matt Cardy/Getty Images)

Most countries have their own currency. To do business internationally, buyers and sellers rely on foreign exchange markets. Why don't companies just accept other countries' currencies as payment?

a bill in euros to a company in Paris. Citibank can draw a bank check payable in euros on its account in Crédit Agricole, a Paris correspondent bank, and then send the check to the French company to which its customer owes the funds. Alternatively, Citibank's customer can request a wire transfer of the funds to the French company. Citibank instructs Crédit Agricole by wire to pay the necessary amount in euros. ●

Letters of Credit

Because buyers and sellers engaged in international business transactions are frequently separated by thousands of miles, special precautions are often taken to ensure performance under the contract. Sellers want to avoid delivering goods for which they might not be paid. Buyers desire the assurance that sellers will not be paid until there is evidence that the goods have been shipped. Thus, **letters of credit** are frequently used to facilitate international business transactions.

Letter of Credit A written instrument, usually issued by a bank on behalf of a customer or other person, in which the issuer promises to honor drafts or other demands for payment by third parties in accordance with the terms of the instrument.

PARTIES TO A LETTER OF CREDIT   In a simple letter-of-credit transaction, the *issuer* (a bank) agrees to issue a letter of credit and to ascertain whether the *beneficiary* (seller) performs certain acts. In return, the *account party* (buyer) promises to reimburse the issuer for the amount paid to the beneficiary. The transaction may also involve an *advising bank* that transmits information and a *paying bank* that expedites payment under the letter of credit. See Exhibit 22–1 for an illustration of a letter-of-credit transaction.

Under a letter of credit, the issuer is bound to pay the beneficiary (seller) when the beneficiary has complied with the terms and conditions of the letter of credit. The beneficiary looks to the issuer, not to the account party (buyer), when it presents the documents required by the letter of credit. Typically, the letter of credit will require that the beneficiary deliver a *bill of lading* to the issuing bank to prove that shipment has been made. A letter of credit assures the beneficiary (seller) of payment and at the same time assures the account party (buyer) that payment will not be made until the beneficiary has complied with the terms and conditions of the letter of credit.

DON'T FORGET A letter of credit is independent of the underlying contract between the buyer and the seller.

THE VALUE OF A LETTER OF CREDIT   The basic principle behind letters of credit is that payment is made against the documents presented by the beneficiary and not against the facts that the documents purport to reflect. Thus, in a letter-of-credit transaction, the issuer does not police the underlying contract; a letter of credit is independent of the underlying contract between the buyer and the seller. Eliminating the need for banks (issuers) to inquire into whether actual contractual conditions have been satisfied greatly reduces the costs of letters of credit. Moreover, the use of a letter of credit protects both buyers and sellers.

 U.S. Laws in a Global Context

The internationalization of business raises questions about the extraterritorial application of a nation's laws—that is, the effect of the country's laws outside its boundaries. To what extent do U.S. domestic laws apply to other nations' businesses? To what extent do U.S. domestic laws apply to U.S. firms doing business abroad? Here, we discuss the extraterritorial application of certain U.S. laws, including antitrust laws, tort laws, and laws prohibiting employment discrimination.

U.S. Antitrust Laws

U.S. antitrust laws (to be discussed in Chapter 32) have a wide application. They may *subject* firms in foreign nations to their provisions, as well as *protect* foreign consumers and competitors from violations committed by U.S. citizens. Section 1 of the Sherman Act—

• *Exhibit* **22–1 A Letter-of-Credit Transaction**

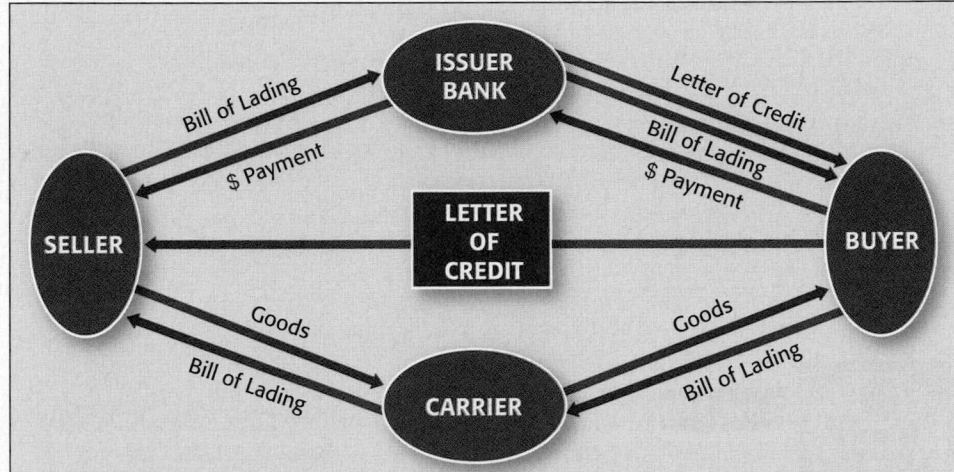

CHRONOLOGY OF EVENTS

1. Buyer contracts with issuer bank to issue a letter of credit; this sets forth the bank's obligation to pay on the letter of credit and buyer's obligation to pay the bank.

2. Letter of credit is sent to seller informing seller that on compliance with the terms of the letter of credit (such as presentment of necessary documents—in this example, a bill of lading), the bank will issue payment for the goods.

3. Seller delivers goods to carrier and receives a bill of lading.

4. Seller delivers the bill of lading to issuer bank and, if the document is proper, receives payment.

5. Issuer bank delivers the bill of lading to buyer.

6. Buyer delivers the bill of lading to carrier.

7. Carrier delivers the goods to buyer.

8. Buyer settles with issuer bank.

the most important U.S. antitrust law—provides for the extraterritorial effect of the U.S. antitrust laws. The United States is a major proponent of free competition in the global economy. Thus, any conspiracy that has a *substantial effect* on U.S. commerce is within the reach of the Sherman Act. The law applies even if the violation occurs outside the United States, and foreign governments as well as businesses can be sued for violations.

Before U.S. courts will exercise jurisdiction and apply antitrust laws, however, it must be shown that the alleged violation had a substantial effect on U.S. commerce. **EXAMPLE 22.7** A number of companies that manufacture and sell paper on the global market meet in Japan on several occasions and reach a price-fixing agreement (an agreement to set prices—see Chapter 32). Although several of the companies are based in foreign nations, they sell paper in the United States through their wholly owned subsidiaries. Thus, the agreement to sell paper at above-normal prices throughout North America has a *substantial restraining effect* on U.S. commerce. In this situation, a U.S. court has jurisdiction over the defendant companies even though all of the price-fixing activities took place outside the United States. •

International Tort Claims

The international application of tort liability is growing in significance and controversy. An increasing number of U.S. plaintiffs are suing foreign (or U.S.) entities for torts that these entities have allegedly committed overseas. Often, these cases involve human rights violations by foreign governments. The Alien Tort Claims Act (ATCA),[8] adopted in 1789, allows even foreign citizens to bring civil suits in U.S. courts for injuries caused by violations of international law or a treaty of the United States.

Since 1980, plaintiffs have increasingly used the ATCA to bring actions against companies operating in other countries. ATCA actions have been brought against companies doing business in nations such as Colombia, Ecuador, Egypt, Guatemala, India, Indonesia, Nigeria, and Saudi Arabia. Some of these cases have involved alleged environmental destruction. In addition, mineral companies in Southeast Asia have been sued for collaborating with oppressive government regimes.

The following case involved claims against hundreds of corporations that allegedly "aided and abetted" the government of South Africa in maintaining its apartheid (racially discriminatory) regime.

Case 22.3   Khulumani v. Barclay National Bank, Ltd.

United States Court of Appeals, Second Circuit, 504 F.3d 254 (2007).[a]

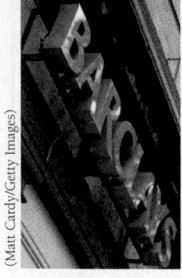

Did hundreds of companies, like Barclays Bank, aid and abet South Africa in apartheid human rights abuse?

FACTS   The Khulumani plaintiffs, along with other plaintiff groups, filed class-action claims on behalf of victims of apartheid-related atrocities, human rights violations, crimes against humanity, and unfair and discriminatory forced-labor practices. The plaintiffs brought this action in federal district court under the Alien Tort Claims Act (ATCA) against a number of corporations, including Bank of America, Barclay National Bank, Citigroup, Credit Suisse Group, General Electric, and IBM. The district court dismissed the plaintiffs' complaints in their entirety. The court held that the plaintiffs had failed to establish subject-matter jurisdiction under the ATCA. The plaintiffs appealed to the U.S. Court of Appeals for the Second Circuit.

ISSUE   Can the plaintiffs bring a claim against U.S. and foreign companies under the ATCA for "aiding and abetting" human rights violations?

DECISION   Yes. The U.S. Court of Appeals for the Second Circuit vacated the district court's dismissal of the plaintiffs' claims and remanded the case for further proceedings. According to the reviewing court, a plaintiff may plead a theory of aiding and abetting liability under the ATCA.

REASON   The court stated that the district court "erred in holding that aiding and abetting violations of a customary international law cannot provide a basis for ATCA jurisdiction." The court reasoned that the United States Supreme Court has instructed courts in this nation to exercise caution and carefully evaluate international norms and potential adverse foreign policy consequences in deciding whether to hear ATCA claims. Thus, "the determination whether a norm is sufficiently definite to support a cause of action should (indeed, inevitably must) involve an element of judgment about the practical consequences of making that cause available to litigants in the federal courts." The court rejected the defendants' argument that an adjudication of the case by the U.S. court "would offend amicable working relationships with a foreign country."

FOR CRITICAL ANALYSIS—Ethical Consideration
Should the companies cited as defendants in this case have refused all business dealings with South Africa during the era of apartheid when the country's white government severely limited the rights of the majority black African population?

a. See also 509 F.3d 148 (2d Cir. 2007), in which the court denied the defendants' motion for a stay; and *American Isuzu Motors, Inc. v. Ntsebeza*, ___ U.S. ___, 128 S.Ct. 2424, 171 L.Ed.2d 225 (2008), in which the United States Supreme Court had to affirm the Second Circuit's decision in this case because it was unable to hear the appeal in the following term.

Ethical Issue   **Should U.S. courts allow "forum-shopping" plaintiffs to sue companies for aiding and abetting global terrorism?** Increasingly, as just described, plaintiffs are bringing claims under the Alien Tort Claims Act (ATCA) for human rights violations that occurred outside the United States. In addition, some plaintiffs are bringing actions in U.S. courts alleging that certain banks and other companies in foreign countries have aided and abetted terrorist activities. Foreign plaintiffs may assert claims for aiding and abetting under the ATCA, while U.S. nationals may also bring claims under the Anti-

8. 28 U.S.C. Section 1350.

Terrorism Act (ATA).[9] Although the ATA is primarily a criminal law, it also allows plaintiffs to file civil actions and recover *treble* damages (three times the amount of actual damages).

In 2009, some 1,600 plaintiffs, including both U.S. and foreign nationals, brought claims against Arab Bank, PLC, alleging that the bank knowingly provided financial services to terrorist organizations that attacked Israel. A U.S. district court held that it had jurisdiction to hear the claims.[10] Although punishing those who aid terrorists is certainly desirable, some have suggested that such rulings may encourage international "forum shopping." Victims of global terrorism may bring lawsuits in U.S. courts against foreign defendants that have little or no contact with the United States because of the potential for large damages awards—and treble damages if the victims are U.S. nationals.

Antidiscrimination Laws

Laws in the United States prohibit discrimination on the basis of race, color, national origin, religion, gender, age, and disability, as will be discussed in Chapter 25. These laws, as they affect employment relationships, generally apply extraterritorially. U.S. employees working abroad for U.S. employers are protected under the Age Discrimination in Employment Act of 1967. The Americans with Disabilities Act of 1990, which requires employers to accommodate the needs of workers with disabilities, also applies to U.S. nationals working abroad for U.S. firms.

In addition, the major law regulating employment discrimination—Title VII of the Civil Rights Act of 1964—also applies extraterritorially to all U.S. employees working for U.S. employers abroad. U.S. employers must abide by U.S. discrimination laws unless to do so would violate the laws of the country where their workplaces are located. This "foreign laws exception" prevents employers from being subjected to conflicting laws.

---

9. 18 U.S.C. Sections 2331 *et seq.*

10. *Almog v. Arab Bank, PLC*, 471 F.Supp.2d 257 (E.D.N.Y. 2007); see also *Litle v. Arab Bank, PLC*, 611 F.Supp.2d 233 (E.D.N.Y. 2009).

 Reviewing . . . International Law in a Global Economy

Robco, Inc., was a Florida arms dealer. The armed forces of Honduras contracted to purchase weapons from Robco over a six-year period. After the government was replaced and a democracy installed, the Honduran government sought to reduce the size of its military, and its relationship with Robco deteriorated. Honduras refused to honor the contract by purchasing the inventory of arms, which Robco could sell only at a much lower price. Robco filed a suit in a federal district court in the United States to recover damages for this breach of contract by the government of Honduras. Using the information provided in the chapter, answer the following questions.

1. Should the Foreign Sovereign Immunities Act preclude this lawsuit? Why or why not?
2. Does the act of state doctrine bar Robco from seeking to enforce the contract? Explain.
3. Suppose that prior to this lawsuit, the new government of Honduras had enacted a law making it illegal to purchase weapons from foreign arms dealers. What doctrine might lead a U.S. court to dismiss Robco's case in that situation?
4. Now suppose that the U.S. court hears the case and awards damages to Robco, but the government of Honduras has no assets in the United States that can be used to satisfy the judgment. Under which doctrine might Robco be able to collect the damages by asking another nation's court to enforce the U.S. judgment?

Linking the Law *to Marketing*
Going Global

Since the end of World War II, international trade in goods and services has grown dramatically. Today, U.S. exports amount to more than 14 percent of the U.S. gross domestic product. In your marketing classes in business school, you will learn about domestic marketing. If you work for many U.S. firms, though, you will also need to know about marketing on a global basis.

Legal and Economic Constraints on Global Marketing Campaigns

If you are the global marketing manager for your company, you will need to be aware of the following legal considerations that we outlined in this chapter:

- **Tariffs**—Before you embark on a marketing campaign in any country, you should determine what tariffs—taxes on imported goods—may be imposed on your company's products. If your company must pay relatively high tariffs and compete against domestic producers who obviously face no tariffs, you may be wasting your time. No matter how good your marketing campaign is, those tariffs could cause your company's products to be priced out of the market.
- **Quotas**—The United States has strict quotas on imports of textiles, sugar, and many dairy products. Other countries have quotas, too. If those quotas are highly restrictive, there is no point in trying to sell your company's products in those countries.
- **Exchange controls**—When your company exports to another country, that country has to pay for those U.S.-made goods in dollars. Sometimes, governments impose restrictions on the amount of dollars that may be purchased in the foreign exchange market to pay for goods from the United States. You may find that some exchange controls are so restrictive that it is not worthwhile to attempt to sell your company's products in a particular country.
- **Trade agreements**—You must also determine whether any trade agreements apply to trade between the United States and the target countries. Some countries may have signed bilateral or international trade agreements that make it particularly attractive for you to attempt to market your company's products in those countries. You should consult a specialist in international trade agreements to find out precisely how those agreements can help your company.

Global Marketing Standardization

In the past, multinational organizations generally employed different marketing strategies for the various countries in which they sold their products. They attempted to adapt the product features, advertising, and packaging to fit the culture of each country. The trend today, according to former Harvard professor Ted Levitt, is toward "global marketing." Levitt, who devised the notion of global marketing standardization, or a global vision, contends that advances in communication and technology have created a "small" world. By this he means that consumers everywhere want the same items that they have seen in popular movies exported from the United States, for example, or featured on the Internet.

Coca-Cola, McDonald's, and Colgate-Palmolive are some of the companies that use global marketing standardization. They produce globally standardized products that are marketed more or less the same way throughout the world.

Global Marketing the Standard Way— Considering Each Culture Separately

No matter how "small" the world has become, countries still have different sets of shared values that affect their citizens' preferences. Therefore, as a global marketing manager, you will have to become intimately acquainted with the cultures of the countries where you conduct marketing campaigns.

Samsonite, for example, found this out the hard way. It used an advertising campaign with an image of its luggage being carried on a magic flying carpet. Only after it conducted focus groups did it learn that most Middle Eastern consumers thought that Samsonite was selling carpets. Green Giant learned to its dismay that it could not use its logo with a man in a green hat in parts of Asia—because in those areas a green hat signifies a man who has an unfaithful wife. Similarly, the translation of names and slogans into other languages is fraught with pitfalls. Toyota had to drop the "2" from its model MR2 in France because the combination of sounds sounded like a French swear word. Mitsubishi Motors had to rename one of its models in Spanish-speaking countries because the original name described a sexual activity.

FOR CRITICAL ANALYSIS

Why should a global marketing manager consult local attorneys in other countries before creating a marketing campaign?

 Key Terms

act of state doctrine 556	choice-of-law clause 564	confiscation 556
choice-of-language clause 563	comity 556	correspondent bank 565

Chapter Summary: International Law in a Global Economy

International Principles and Doctrines (See pages 556–557.)	1. *The principle of comity*—Under this principle, nations give effect to the laws and judicial decrees of other nations for reasons of courtesy and international harmony. 2. *The act of state doctrine*—A doctrine under which U.S. courts avoid passing judgment on the validity of public acts committed by a recognized foreign government within its own territory. 3. *The doctrine of sovereign immunity*—When certain conditions are satisfied, foreign nations are immune from U.S. jurisdiction under the Foreign Sovereign Immunities Act of 1976. Exceptions are made when a foreign state (a) has waived its immunity either explicitly or by implication, (b) has engaged in commercial activity within the United States, or (c) has committed a tort within the United States.
Doing Business Internationally (See pages 557–559.)	U.S. domestic firms may engage in international business transactions in several ways including (a) exporting, which may involve foreign agents or distributors, and (b) manufacturing abroad through licensing arrangements, franchising operations, wholly owned subsidiaries, or joint ventures.
Regulation of Specific Business Activities (See pages 559–562.)	In the interests of their economies, foreign policies, domestic policies, or other national priorities, nations impose laws that restrict or facilitate international business. Such laws regulate foreign investments, exporting, and importing. The World Trade Organization attempts to minimize trade barriers among nations, as do regional trade agreements and associations, including the European Union and the North American Free Trade Agreement.
Commercial Contracts in an International Setting (See pages 563–565.)	International business contracts often include choice-of-language, forum-selection, and choice-of-law clauses to reduce the uncertainties associated with interpreting the language of the agreement and dealing with legal differences. Most domestic and international contracts include *force majeure* clauses. They commonly stipulate that acts of God and certain other events may excuse a party from liability for nonperformance of the contract. Arbitration clauses are also frequently found in international contracts.
Payment Methods for International Transactions (See pages 565–566.)	1. *Currency conversion*—Because nations have different monetary systems, payment on international contracts requires currency conversion at a rate specified in a foreign exchange market. 2. *Correspondent banking*—Correspondent banks facilitate the transfer of funds from a buyer in one country to a seller in another. 3. *Letters of credit*—Letters of credit facilitate international transactions by ensuring payment to sellers and assuring buyers that payment will not be made until the sellers have complied with the terms of the letters of credit. Typically, compliance occurs when a bill of lading is delivered to the issuing bank.
U.S. Laws in a Global Context (See pages 566–569.)	1. *Antitrust laws*—U.S. antitrust laws may be applied beyond the borders of the United States. Any conspiracy that has a substantial effect on commerce within the United States may be subject to the Sherman Act, even if the violation occurs outside the United States. 2. *Antidiscrimination laws*—The major U.S. laws prohibiting employment discrimination, including Title VII of the Civil Rights Act of 1964, the Age Discrimination in Employment Act of 1967, and the Americans with Disabilities Act of 1990, cover U.S. employees working abroad for U.S. firms—*unless* to apply the U.S. laws would violate the laws of the host country.

ExamPrep

ISSUE SPOTTERS

1 Café Rojo, Ltd., an Ecuadoran firm, agrees to sell coffee beans to Dark Roast Coffee Company, a U.S. firm. Dark Roast accepts the beans but refuses to pay. Café Rojo sues Dark Roast in an Ecuadoran court and is awarded damages, but

Dark Roast's assets are in the United States. Under what circumstances would a U.S. court enforce the judgment of the Ecuadoran court?

2 Gems International, Ltd., is a foreign firm that has a 12 percent share of the U.S. market for diamonds. To capture a larger share, Gems offers its products at a below-cost discount to U.S. buyers (and inflates the prices in its own country to make up the difference). How can this attempt to undersell U.S. businesses be defeated?

BEFORE THE TEST

Check your answers to the Issue Spotters, and at the same time, take the interactive quiz for this chapter. Go to **www.cengage.com/blaw/blt** and click on "Chapter 22." First, click on "Answers to Issue Spotters" to check your answers. Next, click on "Interactive Quiz" to assess your mastery of the concepts in this chapter. Then click on "Flashcards" to review this chapter's Key Term definitions.

▶ For Review

Answers for the even-numbered questions in this For Review *section can be found on this text's accompanying Web site at* **www.cengage.com/blaw/blt**. *Select "Chapter 22" and click on "For Review."*

1 What is the principle of comity, and why do courts deciding disputes involving a foreign law or judicial decree apply this principle?

2 What is the act of state doctrine? In what circumstances is this doctrine applied?

3 Under the Foreign Sovereign Immunities Act of 1976, on what bases might a foreign state be considered subject to the jurisdiction of U.S. courts?

4 In what circumstances will U.S. antitrust laws be applied extraterritorially?

5 Do U.S. laws prohibiting employment discrimination apply in all circumstances to U.S. employees working for U.S. employers abroad?

▶ Hypothetical Scenarios and Case Problems

22–1 Letters of Credit. The Swiss Credit Bank issued a letter of credit in favor of Antex Industries to cover the sale of 92,000 electronic integrated circuits manufactured by Electronic Arrays. The letter of credit specified that the chips would be transported to Tokyo by ship. Antex shipped the circuits by air. Payment on the letter of credit was dishonored because the shipment by air did not fulfill the precise terms of the letter of credit. Should a court compel payment? Explain.

22–2 **Hypothetical Question with Sample Answer** The U.S. pineapple industry alleged that producers of canned pineapple from the Philippines were selling their canned pineapple in the United States for less than its fair market value (dumping). The Philippine producers also exported other products, such as pineapple juice and juice concentrate, which used separate parts of the same fresh pineapple, so they shared raw material costs, according to the producers' own financial records. To determine fair value and antidumping duties, the plaintiffs argued that a court should calculate the Philippine producers' cost of production and allocate a portion of the shared fruit costs to the canned fruit. The result of this allocation showed that more than 90 percent of the canned fruit sales were below the cost of production. Is this a reasonable approach to determining the production costs and fair

market value of canned pineapple in the United States? Why or why not?

—For a sample answer to Question 22–2, go to Appendix E at the end of this text.

22–3 Comity. E&L Consulting, Ltd., is a U.S. corporation that sells lumber products in New Jersey, New York, and Pennsylvania. Doman Industries, Ltd., is a Canadian corporation that also sells lumber products, including green hem-fir, a durable product used for homebuilding. Doman supplies more than 95 percent of the green hem-fir for sale in the northeastern United States. In 1990, Doman contracted to sell green hem-fir through E&L, which received monthly payments plus commissions. In 1998, Sherwood Lumber Corp., a New York firm and an E&L competitor, approached E&L about a merger. The negotiations were unsuccessful. According to E&L, Sherwood and Doman then conspired to monopolize the green hem-fir market in the United States. When Doman terminated its contract with E&L, the latter filed a suit in a federal district court against Doman, alleging violations of U.S. antitrust law. Doman filed for bankruptcy in a Canadian court and asked the U.S. court to dismiss E&L's suit under the principle of comity, among other things. What is the "principle of comity"? On what basis would it apply in this case? What would be the likely result? Discuss. [*E&L Consulting, Ltd. v. Doman Industries, Ltd.,* 360 F.Supp.2d 465 (E.D.N.Y. 2005)]

22–4 Dumping. A newspaper printing press system is more than one hundred feet long, stands four or five stories tall, and weighs 2 million pounds. Only about ten of the systems are sold each year in the United States. Because of the size and cost, a newspaper may update its system, rather than replace it, by buying "additions." By the 1990s, Goss International Corp. was the only domestic maker of the equipment in the United States and represented the entire U.S. market. Tokyo Kikai Sei-sakusho (TKSC), a Japanese corporation, makes the systems in Japan. In the 1990s, TKSC began to compete in the U.S. market, forcing Goss to cut its prices below cost. TKSC's tactics included offering its customers "secret" rebates on prices that were ultimately substantially less than the products' actual market value in Japan. According to TKSC office memos, the goal was to "win completely this survival game" against Goss, the "enemy." Goss filed a suit in a federal district court against TKSC and others, alleging illegal dumping. At what point does a foreign firm's attempt to compete with a domestic manufacturer in the United States become illegal dumping? Was that point reached in this case? Discuss. [*Goss International Corp. v. Man Roland Druckmaschinen Aktiengesellschaft,* 434 F.3d 1081 (8th Cir. 2006)]

22–5 Case Problem with Sample Answer Jan Voda, M.D., a resident of Oklahoma City, Oklahoma, owns three U.S. patents related to guiding catheters for use in interventional cardiology, as well as corresponding foreign patents issued by the European Patent Office, Canada, France, Germany, and Great Britain. Voda filed a suit in a federal district court against Cordis Corp., a U.S. firm, alleging infringement of the U.S. patents under U.S. patent law and of the corresponding foreign patents under the patent law of the various foreign countries. Cordis admitted, "[T]he XB catheters have been sold domestically and internationally since 1994. The XB catheters were manufactured in Miami Lakes, Florida, from 1993 to 2001 and have been manufactured in Juarez, Mexico, since 2001." Cordis argued, however, that Voda could not assert infringement claims under foreign patent law because the court did not have jurisdiction over such claims. Which of the important international legal principles discussed in this chapter would be most likely to apply in this case? How should the court apply it? Explain. [*Voda v. Cordis Corp.,* 476 F.3d 887 (Fed.Cir. 2007)]

—**After you have answered Problem 22–5, compare your answer with the sample answer given on the Web site that accompanies this text. Go to www.cengage.com/blaw/blt, select "Chapter 22," and click on "Case Problem with Sample Answer."**

22–6 Sovereign Immunity. When Ferdinand Marcos was president of the Republic of the Philippines, he put assets into a company called Arelma. Its holdings are in New York. A group of plaintiffs, referred to as the Pimentel class, brought a class-action suit in a U.S. district court for human rights violations by Marcos. They won a judgment of $2 billion and sought to

attach Arelma's assets to help pay the judgment. At the same time, the Republic of the Philippines established a commission to recover property wrongfully taken by Marcos. A court in the Philippines was determining whether Marcos's property, including Arelma, should be forfeited to the Republic or to other parties. The Philippine government, in opposition to the Pimentel judgment, moved to dismiss the U.S. court proceedings. The district court refused, and the U.S. Court of Appeals for the Ninth Circuit agreed that the Pimentel class should take the assets. The Republic of the Philippines appealed. What are the key international legal issues? [*Republic of the Philippines v. Pimentel,* __ U.S. __,128 S.Ct. 2180, 171 L.Ed.2d 131 (2008)]

22–7 Dumping. The fuel for nuclear power plants is low enriched uranium (LEU). LEU consists of feed uranium enriched by energy to a certain assay—its percentage of the isotope necessary for a nuclear reaction. The amount of energy is described by an industry standard as a "separative work unit" (SWU). A nuclear utility may buy LEU from an enricher, or the utility may provide an enricher with feed uranium and pay for the SWUs necessary to produce LEU. Under an SWU contract, the LEU returned to the utility may not be exactly the particular uranium the utility provided. This is because feed uranium is fungible and trades like a commodity (such as wheat or corn), and profitable enrichment requires the constant processing of undifferentiated stock. LEU imported from foreign enrichers, including Eurodif, S.A., was purportedly being sold in the United States for "less than fair value." Does this constitute dumping? Explain. If so, what could be done to prevent it? [*United States v. Eurodif, S.A.,* __ U.S. __, 129 S.Ct. 878, 172 L.Ed.2d 679 (2009)]

22–8 A Question of Ethics On December 21, 1988, Pan Am Flight 103 exploded 31,000 feet in the air over Lockerbie, Scotland, killing all 259 passengers and crew on board and 11 people on the ground. Among those killed was Roger Hurst, a U.S. citizen. An investigation determined that a portable radio-cassette player packed in a brown Samsonite suitcase smuggled onto the plane was the source of the explosion. The explosive device was constructed with a digital timer specially made for, and bought by, Libya. Abdel Basset Ali Al-Megrahi, a Libyan government official and an employee of the Libyan Arab Airline (LAA), was convicted by the Scottish High Court of Justiciary on criminal charges that he planned and executed the bombing in association with members of the Jamahiriya Security Organization (JSO)—an agency of the Libyan government that performs security and intelligence functions—or the Libyan military. Members of the victims' families filed a suit in a U.S. federal district court against the JSO, the LAA, Al-Megrahi, and others. The plaintiffs claimed violations of U.S. federal law, including the Anti-Terrorism Act, and state law, including the intentional infliction of emotional distress. [*Hurst v. Socialist People's Libyan Arab Jamahiriya,* 474 F.Supp.2d 19 (D.D.C. 2007)]

1 Under what doctrine, codified in which federal statute, might the defendants claim to be immune from the jurisdiction of a U.S. court? Should this law include an exception for "state-sponsored terrorism"? Why or why not?

2 The defendants agreed to pay $2.7 billion, or $10 million per victim, to settle all claims for "compensatory death damages." The families of eleven victims, including Hurst, were excluded from the settlement because they were "not wrongful death beneficiaries under applicable state law." These plaintiffs continued the suit. The defendants filed a motion to dismiss. Should the motion be granted on the ground that the settlement bars the plaintiffs' claims? Explain.

 Critical Thinking and Writing Assignments

22–9 **Video Question** Go to this text's Web site at **www.cengage.com/blaw/blt** and select "Chapter 22." Click on "Video Questions" and view the video titled *International: Letter of Credit.* Then answer the following questions.

1 Do banks always require the same documents to be presented in letter-of-credit transactions? If not, who dictates what documents will be required in the letter of credit?

2 At what point does the seller receive payment in a letter-of-credit transaction?

3 What assurances does a letter of credit provide to the buyer and the seller involved in the transaction?

 Practical Internet Exercises

Go to this text's Web site at **www.cengage.com/blaw/blt**, select "Chapter 22," and click on "Practical Internet Exercises." There you will find the following Internet research exercises that you can perform to learn more about the topics covered in this chapter.

Practical Internet Exercise 22–1: Legal Perspective—The World Trade Organization
Practical Internet Exercise 22–2: Management Perspective—Overseas Business Opportunities

Sonja owns a bakery in San Francisco.

1. Sonja orders two new model X23 McIntyre ovens from a local company, Western Heating Appliances. The purchase price of the two ovens is $16,000. Sonja and Western Heating agree orally, via the telephone, that Western will deliver the ovens within two weeks and that Sonja will pay for the ovens when they are delivered. Two days later, Sonja receives a fax from Western confirming her order. Shortly thereafter, but before Western delivers the ovens, Sonja learns that she can obtain model X23 McIntyre ovens from another company at a much lower price. Sonja asks Western if she can cancel her order, but Western states that it intends to enforce the contract. Is the contract enforceable against Sonja? Explain.

2. One day, Sonja is baking a batch of croissants. When she opens the door to one of the new ovens, part of the door detaches from the oven. As she struggles with the door, Sonja's hands are badly burned, and she is unable to do any baking for several months. Sonja later learns that the hinge mechanism on the door was improperly installed. Sonja wants to sue the oven's manufacturer to recover damages, including consequential damages for lost profits. In a product liability suit against the manufacturer, under what legal principles and doctrines might Sonja be able to recover damages? Discuss fully.

3. To pay Milled Grains Co., a supplier, Sonja issues a check in the amount due to Milled Grains. The check is drawn on United First Bank. A Milled Grains employee, with authorization, indorses the check and transfers it to Milled Grains' financial institution, Second Federal Bank. Second Federal puts the check into the regular bank collection process. If United First refuses to cash the check, who will ultimately suffer the loss? Could Sonja be subject to criminal prosecution if United First refuses to cash the check?

4. Sonja wants to borrow $40,000 from Credit National Bank to buy coffee brewing equipment. To secure the loan, Credit National could accept Sonja's equipment as collateral. If so, how would Credit National let other potential creditors know of its interest? If Credit National secures its loan with the equipment, and Sonja fails to repay the loan, what are Credit National's alternatives with respect to collecting the amount due?

5. Sonja borrows $20,000 from Ace Loan Co. to make physical improvements to the bakery. Sonja gives the money to Jones Construction, a contractor, to do the work. The amount covers only half of the cost, but when Jones finishes the work, Sonja fails to pay the rest. Sonja also does not repay Ace for the loan. What can Jones do to collect what it is owed? What can Ace do?

As discussed in Chapter 15, in contrast to the rule under the common law of contracts, a contract for a sale of goods will not fail for indefiniteness even if one or more of its terms are left open. For example, under Section 2–305(1) of the Uniform Commercial Code (UCC), if the parties have not agreed on a price, a court will determine a "reasonable price at the time for delivery." If either the buyer or the seller is to determine the price, the price is to be set in good faith [UCC 2–305(2)]. In this context, good faith means "honesty in fact and the observance of reasonable commercial standards of fair dealing in the trade" [UCC 2–103(1)(b)].

In this Extended Case Study, we review the case of Casserlie v. Shell Oil Co.,[1] in which a group of service station dealers brought an action against a gasoline distributor, claiming that the distributor engaged in bad faith in setting the price of gas under the open term provision of their contracts. Is a subjective inquiry into the distributor's motive required to make this determination?

[1]. 121 Ohio St.3d 55, 902 N.E.2d 1 (2009). This opinion can be read online at www.sconet.state.oh.us. In the right-hand column, click on the "Ohio Court Opinions" link. On that page, in the "Ohio Court Opinions" box, in the pull-down menus, select "Supreme Court of Ohio" and "In the Year 2009." In the "WebCite No" box, type "2009-Ohio-3." Click on "Submit." In the result, click on the name of the case to access the opinion. The Supreme Court of Ohio maintains this Web site.

Continued

CASE BACKGROUND

Donald Casserlie is one of a group of independent Shell Oil Company service station lessee-dealers in Cleveland, Ohio. The dealers lease gas stations, including equipment and land, from Shell.

In the 1990s, they contracted to buy gas only from Shell at a price set by Shell at the time of delivery. Shell charged the dealers a price that was based on such factors as the price of its competitor British Petroleum and the street price of gas in Cleveland. The price was referred to as the dealer-tank-wagon (DTW) price because it included the cost of delivery of the gas to the stations. Shell also sells gas to jobbers, which are independent companies operating non-Shell-owned gas stations. Jobbers buy gas at the oil company's terminal and thus pay the "rack price," which does not include delivery costs.

Casserlie and other dealers filed a suit in an Ohio state court against Shell, alleging that the DTW prices were being set in bad faith. The dealers contended that the pricing was commercially unreasonable and part of a plan to drive them out of business. They charged that Shell's goal was to take over the gas stations to profit from all of the sales, including nonfuel sales, not just from wholesale gas sales and rental income. The court issued a summary judgment in Shell's favor. A state intermediate appellate court affirmed the judgment. The dealers appealed to the Ohio Supreme Court.

MAJORITY OPINION

MOYER, C.J.

* * * *

It is not disputed that the latter half of the definition of good faith, "the observance of reasonable commercial standards of fair dealing in the trade," requires only an objective analysis. The issue before us is whether there is room for a subjective inquiry within the honesty-in-fact analysis in these circumstances.

The UCC does not define the term "honesty in fact."

Comment 3 to UCC 2–305 * * * provides, * * * "In the normal case a 'posted price' or a future seller's or buyer's 'given price,' 'price in effect,' 'market price,' or the like satisfies the good faith requirement."

Comment 3 * * * provides a safe harbor where a "posted price" satisfies good faith in its entirety.

* * * *

* * * By its language, the safe harbor does not apply when it is not the "normal case" or when the price setter is not imposing a "posted price," "given price," "price in effect," "market price," or the like. *As long as a price is commercially reasonable, it qualifies as the "normal case."* The touchstone of prices set through open-price-term contracts under UCC 2–305(2) is reasonableness. *A price that is nondiscriminatory among similarly situated buyers correspondingly qualifies as a "posted price" or the like.* A discriminatory price could not be considered a "posted" or "market" price, because, in effect, the seller is not being "honest in fact" about the price that it is charging as a posted price, since it is charging a different price to other buyers. [Emphasis added.]

Therefore, a price that is both commercially reasonable and nondiscriminatory fits within the limits of the safe harbor and complies with the statute's good-faith requirement.

* * * *

The facts of this case demonstrate that the prices set by Shell were both commercially reasonable and nondiscriminatory. * * * The only evidence of bad faith was that the prices set were too high for dealers to remain profitable and compete with jobbers in the Cleveland area. However, Shell is not required to sell gasoline at a price that is profitable for buyers. A good-faith price under UCC 2–305 is not synonymous with a fair market price or the lowest price available. * * * The DTW prices set by the company were within the range set by its competitors.

* * * *

* * * The only other argument of discrimination put forth by the dealers is that jobbers were charged significantly less, specifically, the rack price rather than the DTW price. Jobbers and dealers are not, however, similarly situated buyers. The price difference is partially explained by the fact that the DTW price includes a delivery charge, while the rack price does not. * * * Jobbers perform additional functions compared to dealers, such as maintaining the properties they own and bearing the risk of environmental liability. Because jobbers relieve Shell of these obligations, they are charged a lower price.

* * * *

When a price that has been left open in a contract is fixed at a price posted by a seller or buyer, and the posted price is both commercially reasonable and nondiscriminatory, the price setter has acted in good faith as required by [UCC 2–305(2)] and a subjective inquiry into the motives of the price setter is not permitted. In this case, the dealers have not provided any evidence that the prices set by Shell were commercially unreasonable or discriminatory. The posted-price safe harbor therefore applies, and we affirm the judgment of the court of appeals.

DISSENTING OPINION

PFEIFER, J., dissenting.

* * * *

"Good faith" is generally treated as incorporating both subjective and objective standards. Although [UCC 2–305] deals exclusively with open-price terms, it does not define "good faith" differently from its customary meaning. Many different jurisdictions in many different contexts, including in the context of an open-price term, define "good faith" as requiring both subjective and objective analysis.

* * * The courts agree that it is not possible to determine whether a party acted in "good faith" without a subjective inquiry.
* * * *

"Good faith" in the context of open-price terms should be subject to both objective and subjective inquiry. Even courts and commentators who have written in favor of the safe-harbor presumption have concluded that an intent to drive a contractual partner out of business might overcome the presumption. I can conceive of situations in which nondiscriminatory pricing could violate "good faith." For instance, in this case, it is alleged that Shell charged all of its similarly situated [dealers] the same price, and it is alleged that that price was set too high for them to profitably operate a gas station. In that situation, even though the pricing was nondiscriminatory, it was designed to drive a contractual partner out of business.

* * * A court's analysis of a merchant's good faith, then, should be both subjective and objective. Furthermore, the safe-harbor presumption * * * only applies in the normal case; at a minimum, the appellants should be allowed to attempt

to establish that this is not a normal case. I would reverse the judgment of the court of appeals and remand the case for further consideration.

QUESTIONS FOR ANALYSIS

1. **Law.** What was the majority's reasoning in this case? How did this affect the outcome?

2. **Law.** Why did the dissent disagree with the majority? If the court had adopted the dissent's position, how would this have affected the result?

3. **Technology.** By what method could the distributor ensure the most immediate payment for its products from the dealers?

4. **Economic Dimensions.** If the distributor granted credit to the dealers, how might it guarantee or secure payment for its products on default?

5. **Implications for the Businessperson.** How might tariffs levied on imported oil affect the price of gas in Cleveland? What does this indicate about the ramifications of global developments for domestic businesses?

Unit Four

Agency and Employment Law

©Svetlana Larina, 2009. Used under license from Shutterstock.com)

Chapter 23

Agency Relationships in Business

(©Marcin Balcerzak, 2009. Used under license from Shutterstock.com)

> "[It] is a universal principle in the law of agency, that the powers of the agent are to be exercised for the benefits of the principal only, and not of the agent or of third parties."
>
> —Joseph Story, 1779–1845
> (Associate Justice of the United States Supreme Court, 1811–1844)

Learning Objectives

After reading this chapter, you should be able to answer the following questions:

1. What is the difference between an employee and an independent contractor?

2. How do agency relationships arise?

3. What duties do agents and principals owe to each other?

4. When is a principal liable for the agent's actions with respect to third parties? When is the agent liable?

5. What are some of the ways in which an agency relationship can be terminated?

Agency   A relationship between two parties in which one party (the agent) agrees to represent or act for the other (the principal).

One of the most common, important, and pervasive legal relationships is that of **agency**. In an agency relationship between two parties, one of the parties, called the *agent,* agrees to represent or act for the other, called the *principal*. The principal has the right to control the agent's conduct in matters entrusted to the agent, and the agent must exercise his or her powers "for the benefit of the principal only," as Justice Joseph Story indicated in the chapter-opening quotation. By using agents, a principal can conduct multiple business operations simultaneously in various locations. Thus, for example, contracts that bind the principal can be made at different places with different persons at the same time.

Agency relationships permeate the business world. Indeed, agency law is essential to the existence and operation of a corporate entity, because only through its agents can a corporation function and enter into contracts. A familiar example of an agent is a corporate officer who serves in a representative capacity for the owners of the corporation. In this capacity, the officer has the authority to bind the principal (the corporation) to a contract.

▶ Agency Relationships

Section 1(1) of the *Restatement (Second) of Agency*[1] defines agency as "the fiduciary relation which results from the manifestation of consent by one person to another that the other shall act in his [or her] behalf and subject to his [or her] control, and consent by the other so to act." In other words, in a principal-agent relationship, the parties have agreed that the agent will act *on behalf and instead of* the principal in negotiating and transacting business with third parties.

The term **fiduciary** is at the heart of agency law. The term can be used both as a noun and as an adjective. When used as a noun, it refers to a person having a duty created by her or his undertaking to act primarily for another's benefit in matters connected with the undertaking. When used as an adjective, as in "fiduciary relationship," it means that the relationship involves trust and confidence.

Agency relationships commonly exist between employers and employees. Agency relationships may sometimes also exist between employers and independent contractors who are hired to perform special tasks or services.

fiduciary As a noun, a person having a duty created by his or her undertaking to ... primarily for another's benefit in matters connected with the undertaking. As an adjective, a relationship founded on trust and confidence.

ON THE WEB For information on the *Restatements of the Law,* including planned revisions, go to the American Law Institute's Web site at **www.ali.org**.

Employer-Employee Relationships

Normally, all employees who deal with third parties are deemed to be agents. A salesperson in a department store, for instance, is an agent of the store's owner (the principal) and acts on the owner's behalf. Any sale of goods made by the salesperson to a customer is binding on the principal. Similarly, most representations of fact made by the salesperson with respect to the goods sold are binding on the principal.

Because employees who deal with third parties are generally deemed to be agents of their employers, agency law and employment law overlap considerably. Agency relationships, though, as will become apparent, can exist outside an employer-employee relationship and thus have a broader reach than employment laws do. Additionally, bear in mind that agency law is based on the common law. In the employment realm, many common law doctrines have been displaced by statutory law and government regulations relating to employment relationships.

Employment laws (state and federal) apply only to the employer-employee relationship. Statutes governing Social Security, withholding taxes, workers' compensation, unemployment compensation, workplace safety, employment discrimination, and the like (see Chapters 24 and 25) are applicable only if employer-employee status exists. *These laws do not apply to an independent contractor.*

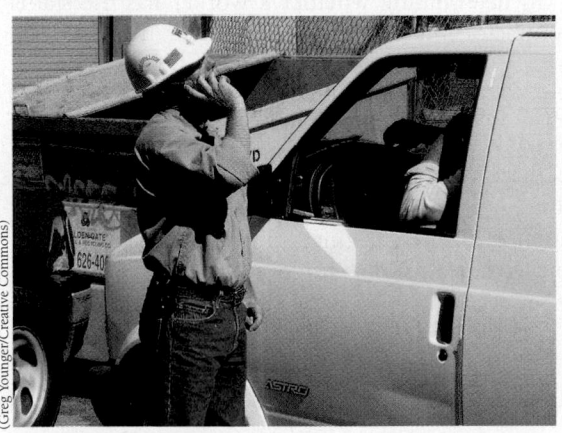

An independent contractor communicates from a building site. What are some significant differences between employees and independent contractors?

Independent Contractor One who works for, and receives payment from, an employer but whose working conditions and methods are not controlled by the employer. An independent contractor is not an employee but may be an agent.

(Greg Younger/Creative Commons)

Employer–Independent Contractor Relationships

Independent contractors are not employees because, by definition, those who hire them have no control over the details of their physical performance. Section 2 of the *Restatement (Second) of Agency* defines an **independent contractor** as follows:

[An independent contractor is] a person who contracts with another to do something for him [or her] but who is not controlled by the other nor subject to the other's right to control with respect to his [or her] physical conduct in the performance of the undertaking. *He [or she] may or may not be an agent.* [Emphasis added.]

---

1. The *Restatement (Second) of Agency* is an authoritative summary of the law of agency and is often referred to by judges and other legal professionals.

"Keep up the good work, whatever it is, whoever you are."

Building contractors and subcontractors are independent contractors; a property owner does not control the acts of either of these professionals. Truck drivers who own their equipment and hire themselves out on a per-job basis are independent contractors, but truck drivers who drive company trucks on a regular basis are usually employees.

The relationship between a person or firm and an independent contractor may or may not involve an agency relationship. To illustrate: An owner of real estate who hires a real estate broker to negotiate a sale of his or her property not only has contracted with an independent contractor (the real estate broker) but also has established an agency relationship for the specific purpose of assisting in the sale of the property. Another example is an insurance agent, who is both an independent contractor and an agent of the insurance company for which she or he sells policies. (Note that an insurance *broker,* in contrast, normally is an agent of the person obtaining insurance and not of the insurance company.)

Determining Employee Status

The courts are frequently asked to determine whether a particular worker is an employee or an independent contractor. How a court decides this issue can have a significant effect on the rights and liabilities of the parties. Employers are required to pay certain taxes, such as Social Security and unemployment taxes, for employees but not for independent contractors.

CRITERIA USED BY THE COURTS   In determining whether a worker has the status of an employee or an independent contractor, the courts often consider the following questions:

1. How much control can the employer exercise over the details of the work? (If an employer can exercise considerable control over the details of the work, this would indicate employee status. This is perhaps the most important factor weighed by the courts in determining employee status.)
2. Is the worker engaged in an occupation or business distinct from that of the employer? (If so, this points to independent-contractor status, not employee status.)
3. Is the work usually done under the employer's direction or by a specialist without supervision? (If the work is usually done under the employer's direction, this would indicate employee status.)
4. Does the employer supply the tools at the place of work? (If so, this would indicate employee status.)
5. For how long is the person employed? (If the person is employed for a long period of time, this would indicate employee status.)
6. What is the method of payment—by time period or at the completion of the job? (Payment by time period, such as once every two weeks or once a month, would indicate employee status.)
7. What degree of skill is required of the worker? (If little skill is required, this may indicate employee status.)

Sometimes, workers may benefit from having employee status—for tax purposes and to be protected under certain employment laws, for example. As mentioned earlier, federal statutes governing employment discrimination apply only when an employer-employee relationship exists. Protection under employment-discrimination statutes provides significant incentive for workers to claim that they are employees rather than independent contractors.

CASE EXAMPLE 23.1 A Puerto Rican television station, WIPR, contracted with a woman to co-host a television show profiling cities in Puerto Rico. The woman signed a new contract for each episode, each of which required her to work a certain number of days. She was under no other commitment to work for WIPR and was free to pursue other opportunities during the weeks between filming. WIPR did not withhold any taxes from the lump-sum amount it paid her for each contract. When the woman became pregnant, WIPR stopped contracting with her. She filed a lawsuit claiming that WIPR was discriminating against her in violation of federal employment-discrimination laws, but the court found in favor of WIPR. Because the parties had structured their relationship through the use of repeated fixed-length contracts and had described the woman as an independent contractor on tax documents, she could not maintain an employment-discrimination suit.[2] ●

Whether a worker is an employee or an independent contractor can also affect the employer's liability for the worker's actions. In the following case, the court had to determine the status of a taxi driver whose passengers were injured in a collision.

Case 23.1 **Lopez v. El Palmar Taxi, Inc.**

Court of Appeals of Georgia, 297 Ga.App. 121, 676 S.E.2d 460 (2009).

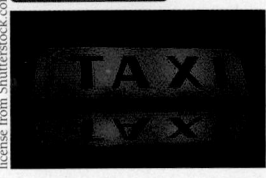

Is a taxi driver who is not subject to the control of the taxi company an independent contractor or an employee?

FACTS El Palmar Taxi, Inc., requires its drivers to supply their own cabs, which must display El Palmar's logo. The drivers pay gas, maintenance, and insurance costs, and a fee to El Palmar. They are expected to follow certain rules—dress neatly, for example—and to comply with the law, including licensing regulations, but they can work when they want for as long as they want. El Palmar might dispatch a driver to pick up a fare, or the driver can look for a fare. Mario Julaju drove a taxi under a contract with El Palmar that described him as an independent contractor. El Palmar sent Julaju to pick up Maria Lopez and her children. During the ride, Julaju's cab collided with a truck. To recover for their injuries, the Lopezes filed a suit in a Georgia state court against El Palmar. The employer argued that it was not liable because Julaju was an independent contractor. The court ruled in El Palmar's favor. The plaintiffs appealed.

ISSUE Is a taxi driver who is not subject to the control of the taxi company considered an independent contractor?

DECISION Yes. A state intermediate appellate court affirmed this part of the lower court's decision. (But the appellate court reversed the

judgment in El Palmar's favor on other grounds and remanded the case for trial.)

REASON An employer normally is not responsible for the actions of an independent contractor with whom the employer contracts. The test to determine if a worker is an independent contractor is whether the employer has the right to control the time, manner, and method of the work. In this case, the only restriction imposed on Julaju was to comply with the law. El Palmar did not own the cab that Julaju was driving at the time of the collision, nor did it exercise control over the time, manner, or method of his work. Julaju could work any time for as long as he wanted. He was not required to accept fares from the company. The cab displayed the El Palmar logo and El Palmar might dispatch him to pick up a passenger, but these factors alone do not create an employer-employee relationship.

WHY IS THIS CASE IMPORTANT? *When an employment contract clearly designates one party as an independent contractor, the relationship between the parties is presumed to be that of employer and independent contractor. But this is only a presumption. Evidence can be introduced to show that the employer exercised sufficient control to establish the other party as an employee. Or, as this case makes clear, the evidence can underscore that the parties' relationship is that of employer and independent contractor.*

CRITERIA USED BY THE IRS The Internal Revenue Service (IRS) has established its own criteria for determining whether a worker is an independent contractor or an employee. Although the IRS once considered twenty factors in determining a worker's status, guidelines that took effect in 1997 encourage IRS examiners to focus on just one of those factors—the degree of control the business exercises over the worker.

---

2. *Alberty-Vélez v. Corporación de Puerto Rico para la Difusión Pública,* 361 F.3d 1 (1st Cir. 2004).

The IRS tends to closely scrutinize a firm's classification of its workers because, as mentioned, employers can avoid certain tax liabilities by hiring independent contractors instead of employees. Even when a firm classifies a worker as an independent contractor, the IRS may decide that the worker is actually an employee. In that situation, the employer will be responsible for paying any applicable Social Security, withholding, and unemployment taxes. Microsoft Corporation, for example, was once ordered to pay back payroll taxes for hundreds of workers that the IRS determined had been misclassified as independent contractors.[3] (The *Business Application* feature at the end of the chapter offers suggestions on using independent contractors.)

EMPLOYEE STATUS AND "WORKS FOR HIRE"   Under the Copyright Act of 1976, any copyrighted work created by an employee within the scope of her or his employment at the request of the employer is a "work for hire," and the *employer* owns the copyright to the work. When an employer hires an independent contractor—a freelance artist, writer, or computer programmer, for example—the independent contractor owns the copyright *unless* the parties agree in writing that the work is a "work for hire" and the work falls into one of nine specific categories, including audiovisual and other works.

EXAMPLE 23.2 Gabe, who marketed DVDs containing compilations of software programs, hired Katlin to create a file-retrieval program that would allow users to access the software on the DVDs. Katlin built into the final version of the program a notice stating that she was the author of the program and owned the copyright. Gabe removed the notice, claiming that Katlin's file-retrieval program was a "work for hire" and that he owned the copyright to the program. In this situation, however, because Katlin was a skilled computer programmer who controlled the manner and method of her work, she was an independent contractor and not an employee for hire. Thus, Katlin owned the copyright to the file-retrieval program. •

▶ How Agency Relationships Are Formed

Agency relationships normally are consensual; that is, they come about by voluntary consent and agreement between the parties. Generally, the agreement need not be in writing,[4] and consideration is not required.

A person must have contractual capacity to be a principal.[5] Those who cannot legally enter into contracts directly should not be allowed to do so indirectly through an agent. Any person can be an agent, though, regardless of whether he or she has the capacity to enter a contract (including minors).

An agency relationship can be created for any legal purpose. An agency relationship that is created for an illegal purpose or that is contrary to public policy is unenforceable. **EXAMPLE 23.3** Sharp (as principal) contracts with McKenzie (as agent) to sell illegal narcotics. This agency relationship is unenforceable because selling illegal narcotics is a felony and is contrary to public policy. • It is also illegal for physicians and other licensed professionals to employ unlicensed agents to perform professional actions.

Generally, an agency relationship can arise in four ways: by agreement of the parties, by ratification, by estoppel, or by operation of law.

ON THE WEB An excellent source for information on agency, including court cases involving agency concepts, is the Legal Information Institute (LII) at Cornell University. You can access the LII's Web page on this topic at **www.law.cornell. edu/wex/index.php/Agency**.

---

3. See *Vizcaino v. U.S. District Court for the Western District of Washington,* 173 F.3d 713 (9th Cir. 1999).

4. The following are two main exceptions to the statement that agency agreements need not be in writing: (1) Whenever agency authority empowers the agent to enter into a contract that the Statute of Frauds requires to be in writing, the agent's authority from the principal must likewise be in writing (this is called the *equal dignity rule,* to be discussed later in this chapter). (2) A power of attorney, which confers authority to an agent, must be in writing.

5. Note that some states allow a minor to be a principal, but any resulting contracts will be voidable by the minor.

Sometimes, a homeowner asks a lawn-care specialist to contract with others for the care of the homeowner's lawn on a regular basis. What type of relationship is established between the homeowner and the lawn-care specialist?

Agency by Agreement

Most agency relationships are based on an express or implied agreement that the agent will act for the principal and that the principal agrees to have the agent so act. An agency agreement can take the form of an express written contract or be created by an oral agreement. **EXAMPLE 23.4** Reese asks Cary, a gardener, to contract with others for the care of his lawn on a regular basis. Cary agrees. An agency relationship is established between Reese and Cary for the lawn care. •

An agency agreement can also be implied by conduct. **EXAMPLE 23.5** A hotel expressly allows only Boris Koontz to park cars, but Boris has no employment contract there. The hotel's manager tells Boris when to work, as well as where and how to park the cars. The hotel's conduct amounts to a manifestation of its willingness to have Boris park its customers' cars, and Boris can infer from the hotel's conduct that he has authority to act as a parking valet. It can be inferred that Boris is an agent-employee for the hotel, his purpose being to provide valet parking services for hotel guests. •

Agency by Ratification

Ratification The act of accepting and giving legal force to an obligation that previously was not enforceable.

On occasion, a person who is in fact not an agent (or who is an agent acting outside the scope of her or his authority) may make a contract on behalf of another (a principal). If the principal approves or affirms that contract by word or by action, an agency relationship is created by **ratification.** Ratification involves a question of intent, and intent can be expressed by either words or conduct. The basic requirements for ratification will be discussed later in this chapter.

Agency by Estoppel

When a principal causes a third person to believe that another person is his or her agent, and the third person deals with the supposed agent, the principal is "estopped to deny" the agency relationship. In such a situation, the principal's actions create the *appearance* of an agency that does not in fact exist. The third person must prove that she or he *reasonably* believed that an agency relationship existed, though.[6] Facts and circumstances must show that an ordinary, prudent person familiar with business practice and custom would have been justified in concluding that the agent had authority.

CASE EXAMPLE 23.6 Marsha and Jerry Wiedmaier owned Wiedmaier, Inc., a corporation that operated a truck stop. Their son, Michael, did not own any interest in the corporation but had worked at the truck stop as a fuel operator. Michael decided to form his own business called Extreme Diecast, LLC. To obtain a line of credit with Motorsport Marketing, Inc., a company that sells racing memorabilia, Michael asked his mother to sign the credit application form. After Marsha had signed as "Secretary-Owner" of Wiedmaier, Inc., Michael added his name to the list of corporate owners and faxed it to Motorsport. Later, when Michael stopped making payments on the merchandise he had ordered, Motorsport sued Wiedmaier for the unpaid balance. The court ruled that Michael was an apparent agent of Wiedmaier, Inc., because the credit application had caused Motorsport to reasonably believe that Michael was acting as Wiedmaier's agent in ordering merchandise.[7] •

Note that the acts or declarations of a purported *agent* in and of themselves do not create an agency by estoppel. Rather, it is the deeds or statements *of the principal* that create

---

6. These concepts also apply when a person who is in fact an agent undertakes an action that is beyond the scope of her or his authority, as will be discussed later in this chapter.

7. *Motorsport Marketing, Inc. v. Wiedmaier, Inc.,* 195 S.W.3d 492 (Mo.App. 2006).

an agency by estoppel. In other words, in Case Example 23.6, if Marsha Wiedmaier had not signed the credit application on behalf of the principal-corporation, then Motorsport would not have been reasonable in believing that Michael was Wiedmaier's agent.

Agency by Operation of Law

The courts may find an agency relationship in the absence of a formal agreement in other situations as well. This can occur in family relationships, such as when one spouse purchases certain basic necessaries and charges them to the other spouse's charge account, for example. The courts will often rule that a spouse is liable to pay for the necessaries, either because of a social policy of promoting the general welfare of the spouse or because of a legal duty to supply necessaries to family members.

Agency by operation of law may also occur in emergency situations, when the agent's failure to act outside the scope of his or her authority would cause the principal substantial loss. If the agent is unable to contact the principal, the courts will often grant this emergency power. For instance, a railroad engineer may contract on behalf of her or his employer for medical care for an injured motorist hit by the train. The *Concept Summary* below reviews the various ways that agencies are formed.

▶ Duties of Agents and Principals

Once the principal-agent relationship has been created, both parties have duties that govern their conduct. As discussed previously, an agency relationship is *fiduciary*—one of trust. In a fiduciary relationship, each party owes the other the duty to act with the utmost good faith. We now examine the various duties of agents and principals.

In general, for every duty of the principal, the agent has a corresponding right, and vice versa. When one party to the agency relationship violates his or her duty to the other party, the remedies available to the nonbreaching party arise out of contract and tort law. These remedies include monetary damages, termination of the agency relationship, an injunction, and required accountings.

Agent's Duties to the Principal

Generally, the agent owes the principal five duties—performance, notification, loyalty, obedience, and accounting.

PERFORMANCE   An implied condition in every agency contract is the agent's agreement to use reasonable diligence and skill in performing the work. When an agent fails entirely

> *"If God had an agent, the world wouldn't be built yet. It'd only be about Thursday."*
>
> Jerry Reynolds, 1940–present
> (National Basketball Association executive)

Concept Summary   How Agency Relationships Are Formed

METHOD OF FORMATION	DESCRIPTION
By Agreement	The agency relationship is formed through express consent (oral or written) or implied by conduct.
By Ratification	The principal either by act or by agreement ratifies the conduct of a person who is not in fact an agent.
By Estoppel	The principal causes a third person to believe that another person is the principal's agent, and the third person acts to his or her detriment in reasonable reliance on that belief.
By Operation of Law	The agency relationship is based on a social duty (such as the need to support family members) or formed in emergency situations when the agent is unable to contact the principal and failure to act outside the scope of the agent's authority would cause the principal substantial loss.

to perform her or his duties, liability for breach of contract normally will result. The degree of skill or care required of an agent is usually that expected of a reasonable person under similar circumstances. Generally, this is interpreted to mean ordinary care. If an agent has represented himself or herself as possessing special skills, however, the agent is expected to exercise the degree of skill or skills claimed. Failure to do so constitutes a breach of the agent's duty.

Not all agency relationships are based on contract. In some situations, an agent acts gratuitously—that is, not for monetary compensation. A gratuitous agent cannot be liable for breach of contract, as there is no contract; he or she is subject only to tort liability. Once a gratuitous agent has begun to act in an agency capacity, he or she has the duty to continue to perform in that capacity in an acceptable manner and is subject to the same standards of care and duty to perform as other agents.

NOTIFICATION   An agent is required to notify the principal of all matters that come to her or his attention concerning the subject matter of the agency. This is the duty of notification, or the duty to inform.   **EXAMPLE 23.7**   Lang, an artist, is about to negotiate a contract to sell a series of paintings to Barber's Art Gallery for $25,000. Lang's agent learns that Barber is insolvent and will be unable to pay for the paintings. The agent has a duty to inform Lang of this fact because it is relevant to the subject matter of the agency—the sale of Lang's paintings. ● Generally, the law assumes that the principal knows of any information acquired by the agent that is relevant to the agency—regardless of whether the agent actually passes on this information to the principal. It is a basic tenet of agency law that notice to the agent is notice to the principal.

LOYALTY   Loyalty is one of the most fundamental duties in a fiduciary relationship. Basically, the agent has the duty to act *solely for the benefit of his or her principal* and not in the interest of the agent or a third party. For example, an agent cannot represent two principals in the same transaction unless both know of the dual capacity and consent to it. The duty of loyalty also means that any information or knowledge acquired through the agency relationship is considered confidential. It would be a breach of loyalty to disclose such information either during the agency relationship or after its termination. Typical examples of confidential information are trade secrets and customer lists compiled by the principal.

In short, the agent's loyalty must be undivided. The agent's actions must be strictly for the benefit of the principal and must not result in any secret profit for the agent. **CASE EXAMPLE 23.8**   Don Cousins contracts with Leo Hodgins, a real estate agent, to negotiate the purchase of an office building as an investment. While working for Cousins, Hodgins discovers that the property owner will sell the building only as a package deal with another parcel. If Hodgins then forms a new company with his brother to buy the two properties and resell the building to Cousins, he has breached his fiduciary duties. As a real estate agent, Hodgins has a duty to communicate all offers to his principal and not to secretly purchase the property and then resell it to his principal. Hodgins is required to act in Cousins's best interests and can become the purchaser in this situation only with Cousins's knowledge and approval.[8] ●

OBEDIENCE   When acting on behalf of a principal, an agent has a duty to follow all lawful and clearly stated instructions of the principal. Any deviation from such instructions is a violation of this duty. During emergency situations, however, when the principal cannot be consulted, the agent may deviate from the instructions without violating this

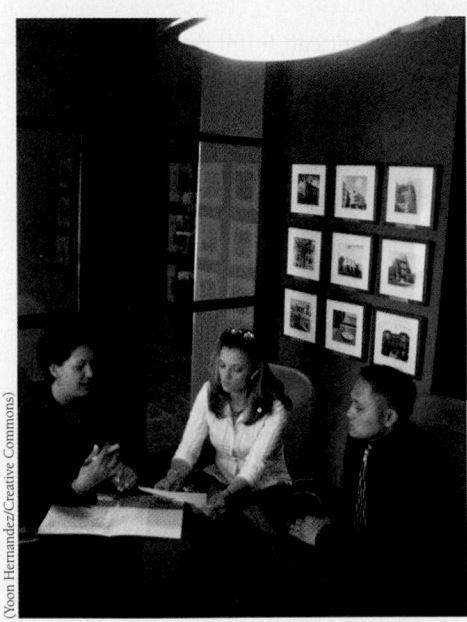

A real estate agent meets with clients in her office. Suppose that the agent knows a buyer who is willing to pay more than the asking price for a property. What duty would the agent breach if she bought the property from the seller and sold it at a profit to that buyer?

BE AWARE   An agent's disclosure of confidential information could constitute the business tort of misappropriation of trade secrets.

---

8. *Cousins v. Realty Ventures, Inc.,* 844 So.2d 860 (La.App. 5 Cir. 2003).

duty. Whenever instructions are not clearly stated, the agent can fulfill the duty of obedience by acting in good faith and in a manner reasonable under the circumstances.

ACCOUNTING   Unless an agent and a principal agree otherwise, the agent has the duty to keep and make available to the principal an account of all property and funds received and paid out on behalf of the principal. This includes gifts from third parties in connection with the agency. For example, a gift from a customer to a salesperson for prompt deliveries made by the salesperson's firm, in the absence of a company policy to the contrary, belongs to the firm. The agent has a duty to maintain separate accounts for the principal's funds and for the agent's personal funds, and the agent must not intermingle these accounts.

Principal's Duties to the Agent

The principal also owes certain duties to the agent. These duties relate to compensation, reimbursement and indemnification, cooperation, and safe working conditions.

COMPENSATION   In general, when a principal requests certain services from an agent, the agent reasonably expects payment. The principal therefore has a duty to pay the agent for services rendered. For example, when an accountant or an attorney is asked to act as an agent, an agreement to compensate the agent for such service is implied. The principal also has a duty to pay that compensation in a timely manner. Except in a gratuitous agency relationship, in which an agent does not act for payment in return, the principal must pay the agreed-on value for an agent's services. If no amount has been expressly agreed on, the principal owes the agent the customary compensation for such services.

Preventing Legal Disputes

Many disputes arise because the principal and agent did not specify how much the agent would be paid. To avoid such disputes, always state in advance, and in writing, the amount or rate of compensation that you will pay your agents. Even when dealing with salespersons, such as real estate agents, who customarily are paid a percentage of the value of the sale, it is best to explicitly state the rate of compensation.

REMEMBER An agent who signs a negotiable instrument on behalf of a principal may be personally liable on the instrument. Liability depends, in part, on whether the identity of the principal is disclosed and whether the parties intend the agent to be bound by her or his signature.

REIMBURSEMENT AND INDEMNIFICATION   Whenever an agent disburses funds to fulfill the request of the principal or to pay for necessary expenses in the course of reasonable performance of his or her agency duties, the principal has the duty to reimburse the agent for these payments. Agents cannot recover for expenses incurred through their own misconduct or negligence, though.

Subject to the terms of the agency agreement, the principal has the duty to compensate, or *indemnify,* an agent for liabilities incurred because of authorized and lawful acts and transactions. For instance, if the principal fails to perform a contract formed by the agent with a third party and the third party then sues the agent, the principal is obligated to compensate the agent for any costs incurred in defending against the lawsuit.

Additionally, the principal must indemnify (pay) the agent for the value of benefits that the agent confers on the principal. The amount of indemnification is usually specified in the agency contract. If it is not, the courts will look to the nature of the business and the type of loss to determine the amount. Note that this rule applies to acts by gratuitous agents as well. If the finder of a dog that becomes sick takes the dog to a veterinarian and pays the required fees for the veterinarian's services, the (gratuitous) agent is entitled to be reimbursed by the dog's owner for those fees.

COOPERATION   A principal has a duty to cooperate with the agent and to assist the agent in performing her or his duties. The principal must do nothing to prevent such performance.

When a principal grants an agent an exclusive territory, for example, the principal creates an *exclusive agency* and cannot compete with the agent or appoint or allow another agent to so compete. If the principal does so, she or he will be exposed to liability for the agent's lost sales or profits. **EXAMPLE 23.9** Akers (the principal) creates an exclusive agency by granting Johnson (the agent) an exclusive territory within which Johnson may sell Akers's products. If Akers begins to sell the products himself within Johnson's territory or permits another agent to do so, Akers has violated the exclusive agency and can be held liable for Johnson's lost sales or profits. ●

SAFE WORKING CONDITIONS   Under the common law, a principal is required to provide safe working premises, equipment, and conditions for all agents and employees. The principal has a duty to inspect the working conditions and to warn agents and employees about any unsafe areas. When the agent is an employee, the employer's liability is frequently covered by state workers' compensation insurance, and federal and state statutes often require the employer to meet certain safety standards (to be discussed in Chapter 24).

▶ Agent's Authority

An agent's authority to act can be either *actual* (express or implied) or *apparent*. If an agent contracts outside the scope of his or her authority, the principal may still become liable by ratifying the contract.

Actual Authority

As indicated, an agent's actual authority can be express or implied. We look here at both of these forms of actual authority.

EXPRESS AUTHORITY   *Express authority* is authority declared in clear, direct, and definite terms. Express authority can be given orally or in writing. In most states, the **equal dignity rule** requires that if the contract being executed is or must be in writing, then the agent's authority must also be in writing. Failure to comply with the equal dignity rule can make a contract voidable *at the option of the principal*. The law regards the contract at that point as a mere offer. If the principal decides to accept the offer, acceptance must be ratified, or affirmed, in writing.

Equal Dignity Rule   In most states, a rule stating that express authority given to an agent must be in writing if the contract to be made on behalf of the principal is required to be in writing.

EXAMPLE 23.10 Lee (the principal) orally asks Parkinson (the agent) to sell a ranch that Lee owns. Parkinson finds a buyer and signs a sales contract (a contract for an interest in realty must be in writing) on behalf of Lee to sell the ranch. The buyer cannot enforce the contract unless Lee subsequently ratifies Parkinson's agency status *in writing*. Once Parkinson's agency status is ratified, either party can enforce rights under the contract. ●

Modern business practice allows an exception to the equal dignity rule. An executive officer of a corporation normally is not required to obtain written authority from the corporation to conduct *ordinary* business transactions. The equal dignity rule does not apply when an agent acts in the presence of a principal or when the agent's act of signing is merely perfunctory (automatic). Thus, if Dickens (the principal) negotiates a contract but is called out of town the day it is to be signed and orally authorizes Santini to sign the contract, the oral authorization is sufficient.

Power of Attorney   A written document, which is usually notarized, authorizing another to act as one's agent; can be special (permitting the agent to do specified acts only) or general (permitting the agent to transact all business for the principal).

POWER OF ATTORNEY   Giving an agent a **power of attorney** confers express authority.[9] The power of attorney normally is a written document and is usually notarized. (A

---

9. An agent who holds the power of attorney is called an *attorney-in-fact* for the principal. The holder does not have to be an attorney-at-law (and often is not).

(Rachael Voorhees/Creative Commons)

Notary publics are those who are authorized by a state to attest to the authenticity of signatures. In most states, there are few restrictions on who can become a notary public.

Notary Public   A public official authorized to attest to the authenticity of signatures.

document is notarized when a **notary public**—a public official authorized to attest to the authenticity of signatures—signs and dates the document and imprints it with his or her seal of authority.) Most states have statutory provisions for creating a power of attorney. A power of attorney can be special (permitting the agent to do specified acts only), or it can be general (permitting the agent to transact all business for the principal). Because a general power of attorney grants extensive authority to an agent to act on behalf of the principal in many ways, it should be used with great caution. Ordinarily, a power of attorney terminates on the incapacity or death of the person giving the power.[10]

IMPLIED AUTHORITY   An agent has the *implied authority* to do what is reasonably necessary to carry out express authority and accomplish the objectives of the agency. Authority can also be implied by custom or inferred from the position the agent occupies. **EXAMPLE 23.11** Mueller is employed by Al's Supermarket to manage one of its stores. Al's has not expressly stated that Mueller has authority to contract with third persons. In this situation, though, authority to manage a business implies authority to do what is reasonably required (as is customary or can be inferred from a manager's position) to operate the business. This includes forming contracts to hire employees, to buy merchandise and equipment, and to advertise the products sold in the store. ●

Ethical Issue ⚖️

Does an agent's breach of loyalty terminate the agent's authority? Suppose that an employee-agent who is authorized to access company trade secrets contained in computer files takes those secrets to a competitor for whom the employee is about to begin working. Clearly, the agent has violated the ethical—and legal—duty of loyalty to the principal. Does this breach of loyalty mean that the employee's act of accessing the trade secrets was unauthorized? The question has significant implications because if the act was unauthorized, the employee will be subject to state and federal laws prohibiting unauthorized access to computer information and data. If the act was authorized, the laws will not apply.

Although a few courts have found that an employee's authority as an agent terminated the moment the employee accessed trade secrets for the purpose of divulging them to a competitor,[11] most courts hold that an agent's authority continues. For example, when Jeff Gast became an employee of Shamrock Foods Company, he signed a confidentiality agreement promising not to disclose trade secrets. In January 2008, Gast e-mailed numerous documents containing Shamrock's confidential proprietary information to himself at his personal e-mail account. That same month, Gast quit his job at Shamrock and went to work for Sysco, a competitor. Shamrock filed a lawsuit in a federal court in Arizona against Gast for violating the Computer Fraud and Abuse Act (CFAA, discussed in Chapter 4). The court held that the phrase "without authorization" in the CFAA was meant to refer to outsiders rather than to agents who had a principal's authority to access the computer information. Gast was initially authorized to access the computer he used at Shamrock and to view the specific files containing the information. Therefore, the court concluded that Gast did not access the information at issue "without authorization" or in a manner that "exceeded authorized access." Although Gast had behaved unethically, the court found that his activity was not actionable under the CFAA and dismissed the lawsuit.[12]

---

10. A *durable* power of attorney, however, continues to be effective despite the principal's incapacity. An elderly person, for example, might grant a durable power of attorney to provide for the handling of property and investments or specific health-care needs should she or he become incompetent.

11. See, for example, *International Airport Centers, LLC v. Citrin,* 440 F.3d 418 (7th Cir. 2006); and *ViChip Corp. v. Lee,* 438 F.Supp.2d 1087 (N.D.Cal. 2006).

12. *Shamrock Foods Co. v. Gast,* 535 F.Supp.2d 962 (D.Ariz. 2008). For a case involving three employee-agents who stole confidential data from their employer-principal, see *Lockheed Martin Corp. v. Speed,* 2006 WL 2683058 (M.D.Fla. 2006).

Apparent Authority

Apparent Authority Authority that is only apparent, not real. In agency law, a person may be deemed to have had the power to act as an agent for another party if the other party's manifestations to a third party led the third party to believe that an agency existed when, in fact, it did not.

Actual authority (express or implied) arises from what the principal manifests *to the agent.* An agent has **apparent authority** when the principal, by either words or actions, causes a *third party* reasonably to believe that an agent has authority to act, even though the agent has no express or implied authority. If the third party changes her or his position in reliance on the principal's representations, the principal may be *estopped* (prevented) from denying that the agent had authority.

Apparent authority usually comes into existence through a principal's pattern of conduct over time. **EXAMPLE 23.12** Bailey is a traveling salesperson with the authority to solicit orders for a principal's goods. Because she does not carry any goods with her, she normally would not have the implied authority to collect payments from customers on behalf of the principal. Suppose that she does accept payments from Corgley Enterprises, however, and submits them to the principal's accounting department for processing. If the principal does nothing to stop Bailey from continuing this practice, a pattern develops over time, and the principal confers apparent authority on Bailey to accept payments from Corgley. ●

At issue in the following case was a question of apparent authority or, as the court referred to it, "ostensible [apparent] agency."

Case 23.2 Ermoian v. Desert Hospital

Court of Appeal of California, Fourth District, 152 Cal.App.4th 475, 61 Cal.Rptr.3d 754 (2007).

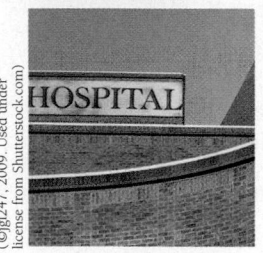

Did clinic physicians have apparent authority to act for the hospital in a negligence claim?

FACTS In 1990, Desert Hospital in California established a comprehensive perinatal services program (CPSP) to provide obstetrical care to women who were uninsured (*perinatal* is often defined as relating to the period from about the twenty-eighth week of pregnancy to around one month after birth). The CPSP was set up in an office suite across from the hospital and named "Desert Hospital Outpatient Maternity Services Clinic." The hospital contracted with a corporation controlled by Dr. Morton Gubin, which employed Dr. Masami Ogata, to provide obstetrical services. In January 1994, Jackie Shahan went to the hospital's emergency room because of cramping and other symptoms. The emergency room physician told Shahan that she was pregnant and referred her to the clinic. Shahan visited the clinic throughout her pregnancy. On May 15, Shahan's baby, Amanda Ermoian, was born with brain abnormalities that left her severely mentally retarded and unable to care for herself. Her conditions could not have been prevented, treated, or cured *in utero.* Through a guardian, Amanda filed a suit in a California state court against the hospital and others, alleging "wrongful life." She claimed that the defendants negligently failed to inform her mother of her abnormalities before her birth, depriving her mother of the opportunity to make an informed choice to terminate the pregnancy. The court ruled in the defendants' favor, holding, among other things, that the hospital was not liable because Drs. Gubin and Ogata were not its employees. Amanda appealed to a state intermediate appellate court, contending, in part, that the physicians were the hospital's "ostensible [apparent] agents."

ISSUE Did the physicians who were working at the clinic during Shahan's pregnancy have apparent authority to act for the hospital?

DECISION Yes. The state intermediate appellate court decided that, contrary to the lower court's finding, the physicians, Gubin and Ogata, were "ostensible [apparent] agents of the Hospital." The appellate court affirmed the lower court's ruling on Amanda's "wrongful life" claim, however, concluding that the physicians were not negligent in failing to advise Shahan to have an elective abortion.

REASON The court pointed out that ostensible agency (apparent agency) can be implied when a principal "by his acts has led others to believe that he has conferred authority upon an agent." Liability for an act of an ostensible agent rests on a doctrine of estoppel. The court noted that a person dealing with an agent must believe in the agent's authority. In this case, the hospital "held out the clinic and the personnel in the clinic as part of the hospital." The clinic used the same name as the hospital and labeled itself as an outpatient clinic. Moreover, personnel in the hospital's emergency room referred Shahan specifically to Dr. Gubin. When Shahan called the hospital, the receptionist told her "that she was calling the Hospital outpatient clinic which was the clinic of Dr. Gubin." The appellate court ruled that the hospital, and those associated with it, created the appearance to Shahan that the hospital was the provider of obstetrical care.

FOR CRITICAL ANALYSIS—Ethical Consideration
Does a principal have an ethical responsibility to inform an unaware third party that an apparent (ostensible) agent does not in fact have authority to act on the principal's behalf?

Ratification

As already mentioned, ratification occurs when the principal affirms an agent's *unauthorized* act. When ratification occurs, the principal is bound to the agent's act, and the act is treated as if it had been authorized by the principal *from the outset*. Ratification can be either express or implied.

If the principal does not ratify the contract, the principal is not bound, and the third party's agreement with the agent is viewed as merely an unaccepted offer. Because the third party's agreement is an unaccepted offer, the third party can revoke the offer at any time, without liability, before the principal ratifies the contract.

The requirements for ratification can be summarized as follows:

1. The agent must have acted on behalf of an identified principal who subsequently ratifies the action.
2. The principal must know of all material facts involved in the transaction. If a principal ratifies a contract without knowing all of the facts, the principal can rescind (cancel) the contract.
3. The principal must affirm the agent's act in its entirety.
4. The principal must have the legal capacity to authorize the transaction at the time the agent engages in the act and at the time the principal ratifies. The third party must also have the legal capacity to engage in the transaction.
5. The principal's affirmation must occur before the third party withdraws from the transaction.
6. The principal must observe the same formalities when approving the act done by the agent as would have been required to authorize it initially.

▶ Liability in Agency Relationships

Frequently, a question arises as to which party, the principal or the agent, should be held liable for contracts formed by the agent or for torts or crimes committed by the agent. We look here at these aspects of agency law.

Liability for Contracts

Liability for contracts formed by an agent depends on how the principal is classified and on whether the actions of the agent were authorized or unauthorized. Principals are classified as disclosed, partially disclosed, or undisclosed.[13]

A **disclosed principal** is a principal whose identity is known by the third party at the time the contract is made by the agent. A **partially disclosed principal** is a principal whose identity is not known by the third party, but the third party knows that the agent is or may be acting for a principal at the time the contract is made. **EXAMPLE 23.13** Sarah has contracted with a real estate agent to sell certain property. She wishes to keep her identity a secret, but the agent makes it perfectly clear to potential buyers of the property that the agent is acting in an agency capacity. In this situation, Sarah is a partially disclosed principal. • An **undisclosed principal** is a principal whose identity is totally unknown by the third party, and the third party has no knowledge that the agent is acting in an agency capacity at the time the contract is made.

AUTHORIZED ACTS   If an agent acts within the scope of her or his authority, normally the principal is obligated to perform the contract regardless of whether the principal was disclosed, partially disclosed, or undisclosed. Whether the agent may also be held liable

---

13. *Restatement (Second) of Agency,* Section 4.

under the contract, however, depends on the disclosed, partially disclosed, or undisclosed status of the principal.

Disclosed or Partially Disclosed Principal.   A disclosed or partially disclosed principal is liable to a third party for a contract made by an agent who is acting within the scope of her or his authority. If the principal is disclosed, an agent has no contractual liability for the nonperformance of the principal or the third party. If the principal is partially disclosed, in most states the agent is also treated as a party to the contract, and the third party can hold the agent liable for contractual nonperformance.[14]

CASE EXAMPLE 23.14   Walgreens leased commercial property to operate a drugstore at a mall owned by Kedzie Plaza Associates. A property management company, Taxman Corporation, signed the lease on behalf of the principal, Kedzie. The lease required the landlord to keep the sidewalks free of snow and ice, so Taxman, on behalf of Kedzie, contracted with another company to remove ice and snow from the sidewalks surrounding the Walgreens store. When a Walgreens employee slipped on ice outside the store and was injured, she sued Walgreens, Kedzie, and Taxman for negligence and ended up settling her claims with the other defendants except Taxman. Because the principal's identity (Kedzie) was fully disclosed in the snow-removal contract, however, the Illinois court ruled that the agent, Taxman, could not be held liable. Taxman did not assume a contractual obligation to remove the snow but merely retained a contractor to do so on behalf of the owner.[15] ●

Undisclosed Principal.   When neither the fact of agency nor the identity of the principal is disclosed, the undisclosed principal is bound to perform just as if the principal had been fully disclosed at the time the contract was made. The agent is also liable as a party to the contract.

When a principal's identity is undisclosed and the agent is forced to pay the third party, the agent is entitled to be indemnified (compensated) by the principal. The principal had a duty to perform, even though his or her identity was undisclosed, and failure to do so will make the principal ultimately liable. Once the undisclosed principal's identity is revealed, the third party generally can elect to hold either the principal or the agent liable on the contract. Conversely, the undisclosed principal can require the third party to fulfill the contract, *unless* (1) the undisclosed principal was expressly excluded as a party in the contract; (2) the contract is a negotiable instrument signed by the agent with no indication of signing in a representative capacity; or (3) the performance of the agent is personal to the contract, allowing the third party to refuse the principal's performance.

UNAUTHORIZED ACTS   If an agent has no authority but nevertheless contracts with a third party, the principal cannot be held liable on the contract. It does not matter whether the principal was disclosed, partially disclosed, or undisclosed. The *agent* is liable, however. **EXAMPLE 23.15**   Scranton signs a contract for the purchase of a truck, purportedly acting as an agent under authority granted by Johnson. In fact, Johnson has not given Scranton any such authority. Johnson refuses to pay for the truck, claiming that Scranton had no authority to purchase it. The seller of the truck is entitled to hold Scranton liable for payment. ●

If the principal is disclosed or partially disclosed, the agent is liable to the third party as long as the third party relied on the agency status. The agent's liability here is based on the breach of an *implied warranty of authority* (an agent impliedly warrants that he or she has the authority to enter a contract on behalf of the principal), not on breach of the contract itself.[16] If the third party knows at the time the contract is made that the agent does

> "*Let every eye negotiate for itself and trust no agent.*"
> William Shakespeare, 1564–1616
> (English dramatist and poet)

---

14. *Restatement (Second) of Agency,* Section 321.

15. *McBride v. Taxman Corp.,* 327 Ill.App.3d 992, 765 N.E.2d 51 (2002).

16. The agent is not liable on the contract because the agent was never intended personally to be a party to the contract.

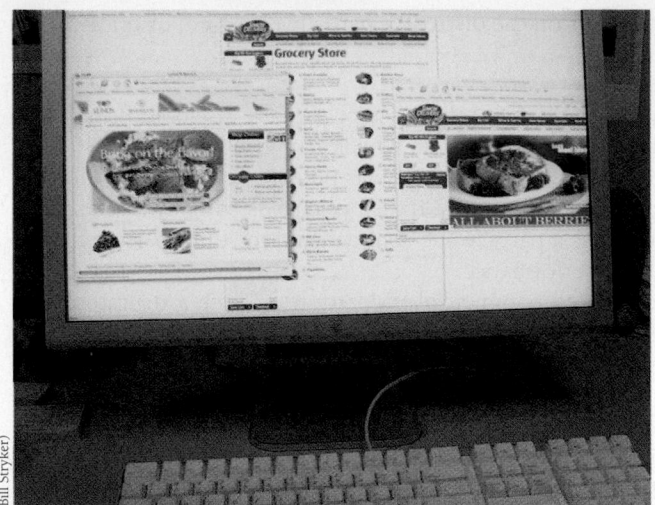

(Bill Stryker)

Today, one can buy an array of products, including groceries, online. What act has taken steps to apply traditional agency principles to online transactions?

E-Agent A computer program that by electronic or other automated means can independently initiate an action or respond to electronic messages or data without review by an individual.

not have authority—or if the agent expresses to the third party *uncertainty* as to the extent of her or his authority—then the agent is not personally liable.

LIABILITY FOR E-AGENTS Although in the past standard agency principles applied only to *human* agents, today these same principles are being applied to electronic agents. An electronic agent, or **e-agent,** is a semiautonomous computer program that is capable of executing specific tasks. E-agents used in e-commerce include software that can search through many databases and retrieve only information that is relevant for the user.

The Uniform Electronic Transactions Act (UETA), which was discussed in Chapter 10 and has been adopted by most states, contains several provisions relating to the principal's liability for the actions of e-agents. Section 15 of the UETA states that e-agents may enter into binding agreements on behalf of their principals. Presumably, then—at least in those states that have adopted the act—the principal will be bound by the terms in a contract entered into by an e-agent. Thus, when you place an order over the Internet, the company (principal) whose system took the order via an e-agent cannot claim that it did not receive your order.

The UETA also stipulates that if an e-agent does not provide an opportunity to prevent errors at the time of the transaction, the other party to the transaction can avoid the transaction. For instance, if an e-agent fails to provide an on-screen confirmation of a purchase or sale, the other party can avoid the effect of any errors.

Liability for Torts and Crimes

Obviously, any person, including an agent, is liable for her or his own torts and crimes. Whether a principal can also be held liable for an agent's torts and crimes depends on several factors, which we examine here. In some situations, a principal may be held liable not only for the torts of an agent but also for the torts committed by an independent contractor.

A serious ski accident occurs under the supervised instruction of a ski resort employee. Are there any circumstances under which the principal (the resort) will not be liable?

(Rob Lee/Creative Commons)

PRINCIPAL'S TORTIOUS CONDUCT A principal conducting an activity through an agent may be liable for harm resulting from the principal's own negligence or recklessness. Thus, a principal may be liable for giving improper instructions, authorizing the use of improper materials or tools, or establishing improper rules that resulted in the agent's committing a tort. **EXAMPLE 23.16** Jack knows that Suki cannot drive but nevertheless tells her to use the company truck to deliver some equipment to a customer. If someone is injured as a result, Jack (the principal) will be liable for his own negligence in giving improper instructions telling Suki to drive. •

PRINCIPAL'S AUTHORIZATION OF AGENT'S TORTIOUS CONDUCT A principal who authorizes an agent to commit a tort may be liable to persons or property injured thereby, because the act is considered to be the principal's. **EXAMPLE 23.17** Selkow directs his agent, Warren, to cut the corn on specific acreage, which neither of them has the right to do. The harvest is therefore a trespass (a tort), and Selkow is liable to the owner of the corn. •

Note also that an agent acting at the principal's direction can be liable as a *tortfeasor* (one who commits a wrong, or tort), along with the principal, for committing the tortious act even if the agent was unaware of the wrongfulness of the act. Assume in the above example that Warren, the agent, did not know that Selkow had no right to harvest the corn. Warren can be held liable to the owner of the field for damages, along with Selkow, the principal.

LIABILITY FOR AGENT'S MISREPRESENTATION   A principal is exposed to tort liability whenever a third person sustains a loss due to the agent's misrepresentation. The principal's liability depends on whether the agent was actually or apparently authorized to make representations and whether the representations were made within the scope of the agency. The principal is always directly responsible for an agent's misrepresentation made within the scope of the agent's authority. **EXAMPLE 23.18**   Bassett is a demonstrator for Moore's products. Moore sends Bassett to a home show to demonstrate the products and to answer questions from consumers. Moore has given Bassett authority to make statements about the products. If Bassett makes only true representations, all is fine; but if he makes false claims, Moore will be liable for any injuries or damages sustained by third parties in reliance on Bassett's false representations. ●

LIABILITY FOR AGENT'S NEGLIGENCE   As mentioned, an agent is liable for his or her own torts. A principal may also be liable for harm an agent caused to a third party under the doctrine of **respondeat superior,**[17] a Latin term meaning "let the master respond." This doctrine, which is discussed in this chapter's *Landmark in the Law* feature on page 597, is similar to the theory of strict liability discussed in Chapters 4 and 17. It imposes **vicarious liability,** or indirect liability, on the employer—that is, liability without regard to the personal fault of the employer—for torts committed by an employee in the course or scope of employment.

When an agent commits a negligent act, can the agent, as well as the principal, be held liable? That was the issue in the following case.

Respondeat Superior   Latin for "let the master respond." A doctrine under which a principal or an employer is held liable for the wrongful acts committed by agents or employees while acting within the course and scope of their agency or employment.

Vicarious Liability   Legal responsibility placed on one person for the acts of another; indirect liability imposed on a supervisory party (such as an employer) for the actions of a subordinate (such as an employee) because of the relationship between the two parties.

17. Pronounced ree-*spahn*-dee-uht soo-*peer*-ee-your.

Case 23.3 **Warner v. Southwest Desert Images, LLC**

Court of Appeals of Arizona, 218 Ariz. 121, 180 P.3d 986 (2008).

Can an employee-agent, as well as the employer, be held liable for negligence in the use of an herbicide?

FACTS   Aegis Communications hired Southwest Desert Images (SDI) to provide landscaping services for its property. SDI employee David Hoggatt was spraying an herbicide to control weeds around the Aegis building one day when he was told that the spray was being sucked into the building by the air-conditioning system and making people sick. The building was evacuated, and employees were treated for breathing problems and itchy eyes. Aegis employee Catherine Warner, who had previously suffered two heart attacks, was taken to the hospital. It was determined that she had suffered a heart attack. She continued experiencing health complications that she blamed on exposure to the spray. Warner sued SDI and Hoggatt for negligence. The trial judge dismissed the suit against Hoggatt. The jury found that SDI was solely liable for Warner's injuries. She was awarded $3,825 in damages. She appealed the decision.

ISSUE   Can Hoggatt, the employee-agent who negligently sprayed the herbicide, be held liable for damages in addition to his employer-principal, SDI?

DECISION   Yes. The appeals court held that Hoggatt should not have been dismissed from the lawsuit.

REASON   The fact that Hoggatt was an agent-employee of SDI did not excuse him from liability for his negligence in spraying. The court reasoned
Case 23.3—Continues next page ➡

Case 23.3—Continued

that there was evidence that Hoggatt had ignored instructions provided by the company that sold SDI the spray. In doing so, he was negligent. An agent (Hoggatt) is not excused from responsibility for tortious conduct just because he is working for a principal (SDI). Although the jury found SDI completely responsible, the dismissal of the suit against Hoggatt denied Warner the right to collect from him as a joint tortfeasor. The appeals court held that Warner should be able to collect from Hoggatt as well.

FOR CRITICAL ANALYSIS—Legal Consideration *How could SDI reduce the likelihood of similar lawsuits occurring in the future?*

Determining the Scope of Employment. The key to determining whether a principal may be liable for the torts of an agent under the doctrine of *respondeat superior* is whether the torts are committed within the scope of the agency or employment. The *Restatement (Second) of Agency,* Section 229, indicates the factors that today's courts will consider in determining whether a particular act occurred within the course and scope of employment. These factors are as follows:

1. Whether the employee's act was authorized by the employer.
2. The time, place, and purpose of the act.
3. Whether the act was one commonly performed by employees on behalf of their employers.
4. The extent to which the employer's interest was advanced by the act.
5. The extent to which the private interests of the employee were involved.
6. Whether the employer furnished the means or instrumentality (for example, a truck or a machine) by which the injury was inflicted.
7. Whether the employer had reason to know that the employee would do the act in question and whether the employee had ever done it before.
8. Whether the act involved the commission of a serious crime.

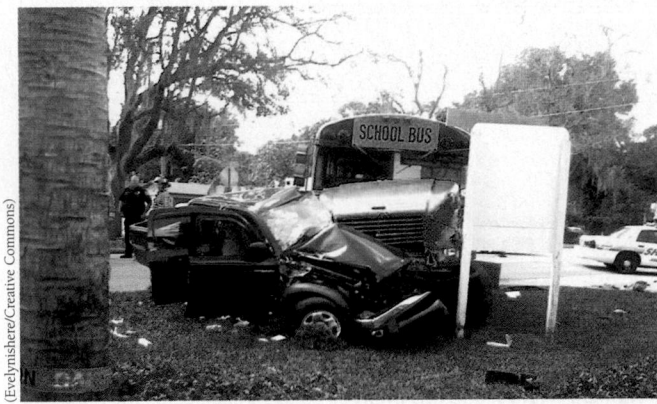

Suppose that the driver of the bus in this photo caused a traffic accident that resulted in property damages and personal injuries. If the driver's employer (the principal) learns that the driver had been drinking alcohol during a break right before the incident, can the principal avoid liability? Why or why not?

The Distinction between a "Detour" and a "Frolic." A useful insight into the "scope of employment" concept may be gained from the judge's classic distinction between a "detour" and a "frolic" in the case of *Joel v. Morison*.[18] In this case, the English court held that if a servant merely took a detour from his master's business, the master will be responsible. If, however, the servant was on a "frolic of his own" and not in any way "on his master's business," the master will not be liable.

EXAMPLE 23.19 Mandel, a traveling salesperson, while driving his employer's vehicle to call on a customer, decides to stop at the post office—which is one block off his route—to mail a personal letter. As Mandel approaches the post office, he negligently runs into a parked vehicle owned by Chan. In this situation, because Mandel's detour from the employer's business is not substantial, he is still acting within the scope of employment, and the employer is liable. The result would be different, though, if Mandel had decided to pick up a few friends for cocktails in another city and in the process had negligently run into Chan's vehicle. In that circumstance, the departure from the employer's business would be substantial, and the employer normally would not be liable to Chan for damages. Mandel would be considered to have been on a "frolic" of his own. ●

---

18. 6 Car. & P. 501, 172 Eng. Reprint 1338 (1834).

Landmark in the Law   The Doctrine of *Respondeat Superior*

The idea that a master (employer) must respond to third persons for losses negligently caused by the master's servant (employee) first appeared in Lord Holt's opinion in *Jones v. Hart* (1698).[a] By the early nineteenth century, this maxim had been adopted by most courts and was referred to as the doctrine of *respondeat superior*.

Theories of Liability The vicarious (indirect) liability of the master for the acts of the servant has been supported primarily by two theories. The first theory rests on the issue of *control,* or *fault:* the master has control over the acts of the servant and is thus responsible for injuries arising out of such service. The second theory is economic in nature: because the master takes the benefits or profits of the servant's service, he or she should also suffer the losses; moreover, the master is better able than the servant to absorb such losses.

The *control* theory is clearly recognized in the *Restatement (Second) of Agency,* which defines a master as "a principal who employs an agent to perform service in his [or her] affairs and who controls, or has the right to control, the physical conduct of the other in the performance of the service." Accordingly, a servant is defined as "an agent employed by a master to perform service in his [or her] affairs whose physical conduct in his [or her] performance of the service is controlled, or is subject to control, by the master."

_____
a. K.B. 642, 90 Eng. Reprint 1255 (1698).

Limitations on the Employer's Liability There are limitations on the master's liability for the acts of the servant, however. An employer (master) is responsible only for the wrongful conduct of an employee (servant) that occurs in "the scope of employment." The criteria used by the courts in determining whether an employee is acting within the scope of employment are set forth in the *Restatement (Second) of Agency* and discussed in the text. Generally, the act must be of a kind the servant was employed to do; must have occurred within "authorized time and space limits"; and must have been "activated, at least in part, by a purpose to serve the master."

● **Application to Today's World** *The courts have accepted the doctrine of* respondeat superior *for nearly two centuries. This theory of vicarious liability is laden with practical implications in all situations in which a principal-agent (master-servant, employer-employee) relationship exists. Today, the small-town grocer with one clerk and the multinational corporation with thousands of employees are equally subject to the doctrinal demand of "let the master respond." (For a further discussion of employers' liability for wrongs committed by their employees, including wrongs committed in the online employment environment, see Chapter 24.)*

● **Relevant Web Sites** To locate information on the Web concerning the doctrine of *respondeat superior,* go to this text's Web site at www.cengage.com/blaw/blt, select "Chapter 23," and click on "URLs for Landmarks."

NOTE An agent-employee going to or from work or meals usually is not considered to be within the scope of employment. An agent-employee whose job requires travel, however, is considered to be within the scope of employment for the entire trip, including the return.

Employee Travel Time. An employee going to and from work or to and from meals is usually considered outside the scope of employment. If travel is part of a person's position, however, such as a traveling salesperson or a regional representative of a company, then travel time is normally considered within the scope of employment. Thus, the duration of the business trip, including the return trip home, is within the scope of employment unless there is a significant departure from the employer's business.

Notice of Dangerous Conditions. The employer is charged with knowledge of any dangerous conditions discovered by an employee and pertinent to the employment situation. **EXAMPLE 23.20** Chad, a maintenance employee in Martin's apartment building, notices a lead pipe protruding from the ground in the building's courtyard. The employee neglects either to fix the pipe or to inform the employer of the danger. John falls on the pipe and is injured. The employer is charged with knowledge of the dangerous condition regardless of whether or not Chad actually informed the employer. That knowledge is imputed to the employer by virtue of the employment relationship. ●

LIABILITY FOR AGENT'S INTENTIONAL TORTS Most intentional torts that employees commit have no relation to their employment; thus, their employers will not be held liable. Nevertheless, under the doctrine of *respondeat superior,* the employer can be liable for intentional torts of the employee that are committed within the course and scope of employment, just as the employer is liable for negligence. For instance, an employer is liable when an employee (such as a "bouncer" at a nightclub or a security guard at a department store) commits the tort of assault and battery or false imprisonment while acting within the scope of employment.

In addition, an employer who knows or should know that an employee has a propensity for committing tortious acts is liable for the employee's acts even if they would not ordinarily be considered within the scope of employment. For example, if the employer hires a bouncer knowing that he has a history of arrests for assault and battery, the employer may be liable if the employee viciously attacks a patron in the parking lot after hours.

An employer may also be liable for permitting an employee to engage in reckless actions that can injure others. **EXAMPLE 23.21** An employer observes an employee smoking while filling containerized trucks with highly flammable liquids. Failure to stop the employee will cause the employer to be liable for any injuries that result if a truck explodes. ● (See this chapter's *Beyond Our Borders* feature for a discussion of another approach to an employer's liability for an employee's acts.)

LIABILITY FOR INDEPENDENT CONTRACTOR'S TORTS   Generally, an employer is not liable for physical harm caused to a third person by the negligent act of an independent contractor in the performance of the contract. This is because the employer does not have the right to control the details of an independent contractor's performance. Exceptions to this rule are made in certain situations, though, such as when unusually hazardous activities are involved. Typical examples of such activities include blasting operations, the transportation of highly volatile chemicals, or the use of poisonous gases. In these situations, an employer cannot be shielded from liability merely by using an independent contractor. Strict liability is imposed on the employer-principal as a matter of law. Also, in some states, strict liability may be imposed by statute.

LIABILITY FOR AGENT'S CRIMES   An agent is liable for his or her own crimes. A principal or employer is not liable for an agent's crime even if the crime was committed within the scope of authority or employment—unless the principal participated by conspiracy or other action. In some jurisdictions, under specific statutes, a principal may be liable for an agent's violation, in the course and scope of employment, of regulations, such as those governing sanitation, prices, weights, and the sale of liquor.

How Agency Relationships Are Terminated

Agency law is similar to contract law in that both an agency and a contract can be terminated by an act of the parties or by operation of law. Once the relationship between the principal and the agent has ended, the agent no longer has the right (*actual* authority) to bind the principal. For an agent's *apparent* authority to be terminated, though, third persons may also need to be notified that the agency has been terminated.

Termination by Act of the Parties

An agency may be terminated by act of the parties in any of the following ways:

1. *Lapse of time.* When an agency agreement specifies the time period during which the agency relationship will exist, the agency ends when that time period expires. If no definite time is stated, then the agency continues for a reasonable time and can be terminated at will by either party. What constitutes a "reasonable time" depends, of course, on the circumstances and the nature of the agency relationship.

Beyond Our Borders   **Islamic Law and *Respondeat Superior***

The doctrine of *respondeat superior* is well established in the legal systems of the United States and most Western countries. As you have already read, under this doctrine employers can be held liable for the acts of their agents, including employees. The doctrine of *respondeat superior* is not universal, however. Most Middle Eastern countries, for example, do not follow this doctrine. Islamic law, as codified in the *sharia,* holds to a strict belief that responsibility for human actions lies with the individual and cannot be vicariously extended to others. This belief and other concepts of Islamic law are based on the writings of Muhammad, the seventh-century prophet whose revelations form the basis of the Islamic religion and, by extension, the *sharia.*

Muhammad's prophecies are documented in the Koran (Qur'an), which is the principal source of the *sharia.*

• For Critical Analysis
How would U.S. society be affected if employers could not be held vicariously liable for their employees' torts?

2. *Purpose achieved.* If an agent is employed to accomplish a particular objective, such as the purchase of stock for a cattle rancher, the agency automatically ends after the cattle have been purchased. If more than one agent is employed to accomplish the same purpose, such as the sale of real estate, the first agent to complete the sale automatically terminates the agency relationship for all the others.

3. *Occurrence of a specific event.* When an agency relationship is to terminate on the happening of a certain event, the agency automatically ends when the event occurs. If Posner appoints Rubik to handle her business affairs while she is away, the agency terminates when Posner returns.

4. *Mutual agreement.* The parties to an agency can cancel (rescind) their contract by mutually agreeing to terminate the agency relationship, whether the agency contract is in writing or whether it is for a specific duration.

5. *Termination by one party.* As a general rule, either party can terminate the agency relationship (the act of termination is called *revocation* if done by the principal and *renunciation* if done by the agent). Although both parties have the *power* to terminate the agency, they may not possess the *right.* Wrongful termination can subject the canceling party to a suit for breach of contract. **EXAMPLE 23.22** Rawlins has a one-year employment contract with Munro to act as an agent in return for $65,000. Although Munro has the *power* to discharge Rawlins before the contract period expires, if he does so, he can be sued for breaching the contract because he had no *right* to terminate the agency. •

When an agency has been terminated by act of the parties, it is the principal's duty to inform any third parties who know of the existence of the agency that it has been terminated (although notice of the termination may be given by others). Although an agent's actual authority ends when the agency is terminated, an agent's *apparent authority* continues until the third party receives notice (from any source) that such authority has been terminated. If the principal knows that a third party has dealt with the agent, the principal is expected to notify that person *directly.* For third parties who have heard about the agency but have not yet dealt with the agent, *constructive notice* is sufficient.[19]

No particular form is required for notice of agency termination to be effective. The principal can personally notify the agent, or the agent can learn of the termination through some other means. **EXAMPLE 23.23** Manning bids on a shipment of steel, and Stone is hired as an agent to arrange transportation of the shipment. When Stone learns that Manning has lost the bid, Stone's authority to make the transportation arrangement terminates. • If the agent's authority is written, however, it normally must be revoked in writing.

---

19. *Constructive notice* is information or knowledge of a fact imputed by law to a person if he or she could have discovered the fact by proper diligence. Constructive notice is often accomplished by newspaper publication.

Termination by Operation of Law

Termination of an agency by operation of law occurs in the circumstances discussed here. Note that when an agency terminates by operation of law, there is no duty to notify third persons.

1. *Death or insanity.* The general rule is that the death or mental incompetence of either the principal or the agent automatically and immediately terminates an ordinary agency relationship. Knowledge of the death is not required. **EXAMPLE 23.24** Geer sends Pyron to China to purchase a rare painting. Before Pyron makes the purchase, Geer dies. Pyron's agent status is terminated at the moment of Geer's death, even though Pyron does not know that Geer has died. ● Some states, however, have enacted statutes changing this common law rule to make knowledge of the principal's death a requirement for agency termination.

2. *Impossibility.* When the specific subject matter of an agency is destroyed or lost, the agency terminates. **EXAMPLE 23.25** Bullard employs Gonzalez to sell Bullard's house. Prior to any sale, the house is destroyed by fire. In this situation, Gonzalez's agency and authority to sell Bullard's house terminate. ● Similarly, when it is impossible for the agent to perform the agency lawfully because of a change in the law, the agency terminates.

3. *Changed circumstances.* When an event occurs that has such an unusual effect on the subject matter of the agency that the agent can reasonably infer that the principal will not want the agency to continue, the agency terminates. **EXAMPLE 23.26** Roberts hires Mullen to sell a tract of land for $20,000. Subsequently, Mullen learns that there is oil under the land and that the land is worth $1 million. The agency and Mullen's authority to sell the land for $20,000 are terminated. ●

4. *Bankruptcy.* If either the principal or the agent petitions for bankruptcy, the agency is *usually* terminated. In certain circumstances, as when the agent's financial status is irrelevant to the purpose of the agency, the agency relationship may continue. Insolvency (defined as the inability to pay debts when they become due or when liabilities exceed assets), as distinguished from bankruptcy, does not necessarily terminate the relationship.

5. *War.* When the principal's country and the agent's country are at war with each other, the agency is terminated. In this situation, the agency is automatically suspended or terminated because there is no way to enforce the legal rights and obligations of the parties.

 Reviewing . . . Agency Relationships in Business

Lynne Meyer, on her way to a business meeting and in a hurry, stopped by a Buy-Mart store for a new pair of nylons to wear to the meeting. There was a long line at one of the checkout counters, but a cashier, Valerie Watts, opened another counter and began loading the cash drawer. Meyer told Watts that she was in a hurry and asked Watts to work faster. Watts, however, only slowed her pace. At this point, Meyer hit Watts. It is not clear from the record whether Meyer hit Watts intentionally or, in an attempt to retrieve the nylons, hit her inadvertently. In response, Watts grabbed Meyer by the hair and hit her repeatedly in the back of the head, while Meyer screamed for help. Management personnel separated the two women and questioned them about the incident. Watts was immediately fired for violating the store's no-fighting policy. Meyer subsequently sued Buy-Mart, alleging that the store was liable for the tort (assault and battery) committed by its employee. Using the information presented in the chapter, answer the following questions.

1. Under what doctrine discussed in this chapter might Buy-Mart be held liable for the tort committed by Watts?
2. What is the key factor in determining whether Buy-Mart is liable under this doctrine?
3. How is Buy-Mart's potential liability affected depending on whether Watts's behavior constituted an intentional tort or a tort of negligence?
4. Suppose that when Watts applied for the job at Buy-Mart, she disclosed in her application that she had previously been convicted of felony assault and battery. Nevertheless, Buy-Mart hired Watts as a cashier. How might this fact affect Buy-Mart's liability for Watts's actions?

Business Application

How Can an Employer Use Independent Contractors?*

As an employer, you may at some time consider hiring an independent contractor. Hiring workers as independent contractors instead of as employees may help you reduce both your potential tort liability and your tax liability.

Minimizing Potential Tort Liability

One reason for using an independent contractor is that employers usually are not liable for torts that an independent contractor commits against third parties. Nevertheless, there are exceptions. If an employer exercises significant control over the activities of the independent contractor, for example, the contractor may be considered an employee, and the employer can then be liable for the contractor's torts.

To minimize even the possibility of being liable for the negligence of an independent contractor, you should check the contractor's qualifications before hiring him or her. The degree to which you should investigate depends, of course, on the nature of the work. For example, hiring an independent contractor to maintain the landscaping around your building should require less investigation than employing an independent contractor to install the electrical systems that you sell. Also, a more thorough investigation is necessary when the contractor's activities present a potential danger to the public (as in delivering explosives).

Generally, it is a good idea to have the independent contractor assume, in a written contract, liability for harms caused to third parties by the contractor's negligence. You should also require that the independent contractor purchase liability insurance to cover the costs of potential lawsuits for harms caused to third persons by the contractor's hazardous activities or negligence.

Reducing Tax Liability and Other Costs

Another reason for hiring independent contractors is that you do not need to pay or withhold Social Security, income, or unemployment taxes on their behalf. The independent contractor is responsible for paying these taxes. Additionally, the independent contractor is not eligible for any retirement or medical plans or other fringe benefits that you provide

for yourself and your employees, and this is a cost saving to you. Make sure that your contract with an independent contractor spells out that the contractor is responsible for paying taxes and is not entitled to any employment benefits.

A word of caution, though: simply designating a person as an independent contractor does not make her or him one. The Internal Revenue Service (IRS) will reclassify individuals as employees if it determines that they are "in fact" employees, regardless of how you have designated them. Keep proper documentation of the independent contractor's business identification number, business cards, and letterhead so that you can show the IRS that the contractor works independently.

If you improperly designate an employee as an independent contractor, the penalty may be high. Usually, you will be liable for back Social Security and unemployment taxes, plus interest and penalties. When in doubt, seek professional assistance in such matters.

CHECKLIST FOR THE EMPLOYER

1. **Check the qualifications of any independent contractor you plan to use to reduce the possibility that you might be legally liable for the contractor's negligence.**
2. **Require in any contract with an independent contractor that the contractor assume liability for harm to a third person caused by the contractor's negligence.**
3. **Require that independent contractors carry liability insurance. Examine the policy to make sure that it is current, particularly when the contractor will be undertaking actions that are more than normally hazardous to the public.**
4. **Do not do anything that would lead a third person to believe that an independent contractor is your employee, and do not allow independent contractors to represent themselves as your employees.**
5. **Regularly inspect the work of the independent contractor to make sure that it is being performed in accordance with contract specifications. Such supervision on your part will not change the worker's status as an independent contractor.**

* This *Business Application* is not meant to substitute for the services of an attorney who is licensed to practice law in your state.

 Key Terms

agency 580	fiduciary 581	ratification 585
apparent authority 591	independent contractor 581	*respondeat superior* 595
disclosed principal 592	notary public 590	undisclosed principal 592
e-agent 594	partially disclosed principal 592	vicarious liability 595
equal dignity rule 589	power of attorney 589	

Chapter Summary: Agency Relationships in Business

Agency Relationships (See pages 581–584.)	In a *principal-agent* relationship, an agent acts on behalf of and instead of the principal in dealing with third parties. An employee who deals with third parties is normally an agent. An independent contractor is not an employee, and the employer has no control over the details of physical performance. An independent contractor may or may not be an agent.
How Agency Relationships Are Formed (See pages 584–586.)	Agency relationships may be formed by agreement, by ratification, by estoppel, and by operation of law—see the *Concept Summary* on page 586.
Duties of Agents and Principals (See pages 586–589.)	1. *Duties of the agent*— a. Performance—The agent must use reasonable diligence and skill in performing her or his duties or use the special skills that the agent has represented to the principal that the agent possesses. b. Notification—The agent is required to notify the principal of all matters that come to his or her attention concerning the subject matter of the agency. c. Loyalty—The agent has a duty to act solely for the benefit of the principal and not in the interest of the agent or a third party. d. Obedience—The agent must follow all lawful and clearly stated instructions of the principal. e. Accounting—The agent has a duty to make available to the principal records of all property and funds received and paid out on behalf of the principal. 2. *Duties of the principal*— a. Compensation—Except in a gratuitous agency relationship, the principal must pay the agreed-on value (or reasonable value) for an agent's services. b. Reimbursement and indemnification—The principal must reimburse the agent for all funds disbursed at the request of the principal and for all funds that the agent disburses for necessary expenses in the course of reasonable performance of his or her agency duties. c. Cooperation—A principal must cooperate with and assist an agent in performing her or his duties. d. Safe working conditions—A principal must provide safe working conditions for the agent-employee.
Agent's Authority (See pages 589–592.)	1. *Express authority*—Can be oral or in writing. Authorization must be in writing if the agent is to execute a contract that must be in writing. 2. *Implied authority*—Authority customarily associated with the position of the agent or authority that is deemed necessary for the agent to carry out expressly authorized tasks. 3. *Apparent authority*—Exists when the principal, by word or action, causes a third party reasonably to believe that an agent has authority to act, even though the agent has no express or implied authority. 4. *Ratification*—The affirmation by the principal of an agent's unauthorized action or promise. For the ratification to be effective, the principal must be aware of all material facts.
Liability in Agency Relationships (See pages 592–598.)	1. *Liability for contracts*—If the principal's identity is disclosed or partially disclosed at the time the agent forms a contract with a third party, the principal is liable to the third party under the contract if the agent acted within the scope of his or her authority. If the principal's identity is undisclosed at the time of contract formation, the agent is personally liable to the third party, but if the agent acted within the scope of his or her authority, the principal is also bound by the contract. 2. *Liability for agent's negligence*—Under the doctrine of *respondeat superior,* the principal is liable for any harm caused to another through the agent's torts if the agent was acting within the scope of her or his employment at the time the harmful act occurred. 3. *Liability for agent's intentional torts*—Usually, employers are not liable for the intentional torts that their agents commit, *unless:* a. The acts are committed within the scope of employment, and thus the doctrine of *respondeat superior* applies. b. The employer knows or should know that the employee has a propensity for committing tortious acts. c. The employer allowed an employee to engage in reckless acts that caused injury to another. 4. *Liability for independent contractor's torts*—A principal is not liable for harm caused by an independent contractor's negligence, unless hazardous activities are involved (in this situation, the principal is strictly liable for any resulting harm) or other exceptions apply.

Chapter Summary: Agency Relationships in Business—Continued

Liability in Agency Relationships —Continued	5. *Liability for agent's crimes—*An agent is responsible for his or her own crimes, even if the crimes were committed while the agent was acting within the scope of authority or employment. A principal will be liable for an agent's crime only if the principal participated by conspiracy or other action or (in some jurisdictions) if the agent violated certain government regulations in the course of employment.
How Agency Relationships Are Terminated (See pages 598–600.)	1. *By act of the parties—* Notice to third parties is required when an agency is terminated by act of the parties. Direct notice is required for those who have previously dealt with the agency; constructive notice will suffice for all other third parties. See pages 598–599 for a list of the ways that an agency may be terminated by act of the parties. 2. *By operation of law—* Notice to third parties is not required when an agency is terminated by operation of law. See page 600 for a list of the ways that an agency can be terminated by operation of law.

ExamPrep

ISSUE SPOTTERS

1 Vivian, owner of Wonder Goods Company, employs Xena as an administrative assistant. In Vivian's absence, and without authority, Xena represents herself as Vivian and signs a promissory note in Vivian's name. In what circumstance is Vivian liable on the note?

2 Davis contracts with Estee to buy a certain horse on her behalf. Estee asks Davis not to reveal her identity. Davis makes a deal with Farmland Stables, the owner of the horse, and makes a down payment. Estee does not pay the rest of the price. Farmland Stables sues Davis for breach of contract. Can Davis hold Estee liable for whatever damages he has to pay? Why or why not?

BEFORE THE TEST

Check your answers to the Issue Spotters, and at the same time, take the interactive quiz for this chapter. Go to **www.cengage.com/blaw/blt** and click on "Chapter 23." First, click on "Answers to Issue Spotters" to check your answers. Next, click on "Interactive Quiz" to assess your mastery of the concepts in this chapter. Then click on "Flashcards" to review this chapter's Key Term definitions.

For Review

Answers for the even-numbered questions in this For Review section can be found on this text's accompanying Web site at **www.cengage.com/blaw/blt**. *Select "Chapter 23" and click on "For Review."*

1 What is the difference between an employee and an independent contractor?
2 How do agency relationships arise?
3 What duties do agents and principals owe to each other?
4 When is a principal liable for the agent's actions with respect to third parties? When is the agent liable?
5 What are some of the ways in which an agency relationship can be terminated?

Hypothetical Scenarios and Case Problems

23–1 Ratification by Principal. Springer was a political candidate running for Congress. He was operating on a tight budget and instructed his campaign staff not to purchase any campaign materials without his explicit authorization. In spite of these instructions, one of his campaign workers ordered Dubychek Printing Co. to print some promotional materials for Springer's campaign. When the printed materials arrived, Springer did not return them but instead used them during his campaign. When Springer failed to pay for the materials, Dubychek sued for recovery of the price. Springer contended that he was not liable on the sales contract because he had not authorized his agent to purchase the printing services.

Dubychek argued that the campaign worker was Springer's agent and that the worker had authority to make the printing contract. Additionally, Dubychek claimed that even if the purchase was unauthorized, Springer's use of the materials constituted ratification of his agent's unauthorized purchase. Is Dubychek correct? Explain.

23–2 **Hypothetical Question with Sample Answer** Paul Gett is a well-known, wealthy financial expert living in the city of Torris. Adam Wade, Gett's friend, tells Timothy Brown that he is Gett's agent for the purchase of rare coins. Wade even shows Brown a local newspaper clipping mentioning Gett's interest in coin collecting. Brown, knowing of Wade's friendship with Gett, contracts with Wade to sell a rare coin valued at $25,000 to Gett. Wade takes the coin and disappears with it. On the payment due date, Brown seeks to collect from Gett, claiming that Wade's agency made Gett liable. Gett does not deny that Wade was a friend, but he claims that Wade was never his agent. Discuss fully whether an agency was in existence at the time the contract for the rare coin was made.

—For a sample answer to Question 23–2, go to Appendix E at the end of this text.

23–3 **Employee versus Independent Contractor.** Stephen Hemmerling was a driver for the Happy Cab Co. Hemmerling paid certain fixed expenses and abided by a variety of rules relating to the use of the cab, the hours that could be worked, and the solicitation of fares, among other things. Rates were set by the state. Happy Cab did not withhold taxes from Hemmerling's pay. While driving the cab, Hemmerling was injured in an accident and filed a claim against Happy Cab in a Nebraska state court for workers' compensation benefits. Such benefits are not available to independent contractors. On what basis might the court hold that Hemmerling is an employee? Explain.

23–4 **Liability for Independent Contractor's Torts.** Dean Brothers Corp. owns and operates a steel drum manufacturing plant. Lowell Wyden, the plant superintendent, hired Best Security Patrol, Inc. (BSP), a security company, to guard Dean property and "deter thieves and vandals." Some BSP security guards, as Wyden knew, carried firearms. Pete Sidell, a BSP security guard, was not certified as an armed guard but nevertheless took his gun, in a briefcase, to work. While working at the Dean plant on October 31, 2010, Sidell fired his gun at Tyrone Gaines, in the belief that Gaines was an intruder. The bullet struck and killed Gaines. Gaines's mother filed a lawsuit claiming that her son's death was the result of BSP's negligence, for which Dean was responsible. What is the plaintiff's best argument that Dean is responsible for BSP's actions? What is Dean's best defense? Explain.

23–5 **Case Problem with Sample Answer** Su Ru Chen owned the Lucky Duck Fortune Cookie Factory in Everett, Massachusetts, which made Chinese-style fortune cookies for restaurants. In November 2001, Chen listed the business for sale with Bob Sun, a real estate broker, for $35,000. Sun's daughter Frances and her fiancé, Chiu Chung Chan, decided that Chan would buy the business. Acting as a broker on Chen's (the seller's) behalf, Frances asked about the Lucky

Duck's finances. Chen said that each month the business sold at least 1,000 boxes of cookies at a $2,000 profit. Frances negotiated a price of $23,000, which Chan (her fiancé) paid. When Chan began to operate the Lucky Duck, it became clear that the demand for the cookies was actually about 500 boxes per month—a rate at which the business would suffer losses. Less than two months later, the factory closed. Chan filed a suit in a Massachusetts state court against Chen, alleging fraud, among other things. Chan's proof included Frances's testimony as to what Chen had said to her. Chen objected to the admission of this testimony. What is the basis for this objection? Should the court admit the testimony? Why or why not? [*Chan v. Chen,* 70 Mass.App.Ct. 79, 872 N.E.2d 1153 (2007)]

—After you have answered Problem 23–5, compare your answer with the sample answer given on the Web site that accompanies this text. Go to **www.cengage.com/blaw/blt**, select "Chapter 23," and click on "Case Problem with Sample Answer."

23–6 **Apparent Authority.** Lee Dennegar and Mark Knutson lived in Dennegar's house in Raritan, New Jersey. Dennegar paid the mortgage and other household expenses. With Dennegar's consent, Knutson managed their household's financial affairs and the "general office functions concerned with maintaining the house." Dennegar allowed Knutson to handle the mail and "to do with it as he chose." Knutson wrote checks for Dennegar to sign, although Knutson signed Dennegar's name to many of the checks with Dennegar's consent. AT & T Universal issued a credit card in Dennegar's name in February 2001. Monthly statements were mailed to Dennegar's house, and payments were sometimes made on those statements. Knutson died in June 2003. The unpaid charges on the card of $14,752.93 were assigned to New Century Financial Services, Inc. New Century filed a suit in a New Jersey state court against Dennegar to collect the unpaid amount. Dennegar claimed that he never applied for or used the card and knew nothing about it. Under what theory could Dennegar be liable for the charges? Explain. [*New Century Financial Services, Inc. v. Dennegar,* 394 N.J.Super. 595, 928 A.2d 48 (A.D. 2007)]

23–7 **Undisclosed Principal.** Homeowners Jim and Lisa Criss hired Kevin and Cathie Pappas, doing business as Outside Creations, to undertake a landscaping project. Kevin signed the parties' contract as "Outside Creations Rep." The Crisses' payments on the contract were by checks payable to Kevin, who deposited them in his personal account—there was no Outside Creations account. Later, alleging breach, the Crisses filed a suit in a Georgia state court against the Pappases. The defendants contended that they could not be liable because the contract was not with them personally. They claimed that they were the agents of Forever Green Landscaping and Irrigation, Inc., which had been operating under the name "Outside Creations" at the time of the contract and had since filed for bankruptcy. The Crisses pointed out that the name "Forever Green" was not in the contract. Can the Pappases be liable on this contract? Why or why not? [*Pappas v. Criss,* 296 Ga.App. 803, 676 S.E.2d 21 (2009)]

23-8 **A Question of Ethics** *Emergency One, Inc. (EO), makes fire and rescue vehicles. Western Fire Truck, Inc., contracted with EO to be its exclusive dealer in Colorado and Wyoming through December 2003. James Costello, a Western salesperson, was authorized to order EO vehicles for his customers. Without informing Western, Costello e-mailed EO about Western's difficulties in obtaining cash to fund its operations. He asked about the viability of Western's contract and his possible employment with EO. On EO's request, and in disregard of Western's instructions, Costello sent some payments for EO vehicles directly to EO. In addition, Costello, with EO's help, sent a competing bid to a potential Western customer. EO's representative e-mailed Costello, "You have my permission to kick [Western's] ass." In April 2002, EO terminated its contract with Western, which, after reviewing Costello's e-mail, fired Costello. Western filed a suit in a Colorado state court against Costello and EO, alleging, among other things, that Costello*

breached his duty as an agent and that EO aided and abetted the breach. [Western Fire Truck, Inc. v. Emergency One, Inc., 134 P.3d 570 (Colo.App. 2006)]

1 Was there an agency relationship between Western and Costello? Western required monthly reports from its sales staff, but Costello did not report regularly. Does this indicate that Costello was *not* Western's agent? In determining whether an agency relationship exists, is the *right* to control or the *fact* of control more important? Explain.

2 Did Costello owe Western a duty? If so, what was the duty? Did Costello breach it? How?

3 A Colorado state statute allows a court to award punitive damages in "circumstances of fraud, malice, or willful and wanton conduct." Did any of these circumstances exist in this case? Should punitive damages be assessed against either defendant? Why or why not?

▶ Critical Thinking and Writing Assignments

23-9 Critical Legal Thinking. What policy is served by the law that employers do not have copyright ownership in works created by independent contractors (unless there is a written "work for hire" agreement)?

▶ Practical Internet Exercises

Go to this text's Web site at **www.cengage.com/blaw/blt**, select "Chapter 23," and click on "Practical Internet Exercises." There you will find the following Internet research exercises that you can perform to learn more about the topics covered in this chapter.

Practical Internet Exercise 23–1: LEGAL PERSPECTIVE—Employees or Independent Contractors?
Practical Internet Exercise 23–2: MANAGEMENT PERSPECTIVE—Liability in Agency Relationships

Employment, Immigration, and Labor Law

Chapter Outline

- Employment at Will
- Wage and Hour Laws
- Layoffs
- Family and Medical Leave
- Worker Health and Safety
- Income Security
- Employee Privacy Rights
- Immigration Law
- Labor Unions

(©Photosani, 2009. Used under license from Shutterstock.com)

Learning Objectives

After reading this chapter, you should be able to answer the following questions:

1. What is the employment-at-will doctrine? When and why are exceptions to this doctrine made?

2. What federal statute governs working hours and wages?

3. Under the Family and Medical Leave Act of 1993, in what circumstances may an employee take family or medical leave?

4. What are the two most important federal statutes governing immigration and employment today?

5. What federal statute gave employees the right to organize unions and engage in collective bargaining?

Until the early 1900s, most employer-employee relationships were governed by the common law. Even today, under the common law *employment-at-will doctrine,* private employers generally are free to hire and fire workers at will, unless doing so violates an employee's contractual or statutory rights. (This is one reason why employers generally get the employees they deserve, as the chapter-opening quotation observed.) Now, however, there are numerous statutes and administrative agency regulations that regulate the workplace. Common law doctrines have thus been displaced to a large extent by statutory law.

In this chapter, we look at the most significant laws regulating employment relationships. We will deal with other important laws regulating the workplace—those that prohibit employment discrimination—in the next chapter.

▶ Employment at Will

Employment at Will A common law doctrine under which either party may terminate an employment relationship at any time for any reason, unless a contract specifies otherwise.

Traditionally, employment relationships have generally been governed by the common law doctrine of **employment at will.** Under the employment-at-will doctrine, either party may terminate the employment relationship at any time and for any reason, unless doing so would violate the provisions of an employment contract. The majority of U.S. workers continue to have the legal status of "employees at will." In other words, this common law doctrine is still in widespread use, and only one state (Montana) does not apply the doctrine.

Nonetheless, as mentioned in the chapter introduction, federal and state statutes governing employment relationships prevent this doctrine from being applied in a number of circumstances. Today, an employer is not permitted to fire an employee if doing so would violate a federal or state employment statute, such as one prohibiting employment termination for discriminatory reasons (see Chapter 25). Note that the distinction made under agency law (discussed in Chapter 23) between employee status and independent-contractor status is important here. The employment laws that are discussed in this chapter and in Chapter 25 apply only to the employer-employee relationship; they do not apply to independent contractors.

Exceptions to the Employment-at-Will Doctrine

Under the employment-at-will doctrine, as mentioned, an employer may hire and fire employees at will (regardless of the employees' performance) without liability, unless doing so violates the terms of an employment contract or statutory law. Because of the harsh effects of the employment-at-will doctrine for employees, the courts have carved out various exceptions to the doctrine. These exceptions are based on contract theory, tort theory, and public policy.

> **REMEMBER** An implied contract may exist if a party furnishes a service expecting to be paid, and the other party, who knows (or should know) of this expectation, has a chance to reject the service and does not.

EXCEPTIONS BASED ON CONTRACT THEORY Some courts have held that an *implied* employment contract exists between an employer and an employee. If an employee is fired outside the terms of the implied contract, he or she may succeed in an action for breach of contract even though no written employment contract exists. **EXAMPLE 24.1** BDI Enterprise's employment manual and personnel bulletin both state that, as a matter of policy, workers will be dismissed only for good cause. If an employee reasonably expects BDI to follow this policy, a court may find that there is an implied contract based on the terms stated in the manual and bulletin.[1] ● Generally, the key factor in determining whether an employment manual creates an implied contractual obligation is the employee's reasonable expectations.

An employer's oral promises to employees regarding discharge policy may also be considered part of an implied contract. If the employer fires a worker in a manner contrary to what was promised, a court may hold that the employer has violated the implied contract and is liable for damages. Most state courts will judge a claim of breach of an implied employment contract by traditional contract standards.

Courts in a few states have gone further and held that all employment contracts contain an implied covenant of good faith. This means that both sides promise to abide by the contract in good faith. If an employer fires an employee for an arbitrary or unjustified reason, the employee can claim that the covenant of good faith was breached and the contract violated.

EXCEPTIONS BASED ON TORT THEORY In a few situations, the discharge of an employee may give rise to an action for wrongful discharge under tort theories. Abusive discharge procedures may result in a suit for intentional infliction of emotional distress or defamation. In addition, some courts have permitted workers to sue their employers under the tort theory of fraud. **EXAMPLE 24.2** Goldfinch, Inc., induces a prospective employee to leave a lucrative job and move to another state by offering "a long-term job with a thriving business." In fact, Goldfinch is not only having significant financial problems but is also planning a merger that will result in the elimination of the position offered to the prospective employee. If the employee takes the job in reliance on Goldfinch's representations and

---

1. See, for example, *Ross v. May Co.*, 377 Ill.App.3d 387, 880 N.E.2d 210 (1 Dist. 2007).

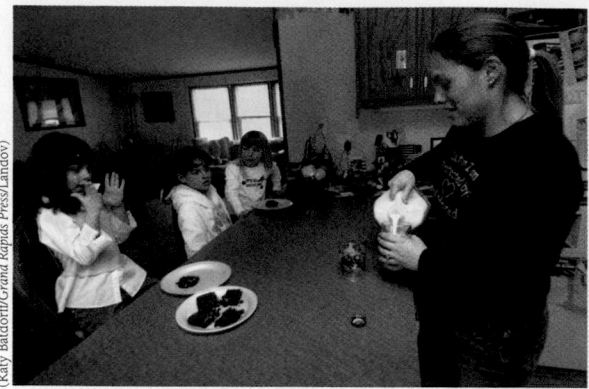

This mother is spending time with her two small children and one of their friends. Working mothers face numerous challenges in attempting to balance family and income-earning activities. The federal Family and Medical Leave Act (FMLA) requires that employees be given up to twelve weeks of unpaid family medical care per year. In some situations, employees are not covered by the FMLA. What is a major limitation on who is covered by the FMLA?

Whistleblowing   An employee's disclosure to government authorities, upper-level managers, or the media that the employer is engaged in unsafe or illegal activities.

Wrongful Discharge   An employer's termination of an employee's employment in violation of the law.

"All I've ever wanted was an honest week's pay for an honest day's work."

Steve Martin, 1945–present
(American actor and comedian)

is fired shortly thereafter, the employee may be able to bring an action against the employer for fraud. ●

EXCEPTIONS BASED ON PUBLIC POLICY   The most common exception to the employment-at-will doctrine is made on the basis of public policy. Courts may apply this exception when an employer fires a worker for reasons that violate a fundamental public policy of the jurisdiction. Generally, the public policy involved must be expressed clearly in the statutory law governing the jurisdiction.

EXAMPLE 24.3   As you will read later in this chapter, employers with fifty or more employees are required by the Family and Medical Leave Act (FMLA) to give employees up to twelve weeks of unpaid family or medical leave per year. Mila's employer, however, has only forty employees and thus is not covered by the federal law. Nonetheless, if Mila is fired from her job because she takes three weeks of unpaid family leave to help her son through a difficult surgery, a court may deem that the employer's actions violated the public policy expressed in the FMLA. ●

An exception may also be made when an employee "blows the whistle" on an employer's wrongdoing. **Whistleblowing** occurs when an employee tells government authorities, upper-level managers, or the media that her or his employer is engaged in some unsafe or illegal activity. Whistleblowers on occasion have been protected from wrongful discharge for reasons of public policy. **CASE EXAMPLE 24.4**   Rebecca Wendeln was the staff coordinator at a nursing home in Nebraska. One of the patients at the home was wheelchair-bound and could be moved only by two persons using a special belt. When Wendeln discovered that the patient had been improperly moved and was injured as a result, she reported the incident to state authorities, as she was required to do by state law. Wendeln's supervisor angrily confronted her about the report, and she was fired shortly after that. Wendeln filed a lawsuit. The court held that although Wendeln was an employee at will, she was protected in this instance from retaliatory firing because a very clear mandate of public policy had been violated.[2] ● Normally, however, whistleblowers seek protection from retaliatory discharge under federal and state statutory laws, such as the Whistleblower Protection Act of 1989.[3]

Wrongful Discharge

Whenever an employer discharges an employee in violation of an employment contract or a statute protecting employees, the employee may bring an action for **wrongful discharge**. Even if an employer's actions do not violate any provisions in an employment contract or a statute, the employer may still be subject to liability under a common law doctrine, such as a tort theory or agency. Note that in today's business world, an employment contract may be established or modified via e-mail exchanges, as discussed in this chapter's *Adapting the Law to the Online Environment* feature.

 Wage and Hour Laws

In the 1930s, Congress enacted several laws regulating the wages and working hours of employees. In 1931, Congress passed the Davis-Bacon Act,[4] which requires contractors and subcontractors working on federal government construction projects to pay "prevailing

---

2. *Wendeln v. The Beatrice Manor, Inc.,* 271 Neb. 373, 712 N.W.2d 226 (2006).
3. 5 U.S.C. Section 1201.
4. 40 U.S.C. Sections 276a–276a-5.

Adapting the Law to the Online Environment

Can Parties Create and Modify Employment Contracts via E-Mail?

E-mail is used in nearly every aspect of the employment environment—from workplace communications to contracts with employees. As you learned in Chapter 12, under the one-year rule of the Statute of Frauds, most employment contracts must be in writing. But electronic communications, including e-mail, instant messages, text messages, and even Twitter, can be used as evidence to show that a contract existed or that the parties modified their contract.

Moreover, although many employment contracts include traditional integration clauses stating that the contract can be modified only by a signed writing, such a clause may not necessarily prevent e-mail modifications. Under the federal E-Sign Act and the Uniform Electronic Transactions Act (both discussed in Chapter 10), what constitutes a signed writing has changed. A court cannot refuse to enforce a contract solely because it is contained in an electronic record, and a name typed at the end of an e-mail can be a signature.

E-Mail Evidence That an Employment Contract Existed

For example, Robert Moroni negotiated a deal to provide consulting services for Medco Health Solutions, Inc., a third party administrator of prescription-drug plans. Medco's agent, Brian Griffin, sent Moroni an e-mail setting forth the details of the parties' agreement. Moroni e-mailed a counteroffer suggesting that he would work on Medco's projects two days a week for thirteen months, in exchange for $17,000 a month ($204,000 annually), plus travel expenses. Medco accepted via e-mail, and Moroni began performing the contract, but Medco refused to pay him. Moroni sued for breach of contract. Medco argued that no enforceable contract existed and that the e-mail showed only an agreement to agree. The court, however, ruled that the e-mail amounted to an agreement to the essential terms of an employment contract.[a]

E-Mail Modifications of Employment Contracts

In another case, Arthur Stevens sold his public relations firm in New York to Publicis, S.A., a French global communications company. (*S.A.*

are the initials for *Société Anonyme,* which is the French equivalent to a corporation in the United States.) The sale involved two contracts: a stock purchase agreement (SPA) and an employment contract. Stevens received an initial payment of more than $3 million under the SPA and stood to receive additional payments of up to $4 million over the next three years, depending on the new company's earnings. The employment contract allowed Stevens to stay on as chief executive officer (CEO) of the new company for three years and contained an integration clause requiring any modification to be in a signed writing.

Within six months of the sale, however, the new company had lost $900,000 and was not meeting revenue and profit targets. Stevens was removed as CEO and given the option of leaving the firm or staying to develop new business. An agent of Publicis, Bob Bloom, then e-mailed Stevens another option, giving him specific information on the responsibilities he could assume. Within a day, Stevens e-mailed a response, "I accept your proposal with total enthusiasm and excitement," and said that he was "psyched" about his new position. Nevertheless, Stevens later sued Publicis, claiming that it had breached the terms of his original employment contract by not keeping him on as CEO. The court, however, held that in the e-mail exchanges, Stevens had accepted the proposed modification of his employment contract in a signed writing. Because the e-mail modification was binding, Stevens could not sue Publicis.[b]

FOR CRITICAL ANALYSIS

Suppose that an employer sends an e-mail to an employee stating that the employee will not be terminated without good cause, but later discharges that employee for no reason. Would that e-mail be sufficient to establish the existence of an employment contract that would allow the employee to sue for damages? Why or why not?

---

a. *Moroni v. Medco Health Solutions, Inc.,* 2008 WL 3539476 (E.D.Mich. 2008).

b. *Stevens v. Publicis, S.A.,* 50 A.D.3d 253, 854 N.Y.S.2d 690 (1 Dept. 2008).

---

wages" to their employees. In 1936, the Walsh-Healey Act[5] was passed. This act requires that a minimum wage, as well as overtime pay at 1.5 times regular pay rates, be paid to employees of manufacturers or suppliers entering into contracts with agencies of the federal government.

In 1938, Congress passed the Fair Labor Standards Act[6] (FLSA). This act extended wage and hour requirements to cover all employers engaged in interstate commerce or in the production of goods for interstate commerce, plus selected types of other businesses. Here, we examine the FLSA's provisions in regard to child labor, maximum hours, and minimum wages.

---

5. 41 U.S.C. Sections 35–45.
6. 29 U.S.C. Sections 201–260.

Child Labor

The FLSA prohibits oppressive child labor. Children under fourteen years of age are allowed to do certain types of work, such as deliver newspapers, work for their parents, and work in the entertainment and (with some exceptions) agricultural areas. Children who are fourteen or fifteen years of age are allowed to work, but not in hazardous occupations. There are also numerous restrictions on how many hours per day (particularly on school days) and per week they can work.

Working times and hours are not restricted for persons between the ages of sixteen and eighteen, but they cannot be employed in hazardous jobs or in jobs detrimental to their health and well-being. None of these restrictions apply to persons over the age of eighteen.

Wages and Hours

Minimum Wage The lowest wage, either by government regulation or union contract, that an employer may pay an hourly worker.

The FLSA provides that a **minimum wage** of a specified amount ($7.25 per hour in 2009) must be paid to employees in covered industries. Congress periodically revises this minimum wage.[7] Under the FLSA, employers who customarily furnish food or lodging to employees can deduct the reasonable cost of those services from the employees' wages.

Under the FLSA, employees who work more than forty hours per week normally must be paid 1.5 times their regular pay for all hours over forty. Note that the FLSA overtime provisions apply only after an employee has worked more than forty hours per *week*. Thus, employees who work for ten hours a day, four days per week, are not entitled to overtime pay because they do not work more than forty hours per week.

Overtime Exemptions

Certain employees—usually executive, administrative, and professional employees, as well as outside salespersons and computer programmers—are exempt from the FLSA's overtime provisions. Employers are not required to pay overtime wages to exempt employees. Employers can voluntarily pay overtime to ineligible employees but cannot waive or reduce the overtime requirements of the FLSA.

"By working faithfully eight hours a day, you may eventually get to be a boss and work twelve hours a day."

Robert Frost, 1875–1963
(American poet)

An executive employee is one whose primary duty is management. An employee's primary duty is determined by what he or she does that is of principal value to the employer, not by how much time the employee spends doing particular tasks. An employer cannot deny overtime wages to an employee based only on the employee's job title, however, and must be able to show that the employee's primary duty qualifies her or him for an exemption.[8]

CASE EXAMPLE 24.5 Starbucks hired Kevin Keevican as a barista (someone who waits on customers, operates the cash register, makes drinks, and cleans and maintains the equipment). Over time, he was promoted to shift supervisor, assistant manager, and then manager. As a manager, Keevican worked 70 hours a week for $650 to $800, a 10 to 20 percent bonus, and fringe benefits, such as paid sick leave, that were not available to baristas. Eventually, Keevican quit and, along with several other former managers, filed a claim against Starbucks for unpaid overtime and other amounts. The plaintiffs admitted that they performed many managerial tasks, but argued that they spent 70 to 80 percent of their time on barista chores and thus were not executive employees. The court, however, found that each plaintiff was "the single highest-ranking employee in his [or her] particular store and was responsible on site for that store's day-to-day overall operations." Therefore, the court

ON THE WEB For more details about the regulations concerning overtime, go to the Web site of the U.S. Department of Labor at **www.dol.gov**.

---

7. Note that many state and local governments also have minimum-wage laws; these laws can provide for higher minimum-wage rates than required by the federal government.

8. See, for example, *Slusser v. Vantage Builders, Inc.,* 576 F.Supp.2d 1207 (D.N.M. 2008).

concluded that each plaintiff's primary duty was management regardless of any other tasks and that Starbucks was not required to pay them overtime.[9] ●

The exemptions to the overtime-pay requirement do not apply to manual laborers or to police, firefighters, licensed nurses, and other public-safety workers. White-collar workers who earn more than $100,000 per year, computer programmers, dental hygienists, and insurance adjusters are typically exempt—though they must also meet certain other criteria.

Ethical Issue ⚖

Should workers get overtime pay for using their BlackBerrys after work hours? Some workers are claiming that they should be paid overtime for the time they spend staying connected to work through their BlackBerrys or other handheld electronic devices. Indeed, many employers require that their employees carry a BlackBerry, iPhone or other smart phone, or PDA (personal digital assistant) to keep in contact. Checking e-mail, responding to text messages, and using other employment-related applications of these handheld devices can be considered work. If employees who are not exempt under the overtime regulations are required to use these devices after office hours, the workers may have a valid claim to overtime wages. In 2009, for example, a maintenance worker in Wisconsin filed a lawsuit against his employer, CB Richard Ellis (CBRE), a property management company. CBRE requires all of its hourly employees to carry BlackBerrys during off hours. The worker is seeking back overtime pay for himself and all the other CBRE employees who are required to carry the device.[10]

ON THE WEB For more information and statistics on employee layoffs in the United States, go to the Mass Layoff Statistics page at the U.S. Bureau of Labor Statistics' Web site at www.bls.gov/mls.

► Layoffs

During the latest economic recession in the United States, hundreds of thousands of workers lost their jobs as many businesses disappeared. Other companies struggling to keep afloat reduced costs by restructuring their operations and downsizing their workforces, which meant layoffs.

Mass layoffs of U.S. workers resulted in high unemployment rates. Later in this chapter, we will discuss unemployment insurance, which helps some workers manage financially until they can find another job. In this section, we discuss the laws pertaining to employee layoffs—an area that is increasingly the subject of litigation.

The Worker Adjustment and Retraining Notification (WARN) Act

Since 1988, federal law has required large employers to provide sixty days' notice before implementing a mass layoff or closing a plant that employs more than fifty full-time workers. The Worker Adjustment and Retraining Notification Act,[11] or WARN Act, applies to employers with at least one hundred full-time employees. It is intended to give workers advance notice so that they can start looking for a new job while they are still employed and to alert state agencies so that they can provide training and other resources for displaced workers.

The WARN Act defines the term *mass layoff* as a reduction in the workforce that, during any thirty-day period, results in an employment loss of either:

1. At least 33 percent of the full-time employees at a single job site *and* at least fifty employees; or
2. At least five hundred full-time employees.

An *employment loss* is defined as a layoff that exceeds six months or a reduction in hours of work of more than 50 percent during each month of any six-month period.

---

9. *Mims v. Starbucks Corp.*, 2007 WL 10369 (S.D.Tex. 2007).
10. "Employee Seeks Class Action in Unpaid Overtime Lawsuit," *The Business Journal of Milwaukee*, March 18, 2009.
11. 29 U.S.C. Sections 2101 *et seq.*

The WARN Act requires that advance notice of the layoff be sent to the affected workers *or* their representative (if the workers are members of a labor union), as well as to state and local government authorities. The state and local authorities are notified so that they can provide resources, such as job training, to displaced workers. Employers must also provide notice to part-time and seasonal employees who are being laid off, even though these workers do not count in determining whether the act's provisions are triggered. Note also that even companies who anticipate filing for bankruptcy normally must provide notice under the WARN Act before implementing a mass layoff.

CRITICISMS AND COMPLIANCE ISSUES   Critics claim that the WARN Act protects too few employees and contains loopholes. Although the U.S. Department of Labor considers a mass layoff to be one that affects fifty or more employees, enforcing the WARN Act rules is not easy. Because the rules depend on the percentage of full-time workers affected at a particular site, employers can avoid the WARN requirements by staggering layoffs over many months or at various locations. Sometimes, employers lay off dozens or even hundreds of workers without having to provide WARN notice. Small employers, of course, never have to provide WARN notice.

REMEDIES FOR WARN ACT VIOLATIONS   If sued, an employer who orders a mass layoff or plant closing in violation of the WARN Act can be fined up to $500 for each day of the violation. Employees can recover back pay for each day of the violation (up to sixty days), plus reasonable attorneys' fees. An employee can also recover benefits under an employee benefit plan, including the cost of medical expenses that would have been covered and were not. Employees who are laid off may also claim that the layoff was in violation of employment discrimination laws (see Chapter 25), if it disproportionately affects members of a protected class, such as minorities, older persons, or women.

State Laws May Also Require Layoff Notices

Many states also have statutes requiring employers to provide notice before initiating mass layoffs, and these laws may have different and even stricter requirements than the WARN Act. In New York, for instance, companies with fifty or more employees must provide ninety days' notice before any layoff that affects twenty-five or more full-time employees. The law in Illinois applies to companies with seventy-five or more employees and requires sixty days' advance notice of any layoff that affects twenty-five or more full-time employees at one plant or 250 employees.

"I stopped carrying a briefcase. I don't like to flaunt my employment."

▶ Family and Medical Leave

In 1993, Congress passed the Family and Medical Leave Act (FMLA)[12] to allow employees to take time off from work for family or medical reasons. A majority of the states also have legislation allowing for a leave from employment for family or medical reasons, and many employers maintain private family-leave plans for their workers. Significant changes to the FMLA regulations that became effective in 2009 created new categories of leave for military caregivers and for qualifying exigencies that arise due to military service.

Coverage and Applicability of the FMLA

The FMLA requires employers who have fifty or more employees to provide employees with up to twelve weeks of unpaid family or medical leave during any twelve-month period. The FMLA expressly covers private and public (government) employees who have worked for

---

12. 29 U.S.C. Sections 2601, 2611–2619, 2651–2654.

A boy leans against his pregnant mother. The mother hopes to take time off from her full-time corporate job when the baby is born. What is required for the Family and Medical Leave Act (FMLA) to apply to her employer? If the employer is covered by the FMLA, how much family leave does the act authorize?

their employers for at least a year.[13] An employee may take *family leave* to care for a newborn baby, an adopted child, or a foster child.[14] An employee can take *medical leave* when the employee or the employee's spouse, child, or parent has a "serious health condition" requiring care.

In addition, an employee caring for a family member with a serious injury or illness incurred as a result of military duty can now take up to *twenty-six weeks of military caregiver leave* within a twelve-month period.[15] Also, an employee can take up to twelve weeks of *qualifying exigency leave* to handle specified *nonmedical* emergencies when a spouse, parent, or child is in, or called to, active military duty.[16] For instance, when a spouse is deployed to Afghanistan, an employee may take exigency leave to arrange for child care or to deal with financial or legal matters.

Benefits and Protections

When an employee takes FMLA leave, the employer must continue the worker's health-care coverage on the same terms as if the employee had continued to work. On returning from FMLA leave, most employees must be restored to their original position or to a comparable position (with nearly equivalent pay and benefits, for example). An important exception allows the employer to avoid reinstating a *key employee*—defined as an employee whose pay falls within the top 10 percent of the firm's workforce.

Employees suffering from addiction to drugs and alcohol pose a special problem under the FMLA. Under what circumstances do days off resulting from the addiction, as opposed to days off for medical treatment in a medical facility, count as part of protected leave? That issue was addressed in the following case.

---

13. Note that changes to the FMLA rules allow employees who have taken a break from their employment to qualify for FMLA leave if they worked a total of twelve months during the previous seven years. See 29 C.F.R. Section 825.110(b)(1-2).

14. The foster care must be state sanctioned before such an arrangement falls within the coverage of the FMLA.

15. 29 C.F.R. Section 825.200.

16. 29 C.F.R. Section 825.126.

Case 24.1   Darst v. Interstate Brands Corp.

United States Court of Appeals, Seventh Circuit, 512 F.3d 903 (2008).

Can FMLA leave for hospitalization mitigate excessive absences that led to the termination of an employee?

FACTS Krzysztof Chalimoniuk worked for Interstate Brands Corporation (IBC) for fifteen years before he was fired for excessive absenteeism. Chalimoniuk, an alcoholic, sought treatment for his condition. He requested leave under the Family and Medical Leave Act (FMLA) from July 29 to August 14, 2000, to deal with the problem. From August 4 to 11, he was hospitalized for treatment of alcohol dependence and withdrawal. When he failed to return to work on August 15, he was fired for being absent. IBC noted that he was also absent from July 29 to August 3, when he was not hospitalized, and those days were counted as improper absences because he was already over the limit for the number of days he could miss under the company's leave policy. Chalimoniuk sued, contending that IBC had violated his FMLA rights. During the course of litigation, Chalimoniuk filed for bankruptcy, and his

claim against IBC became part of the bankruptcy estate. Richard Darst, as trustee for the estate, continued to prosecute the claim. The district court granted summary judgment in favor of IBC. Darst appealed.

ISSUE Was Chalimoniuk entitled to FMLA leave from July 29 through August 3, before he was hospitalized for treatment of alcoholism?

DECISION No. The appeals court affirmed the lower court's ruling. IBC had not violated Chalimoniuk's rights under the FMLA by firing him for excessive absences. FMLA leave covered the days he was receiving medical treatment, but not the days he missed work before and after treatment.

REASON Chalimoniuk was entitled to FMLA leave to obtain treatment for alcoholism, but not because he was incapacitated by his condition and could not, or would not, come to work. Treatment for a serious

Case 24.1–Continues next page ➡

Case 24.1–Continued

health condition qualifies for FMLA leave, but absence from work because of the employee's abuse of a substance does not. Furthermore, contrary to Chalimoniuk's assertion, IBC had the right to determine the dates during which Chalimoniuk was to receive treatment for alcoholism. The employer is allowed this right unless it interferes with or denies the worker's exercise of his or her rights under the FMLA.

FOR CRITICAL ANALYSIS—Ethical Consideration   *Did IBC take unfair advantage of the "letter of the law" by not granting Chalimoniuk a little more leave time, given that he was dealing with his problem? Explain your answer.*

Violations of the FMLA

An employer that violates the FMLA can be required to provide various remedies, including (1) damages to compensate an employee for lost benefits, denied compensation, and actual monetary losses (such as the cost of providing for care of the family member) up to an amount equivalent to the employee's wages for twelve weeks (twenty-six weeks for military caregiver leave); (2) job reinstatement; and (3) promotion, if a promotion has been denied. A successful plaintiff is entitled to court costs; attorneys' fees; and, in cases involving bad faith on the part of the employer, two times the amount of damages awarded by a judge or jury. Supervisors can also be held personally liable, as employers, for violations of the act.

Employers generally are required to notify employees when an absence will be counted against leave authorized under the act. If an employer fails to provide such notice, and the employee consequently suffers an injury because he or she did not receive notice, the employer may be sanctioned.[17]

 ON THE WEB An excellent Web site for information on employee benefits—including the full text of relevant statutes, such as the FMLA and COBRA, as well as case law and current articles—is BenefitsLink. Go to **www.benefitslink. com/index.shtml**.

▶ Worker Health and Safety

Under the common law, employees who were injured on the job had to file lawsuits against their employers to obtain recovery. Today, numerous state and federal statutes protect employees and their families from the risk of accidental injury, death, or disease resulting from their employment. This section discusses the primary federal statute governing health and safety in the workplace, along with state workers' compensation laws.

The Occupational Safety and Health Act

At the federal level, the primary legislation protecting employees' health and safety is the Occupational Safety and Health Act of 1970,[18] which is administered by the Occupational Safety and Health Administration (OSHA). Congress passed this act in an attempt to ensure safe and healthful working conditions for practically every employee in the country. The act imposes on employers a general duty to keep workplaces safe. To this end, OSHA has established specific safety standards that employers must follow depending on the industry. For instance, OSHA regulations require the use of safety guards on certain mechanical equipment and set maximum exposure levels to substances in the workplace that may be harmful to a worker's health.

The act also imposes record-keeping and reporting requirements and requires that employers post certain notices in the workplace. OSHA compliance officers may enter and

---

17. *Ragsdale v. Wolverine World Wide, Inc.*, 535 U.S. 81, 122 S.Ct. 1155, 152 L.Ed.2d 167 (2002).
18. 29 U.S.C. Sections 553, 651–678.

inspect facilities of any establishment covered by the Occupational Safety and Health Act.[19] Employees may also file complaints of violations and cannot be fired by their employers for doing so. Employers with eleven or more employees are required to keep occupational injury and illness records for each employee. Each record must be made available for inspection when requested by an OSHA inspector.

ON THE WEB   A good source for information relating to workplace health and safety is OSHA's Web site. Go to www.osha.gov.

Whenever a work-related injury or disease occurs, employers must make reports directly to OSHA. If an employee dies or five or more employees are hospitalized, the employer must notify the U.S. Department of Labor within forty-eight hours. A company that fails to do so will be fined. Following the accident, a complete inspection of the premises is mandatory. Criminal penalties for willful violation of the Occupational Safety and Health Act are limited. Employers may also be prosecuted under state laws, however. In other words, the act does not preempt state and local criminal laws.[20]

State Workers' Compensation Laws

Workers' Compensation Laws   State statutes establishing an administrative procedure for compensating workers for injuries that arise out of—or in the course of—their employment, regardless of fault.

State **workers' compensation laws** establish an administrative procedure for compensating workers injured on the job. Instead of suing, an injured worker files a claim with the administrative agency or board that administers local workers' compensation claims.

Most workers' compensation statutes are similar. No state covers all employees. Typically, domestic workers, agricultural workers, temporary employees, and employees of common carriers (companies that provide transportation services to the public) are excluded, but minors are covered. Usually, the statutes allow employers to purchase insurance from a private insurer or a state fund to pay workers' compensation benefits in the event of a claim. Most states also allow employers to be self-insured—that is, employers that show an ability to pay claims do not need to buy insurance.

This former employee of Quality Pork Processors believed that she had contracted a neurological illness while working at the processing plant, and she filed a workers' compensation claim. Her claim was approved. What are the requirements for receiving workers' compensation benefits?

REQUIREMENTS FOR RECEIVING WORKERS' COMPENSATION   In general, the only requirements to recover benefits under state workers' compensation laws are:

1. The existence of an employment relationship; and
2. An *accidental* injury that *occurred on the job or in the course of employment,* regardless of fault. (If an injury occurs while an employee is commuting to or from work, it usually will not be considered to have occurred on the job or in the course of employment and hence will not be covered.)

An injured employee must notify her or his employer promptly (usually within thirty days of the accident). Generally, an employee must also file a workers' compensation claim with the appropriate state agency or board within a certain period (sixty days to two years) from the time the injury is first noticed, rather than from the time of the accident.

WORKERS' COMPENSATION VERSUS LITIGATION   An employee's acceptance of workers' compensation benefits bars the employee from suing for injuries caused by the employer's negligence. By barring lawsuits for negligence, workers' compensation laws also

---

19. Initially, warrantless inspections were conducted. In 1978, however, the United States Supreme Court held that warrantless inspections violated the warrant clause of the Fourth Amendment to the U.S. Constitution. See *Marshall v. Barlow's, Inc.,* 436 U.S. 307, 98 S.Ct. 1816, 56 L.Ed.2d 305 (1978).

20. *Pedraza v. Shell Oil Co.,* 942 F.2d 48 (1st Cir. 1991); *cert.* denied, *Shell Oil Co. v. Pedraza,* 502 U.S. 1082, 112 S.Ct. 993, 117 L.Ed.2d 154 (1992).

prevent employers from raising common law defenses to negligence, such as contributory negligence, assumption of risk, or injury caused by a "fellow servant" (another employee). A worker may sue an employer who *intentionally* injures the worker, however.

▶ Income Security

Federal and state governments participate in insurance programs designed to protect employees and their families by covering the financial impact of retirement, disability, death, hospitalization, and unemployment. The key federal law on this subject is the Social Security Act of 1935.[21]

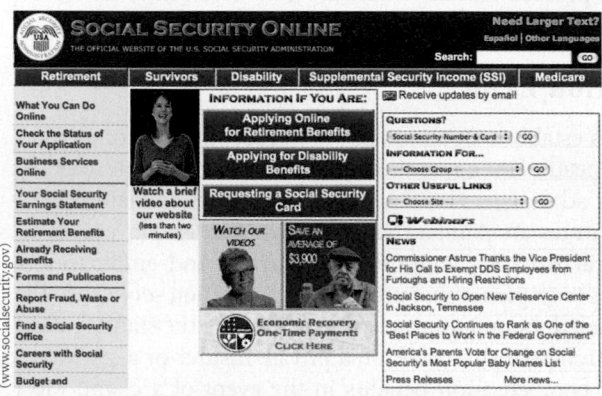

(www.socialsecurity.gov)

This is the home page of the Social Security Administration. Who might wish to consult this Web site?

NOTE Social Security covers almost all jobs in the United States. Nine out of ten workers "contribute" to this protection for themselves and their families.

Social Security

The Social Security Act provides for old-age (retirement), survivors', and disability insurance. The act is therefore often referred to as OASDI. Both employers and employees must "contribute" under the Federal Insurance Contributions Act (FICA)[22] to help pay for benefits that will partially make up for the employees' loss of income on retirement.

The basis for the employee's and the employer's contributions is the employee's annual wage base—the maximum amount of the employee's wages that are subject to the tax. The employer withholds the employee's FICA contribution from the employee's wages and then matches this contribution. (In 2009, employers were required to withhold 6.2 percent of each employee's wages, up to a maximum wage base of $106,800, and to match this contribution.)

Retired workers are then eligible to receive monthly payments from the Social Security Administration, which administers the Social Security Act. Social Security benefits are fixed by statute but increase automatically with increases in the cost of living.

Medicare

Medicare, a federal government health-insurance program, is administered by the Social Security Administration for people sixty-five years of age and older and for some under the age of sixty-five who are disabled. It originally had two parts, one pertaining to hospital costs and the other to nonhospital medical costs, such as visits to physicians' offices. Medicare now offers additional coverage options and a prescription-drug plan. People who have Medicare hospital insurance can also obtain additional federal medical insurance if they pay small monthly premiums, which increase as the cost of medical care increases.

As with Social Security contributions, both the employer and the employee "contribute" to Medicare, but unlike Social Security, there is no cap on the amount of wages subject to the Medicare tax. In 2009, both the employer and the employee were required to pay 1.45 percent of *all* wages and salaries to finance Medicare. Thus, for Social Security and Medicare together, in 2009 the employer and the employee each paid 7.65 percent of the first $106,800 of income (6.2 percent for Social Security + 1.45 percent for Medicare) for a combined total of 15.3 percent. In addition, all wages and salaries above $106,800 were taxed at a combined (employer and employee) rate of 2.9 percent for Medicare. Self-employed persons pay both the employer and the employee portions of the Social Security

---

21. 42 U.S.C. Sections 301–1397e.
22. 26 U.S.C. Sections 3101–3125.

and Medicare taxes (15.3 percent of income up to $106,800 and 2.9 percent of income above that amount in 2009).

Private Pension Plans

The major federal act regulating employee retirement plans is the Employee Retirement Income Security Act (ERISA) of 1974.[23] This act empowers a branch of the U.S. Department of Labor to enforce its provisions governing employers who have private pension funds for their employees. ERISA created the Pension Benefit Guaranty Corporation (PBGC), an independent federal agency, to provide timely and uninterrupted payment of voluntary private pension benefits. The pension plans pay annual insurance premiums (at set rates adjusted for inflation) to the PBGC, which then pays benefits to participants in the event that a plan is unable to do so. Under the Pension Protection Act of 2006,[24] the director of the PBGC is appointed by the president and confirmed by the U.S. Senate.

ERISA does not require an employer to establish a pension plan. When a plan exists, however, ERISA specifies standards for its management. A key provision of ERISA concerns vesting. **Vesting** gives an employee a legal right to receive pension benefits at some future date when he or she stops working. Before ERISA was enacted, some employees who had worked for companies for as long as thirty years received no pension benefits when their employment terminated, because those benefits had not vested. ERISA establishes complex vesting rules. Generally, however, all employee contributions to pension plans vest immediately, and employee rights to employer contributions to a plan vest after five years of employment.

In an attempt to prevent mismanagement of pension funds, ERISA has established rules on how they must be invested. Pension managers must be cautious in choosing investments and must diversify the plan's investments to minimize the risk of large losses. ERISA also imposes detailed record-keeping and reporting requirements.

Vesting The creation of an absolute or unconditional right or power.

Unemployment Insurance

Long lines of those searching for employment are often seen in front of so-called job fairs throughout the country. When they become unemployed, do the formerly employed workers receive payments from the federal government or the state government?

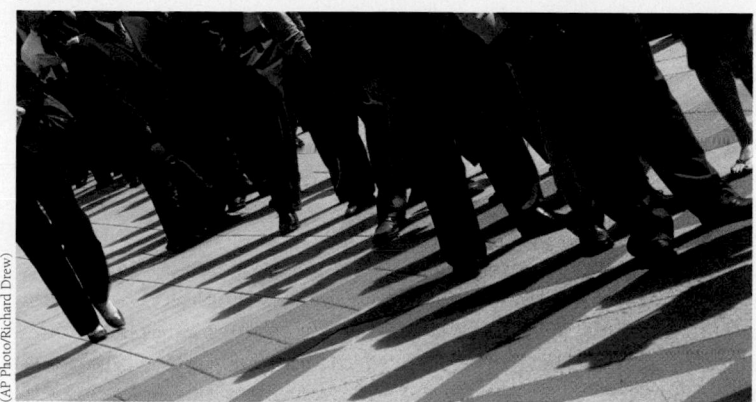

(AP Photo/Richard Drew)

To ease the financial impact of unemployment, the United States has a system of unemployment insurance. The Federal Unemployment Tax Act (FUTA) of 1935[25] created a state-administered system that provides unemployment compensation to eligible individuals. Under this system, employers pay into a fund, and the proceeds are paid out to qualified unemployed workers. The FUTA and state laws require employers that fall under the provisions of the act to pay unemployment taxes at regular intervals.

To be eligible for unemployment compensation, a worker must be willing and able to work. Workers who have been fired for misconduct or who have voluntarily left their jobs are not eligible for benefits. In the past, workers had to be actively seeking employment to continue receiving benefits. Due to the high unemployment rates in 2009, however, President Barack Obama announced new measures that allow jobless persons

---

23. 29 U.S.C. Sections 1001 *et seq.*
24. The Pension Protection Act amended 26 U.S.C. Sections 430–432, 436, 4966, 4967, 6039I, 6050U, 6050V, 6695A, 6720B, 7443B; and 29 U.S.C. Sections 1082–1085, 1202a.
25. 26 U.S.C. Sections 3301–3310.

WATCH OUT If an employer does not pay unemployment taxes, a state government can place a lien (claim) on the business's property to secure the debt. (Liens were discussed in Chapter 21.)

to retain their unemployment benefits while pursuing additional education and training (rather than seeking employment).

COBRA

For workers whose jobs have been terminated—and who are thus no longer eligible for group health-insurance plans—federal law also provides a right to continue their health-care coverage. The Consolidated Omnibus Budget Reconciliation Act (COBRA) of 1985[26] prohibits an employer from eliminating a worker's medical, optical, or dental insurance on the voluntary or involuntary termination of the worker's employment. Employers, with some exceptions, must inform an employee of COBRA's provisions when that worker faces termination or a reduction of hours that would affect his or her eligibility for coverage under the plan. Only workers fired for gross misconduct are excluded from protection.

PROCEDURES A worker has sixty days (beginning with the date that the group coverage would stop) to decide whether to continue with the employer's group insurance plan. If the worker chooses to discontinue the coverage, the employer has no further obligation. If the worker chooses to continue coverage, though, the employer is obligated to keep the policy active for up to eighteen months (or twenty-nine months if the worker is disabled). The coverage provided must be the same as that enjoyed by the worker prior to the termination or reduction of work. If family members were originally included, for instance, COBRA prohibits their exclusion.

PAYMENT The worker does not receive the insurance coverage for free, however. Generally, an employer can require the employee to pay all of the premiums, plus a 2 percent administrative charge. In 2009, however, the law was changed to provide for certain workers who involuntarily lost their jobs between September 2008 and December 2009.[27] For these employees, the employer can only require the worker to pay up to 35 percent of the premiums. The employer is reimbursed for the remaining 65 percent of the premiums through a tax credit.

If the worker fails to pay the required amount of the premiums (or if the employer completely eliminates its group benefit plan), the employer is relieved of further responsibility. An employer that does not comply with COBRA risks substantial penalties, such as a tax of up to 10 percent of the annual cost of the group plan or $500,000, whichever is less.

Employer-Sponsored Group Health Plans

The Health Insurance Portability and Accountability Act (HIPAA),[28] which was discussed in Chapter 2 in the context of privacy protections, contains provisions that affect employer-sponsored group health plans. HIPAA does not require employers to provide health insurance, but it does establish requirements for those that do provide such coverage. For instance, HIPAA strictly limits an employer's ability to exclude coverage for *preexisting conditions,* except pregnancy.

In addition, HIPAA restricts the manner in which covered employers collect, use, and disclose the health information of employees and their families. Employers must train employees, designate privacy officials, and distribute privacy notices to ensure that employees' health information is not disclosed to unauthorized parties. Failure to comply with HIPAA regulations can result in civil penalties of up to $100 per person per violation (with

---

26. 29 U.S.C. Sections 1161–1169.
27. These changes were made by the American Recovery and Reinvestment Act (ARRA) of 2009, Pub. L. No. 111-5, 123 Stat. 115 (February 17, 2009).
28. 29 U.S.C.A. Sections 1181 *et seq.*

a cap of $25,000 per year). The employer is also subject to criminal prosecution for certain types of HIPAA violations and can face up to $250,000 in criminal fines and imprisonment for up to ten years if convicted.

▶ Employee Privacy Rights

In the last thirty years, concerns about the privacy rights of employees have arisen in response to the sometimes invasive tactics used by employers to monitor and screen workers. Perhaps the greatest privacy concern in today's employment arena has to do with electronic performance monitoring.

Electronic Monitoring in the Workplace

According to a survey by the American Management Association, more than half of employers engage in some form of surveillance of their employees. Types of monitoring include reviewing employees' e-mail, blogs, instant messages, Twitters, Internet use, and computer files; video recording of employee job performance; and recording and reviewing telephone conversations, voice mail, and text messages. (See the *Business Application* feature at the end of this chapter for a discussion of how employers should develop an Internet policy for the workplace.)

Employers are increasingly using sophisticated surveillance systems to monitor their employees' conduct in the workplace. What legitimate interests might employers have for using surveillance cameras?

("Redjar"/Creative Commons)

Various specially designed software products have made it easier for employers to track employees' Internet use, including the specific Web sites visited and the time spent surfing the Web. Indeed, inappropriate Web surfing seems to be a primary concern for employers. More than 75 percent of them are monitoring workers' Web connections. Filtering software, which was discussed in Chapter 2, is also being used to prevent employees from accessing certain Web sites, such as sites containing pornographic or sexually explicit images. Private employers generally are free to use filtering software to block access to certain Web sites because the First Amendment's protection of free speech prevents only *government employers* from restraining speech by blocking Web sites.

EMPLOYEE PRIVACY RIGHTS UNDER CONSTITUTIONAL AND TORT LAW

Recall from Chapter 2 that the U.S. Constitution does not contain a provision that explicitly guarantees a right to privacy. A personal right to privacy, however, has been inferred from other constitutional guarantees provided by the First, Third, Fourth, Fifth, and Ninth Amendments to the Constitution. Tort law (see Chapter 4), state constitutions, and a number of state and federal statutes also provide for privacy rights.

When determining whether an employer should be held liable for violating an employee's privacy rights, the courts generally weigh the employer's interests against the employee's reasonable expectation of privacy. Normally, if employees have been informed that their communications are being monitored, they cannot reasonably expect those communications to be private. If employees are not informed that certain communications are being monitored, however, the employer may be held liable for invading their privacy. For this reason, most employers notify their employees about electronic monitoring.

Nevertheless, establishing general policies or notifying employees about e-mail monitoring may not sufficiently protect an employer who monitors text messages or other forms of communications not specifically mentioned. (For an example of a situation in which a general e-mail policy did not protect the employer, see Case Example 24.6 on the next page.)

ON THE WEB The American Civil Liberties Union (ACLU) has a page on its Web site devoted to employee privacy rights with respect to electronic monitoring. Go to www.aclu.org/privacy/workplace/index.html.

THE ELECTRONIC COMMUNICATIONS PRIVACY ACT   Employers must comply with the Electronic Communications Privacy Act (ECPA) of 1986.[29] This act amended existing federal wiretapping law to cover electronic forms of communications, such as communications via cell phones or e-mail. The ECPA prohibits the intentional interception of any wire or electronic communication and the intentional disclosure or use of the information obtained by the interception. Excluded from coverage, however, are any electronic communications through devices that are "furnished to the subscriber or user by a provider of wire or electronic communication service" and that are being used by the subscriber or user, or by the provider of the service, "in the ordinary course of its business."

This "business-extension exception" to the ECPA permits employers to monitor employees' electronic communications made in the ordinary course of business. It does not, however, permit employers to monitor employees' personal communications. Under another exception to the ECPA, however, an employer may avoid liability under the act if the employees consent to having their electronic communications intercepted by the employer. Thus, an employer may be able to avoid liability under the ECPA by requiring employees to sign forms indicating that they consent to the monitoring of personal as well as business communications.

STORED COMMUNICATIONS   Part of the ECPA is known as the Stored Communications Act (SCA).[30] The SCA prohibits intentional and unauthorized access to *stored* electronic communications and sets forth criminal and civil sanctions for violators. A person can violate the SCA by intentionally accessing a stored electronic communication or by intentionally exceeding the authorization given to access the communication.

CASE EXAMPLE 24.6   Arch Wireless Operating Company contracted with the city of Ontario, California, to provide wireless text-messaging services via two-way alphanumeric pagers. The city distributed the pagers to its employees, including Police Sergeant Jeff Quon. The city had a general policy concerning the use of computers, Internet, and e-mail, which stated that these should not be used for personal matters and that any communications were not confidential. The policy did not expressly mention the pagers or text messaging, however.

Under the city's contract with Arch Wireless, each pager was allotted 25,000 characters, after which the city was required to pay overage charges. If an employee exceeded the character limit, the city asked the employee to pay the overage charges. Quon had exceeded the limit on several occasions and had paid overage charges for text messaging on his pager. Without Quon's knowledge, his supervisors requested transcripts of his stored text messages from Arch Wireless and read them to determine whether the texts were exclusively work related or personal. When Quon found out that the city had read his personal (and sexually explicit) text messages to his wife, he filed a lawsuit against the city and Arch Wireless for violating his privacy rights. Although the lower court found in the defendants' favor, Quon won on appeal. The federal appellate court ruled that Quon had a reasonable expectation of privacy with regard to text messages that were temporarily stored by Arch Wireless, a third party provider. Quon's text messages were protected from the employer, and Arch Wireless should not have accessed them and provided transcripts to the city without his authorization.[31] ●

> *"We are rapidly entering the age of no privacy, where everyone is open to surveillance at all times; where there are no secrets."*
> William O. Douglas, 1898–1980
> (Associate justice of the United States Supreme Court, 1939–1975)

---

29. 18 U.S.C. Sections 2510–2521.

30. 18 U.S.C. Sections 2701–2711.

31. *Quon v. Arch Wireless Operating Co.,* 529 F.3d 892 (9th Cir. 2008); rehearing denied, 554 F.3d 769 (9th Cir. 2009).

Preventing Legal Disputes

To avoid legal disputes, exercise caution when monitoring employees and make sure that any monitoring is conducted in a reasonable place and manner. Establish written policies that include all types of electronic devices used by your employees, and notify employees of how and when they may be monitored on these devices. Consider informing employees of the reasons for the monitoring. Explain what the concern is, what job repercussions could result, and what recourse employees have in the event that a negative action is taken against them. By providing more privacy protection to employees than is legally required, you can both avoid potential privacy complaints and give employees a sense that they retain some degree of privacy in their workplace, which can lead to greater job satisfaction.

Other Types of Monitoring

In addition to monitoring their employees' online activities, employers also engage in other types of employee screening and monitoring. These practices, which have included lie-detector tests, drug tests, genetic testing, and employment screening, have often been subject to challenge as violations of employee privacy rights.

LIE-DETECTOR TESTS At one time, many employers required employees or job applicants to take lie-detector (polygraph) tests in connection with their employment. In 1988, Congress passed the Employee Polygraph Protection Act,[32] which generally prohibits employers from requiring or causing employees or job applicants to take lie-detector tests or suggesting or requesting that they do so. The act also restricts employers' ability to use or ask about the results of any lie-detector test or to take any negative employment action based on the results.

Employers excepted from these prohibitions include federal, state, and local government employers; certain security service firms; and companies manufacturing and distributing controlled substances. Other employers may use lie-detector tests when investigating losses attributable to theft, including embezzlement and the theft of trade secrets.

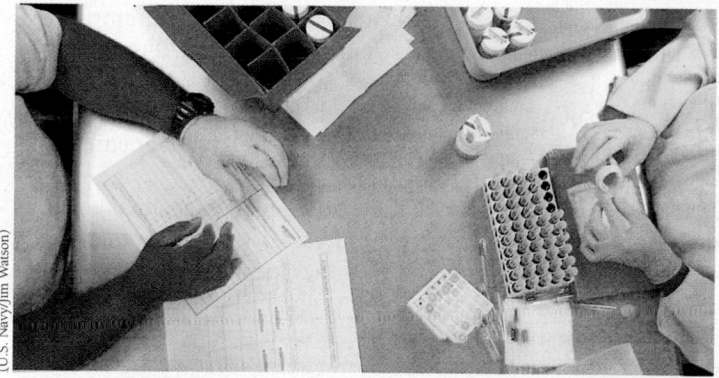

(U.S. Navy/Jim Watson)

Workers at a toxicology lab place employees' urine samples in barcoded test tubes before screening the samples for drugs. Many private employers today routinely require their employees to submit to drug testing. What recourse, if any, does an employee who does not consent to a drug test have against the employer?

DRUG TESTING In the interests of public safety, many employers, including the government, require their employees to submit to drug testing. Government (public) employers are constrained in drug testing by the Fourth Amendment to the U.S. Constitution, which prohibits unreasonable searches and seizures (see Chapter 6). Drug testing of public employees is allowed by statute for transportation workers and is normally upheld by the courts when drug use in a particular job may threaten public safety. Also, when there is a reasonable basis for suspecting government employees of using drugs, courts often find that drug testing does not violate the Fourth Amendment.

The Fourth Amendment does not apply to drug testing conducted by private employers. Hence, the privacy rights and drug testing of private-sector employees are governed by state law, which varies widely. Many states have statutes that allow drug testing by private employers but place restrictions on when and how the testing may be performed. A collective bargaining agreement may also provide protection against drug testing (or authorize drug testing under certain conditions). The permissibility of a private employer's drug tests typically hinges

32. 29 U.S.C. Sections 2001 *et seq.*

on the determination of whether the testing was reasonable. Random drug tests and even "zero-tolerance" policies (that deny a "second chance" to employees who test positive for drugs) have been held to be reasonable.[33]

GENETIC TESTING   A serious privacy issue arose when some employers began conducting genetic testing of employees or prospective employees in an effort to identify individuals who might develop significant health problems in the future. To date, however, only a few cases involving this issue have come before the courts. **CASE EXAMPLE 24.7** Lawrence Berkeley Laboratory screened prospective employees for the gene that causes sickle-cell anemia, although the applicants were not informed of this. In a lawsuit subsequently brought by the prospective employees, a federal appellate court held that they had a cause of action for violation of their privacy rights.[34] The case was later settled for $2.2 million. ●

To prevent the improper use of genetic information in employment and health insurance, in 2008 Congress passed the Genetic Information Nondiscrimination Act (GINA).[35] Under GINA, employers cannot make decisions about hiring, firing, job placement, or promotion based on the results of genetic testing. GINA also prohibits group health plans and insurers from denying coverage or charging higher premiums based solely on a genetic predisposition to developing a specific disease in the future.

SCREENING PROCEDURES   Preemployment screening procedures are another area of concern to potential employees. What kinds of questions are permissible on an employment application or a preemployment test? What kinds of questions go too far in invading the applicant's privacy? Is it an invasion of privacy, for example, to ask questions about the prospective employee's sexual orientation or religious convictions? Generally, questions on an employment application must have a reasonable nexus, or connection, with the job for which the person is applying.

Another issue that has arisen with employment screening involves health-risk-assessment and wellness programs. Many employers today, mindful of the rising cost of health care, are assessing their employees' overall health and instituting mandatory wellness programs at the workplace. Some of these programs require health exams and record employees' weight, blood sugar, blood pressure, cholesterol levels, and tobacco use. Other programs require employees to participate in health-risk assessments to get health-insurance coverage or charge them higher premiums if they refuse to take part in health-risk assessments. Some employers have banned tobacco use both on and off the job, and test their employees for nicotine.

> **KEEP IN MIND** An employer may act on the basis of any professionally developed test, provided the test relates to the employment and does not violate the law.

Employers clearly have an economic interest in having their employees maintain healthful lifestyles and implementing mandatory wellness and health assessment programs. These efforts can be legally problematic, however, particularly if they penalize employees who fail to meet health goals. Employees can claim that these programs violate their privacy rights.[36] Although the courts have not yet decided many cases alleging privacy violations from health screening, litigation in this area is expected to increase. These programs may also violate the Americans with Disabilities Act (ADA, which will be discussed in Chapter 25) if employers discriminate against persons with, say, diabetes or obesity. In addition, a number of states have passed lifestyle discrimination laws that prohibit employers from taking adverse employment action against employees for lawful conduct outside of work.

---

33. See, for example, *CITGO Asphalt Refining Co. v. Paper, Allied-Industrial, Chemical, and Energy Workers International Union Local No. 2-991,* 385 F.3d 809 (3d Cir. 2004).

34. *Norman-Bloodsaw v. Lawrence Berkeley Laboratory,* 135 F.3d 1260 (9th Cir. 1998).

35. 26 U.S.C. Section 9834; 42 U.S.C. Sections 300gg-53, 1320d-9, 2000ff-1 to 2000ff-11.

36. See, for example, *Anderson v. City of Taylor,* 2006 WL 1984104 (E.D.Mich. 2006).

▶ Immigration Law

"Immigration is the sincerest form of flattery."

Jack Paar, 1918–2004
(American entertainer)

The United States had no laws restricting immigration until the late nineteenth century. Today, the most important laws governing immigration and employment are the Immigration Reform and Control Act (IRCA) of 1986[37] and the Immigration Act of 1990.[38] The IRCA provided amnesty to certain groups of illegal aliens then living in the United States and also established a system that sanctions employers who hire illegal immigrants lacking work authorization. As immigration has grown in recent years, an understanding of the related legal requirements for business has become increasingly important. Employers must take steps to avoid hiring illegal immigrants or face serious penalties.

There are an estimated 11 to 12 million illegal immigrants living and usually working in the United States today. Some of these Latino workers in Washington State, shown here, are in the United States legally, and others are not. What to do about illegal immigrants is a political hot potato. Some believe that all illegal immigrants should be given amnesty and a chance to become citizens. Others believe that they should all be arrested and returned to their countries of origin. What are the roadblocks against the latter solution?

I-9 Verification   A process that all employers in the United States must perform within three business days of hiring a new worker to verify the employment eligibility and identity of the worker by completing an I-9 Employment Eligibility Verification form.

Immigration Reform and Control Act (IRCA)

An estimated 11 to 12 million illegal immigrants live in the United States today and are the subject of considerable controversy. The IRCA makes it illegal to hire, recruit, or refer for a fee someone not authorized to work in this country. The federal government—through Immigration and Customs Enforcement officers—conducts random compliance audits and engages in enforcement actions against employers who hire illegal immigrants. This section sets out the compliance requirements for employers.

I-9 Employment Verification   To comply with current law (based on the 1986 act), an employer must perform **I-9 verifications** for new hires, including those hired as "contractors" or "day workers" if they work under the employer's direct supervision. Form I-9, Employment Eligibility Verification, which is available from U.S. Citizenship and Immigration Services,[39] must be completed within three days of a worker's commencement of employment. The three-day period is to allow the employer to check the form's accuracy and to review and verify documents establishing the prospective worker's identity and eligibility for employment in the United States.

The employer must attest, under penalty of perjury, that an employee produced documents establishing his or her identity and legal employability. Acceptable documents include a U.S. passport establishing the person's citizenship or a document authorizing a foreign citizen to work in the United States, such as a Permanent Resident Card or an Alien Registration Receipt (discussed on page 625).

Note that most legal actions alleging violations of I-9 rules are brought against employees. An employee must state that she or he is a U.S. citizen or otherwise authorized to work in the United States. If the employee enters false information on an I-9 form or presents false documentation, the employer can fire the worker, who then may be subject to deportation.

---

37. 29 U.S.C. Section 1802.
38. This act amended various provisions of the Immigration and Nationality Act of 1952, 8 U.S.C. Sections 1101 *et seq.*
39. U.S. Citizenship and Immigration Services is a federal agency that is part of the U.S. Department of Homeland Security.

The IRCA prohibits "knowing" violations, including situations in which an employer "should have known" that the worker was unauthorized. Good faith is a defense under the statute, and employers are legally entitled to rely on a document authorizing a person to work that reasonably appears on its face to be genuine, even if it is later established to be counterfeit.

ENFORCEMENT   U.S. Immigration and Customs Enforcement (ICE) was established in 2003 as the largest investigative arm of the U.S. Department of Homeland Security. ICE has a general inspection program that conducts random compliance audits. Other audits may occur if the agency receives a written complaint alleging an employer's violations. Government inspections include a review of an employer's file of I-9 forms. The government does not need a subpoena or a warrant to conduct such an inspection.

If an investigation reveals a possible violation, ICE will bring an administrative action and issue a Notice of Intent to Fine, which sets out the charges against the employer. The employer has a right to a hearing on the enforcement action if it files a request within thirty days. This hearing is conducted before an *administrative law judge* (see Chapter 1), and the employer has a right to counsel and to *discovery* (see Chapter 3). The typical defense in such actions is good faith or substantial compliance with the documentation provisions. As Exhibit 24–1 indicates, the federal government increased its enforcement efforts significantly during the Bush administration. In fiscal year 2008, ICE made more than 5,100 administrative arrests and 1,100 criminal arrests. In 2009, however, the Obama administration announced that its focus would shift from conducting enforcement actions to reforming immigration laws.

PENALTIES   An employer who violates the law by hiring an unauthorized alien is subject to substantial penalties. The employer may be fined up to $2,200 for each unauthorized employee for a first offense, $5,000 per employee for a second offense, and up to $11,000 for subsequent offenses. Criminal penalties, including additional fines and imprisonment for up to ten years, apply to employers who have engaged in a "pattern or practice of violations." A company may also be barred from future government contracts for violations. In determining the penalty, ICE considers the seriousness of the violation (such as intentional falsification of documents) and the employer's past compliance. ICE regulations also

• *Exhibit* **24–1 Worksite Enforcement Arrests by U.S. Immigration and Customs Enforcement**

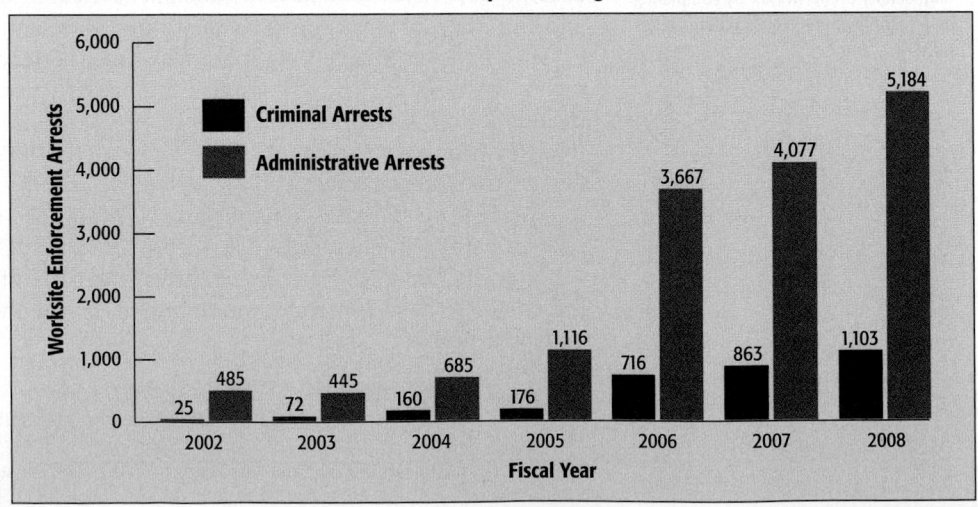

provide for mitigation or aggravation of the penalty under certain circumstances, such as whether the employer cooperated in the investigation or is a small business.

The Immigration Act

Often, U.S. businesses find that they cannot hire sufficient domestic workers with specialized skills. For this reason, U.S. immigration laws have long made provisions for businesses to hire especially qualified foreign workers. The Immigration Act of 1990 placed caps on the number of visas (entry permits) that can be issued to immigrants each year.

Most temporary visas are set aside for workers who can be characterized as "persons of extraordinary ability," members of the professions holding advanced degrees, or other skilled workers and professionals. To hire these individuals, employers must submit a petition to Citizenship and Immigration Services, which determines whether the job candidate meets the legal standards. Each visa is for a specific job, and there are legal limits on the employee's ability to switch jobs once in the United States.

I-551 Alien Registration Receipts A company seeking to hire a noncitizen worker may do so if the worker is self-authorized. This means that the worker either is a lawful permanent resident or has a valid temporary Employment Authorization Document. A lawful permanent resident can prove his or her status to an employer by presenting an **I-551 Alien Registration Receipt**, known as a "green card," or a properly stamped foreign passport. Many immigrant workers are not already self-authorized, and employers may obtain labor certification, or green cards, for those immigrants whom they wish to hire. Approximately fifty thousand new green cards are issued each year. A green card can be obtained only for a person who is being hired for a permanent, full-time position. (A separate authorization system provides for the temporary entry and hiring of nonimmigrant visa workers.)

To gain authorization for hiring a foreign worker, the employer must show that no U.S. worker is qualified, willing, and able to take the job. The employer must advertise the job opening in suitable newspapers or professional journals within six months of the hiring action. The government has detailed regulations governing this advertising requirement as well as the certification process.[40] Any U.S. applicants who meet the stated job qualifications must be interviewed for the position. The employer must also be able to show that the qualifications required for the job are a business necessity. A panel of administrative law judges rejected one company's notice for hiring kitchen supervisors because the company required that the applicants speak Spanish.[41]

The H-1B Visa Program The most common and controversial visa program today is the H-1B visa system. Individuals with H-1B visas can stay in the United States for three to six years and can work only for the sponsoring employer. The recipients of these visas include many high-tech workers, such as computer programmers and electronics specialists. Sixty-five thousand H-1B visas are set aside each year for new immigrants. In recent years, the total allotment of H-1B visas has been filled within the first few weeks of the year, leaving no slots available for the remaining eleven months. Consequently, many businesses, such as Microsoft, have lobbied Congress to expand the number of H-1B visas available to immigrants.

To obtain an H-1B visa, the potential employee must be qualified in a "specialty occupation," which is defined as involving highly specialized knowledge and the attainment of a bachelor's or higher degree or its equivalent. In one 2006 ruling, ICE found that the

I-551 Alien Registration Receipt
A document, commonly known as a "green card," that shows that a foreign-born individual has been lawfully admitted for permanent residency in the United States. Persons seeking employment can prove to prospective employers that they are legally within the United States by showing this receipt.

---

40. The most relevant regulations can be found at 20 C.F.R. Section 655 (for temporary employment) and 20 C.F.R. Section 656 (for permanent employment).
41. *In the Matter of Malnati Organization, Inc.*, 2007-INA-00035 (Bd. Alien Lab. Cert. App. 2007).

position of "accountant" did not qualify as a specialty occupation because the American Council for Accountancy and Taxation did not require a degree for an individual to have this credential.

LABOR CERTIFICATION   Before an employer can submit an H-1B application, it must file a Labor Certification application on a form known as ETA 9035. The employer must agree to provide a wage level at least equal to the wages offered to other individuals with similar experience and qualifications and attest that the hiring will not adversely affect other workers similarly employed. The employer must inform U.S. workers of the intent to hire a foreign worker by posting the form. The U.S. Department of Labor reviews the applications and may reject them for omissions or inaccuracies. **EXAMPLE 24.8** In 2002, a former employee of Sun Microsystems complained to the U.S. Justice Department that the company was discriminating against U.S. workers in favor of H-1B visa holders. Sun had laid off nearly four thousand domestic workers while applying for thousands of temporary visa employees. A court ultimately found that Sun had violated minor technical requirements and ordered it only to change its posting practices for applicants for open positions. ●

H-2, O, L, AND E VISAS   Other specialty temporary visas are available for other categories of employees. H-2 visas provide for workers performing agricultural labor of a seasonal nature. O visas provide entry for persons who have "extraordinary ability in the sciences, arts, education, business or athletics which has been demonstrated by sustained national or international acclaim." L visas allow a company's foreign managers or executives to work inside the United States. E visas permit the entry of certain foreign investors or entrepreneurs.

H-2B visas are available for temporary foreign guest workers in housekeeping, maintenance, and hotel-clerk positions. Are guest workers or their employers liable for the workers' recruitment, transportation, and visa expenses? That was the question in the following case.

Case 24.2   Castellanos-Contreras v. Decatur Hotels, LLC

United States Court of Appeals, Fifth Circuit, 559 F.3d 332 (2009).
www.ca5.uscourts.gov[a]

HISTORICAL AND ENVIRONMENTAL SETTING
According to the National Hurricane Center, Hurricane Katrina, which struck in August 2005, was "one of the most devastating natural disasters" in history. With maximum winds extending across a thirty-mile radius and spawning forty-three tornadoes, the storm swept across Florida and the Gulf Coast states, causing $81 billion in damage and more than 1,800 deaths, including 1,577 in Louisiana. A storm surge of up to twenty-eight feet in a twenty-mile-wide swath flooded parts of Mississippi and Alabama, and burst through levees surrounding the city of New Orleans. More than one million people were evacuated from the afflicted area.

FACTS   Decatur Hotels, LLC, operates luxury hotels in New Orleans. After Hurricane Katrina, Decatur lost 85 percent of its staff. Unable to recruit local residents, Decatur accepted the offer of Accent Personnel Services, Inc., to guide the hotelier through the H-2B visa process to hire temporary foreign workers. Accent sold the information about Decatur's

(Jerry/Creative Commons)

In the aftermath of Hurricane Katrina, a company that operates several luxury hotels in New Orleans needed to hire temporary foreign workers. Who should pay for their recruitment and travel expenses?

positions—for $900 per job—to recruitment companies representing foreign workers. Each worker paid a recruitment company $1,700 to $2,000 to guide him or her through the H-2B visa process and arrange transportation to the United States. The workers also paid the related fees and expenses for an added $1,000 to $3,000. Decatur paid its guest workers between $6.02 and $7.79 per hour but did not reimburse their recruitment, transportation, or visa expenses. Daniel Castellanos-Contreras and other workers filed a suit in a federal district court against Decatur to recover these costs. The court denied the hotelier's motion for summary judgment. Decatur appealed.

ISSUE   Are guest workers liable for their own recruitment, transportation, and visa expenses if these are incurred without their employer's knowledge?

---

a. In the left-hand column, in the "Opinions" column, click on "Opinions Page." On that page, in the "and/or Docket number is:" box, type "07-30942" and click on "Search." In the result, click on the docket number to access the opinion.

Case 24.2–Continued

DECISION   Yes. The U.S. Court of Appeals for the Fifth Circuit held that these fees did not constitute business expenses of the employer, who was therefore not required to reimburse the workers. The court reversed the lower court's ruling and remanded the case to be dismissed.

REASON   Decatur did not know about the foreign recruitment companies or that the companies charged each worker a fee to receive an offer of employment. For these fees—which were most likely incurred before the workers knew about Decatur—applicants received the recruitment companies' guidance in applying for H-2B visas and arranging transportation. The

workers may not have known of any other way to obtain jobs with Decatur other than to apply through the recruitment companies, and in fact there may not have been any other way. But Decatur did not require or approve the payment by a guest worker of any fee to anyone as a condition of an H-2B job offer or employment. "Furthermore, the expenses were not business expenses of Decatur's by custom or practice of Decatur's industry."

FOR CRITICAL ANALYSIS—Global Consideration
Could the guest workers have circumvented the fees by applying directly to Decatur or Accent for the positions? Discuss.

▶ Labor Unions

In the 1930s, in addition to wage-hour laws, the government also enacted the first of several labor laws. These laws protect employees' rights to join labor unions, to bargain with management over the terms and conditions of employment, and to conduct strikes.

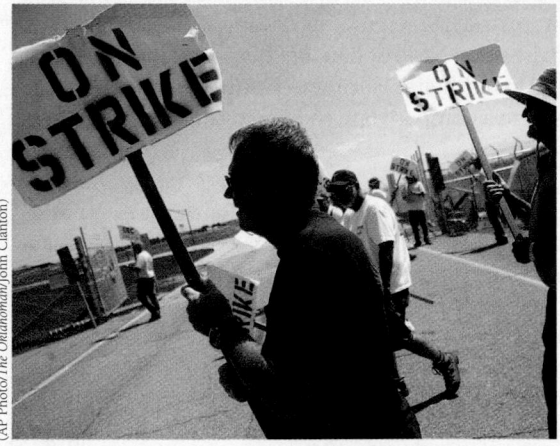

(AP Photo/*The Oklahoman*/John Clanton)

These aircraft mechanics are on strike in Enid, Oklahoma. They walked off the job after negotiators could not reach an agreement on a new contract. Under what circumstances does it make sense for union employees to go on strike? What are the costs of going on strike?

Federal Labor Laws

Federal labor laws governing union-employer relations have developed considerably since the first law was enacted in 1932. Initially, the laws were concerned with protecting the rights and interests of workers. Subsequent legislation placed some restraints on unions and granted rights to employers. We look here at four major federal statutes regulating union-employer relations.

NORRIS-LAGUARDIA ACT   In 1932, Congress protected peaceful strikes, picketing, and boycotts in the Norris-LaGuardia Act.[42] The statute restricted the power of federal courts to issue injunctions against unions engaged in peaceful strikes. In effect, this act established a national policy permitting employees to organize.

NATIONAL LABOR RELATIONS ACT   One of the foremost statutes regulating labor is the National Labor Relations Act (NLRA) of 1935.[43] This act established the rights of employees to engage in collective bargaining and to strike. The act also specifically defined a number of employer practices as unfair to labor:

1. Interference with the efforts of employees to form, join, or assist labor organizations or with the efforts of employees to engage in concerted activities for their mutual aid or protection.
2. An employer's domination of a labor organization or contribution of financial or other support to it.
3. Discrimination in the hiring or awarding of tenure to employees based on union affiliation.

---

42. 29 U.S.C. Sections 101–110, 113–115.
43. 20 U.S.C. Section 151.

4. Discrimination against employees for filing charges under the act or giving testimony under the act.

5. Refusal to bargain collectively with the duly designated representative of the employees.

The National Labor Relations Board (NLRB). The NLRA also created the National Labor Relations Board to oversee union elections and to prevent employers from engaging in unfair and illegal union activities and unfair labor practices. The NLRB has the authority to investigate employees' charges of unfair labor practices and to file complaints against employers in response to these charges. When violations are found, the NLRB may also issue a cease-and-desist order compelling the employer to stop engaging in the unfair practices. Cease-and-desist orders can be enforced by a federal appellate court if necessary. After the NLRB rules on claims of unfair labor practices, its decision may be appealed to a federal court.

Under the NLRA, employers and unions have a duty to bargain in good faith. Bargaining over certain subjects is mandatory, and a party's refusal to bargain over these subjects is an unfair labor practice that can be reported to the NLRB. In one case, for example, an employer was required to bargain with the union over the use of hidden video surveillance cameras.[44]

Workers Protected by the NLRA. To be protected under the NLRA, an individual must be an *employee,* as that term is defined in the statute. Courts have long held that job applicants fall within the definition (otherwise, the NLRA's ban on discrimination in hiring would mean nothing). Additionally, the United States Supreme Court has held that individuals who are hired by a union to organize a company are to be considered employees of the company for NLRA purposes.[45]

LABOR-MANAGEMENT RELATIONS ACT The Labor-Management Relations Act (LMRA) of 1947[46] was passed to proscribe certain unfair union practices, such as the *closed shop.* A **closed shop** requires union membership by its workers as a condition of employment. Although the act made the closed shop illegal, it preserved the legality of the union shop. A **union shop** does not require membership as a prerequisite for employment but can, and usually does, require that workers join the union after a specified amount of time on the job.

The LMRA also prohibited unions from refusing to bargain with employers, engaging in certain types of picketing, and *featherbedding*—causing employers to hire more employees than necessary. The act also allowed individual states to pass their own **right-to-work laws,** which make it illegal for union membership to be required for *continued* employment in any establishment. Thus, union shops are technically illegal in the twenty-three states that have right-to-work laws.

LABOR-MANAGEMENT REPORTING AND DISCLOSURE ACT In 1959, Congress enacted the Labor-Management Reporting and Disclosure Act (LMRDA).[47] The act established an employee bill of rights and reporting requirements for union activities. The act strictly regulates unions' internal business procedures, including union elections. For example, the LMRDA requires a union to hold regularly scheduled elections of officers using secret ballots. Ex-convicts are prohibited from holding union office. Moreover, union officials are

Closed Shop A firm that requires union membership by its workers as a condition of employment. The closed shop was made illegal by the Labor-Management Relations Act of 1947.

Union Shop A firm that requires all workers, once employed, to become union members within a specified period of time as a condition of their continued employment.

Right-to-Work Law A state law providing that employees may not be required to join a union as a condition of retaining employment.

---

44. *National Steel Corp. v. NLRB,* 324 F.3d 928 (7th Cir. 2003).
45. *NLRB v. Town & Country Electric, Inc.,* 516 U.S. 85, 116 S.Ct. 450, 133 L.Ed.2d 371 (1995).
46. 29 U.S.C. Sections 141 *et seq.*
47. 29 U.S.C. Sections 401 *et seq.*

Hot-Cargo Agreement An agreement in which employers voluntarily agree with unions not to handle, use, or deal in other employers' goods that were not produced by union employees; a type of secondary boycott explicitly prohibited by the Labor-Management Reporting and Disclosure Act of 1959.

Secondary Boycott A union's refusal to work for, purchase from, or handle the products of a secondary employer, with whom the union has no dispute, in order to force that employer to stop doing business with the primary employer, with whom the union has a labor dispute.

Authorization Card A card signed by an employee that gives a union permission to act on his or her behalf in negotiations with management.

accountable for union property and funds. Members have the right to attend and to participate in union meetings, to nominate officers, and to vote in most union proceedings.

The act also outlawed **hot-cargo agreements,** in which employers voluntarily agree with unions not to handle, use, or deal in goods produced by nonunion employees working for other employers. The act made all such boycotts (called **secondary boycotts**) illegal.

Union Organization

Typically, the first step in organizing a union at a particular firm is to have the workers sign authorization cards. An **authorization card** usually states that the worker desires to have a certain union, such as the United Auto Workers, represent the workforce. If a majority of the workers sign authorization cards, the union organizers (unionizers) present the cards to the employer and ask for formal recognition of the union. The employer is not required to recognize the union at this point in the process, but it may do so voluntarily on a showing of majority support. (Under legislation that was proposed in 2007 and reintroduced in the U.S. Congress in 2009, the employer would be required to recognize the union as soon as a majority of the workers had signed authorization cards—without holding an election, as described next.)[48]

UNION ELECTIONS If the employer refuses to voluntarily recognize the union after a majority of the workers sign authorization cards—or if fewer than 50 percent of the workers sign authorization cards—the union organizers present the cards to the NLRB with a petition for an election. For an election to be held, the unionizers must demonstrate that at least 30 percent of the workers to be represented support a union or an election on unionization. The proposed union must also represent an *appropriate bargaining unit.* Not every group of workers can form a single union. One key requirement of an appropriate bargaining unit is a *mutuality of interest* among all the workers to be represented by the union. Factors considered in determining whether there is a mutuality of interest include the *similarity of the jobs* of all the workers to be unionized and their physical location.

If all of these requirements are met, an election is held. The NLRB supervises the election and ensures secret voting and voter eligibility. If the proposed union receives majority support in a fair election, the NLRB certifies the union as the bargaining representative for the employees.

UNION ELECTION CAMPAIGNS Many disputes between labor and management arise during union election campaigns. Generally, the employer has control over unionizing activities that take place on company property during working hours. Employers may thus limit the campaign activities of union supporters as long as the employer has a legitimate business reason for doing so. The employer may also reasonably limit the times and places that union solicitation occurs so long as the employer is not discriminating against the union.

EXAMPLE 24.9 A union is seeking to organize clerks at a department store owned by Amanti Enterprises. Amanti can prohibit all union solicitation in areas of the store open to the public because that activity could seriously interfere with the store's business. If Amanti allows solicitation for charitable causes in the workplace, however, it may not prohibit union solicitation. •

An employer may campaign among its workers against the union, but the NLRB carefully monitors and regulates the tactics used by management. Otherwise, management might use its economic power to coerce the workers into voting against unionization. If the employer issued threats ("If the union wins, you'll all be fired") or engaged in other unfair

---

48. If the proposed Employee Free Choice Act becomes law, some of the information stated here may change.

labor practices, the NLRB may certify the union even though it lost the election. Alternatively, the NLRB may ask a court to order a new election.

In the following case, the question was whether managers' brief interruptions of unionizing activities constituted illegal surveillance in violation of the National Labor Relations Act.

Case 24.3 Local Joint Executive Board of Las Vegas v. National Labor Relations Board

United States Court of Appeals, Ninth Circuit, 515 F.3d 942 (2008).

Were managers at the Aladdin casino engaged in "illegal surveillance" of union-organizing activities?

(Smmeale/Creative Commons)

FACTS Aladdin Gaming, LLC, operates a hotel and casino in Las Vegas, Nevada. On May 30, 2003, Local Joint Executive Board of Las Vegas and two other unions (the Unions) began an open campaign to organize Aladdin's housekeeping, food, and beverage departments. On two occasions during this campaign, human resources managers at Aladdin (Tracy Sapien and Stacey Briand) approached union organizers who were discussing unionization with employees in an employee dining room during a lunch break. Sapien and Briand interrupted the organizers while they were obtaining signatures on authorization cards and asked whether the employees were fully informed of the facts before signing. The Unions filed a complaint with the National Labor Relations Board (NLRB) claiming that the managers' actions were illegal surveillance in violation of the National Labor Relations Act (NLRA). The NLRB ruled in favor of Aladdin, and the Unions appealed.

ISSUE Did the managers' conduct violate the NLRA?

DECISION No. The federal appellate court denied the Unions' petition for review, concluding that the managers' brief interruptions of organizing activity did not constitute illegal surveillance.

REASON The NLRA states that an observation of union activity becomes unlawful when that surveillance "goes beyond casual and becomes unduly intrusive." The court found no evidence that Sapien and Briand used threats or other blatant, coercive means to strip union organizers of their rights under the act. The court noted that in both instances Sapien and Briand only attempted to give workers additional information to consider before signing the union cards. Once they were finished speaking to the employees, they left the area.

WHAT IF THE FACTS WERE DIFFERENT?   *If management employees had interrupted union-organizing activities twenty-five times rather than just twice, would the outcome of this case have been different? Why or why not?*

Collective Bargaining

Collective Bargaining The process by which labor and management negotiate the terms and conditions of employment, including working hours and workplace conditions.

If the NLRB certifies the union, the union becomes the *exclusive bargaining representative* of the workers. The central legal right of a union is to engage in collective bargaining on the members' behalf. **Collective bargaining** is the process by which labor and management negotiate the terms and conditions of employment, including wages, benefits, working conditions, and other matters. Collective bargaining allows union representatives elected by union members to speak on behalf of the members at the bargaining table.

When a union is officially recognized, it may demand to bargain with the employer and negotiate new terms or conditions of employment. In collective bargaining, as in most other business negotiations, each side uses its economic power to pressure or persuade the other side to grant concessions.

Bargaining does not mean that one side must give in to the other or that compromises must be made. It does mean that a demand to bargain with the employer must be taken seriously and that both sides must bargain in "good faith." Good faith bargaining means that management, for instance, must be willing to meet with union representatives and consider the union's wishes when negotiating a contract. Examples of bad faith bargaining on the part of management include engaging in a campaign to undermine the union among workers, constantly shifting positions on disputed contract terms, and sending bargainers who lack authority to commit the company to a contract. If an employer (or a union) refuses to bargain in good faith without justification, it has committed an unfair labor practice, and the other party may petition the NLRB for an order requiring good faith bargaining.

Strikes

Even when labor and management have bargained in good faith, they may be unable to reach a final agreement. When extensive collective bargaining has been conducted and an impasse results, the union may call a strike against the employer to pressure it into making concessions. In a **strike,** the unionized workers leave their jobs and refuse to work. The workers also typically picket the workplace, standing outside the facility with signs stating their complaints.

> **Strike** An action undertaken by unionized workers when collective bargaining fails; the workers leave their jobs, refuse to work, and (typically) picket the employer's workplace.

A strike is an extreme action. Striking workers lose their rights to be paid, and management loses production and may lose customers when orders cannot be filled. Labor law regulates the circumstances and conduct of strikes. Most strikes take the form of "economic strikes," which are initiated because the union wants a better contract. **EXAMPLE 24.10** In 2007, the United Auto Workers engaged in an economic strike when General Motors (GM) proposed that its workers accept wage cuts and pay much higher monthly premiums for health care. Approximately 73,000 GM employees walked off the job, shutting down several plants in the United States and Canada. Although the strike was settled quickly, it nevertheless resulted in lost production and profits for the company, its suppliers, and its contractors, as well as lost wages for the strikers. ●

> *"Show me the country in which there are no strikes, and I'll show you the country in which there is no liberty."*
>
> Samuel Gompers 1850–1924
> (American labor leader)

THE RIGHT TO STRIKE The right to strike is guaranteed by the NLRA, within limits, and strike activities, such as picketing, are protected by the free speech guarantee of the First Amendment to the U.S. Constitution. Nonworkers have a right to participate in picketing an employer. The NLRA also gives workers the right to refuse to cross a picket line of fellow workers who are engaged in a lawful strike. Employers are permitted to hire replacement workers to substitute for the workers who are on strike.

THE RIGHTS OF STRIKERS AFTER A STRIKE ENDS An important issue concerns the rights of strikers after the strike ends. In a typical economic strike over working conditions, the employer has a right to hire permanent replacements during the strike and need not terminate the replacement workers when the economic strikers seek to return to work. In other words, striking workers are not guaranteed the right to return to their jobs after the strike if satisfactory replacement workers have been found.

If the employer has not hired replacement workers to fill the strikers' positions, however, then the employer must rehire the economic strikers to fill any vacancies. Employers may not discriminate against former economic strikers, and those who are rehired retain their seniority rights. Different rules apply when a union strikes because the employer has engaged in unfair labor practices. In this situation, the employer may still hire replacements but must give the strikers back their jobs once the strike is over.

 Reviewing . . . Employment, Immigration, and Labor Law

Rick Saldona began working as a traveling salesperson for Aimer Winery in 1987. Sales constituted 90 percent of Saldona's work time. Saldona worked an average of fifty hours per week but received no overtime pay. In June 2010, Saldona's new supervisor, Caesar Braxton, claimed that Saldona had been inflating his reported sales calls and required Saldona to submit to a polygraph test. Saldona reported Braxton to the U.S. Department of Labor, which prohibited Aimer from requiring Saldona to take a polygraph test for this purpose. In August 2010, Saldona's wife, Venita, fell from a ladder and sustained a head injury while employed as a full-time agricultural harvester. Saldona delivered to Aimer's human resources department a letter from his wife's physician indicating that she would need daily care for several months, and Saldona took leave until December 2010. Aimer had sixty-three employees at that time. When Saldona returned to Aimer, he was informed that his position had been eliminated because his sales territory had been combined with an adjacent territory. Using the information presented in the chapter, answer the following questions.

1. Would Saldona have been legally entitled to receive overtime pay at a higher rate? Why or why not?
2. What is the maximum length of time Saldona would have been allowed to take leave to care for his injured spouse?
3. Under what circumstances would Aimer have been allowed to require an employee to take a lie-detector test?
4. Would Aimer likely be able to avoid reinstating Saldona under the *key employee* exception? Why or why not?

Business Application

How to Develop an Employee Internet Policy*

Most businesses provide their employees with access to computer systems and other electronic devices. Employers that make electronic communications systems (such as access to the Internet and e-mail) available to their employees face some obvious risks, though. An employee could use e-mail to harass other employees or subject the employer to liability by reproducing, without authorization, copyright-protected materials found on the Internet. Another risk is that an outside party might intercept confidential information contained in e-mail messages transmitted via the Internet. Finally, by monitoring employees' Internet use and e-mail in an attempt to avoid these problems, the employer may risk being held liable for violating the employees' privacy rights. If you are an employer and find it prudent to monitor employees' Internet use, you should take certain precautions.

Remember that a small company can be bankrupted by just one successful lawsuit against it. Even if your company wins the suit, the legal fees incurred to defend against the claim could be devastating for your profits.

Inform Your Employees of the Monitoring and Obtain Their Consent

First, you should notify your employees that you will be monitoring their Internet communications, including their e-mail. Second, you should ask your employees to consent, in writing, to such actions. Generally, as discussed earlier in this chapter, if employees consent to employer monitoring, they cannot claim that the employer has invaded their privacy rights. You will find it easier to obtain employees' consent to monitoring

if you explain why it is necessary or desirable and let them know what methods will be used to monitor Internet communications. As a rule, when employees are told the reasons for monitoring and clearly understand their rights and duties with respect to the company's communications system, they are less offended by the surveillance.

Spell Out Permissible and Impermissible Internet Uses

Employees should be told which uses of the firm's communications system are permissible and which uses are prohibited. To make sure that employees understand your policy, develop a comprehensive statement setting forth your standards for Internet use and provide specific examples of impermissible activities. It is also important to let employees know what will happen if they violate the policy. The policy might state, for example, that any employee who violates the policy will be subject to disciplinary actions, including termination.

CHECKLIST FOR THE EMPLOYER

1. **Inform employees that their Internet communications will be monitored, explain why monitoring is necessary or desirable, and indicate how it will be conducted.**
2. **Obtain employees' written consent to having their electronic communications monitored.**
3. **Develop a comprehensive policy statement that explains how Internet communications should and should not be used and indicates the consequences of misusing the firm's communications system.**

* This *Business Application* is not meant to substitute for the services of an attorney who is licensed to practice law in your state.

 Key Terms

Chapter Summary: Employment, Immigration, and Labor Law

Employment at Will (See pages 606–608.)	1. *Employment-at-will doctrine*—Under this common law doctrine, either party may terminate the employment relationship at any time and for any reason ("at will"). This doctrine is still in widespread use throughout the United States, although federal and state statutes prevent it from being applied in certain circumstances. 2. *Exceptions to the employment-at-will doctrine*—To protect employees from some of the harsh results of the employment-at-will doctrine, courts have made exceptions to the doctrine on the basis of contract theory, tort theory, and public policy. Whistleblowers have occasionally received protection under the common law for reasons of public policy. 3. *Wrongful discharge*—Whenever an employer discharges an employee in violation of an employment contract or statutory law protecting employees, the employee may bring a suit for wrongful discharge.
Wage and Hour Laws (See pages 608–611.)	1. *Davis-Bacon Act (1931)*—Requires contractors and subcontractors working on federal government construction projects to pay their employees "prevailing wages." 2. *Walsh-Healey Act (1936)*—Requires firms that contract with federal agencies to pay their employees a minimum wage and overtime pay. 3. *Fair Labor Standards Act (1938)*—Extended wage and hour requirements to cover all employers whose activities affect interstate commerce plus certain other businesses. The act has specific requirements in regard to child labor, maximum hours, and minimum wages.
Layoffs (See pages 611–612.)	1. *The Worker Adjustment and Retraining Notification (WARN) Act*—Applies to employers with at least one hundred full-time employees and requires that sixty days' advance notice of mass layoffs (defined on page 611) be given to affected employees or their representative (if workers are in a labor union). Employers who violate the WARN Act can be fined up to $500 for each day of the violation and may also have to pay damages and attorneys' fees to the laid-off employees affected by the failure to warn. 2. *State layoff notice requirements*—Many states have statutes requiring employers to provide notice before initiating mass layoffs, and these laws may have different and even stricter requirements than the WARN Act.
Family and Medical Leave (See pages 612–614.)	The Family and Medical Leave Act (FMLA) requires employers with fifty or more employees to provide their employees with up to twelve weeks of unpaid leave (twenty-six weeks for military caregiver leave) during any twelve-month period. The FMLA authorizes leave for the following reasons: 1. *Family leave*—May be taken to care for a newborn baby, an adopted child, or a foster child. 2. *Medical leave*—May be taken when the employee or the employee's spouse, child, or parent has a serious health condition requiring care. 3. *Military caregiver leave*—May be taken when the employee is caring for a family member with a serious injury or illness incurred as a result of military duty. 4. *Qualifying exigency leave*—May be taken by an employee to handle specified nonmedical emergencies when a spouse, parent, or child is in, or is called to, active military duty.
Worker Health and Safety (See pages 614–616.)	1. *Occupational Safety and Health Act (1970)*—Requires employers to meet specific safety and health standards that are established and enforced by the Occupational Safety and Health Administration (OSHA). 2. *State workers' compensation laws*—Establish an administrative procedure for compensating workers who are injured in accidents that occur on the job, regardless of fault.
Income Security (See pages 616–619.)	1. *Social Security and Medicare*—The Social Security Act of 1935 provides for old-age (retirement), survivors', and disability insurance. Both employers and employees must make contributions under the Federal Insurance Contributions Act (FICA) to help pay for benefits that will partially make up for the employees' loss of income on retirement. The Social Security Administration also administers Medicare, a health-insurance program for older or disabled persons. 2. *Private pension plans*—The federal Employee Retirement Income Security Act (ERISA) of 1974 establishes standards for the management of employer-provided pension plans. 3. *Unemployment insurance*—The Federal Unemployment Tax Act of 1935 created a system that provides unemployment compensation to eligible individuals. Covered employers are taxed to help defray the costs of unemployment compensation. 4. *COBRA*—The Consolidated Omnibus Budget Reconciliation Act (COBRA) of 1985 requires employers to give employees, on termination of employment, the option of continuing their medical, optical, or dental insurance coverage for a certain period.

Continued

Chapter Summary: Employment, Immigration, and Labor Law—Continued

Income Security—Continued	5. *HIPAA*—The Health Insurance Portability and Accountability Act (HIPAA) establishes certain requirements for employer-sponsored health insurance. Employers must comply with a number of administrative, technical, and procedural safeguards to ensure the privacy of employees' health information.
Employee Privacy Rights (See pages 619–622.)	A right to privacy has been inferred from guarantees provided by the First, Third, Fourth, Fifth, and Ninth Amendments to the U.S. Constitution. State laws may also provide for privacy rights. Employer practices that are often challenged by employees as invasive of their privacy rights include electronic performance monitoring, lie-detector tests, drug testing, genetic testing, and screening procedures.
Immigration Law (See pages 623–627.)	1. *Immigration Reform and Control Act (1986)*—Prohibits employers from hiring illegal immigrants; administered by U.S. Citizenship and Immigration Services. Compliance audits and enforcement actions are conducted by U.S. Immigration and Customs Enforcement. 2. *Immigration Act (1990)*—Limits the number of legal immigrants entering the United States by capping the number of visas (entry permits) that are issued each year.

Labor Unions (See pages 627–631.)	1. *Federal labor laws*—
	   a. Norris-LaGuardia Act (1932)—Protects peaceful strikes, picketing, and primary boycotts.
	   b. National Labor Relations Act (1935)—Established the rights of employees to engage in collective bargaining and to strike; also defined specific employer practices as unfair to labor. The National Labor Relations Board (NLRB) was created to administer and enforce the act.
	   c. Labor-Management Relations Act (1947)—Proscribes certain unfair union practices, such as the closed shop.
	   d. Labor-Management Reporting and Disclosure Act (1959)—Established an employee bill of rights and reporting requirements for union activities.
	 2. *Union organization*—Union campaign activities and elections must comply with the requirements established by federal labor laws and the NLRB.
	 3. *Collective bargaining*—The process by which labor and management negotiate the terms and conditions of employment (such as wages, benefits, and working conditions). The central legal right of a labor union is to engage in collective bargaining on the members' behalf.
	 4. *Strikes*—When collective bargaining reaches an impasse, union members may use their ultimate weapon in labor-management struggles—the strike. A strike occurs when unionized workers leave their jobs and refuse to work.

 ExamPrep

ISSUE SPOTTERS

1 Erin, an employee of Fine Print Shop, is injured on the job. For Erin to obtain workers' compensation, does her injury have to have been caused by Fine Print's negligence? Does it matter whether the action causing the injury was intentional? Explain.

2 Onyx applies for work with Precision Design Company, which tells her that it requires union membership as a condition of employment. She applies for work with Quality Engineering, Inc., which does not require union membership as a condition of employment but requires employees to join a union after six months on the job. Are these conditions legal? Why or why not?

BEFORE THE TEST

Check your answers to the Issue Spotters, and at the same time, take the interactive quiz for this chapter. Go to **www.cengage.com/blaw/blt** and click on "Chapter 24." First, click on "Answers to Issue Spotters" to check your answers. Next, click on "Interactive Quiz" to assess your mastery of the concepts in this chapter. Then click on "Flashcards" to review this chapter's Key Term definitions.

For Review

Answers for the even-numbered questions in this For Review *section can be found on this text's accompanying Web site at* **www.cengage.com/blaw/blt**. *Select "Chapter 24" and click on "For Review."*

1 What is the employment-at-will doctrine? When and why are exceptions to this doctrine made?

2 What federal statute governs working hours and wages?

3 Under the Family and Medical Leave Act of 1993, in what circumstances may an employee take family or medical leave?

4 What are the two most important federal statutes governing immigration and employment today?

5 What federal statute gave employees the right to organize unions and engage in collective bargaining?

Hypothetical Scenarios and Case Problems

24–1 Wages and Hours. Calzoni Boating Co. is an interstate business engaged in manufacturing and selling boats. The company has five hundred nonunion employees. Representatives of these employees are requesting a four-day, ten-hours-per-day workweek, and Calzoni is concerned that this would require paying time and a half after eight hours per day. Which federal act is Calzoni thinking of that might require this? Will the act in fact require paying time and a half for all hours worked over eight hours per day if the employees' proposal is accepted? Explain.

24–2 Hypothetical Question with Sample Answer Denton and Carlo were employed at an appliance plant. Their job required them to do occasional maintenance work while standing on a wire mesh twenty feet above the plant floor. Other employees had fallen through the mesh; one was killed by the fall. When Denton and Carlo were asked by their supervisor to do work that would likely require them to walk on the mesh, they refused due to their fear of bodily harm or death. Because of their refusal to do the requested work, the two employees were fired from their jobs. Was their discharge wrongful? If so, under what federal employment law? To what federal agency or department should they turn for assistance?

—For a sample answer to Question 24–2, go to Appendix E at the end of this text.

24–3 Collective Bargaining. Visco, Inc., provides Internet services. Visco and the Internet Workers of America (IWA) have entered into a collective bargaining agreement covering installation and maintenance employees. At one time, Visco supported annual blood drives and worked with IWA and charitable organizations to jointly set dates, arrange appointments, and adjust work schedules for the drives. For each drive, about a thousand employees, including managers, spent up to four hours traveling to a donor site, giving blood, recovering, and returning to their jobs. Employees received full pay for the time. In 2010, Visco told IWA that due to economic conditions, it would no longer allow employees to participate in the drives "on Company time." IWA filed a complaint with the National Labor Relations Board (NLRB), asking that Visco be ordered to bargain over the decision. Did Visco commit an unfair labor practice? Should the NLRB grant IWA's request? Why or why

not? [*Visco New York, Inc. v. National Labor Relations Board*, 360 F.3d 206 (D.C.Cir. 2004)]

24–4 FMLA. Jennifer Willis worked for Coca-Cola Enterprises, Inc. (CCE), in Louisiana as a senior account manager. On a Monday in May 2003, Willis called her supervisor to tell him that she was sick and would not be able to work that day. She also said that she was pregnant, but she did not say she was sick *because* of the pregnancy. On Tuesday, she called to ask where to report to work and was told that she could not return without a doctor's release. She said that she had a doctor's appointment on "Wednesday," which her supervisor understood to be the next day. Willis meant the *following* Wednesday. More than a week later, during which time Willis did not contact CCE, she was told that she had violated CCE's "No Call/No Show" policy. Under this policy "an employee absent from work for three consecutive days without notifying the supervisor during that period will be considered to have voluntarily resigned." She was fired. Willis filed a suit in a federal district court against CCE under the Family and Medical Leave Act (FMLA). To be eligible for FMLA leave, an employee must inform the employer of the reason for the leave. Did Willis meet this requirement? Did CCE's response to Willis's absence violate the FMLA? Explain. [*Willis v. Coca-Cola Enterprises, Inc.*, 445 F.3d 413 (5th Cir. 2006)]

24–5 Unemployment Insurance. Mary Garas, a chemist, sought work in Missouri through Kelly Services, Inc. Kelly is a staffing agency that places individuals in jobs of varying duration with other companies. Through Kelly, Garas worked at Merial Co. from April 2005 to February 2006. After the assignment ended, Garas asked Kelly for more work. Meanwhile, she filed a claim for unemployment benefits with the Missouri Division of Employment Security (DES). In March, Kelly recruiter Rebecca Cockrum told Garas about a temporary assignment with Celsis Laboratory. Garas said that she would prefer a "more stable position," but later asked Cockrum to submit her résumé to Celsis. Before the employer responded, Kelly told the DES that Garas had refused suitable work. Under a Missouri state statute, a claim for unemployment benefits must be denied if "the claimant failed without good cause . . . to accept suitable work when offered the claimant . . . by an employer by whom the individual was formerly employed." The DES denied Garas's claim for benefits. She filed an appeal with a state court. Was the DES's denial right or wrong? Why? [*Garas v. Kelly Services, Inc.,* 211 S.W.3d 149 (Mo.App.E.D. 2007)]

24–6   **Case Problem with Sample Answer** Nicole Tipton and Sadik Seferi owned and operated a restaurant in Iowa. Acting on a tip from the local police, agents of Immigration and Customs Enforcement executed search warrants at the restaurant and at an apartment where some restaurant workers lived. The agents discovered six undocumented aliens working at the restaurant and living together. When the I-9 forms for the restaurant's employees were reviewed, none were found for the six aliens. They were paid in cash while other employees were paid by check. The jury found Tipton and Seferi guilty of hiring and harboring illegal aliens. Both were given prison terms. The defendants challenged the conviction, contending that they did not violate the law because they did not know that the workers were unauthorized aliens. Was that argument credible? Why or why not? [*United States v. Tipton,* 518 F.3d 591 (8th Cir. 2008)]

—After you have answered Problem 24–6, compare your answer with the sample answer given on the Web site that accompanies this text. Go to **www.cengage.com/blaw/blt**, select "Chapter 24," and click on "Case Problem with Sample Answer."

24–7 **Immigration Work Status.** Mohammad Hashmi, a citizen of Pakistan, entered the United States in 2002 on a student visa. Two years later, when he applied for a job at CompuCredit, he completed an I-9 form and checked the box to indicate that he was "a citizen or national of the United States." Soon after submitting that form, he married a U.S. citizen. Several months later, the federal immigration services claimed that he had misrepresented himself as a U.S. citizen. Hashmi contended that he had not misrepresented himself. At an administrative hearing, he testified that when he filled out the I-9 form he believed that he was a "national of the United States" because he was legally in the country under a student visa and was going to marry a U.S. citizen. He requested that his immigration status be adjusted to account for the fact that he was employed and married to an American. The immigration judge rejected that request and found that Hashmi had made a false claim on the I-9 form. He ruled that Hashmi was "inadmissible" to the United States and that his legal status in the country could not be amended because of his marriage or employment. Hashmi appealed. Do you think it was reasonable for Hashmi to think he was a U.S. national? Should his visa status be changed because of his marriage and employment? Why or why not? [*Hashmi v. Mukasey,* 533 F.3d 700 (8th Cir. 2008)]

24–8 **Vesting.** The United Auto Workers (UAW) represents workers at Caterpillar, Inc., and negotiates labor contracts on their behalf. A 1988 labor agreement provided lifetime no-cost medical benefits for retirees but did not state when the employees' rights to those benefits vested. This agreement expired in 1991. Caterpillar and the UAW did not reach a new agreement until 1998. Under the new agreement, retiree medical benefits were subject to certain limits, and retirees were to be responsible for paying some of the costs. Workers who retired during the period when no agreement was in force filed a suit in a federal district court to obtain benefits under the 1988 agreement. Review the Employee Retirement Income Security Act vesting rules for private pension plans on page 617. What is the most plausible application of those rules by analogy to these facts? Discuss. [*Winnett v. Caterpillar, Inc.,* 553 F.3d 1000 (6th Cir. 2009)]

24–9 **A Question of Ethics** *Beverly Tull had worked for Atchison Leather Products, Inc., in Kansas for ten years when, in 1999, she began to complain of hand, wrist, and shoulder pain. Atchison recommended that she contact a certain physician, who in April 2000 diagnosed the condition as carpal tunnel syndrome "severe enough" for surgery. In August, Tull filed a claim with the state workers' compensation board. Because Atchison changed workers' compensation insurance companies every year, a dispute arose as to which company should pay Tull's claim. Fearing liability, no insurer would authorize treatment, and Tull was forced to delay surgery until December. The board granted her temporary total disability benefits for the subsequent six weeks that she missed work. On April 23, 2002, Berger Co. bought Atchison. The new employer adjusted Tull's work to be less demanding and stressful, but she continued to suffer pain. In July, a physician diagnosed her condition as permanent. The board granted her permanent partial disability benefits. By May 2005, the bickering over the financial responsibility for Tull's claim involved five insurers—four of which had each covered Atchison for a single year and one of which covered Berger.* [*Tull v. Atchison Leather Products, Inc.,* 37 Kan.App.2d 87, 150 P.3d 316 (2007)]

1 When an injured employee files a claim for workers' compensation, there is a proceeding to assess the injury and determine the amount of compensation. Should a dispute between insurers over the payment of the claim be resolved in the same proceeding? Why or why not?

2 The board designated April 23, 2002, as the date of Tull's injury. What is the reason for determining the date of a worker's injury? Should the board in this case have selected this date or a different date? Why?

3 How should the board assess liability for the payment of Tull's medical expenses and disability benefits? Would it be appropriate to impose joint and several liability on the insurers, or should the individual liability of each of them be determined? Explain.

Critical Thinking and Writing Assignments

24–10 Critical Legal Thinking. Employees have a right to privacy, but employers also have a right to create and maintain an efficient and safe workplace. Do you think that existing laws strike an appropriate balance between employers' rights and employees' rights? Why or why not?

24–11 **Video Question** Go to this text's Web site at **www.cengage.com/blaw/blt** and select "Chapter 24." Click on "Video Questions" and view the video titled *Employment at Will.* Then answer the following questions.

1 In the video, Laura asserts that she can fire Ray "For any reason. For no reason." Is this true? Explain your answer.

2 What exceptions to the employment-at-will doctrine are discussed in the chapter? Does Ray's situation fit into any of these exceptions?

3 Would Ray be protected from wrongful discharge under whistleblowing statutes? Why or why not?

4 Assume that you are the employer in this scenario. What arguments can you make that Ray should not be able to sue for wrongful discharge in this situation?

 Practical Internet Exercises

Go to this text's Web site at **www.cengage.com/blaw/blt**, select "Chapter 24," and click on "Practical Internet Exercises." There you will find the following Internet research exercises that you can perform to learn more about the topics covered in this chapter.

Practical Internet Exercise 24–1: LEGAL PERSPECTIVE—Workers' Compensation
Practical Internet Exercise 24–2: MANAGEMENT PERSPECTIVE—Workplace Monitoring and Surveillance
Practical Internet Exercise 24–3: HISTORICAL PERSPECTIVE—Labor Unions and Labor Law

Chapter 25

Employment Discrimination

(Getty Images)

"Equal rights
for all, special
privileges for none."

—Thomas Jefferson, 1743–1826
(Third president of the United States,
1801–1809)

Chapter Outline

- Title VII of the Civil Rights Act of 1964
- Discrimination Based on Age
- Discrimination Based on Disability
- Defenses to Employment Discrimination
- Affirmative Action
- State Statutes

Learning Objectives

After reading this chapter, you should be able to answer the following questions:

1. Generally, what kind of conduct is prohibited by Title VII of the Civil Rights Act of 1964, as amended?

2. What is the difference between disparate-treatment discrimination and disparate-impact discrimination?

3. What remedies are available under Title VII of the 1964 Civil Rights Act, as amended?

4. What federal acts prohibit discrimination based on age and discrimination based on disability?

5. What are three defenses to claims of employment discrimination?

Protected Class A group of persons protected by specific laws because of the group's defining characteristics. Under laws prohibiting employment discrimination, these characteristics include race, color, religion, national origin, gender, age, and disability.

Employment Discrimination Treating employees or job applicants unequally on the basis of race, color, national origin, religion, gender, age, or disability; prohibited by federal statutes.

Out of the 1960s civil rights movement to end racial and other forms of discrimination grew a body of law protecting employees against discrimination in the workplace. This protective legislation further eroded the employment-at-will doctrine, which was discussed in the previous chapter. In the past several decades, judicial decisions, administrative agency actions, and legislation have restricted the ability of both employers and unions to discriminate against workers on the basis of race, color, religion, national origin, gender, age, or disability. A class of persons defined by one or more of these criteria is known as a **protected class.** The laws designed to protect these individuals embody the sentiment expressed by Thomas Jefferson in the chapter-opening quotation.

Several federal statutes prohibit **employment discrimination** against members of protected classes. The most important statute is Title VII of the Civil Rights Act of 1964.[1] Title VII prohibits discrimination on the basis of race, color, religion, national origin, or gender at any stage of employment. The Age Discrimination in Employment Act of 1967[2] and the Americans with Disabilities Act of 1990[3] prohibit discrimination on the basis of age and disability, respectively.

---

1. 42 U.S.C. Sections 2000e–2000e-17.
2. 29 U.S.C. Sections 621–634.
3. 42 U.S.C. Sections 12102–12118.

This chapter focuses on the kinds of discrimination prohibited by these federal statutes. Note, though, that discrimination against employees on the basis of any of these criteria may also violate state human rights statutes or other state laws or public policies prohibiting discrimination.

▶ Title VII of the Civil Rights Act of 1964

Title VII of the Civil Rights Act of 1964 and its amendments prohibit job discrimination against employees, applicants, and union members on the basis of race, color, national origin, religion, or gender at any stage of employment. Title VII applies to employers with fifteen or more employees, labor unions with fifteen or more members, labor unions that operate hiring halls (to which members go regularly to be rationed jobs as they become available), employment agencies, and state and local governing units or agencies. The United States Supreme Court has also ruled that an employer with fewer than fifteen employees is not automatically shielded from a lawsuit filed under Title VII.[4] A special section of the act prohibits discrimination in most federal government employment.

The Equal Employment Opportunity Commission

Compliance with Title VII is monitored by the Equal Employment Opportunity Commission (EEOC). A victim of alleged discrimination must file a claim with the EEOC before bringing a suit against the employer. The EEOC may investigate the dispute and attempt to obtain the parties' voluntary consent to an out-of-court settlement. If a voluntary agreement cannot be reached, the EEOC may then file a suit against the employer on the employee's behalf. If the EEOC decides not to investigate the claim, the victim may bring her or his own lawsuit against the employer.

The EEOC does not investigate every claim of employment discrimination, regardless of the merits of the claim. Generally, it investigates only "priority cases," such as cases involving retaliatory discharge (firing an employee in retaliation for submitting a claim to the EEOC) and cases involving types of discrimination that are of particular concern to the EEOC.

Intentional and Unintentional Discrimination

Title VII prohibits both intentional and unintentional discrimination.

INTENTIONAL DISCRIMINATION　Intentional discrimination by an employer against an employee is known as **disparate-treatment discrimination.** Because intent may sometimes be difficult to prove, courts have established certain procedures for resolving disparate-treatment cases. **EXAMPLE 25.1** A woman applies for employment with a construction firm and is rejected. If she sues on the basis of disparate-treatment discrimination in hiring, she must show that (1) she is a member of a protected class, (2) she applied and was qualified for the job in question, (3) she was rejected by the employer, and (4) the employer continued to seek applicants for the position or filled the position with a person not in a protected class. ●

ON THE WEB You can find the complete text of Title VII and information about the activities of the EEOC at that agency's Web site. Go to **www.eeoc.gov**.

Disparate-Treatment Discrimination　A form of employment discrimination that results when an employer intentionally discriminates against employees who are members of protected classes.

Lyndon B. Johnson signs the Civil Rights Act of 1964. Among the guests behind him is Martin Luther King, Jr.

(Lyndon Baines Johnson Presidential Library and Museum)

---

4. *Arbaugh v. Y&H Corp.*, 546 U.S. 500, 126 S.Ct. 1235, 163 L.Ed.2d 1097 (2006).

Prima Facie Case A case in which the plaintiff has produced sufficient evidence of his or her claim that the case can go to a jury; a case in which the evidence compels a decision for the plaintiff if the defendant produces no affirmative defense or evidence to disprove the plaintiff's assertion.

If the woman can meet these relatively easy requirements, she has made out a *prima facie case* of illegal discrimination. *Prima facie* is Latin for "at first sight." Legally, it refers to a fact that is presumed to be true unless contradicted by evidence. Making out a *prima facie* case of discrimination means that the plaintiff has met her initial burden of proof and will win in the absence of a legally acceptable employer defense. (Defenses will be discussed later in this chapter.) The burden then shifts to the employer-defendant, who must articulate a legal reason for not hiring the plaintiff. To prevail, the plaintiff must then show that the employer's reason is a *pretext* (not the true reason) and that discriminatory intent actually motivated the employer's decision.

UNINTENTIONAL DISCRIMINATION Employers often use interviews and testing procedures to choose from among a large number of applicants for job openings. Minimum educational requirements are also common. These practices and procedures may have an unintended discriminatory impact on a protected class. (For tips on how human resources managers can prevent these types of discrimination claims, see the *Linking the Law to Management* feature on pages 658 and 659.)

Disparate-Impact Discrimination A form of employment discrimination that results from certain employer practices or procedures that, although not discriminatory on their face, have a discriminatory effect.

Disparate-impact discrimination occurs when a protected group of people is adversely affected by an employer's practices, procedures, or tests, even though they do not appear to be discriminatory. In a disparate-impact discrimination case, the complaining party must first show statistically that the employer's practices, procedures, or tests are discriminatory in effect. Once the plaintiff has made out a *prima facie* case, the burden of proof shifts to the employer to show that the practices or procedures in question were justified. There are two ways of proving that disparate-impact discrimination exists, as discussed next.

Pool of Applicants. A plaintiff can prove a disparate impact by comparing the employer's workforce to the pool of qualified individuals available in the local labor market. The plaintiff must show that as a result of educational or other job requirements or hiring procedures, the percentage of nonwhites, women, or members of other protected classes in the employer's workforce does not reflect the percentage of that group in the pool of qualified applicants. If a person challenging an employment practice can show a connection between the practice and the disparity, he or she has made out a *prima facie* case and need not provide evidence of discriminatory intent.

Rate of Hiring. A plaintiff can prove disparate-impact discrimination by comparing the selection rates of whites and nonwhites (or members of another protected class), regardless of the racial balance in the employer's workforce. When an educational or other job requirement or hiring procedure excludes members of a protected class from an employer's workforce at a substantially higher rate than nonmembers, discrimination occurs.

The EEOC has devised a test, called the "four-fifths rule," to determine whether an employment examination is discriminatory on its face. Under this rule, a selection rate for protected classes that is less than four-fifths, or 80 percent, of the rate for the group with the highest rate will generally be regarded as evidence of disparate impact. **EXAMPLE 25.2** One hundred white applicants take an employment test, and fifty pass the test and are hired. One hundred minority applicants take the test, and twenty pass the test and are hired. Because twenty is less than four-fifths (80 percent) of fifty, the test would be considered discriminatory under the EEOC guidelines. ●

Discrimination Based on Race, Color, and National Origin

Title VII prohibits employers from discriminating against employees or job applicants on the basis of race, color, or national origin. If an employer's standards or policies for selecting or promoting employees have a discriminatory effect on employees or job applicants in these protected classes, then a presumption of illegal discrimination arises. To avoid liability, the employer must then show that its standards or policies have a substantial, demonstrable relationship to realistic qualifications for the job in question.

EXAMPLE 25.3 Silver City fires Cheng Mai, a Chinese American, who has worked in the city's planning department for two years. Mai claims that he was fired because of his national origin and presents evidence that the city's "residents only" policy has a discriminatory effect on Chinese Americans. The policy requires that all city employees become residents of the city within a reasonable time after being hired. Cheng Mai has not moved to the city but instead has continued to live with his wife and children in a nearby town where a number of other Chinese Americans live. Although residency requirements sometimes violate antidiscrimination laws, if the city can show that its residency requirement has a substantial, demonstrable relationship to realistic qualifications for the job in question, then it normally will not be illegal. •

REVERSE DISCRIMINATION   Note that discrimination based on race can also take the form of *reverse discrimination,* or discrimination against "majority" individuals, such as white males. **CASE EXAMPLE 25.4** An African American woman fired four white men from their management positions at a school district. The men filed a lawsuit for racial discrimination, alleging that the woman was trying to eliminate white males from the department. The woman claimed that the terminations were part of a reorganization plan to cut costs in the department. The jury sided with the men and awarded them nearly $3 million in damages. The verdict was upheld on appeal (though the damages award was reduced slightly).[5] •

In 2009, the United States Supreme Court issued a decision that will have a significant impact on disparate-impact discrimination litigation. **CASE EXAMPLE 25.5** The fire department in New Haven, Connecticut, administered a test to determine which firefighters were eligible for promotions. No African Americans and only two Hispanic firefighters passed the test. Fearing that it would be sued for racial discrimination if it used the test results for promotions, the city refused to certify (and basically discarded) the results. The white firefighters (and one Hispanic) who had passed the test then sued the city, claiming reverse discrimination. The lower courts found in favor of the city, but the United States Supreme Court reversed.

The Court held that an employer can engage in intentional discrimination to remedy an unintentional disparate-impact only if the employer has "a strong basis in evidence" to believe that it will be successfully sued for disparate-impact discrimination "if it fails to take the race-conscious, discriminatory action." In this case, said the Court, mere fear of litigation was not a sufficient reason for the city to discard its test results.[6] • The Court's ruling has been criticized as confusing for employers because although the New Haven officials tried to avoid discrimination, the Court found that throwing out the test was discriminatory.

POTENTIAL "SECTION 1981" CLAIMS   Victims of racial or ethnic discrimination may also have a cause of action under 42 U.S.C. Section 1981. This section, which was enacted as part of the Civil Rights Act of 1866 to protect the rights of freed slaves, prohibits discrimination on the basis of race or ethnicity in the formation or enforcement of contracts. Because employment is often a contractual relationship, Section 1981 can provide an alternative basis for a plaintiff's action and is potentially advantageous because it does not place a cap on damages.[7]

Discrimination Based on Religion

Title VII of the Civil Rights Act of 1964 also prohibits government employers, private employers, and unions from discriminating against persons because of their religion.

---

5. *Johnston v. School District of Philadelphia,* ___ F.Supp.2d ___ (E.D.Pa. 2006).
6. *Ricci v. DeStefano,* ___ U.S. ___, 129 S.Ct. 2658, ___ L.Ed.2d ___ (2009).
7. See, for example, *EEOC v. Sephora USA, LLC,* 419 F.Supp.2d 408 (S.D.N.Y. 2005).

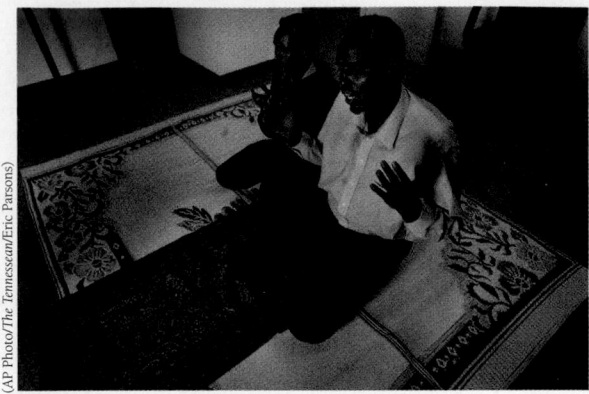

Two Muslims, originally from Somalia, perform religious acts in the evening in Nashville, Tennessee. Under Title VII of the Civil Rights Act, do employers have to accommodate the religious practices of their employees?

> *"A sign that says 'men only' looks very different on a bathroom door than a courthouse door."*
>
> Thurgood Marshall, 1908–1993
> (Associate justice of the United States Supreme Court, 1967–1991)

Employers cannot treat their employees more or less favorably based on their religious beliefs or practices and cannot require employees to participate in any religious activity (or forbid them from participating in one). **EXAMPLE 25.6** Three fifty-year-old men were dismissed from their jobs at a Florida car dealership. The men filed a complaint with the EEOC alleging religious, as well as age, discrimination. They claimed that the employer targeted them for not attending the weekly prayer meetings of dealership employees. If the dealership did require its employees to attend prayer gatherings and fired the men for not attending, they will have a valid case of religious discrimination.[8] •

An employer must "reasonably accommodate" the religious practices of its employees, unless to do so would cause undue hardship to the employer's business. If an employee's religion prohibits him or her from working on a certain day of the week or at a certain type of job, for instance, the employer must make a reasonable attempt to accommodate these religious requirements. Employers must reasonably accommodate an employee's religious belief even if the belief is not based on the doctrines of a traditionally recognized religion, such as Christianity or Judaism, or a denomination, such as Baptist. The only requirement is that the belief be sincerely held by the employee.

Discrimination Based on Gender

Under Title VII, as well as other federal acts (including the Equal Pay Act of 1963, which we also discuss here), employers are forbidden from discriminating against employees on the basis of gender. Employers are prohibited from classifying jobs as male or female and from advertising in help-wanted columns that are designated male or female unless the employer can prove that the gender of the applicant is essential to the job. Employers also cannot have separate male and female seniority lists or refuse to promote employees based on gender.

Generally, to succeed in a suit for gender discrimination, a plaintiff must demonstrate that gender was a determining factor in the employer's decision to fire or refuse to hire or promote her or him. Typically, this involves looking at all of the surrounding circumstances. **CASE EXAMPLE 25.7** In 2009, the EEOC filed a lawsuit against an Indiana plastics manufacturer, Polycon Industries, Inc., and its parent company, Crown Packaging International, Inc. The EEOC alleged that the companies reserved higher-paying production jobs for male employees and refused to promote female workers to these jobs because of their gender. The EEOC decided to pursue the case when it received complaints from women who had applied for production jobs but who were never even interviewed.[9] •

The Pregnancy Discrimination Act of 1978,[10] which amended Title VII, expanded the definition of gender discrimination to include discrimination based on pregnancy. Women affected by pregnancy, childbirth, or related medical conditions must be treated—for all employment-related purposes, including the receipt of benefits under employee benefit programs—the same as other persons not so affected but similar in ability to work.

---

8. The EEOC has stated that employees cannot be forced to participate—or not to participate—in a religious activity as a condition of employment. For more information, see **www.eeoc/gov/types/religion.html**.

9. Case No. 2:09-cv-00141-RL-PRC, filed in the U.S. District Court for the Northern District of Indiana, Hammond Division; see also EEOC Press Release, May 13, 2009.

10. 42 U.S.C. Section 2000e(k).

Ethical Issue ⚖

A human resources specialist from the city of West Hollywood, California, discusses job opportunities with two transgender individuals.

(Jason Redmond/Reuters/Landov)

Does the law prohibit discrimination against transgender persons? Although some states have laws that specifically ban discrimination based on gender identity, most courts have held that federal law (Title VII) does *not* protect transgender persons from discrimination. That may be changing, however, now that one federal court has extended Title VII protection against gender discrimination to transsexuals. Diane Schroer (previously David Schroer) was born male but always identified with the female gender. Schroer, who has master's degrees in history and international relations, served twenty-five years in the military and was a commander of special forces. After retiring with top-secret clearance, she applied for a terrorism specialist position at the Library of Congress. At the job interview, Schroer dressed as a man and received the highest interview score of all eighteen candidates. The selection committee unanimously voted to offer her the job.

Schroer then met with Charlotte Preece, Schroer's future boss, and said that she had been diagnosed with gender identity disorder and was planning to have sex reassignment surgery. The next day, the Library of Congress withdrew its offer to hire Schroer. When Schroer sued alleging gender discrimination, the Library of Congress claimed that it had withdrawn its offer because Schroer was untrustworthy and would be unable to receive the needed security clearance. The court, however, found that these reasons were pretexts (excuses) and ruled in favor of Schroer. The court held that the Library of Congress had refused to hire Schroer because her appearance and background did not comport with the selection committee's stereotypes about how women and men should act and appear. The court concluded that the revocation of the job offer violated Title VII because it was discrimination "because of sex" even though Title VII does not include transsexuals as a protected class.[11] In 2009, Schroer was awarded nearly $500,000 in back pay and damages.

EQUAL PAY ACT The Equal Pay Act of 1963, which amended the Fair Labor Standards Act of 1938 (discussed in Chapter 24), prohibits employers from gender-based wage discrimination. For the act's equal pay requirements to apply, the male and female employees must work at the same establishment doing similar work (a barber and a beautician, for example). To determine whether the Equal Pay Act has been violated, a court will look to the primary duties of the two jobs. It is the job content rather than the job description that controls in all cases. If a court finds that the wage differential is due to any factor other than gender, such as a seniority or merit system, then it does not violate the Equal Pay Act.

2009 EQUAL PAY LEGISLATION Forty-five years after the Equal Pay Act was enacted, there was still a significant gap between the wages earned by male and female employees. Women in the United States typically earn about three-quarters of what men earn. This continuing disparity prompted Congress to pass the Paycheck Fairness Act of 2009, which closed some of the loopholes in the Equal Pay Act. Because the courts had interpreted the defense of "any factor other than sex" so broadly, employers had been able to justify alleged wage discrimination simply by not using the word *gender* or *sex*. The Paycheck Fairness Act clarified employers' defenses and prohibited the use of gender-based differentials in assessing an employee's education, training, or experience. The act also provided additional remedies for wage discrimination, including compensatory and punitive damages, which are available as remedies for discrimination based on race and national origin.

In 2009, Congress also overturned a 2007 decision by the United States Supreme Court, which had required a plaintiff alleging wage discrimination to file a complaint within 180

ON THE WEB The National Women's Law Center maintains a Web site that provides state-by-state statistics on the disparity in pay between female and male employees. Go to **www.nwlc.org/fairpay/statefacts.html**.

---

11. *Schroer v. Billington,* 577 F.Supp.2d 293 (D.D.C. 2008).

President Barack Obama signed the Lilly Ledbetter Fair Pay Act on January 29, 2009. Who will benefit from this law?

Constructive Discharge   A termination of employment brought about by making the employee's working conditions so intolerable that the employee reasonably feels compelled to leave.

days of the decision that set the discriminatory pay.[12] Congress rejected this limit when it enacted the Lilly Ledbetter Fair Pay Act of 2009.[13] The act made discriminatory wages actionable under federal law regardless of when the discrimination began. Each time a person is paid discriminatory wages, benefits, or other compensation, a cause of action arises (and the plaintiff has 180 days from that date to file a complaint). In other words, if a plaintiff continues to work for the employer while receiving discriminatory wages, the time period for filing a complaint is basically unlimited.

Constructive Discharge

The majority of Title VII complaints involve unlawful discrimination in decisions to hire or fire employees. In some situations, however, employees who leave their jobs voluntarily can claim that they were "constructively discharged" by the employer. **Constructive discharge** occurs when the employer causes the employee's working conditions to be so intolerable that a reasonable person in the employee's position would feel compelled to quit.

PROVING CONSTRUCTIVE DISCHARGE   The plaintiff must present objective proof of intolerable working conditions, which the employer knew or had reason to know about yet failed to correct within a reasonable time period. Courts generally also require the employee to show causation—that the employer's unlawful discrimination caused the working conditions to be intolerable. Put a different way, the employee's resignation must be a foreseeable result of the employer's discriminatory action.

EXAMPLE 25.8   Khalil's employer humiliates him in front of his co-workers by informing him that he is being demoted to an inferior position. Khalil's co-workers then continually insult and harass him about his national origin (he is from Iran). The employer is aware of this discriminatory treatment but does nothing to remedy the situation, despite repeated complaints from Khalil. After several months, Khalil quits his job and files a Title VII claim. In this situation, Khalil would likely have sufficient evidence to maintain an action for constructive discharge in violation of Title VII. ● Although courts weigh the facts on a case-by-case basis, employee demotion is one of the most frequently cited reasons for a finding of constructive discharge, particularly when the employee was subjected to humiliation.

APPLIES TO ALL TITLE VII DISCRIMINATION   Note that constructive discharge is a theory that plaintiffs can use to establish any type of discrimination claims under Title VII, including race, color, national origin, religion, gender, pregnancy, and sexual harassment. Constructive discharge has also been successfully used in situations that involve discrimination based on age or disability (both of which will be discussed later in this chapter). Constructive discharge is most commonly asserted in cases involving sexual harassment, however.

When constructive discharge is claimed, the employee can pursue damages for loss of income, including back pay. These damages ordinarily are not available to an employee who left a job voluntarily.

Sexual Harassment

Sexual Harassment   In the employment context, the demanding of sexual favors in return for job promotions or other benefits, or language or conduct that is so sexually offensive that it creates a hostile working environment.

Title VII also protects employees against **sexual harassment** in the workplace. Sexual harassment can take two forms: *quid pro quo* harassment and hostile-environment harassment. *Quid pro quo* is a Latin phrase that is often translated to mean "something in exchange for something else." *Quid pro quo* harassment occurs when sexual favors

---

12. *Ledbetter v. Goodyear Tire Co.*, 550 U.S. 618, 127 S.Ct. 2162, 167 L.Ed.2d 982 (2007).
13. Pub. L. No. 111-2, 123 Stat. 5 (January 5, 2009), amending 42 U.S.C. Section 2000e-5[e].

(Charles Eckert/MCT/Landov)

A federal jury decided that Madison Square Garden in New York City had to pay $11.6 million in damages for sexual harassment to fired executive Anucha Browne Sanders (center).

are demanded in return for job opportunities, promotions, salary increases, and the like. According to the United States Supreme Court, hostile-environment harassment occurs when "the workplace is permeated with discriminatory intimidation, ridicule, and insult, that is sufficiently severe or pervasive to alter the conditions of the victim's employment and create an abusive working environment."[14]

The courts determine whether the sexually offensive conduct was sufficiently severe or pervasive as to create a hostile environment on a case-by-case basis. Typically, a single incident of sexually offensive conduct is not enough to create a hostile environment (although there have been exceptions when the conduct was particularly objectionable). Note also that if the employee who is alleging sexual harassment has signed an arbitration clause (see Chapter 3), she or he will most likely be required to arbitrate the claim.[15]

Preventing Legal Disputes

To avoid sexual-harassment complaints, you should be proactive in preventing sexual harassment in the workplace. Establish written policies, distribute them to employees, and review them annually. Make it clear that the policies prohibiting harassment and discrimination apply to everyone at all levels of your organization. Provide training. Assure employees that no one will be punished for making a complaint. If you receive complaints, always take them seriously and investigate—no matter how trivial they might seem. Prompt remedial action is key, but it must not include any adverse action against the complainant (such as immediate termination). Also, never discourage employees from seeking the assistance of government agencies (such as the EEOC) or threaten or punish them for doing so. It is generally best to obtain the advice of counsel when you receive a serious sexual-harassment complaint.

HARASSMENT BY SUPERVISORS   For an employer to be held liable for a supervisor's sexual harassment, the supervisor normally must have taken a tangible employment action against the employee. A **tangible employment action** is a significant change in employment status or benefits, such as when an employee is fired, refused a promotion, demoted, or reassigned to a position with significantly different responsibilities. Only a supervisor, or another person acting with the authority of the employer, can cause this sort of injury. A constructive discharge also qualifies as a tangible employment action.[16]

Tangible Employment Action   A significant change in employment status, such as a change brought about by firing or failing to promote an employee; reassigning the employee to a position with significantly different responsibilities; or effecting a significant change in employment benefits.

THE *ELLERTH/FARAGHER* AFFIRMATIVE DEFENSE   In 1998, the United States Supreme Court issued several important rulings that have had a lasting impact on cases alleging sexual harassment by supervisors.[17] The Court held that an employer (a city) was liable for a supervisor's harassment of employees even though the employer was unaware of the behavior. Although the city had a written policy against sexual harassment, it had not distributed the policy to its employees and had not established any complaint procedures for employees who felt that they had been sexually harassed. In another case, the Court held that an employer can be liable for a supervisor's sexual harassment even though the employee does not suffer adverse job consequences.

14. *Harris v. Forklift Systems,* 510 U.S. 17, 114 S.Ct. 367, 126 L.Ed.2d 295 (1993); see also *Billings v. Town of Grafton,* 515 F.3d 39 (1st Cir. 2008).

15. See, for example, *EEOC v. Cheesecake Factory, Inc.,* 2009 WL 1259359 (D.Ariz. 2009).

16. See, for example, *Pennsylvania State Police v. Suders,* 542 U.S. 129, 124 S.Ct. 2342, 159 L.Ed.2d 204 (2004).

17. *Burlington Industries, Inc. v. Ellerth,* 524 U.S. 742, 118 S.Ct. 2257, 141 L.Ed.2d 633 (1998); and *Faragher v. City of Boca Raton,* 524 U.S. 775, 118 S.Ct. 2275, 141 L.Ed.2d 662 (1998).

The Court's decisions in these cases established what has become known as the "*Ellerth/ Faragher* affirmative defense" to charges of sexual harassment. The defense has two elements:

1. That the employer has taken reasonable care to prevent and promptly correct any sexually harassing behavior (by establishing effective antiharassment policies and complaint procedures, for example).
2. That the plaintiff-employee unreasonably failed to take advantage of any preventive or corrective opportunities provided by the employer to avoid harm.

An employer that can prove both elements will not be liable for a supervisor's harassment.

RETALIATION BY EMPLOYERS   Employers sometimes retaliate against employees who complain about sexual harassment or other Title VII violations. Retaliation can take many forms. An employer might demote or fire the person, or otherwise change the terms, conditions, and benefits of his or her employment. Title VII prohibits retaliation, and employees can sue their employers. In a *retaliation claim,* an individual asserts that she or he has suffered a harm as a result of making a charge, testifying, or participating in a Title VII investigation or proceeding.

In 2006, the United States Supreme Court made it easier to bring retaliation claims by ruling that plaintiffs do not have to prove that the challenged action adversely affected their workplace or employment.[18] Instead, to prove retaliation, plaintiffs must show that the challenged action was one that would likely have dissuaded a reasonable worker from making or supporting a charge of discrimination.

In 2009, the Court again strengthened Title VII protections against retaliation. The Court held that the law's retaliation protection extends to an employee who speaks out about discrimination not on her or his own initiative, but in answering questions during an employer's internal investigation of another employee's complaint.[19]

HARASSMENT BY CO-WORKERS AND NONEMPLOYEES   When the harassment of co-workers, rather than supervisors, creates a hostile working environment, an employee may still have a cause of action against the employer. Normally, though, the employer will be held liable only if the employer knew, or should have known, about the harassment and failed to take immediate remedial action.

Occasionally, a court may also hold an employer liable for harassment by *nonemployees* if the employer knew about the harassment and failed to take corrective action. **EXAMPLE 25.9** Gordon, who owns and manages a Great Bites restaurant, knows that one of his regular customers, Dean, repeatedly harasses Sharon, a waitress. If Gordon does nothing and permits the harassment to continue, he may be liable under Title VII even though Dean is not an employee of the restaurant. ●

SAME-GENDER HARASSMENT   In *Oncale v. Sundowner Offshore Services, Inc.,*[20] the United States Supreme Court held that Title VII protection extends to situations in which individuals are sexually harassed by members of the same gender. **CASE EXAMPLE 25.10** James Tepperwien was a security officer for three and a half years at a nuclear power plant owned by Entergy Nuclear Operations. During that time, Tepperwien twice reported to his superiors that Vito Messina, another security officer who was allegedly gay, had sexu-

ON THE WEB The New York State Governor's Office of Employee Relations maintains an interactive site on sexual harassment and how to prevent it in the workplace. Go to **www.goer.state.ny.us/ Train/onlinelearning/SH/intro.html**.

"Sexual harassment at work: Is it a problem for the self-employed?"

Victoria Wood, 1953–present
(English comedian and actor)

---

18. *Burlington Northern and Santa Fe Railroad Co. v. White,* 548 U.S. 53, 126 S.Ct. 2405, 165 L.Ed.2d 345 (2006) (see the *Case Analysis Question* on page 662).
19. *Crawford v. Metropolitan Government of Nashville and Davidson County, Tennessee,* ___ U.S. ___, 129 S.Ct. 846, 172 L.Ed.2d 650 (2009).
20. 523 U.S. 75, 118 S.Ct. 998, 140 L.Ed.2d 207 (1998).

ally harassed him. After the first incident, Entergy made all the security officers read and sign its no-tolerance antiharassment policy. After the second incident, Messina was placed on administrative leave for ten weeks. After Messina returned to work, Tepperwien was disciplined for failing to report some missing equipment. He then filed another harassment complaint and quit his job, claiming that he had been constructively discharged and that Entergy had not taken sufficient steps to prevent further harassment. The court noted that a male victim of same-gender harassment must show that he was harassed because he was male. The court found that Tepperwien had presented credible evidence that Messina was a homosexual and had made sexual advances toward other security officers. This evidence was sufficient to establish a *prima facie* case of hostile-environment sexual harassment, so the case could go forward to trial, but it was not enough to show the intolerable conditions required for a finding of constructive discharge.[21] ●

PROOF OF SAME-GENDER HARASSMENT   It can be difficult to prove that the harassment in same-gender cases is "based on sex." It is easier to establish a case of same-gender harassment when the harasser is homosexual, as in Case Example 25.10 just presented above. When the victim is homosexual, some courts have found that the harasser's conduct does not qualify as sexual harassment under Title VII because it was based on the employee's sexual orientation, not on his "sex."[22]

Although federal law (Title VII) does not prohibit discrimination or harassment based on a person's sexual orientation, a growing number of states have enacted laws that prohibit sexual orientation discrimination in private employment. Also, many companies have voluntarily established nondiscrimination policies that include sexual orientation. (Workers in the United States often have more protection against sexual harassment in the workplace than workers in other countries, as this chapter's *Beyond Our Borders* feature on the following page explains.)

Online Harassment

Employees' online activities can create a hostile working environment in many ways. Racial jokes, ethnic slurs, or other comments contained in e-mail, text or instant messages, and blog posts can become the basis for a claim of hostile-environment harassment or other forms of discrimination. A worker who sees sexually explicit images on a co-worker's computer screen may find the images offensive and claim that they create a hostile working environment.[23]

Nevertheless, employers may be able to avoid liability for online harassment if they take prompt remedial action. **CASE EXAMPLE 25.11**   While working at WorldCom, Inc., Angela Daniels received racially harassing e-mailed jokes from another employee. Shortly afterward, the company issued a warning to the offending employee about the proper use of the e-mail system and held two meetings to discuss company policy on the use of the system. In Daniels's suit against WorldCom for racial discrimination, a federal district court concluded that the employer was not liable for its employee's racially harassing e-mails because the employer took prompt remedial action.[24] ●

Remedies under Title VII

Employer liability under Title VII may be extensive. If the plaintiff successfully proves that unlawful discrimination occurred, he or she may be awarded reinstatement, back pay, retroactive promotions, and damages. Compensatory damages are available only in cases of

---

21. *Tepperwien v. Entergy Nuclear Operations, Inc.,* 606 F.Supp.2d 427 (S.D.N.Y. 2009).
22. See, for example, *McCown v. St. John's Health System,* 349 F.3d 540 (8th Cir. 2003); and *Rene v. MGM Grand Hotel, Inc.,* 305 F.3d 1061 (9th Cir. 2002).
23. See, for example, *Doe v. XYC Corp.,* 382 N.J.Super. 122 (App.Div. 2005).
24. *Daniels v. WorldCom, Inc.,* 1998 SL 91261 (N.D.Tex. 1998). See also *Musgrove v. Mobil Oil Corp.,* 2003 WL 21653125 (N.D.Tex. 2003).

Beyond Our Borders   **Sexual Harassment in Other Nations**

The problem of sexual harassment in the workplace is not confined to the United States. Indeed, it is a worldwide problem for female workers. In Argentina, Brazil, Egypt, Turkey, and many other countries, there is no legal protection against any form of employment discrimination. Even in those countries that do have laws prohibiting discriminatory employment practices, including gender-based discrimination, those laws often do not specifically include sexual harassment as a discriminatory practice. Several countries have attempted to

remedy this omission by passing new laws or amending others to specifically prohibit sexual harassment in the workplace. Japan, for example, has amended its Equal Employment Opportunity Law to include a provision making sexual harassment illegal. Thailand has also passed its first sexual-harassment law. The European Union has adopted a directive that specifically identifies sexual harassment as a form of discrimination. Nevertheless, women's groups throughout Europe contend that corporations in European countries tend to view

sexual harassment with "quiet tolerance." They contrast this attitude with that of most U.S. corporations, which have implemented specific procedures to deal with harassment claims.

• For Critical Analysis
Why do you think U.S. corporations are more aggressive than European companies in taking steps to prevent sexual harassment in the workplace?

intentional discrimination. Punitive damages may be recovered against a private employer only if the employer acted with malice or reckless indifference to an individual's rights. The statute limits the total amount of compensatory and punitive damages that the plaintiff can recover from specific employers—ranging from $50,000 against employers with one hundred or fewer employees to $300,000 against employers with more than five hundred employees.

 Discrimination Based on Age

Age discrimination is potentially the most widespread form of discrimination, because anyone—regardless of race, color, national origin, or gender—could be a victim at some point in life. The Age Discrimination in Employment Act (ADEA) of 1967, as amended, prohibits employment discrimination on the basis of age against individuals forty years of age or older. The act also prohibits mandatory retirement for nonmanagerial workers. For the act to apply, an employer must have twenty or more employees, and the employer's business activities must affect interstate commerce. The EEOC administers the ADEA, but the act also permits private causes of action against employers for age discrimination.

The ADEA includes a provision that extends protections against age discrimination to federal government employees.[25] In 2008, the United States Supreme Court ruled that this provision encompasses not only claims of age discrimination, but also claims of retaliation for complaining about age discrimination, which are not specifically mentioned in the statute.[26] Thus, the ADEA protects federal and private-sector employees from retaliation based on age-related complaints.

Procedures under the ADEA

The burden-shifting procedure under the ADEA is similar to that under Title VII. If a plaintiff can establish that she or he (1) was a member of the protected age group, (2) was qualified for the position from which she or he was discharged, and (3) was discharged under circumstances that give rise to an inference of discrimination, the plaintiff has established a *prima facie* case of unlawful age discrimination. The burden then shifts to the employer, who must articulate a legitimate reason for the discrimination. If the plaintiff can prove

"Growing old is like being increasingly penalized for a crime you have not committed."

Anthony Powell, 1905–2000
(English novelist)

REMEMBER   The Fourteenth Amendment prohibits any state from denying any person "the equal protection of the laws." This prohibition applies to the *federal* government through the due process clause of the Fifth Amendment.

---

25. See 29 U.S.C. Section 632(a) (2000 ed., Supp. V).
26. *Gomez-Perez v. Potter,* ___ U.S. ___, 128 S.Ct. 1931, 170 L.Ed.2d 887 (2008).

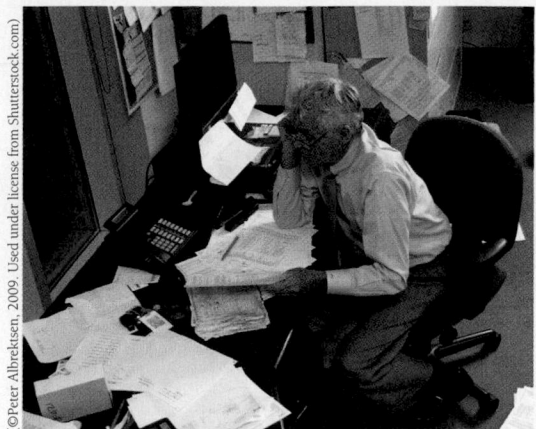

This sixty-year-old worker has just been informed that his position is being eliminated because of company restructuring. How can he establish that his firing was based on his age rather than on the restructuring?

that the employer's reason is only a pretext (excuse) and that the plaintiff's age was a determining factor in the employer's decision, the employer will be held liable under the ADEA.[27]

Replacing Older Workers with Younger Workers

Numerous age discrimination cases have been brought against employers who, to cut costs, replaced older, higher-salaried employees with younger, lower-salaried workers. Whether a firing is discriminatory or simply part of a rational business decision to prune the company's ranks is not always clear. Companies often defend a decision to discharge a worker by asserting that the worker could no longer perform his or her duties or that the worker's skills were no longer needed.

The employee must prove that the discharge was motivated, at least in part, by age bias. Proof that qualified older employees generally were discharged before younger employees or that co-workers continually made unflattering age-related comments about the discharged worker may be enough. **CASE EXAMPLE 25.12** Meenan Oil Company fired Louis Ceccoli, a seventy-one-year-old sales representative. Ceccoli's manager had made several derogatory comments about older workers and had repeatedly asked Ceccoli about his retirement plans. The EEOC filed an ADEA lawsuit. Meenan was eventually required to pay Ceccoli $80,000 and to provide antidiscrimination training to its supervisors and managers.[28] ●

The plaintiff need not prove that he or she was replaced by a person outside the protected class (under the age of forty years) as long as the person is younger than the plaintiff. The issue in all ADEA cases is whether age discrimination has, in fact, occurred, regardless of the age of the replacement worker. Nevertheless, the bigger the age gap, the more likely the individual will succeed in showing age discrimination.

When an older worker who is laid off as part of a restructuring subsequently files a suit against the company for age discrimination, a court must decide what testimony concerning the company's attitudes toward workers' ages will be allowed as evidence at trial. This issue was at the heart of the following case.

---

27. See, for example, *Cash Distributing Co. v. Neely*, 947 So.2d 286 (Miss. Sup.Ct. 2007).
28. See the EEOC press release at **www.eeoc.ogv/press/5-13-09.html**.

Case 25.1 Sprint/United Management Co. v. Mendelsohn

Supreme Court of the United States, ___ U.S. ___ , 128 S.Ct. 1140, 170 L.Ed.2d 1 (2008).

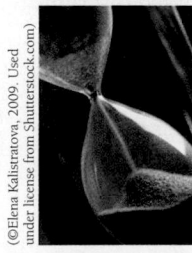

In an age discrimination case, is the testimony of other employees with similar claims admissible?

FACTS Ellen Mendelsohn worked for Sprint/United Management Company (Sprint) from 1989 to 2002, when Sprint fired her during a companywide reduction in the workforce. She sued under the ADEA, alleging disparate treatment based on her age (fifty-one). Five other former Sprint employees testified that they had also suffered discrimination based on age. Three said that they had heard managers make remarks belittling older workers and indicating that age was a factor in deciding who would be fired during the restructuring. None of the five witnesses worked in the same part of the company as Mendelsohn, however, and none could testify about her supervisors. The district court excluded their testimony as to the

impact on Mendelsohn because the witnesses were not "similarly situated" in the company. The appeals court held that the testimony was not *per se* irrelevant and remanded the case with instructions to admit the challenged testimony. Sprint appealed to the United States Supreme Court.

ISSUE Was the testimony of witnesses concerning the company's general attitude toward age discrimination *per se* irrelevant and *per se* inadmissible, even though they did not work in the same department as the plaintiff?

DECISION No. The United States Supreme Court vacated the appellate court's decision and remanded the case to the district court so that the trial court could clarify its ruling.

Case 25.1–Continues next page ➡

Case 25.1–Continued

REASON The Court reasoned that the trial court had gone too far in excluding the challenged testimony and that the appellate court had erred in telling the lower court to admit the testimony. The testimony is not necessarily *per se* admissible or *per se* inadmissible. According to federal rules, the relevance of such evidence is fact based and depends on many factors. The district (trial) court should study the evidence in more detail and determine if the witnesses were providing credible evidence of a discriminatory policy at Sprint that was played

out through the reduction in the workforce. The court had to assess the value of such evidence. It could not simply reject evidence that did not directly address the attitude of Mendelsohn's immediate supervisors.

FOR CRITICAL ANALYSIS—Legal Consideration *What steps should employers take to reduce the likelihood that supervisors will make negative comments about workers' ages?*

State Employees Not Covered by the ADEA

ON THE WEB The Employment Law Information Network provides access to many articles on age discrimination and other employment issues at www.elinfonet.com/fedindex/2.

Generally, the states are immune from lawsuits brought by private individuals in federal court—unless a state consents to the suit. This immunity stems from the United States Supreme Court's interpretation of the Eleventh Amendment (the text of this amendment is included in Appendix B). **CASE EXAMPLE 25.13** In two Florida cases, professors and librarians contended that their employers—two Florida state universities—denied them salary increases and other benefits because they were getting old and their successors could be hired at lower cost. The universities claimed that as agencies of a sovereign state, they could not be sued in federal court without the state's consent. The cases ultimately reached the United States Supreme Court, which held that the Eleventh Amendment bars private parties from suing state employers for violations of the ADEA.[29] ●

State immunity under the Eleventh Amendment is not absolute, however, as the Supreme Court explained in 2004. In some situations, such as when fundamental rights are at stake, Congress has the power to abrogate (abolish) state immunity to private suits through legislation that unequivocally shows Congress's intent to subject states to private suits.[30] As a general rule, though, the Court has found that state employers are immune from private suits brought by employees under the ADEA (for age discrimination, as noted above), the Americans with Disabilities Act[31] (for disability discrimination), and the Fair Labor Standards Act[32] (which relates to wages and hours—see Chapter 24). In contrast, states are not immune from the requirements of the Family and Medical Leave Act[33] (see Chapter 24).

▶ Discrimination Based on Disability

"Jobs are physically easier, but the worker now takes home worries instead of an aching back."

Homer Bigart, 1907–1991
(American journalist)

The Americans with Disabilities Act (ADA) of 1990 was designed to eliminate discriminatory employment practices that prevent otherwise qualified workers with disabilities from fully participating in the national labor force. The ADA prohibits disability-based discrimination in workplaces with fifteen or more workers (with the exception of state government employers, who are generally immune under the Eleventh Amendment, as was just discussed). Basically, the ADA requires that employers "reasonably accommodate" the needs of persons with disabilities unless to do so would cause the employer to suffer an "undue hardship." In 2008, Congress enacted the ADA Amendments Act,[34] which broadened the coverage of the ADA's protections, as will be discussed shortly.

---

29. *Kimel v. Florida Board of Regents,* 528 U.S. 62, 120 S.Ct. 631, 145 L.Ed.2d 522 (2000).
30. *Tennessee v. Lane,* 541 U.S. 509, 124 S.Ct. 1978, 158 L.Ed.2d 820 (2004).
31. *Board of Trustees of the University of Alabama v. Garrett,* 531 U.S. 356, 121 S.Ct. 955, 148 L.Ed.2d 866 (2001).
32. *Alden v. Maine,* 527 U.S. 706, 119 S.Ct. 2240, 144 L.Ed.2d 636 (1999).
33. *Nevada Department of Human Resources v. Hibbs,* 538 U.S. 721, 123 S.Ct. 1972, 155 L.Ed.2d 953 (2003).
34. 42 U.S.C. Sections 12103 and 12205a.

Procedures under the ADA

To prevail on a claim under the ADA, a plaintiff must show that he or she (1) has a disability, (2) is otherwise qualified for the employment in question, and (3) was excluded from the employment solely because of the disability. As in Title VII cases, a plaintiff must pursue her or his claim through the EEOC before filing an action in court for a violation of the ADA. The EEOC may decide to investigate and perhaps even sue the employer on behalf of the employee. If the EEOC decides not to sue, then the employee is entitled to sue in court.

Significantly, the United States Supreme Court held in 2002 that the EEOC could bring a suit against an employer for disability-based discrimination even though the employee had agreed to submit any job-related disputes to arbitration (see Chapter 3). The Court reasoned that because the EEOC was not a party to the arbitration agreement, the agreement was not binding on the EEOC.[35]

Plaintiffs in lawsuits brought under the ADA may obtain many of the same remedies available under Title VII. These include reinstatement, back pay, a limited amount of compensatory and punitive damages (for intentional discrimination), and certain other forms of relief. Repeat violators may be ordered to pay fines of up to $100,000.

What Is a Disability?

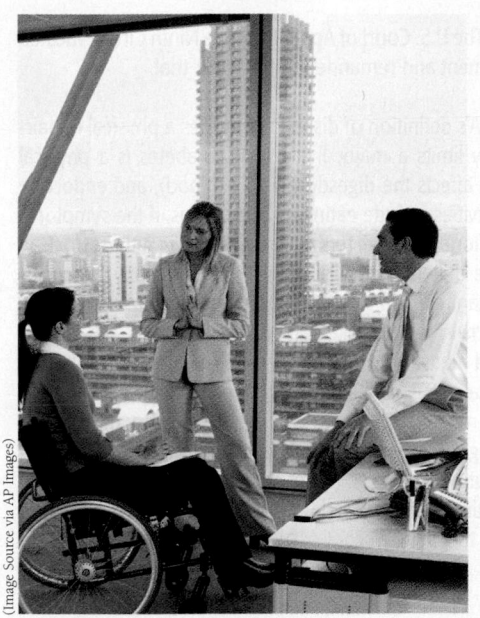

Co-workers discuss business matters. What is a disability under the Americans with Disabilities Act?

The ADA is broadly drafted to cover persons with a wide range of disabilities. Specifically, the ADA defines *disability* as "(1) a physical or mental impairment that substantially limits one or more of the major life activities of such individuals; (2) a record of such impairment; or (3) being regarded as having such an impairment." Health conditions that have been considered disabilities under the federal law include blindness, alcoholism, heart disease, cancer, muscular dystrophy, cerebral palsy, paraplegia, diabetes, acquired immune deficiency syndrome (AIDS), testing positive for the human immunodeficiency virus (HIV), and morbid obesity (defined as existing when an individual's weight is two times the normal weight for his or her height). The ADA excludes from coverage certain conditions, such as kleptomania (the obsessive desire to steal).

THE SUPREME COURT NARROWLY INTERPRETED THE ADA   Although the ADA's definition of disability is broad, United States Supreme Court rulings from 1999 to 2007 interpreted that definition narrowly and made it harder for employees to establish a disability under the act. In 1999, the Court held that severe myopia, or nearsightedness, which can be corrected with lenses, does not qualify as a disability under the ADA.[36] In 2002, the Court held that repetitive-stress injuries (such as carpal tunnel syndrome) ordinarily do not constitute a disability under the ADA.[37] After that, the courts began focusing on how the person functioned when using corrective devices or taking medication, not on how the person functioned without these measures.[38]

2008 AMENDMENTS REVERSE PRIOR SUPREME COURT CASES   In response to the Supreme Court's limiting decisions, Congress decided to amend the ADA in 2008. Basically, the amendments reverse the Court's restrictive interpretation of disability under the ADA and prohibit employers from considering mitigating measures or medications when

---

35. *EEOC v. Waffle House, Inc.,* 534 U.S. 279, 122 S.Ct. 754, 151 L.Ed.2d 755 (2002).

36. *Sutton v. United Airlines, Inc.,* 527 U.S. 471, 119 S.Ct. 2139, 144 L.Ed.2d 450 (1999).

37. *Toyota Motor Manufacturing, Kentucky, Inc. v. Williams,* 534 U.S. 184, 122 S.Ct. 681, 151 L.Ed.2d 615 (2002). This case was invalidated by the 2008 amendments to the ADA.

38. See, for example, *Orr v. Wal-Mart Stores, Inc.,* 297 F.3d 720 (8th Cir. 2002).

determining if an individual has a disability. In other words, disability is now determined on a case-by-case basis.

A condition may fit the definition of disability in one set of circumstances, but not in another. What makes the difference in an individual situation? The court in the following case answered that question.

Case 25.2   Rohr v. Salt River Project Agricultural Improvement and Power District

United States Court of Appeals, Ninth Circuit, 555 F.3d 850 (2009).
www.ca9.uscourts.gov[a]

HISTORICAL AND SOCIAL SETTING   *Diabetes is a chronic and incurable disease associated with an increased risk of heart disease, stroke, high blood pressure, blindness, kidney disease, nervous system disease, amputations, dental disease, complications of pregnancy, and sexual dysfunction. Type 1 diabetes, or juvenile diabetes, results from the body's failure to produce insulin—a hormone that is needed to convert food into energy. Type 2 results from the body's failure to properly use insulin. If left untreated, type 2 can cause seizures and a coma. In the United States, approximately 23.6 million children and adults, or 7.8 percent of the population, have diabetes.*

Is diabetes a disability under the Americans with Disabilities Act?

FACTS   Larry Rohr has type 2 diabetes. He tires quickly and suffers from high blood pressure, deteriorating vision, and loss of feeling in his hands and feet. Insulin injections, other medicine, blood tests, and a strict diet are fixtures of his daily life. If he fails to follow this regimen, his blood sugar rises to a level that aggravates his disease. At the time of his diagnosis, he was a welding metallurgy specialist for the Salt River Project Agricultural Improvement and Power District, which provides utility services to homes in Arizona. Due to the effort required to manage his diabetes, particularly his strict diet schedule, Rohr's physician forbade his assignment to tasks involving overnight, out-of-town travel. Salt River told Rohr that this would prevent him from performing the essential functions of his job, such as responding to

power outages. Rohr was asked to transfer, apply for disability benefits, or take early retirement. He filed a suit in a federal district court against Salt River, alleging discrimination. The court issued a summary judgment in the employer's favor. Rohr appealed.

ISSUE   Is diabetes a disability under the ADA if it significantly restricts an individual's eating?

DECISION   Yes. The U.S. Court of Appeals for the Ninth Circuit vacated the lower court's judgment and remanded the case for trial.

REASON   The ADA's definition of disability includes a physical impairment that substantially limits a major life activity. Diabetes is a physical impairment because it affects the digestive, hemic (blood), and endocrine systems. Major life activities include eating patterns. Thus, if the symptoms of diabetes and the efforts to manage the disease significantly restrict an individual's eating, the definition of disability is met. In many instances, failure to take insulin can result in severe health problems and even death. Determining how much insulin to take can require frequent, self-administered blood tests and adjustments in activity and food levels. Rohr must follow these steps. Because insulin alone does not stabilize his blood sugar levels, he must strictly monitor what, and when, he eats every day. Failure to do so would endanger his health. "Straying from a diet for more than one or two meals is not a cause for medical concern for most people, and skipping a meal, or eating a large one, does not expose them to the risk of fainting." But for Rohr, the effort to control his diet is substantially limiting.

FOR CRITICAL ANALYSIS—Technological Consideration   *If Rohr could monitor his condition and regimen through a cell phone or other portable Internet connection, would the result in this case likely have been affected? Explain.*

---

a. In the left-hand column, in the "Decisions" pull-down menu, click on "Opinions." On that page, click on "Advanced Search." In the "by Case No.:" box, type "06-16527" and click on "Search." In the result, click on the case title to access the opinion.

Reasonable Accommodation

The ADA does not require that employers accommodate the needs of job applicants or employees with disabilities who are not otherwise qualified for the work. If a job applicant or an employee with a disability, with reasonable accommodation, can perform essential job functions, however, the employer must make the accommodation. Required modifications may include installing ramps for a wheelchair, establishing more flexible working hours, creating or modifying job assignments, and creating or improving training materials and procedures. Generally, employers should give primary consideration to employees' preferences in deciding what accommodations should be made.

(©Sergey Lavrentev, 2009. Used under license from Shutterstock.com)

(Paul Tople/MCT/Landov)

This paraplegic employee has a customized van that he parks in the handicap parking area outside his workplace. In general, providing such parking for employees who have a disability is considered a reasonable accommodation that employers must make.

DON'T FORGET Preemployment screening procedures must be applied equally in regard to all job applicants.

ON THE WEB The Equal Employment Opportunity Commission posts a manual that provides guidance on reasonable accommodation and undue hardship under the ADA. Go to **www.eeoc.gov/ policy/docs/accommodation.html**.

UNDUE HARDSHIP Employers who do not accommodate the needs of persons with disabilities must demonstrate that the accommodations will cause "undue hardship" in terms of being significantly difficult or expensive for the employer. Usually, the courts decide whether an accommodation constitutes an undue hardship on a case-by-case basis by looking at the employer's resources in relation to the specific accommodation.

EXAMPLE 25.14 Bryan Lockhart, who uses a wheelchair, works for a cell phone company that provides parking for its employees. Lockhart informs the company supervisors that the parking spaces are so narrow that he is unable to extend the ramp on his van that allows him to get in and out of the vehicle. Lockhart therefore requests that the company reasonably accommodate his needs by paying a monthly fee for him to use a larger parking space in an adjacent lot. In this situation, a court would likely find that it would not be an undue hardship for the employer to pay for additional parking for Lockhart. •

JOB APPLICATIONS AND PREEMPLOYMENT PHYSICAL EXAMS Employers must modify their job-application process so that those with disabilities can compete for jobs with those who do not have disabilities. For instance, a job announcement might be modified to allow job applicants to respond by e-mail or letter, as well as by telephone, so that it does not discriminate against potential applicants with hearing impairments.

Employers are restricted in the kinds of questions they may ask on job-application forms and during preemployment interviews. Furthermore, they cannot require persons with disabilities to submit to preemployment physicals unless such exams are required of all other applicants. Employers can condition an offer of employment on the applicant's successfully passing a medical examination, but can disqualify the applicant only if the medical problems they discover would render the applicant unable to perform the job.

CASE EXAMPLE 25.15 When filling the position of delivery truck driver, a company cannot screen out all applicants who are unable to meet the U.S. Department of Transportation's hearing standard. The company would first have to prove that drivers who are deaf are not qualified to perform the essential job function of driving safely and pose a higher risk of accidents than drivers who are not deaf.[39] •

SUBSTANCE ABUSERS Drug addiction is a disability under the ADA because drug addiction is a substantially limiting impairment. Those who are actually using illegal drugs are not protected by the act, however. The ADA protects only persons with *former* drug addictions—those who have completed or are now in a supervised drug-rehabilitation program. Individuals who have used drugs casually in the past are not protected under the act. They are not considered addicts and therefore do not have a disability (addiction).

People suffering from alcoholism are protected by the ADA. Employers cannot legally discriminate against employees simply because they are suffering from alcoholism and must treat them in the same way they treat other employees. Of course, employers have the right to prohibit the use of alcohol in the workplace and can require that employees not be under the influence of alcohol while working. Employers can also fire or refuse to hire a person who is an alcoholic if he or she poses a substantial risk of harm either to himself or herself or to others and the risk cannot be reduced by reasonable accommodation.

HEALTH INSURANCE PLANS Workers with disabilities must be given equal access to any health insurance provided to other employees. Employers can exclude from coverage preexisting health conditions and certain types of diagnostic or surgical procedures, though. An employer can also put a limit, or cap, on health-care payments under its particular group health policy—as long as such caps are "applied equally to all insured employees" and do not "discriminate on the basis of disability." Whenever a group health-care plan

---

39. *Bates v. United Parcel Service, Inc.,* 465 F.3d 1069 (9th Cir. 2006).

makes a disability-based distinction in its benefits, the plan violates the ADA (unless the employer can justify its actions under the *business necessity* defense, which will be discussed shortly).

Association Discrimination

The ADA contains an "association provision" that protects qualified individuals from employment discrimination based on an identified disability of a person with whom the qualified individual is known to have a relationship or an association.[40] The purpose of this provision is to prevent employers from taking adverse employment actions based on stereotypes or assumptions about individuals who associate with people who have disabilities. An employer cannot, for instance, refuse to hire the parent of a child with a disability based on the assumption that the person will miss work too often or be unreliable.

To establish a *prima facie* case of association discrimination under the ADA, the plaintiff must show that she or he (1) was qualified for the job, (2) was subjected to adverse employment action, and (3) was known by her or his employer to have a relative or an associate with a disability. In addition, the plaintiff must show that the adverse employment action occurred under circumstances raising a reasonable inference that the disability of the relative or associate was a determining factor in the employer's decision.

In the following case, a man claimed that his employer unlawfully discriminated against him based on his wife's disability. Although the case involved a state law that offers slightly more protection than the ADA, the opinion shows how courts analyze association discrimination claims.

---

40. 42 U.S.C. Section 12112(b)(4).

Case 25.3   Francin v. Mosby, Inc.

Missouri Court of Appeals, 248 S.W.3d 619 (2008).
www.courts.mo.gov[a]

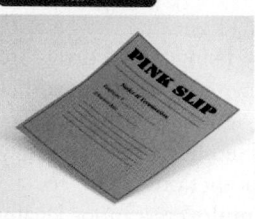

Was an employee fired because of a spouse's illness?

FACTS   Randall Francin began working at Mosby, Inc. (doing business as Elsevier), in 1991. He worked as a production assistant until 2002, when his position was eliminated due to organizational restructuring. Francin was rehired soon after as an associate editor. In this new position, Francin updated drug information and proofread information contained in drug inserts. In 2003, Francin's wife was diagnosed with amyotrophic lateral sclerosis. He discussed his rights for leave under the Family and Medical Leave Act (discussed in Chapter 24) with a company human resources representative. Early in 2004, Francin received a "merit award increase" in salary, and his supervisor resigned. During an interview with his new boss, Francin discussed his wife's illness. On September 21, 2004, Francin was fired. Francin filed a suit under the Missouri Human Rights Act, alleging that Elsevier discriminated against him because of his association with a person with a disability. Elsevier filed a

motion for summary judgment, which was granted by the trial court. On appeal, Francin claimed that the trial court erred in granting summary judgment because there was a genuine issue of material fact concerning whether his wife's disability was a contributing factor in the decision to terminate his employment.

ISSUE   Did the trial court err in granting summary judgment to Elsevier because there was a genuine dispute of material fact?

DECISION   Yes. The Missouri intermediate appellate court reversed the trial court's decision and remanded the case for further proceedings.

REASON   Summary judgment is appropriate only when there are no genuine disputes of material fact. The appellate court found sufficient evidence that Francin's wife's illness was a contributing factor to his termination and thus was a material fact in this case. In particular, the court cited the contradictory evidence of Francin's positive job performance with the close timing of his termination after disclosing his wife's condition to his new boss.

WHAT IF THE FACTS WERE DIFFERENT?   *Assume that Francin had only discussed his wife's illness with a human resources officer in the company and had never mentioned it to his new boss. Would the outcome of the appeal have been different? Explain.*

---

a. Click on "Opinions & Minutes" under the "Quick Links" menu. Select the link for opinions from the Missouri Court of Appeals, Eastern District, and using the "Search Opinions" function, enter "Randall Francin." Click on the case title to access this opinion. This is the official Web site of the Missouri courts.

Hostile-Environment Claims under the ADA

As discussed earlier in this chapter, under Title VII of the Civil Rights Act of 1964, an employee may base certain types of employment-discrimination causes of action on a hostile-environment theory. Using this theory, a worker may successfully sue her or his employer, even if the worker was not fired or otherwise discriminated against.

Although the ADA does not expressly provide for hostile-environment claims, a number of courts have allowed such actions. Only a few plaintiffs have been successful, however. For a claim to succeed, the conduct complained of must be sufficiently severe or pervasive to permeate the workplace and alter the conditions of employment such that a reasonable person would find the environment hostile or abusive. **CASE EXAMPLE 25.16** Lester Wenigar was a fifty-seven-year-old man with a low IQ and limited mental capacity who worked at a farm doing manual labor and as a night watchman. His employer frequently shouted at him and called him names, did not allow him to take breaks, and provided him with substandard living quarters (a storeroom over a garage without any heat or windows). In this situation, because the employer's conduct was severe and offensive, a court would likely find that the working conditions constituted a hostile environment under the ADA.[41] •

▶ Defenses to Employment Discrimination

The first line of defense for an employer charged with employment discrimination is, of course, to assert that the plaintiff has failed to meet his or her initial burden of proving that discrimination occurred. Once a plaintiff succeeds in proving that discrimination occurred, the burden shifts to the employer to justify the discriminatory practice. Often, employers attempt to justify the discrimination by claiming that it was the result of a business necessity, a bona fide occupational qualification, or a seniority system. In some cases, as noted earlier, an effective antiharassment policy and prompt remedial action when harassment occurs may shield employers from liability for sexual harassment under Title VII.

Business Necessity

Business Necessity A defense to allegations of employment discrimination in which the employer demonstrates that an employment practice that discriminates against members of a protected class is related to job performance.

An employer may defend against a claim of disparate-impact (unintentional) discrimination by asserting that a practice that has a discriminatory effect is a **business necessity.** **EXAMPLE 25.17** If requiring a high school diploma is shown to have a discriminatory effect, an employer might argue that a high school education is necessary for workers to perform the job at a required level of competence. If the employer can demonstrate to the court's satisfaction that a definite connection exists between a high school education and job performance, the employer normally will succeed in this business necessity defense. •

Bona Fide Occupational Qualification

Bona Fide Occupational Qualification (BFOQ) Identifiable characteristics reasonably necessary to the normal operation of a particular business. These characteristics can include gender, national origin, and religion, but not race.

Another defense applies when discrimination against a protected class is essential to a job—that is, when a particular trait is a **bona fide occupational qualification (BFOQ).** Race, however, can never be a BFOQ. Generally, courts have restricted the BFOQ defense to instances in which the employee's gender is essential to the job. **EXAMPLE 25.18** A women's clothing store might legitimately hire only female sales attendants if part of an attendant's job involves assisting clients in the store's dressing rooms. Similarly, the Federal Aviation Administration can legitimately impose age limits for airline pilots—but an airline cannot impose weight limits only on female flight attendants. •

---

41. *Wenigar v. Johnson,* 712 N.W.2d 190 (Minn.App. 2006). This case involved a hostile-environment claim under the Minnesota disability statute rather than the ADA, but the court relied on another court's decision under the ADA.

Seniority Systems

An employer with a history of discrimination might have no members of protected classes in upper-level positions. Even if the employer now seeks to be unbiased, it may face a lawsuit in which the plaintiff asks a court to order that minorities be promoted ahead of schedule to compensate for past discrimination. If no present intent to discriminate is shown, however, and if promotions or other job benefits are distributed according to a fair **seniority system** (in which workers with more years of service are promoted first or laid off last), the employer normally has a good defense against the suit.

According to the United States Supreme Court, this defense may also apply to alleged discrimination under the ADA. The case involved a baggage handler who had injured his back and requested an assignment to a position at U.S. Airways, Inc. The airline refused to give the employee the position because another employee had seniority. The Court sided with U.S. Airways. If an employee with a disability requests an accommodation that conflicts with an employer's seniority system, the accommodation generally will not be considered "reasonable" under the act.[42]

> **Seniority System** In regard to employment relationships, a system in which those who have worked longest for the employer are first in line for promotions, salary increases, and other benefits. They are also the last to be laid off if the workforce must be reduced.

After-Acquired Evidence of Employee Misconduct

In some situations, employers have attempted to avoid liability for employment discrimination on the basis of "after-acquired evidence"—that is, evidence that the employer discovers after a lawsuit is filed—of an employee's misconduct. **EXAMPLE 25.19** An employer fires a worker who then sues the employer for employment discrimination. During pretrial investigation, the employer learns that the employee made material misrepresentations on his employment application—misrepresentations that, had the employer known about them, would have served as grounds to fire the individual. •

According to the United States Supreme Court, after-acquired evidence of wrongdoing cannot be used to shield an employer entirely from liability for employment discrimination. It may, however, be used to limit the amount of damages for which the employer is liable.[43]

▶ Affirmative Action

Federal statutes and regulations providing for equal opportunity in the workplace were designed to reduce or eliminate discriminatory practices with respect to hiring, retaining, and promoting employees. **Affirmative action** programs go a step further and attempt to "make up" for past patterns of discrimination by giving members of protected classes preferential treatment in hiring or promotion. During the 1960s, all federal and state government agencies, private companies that contracted to do business with the federal government, and institutions that received federal funding were required to implement affirmative action policies.

> **Affirmative Action** Job-hiring policies that give special consideration to members of protected classes in an effort to overcome present effects of past discrimination.

Title VII of the Civil Rights Act of 1964 neither requires nor prohibits affirmative action. Thus, most private firms have not been required to implement affirmative action policies, though many have voluntarily done so. Affirmative action programs have been controversial, however, particularly when they have resulted in reverse discrimination (which was discussed on page 641).

Constitutionality of Affirmative Action Programs

Because of their inherently discriminatory nature, affirmative action programs may violate the equal protection clause of the Fourteenth Amendment to the U.S. Constitution. The United States Supreme Court has held that any federal, state, or local affirmative action

> **ON THE WEB** The American Association for Affirmative Action provides a wealth of information about affirmative action at its Web site. Go to www.affirmativeaction.org/resources.html.

---

42. *U.S. Airways, Inc. v. Barnett,* 535 U.S. 391, 122 S.Ct. 1516, 152 L.Ed.2d 589 (2002).
43. *McKennon v. Nashville Banner Publishing Co.,* 513 U.S. 352, 115 S.Ct. 879, 130 L.Ed.2d 852 (1995).

Some high schools in Seattle, Washington, make their student selections based on diversity criteria, rather than on pure past scholastic achievement. Under what circumstances is this constitutional?

program that uses racial or ethnic classifications as the basis for making decisions is subject to strict scrutiny by the courts.[44] Recall from Chapter 2 that strict scrutiny is the highest standard, which means that most programs do not survive a court's analysis under this test.

Today, an affirmative action program normally is constitutional only if it attempts to remedy past discrimination and does not make use of quotas or preferences. Furthermore, once such a program has succeeded in the goal of remedying past discrimination, it must be changed or dropped.

Affirmative Action in Schools

Most of the affirmative action cases that have reached the United States Supreme Court in the last twenty years have been in the context of university admissions programs and schools, rather than employment. Generally, the Court has found that a school admissions policy that *automatically* awards minority applicants a specified number of points needed to guarantee admission violates the equal protection clause.[45] A school can, however, "consider race or ethnicity more flexibly as a 'plus' factor in the context of individualized consideration of each and every applicant."[46] In other words, it is unconstitutional for schools to apply a mechanical formula that gives "diversity bonuses" based on race or ethnicity.

CASE EXAMPLE 25.20 In 2007, the United States Supreme Court ruled on two cases involving the use of racial classifications in assigning students to schools in Seattle, Washington, and Jefferson County, Kentucky. Both school districts had adopted student assignment plans that relied on race to determine which schools certain children would attend. The Seattle school district plan classified children as "white" or "nonwhite" and used the racial classifications as a "tiebreaker" to determine which high school the students would attend. The school district in Jefferson County classified students as "black" or "other" to assign children to elementary schools. Parent groups from the relevant public schools filed lawsuits claiming that the racial preferences violated the equal protection clause. The Court held that the school districts failed to show that the use of racial classifications in their student assignment plans was necessary to achieve their stated goal of racial diversity. Hence, the Court found that the affirmative action programs of both school districts were unconstitutional.[47] •

▶ State Statutes

Although the focus of this chapter has been on federal legislation, most states also have statutes that prohibit employment discrimination. Generally, the same kinds of discrimination are prohibited under federal and state legislation. In addition, state statutes often provide protection for certain individuals who are not protected under federal laws. For example, anyone over the age of eighteen is entitled to sue for age discrimination under New Jersey state law, which specifies no threshold age limit.

Furthermore, as mentioned in Chapter 24, state laws prohibiting discrimination may apply to firms with fewer employees than the threshold number required under federal statutes, thus offering protection to more workers. State laws may also allow for additional damages, such as damages for emotional distress, which are not available under federal

---

44. See the landmark decision in *Adarand Constructors, Inc. v. Peña,* 515 U.S. 200, 115 S.Ct. 2097, 132 L.Ed.2d 158 (1995).

45. *Gratz v. Bollinger,* 539 U.S. 244, 123 S.Ct. 2411, 156 L.Ed.2d 257 (2003).

46. *Grutter v. Bollinger,* 539 U.S. 306, 123 S.Ct. 2325, 156 L.Ed.2d 304 (2003).

47. The Court consolidated the two cases and issued one opinion for both. See *Parents Involved in Community Schools v. Seattle School District No. 1,* 551 U.S. 701, 127 S.Ct. 2738, 168 L.Ed.2d 508 (2007).

statutes.[48] Finally, some states, including California and Washington, have passed laws that end affirmative action programs in that state or modify admissions policies at state-sponsored universities.

---

48. For a reverse discrimination case in which a former police officer was awarded nearly $80,000 in emotional distress damages based on a violation of New Jersey's law against discrimination, see *Klawitter v. City of Trenton*, 395 N.J.Super. 302, 928 A.2d 900 (2007).

 Reviewing . . . Employment Discrimination

Amaani Lyle, an African American woman, took a job as a scriptwriters' assistant at Warner Brothers Television Productions. She worked for the writers of *Friends,* a popular, adult-oriented television series. One of her essential job duties was to type detailed notes for the scriptwriters during brainstorming sessions in which they discussed jokes, dialogue, and story lines. The writers then combed through Lyle's notes after the meetings for script material. During these meetings, the three male scriptwriters told lewd and vulgar jokes and made sexually explicit comments and gestures. They often talked about their personal sexual experiences and fantasies, and some of these conversations were then used in episodes of *Friends*.

During the meetings, Lyle never complained that she found the writers' conduct offensive. After four months, she was fired because she could not type fast enough to keep up with the writers' conversations during the meetings. She filed a suit against Warner Brothers alleging sexual harassment and claiming that her termination was based on racial discrimination. Using the information presented in the chapter, answer the following questions.

1. Would Lyle's claim of racial discrimination be for intentional (disparate treatment) or unintentional (disparate impact) discrimination? Explain.
2. Can Lyle establish a *prima facie* case of racial discrimination? Why or why not?
3. Lyle was told when she was hired that typing speed was extremely important to her position. At the time, she maintained that she could type eighty words per minute, so she was not given a typing test. It later turned out that Lyle could type only fifty words per minute. What impact might typing speed have on Lyle's lawsuit?
4. Lyle's sexual-harassment claim is based on the hostile work environment created by the writers' sexually offensive conduct at meetings that she was required to attend. The writers, however, argue that their behavior was essential to the "creative process" of writing *Friends*, a show that routinely contained sexual innuendos and adult humor. Which defense discussed in the chapter might Warner Brothers assert using this argument?

Linking the Law *to Management*
Human Resource Management Comes to the Fore

In the good old days (at least according to company old-timers), the boss determined that the company needed additional workers. So the boss would put an ad in the newspaper, interview job applicants, and pick the ones he or she liked. If the new hires did not work out, they would simply be fired, and the process would start over again. In big companies, a personnel officer would do the hiring and firing. The point is that for much of the business history of the United States, there were no rules, regulations, or laws that placed constraints on the hiring or firing process.

As you learned in this chapter, in today's business environment an ill-conceived hiring and firing process can land a company in court facing a discrimination lawsuit. Moreover, managers today have to make sure that those who work under them do not engage in discriminatory behavior while on the job. Enter the human resource management specialist.

What Is Human Resource Management?

Human resource management (HRM) encompasses the activities required to acquire, maintain, and develop an organization's employees. HRM involves the design and application of formal systems in an organization to ensure the effective and efficient use of human talent to accomplish organizational goals.

Some of you reading this may end up in a human resources department. If so, you will need to be aware of the legal issues that you learned in this chapter (and in Chapters 23 and 24). In addition, all managers in large organizations have to be skilled in the basics of HRM. So-called flat organizations require that managers play an active role in recruiting and selecting the right personnel, as well as developing effective training programs.

The Acquisition Phase of HRM

Acquiring talented employees is the first step in an HRM system. All recruitment must be done without violating any of the laws and regulations outlined in this chapter. Obviously, recruitment must be colorblind, as well as indifferent to gender, religion, national origin, and age. A skilled HRM professional must devise recruitment methods that do not have even the slightest hint of discriminatory basis. Recruitment methods must also give an equal chance to people with disabilities. If a candidate with a disability must be rejected, the HRM professional must make sure that the rejection is based on the applicant's lack of training or ability, not on his or her disability.

On-the-Job HRM Issues

In addition, the HRM professional must monitor the on-the-job working environment. As you learned in this chapter, if some employees harass a co-worker, the courts could decide that such actions constituted constructive discharge. Sexual harassment is another major issue to consider. An HRM professional must work closely with an employment law specialist to develop a set of antiharassment rules and make sure that all employees are familiar with them. In addition, the HRM professional must create and supervise a grievance system so that any harassment can be stopped before it becomes actionable.

HRM Issues Concerning Employee Termination

In many states, employment is at will. In principle, a company can fire any employee for cause or no cause at any time. In reality, even in employment-at-will jurisdictions, lawsuits can arise for improper termination. An informed HRM specialist will develop a system to protect her or his company from termination lawsuits. There should be well-documented procedures that outline how the company will deal with an employee's improper or incompetent behavior. The company should also have an established policy about the amount of severance pay that terminated employees will receive. Sometimes, it is better to err on the side of generosity to maintain the goodwill of terminated employees.

FOR CRITICAL ANALYSIS

What are some types of actions that an HRM professional can take to reduce the probability of harassment lawsuits against her or his company?

 ## Key Terms

affirmative action 656
bona fide occupational
   qualification (BFOQ) 655
business necessity 655
constructive discharge 644

disparate-impact discrimination 640
disparate-treatment discrimination 639
employment discrimination 638
prima facie case 640
protected class 638

seniority system 656
sexual harassment 644
tangible employment
   action 645

 ## Chapter Summary: Employment Discrimination

Title VII of the Civil Rights Act of 1964 (See pages 639–648.)	Title VII prohibits employment discrimination based on race, color, national origin, religion, or gender.
	1. *Procedures*—Employees must file a claim with the Equal Employment Opportunity Commission (EEOC). The EEOC may sue the employer on the employee's behalf; if not, the employee may sue the employer directly.
	2. *Types of discrimination*—Title VII prohibits both intentional (disparate-treatment) and unintentional (disparate-impact) discrimination. Disparate-impact discrimination occurs when an employer's practice, such as hiring only persons with a certain level of education, has the effect of discriminating against a class of persons protected by Title VII. Title VII also extends to discriminatory practices, such as various forms of harassment, in the online environment.
	3. *Remedies for discrimination under Title VII*—If a plaintiff proves that unlawful discrimination occurred, he or she may be awarded reinstatement, back pay, and retroactive promotions. Damages (both compensatory and punitive) may be awarded for intentional discrimination.
Discrimination Based on Age (See pages 648–650.)	The Age Discrimination in Employment Act (ADEA) of 1967 prohibits employment discrimination on the basis of age against individuals forty years of age or older. Procedures for bringing a case under the ADEA are similar to those for bringing a case under Title VII.

Continued

Chapter Summary: Employment Discrimination—Continued

Discrimination Based on Disability (See pages 650–655.)	The Americans with Disabilities Act (ADA) of 1990 prohibits employment discrimination against persons with disabilities who are otherwise qualified to perform the essential functions of the jobs for which they apply. 1. *Procedures and remedies*—To prevail on a claim under the ADA, the plaintiff must show that she or he has a disability, is otherwise qualified for the employment in question, and was excluded from the employment solely because of the disability. Procedures under the ADA are similar to those required in Title VII cases; remedies are also similar to those under Title VII. 2. *Definition of disability*—The ADA defines the term *disability* as a physical or mental impairment that substantially limits one or more major life activities, a record of such impairment, or being regarded as having such an impairment. 3. *Reasonable accommodation*—Employers are required to reasonably accommodate the needs of persons with disabilities. Reasonable accommodations may include altering job-application procedures, modifying the physical work environment, and permitting more flexible work schedules. Employers are not required to accommodate the needs of all workers with disabilities. For example, employers need not accommodate workers who pose a definite threat to health and safety in the workplace or those who are not otherwise qualified for their jobs.
Defenses to Employment Discrimination (See pages 655–656.)	If a plaintiff proves that employment discrimination occurred, employers may avoid liability by successfully asserting certain defenses. Employers may assert that the discrimination was required for reasons of business necessity, to meet a bona fide occupational qualification, or to maintain a legitimate seniority system. Evidence of prior employee misconduct acquired after the employee has been fired is not a defense to discrimination.
Affirmative Action (See pages 656–657.)	Affirmative action programs attempt to "make up" for past patterns of discrimination by giving members of protected classes preferential treatment in hiring or promotion. Such programs are subject to strict scrutiny by the courts and are often struck down for violating the Fourteenth Amendment.
State Statutes (See pages 657–658.)	Generally, state laws also prohibit the kinds of discrimination prohibited by federal statutes. State laws may provide for more extensive protection and remedies than federal laws. Also, some states, such as California and Washington, have banned state-sponsored affirmative action programs.

 ExamPrep

ISSUE SPOTTERS

1   Ruth is a supervisor for Subs & Suds, a restaurant. Tim is a Subs & Suds employee. The owner announces that some employees will be discharged. Ruth tells Tim that if he has sex with her, he can keep his job. Is this sexual harassment? Why or why not?

2   Koko, a person with a disability, applies for a job at Lively Sales Corporation for which she is well qualified, but she is rejected. Lively continues to seek applicants and eventually fills the position with a person who does not have a disability. Could Koko succeed in a suit against Lively for discrimination? Explain.

BEFORE THE TEST

Check your answers to the Issue Spotters, and at the same time, take the interactive quiz for this chapter. Go to **www.cengage.com/blaw/blt** and click on "Chapter 25." First, click on "Answers to Issue Spotters" to check your answers. Next, click on "Interactive Quiz" to assess your mastery of the concepts in this chapter. Then click on "Flashcards" to review this chapter's Key Term definitions.

 For Review

Answers for the even-numbered questions in this For Review section can be found on this text's accompanying Web site at **www.cengage.com/blaw/blt**. *Select "Chapter 25" and click on "For Review."*

1 Generally, what kind of conduct is prohibited by Title VII of the Civil Rights Act of 1964, as amended?
2 What is the difference between disparate-treatment discrimination and disparate-impact discrimination?
3 What remedies are available under Title VII of the 1964 Civil Rights Act, as amended?
4 What federal acts prohibit discrimination based on age and discrimination based on disability?
5 What are three defenses to claims of employment discrimination?

▶ Hypothetical Scenarios and Case Problems

25–1 Title VII Violations. Discuss fully whether either of the following actions would constitute a violation of Title VII of the 1964 Civil Rights Act, as amended.

  1 Tennington, Inc., is a consulting firm and has ten employees. These employees travel on consulting jobs in seven states. Tennington has an employment record of hiring only white males.

  2 Novo Films, Inc., is making a film about Africa and needs to employ approximately one hundred extras for this picture. To hire these extras, Novo advertises in all major newspapers in Southern California. The ad states that only African Americans need apply.

25–2 Hypothetical Question with Sample Answer Chinawa, a major processor of cheese sold throughout the United States, employs one hundred workers at its principal processing plant. The plant is located in Heartland Corners, which has a population that is 50 percent white and 25 percent African American, with the balance Hispanic American, Asian American, and others. Chinawa requires a high school diploma as a condition of employment for its cleaning crew. Three-fourths of the white population complete high school, compared with only one-fourth of those in the minority groups. Chinawa has an all-white cleaning crew. Has Chinawa violated Title VII of the Civil Rights Act of 1964? Explain.

—For a sample answer to Question 25–2, go to Appendix E at the end of this text.

25–3 Religious Discrimination. Gina Gomez, a devout Roman Catholic, worked for Sam's Department Stores, Inc., in Phoenix, Arizona. Sam's considered Gomez a productive employee because her sales exceeded $200,000 per year. At the time, the store gave its managers the discretion to grant unpaid leave to employees but prohibited vacations or leave during the holiday season—October through December. Gomez felt that she had a "calling" to go on a "pilgrimage" in October 2009 to Medjugorje, Bosnia and Herzegovina, where some persons claimed to have had visions of the Virgin Mary. The Catholic Church had not designated the site an official pilgrimage site, the visions were not expected to be stronger in October, and tours were available at other times. The store managers denied Gomez's request for leave, but she had a nonrefundable ticket and left anyway. Sam's terminated her employment, and she could not find another job. Can Gomez establish a *prima facie* case of religious discrimination? Explain.

25–4 Case Problem with Sample Answer For twenty years, Darlene Jespersen worked as a bartender at Harrah's Casino in Reno, Nevada. In 2000, Harrah's implemented a "Personal Best" program that included new grooming standards. Among other requirements, women were told to wear makeup "applied neatly in complimentary colors." Jespersen, who never wore makeup off the job, felt so uncomfortable wearing it on the job that it interfered with her ability to perform. Unwilling to wear makeup and not qualifying for another position at Harrah's with similar compensation, Jespersen quit the casino. She filed a suit in a federal district court against Harrah's Operating Co., the casino's owner, alleging that the makeup policy discriminated against women in violation of Title VII of the Civil Rights Act of 1964. Harrah's argued that any burdens under the new program fell equally on both genders, citing the "Personal Best" short-hair standard that applied only to men. Jespersen responded by describing her personal reaction to the makeup policy and emphasizing her exemplary record during her tenure at Harrah's. In whose favor should the court rule? Why? [*Jespersen v. Harrah's Operating Co.*, 444 F.3d 1104 (9th Cir. 2006)]

—After you have answered Problem 25–4, compare your answer with the sample answer given on the Web site that accompanies this text. Go to **www.cengage.com/blaw/blt**, select "Chapter 25," and click on "Case Problem with Sample Answer."

25–5 Discrimination Based on Disability. Cerebral palsy limits Steven Bradley's use of his legs. He uses forearm crutches for short-distance walks and a wheelchair for longer distances. Standing for more than ten or fifteen minutes is difficult. With support, however, Bradley can climb stairs and get on and off a stool. His condition also restricts the use of his fourth finger to, for example, type, but it does not limit his ability to write—he completed two years of college. His grip strength is normal, and he can lift heavy objects. In 2001, Bradley applied for a "greeter" or "cashier" position at a Wal-Mart Stores, Inc., Supercenter in Richmond, Missouri. The job descriptions stated, "No experience or qualification is required." Bradley indicated that he was available for full- or part-time work from 4:00 P.M. to 10:00 P.M. any evening. His employment history showed that he currently worked as a proofreader and that he had previously worked as an administrator. His application was rejected, according to Janet Daugherty, the personnel manager, based on his "work history" and the "direct threat" that he posed to the safety of himself and others. Bradley claimed, however, that the store refused to hire him due to his disability. What steps must Bradley follow to pursue his claim? What does he need to show to prevail? Is he likely to meet these requirements? Discuss. [*EEOC v. Wal-Mart Stores, Inc.*, 477 F.3d 561 (8th Cir. 2007)]

25–6 Discrimination Based on Gender. The Milwaukee County Juvenile Detention Center established a new policy that required each unit of the facility to be staffed at all times by at least one officer of the same gender as the detainees housed at a unit. The purpose of the policy, administrators said, was to reduce the likelihood of sexual abuse of juveniles by officers of the other gender. Because there were many more male units in the center than female units, the policy had the effect of reducing the number of shifts available for women officers and increasing the number of shifts for men. Two female officers sued for gender discrimination. The district court held for the county, finding that the policy of assignment was based on a bona fide occupational qualification (BFOQ) and so was not illegal gender discrimination. The officers appealed. What would be evidence that the county had a valid BFOQ? [*Henry v. Milwaukee County*, 539 F.3d 573 (7th Cir. 2008)]

25–7 Sexual Harassment. The Metropolitan Government of Nashville and Davidson County, Tennessee (Metro), began looking into rumors of sexual harassment by the Metro School District's employee relations director, Gene Hughes. Veronica Frazier, a Metro human resources officer, asked Vicky Crawford, a Metro employee, whether she had witnessed "inappropriate behavior" by Hughes. Crawford described several instances of sexually harassing behavior. Two other employees also reported being sexually harassed by Hughes. Metro took no action against Hughes, but soon after completing the investigation, Metro accused Crawford of embezzlement and fired her. The two other employees were also fired. Crawford filed a suit in a federal district court against Metro, claiming retaliation under Title VII. What arguments can be made that Crawford's situation does or does not qualify as a retaliation claim under Title VII? Discuss. [*Crawford v. Metropolitan Government of Nashville and Davidson County, Tennessee*, __ U.S. __, 129 S.Ct. 846, 172 L.Ed.2d 650 (2009)]

25–8 A Question of Ethics *Titan Distribution, Inc., employed Quintak, Inc., to run its tire mounting and distribution operation in Des Moines, Iowa. Robert Chalfant worked for Quintak as a second-shift supervisor at Titan. He suffered a heart attack in 1992 and underwent heart bypass surgery in 1997. He also had arthritis. In July 2002, Titan decided to terminate Quintak. Chalfant applied to work at Titan. On his application, he described himself as having a disability. After a physical exam, Titan's doctor concluded that Chalfant could work in his current capacity, and he was notified that he would be hired. Despite the notice, Nadis Barucic, a Titan employee, wrote "not pass px" at the top of Chalfant's application, and he was not hired. He took a job with AMPCO Systems, a parking ramp management company. This work involved walking up to five miles a day and lifting more weight than he had at Titan. In September, Titan eliminated its second shift. Chalfant filed a suit in a federal district court against Titan, in part, under the Americans with Disabilities Act (ADA). Titan argued that the reason it had not hired Chalfant was not that he did not pass the physical, but no one—including Barucic—could explain why she had written "not pass px" on his application. Later, Titan claimed that Chalfant was not hired because the entire second shift was going to be eliminated. [Chalfant v. Titan Distribution, Inc., 475 F.3d 982 (8th Cir. 2007)]*

1 What must Chalfant establish to make his case under the ADA? Can he meet these requirements? Explain.

2 In employment-discrimination cases, punitive damages can be appropriate when an employer acts with malice or reckless indifference to an employee's protected rights. Would an award of punitive damages to Chalfant be appropriate in this case? Discuss.

▶ Critical Thinking and Writing Assignments

25–9 Critical Legal Thinking. Why has the federal government limited the application of the statutes discussed in this chapter to firms with a specified number of employees, such as fifteen or twenty? Should these laws apply to all employers, regardless of size? Why or why not?

25–10 Case Analysis Question Go to Appendix F at the end of this text and examine Case No. 5 [*Burlington Northern and Santa Fe Railway Co. v. White*, 548 U.S. 53, 126 S.Ct. 2405, 165 L.Ed.2d 345 (2006)]. This case has been excerpted there in great detail. Review and then brief the case, making sure that your brief answers the following questions.

1 Issue: What was the plaintiff's complaint, the defendant's response, and the chief legal dispute between them?

2 Rule of Law: Which provisions of Title VII did the Court consider here, and which rule of statutory interpretation governed the Court's consideration?

3 Applying the Rule of Law: How did the Court interpret these provisions, and how did that interpretation apply to the circumstances in this case?

4 Conclusion: Based on its application of the principles in this case, what did the Court conclude?

Practical Internet Exercises

Go to this text's Web site at **www.cengage.com/blaw/blt**, select "Chapter 25," and click on "Practical Internet Exercises." There you will find the following Internet research exercises that you can perform to learn more about the topics covered in this chapter.

Practical Internet Exercise 25–1: LEGAL PERSPECTIVE—Americans with Disabilities
Practical Internet Exercise 25–2: MANAGEMENT PERSPECTIVE—Equal Employment Opportunity
Practical Internet Exercise 25–3: SOCIAL PERSPECTIVE—Religious and National-Origin Discrimination

Cumulative Business Hypothetical

Two brothers, Ray and Paul Ashford, start a business—Ashford Brothers, Inc.—manufacturing a new type of battery system for hybrid automobiles. The batteries hit the market at the perfect time and are in great demand.

1. Loren, one of Ashford's salespersons, anxious to make a sale, intentionally quotes a price to a customer that is $500 lower than Ashford had authorized for that particular product. The customer purchases the product at the quoted price. When Ashford learns of the deal, it claims that it is not legally bound to the sales contract because it did not authorize Loren to sell the product at that price. Is Ashford bound to the contract? Discuss fully.

2. One day Gina, an Ashford employee, suffered a serious burn when she accidentally spilled some acid on her hand. The accident occurred because another employee, who was suspected of using illegal drugs, carelessly bumped into her. The hand required a series of skin-graft operations before it healed sufficiently to allow Gina to return to work. Gina wants to obtain compensation for her lost wages and medical expenses. Can she do that? If so, how?

3. After Gina's injury, Ashford decides to conduct random drug tests on all of its employees. Several employees claim that the testing violates their privacy rights. If the dispute is litigated, what factors will the court consider in deciding whether the random drug testing is legally permissible?

4. Ashford provides health insurance for its two hundred employees, including Dan. For personal medical reasons, Dan takes twelve weeks' leave. During this period, can Dan continue his coverage under Ashford's health-insurance plan? After Dan returns to work, Ashford closes Dan's division and terminates the employees, including Dan. Can Dan continue his coverage under Ashford's health-insurance plan? If so, at whose expense?

5. Aretha, another employee at Ashford, is disgusted by the sexually offensive behavior of several male employees. She has complained to her supervisor on several occasions about the offensive behavior, but the supervisor merely laughs at her concerns. Aretha decides to bring a legal action against the company for sexual harassment. Does Aretha's complaint concern *quid pro quo* harassment or hostile-environment harassment? What federal statute protects employees from sexual harassment? What remedies are available under that statute? What procedures must Aretha follow in pursuing her legal action?

Extended Case Study: *Media General Operations, Inc. v. National Labor Relations Board*

The National Labor Relations Act (NLRA), which was discussed in Chapter 24, ensures that employees are not discriminated against for engaging in collective action in the workplace. It protects the rights of employees to organize and engage in collective bargaining and related activities. This protection prevents employers from retaliating against workers for participating in "concerted activities" and provides a process for enforcing of the rights that the NLRA guarantees.

In this Extended Case Study, we review the case of Media General Operations, Inc. v. National Labor Relations Board,[1] *which involved a worker who was fired for making a profane reference to a company executive during collective bargaining contract negotiations between the employer and the employees' union. Was the worker's derogatory remark a protected "concerted activity" under the NLRA or an unprotected "attack"?*

---

1. 560 F.3d 181 (4th Cir. 2009).

Extended Case Study: *Media General Operations, Inc. v. National Labor Relations Board—Continued*

CASE BACKGROUND

Gregg McMillen was a journeyman pressman for *The Tampa Tribune,* a newspaper published by Media General Operations, Inc., which does business as *The Tampa Tribune.* The Graphic Communications Conference of the International Brotherhood of Teamsters, Local 180 represented McMillen and the other pressroom employees.

Negotiations between the union and the publisher over a contract to cover the employees had failed to yield results more than a year after the previous contract expired. Bill Barker, vice president of the Tribune, wrote to the pressroom workers, accusing the union of delaying the process. About two dozen employees, including McMillen, protested in a letter to Barker.

Barker responded with a letter that repeated his view. During a subsequent shift, McMillen walked into the pressroom office where Glenn Lerro, the pressroom foreman, and Joel Bridges, the assistant foreman, asked him whether he had seen the letter. He said no, referring to the company executive as "that f * * * ing idiot." He later apologized to Lerro for the remark. Three days later, he was fired for violating a workplace rule that bars the use of "threatening, abusive, or harassing language."

McMillen filed a charge with the National Labor Relations Board (NLRB), which concluded that McMillen's discharge violated the NLRA. On appeal, an administrative law judge (ALJ) found that McMillen's remark was not a protected act. The NLRB reversed this decision. The publisher appealed to the U.S. Court of Appeals for the Fourth Circuit.

MAJORITY OPINION

DUNCAN, Circuit Judge:

* * * *

* * * *Four factors * * * determine whether the Act's protection applies: (1) the place of the discussion; (2) the subject matter of the discussion; (3) the nature of the employee's outburst; and (4) whether the outburst was, in any way, provoked by an employer's unfair labor practice. If the balance is such that the conduct crosses the line from protected activity * * * to opprobrious [despicable] conduct, the worker loses the protection of the Act.* [Emphasis added.]

In the instant case, the ALJ found and the Board agreed that the first two factors weighed in favor of McMillen retaining the Act's protections. The discussion during which the derogatory remark was made took place away from the pressroom floor in an office that was used by pressroom supervisors and thus was at least semi-private. In addition, McMillen's comment occurred in the context of a discussion of Barker's letters, and those letters dealt with the ongoing contract negotiations between the Tribune and the Union. The Board also agreed with the ALJ that the fourth factor militated against extending the protection of the Act, since McMillen never claimed that he was responding to an unfair labor practice. Instead, his outburst was in response to a series of admittedly legal and truthful letters written by Barker.

Where the two adjudicators parted ways was on the significance of the third factor. The ALJ determined that the nature of the outburst was "so egregious [offensive]" that it removed McMillen's statement from the Act's protection. The Board disagreed. Analyzing the record, it found that the nature of the remark was only moderately prejudicial to McMillen's retention of the Act's protection. The Board based this determination on the fact that the remark was not made directly to Barker, that it was an isolated statement for which McMillen later apologized, and that it was neither a direct challenge to Barker's authority nor did it undermine employee discipline. Because of this different weighting of the third factor, the Board overturned the ALJ's conclusion and found that on the balance of the factors McMillen was entitled to the protection of the Act.

We disagree. The Board overreached as a matter of law in finding that the conduct in question was not so egregious as to forfeit the protection of the Act.

The lack of concurrence between Barker's lawful letter and McMillen's comment particularly disfavors protection. This was not a spontaneous outburst in response to an illegal threat but an *ad hominem* [appealing to people's emotions] attack made in the context of a discussion McMillen initiated with two supervisors. It was a response to an undisputedly legal letter issued in exercise of the company's rights. In addition, McMillen had not even read the letter in question, which further divorces his derogatory remark from the context of the ongoing labor dispute and thus makes the remark of a nature less eligible for protection. Insulting, obscene personal attacks by an employee against a supervisor need not be tolerated, even when they occur during otherwise protected activity.

It is also of particular significance * * * that McMillen made his derogatory remark in response to a series of *lawful* letters sent by his employer. Thus, the fourth factor of the * * * test weighs more than slightly against extending the Act's protection.

* * * McMillen's opprobrious *ad hominem* attack on a supervisor made at a point temporally remove[d] from and concerned only with lawful behavior by the employer falls outside the zone of protection.

* * * *

* * * We therefore reverse the judgment of the Board and reinstate the opinion of [the] ALJ.

DISSENTING OPINION

KING, Circuit Judge, dissenting.

* * * *

* * * The panel majority * * * seems to reject the Board's analysis of at least two * * * factors (factors one and three). The

Continued

majority's analysis of these factors, however, is * * * problematic and unconvincing * * * . For example, the majority suggests that factor one, i.e., the place of the discussion, should weigh against the Act's protection because McMillen's comment was made in a "setting * * * physically * * * removed from the site of the ongoing collective bargaining negotiations." * * * The majority's apparent view—that only employee conduct occurring at the physical site of labor negotiations should be accorded protection—is not only grossly unfair, but also completely at odds with precedent. That is, the typical factor one assessment focuses on whether the employee conduct, because of the place where it occurred, somehow undermined workplace discipline. Here, the majority does not—and cannot—identify anything in this record supportive of the notion that McMillen's comment undermined workplace discipline.

The panel majority further suggests that factor three—the nature of the employee's outburst—should be given more than the "moderate" weight against protection assigned to it by the Board. More specifically, the majority * * * [indicates] that insulting, obscene personal attacks by an employee against a supervisor need not be tolerated * * * . [But] care must be exercised in evaluating employee language uttered in the course of engaging in activity protected by * * * the Act, and * * * an employee's exercise of rights under the Act must not be stifled by the threat of liability for the over enthusiastic use of rhetoric. Strikingly, * * *

it has been held that calling an employer's president a "son-of-a-bitch" was not so outrageous as to justify discharge. In light of this and other precedent, it was entirely rational and consistent with the Act for the Board to rule that McMillen's comment should weigh only moderately against the Act's protection.

* * * The Board's disposition of this dispute was well within the parameters of its legal authority and binding precedent, and it is instead the panel majority that has reached beyond its bounds.

QUESTIONS FOR ANALYSIS

1. **Law.** What was the majority's decision in this case? On what was this decision based?
2. **Law.** What was the dissent's position with respect to the majority's reasoning and decision? If the majority of the court had agreed with the dissent, what would have resulted?
3. **Technology.** Would the decision in this case likely have been different if the employee had made the derogatory remark online?
4. **Cultural Dimensions.** What is the possible effect on an employee who is aware of the outcome in this case?
5. **Implications for the Investor.** What does the outcome in this case suggest to an employer engaged in collective bargaining negotiations with an employees' union?

Unit Five

Business Organizations

▶ *Unit Contents*

(Othermore/Creative Commons)

Sole Proprietorships and Private Franchises

"Why not go out on a limb? Isn't that where the fruit is?"

—Frank Scully, 1892–1964
(American author)

Chapter Outline

- Sole Proprietorships
- Franchises
- The Franchise Contract
- Termination of the Franchise

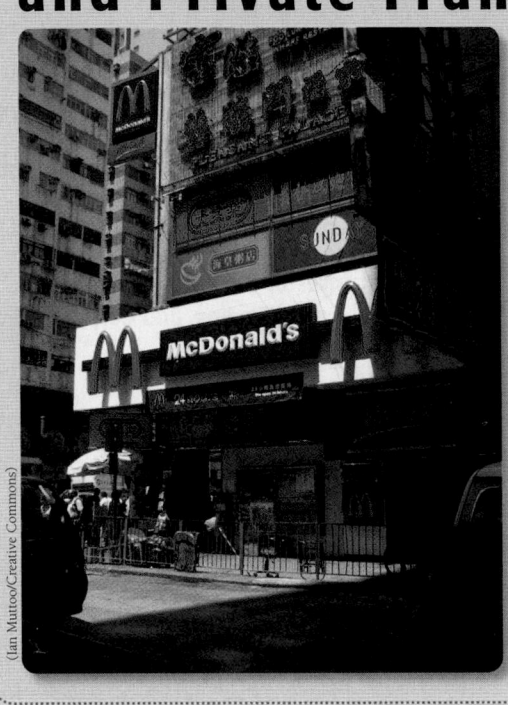

(Ian Muttoo/Creative Commons)

Learning Objectives

After reading this chapter, you should be able to answer the following questions:

1. What advantages and disadvantages are associated with the sole proprietorship?

2. What is a franchise? What are the most common types of franchises?

3. What laws govern a franchising relationship?

4. What terms and conditions are typically included in a franchise contract?

5. What is wrongful termination? In what types of situations do courts typically find that a franchisor has wrongfully terminated a franchise?

Entrepreneur One who initiates and assumes the financial risk of a new business enterprise and undertakes to provide or control its management.

Many Americans would agree with Frank Scully's comment in the chapter-opening quotation that to succeed in business one must "go out on a limb." Certainly, an entrepreneur's primary motive for undertaking a business enterprise is to make profits. An **entrepreneur** is by definition one who initiates and assumes the financial risks of a new enterprise and undertakes to provide or control its management.

One of the questions faced by anyone who wishes to start a business is what form of business organization should be chosen for the endeavor. In making this determination, the entrepreneur needs to consider a number of important factors, including (1) ease of creation, (2) the liability of the owners, (3) tax considerations, and (4) the need for capital. In studying this unit on business organizations, keep these factors in mind as you read about the various business organizational forms available to entrepreneurs.

Traditionally, entrepreneurs have used three major forms to structure their business enterprises—the sole proprietorship, the partnership, and the corporation. In this chapter, we examine sole proprietorships and discuss franchises as well. Although the franchise is not really a business organizational form, it is widely used today by entrepreneurs seeking to make profits.

▶ Sole Proprietorships

Sole Proprietorship The simplest form of business organization, in which the owner is the business. The owner reports business income on his or her personal income tax return and is legally responsible for all debts and obligations incurred by the business.

The simplest form of business organization is a **sole proprietorship.** In this form, the owner is the business; thus, anyone who does business without creating a separate business organization has a sole proprietorship. More than two-thirds of all U.S. businesses are sole proprietorships. They are usually small enterprises—about 99 percent of the sole proprietorships in the United States have revenues of less than $1 million per year. Sole proprietors can own and manage any type of business, ranging from an informal, home-office undertaking to a large restaurant or construction firm.

Advantages of the Sole Proprietorship

A major advantage of the sole proprietorship is that the proprietor owns the entire business and has a right to receive all of the profits (because he or she assumes all of the risk). In addition, it is often easier and less costly to start a sole proprietorship than to start any other kind of business, as few legal formalities are involved.[1] No documents need to be filed with the government to start a sole proprietorship (though a state business license may be required to operate certain types of businesses).

This form of business organization also offers more flexibility than does a partnership or a corporation. The sole proprietor is free to make any decision she or he wishes concerning the business—including whom to hire, when to take a vacation, and what kind of business to pursue. In addition, the proprietor can sell or transfer all or part of the business to another party at any time and does not need approval from anyone else (as would be required from partners in a partnership or normally from shareholders in a corporation).

A sole proprietor pays only personal income taxes (including Social Security and Medicare taxes) on the business's profits, which are reported as personal income on the proprietor's personal income tax return. Sole proprietors are also allowed to establish certain retirement accounts that are tax-exempt until the funds are withdrawn.

Disadvantages of the Sole Proprietorship

The major disadvantage of the sole proprietorship is that the proprietor alone bears the burden of any losses or liabilities incurred by the business enterprise. In other words, the sole proprietor has unlimited liability, or legal responsibility, for all obligations incurred in doing business. Any lawsuit against the business or its employees can lead to unlimited personal liability for the owner of a sole proprietorship. Creditors can go after the owner's personal assets to satisfy any business debts. This unlimited liability is a major factor to be considered in choosing a business form.

EXAMPLE 26.1 Sheila Fowler operates a golf shop as a sole proprietorship. The business is located near a major golf course. A professional golfer, Dean Maheesh, is seriously injured when a display of golf clubs, which one of Fowler's employees had failed to secure, falls on him. If Maheesh sues Fowler's shop (a sole proprietorship) and wins, her personal liability could easily exceed the limits of her insurance policy. In this situation, Fowler could lose not only her business, but also her house, car, and any other personal assets that can be attached to pay the judgment. ●

The sole proprietorship also has the disadvantage of lacking continuity on the death of the proprietor. When the owner dies, so does the business—it is automatically dissolved. Another disadvantage is that the proprietor's opportunity to raise capital is limited to personal funds and the funds of those who are willing to make loans.

This woman owns a gift shop. She owns the business by herself. What are the advantages of doing business as a sole proprietorship?

(Tay Rees/Stone/Getty Images)

> *"Always tell yourself: The difference between running a business and ruining a business is I."*
>
> Anonymous

---

1. Although starting a sole proprietorship involves relatively few legal formalities compared with other business organizational forms, even small sole proprietorships may need to comply with certain zoning requirements, obtain appropriate licenses, and the like.

The personal liability of a sole proprietorship's owner was at issue in the following case. The case involved the federal Cable Communications Act, which prohibits a commercial establishment from broadcasting television programs to its patrons without authorization. The court had to decide whether the owner of the sole proprietorship that had installed a satellite television system was personally liable for violating this act by identifying a restaurant as a "residence" for billing purposes.

Case 26.1 Garden City Boxing Club, Inc. v. Dominguez

United States District Court, Northern District of Illinois, Eastern Division, __ F.Supp.2d __ (2006).

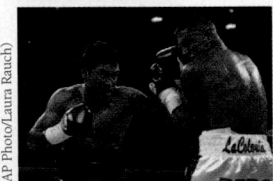

Who is liable for paying the fee for closed-circuit broadcast rights to a prizefight when the end-user is misidentified, causing revenue reduction?

FACTS Garden City Boxing Club, Inc. (GCB), which is based in San Jose, California, owned the exclusive right to broadcast several prizefights via closed-circuit television, including the match between Oscar De La Hoya and Fernando Vargas on September 14, 2002. GCB sold the right to receive the broadcasts to bars and other commercial venues. The fee was $20 multiplied by an establishment's maximum fire code occupancy. Antenas Enterprises in Chicago, Illinois, sells and installs satellite television systems under a contract with DISH Network. After installing a system, Antenas sends the buyer's address and other identifying information to DISH. In January 2002, Luis Garcia, an Antenas employee, identified a new customer as José Melendez at 220 Hawthorn Commons in Vernon Hills. The address was a restaurant—Mundelein Burrito—but Garcia designated the account as residential. Mundelein's patrons watched the De La Hoya–Vargas match, as well as three other fights on other dates, for which the restaurant paid only the residential rate to DISH and nothing to GCB. GCB filed a suit in a federal district court against Luis Dominguez, the sole proprietor of Antenas, to collect the fee.

ISSUE Is Dominguez personally liable for the restaurant's commercial fee to GCB?

DECISION Yes. The court issued a summary judgment in GCB's favor, holding that the plaintiff was entitled to the amount of the fee, plus damages and attorneys' fees.

REASON The court found that Mundelein Burrito was clearly a commercial establishment. "The structure of the building, an exterior identification sign, and its location in a strip mall made this obvious." Under the Cable Communications Act, "an authorized intermediary of a communication violates the Act when it divulges communication through an electronic channel to one other than the addressee." Antenas's improper designation of Mundelein Burrito as residential allowed the unauthorized broadcast of four prizefights to the restaurant. Antenas is a sole proprietorship. Furthermore, a sole proprietorship has no legal identity apart from that of the individual who owns it. A sole proprietor is personally responsible for the acts that his or her employees commit within the scope of their employment. Dominguez owns Antenas, and Garcia is Dominguez's employee. "Accordingly, Dominguez is personally liable for the damages caused by the violation of * * * the [Cable Communications] Act."

WHAT IF THE FACTS WERE DIFFERENT? *If Mundelein Burrito had identified itself as a residence when ordering the satellite system, how might the result in this case have been different?*

▶ Franchises

Franchise Any arrangement in which the owner of a trademark, trade name, or copyright licenses another to use that trademark, trade name, or copyright in the selling of goods or services.

Franchisee One receiving a license to use another's (the franchisor's) trademark, trade name, or copyright in the sale of goods and services.

Franchisor One licensing another (the franchisee) to use the owner's trademark, trade name, or copyright in the selling of goods or services.

Instead of setting up a business form through which to market their own products or services, many entrepreneurs opt to purchase a franchise. A **franchise** is defined as any arrangement in which the owner of a trademark, a trade name, or a copyright licenses others to use the trademark, trade name, or copyright in the selling of goods or services. A **franchisee** (a purchaser of a franchise) is generally legally independent of the **franchisor** (the seller of the franchise). At the same time, the franchisee is economically dependent on the franchisor's integrated business system. In other words, a franchisee can operate as an independent businessperson but still obtain the advantages of a regional or national organization.

Today, franchising companies and their franchisees account for a significant portion of all retail sales in this country. Well-known franchises include McDonald's, 7-Eleven, and Burger King. Franchising has also become a popular way for businesses to expand their operations internationally, as will be discussed in this chapter's *Beyond Our Borders* feature on page 675.

Types of Franchises

KEEP IN MIND Because a franchise involves the licensing of a trademark, a trade name, or a copyright, the law governing intellectual property may apply in some situations.

Many different kinds of businesses now sell franchises, and numerous types of franchises are available. Generally, though, the majority of franchises fall into one of three classifications: distributorships, chain-style business operations, or manufacturing or processing-plant arrangements.

DISTRIBUTORSHIP In a *distributorship,* a manufacturer (the franchisor) licenses a dealer (the franchisee) to sell its product. Often, a distributorship covers an exclusive territory. An example of this type of franchise is an automobile dealership or beer distributorship.

EXAMPLE 26.2 Black Butte Beer Company distributes its brands of beer through a network of authorized wholesale distributors, each with an assigned territory. Marik signs a distributorship contract for the area from Gainesville to Ocala, Florida. If the contract states that Marik is the exclusive distributor in that area, then no other franchisee may distribute Black Butte beer in that region. ●

CHAIN-STYLE BUSINESS OPERATION In a *chain-style business operation,* a franchise operates under a franchisor's trade name and is identified as a member of a select group of dealers that engage in the franchisor's business. The franchisee is generally required to follow standardized or prescribed methods of operation. Often, the franchisor requires that the franchisee maintain certain standards of operation. In addition, the franchisee may be required to obtain materials and supplies exclusively from the franchisor. McDonald's and most other fast-food chains are examples of this type of franchise. Chain-style franchises are also common in service-related businesses, including real estate brokerage firms such as Century 21 and tax-preparing services such as H&R Block, Inc.

MANUFACTURING OR PROCESSING-PLANT ARRANGEMENT In a *manufacturing or processing-plant arrangement,* the franchisor transmits to the franchisee the essential ingredients or formula to make a particular product. The franchisee then markets the product either at wholesale or at retail in accordance with the franchisor's standards. Examples of this type of franchise are Pepsi-Cola and other soft-drink bottling companies.

Laws Governing Franchising

Because a franchise relationship is primarily a contractual relationship, it is governed by contract law. If the franchise exists primarily for the sale of products manufactured by the franchisor, the law governing sales contracts as expressed in Article 2 of the Uniform Commercial Code applies (see Chapters 15 through 17). Additionally, the federal government and most states have enacted laws governing certain aspects of franchising. Generally, these laws are designed to protect prospective franchisees from dishonest franchisors and to prohibit franchisors from terminating franchises without good cause.

FEDERAL REGULATION OF FRANCHISING The federal government regulates franchising through laws that apply to specific industries and through the Franchise Rule, created by the Federal Trade Commission (FTC).

Industry-Specific Standards. Congress has enacted laws that protect franchisees in certain industries, such as automobile dealerships and service stations. These laws protect the franchisee from unreasonable demands and bad faith terminations of the franchise by the franchisor. If an automobile manufacturer-franchisor terminates a franchise because of a

"Hi. Would you guys be interested in a Starbux franchise?"

dealer-franchisee's failure to comply with unreasonable demands (for example, failure to attain an unrealistically high sales quota), the manufacturer may be liable for damages.[2] Similarly, federal law prescribes the conditions under which a franchisor of service stations can terminate the franchise.[3] Federal antitrust laws (to be discussed in Chapter 32) also apply in certain circumstances to prohibit certain types of anticompetitive agreements.

> *"Business opportunities are like buses, there's always another one coming."*
>
> Richard Branson, 1950–present
> (British entrepreneur)

The Franchise Rule.   The FTC's Franchise Rule requires franchisors to disclose certain material facts that a prospective franchisee needs to make an informed decision concerning the purchase of a franchise.[4] The rule was designed to enable potential franchisees to weigh the risks and benefits of an investment. The rule requires the franchisor to make numerous written disclosures to prospective franchisees. For example, if a franchisor provides projected earnings figures, the franchisor must indicate whether the figures are based on actual data or hypothetical examples. If a franchisor makes sales or earnings projections based on actual data for a specific franchise location, the franchisor must disclose the number and percentage of its existing franchises that have achieved this result.

All representations made to a prospective franchisee must have a reasonable basis. Franchisors are also required to explain termination, cancellation, and renewal provisions of the franchise contract to potential franchisees before the agreement is signed. Those who violate the Franchise Rule are subject to substantial civil penalties, and the FTC can sue on behalf of injured parties to recover damages.

Can a franchisor satisfy the Franchise Rule by providing disclosures via the Internet? See this chapter's *Adapting the Law to the Online Environment* feature for a discussion of this topic.

Ethical Issue ⚖️

Should the law require franchisors to give prospective franchisees information about potential earnings? The most common question that entrepreneurs who are thinking about starting a franchise ask is, "How much will I make?" Surprisingly, the law does not require franchisors to provide any estimate of, or actual data on, the earnings potential of a franchise. Franchisors can voluntarily choose to provide earnings data on their uniform disclosure documents but are not required to do so. If franchisors do make earnings claims, as previously mentioned, they must specify whether these figures are actual or hypothetical, follow specific rules, and have a reasonable basis for these claims. About 75 percent of franchisors choose not to provide information about earnings potential (which is Item 19 on the disclosure form).

The failure of the latest version of the FTC's Franchise Rule to require disclosure of earnings potential has led to many complaints from franchisees.[5] After all, some franchisees invest their life savings in franchises that ultimately fail because of unrealistic earnings expectations. Moreover, the franchisee may be legally responsible to continue operating and paying the franchisor even when the business is not turning a profit. For instance, Thomas Anderson asked the franchisor, Rocky Mountain Chocolate Factory, Inc. (RMCF), and five of its franchisees for earnings information before he entered into a franchise agreement, but he did not receive any data. When his chocolate franchise failed to become profitable, Anderson and his partner were ordered by a court to pay $33,109 in past due royalties and interest to RMCF (plus court costs and expenses).[6]

---

2. Automobile Dealers' Franchise Act of 1965, also known as the Automobile Dealers' Day in Court Act, 15 U.S.C. Sections 1221 *et seq.*

3. Petroleum Marketing Practices Act (PMPA) of 1979,15 U.S.C. Sections 2801 *et seq.*

4. 16 C.F.R. Part 436.

5. For example, Beth Tomei and nine other franchisees filed a class-action arbitration claim against their franchisor, Butterfly Life, a women's fitness company, for failure to disclose financial information. The arbitration was dismissed in 2009, however, because the plaintiff-franchisees reportedly failed to pay their allocated share of the arbitration fees.

6. *Rocky Mountain Chocolate Factory, Inc. v. SDMS, Inc.*, 2009 WL 579516 (D.Colo. 2009).

Adapting the Law to the Online Environment

Satisfying the FTC's Franchise Rule in the Internet Age

The Federal Trade Commission (FTC) issued its Franchise Rule in 1978, when the normal medium for transmission of information in a permanent form was on paper. When the Internet became a reality for a large number of people in the 1990s, the FTC was faced with the possibility that franchisors might use Web sites to provide downloadable information to prospective franchisees. Was such online information the equivalent of an offer that requires compliance with the FTC's Franchise Rule? The FTC said yes.

In the 1990s, the FTC issued advisory opinions allowing electronic disclosures by CD-ROM and DVD, as long as the prospective franchisee was given the option of receiving the disclosure in electronic or paper format and chose electronic. The CD-ROM or DVD had to have a label indicating that it contained the disclosures required by the FTC and the date when it was issued. In 1999, the FTC began its formal rulemaking process (see Chapter 1) to create regulations that would apply to online disclosures.[a]

Franchise.com and Others Get the Green Light

In 2001, Franchise.com, a marketer of existing franchises, became the first Web-based franchise operation to win the FTC's approval of its plan to provide electronic disclosure services for all of its franchisor advertisers. Franchise.com requires any franchisor that wishes to advertise on its Web site to provide a disclosure document containing the FTC's proposed cover-page statement regarding electronic disclosures. When a prospective franchisee comes to the Franchise.com Web site, he or she must agree to receive disclosures electronically by clicking on the appropriate button. The prospect can then obtain information on a particular

franchise through the Web site. Whenever prospective franchisees access their accounts at the Web site, there are hyperlinks to written summary documents. Each time a prospective franchisee clicks on the hyperlinks, she or he is advised to download or print the disclosure document for future reference.

In 2003, McGarry Internet, Ltd., of Dublin, Ireland, received similar approval. This company sends each prospective franchisee a Uniform Franchise Offering Circular via e-mail. In 2005, the FTC approved the request of VaultraNet, which had developed an Internet-based file delivery and signature system that it uses to provide disclosure documents to prospective franchisees.

Amendments to the Franchise Rule

In 2007, amendments to the Franchise Rule allowed franchisors to provide online disclosure documents as long as they met certain requirements. In 2008, the final amended version of the rule became mandatory. Prospective franchisees must be able to download or save all electronic disclosure documents. Additional disclosures are required about lawsuits that the franchisor has filed and any past settlement agreements. A franchisor must also disclose whether the franchisor or an affiliate has the right to use other channels of distribution, such as the Internet, to make sales within the franchisee's territory. These amendments bring the federal rule into closer alignment with state franchise disclosure laws.

FOR CRITICAL ANALYSIS

Why do you think it took so long for the FTC to issue final rules about franchisors using the Internet?

a. 16 C.F.R. Part 436, 64 Fed.Reg. 57,294 (October 22, 1999).

STATE REGULATION OF FRANCHISING   State legislation varies but often is aimed at protecting franchisees from unfair practices and bad faith terminations by franchisors. Approximately fifteen states have laws similar to the federal rules requiring franchisors to provide presale disclosures to prospective franchisees.[7]

State laws may also require that a disclosure document (known as the Franchise Disclosure Document, or FDD) be registered or filed with a state official, or they may require that the franchisor's advertising be submitted to the state for review or approval. To protect franchisees, a state law might require the disclosure of information such as the actual costs of operation, recurring expenses, and profits earned, along with data substantiating these figures. State deceptive trade practices acts (see Chapter 33) may also apply and prohibit certain types of actions on the part of franchisors.

To prevent arbitrary or bad faith terminations, state law may prohibit termination without "good cause" or require that certain procedures be followed in terminating a franchising relationship. **CASE EXAMPLE 26.3** FMS, Inc., entered into a franchise agreement with Samsung

ON THE WEB For information about the FTC's regulations on franchising, as well as state laws regulating franchising, go to **www.ftc.gov/bcp/franchise/netfran.htm**.

7. These states include California, Hawaii, Illinois, Indiana, Maryland, Michigan, Minnesota, New York, North Dakota, Oregon, Rhode Island, South Dakota, Virginia, Washington, and Wisconsin.

Construction Equipment North America to become an authorized dealership for the sale of Samsung brand construction equipment. Then Samsung sold its construction-equipment business to Volvo Construction Equipment North America, Inc., which was to continue selling Samsung brand equipment. Volvo did so for a while but then started modifying and rebranding construction equipment under its own name.

When Volvo canceled FMS's franchise agreement, FMS filed a lawsuit alleging that Volvo, among other things, had violated Maine's franchise law, which prohibits termination of a franchise without "good cause." A federal appellate court, however, found that because Volvo was no longer manufacturing the Samsung brand equipment, it did have good cause to terminate FMS's franchise. If Volvo had continued making the Samsung brand equipment, the statute would have prevented it from terminating the FMS franchise, but the statute did not prohibit it from discontinuing the dealership as to the rebranded equipment.[8] ●

▶ The Franchise Contract

The franchise relationship is defined by a contract between the franchisor and the franchisee. The franchise contract specifies the terms and conditions of the franchise and spells out the rights and duties of the franchisor and the franchisee. If either party fails to perform the contractual duties, that party may be subject to a lawsuit for breach of contract. Generally, statutes and case law governing franchising tend to emphasize the importance of good faith and fair dealing in franchise relationships.

ON THE WEB A good source for information on the purchase and sale of franchises is Franchising.org, at www.franchising.org.

Because each type of franchise relationship has its own characteristics, it is difficult to describe the broad range of details a franchising contract may include. In the remaining pages of this chapter, we will look at some of the major issues that typically are addressed in a franchise contract. The *Business Application* feature at the end of this chapter describes some steps a franchisee can take to avoid problems common in franchise agreements.

Payment for the Franchise

The franchisee ordinarily pays an initial fee or lump-sum price for the franchise license (the privilege of being granted a franchise). This fee is separate from the various products that the franchisee purchases from or through the franchisor. In some industries, the franchisor relies heavily on the initial sale of the franchise for realizing a profit. In other industries, the continued dealing between the parties brings profit to both. In most situations, the franchisor will receive a stated percentage of the annual (or monthly) sales or annual volume of business done by the franchisee. The franchise agreement may also require the franchisee to pay a percentage of advertising costs and certain administrative expenses.

Business Premises

The franchise agreement may specify whether the premises for the business must be leased or purchased outright. In some cases, a building must be constructed or remodeled to meet the terms of the agreement. The agreement usually will specify whether the franchisor supplies equipment and furnishings for the premises or whether this is the responsibility of the franchisee.

Location of the Franchise

Typically, the franchisor will determine the territory to be served. Some franchise contracts give the franchisee exclusive rights, or "territorial rights," to a certain geographic area. Other franchise contracts, though they define the territory allotted to a particular franchise,

---

8. *FMS, Inc. v. Volvo Construction Equipment North America, Inc.,* 557 F.3d 758 (7th Cir. 2009).

Beyond Our Borders | Franchising in Foreign Nations

In the last twenty years, many U.S. companies (particularly fast-food chains and coffeehouses) have successfully expanded through franchising in nations around the globe. Franchises offer businesses a way to expand internationally without violating the legal restrictions that many nations impose on foreign ownership of businesses. Although Canada has been the most popular location for franchises in the past, during the last few years, franchisors have expanded their target locations to Asia, South America, Central America, and Mexico.

Cultural and Legal Differences Are Important

Businesspersons must exercise caution when entering international franchise relationships—perhaps even more so than when entering other types of international contracts. Differences in language, culture, laws, and business practices can seriously complicate the franchis-

ing relationship. If a U.S. franchisor has quality control standards that do not mesh with local business practices, for example, how can the franchisor maintain the quality of its product and protect its good reputation? If the law in China, for example, does not provide for the same level of intellectual property protection, how can a U.S. franchisor protect its trademark rights or prevent its "secret recipe or formula" from being copied?

The Need to Adequately Assess the Market

Because of the complexities of international franchising, successful franchisors recommend that a company seeking to franchise overseas conduct thorough research to determine whether its particular type of business will be well received in that location. It is important to know the political and cultural climate of the target country, as well as the economic trends.

Marketing surveys to assess the potential success of the franchise location are crucial in international markets. Also, because complying with U.S. disclosure laws may not satisfy the legal requirements of other nations, most successful franchisors retain counsel knowledgeable in the laws of the target location. Competent counsel can draft dispute-settlement provisions (such as an arbitration clause) for international franchising contracts and advise the parties about the tax implications of operating a foreign franchise (such as import taxes and customs duties).

• **For Critical Analysis** *Should a U.S.-based franchisor be allowed to impose contract terms and quality control standards on franchisees in foreign nations that are different from those imposed on domestic franchisees? Why or why not?*

The RJ Corporation of India signed a franchise agreement with Disney Consumer Products. What do you think some of the elements of that agreement were?

RECALL Under the doctrine of *respondeat superior,* an employer may be liable for the torts of employees if they occur within the scope of employment, without regard to the personal fault of the employer.

either specifically state that the franchise is nonexclusive or are silent on the issue of territorial rights.

Many franchise cases involve disputes over territorial rights, and the implied covenant of good faith and fair dealing often comes into play in this area of franchising. If the franchise contract does not grant exclusive territorial rights to a franchisee and the franchisor allows a competing franchise to be established nearby, the franchisee may suffer a significant loss in profits. In this situation, a court may hold that the franchisor's actions breached an implied covenant of good faith and fair dealing.

Quality Control by the Franchisor

Although the day-to-day operation of the franchise business is normally left to the franchisee, the franchise agreement may provide for the amount of supervision and control agreed on by the parties. When the franchisee prepares a product, such as food, or provides a service, such as a motel, the contract often provides that the franchisor will establish certain standards for the facility. Typically, the contract will state that the franchisor is permitted to make periodic inspections to ensure that the standards are being maintained so as to protect the franchise's name and reputation.

As a general rule, the validity of a provision permitting the franchisor to establish and enforce certain quality standards is unquestioned. Because the franchisor has a legitimate interest in maintaining the quality of the product or service to protect its name and reputation, it can exercise greater control in this area than would otherwise be tolerated.

Pricing Arrangements

Franchises provide the franchisor with an outlet for the firm's goods and services. Depending on the nature of the business, the franchisor may require the franchisee to purchase certain supplies from the franchisor at an established price.[9] A franchisor cannot, however, set the prices at which the franchisee will resell the goods because such price setting may be a violation of state or federal antitrust laws, or both. A franchisor can suggest retail prices but cannot mandate them.

▶ Termination of the Franchise

The duration of the franchise is a matter to be determined between the parties. Sometimes, a franchise will start out for a short period, such as a year, so that the franchisor can determine whether it wants to stay in business with the franchisee. Other times, the duration of the franchise contract correlates with the term of the lease for the business premises, and both are renewable at the end of that period.

Usually, the franchise agreement will specify that termination must be "for cause," such as death or disability of the franchisee, insolvency of the franchisee, breach of the franchise agreement, or failure to meet specified sales quotas. Most franchise contracts provide that notice of termination must be given. If no set time for termination is specified, then a reasonable time, with notice, will be implied. A franchisee must be given reasonable time to wind up the business—that is, to do the accounting and return the copyright or trademark or any other property of the franchisor.

A franchise agreement may grant the franchisee the opportunity to cure an ordinary, curable breach within a certain period of time after notice to forestall, or even avoid, the termination of the contract. Could a franchisee's conduct so seriously undermine the requirements of the agreement that the franchisor could cancel the contract despite a notice-and-cure provision? That was the issue in the following case.

9. Although a franchisor can require franchisees to purchase supplies from it, requiring a franchisee to purchase exclusively from the franchisor may violate federal antitrust laws (see Chapter 32).

Case 26.2   LJL Transportation, Inc. v. Pilot Air Freight Corp.

Supreme Court of Pennsylvania, 599 Pa. 546, 962 A.2d 639 (2009).
www.pacourts.us/T/SupremeCourt[a]

Does a franchisee's diversion of air transportation to a company other than the one stipulated in the franchise agreement warrant its termination?

FACTS Pilot Air Freight Corporation moves freight through a network of company-owned and company-franchised locations at airports and other sites. Franchisees included LJL Transportation Inc., which is owned by Louis Pektor and Leo Decker. The franchise agreement required LJL to assign all shipments to the Pilot network. The agreement also provided that "Pilot shall allow Franchisee an opportunity to cure a default within ninety (90) days of receipt of written notice." After eight years as a Pilot franchisee, LJL began to divert shipments to Northeast Transportation, a competing service owned by Pektor and Decker. On learning of the diversions, Pilot terminated the franchise agreement. LJL filed a suit in a Pennsylvania state court against Pilot, alleging breach of contract and asserting a right to cure. The court issued a summary judgment in Pilot's favor, and a state intermediate appellate court affirmed. LJL appealed.

ISSUE Can a franchisee's conduct justify the immediate termination of a franchise agreement even if it includes a "right-to-cure" clause?

DECISION Yes. The Pennsylvania Supreme Court affirmed the lower court's judgment. A franchise agreement may be terminated immediately "when there is a material breach of the contract so serious it goes directly to the heart and essence of the contract, rendering the breach incurable."

a. In the "Conducting Business with the Court" section, click on "Supreme Court Opinions." On that page, in the "Caption" box type "LJL"; in the "Month" pull-down menu, select "January"; in the "Year" pull-down menu, choose "2009"; and click on "Search." In the result, click on the link to access the opinion. The Unified Judicial System of Pennsylvania maintains this Web site.

Case 26.2–Continued

REASON Good faith and honesty are requirements for the performance and enforcement of a contract. Self-dealing contravenes (disregards) those requirements, violating the trust on which an agreement is based. A franchisee's breach of these duties goes to the contract's "heart." Allowing the franchisee to attempt to undo such conduct through the exercise of a right-to-cure clause would be an inadequate remedy because it could not effectively right the wrong. "Such a breach is so fundamentally destructive, it understandably and inevitably causes the trust that is the bedrock foundation and veritable lifeblood of the parties' contractual relationship to essentially evaporate." In this situation, a franchisor can terminate the franchise agreement without notice despite any right-to-cure provision.

FOR CRITICAL ANALYSIS—Ethical Consideration *From an ethical perspective, if LJL had been allowed to invoke the right-to-cure provision, could it have undone its wrongdoing so that the franchise relationship could have continued? Why or why not?*

WHY IS THIS CASE IMPORTANT? *This was a case of "first impression" for this jurisdiction—Pennsylvania. The court reviewed the decisions of courts in other jurisdictions in cases involving similar facts and applied their reasoning to reach the same conclusion in this case. These holdings emphasize that a party to a contract cannot breach it in an egregious manner and still expect to take advantage of its provisions to avoid the consequences.*

Wrongful Termination

Because a franchisor's termination of a franchise often has adverse consequences for the franchisee, much franchise litigation involves claims of wrongful termination. Generally, the termination provisions of contracts are more favorable to the franchisor. This means that the franchisee, who normally invests a substantial amount of time and funds to make the franchise operation successful, may receive little or nothing for the business on termination. The franchisor owns the trademark and hence the business.

It is in this area that statutory and case law become important. The federal and state laws discussed earlier attempt, among other things, to protect franchisees from the arbitrary or unfair termination of their franchises by the franchisors. Generally, both statutory and case law emphasize the importance of good faith and fair dealing in terminating a franchise relationship.

Preventing Legal Disputes

To avoid potential disputes regarding franchise termination, always do preliminary research on a franchisor before agreeing to enter into a franchise contract. Find out whether the franchisor has terminated franchises in the past, how many times, and for what reasons. Contact five to ten franchisees of the same franchisor and ask questions about their relationships and any problems. If the franchisor has been honest, reliable, and reasonable with its franchisees in the past, you will have a better chance of avoiding disputes over wrongful termination in the future.

The Importance of Good Faith and Fair Dealing

In determining whether a franchisor has acted in good faith when terminating a franchise agreement, the courts generally try to balance the rights of both parties. If a court perceives that a franchisor has arbitrarily or unfairly terminated a franchise, the franchisee will be provided with a remedy for wrongful termination. If a franchisor's decision to terminate a franchise was made in the normal course of the franchisor's business operations, however, and reasonable notice of termination was given to the franchisee, generally a court will not consider termination wrongful.

At issue in the following case was whether General Motors Corporation acted wrongfully in terminating its franchise with a motor vehicle dealer in Connecticut.

Case 26.3 **Chic Miller's Chevrolet, Inc. v. General Motors Corp.**

United States District Court, District of Connecticut, 352 F.Supp.2d 251 (2005).

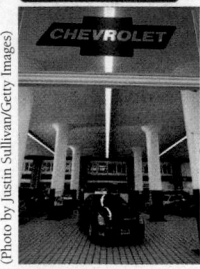

(Photo by Justin Sullivan/Getty Images)

Did GM act wrongfully in terminating a Chevrolet dealership's franchise?

FACTS Chapin Miller began work as a mail clerk with General Motors Acceptance Corporation (GMAC). By 1967, Miller had succeeded sufficiently within the organization to acquire Chic Miller's Chevrolet, a General Motors Corporation (GM) dealership, in Bristol, Connecticut. As part of its operations, Chic Miller's entered into lending agreements, commonly known as floor plan financing, to enable it to buy new vehicles from GM. At first, the dealership had floor plan financing through GMAC. In 2001, however, Miller believed that GMAC was charging interest "at an inappropriately high rate" and negotiated a lower rate from Chase Manhattan Bank. In November 2002, Chase declined to provide further financing. Unable to obtain a loan from any other lender, Chic Miller's contacted GMAC, which also refused to make a deal. Under the parties' "Dealer Sales and Service Agreement," GM could terminate a dealership for "Failure of Dealer to maintain the line of credit." GM sent several notices of termination, but Chic Miller's remained open until March 2003, when it closed for seven days. GM sent a final termination notice. Chic Miller's filed a suit in a federal district court against GM, alleging, among other things, a failure to act in good faith in terminating the franchise. GM filed a motion for summary judgment.

ISSUE Did GM act wrongfully in terminating its franchise with Chic Miller's?

DECISION No. The court granted GM's motion for summary judgment. GM acted in good faith, with good cause under the applicable state statute, in terminating Chic Miller's franchise.

REASON The court stated that to terminate a franchise under the Connecticut Franchise Act, "a franchisor must: provide notice that complies with statutory requirements; have 'good cause' for the termination; and act 'in good faith.'" The court explained that there is "good cause" under the statute "if there is a failure by the dealer to comply with a provision of the franchise which is both reasonable and of material significance to the franchise relationship." In this case, the dealer failed to maintain floor plan financing, a material requirement under the franchise agreement. "[W]ithout floor plan financing, a dealership is unable to purchase motor vehicle inventory, which, in turn, severely limits a dealership's ability to earn income from vehicle sales." The dealership "will eventually lose its ability to generate revenues and become financially insolvent, and will not be able to conduct customary sales and service operations." Here, the dealer also failed to conduct sales and service operations for seven consecutive business days, another material requirement under the parties' contract.

WHAT IF THE FACTS WERE DIFFERENT? *Suppose that in March 2003, Chic Miller's had placed one newspaper ad promoting its services and had sold one car. Would the result have been different? Why or why not?*

 Reviewing . . . Sole Proprietorships and Private Franchises

Carlos Del Rey decided to open a fast-food Mexican restaurant and signed a franchise contract with a national chain called La Grande Enchilada. Under the franchise agreement, Del Rey purchased the building, and La Grande Enchilada supplied the equipment. The contract required the franchisee to strictly follow the franchisor's operating manual and stated that failure to do so would be grounds for terminating the franchise contract. The manual set forth detailed operating procedures and safety standards, and provided that a La Grande Enchilada representative would inspect the restaurant monthly to ensure compliance. Nine months after Del Rey began operating his La Grande Enchilada, a spark from the grill ignited an oily towel in the kitchen. No one was injured, but by the time firefighters were able to put out the fire, the kitchen had sustained extensive damage. The cook told the fire department that the towel was "about two feet from the grill" when it caught fire, which was in compliance with the franchisor's manual that required towels to be at least one foot from the grills. Nevertheless, the next day La Grande Enchilada notified Del Rey that his franchise would terminate in thirty days for failure to follow the prescribed safety procedures. Using the information presented in the chapter, answer the following questions.

1. What type of franchise was Del Rey's La Grande Enchilada restaurant?
2. If Del Rey operates the restaurant as a sole proprietorship, then who bears the loss for the damaged kitchen? Explain.
3. Assume that Del Rey files a lawsuit against La Grande Enchilada, claiming that his franchise was wrongfully terminated. What is the main factor a court would consider in determining whether the franchise was wrongfully terminated?
4. Would a court be likely to rule that La Grande Enchilada had good cause to terminate Del Rey's franchise in this situation? Why or why not?

Business Application
What Problems Can a Franchisee Anticipate?*

A franchise arrangement appeals to many prospective businesspersons for several reasons. Entrepreneurs who purchase franchises can operate independently and without the risks associated with products that have never before been marketed. Additionally, the franchisee can usually rely on the assistance and guidance of a management network that is regional or national in scope and has been in place for some time. Franchisees do face potential problems, however. Generally, to avoid possibly significant economic and legal difficulties, it is imperative that you obtain all relevant details about the business and that you have an attorney evaluate the franchise contract for possible pitfalls.

The Franchise Fee

Almost all franchise contracts require a franchise fee payable up front or in installments. This fee often ranges between $10,000 and $50,000. For nationally known franchises, such as McDonald's, the fee may be $500,000 or more. To calculate the true cost of the franchise, however, you must also include the fees that are paid once the franchise opens for business. For example, as a franchisee, you would probably pay 2 to 8 percent of your gross sales as royalties to the franchisor (for the use of the franchisor's trademark, for example). Another 1 to 2 percent of gross sales might go to the franchisor to cover advertising costs. Although your business would benefit from the advertising, the cost of that advertising might exceed the benefits you would realize.

Electronic Encroachment and Termination Provisions

Even when the franchise contract gives the franchisee exclusive territorial rights, a problem that many franchisees do not anticipate is the adverse effects on their businesses of so-called electronic encroachment. For example, a franchise contract may give the franchisee exclusive rights to operate a franchise in a certain territory but include no provisions to prevent the franchisor from selling its products to customers located within the franchisee's territory via telemarketing, mail-order catalogues, or online services over the Internet. As a prospective franchisee, you should make sure that your franchise contract covers such contingencies and protects you against any losses you might incur from these types of competition in your area.

A major economic consequence, usually of a negative nature, will occur if the franchisor can or does terminate your franchise agreement. Before you sign a franchise contract, make sure that the contract provisions regarding termination are reasonable, are clearly specified, and provide you with adequate notice and sufficient time to wind up business.

CHECKLIST FOR THE FRANCHISEE

1. **Find out all you can about the franchisor: How long has the franchisor been in business? How profitable is the business? Is there a growing market for the product?**
2. **Obtain the most recent financial statement from the franchisor and a complete description of the business.**
3. **Obtain a clear and complete statement of all fees that you will be required to pay.**
4. **Determine whether the franchisor will help you find a suitable location, train management and employees, assist with promotion and advertising, and supply capital or credit.**
5. **Visit other franchisees in the same business. Ask them about their profitability and their experiences with the product, the market, and the franchisor.**
6. **Evaluate your training and experience in the business on which you are about to embark. Are they sufficient to ensure success as a franchisee?**
7. **Carefully examine the franchise contract provisions relating to termination of the franchise agreement. Are they specific enough to allow you to sue for breach of contract in the event the franchisor wrongfully terminates the contract? Find out how many franchises have been terminated in the past several years.**
8. **Will you have an exclusive geographic territory and, if so, for how many years? Does the franchisor have a right to engage in telemarketing, electronic marketing, and Internet or mail-order sales to customers within this territory?**
9. **Finally, the most important way to protect yourself is to have an attorney familiar with franchise law examine the contract before you sign it.**

* This *Business Application* is not meant to substitute for the services of an attorney who is licensed to practice law in your state.

 Key Terms

entrepreneur 668	franchisee 670	sole proprietorship 669
franchise 670	franchisor 670	

Chapter Summary: Sole Proprietorships and Private Franchises

Sole Proprietorships (See pages 669–670.)	The simplest form of business organization; used by anyone who does business without creating a separate organization. The owner is the business. The owner pays personal income taxes on all profits and is personally liable for all business debts.

Franchises (See pages 670–674.)	1. *Types of franchises–*
	   a. Distributorship (for example, automobile dealerships).
	   b. Chain-style operation (for example, fast-food chains).
	   c. Manufacturing/processing-plant arrangement (for example, soft-drink bottling companies, such as Pepsi-Cola).
	2. *Laws governing franchising–*
	   a. Franchises are governed by contract law.
	   b. Franchises are also governed by federal and state statutory laws and agency regulations.

The Franchise Contract (See pages 674–676.)	The franchise relationship is defined by a contract between the franchisor and the franchisee. The contract normally spells out the following terms: 1. *Payment for the franchise–*Ordinarily, the contract requires the franchisee (purchaser) to pay an initial fee or lump-sum price for the franchise license. 2. *Business premises–*Specifies whether the business premises will be leased or purchased by the franchisee. 3. *Location of the franchise–*Specifies the territory to be served by the franchisee. 4. *Business organization–*The franchisor may specify particular requirements for the form and capital structure of the business. 5. *Quality control–*The franchisor may require the franchisee to abide by certain standards of quality relating to the product or service offered. 6. *Pricing arrangements–*The franchisor may require the franchisee to purchase certain supplies from the franchisor at an established price but cannot set retail resale prices.
Termination of the Franchise (See pages 676–678.)	Usually, the contract provides for the date and/or conditions of termination of the franchise arrangement. Both federal and state statutes attempt to protect franchisees from franchisors who unfairly or arbitrarily terminate franchises.

 ExamPrep

ISSUE SPOTTERS

1 Frank plans to open a sporting goods store and to hire Gogi and Hap. Frank will invest only his own money. He expects that he will not make a profit for at least eighteen months and will make only a small profit in the three years after that. He hopes to expand eventually. Which form of business organization would be most appropriate?

2 Thirsty Bottling Company and U.S. Beverages, Inc. (USB), enter into a franchise agreement that states the franchise may be terminated at any time "for cause." Thirsty fails to meet USB's specified sales quota. Does this constitute "cause" for termination? Why or why not?

BEFORE THE TEST

Check your answers to the Issue Spotters, and at the same time, take the interactive quiz for this chapter. Go to **www.cengage.com/blaw/blt** and click on "Chapter 26." First, click on "Answers to Issue Spotters" to check your answers. Next, click on "Interactive Quiz" to assess your mastery of the concepts in this chapter. Then click on "Flashcards" to review this chapter's Key Term definitions.

 For Review

Answers for the even-numbered questions in this For Review *section can be found on this text's accompanying Web site at* **www.cengage.com/blaw/blt**. *Select "Chapter 26" and click on "For Review."*

1 What advantages and disadvantages are associated with the sole proprietorship?

2 What is a franchise? What are the most common types of franchises?

3 What laws govern a franchising relationship?

4 What terms and conditions are typically included in a franchise contract?

5 What is wrongful termination? In what types of situations do courts typically find that a franchisor has wrongfully terminated a franchise?

▶ Hypothetical Scenarios and Case Problems

26–1 Control of a Franchise. National Foods, Inc., sells franchises to its fast-food restaurants, known as Chicky-D's. Under the franchise agreement, franchisees agree to hire and train employees strictly according to Chicky-D's standards. The regional supervisors at Chicky-D's are required to approve all job candidates before they are hired and all general policies affecting those employees. Chicky-D's reserves the right to terminate a franchise for violating the franchisor's rules. In practice, however, Chicky-D's regional supervisors routinely approve new employees and individual franchisees' policies. After several incidents of racist comments and conduct by Tim, a recently hired assistant manager at a Chicky-D's, Sharon, a counterperson at the restaurant, resigns. Sharon files a suit in a federal district court against National. National files a motion for summary judgment, arguing that it is not liable for harassment by franchise employees. Will the court grant National's motion? Why or why not?

26–2 **Hypothetical Question with Sample Answer** Omega Computers, Inc., is a franchisor that grants exclusive physical territories to its franchisees with retail locations, including Pete's Digital Products. Omega sells more than two hundred of the franchises before establishing an interactive Web site. On the site, a customer can order Omega's products directly from the franchisor. When Pete's sets up a Web site through which a customer can also order Omega's products, Omega and Pete's file suits against each other, alleging that each is in violation of the franchise relationship. To decide this issue, what factors should the court consider? How might these parties have avoided this conflict? Discuss.

—For a sample answer to Question 26–2, go to Appendix E at the end of this text.

26–3 Franchising. Maria, Pablo, and Vicky are recent college graduates who would like to go into business for themselves. They are considering purchasing a franchise. If they enter into a franchising arrangement, they would have the support of a large company that could answer any questions they might have. Also, a firm that has been in business for many years would be experienced in dealing with some of the problems that novice businesspersons might encounter. These and other attributes of franchises can lessen some of the risks of the marketplace. What other aspects of franchising—positive and negative—should Maria, Pablo, and Vicky consider before committing themselves to a particular franchise?

26–4 Franchise Termination. J.C., Inc., operated McDonald's restaurants in Lancaster, Ohio, under a franchise agreement with McDonald's Corp. The agreement required J.C. to make monthly payments of certain percentages of the gross sales to McDonald's. If any payment was more than thirty days late, McDonald's had the right to terminate the franchise. The agreement stated, "No waiver by [McDonald's] of any breach . . . shall constitute a waiver of any subsequent breach." McDonald's sometimes accepted J.C.'s late payments, but when J.C. defaulted on the payments in July 2010, McDonald's gave notice of thirty days to comply or surrender possession of the restaurants. J.C. missed the deadline. McDonald's demanded that J.C. vacate the restaurants. J.C. refused. McDonald's alleged that J.C. had violated the franchise agreement. J.C. claimed that McDonald's had breached the implied covenant of good faith and fair dealing. Which party should prevail and why? [*McDonald's Corp. v. C.B. Management Co.,* 13 F.Supp.2d 705 (N.D.Ill. 1998)]

26–5 Sole Proprietorship. James Ferguson operates "Jim's 11-E Auto Sales" in Jonesborough, Tennessee, as a sole proprietorship. In 1999, Consumers Insurance Co. issued a policy to "Jim Ferguson, Jim's 11E Auto Sales" covering "Owned 'Autos' Only." *Auto* was defined to include "a land motor vehicle," which was not further explained in the policy. Coverage included damage caused by the owner or driver of an underinsured motor vehicle. In 2000, Ferguson bought and titled in his own name a 1976 Harley-Davidson motorcycle, intending to repair and sell the cycle through his dealership. In October 2001, while riding the motorcycle, Ferguson was struck by an auto driven by John Jenkins. Ferguson filed a suit in a Tennessee state court against Jenkins—who was underinsured with respect to Ferguson's medical bills—and Consumers. The insurer argued, among other things, that because the motorcycle was bought and titled in Ferguson's own name, and he was riding it at the time of the accident, it was his personal vehicle and thus was not covered under the dealership's policy. What is the relationship between a sole proprietor and a sole proprietorship? How might this status affect the court's decision in this case? [*Ferguson v. Jenkins,* 204 S.W.3d 779 (Tenn.App. 2006)]

26–6 **Case Problem with Sample Answer** Walid Elkhatib, a Palestinian Arab, emigrated to the United States in 1971 and became a U.S. citizen. Eight years later, Elkhatib bought a Dunkin' Donuts, Inc., franchise in Bellwood, Illinois. Dunkin' Donuts began offering breakfast sandwiches with bacon, ham, or sausage through its franchises in 1984, but Elkhatib refused to sell these items at his store on the ground that his religion forbade the handling of pork. In 1995, Elkhatib opened a second franchise in Berkeley, Illinois, at which he also refused to sell pork products. The next year, at both locations, Elkhatib began selling meatless sandwiches. In 1998, Elkhatib opened a third franchise in Westchester, Illinois. When he proposed to relocate this franchise, Dunkin' Donuts refused to approve the new location and added that it would not renew any of his franchise agreements because he did not carry the full sandwich line. Elkhatib filed a suit in a federal district court against Dunkin' Donuts and others. The defendants filed a motion for summary judgment. Did Dunkin' Donuts act in good faith in its relationship with Elkhatib? Explain. [*Elkhatib v. Dunkin' Donuts, Inc.,* 493 F.3d 827 (7th Cir. 2007)]

—**After you have answered Problem 26–6, compare your answer with the sample answer given on the Web site that accompanies this text. Go to www.cengage.com/blaw/blt, select "Chapter 26," and click on "Case Problem with Sample Answer."**

26–7 Sole Proprietorship. Julie Anne Gaskill is an oral and maxillofacial surgeon in Bowling Green, Kentucky. Her medical practice is a sole proprietorship consisting of her as the sole surgeon, with office staff. She sees every patient, exercises all professional judgment and skill, and manages the business. When Gaskill and her spouse, John Robbins, initiated divorce proceedings in a Kentucky state court, her accountant estimated the value of the practice at $221,610, excluding goodwill. Robbins's accountant estimated the value at $669,075, including goodwill. Goodwill is the ability or reputation of a business to draw customers, get them to return, and contribute to future profitability. How can a sole proprietor's reputation, skill, and relationships with customers be valued? Could these qualities be divided into "enterprise" and "personal" goodwill, with some goodwill associated with the business and some

solely due to the personal qualities of the proprietor? If so, what might comprise each type? Is this an effective method for valuing Gaskill's practice? Discuss. [*Gaskill v. Robbins,* 282 S.W.3d 306 (Ky. 2009)]

26–8 **A Question of Ethics** *In August 2004, Ralph Vilardo contacted Travel Center, Inc., in Cincinnati, Ohio, to buy a trip to Florida in December for his family to celebrate his fiftieth wedding anniversary. Vilardo paid $6,900 to David Sheets, the sole proprietor of Travel Center. Vilardo also paid $195 to Sheets for a separate trip to Florida in February 2005. Sheets assured Vilardo that everything was set, but in fact no arrangements were made. Later, two unauthorized charges for travel services totaling $1,182.35 appeared on Vilardo's credit-card statement. Vilardo filed a suit in an Ohio state court against Sheets and his business, alleging, among other things, fraud and violations of the state consumer protection law. Vilardo served Sheets and Travel Center with copies of the complaint, the summons, a request for admissions, and other documents filed with the court, including a motion for summary judgment. Responses to each of these filings were subject to certain time limits. Sheets responded once on his own behalf with a denial of all of Vilardo's claims. Travel Center did not respond.* [*Vilardo v. Sheets, __ N.E.2d __ (12 Dist. 2006)*]

1 Almost four months after Vilardo filed his complaint, Sheets decided that he was unable to adequately represent himself and retained an attorney who asked the court for more time. Should the court grant this request? Why or why not? Ultimately, what should the court rule in this case?

2 Sheets admitted that "Travel Center" was a sole proprietorship. He also argued that liability might be imposed on his business but not on himself. How would you rule with respect to this argument? Would there be anything unethical about allowing Sheets to avoid liability on this basis? Explain.

▶ Critical Thinking and Writing Assignments

26–9 Critical Legal Thinking. Suppose that a franchisor requires the franchisee to purchase a particular type of van that will be used to deliver the franchised carpet-cleaning services to the public. If the van is involved in an accident that causes injury to a person, should the franchisor be held liable for the injuries? What are the arguments for and against holding the franchisor liable under the circumstances?

26–10 Critical Thinking and Writing Assignment for Business. Jordan Mendelson is interested in starting a kitchen franchise business. Customers will come to the business to assemble gour-

met dinners and then take the prepared meals to their homes for cooking. The franchisor requires each store to use a specific layout and provides the recipes for various dinners, but the franchisee is not required to purchase the food products from the franchisor. What general factors should Mendelson consider before entering a contract to start such a franchise? Is location important? Are there any laws that Mendelson should consider due to the fact that this franchise involves food preparation and sales? Should Mendelson operate this business as a sole proprietorship? Why or why not?

▶ Practical Internet Exercises

Go to this text's Web site at **www.cengage.com/blaw/blt**, select "Chapter 26," and click on "Practical Internet Exercises." There you will find the following Internet research exercises that you can perform to learn more about the topics covered in this chapter.

Practical Internet Exercise 26–1: LEGAL PERSPECTIVE—Starting a Business

Practical Internet Exercise 26–2: MANAGEMENT PERSPECTIVE—Franchises

All Forms of Partnership

> **"All men's gains . . . are the fruit of venturing."**
>
> —Herodotus, fifth century B.C.E.
> (Greek historian)

Chapter Outline

- Basic Partnership Concepts
- Partnership Formation
- Partnership Operation, Dissociation, and Termination
- Limited Liability Partnerships
- Limited Partnerships

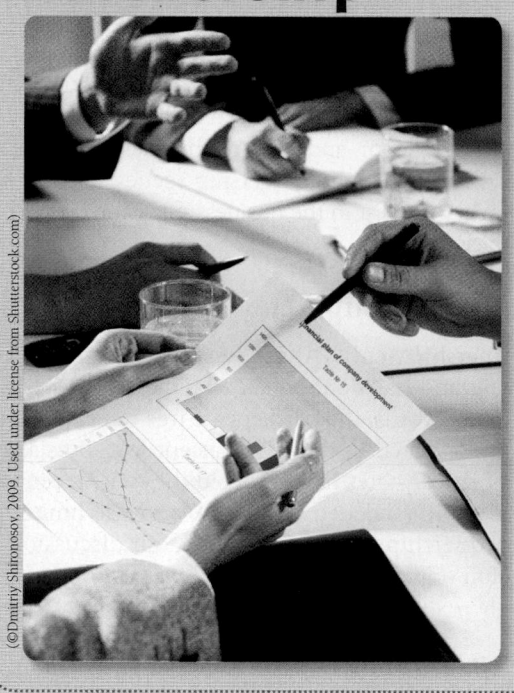

Learning Objectives

After reading this chapter, you should be able to answer the following questions:

1. What are the three essential elements of a partnership?

2. What are the rights and duties of partners in an ordinary partnership?

3. What is meant by joint and several liability? Why is this often considered to be a disadvantage of the partnership form of business?

4. What advantages do limited liability partnerships offer to businesspersons that are not offered by general partnerships?

5. What are the key differences between the rights and liabilities of general partners and those of limited partners?

Traditionally, the two most common forms of business organization selected by two or more persons entering into business together are the partnership and the corporation. A *partnership* arises from an agreement, express or implied, between two or more persons to carry on a business for profit. Partners are co-owners of a business and have joint control over its operation and the right to share in its profits. In this chapter, we focus on partnerships. (Corporations will be discussed in Chapters 28 through 30.)

We open the chapter with an examination of ordinary partnerships, or *general partnerships,* and the rights and duties of partners in this traditional business entity. We then examine some special forms of partnerships known as *limited liability partnerships* and *limited partnerships,* which receive different treatment under the law. As the chapter-opening quotation indicates, all gains are the "fruit of venturing," and partnerships—to the extent that they encourage business ventures—contribute to those gains.

▶ Basic Partnership Concepts

Partnerships are governed both by common law concepts—in particular, those relating to agency—and by statutory law. As in so many other areas of business law, the National Conference of Commissioners on Uniform State Laws has drafted uniform laws for partnerships, and these uniform laws have been widely adopted by the states.

Agency Concepts and Partnership Law

When two or more persons agree to do business as partners, they enter into a special relationship with one another. To an extent, their relationship is similar to an agency relationship because each partner is deemed to be the agent of the other partners and of the partnership. The common law agency concepts outlined in Chapter 23 thus apply—specifically, the imputation of knowledge of, and responsibility for, acts done within the scope of the partnership relationship. In their relationships with one another, partners, like agents, are bound by fiduciary ties.

In one important way, however, partnership law is distinct from agency law. A partnership is based on a voluntary contract between two or more competent persons who agree to commit financial capital, labor, and skill to a business with the understanding that profits and losses will be shared. In a nonpartnership agency relationship, the agent usually does not have an ownership interest in the business nor is he or she obliged to bear a portion of the ordinary business losses.

The Uniform Partnership Act

ON THE WEB You can find summaries, texts, and the legislative history of numerous uniform acts, including the UPA, at the Web site of the National Conference of Commissioners on Uniform State Laws at **www.nccusl.org**.

The Uniform Partnership Act (UPA) governs the operation of partnerships *in the absence of express agreement* and has done much to reduce controversies in the law relating to partnerships. In other words, the partners are free to establish rules for their partnership that differ from those stated in the UPA. Except for Louisiana, every state has adopted the UPA. The majority of states have adopted the most recent version of the UPA, which was issued in 1994 and amended in 1997 to provide limited liability for partners in a limited liability partnership.[1] We therefore base our discussion of the UPA in this chapter on the 1997 version of the act and refer to older versions of the UPA in footnotes when appropriate.

Definition of Partnership

Partnership An agreement by two or more persons to carry on, as co-owners, a business for profit.

Parties sometimes find themselves in conflict over whether their business enterprise is a legal partnership, especially in the absence of a formal, written partnership agreement. The UPA defines a **partnership** as "an association of two or more persons to carry on as co-owners a business for profit" [UPA 101(6)]. Note that the UPA's definition of *person* includes corporations, so a corporation can be a partner in a partnership [UPA 101(10)]. The *intent* to associate is a key element of a partnership, and a person cannot join a partnership unless all of the other partners consent [UPA 401(i)].

When Does a Partnership Exist?

KEEP IN MIND Two or more persons are required to form a partnership. Other forms of business can be organized by a single individual.

In resolving disputes over whether partnership status exists, courts will usually look for the following three essential elements, which are implicit in the UPA's definition of a general partnership:

1. A sharing of profits and losses.
2. A joint ownership of the business.
3. An equal right to be involved in the management of the business.

Joint ownership of property does not in and of itself create a partnership. In fact, the sharing of gross revenues and even profits from such ownership is usually not enough

---

1. At the time this book went to press, two-thirds of the states, as well as the District of Columbia, Puerto Rico, and the U.S. Virgin Islands, had adopted the UPA with the 1997 amendments. Excerpts from the latest version of the UPA are presented on the Web site that accompanies this text.

"Oh, thank you, Lord! Do I have to tell my partner?"

to create a partnership [UPA 202(c)(1), (2)].   **EXAMPLE 27.1**   Chiang and Burke jointly own a piece of rural property. They lease the land to a farmer with the understanding that—in lieu of set rental payments—they will receive a share of the profits from the farming operation conducted by the farmer. This arrangement normally would not make Chiang, Burke, and the farmer partners. ●

Note, though, that while the sharing of profits from ownership of property does not prove the existence of a partnership, sharing *both profits and losses* usually does.   **EXAMPLE 27.2**   Two sisters, Zoe and Cienna, buy a restaurant together, open a joint bank account from which they pay for expenses and supplies, and share the net profits (or losses) that the restaurant generates. Zoe manages the restaurant and Cienna handles the bookkeeping. After eight years, Cienna stops doing the bookkeeping and does no other work for the restaurant. Zoe, who is now operating the restaurant by herself, no longer wants to share the profits with Cienna. Zoe claims that she and Cienna did not establish a partnership. In this situation, a court would find that a partnership existed because the sisters shared management responsibilities, had a joint bank account, and shared the profits and losses of the restaurant equally. ●

Entity versus Aggregate Theory of Partnerships

At common law, a partnership was treated only as an aggregate of individuals and never as a separate legal entity. Thus, at common law a lawsuit could never be brought by or against the firm in its own name; each individual partner had to sue or be sued.

Today, in contrast, a majority of the states follow the UPA and treat a partnership as an entity for most purposes. For example, a partnership usually can sue or be sued, collect judgments, and have all accounting procedures in the name of the partnership entity [UPA 201, 307(a)]. As an entity, a partnership may hold the title to real or personal property in its name rather than in the names of the individual partners. Additionally, federal procedural laws permit the partnership to be treated as an entity in suits in federal courts and bankruptcy proceedings.

For federal income tax purposes, however, the partnership is treated as an aggregate of the individual partners rather than as a separate legal entity. The partnership is a pass-through entity and not a tax-paying entity. A **pass-through entity** is a business entity that has no tax liability; the entity's income is passed through to the owners of the entity, who pay taxes on it. Thus, the income or losses the partnership incurs are "passed through" the entity framework and attributed to the partners on their individual tax returns. The partnership itself has no tax liability and is responsible only for filing an **information return** with the Internal Revenue Service. The firm itself pays no taxes. A partner's profit from the partnership (whether distributed or not) is taxed as individual income to the individual partner.

Pass-Through Entity   A business entity that has no tax liability. The entity's income is passed through to the owners, and the owners pay taxes on the income.

Information Return   A tax return submitted by a partnership that only reports the income and losses earned by the business. The partnership as an entity does not pay taxes on the income received by the partnership.

Articles of Partnership   A written agreement that sets forth each partner's rights and obligations with respect to the partnership.

▶ Partnership Formation

As a general rule, agreements to form a partnership can be *oral, written,* or *implied by conduct.* Some partnership agreements, however, must be in writing (or an electronic record) to be legally enforceable under the Statute of Frauds (see Chapter 12 for details).

A partnership agreement, called **articles of partnership,** can include any terms that the parties wish, unless they are illegal or contrary to public policy or statute [UPA 103]. The terms commonly included in a partnership agreement are listed in Exhibit 27–1 on the following page. (Creating a partnership agreement in another country may involve additional requirements, as this chapter's *Beyond Our Borders* feature on page 687 explains.)

• *Exhibit* **27–1 Common Terms Included in a Partnership Agreement**

Basic structure	1. Name of the partnership. 2. Names of the partners. 3. Location of the business and the state law under which the partnership is organized. 4. Purpose of the partnership. 5. Duration of the partnership.
Capital contributions	1. Amount of capital that each partner is contributing. 2. The agreed-on value of any real or personal property that is contributed instead of cash. 3. How losses and gains on contributed capital will be allocated and whether contributions will earn interest.
Sharing of profits and losses	1. Percentage of the profits and losses of the business that each partner will receive. 2. When distributions of profit will be made and how net profit will be calculated.
Management and control	1. How management responsibilities will be divided among the partners. 2. Name(s) of the managing partner or partners and whether other partners have voting rights.
Accounting and partnership records	1. Name of the bank in which the partnership will maintain its business and checking accounts. 2. Statement that an accounting of partnership records will be maintained and that any partner, or her or his agent, can review these records at any time. 3. The dates of the partnership's fiscal year (if used) and when the annual audit of the books will take place.
Dissociation and dissolution	1. Events that will cause the dissociation of a partner or dissolve the partnership, such as the retirement, death, or incapacity of any partner. 2. How partnership property will be valued and apportioned on dissociation and dissolution. 3. Whether an arbitrator will determine the value of partnership property on dissociation and dissolution and whether that determination will be binding.
Arbitration	1. Whether arbitration is required for any dispute relating to the partnership agreement.

Duration of the Partnership

The partnership agreement can specify the duration of the partnership by stating that it will continue until a certain date or the completion of a particular project. A partnership that is specifically limited in duration is called a *partnership for a term*. Generally, withdrawing from a partnership for a term prematurely (before the expiration date) constitutes a breach of the agreement, and the responsible partner can be held liable for any resulting losses [UPA 602(b)(2)]. If no fixed duration is specified, the partnership is a *partnership at will*.

Partnership by Estoppel

Occasionally, persons who are not partners may nevertheless hold themselves out as partners and make representations that third parties rely on in dealing with them. In such a situation, a court may conclude that a *partnership by estoppel* exists. The law does not confer any partnership rights on these persons, but it may impose liability on them. This is also

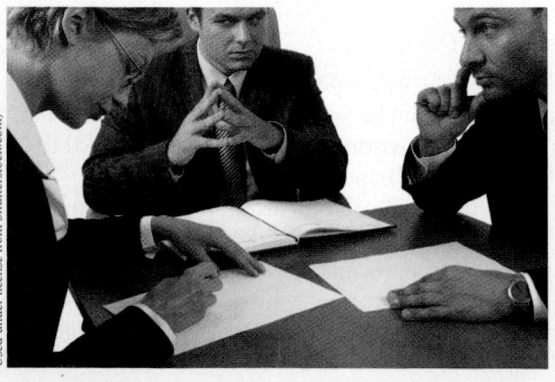

An attorney is having two partners sign a formal partnership agreement. What might be included in this agreement?

U.S. businesspersons who wish to operate a partnership in another country often discover that the country requires local participation. This means that nationals of the host country must own a specific share of the business. In other words, the partnership will have to include one or more partners who live in the host country. Sometimes, U.S. businesspersons are reluctant to establish partnerships in a country that requires local participation. They fear that if the partnership breaks up, the technology and expertise developed by the partnership business may end up in the hands of a future competitor. In that event, the U.S. parties may have little recourse under the host country's laws against their former partners' use of the intellectual property.

• For Critical Analysis
Do local participation rules benefit countries in the long run? Explain.

true when a partner represents, expressly or impliedly, that a nonpartner is a member of the firm. Whenever a third person has reasonably and detrimentally relied on the representation that a nonpartner was part of the partnership, a partnership by estoppel is deemed to exist. When this occurs, the nonpartner is regarded as an agent whose acts are binding on the partnership [UPA 308].

CASE EXAMPLE 27.3 Gary Chavers operated Chavers Welding and Construction (CWC). His sons Reggie and Mark worked in the business as well. CWC contracted with Epsco, Inc., to provide payroll and employee services. Initially, Epsco collected payments for its services each week, but later Epsco extended credit to CWC, which the Chaverses had represented was a partnership. Eventually, when CWC's account was more than $80,000 delinquent, Epsco filed a lawsuit to recover payment. Gary filed for bankruptcy, and his obligation to Epsco was discharged. Reggie and Mark claimed that their father owned CWC as a sole proprietor and that they were not partners in the business. The court, however, held that the sons were liable for CWC's debts based on partnership by estoppel. Because the Chaverses had represented to Epsco that CWC was a partnership and Epsco had relied on this representation when extending credit, the sons could not claim that no partnership existed.[2] •

 Partnership Operation, Dissociation, and Termination

The rights and duties of partners are governed largely by the specific terms of their partnership agreement. In the absence of provisions to the contrary in the partnership agreement, the law imposes the rights and duties discussed here. The character and nature of the partnership business generally influence the application of these rights and duties.

Rights of Partners

The rights of partners in a partnership relate to the following areas: management, interest in the partnership, compensation, inspection of books, accounting, and property.

MANAGEMENT RIGHTS In a general partnership, all partners have equal rights in managing the partnership [UPA 401(f)]. Unless the partners agree otherwise, each partner has one vote in management matters *regardless of the proportional size of his or her interest in the firm*. Often, in a large partnership, partners will agree to delegate daily management responsibilities to a management committee made up of one or more of the partners.

The majority rule controls decisions in ordinary matters connected with partnership business, unless otherwise specified in the agreement. Decisions that significantly affect the

---

2. *Chavers v. Epsco, Inc.,* 352 Ark. 65, 98 S.W.3d 421 (2003).

nature of the partnership or that are not apparently for carrying on the ordinary course of the partnership business, or business of the kind, however, require the *unanimous* consent of the partners [UPA 301(2), 401(i), (j)].

Unanimous consent is likely to be required for a decision to undertake any of the following actions:

1. To alter the essential nature of the firm's business as expressed in the partnership agreement or to alter the capital structure of the partnership.
2. To admit new partners or to enter a wholly new business.
3. To assign partnership property to a trust for the benefit of creditors.
4. To dispose of the partnership's goodwill.
5. To confess judgment against the partnership or to submit partnership claims to arbitration. (A **confession of judgment** is the act of a debtor permitting a judgment to be entered against her or him by a creditor, for an agreed sum, without the institution of legal proceedings.)
6. To undertake any act that would make further conduct of partnership business impossible.
7. To amend the partnership agreement.

INTEREST IN THE PARTNERSHIP   Each partner is entitled to the proportion of business profits and losses designated in the partnership agreement. If the agreement does not apportion profits (indicate how the profits will be shared), the UPA provides that profits will be shared equally. If the agreement does not apportion losses, losses will be shared in the same ratio as profits [UPA 401(b)].

EXAMPLE 27.4   The partnership agreement for Rico and Brent provides for capital contributions of $60,000 from Rico and $40,000 from Brent, but it is silent as to how Rico and Brent will share profits or losses. In this situation, Rico and Brent will share both profits and losses equally. If their partnership agreement provided for profits to be shared in the same ratio as capital contributions, however, 60 percent of the profits would go to Rico, and 40 percent would go to Brent. If their partnership agreement was silent as to losses, losses would be shared in the same ratio as profits (60 percent and 40 percent, respectively). ●

COMPENSATION   Devoting time, skill, and energy to partnership business is a partner's duty and generally is not a compensable service. Rather, as mentioned, a partner's income from the partnership takes the form of a distribution of profits according to the partner's share in the business. Partners can, of course, agree otherwise. For example, the managing partner of a law firm often receives a salary in addition to her or his share of profits for performing special administrative or managerial duties.

INSPECTION OF BOOKS   Partnership books and records must be kept accessible to all partners. Each partner has the right to receive (and the corresponding duty to produce) full and complete information concerning the conduct of all aspects of partnership business [UPA 403]. Each firm keeps books for recording and preserving such information. Partners contribute the information, and a bookkeeper or an accountant typically has the duty to preserve it. The books must be kept at the firm's principal business office and cannot be removed without the consent of all of the partners. Every partner, whether active or inactive, is entitled to inspect all books and records on demand and can make copies of the materials. The personal representative of a deceased partner's estate has the same right of access to partnership books and records that the decedent would have had [UPA 403].

ACCOUNTING OF PARTNERSHIP ASSETS OR PROFITS   An accounting of partnership assets or profits is required to determine the value of each partner's share in the partner-

---

Confession of Judgment   The act or agreement of a debtor permitting a judgment to be entered against him or her by a creditor, for an agreed sum, without the institution of legal proceedings.

"Forty for you, sixty for me—and equal partners we will be."

Anonymous

ship. An accounting can be performed voluntarily, or it can be compelled by court order. Under UPA 405(b), a partner has the right to bring an action for an accounting during the term of the partnership, as well as on the firm's *dissolution* and *winding up* (see pages 694 and 695).

PROPERTY RIGHTS Property acquired *by* a partnership is the property of the partnership and not of the partners individually [UPA 203]. Partnership property includes all property that was originally contributed to the partnership and anything later purchased by the partnership or in the partnership's name (except in rare circumstances) [UPA 204]. A partner may use or possess partnership property only on behalf of the partnership [UPA 401(g)]. A partner is *not* a co-owner of partnership property and has no right to sell, mortgage, or transfer partnership property to another.[3]

In other words, partnership property is owned by the partnership as an entity and not by the individual partners. Thus, a creditor of an individual partner cannot seek to use partnership property to satisfy the partner's debt. Such a creditor can, however, petition a court for a **charging order** to attach the individual partner's interest in the partnership (her or his proportionate share of the profits and losses and right to receive distributions) to satisfy the partner's obligation. (A partner can also assign her or his right to a share of the partnership profits to another to satisfy a debt.)

Charging Order In partnership law, an order granted by a court to a judgment creditor that entitles the creditor to attach profits or assets of a partner on the dissolution of the partnership.

Duties and Liabilities of Partners

The duties and liabilities of partners are basically derived from agency law. Each partner is an agent of every other partner and acts as both a principal and an agent in any business transaction within the scope of the partnership agreement. Each partner is also a general agent of the partnership in carrying out the usual business of the firm "or business of the kind carried on by the partnership" [UPA 301(1)]. Thus, every act of a partner concerning partnership business, or "business of the kind," and every contract signed in the partnership's name bind the firm.

FIDUCIARY DUTIES The fiduciary duties a partner owes to the partnership and the other partners are the *duty of loyalty* and the *duty of care* [UPA 404(a)]. The duty of loyalty requires a partner to account to the partnership for "any property, profit, or benefit" derived by the partner from the partnership's business or the use of its property [UPA 404(b)]. A partner must also refrain from competing with the partnership in business or dealing with the firm as an adverse party.

A partner's duty of care involves refraining from "grossly negligent or reckless conduct, intentional misconduct, or a knowing violation of law" [UPA 404(c)].[4] A partner is not liable to the partnership for simple negligence or honest errors in judgment in conducting partnership business, though.

These duties may not be waived or eliminated in the partnership agreement, and in fulfilling them each partner must act consistently with the obligation of good faith and fair dealing, which applies to all contracts, including partnership agreements [UPA 103(b), 404(d)]. The agreement can specify acts that the partners agree will violate a fiduciary duty.

Note that a partner may pursue his or her own interests without automatically violating these duties [UPA 404(e)]. The key is whether the partner has disclosed the interest to the other partners. **EXAMPLE 27.5** Jayne Trell, a partner at Jacoby & Meyers, owns a shopping mall. Trell may vote against a partnership proposal to open a competing mall, provided that

> "Surround yourself with partners who are better than you are."
> David Ogilvy, 1911–1999
> (Scottish advertising executive)

---

3. Under the previous version of the UPA, partners were *tenants in partnership,* and every partner was a co-owner with all other partners of the partnership property. The current UPA does not recognize this concept.

4. The previous version of the UPA touched only briefly on the duty of loyalty and left the details of the partners' fiduciary duties to be developed under the law of agency.

she has fully disclosed her interest in the shopping mall to the other partners at the firm. ●
A partner cannot make secret profits or put self-interest before his or her duty to the interest of the partnership, however.

AUTHORITY OF PARTNERS   The UPA affirms general principles of agency law that pertain to the authority of a partner to bind a partnership in contract. A partner may also subject the partnership to tort liability under agency principles. When a partner is carrying on partnership business or business of the kind with third parties in the usual way, both the partner and the firm share liability.

The partnership will not be liable, however, if the third parties know that the partner has no such authority. **EXAMPLE 27.6**   Patricia, a partner in Heise, Green, and Stevens, applies for a loan on behalf of the partnership without authorization from the other partners. The bank manager knows that Patricia has no authority. If the bank manager grants the loan, Patricia will be personally bound, but the firm will not be liable. ●

A partnership may file in a designated state office a "statement of partnership authority" to limit the capacity of a partner to act as the firm's agent or transfer property on its behalf [UPA 105, 303]. Any limit on a partner's authority, however, normally does not affect a third party who does not know about the statement (except in real estate transactions when the statement has been recorded with the appropriate state office).

Agency concepts relating to actual (express and implied) authority, apparent authority, and ratification are also applicable to partnerships. The extent of *implied authority* is generally broader for partners than for ordinary agents, though.

The Scope of Implied Powers.   The character and scope of the partnership business and the customary nature of the particular business operation determine the implied powers of the partners. For example, a *trading partnership* is a business that has goods in inventory and makes profits buying and selling those goods. A partner in a trading partnership has a wide range of implied powers, such as to advertise products, hire employees, and extend the firm's credit by issuing or signing checks (see Chapters 18 and 19).

In an ordinary partnership, the partners can exercise all implied powers reasonably necessary and customary to carry on that particular business. Some customarily implied powers include the authority to make warranties on goods in the retail sales business and the power to enter into contracts consistent with the firm's regular course of business. Most partners also have the implied authority to make representations to others concerning partnership affairs, and these statements may be admissible as evidence against the partnership. A partner might also have the implied power to convey real property in the firm's name when such conveyances are part of the ordinary course of partnership business.

Authorized versus Unauthorized Actions.   If a partner acts within the scope of authority, the partnership is legally bound to honor the partner's commitments to third parties. For instance, a partner's authority to sell partnership products carries with it the implied authority to transfer title and to make the usual warranties. **EXAMPLE 27.7**   Jamie Schwab is a partner in a firm that operates a retail tire store. When Schwab negotiates a contract with a customer for the sale of a set of tires, he promises that "each tire will be warranted for normal wear for 40,000 miles." Because Schwab has authority to make warranties, the partnership is bound to honor the warranty. Schwab would not, however, have the authority to sell the partnership's office equipment, fixtures, or other property without the consent of all of the other partners. ●

In addition, because partnerships are formed to generate profits, a partner generally does not have the authority to make charitable contributions without the consent of the other partners. Such actions are not binding on the partnership unless they are ratified by all of the other partners.

LIABILITY OF PARTNERS   One significant disadvantage associated with a traditional partnership is that partners are *personally* liable for the debts of the partnership. Moreover, in most states the liability is essentially unlimited because the acts of one partner in the ordinary course of business subject the other partners to personal liability [UPA 305]. The following subsections explain the rules on a partner's liability. The *Business Application* feature at the end of this chapter discusses the effect that liability rules are having on the rate of partnership formation.

Joint Liability.   At one time, each partner in a partnership generally was jointly liable for the partnership's obligations. **Joint liability** means that a third party must sue all of the partners as a group, but each partner can be held liable for the full amount.[5] If a third party sued the partnership on a contractual debt, the lawsuit had to name all of the partners as defendants to seek partnership assets to pay any judgment. With joint liability, the partnership's assets must be exhausted before creditors can reach the partners' individual assets.[6]

Joint and Several Liability.   In the majority of states, under UPA 306(a), partners are jointly and severally (separately or individually) liable for all partnership obligations, including contracts, torts, and breaches of trust. **Joint and several liability** means that a third party may sue all of the partners together (jointly) or one or more of the partners separately (severally) at his or her option. This is true even if the partner did not participate in, ratify, or know about whatever it was that gave rise to the cause of action. Normally, though, the partnership's assets must be exhausted before a creditor can enforce a judgment against a partner's separate assets [UPA 307(d)].

A judgment against one partner severally (separately) does not extinguish the others' liability. (Similarly, a release of one partner does not discharge the partners' several liability.) Those partners not sued in the first action may be sued subsequently, unless the first action was conclusive on the question of the partnership's liability. In other words, if an action is brought against one partner and the court holds that the partnership was in no way liable, the third party cannot bring an action against another partner and succeed on the issue of the partnership's liability.

Liability of an Incoming Partner.   A partner newly admitted to an existing partnership is not personally liable for any partnership obligations incurred before the person became a partner [UPA 306(b)]. The new partner's liability to existing creditors of the partnership is limited to her or his capital contribution to the firm. **EXAMPLE 27.8** Smartclub, an existing partnership with four members, admits a new partner, Alex Jaff. He contributes $100,000 to the partnership. Smartclub has debts amounting to $600,000 at the time Jaff joins the firm. Although Jaff's capital contribution of $100,000 can be used to satisfy Smartclub's prior obligations, Jaff is not personally liable for partnership debts that were incurred before he became a partner. Thus, his personal assets cannot be used to satisfy the partnership's preexisting debt. If, however, the managing partner at Smartclub borrows funds for the partnership after Jaff becomes a partner, Jaff will be personally liable for those amounts. ●

Joint Liability   Shared liability. In partnership law, partners incur joint liability for partnership obligations and debts. For example, if a third party sues a partner on a partnership debt, the partner has the right to insist that the other partners be sued with him or her.

Joint and Several Liability   In partnership law, a doctrine under which a plaintiff may sue, and collect a judgment from, all of the partners together (jointly) or one or more of the partners separately (severally, or individually). This is true even if one of the partners sued did not participate in, ratify, or know about whatever it was that gave rise to the cause of action.

---

5. Under the previous version of the UPA, which is still in effect in a few states, partners were subject to *joint liability* on partnership debts arising from contracts, but not on partnership debts arising from torts. States that still follow the previous version of the UPA include Connecticut, West Virginia, and Wyoming.

6. For a case applying joint liability to a partnership, see *Shar's Cars, LLC v. Elder,* 97 P.3d 724 (Utah App. 2004).

Partner's Dissociation

Dissociation The severance of the relationship between a partner and a partnership when the partner ceases to be associated with the carrying on of the partnership business.

Dissociation occurs when a partner ceases to be associated in the carrying on of the partnership business. Although a partner always has the *power* to dissociate from the firm, he or she may not have the *right* to dissociate. Dissociation normally entitles the partner to have his or her interest purchased by the partnership and terminates his or her actual authority to act for the partnership and to participate with the partners in running the business. Otherwise, the partnership continues to do business without the dissociating partner.[7]

EVENTS CAUSING DISSOCIATION   Under UPA 601, a partner can be dissociated from a partnership in any of the following ways:

1. By the partner's voluntarily giving notice of and "express will to withdraw."
2. By the occurrence of an event agreed to in the partnership agreement.
3. By a unanimous vote of the other partners under certain circumstances, such as when a partner transfers substantially all of her or his interest in the partnership, or when it becomes unlawful to carry on partnership business with that partner.
4. By order of a court or arbitrator if the partner has engaged in wrongful conduct that affects the partnership business, breached the partnership agreement or violated a duty owed to the partnership or the other partners, or engaged in conduct that makes it "not reasonably practicable to carry on the business in partnership with the partner" [UPA 601(5)].
5. By the partner's declaring bankruptcy, assigning his or her interest in the partnership for the benefit of creditors, or becoming physically or mentally incapacitated, or by the partner's death. Note that although the bankruptcy or death of a partner represents that partner's "dissociation" from the partnership, it is not an *automatic* ground for the partnership's dissolution (*dissolution* will be discussed on page 694).

WRONGFUL DISSOCIATION   As mentioned, a partner has the power to dissociate from a partnership at any time, but if she or he lacks the right to dissociate, then the dissociation is considered wrongful under the law [UPA 602]. When a partner's dissociation is in breach of the partnership agreement, for instance, it is wrongful. **EXAMPLE 27.9** Jensen & Whalen's partnership agreement states that it is a breach of the agreement for any partner to assign partnership property to a creditor without the consent of the other partners. If Janis, a partner, makes such an assignment, she not only has breached the agreement but has also wrongfully dissociated from the partnership. ● Similarly, if a partner refuses to perform duties required by the partnership agreement—such as accounting for profits earned from the use of partnership property—this breach can be treated as a wrongful dissociation. A partner who wrongfully dissociates is liable to the partnership and to the other partners for damages caused by the dissociation.

EFFECTS OF DISSOCIATION   Dissociation (rightful or wrongful) terminates some of the rights of the dissociated partner, requires that the partnership purchase his or her interest, and alters the liability of the parties to third parties. On a partner's dissociation, his or her right to participate in the management and conduct of the partnership business terminates [UPA 603]. The partner's duty of loyalty also ends.

A partner's duty of care continues only with respect to events that occurred before dissociation, unless the partner participates in *winding up* the partnership's business (to be

---

7. Under the previous version of the UPA, when a partner withdrew from a partnership, the partnership was considered dissolved, its business had to be wound up, and the proceeds had to be distributed to creditors and among the partners. The new UPA dramatically changed the law governing partnership breakups and does not require that a partnership be dissolved just because one partner has left the firm.

discussed shortly). **EXAMPLE 27.10** Debbie Pearson, a partner who leaves an accounting firm, Bubb & Pearson, can immediately compete with that firm for new clients. She must exercise care in completing ongoing client transactions, however, and must account to Bubb & Pearson for any fees received from the former clients based on those transactions. ●

After a partner's dissociation, his or her interest in the partnership must be purchased according to the rules in UPA 701. The **buyout price** is based on the amount that would have been distributed to the partner if the partnership were wound up on the date of dissociation. Offset against the price are amounts owed by the partner to the partnership, including any damages for the partner's wrongful dissociation. In the following case, the court had to decide how the buyout price of a partner's interest should be determined on his dissociation from his family's ranch business.

Buyout Price The amount payable to a partner on his or her dissociation from a partnership, based on the amount distributable to that partner if the firm were wound up on that date, and offset by any damages for wrongful dissociation.

Case 27.1 Warnick v. Warnick

Supreme Court of Wyoming, 2006 WY 58, 133 P.3d 997 (2006).

Does the buyout price of a partner in a ranch include the expenses of a hypothetical sale?

FACTS In 1978, Wilbur and Dee Warnick and their son Randall bought a ranch in Sheridan County, Wyoming, for $335,000. To operate the ranch, they formed a partnership—Warnick Ranches. The partners' initial capital contributions totaled $60,000, of which Wilbur paid 36 percent, Dee paid 30 percent, and Randall paid 34 percent. Wilbur and Dee moved onto the ranch in 1981. Randall lived and worked on the ranch during the 1981 and 1982 summer haying seasons and again from 1991 to 1998. The partners each contributed funds to the operation and received cash distributions from the partnership. In 1999, Randall dissociated from the partnership. When the parties could not agree on a buyout price, Randall filed a suit in a Wyoming state court against the other partners and the partnership to recover what he believed to be a fair buyout price. The court awarded Randall $115,783.13—the amount of his cash contributions, plus 34 percent of the increase in the value of the partnership's assets above all partners' cash contributions, with interest from the date of his dissociation. The defendants appealed to the Wyoming Supreme Court, arguing that, in the calculation, $50,000 should be deducted from the appraised value of the ranch, its livestock, and its equipment for the estimated expenses of selling these assets.

ISSUE In determining the buyout price of a dissociated partner, do the costs of liquidating partnership assets include the expenses of a hypothetical sale?

DECISION No. The court affirmed the judgment of the lower court, holding that "purely hypothetical costs of sale are not a required deduction in valuing partnership assets."

REASON The state supreme court explained that under Wyoming Statutes Section 17-21-701 (Wyoming's version of UPA 701), the buyout price is "the amount that would have been paid to the dissociating partner following a settlement of partnership accounts upon the winding up of the partnership, if, on the date of dissociation, the assets of the partnership were sold at a price equal to the greater of the liquidation value or the value based on a sale of the business as a going concern without the dissociating partner." The first step in the calculation is to value the partnership's assets according to the two methods. In making the determination in this case, the defendants "assume that the liquidation value of the ranch is the amount of cash that would remain following a sale." But liquidation value refers to the prices of assets if they are sold separately, as opposed to the value of the business as a whole. For this purpose, an asset's price is the amount that "a willing and informed buyer would pay a willing and informed seller, with neither being under any compulsion to deal." Such a seller would factor the cost of a sale into the price, as the appraiser and the lower court likely did here. Besides "the assets of this partnership were not, in fact, liquidated. Instead, * * * the assets were retained by Warnick Ranches."

FOR CRITICAL ANALYSIS—Economic Consideration
How and why might the value of a partnership interest in a going concern differ from the value of the same interest as a result of a liquidation?

LIABILITY TO THIRD PARTIES

For two years after a partner dissociates from a continuing partnership, the partnership may be bound by the acts of the dissociated partner based on apparent authority [UPA 702]. In other words, the partnership may be liable to a third party with whom a dissociated partner enters into a transaction if the third party reasonably believed that the dissociated partner was still a partner. Similarly, a dissociated partner may be liable for partnership obligations entered into during a two-year period following dissociation [UPA 703]. To avoid this possible liability, a partnership should notify its creditors, customers, and clients of a partner's dissociation. Also, either the partnership or the dissociated partner can file a statement of dissociation in the appropriate state office to limit the dissociated partner's authority to ninety days after the filing [UPA 704].

Partnership Termination

The same events that cause dissociation can result in the end of the partnership if the remaining partners no longer wish to (or are unable to) continue the partnership business. The termination of a partnership is referred to as **dissolution,** which essentially means the commencement of the winding up process. **Winding up** is the actual process of collecting, liquidating, and distributing the partnership assets.[8]

Dissolution   The formal disbanding of a partnership or a corporation. It can take place by (1) acts of the partners or, in a corporation, acts of the shareholders and board of directors; (2) the subsequent illegality of the firm's business; (3) the expiration of a time period stated in a partnership agreement or a certificate of incorporation; or (4) judicial decree.

Winding Up   The second of two stages in the termination of a partnership or corporation. Once the firm is dissolved, it continues to exist legally until the process of winding up all business affairs (collecting and distributing the firm's assets) is complete.

DISSOLUTION   Dissolution of a partnership generally can be brought about by acts of the partners, by operation of law, or by judicial decree [UPA 801]. Any partnership (including one for a fixed term) can be dissolved by the partners' agreement. Similarly, if the partnership agreement states that it will dissolve on a certain event, such as a partner's death or bankruptcy, then the occurrence of that event will dissolve the partnership. A partnership for a fixed term or a particular undertaking is dissolved by operation of law at the expiration of the term or on the completion of the undertaking. Under the UPA, a court may order dissolution when it becomes obviously impractical for the firm to continue—for example, if the business can only be operated at a loss [UPA 801(5)].

Even when one partner has brought a court action seeking to dissolve a partnership, the partnership continues to exist until it is legally dissolved by the court or by the parties' agreement. **CASE EXAMPLE 27.11**   Ellin Curley and Lawrence Kaiser were a married couple when they formed a general partnership, K&K Associates. Later, Curley and Kaiser divorced and entered into an amended partnership agreement that stated that Curley owned 80 percent of the firm and Kaiser owned 20 percent. K&K invested capital in Alpine Focus Fund, LP, but the investment suffered losses. Curley attempted to collect from Kaiser his share of the amount lost, but Kaiser refused to pay. Curley then filed a suit for breach of contract and requested judicial dissolution of K&K.

While the lawsuit was pending, Kaiser died, and his new wife was substituted as the defendant. A provision in the amended agreement stated that if Kaiser died while still a partner, K&K would terminate and the value of Kaiser's ownership interest in the closing capital account would be zero. The defense argued that the court should not enforce this provision because the partnership no longer existed. The court ruled that although the court proceeding had started the dissolution process, the partnership still existed at the time of Kaiser's death. Therefore, the provision in the amended agreement effectively terminated the partnership and reduced Kaiser's interest in the closing capital account to zero.[9] ●

Ethical Issue ⚖️ .... *Do former partners remain jointly and severally liable for a partnership's obligations even after the partnership has been dissolved?* Generally, dissolution has no effect on a partnership's liabilities to third parties. Partners remain liable for partnership debts even after the partnership has ceased to exist. For example, in one case the plaintiff alleged that when he was about twelve years old, Nelson Faerber, Jr., a school board member and prominent attorney, began sexually molesting him. For almost six years, Faerber, who was a partner at a Florida law firm, purportedly molested the boy on numerous occasions and at various locations, including the law firm's offices and the plaintiff's

---

8. Although "winding down" would seem to more accurately describe the process of settling accounts and liquidating the assets of a partnership, "winding up" has been traditionally used in English and U.S. statutory and case law to denote this final stage of a partnership's existence.

9. *Curley v. Kaiser,* 112 Conn.App. 213, 962 A.2d 167 (2009).

middle school. Faerber had died before the plaintiff filed the lawsuit, so the suit named several other defendants, including Faerber's wife, the school, and members of Faerber's former law firm. The law firm argued that the court should dismiss the case against it because the firm no longer existed. The court disagreed, however, holding that "under Florida law, partners remain jointly and severally liable for partnership liability, notwithstanding dissolution and division of property."[10] Although the holding in this case might seem unfair, it illustrates how unlimited liability in general partnerships can extend even beyond the partnership's termination.

WINDING UP   After dissolution, the partnership continues for the limited purpose of the winding up process. The partners cannot create new obligations on behalf of the partnership. They have authority only to complete transactions begun but not finished at the time of dissolution and to wind up the business of the partnership [UPA 803, 804(1)]. Winding up includes collecting and preserving partnership assets, discharging liabilities (paying debts), and accounting to each partner for the value of her or his interest in the partnership. Partners continue to have fiduciary duties to one another and to the firm during this process. UPA 401(h) provides that a partner is entitled to compensation for services in winding up partnership affairs (and reimbursement for expenses incurred in the process) above and apart from his or her share in the partnership profits.

> **DON'T FORGET** Secured creditors have priority over unsecured creditors to any assets that serve as collateral for a partnership's debts.

Both creditors of the partnership and creditors of the individual partners can make claims on the partnership's assets. In general, partnership creditors share proportionately with the partners' individual creditors in the assets of the partners' estates, which include their interests in the partnership. A partnership's assets are distributed according to the following priorities [UPA 807]:

1. Payment of debts, including those owed to partner and nonpartner creditors.
2. Return of capital contributions and distribution of profits to partners.[11]

If the partnership's liabilities are greater than its assets, the partners bear the losses—in the absence of a contrary agreement—in the same proportion in which they shared the profits (rather than, for example, in proportion to their contributions to the partnership's capital).

 Preventing Legal Disputes

Before entering a partnership, agree on how the assets will be valued and divided in the event the partnership dissolves. Make express arrangements that will provide for a smooth dissolution. You and your partners can enter a buy-sell, or buyout, agreement, which provides that one or more partners will buy out the other or others, should the relationship deteriorate. Agreeing beforehand on who buys what, under what circumstances, and, if possible, at what price may eliminate costly negotiations or litigation later. Alternatively, your agreement can specify that one or more partners will determine the value of the interest being sold and that the other or others will decide whether to buy or sell.

> **Limited Liability Partnership (LLP)**
> A hybrid form of business organization that is used mainly by professionals who normally do business in a partnership. An LLP is a pass-through entity for tax purposes, but the personal liability of the partners is limited.

▶ Limited Liability Partnerships

The **limited liability partnership (LLP)** is a hybrid form of business designed mostly for professionals who normally do business as partners in a partnership. The first state to enact an LLP statute was Texas, in 1991. Other states quickly followed suit, and by 1997, almost all of the states had enacted LLP statutes.

---

10. *Doe v. Faerber,* 446 F.Supp.2d 1311 (M.D.Fla. 2006). See also *Red River Wings, Inc. v. Hoot, Inc.,* 751 N.W.2d 206 (N.D. 2008).
11. Under the previous version of the UPA, creditors of the partnership had priority over creditors of the individual partners. Also, in distributing partnership assets, third party creditors were paid before partner creditors, and capital contributions were returned before profits.

The major advantage of the LLP is that it allows a partnership to continue as a pass-through entity for tax purposes but limits the personal liability of the partners. The LLP is especially attractive for two categories of businesses: professional service firms and family businesses. In fact, all of the "Big Four" accounting firms—the four largest international accountancy and professional services firms—are organized as LLPs, including Ernst & Young, LLP, and PricewaterhouseCoopers, LLP.

Formation of an LLP

LLPs must be formed and operated in compliance with state statutes, which may include provisions of the UPA. The appropriate form must be filed with a central state agency, usually the secretary of state's office, and the business's name must include either "Limited Liability Partnership" or "LLP" [UPA 1001, 1002]. In addition, an LLP must file an annual report with the state to remain qualified as an LLP in that state [UPA 1003].

In most states, it is relatively easy to convert a traditional partnership into an LLP because the firm's basic organizational structure remains the same. Additionally, all of the statutory and common law rules governing partnerships still apply (apart from those modified by the LLP statute). Normally, LLP statutes are simply amendments to a state's already existing partnership law.

Liability in an LLP

An LLP allows professionals, such as attorneys and accountants, to avoid personal liability for the malpractice of other partners. A partner in an LLP is still liable for her or his own wrongful acts, such as negligence, however. Also liable is the partner who supervised the individual who committed a wrongful act. This generally is true for all types of partners and partnerships, not just LLPs.

EXAMPLE 27.12   A group of five lawyers is operating as a partnership. One of the attorneys, Dan Kolcher, is sued for malpractice and loses. If the firm was organized as a general partnership and the firm did not have sufficient malpractice insurance to pay the judgment, the personal assets of the other attorneys could be used to satisfy the obligation. Because the firm is organized as an LLP, however, no other partner at the law firm can be held *personally* liable for Kolcher's malpractice, unless she or he acted as Kolcher's supervisor. In the absence of a supervisor, only Kolcher's personal assets can be used to satisfy the judgment (to the extent that it exceeds the liability insurance coverage). ●

Although LLP statutes vary from state to state, generally each state statute limits the liability of partners in some way. For example, Delaware law protects each innocent partner from the "debts and obligations of the partnership arising from negligence, wrongful acts, or misconduct." The UPA more broadly exempts partners from personal liability for any partnership obligation, "whether arising in contract, tort, or otherwise" [UPA 306(c)]. Although the language of some of these statutes may seem to apply specifically to attorneys, any group of professionals can organize as an LLP.

LIABILITY OUTSIDE THE STATE OF FORMATION   When an LLP formed in one state wants to do business in another state, it may be required to register in the second state—for example, by filing a statement of foreign qualification [UPA 1102]. Because state LLP statutes are not uniform, a question arises in this situation. If the LLP statutes in the two states provide different liability protection, which law applies? Most states apply the law of the state in which the LLP was formed, even when the firm does business in another state, which is also the rule under UPA 1101.

SHARING LIABILITY AMONG PARTNERS   When more than one partner in an LLP is negligent, there is a question as to how liability is to be shared. Is each partner jointly and

ON THE WEB For an example of a state law (that of Iowa) governing limited liability partnerships, go to www.sos.state.ia.us/business/limliabpart.html.

severally liable for the entire result, as a general partner would be in most states? Some states provide for proportionate liability—that is, for separate determinations of the negligence of the partners. **EXAMPLE 27.13** Accountants Don and Jane are partners in an LLP, with Don supervising Jane. Jane negligently fails to file tax returns for their client, Centaur Tools. Centaur files a suit against Don and Jane. In a state that does not allow for proportionate liability, Don can be held liable for the entire loss. Under a proportionate liability statute, Don will be liable for no more than his portion of the responsibility for the missed tax deadline. (Even if Jane settles the case quickly, Don will still be liable for his portion.) •

Family Limited Liability Partnerships

Family Limited Liability Partnership (FLLP) A type of limited liability partnership owned by family members or fiduciaries of family members.

A **family limited liability partnership (FLLP)** is a limited liability partnership in which the partners are persons related to each other, essentially as spouses, parents, grandparents, siblings, cousins, nephews, or nieces. A person acting in a fiduciary capacity for persons so related can also be a partner. All of the partners must be natural persons or persons acting in a fiduciary capacity for the benefit of natural persons.

Probably the most significant use of the FLLP form of business organization is in agriculture.[12] Family-owned farms sometimes find this form to their benefit. The FLLP offers the same advantages as other LLPs with some additional advantages, such as, in Iowa, an exemption from real estate transfer taxes when partnership real estate is transferred among partners.[13]

 Limited Partnerships

Limited Partnership A partnership consisting of one or more general partners (who manage the business and are liable to the full extent of their personal assets for debts of the partnership) and one or more limited partners (who contribute only assets and are liable only up to the extent of their contributions).

We now look at a business organizational form that limits the liability of *some* of its owners—the **limited partnership.** Limited partnerships originated in medieval Europe and have been in existence in the United States since the early 1800s. In many ways, limited partnerships are like the general partnerships discussed at the outset of this chapter, but they differ from general partnerships in several ways. Because of this, they are sometimes referred to as *special partnerships*.

General Partner In a limited partnership, a partner who assumes responsibility for the management of the partnership and liability for all partnership debts.

A limited partnership consists of at least one **general partner** and one or more **limited partners.** A general partner assumes management responsibility for the partnership and so has full responsibility for the partnership and for all debts of the partnership. A limited partner contributes cash or other property and owns an interest in the firm but does not undertake any management responsibilities and is not personally liable for partnership debts beyond the amount of his or her investment. A limited partner can forfeit limited liability by taking part in the management of the business. Exhibit 27–2 on the following page compares characteristics of general and limited partnerships.[14]

Limited Partner In a limited partnership, a partner who contributes capital to the partnership but has no right to participate in the management and operation of the business. The limited partner assumes no liability for partnership debts beyond the capital contributed.

Until 1976, the law governing limited partnerships in all states except Louisiana was the Uniform Limited Partnership Act (ULPA). Since 1976, most states and the District of Columbia have adopted the revised version of the ULPA, known as the Revised Uniform Limited Partnership Act (RULPA). Because the RULPA is the dominant law governing limited partnerships in the United States, we will refer to the RULPA in the following discussion of limited partnerships. Note, however, that amendments to make the RULPA more flexible were proposed to the states in 2001 and fifteen states have adopted the 2001 version of this uniform law.

---

12. For a case example, see *Cannon v. Bertrand*, 2 So.3d 393 (La. 2009).

13. Iowa Statutes Section 428A.2.

14. Under the UPA, a general partnership can be converted into a limited partnership and vice versa [UPA 902, 903]. The UPA also provides for the merger of a general partnership with one or more general or limited partnerships under rules that are similar to those governing corporate mergers [UPA 905].

• *Exhibit* **27–2** A Comparison of General Partnerships and Limited Partnerships

CHARACTERISTIC	GENERAL PARTNERSHIP (UPA)	LIMITED PARTNERSHIP (RULPA)
Creation	By agreement of two or more persons to carry on a business as co-owners for profit.	By agreement of two or more persons to carry on a business as co-owners for profit. Must include one or more general partners and one or more limited partners. Filing of a certificate with the secretary of state is required.
Sharing of profits and losses	By agreement; or, in the absence of agreement, profits are shared equally by the partners, and losses are shared in the same ratio as profits.	Profits are shared as required in the certificate agreement, and losses are shared likewise, up to the amount of the limited partners' capital contributions. In the absence of a provision in the certificate agreement, profits and losses are shared on the basis of percentages of capital contributions.
Liability	Unlimited personal liability of all partners.	Unlimited personal liability of all general partners; limited partners liable only to the extent of their capital contributions.
Capital contribution	No minimum or mandatory amount; set by agreement.	Set by agreement.
Management	By agreement, or in the absence of agreement, all partners have an equal voice.	General partner or partners only. Limited partners have no voice or else are subject to liability as general partners (but only if a third party has reason to believe that the limited partner is a general partner). A limited partner may act as an agent or employee of the partnership and vote on amending the certificate or on the sale or dissolution of the partnership.
Duration	Terminated by agreement of the partners, but can continue to do business even when a partner dissociates from the partnership.	Terminated by agreement in the certificate or by retirement, death, or mental incompetence of a general partner in the absence of the right of the other general partners to continue the partnership. Death of a limited partner, unless he or she is the only remaining limited partner, does not terminate the partnership.
Distribution of assets on liquidation— Order of priorities	1. Payment of debts, including those owed to partner and nonpartner creditors. 2. Return of capital contributions and distribution of profit to partners.	1. Outside creditors and partner creditors. 2. Partners and former partners entitled to distributions of partnership assets. 3. Unless otherwise agreed, return of capital contributions and distribution of profit to partners.

Formation of a Limited Partnership

In contrast to the informal, private, and voluntary agreement that usually suffices for a general partnership, the formation of a limited partnership is a public and formal proceeding that must follow statutory requirements. A limited partnership must have at least one general partner and one limited partner, as mentioned previously. Additionally, the partners must sign a **certificate of limited partnership,** which requires information similar to that found in a corporate charter (see Chapter 28). The certificate must be filed with the designated state official—under the RULPA, the secretary of state. The certificate is usually open to public inspection.

Certificate of Limited Partnership The basic document filed with a designated state official by which a limited partnership is formed.

Liabilities of Partners in a Limited Partnership

General partners, unlike limited partners, are personally liable to the partnership's creditors; thus, at least one general partner is necessary in a limited partnership so that someone has personal liability. This policy can be circumvented in states that allow a corporation to be the general partner in a partnership. Because the corporation has limited liability by virtue of corporate laws, if a corporation is the general partner, no one in the limited partnership has personal liability.

In contrast to the personal liability of general partners, the liability of a limited partner is limited to the capital that she or he contributes or agrees to contribute to the partnership [RULPA 502]. Limited partners enjoy this limited liability only so long as they do not participate in management [RULPA 303]. A limited partner who participates in management will be just as liable as a general partner to any creditor who transacts business with the limited partnership and believes, based on the limited partner's conduct, that the limited partner is a general partner [RULPA 303]. The extent of review and advisement a limited partner can engage in before being exposed to liability remains rather vague, though.

NOTE A limited partner is liable only to the extent of any contribution that she or he made to the partnership, but can lose this limited liability by participating in management.

Rights and Duties in a Limited Partnership

With the exception of the right to participate in management, limited partners have essentially the same rights as general partners. Limited partners have a right of access to the partnership's books and to information regarding partnership business.

General and limited partners also owe each other a fiduciary duty to exercise good faith in transactions related to the partnership. Can this duty be waived through a provision in the partnership agreement? That was the issue in the following case.

Case 27.2   1515 North Wells, LP v. 1513 North Wells, LLC

Appellate Court of Illinois, First District, 392 Ill.App.3d 863 (Ill.App. 1 Dist 2009).
www.state.il.us/court/default.asp[a]

A limited partnership agreement to build condominiums allowed partners to engage in "whatever activities" they chose. Can that excuse the breach of fiduciary duties of the partners?

FACTS   Thomas Bracken (owner of 1513 North Wells, LLC), Mark Sutherland, and Alex Pearsall were limited partners in 1515 North Wells, LP. Sutherland and Pearsall's company, SP Development Corporation, was 1515's general partner. The partnership was formed to build a condominium with residential and commercial space. SP chose another Sutherland and Pearsall company, Sutherland and Pearsall Development, to be the general contractor for the 1515 project. Meanwhile, Bracken borrowed $250,000 from 1515. When he did not repay the loan, 1515 filed a suit in an Illinois state court to collect. In response, Bracken filed a claim that included SP Development Corporation, alleging breach of fiduciary duty. The court ordered Bracken to repay the loan and SP to pay Bracken $900,000. SP appealed, arguing that a provision in 1515's partnership agreement, which allowed all partners to engage in "whatever activities they choose," effectively "relaxed" SP's fiduciary duty.

ISSUE   Can a general partner breach a fiduciary duty to a limited partner even if their agreement allows partners to engage in "whatever activities they choose"?

DECISION   Yes. The state intermediate appellate court affirmed the lower court's judgment. A partnership agreement cannot "contract away" the fiduciary duty that a general partner owes to limited partners.

REASON   Under UPA 103(b)(3), a partnership agreement cannot "eliminate or reduce a partner's fiduciary duties." An agreement can permit the partners to engage in activities within or outside the areas of partnership business. But this does not allow them to conduct deals at the expense of the other partners. The provision in 1515's partnership agreement that allowed the partners to engage in "whatever activities" thus could not excuse their liability for a breach of fiduciary duty. To establish a successful claim on this basis, a partner must prove a fiduciary duty, a breach of the duty, and damages caused by the breach. In this case, "there was ample evidence to support the court's finding of a breach of fiduciary duty." The court cited the contract that SP awarded to Sutherland and Pearsall Development. SP had chosen this company even though it had submitted the only bid, which consisted of a "cost plus fee" contract (it did not state a maximum price). SP had also granted the contractor—not 1515—the right to keep any revenue generated by the sales of condominium upgrades.

FOR CRITICAL ANALYSIS—Ethical Consideration   *Did any of the parties involved in this case commit an ethical violation? Discuss.*

a. In the "Documents" pull-down menu, click on "Court Opinions." On that page, click on "Supreme and Appellate Court Opinion Archive." In the result, in the "Select a Court" column, select "1st District Appellate"; in the "Select an Archive Year" column, choose "2009"; and click on "Get Opinions." In that result, scroll to the name of the case and click on it to access the opinion. The Administrative Office of the Illinois Courts maintains this Web site.

Dissociation and Dissolution

> "A friendship founded on business is a good deal better than a business founded on friendship."
>
> John D. Rockefeller, 1839–1937
> (American industrialist)

A general partner has the power to voluntarily dissociate, or withdraw, from a limited partnership unless the partnership agreement specifies otherwise. A limited partner theoretically can withdraw from the partnership by giving six months' notice unless the partnership agreement specifies a term, which most do. Also, some states have passed laws prohibiting the withdrawal of limited partners.

In a limited partnership, a general partner's voluntary dissociation from the firm normally will lead to dissolution *unless* all partners agree to continue the business. Similarly, the bankruptcy, retirement, death, or mental incompetence of a general partner will cause the dissociation of that partner and the dissolution of the limited partnership unless the other members agree to continue the firm [RULPA 801]. Bankruptcy of a limited partner, however, does not dissolve the partnership unless it causes the bankruptcy of the firm. Death or an assignment of the interest of a limited partner does not dissolve a limited partnership [RULPA 702, 704, 705]. A limited partnership can be dissolved by court decree [RULPA 802].

On dissolution, creditors' claims, including those of partners who are creditors, take first priority. After that, partners and former partners receive unpaid distributions of partnership assets and, except as otherwise agreed, amounts representing returns on their contributions and amounts proportionate to their shares of the distributions [RULPA 804].

In the following case, two limited partners wanted the business of the partnership to be sold on its dissolution, while another limited partner (actor Kevin Costner) and the general partner wanted it to continue.

Case 27.3 In re Dissolution of Midnight Star Enterprises, LP

Supreme Court of South Dakota, 2006 SD 98, 724 N.W.2d 334 (2006).

Actor Kevin Costner wanted a partnership to continue doing business. Can another partner force the sale of the business?

FACTS Midnight Star Enterprises, LP, consists of a casino, bar, and restaurant in Deadwood, South Dakota. The owners are Midnight Star Enterprises, Limited (MSEL), the general partner, which owns 22 partnership units; actor Kevin Costner, a limited partner, who owns 71.50 partnership units; and Carla and Francis Caneva, limited partners, who own 3.25 partnership units each. Costner also owns MSEL and thus controls 93.5 partnership units. The Canevas were the business's managers, for which they received salaries and bonuses. When MSEL voiced concerns about the management, communication among the partners broke down. MSEL filed a petition in a South Dakota state court to dissolve the partnership. MSEL hired Paul Thorstenson, an accountant, to determine the firm's fair market value, which he calculated to be $3.1 million. The Canevas solicited a competitor's offer to buy the business for $6.2 million, which the court ruled was the appropriate amount. At the Canevas' request, the court ordered MSEL and Costner to buy the business for that price within ten days or sell it on the open market to the highest bidder. MSEL appealed to the South Dakota Supreme Court.

ISSUE Can a partner force the sale of a limited partnership when the other partners want to continue the business?

DECISION No. The South Dakota Supreme Court reversed the judgment of the lower court and remanded the case to allow MSEL and Costner to pay the Canevas the value of their 6.5 partnership units after a revaluation of the partnership.

REASON The state supreme court concluded that the partnership agreement did not require the business to be sold on the open market on the partnership's dissolution. Under the agreement, during liquidation, the firm's property could be distributed in kind among the partners if it was first offered for sale to a third party. In other words, only a decision to make an in-kind distribution of assets required that the business be offered for sale on the open market. The court also concluded that the correct value of the business was the accountant's figure, which was based on a fair market value analysis using a hypothetical buyer. This analysis provided a reasonable basis for determining value "by removing the irrationalities, strategies, and emotions" that exist in an actual offer. Besides, the partnership agreement required a "fair market value" of the assets. Finally, "[s]ince it was error for the [lower] court to value Midnight Star at $6.2 million, it was also error to force the general partners to buy the business for $6.2 million or

Case 27.3—Continued

sell the business." The state supreme court reasoned that "forced sales typically end up in economic waste." A buyout is an acceptable alternative, as long as the partners receive the fair value of their property interest. "Instead of ordering the majority partners to purchase the whole partnership for the appraised value, the majority partners should only be required to pay any interests the withdrawing partner is due."

FOR CRITICAL ANALYSIS—Ethical Consideration
Under what circumstances on the dissolution of a limited partnership might a forced sale of its property be appropriate?

Limited Liability Limited Partnerships

Limited Liability Limited Partnership (LLLP) A type of limited partnership in which the liability of all of the partners, including general partners, is limited to the amount of their investments.

A **limited liability limited partnership (LLLP)** is a type of limited partnership. An LLLP differs from a limited partnership in that a general partner in an LLLP has the same liability as a limited partner in a limited partnership. In other words, the liability of *all* partners is limited to the amount of their investments in the firm.

A few states provide expressly for LLLPs.[15] In states that do not provide for LLLPs but do allow for limited partnerships and limited liability partnerships, a limited partnership should probably still be able to register with the state as an LLLP.

_____

15. See, for example, Colorado Revised Statutes Annotated Section 7-62-109. Other states that provide expressly for limited liability limited partnerships include Delaware, Florida, Missouri, Pennsylvania, Texas, and Virginia.

Reviewing . . . All Forms of Partnership

Grace Tarnavsky and her sons, Manny and Jason, bought a ranch known as the Cowboy Palace in March 2006, and the three orally agreed to share the business for five years. Grace contributed 50 percent of the investment, and each son contributed 25 percent. Manny agreed to handle the livestock, and Jason agreed to do the bookkeeping. The Tarnavskys took out joint loans and opened a joint bank account into which they deposited the ranch's proceeds and from which they made payments toward property, cattle, equipment, and supplies. In September 2010, Manny severely injured his back while baling hay and became permanently unable to handle livestock. Manny therefore hired additional laborers to tend the livestock, causing the Cowboy Palace to incur significant debt. In September 2011, Al's Feed Barn filed a lawsuit against Jason to collect $12,400 in unpaid debts. Using the information presented in the chapter, answer the following questions.

1. Was this relationship a partnership for a term or a partnership at will?
2. Did Manny have the authority to hire additional laborers to work at the ranch after his injury? Why or why not?
3. Under the UPA, can Al's Feed Barn bring an action against Jason individually for Cowboy Palace's debt? Why or why not?
4. Suppose that after his back injury in 2010, Manny sent his mother and brother a notice indicating his intent to withdraw from the partnership. Can he still be held liable for the debt to Al's Feed Barn? Why or why not?

Business Application

Why Are General Partnerships Declining in Popularity?*

Forty years ago, there were three basic forms of business organization—the sole proprietorship, the general partnership, and the corporation. When several people wanted to join together to create a business, they formed

a general partnership. General partnerships are easy to form through a simple agreement and allow two or more persons to pool their capital and individual expertise for the benefit of all. The partners in a general

*This *Business Application* is not meant to substitute for the services of an attorney who is licensed to practice law in your state.

Continued

partnership do not need to file documents with the state to form their business or obtain any certificate (except perhaps a business license).

Traditional partnerships are also flexible. They can be limited to a specified purpose or stated time period, or they can continue until one or more of the partners decide to terminate the business. The partners themselves can decide how to split the profits and losses of the business, and partnerships can obtain credit from lenders more easily than sole proprietorships can.

Another advantage is that the partnership entity itself has no income tax liability. Instead, the individual partners pay taxes on the profits derived from the partnership. Thus, partnerships avoid double taxation, which occurs with corporations, as you will learn in Chapter 29.

A Distinct Disadvantage—Unlimited Personal Liability

Despite their many advantages, general partnerships have one very important disadvantage—the unlimited personal liability of the individual partners. Partners in a general partnership are personally liable not only for the firm's debts, but also for the acts of other partners committed within the scope of the partnership business. Because partners have joint and several liability, a partner's personal assets can be in jeopardy even though he or she was not involved in the act that gave rise to the liability. Reportedly, Mark Twain (1835–1910), the author of *The Adventures of Huckleberry Finn,* lost more than one small fortune due to his participation in unsuccessful partnerships. In today's business world, liability for a partner's misconduct—including the Twitters and Tweets of another partner that lead to a defamation lawsuit and a substantial damages award—can be particularly devastating.

General partnerships have some other disadvantages as well. They cannot receive a Chapter 7 discharge in bankruptcy, for example, and

one partner's death can sometimes result in the firm's dissolution. Nevertheless, these problems are minor compared to the unlimited personal liability.

A Possible Solution—Limited Liability Entities

Not surprisingly, the disadvantageous liability of general partnerships has created a demand for business organizational forms that offer the benefits of partnerships while providing limited liability as well. These forms include the limited partnership, the limited liability partnership, the limited liability limited partnership (discussed in this chapter); the limited liability company (see Chapter 28); and the S corporation (see Chapter 29). These limited liability entities have increased dramatically in popularity in recent years at the expense of general partnerships.

CHECKLIST FOR FORMING A GENERAL PARTNERSHIP

1. **Decide how important ease and informality are to the creation of your business organization. For example, to accomplish a single project within a limited time, a general partnership may be the ideal business form.**
2. **Choose your partners carefully. Remember that you can be personally liable for their actions.**
3. **The partnership should carry sufficient insurance to protect against third parties reaching each partner's individual assets and to allow the partnership to continue on after a partner's death.**
4. **Before you form a partnership, decide how profits and losses are to be shared and the amount of each partner's capital contribution. Express these decisions in a written partnership agreement.**

 Key Terms

articles of partnership 685	family limited liability partnership (FLLP) 697	limited liability partnership (LLP) 695
buyout price 693	general partner 697	limited partner 697
certificate of limited partnership 698	information return 685	limited partnership 697
charging order 689	joint and several liability 691	partnership 684
confession of judgment 688	joint liability 691	pass-through entity 685
dissociation 692	limited liability limited	winding up 694
dissolution 694	partnership (LLLP) 701	

 Chapter Summary: All Forms of Partnership

Partnerships (See pages 683–695.)	1. A partnership is created by agreement of the parties.
	2. A partnership is treated as an entity except for limited purposes.
	3. Each partner pays a proportionate share of income taxes on the net profits of the partnership, whether or not they are distributed; the partnership files only an information return with the Internal Revenue Service.
	4. Each partner has an equal voice in management unless the partnership agreement provides otherwise.
	5. In the absence of an agreement, partners share profits equally and share losses in the same ratio as they share profits.

Chapter Summary: All Forms of Partnership—Continued

Partnerships—Continued	6. The capital contribution of each partner is determined by agreement.
	7. Partners have unlimited liability for partnership debts.
	8. A partnership can be terminated by agreement or can be dissolved by action of the partners (dissociation from a partnership at will), operation of law (subsequent illegality), or court decree.
Limited Liability Partnerships (LLPs) (See pages 695–697.)	1. *Formation*—The appropriate form must be filed with a state agency, usually the secretary of state's office. Typically, an LLP is formed by professionals who work together as partners in a partnership. Under most state LLP statutes, it is relatively easy to convert a traditional partnership into an LLP.
	2. *Liability of partners*—LLP statutes vary, but under the UPA, professionals generally can avoid personal liability for acts committed by other partners. The extent to which partners' limited liability will be recognized when the partnership does business in another state depends on the other state's laws. Partners in an LLP continue to be liable for their own wrongful acts and for the wrongful acts of those whom they supervise.
	3. *Family limited liability partnership (FLLP)*—A form of LLP in which all of the partners are family members or fiduciaries of family members; the most significant use of the FLLP is by families engaged in agricultural enterprises.
Limited Partnerships (See pages 697–701.)	1. *Formation*—A certificate of limited partnership must be filed with the secretary of state's office or other designated state official. The certificate must include information about the business, similar to the information included in a corporate charter. The partnership consists of one or more general partners and one or more limited partners.
	2. *Rights and liabilities of partners*—With some exceptions, the rights of partners are the same as the rights of partners in a general partnership. General partners have unlimited liability for partnership obligations; limited partners are liable only to the extent of their contributions.
	3. *Limited partners and management*—Only general partners can participate in management. Limited partners have no voice in management; if they do participate in management activities, they risk having general-partner liability.
	4. *Dissolution*—Generally, a limited partnership can be dissolved in much the same way as an ordinary partnership. The death or assignment of the interest of a limited partner does not dissolve the partnership; bankruptcy of a limited partner also will not dissolve the partnership unless it causes the bankruptcy of the firm.
	5. *Limited liability limited partnerships (LLLPs)*—A special type of limited partnership in which the liability of all partners, including general partners, is limited to the amount of their investments.

 ExamPrep

ISSUE SPOTTERS

1 Darnell and Eliana are partners in D&E Designs, an architectural firm. When Darnell dies, his widow claims that as Darnell's heir, she is entitled to take his place as Eliana's partner or to receive a share of the firm's assets. Is she right? Why or why not?

2 Finian and Gloria are partners in F&G Delivery Service. When business is slow, without Gloria's knowledge, Finian leases the delivery vehicles as moving vans. Because the vehicles would otherwise be sitting idle in a parking lot, can Finian keep the income resulting from the leasing of the delivery vehicles? Explain your answer.

BEFORE THE TEST

Check your answers to the Issue Spotters, and at the same time, take the interactive quiz for this chapter. Go to **www.cengage.com/blaw/blt** and click on "Chapter 27." First, click on "Answers to Issue Spotters" to check your answers. Next, click on "Interactive Quiz" to assess your mastery of the concepts in this chapter. Then click on "Flashcards" to review this chapter's Key Term definitions.

▶ For Review

Answers for the even-numbered questions in this **For Review** *section can be found on this text's accompanying Web site at* **www.cengage.com/blaw/blt**. *Select "Chapter 27" and click on "For Review."*

1 What are the three essential elements of a partnership?

2 What are the rights and duties of partners in an ordinary partnership?

3 What is meant by joint and several liability? Why is this often considered to be a disadvantage of the partnership form of business?

4 What advantages do limited liability partnerships offer to businesspersons that are not offered by general partnerships?

5 What are the key differences between the rights and liabilities of general partners and those of limited partners?

▶ Hypothetical Scenarios and Case Problems

27–1 Partnership Formation. Daniel is the owner of a chain of shoe stores. He hires Rubya to be the manager of a new store, which is to open in Grand Rapids, Michigan. Daniel, by written contract, agrees to pay Rubya a monthly salary and 20 percent of the profits. Without Daniel's knowledge, Rubya represents himself to Classen as Daniel's partner, showing Classen the agreement to share profits. Classen extends credit to Rubya. Rubya defaults. Discuss whether Classen can hold Daniel liable as a partner.

27–2 **Hypothetical Question with Sample Answer** Dorinda, Luis, and Elizabeth form a limited partnership. Dorinda is a general partner, and Luis and Elizabeth are limited partners. Discuss fully whether each of the separate events below constitutes a dissolution of the limited partnership.

1 Luis assigns his partnership interest to Ashley.

2 Elizabeth is petitioned into involuntary bankruptcy.

3 Dorinda dies.

—**For a sample answer to Question 27–2, go to Appendix E at the end of this text.**

27–3 Distribution of Partnership Assets. Shawna and David formed a partnership. At the time of the partnership's formation, Shawna's capital contribution was $10,000, and David's was $15,000. Later, Shawna made a $10,000 loan to the partnership when it needed working capital. The partnership agreement provided that profits were to be shared with 40 percent for Shawna and 60 percent for David. The partnership was dissolved after David's death. At the end of the dissolution and the winding up of the partnership, the partnership's assets were $50,000, and the partnership's debts were $8,000. Discuss fully how the assets should be distributed.

27–4 Indications of Partnership. At least six months before the 1996 Summer Olympic Games in Atlanta, Georgia, Stafford Fontenot, Steve Turner, Mike Montelaro, Joe Sokol, and Doug Brinsmade agreed to sell Cajun food at the games and began making preparations. Calling themselves "Prairie Cajun Seafood Catering of Louisiana," on May 19 the group applied for a license with the Fulton County, Georgia, Department of Public Health–Environmental Health Services. Later, Ted Norris sold a mobile kitchen for an $8,000 check drawn on the "Prairie Cajun Seafood Catering of Louisiana" account and two promissory notes, one for $12,000 and the other for $20,000. The notes, which were dated June 12, listed only Fontenot "d/b/a Prairie Cajun Seafood" as the maker (*d/b/a* is an abbreviation for "doing business as"). On July 31, Fontenot and his friends signed a partnership agreement, which listed specific percentages of profits and losses. They drove the mobile kitchen to Atlanta, but business was "disastrous." When the notes were not paid, Norris filed a suit in a Louisiana state court against Fontenot, seeking payment. What are the elements of a partnership? Was there a partnership among Fontenot and the others? Who is liable on the notes? Explain. [*Norris v. Fontenot*, 867 So.2d 179 (La.App. 3 Cir. 2004)]

27–5 **Case Problem with Sample Answer** In August 2003, Tammy Duncan began working as a waitress at Bynum's Diner, which was owned by her mother, Hazel Bynum, and her stepfather, Eddie Bynum, in Valdosta, Georgia. Less than a month later, the three signed an agreement under which Eddie was to relinquish his management responsibilities, allowing Tammy to be co-manager. At the end of this six-month period, Eddie would revisit this agreement and could then extend it for another six-month period. The diner's bank account was to remain in Eddie's name. There was no provision with regard to the diner's profit, if any, and the parties did not change the business's tax information. Tammy began doing the bookkeeping, as well as waiting tables and performing other duties. On October 30, she slipped off a ladder and injured her knees. At the end of the six-month term, Tammy quit working at the diner. The Georgia State Board of Workers' Compensation determined that she had been the diner's employee and awarded her benefits under the diner's workers' compensation policy with Cypress Insurance Co. Cypress filed a suit in a Georgia state court against Tammy, arguing that she was not an employee, but a co-owner. What are the essential elements of a partnership? Was Tammy a partner in the business of the diner? Explain. [*Cypress Insurance Co. v. Duncan*, 281 Ga.App. 469, 636 S.E.2d 159 (2006)]

—**After you have answered Problem 27–5, compare your answer with the sample answer given on the Web site that accompanies this text. Go to** **www.cengage.com/blaw/blt**, **select "Chapter 27," and click on "Case Problem with Sample Answer."**

27-6 Partnership Dissolution. Nine minority partners each owned one-half of 1 percent of J&J Celcom, a partnership with AT&T, which owned the rest. AT&T, using its majority power, voted to buy out the minority partners. It offered each partner a price that was slightly higher than the price provided by a third party's appraisal. Some of the partners accepted the offer, but others did not. AT&T then voted to dissolve the partnership, forcing the remaining minority partners to accept the appraisal price. Those partners sued. The trial court held for AT&T, and the minority partners appealed. The appeals court held that the price offered was the fair market price, but certified the following question to Washington State's highest court: "Does a controlling partner violate the duty of loyalty to the partnership or to dissenting minority partners where the controlling partner causes the partnership to sell all its assets" to another party? Why or why not? [*J&J Celcom v. AT&T Wireless Services, Inc.*, 162 Wash.2d 102, 169 P.3d 823 (Sup.Ct. 2007)]

27-7 Limited Partnership. James Carpenter contracted with Austin Estates, LP, to buy property in Texas. Carpenter asked Sandra McBeth to invest in the deal. He admitted that a dispute had arisen with the city of Austin over water for the property, but he assured her that it would not be a significant obstacle. McBeth agreed to invest $800,000 to hold open the option to buy the property. She became a limited partner in StoneLake Ranch, LP. Carpenter acted as the firm's general partner. Despite his statements to McBeth, the purchase was delayed due to the water dispute. Unable to complete the purchase timely, Carpenter paid the $800,000 to Austin Estates without notifying McBeth. Later, Carpenter and others—*excluding* McBeth—bought the property and sold it at a profit. McBeth filed a suit in a Texas state court against Carpenter. What is the nature of the fiduciary duty that a general partner owes a limited partner? Did

Carpenter breach that duty in this case? Explain. [*McBeth v. Carpenter*, 565 F.3d 171 (5th Cir. 2009)]

27-8 **A Question of Ethics** *In 1991, Hassan Mardanlou and Ali Ghaffarian signed a lease for 3960 South State Street in Salt Lake City, Utah. Ghaffarian paid $6,000 for the first and last months' rent, and said to Mardanlou, "We are in this together, partner." Mardanlou bought business cards for "Access Auto" with his and Ghaffarian's names on the cards. Both men were listed on Access Auto's insurance policy. Mardanlou bought the firm's furniture. Ghaffarian did the bookkeeping and bought the inventory. Mardanlou did not have access to the books but wrote checks on the firm's account, sold its inventory, and managed the sales staff. In March 1993, Ghaffarian gave Mardanlou a check for $10,000. Otherwise, Mardanlou was paid a fixed amount each month. Later that year, without telling Mardanlou, Ghaffarian bought the leased property with the firm's funds but titled it in his name. In 1995, Mardanlou learned of this deal and confronted Ghaffarian, who said, "Don't worry, we're partners." Ghaffarian filed the firm's tax returns in his name only, despite Mardanlou's repeated objections. Finally, in 1997, Mardanlou quit the firm and filed a suit in a Utah state court against Ghaffarian to dissolve the partnership and obtain a share of the profits. [Mardanlou v. Ghaffarian, 2006 UT App 165, 135 P.3d 904 (2006)]*

1 What factors indicate that Mardanlou and Ghaffarian were partners? What factors indicate that they were not partners? If you were the judge, how would you resolve this dispute?

2 Is Mardanlou entitled to a share of the value of the real property that Ghaffarian bought in his own name? If so, how much? From an ethical point of view, what solution appears to be the fairest? Discuss.

3 Is Mardanlou entitled to a share of Access Auto's profits? Why or why not?

▶ Critical Thinking and Writing Assignments

27-9 Critical Thinking and Writing Assignment for Business. Sandra Lerner and Patricia Holmes were friends. One evening, while applying nail polish to Lerner, Holmes layered a raspberry color over black to produce a new color, which Lerner liked. Later, the two created other colors with names like "Bruise," "Smog," and "Oil Slick," and titled their concept "Urban Decay." Lerner and Holmes started a firm to produce and market the polishes but never discussed the sharing of profits and losses. They agreed to build the business and then sell it. Together, they did market research, worked on a logo and advertising, obtained

capital, and hired employees. Then Lerner began working to edge Holmes out of the firm.

1 Lerner claimed that there was no partnership agreement because there was no provision on how to divide profits. Was she right? Why or why not?

2 Suppose that Lerner, but not Holmes, had contributed a significant amount of personal funds into developing and marketing the new nail polish. Would this entitle Lerner to receive more of the profit? Explain.

3 Did Lerner violate her fiduciary duty? Why or why not?

▶ Practical Internet Exercises

Go to this text's Web site at **www.cengage.com/blaw/blt**, select "Chapter 27," and click on "Practical Internet Exercises." There you will find the following Internet research exercises that you can perform to learn more about the topics covered in this chapter.

Practical Internet Exercise 27–1: LEGAL PERSPECTIVE—Liability of Dissociated Partners

Practical Internet Exercise 27–2: ECONOMIC PERSPECTIVE—Taxation of Partnerships

Practical Internet Exercise 27–3: MANAGEMENT PERSPECTIVE—Limited Partnerships and Limited Liability Partnerships

Chapter 28

Limited Liability Companies and Special Business Forms

Chapter Outline

- Limited Liability Companies
- LLC Operation and Management
- Dissociation and Dissolution of an LLC
- Special Business Forms

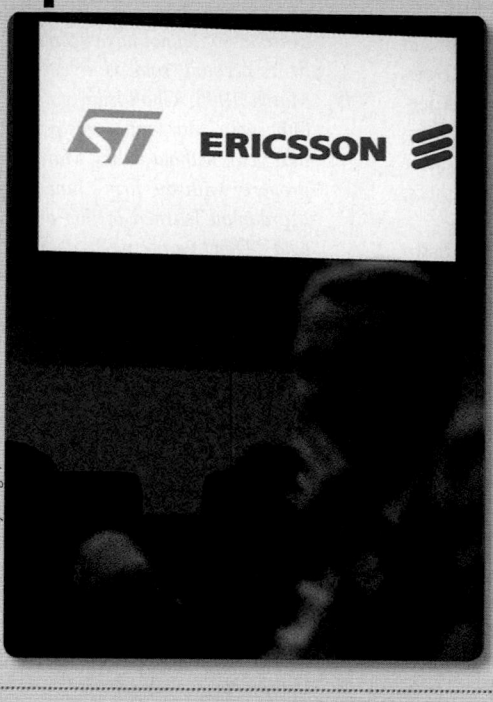

(Leon Neal/AFP/Getty Images)

Learning Objectives

After reading this chapter, you should be able to answer the following questions:

1. What advantages do limited liability companies offer to businesspersons that are not offered by sole proprietorships or partnerships?

2. How are limited liability companies formed, and who decides how they will be managed and operated?

3. What are the two options for managing limited liability companies?

4. What is a joint venture? How is it similar to a partnership? How is it different?

5. What are the essential characteristics of joint stock companies, syndicates, business trusts, and cooperatives, respectively?

In the United States, public policy encourages trade and commerce. To promote commerce and profit-making activities, our government allows entrepreneurs to choose from a variety of business organizational forms when undertaking their business ventures. Many businesspersons would agree with the chapter-opening quotation that in business "to play it safe is not to play." Because risk is associated with the potential for higher profits, businesspersons are motivated to choose organizational forms that limit their liability while allowing them to take risks that may maximize their profit.

In the preceding chapters, we examined sole proprietorships and various partnership forms. Here, we examine a relatively new form of business organization, the **limited liability company (LLC).** The LLC is a hybrid that combines the limited liability aspects of a corporation and the tax advantages of a partnership. We examine the origins and evolution of the LLC in the *Landmark in the Law* feature. Then we look at important characteristics of the LLC, including formation, jurisdictional requirements, and the advantages and disadvantages of choosing to do business as an LLC. Next, we examine the operation and management options in an LLC. The chapter concludes with a discussion of various other special business forms, including joint ventures, syndicates, joint stock companies, business trusts, and cooperatives.

Limited Liability Company (LLC)
A hybrid form of business enterprise that offers the limited liability of a corporation and the tax advantages of a partnership.

Landmark in the Law   Limited Liability Company (LLC) Statutes

In 1977, Wyoming became the first state to pass legislation authorizing the creation of a limited liability company (LLC). Although LLCs emerged in the United States in the late 1970s, they have been used for more than a century in other foreign jurisdictions, including several European and South American nations.

Taxation of LLCs   Despite Wyoming's adoption of an LLC statute, the tax status of LLCs in the United States was not clear until 1988, when the Internal Revenue Service (IRS) ruled that Wyoming LLCs would be taxed as partnerships instead of as corporations, providing that certain requirements were met. Before this ruling, only one additional state–Florida, in 1982–had authorized LLCs. The 1988 IRS ruling encouraged other states to enact LLC statutes, and in less than a decade, all states had done so.

IRS rules that went into effect in 1997 also encouraged more widespread use of LLCs in the business world. Under these rules, any unincorporated business is automatically taxed as a partnership unless it indicates otherwise on the tax form. The exceptions involve publicly traded companies, companies formed under a state incorporation statute, and certain foreign-owned companies. If a business chooses to be taxed as a corporation, it can indicate this preference by checking a box on the IRS form.

Foreign Entities May Be LLC Members   Part of the impetus behind the creation of LLCs in this country is that foreign investors are allowed to become LLC members. Generally, in an era increasingly characterized by global business efforts and investments, the LLC offers U.S. firms and potential investors from other countries greater flexibility and opportunities than are available through partnerships or corporations.

• Application to Today's World   *Once it became clear that LLCs could be taxed as partnerships, the LLC form of business organization was widely adopted. Members could avoid the personal liability associated with the partnership form of business as well as the double taxation of the corporate form of business (see Chapter 29). Today, LLCs are a common form of business organization.*

• Relevant Web Sites   To locate information on the Web concerning limited liability company statutes, go to this text's Web site at www.cengage.com/blaw/blt, select "Chapter 28," and click on "URLs for Landmarks."

▶ Limited Liability Companies

Member   A person who has an ownership interest in a limited liability company.

Flight Options, LLC, offers charter jet services. Why did the company choose to organize as an LLC?

(Michael Brands/*The New York Times*/Redux)

Limited liability companies are governed by state LLC statutes. These laws vary, of course, from state to state. In an attempt to create more uniformity among the states in this respect, in 1995 the National Conference of Commissioners on Uniform State Laws (NCCUSL) issued the Uniform Limited Liability Company Act (ULLCA), but less than one-fifth of the states adopted it.[1] In 2006, the NCCUSL issued a revised version of this uniform law (the Re-ULLCA), which has been adopted in a few states. Thus, the law governing LLCs remains far from uniform. Some provisions are common to most state statutes, however, and we base our discussion of LLCs in this section on these common elements.

The Nature of the LLC

Limited liability companies share many characteristics with corporations. Like corporations, LLCs are creatures of the state. In other words, they must be formed and operated in compliance with state law. Like shareholders in a corporation, owners of an LLC, who are called **members,** enjoy limited liability [ULLCA 303]. Also like corporations, LLCs are legal entities apart from their members. As a legal person, the LLC can sue or be sued, enter into contracts, and hold title to property [ULLCA 201]. The terminology used to describe LLCs formed in other states or nations is

---

1. Excerpts from the Uniform Limited Liability Company Act (ULLCA) are presented on the Web site that accompanies this text.

also similar to the terminology used in corporate law. For example, an LLC formed in one state but doing business in another state is referred to in the second state as a *foreign LLC*.

If an LLC is sued for wrongful discharge, can its members, managers, and agents be held liable, based on their status in the LLC, even though they did not participate in the dismissal that led to the lawsuit? That was the question in the following case.

Case 28.1 **McFarland v. Virginia Retirement Services of Chesterfield, LLC**

United States District Court, Eastern District of Virginia, 477 F.Supp.2d 727 (2007).

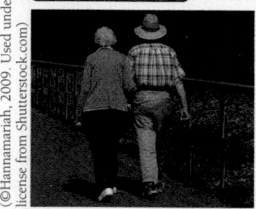

Staff members at a retirement community LLC have elderly residents walk in ninety-five-degree heat. What factors determine accountability and liability?

FACTS Virginia Retirement Services of Chesterfield, LLC, does business as Magnolias of Chesterfield (Magnolia), a retirement community. In 2005, Penny McFarland became Magnolia's activities director. McFarland was responsible for coordinating and conducting resident activities. In 2006, Effie Stovall, McFarland's supervisor, told the staff to take the residents outside for a walk. The temperature was ninety-five degrees. Out of concern for the residents, someone complained to the state licensing board. An inspector contacted McFarland, who immediately told Stovall. When Mary Dunmoyer, Magnolia's executive director, learned of the contact, she had Stovall discharge McFarland for trying to "sabotage" the community. McFarland filed a suit in a federal district court against Magnolia, Dunmoyer, and other individual defendants, alleging, among other things, wrongful discharge—that she was terminated because she had provided information regarding the health and safety of Magnolia's residents in response to the inspector's inquiry. The individual defendants, who were members, managers, or agents of Magnolia, filed a motion to be dismissed from the suit.

ISSUE Can a member, manager, or agent of an LLC be held responsible for its contractual obligations or tort liability based *solely* on the individual's position in the LLC?

DECISION No. The district court dismissed the individual defendants, except for Dunmoyer, from McFarland's suit.

REASON Under Virginia state law, members, managers, and agents of an LLC are not responsible for its liabilities "solely" by virtue of their status. The district court pointed out that only "officers or agents who have played a key role in contributing to the company's tortious conduct" can be part of a wrongful discharge claim. With the exception of Dunmoyer, none of the other individual defendants were alleged to have personally participated in McFarland's discharge. Thus, the court found that they should be dropped from the suit.

FOR CRITICAL ANALYSIS—Legal Consideration *Why is the liability of the members of an LLC limited with respect to the firm's debts and other obligations?*

LLC Formation

Articles of Organization The document filed with a designated state official by which a limited liability company is formed.

To form an LLC, **articles of organization** must be filed with a central state agency—usually the secretary of state's office [ULLCA 202].[2] Typically, the articles are required to include such information as the name of the business, its principal address, the name and address of a registered agent, the names of the members, and information on how the LLC will be managed [ULLCA 203]. The business's name must include the words *Limited Liability Company* or the initials *LLC* [ULLCA 105(a)]. Although a majority of the states permit one-member LLCs, some states require at least two members.

Businesspersons sometimes enter into contracts on behalf of a business organization that is not yet formed. As you will read in Chapter 29, persons who are forming a corporation may enter into contracts during the process of incorporation but before the corporation becomes a legal entity. These contracts are referred to as preincorporation contracts. Once the corporation is formed and adopts the preincorporation contract (by means of a *novation*, discussed in Chapter 13), it can enforce the contract terms.

Where must an LLC's articles of organization be filed?

---

2. In addition to requiring the filing of articles of organization, a few states require that a notice of the intention to form an LLC be published in a local newspaper.

ON THE WEB You can find information on how to form an LLC, including the fees charged in each state for filing LLC articles of organization, at the Web site of Bizcorp, Inc. Go to **www.bizcorp.com**.

In the following case, the question was whether the same principle extends to LLCs. A person in the process of forming an LLC entered into a preorganization contract under which it would be obligated to purchase the Park Plaza Hotel in Hollywood, California. Once the LLC legally existed, the owners of the hotel refused to sell the property to the LLC, claiming that the contract was unenforceable.

Case 28.2   02 Development, LLC v. 607 South Park, LLC

Court of Appeal of California, Second District, 159 Cal.App.4th 609, 71 Cal.Rptr.3d 608 (2008).

(Creative Commons)

Can a purchase agreement for a hotel be assigned to an LLC before its organization?

FACTS In March 2004, 607 South Park, LLC, entered into a written agreement to sell Park Plaza Hotel to 607 Park View Associates, Ltd., for $8.7 million. The general partner of 607 Park View Associates was Creative Environments of Hollywood, Inc. In February 2005, Creative Environments assigned the rights to the hotel purchase to another company, 02 Development, LLC. At the time, 02 Development did not yet exist; it was legally created several months later. When 607 South Park refused to sell the hotel, 02 Development sued for breach of the hotel purchase agreement. 607 South Park moved for summary judgment, arguing that no enforceable contract existed because at the time of the assignment, 02 Development did not yet legally exist. Furthermore, 607 South Park argued, 02 Development suffered no damages because it was "not ready, willing, and able to fund the purchase of the hotel." The trial court granted the motion and entered judgment in favor of 607 South Park. 02 Development appealed.

ISSUE Can an LLC enforce a contract that had been assigned to it prior to the date of its legal formation?

DECISION Yes. A state intermediate appellate court reversed the judgment and directed the trial court to enter an order denying 607 South

Park's motion for summary judgment. According to the appellate court, LLCs should be treated the same as corporations with respect to preorganization contracts.

REASON South Park's primary argument was that 02 Development did not exist at the time of the contract and was not a party to the contract. The court, however, reasoned that it is established law that corporations are liable on preincorporation contracts and that the same principle should extend to LLCs. "When the assignment agreement was executed, 02 Development did not exist so it was not then a party to the agreement. But once 02 Development came into existence, it could enforce any preorganization contract made on its behalf, such as the assignment agreement, if it adopted or ratified it." 607 South Park had not argued that LLCs should be treated differently than corporations. Instead, 607 South Park had argued that 02 Development was required to present admissible evidence that it would have been financially able to close the transaction, but the court rejected this notion. "607 South Park presented no evidence that 02 Development would have been unable to arrange for the necessary funding to close the transaction on time if 607 South Park had given it the opportunity instead of repudiating a contract in advance." Consequently, the trial court erred when it granted 607 South Park's motion for summary judgment.

FOR CRITICAL ANALYSIS—Social Consideration *Why was it unimportant to the appellate court that the trial court did not require 02 Development to prove that it had funding commitments for $8.7 million?*

Jurisdictional Requirements

One of the significant differences between LLCs and corporations involves federal jurisdictional requirements. The federal jurisdiction statute provides that a corporation is deemed to be a citizen of the state where it is incorporated and maintains its principal place of business. The statute does not mention the citizenship of partnerships, LLCs, and other unincorporated associations, but the courts have tended to regard these entities as citizens of every state in which their members are citizens.

The state citizenship of LLCs may come into play when a party sues an LLC based on diversity of citizenship. Remember from Chapter 3 that in some circumstances, such as when parties to a lawsuit are from different states, a federal court can exercise diversity jurisdiction in cases in which the amount in controversy exceeds $75,000. *Total* diversity of citizenship must exist, however. **EXAMPLE 28.1** Fong, a citizen of New York, wishes to bring a lawsuit against Skycel, an LLC formed under the laws of Connecticut. One of Skycel's members also lives in New York. Fong will not be able to bring the action against Skycel in federal court—on the basis of diversity jurisdiction—because the defendant LLC is also impliedly a citizen of New York. The same would be true if Fong was filing a suit against multiple defendants and one of the defendants lived in New York. ●

Advantages of the LLC

The LLC offers many advantages to businesspersons, which is why this form of business organization has become increasingly popular. See the *Business Application* feature at the end of this chapter for a discussion of the factors that entrepreneurs need to consider when choosing between LLCs and limited liability partnerships (LLPs).

LIMITED LIABILITY   A key advantage of the LLC is that the liability of members is limited to the amount of their investments. Although the LLC as an entity can be held liable for any loss or injury caused by the wrongful acts or omissions of its members, the members themselves generally are not personally liable.

The focus in the following case was on a member's personal liability for the alleged "acts" of his firm.

Case 28.3 Allen v. Dackman

Court of Special Appeals of Maryland, 184 Md.App. 1, 964 A.2d 210 (2009).
www.courts.state.md.us/index.html[a]

HISTORICAL AND ENVIRONMENTAL SETTING *Lead is a toxic metal that was used for centuries in water pipes and other products. Lead can be emitted into the air from motor vehicles and industrial sources, and it can leach into drinking water from plumbing. One of the most common sources of lead is deteriorating lead-based paint. This paint can be found in many houses and apartments built before 1978, the year that the federal government banned lead-based paint in housing. If ingested, lead can cause various harmful health effects, ranging from behavioral problems and learning disabilities to seizures and death. Children six years old and under are especially at risk.*

Can a member of an LLC be held personally liable for illness sustained from lead paint in a rental property?

FACTS   When Monica Allen and Shantese Thomas were three years old and one year old, respectively, they came to live with their grandmother, Tracy Allen, at 3143 Elmora Avenue in Baltimore, Maryland. Allen leased the dwelling from Mildred Thompkins. Less than a year later, after Thompkins failed to pay the taxes on the property, Hard Assets, LLC, acquired it. For fifteen years, the firm had bought and sold tax-delinquent properties. Jay Dackman, a member of the LLC, ran the business. Hard Assets intended to sell the property, rather than keep it as a rental, so Allen and her grandchildren were asked to vacate the premises.

Within a few months, the property was sold. While living there, Monica and Shantese were allegedly injured from exposure to lead-based paint. To recover, their mother, Monica Allen, filed a suit in a Maryland state court against Dackman, alleging violations of the city's housing code and negligence. The court issued a judgment in Dackman's favor. Allen appealed.

ISSUE   Can a member of an LLC avoid personal liability for the alleged injuries of residents who live on property owned by the LLC?

DECISION   Yes. A state intermediate appellate court affirmed the lower court's judgment. Dackman, as a member of Hard Assets, could not be held personally liable for the LLC's asserted obligations or liabilities.

REASON   Under the city's housing code, an "owner" is a person who "controls" the title to property, and an "operator" is a person who has control of a building in which "dwelling units * * * are let." Dackman was not an "owner" within this definition because he did not personally "control" the property. He ran Hard Assets' business, but he lacked the right, as an individual, to transfer the title to the property. He was not an "operator" because Hard Assets did not offer the property for lease and did not receive rent, or attempt to collect rent, from the Allens. Dackman could not be liable on the negligence claim because, under Maryland's Limited Liability Company Act, "no member shall be personally liable for the obligations of the limited liability company, whether arising in contract, tort or otherwise, solely by reason of being a member of the limited liability company."

FOR CRITICAL ANALYSIS—Social Consideration *Is Hard Assets liable for the alleged injuries to Monica and Shantese? Explain.*

a. In the "Appellate Courts" section, click on "reported opinions." On that page, in the "Court" box choose "Court of Special Appeals"; in the "Filing Year" box, select "2009"; in the "Sorting Order" box, choose "by appellant's (or first party's) name"; and click on "Submit." In the result, click on the link to access the opinion. The Maryland Judiciary maintains this Web site.

Stan Ovshinsky, founder of Ovonic Hydrogen Systems, LLC, a developer of alternative energy technologies. What are some of the advantages of doing business as an LLC instead of a corporation? Are there any disadvantages?

(Photo Courtesy of ECD Ovonics)

REMEMBER A uniform law is a "model" law. It does not become the law of any state until the state legislature adopts it, either in part or in its entirety.

Operating Agreement In a limited liability company, an agreement in which the members set forth the details of how the business will be managed and operated. State statutes typically give the members wide latitude in deciding for themselves the rules that will govern their organization.

TAXATION   Another advantage is the flexibility of the LLC in regard to taxation. An LLC that has *two or more members* can choose to be taxed either as a partnership or as a corporation. As you will read in Chapter 29, a corporate entity must pay income taxes on its profits, and the shareholders pay personal income taxes on profits distributed as dividends. An LLC that wants to distribute profits to its members may prefer to be taxed as a partnership to avoid the "double taxation" that is characteristic of the corporate entity.

Unless an LLC indicates that it wishes to be taxed as a corporation, the IRS automatically taxes it as a partnership. This means that the LLC as an entity pays no taxes; rather, as in a partnership, profits are "passed through" the LLC to the members who then personally pay taxes on the profits. If an LLC's members want to reinvest the profits in the business, however, rather than distribute the profits to members, they may prefer that the LLC be taxed as a corporation. Corporate income tax rates may be lower than personal tax rates. Part of the attractiveness of the LLC is this flexibility with respect to taxation.

For federal income tax purposes, one-member LLCs are automatically taxed as sole proprietorships unless they indicate that they wish to be taxed as corporations. With respect to state taxes, most states follow the IRS rules.

MANAGEMENT AND FOREIGN INVESTORS   Still another advantage of the LLC for businesspersons is the flexibility it offers in terms of business operations and management—as will be discussed shortly. Finally, because foreign investors can participate in an LLC, the LLC form of business is attractive as a way to encourage investment. For a discussion of business organizations in other nations that are similar to the LLC, see this chapter's *Beyond Our Borders* feature on the following page.

Disadvantages of the LLC

The main disadvantage of the LLC is that state LLC statutes are not uniform. Therefore, businesses that operate in more than one state may not receive consistent treatment in these states. Generally, though, most states apply to a foreign LLC (an LLC formed in another state) the law of the state where the LLC was formed. Difficulties can arise, nonetheless, when one state's court must interpret and apply another state's laws.

▶ LLC Operation and Management

As mentioned, an advantage of the LLC form of business is the flexibility it offers in terms of operation and management. We discuss the operating agreement, management options, and general operating procedures of LLCs next.

The LLC Operating Agreement

The members of an LLC can decide how to operate the various aspects of the business by forming an **operating agreement** [ULLCA 103(a)]. Operating agreements typically contain provisions relating to management, how profits will be divided, the transfer of membership interests, whether the LLC will be dissolved on the death or departure of a member, and other important issues.

A WRITING IS PREFERRED   In many states, an operating agreement is not required for an LLC to exist, and if there is one, it need not be in writing. Generally, though, LLC members should protect their interests by creating a written operating agreement. As in any business, disputes may arise over any number of issues. If there is no agreement covering the topic under dispute, such as how profits will be divided, the state LLC statute will govern the outcome. For example, most LLC statutes provide that if the members have not specified how profits will be divided, they will be divided equally among the members.

Beyond Our Borders   Limited Liability Companies in Other Nations

Limited liability companies are not unique to the United States. Many nations have business forms that provide limited liability, although these organizations may differ significantly from domestic LLCs. In Germany, for example, the *GmbH,* or *Gesellschaft mit beschränkter Haftung* (which means "company with limited liability"), is a type of business entity that has been available since 1892. The GmbH is now the most widely used business form in Germany. A GmbH, however, is owned by shareholders and thus resembles a U.S. corporation in certain respects. German laws also impose numerous restrictions on the operations and business transactions of GmbHs, whereas LLCs

in the United States are not even required to have an operating agreement.

Business forms that limit the liability of owners can also be found in various other countries. Limited liability companies known as *limitadas* are common in many Latin American nations. In France, a *société à responsabilité limitée* (meaning "society with limited liability") is an entity that provides business owners with limited liability. Although laws in the United Kingdom and Ireland use the term *limited liability partnership,* the entities are similar to our domestic LLCs. In 2006, Japan enacted legislation that created a new type of business organization, called the *godo kaisha (GK),*

which is also quite similar to a U.S. LLC. In most nations, some type of document that is similar to the LLC's articles of organization must be filed with the government to form the business. Many countries limit the number of owners that such businesses may have, and some also require the member-owners to choose one or more persons who will manage the business affairs.

• **For Critical Analysis**
Clearly, limited liability is an important aspect of doing business globally. Why might a nation limit the number of member-owners in a limited liability entity?

PARTNERSHIP LAW MAY APPLY   When an issue, such as the authority of individual members, is not covered by an operating agreement or by an LLC statute, the courts often apply principles of partnership law. These principles can give the members of an LLC broad authority to bind the LLC unless an operating agreement provides otherwise. **CASE EXAMPLE 28.2**   Clifford Kuhn, Jr., and Joseph Tumminelli formed Touch of Class Limousine Service as an LLC. They did not create a written operating agreement but orally agreed that Kuhn would provide the financial backing and procure customers, and that Tumminelli would manage the company's day-to-day operations. Tumminelli embezzled $283,000 from the company after cashing customers' checks at Quick Cash, Inc., a local check-cashing service. Kuhn filed a lawsuit against Tumminelli, the banks, and others in a New Jersey state court to recover the embezzled funds. He argued that Quick Cash and the banks were liable because Tumminelli did not have the authority to cash the company's checks and convert the funds. The court, however, held that in the absence of a written operating agreement to the contrary, a member of an LLC, like a partner in a partnership, does have the authority to cash the firm's checks.[3] ●

Management of an LLC

> *"Business is the salt of life."*
>
> Voltaire, 1694–1778
> (French author and philosopher)

Basically, the members of an LLC have two options for managing the firm. It can be either a "member-managed" LLC or a "manager-managed" LLC. Most LLC statutes and the ULLCA provide that unless the articles of organization specify otherwise, an LLC is assumed to be member managed [ULLCA 203(a)(6)].

In a *member-managed* LLC, all of the members participate in management, and decisions are made by majority vote [ULLCA 404(a)]. In a *manager-managed* LLC, the members designate a group of persons to manage the firm. The management group may consist of only members, both members and nonmembers, or only nonmembers.

Under the ULLCA, managers in a manager-managed LLC owe fiduciary duties (the duty of loyalty and the duty of care) to the LLC and its members, just as corporate directors and officers owe fiduciary duties to the corporation and its shareholders [ULLCA 409(a), (h)].

---

3. *Kuhn v. Tumminelli,* 366 N.J.Super. 431, 841 A.2d 496 (2004).

But because not all states have adopted the ULLCA, some state statutes provide that managers owe fiduciary duties only to the LLC and not to the other members. Although to whom the duty is owed may seem insignificant at first glance, it actually can have a dramatic effect on the outcome of litigation.

Do managers in a manager-managed LLC owe fiduciary duties to other members? Fiduciary duties, such as the duty of loyalty and the duty of care, have an ethical component because they require a person to act honestly and faithfully toward another. In states that have adopted the ULLCA, the managers of a manager-managed LLC owe fiduciary duties to the members and thus basically are required to behave ethically toward them. In other states, however, the LLC statutes may not include such a requirement. Consequently, even when a manager-member has acted unfairly and unethically toward other members, the members may not be able to sue the manager for a breach of fiduciary duties.

In North Carolina and Virginia, for example, the LLC statutes do not explicitly create fiduciary duties for managers to members. Instead, the statutes require that a manager exercise good business judgment in the best interests of the company. Because the statutes are silent on the manager's duty to members, in 2009 courts in those two states held that a manager-member owed fiduciary duties only to the LLC and not to the members.[4] In contrast, in two other 2009 cases, courts in Idaho and Kentucky held that a manager-member owes fiduciary duties to the LLC's members and that the members can sue the manager for breaching fiduciary duties.[5]

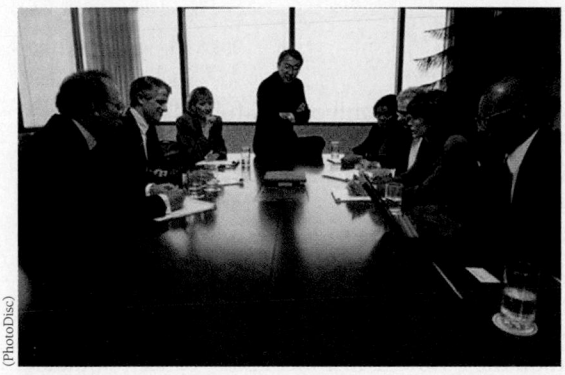

(PhotoDisc)

Members of a manager-managed LLC hold a formal members' meeting. What is the difference between a member-managed LLC and a manager-managed LLC? How are managers typically chosen?

Operating Procedures

The members of an LLC can also set forth in their operating agreement provisions governing decision-making procedures. For instance, the agreement can include procedures for choosing or removing managers. Although most LLC statutes are silent on this issue, the ULLCA provides that members may choose and remove managers by majority vote [ULLCA 404(b)(3)].

The members are also free to include in the agreement provisions designating when and for what purposes they will hold formal members' meetings. In contrast to the state laws governing corporations, which generally provide for shareholders' meetings (see Chapter 29), most state LLC statutes have no provisions regarding members' meetings.

Members may also specify in their agreement how voting rights will be apportioned. If they do not, LLC statutes in most states provide that voting rights are apportioned according to each member's capital contributions. Some states provide that, in the absence of an agreement to the contrary, each member has one vote.

▶ Dissociation and Dissolution of an LLC

Recall from Chapter 27 that in the context of partnerships, *dissociation* occurs when a partner ceases to be associated in the carrying on of the business. The same concept applies to LLCs. A member of an LLC has the *power* to dissociate from the LLC at any time, but she or he may not have the *right* to dissociate. Under the ULLCA, the events that trigger a member's dissociation from an LLC are similar to the events causing a partner to be dissociated

---

4. *Remora Investments, LLC v. Orr,* 277 Va. 316, 673 S.E.2d 845 (2009); Virginia Code Sections 13.1–1024.1; and *Kaplan v. O.K. Technologies, LLC,* 675 S.E.2d 133 (N.C.App. 2009); North Carolina General Statutes Section 57C-3-22(b).

5. *Bushi v. Sage Health Care, LLC,* 146 Idaho 764, 203 P.3d 694 (2009); Idaho Code Sections 30-6-101 *et seq.*; and *Patmon v. Hobbs,* 280 S.W.3d 589 (Ky.App. 2009); Kentucky Revised Statutes Section 275.170.

under the Uniform Partnership Act (UPA). These include voluntary withdrawal, expulsion by other members or by court order, bankruptcy, incompetence, and death. Generally, even if a member dies or otherwise dissociates from an LLC, the other members may continue to carry on the LLC's business, unless the operating agreement provides otherwise.

The Effect of Dissociation

When a member dissociates from an LLC, he or she loses the right to participate in management and the right to act as an agent for the LLC. The member's duty of loyalty to the LLC also terminates, and the duty of care continues only with respect to events that occurred before dissociation. Generally, the dissociated member also has a right to have his or her interest in the LLC bought out by the other members. The LLC's operating agreement may contain provisions establishing a buyout price, but if it does not, the member's interest is usually purchased at a fair value. In states that have adopted the ULLCA, the LLC must purchase the interest at "fair" value within 120 days after the dissociation.

If the member's dissociation violates the LLC's operating agreement, it is considered legally wrongful, and the dissociated member can be held liable for damages caused by the dissociation. **EXAMPLE 28.3** Chadwick and Barrel are members in an LLC. Chadwick manages the accounts, and Barrel, who has many connections in the community and is a skilled investor, brings in the business. If Barrel wrongfully dissociates from the LLC, the LLC's business will suffer, and Chadwick can hold Barrel liable for the loss of business resulting from her withdrawal. •

Dissolution

Regardless of whether a member's dissociation was wrongful or rightful, normally the dissociated member has no right to force the LLC to dissolve. The remaining members can opt to either continue or dissolve the business. Members can also stipulate in their operating agreement that certain events will cause dissolution, or they can agree that they have the power to dissolve the LLC by vote. As with partnerships, a court can order an LLC to be dissolved in certain circumstances, such as when the members have engaged in illegal or oppressive conduct, or when it is no longer feasible to carry on the business.

When an LLC is dissolved, any members who did not wrongfully dissociate may participate in the winding up process. To wind up the business, members must collect, liquidate, and distribute the LLC's assets. Members may preserve the assets for a reasonable time to optimize their return, and they continue to have the authority to perform reasonable acts in conjunction with winding up. In other words, the LLC will be bound by the reasonable acts of its members during the winding up process. Once all the LLC's assets have been sold, the proceeds are distributed to pay off debts to creditors first (including debts owed to members who are creditors of the LLC). The member's capital contributions are returned next, and any remaining amounts are then distributed to members in equal shares or according to their operating agreement.

Preventing Legal Disputes

When forming an LLC, carefully draft the operating agreement. Stipulate the events that will cause dissociation and how the fair-value buyout price will be calculated. Set a time limit within which the LLC must pay the dissociated member (or her or his estate) in the event of withdrawal, disability, or death. Include provisions that clearly limit the authority of dissociated members to act on behalf of the LLC and provide a right to seek damages from members who exceed the agreed-on parameters. Also, notify third parties if any member dissociates and file a notice of dissociation with the state to limit the extent of the former member's apparent authority to act on behalf of the LLC. The operating agreement should specify any events that will automatically cause a dissolution, as well as which members will have a right to participate in—or make decisions about—the winding up.

Special Business Forms

Besides the traditional business forms and limited liability companies discussed in this unit, several other forms can be used to organize a business. For the most part, these special business forms are hybrid organizations—that is, they have characteristics similar to those of partnerships or corporations or combine features of both. These forms include joint ventures, syndicates, joint stock companies, business trusts, and cooperatives.

Joint Ventures

Joint Venture A joint undertaking of a specific commercial enterprise by an association of persons. A joint venture normally is not a legal entity and is treated like a partnership for federal income tax purposes.

A **joint venture,** sometimes referred to as a *joint adventure,* is a relationship in which two or more persons or business entities combine their efforts or their property for a single transaction or project or a related series of transactions or projects. Unless otherwise agreed, joint venturers share profits and losses equally. For instance, when several contractors combine their resources to build and sell houses in a single development, their relationship is a joint venture.

Joint ventures range in size from very small activities to huge, multimillion-dollar joint actions carried out by some of the world's largest corporations. Large organizations often investigate new markets or new ideas by forming joint ventures with other enterprises. For instance, Intel Corporation and Micron Technology, Inc., formed a joint venture to manufacture NAND flash memory, a data-storage chip widely used in digital cameras, cell phones, and portable music players, including some iPods made by Apple, Inc. Similarly, Mitsubishi Chemical Corporation formed a joint venture with Exxon Chemical Corporation to start Mytex Polymers, a company that produces certain plastic compounds used by automakers in the United States and Japan.

SIMILARITIES TO PARTNERSHIPS The joint venture resembles a partnership and is taxed like a partnership. For this reason, most courts apply the same principles to joint ventures as they apply to partnerships. Joint venturers owe to each other the same fiduciary duties, including the duty of loyalty, that partners owe each other. If one of the venturers secretly buys land that was to be acquired by the joint venture, the other joint venturers may be awarded damages for the breach of loyalty. A joint venturer can also be held personally liable for the venture's debts (because joint venturers share profits and *losses*). Like partners, joint venturers have equal rights to manage the activities of the enterprise, but they can agree to give control of the operation to one of the members.

"*Business without profit is not business any more than a pickle is candy.*"

Charles Abbott, 1762–1832
(British jurist)

Joint venturers also have authority as agents to enter into contracts for the business that will bind the joint venture. **CASE EXAMPLE 28.4** Murdo Cameron developed components to make replicas of vintage P-51 Mustang planes. Cameron agreed in writing with Douglas Anderson to collaborate on the design and manufacture of one P-51 for each of them. They agreed that Anderson would build the first plane and that Cameron would provide an engine, which Anderson would pay for after the plane's first flight. Without Cameron's knowledge, Anderson borrowed funds from SPW Associates, LLP, to finance the construction, using the first plane as security for the loan. After Anderson built one plane, he defaulted on the loan. SPW filed a lawsuit asking a state court to declare that SPW was entitled to the aircraft. The court ruled that Anderson and Cameron had entered into a joint venture and that the plane was the venture's property. Under partnership law, partners have the power as agents to bind the partnership. Because this principle applies to joint ventures, Anderson had the authority to grant SPW a security interest in the plane, and SPW was entitled to its possession.[6] •

6. *SPW Associates, LLP v. Anderson,* 2006 ND 159, 718 N.W.2d 580 (N.D.Sup.Ct. 2006).

CONTRAST A partnership involves a continuing relationship of the partners. A joint venture is often a one-time association.

DIFFERENCES FROM PARTNERSHIPS Joint ventures differ from partnerships in several important ways. The members of a joint venture have less implied and apparent authority than the partners in a partnership. As discussed in Chapter 27, each partner is treated as an agent of the other partners. Because the activities of a joint venture are more limited than the business of a partnership, the members of a joint venture are presumed to have less power to bind their co-venturers. In Case Example 28.4 on the previous page, for instance, if Anderson's contract had not been directly related to the business of building vintage planes, the court might have concluded that Anderson lacked the authority to bind the joint venture. Also, unlike most partnerships, a joint venture normally terminates when the project or the transaction for which it was formed has been completed, though the members can specify how long the relationship will last.

Syndicates

Syndicate A group of individuals or firms brought together for the purpose of financing a project that they would not or could not undertake independently; also called an *investment group.*

A group of individuals or firms that get together to finance a particular project, such as the building of a shopping center or the purchase of a professional basketball franchise, is called a **syndicate** or an *investment group.* The form of such groups varies considerably. A syndicate may exist as a corporation or as a general or limited partnership. In some instances, the members do not have a legally recognized business arrangement but merely purchase and own property jointly.

Joint Stock Companies

Joint Stock Company A hybrid form of business organization that combines characteristics of a corporation and a partnership. Usually, a joint stock company is regarded as a partnership for tax and other legal purposes.

A **joint stock company** is a true hybrid of a partnership and a corporation. It has many characteristics of a corporation in that (1) its ownership is represented by transferable shares of stock, (2) it is usually managed by directors and officers of the company or association, and (3) it can have a perpetual existence. Most of its other features, however, are more characteristic of a partnership, and it is usually treated like a partnership. As with a partnership, a joint stock company is formed by agreement (not statute), property is usually held in the names of the members, shareholders have personal liability, and the company generally is not treated as a legal entity for purposes of a lawsuit. In a joint stock company, however, shareholders are not considered to be agents of one another, as would be the case if the company were a true partnership (see Chapter 27).

Business Trusts

Business Trust A form of business organization in which investors (trust beneficiaries) transfer cash or property to trustees in exchange for trust certificates that represent their investment shares. The certificate holders share in the trust's profits but have limited liability.

A **business trust** is created by a written trust agreement that sets forth the interests of the beneficiaries and the obligations and powers of the trustees. With a business trust, legal ownership and management of the property of the business stay with one or more of the trustees, and the profits are distributed to the beneficiaries.

The business trust was started in Massachusetts in an attempt to obtain the limited liability advantage of corporate status while avoiding certain restrictions on a corporation's ownership of, and ability to develop, real property. A business trust resembles a corporation in many respects. Beneficiaries of the trust, for example, are not personally responsible for the debts or obligations of the business trust. In fact, in a number of states, business trusts must pay corporate taxes.

Cooperatives

Cooperative An association, which may or may not be incorporated, that is organized to provide an economic service to its members. Unincorporated cooperatives are often treated like partnerships for tax and other legal purposes. Examples of cooperatives include consumer purchasing cooperatives, credit cooperatives, and farmers' cooperatives.

A **cooperative** is an association that is organized to provide an economic service to its members (or shareholders); it may or may not be incorporated. Most cooperatives are organized under state statutes for cooperatives, general business corporations, or LLCs. Generally, an incorporated cooperative will distribute dividends, or profits, to its owners on the basis of their transactions with the cooperative rather than on the basis of the amount of capital they contributed. Members of incorporated cooperatives have limited liability, as do shareholders of corporations and members of LLCs. Cooperatives that are unincorporated are often treated like partnerships. The members have joint liability for the cooperative's acts.

This form of business generally is adopted by groups of individuals who wish to pool their resources to gain some advantage in the marketplace. Consumer purchasing co-ops are formed to obtain lower prices through quantity discounts. Seller marketing co-ops are formed to control the market and thereby enable members to sell their goods at higher prices. Co-ops range in size from small, local, consumer cooperatives to national businesses such as Ace Hardware and Land O' Lakes, a well-known producer of dairy products.

 Reviewing . . . Limited Liability Companies and Special Business Forms

The city of Papagos, Arizona, had a deteriorating bridge in need of repair on a prominent public roadway. The city posted notices seeking proposals for an artistic bridge design and reconstruction. Davidson Masonry, LLC—owned and managed by Carl Davidson and his wife, Marilyn Rowe—decided to submit a bid for a decorative concrete project that incorporated artistic metalwork. They contacted Shana Lafayette, a local sculptor who specialized in large-scale metal creations, to help them design the bridge. The city selected their bridge design and awarded them the contract for a commission of $184,000. Davidson Masonry and Lafayette then entered into an agreement to work together on the bridge project. Davidson Masonry agreed to install and pay for concrete and structural work, and Lafayette agreed to install the metalwork at her expense. They agreed that overall profits would be split, with 25 percent going to Lafayette and 75 percent going to Davidson Masonry. Lafayette designed numerous metal salmon sculptures that were incorporated into colorful decorative concrete forms designed by Rowe, while Davidson performed the structural engineering. The group worked together successfully until the completion of the project. Using the information presented in the chapter, answer the following questions.

1. Would Davidson Masonry automatically be taxed as a partnership or a corporation? Why or why not?
2. Is Davidson Masonry member managed or manager managed?
3. When Davidson Masonry and Lafayette entered into an agreement to work together, what kind of special business form was created? Explain.
4. Suppose that during construction, Lafayette had entered into an agreement to rent space in a warehouse that was close to the bridge so that she could work on her sculptures near the location at which they would eventually be installed. She entered into the contract without the knowledge or consent of Davidson Masonry. In this situation, would a court be likely to hold that Davidson Masonry was bound by the contract that Lafayette entered? Why or why not?

Business Application
How Do You Choose between LLCs and LLPs?*

One of the most important decisions that an entrepreneur makes is the selection of the form in which to do business. To make the best decision, a businessperson needs to understand all aspects of the various forms, including legal, tax, licensing, and business considerations. In addition, all of the participants in the business should understand their actual relationship, regardless of the organizational structure.

Number of Participants

During the last fifteen years, new forms of business organizations, including limited liability partnerships (LLPs—discussed in Chapter 27) and limited liability companies (LLCs), have been added to the options for business entities. An initial consideration in choosing between these forms

*This *Business Application* is not meant to substitute for the services of an attorney who is licensed to practice law in your state.

Continued

is the number of participants. An LLP must have two or more partners, but in many states, an LLC can have a single member (owner).

Liability Considerations

The members of an LLC are not liable for the obligations of the organization. Members' liability is limited to the amount of their property (investment) interest. The liability of the partners in an LLP varies from state to state. About half of the states exempt the partners from liability for any obligation of the firm. In some states, the partners are individually liable for the contractual obligations of the firm but are not liable for obligations arising from the torts of others. In either situation, each partner may be on his or her own with respect to liability unless the other partners agree to help.

Distributions from the Firm

Members and partners generally are paid by allowing them to withdraw funds from the firm against their share of the profits. In many states, a member of an LLC must repay so-called wrongful distributions even if she or he did not know that the distributions were wrongful (wrongful distributions include those made when the LLC is insolvent). Under most LLP statutes, by contrast, the partners must repay only distributions that were fraudulent.

Management Structure

Both LLPs and LLCs can set up whatever management structure the participants desire. Also, all unincorporated business organizations, including LLPs and LLCs with two or more members, are treated as partnerships for federal income tax purposes (unless an LLC elects to be treated as a corporation[a]). This means that the firms are not taxed at the

---

a. The chief benefits of electing corporate status for tax purposes are that the members generally are not subject to self-employment taxes and that fringe benefits may be provided to employee-members on a tax-reduced basis. The tax laws are complicated, however, and a professional should be consulted about the details.

entity level. Their income is passed through to the partners or members, who report it on their individual income tax returns. Some states impose additional taxes on LLCs.

The Nature of the Business

The business in which a firm engages is another factor to consider in choosing a business form. For example, with a few exceptions, professionals, such as accountants, attorneys, and physicians, may organize as either an LLP or an LLC in any state. In many states, however, the organizational form of an entity that engages in a certain profession and the liability of the owners are prescribed by state law.

Financial and Personal Relationships

Although the legal consequences of choosing a business form are certainly important, they are often secondary to the financial and personal relationships among the participants. Work effort, motivation, ability, and other personal attributes can be significant factors, as may fundamental business concerns such as the expenses and debts of the firm—and the extent of personal liability for these obligations. Another practical factor to consider is the willingness of others to do business with an LLP or an LLC. A supplier, for example, may not be willing to extend credit to a firm whose partners or members will not accept personal liability for the debt.

CHECKLIST FOR CHOOSING A LIMITED LIABILITY BUSINESS FORM

1. **Determine the number of participants, the forms a state allows, and the limits on liability the state provides for the participants.**
2. **Evaluate the tax considerations.**
3. **Consider the business in which the firm engages, or will engage, and any restrictions imposed on that type of business.**
4. **Weigh such practical concerns as the financial and personal relationships among the participants and the willingness of others to do business with a particular organizational form.**

 ## Key Terms

articles of organization 708	joint stock company 716	member 707
business trust 716	joint venture 715	operating agreement 711
cooperative 716	limited liability company (LLC) 706	syndicate 716

 ## Chapter Summary: Limited Liability Companies and Special Business Forms

Limited Liability Companies (LLCs) (See pages 707–711.)	1. *Formation*—Articles of organization must be filed with the appropriate state office—usually the office of the secretary of state—setting forth the name of the business, its principal address, the names of the owners (called *members*), and other relevant information.

Chapter Summary: Limited Liability Companies and Special Business Forms—Continued

Limited Liability Companies (LLCs)— Continued	2. *Advantages and disadvantages of the LLC*—Advantages of the LLC include limited liability, the option to be taxed as a partnership or as a corporation, and flexibility in deciding how the business will be managed and operated. The main disadvantage is the absence of uniformity in state LLC statutes.
LLC Operation and Management (See pages 711–713.)	1. *Operating agreement*—When an LLC is formed, the members decide, in an operating agreement, how the business will be managed and what rules will apply to the organization. 2. *Management*—An LLC may be managed by members only, by some members and some nonmembers, or by nonmembers only.
Dissociation and Dissolution of an LLC (See pages 713–714.)	Members of an LLC have the power to dissociate from the LLC at any time, but they may not have the right to dissociate. Dissociation does not always result in the dissolution of an LLC; the remaining members can choose to continue the business. Dissociated members have a right to have their interest purchased by the other members. If the LLC is dissolved, the business must be wound up and the assets sold. Creditors are paid first; then members' capital investments are returned. Any remaining proceeds are distributed to members.
Special Business Forms (See pages 715–717.)	1. *Joint venture*—An organization created by two or more persons in contemplation of a limited activity or a single transaction; similar to a partnership in many respects. 2. *Syndicate*—An investment group that undertakes to finance a particular project; may exist as a corporation or as a general or limited partnership. 3. *Joint stock company*—A business form similar to a corporation in some respects (transferable shares of stock, management by directors and officers, perpetual existence) but otherwise resembling a partnership. 4. *Business trust*—A business form created by a written trust agreement that sets forth the interests of the beneficiaries and the obligations and powers of the trustee(s); similar to a corporation in many respects. Beneficiaries are not personally liable for the debts or obligations of the business trust. 5. *Cooperative*—An association organized to provide an economic service, without profit, to its members; may take the form of a corporation or a partnership.

 ExamPrep

ISSUE SPOTTERS

1 Gomer, Harry, and Ida are members of Jeweled Watches, LLC. What are their options with respect to the management of their firm?

2 Greener Delivery Company and Hiway Trucking, Inc., form a business trust. Insta Equipment Company and Jiffy Supply Corporation form a joint stock company. Kwik Mart, Inc., and Luscious Produce, Inc., form an incorporated cooperative. What do these forms of business organization have in common?

BEFORE THE TEST

Check your answers to the Issue Spotters, and at the same time, take the interactive quiz for this chapter. Go to **www.cengage.com/blaw/blt** and click on "Chapter 28." First, click on "Answers to Issue Spotters" to check your answers. Next, click on "Interactive Quiz" to assess your mastery of the concepts in this chapter. Then click on "Flashcards" to review this chapter's Key Term definitions.

 For Review

Answers for the even-numbered questions in this For Review section can be found on this text's accompanying Web site at **www.cengage.com/blaw/blt**. *Select "Chapter 28" and click on "For Review."*

1 What advantages do limited liability companies offer to businesspersons that are not offered by sole proprietorships or partnerships?

2 How are limited liability companies formed, and who decides how they will be managed and operated?

3 What are the two options for managing limited liability companies?

4 What is a joint venture? How is it similar to a partnership? How is it different?

5 What are the essential characteristics of joint stock companies, syndicates, business trusts, and cooperatives, respectively?

▶ Hypothetical Scenarios and Case Problems

28–1 Limited Liability Companies. John, Lesa, and Trevor form a limited liability company. John contributes 60 percent of the capital, and Lesa and Trevor each contribute 20 percent. Nothing is decided about how profits will be divided. John assumes that he will be entitled to 60 percent of the profits, in accordance with his contribution. Lesa and Trevor, however, assume that the profits will be divided equally. A dispute over the profits arises, and ultimately a court has to decide the issue. What law will the court apply? In most states, what will result? How could this dispute have been avoided in the first place? Discuss fully.

28–2 **Hypothetical Question with Sample Answer** Faraway Corp. is considering entering into two contracts, one with a joint stock company that distributes home products east of the Mississippi River and the other with a business trust formed by a number of sole proprietors who are sellers of home products on the West Coast. Both contracts involve large capital outlays for Faraway, which will supply each business with soft-drink dispensers. In both business organizations, at least two shareholders or beneficiaries are personally wealthy, but each organization has limited financial resources. The owner-managers of Faraway are not familiar with either form of business organization. Because each form resembles a corporation, they are concerned about whether they will be able to collect payments from the wealthy members of the business organizations in the event that either organization breaches the contract by failing to make the payments. Discuss fully Faraway's concern.

—For a sample answer to Question 28–2, go to Appendix E at the end of this text.

28–3 Limited Liability Companies. Joe, a resident of New Jersey, wants to open a restaurant. He asks his friend Kay, who is an experienced attorney and a New Yorker, for her business and legal advice in exchange for a 20 percent ownership interest in the restaurant. Kay helps Joe negotiate a lease for the restaurant premises and advises Joe to organize the business as a limited liability company (LLC). Joe forms Café Olé, LLC, and, with Kay's help, obtains financing. Then, the night before the restaurant opens, Joe tells Kay that he is "cutting her out of the deal." The restaurant proves to be a success. Kay wants to file a suit in a federal district court against Joe and the LLC. Can a federal court exercise jurisdiction over the parties based on diversity of citizenship? Explain.

28–4 Foreign Limited Liability Companies. Whalen Murdock and Cary Hansen organized Capital Care, LLC, in Nebraska. Capital Care operated, and Murdock and Hansen managed, Heartland Care Center in Abilene, Kansas. Burk Properties, Inc., held a mortgage on the Heartland facilities. When Heartland failed as a business, its residents were transferred to other facilities. Heartland employees who provided care to the residents for five days during the transfers were not paid wages. The employees filed claims with the Kansas Department of Human Resources for the unpaid wages. Kansas state law provides that a *corporate* officer or manager may be liable for a firm's unpaid wages, but protects LLC members from personal liability generally and states that an LLC cannot be construed as a corporation. Under Nebraska state law, the members of an LLC can be personally liable for wages due the LLC's employees. Should Murdock and Hansen be held personally liable for the unpaid wages? Explain.

28–5 **Case Problem with Sample Answer** Westbury Properties, Inc., and others (collectively the Westbury group) owned, managed, and developed real property. Jerry Stoker and the Stoker Group, Inc. (the Stokers), also developed real property. The Westbury group entered into agreements with the Stokers concerning a large tract of property in Houston County, Georgia. The parties formed limited liability companies (LLCs), including Bellemeade, LLC (the LLC group), to develop various parcels of the tract for residential purposes. The operating agreements provided that "no Member shall be accountable to the [LLC] or to any other Member with respect to [any other] business or activity even if the business or activity competes with the [LLC's] business." The Westbury group entered into agreements with other parties to develop additional parcels within the tract in competition with the LLC group. The Stokers filed a suit in a Georgia state court against the Westbury group, alleging, among other things, breach of fiduciary duty. What duties do the members of an LLC owe to each other? Under what principle might the terms of an operating agreement alter these duties? In whose favor should the court rule? Discuss. [*Stoker v. Bellemeade, LLC*, 272 Ga.App. 817, 615 S.E.2d 1 (2005)]

—After you have answered Problem 28–5, compare your answer with the sample answer given on the Web site that accompanies this text. Go to **www.cengage.com/blaw/blt**, select "Chapter 28," and click on "Case Problem with Sample Answer."

28–6 Limited Liability Companies. A limited liability company (LLC) owned a Manhattan apartment building that was sold. The owners of 25 percent of the membership interests in the LLC filed a lawsuit on behalf of the company (the LLC)—called a derivative suit—claiming that those in majority control of the LLC sold the building for less than its market value and personally profited from the deal. The trial court dismissed the suit, holding that the plaintiffs individually could not bring a derivative suit "to redress wrongs suffered by the corporation" because such actions were permitted only for corporations and could not be brought for a LLC. The appellate court reversed, holding that derivative suits on behalf of LLCs are permitted. That decision was appealed. A key problem was that the state law governing LLCs did not address the issue. How should such matters logically be resolved? Are the minority owners in an LLC at the mercy of the decisions of the majority owners? [*Tzolis v. Wolff*, 10 N.Y.3d 100, 884 N.E.2d 1005 (2008)]

28–7 Joint Venture. Holiday Isle Resort & Marina, Inc., operated four restaurants, five bars, and various food kiosks at its resort in Islamorada, Florida. Holiday entered into a "joint venture agreement" with Rip Tosun to operate a fifth restaurant called Rip's—A Place For Ribs. The agreement gave Tosun authority over the employees and "full authority as to the conduct of the business." It also prohibited Tosun from competing with Rip's without Holiday's approval but did not prevent Holiday from competing. Later, Tosun sold half of his interest in Rip's to Thomas Hallock. Soon, Tosun and Holiday opened the Olde Florida Steakhouse next to Rip's. Holiday stopped serving breakfast at Rip's and diverted employees and equipment from Rip's to the Steakhouse, which then started offering breakfast. Hallock filed a suit in a Florida state court against Holiday. Did Holiday breach the joint venture agreement? Did it breach the duties that joint venturers owe each other? Explain. [*Hallock v. Holiday Isle Resort & Marina, Inc.*, 4 So.3d 17 (Fla.App. 3 Dist. 2009)]

28–8 **A Question of Ethics** *Blushing Brides, LLC, a publisher of wedding planning magazines in Columbus, Ohio, opened an account with Gray Printing Co. in July 2000. On behalf of Blushing Brides, Louis Zacks, the firm's member-manager, signed a credit agreement that identified the firm as the "purchaser" and required payment within thirty days. Despite the agreement, Blushing Brides typically took up to six months to pay the full amount for its orders. Gray printed and shipped 10,000 copies of a fall/winter 2001 issue for Blushing Brides but had not been paid when the firm ordered 15,000 copies of a spring/summer 2002 issue. Gray refused to print the new order without an assurance of payment. Zacks signed a promissory note for $14,778, plus interest at 6 percent per year, payable to Gray on June 22. Gray printed the new order but by October had been paid only $7,500. Gray filed a suit in an Ohio state court against Blushing Brides and Zacks to collect the balance. [Gray Printing Co. v. Blushing Brides, LLC, __ N.E.2d __ (10 Dist. 2006)]*

1 Under what circumstances is a member of an LLC liable for the firm's debts? In this case, is Zacks personally liable under the credit agreement for the unpaid amount on Blushing Brides' account? Did Zacks's promissory note affect the parties' liability on the account? Explain.

2 Should a member of an LLC assume an ethical responsibility to meet the obligations of the firm? Discuss.

3 Gray shipped only 10,000 copies of the spring/summer 2002 issue of Blushing Brides' magazine, waiting for the publisher to identify a destination for the other 5,000 copies. The magazine had a retail price of $4.50 per copy. Did Gray have a legal or ethical duty to "mitigate the damages" by attempting to sell or otherwise distribute these copies itself? Why or why not?

Critical Thinking and Writing Assignments

28–9 Critical Legal Thinking. Although a limited liability entity may be the best organizational form for most businesses, a significant number of firms may be better off as a corporation or some other form of organization. How does the fact that most of the limited liability entities are new forms for doing business affect the reasons for choosing another form of organization in which to do business? Explain.

Practical Internet Exercises

Go to this text's Web site at **www.cengage.com/blaw/blt**, select "Chapter 28," and click on "Practical Internet Exercises." There you will find the following Internet research exercises that you can perform to learn more about the topics covered in this chapter.

Practical Internet Exercise 28–1: LEGAL PERSPECTIVE—**Limited Liability Companies**

Practical Internet Exercise 28–2: MANAGEMENT PERSPECTIVE—**Joint Ventures**

Chapter 29

Corporate Formation, Merger, and Termination

(AP Photo/Don Ryan)

> "A corporation is an artificial being, invisible, intangible, and existing only in contemplation of law."
>
> —John Marshall, 1755–1835
> (Chief Justice of the United States Supreme Court, 1801–1835)

Chapter Outline

- Corporate Nature and Classification
- Corporate Formation and Powers
- Defects in Formation and Corporate Status
- Corporate Financing
- Mergers and Acquisitions
- Termination

Learning Objectives

After reading this chapter, you should be able to answer the following questions:

1. What steps are involved in bringing a corporation into existence?

2. What is the difference between a *de jure* corporation and a *de facto* corporation?

3. In what circumstances might a court disregard the corporate entity ("pierce the corporate veil") and hold the shareholders personally liable?

4. What are the basic differences between a merger, a consolidation, and a share exchange?

5. What are the two ways in which a corporation can be voluntarily dissolved?

The corporation is a creature of statute. As John Marshall indicated in the chapter-opening quotation, a corporation is an artificial being, existing only in law and neither tangible nor visible. Its existence generally depends on state law, although some corporations, especially public organizations, can be created under state or federal law.

Each state has its own body of corporate law, and these laws are not entirely uniform. The Model Business Corporation Act (MBCA) is a codification of modern corporation law that has been influential in the drafting and revision of state corporation statutes. Today, the majority of state statutes are guided by the revised version of the MBCA, which is often referred to as the Revised Model Business Corporation Act (RMBCA).[1] You should keep in mind, however, that there is considerable variation among the statutes of the states that have used the MBCA or the RMBCA as a basis for their statutes, and several states do not follow either act. Consequently, individual state corporation laws should be relied on rather than the MBCA or the RMBCA.

In this chapter, we examine the nature of the corporate form of business enterprise, the various classifications of corporations, and the formation and financing of today's corporations. We also discuss how a corporation can expand its operations by combining with

---

1. Excerpts from the Revised Model Business Corporation Act (RMBCA) are presented on the Web site that accompanies this text.

another corporation through a merger, a consolidation, a purchase of assets, or a purchase of a controlling interest in the other corporation. The last part of this chapter will discuss the typical reasons for—and methods used in—terminating a corporation's existence.

▶ Corporate Nature and Classification

Corporation A legal entity formed in compliance with statutory requirements that is distinct from its shareholder-owners.

A **corporation** is a legal entity created and recognized by state law. It can consist of one or more *natural persons* (as opposed to the artificial *legal person* of the corporation) identified under a common name. A corporation can be owned by a single person, or it can have hundreds, thousands, or even millions of owners (shareholders). The corporation substitutes itself for its shareholders in conducting corporate business and in incurring liability, yet its authority to act and the liability for its actions are separate and apart from the individuals who own it.

(AP Photo/Paul Sakuma)

Yahoo! has a shareholders' meeting once a year. To what extent do those attending have any say over what direction the company takes?

The shareholder form of business organization emerged in Europe at the end of the seventeenth century. These organizations, called joint stock companies (see Chapter 28), frequently collapsed because their organizers absconded with the funds or proved to be incompetent. Because of this history of fraud and collapse, organizations resembling corporations were regarded with suspicion in the United States during its early years. Although several business corporations were formed after the Revolutionary War, the corporation did not come into common use for private business until the nineteenth century.

Corporate Personnel

In a corporation, the responsibility for the overall management of the firm is entrusted to a *board of directors*, whose members are elected by the shareholders. The board of directors hires *corporate officers* and other employees to run the daily business operations of the corporation.

CONTRAST The death of a sole proprietor results in the dissolution of a business. The death of a corporate shareholder, however, rarely causes the dissolution of a corporation.

When an individual purchases a share of stock in a corporation, that person becomes a shareholder and thus an owner of the corporation. Unlike the members of a partnership, the body of shareholders can change constantly without affecting the continued existence of the corporation. A shareholder can sue the corporation, and the corporation can sue a shareholder. Also, under certain circumstances, a shareholder can sue on behalf of a corporation. The rights and duties of corporate personnel will be examined in detail in Chapter 30.

Very large corporations have numerous directors. What does a board of directors do?

(©bonsai, 2009. Used under license from Shutterstock.com)

The Constitutional Rights of Corporations

A corporation is recognized as a "person," and it has many of the same rights and privileges under state and federal law that U.S. citizens enjoy. The Bill of Rights guarantees persons certain protections, and corporations are considered persons in most instances. Under the First Amendment, corporations are entitled to freedom of speech, although commercial speech (such as advertising) and political speech (such as contributions to political causes or candidates) receive significantly less protection than noncommercial speech. A corporation has the same right of access to the courts as a natural person and can sue or be sued. It also has a right to due process (see Chapter 2), as well as freedom from unreasonable searches and seizures (see Chapter 6) and from double jeopardy.

Generally, though, a corporation is not entitled to claim the Fifth Amendment privilege against self-incrimination. Agents or officers of the corporation therefore cannot refuse to produce corporate records on the ground that doing so might incriminate them. Additionally, the privileges and immunities clause of the U.S. Constitution, which requires each state to treat citizens of other states equally with respect to certain rights, such as travel, does not apply to corporations.

The Limited Liability of Shareholders

One of the key advantages of the corporate form is the limited liability of its owners (shareholders). Corporate shareholders normally are not personally liable for the obligations of the corporation beyond the extent of their investments. In certain limited situations, however, a court can pierce the "corporate veil" and impose liability on shareholders for the corporation's obligations—a concept that will be explained later in this chapter. Additionally, to enable the firm to obtain credit, shareholders in small companies sometimes voluntarily assume personal liability, as guarantors, for corporate obligations.

Corporate Earnings and Taxation

When a corporation earns profits, it can either pass them on to shareholders in the form of **dividends** or retain them as profits. These **retained earnings,** if invested properly, will yield higher corporate profits in the future and thus cause the price of the company's stock to rise. Individual shareholders can then reap the benefits of these retained earnings in the capital gains that they receive when they sell their stock.

CORPORATE TAXATION   Whether a corporation retains its profits or passes them on to the shareholders as dividends, those profits are subject to income tax by various levels of government. As you will read later in this chapter, failure to pay taxes can lead to severe consequences. The state can suspend the entity's corporate status until the taxes are paid or even dissolve the corporation for failing to pay taxes.

Another important aspect of corporate taxation is that corporate profits can be subject to double taxation. The company pays tax on its profits, and then if the profits are passed on to the shareholders as dividends, the shareholders must also pay income tax on them. The corporation normally does not receive a tax deduction for dividends it distributes to shareholders. This double-taxation feature is one of the major disadvantages of the corporate business form.

A taxation issue of increasing importance to corporations is whether they are required to collect state sales taxes on goods or services sold to consumers via the Internet. See this chapter's *Adapting the Law to the Online Environment* feature for a discussion of this issue.

HOLDING COMPANIES   Some U.S. corporations use holding companies to reduce—or at least defer—their U.S. income taxes. At its simplest, a **holding company** (sometimes referred to as a *parent company*) is a company whose business activity consists of holding shares in another company. Typically, the holding company is established in a low-tax or no-tax offshore jurisdiction, such as those shown in Exhibit 29–1 on page 726. Among the best known are the Cayman Islands, Dubai, Hong Kong, Luxembourg, Monaco, and Panama.

Sometimes, a U.S. corporation sets up a holding company in a low-tax offshore environment and then transfers its cash, bonds, stocks, and other investments to the holding company. In general, any profits received by the holding company on these investments are taxed at the rate of the offshore jurisdiction where the company is registered, not the rates applicable to the parent company or its shareholders in their country of residence. Thus, deposits of cash, for example, may earn interest that is taxed at only a minimal rate. Once the profits are brought "onshore," though, they are taxed at the federal corporate income tax rate, and any payments received by the shareholders are also taxable at the full U.S. rates.

ON THE WEB Corporate statutes for all but a few states are now online at topics.law.cornell.edu/wex/ table_corporations.

Dividend A distribution to corporate shareholders of corporate profits or income, disbursed in proportion to the number of shares held.

Retained Earnings The portion of a corporation's profits that has not been paid out as dividends to shareholders.

Holding Company A company whose business activity is holding shares in another company.

Adapting the Law to the Online Environment

Economic Recession Fuels the Internet Taxation Debate

As discussed in the *Adapting the Law to the Online Environment* feature in Chapter 15 on page 363, governments at the state and federal levels have long debated whether states should be able to collect sales taxes on online sales to in-state customers. State governments claim that their inability to tax online sales has caused them to lose billions of dollars in sales tax revenue. The issue has taken on new urgency as the states search desperately for revenue in the wake of the economic recession that began in December 2007.

Supreme Court Precedent Requires Physical Presence

In 1992, the United States Supreme Court ruled that no individual state can compel an out-of-state business that lacks a substantial physical presence (such as a warehouse, office, or retail store) within that state to collect and remit state taxes.[a] The Court recognized that Congress has the power to pass legislation requiring out-of-state corporations to collect and remit state sales taxes, but Congress so far has chosen not to tax Internet transactions. In fact, Congress temporarily prohibited the states from taxing Internet sales, and that ban was extended until 2014.[b] Thus, only online retailers that also have a physical presence within a state must collect state taxes on any Web sales made to residents of that state. (Otherwise, state residents are required to self-report their purchases and pay use taxes to the state, which rarely happens.)

New York Changed Its Definition of Physical Presence

In an effort to collect taxes on Internet sales made by out-of-state corporations, New York changed its tax laws in 2008 to redefine *physical presence.* Under the new law, if an online retailer pays any party within the state to solicit business for its products, that retailer has a physical presence in the state and must collect state taxes.[c] For example, Amazon.com, America's largest online retailer, pays thousands of associates in New York to post ads that link to Amazon's Web site. Consequently, the law requires Amazon to collect tax on any sales to New York residents.

Both Amazon and Overstock.com, a Utah corporation, filed lawsuits in 2009 claiming that the new law was unconstitutional. A New York court dismissed Amazon's case, finding that the law provided a sufficient basis for requiring collection of New York taxes. As long as the seller has a substantial connection with the state, the taxes need not derive from in-state activity. The court also observed that "out-of-state sellers can shield themselves from a tax-collection obligation by altogether prohibiting in-state solicitation activities . . . on their behalf."[d] As a result, Amazon now collects and pays state sales taxes on shipments to New York.

Overstock also lost its lawsuit, but it is appealing the decision.[e] In the meantime, to avoid having to collect the sales tax, Overstock canceled agreements with its New York affiliates that were being paid to direct traffic to its Web site. In 2009, Amazon ended its arrangements with affiliates in Rhode Island and North Carolina for the same reason.

FOR CRITICAL ANALYSIS

Should the fact that an out-of-state corporation pays affiliates in a state to direct consumers to its Web site be sufficient to require the corporation to collect taxes on Web sales to state residents? Why or why not?

a. See *Quill Corp. v. North Dakota,* 504 U.S. 298, 112 S.Ct. 1904, 119 L.Ed.2d 91 (1992).
b. Internet Tax Freedom Act, Pub. L. No. 105-277; 47 U.S.C. Section 151 note (1998); extended to 2014 by Pub. L. No. 110-108.
c. New York Tax Law Section 1101(b)(8)(vi).
d. *Amazon.com, LLC v. New York State Department of Taxation and Finance,* 23 Misc.3d 418, 877 N.Y.S.2d 842 (2009).
e. *Overstock.com, Inc. v. New York State Department of Taxation and Finance,* 2009 WL 1259061 (2009).

Ethical Issue ⚖

Is it ethical for a corporation to establish an offshore holding company to reduce U.S. taxes? The use of offshore holding companies and other methods of reducing tax liability has come under criticism in recent years. In 2008, a study by the Government Accountability Office found that nearly two-thirds of U.S. corporations paid no federal income taxes between 1998 and 2005. Moreover, some of the corporations that received substantial amounts of federal bailout funds during the credit crisis had numerous subsidiaries in offshore tax havens—for example, Citigroup had 427 and Bank of America had 115.[2]

Although the use of offshore holding companies to defer or reduce tax liability is often decried as both unethical and unpatriotic, some observers are not so sure. They point out that those who run corporations have a duty to minimize (legally, of course) taxes owed by the corporation and by its shareholders. Nevertheless, given the nation's weak economic forecast, some politicians are seeking

---

2. Lynnley Browning, "Many U.S. Firms Operate in Tax Havens Abroad, Study Says," *The New York Times, Business Edition,* January 17, 2009.

• *Exhibit* 29–1 Offshore Low-Tax Jurisdictions

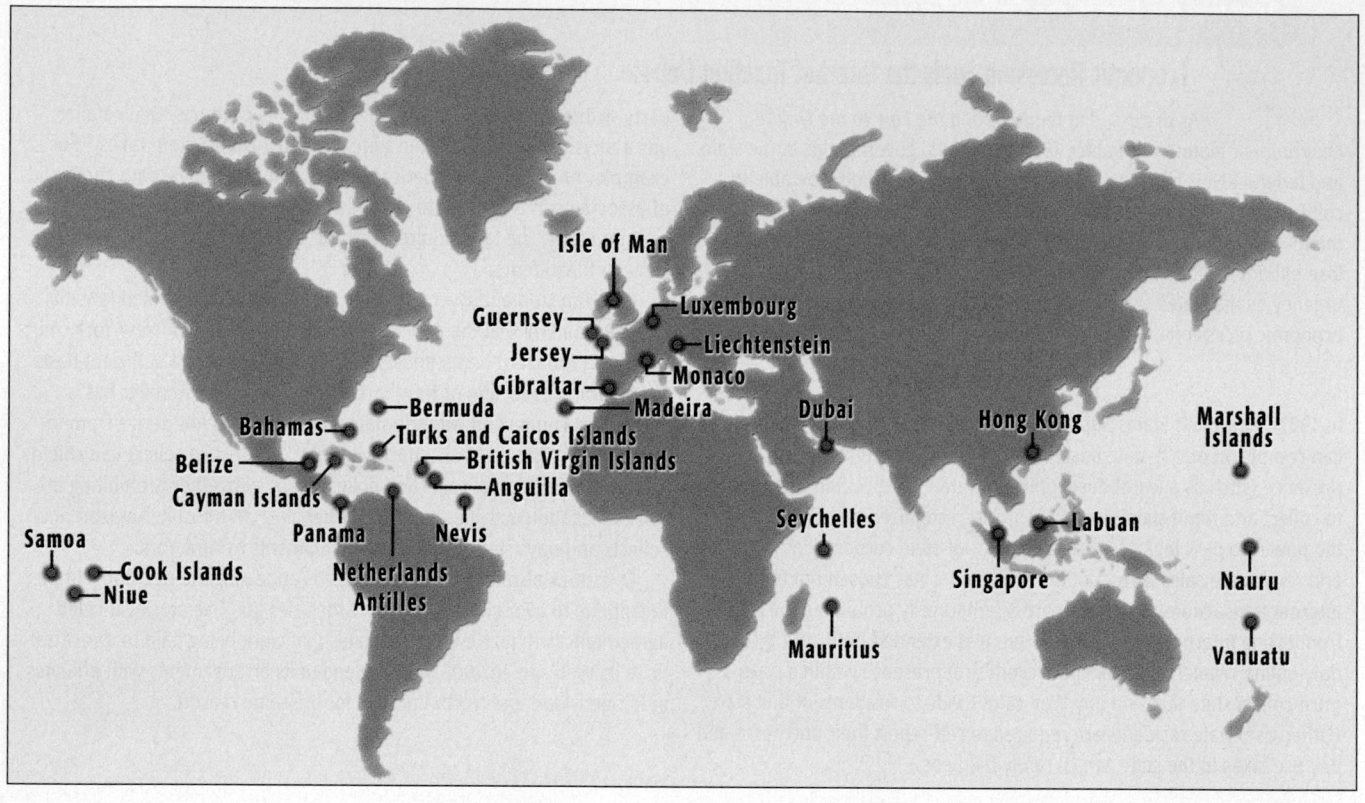

to crack down on these offshore tax havens and force corporations to pay larger amounts of taxes. In 2009, President Barack Obama proposed measures to restrict multinational companies from deferring the payment of taxes on profits earned overseas. The plan would also prevent corporations from inflating the amount of foreign taxes they paid in order to cut their U.S. tax bill and would prohibit wealthy Americans from establishing offshore bank accounts to evade U.S. taxes.

Torts and Criminal Acts

A corporation is liable for the torts committed by its agents or officers within the course and scope of their employment. This principle applies to a corporation exactly as it applies to the ordinary agency relationships discussed in Chapter 23. It follows the doctrine of *respondeat superior.*

Recall from Chapter 6 that under modern criminal law, a corporation may be held liable for the criminal acts of its agents and employees, provided the punishment is one that can be applied to the corporation. Although corporations cannot be imprisoned, they can be fined. (Of course, corporate directors and officers can be imprisoned, and many have been in recent years.) In addition, under sentencing guidelines for crimes committed by corporate employees (white-collar crimes), corporate lawbreakers can face fines amounting to hundreds of millions of dollars.[3]

---

3. Note that the Sarbanes-Oxley Act of 2002, discussed in Chapter 8, stiffened the penalties for certain types of corporate crime and ordered the U.S. Sentencing Commission to revise the sentencing guidelines accordingly.

CASE EXAMPLE 29.1   Brian Gauthier was a truck driver who worked for Angelo Todesca Corporation. Gauthier drove the AT-56, a ten-wheel dump truck. Although Angelo's safety manual required its trucks to be equipped with back-up alarms that automatically sounded when the trucks were put into reverse, the AT-56's alarm was missing. Angelo ordered a new alarm but allowed Gauthier to continue driving the AT-56. At a worksite, when Gauthier backed up the AT-56 to dump its load, he struck and killed a police officer who was directing traffic through the site and facing away from the truck. The state charged Angelo and Gauthier with the crime of vehicular homicide. Angelo argued that a "corporation" could not be guilty of vehicular homicide because it cannot "operate" a vehicle. The court ruled that if an employee commits a crime "while engaged in corporate business that the employee has been authorized to conduct," a corporation can be held liable for the crime. Hence, the court held that Angelo was liable for Gauthier's negligent operation of its truck, which resulted in a person's death.[4] ●

Classification of Corporations

Corporations can be classified in several ways. The classification of a corporation normally depends on its location, purpose, and ownership characteristics, as described in the following subsections.

DOMESTIC, FOREIGN, AND ALIEN CORPORATIONS   A corporation is referred to as a **domestic corporation** by its home state (the state in which it incorporates). A corporation formed in one state but doing business in another is referred to in the second state as a **foreign corporation.** A corporation formed in another country (say, Mexico) but doing business in the United States is referred to in the United States as an **alien corporation.**

> **Domestic Corporation**   In a given state, a corporation that does business in, and is organized under the law of, that state.
>
> **Foreign Corporation**   In a given state, a corporation that does business in the state without being incorporated therein.
>
> **Alien Corporation**   A designation in the United States for a corporation formed in another country but doing business in the United States.

A corporation does not have an automatic right to do business in a state other than its state of incorporation. In some instances, it must obtain a *certificate of authority* in any state in which it plans to do business. Once the certificate has been issued, the corporation generally can exercise in that state all of the powers conferred on it by its home state. If a foreign corporation does business in a state without obtaining a certificate of authority, the state can impose substantial fines and sanctions on the corporation, and sometimes even on its officers, directors, or agents. Note that most state statutes specify certain activities, such as soliciting orders via the Internet, that are not considered doing business within the state. Thus, a foreign corporation normally does not need a certificate of authority to sell goods or services via the Internet or by mail.

AMTRAK is a public corporation. How does a public corporation differ from a private corporation?

(Paul Sullivan/Creative Commons)

PUBLIC AND PRIVATE CORPORATIONS   A public corporation is one formed by the government to meet some political or governmental purpose. Cities and towns that incorporate are common examples. In addition, many federal government organizations, such as the U.S. Postal Service, the Tennessee Valley Authority, and AMTRAK, are public corporations. Note that a public corporation is not the same as a *publicly held* corporation (often called a *public company*). A publicly held corporation is any corporation whose shares are publicly traded in securities markets, such as the New York Stock Exchange or the over-the-counter market.

In contrast to public corporations (*not* public companies), private corporations are created either wholly or in part for private benefit. Most corporations are private. Although they may serve a public

---

4. *Commonwealth v. Angelo Todesca Corp.,* 446 Mass. 128, 842 N.E.2d 930 (2006).

NOTE A private corporation is a voluntary association, but a public corporation is not.

purpose, as a public electric or gas utility does, they are owned by private persons rather than by the government.[5]

NONPROFIT CORPORATIONS

Corporations formed for purposes other than making a profit are called *nonprofit* or *not-for-profit* corporations. Private hospitals, educational institutions, charities, and religious organizations, for example, are frequently organized as nonprofit corporations. The nonprofit corporation is a convenient form of organization that allows various groups to own property and to form contracts without exposing the individual members to personal liability.

CLOSE CORPORATIONS

Close Corporation A corporation whose shareholders are limited to a small group of persons, often only family members. In a close corporation, the shareholders' rights to transfer shares to others are usually restricted.

Most corporate enterprises in the United States fall into the category of close corporations. A **close corporation** is one whose shares are held by members of a family or by relatively few persons. Close corporations are also referred to as *closely held, family,* or *privately held* corporations. Usually, the members of the small group constituting a close corporation are personally known to one another. Because the number of shareholders is so small, there is no trading market for the shares.

In practice, a close corporation is often operated like a partnership. Some states have enacted special statutory provisions that apply to close corporations. These provisions expressly permit close corporations to depart significantly from certain formalities required by traditional corporation law.[6]

Additionally, a provision added to the RMBCA in 1991 gives close corporations a substantial amount of flexibility in determining the rules by which they will operate [RMBCA 7.32]. If all of a corporation's shareholders agree in writing, the corporation can operate without directors, bylaws, annual or special shareholders' or directors' meetings, stock certificates, or formal records of shareholders' or directors' decisions.[7]

Management of Close Corporations. A close corporation has a single shareholder or a closely knit group of shareholders, who usually hold the positions of directors and officers. Management of a close corporation resembles that of a sole proprietorship or a partnership. As a corporation, however, the firm must meet all specific legal requirements set forth in state statutes.

To prevent a majority shareholder from dominating a close corporation, the corporation may require that more than a simple majority of the directors approve any action taken by the board. Typically, this would apply only to extraordinary actions, such as changing the amount of dividends or dismissing an employee-shareholder, and not to ordinary business decisions.

Transfer of Shares in Close Corporations. By definition, a close corporation has a small number of shareholders. Thus, the transfer of one shareholder's shares to someone else can cause serious management problems. The other shareholders may find themselves required to share control with someone they do not know or like.

EXAMPLE 29.2 Three brothers—Terry, Damon, and Henry Johnson—are the only shareholders of Johnson's Car Wash, Inc. Terry and Damon do not want Henry to sell

---

5. The United States Supreme Court first recognized the property rights of private corporations and clarified the distinction between public and private corporations in the landmark case *Trustees of Dartmouth College v. Woodward,* 17 U.S. (4 Wheaton) 518, 4 L.Ed. 629 (1819).

6. For example, in some states (such as Maryland), a close corporation need not have a board of directors.

7. Shareholders cannot agree, however, to eliminate certain rights of shareholders, such as the right to inspect corporate books and records or the right to bring *derivative actions* (lawsuits on behalf of the corporation—see Chapter 30).

his shares to an unknown third person. To avoid this situation, the corporation could restrict the transferability of shares to outside persons. Shareholders could be required to offer their shares to the corporation or the other shareholders before selling them to an outside purchaser. In fact, a few states have statutes that prohibit the transfer of close corporation shares unless certain persons—including shareholders, family members, and the corporation—are first given the opportunity to purchase the shares for the same price. ●

Control of a close corporation can also be stabilized through the use of a *shareholder agreement.* A shareholder agreement can provide that when one of the original shareholders dies, her or his shares of stock in the corporation will be divided in such a way that the proportionate holdings of the survivors, and thus their proportionate control, will be maintained. Courts are generally reluctant to interfere with private agreements, including shareholder agreements.

Misappropriation of Close Corporation Funds.   Sometimes, a majority shareholder in a close corporation takes advantage of his or her position and misappropriates company funds. In such situations, the normal remedy for the injured minority shareholders is to have their shares appraised and to be paid the fair market value for them. In the following case, two wronged minority shareholders pursued an additional remedy.

Case 29.1   Williams v. Stanford

District Court of Appeal of Florida, First District, 977 So.2d 722 (2008).

A majority shareholder in a construction close corporation mismanaged funds. What rights do minority sharholders have when adverse events occur?

FACTS   Two brothers, Paul and James Williams, together held 30 percent of the stock in Brown and Standard (B&S), Inc., a construction company. John Stanford owned the other 70 percent of the close corporation shares. The Williams brothers worked for B&S for five years when they became suspicious of Stanford's financial management. Stanford reported net losses for the company. When the brothers asked to see the B&S books, they were fired. Later, it was shown that Stanford had misappropriated at least $250,000 in B&S funds for his personal use. The Williams brothers brought a *shareholder's derivative suit* (see Chapter 30) on behalf of B&S, naming Stanford as the defendant and accusing him of a breach of fiduciary duty. Before trial, Stanford resigned from B&S and closed the company. He gave the assets and liabilities of B&S to a new company he formed and owned, J. C. Stanford & Sons. He offered the Williams brothers $25,000 each for their stock in B&S. They responded with a request for $125,000 each. The trial court held that by law the Williams brothers, by making a counteroffer, gave up their rights to bring a suit against the company. Hence, the court granted summary judgment for Stanford. The Williams brothers appealed.

ISSUE   If the majority shareholder in a close corporation was misappropriating and mismanaging corporate funds, can the minority sharehold-

ers seek to rescind the transfer of corporate assets in addition to appraisal rights?

DECISION   Yes. The appeals court reversed the trial court's ruling and held that the Williams brothers were entitled to a trial to determine if they could prove abuse of the company by Stanford. Although this did not follow the usual procedure for appraisal of minority shares, given the strong suspicion of fraud in this instance, the court was willing to allow for greater review.

REASON   The minority shareholders claimed that their shares were worth more than the $25,000 Stanford offered. When dissenting shareholders seek more than an appraisal of their shares in the wake of dubious transactions, the courts must balance the principle that an adequate remedy should exist for the shareholders against the consideration that courts should not become bogged down in a wide range of disputes about the fairness of cash-out prices offered to minority shareholders. When shareholders point to specific acts of self-dealing or misrepresentation, they are entitled to equitable remedies beyond the normal appraisal option that dissenting shareholders must accept.

FOR CRITICAL ANALYSIS—Ethical Consideration   *Was it ethical for the Williams brothers to demand $125,000 each for their shares? Why or why not?*

S Corporation A close business corporation that has met certain requirements set out in the Internal Revenue Code and thus qualifies for special income tax treatment. Essentially, an S corporation is taxed the same as a partnership, but its owners enjoy the privilege of limited liability.

S CORPORATIONS A close corporation that meets the qualifying requirements specified in Subchapter S of the Internal Revenue Code can operate as an **S corporation.** If a corporation has S corporation status, it can avoid the imposition of income taxes at the corporate level while retaining many of the advantages of a corporation, particularly limited liability. Among the numerous requirements for S corporation status, the following are the most important:

1. The corporation must be a domestic corporation.
2. The corporation must not be a member of an affiliated group of corporations.
3. The shareholders of the corporation must be individuals, estates, or certain trusts. Partnerships and nonqualifying trusts cannot be shareholders. Corporations can be shareholders under certain circumstances.
4. The corporation must have no more than one hundred shareholders.
5. The corporation must have only one class of stock, although all shareholders do not have to have the same voting rights.
6. No shareholder of the corporation may be a nonresident alien.

An S corporation is treated differently from a regular corporation for tax purposes. An S corporation is taxed like a partnership, so the corporate income passes through to the shareholders, who pay personal income tax on it. This treatment enables the S corporation to avoid the double taxation that is imposed on regular corporations. In addition, the shareholders' tax brackets may be lower than the tax bracket that the corporation would have been in if the tax had been imposed at the corporate level. This tax saving is particularly attractive when the corporation wants to accumulate earnings for some future business purpose. If the corporation has losses, the S election allows the shareholders to use the losses to offset other taxable income. Nevertheless, because the limited liability company (see Chapter 28) and the limited liability partnership (see Chapter 27) offer similar tax advantages and greater flexibility, the S corporation has lost some of its significance.

CONTRAST Unlike the shareholders of most other corporations, the shareholders of professional corporations generally must be licensed professionals.

PROFESSIONAL CORPORATIONS Professionals such as physicians, lawyers, dentists, and accountants can incorporate. Professional corporations typically are identified by the letters *S.C.* (service corporation), *P.C.* (professional corporation), or *P.A.* (professional association).

In general, the laws governing the formation and operation of professional corporations are similar to those governing ordinary business corporations. There are some differences in terms of liability, however, because the shareholder-owners are professionals who are held to a higher standard of conduct. For liability purposes, some courts treat a professional corporation somewhat like a partnership and hold each professional liable for any malpractice committed within the scope of the business by the others in the firm. With the exception of malpractice or a breach of duty to clients or patients, a shareholder in a professional corporation generally cannot be held liable for the torts committed by other professionals at the firm.

▶ **Corporate Formation and Powers**

Up to this point, we have discussed some of the general characteristics of corporations. We now examine the process by which corporations come into existence. Incorporating a business is much simpler today than it was twenty years ago, and many states allow businesses to incorporate via the Internet. If the owners of a partnership or sole proprietorship wish to expand the business, they may decide to incorporate because a corporation can obtain more capital by issuing shares of stock.

Promotional Activities

In the past, preliminary steps were taken to organize and promote the business prior to incorporating. Contracts were made with investors and others on behalf of the future corporation. Today, due to the relative ease of forming a corporation in most states, persons incorporating their business rarely, if ever, engage in preliminary promotional activities. Nevertheless, it is important for businesspersons to understand that they are personally liable for all preincorporation contracts made with investors, accountants, or others on behalf of the future corporation. This personal liability continues until the corporation assumes the preincorporation contracts by *novation* (discussed in Chapter 13).

EXAMPLE 29.3 Jade Sorrel contracts with an accountant, Ray Cooper, to provide tax advice for a proposed corporation, Blackstone, Inc. Cooper provides the services to Sorrel, knowing that the corporation has not yet been formed. Once Blackstone, Inc., is formed, Cooper sends an invoice to the corporation and to Sorrel personally, but the bill is not paid. Because Sorrel is personally liable for the preincorporation contract, Cooper can file a lawsuit against Sorrel for breaching the contract for accounting services. Cooper cannot seek to hold Blackstone, Inc., liable unless he has entered into a novation contract with the corporation. ●

Incorporation Procedures

Exact procedures for incorporation differ among states, but the basic steps are as follows: (1) select a state of incorporation, (2) secure the corporate name by confirming its availability, (3) prepare the articles of incorporation, and (4) file the articles of incorporation with the secretary of state accompanied by payment of the specified fees. These steps are discussed in more detail in the following subsections.

ON THE WEB For answers to "frequently asked questions" on the topic of incorporation, go to **www.bizfilings. com/products/ccorp_FAQ.asp**.

SELECTING THE STATE OF INCORPORATION   The first step in the incorporation process is to select a state in which to incorporate. Because state corporation laws differ, individuals may look for the states that offer the most advantageous tax or other provisions. Another consideration is the fee that a particular state charges to incorporate, as well as the annual fees and the fees for specific transactions (such as stock transfers).

Delaware has historically had the least restrictive laws and provisions that favor corporate management. Consequently, many corporations, including a number of the largest, have incorporated there. Delaware's statutes permit firms to incorporate in that state and conduct business and locate their operating headquarters elsewhere. Most other states now permit this as well. Note, though, that closely held corporations, particularly those of a professional nature, generally incorporate in the state where their principal shareholders live and work. For reasons of convenience and cost, businesses often choose to incorporate in the state in which the corporation's business will primarily be conducted.

Each corporation must select a name that is not already in use and that could not be confused with an existing corporate name. What level of government usually approves corporate names?

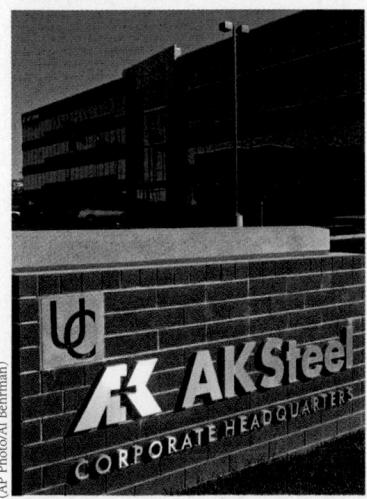

(AP Photo/Al Behrman)

SECURING THE CORPORATE NAME   The choice of a corporate name is subject to state approval to ensure against duplication or deception. State statutes usually require that the secretary of state run a check on the proposed name in the state of incorporation. Some states require that the persons incorporating a firm, at their own expense, run a check on the proposed name, which can often be accomplished via Internet-based services. Once cleared, a name can be reserved for a short time, for a fee, pending the completion of the articles of incorporation. All corporate statutes require the corporation name to include the word *Corporation, Incorporated, Company,* or *Limited,* or abbreviations of these terms.

A new corporation's name cannot be the same as (or deceptively similar to) the name of an existing corporation doing business within the state. The name should also be one that can be used as the business's Internet domain name. **EXAMPLE 29.4** If an existing corporation is named Digital Synergy, Inc., you cannot choose the name Digital Synergy Company because that name is deceptively similar to the first. The state will be unlikely to allow the corporate name because it could impliedly transfer a part of the goodwill established by the first corporate user to the second corporation. In addition, you would not want to choose the name Digital Synergy Company because you would be unable to acquire an Internet domain name using even part of the name of the business. ●

If those incorporating a firm contemplate doing business in other states—or over the Internet—they also need to check on existing corporate names in those states as well. Otherwise, if the firm does business under a name that is the same as or deceptively similar to an existing company's name, it may be liable for trade name infringement.

Preventing Legal Disputes ⚖

Be cautious when choosing a corporate name. Recognize that even if a particular state does not require the incorporator to run a name check, doing so can help prevent future disputes. Many states provide online search capabilities, but these searches usually are limited and will only compare the proposed name to the names of active corporations within that state. Trade name disputes may also arise, however, if you use a business name that is deceptively similar to the name of a partnership or limited liability company. Disputes are even more likely to arise among online firms. Always check on the availability of a particular domain name before selecting a corporate name. It pays to be overly cautious and incur some additional cost to hire a professional to conduct a name search.

Articles of Incorporation The document filed with the appropriate governmental agency, usually the secretary of state, when a business is incorporated. State statutes usually prescribe what kind of information must be contained in the articles of incorporation.

ON THE WEB For sample articles of incorporation, go to **www.samplearticleofincorporation.com**.

Bylaws A set of governing rules adopted by a corporation or other association.

PREPARING THE ARTICLES OF INCORPORATION The primary document needed to incorporate a business is the **articles of incorporation.** The articles include basic information about the corporation and serve as a primary source of authority for its future organization and business functions. The person or persons who execute (sign) the articles are called *incorporators*. Generally, the articles of incorporation *must* include the following information [RMBCA 2.02]:

1. The name of the corporation.
2. The number of shares the corporation is authorized to issue.
3. The name and address of the corporation's initial registered agent.
4. The name and address of each incorporator.

In addition, the articles *may* set forth other information, such as the names and addresses of the initial board of directors, the duration and purpose of the corporation, a par value of shares of the corporation, and any other information pertinent to the rights and duties of the corporation's shareholders and directors. Articles of incorporation vary widely depending on the size and type of corporation and the jurisdiction. Frequently, the articles do not provide much detail about the firm's operations, which are spelled out in the company's **bylaws** (internal rules of management adopted by the corporation at its first organizational meeting).

Shares of the Corporation. The articles must specify the number of shares of stock authorized for issuance. For instance, a company might state that the aggregate number of shares that the corporation has the authority to issue is five thousand. Large corporations often state a par value of each share, such as twenty cents per share, and specify the various types or classes of stock authorized for issuance (see the discussion of *common* and *preferred stock* later in this chapter). Sometimes, the articles set forth the capital structure of the corporation and other relevant information concerning equity, shares, and credit.

Registered Office and Agent. The corporation must indicate the location and address of its registered office within the state. Usually, the registered office is also the principal office of the corporation. The corporation must also give the name and address of a specific person who has been designated as an *agent* and can receive legal documents (such as orders to appear in court) on behalf of the corporation.

Incorporators.   Each incorporator must be listed by name and address. The incorporators need not have any interest at all in the corporation, and sometimes signing the articles is their only duty. Many states do not have residency or age requirements for incorporators. States vary on the required number of incorporators; it can be as few as one or as many as three. Incorporators frequently participate in the first organizational meeting of the corporation.

Duration and Purpose.   A corporation has perpetual existence unless the articles state otherwise. The RMBCA does not require a specific statement of purpose to be included in the articles. A corporation can be formed for any lawful purpose. Some incorporators choose to include a general statement of purpose "to engage in any lawful act or activity," while others opt to specify the intended business activities ("to engage in the production and sale of agricultural products," for example). It is increasingly common for the articles to state that the corporation is organized for "any legal business," with no mention of specifics, to avoid the need for future amendments to the corporate articles.

Internal Organization.   The articles can describe the internal management structure of the corporation, although this is usually included in the bylaws adopted after the corporation is formed. The articles of incorporation commence the corporation; the bylaws are formed after commencement by the board of directors. Bylaws cannot conflict with the corporation statute or the articles of incorporation [RMBCA 2.06].

> **KEEP IN MIND**   Unlike the articles of incorporation, bylaws do not need to be filed with a state official.

Under the RMBCA, shareholders may amend or repeal the bylaws. The board of directors may also amend or repeal the bylaws unless the articles of incorporation or provisions of the corporation statute reserve this power to the shareholders exclusively [RMBCA 10.20]. Typical bylaw provisions describe such matters as voting requirements for shareholders, the election of the board of directors, the methods of replacing directors, and the manner and time of holding shareholders' and board meetings (these corporate activities will be discussed in Chapter 30).

FILING THE ARTICLES WITH THE STATE   Once the articles of incorporation have been prepared, signed, and authenticated by the incorporators, they are sent to the appropriate state official, usually the secretary of state, along with the required filing fee. In most states, the secretary of state then stamps the articles as "Filed" and returns a copy of the articles to the incorporators. Once this occurs, the corporation officially exists. (Note that some states issue a *certificate of incorporation,* which is similar to articles of incorporation, representing the state's authorization for the corporation to conduct business. This procedure was typical under the unrevised MBCA.)

First Organizational Meeting to Adopt Bylaws

After incorporation, the first organizational meeting must be held. Usually, the most important function of this meeting is the adoption of bylaws—the internal rules of management for the corporation. If the articles of incorporation named the initial board of directors, then the directors, by majority vote, call the meeting to adopt the bylaws and complete the company's organization. If the articles did not name the directors (as is typical), then the incorporators hold the meeting to elect the directors, adopt bylaws, and complete the routine business of incorporation (authorizing the issuance of shares and hiring employees, for example). The business transacted depends on the requirements of the state's corporation statute, the nature of the corporation, the provisions made in the articles, and the desires of the incorporators.

Corporate Powers

When a corporation is created, the express and implied powers necessary to achieve its purpose also come into existence. The express powers of a corporation are found in its articles of incorporation, in the law of the state of incorporation, and in the state and federal constitutions.

ON THE WEB For an example of one state's (Minnesota's) statute governing corporations, go to www.revisor.leg. state.mn.us/statutes/?id=302A.

Corporate bylaws also establish the express powers of the corporation. Because state corporation statutes frequently provide default rules that apply if the company's bylaws are silent on an issue, it is important that the bylaws set forth the specific operating rules of the corporation. In addition, after the bylaws are adopted, the corporation's board of directors will pass resolutions that also grant or restrict corporate powers.

The following order of priority is used when conflicts arise among documents involving corporations:

1. The U.S. Constitution
2. State constitutions
3. State statutes
4. The articles of incorporation
5. Bylaws
6. Resolutions of the board of directors

IMPLIED POWERS   When a corporation is created, it acquires certain implied powers. Barring express constitutional, statutory, or other prohibitions, the corporation has the implied power to perform all acts reasonably appropriate and necessary to accomplish its corporate purposes. For this reason, a corporation has the implied power to borrow funds within certain limits, to lend funds, and to extend credit to those with whom it has a legal or contractual relationship.

To borrow funds, the corporation acts through its board of directors to authorize the loan. Most often, the president or chief executive officer of the corporation will execute the necessary papers on behalf of the corporation. In so doing, corporate officers have the implied power to bind the corporation in matters directly connected with the *ordinary* business affairs of the enterprise. There is a limit to what a corporate officer can do, though. A corporate officer does not have the authority to bind the corporation to an action that will greatly affect the corporate purpose or undertaking, such as the sale of substantial corporate assets.

Ultra Vires   A Latin term meaning "beyond the powers"; in corporate law, acts of a corporation that are beyond its express and implied powers to undertake.

ULTRA VIRES DOCTRINE   The term ***ultra vires*** means "beyond the powers." In corporate law, acts of a corporation that are beyond its express and implied powers are *ultra vires* acts. Most cases dealing with *ultra vires* acts have involved contracts made for unauthorized purposes. **EXAMPLE 29.5** Suarez is the chief executive officer of SOS Plumbing, Inc. The stated purpose of SOS is to install and repair plumbing. If Suarez enters into a contract with Carlini for SOS to purchase ten cases of brandy, this contract would likely be *ultra vires* because it is not reasonably related to the corporation's purpose. ●

Under Section 3.04 of the RMBCA, the shareholders can seek an injunction from a court to prevent (or stop) the corporation from engaging in *ultra vires* acts. The attorney general in the state of incorporation can also bring an action to obtain an injunction against the *ultra vires* transactions or to institute dissolution proceedings against the corporation on the basis of *ultra vires* acts. The corporation or its shareholders (on behalf of the corporation) can seek damages from the officers and directors who were responsible for the *ultra vires* acts. As mentioned previously, most corporations today are organized for "any legal business" and do not state a specific purpose; thus, the importance of the *ultra vires* doctrine has declined in recent years.

Defects in Formation and Corporate Status

The procedures for incorporation are very specific. If they are not followed precisely, others may be able to challenge the existence of the corporation. Errors in the incorporation procedures can become important when, for example, a third party who is attempting to enforce a contract or bring a suit for a tort injury learns of them. On the basis of improper incorporation, the plaintiff could attempt to hold the would-be shareholders personally liable. Additionally, when the corporation seeks to enforce a contract against a defaulting party, that party may be able to avoid liability on the ground of a defect in the incorporation procedure.

To prevent injustice, courts will sometimes attribute corporate status to an improperly formed corporation by holding it to be a *de jure* corporation or a *de facto* corporation. Occasionally, a corporation may be held to exist by estoppel. Additionally, in certain circumstances involving abuse of the corporate form, a court may disregard the corporate entity and hold the shareholders personally liable.

De Jure and De Facto Corporations

If a corporation has substantially complied with all conditions precedent to incorporation, the corporation is said to have *de jure* (rightful and lawful) existence. In most states and under the RMBCA, the secretary of state's filing of the articles of incorporation is conclusive proof that all mandatory statutory provisions have been met [RMBCA 2.03(b)]. Because a *de jure* corporation is one that is properly formed, neither the state nor a third party can attack its existence.[8]

Sometimes, there is a defect in complying with statutory mandates—for example, the corporation failed to hold an organizational meeting. Under these circumstances, the corporation may have *de facto* (actual) status, meaning that it will be treated as a legal corporation despite the defect in its formation. A corporation with *de facto* status cannot be challenged by third persons (only by the state). In other words, the shareholders of a *de facto* corporation are still protected by limited liability (provided they are unaware of the defect). The following elements are required for *de facto* status:

1. There must be a state statute under which the corporation can be validly incorporated.
2. The parties must have made a good faith attempt to comply with the statute.
3. The enterprise must already have undertaken to do business as a corporation.

Corporation by Estoppel

If a business association holds itself out to others as being a corporation but has made no attempt to incorporate, the firm normally will be estopped (prevented) from denying corporate status in a lawsuit by a third party. This usually occurs when a third party contracts with an entity that claims to be a corporation but has not filed articles of incorporation—or contracts with a person claiming to be an agent of a corporation that does not in fact exist. When justice requires, the courts treat an alleged corporation as if it were an actual corporation for the purpose of determining the rights and liabilities of its officers and directors involved in a particular situation. A corporation by estoppel is thus determined by the situation. Recognition of its corporate status does not extend beyond the resolution of the problem at hand.

In the following case, a party sought to avoid liability on a contract with a firm that had not yet filed its articles of incorporation. Could the party escape liability on the ground that the corporation did not exist at the time of the contract?

---

8. There is an exception: a few states allow state authorities, in a *quo warranto* proceeding, to bring an action against the corporation for noncompliance with a necessary condition *subsequent* to incorporation. This might occur if the corporation fails to file annual reports, for example.

Case 29.2 Brown v. W.P. Media, Inc.

Supreme Court of Alabama, ___ So.2d ___ (2009).

HISTORICAL AND TECHNOLOGICAL SETTING *The term* wireless network *commonly refers to a telecommunications network whose interconnection is accomplished without wires. As early as World War II, wireless networks using radio waves transmitted information long distances, overseas, or behind enemy lines. Today's wireless networks are computer networks. Cell phones communicate through wide-ranging wireless networks. Businesses use wireless networks to exchange data quickly. Wireless networks can also be a relatively inexpensive and fast method to connect to the Internet.*

(©Phillips, 2009. Used under license from Shutterstock.com)

When a joint venture to build a wireless network fails, does liability exist when the articles of incorporation were filed after the original obligations were made?

FACTS In 2001, W.P. Media, Inc., and Alabama MBA, Inc., agreed to a joint venture—to be called Alabaster Wireless MBA, LLC—to provide wireless Internet services to consumers. W.P. Media was to create a wireless network and provide ongoing technical support. Alabama MBA was to contribute capital of $79,300, and W.P. Media was to contribute "proprietary technology" in the same amount. Hugh Brown signed the parties' contract on Alabama MBA's behalf as the chairman of its board. At the time, however, Alabama MBA's articles of incorporation had not yet been filed. Brown filed the articles of incorporation in 2002. Later, Brown and Alabama MBA filed a suit in an Alabama state court, alleging that W.P. Media had breached their contract by not building the wireless network. The court issued a summary judgment in the defendant's favor. The plaintiffs appealed.

ISSUE Can a party be liable on an obligation to a firm that had not filed its articles of incorporation when the obligation arose?

DECISION Yes. The Alabama Supreme Court reversed the lower court's judgment and remanded the case. Under the principle of estoppel, W.P. Media could not deny Alabama MBA's corporate existence.

REASON A firm that represents itself as a corporation in contracting with a third party may be estopped (prevented) from denying corporate status to avoid liability even if the firm was not incorporated at the time of the contract. Likewise, a third party that recognizes an organization as a corporation may be estopped from denying its corporate status. Here, Alabama MBA was represented as "a viable, legal corporation." The parties' contract identified Alabama MBA as a corporation, and Brown signed the contract as Alabama MBA's "chairman of the board." W.P. Media did not act as though it doubted that representation. It agreed to operate Alabaster and participated in the venture before and after Alabama MBA filed its articles of incorporation. W.P. Media did not challenge the validity of the contract until after it was sued for breaching it. Because W.P. Media treated Alabama MBA as a corporation, W.P. Media is estopped from denying Alabama MBA's corporate existence.

WHAT IF THE FACTS WERE DIFFERENT? *Would the result in this case have been different if the parties' contract to build and operate a wireless network had been negotiated and agreed to entirely online? Discuss.*

Piercing the Corporate Veil

Piercing the Corporate Veil An action in which a court disregards the corporate entity and holds the shareholders personally liable for corporate debts and obligations.

Occasionally, the owners use a corporate entity to perpetrate a fraud, circumvent the law, or in some other way accomplish an illegitimate objective. In these situations, the court will ignore the corporate structure by **piercing the corporate veil** and exposing the shareholders to personal liability. Generally, when the corporate privilege is abused for personal benefit or when the corporate business is treated so carelessly that the corporation and the controlling shareholder are no longer separate entities, the court will require the owner to assume personal liability to creditors for the corporation's debts. In short, when the facts show that great injustice would result from the use of a corporation to avoid individual responsibility, a court will look behind the corporate structure to the individual shareholder.

FACTORS THAT LEAD COURTS TO PIERCE THE CORPORATE VEIL The following are some of the factors that frequently cause the courts to pierce the corporate veil:

1. A party is tricked or misled into dealing with the corporation rather than the individual.
2. The corporation is set up never to make a profit or always to be insolvent, or it is too "thinly" capitalized—that is, it has insufficient capital at the time of formation to meet its prospective debts or other potential liabilities.

Commingle To put funds or goods together into one mass so that they are mixed to such a degree that they no longer have separate identities. In corporate law, if personal and corporate interests are commingled to the extent that the corporation has no separate identity, a court may "pierce the corporate veil" and expose the shareholders to personal liability.

3. Statutory corporate formalities, such as holding required corporation meetings, are not followed.

4. Personal and corporate interests are **commingled** (mixed together) to such an extent that the corporation has no separate identity.

A POTENTIAL PROBLEM FOR CLOSE CORPORATIONS The potential for corporate assets to be used for personal benefit is especially great in a close corporation, in which the shares are held by a single person or by only a few individuals, usually family members. In such a situation, the separate status of the corporate entity and the sole shareholder (or family-member shareholders) must be carefully preserved. Certain practices invite trouble for the one-person or family-owned corporation: the commingling of corporate and personal funds, the failure to hold board of directors' meetings and record the minutes, or the shareholders' continuous personal use of corporate property (for example, vehicles).

In the following case, when a close corporation's creditors sought payment of its debts, the owners took the small value in the business for themselves, filed a bankruptcy petition for the firm, and incorporated under a new name to continue the business. Could the court recover the business assets from the new corporation for distribution to the original firm's creditors?

Case 29.3 In re Aqua Clear Technologies, Inc.

United States Bankruptcy Court, Southern District of Florida, 361 Bankr. 567 (2007).

Can a water-softener company that has already filed for bankruptcy simply create a new company with the assets from the first corporation without paying its debts?

FACTS Harvey and Barbara Jacobson owned Aqua Clear Technologies, Inc., a small Florida business that installed and serviced home water-softening systems. Barbara was Aqua's president, and Sharon, the Jacobsons' daughter, was an officer, but neither participated in the business. Although Harvey controlled the day-to-day operations, he was not an Aqua officer, director, or employee, but an independent contractor in service to the company. Aqua had no compensation agreement with the Jacobsons. Instead, whenever Harvey decided that there were sufficient funds, they took funds out of the business for their personal expenses, including the maintenance of their home and payments for their cars, health-insurance premiums, and charges on their credit cards. In December 2004, Aqua filed a bankruptcy petition in a federal bankruptcy court. Three weeks later, Harvey incorporated Discount Water Services, Inc., and continued to service water-softening systems for Aqua's customers. Discount appropriated Aqua's equipment and inventory without a formal transfer and advertised Aqua's phone number as Discount's. Kenneth Welt, Aqua's trustee, initiated a proceeding against Discount, seeking, among other things, to recover Aqua's assets. The trustee contended that Discount was Aqua's "alter ego." (An *alter ego* is the double of something—in this case, the original company.)

ISSUE Can a firm's owners file for corporate bankruptcy and then open another corporation that engages in substantially the same business with the same equipment without paying the first corporation's debts?

DECISION No. The court issued a judgment against Discount, and in the trustee's favor, for $108,732.64, which represented the amount of the claims listed in Aqua Clear's bankruptcy schedules. The court also agreed to add the administrative expenses and all other claims allowed against Aqua Clear once those amounts were determined.

REASON The bankruptcy court pointed out that Aqua Clear—the debtor—and Discount Water "were in substantially the same business. They used the same telephone number. They operated from the same business location. They serviced the same geographic area and many of the same customers." Furthermore, the debtor and Discount Water had identical officers and directors. Consequently, "the Court may presume fraud when a transfer occurs between two corporations controlled by the same officers and directors." The court then pointed out that Aqua Clear had sent a letter to its health-insurance carrier stating that it was simply changing its name to Discount Water Services, Inc. Most of the Jacobsons' actions were designed to interfere with the collection efforts of judgment creditors. "The bottom line question is whether each entity has run its own race, or whether there has been a relay-style passing of the baton from one to the other."

FOR CRITICAL ANALYSIS—Global Consideration *If the Jacobsons' business had been global in scope, should the court have issued a different judgment? Explain.*

Corporate Financing

Part of the process of corporate formation involves corporate financing. (See the *Linking the Law to Finance* feature on pages 746 and 747 for details on how a start-up company can obtain financing for expanding the business through incorporation.) Corporations are financed by the issuance and sale of corporate securities. **Securities** (stocks and bonds) evidence the right to participate in earnings and the distribution of corporate property or the obligation to pay funds.

Stocks, or *equity securities,* represent the purchase of ownership in the business firm. Bonds (debentures), or *debt securities,* represent the borrowing of funds by firms (and governments). Of course, not all debt is in the form of debt securities. For example, some debt is in the form of accounts payable and notes payable, which typically are short-term debts. Bonds are simply a way for the corporation to split up its long-term debt so that it can be more easily marketed.

Bonds

Bonds are issued by business firms and by governments at all levels as evidence of the funds they are borrowing from investors. Bonds normally have a designated *maturity date*—the date when the principal, or face, amount of the bond is returned to the investor. They are sometimes referred to as *fixed-income securities* because their owners (that is, the creditors) receive fixed-dollar interest payments, usually semiannually, during the period of time prior to maturity.

Because debt financing represents a legal obligation on the part of the corporation, various features and terms of a particular bond issue are specified in a lending agreement called a **bond indenture.** A corporate trustee, often a commercial bank trust department, represents the collective well-being of all bondholders in ensuring that the corporation meets the terms of the bond issue. The bond indenture specifies the maturity date of the bond and the pattern of interest payments until maturity. The different types of corporate bonds are described in Exhibit 29–2.

Securities   Generally, stocks, bonds, notes, debentures, warrants, or other items that evidence an ownership interest in a corporation or a promise of repayment by a corporation.

Stock   An equity (ownership) interest in a corporation, measured in units of shares.

Bond   A security that evidences a corporate (or government) debt. It does not represent an ownership interest in the issuing entity.

"Gentlemen prefer bonds."
Andrew Mellon, 1855–1937
(American banker)

• *Exhibit* 29–2 Types of Corporate Bonds

Debenture bonds	Bonds for which no specific assets of the corporation are pledged as backing. Rather, they are backed by the general credit rating of the corporation, plus any assets that can be seized if the corporation allows the debentures to go into default.
Mortgage bonds	Bonds that pledge specific property. If the corporation defaults on the bonds, the bondholders can take the property.
Convertible bonds	Bonds that can be exchanged for a specified number of shares of common stock under certain conditions.
Callable bonds	Bonds that may be called in and the principal repaid at specified times or under conditions specified in the bonds when they are issued.

Stocks

Bond Indenture   A contract between the issuer of a bond and the bondholder.

Issuing stocks is another way that corporations can obtain financing. The ways in which stocks differ from bonds are summarized in Exhibit 29–3. Basically, as mentioned, stocks represent ownership in a business firm, whereas bonds represent borrowing by the firm.

Exhibit 29–4 on page 740 summarizes the types of stocks issued by corporations. We look now at the two major types of stock—*common stock* and *preferred stock.*

Common Stock   Shares of ownership in a corporation that give the owner of the stock a proportionate interest in the corporation with regard to control, earnings, and net assets. Shares of common stock are lowest in priority with respect to payment of dividends and distribution of the corporation's assets on dissolution.

COMMON STOCK   The true ownership of a corporation is represented by **common stock.** Common stock provides a proportionate interest in the corporation with regard to (1) control, (2) earnings, and (3) net assets. A shareholder's interest is generally in proportion to the number of shares he or she owns out of the total number of shares issued.

Voting rights in a corporation apply to the election of the firm's board of directors and to any proposed changes in the ownership structure of the firm. For example, a holder of common stock generally has the right to vote in a decision on a proposed merger, as mergers

• *Exhibit* 29–3 How Do Stocks and Bonds Differ?

STOCKS	BONDS
1. Stocks represent ownership.	1. Bonds represent debt.
2. Stocks (common) do not have a fixed dividend rate.	2. Interest on bonds must always be paid, whether or not any profit is earned.
3. Stockholders can elect the board of directors, which controls the corporation.	3. Bondholders usually have no voice in, or control over, management of the corporation.
4. Stocks do not have a maturity date; the corporation usually does not repay the stockholder.	4. Bonds have a maturity date, when the corporation is to repay the bondholder the face value of the bond.
5. All corporations issue or offer to sell stocks. This is the usual definition of a corporation.	5. Corporations do not necessarily issue bonds.
6. Stockholders have a claim against the property and income of a corporation after all creditors' claims have been met.	6. Bondholders have a claim against the property and income of a corporation that must be met *before* the claims of stockholders.

can change the proportion of ownership. State corporation law specifies the types of actions for which shareholder approval must be obtained.

Firms are not obligated to return a principal amount per share to each holder of common stock because no firm can ensure that the market price per share of its common stock will not decline over time. The issuing firm also does not have to guarantee a dividend; indeed, some corporations never pay dividends.

Holders of common stock are investors who assume a *residual* position in the overall financial structure of a business. In terms of receiving payment for their investments, they are last in line. They are entitled to the earnings that are left after preferred stockholders, bondholders, suppliers, employees, and other groups have been paid. Once those groups are paid, however, the owners of common stock may be entitled to *all* the remaining earnings as dividends. (The board of directors normally is not under any duty to declare the remaining earnings as dividends, however.)

Preferred Stock Classes of stock that have priority over common stock as to both payment of dividends and distribution of assets on the corporation's dissolution.

PREFERRED STOCK   **Preferred stock** is stock with *preferences*. Usually, this means that holders of preferred stock have priority over holders of common stock as to dividends and as to payment on dissolution of the corporation. Holders of preferred stock may or may not have the right to vote.

Preferred stock is not included among the liabilities of a business because it is equity. Like other equity securities, preferred shares have no fixed maturity date on which the firm must pay them off. Although firms occasionally buy back preferred stock, they are not legally obligated to do so. Holders of preferred stock are investors who have assumed a rather cautious position in their relationship to the corporation. They have a stronger position than common shareholders with respect to dividends and claims on assets, but they will not share in the full prosperity of the firm if it grows successfully over time. This is because the value of preferred shares will not rise as rapidly as that of common shares during a period of financial success. Preferred stockholders do receive fixed dividends periodically, however, and they may benefit to some extent from changes in the market price of the shares.

The return and the risk for preferred stock lie somewhere between those for bonds and those for common stock. Preferred stock is more similar to bonds than to common stock, even though preferred stock appears in the ownership section of the firm's balance sheet. As a result, preferred stock is often categorized with corporate bonds as a fixed-income security, even though the legal status is not the same.

Venture Capital and Private Equity Capital

As discussed, corporations traditionally obtain financing through issuing and selling securities (stocks and bonds) in the capital market. In reality, however, many investors do not want to purchase stock in a business that lacks a track record, and banks are generally reluctant to extend loans to high-risk enterprises. Numerous corporations fail because they are

• *Exhibit 29–4* Types of Stocks

Common stock	Voting shares that represent ownership interest in a corporation. Common stock has the lowest priority with respect to payment of dividends and distribution of assets on the corporation's dissolution.
Preferred stock	Shares of stock that have priority over common-stock shares as to payment of dividends and distribution of assets on dissolution. Dividend payments are usually a fixed percentage of the face value of the share.
Cumulative preferred stock	Preferred shares on which required dividends not paid in a given year must be paid in a subsequent year before any common-stock dividends are paid.
Participating preferred stock	Preferred shares entitling the owner to receive the preferred-stock dividend and additional dividends if the corporation has paid dividends on common stock.
Convertible preferred stock	Preferred shares that, under certain conditions, can be converted into a specified number of common shares either in the issuing corporation or, sometimes, in another corporation.
Redeemable, or callable, preferred stock	Preferred shares issued with the express condition that the issuing corporation has the right to repurchase the shares as specified.

Venture Capital Capital (funds and other assets) provided by professional, outside investors (*venture capitalists,* usually groups of wealthy investors and securities firms) to start new business ventures.

Private Equity Capital Private equity capital is a financing method by which a company sells equity in an existing business to a private or institutional investor.

Merger A contractual and statutory process in which one corporation (the surviving corporation) acquires all of the assets and liabilities of another corporation (the merged corporation).

undercapitalized. Therefore, to obtain sufficient financing, many entrepreneurs seek alternative financing.

VENTURE CAPITAL   Start-up businesses and high-risk enterprises often obtain venture capital financing. **Venture capital** is capital provided by professional, outside investors (*venture capitalists,* usually groups of wealthy investors and securities firms) to new business ventures. Venture capital investments are high risk—the investors must be willing to lose all of their invested funds—but offer the potential for well-above-average returns at some point in the future.

To obtain venture capital financing, the start-up business typically gives up a share of its ownership to the venture capitalists. In addition to funding, venture capitalists may provide managerial and technical expertise, and they nearly always are given some control over the new company's decisions. Many Internet-based companies, such as Google, were initially financed by venture capital.

PRIVATE EQUITY CAPITAL   Private equity firms obtain their capital from wealthy investors in private markets. The firms use their **private equity capital** to invest in existing—often, publicly traded—corporations. Usually, they buy an entire corporation and then reorganize it. Sometimes, divisions of the purchased company are sold off to pay down debt. Ultimately, the private equity firm may sell shares in the reorganized (and perhaps more profitable) company to the public in an *initial public offering* (usually called an IPO—see Chapter 31). In this way, the private equity firm can make profits by selling its shares in the company to the public.

 Mergers and Acquisitions

A corporation typically extends its operations by combining with another corporation through a merger, a consolidation, a share exchange, a purchase of assets, or a purchase of a controlling interest in the other corporation. The terms *merger* and *consolidation* traditionally referred to two legally distinct proceedings. Today, however, the term *consolidation* generally is used as a generic term to refer to all types of combinations, including mergers and acquisitions. Whether a combination is a merger, a consolidation, or a share exchange, the rights and liabilities of shareholders, the corporation, and the corporation's creditors are the same.

Merger

A **merger** involves the legal combination of two or more corporations in such a way that only one of the corporations continues to exist. **EXAMPLE 29.6** Corporation A and Corporation B decide to merge. They agree that A will absorb B. Therefore, on merging, B ceases to exist as a separate entity, and A continues as the *surviving corporation.* • Exhibit 29–5 graphically illustrates this process.

After the merger, Corporation A is recognized as a single corporation, possessing all the rights, privileges, and powers of itself and Corporation B. It automatically acquires all of

● *Exhibit* **29-5 Merger**
Corporation A and Corporation B decide to merge. They agree that A will absorb B, so after the merger, B no longer exists as a separate entity, and A continues as the surviving corporation.

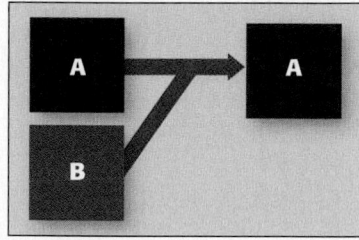

Consolidation A contractual and statutory process in which two or more corporations join to become a completely new corporation. The original corporations cease to exist, and the new corporation acquires all their assets and liabilities.

● *Exhibit* **29-6 Consolidation**
Corporation A and Corporation B consolidate to form an entirely new organization, Corporation C. In the process, A and B terminate.

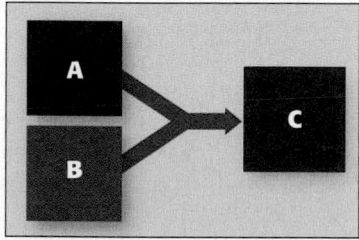

Share Exchange In a share exchange, some or all of the shares of one corporation are exchanged for some or all of the shares of another corporation, but both corporations continue to exist. Share exchanges are often used to create *holding companies* (companies that own part or all of other companies' stock).

B's property and assets without the necessity of a formal transfer. Additionally, A becomes liable for all of B's debts and obligations.[9] Finally, A's articles of incorporation are deemed amended to include any changes that are stated in the *articles of merger* (a document setting forth the terms and conditions of the merger that is filed with the secretary of state).

In a merger, the surviving corporation inherits the disappearing corporation's preexisting legal rights and obligations. If the disappearing corporation had a right of action against a third party under tort or property law, for example, the surviving corporation can bring a suit after the merger to recover the disappearing corporation's damages.

Consolidation

In a **consolidation,** two or more corporations combine in such a way that each corporation ceases to exist and a new one emerges. **EXAMPLE 29.7** Corporation A and Corporation B consolidate to form an entirely new organization, Corporation C. In the process, A and B both terminate, and C comes into existence as an entirely new entity. ● Exhibit 29–6 graphically illustrates this process.

The results of a consolidation are essentially the same as the results of a merger. C is recognized as a new corporation and a single entity; A and B cease to exist. C inherits all of the rights, privileges, and powers previously held by A and B. Title to any property and assets owned by A and B passes to C without a formal transfer. C assumes liability for all of the debts and obligations owed by A and B. The *articles of consolidation,* which state the terms of the consolidation, take the place of A's and B's original corporate articles and are thereafter regarded as C's corporate articles.

When a merger or consolidation takes place, the surviving corporation or newly formed corporation will issue shares or pay some fair consideration to the shareholders of the corporation or corporations that cease to exist. True consolidations have become less common among for-profit corporations because it is often advantageous for one of the firms to survive. In contrast, nonprofit corporations and associations may prefer consolidation because it suggests a new beginning in which neither of the two initial entities is dominant.

Share Exchange

In a **share exchange,** some or all of the shares of one corporation are exchanged for some or all of the shares of another corporation, but both of these companies continue to exist. Share exchanges are often used to create holding companies (discussed earlier in this chapter). For example, UAL Corporation is a large holding company that owns United Airlines. If one corporation owns *all* of the shares of another corporation, it is referred to as the *parent corporation,* and the wholly owned company is the *subsidiary corporation.*

Merger, Consolidation, or Share Exchange Procedures

All states have statutes authorizing mergers, consolidations, and share exchanges for domestic (in-state) and foreign (out-of-state) corporations. The procedures vary somewhat among jurisdictions. In some states, a consolidation resulting in an entirely new corporation simply follows the initial incorporation procedures discussed earlier in this chapter, whereas other business combinations must follow the procedures outlined below.

The RMBCA sets forth the following basic requirements [RMBCA 11.01–11.07]:

1. The board of directors of *each* corporation involved must approve the merger or consolidation plan.
2. The plan must specify any terms and conditions of the merger. It also must state how the value of the shares of each merging corporation will be determined and how they

9. See, for example, *Rodriguez v. Tech Credit Union Corp.,* 824 N.E.2d 442 (Ind.App. 2005).

The chairman of Chrysler discusses that company's merger with Fiat in 2009.

will be converted into shares or other securities, cash, property, or other interests in another corporation.

3. The majority of the shareholders of *each* corporation must vote to approve the plan at a shareholders' meeting. If any class of stock is entitled to vote as a separate group, the majority of each separate voting group must approve the plan. Although RMBCA 11.04(e) requires only a simple majority of the shareholders entitled to vote once a quorum is present, frequently a corporation's articles of incorporation or bylaws require greater than a majority approval (Chapter 30 will discuss *quorums* and other voting requirements). In addition, some state statutes require the approval of two-thirds of the outstanding shares of voting stock, and others require a four-fifths vote.

4. Once approved by the directors and the shareholders of both corporations, the surviving corporation files the plan (articles of merger, consolidation, or share exchange) with the appropriate official, usually the secretary of state.

5. When state formalities are satisfied, the state issues a certificate of merger to the surviving corporation or a certificate of consolidation to the newly consolidated corporation.

Short-Form Mergers

RMBCA 11.04 provides a simplified procedure for the merger of a substantially owned subsidiary corporation into its parent corporation. Under these provisions, a **short-form merger**—also referred to as a *parent-subsidiary merger*—can be accomplished *without* the approval of the shareholders of either corporation. The short-form merger can be used only when the parent corporation owns at least 90 percent of the outstanding shares of each class of stock of the subsidiary corporation. Once the board of directors of the parent corporation approves the plan, it is filed with the state, and copies are sent to each shareholder of record in the subsidiary corporation.

Shareholder Approval

As mentioned, except in a short-form merger, the shareholders of both corporations must approve a merger or consolidation plan. Shareholders invest in a corporation with the expectation that the board of directors will manage the enterprise and make decisions on ordinary business matters. For *extraordinary* matters, normally both the board of directors and the shareholders must approve of the transaction.

Mergers and other combinations are extraordinary business matters, meaning that the board of directors must normally obtain the shareholders' approval and provide appraisal rights (discussed next). Amendments to the articles of incorporation and the dissolution of the corporation also generally require shareholder approval. Sometimes, a transaction can be structured in such a way that shareholder approval is not required, but if the shareholders challenge the transaction, a court might use its equity powers to require shareholder approval. For this reason, the board of directors may request shareholder approval even when it might not be legally required.

Appraisal Rights

What if a shareholder disapproves of a merger or a consolidation but is outvoted by the other shareholders? The law recognizes that a dissenting shareholder should not be forced to become an unwilling shareholder in a corporation that is new or different from the one in which the shareholder originally invested. Dissenting shareholders therefore are given a statutory right to be paid the fair value of the shares they held on the date of the merger or consolidation. This right is referred to as the shareholder's **appraisal right**. So long as the

Short-Form (Parent-Subsidiary) Merger A merger of companies in which one company (the parent corporation) owns at least 90 percent of the outstanding shares of each class of stock of the other corporation (the subsidiary corporation). The merger can be accomplished without the approval of the shareholders of either corporation.

REMEMBER   State statutes, articles of incorporation, and corporate bylaws can require the approval of more than a majority of shares for some extraordinary matters.

Appraisal Right   The right of a dissenting shareholder, who objects to an extraordinary transaction of the corporation (such as a merger or a consolidation), to have his or her shares appraised and to be paid the fair value of those shares by the corporation.

transaction does not involve fraud or other illegal conduct, appraisal rights are the exclusive remedy for a shareholder who is dissatisfied with the price received for the stock.

Appraisal rights normally extend to regular mergers, consolidations, share exchanges, short-form mergers, and sales of substantially all of the corporate assets not in the ordinary course of business. Such rights can be particularly important in a short-form merger because the minority stockholders do not receive advance notice of the merger, the directors do not consider or approve it, and there is no vote. Appraisal rights are often the only recourse available to shareholders who object to parent-subsidiary mergers.

Each state establishes the procedures for asserting appraisal rights in that jurisdiction. Shareholders may lose their appraisal rights if they do not adhere precisely to the procedures prescribed by statute. When they lose the right to an appraisal, dissenting shareholders must go along with the transaction despite their objections.

Purchase of Assets

When a corporation acquires all or substantially all of the assets of another corporation by direct purchase, the purchasing, or *acquiring,* corporation simply extends its ownership and control over more physical assets. Because no change in the legal entity occurs, the acquiring corporation is not required to obtain shareholder approval for the purchase.[10] The U.S. Department of Justice and the Federal Trade Commission, however, have issued guidelines that significantly constrain and often prohibit mergers that could result from a purchase of assets, including takeover bids. (These guidelines are part of the federal antitrust laws that will be discussed in Chapter 32.)

Note that the corporation that is *selling* all of its assets is substantially changing its business position and perhaps its ability to carry out its corporate purposes. For that reason, the corporation whose assets are being sold must obtain the approval of both the board of directors and the shareholders. In most states and under RMBCA 13.02, a dissenting shareholder of the selling corporation can demand appraisal rights.

Potential Liability in Purchases of Assets

Generally, a corporation that purchases the assets of another corporation is not responsible for the liabilities of the selling corporation. Exceptions to this rule are made in certain circumstances, however. In any of the following situations, the acquiring corporation will be held to have assumed *both* the assets and the liabilities of the selling corporation.

1. When the purchasing corporation impliedly or expressly assumes the seller's liabilities.
2. When the sale transaction is actually a merger or consolidation of the two companies.
3. When the purchaser continues the seller's business and retains the same personnel (same shareholders, directors, and officers).
4. When the sale is fraudulently executed to escape liability.

Purchase of Stock and Tender Offers

An alternative to the purchase of another corporation's assets is the purchase of a substantial number of the voting shares of its stock. This enables the acquiring corporation to control the **target corporation** (the corporation being acquired). The process of acquiring control over a corporation in this way is commonly referred to as a corporate **takeover.**

"There are two times in a man's life when he should not speculate: when he can't afford it and when he can."

Samuel Clemens (Mark Twain),
1835–1919
(American author and humorist)

RECALL In a merger or consolidation, the surviving corporation inherits the disappearing corporation's rights *and* obligations.

Target Corporation The corporation to be acquired in a corporate takeover; a corporation whose shareholders receive a tender offer.

Takeover The acquisition of control over a corporation through the purchase of a substantial number of the voting shares of the corporation.

---

10. Shareholder approval may be required in a few situations. If the acquiring corporation plans to pay for the assets with its own corporate stock and not enough authorized unissued shares are available, the shareholders must vote to approve the issuance of additional shares by amendment of the corporate articles. Also, if the acquiring corporation is a company whose stock is traded on a national stock exchange and it will be issuing a significant number (at least 20 percent) of its outstanding shares, shareholder approval can be required.

Tender Offer An offer made by one company directly to the shareholders of another (target) company to purchase their shares of stock; sometimes referred to as a *takeover bid.*

"In the takeover business, if you want a friend, you buy a dog."

Carl Icahn, 1936–present
(American financier)

The acquiring corporation deals directly with the target company's shareholders in seeking to purchase the shares they hold. It does this by making a **tender offer** to all of the shareholders of the target corporation. The tender offer can be conditioned on receiving a specified number of shares by a certain date. The price offered is generally higher than the market price of the target corporation's stock prior to the announcement of the tender offer as a means of inducing shareholders to accept the offer. **EXAMPLE 29.8** In the 2009 merger of two Fortune 500 pharmaceutical companies, Pfizer, Inc., paid $68 billion to acquire its rival Wyeth. Wyeth shareholders reportedly received approximately $50.19 per share (part in cash and part in Pfizer stock), which amounted to a 15 percent premium over the market price of the stock. • Federal securities laws strictly control the terms, duration, and circumstances under which most tender offers are made. In addition, many states have passed antitakeover statutes.

Responses to Tender Offers

A firm may respond to a tender offer in numerous ways. Sometimes, a target firm's board of directors will see a tender offer as favorable and will recommend to the shareholders that they accept it. To resist a takeover, a target company can make a *self-tender,* which is an offer to acquire stock from its own shareholders and thereby retain corporate control.

Alternatively, a target corporation might resort to one of several other defensive tactics to resist a takeover (see Exhibit 29–7). In one commonly used tactic, known as a "poison pill," a target company gives its shareholders rights to purchase additional shares at low prices when there is a takeover attempt. The use of poison pills is an attempt to prevent takeovers by making a takeover prohibitively expensive.

 Termination

Dissolution The formal disbanding of a partnership or a corporation. Dissolution of a corporation can take place by (1) an act of the state, (2) agreement of the shareholders and the board of directors, (3) the expiration of a time period stated in the certificate of incorporation, or (4) court order.

The termination of a corporation's existence has two phases—dissolution and winding up. **Dissolution** is the legal death of the artificial "person" of the corporation. *Winding up* is the process by which corporate assets are liquidated, or converted into cash and distributed among creditors and shareholders.[11]

---

11. Some prefer to call this phase *liquidation,* but we use the term *winding up* to mean all acts needed to bring the legal and financial affairs of the business to an end, including liquidating the assets and distributing them among creditors and shareholders. See RMBCA 14.05.

• *Exhibit* **29–7 The Terminology of Takeover Defenses**

TERM	DEFINITION
Crown jewel	When threatened with a takeover, management makes the company less attractive to the raider by selling the company's most valuable asset (the "crown jewel") to a third party.
Golden parachute	When a takeover is successful, top management usually is changed. With this in mind, a company may establish special termination or retirement benefits that must be paid to top managers if they are "retired." In other words, a departing high-level manager's parachute will be "golden" when he or she is forced to "bail out" of the company.
Greenmail	To regain control, a target company may pay a higher-than-market price to repurchase the stock that the acquiring corporation bought. When a takeover is attempted through a gradual accumulation of target stock rather than a tender offer, the intent may be to get the target company to buy back the shares at a premium price—a concept similar to blackmail.
Pac-Man	Named after the Atari video game, this is an aggressive defense in which the target corporation attempts its own takeover of the acquiring corporation.
Poison pill	The target corporation issues to its stockholders rights to purchase additional shares at low prices when there is a takeover attempt. This makes the takeover undesirably or even prohibitively expensive for the acquiring corporation.
White knight	The target corporation solicits a merger with a third party, which then makes a better (often simply a higher) tender offer to the target's shareholders. The third party that "rescues" the target is the "white knight."

Voluntary Dissolution

Dissolution can be brought about voluntarily by the directors and the shareholders. State corporation statutes establish the procedures required to voluntarily dissolve a corporation. Basically, there are two possible methods: (1) by the shareholders' unanimous vote to initiate dissolution proceedings[12] or (2) by a proposal of the board of directors that is submitted to the shareholders at a shareholders' meeting.

When a corporation is dissolved voluntarily, the corporation must file *articles of dissolution* with the state and notify its creditors of the dissolution. The corporation must also establish a date (at least 120 days after the date of dissolution) by which all claims against the corporation must be received [RMBCA 14.06].

If a corporation is dissolved and its assets are liquidated without notice to a party who has a claim against the firm, shareholders of the former corporation can be held personally liable for the debt. **CASE EXAMPLE 29.9**   Christine Parent leased an automobile from Amity Autoworld, Ltd. Soon after that, Amity sold all of its automobile-franchising assets to another company named Atlantic. Parent made a written claim for monetary damages to Amity one month after the sale of its assets. Parent then filed a small claims action against Amity and obtained a $2,643 judgment, but she was unable to collect the amount because Amity had been sold to Atlantic. Parent knew that Amity's principal shareholder and chief executive officer, John Staluppi, Jr., was the son of Atlantic's principal shareholder, John Staluppi, Sr., so she filed a claim against Staluppi, Jr., personally. A state court ruled that because Amity was liquidated and dissolved without any notice to creditors, those creditors (including Parent) could hold Amity's principal shareholder, Staluppi, Jr., liable.[13] ●

Involuntary Dissolution

Because corporations are creatures of statute, the state can also dissolve a corporation in certain circumstances. The secretary of state or the state attorney general can bring an action to dissolve a corporation that has failed to pay its annual taxes or to submit required annual reports, for example. A state court can also dissolve a corporation that has engaged in *ultra vires* acts or committed fraud or misrepresentation to the state during incorporation.

Sometimes, a shareholder or a group of shareholders petitions a court for corporate dissolution. A court may dissolve a corporation if the controlling shareholders or directors have engaged in fraudulent, illegal, or oppressive conduct. **CASE EXAMPLE 29.10** Mt. Princeton Trout Club, Inc. (MPTC), was formed to own land in Colorado and provide fishing and other recreational benefits to its shareholders. The articles of incorporation prohibited MPTC from selling or leasing any of the property and assets of the corporation without the approval of a majority of the directors. Despite this provision, MPTC officers entered into leases and contracts to sell corporate property without even notifying the directors. When a shareholder, Sam Colt, petitioned for dissolution, the court dissolved MPTC based on a finding that its officers had engaged in illegal, oppressive, and fraudulent conduct.[14] ● Shareholders may also petition a court for dissolution when the board of directors is deadlocked and the affairs of the corporation can no longer be conducted because of the deadlock.[15]

---

12. Only some states allow shareholders to initiate corporate dissolution. See, for example, Delaware Code Section 275(c).

13. *Parent v. Amity Autoworld, Ltd.*, 15 Misc.3d 633, 832 N.Y.S.2d 775 (2007).

14. *Colt v. Mt. Princeton Trout Club, Inc.*, 78 P.3d 1115 (Colo.App. 2003).

15. See, for example, *Sartori v. S&S Trucking, Inc.*, 2006 MT 164, 322 Mont. 503, 139 P.3d 806 (2006).

Winding Up

When dissolution takes place by voluntary action, the members of the board of directors act as trustees of the corporate assets. As trustees, they are responsible for winding up the affairs of the corporation for the benefit of corporate creditors and shareholders. This makes the board members personally liable for any breach of their fiduciary trustee duties.

When the dissolution is involuntary—or if board members do not wish to act as trustees of the assets—the court will appoint a **receiver** to wind up the corporate affairs and liquidate corporate assets. Courts may also appoint a receiver when shareholders or creditors can show that the board of directors should not be permitted to act as trustees of the corporate assets.

Receiver In a corporate dissolution, a court-appointed person who winds up corporate affairs and liquidates corporate assets.

Reviewing . . . Corporate Formation, Merger, and Termination

Mario Bonsetti and Rico Sanchez incorporated Gnarly Vulcan Gear, Inc. (GVG), to manufacture windsurfing equipment. Bonsetti owned 60 percent of the corporation's stock, and Sanchez owned 40 percent; both men served on the board of directors. Hula Boards, Inc., owned solely by Mai Jin Li, made a public offer to Bonsetti and Sanchez to buy GVG stock. Hula offered 30 percent more than the market price per share for the GVG stock, and Bonsetti and Sanchez each sold 20 percent of their stock to Hula. Jin Li became the third member of the GVG board of directors. An irreconcilable dispute soon arose between Bonsetti and Sanchez over design modifications of their popular Baked Chameleon board. Despite Bonsetti's dissent, Sanchez and Jin Li voted to merge GVG with Hula Boards under the latter name, Gnarly Vulcan Gear was dissolved, and production of the Baked Chameleon ceased. Using the information presented in the chapter, answer the following questions.

1. What rights does Bonsetti have (in most states) as a minority shareholder dissenting to the merger of GVG and Hula Boards?
2. Could the parties have used a short-form merger procedure in this situation? Why or why not?
3. What is the term used for Hula's offer to purchase GVG stock?
4. Suppose that after the merger, a person who was injured on the Baked Chameleon board sued Hula (the surviving corporation). Can Hula be held liable for the injury? Why or why not?

Linking the Law *to Finance*
Sources of Funds

This chapter explained corporate formation and corporate financing. When you complete your education, you may work in corporate finance directly, or you may become involved in starting a sole proprietorship. When the start-up is up and running and sales revenues are sufficient to pay for operating expenses, you may consider incorporating the business and then seeking financing for expansion. As you learned in your finance courses, a finance manager helps directors and upper management decide on the sources of additional funding for ongoing expenses or for growth.

Difficulties Facing Finance Managers in Times of Crisis

During the recent economic crisis, many businesses experienced severe financial pressures because their traditional sources of financing dried up. In particular, commercial banks abruptly cut off lines of credit even

for corporations that had solid balance sheets and stable profits. A number of corporations that were preparing to sell shares in an initial public offering (IPO) were told that there was no market for new shares, and the IPOs were canceled. Some large corporations that were considering secondary issues of additional stock found that there were no buyers for those shares either.

During the economic crisis, some finance managers had to deal with the bankruptcy of their companies. Other finance managers of troubled firms sought mergers with stronger competitors, even though those mergers meant that the value of the shares held by the current owners would be severely reduced. Some finance managers turned to the remaining players in the private equity market. The managers offered large stakes in their companies at attractive prices—anything to obtain the financing needed to avoid going under.

Sources of Funds in More Normal Times

Fortunately, during normal business periods, finance managers have a variety of options for financing. These include obtaining financing from a bank and issuing bonds or stock. When there is no financial crisis, commercial banks are ready to lend to businesses. Successful corporations typically obtain lines of credit that can be drawn down at any time and then repaid when their cash flows warrant.

In most situations, though, issuing bonds will be a less expensive option than depending on a line of credit at a commercial bank. Corporate finance managers will then have to consider the trade-off between issuing more debt or selling more common shares (equity). Although the sale of common stock does not obligate the corporation to make fixed interest payments every year, as bonds do, increasing the amount of common stock dilutes the current shareholders.

Another possibility is to sell preferred stock, which, as you learned in this chapter, has preferences. Holders of preferred stock have priority over holders of common stock with respect to dividends and to payment on the dissolution of the corporation.

Self-Financing

Sometimes, finance managers decide that the best type of financing is self-financing. That is to say, the corporation retains earnings and invests them in order to grow. Do not get the impression, though, that the use of retained earnings is costless. There is an *opportunity cost,* which, as you learned in your economics classes, is what the company could have earned if it had invested those retained earnings in, say, U.S. Treasury bonds. Alternatively, the retained earnings could be distributed to the shareholders as dividends.

FOR CRITICAL ANALYSIS

What is the benefit of paying dividends to shareholders rather than using retained earnings to expand?

 ## Key Terms

alien corporation 727	dissolution 744	S corporation 730
appraisal right 742	dividend 724	securities 738
articles of incorporation 732	domestic corporation 727	share exchange 741
bond 738	foreign corporation 727	short-form (parent-subsidiary) merger 742
bond indenture 738	holding company 724	stock 738
bylaws 732	merger 740	takeover 743
close corporation 728	piercing the corporate veil 736	target corporation 743
commingle 737	preferred stock 739	tender offer 744
common stock 738	private equity capital 740	*ultra vires* 734
consolidation 741	receiver 746	venture capital 740
corporation 723	retained earnings 724	

 ## Chapter Summary: Corporate Formation, Merger, and Termination

Corporate Nature and Classification (See pages 723–730.)	A corporation is a legal entity distinct from its owners. Formal statutory requirements, which vary somewhat from state to state, must be followed in forming a corporation. 1. *Corporate parties*—The shareholders own the corporation. They elect a board of directors to govern the corporation. The board of directors hires corporate officers and other employees to run the daily business of the firm. 2. *Corporate taxation*—The corporation pays income tax on net profits; shareholders pay income tax on the disbursed dividends that they receive from the corporation (double-taxation feature). 3. *Torts and criminal acts*—The corporation is liable for the torts committed by its agents or officers within the course and scope of their employment (under the doctrine of *respondeat superior*). In some circumstances, a corporation can be held liable (and be fined) for the criminal acts of its agents and employees. In certain situations, corporate officers may be held personally liable for corporate crimes.

Continued

Chapter Summary: Corporate Formation, Merger, and Termination—Continued

Corporate Nature and Classification—Continued	4. *Domestic, foreign, and alien corporations*—A corporation is referred to as a *domestic corporation* within its home state (the state in which it incorporates). A corporation is referred to as a *foreign corporation* by any state that is not its home state. A corporation is referred to as an *alien corporation* if it originates in another country but does business in the United States.
	5. *Public and private corporations*—A public corporation is one formed by a government (for example, cities, towns, and public projects). A private corporation is one formed wholly or in part for private benefit. Most corporations are private corporations.
	6. *Nonprofit corporations*—Corporations formed without a profit-making purpose (for example, charitable, educational, and religious organizations and hospitals).
	7. *Close corporations*—Corporations owned by a family or a relatively small number of individuals. Transfer of shares is usually restricted, and the corporation cannot make a public offering of its securities.
	8. *S corporations*—Small domestic corporations (with no more than one hundred shareholders) that, under Subchapter S of the Internal Revenue Code, are given special tax treatment. These corporations allow shareholders to enjoy the limited legal liability of the corporate form but avoid its double-taxation feature.
	9. *Professional corporations*—Corporations formed by professionals (for example, physicians and lawyers) to obtain the benefits of incorporation (such as limited liability). In most situations, the professional corporation is treated like other corporations, but sometimes the courts will disregard the corporate form and treat the shareholders as partners.
Corporate Formation and Powers (See pages 730–734.)	1. *Promotional activities*—Preliminary promotional activities are rarely if ever taken today. A person who enters contracts with investors and others on behalf of the future corporation is personally liable on all preincorporation contracts. Liability remains until the corporation is formed and assumes the contract by novation.
	2. *Incorporation procedures*—Exact procedures for incorporation differ among states, but the basic steps are as follows: (a) select a state of incorporation, (b) secure the corporate name by confirming its availability, (c) prepare the articles of incorporation, and (d) file the articles of incorporation with the secretary of state accompanied by payment of the specified fees.
	3. *Articles of incorporation*—The articles of incorporation must include the corporate name, the number of shares of stock the corporation is authorized to issue, the registered office and agent, and the names and addresses of the incorporators. The articles may (but are not required to) include additional information about the corporation's nature and purpose, duration, and internal organization. The state's filing of the articles of incorporation authorizes the corporation to conduct business.
	4. *The first organizational meeting*—A meeting is held after incorporation. The usual purpose of this meeting is to adopt the bylaws, or internal rules of the corporation, but other business, such as election of the board of directors may also take place.
	5. *Express powers*—The express powers of a corporation are granted by the following laws and documents (listed according to their priority): federal constitution, state constitutions, state statutes, articles of incorporation, bylaws, and resolutions of the board of directors.
	6. *Implied powers*—Barring express constitutional, statutory, or other prohibitions, the corporation has the implied power to do all acts reasonably appropriate and necessary to accomplish its corporate purposes.
	7. *Ultra vires doctrine*—Any act of a corporation that is beyond its express or implied powers to undertake is an *ultra vires* act and may lead to a lawsuit by the shareholders, corporation, or state attorney general to enjoin or recover damages for the *ultra vires* acts.
Defects in Formation and Corporate Status (See pages 735–737.)	1. *De jure or de facto corporation*—If a corporation has been improperly incorporated, the courts will sometimes impute corporate status to the firm by holding that it is a *de jure* corporation (cannot be challenged by the state or third persons) or a *de facto* corporation (can be challenged by the state but not by third persons).
	2. *Corporation by estoppel*—If a firm is neither a *de jure* nor a *de facto* corporation but represents itself to be a corporation and is sued as such by a third party, it may be held to be a corporation by estoppel.
	3. *Piercing the corporate veil*—To avoid injustice, courts may "pierce the corporate veil" and hold a shareholder or shareholders personally liable for a judgment against the corporation. This usually occurs only when the corporation was established to circumvent the law, when the corporate form is used for an illegitimate or fraudulent purpose, or when the controlling shareholder commingles his or her own interests with those of the corporation to such an extent that the corporation no longer has a separate identity.

Chapter Summary: Corporate Formation, Merger, and Termination—Continued

Corporate Financing (See pages 738–740.)	1. *Bonds*—Corporate bonds are securities representing *corporate debt*—funds borrowed by a corporation. See Exhibit 29–2 on page 738 for a description of the various types of corporate bonds. 2. *Stocks*—Stocks are equity securities issued by a corporation that represent the purchase of ownership in the business firm. Exhibit 29–3 on page 739 describes how stocks differ from bonds, and Exhibit 29–4 on page 740 describes the various types of stocks issued by corporations, including the two main types—common stock and preferred stock.

Mergers and Acquisitions (See pages 740–744.)	1. *Merger*—The legal combination of two or more corporations, with the result that the surviving corporation acquires all the assets and obligations of the other corporation, which then ceases to exist.
	2. *Consolidation*—The legal combination of two or more corporations, with the result that each corporation ceases to exist and a new one emerges. The new corporation assumes all the assets and obligations of the former corporations.
	3. *Share exchange*—Some or all of the shares of one corporation are exchanged for some or all of the shares of another corporation, but both corporations continue to exist.
	4. *Procedure*—Determined by state statutes. The basic requirements are listed on pages 741 and 742.
	5. *Short-form (parent-subsidiary) merger*—Possible when the parent corporation owns at least 90 percent of the outstanding shares of each class of stock of the subsidiary corporation. Shareholder approval is not required. The merger need be approved only by the board of directors of the parent corporation.
	6. *Appraisal rights*—Rights of dissenting shareholders (given by state statute) to receive the *fair value* for their shares when a merger or consolidation takes place.
	7. *Purchase of assets*—A purchase of assets occurs when one corporation acquires all or substantially all of the assets of another corporation.
	  a. The acquiring (purchasing) corporation is not required to obtain shareholder approval; the corporation is merely increasing its assets, and no fundamental business change occurs.
	  b. The acquired (purchased) corporation is required to obtain the approval of both its directors and its shareholders for the sale of its assets, because the sale will substantially change the corporation's business position.
	8. *Purchase of stock*—A purchase of stock occurs when one corporation acquires a substantial number of the voting shares of the stock of another (target) corporation.
	9. *Tender offer*—A public offer to all shareholders of the target corporation to purchase its stock at a price that generally is higher than the market price of the target stock prior to the announcement of the tender offer. Federal and state securities laws strictly control the terms, duration, and circumstances under which most tender offers are made.
	10. *Target responses*—Target corporations may respond to takeover bids in various ways, including self-tender (the target firm's offer to acquire its own shareholders' stock) and the strategies listed in Exhibit 29–7 on page 744.

Termination (See pages 744–746.)	The termination of a corporation involves the following two phases: 1. *Dissolution*—The legal death of the artificial "person" of the corporation. Dissolution can be brought about voluntarily by the directors and shareholders or involuntarily by the state or through a court order. 2. *Winding up (liquidation)*—The process by which corporate assets are converted into cash and distributed to creditors and shareholders according to specified rules of preference. May be supervised by members of the board of directors (when dissolution is voluntary) or by a receiver appointed by the court to wind up corporate affairs.

 ExamPrep

ISSUE SPOTTERS

1 Name Brand, Inc., is a small business. Twelve members of a single family own all of its stock. Ordinarily, corporate income is taxed at the corporate and shareholder levels. How can Name Brand avoid this double taxation of income?

2 ABC Corporation combines with DEF, Inc. ABC ceases to exist. DEF is the surviving firm. Global Corporation and Hometown Company combine. Afterwards, Global and Hometown cease to exist. GH, Inc., a new firm, functions in their place. Which of these combinations is a merger and which is a consolidation?

BEFORE THE TEST

Check your answers to the Issue Spotters, and at the same time, take the interactive quiz for this chapter. Go to **www.cengage.com/blaw/blt** and click on "Chapter 29." First, click on "Answers to Issue Spotters" to check your answers. Next, click on "Interactive Quiz" to assess your mastery of the concepts in this chapter. Then click on "Flashcards" to review this chapter's Key Term definitions.

▶ ## For Review

Answers for the even-numbered questions in this For Review *section can be found on this text's accompanying Web site at* **www.cengage.com/blaw/blt**. *Select "Chapter 29" and click on "For Review."*

1 What steps are involved in bringing a corporation into existence?

2 What is the difference between a *de jure* corporation and a *de facto* corporation?

3 In what circumstances might a court disregard the corporate entity ("pierce the corporate veil") and hold the shareholders personally liable?

4 What are the basic differences between a merger, a consolidation, and a share exchange?

5 What are the two ways in which a corporation can be voluntarily dissolved?

▶ ## Hypothetical Scenarios and Case Problems

29–1 Corporate Status. Three brothers inherited a small paper-supply business from their father, who had operated the business as a sole proprietorship. The brothers decided to incorporate under the name Gomez Corp. and retained an attorney to draw up the necessary documents. The attorney drew up the papers and had the brothers sign them, but she neglected to file the articles of incorporation with the secretary of state's office. The brothers assumed that all necessary legal work had been completed, so they proceeded to do business as Gomez Corp. One day, a Gomez Corp. employee, while making a delivery to a customer, negligently ran a red light and caused an accident. Baxter, the driver of the other vehicle, was injured and sued Gomez Corp. for damages. Baxter then learned that no state authorization had ever been issued to Gomez Corp., so he sued each of the brothers personally for damages. Can the brothers avoid personal liability for the tort of their employee? Explain.

29–2 **Hypothetical Question with Sample Answer** Jolson is the chair of the board of directors of Artel, Inc., and Douglas is the chair of the board of directors of Fox Express, Inc. Artel is a manufacturing corporation, and Fox Express is a transportation corporation. Jolson and Douglas meet to consider the possibility of combining their corporations and activities into a single corporate entity. They consider two alternative courses of action: Artel could acquire all of the stock and assets of Fox Express, or the corporations could combine to form a new corporation, called A&F Enterprises, Inc. Both Jolson and Douglas are concerned about the necessity of a formal transfer of property, liability for existing debts, and the need to amend the articles of incorporation. Discuss what the two proposed combinations are called and the legal effect each has on the transfer of property, the liabilities of the

combined corporations, and the need to amend the articles of incorporation.

—For a sample answer to Question 29–2, go to Appendix E at the end of this text.

29–3 Corporate Powers. Kora Nayenga and two business associates formed a corporation called Nayenga Corp. for the purpose of selling computer services. Kora, who owned 50 percent of the corporate shares, served as the corporation's president. Kora wished to obtain a personal loan from his bank for $250,000, but the bank required the note to be cosigned by a third party. Kora cosigned the note in the name of the corporation. Later, Kora defaulted on the note, and the bank sued the corporation for payment. The corporation asserted, as a defense, that Kora had exceeded his authority when he cosigned the note. Had he? Explain.

29–4 **Case Problem with Sample Answer** Thomas Persson and Jon Nokes founded Smart Inventions, Inc., in 1991 to market household consumer products. The success of their first product, the Smart Mop, continued with later products, which were sold through infomercials and other means. Persson and Nokes were the firm's officers and equal shareholders, with Persson responsible for product development and Nokes operating the day-to-day activities. By 1998, they had become dissatisfied with each other's efforts. Nokes represented the firm as financially "dying," "in a grim state, . . . worse than ever," and offered to buy all of Persson's shares for $1.6 million. Persson accepted. On the day that they signed the agreement to transfer the shares, Smart Inventions began marketing a new product—the Tap Light. It was an instant success, generating millions of dollars in revenues. In negotiating with Persson, Nokes had intentionally kept the Tap Light a secret. Persson filed a suit in a California state court against

Smart Inventions and others, asserting fraud and other claims. Under what principle might Smart Inventions be liable for Nokes's fraud? Is Smart Inventions liable in this case? Explain. [*Persson v. Smart Inventions, Inc.,* 125 Cal.App.4th 1141, 23 Cal.Rptr.3d 335 (2 Dist. 2005)]

—After you have answered Problem 29–4, compare your answer with the sample answer given on the Web site that accompanies this text. Go to www.cengage.com/blaw/blt, select "Chapter 29," and click on "Case Problem with Sample Answer."

29–5 Dissolution. Clara Mahaffey operated Mahaffey's Auto Salvage, Inc., in Dayton, Ohio, as a sole proprietorship. In 1993, Kenneth Stumpff and Mahaffey's son, Richard Harris, joined the firm. Stumpff ran the wrecker and bought the vehicles for salvage. Harris handled the day-to-day operations and the bookkeeping. They became the company's equal 50 percent shareholders on Mahaffey's death in 2002. Harris, who inherited the land on which the firm was located, increased the rent to $1,500 per month. Within two years of Mahaffey's death, and without consulting Stumpff, Harris raised the rent to $2,500. Stumpff's wife died, and he took a leave of absence, during which the company paid him $2,500 a month and provided health insurance. After two years, Harris stopped the payments, discontinued the health benefits, and fired Stumpff, threatening to call the police if he came on the premises. Stumpff withdrew $16,000 from the firm's account, leaving a balance of $113. Harris offered to buy Stumpff's interest in the business, but Stumpff refused and filed a suit in an Ohio state court against Harris. A state statute permits the dissolution of a corporation if the owners are deadlocked in its management. Should the court order the dissolution of Mahaffey's? Why or why not? [*Stumpff v. Harris,* __ N.E.2d __ (Ohio App.2 Dist. 2006)]

29–6 Improper Incorporation. Denise Rubenstein and Christopher Mayor agreed to form Bayshore Sunrise Corp. (BSC) in New York to rent certain premises and operate a laundromat. BSC entered into a twenty-year commercial lease with Bay Shore Property Trust on April 15, 1999. Mayor signed the lease as the president of BSC. The next day—April 16—BSC's certificate of incorporation was filed with New York's secretary of state. Three years later, BSC defaulted on the lease, which resulted in its termination. Rubenstein and BSC filed a suit in a New York state court against Mayor, his brother-in-law Thomas Castellano, and Planet Laundry, Inc., claiming wrongful interference with a contractual relationship. The plaintiffs alleged that Mayor and Castellano conspired to squeeze Rubenstein out of BSC and arranged the default on the lease so that Mayor and Castellano could form and operate their own business, Planet Laundry, at the same address. The defendants argued that they could not be liable on the plaintiffs' claim because there had never been an enforceable lease—BSC lacked the capacity to enter into contracts on April 15. What theory might Rubenstein and BSC assert to refute this argument? Discuss. [*Rubenstein v. Mayor,* 41 A.D.3d 826, 839 N.Y.S.2d 170 (2 Dept. 2007)]

29–7 Involuntary Dissolution. Charles Brooks began working as an independent supplier for Georgia-Pacific, LLC, when the paper products manufacturer acquired a mill in Crossett, Arkansas. Brooks soon organized Charles Brooks Co. in corporate form. Each of the parties' contracts provided, "there is absolutely no guarantee as to the amount of work to be performed." Charles Brooks Co. borrowed funds to buy new equipment. When Georgia-Pacific reduced the quantity of timber that it bought from the supplier, the firm was unable to pay its loans. In 2002, some of the new equipment was returned to the seller. The rest was sold, but the proceeds were not enough to eliminate the debt. The same year, the Arkansas secretary of state revoked Charles Brooks Co.'s corporate status for nonpayment of franchise taxes. In 2006, Charles Brooks Co. filed a suit in a federal district court against Georgia-Pacific, alleging breach of contract. Can the plaintiff maintain this suit? Explain. [*Charles Brooks Co. v. Georgia-Pacific, LLC,* 552 F.3d 718 (8th Cir. 2009)]

29–8 **A Question of Ethics** *Mike Lyons incorporated Lyons Concrete, Inc., in Montana, but did not file its first annual report, so the state involuntarily dissolved the firm in 1996. Unaware of the dissolution, Lyons continued to do business as Lyons Concrete. In 2003, he signed a written contract with William Weimar to form and pour a certain amount of concrete on Weimar's property in Lake County for $19,810. Weimar was in a rush to complete the entire project, and he and Lyons orally agreed to additional work on a time-and-materials basis. When scheduling conflicts arose, Weimar had his own employees set some of the forms, which proved deficient. Weimar also directed Lyons to pour concrete in the rain, which undercut its quality. Mid-project, Lyons submitted an invoice for $14,389, which Weimar paid. After the work was complete, Lyons invoiced Weimar for $25,731, but he refused to pay, claiming that the $14,389 covered everything. To recover the unpaid amount, Lyons filed a mechanic's lien as "Mike Lyons d/b/a Lyons Concrete, Inc." against Weimar's property. Weimar filed a suit in a Montana state court to strike the lien, which Lyons filed a counterclaim to reassert. [Weimar v. Lyons, 338 Mont. 242, 164 P.3d 922 (2007)]*

1 Before the trial, Weimar asked for a change of venue on the ground that a sign on the courthouse lawn advertised "Lyons Concrete." How might the sign affect a trial on the parties' dispute? Should the court grant this request?

2 Weimar asked the court to dismiss the counterclaim on the ground that the state had dissolved Lyons Concrete in 1996. Lyons immediately filed new articles of incorporation for "Lyons Concrete, Inc." Under what doctrine might the court rule that Weimar could not deny the existence of Lyons Concrete? What ethical values underlie this doctrine? Should the court make this ruling?

3 At the trial, Weimar argued in part that there was no "fixed price" contract between the parties and that even if there was, the poor quality of the work, which required repairs, amounted to a breach, excusing Weimar's further performance. Should the court rule in Weimar's favor on this basis?

Critical Thinking and Writing Assignments

29–9 Critical Legal Thinking. If you had started a business, under what circumstances would you be willing to give up a substantial percentage of its ownership to obtain venture capital financing?

29–10 **Video Question** Go to this text's Web site at **www.cengage.com/blaw/blt** and select "Chapter 29." Click on "Video Questions" and view the video titled *Corporation or LLC: Which Is Better?* Then answer the following questions.

1 Compare the liability that Anna and Caleb would be exposed to as shareholders/owners of a corporation versus as members of a limited liability company (LLC).

2 How does the taxation of corporations different from that of LLCs?

3 Given that Anna and Caleb conduct their business (Wizard Internet) over the Internet, can you think of any drawbacks to forming an LLC?

4 If you were in the position of Anna and Caleb, would you choose to create a corporation or an LLC? Why?

Practical Internet Exercises

Go to this text's Web site at **www.cengage.com/blaw/blt**, select "Chapter 29," and click on "Practical Internet Exercises." There you will find the following Internet research exercises that you can perform to learn more about the topics covered in this chapter.

Practical Internet Exercise 29–1: LEGAL PERSPECTIVE—**Mergers**
Practical Internet Exercise 29–2: MANAGEMENT PERSPECTIVE—**Online Incorporation**

Chapter 30

Corporate Directors, Officers, and Shareholders

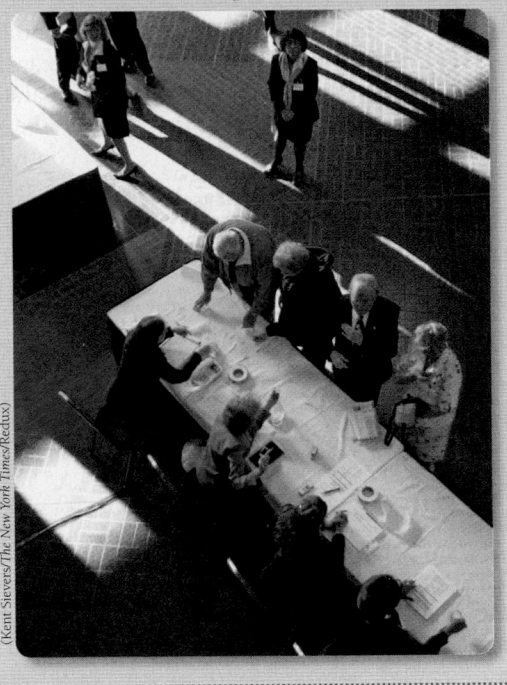

(Kent Sievers/*The New York Times*/Redux)

"They [corporations] cannot commit treason, nor be outlawed nor excommunicated, because they have no soul."

—Sir Edward Coke, 1552–1634
(English jurist and legal scholar)

Chapter Outline

- Roles of Directors and Officers
- Duties and Liabilities of Directors and Officers
- Role of Shareholders
- Rights of Shareholders
- Duties and Liabilities of Shareholders
- Major Business Forms Compared

Learning Objectives

After reading this chapter, you should be able to answer the following questions:

1. What are the duties of corporate directors and officers?

2. Directors are expected to use their best judgment in managing the corporation. What must directors do to avoid liability for honest mistakes of judgment and poor business decisions?

3. What is a voting proxy? What is cumulative voting?

4. If a group of shareholders perceives that the corporation has suffered a wrong and the directors refuse to take action, can the shareholders compel the directors to act? If so, how?

5. From what sources may dividends be paid legally? In what circumstances is a dividend illegal? What happens if a dividend is illegally paid?

When Sir Edward Coke observed, in the chapter-opening quotation, that a corporation has no "soul," he was referring to the fact that a corporation is not a "natural" person but a legal fiction. No one individual shareholder or director bears sole responsibility for the corporation and its actions. Rather, a corporation joins the efforts and resources of a large number of individuals for the purpose of producing greater returns than those persons could have obtained individually.

Sometimes, actions that benefit the corporation as a whole do not coincide with the separate interests of the individuals making up the corporation. In such situations, it is important to know the rights and duties of all participants in the corporate enterprise. This chapter focuses on the rights and duties of directors, officers, and shareholders and the ways in which conflicts among them are resolved.

▶ Roles of Directors and Officers

The board of directors is the ultimate authority in every corporation. Directors have responsibility for all policymaking decisions necessary to the management of all corporate affairs. The board selects and removes the corporate officers, determines the capital structure of the corporation, and declares dividends. Each director has one vote, and customarily the majority rules. The general areas of responsibility of the board of directors are shown in Exhibit 30–1 on the following page.

• *Exhibit* 30-1 Directors' Management Responsibilities

AUTHORIZE MAJOR CORPORATE POLICY DECISIONS	SELECT AND REMOVE CORPORATE OFFICERS AND OTHER MANAGERIAL EMPLOYEES, AND DETERMINE THEIR COMPENSATION	MAKE CORPORATE FINANCIAL DECISIONS
Examples: • Oversee major contract negotiations and management-labor negotiations. • Initiate negotiations on the sale or lease of corporate assets outside the regular course of business. • Decide whether to pursue new product lines or business opportunities.	*Examples:* • Search for and hire corporate executives and determine the elements of their compensation packages, including stock options. • Supervise managerial employees and make decisions regarding their termination.	*Examples:* • Make decisions regarding the issuance of authorized shares and bonds. • Decide when to declare dividends that are to be paid to shareholders.

Directors are sometimes inappropriately characterized as *agents* because they act on behalf of the corporation. No *individual* director, however, can act as an agent to bind the corporation; and as a group, directors collectively control the corporation in a way that no agent is able to control a principal. In addition, although directors occupy positions of trust and control over the corporation, they are not *trustees* because they do not hold title to property for the use and benefit of others.

There are few legal requirements concerning directors' qualifications. Only a handful of states impose minimum age and residency requirements. A director may be a shareholder, but this is not necessary (unless the articles of incorporation or bylaws require ownership).

Election of Directors

Subject to statutory limitations, the number of directors is set forth in the corporation's articles or bylaws. Historically, the minimum number of directors has been three, but today many states permit fewer. Normally, the incorporators appoint the first board of directors at the time the corporation is created. The initial board serves until the first annual shareholders' meeting. Subsequent directors are elected by a majority vote of the shareholders.

A director usually serves for a term of one year—from annual meeting to annual meeting. Most state statutes permit longer and staggered terms. A common practice is to elect one-third of the board members each year for a three-year term. In this way, there is greater management continuity.

ON THE WEB One of the best sources on the Web for information on publicly traded corporations, including their directors, is the EDGAR database of the Securities and Exchange Commission at www.sec.gov/edgar.shtml.

BE AWARE The articles of incorporation may provide that a director can be removed only for cause.

REMOVAL OF DIRECTORS   A director can be removed *for cause*—that is, for failing to perform a required duty—either as specified in the articles or bylaws or by shareholder action. The board of directors may also have the power to remove a director for cause, subject to shareholder review. In most states, a director cannot be removed without cause unless the shareholders have reserved the right to do so at the time of his or her election.

VACANCIES ON THE BOARD OF DIRECTORS   If a director dies or resigns or if a new position is created through amendment of the articles or bylaws, either the shareholders or the board itself can fill the vacant position, depending on state law or the provisions of the bylaws. Note, however, that even when an election appears to be authorized by the bylaws, a court can invalidate it if the directors were attempting to manipulate the election in order to reduce the shareholders' influence.

CASE EXAMPLE 30.1   The bylaws of Liquid Audio, a Delaware corporation, authorized a board of five directors. Two directors on the board were elected each year. Another company offered to buy all of Liquid Audio's stock, but the board of directors rejected this offer. An election was coming up, and the directors feared that the shareholders would elect new directors who would allow the sale. The directors, therefore, amended the bylaws to increase the number of directors to seven, thereby diminishing the shareholders' influence in the vote. The shareholders filed an action challenging the election. The Delaware Supreme Court ruled that the directors' action was illegal because they had attempted to diminish the shareholders' right to vote effectively in an election of directors.[1] •

Compensation of Directors

In the past, corporate directors rarely were compensated, but today they are often paid at least nominal sums and may receive more substantial compensation in large corporations because of the time, work, effort, and especially risk involved. Most states permit the corporate articles or bylaws to authorize compensation for directors. In fact, the Revised Model Business Corporation Act (RMBCA) states that unless the articles or bylaws provide otherwise, the directors may set their own compensation [RMBCA 8.11]. Directors also gain through indirect benefits, such as business contacts and prestige, and other rewards, such as stock options.

In many corporations, directors are also chief corporate officers (president or chief executive officer, for example) and receive compensation in their managerial positions. A director who is also an officer of the corporation is referred to as an **inside director,** whereas a director who does not hold a management position is an **outside director.** Typically, a corporation's board of directors includes both inside and outside directors.

Board of Directors' Meetings

The board of directors conducts business by holding formal meetings with recorded minutes. The dates of regular meetings are usually established in the articles or bylaws or by board resolution, and ordinarily no further notice is required. Special meetings can be called, with notice sent to all directors. Today, most states allow directors to participate in board of directors' meetings from remote locations via telephone or Web conferencing, provided that all the directors can simultaneously hear each other during the meeting [RMBCA 8.20].

Unless the articles of incorporation or bylaws specify a greater number, a majority of the board of directors normally constitutes a quorum [RMBCA 8.24]. (A **quorum** is the minimum number of members of a body of officials or other group that must be present in order for business to be validly transacted.) Some state statutes specifically allow corporations to set a quorum as less than a majority but not less than one-third of the directors.[2]

Once a quorum is present, the directors transact business and vote on issues affecting the corporation. Each director present at the meeting has one vote.[3] Ordinary matters generally require a simple majority vote; certain extraordinary issues may require a greater-than-majority vote.

Rights of Directors

A corporate director must have certain rights to function properly in that position and make informed policy decisions for the company. The *right to participation* means that directors are entitled to participate in all board of directors' meetings and have a right to be notified of these meetings. Because the dates of regular board meetings are usually specified in the bylaws, as noted earlier, no notice of these meetings is required. If special meetings are called, however, notice is required unless waived by the director.

Inside Director A person on the board of directors who is also an officer of the corporation.

Outside Director A person on the board of directors who does not hold a management position at the corporation.

ON THE WEB You can find definitions for terms used in corporate law, as well as court decisions and articles on corporate law topics, at www.law.com.

Quorum The number of members of a decision-making body that must be present before business may be transacted.

---

1. *MM Companies v. Liquid Audio, Inc.,* 813 A.2d 1118 (Del.Sup. 2003).
2. See, for example, Delaware Code Annotated Title 8, Section 141(b); and New York Business Corporation Law Section 707.
3. Except in Louisiana, which allows a director to authorize another person to cast a vote in his or her place under certain circumstances.

A director also has the *right of inspection,* which means that each director can access the corporation's books and records, facilities, and premises. Inspection rights are essential for directors to make informed decisions and to exercise the necessary supervision over corporate officers and employees. This right of inspection is almost absolute and cannot be restricted (by the articles, bylaws, or any act of the board).

When a director becomes involved in litigation by virtue of her or his position or actions, the director may also have a right to indemnification (reimbursement) for legal costs, fees, and damages incurred. Most states allow corporations to indemnify and purchase liability insurance for corporate directors [RMBCA 8.51].

Preventing Legal Disputes

If you serve as a corporate director or officer, be aware that you may at some point become involved in litigation as a result. To protect against personal liability, make sure that the corporate bylaws explicitly give directors and officers a right to indemnification (reimbursement) for any costs incurred, as well as for any judgments or settlements. Also, have the corporation purchase directors' and officers' liability insurance (D&O insurance). Having D&O insurance policies enables the corporation to avoid paying the substantial costs involved in defending a particular director or officer. Because most D&O policies have maximum coverage limits, make sure that the corporation is required to indemnify you in the event that the costs exceed the policy limits.

"I often feel like the director of a cemetery. I have a lot of people under me, but nobody listens!"

General James Gavin, 1907–1990
(U.S. Army lieutenant general)

Committees of the Board of Directors

When a board of directors has a large number of members and must deal with myriad complex business issues, meetings can become unwieldy. Therefore, the boards of large, publicly held corporations typically create committees, appoint directors to serve on individual committees, and delegate certain tasks to these committees. Committees focus on individual subjects and increase the efficiency of the board. The most common types of committees include the following:

1. *Executive committee.* The board members often elect an executive committee to handle interim management decisions between board meetings. The committee is limited to making decisions about ordinary business matters and conducting preliminary investigations into proposals. It cannot declare dividends, authorize the issuance of shares, amend the bylaws, or initiate any actions that require shareholder approval.

2. *Audit committee.* The audit committee is responsible for the selection, compensation, and oversight of the independent public accountants that audit the corporation's financial records. The Sarbanes-Oxley Act of 2002 requires all publicly held corporations to have an audit committee (as will be discussed in Chapters 31 and 34).

3. *Nominating committee.* This committee chooses the candidates for the board of directors that management wishes to submit to the shareholders in the next election. The committee can nominate but cannot select directors to fill vacancies on the board [RMBCA 8.25].

4. *Compensation committee.* The compensation committee reviews and decides the salaries, bonuses, stock options, and other benefits that are given to the corporation's top executives. The committee may also determine the compensation of directors.

5. *Litigation committee.* This committee decides whether the corporation should pursue requests by shareholders to file a lawsuit against some party that has allegedly harmed the corporation. The committee members investigate the allegations and weigh the costs and benefits of litigation.

In addition to appointing committees, the board of directors can also delegate some of its functions to corporate officers. In doing so, the board is not relieved of its overall responsibility for directing the affairs of the corporation. Instead, corporate officers and

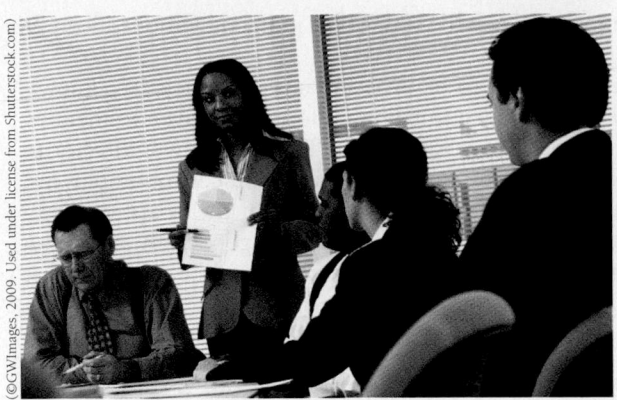

Who hires corporate officers?

managerial personnel are empowered to make decisions relating to ordinary, daily corporate activities within well-defined guidelines.

Corporate Officers and Executives

Corporate officers and other executive employees are hired by the board of directors. At a minimum, most corporations have a president, one or more vice presidents, a secretary, and a treasurer. In most states, an individual can hold more than one office, such as president and secretary, and can be both an officer and a director of the corporation. In addition to carrying out the duties articulated in the bylaws, corporate and managerial officers act as agents of the corporation, and the ordinary rules of agency (discussed in Chapter 23) normally apply to their employment.

Corporate officers and other high-level managers are employees of the company, so their rights are defined by employment contracts. The board of directors, though, normally can remove corporate officers at any time with or without cause and regardless of the terms of the employment contracts—although in so doing, the corporation may be liable for breach of contract.

The duties of corporate officers are the same as those of directors because both groups are involved in decision making and are in similar positions of control. Hence, officers are viewed as having the same fiduciary duties of care and loyalty in their conduct of corporate affairs as directors.

▶ Duties and Liabilities of Directors and Officers

Directors and officers are deemed fiduciaries of the corporation because their relationship with the corporation and its shareholders is one of trust and confidence. As fiduciaries, directors and officers owe ethical—and legal—duties to the corporation and to the shareholders as a whole. These fiduciary duties include the duty of care and the duty of loyalty. (Directors and officers also have a duty not to destroy evidence in the event of a lawsuit involving the corporation. The *Business Application* feature at the end of this chapter discusses how due care can be exercised to preserve electronic evidence by creating a retention policy for e-documents.)

Duty of Care

CONTRAST Shareholders own the corporation and directors make policy decisions, but the officers who run the corporation's daily business often have significant decision-making power.

Directors and officers must exercise due care in performing their duties. The standard of *due care* has been variously described in judicial decisions and codified in many state corporation codes. Generally, a director or officer is expected to act in good faith, to exercise the care that an ordinarily prudent person would exercise in similar circumstances, and to act in what he or she considers to be the best interests of the corporation [RMBCA 8.30]. Directors and officers whose failure to exercise due care results in harm to the corporation or its shareholders can be held liable for negligence (unless the *business judgment rule* applies, as will be discussed shortly).

DUTY TO MAKE INFORMED AND REASONABLE DECISIONS Directors and officers are expected to be informed on corporate matters and to conduct a reasonable investigation of the situation before making a decision. This means that they must do what is necessary to keep adequately informed: attend meetings and presentations, ask for information from those who have it, read reports, and review other written materials. In other words, directors and officers must investigate, study, and discuss matters and evaluate alternatives before making a decision. They cannot decide on the spur of the moment without adequate research.

Although directors and officers are expected to act in accordance with their own knowledge and training, they are also normally entitled to rely on information given to them by certain other persons. Most states and Section 8.30(b) of the RMBCA allow a director to make decisions in reliance on information furnished by competent officers or employees, professionals such as attorneys and accountants, and committees of the board of directors (on which the director does not serve). The reliance must be in good faith, of course, to insulate a director from liability if the information later proves to be inaccurate or unreliable.

> *"Executive ability is deciding quickly and getting somebody else to do the work."*
>
> J. C. Pollard, 1946–present
> (British businessman)

DUTY TO EXERCISE REASONABLE SUPERVISION   Directors are also expected to exercise a reasonable amount of supervision when they delegate work to corporate officers and employees. **EXAMPLE 30.2** Dale, a corporate bank director, fails to attend any board of directors' meetings for five years. In addition, Dale never inspects any of the corporate books or records and generally fails to supervise the efforts of the bank president and the loan committee. Meanwhile, Brennan, the bank president, who is a corporate officer, makes various improper loans and permits large overdrafts. In this situation, Dale (the corporate director) can be held liable to the corporation for losses resulting from the unsupervised actions of the bank president and the loan committee. •

DISSENTING DIRECTORS   Directors are expected to attend board of directors' meetings, and their votes should be entered into the minutes of the meetings. Sometimes, an individual director disagrees with the majority's vote (which becomes an act of the board of directors). Unless a dissent is entered, the director is presumed to have assented. If a decision later leads to the directors being held liable for mismanagement, dissenting directors are rarely held individually liable to the corporation. For this reason, a director who is absent from a given meeting sometimes registers a dissent to actions taken at the meeting with the secretary of the board.

The Business Judgment Rule

Directors and officers are expected to exercise due care and to use their best judgment in guiding corporate management, but they are not insurers of business success. Under the **business judgment rule**, a corporate director or officer will not be liable to the corporation or to its shareholders for honest mistakes of judgment and bad business decisions.

> **Business Judgment Rule** A rule that immunizes corporate management from liability for actions that result in corporate losses or damages if the actions are undertaken in good faith and are within both the power of the corporation and the authority of management to make.

Courts give significant deference to the decisions of corporate directors and officers, and consider the reasonableness of a decision at the time it was made, without the benefit of hindsight. Thus, corporate decision makers are not subjected to second-guessing by shareholders or others in the corporation. The business judgment rule will apply as long as the director or officer:

1. Took reasonable steps to become informed about the matter.
2. Had a rational basis for his or her decision.
3. Did not have a conflict of interest between his or her personal interest and that of the corporation.

In fact, unless there is evidence of bad faith, fraud, or a clear breach of fiduciary duties, most courts will apply the rule and protect directors and officers who make bad business decisions from liability for those choices. Consequently, if there is a reasonable basis for a business decision, a court is unlikely to interfere with that decision, even if the corporation suffers as a result.

Does the business judgment rule go too far in protecting directors and officers from liability?
The business judgment rule generally insulates corporate decision makers from liability for bad decisions even though this may seem to contradict the goal of greater corporate accountability. Is the rule fair to shareholders? In 2009, a Delaware court ruled against shareholders of Citigroup, Inc., who claimed that the bank's directors had breached their fiduciary duties. The shareholders alleged that the directors caused Citigroup to engage in subprime lending (discussed in Chapter 21) even in the face of "red flags" that should have warned the bank to change its practices. Those red flags included the steady decline of the housing market, the dramatic increase in foreclosures, and the collapse of other subprime lenders. The shareholders claimed that the directors' failure to adequately protect the corporation's exposure to risk given those warning signs was a breach of their duties and resulted in significant losses to Citigroup. The court, however, found "the warning signs alleged by plaintiffs are not evidence that the directors consciously disregarded their duties or otherwise acted in bad faith; at most they evidence that the directors made bad business decisions." Thus, under the business judgment rule, the court dismissed the shareholders' claims of breach of fiduciary duty.[4]

Another 2009 case also involved the business judgment rule. Early in 2007, a foreign firm had announced its intention to acquire Lyondell Chemical Company. Over the next several months, Lyondell's directors did nothing to prepare for a possible merger. They failed to research Lyondell's market value and made no attempt to seek out other potential buyers. The $13 billion cash merger was negotiated and finalized in less than one week in July 2007, during which time the directors met for a total of only seven hours to discuss it. Shortly afterward, shareholders filed a lawsuit alleging that the directors had breached their fiduciary duties by failing to maximize the sale price of the corporation. The Delaware Supreme Court ruled that the directors were protected by the business judgment rule.[5]

Duty of Loyalty

Loyalty can be defined as faithfulness to one's obligations and duties. In the corporate context, the duty of loyalty requires directors and officers to subordinate their personal interests to the welfare of the corporation. Directors cannot use corporate funds or confidential corporate information for personal advantage and must refrain from self-dealing. For instance, a director should not oppose a tender offer (see Chapter 29) that is in the corporation's best interest simply because its acceptance may cost the director her or his position. Cases dealing with the duty of loyalty typically involve one or more of the following:

1. Competing with the corporation.
2. Usurping (taking advantage of) a corporate opportunity.
3. Having an interest that conflicts with the interest of the corporation.
4. Engaging in insider trading (using information that is not public to make a profit trading securities, as will be discussed in Chapter 31).
5. Authorizing a corporate transaction that is detrimental to minority shareholders.
6. Selling control over the corporation.

The following classic case illustrates the conflict that can arise between a corporate official's personal interest and his or her duty of loyalty.

---

4. *In re Citigroup, Inc., Shareholder Derivative Litigation*, 964 A.2d 106 (Del.Ch. 2009). The court did allow the shareholders to maintain a claim for waste based on the directors' approval of a chief executive officer compensation package, however.
5. *Lyondell Chemical Co. v. Ryan*, 970 A.2d 235 (Del.Sup. 2009).

Classic Case 30.1 Guth v. Loft, Inc.

Supreme Court of Delaware, 23 Del.Ch. 255, 5 A.2d 503 (1939).

HISTORICAL SETTING   *In the 1920s, Loft Candy Company (Loft, Inc.), based in Long Island City, New York, was a publicly held company with a $13 million candy-and-restaurant chain. The company manufactured its own candies, syrups, and beverages and sold its products in its more than one hundred retail locations throughout the Northeast. The retail stores featured old-fashioned soda fountains and were very popular. In 1930, Charles Guth became Loft's president after a contentious stockholders' meeting. His position there set the stage for the rise of the soft drink Pepsi-Cola.*

Pepsi-Cola got its start when the head of Loft Candy Company usurped a corporate opportunity.

FACTS   At the time Charles Guth became Loft's president, Guth and his family owned Grace Company, which made syrups for soft drinks in a plant in Baltimore, Maryland. Coca-Cola Company supplied Loft with cola syrup. Unhappy with what he felt was Coca-Cola's high price, Guth entered into an agreement with Roy Megargel to acquire the trademark and formula for Pepsi-Cola and form Pepsi-Cola Corporation. Neither Guth nor Megargel could finance the new venture, however, and Grace Company was insolvent. Without the knowledge of Loft's board of directors, Guth used Loft's capital, credit, facilities, and employees to further the Pepsi enterprise. At Guth's direction, a Loft employee made the concentrate for the syrup, which was sent to Grace Company to add sugar and water. Loft charged Grace Company for the concentrate but allowed forty months' credit. Grace charged Pepsi for the syrup but also granted substantial credit. Grace sold the syrup to Pepsi's customers, including Loft, which paid on delivery or within thirty days. Loft also paid for Pepsi's advertising. Finally, losing profits at its stores as a result of switching from Coca-Cola, Loft filed a suit in a Delaware state court against Guth, Grace, and Pepsi, seeking their Pepsi stock and an accounting. The court entered a judgment in the plaintiff's favor. The defendants appealed to the Delaware Supreme Court.

ISSUE   Did Guth violate his duty of loyalty to Loft, Inc., by acquiring the Pepsi-Cola trademark and formula for himself without the knowledge of Loft's board of directors?

DECISION   Yes. The Delaware Supreme Court upheld the judgment of the lower court. The state supreme court was "convinced that the oppor-

tunity to acquire the Pepsi-Cola trademark and formula, goodwill and business belonged to [Loft], and that Guth, as its president, had no right to appropriate the opportunity to himself."

REASON   The court pointed out that the officers and directors of a corporation stand in a fiduciary relationship to that corporation and to its shareholders. Corporate officers and directors must protect the corporation's interest at all times. They must also "refrain from doing anything that works injury to the corporation." In other words, corporate officers and directors must provide undivided and unselfish loyalty to the corporation, and "there should be no conflict between duty and self-interest." Whenever an opportunity is presented to the corporation, officers and directors with knowledge of that opportunity cannot seize it for themselves. "The corporation may elect to claim all of the benefits of the transaction for itself, and the law will impress a trust in favor of the corporation upon the property, interest, and profits required." Guth clearly created a conflict between his self-interest and his duty to Loft—the corporation for which he was president and director. Guth illegally appropriated the Pepsi-Cola opportunity for himself and thereby placed himself in a competitive position with the company for which he worked.

WHAT IF THE FACTS WERE DIFFERENT?   *Suppose that Loft's board of directors had approved Pepsi-Cola's use of its personnel and equipment. Would the court's decision have been different? Discuss.*

IMPACT OF THIS CASE ON TODAY'S LAW   *This early Delaware decision was one of the first to set forth a test for determining when a corporate officer or director has breached the duty of loyalty. The test has two basic parts—whether the opportunity was reasonably related to the corporation's line of business, and whether the corporation was financially able to undertake the opportunity. The court also considered whether the corporation had an interest or expectancy in the opportunity and recognized that when the corporation had "no interest or expectancy, the officer or director is entitled to treat the opportunity as his own."*

RELEVANT WEB SITES   *To locate information on the Web concerning the* Guth v. Loft *decision, go to this text's Web site at* www.cengage.com/blaw/blt. *Select "Chapter 30" and click on "Classic Cases."*

Conflicts of Interest

Corporate directors often have many business affiliations, and a director may sit on the board of more than one corporation. Of course, directors are precluded from entering into or supporting businesses that operate in direct competition with corporations on whose boards they serve. Their fiduciary duty requires them to make a full disclosure of any potential conflicts of interest that might arise in any corporate transaction [RMBCA 8.60].

> *"If it is not in the interest of the public, it is not in the interest of the business."*
>
> Joseph H. Defrees, 1812–1885
> (U.S. congressman)

Sometimes, a corporation enters into a contract or engages in a transaction in which an officer or director has a personal interest. The director or officer must make a *full disclosure* of that interest and must abstain from voting on the proposed transaction.

EXAMPLE 30.3 Southwood Corporation needs office space. Lambert Alden, one of its five directors, owns the building adjoining the corporation's main office building. He negotiates a lease with Southwood for the space, making a full disclosure to Southwood and the other four board directors. The lease arrangement is fair and reasonable, and it is unanimously approved by the other four directors. In this situation, Alden has not breached his duty of loyalty to the corporation, and thus the contract is valid. If it were otherwise, directors would be prevented from ever transacting business with the corporations they serve. •

Liability of Directors and Officers

Directors and officers are exposed to liability on many fronts. Corporate directors and officers may be held liable for the crimes and torts committed by themselves or by corporate employees under their supervision, as discussed in Chapter 6 and Chapter 23, respectively. Additionally, if shareholders perceive that the corporate directors are not acting in the best interests of the corporation, they may sue the directors, in what is called a *shareholder's derivative suit,* on behalf of the corporation. (This type of action will be discussed later in this chapter, in the context of shareholders' rights.) Directors and officers also can be held personally liable under a number of statutes, such as statutes enacted to protect consumers or the environment (see Chapter 33).

▶ Role of Shareholders

BE AWARE Shareholders normally are not agents of the corporation.

Starbucks chairman and chief executive officer Howard Schultz speaks to shareholders at the company's annual shareholders' meeting in Seattle, Washington. Do shareholders have any power over the actions of a corporation's board of directors?

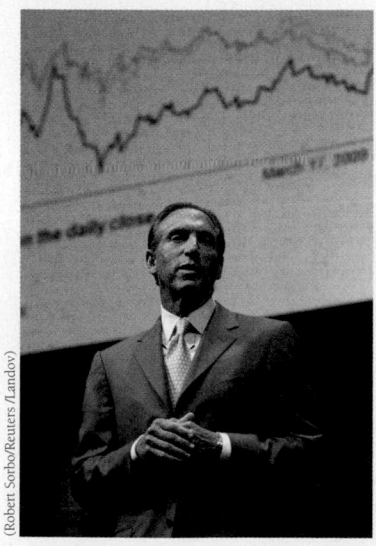

(Robert Sorbo/Reuters/Landov)

The acquisition of a share of stock makes a person an owner and shareholder in a corporation. Shareholders thus own the corporation. Although they have no legal title to corporate property, such as buildings and equipment, they do have an equitable (ownership) interest in the firm.

As a general rule, shareholders have no responsibility for the daily management of the corporation, even if they are ultimately responsible for choosing the board of directors, which does have such control. Ordinarily, corporate officers and directors owe no duty to individual shareholders unless some contract or special relationship exists between them in addition to the corporate relationship. Their duty is to act in the best interests of the corporation and its shareholder-owners as a whole. In turn, as you will read later in this chapter, controlling shareholders owe a fiduciary duty to minority shareholders. Normally, there is no legal relationship between shareholders and creditors of the corporation. Shareholders can be creditors of the corporation, though, and they have the same rights of recovery against the corporation as any other creditor.

In this section, we look at the powers and voting rights of shareholders, which are generally established in the articles of incorporation and by the state's general corporation law.

Shareholders' Powers

Shareholders must approve fundamental changes affecting the corporation before the changes can be implemented. Hence, shareholders are empowered to amend the articles of incorporation (charter) and bylaws, approve a merger or the dissolution of the corporation, and approve the sale of all or substantially all of the corporation's assets. Some of these powers are subject to prior board approval.

Members of the board of directors are elected and removed by a vote of the shareholders. The first board of directors is either named in the articles of incorporation or chosen by the incorporators to serve until the first shareholders' meeting. From that time on, the selection and retention of directors are exclusively shareholder functions.

Directors usually serve their full terms; if the shareholders judge them unsatisfactory, they are simply not reelected. Shareholders have the inherent power, however, to remove a director from office for cause (such as for breach of duty or misconduct) by a majority vote.[6] As mentioned earlier, some state statutes (and some corporate articles) permit removal of directors without cause by the vote of a majority of the holders of outstanding shares entitled to vote.

Shareholders' Meetings

Shareholders' meetings must occur at least annually. In addition, special meetings can be called to deal with urgent matters.

NOTICE OF MEETINGS   A corporation must notify its shareholders of the date, time, and place of an annual or special shareholders' meeting at least ten days, but not more than sixty days, before the meeting date [RMBCA 7.05].[7] Notice of a special meeting must include a statement of the purpose of the meeting, and business transacted at the meeting is limited to that purpose.

PROXIES   It is usually not practical for owners of only a few shares of stock of publicly traded corporations to attend shareholders' meetings. Therefore, the law allows stockholders to either vote in person or appoint another person as their agent to vote their shares at the meeting. The signed appointment form or electronic transmission authorizing an agent to vote the shares is called a **proxy** (from the Latin *procurare,* meaning "to manage, take care of").

Management often solicits proxies, but any person can solicit proxies to concentrate voting power. Proxies have been used by a group of shareholders as a device for taking over a corporation (corporate takeovers were discussed in Chapter 29). Proxies normally are revocable (that is, they can be withdrawn), unless they are specifically designated as irrevocable. Under RMBCA 7.22(c), proxies last for eleven months, unless the proxy agreement provides for a longer period.

PROXY MATERIALS AND SHAREHOLDER PROPOSALS   When shareholders want to change a company policy, they can put their idea up for a shareholder vote. They can do this by submitting a shareholder proposal to the board of directors and asking the board to include the proposal in the proxy materials that are sent to all shareholders before meetings.

The Securities and Exchange Commission (SEC), which regulates the purchase and sale of securities (see Chapter 31), has special provisions relating to proxies and shareholder proposals. SEC Rule 14a-8 provides that all shareholders who own stock worth at least $1,000 are eligible to submit proposals for inclusion in corporate proxy materials. The corporation is required to include information on whatever proposals will be considered at the shareholders' meeting along with proxy materials. Only those proposals that relate to significant policy considerations rather than ordinary business operations must be included. For a discussion of how the SEC is adapting its rules regarding proxies to take advantage of today's communications technology, see this chapter's *Adapting the Law to the Online Environment* feature.

Proxy   In corporate law, a written agreement between a stockholder and another party in which the stockholder authorizes the other party to vote the stockholder's shares in a certain manner.

ON THE WEB   To read an article on the SEC's new e-proxy rules, go to **blogs. law.harvard.edu/corpgov/2009/01/03/ e-proxy-rules-take-effect-for-all- public-companies**.

---

6. A director can often demand court review of removal for cause.

7. A shareholder can waive the requirement of written notice by signing a waiver form. In some states, a shareholder who does not receive written notice, but who learns of the meeting and attends without protesting the lack of notice, is said to have waived notice by such conduct. State statutes and corporate bylaws typically set forth the time within which notice must be sent, what methods can be used, and what the notice must contain.

Adapting the Law to the Online Environment

Moving Company Information to the Internet

Anyone who has ever owned shares in a public company knows that such companies often are required to distribute voluminous documents relating to proxies to all shareholders. Traditionally, large packets of paper documents were sent to shareholders, but in 2007 the Securities and Exchange Commission (SEC) permitted publicly held companies to voluntarily distribute electronic proxy (e-proxy) materials. In 2009, the SEC's e-proxy rules became mandatory. Now, all public companies must post their proxy materials on the Internet, although they may still choose among several options—including paper documents sent by mail—for actually delivering the materials to shareholders.[a]

Notice and Access: E-Proxy Rules

Companies that want to distribute proxy materials only via the Internet can choose the notice and access delivery option. Under this model, the corporation posts the proxy materials on a Web site and notifies the shareholders that the proxy materials are available online.

The notice and access model involves the following steps:

1. The company posts the proxy materials on its publicly accessible Web site.
2. Subsequently, the company sends a (paper) notice to each shareholder at least forty calendar days before the date of the shareholders' meeting for which the proxy is being solicited.
3. No other materials can be sent along with the initial notice (unless the proxy is being combined with the meeting notice required by state law).
4. The notice must be written in plain English, and it must include a prominent statement of the following: the date, time, and location of the shareholders' meeting; the specific Web site at which shareholders can access the proxy materials; an explanation of how they can obtain paper copies of the proxy materials at no cost; and a clear and impartial description of each matter to be considered at the shareholders' meeting.
5. Next, the company must wait at least ten days before sending a "paper" proxy card to the shareholders. This ten-day waiting period provides shareholders with sufficient time to access the proxy materials online or to request paper copies.
6. If a shareholder requests paper proxy materials, the company must send them within three business days.
7. After receiving the initial paper notice, a shareholder can permanently elect to receive all future proxy materials on paper or by e-mail.

Other Delivery Options

Rather than using notice and access delivery, public companies can choose to deliver the full set of proxy materials to the shareholders in paper or electronic form, such as on a CD or DVD. They can also use a blend of these two options, as long as they also post the materials on a Web site. Many corporations choose one option for certain shareholders and another option for other shareholders, depending on the number of shares owned or whether the shareholders are domestic or foreign. The shareholder can always choose to receive paper documents rather than accessing materials online.

Some corporate executives want the SEC to go even further and allow corporations to disseminate important information to the public via CEO blogs. Thus far, however, the SEC has not allowed companies to distribute proxy materials (or disclose material information to the public as required before issuing shares—see Chapter 31) via blogs.

FOR CRITICAL ANALYSIS

Why might a company or other party choose to solicit proxies the old-fashioned way—by providing paper documents instead of Internet access—despite the added costs?

---

a.   17 C.F.R. Parts 240, 249, and 274.

Shareholder Voting

Shareholders exercise ownership control through the power of their votes. Corporate business matters are presented in the form of *resolutions,* which shareholders vote to approve or disapprove. Each common shareholder is entitled to one vote per share, although the voting techniques to be discussed shortly all enhance the power of the shareholder's vote. The articles of incorporation can exclude or limit voting rights, particularly for certain classes of shares. For example, owners of preferred shares are usually denied the right to vote [RMBCA 7.21]. If a state statute requires specific voting procedures, the corporation's articles or bylaws must be consistent with the statute.

BE CAREFUL   Once a quorum is present, a vote can be taken even if some shareholders leave without casting their votes.

QUORUM REQUIREMENTS   For shareholders to conduct business at a meeting, a quorum must be present. Generally, a quorum exists when shareholders holding more than

Shareholders in Wachovia Corporation leave a shareholders' meeting during which they voted on that company's takeover (see Chapter 29) by Wells Fargo. Do shareholders who oppose takeovers have any rights?

50 percent of the outstanding shares are present. In some states, obtaining the unanimous written consent of shareholders is a permissible alternative to holding a shareholders' meeting [RMBCA 7.25].

Once a quorum is present, voting can proceed. A majority vote of the shares represented at the meeting usually is required to pass resolutions. **EXAMPLE 30.4** Novo Pictures, Inc., has 10,000 outstanding shares of voting stock. Its articles of incorporation set the quorum at 50 percent of outstanding shares and provide that a majority vote of the shares present is necessary to pass resolutions concerning ordinary matters. Therefore, for this firm, a quorum of shareholders representing 5,000 outstanding shares must be present at a shareholders' meeting to conduct business. If exactly 5,000 shares are represented at the meeting, a vote of at least 2,501 of those shares is needed to pass a resolution. If 6,000 shares are represented, a vote of 3,001 will be required. •

At times, more than a simple majority vote will be required either by a state statute or by the corporate articles. Extraordinary corporate matters, such as a merger, consolidation, or dissolution of the corporation (as discussed in Chapter 29), require a higher percentage of all corporate shares entitled to vote [RMBCA 7.27].

VOTING LISTS   The corporation prepares voting lists prior to each meeting of the shareholders. Ordinarily, only persons whose names appear on the corporation's shareholder records as owners are entitled to vote.[8] The voting list contains the name and address of each shareholder as shown on the corporate records on a given cutoff, or record, date. (Under RMBCA 7.07, the record date may be as much as seventy days before the meeting.) The voting list also includes the number of voting shares held by each owner. The list is usually kept at the corporate headquarters and is available for shareholder inspection [RMBCA 7.20].

CUMULATIVE VOTING   Most states permit, and some require, shareholders to elect directors by *cumulative voting,* which is a voting method designed to allow minority shareholders to be represented on the board of directors.[9] With cumulative voting, each shareholder is entitled to a total number of votes equal to the number of board members to be elected multiplied by the number of voting shares a shareholder owns. The shareholder can cast all of these votes for one candidate or split them among several nominees for director. All nominees stand for election at the same time. When cumulative voting is not required either by statute or under the articles, the entire board can be elected by a simple majority of shares at a shareholders' meeting.

Cumulative voting can best be understood by an example. **EXAMPLE 30.5** A corporation has 10,000 shares issued and outstanding. The minority shareholders hold 3,000 shares, and the majority shareholders hold the other 7,000 shares. Three members of the board are to be elected. The majority shareholders' nominees are Acevedo, Barkley, and Craycik. The minority shareholders' nominee is Drake. Can Drake be elected by the minority shareholders?

If cumulative voting is allowed, the answer is yes. Together, the minority shareholders have 9,000 votes (the number of directors to be elected times the number of shares held by the minority shareholders equals 3 times 3,000, which equals 9,000 votes). All of these

---

8. When the legal owner is bankrupt, incompetent, deceased, or in some other way under a legal disability, his or her vote can be cast by a person designated by law to control and manage the owner's property.

9. See, for example, California Corporations Code Section 708. Under RMBCA 7.28, however, no cumulative voting rights exist unless the articles of incorporation so provide.

• *Exhibit* 30–2 Results of Cumulative Voting

BALLOT	MAJORITY SHAREHOLDERS' VOTES			MINORITY SHAREHOLDERS' VOTES	DIRECTORS ELECTED
	Acevedo	Barkley	Craycik	Drake	
1	10,000	10,000	1,000	9,000	Acevedo/Barkley/Drake
2	9,001	9,000	2,999	9,000	Acevedo/Barkley/Drake
3	6,000	7,000	8,000	9,000	Barkley/Craycik/Drake

votes can be cast to elect Drake. The majority shareholders have 21,000 votes (3 times 7,000 equals 21,000 votes), but these votes have to be distributed among their three nominees. The principle of cumulative voting is that no matter how the majority shareholders cast their 21,000 votes, they will not be able to elect all three directors if the minority shareholders cast all of their 9,000 votes for Drake, as illustrated in Exhibit 30–2. •

OTHER VOTING TECHNIQUES   Before a shareholders' meeting, a group of shareholders can agree in writing to vote their shares together in a specified manner. Such agreements, called *shareholder voting agreements,* usually are held to be valid and enforceable. A shareholder can also appoint a voting agent and vote by proxy.

In the following case, corporate management was concerned about losing a proxy contest. The corporation's chief executive officer then entered into an agreement with a shareholder who would support management's candidates in return for a seat on the board of directors. A shareholder who opposed the deal filed a lawsuit claiming that this agreement was illegal and a breach of the officer's fiduciary duty.

Case 30.2 Portnoy v. Cryo-Cell International, Inc.

Court of Chancery of Delaware, 940 A.2d 43 (2008).

To avoid the possibility of a shareholders' vote replacing the board of directors, did the chief executive officer of a stem cell services company breach her fiduciary duties?

FACTS Cryo-Cell International, Inc., a small public company, was struggling to survive. Several of its shareholders, including David Portnoy, mounted a proxy contest in an effort to replace the board of directors at the annual shareholders' meeting. Another shareholder, Andrew Filipowski, used management's fear of being replaced if the dissident shareholders won to create a deal for himself—he would support management in exchange for being included in management's slate of directors. The company's chief executive officer, Mercedes Walton, devised a plan that would allow management and Filipowski to win the proxy contest. Under this plan, Walton would act as a "matchmaker" and find shareholders willing to sell their shares to Filipowski. Walton promised Filipowski that if management's slate won, Cryo-Cell's board of directors would add another board seat that a Filipowski designee would fill. Walton's side deal was not made known to the shareholders when they voted. After management won the election, Walton prepared to add Filipowski's designee to the board. Portnoy then filed a lawsuit, claiming that the election results should be overturned. Portnoy argued that all of the

dealings between Cryo-Cell and Filipowski were tainted by fiduciary misconduct and that the agreement to add Filipowski to the management slate in exchange for his support was not created in the company's best interests and constituted an "illegal vote-buying arrangement."

ISSUE Did the chief executive officer's promise to change the corporate bylaws and expand the number of directors after a vote constitute a breach of fiduciary duties and taint the election?

DECISION Yes. The court ruled that the incumbent board's actions and the side agreement with the company's chief executive officer (Walton) constituted serious breaches of fiduciary duty that tainted the election. The court, therefore, ordered a special shareholders' meeting at which a new election would be held. The court did not, however, find that the agreement to add Filipowski to management's slate of directors was improper.

REASON The court reasoned that a mere offer of a position on a management slate should not be considered a vote-buying agreement. "When stockholders can decide for themselves whether to see the candidate who obtained a place on a management slate by way of [bargaining

Case 30.2–Continues next page ➡

Case 30.2–Continued

with management], it seems unwise to formulate a standard that involves the potential for excessive and imprecise judicial involvement." Such an arrangement is not vote buying. In contrast, the side agreement that guaranteed Filipowski's designee an additional seat on the board was a breach of fiduciary duty. Walton had promised "she and her incumbent colleagues would use their powers as directors of Cryo-Cell to increase the size of the board and to seat [Filipowski's designee]. This was therefore a promise that

would not be, for the duration of the term, subject to prior approval by the electorate." Thus, it was improper.

FOR CRITICAL ANALYSIS—Ethical Consideration *If Filipowski had promised to bring additional funding to keep Cryo-Cell from failing due to lack of capital, would the actions described in this case have been considered ethical? Explain your answer.*

▶ Rights of Shareholders

Shareholders possess numerous rights. A significant right—the right to vote their shares—has already been discussed. We now look at some additional rights of shareholders.

(PhotoDisc)

Stock certificates are displayed. To be a shareholder, is it necessary to have physical possession of a certificate? Why or why not?

Stock Certificate A certificate issued by a corporation evidencing the ownership of a specified number of shares in the corporation.

Preemptive Rights Rights held by shareholders that entitle them to purchase newly issued shares of a corporation's stock, equal in percentage to shares already held, before the stock is offered to any outside buyers. Preemptive rights enable shareholders to maintain their proportionate ownership and voice in the corporation.

Stock Certificates

A **stock certificate** is a certificate issued by a corporation that evidences ownership of a specified number of shares in the corporation. In jurisdictions that require the issuance of stock certificates, shareholders have the right to demand that the corporation issue certificates. In most states and under RMBCA 6.26, boards of directors may provide that shares of stock will be uncertificated—that is, no actual, physical stock certificates will be issued. When shares are uncertificated, the corporation may be required to send each shareholder a letter or some other form of notice that contains the same information that would normally appear on the face of stock certificates.

Stock is intangible personal property, and the ownership right exists independently of the certificate itself. If a stock certificate is lost or destroyed, ownership is not destroyed with it. A new certificate can be issued to replace one that has been lost or destroyed. Notice of shareholders' meetings, dividends, and operational and financial reports are all distributed according to the recorded ownership listed in the corporation's books, not on the basis of possession of the certificate.

Preemptive Rights

Sometimes, the articles of incorporation grant preemptive rights to shareholders [RMBCA 6.30]. With **preemptive rights,** a shareholder receives a preference over all other purchasers to subscribe to or purchase a prorated share of a new issue of stock. In other words, a shareholder who is given preemptive rights can purchase the same percentage of the new shares being issued as she or he already holds in the company. This allows each shareholder to maintain her or his proportionate control, voting power, or financial interest in the corporation. Generally, preemptive rights apply only to additional, newly issued stock sold for cash, and the preemptive rights must be exercised within a specified time period, which is usually thirty days.

EXAMPLE 30.6 Tran Corporation authorizes and issues 1,000 shares of stock. Lebow purchases 100 shares, making her the owner of 10 percent of the company's stock. Subsequently, Tran, by vote of its shareholders, authorizes the issuance of another 1,000 shares (by amending the articles of incorporation). This increases its capital stock to a total of

2,000 shares. If preemptive rights have been provided, Lebow can purchase one additional share of the new stock being issued for each share she already owns—or 100 additional shares. Thus, she can own 200 of the 2,000 shares outstanding, and she will maintain her relative position as a shareholder. If preemptive rights are not allowed, her proportionate control and voting power may be diluted from that of a 10 percent shareholder to that of a 5 percent shareholder because of the issuance of the additional 1,000 shares. ●

Preemptive rights are most important in close corporations because each shareholder owns a relatively small number of shares but controls a substantial interest in the corporation. Without preemptive rights, it would be possible for a shareholder to lose his or her proportionate control over the firm.

Stock Warrants

Stock Warrant   A certificate that grants the owner the option to buy a given number of shares of stock, usually within a set time period.

Stock warrants are rights to buy stock at a stated price by a specified date that are created by the company. Usually, when preemptive rights exist and a corporation is issuing additional shares, it issues its shareholders stock warrants. Warrants are often publicly traded on securities exchanges.

Dividends

As mentioned in Chapter 29, a *dividend* is a distribution of corporate profits or income *ordered by the directors* and paid to the shareholders in proportion to their respective shares in the corporation. Dividends can be paid in cash, property, stock of the corporation that is paying the dividends, or stock of other corporations.[10]

State laws vary, but each state determines the general circumstances and legal requirements under which dividends are paid. State laws also control the sources of revenue to be used; only certain funds are legally available for paying dividends. Depending on state law, dividends may be paid from the following sources:

1. *Retained earnings.* All states allow dividends to be paid from the undistributed net profits earned by the corporation, including capital gains from the sale of fixed assets. As mentioned in Chapter 29, the undistributed net profits are called *retained earnings.*
2. *Net profits.* A few states allow dividends to be issued from current net profits without regard to deficits in prior years.
3. *Surplus.* A number of states allow dividends to be paid out of any kind of surplus.

ILLEGAL DIVIDENDS   Sometimes, dividends are improperly paid from an unauthorized account, or their payment causes the corporation to become insolvent. Generally, shareholders must return illegal dividends only if they knew that the dividends were illegal when the payment was received (or if the dividends were paid when the corporation was insolvent). Whenever dividends are illegal or improper, the board of directors can be held personally liable for the amount of the payment.

DIRECTORS' FAILURE TO DECLARE A DIVIDEND   When directors fail to declare a dividend, shareholders can ask a court to compel the directors to meet and to declare a dividend. To succeed, the shareholders must show that the directors have acted so unreasonably in withholding the dividend that their conduct is an abuse of their discretion.

Often, a corporation accumulates large cash reserves for a legitimate corporate purpose, such as expansion or research. The mere fact that the firm has sufficient earnings or surplus available to pay a dividend is not enough to compel directors to distribute funds that, in the

---

10. Technically, dividends paid in stock are not dividends. They maintain each shareholder's proportionate interest in the corporation. On one occasion, a distillery declared and paid a "dividend" in bonded whiskey.

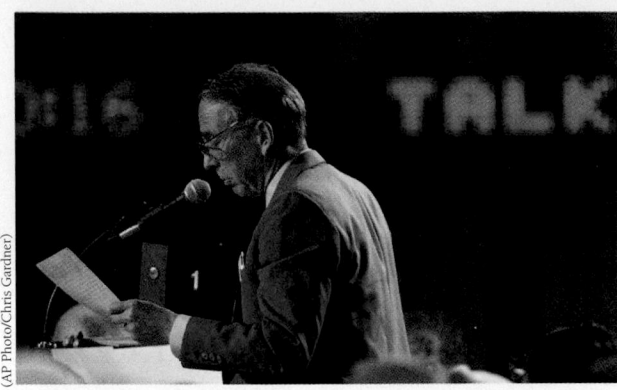

A General Motors shareholder asks a question at the company's annual stockholders' meeting. Shareholders also have a limited right to inspect and copy corporate books and records, provided the request is made in advance and is not impromptu in an open forum like a shareholders' meeting. What other limitations are placed on shareholders' inspection rights?

board's opinion, should not be distributed. The courts are reluctant to interfere with corporate operations and will not compel directors to declare dividends unless abuse of discretion is clearly shown.

Inspection Rights

Shareholders in a corporation enjoy both common law and statutory inspection rights. The RMBCA provides that every shareholder is entitled to examine specified corporate records. The shareholder's right of inspection is limited, however, to the inspection and copying of corporate books and records for a *proper purpose,* provided the request is made in advance. The shareholder can inspect in person, or an attorney, accountant, or other authorized assistant can do so as the shareholder's agent.

The power of inspection is fraught with potential abuses, and the corporation is allowed to protect itself from them. For instance, a shareholder can properly be denied access to corporate records to prevent harassment or to protect trade secrets or other confidential corporate information. Some states require that a shareholder must have held his or her shares for a minimum period of time immediately preceding the demand to inspect or must hold a minimum number of outstanding shares. A shareholder who is denied the right of inspection can seek a court order to compel the inspection.

Transfer of Shares

Do shareholders have to sign stock certificates in order to transfer their shares to someone else?

Corporate stock represents an ownership right in intangible personal property. The law generally recognizes the right to transfer stock to another person unless there are valid restrictions on its transferability. Although stock certificates are negotiable and freely transferable by indorsement and delivery, transfer of stock in closely held corporations usually is restricted. These restrictions must be reasonable and may be set out in the bylaws or in a shareholder agreement. The existence of any restrictions on transferability must always be indicated on the face of the stock certificate.

When shares are transferred, a new entry is made in the corporate stock book to indicate the new owner. Until the corporation is notified and the entry is complete, all rights—including voting rights, the right to notice of shareholders' meetings, and the right to dividend distributions—remain with the current record owner.

Rights on Dissolution

When a corporation is dissolved and its outstanding debts and the claims of its creditors have been satisfied, the remaining assets are distributed to the shareholders in proportion to the percentage of shares owned by each shareholder. Certain classes of preferred stock can be given priority. If no class of stock has been given preferences in the distribution of assets on liquidation, then all of the stockholders share the remaining assets.

As noted in Chapter 29, in some situations, shareholders can petition a court to have the corporation dissolved. The RMBCA permits any shareholder to initiate a dissolution proceeding in any of the following circumstances [RMBCA 14.30]:

1. The directors are deadlocked in the management of corporate affairs. The shareholders are unable to break that deadlock, and irreparable injury to the corporation is being suffered or threatened.

2. The acts of the directors or those in control of the corporation are illegal, oppressive, or fraudulent.

3. Corporate assets are being misapplied or wasted.

4. The shareholders are deadlocked in voting power and have failed, for a specified period (usually two annual meetings), to elect successors to directors whose terms have expired or would have expired with the election of successors.

The Shareholder's Derivative Suit

Shareholder's Derivative Suit A suit brought by a shareholder to enforce a corporate cause of action against a third person.

When the corporation is harmed by the actions of a third party, the directors can bring a lawsuit in the name of the corporation against that party. If the corporate directors fail to bring a lawsuit, shareholders can do so "derivatively" in what is known as a **shareholder's derivative suit.** A shareholder cannot bring a derivative suit until ninety days after making a written demand on the corporation (the board of directors) to take suitable action [RMBCA 7.40]. Only if the directors refuse to take appropriate action can the derivative suit go forward.

The right of shareholders to bring a derivative action is especially important when the wrong suffered by the corporation results from the actions of corporate directors or officers. This is because the directors and officers would probably be unwilling to take any action against themselves. Nevertheless, a court will dismiss a derivative suit if the majority of directors or an independent panel determines in good faith that the lawsuit is not in the best interests of the corporation [RMBCA 7.44].

When shareholders bring a derivative suit, they are not pursuing rights or benefits for themselves personally but are acting as guardians of the corporate entity. Therefore, if the suit is successful, any damages recovered normally go into the corporation's treasury, not to the shareholders personally.[11] **EXAMPLE 30.7** Zeon Corporation is owned by two shareholders, each holding 50 percent of the corporate shares. One of the shareholders wants to sue the other for misusing corporate assets or usurping corporate opportunities. In this situation, the plaintiff-shareholder will have to bring a shareholder's derivative suit (not a suit in his or her own name) because the alleged harm was suffered by Zeon, not by the plaintiff personally. Any damages awarded will go to the corporation, not to the plaintiff-shareholder. • (Derivative actions are less common in other countries than in the United States, as this chapter's *Beyond Our Borders* feature explains.)

 Duties and Liabilities of Shareholders

One of the hallmarks of the corporate form of business organization is that shareholders are not personally liable for the debts of the corporation. If the corporation fails, shareholders can lose their investments, but generally that is the limit of their liability. As discussed in Chapter 29, in certain instances of fraud, undercapitalization, or careless observance of corporate formalities, a court will pierce the corporate veil (disregard the corporate entity)

---

11. The shareholders may be entitled to reimbursement for reasonable expenses involved in the derivative suit, however, including attorneys' fees.

 Beyond Our Borders **Derivative Actions in Other Nations**

Today, most of the claims brought against directors and officers in the United States are those alleged in shareholders' derivative suits. Other nations, however, put more restrictions on the use of such suits. German law, for example, does not provide for derivative litigation, and a corporation's duty to its employees is just as significant as its duty to its shareholder-owners. The United Kingdom has no statute authorizing derivative actions, which are permitted only to challenge directors' actions that the shareholders could not legally ratify. Japan authorizes derivative actions but also permits a company to sue the plaintiff-shareholder for damages if the action is unsuccessful.

• For Critical Analysis
Do corporations benefit from shareholders' derivative suits? If so, how?

and hold the shareholders individually liable. These situations are the exception, however, not the rule. A shareholder can also be personally liable in certain other rare instances. One relates to illegal dividends, which were discussed previously. Another relates to *watered stock*. Finally, in certain instances, a majority shareholder who engages in oppressive conduct or attempts to exclude minority shareholders from receiving certain benefits can be held personally liable.

Watered Stock

Watered Stock Shares of stock issued by a corporation for which the corporation receives, as payment, less than the stated value of the shares.

When a corporation issues shares for less than their fair market value, the shares are referred to as **watered stock**.[12] Usually, the shareholder who receives watered stock must pay the difference to the corporation (the shareholder is personally liable). In some states, the shareholder who receives watered stock may be liable to creditors of the corporation for unpaid corporate debts.

EXAMPLE 30.8 During the formation of a corporation, Gomez, one of the incorporators, transfers his property, Sunset Beach, to the corporation for 10,000 shares of stock. The stock has a specific face value (*par value*) of $100 per share, and thus the total price of the 10,000 shares is $1 million. After the property is transferred and the shares are issued, Sunset Beach is carried on the corporate books at a value of $1 million. On appraisal, it is discovered that the market value of the property at the time of transfer was only $500,000. The shares issued to Gomez are therefore watered stock, and he is liable to the corporation for the difference between the value of the shares and the value of the property. •

Duties of Majority Shareholders

In some instances, a majority shareholder is regarded as having a fiduciary duty to the corporation and to the minority shareholders. This occurs when a single shareholder (or a few shareholders acting in concert) owns a sufficient number of shares to exercise *de facto* (actual) control over the corporation. In these situations, majority shareholders owe a fiduciary duty to the minority shareholders. When a majority shareholder breaches her or his fiduciary duty to a minority shareholder, the minority shareholder can sue for damages. How egregious should majority shareholders' misbehavior be to warrant—in addition to compensatory damages—an award of punitive damages? The court in the following case set out the factors to consider and then weighed the majority shareholders' acts against these standards.

---

12. The phrase *watered stock* was originally used to describe cattle that were kept thirsty during a long drive and then were allowed to drink large quantities of water just prior to their sale. The increased weight of the "watered stock" allowed the seller to reap a higher profit.

Case 30.3 Mazloom v. Mazloom

Court of Appeals of South Carolina, 382 S.C. 307, 675 S.E.2d 746 (2009).

(TheTruthAbout/ Creative Commons)

A Mini Mart was part of assets sold without payment to a legitimate owner. What duty was breached?

FACTS Four brothers—Iraj, Ahmad, Manooch, and Aboli Mazloom—incorporated a business known as AMBI, Inc. AMBI owned real estate in South Carolina on which the brothers operated a Mini Mart, a liquor store, and a one-bedroom apartment. Each brother had a 25 percent interest in AMBI. After seventeen years, Ahmad, Manooch, and Aboli dissolved AMBI, filed articles of organization for a new firm—AMA, LLC—and transferred AMBI's assets to AMA for five dollars. When Iraj learned of the changes, he had Manooch and

Aboli file an amendment to AMA's articles stating that "Iraj Mazloom owns 25% (or 1/4) shares of stock in AMA." Less than five months later, Ahmad sold his interest in AMA to Manooch and Aboli, who then sold AMA's assets to Ganesh Mini Mart, LLC, for $345,000. They paid Iraj nothing. He filed a suit in a South Carolina state court against Manooch and Aboli, claiming breach of fiduciary duty. The brothers asserted that Iraj did not own shares in AMBI or AMA. The court awarded Iraj 25 percent of the proceeds from the sale of AMA's assets and other amounts, including punitive damages of $50,000. Manooch and Aboli appealed.

ISSUE Can a majority shareholders' breach of fiduciary duty to a minority shareholder support an award of punitive damages?

Case 30.3–Continued

DECISION Yes. The state intermediate appellate court affirmed the award of punitive damages to Iraj for Manooch and Aboli's breach of their duty.

REASON Factors considered in reviewing an award of punitive damages include the misconduct on which the award was based, the knowledge and culpability of the parties against whom the award was assessed, the relationship of the harm to the award, the effect that the award might have in deterring the wrongdoers and others from similar misconduct, and the wrongdoers' ability to pay. In this case, the misconduct included the brothers' failure to notify Iraj before the sale of AMBI's assets, AMBI's dissolution, and the sale of AMA's assets to a third party; the brothers' denial of Iraj's 25 percent interest in the business; and their failure to tender his share of the proceeds from the sale of the assets. The brothers were aware of their misconduct and were entirely culpable. The award was likely to deter them

from similar misconduct. Furthermore, they had sufficient personal assets, including their proceeds from the AMA sale, to pay the award.

FOR CRITICAL ANALYSIS—Social Consideration *An award of punitive damages is almost completely at the discretion of a jury and trial judge. Why is that?*

WHY IS THIS CASE IMPORTANT? *Why did the three brothers attempt to cheat their sibling out of his share of the family's jointly owned business? The brothers did not plead their motive in defense. The court did not ask for it. It did not affect the consideration of their legal dispute. This case makes it clear that, regardless of the personal motivation underlying a party's actions, he or she will be held to the legal obligations arising out of a business relationship and liability will be assessed for any breach.*

 Major Business Forms Compared

As mentioned in Chapter 26, when deciding which form of business organization would be most appropriate, businesspersons normally take into account several factors, including ease of creation, the liability of the owners, tax considerations, and the need for capital. Each major form of business organization offers distinct advantages and disadvantages with respect to these and other factors. Exhibit 30–3 summarizes the essential advantages and disadvantages of each of the forms of business organization discussed in Chapters 26 through 30.

• *Exhibit* **30–3 Major Forms of Business Compared**

CHARACTERISTIC	SOLE PROPRIETORSHIP	PARTNERSHIP	CORPORATION
Method of creation	Created at will by owner.	Created by agreement of the parties.	Authorized by the state under the state's corporation law.
Legal position	Not a separate entity; owner is the business.	Is a separate legal entity in most states.	Always a legal entity separate and distinct from its owners—a legal fiction for the purposes of owning property and being a party to litigation.
Liability	Unlimited liability.	Unlimited liability.	Limited liability of shareholders—shareholders are not liable for the debts of the corporation.
Duration	Determined by owner; automatically dissolved on owner's death.	Terminated by agreement of the partners, but can continue to do business even when a partner dissociates from the partnership.	Can have perpetual existence.
Transferability of interest	Interest can be transferred, but individual's proprietorship then ends.	Although partnership interest can be assigned, assignee does not have full rights of a partner.	Shares of stock can be transferred.
Management	Completely at owner's discretion.	Each general partner has a direct and equal voice in management unless expressly agreed otherwise in the partnership agreement.	Shareholders elect directors, who set policy and appoint officers.

Continued

● *Exhibit* 30-3 Major Forms of Business Compared—Continued

CHARACTERISTIC	SOLE PROPRIETORSHIP	PARTNERSHIP	CORPORATION
Taxation	Owner pays personal taxes on business income.	Each partner pays pro rata share of income taxes on net profits, whether or not they are distributed.	Double taxation—corporation pays income tax on net profits, with no deduction for dividends, and shareholders pay income tax on disbursed dividends they receive.
Organizational fees, annual license fees, and annual reports	None or minimal.	None or minimal.	All required.
Transaction of business in other states	Generally no limitation.	Generally no limitation.[a]	Normally must qualify to do business and obtain certificate of authority.

CHARACTERISTIC	LIMITED PARTNERSHIP	LIMITED LIABILITY COMPANY	LIMITED LIABILITY PARTNERSHIP
Method of creation	Created by agreement to carry on a business for a profit. At least one party must be a general partner and the other(s) limited partner(s). Certificate of limited partnership is filed. Charter must be issued by the state.	Created by an agreement of the member-owners of the company. Articles of organization are filed. Charter must be issued by the state.	Created by agreement of the partners. A statement of qualification for the limited liability partnership is filed.
Legal position	Treated as a legal entity.	Treated as a legal entity.	Generally, treated same as a general partnership.
Liability	Unlimited liability of all general partners; limited partners are liable only to the extent of capital contributions.	Member-owners' liability is limited to the amount of capital contributions or investments.	Varies, but under the Uniform Partnership Act, liability of a partner for acts committed by other partners is limited.
Duration	By agreement in certificate, or by termination of the last general partner (retirement, death, and the like) or last limited partner.	Unless a single-member LLC, can have perpetual existence (same as a corporation).	Remains in existence until cancellation or revocation.
Transferability of interest	Interest can be assigned (same as general partnership), but if assignee becomes a member with consent of other partners, certificate must be amended.	Member interests are freely transferable.	Interest can be assigned same as in a traditional partnership.
Management	General partners have equal voice or by agreement. Limited partners may not retain limited liability if they actively participate in management.	Member-owners can fully participate in management or can designate a group of persons to manage on behalf of the members.	Same as a traditional partnership.
Taxation	Generally taxed as a partnership.	LLC is not taxed, and members are taxed personally on profits "passed through" the LLC.	Same as a traditional partnership.
Organizational fees, annual license fees, and annual reports	Organizational fee required; usually not others.	Organizational fee required; others vary with states.	Fees are set by each state for filing statements of qualification, foreign qualification, and annual reports.
Transaction of business in other states	Generally no limitations.	Generally no limitation, but may vary depending on state.	Must file a statement of foreign qualification before doing business in another state.

a. A few states have enacted statutes requiring that foreign partnerships qualify to do business there.

▶ Reviewing . . . Corporate Directors, Officers, and Shareholders

David Brock is on the board of directors of Firm Body Fitness, Inc., which owns a string of fitness clubs in New Mexico. Brock owns 15 percent of the Firm Body stock, and he is also employed as a tanning technician at one of the fitness clubs. After the January financial report showed that Firm Body's tanning division was operating at a substantial net loss, the board of directors, led by Marty Levinson, discussed terminating the tanning operations. Brock successfully convinced a majority of the board that the tanning division was necessary to market the club's overall fitness package. By April, the tanning division's financial losses had risen. The board hired a business analyst who conducted surveys and determined that the tanning operations did not significantly increase membership. A shareholder, Diego Peñada, discovered that Brock owned stock in Sunglow, Inc., the company from which Firm Body purchased its tanning equipment. Peñada notified Levinson, who privately reprimanded Brock. Shortly afterwards, Brock and Mandy Vail, who owned 37 percent of the Firm Body stock and also held shares of Sunglow, voted to replace Levinson on the board of directors. Using the information presented in the chapter, answer the following questions.

1 What duties did Brock, as a director, owe to Firm Body?
2 Does the fact that Brock owned shares in Sunglow establish a conflict of interest? Why or why not?
3 Suppose that Firm Body brought an action against Brock claiming that he had breached the duty of loyalty by not disclosing his interest in Sunglow to the other directors. What theory might Brock use in his defense?
4 Now suppose that Firm Body did not bring an action against Brock. What type of lawsuit might Peñada be able to bring based on these facts?

Business Application
Creating an E-Document-Retention Policy*

If a corporation becomes the target of a civil lawsuit or criminal investigation, the company may be required to turn over any documents in its files relating to the matter during the discovery stage of litigation. These documents may include legal documents, contracts, e-mail, faxes, letters, interoffice memorandums, notebooks, diaries, and other materials, even if they are kept in personal files in the homes of directors or officers. Under the current Federal Rules of Civil Procedure, which govern civil litigation procedures (see Chapter 3), a defendant in a lawsuit must disclose all relevant electronic data compilations and documents, as well as all relevant paper documents.

Although certain documents or data might free a company of any liability arising from a claim, others might serve to substantiate a civil claim or criminal charge. It is also possible that information contained in a document—an interoffice e-mail memo, for example (or even a memo referring to that memo)—could be used to convince a jury that the company or its directors or officers had condoned a certain action that they later denied condoning.

Which E-Documents Should Be Retained?

How does a company decide which e-documents should be retained and which should be destroyed? By law, corporations are required to keep certain types of documents, such as those specified in the *Code of Federal Regulations* and in regulations issued by government agencies, such as the Occupational Safety and Health Administration. Most businesses

today have a document-retention policy. Generally, any records that the company is not legally required to keep or that the company is sure it will have no legal need for should be removed from the files and destroyed. A partnership agreement, for example, should be kept. A memo about last year's company picnic should not.

Modifications May Be Necessary During an Investigation

Companies that are under investigation usually must modify their document-retention policy until the investigation has been completed. After receiving a subpoena to produce specific types of documents, company officers should instruct the appropriate employees not to destroy relevant papers or e-documents that would otherwise be disposed of as part of the company's normal document-retention program.

To avoid being charged with obstruction of justice, company officials must always exercise good faith in deciding which documents should or should not be destroyed when attempting to comply with a subpoena. The specter of criminal prosecution would appear to encourage the retention of even those documents that are only remotely related to the dispute—at least until it has been resolved.

CHECKLIST FOR AN E-DOCUMENT-RETENTION POLICY

1. Develop guidelines that let employees know not only which e-documents should be retained and deleted but also which types of documents should not be created in the first place.

*This *Business Application* is not meant to substitute for the services of an attorney who is licensed to practice law in your state.

Continued

2. Find out which documents must be retained under the *Code of Federal Regulations* and other government agency regulations to which your corporation is subject.

3. Retain other e-documents only if their retention is in the corporation's interest.

4. If certain corporate documents are subpoenaed, modify your document-retention policy to keep any documents that are even remotely related to the dispute until it has been resolved.

 Key Terms

business judgment rule 758
inside director 755
outside director 755
preemptive right 766

proxy 762
quorum 755
shareholder's derivative suit 769
stock certificate 766

stock warrant 767
watered stock 770

 Chapter Summary: Corporate Directors, Officers, and Shareholders

Roles of Directors and Officers (See pages 753–757.)	1. *Directors' qualifications*—Few qualifications are required; a director may be a shareholder but is not required to be. Directors are responsible for all policymaking decisions necessary to the management of all corporate affairs (see Exhibit 30–1 on page 754). 2. *Election of directors*—The first board of directors is usually appointed by the incorporators; thereafter, directors are elected by the shareholders. Directors usually serve a one-year term, although their terms can be longer or staggered. Compensation is usually specified in the corporate articles or bylaws. 3. *Board of directors' meetings*—The board of directors conducts business by holding formal meetings with recorded minutes. The date of regular meetings is usually established in the corporate articles or bylaws; special meetings can be called, with notice sent to all directors. Quorum requirements vary from state to state; usually, a quorum is a majority of the directors. Voting usually must be done in person, and in ordinary matters only a majority vote is required. 4. *Rights of directors*—Directors' rights include the rights of participation, inspection, compensation, and indemnification. 5. *Directors' committees*—A board of directors may create committees of directors and delegate various responsibilities to them. Common types of committees are listed and described on page 756. 6. *Corporate officers and executives*—Corporate officers and other executive employees are normally hired by the board of directors and have the rights defined by their employment contracts. The duties of corporate officers are the same as those of directors.
Duties and Liabilities of Directors and Officers (See pages 757–761.)	1. *Duty of care*—Directors and officers are obligated to act in good faith, to use prudent business judgment in the conduct of corporate affairs, and to act in the corporation's best interests. If a director fails to exercise this duty of care, she or he can be answerable to the corporation and to the shareholders for breaching the duty. 2. *The business judgment rule*—This rule immunizes directors and officers from liability when they acted in good faith, acted in the best interests of the corporation, and exercised due care. For the rule to apply, the directors and officers must have made an informed, reasonable, and loyal decision. 3. *Duty of loyalty*—Directors and officers have a fiduciary duty to subordinate their own interests to those of the corporation in matters relating to the corporation. 4. *Conflicts of interest*—To fulfill their duty of loyalty, directors and officers must make a full disclosure of any potential conflicts between their personal interests and those of the corporation. 5. *Liability of directors and officers*—Corporate directors and officers are personally liable for their own torts and crimes. Additionally, they may be held personally liable for the torts and crimes committed by corporate personnel under their supervision (see Chapters 6 and 23).

Chapter Summary: Corporate Directors, Officers, and Shareholders

Role of Shareholders
(See pages 761–766.)
	1. *Shareholders' powers*—Shareholders' powers include the approval of all fundamental changes affecting the corporation and the election of the board of directors.
	2. *Shareholders' meetings*—Shareholders' meetings must occur at least annually; special meetings can be called when necessary. Notice of the date, time, and place of the meeting (and its purpose, if it is specially called) must be sent to shareholders. Shareholders may vote by proxy (authorizing someone else to vote their shares) and may submit proposals to be included in the company's proxy materials sent to shareholders before meetings.
	3. *Shareholder voting*—Shareholder voting requirements and procedures are as follows:
	  a. A minimum number of shareholders (a quorum—generally, more than 50 percent of shares held) must be present at a meeting for business to be conducted; resolutions are passed (usually) by simple majority vote.
	  b. The corporation must prepare voting lists of shareholders of record prior to each shareholders' meeting.
	  c. Cumulative voting may or may not be required or permitted. Cumulative voting gives minority shareholders a better chance to be represented on the board of directors.
	  d. A shareholder voting agreement (an agreement of shareholders to vote their shares together) is usually held to be valid and enforceable.

Rights of Shareholders **(See pages 766–769.)**	Shareholders have numerous rights, which may include the following: 1. The right to a stock certificate, preemptive rights, and the right to stock warrants (depending on the articles of incorporation). 2. The right to obtain a dividend (at the discretion of the directors). 3. Voting rights. 4. The right to inspect the corporate records. 5. The right to transfer shares (this right may be restricted in close corporations). 6. The right to a share of corporate assets when the corporation is dissolved. 7. The right to sue on behalf of the corporation (bring a shareholder's derivative suit) when the directors fail to do so.
Duties and Liabilities **of Shareholders** **(See pages 769–771.)**	1. Shareholders may be liable for the retention of illegal dividends and for the value of watered stock. 2. In certain situations, majority shareholders may be regarded as having a fiduciary duty to minority shareholders and will be liable if that duty is breached.

 ExamPrep

ISSUE SPOTTERS

1 Wonder Corporation has an opportunity to buy stock in XL, Inc. The directors decide that instead of Wonder buying the stock, the directors will buy it. Yvon, a Wonder shareholder, learns of the purchase and wants to sue the directors on Wonder's behalf. Can she do it? Explain.

2 Nico is Omega Corporation's majority shareholder. He owns enough stock in Omega that if he were to sell it, the sale would be a transfer of control of the firm. Discuss whether Nico owes a duty to Omega or the minority shareholders in selling his shares.

BEFORE THE TEST

Check your answers to the Issue Spotters, and at the same time, take the interactive quiz for this chapter. Go to **www.cengage.com/blaw/blt** and click on "Chapter 30." First, click on "Answers to Issue Spotters" to check your answers. Next, click on "Interactive Quiz" to assess your mastery of the concepts in this chapter. Then click on "Flashcards" to review this chapter's Key Term definitions.

 For Review

Answers for the even-numbered questions in this For Review *section can be found on this text's accompanying Web site at* **www.cengage.com/blaw/blt**. *Select "Chapter 30" and click on "For Review."*

1 What are the duties of corporate directors and officers?

2 Directors are expected to use their best judgment in managing the corporation. What must directors do to avoid liability for honest mistakes of judgment and poor business decisions?

3 What is a voting proxy? What is cumulative voting?

4 If a group of shareholders perceives that the corporation has suffered a wrong and the directors refuse to take action, can the shareholders compel the directors to act? If so, how?

5 From what sources may dividends be paid legally? In what circumstances is a dividend illegal? What happens if a dividend is illegally paid?

▶ Hypothetical Scenarios and Case Problems

30–1 Voting Techniques. Algonquin Corp. has issued and has outstanding 100,000 shares of common stock. Four stockholders own 60,000 of these shares, and for the past six years they have nominated a slate of candidates for membership on the board, all of whom have been elected. Sergio and twenty other shareholders, owning 20,000 shares, are dissatisfied with corporate management and want a representative on the board who shares their views. Explain under what circumstances Sergio and the twenty other shareholders can elect their representative to the board.

30–2 Hypothetical Question with Sample Answer Starboard, Inc., has a board of directors consisting of three members (Ellsworth, Green, and Morino) and approximately five hundred shareholders. At a regular meeting of the board, the board selects Tyson as president of the corporation by a two-to-one vote, with Ellsworth dissenting. The minutes of the meeting do not register Ellsworth's dissenting vote. Later, during an audit, it is discovered that Tyson is a former convict and has openly embezzled $500,000 from Starboard. This loss is not covered by insurance. The corporation wants to hold directors Ellsworth, Green, and Morino liable. Ellsworth claims no liability. Discuss the personal liability of the directors to the corporation.

—For a sample answer to Question 30–2, go to Appendix E at the end of this text.

30–3 Rights of Shareholders. Lucia has acquired one share of common stock of a multimillion-dollar corporation with more than 500,000 shareholders. Lucia's ownership is so small that she is wondering what her rights are as a shareholder. For example, she wants to know whether owning this one share entitles her to (1) attend and vote at shareholders' meetings, (2) inspect the corporate books, and (3) receive yearly dividends. Discuss Lucia's rights in these three matters.

30–4 Duties of Directors and Officers. In 1978, David Brandt and Dean Somerville incorporated Posilock Puller, Inc. (PPI), to make and market bearing pullers. Each received half of the stock. Initially operating out of McHenry, North Dakota, PPI moved to Cooperstown, North Dakota, in 1984 into a building owned by Somerville. After the move, Brandt's participation in PPI diminished, and Somerville's increased. In 1998, Somerville formed PL MFG as his own business to make components for the bearing pullers and sell the parts to PPI. The start-up costs included a $450,000 loan from Sheyenne Valley Electric Cooperative. PPI executed the loan documents and indorsed the check. The proceeds were deposited into an account for PL MFG, which did

not sign a promissory note payable to PPI until 2000. When Brandt learned of PL MFG and the loan, he filed a suit in a North Dakota state court against Somerville, alleging, in part, a breach of fiduciary duty. What fiduciary duty does a director owe to his or her corporation? What does this duty require? Should the court hold Somerville liable? Why or why not? [*Brandt v. Somerville*, 2005 ND 35, 692 N.W.2d 144 (2005)]

30–5 Duties of Majority Shareholders. Steve and Marie Venturini were involved in the operation of Steve's Sizzling Steakhouse in Carlstadt, New Jersey, from the day their parents opened it in the 1930s. By the 1980s, Steve, Marie, and her husband, Joe, were running it. The business was a corporation with Steve and Marie each owning half of the stock. Steve died in 2001, leaving his stock in equal shares to his sons Steve and Gregg. Son Steve had never worked there. Gregg did occasional maintenance work until his father's death. Despite their lack of participation, the sons were paid more than $750 per week each. In 2002, Marie's son Blaise, who had obtained a college degree in restaurant management while working part-time at the steakhouse, took over its management. When his cousins became threatening, he denied them access to the business and its books. Marie refused Gregg and Steve's offer of about $1.4 million for her stock in the restaurant, and they refused her offer of about $800,000 for theirs. They filed a suit in a New Jersey state court against her, claiming, among other things, a breach of fiduciary duty. Should the court order the aunt to buy out the nephews or the nephews to buy out the aunt, or neither? Why? [*Venturini v. Steve's Steakhouse, Inc.*, ___ N.J.Super. ___, ___ A.2d ___ (Ch.Div. 2006)]

30–6 Case Problem with Sample Answer Harry Hoaas and Larry Griffiths were shareholders in Grand Casino, Inc., which owned and operated a casino in Watertown, South Dakota. Griffiths owned 51 percent of the stock and Hoaas 49 percent. Hoaas managed the casino, which Griffiths typically visited once a week. At the end of 1997, an accounting showed that the cash on hand was less than the amount posted in the casino's books. Later, more shortfalls were discovered. In October 1999, Griffiths did a complete audit. Hoaas was unable to account for $135,500 in missing cash. Griffiths then kept all of the casino's most recent profits, including Hoaas's $9,447.20 share, and, without telling Hoaas, sold the casino for $100,000 and kept all of the proceeds. Hoaas filed a suit in a South Dakota state court against Griffiths, asserting, among other things, a breach of fiduciary duty. Griffiths countered with evidence of Hoaas's misappropriation of corporate cash. What duties did these parties owe each other? Did either Griffiths or Hoaas, or both of them, breach those duties? How should their dispute be resolved? How should their finances be reconciled? Explain. [*Hoaas v. Griffiths,* 2006 SD 27, 714 N.W.2d 61 (2006)]

—After you have answered Problem 30–6, compare your answer with the sample answer given on the Web site that accompanies this text. Go to **www.cengage.com/blaw/blt**, select "Chapter 30," and click on "Case Problem with Sample Answer."

30–7 Role of Directors. The board of directors of a property management corporation in Oregon meets on a regular basis. The company paid the directors $6,000 each in the third quarter of 2003. It did not report the payments as part of its payroll and did not pay unemployment tax on the payments. The Oregon Employment Department contended that the company owed $700 in unemployment taxes on the payments to the directors. The company protested. The administrative law judge (ALJ) for the Employment Department held that the company owed the taxes because directors' fees are the same as wages for employment. The company appealed. The court of appeals affirmed the ALJ's ruling. The company appealed again. Are payments to directors the same as wages for tax purposes? Explain. [*Necanicum Investment Co. v. Employment Department,* 345 Or. 138, 190 P.3d 368 (2008)]

30–8 Duties of Directors and Officers. First Niles Financial, Inc., is a company whose sole business is to own and operate a bank, Home Federal Savings and Loan Association of Niles, Ohio. First Niles's directors include bank officers William Stephens, Daniel Csontos, and Lawrence Safarek; James Kramer, president of an air-conditioning company that services the bank; and Ralph Zuzolo, whose law firm serves the bank and whose title company participates in most of its real estate deals. First Niles's board put the bank up for sale. There were three bids. Farmers National Bank Corp. stated that it would not retain the board. Cortland Bancorp indicated that it would terminate the directors but consider them for future service. First Financial Corp. said nothing about the directors. The board did not pursue Farmers' offer, failed to respond timely to Cortland's request, and rejected First Financial's bid. Leonard Gantler and other First Niles shareholders filed a suit in a Delaware state court against Stephens and the others. What duties do directors and officers owe to a corporation and its shareholders? How might those duties have been breached here? Discuss. [*Gantler v. Stephens,* 965 A.2d 695 (Del.Sup. 2009)]

30–9 **A Question of Ethics** *New Orleans Paddlewheels, Inc. (NOP), is a Louisiana corporation formed in 1982, when James Smith, Sr., and Warren Reuther were its only shareholders, with each holding 50 percent of the stock. NOP is part of a sprawling enterprise of tourism and hospitality companies in New Orleans. The positions on the board of each company were split equally between the Smith and Reuther families. At Smith's request, his son James Smith, Jr. (JES), became involved in the businesses. In 1999, NOP's board elected JES as president, in charge of day-to-day operations, and Reuther as chief executive officer (CEO), in charge of marketing and development. Over the next few years, animosity developed between Reuther and JES. In October 2001, JES terminated Reuther as CEO and denied him access to the offices and books of NOP and the other companies, literally changing the locks on the doors. At the next meetings of the boards of NOP and the overall enterprise, deadlock ensued, with the directors voting along family lines on every issue. Complaining that the meetings were a "waste of time," JES began to run the entire enterprise by taking advantage of an unequal balance of power on the companies' executive committees. In NOP's subsequent bankruptcy proceeding, Reuther filed a motion for the appointment of a trustee to formulate a plan for the firm's reorganization, alleging, among other things, misconduct by NOP's management.* [*In re New Orleans Paddlewheels, Inc.,* 350 Bankr. 667 (E.D.La. 2006)]

1 Was Reuther legally entitled to have access to the books and records of NOP and the other companies? JES maintained, among other things, that NOP's books were "a mess." Was JES's denial of that access unethical? Explain.

2 How would you describe JES's attempt to gain control of NOP and the other companies? Were his actions deceptive and self-serving in the pursuit of personal gain or legitimate and reasonable in the pursuit of a business goal? Discuss.

 Critical Thinking and Writing Assignments

30–10 Critical Legal Thinking. In general, courts are reluctant to grant shareholders' petitions for corporate dissolution except in extreme circumstances, such as when corporate directors or shareholders are deadlocked and the corporation suffers as a result. Instead, a court will attempt to "save" the corporate entity whenever possible. Why is this?

 Practical Internet Exercises

Go to this text's Web site at **www.cengage.com/blaw/blt**, select "Chapter 30," and click on "Practical Internet Exercises." There you will find the following Internet research exercises that you can perform to learn more about the topics covered in this chapter.

Practical Internet Exercise 30–1: Legal Perspective—Liability of Directors and Officers
Practical Internet Exercise 30–2: Management Perspective—D&O Insurance

Chapter 31

Investor Protection, Insider Trading, and Corporate Governance

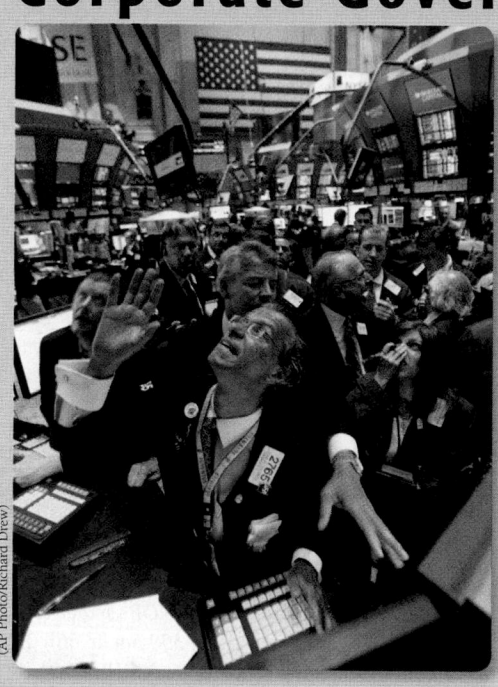

(AP Photo/Richard Drew)

Chapter Outline

- Securities Act of 1933
- Securities Exchange Act of 1934
- State Securities Laws
- Corporate Governance
- Online Securities Fraud

Learning Objectives

After reading this chapter, you should be able to answer the following questions:

1. What is meant by the term *securities?*

2. What are the two major statutes regulating the securities industry?

3. What is insider trading? Why is it prohibited?

4. What are some of the features of state securities laws?

5. What certification requirements does the Sarbanes-Oxley Act impose on corporate executives?

Security Generally, a stock certificate, bond, note, debenture, warrant, or other document or record evidencing an ownership interest in a corporation or a promise of repayment of debt by a corporation.

After the stock market crash of 1929, Congress enacted legislation to regulate securities markets. **Securities** generally are defined as any documents or records evidencing corporate ownership (stock) or debts (bonds). The goal of regulation was to provide investors with more information to help them make buying and selling decisions about securities and to prohibit deceptive, unfair, and manipulative practices. Today, the sale and transfer of securities are heavily regulated by federal and state statutes and by government agencies, and the Obama administration has proposed even more regulations. As we have seen in recent years, General MacArthur's observation in the chapter-opening quotation that people are remembered for the rules that they break certainly holds true with regard to securities law violations.

This chapter discusses the nature of federal securities regulation and its effect on the business world. We first examine the major traditional laws governing securities offerings and trading. We then discuss corporate governance and the Sarbanes-Oxley Act of 2002,[1]

---

1. 15 U.S.C. Sections 7201 *et seq.*

which affects certain types of securities transactions. Finally, we look at the problem of online securities fraud. Before we begin, though, the important role played by the Securities and Exchange Commission (SEC) in the regulation of federal securities laws requires some attention. We examine the origin and functions of the SEC in this chapter's *Landmark in the Law* feature on the following page.

During the stock market crash of 1929, hordes of investors crowded Wall Street to find out the latest news. How did the "crash" affect stock trading in the years thereafter?

(National Archives)

▶ Securities Act of 1933

The Securities Act of 1933[2] governs initial sales of stock by businesses. The act was designed to prohibit various forms of fraud and to stabilize the securities industry by requiring that all essential information concerning the issuance of securities be made available to the investing public. Basically, the purpose of this act is to require disclosure. The 1933 act provides that all securities transactions must be registered with the SEC or be exempt from registration requirements.

What Is a Security?

Section 2(1) of the Securities Act of 1933 contains a broad definition of securities, which generally include the following:[3]

1. Instruments and interests commonly known as securities, such as preferred and common stocks, treasury stocks, bonds, debentures, and stock warrants.
2. Any interests in securities, such as stock options, puts, calls, or other types of privilege on a security or on the right to purchase a security or a group of securities in a national security exchange.
3. Notes, instruments, or other evidence of indebtedness, including certificates of interest in a profit-sharing agreement and certificates of deposit.
4. Any fractional undivided interest in oil, gas, or other mineral rights.
5. Investment contracts, which include interests in limited partnerships and other investment schemes.

Investment Contract In securities law, a transaction in which a person invests in a common enterprise reasonably expecting profits that are derived primarily from the efforts of others.

In interpreting the act, the United States Supreme Court has held that an **investment contract** is any transaction in which a person (1) invests (2) in a common enterprise (3) reasonably expecting profits (4) derived *primarily* or *substantially* from others' managerial or entrepreneurial efforts. Known as the *Howey* test, this definition continues to guide the determination of what types of contracts can be considered securities.[4]

For our purposes, it is probably convenient to think of securities in their most common forms—stocks and bonds issued by corporations. Bear in mind, though, that securities can take many forms, including interests in whiskey, cosmetics, worms, beavers, boats, vacuum cleaners, muskrats, and cemetery lots. Almost any stake in the ownership or debt of a company can be considered a security. Investment contracts in condominiums, franchises, limited partnerships in real estate, and oil or gas or other mineral rights have qualified as securities. **CASE EXAMPLE 31.1** Alpha Telcom sold, installed, and maintained pay-phone systems. As part of its pay-phone program, Alpha guaranteed buyers a 14 percent return on the amount of their purchase. Alpha was operating at a net loss,

---

2. 15 U.S.C. Sections 77–77aa.
3. 15 U.S.C. Section 77b(1). Amendments in 1982 added stock options.
4. *SEC v. W. J. Howey Co.*, 328 U.S. 293, 66 S.Ct. 1100, 90 L.Ed. 1244 (1946).

Landmark in the Law   The Securities and Exchange Commission

In 1931, the U.S. Senate passed a resolution calling for an extensive investigation of securities trading. The investigation led, ultimately, to the passage by Congress of the Securities Act of 1933, which is also known as the *truth-in-securities* bill. In the following year, Congress passed the Securities Exchange Act. This 1934 act created the Securities and Exchange Commission (SEC).

Major Responsibilities of the SEC   The SEC was created as an independent regulatory agency with the function of administering the 1933 and 1934 acts. Its major responsibilities in this respect are as follows:

1. Interprets federal securities laws and investigates securities law violations.
2. Issues new rules and amends existing rules.
3. Oversees the inspection of securities firms, brokers, investment advisers, and ratings agencies.
4. Oversees private regulatory organizations in the securities, accounting, and auditing fields.
5. Coordinates U.S. securities regulation with federal, state, and foreign authorities.

The SEC's Expanding Regulatory Powers   Since its creation, the SEC's regulatory functions have gradually been increased by legislation granting it authority in different areas. For example, to curb further securities fraud, the Securities Enforcement Remedies and Penny Stock Reform Act of 1990[a] was enacted to expand the SEC's enforcement options and allow SEC administrative law judges to hear cases involving more types of alleged securities law violations. In addition, the act provides that courts can prevent persons who have engaged in securities fraud from serving as officers and directors of publicly held corporations. The Securities Acts Amendments of 1990 authorized the SEC to seek sanctions against those who violate foreign securities laws.[b]

IN TODAY'S MARKET NEWS, GREED ROARED BACK.

(©Harley Schwadron)

The National Securities Markets Improvement Act of 1996 expanded the power of the SEC to exempt persons, securities, and transactions from the requirements of the securities laws.[c] (This part of the act is also known as the Capital Markets Efficiency Act.) The act also limited the authority of the states to regulate certain securities transactions and particular investment advisory firms.[d] The Sarbanes-Oxley Act of 2002,[e] which you will read about later in this chapter, further expanded the authority of the SEC by directing the agency to issue new rules relating to corporate disclosure requirements and by creating an oversight board to regulate public accounting firms.

• Application to Today's World   *The SEC is working to make the regulatory process more efficient and more relevant to today's securities trading practices. To this end, the SEC has embraced modern technology and communications methods, especially the Internet, more completely than many other federal agencies have. For example, the agency now requires—not just allows—companies to file certain information electronically so that it can be posted on the SEC's EDGAR (Electronic Data Gathering, Analysis, and Retrieval) database.*

• Relevant Web Sites   *To locate information on the Web concerning the SEC, go to this text's Web site at www.cengage.com/blaw/blt, select "Chapter 31," and click on "URLs for Landmarks."*

---

a. 15 U.S.C. Section 77g.
b. 15 U.S.C. Section 78a.

c. 15 U.S.C. Sections 77z-3, 78mm.
d. 15 U.S.C. Section 80b-3a.
e. 15 U.S.C. Sections 7201 *et seq.*

---

however, and continually borrowed funds to pay investors the fixed rate of return it had promised. Eventually, the company filed for bankruptcy, and the SEC brought an action alleging that Alpha had violated the Securities Act of 1933. In this situation, a federal court concluded that the pay-phone program was a security because it involved an investment contract.[5] •

---

5. *SEC v. Alpha Telcom, Inc.*, 187 F.Supp.2d 1250 (2002). See also *SEC v. Edwards*, 540 U.S. 389, 124 S.Ct. 892, 157 L.Ed.2d 813 (2004), in which the United States Supreme Court held that an investment scheme offering contractual entitlement to a fixed rate of return can be an investment contract and therefore can be considered a security under federal law.

Preventing Legal Disputes

Securities are not limited to stocks and bonds but can encompass a wide variety of legal claims. The analysis hinges on the nature of the transaction rather than on the particular instrument or rights involved. Because Congress enacted securities laws to regulate investments, in whatever form and by whatever name they are called, almost any type of security that might be sold as an investment can be subject to securities laws. When in doubt about whether an investment transaction involves securities, seek the advice of a specialized attorney.

Registration Statement

Section 5 of the Securities Act of 1933 broadly provides that a security must be *registered* before being offered to the public unless it qualifies for an exemption. The issuing corporation must file a *registration statement* with the SEC and must provide all investors with a *prospectus*. A **prospectus** is a written disclosure document that describes the security being sold, the financial operations of the issuing corporation, and the investment or risk attaching to the security. The prospectus also serves as a selling tool for the issuing corporation. The SEC now allows an issuer to deliver its prospectus to investors electronically via the Internet.[6] In principle, the registration statement and the prospectus supply sufficient information to enable unsophisticated investors to evaluate the financial risk involved.

Prospectus A written document, required by securities laws, that describes the security being sold, the financial operations of the issuing corporation, and the investment or risk attaching to the security. It is designed to provide sufficient information to enable investors to evaluate the risk involved in purchasing the security.

CONTENTS OF THE REGISTRATION STATEMENT The registration statement must be written in plain English and fully describe the following:

1. The securities being offered for sale, including their relationship to the registrant's other capital securities.
2. The corporation's properties and business (including a financial statement certified by an independent public accounting firm).
3. The management of the corporation, including managerial compensation, stock options, pensions, and other benefits. Any interests of directors or officers in any material transactions with the corporation must be disclosed.
4. How the corporation intends to use the proceeds of the sale.
5. Any pending lawsuits or special risk factors.

DON'T FORGET The purpose of the Securities Act of 1933 is disclosure—the SEC does not consider whether a security is worth the investment price.

All companies, both domestic and foreign, must file their registration statements electronically so that they can be posted on the SEC's EDGAR (Electronic Data Gathering, Analysis, and Retrieval) database. The EDGAR database includes material on initial public offerings, proxy statements, corporations' annual reports, registration statements, and other documents that have been filed with the SEC. Investors can access the database via the Internet to obtain information that can be used to make investment decisions.

ON THE WEB The SEC's EDGAR system contains information about the SEC's operations, the statutes it implements, its proposed and final rules, and its enforcement actions, as well as corporate financial information. Go to **www.sec. gov/edgar.shtml**.

REGISTRATION PROCESS The registration statement does not become effective until after it has been reviewed and approved by the SEC (unless it is filed by a *well-known seasoned issuer*, as will be discussed shortly). The 1933 act restricted the types of activities that an issuer can engage in at each stage in the registration process. During the *prefiling period* (before filing the registration statement), the issuer normally cannot either sell or offer to sell the securities. Once the registration statement has been filed, a waiting period begins while the SEC reviews the registration statement for completeness.[7]

---

6. Basically, an electronic prospectus must meet the same requirements as a printed prospectus. The SEC has special rules that address situations in which the graphics, images, or audio files in a printed prospectus cannot be reproduced in an electronic form. 17 C.F.R. Section 232.304.
7. The waiting period must last at least twenty days but always extends much longer because the SEC inevitably requires numerous changes and additions to the registration statement.

Free-Writing Prospectus   A free-writing prospectus is any type of written, electronic, or graphic offer that describes the issuing corporation or its securities and includes a legend indicating that the investor may obtain the prospectus at the Securities and Exchange Commission's Web site.

During the *waiting period,* the securities can be offered for sale but cannot be sold by the issuing corporation. Only certain types of offers are allowed. All issuers can distribute a *preliminary prospectus,* which contains most of the information that will be included in the final prospectus but often does not include a price. Most issuers can also use a *free-writing prospectus* during this period (although some inexperienced issuers will need to file a preliminary prospectus first).[8] A **free-writing prospectus** is any type of written, electronic, or graphic offer that describes the issuer or its securities and includes a legend indicating that the investor may obtain the prospectus at the SEC's Web site.

Once the SEC has reviewed and approved the registration statement and the waiting period is over, the registration is effective, and the *posteffective period* begins. The issuer can now offer and sell the securities without restrictions. If the company issued a preliminary or free-writing prospectus to investors, it must provide those investors with a final prospectus either before or at the time they purchase the securities. The issuer can require investors to download the final prospectus from a Web site if it notifies them of the appropriate Internet address.

RESTRICTIONS RELAXED FOR WELL-KNOWN SEASONED ISSUERS   In 2005, the SEC revised the registration process and loosened some of the restrictions on large experienced issuers.[9] The rules created new categories of issuers depending on their size and presence in the market and provided a simplified registration process for these issuers. The large, well-known securities firms that issue most securities have the greatest flexibility. A *well-known seasoned issuer* (WKSI) is a firm that has issued at least $1 billion in securities in the previous three years or has at least $700 million of value of outstanding stock in the hands of the public. WKSIs can file registration statements the day they announce a new offering and are not required to wait for SEC review and approval. They can also use a free-writing prospectus at any time, even during the prefiling period.

Exempt Securities and Transactions

Certain types of securities are exempt from the registration requirements of the Securities Act of 1933. These securities—which generally can also be resold without being registered—are summarized in Exhibit 31–1 under the "Exempt Securities" heading.[10] The exhibit also lists and describes certain transactions that are exempt from registration requirements under various SEC regulations.

The Center for Corporate Law at the University of Cincinnati College of Law offers a Securities Lawyer's Deskbook online that examines all of the laws and legal terms discussed in this chapter. Go to **www.law.uc.edu/CCL**.

The transaction exemptions are the most important because they are very broad and can enable an issuer to avoid the high cost and complicated procedures associated with registration. Because the coverage of the exemptions overlaps somewhat, an offering may qualify for more than one. Therefore, many sales of securities occur without registration. Even when a transaction is exempt from the registration requirements, the offering is still subject to the antifraud provisions of the 1933 act (as well as those of the 1934 act, to be discussed later in this chapter).

BE AWARE   The issuer of an exempt security does not have to disclose the same information that other issuers do.

REGULATION A OFFERINGS   Securities issued by an issuer that has offered less than $5 million in securities during any twelve-month period are exempt from registration.[11] Under Regulation A,[12] the issuer must file with the SEC a notice of the issue and an offering circular, which must also be provided to investors before the sale. This is a much simpler and less expensive process than the procedures associated with full registration. Companies are

---

8. See SEC Rules 164 and 433.
9. Securities Offering Reform, codified at 17 C.F.R. Sections 200, 228, 229, 230, 239, 240, 243, 249, and 274.
10. 15 U.S.C. Section 77c.
11. 15 U.S.C. Section 77c(b).
12. 17 C.F.R. Sections 230.251–230.263.

● *Exhibit* 31–1 Exemptions for Securities Offerings under the 1933 Securities Act

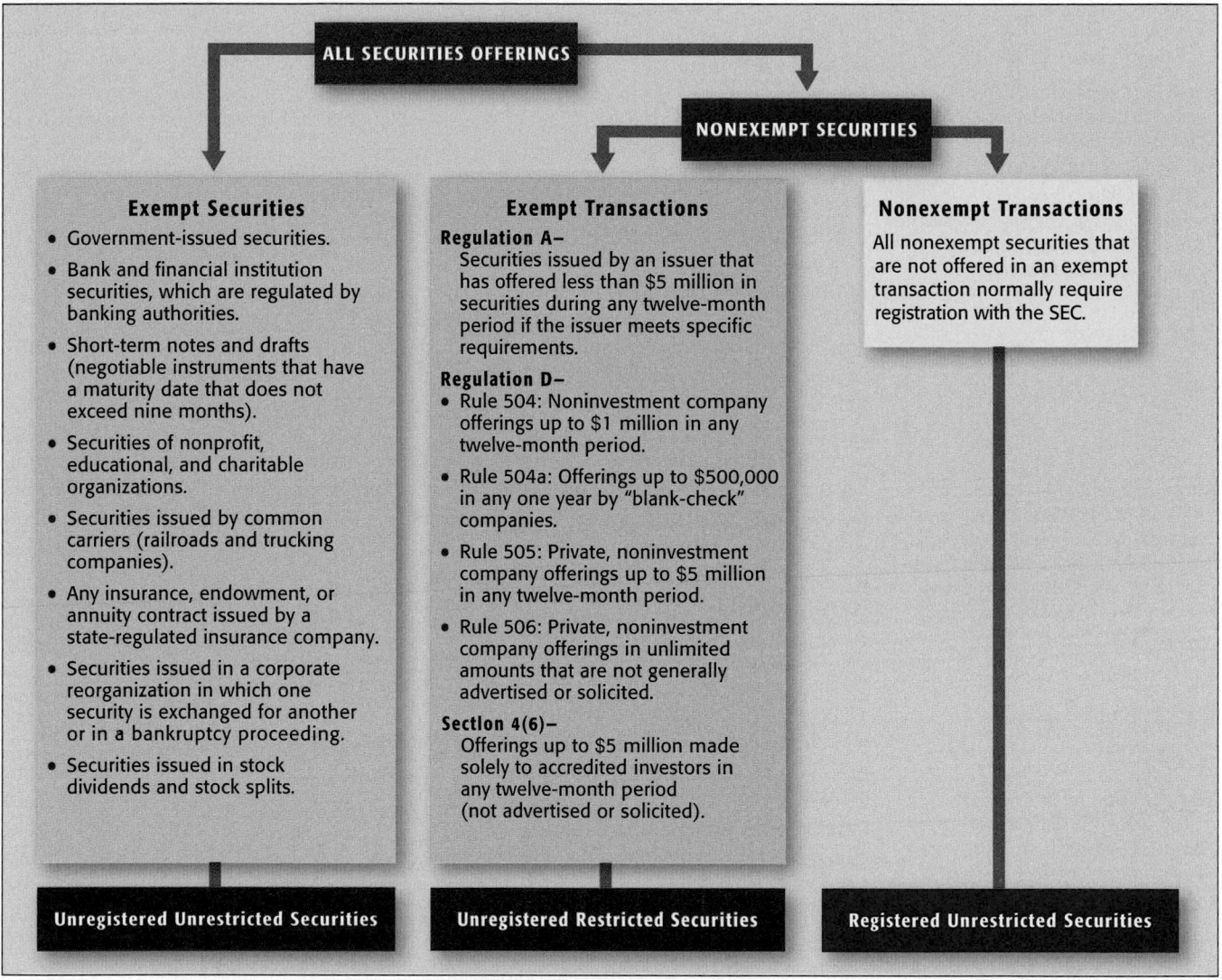

allowed to "test the waters" for potential interest before preparing the offering circular. To *test the waters* means to determine potential interest without actually selling any securities or requiring any commitment on the part of those who express interest. Small-business issuers (companies with annual revenues of less than $25 million) can also use an integrated registration and reporting system that uses simpler forms than the full registration system.

Some companies have sold their securities via the Internet using Regulation A. **EXAMPLE 31.2** The Spring Street Brewing Company became the first company to sell securities via an online initial public offering (IPO). Spring Street raised about $1.6 million— without having to pay any commissions to brokers or underwriters. **●** Such online IPOs are particularly attractive to small companies and start-up ventures that may find it difficult to raise capital from institutional investors or through underwriters.

SMALL OFFERINGS—REGULATION D The SEC's Regulation D contains several exemptions from registration requirements (Rules 504, 504a, 505, and 506) for offers that

ON THE WEB The SEC provides a list of downloadable forms pertinent to securities filings. Go to **www.sec.gov/about/forms/secforms.htm**.

either involve a small dollar amount or are made in a limited manner. Rule 504 is the exemption used by most small businesses. It provides that noninvestment company offerings up to $1 million in any twelve-month period are exempt. Noninvestment companies are firms that are not engaged primarily in the business of investing or trading in securities. (In contrast, an **investment company** is a firm that buys a large portfolio of securities and professionally manages it on behalf of many smaller shareholders/owners. A **mutual fund** is a type of investment company.)

Investment Company A company that acts on the behalf of many smaller shareholders/owners by buying a large portfolio of securities and professionally managing that portfolio.

Mutual Fund A specific type of investment company that continually buys or sells to investors shares of ownership in a portfolio.

EXAMPLE 31.3 Zeta Enterprises is a limited partnership that develops commercial property. Zeta intends to offer $600,000 of its limited partnership interests for sale between June 1 and next May 31. Because an interest in a limited partnership meets the definition of a security (discussed earlier in this chapter), its sale would be subject to the registration and prospectus requirements of the Securities Act of 1933. Under Rule 504, however, the sales of Zeta's interests are exempt from these requirements because Zeta is a noninvestment company making an offering of less than $1 million in a twelve-month period. Therefore, Zeta can sell its limited partnership interests without filing a registration statement with the SEC or issuing a prospectus to any investor. ●

Another exemption is available under Rule 505 for private, noninvestment company offerings up to $5 million in any twelve-month period. The offer may be made to an unlimited number of *accredited investors* and up to thirty-five unaccredited investors. **Accredited investors** include banks, insurance companies, investment companies, employee benefit plans, the issuer's executive officers and directors, and persons whose income or net worth exceeds a certain threshold. The SEC must be notified of the sales, and precautions must be taken because these restricted securities may be resold only by registration or in an exempt transaction. No general solicitation or advertising is allowed. The issuer must provide any unaccredited investors with disclosure documents that generally are the same as those used in registered offerings.

Accredited Investor In the context of securities offerings, "sophisticated" investors, such as banks, insurance companies, investment companies, the issuer's executive officers and directors, and persons whose income or net worth exceeds certain limits.

PRIVATE PLACEMENT EXEMPTION   Private, noninvestment company offerings in unlimited amounts that generally are not solicited or advertised are exempt under Rule 506. This exemption is often referred to as the *private placement* exemption because it exempts "transactions not involving any public offering."[13] To qualify for the exemption, the issuer must believe that each unaccredited investor has sufficient knowledge or experience in financial matters to be capable of evaluating the investment's merits and risks.[14]

KEEP IN MIND An investor can be "sophisticated" by virtue of his or her education and experience or by investing through a knowledgeable, experienced representative.

The private placement exemption is perhaps most important to firms that want to raise funds through the sale of securities without registering them. **EXAMPLE 31.4** Citco Corporation needs to raise capital to expand its operations. Citco decides to make a private $10 million offering of its common stock directly to two hundred accredited investors and thirty highly sophisticated, but unaccredited, investors. Citco provides all of these investors with a prospectus and material information about the firm, including its most recent financial statements. As long as Citco notifies the SEC of the sale, this offering will likely qualify for the private placement exemption. The offering is nonpublic and not generally advertised. There are fewer than thirty-five unaccredited investors, and each of them possesses sufficient knowledge and experience to evaluate the risks involved. The issuer has provided all purchasers with the material information. Thus, Citco will *not* be required to comply with the registration requirements of the Securities Act of 1933. ●

RESALES   Most securities can be resold without registration. The Securities Act of 1933 provides exemptions for resales by most persons other than issuers or underwriters. The average investor who sells shares of stock does not have to file a registration statement with the SEC. Resales of restricted securities, however, trigger the registration requirements

---

13. 15 U.S.C. Section 77d(2).
14. 7 C.F.R. Section 230.506.

unless the party selling them complies with Rule 144 or Rule 144A. These rules are sometimes referred to as "safe harbors."

Rule 144. Rule 144 exempts restricted securities from registration on resale if all of the following conditions are met:

1. There is adequate current public information about the issuer. ("Adequate current public information" refers to the reports that certain companies are required to file under the Securities Exchange Act of 1934.)
2. The person selling the securities has owned them for at least six months if the issuer is subject to the reporting requirements of the 1934 act.[15] If the issuer is not subject to the 1934 act's reporting requirements, the seller must have owned the securities for at least one year.
3. The securities are sold in certain limited amounts in unsolicited brokers' transactions.
4. The SEC is notified of the resale.[16]

• *Exhibit* **31–2 A Sample Restricted Stock Certificate**

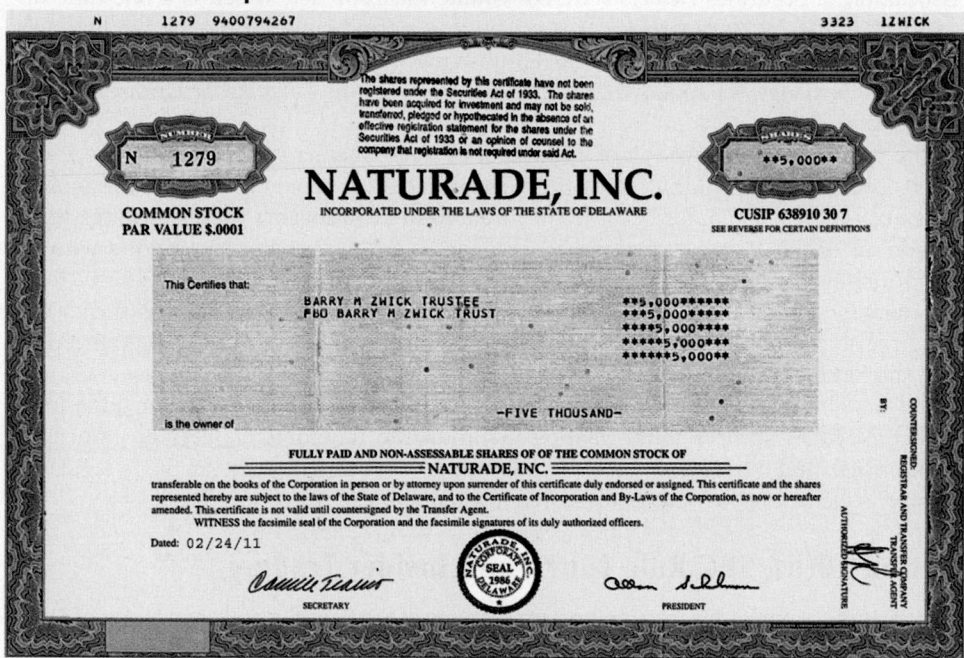

Rule 144A. Securities that at the time of issue are not of the same class as securities listed on a national securities exchange or quoted in a U.S. automated inter-dealer quotation system may be resold under Rule 144A.[17] They may be sold only to a qualified institutional buyer (an institution, such as an insurance company or a bank that owns and invests at least $100 million in securities). The seller must take reasonable steps to ensure that the buyer knows that the seller is relying on the exemption under Rule 144A. A sample restricted stock certificate is shown in Exhibit 31–2.

Violations of the 1933 Act

It is a violation of the Securities Act of 1933 to intentionally defraud investors by misrepresenting or omitting facts in a registration statement or prospectus. Liability is also imposed on those who are negligent for not discovering the fraud. Selling securities before the effective date of the registration statement or under an exemption for which the securities do not qualify results in liability.

Criminal violations are prosecuted by the U.S. Department of Justice. Violators may be fined up to $10,000, imprisoned for up to five years, or both. The SEC is authorized

CONTRAST Securities do not have to be held for a specific period (six months or one year) to be exempt from registration on a resale under Rule 144A, as they do under Rule 144.

---

15. Before 2008, when amendments to Rule 144 became effective, the holding period was one year if the issuer was subject to the reporting requirements of the 1934 act. See the revised SEC Rules and Regulations at 72 Federal Rules 71546-01, 2007 WL 4368599, Release No. 33-8869. This reduced holding period allows non-public issuers to raise capital electronically from private and overseas sources more quickly.
16. 17 C.F.R. Section 230.144.
17. 17 C.F.R. Section 230.144A.

to seek civil sanctions against those who willfully violate the 1933 act. It can request an injunction to prevent further sales of the securities involved or ask the court to grant other relief, such as an order to a violator to refund profits. Parties who purchase securities and suffer harm as a result of false or omitted statements may also bring suits in a federal court to recover their losses and other damages.

There are three basic defenses to charges of violations under the 1933 act. A defendant can avoid liability by proving that (1) the statement or omission was not material, (2) the plaintiff knew about the misrepresentation at the time of purchasing the stock, or (3) the defendant exercised *due diligence* in preparing the registration and reasonably believed at the time that the statements were true.

► Securities Exchange Act of 1934

The Securities Exchange Act of 1934 provides for the regulation and registration of securities exchanges, brokers, dealers, and national securities associations, such as the National Association of Securities Dealers (NASD). Unlike the 1933 act, which is a one-time disclosure law, the 1934 act provides for continuous periodic disclosures by publicly held corporations to enable the SEC to regulate subsequent trading. For a discussion of how the Securities Exchange Act applies in the online context, see the *Adapting the Law to the Online Environment* feature.

The Securities Exchange Act of 1934 applies to companies that have assets in excess of $10 million and five hundred or more shareholders. These corporations are referred to as Section 12 companies because they are required to register their securities under Section 12 of the 1934 act. Section 12 companies are required to file reports with the SEC annually and quarterly, and sometimes even monthly if specified events occur (such as a merger). Other provisions in the 1934 act require all securities brokers and dealers to be registered, to keep detailed records of their activities, and to file annual reports with the SEC.

The act also authorizes the SEC to engage in market surveillance to deter undesirable market practices such as fraud, market manipulation (attempts at illegally influencing stock prices), and misrepresentation. In addition, the act provides for the SEC's regulation of proxy solicitations for voting (discussed in Chapter 30).

SEC Rule 10b-5   A rule of the Securities and Exchange Commission that makes it unlawful, in connection with the purchase or sale of any security, to make any untrue statement of a material fact or to omit a material fact if such omission causes the statement to be misleading.

Section 10(b), SEC Rule 10b-5, and Insider Trading

Section 10(b) is one of the more important sections of the Securities Exchange Act of 1934. This section proscribes the use of any manipulative or deceptive device in violation of SEC rules and regulations. Among the rules that the SEC has promulgated pursuant to the 1934 act is **SEC Rule 10b-5,** which prohibits the commission of fraud in connection with the purchase or sale of any security.

APPLICABILITY OF SEC RULE 10B-5   SEC Rule 10b-5 applies to almost all trading of securities, whether on organized exchanges, in over-the-counter markets, or in private transactions. Generally, the rule covers just about any form of security, including, among other things, notes, bonds, agreements to form a corporation, and joint-venture agreements. The securities need not be registered under the 1933 act for the 1934 act to apply.

SEC Rule 10b-5 applies only when the requisites of federal jurisdiction—such as the use of stock exchange facilities, U.S. mail, or any means of interstate commerce—are present, but this requirement is easily met because almost every commercial transaction involves interstate contacts. In addition, the states have corporate securities laws, many of which include provisions similar to SEC Rule 10b-5.

FBI agents escort Joseph Contorinis from FBI headquarters in New York in 2009. He was accused of making several million dollars from insider tips provided by an investment banker.

(AP Photo/Louis Lanzano)

Adapting the Law to the Online Environment

Corporate Blogs and Tweets Must Comply with the Securities Exchange Act

In the fast-paced world of securities trading, there is great demand for the latest information about companies, earnings, and market conditions. Corporations are meeting this demand by establishing Web sites and blogs, and using other interactive online media, such as Twitter and online shareholder forums. Nearly 20 percent of Fortune 500 companies now sponsor blogs. Corporations that use the Internet to distribute information to investors, however, must make sure that they comply with SEC regulations. For purposes of federal securities laws, the SEC treats statements by employees on online media, such as blogs and Twitter, the same as any other company statements.

Beware of Tweets Containing Financial Information

Some corporate blogs include links to corporate employees' Twitter accounts so that readers can communicate directly with, and get updates from, the individual who posted the information. For example, eBay, Inc., launched its corporate blog in 2008. A few months later, Richard Brewer-Hay, a seasoned blogger whom eBay hired to report online about the company, began *tweeting* (posting updates on Twitter) about eBay's quarterly earnings and what took place at Silicon Valley technology conferences. Brewer-Hay's tweets gained him a following, but then eBay's lawyers required him to include a regulatory disclaimer with certain posts to avoid problems with the SEC. Many members of his audience were disappointed by the company's supervision, which curbed his spontaneity. Brewer-Hay is now much more reserved in his tweets on financial matters and often simply repeats eBay executives' statements verbatim.[a]

A 2008 SEC Release Provides Guidance

The reaction of eBay's lawyers to Brewer-Hay's tweets was prompted, in part, by an interpretive release issued by the SEC in August 2008. As noted earlier in this chapter, the SEC generally embraces new technology and encourages companies to use it. In the release, the SEC noted that, in some circumstances, posting information on a company's Web site may be a "sufficient method of public disclosure."

The release also acknowledged that company-sponsored blogs, electronic shareholders' forums, and other interactive Web features can be a useful means of ongoing communications among companies, their shareholders, and other stakeholders. The SEC cautioned, though, that all communications made by or on behalf of a company are subject to the antifraud provisions of federal securities laws. "While blogs or forums can be informal and conversational in nature, statements made there . . . will not be treated differently from other company statements." In addition, the release stated that companies cannot require investors to waive protections under federal securities laws as a condition of participating in a blog or forum. The release also warned companies that they can, in some situations, be liable for providing hyperlinks to third party information or inaccurate summaries of financial information on their Web sites.[b]

FOR CRITICAL ANALYSIS

Would Brewer-Hay's tweets about what had transpired at technology conferences require SEC disclosures? Why or why not?

---

a. Cari Tuna, "Corporate Blogs and 'Tweets' Must Keep SEC in Mind," *Wall Street Journal Online*, April 27, 2009.

b. SEC Release Nos. 34–58288, IC–28351, File No. S7–23–08, Commission Guidance on the Use of Company Web Sites.

Insider Trading The purchase or sale of securities on the basis of information that has not been made available to the public.

INSIDER TRADING One of the major goals of Section 10(b) and SEC Rule 10b-5 is to prevent so-called **insider trading,** which occurs when persons buy or sell securities on the basis of information that is not available to the public. Corporate directors, officers, and others such as majority shareholders, for instance, often have advance inside information that can affect the future market value of the corporate stock. Obviously, if they act on this information, their positions give them a trading advantage over the general public and other shareholders. The 1934 Securities Exchange Act defines inside information and extends liability to those who take advantage of such information in their personal transactions when they know that the information is unavailable to those with whom they are dealing. Section 10(b) of the 1934 act and SEC Rule 10b-5 apply to anyone who has access to or receives information of a nonpublic nature on which trading is based—not just to corporate "insiders."

DISCLOSURE UNDER SEC RULE 10B-5 Any material omission or misrepresentation of material facts in connection with the purchase or sale of a security may violate not only the Securities Act of 1933 but also the antifraud provisions of Section 10(b) of the 1934 act and SEC Rule 10b-5. The key to liability (which can be civil or criminal) under Section 10(b) and SEC Rule 10b-5 is whether the insider's information is *material.*

The following are some examples of material facts calling for disclosure under SEC Rule 10b-5:

1. Fraudulent trading in the company stock by a broker-dealer.
2. A dividend change (whether up or down).
3. A contract for the sale of corporate assets.
4. A new discovery, a new process, or a new product.
5. A significant change in the firm's financial condition.
6. Potential litigation against the company.

Note that any one of these facts, by itself, is not *automatically* considered a material fact. Rather, it will be regarded as a material fact if it is significant enough that it would likely affect an investor's decision as to whether to purchase or sell the company's securities. **EXAMPLE 31.5** Sheen, Inc., is the defendant in a class-action product liability suit that its attorney, Paula Frasier, believes that the company will lose. Frasier has advised Sheen's directors, officers, and accountants that the company will likely have to pay a substantial damages award. Sheen plans to make a $5 million offering of newly issued stock before the date when the trial is expected to end. Sheen's potential liability and the financial consequences to the firm are material facts that must be disclosed because they are significant enough to affect an investor's decision as to whether to purchase the stock. ●

The following is one of the classic cases interpreting materiality under SEC Rule 10b-5.

Classic Case 31.1   Securities and Exchange Commission v. Texas Gulf Sulphur Co.

United States Court of Appeals, Second Circuit, 401 F.2d 833 (1968).

HISTORICAL AND ENVIRONMENTAL SETTING *In 1957, the Texas Gulf Sulphur Company (TGS) began exploring for minerals in eastern Canada. In March 1959, aerial geophysical surveys were conducted over more than fifteen thousand square miles of the area. The operations revealed numerous variations in the conductivity of the rock, which indicated a remarkable concentration of commercially exploitable minerals. One site of such variations was near Timmins, Ontario. On October 29 and 30, 1963, a ground survey of the site near Timmins indicated a need to drill for further evaluation.*

After sample drilling revealed potential mineral deposits, company executives made substantial stock purchases. Did they violate insider-trading laws?

FACTS On November 12, 1963, the Texas Gulf Sulphur Company drilled a hole that appeared to yield a core with an exceedingly high mineral content, although further drilling would be necessary to establish whether there was enough ore to be mined commercially. TGS kept secret the results of the core sample. After learning of the ore discovery, officers and employees of the company made substantial purchases of TGS's stock or accepted stock options (rights to purchase stock). On April 11, 1964, an unauthorized report of the mineral find appeared in the newspapers. On the following day, April 12, TGS issued a press release that played down the discovery and stated that it was too early to tell whether the ore find would be significant. Later on, TGS announced a strike of at least

25 million tons of ore. The news led to a substantial increase in the price of TGS stock. The Securities and Exchange Commission (SEC) brought a suit in a federal district court against the officers and employees of TGS for violating the insider-trading prohibition of SEC Rule 10b-5. The officers and employees argued that the prohibition did not apply. They reasoned that the information on which they had traded was not material, as the find had not been commercially proved. The trial court held that most of the defendants had not violated SEC Rule 10b-5, and the SEC appealed.

ISSUE Did the officers and employees of TGS violate SEC Rule 10b-5 by buying the stock, even though they did not know the full extent and profit potential of the ore discovery at the time of their purchases?

DECISION Yes. The U.S. Court of Appeals for the Second Circuit reversed the lower court's decision and remanded the case for further proceedings, holding that the employees and officers had violated SEC Rule 10b-5's prohibition against insider trading.

REASON For SEC Rule 10b-5 purposes, the test of materiality is whether the information would affect the judgment of reasonable investors. Reasonable investors include speculative as well as conservative investors. "A major factor in determining whether the * * * discovery [of the ore] was a material fact is the importance attached to the drilling results by those who knew about it. * * * The timing by those who knew of it of their stock purchases and their purchases of short-term calls [rights to buy shares at a specified price within a specified time period]—purchases in

Case 31.1–Continued

some cases by individuals who had never before purchased calls or even TGS stock—virtually compels the inference that the insiders were influenced by the drilling results. * * * We hold, therefore, that all transactions in TGS stock or calls by individuals apprised of the drilling results * * * were made in violation of Rule 10b-5."

IMPACT OF THIS CASE ON TODAY'S LAW *This landmark case affirmed the principle that the test of whether information is "material," for SEC Rule 10b-5 purposes, is whether it would affect the judgment of reasonable investors. The corporate insiders' purchases of stock and*

stock options indicated that they were influenced by the results and that the information about the results was material. The courts continue to cite this case when applying SEC Rule 10b-5 to other cases of alleged insider trading.

RELEVANT WEB SITES *To locate information on the Web concerning the* Securities and Exchange Commission v. Texas Gulf Sulphur Co. *decision, go to this text's Web site at* www.cengage.com/blaw/blt. *Select "Chapter 31" and click on "Classic Cases."*

THE PRIVATE SECURITIES LITIGATION REFORM ACT OF 1995 One of the unintended effects of SEC Rule 10b-5 was to deter the disclosure of forward-looking information. To understand why, consider an example. **EXAMPLE 31.6** QT Company announces that its projected earnings in a future time period will be a certain amount, but the forecast turns out to be wrong. The earnings are in fact much lower, and the price of QT's stock is affected—negatively. The shareholders then bring a class-action suit against the company, alleging that the directors violated SEC Rule 10b-5 by disclosing misleading financial information. ●

In an attempt to rectify this problem and promote disclosure, Congress passed the Private Securities Litigation Reform Act of 1995. The act provides a "safe harbor" for publicly held companies that make forward-looking statements, such as financial forecasts. Those who make such statements are protected against liability for securities fraud as long as the statements are accompanied by "meaningful cautionary statements identifying important factors that could cause actual results to differ materially from those in the forward-looking statement."[18]

After the 1995 act was passed, a number of securities class-action suits were filed in state courts to skirt the requirements of the 1995 federal act. In response to this problem, Congress passed the Securities Litigation Uniform Standards Act of 1998 (SLUSA).[19] The act placed stringent limits on the ability of plaintiffs to bring class-action suits in state courts against firms whose securities are traded on national stock exchanges. SLUSA not only prevents the purchasers and sellers of securities from bringing class-action fraud claims under state securities laws, but also applies to investors who are fraudulently induced to hold on to their securities.[20]

OUTSIDERS AND SEC RULE 10B-5 The traditional insider-trading case involves true insiders—corporate officers, directors, and majority shareholders who have access to (and trade on) inside information. Increasingly, liability under Section 10(b) of the 1934 act and SEC Rule 10b-5 is being extended to certain "outsiders"—those persons who trade on inside information acquired indirectly. As will be discussed shortly, two theories have been developed under which outsiders may be held liable for insider trading: the *tipper/tippee theory* and the *misappropriation theory.*

In the following case, the plaintiffs attempted to assert a third theory—scheme liability. Can Section 10(b) and SEC Rule 10b-5 apply to outsiders—suppliers and customers—who seemingly "aid and abet" a scheme to show inflated sales revenue figures for a publicly traded company?

---

18. 15 U.S.C. Sections 77z-2, 78u-5.

19. Pub. L. No. 105-353. This act amended many sections of Title 15 of the *United States Code.*

20. *Merrill Lynch, Pierce, Fenner & Smith, Inc. v. Dabit,* 547 U.S. 71, 126 S.Ct. 1503, 164 L.Ed.2d 179 (2006). This Supreme Court decision forms the basis of the *Case Analysis Question* on page 807.

Case 31.2   Stoneridge Investment Partners, LLC v. Scientific-Atlanta, Inc.

Supreme Court of the United States, 552 U.S. 148, 128 S.Ct. 761, 169 L.Ed.2d 627 (2008).
www.supremecourtus.gov/opinions/opinions.html[a]

A cable TV operator, in a scheme to report higher earnings, asked its set-top box suppliers to overcharge them. Can investors in the cable company sue the set-top box suppliers for their role in the scheme?

FACTS   In 2000, the cable operator Charter Communications wanted to satisfy stock analysts' expectations about its revenue growth and thereby keep its stock price high. When it became apparent that revenues were not growing as projected, Charter's management devised an accounting scheme that would artificially inflate its reported revenues. The scheme involved Charter's digital cable converter (set top) box suppliers, Scientific-Atlanta and Motorola. They agreed to overcharge Charter for the cable boxes in exchange for additional advertising on Charter's cable network. A group of investors, represented in this case by Stoneridge Investment Partners, sued Scientific-Atlanta and Motorola, alleging violation of Section 10(b) of the Securities Exchange Act of 1934 and of SEC Rule 10b-5. At trial, the district court dismissed the case. On appeal, the U.S. Court of Appeals for the Eighth Circuit upheld this ruling. Stoneridge then appealed to the United States Supreme Court.

ISSUE   Can Charter investors sue third-party suppliers and customers (Scientific-Atlanta and Motorola) for participating in a scheme to overcharge Charter for cable boxes so that Charter could report inflated sales revenue figures?

a. Click on "2007 Term Opinions of the Court" and scroll down to "1/15/08" to access this case's opinion.

DECISION   No. The United States Supreme Court affirmed the federal appellate court's decision that dismissed the case against Scientific-Atlanta and Motorola. Section 10(b)'s private right of action cannot be applied to a supplier or customer. Investors did not rely on Scientific-Atlanta's and Motorola's statements or representations.

REASON   The Court pointed out that Scientific-Atlanta and Motorola had no role in preparing or disseminating Charter's financial statements. The financial statements of both Scientific-Atlanta and Motorola were correct. The $20 per cable set top box that they received from Charter was offset by their agreeing to spend the equivalent of $20 per cable set-top box in additional advertising. They "booked the transactions as a wash, under generally accepted accounting practices." To bring a Section 10(b) private action, the plaintiff must have relied on the defendant's deceptive acts. There has to be the "requisite causal connection between a defendant's misrepresentation and a plaintiff's injury" in order to assess liability against the defendant. But in this case, neither Scientific-Atlanta nor Motorola had a duty to disclose, and their deceptive acts were not communicated to the public. "No member of the investing public had knowledge, either actual or presumed, of [their] deceptive acts during the relevant times." Consequently, Stoneridge was unable to show reliance upon any of the actions of Scientific-Atlanta and Motorola "except in an indirect chain" that the Court found too remote to justify liability.

FOR CRITICAL ANALYSIS—Global Consideration   *The Court noted that a ruling in favor of the investors bringing the suit would have had negative effects on foreign companies doing business within the United States. Explain the logic behind this line of reasoning.*

Tippee   A person who receives inside information.

Tipper/Tippee Theory.   Anyone who acquires inside information as a result of a corporate insider's breach of his or her fiduciary duty can be liable under SEC Rule 10b-5. This liability extends to **tippees** (those who receive "tips" from insiders) and even remote tippees (tippees of tippees).

The key to liability under this theory is that the inside information must be obtained as a result of someone's breach of a fiduciary duty to the corporation whose shares are involved in the trading. The tippee is liable under this theory only if (1) there is a breach of a duty not to disclose inside information, (2) the disclosure is in exchange for personal benefit, and (3) the tippee knows (or should know) of this breach and benefits from it.[21]

Misappropriation Theory.   Liability for insider trading may also be established under the misappropriation theory. This theory holds that an individual who wrongfully obtains (misappropriates) inside information and trades on it for her or his personal gain should be held liable because, in essence, she or he stole information rightfully belonging to another.

---

21. See, for example, *Chiarella v. United States*, 445 U.S. 222, 100 S.Ct. 1108, 63 L.Ed.2d 348 (1980); and *Dirks v. SEC*, 463 U.S. 646, 103 S.Ct. 3255, 77 L.Ed.2d 911 (1983).

The misappropriation theory has been controversial because it significantly extends the reach of SEC Rule 10b-5 to outsiders who ordinarily would *not* be deemed fiduciaries of the corporations in whose stock they trade. The United States Supreme Court, however, has held that liability under SEC Rule 10b-5 can be based on the misappropriation theory.[22]

It is not always wrong to disclose material, nonpublic information about a company to another person. Nevertheless, a person who obtains the information and trades securities on it can be liable. **CASE EXAMPLE 31.7**   Patricia Rocklage was the wife of Scott Rocklage, the chair and chief executive officer of Cubist Pharmaceuticals, Inc. Scott had sometimes disclosed material, nonpublic information about Cubist to Patricia, and she had always kept the information confidential. In December 2001, however, when Scott told Patricia that one of Cubist's key drugs had failed its clinical trial and reminded her not to tell anyone, Patricia refused to keep the information secret. She then warned her brother, William Beaver, who owned Cubist stock. William sold his 5,583 Cubist shares and tipped his friend David Jones, who sold his 7,500 shares.

On January 16, 2002, Cubist publicly announced the trial results, and the price of its stock dropped. William and David had avoided losses of $99,527 and $133,222, respectively, by selling when they did. The SEC filed a lawsuit against Patricia, William, and David, alleging insider trading. The defendants claimed that because Patricia had told Scott that she was going to tell William about the failed trial, they had not "misappropriated" the information. The court, however, determined that Patricia had "engaged in deceptive devices," because she "tricked her husband into revealing confidential information to her so that she could, and did, assist her brother with the sale of his Cubist stock." The court therefore found all three defendants guilty of insider trading under the misappropriation theory.[23] ●

INSIDER REPORTING AND TRADING—SECTION 16(B)   Section 16(b) of the 1934 act provides for the recapture by the corporation of all profits realized by an insider on any purchase and sale or sale and purchase of the corporation's stock within any six-month period.[24] It is irrelevant whether the insider actually uses inside information; *all such* **short-swing profits** *must be returned to the corporation.* In this context, *insiders* means officers, directors, and large stockholders of Section 12 corporations (those owning at least 10 percent of the class of equity securities registered under Section 12 of the 1934 act). To discourage such insiders from using nonpublic information about their companies for their personal benefit in the stock market, they must file reports with the SEC concerning their ownership and trading of the corporation's securities.

Section 16(b) applies not only to stock but also to warrants, options, and securities convertible into stock. In addition, the courts have fashioned complex rules for determining profits. Note that the SEC exempts a number of transactions under Rule 16b-3.[25] For all of these reasons, corporate insiders are wise to seek specialized counsel before trading in the corporation's stock. Exhibit 31–3 on the following page compares the effects of SEC Rule 10b-5 and Section 16(b).

Regulation of Proxy Statements

Section 14(a) of the Securities Exchange Act of 1934 regulates the solicitation of proxies (see Chapter 30) from shareholders of Section 12 companies. The SEC regulates the content of proxy statements. Whoever solicits a proxy must fully and accurately disclose in the proxy statement all of the facts that are pertinent to the matter on which the shareholders

Short-Swing Profits   Profits earned by a purchase and sale, or sale and purchase, of the same security within a six-month period; under Section 16(b) of the 1934 Securities Exchange Act, must be returned to the corporation if earned by company insiders from transactions in the company's stock.

ON THE WEB   For information on investor protection, including answers to frequently asked questions on the topic of securities fraud, go to **www.securitieslaw.com**.

---

22. *United States v. O'Hagan,* 521 U.S. 642, 117 S.Ct. 2199, 138 L.Ed.2d 724 (1997).
23. *SEC v. Rocklage,* 470 F.3d 1 (1st Cir. 2006).
24. A person who expects the price of a particular stock to decline can realize profits by "selling short"—selling at a high price and repurchasing later at a lower price to cover the "short sale."
25. 17 C.F.R. Section 240.16b-3.

● *Exhibit* 31–3 Comparison of Coverage, Application, and
Liability under SEC Rule 10b-5 and Section 16(b)

AREA OF COMPARISON	SEC RULE 10b-5	SECTION 16(b)
What is the subject matter of the transaction?	Any security (does not have to be registered).	Any security (does not have to be registered).
What transactions are covered?	Purchase or sale.	Short-swing purchase and sale or short-swing sale and purchase.
Who is subject to liability?	Almost anyone with inside information under a duty to disclose—including officers, directors, controlling shareholders, and tippees.	Officers, directors, and certain shareholders who own 10 percent or more.
Is omission or misrepresentation necessary for liability?	Yes.	No.
Are there any exempt transactions?	No.	Yes, there are a number of exemptions.
Who may bring an action?	A person transacting with an insider, the SEC, or a purchaser or seller damaged by a wrongful act.	A corporation or a shareholder by derivative action.

are to vote. SEC Rule 14a-9 is similar to the antifraud provisions of SEC Rule 10b-5. Remedies for violations are extensive, ranging from injunctions to prevent a vote from being taken to monetary damages.

Violations of the 1934 Act

As mentioned earlier, violations of Section 10(b) of the Securities Exchange Act of 1934 and SEC Rule 10b-5, including insider trading, may be subject to criminal or civil liability. For either criminal or civil sanctions to be imposed, however, *scienter* must exist—that is, the violator must have had an intent to defraud or knowledge of her or his misconduct (see Chapter 11). *Scienter* can be proved by showing that the defendant made false statements or wrongfully failed to disclose material facts.

Violations of Section 16(b) include the sale by insiders of stock acquired less than six months before the sale (or less than six months after the sale if selling short). These violations are subject to civil sanctions. Liability under Section 16(b) is strict liability. Neither *scienter* nor negligence is required.

Ethical Issue ⚖

When a company is held liable for a Section 10(b) violation, should its accounting firm also be held liable? Royal Ahold, N.V., a Dutch corporation, and its Maryland-based subsidiary, U.S. Foodservice, Inc. (USF), own and operate food service companies in the United States and elsewhere. From 1990 through 2003, Ahold perpetrated two frauds that resulted in its earnings being overstated by at least $500 million. Ahold and USF were later found liable for securities fraud, and Ahold shareholders brought a class-action suit against Deloitte & Touche, LLP, the accounting firm that had advised Ahold and USF.

One of Ahold's frauds had involved the accounting treatment of income from various joint ventures. Deloitte had been involved with Ahold since 1992 and had provided advice on the consolidation of the financial reports of joint ventures before the first venture was formed. None of Ahold's joint-venture agreements gave it the control necessary to consolidate their financial reports, but Ahold represented to Deloitte that it had sufficient control. Deloitte did not verify Ahold's control and only later discovered that Ahold's stake in the ventures was insufficient for consolidation. The second fraud involved USF's internal system for promotional allowances (PAs). Before Ahold had acquired USF in 2000, Deloitte performed a due diligence investigation and reported that USF's internal system for PAs was fraudulent and required a restatement of $11 million of PA income. In a 2001 audit, Deloitte reported that it "was unable to obtain supporting documentation" for some of the PA statistical samples. By 2003, Deloitte concluded that USF's system had been fraudulently inflating its PA income.

The class-action plaintiffs argued that Deloitte should be liable for the fraudulent accounting practices because of the "red flags" raised by the treatment of the joint-venture revenues and the PA income. The court, however, dismissed the suit. The court said that to establish liability for securities fraud, there must be evidence that leads to a strong inference of *scienter* on the part of the defendant. Here, such evidence was lacking. Instead, said the court, "the stronger and more plausible inference" is that the acountants "were, like the plaintiffs, victims of Ahold's fraud rather than its enablers."[26]

CRIMINAL PENALTIES For violations of Section 10(b) and Rule 10b-5, an individual may be fined up to $5 million, imprisoned for up to twenty years, or both. A partnership or a corporation may be fined up to $25 million. Under Section 807 of the Sarbanes-Oxley Act of 2002, for a *willful* violation of the 1934 act the violator may, in addition to being subject to a fine, be imprisoned for up to twenty-five years.

For a defendant to be convicted in a criminal prosecution under the securities laws, there can be no reasonable doubt that the defendant knew he or she was acting wrongfully—a jury is not allowed merely to speculate that the defendant may have acted willfully. **CASE EXAMPLE 31.8** Martha Stewart, founder of a well-known media and homemaking empire, was once charged with intentionally deceiving investors based on statements she made at a Martha Stewart Living Omnimedia (MSLO) conference. In December 2001, Stewart's stockbroker allegedly had informed Stewart that the head of ImClone Systems, Inc., was selling his shares in that company. Stewart then sold her ImClone shares. The next day, ImClone announced that the U.S. Food and Drug Administration had failed to approve Erbitux, the company's greatly anticipated medication.

The government began to investigate Stewart's ImClone trades, the media began to report on the investigation, and the value of MSLO stock began to fall. In June 2002, Stewart publicly stated at an MSLO conference that she had previously instructed her stockbroker to sell her ImClone stock if the price fell to $60 per share. The government filed a lawsuit and argued that Stewart's statement represented an intent to deceive because it was deliberately directed to investors at a time when she was aware that the negative publicity was affecting the market value of MSLO securities. The court, however, acquitted Stewart on this charge because "to find the essential element of criminal intent beyond a reasonable doubt, a rational juror would have to speculate."[27] Stewart was later convicted on other charges relating to her ImClone trading that did not require proof of intent. •

CIVIL SANCTIONS The SEC can also bring suit in a federal district court against anyone violating or aiding in a violation of the 1934 act or SEC rules by purchasing or selling a security while in the possession of material nonpublic information.[28] The violation must occur on or through the facilities of a national securities exchange or from or through a broker or dealer. The court may assess a penalty for as much as triple the profits gained or the

---

26. *Public Employees' Retirement Association of Colorado v. Deloitte & Touche, LLP,* 551 F.3d 305 (4th Cir. 2009).
27. *United States v. Stewart,* 305 F.Supp.2d 368 (S.D.N.Y. 2004).
28. The Insider Trading Sanctions Act of 1984, 15 U.S.C. Section 78u(d)(2)(A).

loss avoided by the guilty party.[29] The Insider Trading and Securities Fraud Enforcement Act of 1988 enlarged the class of persons who may be subject to civil liability for insider trading and gave the SEC authority to give monetary rewards to informants.[30]

Private parties may also sue violators of Section 10(b) and Rule 10b-5. A private party may obtain rescission (cancellation) of a contract to buy securities or damages to the extent of the violator's illegal profits. Those found liable have a right to seek contribution from those who share responsibility for the violations, including accountants, attorneys, and corporations. For violations of Section 16(b), a corporation can bring an action to recover the short-swing profits.

Recall from Chapter 12 that a required element of fraud is reliance; the innocent party must justifiably have relied on the misrepresentation. If an investor is aware of misrepresentations by corporate management and purchases shares in the firm anyway, can the investor still bring a lawsuit against the corporation for a violation of Rule 10b-5? That was the question in the following case.

---

29. Profit or loss is defined as "the difference between the purchase or sale price of the security and the value of that security as measured by the trading price of the security at a reasonable period of time after public dissemination of the nonpublic information." 15 U.S.C. Section 78u(d)(2)(C).

30. 15 U.S.C. Section 78u-1.

Case 31.3   Stark Trading v. Falconbridge, Ltd.

United States Court of Appeals, Seventh Circuit, 552 F.3d 568 (2009).
www.ca7.uscourts.gov[a]

COMPANY PROFILE   *Brian Stark's interest in investing began in high school when he worked for his father, an independent accountant. Together, they invested in the financial markets. Stark tested his own investment theories throughout college and law school, where he met Mike Roth. In 1992, Stark and Roth formed Stark Trading. Known today as Stark Investments (www.starkinvestments.com), the firm invests in commodities, real estate, equity, and other markets. Its principals apply hedging and portfolio management techniques on behalf of their investors, including institutions, investment funds, and wealthy individuals. The firm has offices in cities around the world, including Hong Kong, London, Singapore, and Toronto.*

In the first decade of the 2000s, many mining companies bought out their competitors.

FACTS   Stark Trading was a minority shareholder in Falconbridge, Inc. Noranda, Inc., owned 59 percent of Falconbridge. Both were Canadian mining companies. Noranda offered its common stockholders preferred stock for their common stock. Noranda also offered to redeem the preferred stock for $25 per share, which exceeded the market value of the common stock. On the same day, Noranda offered minority shareholders in Falconbridge 1.77 shares of Noranda common stock for each share of Falconbridge common stock. Stark knew that

Noranda's value was overstated in the offer to its common stockholders. Stark thought that the Falconbridge stock was undervalued in the market. This meant that Noranda was buying out Falconbridge's shareholders at a reduced price. Stark sent a letter explaining this to the Ontario Securities Commission. Nonetheless, Stark exchanged its Falconbridge shares for Noranda stock. Later, Noranda and Falconbridge merged to become Falconbridge, Ltd. Stark and others filed a suit in a federal district court against the new firm, alleging a violation of Rule 10b-5. The court dismissed the suit. The plaintiffs appealed.

ISSUE   Should the investors' claim under Rule 10b-5 be dismissed if the investors were not deceived by a purported dishonest tender offer?

DECISION   Yes. The U.S. Court of Appeals for the Seventh Circuit upheld the lower court's decision. "So implausible is an inference of reliance from the complaint in this case * * * that the dismissal of the 10b-5 claim must be affirmed."

REASON   A suit can be brought under Rule 10b-5 if a party buys stock at a price inflated by the misrepresentations of its issuer and sells the stock at a loss when the truth is revealed and the price drops. In this case, the plaintiffs argued that Noranda's offer to trade its stock for Falconbridge's stock inflated the value of Noranda's stock. But the plaintiffs were not fooled. As they explained in their letter to the Ontario Securities Commission, they were aware of what Noranda was trying to do. Thus, reliance is missing from the plaintiffs' claim for fraud as a violation of Rule 10b-5. "Sophisticated investors, they must have considered the combination of the tender offer and a later suit (this suit) against the defendants a better

---

a. In the left-hand column, click on "Opinions." On that page, in the "Case Number:" boxes, type "08" and "1327," and click on "List Case(s)." In the result, click on the appropriate link to access the opinion.

Case 31.3–Continued

deal than holding on to their shares"–because Canadian law might have applied and would not have provided the same remedy as U.S. law–but "this is not a strategy that the courts should reward in the name of rectifying securities fraud."

FOR CRITICAL ANALYSIS—Global Consideration
Noranda and Falconbridge were Canadian companies. Falconbridge, Ltd., was later bought by Xstrata, a Swiss mining company. On what basis could a U.S. court exercise jurisdiction in this case?

 State Securities Laws

Today, every state has its own corporate securities laws, or "blue sky laws," that regulate the offer and sale of securities within its borders. (As mentioned in Chapter 11, the phrase *blue sky laws* dates to a 1917 decision by the United States Supreme Court in which the Court declared that the purpose of such laws was to prevent "speculative schemes which have no more basis than so many feet of 'blue sky.'")[31] Article 8 of the Uniform Commercial Code, which has been adopted by all of the states, also imposes various requirements relating to the purchase and sale of securities.

BE AWARE Federal securities laws do not take priority over state securities laws.

Requirements under State Securities Laws

Typically, state laws have disclosure requirements and antifraud provisions, many of which are patterned after Section 10(b) of the Securities Exchange Act of 1934 and SEC Rule 10b-5. State laws also provide for the registration of securities offered or issued for sale within the state and impose disclosure requirements. Methods of registration, required disclosures, and exemptions from registration vary among states. Unless an exemption from registration is applicable, issuers must register or qualify their stock with the appropriate state official, often called a *corporations commissioner.* Additionally, most state securities laws regulate securities brokers and dealers.

Concurrent Regulation

State securities laws apply mainly to intrastate transactions. Since the adoption of the 1933 and 1934 federal securities acts, the state and federal governments have regulated securities concurrently. Issuers must comply with both federal and state securities laws, and exemptions from federal law are not exemptions from state laws.

The dual federal and state system has not always worked well, particularly during the early 1990s, when the securities markets underwent considerable expansion. In response, Congress passed the National Securities Markets Improvement Act of 1996, which eliminated some of the duplicate regulations and gave the SEC exclusive power to regulate most national securities activities. The National Conference of Commissioners on Uniform State Laws then substantially revised the Uniform Securities Act to coordinate state and federal securities regulation and enforcement efforts. The new version was offered to the states for adoption in 2002. Seventeen states have adopted the Uniform Securities Act, and other states are considering adoption.[32]

---

31. *Hall v. Geiger-Jones Co.,* 242 U.S. 539, 37 S.Ct. 217, 61 L.Ed. 480 (1917).
32. At the time this book went to press, the Uniform Securities Act had been adopted in Georgia, Hawaii, Idaho, Indiana, Iowa, Kansas, Maine, Michigan, Minnesota, Mississippi, Missouri, New Mexico, Oklahoma, South Carolina, South Dakota, Vermont, and Wisconsin, as well as in the U.S. Virgin Islands. Adoption legislation was pending in Indiana and Washington State. You can find current information on state adoptions at www.nccusl.com.

▶ Corporate Governance

Corporate Governance   A set of policies or procedures affecting the way a corporation is directed or controlled.

Corporate governance can be narrowly defined as the relationship between a corporation and its shareholders. Some argue for a broader definition—that corporate governance specifies the rights and responsibilities among different participants in the corporation, such as the board of directors, managers, shareholders, and other stakeholders, and spells out the rules and procedures for making decisions on corporate affairs. Regardless of the way it is defined, effective corporate governance requires more than just compliance with laws and regulations. (For a discussion of corporate governance in other nations, see this chapter's *Beyond Our Borders* feature.)

Effective corporate governance is essential in large corporations because corporate ownership (by shareholders) is separated from corporate control (by officers and managers). Under these circumstances, officers and managers may attempt to advance their own interests at the expense of the shareholders. The well-publicized corporate scandals in the early 2000s clearly illustrate the reasons for concern about managerial opportunism.

Attempts at Aligning the Interests of Officers with Those of Shareholders

Stock Option   A right to buy a given number of shares of stock at a set price, usually within a specified time period.

Some corporations have sought to align the financial interests of their officers with those of the company's shareholders by providing the officers with **stock options,** which enable them to purchase shares of the corporation's stock at a set price. When the market price rises above that level, the officers can sell their shares for a profit. Because a stock's market price generally increases as the corporation prospers, the options give the officers a financial stake in the corporation's well-being and supposedly encourage them to work hard for the benefit of the shareholders.

Options have turned out to be an imperfect device for providing effective governance, however. Executives in some companies have been tempted to "cook" the company's books in order to keep share prices higher so that they could sell their stock for a profit. Executives in other corporations have experienced no losses when share prices dropped; instead, their options were "repriced" so that they did not suffer from the share price decline and could still profit from future increases above the lowered share price. Thus, although stock options theoretically can motivate officers to protect shareholder interests, stock option plans have often become a way for officers to take advantage of shareholders.

With stock options generally failing to work as planned and numerous headline-making scandals occurring within major corporations, there has been an outcry for more "outside" directors (those with no formal employment affiliation with the company). The theory is that independent directors will more closely monitor the actions of corporate officers. Hence, today we see more boards with outside directors. Note, though, that outside directors may not be truly independent of corporate officers; they may be friends or business associates of the leading officers.

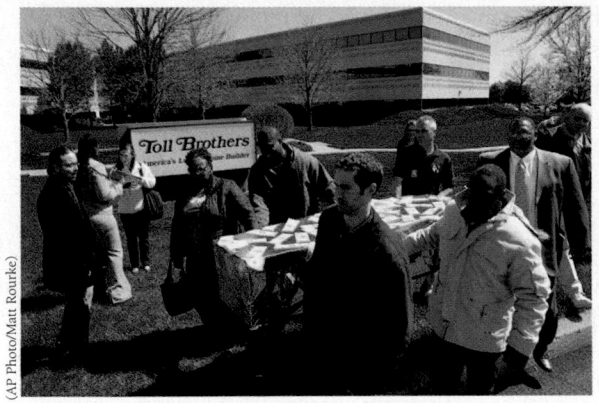

AFL-CIO officials and union members carry a decorated coffin as they conclude a mock funeral at the headquarters of Toll Brothers, Inc. The protesters were demonstrating against benefits and stock options granted to Toll Brothers, Inc., founding chairman and chief executive Robert Toll.

Corporate Governance and Corporate Law

Effective corporate governance standards are designed to address problems (such as those briefly discussed above) and to motivate officers to make decisions that promote the financial interests of the company's shareholders. Generally, corporate governance entails corporate decision-making structures that monitor employees (particularly officers) to ensure that they are acting for the benefit of the shareholders. Thus, corporate governance involves, at a minimum:

Beyond Our Borders | Corporate Governance in Other Nations

Corporate governance has become an issue of concern not only for U.S. corporations, but also for corporate entities around the world. With the globalization of business, a corporation's bad acts (or lack of control systems) can have far-reaching consequences. Different models of corporate governance exist, often depending on the degree of capitalism in the particular nation. In the United States, corporate gover- nance tends to give priority to shareholders' interests. This approach encourages significant innovation and cost and quality competition. In contrast, the coordinated model of governance that prevails in continental Europe and Japan considers the interests of so-called stakehold- ers—employees, managers, suppliers, custom- ers, and the community—to be a priority. The coordinated model still encourages innovation and cost and quality competition, but not to the same extent as the U.S. model.

• For Critical Analysis
Why does the presence of a capitalist system affect a nation's perspective on corporate governance?

1. The audited reporting of financial progress at the corporation, so managers can be evaluated.
2. Legal protections for shareholders, so violators of the law, who attempt to take advan- tage of shareholders, can be punished for misbehavior and victims may recover damages for any associated losses.

THE PRACTICAL SIGNIFICANCE OF GOOD CORPORATE GOVERNANCE Effective cor- porate governance may have considerable practical significance. A study by researchers at Harvard University and the Wharton School of Business found that firms providing greater shareholder rights had higher profits, higher sales growth, higher firm value, and other economic advantages.[33] Thus, a corporation that provides better corporate governance in the form of greater accountability to investors may also have a higher valuation than a cor- poration that is less concerned about governance.

"Honesty is the single most important factor having a direct bearing on the final success of an individual, corporation, or product."

Ed McMahon, 1923–2009
(American entertainer)

GOVERNANCE AND CORPORATION LAW Corporate governance is the essential pur- pose of corporation law in the United States. These statutes set up the legal framework for corporate governance. Under the corporate law of Delaware, where most major companies incorporate, all corporations must have in place certain structures of corporate governance. The key structure of corporate law is, of course, the board of directors.

THE BOARD OF DIRECTORS Some argue that shareholder democracy is key to improv- ing corporate governance. If shareholders could vote on major corporate decisions, share- holders could presumably have more control over the corporation. Essential to shareholder democracy is the election of the board of directors, usually at the corporation's annual meeting. Under corporate law, a corporation must have a board of directors elected by the shareholders. Almost anyone can become a director, though some organizations, such as the New York Stock Exchange, require certain standards of service for directors of their listed corporations.

Directors are responsible for ensuring that the corporation's officers are operating wisely and in the exclusive interest of shareholders. The directors receive reports from the officers and give them managerial directions. In reality, though, corporate directors devote a rela- tively small amount of time to monitoring officers.

Ideally, shareholders would monitor the directors' supervision of the officers. As one leading board monitor commented, "Boards of directors are like subatomic particles—

---

33. Paul A. Gompers, Joy L. Ishii, and Andrew Metrick, "Corporate Governance and Equity Prices," *Quarterly Journal of Economics*, Vol. 118 (2003), p. 107.

they behave differently when they are observed." In practice, however, it can be difficult for shareholders to monitor directors and hold them responsible for corporate failings. Although the directors can be sued for failing to do their jobs effectively, directors are rarely held personally liable (as discussed in Chapter 30's *Ethical Issue* on page 759).

IMPORTANCE OF THE AUDIT COMMITTEE   One crucial board committee is the *audit committee,* which oversees the corporation's accounting and financial reporting processes, including both internal and outside auditors. Unless the committee members have sufficient expertise and are willing to spend the time to carefully examine the corporation's bookkeeping methods, however, the audit committee may be ineffective.

The audit committee also oversees the corporation's "internal controls." These are the measures taken to ensure that reported results are accurate; they are carried out largely by the company's internal auditing staff. As an example, these controls help to determine whether a corporation's debts are collectible. If the debts are not collectible, it is up to the audit committee to make sure that the corporation's financial officers do not simply pretend that payment will eventually be made. (The *Linking the Law to Taxation* feature on pages 802 and 803 discusses how corporations, at least during the next few years, might benefit from *deleveraging,* or repurchasing, their debts.)

THE ROLE OF THE COMPENSATION COMMITTEE   Another important committee of the board of directors is the *compensation committee.* This committee monitors and determines the compensation the company's officers are paid. As part of this process, it is responsible for assessing the officers' performance and for designing a compensation system that will better align the officers' interests with those of shareholders.

(Fred Prouser/Reuters/Landov)

Michael Oxley is a former member of the U.S. House of Representatives and vice president of NASDAQ, the over-the-counter stock exchange. When in Congress, he cosponsored legislation that imposed large compliance costs on publicly held companies. What is the name of that legislation?

The Sarbanes-Oxley Act of 2002

As discussed in Chapter 8, in 2002 following a series of corporate scandals, Congress passed the Sarbanes-Oxley Act. The act separately addresses certain issues relating to corporate governance. Generally, the act attempts to increase corporate accountability by imposing strict disclosure requirements and harsh penalties for violations of securities laws. Among other things, the act requires chief corporate executives to take responsibility for the accuracy of financial statements and reports that are filed with the SEC.

Additionally, the act requires that certain financial and stock-transaction reports be filed with the SEC earlier than was required under the previous rules. The act also created a new entity, called the Public Company Accounting Oversight Board, which regulates and oversees public accounting firms. Other provisions of the act establish private civil actions and expand the SEC's remedies in administrative and civil actions.

Because of the importance of this act for corporate leaders and for those dealing with securities transactions, we present excerpts and explanatory comments in Appendix D at the end of this text. We also highlight some of its key provisions relating to corporate accountability in Exhibit 31–4.

MORE INTERNAL CONTROLS AND ACCOUNTABILITY   The Sarbanes-Oxley Act includes some traditional securities law provisions but also introduces direct *federal* corporate governance requirements for public companies (companies whose shares are traded in the public securities markets). The law addresses many of the corporate governance procedures just discussed and creates new requirements in an attempt to make the system work more effectively. The requirements deal with independent monitoring of company officers by both the board of directors and auditors.

● *Exhibit* **31–4 Some Key Provisions of the Sarbanes-Oxley Act of 2002 Relating to Corporate Accountability**

Certification Requirements—Under Section 906 of the Sarbanes-Oxley Act, the chief executive officers (CEOs) and chief financial officers (CFOs) of most major companies listed on public stock exchanges must certify financial statements that are filed with the SEC. CEOs and CFOs have to certify that filed financial reports "fully comply" with SEC requirements and that all of the information reported "fairly represents in all material respects, the financial conditions and results of operations of the issuer."

Under Section 302 of the act, CEOs and CFOs of reporting companies are required to certify that a signing officer reviewed each quarterly and annual filing with the SEC and that it contains no untrue statements of material fact. Also, the signing officer or officers must certify that they have established an internal control system to identify all material information and that any deficiencies in the system were disclosed to the auditors.

Loans to Directors and Officers—Section 402 prohibits any reporting company, as well as any private company that is filing an initial public offering, from making personal loans to directors and executive officers (with a few limited exceptions, such as for certain consumer and housing loans).

Protection for Whistleblowers—Section 806 protects "whistleblowers"—employees who report ("blow the whistle" on) securities violations by their employers—from being fired or in any way discriminated against by their employers.

Blackout Periods—Section 306 prohibits certain types of securities transactions during "blackout periods"—periods during which the issuer's ability to purchase, sell, or otherwise transfer funds in individual account plans (such as pension funds) is suspended.

Enhanced Penalties for—

• *Violations of Section 906 Certification Requirements*—A CEO or CFO who certifies a financial report or statement filed with the SEC knowing that the report or statement does not fulfill all of the requirements of Section 906 will be subject to criminal penalties of up to $1 million in fines, ten years in prison, or both. *Willful* violators of the certification requirements may be subject to $5 million in fines, twenty years in prison, or both.

• *Violations of the Securities Exchange Act of 1934*—Penalties for securities fraud under the 1934 act were also increased (as discussed earlier in this chapter). Individual violators may be fined up to $5 million, imprisoned for up to twenty years, or both. *Willful* violators may be imprisoned for up to twenty-five years in addition to being fined.

• *Destruction or Alteration of Documents*—Anyone who alters, destroys, or conceals documents or otherwise obstructs any official proceeding will be subject to fines, imprisonment for up to twenty years, or both.

• *Other Forms of White-Collar Crime*—The act stiffened the penalties for certain criminal violations, such as federal mail and wire fraud, and ordered the U.S. Sentencing Commission to revise the sentencing guidelines for white-collar crimes (see Chapter 6).

Statute of Limitations for Securities Fraud—Section 804 provides that a private right of action for securities fraud may be brought no later than two years after the discovery of the violation or five years after the violation, whichever is earlier.

Sections 302 and 404 of Sarbanes-Oxley require high-level managers (the most senior officers) to establish and maintain an effective system of internal controls. Moreover, senior management must reassess the system's effectiveness annually. Some companies already had strong and effective internal control systems in place before the passage of the act, but others had to take expensive steps to bring their internal controls up to the new federal standard. These include "disclosure controls and procedures" to ensure that company financial reports are accurate and timely. Assessment must involve the documenting of financial results and accounting policies before reporting the results. After the act was passed, hundreds of companies reported that they had identified and corrected shortcomings in their internal control systems.

CERTIFICATION AND MONITORING REQUIREMENTS   Section 906 requires that chief executive officers (CEOs) and chief financial officers (CFOs) certify that the information in the corporate financial statements "fairly represents in all material respects, the financial conditions and results of operations of the issuer." These corporate officers are subject to both civil and criminal penalties for violation of this section. This requirement makes officers directly accountable for the accuracy of their financial reporting and avoids any "ignorance defense" if shortcomings are later discovered.

Sarbanes-Oxley also includes requirements to improve directors' monitoring of officers' activities. All members of the corporate audit committee for public companies must be outside directors. The New York Stock Exchange (NYSE) has a similar rule that also extends to the board's compensation committee. The audit committee must have a written charter that sets out its duties and provides for performance appraisal. At least one "financial expert" must serve on the audit committee, which must hold executive meetings without company officers being present. The audit committee must establish procedures to encourage "whistleblowers" to report violations. In addition to reviewing the internal controls, the committee also monitors the actions of the outside auditor.

▶ Online Securities Fraud

A major problem facing the SEC today is how to enforce the antifraud provisions of the securities laws in the online environment. In 1999, in the first cases involving illegal online securities offerings, the SEC filed suit against three individuals for illegally offering securities on an Internet auction site.[34] In essence, all three indicated that their companies would go public soon and attempted to sell unregistered securities via the Web auction site. All of these actions were in violation of Sections 5, 17(a)(1), and 17(a)(3) of the 1933 Securities Act. Since then, the SEC has brought a variety of Internet-related fraud cases and regularly issues interpretive releases to explain how securities laws apply in the online environment.

Investment Scams

"Make money your God and it will plague you like the devil."

Henry Fielding, 1707–1754
(English author)

An ongoing problem is how to curb online investment scams. As discussed in Chapter 7, the Internet has created a new vehicle for criminals to use to commit fraud and has provided them with new ways of targeting innocent investors. The criminally inclined can use spam, online newsletters and bulletin boards, chat rooms, blogs, and tweets to spread false information and perpetrate fraud. For a relatively small cost, criminals can even build sophisticated Web pages to facilitate their investment scams.

There are countless variations of investment scams, most of which promise spectacular returns for small investments. A person might receive spam e-mail, for example, that falsely claims the earnings potential of a home business can "turn $5 into $60,000 in just three to six weeks." Another popular investment scam claims "your stimulus package has arrived" and promises you can make $100,000 a year using your home computer. Although most people today are dubious of the bogus claims made in spam messages, such offers can be more attractive during times of economic recession. Often, investment scams are simply the electronic version of pyramid schemes in which the participants attempt to profit solely by recruiting new participants.

Online Investment Newsletters and Forums

Hundreds of online investment newsletters provide free information on stocks. Legitimate online newsletters can help investors gather valuable information, but some of these newsletters are used for fraud. The law allows companies to pay people who write these newsletters to tout their securities, but the newsletters are required to disclose who paid for the advertising. Many fraudsters either fail to disclose or lie about who paid them. Thus, an investor reading an online newsletter may believe that the information is unbiased, when in fact the fraudsters will directly profit by convincing investors to buy or sell particular stocks.

---

34. *In re Davis,* SEC Administrative File No. 3-10080 (October 20, 1999); *In re Haas,* SEC Administrative File No. 3-10081 (October 20, 1999); *In re Sitaras,* SEC Administrative File No. 3-10082 (October 20, 1999).

The same deceptive tactics can be used on online bulletin boards (such as newsgroups and usenet groups), blogs, and social networking sites, including Twitter. While hiding their true identity, fraudsters may falsely pump up a company or reveal some "inside" information about a new product or lucrative contract to convince people to invest. By using multiple aliases on an online forum, a single person can easily create the illusion of widespread interest in a small stock.

Ponzi Schemes

In recent years, the SEC has filed an increasing number of enforcement actions against perpetrators of Ponzi schemes. In these scams, named after swindler Charles Ponzi, the fraudster promises high returns to investors and then uses their funds to pay previous investors.

OFFSHORE FRAUD   Ponzi schemes sometimes target U.S. residents and convince them to invest in offshore companies or banks. **EXAMPLE 31.9**   In 2009, Texas billionaire R. Allen Stanford, of the Stanford Financial Group, was indicted for allegedly orchestrating a $7 billion scheme to defraud more than five thousand investors. For about ten years, Stanford advised clients to buy certificates of deposit with improbably high interest rates from his Antigua-based Stanford International Bank. Some early investors were paid returns from the funds provided by later investors, but Stanford allegedly used $1.6 billion of the funds for personal purchases. He also falsified financial statements that were filed with the SEC and reportedly paid more than $100,000 in bribes to an Antigua official to ensure that the bank would not be audited. ●

"RISK-FREE" FRAUD   Another type of online fraud scheme offers risk-free or low-risk investments to lure investors. **CASE EXAMPLE 31.10**   Michael C. Regan used his firm, Regan & Company, to fraudulently obtain at least $15.9 million from dozens of investors by selling securities in his River Stream Fund. Regan told investors that he had a "proven track record" of successful securities trading and showed them falsified account statements and tax returns that showed artificially high account balances.

In reality, Regan was not a registered investment adviser, had not traded any securities for several years, and had suffered substantial losses on investments he did make. Regan promised investors returns averaging 20 percent with minimal risk to their principal and claimed to be using an investment strategy based on "short-term price trends." He used less than half of the funds entrusted to him for trading purposes and spent at least $2.4 million for his personal and family expenses. In 2009, the SEC filed a complaint alleging that Regan and his company had engaged in a multimillion-dollar Ponzi scheme. Regan agreed to settle the case and return more than $8.7 million (plus interest) of the wrongfully acquired funds.[35] ●

Hacking into Online Stock Accounts

Millions of people now buy and sell investments online through online brokerage companies such as E*Trade and TD Ameritrade. Sophisticated hackers have learned to use online investing to their advantage. By installing keystroke-monitoring software on computer terminals in public places, such as hotels, libraries, and airports, hackers can gain access to online account information. All they have to do is wait for a person to access an online trading account and then monitor the next several dozen keystrokes to determine the customer's account number and password. Once they have the log-in information, they can access the customer's account and liquidate her or his existing stock holdings.

---

35. You can read the SEC's complaint against Regan at **www.sec.gov/litigation/complaints/2009/comp21102.pdf**.

The hackers then use the customer's funds to purchase thinly traded, microcap securities, also known as penny stocks. The goal is to boost the price of a stock that the hacker has already purchased at a lower price. Then, when the stock price goes up, the hacker sells all the stock and wires the funds to either an offshore account or a dummy corporation, making it difficult for the SEC to trace the transactions and prosecute the offender.

EXAMPLE 31.11 Aleksey Kamardin, a twenty-one-year-old Florida college student, purchased 55,000 shares of stock in Fuego Entertainment using an E*Trade account in his own name. Kamardin then hacked into other customers' accounts at E*Trade, TD Ameritrade, Charles Schwab, and other brokerage companies, and used their funds to purchase a total of 458,000 shares of Fuego stock. When the stock price rose from $0.88 per share to $1.28 per share, Kamardin sold all of his shares of Fuego, making a profit of $9,164.28 in about three hours. Kamardin did this with other thinly traded stocks as well, allegedly making $82,960 in about five weeks. The SEC filed charges against him in 2007, and he was later ordered to return the profits, plus interest.[36] ●

---

36. You can read about the judgment against Kamardin by going to the SEC's Web site at www.sec.gov, clicking on the link to litigation releases, and selecting "LR-20190."

Reviewing . . . Investor Protection, Insider Trading, and Corporate Governance

Dale Emerson served as the chief financial officer for Reliant Electric Company, a distributor of electricity serving portions of Montana and North Dakota. Reliant was in the final stages of planning a takeover of Dakota Gasworks, Inc., a natural gas distributor that operated solely within North Dakota. Emerson went on a weekend fishing trip with his uncle, Ernest Wallace. Emerson mentioned to Wallace that he had been putting in a lot of extra hours at the office planning a takeover of Dakota Gasworks. When he returned from the fishing trip, Wallace purchased $20,000 worth of Reliant stock. Three weeks later, Reliant made a tender offer to Dakota Gasworks stockholders and purchased 57 percent of Dakota Gasworks stock. Over the next two weeks, the price of Reliant stock rose 72 percent before leveling out. Wallace then sold his Reliant stock for a gross profit of $14,400. Using the information presented in the chapter, answer the following questions.

1 Would registration with the SEC be required for Dakota Gasworks securities? Why or why not?
2 Did Emerson violate Section 10(b) of the Securities Exchange Act of 1934 and SEC Rule 10b-5? Why or why not?
3 What theory or theories might a court use to hold Wallace liable for insider trading?
4 Under the Sarbanes-Oxley Act of 2002, who would be required to certify the accuracy of financial statements filed with the SEC?

Linking the Law *to Taxation*

The Tax Consequences of Deleveraging during an Economic Crisis

Part of corporate governance involves making sure that the corporation effectively examines trade-offs involved in any future action. When corporate boards or upper management makes decisions, those decisions affect employees, customers, and shareholders. In a time of economic crisis, *deleveraging,* or repurchasing debt, is one possible action that a corporation may take to reduce its debt.

Why Companies Leverage

Corporations engage in leveraging—borrowing on a large scale in order to make additional investments—particularly in boom times. Leverage in capital structure is neither good nor bad. Companies in volatile industries avoid taking on too much debt, but other companies have found that debt is an important part of their capital structure. In any event, corporations have to be flexible in their ratio of debt to equity as market conditions change.

Recessions, such as the one that may still be going on as you read this, create uncertainty. Uncertainty is the enemy of capital markets. Formerly routine credit transactions become unavailable, even to solvent firms, and companies that have leveraged—have large debt loads—may find that credit has disappeared altogether. Suppliers may refuse to ship goods to such corporations unless they agree to pay cash on delivery. This pessimism ripples through the economy. Today, not only have auto manufacturers suffered, but so too have community hospitals, restaurants, hotels, and a host of firms in other industries.

The Downside of Deleveraging

Many corporations' publicly traded debt instruments have been selling at very deep discounts. One way for a company to improve its balance sheet and to reassure suppliers that it will be able to pay its bills is to retire that debt (at deep discounts). Some corporations could do this by issuing additional shares of stock to obtain the financing for such debt retirement. Moreover, repurchasing corporate debt may be a beneficial use of cash for corporations when consumer demand slows and alternative capital investments do not offer immediate returns.

Until 2009, however, corporate finance officers faced a daunting cost for such debt retirement plans. Under tax code and regulatory changes made in the 1980s, the difference between the original issue price of debt and the lower price for which it was repurchased was treated as taxable income. Finance managers call this a tax liability on "phantom income"

(calculated as the difference between the issued price and the repurchase price of corporate debt). Such tax liabilities have prevented many corporations from necessary capital restructuring. Additionally, the tax liability on phantom income helped to create a perverse preference for bankruptcy. To avoid the tax liability, a heavily leveraged firm might choose bankruptcy over debt retirement even though bankruptcy destroys asset values, customer relations, and, most of all, jobs.

A New Tax Incentive for Finance Managers to Consider

In 2009, as part of the economic stimulus bill, the Obama administration created a new tax break that applies to the retirement of heavily discounted debt instruments by corporations. Under this provision, tax liabilities on phantom income will not trigger corporate income taxes until 2014. At that time, corporations that have retired discounted debt will be able to spread out their tax liabilities over a five-year period.

Immediately, homebuilder Hovnanian Enterprises paid $105 million to repurchase $315 million of its unsecured debt. That $210 million of phantom income will not be taxable until 2014. At about the same time, GE Capital, a unit of General Electric, offered to buy back $1.46 billion of its bonds.

FOR CRITICAL ANALYSIS

If you were a finance manager in a large corporation, under what circumstances might you argue that the corporation should deleverage?

 Key Terms

accredited investor 784	investment contract 779	short-swing profits 791
corporate governance 796	mutual fund 784	stock option 796
free-writing prospectus 782	prospectus 781	tippee 790
insider trading 787	SEC Rule 10b-5 786	
investment company 784	security 778	

 Chapter Summary: Investor Protection, Insider Trading, and Corporate Governance

Securities Act of 1933 (See pages 779–786.)	Prohibits fraud and stabilizes the securities industry by requiring disclosure of all essential information relating to the issuance of securities to the investing public. 1. *Registration requirements*—Securities, unless exempt, must be registered with the SEC before being offered to the public. The *registration statement* must include detailed financial information about the issuing corporation; the intended use of the proceeds of the securities being issued; and certain disclosures, such as interests of directors or officers and pending lawsuits. 2. *Prospectus*—The issuer must provide investors with a *prospectus* that describes the security being sold, the issuing corporation, and the risk attaching to the security.

Continued

Chapter Summary: Investor Protection, Insider Trading, and Corporate Governance—Continued

Securities Act of 1933—Continued	3. *Exemptions*—The SEC has exempted certain offerings from the requirements of the Securities Act of 1933. Exemptions may be determined on the basis of the size of the issue, whether the offering is private or public, and whether advertising is involved. Exemptions are summarized in Exhibit 31–1 on page 783.

Securities Exchange Act of 1934 (See pages 786–795.)	Provides for the regulation and registration of securities exchanges, brokers, dealers, and national securities associations (such as the NASD). Maintains a continuous disclosure system for all corporations with securities on the securities exchanges and for those companies that have assets in excess of $10 million and five hundred or more shareholders (Section 12 companies).
	1. *SEC Rule 10b-5 [under Section 10(b) of the 1934 act]*—
	  a. Applies to almost all trading of securities—a firm's securities do not have to be registered under the 1933 act for the 1934 act to apply.
	  b. Applies only when the requisites of federal jurisdiction (such as use of the mails, stock exchange facilities, or any facility of interstate commerce) are present.
	  c. Applies to insider trading by corporate officers, directors, majority shareholders, and any persons receiving inside information (information not available to the public) who base their trading on this information.
	  d. Liability for violations can be civil or criminal.
	  e. May be violated by failing to disclose "material facts" that must be disclosed under this rule.
	  f. Liability may be based on the tipper/tippee or the misappropriation theory.
	2. *Insider trading [under Section 16(b) of the 1934 act]*—To prevent corporate insiders from taking advantage of inside information, the 1934 act requires officers, directors, and shareholders owning 10 percent or more of the issued stock of a corporation to turn over to the corporation all short-term profits (called *short-swing profits*) realized from the purchase and sale or sale and purchase of corporate stock within any six-month period.
	3. *Regulation of proxies*—The SEC regulates the content of proxy statements sent to shareholders of Section 12 companies. Section 14(a) is essentially a disclosure law, with provisions similar to the antifraud provisions of SEC Rule 10b-5.

State Securities Laws (See page 795.)	All states have corporate securities laws *(blue sky laws)* that regulate the offer and sale of securities within state borders; these laws are designed to prevent "speculative schemes which have no more basis than so many feet of 'blue sky.'" States regulate securities concurrently with the federal government. The Uniform Securities Act of 2002, which has been adopted by seventeen states and is being considered by several others, is designed to promote coordination and reduce duplication between state and federal securities regulation.
Corporate Governance (See pages 796–800.)	1. *Definition*—Corporate governance is the system by which business corporations are governed, including policies and procedures for making decisions on corporate affairs. 2. *The need for corporate governance*—Corporate governance is necessary in large corporations because corporate ownership (by the shareholders) is separated from corporate control (by officers and managers). This separation of corporate ownership and control can often result in conflicting interests. Corporate governance standards address such issues. 3. *Sarbanes-Oxley Act of 2002*—This act attempts to increase corporate accountability by imposing strict disclosure requirements and harsh penalties for violations of securities laws.
Online Securities Fraud (See pages 800–802.)	A major problem facing the SEC today is how to enforce the antifraud provisions of the securities laws in the online environment. Internet-related forms of securities fraud include numerous types of investment scams, Ponzi schemes, pumping and dumping, and hacking into online trading accounts.

 ExamPrep

ISSUE SPOTTERS

1 When a corporation wishes to issue certain securities, it must provide sufficient information for an unsophisticated investor to evaluate the financial risk involved. Specifically, the law imposes liability for making a false statement or omission that is "material." What sort of information would an investor consider material?

2 Lee is an officer of Magma Oil, Inc. Lee knows that a Magma geologist has just discovered a new deposit of oil. Can Lee take advantage of this information to buy and sell Magma stock? Why or why not?

BEFORE THE TEST

Check your answers to the Issue Spotters, and at the same time, take the interactive quiz for this chapter. Go to **www.cengage.com/blaw/blt** and click on "Chapter 31." First, click on "Answers to Issue Spotters" to check your answers. Next, click on "Interactive Quiz" to assess your mastery of the concepts in this chapter. Then click on "Flashcards" to review this chapter's Key Term definitions.

▶ For Review

Answers for the even-numbered questions in this For Review *section can be found on this text's accompanying Web site at* **www.cengage.com/blaw/blt**. *Select "Chapter 31" and click on "For Review."*

1 What is meant by the term *securities?*
2 What are the two major statutes regulating the securities industry?
3 What is insider trading? Why is it prohibited?
4 What are some of the features of state securities laws?
5 What certification requirements does the Sarbanes-Oxley Act impose on corporate executives?

▶ Hypothetical Scenarios and Case Problems

31–1 Registration Requirements. Langley Brothers, Inc., a corporation incorporated and doing business in Kansas, decides to sell common stock worth $1 million to the public. The stock will be sold only within the state of Kansas. Joseph Langley, the chairman of the board, says the offering need not be registered with the Securities and Exchange Commission. His brother, Harry, disagrees. Who is right? Explain.

31–2 **Hypothetical Question with Sample Answer** Huron Corp. has 300,000 common shares outstanding. The owners of these outstanding shares live in several different states. Huron has decided to split the 300,000 shares two for one. Will Huron Corp. have to file a registration statement and prospectus on the 300,000 new shares to be issued as a result of the split? Explain.

—For a sample answer to Question 31–2, go to Appendix E at the end of this text.

31–3 Insider Trading. David Gain was chief executive officer (CEO) of Forest Media Corp., which became interested in acquiring RS Communications, Inc., in 2010. To initiate negotiations, Gain met with RS's CEO, Gill Raz, on Friday, July 12. Two days later, Gain phoned his brother Mark, who, on Monday, bought 3,800 shares of RS stock. Mark discussed the deal with their father, Jordan, who bought 20,000 RS shares on Thursday. On July 25, the day before the RS bid was due, Gain phoned his parents' home, and Mark bought another 3,200 RS shares. The same routine was followed over the next few days, with Gain periodically phoning Mark or Jordan, both of whom continued to buy RS shares. Forest's bid was refused, but on August 5, RS announced its merger with another company. The price of RS stock rose 30 percent, increasing the value of Mark and Jordan's shares by $664,024 and $412,875, respectively. Did Gain engage in insider trading? What is required to impose sanctions for this offense? Could a court hold Gain liable? Why or why not?

31–4 Securities Trading. Between 1994 and 1998, Richard Svoboda, a credit officer for NationsBank N.A., in Dallas, Texas, evaluated and approved his employer's extensions of credit to clients. These responsibilities gave Svoboda access to nonpublic information about the clients' earnings, performance, acquisitions, and business plans in confidential memos, e-mail, credit applications, and other sources. Svoboda devised a scheme with Michael Robles, an independent accountant, to use this information to trade securities. Pursuant to their scheme, Robles traded in the securities of more than twenty different companies and profited by more than $1 million. Svoboda also executed trades for his own profit of more than $200,000, despite their agreement that Robles would do all of the trading. Aware that their scheme violated NationsBank's policy, they attempted to conduct their trades to avoid suspicion. When NationsBank questioned Svoboda about his actions, he lied, refused to cooperate, and was fired. Did Svoboda or Robles commit any crimes? Are they subject to civil liability? If so, who could file a suit and on what ground? What are the possible sanctions? What might be a defense? How should a court rule? Discuss. [*SEC v. Svoboda,* 409 F.Supp.2d 331 (S.D.N.Y. 2006)]

31–5 **Case Problem with Sample Answer** In 1997, WTS Transnational, Inc., required financing to develop a prototype of an unpatented fingerprint-verification system. At the time, WTS had no revenue, $655,000 in liabilities, and only $10,000 in assets. Thomas Cavanagh and Frank Nicolois, who operated an investment banking company called U.S. Milestone (USM), arranged the financing using Curbstone Acquisition Corp. Curbstone had no assets but had registered approximately 3.5 million shares of stock with the Securities and Exchange Commission (SEC). Under the terms of the deal, Curbstone acquired WTS, and the resulting entity was named Electro-Optical Systems Corp. (EOSC). New EOSC shares were issued to all of the WTS shareholders. Only Cavanagh and others affiliated with USM could sell EOSC stock to the public, however. Over the next few months, these individuals issued false press releases, made small deceptive purchases of EOSC shares at high prices, distributed hundreds of thousands of shares to friends and relatives, and sold their own shares at inflated prices through third party companies they owned. When the SEC began to investigate, the share price fell to its actual value, and innocent investors lost more than $15 million. Were any securities laws violated in this case? If so, what might be an appropriate remedy? [*SEC v. Cavanagh*, 445 F.3d 105 (2d Cir. 2006)]

—After you have answered Problem 31–5, compare your answer with the sample answer given on the Web site that accompanies this text. Go to **www.cengage.com/blaw/blt**, select "Chapter 31," and click on "Case Problem with Sample Answer."

31–6 Duty to Disclose. Orphan Medical, Inc., was a pharmaceutical company that focused on central nervous system disorders. Its major product was the drug Xyrem. In June 2004, Orphan merged with Jazz, and Orphan shareholders received $10.75 per share for their stock. Before the merger was final, Orphan completed a phase of testing of Xyrem that indicated that the U.S. Food and Drug Administration (FDA) would allow the drug to go to the next stage of testing, which was necessary for the drug to be widely marketed. If that happened, the value of the drug and Orphan would go up, and the stock would have been worth more than $10.75. Little Gem Life Sciences, LLC, was an Orphan shareholder that received $10.75 a share. It sued, claiming violations of federal securities laws because shareholders were not told, during the merger process, that the current stage of FDA tests had been successful. Little Gem claimed that if the information had been public, the stock price would have been higher. The district court dismissed the suit, holding that it did not meet the standards required by the Private Securities Litigation Reform Act. Little Gem appealed. Did Orphan's directors have a duty to reveal all relevant drug-testing information to shareholders? Why or why not? [*Little Gem Life Sciences, LLC v. Orphan Medical, Inc.*, 537 F.3d 913 (8th Cir. 2008)]

31–7 Violations of the 1934 Act. To comply with accounting principles, a company that engages in software development must either "expense" the cost (record it immediately on the com-

pany's financial statement) or "capitalize" it (record it as a cost incurred in increments over time). If the project is in the pre- or post-development stage, the cost must be expensed. Otherwise it may be capitalized. Capitalizing a cost makes a company look more profitable in the short term. Digimarc Corp., which provides secure personal identification documents such as drivers' licenses using digital watermark technology, announced that it had improperly capitalized software development costs over at least the previous eighteen months. The errors resulted in $2.7 million in overstated earnings, requiring a restatement of prior financial statements. Zucco Partners, LLC, which had bought Digimarc stock within the relevant period, filed a suit in a federal district court against the firm. Zucco claimed that it could show that there had been disagreements within Digimarc over its accounting. Is this sufficient to establish a violation of SEC Rule 10b-5? Why or why not? [*Zucco Partners, LLC v. Digimarc Corp.*, 552 F.3d 981 (9th Cir. 2009)]

31–8 **A Question of Ethics** *Melvin Lyttle told John Montana and Paul Knight about a "Trading Program" that purportedly would buy and sell securities in deals that were fully insured, as well as monitored and controlled by the Federal Reserve Board. Without checking the details or even verifying whether the Program existed, Montana and Knight, with Lyttle's help, began to sell interests in the Program to investors. For a minimum investment of $1 million, the investors were promised extraordinary rates of return—from 10 percent to as much as 100 percent per week—without risk. They were told, among other things, that the Program would "utilize banks that can ensure full bank integrity of The Transaction whose undertaking[s] are in complete harmony with international banking rules and protocol and who [sic] guarantee maximum security of a Funder's Capital Placement Amount." Nothing was required but the investors' funds and their silence— the Program was to be kept secret. Over a four-month period in 1999, Montana raised approximately $23 million from twenty-two investors. The promised gains did not accrue, however. Instead, Montana, Lyttle, and Knight depleted the investors' funds in high-risk trades or spent the funds on themselves. [SEC v. Montana, 464 F.Supp.2d 772 (S.D.Ind. 2006)]*

1 The Securities and Exchange Commission (SEC) filed a suit in a federal district court against Montana and the others, seeking an injunction, civil penalties, and disgorgement with interest. The SEC alleged, among other things, violations of Section 10(b) of the Securities Exchange Act of 1934 and SEC Rule 10b-5. What is required to establish a violation of these laws? Explain how and why the facts in this case meet, or fail to meet, these requirements.

2 It is often remarked, "There's a sucker born every minute!" Does that phrase describe the Program's investors? Ultimately, about half of the investors recouped the amount they invested. Should the others be considered at least partly responsible for their own losses? Why or why not?

Critical Thinking and Writing Assignments

31-9 Critical Thinking and Writing Assignment for Business. Insider trading, as you learned, is illegal. Not everyone agrees that it should be, though. A small group of legal scholars believes that insider trading should be completely legal. They argue that if insider trading was more widespread, it would cause stock prices to adjust almost instantly to new information. They further argue that insiders, if able to make profits from insider trading, would therefore accept lower salaries and benefits.

1 Why is insider trading illegal in the first place? Who is supposed to be protected and why?

2 What is wrong with the argument advanced by the legal scholars who want insider trading made legal? Or are they right? Explain your answer.

31-10 **Case Analysis Question** Go to Appendix F at the end of this text and examine Case No. 6 [*Merrill Lynch, Pierce, Fenner & Smith, Inc. v. Dabit,* 547 U.S. 71, 126 S.Ct. 1503, 164 L.Ed.2d 179 (2006)]. This case has been excerpted there in great detail. Review and then brief the case, making sure that your brief answers the following questions.

1 **Issue:** The dispute in this case centered on whether a certain federal statute covered the claims of a certain class of investors who had allegedly been the victims of fraud. What was the statute, who were the investors, and how were they allegedly defrauded?

2 **Rule of Law:** On what "requisite showing" did the United States Supreme Court base its decision?

3 **Applying the Rule of Law:** What were the reasons for the Court's conclusion? What rule of statutory interpretation supported this reasoning? How did the purpose of the statute influence its application?

4 **Conclusion:** How did the Court's ruling affect the investors' claims?

31-11 **Video Question** Go to this text's Web site at **www.cengage.com/blaw/blt** and select "Chapter 31." Click on "Video Questions" and view the video titled *Mergers and Acquisitions*. Then answer the following questions.

1 Analyze whether the purchase of Onyx Advertising is a material fact that the Quigley Company had a duty to disclose under SEC Rule 10b-5.

2 Does it matter whether Quigley personally knew about or authorized the company spokesperson's statements? Why or why not?

3 Who else might be able to bring a suit against the Quigley Company for insider trading under SEC Rule 10b-5?

 Practical Internet Exercises

Go to this text's Web site at **www.cengage.com/blaw/blt**, select "Chapter 31," and click on "Practical Internet Exercises." There you will find the following Internet research exercises that you can perform to learn more about the topics covered in this chapter.

Practical Internet Exercise 31-1: LEGAL PERSPECTIVE—**Electronic Delivery**
Practical Internet Exercise 31-2: MANAGEMENT PERSPECTIVE—**The SEC's Role**

Cumulative Business Hypothetical

John leases an office and buys computer equipment. Initially, to pay for the lease and the equipment, he goes into the business of designing Web pages. He also has an idea for a new software product that he hopes will be more profitable than designing Web pages. Whenever he has time, he works on the software.

1. After six months, Mary and Paul come to work in the office to help develop John's idea. John continues to pay the rent and other expenses, including salaries for Mary and Paul. John does not expect to make a profit until the software is developed, which could take months; even then, there may be very little profit unless the product is marketed successfully. If the software is successful, though, John believes that the firm will be able to follow up with other products. In choosing a form of business organization for this firm, what are the important considerations? What are the advantages and disadvantages of each basic option?

2. It is decided that the organizational form for this firm should provide limited liability for the owners. The owners will include John, Mary, Paul, and some members of their respective families. One of the features of the corporate form is limited liability. Ordinarily, however, corporate income is taxed at both the corporate level and the shareholder level. Which corporate form could the firm use to avoid this double taxation? Which other forms of business organization provide limited liability? What factors, other than liability and taxation, influence a firm's choice among these forms?

3. The firm is incorporated as Digital Software, Inc. (DSI). The software is developed and marketed successfully, and DSI prospers. John, Mary, and Paul become directors of DSI. At a board meeting, Paul proposes a marketing strategy for DSI's next product, and John and Mary approve it. Implementing the strategy causes DSI's profits to drop. If the shareholders accuse Paul of breaching his fiduciary duty to DSI, what is Paul's most likely defense? If the shareholders accuse John and Mary of the same breach, what is their best defense? In either case, if the shareholders file a suit, how is a court likely to rule?

4. International Investments, Inc., makes a public offer to buy the stock of DSI. The price of the offer is higher than the market price of the stock, but DSI's board believes that the offer should not be accepted and that International's attempt to take over DSI should be resisted. What steps can DSI take to resist the takeover?

5. Mary and Paul withdraw from DSI to set up their own firm. To obtain operating capital, they solicit investors who agree to become "general partners." Mary and Paul designate themselves "managing partners." The investors are spread over a wide area geographically and do not know anything about Mary and Paul's business until they are contacted. Are Mary and Paul truly soliciting partners, or are they selling securities? What are the criteria for determining whether an investment is a security? What are the advantages and disadvantages of selling securities versus soliciting partners?

Extended Case Study: *Notz v. Everett Smith Group, Ltd.*

This Extended Case Study examines Notz v. Everett Smith Group, Ltd.,[1] *in which a minority shareholder was allegedly excluded from some of the benefits of participating in the corporation. The shareholder claimed that the majority shareholder and the board of directors, which was controlled by the majority shareholder, had breached their fiduciary duties to the minority shareholder and to the firm (see Chapter 30 on the fiduciary duties of majority shareholders and directors). The court had to decide, among other things, whether the minority shareholder could bring a suit directly to recover personally from the directors or whether he was limited to bringing a shareholder's derivative suit on behalf of the corporation (see the discussion of the options of shareholders with respect to appraisal rights in Chapter 29, as well as the discussion of shareholders' derivative suits in Chapter 30).*

1. 316 Wis.2d 640, 764 N.W.2d 904 (2009). To read this case online, go to **www.wicourts.gov**. In the "opinions & rules" pull-down menu, click on "Supreme Court." In the result, in the "Opinions and dispositional orders" section, click on "Search for opinions and dispositional orders." On that page, in the "Docket number:" box, type "2006AP3156" and click on "Search." In that result, select the appropriate "view" and click on the link to read the case. The Wisconsin court system maintains this Web site.

CASE BACKGROUND

Albert Trostel & Sons (ATS) began as a tannery in Milwaukee, Wisconsin, in the 1800s. Over the decades, ATS acquired subsidiaries and expanded into the production of rubber and plastics. Everett Smith came to work for ATS in 1938, later became its president, and eventually gained control of the company. Smith formed Everett Smith Group, Ltd., which owned 88.9 percent of ATS by 2003. Edward Notz owned 5.5 percent, and others owned the rest. All of the members of ATS's board of directors were either officers or directors of the Smith Group.

In 2004, ATS had an opportunity to acquire Dickten & Masch, a competing thermoplastics maker. The ATS board chose not to act. Instead, the Smith Group, which had no direct holdings in the plastics field, acquired Dickten & Masch. Within months, the Smith Group's new affiliate bought the assets of ATS's plastics subsidiary, Trostel Specialty Elastomers Group, Inc. (Trostel SEG), from ATS.

Notz filed a suit in a Wisconsin state court against the Smith Group, alleging breach of fiduciary duty for stripping ATS of its most important assets and diverting the corporate opportunity to buy Dickten & Masch. The court dismissed the claim, and a state intermediate appellate court affirmed. Notz appealed to the Wisconsin Supreme Court.

MAJORITY OPINION

N. PATRICK CROOKS, J.:

* * * *

Notz's claims of breach of fiduciary duty are primarily based on the series of transactions in which the Smith Group acquired two plastics companies. The allegations are that the Smith Group, as ATS's majority shareholder, rejected the opportunity ATS had to buy Dickten & Masch; the Smith Group subsequently bought Dickten & Masch itself; and the Smith Group, in its capacity as majority shareholder, orchestrated the sale of ATS's valuable plastics group, Trostel SEG, to its own new acquisition.

The question is whether those allegations support direct claims for breach of fiduciary duty to a minority shareholder. * * * The Smith Group argues that * * * these are derivative claims; Notz argues that * * * these are direct claims.

* * * *Though each shareholder has an individual right to be treated fairly by the board of directors, when the injury from such actions is primarily to the corporation, there can be no direct claim by minority shareholders.* [Emphasis added.]

* * * It is true the fiduciary duty of a director is owed to the individual stockholders as well as to the corporation. Directors in this state may not use their position of trust to further their private interests. Thus, where some individual right of a stockholder is being impaired by the improper acts of a director, the stockholder can bring a direct suit on his own behalf because it is his individual right that is being violated. However, a right of action that belongs to the corporation cannot be pursued as a direct claim by an individual stockholder. * * * *Even where the injury to the corporation results in harm to a shareholder, it won't transform an action from a derivative to a direct one* * * *. That such primary and direct injury to a corporation may have a subsequent impact on the value of the stockholders' shares is clear, but that is not enough to create a right to bring a direct, rather than derivative, action. Where the injury to the corporation is the primary injury, and any injury to stockholders secondary, it is the derivative action alone that can be brought and maintained. That is the general rule, and, if it were to be abandoned, there would be no reason left for the concept of derivative actions for the redress of wrongs to a corporation. [Emphasis added.]

* * * *

Notz alleges self-dealing on the part of the majority shareholder, but * * * a shareholder-director's self-dealing [does not] transform an action that primarily injures the corporation into one that primarily injures a shareholder.

We agree with the Smith Group that breach of fiduciary duty claims, based on the lost opportunity to purchase one company and the sale of a subsidiary with great growth potential, are [derivative claims]. Our analysis * * * centers on a determination of whether the primary injury is to the corporation or to the shareholder. * * * An injury primarily * * * to an individual shareholder [is] one which affects a shareholder's rights in a manner distinct from the effect upon other shareholders. We agree with the court of appeals that the allegations here are essentially that the Smith Group stripped ATS of its most important assets and engaged in various acts of self-dealing, and that those are allegations of injury primarily to ATS. * * * All of the shareholders of ATS were affected equally by the loss of the opportunity to acquire Dickten & Masch and by the sale of Trostel SEG, the plastics division.

* * * *

* * * We agree with the court of appeals that the claims of harm alleged—the loss of a corporate opportunity and the sale of a subsidiary with high growth potential—caused harm primarily to the corporation, and thus we affirm the dismissal of Notz's direct claim of breach of fiduciary duty as to those allegations.

DISSENTING OPINION

ANN WALSH BRADLEY, J. (* * * dissenting * * *).

* * * *

* * * I disagree with the majority * * * that Notz's claim for breach of fiduciary duty arising out of corporate usurpation is a derivative rather than a direct claim and that it thus must be dismissed.

Continued

Instead, * * * I conclude that Notz states a direct claim for breach of fiduciary duty arising out of the defendants' usurpation of a corporate opportunity.

* * * *

* * * Officers and directors owe a fiduciary duty to shareholders to act in good faith and to treat each shareholder fairly. The directors and officers of a corporation owe a fiduciary duty to not use their positions for their own personal advantage * * * to the detriment of the interests of the stockholders of the corporation.

That same fiduciary duty is also owed by majority shareholders to minority shareholders.

Officers, directors, and controlling shareholders breach their fiduciary duties when they treat minority shareholders differently, and inequitably, or when they use their position of trust to further their private interests. If through that control a sale of the corporate property is made and the property acquired by the majority, the minority may not be excluded from a fair participation in the fruits of the sale.

* * * *

[The majority's] conclusion is antithetical to the facts. It is true that all shareholders suffered a common injury in that the value of their investment in ATS depreciated. Nonetheless, Notz suffered an additional injury that was unique to the minority shareholders. The Smith Group who planned and executed these transactions received a net gain, but Notz suffered a net loss. * * * Notz's injury was distinct from the injury to the controlling shareholder—unlike the defendants, Notz was denied continued participation in a thriving growth industry.

QUESTIONS FOR ANALYSIS

1. **Law.** What did the majority rule with respect to the dispute before the court? On what reasoning did the majority base its ruling?
2. **Law.** What was the dissent's interpretation of the facts in this case? How would the dissent have applied the law to these facts? Why?
3. **Ethics.** From an ethical perspective, should ATS's directors have made different decisions on the choices that came before the board? Discuss.
4. **Economic Dimensions.** Could a shareholder in the position of the minority shareholder in this case seek a judicial dissolution? If so, what would be the likely result?
5. **Implications for the Shareholder.** Can a shareholder pursue a derivative claim on behalf of a corporation? If so, what steps must the shareholder take? Why might a shareholder be reluctant to take these steps?

Government Regulation

(Moody75/Creative Commons)

Chapter 32

Promoting Competition

(Photo by ChinaFotoPress/Getty Images)

Chapter Outline

- The Sherman Antitrust Act
- Section 1 of the Sherman Act
- Section 2 of the Sherman Act
- The Clayton Act
- Enforcement and Exemptions
- U.S. Antitrust Laws in the Global Context

Learning Objectives

After reading this chapter, you should be able to answer the following questions:

1. What is a monopoly? What is market power? How do these concepts relate to each other?

2. What type of activity is prohibited by Section 1 of the Sherman Act? What type of activity is prohibited by Section 2 of the Sherman Act?

3. What are the four major provisions of the Clayton Act, and what types of activities do these provisions prohibit?

4. What agencies of the federal government enforce the federal antitrust laws?

5. What are four activities that are exempt from the antitrust laws?

Today's antitrust laws are the direct descendants of common law actions intended to limit *restraints of trade* (agreements between firms that have the effect of reducing competition in the marketplace). Such actions date to the fifteenth century in England. In the United States, concern over monopolistic practices arose following the Civil War with the growth of large corporate enterprises and their attempts to reduce competition. To thwart competition, they legally tied themselves together in business trusts. As discussed in Chapter 28, a business trust is a form of business organization in which trustees hold title to property for the benefit of others. The most powerful of these trusts, the Standard Oil trust, is examined in this chapter's *Landmark in the Law* feature on page 814.

Many states tried to curb such monopolistic behavior by enacting statutes outlawing the use of trusts. That is why all the laws regulating economic competition in the United States today are referred to as **antitrust laws.** At the national level, Congress passed the Sherman Antitrust Act in 1890.[1] In 1914, Congress passed the Clayton Act[2] and the Federal Trade Commission Act[3] to further curb anticompetitive or unfair business practices. Congress later amended the 1914 acts to broaden and strengthen their coverage.

Antitrust Law Laws protecting commerce from unlawful restraints.

---

1. 15 U.S.C. Sections 1–7.
2. 15 U.S.C. Sections 12–27.
3. 15 U.S.C. Sections 41–58.

This chapter examines these major antitrust statutes, focusing particularly on the Sherman Act and the Clayton Act, as amended, and the types of activities they prohibit. Remember in reading this chapter that the basis of antitrust legislation is the desire to foster competition. Antitrust legislation was initially created—and continues to be enforced—because of our society's belief that competition leads to lower prices, generates more product information, and results in a more equitable distribution of wealth between consumers and producers. As President Herbert Hoover indicated in the chapter-opening quotation, competition not only protects the consumer, but also provides "the incentive to progress." Consumers and society as a whole benefit when producers strive to develop better products that they can sell at lower prices to beat the competition.

▶ The Sherman Antitrust Act

In 1890, Congress passed "An Act to Protect Trade and Commerce against Unlawful Restraints and Monopolies"—commonly known as the Sherman Antitrust Act or, more simply, as the Sherman Act. The Sherman Act was and remains one of the government's most powerful weapons in the effort to maintain a competitive economy.

Major Provisions of the Sherman Act

Sections 1 and 2 contain the main provisions of the Sherman Act:

1. Every contract, combination in the form of trust or otherwise, or conspiracy, in restraint of trade or commerce among the several States, or with foreign nations, is hereby declared to be illegal [and is a felony punishable by a fine and/or imprisonment].

2. Every person who shall monopolize, or attempt to monopolize, or combine or conspire with any other person or persons, to monopolize any part of the trade or commerce among the several States, or with foreign nations, shall be deemed guilty of a felony [and is similarly punishable].

Differences between Section 1 and Section 2

These two sections of the Sherman Act are quite different. Violation of Section 1 requires two or more persons, as a person cannot contract or combine or conspire alone. Thus, the essence of the illegal activity is *the act of joining together.* Section 2, though, can apply either to one person or to two or more persons because it refers to "every person." Thus, unilateral conduct can result in a violation of Section 2.

The cases brought to court under Section 1 of the Sherman Act differ from those brought under Section 2. Section 1 cases are often concerned with finding an agreement (written or oral) that leads to a restraint of trade. Section 2 cases deal with the structure of a monopoly that already exists in the marketplace. The term **monopoly** generally is used to describe a market in which there is a single seller or a very limited number of sellers.

ON THE WEB The Web site of Cornell University's Legal Information Institute contains the text of federal statutes relating to commerce and trade, including the Sherman Antitrust Act, at **www4.law. cornell.edu/uscode/15/1.html**.

Monopoly A term generally used to describe a market in which there is a single seller or a very limited number of sellers.

One of Standard Oil's refineries in Richmond, California, around 1900.

(Library of Congress)

Landmark in the Law   The Sherman Antitrust Act of 1890

The author of the Sherman Antitrust Act of 1890, Senator John Sherman, was the brother of the famous Civil War general William Tecumseh Sherman and a recognized financial authority. Sherman had been concerned for years about what he saw as diminishing competition within U.S. industry and the emergence of monopolies, such as the Standard Oil trust.

The Standard Oil Trust   By 1890, the Standard Oil trust had become the foremost petroleum refining and marketing combination in the United States. Streamlined, integrated, and centrally controlled, Standard Oil maintained an indisputable monopoly over the industry. The trust controlled 90 percent of the U.S. market for refined petroleum products, making it impossible for small producers to compete with such a leviathan.

   The increasing consolidation in U.S. industry, and particularly the Standard Oil trust, came to the attention of the public in March 1881. Henry Demarest Lloyd, a young journalist from Chicago, published an article in the *Atlantic Monthly* entitled "The Story of a Great Monopoly." The article attempted to demonstrate that the U.S. petroleum industry was dominated by one firm—Standard Oil. Lloyd's article was so popular that the issue was reprinted six times. It marked the beginning of the U.S. public's growing concern over the rise of monopolies.

The Passage of the Sherman Antitrust Act   The common law regarding trade regulation was not always consistent. Certainly, it was not very familiar to the members of Congress. The public concern over large business integrations and trusts was familiar, however. In 1888, 1889, and again in 1890, Senator Sherman introduced in Congress bills designed to destroy the large combinations of capital that, he felt, were creating a lack

of balance within the nation's economy. Sherman told Congress that the Sherman Act "does not announce a new principle of law, but applies old and well-recognized principles of the common law."[a] In 1890, the Fifty-First Congress enacted the bill into law. Generally, the act prohibits business combinations and conspiracies that restrain trade and commerce, as well as certain monopolistic practices.

• **Application to Today's World**   *The Sherman Antitrust Act remains very relevant to today's world. Since the widely publicized monopolization case against Microsoft Corporation in 2001,[b] the U.S. Department of Justice and state attorneys general have brought numerous Sherman Act cases against other corporations, including eBay, Intel, and Philip Morris.[c]*

• **Relevant Web Sites**   To locate information on the Web concerning the Sherman Antitrust Act, go to this text's Web site at www.cengage.com/blaw/blt, select "Chapter 32," and click on "URLs for Landmarks."

---

a. 21 Congressional Record 2456 (1890).
b. *United States v. Microsoft Corp.,* 253 F.3d 34 (D.C.Cir. 2001). This case will be discussed in Case Example 32.6 on page 820. See also *New York v. Microsoft Corp.,* 531 F.Supp.2d 141 (D.D.C. 2008); and *Massachusetts v. Microsoft Corp.,* 379 F.3d 1199 (D.C.Cir. 2004).
c. See, for example, *United States v. Philip Morris USA, Inc.,* 566 F.3d 1095 (D.C.Cir. 2009); *In re eBay Seller Antitrust Litigation,* 545 F.Supp.2d 1027 (N.D.Cal. 2008); and *In re Intel Corp. Microprocessor Antitrust Litigation,* 2007 WL 137152 (D.Del. 2007).

Monopoly Power   The ability of a monopoly to dictate what takes place in a given market.

Market Power   The power of a firm to control the market price of its product. A monopoly has the greatest degree of market power.

> *"I don't know what a monopoly is until somebody tells me."*
>
> Steve Ballmer, 1956–present
> (Chief executive officer of Microsoft Corporation)

Whereas Section 1 focuses on agreements that are restrictive—that is, agreements that have a wrongful purpose—Section 2 looks at the so-called misuse of **monopoly power** in the marketplace.

   Monopoly power exists when a firm has an extreme amount of **market power**—the power to affect the market price of its product. Both Section 1 and Section 2 seek to curtail market practices that result in undesired monopoly pricing and output behavior. For a case to be brought under Section 2, however, the "threshold" or "necessary" amount of monopoly power must already exist. We will return to a discussion of these two sections of the Sherman Act after we look at the act's jurisdictional requirements.

Jurisdictional Requirements

The Sherman Act applies only to restraints that have a substantial impact on interstate commerce. Courts generally have held that any activity that substantially affects interstate commerce falls within the scope of the Sherman Act. As will be discussed later in this chapter, the Sherman Act also extends to U.S. nationals abroad who are engaged in activities that have an effect on U.S. foreign commerce. State laws regulate local restraints on competition.

Section 1 of the Sherman Act

The underlying assumption of Section 1 of the Sherman Act is that society's welfare is harmed if rival firms are permitted to join in an agreement that consolidates their market power or otherwise restrains competition. The types of trade restraints that Section 1 of the Sherman Act prohibits generally fall into two broad categories: *horizontal restraints* and *vertical restraints,* both of which will be discussed shortly. First, though, we look at the rules that the courts may apply when assessing the anticompetitive impact of alleged restraints on trade.

Per Se Violations versus the Rule of Reason

Per Se Violation   A type of anticompetitive agreement that is considered to be so injurious to the public that there is no need to determine whether it actually injures market competition. Rather, it is in itself *(per se)* a violation of the Sherman Act.

Rule of Reason   A test by which a court balances the positive effects (such as economic efficiency) of an agreement against its potentially anticompetitive effects. In antitrust litigation, many practices are analyzed under the rule of reason.

Some restraints are so blatantly and substantially anticompetitive that they are deemed *per se* violations—illegal *per se* (on their face, or inherently)—under Section 1. Other agreements, however, even though they result in enhanced market power, do not *unreasonably* restrain trade. Using what is called the **rule of reason,** the courts analyze anticompetitive agreements that allegedly violate Section 1 of the Sherman Act to determine whether they may, in fact, constitute reasonable restraints on trade.

The need for a rule-of-reason analysis of some agreements in restraint of trade is obvious—if the rule of reason had not been developed, almost any business agreement could conceivably be held to violate the Sherman Act. Justice Louis Brandeis effectively phrased this sentiment in *Chicago Board of Trade v. United States,* a case decided in 1918:

> Every agreement concerning trade, every regulation of trade, restrains. To bind, to restrain, is of their very essence. The true test of legality is whether the restraint imposed is such as merely regulates and perhaps thereby promotes competition or whether it is such as may suppress or even destroy competition.[4]

ON THE WEB You can find links to discussions of the *per se* rule and the rule of reason, as well as to antitrust laws, at **www.findlaw. com/01topics/01antitrust/index.html**.

When analyzing an alleged Section 1 violation under the rule of reason, a court will consider several factors. These factors include the purpose of the agreement, the parties' power to implement the agreement to achieve that purpose, and the effect or potential effect of the agreement on competition. Another factor that a court might consider is whether the parties could have relied on less restrictive means to achieve their purpose.

Horizontal Restraints

Horizontal Restraint   Any agreement that in some way restrains competition between rival firms competing in the same market.

The term **horizontal restraint** is encountered frequently in antitrust law. A horizontal restraint is any agreement that in some way restrains competition between rival firms competing in the same market.

Price-Fixing Agreement   An agreement between competitors to fix the prices of products or services at a certain level.

PRICE FIXING   Any **price-fixing agreement**—an agreement among competitors to fix prices—constitutes a *per se* violation of Section 1. Perhaps the definitive case regarding price-fixing agreements is still the 1940 case of *United States v. Socony-Vacuum Oil Co.*[5] In that case, a group of independent oil producers in Texas and Louisiana were caught between falling demand due to the Great Depression of the 1930s and increasing supply from newly discovered oil fields in the region. In response to these conditions, a group of major refining companies agreed to buy "distress" gasoline (excess supplies) from the independents so as to dispose of it in an "orderly manner." Although there was no explicit agreement as to price, it was clear that the purpose of the agreement was to limit the supply of gasoline on the market and thereby raise prices.

There may have been good business reasons for the agreement. Nonetheless, the United States Supreme Court recognized the dangerous effects that such an agreement could have

---

4. 246 U.S. 231, 38 S.Ct. 242, 62 L.Ed. 683 (1918).
5. 310 U.S. 150, 60 S.Ct. 811, 84 L.Ed. 1129 (1940).

(Yoshikazu Tsuno/AFP/Getty Images)

Asian LCD flat-screen makers were fined $600 million by the U.S. Department of Justice for price fixing.

Group Boycott The refusal by a group of competitors to deal with a particular person or firm; prohibited by the Sherman Act.

ON THE WEB The Bureau of Competition of the Federal Trade Commission (FTC) offers an abundance of information on antitrust law at its Web site. Go to **www.ftc.gov/bc/antitrust/index.shtm**.

Concentrated Industry An industry in which a large percentage of market sales is controlled by either a single firm or a small number of firms.

on open and free competition. The Court held that the reasonableness of a price-fixing agreement is never a defense; any agreement that restricts output or artificially fixes price is a *per se* violation of Section 1. The rationale of the *per se* rule was best stated in what is now the most famous portion of the Court's opinion—footnote 59. In that footnote, Justice William O. Douglas compared a freely functioning price system to a body's central nervous system, condemning price-fixing agreements as threats to "the central nervous system of the economy."

CASE EXAMPLE 32.1   The manufacturer of the prescription drug Cardizem CD, which can help prevent heart attacks, was about to lose its patent on the drug. Another company developed a generic version in anticipation of the patent expiring. After the two firms became involved in litigation over the patent, the first company agreed to pay the second company $40 million per year not to market the generic version until their dispute was resolved. This agreement was held to be a *per se* violation of the Sherman Act because it restrained competition between rival firms and delayed the entry of generic versions of Cardizem into the market.[6] •

GROUP BOYCOTTS   A **group boycott** is an agreement by two or more sellers to refuse to deal with (boycott) a particular person or firm. Such group boycotts have been held to constitute *per se* violations of Section 1 of the Sherman Act. Section 1 has been violated if it can be demonstrated that the boycott or joint refusal to deal was undertaken with the intention of eliminating competition or preventing entry into a given market. Some boycotts, such as group boycotts against a supplier for political reasons, may be protected under the First Amendment right to freedom of expression, however.

HORIZONTAL MARKET DIVISION   It is a *per se* violation of Section 1 of the Sherman Act for competitors to divide up territories or customers. **EXAMPLE 32.2** Manufacturers A, B, and C compete against each other in the states of Kansas, Nebraska, and Oklahoma. By agreement, A sells products only in Kansas, B sells only in Nebraska, and C sells only in Oklahoma. This concerted action not only reduces marketing costs but also allows all three (assuming there is no other competition) to raise the price of the goods sold in their respective states. The same violation would take place if A, B, and C agreed that A would sell only to institutional purchasers (such as school districts, universities, state agencies and departments, and cities) in all three states, B only to wholesalers, and C only to retailers. •

TRADE ASSOCIATIONS   Businesses in the same general industry or profession frequently organize trade associations to pursue common interests. A trade association may engage in various joint activities such as exchanging information, representing the members' business interests before governmental bodies, conducting advertising campaigns, and setting regulatory standards to govern the industry or profession. Generally, the rule of reason is applied to many of these horizontal actions. If a court finds that a trade association practice or agreement that restrains trade is sufficiently beneficial both to the association and to the public, it may deem the restraint reasonable.

A **concentrated industry** is one in which either a single firm or a small number of firms control a large percentage of market sales. In concentrated industries, trade associations can be, and have been, used as a means to facilitate anticompetitive actions, such as fixing prices or allocating markets. When trade association agreements have substantially anticompetitive effects, a court will consider them to be in violation of Section 1 of the Sherman Act.

---

6. *In re Cardizem CD Antitrust Litigation,* 332 F.3d 896 (6th Cir. 2003).

Vertical Restraints

Vertical Restraint Any restraint of trade created by agreements between firms at different levels in the manufacturing and distribution process.

A **vertical restraint** of trade results from an agreement between firms at different levels in the manufacturing and distribution process. In contrast to horizontal relationships, which occur at the same level of operation, vertical relationships encompass the entire chain of production. The chain of production normally includes the purchase of inventory, basic manufacturing, distribution to wholesalers, and eventual sale of a product at the retail level. For some products, these distinct phases may be carried out by different firms. In other instances, a single firm carries out two or more of the separate functional phases. Such enterprises are considered to be **vertically integrated firms.**

Vertically Integrated Firm A firm that carries out two or more functional phases (manufacture, distribution, and retailing, for example) of the chain of production.

Even though firms operating at different functional levels are not in direct competition with one another, they are in competition with other firms. Thus, agreements between firms standing in a vertical relationship may affect competition. Some vertical restraints are *per se* violations of Section 1; others are judged under the rule of reason.

TERRITORIAL OR CUSTOMER RESTRICTIONS In arranging for the distribution of its products, a manufacturing firm often wishes to insulate dealers from direct competition with other dealers selling the product. To this end, it may institute territorial restrictions or attempt to prohibit wholesalers or retailers from reselling the product to certain classes of buyers, such as competing retailers.

A firm may have legitimate reasons for imposing such territorial or customer restrictions. **EXAMPLE 32.3** A computer manufacturer may wish to prevent a dealer from cutting costs and undercutting rivals by selling computers without promotion or customer service, while relying on nearby dealers to provide these services. In this situation, the cost-cutting dealer reaps the benefits (sales of the product) paid for by other dealers who undertake promotion and arrange for customer service. By not providing customer service, the cost-cutting dealer may also harm the manufacturer's reputation. ●

> "The idea of imposing restrictions on a free economy to assure freedom of competition is like breaking a man's leg to make him run faster."
> Morris R. Sayre, 1946–present
> (American politician)

Territorial and customer restrictions are judged under the rule of reason. In *United States v. Arnold, Schwinn & Co.,*[7] a case decided in 1967, a bicycle manufacturer, Schwinn, was assigning specific territories to its wholesale distributors and authorizing certain retail dealers only if they agreed to advertise Schwinn bikes and give them the same prominence as other brands. The United States Supreme Court held that these vertical territorial and customer restrictions were *per se* violations of Section 1 of the Sherman Act. Ten years later, however, in *Continental T.V., Inc. v. GTE Sylvania, Inc.,*[8] a case involving similar restrictions imposed on retailers by a television manufacturer, the Supreme Court overturned the *Schwinn* decision. In the *Continental* decision, the Court held that such vertical restrictions should be judged under the rule of reason, and this rule is still applied in most vertical restraint cases.[9] The *Continental* case marked a definite shift from rigid characterization of these kinds of vertical restraints to a more flexible, economic analysis of the restraints under the rule of reason.

Resale Price Maintenance Agreement An agreement between a manufacturer and a retailer in which the manufacturer specifies what the retail prices of its products must be.

RESALE PRICE MAINTENANCE AGREEMENTS An agreement between a manufacturer and a distributor or retailer in which the manufacturer specifies what the retail prices of its products must be is referred to as a **resale price maintenance agreement.** Such agreements were once considered to be *per se* violations of Section 1, but in 1997 the United States Supreme Court ruled that *maximum* resale price maintenance agreements should be judged under the rule of reason.[10] The setting of a maximum price that retailers and

---

7. 388 U.S. 365, 87 S.Ct. 1856, 18 L.Ed.2d 1249 (1967).

8. 433 U.S. 36, 97 S.Ct. 2549, 53 L.Ed.2d 568 (1977).

9. Note that there is some disagreement in the case law on when a vertical restraint should be considered unreasonable. See, for example, *State of New York by Abrams v. Anheuser-Busch,* 811 F.Supp. 848 (E.D.N.Y. 1993), which calls into doubt one of the holdings of the *Continental* case.

10. *State Oil Co. v. Khan,* 522 U.S. 3, 118 S.Ct. 275, 139 L.Ed.2d 199 (1997).

distributors can charge for a manufacturer's products may sometimes increase competition and benefit consumers.

The question before the Court in the following case was whether *minimum* resale price maintenance agreements should be treated as *per se* unlawful.

Case 32.1   Leegin Creative Leather Products, Inc. v. PSKS, Inc.

Supreme Court of the United States, 551 U.S. 877, 127 S.Ct. 2705, 168 L.Ed.2d 623 (2007).
supct.law.cornell.edu/supct/index.html[a]

When a company mandated a minimum price to the retailers of its leather products, did it violate antitrust laws?

FACTS Leegin Creative Leather Products, Inc., designs, manufactures, and distributes leather goods and accessories. One of its brand names is Brighton. Kay's Kloset, owned by PSKS, Inc., started purchasing Brighton goods from Leegin in 1995. As part of a resale price maintenance program, Leegin required resellers of Brighton goods to charge customers a minimum price. When Leegin discovered that Kay's Kloset had been discounting Brighton products by 20 percent, Leegin stopped selling Brighton products to the store. PSKS sued Leegin in federal court, claiming that Leegin had violated antitrust law when it imposed minimum prices. The district court entered a judgment against Leegin in the amount of almost $4 million. The U.S. Court of Appeals for the Fifth Circuit affirmed, and Leegin appealed to the United States Supreme Court.

ISSUE Did Leegin violate antitrust law when it required resellers of its goods to charge customers a minimum price?

a. In the "Archive of Decisions" section, in the "By party" subsection, click on "1990-present." In the result, in the "2006-2007" row, click on "1st party." On the next page, scroll to the name of the case and click on it. On the next page, click on the appropriate link to access the opinion.

DECISION No. The United States Supreme Court reversed the judgment of the court of appeals and remanded the case for proceedings consistent with its opinion.

REASON The Court pointed out that a *per se* rule should be confined to restraints of trade that "would always or almost always tend to restrict competition and decrease output. To justify a *per se* prohibition, a restraint must have manifestly anticompetitive effects, and lack * * * any redeeming virtue." The Court did not believe that a *per se* rule should apply to minimum resale prices. "Minimum resale price maintenance can stimulate interbrand competition * * * by reducing intrabrand competition * * * . Resale price maintenance * * * has the potential to give consumers more options so that they can choose among low-price, low-service brands; high-price, high-service brands; and brands that fall in between." Consequently, the Court concluded that minimum resale price maintenance does not necessarily restrict competition and decrease output. "As the [*per se*] rule would proscribe a significant amount of procompetitive conduct, these agreements appear ill suited for *per se* condemnation."

FOR CRITICAL ANALYSIS—Global Consideration *If a product competes mainly with the products of major foreign companies, is resale price maintenance more or less likely to lessen competition and restrict output than if the competitors were all U.S. firms? Explain.*

▶ Section 2 of the Sherman Act

Section 1 of the Sherman Act proscribes certain concerted, or joint, activities that restrain trade. In contrast, Section 2 condemns "every person who shall monopolize, or attempt to monopolize." Thus, two distinct types of behavior are subject to sanction under Section 2: *monopolization* and *attempts to monopolize*. One tactic that may be involved in either offense is **predatory pricing**. Predatory pricing involves an attempt by one firm to drive its competitors from the market by selling its product at prices substantially *below* the normal costs of production. Once the competitors are eliminated, the firm will attempt to recapture its losses and go on to earn higher profits by driving prices up far above their competitive levels.

Predatory Pricing The pricing of a product below cost with the intent to drive competitors out of the market.

Monopolization

Monopolization The possession of monopoly power in the relevant market and the willful acquisition or maintenance of that power, as distinguished from growth or development as a consequence of a superior product, business acumen, or historic accident.

The United States Supreme Court has defined the offense of **monopolization** as involving the following two elements: "(1) the possession of monopoly power in the relevant market and (2) the willful acquisition or maintenance of [that] power as distinguished from growth or development as a consequence of a superior product, business acumen, or historic accident."[11] A violation of Section 2 requires that both these elements—monopoly power and an intent to monopolize—be established.

ON THE WEB The American Antitrust Institute maintains a Web site that is devoted entirely to the topic of antitrust law. To access this site, go to www.antitrustinstitute.org.

MONOPOLY POWER   The Sherman Act does not define *monopoly*. In economic theory, monopoly refers to control of a single market by a single entity. It is well established in antitrust law, however, that a firm may be deemed a monopolist even though it is not the sole seller in a market. Additionally, size alone does not determine whether a firm is a monopoly. **EXAMPLE 32.4** A "mom and pop" grocery located in the isolated town of Happy Camp, Idaho, is a monopolist if it is the only grocery serving that particular market. Size in relation to the market is what matters because monopoly involves the power to affect prices. ●

Monopoly power may be proved by direct evidence that the firm used its power to control prices and restrict output.[12] Usually, however, there is not enough evidence to show that the firm was intentionally controlling prices, so the plaintiff has to offer indirect, or circumstantial, evidence of monopoly power. To prove monopoly power indirectly, the plaintiff must show that the firm has a dominant share of the relevant market and that there are significant barriers for new competitors entering that market.

RELEVANT MARKET   Before a court can determine whether a firm has a dominant market share, it must define the relevant market. The relevant market consists of two elements: a relevant product market and a relevant geographic market.

Relevant Product Market.   The relevant product market includes all products that, although produced by different firms, have identical attributes, such as sugar. It also includes products that are reasonably interchangeable for the purpose for which they are produced. Products will be considered reasonably interchangeable if consumers treat them as acceptable substitutes.[13]

What should the relevant product market include? This is often a key issue in monopolization cases because the way the market is defined may determine whether a firm has monopoly power. In defining the relevant product market, the key issue is the degree of interchangeability between products. If one product is a sufficient substitute for another, the two products are considered to be part of the same product market. **CASE EXAMPLE 32.5** In 2007, the Federal Trade Commission (FTC) filed a Section 2 claim against Whole Foods Market, Inc., which owns a nationwide chain of natural and organic food stores. The FTC was seeking to prevent Whole Foods from merging with Wild Oats Markets, Inc., its main competitor in nationwide high-end organic food supermarkets.

The FTC argued that the relevant product market consisted of only "premium natural and organic supermarkets (PNOS)" rather than all supermarkets. By defining the product market narrowly, the degree of a firm's market power is enhanced. Although a federal court originally ruled against the FTC and allowed the merger to go forward, the FTC won on appeal, convincing the appellate court that an injunction should have been granted. On remand, the lower court had to decide what remedies were appropriate as the merger had already taken place.[14] ●

The Federal Trade Commission fought Whole Foods Market's merger with competitor Wild Oats Markets, Inc., claiming that such a merger would lessen competition in the organic food market. Given the fact that most major supermarket chains now offer high-end organic foods, wouldn't that indicate Whole Foods has numerous competitors?

(Karl Sullivan/Creative Commons)

11. *United States v. Grinnell Corp.*, 384 U.S. 563, 86 S.Ct. 1698, 16 L.Ed.2d 778 (1966).
12. See, for example, *Broadcom Corp. v. Qualcomm, Inc.*, 501 F.3d 297 (3d Cir. 2007).
13. See, for example, *HDC Medical, Inc. v. Minntech Corp.*, 474 F.3d 543 (8th Cir. 2007).
14. *FTC v. Whole Foods Market, Inc.*, 548 F.3d 1028 (D.C.Cir. 2008); and 592 F.Supp.2d 107 (D.D.C. 2009).

Relevant Geographic Market.   The second component of the relevant market is the geographic boundaries of the market. For products that are sold nationwide, the geographic boundaries of the market encompass the entire United States. If transportation costs are significant or a producer and its competitors sell in only a limited area (one in which customers have no access to other sources of the product), the geographic market is limited to that area. A national firm may thus compete in several distinct areas and have monopoly power in one area but not in another.

Generally, the geographic market is that section of the country within which a firm can increase its price a bit without attracting new sellers or without losing many customers to alternative suppliers outside that area. Of course, the Internet is changing the notion of the size and limits of a geographic market. It may become difficult to perceive any geographic market as local, except for products that are not easily transported, such as concrete.

THE INTENT REQUIREMENT   Monopoly power, in and of itself, does not constitute the offense of monopolization under Section 2 of the Sherman Act. The offense also requires an *intent* to monopolize. A dominant market share may be the result of business acumen or the development of a superior product. It may simply be the result of a historic accident. In these situations, the acquisition of monopoly power is not an antitrust violation. Indeed, it would be contrary to society's interest to condemn every firm that acquired a position of power because it was well managed and efficient and marketed a product desired by consumers.

> **KEEP IN MIND**   Section 2 of the Sherman Act essentially condemns the act of monopolizing, not the possession of monopoly power.

If a firm possesses market power as a result of carrying out some purposeful act to acquire or maintain that power through anticompetitive means, then it is in violation of Section 2. In most monopolization cases, intent may be inferred from evidence that the firm had monopoly power and engaged in anticompetitive behavior.

CASE EXAMPLE 32.6   Navigator, the first popular graphical Internet browser, used Java technology that was able to run on a variety of platforms. When Navigator was introduced, Microsoft perceived a threat to its dominance of the operating-system market. Microsoft developed a competing browser, Internet Explorer, and then began to require computer makers that wanted to install the Windows operating system to also install Explorer and exclude Navigator. In addition, Microsoft included codes in Windows that would cripple the operating system if Explorer was deleted, and it also paid Internet service providers to distribute Explorer and exclude Navigator. Because of this pattern of exclusionary conduct, a court found that Microsoft was guilty of monopolization in violation of Section 2 of the Sherman Act. The court reasoned that Microsoft's pattern of conduct could be rational only if the firm knew that it possessed monopoly power.[15] ●

Preventing Legal Disputes ✍

Because exclusionary conduct can have legitimate efficiency-enhancing effects, it can be difficult to determine when conduct will be viewed as anticompetitive and a violation of Section 2 of the Sherman Act. Thus, a business that possesses monopoly power must be careful that its actions cannot be inferred to be evidence of intent to monopolize. Even if your business does not have a dominant market share, you would be wise to take precautions. Make sure that you can articulate clear, legitimate reasons for the particular conduct or contract and that you do not provide any direct evidence (damaging e-mails, for example) of an intent to exclude competitors. A court will be less likely to infer the intent to monopolize if the specific conduct was aimed at increasing output and lowering per-unit costs, improving product quality, or protecting a patented technology or innovation. Exclusionary conduct and agreements that have no redeeming qualities are much more likely to be deemed illegal.

---

15. *United States v. Microsoft Corp.*, 253 F.3d 34 (D.C.Cir. 2001). Microsoft has faced numerous antitrust claims and has settled a number of lawsuits in which it was accused of antitrust violations and anticompetitive tactics.

UNILATERAL REFUSALS TO DEAL As discussed previously, joint refusals to deal (group boycotts) are subject to close scrutiny under Section 1 of the Sherman Act. A single manufacturer acting unilaterally, though, normally is free to deal, or not to deal, with whomever it wishes.[16]

Nevertheless, in limited circumstances, a unilateral refusal to deal will violate antitrust laws. These instances involve offenses proscribed under Section 2 of the Sherman Act and occur only if (1) the firm refusing to deal has—or is likely to acquire—monopoly power and (2) the refusal is likely to have an anticompetitive effect on a particular market. **CASE EXAMPLE 32.7** The owner of three of the four major downhill ski areas in Aspen, Colorado, refused to continue participating in a jointly offered six-day "all Aspen" lift ticket. The Supreme Court ruled that the owner's refusal to cooperate with its smaller competitor was a violation of Section 2 of the Sherman Act. Because the company owned three-fourths of the local ski areas, it had monopoly power, and thus its unilateral refusal had an anticompetitive effect on the market.[17] ●

Attempts to Monopolize

Attempted Monopolization Any action by a firm to eliminate competition and gain monopoly power.

Section 2 also prohibits **attempted monopolization** of a market. Any action challenged as an attempt to monopolize must have been specifically intended to exclude competitors and garner monopoly power. The attempt must also have had a "dangerous" probability of success—only *serious* threats of monopolization are condemned as violations. The probability cannot be dangerous unless the alleged offender possesses some degree of market power.

As mentioned earlier, predatory pricing is a form of anticompetitive conduct that, in theory, could be used by firms that are attempting to monopolize. (Predatory pricing may also lead to claims of price discrimination, to be discussed shortly.) Predatory bidding involves the acquisition and use of *monopsony power,* which is market power on the *buy* side of a market. This may occur when a buyer bids up the price of an input too high for its competitors to pay, causing them to leave the market. The predatory bidder may then attempt to drive down input prices to reap above-competitive profits and recoup any losses it suffered in bidding up the prices.

The question in the following case was whether a claim of predatory bidding is sufficiently similar to a claim of predatory pricing that the same test should apply to both.

16. See, for example, *Pacific Bell Telephone Co. v. Linkline Communications, Inc.,* ___ U.S. ___, 129 S.Ct. 1109, 172 L.Ed.2d 836 (2009).

17. *Aspen Skiing Co. v. Aspen Highlands Skiing Corp.,* 472 U.S. 585, 105 S.Ct. 2847, 86 L.Ed.2d 467 (1985). See also *America Channel, LLC v. Time Warner Cable, Inc.,* 2007 WL 142173 (D.Minn. 2007).

Case 32.2 Weyerhaeuser Co. v. Ross-Simmons Hardwood Lumber Co.

Supreme Court of the United States, 549 U.S. 312, 127 S.Ct. 1069, 166 L.Ed.2d 911 (2007).
www.findlaw.com/casecode/supreme.html[a]

(Claire L. Evans/Creative Commons)

Was predatory bidding on the price of alder logs tantamount to predatory pricing and therefore illegal?

FACTS Weyerhaeuser Company entered the Pacific Northwest's hardwood lumber market in 1980. By 2000, Weyerhaeuser owned six mills processing 65 percent of the red alder logs in the region. Meanwhile, Ross-Simmons Hardwood Lumber Company operated a single competing mill. When the prices of the logs rose and those for the lumber fell, Ross-Simmons suffered heavy losses.

Several million dollars in debt, the mill closed in 2001. Ross-Simmons filed a suit in a federal district court against Weyerhaeuser, alleging attempted monopolization under Section 2 of the Sherman Act. Ross-Simmons claimed that Weyerhaeuser used its dominant position in the market to bid up the prices of logs and prevent its competitors from being profitable. Weyerhaeuser argued that the antitrust test for predatory pricing applies to a claim of predatory bidding and that Ross-Simmons had not met this standard. The district court ruled in favor of the plaintiff, the U.S. Court of Appeals for the Ninth Circuit affirmed, and Weyerhaeuser appealed to the United States Supreme Court.

a. In the "Browse Supreme Court Opinions" section, click on "2007." On that page, scroll to the name of the case and click on it to access the opinion.

Case 32.2—Continues next page ➡

Case 32.2–Continued

ISSUE   Does the antitrust test that applies to a claim of predatory pricing also apply to a claim of predatory bidding?

DECISION   Yes. Because Ross-Simmons conceded that it had not met this standard, the Court vacated the lower court's judgment and remanded the case.

REASON   Both predatory pricing and predatory bidding involve a company's intentional use of pricing for an anticompetitive purpose. Both actions require a company to incur a short-term loss on the possibility of later making a "supracompetitive" profit. Because a "rational" firm is unlikely to "make this sacrifice," both schemes are "rarely tried and even more rarely successful." A failed scheme of either type can benefit consumers. Thus, the two-part predatory-pricing test should apply to predatory-bidding claims. A plaintiff alleging predatory bidding must then prove that the defendant's "bidding on the buy side caused the cost of the relevant output to rise above the revenues generated in the sale of those outputs." The plaintiff must also prove that "the defendant has a dangerous prob-

ability of recouping the losses incurred in bidding up input prices through the exercise of monopsony power."

FOR CRITICAL ANALYSIS—Economic Consideration
Why does a plaintiff alleging predatory bidding have to prove that the defendant's "bidding on the buy side caused the cost of the relevant output to rise above the revenues generated in the sale of those outputs"?

WHY IS THIS CASE IMPORTANT?   *Predatory-bidding schemes of the type that Ross-Simmons alleged Weyerhaeuser had committed are rare. Under the standard that the Court imposed in this case, a plaintiff's success in pursuing such a claim will likely be even more rare. But this may not be a negative development, at least for consumers. A predatory-bidding scheme can actually benefit consumers—a predator's high bidding can lead to its acquisition of more inputs, which can lead to the manufacture of more outputs, and increases in output generally result in lower prices to consumers.*

 Ethical Issue

Are we destined for more monopolies in the future? Knowledge and information form the building blocks of the so-called new economy. Some observers believe that the nature of this new economy means that we will see an increasing number of monopolies similar to Microsoft. Consider that the justification for all antitrust law is that monopoly leads to restricted output and hence higher prices for consumers. That is how a monopolist maximizes profits relative to a competitive firm. In the knowledge-based sector, however, firms face *economies of scale* (defined as decreases in long-run average costs resulting from increases in output), so they will do the exact opposite of a traditional monopolist—they will increase output and reduce prices. That is exactly what Microsoft has done over the years—the prices of its operating system and applications have fallen, particularly when corrected for inflation.

    This characteristic of knowledge-based monopolies may mean that antitrust authorities will have to have greater tolerance for these monopolies to allow them to benefit from full economies of scale. After all, consumers are the ultimate beneficiaries of such economies of scale. In the early 1900s, economist Joseph Schumpeter argued in favor of allowing monopolies. According to his theory of "creative destruction," monopolies stimulate innovation and economic growth because firms that capture monopoly profits have a greater incentive to innovate. Those that do not survive—the firms that are "destroyed"—leave room for the more efficient firms that will survive.

▶ The Clayton Act

In 1914, Congress attempted to strengthen federal antitrust laws by enacting the Clayton Act. The Clayton Act was aimed at specific anticompetitive or monopolistic practices that the Sherman Act did not cover. The substantive provisions of the act deal with four distinct forms of business behavior, which are declared illegal but not criminal. In each instance, the act states that the behavior is illegal only if it tends to substantially lessen competition or to create monopoly power. The major offenses under the Clayton Act are set out in Sections 2, 3, 7, and 8 of the act.

Price Discrimination   Setting prices in such a way that two competing buyers pay two different prices for an identical product or service.

Section 2 (The Robinson-Patman Act)—Price Discrimination

Section 2 of the Clayton Act prohibits **price discrimination**, which occurs when a seller charges different prices to competing buyers for identical goods or services. Congress strengthened this section by amending it with the passage of the Robinson-Patman Act in 1936. As amended, Section 2 prohibits price discrimination that cannot be justified by differences in production costs, transportation costs, or cost differences due to other reasons. In short, a seller is prohibited from charging a lower price to one buyer than is charged to that buyer's competitor.

REQUIREMENTS   To violate Section 2, the seller must be engaged in interstate commerce, the goods must be of like grade and quality, and goods must have been sold to two or more purchasers. In addition, the effect of the price discrimination must be to substantially lessen competition, to tend to create a monopoly, or to otherwise injure competition. Without proof of an actual injury resulting from the price discrimination, the plaintiff cannot recover damages.

Note that price discrimination claims can arise from discounts, offsets, rebates, or allowances given to one buyer over another. Moreover, giving favorable credit terms, delivery, or freight charges to only some buyers can also lead to allegations of price discrimination. For example, offering goods to different customers at the same price but including free delivery for certain buyers may violate Section 2 in some circumstances.

DEFENSES   There are several statutory defenses to liability for price discrimination.

1. *Cost justification.* If the seller can justify the price reduction by demonstrating that a particular buyer's purchases saved the seller costs in producing and selling the goods, the seller will not be liable for price discrimination.
2. *Meeting the price of competition.* If the seller charged the lower price in a good faith attempt to meet an equally low price of a competitor, the seller will not be liable for price discrimination. **CASE EXAMPLE 32.8**   Water Craft was a retail dealership of Mercury Marine outboard motors in Baton Rouge, Louisiana. Mercury Marine also sold its motors to other dealers in the Baton Rouge area. When Water Craft discovered that Mercury was selling its outboard motors at a substantial discount to Water Craft's largest competitor, it filed a price discrimination lawsuit against Mercury. In this situation, the court held that Mercury Marine had shown that the discounts given to Water Craft's competitor were made in good faith to meet the low price charged by another manufacturer of marine motors.[18] •
3. *Changing market conditions.* A seller may lower its price on an item in response to changing conditions affecting the market for or the marketability of the goods concerned. Sellers are allowed to readjust their prices to meet the realities of the market without liability for price discrimination. Thus, if an advance in technology makes a particular product less marketable than it was previously, a seller can lower the product's price.

Section 3—Exclusionary Practices

Under Section 3 of the Clayton Act, sellers or lessors cannot sell or lease goods "on the condition, agreement or understanding that the . . . purchaser or lessee thereof shall not use or deal in the goods . . . of a competitor or competitors of the seller." In effect, this section prohibits two types of vertical agreements involving exclusionary practices—exclusive-dealing contracts and tying arrangements.

EXCLUSIVE-DEALING CONTRACTS   A contract under which a seller forbids a buyer to purchase products from the seller's competitors is called an **exclusive-dealing contract.** A seller is prohibited from making an exclusive-dealing contract under Section 3 if the effect of the contract is "to substantially lessen competition or tend to create a monopoly."

> "Becoming number one is easier than remaining number one."
>
> Bill Bradley, 1943–present
> (American politician and athlete)

Exclusive-Dealing Contract   An agreement under which a seller forbids a buyer to purchase products from the seller's competitors.

---

18. *Water Craft Management, LLC v. Mercury Marine,* 457 F.3d 484 (5th Cir. 2006).

CASE EXAMPLE 32.9 In a classic case decided by the United States Supreme Court in 1949, Standard Oil Company, the largest gasoline seller in the nation at that time, made exclusive-dealing contracts with independent stations in seven Western states. The contracts involved 16 percent of all retail outlets, with sales amounting to approximately 7 percent of all retail sales in that market. The Court noted that the market was substantially concentrated because the seven largest gasoline suppliers all used exclusive-dealing contracts with their independent retailers. Together, these suppliers controlled 65 percent of the market. Looking at market conditions after the arrangements were instituted, the Court found that market shares were extremely stable and that entry into the market was apparently restricted. Thus, the Court held that Section 3 of the Clayton Act had been violated because competition was "foreclosed in a substantial share" of the relevant market.[19] ●

Note that since the Supreme Court's 1949 decision, a number of subsequent decisions have called the holding in this case into doubt.[20] Today, it is clear that to violate antitrust law, an exclusive-dealing agreement (or *tying arrangement,* discussed next) must qualitatively and substantially harm competition. To prevail, a plaintiff must present affirmative evidence that the performance of the agreement will foreclose competition and harm consumers.

Tying Arrangement An agreement between a buyer and a seller in which the buyer of a specific product or service becomes obligated to purchase additional products or services from the seller.

TYING ARRANGEMENTS

In a **tying arrangement,** or *tie-in sales agreement,* a seller conditions the sale of a product (the tying product) on the buyer's agreement to purchase another product (the tied product) produced or distributed by the same seller. The legality of a tie-in agreement depends on many factors, particularly the purpose of the agreement and its likely effect on competition in the relevant markets (the market for the tying product and the market for the tied product).

CASE EXAMPLE 32.10 In 1936, the United States Supreme Court held that International Business Machines and Remington Rand had violated Section 3 of the Clayton Act by requiring the purchase of their own machine cards (the tied product) as a condition for leasing their tabulation machines (the tying product). Because only these two firms sold completely automated tabulation machines, the Court concluded that each possessed market power sufficient to "substantially lessen competition" through the tying arrangements.[21] ●

Section 3 of the Clayton Act has been held to apply only to commodities, not to services. Tying arrangements, however, can also be considered agreements that restrain trade in violation of Section 1 of the Sherman Act. Thus, cases involving tying arrangements of services have been brought under Section 1 of the Sherman Act. Although earlier cases condemned tying arrangements as illegal *per se,* courts now evaluate tying agreements under the rule of reason.[22]

Section 7—Mergers

Under Section 7 of the Clayton Act, a person or business organization cannot hold stock and/or assets in another entity "where the effect . . . may be to substantially lessen competition." Section 7 is the statutory authority for preventing mergers or acquisitions that could result in monopoly power or a substantial lessening of competition in the marketplace. Section 7 applies to horizontal mergers and vertical mergers, both of which we discuss in the following subsections.

Market Concentration The degree to which a small number of firms control a large percentage share of a relevant market; determined by calculating the percentages held by the largest firms in that market.

A crucial consideration in most merger cases is the **market concentration** of a product or business. Determining market concentration involves allocating percentage market

---

19. *Standard Oil Co. of California v. United States,* 337 U.S. 293, 69 S.Ct. 1051, 93 L.Ed. 1371 (1949).
20. See, for example, *Illinois Tool Works, Inc. v. Independent Ink, Inc.,* 547 U.S. 28, 126 S.Ct. 1281, 164 L.Ed.2d 26 (2006); and *Stop & Shop Supermarket Co. v. Blue Cross & Blue Shield of Rhode Island,* 373 F.3d 57 (1st Cir. 2004).
21. *International Business Machines Corp. v. United States,* 298 U.S. 131, 56 S.Ct. 701, 80 L.Ed. 1085 (1936).
22. See, for example, *Illinois Tool Works, Inc. v. Independent Ink, Inc.,* cited in Footnote 20.

shares among the various companies in the relevant market. When a small number of companies control a large share of trade market, the market is concentrated. If the four largest grocery stores in Chicago accounted for 80 percent of all retail food sales, for example, the market clearly would be concentrated in those four firms.

Competition, however, is not necessarily diminished solely as a result of market concentration, and courts will consider other factors in determining whether a merger will violate Section 7. One factor of particular importance in evaluating the effects of a merger is whether the merger will make it more difficult for *potential* competitors to enter the relevant market.

Horizontal Merger A merger between two firms that are competing in the same marketplace.

HORIZONTAL MERGERS Mergers between firms that compete with each other in the same market are called **horizontal mergers.** If a horizontal merger creates an entity with a significant market share, the merger will be presumed illegal because it increases market concentration. When analyzing the legality of a horizontal merger, the courts also consider three other factors: the overall concentration of the relevant product market, the relevant market's history of tending toward concentration, and whether the apparent design of the merger is to establish market power or to restrict competition.

The Federal Trade Commission (FTC) and the U.S. Department of Justice (DOJ) have established guidelines indicating which mergers will be challenged. Under the guidelines, the first factor to be considered is the degree of concentration in the relevant market. In determining market concentration, the FTC and the DOJ employ what is known as the **Herfindahl-Hirschman Index (HHI).** The HHI is computed by summing the squares of the percentage market shares of the firms in the relevant market. If there are four firms with shares of 30 percent, 30 percent, 20 percent, and 20 percent, respectively, then the HHI equals 2,600 (900 + 900 + 400 + 400 = 2,600).

Herfindahl-Hirschman Index (HHI) An index of market power used to calculate whether a merger of two businesses will result in sufficient monopoly power to violate antitrust laws.

If the premerger HHI is less than 1,000, then the market is unconcentrated, and the merger is unlikely to be challenged. If the premerger HHI is between 1,000 and 1,800, the industry is moderately concentrated, and the merger will be challenged only if it increases the HHI by 100 points or more.[23] If the HHI is greater than 1,800, the market is highly concentrated. In a highly concentrated market, a merger that produces an increase in the HHI of between 50 and 100 points raises "significant" competitive concerns. Mergers that produce an increase in the HHI of more than 100 points in a highly concentrated market are deemed likely to enhance market power. HHI figures were a factor in the following case.

---

23. Compute the change in the index by doubling the product of the merging firms' premerger market shares. For example, a merger between a firm with a 5 percent share and one with a 6 percent share will increase the HHI by $2 \times (5 \times 6) = 60$.

Case 32.3 Chicago Bridge & Iron Co. v. Federal Trade Commission

United States Court of Appeals, Fifth Circuit, 534 F.3d 410 (2008).
www.ca5.uscourts.gov[a]

The market-dominant manufacturer of industrial-storage tanks acquires its largest competitor. Did the FTC correctly rule the acquisition illegal?

FACTS Chicago Bridge & Iron Company designs and constructs industrial-storage tanks for liquefied natural gas (LNG), liquefied petroleum gas (LPG), and liquid atmospheric gases, such as nitrogen, oxygen, and argon (LIN/LOX), as well as thermal vacuum chambers (TVCs) for testing aerospace satellites. In these four separate markets, Chicago Bridge and another company, Pitt–Des Moines, Inc., have been the dominant firms. In 2001, Chicago Bridge acquired all of Pitt–Des Moines's assets for $84 million. The Federal Trade Commission (FTC) charged that Chicago Bridge's acquisition violated Section 7 of the Clayton Act and Section 5 of the Federal Trade Commission Act. An administrative law judge concurred, finding that the acquisition resulted in an undue increase in Chicago Bridge's market power that would

a. On the left, click on "Opinions Page." In the resulting page, under "Search for opinions where:" type "Chicago Bridge" in the "and/or Title contains text:" box. Then click on the docket number from 7/15/2008 to download this court opinion.

Case 32.3–Continues next page ➡

Case 32.3–Continued

not be constrained by timely entry of new competitors. At issue was the use of the Herfindahl-Hirschman Index (HHI). The FTC calculated the HHI over a several-year period rather than on an annualized basis. Chicago Bridge appealed.

ISSUE Did the FTC's calculations of the HHI correctly determine that the proposed merger would be a violation of antitrust laws?

DECISION Yes. The U.S. Court of Appeals for the Fifth Circuit affirmed the FTC's ruling that Chicago Bridge must divest itself of its former competitor, Pitt–Des Moines.

REASON The reviewing court pointed out that merger guidelines create a presumption of adverse competitive consequences when the postmerger HHI exceeds 1,800 and the merger produces an increase in the HHI of more than 100 points. When Chicago Bridge purchased the assets of Pitt–Des Moines, the postmerger *increases* in the HHI ranged from a low of 2,635 for the LIN/LOX storage-tank market to a high of almost 5,000 for the

TVC storage-tank market. Indeed, if the merger took place, Chicago Bridge would have a complete monopoly in both the TVC market and the LNG market. The reviewing court was unimpressed with Chicago Bridge's contention that the FTC should not have used sales data over an eleven-year period. The court stated, "When sales data are sporadic, a longer historical perspective may be necessary. . . . We find that the record contains substantial evidence to support the Commission's finding that the HHIs are not completely irrelevant in three of the four markets. Instead of ignoring HHIs, we agree with the Commission that they should be viewed with caution and within the larger picture of long-term trends in the market." Further, "the Government's other evidence favors what the HHIs also indicate; the proposed merger will substantially lessen competition."

FOR CRITICAL ANALYSIS—Global Consideration *Assume that just before Chicago Bridge acquired its only U.S. competitor, a multinational company based in Indonesia announced that it intended to enter all four of the markets mentioned in this case. How might this announcement affect the reasoning behind this case, if at all?*

Vertical Merger The acquisition by a company at one level in a marketing chain of a company at a higher or lower level in the chain (such as a company merging with one of its suppliers or retailers).

VERTICAL MERGERS A **vertical merger** occurs when a company at one stage of production acquires a company at a higher or lower stage of production. An example of a vertical merger is a company merging with one of its suppliers or retailers. In the past, courts focused almost exclusively on "foreclosure" in assessing vertical mergers. Foreclosure may occur because competitors of the merging firms lose opportunities to sell or buy products from the merging firms.

Today, whether a vertical merger will be deemed illegal generally depends on several factors, such as whether the merger would produce a firm controlling an undue percentage share of the relevant market. The courts also analyze whether the merger would result in a significant increase in the concentration of firms in that market, the barriers to entry into the market, and the apparent intent of the merging parties.[24] Mergers that do not prevent competitors of either merging firm from competing in a segment of the market will not be condemned as "foreclosing" competition and are legal.

Section 8—Interlocking Directorates

Section 8 of the Clayton Act deals with *interlocking directorates*—that is, the practice of having individuals serve as directors on the boards of two or more competing companies simultaneously. Specifically, no person may be a director in two or more competing corporations at the same time if either of the corporations has capital, surplus, or undivided profits aggregating more than $26,161,000 or competitive sales of $2,616,100 or more. The FTC adjusts the threshold amounts each year. (The amounts given here are those announced by the FTC in 2009.)

CONTRAST Section 5 of the Federal Trade Commission Act is broader than the other antitrust laws. It covers nearly all anticompetitive behavior, including conduct that does not violate either the Sherman Act or the Clayton Act.

 Enforcement and Exemptions

The federal agencies that enforce the federal antitrust laws are the U.S. Department of Justice (DOJ) and the Federal Trade Commission (FTC). The FTC was established by the Federal Trade Commission Act of 1914. Section 5 of that act condemns all forms of anticompetitive behavior that are not covered under other federal antitrust laws.

---

24. See, for example, *United States v. Dairy Farmers of America, Inc.*, 425 F.3d 850 (6th Cir. 2005).

Agency Actions

Only the DOJ can prosecute violations of the Sherman Act, which can be either criminal or civil offenses. Either the DOJ or the FTC can enforce the Clayton Act, but violations of that statute are not crimes and can be pursued only through civil proceedings. The DOJ or the FTC may ask the courts to impose various remedies, including **divestiture** (making a company give up one or more of its operating functions) and dissolution. A meatpacking firm, for example, might be forced to divest itself of control or ownership of butcher shops. (To find out how you can avoid antitrust problems, see the *Business Application* feature at the end of this chapter.)

The FTC has the sole authority to enforce violations of Section 5 of the Federal Trade Commission Act. FTC actions are effected through administrative orders, but if a firm violates an FTC order, the FTC can seek court sanctions for the violation.

Divestiture The act of selling one or more of a company's divisions or parts, such as a subsidiary or plant; often mandated by the courts in merger or monopolization cases.

Private Actions

A private party who has been injured as a result of a violation of the Sherman Act or the Clayton Act can sue for damages and attorneys' fees. In some instances, private parties may also seek injunctive relief to prevent antitrust violations. The courts have determined that the ability to sue depends on the directness of the injury suffered by the would-be plaintiff. Thus, a person wishing to sue under the Sherman Act must prove (1) that the antitrust violation either caused or was a substantial factor in causing the injury that was suffered and (2) that the unlawful actions of the accused party affected business activities of the plaintiff that were protected by the antitrust laws.

ON THE WEB You can find links to the home pages for federal government agencies, including the Department of Justice and the Federal Trade Commission, at www.usa.gov.

Treble Damages

In recent years, more than 90 percent of all antitrust actions have been brought by private plaintiffs. One reason for this is that successful plaintiffs may recover **treble damages—** three times the damages that they have suffered as a result of the violation. In a situation involving a price-fixing agreement, normally each competitor is jointly and severally liable for the total amount of any damages, including treble damages if they are imposed.

Treble Damages Damages that, by statute, are three times the amount that the fact finder determines is owed.

Exemptions from Antitrust Laws

There are many legislative and constitutional limitations on antitrust enforcement. Most of the statutory or judicially created exemptions to antitrust laws apply in such areas as labor, insurance, and foreign trade, and are listed in Exhibit 32–1 on the following page. One of the most significant of these exemptions covers joint efforts by businesspersons to obtain legislative, judicial, or executive action. Under this exemption, DVD producers can jointly lobby Congress to change the copyright laws without being held liable for attempting to restrain trade. Another exemption covers professional baseball teams.

▶ U.S. Antitrust Laws in the Global Context

U.S. antitrust laws have a broad application. Not only may persons in foreign nations be subject to their provisions, but the laws may also be applied to protect foreign consumers and competitors from violations committed by U.S. business firms. Consequently, *foreign persons,* a term that by definition includes foreign governments, may sue under U.S. antitrust laws in U.S. courts.

The Extraterritorial Application of U.S. Antitrust Laws

Section 1 of the Sherman Act provides for the extraterritorial effect of the U.S. antitrust laws. The United States is a major proponent of free competition in the global economy,

• *Exhibit* 32–1 Exemptions to Antitrust Enforcement

EXEMPTION	SOURCE AND SCOPE
Labor	Clayton Act—Permits unions to organize and bargain without violating antitrust laws and specifies that strikes and other labor activities normally do not violate any federal law.
Agricultural associations	Clayton Act and Capper-Volstead Act of 1922—Allow agricultural cooperatives to set prices.
Fisheries	Fisheries Cooperative Marketing Act of 1976—Allows the fishing industry to set prices.
Insurance companies	McCarran-Ferguson Act of 1945—Exempts the insurance business in states in which the industry is regulated.
Exporters	Webb-Pomerene Act of 1918—Allows U.S. exporters to engage in cooperative activity to compete with similar foreign associations. Export Trading Company Act of 1982—Permits the U.S. Department of Justice to exempt certain exporters.
Professional baseball	The United States Supreme Court has held that professional baseball is exempt because it is not "interstate commerce."[a]
Oil marketing	Interstate Oil Compact of 1935—Allows states to set quotas on oil to be marketed in interstate commerce.
Defense activities	Defense Production Act of 1950—Allows the president to approve, and thereby exempt, certain activities to further the military defense of the United States.
Small businesses' cooperative research	Small Business Administration Act of 1958—Allows small firms to undertake cooperative research.
State actions	The United States Supreme Court has held that actions by a state are exempt if the state clearly articulates and actively supervises the policy behind its action.[b]
Regulated industries	Industries (such as airlines) are exempt when a federal administrative agency (such as the Federal Aviation Administration) has primary regulatory authority.
Businesspersons' joint efforts to seek government action	Cooperative efforts by businesspersons to obtain legislative, judicial, or executive action are exempt unless it is clear that an effort is "objectively baseless" and is an attempt to make anticompetitive use of government processes.[c]

a. *Federal Baseball Club of Baltimore, Inc. v. National League of Professional Baseball Clubs,* 259 U.S. 200, 42 S.Ct. 465, 66 L.Ed. 898 (1922). A federal district court has held that this exemption applies only to the game's reserve system. (Under the reserve system, teams hold players' contracts for the players' entire careers. The reserve system generally is being replaced by the free agency system.) See *Piazza v. Major League Baseball,* 831 F.Supp. 420 (E.D.Pa. 1993).
b. See *Parker v. Brown,* 317 U.S. 341, 63 S.Ct. 307, 87 L.Ed. 315 (1943).
c. *Eastern Railroad Presidents Conference v. Noerr Motor Freight, Inc.,* 365 U.S. 127, 81 S.Ct. 523, 5 L.Ed.2d 464 (1961); and *United Mine Workers of America v. Pennington,* 381 U.S. 657, 89 S.Ct. 1585, 14 L.Ed.2d 626 (1965).

and thus any conspiracy that has a *substantial effect* on U.S. commerce is within the reach of the Sherman Act. The violation may even occur outside the United States, and foreign governments as well as persons can be sued for violation of U.S. antitrust laws. Before U.S. courts will exercise jurisdiction and apply antitrust laws, it must be shown that the alleged violation had a substantial effect on U.S. commerce. U.S. jurisdiction is automatically invoked, however, when a *per se* violation occurs.

If a domestic firm, for example, joins a foreign cartel to control the production, price, or distribution of goods, and this cartel has a *substantial effect* on U.S. commerce, a *per se* violation may exist. Hence, both the domestic firm and the foreign cartel could be sued for violation of the U.S. antitrust laws. Likewise, if a foreign firm doing business in the United States enters into a price-fixing or other anticompetitive agreement to control a portion of U.S. markets, a *per se* violation may exist.

The Application of Foreign Antitrust Laws

Large U.S. companies increasingly need to worry about the application of foreign antitrust laws as well. The European Union, in particular, has stepped up its enforcement actions against antitrust violators, as discussed in this chapter's *Beyond Our Borders* feature.

ON THE WEB For information on the European Union's antitrust legislation, investigations, and enforcement actions, go to the Web site of the European Commission on Competition at **ec.europa.eu/competition**.

Beyond Our Borders   The European Union's Expanding Role in Antitrust Litigation

The European Union (EU) has laws promoting competition that are stricter in many respects than those of the United States. Although the EU's laws provide only for civil, rather than criminal, penalties, the rules exhibit a different philosophy and define more conduct as anticompetitive than U.S. laws do. The EU issued strict enforcement guidelines in December 2008, signaling its intent to bring more actions against individual companies and cartels that engage in monopolistic conduct. The guidelines define what it means for a dominant company to harm competition by abusing its market power. They also include detailed provisions to prohibit dominant companies from requiring their customers to buy products solely

from them or requiring customers to buy bundles of products.[a]

The EU actively pursues antitrust violators. It entered into its own antitrust settlement with Microsoft Corporation in 2004, with remedies (including fines of more than $600 million) that went beyond those imposed in the United States. When Microsoft continued to bundle its browser (Internet Explorer) with the Windows operating systems sold in Europe, the EU brought another case and imposed additional fines. By 2009, the EU had fined Microsoft more than $2 billion. As a result, Microsoft announced in 2009 that all versions of Windows 7 sold in Europe will not include Internet Explorer 8.

a. Sheri Qualters, "Europe Gets Tough on Antitrust," *The National Law Journal,* December 22, 2008.

Also in 2009, the EU fined chip-making giant Intel, Inc., $1.44 billion in an antitrust case. According to European regulators, Intel offered computer manufacturers and retailers price discounts and marketing subsidies if they agreed to buy Intel's chips rather than the chips produced by Intel's main competitor in Europe.

• **For Critical Analysis**
Some commentators argue that EU regulators are too focused on reining in powerful U.S. technology companies, such as Microsoft and Intel. How might the large fines imposed by the EU on successful U.S. technology firms affect competition in the United States?

Many other nations also have laws that promote competition and prohibit trade restraints. For instance, Japanese antitrust laws forbid unfair trade practices, monopolization, and restrictions that unreasonably restrain trade. In 2008, China enacted its first antitrust rules, which restrict monopolization and price fixing (although China has claimed that the government may set prices on exported goods without violating these rules).[25] Indonesia, Malaysia, South Korea, and Vietnam all have statutes protecting competition. Argentina, Brazil, Chile, Peru, and several other Latin American countries have adopted modern antitrust laws as well.

Most of these antitrust laws apply extraterritorially, as U.S. antitrust laws do. This means that a U.S. company may be subject to another nation's antitrust laws if the company's conduct has a substantial effect on that nation's commerce. For instance, in 2008 South Korea fined Intel, Inc., the world's largest semiconductor chip maker, $25 million for antitrust violations; Japan settled an antitrust case against Intel in 2005.

25. John R. Wilke, "Beijing Defends Vitamin Makers," *The Wall Street Journal,* November 26, 2008.

Reviewing . . . Promoting Competition

The Internet Corporation for Assigned Names and Numbers (ICANN) is a nonprofit entity that organizes Internet domain names. It is governed by a board of directors elected by various groups with commercial interests in the Internet. One of ICANN's functions is to authorize an entity to serve as a registrar for certain "top level domains" (TLDs). ICANN entered into an agreement with VeriSign to provide registry services for the ".com" TLD in accordance with ICANN's specifications. VeriSign complained that ICANN was restricting the services that it could make available as a registrar and was blocking new services, imposing unnecessary conditions on those services, and setting prices at which the services were offered. VeriSign claimed that ICANN's control of the registry services for domain names violated Section 1 of the Sherman Act. Using the information presented in the chapter, answer the following questions.

1. Should ICANN's actions be judged under the rule of reason or be deemed a *per se* violation of Section 1 of the Sherman Act?
2. Should ICANN's action be viewed as a horizontal or a vertical restraint of trade?
3. Does it matter that ICANN's directors are chosen by groups with a commercial interest in the Internet?
4. If the dispute is judged under the rule of reason, what might be ICANN's defense for having a standardized set of registry services that must be used?

Business Application

How Can You Avoid Antitrust Problems?*

Business managers need to be aware of how antitrust legislation may affect their activities. In addition to the federal antitrust laws covered in this chapter, the states also have antitrust and unfair competition laws. Moreover, state authorities have the power to bring civil lawsuits to enforce federal antitrust laws. Additionally, antitrust law is subject to various interpretations by the courts. Unless a businessperson exercises caution, a court may decide that his or her actions are in violation of a federal or state statute.

Pricing Issues

Almost all businesses have competitors and want to outsell those competitors. The pricing of a business's goods or services is extremely important not only for its volume of sales, but also for its bottom-line profit. When setting or changing a price, businesses frequently hire a cost accountant to perform an analysis. This is only a start because a firm must also consider the price of a competitor's similar or identical products. Most businesses do not want a "price war" with rapidly declining prices. Thus, it is not uncommon for a business to charge basically the same price as its competitors. A problem arises when there is an agreement (express or implied) to fix the price. This is a *per se* violation of Section 1 of the Sherman Act and can result in criminal or civil actions (including treble damages).

Knowing the price a competitor charges—and meeting that price—is not a violation in and of itself. Frequently, its legality depends on how the information was obtained. Violations occur when there is a communication (regardless of purpose) between a business owner (or employee) and a direct competitor. If concerned that a communication may cause antitrust pricing problems, businesspersons should consult with an attorney who can explain what is legal when dealing with competitors.

Another problem in pricing can occur when a business wants to have some control over the price that its retailers charge when selling its product to customers. Historically, resale price maintenance agreements were automatically deemed illegal as vertical restraints of trade. Today, the courts use the rule of reason to test for illegality. There are a variety of legitimate reasons for price maintenance agreements, including product image and resale value. For example, a BMW automobile has both a price and a value image, and to sell it at a Hyundai's price could seriously damage BMW's image.

Implications of Foreign Law

Antitrust issues are not limited to domestic firms doing business in the United States. In today's global economy, many companies conduct business in other nations and with foreign businesses. Antitrust laws in other countries differ from U.S. law and can apply to a U.S. firm that has dealings with businesses located in a foreign nation even though the firm does not have a physical presence there. Always be aware of the antitrust laws of any country in which you are doing business. Generally, any businessperson who is considering doing business overseas should seek counsel from a competent attorney concerning potential antitrust violations.

CHECKLIST FOR AVOIDING ANTITRUST PROBLEMS
1. **Exercise caution when communicating and dealing with competitors.**
2. **Seek the advice of an attorney specializing in antitrust law to ensure that your business practices and agreements do not violate antitrust laws.**
3. **If you conduct business in other nations, obtain the advice of an attorney who is familiar with the antitrust laws of those nations.**

* This *Business Application* is not meant to substitute for the services of an attorney who is licensed to practice law in your state.

 Key Terms

antitrust law 812	concentrated industry 816	exclusive-dealing contract 823
attempted monopolization 821	divestiture 827	group boycott 816

Chapter Summary: Promoting Competition

The Sherman Antitrust Act (1890) (See pages 813–822.)	1. *Major provisions–*
	  a. Section 1–Prohibits contracts, combinations, and conspiracies in restraint of trade.
	    (1) Horizontal restraints subject to Section 1 include price-fixing agreements, group boycotts (joint refusals to deal), horizontal market divisions, and trade association agreements.
	    (2) Vertical restraints subject to Section 1 include territorial or customer restrictions, resale price maintenance agreements, and refusals to deal.
	  b. Section 2–Prohibits monopolies and attempts to monopolize.
	2. *Jurisdictional requirements–*The Sherman Act applies only to activities that have a significant impact on interstate commerce.
	3. *Interpretive rules–*
	  a. *Per se* rule–Applied to restraints on trade that are so inherently anticompetitive that they cannot be justified and are deemed illegal as a matter of law.
	  b. Rule of reason–Applied when an anticompetitive agreement may be justified by legitimate benefits. Under the rule of reason, the lawfulness of a trade restraint will be determined by the purpose and effects of the restraint.

The Clayton Act (1914) (See pages 822–826.)	The major provisions are as follows:
	1. *Section 2–*As amended in 1936 by the Robinson-Patman Act, prohibits price discrimination that substantially lessens competition and prohibits a seller engaged in interstate commerce from selling to two or more buyers goods of similar grade and quality at different prices when the result is a substantial lessening of competition or the creation of a competitive injury.
	2. *Section 3–*Prohibits exclusionary practices, such as exclusive-dealing contracts and tying arrangements, when the effect may be to substantially lessen competition.
	3. *Section 7–*Prohibits mergers when the effect may be to substantially lessen competition or to tend to create a monopoly.
	  a. Horizontal merger–The acquisition by merger or consolidation of a competing firm engaged in the same relevant market. Will be presumed unlawful if the entity created by the merger will have more than a small percentage market share.
	  b. Vertical merger–The acquisition by a seller of one of its buyers or vice versa. Will be unlawful if the merger prevents competitors of either merging firm from competing in a segment of the market that otherwise would be open to them, resulting in a substantial lessening of competition.
	4. *Section 8–*Prohibits interlocking directorates.

Enforcement and Exemptions (See pages 826–827.)	1. *Enforcement–*Federal agencies that enforce antitrust laws are the U.S. Department of Justice and the Federal Trade Commission, which was established by the Federal Trade Commission Act of 1914. Private parties who have been injured as a result of violations of the Sherman Act or Clayton Act may also bring civil suits. In recent years, many private parties have filed such suits largely because, if successful, they may be awarded treble damages and attorneys' fees. 2. *Exemptions–*Numerous exemptions from antitrust enforcement have been created. See Exhibit 32–1 on page 828 for a list of significant exemptions.

Continued

Chapter Summary: Promoting Competition—Continued

U.S. Antitrust Laws in the Global Context (See pages 827–829.)	1. *Application of U.S. laws*—U.S. antitrust laws are broad and can be applied in foreign nations to protect foreign consumers and competitors. Foreign governments and persons can also bring actions under U.S. antitrust laws. Section 1 of the Sherman Act applies to any conspiracy that has a substantial effect on U.S. commerce. 2. *Application of foreign laws*—Many other nations also have laws that promote competition and prohibit trade restraints, and some are more restrictive than U.S. laws. These foreign antitrust laws are increasingly being applied to U.S. firms.

ExamPrep

ISSUE SPOTTERS

1 Under what circumstances would Pop's Market, a small store in a small, isolated town, be considered a monopolist? If Pop's is a monopolist, is it in violation of Section 2 of the Sherman Act? Why or why not?

2 Maple Corporation conditions the sale of its syrup on the buyer's agreement to buy Maple's pancake mix. What factors would a court consider to decide whether this arrangement violates the Clayton Act?

BEFORE THE TEST

Check your answers to the Issue Spotters, and at the same time, take the interactive quiz for this chapter. Go to **www.cengage.com/blaw/blt** and click on "Chapter 32." First, click on "Answers to Issue Spotters" to check your answers. Next, click on "Interactive Quiz" to assess your mastery of the concepts in this chapter. Then click on "Flashcards" to review this chapter's Key Term definitions.

For Review

Answers for the even-numbered questions in this For Review *section can be found on this text's accompanying Web site at* **www.cengage.com/blaw/blt**. *Select "Chapter 32" and click on "For Review."*

1 What is a monopoly? What is market power? How do these concepts relate to each other?

2 What type of activity is prohibited by Section 1 of the Sherman Act? What type of activity is prohibited by Section 2 of the Sherman Act?

3 What are the four major provisions of the Clayton Act, and what types of activities do these provisions prohibit?

4 What agencies of the federal government enforce the federal antitrust laws?

5 What are four activities that are exempt from the antitrust laws?

Hypothetical Scenarios and Case Problems

32–1 Sherman Act. An agreement that is blatantly and substantially anticompetitive is deemed a *per se* violation of Section 1 of the Sherman Act. Under what rule is an agreement analyzed if it appears to be anticompetitive but is not a *per se* violation? In making this analysis, what factors will a court consider?

32–2 Hypothetical Question with Sample Answer Allitron, Inc., and Donovan, Ltd., are interstate competitors selling similar appliances, principally in the states of Illinois, Indiana, Kentucky, and Ohio. Allitron and Donovan agree that Allitron will no longer sell in Indiana and Ohio and that Donovan will no longer sell in Illinois and Kentucky. Have Allitron and Donovan violated any antitrust laws? If so, which law? Explain.

—**For a sample answer to Question 32–2, go to Appendix E at the end of this text.**

32–3 Exclusionary Practices. Instant Foto Corp. is a manufacturer of photography film. At the present time, Instant Foto has approximately 50 percent of the market. Instant Foto advertises that the purchase price for its film includes photo processing by Instant Foto Corp. Instant Foto claims that its film processing is specially designed to improve the quality of photos taken with Instant Foto film. Is Instant Foto's combination of film and film processing an antitrust violation? Explain.

32–4 Price Fixing. Texaco, Inc., and Shell Oil Co. are competitors in the national and international oil and gasoline markets. They refine crude oil into gasoline and sell it to service station owners and others. Between 1998 and 2002, Texaco and Shell engaged in two joint ventures—Equilon Enterprises, which consolidated their operations in the western United States, and Motiva Enterprises, which performed the same function in the eastern United States. Consequently, Texaco and Shell ended their competition in the domestic refining and marketing of gasoline. As part of the ventures, Texaco and Shell agreed to pool their resources and share the risks and profits of their joint activities. The Federal Trade Commission and several states approved the formation of these entities without restricting the pricing of their gasoline, which the ventures began to sell at a single price under the original Texaco and Shell brand names. Fouad Dagher and other station owners filed a suit in a federal district court against Texaco and Shell, alleging that the defendants were engaged in illegal price fixing. Do the circumstances in this case fit the definition of a price-fixing agreement? Explain. [*Texaco Inc. v. Dagher,* 547 U.S. 1, 126 S.Ct. 1276, 164 L.Ed.2d 1 (2006)]

32–5 Restraint of Trade. In 1999, residents of the city of Madison, Wisconsin, became concerned that over-consumption of liquor seemed to be increasing near the campus of the University of Wisconsin–Madison (UW), leading to more frequent use of detoxification facilities and calls for police services in the campus area. Under pressure from UW, which shared these concerns, the city initiated a new policy, imposing conditions on area taverns to discourage price reduction "specials" believed to encourage high-volume and dangerous drinking. In 2002, the city began to draft an ordinance to ban all drink specials. Tavern owners responded by announcing that they had "voluntarily" agreed to discontinue drink specials on Friday and Saturday nights after 8 P.M. The city put its ordinance on hold. UW student Nic Eichenseer and others filed a suit in a Wisconsin state court against the Madison–Dane County Tavern League, Inc. (an association of local tavern owners), and others, alleging violations of antitrust law. On what might the plaintiffs base a claim for relief? Are the defendants in this case exempt from the antitrust laws? What should the court rule? Why? [*Eichenseer v. Madison–Dane County Tavern League, Inc.,* 2006 WI App. 226, 725 N.W.2d 274 (2006)]

32–6 Tying Arrangement. John Sheridan owned a Marathon gas station franchise. He sued Marathon Petroleum Co. under Section 1 of the Sherman Act and Section 3 of the Clayton Act, charging it with illegally tying the processing of credit-card sales to the gas station. As a condition of obtaining a Marathon dealership, dealers had to agree to let the franchisor process credit cards. They could not shop around to see if credit-card processing could be obtained at a lower price from another source. The district court dismissed the case for failure to state a claim. Sheridan appealed. Is there a tying arrangement? If so,

does it violate the law? [*Sheridan v. Marathon Petroleum Co.,* 530 F.3d 590 (7th Cir. 2008)]

32–7 Case Problem with Sample Answer When Deer Valley Resort Co. (DVRC) was developing its ski resort in the Wasatch Mountains near Park City, Utah, it sold parcels of land in the resort village to third parties. Each sales contract reserved the right of approval over the conduct of certain businesses on the property, including ski rentals. For fifteen years, DVRC permitted Christy Sports, LLC, to rent skis in competition with DVRC's ski rental outlet. When DVRC opened a new midmountain ski rental outlet, it revoked Christy's permission to rent skis. This meant that most skiers who flew into Salt Lake City and shuttled to Deer Valley had few choices: they could carry their ski equipment onto their flights, take a shuttle into Park City and look for cheaper ski rentals there, or rent from DVRC. Christy filed a suit in a federal district court against DVRC. Was DVRC's action an attempt to monopolize in violation of Section 2 of the Sherman Act? Why or why not? [*Christy Sports, LLC v. Deer Valley Resort Co.,* 555 F.3d 1188 (10th Cir. 2009)]

—After you have answered Problem 32–7, compare your answer with the sample answer given on the Web site that accompanies this text. Go to **www.cengage.com/blaw/blt**, select "Chapter 32," and click on "Case Problem with Sample Answer."

32–8 A Question of Ethics *In the 1990s, DuCoa, LP, made choline chloride, a B-complex vitamin essential for the growth and development of animals. The U.S. market for choline chloride was divided into thirds among DuCoa, Bioproducts, Inc., and Chinook Group, Ltd. To stabilize the market and keep the price of the vitamin higher than it would otherwise be, the companies agreed to fix the price and allocate market share by deciding which of them would offer the lowest price to each customer. At times, however, the companies disregarded the agreement. During an increase in competitive activity in August 1997, Daniel Rose became president of DuCoa. The next month, a subordinate advised him of the conspiracy. By February 1998, Rose had begun to implement a strategy to persuade DuCoa's competitors to rejoin the conspiracy. By April, the three companies had reallocated their market shares and increased their prices. In June, the U.S. Department of Justice began to investigate allegations of price fixing in the vitamin market. Ultimately, a federal district court convicted Rose of conspiracy to violate Section 1 of the Sherman Act. [United States v. Rose, 449 F.3d 627 (5th Cir. 2006)]*

1 The court "enhanced" Rose's sentence to thirty months' imprisonment, one year of supervised release, and a $20,000 fine based on, among other things, his role as "a manager or supervisor" in the conspiracy. Rose appealed this enhancement to the U.S. Court of Appeals for the Fifth Circuit. Was it fair to increase Rose's sentence on this ground? Why or why not?

2 Was Rose's participation in the conspiracy unethical? If so, how might Rose have behaved ethically instead? If not, could any of the participants' conduct be considered unethical? Explain.

Critical Thinking and Writing Assignments

32–9 Critical Legal Thinking. Critics of antitrust law claim that in the long run, competitive market forces will eliminate private monopolies unless they are fostered by government regulation. Can you think of any examples of monopolies that continue to be fostered by government in the United States?

32–10 Critical Thinking and Writing Assignment for Business. In what ways might antitrust laws place too great a burden on commerce in the global marketplace?

Practical Internet Exercises

Go to this text's Web site at **www.cengage.com/blaw/blt**, select "Chapter 32," and click on "Practical Internet Exercises." There you will find the following Internet research exercises that you can perform to learn more about the topics covered in this chapter.

Practical Internet Exercise 32–1: LEGAL PERSPECTIVE—The Standard Oil Trust
Practical Internet Exercise 32–2: MANAGEMENT PERSPECTIVE—Avoiding Antitrust Problems

Chapter 33

Consumer and Environmental Law

(©SergioZ, 2009. Used under license from Shutterstock.com)

Chapter Outline

- Consumer Law
- Environmental Law

Learning Objectives

After reading this chapter, you should be able to answer the following questions:

1. When will advertising be deemed deceptive?

2. What are the major federal statutes providing for consumer protection in credit transactions?

3. Under what common law theories can polluters be held liable?

4. What is contained in an environmental impact statement, and who must file one?

5. What major federal statutes regulate air and water pollution? What is Superfund, and who is potentially liable under Superfund?

During the heyday of the consumer movement in the 1960s and 1970s, Congress enacted a substantial amount of legislation to protect "the good of the people," to borrow a phrase from Marcus Tullius Cicero. All statutes, agency rules, and common law judicial decisions that serve to protect the interests of consumers are classified as *consumer law*. While the consumer movement has abated somewhat in recent years, efforts to protect the environment have taken on increasing importance in the global community. In the first part of this chapter, we examine some of the major laws and regulations protecting consumers. We then turn to a discussion of *environmental law*, which consists of all of the laws and regulations designed to protect and preserve our environmental resources.

▶ Consumer Law

Sources of consumer protection exist at all levels of government. At the federal level, a number of laws have been passed to define the duties of sellers and the rights of consumers. Exhibit 33–1 on the next page indicates many of the areas of consumer law that are regulated by statutes. Federal administrative agencies, such as the Federal Trade Commission (FTC), also provide an important source of consumer protection. Nearly every agency and

• *Exhibit* 33–1 Selected Areas of Consumer Law Regulated by Statutes

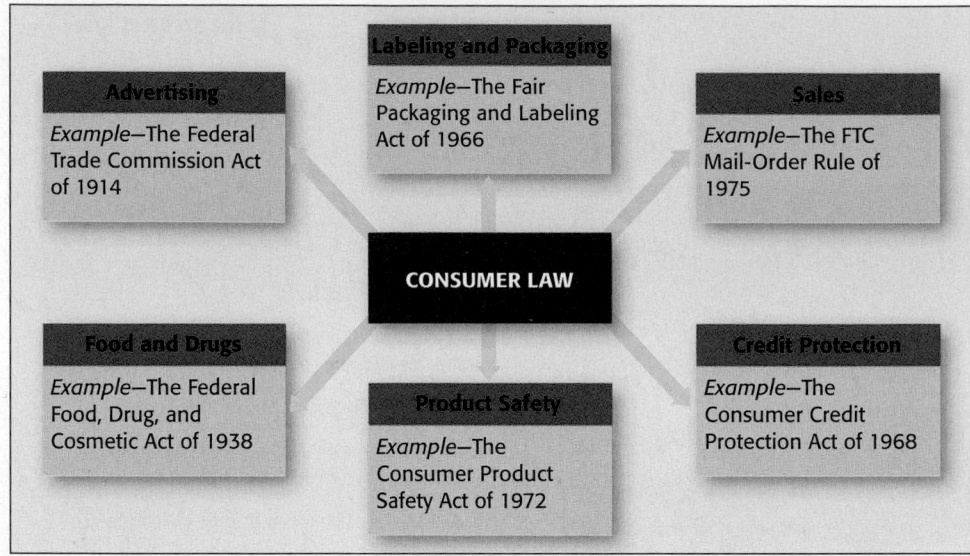

Advertising

Example—The Federal Trade Commission Act of 1914

Labeling and Packaging

Example—The Fair Packaging and Labeling Act of 1966

Sales

Example—The FTC Mail-Order Rule of 1975

CONSUMER LAW

Food and Drugs

Example—The Federal Food, Drug, and Cosmetic Act of 1938

Product Safety

Example—The Consumer Product Safety Act of 1972

Credit Protection

Example—The Consumer Credit Protection Act of 1968

department of the federal government has an office of consumer affairs, and most states have one or more such offices, including the offices of state attorneys general, to assist consumers.

Because of the wide variation among state consumer protection laws, our primary focus here will be on federal legislation—specifically, on legislation governing deceptive advertising, telemarketing and electronic advertising, labeling and packaging, sales, health protection, product safety, and credit protection. Realize, though, that state laws often provide more sweeping and significant protections for the consumer than do federal laws.

Deceptive Advertising

One of the earliest—and still one of the most important—federal consumer protection laws is the Federal Trade Commission Act of 1914 (mentioned in Chapter 32). The act created the FTC to carry out the broadly stated goal of preventing unfair and deceptive trade practices, including deceptive advertising, within the meaning of Section 5 of the act.

Generally, **deceptive advertising** occurs if a reasonable consumer would be misled by the advertising claim. Vague generalities and obvious exaggerations are permissible. These claims are known as puffery. Recall from the discussion of warranties on page 416 in Chapter 17 that puffery consists of statements about a product that a reasonable person would not believe to be literally true. When a claim takes on the appearance of literal authenticity, however, it may create problems. Advertising that *appears* to be based on factual evidence but that in fact cannot be scientifically supported will be deemed deceptive. A classic example occurred in a 1944 case in which the claim that a skin cream would restore youthful qualities to aged skin was deemed deceptive.[1]

Some advertisements contain "half-truths," meaning that the presented information is true but incomplete and, therefore, leads consumers to a false conclusion. **EXAMPLE 33.1** The maker of Campbell's soups advertised that "most" Campbell's soups were low in fat and cholesterol and thus were helpful in fighting heart disease. What the ad did not say was that Campbell's soups were also high in sodium and that high-sodium diets may increase the risk of heart disease. Hence, the FTC ruled that the company's claims were deceptive. • Advertising featuring an endorsement by a celebrity may be deemed deceptive if the celebrity does not actually use the product.

Even before the FTC brought the following case, *Wired* magazine had already put the product in question on its list of the top ten "snake-oil gadgets."

Deceptive Advertising Advertising that misleads consumers, either by making unjustified claims concerning a product's performance or by omitting a material fact concerning the product's composition or performance.

When Campbell's advertised that its soups helped fight heart disease, what important fact did the ads not include?

(Tanjila/Creative Commons)

---

1. *Charles of the Ritz Distributors Corp. v. Federal Trade Commission,* 143 F.2d 676 (2d Cir. 1944).

Case 33.1 Federal Trade Commission v. QT, Inc.

United States Court of Appeals, Seventh Circuit, 512 F.3d 858 (2008).
www.ca7.uscourts.gov[a]

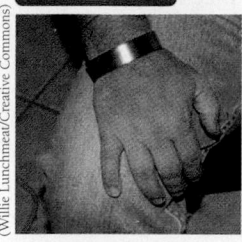

Did a company's claims that a metal bracelet cured chronic pain constitute deceptive advertising?

FACTS QT, Inc., heavily promoted the Q-Ray Ionized Bracelet on television infomercials and on its Web site. In its promotions, the company claimed that the bracelets offered immediate and significant or complete pain relief and could cure chronic pain. At trial, the U.S. district court labeled all such claims fraudulent, forbade further promotional claims, and ordered the company to pay $16 million, plus interest, into a fund to be distributed to customers. QT appealed to the U.S. Court of Appeals for the Seventh Circuit.

ISSUE Was the lower court correct in finding that the defendant's advertising of the Ionized Bracelet was deceptive?

DECISION Yes. The U.S. Court of Appeals for the Seventh Circuit affirmed the district court's decision. QT, Inc., was required to stop its deceptive advertising and to pay the $16 million, plus interest, so that its customers could be reimbursed.

REASON The appellate court stated that "almost everything that defendants have said about the bracelet is false." It had no therapeutic effect. No bracelet had a memory cycle specific to each individual wearer, as the company had claimed. The judge presiding over the trial "did not commit a clear error, or abuse his discretion, in concluding that the defendants set out to bilk unsophisticated persons who found themselves in pain from arthritis and other chronic conditions." All statements about how the product worked were pure fiction. "Proof is what separates an effect new to science from a swindle." Although the defendants told customers that the bracelet's efficiency had been "test proven," it had not. What remained were testimonials, which are not a form of proof. "Physicians know how to treat pain. Why pay $200 for a Q-Ray Ionized Bracelet when you can get relief from an aspirin tablet that costs [one cent]?"

WHAT IF THE FACTS WERE DIFFERENT? *Assume that the defendant had actually conducted scientific studies, but the results were inconclusive. How might the judge have ruled in that situation?*

---

a. Click on "Opinions" in the left-hand column. In the boxes for the case number, type "07" and "1662," and then click on "List Case." Follow the links to access this case opinion. The U.S. Court of Appeals for the Seventh Circuit maintains this Web site.

Bait-and-Switch Advertising Advertising a product at a very attractive price (the bait) and then, once the consumer is in the store, saying that the advertised product either is not available or is of poor quality. The customer is then urged to purchase (switched to) a more expensive item.

BAIT-AND-SWITCH ADVERTISING The FTC has issued rules that govern specific advertising techniques. One of the more important rules is contained in the FTC's "Guides Against Bait Advertising."[2] The rule is designed to prevent **bait-and-switch advertising**— that is, advertising a very low price for a particular item that will likely be unavailable to the consumer and then encouraging him or her to purchase a more expensive item. The low price is the "bait" to lure the consumer into the store. The salesperson is instructed to "switch" the consumer to a different, more expensive item. According to the FTC guidelines, bait-and-switch advertising occurs if the seller refuses to show the advertised item, fails to have reasonable quantities of it available, fails to promise to deliver the advertised item within a reasonable time, or discourages employees from selling the item.

> "*Ads are the cave art of the twentieth century.*"
> Marshall McLuhan, 1911–1980
> (Canadian academic and commentator)

ONLINE DECEPTIVE ADVERTISING Deceptive advertising can occur in the online environment as well. The FTC actively monitors online advertising and has identified hundreds of Web sites that have made false or deceptive claims for products ranging from medical treatments for various diseases to exercise equipment and weight-loss aids.

The FTC has issued guidelines to help online businesses comply with existing laws prohibiting deceptive advertising.[3] These guidelines include the following three basic requirements:

1. All ads—both online and offline—must be truthful and not misleading.
2. The claims made in an ad must be substantiated; that is, advertisers must have evidence to back up their claims.

---

2. 16 C.F.R. Section 288.

3. *Advertising and Marketing on the Internet: Rules of the Road,* September 2000, available at **www.ftc.gov/bcp/conline/pubs/buspubs/ruleroad.htm**. Also see the FTC's guidelines on behavioral advertising, which targets specific individuals based on their Web-browsing behavior, at **www.ftc.gov/opa/2009/02/behavad.shtm**.

3. Ads cannot be unfair, which the FTC defines as "likely to cause substantial consumer injury that consumers could not reasonably avoid and that is not outweighed by the benefit to consumers or competition."

The guidelines also call for "clear and conspicuous" disclosure of any qualifying or limiting information. The overall impression of the ad is important in meeting this requirement. The FTC suggests that advertisers should assume that consumers will not read an entire Web page. Therefore, to satisfy the "clear and conspicuous" requirement, advertisers should place the disclosure as close as possible to the claim being qualified or include the disclosure within the claim itself. If such placement is not feasible, the next-best location is on a section of the page to which a consumer can easily scroll. Generally, hyperlinks to a disclosure are recommended only for lengthy disclosures or for disclosures that must be repeated in a variety of locations on the Web page.

FTC ACTIONS AGAINST DECEPTIVE ADVERTISING   The FTC receives complaints from many sources, including competitors of alleged violators, consumers, consumer organizations, trade associations, Better Business Bureaus, government organizations, and state and local officials. If it receives numerous and widespread complaints about a problem, the FTC will investigate. If the FTC concludes that a given advertisement is unfair or deceptive, it sends a formal complaint to the alleged offender. The company may agree to settle the complaint without further proceedings; if not, the FTC can conduct a hearing before an administrative law judge (discussed in Chapter 1) in which the company can present its defense.

If the FTC succeeds in proving that an advertisement is unfair or deceptive, it usually issues a **cease-and-desist order** requiring the company to stop the challenged advertising. In some circumstances, it may also require **counteradvertising** in which the company advertises anew—in print, on the Internet, on radio, and on television—to inform the public about the earlier misinformation. The FTC sometimes institutes a **multiple product order,** which requires a firm to cease and desist from false advertising in regard to all of its products, not just the product that was the subject of the action.

When a company's deceptive ad involves wrongful charges to consumers, the FTC may seek other remedies, including restitution. **CASE EXAMPLE 33.2** Verity International, Ltd., billed phone-line subscribers who accessed certain online pornography sites at the rate for international calls to Madagascar. When consumers complained about the charges, Verity employees told them that the charges were valid and had to be paid, or the consumers would face further collection activity. A federal appellate court held that this representation of "uncontestability" was deceptive and a violation of the FTC Act and ordered Verity to pay nearly $18 million in restitution to consumers.[4] ●

Telemarketing and Fax Advertising

The pervasive use of telemarketing led Congress to pass the Telephone Consumer Protection Act (TCPA) of 1991.[5] The act prohibits telephone solicitation using an automatic telephone dialing system or a prerecorded voice. Most states also have laws regulating telephone solicitation. The TCPA also makes it illegal to transmit ads via fax without first obtaining the recipient's permission.

The Federal Communications Commission (FCC) enforces the act. The FCC imposes substantial fines ($11,000 each day) on companies that violate the junk fax provisions of the TCPA and has fined one company as much as $5.4 million for violations.[6] The TCPA

Cease-and-Desist Order An administrative or judicial order prohibiting a person or business firm from conducting activities that an agency or court has deemed illegal.

Counteradvertising New advertising that is undertaken pursuant to a Federal Trade Commission order for the purpose of correcting earlier false claims that were made about a product.

Multiple Product Order An order issued by the Federal Trade Commission to a firm that has engaged in deceptive advertising by which the firm is required to cease and desist from false advertising not only in regard to the product that was the subject of the action but also in regard to all the firm's other products.

---

4. *Federal Trade Commission v. Verity International, Ltd.,* 443 F.3d 48 (2d Cir. 2006).

5. 47 U.S.C. Sections 227 *et seq.,* as modified by the Junk Fax Protection Act of 2005.

6. See *Missouri ex rel. Nixon v. American Blast Fax, Inc.,* 323 F.3d 649 (8th Cir. 2003); *cert.* denied, 540 U.S. 1104, 124 S.Ct. 1043, 157 L.Ed.2d 888 (2004). The term *ex rel.* in the case title means that the government brought this action on behalf of an individual (Nixon).

also gives consumers a right to sue for either the actual monetary loss resulting from a violation of the act or $500 in damages for each violation, whichever is greater. If a court finds that a defendant willfully or knowingly violated the act, the court has the discretion to triple the damages that are awarded.

The Telemarketing and Consumer Fraud and Abuse Prevention Act of 1994[7] directed the FTC to establish rules governing telemarketing and to bring actions against fraudulent telemarketers. The FTC's Telemarketing Sales Rule of 1995[8] requires a telemarketer to identify the seller; describe the product being sold; and disclose all material facts related to the sale, including the total cost of the goods being sold, any restrictions on obtaining or using the goods, and whether a sale will be considered final and nonrefundable. The act makes it illegal for telemarketers to misrepresent information (including facts about their goods or services and earnings potential, for example). A telemarketer must also remove a consumer's name from its list of potential contacts if the consumer so requests. (For a discussion of how this rule applies to foreign telemarketers, see this chapter's *Beyond Our Borders* feature on the following page.) An amendment to the Telemarketing Sales Rule established the national Do Not Call Registry. Telemarketers must refrain from calling consumers who have placed their names on the list.

REMEMBER Changes in technology often require changes in the law.

Preventing Legal Disputes

Advertising is essential to business. Before you advertise via faxes, however, you should know the applicable rules and be aware that the FCC aggressively enforces these rules. Make sure that all fax advertisements comply with the Telephone Consumer Protection Act and any state laws on faxes. Educate and train your employees about these laws. Do not send faxes without first obtaining the recipient's permission, and develop effective opt-out procedures so that anyone who no longer wants to receive faxes can notify you. Keep reliable records of the faxes you send and maintain these records for at least four years. Do not purchase lists of fax numbers from outsiders. Avoiding consumer complaints about unwanted faxes and phone calls is the best way to avoid potentially significant liability.

Why would some consumer legislation require that the fiber content of certain products be clearly stated?

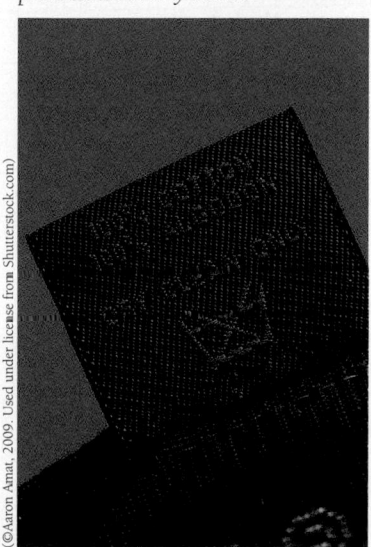

(©Aaron Amat, 2009. Used under license from Shutterstock.com)

Labeling and Packaging

A number of federal and state laws deal specifically with the information given on labels and packages. In general, labels must be accurate, and they must use words that are understood by the ordinary consumer. In some instances, labels must specify the raw materials used in the product, such as the percentage of cotton, nylon, or other fibers used in a garment. In other instances, the products must carry a warning, such as those required on cigarette packages and advertising.[9]

The Fair Packaging and Labeling Act requires that food product labels identify (1) the product; (2) the net quantity of the contents and, if the number of servings is stated, the size of a serving; (3) the manufacturer; and (4) the packager or distributor.[10] The act also provides for additional requirements concerning descriptions on packages, savings claims, components of nonfood products, and standards for the partial filling of packages.

The Nutrition Labeling and Education Act of 1990 requires food labels to provide standard nutrition facts (including the amount and type of fat that the food contains) and regulates the use of such terms as *fresh* and *low fat*. The U.S. Food and Drug Administration and the U.S. Department of Agriculture (USDA) are the primary agencies that publish regulations on food labeling in the *Federal Register*. These rules are updated annually. New rules that became effective in 2009 require the labels on fresh meats, vegetables,

---

7. 15 U.S.C. Sections 6101–6108.
8. 16 C.F.R. Sections 310.1–310.8.
9. 15 U.S.C. Sections 1331 *et seq.*
10. 15 U.S.C. Sections 4401–4408.

Beyond Our Borders   **Protecting U.S. Consumers from Cross-Border Telemarketers**

One of the problems that the Federal Trade Commission (FTC) faces in protecting consumers from scams is that those involved in the illegal operations frequently are located outside the United States. Nevertheless, the FTC has had some success in bringing cases under the Telemarketing Sales Rule (TSR) against telemarketers who violate the law from foreign locations. As discussed in the text, the TSR requires telemarketers to disclose all material facts about the goods or services being offered and prohibits the telemarketers from misrepresenting information. Significantly, the TSR applies to any offer made to consumers in the United States—even if the offer comes from a foreign firm.

A Telemarketing Scam from Canada

Oleg Oks and Aleksandr Oks, along with several other residents of Canada, set up a number of sham corporations in Ontario. Through these businesses, they placed unsolicited outbound telephone calls to consumers in the United States. The telemarketers offered preapproved Visa or MasterCard credit cards to consumers who agreed to permit their bank accounts to be electronically debited for an advance fee of $319.

The telemarketers frequently promised that the consumers would receive other items—such

"I just got home. Can you call back tomorrow when I'm still at work?"

as a cell phone, satellite dish system, vacation package, or home security system—at no additional cost. In fact, *no consumers* who paid the advance fee received either a credit card or any of the promised gifts. Instead, consumers received a "member benefits" package that included items such as booklets on how to improve their creditworthiness or merchandise cards that could be used only to purchase goods from the catalogue provided.

Joint Cooperation to Prosecute the Telemarketers

The FTC, working in conjunction with the U.S. Postal Service and various Canadian

government and law enforcement agencies, conducted an investigation that lasted several years. Ultimately, in 2007 Oleg and Aleksandr Oks pleaded guilty in Canada to criminal charges for deceptive advertising. They were barred from telemarketing for ten years.[a]

In addition, the FTC filed a civil lawsuit against the Okses and other Canadian defendants in a federal court in Illinois. The court found that the defendants had violated the FTC Act and the TSR and ordered them to pay nearly $5 million in damages.[b]

• For Critical Analysis

Suppose that this scam had originated in a country that was not as friendly and cooperative as Canada is with the United States. In that situation, how would the FTC obtain sufficient evidence to prosecute the foreign telemarketers? Is the testimony of U.S. consumers regarding the phone calls that they received sufficient proof? Why or why not?

a. Oleg was also sentenced to a year in jail and two years' probation.
b. *Federal Trade Commission v. Oks,* 2007 WL 3307009 (N.D.Ill. 2007). The court entered its final judgment on March 18, 2008.

ON THE WEB You can find current articles concerning consumer issues at the "Consumer Law Page" of the law firm Alexander Hawes, LLP. Go to **consumerlawpage.com**.

and fruits to indicate where the food originated so that consumers can know whether it was imported.

Sales

A number of statutes protect consumers by requiring the disclosure of certain terms in sales transactions and providing rules governing home or door-to-door sales, mail-order transactions, referral sales, and unsolicited merchandise. The Federal Reserve Board of Governors, for example, has issued **Regulation Z,** which governs credit provisions associated with sales contracts (discussed later in this chapter). Many states and the FTC have **"cooling-off" laws** that permit the buyers of goods sold door to door to cancel their contracts within three business days. The FTC rule further requires that consumers be notified in Spanish of this right if the oral negotiations for the sale were in that language.

TELEPHONE AND MAIL-ORDER SALES   The FTC's Mail or Telephone Order Merchandise Rule of 1993 amended the FTC's Mail-Order Rule of 1975.[11] The rule provides specific

Regulation Z   A set of rules issued by the Federal Reserve Board of Governors to implement the provisions of the Truth-in-Lending Act.

"Cooling-off" Laws   Laws that allow buyers a period of time, such as three business days, in which to cancel door-to-door sales contracts.

---

11. 16 C.F.R. Sections 435.1–435.2.

What are the FTC's Mail-Order Rule requirements with respect to when merchants must ship goods?

(©Stephen Coburn, 2009.
Used under license from Shutterstock.com)

ON THE WEB The federal government provides practical tips to guard against online fraud and protect a consumer's personal information at the following Web site:
www.onguardonline.gov/default.aspx.

BE AWARE The U.S. Food and Drug Administration is authorized to obtain, among other things, orders for the recall and seizure of certain products.

protections for consumers who purchase goods over the phone, through the mail, or via a computer (Internet) or fax machine. For instance, merchants are required to ship orders within the time promised in their advertisements and to notify consumers when orders cannot be shipped on time. The rule also requires merchants to issue a refund within a specified period of time when a consumer cancels an order.

In addition, under the Postal Reorganization Act of 1970[12] a consumer who receives *unsolicited* merchandise sent by U.S. mail can keep it, throw it away, or dispose of it in any manner that she or he sees fit. The recipient will not be obligated to the sender.

ONLINE SALES The FTC and other federal agencies have brought numerous enforcement actions against those who perpetrate online fraud. Nonetheless, protecting consumers from fraudulent and deceptive sales practices conducted via the Internet has proved to be a challenging task. Faced with economic recession, job losses, mounting debt, and dwindling savings, many consumers are looking for any source of income. The number of consumers who have fallen prey to Internet fraud has actually grown in recent years. Complaints to the FTC about the sale of business opportunities, such as work-at-home offers, nearly doubled from 2007 to 2008 and tripled in the first six months of 2009.

Health and Safety

Although labeling and packaging laws (discussed earlier) promote consumer health and safety, there is a significant distinction between regulating the information dispensed about a product and regulating the actual content of the product. The classic example is tobacco products. Producers of tobacco products are required to warn consumers about the hazards associated with the use of their products, but the sale of tobacco products has not been subjected to significant restrictions or banned outright despite the obvious dangers to health. We now examine various laws that regulate the actual products made available to consumers.

FOOD AND DRUGS The first federal legislation regulating food and drugs was enacted in 1906 as the Pure Food and Drugs Act.[13] That law, as amended in 1938, exists now as the Federal Food, Drug, and Cosmetic Act (FDCA).[14] The act protects consumers against adulterated and misbranded foods and drugs. As to foods, the act establishes food standards, specifies safe levels of potentially hazardous food additives, and sets classifications of food and food advertising. Most of these statutory requirements are monitored and enforced by the U.S. Food and Drug Administration (FDA).

The FDCA also charges the FDA with the responsibility of ensuring that drugs are safe before they are marketed to the public. Under an extensive set of procedures established by the FDA, drugs must be shown to be safe, as well as effective, before they may be marketed to the public. **CASE EXAMPLE 33.3** A group of terminally ill patients claimed that they were entitled, under the U.S. Constitution, to better access to experimental drugs before the FDA completed its clinical tests. The court, however, found that the FDA's policy of limiting access to drugs that were undergoing tests was rationally related to protecting patients from potentially unsafe drugs. Therefore, the court held that terminally ill patients do not have a fundamental constitutional right of access to experimental drugs.[15] ● A 1976

---

12. 39 U.S.C. Section 3009.
13. 21 U.S.C. Sections 1–5, 7–15.
14. 21 U.S.C. Section 301.
15. *Abigail Alliance for Better Access to Developmental Drugs v. von Eschenbach,* 495 F.3d 695 (D.C.Cir. 2007).

amendment to the FDCA[16] authorizes the FDA to regulate medical devices, such as pacemakers, and to withdraw from the market any such device that is mislabeled.

CONSUMER PRODUCT SAFETY   In 1972, Congress enacted the Consumer Product Safety Act,[17] which created the first comprehensive scheme of regulation over matters concerning consumer safety. The act also established the Consumer Product Safety Commission (CPSC) and gave it far-reaching authority over consumer safety.

The CPSC's Authority.   The CPSC conducts research on the safety of individual products and maintains a clearinghouse on the risks associated with various products. The Consumer Product Safety Act authorizes the CPSC to do the following:

ON THE WEB The Web site of the Consumer Product Safety Commission offers a business information page that provides the text of regulations and laws, notices in the *Federal Register,* and other information. Go to **www.cpsc.gov/businfo/businfo.html**.

1. Set safety standards for consumer products.
2. Ban the manufacture and sale of any product that the commission believes poses an "unreasonable risk" to consumers. (Products banned by the CPSC have included various types of fireworks, cribs, and toys, as well as many products containing asbestos or vinyl chloride.)
3. Remove from the market any products it believes to be imminently hazardous. The CPSC frequently works in conjunction with manufacturers to voluntarily recall defective products from stores. **EXAMPLE 33.4** In 2009, in cooperation with the CPSC, Kolcraft Enterprises, Inc., recalled one million infant play yards because of a defective latch that could cause a rail to fall, posing a risk to children. •
4. Require manufacturers to report on any products already sold or intended for sale if the products have proved to be hazardous.
5. Administer other product-safety legislation, including the Child Protection and Toy Safety Act of 1969[18] and the Federal Hazardous Substances Act of 1960.[19]

(AP Photo/Kelley McCall)

The CPSC passed a rule requiring that any product sold to children cannot contain lead. How could children be harmed if some lead was used in the manufacturing of dirt bikes?

Notification Requirements.   The Consumer Product Safety Act imposes notification requirements on distributors of consumer products. Distributors must immediately notify the CPSC when they receive information that a product "contains a defect which . . . creates a substantial risk to the public" or "an unreasonable risk of serious injury or death."

CASE EXAMPLE 33.5 A company that sold juicers began receiving letters from customers complaining that during operation the juicer suddenly exploded, sending pieces of glass and razor-sharp metal across the room. The company received twenty-three letters from angry consumers about the exploding juicer but waited more than six months before notifying the CPSC that the product posed a significant risk to the public. In a case filed by the federal government, the court held that when a company first receives information regarding a threat, the company is required to report the problem within twenty-four hours to the CPSC. Even if the company had to investigate the allegations, it should not have taken more than ten days to verify the information and report the problem. The court therefore found that the company had violated the law and ordered it to pay damages.[20] •

Credit Protection

Credit protection is one of the most important aspects of consumer protection legislation. Nearly 80 percent of U.S. consumers have credit cards, and most carry a balance on these cards, amounting to about $2.5 trillion of debt nationwide.

---

16. 21 U.S.C. Sections 352(o), 360(j), 360(k), and 360c–360k.
17. 15 U.S.C. Section 2051.
18. 15 U.S.C. Section 1262(e).
19. 15 U.S.C. Sections 1261–1273.
20. *United States v. Mirama Enterprises, Inc.,* 185 F.Supp.2d 1148 (S.D.Cal. 2002).

A key statute regulating the credit and credit-card industries is the Truth-in-Lending Act (TILA), the name commonly given to Title 1 of the Consumer Credit Protection Act (CCPA),[21] which was passed by Congress in 1968. The TILA has been amended several times, most recently in 2009, when Congress passed sweeping reforms to strengthen its consumer protections.[22]

TRUTH IN LENDING   The TILA is basically a *disclosure law*. It is administered by the Federal Reserve Board and requires sellers and lenders to disclose credit terms or loan terms so that individuals can shop around for the best financing arrangements. TILA requirements apply only to persons who, in the ordinary course of business, lend funds, sell on credit, or arrange for the extension of credit. Thus, sales or loans made between two consumers do not come under the protection of the act. Additionally, this law protects only debtors who are *natural* persons (as opposed to the artificial "person" of a corporation); it does not extend to other legal entities.

The disclosure requirements are found in Regulation Z. If the contracting parties are subject to the TILA, the requirements of Regulation Z apply to any transaction involving an installment sales contract that calls for payment to be made in more than four installments. Transactions subject to Regulation Z typically include installment loans, retail and installment sales, car loans, home-improvement loans, and certain real estate loans if the amount of financing is less than $25,000.

Under the provisions of the TILA, all of the terms of a credit instrument must be clearly and conspicuously disclosed. A lender must disclose the annual percentage rate (APR), finance charge, amount financed, and total payments (the sum of the amount loaned, plus any fees, finance charges, and interest at the end of the loan). The TILA provides for contract rescission (cancellation) if a creditor fails to follow the exact procedures required by the act.[23]

Equal Credit Opportunity.   In 1974, Congress enacted, as an amendment to the TILA, the Equal Credit Opportunity Act (ECOA). The ECOA prohibits the denial of credit solely on the basis of race, religion, national origin, color, gender, marital status, or age. The act also prohibits credit discrimination on the basis of whether an individual receives certain forms of income, such as public-assistance benefits.

Under the ECOA, a creditor may not require the signature of an applicant's spouse, or a cosigner, on a credit instrument if the applicant qualifies under the creditor's standards of creditworthiness for the amount requested. **CASE EXAMPLE 33.6**   Tonja, an African American, applied for financing with a used-car dealer. The dealer reviewed Tonja's credit report and, without submitting the application to the lender, decided that she would not qualify. Instead of informing Tonja that she did not qualify, the dealer told her that she needed a cosigner on the loan to purchase the car. According to a federal appellate court, the dealership qualified as a creditor in this situation because it unilaterally denied credit. Thus, the dealer could be held liable under the ECOA.[24] ●

NOTE The Federal Reserve Board is part of the Federal Reserve System, which influences the lending and investing activities of commercial banks and the cost and availability of credit.

"Credit is a system whereby a person who can't pay gets another person who can't pay to guarantee that he can pay."

Charles Dickens, 1812–1870
(English novelist)

---

21. 15 U.S.C. Sections 1601–1693r.

22. The TILA was amended in 1980 by the Truth-in-Lending Simplification and Reform Act; and significantly amended again in 2009 by the Credit Card Accountability Responsibility and Disclosure Act of 2009, Pub. L. No. 111-24, 123 Stat. 1734, enacting 15 U.S.C. Sections 1616, 1651, 1665c to 1665e, 1666i-1, 1666i-2, 1666b, and 1693l-1, and 16 U.S.C. Section 1a-7b, as well as amending many other provisions of the TILA.

23. Note, though, that amendments to the TILA enacted in 1995 prevent borrowers from rescinding loans because of minor clerical errors in the final documents that were signed [15 U.S.C. Sections 1605, 1631, 1635, 1640, and 1641].

24. *Treadway v. Gateway Chevrolet Oldsmobile, Inc.,* 362 F.3d 971 (7th Cir. 2004).

Assume that your credit card is stolen, but you do not report the theft to the credit-card issuer. What is the maximum dollar liability you face?

Credit-Card Rules. The TILA also contains provisions regarding credit cards. One provision limits the liability of a cardholder to $50 per card for unauthorized charges made before the creditor is notified that the card has been lost. If a consumer received an *unsolicited* credit card in the mail that is later stolen, the company that issued the card cannot charge the consumer for any unauthorized charges. Another provision requires credit-card companies to disclose the balance computation method that is used to determine the outstanding balance, and to state when finance charges begin to accrue. Other provisions set forth procedures for resolving billing disputes with the credit-card company. These procedures may be used if, for example, a cardholder thinks that an error has occurred in billing or wishes to withhold payment for a faulty product purchased by credit card.

In 2009, President Barack Obama signed into law amendments to the credit-card protections of the TILA that became effective in 2010. The most significant provisions of the new rules are as follows:

1. Protect consumers from retroactive increases in interest rates on existing card balances unless the account is sixty days delinquent.
2. Require companies to provide forty-five days' advance notice to consumers before making changes to the credit-card terms.
3. Require companies to send out monthly bills to cardholders twenty-one days before the due date.
4. Prevent companies from increasing the interest rate charged on a customer's credit-card balance except in specific situations, such as when a promotional rate ends.
5. Prevent companies from charging over-limit fees except in specified situations.
6. Require companies to apply payments in excess of the minimum amount due to the customer's higher-interest balances first when the borrower has balances with different rates (such as the higher interest rates commonly charged for cash advances).
7. Prevent companies from computing finance charges based on the previous billing cycle (known as double-cycle billing, which hurts consumers because they are charged interest for the previous cycle even though they have paid the bill in full).

Consumer Leases. The Consumer Leasing Act (CLA) of 1988[25] amended the TILA to provide protection for consumers who lease automobiles and other goods. The CLA applies to those who lease or arrange to lease consumer goods in the ordinary course of their business. The act applies only if the goods are priced at $25,000 or less and if the lease term exceeds four months. The CLA and its implementing regulation, Regulation M,[26] require lessors to disclose in writing all of the material terms of the lease.

FAIR CREDIT REPORTING In 1970, to protect consumers against inaccurate credit reporting, Congress enacted the Fair Credit Reporting Act (FCRA).[27] The act provides that consumer credit reporting agencies may issue credit reports to users only for specified purposes, including the extension of credit, the issuance of insurance policies, compliance with a court order, and compliance with a consumer's request for a copy of her or his own credit report. Any time a consumer is denied credit or insurance on the basis of his or her credit report, the consumer must be notified of that fact and of the name

ON THE WEB The Consumer Action Web site offers useful information and links to consumer protection agencies at the city, county, and state level. Go to **www.consumeraction.gov**.

---

25. 15 U.S.C. Sections 1667–1667e.
26. 12 C.F.R. Part 213.
27. 15 U.S.C. Sections 1681 *et seq.*

and address of the credit reporting agency that issued the report. The same notice must be sent to consumers who are charged more than others ordinarily would be for credit or insurance because of their credit reports.

Under the FCRA, consumers can request the source of any information used by the credit agency, as well as the identity of anyone who has received an agency's report. Consumers are also permitted to have access to the information contained about them in a credit reporting agency's files. If a consumer discovers that the agency's files contain inaccurate information about his or her credit standing, the agency, on the consumer's written request, must investigate the disputed information. Any unverifiable or erroneous information must be deleted within a reasonable period of time.

An agency that fails to comply with the act is liable for actual damages, plus additional damages not to exceed $1,000 and attorneys' fees.[28] The FCRA also allows a court to award punitive damages for a "willful" violation. In 2007, the United States Supreme Court held that an insurance company's failure to notify new customers that they were paying higher insurance rates as a result of their credit scores was a *willful* violation of the FCRA.[29]

FAIR AND ACCURATE CREDIT TRANSACTIONS ACT

In an effort to combat rampant identity theft (discussed in Chapter 7), Congress passed the Fair and Accurate Credit Transactions (FACT) Act of 2003.[30] The act established a national fraud alert system so that consumers who suspect that they have been or may be victimized by identity theft can place an alert in their credit files. The FACT Act also requires the major credit reporting agencies to provide consumers with a free copy of their credit reports every twelve months. Another provision requires account numbers on credit-card receipts to be truncated (shortened) so that merchants, employees, and others who have access to the receipts cannot obtain a consumer's name and full credit-card number. The act also mandates that financial institutions work with the FTC to identify "red flag" indicators of identity theft and to develop rules for disposing of sensitive credit information.

The FACT Act also gives consumers who have been victimized by identity theft some assistance in rebuilding their credit reputations. For example, credit reporting agencies must stop reporting allegedly fraudulent account information once the consumer establishes that identify theft has occurred. Business owners and creditors are required to provide a consumer with copies of any records that can help the consumer prove that a particular account or transaction is fraudulent (records showing that an account was created with a fraudulent signature, for example). In addition, to help prevent the spread of erroneous credit information, the act allows consumers to report the accounts affected by identity theft directly to the creditors.

ON THE WEB For information on the Fair and Accurate Credit Transactions Act, including transcripts of congressional hearings concerning the act, go to www.ftc.gov/opa/2004/06/factaidt.htm.

FAIR DEBT-COLLECTION PRACTICES

In 1977, Congress enacted the Fair Debt Collection Practices Act (FDCPA)[31] in an attempt to curb what were perceived to be abuses by collection agencies. The act applies only to specialized debt-collection agencies and attorneys who regularly attempt to collect debts on behalf of someone else, usually for a percentage of the amount owed. Creditors attempting to collect debts are not covered by the act unless, by misrepresenting themselves, they cause the debtors to believe that they are collection agencies.

The act prohibits a collection agency from using certain offensive tactics to collect the debt. For instance, a collection agency may not contact the debtor at his or her place of employment if the employer objects and may not contact the debtor's family members or other third parties about payment. The agency also may not harass or intimidate the

28. 15 U.S.C. Section 1681n.
29. *Safeco Insurance Co. of America v. Burr,* 551 U.S. 47, 127 S.Ct. 2201, 167 L.Ed.2d 1045 (2007).
30. Pub. L. No. 108-159, 117 Stat. 1952 (December 4, 2003).
31. 15 U.S.C. Section 1692.

debtor, or make false or misleading statements (such as posing as a police officer). A debt collector who fails to comply with the act is liable for actual damages, plus additional damages not to exceed $1,000[32] and attorneys' fees.

 Environmental Law

To this point, this chapter has dealt with government regulation of business in the interest of protecting consumers. We now turn to a discussion of the various ways in which businesses are regulated by the government in the interest of protecting the environment. Concern over the degradation of the environment has increased over time in response to the environmental effects of population growth, urbanization, and industrialization. Environmental protection is not without a price, however. For many businesses, the costs of complying with environmental regulations are high, and for some they may seem too high. (See the *Business Application* feature at the end of this chapter for information on how to avoid facing penalties for violating environmental laws.) A constant tension exists between the desirability of increasing profits and productivity and the need to protect the environment.

To a great extent, environmental law consists of statutes passed by federal, state, or local governments and regulations issued by administrative agencies. Before examining statutory and regulatory environmental laws, however, we look at the remedies against environmental pollution that are available under the common law.

Common Law Actions

Common law remedies against environmental pollution originated centuries ago in England. Those responsible for operations that created dirt, smoke, noxious odors, noise, or toxic substances were sometimes held liable under common law theories of nuisance or negligence. Today, injured individuals continue to rely on the common law to obtain damages and injunctions against business polluters.

Nuisance A common law doctrine under which persons may be held liable for using their property in a manner that unreasonably interferes with others' rights to use or enjoy their own property.

NUISANCE   Under the common law doctrine of **nuisance**, persons may be held liable if they use their property in a manner that unreasonably interferes with others' rights to use or enjoy their own property. In these situations, the courts commonly balance the harm caused by the pollution against the costs of stopping it.

Courts have often denied injunctive relief on the ground that the hardships that would be imposed on the polluter and on the community are relatively greater than the hardships suffered by the plaintiff. **EXAMPLE 33.7** A factory that causes neighboring landowners to suffer from smoke, soot, and vibrations may be left in operation if it is the core of the local economy. The injured parties may be awarded only monetary damages, which may include compensation for the decrease in the value of their property caused by the factory's operation. ●

A property owner may be given relief from pollution if she or he can identify a distinct harm separate from that affecting the general public. This harm is referred to as a "private" nuisance. Under the common law, individuals were denied standing (access to the courts—see Chapter 3) unless they suffered a harm distinct from the harm suffered by the public at large. Some states still require this. A public authority (such as a state's attorney general), though, can sue to abate a "public" nuisance.

NEGLIGENCE AND STRICT LIABILITY   An injured party may sue a business polluter in tort under the negligence and strict liability theories discussed in Chapter 4. The basis for a negligence action is the business's alleged failure to use reasonable care toward the party

---

32. According to the U.S. Court of Appeals for the Sixth Circuit, the $1,000 limit on damages applies to each lawsuit, not to each violation. See *Wright v. Finance Service of Norwalk, Inc.*, 22 F.3d 647 (6th Cir. 1994).

whose injury was foreseeable and, of course, caused by the lack of reasonable care. For instance, employees might sue an employer whose failure to use proper pollution controls contaminated the air and caused the employees to suffer respiratory illnesses. Lawsuits for personal injuries caused by exposure to a toxic substance, such as asbestos, radiation, or hazardous waste, have given rise to a growing body of tort law known as **toxic torts.**

Toxic Tort A civil wrong arising from exposure to a toxic substance, such as asbestos, radiation, or hazardous waste.

Businesses that engage in ultrahazardous activities—such as the transportation of radioactive materials—are strictly liable for any injuries the activities cause. In a strict liability action, the injured party does not need to prove that the business failed to exercise reasonable care.

State and Local Regulation

In addition to the federal regulation to be discussed shortly, many states have enacted laws to protect the environment. State laws may restrict a business's discharge of chemicals into the air or water or regulate its disposal of toxic wastes. States may also regulate the disposal or recycling of other wastes, including glass, metal, plastic containers, and paper. Additionally, states may restrict emissions from motor vehicles.

City, county, and other local governments also regulate some aspects of the environment. For instance, local zoning laws may be designed to inhibit or regulate the growth of cities and suburbs or to protect the natural environment. In the interest of safeguarding the environment, such laws may prohibit certain land uses. Even when zoning laws permit a business's proposed development, the proposal may have to be altered to lessen the development's impact on the environment. In addition, cities and counties may impose rules regulating methods of waste removal, the appearance of buildings, the maximum noise level, and other aspects of the local environment.

State and local regulatory agencies also play a significant role in implementing federal environmental legislation. Typically, the federal government relies on state and local governments to enforce federal environmental statutes and regulations such as those regulating air quality.

Federal Regulation

Congress has enacted a number of statutes to control the impact of human activities on the environment. Some of these laws have been passed in an attempt to improve the quality of air and water. Other laws specifically regulate toxic chemicals, including pesticides, herbicides, and hazardous wastes.

ENVIRONMENTAL REGULATORY AGENCIES The primary agency regulating environmental law is, of course, the Environmental Protection Agency (EPA), which was created in 1970 to coordinate federal environmental responsibilities. Other federal agencies with authority to regulate specific environmental matters include the Department of the Interior, the Department of Defense, the Department of Labor, the Food and Drug Administration, and the Nuclear Regulatory Commission. All agencies of the federal government must take environmental factors into consideration when making significant decisions. In addition, as mentioned, state and local agencies play an important role in enforcing federal environmental legislation.

Most federal environmental laws provide that private parties can sue to enforce environmental regulations if government agencies fail to do so—or if agencies go too far in their enforcement actions. Typically, a threshold hurdle in such suits is meeting the requirements for standing to sue.

Environmental Impact Statement (EIS) A statement required by the National Environmental Policy Act for any major federal action that will significantly affect the quality of the environment. The statement must analyze the action's impact on the environment and explore alternative actions that might be taken.

ENVIRONMENTAL IMPACT STATEMENTS The National Environmental Policy Act (NEPA) of 1969[33] requires that an **environmental impact statement (EIS)** be prepared for

---

33. 42 U.S.C. Sections 4321–4370d.

every major federal action that significantly affects the quality of the environment. An EIS must analyze (1) the impact on the environment that the action will have, (2) any adverse effects on the environment and alternative actions that might be taken, and (3) irreversible effects the action might generate.

An action qualifies as "major" if it involves a substantial commitment of resources (monetary or otherwise). An action is "federal" if a federal agency has the power to control it. Construction by a private developer of a ski resort on federal land, for example, may require an EIS. Building or operating a nuclear plant, which requires a federal permit, requires an EIS. If an agency decides that an EIS is unnecessary, it must issue a statement supporting this conclusion. Private individuals, consumer interest groups, businesses, and others who believe that a federal agency's actions threaten the environment often use EISs as a means of challenging those actions.

Air Pollution

Federal involvement with air pollution goes back to the 1950s and 1960s, when Congress authorized funds for air-pollution research and enacted the Clean Air Act to address multi-state air pollution.[34] The Clean Air Act provides the basis for issuing regulations to control pollution coming both from mobile sources (such as automobiles and other vehicles) and from stationary sources (such as electric utilities and industrial plants).

MOBILE SOURCES OF POLLUTION   Regulations governing air pollution from automobiles and other mobile sources specify pollution standards and establish time schedules for meeting the standards. Under the 1990 amendments to the Clean Air Act, automobile manufacturers were required to cut new automobiles' exhaust emissions of nitrogen oxide by 60 percent and of other pollutants by 35 percent by 1998. Beginning with 2004 model cars, regulations required nitrogen oxide tailpipe emissions to be cut nearly 10 percent by 2007. For the first time, sport utility vehicles (SUVs) and light trucks had to meet the same standards as automobiles. The amendments also required service stations to sell gasoline with a higher oxygen content in certain cities and to sell even cleaner-burning gasoline in the most polluted urban areas. In 2009, the Obama administration announced that it will seek to amend these standards to reduce emissions by 80 percent by 2050.

UPDATING POLLUTION-CONTROL STANDARDS   The EPA attempts to update pollution-control standards when new scientific information becomes available. For instance, studies conducted in the 1990s showed that very small particles (2.5 microns, or about one-thirtieth the width of a human hair) of soot might affect our health as significantly as larger particles. Based on this evidence, in 1997 the EPA issued new particulate standards for motor vehicle exhaust systems and other sources of pollution. The EPA also instituted a more rigorous standard for ozone (the basic ingredient of smog), which is formed when sunlight combines with pollutants from cars and other sources. The United States Supreme Court has upheld the EPA's authority to issue emission standards under the Clean Air Act without taking economic costs into account when creating new rules.[35]

In 2006, the EPA again re-evaluated its particulate standards and found that more than two hundred counties were not meeting the standards set in 1997. The EPA issued new regulations for daily (twenty-four-hour) exposure to particles of soot but did not change the annual particulate standards.[36]

ON THE WEB For information on EPA standards, guidelines, and regulations, go to the EPA's Web site at **www.epa.gov**.

> *"There's so much pollution in the air now that if it weren't for our lungs, there'd be no place to put it all."*
> Robert Orben, 1927–present
> (American comedian)

---

34. 42 U.S.C. Sections 7401 *et seq.*
35. *Whitman v. American Trucking Associations,* 531 U.S. 457, 121 S.Ct. 903, 149 L.Ed.2d 1 (2001).
36. 40 C.F.R. Part 50.

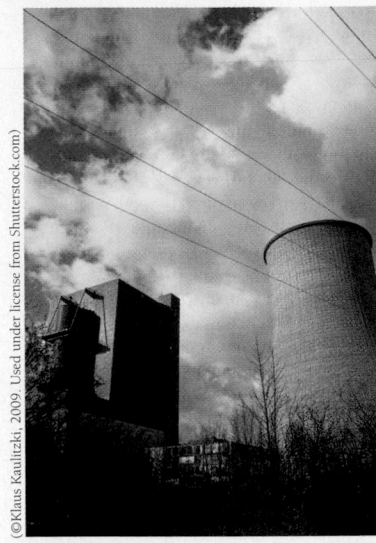

The most common stationary sources of air pollution are factories and electricity-generating facilities. For the application of the EPA's ambient standards, does it matter where the factory or electricity-generating facility is located? Why or why not?

STATIONARY SOURCES OF POLLUTION   The Clean Air Act authorizes the EPA to establish air-quality standards for stationary sources (such as manufacturing plants) but recognizes that the primary responsibility for preventing and controlling air pollution rests with state and local governments. The standards are aimed at controlling hazardous air pollutants—those likely to cause death or serious irreversible or incapacitating illness such as cancer or neurological and reproductive damage. In all, 189 substances, including asbestos, benzene, beryllium, cadmium, and vinyl chloride, have been classified as hazardous. They are emitted from stationary sources by a variety of business activities, including smelting (melting ore to produce metal), dry cleaning, house painting, and commercial baking.

Mercury was added to the list of hazardous substances in 2000. **CASE EXAMPLE 33.8**   In 2005, the EPA published a rule (the Delisting Rule) stating that it was removing mercury from its list of hazardous emissions from steam-generated electricity plants. New Jersey and fourteen other states filed a lawsuit challenging the EPA's action. The EPA argued that it had the authority to remove mercury from the list because its inclusion on the list was not a final agency action and because mercury was more appropriately regulated under other provisions. In 2008, a federal appellate court ruled that the EPA had exceeded its authority and required it to return mercury to the list of hazardous air pollutants.[37] ●

The EPA sets primary and secondary levels of ambient standards—that is, the maximum levels of certain pollutants—and the states formulate plans to achieve those standards. Different standards apply depending on whether the sources of pollution are located in clean areas or polluted areas and whether they are already existing sources or major new sources. Major new sources include existing sources modified by a change in a method of operation that increases emissions. Performance standards for major sources require the use of the *maximum achievable control technology,* or MACT, to reduce emissions. The EPA issues guidelines as to what equipment meets this standard.[38]

VIOLATIONS OF THE CLEAN AIR ACT   For violations of emission limits under the Clean Air Act, the EPA can assess civil penalties of up to $25,000 per day. Additional fines of up to $5,000 per day can be assessed for other violations, such as failing to maintain the required records. To penalize those who find it more cost-effective to violate the act than to comply with it, the EPA is authorized to obtain a penalty equal to the violator's economic benefits from noncompliance. Persons who provide information about violators may be paid up to $10,000. Private individuals can also sue violators.

Those who knowingly violate the act may be subject to criminal penalties, including fines of up to $1 million and imprisonment for up to two years (for false statements or failures to report violations). Corporate officers are among those who may be subject to these penalties.

Water Pollution

Water pollution stems mostly from industrial, municipal, and agricultural sources. Pollutants entering streams, lakes, and oceans include organic wastes, heated water, sediments from soil runoff, nutrients (including fertilizers and human and animal wastes), and toxic chemicals and other hazardous substances. We look here at laws and regulations governing water pollution.

Federal regulations governing the pollution of water can be traced back to the Rivers and Harbors Appropriations Act of 1899.[39] These regulations prohibited ships and manufacturers from discharging or depositing refuse in navigable waterways without a permit. In

---

37. *New Jersey v. Environmental Protection Agency,* 517 F.3d 574 (D.C.Cir. 2008).

38. The EPA has also issued rules to regulate hazardous air pollutants emitted by landfills. See 40 C.F.R. Sections 60.750–60.759.

39. 33 U.S.C. Sections 401–418.

1948, Congress passed the Federal Water Pollution Control Act (FWPCA),[40] but its regulatory system and enforcement powers proved to be inadequate.

THE CLEAN WATER ACT   In 1972, amendments to the FWPCA—known as the Clean Water Act (CWA)—established the following goals: (1) make waters safe for swimming, (2) protect fish and wildlife, and (3) eliminate the discharge of pollutants into the water. The amendments set specific time schedules, which were extended by amendment in 1977 and by the Water Quality Act of 1987.[41] Under these schedules, the EPA limits the discharge of various types of pollutants based on the technology available for controlling them.

The CWA established a permit system, called the *National Pollutant Discharge Elimination System* (NPDES), for regulating discharges from "point sources" of pollution that include industrial, municipal (such as pipes and sewage treatment plants), and agricultural facilities.[42] Under this system, industrial, municipal, and agricultural polluters must apply for permits before discharging wastes into surface waters. NPDES permits can be issued by the EPA and authorized state agencies and Indian tribes, but only if the discharge will not violate water-quality standards. NPDES permits must be reissued every five years. Although initially the NPDES system focused mainly on industrial wastewater, it was later expanded to cover storm water discharges.

The EPA must take into account many factors when issuing and updating the rules that impose standards to attain the goals of the CWA. Some provisions of the act instruct the EPA to weigh the cost of the technology applied against the benefits achieved. The statute that covers power plants, however, neither requires nor prohibits a comparison of the economic costs and benefits. The question in the following case was whether the EPA could make this comparison anyway.

> "Among the treasures of our land is water—fast becoming our most valuable, most prized, most critical resource."
>
> Dwight D. Eisenhower, 1890–1969
> (Thirty-fourth president of the United States, 1953–1961)

40. 33 U.S.C. Sections 1251–1387.
41. This act amended 33 U.S.C. Section 1251.
42. 33 U.S.C. Section 1342.

Case 33.2 Entergy Corp. v. Riverkeeper, Inc.

Supreme Court of the United States, __ U.S. __, 129 S.Ct. 1498, 173 L.Ed.2d 369 (2009).
www.findlaw.com/casecode/supreme.html[a]

HISTORICAL AND ENVIRONMENTAL SETTING   *In generating electricity, a power plant produces heat. To cool the operating machinery, the plant can use water pulled from a nearby source through a cooling water intake structure. The structure affects the environment by squashing aquatic organisms against intake screens or sucking the organisms into the cooling system. The Clean Water Act mandates that "cooling water intake structures reflect the best technology available for minimizing adverse environmental impact." For more than thirty years, the EPA made the "best technology available" determination on a case-by-case basis. In 2001 and 2004, the EPA adopted "Phase I" and "Phase II" rules for power plants.*

FACTS   Phase I rules require new power plants to restrict their inflow of water "to a level commensurate with that which can be attained by a closed-cycle recirculating cooling water system." Phase II rules apply "national performance standards" to more than five hundred existing plants but do not require closed-cycle cooling systems. The EPA found that converting these facilities to closed-cycle operations would cost $3.5 billion per year. The

Can the EPA use cost-versus-benefit analyses to determine whether power plants are implementing the best technological method for minimal environmental impact when cooling water?

(Jason Tessmann/Creative Commons)

facilities would then produce less power while burning the same amount of coal. Moreover, other technologies can attain nearly the same results as closed-cycle systems. Phase II rules also allow a variance from the national performance standards if a facility's cost of compliance "would be significantly greater than the benefits." Environmental organizations, including Riverkeeper, Inc., challenged the Phase II regulations, arguing that existing plants should be required to convert to closed-cycle systems. The U.S. Court of Appeals for the Second Circuit issued a ruling in the plaintiffs' favor. Power-generating companies, including Entergy Corporation, appealed.

ISSUE   Can the EPA compare costs with benefits to determine the "best technology available for minimizing adverse environmental impact" at cooling water intake structures?

---

a. In the "Browse Supreme Court Opinions" section, click on "2009." On that page, scroll to the name of the case and click on it to access the opinion.

Case 33.2–Continued

DECISION Yes. The United States Supreme Court reversed the lower court's decision. The EPA can rely on a cost-benefit analysis to set national performance standards and allow for variances from those standards as part of the Phase II regulations.

REASON "Best technology" can mean the technology that achieves the greatest reduction in adverse environmental impacts, but it can also describe the technology that "most efficiently" achieves a reduction, even if the result is less than other technologies might achieve. The use of the word *minimizing* in the controlling statute indicates that the intended objective was not the greatest possible reduction. When Congress wanted to set that as the goal in other parts of the Clean Water Act, it did so in "plain lan-

guage." This suggests that the EPA has some discretion to determine the extent of the reduction under this provision. Other provisions order the EPA to consider costs and benefits in some situations. This shows that "cost-benefit analysis is not categorically forbidden." Also, in imposing standards on power plants, the EPA has been weighing costs against benefits for more than thirty years. This suggests that the practice is "reasonable and hence legitimate."

FOR CRITICAL ANALYSIS—Political Consideration *Is a comparison of costs and benefits always an effective method for choosing among alternatives? Why or why not?*

VIOLATIONS OF THE CLEAN WATER ACT Under the CWA, violators are subject to a variety of civil and criminal penalties. Depending on the violation, civil penalties range from $10,000 per day to $25,000 per day, but not more than $25,000 per violation. Criminal penalties, which apply only if a violation was intentional, range from a fine of $2,500 per day and imprisonment for up to one year to a fine of $1 million and fifteen years' imprisonment. Injunctive relief and damages can also be imposed. The polluting party can be required to clean up the pollution or pay for the cost of doing so.

Wetlands Water-saturated areas of land that are designated by a government agency (such as the Army Corps of Engineers or the Environmental Protection Agency) as protected areas that support wildlife and therefore cannot be filled in or dredged by private contractors or parties without a permit.

WETLANDS The Clean Water Act prohibits the filling or dredging of **wetlands** unless a permit is obtained from the Army Corps of Engineers. The EPA defines *wetlands* as "those areas that are inundated or saturated by surface or ground water at a frequency and duration sufficient to support . . . vegetation typically adapted for life in saturated soil conditions." Wetlands are thought to be vital to the ecosystem because they filter streams and rivers and provide habitat for wildlife. Although in the past the EPA's broad interpretation of what constitutes a wetland generated substantial controversy, the courts have considerably scaled back the CWA's protection of wetlands in recent years.[43]

DRINKING WATER The Safe Drinking Water Act of 1974[44] requires the EPA to set maximum levels for pollutants in public water systems. Public water system operators must come as close as possible to meeting the EPA's standards by using the best available technology that is economically and technologically feasible. The EPA is particularly concerned about contamination from underground sources, such as pesticides and wastes leaked from landfills or disposed of in underground injection wells. Many of these substances are associated with cancer and may cause damage to the central nervous system, liver, and kidneys.

The act was amended in 1996 to give the EPA more flexibility in setting regulatory standards. These amendments also imposed requirements on suppliers of drinking water. Each supplier must send to every household it supplies with water an annual statement describing the source of its water, the level of any contaminants contained in the water, and any possible health concerns associated with the contaminants.

Ethical Issue ⚖️

Should the government begin regulating the presence of pharmaceuticals in drinking water? The amount of pharmaceuticals used by the American public and in agriculture (antibiotics and hormones given to livestock) has grown substantially in recent years. Now trace amounts of many drugs have been detected in our nation's water supply. In 2008, for example, the drinking water of

---

43. See, for example, *Rapanos v. United States*, 547 U.S. 715, 126 S.Ct. 2208, 165 L.Ed.2d 159 (2006).
44. 42 U.S.C. Sections 300f to 300j-25.

at least 41 million Americans in twenty-four regions across the country was found to contain small amounts of prescription drugs. Some of these trace amounts came from unmetabolized drugs that had passed through the humans and animals that ingested them, but the rest had been flushed down the toilet. For years, pharmacists, physicians, and the federal government have recommended that people dispose of unused medications by flushing them away. This prevents children from accidentally ingesting the drugs and keeps controlled substances, such as the painkillers oxycodone and morphine, from falling into the hands of people who might abuse them. In making these recommendations, however, no one considered the long-term effect on the environment of adding pharmaceuticals to the water supply.

Clearly, the quantities present in water now are far below medicinal doses, but no one knows how long-term exposure to random combinations of drugs will affect humans or wildlife. As yet there is little scientific evidence about the long-term effects. The federal government does not require drinking water to be tested for drugs, so Americans do not know whether their drinking water is contaminated. Requiring that water be tested and that all traces of drugs be filtered from it would be enormously expensive. In a time of economic recession, should the government wait until there is scientific proof of the harmful effects on humans and wildlife before regulating? Or should the government enact legislation to address the problem now—before it becomes worse?

OCEAN DUMPING   The Marine Protection, Research, and Sanctuaries Act of 1972[45] (popularly known as the Ocean Dumping Act), as amended in 1983, regulates the transportation and dumping of material into ocean waters. It prohibits entirely the ocean dumping of radiological, chemical, and biological warfare agents and high-level radioactive waste. The act also established a permit program for transporting and dumping other materials, and designated certain areas as marine sanctuaries. Each violation of any provision in the Ocean Dumping Act may result in a civil penalty of up to $50,000. A knowing violation is a criminal offense that may result in a $50,000 fine, imprisonment for not more than a year, or both. A court may also grant an injunction to prevent an imminent or continuing violation of the Ocean Dumping Act.

OIL POLLUTION   In response to the worst oil spill in North American history—more than 10 million gallons of oil that leaked into Alaska's Prince William Sound from the *Exxon Valdez* supertanker—Congress passed the Oil Pollution Act of 1990.[46] Under this act, any onshore or offshore oil facility, oil shipper, vessel owner, or vessel operator that discharges oil into navigable waters or onto an adjoining shore can be liable for clean-up costs, as well as damages.

Under the act, damage to natural resources, private property, and the local economy, including the increased cost of providing public services, is compensable. The penalties range from $2 million to $350 million, depending on the size of the vessel and on whether the oil spill came from a vessel or an offshore facility. The party held responsible for the clean-up costs can bring a civil suit for contribution from other potentially liable parties. The act also mandated that by the year 2011, oil tankers using U.S. ports must be double hulled to limit the severity of accidental spills.

Toxic Chemicals

Originally, most environmental clean-up efforts were directed toward reducing smog and making water safe for fishing and swimming. Today, the control of toxic chemicals used in agriculture and in industry has become increasingly important.

---

45. 16 U.S.C. Sections 1401–1445.
46. 33 U.S.C. Sections 2701–2761.

PESTICIDES AND HERBICIDES   The Federal Insecticide, Fungicide, and Rodenticide Act (FIFRA) of 1947 regulates pesticides and herbicides.[47] Under FIFRA, pesticides and herbicides must be (1) registered before they can be sold, (2) certified and used only for approved applications, and (3) used in limited quantities when applied to food crops. The EPA can cancel or suspend registration of substances that are identified as harmful and may also inspect factories where the chemicals are made. Under 1996 amendments to FIFRA, there must be no more than a one-in-a-million risk to people of developing cancer from any kind of exposure to the substance, including eating food that contains pesticide residues.[48]

It is a violation of FIFRA to sell a pesticide or herbicide that is either unregistered or has had its registration canceled or suspended. It is also a violation to sell a pesticide or herbicide with a false or misleading label or to destroy or deface any labeling required under the act. Penalties for commercial dealers include imprisonment for up to one year and a fine of no more than $25,000. Farmers and other private users of pesticides or herbicides who violate the act are subject to a $1,000 fine and incarceration for up to thirty days.

Note that a state can also regulate the sale and use of federally registered pesticides. **CASE EXAMPLE 33.9**   The EPA conditionally registered Strongarm, a weed-killing pesticide, in 2000. Dow Agrosciences, LLC, immediately sold Strongarm to Texas peanut farmers. When the farmers applied it, however, Strongarm damaged their crops while failing to control the growth of weeds. The farmers sued Dow, but the lower courts ruled that FIFRA preempted their claims. The farmers appealed to the United States Supreme Court. The Supreme Court held that under a specific provision of FIFRA, a state can regulate the sale and use of federally registered pesticides so long as the regulation does not permit anything that FIFRA prohibits.[49] ●

TOXIC SUBSTANCES   The first comprehensive law covering toxic substances was the Toxic Substances Control Act of 1976.[50] The act was passed to regulate chemicals and chemical compounds that are known to be toxic—such as asbestos and polychlorinated biphenyls, popularly known as PCBs—and to institute investigation of any possible harmful effects from new chemical compounds. The regulations authorize the EPA to require that manufacturers, processors, and other organizations planning to use chemicals first determine their effects on human health and the environment. The EPA can regulate substances that potentially pose an imminent hazard or an unreasonable risk of injury to health or the environment. The EPA may require special labeling, limit the use of a substance, set production quotas, or prohibit the use of a substance altogether.

Hazardous Waste Disposal

Some industrial, agricultural, and household wastes pose more serious threats than others. If not properly disposed of, these toxic chemicals may present a substantial danger to human health and the environment. If released into the environment, they may contaminate public drinking water resources.

RESOURCE CONSERVATION AND RECOVERY ACT   In 1976, Congress passed the Resource Conservation and Recovery Act (RCRA)[51] in reaction to concern over the effects of hazardous waste materials on the environment. The RCRA required the EPA to determine which forms of solid waste should be considered hazardous and to establish regulations

---

47. 7 U.S.C. Sections 135–136y.
48. 21 U.S.C. Section 346a.
49. *Bates v. Dow Agrosciences, LLC*, 544 U.S. 431, 125 S.Ct. 1788, 161 L.Ed.2d 687 (2005).
50. 15 U.S.C. Sections 2601–2692.
51. 42 U.S.C. Sections 6901 *et seq.*

to monitor and control hazardous waste disposal. The act also requires all producers of hazardous waste materials to label and package properly any hazardous waste to be transported. The RCRA was amended in 1984 and 1986 to decrease the use of land containment in the disposal of hazardous waste and to require smaller generators of hazardous waste to comply with the act.

Under the RCRA, a company may be assessed a civil penalty of up to $25,000 for each violation.[52] Penalties are based on the seriousness of the violation, the probability of harm, and the extent to which the violation deviates from RCRA requirements. Criminal penalties include fines of up to $50,000 for each day of violation, imprisonment for up to two years (in most instances), or both.[53] Criminal fines and the period of imprisonment can be doubled for certain repeat offenders.

SUPERFUND　　In 1980, Congress passed the Comprehensive Environmental Response, Compensation, and Liability Act (CERCLA),[54] commonly known as Superfund, to regulate the clean-up of leaking hazardous waste–disposal sites. A special federal fund was created for that purpose.

CERCLA, as amended in 1986, has four primary elements:

1. It established an information-gathering and analysis system that enables the government to identify chemical dump sites and determine the appropriate action.
2. It authorized the EPA to respond to hazardous substance emergencies and to arrange for the clean-up of a leaking site directly if the persons responsible for the problem fail to clean up the site.
3. It created a Hazardous Substance Response Trust Fund (Superfund) to pay for the clean-up of hazardous sites using funds obtained through taxes on certain businesses.
4. It allowed the government to recover the cost of clean-up from the persons who were (even remotely) responsible for hazardous substance releases.

Potentially Responsible Parties under Superfund.　　Superfund provides that when a release or a threatened release of hazardous chemicals from a site occurs, the EPA can clean up the site and recover the cost of the clean-up from the following persons: (1) the person who generated the wastes disposed of at the site, (2) the person who transported the wastes to the site, (3) the person who owned or operated the site at the time of the disposal, or (4) the current owner or operator. A person falling within one of these categories is referred to as a **potentially responsible party (PRP)**.

Joint and Several Liability under Superfund.　　Liability under Superfund is usually joint and several—that is, a person who generated *only a fraction of the hazardous waste* disposed of at the site may nevertheless be liable for *all* of the clean-up costs. CERCLA authorizes a party who has incurred clean-up costs to bring a "contribution action" against any other person who is liable or potentially liable for a percentage of the costs.

Potentially Responsible Party (PRP)
A party liable for the costs of cleaning up a hazardous waste-disposal site under the Comprehensive Environmental Response, Compensation, and Liability Act. Any person who generated the hazardous waste, transported it, owned or operated the waste site at the time of disposal, or owns or operates the site at the present time may be responsible for some or all of the clean-up costs.

52. 42 U.S.C. Section 6928(a).
53. 42 U.S.C. Section 6928(d).
54. 42 U.S.C. Sections 9601–9675.

 Reviewing . . . Consumer and Environmental Law

Leota Sage saw a local motorcycle dealer's advertisement in a newspaper offering a MetroRider EZ electric scooter for $1,699. When she went to the dealership, however, she learned that the EZ model was sold out. The salesperson told Sage that he still had the higher-end MetroRider FX model in stock for $2,199 and would sell her one for $1,999. Sage was disappointed but decided to purchase the FX model. Sage told the sales representative that she wished to purchase the scooter on credit and was directed to the dealer's credit department. As she filled out the credit forms, the clerk told Sage, an African American, that she would need a cosigner. Sage could not understand why she would need a cosigner and asked to speak to the manager. The manager apologized, told her that the clerk was mistaken, and said that he would "speak to" the clerk. The manager completed Sage's credit application, and Sage then rode the scooter home. Seven months later, Sage received a letter from the Federal Trade Commission (FTC) asking questions about her transaction with the motorcycle dealer and indicating that it had received complaints from other consumers. Using the information presented in the chapter, answer the following questions.

1. Did the dealer engage in deceptive advertising? Why or why not?
2. Suppose that Sage had ordered the scooter through the dealer's Web site but the dealer had been unable to deliver it by the date promised. What would the FTC have required the merchant to do in that situation?
3. Assuming that the clerk required a cosigner based on Sage's race or gender, what act prohibits such credit discrimination?
4. What organization has the authority to ban the sale of scooters based on safety concerns?

Business Application

How Can You Keep Abreast of Environmental Laws?*

Businesspersons today increasingly face the threat of severe civil or criminal penalties if they violate environmental laws and regulations. Thus, it is crucial to be aware of what those laws and regulations are, how to monitor changes in them, and when to consult with an attorney during the normal course of business. Consider some areas of concern that affect businesses.

Factors to Consider When Purchasing Business Property

When purchasing business property, keep in mind the environmental problems that may arise. Realize that it is up to you as a purchaser of the property to raise environmental issues—sellers, title insurance companies, and real estate brokers will rarely pursue such matters. (A bank financing the property may worry about the potential environmental hazards of the property, however.)

As a purchaser of business property, you should find out whether there are any restrictions on the use of the land, such as whether it can be cleared of trees for construction purposes. The most important environmental concern, though, is whether the property has been contaminated by hazardous wastes created by the previous owners.

Investigate Land-Use History

Purchasers of property can be held liable under Superfund for the clean-up of hazardous wastes dumped by previous property owners. Although current property owners who pay clean-up costs can sue the previous owners for contribution, such litigation is expensive and the outcome uncertain. Clearly, a more prudent course is to investigate the history of the use of the land before purchasing the property. You might even want to hire a private environmental site inspector to determine, at a minimum, whether the land has any obvious signs of former contamination.

Investigate and Correct Environmental Violations

Today's companies have an incentive to discover their own environmental wrongdoings. As mentioned in Chapter 6, the federal sentencing guidelines encourage companies to promptly detect, disclose, and correct wrongdoing, including environmental crimes. Companies that do so are subject to lighter penalties for violations of environmental laws. Thus, a company would be well advised to conduct environmental compliance audits regularly.

Small businesses (those with up to one hundred employees) will find it particularly advantageous to investigate and correct environmental violations. Under EPA guidelines, the EPA will waive all fines if a small company corrects environmental violations within 180 days after being notified of the violations (or 360 days if pollution-prevention techniques are involved). The policy does not apply to criminal violations of environmental laws or to actions that pose a significant threat to public health, safety, or the environment.

CHECKLIST FOR THE BUSINESSPERSON

1. **If you are going to purchase real estate, consult your attorney to find out whether there are any restrictions on the use of the property and investigate its history to check for previous contamination.**
2. **If you want to avoid liability for violating environmental regulations or statutes, conduct environmental compliance audits on a regular basis.**
3. **If you are ever charged with violating an environmental regulation or law, immediately cease the activity you are being charged with and contact your attorney.**
4. **In general, environmental law is sufficiently complex that you should never attempt to deal with it without the help of an attorney.**

* This *Business Application* is not meant to substitute for the services of an attorney who is licensed to practice law in your state.

Key Terms

bait-and-switch advertising 837
cease-and-desist order 838
"cooling-off" laws 840
counteradvertising 838

deceptive advertising 836
environmental impact statement (EIS) 847
multiple product order 838
nuisance 846

potentially responsible party (PRP) 854
Regulation Z 840
toxic tort 847
wetlands 851

 Chapter Summary: Consumer and Environmental Law

CONSUMER LAW	

Deceptive Advertising
(See pages 836–838.)
	1. *Definition of deceptive advertising*—Generally, an advertising claim will be deemed deceptive if it would mislead a reasonable consumer.
	2. *Bait-and-switch advertising*—Advertising a lower-priced product (the bait) when the intention is not to sell the advertised product but to lure consumers into the store and convince them to buy a higher-priced product (the switch) is prohibited by the FTC.
	3. *Online deceptive advertising*—The FTC has issued guidelines to help online businesses comply with existing laws prohibiting deceptive advertising.
	4. *FTC actions against deceptive advertising*—
	  a. Cease-and-desist orders—Requiring the advertiser to stop the challenged advertising.
	  b. Counteradvertising—Requiring the advertiser to advertise to correct the earlier misinformation.

Telemarketing and Fax Advertising (See pages 838–839.)	The Telephone Consumer Protection Act of 1991 prohibits telephone solicitation using an automatic telephone dialing system or a prerecorded voice, as well as the transmission of advertising materials via fax without first obtaining the recipient's permission.
Labeling and Packaging (See pages 839–840.)	Manufacturers must comply with the labeling or packaging requirements for their specific products. In general, all labels must be accurate and not misleading.
Sales (See pages 840–841.)	1. *Telephone and mail-order sales*—Federal and state statutes and regulations govern certain practices of sellers who solicit over the telephone or through the mails and prohibit the use of the mails to defraud individuals. 2. *Online sales*—Both state and federal laws protect consumers to some extent against fraudulent and deceptive online sales practices.
Health and Safety (See pages 841–842.)	1. *Food and drugs*—The Federal Food, Drug, and Cosmetic Act of 1916, as amended in 1938, protects consumers against adulterated and misbranded foods and drugs. The act establishes food standards, specifies safe levels of potentially hazardous food additives, and sets classifications of food and food advertising. 2. *Consumer product safety*—The Consumer Product Safety Act of 1972 seeks to protect consumers from risk of injury from hazardous products. The Consumer Product Safety Commission has the power to remove products that are deemed imminently hazardous from the market and to ban the manufacture and sale of hazardous products.

Credit Protection
(See pages 842–846.)
	1. *Consumer Credit Protection Act, Title I (Truth-in-Lending Act, or TILA)*—A disclosure law that requires sellers and lenders to disclose credit terms or loan terms in certain transactions, including retail and installment sales and loans, car loans, home-improvement loans, and certain real estate loans. Additionally, the TILA provides for the following:
	  a. Equal credit opportunity—Creditors are prohibited from discriminating on the basis of race, religion, marital status, gender, national origin, color, or age.
	  b. Credit-card protection—Liability of cardholders for unauthorized charges is limited to $50, providing notice requirements are met; consumers are not liable for unauthorized charges made on unsolicited credit cards. The act also sets out procedures to be used in settling disputes between credit-card companies and their cardholders.
	  c. Consumer leases—The Consumer Leasing Act (CLA) of 1988 protects consumers who lease automobiles and other goods priced at $25,000 or less if the lease term exceeds four months.

Chapter Summary: Consumer and Environmental Law–Continued

Credit Protection–Continued	2. *Fair Credit Reporting Act*–Entitles consumers to request verification of the accuracy of a credit report and to have unverified or false information removed from their files. 3. *Fair and Accurate Credit Transaction Act*–Attempts to combat identity theft by establishing a national fraud alert system. Requires account numbers to be truncated and credit reporting agencies to provide one free credit report per year to consumers. Assists victims of identity theft in rebuilding their credit. 4. *Fair Debt Collection Practices Act*–Prohibits debt collectors from using unfair debt-collection practices, such as contacting the debtor at his or her place of employment if the employer objects or at unreasonable times, contacting third parties about the debt, and harassing the debtor.
ENVIRONMENTAL LAW	
Common Law Actions **(See pages 846–847.)**	1. *Nuisance*–A common law doctrine under which actions against pollution-causing activities may be brought. An action is permissible only if an individual suffers a harm separate and distinct from that of the general public. 2. *Negligence and strict liability*–Parties may recover damages for injuries sustained as a result of a firm's pollution-causing activities if they can demonstrate that the harm was a foreseeable result of the firm's failure to exercise reasonable care (negligence); businesses engaging in ultrahazardous activities are liable for whatever injuries the activities cause, regardless of whether the firms exercise reasonable care.
State and Local Regulation **(See page 847.)**	Activities affecting the environment are controlled at the local and state levels through regulations relating to land use, the disposal and recycling of garbage and waste, and pollution-causing activities in general.

Federal Regulation
(See pages 847–854.)
	1. *Environmental protection agencies*–The primary agency regulating environmental law is the federal Environmental Protection Agency (EPA), which was created in 1970 to coordinate federal environmental programs. The EPA administers most federal environmental policies and statutes.
	2. *Assessing environmental impact*–The National Environmental Policy Act of 1969 imposes environmental responsibilities on all federal agencies and requires the preparation of an environmental impact statement (EIS) for every major federal action. An EIS must analyze the action's impact on the environment, its adverse effects and possible alternatives, and its irreversible effects on environmental quality.
	3. *Important areas regulated by the federal government*–Important areas regulated by the federal government include the following:
	  a. Air pollution–Regulated under the authority of the Clean Air Act and its amendments.
	  b. Water pollution–Regulated under the authority of the Rivers and Harbors Appropriations Act of 1899, as amended, and the Federal Water Pollution Control Act of 1948, as amended by the Clean Water Act of 1972.
	  c. Toxic chemicals and hazardous waste–Pesticides and herbicides, toxic substances, and hazardous waste are regulated under the authority of the Federal Insecticide, Fungicide, and Rodenticide Act of 1947, the Toxic Substances Control Act of 1976, and the Resource Conservation and Recovery Act of 1976, respectively. The Comprehensive Environmental Response, Compensation, and Liability Act (CERCLA) of 1980, as amended, regulates the clean-up of hazardous waste–disposal sites.

 ExamPrep

ISSUE SPOTTERS

1 Gert buys a notebook computer from EZ Electronics. She pays for it with her credit card. When the computer proves defective, she asks EZ to repair or replace it, but EZ refuses. What can Gert do?

2 Resource Refining Company's plant emits smoke and fumes. Resource's operation includes a short railway system, and trucks enter and exit the grounds continuously. Constant vibrations from the trains and trucks rattle nearby residential neighborhoods. The residents sue Resource. Are there any reasons that the court might refuse to enjoin Resource's operation? Explain.

BEFORE THE TEST

Check your answers to the Issue Spotters, and at the same time, take the interactive quiz for this chapter. Go to **www.cengage.com/blaw/blt** and click on "Chapter 33." First, click on "Answers to Issue Spotters" to check your answers. Next, click on "Interactive Quiz" to assess your mastery of the concepts in this chapter. Then click on "Flashcards" to review this chapter's Key Term definitions.

For Review

Answers for the even-numbered questions in this For Review *section can be found on this text's accompanying Web site at* www.cengage.com/blaw/blt. *Select "Chapter 33" and click on "For Review."*

1 When will advertising be deemed deceptive?

2 What are the major federal statutes providing for consumer protection in credit transactions?

3 Under what common law theories can polluters be held liable?

4 What is contained in an environmental impact statement, and who must file one?

5 What major federal statutes regulate air and water pollution? What is Superfund, and who is potentially liable under Superfund?

 Hypothetical Scenarios and Case Problems

33–1 Clean Air Act. Current scientific knowledge indicates that there is no safe level of exposure to a cancer-causing agent. In theory, even one molecule of such a substance has the potential for causing cancer. Section 112 of the Clean Air Act requires that all cancer-causing substances be regulated to ensure a margin of safety. Some environmental groups have argued that all emissions of such substances must be eliminated if a margin of safety is to be reached. Such a total elimination would likely shut down many major U.S. industries. Should the Environmental Protection Agency totally eliminate all emissions of cancer-causing chemicals? Discuss.

33–2 Hypothetical Question with Sample Answer Maria Ochoa receives two new credit cards on May 1. She had solicited one of them from Midtown Department Store, and the other arrived unsolicited from High-Flying Airlines. During the month of May, Ochoa makes numerous credit-card purchases from Midtown Department Store, but she does not use the High-Flying Airlines card. On May 31, a burglar breaks into Ochoa's home and steals both credit cards, along with other items. Ochoa notifies Midtown Department Store of the theft on June 2, but she fails to notify High-Flying Airlines. Using the Midtown credit card, the burglar makes a $500 purchase on June 1 and a $200 purchase on June 3. The burglar then charges a vacation flight on the High-Flying Airlines card for $1,000 on June 5. Ochoa receives the bills for these charges and refuses to pay them. Discuss Ochoa's liability in these situations.

—**For a sample answer to Question 33–2, go to Appendix E at the end of this text.**

33–3 Environmental Laws. Fruitade, Inc., is a processor of a soft drink called Freshen Up. Fruitade uses returnable bottles, which it cleans with a special acid to allow for further beverage processing. The acid is diluted with water and then allowed to pass into a navigable stream. Fruitade crushes its broken bottles and throws the crushed glass into the stream. Discuss fully any environmental laws that Fruitade has violated.

33–4 Clean Water Act. The Anacostia River, which flows through Washington, D.C., is one of the ten most polluted rivers in the country. For bodies of water such as the Anacostia, the Clean Water Act requires states (which, under the act, include the District of Columbia) to set a "total maximum daily load"

(TMDL) for pollutants. A TMDL is to be set "at a level necessary to implement the applicable water-quality standards with seasonal variations." The Anacostia contains biochemical pollutants that consume oxygen, putting the river's aquatic life at risk for suffocation. In addition, the river is murky, stunting the growth of plants that rely on sunlight and impairing recreational use. The Environmental Protection Agency (EPA) approved one TMDL limiting the *annual* discharge of oxygen-depleting pollutants and a second limiting the *seasonal* discharge of pollutants contributing to turbidity. Neither TMDL limited daily discharges. Friends of the Earth, Inc. (FoE), asked a federal district court to review the TMDLs. What is FoE's best argument in this dispute? What is the EPA's likely response? What should the court rule, and why? [*Friends of the Earth, Inc. v. Environmental Protection Agency,* 446 F.3d 140 (D.C.Cir. 2006)]

33–5 Environmental Impact Statement. The fourth largest crop in the United States is alfalfa, of which 5 percent is exported to Japan. RoundUp Ready alfalfa is genetically engineered to resist glyphosate, the active ingredient in the herbicide RoundUp. The U.S. Department of Agriculture (USDA) regulates genetically engineered agricultural products through the Animal and Plant Health Inspection Service (APHIS). APHIS concluded that RoundUp Ready alfalfa does not have any harmful effects on the health of humans or livestock and deregulated it. Geertson Seed Farms and others filed a suit in a federal district court against Mike Johanns (the secretary of the USDA) and others, asserting that APHIS's decision required the preparation of an environmental impact statement (EIS). The plaintiffs argued, among other things, that the introduction of RoundUp Ready alfalfa might significantly decrease the availability of, or even eliminate, all nongenetically engineered varieties. The plaintiffs were concerned that the RoundUp Ready alfalfa might contaminate standard alfalfa because alfalfa is pollinated by bees, which can travel as far as two miles from a pollen source. If contamination occurred, farmers would not be able to market "contaminated" varieties as "organic," which would affect the sales of "organic" livestock and exports to Japan, which does not allow the import of glyphosate-resistant alfalfa. Should an EIS be prepared in this case? Why or why not? [*Geertson Seed Farms v. Johanns,* __ F.Supp.2d __ (N.D.Cal. 2007)]

33–6 Case Problem with Sample Answer The Nutrition Labeling and Education Act (NLEA) requires packaged food to have a "Nutrition Facts" panel that sets out "nutrition information," including "the total number of calories" per serving. Restaurants are exempt from this requirement. The NLEA also regulates nutrition-content claims, such as "low sodium," that a purveyor might choose to add to a label. The NLEA permits a state or local law to require restaurants to disclose nutrition information about the food they serve, but expressly preempts state or local attempts to regulate nutrition-content claims. New York City Health Code Section 81.50 requires 10 percent of the restaurants in the city, including McDonald's, Burger King, and Kentucky Fried Chicken, to post calorie content information on their menus. The New York State Restaurant Association (NYSRA) filed a suit in a federal district court, contending that the NLEA preempts Section 81.50. (Under the U.S. Constitution, state or local laws that conflict with federal laws are preempted.) Is the NYSRA correct? Explain. [*New York State Restaurant Association v. New York City Board of Health,* 556 F.3d 114 (2d Cir. 2009)]

—**After you have answered Problem 33–6, compare your answer with the sample answer given on the Web site that accompanies this text. Go to www.cengage.com/blaw/blt, select "Chapter 33," and click on "Case Problem with Sample Answer."**

33–7 A Question of Ethics *In the Clean Air Act, Congress allowed California, which has particular problems with clean air, to adopt its own standard for emissions from cars and trucks, subject to the approval of the Environmental Protection Agency (EPA) according to certain criteria. Congress also allowed* other states to adopt California's standard after the EPA's approval. *In 2004, in an effort to address global warming, the California Air Resources Board amended the state's standard to attain "the maximum feasible and cost-effective reduction of GHG [greenhouse gas] emissions from motor vehicles." The regulation, which applies to new passenger vehicles and light-duty trucks for 2009 and later, imposes decreasing limits on emissions of carbon dioxide through 2016. While EPA approval was pending, Vermont and other states adopted similar standards. Green Mountain Chrysler Plymouth Dodge Jeep and other auto dealers, automakers, and associations of automakers filed a suit in a federal district court against George Crombie (secretary of the Vermont Agency of Natural Resources) and others, seeking relief from the state regulations. [Green Mountain Chrysler Plymouth Dodge Jeep v. Crombie, __ F.Supp.2d __ (D.Vt. 2007)]*

1 Under the Environmental Policy and Conservation Act (EPCA) of 1975, the National Highway Traffic Safety Administration sets fuel economy standards for new cars. The plaintiffs argued, among other things, that the EPCA, which prohibits states from adopting fuel economy standards, preempts Vermont's GHG regulation. Do the GHG rules equate to the fuel economy standards? Discuss.

2 Do Vermont's rules tread on the efforts of the federal government to address global warming internationally? Who should regulate GHG emissions? The federal government? The state governments? Both? Neither? Why?

3 The plaintiffs claimed that they would go bankrupt if they were forced to adhere to the state's GHG standards. Should they be granted relief on this basis? Does history support their claim? Explain.

Critical Thinking and Writing Assignments

33–8 **Critical Legal Thinking.** It has been estimated that for every dollar spent cleaning up hazardous waste sites, administrative agencies spend seven dollars in overhead. Can you think of any way to trim these administrative costs? Explain.

33–9 **Critical Thinking and Writing Assignment for Business.** Many states have enacted laws that go even further than federal law to protect consumers. These laws vary tremendously from state to state. Generally, is having different laws fair to sellers who may be prohibited from engaging in a practice in one state that is legal in another? How might these different laws affect a business? Is it fair that residents of one state have more protection than residents of another?

33–10 **Video Question** Go to this text's Web site at **www.cengage.com/blaw/blt** and select "Chapter 33." Click on "Video Questions" and view the video titled *Advertising Communication Law: Bait and Switch.* Then answer the following questions.

1 Is the auto dealership's advertisement for the truck in the video deceptive? Why or why not?

2 Is the advertisement for the truck an offer to which the dealership is bound? Does it matter if Betty detrimentally relied on the advertisement?

3 Is Tony committed to buying Betty's trade-in truck for $3,000 because that is what he told her over the phone?

 ## Practical Internet Exercises

Go to this text's Web site at **www.cengage.com/blaw/blt**, select "Chapter 33," and click on "Practical Internet Exercises." There you will find the following Internet research exercises that you can perform to learn more about the topics covered in this chapter.

Practical Internet Exercise 33–1: LEGAL PERSPECTIVE—The Food and Drug Administration
Practical Internet Exercise 33–2: SOCIAL PERSPECTIVE—Nuisance Law
Practical Internet Exercise 33–3: MANAGEMENT PERSPECTIVE—Complying with Environmental Regulations

Chapter 34

Liability of Accountants and Other Professionals

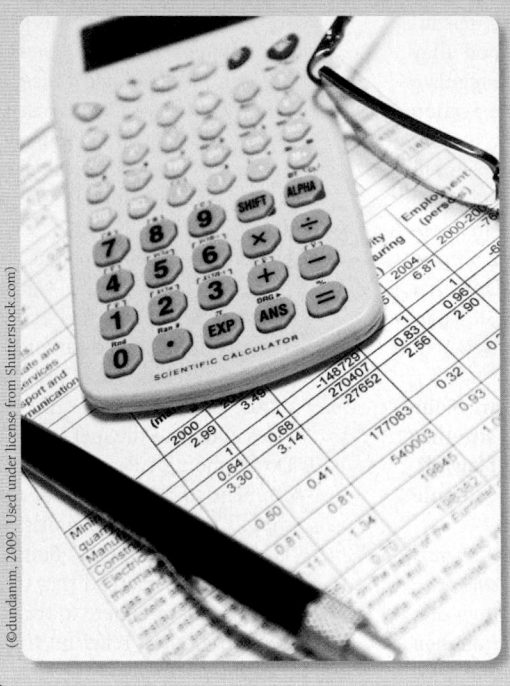

(©dundanim, 2009. Used under license from Shutterstock.com)

> "A member should observe the profession's technical and ethical standard . . . and discharge professional responsibility to the best of the member's ability."
>
> —Article V, *Code of Professional Conduct*, American Institute of Certified Public Accountants

Learning Objectives

After reading this chapter, you should be able to answer the following questions:

1. Under what common law theories may professionals be liable to clients?

2. What are the rules concerning an auditor's liability to third parties?

3. How might an accountant violate federal securities laws?

4. What crimes might an accountant commit under the Internal Revenue Code?

5. What constrains professionals to keep communications with their clients confidential?

The standard of due care to which the members of the American Institute of Certified Public Accountants are expected to adhere is set out in the chapter-opening quotation. Accountants, attorneys, physicians, and other professionals have found themselves increasingly subject to liability in the past decade or so. This more extensive liability has resulted in large part from a greater public awareness of the fact that professionals are required to deliver competent services and are obligated to adhere to standards of performance commonly accepted within their professions.

Certainly, the dizzying collapse of Enron Corporation and the failure of other major companies, including WorldCom, Inc., in the early 2000s called attention to the importance of abiding by professional accounting standards. Arthur Andersen, LLP, one of the world's leading public accounting firms, ended up being indicted on criminal charges for its role in thwarting the government's investigation into Enron's accounting practices.[1] As a result, Arthur Andersen ceased to exist and roughly 85,000 employees lost their jobs. Moreover, under the Sarbanes-Oxley Act of 2002, which Congress passed in response to these events, public accounting firms throughout the nation will feel the effects for years to

---

1. Although Arthur Andersen, LLP, was subsequently convicted in a federal district court on the charge of obstructing justice, the United States Supreme Court reversed and remanded the case in 2005 due to erroneous jury instructions. *Arthur Andersen, LLP v. United States,* 544 U.S. 696, 125 S.Ct. 2129, 161 L.Ed.2d 1008 (2005).

come. Among other things, the act imposed stricter regulation and oversight on the public accounting industry.

Considering the many potential sources of legal liability that they face, accountants, attorneys, and other professionals should be very aware of their legal obligations. In this chapter, we look at the potential common law liability of professionals and then examine the potential liability of accountants under securities laws and the Internal Revenue Code. The chapter concludes with a brief examination of the relationship of professionals, particularly accountants and attorneys, with their clients.

▶ Potential Common Law Liability to Clients

Under the common law, professionals may be liable to clients for breach of contract, negligence, or fraud.

Liability for Breach of Contract

Accountants and other professionals face liability under the common law for any breach of contract. A professional owes a duty to his or her client to honor the terms of their contract and to perform the contract within the stated time period. If the professional fails to perform as agreed in the contract, then he or she has breached the contract, and the client has the right to recover damages from the professional. A professional may be held liable for expenses incurred by the client in securing another professional to provide the contracted-for services, for penalties imposed on the client for failure to meet time deadlines, and for any other reasonable and foreseeable monetary losses that arise from the professional's breach.

Liability for Negligence

Accountants and other professionals may also be held liable under the common law for negligence in the performance of their services. The elements that must be proved to establish negligence on the part of a professional are as follows:

1. A duty of care existed.
2. That duty of care was breached.
3. The plaintiff suffered an injury.
4. The injury was proximately caused by the defendant's breach of the duty of care.

All professionals are subject to standards of conduct established by codes of professional ethics, by state statutes, and by judicial decisions. They are also governed by the contracts they enter into with their clients. In their performance of contracts, professionals must exercise the established standards of care, knowledge, and judgment generally accepted by members of their professional group. Here, we look at the duty of care owed by two groups of professionals that frequently perform services for business firms: accountants and attorneys.

ACCOUNTANT'S DUTY OF CARE   Accountants play a major role in a business's financial system. Accountants have the necessary expertise and experience to establish and maintain accurate financial records; design, control, and audit record-keeping systems; prepare reliable statements that reflect an individual's or a business's financial status; and give tax advice and prepare tax returns.

GAAP and GAAS.   In the performance of their services, accountants must comply with **generally accepted accounting principles (GAAP)** and **generally accepted auditing standards (GAAS).** The Financial Accounting Standards Board (FASB, usually pronounced

Generally Accepted Accounting Principles (GAAP)   The conventions, rules, and procedures that define accepted accounting practices at a particular time. The source of the principles is the Financial Accounting Standards Board.

Generally Accepted Auditing Standards (GAAS)   Standards concerning an auditor's professional qualities and the judgment exercised by him or her in the performance of an audit and report. The source of the standards is the American Institute of Certified Public Accountants.

Defalcation Embezzlement; the misappropriation of funds by a party, such as a corporate officer or public official, in a fiduciary relationship with another.

"Never call an accountant a credit to his profession; a good accountant is a debit to his profession."

Attributed to Charles J. C. Lyall,
1943–1996
(American commentator)

"faz-bee") determines what accounting conventions, rules, and procedures constitute GAAP at a given point in time. GAAS are standards concerning an auditor's professional qualities and the judgment that he or she exercises in performing an audit and report. GAAS are established by the American Institute of Certified Public Accountants. As long as an accountant conforms to GAAP and acts in good faith, he or she normally will not be held liable to the client for incorrect judgment. (For a discussion of how GAAP will be replaced by global accounting rules in the future, see this chapter's *Landmark in the Law* feature.)

As a general rule, an accountant is not required to discover every impropriety, **defalcation**[2] (embezzlement), or fraud, in her or his client's books. If, however, the impropriety, defalcation, or fraud has gone undiscovered because of the accountant's negligence or failure to perform an express or implied duty, the accountant will be liable for any resulting losses suffered by the client. Therefore, an accountant who uncovers suspicious financial transactions and fails to investigate the matter fully or to inform the client of the discovery can be held liable to the client for the resulting loss.

A violation of GAAP and GAAS is considered *prima facie* evidence of negligence on the part of the accountant. Compliance with GAAP and GAAS, however, does not *necessarily* relieve an accountant from potential legal liability. An accountant may be held to a higher standard of conduct established by state statute and by judicial decisions.

Audits, Qualified Opinions, and Disclaimers. One of the most important tasks that an accountant may perform for a business is an audit. An *audit* is a systematic inspection, by analyses and tests, of a business's financial records. (For a discussion of the use of statistical sampling in audits, see this chapter's *Linking the Law to Business Statistics* feature on page 875.)

The purpose of an audit is to provide the auditor with evidence to support an opinion on the reliability of the business's financial statements. A normal audit is not intended to uncover fraud or other misconduct. Nevertheless, an accountant may be liable for failing to detect misconduct if a normal audit would have revealed it. Also, if the auditor agreed to examine the records for evidence of fraud or other obvious misconduct and then failed to detect it, he or she may be liable. After performing an audit, the auditor issues an opinion letter stating whether, in his or her opinion, the financial statements fairly present the business's financial position.

In issuing an opinion letter, an auditor may *qualify* the opinion or include a disclaimer. An opinion that disclaims any liability for false or misleading financial statements is too general, however. A qualified opinion or a disclaimer must be specific and identify the reason for the qualification or disclaimer. **EXAMPLE 34.1** Richard Zehr performs an audit of Lacey Corporation. In the opinion letter, Zehr qualifies his opinion by stating that there is uncertainty about how a lawsuit against the firm will be resolved. In this situation, Zehr will not be liable if the outcome of the suit is unfavorable for the firm. Zehr could still be liable, however, for failing to discover other problems that an audit in compliance with GAAS and GAAP would have revealed. ● In a disclaimer, the auditor basically is stating that she or he does not have sufficient information to issue an opinion. Again, the auditor must identify the problem and indicate what information is lacking.

Unaudited Financial Statements. Sometimes, accountants are hired to prepare unaudited financial statements. (A financial statement is considered unaudited if incomplete auditing procedures have been used in its preparation or if insufficient procedures have been used to justify an opinion.) Accountants may be subject to liability for failing, in accor-

---

2. This term, pronounced deh-fal-*kay*-shun, is derived from the Latin *de* ("off") and *falx* ("sickle"—a tool for cutting grain or tall grass). In law, the term refers to the act of a defaulter or of an embezzler. As used here, it means embezzlement.

Landmark in the Law   The SEC Adopts Global Accounting Rules

At one time, investors and companies considered the U.S. accounting rules, known as generally accepted accounting principles (GAAP), to be the gold standard—the best system for reporting earnings and other financial information. Then came the subprime mortgage meltdown and the global economic crisis, which caused many to question the effectiveness and superiority of GAAP.

In 2008, the Securities and Exchange Commission (SEC) unanimously approved a plan to require U.S. companies to use a set of global accounting rules, known as International Financial Reporting Standards (IFRS), for all of the financial reports that they must file with the Commission. Under the plan, the use of GAAP will be phased out, with final approval of rules implementing the IFRS scheduled for 2011.

Why Shift to Global Accounting Standards?   The SEC decided to replace the rules-based GAAP with the principles-based IFRS for several reasons. GAAP rules are detailed and fill nearly 25,000 pages. The IFRS are simpler and more straightforward, spanning only 2,500 pages, and they focus more on overriding principles than on specific rules.

Consequently, companies should eventually find it less difficult to comply with the international rules, and this should lead to cost savings. Another benefit is that investors will find it easier to make cross-country comparisons between, say, a technology company in the Silicon Valley and one in Germany or Japan.

Furthermore, having uniform accounting rules that apply to all nations makes sense in a global economy. The European Union and 113 other nations, including Australia, Canada, China, India, and Mexico, have already adopted the IFRS. In fact, most of the United States' trading partners use the global rules. The widespread use of the IFRS is why some large multinational firms embraced the SEC's decision. By switching to the IFRS, multinational companies will no longer have to prepare different financial reports for their subsidiaries located in various countries around the world.

The Downside to Adopting Global Rules   Despite these benefits, the shift to the global rules has some drawbacks. For one thing, the switch will be both costly and time consuming. Companies will have to upgrade their communications and software systems, study and implement the new rules, and train their employees, accountants, and tax attorneys. To ease the transition, the SEC has set up a multiyear timetable for converting to the IFRS. Although 110 of the largest multinational companies began using the IFRS in 2009, they are not legally required to do so until 2014. Smaller firms will make the change in 2015, and the smallest publicly reporting companies will be required to shift by 2016. Nonetheless, some of the smaller U.S. firms may find it difficult to absorb the costs of converting to the IFRS.

Another issue is that although the IFRS rules are simpler, they may not be better than GAAP. Because the global rules are broader and less detailed, they give companies more leeway in reporting, so less financial information may be disclosed. Reports have also indicated that using the IFRS can lead to wide variances in profit reporting and tends to boost earnings above what they would have been under GAAP. Finally, the role of the U.S. Financial Accounting Standards Board and the SEC in shaping and overseeing accounting standards will necessarily be reduced because the London-based International Accounting Standards Board sets the IFRS.

• **Application to Today's World**   *The shift to the IFRS has received broad bipartisan political support even in the face of the current economic crisis. Nevertheless, it will take years for U.S. companies to completely implement the global accounting rules. Business students should study and understand the global accounting rules so that they will be prepared to use these rules in their future careers.*

• **Relevant Web Sites**   To locate information on the Web concerning the SEC's adoption of the International Financial Reporting Standards, go to this text's Web site at www.cengage.com/blaw/blt, select "Chapter 34," and click on "URLs for Landmarks."

dance with standard accounting procedures, to designate a balance sheet as "unaudited." An accountant will also be held liable for failure to disclose to a client the facts or circumstances that give reason to believe that misstatements have been made or that a fraud has been committed.

Defenses to Negligence.   If an accountant is found guilty of negligence, the client can collect damages for losses that arose from the accountant's negligence. An accountant facing a claim of negligence, however, has several possible defenses, including the following:

1. The accountant was not negligent.
2. If the accountant was negligent, this negligence was not the proximate cause of the client's losses.
3. The client was also negligent (depending on whether state law allows contributory negligence as a defense).

ATTORNEY'S DUTY OF CARE   The conduct of attorneys is governed by rules established by each state and by the American Bar Association's Code of Professional Responsibility and Model Rules of Professional Conduct. All attorneys owe a duty to provide competent and diligent representation. Attorneys are required to be familiar with well-settled principles of law applicable to a case and to discover law that can be found through a reasonable amount of research. The lawyer must also investigate and discover facts that could materially affect the client's legal rights.

In judging an attorney's performance, the standard used will normally be that of a reasonably competent general practitioner of ordinary skill, experience, and capacity. If the attorney holds himself or herself out as having expertise in a particular area of law, the standard is that of a reasonably competent specialist of ordinary skill, experience, and capacity in that area of the law.

When an attorney fails to exercise reasonable care and professional judgment, she or he breaches the duty of care. The plaintiff must then prove that the breach actually caused him or her some injury. **EXAMPLE 34.2**   Attorney Lynette Boehmer allows the statute of limitations to lapse on the claim of Karen Anderson, a client. Boehmer can be held liable for **malpractice** (professional negligence) because Anderson can no longer pursue her claim and has lost a potential award of damages. •

Malpractice Professional misconduct or unreasonable lack of skill; the failure of a professional to use the skills and learning common to the average reputable members of the profession or the skills and learning the professional claims to possess, resulting in injury, loss, or damage to those relying on the professional.

Liability for Fraud

An accountant may be found liable for either actual fraud or constructive fraud. Recall from Chapter 12 that fraud, or misrepresentation, involves the following elements:

1. A misrepresentation of a material fact has occurred.
2. There is an intent to deceive.
3. The innocent party has justifiably relied on the misrepresentation.
4. To obtain damages, the innocent party must have been injured.

A professional may be held liable for *actual fraud* when he or she intentionally misstates a material fact to mislead a client and the client is injured as a result of her or his justifiable reliance on the misstated fact. A material fact is one that a reasonable person would consider important in deciding whether to act.

In contrast, a professional may be held liable for *constructive* fraud whether or not he or she acted with fraudulent intent. **EXAMPLE 34.3**   Paula, an accountant, is conducting an audit of National Computing Company (NCC). Paula accepts the explanations of Ron, an NCC officer, regarding certain financial irregularities, despite evidence that contradicts those explanations and indicates that the irregularities may be illegal. Paula's conduct could be characterized as an intentional failure to perform a duty in reckless disregard of the consequences of such failure. This would constitute gross negligence and could be held to be constructive fraud. • Both actual and constructive fraud are potential sources of legal liability for an accountant or other professional.

For fraudulent conduct, an accountant may also suffer penalties imposed by a state board of accountancy, as the following case illustrates.

Case 34.1 Walsh v. State

Nebraska Supreme Court, 276 Neb. 1034, 759 N.W.2d 100 (2009).

FACTS   Stephen Teiper wrote a letter to the Nebraska Board of Public Accountancy to accuse his brother-in-law, Michael Walsh, a certified public accountant (CPA), of impersonating Teiper on the phone to obtain financial information from Teiper's insurance company. The board filed a complaint against Walsh for a violation of its rules. At a hearing, Walsh admitted that he had impersonated Teiper, but argued that Teiper had provided his personal

Case 34.1–Continued

©Sasha Radosavljevich, 2009. Used under license from Shutterstock.com

Did a CPA who impersonated someone on the phone to obtain financial information breach his professional standards?

information to Walsh for this purpose. The board found that Walsh had committed a "discreditable act" and concluded that his conduct was reprehensible and reflected adversely on his fitness to engage in the practice of public accountancy. As sanctions, the board reprimanded Walsh, placed him on probation for three months, and ordered him to attend four hours of continuing education in ethics. The board also ordered him to pay the costs of the hearing. Walsh petitioned a Nebraska state court, which affirmed the orders. Walsh appealed.

ISSUE Is there a sufficient connection between the practice of public accountancy and Walsh's conduct to allow the board to discipline him?

DECISION Yes. The Nebraska Supreme Court affirmed the lower court's decision. Walsh's actions reflected adversely on the accountancy profession, which demands a high level of honesty and integrity.

REASON A CPA cannot impersonate another person and "make false statements," or otherwise commit fraud, without "tainting" the CPA's reputation and the reputation of the accountancy profession. Like attorneys and other professionals, CPAs are held to "a high degree of moral and ethical integrity" because laypersons depend on their "honesty, integrity, sound professional judgment, and compliance with government regulations." The Nebraska Board of Public Accountancy has the authority to issue rules to "establish and maintain a high standard of integrity and dignity in the profession of public accountancy." Under these rules, a CPA "shall not commit an act that reflects adversely" on his or her fitness to practice the profession. The board can discipline CPAs who do not follow these standards and can impose various sanctions, including those levied on Walsh.

FOR CRITICAL ANALYSIS—Ethical Consideration *Was the specific reason for Walsh's impersonation significant to the result in this case? Why or why not?*

▶ Potential Liability to Third Parties

Traditionally, an accountant or other professional did not owe any duty to a third person with whom she or he had no direct contractual relationship—that is, to any person not in *privity of contract.* A professional's duty was only to her or his client. Violations of statutory laws, fraud, and other intentional or reckless acts of wrongdoing were the only exceptions to this general rule.

Today, numerous third parties—including investors, shareholders, creditors, corporate managers and directors, and regulatory agencies—rely on professional opinions, such as those of auditors, when making decisions. In view of this extensive reliance, many courts have all but abandoned the privity requirement in regard to accountants' liability to third parties.

In this section, we focus primarily on the potential liability of auditors to third parties. Understanding an auditor's common law liability to third parties is critical because often, when a business fails, its independent auditor (accountant) is one of the few potentially solvent defendants. The majority of courts now hold that auditors can be held liable to third parties for negligence, but the standard for the imposition of this liability varies. There generally are three different views of accountants' liability to third parties, each of which we discuss below.

The *Ultramares* Rule

The traditional rule regarding an accountant's liability to third parties was enunciated by Chief Judge Benjamin Cardozo in *Ultramares Corp. v. Touche,* a case decided in 1931.[3] **CASE EXAMPLE 34.4** Fred Stern & Company hired the public accounting firm of Touche, Niven & Company to review Stern's financial records and prepare a balance sheet for the year ending December 31, 1923.[4] Touche prepared the balance sheet and supplied Stern with thirty-two certified copies. According to the certified balance sheet, Stern had a net worth (assets less

---

3. 255 N.Y. 170, 174 N.E. 441 (1931).

4. Banks, creditors, stockholders, purchasers, or sellers often rely on a balance sheet as a basis for making decisions relating to a company's business.

liabilities) of $1,070,715.26. In reality, however, Stern's liabilities exceeded its assets—the company's records had been falsified by insiders at Stern to reflect a positive net worth (assets exceed liabilities). In reliance on the certified balance sheets, Ultramares Corporation loaned substantial amounts to Stern. After Stern was declared bankrupt, Ultramares brought an action against Touche for negligence in an attempt to recover damages. ●

THE REQUIREMENT OF PRIVITY   The New York Court of Appeals (that state's highest court) refused to impose liability on the Touche accountants and concluded that they owed a duty of care only to those persons for whose "primary benefit" the statements were intended. In this case, Stern was the only person for whose primary benefit the statements were intended. The court held that in the absence of privity or a relationship "so close as to approach that of privity," a party could not recover from an accountant. The court's requirement of privity has since been referred to as the *Ultramares* rule, or the New York rule.

CASE EXAMPLE 34.5   Toro Company supplied equipment and credit to Summit Power Equipment Distributors and required Summit to submit audited reports so that Toro could evaluate the distributor's financial condition. Summit supplied Toro with reports prepared by accountants at Krouse, Kern & Company, which allegedly contained mistakes and omissions regarding Summit's financial condition. Toro extended and renewed large amounts of credit to Summit in reliance on the audited reports, but Summit was unable to repay these amounts. Toro brought a negligence action against the accounting firm and proved that accountants at Krouse knew the reports it furnished would be used by Summit to induce Toro to extend credit. Nevertheless, under the *Ultramares* rule, the court refused to hold the accounting firm liable because the firm was not in privity with Toro.[5] ●

MODIFIED TO ALLOW "NEAR PRIVITY"   The *Ultramares* rule was restated and somewhat modified in a 1985 New York case, *Credit Alliance Corp. v. Arthur Andersen & Co.*[6] In that case, the court held that if a third party has a sufficiently close relationship or nexus (link or connection) with an accountant, then the *Ultramares* privity requirement may be satisfied even if no accountant-client relationship is established. The rule enunciated in the *Credit Alliance* case is often referred to as the "near privity" rule. Only a minority of states have adopted this rule of accountants' liability to third parties.

The *Restatement* Rule

The *Ultramares* rule has been severely criticized because much of the work performed by auditors is intended for use by persons who are not parties to the contract. Thus, it is asserted that the auditors owe a duty to these third parties. Consequently, there has been an erosion of the *Ultramares* rule, and accountants have increasingly been exposed to potential liability to third parties. The majority of courts have adopted the position taken by the *Restatement (Second) of Torts*, which states that accountants are subject to liability for negligence not only to their clients but also to foreseen, or *known*, users—or classes of users—of their reports or financial statements.

Under Section 552(2) of the *Restatement (Second) of Torts*, an accountant's liability extends to

1. Persons for whose benefit and guidance the accountant intends to supply the information or knows that the recipient intends to supply it, and
2. Persons whom the accountant intends the information to influence or knows that the recipient so intends.

---

5. *Toro Co. v. Krouse, Kern & Co.*, 827 F.2d 155 (7th Cir. 1987).

6. 65 N.Y.2d 536, 483 N.E.2d 110 (1985). A "relationship sufficiently intimate to be equated with privity" is enough for a third party to sue another's accountant for negligence.

EXAMPLE 34.6   Steve, an accountant, prepares a financial statement for Tech Software, Inc., a client, knowing that the client will submit that statement to First National Bank to secure a loan. If Steve makes negligent misstatements or omissions in the statement, he may be held liable by the bank because he knew that the bank would rely on his work product when deciding whether to make the loan. •

Liability to Reasonably Foreseeable Users

A small minority of courts hold accountants liable to any users whose reliance on an accountant's statements or reports was *reasonably foreseeable*. This standard has been criticized as extending liability too far and exposing accountants to massive liability.

The majority of courts have concluded that the *Restatement's* approach is more reasonable because it allows accountants to control their exposure to liability. Liability is "fixed by the accountants' particular knowledge at the moment the audit is published," not by the foreseeability of the harm that might occur to a third party after the report is released.

Liability of Attorneys

Like accountants, attorneys may be held liable under the common law to third parties who rely on legal opinions to their detriment. Generally, an attorney is not liable to a nonclient unless there is fraud (or malicious conduct) by the attorney. The liability principles stated in Section 552 of the *Restatement (Second) of Torts,* however, may apply to attorneys as well as to accountants.

The Sarbanes-Oxley Act of 2002

As previously mentioned, in 2002 Congress enacted the Sarbanes-Oxley Act. The act imposes a number of strict requirements on both domestic and foreign public accounting firms that provide auditing services to companies ("issuers") whose securities are sold to public investors. The act defines the term *issuer* as a company that has securities that are registered under Section 12 of the Securities Exchange Act of 1934, that is required to file reports under Section 15(d) of the 1934 act, or that files—or has filed—a registration statement that has not yet become effective under the Securities Act of 1933 (see Chapter 31).

The Public Company Accounting Oversight Board

Among other things, the Sarbanes-Oxley Act increased the degree of government oversight of public accounting practices by creating the Public Company Accounting Oversight Board, which reports to the Securities and Exchange Commission. The board consists of a chair and four other members. The purpose of the board is to oversee the audit of public companies that are subject to securities laws. The goal is to protect public investors and to ensure that public accounting firms comply with the provisions of the Sarbanes-Oxley Act.

Applicability to Public Accounting Firms

Titles I and II of the act set forth the key provisions relating to the duties of the oversight board and the requirements relating to *public accounting firms*—defined by the act as firms and associated persons that are "engaged in the practice of public accounting or preparing or issuing audit reports." These provisions are summarized in Exhibit 34–1 on the next page. (Provisions relating to corporate fraud and the responsibilities of corporate officers and directors were described in Chapter 31 and listed in Exhibit 31–4 on page 799.)

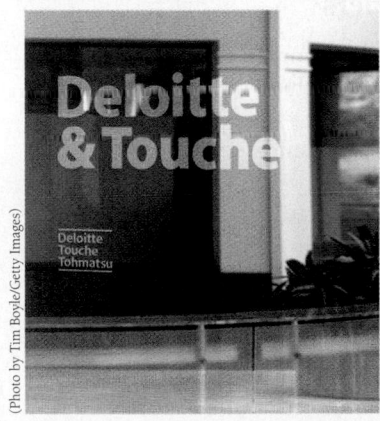

To the extent that Deloitte & Touche engages in auditing public companies, its procedures are overseen by the Public Company Accounting Oversight Board.

(Photo by: Tim Boyle/Getty Images)

● *Exhibit* 34–1 Key Provisions of the Sarbanes-Oxley Act of 2002 Relating to Public Accounting Firms

AUDITOR INDEPENDENCE

To help ensure that auditors remain independent of the firms that they audit, Title II of the Sarbanes-Oxley Act does the following:

- Makes it unlawful for Registered Public Accounting Firms (RPAFs) to perform both audit and nonaudit services for the same company at the same time. Nonaudit services include the following:

  1. Bookkeeping or other services related to the accounting records or financial statements of the audit client.
  2. Financial information systems design and implementation.
  3. Appraisal or valuation services.
  4. Fairness opinions.
  5. Management functions.
  6. Broker or dealer, investment adviser, or investment banking services.

- Requires preapproval for most auditing services from the issuer's (the corporation's) audit committee.

- Requires audit partner rotation by prohibiting RPAFs from providing audit services to an issuer if either the lead audit partner or the audit partner responsible for reviewing the audit has provided such services to that corporation in each of the prior five years.

- Requires RPAFs to make timely reports to the audit committees of the corporations. The report must indicate all critical accounting policies and practices to be used; all alternative treatments of financial information within generally accepted accounting principles that have been discussed with the corporation's management officials, the ramifications of the use of such alternative treatments, and the treatment preferred by the auditor; and other material written communications between the auditor and the corporation's management.

- Makes it unlawful for an RPAF to provide auditing services to an issuer if the corporation's chief executive officer, chief financial officer, chief accounting officer, or controller was previously employed by the auditor and participated in any capacity in the audit of the corporation during the one-year period preceding the date that the audit began.

DOCUMENT RETENTION AND DESTRUCTION

- The Sarbanes-Oxley Act provides that anyone who destroys, alters, or falsifies records with the intent to obstruct or influence a federal investigation or in relation to bankruptcy proceedings can be criminally prosecuted and sentenced to a fine, imprisonment for up to twenty years, or both.

- The act also requires accountants who audit or review publicly traded companies to retain all working papers related to the audit or review for a period of five years (now amended to seven years). Violators can be sentenced to a fine, imprisonment for up to ten years, or both.

Requirements for Maintaining Working Papers

Working Papers The various documents used and developed by an accountant during an audit. Working papers include notes, computations, memoranda, copies, and other papers that make up the work product of an accountant's services to a client.

Performing an audit for a client involves an accumulation of **working papers**—the various documents used and developed during the audit. These include notes, computations, memoranda, copies, and other papers that make up the work product of an accountant's services to a client. Under the common law, which in this instance has been codified in a number of states, working papers remain the accountant's property. It is important for accountants to retain such records in the event that they need to defend against lawsuits for negligence or other actions in which their competence is challenged. The client also has a right to access an accountant's working papers because they reflect the client's financial situation. On a client's request, an accountant must return to the client any of the client's records or journals, and failure to do so may result in liability.

"Destroy the old files, but make copies first."

Samuel Goldwyn, 1879–1974
(American motion picture producer)

Section 802(a)(1) of the Sarbanes-Oxley Act provides that accountants must maintain working papers relating to an audit or review for five years—subsequently increased to seven years—from the end of the fiscal period in which the audit or review was concluded. A knowing violation of this requirement will subject the accountant to a fine, imprisonment for up to ten years, or both.

Ethical Issue ⚖ ·········

> ***Are the high costs of complying with the Sarbanes-Oxley Act justified by more ethical conduct?***
> Since its enactment, critics have complained that the costs of complying with the Sarbanes-Oxley Act greatly outweigh the perceived benefits. In fact, studies estimate that a public company spends, on average, at least $2.9 million annually complying with the act's provisions. These funds could otherwise have been distributed as dividends to shareholders or reinvested to finance the company's growth and thereby provide more jobs. The burdens of complying with the Sarbanes-Oxley Act have also led many companies to go private, turning over control to private equity firms (businesses that own shares in companies that are not listed on a public stock exchange). There is also some doubt as to whether the act has been effective in improving corporate ethics and accountability.

▶ Potential Statutory Liability of Accountants under Securities Laws

Both civil and criminal liability may be imposed on accountants under the Securities Act of 1933, the Securities Exchange Act of 1934, and the Private Securities Litigation Reform Act of 1995.[7]

Liability under the Securities Act of 1933

The Securities Act of 1933 requires registration statements to be filed with the Securities and Exchange Commission (SEC) prior to an offering of securities (see Chapter 31).[8] Accountants frequently prepare and certify the issuer's financial statements that are included in the registration statement.

LIABILITY UNDER SECTION 11 Section 11 of the Securities Act of 1933 imposes civil liability on accountants for misstatements and omissions of material facts in registration statements. An accountant may be liable if he or she prepared any financial statements included in the registration statement that "contained an untrue statement of a material fact or omitted to state a material fact required to be stated therein or necessary to make the statements therein not misleading."[9]

Under Section 11, an accountant's liability for a misstatement or omission of a material fact in a registration statement extends to anyone who acquires a security covered by the registration statement. A purchaser of a security need only demonstrate that she or he has suffered a loss on the security. Proof of reliance on the materially false statement or misleading omission ordinarily is not required. Nor is there a requirement of privity between the accountant and the security purchasers.

Due Diligence A required standard of care that certain professionals, such as accountants, must meet to avoid liability for securities violations.

The Due Diligence Standard. Section 11 imposes a duty on accountants to use **due diligence** in preparing the financial statements included in the filed registration statements. After a purchaser has proved a loss on the security, the accountant has the burden of showing that he or she exercised due diligence in preparing the financial statements. To avoid liability, the accountant must show that he or she had, "after reasonable investigation, reasonable grounds to believe and did believe, at the time such part of the registration statement became effective, that the statements therein were true and that there was no omission of a material fact required to be stated therein or necessary to make the statements therein not misleading."[10] Failure to follow GAAP and GAAS is also proof of a lack of due diligence.

---

7. Civil and criminal liability may also be imposed on accountants and other professionals under other statutes, including the Racketeer Influenced and Corrupt Organizations Act (RICO). RICO was discussed in Chapter 6.

8. Many securities and transactions are expressly exempted from the 1933 act.

9. 15 U.S.C. Section 77k(a).

10. 15 U.S.C. Section 77k(b)(3).

In particular, the due diligence standard places a burden on accountants to verify information furnished by a corporation's officers and directors. The burden of proving due diligence requires an accountant to demonstrate that she or he is free from negligence or fraud. Merely asking questions is not always sufficient to satisfy the requirement. Accountants can be held liable for failing to detect danger signals in documents furnished by corporate officers that, under GAAS, require further investigation under the circumstances.[11]

Preventing Legal Disputes

When "danger signals" exist, you must investigate the situation further. Remember that persons other than accountants, such as corporate directors, officers, and managers, can also be liable for failing to perform due diligence. Courts are more likely to impose liability when someone has ignored warning signs or red flags that suggest accounting errors or misstatements are present. To avoid liability, always investigate the facts underlying financial statements that appear "too good to be true." Compare recent financial statements with earlier ones, read minutes of shareholders' and directors' meetings, and inspect changes in material contracts, bad debts, and newly discovered liabilities. Know what is required to meet due diligence standards in the particular jurisdiction and conduct yourself in a manner that is above reproach.

Defenses to Liability.   Besides proving that he or she has acted with due diligence, an accountant can raise the following defenses to Section 11 liability:

1. There were no misstatements or omissions.
2. The misstatements or omissions were not of material facts.
3. The misstatements or omissions had no causal connection to the plaintiff's loss.
4. The plaintiff-purchaser invested in the securities knowing of the misstatements or omissions.

LIABILITY UNDER SECTION 12(2)   Section 12(2) of the Securities Act of 1933 imposes civil liability for fraud in relation to offerings or sales of securities.[12] Liability is based on communication to an investor, whether orally or in the written prospectus,[13] of an untrue statement or omission of a material fact.

PENALTIES AND SANCTIONS FOR VIOLATIONS   Those who purchase securities and suffer harm as a result of a false or omitted statement, or some other violation, may bring a suit in a federal court to recover their losses and other damages. The U.S. Department of Justice brings criminal actions against those who commit willful violations. The penalties include fines of up to $10,000, imprisonment for up to five years, or both. The SEC is authorized to seek an injunction against a willful violator to prevent further violations. The SEC can also ask a court to grant other relief, such as an order to a violator to refund profits derived from an illegal transaction.

Liability under the Securities Exchange Act of 1934

Under Sections 18 and 10(b) of the Securities Exchange Act of 1934 and SEC Rule 10b-5, an accountant may be found liable for fraud. A plaintiff has a substantially heavier burden of proof under the 1934 act than under the 1933 act, because under the 1934 act an accountant does not have to prove due diligence to escape liability.

---

11. See *In re Cardinal Health, Inc. Securities Litigation,* 426 F.Supp.2d 688 (S.D. Ohio 2006); and *In re WorldCom, Inc. Securities Litigation,* 352 F.Supp.2d 472 (S.D.N.Y. 2005).
12. 15 U.S.C. Section 77l.
13. As discussed in Chapter 31, a *prospectus* contains financial disclosures about the corporation for the benefit of potential investors.

LIABILITY UNDER SECTION 18   Section 18 of the 1934 act imposes civil liability on an accountant who makes or causes to be made in any application, report, or document a statement that at the time and in light of the circumstances was false or misleading with respect to any material fact.[14]

Section 18 liability is narrow in that it applies only to applications, reports, documents, and registration statements filed with the SEC. This remedy is further limited in that it applies only to sellers and purchasers. Under Section 18, a seller or purchaser must prove one of the following:

1. That the false or misleading statement affected the price of the security.
2. That the purchaser or seller relied on the false or misleading statement in making the purchase or sale and was not aware of the inaccuracy of the statement.

An accountant will not be liable for violating Section 18 if he or she acted in good faith in preparing the financial statement. To demonstrate good faith, an accountant must show that he or she had no knowledge that the financial statement was false and misleading. Acting in good faith also requires that the accountant lacked any intent to deceive, manipulate, defraud, or seek unfair advantage over another party. (Note that "mere" negligence in preparing a financial statement does not lead to liability under the 1934 act. This differs from the 1933 act, under which an accountant is liable for *all* negligent acts.)

In addition to the good faith defense, accountants can escape liability by proving that the buyer or seller of the security in question knew the financial statement was false and misleading. Sellers and purchasers must bring a cause of action "within one year after the discovery of the facts constituting the cause of action and within three years after such cause of action accrued."[15] A court also has the discretion to assess reasonable costs, including attorneys' fees, against accountants who violate this section.

LIABILITY UNDER SECTION 10(B) AND RULE 10B-5   Accountants additionally face potential legal liability under the antifraud provisions contained in the Securities Exchange Act of 1934 and SEC Rule 10b-5. The scope of these antifraud provisions is very broad and allows private parties to bring civil actions against violators.

Section 10(b) makes it unlawful for any person, including accountants, to use, in connection with the purchase or sale of any security, any manipulative or deceptive device or contrivance in contravention of SEC rules and regulations.[16] Rule 10b-5 further makes it unlawful for any person, by use of any means or instrumentality of interstate commerce, to do the following:

1. Employ any device, scheme, or artifice (pretense) to defraud.
2. Make any untrue statement of a material fact or omit to state a material fact necessary to make the statements made, in light of the circumstances, not misleading.
3. Engage in any act, practice, or course of business that operates or would operate as a fraud or deceit on any person, in connection with the purchase or sale of any security.[17]

Accountants may be held liable only to sellers or purchasers of securities under Section 10(b) and Rule 10b-5. Privity is not necessary for a recovery. An accountant may be found liable not only for fraudulent misstatements of material facts in written material filed with the SEC, but also for any fraudulent oral statements or omissions made in connection with the purchase or sale of any security.

---

14. 15 U.S.C. Section 78r(a).
15. 15 U.S.C. Section 78r(c).
16. 15 U.S.C. Section 78j(b)
17. 17 C.F.R. Section 240.10b-5.

For a plaintiff to succeed in recovering damages under these antifraud provisions, however, he or she must prove intent (*scienter*) to commit the fraudulent or deceptive act. Ordinary negligence is not enough.

Do accountants have a duty to correct misstatements that they discover in *previous* financial statements? What if they know that potential investors are relying on those statements? Those were the questions in the following case.

Case 34.2   Overton v. Todman & Co., CPAs, P.C.

United States Court of Appeals, Second Circuit, 478 F.3d 479 (2007).

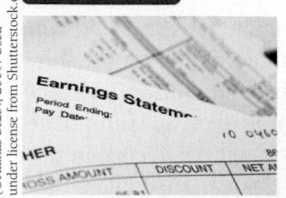

Must an accounting firm make public its new knowledge of prior misstatements?

FACTS From 1999 through 2002, Todman & Company, CPAs, P.C., audited the financial statements of Direct Brokerage, Inc. (DBI), a broker-dealer in New York registered with the Securities and Exchange Commission (SEC). Each year, Todman issued an unqualified opinion that DBI's financial statements were accurate. DBI filed its statements and Todman's opinions with the SEC. Despite the certifications of accuracy, Todman made significant errors that concealed DBI's largest liability—its payroll taxes—in the 1999 and 2000 audits. The errors came to light in 2003 when the New York State Division of Taxation subpoenaed DBI's payroll records, and it became clear that the company had not filed or paid its payroll taxes for 1999 and 2000. This put DBI in a precarious financial position, owing the state more than $3 million in unpaid taxes, interest, and penalties. To meet its needs, DBI sought outside investors, including David Overton, who relied on DBI's statements and Todman's opinion for 2002 to invest in DBI. When DBI collapsed under the weight of its liabilities in 2004, Overton and others filed a suit in a federal district court against Todman, asserting, among other things, fraud under Section 10(b) and Rule 10b-5. The court dismissed the complaint. The plaintiffs appealed to the U.S. Court of Appeals for the Second Circuit.

ISSUE Is an accountant liable for securities fraud if the accountant certified a financial statement containing a misstatement and later learned of the misstatement but failed to correct it, even though the accountant knew that investors were relying on the statement?

DECISION Yes. The U.S. Court of Appeals for the Second Circuit held that an accountant is liable in these circumstances under Section 10(b) and Rule 10b-5. The court vacated the lower court's dismissal and remanded the case "for further proceedings consistent with this opinion."

REASON The appellate court pointed out that "[a]ny person or entity," including an accountant, "who employs a manipulative device or makes a material misstatement (or omission) on which a purchaser or seller of securities relies may be liable as a primary violator under [Section] 10b-5, assuming all of the requirements for primary liability under Rule 10b-5 are met." To be liable, one of the requirements is a "duty to speak." Such a duty arises "when one party has information that the other party is entitled to know because of a fiduciary or other similar relation of trust and confidence between them." When accountants issue a certified opinion, they create the required special relationship with investors. Thus, accountants have a duty to take reasonable steps to correct misstatements that they discover in previous financial statements on which they know the public is relying. Silence in this situation can constitute a false or misleading statement under Section 10(b) and Rule 10b-5. Among other authorities, the court cited Section 10(b), which covers "any person," and a United States Supreme Court decision that "labeled a critical element under [Section] 10(b) and Rule 10b-5: reliance by potential investors on the accountant's omission."[a]

WHAT IF THE FACTS WERE DIFFERENT? *If Todman had conducted an audit for DBI but had not issued a certified opinion about DBI's financial statements, would the result in this case have been the same? Explain.*

a. *Central Bank of Denver v. First Interstate Bank of Denver,* 511 U.S. 164, 114 S.Ct. 1439, 128 L.Ed.2d 119 (1994).

The Private Securities Litigation Reform Act of 1995

The Private Securities Litigation Reform Act of 1995 made some changes to the potential liability of accountants and other professionals in securities fraud cases. Among other things, the act imposed a new statutory obligation on accountants. An auditor must use adequate procedures in an audit to detect any illegal acts of the company being audited. If something illegal is detected, the auditor must disclose it to the company's board of directors, the audit committee, or the SEC, depending on the circumstances.[18]

---

18. 15 U.S.C. Section 78j-1.

The 1995 act also provides that, in most situations, a party is liable only for the proportion of damages for which he or she is responsible.[19] An accountant who participates in, but is unaware of, illegal conduct may not be liable for the entire loss caused by the illegality.

EXAMPLE 34.7 Nina, an accountant, helps the president and owner of Midstate Trucking Company draft financial statements that misrepresent Midstate's financial condition, but Nina is not actually aware of the fraud. Nina might be held liable, but the amount of her liability could be proportionately less than the entire loss. ●

If an accountant knowingly aids and abets a primary violator, the SEC can seek an injunction or monetary damages. **EXAMPLE 34.8** Smith & Jones, an accounting firm, performs an audit for ABC Sales Company that is so inadequate as to constitute gross negligence. ABC uses the materials provided by Smith & Jones as part of a scheme to defraud investors. When the scheme is uncovered, the SEC can bring an action against Smith & Jones for aiding and abetting on the ground that the firm knew or should have known of the material misrepresentations that were in its audit and on which investors were likely to rely. ●

▶ Potential Criminal Liability

The Securities and Exchange Acts of 1933 and 1934 created accountants' violations that can be criminally prosecuted.

An accountant may be found criminally liable for violations of the Securities Act of 1933, the Securities Exchange Act of 1934, the Internal Revenue Code, and both state and federal criminal codes. Under both the 1933 act and the 1934 act, accountants may be subject to criminal penalties for *willful* violations—imprisonment for up to five years and/or a fine of up to $10,000 under the 1933 act and imprisonment for up to ten years and a fine of $100,000 under the 1934 act. Under the Sarbanes-Oxley Act of 2002, for a securities filing that is accompanied by an accountant's false or misleading certified audit statement, the accountant may be fined up to $5 million, imprisoned for up to twenty years, or both.

The Internal Revenue Code makes aiding or assisting in the preparation of a false tax return a felony punishable by a fine of $100,000 ($500,000 in the case of a corporation) and imprisonment for up to three years.[20] This provision applies to anyone who prepares tax returns for others for compensation, and not just to accountants.[21] A penalty of $250 per tax return is levied on tax preparers for negligent understatement of the client's tax liability. For willful understatement of tax liability or reckless or intentional disregard of rules or regulations, a penalty of $1,000 is imposed.[22]

A tax preparer may also be subject to penalties for failing to furnish the taxpayer with a copy of the return, failing to sign the return, or failing to furnish the appropriate tax identification numbers.[23] In addition, those who prepare tax returns for others may be fined $1,000 per document for aiding and abetting another's understatement of tax liability (the penalty is increased to $10,000 in corporate cases).[24] The tax preparer's liability is limited to one penalty per taxpayer per tax year.

In most states, criminal penalties may be imposed for such actions as knowingly certifying false or fraudulent reports; falsifying, altering, or destroying books of account; and obtaining property or credit through the use of false financial statements.

---

19. 15 U.S.C. Section 78u-4(g).
20. 26 U.S.C. Section 7206(2).
21. 26 U.S.C. Section 7701(a)(36).
22. 26 U.S.C. Section 6694.
23. 26 U.S.C. Section 6695.
24. 26 U.S.C. Section 6701.

Confidentiality and Privilege

Professionals are restrained by the ethical tenets of their professions to keep all communications with their clients confidential.

Attorney-Client Relationships

The confidentiality of attorney-client communications is protected by law, which confers a privilege on such communications. This privilege is granted because of the need for full disclosure to the attorney of the facts of a client's case. To encourage frankness, confidential attorney-client communications relating to representation are normally held in strictest confidence and protected by law. The attorney and her or his employees may not discuss the client's case with anyone—even under court order—without the client's permission. The client holds the privilege, and only the client may waive it—by disclosing privileged information to someone outside the privilege, for example.

Note, however, that since the Sarbanes-Oxley Act was enacted in 2002, the SEC has implemented new rules requiring attorneys who become aware that a client has violated securities laws to report the violation to the SEC. Reporting a client's misconduct could be a breach of the attorney-client privilege, however, an issue that has caused controversy in the legal community.

Accountant-Client Relationships

In a few states, accountant-client communications are privileged by state statute. In these states, accountant-client communications may not be revealed even in court or in court-sanctioned proceedings without the client's permission. The majority of states, however, abide by the common law, which provides that, if a court so orders, an accountant must disclose information about his or her client to the court. Physicians and other professionals may similarly be compelled to disclose in court information given to them in confidence by patients or clients.

Communications between professionals and their clients—other than those between an attorney and her or his client—are not privileged under federal law. In cases involving federal law, state-provided rights to confidentiality of accountant-client communications are not recognized. Thus, in those cases, in response to a court order, an accountant must provide the information sought.

 Reviewing . . . Liability of Accountants and Other Professionals

Superior Wholesale Corporation planned to purchase Regal Furniture, Inc., and wished to determine Regal's net worth. Superior hired Lynette Shuebke, of the accounting firm Shuebke Delgado, to review an audit that had been prepared by Norman Chase, the accountant for Regal. Shuebke advised Superior that Chase had performed a high-quality audit and that Regal's inventory on the audit dates was stated accurately on the general ledger. As a result of these representations, Superior went forward with its purchase of Regal. After the purchase, Superior discovered that the audit by Chase had been materially inaccurate and misleading, primarily because the inventory had been grossly overstated on the balance sheet. Later, a former Regal employee who had begun working for Superior exposed an e-mail exchange between Chase and former Regal chief executive officer Buddy Gantry. The exchange revealed that Chase had cooperated in overstating the inventory and understating Regal's tax liability. Using the information presented in the chapter, answer the following questions.

1. If Shuebke's review was conducted in good faith and conformed to generally accepted accounting principles, could Superior hold Shuebke Delgado liable for negligently failing to detect material omissions in Chase's audit? Why or why not?

2. According to the rule adopted by the majority of courts to determine accountants' liability to third parties, could Chase be liable to Superior?
3. Generally, what requirements must be met before Superior can recover damages under Section 10(b) of the Securities Exchange Act of 1934 and SEC Rule 10b-5? Can Superior meet these requirements?
4. Suppose that a court determined that Chase had aided Regal in willfully understating its tax liability. What is the maximum penalty that could be imposed on Chase?

Linking the Law *to Business Statistics*
Statistical Sampling When Conducting Audits

Some of you taking this business law or legal environment course are doing so as part of your business school curriculum to become certified public accountants (CPAs). Eventually, you may be part of an audit team that regularly examines company statistics to determine whether generally accepted accounting principles have been used to state each firm's net income and net worth. Even if you do not become part of an auditing team, it will be helpful for you to understand how auditors use statistical sampling in their work.

What Statistical Sampling Means

Most of you are familiar with opinion polls, particularly during presidential campaigns. Obviously, pollsters cannot query every potential voter. Instead, they take a statistical sample of potential voters to determine the likely outcome of an election. Such samples are supposed to be random—they should not prejudice the outcome of the poll. Pollsters attempt to sample all types of demographic groups—rural, urban, poor, middle class, rich, African American, Hispanic, white, and more.

Many of the "facts" that are reported about businesses are also based on statistical sampling. If you read that the average automotive cash rebate last year was $4,000 per vehicle, you can be sure that the person citing that number did not examine every single cash rebate in the industry. Rather, a random sampling of rebates was used to arrive at the number.

How Public Accounting Firms Use Statistical Sampling

Public accountants use statistical sampling. Assume that you are working with an audit team and you wish to determine whether the total accounts receivable shown on a client's balance sheet are accurate. Of course, if the business is very small, you could actually look at every single accounts receivable. In large corporations, however, statistical sampling must be used. As an auditor, you would select a subset of accounts receivable and check the validity of each actual account within that small sample. You might take additional samples to confirm your results. In any event, you would draw a conclusion as to whether the amount shown for total accounts receivable on the client's balance sheet was acceptably accurate.

Your Work as an Internal Auditor

As a CPA, you may be hired by a large corporation to be an internal auditor. Your job would involve regular reviews of the same types of financial data that external auditors examine. Thus, you too would have to engage in statistical sampling to make sure that the company's books were accurate.

Assume that your company extends equipment leases to tens of thousands of businesses. Of course, you could access every lease record to determine what percentage of lease payments are being timely paid. Such a task could take more time than you have allocated, however. Instead, you could take a random sample of lease payment data to come up with a relatively accurate estimate of the percentage of lease payments that are being made on time.

In all statistical sampling, assuming that it is random, the larger the sample size, the greater the accuracy. The most accurate sample is not a sample at all—it is the entire universe of whatever you are studying.

FOR CRITICAL ANALYSIS
How does an auditor determine the appropriate size of the sample?

 Key Terms

defalcation 862
due diligence 869
generally accepted accounting principles (GAAP) 861

generally accepted auditing standards (GAAS) 861
malpractice 864

working papers 868

Chapter Summary: Liability of Accountants and Other Professionals

COMMON LAW LIABILITY	
Potential Common Law Liability to Clients (See pages 861–865.)	1. *Breach of contract*–An accountant or other professional who fails to perform according to his or her contractual obligations can be held liable for breach of contract and resulting damages. 2. *Negligence*–An accountant, attorney, or other professional, in performance of her or his duties, must use the care, knowledge, and judgment generally used by professionals in the same or similar circumstances. Failure to do so is negligence. An accountant's violation of generally accepted accounting principles and generally accepted auditing standards is *prima facie* evidence of negligence. 3. *Fraud*–Intentionally misrepresenting a material fact to a client, when the client relies on the misrepresentation, is actual fraud. Gross negligence in performance of duties is constructive fraud.
Potential Liability to Third Parties (See pages 865–867.)	An accountant may be liable for negligence to any third person the accountant knows or should have known will benefit from the accountant's work. The standard for imposing this liability varies, but generally courts follow one of the following rules: 1. *Ultramares rule*–Liability will be imposed only if the accountant is in privity, or near privity, with the third party. 2. *Restatement rule*–Liability will be imposed only if the third party's reliance is foreseen, or known, or if the third party is among a class of foreseen, or known, users. The majority of courts have adopted this rule. 3. *"Reasonably foreseeable user" rule*–Liability will be imposed if the third party's use was reasonably foreseeable.
STATUTORY LIABILITY	
The Sarbanes–Oxley Act of 2002 (See pages 867–869.)	1. *Purpose*–This act imposed requirements on public accounting firms that provide auditing services to companies whose securities are sold to public investors. 2. *Government oversight*–Among other things, the act created the Public Company Accounting Oversight Board to provide government oversight over public accounting practices. 3. *Working papers*–The act requires accountants to maintain working papers relating to an audit or review for seven years from the end of the fiscal period in which the audit or review was concluded. 4. *Other requirements*–See Exhibit 34–1 on page 868.
Securities Act of 1933, Section 11 (See pages 869–870.)	An accountant who makes a false statement or omits a material fact in audited financial statements required for registration of securities under the law may be liable to anyone who acquires securities covered by the registration statement. The accountant's defense is basically the use of due diligence and the reasonable belief that the work was complete and correct. The burden of proof is on the accountant. Willful violations of this act may be subject to criminal penalties.
Securities Act of 1933, Section 12(2) (See page 870.)	An accountant may be liable for aiding and abetting the seller or offeror of securities when a prospectus or communication presented to an investor contained an untrue statement or omission of a material fact. To be liable, the accountant must have known, or at least should have known, that an untrue statement or omission of material fact existed in the offer to sell the security.
Securities Exchange Act of 1934, Sections 10(b) and 18 (See pages 870–873.)	Accountants may be held liable for false and misleading applications, reports, and documents required under the act. The burden is on the plaintiff, and the accountant has numerous defenses, including good faith and lack of knowledge that what was submitted was false.
Potential Criminal Liability (See page 873.)	1. Willful violations of the Securities Act of 1933 and the Securities Exchange Act of 1934 may be subject to criminal penalties. 2. Aiding or assisting in the preparation of a false tax return is a felony. Aiding and abetting an individual's understatement of tax liability is a separate crime. 3. Tax preparers who negligently or willfully understate a client's tax liability or who recklessly or intentionally disregard Internal Revenue rules or regulations are subject to criminal penalties. 4. Tax prepares who fail to provide a taxpayer with a copy of the return, fail to sign the return, or fail to furnish the appropriate tax identification numbers may also be subject to criminal penalties.

ExamPrep

ISSUE SPOTTERS

1 Dave, an accountant, prepares a financial statement for Excel Company, a client, knowing that Excel will use the statement to obtain a loan from First National Bank. Dave makes negligent omissions in the statement that result in a loss to the bank. Can the bank successfully sue Dave? Why or why not?

2 Nora, an accountant, prepares a financial statement as part of a registration statement that Omega, Inc., files with the Securities and Exchange Commission before making a public offering of securities. The statement contains a misstatement of material fact that is not attributable to Nora's fraud or negligence. Pat relies on the misstatement, buys some of the securities, and suffers a loss. Can Nora be held liable to Pat? Explain.

BEFORE THE TEST

Check your answers to the Issue Spotters, and at the same time, take the interactive quiz for this chapter. Go to **www.cengage.com/blaw/blt** and click on "Chapter 34." First, click on "Answers to Issue Spotters" to check your answers. Next, click on "Interactive Quiz" to assess your mastery of the concepts in this chapter. Then click on "Flashcards" to review this chapter's Key Term definitions.

 For Review

Answers for the even-numbered questions in this For Review *section can be found on this text's accompanying Web site at* **www.cengage.com/blaw/blt**. *Select "Chapter 34" and click on "For Review."*

1 Under what common law theories may professionals be liable to clients?
2 What are the rules concerning an auditor's liability to third parties?
3 How might an accountant violate federal securities laws?
4 What crimes might an accountant commit under the Internal Revenue Code?
5 What constrains professionals to keep communications with their clients confidential?

 Hypothetical Scenarios and Case Problems

34–1 The *Ultramares* Rule. Larkin, Inc., retains Howard Perkins to manage its books and prepare its financial statements. Perkins, a certified public accountant, lives in Indiana and practices there. After twenty years, Perkins has become a bit bored with generally accepted accounting principles (GAAP) and has adopted more creative accounting methods. Now, though, Perkins has a problem, as he is being sued by Molly Tucker, one of Larkin's creditors. Tucker alleges that Perkins either knew or should have known that Larkin's financial statements would be distributed to various individuals. Furthermore, she asserts that these financial statements were negligently prepared and seriously inaccurate. What are the consequences of Perkins's failure to follow GAAP? Under the traditional *Ultramares* rule, can Tucker recover damages from Perkins? Explain.

34–2 **?** **Hypothetical Question with Sample Answer** The accounting firm of Goldman, Walters, Johnson & Co. prepared financial statements for Lucy's Fashions, Inc. After reviewing the various financial statements, Happydays

State Bank agreed to loan Lucy's Fashions $35,000 for expansion. When Lucy's Fashions declared bankruptcy under Chapter 11 six months later, Happydays State Bank promptly filed an action against Goldman, Walters, Johnson & Co., alleging negligent preparation of financial statements. Assuming that the court has abandoned the *Ultramares* approach, what is the result? What are the policy reasons for holding accountants liable to third parties with whom they are not in privity?
—**For a sample answer to Question 34–2, go to Appendix E at the end of this text.**

34–3 Accountant's Liability under Rule 10b-5. In early 2010, Bennett, Inc., offered a substantial number of new common shares to the public. Harvey Helms had a long-standing interest in Bennett because his grandfather had once been president of the company. On receiving a prospectus prepared and distributed by Bennett, Helms was dismayed by the pessimism it embodied. Helms decided to delay purchasing stock in the company. Later, Helms asserted that the prospectus prepared by the accountants was overly pessimistic and contained materially misleading statements. Discuss fully how successful Helms would be in bringing a cause of action under Rule 10b-5 against the accountants of Bennett, Inc.

34–4 Case Problem with Sample Answer In October 1993, Marilyn Greenen, a licensed certified public accountant (CPA), began working at the Port of Vancouver, Washington (the Port), as an account manager. She was not directly engaged in public accounting at the Port, but she oversaw the preparation of financial statements and supervised employees with accounting duties. At the start of her employment, she enrolled her husband for benefits under the Port's medical plan. Her marriage was dissolved in November, but she did not notify the Port of the change. In May 1998 and April 1999, the Port confronted her about the divorce, but she did not update her insurance information. After she was terminated, she reimbursed the Port for the additional premiums it had paid for unauthorized coverage for her former spouse. The Washington State Board of Accountancy imposed sanctions on Greenen for "dishonesty and misleading representations" while, in the words of an applicable state statute, "representing oneself as a CPA." Greenen asked a Washington state court to review the case. What might be an appropriate sanction in this case? What might be Greenen's best argument against the board's action? On what reasoning might the court uphold the decision? [*Greenen v. Washington State Board of Accountancy*, 824 Wash. App. 126, 110 P.3d 224 (Div. 2 2005)]

—**After you have answered Problem 34–4, compare your answer with the sample answer given on the Web site that accompanies this text. Go to www.cengage.com/blaw/blt, select "Chapter 34," and click on "Case Problem with Sample Answer."**

34–5 **Confidentiality and Privilege.** Napster, Inc., offered a service that allowed its users to browse digital music files on other users' computers and download selections for free. Music industry principals filed a suit in a federal district court against Napster, alleging copyright infringement. The court ordered Napster to remove from its service files that were identified as infringing. Napster failed to comply and was shut down in July 2001. In October, Bertelsmann AG, a German corporation, loaned Napster $85 million to fund its anticipated transition to a licensed digital music distribution system. The terms allowed Napster to spend the loan on "general, administrative and overhead expenses." In an e-mail, Hank Barry, Napster's chief executive officer, referred to a "side deal" under which Napster could use up to $10 million of the loan to pay litigation expenses. Napster failed to launch the new system before declaring bankruptcy in June 2002. Some of the plaintiffs filed a suit in a federal district court against Bertelsmann, charging that by its loan, it prolonged Napster's infringement. The plaintiffs asked the court to order the disclosure of all attorney-client communications related to the loan. What principle could Bertelsmann assert to protect these communications? What is the purpose of this protection? Should this principle protect a client who consults an attorney for advice that will help the client

commit fraud? Should the court grant the plaintiffs' request? Discuss. [*In re Napster, Inc. Copyright Litigation*, 479 F.3d 1078 (9th Cir. 2007)]

34–6 **Accountant's Liability for Audit.** A West Virginia bank ran its asset value from $100 million to $1 billion over seven years by aggressively marketing subprime loans. The Office of the Comptroller of the Currency, a federal regulator, audited the bank and discovered that the books had been falsified for several years and that the bank was insolvent. The Comptroller closed the bank and brought criminal charges against its managers. The Comptroller fined Grant Thornton, the bank's accounting firm, $300,000 for recklessly failing to meet generally accepted auditing standards during the years it audited the bank. The Comptroller claimed Thornton violated federal law by "participating in . . . unsafe and unsound banking practice." Thornton appealed, contending that it was not involved in bank operations to that extent based on its audit function. What would be the key to determining if the accounting firm could be held liable for that violation of federal law? [*Grant Thornton, LLP v. Office of the Comptroller of the Currency*, 514 F.3d 1328 (D.C.Cir. 2008)]

34–7 **Professional's Liability.** Soon after Teresa DeYoung's husband died, her mother-in-law also died, leaving an inheritance of more than $400,000 for DeYoung's children. DeYoung hired John Ruggerio, an attorney, to ensure that her children would receive it. Ruggerio advised her to invest the funds in his real estate business. She declined. A few months later, $300,000 of the inheritance was sent to Ruggerio. Without telling DeYoung, he deposited the $300,000 in his account and began to use the funds in his real estate business. Nine months later, $109,000 of the inheritance was sent to Ruggerio. He paid this to DeYoung. She asked about the remaining amount. Ruggerio lied to hide his theft. Unable to access these funds, DeYoung's children changed their college plans to attend less expensive institutions. Nearly three years later, DeYoung learned the truth. Can she bring a suit against Ruggerio? If so, on what ground? If not, why not? Did Ruggerio violate any standard of professional ethics? Discuss. [*DeYoung v. Ruggerio*, 2009 VT 9, 971 A.2d 627 (2009)]

34–8 **A Question of Ethics** *Portland Shellfish Co. processes live shellfish in Maine. As one of the firm's two owners, Frank Wetmore held 300 voting and 150 nonvoting shares of the stock. Donna Holden held the other 300 voting shares. Donna's husband, Jeff, managed the company's daily operations, including production, procurement, and sales. The board of directors consisted of Frank and Jeff. In 2001, disagreements arose over the company's management. The Holdens invoked the "Shareholders' Agreement," which provided that "[i]n the event of a deadlock, the directors shall hire an accountant at [MacDonald, Page, Schatz, Fletcher & Co., LLC] to determine the value of the outstanding shares. . . . [E]ach shareholder shall have the right to buy out the other shareholder(s)' interest." MacDonald Page estimated the stock's "fair market value" to be $1.09 million. Donna offered to buy Frank's shares at a price equal to his proportionate share. Frank countered by offering $1.25 million for Donna's shares. Donna rejected Frank's offer and insisted* *that he sell his shares to her or she would sue. In the face of this threat, Frank sold his shares to Donna for $750,705. Believing the stock to be worth more than twice MacDonald Page's estimate, Frank filed a suit in a federal district court against the accountant. [Wetmore v. MacDonald, Page, Schatz, Fletcher & Co., LLC, 476 F.3d 1 (1st Cir. 2007)]*

1 Frank claimed that in valuing the stock, the accountant disregarded "commonly accepted and reliable methods of valuation in favor of less reliable methods." He alleged negligence, among other things. MacDonald Page filed a motion to dismiss the complaint. What are the elements that establish negligence? Which is the most critical element in this case?

2 MacDonald Page evaluated the company's stock by identifying its "fair market value," defined as "[t]he price at which

the property would change hands between a willing buyer and a willing seller, neither being under a compulsion to buy or sell and both having reasonable knowledge of relevant facts." The accountant knew that the shareholders would use its estimate to determine the price that one would pay to the other. Under these circumstances, was Frank's injury foreseeable? Explain.

3 What factor might have influenced Frank to sell his shares to Donna even if he thought that MacDonald Page's "fair market value" figure was less than half what it should have been? Does this factor represent an unfair, or unethical, advantage? Why or why not?

Critical Thinking and Writing Assignments

34–9 Critical Legal Thinking. In cases involving third parties who have suffered losses in reliance on negligent misrepresentations in accountants' financial reports, the courts apply different standards to assess liability. Some courts impose liability only when there is privity between the accountant and the party seeking recovery. Other courts impose liability under a foreseeability rule. What are the implications of imposing liability on accountants for losses suffered by third parties on the basis of foreseeability rather than privity?

34–10 Video Question Go to this text's Web site at **www.cengage.com/blaw/blt** and select "Chapter 34." Click on "Video Questions" and view the video

titled *Accountant's Liability.* Then answer the following questions.

1 Should Ray prepare a financial statement that values a list of assets provided by the advertising firm without verifying that the firm actually owns these assets?

2 Discuss whether Ray is in privity with the company interested in buying Laura's advertising firm.

3 Under the *Ultramares* rule, to whom does Ray owe a duty?

4 Assume that Laura did not tell Ray that she intended to give the financial statement to the potential acquirer. Would this fact change Ray's liability under the *Ultramares* rule? Explain.

Practical Internet Exercises

Go to this text's Web site at **www.cengage.com/blaw/blt**, select "Chapter 34," and click on "Practical Internet Exercises." There you will find the following Internet research exercises that you can perform to learn more about the topics covered in this chapter.

Practical Internet Exercise 34–1: Legal Perspective—The Sarbanes-Oxley Act of 2002
Practical Internet Exercise 34–2: Management Perspective—Avoiding Legal Liability

Unit Six — Cumulative Business Hypothetical

Alpha Software, Inc., and Beta Products Corporation—both small firms—are competitors in the business of software research, development, and production.

1. Alpha and Beta form a joint venture to research, develop, and produce new software for a particular line of computers. Does this business combination violate the antitrust laws? If so, is it a per se violation, or is it subject to the rule of reason? Alpha and Beta decide to merge. After the merger, Beta is the surviving firm. What aspect of this firm's presence in the market will be assessed to decide whether this merger is in violation of any antitrust laws?

2. To market its products profitably, Beta considers a number of advertising and labeling proposals. One proposal is that Beta suggest in its advertising that one of its software products has a certain function even though the product does not actually have that capability. Another suggestion is that Beta sell half of a certain program in packaging that misleads the buyer into believing the entire program is included. To obtain the entire program, customers would need to buy a second product. Can Beta implement these suggestions or otherwise market its products in any way it likes? If not, why not?

3. The production part of Beta's operations generates hazardous waste. Gamma Transport Company transports the waste to Omega Waste Corporation, which owns and operates a hazardous waste–disposal site. At the site, some containers leak hazardous waste, and the Environmental Protection Agency (EPA) cleans it up. From whom can the EPA recover the cost of the clean-up?

4. Beta hires a certified public accountant, Aaron Schleger, to prepare its financial reports and issue opinion letters based on those reports. One year, Beta falls into serious financial trouble, but this is not reflected in Schleger's reports and opinion letters. Relying on Schleger's portrayal of the company's fiscal health, Beta borrows substantial amounts to develop a new product. The bank, in lending funds to Beta, relies on an opinion letter from Schleger, and Schleger is aware of the bank's reliance. Assuming that Schleger was negligent but did not engage in intentional fraud, what is his potential liability in this situation? Discuss fully.

Unit Six — Extended Case Study: *McCoy v. Chase Manhattan Bank, USA*

As Chapter 33 described, credit-card agreements are governed by the Truth-in-Lending Act (TILA) and by Regulation Z, which was adopted by the Federal Reserve Board to implement the TILA. An important part of any credit-card agreement is the rate of interest that will be charged. In this Extended Case Study, we look at McCoy v. Chase Manhattan Bank, USA,[1] in which a cardholder challenged the credit–card issuer's rate increase, claiming that he had not been notified as required by the TILA. The issuer claimed that its "Card-member Agreement" provided advance notice of the rate increase. The issue for the court was whether the increase also required contemporaneous notice under the TILA and Regulation Z.

1. 559 F.3d 963 (9th Cir. 2009). To read this case online, go to **www.ca9.uscourts.gov**. In the left-hand column, in the "Decisions" pull-down menu, click on "Opinions." On that page, click on "Advanced Search"; then, in the "by Case No.:" box, type "06-56278" and click on "Search." In the result, click on the appropriate link to access the opinion.

CASE BACKGROUND

James McCoy held a credit card issued by Chase Manhattan Bank, USA, N.A., a national bank located in Delaware. Chase closed McCoy's account to new transactions after he made a late payment. Chase also increased the interest rate on McCoy's card retroactively to the beginning of his payment cycle. The bank did not notify him of the increase, however, until the following periodic statement, after the increase had already taken effect.

McCoy filed a suit in a federal district court against Chase, on behalf of himself and other cardholders similarly situated, claiming that the rate increase without notice violated the TILA. The court dismissed McCoy's complaint, holding that no notice was required. McCoy appealed to the U.S. Court of Appeals for the Ninth Circuit.

MAJORITY OPINION

HAWKINS, Circuit Judge:

* * * *

Congress enacted TILA to "assure a meaningful disclosure of credit terms * * * ." Regulation Z * * * addresses when and how notice of changes in terms must be given:

> * * * Whenever any term required to be disclosed under [12 Code of Federal Regulations] Section 226.6 is changed or the required minimum periodic payment is increased, the creditor shall mail or deliver written notice of the change to each consumer who may be affected. * * *

Section 226.6 requires that a creditor disclose * * * "each periodic rate that may be used to compute the finance charge."

The parties dispute the meaning of the phrase "any term required to be disclosed under Section 226.6." Chase argues that the phrase applies only to the contractual terms of Chase's Card-member Agreement. McCoy suggests the phrase also applies to the list of specific "items" Section 226.6(a)(2) requires be disclosed, which includes the interest rate that may be used.

* * * *

Chase argues that the Federal Reserve Board ("FRB")'s Official Staff Commentary interprets Regulation Z to require no notice in this case.

Comment 3 is the most salient [important] Official Staff Commentary to [Regulation Z] and, when describing the amount of notice required for different kinds of changes, provides that "a notice of change in terms is required, but may be mailed or delivered as late as the effective date of the change * * * if there is an increased periodic rate or any other finance charge attributable to the consumer's delinquency or default." The plain-meaning of Comment 3 is to require notice when a cardholder's interest rates increase because of a default * * * . Under Comment 3, McCoy has stated a claim.

Chase argues that * * * a different portion of the Official Staff Commentary, Comment 1, should govern instead. Comment 3's specific reference to interest rate increases attributable to the consumer's delinquency or default is directly on point and therefore governs.

Comment 1 * * * describes the circumstances in which Regulation Z requires no notice of a change in terms:

* * * No notice of a change in terms need be given if the specific change is set forth initially * * * . In contrast, notice must be given if the contract allows the creditor to increase the rate at its discretion but does not include specific terms for an increase.

* * * *

* * * Chase's "contract allows the creditor to increase the rate at its discretion" and does not specify the relevant terms, including the conditions that are necessary and sufficient for an increase to occur and the actual amount of the increase that will occur. * * * *An interpretation of Comment 1 as eliminating Regulation Z's notice requirement even where consumers do not have sufficient information to determine whether their interest rate will be raised, or by how much, dilutes the meaning of the word "specific" beyond recognition.* [Emphasis added.]

Chase argues that we must nevertheless interpret Regulation Z to require no notice in this case because we must defer to [an] Advance Notice of Proposed Rule-making, [ANPR] promulgated * * * by the Federal Reserve in 2007, which briefly characterizes existing law in the process of explaining a proposal to amend Regulation Z. [The final rule amended Regulation Z to require forty-five days' notice for interest rate increases effective July 1, 2010.]

Consideration of the 2007 ANPR does not lead us to change our interpretation of the FRB's Official Staff Commentary. Chase observes that the 2007 ANPR includes as an example of when a "change-in-terms notice" is not required, "some credit card account agreements that permit the card issuer to increase the periodic rate if the consumer makes a late payment" * * * . The effect of this language is ambiguous, however, because the term "change-in-terms notice" could * * * refer to contemporaneous notice required for changes in interest rates, but might instead refer only to the * * * advance notice required for changes in contractual terms.

* * * FRB chose to remove the ambiguous language entirely when it issued a Final Rule and Supplementary Information amending Regulation Z.

* * * The primary purpose of the 2007 ANPR * * * was to announce proposed amendments to Regulation Z and solicit comment, not to offer additional staff commentary on Regulation Z's current requirements.

* * * Our own consideration of the FRB's Official Staff Commentary, unofficial [ANPR], and the Supplementary

Continued

Information accompanying its recent amendment of Regulation Z *leaves us firmly convinced of the FRB's intent to require contemporaneous notice when rates are raised because of a consumer's delinquency or default,* as McCoy alleges occurred in this case. [Emphasis added.]

    * * * *

    * * * Having concluded that McCoy has stated a claim * * * , we reverse and remand to the district court.

DISSENTING OPINION

CUDAHY, Circuit Judge, dissenting:

    * * * *

    The claims made by Mr. McCoy have been raised in many other forums * * * . In all of those cases the result was the opposite of the one reached here. In one case the court did at first indicate that it was inclined to rule in favor of the plaintiffs but reversed course when it was made aware of the Advance Notice of Proposed Rulemaking (ANPR) issued by the expert agency, the Federal Reserve Board (FRB or the Board), which quite clearly showed that the Board disagreed with their interpretation.

    * * * So the question becomes the following: did [Regulation Z] require Chase to provide contemporaneous notice to McCoy of an increase in his interest rate due to his default when that increase was an implementation of the existing terms of his agreement with Chase? The majority says that * * * the FRB's

Official Staff Commentary to [Regulation Z] makes the answer a clear "yes." The majority feels no need to give any deference to the Board's views expressed in its [ANPR], which [leads] to the opposite conclusion and which [is] reinforced by every other court that has considered the question.

    * * * *

    * * * I would find that McCoy has not stated a claim for a violation of TILA.

QUESTIONS FOR ANALYSIS

1. **Law.** What conclusion did the majority reach on the question in this case? What points supported this conclusion?
2. **Law.** What was the dissent's view with regard to the majority's analysis?
3. **Ethics.** Suppose that Chase's card-member agreement was written by an accountant or an attorney. Could that individual be found to be in breach of her or his profession's ethics? Why or why not?
4. **Social Dimensions.** Under the TILA, credit terms must be clearly disclosed. Can any credit-card agreement meet this requirement? Explain.
5. **Implications for the Consumer.** What do the circumstances of this case suggest to current and potential cardholders concerning the management of their personal finances? Discuss.

Property and Its Protection

Chapter 35

Personal Property and Bailments

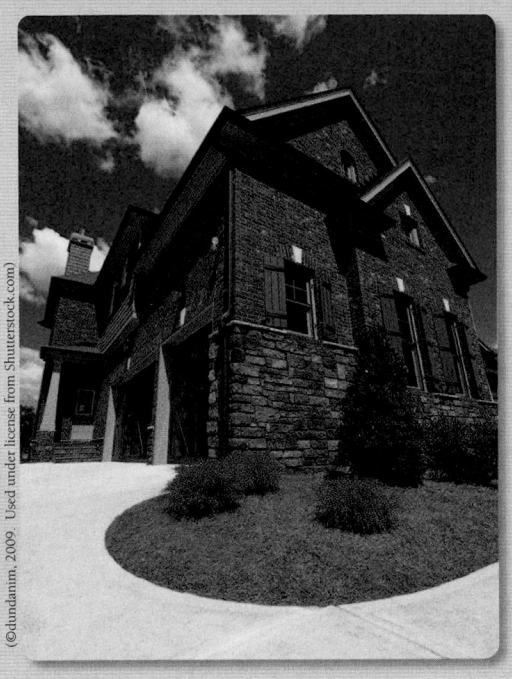

(©dundanim, 2009. Used under license from Shutterstock.com)

Chapter Outline

- Property Ownership
- Acquiring Ownership of Personal Property
- Mislaid, Lost, and Abandoned Property
- Bailments

Learning Objectives

After reading this chapter, you should be able to answer the following questions:

1. What is real property? What is personal property?
2. What is the difference between a joint tenancy and a tenancy in common?
3. What are the three elements necessary for an effective gift?
4. What are the three elements of a bailment?
5. What are the basic rights and duties of a bailee? What are the rights and duties of a bailor?

Property Legally protected rights and interests in anything with an ascertainable value that is subject to ownership.

Property consists of the legally protected rights and interests a person has in anything with an ascertainable value that is subject to ownership. Property would have little value (and the word would have little meaning) if the law did not define the right to use it, to sell or dispose of it, and to prevent trespass on it. Indeed, John Locke, as indicated in the chapter-opening quotation, considered the preservation of property to be the primary reason for the establishment of government.

Real Property Land and everything attached to it, such as trees and buildings.

Personal Property Property that is movable; any property that is not real property.

Chattel All forms of personal property.

Property is divided into real property and personal property. **Real property** (sometimes called *realty* or *real estate*) means the land and everything permanently attached to it. Everything else is **personal property,** or *personalty.* Attorneys sometimes refer to personal property as **chattel,** a term used under the common law to denote all forms of personal property. Personal property can be tangible or intangible. *Tangible* personal property, such as a television set or a car, has physical substance. *Intangible* personal property represents some set of rights and interests but has no real physical existence. Stocks and bonds, patents, and copyrights are examples of intangible personal property.

Property Ownership

Ownership of property—both real and personal property—can be viewed as a bundle of rights, including the right to possess the property and to dispose of it by sale, gift, lease, or other means. As discussed in Chapter 15, the right of ownership in property is often referred to as *title*.

Fee Simple

Fee Simple An absolute form of property ownership entitling the property owner to use, possess, or dispose of the property as he or she chooses during his or her lifetime. On death, the interest in the property descends to the owner's heirs.

A person who holds the entire bundle of rights to property is said to be the owner in **fee simple.** The owner in fee simple is entitled to use, possess, or dispose of the property as he or she chooses during his or her lifetime, and on this owner's death, the interests in the property descend to his or her heirs. We will return to this form of property ownership in Chapter 36, in the context of ownership rights in real property.

Concurrent Ownership

Concurrent Ownership Joint ownership.

Persons who share ownership rights simultaneously in a particular piece of property are said to be *concurrent* owners. There are two principal types of **concurrent ownership:** *tenancy in common* and *joint tenancy.* Additionally, in some states, married persons can hold property together as *community property.*

Tenancy in Common Co-ownership of property in which each party owns an undivided interest that passes to her or his heirs at death.

TENANCY IN COMMON The term **tenancy in common** refers to a form of co-ownership in which each of two or more persons owns an *undivided* interest in the property. The interest is undivided because each tenant has rights in the *whole* property. On the death of a tenant in common, that tenant's interest in the property passes to her or his heirs.

EXAMPLE 35.1 Sofia and Greg own a rare stamp collection together as tenants in common. This means that Sofia and Greg each have rights in the *entire* collection. (If Sofia owned some of the stamps and Greg owned others, then the interest would be *divided*.) In the event that Sofia dies before Greg, a one-half interest in the stamp collection will become the property of Sofia's heirs. If Sofia sells her interest to Jorge before she dies, Jorge and Greg will be co-owners as tenants in common. If Jorge dies, his interest in the personal property will pass to his heirs, and they in turn will own the property with Greg as tenants in common. ●

Joint Tenancy The joint ownership of property by two or more co-owners in which each co-owner owns an undivided portion of the property. On the death of one of the joint tenants, his or her interest automatically passes to the surviving joint tenant(s).

JOINT TENANCY In a **joint tenancy,** each of two or more persons owns an undivided interest in the property, but a deceased joint tenant's interest passes to the surviving joint tenant or tenants.[1] The rights of a surviving joint tenant to inherit a deceased joint tenant's ownership interest—which are referred to as *survivorship rights*—distinguish the joint tenancy from the tenancy in common. A joint tenancy can be terminated before a joint tenant's death by gift or by sale; in this situation, the person who receives the property as a gift or who purchases the property becomes a tenant in common, not a joint tenant.

EXAMPLE 35.2 In the preceding example, suppose that Sofia and Greg held their stamp collection in a joint tenancy. In that situation, if Sofia died before Greg, the entire collection would become the property of Greg; Sofia's heirs would receive absolutely no interest in the collection. If Sofia, while living, sold her interest to Jorge, however, the sale would terminate the joint tenancy, and Jorge and Greg would become owners as tenants in common. ●

Generally, it is presumed that a co-tenancy is a tenancy in common unless there is a clear intention to establish a joint tenancy. Thus, language such as "to Jerrold and Eva as joint

---

1. See, for example, *In re Estate of Grote*, 766 N.W.2d 82 (Minn.App. 2009).

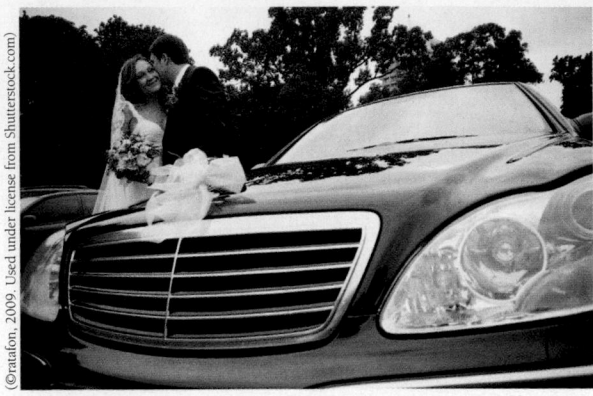
(©atafon, 2009. Used under license from Shutterstock.com)

Does this couple necessarily share equally in all income earned during the marriage?

Community Property A form of concurrent ownership of property in which each spouse technically owns an undivided one-half interest in property acquired during the marriage. This form of joint ownership occurs in only ten states and Puerto Rico.

"In no country in the world is the love of property more active and more anxious than in the United States."

Alexis de Tocqueville, 1805–1859
(French historian and statesman)

tenants with right of survivorship, and not as tenants in common," would be necessary to create a joint tenancy.

COMMUNITY PROPERTY   A married couple is allowed to own property as **community property** in a limited number of states.[2] If property is held as community property, each spouse technically owns an undivided one-half interest in property acquired during the marriage. Generally, community property does *not* include property acquired before the marriage or property acquired by gift or inheritance as separate property during the marriage. After a divorce, community property is divided equally in some states and according to the discretion of the court in other states.

The *Concept Summary* below illustrates the primary types of property ownership.

 Acquiring Ownership of Personal Property

The most common way of acquiring personal property is by purchasing it. We have already discussed the purchase and sale of personal property (goods) in Chapters 15 through 17. Often, property is acquired by will or inheritance, a topic we will cover in Chapter 37. Here, we look at additional ways in which ownership of personal property can be acquired, including acquisition by possession, production, gifts, accession, and confusion.

Possession

Sometimes, a person can become the owner of personal property merely by possessing it. One example of acquiring ownership by possession is the capture of wild animals. Wild animals belong to no one in their natural state, and the first person to take possession of a wild animal normally owns it. A hunter who kills a deer, for instance, has assumed ownership of it (unless he or she acted in violation of the law).

---

2. These states include Alaska, Arizona, California, Idaho, Louisiana, Nevada, New Mexico, Texas, Washington, and Wisconsin. Puerto Rico allows property to be owned as community property as well.

Concept Summary **Common Types of Property Ownership**	
CONCEPT	**DESCRIPTION**
Fee Simple	Owners of property in fee simple have the fullest ownership rights in property. They have the right to use, possess, or dispose of the property as they choose during their lifetimes and to pass on the property to their heirs at death.
Tenancy in Common	Co-ownership in which two or more persons own an undivided interest in property; on one tenant's death, that tenant's property interest passes to his or her heirs.
Joint Tenancy	Co-ownership in which two or more persons own an undivided interest in property; on the death of a joint tenant, that tenant's property interest transfers to the remaining tenant(s), *not* to the heirs of the deceased.
Community Property	A form of co-ownership between a husband and wife in which each spouse technically owns an undivided one-half interest in property acquired during the marriage. This type of ownership exists in only some states.

How does a person acquire ownership of wild animals?

Gift Any voluntary transfer of property made without consideration, past or present.

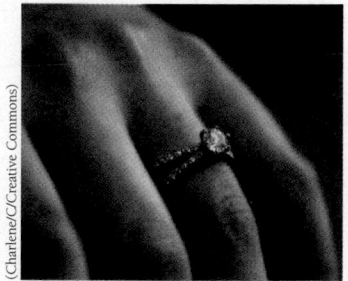

Can a woman keep her engagement ring if the wedding is called off?

Those who find lost or abandoned property can also acquire ownership rights through mere possession of the property, as will be discussed later in the chapter. (Ownership rights in real property can also be acquired through possession, such as adverse possession—see Chapter 36.)

Production

Production—the fruits of labor—is another means of acquiring ownership of personal property. For instance, writers, inventors, and manufacturers all produce personal property and thereby acquire title to it. (In some situations, though, as when a researcher is hired to invent a new product or technique, the researcher-producer may not own what is produced—see Chapter 23.)

Gifts

A **gift** is another fairly common means of acquiring and transferring ownership of real and personal property. A gift is essentially a *voluntary* transfer of property ownership for which no consideration is given. As discussed in Chapter 11, the presence of consideration is what distinguishes a contract from a gift.

For a gift to be effective, three requirements must be met: (1) donative intent on the part of the *donor* (the one giving the gift), (2) delivery, and (3) acceptance by the *donee* (the one receiving the gift). We examine each of these requirements here, as well as the requirements of a gift made in contemplation of imminent death. Until these three requirements are met, no effective gift has been made. **EXAMPLE 35.3** Your aunt tells you that she *intends* to give you a new Mercedes-Benz for your next birthday. This is simply a promise to make a gift. It is not considered a gift until the Mercedes-Benz is delivered and accepted. ●

Ethical Issue ⚖️

Who owns the engagement ring? Often, when two people decide to marry, one party (traditionally the man in an opposite-sex relationship) gives the other an engagement ring. What if the engagement is called off? Etiquette authorities routinely counsel that if the woman breaks the engagement, she should return the ring, but if the man calls the wedding off, the woman is entitled to keep the ring. When the party who gave the ring (the donor) sues for its return after a breakup, the courts are split. Courts in a majority of states, including Kansas, Michigan, New York, and Ohio, hold that an engagement ring is not a real gift. Rather, it is a "conditional gift" that becomes final only if the marriage occurs. If the marriage does not take place, the ring is returned to the donor regardless of who broke the engagement. This position is actually similar to the law of ancient Rome, which mandated that when an engagement was broken, the woman had to return the ring, as a penalty, regardless of who was at fault. Some judges, however, disagree with the conditional-gift theory and contend that an engagement ring is a gift and, as such, it belongs to the donee, even if the engagement is broken.

DONATIVE INTENT When a gift is challenged in court, the court will determine whether donative intent exists by looking at the language of the donor and the surrounding circumstances. A court may look at the relationship between the parties and the size of the gift in relation to the donor's other assets. When a person has given away a large portion of her or his assets, the court will scrutinize the transaction closely to determine the donor's mental capacity and look for indications of fraud or duress.

DELIVERY The gift must be delivered to the donee. Delivery may be accomplished by means of a third person who is the agent of either the donor or the donee. Naturally, no delivery is necessary if the gift is already in the hands of the donee (provided there is donative intent and acceptance). Delivery is obvious in most cases, but some objects cannot be relinquished physically. Then the question of delivery depends on the surrounding circumstances.

Constructive Delivery.   When the object itself cannot be physically delivered, a symbolic, or constructive, delivery will be sufficient. **Constructive delivery** does not confer actual possession of the object in question, only the right to take actual possession. Thus, constructive delivery is a general term used to describe an action that the law holds to be the equivalent of real delivery. **EXAMPLE 35.4** You want to make a gift of various rare coins that you have stored in a safe-deposit box at your bank. You certainly cannot deliver the box itself to the donee, and you do not want to take the coins out of the bank. In this situation, you can simply deliver the key to the box to the donee and authorize the donee's access to the box and its contents. This action constitutes a constructive delivery of the contents of the box. ●

The delivery of intangible property—such as stocks, bonds, insurance policies, and contracts, for example—must always be accomplished by symbolic, or constructive, delivery. This is because the documents represent rights and are not, in themselves, the true property.

Relinquishing Dominion and Control.   An effective delivery also requires giving up complete control and **dominion** (ownership rights) over the subject matter of the gift. The outcome of disputes often turns on whether control has actually been relinquished. The Internal Revenue Service scrutinizes transactions between relatives, especially when one claims to have given income-producing property to another who is in a lower marginal tax bracket. Unless complete control over the property has been relinquished, the "donor"— not the family member who received the "gift"—will have to pay taxes on the income from that property.

In the following classic case, the court focused on the requirement that a donor must relinquish complete control and dominion over property given to the donee before a gift can be effectively delivered.

Constructive Delivery   An act equivalent to the actual, physical delivery of property that cannot be physically delivered because of difficulty or impossibility. For example, the transfer of a key to a safe constructively delivers the contents of the safe.

Dominion   Ownership rights in property, including the right to possess and control the property.

Classic **Case 35.1** **In re Estate of Piper**

Missouri Court of Appeals, 676 S.W.2d 897 (1984).

How can two diamond rings be gifted if they remain in the owner's purse after her death?

FACTS Gladys Piper died intestate (without a will) in 1982. At her death, she owned miscellaneous personal property worth $5,000 and had in her purse $200 in cash and two diamond rings, known as the Andy Piper rings. The contents of her purse were taken by her niece Wanda Brown, allegedly to preserve them for the estate. Clara Kaufmann, a friend of Piper's, filed a claim against the estate for $4,800. From October 1974 until Piper's death, Kaufmann had taken Piper to the doctor, beauty shop, and grocery store; had written her checks to pay her bills; and had helped her care for her home. Kaufmann maintained that Piper had promised to pay her for these services and had given her the diamond rings as a gift. A Missouri state trial court denied her request for payment; the court found that her services had been voluntary. Kaufmann then filed a petition for delivery of personal property—the rings—which

was granted by the trial court. Brown, other heirs, and the administrator of Piper's estate appealed.

ISSUE Had Gladys Piper made an effective gift of the rings to Clara Kaufmann?

DECISION No. The state appellate court reversed the judgment of the trial court on the ground that Piper had never delivered the rings to Kaufmann.

REASON Kaufmann claimed that the rings belonged to her by reason of a "consummated gift long prior to the death of Gladys Piper." Two witnesses testified at the trial that Piper had told them that she was going to wear the rings until she died but that the rings belonged to Kaufmann. The appellate court, however, found "no evidence of any actual delivery." The court pointed out that the essentials of a gift are (1) a present intention to make a gift on the part of the donor, (2) a delivery of the property

Case 35.1–Continued

by the donor to the donee, and (3) an acceptance by the donee. Here, the evidence showed only an intent to make a gift. Because there was no delivery—either actual or constructive—a valid gift was not made. For Piper to have made a gift, she would have had to execute her intention by the complete and unconditional delivery of the property or the delivery of a proper written instrument evidencing the gift. As this did not occur, the court found that there had been no gift.

WHAT IF THE FACTS WERE DIFFERENT? *Suppose that Gladys Piper had told Clara Kaufmann that she was giving the rings to Clara but wished to keep them in her possession for a few more days. Would this have affected the court's decision in this case? Explain.*

IMPACT OF THIS CASE ON TODAY'S LAW *This case clearly illustrates the delivery requirement when making a gift. Assuming that Piper did, indeed, intend for Kaufmann to have the rings, it was unfortunate that Kaufmann had no right to receive them after Piper's death. Yet the alternative could lead to perhaps even more unfairness. The policy behind the delivery requirement is to protect alleged donors and their heirs from fraudulent claims based solely on parol evidence. If not for this policy, an alleged donee could easily claim that a gift was made when, in fact, it was not.*

RELEVANT WEB SITES *To locate information on the Web concerning the* Piper *decision, go to this text's Web site at* www.cengage.com/blaw/blt. *Select "Chapter 35" and click on "Classic Cases."*

ACCEPTANCE The final requirement of a valid gift is acceptance by the donee. This rarely presents any problem, as most donees readily accept their gifts. The courts generally assume acceptance unless the circumstances indicate otherwise.

GIFTS *INTER VIVOS* AND GIFTS *CAUSA MORTIS* A gift made during one's lifetime is termed a **gift *inter vivos*. Gifts *causa mortis*** (so-called *deathbed gifts*), in contrast, are made in contemplation of imminent death. A gift *causa mortis* does not become absolute until the donor dies from the contemplated illness, and it is automatically revoked if the donor recovers from that illness. The gift is also revoked if the prospective donee dies before the donor. To be effective, a gift *causa mortis* must also meet the three requirements discussed earlier—donative intent, delivery, and acceptance by the donee.

Gift *Inter Vivos* A gift made during one's lifetime and not in contemplation of imminent death, in contrast to a gift *causa mortis*.

Gift *Causa Mortis* A gift made in contemplation of death. If the donor does not die of that ailment, the gift is revoked.

EXAMPLE 35.5 Yang, who is about to undergo surgery to remove a cancerous tumor, delivers an envelope to Chao, a close business associate. The envelope contains a letter saying, "I realize my days are numbered, and I want to give you this check for $1 million in the event of my death from this operation." Chao cashes the check. The surgeon performs the operation and removes the tumor. Yang recovers fully. Several months later, Yang dies from a heart attack that is totally unrelated to the operation. If Yang's personal representative (the party charged with administering Yang's estate) tries to recover the $1 million, she normally will succeed. The gift *causa mortis* to Chao is automatically revoked if Yang recovers. The *specific event* that was contemplated in making the gift was death from a particular operation. Because Yang's death was not the result of this event, the gift is revoked, and the $1 million passes to Yang's estate. Similarly, even if Yang had died during the operation, the gift would have been revoked if Chao had died a few minutes earlier. In that event, the $1 million would have passed to Yang's estate, and not to Chao's heirs. ●

Accession

Accession Occurs when an individual adds value to personal property by the use of either labor or materials. In some situations, a person may acquire ownership rights in another's property through accession.

Accession means "something added." Accession occurs when someone adds value to an item of personal property by the use of either labor or materials. Generally, there is no dispute about who owns the property after the accession occurs, especially when the accession is accomplished with the owner's consent. **EXAMPLE 35.6** Hoshi buys all the materials necessary to customize his Corvette. He hires Zach, a customizing specialist, to come to his house to perform the work. Hoshi pays Zach for the value of the labor, obviously retaining title to the property. ●

If the improvement was made wrongfully—without the permission of the owner—the owner retains title to the property and normally does not have to pay for the improvement.

This is true even if the accession increased the value of the property substantially. **EXAMPLE 35.7** Patti steals a car and puts expensive new tires on it. If the rightful owner later recovers the car, he obviously will not be required to compensate Patti, a car thief, for the value of the new tires. ●

If the accession is performed in good faith—and the improvement was made due to an honest mistake of judgment—the owner normally still retains title to the property but usually must pay for the improvement. In rare instances, when the improvement greatly increases the value of the property or changes its identity, the court may rule that ownership has passed to the improver. In those rare situations, the improver must compensate the original owner for the value of the property before the accession occurred.

Confusion

Confusion is the commingling (mixing together) of goods to such an extent that one person's personal property cannot be distinguished from another's. Confusion frequently occurs with *fungible goods,* such as grain or oil, which consist of identical units.

If confusion occurs as a result of agreement, an honest mistake, or the act of some third party, the owners share ownership as tenants in common and will share any loss in proportion to their ownership interests in the property. **EXAMPLE 35.8** Five farmers in a small Iowa community enter into a cooperative arrangement. Each fall, the farmers harvest the same amount of number 2–grade yellow corn and store it in silos that are held by the cooperative. Each farmer thus owns one-fifth of the total corn in the silos. If a fire burns down one of the silos, each farmer will bear one-fifth of the loss. ● When goods are confused due to an intentional wrongful act, then the innocent party ordinarily acquires title to the whole.

▶ Mislaid, Lost, and Abandoned Property

As already mentioned, one of the methods of acquiring ownership of property is to possess it. Simply finding something and holding on to it, however, does not necessarily give the finder any legal rights in the property. Different rules apply, depending on whether the property was mislaid, lost, or abandoned.

Mislaid Property

Property that has voluntarily been placed somewhere by the owner and then inadvertently forgotten is **mislaid property.** A person who finds mislaid property does not obtain title to the goods. Instead, the owner of the place where the property was mislaid becomes the caretaker of the property because it is highly likely that the true owner will return.[3] **EXAMPLE 35.9** You go to a movie theater. While paying for popcorn at the concessions stand, you set your iPhone on the counter and then leave it there. The iPhone is mislaid property, and the theater owner is entrusted with the duty of reasonable care for it. ●

Lost Property

Property that is *involuntarily* left is **lost property.** A finder of the property can claim title to the property against the whole world—*except the true owner.*[4] The well-known children's adage "Finders keepers, losers weepers" is actually written into law—provided that the loser (the rightful owner) cannot be found. If the true owner is identified and demands that the lost property be returned, the finder must return it. In contrast, if a third party

---

Confusion The mixing together of goods belonging to two or more owners to such an extent that the separately owned goods cannot be identified.

Mislaid Property Property with which the owner has voluntarily parted and then cannot find or recover.

Lost Property Property with which the owner has involuntarily parted and then cannot find or recover.

---

3. The finder of mislaid property is an involuntary bailee (to be discussed later in this chapter).
4. For a classic English case establishing this principle, see *Armory v. Delamirie,* 93 Eng.Rep. 664 (K.B. [King's Bench] 1722).

attempts to take possession of the lost property, the finder will have a better title than the third party.

EXAMPLE 35.10   Khalia works in a large library at night. As she crosses the courtyard on her way home, she finds a gold bracelet set with what seem to be precious stones. She takes the bracelet to a jeweler to have it appraised. While pretending to weigh the bracelet, the jeweler's employee removes several of the stones. If Khalia brings an action to recover the stones from the jeweler, she normally will win because she found lost property and holds title against everyone *except the true owner.* ●

CONVERSION OF LOST PROPERTY   When a finder of lost property knows the true owner and fails to return the property to that person, the finder is guilty of the tort of *conversion* (the wrongful taking of another's property—see Chapter 4). **EXAMPLE 35.11**   In Example 35.10, suppose that Khalia knows that the gold bracelet she found belongs to Geneva. If Khalia does not return Geneva's bracelet, she is guilty of conversion. ●   Many states require the finder to make a reasonably diligent search to locate the true owner of lost property. (The *Business Application* feature at the end of this chapter discusses the obligations that states often impose on finders of lost property.)

ESTRAY STATUTES   Many states have **estray statutes,** which encourage and facilitate the return of property to its true owner and then reward the finder for honesty if the property remains unclaimed. These laws provide an incentive for finders to report their discoveries by making it possible for them, after the passage of a specified period of time, to acquire legal title to the property they have found. Generally, the item must be lost property, not merely mislaid property, for estray statutes to apply. Estray statutes usually require the finder or the county clerk to advertise the property in an attempt to help the owner recover what has been lost.

CASE EXAMPLE 35.12   To avoid U.S. Customs authorities, drug smugglers often enter the United States illegally from Canada via a frozen river that flows through Van Buren, Maine. When two railroad employees walking near the railroad tracks in Van Buren found a duffel bag that contained $165,580 in cash, they reported their find to U.S. Customs agents, who took custody of the bag and cash. The next day, a drug-sniffing dog gave a positive alert on the bag for the scent of drugs. The federal government filed a lawsuit claiming title to the property under forfeiture laws, which provide that cash and property involved in illegal drug transactions are forfeited to the government. The two employees argued that they were entitled to the $165,580 under Maine's estray statute. The statute required finders to (1) provide written notice to the town clerk within seven days after finding the property, (2) post a public notice in the town, and (3) advertise in the town's newspaper for one month. Because the employees had not fulfilled these requirements, the court ruled that they had not acquired title to the property. Thus, the federal government had a right to seize the cash.[5] ●

Abandoned Property

Property that has been discarded by the true owner, who has no intention of reclaiming title to it, is **abandoned property.** Someone who finds abandoned property acquires title to it that is good against the whole world, *including the original owner.* The owner of lost property who eventually gives up any further attempt to find it is frequently held to have abandoned the property. If a person finds abandoned property while trespassing on the property of another, title vests in the owner of the land, not in the finder.

BE AWARE   A finder who appropriates the personal property of another, knowing who the true owner is, can be guilty of conversion.

Estray Statute   A statute defining finders' rights in property when the true owners are unknown.

ON THE WEB   Some states and government agencies post lists of unclaimed property on their Web sites. For an example of the various types of property that may go unclaimed, go to the following Web page, which is part of the state of Delaware's Web site: **revenue.delaware. gov/information/Escheat.shtml**.

Abandoned Property   Property that has been discarded by the owner, who has no intention of reclaiming it.

5. *United States v. One Hundred Sixty-Five Thousand Five Hundred Eighty Dollars ($165,580) in U.S. Currency,* 502 F.Supp.2d 114 (D.Me 2007).

EXAMPLE 35.13 As Aleka is driving on the freeway, her valuable scarf blows out the window. She retraces her route and searches for the scarf but cannot find it. She finally gives up her search and proceeds to her destination five hundred miles away. When Frye later finds the scarf, he acquires title to it that is good even against Aleka. By completely giving up her search, Aleka abandoned the scarf just as effectively as if she had intentionally discarded it. •

The *Concept Summary* below reviews the rules relating to mislaid, lost, and abandoned property.

Bailments

Bailment   A situation in which the personal property of one person (a bailor) is entrusted to another (a bailee), who is obligated to return the bailed property to the bailor or dispose of it as directed.

Bailor   One who entrusts goods to a bailee.

Bailee   One to whom goods are entrusted by a bailor.

Many routine personal and business transactions involve bailments. A **bailment** is formed by the delivery of personal property, without transfer of title, by one person, called a **bailor**, to another, called a **bailee**, usually under an agreement for a particular purpose—for example, to loan, lease, store, repair, or transport the property. The distinguishing characteristic of a bailment compared with a sale or a gift is that there is no passage of title and no intent to transfer title. On completion of the purpose, the bailee is obligated to return the bailed property in the same or better condition to the bailor or a third person or to dispose of it as directed.

Bailments usually are created by agreement, but not necessarily by contract, because in many bailments not all of the elements of a contract (such as mutual assent and consideration) are present. **EXAMPLE 35.14** If you lend your bicycle to a friend, a bailment is created, but not by contract, because there is no consideration. Many commercial bailments, such as the delivery of clothing to the cleaners for dry cleaning, are based on contract, though. •

Preventing Legal Disputes

The law of bailments applies to many routine personal and business transactions. When a transaction involves a bailment, whether you realize it or not, you are subject to the obligations and duties that arise from the bailment relationship. Consequently, knowing how bailment relationships are created, and what rights, duties, and liabilities flow from ordinary bailments, is critical in avoiding legal disputes. Also important is understanding that bailees can limit the dollar amount of their liability by contract.

Elements of a Bailment

Not all transactions involving the delivery of property from one person to another create a bailment. For such a transfer to become a bailment, the following three elements must be present:

1. Personal property.
2. Delivery of possession (without title).
3. Agreement that the property will be returned to the bailor or otherwise disposed of according to its owner's directions.

Concept Summary	Mislaid, Lost, and Abandoned Property
CONCEPT	**DESCRIPTION**
Mislaid Property	Property that is placed somewhere voluntarily by the owner and then inadvertently forgotten. A finder of mislaid property will not acquire title to the goods, and the owner of the place where the property was mislaid becomes a caretaker of the mislaid property.
Lost Property	Property that is involuntarily left and forgotten. A finder of lost property can claim title to the property against the whole world *except the true owner.*
Abandoned Property	Property that has been discarded by the true owner, who has no intention of claiming title to the property in the future. A finder of abandoned property can claim title to it against the whole world, *including the original owner.*

(Waving at You/Creative Commons)

Is the bailment relationship between your dry cleaner and you based on contract?

PERSONAL PROPERTY REQUIREMENT Only personal property, not real property or persons, can be the subject of a bailment. Although bailments commonly involve *tangible* items—jewelry, cattle, automobiles, and the like—*intangible* personal property, such as promissory notes and shares of corporate stock, may also be bailed.

DELIVERY OF POSSESSION *Delivery of possession* means the transfer of possession of the property to the bailee. For delivery to occur, the bailee must be given exclusive possession and control over the property, and the bailee must *knowingly* accept the personal property.[6] In other words, the bailee must *intend* to exercise control over it.

If either delivery of possession or knowing acceptance is lacking, there is no bailment relationship. **EXAMPLE 35.15** Kim goes to a five-star restaurant and checks her coat at the door. In the pocket of the coat is a diamond necklace worth $20,000. In accepting the coat, the bailee does not *knowingly* also accept the necklace. Thus, a bailment of the coat exists—because the restaurant has exclusive possession and control over the coat and knowingly accepted it—but not a bailment of the necklace. ●

Physical versus Constructive Delivery. Either *physical* or *constructive* delivery will result in the bailee's exclusive possession of and control over the property. As discussed earlier in the context of gifts, constructive delivery is a substitute, or symbolic, delivery. What is delivered to the bailee is not the actual property bailed (such as a car) but something so related to the property (such as the car keys) that the requirement of delivery is satisfied.

Involuntary Bailments. In certain situations, a bailment is found despite the apparent lack of the requisite elements of control and knowledge. One example of such a situation occurs when the bailee acquires the property accidentally or by mistake—as in finding someone else's lost or mislaid property. A bailment is created even though the bailor did not voluntarily deliver the property to the bailee. Such bailments are called *constructive* or *involuntary* bailments.

EXAMPLE 35.16 Several corporate managers are asked to attend an urgent meeting at the law firm of Jacobs & Matheson. One of the corporate officers, Kyle Gustafson, inadvertently leaves his briefcase at the firm at the conclusion of the meeting. In this situation, a court could find that an involuntary bailment was created, even though Gustafson did not voluntarily deliver the briefcase and the law firm did not intentionally accept it. If an involuntary bailment existed, the firm would be responsible for taking care of the briefcase and returning it to Gustafson. ●

BAILMENT AGREEMENT A bailment agreement can be express or implied. Although a written contract is not required for bailments of less than one year (that is, the Statute of Frauds does not apply—see Chapter 12), it is a good idea to have one, especially when valuable property is involved.

The bailment agreement expressly or impliedly provides for the return of the bailed property to the bailor or to a third person, or for the disposal of the property by the bailee. The agreement presupposes that the bailee will return the identical goods originally given by the bailor. In certain types of bailments, though, such as bailments of fungible goods, the property returned need only be equivalent property.

---

6. We are dealing here with *voluntary bailments*. This does not apply to *involuntary bailments*.

EXAMPLE 35.17 If Holman stores his grain (fungible goods) in Joe's Warehouse, a bailment is created. At the end of the storage period, however, the warehouse is not obligated to return to Holman exactly the same grain that he stored. As long as the warehouse returns grain of the same *type, grade,* and *quantity,* the warehouse—the bailee—has performed its obligation. •

Ordinary Bailments

Bailments are either *ordinary* or *special (extraordinary)*. There are three types of ordinary bailments. They are distinguished according to *which party receives a benefit from the bailment.* This factor will dictate the rights and liabilities of the parties, and the courts use it to determine the standard of care required of the bailee in possession of the personal property. The three types of ordinary bailments are as follows:

1. *Bailment for the sole benefit of the bailor.* This is a gratuitous bailment (a bailment without consideration) for the convenience and benefit of the bailor. Basically, the bailee is caring for the bailor's property as a favor. **EXAMPLE 35.18** Allen asks his friend, Sumi, to store his car in her garage while he is away. If Sumi agrees to do so, then this is a gratuitous bailment because the bailment of the car is for the sole benefit of the bailor (Allen). •
2. *Bailment for the sole benefit of the bailee.* This type of bailment typically occurs when one person lends an item to another person (the bailee) solely for the bailee's convenience and benefit. **EXAMPLE 35.19** Allen asks to borrow Sumi's boat so that he can go sailing over the weekend. The bailment of the boat is for Allen's (the bailee's) sole benefit. •
3. *Bailment for the mutual benefit of the bailee and the bailor.* This is the most common kind of bailment and involves some form of compensation for storing items or holding property while it is being serviced. It is a contractual bailment and may be referred to as a *bailment for hire* or a *commercial bailment.* **EXAMPLE 35.20** Allen leaves his car at a service station for an oil change. Because the service station will be paid to change Allen's oil, this is a mutual-benefit bailment. • Many lease arrangements in which the lease involves goods (leases were discussed in Chapters 15 through 17) also fall into this category of bailment once the lessee takes possession.

RIGHTS OF THE BAILEE   Certain rights are implicit in the bailment agreement. Generally, the bailee has the right to take possession of the property, to utilize the property for accomplishing the purpose of the bailment, to receive some form of compensation, and to limit her or his liability for the bailed goods. These rights of the bailee are present (with some limitations) in varying degrees in all bailment transactions.

ON THE WEB For a discussion of the origins of the term *bailment* and how bailment relationships have been defined, go to www.lectlaw.com/def/b005.htm.

Right of Possession.   A hallmark of the bailment agreement is that the bailee acquires the *right to control and possess the property temporarily.* The bailee's right of possession permits the bailee to recover damages from any third person for damage or loss of the property. **EXAMPLE 35.21** No-Spot Dry Cleaners sends all suede leather garments to Cleanall Company for special processing. If Cleanall loses or damages any leather goods, No-Spot has the right to recover against Cleanall. • If the bailed property is stolen, the bailee has a legal right to regain possession of it or to recover damages.

Right to Use Bailed Property.   Depending on the type of bailment and the terms of the bailment agreement, a bailee may also have a right to use the bailed property. When no provision is made, the extent of use depends on how necessary it is for the goods to be at the bailee's disposal for the ordinary purpose of the bailment to be carried out. **EXAMPLE 35.22** If you borrow a friend's car to drive to the airport, you, as the bailee, would obviously be expected to use the car. In a bailment involving the long-term storage of a car, however, the bailee is not expected to use the car because the ordinary purpose of a storage bailment does not include use of the property. •

Right of Compensation.   Except in a gratuitous bailment, a bailee has a right to be compensated as provided for in the bailment agreement. The bailee also has a right to be reimbursed for costs incurred and services rendered in the keeping of the bailed property—even in a gratuitous bailment. **EXAMPLE 35.23** Margo loses her pet dog, and Justine finds it. Justine takes Margo's dog to her home and feeds it. Even though she takes good care of the dog, it becomes ill and she takes it to a veterinarian. Justine pays the bill for the veterinarian's services and the medicine. Justine normally will be entitled to be reimbursed by Margo for all reasonable costs incurred in the keeping of Margo's dog. •

To enforce the right of compensation, the bailee has a right to place a *possessory lien* on the specific bailed property until he or she has been fully compensated. A lien on bailed property is referred to as a **bailee's lien,** or artisan's lien (discussed in Chapter 21). If the bailor refuses to pay or cannot pay the charges (compensation), in most states the bailee is entitled to foreclose on the lien and sell the property to recover the amount owed.

Bailee's Lien   A possessory lien, or claim, that a bailee entitled to compensation can place on the bailed property to ensure that he or she will be paid for the services provided. The lien is effective as long as the bailee retains possession of the bailed goods and has not agreed to extend credit to the bailor. Sometimes referred to as an artisan's lien.

Right to Limit Liability.   In ordinary bailments, bailees have the right to limit their liability, provided that the limitations are called to the attention of the bailor and are not against public policy. It is essential that the bailor be informed of the limitation in some way.

Even when the bailor knows of the limitation, courts consider certain types of disclaimers of liability to be against public policy and therefore illegal. The courts carefully scrutinize *exculpatory clauses,* or clauses that limit a person's liability for her or his own wrongful acts, and in bailments they are often held to be illegal. This is particularly true in bailments for the mutual benefit of the bailor and the bailee. **EXAMPLE 35.24** A receipt from a parking garage expressly disclaims liability for any damage to parked cars, regardless of the cause. Because the bailee has attempted to exclude liability for the bailee's own negligence, including the parking attendant's negligence, the clause will likely be deemed unenforceable because it is against public policy. •

DUTIES OF THE BAILEE   The bailee has two basic responsibilities: (1) to take appropriate care of the property and (2) to surrender the property to the bailor or dispose of it in accordance with the bailor's instructions at the end of the bailment.

The Duty of Care.   The bailee must exercise reasonable care in preserving the bailed property. What constitutes reasonable care in a bailment situation normally depends on the nature and specific circumstances of the bailment.

The courts determine the appropriate standard of care on the basis of the type of bailment involved. In a bailment for the sole benefit of the bailor, the bailee need exercise only a slight degree of care. In a bailment for the sole benefit of the bailee, however, the bailee must exercise great care. In a mutual-benefit bailment, courts normally impose a reasonable standard of care—that is, the bailee must exercise the degree of care that a reasonable and prudent person would exercise in the same circumstances. Exhibit 35–1 illustrates these concepts. A bailee's failure to exercise appropriate care in handling the bailor's property results in tort liability.

• *Exhibit* 35–1 Degree of Care Required of a Bailee

Bailment for the Sole Benefit of the Bailor	Mutual-Benefit Bailment	Bailment for the Sole Benefit of the Bailee
DEGREE OF CARE →		
SLIGHT	REASONABLE	GREAT

Duty to Return Bailed Property. At the end of the bailment, the bailee normally must hand over the original property to either the bailor or someone the bailor designates, or must otherwise dispose of it as directed. This is usually a *contractual* duty arising from the bailment agreement (contract). Failure to give up possession at the time the bailment ends is a breach of contract and could result in the tort of conversion or an action based on bailee negligence.

If the bailed property has been lost or is returned damaged, a court will presume that the bailee was negligent. The bailee's obligation is excused, however, if the goods or chattels were destroyed, lost, or stolen through no fault of the bailee (or claimed by a third party with a superior claim).

Because the bailee has a duty to return the bailed goods to the bailor, a bailee may be liable for conversion or misdelivery if the goods being held or delivered are given to the wrong person. Hence, a bailee must be satisfied that the person (other than the bailor) to whom the goods are being delivered is the actual owner or has authority from the owner to take possession of the goods.

A bailee's alleged negligence was at the heart of the following case.

Case 35.2 LaPlace v. Briere

New Jersey Superior Court, Appellate Division, 404 N.J.Super. 585, 962 A.2d 1139 (2009).
www.lawlibrary.rutgers.edu/search.shtml[a]

HISTORICAL AND CULTURAL SETTING *The earliest direct ancestor of the horse lived about 50 million years ago. First domesticated by central Asians nearly five thousand years ago, horses were originally used primarily in warfare and to provide transportation for the nobility and royalty. Modern horses, including the American Quarter Horse, descended from the Arabian horse. Today, horses are used mainly for racing, recreational riding, and showing. To exercise a horse, its handler often uses a technique known as lunging—that is, having the horse walk, trot, or canter in a circle while it is secured to a lunge line held by the handler who stands in the center of the circle. Lunging can be part of a horse's daily routine and usually is not considered dangerous.*

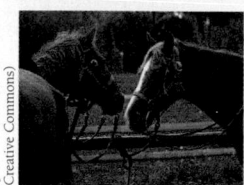

(Jason Wehrmhoener/Creative Commons)

Without proof of negligence, can a bailee's liability for a horse's death be established?

FACTS Michael LaPlace boarded his horses, including a trained Quarter Horse named Park Me In First, at Pierre Briere's stable in New Jersey. Charlene Bridgwood also boarded a horse at the stable. About a dozen years earlier, LaPlace had boarded horses at the farm owned by Bridgwood's husband. Bridgwood had often lunged the horses, including those owned by LaPlace. In 2006, after a snowy night while LaPlace and Briere were at a horse show, Bridgwood offered to help Briere's shorthanded staff by lunging the horses, even though she was not an employee of the stable. During the exercise, Park Me In First suddenly reared up on his hind legs. He then collapsed with blood pumping from his nose

and died. The veterinarian could not determine the cause of death without performing a necropsy (autopsy). Briere and Bridgwood offered to pay for the procedure, but none was performed because LaPlace did not authorize it until after the horse's remains had been removed. LaPlace filed a suit in a New Jersey state court against Briere, claiming negligence. The court issued a summary judgment in the defendant's favor. LaPlace appealed.

ISSUE Without proof of negligence, can a bailee (Briere) be absolved of liability on a claim for the loss of bailed goods (Park Me In First)?

DECISION Yes. The state intermediate appellate court affirmed the lower court's judgment.

REASON A bailee has a duty to take reasonable care of bailed property and is liable for any loss caused by a failure to do so. If the property is damaged in the care of the bailee, a presumption of negligence arises. But this presumption may be rebutted by proof that the loss was not caused by the bailee's negligence or that he or she exercised due care. In this case, LaPlace's horse, Park Me In First, died in Briere's care during its bailment, giving rise to a presumption of negligence. Briere showed, however, that at the time the horse died, Bridgwood, who was experienced in handling horses, was exercising the horse in an ordinary manner. This proof is "devoid of any evidence of negligence causing the death of the horse, and thus rebuts the presumption of negligence." LaPlace did not offer any additional proof of negligence, and "determining the cause of death was uniquely within the control of plaintiff," whose permission was required for a necropsy.

FOR CRITICAL ANALYSIS—Social Consideration *As a bailee, was Briere liable in conversion for the death of Park Me In First? Explain. (Hint: Did Briere wrongfully possess or use the horse without permission and without just cause?)*

---

a. In the "Search the N.J. Courts Decisions" section, in the "Please enter your search term(s) below:" box, type "LaPlace" and click on "Search!" In the result, click on the name of the case to access the opinion.

DUTIES OF THE BAILOR   The duties of a bailor are essentially the same as the rights of a bailee. A bailor has a duty to compensate the bailee either as agreed or as reimbursement for costs incurred by the bailee in keeping the bailed property. A bailor also has an all-encompassing duty to provide the bailee with goods or chattels that are free from known defects that could cause injury to the bailee.

Bailor's Duty to Reveal Defects.   The bailor's duty to reveal defects to the bailee translates into two rules:

1. In a *mutual-benefit bailment,* the bailor must notify the bailee of all known defects and any hidden defects that the bailor knows of or could have discovered with reasonable diligence and proper inspection.
2. In a *bailment for the sole benefit of the bailee,* the bailor must notify the bailee of any known defects.

The bailor's duty to reveal defects is based on a negligence theory of tort law. A bailor who fails to give the appropriate notice is liable to the bailee and to any other person who might reasonably be expected to come into contact with the defective article.

EXAMPLE 35.25   Rentco (the bailor) rents a tractor to Hal Iverson. Unknown to Rentco, the brake mechanism on the tractor is defective at the time the bailment is made. Although Rentco was unaware of the defect, it would have been discovered on reasonable inspection. Iverson uses the defective tractor without knowledge of the brake problem and is injured, along with two other field workers, when the tractor rolls out of control down an incline after failing to stop. In this situation, Rentco is liable for the injuries sustained by Iverson and the other workers because it negligently failed to discover the defect and notify Iverson. ●

Warranty Liability for Defective Goods.   A bailor can also incur *warranty liability* based on contract law (see Chapter 17) for injuries resulting from the bailment of defective articles. Property leased by a bailor must be *fit for the intended purpose of the bailment.* Warranties of fitness arise by law in sales contracts and leases, and judges have extended these warranties to situations in which the bailees are compensated for the bailment (such as when one leaves a car with a parking attendant). Article 2A of the Uniform Commercial Code (UCC) extends the implied warranties of merchantability and fitness for a particular purpose to bailments whenever the bailments include rights to use the bailed goods.[7]

Special Types of Bailments

Although many bailments are the ordinary bailments that we have just discussed, a business is also likely to engage in some special types of bailment transactions. These include bailments in which the bailee's duty of care is *extraordinary*—that is, the bailee's liability for loss or damage to the property is absolute—as is generally true in bailments involving common carriers and innkeepers. Warehouse companies have the same duty of care as ordinary bailees, but, like carriers, they are subject to extensive regulation under federal and state laws, including Article 7 of the UCC.

COMMON CARRIERS   *Common carriers* are publicly licensed to provide transportation services to the general public. They are distinguished from private carriers, which operate transportation facilities for a select clientele. A private carrier is not required to provide

7. UCC 2A–212, 2A–213.

service to every person or company making a request. A common carrier, however, must arrange carriage for all who apply, within certain limitations.[8]

The delivery of goods to a common carrier creates a bailment relationship between the shipper (bailor) and the common carrier (bailee). Unlike ordinary bailees, the common carrier is held to a standard of care based on *strict liability,* rather than reasonable care, in protecting the bailed personal property. This means that the common carrier is absolutely liable, regardless of due care, for all loss or damage to goods except damage caused by one of the following common law exceptions: (1) an act of God, (2) an act of a public enemy, (3) an order of a public authority, (4) an act of the shipper, or (5) the inherent nature of the goods.

Common carriers cannot contract away their liability for damaged goods. Subject to government regulations, however, they are permitted to limit their dollar liability to an amount stated on the shipment contract or rate filing.[9] This point is illustrated in the following case.

8. A common carrier is not required to take any and all property anywhere in all instances. Public regulatory agencies govern common carriers, and carriers can be restricted to geographic areas. They can also be limited to carrying certain kinds of goods or to providing only special types of transportation equipment.

9. Federal laws require common carriers to offer shippers the opportunity to obtain higher dollar limits for loss by paying a higher fee for the transport.

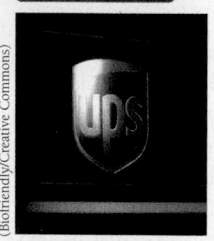

Case 35.3 Treiber & Straub, Inc. v. United Parcel Service, Inc.

United States Court of Appeals, Seventh Circuit, 474 F.3d 379 (2007).

Was a disclaimer that UPS refuses to ship items valued at more than $50,000 sufficient to protect the company from liability after losing a diamond ring?

FACTS   Michael Straub is the president of Treiber & Straub, Inc., a fine-jewelry store in Wisconsin. To return a diamond ring to Norman Silverman Company, a wholesaler in California, Straub chose United Parcel Service, Inc. (UPS), and, through www.ups.com, arranged to ship the ring via "Next Day Air." To ship a package using the Web site, a customer has to click on two on-screen boxes to agree to "My UPS Terms and Conditions." Among these terms, UPS and its insurer, UPS Capital Insurance Agency, Inc., limit their liability and the amount of insurance coverage on packages to $50,000. UPS refuses to ship items of "unusual value"—those worth more than $50,000. The carrier and its insurer disclaim liability *entirely* for such items. The ring was worth $105,000. Undeterred, Straub opted for the maximum coverage and indicated on the air bill that the value was "$50,000 or less." UPS lost the ring. Treiber & Straub reimbursed the wholesaler for the full loss and filed a suit in a federal district court against UPS and its insurer to recover $50,000 under the insurance policy. The court issued a summary judgment in the defendants' favor based on the disclaimer. The plaintiff appealed to the U.S. Court of Appeals for the Seventh Circuit, arguing, among other things, that the disclaimer was "literally buried among all the other extensive terms and conditions on the vast UPS Web site."

ISSUE   Was the carrier's disclaimer enforceable?

DECISION   Yes. The U.S. Court of Appeals for the Seventh Circuit affirmed the judgment of the lower court. The appellate court held that the carrier's disclaimer was prominent enough.

REASON   The court examined the relevant pages on the UPS Web site. On those pages, UPS initially limits its liability to $100 but offers customers an opportunity to buy insurance for coverage up to $50,000. If a customer wants to ship a package with a value of more than $50,000, UPS refuses to accept it or to insure it. UPS does not explain all of the details about these limits on a single page, but the court ruled that this "does not call for a different result in light of everything else that was available to the shipper." The limitation and the disclaimer are repeated several times on the Web site. This ensures "clear and reasonable notice" of the terms, to which a customer has to click twice in agreement to arrange a shipment. Further, the court reasoned that if UPS accepted packages with values greater than $50,000 but insured them for no more than that amount, "it would distort the mix of claims it is insuring, skewing it toward the high-value end, necessitating a significant change in premiums. The risk of theft would also increase for packages with higher declared values." The court also pointed out that in this case, "by indicating on the air bill the insured value (of $50,000 or less) rather than the actual value" of the ring, "Treiber & Straub effectively breached the shipping contract."

WHAT IF THE FACTS WERE DIFFERENT?   *If Straub had claimed that he had not read the terms, would the result in this case have been different? Why or why not?*

WAREHOUSE COMPANIES   *Warehousing* is the business of providing storage of property for compensation.[10] Like ordinary bailees, warehouse companies are liable for loss or damage to property resulting from *negligence*. A warehouse company, though, is a professional bailee and is therefore expected to exercise a high degree of care to protect and preserve the goods. A warehouse company can limit the dollar amount of its liability, but the bailor must be given the option of paying an increased storage rate for an increase in the liability limit.

Unlike ordinary bailees, a warehouse company can issue *documents of title*—in particular, *warehouse receipts*—and is subject to extensive government regulation, including Article 7 of the UCC.[11] A warehouse receipt describes the bailed property and the terms of the bailment contract. It can be negotiable or nonnegotiable, depending on how it is written. It is negotiable if its terms provide that the warehouse company will deliver the goods "to the bearer" of the receipt or "to the order of" a person named on the receipt.[12] The warehouse receipt represents the goods (that is, it indicates title) and hence has value and utility in financing commercial transactions.

EXAMPLE 35.26   Ossip delivers 6,500 cases of canned corn to Chaney, the owner of a warehouse. Chaney issues a negotiable warehouse receipt payable "to bearer" and gives it to Ossip. Ossip sells and delivers the warehouse receipt to Better Foods, Inc. Better Foods is now the owner of the corn and has the right to obtain the cases by simply presenting the warehouse receipt to Chaney. •

INNKEEPERS   At common law, innkeepers and hotel owners were strictly liable for the loss of any cash or property that guests brought into their rooms. Today, only those who provide lodging to the public for compensation as a *regular* business are covered under this rule of strict liability. Moreover, the rule applies only to those who are guests, as opposed to lodgers, who are persons that permanently reside at the hotel or inn.

In many states, innkeepers can avoid strict liability for loss of guests' cash and valuables by (1) providing a safe in which to keep them and (2) notifying guests that a safe is available. In addition, statutes often limit the liability of innkeepers with regard to articles that are not kept in the safe and may limit the availability of damages in the absence of innkeeper negligence. Most statutes require that the innkeeper post these limitations or otherwise notify the guest. Such postings, or notices, are frequently found on the doors of the rooms in motels and hotels.

EXAMPLE 35.27   Joyce stays for a night at the Harbor Hotel. When she returns from eating breakfast in the hotel restaurant, she discovers that her suitcase has been stolen and sees that the lock on the door between her room and the room next door was forced open. Joyce claims that the hotel is liable for her loss. Because the hotel was not negligent, however, it normally is not liable under state law. •

---

10. UCC 7–102(h) refers to the person engaged in the storing of goods for hire as a "warehouseman."

11. A *document of title* is defined in UCC 1–201(15) as any "document which in the regular course of business or financing is treated as adequately evidencing that the person in possession of it is entitled to receive, hold, and dispose of the document and the goods it covers." A *warehouse receipt* is a document of title issued by a person engaged for hire in the business of storing goods for hire.

12. UCC 7–104.

 ## Reviewing . . . Personal Property and Bailments

Vanessa Denai owned forty acres of land in rural Louisiana with a 1,600-square-foot house on it and a metal barn near the house. Denai later met Lance Finney, who had been seeking a small plot of rural property to rent. After several meetings, Denai invited Finney to live on a corner of her land in exchange for Finney's assistance in cutting wood and tending her property. Denai agreed to store Finney's sailboat in her barn. With Denai's consent,

Finney constructed a concrete and oak foundation on Denai's property and purchased a 190-square-foot dome from Dome Baja for $3,395. The dome was shipped by Doty Express, a transportation company licensed to serve the public. When it arrived, Finney installed the dome frame and fabric exterior so that the dome was detachable from the foundation. A year after Finney installed the dome, Denai wrote Finney a note stating, "I've decided to give you four acres of land surrounding your dome as drawn on this map." This gift violated no local land-use restrictions. Using the information presented in the chapter, answer the following questions.

1. Is the dome real property or personal property? Explain.
2. Is Denai's gift of land to Finney a testamentary gift, a gift *causa mortis*, or a gift *inter vivos*?
3. What type of bailment relationship was created when Denai agreed to store Finney's boat? What degree of care was Denai required to exercise in storing the boat?
4. What standard of care applied to the shipment of the dome by Doty Express?

Business Application
What Should You Do with Lost Property?*

If you are walking down a street in New York City and come across a valuable diamond ring lying in the gutter, what should you do? You might be tempted to keep the ring or sell it and enjoy the proceeds, but that would be unethical. It would also be illegal under New York law—and under the laws of many other states as well.

An Example—New York Laws

New York law defines *lost property* to include lost property, mislaid property, and abandoned property, whether it is cash, goods, or some other type of tangible personal property. Generally, the finder of property worth $20 or more must either return it to the rightful owner or report the find to the police and deposit the property at a police station within ten days. Failure to do so is a misdemeanor, subject to a fine and imprisonment for not more than six months. When the finder delivers the property to the authorities, he or she is given a receipt, and the statutory waiting period begins (ranging from three months for property valued at less than $100 to three years for property valued at more than $5,000). The police then attempt to find the rightful owner.

Other States' Lost-Property Laws

Many other states have also enacted lost-property statutes. The statutes differ greatly from state to state, but typically they eliminate the distinctions among lost property, mislaid property, and abandoned property, as the

New York statute does. Many statutes also require the finder to deposit found property with local authorities, although the penalty imposed for failure to do so may not be as severe as under New York's statute. Lost-property statutes also typically require the police to attempt to find the true owner through such measures as calling the owner or person in charge of the premises where the property was found. Sometimes, the finder must advertise the property and its discovery through the county court.

Generally, if the true owner cannot be located within a certain period of time, which varies depending on the value of the property and whether the property is perishable, the finder gets the property. If the finder does not appear after the period of time has lapsed, the property may be sold and the proceeds disposed of as specified by statute. In California, for instance, the proceeds from such a sale go into a state abandoned-property fund (if the state police had custody of the lost property) or become the property of the city, county, town, or village (if other police had custody).

CHECKLIST FOR THE FINDER OF LOST PROPERTY

1. **To maximize your chances of legally keeping lost property, take the found property to the nearest police station.**
2. **Make sure you follow the statutory requirements of the jurisdiction, which may require you to advertise the found property.**

* This *Business Application* is not meant to substitute for the services of an attorney who is licensed to practice law in your state.

 Key Terms

Chapter Summary: Personal Property and Bailments

PERSONAL PROPERTY	
Definition of Personal Property (See page 884.)	Personal property (personalty) includes all property not classified as real property (realty). Personal property can be tangible (such as a TV or a car) or intangible (such as stocks or bonds). Personal property may be referred to legally as *chattel*—a term used under the common law to denote all forms of personal property.
Property Ownership (See pages 885–886.)	Having the fullest ownership rights in property is called *fee simple* ownership. There are various ways of co-owning property, including *tenancy in common, joint tenancy,* and *community property.* Each of these types of property ownership is described in the *Concept Summary* on page 886.

Acquiring Ownership of Personal Property (See pages 886–890.)	The most common way of acquiring ownership in personal property is by purchasing it (see Chapters 15 through 17). Another way in which personal property is often acquired is by will or inheritance (see Chapter 37). The following are additional methods of acquiring personal property:
	 1. *Possession*—Ownership may be acquired by possession if no other person has ownership title (for example, capturing wild animals or finding abandoned property).
	 2. *Production*—Any product or item produced by an individual (with minor exceptions) becomes the property of that individual.
	 3. *Gifts*—A gift is effective when the following conditions exist:
	    a. There is evidence of *intent* to make a gift of the property in question.
	    b. The gift is *delivered* (physically or constructively) to the donee or the donee's agent.
	    c. The gift is *accepted* by the donee.
	 4. *Accession*—When someone adds value to an item of personal property by the use of labor or materials, the added value generally becomes the property of the owner of the original property (although the owner sometimes must pay for good faith accessions). In rare situations, good faith accessions that substantially increase the property's value or change the identity of the property may cause title to pass to the improver.
	 5. *Confusion*—If a person wrongfully and willfully commingles fungible goods with those of another in order to render them indistinguishable, the innocent party acquires title to the whole. Otherwise, the owners become tenants in common of the commingled goods.

Mislaid, Lost, and Abandoned Property (See pages 890–892.)	The finder of property acquires different rights depending on whether the property was mislaid, lost, or abandoned, as described in the *Concept Summary* on page 892.

BAILMENTS	
Elements of a Bailment (See pages 892–894.)	1. *Personal property*—Bailments involve only personal property. 2. *Delivery of possession*—For an effective bailment to exist, the bailee (the one receiving the property) must be given exclusive possession and control over the property, and in a voluntary bailment, the bailee must knowingly accept the personal property. 3. *The bailment agreement*—Expressly or impliedly provides for the return of the bailed property to the bailor or a third party, or for the disposal of the bailed property by the bailee.

Ordinary Bailments (See pages 894–897.)	1. *Types of bailments*—
	    a. Bailment for the sole benefit of the bailor—A gratuitous bailment undertaken for the sole benefit of the bailor (for example, as a favor to the bailor).
	    b. Bailment for the sole benefit of the bailee—A gratuitous loan of an article to a person (the bailee) solely for the bailee's benefit.

Continued

Chapter Summary: Personal Property and Bailments—Continued

Ordinary Bailments— Continued	c. Mutual-benefit (contractual) bailment—The most common kind of bailment; involves compensation between the bailee and bailor for the service provided.
	 2. *Rights of a bailee (duties of a bailor)*—
	   a. The right of possession—Allows a bailee to sue any third persons who damage, lose, or convert the bailed property.
	   b. The right to be compensated and reimbursed for expenses—In the event of nonpayment, the bailee has the right to place a possessory (bailee's) lien on the bailed property.
	   c. The right to limit liability—An ordinary bailee can limit his or her liability for loss or damage, provided proper notice is given and the limitation is not against public policy. In special bailments, limitations on liability for negligence or on types of losses usually are not allowed, but limitations on the monetary amount of liability are permitted.
	 3. *Duties of a bailee (rights of a bailor)*—
	   a. A bailee must exercise appropriate care over property entrusted to her or him. What constitutes appropriate care normally depends on the nature and circumstances of the bailment. See Exhibit 35–1 on page 895.
	   b. Bailed goods in a bailee's possession must be either returned to the bailor or disposed of according to the bailor's directions. A bailee's failure to return the bailed property creates a presumption of negligence and constitutes a breach of contract or the tort of conversion of goods.

Special Types of Bailments (See pages 897–899.)	1. *Common carriers*—Carriers that are publicly licensed to provide transportation services to the general public. A common carrier is held to a standard of care based on *strict liability* unless the bailed property is lost or destroyed due to (a) an act of God, (b) an act of a public enemy, (c) an order of a public authority, (d) an act of the shipper, or (e) the inherent nature of the goods. 2. *Warehouse companies*—Professional bailees differ from ordinary bailees in that they (a) can issue documents of title (warehouse receipts) and (b) are subject to state and federal statutes, including Article 7 of the UCC (as are common carriers). They must exercise a high degree of care over the bailed property and are liable for loss of or damage to property if they fail to do so. 3. *Innkeepers (hotel operators)*—Those who provide lodging to the public for compensation as a *regular* business. The common law strict liability standard to which innkeepers were once held is limited today by state statutes, which vary from state to state.

 ExamPrep

ISSUE SPOTTERS

1 Quintana Corporation sends important documents to Regal Nursery, Inc., via Speedy Messenger Service. While the documents are in Speedy's care, a third party causes an accident to Speedy's delivery vehicle that results in the loss of the documents. Does Speedy have a right to recover from the third party for the loss of the documents? Why or why not?

2 Rosa de la Mar Corporation ships a load of goods via Southeast Delivery Company. The load of goods is lost in a hurricane in Florida. Who suffers the loss? Explain your answer.

BEFORE THE TEST

Check your answers to the Issue Spotters, and at the same time, take the interactive quiz for this chapter. Go to **www.cengage.com/blaw/blt** and click on "Chapter 35." First, click on "Answers to Issue Spotters" to check your answers. Next, click on "Interactive Quiz" to assess your mastery of the concepts in this chapter. Then click on "Flashcards" to review this chapter's Key Term definitions.

 For Review

Answers for the even-numbered questions in this For Review *section can be found on this text's accompanying Web site at* **www.cengage.com/blaw/blt**. *Select "Chapter 35" and click on "For Review."*

1   What is real property? What is personal property?
2   What is the difference between a joint tenancy and a tenancy in common?
3   What are the three elements necessary for an effective gift?
4   What are the three elements of a bailment?
5   What are the basic rights and duties of a bailee? What are the rights and duties of a bailor?

 Hypothetical Scenarios and Case Problems

35–1 Duties of the Bailee. Discuss the standard of care traditionally required of the bailee for the bailed property in each of the following situations, and determine whether the bailee breached that duty.

1   Ricardo borrows Steve's lawn mower because his own lawn mower needs repair. Ricardo mows his front yard. To mow the backyard, he needs to move some hoses and lawn furniture. He leaves the mower in front of his house while doing so. When he returns to the front yard, he discovers that the mower has been stolen.

2   Alicia owns a valuable speedboat. She is going on vacation and asks her neighbor, Maureen, to store the boat in one stall of Maureen's double garage. Maureen consents, and the boat is moved into the garage. Maureen needs some grocery items for dinner and drives to the store. She leaves the garage door open while she is gone, as is her custom, and the speedboat is stolen during that time.

35–2 Gifts. Jaspal has a severe heart attack and is taken to the hospital. He is aware that he is not expected to live. Because he is a bachelor with no close relatives nearby, Jaspal gives his car keys to his close friend, Friedrich, telling Friedrich that he is expected to die and that the car is Friedrich's. Jaspal survives the heart attack, but two months later he dies from pneumonia. Sam, Jaspal's uncle and the executor of his estate, wants Friedrich to return the car. Friedrich refuses, claiming that the car was given to him by Jaspal as a gift. Discuss whether Friedrich will be required to return the car to Jaspal's estate.

35–3 ![?] **Hypothetical Question with Sample Answer** Curtis is an executive on a business trip to the West Coast. He has driven his car on this trip and checks into the Hotel Ritz. The hotel has a guarded underground parking lot. Curtis gives his car keys to the parking lot attendant but fails to notify the attendant that his wife's $10,000 fur coat is in a box in the trunk. The next day, on checking out, he discovers that his car has been stolen. Curtis wants to hold the hotel liable for both the car and the coat. Discuss the probable success of his claim.

—**For a sample answer to Question 35–3, go to Appendix E at the end of this text.**

35–4 Found Property. A. D. Lock owned Lock Hospitality, Inc., which in turn owned the Best Western Motel in Conway, Arkansas. Joe Terry and David Stocks were preparing the motel for renovation. As they were removing the ceiling tiles in room 118, with Lock present in the room, they noticed a dusty cardboard box near the heating and air-supply vent where it had

apparently been concealed. Terry climbed a ladder to reach the box, opened it, and handed it to Stocks. The box was filled with more than $38,000 in old currency. Lock took possession of the box and its contents. Terry and Stocks filed a suit in an Arkansas state court against Lock and his corporation to obtain the currency. Should the cash be characterized as lost, mislaid, or abandoned property? To whom should the court award it? Explain. [*Terry v. Lock,* 343 Ark. 452, 37 S.W.3d 202 (2001)]

35–5 ![gavel] **Case Problem with Sample Answer** Vincent Slavin was a partner at Cantor Fitzgerald Securities in the World Trade Center (WTC) in New York City. In 1998, Slavin and Anna Baez became engaged and began living together. They placed both of their names on three accounts at Chase Manhattan Bank according to the bank's terms, which provided that "accounts with multiple owners are joint, payable to either owner or the survivor." Slavin arranged for the direct deposit of his salary and commissions into one of the accounts. On September 11, 2001, Slavin died when two planes piloted by terrorists crashed into the WTC towers, causing their collapse. At the time, the balance in the three accounts was $656,944.36. On September 14, Cantor Fitzgerald deposited an additional $58,264.73 into the direct-deposit account. Baez soon withdrew the entire amount from all of the accounts. Mary Jelnek, Slavin's mother, filed a suit in a New York state court against Baez to determine the ownership of the funds that had been in the accounts. In what form of ownership were the accounts held? Who is entitled to which of the funds, and why? [*In re Jelnek,* 3 Misc.3d 725, 777 N.Y.S.2d 871 (2004)]

—**After you have answered Problem 35–5, compare your answer with the sample answer given on the Web site that accompanies this text. Go to www.cengage.com/blaw/blt, select "Chapter 35," and click on "Case Problem with Sample Answer."**

35–6 Concurrent Ownership. In July 2003, Chester Dellinger and his son Michael opened a joint bank account with Advancial Federal Credit Union in Dallas, Texas. Both of them signed the "Account Application," which designated Chester as a "member" and Michael as a "joint owner." Both of them received a copy of the "Account Agreement, Disclosures and Privacy Policy," which provided that "a multiple party account includes rights of survivorship." Chester died in February 2005. His will designated Michael as the executor of the estate, most of which was to be divided equally between Michael and his brother, Joseph, Chester's other son. Michael determined the value of the estate to be about $117,000. He did not include the Advancial account balance, which was about $234,000. Joseph filed a suit in a Texas state court against Michael, contending that the funds in the Advancial account should be included in the estate. Michael filed a motion for summary judgment. Who owned the Advancial account when Chester was alive? Who owned it after he died? What should the court rule? Explain. [*In re Estate of Dellinger*, 224 S.W.3d 434 (Tex. App.—Dallas 2007)]

35–7 Gifts. John Wasniewski opened a brokerage account with Quick and Reilly, Inc., in his son James's name. Twelve years later, when the balance was $52,085, the account was closed, and the funds were transferred to a joint account in the names of John and James's brother. Only after the transfer, when James received a tax form for the prior account's final year, did James learn of its existence. He filed a suit in a Connecticut state court against Quick and Reilly, alleging breach of contract and seeking to recover the account's principal and interest. What are the elements of a valid gift? Did John's opening of the account with Quick and Reilly constitute a gift to James? What is the likely result in this case, and why? [*Wasniewski v. Quick and Reilly, Inc.*, 292 Conn. 98, 971 A.2d 8 (Conn. 2009)]

35–8 **A Question of Ethics** *Marcella Lashmett was engaged in the business of farming in Illinois. Her daughter Christine Montgomery was also a farmer. Christine often borrowed Marcella's farm equipment. More than once, Christine used the equipment as a trade-in on the purchase of new equipment titled in* Christine's name alone. After each transaction, Christine paid Marcella an agreed-to sum of money, and Marcella filed a gift tax return. Marcella died on December 19, 1999. Her heirs included Christine and Marcella's other daughter, Cheryl Thomas. Marcella's will gave whatever farm equipment remained on her death to Christine. If Christine chose to sell or trade any of the items, however, the proceeds were to be split equally with Cheryl. The will designated Christine to handle the disposition of the estate, but she did nothing. Eventually, Cheryl filed a petition with an Illinois state court, which appointed her to administer the will. Cheryl then filed a suit against her sister to discover what assets their mother had owned. [*In re Estate of Lashmett*, 369 Ill.App.3d 1013, 874 N.E.2d 65 (4 Dist. 2007)]

1 Cheryl learned that three months before Marcella's death, Christine had used Marcella's tractor as a trade-in on the purchase of a new tractor. The trade-in credit had been $55,296.28. Marcella had been paid nothing, and no gift tax return had been filed. Christine claimed, among other things, that the old tractor had been a gift. What is a "gift"? What are the elements of a gift? What do the facts suggest on this claim? Discuss.

2 Christine also claimed that she had tried to pay Marcella $20,000 on the trade-in of the tractor but that her mother had refused to accept it. Christine showed a check made out to Marcella for that amount and marked "void." Would you rule in Christine's favor on this claim? Why or why not?

▶ Critical Thinking and Writing Assignments

35–9 Critical Legal Thinking. Suppose that a certificate of deposit (CD) owned by two joint tenants (with the right of survivorship) is given by one of the joint tenants as security for a loan (without the other joint tenant's knowledge). Further suppose that the joint tenant dies after defaulting on the loan. Who has superior rights in the CD, the creditor or the other surviving joint tenant? Explain.

35–10 Video Question Go to this text's Web site at **www.cengage.com/blaw/blt** and select "Chapter 35."

Click on "Video Questions" and view the video titled *Personal Property and Bailments.* Then answer the following questions.

1 What type of bailment is discussed in the video?

2 What were Vinny's duties with regard to the rug-cleaning machine? What standard of care should apply?

3 Did Vinny exercise the appropriate degree of care? Why or why not? How would a court decide this issue?

▶ Practical Internet Exercises

Go to this text's Web site at **www.cengage.com/blaw/blt**, select "Chapter 35," and click on "Practical Internet Exercises." There you will find the following Internet research exercises that you can perform to learn more about the topics covered in this chapter.

Practical Internet Exercise 35–1: LEGAL PERSPECTIVE—Lost Property

Practical Internet Exercise 35–2: MANAGEMENT PERSPECTIVE—Bailments

Chapter 36

Real Property and Landlord-Tenant Law

(Jorge Michel/Creative Commons)

> "The right of property is the most sacred of all the rights of citizenship."
>
> —Jean-Jacques Rousseau, 1712–1778
> (French writer and philosopher)

Learning Objectives

After reading this chapter, you should be able to answer the following questions:

1. What can a person who holds property in fee simple absolute do with the property?

2. What are the requirements for acquiring property by adverse possession?

3. What limitations may be imposed on the rights of property owners?

4. What is a leasehold estate? What types of leasehold estates, or tenancies, can be created when real property is leased?

5. What are the respective duties of the landlord and the tenant concerning the use and maintenance of leased property?

From earliest times, property has provided a means for survival. Primitive peoples lived off the fruits of the land, eating the vegetation and wildlife. Later, as the vegetation was cultivated and the wildlife domesticated, property provided farmland and pasture. Throughout history, property has continued to be an indicator of family wealth and social position. Indeed, an individual's right to his or her property has become, in the words of Jean-Jacques Rousseau, one of the "most sacred of all the rights of citizenship."

In this chapter, we first examine the nature of real property. We then look at the various ways in which real property can be owned and at how ownership rights in real property are transferred from one person to another. We conclude the chapter with a discussion of leased property and landlord-tenant relationships.

▶ The Nature of Real Property

Real property consists of land and the buildings, plants, and trees that are on it. Real property also includes subsurface and airspace rights, as well as personal property that has become permanently attached to real property. Whereas personal property is movable, real property—also called *real estate* or *realty*—is immovable.

Land

Land includes the soil on the surface of the earth and the natural or artificial structures that are attached to it. It further includes all the waters contained on or under the surface and much, but not necessarily all, of the airspace above it. The exterior boundaries of land extend down to the center of the earth and up to the farthest reaches of the atmosphere (subject to certain qualifications).

ON THE WEB For links to numerous online legal sources relating to real property, go to www.findlaw.com/01topics/index.html and click on "Property Law."

Airspace and Subsurface Rights

The owner of real property has rights to the airspace above the land, as well as to the soil and minerals underneath it. Limitations on either airspace rights or subsurface rights normally must be indicated on the document that transfers title at the time of purchase. When no such limitations, or *encumbrances,* are noted, a purchaser generally can expect to have an unlimited right to possession of the property.

AIRSPACE RIGHTS   Disputes concerning airspace rights may involve the right of commercial and private planes to fly over property and the right of individuals and governments to seed clouds and produce rain artificially. Flights over private land normally do not violate property rights unless the flights are so low and so frequent that they directly interfere with the owner's enjoyment and use of the land.[1] Leaning walls or buildings and projecting eave spouts or roofs may also violate the airspace rights of an adjoining property owner.

SUBSURFACE RIGHTS   In many states, land ownership may be separated, in that the surface of a piece of land and the subsurface may have different owners. Subsurface rights can be extremely valuable, as these rights include the ownership of minerals, oil, and natural gas. Subsurface rights would be of little value, however, if the owner could not use the surface to exercise those rights. Hence, a subsurface owner has a right (called a *profit,* to be discussed later in this chapter) to go onto the surface of the land to, for example, discover and mine minerals.

When ownership is separated into surface and subsurface rights, each owner can pass title to what she or he owns without the consent of the other owner. Of course, conflicts can arise between the surface owner's use of the property and the subsurface owner's need to extract minerals, oil, or natural gas. In that situation, one party's interest may become subservient (secondary) to the other party's interest either by statute or by case law. If the owners of the subsurface rights excavate (dig), they are absolutely liable if their excavation causes the surface to collapse. Many states have statutes that also make the excavators liable for any damage to structures on the land. Typically, these statutes provide precise requirements for excavations of various depths.

"The meek shall inherit the earth, but not the mineral rights."
J. Paul Getty, 1892–1976
(American entrepreneur and industrialist)

Plant Life and Vegetation

Plant life, both natural and cultivated, is also considered to be real property. In many instances, the natural vegetation, such as trees, adds greatly to the value of the realty. When a parcel of land is sold and the land has growing crops on it, the sale includes the crops, unless otherwise specified in the sales contract. When crops are sold by themselves, however, they are considered to be personal property or goods. Consequently, the sale of crops is a sale of goods and thus is governed by the Uniform Commercial Code (UCC) rather than by real property law.[2]

---

1. *United States v. Causby,* 328 U.S. 256, 66 S.Ct. 1062, 90 L.Ed. 1206 (1946).
2. See UCC 2–107(2), discussed in Chapters 15 and 16.

Fixtures

Fixture An item that was once personal property but has become attached to real property in such a way that it takes on the characteristics of real property and becomes part of that real property.

Certain personal property can become so closely associated with the real property to which it is attached that the law views it as real property. Such property is known as a **fixture**—an item *affixed* to realty, meaning that it is attached to the real property by roots; embedded in it; permanently situated on it; or permanently attached by means of cement, plaster, bolts, nails, or screws. The fixture can be physically attached to real property, be attached to another fixture, or even be without any actual physical attachment to the land (such as a statue). As long as the owner intends the property to be a fixture, normally it will be a fixture.

Fixtures are included in the sale of land if the sales contract does not provide otherwise. The sale of a house includes the land and the house and the garage on the land, as well as the cabinets, plumbing, and windows. Because these are permanently affixed to the property, they are considered to be a part of it. Certain items, such as drapes and window-unit air conditioners, are difficult to classify. Thus, a contract for the sale of a house or commercial realty should indicate which items of this sort are included in the sale.

Under what circumstances will a farming irrigation system be considered a fixture?

(Kevin Dooley/Creative Commons)

CASE EXAMPLE 36.1 A farm had an eight-tower center-pivot irrigation system bolted to a cement slab and connected to an underground well. The bank held a mortgage note on the farm secured by "all buildings, improvements, and fixtures." The farm's owners had also used the property as security for other loans, but the contracts for those loans did not specifically mention fixtures or the irrigation system. Later, when the farmers were unable to repay their debts and filed for bankruptcy, a dispute arose between the bank and another creditor over the irrigation system. Ultimately, a court held that the irrigation system was a fixture because it was firmly attached to the land and integral to the operation of the farm. Therefore, the bank's security interest had priority over the other creditor's interest.[3] ●

Preventing Legal Disputes When real property is being sold, transferred, or subjected to a security interest, make sure that any contract specifically lists which fixtures are to be included. Without such a list, the parties may have very different ideas as to what is being transferred with the real property (or included as collateral for a loan). It is much simpler and less expensive to itemize fixtures in a contract than to engage in litigation.

▶ Ownership Interests in Real Property

Ownership of property is an abstract concept that cannot exist independently of the legal system. No one can actually possess or *hold* a piece of land, the airspace above it, the earth below it, and all the water contained on it. The legal system therefore recognizes certain rights and duties that constitute ownership interests in real property.

Recall from Chapter 35 that property ownership is often viewed as a bundle of rights. One who possesses the entire bundle of rights is said to hold the property in *fee simple,* which is the most complete form of ownership. When only some of the rights in the bundle are transferred to another person, the effect is to limit the ownership rights of both the transferor of the rights and the recipient.

"Few . . . men own their property. The property owns them."
Robert G. Ingersoll, 1833–1899
(American politician and lecturer)

---

3. *In re Sand & Sage Farm & Ranch, Inc.,* 266 Bankr. 507 (D.Kans. 2001).

Ownership in Fee Simple

Fee Simple Absolute   An ownership interest in land in which the owner has the greatest possible aggregation of rights, privileges, and power. Ownership in fee simple absolute is assigned forever to a person and her or his heirs without limitation.

In a **fee simple absolute,** the owner has the greatest aggregation of rights, privileges, and power possible. The owner can give the property away or dispose of the property by *deed* (the instrument used to transfer property, as will be discussed later in this chapter) or by will. When there is no will, the fee simple ownership interest passes to the owner's legal heirs on her or his death. A fee simple is potentially infinite in duration and is assigned forever to a person and her or his heirs without limitation or condition. The owner has the rights of *exclusive* possession and use of the property.

The rights that accompany a fee simple include the right to use the land for whatever purpose the owner sees fit. Of course, other laws, including applicable zoning, noise, and environmental laws, may limit the owner's ability to use the property in certain ways. A person who uses his or her property in a manner that unreasonably interferes with others' right to use or enjoy their own property can be liable for the tort of *nuisance* (discussed in Chapter 33).

In the following case, the court had to decide whether the noise—rock and roll music, conversation, and clacking pool balls—coming from a local bar (called a "saloon" during the days of cowboys in the United States) unreasonably interfered with a neighboring property owner's rights.

Case 36.1   Biglane v. Under the Hill Corp.

Mississippi Supreme Court, 949 So.2d 9 (2007).
www.mssc.state.ms.us[a]

(Christopher Thompson/Creative Commons)

When does the noise from a saloon interfere with the neighbors' property rights?

FACTS   In 1967, Nancy and James Biglane bought and refurbished a building at 27 Silver Street in Natchez, Mississippi, and opened the lower portion as a gift shop. In 1973, Andre Farish and Paul O'Malley bought the building next door, at 25 Silver Street, and opened the Natchez Under the Hill Saloon (the Saloon). Later, the Biglanes converted the upper floors of their building into an apartment and moved into it. Even though the Biglanes installed insulated walls and windows, located their bedroom on the side of the building away from the Saloon, and placed the air-conditioning unit on the side nearest the Saloon, the noise from the Saloon kept them awake at night. During the summer, the Saloon, which had no air-conditioning, opened its windows and doors, and live music echoed up and down the street. After the Biglanes complained about the noise, the Saloon installed thicker windows, replaced the loudest band, and asked the other bands to keep their output below a certain level of decibels. Still dissatisfied, the Biglanes filed a suit in a Mississippi state court against the Saloon. The court enjoined (prevented) the defendant from opening doors or windows when music was playing and ordered it to

prevent its patrons from loitering in the street. Both parties appealed to the Mississippi Supreme Court.

ISSUE   Did the Saloon's noise unreasonably interfere with the Biglanes' property rights?

DECISION   Yes. The Mississippi Supreme Court affirmed the lower court's injunction: "One landowner may not use his land so as to unreasonably annoy, inconvenience, or harm others."

REASON   The state supreme court pointed out that an owner may be subject to liability when the owner's conduct is "an invasion of another's interest in the private use and enjoyment of land and that invasion is * * * intentional and unreasonable." Reasonable use of property does not include "obnoxious noises, which in turn result in a material injury to owners of property in the vicinity, causing them to suffer substantial annoyance, inconvenience, and discomfort." An owner does not have to be driven from his or her property. The interference can be sufficient if "the enjoyment of life and property is rendered materially uncomfortable and annoying." Each case is to be decided on its own facts, including the location of the property and the surrounding circumstances. Here, the court balanced the interests of the Biglanes and the Saloon "in a quest for an equitable remedy that allowed the couple to enjoy their private apartment * * * while protecting a popular business and tourist attraction from over-regulation."

FOR CRITICAL ANALYSIS—Ethical Consideration   *At one point in their dispute, the Biglanes blocked off two parking lots that served the Saloon. Was this an unreasonable interference with the Saloon's rights? Explain.*

---

a. Under "Quick Links" at the right-hand side of the page, click on "Decisions Search." When that page opens, select "Natural Language" and then enter "Biglane" in the box and click on "Search." Select the file from the Mississippi Supreme Court (decided 2/27/07) to view the decision. The Mississippi judiciary maintains this Web site.

Life Estates

A **life estate** is an estate that lasts for the life of some specified individual. A **conveyance**, or transfer of real property, "to A for his life" creates a life estate. In a life estate, the life tenant's ownership rights cease to exist on the life tenant's death.[4] The life tenant has the right to use the land, provided that he or she commits no waste (injury to the land). In other words, the life tenant cannot use the land in a manner that would adversely affect its value. The life tenant is entitled to any rents generated by the land and can harvest crops from the land. If mines and oil wells are already on the land, the life tenant can extract minerals and oil and is entitled to the royalties, but he or she cannot exploit the land by creating new wells or mines.

The life tenant can create liens, *easements* (discussed below), and leases, but none can extend beyond the life of the tenant. In addition, with few exceptions, the owner of a life estate has an exclusive right to possession during her or his life.

Along with these rights, the life tenant also has some duties—to keep the property in repair and to pay property taxes. In short, the owner of the life estate has the same rights as a fee simple owner except that the life tenant must maintain the value of the property during her or his tenancy.

Nonpossessory Interests

In contrast to the types of property interests just described, some interests in land do not include any rights to possess the property. These interests, known as **nonpossessory interests,** include easements, profits, and licenses.

An **easement** is the right of a person to make limited use of another person's real property without taking anything from the property. An easement, for instance, can be the right to walk or drive across another's property. In contrast, a **profit**[5] is the right to go onto land owned by another and take away some part of the land itself or some product of the land. **EXAMPLE 36.2** Akmed owns Sandy View. Akmed gives Carmen the right to go there to remove all the sand and gravel that she needs for her cement business. Carmen has a profit. ●

Easements and profits can be classified as either *appurtenant* or *in gross*. Because easements and profits are similar and the same rules apply to both, we discuss them together.

EASEMENT OR PROFIT APPURTENANT An easement or profit *appurtenant* arises when the owner of one piece of land has a right to go onto (or remove something from) an adjacent piece of land owned by another. The land that is benefited by the easement is called the *dominant estate,* and the land that is burdened is called the *servient estate.* Because easements appurtenant are intended to *benefit the land,* they run (are conveyed) with the land when it is transferred. **EXAMPLE 36.3** Acosta has a right to drive his car across Green's land, which is adjacent to Acosta's land. This right-of-way over Green's property is an easement appurtenant to Acosta's property and can be used only by Acosta. If Acosta sells his land, the easement runs with the land to benefit the new owner. ●

EASEMENT OR PROFIT IN GROSS In an easement or profit *in gross,* the right to use or take things from another's land is given to one who does not own an adjacent tract of land. These easements are intended to *benefit a particular person or business,* not a particular piece of land,

---

4. Because a life tenant's rights in the property cease at death, life estates frequently are used to avoid probate proceedings—see Chapter 37. The person who owns the property deeds it to the person who would eventually inherit the property and reserves a life estate for herself or himself. That way, the property owner can live there until death, and the property then passes to the intended heir without the need for legal proceedings.

5. The term *profit,* as used here, does not refer to the profits made by a business firm. Rather, it means a gain or an advantage.

CONTRAST An easement appurtenant requires two adjacent pieces of land owned by two different persons, but an easement in gross needs only one piece of land owned by someone other than the owner of the easement.

and cannot be transferred. **EXAMPLE 36.4** Avery owns a parcel of land with a marble quarry. Avery conveys (transfers) to Classic Stone Corporation the right to come onto her land and remove up to five hundred pounds of marble per day. Classic Stone owns a profit in gross and cannot transfer this right to another. ● Similarly, when a utility company is granted an easement to run its power lines across another's property, it obtains an easement in gross.

CREATION OF AN EASEMENT OR PROFIT Most easements and profits are created by an express grant in a contract, deed (discussed shortly), or will (see Chapter 37). This allows the parties to include terms defining the extent and length of time of use. In some situations, an easement or profit can also be created without an express agreement.

An easement or profit may arise by *implication* when the circumstances surrounding the division of a parcel of property imply its existence. **EXAMPLE 36.5** Barrow divides a parcel of land that has only one well for drinking water. If Barrow conveys the half without a well to Jarad, a profit by implication arises because Jarad needs drinking water. ●

An easement may also be created by *necessity*. An easement by necessity does not require a division of property for its existence. A person who rents an apartment, for example, has an easement by necessity in the private road leading up to it.

An easement arises by *prescription* when one person exercises an easement, such as a right-of-way, on another person's land without the landowner's consent, and the use is apparent and continues for the length of time required by the applicable statute of limitations. (In much the same way, title to property may be obtained by *adverse possession*, as will be discussed later in this chapter.)

TERMINATION OF AN EASEMENT OR PROFIT An easement or profit can be terminated or extinguished in several ways. The simplest way is to deed it back to the owner of the land that is burdened by it. Another way is to abandon it and create evidence of intent to relinquish the right to use it. Mere nonuse will not extinguish an easement or profit *unless the nonuse is accompanied by an overt act showing the intent to abandon.* Also, if the owner of an easement or profit becomes the owner of the property burdened by it, then it is merged into the property.

License A revocable right or privilege of a person to come onto another person's land.

LICENSE In the context of real property, a **license** is the revocable right of a person to come onto another person's land. It is a personal privilege that arises from the consent of the owner of the land and can be revoked by the owner. A ticket to attend a movie at a theater is an example of a license. **EXAMPLE 36.6** The owner of a Broadway theater issues Alena a ticket to see a play. If Alena is refused entry into the theater because she is improperly dressed, she has no right to force her way into the theater. The ticket is only a revocable license and not a conveyance of an interest in property. ●

In essence, a license grants a person the authority to enter the land of another and perform a specified act or series of acts without obtaining any permanent interest in the land. What happens when a person with a license exceeds the authority granted and undertakes an action that is not permitted? That was the central issue in the following case.

Case 36.2 **Roman Catholic Church of Our Lady of Sorrows v. Prince Realty Management, LLC**

New York Supreme Court, Appellate Division, 47 A.D.3d 909, 850 N.Y.S.2d 569 (2008).

FACTS The Roman Catholic Church of Our Lady of Sorrows (the Church) and Prince Realty Management, LLC (Prince), own adjoining property in Queens County, New York. In 2005, the parties entered into an agreement by which the Church granted Prince a three-month license to use a

three-foot strip of its property immediately adjacent to Prince's property. The license specifically authorized Prince to remove an existing chain-link fence on the licensed strip and to "put up plywood panels surrounding the construction site, including the [licensed strip]." The license also required

Case 36.2–Continued

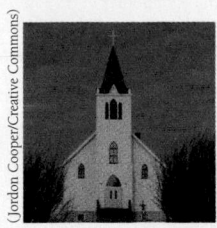

Did an adjoining property owner violate a license agreement with a church for temporary use of its property?

that Prince restore the boundary line between the properties with a new brick fence. The purpose of the license was to allow Prince to erect a temporary plywood fence to protect Prince's property during the construction of a new building. During the license's term, Prince installed structures consisting of steel piles and beams on the licensed property. The Church objected to these structures and repeatedly demanded that they be removed. The Church commenced an action to recover damages for breach of the license. The trial court concluded that the Church had made a *prima facie* case showing that structures were placed on its property by the defendant in violation of the license and that Prince had failed to dispute the plaintiff's claim that it had violated the agreement. Prince appealed.

ISSUE   Does a license that conveys the right to construct a temporary plywood fence on a three-foot strip of land during a construction project also convey the right to install steel piles and beams on the property?

DECISION   No. The state appellate court held that the license did not permit the adjoining property owner to install structures consisting of steel piles and beams on the licensed strip of property. The court found that by exceeding the authority granted in the license, the defendant's actions constituted trespass.

REASON   The reviewing court pointed out that "a license, within the context of real property law, grants the licensee a revocable non-assignable privilege to do one or more acts upon the land of a licensor, without granting possession of any interest herein. A license is the authority to do a particular act or series of acts upon another's land, which would amount to a trespass without such permission." The evidence was clear that the license allowed only for temporary structures. The defendant nonetheless installed structures consisting of steel piles and beams on the licensed property. "The plaintiff * * * established as a matter of law that the defendant's installation of these structures constituted a trespass regardless of whether they were subsequently removed."

FOR CRITICAL ANALYSIS—Legal Consideration   *The Church sued for damages. What would be an appropriate way of calculating those damages?*

▶ Transfer of Ownership

Ownership interests in real property are frequently transferred (conveyed) by sale, and the terms of the transfer are specified in a real estate sales contract. Often, real estate brokers or agents who are licensed by the state assist the buyers and sellers during the sales transaction. Real property ownership can also be transferred by gift, by will or inheritance, by possession, or by *eminent domain*. When ownership rights in real property are transferred, the type of interest being transferred and the conditions of the transfer normally are set forth in a *deed* executed by the person who is conveying the property.

Deeds

Deed   A document by which title to property (usually real property) is passed.

Possession and title to land are passed from person to person by means of a **deed**—the instrument of conveyance of real property. A deed is a writing signed by an owner of real property that transfers title to another. Deeds must meet certain requirements, but unlike a contract, a deed does not have to be supported by legally sufficient consideration. Gifts of real property are common, and they require deeds even though there is no consideration for the gift. To be valid, a deed must include the following:

1. The names of the *grantor* (the giver or seller) and the *grantee* (the donee or buyer).
2. Words evidencing an intent to convey the property (for example, "I hereby bargain, sell, grant, or give").
3. A legally sufficient description of the land.
4. The grantor's (and usually her or his spouse's) signature.
5. Delivery of the deed.

Warranty Deed   A deed in which the grantor assures (warrants to) the grantee that the grantor has title to the property conveyed in the deed, that there are no encumbrances on the property other than what the grantor has represented, and that the grantee will enjoy quiet possession of the property; a deed that provides the greatest amount of protection for the grantee.

WARRANTY DEEDS   Different types of deeds provide different degrees of protection against defects of title. A **warranty deed** makes the greatest number of warranties and thus provides the greatest protection against defects of title. In most states, special language is required to create a general warranty deed.

Warranty deeds commonly include a number of *covenants,* or promises, that the grantor makes to the grantee. These covenants include a covenant that the grantor has the title to, and the power to convey, the property; a covenant of quiet enjoyment (a warranty that the buyer will not be disturbed in her or his possession of the land); and a covenant that transfer of the property is made without knowledge of adverse claims of third parties. Generally, the warranty deed makes the grantor liable for all defects of title by the grantor and previous titleholders.

EXAMPLE 36.7 Julio sells a two-acre lot and office building by warranty deed. Subsequently, a third person shows up who has better title than Julio had and forces the buyer off the property. Here, the covenant of quiet enjoyment has been breached. The buyer can sue Julio to recover the purchase price of the land, plus any other damages incurred as a result. •

Special Warranty Deed A deed in which the grantor warrants only that the grantor or seller held good title during his or her ownership of the property and does not warrant that there were no defects of title when the property was held by previous owners.

SPECIAL WARRANTY DEEDS In contrast to a warranty deed, a **special warranty deed,** which is also referred to as a *limited warranty deed,* warrants only that the grantor or seller held good title during his or her ownership of the property. In other words, the grantor is not warranting that there were no defects of title when the property was held by previous owners.

If the special warranty deed discloses all liens or other encumbrances, the seller will not be liable to the buyer if a third person subsequently interferes with the buyer's ownership. If the third person's claim arises out of, or is related to, some act of the seller, however, the seller will be liable to the buyer for damages.

Implied Warranty of Habitability An implied promise by a seller of a new house that the house is fit for human habitation—that is, in a condition that is safe and suitable for people to live there. Also, the implied promise by a landlord that rented residential premises are habitable.

Note, however, that most states now imply a warranty—the **implied warranty of habitability**—in the sale of *new homes.* The seller of a new house warrants that it will be fit for human habitation even if the deed or contract of sale does not include such a warranty. Essentially, the seller is warranting that the house is in reasonable working order and is of reasonably sound construction. Under this theory, the seller of a new home can be liable if the home is defective. In some states, the warranty protects not only the first purchaser but any subsequent purchaser as well.

Quitclaim Deed A deed intended to pass any title, interest, or claim that the grantor may have in the property without warranting that such title is valid. A quitclaim deed offers the least amount of protection against defects of title.

QUITCLAIM DEEDS A **quitclaim deed** offers the least amount of protection against defects of title. Basically, a quitclaim deed conveys to the grantee whatever interest the grantor had; so, if the grantor had no interest, then the grantee receives no interest. Naturally, if the grantor had a defective title or no title at all, a conveyance by warranty deed or special warranty deed would not cure the defects. Such deeds, however, will give the buyer a cause of action to sue the seller.

A quitclaim deed can and often does serve as a release of the grantor's interest in a particular parcel of property. **EXAMPLE 36.8** After ten years of marriage, Sandi and Jim are getting a divorce. During the marriage, Sandi purchased a parcel of waterfront property next to her grandparents' home in Louisiana. Jim helped make some improvements to the property, but he is not sure what ownership interests, if any, he has in the property because Sandi used her own funds (acquired before the marriage) to purchase the lot. Jim agrees to quitclaim the property to Sandi as part of the divorce settlement, releasing any interest he might have in that piece of property. •

Recording Statutes Statutes that allow deeds, mortgages, and other real property transactions to be recorded so as to provide notice to future purchasers or creditors of an existing claim on the property.

RECORDING STATUTES Every jurisdiction has **recording statutes,** which allow deeds to be recorded for a fee. The grantee normally pays this fee because he or she is the one who will be protected by recording the deed.

Recording a deed gives notice to the public that a certain person is now the owner of a particular parcel of real estate. Thus, prospective buyers can check the public records to see whether there have been earlier transactions creating interests or rights in specific parcels of real property. Putting everyone on notice as to the identity of the true owner is intended to prevent the previous owners from fraudulently conveying the land to other purchasers. Deeds are recorded in the county where the property is located. Many state statutes require that the grantor sign the deed in the presence of two witnesses before it can be recorded.

Will or Inheritance

Property that is transferred on an owner's death is passed either by will or by state inheritance laws. If the owner of land dies with a will, the land passes in accordance with the terms of the will. If the owner dies without a will, state inheritance statutes prescribe how and to whom the property will pass. Transfers of property by will or inheritance will be examined in detail in Chapter 37.

Adverse Possession

Adverse Possession The acquisition of title to real property by occupying it openly, without the consent of the owner, for a period of time specified by a state statute. The occupation must be actual, open, continuous, exclusive, and in opposition to all others, including the owner.

Adverse possession is a means of obtaining title to land without delivery of a deed. Essentially, when one person possesses the property of another for a certain statutory period of time (three to thirty years, with ten years being most common), that person, called the *adverse possessor,* acquires title to the land and cannot be removed from it by the original owner. The adverse possessor may ultimately obtain a perfect title just as if there had been a conveyance by deed.

REQUIREMENTS FOR ADVERSE POSSESSION   For property to be held adversely, four elements must be satisfied:

1. Possession must be *actual and exclusive;* that is, the possessor must take sole physical occupancy of the property.
2. The possession must be *open, visible, and notorious,* not secret or clandestine. The possessor must occupy the land for all the world to see.
3. Possession must be *continuous and peaceable for the required period of time.* This requirement means that the possessor must not be interrupted in the occupancy by the true owner or by the courts.
4. Possession must be *hostile and adverse.* In other words, the possessor must claim the property as against the whole world. He or she cannot be living on the property with the permission of the owner.

CASE EXAMPLE 36.9   In the late 1960s, Bessie Otwell Sanders and her husband, William, acquired title from her grandmother to 24 acres of land in Louisiana known as the "Terry Brown Estate." This included 3.12 acres between Hemphill's Creek and the "old slough," a natural feature that appeared to have been the creek's original bed. William managed the timber on the land and marked at least two hundred trees with his wife's registered brand with the intent to show "that this property was occupied by someone."

In 2001, Jesse Moffett sold the timber on the 3.12 acres to B&S Timber, Inc. The Sanderses filed a trespass lawsuit against Moffett, who claimed that he had held title to the land in dispute since 1955. The court ruled that the Sanderses had proved all the requirements for adverse possession, even if they could not prove they owned the land initially. They had taken actual and sole possession of the property, run off trespassers, created a riding trail, shot hogs, hunted wood ducks, harvested berries, posted hunting signs, and erected deer stands. Moffett knew "as early as 1966 that Mr. and Mrs. Sanders intended to claim the property," yet he did not take any action. Thus, the court found that the Sanderses were the legal owners of the disputed property and ordered Moffett to pay them damages for taking the timber.[6] ●

6. *Otwell v. Diversified Timber Services, Inc.,* 896 So.2d 222 (La.App. 3d Cir. 2005).

PURPOSE OF THE DOCTRINE   There are a number of public-policy reasons for the adverse possession doctrine. These include society's interest in resolving boundary disputes, determining title when title to property is in question, and ensuring that real property remains in the stream of commerce. More fundamentally, policies behind the doctrine include rewarding possessors for putting land to productive use and punishing owners who sit on their rights too long and do not take action when they see adverse possession.

Eminent Domain

Even ownership in fee simple absolute is limited by a superior ownership. Just as in medieval England the king was the ultimate landowner, so in the United States the government has an ultimate ownership right in all land. This right, known as **eminent domain**, is sometimes referred to as the *condemnation power* of government to take land for public use. It gives the government the right to acquire possession of real property in the manner directed by the U.S. Constitution and the laws of the state whenever the public interest requires it. Property may be taken only for public use, not for private benefit.

EXAMPLE 36.10   When a new public highway is to be built, the government must decide where to build it and how much land to condemn. After the government determines that a particular parcel of land is necessary for public use, it will first offer to buy the property. If the owner refuses the offer, the government brings a judicial (**condemnation**) proceeding to obtain title to the land. Then, in another proceeding, the court determines the *fair value* of the land, which usually is approximately equal to its market value. ●

When the government uses its power of eminent domain to acquire land owned by a private party, a **taking** occurs. Under the *takings clause* of the Fifth Amendment to the U.S. Constitution, the government must pay "just compensation" to the property owner. State constitutions contain similar provisions.

Does the government engage in a taking when it diverts water across private property during an emergency? That was the question in the following case.

> **Eminent Domain**   The power of a government to take land from private citizens for public use on the payment of just compensation.

> **Condemnation**   The process of taking private property for public use through the government's power of eminent domain.

> **Taking**   The taking of private property by the government for public use. The government may not take private property for public use without "just compensation."

Case 36.3   Drake v. Walton County

District Court of Appeal of Florida, First District, 6 So.3d 717 (2009).
www.1dca.org[a]

(Ange Soleil/Creative Commons)

Did Walton County's reconfiguration of the drainage pattern of a lake result in the taking of property?

FACTS   In Walton County, Florida, water flows through a ditch from Oyster Lake to the Gulf of Mexico. To prevent the water from overflowing onto private property, the outflow was stabilized with the help of the Florida Department of Environmental Regulation. This made the land available for development. William and Patricia Hemby bought it. When Hurricane Opal caused the water to rise in Oyster Lake, Walton County reconfigured the drainage to divert the overflow onto the Hembys' property. The flow was eventually restored to pre-Opal conditions, but during a later emer-

gency, water was diverted onto the property to protect a neighbor's home. This diversion was not restored. The Hembys filed a suit against the county. After their deaths, their daughter Cozette Drake pursued the claim. The court entered a final judgment for the defendant. Drake appealed.

ISSUE   Did Walton County's reconfiguration of Oyster Lake's drainage pattern result in a taking of the Hembys' property?

DECISION   Yes. A state intermediate appellate court reversed the lower court's judgment and remanded the case for the entry of a judgment in Drake's favor and a determination of the amount of compensation to be paid.

REASON   Before the Hembys bought their property, the ditch draining Oyster Lake was stabilized, and water did not flow across the property. The Hembys reasonably relied on this drainage pattern when they bought the land. Walton County changed the flow to alleviate or prevent the flooding of other property during emergencies. This "may have been prudent and

---

a.   In the left column, in the "DCA Links" section, click on "Archived Opinions." On that page, in the "April 2009" section, click on "April 14." In the result, click on the name of the case to access the opinion. The First District Court of Appeal of Florida maintains this Web site.

Case 36.3–Continued

commendable," but the county's actions caused the Hembys' property to flood. "A county takes private property when it directs a concentrated flow of water from one property onto another, permanently depriving the owner[s] of all beneficial enjoyment of their property." After the latest emergency, the county allowed the diversion to remain, and it became a "continuous physical invasion of Appellant's property, rendering it useless."

WHY IS THIS CASE IMPORTANT?   *For decades, Oyster Lake sometimes overflowed onto nearby property until the drainage ditch at*

the heart of this case was excavated and the outflow was stabilized. A Florida statute authorizes local governments to divert water under the state's police power in an emergency. Hurricane Opal created emergency conditions to which the county responded, restoring the natural overflow drainage pattern to confer a public benefit on some property owners. The county argued that these facts immunized it from liability on a takings claim. A ruling in the county's favor on any of these arguments would have set a costly precedent for private property owners.

Ethical Issue ⚖

Should eminent domain be used to promote private development? Issues of fairness often arise when the government takes private property for public use. One issue is whether it is fair for a government to take property by eminent domain and then convey it to private developers. For example, suppose that a city government decides that it is in the public interest to have a larger parking lot for a local, privately owned sports stadium or to have a manufacturing plant locate in the city to create more jobs. The government may condemn certain tracts of existing housing or business property and then convey the land to the privately owned stadium or manufacturing plant. Such actions may bring in private developers and businesses that provide jobs and increase tax revenues, thus revitalizing communities. But is the land really being taken for "public use," as required by the Fifth Amendment to the U.S. Constitution?

Although the United States Supreme Court has approved this type of taking, the Court also recognized that individual states have the right to pass laws that prohibit takings for economic development.[7] Thirty-five states have done exactly that, limiting the government's ability to take private property and give it to private developers. At least eight states have amended their state constitutions, and a number of other states have passed ballot measures. Thus, the debate over whether it is fair for a government to take its citizens' property for economic redevelopment continues. (See the *Linking the Law to Economics* feature on page 919 for additional information on this topic.)

▶ **Leasehold Estates**

Leasehold Estate   An interest in real property that is held by a tenant for only a limited time under a lease. In every leasehold estate, the tenant has a qualified right to possess and/or use the land.

A **leasehold estate** is created when a real property owner or lessor (landlord) agrees to convey the right to possess and use the property to a lessee (tenant) for a certain period of time. In every leasehold estate, the tenant has a *qualified* right to exclusive possession (qualified by the right of the landlord to enter on the premises to ensure that waste is not being committed). The *temporary* nature of possession, under a lease, is what distinguishes a tenant from a purchaser, who acquires title to the property. The tenant can use the land—for example, by harvesting crops—but cannot injure it by such activities as cutting down timber for sale or extracting oil.

Fixed-Term Tenancy   A type of tenancy under which property is leased for a specified period of time, such as a month, a year, or a period of years; also called a tenancy for years.

Fixed-Term Tenancy

A **fixed-term tenancy**, also called a *tenancy for years,* is created by an express contract by which property is leased for a specified period of time, such as a day, a month, a year,

---

7. See *Kelo v. City of New London, Connecticut,* 545 U.S. 469, 125 S.Ct. 2655, 162 L.Ed.2d 439 (2005). The *Kelo* case forms the basis of the *Case Analysis Question* on page 923, and an excerpt of the case appears in Appendix F.

or a period of years. Signing a one-year lease to occupy an apartment, for instance, creates a fixed-term tenancy. Note that the term need not be specified by date and can be conditioned on the occurrence of an event, such as leasing a cabin for the summer or an apartment during Mardi Gras. At the end of the period specified in the lease, the lease ends (without notice), and possession of the property returns to the lessor. If the tenant dies during the period of the lease, the lease interest passes to the tenant's heirs as personal property. Often, leases include renewal or extension provisions.

Periodic Tenancy

Periodic Tenancy   A lease interest in land for an indefinite period involving payment of rent at fixed intervals, such as week to week, month to month, or year to year.

A **periodic tenancy** is created by a lease that does not specify how long it is to last but does specify that rent is to be paid at certain intervals. This type of tenancy is automatically renewed for another rental period unless properly terminated. **EXAMPLE 36.11** Kayla enters into a lease with Capital Properties. The lease states, "Rent is due on the tenth day of every month." This provision creates a periodic tenancy from month to month. ● This type of tenancy can also extend from week to week or from year to year.

Under the common law, to terminate a periodic tenancy, the landlord or tenant must give at least one period's notice to the other party. If the tenancy extends from month to month, for example, one month's notice must be given prior to the last month's rent payment. State statutes may require a different period for notice of termination in a periodic tenancy, however.

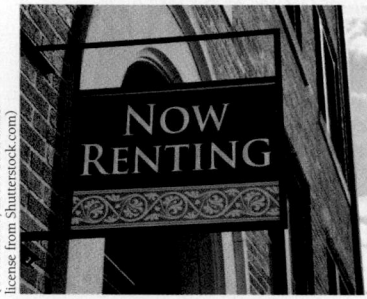

Does a periodic tenancy terminate at a specific date by contract?

Tenancy at Will

Tenancy at Will   A type of tenancy that either party can terminate without notice; can arise when a landowner allows a person to live on the premises without paying rent.

With a **tenancy at will**, either party can terminate the tenancy without notice. This type of tenancy can arise if a landlord rents property to a tenant "for as long as both agree" or allows a person to live on the premises without paying rent. Tenancies at will are rare today because most state statutes require a landlord to provide some period of notice to terminate a tenancy (as previously noted). States may also require a landowner to have sufficient cause (reason) to end a residential tenancy. Certain events, such as the death of either party or the voluntary commission of waste by the tenant, automatically terminate a tenancy at will.

Tenancy at Sufferance

Tenancy at Sufferance   A type of tenancy under which a tenant who, after rightfully being in possession of leased premises, continues (wrongfully) to occupy the property after the lease has terminated. The tenant has no rights to possess the property and occupies it only because the person entitled to evict the tenant has not done so.

The mere possession of land without right is called a **tenancy at sufferance.** A tenancy at sufferance is not a true tenancy because it is created when a tenant *wrongfully* retains possession of property. Whenever a tenancy for years or a periodic tenancy ends and the tenant continues to retain possession of the premises without the owner's permission, a tenancy at sufferance is created.

When a commercial or residential tenant wrongfully retains possession, the landlord is entitled to damages. Typically, the damages are based on the fair market rental value of the premises after the expiration of the lease. If the landlord has increased the rent for the premises, and the tenant does not agree to pay the higher rent and does not vacate the premises, then the proper standard of damages may be an issue. A court has to determine whether another tenant was willing to pay the higher rent during the time the existing tenant retained possession. If the landlord cannot show that another tenant was ready to rent the property at the higher rent, the proper standard of damages is the existing rental rate (rather than the higher rate).

▶ Landlord-Tenant Relationships

A landlord-tenant relationship is established by a lease contract. As mentioned, a lease contract arises when a property owner (landlord) agrees to give another party (the tenant) the exclusive right to possess the property—usually for a price and for a specified term. In most states, statutes require leases for terms exceeding one year to be in writing. The lease

ON THE WEB   You can find online links to most uniform laws, including the Uniform Residential Landlord and Tenant Act (URLTA), at www.lawsource.com.

NOTE Sound business practice dictates that a lease for commercial property should be written carefully and should clearly define the parties' rights and obligations.

"Give a landlord an inch and he'll build an apartment house."

Saul Antin, 1949–present
(American businessman)

Eviction A landlord's act of depriving a tenant of possession of the leased premises.

Constructive Eviction A form of eviction that occurs when a landlord fails to perform adequately any of the duties (such as providing heat in the winter) required by the lease, thereby making the tenant's further use and enjoyment of the property exceedingly difficult or impossible.

ON THE WEB Many Web sites now provide information on laws and other topics relating to landlord-tenant relationships. One of them is TenantNet™ at **www.tenant.net**.

should describe the property and indicate the length of the term, the amount of the rent, and how and when it is to be paid.

State or local law often dictates permissible lease terms. For example, a statute or ordinance might prohibit the leasing of a structure that is in a certain physical condition or is not in compliance with local building codes. In 1972, in an effort to create more uniformity in the law governing landlord-tenant relationships, the National Conference of Commissioners on Uniform State Laws issued the Uniform Residential Landlord and Tenant Act (URLTA). Twenty-one states have adopted variations of the URLTA.

In the past forty years, landlord-tenant relationships, which were traditionally governed by contract law, have become much more complex, as has the law governing them. We look now at the respective rights and duties of landlords and tenants.

Rights and Duties

The rights and duties of landlords and tenants generally pertain to four broad areas of concern—the possession, use, maintenance, and, of course, rent of leased property.

POSSESSION   A landlord is obligated to give a tenant possession of the property that the tenant has agreed to lease. After obtaining possession, the tenant retains the property exclusively until the lease expires, unless the lease states otherwise.

The covenant of quiet enjoyment mentioned previously also applies to leased premises. Under this covenant, the landlord promises that during the lease term, neither the landlord nor anyone having a superior title to the property will disturb the tenant's use and enjoyment of the property. This covenant forms the essence of the landlord-tenant relationship, and if it is breached, the tenant can terminate the lease and sue for damages.

If the landlord deprives the tenant of possession of the leased property or interferes with the tenant's use or enjoyment of it, an eviction occurs. An **eviction** arises, for instance, when the landlord changes the lock and refuses to give the tenant a new key. A **constructive eviction** occurs when the landlord wrongfully performs or fails to perform any of the duties the lease requires, thereby making the tenant's further use and enjoyment of the property exceedingly difficult or impossible. Examples of constructive eviction include a landlord's failure to provide heat in the winter, electricity, or other essential utilities.

USE AND MAINTENANCE OF THE PREMISES   If the parties do not limit by agreement the uses to which the property may be put, the tenant may make any use of it, as long as the use is legal and reasonably relates to the purpose for which the property is adapted or ordinarily used and does not injure the landlord's interest.

The tenant is responsible for any damage to the premises that he or she causes, intentionally or negligently, and may be held liable for the cost of returning the property to the physical condition it was in at the lease's inception. Also, the tenant is not entitled to create a *nuisance* by substantially interfering with others' quiet enjoyment of their property rights (nuisance was discussed in Chapter 33 and is illustrated in Case 36.1 on page 908). Unless the parties have agreed otherwise, the tenant is not responsible for ordinary wear and tear and the property's consequent depreciation in value.

In some jurisdictions, landlords of residential property are required by statute to maintain the premises in good repair. Landlords must also comply with any applicable state statutes and city ordinances regarding maintenance and repair of buildings.

IMPLIED WARRANTY OF HABITABILITY   The *implied warranty of habitability,* which was discussed earlier in this chapter in the context of the sale of new homes, also applies to residential leases. It requires a landlord who leases residential property to ensure that the premises are habitable—that is, safe and suitable for people to live in. Also, the landlord must make repairs to maintain the premises in that condition for the lease's duration.

Generally, this warranty applies to major, or *substantial,* physical defects that the landlord knows or should know about and has had a reasonable time to repair—for example, a large hole in the roof.

RENT   *Rent* is the tenant's payment to the landlord for the tenant's occupancy or use of the landlord's real property. Usually, the tenant must pay the rent even if she or he refuses to occupy the property or moves out, as long as the refusal or the move is unjustified and the lease is in force. Under the common law, if the leased premises were destroyed by fire or flood, the tenant still had to pay rent. Today, however, if an apartment building burns down, most state's laws do not require tenants to continue to pay rent.

In some situations, such as when a landlord breaches the implied warranty of habitability, a tenant may be allowed to withhold rent as a remedy. When rent withholding is authorized under a statute, the tenant must usually put the amount withheld into an *escrow account.* This account is held in the name of the depositor (the tenant) and an *escrow agent* (usually the court or a government agency), and the funds are returnable to the depositor if the third person (the landlord) fails to make the premises habitable.

Transferring Rights to Leased Property

Either the landlord or the tenant may wish to transfer her or his rights to the leased property during the term of the lease. If a landlord transfers complete title to the leased property to another, the tenant becomes the tenant of the new owner. The new owner may collect subsequent rent but must abide by the terms of the existing lease.

ASSIGNMENT   The tenant's transfer of his or her entire interest in the leased property to a third person is an *assignment of the lease.* Many leases require that an assignment have the landlord's written consent. An assignment that lacks consent can be avoided (nullified) by the landlord. State statutes may specify that the landlord may not unreasonably withhold consent, though. Also, a landlord who knowingly accepts rent from the assignee may be held to have waived the consent requirement.

When an assignment is valid, the assignee acquires all of the tenant's rights under the lease. An assignment, however, does not release the original tenant (the assignor) from the obligation to pay rent should the assignee default. Also, if the assignee exercises an option under the original lease to extend the term, the assigning tenant remains liable for the rent during the extension, unless the landlord agrees otherwise.

SUBLEASES   The tenant's transfer of all or part of the premises for a period shorter than the lease term is a **sublease.** Many leases also require the landlord's written consent for a sublease. If the landlord's consent is required, a sublease without such permission is ineffective. Also, like an assignment, a sublease does not release the tenant from her or his obligations under the lease.

EXAMPLE 36.12   Derek, a student, leases an apartment for a two-year period. Although Derek had planned on attending summer school, he decides to accept a job offer in Europe for the summer months instead. Derek therefore obtains his landlord's consent to sublease the apartment to Ava. Ava is bound by the same terms of the lease as Derek, and the landlord can hold Derek liable if Ava violates the lease terms. ●

 ## Reviewing . . . Real Property and Landlord-Tenant Law

Vern Shoepke purchased a two-story home from Walter and Eliza Bruster in the town of Roche, Maine. The warranty deed did not specify what covenants would be included in the conveyance. The property was adjacent to a public park that included a popular Frisbee golf course. (Frisbee golf is a sport similar to golf but using Frisbees.) Wayakichi Creek ran along the north end of the park and along Shoepke's property. The deed allowed Roche citizens the right to walk across a five-foot-wide section of the lot beside Wayakichi Creek as part of a two-mile public trail system. Teenagers regularly

---

NOTE   Options that may be available to a tenant on a landlord's breach of the implied warranty of habitability include repairing the defect and deducting the cost from the rent, canceling the lease, and suing for damages.

"Even in hell the peasant will have to serve the landlord, for, while the landlord is boiling in a cauldron, the peasant will have to put wood under it."

Russian Proverb

Sublease   A lease executed by the lessee of real estate to a third person, conveying the same interest that the lessee enjoys but for a shorter term than that held by the lessee.

threw Frisbee golf discs from the walking path behind Shoepke's property over his yard to the adjacent park. Shoepke habitually shouted and cursed at the teenagers, demanding that they not throw the discs over his yard. Two months after moving into his Roche home, Shoepke leased the second floor to Lauren Slater for nine months. (The lease agreement did not specify that Shoepke's consent would be required to sublease the second floor.) After three months of tenancy, Slater sublet the second floor to a local artist, Javier Indalecio. Over the remaining six months, Indalecio's use of oil paints damaged the carpeting in Shoepke's home. Using the information presented in the chapter, answer the following questions.

1. What is the term for the right of Roche citizens to walk across Shoepke's land on the trail?
2. What covenants would most courts infer were included in the warranty deed that was used in the property transfer from the Brusters to Shoepke?
3. Can Shoepke hold Slater financially responsible for the damage to the carpeting caused by Indalecio?
4. Suppose that Slater—to offset her liability for the carpet damage caused by Indalecio—files a counterclaim against Shoepke for breach of the covenant of quiet enjoyment. Could the fact that teenagers continually throw Frisbees over the leased property arguably be a breach of the covenant of quiet enjoyment? Why or why not?

Linking the Law *to Economics*
Eminent Domain

As you learned in this chapter, private ownership of land is always limited by the government's power to take private property for public use through eminent domain. The U.S. Constitution allows private property to be condemned so that it can used for public benefit.

You may have already learned in an economics course that when an exchange is voluntary, both parties by definition are better off—otherwise, they would not engage in the exchange. In contrast, an involuntary exchange occurs when, for example, a robber puts a gun to your head and says, "Your wallet or your life." Voluntary exchange is the basis of all market economic systems. Indeed, some economists argue that the only way a nation can experience economic growth is through voluntary exchange because both parties to such exchanges always benefit.

In this country, much real property is privately owned and is transferred through voluntary exchange. The owner exchanges property for a payment that the purchaser agrees to make. If the owner thinks that the offered payment is not sufficient, then the sale does not occur.

The Government Can Force Involuntary Transfers

When a government exercises its right to obtain private property through eminent domain, however, the exchange is not voluntary. The government is forcing the property owner to sell his or her property. When property is sold involuntarily, though, the seller is worse off. The justification for allowing the government to take property through involuntary transfers is that the government will put the property to a use that will benefit the community more than the transaction will hurt the previous property owner. For example, the property owners whose homes are condemned so that land can be used for a new school will suffer less than the community will benefit from having well-educated children.

When Government Does Not Use Eminent Domain for a Public Purpose

In recent years, some local governments have used the power of eminent domain to obtain private property in order to resell it to another

private party. In addition to raising ethical questions (see this chapter's *Ethical Issues* feature on page 915), such transactions have economic consequences.

Consider, for example, how private real estate developers operate. If an area of town appears undervalued, the developers will calculate the costs of buying the land, including the houses from the homeowners, tearing the houses down, and building a shopping mall on the site. In making these financial projections, the developers have to determine whether, when all costs are included, the projected revenues will yield a profit.

Now suppose that the municipal government forces those same homeowners to sell their land to the government, which then resells it to the developers. Obviously, the developers obtain the land at a lower cost than they would have had to pay if they had acquired it directly from the homeowners. In essence, the local government is forcing current homeowners to subsidize private developers so that they can put up a shopping mall.

Although some people argue that the local government is providing the subsidy, that is not the situation. The subsidy is coming from those homeowners who were forced to sell because the government condemned their property. As this example illustrates, any use of eminent domain to take private property to be sold to other private companies has adverse consequences that may not be completely justified on any grounds.

FOR CRITICAL ANALYSIS

Under what circumstances is it cheaper for private developers to obtain formerly private property through the government's use of eminent domain?

Key Terms

adverse possession 913	fixed-term tenancy 915	quitclaim deed 912
condemnation 914	fixture 907	recording statutes 912
constructive eviction 917	implied warranty of habitability 912	special warranty deed 912
conveyance 909	leasehold estate 915	sublease 918
deed 911	license 910	taking 914
easement 909	life estate 909	tenancy at sufferance 916
eminent domain 914	nonpossessory interest 909	tenancy at will 916
eviction 917	periodic tenancy 916	warranty deed 911
fee simple absolute 908	profit 909	

Chapter Summary: Real Property and Landlord-Tenant Law

The Nature of Real Property (See pages 905–907.)	Real property (also called real estate or realty) is immovable. It includes land, subsurface and airspace rights, plant life and vegetation, and fixtures.
Ownership Interests in Real Property (See pages 907–911.)	1. *Fee simple absolute*—The most complete form of ownership. 2. *Life estate*—An estate that lasts for the life of a specified individual, during which time the individual is entitled to possess, use, and benefit from the estate; the life tenant's ownership rights in the life estate cease to exist on her or his death. 3. *Nonpossessory interest*—An interest that involves the right to use real property but not to possess it. Easements, profits, and licenses are nonpossessory interests.
Transfer of Ownership (See pages 911–915.)	1. *By deed*—When real property is sold or transferred as a gift, title to the property is conveyed by means of a deed. A deed must meet specific legal requirements. A *warranty deed* provides the most extensive protection against defects of title. A *quitclaim deed* conveys to the grantee only whatever interest the grantor had in the property. A deed may be recorded in the manner prescribed by *recording statutes* in the appropriate jurisdiction to give third parties notice of the owner's interest. 2. *By will or inheritance*—If the owner dies after having made a valid will, the land passes as specified in the will. If the owner dies without having made a will, the heirs inherit according to state inheritance statutes. 3. *By adverse possession*—When a person possesses the property of another for a statutory period of time (ten years is the most common), that person acquires title to the property, provided the possession is actual and exclusive, open and visible, continuous and peaceable, and hostile and adverse (without the permission of the owner). 4. *By eminent domain*—The government can take land for public use, with just compensation, when the public interest requires the taking.
Leasehold Estates (See pages 915–916.)	A leasehold estate is an interest in real property that is held for only a limited period of time, as specified in the lease agreement. Types of tenancies include the following: 1. *Fixed-term tenancy*—Tenancy for a period of time stated by express contract. 2. *Periodic tenancy*—Tenancy for a period determined by the frequency of rent payments; automatically renewed unless proper notice is given. 3. *Tenancy at will*—Tenancy for as long as both parties agree; no notice of termination is required. 4. *Tenancy at sufferance*—Possession of land without legal right.
Landlord-Tenant Relationships (See pages 916–918.)	1. *Lease agreement*—The landlord-tenant relationship is created by a lease agreement. State or local laws may dictate whether the lease must be in writing and what lease terms are permissible. 2. *Rights and duties*—The rights and duties that arise under a lease agreement generally pertain to the following areas: a. Possession—The tenant has an exclusive right to possess the leased premises. Under the covenant of quiet enjoyment, the landlord promises that during the lease term neither the landlord nor anyone having superior title to the property will disturb the tenant's use and enjoyment of the property.

Chapter Summary: Real Property and Landlord-Tenant Law—Continued

Landlord-Tenant Relationships—Continued	b. Use and maintenance of the premises—Unless the parties agree otherwise, the tenant may make any legal use of the property. The tenant is responsible for any damage that he or she causes. The landlord must comply with laws that set specific standards for the maintenance of real property. The implied warranty of habitability requires that a landlord furnish and maintain residential premises in a habitable condition (that is, in a condition safe and suitable for human life).
	c. Rent—The tenant must pay the rent as long as the lease is in force, unless the tenant justifiably refuses to occupy the property or withholds the rent because of the landlord's failure to maintain the premises properly.
	3. *Transferring rights to leased property—*
	a. If the landlord transfers complete title to the leased property, the tenant becomes the tenant of the new owner. The new owner may then collect the rent but must abide by the existing lease.
	b. Generally, in the absence of an agreement to the contrary, tenants may assign their rights (but not their duties) under a lease contract to a third person. Tenants may also sublease leased property to a third person, but the original tenant is not relieved of any obligations to the landlord under the lease. In either situation, the landlord's consent may be required, but statutes may prohibit the landlord from unreasonably withholding consent.

 ExamPrep

ISSUE SPOTTERS

1. Bernie sells his house to Consuela under a warranty deed. Later, Delmira appears, holding a better title to the house than Consuela has. Delmira wants Consuela off the property. What can Consuela do?

2. Grey owns a commercial building in fee simple. Grey transfers temporary possession of the building to Haven Corporation (HC). Can HC transfer possession for even less time to Idyll Company? Explain.

BEFORE THE TEST

Check your answers to the Issue Spotters, and at the same time, take the interactive quiz for this chapter. Go to **www.cengage.com/blaw/blt** and click on "Chapter 36." First, click on "Answers to Issue Spotters" to check your answers. Next, click on "Interactive Quiz" to assess your mastery of the concepts in this chapter. Then click on "Flashcards" to review this chapter's Key Term definitions.

 For Review

Answers for the even-numbered questions in this For Review *section can be found on this text's accompanying Web site at* **www.cengage.com/blaw/blt**. *Select "Chapter 36" and click on "For Review."*

1 What can a person who holds property in fee simple absolute do with the property?
2 What are the requirements for acquiring property by adverse possession?
3 What limitations may be imposed on the rights of property owners?
4 What is a leasehold estate? What types of leasehold estates, or tenancies, can be created when real property is leased?
5 What are the respective duties of the landlord and the tenant concerning the use and maintenance of leased property?

 Hypothetical Scenarios and Case Problems

36–1 Property Ownership. Twenty-two years ago, Lorenz was a wanderer. At that time, he decided to settle down on an unoccupied, three-acre parcel of land that he did not own. People in the area told him that they had no idea who owned the property. Lorenz built a house on the land, got married, and raised three children while living there. He fenced in the land, installed a gate with a sign above it that read "Lorenz's Homestead," and removed trespassers. Lorenz is now confronted by Joe Reese, who has a deed in his name as owner of the property. Reese, claiming ownership of the land, orders Lorenz and his family off the property. Discuss who has the better "title" to the property.

36–2 **Hypothetical Question with Sample Answer** Wiley and Gemma are neighbors. Wiley's lot is extremely large, and his present and future use of it will not involve the entire area. Gemma wants to build a single-car garage and driveway along the present lot boundary. Because the placement of her existing structures makes it impossible for her to comply with an ordinance requiring buildings to be set back fifteen feet from an adjoining property line, Gemma cannot build the garage. Gemma contracts to purchase ten feet of Wiley's property along their boundary line for $3,000. Wiley is willing to sell but will give Gemma only a quitclaim deed, whereas Gemma wants a warranty deed. Discuss the differences between these deeds as they would affect the rights of the parties if the title to this ten feet of land later proves to be defective.

—For a sample answer to Question 36–2, go to Appendix E at the end of this text.

36–3 **Easements.** The Wallens family owned a cabin on Lummi Island in the state of Washington. A driveway ran from the cabin across their property to South Nugent Road. In 1952, Floyd Massey bought the adjacent lot and built a cabin. To gain access to his property, he used a bulldozer to extend the driveway, without the Wallenses' permission but also without their objection. In 1975, the Wallenses sold their property to Wright Fish Co. Massey continued to use and maintain the driveway without permission or objection. In 1984, Massey sold his property to Robert Drake. Drake and his employees continued to use and maintain the driveway without permission or objection, although Drake knew it was located largely on Wright's property. In 1997, Wright sold its lot to Robert Smersh. The next year, Smersh told Drake to stop using the driveway. Drake filed a suit in a Washington state court against Smersh, claiming an easement by prescription (which is created by meeting the same requirements as adverse possession). Does Drake's use of the driveway meet all of the requirements? What should the court rule? Explain. [*Drake v. Smersh*, 122 Wash.App. 147, 89 P.3d 726 (Div. 1 2004)]

36–4 **Case Problem with Sample Answer** The Hope Partnership for Education, a religious organization, proposed to build a private independent middle school in a blighted neighborhood in Philadelphia, Pennsylvania. In 2002, the Hope Partnership asked the Redevelopment Authority of the City of Philadelphia to acquire specific land for the project and sell it to the Hope Partnership for a nominal price. The land included a house at 1839 North Eighth Street owned by Mary Smith, whose daughter Veronica lived there with her family. The Authority offered Smith $12,000 for the house and initiated a taking of the property. Smith filed a suit in a Pennsylvania state court against the Authority, admitting that the house was a "substandard structure in a blighted area," but arguing that the taking was unconstitutional because its beneficiary was private. The Authority asserted that only the public purpose of the taking should be considered, not the status of the property's developer. On what basis can a government entity use the power of eminent domain to take property? What are the limits to this power? How should the court rule? Why? [*In re Redevelopment Authority of City of Philadelphia*, 588 Pa. 789, 906 A.2d 1197 (2006)]

—After you have answered Problem 36–4, compare your answer with the sample answer given on the Web site that accompanies this text. Go to **www.cengage.com/blaw/blt**, select "Chapter 36," and click on "Case Problem with Sample Answer."

36–5 **Ownership in Fee Simple.** Thomas and Teresa Cline built a house on a 76-acre parcel of real estate next to Roy Berg's home and property in Augusta County, Virginia. The homes were about 1,800 feet apart but in view of each other. After several disagreements between the parties, Berg equipped an 11-foot tripod with motion sensors and floodlights that intermittently illuminated the Clines' home. Berg also installed surveillance cameras that tracked some of the movement on the Clines' property. The cameras transmitted on an open frequency, which could be received by any television within range. The Clines asked Berg to turn off, or at least redirect, the lights. When he refused, they erected a fence for 200 feet along the parties' common property line. The 32-foot-high fence consisted of 20 utility poles spaced 10 feet apart with plastic wrap stretched between the poles. This effectively blocked the lights and cameras. Berg filed a suit against the Clines in a Virginia state court, complaining that the fence interfered unreasonably with his use and enjoyment of his property. He asked the court to order the Clines to take the fence down. What are the limits on an owner's use of property? How should the court rule in this case? Why? [*Cline v. Berg*, 273 Va. 142, 639 S.E.2d 231 (2007)]

36–6 **Tenancy at Sufferance Damages.** S&V Liquor, Inc., leased commercial retail space from the Charles Downey Family Limited Partnership for five years at a monthly rent of $3,333.33. The lease provided that S&V could renew for another five years if it gave Downey notice of intent to renew no later than 120 days before the lease expired. S&V did not send notice of intent to renew when the lease was coming to an end. Downey sent a letter offering to renew the lease at a new rate of $9,167.67 per month. S&V did not respond. Five days before the lease was to expire, S&V wrote that it intended to remain as a tenant for another six months, after which, it would move to a new location. Downey refused and sued S&V for damages of $9,167.67 per month during the six-month period, rather than the original rent paid by S&V. The trial court awarded Downey monthly rent at the original rate for the six-month period. Downey appealed, contending that it should have been awarded the higher lease rate as damages. Which monthly rental rate should apply? Why? [*Charles Downey Family Limited Partnership v. S&V Liquor, Inc.*, 880 N.E.2d 322 (Ind.Ct. App. 2008)]

36–7 Commercial Lease Terms. Gi Hwa Park entered into a lease with Landmark HHH, LLC, for retail space in the Plaza at Landmark, a shopping center in Virginia. The lease required that the landlord keep the roof "in good repair" and that the tenant obtain insurance on her inventory and absolve the landlord from any losses to the extent of the insurance proceeds. Park opened a store—The Four Seasons—in the space, specializing in imported men's suits and accessories. Within a month of the opening and continuing for nearly eight years, water intermittently leaked through the roof, causing damage. Landmark eventually had a new roof installed, but water continued to leak into The Four Seasons. On a night of record rainfall, the store suffered substantial water damage, and Park was forced to close the store. On what basis might Park seek to recover from Landmark? What might Landmark assert in response? Which party's argument is more likely to succeed, and why? [*Landmark HHH, LLC v. Gi Hwa Park*, 277 Va. 50, 671 S.E.2d 143 (2009)]

36–8 **A Question of Ethics** *In 1999, Stephen and Linda Kailin bought the Monona Center, a mall in Madison, Wisconsin, from Perry Armstrong for $760,000. The contract provided,*

"Seller represents to Buyer that as of the date of acceptance Seller had no notice or knowledge of conditions affecting the Property or transaction" other than certain items disclosed at the time of the offer. Armstrong told the Kailins of the Center's eight tenants, their lease expiration dates, and the monthly and annual rent due under each lease. One of the lessees, Ring's All-American Karate, occupied about a third of the Center's space under a five-year lease. Because of Ring's financial difficulties, Armstrong had agreed to reduce its rent for nine months in 1997. By the time of the sale to the Kailins, Ring owed $13,910 in unpaid rent, but Armstrong did not tell the Kailins, who did not ask. Ring continued to fail to pay rent and finally vacated the Center. The Kailins filed a suit in a Wisconsin state court against Armstrong and others, alleging, among other things, misrepresentation. [Kailin v. Armstrong, 2002 WI App. 70, 252 Wis.2d 676, 643 N.W.2d 132 (2002)]

1 Did Armstrong have a duty to disclose Ring's delinquency and default to the Kailins? Explain.

2 What obligation, if any, did Ring have to the Kailins or Armstrong after failing to pay the rent and eventually defaulting on the lease? Why?

▶ **Critical Thinking and Writing Assignments**

36–9 Critical Thinking and Writing Assignment for Business. Garza Construction Co. erects a silo (a grain storage facility) on Reeve's ranch. Garza also lends Reeve funds to pay for the silo under an agreement providing that the silo is not to become part of the land until Reeve completes the loan payments. Before the silo is paid for, Metropolitan State Bank, the mortgage holder on Reeve's land, forecloses on the property. Metropolitan contends that the silo is a fixture to the realty and that the bank is therefore entitled to the proceeds from its sale. Garza argues that the silo is personal property and that the proceeds should therefore go to Garza. Is the silo a fixture? Why or why not?

36–10 **Case Analysis Question** Go to Appendix F at the end of this text and examine Case No. 7 [*Kelo v. City of New*

London, Connecticut, 545 U.S. 469, 125 S.Ct. 2655, 162 L. Ed.2d 439 (2005)]. This case has been excerpted there in great detail. Review and then brief the case, making sure that your brief answers the following questions.

1 Issue: On what issue did the Court focus in this case?

2 Rule of Law: What does the Fifth Amendment to the U.S. Constitution, which the Court applied, require with respect to the legal issue in this case?

3 Applying the Rule of Law: How did the Court apply the rule of law to the facts of this case?

4 Conclusion: What was the Court's conclusion concerning the issue in this case?

▶ **Practical Internet Exercises**

Go to this text's Web site at **www.cengage.com/blaw/blt**, select "Chapter 36," and click on "Practical Internet Exercises." There you will find the following Internet research exercises that you can perform to learn more about the topics covered in this chapter.

Practical Internet Exercise 36–1: LEGAL PERSPECTIVE—**Eminent Domain**
Practical Internet Exercise 36–2: MANAGEMENT PERSPECTIVE—**Fair Housing**
Practical Internet Exercise 36–3: SOCIAL PERSPECTIVE—**The Rights of Tenants**

Chapter 37

Insurance, Wills, and Trusts

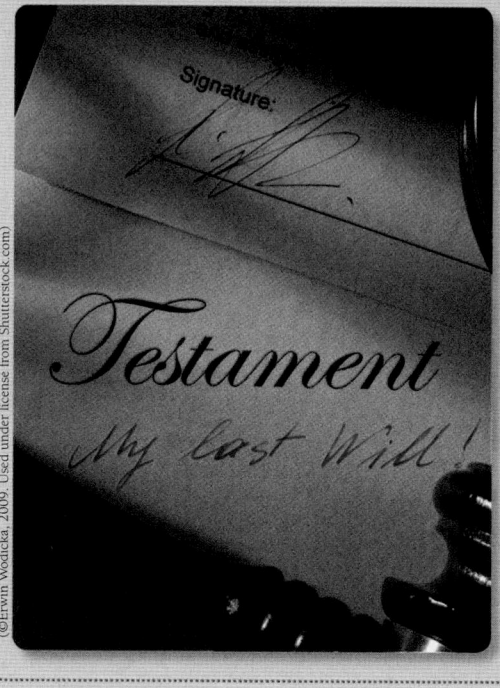
(©Erwin Wodicka, 2009. Used under license from Shutterstock.com)

"Insurance is part charity and part business, but all common sense."

—Calvin Coolidge, 1872–1933
(Thirtieth president of the United States, 1923–1929)

Learning Objectives

After reading this chapter, you should be able to answer the following questions:

1. What is an insurable interest? When must an insurable interest exist—at the time the insurance policy is obtained, at the time the loss occurs, or both?

2. Is an insurance broker the agent of the insurance applicant or the agent of the insurer?

3. What are the basic requirements for executing a will? How may a will be revoked?

4. What is the difference between a *per stirpes* distribution and a *per capita* distribution of an estate to the grandchildren of the deceased?

5. What are the four essential elements of a trust? What is the difference between an express trust and an implied trust?

Most individuals insure both real and personal property (as well as their lives). As Calvin Coolidge asserted in the chapter-opening quotation, insurance is "all common sense"—by insuring our property, we protect ourselves against damage and loss.

The first part of this chapter focuses on insurance, which is a foremost concern of all property owners. We then examine how property is transferred on the death of its owner. Certainly, the laws of succession of property are a necessary corollary to the concept of private ownership of property. Our laws require that on death, title to the property of the decedent (one who has recently died) must be delivered in full somewhere. In this chapter, we see that this can be done by will, through trusts, or through state laws prescribing distribution of property among heirs or next of kin.

▶ Insurance

Many precautions may be taken to protect against the hazards of life. For instance, an individual may wear a seat belt to protect against injuries from automobile accidents or install smoke detectors to guard against injury from fire. Of course, no one can predict whether an accident or a fire will ever occur, but individuals and businesses must establish plans

Insurance A contract in which, for a stipulated consideration, one party agrees to compensate the other for loss on a specific subject by a specified peril.

oncerning potential loss
nown factors.

Risk Management Planning that is undertaken to protect one's interest should some event threaten to undermine its security. In the context of insurance, risk management involves transferring certain risks from the insured to the insurance company.

to protect their personal and financial interests should some event threaten to undermine their security.

Insurance is a contract by which the insurance company (the insurer) promises to pay an amount or to give something of value to another (either the insured or the beneficiary) in the event that the insured is injured, dies, or sustains damage to her or his property as a result of particular, stated contingencies. Basically, insurance is an arrangement for *transferring and allocating risk*. In many instances, **risk** can be described as a prediction concerning potential loss based on known and unknown factors. Insurance, however, involves much more than a game of chance.

Risk management normally involves the transfer of certain risks from the individual to the insurance company by a contractual agreement. The insurance contract and its provisions will be examined shortly. First, however, we look at the different types of insurance that can be obtained, insurance terminology, and the concept of insurable interest.

Classifications of Insurance

Insurance is classified according to the nature of the risk involved. For instance, fire insurance, casualty insurance, life insurance, and title insurance apply to different types of risk. Furthermore, policies of these types protect different persons and interests. This is reasonable because the types of losses that are expected and that are foreseeable or unforeseeable vary with the nature of the activity. Exhibit 37–1 on the next two pages presents a list of insurance classifications. (For a discussion of insurance policies designed to cover the special kinds of risks faced by online businesses, see the *Business Application* feature at the end of this chapter.)

Insurance Terminology

Policy In insurance law, a contract between the insurer and the insured in which, for a stipulated consideration, the insurer agrees to compensate the insured for loss on a specific subject by a specified peril.

Premium In insurance law, the price paid by the insured for insurance protection for a specified period of time.

Underwriter In insurance law, the insurer, or the one assuming a risk in return for the payment of a premium.

An insurance contract is called a **policy**; the consideration paid to the insurer is called a **premium**; and the insurance company is sometimes called an **underwriter**. The parties to an insurance policy are the *insurer* (the insurance company) and the *insured* (the person covered by its provisions or the holder of the policy).

Insurance contracts are usually obtained through an *agent*, who ordinarily works for the insurance company, or through a *broker*, who is ordinarily an *independent contractor*. When a broker deals with an applicant for insurance, the broker is, in effect, the applicant's agent and not an agent of the insurance company. In contrast, an insurance agent is an agent of the insurance company, not of the applicant. Thus, the agent owes fiduciary duties to the insurer (the insurance company), but not to the person who is applying for insurance. As a general rule, the insurance company is bound by the acts of its insurance agents when they act within the agency relationship (discussed in Chapter 23). In most situations, state law determines the status of all parties writing or obtaining insurance.

Insurable Interest

Insurable Interest An interest either in a person's life or well-being or in property that is sufficiently substantial that insuring against injury to (or the death of) the person or against damage to the property does not amount to a mere wagering (betting) contract.

A person can insure anything in which she or he has an **insurable interest**. In regard to real and personal property, an insurable interest exists when the insured derives a pecuniary benefit (a benefit consisting of or relating to money) from the preservation and continued existence of the property. Put another way, one has an insurable interest in property when one would sustain a financial loss from its destruction. Without an insurable interest, there is no enforceable contract, and a transaction to purchase insurance coverage would have to be treated as a wager.

LIFE INSURANCE In regard to life insurance, a person must have a reasonable expectation of benefit from the continued life of another in order to have an insurable interest

● *Exhibit 37–1* Insurance Classifications

TYPE OF INSURANCE	COVERAGE
Accident	Covers expenses, losses, and suffering incurred by the insured because of accidents causing physical injury and any consequent disability; sometimes includes a specified payment to heirs of the insured if death results from an accident.
All-risk	Covers all losses that the insured may incur except those that are specifically excluded. Typical exclusions are war, pollution, earthquakes, and floods.
Automobile	May cover damage to automobiles resulting from specified hazards or occurrences (such as fire, vandalism, theft, or collision); normally provides protection against liability for personal injuries and property damage resulting from the operation of the vehicle.
Casualty	Protects against losses incurred by the insured as a result of being held liable for personal injuries or property damage sustained by others.
Credit	Pays to a creditor the balance of a debt on the disability, death, insolvency, or bankruptcy of the debtor; often offered by lending institutions.
Decreasing-term life	Provides life insurance; requires uniform payments over the life (term) of the policy, but with a decreasing face value (amount of coverage).
Disability	Replaces a portion of the insured's monthly income from employment in the event that illness or injury causes a short- or long-term disability. Some states require employers to provide short-term disability insurance. Benefits typically last a set period of time, such as six months for short-term coverage or five years for long-term coverage.
Employer's liability	Insures an employer against liability for injuries or losses sustained by employees during the course of their employment; covers claims not covered under workers' compensation insurance.
Fidelity or guaranty	Provides indemnity against losses in trade or losses caused by the dishonesty of employees, the insolvency of debtors, or breaches of contract.
Fire	Covers losses incurred by the insured as a result of fire.
Floater	Covers movable property, as long as the property is within the territorial boundaries specified in the contract.
Group	Provides individual life, medical, or disability insurance coverage but is obtainable through a group of persons, usually employees. The policy premium is paid either entirely by the employer or partially by the employer and partially by the employee.

in that person's life. The insurable interest must exist *at the time the policy is obtained.* The benefit may be pecuniary (as with so-called *key-person insurance,* which insures the lives of important employees, usually in small companies), or it may be founded on the relationship between the parties (by blood or affinity).

Ethical Issue ⚖️

Is it ethical for companies to take out life insurance policies on rank-and-file employees?
Nearly 20 percent of the life insurance policies issued each year are sold to corporations to cover the lives of their employees. These policies—known as *dead peasant policies, corporate-owned life insurance* (COLI), or *bank-owned life insurance* (BOLI)—cover rank-and-file employees rather than key employees. Since the 1990s, insurance companies have marketed COLI plans as a way for businesses to reap profits and significant tax deductions from a small investment. The businesses used the profits from the plans to fund employee benefits. For years, employers were allowed to take out dead peasant policies without notifying the employees whose lives were being insured. Then, some employees (or their families if the employees were deceased) who had been insured through these plans started bringing lawsuits, claiming that their employers lacked an insurable interest and had obtained the policies without the employees' consent. For example, Wal-Mart Stores, Inc., which purchased more than 350,000 COLI policies between 1993 and 1995, has faced numerous lawsuits (and no longer obtains COLI policies). Wal-Mart settled one class-action suit in 2004 for $10.3 million and another in 2006 for $5 million, including $1.7 million in attorneys' fees.[1]

---

1. See *Lewis v. Wal-Mart Stores, Inc.,* 2006 WL 3505851 (N.D.Okla. 2006), and 232 Federal Rules Decision 687 (N.D.Okla. 2005); *Mayo v. Hartford Life Insurance Co.,* 354 F.3d 400 (S.D.Tex. 2004).

• *Exhibit* 37–1 Insurance Classifications—Continued

TYPE OF INSURANCE	COVERAGE
Health	Covers expenses incurred by the insured as a result of physical injury or illness and other expenses relating to health and life maintenance.
Homeowners'	Protects homeowners against some or all risks of loss to their residences and the residences' contents or liability arising from the use of the property.
Key-person	Protects a business in the event of the death or disability of a key employee.
Liability	Protects against liability imposed on the insured as a result of injuries to the person or property of another.
Life	Covers the death of the policyholder. On the death of the insured, the insurer pays the amount specified in the policy to the insured's beneficiary.
Major medical	Protects the insured against major hospital, medical, or surgical expenses.
Malpractice	Protects professionals (physicians, lawyers, and others) against malpractice claims brought against them by their patients or clients; a form of liability insurance.
Marine	Covers movable property (including ships, freight, and cargo) against certain perils or navigation risks during a specific voyage or time period.
Mortgage	Covers a mortgage loan. The insurer pays the balance of the mortgage to the creditor on the death or disability of the debtor.
No-fault auto	Covers personal injuries and (sometimes) property damage resulting from automobile accidents. The insured submits his or her claims to his or her own insurance company, regardless of who was at fault. A person may sue the party at fault or that party's insurer only when an accident results in serious medical injury and consequent high medical costs. Governed by state "no-fault" statutes.
Term life	Provides life insurance for a specified period of time (term) with no cash surrender value; usually renewable.
Title	Protects against any defects in title to real property and any losses incurred as a result of existing claims against or liens on the property at the time of purchase.

In 2006, Congress responded to the controversy by enacting a law that requires an employer to obtain an employee's consent before purchasing life insurance on her or him and to notify the employee of the maximum amount of the policy. Litigation over COLI policies continues, however. In 2009, Wal-Mart lost an appeal in a class-action case filed by a Louisiana widow whose late husband had been covered by a COLI plan.[2] Another case against Wal-Mart was dismissed in 2009, however, on procedural grounds. The federal district court found that Wal-Mart had lacked an insurable interest in the life of Rita Atkinson, a rank-and-file employee, and therefore the $66,000 insurance policy on her life was void. Consequently, the amount in controversy did not exceed $75,000, as is required for a federal court to exercise diversity jurisdiction.[3]

PROPERTY INSURANCE   For property insurance, the insurable interest must exist at the time the loss occurs but need not exist when the policy is purchased. The existence of an insurable interest is a primary concern in determining liability under an insurance policy.

CASE EXAMPLE 37.1   ABM Industries, Inc., an engineering, lighting, and janitorial service contractor, leased office and storage space in the World Trade Center (WTC) in New York City in 2001. ABM also ran the building's heating, ventilation, and air-condition systems, and maintained all of the WTC's common areas. At the time, ABM employed more than eight hundred workers at the WTC. Zurich American Insurance Company insured ABM against losses resulting from "business interruption" caused by direct physical loss or

---

2. *Richard v. Wal-Mart Stores, Inc.*, 559 F.3d 341 (5th Cir. 2009). The case was remanded for trial and had not yet been fully resolved when this book went to press.
3. *Atkinson v. Wal-Mart Stores, Inc.*, 2009 WL 1458020 (M.D.Fla. 2009).

damage "to property owned, controlled, used, leased or intended for use" by ABM. After the terrorist attacks on September 11, 2001, ABM filed a claim with Zurich to recover for the loss of all income derived from ABM's WTC operations. Zurich argued that ABM's recovery should be limited to the income lost as a result of the destruction of ABM's office and storage space and supplies. A federal appellate court, however, ruled that ABM was entitled to compensation for the loss of all of its WTC operations. The court reasoned that the "policy's scope expressly includes real or personal property that the insured 'used,' 'controlled,' or 'intended for use.'" Because ABM's income depended on "the common areas and leased premises in the WTC complex," it had an insurable interest in that property at the time of the loss.[4] ●

The Insurance Contract

An insurance contract is governed by the general principles of contract law, although the insurance industry is heavily regulated by each state. Here, we discuss the application for insurance, the date when the contract takes effect, and some of the important provisions typically found in insurance contracts. We will also discuss the cancellation of an insurance policy and defenses that insurance companies can raise against payment on a policy.

APPLICATION   The filled-in application form for insurance is usually attached to the policy and made a part of the insurance contract. Thus, an insurance applicant is bound by any false statements that appear in the application (subject to certain exceptions). Because the insurance company evaluates the risk factors based on the information included in the insurance application, misstatements or misrepresentations can void a policy, especially if the insurance company can show that it would not have extended insurance if it had known the true facts.

EFFECTIVE DATE   The effective date of an insurance contract—that is, the date on which the insurance coverage begins—is important. In some situations, the insurance applicant is not protected until a formal written policy is issued. For instance, if the parties agree that the policy will be issued and delivered at a later time, the contract is not effective until the policy is issued and delivered. Thus, any loss sustained between the time of application and the delivery of the policy is not covered. Also, when a person hires a broker to obtain insurance, the broker is merely the agent of the applicant. Therefore, if the broker fails to procure a policy, the applicant normally is not insured.

In other situations, the applicant is protected between the time the application is received and the time the insurance company either accepts or rejects it. A person who seeks insurance from an insurance company's agent is usually protected from the moment the application is made, provided—for life insurance—that some form of premium has been paid. Usually, the agent will write a memorandum, or **binder**, indicating that a policy is pending and stating its essential terms.

Parties may agree that a life insurance policy will be binding at the time the insured pays the first premium, or the policy may be expressly contingent on the applicant's passing a physical examination. If the applicant pays the premium but dies before having the physical examination, then in order to collect, the applicant's estate normally must show that the applicant *would have passed* the examination had he or she not died.

COINSURANCE CLAUSES   Often, when taking out fire insurance policies, property owners insure their property for less than full value because most fires do not result in a total loss. To encourage owners to insure their property for an amount as close to full value

---

NOTE The federal government has the power to regulate the insurance industry under the commerce clause of the U.S. Constitution. Instead of exercising this power itself, Congress allows the states to regulate insurance.

Binder   A written, temporary insurance policy.

---

4. *Zurich American Insurance Co. v. ABM Industries, Inc.,* 397 F.3d 158 (2d Cir. 2005).

as possible, fire insurance policies commonly include a coinsurance clause. Typically, a *coinsurance clause* provides that if the owner insures the property up to a specified percentage—usually 80 percent—of its value, she or he will recover any loss up to the face amount of the policy. If the insurance is for less than the fixed percentage, the owner is responsible for a proportionate share of the loss.

Coinsurance applies only in instances of partial loss. The amount of the recovery is calculated by using the following formula:

$$\text{Loss} \times \left(\frac{\text{Amount of Insurance Coverage}}{\text{Coinsurance Percentage} \times \text{Property Value}} \right) = \text{Amount of Recovery}$$

EXAMPLE 37.2 The owner of property valued at $200,000 takes out a policy in the amount of $100,000. If the owner then suffers a loss of $80,000, the recovery will be $50,000. The owner will be responsible for (coinsure) the balance of the loss, or $30,000.

$$\$80,000 \times \left(\frac{\$100,000}{0.8 \times \$200,000} \right) = \$50,000$$

If the owner had taken out a policy in the amount of 80 percent of the value of the property, or $160,000, then according to the same formula, the owner would have recovered the full amount of the loss (the face amount of the policy). ●

INCONTESTABILITY CLAUSES Statutes commonly require that a policy for life or health insurance provide that after the policy has been in force for a specified length of time—often two or three years—the insurer cannot contest statements made in the application. This is known as an **incontestability clause.** Once a policy becomes incontestable, the insurer cannot later avoid a claim on the basis of, for example, fraud on the part of the insured, unless the clause provides an exception for that circumstance.

Some other important provisions and clauses contained in insurance contracts are listed and defined in Exhibit 37–2.

Incontestability Clause A clause within a life or health insurance policy that states after the policy has been in force for a specified length of time—most often two or three years—the insurer cannot contest statements made in the policyholder's application.

● *Exhibit* **37–2 Insurance Contract Provisions and Clauses**

Antilapse clause	An antilapse clause provides that the policy will not automatically lapse if no payment is made on the date due. Ordinarily, under such a provision, the insured has a *grace period* of thirty or thirty-one days within which to pay an overdue premium before the policy is canceled.
Appraisal clause	Insurance policies frequently provide that if the parties cannot agree on the amount of a loss covered under the policy or the value of the property lost, an appraisal, or estimate, by an impartial and qualified third party can be demanded.
Arbitration clause	Many insurance policies include clauses that call for arbitration of disputes that may arise between the insurer and the insured concerning the settlement of claims.
Incontestability clause	An incontestability clause provides that after a policy has been in force for a specified length of time—usually two or three years—the insurer cannot contest statements made in the application.
Multiple insurance	Many insurance policies include a clause providing that if the insured has multiple insurance policies that cover the same property and the amount of coverage exceeds the loss, the loss will be shared proportionately by the insurance companies.

INTERPRETING THE INSURANCE CONTRACT   The courts are aware that most people do not have the special training necessary to understand the intricate terminology used in insurance policies. Therefore, when disputes arise, the courts will interpret the words used in an insurance contract according to their ordinary meanings in light of the nature of the coverage involved.

When there is an ambiguity in the policy, the provision generally is interpreted against the insurance company. Also, when it is unclear whether an insurance contract actually exists because the written policy has not been delivered, the uncertainty normally is resolved against the insurance company. The court presumes that the policy is in effect unless the company can show otherwise. Similarly, an insurer must make sure that the insured is adequately notified of any change in coverage under an existing policy.

Disputes over insurance often focus on the interpretation of an ambiguous provision in the policy. Words that can be interpreted differently, such as *accidental* or *physical*, often lead to litigation. **CASE EXAMPLE 37.3**   The computer operating system of an employment agency, Lambrecht & Associates, Inc., was attacked by a virus. The virus caused the entire system to freeze up, and all of the information that had previously been stored on the system was deleted. Lambrecht's employees were unable to use their computers to communicate with clients, and the business lost income. In addition, Lambrecht had to replace its server, buy a new operating system and new software, and manually reenter a large amount of data. Lambrecht had a business insurance policy with State Farm Lloyd's that provided coverage for "accidental direct physical loss to business personal property."

When Lambrecht filed a claim, however, State Farm denied coverage on the ground that the damage was not accidental—because the hacker's act of infecting Lambrecht's computer system with a virus was voluntary and intentional. A state appellate court disagreed and held that the question of whether an occurrence was "accidental" should be determined by looking at the incident from the perspective of the insured. Because there was no evidence that Lambrecht was involved in any voluntary or intentional conduct that caused its loss, the court concluded that the damage was accidental.[5] ●

CANCELLATION   The insured can cancel a policy at any time, and the insurer can cancel under certain circumstances. When an insurance company can cancel its insurance contract, the policy or a state statute usually requires that the insurer give advance written notice of the cancellation to the insured. The same requirement applies when only part of a policy is canceled. Any premium paid in advance may be refundable on the policy's cancellation. The insured may also be entitled to a life insurance policy's cash surrender value.

The insurer may cancel an insurance policy for various reasons, depending on the type of insurance. For example, automobile insurance can be canceled for nonpayment of premiums or suspension of the insured's driver's license. Property insurance can be canceled for nonpayment of premiums or for other reasons, including the insured's fraud or misrepresentation, conviction for a crime that increases the hazard insured against, or gross negligence that increases the risk assumed by the insurer. Life and health policies can be canceled because of false statements made by the insured in the application, but the cancellation must take place before the effective date of an incontestability clause. An insurer cannot cancel—or refuse to renew—a policy for discriminatory reasons or other reasons that violate public policy, or because the insured has appeared as a witness in a case against the company.

GOOD FAITH OBLIGATIONS   Both parties to an insurance contract are responsible for the obligations they assume under the contract (contract law was discussed in Chapters 9 through 14). In addition, both the insured and the insurer have an implied duty to act in good faith.

ON THE WEB The Web site of the Insurance Information Institute provides a wealth of news and information on insurance-related issues, including statistical data, a glossary of insurance terms, and various PowerPoint presentations. Go to www.iii.org.

---

5. *Lambrecht & Associates, Inc. v. State Farm Lloyd's,* 119 S.W.3d 16 (Tex.App. 2003).

Good faith requires the party who is applying for insurance to reveal everything necessary for the insurer to evaluate the risk. In other words, the applicant must disclose all material facts, including all facts that an insurer would consider in determining whether to charge a higher premium or to refuse to issue a policy altogether. Many insurance companies today require that an applicant give the company permission to access other information, such as private medical records and credit ratings, for the purpose of evaluating the risk.

Once the insurer has accepted the risk and some event occurs that gives rise to a claim, the insurer has a duty to investigate to determine the facts. When a policy provides insurance against third party claims, the insurer is obligated to make reasonable efforts to settle such a claim. If a settlement cannot be reached, then regardless of the claim's merit, the insurer must defend any suit against the insured. Usually, a policy provides that in this situation the insured must cooperate in the defense and attend hearings and trials if necessary.

An insurer has a duty to provide or pay an attorney to defend its insured when a complaint alleges facts that could, if proved, impose liability on the insured within the policy's coverage. In the following case, the question was whether a policy covered a dentist's potential liability arising from a practical joke that he played on an employee while performing a dental procedure.

Case 37.1   Woo v. Fireman's Fund Insurance Co.

Supreme Court of Washington, 161 Wash.2d 43, 164 P.3d 454 (2007).

(©Gelpi, 2009. Used under license from Shutterstock.com)

Is an insurance company obligated to defend a dentist in a lawsuit resulting from a practical joke he performed on a patient?

FACTS   Tina Alberts worked for Robert Woo as a dental surgical assistant. Her family raised potbellied pigs, and she often talked about them at work. Sometimes, Woo mentioned the pigs, intending to encourage a "friendly working environment." Alberts interpreted the comments as offensive. Alberts asked Woo to replace two of her teeth with implants. The procedure required the installation of temporary partial bridges called "flippers." While Alberts was anesthetized, Woo installed a set of flippers shaped like boar tusks, as a joke, and took photos. Before Alberts regained consciousness, he inserted the normal flippers. A month later, Woo's staff gave Alberts the photos at a gathering to celebrate her birthday. Stunned, Alberts refused to return to work. Woo tried to apologize. Alberts filed a suit in a Washington state court against him, alleging battery and other torts. He asked Fireman's Fund Insurance Company to defend him, claiming coverage under his policy. The insurer refused. Woo settled the suit with Alberts for $250,000 and filed a suit against Fireman's, claiming that it had breached its duty to defend him. The court awarded him $750,000 in damages, plus the amount of the settlement and attorneys' fees and costs. A state intermediate appellate court reversed the award. Woo appealed to the state's supreme court.

ISSUE   Did the insurance company have an obligation to defend a customer-dentist who, as a practical joke, temporarily installed a set of boar-tusk flippers into his patient-employee's mouth during a routine dental procedure?

DECISION   Yes. The Washington Supreme Court reversed the decision of the lower court. The court held that Fireman's had a duty to defend Woo under the professional liability provision of his policy.

REASON   The court pointed out that the professional liability provision in Woo's policy stated that Fireman's would defend any claim brought against the insured "even if the allegations of the claim are groundless, false or fraudulent." Furthermore, the policy defined *dental services* as "all services which are performed in the practice of the dentistry profession as defined in the business and professional codes of the state where [the dentist is licensed]." Washington State law defines the practice of dentistry quite broadly, and Woo's practical joke took place while Woo was conducting his dental practice. Therefore, the court concluded that the insertion of the boar-tusk flippers into Alberts's mouth conceivably fell within the policy's broad definition of the practice of dentistry. The insertion of boar-tusk flippers was also intertwined with Woo's dental practice because it involved an interaction with an employee.

FOR CRITICAL ANALYSIS—Legal Consideration   *In determining if an insurer has a duty to defend an insured, should a court ask whether the insured had a "reasonable expectation" of coverage? Explain.*

BAD FAITH ACTIONS Although the law of insurance generally follows contract law, most states now recognize a "bad faith" tort action against insurers. Thus, if an insurer in bad faith denies coverage of a claim, the insured may recover in tort in an amount exceeding the policy's coverage limits and may also recover punitive damages. Some courts have held insurers liable for bad faith refusals to settle claims for reasonable amounts within the policy limits.

DEFENSES AGAINST PAYMENT An insurance company can raise any of the defenses that would be valid in an ordinary action on a contract, as well as some defenses that do not apply in ordinary contract actions.

1. If the insurance company can show that the policy was procured by fraud or misrepresentation, it may have a valid defense for not paying on a claim. (The insurance company may also have the right to disaffirm or rescind the insurance contract.)
2. An absolute defense exists if the insurer can show that the insured lacked an insurable interest—thus rendering the policy void from the beginning.
3. Improper actions, such as those that are against public policy or that are otherwise illegal, can also give the insurance company a defense against the payment of a claim or allow it to rescind the contract.

An insurance company can be prevented, or estopped, from asserting some defenses that are normally available, however. For instance, an insurance company normally cannot escape payment on the death of an insured on the ground that the person's age was stated incorrectly on the application. Also, incontestability clauses prevent the insurer from asserting certain defenses.

Will An instrument directing what is to be done with the testator's property on his or her death, made by the testator and revocable during his or her lifetime. No interests in the testator's property pass until the testator dies.

Testate Having left a will at death.

Intestate As a noun, one who has died without having created a valid will; as an adjective, the state of having died without a will.

Intestacy Laws State statutes that specify how property will be distributed when a person dies intestate (without a valid will); also called *statutes of descent and distribution.*

What term describes those who die after having made a valid will?

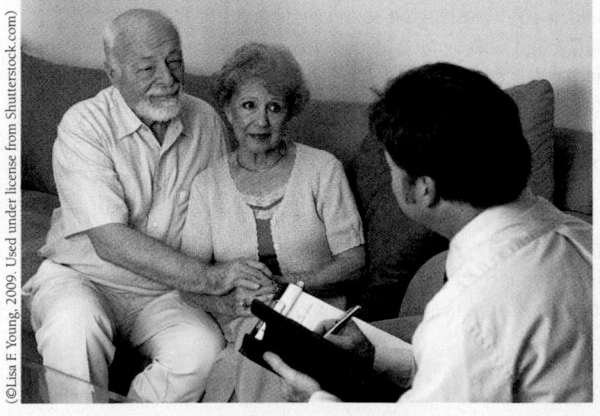

▶ Wills

Not only do the owners of property want to protect it during their lifetime through insurance coverage, but they also wish to transfer it to their loved ones at the time of their death. A **will** is the final declaration of how a person desires to have her or his property disposed of after death. It is a formal instrument that must follow exactly the requirements of state law to be effective. A will is referred to as a *testamentary disposition* of property, and one who dies after having made a valid will is said to have died **testate.**

A will can serve other purposes besides the distribution of property. It can appoint a guardian for minor children or incapacitated adults. It can also appoint a personal representative to settle the affairs of the deceased. Exhibit 37–3 presents excerpts from the will of Michael Jackson, the "King of Pop," who died from cardiac arrest in 2009 at the age of fifty. Jackson held a substantial amount of tangible and intangible property, including the publishing rights to most of The Beatles' music catalogue. The will is a "pour-over" will, meaning that it transfers all of his property (that is not already held in the name of the trust) into the Michael Jackson Family Trust (*trusts* will be discussed later in the chapter). Jackson's will also appoints his mother, Katherine Jackson, as the guardian of his three minor children.

A person who dies without having created a valid will is said to have died **intestate.** In this situation, state **intestacy laws** prescribe the distribution of the property among heirs or next of kin. If no heirs or kin can be found, title to the property will be transferred to the state.

• *Exhibit* **37-3 Excerpts from Michael Jackson's Will**

LAST WILL OF MICHAEL JOSEPH JACKSON

I, MICHAEL JOSEPH JACKSON, a resident of the State of California, declare this to be my last Will, and do hereby revoke all former wills and codicils made by me.

I. I declare that I am not married. My marriage to DEBORAH JEAN ROWE JACKSON has been dissolved. I have three children now living, PRINCE MICHAEL JACKSON, JR., PARIS MICHAEL KATHERINE JACKSON and PRINCE MICHAEL JOSEPH JACKSON, II. I have no other children, living or deceased.

II. It is my intention by this Will to dispose of all property which I am entitled to dispose of by will. I specifically refrain from exercising all powers of appointment that I may possess at the time of my death.

III. I give my entire estate to the Trustee or Trustees then acting under that certain Amended and Restated Declaration of Trust executed on March 22, 2002 by me as Trustee and Trustor which is called the MICHAEL JACKSON FAMILY TRUST, giving effect to any amendments thereto made prior to my death. All such assets shall be held, managed and distributed as a part of said Trust according to its terms and not as a separate testamentary trust.

If for any reason this gift is not operative or is invalid, or if the aforesaid Trust fails or has been revoked, I give my residuary estate to the Trustee or Trustees named to act in the MICHAEL JACKSON FAMILY TRUST, as Amended and Restated on March 22, 2002, and I direct said Trustee or Trustees to divide, administer, hold and distribute the trust estate pursuant to the provisions of said Trust * * * .

* * * *

IV. I direct that all federal estate taxes and state inheritance or succession taxes payable upon or resulting from or by reason of my death (herein "Death Taxes") attributable to property which is part of the trust estate of the MICHAEL JACKSON FAMILY TRUST, including property which passes to said trust from my probate estate shall be paid by the Trustee of said trust in accordance with its terms. Death Taxes attributable to property passing outside this Will, other than property constituting the trust estate of the trust mentioned in the preceding sentence, shall be charged against the taker of said property.

V. I appoint JOHN BRANCA, JOHN McCLAIN and BARRY SIEGEL as co-Executors of this Will. In the event of any of their deaths, resignations, inability, failure or refusal to serve or continue to serve as a co-Executor, the other shall serve and no replacement need be named. The co-Executors serving at any time after my death may name one or more replacements to serve in the event that none of the three named individuals is willing or able to serve at any time.

The term "my executors" as used in this Will shall include any duly acting personal representative or representatives of my estate. No individual acting as such need past a bond.

I hereby give to my Executors, full power and authority at any time or times to sell, lease, mortgage, pledge, exchange or otherwise dispose of the property, whether real or personal comprising my estate, upon such terms as my Executors shall deem best, to continue any business enterprises, to purchase assets from my estate, to continue in force and pay any insurance policy * * * .

VI. Except as otherwise provided in this Will or in the Trust referred to in Article III hereof, I have intentionally omitted to provide for my heirs. I have intentionally omitted to provide for my former wife, DEBORAH JEAN ROWE JACKSON.

* * * *

VIII. If any of my children are minors at the time of my death, I nominate my mother, KATHERINE JACKSON as guardian of the persons and estates of such minor children. If KATHERINE JACKSON fails to survive me, or is unable or unwilling to act as guardian, I nominate DIANA ROSS as guardian of the persons and estates of such minor children.

* * * *

Testator One who makes and executes a will.

Executor A person appointed by a testator in a will to see that her or his will is administered appropriately.

Administrator One who is appointed by a court to handle the probate (disposition) of a person's estate if that person dies intestate (without a valid will) or if the executor named in the will cannot serve.

Terminology of Wills

A person who makes out a will is known as a **testator** (from the Latin *testari*, "to make a will"). The court responsible for administering any legal problems surrounding a will is called a *probate court*, as mentioned in Chapter 3. When a person dies, a personal representative administers the estate and settles finally all of the decedent's (deceased person's) affairs. An **executor** is a personal representative named in the will; an **administrator** is a personal representative appointed by the court for a decedent who dies without a will.

The court will also appoint an administrator if the will does not name an executor or if the named person lacks the capacity to serve as an executor.

A gift of real estate by will is generally called a **devise**, and a gift of personal property by will is called a **bequest**, or **legacy**. The recipient of a gift by will is a **devisee** or a **legatee**, depending on whether the gift was a devise or a legacy.

Devise   As a noun, a gift of real property by will; as a verb, to make a gift of real property by will.

Bequest   A gift of personal property by will (from the verb to bequeath).

Legacy   A gift of personal property under a will.

Devisee   One designated in a will to receive a gift of real property.

Legatee   One designated in a will to receive a gift of personal property.

Types of Gifts

Gifts by will can be specific, general, or residuary. A *specific* devise or bequest (legacy) describes particular property (such as "Eastwood Estate" or "my gold pocket watch") that can be distinguished from all the rest of the testator's property. A *general* devise or bequest (legacy) uses less restrictive terminology. For instance, "I devise all my lands" is a general devise. A general bequest often specifies a sum of money instead of a particular item of property, such as a watch or an automobile. "I give to my nephew, Carleton, $30,000," for example, is a general bequest.

If this gold watch is listed as a specific gift in a will, what is it called?

(Nic McPhee/Creative Commons)

If the assets of an estate are insufficient to pay in full all general bequests provided for in the will, an *abatement* takes place, meaning the legatees receive reduced benefits. **EXAMPLE 37.4** Yusuf's will leaves $15,000 each to his children, Tamara and Kwame. On Yusuf's death, only $10,000 is available to honor these bequests. By abatement, each child will receive $5,000. ● If bequests are more complicated, abatement may be more complex. The testator's intent, as expressed in the will, controls.

Sometimes, a will provides that any assets remaining after the estate's debts have been paid and specific gifts have been made—called the *residuary* (or *residuum*)—are to be distributed in a specific way, such as to the testator's spouse or descendants. Such a clause, called a *residuary clause,* is often used when the exact amount to be distributed cannot be determined until all of the other gifts and payouts have been made. If the testator has not indicated what party or parties should receive the residuary of the estate, the residuary passes according to state laws of intestacy.

ON THE WEB   Estate planning—preparing for the transfer of assets to others on one's death—involves a number of tools, including wills and trusts. These and other devices that can be used in estate planning are described by the American Academy of Estate Planning Attorneys on its Web site at **www.aaepa.com**.

Requirements for a Valid Will

A will must comply with statutory formalities designed to ensure that the testator understood his or her actions at the time the will was made. These formalities are intended to help prevent fraud. Unless they are followed, the will is declared void, and the decedent's property is distributed according to the laws of intestacy of that state.

Although the required formalities vary among jurisdictions, most states uphold certain basic requirements for executing a will. In 1969, to promote more uniformity among the states, the National Conference of Commissioners on Uniform State Laws issued the Uniform Probate Code (UPC). Almost half of the states have enacted some part of the UPC and incorporated it into their own probate codes. Several states have adopted amendments to the UPC that were issued in 2008. We now look at the basic requirements for a valid will, including references to the UPC where appropriate.

RECALL   In most states, the age of majority for contractual purposes is also eighteen years.

TESTAMENTARY CAPACITY AND INTENT   For a will to be valid, the testator must have testamentary capacity—that is, the testator must be of legal age and sound mind *at the time the will is made.* The legal age for executing a will varies, but in most states and under the UPC, the minimum age is eighteen years [UPC 2–501]. Thus, the will of a twenty-one-year-old decedent written when the person was sixteen is invalid if, under state law, the legal age for executing a will is eighteen.

"If you want to see a man's true character, watch him divide an estate."

Benjamin Franklin, 1706–1790
(American diplomat, author, and scientist)

The "Sound-Mind" Requirement.   The concept of "being of sound mind" refers to the testator's ability to formulate and to comprehend a personal plan for the disposition of property. Generally, a testator must (1) intend the document to be his or her last will and testament, (2) comprehend the kind and character of the property being distributed, and (3) comprehend and remember the "natural objects of his or her bounty" (usually, family members and persons for whom the testator has affection).

Intent.   A valid will is one that represents the maker's intention to transfer and distribute her or his property. When it can be shown that the decedent's plan of distribution was the result of fraud or of undue influence, the will is declared invalid. A court may sometimes infer undue influence when the named beneficiary was in a position to influence the making of the will. If the testator ignored blood relatives and named as a beneficiary a nonrelative who was in constant close contact with the testator, for instance, a court might infer undue influence. **EXAMPLE 37.5** Frieda is a nurse who was responsible for caring for Julie, the testator, during the last years of her life. After Julie's death, her family discovers that her will names Frieda as a beneficiary and excludes all family members. If Julie's family challenges the validity of the will on the basis of undue influence, the court might infer that Frieda unduly influenced Julie and declare the will invalid. •

WRITING REQUIREMENTS   Generally, a will must be in writing. The writing itself can be informal as long as it substantially complies with the statutory requirements. In some states, a will can be handwritten in crayon or ink. It can be written on a sheet or scrap of paper, on a paper bag, or on a piece of cloth. A will that is completely in the handwriting of the testator is called a **holographic will** (sometimes referred to as an *olographic will*).

In some instances, a court may find an oral will valid. A **nuncupative will** is an oral will made before witnesses. It is not permitted in most states. Where authorized by statute, such wills are generally valid only if made during the last illness of the testator and are therefore sometimes referred to as *deathbed wills*. Normally, only personal property can be transferred by a nuncupative will. Statutes frequently permit members of the military to make nuncupative wills when on active duty.

Holographic Will   A will written entirely in the signer's handwriting and usually not witnessed.

Nuncupative Will   An oral will (often called a *deathbed will*) made before witnesses; usually limited to transfers of personal property.

SIGNATURE REQUIREMENTS   A fundamental requirement is that the testator's signature must appear on the will, generally at the end. Each jurisdiction dictates by statute and court decision what constitutes a signature. Initials, an X or other mark, and words such as "Mom" have all been upheld as valid when it was shown that the testators *intended* them to be signatures.

WITNESS REQUIREMENTS   A will normally must be attested (sworn to) by two, and sometimes three, witnesses. The number of witnesses, their qualifications, and the manner in which the witnessing must be done are generally set out in a statute. A witness can be required to be disinterested—that is, not a beneficiary under the will. The UPC, however, provides that a will is valid even if it is attested by an interested witness [UPC 2–505]. There are no age requirements for witnesses, but they must be mentally competent.

The purpose of the witnesses is to verify that the testator actually executed (signed) the will and had the requisite intent and capacity at the time. A witness does not have to read the contents of the will. Usually, the testator and all witnesses must sign in the sight or the presence of one another, but there are exceptions.[6] The UPC does not require all parties to sign in the presence of one another and deems it sufficient if the testator acknowledges her or his signature to the witnesses [UPC 2–502].

------

6. See, for example, *Slack v. Truitt,* 368 Md. 2, 791 A.2d 129 (2000). Also, note that the 2008 amendments to the UPC provide an alternative to traditional witnesses—the signature may be acknowledged by the testator before a notary public [amended UPC 2–502].

PUBLICATION REQUIREMENTS   A will is *published* by an oral declaration by the maker to the witnesses that the document they are about to sign is his or her "last will and testament." Publication is becoming an unnecessary formality in most states, and it is not required under the UPC.

Revocation of Wills

An executed will is revocable by the maker at any time during the maker's lifetime. The maker may revoke a will by a physical act, such as tearing up the will, or by a subsequent writing. Wills can also be revoked by operation of law. Revocation can be partial or complete, and it must follow certain strict formalities.

REVOCATION BY A PHYSICAL ACT OF THE MAKER   A testator may revoke a will by *intentionally* burning, tearing, canceling, obliterating, or otherwise destroying it, or by having someone else do so in the presence of the maker and at the maker's direction.[7] In some states, partial revocation by physical act of the maker is recognized. Thus, those portions of a will lined out or torn away are dropped, and the remaining parts of the will are valid. In no circumstances, however, can a provision be crossed out and an additional or substitute provision written in. Such altered portions require reexecution (re-signing) and reattestation (rewitnessing).

To revoke a will by physical act, it is necessary to follow the mandates of a state statute exactly. When a state statute prescribes the specific methods for revoking a will by physical act, only those methods can be used to revoke the will.

REVOCATION BY A SUBSEQUENT WRITING   A will may also be wholly or partially revoked by a **codicil,** a written instrument separate from the will that amends or revokes provisions in the will. A codicil eliminates the necessity of redrafting an entire will merely to add to it or amend it. A codicil can also be used to revoke an entire will. The codicil must be executed with the same formalities required for a will, and it must refer expressly to the will. In effect, it updates a will because the will is "incorporated by reference" into the codicil.

A new will (second will) can be executed that may or may not revoke the first or a prior will, depending on the language used. To revoke a prior will, the second will must use language specifically revoking other wills, such as "This will hereby revokes all prior wills." If the second will is otherwise valid and properly executed, it will revoke all prior wills. If the express *declaration of revocation* is missing, then both wills are read together. If there are any discrepancies between the wills, the second will controls.

REVOCATION BY OPERATION OF LAW   Revocation by *operation of law* occurs when marriage, divorce or annulment, or the birth of a child takes place after a will has been executed. In most states, when a testator marries after executing a will that does not include the new spouse, on the testator's death the spouse can still receive the amount he or she would have taken had the testator died intestate—that is, without a will (how an intestate's property is distributed under state laws will be discussed shortly). In effect, the will is revoked to the point of providing the spouse with an intestate share. The rest of the estate is passed under the will [UPC 2–301, 2–508]. If, however, the new spouse is otherwise provided for in the will (or by transfer of property outside the will), he or she will not be given an intestate amount.

Codicil   A written supplement or modification to a will. A codicil must be executed with the same formalities as a will.

Is tearing up a will a legally recognized method of revoking that will?

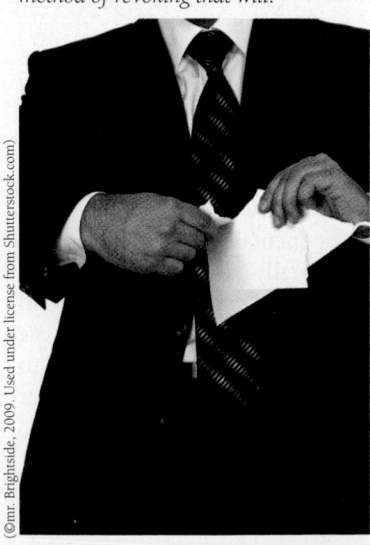

---

7. The destruction cannot be inadvertent. The maker's intent to revoke must be shown. Consequently, when a will has been burned or torn accidentally, the maker should normally have a new document created to avoid any suggestion that the maker intended to revoke the will.

At common law and under the UPC, divorce does not necessarily revoke the entire will.[8] A divorce or an annulment occurring after a will has been executed revokes those dispositions of property made under the will to the former spouse [UPC 2–508]. Note also that a married person who makes a will generally cannot avoid leaving a certain portion of the estate to the surviving spouse (unless there is a valid prenuptial agreement—see Chapter 11). In most states, this is called an elective share, or a forced share, and it is often one-third of the estate or an amount equal to a spouse's share under intestacy laws.

If a child is born after a will has been executed and if it appears that the deceased parent would have made a provision for the child, that child may be entitled to a portion of the estate. Most state laws allow a child to receive some portion of a parent's estate even if no provision is made in the parent's will. This is true unless it is clear from the will's terms that the testator intended to disinherit the child. Under the UPC, the rule is the same.

Probate Procedures

Probate The process of proving and validating a will and settling all matters pertaining to an estate.

To **probate** a will means to establish its validity and to carry the administration of the estate through a court process. Probate laws vary from state to state. Typically, the procedure depends on the size of the decedent's estate.

INFORMAL PROBATE For smaller estates, most state statutes provide for the distribution of assets without formal probate proceedings. Faster and less expensive methods are then used. Property can be transferred by *affidavit* (a written statement taken before a person who has authority to affirm it), and problems or questions can be handled during an administrative hearing. Some state statutes allow title to cars, savings and checking accounts, and certain other property to be transferred simply by filling out forms.

A majority of states also provide for *family settlement agreements*, which are private agreements among the beneficiaries. Once a will is admitted to probate, the family members can agree to settle among themselves the distribution of the decedent's assets. Although a family settlement agreement speeds the settlement process, a court order is still needed to protect the estate from future creditors and to clear title to the assets involved. The use of these and other types of summary procedures in estate administration can save time and expenses.

ON THE WEB To learn more about wills and probate procedures in those states that have adopted parts of the Uniform Probate Code, go to **www.law.cornell.edu/uniform/probate.html**.

FORMAL PROBATE For larger estates, formal probate proceedings normally are undertaken, and the probate court supervises every aspect of the settlement of the decedent's estate. Additionally, in some situations—such as when a guardian for minor children must be appointed—more formal probate procedures cannot be avoided. Formal probate proceedings may take several months or several years to complete, depending on the size and complexity of the estate and whether the will is contested. As a result, a sizable portion of the decedent's assets (as much as 10 percent) may go toward payment of court costs and fees charged by attorneys and personal representatives.

Will Substitutes Various documents that attempt to dispose of an estate in the same or similar manner as a will, such as trusts or life insurance plans.

PROPERTY TRANSFERS OUTSIDE THE PROBATE PROCESS In the ordinary situation, a person can employ various **will substitutes** to avoid the cost of probate—for example, *living trusts* (which will be discussed later in this chapter), life insurance policies or individual retirement accounts (IRAs) with named beneficiaries, or joint-tenancy arrangements.[9] Not all alternatives to formal probate administration are suitable to every estate, however.

---

8. Note that the 2008 amendments to the UPC, which have been adopted by only a few states, do provide for automatic revocation of testamentary devises on divorce [amended UPC 2–804].

9. Recall from Chapters 35 and 36 that in a joint tenancy, when one joint tenant dies, the other joint tenant or tenants automatically inherit the deceased tenant's share of the property.

For most people, estate planning involves not only ensuring that, after they die, their property goes to the intended recipients, but also avoiding probate and maximizing their estates. To this end, many choose to set up a living trust, arrange for a joint tenancy, or name beneficiaries of an IRA or an insurance policy. If you use these will substitutes, though, you should be aware that a court will not apply the same principles in reviewing a transfer outside the probate process as it would apply to a testamentary transfer. Therefore, any such arrangements must be carefully drafted by your attorney and must comply with all legal requirements. To avoid disputes between beneficiaries after your death, make sure that your words and actions in such property transfers are clear and represent the final expression of your intent.

"You cannot live without the lawyers, and certainly you cannot die without them."

Joseph H. Choate, 1832–1917
(American lawyer and diplomat)

Intestacy Laws

As mentioned, each state regulates by statute how property will be distributed when a person dies intestate (without a valid will). Intestacy laws attempt to carry out the likely intent and wishes of the decedent. These laws assume that deceased persons would have intended that their natural heirs (spouses, children, grandchildren, or other family members) inherit their property. Therefore, intestacy statutes set out rules and priorities under which these heirs inherit the property. If no heirs exist, the state will assume ownership of the property. The rules of descent vary widely from state to state.

SURVIVING SPOUSE AND CHILDREN   Usually, state statutes provide that first the debts of the decedent must be satisfied out of the estate; then the remaining assets pass to the surviving spouse and to the children. A surviving spouse usually receives only a share of the estate—one-half if there is also a surviving child and one-third if there are two or more children. Only if no children or grandchildren survive the decedent will a surviving spouse be entitled to the entire estate.

EXAMPLE 37.6   Allen dies intestate and is survived by his wife, Beth, and his children, Duane and Tara. Allen's property passes according to intestacy laws. After his outstanding debts are paid, Beth will receive the homestead (either in fee simple or as a life estate) and ordinarily a one-third interest in all other property. The remaining real and personal property will pass to Duane and Tara in equal portions. ● Under most state intestacy laws and under the UPC, in-laws do not share in an estate. If a child dies before his or her parents, the child's spouse will not receive an inheritance on the parents' death. For instance, if Duane died before his father (Allen), Duane's spouse would not inherit Duane's share of Allen's estate.

When there is no surviving spouse or child, the order of inheritance is grandchildren, then brothers and sisters, and, in some states, parents of the decedent. These relatives are usually called *lineal descendants*. If there are no lineal descendants, then *collateral heirs*—nieces, nephews, aunts, and uncles of the decedent—make up the next group to share. If there are no survivors in any of these groups, most statutes provide for the property to be distributed among the next of kin of the collateral heirs.

STEPCHILDREN, ADOPTED CHILDREN, AND ILLEGITIMATE CHILDREN   Under intestacy laws, stepchildren are not considered kin. Legally adopted children, however, are recognized as lawful heirs of their adoptive parents (as are children who are in the process of being adopted at the time of death). Statutes vary from state to state in regard to the inheritance rights of illegitimate children (children born out of wedlock). Generally, an illegitimate child is treated as the child of the mother and can inherit from her and her relatives. Traditionally, the child usually was not regarded as the legal child of the father for inheritance purposes—unless paternity was established through some legal proceeding.

- *Exhibit* **37–4** *Per Stirpes* **Distribution**

Under this method of distribution, an heir takes the share that his or her deceased parent would have been entitled to inherit, had the parent lived. This may mean that a class of distributees—the grandchildren in this example—will not inherit in equal portions. Note that Becky and Holly receive only one-fourth of Michael's estate while Paul inherits one-half.

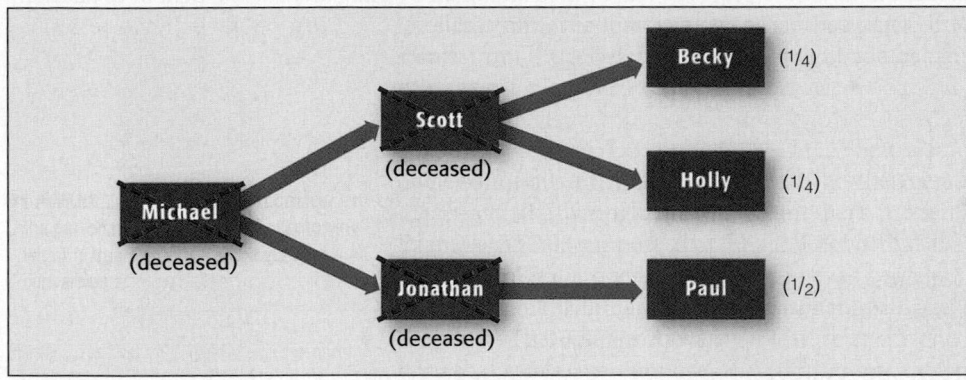

- *Exhibit* **37–5** *Per Capita* **Distribution**

Under this method of distribution, all heirs in a certain class—in this example, the grandchildren—inherit equally. Note that Becky and Holly in this situation each inherit one-third, as does Paul.

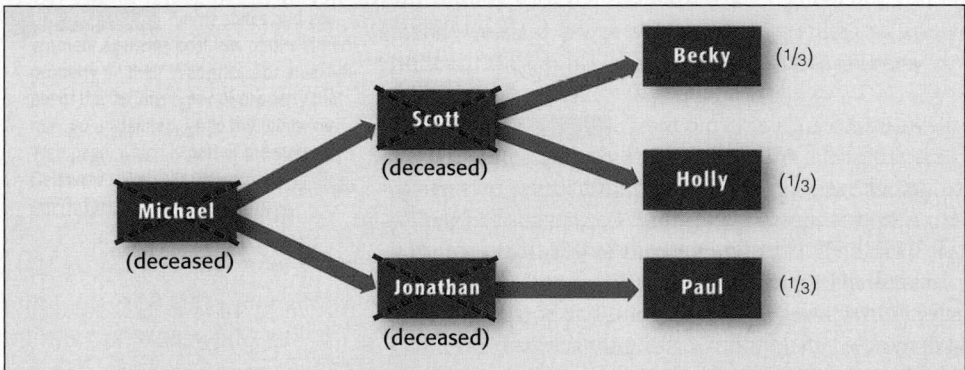

Given the dramatic increase in the number of children born out of wedlock in society today, many states have relaxed their laws of inheritance. A majority of states now consider a child born of any union that has the characteristics of a formal marriage relationship (such as unmarried parents who cohabit) to be legitimate. Under the revised UPC, a child is the child of his or her natural (biological) parents, regardless of their marital status, as long as the natural parent has openly treated the child as her or his child [UPC 2–114]. Although illegitimate children may have inheritance rights in most states, their rights are not necessarily identical to those of legitimate children.

DISTRIBUTION TO GRANDCHILDREN Usually, a will provides for how the decedent's estate will be distributed to descendants of deceased children—that is, to the decedent's grandchildren. If a will does not include such a provision— or if a person dies intestate—the question arises as to what share the grandchildren of the decedent will receive. Each state designates one of two methods of distributing the assets of intestate decedents.

One method of dividing an intestate's estate is *per stirpes*.[10] Under this method, within a class or group of distributees (for example, grandchildren), the children of any one descendant take the share that their deceased parent *would have been* entitled to inherit. **EXAMPLE 37.7** Michael, a widower, has two children, Scott and Jonathan. Scott has two children (Becky and Holly), and Jonathan has one child (Paul). Scott and Jonathan die before their father, and then Michael dies. If Michael's estate is distributed *per stirpes*, Becky and Holly each receive one-fourth of the estate (dividing Scott's one-half share). Paul receives one-half of the estate (taking Jonathan's one-half share). Exhibit 37–4 illustrates the *per stirpes* method of distribution. ●

An estate may also be distributed on a *per capita*[11] basis, which means that each person in a class or group takes an equal share of the estate. If Michael's estate is distributed *per capita*, Becky, Holly, and Paul each receive a one-third share. Exhibit 37–5 illustrates the *per capita* method of distribution.

Per Stirpes A Latin term meaning "by the roots." In the law governing estate distribution, a method of distributing an intestate's estate so that each heir in a certain class (such as grandchildren) takes the share to which her or his deceased ancestor (such as a mother or father) would have been entitled.

Per Capita A Latin term meaning "per person." In the law governing estate distribution, a method of distributing the property of an intestate's estate so that each heir in a certain class (such as grandchildren) receives an equal share.

---

10. *Per stirpes* is a Latin term meaning "by the roots" or "by stock." When used in estate law, it means proportionally divided between beneficiaries according to their deceased ancestor's share.

11. *Per capita* is a Latin term meaning "per person" or "for each head." When used in estate law, it means equally divided between beneficiaries.

▶ Trusts

Trust An arrangement in which title to property is held by one person (a trustee) for the benefit of another (a beneficiary).

A **trust** is any arrangement through which property is transferred from one person to a trustee to be administered for the transferor's or another party's benefit. It can also be defined as a right of property, real or personal, held by one party for the benefit of another. A trust can be created for any purpose that is not illegal or against public policy. Its essential elements are as follows:

1. A designated beneficiary.
2. A designated trustee.
3. A fund sufficiently identified to enable title to pass to the trustee.
4. Actual delivery by the *settlor* or *grantor* (the person creating the trust) to the trustee with the intention of passing title.

Numerous types of trusts can be established. In this section, we look at some of the types of trusts and their characteristics.

Express Trusts

An express trust is created or declared in explicit terms, usually in writing. There are many types of express trusts, each with its own special characteristics.

Inter Vivos Trust A trust created by the grantor (settlor) and effective during the grantor's lifetime; a trust not established by a will.

LIVING TRUSTS A living trust—or **inter vivos trust** (*inter vivos* is Latin for "between or among the living")—is a trust created by a grantor during her or his lifetime. Living trusts have become a popular estate-planning option because at the grantor's death, assets held in a living trust can pass to the heirs without going through probate. Note, however, that living trusts do not shelter assets from estate taxes, and the grantor may still have to pay income taxes on trust earnings—depending on whether the trust is revocable or irrevocable.

Revocable Living Trusts. Living trusts can be revocable or irrevocable. In a *revocable* living trust, which is the most common type, the grantor retains control over the trust property during her or his lifetime. The grantor deeds the property to the trust but retains the power to amend, alter, or revoke the trust during her or his lifetime. The grantor may also serve as a trustee or co-trustee and can arrange to receive income earned by the trust assets during her or his lifetime. Because the grantor is in control of the funds, she or he is required to pay income taxes on the trust earnings. Unless the trust is revoked, the principal of the trust is transferred to the trust beneficiary on the grantor's death.

EXAMPLE 37.8 James Cortez owns and operates a large farm. After his wife dies, James decides to create a living trust for the benefit of his three children, Alicia, Emma, and Jayden. He contacts his attorney, who prepares the documents creating the trust, executes a deed conveying the farm to the trust, and transfers the farm's bank accounts into the name of the trust. The trust designates James as the trustee and names his son Jayden as the *successor trustee,* who will take over the management of the trust when James dies or becomes incapacitated. Each of the children will receive income from the trust while James is alive, and when James dies, the farm will pass to them without having to go through probate. By holding the property in a revocable living trust, James still has control over the farm during his life. This trust arrangement is illustrated in Exhibit 37–6. ●

Irrevocable Living Trusts. In an *irrevocable* living trust, in contrast, the grantor permanently gives up control over the property to the

● *Exhibit* **37–6 A Revocable Living Trust Arrangement**

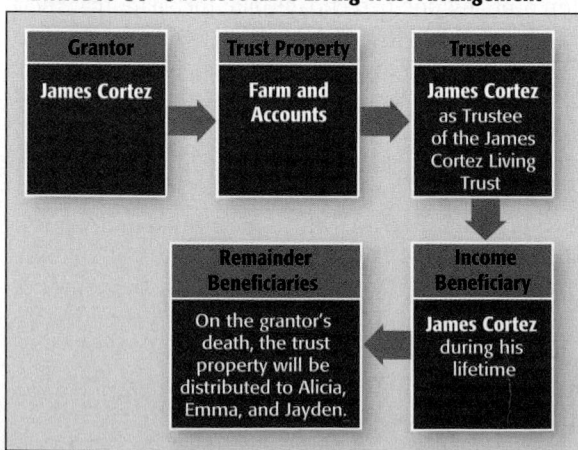

trustee. The grantor executes a trust deed, and legal title to the trust property passes to the named trustee. The trustee has a duty to administer the property as directed by the grantor for the benefit and in the interest of the beneficiaries. The trustee must preserve the trust property; make it productive; and, if required by the terms of the trust agreement, pay income to the beneficiaries, all in accordance with the terms of the trust. Because the grantor has, in effect, given over the property for the benefit of the beneficiaries, he or she is no longer responsible for paying income taxes on the trust earnings.

Testamentary Trust A trust that is created by will and therefore does not take effect until the death of the testator.

TESTAMENTARY TRUSTS A **testamentary trust** is created by will and comes into existence on the settlor's death. Although a testamentary trust has a trustee who maintains legal title to the trust property, the trustee's actions are subject to judicial approval. This trustee can be named in the will or be appointed by the court. Thus, a testamentary trust does not fail because a trustee has not been named in the will. The legal responsibilities of the trustee are the same as in an *inter vivos* trust.

If a court finds that the will setting up a testamentary trust is invalid, then the trust will also be invalid. The property that was supposed to be in the trust will then pass according to intestacy laws, not according to the terms of the trust.

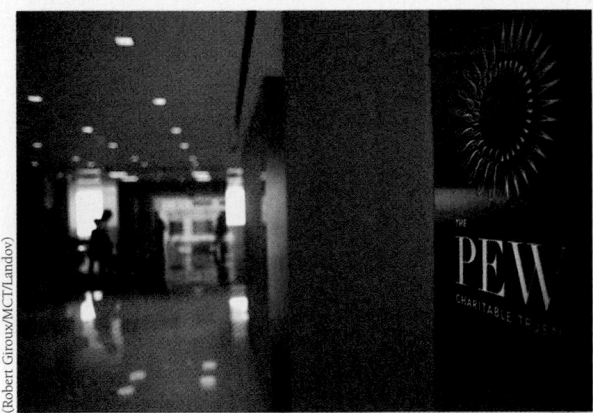

What are the typical purposes of a charitable trust?

CHARITABLE TRUSTS A **charitable trust** is an express trust designed for the benefit of a segment of the public or the public in general. It differs from other types of trusts in that the identities of the beneficiaries are uncertain and it can be established to last indefinitely. Usually, to be deemed a charitable trust, a trust must be created for charitable, educational, religious, or scientific purposes.

Charitable Trust A trust in which the property held by the trustee must be used for a charitable purpose, such as the advancement of health, education, or religion.

Spendthrift Trust A trust created to protect the beneficiary from spending all the funds to which she or he is entitled. Only a certain portion of the total amount is given to the beneficiary at any one time, and most states prohibit creditors from attaching assets of the trust.

SPENDTHRIFT TRUSTS A **spendthrift trust** is created to provide for the maintenance of a beneficiary by preventing him or her from being careless with the bestowed funds. Unlike the beneficiaries of other trusts, the beneficiary in a spendthrift trust is not permitted to transfer or assign his or her right to the trust's principal or future payments from the trust (*assignments* were discussed in Chapter 13). Essentially, the beneficiary can withdraw only a certain portion of the total amount to which he or she is entitled at any one time. The majority of states allow spendthrift trust provisions that prohibit creditors from attaching such trusts.

Totten Trust A trust created when a person deposits funds in his or her own name as a trustee for another. It is a tentative trust, revocable at will until the depositor dies or completes the gift in his or her lifetime by some unequivocal act or declaration.

TOTTEN TRUSTS A **Totten trust**[12] is created when one person deposits funds in her or his own name with instructions that on the settlor's death, whatever is in that account should go to a specific beneficiary. This trust is revocable at will until the depositor dies or completes the gift during her or his lifetime (by delivering the funds to the intended beneficiary, for example). The beneficiary has no access to the funds until the depositor's death, when the beneficiary obtains property rights to the balance on hand.

Resulting Trust An implied trust arising from the conduct of the parties. A trust in which a party holds the actual legal title to another's property but only for that person's benefit.

Implied Trusts

Sometimes, a trust will be imposed (implied) by law, even in the absence of an express trust. Implied trusts include resulting trusts and constructive trusts.

A **resulting trust** arises from the conduct of the parties. The trust results, or is created, when circumstances raise an inference that the party holding legal title to the property does so for the benefit of another. **EXAMPLE 37.9** Garrison wants to put one acre of land she owns

---

12. This type of trust derives its unusual name from the case, *In re Totten,* 179 N.Y. 112, 71 N.E. 748 (1904).

on the market for sale. Because she is going out of the country for two years and will not be able to deed the property to a buyer during that period, Garrison conveys (transfers) the property to her good friend Oswald. Oswald can then attempt to sell the property while Garrison is gone. Because the intent of the transaction in which Garrison conveyed the property to Oswald is neither a sale nor a gift, the property will be held in trust (a resulting trust) by Oswald for the benefit of Garrison. Therefore, on Garrison's return, Oswald will be required either to deed back the property to Garrison or, if the property has been sold, to turn over the proceeds (held in trust) to her. ●

Constructive Trust An equitable trust that is imposed in the interests of fairness and justice when someone wrongfully holds legal title to property. A court may require the owner to hold the property in trust for the person or persons who should rightfully own the property.

A **constructive trust** is an equitable trust imposed by a court in the interests of fairness and justice. In a constructive trust, the owner is declared to be a trustee for the parties who are, in equity, actually entitled to the benefits that flow from the trust. If someone wrongfully holds legal title to property—because the property was obtained through fraud or in breach of a legal duty, for example—a court may impose a constructive trust. Courts often impose constructive trusts when someone who is in a confidential or fiduciary relationship with another person, such as a guardian to a ward, has breached a duty to that person.

In the following case, bank accounts and other financial assets with a value of about $500,000 were at the heart of a dispute over the imposition of a constructive trust.

Case 37.2   Garrigus v. Viarengo

Appellate Court of Connecticut, 112 Conn.App. 655, 963 A.2d 1065 (2009).
www.jud.state.ct.us/index.html[a]

A joint owner of assets removes valuables from the decedent's safe and refuses to disclose details to heirs. Can a court impose a constructive trust?

FACTS Stella Jankowski added her niece Genevieve Viarengo as a joint owner on several savings and checking accounts, certificates of deposit, and savings bonds. In executing a will, Jankowski told her attorney John Wabiszczewicz that she wanted her estate divided equally among her ten nieces, nephews, and cousins. She named Viarengo and Richard Golebiewski as coexecutors. Wabiszczewicz was not aware of the jointly held accounts and neither Jankowski nor Viarengo mentioned them. Jankowski died in 2001. Within days, Viarengo emptied Jankowski's safe and removed her financial records. Despite requests from Golebiewski and Wabiszczewicz, Viarengo did not reveal the contents of the safe or the records. Jankowski's estate—jewelry; a home in Waterbury, Connecticut; and the jointly held accounts—totaled about $600,000. The jointly owned assets were valued at about $500,000. Viarengo claimed that those accounts were hers. Diane Garrigus and other relatives filed a suit in a Connecticut state

court against Viarengo. The court imposed a constructive trust. Viarengo appealed.

ISSUE Can a court impose a constructive trust in the absence of a confidential relationship?

DECISION Yes. A state intermediate appellate court affirmed the lower court's judgment.

REASON A constructive trust is imposed against a party who obtains property by fraud or other misconduct. Here, the court found that Viarengo committed fraud in obtaining the assets that she had held jointly with Jankowski and would be unjustly enriched if she were allowed to retain them. Jankowski wanted the assets divided among her ten nieces, nephews, and cousins, and Viarengo did not do that. Viarengo argued that to impose a constructive trust, the court had to find a confidential relationship between Jankowski and herself, as well as fraud. But "our case law does not support that position." The imposition of a constructive trust requires proof of fraud *or* other wrongdoing, including abuse of confidential relations. "If fraud is established by clear and convincing evidence, which it was in this case, there is no additional requirement to prove the existence of a confidential relationship."

FOR CRITICAL ANALYSIS—Social Consideration *What are the elements of fraud? Which facts in this case support the court's finding of fraud?*

---

a. In the left-hand column, in the "Opinions" pullout menu, select "Appellate Court." On that page, in the "Search the Archives:" section, click on "Appellate Court Archive." In the result, click on "2009." On that page, scroll to the "Published in Connecticut Law Journal – 2/17/09:" section and click on the name of the case to access the opinion. The State of Connecticut Judicial Branch maintains this Web site.

The Trustee

The *trustee* is the person holding the trust property. Anyone legally capable of holding title to, and dealing in, property can be a trustee. If the settlor of a trust fails to name a trustee, or if a named trustee cannot or will not serve, the trust does not fail—an appropriate court can appoint a trustee.

TRUSTEE'S DUTIES   A trustee must act with honesty, good faith, and prudence in administering the trust and must exercise a high degree of loyalty toward the trust beneficiary. The general standard of care is the degree of care a prudent person would exercise in his or her personal affairs.[13] The duty of loyalty requires that the trustee act in the exclusive interest of the beneficiary.

Among specific duties, a trustee must keep clear and accurate accounts of the trust's administration and furnish complete and correct information to the beneficiary. A trustee must keep trust assets separate from her or his own assets. A trustee has a duty to pay to an income beneficiary the net income of the trust assets at reasonable intervals. A trustee also has a duty to distribute the risk of loss from investments by reasonable diversification and to dispose of assets that do not represent prudent investments. Depending on the particular circumstances, prudent investment choices might include federal, state, or municipal bonds; corporate bonds; and shares of preferred or common stock.

> "*Put not your trust in money, but put your money in trust.*"
>
> Oliver Wendell Holmes, Jr., 1841–1935
> (Associate justice of the United States Supreme Court, 1902–1932)

TRUSTEE'S POWERS   When a settlor creates a trust, he or she may set forth the trustee's powers and performance. State law governs in the absence of specific terms in the trust, and the states often restrict the trustee's investment of trust funds.

Typically, statutes confine trustees to investments in conservative debt securities such as government, utility, and railroad bonds. Frequently, though, a settlor grants a trustee discretionary investment power. In that circumstance, any statute may be considered only advisory, with the trustee's decisions subject in most states to the prudent person rule. Of course, a trustee is responsible for carrying out the purposes of the trust. If the trustee fails to comply with the terms of the trust or the controlling statute, he or she is personally liable for any loss.

ALLOCATIONS BETWEEN PRINCIPAL AND INCOME   Often, a settlor will provide one beneficiary with a life estate and another beneficiary with the remainder interest in a trust. A farmer, for example, may create a testamentary trust providing that the farm's income be paid to her surviving spouse and that on the surviving spouse's death, the farm be given to their children. In this example, the surviving spouse has a *life estate* in the farm's income, and the children have a *remainder interest* in the farm (the principal). When a trust is set up in this manner, questions may arise among the income and principal beneficiaries as to how the receipts and expenses for the farm's management and the trust's administration should be allocated between income and principal.

When a trust instrument does not provide instructions, a trustee must refer to applicable state law. The general rule is that ordinary receipts and expenses are chargeable to the income beneficiary, whereas extraordinary receipts and expenses are allocated to the principal beneficiaries.[14] For example, the receipt of rent from trust realty would be ordinary, as would the expense of paying the property's taxes. The cost of long-term improvements and proceeds from the property's sale, however, would be extraordinary.

---

13. Revised Uniform Principal and Income Act, Section 2(a)(3); *Restatement (Third) of Trusts (Prudent Investor Rule)* Section 227. This rule is in force in the majority of states by statute and in a small number of states under the common law.
14. Revised Uniform Principal and Income Act, Sections 3, 6, 8, and 13; *Restatement (Second) of Trusts,* Section 233.

Reviewing . . . Insurance, Wills, and Trusts

In June 2010, Bernard Ramish set up a $48,000 trust fund through West Plains Credit Union to provide tuition for his nephew, Nathan Covacek, to attend Tri-State Polytechnic Institute. The trust was established under Ramish's control and went into effect that August. In December, Ramish suffered a brain aneurysm that caused frequent, severe headaches but no other symptoms. In August 2011, Ramish developed heat stroke and collapsed on the golf course at La Prima Country Club. After recuperating at the clubhouse, Ramish quickly wrote his will on the back of a wine list. It stated, "My last will and testament: Upon my death, I give all of my personal property to my friend Bernard Eshom and my home to Lizzie Johansen." He signed the will at the bottom in the presence of five men in the La Prima clubhouse, and all five men signed as witnesses. A week later, Ramish suffered a second aneurysm and died in his sleep. He was survived by his mother, Dorris Ramish; his nephew, Nathan Covacek; his son-in-law, Bruce Lupin; and his granddaughter, Tori Lupin. Using the information presented in the chapter, answer the following questions.

1. Does Ramish's testament on the back of the wine list meet the requirements for a valid will?
2. Suppose that after Ramish's first aneurysm in 2010, Covacek contacted an insurance company to obtain a life insurance policy on Ramish's life. Would Covacek have had an insurable interest in his uncle's life? Why or why not?
3. What would the order of inheritance have been if Ramish had died intestate?
4. What will most likely happen to the trust fund established for Covacek on Ramish's death?

Business Application

How Can You Manage Risk in Cyberspace?*

As mentioned elsewhere, companies doing business online face many risks that are not covered by traditional types of insurance (see Exhibit 37–1 on pages 926 and 927). Not surprisingly, a growing number of companies are now offering policies designed to cover Web-related risks.

Insurance Coverage for Web-Related Risks

Insurance to cover Web-related incidents is frequently referred to as *network intrusion insurance.* Such insurance protects companies from losses stemming from hacking and computer viruses; programming errors; network and Web site disruptions; theft of electronic data and assets, including intellectual property; Web-related defamation, copyright infringement, and false advertising; and violations of users' privacy rights.

InsureTrust.com, an insurer affiliated with three leading insurance companies—American International Group, Lloyd's of London, and Reliance National—is a leading provider of cyberinsurance coverage. Other insurers, such as Hartford Insurance and the Chubb Group of Insurance Companies, have also added insurance for Web-related perils to their offerings. Clearly, the market for these types of insurance coverage is rapidly evolving, and new policies will continue to appear.

Customized Policies

Unlike traditional insurance policies, which are generally drafted by insurance companies and presented to insurance applicants on a take-it-or-leave-it basis, cyberinsurance policies are usually customized to provide protection against specific risks faced by a particular type of business. For example, an Internet service provider will face different risks than an online merchant, and a banking institution will face different risks than a law firm. The specific business-related risks are taken into consideration when determining the policy premium.

Qualifying Criteria

Many companies that offer network intrusion insurance require applicants to meet high security standards. In other words, to qualify for a policy under an insurance company's risk management processes, a business must have Web-related security measures in place. Several companies assess the applicant's security system before underwriting a policy. For example, an insurer might assess the applicant's security measures and refuse to provide coverage unless the business scores higher than 60 percent. If the business does not score that high, it can contract with the company to improve its Web-related security.

CHECKLIST FOR THE BUSINESSPERSON

1. **Determine the types of risks that your Web business is exposed to and try to obtain an insurance policy that protects you against those specific risks.**
2. **As when procuring any type of insurance coverage, read the policy carefully, including any exclusions contained in the fine print, before committing to it.**
3. **Do not be "penny wise and pound foolish" when it comes to insurance protection. Though insurance coverage may seem expensive, it may be much less costly than the loss of intellectual property or the cost of defending against a lawsuit. Opting for a higher deductible can reduce the amount you pay in premiums.**
4. **Find out what the company's underwriting standards are and determine whether your Web security measures meet its standards.**

* This *Business Application* is not meant to substitute for the services of an attorney who is licensed to practice law in your state.

Key Terms

 Chapter Summary: Insurance, Wills, and Trusts

INSURANCE	
Classifications (See page 925.)	See Exhibit 37–1 on pages 926 and 927.
Terminology (See page 925.)	1. *Policy*—The insurance contract. 2. *Premium*—The consideration paid to the insurer for a policy. 3. *Underwriter*—The insurance company. 4. *Parties*—Include the insurer (the insurance company), the insured (the person covered by insurance), an agent (a representative of the insurance company) or a broker (ordinarily an independent contractor), and a beneficiary (a person to receive proceeds under the policy).
Insurable Interest (See pages 925–928.)	An insurable interest exists whenever an individual or entity benefits from the preservation of the health or life of the insured or the property to be insured. For life insurance, an insurable interest must exist at the time the policy is issued. For property insurance, an insurable interest must exist at the time of the loss.
The Insurance Contract (See pages 928–932.)	1. *Laws governing*—The general principles of contract law are applied; the insurance industry is also heavily regulated by the states. 2. *Application*—An insurance applicant is bound by any false statements that appear in the application (subject to certain exceptions), which is part of the insurance contract. Misstatements or misrepresentations may be grounds for voiding the policy. 3. *Effective date*—Coverage on an insurance policy can begin when a *binder* (a written memorandum indicating that a formal policy is pending and stating its essential terms) is written; when the policy is issued; at the time of contract formation; or depending on the terms of the contract, when certain conditions are met. 4. *Provisions and clauses*—See Exhibit 37–2 on page 929. Words will be given their ordinary meanings, and any ambiguity in the policy will be interpreted against the insurance company. When the written policy has not been delivered and it is unclear whether an insurance contract actually exists, the uncertainty will be resolved against the insurance company. The court will presume that the policy is in effect unless the company can show otherwise. 5. *Defenses against payment to the insured*—Defenses include misrepresentation or fraud by the applicant.
WILLS	
Terminology (See pages 933–934.)	1. *Intestate*—One who dies without a valid will. 2. *Testator*—A person who makes out a will. 3. *Personal representative*—A person appointed in a will or by a court to settle the affairs of a decedent. A personal representative named in the will is an executor; a personal representative appointed by the court for an intestate decedent is an *administrator*.

Continued

Chapter Summary: Insurance, Wills, and Trusts—Continued

Terminology—Continued	4. *Devise*—A gift of real estate by will; may be general or specific. The recipient of a devise is a *devisee*.
	5. *Bequest, or legacy*—A gift of personal property by will; may be general or specific. The recipient of a bequest (legacy) is a *legatee*.
Requirements for a Valid Will (See pages 934–936.)	1. The testator must have testamentary capacity (be of legal age and sound mind at the time the will is made).
	2. A will must be in writing (except for nuncupative wills). A holographic will is completely in the handwriting of the testator.
	3. A will must be signed by the testator; what constitutes a signature varies from jurisdiction to jurisdiction.
	4. A nonholographic will (an attested will) must be witnessed in the manner prescribed by state statute.
	5. A will may have to be *published*—that is, the testator may be required to announce to witnesses that this is his or her "last will and testament"; not required under the Uniform Probate Code.
Revocation of Wills (See pages 936–937.)	1. *By physical act of the maker*—Tearing up, canceling, obliterating, or deliberately destroying part or all of a will.
	2. *By subsequent writing*—
	a. Codicil—A formal, separate document to amend or revoke an existing will.
	b. Second will or new will—A new, properly executed will expressly revoking the existing will.
	3. *By operation of law*—
	a. Marriage—Generally revokes part of a will written before the marriage.
	b. Divorce or annulment—Revokes dispositions of property made under a will to a former spouse.
	c. Subsequently born child—It is *inferred* that the child is entitled to receive the portion of the estate granted under intestacy distribution laws.
Probate Procedures (See pages 937–938.)	To probate a will means to establish its validity and to carry the administration of the estate through a court process. Probate laws vary from state to state. Probate procedures may be informal or formal, depending on the size of the estate and other factors, such as whether a guardian for minor children must be appointed.
Intestacy Laws (See pages 938–939.)	1. Intestacy laws vary widely from state to state. Usually, the law provides that the surviving spouse and children inherit the property of the decedent (after the decedent's debts are paid). The spouse usually inherits the entire estate if there are no children, one-half of the estate if there is one child, and one-third of the estate if there are two or more children.
	2. If there is no surviving spouse or child, then, in order, lineal descendants (grandchildren, brothers and sisters, and—in some states—parents of the decedent) inherit. If there are no lineal descendants, then collateral heirs (nieces, nephews, aunts, and uncles of the decedent) inherit.

TRUSTS	
Definition (See page 940.)	A trust is any arrangement through which property is transferred from one person to a trustee to be administered for another party's benefit. The essential elements of a trust are (1) a designated beneficiary, (2) a designated trustee, (3) a fund sufficiently identified to enable title to pass to the trustee, and (4) actual delivery to the trustee with the intention of passing title.
Express Trusts (See pages 940–941.)	Express trusts are created by explicit terms, usually in writing, and include the following:
	1. *Living (inter vivos) trust*—A trust created by a grantor during her or his lifetime.
	2. *Testamentary trust*—A trust that is created by will and comes into existence on the death of the grantor.
	3. *Charitable trust*—A trust designed for the benefit of a public group or the public in general.
	4. *Spendthrift trust*—A trust created to provide for the maintenance of a beneficiary and to protect him or her from spending all the funds to which he or she is entitled. The beneficiary is allowed to withdraw only a certain amount at any one time.
	5. *Totten trust*—A trust created when one person deposits funds in his or her own name as a trustee for another.
Implied Trusts (See pages 941–943.)	Implied trusts, which are imposed by law in the interests of fairness and justice, include the following:
	1. *Resulting trust*—Arises from the conduct of the parties when an apparent intention to create a trust is present.
	2. *Constructive trust*—Arises by operation of law when a person wrongfully takes title to property. A court may require the owner to hold the property in trust for those who, in equity, are entitled to enjoy the beneficial interest therein.

ExamPrep

ISSUE SPOTTERS

1 Sheila makes out a will, leaving her property in equal thirds to Toby and Umeko, her children, and Velda, her niece. Two years later, Sheila is adjudged mentally incompetent, and that same year, she dies. Can Toby and Umeko have Sheila's will revoked on the ground that she did not have the capacity to make a will? Why or why not?

2 Ralph dies without having made a will. He is survived by many relatives—a spouse, children, adopted children, sisters, brothers, uncles, aunts, cousins, nephews, and nieces. What determines who gets what?

BEFORE THE TEST

Check your answers to the Issue Spotters, and at the same time, take the interactive quiz for this chapter. Go to **www.cengage.com/blaw/blt** and click on "Chapter 37." First, click on "Answers to Issue Spotters" to check your answers. Next, click on "Interactive Quiz" to assess your mastery of the concepts in this chapter. Then click on "Flashcards" to review this chapter's Key Term definitions.

 For Review

Answers for the even-numbered questions in this For Review *section can be found on this text's accompanying Web site at* **www.cengage.com/blaw/blt**. *Select "Chapter 37" and click on "For Review."*

1 What is an insurable interest? When must an insurable interest exist—at the time the insurance policy is obtained, at the time the loss occurs, or both?

2 Is an insurance broker the agent of the insurance applicant or the agent of the insurer?

3 What are the basic requirements for executing a will? How may a will be revoked?

4 What is the difference between a *per stirpes* distribution and a *per capita* distribution of an estate to the grandchildren of the deceased?

5 What are the four essential elements of a trust? What is the difference between an express trust and an implied trust?

 Hypothetical Scenarios and Case Problems

37–1 Timing of Insurance Coverage. On October 10, Joleen Vora applied for a $50,000 life insurance policy with Magnum Life Insurance Co.; she named her husband, Jay, as the beneficiary. Joleen paid the insurance company the first year's policy premium on making the application. Two days later, before she had a chance to take the physical examination required by the insurance company and before the policy was issued, Joleen was killed in an automobile accident. Jay submitted a claim to the insurance company for the $50,000. Can Jay collect? Explain.

37–2 **Hypothetical Question with Sample Answer** Benjamin is a widower who has two married children, Edward and Patricia. Patricia has two children, Perry and Paul. Edward has no children. Benjamin dies, and his will leaves all his property equally to his children, Edward and Patricia, and provides that should a child predecease him, the grandchildren are to take *per stirpes*. The will was witnessed by Patricia and by Benjamin's lawyer and was signed by Benjamin in their presence. Patricia has predeceased Benjamin. Edward claims the will is invalid.

1 Discuss whether the will is valid.

2 Discuss the distribution of Benjamin's estate if the will is invalid.

3 Discuss the distribution of Benjamin's estate if the will is valid.

—**For a sample answer to Question 37–2, go to Appendix E at the end of this text.**

37–3 Insurer's Defenses. Patrick contracts with an Ajax Insurance Co. agent for a $50,000 ordinary life insurance policy. The application form is filled in to show Patrick's age as thirty-two. In addition, the application form asks whether Patrick has ever had any heart ailments or problems. Patrick answers no, forgetting that as a young child he was diagnosed as having a slight heart murmur. A policy is issued. Three years later, Patrick becomes seriously ill and dies. A review of the policy discloses that Patrick was actually thirty-three at the time of the application and the issuance of the policy and that he erred in answering the question about a history of heart ailments. Discuss whether Ajax can void the policy and escape liability on Patrick's death.

37–4 Insurance Contract. Richard Vanderbrook's home in New Orleans, Louisiana, was insured through Unitrin Preferred

Insurance Co. His policy excluded coverage for, among other things, "[f]lood, surface water, waves, tidal water, overflow of a body of water, or spray from any of these, whether or not driven by wind." The policy did not define the term *flood*. In August 2005, Hurricane Katrina struck along the coast of the Gulf of Mexico, devastating portions of Louisiana. In New Orleans, some of the most significant damage occurred when the levees along three canals—the 17th Street Canal, the Industrial Canal, and the London Avenue Canal—ruptured, and water submerged about 80 percent of the city, including Vanderbrook's home. He filed a claim for the loss, but Unitrin refused to pay. Vanderbrook and others whose policies contained similar exclusions asked a federal district court to order their insurers to pay. They contended that their losses were due to the negligent design, construction, and maintenance of the levees and that the policies did not clearly exclude coverage for an inundation of water induced by negligence. On what does a decision in this case hinge? What reasoning supports a ruling in the plaintiffs' favor? In the defendants' favor? [*In re Katrina Canal Breaches Litigation*, 495 F.3d 191 (5th Cir. 2007)]

37–5 **Case Problem with Sample Answer** James Lillard's first wife had a child whom James adopted when he married the child's mother. James fathered other children with her until they divorced in the early 1970s. In 1975, James married his second wife. During this marriage, neither spouse adopted the other's children, so each spouse's biological children remained the other's stepchildren. James's second wife died in 2002, and he was diagnosed with terminal cancer in January 2004. In February, he executed a will that divided his property equally among all of his children and stepchildren. By October, James was living with his children, who managed his finances and administered his prescribed drugs, which impaired him mentally and physically. A hospice worker noted that on October 5 James had difficulty completing sentences and was forgetful. A visitor two days later described him as "morphined up." On this same day, he tore his first will in half and executed a new will that left most of his property to his children. James died on October 19. His children submitted the second will to a Georgia state court for probate. His stepchildren objected, alleging, in part, that at the time of the second will's execution, James lacked testamentary capacity. His children responded that the first will had been validly revoked. Which will should be declared valid? Why? [*Lillard v. Owens*, 281 Ga. 619, 641 S.E.2d 511 (2007)]

—After you have answered Problem 37–5, compare your answer with the sample answer given on the Web site that accompanies this text. Go to **www.cengage.com/blaw/blt**, select "Chapter 37," and click on "Case Problem with Sample Answer."

37–6 **Insurance Coverage.** PAJ, Inc., a jewelry company, had a commercial general liability (CGL) policy from Hanover Insurance Co. It covered, among other things, liability for advertising injury. The policy required PAJ to notify Hanover of any claim or suit against PAJ "as soon as practicable." Yurman Designs

sued PAJ for copyright infringement because of the design of a particular jewelry line. Unaware that the CGL policy applied to this matter, PAJ did not notify Hanover of the suit until four to six months after litigation began. Hanover contended that the policy did not apply to this incident because the late notification had violated its terms. PAJ sued Hanover, seeking a declaration that it was obligated to defend and indemnify PAJ. The trial court held for Hanover, as did the appeals court. PAJ appealed. Does Hanover have an obligation to provide PAJ with assistance, or did PAJ violate the insurance contract? [*PAJ, Inc. v. The Hanover Insurance Co.*, 243 S.W.3d 630 (Sup.Ct.Tex. 2008)]

37–7 **Intestacy Laws.** A Florida statute provides that the right of election of a surviving spouse can be waived by written agreement: "A waiver of 'all rights,' or equivalent language, in the property or estate of a present or prospective spouse * * * is a waiver of all rights to elective share." The day before Mary Ann Taylor married Louis Taylor in Florida, they entered into a prenuptial agreement. The agreement stated that all property belonging to each spouse would "forever remain his or her personal estate," "said property shall remain forever free of claim by the other," and the parties would retain "full rights and authority" over their property as they would have as "if not married." After Louis's death, his only child, Joshua Taylor, filed a petition in a Florida state court for a determination of the beneficiaries of Louis's estate. How much of the estate can Mary Ann elect to receive? Explain. [*Taylor v. Taylor*, 1 So.3d 348 (Fla.App. 1 Dist. 2009)]

37–8 **A Question of Ethics** *Vickie Lynn Smith, an actress and model also known as Anna Nicole Smith, met J. Howard Marshall II in 1991. During their courtship, J. Howard lavished gifts and large sums of money on Anna Nicole, and they married on June 27, 1994. J. Howard died on August 4, 1995. According to Anna Nicole, J. Howard intended to provide for her financial security through a trust, but under the terms of his will, all of his assets were transferred to a trust for the benefit of E. Pierce Marshall, one of J. Howard's sons. While J. Howard's estate was subject to probate proceedings in a Texas state court, Anna Nicole filed for bankruptcy in a federal bankruptcy court. Pierce filed a claim in the bankruptcy proceeding, alleging that Anna Nicole had defamed him when her lawyers told the media that Pierce had engaged in forgery and fraud to gain control of his father's assets. Anna Nicole filed a counterclaim, alleging that Pierce prevented the transfer of his father's assets to a trust for her by, among other things, imprisoning J. Howard against his wishes, surrounding him with security guards to prevent contact with her, and transferring property against his wishes. [Marshall v. Marshall, 547 U.S. 293, 126 S.Ct. 1735, 164 L.Ed.2d 480 (2006)]*

1 What is the purpose underlying the requirements for a valid will? Which of these requirements might be at issue in this case? How should it apply here? Why?

2 State courts generally have jurisdiction over the probate of a will and the administration of an estate. Does the Texas state court thus have the sole authority to adjudicate all of the claims in this case? Why or why not?

3 How should Pierce's claim against Anna Nicole and her counterclaim be resolved?

4 Anna Nicole executed her will in 2001. The beneficiary—Daniel, her son, who was not J. Howard's child—died in 2006, shortly after Anna Nicole gave birth to a daughter, Dannielynn. In 2007, before executing a new will, Anna Nicole died. What happens if a will's beneficiary dies before the testator? What happens if a child is born after a will is executed?

 ## Critical Thinking and Writing Assignments

37–9 Critical Legal Thinking. Statistics show that the extent of risk assumed by insurance companies varies depending on the gender of the insured. Many people contend that laws prohibiting gender-based insurance rates are thus fundamentally unfair.

Why might gender discrimination be fair when it comes to insurance premiums when it is clearly unfair (and illegal) in housing or employment?

 ## Practical Internet Exercises

Go to this text's Web site at **www.cengage.com/blaw/blt**, select "Chapter 37," and click on "Practical Internet Exercises." There you will find the following Internet research exercises that you can perform to learn more about the topics covered in this chapter.

Practical Internet Exercise 37–1: Social Perspective—Disappearing Decisions
Practical Internet Exercise 37–2: Legal Perspective—Wills and Trusts
Practical Internet Exercise 37–3: Management Perspective—Risk Management in Cyberspace

Dave graduates from State University with an engineering degree and goes into business as a self-employed computer programmer.

1. To advertise his services on the Internet, Dave creates and produces a short digital video. Hollywood Films, Inc., sees the video and hires Dave to program the special effects for a short sequence in a Hollywood movie. Their contract states that all rights to the sequence belong to Hollywood. Does the digital video, the movie sequence, both, or neither belong to Dave?

2. Dave leases an office in Carl's Riverside Plaza office building for a two-year term. What is Dave's obligation for the rent if he moves out before the end of the term? If Dave dies during the term, who is entitled to possession of the office? What is Dave's obligation for the rent if Carl sells the building to Commercial Investments, Inc., before Dave's lease is up?

3. At the end of the lease term, Dave buys the office building from Carl, who gives Dave a warranty deed. Commercial Investments later challenges Dave's ownership of the building and presents its own allegedly valid deed. What will it mean if a court rules that Dave owns the building in fee simple? If Commercial Investments is successful, can Dave recover anything from Carl? Explain.

4. Dave's programming business expands, and he hires Mary as an employee. Mary becomes invaluable to the business, and Dave obtains a key-person insurance policy on her life. She dies six years later. If the insurance company discovers that Dave understated Mary's age when applying for the policy (which includes an incontestability clause), can the insurer legitimately refuse payment? If Mary had resigned to start her own programming firm one year before she died, can Dave collect payment under the policy? Why or why not?

5. Over time, Dave acquires other commercial property, which eventually becomes the most lucrative part of his business. Dave wants his adult children, Frank and Terry, to get the benefit of this property when he dies. Dave does not think that Frank and Terry can manage the property, however, because they have their own careers and live in other states. How can Dave provide for them to get the benefit of the property under someone else's management? In his will, Dave designates Hal, his attorney, as executor. What does an executor do?

When a couple divorces, the division of the marital estate—all of the property that the parties accumulated during their marriage—often leads to disputes. Questions of ownership frequently arise in divorce proceedings: Who owned what property, and how did she or he acquire it? If property was allegedly acquired by gift, did the transfer satisfy the requirements for a valid gift? Those questions arose in Kovarik v. Kovarik,[1] which we examine in this Extended Case Study. During a divorce, a dispute arose over whether the couple's marital estate included several certificates of deposit (discussed in Chapter 18) worth about $60,000 in which one spouse allegedly had an interest. The acquisition, division, and transfer of ownership of personal property were discussed in Chapter 35, and other types of property transfers were covered in Chapter 36.

1. 2009 ND 82, 765 N.W.2d 511 (2009). To read this case online, go to www.ndcourts.gov. In the left-hand column, click on "Opinions." On that page, in the "Citation:" boxes, type "2009" ND "82" or "765" N.W.2d "511" and click on "Execute." In the result, click on the appropriate link to access the opinion. The North Dakota Supreme Court maintains this Web site.

CASE BACKGROUND

Jennifer Stahl and Bradly Kovarik were married in North Dakota in July 2001. A few months later, Bradly's parents, Dennis and Marlene, liquidated their farm business and equipment, and invested the proceeds in certificates of deposit (CDs). Four of the CDs were in the names of Kovarik and his sister, Wanda Morstad, but were retained by their parents.

Jennifer and Bradly separated in August 2007. Jennifer filed for divorce in a North Dakota state court. In a list of their marital property, she included the four CDs. Bradly denied any interest in those items.

At the trial, Bradly testified that he learned about the CDs from his sister, who cashed one without giving him any of the proceeds after Jennifer filed for divorce. At their mother's

request, his sister also negotiated the other three CDs before the divorce trial. The court did not include the CDs in valuing and distributing the Kovariks' marital estate. Jennifer appealed to the North Dakota Supreme Court, arguing that Bradly's interest in the CDs should have been included.

MAJORITY OPINION

SANDSTROM, Justice:

* * * *

A [trial] court's decisions regarding the division of marital property are findings of fact and may be reversed on appeal only if clearly erroneous. A finding of fact is clearly erroneous if it is induced by an erroneous view of the law, if there is no evidence to support it, or if, after reviewing the entirety of the evidence, this Court is left with a definite and firm conviction a mistake has been made. A [trial] court's findings of fact are presumed correct, and we view the evidence in the light most favorable to its findings.

Division of marital property upon divorce must be equitable. Although the division does not have to be equal, a substantial disparity must be explained. *All of the real and personal property accumulated by the parties, regardless of source, must be included in the marital estate.* [Emphasis added.]

* * * *

A * * * court may consider property to be part of the marital estate, if supported by evidence, even if a party claims it is owned by a nonparty. The principles applicable to *inter vivos* gifts in general apply as well to purported gifts of certificates of deposit. A valid gift made during the donor's lifetime must satisfy certain requirements—donative intent, delivery, actual or constructive, and acceptance by donee. A donor's intent is a question of fact. The actual or constructive delivery must be of a nature sufficient to divest the owner of all dominion [control] over the property and to invest the donee therewith.

Bradly Kovarik's parents testified that after liquidating their farm and equipment * * * , they placed four certificates of deposit in Bradly Kovarik's and his sister's names—"Wanda Morstad or Bradly Kovarik." They also testified they did not intend to give Bradly Kovarik and Morstad any present interest in the certificates. Moreover, Bradly Kovarik's father testified that the certificates, prior to having been cashed out, had been locked in a safe in their home and neither Bradly Kovarik nor his sister could just come and take the certificates.

Bradly Kovarik testified he had no knowledge of the certificates' existence until his sister told him she cashed one out and used some of the proceeds for home repairs. He also testified he did not receive any of the remaining proceeds. Wanda Morstad testified she did not expect the certificates of deposit to belong to her. When requested, she assisted her parents in cashing out the certificates, which she did with respect to the remaining three certificates.

The [trial] court found Bradly Kovarik's parents did not intend to gift the certificates to him and his sister. The court further found the certificates were never delivered to either Bradly Kovarik or his sister but were retained in their parents' possession. The record does not reflect donative intent or delivery of the certificates to Bradly Kovarik, either actual or constructive. *In the absence of a donative intent and delivery, the [trial] court's finding that there was no valid gift is not clearly erroneous.* [Emphasis added.]

* * * *

We hold the [trial] court's property distribution and property valuation is not clearly erroneous, and affirm.

DISSENTING OPINION

MARING, Justice, dissenting:

I respectfully dissent from * * * the Majority opinion because the [trial] court * * * erred in concluding Bradly Kovarik's parents never gave him the certificates of deposit.

* * * *

First, the [trial] court found Bradly Kovarik's parents did not intend to give the certificates of deposit to Bradly Kovarik or his sister. This finding is not supported by the record. Bradly Kovarik admits that he and his sister were the co-owners of the certificates of deposit. Bradly Kovarik's sister also testified * * * that she was the co-owner of the certificates of deposit with her brother.

* * * *

Dennis Kovarik's testimony establishes that he knew Bradly Kovarik was a joint owner of the certificates of deposit * * * . Marlene Kovarik's testimony establishes that Bradly Kovarik was the joint owner of the certificates of deposit.

Continued

These admissions by Bradly Kovarik and his family that he owned the certificates of deposits are supported by the law. The parties do not dispute that Bradly Kovarik's name was on the certificate of deposit together with his sister's name or that neither of his parents' names were on the certificates of deposit. It is presumed that a certificate of deposit belongs to the person whose name appears on the certificate. * * * Bradly Kovarik's parents gave up their exclusive dominion and control over their assets when they placed the money in certificates of deposit in their children's names.

* * * *

The [trial] court found the certificates of deposit were never delivered to Bradly Kovarik or his sister because the parents kept possession of the certificates of deposit. This finding is not supported by the record.

* * * *

* * * Bradly Kovarik's parents divested themselves of the control of the certificates of deposit by first solely placing their children's names on the certificates of deposit and then delivering the certificates of deposit to Wanda Morstad to be cashed.

* * * *

In conclusion, I dissent because the certificates of deposit were completed gifts to Bradly Kovarik and must be included in the marital estate.

QUESTIONS FOR ANALYSIS

1. **Law.** How does the majority respond to the appellant's argument in this case? What is the majority's reasoning?
2. **Law.** How does the dissent analyze the issue before the court?
3. **Ethics.** According to Marlene Kovarik, the CDs were obtained in her children's names in an effort to avoid the parents' tax obligations, rather than to give the funds to the children. Is this ethical? Explain.
4. **Social Dimensions.** If the Kovariks had invested their funds in real estate in their children's names, instead of CDs, would the result in this case have been the same? Why or why not?
5. **Implications for the Estate Planner.** How might Marlene and Dennis Kovarik have avoided the question that Jennifer raised here? Discuss.

How to Brief Cases and Analyze Case Problems

How to Brief Cases

To fully understand the law with respect to business, you need to be able to read and understand court decisions. To make this task easier, you can use a method of case analysis that is called *briefing*. There is a fairly standard procedure that you can follow when you "brief" any court case. You must first read the case opinion carefully. When you feel you understand the case, you can prepare a brief of it.

Although the format of the brief may vary, typically it will present the essentials of the case under headings such as those listed below.

1. **Citation.** Give the full citation for the case, including the name of the case, the date it was decided, and the court that decided it.
2. **Facts.** Briefly indicate (a) the reasons for the lawsuit; (b) the identity and arguments of the plaintiff(s) and defendant(s), respectively; and (c) the lower court's decision—if appropriate.
3. **Issue.** Concisely phrase, in the form of a question, the essential issue before the court. (If more than one issue is involved, you may have two—or even more—questions here.)
4. **Decision.** Indicate here—with a "yes" or "no," if possible—the court's answer to the question (or questions) in the Issue section above.
5. **Reason.** Summarize as briefly as possible the reasons given by the court for its decision (or decisions) and the case or statutory law relied on by the court in arriving at its decision.

For a case-specific example of what should be included under each of the above headings when briefing a case, see the review of the sample court case presented in the appendix to Chapter 1 of this text on pages 30 and 31.

Analyzing Case Problems

In addition to learning how to brief cases, students of business law and the legal environment also find it helpful to know how to analyze case problems. Part of the study of business law and the legal environment usually involves analyzing case problems, such as those included in this text at the end of each chapter.

For each case problem in this book, we provide the relevant background and facts of the lawsuit and the issue before the court. When you are assigned one of these problems, your job will be to determine how the court should decide the issue, and why. In other words, you will need to engage in legal analysis and reasoning. Here, we offer some suggestions on how to make this task less daunting. We begin by presenting a sample case problem:

> While Janet Lawson, a famous pianist, was shopping in Quality Market, she slipped and fell on a wet floor in one of the aisles. The floor had recently been mopped by one of the store's employees, but there were no signs warning customers that the floor in that area was wet. As a result of the fall, Lawson injured her right arm and was unable to perform piano concerts for the next six months. Had she been able to perform the scheduled concerts, she would have earned approximately $60,000 over that period of time. Lawson sued Quality Market for this amount, plus another $10,000 in medical expenses. She claimed that the store's failure to warn customers of the wet floor constituted negligence and therefore the market was liable for her injuries. Will the court agree with Lawson? Discuss.

Understand the Facts

This may sound obvious, but before you can analyze or apply the relevant law to a specific set of facts, you must clearly understand those facts. In other words, you should read through the case problem carefully—more than once, if necessary—to make sure you understand the identity of the plaintiff(s) and defendant(s) in the case and the progression of events that led to the lawsuit.

In the sample case problem just given, the identity of the parties is fairly obvious. Janet Lawson is the one bringing the suit; therefore, she is the plaintiff. Lawson is bringing the suit against Quality Market, so it is the defendant. Some of the case problems you may work on have multiple plaintiffs or defendants. Often, it is helpful to use abbreviations for the parties. To indicate a reference to a plaintiff, for example, the *pi* symbol—π—is often used, and a defendant is denoted by a *delta*—Δ—a triangle.

The events leading to the lawsuit are also fairly straightforward. Lawson slipped and fell on a wet floor, and she contends that Quality Market should be liable for her injuries because it was negligent in not posting a sign warning customers of the wet floor.

When you are working on case problems, realize that the facts should be accepted as they are given. For instance, in our sample problem, it should be accepted that the floor was wet and that there was no sign. In other words, avoid making conjectures, such as "Maybe the floor wasn't too wet," or "Maybe an employee was getting a sign to put up," or "Maybe someone stole the sign." Questioning the facts as they are presented only adds confusion to your analysis.

Legal Analysis and Reasoning

Once you understand the facts given in the case problem, you can begin to analyze the case. Recall from Chapter 1 that the **IRAC method** is a helpful tool to use in the legal analysis and reasoning process. IRAC is an acronym for **I**ssue, **R**ule, **A**pplication, **C**onclusion. Applying this method to our sample problem would involve the following steps:

1. First, you need to decide what legal **issue** is involved in the case. In our sample case, the basic issue is whether Quality Market's failure to warn customers of the wet floor constituted negligence. As discussed in Chapter 4 negligence is a *tort*—a civil wrong. In a tort lawsuit, the plaintiff seeks to be compensated for another's wrongful act. A defendant will be deemed negligent if he or she breached a duty of care owed to the plaintiff and the breach of that duty caused the plaintiff to suffer harm.

2. Once you have identified the issue, the next step is to determine what **rule of law** applies to the issue. To make this determination, you will want to carefully review the text discussion relating to the issue involved in the problem. Our sample case problem involves the tort of negligence, which is covered in Chapter 4. The applicable rule of law is the tort law principle that business owners owe a duty to exercise reasonable care to protect their customers (*business invitees*). Reasonable care, in this context, includes either removing—or warning customers of—*foreseeable* risks about which the owner *knew* or *should have known*. Business owners need not warn customers of "open and obvious" risks, however. If a business owner breaches this duty of care (fails to exercise the appropriate degree of care toward customers), and the breach of duty causes a customer to be injured, the business owner will be liable to the customer for the customer's injuries.

3. The next—and usually the most difficult—step in analyzing case problems is the **application** of the relevant rule of law to the specific facts of the case you are studying. In our sample problem, applying the tort law principle just discussed presents few difficulties. An employee of the store had mopped the floor in the aisle where Lawson slipped and fell, but no sign was present indicating that the floor was wet. That a customer might fall on a wet floor is clearly a foreseeable risk. Therefore, the failure to warn customers about the wet floor was a breach of the duty of care owed by the business owner to the store's customers.

4. Once you have completed Step 3 in the IRAC method, you should be ready to draw your **conclusion.** In our sample problem, Quality Market is liable to Lawson for her injuries because the market's breach of its duty of care caused Lawson's injuries.

The fact patterns in the case problems presented in this text are not always as simple as those presented in our sample problem. Often, a case has more than one plaintiff or defendant. A case may also involve more than one issue and have more than one applicable rule of law. Furthermore, in some case problems the facts may indicate that the general rule of law should not apply. Suppose that a store employee told Lawson about the wet floor and advised her not to walk in that aisle, but Lawson decided to walk there anyway. This fact could alter the outcome of the case because the store could then raise the defense of *assumption of risk* (see Chapter 4). Nonetheless, a careful review of the chapter should always provide you with the knowledge you need to analyze the problem thoroughly and arrive at accurate conclusions.

The Constitution of the United States

Preamble

We the People of the United States, in Order to form a more perfect Union, establish Justice, insure domestic Tranquility, provide for the common defence, promote the general Welfare, and secure the Blessings of Liberty to ourselves and our Posterity, do ordain and establish this Constitution for the United States of America.

Article I

Section 1. All legislative Powers herein granted shall be vested in a Congress of the United States, which shall consist of a Senate and House of Representatives.

Section 2. The House of Representatives shall be composed of Members chosen every second Year by the People of the several States, and the Electors in each State shall have the Qualifications requisite for Electors of the most numerous Branch of the State Legislature.

No Person shall be a Representative who shall not have attained to the Age of twenty five Years, and been seven Years a Citizen of the United States, and who shall not, when elected, be an Inhabitant of that State in which he shall be chosen.

Representatives and direct Taxes shall be apportioned among the several States which may be included within this Union, according to their respective Numbers, which shall be determined by adding to the whole Number of free Persons, including those bound to Service for a Term of Years, and excluding Indians not taxed, three fifths of all other Persons. The actual Enumeration shall be made within three Years after the first Meeting of the Congress of the United States, and within every subsequent Term of ten Years, in such Manner as they shall by Law direct. The Number of Representatives shall not exceed one for every thirty Thousand, but each State shall have at Least one Representative; and until such enumeration shall be made, the State of New Hampshire shall be entitled to chuse three, Massachusetts eight, Rhode Island and Providence Plantations one, Connecticut five, New York six, New Jersey four, Pennsylvania eight, Delaware one, Maryland six, Virginia ten, North Carolina five, South Carolina five, and Georgia three.

When vacancies happen in the Representation from any State, the Executive Authority thereof shall issue Writs of Election to fill such Vacancies.

The House of Representatives shall chuse their Speaker and other Officers; and shall have the sole Power of Impeachment.

Section 3. The Senate of the United States shall be composed of two Senators from each State, chosen by the Legislature thereof, for six Years; and each Senator shall have one Vote.

Immediately after they shall be assembled in Consequence of the first Election, they shall be divided as equally as may be into three Classes. The Seats of the Senators of the first Class shall be vacated at the Expiration of the second Year, of the second Class at the Expiration of the fourth Year, and of the third Class at the Expiration of the sixth Year, so that one third may be chosen every second Year; and if Vacancies happen by Resignation, or otherwise, during the Recess of the Legislature of any State, the Executive thereof may make temporary Appointments until the next Meeting of the Legislature, which shall then fill such Vacancies.

No Person shall be a Senator who shall not have attained to the Age of thirty Years, and been nine Years a Citizen of the United States, and who shall not, when elected, be an Inhabitant of that State for which he shall be chosen.

The Vice President of the United States shall be President of the Senate, but shall have no Vote, unless they be equally divided.

The Senate shall chuse their other Officers, and also a President pro tempore, in the Absence of the Vice President, or when he shall exercise the Office of President of the United States.

The Senate shall have the sole Power to try all Impeachments. When sitting for that Purpose, they shall be on Oath or Affirmation. When the President of the United States is tried, the Chief Justice shall preside: And no Person shall be convicted without the Concurrence of two thirds of the Members present.

Judgment in Cases of Impeachment shall not extend further than to removal from Office, and disqualification to hold and enjoy any Office of honor, Trust, or Profit under the United States: but the Party convicted shall nevertheless be liable and subject to Indictment, Trial, Judgment, and Punishment, according to Law.

Section 4. The Times, Places and Manner of holding Elections for Senators and Representatives, shall be prescribed in each State by the Legislature thereof; but the Congress may at any time by Law make or alter such Regulations, except as to the Places of chusing Senators.

The Congress shall assemble at least once in every Year, and such Meeting shall be on the first Monday in December, unless they shall by Law appoint a different Day.

Section 5. Each House shall be the Judge of the Elections, Returns, and Qualifications of its own Members, and a Majority of each shall constitute a Quorum to do Business; but a smaller Number may adjourn from day to day, and may be authorized to compel the Attendance of absent Members, in such Manner, and under such Penalties as each House may provide.

Each House may determine the Rules of its Proceedings, punish its Members for disorderly Behavior, and, with the Concurrence of two thirds, expel a Member.

Each House shall keep a Journal of its Proceedings, and from time to time publish the same, excepting such Parts as may in their Judgment require Secrecy; and the Yeas and Nays of the Members of either House on any question shall, at the Desire of one fifth of those Present, be entered on the Journal.

Neither House, during the Session of Congress, shall, without the Consent of the other, adjourn for more than three days, nor to any other Place than that in which the two Houses shall be sitting.

Section 6. The Senators and Representatives shall receive a Compensation for their Services, to be ascertained by Law, and paid out of the Treasury of the United States. They shall in all Cases, except Treason, Felony and Breach of the Peace, be privileged from Arrest during their Attendance at the Session of their respective Houses, and in going to and returning from the same; and for any Speech or Debate in either House, they shall not be questioned in any other Place.

No Senator or Representative shall, during the Time for which he was elected, be appointed to any civil Office under the Authority of the United States, which shall have been created, or the Emoluments whereof shall have been increased during such time; and no Person holding any Office under the United States, shall be a Member of either House during his Continuance in Office.

Section 7. All Bills for raising Revenue shall originate in the House of Representatives; but the Senate may propose or concur with Amendments as on other Bills.

Every Bill which shall have passed the House of Representatives and the Senate, shall, before it become a Law, be presented to the President of the United States; If he approve he shall sign it, but if not he shall return it, with his Objections to the House in which it shall have originated, who shall enter the Objections at large on their Journal, and proceed to reconsider it. If after such Reconsideration two thirds of that House shall agree to pass the Bill, it shall be sent together with the Objections, to the other House, by which it shall likewise be reconsidered, and if approved by two thirds of that House, it shall become a Law. But in all such Cases the Votes of both Houses shall be determined by Yeas and Nays, and the Names of the Persons voting for and against the Bill shall be entered on the Journal of each House respectively. If any Bill shall not be returned by the President within ten Days (Sundays excepted) after it shall have been presented to him, the Same shall be a Law, in like Manner as if he had signed it, unless the Congress by their Adjournment prevent its Return in which Case it shall not be a Law.

Every Order, Resolution, or Vote, to which the Concurrence of the Senate and House of Representatives may be necessary (except on a question of Adjournment) shall be presented to the President of the United States; and before the Same shall take Effect, shall be approved by him, or being disapproved by him, shall be repassed by two thirds of the Senate and House of Representatives, according to the Rules and Limitations prescribed in the Case of a Bill.

Section 8. The Congress shall have Power To lay and collect Taxes, Duties, Imposts and Excises, to pay the Debts and provide for the common Defence and general Welfare of the United States; but all Duties, Imposts and Excises shall be uniform throughout the United States;

To borrow Money on the credit of the United States;

To regulate Commerce with foreign Nations, and among the several States, and with the Indian Tribes;

To establish an uniform Rule of Naturalization, and uniform Laws on the subject of Bankruptcies throughout the United States;

To coin Money, regulate the Value thereof, and of foreign Coin, and fix the Standard of Weights and Measures;

To provide for the Punishment of counterfeiting the Securities and current Coin of the United States;

To establish Post Offices and post Roads;

To promote the Progress of Science and useful Arts, by securing for limited Times to Authors and Inventors the exclusive Right to their respective Writings and Discoveries;

To constitute Tribunals inferior to the supreme Court;

To define and punish Piracies and Felonies committed on the high Seas, and Offenses against the Law of Nations;

To declare War, grant Letters of Marque and Reprisal, and make Rules concerning Captures on Land and Water;

To raise and support Armies, but no Appropriation of Money to that Use shall be for a longer Term than two Years;

To provide and maintain a Navy;

To make Rules for the Government and Regulation of the land and naval Forces;

To provide for calling forth the Militia to execute the Laws of the Union, suppress Insurrections and repel Invasions;

To provide for organizing, arming, and disciplining, the Militia, and for governing such Part of them as may be employed in the Service of the United States, reserving to the States respectively, the Appointment of the Officers, and the Authority of training the Militia according to the discipline prescribed by Congress;

To exercise exclusive Legislation in all Cases whatsoever, over such District (not exceeding ten Miles square) as may, by Cession of particular States, and the Acceptance of Congress, become the Seat of the Government of the United States, and to exercise like Authority over all Places purchased by the Consent of the Legislature of the State in which the Same shall be, for the Erection of Forts, Magazines, Arsenals, dock-Yards, and other needful Buildings;—And

To make all Laws which shall be necessary and proper for carrying into Execution the foregoing Powers, and all other Powers vested by this Constitution in the Government of the United States, or in any Department or Officer thereof.

Section 9. The Migration or Importation of such Persons as any of the States now existing shall think proper to admit, shall not be prohibited by the Congress prior to the Year one thousand eight hundred and eight, but a Tax or duty may be imposed on such Importation, not exceeding ten dollars for each Person.

The privilege of the Writ of Habeas Corpus shall not be suspended, unless when in Cases of Rebellion or Invasion the public Safety may require it.

No Bill of Attainder or ex post facto Law shall be passed.

No Capitation, or other direct, Tax shall be laid, unless in Proportion to the Census or Enumeration herein before directed to be taken.

No Tax or Duty shall be laid on Articles exported from any State.

No Preference shall be given by any Regulation of Commerce or Revenue to the Ports of one State over those of another: nor shall Vessels bound to, or from, one State be obliged to enter, clear, or pay Duties in another.

No Money shall be drawn from the Treasury, but in Consequence of Appropriations made by Law; and a regular Statement and Account of the Receipts and Expenditures of all public Money shall be published from time to time.

No Title of Nobility shall be granted by the United States: And no Person holding any Office of Profit or Trust under them, shall, without the Consent of the Congress, accept of any present, Emolument, Office, or Title, of any kind whatever, from any King, Prince, or foreign State.

Section 10. No State shall enter into any Treaty, Alliance, or Confederation; grant Letters of Marque and Reprisal; coin Money; emit Bills of Credit; make any Thing but gold and silver Coin a Tender in Payment of Debts; pass any Bill of Attainder, ex post facto Law, or Law impairing the Obligation of Contracts, or grant any Title of Nobility.

No State shall, without the Consent of the Congress, lay any Imposts or Duties on Imports or Exports, except what may be absolutely necessary for executing its inspection Laws: and the net Produce of all Duties and Imposts, laid by any State on Imports or Exports, shall be for the Use of the Treasury of the United States; and all such Laws shall be subject to the Revision and Controul of the Congress.

No State shall, without the Consent of Congress, lay any Duty of Tonnage, keep Troops, or Ships of War in time of Peace, enter into any Agreement or Compact with another State, or with a foreign Power, or engage in War, unless actually invaded, or in such imminent Danger as will not admit of delay.

Article II

Section 1. The executive Power shall be vested in a President of the United States of America. He shall hold his Office during the Term of four Years, and, together with the Vice President, chosen for the same Term, be elected, as follows:

Each State shall appoint, in such Manner as the Legislature thereof may direct, a Number of Electors, equal to the whole Number of Senators and Representatives to which the State may be entitled in the Congress; but no Senator or Representative, or Person holding an Office of Trust or Profit under the United States, shall be appointed an Elector.

The Electors shall meet in their respective States, and vote by Ballot for two Persons, of whom one at least shall not be an Inhabitant of the same State with themselves. And they shall make a List of all the Persons voted for, and of the Number of Votes for each; which List they shall sign and certify, and transmit sealed to the Seat of the Government of the United States, directed to the President of the Senate. The President of the Senate shall, in the Presence of the Senate and House of Representatives, open all the Certificates, and the Votes shall then be counted. The Person having the greatest Number of Votes shall be the President, if such Number be a Majority of the whole Number of Electors appointed; and if there be more than one who have such Majority, and have an equal Number of Votes, then the House of Representatives shall immediately chuse by Ballot one of them for President; and if no Person have a Majority, then from the five highest on the List the said House shall in like Manner chuse the President. But in chusing the President, the Votes shall be taken by States, the Representation from each State having one Vote; A quorum for this Purpose shall consist of a Member or Members from two thirds of the States, and a Majority of all the States shall be necessary to a Choice. In every Case, after the Choice of the President, the Person having the greater Number of Votes of the Electors shall be the Vice President. But if there should remain two or more who have equal Votes, the Senate shall chuse from them by Ballot the Vice President.

The Congress may determine the Time of chusing the Electors, and the Day on which they shall give their Votes; which Day shall be the same throughout the United States.

No person except a natural born Citizen, or a Citizen of the United States, at the time of the Adoption of this Constitution, shall be eligible to the Office of President; neither shall any Person be eligible to that Office who shall not have attained to the Age of thirty five Years, and been fourteen Years a Resident within the United States.

In Case of the Removal of the President from Office, or of his Death, Resignation or Inability to discharge the Powers and Duties of the said Office, the same shall devolve on the Vice President, and the Congress may by Law provide for the Case of Removal, Death, Resignation or Inability, both of the President and Vice President, declaring what Officer shall then act as President, and such Officer shall act accordingly, until the Disability be removed, or a President shall be elected.

The President shall, at stated Times, receive for his Services, a Compensation, which shall neither be increased nor diminished during the Period for which he shall have been elected, and he shall not receive within that Period any other Emolument from the United States, or any of them.

Before he enter on the Execution of his Office, he shall take the following Oath or Affirmation: "I do solemnly swear (or affirm) that I will faithfully execute the Office of President of the United States, and will to the best of my Ability, preserve, protect and defend the Constitution of the United States."

Section 2. The President shall be Commander in Chief of the Army and Navy of the United States, and of the Militia of the several States, when called into the actual Service of the United States; he may require the Opinion, in writing, of the principal Officer in each of the executive Departments, upon any Subject relating to the Duties of their respective Offices, and he shall have Power to grant Reprieves and Pardons for Offenses against the United States, except in Cases of Impeachment.

He shall have Power, by and with the Advice and Consent of the Senate to make Treaties, provided two thirds of the Senators present concur; and he shall nominate, and by and with the Advice and Consent of the Senate, shall appoint Ambassadors, other public Ministers and Consuls, Judges of the supreme Court, and all other Officers of the United States, whose Appointments are not herein otherwise provided for, and which shall be established by Law; but the Congress may by Law vest the Appointment of such inferior Officers, as they think proper, in the President alone, in the Courts of Law, or in the Heads of Departments.

The President shall have Power to fill up all Vacancies that may happen during the Recess of the Senate, by granting Commissions which shall expire at the End of their next Session.

Section 3. He shall from time to time give to the Congress Information of the State of the Union, and recommend to their Consideration such Measures as he shall judge necessary and expedient; he may, on extraordinary Occasions, convene both Houses, or either of them, and in Case of Disagreement between them, with Respect to the Time of Adjournment, he may adjourn them to such Time as he shall think proper; he shall receive Ambassadors and other public Ministers; he shall take Care that the Laws be faithfully executed, and shall Commission all the Officers of the United States.

Section 4. The President, Vice President and all civil Officers of the United States, shall be removed from Office on Impeachment for, and Conviction of, Treason, Bribery, or other high Crimes and Misdemeanors.

Article III

Section 1. The judicial Power of the United States, shall be vested in one supreme Court, and in such inferior Courts as the Congress may from time to time ordain and establish. The Judges, both of the supreme and inferior Courts, shall hold their Offices during good Behaviour, and shall, at stated Times, receive for their Services a Compensation, which shall not be diminished during their Continuance in Office.

Section 2. The judicial Power shall extend to all Cases, in Law and Equity, arising under this Constitution, the Laws of the United States, and Treaties made, or which shall be made, under their Authority;—to all Cases affecting Ambassadors, other public Ministers and Consuls;—to all Cases of admiralty and maritime Jurisdiction;—to Controversies to which the United States shall be a Party;—to Controversies between two or more States;—between a State and Citizens of another State;—between Citizens of different States;—between Citizens of the same State claiming Lands under Grants of different States, and between a State, or the Citizens thereof, and foreign States, Citizens or Subjects.

In all Cases affecting Ambassadors, other public Ministers and Consuls, and those in which a State shall be a Party, the supreme Court shall have original Jurisdiction. In all the other Cases before mentioned, the supreme Court shall have appellate Jurisdiction, both as to Law and Fact, with such Exceptions, and under such Regulations as the Congress shall make.

The Trial of all Crimes, except in Cases of Impeachment, shall be by Jury; and such Trial shall be held in the State where the said Crimes shall have been committed; but when not committed within any State, the Trial shall be at such Place or Places as the Congress may by Law have directed.

Section 3. Treason against the United States, shall consist only in levying War against them, or, in adhering to their Enemies, giving them Aid and Comfort. No Person shall be convicted of Treason unless on the Testimony of two Witnesses to the same overt Act, or on Confession in open Court.

The Congress shall have Power to declare the Punishment of Treason, but no Attainder of Treason shall work Corruption of Blood, or Forfeiture except during the Life of the Person attainted.

Article IV

Section 1. Full Faith and Credit shall be given in each State to the public Acts, Records, and judicial Proceedings of every other State. And the Congress may by general Laws prescribe the Manner in which such Acts, Records and Proceedings shall be proved, and the Effect thereof.

Section 2. The Citizens of each State shall be entitled to all Privileges and Immunities of Citizens in the several States.

A Person charged in any State with Treason, Felony, or other Crime, who shall flee from Justice, and be found in another State, shall on Demand of the executive Authority of the State from which he fled, be delivered up, to be removed to the State having Jurisdiction of the Crime.

No Person held to Service or Labour in one State, under the Laws thereof, escaping into another, shall, in Consequence of any Law or Regulation therein, be discharged from such Service or Labour, but shall be delivered up on Claim of the Party to whom such Service or Labour may be due.

Section 3. New States may be admitted by the Congress into this Union; but no new State shall be formed or erected within the Jurisdiction of any other State; nor any State be formed by the Junction of two or more States, or Parts of States, without the Consent of the Legislatures of the States concerned as well as of the Congress.

The Congress shall have Power to dispose of and make all needful Rules and Regulations respecting the Territory or other Property belonging to the United States; and nothing in this Constitution shall be so construed as to Prejudice any Claims of the United States, or of any particular State.

Section 4. The United States shall guarantee to every State in this Union a Republican Form of Government, and shall protect each of them against Invasion; and on Application of the Legislature, or of the Executive (when the Legislature cannot be convened) against domestic Violence.

Article V

The Congress, whenever two thirds of both Houses shall deem it necessary, shall propose Amendments to this Constitution, or, on the Application of the Legislatures of two thirds of the several States, shall call a Convention for proposing Amendments, which, in either Case, shall be valid to all Intents and Purposes, as part of this Constitution, when ratified by the Legislatures of three fourths of the several States, or by Conventions in three fourths thereof, as the one or the other Mode of Ratification may be proposed by the Congress; Provided that no Amendment which may be made prior to the Year One thousand eight hundred and eight shall in any Manner affect the first and fourth Clauses in the Ninth Section of the first Article; and that no State, without its Consent, shall be deprived of its equal Suffrage in the Senate.

Article VI

All Debts contracted and Engagements entered into, before the Adoption of this Constitution shall be as valid against the United States under this Constitution, as under the Confederation.

This Constitution, and the Laws of the United States which shall be made in Pursuance thereof; and all Treaties made, or which shall be made, under the Authority of the United States, shall be the supreme Law of the Land; and the Judges in every State shall be bound thereby, any Thing in the Constitution or Laws of any State to the Contrary notwithstanding.

The Senators and Representatives before mentioned, and the Members of the several State Legislatures, and all executive and judicial Officers, both of the United States and of the several States, shall be bound by Oath or Affirmation, to support this Constitution; but no religious Test shall ever be required as a Qualification to any Office or public Trust under the United States.

Article VII

The Ratification of the Conventions of nine States shall be sufficient for the Establishment of this Constitution between the States so ratifying the Same.

Amendment I [1791]

Congress shall make no law respecting an establishment of religion, or prohibiting the free exercise thereof; or abridging the freedom of speech, or of the press; or the right of the people peaceably to assembly, and to petition the Government for a redress of grievances.

Amendment II [1791]

A well regulated Militia, being necessary to the security of a free State, the right of the people to keep and bear Arms, shall not be infringed.

Amendment III [1791]

No Soldier shall, in time of peace be quartered in any house, without the consent of the Owner, nor in time of war, but in a manner to be prescribed by law.

Amendment IV [1791]

The right of the people to be secure in their persons, houses, papers, and effects, against unreasonable searches and seizures, shall not be violated, and no Warrants shall issue, but upon probable cause, supported by Oath or affirmation, and particularly describing the place to be searched, and the persons or things to be seized.

Amendment V [1791]

No person shall be held to answer for a capital, or otherwise infamous crime, unless on a presentment or indictment of a Grand Jury, except in cases arising in the land or naval forces, or in the Militia, when in actual service in time of War or public danger; nor shall any person be subject for the same offence to be twice put in jeopardy of life or limb; nor shall be compelled in any criminal case to be a witness against himself, nor be deprived of life, liberty, or property, without due process of law; nor shall private property be taken for public use, without just compensation.

Amendment VI [1791]

In all criminal prosecutions, the accused shall enjoy the right to a speedy and public trial, by an impartial jury of the State and district wherein the crime shall have been committed, which district shall have been previously ascertained by law, and to be informed of the nature and cause of the accusation; to be confronted with the witnesses against him; to have compulsory process for obtaining witnesses in his favor, and to have the Assistance of Counsel for his defence.

Amendment VII [1791]

In Suits at common law, where the value in controversy shall exceed twenty dollars, the right of trial by jury shall be preserved, and no fact tried by jury, shall be otherwise re-examined in any Court of the United States, than according to the rules of the common law.

Amendment VIII [1791]

Excessive bail shall not be required, nor excessive fines imposed, nor cruel and unusual punishments inflicted.

Amendment IX [1791]

The enumeration in the Constitution, of certain rights, shall not be construed to deny or disparage others retained by the people.

Amendment X [1791]

The powers not delegated to the United States by the Constitution, nor prohibited by it to the States, are reserved to the States respectively, or to the people.

Amendment XI [1798]

The Judicial power of the United States shall not be construed to extend to any suit in law or equity, commenced or prosecuted against one of the United States by Citizens of another State, or by Citizens or Subjects of any Foreign State.

Amendment XII [1804]

The Electors shall meet in their respective states, and vote by ballot for President and Vice-President, one of whom, at least, shall not be an inhabitant of the same state with themselves; they shall name in their ballots the person voted for as President, and in distinct ballots the person voted for as Vice-President, and they shall make distinct lists of all persons voted for as President, and of all persons voted for as Vice-President, and of the number of votes for each, which lists they shall sign and certify, and transmit sealed to the seat of the government of the United States, directed to the President of the Senate;— The President of the Senate shall, in the presence of the Senate and House of Representatives, open all the certificates and the votes shall then be counted;—The person having the greatest number of votes for President, shall be the President, if such number be a majority of the whole number of Electors appointed; and if no person have such majority, then from the persons having the highest numbers not exceeding three on the list of those voted for as President, the House of Representatives shall choose immediately, by ballot, the President. But in choosing the President, the votes shall be taken by states, the representation from each state having one vote; a quorum for this purpose shall consist of a member or members from two-thirds of the states, and a majority of all states shall be necessary to a choice. And if the House of Representatives shall not choose a President whenever the right of choice shall devolve upon them, before the fourth day of March next following, then the Vice-President shall act as President, as in the case of the death or other constitutional disability of the President.—The person having the greatest number of votes as Vice-President, shall be the Vice-President, if such number be a majority of the whole number of Electors appointed, and if no person have a majority, then from the two highest numbers on the list, the Senate shall choose the Vice-President; a quorum for the purpose shall consist of two-thirds of the whole number of Senators, and a majority of the whole number shall be necessary to a choice. But no person constitutionally ineligible to the office of President shall be eligible to that of Vice-President of the United States.

Amendment XIII [1865]

Section 1. Neither slavery nor involuntary servitude, except as a punishment for crime whereof the party shall have been duly convicted, shall exist within the United States, or any place subject to their jurisdiction.

Section 2. Congress shall have power to enforce this article by appropriate legislation.

Amendment XIV [1868]

Section 1. All persons born or naturalized in the United States, and subject to the jurisdiction thereof, are citizens of the United States and of the State wherein they reside. No State shall make or enforce any law which shall abridge the privileges or immunities of citizens of the United States; nor shall any State deprive any person of life, liberty, or property, without due process of law; nor deny to any person within its jurisdiction the equal protection of the laws.

Section 2. Representatives shall be apportioned among the several States according to their respective numbers, counting the whole number of persons in each State, excluding Indians not taxed. But when the right to vote at any election for the choice of electors for President and Vice President of the United States, Representatives in Congress, the Executive and Judicial officers of a State, or the members of the Legislature thereof, is denied to any of the male inhabitants of such State, being twenty-one years of age, and citizens of the United States, or in any way abridged, except for participation in rebellion, or other crime, the basis of representation therein shall be reduced in the proportion which the number of such male citizens shall bear to the whole number of male citizens twenty-one years of age in such State.

Section 3. No person shall be a Senator or Representative in Congress, or elector of President and Vice President, or hold any office, civil or military, under the United States, or under any State, who having previously taken an oath, as a member of Congress, or as an officer of the United States, or as a member of any State legislature, or as an executive or judicial officer of any State, to support the Constitution of the United States, shall have engaged in insurrection or rebellion against the same, or given aid or comfort to the enemies thereof. But Congress may by a vote of two-thirds of each House, remove such disability.

Section 4. The validity of the public debt of the United States, authorized by law, including debts incurred for payment of pensions and bounties for services in suppressing insurrection or rebellion, shall not be questioned. But neither the United States nor any State shall assume or pay any debt or obligation incurred in aid of insurrection or rebellion against the United States, or any claim for the loss or emancipation of any slave; but all such debts, obligations and claims shall be held illegal and void.

Section 5. The Congress shall have power to enforce, by appropriate legislation, the provisions of this article.

Amendment XV [1870]

Section 1. The right of citizens of the United States to vote shall not be denied or abridged by the United States or by any State on account of race, color, or previous condition of servitude.

Section 2. The Congress shall have power to enforce this article by appropriate legislation.

Amendment XVI [1913]

The Congress shall have power to lay and collect taxes on incomes, from whatever source derived, without apportionment among the several States, and without regard to any census or enumeration.

Amendment XVII [1913]

Section 1. The Senate of the United States shall be composed of two Senators from each State, elected by the people thereof, for six years; and each Senator shall have one vote. The electors in each State shall have the qualifications requisite for electors of the most numerous branch of the State legislatures.

Section 2. When vacancies happen in the representation of any State in the Senate, the executive authority of such State shall issue writs of election to fill such vacancies: Provided, That the legislature of any State may empower the executive thereof to make temporary appointments until the people fill the vacancies by election as the legislature may direct.

Section 3. This amendment shall not be so construed as to affect the election or term of any Senator chosen before it becomes valid as part of the Constitution.

Amendment XVIII [1919]

Section 1. After one year from the ratification of this article the manufacture, sale, or transportation of intoxicating liquors within, the importation thereof into, or the exportation thereof from the United States and all territory subject to the jurisdiction thereof for beverage purposes is hereby prohibited.

Section 2. The Congress and the several States shall have concurrent power to enforce this article by appropriate legislation.

Section 3. This article shall be inoperative unless it shall have been ratified as an amendment to the Constitution by the legislatures of the several States, as provided in the Constitution, within seven years from the date of the submission hereof to the States by the Congress.

Amendment XIX [1920]

Section 1. The right of citizens of the United States to vote shall not be denied or abridged by the United States or by any State on account of sex.

Section 2. Congress shall have power to enforce this article by appropriate legislation.

Amendment XX [1933]

Section 1. The terms of the President and Vice President shall end at noon on the 20th day of January, and the terms of Senators and Representatives at noon on the 3d day of January, of the years in which such terms would have ended if this article had not been ratified; and the terms of their successors shall then begin.

Section 2. The Congress shall assemble at least once in every year, and such meeting shall begin at noon on the 3d day of January, unless they shall by law appoint a different day.

Section 3. If, at the time fixed for the beginning of the term of the President, the President elect shall have died, the Vice President elect shall become President. If the President shall not have been chosen before the time fixed for the beginning of his term, or if the President elect shall have failed to qualify, then the Vice President elect shall act as President until a President shall have qualified; and the Congress may by law provide for the case wherein neither a President elect nor a Vice President elect shall have qualified, declaring who shall then act as President, or the manner in which one who is to act shall be selected, and such person shall act accordingly until a President or Vice President shall have qualified.

Section 4. The Congress may by law provide for the case of the death of any of the persons from whom the House of Representatives may choose a President whenever the right of choice shall have devolved upon them, and for the case of the death of any of the persons from whom the Senate may choose a Vice President whenever the right of choice shall have devolved upon them.

Section 5. Sections 1 and 2 shall take effect on the 15th day of October following the ratification of this article.

Section 6. This article shall be inoperative unless it shall have been ratified as an amendment to the Constitution by the legislatures of three-fourths of the several States within seven years from the date of its submission.

Amendment XXI [1933]

Section 1. The eighteenth article of amendment to the Constitution of the United States is hereby repealed.

Section 2. The transportation or importation into any State, Territory, or possession of the United States for delivery or use therein of intoxicating liquors, in violation of the laws thereof, is hereby prohibited.

Section 3. This article shall be inoperative unless it shall have been ratified as an amendment to the Constitution by conventions in the several States, as provided in the Constitution, within seven years from the date of the submission hereof to the States by the Congress.

Amendment XXII [1951]

Section 1. No person shall be elected to the office of the President more than twice, and no person who has held the office of President, or acted as President, for more than two years of a term to which some other person was elected President shall be elected to the office of President more than once. But this Article shall not apply to any person holding the office of President when this Article was proposed by the Congress, and shall not prevent any person who may be holding the office of President, or acting as President, during the term within which this Article becomes operative from holding the office of President or acting as President during the remainder of such term.

Section 2. This article shall be inoperative unless it shall have been ratified as an amendment to the Constitution by the legislatures of three-fourths of the several States within seven years from the date of its submission to the States by the Congress.

Amendment XXIII [1961]

Section 1. The District constituting the seat of Government of the United States shall appoint in such manner as the Congress may direct:

A number of electors of President and Vice President equal to the whole number of Senators and Representatives in Congress to which the District would be entitled if it were a State, but in no event more than the least populous state; they shall be in addition to those appointed by the states, but they shall be considered, for the purposes of the election of President and Vice President, to be electors appointed by a state; and they shall meet in the District and perform such duties as provided by the twelfth article of amendment.

Section 2. The Congress shall have power to enforce this article by appropriate legislation.

Amendment XXIV [1964]

Section 1. The right of citizens of the United States to vote in any primary or other election for President or Vice President, for electors for President or Vice President, or for Senator or Representative in Congress, shall not be denied or abridged by the United States, or any State by reason of failure to pay any poll tax or other tax.

Section 2. The Congress shall have power to enforce this article by appropriate legislation.

Amendment XXV [1967]

Section 1. In case of the removal of the President from office or of his death or resignation, the Vice President shall become President.

Section 2. Whenever there is a vacancy in the office of the Vice President, the President shall nominate a Vice President who shall take office upon confirmation by a majority vote of both Houses of Congress.

Section 3. Whenever the President transmits to the President pro tempore of the Senate and the Speaker of the House of Representatives his written declaration that he is unable to discharge the powers and duties of his office, and until he transmits to them a written declaration to the contrary, such powers and duties shall be discharged by the Vice President as Acting President.

Section 4. Whenever the Vice President and a majority of either the principal officers of the executive departments or of such other body as Congress may by law provide, transmit to the President pro tempore of the Senate and the Speaker of the House of Representatives their written declaration that the President is unable to discharge the powers and duties of his office, the Vice President shall immediately assume the powers and duties of the office as Acting President.

Thereafter, when the President transmits to the President pro tempore of the Senate and the Speaker of the House of Representatives his written declaration that no inability exists, he shall resume the powers and duties of his office unless the Vice President and a majority of either the principal officers of the executive department or of such other body as Congress may by law provide, transmit within four days to the President pro tempore of the Senate and the Speaker of the House of Representatives their written declaration that the President is unable to discharge the powers and duties of his office. Thereupon Congress shall decide the issue, assembling within forty-eight hours for that purpose if not in session. If the Congress, within twenty-one days after receipt of the latter written declaration, or, if Congress is not in session, within twenty-one days after Congress is required to assemble, determines by two-thirds vote of both Houses that the President is unable to discharge the powers and duties of his office, the Vice President shall continue to discharge the same as Acting President; otherwise, the President shall resume the powers and duties of his office.

Amendment XXVI [1971]

Section 1. The right of citizens of the United States, who are eighteen years of age or older, to vote shall not be denied or abridged by the United States or by any State on account of age.

Section 2. The Congress shall have power to enforce this article by appropriate legislation.

Amendment XXVII [1992]

No law, varying the compensation for the services of the Senators and Representatives, shall take effect, until an election of Representatives shall have intervened.

Appendix C

The Uniform Commercial Code (Excerpts)

(Adopted in fifty-two jurisdictions; all fifty States, although Louisiana has adopted only Articles 1, 3, 4, 7, 8, and 9; the District of Columbia; and the Virgin Islands.)

The Uniform Commercial Code consists of the following articles:

1. **General Provisions**
2. **Sales**
2A. **Leases**
3. **Negotiable Instruments**
4. **Bank Deposits and Collections**
4A. **Fund Transfers**
5. **Letters of Credit**
6. **Repealer of Article 6—Bulk Transfers and [Revised] Article 6—Bulk Sales**
7. **Warehouse Receipts, Bills of Lading and Other Documents of Title**
8. **Investment Securities**
9. **Secured Transactions**
10. **Effective Date and Repealer**
11. **Effective Date and Transition Provisions**

Article 1
GENERAL PROVISIONS

Part 1   General Provisions

§ 1–101.   Short Titles.

(a) This [Act] may be cited as Uniform Commercial Code.

(b) This article may be cited as Uniform Commercial Code-Uniform Provisions.

§ 1–102.   Scope of Article.

This article applies to a transaction to the extent that it is governed by another article of [the Uniform Commercial Code].

§ 1–103.   Construction of [Uniform Commercial Code] to Promote Its Purpose and Policies; Applicability of Supplemental Principles of Law.

(a) [The Uniform Commercial Code] must be liberally construed and applied to promote its underlying purposes and policies, which are:

(1) to simplify, clarify, and modernize the law governing commercial transactions;

(2) to permit the continued expansion of commercial practices through custom, usage, and agreement of the parties; and

(3) to make uniform the law among the various jurisdictions.

(b) Unless displaced by the particular provisions of [the Uniform Commercial Code], the principles of law and equity, including the law merchant and the law relative to capacity to contract, principal and agent, estoppel, fraud, misrepresentation, duress, coercion, mistake, bankruptcy, and other validating or invalidating cause, supplement its provisions.

§ 1–104.   Construction Against Implicit Repeal.

This Act being a general act intended as a unified coverage of its subject matter, no part of it shall be deemed to be impliedly repealed by subsequent legislation if such construction can reasonably be avoided.

§ 1–105.   Severability.

If any provision or clause of [the Uniform Commercial Code] or its application to any person or circumstance is held invalid, the invalidity does not affect other provisions or applications of [the Uniform Commercial Code] which can be given effect without the invalid provision or application, and to this end the provisions of [the Uniform Commercial Code] are severable.

§ 1–106.   Use of Singular and Plural; Gender.

In [the Uniform Commercial Code], unless the statutory context otherwise requires:

(1) words in the singular number include the plural, and those in the plural include the singular; and

(2) words of any gender also refer to any other gender.

§ 1–107.   Section Captions.

Section captions are part of [the Uniform Commercial Code].

§ 1–108.   Relation to Electronic Signatures in Global and National Commerce Act.

This article modifies, limits, and supersedes the Federal Electronic Signatures in Global and National Commerce Act, 15 U.S.C. Sections 7001 et seq., except that nothing in this article modifies, limits, or supersedes section 7001(c) of that act or authorizes electronic delivery of any of the notices described in section 7003(b) of that Act.

Part 2   General Definitions and Principles of Interpretation

§ 1–201.   General Definitions.

Subject to additional definitions contained in the subsequent Articles of this Act which are applicable to specific Articles or Parts thereof, and unless the context otherwise requires, in this Act:

(1) "Action", in the sense of a judicial proceeding, includes recoupment, counterclaim, set-off, suit in equity, and any other proceedings in which rights are determined.

(2) "Aggrieved party" means a party entitled to resort to a remedy.

(3) "Agreement", as distinguished from "contract", means the bargain of the parties in fact, as found in their language or by implication from other circumstances, including course of performance, course of dealing, or usage of trade as provided in Section 1-303.

(4) "Bank" means a person engaged in the business of banking and includes a savings bank, savings and loan association, credit union, and trust company.

(5) "Bearer" means a person in control of a negotiable electronic document of title or a person in possession of a negotiable instrument, negotiable tangible document of title, or certificated security that is payable to bearer or indorsed in blank.

(6) "Bill of lading" means a document of title evidencing the receipt of goods for shipment issued by a person engaged in the business of directly or indirectly transporting or forwarding goods. The term does not include a warehouse receipt.

(7) "Branch" includes a separately incorporated foreign branch of a bank.

(8) "Burden of establishing" a fact means the burden of persuading the trier of fact that the existence of the fact is more probable than its nonexistence.

(9) "Buyer in ordinary course of business" means a person that buys goods in good faith, without knowledge that the sale violates the rights of another person in the goods, and in the ordinary course from a person, other than a pawnbroker, in the business of selling goods of that kind. A person buys goods in the ordinary course if the sale to the person comports with the usual or customary practices in the kind of business in which the seller is engaged or with the seller's own usual or customary practices. A person that sells oil, gas, or other minerals at the wellhead or minehead is a person in the business of selling goods of that kind. A buyer in ordinary course of business may buy for cash, by exchange of other property, or on secured or unsecured credit, and may acquire goods or documents of title under a pre-existing contract for sale. Only a buyer that takes possession of the goods or has a right to recover the goods from the seller under Article 2 may be a buyer in ordinary course of business. A person that acquires goods in a transfer in bulk or as security for or in total or partial satisfaction of a money debt is not a buyer in ordinary course of business.

(10) "Conspicuous", with reference to a term, means so written, displayed, or presented that a reasonable person against which it is to operate ought to have noticed it. Whether a term is "conspicuous" or not is a decision for the court. Conspicuous terms include the following:

(A) a heading in capitals equal to or greater in size than the surrounding text, or in contrasting type, font, or color to the surrounding text of the same or lesser size; and

(B) language in the body of a record or display in larger type than the surrounding text, or in contrasting type, font, or color to the surrounding text of the same size, or set off from surrounding text of the same size by symbols or other marks that call attention to the language.

(11) "Consumer" means an individual who enters into a transaction primarily for personal, family, or household purposes.

(12) "Contract", as distinguished from "agreement", means the total legal obligation that results from the parties' agreement as determined by [the Uniform Commercial Code] as supplemented by any other laws.

(13) "Creditor" includes a general creditor, a secured creditor, a lien creditor and any representative of creditors, including an assignee for the benefit of creditors, a trustee in bankruptcy, a receiver in equity and an executor or administrator of an insolvent debtor's or assignor's estate.

(14) "Defendant" includes a person in the position of defendant in a counterclaim, cross-action, or third-party claim.

(15) "Delivery" with respect to an electronic document of title means voluntary transfer of control and with respect to an instrument, a tangible document of title, or chattel paper means voluntary transfer of possession.

(16) "Document of title" means a record (i) that in regular course of business or financing is treated as adequately evidencing that the person in possession or control of the record is entitled to receive, control, hold, and dispose of the record and the goods the record covers and (ii) that purports to be issued by or addressed to a bailee and to cover goods in the bailee's possession which are either identified or are fungible portions of an identified mass. The term includes a bill of lading, transport document, dock warrant, dock receipt, warehouse receipt, and order for delivery of goods. An electronic document of title means a document of title evidenced by a record consisting of information stored in an electronic medium. A tangible document of title means a document of title evidenced by a record consisting of information that is inscribed on a tangible medium.

(17) "Fault" means a default, breach, or wrongful act or omission.

(18) "Fungible goods" means:

(A) goods of which any unit, by nature or usage of trade, is the equivalent of any other like unit; or

(B) goods that by agreement are treated as equivalent.

(19) "Genuine" means free of forgery or counterfeiting.

(20) "Good faith," except as otherwise provided in Article 5, means honesty in fact and the observance of reasonable commercial standards of fair dealing.

(21) "Holder" means:

(A) the person in possession of a negotiable instrument that is payable either to bearer or to an identified person that is the person in possession;

(B) the person in possession of a negotiable tangible document of title if the goods are deliverable either to bearer or to the order of the person in possession; or

(C) the person in control of a negotiable electronic document of title.

(22) "Insolvency proceeding" includes an assignment for the benefit of creditors or other proceeding intended to liquidate or rehabilitate the estate of the person involved.

(23) "Insolvent" means:

(A) having generally ceased to pay debts in the ordinary course of business other than as a result of bona fide dispute;

(B) being unable to pay debts as they become due; or

(C) being insolvent within the meaning of federal bankruptcy law.

(24) "Money" means a medium of exchange currently authorized or adopted by a domestic or foreign government. The term includes a

monetary unit of account established by an intergovernmental organization or by agreement between two or more countries.

(25) "Organization" means a person other than an individual.

(26) "Party", as distinguished from "third party", means a person that has engaged in a transaction or made an agreement subject to [the Uniform Commercial Code].

(27) "Person" means an individual, corporation, business trust, estate, trust, partnership, limited liability company, association, joint venture, government, governmental subdivision, agency, or instrumentality, public corporation, or any other legal or commercial entity.

(28) "Present value" means the amount as of a date certain of one or more sums payable in the future, discounted to the date certain by use of either an interest rate specified by the parties if that rate is not manifestly unreasonable at the time the transaction is entered into or, if an interest rate is not so specified, a commercially reasonable rate that takes into account the facts and circumstances at the time the transaction is entered into.

(29) "Purchase" means taking by sale, lease, discount, negotiation, mortgage, pledge, lien, security interest, issue or reissue, gift, or any other voluntary transaction creating an interest in property.

(30) "Purchaser" means a person that takes by purchase.

(31) "Record" means information that is inscribed on a tangible medium or that is stored in an electronic or other medium and is retrievable in perceivable form.

(32) "Remedy" means any remedial right to which an aggrieved party is entitled with or without resort to a tribunal.

(33) "Representative" means a person empowered to act for another, including an agent, an officer of a corporation or association, and a trustee, executor, or administrator of an estate.

(34) "Right" includes remedy.

(35) "Security interest" means an interest in personal property or fixtures which secures payment or performance of an obligation. "Security interest" includes any interest of a consignor and a buyer of accounts, chattel paper, a payment intangible, or a promissory note in a transaction that is subject to Article 9. "Security interest" does not include the special property interest of a buyer of goods on identification of those goods to a contract for sale under Section 2-401, but a buyer may also acquire a "security interest" by complying with Article 9. Except as otherwise provided in Section 2-505, the right of a seller or lessor of goods under Article 2 or 2A to retain or acquire possession of the goods is not a "security interest", but a seller or lessor may also acquire a "security interest" by complying with Article 9. The retention or reservation of title by a seller of goods notwithstanding shipment or delivery to the buyer under Section 2-401 is limited in effect to a reservation of a "security interest." Whether a transaction in the form of a lease creates a "security interest" is determined pursuant to Section 1-203.

(36) "Send" in connection with a writing, record, or notice means:

(A) to deposit in the mail or deliver for transmission by any other usual means of communication with postage or cost of transmission provided for and properly addressed and, in the case of an instrument, to an address specified thereon or otherwise agreed, or if there be none to any address reasonable under the circumstances; or

(B) in any other way to cause to be received any record or notice within the time it would have arrived if properly sent.

(37) "Signed" includes using any symbol executed or adopted with present intention to adopt or accept a writing.

(38) "State" means a State of the United States, the District of Columbia, Puerto Rico, the United States Virgin Islands, or any territory or insular possession subject to the jurisdiction of the United States.

(39) "Surety" includes a guarantor or other secondary obligor.

(40) "Term" means a portion of an agreement that relates to a particular matter.

(41) "Unauthorized signature" means a signature made without actual, implied, or apparent authority. The term includes a forgery.

(42) "Warehouse receipt" means a document of title issued by a person engaged in the business of storing goods for hire.

(43) "Writing" includes printing, typewriting, or any other intentional reduction to tangible form. "Written" has a corresponding meaning.

As amended in 2003.

* * * *

§ 1–205.   Reasonable Time; Seasonableness.

(a) Whether a time for taking an action required by [the Uniform Commercial Code] is reasonable depends on the nature, purpose, and circumstances of the action.

(b) An action is taken seasonably if it is taken at or within the time agreed or, if no time is agreed, at or within a reasonable time.

* * * *

Part 3   Territorial Applicability and General Rules

* * * *

§ 1–303.   Course of Performance, Course of Dealing, and Usage of Trade.

(a) A "course of performance" is a sequence of conduct between the parties to a particular transaction that exists if:

(1) the agreement of the parties with respect to the transaction involves repeated occasions for performance by a party; and

(2) the other party, with knowledge of the nature of the performance and opportunity for objection to it, accepts the performance or acquiesces in it without objection.

(b) A "course of dealing" is a sequence of conduct concerning previous transactions between the parties to a particular transaction that is fairly to be regarded as establishing a common basis of understanding for interpreting their expressions and other conduct.

(c) A "usage of trade" is any practice or method of dealing having such regularity of observance in a place, vocation, or trade as to justify an expectation that it will be observed with respect to the transaction in question. The existence and scope of such a usage must be proved as facts. If it is established that such a usage is embodied in a trade code or similar record, the interpretation of the record is a question of law.

(d) A course of performance or course of dealing between the parties or usage of trade in the vocation or trade in which they are engaged or of which they are or should be aware is relevant in ascertaining the meaning of the parties' agreement, may give particular meaning to specific terms of the agreement, and may supplement or qualify the terms of the agreement. A usage of trade applicable in the place in which part of the performance under the agreement is to occur may be so utilized as to that part of the performance.

(e) Except as otherwise provided in subsection (f), the express terms of an agreement and any applicable course of performance, course of dealing, or usage of trade must be construed whenever reasonable as consistent with each other. If such a construction is unreasonable:

    (1) express terms prevail over course of performance, course of dealing, and usage of trade;

    (2) course of performance prevails over course of dealing and usage of trade; and

    (3) course of dealing prevails over usage of trade.

(f) Subject to Section 2-209 and Section 2A-208, a course of performance is relevant to show a waiver or modification of any term inconsistent with the course of performance.

(g) Evidence of a relevant usage of trade offered by one party is not admissible unless that party has given the other party notice that the court finds sufficient to prevent unfair surprise to the other party.

§ 1–304. Obligation of Good Faith.

Every contract or duty within [the Uniform Commercial Code] imposes an obligation of good faith in its performance and enforcement.

* * * *

§ 1–309. Option to Accelerate at Will.

A term providing that one party or that party's successor in interest may accelerate payment or performance or require collateral or additional collateral "at will" or when the party "deems itself insecure," or words of similar import, means that the party has power to do so only if that party in good faith believes that the prospect of payment or performance is impaired. The burden of establishing lack of good faith is on the party against which the power has been exercised.

§ 1–310. Subordinated Obligations.

An obligation may be issued as subordinated to performance of another obligation of the person obligated, or a creditor may subordinate its right to performance of an obligation by agreement with either the person obligated or another creditor of the person obligated. Subordination does not create a security interest as against either the common debtor or a subordinated creditor.

Article 2
SALES

Part 1 Short Title, General Construction and Subject Matter

§ 2–101. Short Title.

This Article shall be known and may be cited as Uniform Commercial Code—Sales.

§ 2–102. Scope; Certain Security and Other Transactions Excluded From This Article.

Unless the context otherwise requires, this Article applies to transactions in goods; it does not apply to any transaction which although in the form of an unconditional contract to sell or present sale is intended to operate only as a security transaction nor does this Article impair or repeal any statute regulating sales to consumers, farmers or other specified classes of buyers.

§ 2–103. Definitions and Index of Definitions.

(1) In this Article unless the context otherwise requires

    (a) "Buyer" means a person who buys or contracts to buy goods.

    (b) "Good faith" in the case of a merchant means honesty in fact and the observance of reasonable commercial standards of fair dealing in the trade.

    (c) "Receipt" of goods means taking physical possession of them.

    (d) "Seller" means a person who sells or contracts to sell goods.

(2) Other definitions applying to this Article or to specified Parts thereof, and the sections in which they appear are:

"Acceptance". Section 2–606.
"Banker's credit". Section 2–325.
"Between merchants". Section 2–104.
"Cancellation". Section 2–106(4).
"Commercial unit". Section 2–105.
"Confirmed credit". Section 2–325.
"Conforming to contract". Section 2–106.
"Contract for sale". Section 2–106.
"Cover". Section 2–712.
"Entrusting". Section 2–403.
"Financing agency". Section 2–104.
"Future goods". Section 2–105.
"Goods". Section 2–105.
"Identification". Section 2–501.
"Installment contract". Section 2–612.
"Letter of Credit". Section 2–325.
"Lot". Section 2–105.
"Merchant". Section 2–104.
"Overseas". Section 2–323.
"Person in position of seller". Section 2–707.
"Present sale". Section 2–106.
"Sale". Section 2–106.
"Sale on approval". Section 2–326.
"Sale or return". Section 2–326.
"Termination". Section 2–106.

(3) The following definitions in other Articles apply to this Article:
"Check". Section 3–104.
"Consignee". Section 7–102.
"Consignor". Section 7–102.
"Consumer goods". Section 9–109.
"Dishonor". Section 3–507.
"Draft". Section 3–104.

(4) In addition Article 1 contains general definitions and principles of construction and interpretation applicable throughout this Article.

As amended in 1994 and 1999.

§ 2–104. Definitions: "Merchant"; "Between Merchants"; "Financing Agency".

(1) "Merchant" means a person who deals in goods of the kind or otherwise by his occupation holds himself out as having knowledge or skill peculiar to the practices or goods involved in the transaction or to whom such knowledge or skill may be attributed by his employment of an agent or broker or other intermediary who by his occupation holds himself out as having such knowledge or skill.

(2) "Financing agency" means a bank, finance company or other person who in the ordinary course of business makes advances against goods or documents of title or who by arrangement with either the seller or the buyer intervenes in ordinary course to make or collect payment due or claimed under the contract for sale, as by purchasing or paying the seller's draft or making advances against it or by merely

taking it for collection whether or not documents of title accompany the draft. "Financing agency" includes also a bank or other person who similarly intervenes between persons who are in the position of seller and buyer in respect to the goods (Section 2–707).

(3) "Between merchants" means in any transaction with respect to which both parties are chargeable with the knowledge or skill of merchants.

§ 2–105. Definitions: Transferability; "Goods"; "Future" Goods; "Lot"; "Commercial Unit".

(1) "Goods" means all things (including specially manufactured goods) which are movable at the time of identification to the contract for sale other than the money in which the price is to be paid, investment securities (Article 8) and things in action. "Goods" also includes the unborn young of animals and growing crops and other identified things attached to realty as described in the section on goods to be severed from realty (Section 2–107).

(2) Goods must be both existing and identified before any interest in them can pass. Goods which are not both existing and identified are "future" goods. A purported present sale of future goods or of any interest therein operates as a contract to sell.

(3) There may be a sale of a part interest in existing identified goods.

(4) An undivided share in an identified bulk of fungible goods is sufficiently identified to be sold although the quantity of the bulk is not determined. Any agreed proportion of such a bulk or any quantity thereof agreed upon by number, weight or other measure may to the extent of the seller's interest in the bulk be sold to the buyer who then becomes an owner in common.

(5) "Lot" means a parcel or a single article which is the subject matter of a separate sale or delivery, whether or not it is sufficient to perform the contract.

(6) "Commercial unit" means such a unit of goods as by commercial usage is a single whole for purposes of sale and division of which materially impairs its character or value on the market or in use. A commercial unit may be a single article (as a machine) or a set of articles (as a suite of furniture or an assortment of sizes) or a quantity (as a bale, gross, or carload) or any other unit treated in use or in the relevant market as a single whole.

§ 2–106. Definitions: "Contract"; "Agreement"; "Contract for Sale"; "Sale"; "Present Sale"; "Conforming" to Contract; "Termination"; "Cancellation".

(1) In this Article unless the context otherwise requires "contract" and "agreement" are limited to those relating to the present or future sale of goods. "Contract for sale" includes both a present sale of goods and a contract to sell goods at a future time. A "sale" consists in the passing of title from the seller to the buyer for a price (Section 2–401). A "present sale" means a sale which is accomplished by the making of the contract.

(2) Goods or conduct including any part of a performance are "conforming" or conform to the contract when they are in accordance with the obligations under the contract.

(3) "Termination" occurs when either party pursuant to a power created by agreement or law puts an end to the contract otherwise than for its breach. On "termination" all obligations which are still executory on both sides are discharged but any right based on prior breach or performance survives.

(4) "Cancellation" occurs when either party puts an end to the contract for breach by the other and its effect is the same as that of "termination" except that the cancelling party also retains any remedy for breach of the whole contract or any unperformed balance.

§ 2–107. Goods to Be Severed From Realty: Recording.

(1) A contract for the sale of minerals or the like (including oil and gas) or a structure or its materials to be removed from realty is a contract for the sale of goods within this Article if they are to be severed by the seller but until severance a purported present sale thereof which is not effective as a transfer of an interest in land is effective only as a contract to sell.

(2) A contract for the sale apart from the land of growing crops or other things attached to realty and capable of severance without material harm thereto but not described in subsection (1) or of timber to be cut is a contract for the sale of goods within this Article whether the subject matter is to be severed by the buyer or by the seller even though it forms part of the realty at the time of contracting, and the parties can by identification effect a present sale before severance.

(3) The provisions of this section are subject to any third party rights provided by the law relating to realty records, and the contract for sale may be executed and recorded as a document transferring an interest in land and shall then constitute notice to third parties of the buyer's rights under the contract for sale.

As amended in 1972.

Part 2 Form, Formation and Readjustment of Contract

§ 2–201. Formal Requirements; Statute of Frauds.

(1) Except as otherwise provided in this section a contract for the sale of goods for the price of $500 or more is not enforceable by way of action or defense unless there is some writing sufficient to indicate that a contract for sale has been made between the parties and signed by the party against whom enforcement is sought or by his authorized agent or broker. A writing is not insufficient because it omits or incorrectly states a term agreed upon but the contract is not enforceable under this paragraph beyond the quantity of goods shown in such writing.

(2) Between merchants if within a reasonable time a writing in confirmation of the contract and sufficient against the sender is received and the party receiving it has reason to know its contents, its satisfies the requirements of subsection (1) against such party unless written notice of objection to its contents is given within ten days after it is received.

(3) A contract which does not satisfy the requirements of subsection (1) but which is valid in other respects is enforceable

(a) if the goods are to be specially manufactured for the buyer and are not suitable for sale to others in the ordinary course of the seller's business and the seller, before notice of repudiation is received and under circumstances which reasonably indicate that the goods are for the buyer, has made either a substantial beginning of their manufacture or commitments for their procurement; or

(b) if the party against whom enforcement is sought admits in his pleading, testimony or otherwise in court that a contract for sale was made, but the contract is not enforceable under this provision beyond the quantity of goods admitted; or

(c) with respect to goods for which payment has been made and accepted or which have been received and accepted (Sec. 2–606).

§ 2–202. Final Written Expression: Parol or Extrinsic Evidence.

Terms with respect to which the confirmatory memoranda of the parties agree or which are otherwise set forth in a writing intended by the parties as a final expression of their agreement with respect to such terms as are included therein may not be contradicted by evidence of any prior agreement or of a contemporaneous oral agreement but may be explained or supplemented

(a) by course of dealing or usage of trade (Section 1–205) or by course of performance (Section 2–208); and

(b) by evidence of consistent additional terms unless the court finds the writing to have been intended also as a complete and exclusive statement of the terms of the agreement.

§ 2–203. Seals Inoperative.

The affixing of a seal to a writing evidencing a contract for sale or an offer to buy or sell goods does not constitute the writing a sealed instrument and the law with respect to sealed instruments does not apply to such a contract or offer.

§ 2–204. Formation in General.

(1) A contract for sale of goods may be made in any manner sufficient to show agreement, including conduct by both parties which recognizes the existence of such a contract.

(2) An agreement sufficient to constitute a contract for sale may be found even though the moment of its making is undetermined.

(3) Even though one or more terms are left open a contract for sale does not fail for indefiniteness if the parties have intended to make a contract and there is a reasonably certain basis for giving an appropriate remedy.

§ 2–205. Firm Offers.

An offer by a merchant to buy or sell goods in a signed writing which by its terms gives assurance that it will be held open is not revocable, for lack of consideration, during the time stated or if no time is stated for a reasonable time, but in no event may such period of irrevocability exceed three months; but any such term of assurance on a form supplied by the offeree must be separately signed by the offeror.

§ 2–206. Offer and Acceptance in Formation of Contract.

(1) Unless other unambiguously indicated by the language or circumstances

(a) an offer to make a contract shall be construed as inviting acceptance in any manner and by any medium reasonable in the circumstances;

(b) an order or other offer to buy goods for prompt or current shipment shall be construed as inviting acceptance either by a prompt promise to ship or by the prompt or current shipment of conforming or nonconforming goods, but such a shipment of non-conforming goods does not constitute an acceptance if the seller seasonably notifies the buyer that the shipment is offered only as an accommodation to the buyer.

(2) Where the beginning of a requested performance is a reasonable mode of acceptance an offeror who is not notified of acceptance within a reasonable time may treat the offer as having lapsed before acceptance.

§ 2–207. Additional Terms in Acceptance or Confirmation.

(1) A definite and seasonable expression of acceptance or a written confirmation which is sent within a reasonable time operates as an acceptance even though it states terms additional to or different from those offered or agreed upon, unless acceptance is expressly made conditional on assent to the additional or different terms.

(2) The additional terms are to be construed as proposals for addition to the contract. Between merchants such terms become part of the contract unless:

(a) the offer expressly limits acceptance to the terms of the offer;

(b) they materially alter it; or

(c) notification of objection to them has already been given or is given within a reasonable time after notice of them is received.

(3) Conduct by both parties which recognizes the existence of a contract is sufficient to establish a contract for sale although the writings of the parties do not otherwise establish a contract. In such case the terms of the particular contract consist of those terms on which the writings of the parties agree, together with any supplementary terms incorporated under any other provisions of this Act.

§ 2–208. Course of Performance or Practical Construction.

(1) Where the contract for sale involves repeated occasions for performance by either party with knowledge of the nature of the performance and opportunity for objection to it by the other, any course of performance accepted or acquiesced in without objection shall be relevant to determine the meaning of the agreement.

(2) The express terms of the agreement and any such course of performance, as well as any course of dealing and usage of trade, shall be construed whenever reasonable as consistent with each other; but when such construction is unreasonable, express terms shall control course of performance and course of performance shall control both course of dealing and usage of trade (Section 1–303).

(3) Subject to the provisions of the next section on modification and waiver, such course of performance shall be relevant to show a waiver or modification of any term inconsistent with such course of performance.

§ 2–209. Modification, Rescission and Waiver.

(1) An agreement modifying a contract within this Article needs no consideration to be binding.

(2) A signed agreement which excludes modification or rescission except by a signed writing cannot be otherwise modified or rescinded, but except as between merchants such a requirement on a form supplied by the merchant must be separately signed by the other party.

(3) The requirements of the statute of frauds section of this Article (Section 2–201) must be satisfied if the contract as modified is within its provisions.

(4) Although an attempt at modification or rescission does not satisfy the requirements of subsection (2) or (3) it can operate as a waiver.

(5) A party who has made a waiver affecting an executory portion of the contract may retract the waiver by reasonable notification received by the other party that strict performance will be required of any term waived, unless the retraction would be unjust in view of a material change of position in reliance on the waiver.

§ 2–210. Delegation of Performance; Assignment of Rights.

(1) A party may perform his duty through a delegate unless otherwise agreed or unless the other party has a substantial interest in having his original promisor perform or control the acts required by the

contract. No delegation of performance relieves the party delegating of any duty to perform or any liability for breach.

(2) Except as otherwise provided in Section 9–406, unless otherwise agreed, all rights of either seller or buyer can be assigned except where the assignment would materially change the duty of the other party, or increase materially the burden or risk imposed on him by his contract, or impair materially his chance of obtaining return performance. A right to damages for breach of the whole contract or a right arising out of the assignor's due performance of his entire obligation can be assigned despite agreement otherwise.

(3) The creation, attachment, perfection, or enforcement of a security interest in the seller's interest under a contract is not a transfer that materially changes the duty of or increases materially the burden or risk imposed on the buyer or impairs materially the buyer's chance of obtaining return performance within the purview of subsection (2) unless, and then only to the extent that, enforcement actually results in a delegation of material performance of the seller. Even in that event, the creation, attachment, perfection, and enforcement of the security interest remain effective, but (i) the seller is liable to the buyer for damages caused by the delegation to the extent that the damages could not reasonably by prevented by the buyer, and (ii) a court having jurisdiction may grant other appropriate relief, including cancellation of the contract for sale or an injunction against enforcement of the security interest or consummation of the enforcement.

(4) Unless the circumstances indicate the contrary a prohibition of assignment of "the contract" is to be construed as barring only the delegation to the assignee of the assignor's performance.

(5) An assignment of "the contract" or of "all my rights under the contract" or an assignment in similar general terms is an assignment of rights and unless the language or the circumstances (as in an assignment for security) indicate the contrary, it is a delegation of performance of the duties of the assignor and its acceptance by the assignee constitutes a promise by him to perform those duties. This promise is enforceable by either the assignor or the other party to the original contract.

(6) The other party may treat any assignment which delegates performance as creating reasonable grounds for insecurity and may without prejudice to his rights against the assignor demand assurances from the assignee (Section 2–609).

As amended in 1999.

Part 3   General Obligation and Construction of Contract

§ 2–301.   General Obligations of Parties.

The obligation of the seller is to transfer and deliver and that of the buyer is to accept and pay in accordance with the contract.

§ 2–302.   Unconscionable Contract or Clause.

(1) If the court as a matter of law finds the contract or any clause of the contract to have been unconscionable at the time it was made the court may refuse to enforce the contract, or it may enforce the remainder of the contract without the unconscionable clause, or it may so limit the application of any unconscionable clause as to avoid any unconscionable result.

(2) When it is claimed or appears to the court that the contract or any clause thereof may be unconscionable the parties shall be afforded a reasonable opportunity to present evidence as to its commercial setting, purpose and effect to aid the court in making the determination.

§ 2–303.   Allocations or Division of Risks.

Where this Article allocates a risk or a burden as between the parties "unless otherwise agreed", the agreement may not only shift the allocation but may also divide the risk or burden.

§ 2–304.   Price Payable in Money, Goods, Realty, or Otherwise.

(1) The price can be made payable in money or otherwise. If it is payable in whole or in part in goods each party is a seller of the goods which he is to transfer.

(2) Even though all or part of the price is payable in an interest in realty the transfer of the goods and the seller's obligations with reference to them are subject to this Article, but not the transfer of the interest in realty or the transferor's obligations in connection therewith.

§ 2–305.   Open Price Term.

(1) The parties if they so intend can conclude a contract for sale even though the price is not settled. In such a case the price is a reasonable price at the time for delivery if

(a) nothing is said as to price; or

(b) the price is left to be agreed by the parties and they fail to agree; or

(c) the price is to be fixed in terms of some agreed market or other standard as set or recorded by a third person or agency and it is not so set or recorded.

(2) A price to be fixed by the seller or by the buyer means a price for him to fix in good faith.

(3) When a price left to be fixed otherwise than by agreement of the parties fails to be fixed through fault of one party the other may at his option treat the contract as cancelled or himself fix a reasonable price.

(4) Where, however, the parties intend not to be bound unless the price be fixed or agreed and it is not fixed or agreed there is no contract. In such a case the buyer must return any goods already received or if unable so to do must pay their reasonable value at the time of delivery and the seller must return any portion of the price paid on account.

§ 2–306.   Output, Requirements and Exclusive Dealings.

(1) A term which measures the quantity by the output of the seller or the requirements of the buyer means such actual output or requirements as may occur in good faith, except that no quantity unreasonably disproportionate to any stated estimate or in the absence of a stated estimate to any normal or otherwise comparable prior output or requirements may be tendered or demanded.

(2) A lawful agreement by either the seller or the buyer for exclusive dealing in the kind of goods concerned imposes unless otherwise agreed an obligation by the seller to use best efforts to supply the goods and by the buyer to use best efforts to promote their sale.

§ 2–307.   Delivery in Single Lot or Several Lots.

Unless otherwise agreed all goods called for by a contract for sale must be tendered in a single delivery and payment is due only on such tender but where the circumstances give either party the right to make or demand delivery in lots the price if it can be apportioned may be demanded for each lot.

§ 2–308.   Absence of Specified Place for Delivery.

Unless otherwise agreed

(a) the place for delivery of goods is the seller's place of business or if he has none his residence; but

(b) in a contract for sale of identified goods which to the knowledge of the parties at the time of contracting are in some other place, that place is the place for their delivery; and

(c) documents of title may be delivered through customary banking channels.

§ 2–309.   Absence of Specific Time Provisions; Notice of Termination.

(1) The time for shipment or delivery or any other action under a contract if not provided in this Article or agreed upon shall be a reasonable time.

(2) Where the contract provides for successive performances but is indefinite in duration it is valid for a reasonable time but unless otherwise agreed may be terminated at any time by either party.

(3) Termination of a contract by one party except on the happening of an agreed event requires that reasonable notification be received by the other party and an agreement dispensing with notification is invalid if its operation would be unconscionable.

§ 2–310.   Open Time for Payment or Running of Credit; Authority to Ship Under Reservation.

Unless otherwise agreed

(a) payment is due at the time and place at which the buyer is to receive the goods even though the place of shipment is the place of delivery; and

(b) if the seller is authorized to send the goods he may ship them under reservation, and may tender the documents of title, but the buyer may inspect the goods after their arrival before payment is due unless such inspection is inconsistent with the terms of the contract (Section 2–513); and

(c) if delivery is authorized and made by way of documents of title otherwise than by subsection (b) then payment is due at the time and place at which the buyer is to receive the documents regardless of where the goods are to be received; and

(d) where the seller is required or authorized to ship the goods on credit the credit period runs from the time of shipment but postdating the invoice or delaying its dispatch will correspondingly delay the starting of the credit period.

§ 2–311.   Options and Cooperation Respecting Performance.

(1) An agreement for sale which is otherwise sufficiently definite (subsection (3) of Section 2–204) to be a contract is not made invalid by the fact that it leaves particulars of performance to be specified by one of the parties. Any such specification must be made in good faith and within limits set by commercial reasonableness.

(2) Unless otherwise agreed specifications relating to assortment of the goods are at the buyer's option and except as otherwise provided in subsections (1)(c) and (3) of Section 2–319 specifications or arrangements relating to shipment are at the seller's option.

(3) Where such specification would materially affect the other party's performance but is not seasonably made or where one party's cooperation is necessary to the agreed performance of the other but is not seasonably forthcoming, the other party in addition to all other remedies

(a) is excused for any resulting delay in his own performance; and

(b) may also either proceed to perform in any reasonable manner or after the time for a material part of his own performance treat the failure to specify or to cooperate as a breach by failure to deliver or accept the goods.

§ 2–312.   Warranty of Title and Against Infringement; Buyer's Obligation Against Infringement.

(1) Subject to subsection (2) there is in a contract for sale a warranty by the seller that

(a) the title conveyed shall be good, and its transfer rightful; and

(b) the goods shall be delivered free from any security interest or other lien or encumbrance of which the buyer at the time of contracting has no knowledge.

(2) A warranty under subsection (1) will be excluded or modified only by specific language or by circumstances which give the buyer reason to know that the person selling does not claim title in himself or that he is purporting to sell only such right or title as he or a third person may have.

(3) Unless otherwise agreed a seller who is a merchant regularly dealing in goods of the kind warrants that the goods shall be delivered free of the rightful claim of any third person by way of infringement or the like but a buyer who furnishes specifications to the seller must hold the seller harmless against any such claim which arises out of compliance with the specifications.

§ 2–313.   Express Warranties by Affirmation, Promise, Description, Sample.

(1) Express warranties by the seller are created as follows:

(a) Any affirmation of fact or promise made by the seller to the buyer which relates to the goods and becomes part of the basis of the bargain creates an express warranty that the goods shall conform to the affirmation or promise.

(b) Any description of the goods which is made part of the basis of the bargain creates an express warranty that the goods shall conform to the description.

(c) Any sample or model which is made part of the basis of the bargain creates an express warranty that the whole of the goods shall conform to the sample or model.

(2) It is not necessary to the creation of an express warranty that the seller use formal words such as "warrant" or "guarantee" or that he have a specific intention to make a warranty, but an affirmation merely of the value of the goods or a statement purporting to be merely the seller's opinion or commendation of the goods does not create a warranty.

§ 2–314.   Implied Warranty: Merchantability; Usage of Trade.

(1) Unless excluded or modified (Section 2–316), a warranty that the goods shall be merchantable is implied in a contract for their sale if the seller is a merchant with respect to goods of that kind. Under this section the serving for value of food or drink to be consumed either on the premises or elsewhere is a sale.

(2) Goods to be merchantable must be at least such as

(a) pass without objection in the trade under the contract description; and

(b) in the case of fungible goods, are of fair average quality within the description; and

(c) are fit for the ordinary purposes for which such goods are used; and

(d) run, within the variations permitted by the agreement, of even kind, quality and quantity within each unit and among all units involved; and

(e) are adequately contained, packaged, and labeled as the agreement may require; and

(f) conform to the promises or affirmations of fact made on the container or label if any.

(3) Unless excluded or modified (Section 2–316) other implied warranties may arise from course of dealing or usage of trade.

§ 2–315. Implied Warranty: Fitness for Particular Purpose.

Where the seller at the time of contracting has reason to know any particular purpose for which the goods are required and that the buyer is relying on the seller's skill or judgment to select or furnish suitable goods, there is unless excluded or modified under the next section an implied warranty that the goods shall be fit for such purpose.

§ 2–316. Exclusion or Modification of Warranties.

(1) Words or conduct relevant to the creation of an express warranty and words or conduct tending to negate or limit warranty shall be construed wherever reasonable as consistent with each other; but subject to the provisions of this Article on parol or extrinsic evidence (Section 2–202) negation or limitation is inoperative to the extent that such construction is unreasonable.

(2) Subject to subsection (3), to exclude or modify the implied warranty of merchantability or any part of it the language must mention merchantability and in case of a writing must be conspicuous, and to exclude or modify any implied warranty of fitness the exclusion must be by a writing and conspicuous. Language to exclude all implied warranties of fitness is sufficient if it states, for example, that "There are no warranties which extend beyond the description on the face hereof."

(3) Notwithstanding subsection (2)

(a) unless the circumstances indicate otherwise, all implied warranties are excluded by expressions like "as is", "with all faults" or other language which in common understanding calls the buyer's attention to the exclusion of warranties and makes plain that there is no implied warranty; and

(b) when the buyer before entering into the contract has examined the goods or the sample or model as fully as he desired or has refused to examine the goods there is no implied warranty with regard to defects which an examination ought in the circumstances to have revealed to him; and

(c) an implied warranty can also be excluded or modified by course of dealing or course of performance or usage of trade.

(4) Remedies for breach of warranty can be limited in accordance with the provisions of this Article on liquidation or limitation of damages and on contractual modification of remedy (Sections 2–718 and 2–719).

§ 2–317. Cumulation and Conflict of Warranties Express or Implied.

Warranties whether express or implied shall be construed as consistent with each other and as cumulative, but if such construction is unreasonable the intention of the parties shall determine which warranty is dominant. In ascertaining that intention the following rules apply:

(a) Exact or technical specifications displace an inconsistent sample or model or general language of description.

(b) A sample from an existing bulk displaces inconsistent general language of description.

(c) Express warranties displace inconsistent implied warranties other than an implied warranty of fitness for a particular purpose.

§ 2–318. Third Party Beneficiaries of Warranties Express or Implied.

Note: If this Act is introduced in the Congress of the United States this section should be omitted. (States to select one alternative.)

Alternative A

A seller's warranty whether express or implied extends to any natural person who is in the family or household of his buyer or who is a guest in his home if it is reasonable to expect that such person may use, consume or be affected by the goods and who is injured in person by breach of the warranty. A seller may not exclude or limit the operation of this section.

Alternative B

A seller's warranty whether express or implied extends to any natural person who may reasonably be expected to use, consume or be affected by the goods and who is injured in person by breach of the warranty. A seller may not exclude or limit the operation of this section.

Alternative C

A seller's warranty whether express or implied extends to any person who may reasonably be expected to use, consume or be affected by the goods and who is injured by breach of the warranty. A seller may not exclude or limit the operation of this section with respect to injury to the person of an individual to whom the warranty extends. As amended 1966.

§ 2–319. F.O.B. and F.A.S. Terms.

(1) Unless otherwise agreed the term F.O.B. (which means "free on board") at a named place, even though used only in connection with the stated price, is a delivery term under which

(a) when the term is F.O.B. the place of shipment, the seller must at that place ship the goods in the manner provided in this Article (Section 2–504) and bear the expense and risk of putting them into the possession of the carrier; or

(b) when the term is F.O.B. the place of destination, the seller must at his own expense and risk transport the goods to that place and there tender delivery of them in the manner provided in this Article (Section 2–503);

(c) when under either (a) or (b) the term is also F.O.B. vessel, car or other vehicle, the seller must in addition at his own expense and risk load the goods on board. If the term is F.O.B. vessel the buyer must name the vessel and in an appropriate case the seller must comply with the provisions of this Article on the form of bill of lading (Section 2–323).

(2) Unless otherwise agreed the term F.A.S. vessel (which means "free alongside") at a named port, even though used only in connection with the stated price, is a delivery term under which the seller must

(a) at his own expense and risk deliver the goods alongside the vessel in the manner usual in that port or on a dock designated and provided by the buyer; and

(b) obtain and tender a receipt for the goods in exchange for which the carrier is under a duty to issue a bill of lading.

(3) Unless otherwise agreed in any case falling within subsection (1)(a) or (c) or subsection (2) the buyer must seasonably give any needed instructions for making delivery, including when the term is F.A.S. or F.O.B. the loading berth of the vessel and in an appropriate case its name and sailing date. The seller may treat the failure of needed instructions as a failure of cooperation under this Article (Section 2–311). He may also at his option move the goods in any reasonable manner preparatory to delivery or shipment.

(4) Under the term F.O.B. vessel or F.A.S. unless otherwise agreed the buyer must make payment against tender of the required documents and the seller may not tender nor the buyer demand delivery of the goods in substitution for the documents.

§ 2–320. C.I.F. and C. & F. Terms.

(1) The term C.I.F. means that the price includes in a lump sum the cost of the goods and the insurance and freight to the named destination. The term C. & F. or C.F. means that the price so includes cost and freight to the named destination.

(2) Unless otherwise agreed and even though used only in connection with the stated price and destination, the term C.I.F. destination or its equivalent requires the seller at his own expense and risk to

(a) put the goods into the possession of a carrier at the port for shipment and obtain a negotiable bill or bills of lading covering the entire transportation to the named destination; and

(b) load the goods and obtain a receipt from the carrier (which may be contained in the bill of lading) showing that the freight has been paid or provided for; and

(c) obtain a policy or certificate of insurance, including any war risk insurance, of a kind and on terms then current at the port of shipment in the usual amount, in the currency of the contract, shown to cover the same goods covered by the bill of lading and providing for payment of loss to the order of the buyer or for the account of whom it may concern; but the seller may add to the price the amount of the premium for any such war risk insurance; and

(d) prepare an invoice of the goods and procure any other documents required to effect shipment or to comply with the contract; and

(e) forward and tender with commercial promptness all the documents in due form and with any indorsement necessary to perfect the buyer's rights.

(3) Unless otherwise agreed the term C. & F. or its equivalent has the same effect and imposes upon the seller the same obligations and risks as a C.I.F. term except the obligation as to insurance.

(4) Under the term C.I.F. or C. & F. unless otherwise agreed the buyer must make payment against tender of the required documents and the seller may not tender nor the buyer demand delivery of the goods in substitution for the documents.

§ 2–321. C.I.F. or C. & F.: "Net Landed Weights"; "Payment on Arrival"; Warranty of Condition on Arrival.

Under a contract containing a term C.I.F. or C. & F.

(1) Where the price is based on or is to be adjusted according to "net landed weights", "delivered weights", "out turn" quantity or quality or the like, unless otherwise agreed the seller must reasonably

estimate the price. The payment due on tender of the documents called for by the contract is the amount so estimated, but after final adjustment of the price a settlement must be made with commercial promptness.

(2) An agreement described in subsection (1) or any warranty of quality or condition of the goods on arrival places upon the seller the risk of ordinary deterioration, shrinkage and the like in transportation but has no effect on the place or time of identification to the contract for sale or delivery or on the passing of the risk of loss.

(3) Unless otherwise agreed where the contract provides for payment on or after arrival of the goods the seller must before payment allow such preliminary inspection as is feasible; but if the goods are lost delivery of the documents and payment are due when the goods should have arrived.

§ 2–322. Delivery "Ex-Ship".

(1) Unless otherwise agreed a term for delivery of goods "ex-ship" (which means from the carrying vessel) or in equivalent language is not restricted to a particular ship and requires delivery from a ship which has reached a place at the named port of destination where goods of the kind are usually discharged.

(2) Under such a term unless otherwise agreed

(a) the seller must discharge all liens arising out of the carriage and furnish the buyer with a direction which puts the carrier under a duty to deliver the goods; and

(b) the risk of loss does not pass to the buyer until the goods leave the ship's tackle or are otherwise properly unloaded.

§ 2–323. Form of Bill of Lading Required in Overseas Shipment; "Overseas".

(1) Where the contract contemplates overseas shipment and contains a term C.I.F. or C. & F. or F.O.B. vessel, the seller unless otherwise agreed must obtain a negotiable bill of lading stating that the goods have been loaded on board or, in the case of a term C.I.F. or C. & F., received for shipment.

(2) Where in a case within subsection (1) a bill of lading has been issued in a set of parts, unless otherwise agreed if the documents are not to be sent from abroad the buyer may demand tender of the full set; otherwise only one part of the bill of lading need be tendered. Even if the agreement expressly requires a full set

(a) due tender of a single part is acceptable within the provisions of this Article on cure of improper delivery (subsection (1) of Section 2–508); and

(b) even though the full set is demanded, if the documents are sent from abroad the person tendering an incomplete set may nevertheless require payment upon furnishing an indemnity which the buyer in good faith deems adequate.

(3) A shipment by water or by air or a contract contemplating such shipment is "overseas" insofar as by usage of trade or agreement it is subject to the commercial, financing or shipping practices characteristic of international deep water commerce.

§ 2–324. "No Arrival, No Sale" Term.

Under a term "no arrival, no sale" or terms of like meaning, unless otherwise agreed,

(a) the seller must properly ship conforming goods and if they arrive by any means he must tender them on arrival but he assumes no obligation that the goods will arrive unless he has caused the non-arrival; and

(b) where without fault of the seller the goods are in part lost or have so deteriorated as no longer to conform to the contract or arrive after the contract time, the buyer may proceed as if there had been casualty to identified goods (Section 2–613).

§ 2–325. "Letter of Credit" Term; "Confirmed Credit".

(1) Failure of the buyer seasonably to furnish an agreed letter of credit is a breach of the contract for sale.

(2) The delivery to seller of a proper letter of credit suspends the buyer's obligation to pay. If the letter of credit is dishonored, the seller may on seasonable notification to the buyer require payment directly from him.

(3) Unless otherwise agreed the term "letter of credit" or "banker's credit" in a contract for sale means an irrevocable credit issued by a financing agency of good repute and, where the shipment is overseas, of good international repute. The term "confirmed credit" means that the credit must also carry the direct obligation of such an agency which does business in the seller's financial market.

§ 2–326. Sale on Approval and Sale or Return; Rights of Creditors.

(1) Unless otherwise agreed, if delivered goods may be returned by the buyer even though they conform to the contract, the transaction is

(a) a "sale on approval" if the goods are delivered primarily for use, and

(b) a "sale or return" if the goods are delivered primarily for resale.

(2) Goods held on approval are not subject to the claims of the buyer's creditors until acceptance; goods held on sale or return are subject to such claims while in the buyer's possession.

(3) Any "or return" term of a contract for sale is to be treated as a separate contract for sale within the statute of frauds section of this Article (Section 2–201) and as contradicting the sale aspect of the contract within the provisions of this Article or on parol or extrinsic evidence (Section 2–202).

As amended in 1999.

§ 2–327. Special Incidents of Sale on Approval and Sale or Return.

(1) Under a sale on approval unless otherwise agreed

(a) although the goods are identified to the contract the risk of loss and the title do not pass to the buyer until acceptance; and

(b) use of the goods consistent with the purpose of trial is not acceptance but failure seasonably to notify the seller of election to return the goods is acceptance, and if the goods conform to the contract acceptance of any part is acceptance of the whole; and

(c) after due notification of election to return, the return is at the seller's risk and expense but a merchant buyer must follow any reasonable instructions.

(2) Under a sale or return unless otherwise agreed

(a) the option to return extends to the whole or any commercial unit of the goods while in substantially their original condition, but must be exercised seasonably; and

(b) the return is at the buyer's risk and expense.

§ 2–328. Sale by Auction.

(1) In a sale by auction if goods are put up in lots each lot is the subject of a separate sale.

(2) A sale by auction is complete when the auctioneer so announces by the fall of the hammer or in other customary manner. Where a bid is made while the hammer is falling in acceptance of a prior bid the auctioneer may in his discretion reopen the bidding or declare the goods sold under the bid on which the hammer was falling.

(3) Such a sale is with reserve unless the goods are in explicit terms put up without reserve. In an auction with reserve the auctioneer may withdraw the goods at any time until he announces completion of the sale. In an auction without reserve, after the auctioneer calls for bids on an article or lot, that article or lot cannot be withdrawn unless no bid is made within a reasonable time. In either case a bidder may retract his bid until the auctioneer's announcement of completion of the sale, but a bidder's retraction does not revive any previous bid.

(4) If the auctioneer knowingly receives a bid on the seller's behalf or the seller makes or procures such as bid, and notice has not been given that liberty for such bidding is reserved, the buyer may at his option avoid the sale or take the goods at the price of the last good faith bid prior to the completion of the sale. This subsection shall not apply to any bid at a forced sale.

Part 4 Title, Creditors and Good Faith Purchasers

§ 2–401. Passing of Title; Reservation for Security; Limited Application of This Section.

Each provision of this Article with regard to the rights, obligations and remedies of the seller, the buyer, purchasers or other third parties applies irrespective of title to the goods except where the provision refers to such title. Insofar as situations are not covered by the other provisions of this Article and matters concerning title became material the following rules apply:

(1) Title to goods cannot pass under a contract for sale prior to their identification to the contract (Section 2–501), and unless otherwise explicitly agreed the buyer acquires by their identification a special property as limited by this Act. Any retention or reservation by the seller of the title (property) in goods shipped or delivered to the buyer is limited in effect to a reservation of a security interest. Subject to these provisions and to the provisions of the Article on Secured Transactions (Article 9), title to goods passes from the seller to the buyer in any manner and on any conditions explicitly agreed on by the parties.

(2) Unless otherwise explicitly agreed title passes to the buyer at the time and place at which the seller completes his performance with reference to the physical delivery of the goods, despite any reservation of a security interest and even though a document of title is to be delivered at a different time or place; and in particular and despite any reservation of a security interest by the bill of lading

(a) if the contract requires or authorizes the seller to send the goods to the buyer but does not require him to deliver them at destination, title passes to the buyer at the time and place of shipment; but

(b) if the contract requires delivery at destination, title passes on tender there.

(3) Unless otherwise explicitly agreed where delivery is to be made without moving the goods,

(a) if the seller is to deliver a document of title, title passes at the time when and the place where he delivers such documents; or

(b) if the goods are at the time of contracting already identified and no documents are to be delivered, title passes at the time and place of contracting.

(4) A rejection or other refusal by the buyer to receive or retain the goods, whether or not justified, or a justified revocation of acceptance revests title to the goods in the seller. Such revesting occurs by operation of law and is not a "sale".

§ 2–402. Rights of Seller's Creditors Against Sold Goods.

(1) Except as provided in subsections (2) and (3), rights of unsecured creditors of the seller with respect to goods which have been identified to a contract for sale are subject to the buyer's rights to recover the goods under this Article (Sections 2–502 and 2–716).

(2) A creditor of the seller may treat a sale or an identification of goods to a contract for sale as void if as against him a retention of possession by the seller is fraudulent under any rule of law of the state where the goods are situated, except that retention of possession in good faith and current course of trade by a merchant-seller for a commercially reasonable time after a sale or identification is not fraudulent.

(3) Nothing in this Article shall be deemed to impair the rights of creditors of the seller

(a) under the provisions of the Article on Secured Transactions (Article 9); or

(b) where identification to the contract or delivery is made not in current course of trade but in satisfaction of or as security for a pre-existing claim for money, security or the like and is made under circumstances which under any rule of law of the state where the goods are situated would apart from this Article constitute the transaction a fraudulent transfer or voidable preference.

§ 2–403. Power to Transfer; Good Faith Purchase of Goods; "Entrusting".

(1) A purchaser of goods acquires all title which his transferor had or had power to transfer except that a purchaser of a limited interest acquires rights only to the extent of the interest purchased. A person with voidable title has power to transfer a good title to a good faith purchaser for value. When goods have been delivered under a transaction of purchase the purchaser has such power even though

(a) the transferor was deceived as to the identity of the purchaser, or

(b) the delivery was in exchange for a check which is later dishonored, or

(c) it was agreed that the transaction was to be a "cash sale", or

(d) the delivery was procured through fraud punishable as larcenous under the criminal law.

(2) Any entrusting of possession of goods to a merchant who deals in goods of that kind gives him power to transfer all rights of the entruster to a buyer in ordinary course of business.

(3) "Entrusting" includes any delivery and any acquiescence in retention of possession regardless of any condition expressed between the parties to the delivery or acquiescence and regardless of whether the procurement of the entrusting or the possessor's disposition of the goods have been such as to be larcenous under the criminal law.

(4) The rights of other purchasers of goods and of lien creditors are governed by the Articles on Secured Transactions (Article 9), Bulk Transfers (Article 6) and Documents of Title (Article 7).

As amended in 1988.

Part 5 Performance

§ 2–501. Insurable Interest in Goods; Manner of Identification of Goods.

(1) The buyer obtains a special property and an insurable interest in goods by identification of existing goods as goods to which the contract refers even though the goods so identified are non-conforming and he has an option to return or reject them. Such identification can be made at any time and in any manner explicitly agreed to by the parties. In the absence of explicit agreement identification occurs

(a) when the contract is made if it is for the sale of goods already existing and identified;

(b) if the contract is for the sale of future goods other than those described in paragraph (c), when goods are shipped, marked or otherwise designated by the seller as goods to which the contract refers;

(c) when the crops are planted or otherwise become growing crops or the young are conceived if the contract is for the sale of unborn young to be born within twelve months after contracting or for the sale of crops to be harvested within twelve months or the next normal harvest season after contracting whichever is longer.

(2) The seller retains an insurable interest in goods so long as title to or any security interest in the goods remains in him and where the identification is by the seller alone he may until default or insolvency or notification to the buyer that the identification is final substitute other goods for those identified.

(3) Nothing in this section impairs any insurable interest recognized under any other statute or rule of law.

§ 2–502. Buyer's Right to Goods on Seller's Insolvency.

(1) Subject to subsections (2) and (3) and even though the goods have not been shipped a buyer who has paid a part or all of the price of goods in which he has a special property under the provisions of the immediately preceding section may on making and keeping good a tender of any unpaid portion of their price recover them from the seller if:

(a) in the case of goods bought for personal, family, or household purposes, the seller repudiates or fails to deliver as required by the contract; or

(b) in all cases, the seller becomes insolvent within ten days after receipt of the first installment on their price.

(2) The buyer's right to recover the goods under subsection (1)(a) vests upon acquisition of a special property, even if the seller had not then repudiated or failed to deliver.

(3) If the identification creating his special property has been made by the buyer he acquires the right to recover the goods only if they conform to the contract for sale.

As amended in 1999.

§ 2–503. Manner of Seller's Tender of Delivery.

(1) Tender of delivery requires that the seller put and hold conforming goods at the buyer's disposition and give the buyer any notification

reasonably necessary to enable him to take delivery. The manner, time and place for tender are determined by the agreement and this Article, and in particular

(a) tender must be at a reasonable hour, and if it is of goods they must be kept available for the period reasonably necessary to enable the buyer to take possession; but

(b) unless otherwise agreed the buyer must furnish facilities reasonably suited to the receipt of the goods.

(2) Where the case is within the next section respecting shipment tender requires that the seller comply with its provisions.

(3) Where the seller is required to deliver at a particular destination tender requires that he comply with subsection (1) and also in any appropriate case tender documents as described in subsections (4) and (5) of this section.

(4) Where goods are in the possession of a bailee and are to be delivered without being moved

(a) tender requires that the seller either tender a negotiable document of title covering such goods or procure acknowledgment by the bailee of the buyer's right to possession of the goods; but

(b) tender to the buyer of a non-negotiable document of title or of a written direction to the bailee to deliver is sufficient tender unless the buyer seasonably objects, and receipt by the bailee of notification of the buyer's rights fixes those rights as against the bailee and all third persons; but risk of loss of the goods and of any failure by the bailee to honor the non-negotiable document of title or to obey the direction remains on the seller until the buyer has had a reasonable time to present the document or direction, and a refusal by the bailee to honor the document or to obey the direction defeats the tender.

(5) Where the contract requires the seller to deliver documents

(a) he must tender all such documents in correct form, except as provided in this Article with respect to bills of lading in a set (subsection (2) of Section 2–323); and

(b) tender through customary banking channels is sufficient and dishonor of a draft accompanying the documents constitutes non-acceptance or rejection.

§ 2–504.   Shipment by Seller.

Where the seller is required or authorized to send the goods to the buyer and the contract does not require him to deliver them at a particular destination, then unless otherwise agreed he must

(a) put the goods in the possession of such a carrier and make such a contract for their transportation as may be reasonable having regard to the nature of the goods and other circumstances of the case; and

(b) obtain and promptly deliver or tender in due form any document necessary to enable the buyer to obtain possession of the goods or otherwise required by the agreement or by usage of trade; and

(c) promptly notify the buyer of the shipment.

Failure to notify the buyer under paragraph (c) or to make a proper contract under paragraph (a) is a ground for rejection only if material delay or loss ensues.

§ 2–505.   Seller's Shipment under Reservation.

(1) Where the seller has identified goods to the contract by or before shipment:

(a) his procurement of a negotiable bill of lading to his own order or otherwise reserves in him a security interest in the goods. His procurement of the bill to the order of a financing agency or of the buyer indicates in addition only the seller's expectation of transferring that interest to the person named.

(b) a non-negotiable bill of lading to himself or his nominee reserves possession of the goods as security but except in a case of conditional delivery (subsection (2) of Section 2–507) a non-negotiable bill of lading naming the buyer as consignee reserves no security interest even though the seller retains possession of the bill of lading.

(2) When shipment by the seller with reservation of a security interest is in violation of the contract for sale it constitutes an improper contract for transportation within the preceding section but impairs neither the rights given to the buyer by shipment and identification of the goods to the contract nor the seller's powers as a holder of a negotiable document.

§ 2–506.   Rights of Financing Agency.

(1) A financing agency by paying or purchasing for value a draft which relates to a shipment of goods acquires to the extent of the payment or purchase and in addition to its own rights under the draft and any document of title securing it any rights of the shipper in the goods including the right to stop delivery and the shipper's right to have the draft honored by the buyer.

(2) The right to reimbursement of a financing agency which has in good faith honored or purchased the draft under commitment to or authority from the buyer is not impaired by subsequent discovery of defects with reference to any relevant document which was apparently regular on its face.

§ 2–507.   Effect of Seller's Tender; Delivery on Condition.

(1) Tender of delivery is a condition to the buyer's duty to accept the goods and, unless otherwise agreed, to his duty to pay for them. Tender entitles the seller to acceptance of the goods and to payment according to the contract.

(2) Where payment is due and demanded on the delivery to the buyer of goods or documents of title, his right as against the seller to retain or dispose of them is conditional upon his making the payment due.

§ 2–508.   Cure by Seller of Improper Tender or Delivery; Replacement.

(1) Where any tender or delivery by the seller is rejected because non-conforming and the time for performance has not yet expired, the seller may seasonably notify the buyer of his intention to cure and may then within the contract time make a conforming delivery.

(2) Where the buyer rejects a non-conforming tender which the seller had reasonable grounds to believe would be acceptable with or without money allowance the seller may if he seasonably notifies the buyer have a further reasonable time to substitute a conforming tender.

§ 2–509.   Risk of Loss in the Absence of Breach.

(1) Where the contract requires or authorizes the seller to ship the goods by carrier

(a) if it does not require him to deliver them at a particular destination, the risk of loss passes to the buyer when the goods are duly delivered to the carrier even though the shipment is under reservation (Section 2–505); but

(b) if it does require him to deliver them at a particular destination and the goods are there duly tendered while in the possession of the carrier, the risk of loss passes to the buyer when the goods are there duly so tendered as to enable the buyer to take delivery.

(2) Where the goods are held by a bailee to be delivered without being moved, the risk of loss passes to the buyer

(a) on his receipt of a negotiable document of title covering the goods; or

(b) on acknowledgment by the bailee of the buyer's right to possession of the goods; or

(c) after his receipt of a non-negotiable document of title or other written direction to deliver, as provided in subsection (4)(b) of Section 2–503.

(3) In any case not within subsection (1) or (2), the risk of loss passes to the buyer on his receipt of the goods if the seller is a merchant; otherwise the risk passes to the buyer on tender of delivery.

(4) The provisions of this section are subject to contrary agreement of the parties and to the provisions of this Article on sale on approval (Section 2–327) and on effect of breach on risk of loss (Section 2–510).

§ 2–510.   Effect of Breach on Risk of Loss.

(1) Where a tender or delivery of goods so fails to conform to the contract as to give a right of rejection the risk of their loss remains on the seller until cure or acceptance.

(2) Where the buyer rightfully revokes acceptance he may to the extent of any deficiency in his effective insurance coverage treat the risk of loss as having rested on the seller from the beginning.

(3) Where the buyer as to conforming goods already identified to the contract for sale repudiates or is otherwise in breach before risk of their loss has passed to him, the seller may to the extent of any deficiency in his effective insurance coverage treat the risk of loss as resting on the buyer for a commercially reasonable time.

§ 2–511.   Tender of Payment by Buyer; Payment by Check.

(1) Unless otherwise agreed tender of payment is a condition to the seller's duty to tender and complete any delivery.

(2) Tender of payment is sufficient when made by any means or in any manner current in the ordinary course of business unless the seller demands payment in legal tender and gives any extension of time reasonably necessary to procure it.

(3) Subject to the provisions of this Act on the effect of an instrument on an obligation (Section 3–310), payment by check is conditional and is defeated as between the parties by dishonor of the check on due presentment.

As amended in 1994.

§ 2–512.   Payment by Buyer Before Inspection.

(1) Where the contract requires payment before inspection non-conformity of the goods does not excuse the buyer from so making payment unless

(a) the non-conformity appears without inspection; or

(b) despite tender of the required documents the circumstances would justify injunction against honor under this Act (Section 5–109(b)).

(2) Payment pursuant to subsection (1) does not constitute an acceptance of goods or impair the buyer's right to inspect or any of his remedies.

As amended in 1995.

§ 2–513.   Buyer's Right to Inspection of Goods.

(1) Unless otherwise agreed and subject to subsection (3), where goods are tendered or delivered or identified to the contract for sale, the buyer has a right before payment or acceptance to inspect them at any reasonable place and time and in any reasonable manner. When the seller is required or authorized to send the goods to the buyer, the inspection may be after their arrival.

(2) Expenses of inspection must be borne by the buyer but may be recovered from the seller if the goods do not conform and are rejected.

(3) Unless otherwise agreed and subject to the provisions of this Article on C.I.F. contracts (subsection (3) of Section 2–321), the buyer is not entitled to inspect the goods before payment of the price when the contract provides

(a) for delivery "C.O.D." or on other like terms; or

(b) for payment against documents of title, except where such payment is due only after the goods are to become available for inspection.

(4) A place or method of inspection fixed by the parties is presumed to be exclusive but unless otherwise expressly agreed it does not postpone identification or shift the place for delivery or for passing the risk of loss. If compliance becomes impossible, inspection shall be as provided in this section unless the place or method fixed was clearly intended as an indispensable condition failure of which avoids the contract.

§ 2–514.   When Documents Deliverable on Acceptance; When on Payment.

Unless otherwise agreed documents against which a draft is drawn are to be delivered to the drawee on acceptance of the draft if it is payable more than three days after presentment; otherwise, only on payment.

§ 2–515.   Preserving Evidence of Goods in Dispute.

In furtherance of the adjustment of any claim or dispute

(a) either party on reasonable notification to the other and for the purpose of ascertaining the facts and preserving evidence has the right to inspect, test and sample the goods including such of them as may be in the possession or control of the other; and

(b) the parties may agree to a third party inspection or survey to determine the conformity or condition of the goods and may agree that the findings shall be binding upon them in any subsequent litigation or adjustment.

Part 6   Breach, Repudiation and Excuse

§ 2–601.   Buyer's Rights on Improper Delivery.

Subject to the provisions of this Article on breach in installment contracts (Section 2–612) and unless otherwise agreed under the sections on contractual limitations of remedy (Sections 2–718 and 2–719), if the goods or the tender of delivery fail in any respect to conform to the contract, the buyer may

(a) reject the whole; or

(b) accept the whole; or

(c) accept any commercial unit or units and reject the rest.

§ 2–602.   Manner and Effect of Rightful Rejection.

(1) Rejection of goods must be within a reasonable time after their delivery or tender. It is ineffective unless the buyer seasonably notifies the seller.

(2) Subject to the provisions of the two following sections on rejected goods (Sections 2–603 and 2–604),

(a) after rejection any exercise of ownership by the buyer with respect to any commercial unit is wrongful as against the seller; and

(b) if the buyer has before rejection taken physical possession of goods in which he does not have a security interest under the provisions of this Article (subsection (3) of Section 2–711), he is under a duty after rejection to hold them with reasonable care at the seller's disposition for a time sufficient to permit the seller to remove them; but

(c) the buyer has no further obligations with regard to goods rightfully rejected.

(3) The seller's rights with respect to goods wrongfully rejected are governed by the provisions of this Article on Seller's remedies in general (Section 2–703).

§ 2–603. Merchant Buyer's Duties as to Rightfully Rejected Goods.

(1) Subject to any security interest in the buyer (subsection (3) of Section 2–711), when the seller has no agent or place of business at the market of rejection a merchant buyer is under a duty after rejection of goods in his possession or control to follow any reasonable instructions received from the seller with respect to the goods and in the absence of such instructions to make reasonable efforts to sell them for the seller's account if they are perishable or threaten to decline in value speedily. Instructions are not reasonable if on demand indemnity for expenses is not forthcoming.

(2) When the buyer sells goods under subsection (1), he is entitled to reimbursement from the seller or out of the proceeds for reasonable expenses of caring for and selling them, and if the expenses include no selling commission then to such commission as is usual in the trade or if there is none to a reasonable sum not exceeding ten per cent on the gross proceeds.

(3) In complying with this section the buyer is held only to good faith and good faith conduct hereunder is neither acceptance nor conversion nor the basis of an action for damages.

§ 2–604. Buyer's Options as to Salvage of Rightfully Rejected Goods.

Subject to the provisions of the immediately preceding section on perishables if the seller gives no instructions within a reasonable time after notification of rejection the buyer may store the rejected goods for the seller's account or reship them to him or resell them for the seller's account with reimbursement as provided in the preceding section. Such action is not acceptance or conversion.

§ 2–605. Waiver of Buyer's Objections by Failure to Particularize.

(1) The buyer's failure to state in connection with rejection a particular defect which is ascertainable by reasonable inspection precludes him from relying on the unstated defect to justify rejection or to establish breach

(a) where the seller could have cured it if stated seasonably; or

(b) between merchants when the seller has after rejection made a request in writing for a full and final written statement of all defects on which the buyer proposes to rely.

(2) Payment against documents made without reservation of rights precludes recovery of the payment for defects apparent on the face of the documents.

§ 2–606. What Constitutes Acceptance of Goods.

(1) Acceptance of goods occurs when the buyer

(a) after a reasonable opportunity to inspect the goods signifies to the seller that the goods are conforming or that he will take or retain them in spite of their nonconformity; or

(b) fails to make an effective rejection (subsection (1) of Section 2–602), but such acceptance does not occur until the buyer has had a reasonable opportunity to inspect them; or

(c) does any act inconsistent with the seller's ownership; but if such act is wrongful as against the seller it is an acceptance only if ratified by him.

(2) Acceptance of a part of any commercial unit is acceptance of that entire unit.

§ 2–607. Effect of Acceptance; Notice of Breach; Burden of Establishing Breach After Acceptance; Notice of Claim or Litigation to Person Answerable Over.

(1) The buyer must pay at the contract rate for any goods accepted.

(2) Acceptance of goods by the buyer precludes rejection of the goods accepted and if made with knowledge of a non-conformity cannot be revoked because of it unless the acceptance was on the reasonable assumption that the non-conformity would be seasonably cured but acceptance does not of itself impair any other remedy provided by this Article for non-conformity.

(3) Where a tender has been accepted

(a) the buyer must within a reasonable time after he discovers or should have discovered any breach notify the seller of breach or be barred from any remedy; and

(b) if the claim is one for infringement or the like (subsection (3) of Section 2–312) and the buyer is sued as a result of such a breach he must so notify the seller within a reasonable time after he receives notice of the litigation or be barred from any remedy over for liability established by the litigation.

(4) The burden is on the buyer to establish any breach with respect to the goods accepted.

(5) Where the buyer is sued for breach of a warranty or other obligation for which his seller is answerable over

(a) he may give his seller written notice of the litigation. If the notice states that the seller may come in and defend and that if the seller does not do so he will be bound in any action against him by his buyer by any determination of fact common to the two litigations, then unless the seller after seasonable receipt of the notice does come in and defend he is so bound.

(b) if the claim is one for infringement or the like (subsection (3) of Section 2–312) the original seller may demand in writing that his buyer turn over to him control of the litigation including settlement or else be barred from any remedy over and if he also agrees to bear all expense and to satisfy any adverse judgment, then unless the buyer after seasonable receipt of the demand does turn over control the buyer is so barred.

(6) The provisions of subsections (3), (4) and (5) apply to any obligation of a buyer to hold the seller harmless against infringement or the like (subsection (3) of Section 2–312).

§ 2–608. Revocation of Acceptance in Whole or in Part.

(1) The buyer may revoke his acceptance of a lot or commercial unit whose non-conformity substantially impairs its value to him if he has accepted it

(a) on the reasonable assumption that its nonconformity would be cured and it has not been seasonably cured; or

(b) without discovery of such non-conformity if his acceptance was reasonably induced either by the difficulty of discovery before acceptance or by the seller's assurances.

(2) Revocation of acceptance must occur within a reasonable time after the buyer discovers or should have discovered the ground for it and before any substantial change in condition of the goods which is not caused by their own defects. It is not effective until the buyer notifies the seller of it.

(3) A buyer who so revokes has the same rights and duties with regard to the goods involved as if he had rejected them.

§ 2–609. Right to Adequate Assurance of Performance.

(1) A contract for sale imposes an obligation on each party that the other's expectation of receiving due performance will not be impaired. When reasonable grounds for insecurity arise with respect to the performance of either party the other may in writing demand adequate assurance of due performance and until he receives such assurance may if commercially reasonable suspend any performance for which he has not already received the agreed return.

(2) Between merchants the reasonableness of grounds for insecurity and the adequacy of any assurance offered shall be determined according to commercial standards.

(3) Acceptance of any improper delivery or payment does not prejudice the party's right to demand adequate assurance of future performance.

(4) After receipt of a justified demand failure to provide within a reasonable time not exceeding thirty days such assurance of due performance as is adequate under the circumstances of the particular case is a repudiation of the contract.

§ 2–610. Anticipatory Repudiation.

When either party repudiates the contract with respect to a performance not yet due the loss of which will substantially impair the value of the contract to the other, the aggrieved party may

(a) for a commercially reasonable time await performance by the repudiating party; or

(b) resort to any remedy for breach (Section 2–703 or Section 2–711), even though he has notified the repudiating party that he would await the latter's performance and has urged retraction; and

(c) in either case suspend his own performance or proceed in accordance with the provisions of this Article on the seller's right to identify goods to the contract notwithstanding breach or to salvage unfinished goods (Section 2–704).

§ 2–611. Retraction of Anticipatory Repudiation.

(1) Until the repudiating party's next performance is due he can retract his repudiation unless the aggrieved party has since the repudiation cancelled or materially changed his position or otherwise indicated that he considers the repudiation final.

(2) Retraction may be by any method which clearly indicates to the aggrieved party that the repudiating party intends to perform, but must include any assurance justifiably demanded under the provisions of this Article (Section 2–609).

(3) Retraction reinstates the repudiating party's rights under the contract with due excuse and allowance to the aggrieved party for any delay occasioned by the repudiation.

§ 2–612. "Installment Contract"; Breach.

(1) An "installment contract" is one which requires or authorizes the delivery of goods in separate lots to be separately accepted, even though the contract contains a clause "each delivery is a separate contract" or its equivalent.

(2) The buyer may reject any installment which is non-conforming if the non-conformity substantially impairs the value of that installment and cannot be cured or if the non-conformity is a defect in the required documents; but if the non-conformity does not fall within subsection (3) and the seller gives adequate assurance of its cure the buyer must accept that installment.

(3) Whenever non-conformity or default with respect to one or more installments substantially impairs the value of the whole contract there is a breach of the whole. But the aggrieved party reinstates the contract if he accepts a non-conforming installment without seasonably notifying of cancellation or if he brings an action with respect only to past installments or demands performance as to future installments.

§ 2–613. Casualty to Identified Goods.

Where the contract requires for its performance goods identified when the contract is made, and the goods suffer casualty without fault of either party before the risk of loss passes to the buyer, or in a proper case under a "no arrival, no sale" term (Section 2–324) then

(a) if the loss is total the contract is avoided; and

(b) if the loss is partial or the goods have so deteriorated as no longer to conform to the contract the buyer may nevertheless demand inspection and at his option either treat the contract as voided or accept the goods with due allowance from the contract price for the deterioration or the deficiency in quantity but without further right against the seller.

§ 2–614. Substituted Performance.

(1) Where without fault of either party the agreed berthing, loading, or unloading facilities fail or an agreed type of carrier becomes unavailable or the agreed manner of delivery otherwise becomes commercially impracticable but a commercially reasonable substitute is available, such substitute performance must be tendered and accepted.

(2) If the agreed means or manner of payment fails because of domestic or foreign governmental regulation, the seller may withhold or stop delivery unless the buyer provides a means or manner of payment which is commercially a substantial equivalent. If delivery has already been taken, payment by the means or in the manner provided by the regulation discharges the buyer's obligation unless the regulation is discriminatory, oppressive or predatory.

§ 2–615. Excuse by Failure of Presupposed Conditions.

Except so far as a seller may have assumed a greater obligation and subject to the preceding section on substituted performance:

(a) Delay in delivery or non-delivery in whole or in part by a seller who complies with paragraphs (b) and (c) is not a breach of his duty under a contract for sale if performance as agreed has been made impracticable by the occurrence of a contingency the nonoccurrence of which was a basic assumption on which the contract was made or by compliance in good faith with any applicable foreign or domestic governmental regulation or order whether or not it later proves to be invalid.

(b) Where the causes mentioned in paragraph (a) affect only a part of the seller's capacity to perform, he must allocate production and deliveries among his customers but may at his option include regular customers not then under contract as well as his own requirements for further manufacture. He may so allocate in any manner which is fair and reasonable.

(c) The seller must notify the buyer seasonably that there will be delay or non-delivery and, when allocation is required under paragraph (b), of the estimated quota thus made available for the buyer.

§ 2-616. Procedure on Notice Claiming Excuse.

(1) Where the buyer receives notification of a material or indefinite delay or an allocation justified under the preceding section he may by written notification to the seller as to any delivery concerned, and where the prospective deficiency substantially impairs the value of the whole contract under the provisions of this Article relating to breach of installment contracts (Section 2-612), then also as to the whole,

(a) terminate and thereby discharge any unexecuted portion of the contract; or

(b) modify the contract by agreeing to take his available quota in substitution.

(2) If after receipt of such notification from the seller the buyer fails so to modify the contract within a reasonable time not exceeding thirty days the contract lapses with respect to any deliveries affected.

(3) The provisions of this section may not be negated by agreement except in so far as the seller has assumed a greater obligation under the preceding section.

Part 7   Remedies

§ 2-701. Remedies for Breach of Collateral Contracts Not Impaired.

Remedies for breach of any obligation or promise collateral or ancillary to a contract for sale are not impaired by the provisions of this Article.

§ 2-702. Seller's Remedies on Discovery of Buyer's Insolvency.

(1) Where the seller discovers the buyer to be insolvent he may refuse delivery except for cash including payment for all goods theretofore delivered under the contract, and stop delivery under this Article (Section 2-705).

(2) Where the seller discovers that the buyer has received goods on credit while insolvent he may reclaim the goods upon demand made within ten days after the receipt, but if misrepresentation of solvency has been made to the particular seller in writing within three months before delivery the ten day limitation does not apply. Except as provided in this subsection the seller may not base a right to reclaim goods on the buyer's fraudulent or innocent misrepresentation of solvency or of intent to pay.

(3) The seller's right to reclaim under subsection (2) is subject to the rights of a buyer in ordinary course or other good faith purchaser under this Article (Section 2-403). Successful reclamation of goods excludes all other remedies with respect to them.

§ 2-703. Seller's Remedies in General.

Where the buyer wrongfully rejects or revokes acceptance of goods or fails to make a payment due on or before delivery or repudiates

with respect to a part or the whole, then with respect to any goods directly affected and, if the breach is of the whole contract (Section 2-612), then also with respect to the whole undelivered balance, the aggrieved seller may

(a) withhold delivery of such goods;

(b) stop delivery by any bailee as hereafter provided (Section 2-705);

(c) proceed under the next section respecting goods still unidentified to the contract;

(d) resell and recover damages as hereafter provided (Section 2-706);

(e) recover damages for non-acceptance (Section 2-708) or in a proper case the price (Section 2-709);

(f) cancel.

§ 2-704. Seller's Right to Identify Goods to the Contract Notwithstanding Breach or to Salvage Unfinished Goods.

(1) An aggrieved seller under the preceding section may

(a) identify to the contract conforming goods not already identified if at the time he learned of the breach they are in his possession or control;

(b) treat as the subject of resale goods which have demonstrably been intended for the particular contract even though those goods are unfinished.

(2) Where the goods are unfinished an aggrieved seller may in the exercise of reasonable commercial judgment for the purposes of avoiding loss and of effective realization either complete the manufacture and wholly identify the goods to the contract or cease manufacture and resell for scrap or salvage value or proceed in any other reasonable manner.

§ 2-705. Seller's Stoppage of Delivery in Transit or Otherwise.

(1) The seller may stop delivery of goods in the possession of a carrier or other bailee when he discovers the buyer to be insolvent (Section 2-702) and may stop delivery of carload, truckload, planeload or larger shipments of express or freight when the buyer repudiates or fails to make a payment due before delivery or if for any other reason the seller has a right to withhold or reclaim the goods.

(2) As against such buyer the seller may stop delivery until

(a) receipt of the goods by the buyer; or

(b) acknowledgment to the buyer by any bailee of the goods except a carrier that the bailee holds the goods for the buyer; or

(c) such acknowledgment to the buyer by a carrier by reshipment or as warehouseman; or

(d) negotiation to the buyer of any negotiable document of title covering the goods.

(3) (a) To stop delivery the seller must so notify as to enable the bailee by reasonable diligence to prevent delivery of the goods.

(b) After such notification the bailee must hold and deliver the goods according to the directions of the seller but the seller is liable to the bailee for any ensuing charges or damages.

(c) If a negotiable document of title has been issued for goods the bailee is not obliged to obey a notification to stop until surrender of the document.

(d) A carrier who has issued a non-negotiable bill of lading is not obliged to obey a notification to stop received from a person other than the consignor.

§ 2–706.   Seller's Resale Including Contract for Resale.

(1) Under the conditions stated in Section 2–703 on seller's remedies, the seller may resell the goods concerned or the undelivered balance thereof. Where the resale is made in good faith and in a commercially reasonable manner the seller may recover the difference between the resale price and the contract price together with any incidental damages allowed under the provisions of this Article (Section 2–710), but less expenses saved in consequence of the buyer's breach.

(2) Except as otherwise provided in subsection (3) or unless otherwise agreed resale may be at public or private sale including sale by way of one or more contracts to sell or of identification to an existing contract of the seller. Sale may be as a unit or in parcels and at any time and place and on any terms but every aspect of the sale including the method, manner, time, place and terms must be commercially reasonable. The resale must be reasonably identified as referring to the broken contract, but it is not necessary that the goods be in existence or that any or all of them have been identified to the contract before the breach.

(3) Where the resale is at private sale the seller must give the buyer reasonable notification of his intention to resell.

(4) Where the resale is at public sale

(a) only identified goods can be sold except where there is a recognized market for a public sale of futures in goods of the kind; and

(b) it must be made at a usual place or market for public sale if one is reasonably available and except in the case of goods which are perishable or threaten to decline in value speedily the seller must give the buyer reasonable notice of the time and place of the resale; and

(c) if the goods are not to be within the view of those attending the sale the notification of sale must state the place where the goods are located and provide for their reasonable inspection by prospective bidders; and

(d) the seller may buy.

(5) A purchaser who buys in good faith at a resale takes the goods free of any rights of the original buyer even though the seller fails to comply with one or more of the requirements of this section.

(6) The seller is not accountable to the buyer for any profit made on any resale. A person in the position of a seller (Section 2–707) or a buyer who has rightfully rejected or justifiably revoked acceptance must account for any excess over the amount of his security interest, as hereinafter defined (subsection (3) of Section 2–711).

§ 2–707.   "Person in the Position of a Seller".

(1) A "person in the position of a seller" includes as against a principal an agent who has paid or become responsible for the price of goods on behalf of his principal or anyone who otherwise holds a security interest or other right in goods similar to that of a seller.

(2) A person in the position of a seller may as provided in this Article withhold or stop delivery (Section 2–705) and resell (Section 2–706) and recover incidental damages (Section 2–710).

§ 2–708.   Seller's Damages for Non-Acceptance or Repudiation.

(1) Subject to subsection (2) and to the provisions of this Article with respect to proof of market price (Section 2–723), the measure of damages for non-acceptance or repudiation by the buyer is the difference between the market price at the time and place for tender and the unpaid contract price together with any incidental damages provided in this Article (Section 2–710), but less expenses saved in consequence of the buyer's breach.

(2) If the measure of damages provided in subsection (1) is inadequate to put the seller in as good a position as performance would have done then the measure of damages is the profit (including reasonable overhead) which the seller would have made from full performance by the buyer, together with any incidental damages provided in this Article (Section 2–710), due allowance for costs reasonably incurred and due credit for payments or proceeds of resale.

§ 2–709.   Action for the Price.

(1) When the buyer fails to pay the price as it becomes due the seller may recover, together with any incidental damages under the next section, the price

(a) of goods accepted or of conforming goods lost or damaged within a commercially reasonable time after risk of their loss has passed to the buyer; and

(b) of goods identified to the contract if the seller is unable after reasonable effort to resell them at a reasonable price or the circumstances reasonably indicate that such effort will be unavailing.

(2) Where the seller sues for the price he must hold for the buyer any goods which have been identified to the contract and are still in his control except that if resale becomes possible he may resell them at any time prior to the collection of the judgment. The net proceeds of any such resale must be credited to the buyer and payment of the judgment entitles him to any goods not resold.

(3) After the buyer has wrongfully rejected or revoked acceptance of the goods or has failed to make a payment due or has repudiated (Section 2–610), a seller who is held not entitled to the price under this section shall nevertheless be awarded damages for non-acceptance under the preceding section.

§ 2–710.   Seller's Incidental Damages.

Incidental damages to an aggrieved seller include any commercially reasonable charges, expenses or commissions incurred in stopping delivery, in the transportation, care and custody of goods after the buyer's breach, in connection with return or resale of the goods or otherwise resulting from the breach.

§ 2–711.   Buyer's Remedies in General; Buyer's Security Interest in Rejected Goods.

(1) Where the seller fails to make delivery or repudiates or the buyer rightfully rejects or justifiably revokes acceptance then with respect to any goods involved, and with respect to the whole if the breach goes to the whole contract (Section 2–612), the buyer may cancel and whether or not he has done so may in addition to recovering so much of the price as has been paid

(a) "cover" and have damages under the next section as to all the goods affected whether or not they have been identified to the contract; or

(b) recover damages for non-delivery as provided in this Article (Section 2–713).

(2) Where the seller fails to deliver or repudiates the buyer may also

(a) if the goods have been identified recover them as provided in this Article (Section 2–502); or

(b) in a proper case obtain specific performance or replevy the goods as provided in this Article (Section 2–716).

(3) On rightful rejection or justifiable revocation of acceptance a buyer has a security interest in goods in his possession or control for any payments made on their price and any expenses reasonably incurred in their inspection, receipt, transportation, care and custody and may hold such goods and resell them in like manner as an aggrieved seller (Section 2–706).

§ 2–712.   "Cover"; Buyer's Procurement of Substitute Goods.

(1) After a breach within the preceding section the buyer may "cover" by making in good faith and without unreasonable delay any reasonable purchase of or contract to purchase goods in substitution for those due from the seller.

(2) The buyer may recover from the seller as damages the difference between the cost of cover and the contract price together with any incidental or consequential damages as hereinafter defined (Section 2–715), but less expenses saved in consequence of the seller's breach.

(3) Failure of the buyer to effect cover within this section does not bar him from any other remedy.

§ 2–713.   Buyer's Damages for Non-Delivery or Repudiation.

(1) Subject to the provisions of this Article with respect to proof of market price (Section 2–723), the measure of damages for non-delivery or repudiation by the seller is the difference between the market price at the time when the buyer learned of the breach and the contract price together with any incidental and consequential damages provided in this Article (Section 2–715), but less expenses saved in consequence of the seller's breach.

(2) Market price is to be determined as of the place for tender or, in cases of rejection after arrival or revocation of acceptance, as of the place of arrival.

§ 2–714.   Buyer's Damages for Breach in Regard to Accepted Goods.

(1) Where the buyer has accepted goods and given notification (subsection (3) of Section 2–607) he may recover as damages for any non-conformity of tender the loss resulting in the ordinary course of events from the seller's breach as determined in any manner which is reasonable.

(2) The measure of damages for breach of warranty is the difference at the time and place of acceptance between the value of the goods accepted and the value they would have had if they had been as warranted, unless special circumstances show proximate damages of a different amount.

(3) In a proper case any incidental and consequential damages under the next section may also be recovered.

§ 2–715.   Buyer's Incidental and Consequential Damages.

(1) Incidental damages resulting from the seller's breach include expenses reasonably incurred in inspection, receipt, transportation and care and custody of goods rightfully rejected, any commercially reasonable charges, expenses or commissions in connection with effecting cover and any other reasonable expense incident to the delay or other breach.

(2) Consequential damages resulting from the seller's breach include

    (a) any loss resulting from general or particular requirements and needs of which the seller at the time of contracting had reason to know and which could not reasonably be prevented by cover or otherwise; and

    (b) injury to person or property proximately resulting from any breach of warranty.

§ 2–716.   Buyer's Right to Specific Performance or Replevin.

(1) Specific performance may be decreed where the goods are unique or in other proper circumstances.

(2) The decree for specific performance may include such terms and conditions as to payment of the price, damages, or other relief as the court may deem just.

(3) The buyer has a right of replevin for goods identified to the contract if after reasonable effort he is unable to effect cover for such goods or the circumstances reasonably indicate that such effort will be unavailing or if the goods have been shipped under reservation and satisfaction of the security interest in them has been made or tendered. In the case of goods bought for personal, family, or household purposes, the buyer's right of replevin vests upon acquisition of a special property, even if the seller had not then repudiated or failed to deliver.

As amended in 1999.

§ 2–717.   Deduction of Damages From the Price.

The buyer on notifying the seller of his intention to do so may deduct all or any part of the damages resulting from any breach of the contract from any part of the price still due under the same contract.

§ 2–718.   Liquidation or Limitation of Damages; Deposits.

(1) Damages for breach by either party may be liquidated in the agreement but only at an amount which is reasonable in the light of the anticipated or actual harm caused by the breach, the difficulties of proof of loss, and the inconvenience or nonfeasibility of otherwise obtaining an adequate remedy. A term fixing unreasonably large liquidated damages is void as a penalty.

(2) Where the seller justifiably withholds delivery of goods because of the buyer's breach, the buyer is entitled to restitution of any amount by which the sum of his payments exceeds

    (a) the amount to which the seller is entitled by virtue of terms liquidating the seller's damages in accordance with subsection (1), or

    (b) in the absence of such terms, twenty per cent of the value of the total performance for which the buyer is obligated under the contract or $500, whichever is smaller.

(3) The buyer's right to restitution under subsection (2) is subject to offset to the extent that the seller establishes

    (a) a right to recover damages under the provisions of this Article other than subsection (1), and

    (b) the amount or value of any benefits received by the buyer directly or indirectly by reason of the contract.

(4) Where a seller has received payment in goods their reasonable value or the proceeds of their resale shall be treated as payments for the purposes of subsection (2); but if the seller has notice of the buyer's breach before reselling goods received in part performance, his resale is subject to the conditions laid down in this Article on resale by an aggrieved seller (Section 2–706).

§ 2–719.   Contractual Modification or Limitation of Remedy.

(1) Subject to the provisions of subsections (2) and (3) of this section and of the preceding section on liquidation and limitation of damages,

(a) the agreement may provide for remedies in addition to or in substitution for those provided in this Article and may limit or alter the measure of damages recoverable under this Article, as by limiting the buyer's remedies to return of the goods and repayment of the price or to repair and replacement of nonconforming goods or parts; and

(b) resort to a remedy as provided is optional unless the remedy is expressly agreed to be exclusive, in which case it is the sole remedy.

(2) Where circumstances cause an exclusive or limited remedy to fail of its essential purpose, remedy may be had as provided in this Act.

(3) Consequential damages may be limited or excluded unless the limitation or exclusion is unconscionable. Limitation of consequential damages for injury to the person in the case of consumer goods is prima facie unconscionable but limitation of damages where the loss is commercial is not.

§ 2–720. Effect of "Cancellation" or "Rescission" on Claims for Antecedent Breach.

Unless the contrary intention clearly appears, expressions of "cancellation" or "rescission" of the contract or the like shall not be construed as a renunciation or discharge of any claim in damages for an antecedent breach.

§ 2–721. Remedies for Fraud.

Remedies for material misrepresentation or fraud include all remedies available under this Article for non-fraudulent breach. Neither rescission or a claim for rescission of the contract for sale nor rejection or return of the goods shall bar or be deemed inconsistent with a claim for damages or other remedy.

§ 2–722. Who Can Sue Third Parties for Injury to Goods.

Where a third party so deals with goods which have been identified to a contract for sale as to cause actionable injury to a party to that contract

(a) a right of action against the third party is in either party to the contract for sale who has title to or a security interest or a special property or an insurable interest in the goods; and if the goods have been destroyed or converted a right of action is also in the party who either bore the risk of loss under the contract for sale or has since the injury assumed that risk as against the other;

(b) if at the time of the injury the party plaintiff did not bear the risk of loss as against the other party to the contract for sale and there is no arrangement between them for disposition of the recovery, his suit or settlement is, subject to his own interest, as a fiduciary for the other party to the contract;

(c) either party may with the consent of the other sue for the benefit of whom it may concern.

§ 2–723. Proof of Market Price: Time and Place.

(1) If an action based on anticipatory repudiation comes to trial before the time for performance with respect to some or all of the goods, any damages based on market price (Section 2–708 or Section 2–713) shall be determined according to the price of such goods prevailing at the time when the aggrieved party learned of the repudiation.

(2) If evidence of a price prevailing at the times or places described in this Article is not readily available the price prevailing within any reasonable time before or after the time described or at any other place which in commercial judgment or under usage of trade would serve as a reasonable substitute for the one described may be used, making any proper allowance for the cost of transporting the goods to or from such other place.

(3) Evidence of a relevant price prevailing at a time or place other than the one described in this Article offered by one party is not admissible unless and until he has given the other party such notice as the court finds sufficient to prevent unfair surprise.

§ 2–724. Admissibility of Market Quotations.

Whenever the prevailing price or value of any goods regularly bought and sold in any established commodity market is in issue, reports in official publications or trade journals or in newspapers or periodicals of general circulation published as the reports of such market shall be admissible in evidence. The circumstances of the preparation of such a report may be shown to affect its weight but not its admissibility.

§ 2–725. Statute of Limitations in Contracts for Sale.

(1) An action for breach of any contract for sale must be commenced within four years after the cause of action has accrued. By the original agreement the parties may reduce the period of limitation to not less than one year but may not extend it.

(2) A cause of action accrues when the breach occurs, regardless of the aggrieved party's lack of knowledge of the breach. A breach of warranty occurs when tender of delivery is made, except that where a warranty explicitly extends to future performance of the goods and discovery of the breach must await the time of such performance the cause of action accrues when the breach is or should have been discovered.

(3) Where an action commenced within the time limited by subsection (1) is so terminated as to leave available a remedy by another action for the same breach such other action may be commenced after the expiration of the time limited and within six months after the termination of the first action unless the termination resulted from voluntary discontinuance or from dismissal for failure or neglect to prosecute.

(4) This section does not alter the law on tolling of the statute of limitations nor does it apply to causes of action which have accrued before this Act becomes effective.

Article 2A
LEASES

Part 1 General Provisions

§ 2A–101. Short Title.

This Article shall be known and may be cited as the Uniform Commercial Code—Leases.

§ 2A–102. Scope.

This Article applies to any transaction, regardless of form, that creates a lease.

§ 2A–103. Definitions and Index of Definitions.

(1) In this Article unless the context otherwise requires:

(a) "Buyer in ordinary course of business" means a person who in good faith and without knowledge that the sale to him [or her] is in violation of the ownership rights or security interest or leasehold interest of a third party in the goods buys in ordinary course from a person in the business of selling goods of that kind but does not include a pawnbroker. "Buying" may be for cash or by exchange of other property or on secured or unsecured credit and includes receiving goods or documents of title under a pre-existing contract for sale but does not include a transfer in bulk or as security for or in total or partial satisfaction of a money debt.

(b) "Cancellation" occurs when either party puts an end to the lease contract for default by the other party.

(c) "Commercial unit" means such a unit of goods as by commercial usage is a single whole for purposes of lease and division of which materially impairs its character or value on the market or in use. A commercial unit may be a single article, as a machine, or a set of articles, as a suite of furniture or a line of machinery, or a quantity, as a gross or carload, or any other unit treated in use or in the relevant market as a single whole.

(d) "Conforming" goods or performance under a lease contract means goods or performance that are in accordance with the obligations under the lease contract.

(e) "Consumer lease" means a lease that a lessor regularly engaged in the business of leasing or selling makes to a lessee who is an individual and who takes under the lease primarily for a personal, family, or household purpose [, if the total payments to be made under the lease contract, excluding payments for options to renew or buy, do not exceed $_____].

(f) "Fault" means wrongful act, omission, breach, or default.

(g) "Finance lease" means a lease with respect to which:

(i) the lessor does not select, manufacture or supply the goods;

(ii) the lessor acquires the goods or the right to possession and use of the goods in connection with the lease; and

(iii) one of the following occurs:

(A) the lessee receives a copy of the contract by which the lessor acquired the goods or the right to possession and use of the goods before signing the lease contract;

(B) the lessee's approval of the contract by which the lessor acquired the goods or the right to possession and use of the goods is a condition to effectiveness of the lease contract;

(C) the lessee, before signing the lease contract, receives an accurate and complete statement designating the promises and warranties, and any disclaimers of warranties, limitations or modifications of remedies, or liquidated damages, including those of a third party, such as the manufacturer of the goods, provided to the lessor by the person supplying the goods in connection with or as part of the contract by which the lessor acquired the goods or the right to possession and use of the goods; or

(D) if the lease is not a consumer lease, the lessor, before the lessee signs the lease contract, informs the lessee in writing (a) of the identity of the person supplying the goods to the lessor, unless the lessee has selected that person and directed the lessor to acquire the goods or the right to possession and use of the goods from that person, (b) that the lessee is entitled under this Article to any promises and warranties, including those of any third party, provided to the lessor by the person supplying the goods in connection with or as part of the contract by which the lessor acquired the goods or the right to possession and use of the goods, and (c) that the lessee may communicate with the person supplying the goods to the lessor and receive an accurate and complete statement of those promises and warranties, including any disclaimers and limitations of them or of remedies.

(h) "Goods" means all things that are movable at the time of identification to the lease contract, or are fixtures (Section 2A–309), but the term does not include money, documents, instruments, accounts, chattel paper, general intangibles, or minerals or the like, including oil and gas, before extraction. The term also includes the unborn young of animals.

(i) "Installment lease contract" means a lease contract that authorizes or requires the delivery of goods in separate lots to be separately accepted, even though the lease contract contains a clause "each delivery is a separate lease" or its equivalent.

(j) "Lease" means a transfer of the right to possession and use of goods for a term in return for consideration, but a sale, including a sale on approval or a sale or return, or retention or creation of a security interest is not a lease. Unless the context clearly indicates otherwise, the term includes a sublease.

(k) "Lease agreement" means the bargain, with respect to the lease, of the lessor and the lessee in fact as found in their language or by implication from other circumstances including course of dealing or usage of trade or course of performance as provided in this Article. Unless the context clearly indicates otherwise, the term includes a sublease agreement.

(l) "Lease contract" means the total legal obligation that results from the lease agreement as affected by this Article and any other applicable rules of law. Unless the context clearly indicates otherwise, the term includes a sublease contract.

(m) "Leasehold interest" means the interest of the lessor or the lessee under a lease contract.

(n) "Lessee" means a person who acquires the right to possession and use of goods under a lease. Unless the context clearly indicates otherwise, the term includes a sublessee.

(o) "Lessee in ordinary course of business" means a person who in good faith and without knowledge that the lease to him [or her] is in violation of the ownership rights or security interest or leasehold interest of a third party in the goods, leases in ordinary course from a person in the business of selling or leasing goods of that kind but does not include a pawnbroker. "Leasing" may be for cash or by exchange of other property or on secured or unsecured credit and includes receiving goods or documents of title under a pre-existing lease contract but does not include a transfer in bulk or as security for or in total or partial satisfaction of a money debt.

(p) "Lessor" means a person who transfers the right to possession and use of goods under a lease. Unless the context clearly indicates otherwise, the term includes a sublessor.

(q) "Lessor's residual interest" means the lessor's interest in the goods after expiration, termination, or cancellation of the lease contract.

(r) "Lien" means a charge against or interest in goods to secure payment of a debt or performance of an obligation, but the term does not include a security interest.

(s) "Lot" means a parcel or a single article that is the subject matter of a separate lease or delivery, whether or not it is sufficient to perform the lease contract.

(t) "Merchant lessee" means a lessee that is a merchant with respect to goods of the kind subject to the lease.

(u) "Present value" means the amount as of a date certain of one or more sums payable in the future, discounted to the date certain. The discount is determined by the interest rate specified by the parties if the rate was not manifestly unreasonable at the time the transaction was entered into; otherwise, the discount is determined by a commercially reasonable rate that takes into account the facts and circumstances of each case at the time the transaction was entered into.

(v) "Purchase" includes taking by sale, lease, mortgage, security interest, pledge, gift, or any other voluntary transaction creating an interest in goods.

(w) "Sublease" means a lease of goods the right to possession and use of which was acquired by the lessor as a lessee under an existing lease.

(x) "Supplier" means a person from whom a lessor buys or leases goods to be leased under a finance lease.

(y) "Supply contract" means a contract under which a lessor buys or leases goods to be leased.

(z) "Termination" occurs when either party pursuant to a power created by agreement or law puts an end to the lease contract otherwise than for default.

(2) Other definitions applying to this Article and the sections in which they appear are:

"Accessions". Section 2A–310(1).

"Construction mortgage". Section 2A–309(1)(d).

"Encumbrance". Section 2A–309(1)(e).

"Fixtures". Section 2A–309(1)(a).

"Fixture filing". Section 2A–309(1)(b).

"Purchase money lease". Section 2A–309(1)(c).

(3) The following definitions in other Articles apply to this Article:

"Accounts". Section 9–106.

"Between merchants". Section 2–104(3).

"Buyer". Section 2–103(1)(a).

"Chattel paper". Section 9–105(1)(b).

"Consumer goods". Section 9–109(1).

"Document". Section 9–105(1)(f).

"Entrusting". Section 2–403(3).

"General intangibles". Section 9–106.

"Good faith". Section 2–103(1)(b).

"Instrument". Section 9–105(1)(i).

"Merchant". Section 2–104(1).

"Mortgage". Section 9–105(1)(j).

"Pursuant to commitment". Section 9–105(1)(k).

"Receipt". Section 2–103(1)(c).

"Sale". Section 2–106(1).

"Sale on approval". Section 2–326.

"Sale or return". Section 2–326.

"Seller". Section 2–103(1)(d).

(4) In addition Article 1 contains general definitions and principles of construction and interpretation applicable throughout this Article.

As amended in 1990 and 1999.

§ 2A–104. Leases Subject to Other Law.

(1) A lease, although subject to this Article, is also subject to any applicable:

(a) certificate of title statute of this State: (list any certificate of title statutes covering automobiles, trailers, mobile homes, boats, farm tractors, and the like);

(b) certificate of title statute of another jurisdiction (Section 2A–105); or

(c) consumer protection statute of this State, or final consumer protection decision of a court of this State existing on the effective date of this Article.

(2) In case of conflict between this Article, other than Sections 2A–105, 2A–304(3), and 2A–305(3), and a statute or decision referred to in subsection (1), the statute or decision controls.

(3) Failure to comply with an applicable law has only the effect specified therein.

As amended in 1990.

§ 2A–105. Territorial Application of Article to Goods Covered by Certificate of Title.

Subject to the provisions of Sections 2A–304(3) and 2A–305(3), with respect to goods covered by a certificate of title issued under a statute of this State or of another jurisdiction, compliance and the effect of compliance or noncompliance with a certificate of title statute are governed by the law (including the conflict of laws rules) of the jurisdiction issuing the certificate until the earlier of (a) surrender of the certificate, or (b) four months after the goods are removed from that jurisdiction and thereafter until a new certificate of title is issued by another jurisdiction.

§ 2A–106. Limitation on Power of Parties to Consumer Lease to Choose Applicable Law and Judicial Forum.

(1) If the law chosen by the parties to a consumer lease is that of a jurisdiction other than a jurisdiction in which the lessee resides at the time the lease agreement becomes enforceable or within 30 days thereafter or in which the goods are to be used, the choice is not enforceable.

(2) If the judicial forum chosen by the parties to a consumer lease is a forum that would not otherwise have jurisdiction over the lessee, the choice is not enforceable.

§ 2A–107. Waiver or Renunciation of Claim or Right After Default.

Any claim or right arising out of an alleged default or breach of warranty may be discharged in whole or in part without consideration by a written waiver or renunciation signed and delivered by the aggrieved party.

§ 2A–108. Unconscionability.

(1) If the court as a matter of law finds a lease contract or any clause of a lease contract to have been unconscionable at the time it was made the court may refuse to enforce the lease contract, or it may enforce the remainder of the lease contract without the unconscionable clause, or it may so limit the application of any unconscionable clause as to avoid any unconscionable result.

(2) With respect to a consumer lease, if the court as a matter of law finds that a lease contract or any clause of a lease contract has been

induced by unconscionable conduct or that unconscionable conduct has occurred in the collection of a claim arising from a lease contract, the court may grant appropriate relief.

(3) Before making a finding of unconscionability under subsection (1) or (2), the court, on its own motion or that of a party, shall afford the parties a reasonable opportunity to present evidence as to the setting, purpose, and effect of the lease contract or clause thereof, or of the conduct.

(4) In an action in which the lessee claims unconscionability with respect to a consumer lease:

(a) If the court finds unconscionability under subsection (1) or (2), the court shall award reasonable attorney's fees to the lessee.

(b) If the court does not find unconscionability and the lessee claiming unconscionability has brought or maintained an action he [or she] knew to be groundless, the court shall award reasonable attorney's fees to the party against whom the claim is made.

(c) In determining attorney's fees, the amount of the recovery on behalf of the claimant under subsections (1) and (2) is not controlling.

§ 2A–109.   Option to Accelerate at Will.

(1) A term providing that one party or his [or her] successor in interest may accelerate payment or performance or require collateral or additional collateral "at will" or "when he [or she] deems himself [or herself] insecure" or in words of similar import must be construed to mean that he [or she] has power to do so only if he [or she] in good faith believes that the prospect of payment or performance is impaired.

(2) With respect to a consumer lease, the burden of establishing good faith under subsection (1) is on the party who exercised the power; otherwise the burden of establishing lack of good faith is on the party against whom the power has been exercised.

Part 2   Formation and Construction of Lease Contract

§ 2A–201.   Statute of Frauds.

(1) A lease contract is not enforceable by way of action or defense unless:

(a) the total payments to be made under the lease contract, excluding payments for options to renew or buy, are less than $1,000; or

(b) there is a writing, signed by the party against whom enforcement is sought or by that party's authorized agent, sufficient to indicate that a lease contract has been made between the parties and to describe the goods leased and the lease term.

(2) Any description of leased goods or of the lease term is sufficient and satisfies subsection (1)(b), whether or not it is specific, if it reasonably identifies what is described.

(3) A writing is not insufficient because it omits or incorrectly states a term agreed upon, but the lease contract is not enforceable under subsection (1)(b) beyond the lease term and the quantity of goods shown in the writing.

(4) A lease contract that does not satisfy the requirements of subsection (1), but which is valid in other respects, is enforceable:

(a) if the goods are to be specially manufactured or obtained for the lessee and are not suitable for lease or sale to others in the ordinary course of the lessor's business, and the lessor, before

notice of repudiation is received and under circumstances that reasonably indicate that the goods are for the lessee, has made either a substantial beginning of their manufacture or commitments for their procurement;

(b) if the party against whom enforcement is sought admits in that party's pleading, testimony or otherwise in court that a lease contract was made, but the lease contract is not enforceable under this provision beyond the quantity of goods admitted; or

(c) with respect to goods that have been received and accepted by the lessee.

(5) The lease term under a lease contract referred to in subsection (4) is:

(a) if there is a writing signed by the party against whom enforcement is sought or by that party's authorized agent specifying the lease term, the term so specified;

(b) if the party against whom enforcement is sought admits in that party's pleading, testimony, or otherwise in court a lease term, the term so admitted; or

(c) a reasonable lease term.

§ 2A–202.   Final Written Expression: Parol or Extrinsic Evidence.

Terms with respect to which the confirmatory memoranda of the parties agree or which are otherwise set forth in a writing intended by the parties as a final expression of their agreement with respect to such terms as are included therein may not be contradicted by evidence of any prior agreement or of a contemporaneous oral agreement but may be explained or supplemented:

(a) by course of dealing or usage of trade or by course of performance; and

(b) by evidence of consistent additional terms unless the court finds the writing to have been intended also as a complete and exclusive statement of the terms of the agreement.

§ 2A–203.   Seals Inoperative.

The affixing of a seal to a writing evidencing a lease contract or an offer to enter into a lease contract does not render the writing a sealed instrument and the law with respect to sealed instruments does not apply to the lease contract or offer.

§ 2A–204.   Formation in General.

(1) A lease contract may be made in any manner sufficient to show agreement, including conduct by both parties which recognizes the existence of a lease contract.

(2) An agreement sufficient to constitute a lease contract may be found although the moment of its making is undetermined.

(3) Although one or more terms are left open, a lease contract does not fail for indefiniteness if the parties have intended to make a lease contract and there is a reasonably certain basis for giving an appropriate remedy.

§ 2A–205.   Firm Offers.

An offer by a merchant to lease goods to or from another person in a signed writing that by its terms gives assurance it will be held open is not revocable, for lack of consideration, during the time stated or, if no time is stated, for a reasonable time, but in no event may the period of irrevocability exceed 3 months. Any such term of assurance on a form supplied by the offeree must be separately signed by the offeror.

§ 2A–206. Offer and Acceptance in Formation of Lease Contract.

(1) Unless otherwise unambiguously indicated by the language or circumstances, an offer to make a lease contract must be construed as inviting acceptance in any manner and by any medium reasonable in the circumstances.

(2) If the beginning of a requested performance is a reasonable mode of acceptance, an offeror who is not notified of acceptance within a reasonable time may treat the offer as having lapsed before acceptance.

§ 2A–207. Course of Performance or Practical Construction.

(1) If a lease contract involves repeated occasions for performance by either party with knowledge of the nature of the performance and opportunity for objection to it by the other, any course of performance accepted or acquiesced in without objection is relevant to determine the meaning of the lease agreement.

(2) The express terms of a lease agreement and any course of performance, as well as any course of dealing and usage of trade, must be construed whenever reasonable as consistent with each other; but if that construction is unreasonable, express terms control course of performance, course of performance controls both course of dealing and usage of trade, and course of dealing controls usage of trade.

(3) Subject to the provisions of Section 2A–208 on modification and waiver, course of performance is relevant to show a waiver or modification of any term inconsistent with the course of performance.

§ 2A–208. Modification, Rescission and Waiver.

(1) An agreement modifying a lease contract needs no consideration to be binding.

(2) A signed lease agreement that excludes modification or rescission except by a signed writing may not be otherwise modified or rescinded, but, except as between merchants, such a requirement on a form supplied by a merchant must be separately signed by the other party.

(3) Although an attempt at modification or rescission does not satisfy the requirements of subsection (2), it may operate as a waiver.

(4) A party who has made a waiver affecting an executory portion of a lease contract may retract the waiver by reasonable notification received by the other party that strict performance will be required of any term waived, unless the retraction would be unjust in view of a material change of position in reliance on the waiver.

§ 2A–209. Lessee under Finance Lease as Beneficiary of Supply Contract.

(1) The benefit of the supplier's promises to the lessor under the supply contract and of all warranties, whether express or implied, including those of any third party provided in connection with or as part of the supply contract, extends to the lessee to the extent of the lessee's leasehold interest under a finance lease related to the supply contract, but is subject to the terms warranty and of the supply contract and all defenses or claims arising therefrom.

(2) The extension of the benefit of supplier's promises and of warranties to the lessee (Section 2A–209(1)) does not: (i) modify the rights and obligations of the parties to the supply contract, whether arising therefrom or otherwise, or (ii) impose any duty or liability under the supply contract on the lessee.

(3) Any modification or rescission of the supply contract by the supplier and the lessor is effective between the supplier and the lessee unless, before the modification or rescission, the supplier has received notice that the lessee has entered into a finance lease related to the supply contract. If the modification or rescission is effective between the supplier and the lessee, the lessor is deemed to have assumed, in addition to the obligations of the lessor to the lessee under the lease contract, promises of the supplier to the lessor and warranties that were so modified or rescinded as they existed and were available to the lessee before modification or rescission.

(4) In addition to the extension of the benefit of the supplier's promises and of warranties to the lessee under subsection (1), the lessee retains all rights that the lessee may have against the supplier which arise from an agreement between the lessee and the supplier or under other law.

As amended in 1990.

§ 2A–210. Express Warranties.

(1) Express warranties by the lessor are created as follows:

(a) Any affirmation of fact or promise made by the lessor to the lessee which relates to the goods and becomes part of the basis of the bargain creates an express warranty that the goods will conform to the affirmation or promise.

(b) Any description of the goods which is made part of the basis of the bargain creates an express warranty that the goods will conform to the description.

(c) Any sample or model that is made part of the basis of the bargain creates an express warranty that the whole of the goods will conform to the sample or model.

(2) It is not necessary to the creation of an express warranty that the lessor use formal words, such as "warrant" or "guarantee," or that the lessor have a specific intention to make a warranty, but an affirmation merely of the value of the goods or a statement purporting to be merely the lessor's opinion or commendation of the goods does not create a warranty.

§ 2A–211. Warranties Against Interference and Against Infringement; Lessee's Obligation Against Infringement.

(1) There is in a lease contract a warranty that for the lease term no person holds a claim to or interest in the goods that arose from an act or omission of the lessor, other than a claim by way of infringement or the like, which will interfere with the lessee's enjoyment of its leasehold interest.

(2) Except in a finance lease there is in a lease contract by a lessor who is a merchant regularly dealing in goods of the kind a warranty that the goods are delivered free of the rightful claim of any person by way of infringement or the like.

(3) A lessee who furnishes specifications to a lessor or a supplier shall hold the lessor and the supplier harmless against any claim by way of infringement or the like that arises out of compliance with the specifications.

§ 2A–212. Implied Warranty of Merchantability.

(1) Except in a finance lease, a warranty that the goods will be merchantable is implied in a lease contract if the lessor is a merchant with respect to goods of that kind.

(2) Goods to be merchantable must be at least such as

(a) pass without objection in the trade under the description in the lease agreement;

(b) in the case of fungible goods, are of fair average quality within the description;

(c) are fit for the ordinary purposes for which goods of that type are used;

(d) run, within the variation permitted by the lease agreement, of even kind, quality, and quantity within each unit and among all units involved;

(e) are adequately contained, packaged, and labeled as the lease agreement may require; and

(f) conform to any promises or affirmations of fact made on the container or label.

(3) Other implied warranties may arise from course of dealing or usage of trade.

§ 2A–213.   Implied Warranty of Fitness for Particular Purpose.

Except in a finance of lease, if the lessor at the time the lease contract is made has reason to know of any particular purpose for which the goods are required and that the lessee is relying on the lessor's skill or judgment to select or furnish suitable goods, there is in the lease contract an implied warranty that the goods will be fit for that purpose.

§ 2A–214.   Exclusion or Modification of Warranties.

(1) Words or conduct relevant to the creation of an express warranty and words or conduct tending to negate or limit a warranty must be construed wherever reasonable as consistent with each other; but, subject to the provisions of Section 2A–202 on parol or extrinsic evidence, negation or limitation is inoperative to the extent that the construction is unreasonable.

(2) Subject to subsection (3), to exclude or modify the implied warranty of merchantability or any part of it the language must mention "merchantability", be by a writing, and be conspicuous. Subject to subsection (3), to exclude or modify any implied warranty of fitness the exclusion must be by a writing and be conspicuous. Language to exclude all implied warranties of fitness is sufficient if it is in writing, is conspicuous and states, for example, "There is no warranty that the goods will be fit for a particular purpose".

(3) Notwithstanding subsection (2), but subject to subsection (4),

(a) unless the circumstances indicate otherwise, all implied warranties are excluded by expressions like "as is" or "with all faults" or by other language that in common understanding calls the lessee's attention to the exclusion of warranties and makes plain that there is no implied warranty, if in writing and conspicuous;

(b) if the lessee before entering into the lease contract has examined the goods or the sample or model as fully as desired or has refused to examine the goods, there is no implied warranty with regard to defects that an examination ought in the circumstances to have revealed; and

(c) an implied warranty may also be excluded or modified by course of dealing, course of performance, or usage of trade.

(4) To exclude or modify a warranty against interference or against infringement (Section 2A–211) or any part of it, the language must be specific, be by a writing, and be conspicuous, unless the circumstances, including course of performance, course of dealing, or usage of trade, give the lessee reason to know that the goods are being leased subject to a claim or interest of any person.

§ 2A–215.   Cumulation and Conflict of Warranties Express or Implied.

Warranties, whether express or implied, must be construed as consistent with each other and as cumulative, but if that construction is unreasonable, the intention of the parties determines which warranty is dominant. In ascertaining that intention the following rules apply:

(a) Exact or technical specifications displace an inconsistent sample or model or general language of description.

(b) A sample from an existing bulk displaces inconsistent general language of description.

(c) Express warranties displace inconsistent implied warranties other than an implied warranty of fitness for a particular purpose.

§ 2A–216.   Third-Party Beneficiaries of Express and Implied Warranties.

Alternative A

A warranty to or for the benefit of a lessee under this Article, whether express or implied, extends to any natural person who is in the family or household of the lessee or who is a guest in the lessee's home if it is reasonable to expect that such person may use, consume, or be affected by the goods and who is injured in person by breach of the warranty. This section does not displace principles of law and equity that extend a warranty to or for the benefit of a lessee to other persons. The operation of this section may not be excluded, modified, or limited, but an exclusion, modification, or limitation of the warranty, including any with respect to rights and remedies, effective against the lessee is also effective against any beneficiary designated under this section.

Alternative B

A warranty to or for the benefit of a lessee under this Article, whether express or implied, extends to any natural person who may reasonably be expected to use, consume, or be affected by the goods and who is injured in person by breach of the warranty. This section does not displace principles of law and equity that extend a warranty to or for the benefit of a lessee to other persons. The operation of this section may not be excluded, modified, or limited, but an exclusion, modification, or limitation of the warranty, including any with respect to rights and remedies, effective against the lessee is also effective against the beneficiary designated under this section.

Alternative C

A warranty to or for the benefit of a lessee under this Article, whether express or implied, extends to any person who may reasonably be expected to use, consume, or be affected by the goods and who is injured by breach of the warranty. The operation of this section may not be excluded, modified, or limited with respect to injury to the person of an individual to whom the warranty extends, but an exclusion, modification, or limitation of the warranty, including any with respect to rights and remedies, effective against the lessee is also effective against the beneficiary designated under this section.

§ 2A–217.   Identification.

Identification of goods as goods to which a lease contract refers may be made at any time and in any manner explicitly agreed to by the parties. In the absence of explicit agreement, identification occurs:

(a) when the lease contract is made if the lease contract is for a lease of goods that are existing and identified;

(b) when the goods are shipped, marked, or otherwise designated by the lessor as goods to which the lease contract refers, if the lease contract is for a lease of goods that are not existing and identified; or

(c) when the young are conceived, if the lease contract is for a lease of unborn young of animals.

§ 2A-218. Insurance and Proceeds.

(1) A lessee obtains an insurable interest when existing goods are identified to the lease contract even though the goods identified are nonconforming and the lessee has an option to reject them.

(2) If a lessee has an insurable interest only by reason of the lessor's identification of the goods, the lessor, until default or insolvency or notification to the lessee that identification is final, may substitute other goods for those identified.

(3) Notwithstanding a lessee's insurable interest under subsections (1) and (2), the lessor retains an insurable interest until an option to buy has been exercised by the lessee and risk of loss has passed to the lessee.

(4) Nothing in this section impairs any insurable interest recognized under any other statute or rule of law.

(5) The parties by agreement may determine that one or more parties have an obligation to obtain and pay for insurance covering the goods and by agreement may determine the beneficiary of the proceeds of the insurance.

§ 2A-219. Risk of Loss.

(1) Except in the case of a finance lease, risk of loss is retained by the lessor and does not pass to the lessee. In the case of a finance lease, risk of loss passes to the lessee.

(2) Subject to the provisions of this Article on the effect of default on risk of loss (Section 2A-220), if risk of loss is to pass to the lessee and the time of passage is not stated, the following rules apply:

    (a) If the lease contract requires or authorizes the goods to be shipped by carrier

        (i) and it does not require delivery at a particular destination, the risk of loss passes to the lessee when the goods are duly delivered to the carrier; but

        (ii) if it does require delivery at a particular destination and the goods are there duly tendered while in the possession of the carrier, the risk of loss passes to the lessee when the goods are there duly so tendered as to enable the lessee to take delivery.

    (b) If the goods are held by a bailee to be delivered without being moved, the risk of loss passes to the lessee on acknowledgment by the bailee of the lessee's right to possession of the goods.

    (c) In any case not within subsection (a) or (b), the risk of loss passes to the lessee on the lessee's receipt of the goods if the lessor, or, in the case of a finance lease, the supplier, is a merchant; otherwise the risk passes to the lessee on tender of delivery.

§ 2A-220. Effect of Default on Risk of Loss.

(1) Where risk of loss is to pass to the lessee and the time of passage is not stated:

    (a) If a tender or delivery of goods so fails to conform to the lease contract as to give a right of rejection, the risk of their loss remains with the lessor, or, in the case of a finance lease, the supplier, until cure or acceptance.

    (b) If the lessee rightfully revokes acceptance, he [or she], to the extent of any deficiency in his [or her] effective insurance cover-

age, may treat the risk of loss as having remained with the lessor from the beginning.

(2) Whether or not risk of loss is to pass to the lessee, if the lessee as to conforming goods already identified to a lease contract repudiates or is otherwise in default under the lease contract, the lessor, or, in the case of a finance lease, the supplier, to the extent of any deficiency in his [or her] effective insurance coverage may treat the risk of loss as resting on the lessee for a commercially reasonable time.

§ 2A-221. Casualty to Identified Goods.

If a lease contract requires goods identified when the lease contract is made, and the goods suffer casualty without fault of the lessee, the lessor or the supplier before delivery, or the goods suffer casualty before risk of loss passes to the lessee pursuant to the lease agreement or Section 2A-219, then:

(a) if the loss is total, the lease contract is avoided; and

(b) if the loss is partial or the goods have so deteriorated as to no longer conform to the lease contract, the lessee may nevertheless demand inspection and at his [or her] option either treat the lease contract as avoided or, except in a finance lease that is not a consumer lease, accept the goods with due allowance from the rent payable for the balance of the lease term for the deterioration or the deficiency in quantity but without further right against the lessor.

Part 3   Effect of Lease Contract

§ 2A-301. Enforceability of Lease Contract.

Except as otherwise provided in this Article, a lease contract is effective and enforceable according to its terms between the parties, against purchasers of the goods and against creditors of the parties.

§ 2A-302. Title to and Possession of Goods.

Except as otherwise provided in this Article, each provision of this Article applies whether the lessor or a third party has title to the goods, and whether the lessor, the lessee, or a third party has possession of the goods, notwithstanding any statute or rule of law that possession or the absence of possession is fraudulent.

§ 2A-303. Alienability of Party's Interest Under Lease Contract or of Lessor's Residual Interest in Goods; Delegation of Performance; Transfer of Rights.

(1) As used in this section, "creation of a security interest" includes the sale of a lease contract that is subject to Article 9, Secured Transactions, by reason of Section 9-109(a)(3).

(2) Except as provided in subsections (3) and Section 9-407, a provision in a lease agreement which (i) prohibits the voluntary or involuntary transfer, including a transfer by sale, sublease, creation or enforcement of a security interest, or attachment, levy, or other judicial process, of an interest of a party under the lease contract or of the lessor's residual interest in the goods, or (ii) makes such a transfer an event of default, gives rise to the rights and remedies provided in subsection (4), but a transfer that is prohibited or is an event of default under the lease agreement is otherwise effective.

(3) A provision in a lease agreement which (i) prohibits a transfer of a right to damages for default with respect to the whole lease contract or of a right to payment arising out of the transferor's due performance of the transferor's entire obligation, or (ii) makes such a transfer an event of default, is not enforceable, and such a transfer is not a transfer that materially impairs the prospect of obtaining return performance by, materially changes the duty of, or materially

increases the burden or risk imposed on, the other party to the lease contract within the purview of subsection (4).

(4) Subject to subsection (3) and Section 9–407:

(a) if a transfer is made which is made an event of default under a lease agreement, the party to the lease contract not making the transfer, unless that party waives the default or otherwise agrees, has the rights and remedies described in Section 2A–501(2);

(b) if paragraph (a) is not applicable and if a transfer is made that (i) is prohibited under a lease agreement or (ii) materially impairs the prospect of obtaining return performance by, materially changes the duty of, or materially increases the burden or risk imposed on, the other party to the lease contract, unless the party not making the transfer agrees at any time to the transfer in the lease contract or otherwise, then, except as limited by contract, (i) the transferor is liable to the party not making the transfer for damages caused by the transfer to the extent that the damages could not reasonably be prevented by the party not making the transfer and (ii) a court having jurisdiction may grant other appropriate relief, including cancellation of the lease contract or an injunction against the transfer.

(5) A transfer of "the lease" or of "all my rights under the lease", or a transfer in similar general terms, is a transfer of rights and, unless the language or the circumstances, as in a transfer for security, indicate the contrary, the transfer is a delegation of duties by the transferor to the transferee. Acceptance by the transferee constitutes a promise by the transferee to perform those duties. The promise is enforceable by either the transferor or the other party to the lease contract.

(6) Unless otherwise agreed by the lessor and the lessee, a delegation of performance does not relieve the transferor as against the other party of any duty to perform or of any liability for default.

(7) In a consumer lease, to prohibit the transfer of an interest of a party under the lease contract or to make a transfer an event of default, the language must be specific, by a writing, and conspicuous.

As amended in 1990 and 1999.

§ 2A–304. Subsequent Lease of Goods by Lessor.

(1) Subject to Section 2A–303, a subsequent lessee from a lessor of goods under an existing lease contract obtains, to the extent of the leasehold interest transferred, the leasehold interest in the goods that the lessor had or had power to transfer, and except as provided in subsection (2) and Section 2A–527(4), takes subject to the existing lease contract. A lessor with voidable title has power to transfer a good leasehold interest to a good faith subsequent lessee for value, but only to the extent set forth in the preceding sentence. If goods have been delivered under a transaction of purchase the lessor has that power even though:

(a) the lessor's transferor was deceived as to the identity of the lessor;

(b) the delivery was in exchange for a check which is later dishonored;

(c) it was agreed that the transaction was to be a "cash sale"; or

(d) the delivery was procured through fraud punishable as larcenous under the criminal law.

(2) A subsequent lessee in the ordinary course of business from a lessor who is a merchant dealing in goods of that kind to whom the goods were entrusted by the existing lessee of that lessor before the interest of the subsequent lessee became enforceable against that lessor obtains, to the extent of the leasehold interest transferred, all of that lessor's and the existing lessee's rights to the goods, and takes free of the existing lease contract.

(3) A subsequent lessee from the lessor of goods that are subject to an existing lease contract and are covered by a certificate of title issued under a statute of this State or of another jurisdiction takes no greater rights than those provided both by this section and by the certificate of title statute.

As amended in 1990.

§ 2A–305. Sale or Sublease of Goods by Lessee.

(1) Subject to the provisions of Section 2A–303, a buyer or sublessee from the lessee of goods under an existing lease contract obtains, to the extent of the interest transferred, the leasehold interest in the goods that the lessee had or had power to transfer, and except as provided in subsection (2) and Section 2A–511(4), takes subject to the existing lease contract. A lessee with a voidable leasehold interest has power to transfer a good leasehold interest to a good faith buyer for value or a good faith sublessee for value, but only to the extent set forth in the preceding sentence. When goods have been delivered under a transaction of lease the lessee has that power even though:

(a) the lessor was deceived as to the identity of the lessee;

(b) the delivery was in exchange for a check which is later dishonored; or

(c) the delivery was procured through fraud punishable as larcenous under the criminal law.

(2) A buyer in the ordinary course of business or a sublessee in the ordinary course of business from a lessee who is a merchant dealing in goods of that kind to whom the goods were entrusted by the lessor obtains, to the extent of the interest transferred, all of the lessor's and lessee's rights to the goods, and takes free of the existing lease contract.

(3) A buyer or sublessee from the lessee of goods that are subject to an existing lease contract and are covered by a certificate of title issued under a statute of this State or of another jurisdiction takes no greater rights than those provided both by this section and by the certificate of title statute.

§ 2A–306. Priority of Certain Liens Arising by Operation of Law.

If a person in the ordinary course of his [or her] business furnishes services or materials with respect to goods subject to a lease contract, a lien upon those goods in the possession of that person given by statute or rule of law for those materials or services takes priority over any interest of the lessor or lessee under the lease contract or this Article unless the lien is created by statute and the statute provides otherwise or unless the lien is created by rule of law and the rule of law provides otherwise.

§ 2A–307. Priority of Liens Arising by Attachment or Levy on, Security Interests in, and Other Claims to Goods.

(1) Except as otherwise provided in Section 2A–306, a creditor of a lessee takes subject to the lease contract.

(2) Except as otherwise provided in subsection (3) and in Sections 2A–306 and 2A–308, a creditor of a lessor takes subject to the lease contract unless the creditor holds a lien that attached to the goods before the lease contract became enforceable.

(3) Except as otherwise provided in Sections 9–317, 9–321, and 9–323, a lessee takes a leasehold interest subject to a security interest held by a creditor of the lessor.

As amended in 1990 and 1999.

§ 2A–308. Special Rights of Creditors.

(1) A creditor of a lessor in possession of goods subject to a lease contract may treat the lease contract as void if as against the creditor retention of possession by the lessor is fraudulent under any statute or rule of law, but retention of possession in good faith and current course of trade by the lessor for a commercially reasonable time after the lease contract becomes enforceable is not fraudulent.

(2) Nothing in this Article impairs the rights of creditors of a lessor if the lease contract (a) becomes enforceable, not in current course of trade but in satisfaction of or as security for a pre-existing claim for money, security, or the like, and (b) is made under circumstances which under any statute or rule of law apart from this Article would constitute the transaction a fraudulent transfer or voidable preference.

(3) A creditor of a seller may treat a sale or an identification of goods to a contract for sale as void if as against the creditor retention of possession by the seller is fraudulent under any statute or rule of law, but retention of possession of the goods pursuant to a lease contract entered into by the seller as lessee and the buyer as lessor in connection with the sale or identification of the goods is not fraudulent if the buyer bought for value and in good faith.

§ 2A–309. Lessor's and Lessee's Rights When Goods Become Fixtures.

(1) In this section:

(a) goods are "fixtures" when they become so related to particular real estate that an interest in them arises under real estate law;

(b) a "fixture filing" is the filing, in the office where a mortgage on the real estate would be filed or recorded, of a financing statement covering goods that are or are to become fixtures and conforming to the requirements of Section 9–502(a) and (b);

(c) a lease is a "purchase money lease" unless the lessee has possession or use of the goods or the right to possession or use of the goods before the lease agreement is enforceable;

(d) a mortgage is a "construction mortgage" to the extent it secures an obligation incurred for the construction of an improvement on land including the acquisition cost of the land, if the recorded writing so indicates; and

(e) "encumbrance" includes real estate mortgages and other liens on real estate and all other rights in real estate that are not ownership interests.

(2) Under this Article a lease may be of goods that are fixtures or may continue in goods that become fixtures, but no lease exists under this Article of ordinary building materials incorporated into an improvement on land.

(3) This Article does not prevent creation of a lease of fixtures pursuant to real estate law.

(4) The perfected interest of a lessor of fixtures has priority over a conflicting interest of an encumbrancer or owner of the real estate if:

(a) the lease is a purchase money lease, the conflicting interest of the encumbrancer or owner arises before the goods become fixtures, the interest of the lessor is perfected by a fixture filing before the goods become fixtures or within ten days thereafter, and the lessee has an interest of record in the real estate or is in possession of the real estate; or

(b) the interest of the lessor is perfected by a fixture filing before the interest of the encumbrancer or owner is of record, the lessor's interest has priority over any conflicting interest of a predecessor in title of the encumbrancer or owner, and the lessee has an interest of record in the real estate or is in possession of the real estate.

(5) The interest of a lessor of fixtures, whether or not perfected, has priority over the conflicting interest of an encumbrancer or owner of the real estate if:

(a) the fixtures are readily removable factory or office machines, readily removable equipment that is not primarily used or leased for use in the operation of the real estate, or readily removable replacements of domestic appliances that are goods subject to a consumer lease, and before the goods become fixtures the lease contract is enforceable; or

(b) the conflicting interest is a lien on the real estate obtained by legal or equitable proceedings after the lease contract is enforceable; or

(c) the encumbrancer or owner has consented in writing to the lease or has disclaimed an interest in the goods as fixtures; or

(d) the lessee has a right to remove the goods as against the encumbrancer or owner. If the lessee's right to remove terminates, the priority of the interest of the lessor continues for a reasonable time.

(6) Notwithstanding paragraph (4)(a) but otherwise subject to subsections (4) and (5), the interest of a lessor of fixtures, including the lessor's residual interest, is subordinate to the conflicting interest of an encumbrancer of the real estate under a construction mortgage recorded before the goods become fixtures if the goods become fixtures before the completion of the construction. To the extent given to refinance a construction mortgage, the conflicting interest of an encumbrancer of the real estate under a mortgage has this priority to the same extent as the encumbrancer of the real estate under the construction mortgage.

(7) In cases not within the preceding subsections, priority between the interest of a lessor of fixtures, including the lessor's residual interest, and the conflicting interest of an encumbrancer or owner of the real estate who is not the lessee is determined by the priority rules governing conflicting interests in real estate.

(8) If the interest of a lessor of fixtures, including the lessor's residual interest, has priority over all conflicting interests of all owners and encumbrancers of the real estate, the lessor or the lessee may (i) on default, expiration, termination, or cancellation of the lease agreement but subject to the agreement and this Article, or (ii) if necessary to enforce other rights and remedies of the lessor or lessee under this Article, remove the goods from the real estate, free and clear of all conflicting interests of all owners and encumbrancers of the real estate, but the lessor or lessee must reimburse any encumbrancer or owner of the real estate who is not the lessee and who has not otherwise agreed for the cost of repair of any physical injury, but not for any diminution in value of the real estate caused by the absence of the goods removed or by any necessity of replacing them. A person entitled to reimbursement may refuse permission to remove until the party seeking removal gives adequate security for the performance of this obligation.

(9) Even though the lease agreement does not create a security interest, the interest of a lessor of fixtures, including the lessor's residual interest, is perfected by filing a financing statement as a fixture filing for leased goods that are or are to become fixtures in accordance with the relevant provisions of the Article on Secured Transactions (Article 9).

As amended in 1990 and 1999.

§ 2A–310. Lessor's and Lessee's Rights When Goods Become Accessions.

(1) Goods are "accessions" when they are installed in or affixed to other goods.

(2) The interest of a lessor or a lessee under a lease contract entered into before the goods became accessions is superior to all interests in the whole except as stated in subsection (4).

(3) The interest of a lessor or a lessee under a lease contract entered into at the time or after the goods became accessions is superior to all subsequently acquired interests in the whole except as stated in subsection (4) but is subordinate to interests in the whole existing at the time the lease contract was made unless the holders of such interests in the whole have in writing consented to the lease or disclaimed an interest in the goods as part of the whole.

(4) The interest of a lessor or a lessee under a lease contract described in subsection (2) or (3) is subordinate to the interest of

   (a) a buyer in the ordinary course of business or a lessee in the ordinary course of business of any interest in the whole acquired after the goods became accessions; or

   (b) a creditor with a security interest in the whole perfected before the lease contract was made to the extent that the creditor makes subsequent advances without knowledge of the lease contract.

(5) When under subsections (2) or (3) and (4) a lessor or a lessee of accessions holds an interest that is superior to all interests in the whole, the lessor or the lessee may (a) on default, expiration, termination, or cancellation of the lease contract by the other party but subject to the provisions of the lease contract and this Article, or (b) if necessary to enforce his [or her] other rights and remedies under this Article, remove the goods from the whole, free and clear of all interests in the whole, but he [or she] must reimburse any holder of an interest in the whole who is not the lessee and who has not otherwise agreed for the cost of repair of any physical injury but not for any diminution in value of the whole caused by the absence of the goods removed or by any necessity for replacing them. A person entitled to reimbursement may refuse permission to remove until the party seeking removal gives adequate security for the performance of this obligation.

§ 2A–311. Priority Subject to Subordination.

Nothing in this Article prevents subordination by agreement by any person entitled to priority.

As added in 1990.

Part 4 Performance of Lease Contract: Repudiated, Substituted and Excused

§ 2A–401. Insecurity: Adequate Assurance of Performance.

(1) A lease contract imposes an obligation on each party that the other's expectation of receiving due performance will not be impaired.

(2) If reasonable grounds for insecurity arise with respect to the performance of either party, the insecure party may demand in writing adequate assurance of due performance. Until the insecure party receives that assurance, if commercially reasonable the insecure party may suspend any performance for which he [or she] has not already received the agreed return.

(3) A repudiation of the lease contract occurs if assurance of due performance adequate under the circumstances of the particular case is not provided to the insecure party within a reasonable time, not to exceed 30 days after receipt of a demand by the other party.

(4) Between merchants, the reasonableness of grounds for insecurity and the adequacy of any assurance offered must be determined according to commercial standards.

(5) Acceptance of any nonconforming delivery or payment does not prejudice the aggrieved party's right to demand adequate assurance of future performance.

§ 2A–402. Anticipatory Repudiation.

If either party repudiates a lease contract with respect to a performance not yet due under the lease contract, the loss of which performance will substantially impair the value of the lease contract to the other, the aggrieved party may:

(a) for a commercially reasonable time, await retraction of repudiation and performance by the repudiating party;

(b) make demand pursuant to Section 2A–401 and await assurance of future performance adequate under the circumstances of the particular case; or

(c) resort to any right or remedy upon default under the lease contract or this Article, even though the aggrieved party has notified the repudiating party that the aggrieved party would await the repudiating party's performance and assurance and has urged retraction. In addition, whether or not the aggrieved party is pursuing one of the foregoing remedies, the aggrieved party may suspend performance or, if the aggrieved party is the lessor, proceed in accordance with the provisions of this Article on the lessor's right to identify goods to the lease contract notwithstanding default or to salvage unfinished goods (Section 2A–524).

§ 2A–403. Retraction of Anticipatory Repudiation.

(1) Until the repudiating party's next performance is due, the repudiating party can retract the repudiation unless, since the repudiation, the aggrieved party has cancelled the lease contract or materially changed the aggrieved party's position or otherwise indicated that the aggrieved party considers the repudiation final.

(2) Retraction may be by any method that clearly indicates to the aggrieved party that the repudiating party intends to perform under the lease contract and includes any assurance demanded under Section 2A–401.

(3) Retraction reinstates a repudiating party's rights under a lease contract with due excuse and allowance to the aggrieved party for any delay occasioned by the repudiation.

§ 2A–404. Substituted Performance.

(1) If without fault of the lessee, the lessor and the supplier, the agreed berthing, loading, or unloading facilities fail or the agreed type of carrier becomes unavailable or the agreed manner of delivery otherwise becomes commercially impracticable, but a commercially reasonable substitute is available, the substitute performance must be tendered and accepted.

(2) If the agreed means or manner of payment fails because of domestic or foreign governmental regulation:

(a) the lessor may withhold or stop delivery or cause the supplier to withhold or stop delivery unless the lessee provides a means or manner of payment that is commercially a substantial equivalent; and

(b) if delivery has already been taken, payment by the means or in the manner provided by the regulation discharges the lessee's obligation unless the regulation is discriminatory, oppressive, or predatory.

§ 2A–405. Excused Performance.

Subject to Section 2A–404 on substituted performance, the following rules apply:

(a) Delay in delivery or nondelivery in whole or in part by a lessor or a supplier who complies with paragraphs (b) and (c) is not a default under the lease contract if performance as agreed has been made impracticable by the occurrence of a contingency the nonoccurrence of which was a basic assumption on which the lease contract was made or by compliance in good faith with any applicable foreign or domestic governmental regulation or order, whether or not the regulation or order later proves to be invalid.

(b) If the causes mentioned in paragraph (a) affect only part of the lessor's or the supplier's capacity to perform, he [or she] shall allocate production and deliveries among his [or her] customers but at his [or her] option may include regular customers not then under contract for sale or lease as well as his [or her] own requirements for further manufacture. He [or she] may so allocate in any manner that is fair and reasonable.

(c) The lessor seasonably shall notify the lessee and in the case of a finance lease the supplier seasonably shall notify the lessor and the lessee, if known, that there will be delay or nondelivery and, if allocation is required under paragraph (b), of the estimated quota thus made available for the lessee.

§ 2A–406. Procedure on Excused Performance.

(1) If the lessee receives notification of a material or indefinite delay or an allocation justified under Section 2A–405, the lessee may by written notification to the lessor as to any goods involved, and with respect to all of the goods if under an installment lease contract the value of the whole lease contract is substantially impaired (Section 2A–510):

(a) terminate the lease contract (Section 2A–505(2)); or

(b) except in a finance lease that is not a consumer lease, modify the lease contract by accepting the available quota in substitution, with due allowance from the rent payable for the balance of the lease term for the deficiency but without further right against the lessor.

(2) If, after receipt of a notification from the lessor under Section 2A–405, the lessee fails so to modify the lease agreement within a reasonable time not exceeding 30 days, the lease contract lapses with respect to any deliveries affected.

§ 2A–407. Irrevocable Promises: Finance Leases.

(1) In the case of a finance lease that is not a consumer lease the lessee's promises under the lease contract become irrevocable and independent upon the lessee's acceptance of the goods.

(2) A promise that has become irrevocable and independent under subsection (1):

(a) is effective and enforceable between the parties, and by or against third parties including assignees of the parties, and

(b) is not subject to cancellation, termination, modification, repudiation, excuse, or substitution without the consent of the party to whom the promise runs.

(3) This section does not affect the validity under any other law of a covenant in any lease contract making the lessee's promises irrevocable and independent upon the lessee's acceptance of the goods.

As amended in 1990.

Part 5 Default
A. In General
§ 2A–501. Default: Procedure.

(1) Whether the lessor or the lessee is in default under a lease contract is determined by the lease agreement and this Article.

(2) If the lessor or the lessee is in default under the lease contract, the party seeking enforcement has rights and remedies as provided in this Article and, except as limited by this Article, as provided in the lease agreement.

(3) If the lessor or the lessee is in default under the lease contract, the party seeking enforcement may reduce the party's claim to judgment, or otherwise enforce the lease contract by self-help or any available judicial procedure or nonjudicial procedure, including administrative proceeding, arbitration, or the like, in accordance with this Article.

(4) Except as otherwise provided in Section 1–106(1) or this Article or the lease agreement, the rights and remedies referred to in subsections (2) and (3) are cumulative.

(5) If the lease agreement covers both real property and goods, the party seeking enforcement may proceed under this Part as to the goods, or under other applicable law as to both the real property and the goods in accordance with that party's rights and remedies in respect of the real property, in which case this Part does not apply.

As amended in 1990.

§ 2A–502. Notice After Default.

Except as otherwise provided in this Article or the lease agreement, the lessor or lessee in default under the lease contract is not entitled to notice of default or notice of enforcement from the other party to the lease agreement.

§ 2A–503. Modification or Impairment of Rights and Remedies.

(1) Except as otherwise provided in this Article, the lease agreement may include rights and remedies for default in addition to or in substitution for those provided in this Article and may limit or alter the measure of damages recoverable under this Article.

(2) Resort to a remedy provided under this Article or in the lease agreement is optional unless the remedy is expressly agreed to be exclusive. If circumstances cause an exclusive or limited remedy to fail of its essential purpose, or provision for an exclusive remedy is unconscionable, remedy may be had as provided in this Article.

(3) Consequential damages may be liquidated under Section 2A–504, or may otherwise be limited, altered, or excluded unless the limitation, alteration, or exclusion is unconscionable. Limitation, alteration, or exclusion of consequential damages for injury to the person in the case of consumer goods is prima facie unconscionable but limitation, alteration, or exclusion of damages where the loss is commercial is not prima facie unconscionable.

(4) Rights and remedies on default by the lessor or the lessee with respect to any obligation or promise collateral or ancillary to the lease contract are not impaired by this Article.

As amended in 1990.

§ 2A-504. Liquidation of Damages.

(1) Damages payable by either party for default, or any other act or omission, including indemnity for loss or diminution of anticipated tax benefits or loss or damage to lessor's residual interest, may be liquidated in the lease agreement but only at an amount or by a formula that is reasonable in light of the then anticipated harm caused by the default or other act or omission.

(2) If the lease agreement provides for liquidation of damages, and such provision does not comply with subsection (1), or such provision is an exclusive or limited remedy that circumstances cause to fail of its essential purpose, remedy may be had as provided in this Article.

(3) If the lessor justifiably withholds or stops delivery of goods because of the lessee's default or insolvency (Section 2A-525 or 2A-526), the lessee is entitled to restitution of any amount by which the sum of his [or her] payments exceeds:

(a) the amount to which the lessor is entitled by virtue of terms liquidating the lessor's damages in accordance with subsection (1); or

(b) in the absence of those terms, 20 percent of the then present value of the total rent the lessee was obligated to pay for the balance of the lease term, or, in the case of a consumer lease, the lesser of such amount or $500.

(4) A lessee's right to restitution under subsection (3) is subject to offset to the extent the lessor establishes:

(a) a right to recover damages under the provisions of this Article other than subsection (1); and

(b) the amount or value of any benefits received by the lessee directly or indirectly by reason of the lease contract.

§ 2A-505. Cancellation and Termination and Effect of Cancellation, Termination, Rescission, or Fraud on Rights and Remedies.

(1) On cancellation of the lease contract, all obligations that are still executory on both sides are discharged, but any right based on prior default or performance survives, and the cancelling party also retains any remedy for default of the whole lease contract or any unperformed balance.

(2) On termination of the lease contract, all obligations that are still executory on both sides are discharged but any right based on prior default or performance survives.

(3) Unless the contrary intention clearly appears, expressions of "cancellation," "rescission," or the like of the lease contract may not be construed as a renunciation or discharge of any claim in damages for an antecedent default.

(4) Rights and remedies for material misrepresentation or fraud include all rights and remedies available under this Article for default.

(5) Neither rescission nor a claim for rescission of the lease contract nor rejection or return of the goods may bar or be deemed inconsistent with a claim for damages or other right or remedy.

§ 2A-506. Statute of Limitations.

(1) An action for default under a lease contract, including breach of warranty or indemnity, must be commenced within 4 years after the cause of action accrued. By the original lease contract the parties may reduce the period of limitation to not less than one year.

(2) A cause of action for default accrues when the act or omission on which the default or breach of warranty is based is or should have been discovered by the aggrieved party, or when the default occurs, whichever is later. A cause of action for indemnity accrues when the act or omission on which the claim for indemnity is based is or should have been discovered by the indemnified party, whichever is later.

(3) If an action commenced within the time limited by subsection (1) is so terminated as to leave available a remedy by another action for the same default or breach of warranty or indemnity, the other action may be commenced after the expiration of the time limited and within 6 months after the termination of the first action unless the termination resulted from voluntary discontinuance or from dismissal for failure or neglect to prosecute.

(4) This section does not alter the law on tolling of the statute of limitations nor does it apply to causes of action that have accrued before this Article becomes effective.

§ 2A-507. Proof of Market Rent: Time and Place.

(1) Damages based on market rent (Section 2A-519 or 2A-528) are determined according to the rent for the use of the goods concerned for a lease term identical to the remaining lease term of the original lease agreement and prevailing at the times specified in Sections 2A-519 and 2A-528.

(2) If evidence of rent for the use of the goods concerned for a lease term identical to the remaining lease term of the original lease agreement and prevailing at the times or places described in this Article is not readily available, the rent prevailing within any reasonable time before or after the time described or at any other place or for a different lease term which in commercial judgment or under usage of trade would serve as a reasonable substitute for the one described may be used, making any proper allowance for the difference, including the cost of transporting the goods to or from the other place.

(3) Evidence of a relevant rent prevailing at a time or place or for a lease term other than the one described in this Article offered by one party is not admissible unless and until he [or she] has given the other party notice the court finds sufficient to prevent unfair surprise.

(4) If the prevailing rent or value of any goods regularly leased in any established market is in issue, reports in official publications or trade journals or in newspapers or periodicals of general circulation published as the reports of that market are admissible in evidence. The circumstances of the preparation of the report may be shown to affect its weight but not its admissibility.

As amended in 1990.

B. Default by Lessor

§ 2A-508. Lessee's Remedies.

(1) If a lessor fails to deliver the goods in conformity to the lease contract (Section 2A-509) or repudiates the lease contract (Section 2A-402), or a lessee rightfully rejects the goods (Section 2A-509) or justifiably revokes acceptance of the goods (Section 2A-517), then with respect to any goods involved, and with respect to all of the goods if under an installment lease contract the value of the whole

lease contract is substantially impaired (Section 2A–510), the lessor is in default under the lease contract and the lessee may:

(a) cancel the lease contract (Section 2A–505(1));

(b) recover so much of the rent and security as has been paid and is just under the circumstances;

(c) cover and recover damages as to all goods affected whether or not they have been identified to the lease contract (Sections 2A–518 and 2A–520), or recover damages for nondelivery (Sections 2A–519 and 2A–520);

(d) exercise any other rights or pursue any other remedies provided in the lease contract.

(2) If a lessor fails to deliver the goods in conformity to the lease contract or repudiates the lease contract, the lessee may also:

(a) if the goods have been identified, recover them (Section 2A–522); or

(b) in a proper case, obtain specific performance or replevy the goods (Section 2A–521).

(3) If a lessor is otherwise in default under a lease contract, the lessee may exercise the rights and pursue the remedies provided in the lease contract, which may include a right to cancel the lease, and in Section 2A–519(3).

(4) If a lessor has breached a warranty, whether express or implied, the lessee may recover damages (Section 2A–519(4)).

(5) On rightful rejection or justifiable revocation of acceptance, a lessee has a security interest in goods in the lessee's possession or control for any rent and security that has been paid and any expenses reasonably incurred in their inspection, receipt, transportation, and care and custody and may hold those goods and dispose of them in good faith and in a commercially reasonable manner, subject to Section 2A–527(5).

(6) Subject to the provisions of Section 2A–407, a lessee, on notifying the lessor of the lessee's intention to do so, may deduct all or any part of the damages resulting from any default under the lease contract from any part of the rent still due under the same lease contract.

As amended in 1990.

§ 2A–509. Lessee's Rights on Improper Delivery; Rightful Rejection.

(1) Subject to the provisions of Section 2A–510 on default in installment lease contracts, if the goods or the tender or delivery fail in any respect to conform to the lease contract, the lessee may reject or accept the goods or accept any commercial unit or units and reject the rest of the goods.

(2) Rejection of goods is ineffective unless it is within a reasonable time after tender or delivery of the goods and the lessee seasonably notifies the lessor.

§ 2A–510. Installment Lease Contracts: Rejection and Default.

(1) Under an installment lease contract a lessee may reject any delivery that is nonconforming if the nonconformity substantially impairs the value of that delivery and cannot be cured or the nonconformity is a defect in the required documents; but if the nonconformity does not fall within subsection (2) and the lessor or the supplier gives adequate assurance of its cure, the lessee must accept that delivery.

(2) Whenever nonconformity or default with respect to one or more deliveries substantially impairs the value of the installment lease contract as a whole there is a default with respect to the whole. But, the aggrieved party reinstates the installment lease contract as a whole if the aggrieved party accepts a nonconforming delivery without seasonably notifying of cancellation or brings an action with respect only to past deliveries or demands performance as to future deliveries.

§ 2A–511. Merchant Lessee's Duties as to Rightfully Rejected Goods.

(1) Subject to any security interest of a lessee (Section 2A–508(5)), if a lessor or a supplier has no agent or place of business at the market of rejection, a merchant lessee, after rejection of goods in his [or her] possession or control, shall follow any reasonable instructions received from the lessor or the supplier with respect to the goods. In the absence of those instructions, a merchant lessee shall make reasonable efforts to sell, lease, or otherwise dispose of the goods for the lessor's account if they threaten to decline in value speedily. Instructions are not reasonable if on demand indemnity for expenses is not forthcoming.

(2) If a merchant lessee (subsection (1)) or any other lessee (Section 2A–512) disposes of goods, he [or she] is entitled to reimbursement either from the lessor or the supplier or out of the proceeds for reasonable expenses of caring for and disposing of the goods and, if the expenses include no disposition commission, to such commission as is usual in the trade, or if there is none, to a reasonable sum not exceeding 10 percent of the gross proceeds.

(3) In complying with this section or Section 2A–512, the lessee is held only to good faith. Good faith conduct hereunder is neither acceptance or conversion nor the basis of an action for damages.

(4) A purchaser who purchases in good faith from a lessee pursuant to this section or Section 2A–512 takes the goods free of any rights of the lessor and the supplier even though the lessee fails to comply with one or more of the requirements of this Article.

§ 2A–512. Lessee's Duties as to Rightfully Rejected Goods.

(1) Except as otherwise provided with respect to goods that threaten to decline in value speedily (Section 2A–511) and subject to any security interest of a lessee (Section 2A–508(5)):

(a) the lessee, after rejection of goods in the lessee's possession, shall hold them with reasonable care at the lessor's or the supplier's disposition for a reasonable time after the lessee's seasonable notification of rejection;

(b) if the lessor or the supplier gives no instructions within a reasonable time after notification of rejection, the lessee may store the rejected goods for the lessor's or the supplier's account or ship them to the lessor or the supplier or dispose of them for the lessor's or the supplier's account with reimbursement in the manner provided in Section 2A–511; but

(c) the lessee has no further obligations with regard to goods rightfully rejected.

(2) Action by the lessee pursuant to subsection (1) is not acceptance or conversion.

§ 2A–513. Cure by Lessor of Improper Tender or Delivery; Replacement.

(1) If any tender or delivery by the lessor or the supplier is rejected because nonconforming and the time for performance has not yet expired, the lessor or the supplier may seasonably notify the lessee of the lessor's or the supplier's intention to cure and may then make a conforming delivery within the time provided in the lease contract.

(2) If the lessee rejects a nonconforming tender that the lessor or the supplier had reasonable grounds to believe would be acceptable with or without money allowance, the lessor or the supplier may have a further reasonable time to substitute a conforming tender if he [or she] seasonably notifies the lessee.

§ 2A-514. Waiver of Lessee's Objections.

(1) In rejecting goods, a lessee's failure to state a particular defect that is ascertainable by reasonable inspection precludes the lessee from relying on the defect to justify rejection or to establish default:

  (a) if, stated seasonably, the lessor or the supplier could have cured it (Section 2A-513); or

  (b) between merchants if the lessor or the supplier after rejection has made a request in writing for a full and final written statement of all defects on which the lessee proposes to rely.

(2) A lessee's failure to reserve rights when paying rent or other consideration against documents precludes recovery of the payment for defects apparent on the face of the documents.

§ 2A-515. Acceptance of Goods.

(1) Acceptance of goods occurs after the lessee has had a reasonable opportunity to inspect the goods and

  (a) the lessee signifies or acts with respect to the goods in a manner that signifies to the lessor or the supplier that the goods are conforming or that the lessee will take or retain them in spite of their nonconformity; or

  (b) the lessee fails to make an effective rejection of the goods (Section 2A-509(2)).

(2) Acceptance of a part of any commercial unit is acceptance of that entire unit.

§ 2A-516. Effect of Acceptance of Goods; Notice of Default; Burden of Establishing Default after Acceptance; Notice of Claim or Litigation to Person Answerable Over.

(1) A lessee must pay rent for any goods accepted in accordance with the lease contract, with due allowance for goods rightfully rejected or not delivered.

(2) A lessee's acceptance of goods precludes rejection of the goods accepted. In the case of a finance lease, if made with knowledge of a nonconformity, acceptance cannot be revoked because of it. In any other case, if made with knowledge of a nonconformity, acceptance cannot be revoked because of it unless the acceptance was on the reasonable assumption that the nonconformity would be seasonably cured. Acceptance does not of itself impair any other remedy provided by this Article or the lease agreement for nonconformity.

(3) If a tender has been accepted:

  (a) within a reasonable time after the lessee discovers or should have discovered any default, the lessee shall notify the lessor and the supplier, if any, or be barred from any remedy against the party notified;

  (b) except in the case of a consumer lease, within a reasonable time after the lessee receives notice of litigation for infringement or the like (Section 2A-211) the lessee shall notify the lessor or be barred from any remedy over for liability established by the litigation; and

  (c) the burden is on the lessee to establish any default.

(4) If a lessee is sued for breach of a warranty or other obligation for which a lessor or a supplier is answerable over the following apply:

  (a) The lessee may give the lessor or the supplier, or both, written notice of the litigation. If the notice states that the person notified may come in and defend and that if the person notified does not do so that person will be bound in any action against that person by the lessee by any determination of fact common to the two litigations, then unless the person notified after seasonable receipt of the notice does come in and defend that person is so bound.

  (b) The lessor or the supplier may demand in writing that the lessee turn over control of the litigation including settlement if the claim is one for infringement or the like (Section 2A-211) or else be barred from any remedy over. If the demand states that the lessor or the supplier agrees to bear all expense and to satisfy any adverse judgment, then unless the lessee after seasonable receipt of the demand does turn over control the lessee is so barred.

(5) Subsections (3) and (4) apply to any obligation of a lessee to hold the lessor or the supplier harmless against infringement or the like (Section 2A-211).

As amended in 1990.

§ 2A-517. Revocation of Acceptance of Goods.

(1) A lessee may revoke acceptance of a lot or commercial unit whose nonconformity substantially impairs its value to the lessee if the lessee has accepted it:

  (a) except in the case of a finance lease, on the reasonable assumption that its nonconformity would be cured and it has not been seasonably cured; or

  (b) without discovery of the nonconformity if the lessee's acceptance was reasonably induced either by the lessor's assurances or, except in the case of a finance lease, by the difficulty of discovery before acceptance.

(2) Except in the case of a finance lease that is not a consumer lease, a lessee may revoke acceptance of a lot or commercial unit if the lessor defaults under the lease contract and the default substantially impairs the value of that lot or commercial unit to the lessee.

(3) If the lease agreement so provides, the lessee may revoke acceptance of a lot or commercial unit because of other defaults by the lessor.

(4) Revocation of acceptance must occur within a reasonable time after the lessee discovers or should have discovered the ground for it and before any substantial change in condition of the goods which is not caused by the nonconformity. Revocation is not effective until the lessee notifies the lessor.

(5) A lessee who so revokes has the same rights and duties with regard to the goods involved as if the lessee had rejected them.

As amended in 1990.

§ 2A-518. Cover; Substitute Goods.

(1) After a default by a lessor under the lease contract of the type described in Section 2A-508(1), or, if agreed, after other default by the lessor, the lessee may cover by making any purchase or lease of or contract to purchase or lease goods in substitution for those due from the lessor.

(2) Except as otherwise provided with respect to damages liquidated in the lease agreement (Section 2A-504) or otherwise determined pursuant to agreement of the parties (Sections 1-102(3) and 2A-503), if a lessee's cover is by lease agreement substantially similar to the original lease agreement and the new lease agreement is made

in good faith and in a commercially reasonable manner, the lessee may recover from the lessor as damages (i) the present value, as of the date of the commencement of the term of the new lease agreement, of the rent under the new lease agreement applicable to that period of the new lease term which is comparable to the then remaining term of the original lease agreement minus the present value as of the same date of the total rent for the then remaining lease term of the original lease agreement, and (ii) any incidental or consequential damages, less expenses saved in consequence of the lessor's default.

(3) If a lessee's cover is by lease agreement that for any reason does not qualify for treatment under subsection (2), or is by purchase or otherwise, the lessee may recover from the lessor as if the lessee had elected not to cover and Section 2A–519 governs.

As amended in 1990.

§ 2A–519. Lessee's Damages for Non-Delivery, Repudiation, Default, and Breach of Warranty in Regard to Accepted Goods.

(1) Except as otherwise provided with respect to damages liquidated in the lease agreement (Section 2A–504) or otherwise determined pursuant to agreement of the parties (Sections 1–102(3) and 2A–503), if a lessee elects not to cover or a lessee elects to cover and the cover is by lease agreement that for any reason does not qualify for treatment under Section 2A–518(2), or is by purchase or otherwise, the measure of damages for non-delivery or repudiation by the lessor or for rejection or revocation of acceptance by the lessee is the present value, as of the date of the default, of the then market rent minus the present value as of the same date of the original rent, computed for the remaining lease term of the original lease agreement, together with incidental and consequential damages, less expenses saved in consequence of the lessor's default.

(2) Market rent is to be determined as of the place for tender or, in cases of rejection after arrival or revocation of acceptance, as of the place of arrival.

(3) Except as otherwise agreed, if the lessee has accepted goods and given notification (Section 2A–516(3)), the measure of damages for non-conforming tender or delivery or other default by a lessor is the loss resulting in the ordinary course of events from the lessor's default as determined in any manner that is reasonable together with incidental and consequential damages, less expenses saved in consequence of the lessor's default.

(4) Except as otherwise agreed, the measure of damages for breach of warranty is the present value at the time and place of acceptance of the difference between the value of the use of the goods accepted and the value if they had been as warranted for the lease term, unless special circumstances show proximate damages of a different amount, together with incidental and consequential damages, less expenses saved in consequence of the lessor's default or breach of warranty.

As amended in 1990.

§ 2A–520. Lessee's Incidental and Consequential Damages.

(1) Incidental damages resulting from a lessor's default include expenses reasonably incurred in inspection, receipt, transportation, and care and custody of goods rightfully rejected or goods the acceptance of which is justifiably revoked, any commercially reasonable charges, expenses or commissions in connection with effecting cover, and any other reasonable expense incident to the default.

(2) Consequential damages resulting from a lessor's default include:

(a) any loss resulting from general or particular requirements and needs of which the lessor at the time of contracting had reason to know and which could not reasonably be prevented by cover or otherwise; and

(b) injury to person or property proximately resulting from any breach of warranty.

§ 2A–521. Lessee's Right to Specific Performance or Replevin.

(1) Specific performance may be decreed if the goods are unique or in other proper circumstances.

(2) A decree for specific performance may include any terms and conditions as to payment of the rent, damages, or other relief that the court deems just.

(3) A lessee has a right of replevin, detinue, sequestration, claim and delivery, or the like for goods identified to the lease contract if after reasonable effort the lessee is unable to effect cover for those goods or the circumstances reasonably indicate that the effort will be unavailing.

§ 2A–522. Lessee's Right to Goods on Lessor's Insolvency.

(1) Subject to subsection (2) and even though the goods have not been shipped, a lessee who has paid a part or all of the rent and security for goods identified to a lease contract (Section 2A–217) on making and keeping good a tender of any unpaid portion of the rent and security due under the lease contract may recover the goods identified from the lessor if the lessor becomes insolvent within 10 days after receipt of the first installment of rent and security.

(2) A lessee acquires the right to recover goods identified to a lease contract only if they conform to the lease contract.

C. Default by Lessee

§ 2A–523. Lessor's Remedies.

(1) If a lessee wrongfully rejects or revokes acceptance of goods or fails to make a payment when due or repudiates with respect to a part or the whole, then, with respect to any goods involved, and with respect to all of the goods if under an installment lease contract the value of the whole lease contract is substantially impaired (Section 2A–510), the lessee is in default under the lease contract and the lessor may:

(a) cancel the lease contract (Section 2A–505(1));

(b) proceed respecting goods not identified to the lease contract (Section 2A–524);

(c) withhold delivery of the goods and take possession of goods previously delivered (Section 2A–525);

(d) stop delivery of the goods by any bailee (Section 2A–526);

(e) dispose of the goods and recover damages (Section 2A–527), or retain the goods and recover damages (Section 2A–528), or in a proper case recover rent (Section 2A–529)

(f) exercise any other rights or pursue any other remedies provided in the lease contract.

(2) If a lessor does not fully exercise a right or obtain a remedy to which the lessor is entitled under subsection (1), the lessor may recover the loss resulting in the ordinary course of events from the lessee's default as determined in any reasonable manner, together with incidental damages, less expenses saved in consequence of the lessee's default.

(3) If a lessee is otherwise in default under a lease contract, the lessor may exercise the rights and pursue the remedies provided in the lease contract, which may include a right to cancel the lease. In addition, unless otherwise provided in the lease contract:

(a) if the default substantially impairs the value of the lease contract to the lessor, the lessor may exercise the rights and pursue the remedies provided in subsections (1) or (2); or

(b) if the default does not substantially impair the value of the lease contract to the lessor, the lessor may recover as provided in subsection (2).

As amended in 1990.

§ 2A–524. Lessor's Right to Identify Goods to Lease Contract.

(1) After default by the lessee under the lease contract of the type described in Section 2A–523(1) or 2A–523(3)(a) or, if agreed, after other default by the lessee, the lessor may:

(a) identify to the lease contract conforming goods not already identified if at the time the lessor learned of the default they were in the lessor's or the supplier's possession or control; and

(b) dispose of goods (Section 2A–527(1)) that demonstrably have been intended for the particular lease contract even though those goods are unfinished.

(2) If the goods are unfinished, in the exercise of reasonable commercial judgment for the purposes of avoiding loss and of effective realization, an aggrieved lessor or the supplier may either complete manufacture and wholly identify the goods to the lease contract or cease manufacture and lease, sell, or otherwise dispose of the goods for scrap or salvage value or proceed in any other reasonable manner.

As amended in 1990.

§ 2A–525. Lessor's Right to Possession of Goods.

(1) If a lessor discovers the lessee to be insolvent, the lessor may refuse to deliver the goods.

(2) After a default by the lessee under the lease contract of the type described in Section 2A–523(1) or 2A–523(3)(a) or, if agreed, after other default by the lessee, the lessor has the right to take possession of the goods. If the lease contract so provides, the lessor may require the lessee to assemble the goods and make them available to the lessor at a place to be designated by the lessor which is reasonably convenient to both parties. Without removal, the lessor may render unusable any goods employed in trade or business, and may dispose of goods on the lessee's premises (Section 2A–527).

(3) The lessor may proceed under subsection (2) without judicial process if that can be done without breach of the peace or the lessor may proceed by action.

As amended in 1990.

§ 2A–526. Lessor's Stoppage of Delivery in Transit or Otherwise.

(1) A lessor may stop delivery of goods in the possession of a carrier or other bailee if the lessor discovers the lessee to be insolvent and may stop delivery of carload, truckload, planeload, or larger shipments of express or freight if the lessee repudiates or fails to make a payment due before delivery, whether for rent, security or otherwise under the lease contract, or for any other reason the lessor has a right to withhold or take possession of the goods.

(2) In pursuing its remedies under subsection (1), the lessor may stop delivery until

(a) receipt of the goods by the lessee;

(b) acknowledgment to the lessee by any bailee of the goods, except a carrier, that the bailee holds the goods for the lessee; or

(c) such an acknowledgment to the lessee by a carrier via reshipment or as warehouseman.

(3) (a) To stop delivery, a lessor shall so notify as to enable the bailee by reasonable diligence to prevent delivery of the goods.

(b) After notification, the bailee shall hold and deliver the goods according to the directions of the lessor, but the lessor is liable to the bailee for any ensuing charges or damages.

(c) A carrier who has issued a nonnegotiable bill of lading is not obliged to obey a notification to stop received from a person other than the consignor.

§ 2A–527. Lessor's Rights to Dispose of Goods.

(1) After a default by a lessee under the lease contract of the type described in Section 2A–523(1) or 2A–523(3)(a) or after the lessor refuses to deliver or takes possession of goods (Section 2A–525 or 2A–526), or, if agreed, after other default by a lessee, the lessor may dispose of the goods concerned or the undelivered balance thereof by lease, sale, or otherwise.

(2) Except as otherwise provided with respect to damages liquidated in the lease agreement (Section 2A–504) or otherwise determined pursuant to agreement of the parties (Sections 1–102(3) and 2A–503), if the disposition is by lease agreement substantially similar to the original lease agreement and the new lease agreement is made in good faith and in a commercially reasonable manner, the lessor may recover from the lessee as damages (i) accrued and unpaid rent as of the date of the commencement of the term of the new lease agreement, (ii) the present value, as of the same date, of the total rent for the then remaining lease term of the original lease agreement minus the present value, as of the same date, of the rent under the new lease agreement applicable to that period of the new lease term which is comparable to the then remaining term of the original lease agreement, and (iii) any incidental damages allowed under Section 2A–530, less expenses saved in consequence of the lessee's default.

(3) If the lessor's disposition is by lease agreement that for any reason does not qualify for treatment under subsection (2), or is by sale or otherwise, the lessor may recover from the lessee as if the lessor had elected not to dispose of the goods and Section 2A–528 governs.

(4) A subsequent buyer or lessee who buys or leases from the lessor in good faith for value as a result of a disposition under this section takes the goods free of the original lease contract and any rights of the original lessee even though the lessor fails to comply with one or more of the requirements of this Article.

(5) The lessor is not accountable to the lessee for any profit made on any disposition. A lessee who has rightfully rejected or justifiably revoked acceptance shall account to the lessor for any excess over the amount of the lessee's security interest (Section 2A–508(5)).

As amended in 1990.

§ 2A–528. Lessor's Damages for Non-acceptance, Failure to Pay, Repudiation, or Other Default.

(1) Except as otherwise provided with respect to damages liquidated in the lease agreement (Section 2A–504) or otherwise determined

pursuant to agreement of the parties (Section 1–102(3) and 2A–503), if a lessor elects to retain the goods or a lessor elects to dispose of the goods and the disposition is by lease agreement that for any reason does not qualify for treatment under Section 2A–527(2), or is by sale or otherwise, the lessor may recover from the lessee as damages for a default of the type described in Section 2A–523(1) or 2A–523(3)(a), or if agreed, for other default of the lessee, (i) accrued and unpaid rent as of the date of the default if the lessee has never taken possession of the goods, or, if the lessee has taken possession of the goods, as of the date the lessor repossesses the goods or an earlier date on which the lessee makes a tender of the goods to the lessor, (ii) the present value as of the date determined under clause (i) of the total rent for the then remaining lease term of the original lease agreement minus the present value as of the same date of the market rent as the place where the goods are located computed for the same lease term, and (iii) any incidental damages allowed under Section 2A–530, less expenses saved in consequence of the lessee's default.

(2) If the measure of damages provided in subsection (1) is inadequate to put a lessor in as good a position as performance would have, the measure of damages is the present value of the profit, including reasonable overhead, the lessor would have made from full performance by the lessee, together with any incidental damages allowed under Section 2A–530, due allowance for costs reasonably incurred and due credit for payments or proceeds of disposition.

As amended in 1990.

§ 2A–529. Lessor's Action for the Rent.

(1) After default by the lessee under the lease contract of the type described in Section 2A–523(1) or 2A–523(3)(a) or, if agreed, after other default by the lessee, if the lessor complies with subsection (2), the lessor may recover from the lessee as damages:

> (a) for goods accepted by the lessee and not repossessed by or tendered to the lessor, and for conforming goods lost or damaged within a commercially reasonable time after risk of loss passes to the lessee (Section 2A–219), (i) accrued and unpaid rent as of the date of entry of judgment in favor of the lessor (ii) the present value as of the same date of the rent for the then remaining lease term of the lease agreement, and (iii) any incidental damages allowed under Section 2A–530, less expenses saved in consequence of the lessee's default; and

> (b) for goods identified to the lease contract if the lessor is unable after reasonable effort to dispose of them at a reasonable price or the circumstances reasonably indicate that effort will be unavailing, (i) accrued and unpaid rent as of the date of entry of judgment in favor of the lessor, (ii) the present value as of the same date of the rent for the then remaining lease term of the lease agreement, and (iii) any incidental damages allowed under Section 2A–530, less expenses saved in consequence of the lessee's default.

(2) Except as provided in subsection (3), the lessor shall hold for the lessee for the remaining lease term of the lease agreement any goods that have been identified to the lease contract and are in the lessor's control.

(3) The lessor may dispose of the goods at any time before collection of the judgment for damages obtained pursuant to subsection (1). If the disposition is before the end of the remaining lease term of the lease agreement, the lessor's recovery against the lessee for damages is governed by Section 2A–527 or Section 2A–528, and the lessor will cause an appropriate credit to be provided against a judgment for damages to the extent that the amount of the judgment exceeds the recovery available pursuant to Section 2A–527 or 2A–528.

(4) Payment of the judgment for damages obtained pursuant to subsection (1) entitles the lessee to the use and possession of the goods not then disposed of for the remaining lease term of and in accordance with the lease agreement.

(5) After default by the lessee under the lease contract of the type described in Section 2A–523(1) or Section 2A–523(3)(a) or, if agreed, after other default by the lessee, a lessor who is held not entitled to rent under this section must nevertheless be awarded damages for non-acceptance under Sections 2A–527 and 2A–528.

As amended in 1990.

§ 2A–530. Lessor's Incidental Damages.

Incidental damages to an aggrieved lessor include any commercially reasonable charges, expenses, or commissions incurred in stopping delivery, in the transportation, care and custody of goods after the lessee's default, in connection with return or disposition of the goods, or otherwise resulting from the default.

§ 2A–531. Standing to Sue Third Parties for Injury to Goods.

(1) If a third party so deals with goods that have been identified to a lease contract as to cause actionable injury to a party to the lease contract (a) the lessor has a right of action against the third party, and (b) the lessee also has a right of action against the third party if the lessee:

> (i) has a security interest in the goods;

> (ii) has an insurable interest in the goods; or

> (iii) bears the risk of loss under the lease contract or has since the injury assumed that risk as against the lessor and the goods have been converted or destroyed.

(2) If at the time of the injury the party plaintiff did not bear the risk of loss as against the other party to the lease contract and there is no arrangement between them for disposition of the recovery, his [or her] suit or settlement, subject to his [or her] own interest, is as a fiduciary for the other party to the lease contract.

(3) Either party with the consent of the other may sue for the benefit of whom it may concern.

§ 2A–532. Lessor's Rights to Residual Interest.

In addition to any other recovery permitted by this Article or other law, the lessor may recover from the lessee an amount that will fully compensate the lessor for any loss of or damage to the lessor's residual interest in the goods caused by the default of the lessee.

As added in 1990.

Revised Article 3
NEGOTIABLE INSTRUMENTS

Part 1 General Provisions and Definitions
§ 3–101. Short Title.

This Article may be cited as Uniform Commercial Code–Negotiable Instruments.

§ 3–102. Subject Matter.

(a) This Article applies to negotiable instruments. It does not apply to money, to payment orders governed by Article 4A, or to securities governed by Article 8.

(b) If there is conflict between this Article and Article 4 or 9, Articles 4 and 9 govern.

(c) Regulations of the Board of Governors of the Federal Reserve System and operating circulars of the Federal Reserve Banks supersede any inconsistent provision of this Article to the extent of the inconsistency.

§ 3–103.   Definitions.

(a) In this Article:

(1) "Acceptor" means a drawee who has accepted a draft.

(2) "Drawee" means a person ordered in a draft to make payment.

(3) "Drawer" means a person who signs or is identified in a draft as a person ordering payment.

(4) "Good faith" means honesty in fact and the observance of reasonable commercial standards of fair dealing.

(5) "Maker" means a person who signs or is identified in a note as a person undertaking to pay.

(6) "Order" means a written instruction to pay money signed by the person giving the instruction. The instruction may be addressed to any person, including the person giving the instruction, or to one or more persons jointly or in the alternative but not in succession. An authorization to pay is not an order unless the person authorized to pay is also instructed to pay.

(7) "Ordinary care" in the case of a person engaged in business means observance of reasonable commercial standards, prevailing in the area in which the person is located, with respect to the business in which the person is engaged. In the case of a bank that takes an instrument for processing for collection or payment by automated means, reasonable commercial standards do not require the bank to examine the instrument if the failure to examine does not violate the bank's prescribed procedures and the bank's procedures do not vary unreasonably from general banking usage not disapproved by this Article or Article 4.

(8) "Party" means a party to an instrument.

(9) "Promise" means a written undertaking to pay money signed by the person undertaking to pay. An acknowledgment of an obligation by the obligor is not a promise unless the obligor also undertakes to pay the obligation.

(10) "Prove" with respect to a fact means to meet the burden of establishing the fact (Section 1–201(8)).

(11) "Remitter" means a person who purchases an instrument from its issuer if the instrument is payable to an identified person other than the purchaser.

(b) [Other definitions' section references deleted.]

(c) [Other definitions' section references deleted.]

(d) In addition, Article 1 contains general definitions and principles of construction and interpretation applicable throughout this Article.

§ 3–104.   Negotiable Instrument.

(a) Except as provided in subsections (c) and (d), "negotiable instrument" means an unconditional promise or order to pay a fixed amount of money, with or without interest or other charges described in the promise or order, if it:

(1) is payable to bearer or to order at the time it is issued or first comes into possession of a holder;

(2) is payable on demand or at a definite time; and

(3) does not state any other undertaking or instruction by the person promising or ordering payment to do any act in addition to the payment of money, but the promise or order may contain (i) an undertaking or power to give, maintain, or protect collateral to secure payment, (ii) an authorization or power to the holder to confess judgment or realize on or dispose of collateral, or (iii) a waiver of the benefit of any law intended for the advantage or protection of an obligor.

(b) "Instrument" means a negotiable instrument.

(c) An order that meets all of the requirements of subsection (a), except paragraph (1), and otherwise falls within the definition of "check" in subsection (f) is a negotiable instrument and a check.

(d) A promise or order other than a check is not an instrument if, at the time it is issued or first comes into possession of a holder, it contains a conspicuous statement, however expressed, to the effect that the promise or order is not negotiable or is not an instrument governed by this Article.

(e) An instrument is a "note" if it is a promise and is a "draft" if it is an order. If an instrument falls within the definition of both "note" and "draft," a person entitled to enforce the instrument may treat it as either.

(f) "Check" means (i) a draft, other than a documentary draft, payable on demand and drawn on a bank or (ii) a cashier's check or teller's check. An instrument may be a check even though it is described on its face by another term, such as "money order."

(g) "Cashier's check" means a draft with respect to which the drawer and drawee are the same bank or branches of the same bank.

(h) "Teller's check" means a draft drawn by a bank (i) on another bank, or (ii) payable at or through a bank.

(i) "Traveler's check" means an instrument that (i) is payable on demand, (ii) is drawn on or payable at or through a bank, (iii) is designated by the term "traveler's check" or by a substantially similar term, and (iv) requires, as a condition to payment, a countersignature by a person whose specimen signature appears on the instrument.

(j) "Certificate of deposit" means an instrument containing an acknowledgment by a bank that a sum of money has been received by the bank and a promise by the bank to repay the sum of money. A certificate of deposit is a note of the bank.

§ 3–105.   Issue of Instrument.

(a) "Issue" means the first delivery of an instrument by the maker or drawer, whether to a holder or nonholder, for the purpose of giving rights on the instrument to any person.

(b) An unissued instrument, or an unissued incomplete instrument that is completed, is binding on the maker or drawer, but nonissuance is a defense. An instrument that is conditionally issued or is issued for a special purpose is binding on the maker or drawer, but failure of the condition or special purpose to be fulfilled is a defense.

(c) "Issuer" applies to issued and unissued instruments and means a maker or drawer of an instrument.

§ 3–106.   Unconditional Promise or Order.

(a) Except as provided in this section, for the purposes of Section 3–104(a), a promise or order is unconditional unless it states (i) an express condition to payment, (ii) that the promise or order is subject to or governed by another writing, or (iii) that rights or obligations with respect to the promise or order are stated in another writing. A reference to another writing does not of itself make the promise or order conditional.

(b) A promise or order is not made conditional (i) by a reference to another writing for a statement of rights with respect to collateral, prepayment, or acceleration, or (ii) because payment is limited to resort to a particular fund or source.

(c) If a promise or order requires, as a condition to payment, a countersignature by a person whose specimen signature appears on the promise or order, the condition does not make the promise or order conditional for the purposes of Section 3–104(a). If the person whose specimen signature appears on an instrument fails to countersign the instrument, the failure to countersign is a defense to the obligation of the issuer, but the failure does not prevent a transferee of the instrument from becoming a holder of the instrument.

(d) If a promise or order at the time it is issued or first comes into possession of a holder contains a statement, required by applicable statutory or administrative law, to the effect that the rights of a holder or transferee are subject to claims or defenses that the issuer could assert against the original payee, the promise or order is not thereby made conditional for the purposes of Section 3–104(a); but if the promise or order is an instrument, there cannot be a holder in due course of the instrument.

§ 3–107. Instrument Payable in Foreign Money.

Unless the instrument otherwise provides, an instrument that states the amount payable in foreign money may be paid in the foreign money or in an equivalent amount in dollars calculated by using the current bank-offered spot rate at the place of payment for the purchase of dollars on the day on which the instrument is paid.

§ 3–108. Payable on Demand or at Definite Time.

(a) A promise or order is "payable on demand" if it (i) states that it is payable on demand or at sight, or otherwise indicates that it is payable at the will of the holder, or (ii) does not state any time of payment.

(b) A promise or order is "payable at a definite time" if it is payable on elapse of a definite period of time after sight or acceptance or at a fixed date or dates or at a time or times readily ascertainable at the time the promise or order is issued, subject to rights of (i) prepayment, (ii) acceleration, (iii) extension at the option of the holder, or (iv) extension to a further definite time at the option of the maker or acceptor or automatically upon or after a specified act or event.

(c) If an instrument, payable at a fixed date, is also payable upon demand made before the fixed date, the instrument is payable on demand until the fixed date and, if demand for payment is not made before that date, becomes payable at a definite time on the fixed date.

§ 3–109. Payable to Bearer or to Order.

(a) A promise or order is payable to bearer if it:

(1) states that it is payable to bearer or to the order of bearer or otherwise indicates that the person in possession of the promise or order is entitled to payment;

(2) does not state a payee; or

(3) states that it is payable to or to the order of cash or otherwise indicates that it is not payable to an identified person.

(b) A promise or order that is not payable to bearer is payable to order if it is payable (i) to the order of an identified person or (ii) to an identified person or order. A promise or order that is payable to order is payable to the identified person.

(c) An instrument payable to bearer may become payable to an identified person if it is specially indorsed pursuant to Section 3–205(a). An instrument payable to an identified person may become payable to bearer if it is indorsed in blank pursuant to Section 3–205(b).

§ 3–110. Identification of Person to Whom Instrument Is Payable.

(a) The person to whom an instrument is initially payable is determined by the intent of the person, whether or not authorized, signing as, or in the name or behalf of, the issuer of the instrument. The instrument is payable to the person intended by the signer even if that person is identified in the instrument by a name or other identification that is not that of the intended person. If more than one person signs in the name or behalf of the issuer of an instrument and all the signers do not intend the same person as payee, the instrument is payable to any person intended by one or more of the signers.

(b) If the signature of the issuer of an instrument is made by automated means, such as a check-writing machine, the payee of the instrument is determined by the intent of the person who supplied the name or identification of the payee, whether or not authorized to do so.

(c) A person to whom an instrument is payable may be identified in any way, including by name, identifying number, office, or account number. For the purpose of determining the holder of an instrument, the following rules apply:

(1) If an instrument is payable to an account and the account is identified only by number, the instrument is payable to the person to whom the account is payable. If an instrument is payable to an account identified by number and by the name of a person, the instrument is payable to the named person, whether or not that person is the owner of the account identified by number.

(2) If an instrument is payable to:

(i) a trust, an estate, or a person described as trustee or representative of a trust or estate, the instrument is payable to the trustee, the representative, or a successor of either, whether or not the beneficiary or estate is also named;

(ii) a person described as agent or similar representative of a named or identified person, the instrument is payable to the represented person, the representative, or a successor of the representative;

(iii) a fund or organization that is not a legal entity, the instrument is payable to a representative of the members of the fund or organization; or

(iv) an office or to a person described as holding an office, the instrument is payable to the named person, the incumbent of the office, or a successor to the incumbent.

(d) If an instrument is payable to two or more persons alternatively, it is payable to any of them and may be negotiated, discharged, or enforced by any or all of them in possession of the instrument. If an instrument is payable to two or more persons not alternatively, it is payable to all of them and may be negotiated, discharged, or enforced only by all of them. If an instrument payable to two or more persons is ambiguous as to whether it is payable to the persons alternatively, the instrument is payable to the persons alternatively.

§ 3–111.   Place of Payment.

Except as otherwise provided for items in Article 4, an instrument is payable at the place of payment stated in the instrument. If no place of payment is stated, an instrument is payable at the address of the drawee or maker stated in the instrument. If no address is stated, the place of payment is the place of business of the drawee or maker. If a drawee or maker has more than one place of business, the place of payment is any place of business of the drawee or maker chosen by the person entitled to enforce the instrument. If the drawee or maker has no place of business, the place of payment is the residence of the drawee or maker.

§ 3–112.   Interest.

(a) Unless otherwise provided in the instrument, (i) an instrument is not payable with interest, and (ii) interest on an interest-bearing instrument is payable from the date of the instrument.

(b) Interest may be stated in an instrument as a fixed or variable amount of money or it may be expressed as a fixed or variable rate or rates. The amount or rate of interest may be stated or described in the instrument in any manner and may require reference to information not contained in the instrument. If an instrument provides for interest, but the amount of interest payable cannot be ascertained from the description, interest is payable at the judgment rate in effect at the place of payment of the instrument and at the time interest first accrues.

§ 3–113.   Date of Instrument.

(a) An instrument may be antedated or postdated. The date stated determines the time of payment if the instrument is payable at a fixed period after date. Except as provided in Section 4–401(c), an instrument payable on demand is not payable before the date of the instrument.

(b) If an instrument is undated, its date is the date of its issue or, in the case of an unissued instrument, the date it first comes into possession of a holder.

§ 3–114.   Contradictory Terms of Instrument.

If an instrument contains contradictory terms, typewritten terms prevail over printed terms, handwritten terms prevail over both, and words prevail over numbers.

§ 3–115.   Incomplete Instrument.

(a) "Incomplete instrument" means a signed writing, whether or not issued by the signer, the contents of which show at the time of signing that it is incomplete but that the signer intended it to be completed by the addition of words or numbers.

(b) Subject to subsection (c), if an incomplete instrument is an instrument under Section 3–104, it may be enforced according to its terms if it is not completed, or according to its terms as augmented by completion. If an incomplete instrument is not an instrument under Section 3–104, but, after completion, the requirements of Section 3–104 are met, the instrument may be enforced according to its terms as augmented by completion.

(c) If words or numbers are added to an incomplete instrument without authority of the signer, there is an alteration of the incomplete instrument under Section 3–407.

(d) The burden of establishing that words or numbers were added to an incomplete instrument without authority of the signer is on the person asserting the lack of authority.

§ 3–116.   Joint and Several Liability; Contribution.

(a) Except as otherwise provided in the instrument, two or more persons who have the same liability on an instrument as makers, drawers, acceptors, indorsers who indorse as joint payees, or anomalous indorsers are jointly and severally liable in the capacity in which they sign.

(b) Except as provided in Section 3–419(e) or by agreement of the affected parties, a party having joint and several liability who pays the instrument is entitled to receive from any party having the same joint and several liability contribution in accordance with applicable law.

(c) Discharge of one party having joint and several liability by a person entitled to enforce the instrument does not affect the right under subsection (b) of a party having the same joint and several liability to receive contribution from the party discharged.

§ 3–117.   Other Agreements Affecting Instrument.

Subject to applicable law regarding exclusion of proof of contemporaneous or previous agreements, the obligation of a party to an instrument to pay the instrument may be modified, supplemented, or nullified by a separate agreement of the obligor and a person entitled to enforce the instrument, if the instrument is issued or the obligation is incurred in reliance on the agreement or as part of the same transaction giving rise to the agreement. To the extent an obligation is modified, supplemented, or nullified by an agreement under this section, the agreement is a defense to the obligation.

§ 3–118.   Statute of Limitations.

(a) Except as provided in subsection (e), an action to enforce the obligation of a party to pay a note payable at a definite time must be commenced within six years after the due date or dates stated in the note or, if a due date is accelerated, within six years after the accelerated due date.

(b) Except as provided in subsection (d) or (e), if demand for payment is made to the maker of a note payable on demand, an action to enforce the obligation of a party to pay the note must be commenced within six years after the demand. If no demand for payment is made to the maker, an action to enforce the note is barred if neither principal nor interest on the note has been paid for a continuous period of 10 years.

(c) Except as provided in subsection (d), an action to enforce the obligation of a party to an unaccepted draft to pay the draft must be commenced within three years after dishonor of the draft or 10 years after the date of the draft, whichever period expires first.

(d) An action to enforce the obligation of the acceptor of a certified check or the issuer of a teller's check, cashier's check, or traveler's check must be commenced within three years after demand for payment is made to the acceptor or issuer, as the case may be.

(e) An action to enforce the obligation of a party to a certificate of deposit to pay the instrument must be commenced within six years after demand for payment is made to the maker, but if the instrument states a due date and the maker is not required to pay before that date, the six-year period begins when a demand for payment is in effect and the due date has passed.

(f) An action to enforce the obligation of a party to pay an accepted draft, other than a certified check, must be commenced (i) within six years after the due date or dates stated in the draft or acceptance if the obligation of the acceptor is payable at a definite time, or (ii) within six years after the date of the acceptance if the obligation of the acceptor is payable on demand.

(g) Unless governed by other law regarding claims for indemnity or contribution, an action (i) for conversion of an instrument, for money had and received, or like action based on conversion, (ii) for breach of warranty, or (iii) to enforce an obligation, duty, or right arising under this Article and not governed by this section must be commenced within three years after the [cause of action] accrues.

§ 3–119. Notice of Right to Defend Action.

In an action for breach of an obligation for which a third person is answerable over pursuant to this Article or Article 4, the defendant may give the third person written notice of the litigation, and the person notified may then give similar notice to any other person who is answerable over. If the notice states (i) that the person notified may come in and defend and (ii) that failure to do so will bind the person notified in an action later brought by the person giving the notice as to any determination of fact common to the two litigations, the person notified is so bound unless after seasonable receipt of the notice the person notified does come in and defend.

Part 2 Negotiation, Transfer, and Indorsement

§ 3–201. Negotiation.

(a) "Negotiation" means a transfer of possession, whether voluntary or involuntary, of an instrument by a person other than the issuer to a person who thereby becomes its holder.

(b) Except for negotiation by a remitter, if an instrument is payable to an identified person, negotiation requires transfer of possession of the instrument and its indorsement by the holder. If an instrument is payable to bearer, it may be negotiated by transfer of possession alone.

§ 3–202. Negotiation Subject to Rescission.

(a) Negotiation is effective even if obtained (i) from an infant, a corporation exceeding its powers, or a person without capacity, (ii) by fraud, duress, or mistake, or (iii) in breach of duty or as part of an illegal transaction.

(b) To the extent permitted by other law, negotiation may be rescinded or may be subject to other remedies, but those remedies may not be asserted against a subsequent holder in due course or a person paying the instrument in good faith and without knowledge of facts that are a basis for rescission or other remedy.

§ 3–203. Transfer of Instrument; Rights Acquired by Transfer.

(a) An instrument is transferred when it is delivered by a person other than its issuer for the purpose of giving to the person receiving delivery the right to enforce the instrument.

(b) Transfer of an instrument, whether or not the transfer is a negotiation, vests in the transferee any right of the transferor to enforce the instrument, including any right as a holder in due course, but the transferee cannot acquire rights of a holder in due course by a transfer, directly or indirectly, from a holder in due course if the transferee engaged in fraud or illegality affecting the instrument.

(c) Unless otherwise agreed, if an instrument is transferred for value and the transferee does not become a holder because of lack of indorsement by the transferor, the transferee has a specifically enforceable right to the unqualified indorsement of the transferor, but negotiation of the instrument does not occur until the indorsement is made.

(d) If a transferor purports to transfer less than the entire instrument, negotiation of the instrument does not occur. The transferee obtains no rights under this Article and has only the rights of a partial assignee.

§ 3–204. Indorsement.

(a) "Indorsement" means a signature, other than that of a signer as maker, drawer, or acceptor, that alone or accompanied by other words is made on an instrument for the purpose of (i) negotiating the instrument, (ii) restricting payment of the instrument, or (iii) incurring indorser's liability on the instrument, but regardless of the intent of the signer, a signature and its accompanying words is an indorsement unless the accompanying words, terms of the instrument, place of the signature, or other circumstances unambiguously indicate that the signature was made for a purpose other than indorsement. For the purpose of determining whether a signature is made on an instrument, a paper affixed to the instrument is a part of the instrument.

(b) "Indorser" means a person who makes an indorsement.

(c) For the purpose of determining whether the transferee of an instrument is a holder, an indorsement that transfers a security interest in the instrument is effective as an unqualified indorsement of the instrument.

(d) If an instrument is payable to a holder under a name that is not the name of the holder, indorsement may be made by the holder in the name stated in the instrument or in the holder's name or both, but signature in both names may be required by a person paying or taking the instrument for value or collection.

§ 3–205. Special Indorsement; Blank Indorsement; Anomalous Indorsement.

(a) If an indorsement is made by the holder of an instrument, whether payable to an identified person or payable to bearer, and the indorsement identifies a person to whom it makes the instrument payable, it is a "special indorsement." When specially indorsed, an instrument becomes payable to the identified person and may be negotiated only by the indorsement of that person. The principles stated in Section 3–110 apply to special indorsements.

(b) If an indorsement is made by the holder of an instrument and it is not a special indorsement, it is a "blank indorsement." When indorsed in blank, an instrument becomes payable to bearer and may be negotiated by transfer of possession alone until specially indorsed.

(c) The holder may convert a blank indorsement that consists only of a signature into a special indorsement by writing, above the signature of the indorser, words identifying the person to whom the instrument is made payable.

(d) "Anomalous indorsement" means an indorsement made by a person who is not the holder of the instrument. An anomalous indorsement does not affect the manner in which the instrument may be negotiated.

§ 3–206. Restrictive Indorsement.

(a) An indorsement limiting payment to a particular person or otherwise prohibiting further transfer or negotiation of the instrument is not effective to prevent further transfer or negotiation of the instrument.

(b) An indorsement stating a condition to the right of the indorsee to receive payment does not affect the right of the indorsee to enforce the instrument. A person paying the instrument or taking it for value or collection may disregard the condition, and the rights and liabilities of that person are not affected by whether the condition has been fulfilled.

(c) If an instrument bears an indorsement (i) described in Section 4–201(b), or (ii) in blank or to a particular bank using the words "for deposit," "for collection," or other words indicating a purpose of having the instrument collected by a bank for the indorser or for a particular account, the following rules apply:

(1) A person, other than a bank, who purchases the instrument when so indorsed converts the instrument unless the amount paid for the instrument is received by the indorser or applied consistently with the indorsement.

(2) A depositary bank that purchases the instrument or takes it for collection when so indorsed converts the instrument unless the amount paid by the bank with respect to the instrument is received by the indorser or applied consistently with the indorsement.

(3) A payor bank that is also the depositary bank or that takes the instrument for immediate payment over the counter from a person other than a collecting bank converts the instrument unless the proceeds of the instrument are received by the indorser or applied consistently with the indorsement.

(4) Except as otherwise provided in paragraph (3), a payor bank or intermediary bank may disregard the indorsement and is not liable if the proceeds of the instrument are not received by the indorser or applied consistently with the indorsement.

(d) Except for an indorsement covered by subsection (c), if an instrument bears an indorsement using words to the effect that payment is to be made to the indorsee as agent, trustee, or other fiduciary for the benefit of the indorser or another person, the following rules apply:

(1) Unless there is notice of breach of fiduciary duty as provided in Section 3–307, a person who purchases the instrument from the indorsee or takes the instrument from the indorsee for collection or payment may pay the proceeds of payment or the value given for the instrument to the indorsee without regard to whether the indorsee violates a fiduciary duty to the indorser.

(2) A subsequent transferee of the instrument or person who pays the instrument is neither given notice nor otherwise affected by the restriction in the indorsement unless the transferee or payor knows that the fiduciary dealt with the instrument or its proceeds in breach of fiduciary duty.

(e) The presence on an instrument of an indorsement to which this section applies does not prevent a purchaser of the instrument from becoming a holder in due course of the instrument unless the purchaser is a converter under subsection (c) or has notice or knowledge of breach of fiduciary duty as stated in subsection (d).

(f) In an action to enforce the obligation of a party to pay the instrument, the obligor has a defense if payment would violate an indorsement to which this section applies and the payment is not permitted by this section.

§ 3–207. Reacquisition.

Reacquisition of an instrument occurs if it is transferred to a former holder, by negotiation or otherwise. A former holder who reacquires the instrument may cancel indorsements made after the reacquirer first became a holder of the instrument. If the cancellation causes the instrument to be payable to the reacquirer or to bearer, the reacquirer may negotiate the instrument. An indorser whose indorsement is canceled is discharged, and the discharge is effective against any subsequent holder.

Part 3 Enforcement of Instruments

§ 3–301. Person Entitled to Enforce Instrument.

"Person entitled to enforce" an instrument means (i) the holder of the instrument, (ii) a nonholder in possession of the instrument who has the rights of a holder, or (iii) a person not in possession of the instrument who is entitled to enforce the instrument pursuant to Section 3–309 or 3–418(d). A person may be a person entitled to enforce the instrument even though the person is not the owner of the instrument or is in wrongful possession of the instrument.

§ 3–302. Holder in Due Course.

(a) Subject to subsection (c) and Section 3–106(d), "holder in due course" means the holder of an instrument if:

(1) the instrument when issued or negotiated to the holder does not bear such apparent evidence of forgery or alteration or is not otherwise so irregular or incomplete as to call into question its authenticity; and

(2) the holder took the instrument (i) for value, (ii) in good faith, (iii) without notice that the instrument is overdue or has been dishonored or that there is an uncured default with respect to payment of another instrument issued as part of the same series, (iv) without notice that the instrument contains an unauthorized signature or has been altered, (v) without notice of any claim to the instrument described in Section 3–306, and (vi) without notice that any party has a defense or claim in recoupment described in Section 3–305(a).

(b) Notice of discharge of a party, other than discharge in an insolvency proceeding, is not notice of a defense under subsection (a), but discharge is effective against a person who became a holder in due course with notice of the discharge. Public filing or recording of a document does not of itself constitute notice of a defense, claim in recoupment, or claim to the instrument.

(c) Except to the extent a transferor or predecessor in interest has rights as a holder in due course, a person does not acquire rights of a holder in due course of an instrument taken (i) by legal process or by purchase in an execution, bankruptcy, or creditor's sale or similar proceeding, (ii) by purchase as part of a bulk transaction not in ordinary course of business of the transferor, or (iii) as the successor in interest to an estate or other organization.

(d) If, under Section 3–303(a)(1), the promise of performance that is the consideration for an instrument has been partially performed, the holder may assert rights as a holder in due course of the instrument only to the fraction of the amount payable under the instrument equal to the value of the partial performance divided by the value of the promised performance.

(e) If (i) the person entitled to enforce an instrument has only a security interest in the instrument and (ii) the person obliged to pay the instrument has a defense, claim in recoupment, or claim to the instrument that may be asserted against the person who granted the security interest, the person entitled to enforce the instrument may assert rights as a holder in due course only to an amount payable under the instrument which, at the time of enforcement of the instrument, does not exceed the amount of the unpaid obligation secured.

(f) To be effective, notice must be received at a time and in a manner that gives a reasonable opportunity to act on it.

(g) This section is subject to any law limiting status as a holder in due course in particular classes of transactions.

§ 3–303. Value and Consideration.

(a) An instrument is issued or transferred for value if:

(1) the instrument is issued or transferred for a promise of performance, to the extent the promise has been performed;

(2) the transferee acquires a security interest or other lien in the instrument other than a lien obtained by judicial proceeding;

(3) the instrument is issued or transferred as payment of, or as security for, an antecedent claim against any person, whether or not the claim is due;

(4) the instrument is issued or transferred in exchange for a negotiable instrument; or

(5) the instrument is issued or transferred in exchange for the incurring of an irrevocable obligation to a third party by the person taking the instrument.

(b) "Consideration" means any consideration sufficient to support a simple contract. The drawer or maker of an instrument has a defense if the instrument is issued without consideration. If an instrument is issued for a promise of performance, the issuer has a defense to the extent performance of the promise is due and the promise has not been performed. If an instrument is issued for value as stated in subsection (a), the instrument is also issued for consideration.

§ 3–304. Overdue Instrument.

(a) An instrument payable on demand becomes overdue at the earliest of the following times:

(1) on the day after the day demand for payment is duly made;

(2) if the instrument is a check, 90 days after its date; or

(3) if the instrument is not a check, when the instrument has been outstanding for a period of time after its date which is unreasonably long under the circumstances of the particular case in light of the nature of the instrument and usage of the trade.

(b) With respect to an instrument payable at a definite time the following rules apply:

(1) If the principal is payable in installments and a due date has not been accelerated, the instrument becomes overdue upon default under the instrument for nonpayment of an installment, and the instrument remains overdue until the default is cured.

(2) If the principal is not payable in installments and the due date has not been accelerated, the instrument becomes overdue on the day after the due date.

(3) If a due date with respect to principal has been accelerated, the instrument becomes overdue on the day after the accelerated due date.

(c) Unless the due date of principal has been accelerated, an instrument does not become overdue if there is default in payment of interest but no default in payment of principal.

§ 3–305. Defenses and Claims in Recoupment.

(a) Except as stated in subsection (b), the right to enforce the obligation of a party to pay an instrument is subject to the following:

(1) a defense of the obligor based on (i) infancy of the obligor to the extent it is a defense to a simple contract, (ii) duress, lack of legal capacity, or illegality of the transaction which, under other law, nullifies the obligation of the obligor, (iii) fraud that induced the obligor to sign the instrument with neither knowledge nor reasonable opportunity to learn of its character or its essential terms, or (iv) discharge of the obligor in insolvency proceedings;

(2) a defense of the obligor stated in another section of this Article or a defense of the obligor that would be available if the person entitled to enforce the instrument were enforcing a right to payment under a simple contract; and

(3) a claim in recoupment of the obligor against the original payee of the instrument if the claim arose from the transaction that gave rise to the instrument; but the claim of the obligor may be asserted against a transferee of the instrument only to reduce the amount owing on the instrument at the time the action is brought.

(b) The right of a holder in due course to enforce the obligation of a party to pay the instrument is subject to defenses of the obligor stated in subsection (a)(1), but is not subject to defenses of the obligor stated in subsection (a)(2) or claims in recoupment stated in subsection (a)(3) against a person other than the holder.

(c) Except as stated in subsection (d), in an action to enforce the obligation of a party to pay the instrument, the obligor may not assert against the person entitled to enforce the instrument a defense, claim in recoupment, or claim to the instrument (Section 3–306) of another person, but the other person's claim to the instrument may be asserted by the obligor if the other person is joined in the action and personally asserts the claim against the person entitled to enforce the instrument. An obligor is not obliged to pay the instrument if the person seeking enforcement of the instrument does not have rights of a holder in due course and the obligor proves that the instrument is a lost or stolen instrument.

(d) In an action to enforce the obligation of an accommodation party to pay an instrument, the accommodation party may assert against the person entitled to enforce the instrument any defense or claim in recoupment under subsection (a) that the accommodated party could assert against the person entitled to enforce the instrument, except the defenses of discharge in insolvency proceedings, infancy, and lack of legal capacity.

§ 3–306. Claims to an Instrument.

A person taking an instrument, other than a person having rights of a holder in due course, is subject to a claim of a property or possessory right in the instrument or its proceeds, including a claim to rescind a negotiation and to recover the instrument or its proceeds. A person having rights of a holder in due course takes free of the claim to the instrument.

§ 3–307. Notice of Breach of Fiduciary Duty.

(a) In this section:

(1) "Fiduciary" means an agent, trustee, partner, corporate officer or director, or other representative owing a fiduciary duty with respect to an instrument.

(2) "Represented person" means the principal, beneficiary, partnership, corporation, or other person to whom the duty stated in paragraph (1) is owed.

(b) If (i) an instrument is taken from a fiduciary for payment or collection or for value, (ii) the taker has knowledge of the fiduciary status of the fiduciary, and (iii) the represented person makes a claim to the instrument or its proceeds on the basis that the transaction of the fiduciary is a breach of fiduciary duty, the following rules apply:

(1) Notice of breach of fiduciary duty by the fiduciary is notice of the claim of the represented person.

(2) In the case of an instrument payable to the represented person or the fiduciary as such, the taker has notice of the breach of fiduciary duty if the instrument is (i) taken in payment of or as security for a debt known by the taker to be the personal debt of the fiduciary, (ii) taken in a transaction known by the taker to be for the personal benefit of the fiduciary, or (iii) deposited to an account other than an account of the fiduciary, as such, or an account of the represented person.

(3) If an instrument is issued by the represented person or the fiduciary as such, and made payable to the fiduciary personally, the taker does not have notice of the breach of fiduciary duty unless the taker knows of the breach of fiduciary duty.

(4) If an instrument is issued by the represented person or the fiduciary as such, to the taker as payee, the taker has notice of the breach of fiduciary duty if the instrument is (i) taken in payment of or as security for a debt known by the taker to be the personal debt of the fiduciary, (ii) taken in a transaction known by the taker to be for the personal benefit of the fiduciary, or (iii) deposited to an account other than an account of the fiduciary, as such, or an account of the represented person.

§ 3–308.   Proof of Signatures and Status as Holder in Due Course.

(a) In an action with respect to an instrument, the authenticity of, and authority to make, each signature on the instrument is admitted unless specifically denied in the pleadings. If the validity of a signature is denied in the pleadings, the burden of establishing validity is on the person claiming validity, but the signature is presumed to be authentic and authorized unless the action is to enforce the liability of the purported signer and the signer is dead or incompetent at the time of trial of the issue of validity of the signature. If an action to enforce the instrument is brought against a person as the undisclosed principal of a person who signed the instrument as a party to the instrument, the plaintiff has the burden of establishing that the defendant is liable on the instrument as a represented person under Section 3–402(a).

(b) If the validity of signatures is admitted or proved and there is compliance with subsection (a), a plaintiff producing the instrument is entitled to payment if the plaintiff proves entitlement to enforce the instrument under Section 3–301, unless the defendant proves a defense or claim in recoupment. If a defense or claim in recoupment is proved, the right to payment of the plaintiff is subject to the defense or claim, except to the extent the plaintiff proves that the plaintiff has rights of a holder in due course which are not subject to the defense or claim.

§ 3–309.   Enforcement of Lost, Destroyed, or Stolen Instrument.

(a) A person not in possession of an instrument is entitled to enforce the instrument if (i) the person was in possession of the instrument and entitled to enforce it when loss of possession occurred, (ii) the loss of possession was not the result of a transfer by the person or a lawful seizure, and (iii) the person cannot reasonably obtain possession of the instrument because the instrument was destroyed, its whereabouts cannot be determined, or it is in the wrongful possession of an unknown person or a person that cannot be found or is not amenable to service of process.

(b) A person seeking enforcement of an instrument under subsection (a) must prove the terms of the instrument and the person's right to enforce the instrument. If that proof is made, Section 3–308 applies to the case as if the person seeking enforcement had produced the instrument. The court may not enter judgment in favor of the person seeking enforcement unless it finds that the person required to pay the instrument is adequately protected against loss that might occur by reason of a claim by another person to enforce the instrument. Adequate protection may be provided by any reasonable means.

§ 3–310.   Effect of Instrument on Obligation for Which Taken.

(a) Unless otherwise agreed, if a certified check, cashier's check, or teller's check is taken for an obligation, the obligation is discharged to the same extent discharge would result if an amount of money equal to the amount of the instrument were taken in payment of the obligation. Discharge of the obligation does not affect any liability that the obligor may have as an indorser of the instrument.

(b) Unless otherwise agreed and except as provided in subsection (a), if a note or an uncertified check is taken for an obligation, the obligation is suspended to the same extent the obligation would be discharged if an amount of money equal to the amount of the instrument were taken, and the following rules apply:

(1) In the case of an uncertified check, suspension of the obligation continues until dishonor of the check or until it is paid or certified. Payment or certification of the check results in discharge of the obligation to the extent of the amount of the check.

(2) In the case of a note, suspension of the obligation continues until dishonor of the note or until it is paid. Payment of the note results in discharge of the obligation to the extent of the payment.

(3) Except as provided in paragraph (4), if the check or note is dishonored and the obligee of the obligation for which the instrument was taken is the person entitled to enforce the instrument, the obligee may enforce either the instrument or the obligation. In the case of an instrument of a third person which is negotiated to the obligee by the obligor, discharge of the obligor on the instrument also discharges the obligation.

(4) If the person entitled to enforce the instrument taken for an obligation is a person other than the obligee, the obligee may not enforce the obligation to the extent the obligation is suspended. If the obligee is the person entitled to enforce the instrument but no longer has possession of it because it was lost, stolen, or destroyed, the obligation may not be enforced to the extent of the amount payable on the instrument, and to that extent the obligee's rights against the obligor are limited to enforcement of the instrument.

(c) If an instrument other than one described in subsection (a) or (b) is taken for an obligation, the effect is (i) that stated in subsection (a) if the instrument is one on which a bank is liable as maker or acceptor, or (ii) that stated in subsection (b) in any other case.

§ 3–311.   Accord and Satisfaction by Use of Instrument.

(a) If a person against whom a claim is asserted proves that (i) that person in good faith tendered an instrument to the claimant as full satisfaction of the claim, (ii) the amount of the claim was unliquidated or subject to a bona fide dispute, and (iii) the claimant obtained payment of the instrument, the following subsections apply.

(b) Unless subsection (c) applies, the claim is discharged if the person against whom the claim is asserted proves that the instrument or an accompanying written communication contained a conspicuous statement to the effect that the instrument was tendered as full satisfaction of the claim.

(c) Subject to subsection (d), a claim is not discharged under subsection (b) if either of the following applies:

(1) The claimant, if an organization, proves that (i) within a reasonable time before the tender, the claimant sent a conspicuous statement to the person against whom the claim is asserted that communications concerning disputed debts, including an instrument tendered as full satisfaction of a debt, are to be sent to a designated person, office, or place, and (ii) the instrument or accompanying communication was not received by that designated person, office, or place.

(2) The claimant, whether or not an organization, proves that within 90 days after payment of the instrument, the claimant tendered repayment of the amount of the instrument to the person against whom the claim is asserted. This paragraph does not apply if the claimant is an organization that sent a statement complying with paragraph (1)(i).

(d) A claim is discharged if the person against whom the claim is asserted proves that within a reasonable time before collection of the instrument was initiated, the claimant, or an agent of the claimant having direct responsibility with respect to the disputed obligation, knew that the instrument was tendered in full satisfaction of the claim.

§ 3–312. Lost, Destroyed, or Stolen Cashier's Check, Teller's Check, or Certified Check.

(a) In this section:

(1) "Check" means a cashier's check, teller's check, or certified check.

(2) "Claimant" means a person who claims the right to receive the amount of a cashier's check, teller's check, or certified check that was lost, destroyed, or stolen.

(3) "Declaration of loss" means a written statement, made under penalty of perjury, to the effect that (i) the declarer lost possession of a check, (ii) the declarer is the drawer or payee of the check, in the case of a certified check, or the remitter or payee of the check, in the case of a cashier's check or teller's check, (iii) the loss of possession was not the result of a transfer by the declarer or a lawful seizure, and (iv) the declarer cannot reasonably obtain possession of the check because the check was destroyed, its whereabouts cannot be determined, or it is in the wrongful possession of an unknown person or a person that cannot be found or is not amenable to service of process.

(4) "Obligated bank" means the issuer of a cashier's check or teller's check or the acceptor of a certified check.

(b) A claimant may assert a claim to the amount of a check by a communication to the obligated bank describing the check with reasonable certainty and requesting payment of the amount of the check, if (i) the claimant is the drawer or payee of a certified check or the remitter or payee of a cashier's check or teller's check, (ii) the communication contains or is accompanied by a declaration of loss of the claimant with respect to the check, (iii) the communication is received at a time and in a manner affording the bank a reasonable time to act on it before the check is paid, and (iv) the claimant provides reasonable identification if requested by the obligated bank. Delivery of a declaration of loss is a warranty of the truth of the statements made in the declaration. If a claim is asserted in compliance with this subsection, the following rules apply:

(1) The claim becomes enforceable at the later of (i) the time the claim is asserted, or (ii) the 90th day following the date of the check, in the case of a cashier's check or teller's check, or the 90th day following the date of the acceptance, in the case of a certified check.

(2) Until the claim becomes enforceable, it has no legal effect and the obligated bank may pay the check or, in the case of a teller's check, may permit the drawee to pay the check. Payment to a person entitled to enforce the check discharges all liability of the obligated bank with respect to the check.

(3) If the claim becomes enforceable before the check is presented for payment, the obligated bank is not obliged to pay the check.

(4) When the claim becomes enforceable, the obligated bank becomes obliged to pay the amount of the check to the claimant if payment of the check has not been made to a person entitled to enforce the check. Subject to Section 4–302(a)(1), payment to the claimant discharges all liability of the obligated bank with respect to the check.

(c) If the obligated bank pays the amount of a check to a claimant under subsection (b)(4) and the check is presented for payment by a person having rights of a holder in due course, the claimant is obliged to (i) refund the payment to the obligated bank if the check is paid, or (ii) pay the amount of the check to the person having rights of a holder in due course if the check is dishonored.

(d) If a claimant has the right to assert a claim under subsection (b) and is also a person entitled to enforce a cashier's check, teller's check, or certified check which is lost, destroyed, or stolen, the claimant may assert rights with respect to the check either under this section or Section 3–309.

Added in 1991.

Part 4   Liability of Parties

§ 3–401.   Signature.

(a) A person is not liable on an instrument unless (i) the person signed the instrument, or (ii) the person is represented by an agent or representative who signed the instrument and the signature is binding on the represented person under Section 3–402.

(b) A signature may be made (i) manually or by means of a device or machine, and (ii) by the use of any name, including a trade or assumed name, or by a word, mark, or symbol executed or adopted by a person with present intention to authenticate a writing.

§ 3–402.   Signature by Representative.

(a) If a person acting, or purporting to act, as a representative signs an instrument by signing either the name of the represented person or the name of the signer, the represented person is bound by the signature to the same extent the represented person would be bound if the signature were on a simple contract. If the represented person is bound, the signature of the representative is the "authorized signature of the represented person" and the represented person is liable on the instrument, whether or not identified in the instrument.

(b) If a representative signs the name of the representative to an instrument and the signature is an authorized signature of the represented person, the following rules apply:

(1) If the form of the signature shows unambiguously that the signature is made on behalf of the represented person who is identified in the instrument, the representative is not liable on the instrument.

(2) Subject to subsection (c), if (i) the form of the signature does not show unambiguously that the signature is made in a representative capacity or (ii) the represented person is not identified in the instrument, the representative is liable on the instrument to a holder in due course that took the instrument without notice that the representative was not intended to be liable on the instrument. With respect to any other person, the representative is liable on the instrument unless the representative proves that the original parties did not intend the representative to be liable on the instrument.

(c) If a representative signs the name of the representative as drawer of a check without indication of the representative status and the check is payable from an account of the represented person who is identified on the check, the signer is not liable on the check if the signature is an authorized signature of the represented person.

§ 3–403. Unauthorized Signature.

(a) Unless otherwise provided in this Article or Article 4, an unauthorized signature is ineffective except as the signature of the unauthorized signer in favor of a person who in good faith pays the instrument or takes it for value. An unauthorized signature may be ratified for all purposes of this Article.

(b) If the signature of more than one person is required to constitute the authorized signature of an organization, the signature of the organization is unauthorized if one of the required signatures is lacking.

(c) The civil or criminal liability of a person who makes an unauthorized signature is not affected by any provision of this Article which makes the unauthorized signature effective for the purposes of this Article.

§ 3–404. Impostors; Fictitious Payees.

(a) If an impostor, by use of the mails or otherwise, induces the issuer of an instrument to issue the instrument to the impostor, or to a person acting in concert with the impostor, by impersonating the payee of the instrument or a person authorized to act for the payee, an indorsement of the instrument by any person in the name of the payee is effective as the indorsement of the payee in favor of a person who, in good faith, pays the instrument or takes it for value or for collection.

(b) If (i) a person whose intent determines to whom an instrument is payable (Section 3–110(a) or (b)) does not intend the person identified as payee to have any interest in the instrument, or (ii) the person identified as payee of an instrument is a fictitious person, the following rules apply until the instrument is negotiated by special indorsement:

(1) Any person in possession of the instrument is its holder.

(2) An indorsement by any person in the name of the payee stated in the instrument is effective as the indorsement of the payee in favor of a person who, in good faith, pays the instrument or takes it for value or for collection.

(c) Under subsection (a) or (b), an indorsement is made in the name of a payee if (i) it is made in a name substantially similar to that of the payee or (ii) the instrument, whether or not indorsed, is deposited in a depositary bank to an account in a name substantially similar to that of the payee.

(d) With respect to an instrument to which subsection (a) or (b) applies, if a person paying the instrument or taking it for value or for collection fails to exercise ordinary care in paying or taking the instrument and that failure substantially contributes to loss resulting from payment of the instrument, the person bearing the loss may recover from the person failing to exercise ordinary care to the extent the failure to exercise ordinary care contributed to the loss.

§ 3–405. Employer's Responsibility for Fraudulent Indorsement by Employee.

(a) In this section:

(1) "Employee" includes an independent contractor and employee of an independent contractor retained by the employer.

(2) "Fraudulent indorsement" means (i) in the case of an instrument payable to the employer, a forged indorsement purporting to be that of the employer, or (ii) in the case of an instrument with respect to which the employer is the issuer, a forged indorsement purporting to be that of the person identified as payee.

(3) "Responsibility" with respect to instruments means authority (i) to sign or indorse instruments on behalf of the employer, (ii) to process instruments received by the employer for bookkeeping purposes, for deposit to an account, or for other disposition, (iii) to prepare or process instruments for issue in the name of the employer, (iv) to supply information determining the names or addresses of payees of instruments to be issued in the name of the employer, (v) to control the disposition of instruments to be issued in the name of the employer, or (vi) to act otherwise with respect to instruments in a responsible capacity. "Responsibility" does not include authority that merely allows an employee to have access to instruments or blank or incomplete instrument forms that are being stored or transported or are part of incoming or outgoing mail, or similar access.

(b) For the purpose of determining the rights and liabilities of a person who, in good faith, pays an instrument or takes it for value or for collection, if an employer entrusted an employee with responsibility with respect to the instrument and the employee or a person acting in concert with the employee makes a fraudulent indorsement of the instrument, the indorsement is effective as the indorsement of the person to whom the instrument is payable if it is made in the name of that person. If the person paying the instrument or taking it for value or for collection fails to exercise ordinary care in paying or taking the instrument and that failure substantially contributes to loss resulting from the fraud, the person bearing the loss may recover from the person failing to exercise ordinary care to the extent the failure to exercise ordinary care contributed to the loss.

(c) Under subsection (b), an indorsement is made in the name of the person to whom an instrument is payable if (i) it is made in a name substantially similar to the name of that person or (ii) the instrument, whether or not indorsed, is deposited in a depositary bank to an account in a name substantially similar to the name of that person.

§ 3–406. Negligence Contributing to Forged Signature or Alteration of Instrument.

(a) A person whose failure to exercise ordinary care substantially contributes to an alteration of an instrument or to the making of a forged signature on an instrument is precluded from asserting the alteration or the forgery against a person who, in good faith, pays the instrument or takes it for value or for collection.

(b) Under subsection (a), if the person asserting the preclusion fails to exercise ordinary care in paying or taking the instrument and that failure substantially contributes to loss, the loss is allocated between the person precluded and the person asserting the preclusion according to the extent to which the failure of each to exercise ordinary care contributed to the loss.

(c) Under subsection (a), the burden of proving failure to exercise ordinary care is on the person asserting the preclusion. Under subsection (b), the burden of proving failure to exercise ordinary care is on the person precluded.

§ 3–407. Alteration.

(a) "Alteration" means (i) an unauthorized change in an instrument that purports to modify in any respect the obligation of a party, or (ii) an unauthorized addition of words or numbers or other change to an incomplete instrument relating to the obligation of a party.

(b) Except as provided in subsection (c), an alteration fraudulently made discharges a party whose obligation is affected by the alteration unless that party assents or is precluded from asserting the alteration. No other alteration discharges a party, and the instrument may be enforced according to its original terms.

(c) A payor bank or drawee paying a fraudulently altered instrument or a person taking it for value, in good faith and without notice of the alteration, may enforce rights with respect to the instrument (i) according to its original terms, or (ii) in the case of an incomplete instrument altered by unauthorized completion, according to its terms as completed.

§ 3–408. Drawee Not Liable on Unaccepted Draft.

A check or other draft does not of itself operate as an assignment of funds in the hands of the drawee available for its payment, and the drawee is not liable on the instrument until the drawee accepts it.

§ 3–409. Acceptance of Draft; Certified Check.

(a) "Acceptance" means the drawee's signed agreement to pay a draft as presented. It must be written on the draft and may consist of the drawee's signature alone. Acceptance may be made at any time and becomes effective when notification pursuant to instructions is given or the accepted draft is delivered for the purpose of giving rights on the acceptance to any person.

(b) A draft may be accepted although it has not been signed by the drawer, is otherwise incomplete, is overdue, or has been dishonored.

(c) If a draft is payable at a fixed period after sight and the acceptor fails to date the acceptance, the holder may complete the acceptance by supplying a date in good faith.

(d) "Certified check" means a check accepted by the bank on which it is drawn. Acceptance may be made as stated in subsection (a) or by a writing on the check which indicates that the check is certified. The drawee of a check has no obligation to certify the check, and refusal to certify is not dishonor of the check.

§ 3–410. Acceptance Varying Draft.

(a) If the terms of a drawee's acceptance vary from the terms of the draft as presented, the holder may refuse the acceptance and treat the draft as dishonored. In that case, the drawee may cancel the acceptance.

(b) The terms of a draft are not varied by an acceptance to pay at a particular bank or place in the United States, unless the acceptance states that the draft is to be paid only at that bank or place.

(c) If the holder assents to an acceptance varying the terms of a draft, the obligation of each drawer and indorser that does not expressly assent to the acceptance is discharged.

§ 3–411. Refusal to Pay Cashier's Checks, Teller's Checks, and Certified Checks.

(a) In this section, "obligated bank" means the acceptor of a certified check or the issuer of a cashier's check or teller's check bought from the issuer.

(b) If the obligated bank wrongfully (i) refuses to pay a cashier's check or certified check, (ii) stops payment of a teller's check, or (iii) refuses to pay a dishonored teller's check, the person asserting the right to enforce the check is entitled to compensation for expenses and loss of interest resulting from the nonpayment and may recover consequential damages if the obligated bank refuses to pay after receiving notice of particular circumstances giving rise to the damages.

(c) Expenses or consequential damages under subsection (b) are not recoverable if the refusal of the obligated bank to pay occurs because (i) the bank suspends payments, (ii) the obligated bank asserts a claim or defense of the bank that it has reasonable grounds to believe is available against the person entitled to enforce the instrument, (iii) the obligated bank has a reasonable doubt whether the person demanding payment is the person entitled to enforce the instrument, or (iv) payment is prohibited by law.

§ 3–412. Obligation of Issuer of Note or Cashier's Check.

The issuer of a note or cashier's check or other draft drawn on the drawer is obliged to pay the instrument (i) according to its terms at the time it was issued or, if not issued, at the time it first came into possession of a holder, or (ii) if the issuer signed an incomplete instrument, according to its terms when completed, to the extent stated in Sections 3–115 and 3–407. The obligation is owed to a person entitled to enforce the instrument or to an indorser who paid the instrument under Section 3–415.

§ 3–413. Obligation of Acceptor.

(a) The acceptor of a draft is obliged to pay the draft (i) according to its terms at the time it was accepted, even though the acceptance states that the draft is payable "as originally drawn" or equivalent terms, (ii) if the acceptance varies the terms of the draft, according to the terms of the draft as varied, or (iii) if the acceptance is of a draft that is an incomplete instrument, according to its terms when completed, to the extent stated in Sections 3–115 and 3–407. The obligation is owed to a person entitled to enforce the draft or to the drawer or an indorser who paid the draft under Section 3–414 or 3–415.

(b) If the certification of a check or other acceptance of a draft states the amount certified or accepted, the obligation of the acceptor is that amount. If (i) the certification or acceptance does not state an amount, (ii) the amount of the instrument is subsequently raised, and (iii) the instrument is then negotiated to a holder in due course, the obligation of the acceptor is the amount of the instrument at the time it was taken by the holder in due course.

§ 3–414. Obligation of Drawer.

(a) This section does not apply to cashier's checks or other drafts drawn on the drawer.

(b) If an unaccepted draft is dishonored, the drawer is obliged to pay the draft (i) according to its terms at the time it was issued or, if not issued, at the time it first came into possession of a holder, or (ii) if the drawer signed an incomplete instrument, according to its terms when completed, to the extent stated in Sections 3–115 and 3–407. The obligation is owed to a person entitled to enforce the draft or to an indorser who paid the draft under Section 3–415.

(c) If a draft is accepted by a bank, the drawer is discharged, regardless of when or by whom acceptance was obtained.

(d) If a draft is accepted and the acceptor is not a bank, the obligation of the drawer to pay the draft if the draft is dishonored by the acceptor is the same as the obligation of an indorser under Section 3–415(a) and (c).

(e) If a draft states that it is drawn "without recourse" or otherwise disclaims liability of the drawer to pay the draft, the drawer is not liable under subsection (b) to pay the draft if the draft is not a check. A disclaimer of the liability stated in subsection (b) is not effective if the draft is a check.

(f) If (i) a check is not presented for payment or given to a depositary bank for collection within 30 days after its date, (ii) the drawee suspends payments after expiration of the 30-day period without paying the check, and (iii) because of the suspension of payments, the drawer is deprived of funds maintained with the drawee to cover payment of the check, the drawer to the extent deprived of funds may discharge its obligation to pay the check by assigning to the person entitled to enforce the check the rights of the drawer against the drawee with respect to the funds.

§ 3–415. Obligation of Indorser.

(a) Subject to subsections (b), (c), and (d) and to Section 3–419(d), if an instrument is dishonored, an indorser is obliged to pay the amount due on the instrument (i) according to the terms of the instrument at the time it was indorsed, or (ii) if the indorser indorsed an incomplete instrument, according to its terms when completed, to the extent stated in Sections 3–115 and 3–407. The obligation of the indorser is owed to a person entitled to enforce the instrument or to a subsequent indorser who paid the instrument under this section.

(b) If an indorsement states that it is made "without recourse" or otherwise disclaims liability of the indorser, the indorser is not liable under subsection (a) to pay the instrument.

(c) If notice of dishonor of an instrument is required by Section 3–503 and notice of dishonor complying with that section is not given to an indorser, the liability of the indorser under subsection (a) is discharged.

(d) If a draft is accepted by a bank after an indorsement is made, the liability of the indorser under subsection (a) is discharged.

(e) If an indorser of a check is liable under subsection (a) and the check is not presented for payment, or given to a depositary bank for collection, within 30 days after the day the indorsement was made, the liability of the indorser under subsection (a) is discharged.

As amended in 1993.

§ 3–416. Transfer Warranties.

(a) A person who transfers an instrument for consideration warrants to the transferee and, if the transfer is by indorsement, to any subsequent transferee that:

(1) the warrantor is a person entitled to enforce the instrument;

(2) all signatures on the instrument are authentic and authorized;

(3) the instrument has not been altered;

(4) the instrument is not subject to a defense or claim in recoupment of any party which can be asserted against the warrantor; and

(5) the warrantor has no knowledge of any insolvency proceeding commenced with respect to the maker or acceptor or, in the case of an unaccepted draft, the drawer.

(b) A person to whom the warranties under subsection (a) are made and who took the instrument in good faith may recover from the warrantor as damages for breach of warranty an amount equal to the loss suffered as a result of the breach, but not more than the amount of the instrument plus expenses and loss of interest incurred as a result of the breach.

(c) The warranties stated in subsection (a) cannot be disclaimed with respect to checks. Unless notice of a claim for breach of warranty is given to the warrantor within 30 days after the claimant has reason to know of the breach and the identity of the warrantor, the liability of the warrantor under subsection (b) is discharged to the extent of any loss caused by the delay in giving notice of the claim.

(d) A [cause of action] for breach of warranty under this section accrues when the claimant has reason to know of the breach.

§ 3–417. Presentment Warranties.

(a) If an unaccepted draft is presented to the drawee for payment or acceptance and the drawee pays or accepts the draft, (i) the person obtaining payment or acceptance, at the time of presentment, and (ii) a previous transferor of the draft, at the time of transfer, warrant to the drawee making payment or accepting the draft in good faith that:

(1) the warrantor is, or was, at the time the warrantor transferred the draft, a person entitled to enforce the draft or authorized to obtain payment or acceptance of the draft on behalf of a person entitled to enforce the draft;

(2) the draft has not been altered; and

(3) the warrantor has no knowledge that the signature of the drawer of the draft is unauthorized.

(b) A drawee making payment may recover from any warrantor damages for breach of warranty equal to the amount paid by the drawee less the amount the drawee received or is entitled to receive from the drawer because of the payment. In addition, the drawee is entitled to compensation for expenses and loss of interest resulting from the breach. The right of the drawee to recover damages under this subsection is not affected by any failure of the drawee to exercise ordinary care in making payment. If the drawee accepts the draft, breach of warranty is a defense to the obligation of the acceptor. If the acceptor makes payment with respect to the draft, the acceptor is entitled to recover from any warrantor for breach of warranty the amounts stated in this subsection.

(c) If a drawee asserts a claim for breach of warranty under subsection (a) based on an unauthorized indorsement of the draft or an alteration of the draft, the warrantor may defend by proving that the indorsement is effective under Section 3–404 or 3–405 or the drawer is precluded under Section 3–406 or 4–406 from asserting against the drawee the unauthorized indorsement or alteration.

(d) If (i) a dishonored draft is presented for payment to the drawer or an indorser or (ii) any other instrument is presented for payment to a party obliged to pay the instrument, and (iii) payment is received, the following rules apply:

(1) The person obtaining payment and a prior transferor of the instrument warrant to the person making payment in good faith that the warrantor is, or was, at the time the warrantor transferred the instrument, a person entitled to enforce the instrument or authorized to obtain payment on behalf of a person entitled to enforce the instrument.

(2) The person making payment may recover from any warrantor for breach of warranty an amount equal to the amount paid plus expenses and loss of interest resulting from the breach.

(e) The warranties stated in subsections (a) and (d) cannot be disclaimed with respect to checks. Unless notice of a claim for breach of warranty is given to the warrantor within 30 days after the claimant has reason to know of the breach and the identity of the warrantor, the liability of the warrantor under subsection (b) or (d) is discharged to the extent of any loss caused by the delay in giving notice of the claim.

(f) A [cause of action] for breach of warranty under this section accrues when the claimant has reason to know of the breach.

§ 3–418. Payment or Acceptance by Mistake.

(a) Except as provided in subsection (c), if the drawee of a draft pays or accepts the draft and the drawee acted on the mistaken belief that (i) payment of the draft had not been stopped pursuant to Section 4–403 or (ii) the signature of the drawer of the draft was authorized, the drawee may recover the amount of the draft from the person to whom or for whose benefit payment was made or, in the case of acceptance, may revoke the acceptance. Rights of the drawee under this subsection are not affected by failure of the drawee to exercise ordinary care in paying or accepting the draft.

(b) Except as provided in subsection (c), if an instrument has been paid or accepted by mistake and the case is not covered by subsection (a), the person paying or accepting may, to the extent permitted by the law governing mistake and restitution, (i) recover the payment from the person to whom or for whose benefit payment was made or (ii) in the case of acceptance, may revoke the acceptance.

(c) The remedies provided by subsection (a) or (b) may not be asserted against a person who took the instrument in good faith and for value or who in good faith changed position in reliance on the payment or acceptance. This subsection does not limit remedies provided by Section 3–417 or 4–407.

(d) Notwithstanding Section 4–215, if an instrument is paid or accepted by mistake and the payor or acceptor recovers payment or revokes acceptance under subsection (a) or (b), the instrument is deemed not to have been paid or accepted and is treated as dishonored, and the person from whom payment is recovered has rights as a person entitled to enforce the dishonored instrument.

§ 3–419. Instruments Signed for Accommodation.

(a) If an instrument is issued for value given for the benefit of a party to the instrument ("accommodated party") and another party to the instrument ("accommodation party") signs the instrument for the purpose of incurring liability on the instrument without being a direct beneficiary of the value given for the instrument, the instrument is signed by the accommodation party "for accommodation."

(b) An accommodation party may sign the instrument as maker, drawer, acceptor, or indorser and, subject to subsection (d), is obliged to pay the instrument in the capacity in which the accommodation party signs. The obligation of an accommodation party may be enforced notwithstanding any statute of frauds and whether or not the accommodation party receives consideration for the accommodation.

(c) A person signing an instrument is presumed to be an accommodation party and there is notice that the instrument is signed for accommodation if the signature is an anomalous indorsement or is accompanied by words indicating that the signer is acting as surety or guarantor with respect to the obligation of another party to the instrument. Except as provided in Section 3–605, the obligation of an accommodation party to pay the instrument is not affected by the fact that the person enforcing the obligation had notice when the instrument was taken by that person that the accommodation party signed the instrument for accommodation.

(d) If the signature of a party to an instrument is accompanied by words indicating unambiguously that the party is guaranteeing collection rather than payment of the obligation of another party to the instrument, the signer is obliged to pay the amount due on the instrument to a person entitled to enforce the instrument only if (i) execution of judgment against the other party has been returned unsatisfied, (ii) the other party is insolvent or in an insolvency proceeding, (iii) the other party cannot be served with process, or (iv) it is otherwise apparent that payment cannot be obtained from the other party.

(e) An accommodation party who pays the instrument is entitled to reimbursement from the accommodated party and is entitled to enforce the instrument against the accommodated party. An accommodated party who pays the instrument has no right of recourse against, and is not entitled to contribution from, an accommodation party.

§ 3–420. Conversion of Instrument.

(a) The law applicable to conversion of personal property applies to instruments. An instrument is also converted if it is taken by transfer, other than a negotiation, from a person not entitled to enforce the instrument or a bank makes or obtains payment with respect to the instrument for a person not entitled to enforce the instrument or receive payment. An action for conversion of an instrument may not be brought by (i) the issuer or acceptor of the instrument or (ii) a payee or indorsee who did not receive delivery of the instrument either directly or through delivery to an agent or a co-payee.

(b) In an action under subsection (a), the measure of liability is presumed to be the amount payable on the instrument, but recovery may not exceed the amount of the plaintiff's interest in the instrument.

(c) A representative, other than a depositary bank, who has in good faith dealt with an instrument or its proceeds on behalf of one who was not the person entitled to enforce the instrument is not liable in conversion to that person beyond the amount of any proceeds that it has not paid out.

Part 5   Dishonor

§ 3–501.   Presentment.

(a) "Presentment" means a demand made by or on behalf of a person entitled to enforce an instrument (i) to pay the instrument made to the drawee or a party obliged to pay the instrument or, in the case of a note or accepted draft payable at a bank, to the bank, or (ii) to accept a draft made to the drawee.

(b) The following rules are subject to Article 4, agreement of the parties, and clearing-house rules and the like:

(1) Presentment may be made at the place of payment of the instrument and must be made at the place of payment if the instrument is payable at a bank in the United States; may be made by any commercially reasonable means, including an oral, written, or electronic communication; is effective when the demand for payment or acceptance is received by the person to whom presentment is made; and is effective if made to any one of two or more makers, acceptors, drawees, or other payors.

(2) Upon demand of the person to whom presentment is made, the person making presentment must (i) exhibit the instrument, (ii) give reasonable identification and, if presentment is made on behalf of another person, reasonable evidence of authority to do so, and (. . .) sign a receipt on the instrument for any payment made or surrender the instrument if full payment is made.

(3) Without dishonoring the instrument, the party to whom presentment is made may (i) return the instrument for lack of a necessary indorsement, or (ii) refuse payment or acceptance for failure of the presentment to comply with the terms of the instrument, an agreement of the parties, or other applicable law or rule.

(4) The party to whom presentment is made may treat presentment as occurring on the next business day after the day of presentment if the party to whom presentment is made has established a cut-off hour not earlier than 2 p.m. for the receipt and processing of instruments presented for payment or acceptance and presentment is made after the cut-off hour.

§ 3–502.   Dishonor.

(a) Dishonor of a note is governed by the following rules:

(1) If the note is payable on demand, the note is dishonored if presentment is duly made to the maker and the note is not paid on the day of presentment.

(2) If the note is not payable on demand and is payable at or through a bank or the terms of the note require presentment, the note is dishonored if presentment is duly made and the note is not paid on the day it becomes payable or the day of presentment, whichever is later.

(3) If the note is not payable on demand and paragraph (2) does not apply, the note is dishonored if it is not paid on the day it becomes payable.

(b) Dishonor of an unaccepted draft other than a documentary draft is governed by the following rules:

(1) If a check is duly presented for payment to the payor bank otherwise than for immediate payment over the counter, the check is dishonored if the payor bank makes timely return of the check or sends timely notice of dishonor or nonpayment under Section 4–301 or 4–302, or becomes accountable for the amount of the check under Section 4–302.

(2) If a draft is payable on demand and paragraph (1) does not apply, the draft is dishonored if presentment for payment is duly made to the drawee and the draft is not paid on the day of presentment.

(3) If a draft is payable on a date stated in the draft, the draft is dishonored if (i) presentment for payment is duly made to the drawee and payment is not made on the day the draft becomes payable or the day of presentment, whichever is later, or (ii) presentment for acceptance is duly made before the day the draft becomes payable and the draft is not accepted on the day of presentment.

(4) If a draft is payable on elapse of a period of time after sight or acceptance, the draft is dishonored if presentment for acceptance is duly made and the draft is not accepted on the day of presentment.

(c) Dishonor of an unaccepted documentary draft occurs according to the rules stated in subsection (b)(2), (3), and (4), except that payment or acceptance may be delayed without dishonor until no later than the close of the third business day of the drawee following the day on which payment or acceptance is required by those paragraphs.

(d) Dishonor of an accepted draft is governed by the following rules:

(1) If the draft is payable on demand, the draft is dishonored if presentment for payment is duly made to the acceptor and the draft is not paid on the day of presentment.

(2) If the draft is not payable on demand, the draft is dishonored if presentment for payment is duly made to the acceptor and payment is not made on the day it becomes payable or the day of presentment, whichever is later.

(e) In any case in which presentment is otherwise required for dishonor under this section and presentment is excused under Section 3–504, dishonor occurs without presentment if the instrument is not duly accepted or paid.

(f) If a draft is dishonored because timely acceptance of the draft was not made and the person entitled to demand acceptance consents to a late acceptance, from the time of acceptance the draft is treated as never having been dishonored.

§ 3–503.   Notice of Dishonor.

(a) The obligation of an indorser stated in Section 3–415(a) and the obligation of a drawer stated in Section 3–414(d) may not be enforced unless (i) the indorser or drawer is given notice of dishonor of the instrument complying with this section or (ii) notice of dishonor is excused under Section 3–504(b).

(b) Notice of dishonor may be given by any person; may be given by any commercially reasonable means, including an oral, written, or electronic communication; and is sufficient if it reasonably identifies the instrument and indicates that the instrument has been dishonored or has not been paid or accepted. Return of an instrument given to a bank for collection is sufficient notice of dishonor.

(c) Subject to Section 3–504(c), with respect to an instrument taken for collection by a collecting bank, notice of dishonor must be given (i) by the bank before midnight of the next banking day following the banking day on which the bank receives notice of dishonor of the instrument, or (ii) by any other person within 30 days following the day on which the person receives notice of dishonor. With respect to any other instrument, notice of dishonor must be given within 30 days following the day on which dishonor occurs.

§ 3–504. Excused Presentment and Notice of Dishonor.

(a) Presentment for payment or acceptance of an instrument is excused if (i) the person entitled to present the instrument cannot with reasonable diligence make presentment, (ii) the maker or acceptor has repudiated an obligation to pay the instrument or is dead or in insolvency proceedings, (iii) by the terms of the instrument presentment is not necessary to enforce the obligation of indorsers or the drawer, (iv) the drawer or indorser whose obligation is being enforced has waived presentment or otherwise has no reason to expect or right to require that the instrument be paid or accepted, or (v) the drawer instructed the drawee not to pay or accept the draft or the drawee was not obligated to the drawer to pay the draft.

(b) Notice of dishonor is excused if (i) by the terms of the instrument notice of dishonor is not necessary to enforce the obligation of a party to pay the instrument, or (ii) the party whose obligation is being enforced waived notice of dishonor. A waiver of presentment is also a waiver of notice of dishonor.

(c) Delay in giving notice of dishonor is excused if the delay was caused by circumstances beyond the control of the person giving the notice and the person giving the notice exercised reasonable diligence after the cause of the delay ceased to operate.

§ 3–505. Evidence of Dishonor.

(a) The following are admissible as evidence and create a presumption of dishonor and of any notice of dishonor stated:

    (1) a document regular in form as provided in subsection (b) which purports to be a protest;

    (2) a purported stamp or writing of the drawee, payor bank, or presenting bank on or accompanying the instrument stating that acceptance or payment has been refused unless reasons for the refusal are stated and the reasons are not consistent with dishonor;

    (3) a book or record of the drawee, payor bank, or collecting bank, kept in the usual course of business which shows dishonor, even if there is no evidence of who made the entry.

(b) A protest is a certificate of dishonor made by a United States consul or vice consul, or a notary public or other person authorized to administer oaths by the law of the place where dishonor occurs. It may be made upon information satisfactory to that person. The protest must identify the instrument and certify either that presentment has been made or, if not made, the reason why it was not made, and that the instrument has been dishonored by nonacceptance or nonpayment. The protest may also certify that notice of dishonor has been given to some or all parties.

Part 6 Discharge and Payment

§ 3–601. Discharge and Effect of Discharge.

(a) The obligation of a party to pay the instrument is discharged as stated in this Article or by an act or agreement with the party which would discharge an obligation to pay money under a simple contract.

(b) Discharge of the obligation of a party is not effective against a person acquiring rights of a holder in due course of the instrument without notice of the discharge.

§ 3–602. Payment.

(a) Subject to subsection (b), an instrument is paid to the extent payment is made (i) by or on behalf of a party obliged to pay the instrument, and (ii) to a person entitled to enforce the instrument. To the extent of the payment, the obligation of the party obliged to pay the instrument is discharged even though payment is made with knowledge of a claim to the instrument under Section 3–306 by another person.

(b) The obligation of a party to pay the instrument is not discharged under subsection (a) if:

    (1) a claim to the instrument under Section 3–306 is enforceable against the party receiving payment and (i) payment is made with knowledge by the payor that payment is prohibited by injunction or similar process of a court of competent jurisdiction, or (ii) in the case of an instrument other than a cashier's check, teller's check, or certified check, the party making payment accepted, from the person having a claim to the instrument, indemnity against loss resulting from refusal to pay the person entitled to enforce the instrument; or

    (2) the person making payment knows that the instrument is a stolen instrument and pays a person it knows is in wrongful possession of the instrument.

§ 3–603. Tender of Payment.

(a) If tender of payment of an obligation to pay an instrument is made to a person entitled to enforce the instrument, the effect of tender is governed by principles of law applicable to tender of payment under a simple contract.

(b) If tender of payment of an obligation to pay an instrument is made to a person entitled to enforce the instrument and the tender is refused, there is discharge, to the extent of the amount of the tender, of the obligation of an indorser or accommodation party having a right of recourse with respect to the obligation to which the tender relates.

(c) If tender of payment of an amount due on an instrument is made to a person entitled to enforce the instrument, the obligation of the obligor to pay interest after the due date on the amount tendered is discharged. If presentment is required with respect to an instrument and the obligor is able and ready to pay on the due date at every place of payment stated in the instrument, the obligor is deemed to have made tender of payment on the due date to the person entitled to enforce the instrument.

§ 3–604. Discharge by Cancellation or Renunciation.

(a) A person entitled to enforce an instrument, with or without consideration, may discharge the obligation of a party to pay the instrument (i) by an intentional voluntary act, such as surrender of the instrument to the party, destruction, mutilation, or cancellation of the instrument, cancellation or striking out of the party's signature, or the addition of words to the instrument indicating discharge, or (ii) by agreeing not to sue or otherwise renouncing rights against the party by a signed writing.

(b) Cancellation or striking out of an indorsement pursuant to subsection (a) does not affect the status and rights of a party derived from the indorsement.

§ 3–605. Discharge of Indorsers and Accommodation Parties.

(a) In this section, the term "indorser" includes a drawer having the obligation described in Section 3–414(d).

(b) Discharge, under Section 3–604, of the obligation of a party to pay an instrument does not discharge the obligation of an indorser or accommodation party having a right of recourse against the discharged party.

(c) If a person entitled to enforce an instrument agrees, with or without consideration, to an extension of the due date of the obligation of a party to pay the instrument, the extension discharges an indorser or accommodation party having a right of recourse against the party whose obligation is extended to the extent the indorser or accommodation party proves that the extension caused loss to the indorser or accommodation party with respect to the right of recourse.

(d) If a person entitled to enforce an instrument agrees, with or without consideration, to a material modification of the obligation of a party other than an extension of the due date, the modification discharges the obligation of an indorser or accommodation party having a right of recourse against the person whose obligation is modified to the extent the modification causes loss to the indorser or accommodation party with respect to the right of recourse. The loss suffered by the indorser or accommodation party as a result of the modification is equal to the amount of the right of recourse unless the person enforcing the instrument proves that no loss was caused by the modification or that the loss caused by the modification was an amount less than the amount of the right of recourse.

(e) If the obligation of a party to pay an instrument is secured by an interest in collateral and a person entitled to enforce the instrument impairs the value of the interest in collateral, the obligation of an indorser or accommodation party having a right of recourse against the obligor is discharged to the extent of the impairment. The value of an interest in collateral is impaired to the extent (i) the value of the interest is reduced to an amount less than the amount of the right of recourse of the party asserting discharge, or (ii) the reduction in value of the interest causes an increase in the amount by which the amount of the right of recourse exceeds the value of the interest. The burden of proving impairment is on the party asserting discharge.

(f) If the obligation of a party is secured by an interest in collateral not provided by an accommodation party and a person entitled to enforce the instrument impairs the value of the interest in collateral, the obligation of any party who is jointly and severally liable with respect to the secured obligation is discharged to the extent the impairment causes the party asserting discharge to pay more than that party would have been obliged to pay, taking into account rights of contribution, if impairment had not occurred. If the party asserting discharge is an accommodation party not entitled to discharge under subsection (e), the party is deemed to have a right to contribution based on joint and several liability rather than a right to reimbursement. The burden of proving impairment is on the party asserting discharge.

(g) Under subsection (e) or (f), impairing value of an interest in collateral includes (i) failure to obtain or maintain perfection or recordation of the interest in collateral, (ii) release of collateral without substitution of collateral of equal value, (iii) failure to perform a duty to preserve the value of collateral owed, under Article 9 or other law, to a debtor or surety or other person secondarily liable, or (iv) failure to comply with applicable law in disposing of collateral.

(h) An accommodation party is not discharged under subsection (c), (d), or (e) unless the person entitled to enforce the instrument knows of the accommodation or has notice under Section 3–419(c) that the instrument was signed for accommodation.

(i) A party is not discharged under this section if (i) the party asserting discharge consents to the event or conduct that is the basis of the discharge, or (ii) the instrument or a separate agreement of the party provides for waiver of discharge under this section either specifically or by general language indicating that parties waive defenses based on suretyship or impairment of collateral.

ADDENDUM TO REVISED ARTICLE 3

Notes to Legislative Counsel

1. If revised Article 3 is adopted in your state, the reference in Section 2–511 to Section 3–802 should be changed to Section 3–310.

2. If revised Article 3 is adopted in your state and the Uniform Fiduciaries Act is also in effect in your state, you may want to consider amending Uniform Fiduciaries Act § 9 to conform to Section 3–307(b)(2)(iii) and (4)(iii). See Official Comment 3 to Section 3–307.

Revised Article 4
BANK DEPOSITS AND COLLECTIONS

Part 1   General Provisions and Definitions

§ 4–101.   Short Title.

This Article may be cited as Uniform Commercial Code—Bank Deposits and Collections.

As amended in 1990.

§ 4–102.   Applicability.

(a) To the extent that items within this Article are also within Articles 3 and 8, they are subject to those Articles. If there is conflict, this Article governs Article 3, but Article 8 governs this Article.

(b) The liability of a bank for action or non-action with respect to an item handled by it for purposes of presentment, payment, or collection is governed by the law of the place where the bank is located. In the case of action or non-action by or at a branch or separate office of a bank, its liability is governed by the law of the place where the branch or separate office is located.

§ 4–103.   Variation by Agreement; Measure of Damages; Action Constituting Ordinary Care.

(a) The effect of the provisions of this Article may be varied by agreement, but the parties to the agreement cannot disclaim a bank's responsibility for its lack of good faith or failure to exercise ordinary care or limit the measure of damages for the lack or failure. However, the parties may determine by agreement the standards by which the bank's responsibility is to be measured if those standards are not manifestly unreasonable.

(b) Federal Reserve regulations and operating circulars, clearing-house rules, and the like have the effect of agreements under subsection (a), whether or not specifically assented to by all parties interested in items handled.

(c) Action or non-action approved by this Article or pursuant to Federal Reserve regulations or operating circulars is the exercise of ordinary care and, in the absence of special instructions, action or non-action consistent with clearing-house rules and the like or with a general banking usage not disapproved by this Article, is prima facie the exercise of ordinary care.

(d) The specification or approval of certain procedures by this Article is not disapproval of other procedures that may be reasonable under the circumstances.

(e) The measure of damages for failure to exercise ordinary care in handling an item is the amount of the item reduced by an amount that could not have been realized by the exercise of ordinary care. If there is also bad faith it includes any other damages the party suffered as a proximate consequence.

As amended in 1990.

§ 4-104. Definitions and Index of Definitions.

(a) In this Article, unless the context otherwise requires:

(1) "Account" means any deposit or credit account with a bank, including a demand, time, savings, passbook, share draft, or like account, other than an account evidenced by a certificate of deposit;

(2) "Afternoon" means the period of a day between noon and midnight;

(3) "Banking day" means the part of a day on which a bank is open to the public for carrying on substantially all of its banking functions;

(4) "Clearing house" means an association of banks or other payors regularly clearing items;

(5) "Customer" means a person having an account with a bank or for whom a bank has agreed to collect items, including a bank that maintains an account at another bank;

(6) "Documentary draft" means a draft to be presented for acceptance or payment if specified documents, certificated securities (Section 8–102) or instructions for uncertificated securities (Section 8–102), or other certificates, statements, or the like are to be received by the drawee or other payor before acceptance or payment of the draft;

(7) "Draft" means a draft as defined in Section 3–104 or an item, other than an instrument, that is an order;

(8) "Drawee" means a person ordered in a draft to make payment;

(9) "Item" means an instrument or a promise or order to pay money handled by a bank for collection or payment. The term does not include a payment order governed by Article 4A or a credit or debit card slip;

(10) "Midnight deadline" with respect to a bank is midnight on its next banking day following the banking day on which it receives the relevant item or notice or from which the time for taking action commences to run, whichever is later;

(11) "Settle" means to pay in cash, by clearing-house settlement, in a charge or credit or by remittance, or otherwise as agreed. A settlement may be either provisional or final;

(12) "Suspends payments" with respect to a bank means that it has been closed by order of the supervisory authorities, that a public officer has been appointed to take it over, or that it ceases or refuses to make payments in the ordinary course of business.

(b) [Other definitions' section references deleted.]

(c) [Other definitions' section references deleted.]

(d) In addition, Article 1 contains general definitions and principles of construction and interpretation applicable throughout this Article.

§ 4-105. "Bank"; "Depositary Bank"; "Payor Bank"; "Intermediary Bank"; "Collecting Bank"; "Presenting Bank".

In this Article:

(1) "Bank" means a person engaged in the business of banking, including a savings bank, savings and loan association, credit union, or trust company;

(2) "Depositary bank" means the first bank to take an item even though it is also the payor bank, unless the item is presented for immediate payment over the counter;

(3) "Payor bank" means a bank that is the drawee of a draft;

(4) "Intermediary bank" means a bank to which an item is transferred in course of collection except the depositary or payor bank;

(5) "Collecting bank" means a bank handling an item for collection except the payor bank;

(6) "Presenting bank" means a bank presenting an item except a payor bank.

§ 4-106. Payable Through or Payable at Bank: Collecting Bank.

(a) If an item states that it is "payable through" a bank identified in the item, (i) the item designates the bank as a collecting bank and does not by itself authorize the bank to pay the item, and (ii) the item may be presented for payment only by or through the bank.

Alternative A

(b) If an item states that it is "payable at" a bank identified in the item, the item is equivalent to a draft drawn on the bank.

Alternative B

(b) If an item states that it is "payable at" a bank identified in the item, (i) the item designates the bank as a collecting bank and does not by itself authorize the bank to pay the item, and (ii) the item may be presented for payment only by or through the bank.

(c) If a draft names a nonbank drawee and it is unclear whether a bank named in the draft is a co-drawee or a collecting bank, the bank is a collecting bank.

As added in 1990.

§ 4-107. Separate Office of Bank.

A branch or separate office of a bank is a separate bank for the purpose of computing the time within which and determining the place at or to which action may be taken or notices or orders shall be given under this Article and under Article 3.

As amended in 1962 and 1990.

§ 4-108. Time of Receipt of Items.

(a) For the purpose of allowing time to process items, prove balances, and make the necessary entries on its books to determine its position for the day, a bank may fix an afternoon hour of 2 p.m. or later as a cutoff hour for the handling of money and items and the making of entries on its books.

(b) An item or deposit of money received on any day after a cutoff hour so fixed or after the close of the banking day may be treated as being received at the opening of the next banking day.

As amended in 1990.

§ 4-109. Delays.

(a) Unless otherwise instructed, a collecting bank in a good faith effort to secure payment of a specific item drawn on a payor other than a bank, and with or without the approval of any person involved, may waive, modify, or extend time limits imposed or permitted by this [act] for a period not exceeding two additional banking days without discharge of drawers or indorsers or liability to its transferor or a prior party.

(b) Delay by a collecting bank or payor bank beyond time limits prescribed or permitted by this [act] or by instructions is excused if (i) the delay is caused by interruption of communication or computer facilities, suspension of payments by another bank, war, emergency conditions, failure of equipment, or other circumstances beyond the control of the bank, and (ii) the bank exercises such diligence as the circumstances require.

§ 4–110. Electronic Presentment.

(a) "Agreement for electronic presentment" means an agreement, clearing-house rule, or Federal Reserve regulation or operating circular, providing that presentment of an item may be made by transmission of an image of an item or information describing the item ("presentment notice") rather than delivery of the item itself. The agreement may provide for procedures governing retention, presentment, payment, dishonor, and other matters concerning items subject to the agreement.

(b) Presentment of an item pursuant to an agreement for presentment is made when the presentment notice is received.

(c) If presentment is made by presentment notice, a reference to "item" or "check" in this Article means the presentment notice unless the context otherwise indicates.

As added in 1990.

§ 4–111. Statute of Limitations.

An action to enforce an obligation, duty, or right arising under this Article must be commenced within three years after the [cause of action] accrues.

As added in 1990.

Part 2   Collection of Items: Depository and Collecting Banks

§ 4–201. Status of Collecting Bank as Agent and Provisional Status of Credits; Applicability of Article; Item Indorsed "Pay Any Bank".

(a) Unless a contrary intent clearly appears and before the time that a settlement given by a collecting bank for an item is or becomes final, the bank, with respect to an item, is an agent or sub-agent of the owner of the item and any settlement given for the item is provisional. This provision applies regardless of the form of indorsement or lack of indorsement and even though credit given for the item is subject to immediate withdrawal as of right or is in fact withdrawn; but the continuance of ownership of an item by its owner and any rights of the owner to proceeds of the item are subject to rights of a collecting bank, such as those resulting from outstanding advances on the item and rights of recoupment or setoff. If an item is handled by banks for purposes of presentment, payment, collection, or return, the relevant provisions of this Article apply even though action of the parties clearly establishes that a particular bank has purchased the item and is the owner of it.

(b) After an item has been indorsed with the words "pay any bank" or the like, only a bank may acquire the rights of a holder until the item has been:

(1) returned to the customer initiating collection; or

(2) specially indorsed by a bank to a person who is not a bank.

As amended in 1990.

§ 4–202. Responsibility for Collection or Return; When Action Timely.

(a) A collecting bank must exercise ordinary care in:

(1) presenting an item or sending it for presentment;

(2) sending notice of dishonor or nonpayment or returning an item other than a documentary draft to the bank's transferor after learning that the item has not been paid or accepted, as the case may be;

(3) settling for an item when the bank receives final settlement; and

(4) notifying its transferor of any loss or delay in transit within a reasonable time after discovery thereof.

(b) A collecting bank exercises ordinary care under subsection (a) by taking proper action before its midnight deadline following receipt of an item, notice, or settlement. Taking proper action within a reasonably longer time may constitute the exercise of ordinary care, but the bank has the burden of establishing timeliness.

(c) Subject to subsection (a)(1), a bank is not liable for the insolvency, neglect, misconduct, mistake, or default of another bank or person or for loss or destruction of an item in the possession of others or in transit.

As amended in 1990.

§ 4–203. Effect of Instructions.

Subject to Article 3 concerning conversion of instruments (Section 3–420) and restrictive indorsements (Section 3–206), only a collecting bank's transferor can give instructions that affect the bank or constitute notice to it, and a collecting bank is not liable to prior parties for any action taken pursuant to the instructions or in accordance with any agreement with its transferor.

§ 4–204. Methods of Sending and Presenting; Sending Directly to Payor Bank.

(a) A collecting bank shall send items by a reasonably prompt method, taking into consideration relevant instructions, the nature of the item, the number of those items on hand, the cost of collection involved, and the method generally used by it or others to present those items.

(b) A collecting bank may send:

(1) an item directly to the payor bank;

(2) an item to a nonbank payor if authorized by its transferor; and

(3) an item other than documentary drafts to a nonbank payor, if authorized by Federal Reserve regulation or operating circular, clearing-house rule, or the like.

(c) Presentment may be made by a presenting bank at a place where the payor bank or other payor has requested that presentment be made.

As amended in 1990.

§ 4–205. Depositary Bank Holder of Unindorsed Item.

If a customer delivers an item to a depositary bank for collection:

(1) the depositary bank becomes a holder of the item at the time it receives the item for collection if the customer at the time of deliv-

ery was a holder of the item, whether or not the customer indorses the item, and, if the bank satisfies the other requirements of Section 3–302, it is a holder in due course; and

(2) the depositary bank warrants to collecting banks, the payor bank or other payor, and the drawer that the amount of the item was paid to the customer or deposited to the customer's account.

As amended in 1990.

§ 4–206. Transfer Between Banks.

Any agreed method that identifies the transferor bank is sufficient for the item's further transfer to another bank.

As amended in 1990.

§ 4–207. Transfer Warranties.

(a) A customer or collecting bank that transfers an item and receives a settlement or other consideration warrants to the transferee and to any subsequent collecting bank that:

(1) the warrantor is a person entitled to enforce the item;

(2) all signatures on the item are authentic and authorized;

(3) the item has not been altered;

(4) the item is not subject to a defense or claim in recoupment (Section 3–305(a)) of any party that can be asserted against the warrantor; and

(5) the warrantor has no knowledge of any insolvency proceeding commenced with respect to the maker or acceptor or, in the case of an unaccepted draft, the drawer.

(b) If an item is dishonored, a customer or collecting bank transferring the item and receiving settlement or other consideration is obliged to pay the amount due on the item (i) according to the terms of the item at the time it was transferred, or (ii) if the transfer was of an incomplete item, according to its terms when completed as stated in Sections 3–115 and 3–407. The obligation of a transferor is owed to the transferee and to any subsequent collecting bank that takes the item in good faith. A transferor cannot disclaim its obligation under this subsection by an indorsement stating that it is made "without recourse" or otherwise disclaiming liability.

(c) A person to whom the warranties under subsection (a) are made and who took the item in good faith may recover from the warrantor as damages for breach of warranty an amount equal to the loss suffered as a result of the breach, but not more than the amount of the item plus expenses and loss of interest incurred as a result of the breach.

(d) The warranties stated in subsection (a) cannot be disclaimed with respect to checks. Unless notice of a claim for breach of warranty is given to the warrantor within 30 days after the claimant has reason to know of the breach and the identity of the warrantor, the warrantor is discharged to the extent of any loss caused by the delay in giving notice of the claim.

(e) A cause of action for breach of warranty under this section accrues when the claimant has reason to know of the breach.

As amended in 1990.

§ 4–208. Presentment Warranties.

(a) If an unaccepted draft is presented to the drawee for payment or acceptance and the drawee pays or accepts the draft, (i) the person obtaining payment or acceptance, at the time of presentment, and (ii) a previous transferor of the draft, at the time of transfer, warrant to the drawee that pays or accepts the draft in good faith that:

(1) the warrantor is, or was, at the time the warrantor transferred the draft, a person entitled to enforce the draft or authorized to obtain payment or acceptance of the draft on behalf of a person entitled to enforce the draft;

(2) the draft has not been altered; and

(3) the warrantor has no knowledge that the signature of the purported drawer of the draft is unauthorized.

(b) A drawee making payment may recover from a warrantor damages for breach of warranty equal to the amount paid by the drawee less the amount the drawee received or is entitled to receive from the drawer because of the payment. In addition, the drawee is entitled to compensation for expenses and loss of interest resulting from the breach. The right of the drawee to recover damages under this subsection is not affected by any failure of the drawee to exercise ordinary care in making payment. If the drawee accepts the draft (i) breach of warranty is a defense to the obligation of the acceptor, and (ii) if the acceptor makes payment with respect to the draft, the acceptor is entitled to recover from a warrantor for breach of warranty the amounts stated in this subsection.

(c) If a drawee asserts a claim for breach of warranty under subsection (a) based on an unauthorized indorsement of the draft or an alteration of the draft, the warrantor may defend by proving that the indorsement is effective under Section 3–404 or 3–405 or the drawer is precluded under Section 3–406 or 4–406 from asserting against the drawee the unauthorized indorsement or alteration.

(d) If (i) a dishonored draft is presented for payment to the drawer or an indorser or (ii) any other item is presented for payment to a party obliged to pay the item, and the item is paid, the person obtaining payment and a prior transferor of the item warrant to the person making payment in good faith that the warrantor is, or was, at the time the warrantor transferred the item, a person entitled to enforce the item or authorized to obtain payment on behalf of a person entitled to enforce the item. The person making payment may recover from any warrantor for breach of warranty an amount equal to the amount paid plus expenses and loss of interest resulting from the breach.

(e) The warranties stated in subsections (a) and (d) cannot be disclaimed with respect to checks. Unless notice of a claim for breach of warranty is given to the warrantor within 30 days after the claimant has reason to know of the breach and the identity of the warrantor, the warrantor is discharged to the extent of any loss caused by the delay in giving notice of the claim.

(f) A cause of action for breach of warranty under this section accrues when the claimant has reason to know of the breach.

As amended in 1990.

§ 4–209. Encoding and Retention Warranties.

(a) A person who encodes information on or with respect to an item after issue warrants to any subsequent collecting bank and to the payor bank or other payor that the information is correctly encoded. If the customer of a depositary bank encodes, that bank also makes the warranty.

(b) A person who undertakes to retain an item pursuant to an agreement for electronic presentment warrants to any subsequent collecting bank and to the payor bank or other payor that retention and presentment of the item comply with the agreement. If a customer of a depositary bank undertakes to retain an item, that bank also makes this warranty.

(c) A person to whom warranties are made under this section and who took the item in good faith may recover from the warrantor as damages for breach of warranty an amount equal to the loss suffered as a result of the breach, plus expenses and loss of interest incurred as a result of the breach.

As added in 1990.

§ 4–210. Security Interest of Collecting Bank in Items, Accompanying Documents and Proceeds.

(a) A collecting bank has a security interest in an item and any accompanying documents or the proceeds of either:

(1) in case of an item deposited in an account, to the extent to which credit given for the item has been withdrawn or applied;

(2) in case of an item for which it has given credit available for withdrawal as of right, to the extent of the credit given, whether or not the credit is drawn upon or there is a right of charge-back; or

(3) if it makes an advance on or against the item.

(b) If credit given for several items received at one time or pursuant to a single agreement is withdrawn or applied in part, the security interest remains upon all the items, any accompanying documents or the proceeds of either. For the purpose of this section, credits first given are first withdrawn.

(c) Receipt by a collecting bank of a final settlement for an item is a realization on its security interest in the item, accompanying documents, and proceeds. So long as the bank does not receive final settlement for the item or give up possession of the item or accompanying documents for purposes other than collection, the security interest continues to that extent and is subject to Article 9, but:

(1) no security agreement is necessary to make the security interest enforceable (Section 9–203(1)(a));

(2) no filing is required to perfect the security interest; and

(3) the security interest has priority over conflicting perfected security interests in the item, accompanying documents, or proceeds.

As amended in 1990 and 1999.

§ 4–211. When Bank Gives Value for Purposes of Holder in Due Course.

For purposes of determining its status as a holder in due course, a bank has given value to the extent it has a security interest in an item, if the bank otherwise complies with the requirements of Section 3–302 on what constitutes a holder in due course.

As amended in 1990.

§ 4–212. Presentment by Notice of Item Not Payable by, Through, or at Bank; Liability of Drawer or Indorser.

(a) Unless otherwise instructed, a collecting bank may present an item not payable by, through, or at a bank by sending to the party to accept or pay a written notice that the bank holds the item for acceptance or payment. The notice must be sent in time to be received on or before the day when presentment is due and the bank must meet any requirement of the party to accept or pay under Section 3–501 by the close of the bank's next banking day after it knows of the requirement.

(b) If presentment is made by notice and payment, acceptance, or request for compliance with a requirement under Section 3–501 is not received by the close of business on the day after maturity or, in the case of demand items, by the close of business on the third banking day after notice was sent, the presenting bank may treat the item as dishonored and charge any drawer or indorser by sending it notice of the facts.

As amended in 1990.

§ 4–213. Medium and Time of Settlement by Bank.

(a) With respect to settlement by a bank, the medium and time of settlement may be prescribed by Federal Reserve regulations or circulars, clearing-house rules, and the like, or agreement. In the absence of such prescription:

(1) the medium of settlement is cash or credit to an account in a Federal Reserve bank of or specified by the person to receive settlement; and

(2) the time of settlement is:

(i) with respect to tender of settlement by cash, a cashier's check, or teller's check, when the cash or check is sent or delivered;

(ii) with respect to tender of settlement by credit in an account in a Federal Reserve Bank, when the credit is made;

(iii) with respect to tender of settlement by a credit or debit to an account in a bank, when the credit or debit is made or, in the case of tender of settlement by authority to charge an account, when the authority is sent or delivered; or

(iv) with respect to tender of settlement by a funds transfer, when payment is made pursuant to Section 4A–406(a) to the person receiving settlement.

(b) If the tender of settlement is not by a medium authorized by subsection (a) or the time of settlement is not fixed by subsection (a), no settlement occurs until the tender of settlement is accepted by the person receiving settlement.

(c) If settlement for an item is made by cashier's check or teller's check and the person receiving settlement, before its midnight deadline:

(1) presents or forwards the check for collection, settlement is final when the check is finally paid; or

(2) fails to present or forward the check for collection, settlement is final at the midnight deadline of the person receiving settlement.

(d) If settlement for an item is made by giving authority to charge the account of the bank giving settlement in the bank receiving settlement, settlement is final when the charge is made by the bank receiving settlement if there are funds available in the account for the amount of the item.

As amended in 1990.

§ 4–214. Right of Charge-Back or Refund; Liability of Collecting Bank: Return of Item.

(a) If a collecting bank has made provisional settlement with its customer for an item and fails by reason of dishonor, suspension of payments by a bank, or otherwise to receive settlement for the item which is or becomes final, the bank may revoke the settlement given by it, charge back the amount of any credit given for the item to its customer's account, or obtain refund from its customer, whether or not it is able to return the item, if by its midnight deadline or within a longer reasonable time after it learns the facts it returns the item or sends notification of the facts. If the return or notice is delayed beyond the bank's midnight deadline or a longer reasonable time after it learns the facts, the bank may revoke the settlement, charge back the credit, or obtain refund from its customer, but it is liable for any loss resulting from the delay. These rights to revoke, charge back, and obtain refund terminate if and when a settlement for the item received by the bank is or becomes final.

(b) A collecting bank returns an item when it is sent or delivered to the bank's customer or transferor or pursuant to its instructions.

(c) A depositary bank that is also the payor may charge back the amount of an item to its customer's account or obtain refund in accordance with the section governing return of an item received by a payor bank for credit on its books (Section 4–301).

(d) The right to charge back is not affected by:

(1) previous use of a credit given for the item; or

(2) failure by any bank to exercise ordinary care with respect to the item, but a bank so failing remains liable.

(e) A failure to charge back or claim refund does not affect other rights of the bank against the customer or any other party.

(f) If credit is given in dollars as the equivalent of the value of an item payable in foreign money, the dollar amount of any charge-back or refund must be calculated on the basis of the bank-offered spot rate for the foreign money prevailing on the day when the person entitled to the charge-back or refund learns that it will not receive payment in ordinary course.

As amended in 1990.

§ 4–215. Final Payment of Item by Payor Bank; When Provisional Debits and Credits Become Final; When Certain Credits Become Available for Withdrawal.

(a) An item is finally paid by a payor bank when the bank has first done any of the following:

(1) paid the item in cash;

(2) settled for the item without having a right to revoke the settlement under statute, clearing-house rule, or agreement; or

(3) made a provisional settlement for the item and failed to revoke the settlement in the time and manner permitted by statute, clearing-house rule, or agreement.

(b) If provisional settlement for an item does not become final, the item is not finally paid.

(c) If provisional settlement for an item between the presenting and payor banks is made through a clearing house or by debits or credits in an account between them, then to the extent that provisional debits or credits for the item are entered in accounts between the presenting and payor banks or between the presenting and successive prior collecting banks seriatim, they become final upon final payment of the item by the payor bank.

(d) If a collecting bank receives a settlement for an item which is or becomes final, the bank is accountable to its customer for the amount of the item and any provisional credit given for the item in an account with its customer becomes final.

(e) Subject to (i) applicable law stating a time for availability of funds and (ii) any right of the bank to apply the credit to an obligation of the customer, credit given by a bank for an item in a customer's account becomes available for withdrawal as of right:

(1) if the bank has received a provisional settlement for the item, when the settlement becomes final and the bank has had a rea-

sonable time to receive return of the item and the item has not been received within that time;

(2) if the bank is both the depositary bank and the payor bank, and the item is finally paid, at the opening of the bank's second banking day following receipt of the item.

(f) Subject to applicable law stating a time for availability of funds and any right of a bank to apply a deposit to an obligation of the depositor, a deposit of money becomes available for withdrawal as of right at the opening of the bank's next banking day after receipt of the deposit.

As amended in 1990.

§ 4–216. Insolvency and Preference.

(a) If an item is in or comes into the possession of a payor or collecting bank that suspends payment and the item has not been finally paid, the item must be returned by the receiver, trustee, or agent in charge of the closed bank to the presenting bank or the closed bank's customer.

(b) If a payor bank finally pays an item and suspends payments without making a settlement for the item with its customer or the presenting bank which settlement is or becomes final, the owner of the item has a preferred claim against the payor bank.

(c) If a payor bank gives or a collecting bank gives or receives a provisional settlement for an item and thereafter suspends payments, the suspension does not prevent or interfere with the settlement's becoming final if the finality occurs automatically upon the lapse of certain time or the happening of certain events.

(d) If a collecting bank receives from subsequent parties settlement for an item, which settlement is or becomes final and the bank suspends payments without making a settlement for the item with its customer which settlement is or becomes final, the owner of the item has a preferred claim against the collecting bank.

As amended in 1990.

Part 3 Collection of Items: Payor Banks

§ 4–301. Deferred Posting; Recovery of Payment by Return of Items; Time of Dishonor; Return of Items by Payor Bank.

(a) If a payor bank settles for a demand item other than a documentary draft presented otherwise than for immediate payment over the counter before midnight of the banking day of receipt, the payor bank may revoke the settlement and recover the settlement if, before it has made final payment and before its midnight deadline, it

(1) returns the item; or

(2) sends written notice of dishonor or nonpayment if the item is unavailable for return.

(b) If a demand item is received by a payor bank for credit on its books, it may return the item or send notice of dishonor and may revoke any credit given or recover the amount thereof withdrawn by its customer, if it acts within the time limit and in the manner specified in subsection (a).

(c) Unless previous notice of dishonor has been sent, an item is dishonored at the time when for purposes of dishonor it is returned or notice sent in accordance with this section.

(d) An item is returned:

(1) as to an item presented through a clearing house, when it is delivered to the presenting or last collecting bank or to the

clearing house or is sent or delivered in accordance with clearing-house rules; or

(2) in all other cases, when it is sent or delivered to the bank's customer or transferor or pursuant to instructions.

As amended in 1990.

§ 4–302. Payor Bank's Responsibility for Late Return of Item.

(a) If an item is presented to and received by a payor bank, the bank is accountable for the amount of:

(1) a demand item, other than a documentary draft, whether properly payable or not, if the bank, in any case in which it is not also the depositary bank, retains the item beyond midnight of the banking day of receipt without settling for it or, whether or not it is also the depositary bank, does not pay or return the item or send notice of dishonor until after its midnight deadline; or

(2) any other properly payable item unless, within the time allowed for acceptance or payment of that item, the bank either accepts or pays the item or returns it and accompanying documents.

(b) The liability of a payor bank to pay an item pursuant to subsection (a) is subject to defenses based on breach of a presentment warranty (Section 4–208) or proof that the person seeking enforcement of the liability presented or transferred the item for the purpose of defrauding the payor bank.

As amended in 1990.

§ 4–303. When Items Subject to Notice, Stop-Payment Order, Legal Process, or Setoff; Order in Which Items May Be Charged or Certified.

(a) Any knowledge, notice, or stop-payment order received by, legal process served upon, or setoff exercised by a payor bank comes too late to terminate, suspend, or modify the bank's right or duty to pay an item or to charge its customer's account for the item if the knowledge, notice, stop-payment order, or legal process is received or served and a reasonable time for the bank to act thereon expires or the setoff is exercised after the earliest of the following:

(1) the bank accepts or certifies the item;

(2) the bank pays the item in cash;

(3) the bank settles for the item without having a right to revoke the settlement under statute, clearing-house rule, or agreement;

(4) the bank becomes accountable for the amount of the item under Section 4–302 dealing with the payor bank's responsibility for late return of items; or

(5) with respect to checks, a cutoff hour no earlier than one hour after the opening of the next banking day after the banking day on which the bank received the check and no later than the close of that next banking day or, if no cutoff hour is fixed, the close of the next banking day after the banking day on which the bank received the check.

(b) Subject to subsection (a), items may be accepted, paid, certified, or charged to the indicated account of its customer in any order.

As amended in 1990.

Part 4 Relationship Between Payor Bank and Its Customer

§ 4–401. When Bank May Charge Customer's Account.

(a) A bank may charge against the account of a customer an item that is properly payable from the account even though the charge creates an overdraft. An item is properly payable if it is authorized by the customer and is in accordance with any agreement between the customer and bank.

(b) A customer is not liable for the amount of an overdraft if the customer neither signed the item nor benefited from the proceeds of the item.

(c) A bank may charge against the account of a customer a check that is otherwise properly payable from the account, even though payment was made before the date of the check, unless the customer has given notice to the bank of the postdating describing the check with reasonable certainty. The notice is effective for the period stated in Section 4–403(b) for stop-payment orders, and must be received at such time and in such manner as to afford the bank a reasonable opportunity to act on it before the bank takes any action with respect to the check described in Section 4–303. If a bank charges against the account of a customer a check before the date stated in the notice of postdating, the bank is liable for damages for the loss resulting from its act. The loss may include damages for dishonor of subsequent items under Section 4–402.

(d) A bank that in good faith makes payment to a holder may charge the indicated account of its customer according to:

(1) the original terms of the altered item; or

(2) the terms of the completed item, even though the bank knows the item has been completed unless the bank has notice that the completion was improper.

As amended in 1990.

§ 4–402. Bank's Liability to Customer for Wrongful Dishonor; Time of Determining Insufficiency of Account.

(a) Except as otherwise provided in this Article, a payor bank wrongfully dishonors an item if it dishonors an item that is properly payable, but a bank may dishonor an item that would create an overdraft unless it has agreed to pay the overdraft.

(b) A payor bank is liable to its customer for damages proximately caused by the wrongful dishonor of an item. Liability is limited to actual damages proved and may include damages for an arrest or prosecution of the customer or other consequential damages. Whether any consequential damages are proximately caused by the wrongful dishonor is a question of fact to be determined in each case.

(c) A payor bank's determination of the customer's account balance on which a decision to dishonor for insufficiency of available funds is based may be made at any time between the time the item is received by the payor bank and the time that the payor bank returns the item or gives notice in lieu of return, and no more than one determination need be made. If, at the election of the payor bank, a subsequent balance determination is made for the purpose of reevaluating the bank's decision to dishonor the item, the account balance at that time is determinative of whether a dishonor for insufficiency of available funds is wrongful.

As amended in 1990.

§ 4–403. Customer's Right to Stop Payment; Burden of Proof of Loss.

(a) A customer or any person authorized to draw on the account if there is more than one person may stop payment of any item drawn on the customer's account or close the account by an order to the bank describing the item or account with reasonable certainty received at a time and in a manner that affords the bank a reasonable opportunity to act on it before any action by the bank with respect to the item described in Section 4–303. If the signature of more than one person is required to draw on an account, any of these persons may stop payment or close the account.

(b) A stop-payment order is effective for six months, but it lapses after 14 calendar days if the original order was oral and was not confirmed in writing within that period. A stop-payment order may be renewed for additional six-month periods by a writing given to the bank within a period during which the stop-payment order is effective.

(c) The burden of establishing the fact and amount of loss resulting from the payment of an item contrary to a stop-payment order or order to close an account is on the customer. The loss from payment of an item contrary to a stop-payment order may include damages for dishonor of subsequent items under Section 4–402.

As amended in 1990.

§ 4–404. Bank Not Obliged to Pay Check More Than Six Months Old.

A bank is under no obligation to a customer having a checking account to pay a check, other than a certified check, which is presented more than six months after its date, but it may charge its customer's account for a payment made thereafter in good faith.

§ 4–405. Death or Incompetence of Customer.

(a) A payor or collecting bank's authority to accept, pay, or collect an item or to account for proceeds of its collection, if otherwise effective, is not rendered ineffective by incompetence of a customer of either bank existing at the time the item is issued or its collection is undertaken if the bank does not know of an adjudication of incompetence. Neither death nor incompetence of a customer revokes the authority to accept, pay, collect, or account until the bank knows of the fact of death or of an adjudication of incompetence and has reasonable opportunity to act on it.

(b) Even with knowledge, a bank may for 10 days after the date of death pay or certify checks drawn on or before the date unless ordered to stop payment by a person claiming an interest in the account.

As amended in 1990.

§ 4–406. Customer's Duty to Discover and Report Unauthorized Signature or Alteration.

(a) A bank that sends or makes available to a customer a statement of account showing payment of items for the account shall either return or make available to the customer the items paid or provide information in the statement of account sufficient to allow the customer reasonably to identify the items paid. The statement of account provides sufficient information if the item is described by item number, amount, and date of payment.

(b) If the items are not returned to the customer, the person retaining the items shall either retain the items or, if the items are destroyed, maintain the capacity to furnish legible copies of the items until the expiration of seven years after receipt of the items. A customer may request an item from the bank that paid the item, and that bank must provide in a reasonable time either the item or, if the item has been destroyed or is not otherwise obtainable, a legible copy of the item.

(c) If a bank sends or makes available a statement of account or items pursuant to subsection (a), the customer must exercise reasonable promptness in examining the statement or the items to determine whether any payment was not authorized because of an alteration of an item or because a purported signature by or on behalf of the customer was not authorized. If, based on the statement or items provided, the customer should reasonably have discovered the unauthorized payment, the customer must promptly notify the bank of the relevant facts.

(d) If the bank proves that the customer failed, with respect to an item, to comply with the duties imposed on the customer by subsection (c), the customer is precluded from asserting against the bank:

   (1) the customer's unauthorized signature or any alteration on the item, if the bank also proves that it suffered a loss by reason of the failure; and

   (2) the customer's unauthorized signature or alteration by the same wrongdoer on any other item paid in good faith by the bank if the payment was made before the bank received notice from the customer of the unauthorized signature or alteration and after the customer had been afforded a reasonable period of time, not exceeding 30 days, in which to examine the item or statement of account and notify the bank.

(e) If subsection (d) applies and the customer proves that the bank failed to exercise ordinary care in paying the item and that the failure substantially contributed to loss, the loss is allocated between the customer precluded and the bank asserting the preclusion according to the extent to which the failure of the customer to comply with subsection (c) and the failure of the bank to exercise ordinary care contributed to the loss. If the customer proves that the bank did not pay the item in good faith, the preclusion under subsection (d) does not apply.

(f) Without regard to care or lack of care of either the customer or the bank, a customer who does not within one year after the statement or items are made available to the customer (subsection (a)) discover and report the customer's unauthorized signature on or any alteration on the item is precluded from asserting against the bank the unauthorized signature or alteration. If there is a preclusion under this subsection, the payor bank may not recover for breach or warranty under Section 4–208 with respect to the unauthorized signature or alteration to which the preclusion applies.

As amended in 1990.

§ 4–407. Payor Bank's Right to Subrogation on Improper Payment.

If a payor has paid an item over the order of the drawer or maker to stop payment, or after an account has been closed, or otherwise under circumstances giving a basis for objection by the drawer or maker, to prevent unjust enrichment and only to the extent necessary to prevent loss to the bank by reason of its payment of the item, the payor bank is subrogated to the rights

   (1) of any holder in due course on the item against the drawer or maker;

   (2) of the payee or any other holder of the item against the drawer or maker either on the item or under the transaction out of which the item arose; and

   (3) of the drawer or maker against the payee or any other holder of the item with respect to the transaction out of which the item arose.

As amended in 1990.

Part 5   Collection of Documentary Drafts

§ 4–501.   Handling of Documentary Drafts; Duty to Send for Presentment and to Notify Customer of Dishonor.

A bank that takes a documentary draft for collection shall present or send the draft and accompanying documents for presentment and, upon learning that the draft has not been paid or accepted in due course, shall seasonably notify its customer of the fact even though it may have discounted or bought the draft or extended credit available for withdrawal as of right.

As amended in 1990.

§ 4–502.   Presentment of "On Arrival" Drafts.

If a draft or the relevant instructions require presentment "on arrival", "when goods arrive" or the like, the collecting bank need not present until in its judgment a reasonable time for arrival of the goods has expired. Refusal to pay or accept because the goods have not arrived is not dishonor; the bank must notify its transferor of the refusal but need not present the draft again until it is instructed to do so or learns of the arrival of the goods.

§ 4–503.   Responsibility of Presenting Bank for Documents and Goods; Report of Reasons for Dishonor; Referee in Case of Need.

Unless otherwise instructed and except as provided in Article 5, a bank presenting a documentary draft:

(1) must deliver the documents to the drawee on acceptance of the draft if it is payable more than three days after presentment, otherwise, only on payment; and

(2) upon dishonor, either in the case of presentment for acceptance or presentment for payment, may seek and follow instructions from any referee in case of need designated in the draft or, if the presenting bank does not choose to utilize the referee's services, it must use diligence and good faith to ascertain the reason for dishonor, must notify its transferor of the dishonor and of the results of its effort to ascertain the reasons therefor, and must request instructions.

However, the presenting bank is under no obligation with respect to goods represented by the documents except to follow any reasonable instructions seasonably received; it has a right to reimbursement for any expense incurred in following instructions and to prepayment of or indemnity for those expenses.

As amended in 1990.

§ 4–504.   Privilege of Presenting Bank to Deal With Goods; Security Interest for Expenses.

(a) A presenting bank that, following the dishonor of a documentary draft, has seasonably requested instructions but does not receive them within a reasonable time may store, sell, or otherwise deal with the goods in any reasonable manner.

(b) For its reasonable expenses incurred by action under subsection (a) the presenting bank has a lien upon the goods or their proceeds, which may be foreclosed in the same manner as an unpaid seller's lien.

As amended in 1990.

Article 4A
FUNDS TRANSFERS

Part 1   Subject Matter and Definitions

§ 4A–101.   Short Title.

This Article may be cited as Uniform Commercial Code—Funds Transfers.

§ 4A–102.   Subject Matter.

Except as otherwise provided in Section 4A–108, this Article applies to funds transfers defined in Section 4A–104.

§ 4A–103.   Payment Order–Definitions.

(a) In this Article:

(1) "Payment order" means an instruction of a sender to a receiving bank, transmitted orally, electronically, or in writing, to pay, or to cause another bank to pay, a fixed or determinable amount of money to a beneficiary if:

(i) the instruction does not state a condition to payment to the beneficiary other than time of payment,

(ii) the receiving bank is to be reimbursed by debiting an account of, or otherwise receiving payment from, the sender, and

(iii) the instruction is transmitted by the sender directly to the receiving bank or to an agent, funds-transfer system, or communication system for transmittal to the receiving bank.

(2) "Beneficiary" means the person to be paid by the beneficiary's bank.

(3) "Beneficiary's bank" means the bank identified in a payment order in which an account of the beneficiary is to be credited pursuant to the order or which otherwise is to make payment to the beneficiary if the order does not provide for payment to an account.

(4) "Receiving bank" means the bank to which the sender's instruction is addressed.

(5) "Sender" means the person giving the instruction to the receiving bank.

(b) If an instruction complying with subsection (a)(1) is to make more than one payment to a beneficiary, the instruction is a separate payment order with respect to each payment.

(c) A payment order is issued when it is sent to the receiving bank.

§ 4A–104.   Funds Transfer–Definitions.

In this Article:

(a) "Funds transfer" means the series of transactions, beginning with the originator's payment order, made for the purpose of making payment to the beneficiary of the order. The term includes any payment order issued by the originator's bank or an intermediary bank intended to carry out the originator's payment order. A funds transfer is completed by acceptance by the beneficiary's bank of a payment order for the benefit of the beneficiary of the originator's payment order.

(b) "Intermediary bank" means a receiving bank other than the originator's bank or the beneficiary's bank.

(c) "Originator" means the sender of the first payment order in a funds transfer.

(d) "Originator's bank" means (i) the receiving bank to which the payment order of the originator is issued if the originator is not a bank, or (ii) the originator if the originator is a bank.

§ 4A–105.   Other Definitions.

(a) In this Article:

(1) "Authorized account" means a deposit account of a customer in a bank designated by the customer as a source of payment of payment orders issued by the customer to the bank. If a customer does not so designate an account, any account of the customer is an authorized account if payment of a payment order from that account is not inconsistent with a restriction on the use of that account.

(2) "Bank" means a person engaged in the business of banking and includes a savings bank, savings and loan association, credit union, and trust company. A branch or separate office of a bank is a separate bank for purposes of this Article.

(3) "Customer" means a person, including a bank, having an account with a bank or from whom a bank has agreed to receive payment orders.

(4) "Funds-transfer business day" of a receiving bank means the part of a day during which the receiving bank is open for the receipt, processing, and transmittal of payment orders and cancellations and amendments of payment orders.

(5) "Funds-transfer system" means a wire transfer network, automated clearing house, or other communication system of a clearing house or other association of banks through which a payment order by a bank may be transmitted to the bank to which the order is addressed.

(6) "Good faith" means honesty in fact and the observance of reasonable commercial standards of fair dealing.

(7) "Prove" with respect to a fact means to meet the burden of establishing the fact (Section 1–201(8)).

(b) Other definitions applying to this Article and the sections in which they appear are:

"Acceptance"	Section 4A–209
"Beneficiary"	Section 4A–103
"Beneficiary's bank"	Section 4A–103
"Executed"	Section 4A–301
"Execution date"	Section 4A–301
"Funds transfer"	Section 4A–104
"Funds-transfer system rule"	Section 4A–501
"Intermediary bank"	Section 4A–104
"Originator"	Section 4A–104
"Originator's bank"	Section 4A–104
"Payment by beneficiary's bank to beneficiary"	Section 4A–405
"Payment by originator to beneficiary"	Section 4A–406
"Payment by sender to receiving bank"	Section 4A–403
"Payment date"	Section 4A–401
"Payment order"	Section 4A–103
"Receiving bank"	Section 4A–103
"Security procedure"	Section 4A–201
"Sender"	Section 4A–103

(c) The following definitions in Article 4 apply to this Article:

"Clearing house"	Section 4–104
"Item"	Section 4–104
"Suspends payments"	Section 4–104

(d) In addition, Article 1 contains general definitions and principles of construction and interpretation applicable throughout this Article.

§ 4A–106. Time Payment Order Is Received.

(a) The time of receipt of a payment order or communication cancelling or amending a payment order is determined by the rules applicable to receipt of a notice stated in Section 1–201(27). A receiving bank may fix a cut-off time or times on a funds-transfer business day for the receipt and processing of payment orders and communications cancelling or amending payment orders. Different cut-off times may apply to payment orders, cancellations, or amendments, or to different categories of payment orders, cancellations, or amendments. A cut-off time may apply to senders generally or different cut-off times may apply to different senders or categories of payment orders. If a payment order or communication cancelling or amending a payment order is received after the close of a funds-transfer business day or after the appropriate cut-off time on a funds-transfer business day, the receiving bank may treat the payment order or communication as received at the opening of the next funds-transfer business day.

(b) If this Article refers to an execution date or payment date or states a day on which a receiving bank is required to take action, and the date or day does not fall on a funds-transfer business day, the next day that is a funds-transfer business day is treated as the date or day stated, unless the contrary is stated in this Article.

§ 4A–107. Federal Reserve Regulations and Operating Circulars.

Regulations of the Board of Governors of the Federal Reserve System and operating circulars of the Federal Reserve Banks supersede any inconsistent provision of this Article to the extent of the inconsistency.

§ 4A–108. Exclusion of Consumer Transactions Governed by Federal Law.

This Article does not apply to a funds transfer any part of which is governed by the Electronic Fund Transfer Act of 1978 (Title XX, Public Law 95–630, 92 Stat. 3728, 15 U.S.C. § 1693 et seq.) as amended from time to time.

Part 2 Issue and Acceptance of Payment Order

§ 4A–201. Security Procedure.

"Security procedure" means a procedure established by agreement of a customer and a receiving bank for the purpose of (i) verifying that a payment order or communication amending or cancelling a payment order is that of the customer, or (ii) detecting error in the transmission or the content of the payment order or communication. A security procedure may require the use of algorithms or other codes, identifying words or numbers, encryption, callback procedures, or similar security devices. Comparison of a signature on a payment order or communication with an authorized specimen signature of the customer is not by itself a security procedure.

§ 4A–202. Authorized and Verified Payment Orders.

(a) A payment order received by the receiving bank is the authorized order of the person identified as sender if that person authorized the order or is otherwise bound by it under the law of agency.

(b) If a bank and its customer have agreed that the authenticity of payment orders issued to the bank in the name of the customer as sender will be verified pursuant to a security procedure, a payment order received by the receiving bank is effective as the order of the customer, whether or not authorized, if (i) the security procedure is a commercially reasonable method of providing security against unauthorized payment orders, and (ii) the bank proves that it accepted the payment order in good faith and in compliance with the security procedure and any written agreement or instruction of the customer restricting acceptance of payment orders issued in the name of the customer. The bank is not required to follow an instruction that violates a written agreement with the customer or notice of which is not received at a time and in a manner affording the bank a reasonable opportunity to act on it before the payment order is accepted.

(c) Commercial reasonableness of a security procedure is a question of law to be determined by considering the wishes of the customer expressed to the bank, the circumstances of the customer known to the bank, including the size, type, and frequency of payment orders normally issued by the customer to the bank, alternative security procedures offered to the customer, and security procedures in general use by customers and receiving banks similarly situated. A security procedure is deemed to be commercially reasonable if (i) the security procedure was chosen by the customer after the bank offered, and the customer refused, a security procedure that was commercially reasonable for that customer, and (ii) the customer expressly agreed in writing to be bound by any payment order, whether or not authorized, issued in its name and accepted by the bank in compliance with the security procedure chosen by the customer.

(d) The term "sender" in this Article includes the customer in whose name a payment order is issued if the order is the authorized order of the customer under subsection (a), or it is effective as the order of the customer under subsection (b).

(e) This section applies to amendments and cancellations of payment orders to the same extent it applies to payment orders.

(f) Except as provided in this section and in Section 4A–203(a)(1), rights and obligations arising under this section or Section 4A–203 may not be varied by agreement.

§ 4A–203. Unenforceability of Certain Verified Payment Orders.

(a) If an accepted payment order is not, under Section 4A–202(a), an authorized order of a customer identified as sender, but is effective as an order of the customer pursuant to Section 4A–202(b), the following rules apply:

(1) By express written agreement, the receiving bank may limit the extent to which it is entitled to enforce or retain payment of the payment order.

(2) The receiving bank is not entitled to enforce or retain payment of the payment order if the customer proves that the order was not caused, directly or indirectly, by a person (i) entrusted at any time with duties to act for the customer with respect to payment orders or the security procedure, or (ii) who obtained access to transmitting facilities of the customer or who obtained, from a source controlled by the customer and without authority of the receiving bank, information facilitating breach of the security procedure, regardless of how the information was obtained or whether the customer was at fault. Information includes any access device, computer software, or the like.

(b) This section applies to amendments of payment orders to the same extent it applies to payment orders.

§ 4A–204. Refund of Payment and Duty of Customer to Report with Respect to Unauthorized Payment Order.

(a) If a receiving bank accepts a payment order issued in the name of its customer as sender which is (i) not authorized and not effective as the order of the customer under Section 4A–202, or (ii) not enforceable, in whole or in part, against the customer under Section 4A–203, the bank shall refund any payment of the payment order received from the customer to the extent the bank is not entitled to enforce payment and shall pay interest on the refundable amount calculated from the date the bank received payment to the date of the refund. However, the customer is not entitled to interest from the bank on the amount to be refunded if the customer fails to exercise ordinary care to determine that the order was not authorized by the customer and to notify the bank of the relevant facts within a reasonable time not exceeding 90 days after the date the customer received notification from the bank that the order was accepted or that the customer's account was debited with respect to the order. The bank is not entitled to any recovery from the customer on account of a failure by the customer to give notification as stated in this section.

(b) Reasonable time under subsection (a) may be fixed by agreement as stated in Section 1–204(1), but the obligation of a receiving bank to refund payment as stated in subsection (a) may not otherwise be varied by agreement.

§ 4A–205. Erroneous Payment Orders.

(a) If an accepted payment order was transmitted pursuant to a security procedure for the detection of error and the payment order (i) erroneously instructed payment to a beneficiary not intended by the sender, (ii) erroneously instructed payment in an amount greater than the amount intended by the sender, or (iii) was an erroneously transmitted duplicate of a payment order previously sent by the sender, the following rules apply:

(1) If the sender proves that the sender or a person acting on behalf of the sender pursuant to Section 4A–206 complied with the security procedure and that the error would have been detected if the receiving bank had also complied, the sender is not obliged to pay the order to the extent stated in paragraphs (2) and (3).

(2) If the funds transfer is completed on the basis of an erroneous payment order described in clause (i) or (iii) of subsection (a), the sender is not obliged to pay the order and the receiving bank is entitled to recover from the beneficiary any amount paid to the beneficiary to the extent allowed by the law governing mistake and restitution.

(3) If the funds transfer is completed on the basis of a payment order described in clause (ii) of subsection (a), the sender is not obliged to pay the order to the extent the amount received by the beneficiary is greater than the amount intended by the sender. In that case, the receiving bank is entitled to recover from the beneficiary the excess amount received to the extent allowed by the law governing mistake and restitution.

(b) If (i) the sender of an erroneous payment order described in subsection (a) is not obliged to pay all or part of the order, and (ii) the sender receives notification from the receiving bank that the order was accepted by the bank or that the sender's account was debited with respect to the order, the sender has a duty to exercise ordinary care, on the basis of information available to the sender, to discover the error with respect to the order and to advise the bank of the relevant facts within a reasonable time, not exceeding 90 days, after the bank's notification was received by the sender. If the bank proves that the sender failed to perform that duty, the sender is liable to the bank for the loss the bank proves it incurred as a result of the failure, but the liability of the sender may not exceed the amount of the sender's order.

(c) This section applies to amendments to payment orders to the same extent it applies to payment orders.

§ 4A–206.   Transmission of Payment Order through Funds-Transfer or Other Communication System.

(a) If a payment order addressed to a receiving bank is transmitted to a funds-transfer system or other third party communication system for transmittal to the bank, the system is deemed to be an agent of the sender for the purpose of transmitting the payment order to the bank. If there is a discrepancy between the terms of the payment order transmitted to the system and the terms of the payment order transmitted by the system to the bank, the terms of the payment order of the sender are those transmitted by the system. This section does not apply to a funds-transfer system of the Federal Reserve Banks.

(b) This section applies to cancellations and amendments to payment orders to the same extent it applies to payment orders.

§ 4A–207.   Misdescription of Beneficiary.

(a) Subject to subsection (b), if, in a payment order received by the beneficiary's bank, the name, bank account number, or other identification of the beneficiary refers to a nonexistent or unidentifiable person or account, no person has rights as a beneficiary of the order and acceptance of the order cannot occur.

(b) If a payment order received by the beneficiary's bank identifies the beneficiary both by name and by an identifying or bank account number and the name and number identify different persons, the following rules apply:

(1) Except as otherwise provided in subsection (c), if the beneficiary's bank does not know that the name and number refer to different persons, it may rely on the number as the proper identification of the beneficiary of the order. The beneficiary's bank need not determine whether the name and number refer to the same person.

(2) If the beneficiary's bank pays the person identified by name or knows that the name and number identify different persons, no person has rights as beneficiary except the person paid by the beneficiary's bank if that person was entitled to receive payment from the originator of the funds transfer. If no person has rights as beneficiary, acceptance of the order cannot occur.

(c) If (i) a payment order described in subsection (b) is accepted, (ii) the originator's payment order described the beneficiary inconsistently by name and number, and (iii) the beneficiary's bank pays the person identified by number as permitted by subsection (b)(1), the following rules apply:

(1) If the originator is a bank, the originator is obliged to pay its order.

(2) If the originator is not a bank and proves that the person identified by number was not entitled to receive payment from the originator, the originator is not obliged to pay its order unless the originator's bank proves that the originator, before acceptance of the originator's order, had notice that payment of a payment order issued by the originator might be made by the beneficiary's bank on the basis of an identifying or bank account number even if it identifies a person different from the named beneficiary. Proof of notice may be made by any admissible evidence. The originator's bank satisfies the burden of proof if it proves that the originator, before the payment order was accepted, signed a writing stating the information to which the notice relates.

(d) In a case governed by subsection (b)(1), if the beneficiary's bank rightfully pays the person identified by number and that person was not entitled to receive payment from the originator, the amount paid may be recovered from that person to the extent allowed by the law governing mistake and restitution as follows:

(1) If the originator is obliged to pay its payment order as stated in subsection (c), the originator has the right to recover.

(2) If the originator is not a bank and is not obliged to pay its payment order, the originator's bank has the right to recover.

§ 4A–208.   Misdescription of Intermediary Bank or Beneficiary's Bank.

(a) This subsection applies to a payment order identifying an intermediary bank or the beneficiary's bank only by an identifying number.

(1) The receiving bank may rely on the number as the proper identification of the intermediary or beneficiary's bank and need not determine whether the number identifies a bank.

(2) The sender is obliged to compensate the receiving bank for any loss and expenses incurred by the receiving bank as a result of its reliance on the number in executing or attempting to execute the order.

(b) This subsection applies to a payment order identifying an intermediary bank or the beneficiary's bank both by name and an identifying number if the name and number identify different persons.

(1) If the sender is a bank, the receiving bank may rely on the number as the proper identification of the intermediary or beneficiary's bank if the receiving bank, when it executes the sender's order, does not know that the name and number identify different persons. The receiving bank need not determine whether the name and number refer to the same person or whether the number refers to a bank. The sender is obliged to compensate the receiving bank for any loss and expenses incurred by the receiving bank as a result of its reliance on the number in executing or attempting to execute the order.

(2) If the sender is not a bank and the receiving bank proves that the sender, before the payment order was accepted, had notice that the receiving bank might rely on the number as the proper identification of the intermediary or beneficiary's bank even if it identifies a person different from the bank identified by name, the rights and obligations of the sender and the receiving bank are governed by subsection (b)(1), as though the sender were a bank. Proof of notice may be made by any admissible evidence. The receiving bank satisfies the burden of proof if it proves that the sender, before the payment order was accepted, signed a writing stating the information to which the notice relates.

(3) Regardless of whether the sender is a bank, the receiving bank may rely on the name as the proper identification of the intermediary or beneficiary's bank if the receiving bank, at the

time it executes the sender's order, does not know that the name and number identify different persons. The receiving bank need not determine whether the name and number refer to the same person.

(4) If the receiving bank knows that the name and number identify different persons, reliance on either the name or the number in executing the sender's payment order is a breach of the obligation stated in Section 4A–302(a)(1).

§ 4A–209. Acceptance of Payment Order.

(a) Subject to subsection (d), a receiving bank other than the beneficiary's bank accepts a payment order when it executes the order.

(b) Subject to subsections (c) and (d), a beneficiary's bank accepts a payment order at the earliest of the following times:

(1) When the bank (i) pays the beneficiary as stated in Section 4A–405(a) or 4A–405(b), or (ii) notifies the beneficiary of receipt of the order or that the account of the beneficiary has been credited with respect to the order unless the notice indicates that the bank is rejecting the order or that funds with respect to the order may not be withdrawn or used until receipt of payment from the sender of the order;

(2) When the bank receives payment of the entire amount of the sender's order pursuant to Section 4A–403(a)(1) or 4A–403(a)(2); or

(3) The opening of the next funds-transfer business day of the bank following the payment date of the order if, at that time, the amount of the sender's order is fully covered by a withdrawable credit balance in an authorized account of the sender or the bank has otherwise received full payment from the sender, unless the order was rejected before that time or is rejected within (i) one hour after that time, or (ii) one hour after the opening of the next business day of the sender following the payment date if that time is later. If notice of rejection is received by the sender after the payment date and the authorized account of the sender does not bear interest, the bank is obliged to pay interest to the sender on the amount of the order for the number of days elapsing after the payment date to the day the sender receives notice or learns that the order was not accepted, counting that day as an elapsed day. If the withdrawable credit balance during that period falls below the amount of the order, the amount of interest payable is reduced accordingly.

(c) Acceptance of a payment order cannot occur before the order is received by the receiving bank. Acceptance does not occur under subsection (b)(2) or (b)(3) if the beneficiary of the payment order does not have an account with the receiving bank, the account has been closed, or the receiving bank is not permitted by law to receive credits for the beneficiary's account.

(d) A payment order issued to the originator's bank cannot be accepted until the payment date if the bank is the beneficiary's bank, or the execution date if the bank is not the beneficiary's bank. If the originator's bank executes the originator's payment order before the execution date or pays the beneficiary of the originator's payment order before the payment date and the payment order is subsequently cancelled pursuant to Section 4A–211(b), the bank may recover from the beneficiary any payment received to the extent allowed by the law governing mistake and restitution.

§ 4A–210. Rejection of Payment Order.

(a) A payment order is rejected by the receiving bank by a notice of rejection transmitted to the sender orally, electronically, or in writing. A notice of rejection need not use any particular words and is sufficient if it indicates that the receiving bank is rejecting the order or will not execute or pay the order. Rejection is effective when the notice is given if transmission is by a means that is reasonable in the circumstances. If notice of rejection is given by a means that is not reasonable, rejection is effective when the notice is received. If an agreement of the sender and receiving bank establishes the means to be used to reject a payment order, (i) any means complying with the agreement is reasonable and (ii) any means not complying is not reasonable unless no significant delay in receipt of the notice resulted from the use of the noncomplying means.

(b) This subsection applies if a receiving bank other than the beneficiary's bank fails to execute a payment order despite the existence on the execution date of a withdrawable credit balance in an authorized account of the sender sufficient to cover the order. If the sender does not receive notice of rejection of the order on the execution date and the authorized account of the sender does not bear interest, the bank is obliged to pay interest to the sender on the amount of the order for the number of days elapsing after the execution date to the earlier of the day the order is cancelled pursuant to Section 4A–211(d) or the day the sender receives notice or learns that the order was not executed, counting the final day of the period as an elapsed day. If the withdrawable credit balance during that period falls below the amount of the order, the amount of interest is reduced accordingly.

(c) If a receiving bank suspends payments, all unaccepted payment orders issued to it are are deemed rejected at the time the bank suspends payments.

(d) Acceptance of a payment order precludes a later rejection of the order. Rejection of a payment order precludes a later acceptance of the order.

§ 4A–211. Cancellation and Amendment of Payment Order.

(a) A communication of the sender of a payment order cancelling or amending the order may be transmitted to the receiving bank orally, electronically, or in writing. If a security procedure is in effect between the sender and the receiving bank, the communication is not effective to cancel or amend the order unless the communication is verified pursuant to the security procedure or the bank agrees to the cancellation or amendment.

(b) Subject to subsection (a), a communication by the sender cancelling or amending a payment order is effective to cancel or amend the order if notice of the communication is received at a time and in a manner affording the receiving bank a reasonable opportunity to act on the communication before the bank accepts the payment order.

(c) After a payment order has been accepted, cancellation or amendment of the order is not effective unless the receiving bank agrees or a funds-transfer system rule allows cancellation or amendment without agreement of the bank.

(1) With respect to a payment order accepted by a receiving bank other than the beneficiary's bank, cancellation or amendment is not effective unless a conforming cancellation or amendment of the payment order issued by the receiving bank is also made.

(2) With respect to a payment order accepted by the beneficiary's bank, cancellation or amendment is not effective unless the order was issued in execution of an unauthorized payment order,

or because of a mistake by a sender in the funds transfer which resulted in the issuance of a payment order (i) that is a duplicate of a payment order previously issued by the sender, (ii) that orders payment to a beneficiary not entitled to receive payment from the originator, or (iii) that orders payment in an amount greater than the amount the beneficiary was entitled to receive from the originator. If the payment order is cancelled or amended, the beneficiary's bank is entitled to recover from the beneficiary any amount paid to the beneficiary to the extent allowed by the law governing mistake and restitution.

(d) An unaccepted payment order is cancelled by operation of law at the close of the fifth funds-transfer business day of the receiving bank after the execution date or payment date of the order.

(e) A cancelled payment order cannot be accepted. If an accepted payment order is cancelled, the acceptance is nullified and no person has any right or obligation based on the acceptance. Amendment of a payment order is deemed to be cancellation of the original order at the time of amendment and issue of a new payment order in the amended form at the same time.

(f) Unless otherwise provided in an agreement of the parties or in a funds-transfer system rule, if the receiving bank, after accepting a payment order, agrees to cancellation or amendment of the order by the sender or is bound by a funds-transfer system rule allowing cancellation or amendment without the bank's agreement, the sender, whether or not cancellation or amendment is effective, is liable to the bank for any loss and expenses, including reasonable attorney's fees, incurred by the bank as a result of the cancellation or amendment or attempted cancellation or amendment.

(g) A payment order is not revoked by the death or legal incapacity of the sender unless the receiving bank knows of the death or of an adjudication of incapacity by a court of competent jurisdiction and has reasonable opportunity to act before acceptance of the order.

(h) A funds-transfer system rule is not effective to the extent it conflicts with subsection (c)(2).

§ 4A-212.   Liability and Duty of Receiving Bank Regarding Unaccepted Payment Order.

If a receiving bank fails to accept a payment order that it is obliged by express agreement to accept, the bank is liable for breach of the agreement to the extent provided in the agreement or in this Article, but does not otherwise have any duty to accept a payment order or, before acceptance, to take any action, or refrain from taking action, with respect to the order except as provided in this Article or by express agreement. Liability based on acceptance arises only when acceptance occurs as stated in Section 4A-209, and liability is limited to that provided in this Article. A receiving bank is not the agent of the sender or beneficiary of the payment order it accepts, or of any other party to the funds transfer, and the bank owes no duty to any party to the funds transfer except as provided in this Article or by express agreement.

Part 3   Execution of Sender's Payment Order by Receiving Bank

§ 4A-301.   Execution and Execution Date.

(a) A payment order is "executed" by the receiving bank when it issues a payment order intended to carry out the payment order received by the bank. A payment order received by the beneficiary's bank can be accepted but cannot be executed.

(b) "Execution date" of a payment order means the day on which the receiving bank may properly issue a payment order in execution of the sender's order. The execution date may be determined by instruction of the sender but cannot be earlier than the day the order is received and, unless otherwise determined, is the day the order is received. If the sender's instruction states a payment date, the execution date is the payment date or an earlier date on which execution is reasonably necessary to allow payment to the beneficiary on the payment date.

§ 4A-302.   Obligations of Receiving Bank in Execution of Payment Order.

(a) Except as provided in subsections (b) through (d), if the receiving bank accepts a payment order pursuant to Section 4A-209(a), the bank has the following obligations in executing the order:

(1) The receiving bank is obliged to issue, on the execution date, a payment order complying with the sender's order and to follow the sender's instructions concerning (i) any intermediary bank or funds-transfer system to be used in carrying out the funds transfer, or (ii) the means by which payment orders are to be transmitted in the funds transfer. If the originator's bank issues a payment order to an intermediary bank, the originator's bank is obliged to instruct the intermediary bank according to the instruction of the originator. An intermediary bank in the funds transfer is similarly bound by an instruction given to it by the sender of the payment order it accepts.

(2) If the sender's instruction states that the funds transfer is to be carried out telephonically or by wire transfer or otherwise indicates that the funds transfer is to be carried out by the most expeditious means, the receiving bank is obliged to transmit its payment order by the most expeditious available means, and to instruct any intermediary bank accordingly. If a sender's instruction states a payment date, the receiving bank is obliged to transmit its payment order at a time and by means reasonably necessary to allow payment to the beneficiary on the payment date or as soon thereafter as is feasible.

(b) Unless otherwise instructed, a receiving bank executing a payment order may (i) use any funds-transfer system if use of that system is reasonable in the circumstances, and (ii) issue a payment order to the beneficiary's bank or to an intermediary bank through which a payment order conforming to the sender's order can expeditiously be issued to the beneficiary's bank if the receiving bank exercises ordinary care in the selection of the intermediary bank. A receiving bank is not required to follow an instruction of the sender designating a funds-transfer system to be used in carrying out the funds transfer if the receiving bank, in good faith, determines that it is not feasible to follow the instruction or that following the instruction would unduly delay completion of the funds transfer.

(c) Unless subsection (a)(2) applies or the receiving bank is otherwise instructed, the bank may execute a payment order by transmitting its payment order by first class mail or by any means reasonable in the circumstances. If the receiving bank is instructed to execute the sender's order by transmitting its payment order by a particular means, the receiving bank may issue its payment order by the means stated or by any means as expeditious as the means stated.

(d) Unless instructed by the sender, (i) the receiving bank may not obtain payment of its charges for services and expenses in connection with the execution of the sender's order by issuing a payment order in an amount equal to the amount of the sender's order less the amount of the charges, and (ii) may not instruct a subsequent receiving bank to obtain payment of its charges in the same manner.

§ 4A–303. Erroneous Execution of Payment Order.

(a) A receiving bank that (i) executes the payment order of the sender by issuing a payment order in an amount greater than the amount of the sender's order, or (ii) issues a payment order in execution of the sender's order and then issues a duplicate order, is entitled to payment of the amount of the sender's order under Section 4A–402(c) if that subsection is otherwise satisfied. The bank is entitled to recover from the beneficiary of the erroneous order the excess payment received to the extent allowed by the law governing mistake and restitution.

(b) A receiving bank that executes the payment order of the sender by issuing a payment order in an amount less than the amount of the sender's order is entitled to payment of the amount of the sender's order under Section 4A–402(c) if (i) that subsection is otherwise satisfied and (ii) the bank corrects its mistake by issuing an additional payment order for the benefit of the beneficiary of the sender's order. If the error is not corrected, the issuer of the erroneous order is entitled to receive or retain payment from the sender of the order it accepted only to the extent of the amount of the erroneous order. This subsection does not apply if the receiving bank executes the sender's payment order by issuing a payment order in an amount less than the amount of the sender's order for the purpose of obtaining payment of its charges for services and expenses pursuant to instruction of the sender.

(c) If a receiving bank executes the payment order of the sender by issuing a payment order to a beneficiary different from the beneficiary of the sender's order and the funds transfer is completed on the basis of that error, the sender of the payment order that was erroneously executed and all previous senders in the funds transfer are not obliged to pay the payment orders they issued. The issuer of the erroneous order is entitled to recover from the beneficiary of the order the payment received to the extent allowed by the law governing mistake and restitution.

§ 4A–304. Duty of Sender to Report Erroneously Executed Payment Order.

If the sender of a payment order that is erroneously executed as stated in Section 4A–303 receives notification from the receiving bank that the order was executed or that the sender's account was debited with respect to the order, the sender has a duty to exercise ordinary care to determine, on the basis of information available to the sender, that the order was erroneously executed and to notify the bank of the relevant facts within a reasonable time not exceeding 90 days after the notification from the bank was received by the sender. If the sender fails to perform that duty, the bank is not obliged to pay interest on any amount refundable to the sender under Section 4A–402(d) for the period before the bank learns of the execution error. The bank is not entitled to any recovery from the sender on account of a failure by the sender to perform the duty stated in this section.

§ 4A–305. Liability for Late or Improper Execution or Failure to Execute Payment Order.

(a) If a funds transfer is completed but execution of a payment order by the receiving bank in breach of Section 4A–302 results in delay in payment to the beneficiary, the bank is obliged to pay interest to either the originator or the beneficiary of the funds transfer for the period of delay caused by the improper execution. Except as provided in subsection (c), additional damages are not recoverable.

(b) If execution of a payment order by a receiving bank in breach of Section 4A–302 results in (i) noncompletion of the funds transfer, (ii) failure to use an intermediary bank designated by the originator, or (iii) issuance of a payment order that does not comply with the terms of the payment order of the originator, the bank is liable to the originator for its expenses in the funds transfer and for incidental expenses and interest losses, to the extent not covered by subsection (a), resulting from the improper execution. Except as provided in subsection (c), additional damages are not recoverable.

(c) In addition to the amounts payable under subsections (a) and (b), damages, including consequential damages, are recoverable to the extent provided in an express written agreement of the receiving bank.

(d) If a receiving bank fails to execute a payment order it was obliged by express agreement to execute, the receiving bank is liable to the sender for its expenses in the transaction and for incidental expenses and interest losses resulting from the failure to execute. Additional damages, including consequential damages, are recoverable to the extent provided in an express written agreement of the receiving bank, but are not otherwise recoverable.

(e) Reasonable attorney's fees are recoverable if demand for compensation under subsection (a) or (b) is made and refused before an action is brought on the claim. If a claim is made for breach of an agreement under subsection (d) and the agreement does not provide for damages, reasonable attorney's fees are recoverable if demand for compensation under subsection (d) is made and refused before an action is brought on the claim.

(f) Except as stated in this section, the liability of a receiving bank under subsections (a) and (b) may not be varied by agreement.

Part 4 Payment

§ 4A–401. Payment Date.

"Payment date" of a payment order means the day on which the amount of the order is payable to the beneficiary by the beneficiary's bank. The payment date may be determined by instruction of the sender but cannot be earlier than the day the order is received by the beneficiary's bank and, unless otherwise determined, is the day the order is received by the beneficiary's bank.

§ 4A–402. Obligation of Sender to Pay Receiving Bank.

(a) This section is subject to Sections 4A–205 and 4A–207.

(b) With respect to a payment order issued to the beneficiary's bank, acceptance of the order by the bank obliges the sender to pay the bank the amount of the order, but payment is not due until the payment date of the order.

(c) This subsection is subject to subsection (e) and to Section 4A–303. With respect to a payment order issued to a receiving bank other than the beneficiary's bank, acceptance of the order by the receiving bank obliges the sender to pay the bank the amount of the sender's order. Payment by the sender is not due until the execution date of the sender's order. The obligation of that sender to pay its payment order is excused if the funds transfer is not completed by acceptance by the beneficiary's bank of a payment order instructing payment to the beneficiary of that sender's payment order.

(d) If the sender of a payment order pays the order and was not obliged to pay all or part of the amount paid, the bank receiving payment is obliged to refund payment to the extent the sender was not obliged to pay. Except as provided in Sections 4A–204 and 4A–304, interest is payable on the refundable amount from the date of payment.

(e) If a funds transfer is not completed as stated in subsection (c) and an intermediary bank is obliged to refund payment as stated in subsection (d) but is unable to do so because not permitted by applicable law or because the bank suspends payments, a sender in the funds transfer that executed a payment order in compliance with an instruction, as stated in Section 4A–302(a)(1), to route the funds transfer through that intermediary bank is entitled to receive or retain payment from the sender of the payment order that it accepted. The first sender in the funds transfer that issued an instruction requiring routing through that intermediary bank is subrogated to the right of the bank that paid the intermediary bank to refund as stated in subsection (d).

(f) The right of the sender of a payment order to be excused from the obligation to pay the order as stated in subsection (c) or to receive refund under subsection (d) may not be varied by agreement.

§ 4A–403. Payment by Sender to Receiving Bank.

(a) Payment of the sender's obligation under Section 4A–402 to pay the receiving bank occurs as follows:

> (1) If the sender is a bank, payment occurs when the receiving bank receives final settlement of the obligation through a Federal Reserve Bank or through a funds-transfer system.

> (2) If the sender is a bank and the sender (i) credited an account of the receiving bank with the sender, or (ii) caused an account of the receiving bank in another bank to be credited, payment occurs when the credit is withdrawn or, if not withdrawn, at midnight of the day on which the credit is withdrawable and the receiving bank learns of that fact.

> (3) If the receiving bank debits an account of the sender with the receiving bank, payment occurs when the debit is made to the extent the debit is covered by a withdrawable credit balance in the account.

(b) If the sender and receiving bank are members of a funds-transfer system that nets obligations multilaterally among participants, the receiving bank receives final settlement when settlement is complete in accordance with the rules of the system. The obligation of the sender to pay the amount of a payment order transmitted through the funds-transfer system may be satisfied, to the extent permitted by the rules of the system, by setting off and applying against the sender's obligation the right of the sender to receive payment from the receiving bank of the amount of any other payment order transmitted to the sender by the receiving bank through the funds-transfer system. The aggregate balance of obligations owed by each sender to each receiving bank in the funds-transfer system may be satisfied, to the extent permitted by the rules of the system, by setting off and applying against that balance the aggregate balance of obligations owed to the sender by other members of the system. The aggregate balance is determined after the right of setoff stated in the second sentence of this subsection has been exercised.

(c) If two banks transmit payment orders to each other under an agreement that settlement of the obligations of each bank to the other under Section 4A–402 will be made at the end of the day or other period, the total amount owed with respect to all orders transmit-

ted by one bank shall be set off against the total amount owed with respect to all orders transmitted by the other bank. To the extent of the setoff, each bank has made payment to the other.

(d) In a case not covered by subsection (a), the time when payment of the sender's obligation under Section 4A–402(b) or 4A–402(c) occurs is governed by applicable principles of law that determine when an obligation is satisfied.

§ 4A–404. Obligation of Beneficiary's Bank to Pay and Give Notice to Beneficiary.

(a) Subject to Sections 4A–211(e), 4A–405(d), and 4A–405(e), if a beneficiary's bank accepts a payment order, the bank is obliged to pay the amount of the order to the beneficiary of the order. Payment is due on the payment date of the order, but if acceptance occurs on the payment date after the close of the funds-transfer business day of the bank, payment is due on the next funds-transfer business day. If the bank refuses to pay after demand by the beneficiary and receipt of notice of particular circumstances that will give rise to consequential damages as a result of non-payment, the beneficiary may recover damages resulting from the refusal to pay to the extent the bank had notice of the damages, unless the bank proves that it did not pay because of a reasonable doubt concerning the right of the beneficiary to payment.

(b) If a payment order accepted by the beneficiary's bank instructs payment to an account of the beneficiary, the bank is obliged to notify the beneficiary of receipt of the order before midnight of the next funds-transfer business day following the payment date. If the payment order does not instruct payment to an account of the beneficiary, the bank is required to notify the beneficiary only if notice is required by the order. Notice may be given by first class mail or any other means reasonable in the circumstances. If the bank fails to give the required notice, the bank is obliged to pay interest to the beneficiary on the amount of the payment order from the day notice should have been given until the day the beneficiary learned of receipt of the payment order by the bank. No other damages are recoverable. Reasonable attorney's fees are also recoverable if demand for interest is made and refused before an action is brought on the claim.

(c) The right of a beneficiary to receive payment and damages as stated in subsection (a) may not be varied by agreement or a funds-transfer system rule. The right of a beneficiary to be notified as stated in subsection (b) may be varied by agreement of the beneficiary or by a funds-transfer system rule if the beneficiary is notified of the rule before initiation of the funds transfer.

§ 4A–405. Payment by Beneficiary's Bank to Beneficiary.

(a) If the beneficiary's bank credits an account of the beneficiary of a payment order, payment of the bank's obligation under Section 4A–404(a) occurs when and to the extent (i) the beneficiary is notified of the right to withdraw the credit, (ii) the bank lawfully applies the credit to a debt of the beneficiary, or (iii) funds with respect to the order are otherwise made available to the beneficiary by the bank.

(b) If the beneficiary's bank does not credit an account of the beneficiary of a payment order, the time when payment of the bank's obligation under Section 4A–404(a) occurs is governed by principles of law that determine when an obligation is satisfied.

(c) Except as stated in subsections (d) and (e), if the beneficiary's bank pays the beneficiary of a payment order under a condition to payment or agreement of the beneficiary giving the bank the right to recover payment from the beneficiary if the bank does not receive payment of the order, the condition to payment or agreement is not enforceable.

(d) A funds-transfer system rule may provide that payments made to beneficiaries of funds transfers made through the system are provisional until receipt of payment by the beneficiary's bank of the payment order it accepted. A beneficiary's bank that makes a payment that is provisional under the rule is entitled to refund from the beneficiary if (i) the rule requires that both the beneficiary and the originator be given notice of the provisional nature of the payment before the funds transfer is initiated, (ii) the beneficiary, the beneficiary's bank, and the originator's bank agreed to be bound by the rule, and (iii) the beneficiary's bank did not receive payment of the payment order that it accepted. If the beneficiary is obliged to refund payment to the beneficiary's bank, acceptance of the payment order by the beneficiary's bank is nullified and no payment by the originator of the funds transfer to the beneficiary occurs under Section 4A-406.

(e) This subsection applies to a funds transfer that includes a payment order transmitted over a funds-transfer system that (i) nets obligations multilaterally among participants, and (ii) has in effect a loss-sharing agreement among participants for the purpose of providing funds necessary to complete settlement of the obligations of one or more participants that do not meet their settlement obligations. If the beneficiary's bank in the funds transfer accepts a payment order and the system fails to complete settlement pursuant to its rules with respect to any payment order in the funds transfer, (i) the acceptance by the beneficiary's bank is nullified and no person has any right or obligation based on the acceptance, (ii) the beneficiary's bank is entitled to recover payment from the beneficiary, (iii) no payment by the originator to the beneficiary occurs under Section 4A-406, and (iv) subject to Section 4A-402(e), each sender in the funds transfer is excused from its obligation to pay its payment order under Section 4A-402(c) because the funds transfer has not been completed.

§ 4A-406. Payment by Originator to Beneficiary; Discharge of Underlying Obligation.

(a) Subject to Sections 4A-211(e), 4A-405(d), and 4A-405(e), the originator of a funds transfer pays the beneficiary of the originator's payment order (i) at the time a payment order for the benefit of the beneficiary is accepted by the beneficiary's bank in the funds transfer and (ii) in an amount equal to the amount of the order accepted by the beneficiary's bank, but not more than the amount of the originator's order.

(b) If payment under subsection (a) is made to satisfy an obligation, the obligation is discharged to the same extent discharge would result from payment to the beneficiary of the same amount in money, unless (i) the payment under subsection (a) was made by a means prohibited by the contract of the beneficiary with respect to the obligation, (ii) the beneficiary, within a reasonable time after receiving notice of receipt of the order by the beneficiary's bank, notified the originator of the beneficiary's refusal of the payment, (iii) funds with respect to the order were not withdrawn by the beneficiary or applied to a debt of the beneficiary, and (iv) the beneficiary would suffer a loss that could reasonably have been avoided if payment had been made by a means complying with the contract. If payment by the originator does not result in discharge under this section, the originator is subrogated to the rights of the beneficiary to receive payment from the beneficiary's bank under Section 4A-404(a).

(c) For the purpose of determining whether discharge of an obligation occurs under subsection (b), if the beneficiary's bank accepts a payment order in an amount equal to the amount of the originator's payment order less charges of one or more receiving banks in the funds transfer, payment to the beneficiary is deemed to be in the amount of the originator's order unless upon demand by the beneficiary the originator does not pay the beneficiary the amount of the deducted charges.

(d) Rights of the originator or of the beneficiary of a funds transfer under this section may be varied only by agreement of the originator and the beneficiary.

Part 5 Miscellaneous Provisions

§ 4A-501. Variation by Agreement and Effect of Funds-Transfer System Rule.

(a) Except as otherwise provided in this Article, the rights and obligations of a party to a funds transfer may be varied by agreement of the affected party.

(b) "Funds-transfer system rule" means a rule of an association of banks (i) governing transmission of payment orders by means of a funds-transfer system of the association or rights and obligations with respect to those orders, or (ii) to the extent the rule governs rights and obligations between banks that are parties to a funds transfer in which a Federal Reserve Bank, acting as an intermediary bank, sends a payment order to the beneficiary's bank. Except as otherwise provided in this Article, a funds-transfer system rule governing rights and obligations between participating banks using the system may be effective even if the rule conflicts with this Article and indirectly affects another party to the funds transfer who does not consent to the rule. A funds-transfer system rule may also govern rights and obligations of parties other than participating banks using the system to the extent stated in Sections 4A-404(c), 4A-405(d), and 4A-507(c).

§ 4A-502. Creditor Process Served on Receiving Bank; Setoff by Beneficiary's Bank.

(a) As used in this section, "creditor process" means levy, attachment, garnishment, notice of lien, sequestration, or similar process issued by or on behalf of a creditor or other claimant with respect to an account.

(b) This subsection applies to creditor process with respect to an authorized account of the sender of a payment order if the creditor process is served on the receiving bank. For the purpose of determining rights with respect to the creditor process, if the receiving bank accepts the payment order the balance in the authorized account is deemed to be reduced by the amount of the payment order to the extent the bank did not otherwise receive payment of the order, unless the creditor process is served at a time and in a manner affording the bank a reasonable opportunity to act on it before the bank accepts the payment order.

(c) If a beneficiary's bank has received a payment order for payment to the beneficiary's account in the bank, the following rules apply:

(1) The bank may credit the beneficiary's account. The amount credited may be set off against an obligation owed by the beneficiary to the bank or may be applied to satisfy creditor process served on the bank with respect to the account.

(2) The bank may credit the beneficiary's account and allow withdrawal of the amount credited unless creditor process with respect

to the account is served at a time and in a manner affording the bank a reasonable opportunity to act to prevent withdrawal.

(3) If creditor process with respect to the beneficiary's account has been served and the bank has had a reasonable opportunity to act on it, the bank may not reject the payment order except for a reason unrelated to the service of process.

(d) Creditor process with respect to a payment by the originator to the beneficiary pursuant to a funds transfer may be served only on the beneficiary's bank with respect to the debt owed by that bank to the beneficiary. Any other bank served with the creditor process is not obliged to act with respect to the process.

§ 4A–503.   Injunction or Restraining Order with Respect to Funds Transfer.

For proper cause and in compliance with applicable law, a court may restrain (i) a person from issuing a payment order to initiate a funds transfer, (ii) an originator's bank from executing the payment order of the originator, or (iii) the beneficiary's bank from releasing funds to the beneficiary or the beneficiary from withdrawing the funds. A court may not otherwise restrain a person from issuing a payment order, paying or receiving payment of a payment order, or otherwise acting with respect to a funds transfer.

§ 4A–504.   Order in Which Items and Payment Orders May Be Charged to Account; Order of Withdrawals from Account.

(a) If a receiving bank has received more than one payment order of the sender or one or more payment orders and other items that are payable from the sender's account, the bank may charge the sender's account with respect to the various orders and items in any sequence.

(b) In determining whether a credit to an account has been withdrawn by the holder of the account or applied to a debt of the holder of the account, credits first made to the account are first withdrawn or applied.

§ 4A–505.   Preclusion of Objection to Debit of Customer's Account.

If a receiving bank has received payment from its customer with respect to a payment order issued in the name of the customer as sender and accepted by the bank, and the customer received notification reasonably identifying the order, the customer is precluded from asserting that the bank is not entitled to retain the payment unless the customer notifies the bank of the customer's objection to the payment within one year after the notification was received by the customer.

§ 4A–506.   Rate of Interest.

(a) If, under this Article, a receiving bank is obliged to pay interest with respect to a payment order issued to the bank, the amount payable may be determined (i) by agreement of the sender and receiving bank, or (ii) by a funds-transfer system rule if the payment order is transmitted through a funds-transfer system.

(b) If the amount of interest is not determined by an agreement or rule as stated in subsection (a), the amount is calculated by multiplying the applicable Federal Funds rate by the amount on which interest is payable, and then multiplying the product by the number of days for which interest is payable. The applicable Federal Funds rate is the average of the Federal Funds rates published by the Federal Reserve Bank of New York for each of the days for which interest

is payable divided by 360. The Federal Funds rate for any day on which a published rate is not available is the same as the published rate for the next preceding day for which there is a published rate. If a receiving bank that accepted a payment order is required to refund payment to the sender of the order because the funds transfer was not completed, but the failure to complete was not due to any fault by the bank, the interest payable is reduced by a percentage equal to the reserve requirement on deposits of the receiving bank.

§ 4A–507.   Choice of Law.

(a) The following rules apply unless the affected parties otherwise agree or subsection (c) applies:

(1) The rights and obligations between the sender of a payment order and the receiving bank are governed by the law of the jurisdiction in which the receiving bank is located.

(2) The rights and obligations between the beneficiary's bank and the beneficiary are governed by the law of the jurisdiction in which the beneficiary's bank is located.

(3) The issue of when payment is made pursuant to a funds transfer by the originator to the beneficiary is governed by the law of the jurisdiction in which the beneficiary's bank is located.

(b) If the parties described in each paragraph of subsection (a) have made an agreement selecting the law of a particular jurisdiction to govern rights and obligations between each other, the law of that jurisdiction governs those rights and obligations, whether or not the payment order or the funds transfer bears a reasonable relation to that jurisdiction.

(c) A funds-transfer system rule may select the law of a particular jurisdiction to govern (i) rights and obligations between participating banks with respect to payment orders transmitted or processed through the system, or (ii) the rights and obligations of some or all parties to a funds transfer any part of which is carried out by means of the system. A choice of law made pursuant to clause (i) is binding on participating banks. A choice of law made pursuant to clause (ii) is binding on the originator, other sender, or a receiving bank having notice that the funds-transfer system might be used in the funds transfer and of the choice of law by the system when the originator, other sender, or receiving bank issued or accepted a payment order. The beneficiary of a funds transfer is bound by the choice of law if, when the funds transfer is initiated, the beneficiary has notice that the funds-transfer system might be used in the funds transfer and of the choice of law by the system. The law of a jurisdiction selected pursuant to this subsection may govern, whether or not that law bears a reasonable relation to the matter in issue.

(d) In the event of inconsistency between an agreement under subsection (b) and a choice-of-law rule under subsection (c), the agreement under subsection (b) prevails.

(e) If a funds transfer is made by use of more than one funds-transfer system and there is inconsistency between choice-of-law rules of the systems, the matter in issue is governed by the law of the selected jurisdiction that has the most significant relationship to the matter in issue.

Revised Article 9
SECURED TRANSACTIONS

Part 1   General Provisions

[Subpart 1. Short Title, Definitions, and General Concepts]

§ 9–101. Short Title.

This article may be cited as Uniform Commercial Code—Secured Transactions.

§ 9–102. Definitions and Index of Definitions.

(a) In this article:

(1) "Accession" means goods that are physically united with other goods in such a manner that the identity of the original goods is not lost.

(2) "Account", except as used in "account for", means a right to payment of a monetary obligation, whether or not earned by performance, (i) for property that has been or is to be sold, leased, licensed, assigned, or otherwise disposed of, (ii) for services rendered or to be rendered, (iii) for a policy of insurance issued or to be issued, (iv) for a secondary obligation incurred or to be incurred, (v) for energy provided or to be provided, (vi) for the use or hire of a vessel under a charter or other contract, (vii) arising out of the use of a credit or charge card or information contained on or for use with the card, or (viii) as winnings in a lottery or other game of chance operated or sponsored by a State, governmental unit of a State, or person licensed or authorized to operate the game by a State or governmental unit of a State. The term includes health-care insurance receivables. The term does not include (i) rights to payment evidenced by chattel paper or an instrument, (ii) commercial tort claims, (iii) deposit accounts, (iv) investment property, (v) letter-of-credit rights or letters of credit, or (vi) rights to payment for money or funds advanced or sold, other than rights arising out of the use of a credit or charge card or information contained on or for use with the card.

(3) "Account debtor" means a person obligated on an account, chattel paper, or general intangible. The term does not include persons obligated to pay a negotiable instrument, even if the instrument constitutes part of chattel paper.

(4) "Accounting", except as used in "accounting for", means a record:

(A) authenticated by a secured party;

(B) indicating the aggregate unpaid secured obligations as of a date not more than 35 days earlier or 35 days later than the date of the record; and

(C) identifying the components of the obligations in reasonable detail.

(5) "Agricultural lien" means an interest, other than a security interest, in farm products:

(A) which secures payment or performance of an obligation for:

(i) goods or services furnished in connection with a debtor's farming operation; or

(ii) rent on real property leased by a debtor in connection with its farming operation;

(B) which is created by statute in favor of a person that:

(i) in the ordinary course of its business furnished goods or services to a debtor in connection with a debtor's farming operation; or

(ii) leased real property to a debtor in connection with the debtor's farming operation; and

(C) whose effectiveness does not depend on the person's possession of the personal property.

(6) "As-extracted collateral" means:

(A) oil, gas, or other minerals that are subject to a security interest that:

(i) is created by a debtor having an interest in the minerals before extraction; and

(ii) attaches to the minerals as extracted; or

(B) accounts arising out of the sale at the wellhead or minehead of oil, gas, or other minerals in which the debtor had an interest before extraction.

(7) "Authenticate" means:

(A) to sign; or

(B) to execute or otherwise adopt a symbol, or encrypt or similarly process a record in whole or in part, with the present intent of the authenticating person to identify the person and adopt or accept a record.

(8) "Bank" means an organization that is engaged in the business of banking. The term includes savings banks, savings and loan associations, credit unions, and trust companies.

(9) "Cash proceeds" means proceeds that are money, checks, deposit accounts, or the like.

(10) "Certificate of title" means a certificate of title with respect to which a statute provides for the security interest in question to be indicated on the certificate as a condition or result of the security interest's obtaining priority over the rights of a lien creditor with respect to the collateral.

(11) "Chattel paper" means a record or records that evidence both a monetary obligation and a security interest in specific goods, a security interest in specific goods and software used in the goods, a security interest in specific goods and license of software used in the goods, a lease of specific goods, or a lease of specific goods and license of software used in the goods. In this paragraph, "monetary obligation" means a monetary obligation secured by the goods or owed under a lease of the goods and includes a monetary obligation with respect to software used in the goods. The term does not include (i) charters or other contracts involving the use or hire of a vessel or (ii) records that evidence a right to payment arising out of the use of a credit or charge card or information contained on or for use with the card. If a transaction is evidenced by records that include an instrument or series of instruments, the group of records taken together constitutes chattel paper.

(12) "Collateral" means the property subject to a security interest or agricultural lien. The term includes:

(A) proceeds to which a security interest attaches;

(B) accounts, chattel paper, payment intangibles, and promissory notes that have been sold; and

(C) goods that are the subject of a consignment.

(13) "Commercial tort claim" means a claim arising in tort with respect to which:

(A) the claimant is an organization; or

(B) the claimant is an individual and the claim:

(i) arose in the course of the claimant's business or profession; and

(ii) does not include damages arising out of personal injury to or the death of an individual.

(14) "Commodity account" means an account maintained by a commodity intermediary in which a commodity contract is carried for a commodity customer.

(15) "Commodity contract" means a commodity futures contract, an option on a commodity futures contract, a commodity option, or another contract if the contract or option is:

(A) traded on or subject to the rules of a board of trade that has been designated as a contract market for such a contract pursuant to federal commodities laws; or

(B) traded on a foreign commodity board of trade, exchange, or market, and is carried on the books of a commodity intermediary for a commodity customer.

(16) "Commodity customer" means a person for which a commodity intermediary carries a commodity contract on its books.

(17) "Commodity intermediary" means a person that:

(A) is registered as a futures commission merchant under federal commodities law; or

(B) in the ordinary course of its business provides clearance or settlement services for a board of trade that has been designated as a contract market pursuant to federal commodities law.

(18) "Communicate" means:

(A) to send a written or other tangible record;

(B) to transmit a record by any means agreed upon by the persons sending and receiving the record; or

(C) in the case of transmission of a record to or by a filing office, to transmit a record by any means prescribed by filing-office rule.

(19) "Consignee" means a merchant to which goods are delivered in a consignment.

(20) "Consignment" means a transaction, regardless of its form, in which a person delivers goods to a merchant for the purpose of sale and:

(A) the merchant:

(i) deals in goods of that kind under a name other than the name of the person making delivery;

(ii) is not an auctioneer; and

(iii) is not generally known by its creditors to be substantially engaged in selling the goods of others;

(B) with respect to each delivery, the aggregate value of the goods is $1,000 or more at the time of delivery;

(C) the goods are not consumer goods immediately before delivery; and

(D) the transaction does not create a security interest that secures an obligation.

(21) "Consignor" means a person that delivers goods to a consignee in a consignment.

(22) "Consumer debtor" means a debtor in a consumer transaction.

(23) "Consumer goods" means goods that are used or bought for use primarily for personal, family, or household purposes.

(24) "Consumer-goods transaction" means a consumer transaction in which:

(A) an individual incurs an obligation primarily for personal, family, or household purposes; and

(B) a security interest in consumer goods secures the obligation.

(25) "Consumer obligor" means an obligor who is an individual and who incurred the obligation as part of a transaction entered into primarily for personal, family, or household purposes.

(26) "Consumer transaction" means a transaction in which (i) an individual incurs an obligation primarily for personal, family, or household purposes, (ii) a security interest secures the obligation, and (iii) the collateral is held or acquired primarily for personal, family, or household purposes. The term includes consumer-goods transactions.

(27) "Continuation statement" means an amendment of a financing statement which:

(A) identifies, by its file number, the initial financing statement to which it relates; and

(B) indicates that it is a continuation statement for, or that it is filed to continue the effectiveness of, the identified financing statement.

(28) "Debtor" means:

(A) a person having an interest, other than a security interest or other lien, in the collateral, whether or not the person is an obligor;

(B) a seller of accounts, chattel paper, payment intangibles, or promissory notes; or

(C) a consignee.

(29) "Deposit account" means a demand, time, savings, passbook, or similar account maintained with a bank. The term does not include investment property or accounts evidenced by an instrument.

(30) "Document" means a document of title or a receipt of the type described in Section 7–201(2).

(31) "Electronic chattel paper" means chattel paper evidenced by a record or records consisting of information stored in an electronic medium.

(32) "Encumbrance" means a right, other than an ownership interest, in real property. The term includes mortgages and other liens on real property.

(33) "Equipment" means goods other than inventory, farm products, or consumer goods.

(34) "Farm products" means goods, other than standing timber, with respect to which the debtor is engaged in a farming operation and which are:

(A) crops grown, growing, or to be grown, including:

(i) crops produced on trees, vines, and bushes; and

(ii) aquatic goods produced in aquacultural operations;

(B) livestock, born or unborn, including aquatic goods produced in aquacultural operations;

(C) supplies used or produced in a farming operation; or

(D) products of crops or livestock in their unmanufactured states.

(35) "Farming operation" means raising, cultivating, propagating, fattening, grazing, or any other farming, livestock, or aquacultural operation.

(36) "File number" means the number assigned to an initial financing statement pursuant to Section 9–519(a).

(37) "Filing office" means an office designated in Section 9–501 as the place to file a financing statement.

(38) "Filing-office rule" means a rule adopted pursuant to Section 9–526.

(39) "Financing statement" means a record or records composed of an initial financing statement and any filed record relating to the initial financing statement.

(40) "Fixture filing" means the filing of a financing statement covering goods that are or are to become fixtures and satisfying Section 9–502(a) and (b). The term includes the filing of a financing statement covering goods of a transmitting utility which are or are to become fixtures.

(41) "Fixtures" means goods that have become so related to particular real property that an interest in them arises under real property law.

(42) "General intangible" means any personal property, including things in action, other than accounts, chattel paper, commercial tort claims, deposit accounts, documents, goods, instruments, investment property, letter-of-credit rights, letters of credit, money, and oil, gas, or other minerals before extraction. The term includes payment intangibles and software.

(43) "Good faith" means honesty in fact and the observance of reasonable commercial standards of fair dealing.

(44) "Goods" means all things that are movable when a security interest attaches. The term includes (i) fixtures, (ii) standing timber that is to be cut and removed under a conveyance or contract for sale, (iii) the unborn young of animals, (iv) crops grown, growing, or to be grown, even if the crops are produced on trees, vines, or bushes, and (v) manufactured homes. The term also includes a computer program embedded in goods and any supporting information provided in connection with a transaction relating to the program if (i) the program is associated with the goods in such a manner that it customarily is considered part of the goods, or (ii) by becoming the owner of the goods, a person acquires a right to use the program in connection with the goods. The term does not include a computer program embedded in goods that consist solely of the medium in which the program is embedded. The term also does not include accounts, chattel paper, commercial tort claims, deposit accounts, documents, general intangibles, instruments, investment property, letter-of-credit rights, letters of credit, money, or oil, gas, or other minerals before extraction.

(45) "Governmental unit" means a subdivision, agency, department, county, parish, municipality, or other unit of the government of the United States, a State, or a foreign country. The term includes an organization having a separate corporate existence if the organization is eligible to issue debt on which interest is exempt from income taxation under the laws of the United States.

(46) "Health-care-insurance receivable" means an interest in or claim under a policy of insurance which is a right to payment of a monetary obligation for health-care goods or services provided.

(47) "Instrument" means a negotiable instrument or any other writing that evidences a right to the payment of a monetary obligation, is not itself a security agreement or lease, and is of a type that in ordinary course of business is transferred by delivery with any necessary indorsement or assignment. The term does not include (i) investment property, (ii) letters of credit, or (iii) writings that evidence a right to payment arising out of the use of a credit or charge card or information contained on or for use with the card.

(48) "Inventory" means goods, other than farm products, which:

(A) are leased by a person as lessor;

(B) are held by a person for sale or lease or to be furnished under a contract of service;

(C) are furnished by a person under a contract of service; or

(D) consist of raw materials, work in process, or materials used or consumed in a business.

(49) "Investment property" means a security, whether certificated or uncertificated, security entitlement, securities account, commodity contract, or commodity account.

(50) "Jurisdiction of organization", with respect to a registered organization, means the jurisdiction under whose law the organization is organized.

(51) "Letter-of-credit right" means a right to payment or performance under a letter of credit, whether or not the beneficiary has demanded or is at the time entitled to demand payment or performance. The term does not include the right of a beneficiary to demand payment or performance under a letter of credit.

(52) "Lien creditor" means:

(A) a creditor that has acquired a lien on the property involved by attachment, levy, or the like;

(B) an assignee for benefit of creditors from the time of assignment;

(C) a trustee in bankruptcy from the date of the filing of the petition; or

(D) a receiver in equity from the time of appointment.

(53) "Manufactured home" means a structure, transportable in one or more sections, which, in the traveling mode, is eight body feet or more in width or 40 body feet or more in length, or, when erected on site, is 320 or more square feet, and which is built on a permanent chassis and designed to be used as a dwelling with or without a permanent foundation when connected to the required utilities, and includes the plumbing, heating, air-conditioning, and electrical systems contained therein. The term includes any structure that meets all of the requirements of this paragraph except the size requirements and with respect to which the manufacturer voluntarily files a certification required by the United States Secretary of Housing and Urban Development and complies with the standards established under Title 42 of the United States Code.

(54) "Manufactured-home transaction" means a secured transaction:

(A) that creates a purchase-money security interest in a manufactured home, other than a manufactured home held as inventory; or

(B) in which a manufactured home, other than a manufactured home held as inventory, is the primary collateral.

(55) "Mortgage" means a consensual interest in real property, including fixtures, which secures payment or performance of an obligation.

(56) "New debtor" means a person that becomes bound as debtor under Section 9–203(d) by a security agreement previously entered into by another person.

(57) "New value" means (i) money, (ii) money's worth in property, services, or new credit, or (iii) release by a transferee of an interest in property previously transferred to the transferee. The term does not include an obligation substituted for another obligation.

(58) "Noncash proceeds" means proceeds other than cash proceeds.

(59) "Obligor" means a person that, with respect to an obligation secured by a security interest in or an agricultural lien on the collateral, (i) owes payment or other performance of the obligation, (ii) has provided property other than the collateral to secure payment or other performance of the obligation, or (iii) is otherwise accountable in whole or in part for payment or other performance of the obligation. The term does not include issuers or nominated persons under a letter of credit.

(60) "Original debtor", except as used in Section 9–310(c), means a person that, as debtor, entered into a security agreement to which a new debtor has become bound under Section 9–203(d).

(61) "Payment intangible" means a general intangible under which the account debtor's principal obligation is a monetary obligation.

(62) "Person related to", with respect to an individual, means:

(A) the spouse of the individual;

(B) a brother, brother-in-law, sister, or sister-in-law of the individual;

(C) an ancestor or lineal descendant of the individual or the individual's spouse; or

(D) any other relative, by blood or marriage, of the individual or the individual's spouse who shares the same home with the individual.

(63) "Person related to", with respect to an organization, means:

(A) a person directly or indirectly controlling, controlled by, or under common control with the organization;

(B) an officer or director of, or a person performing similar functions with respect to, the organization;

(C) an officer or director of, or a person performing similar functions with respect to, a person described in subparagraph (A);

(D) the spouse of an individual described in subparagraph (A), (B), or (C); or

(E) an individual who is related by blood or marriage to an individual described in subparagraph (A), (B), (C), or (D) and shares the same home with the individual.

(64) "Proceeds", except as used in Section 9–609(b), means the following property:

(A) whatever is acquired upon the sale, lease, license, exchange, or other disposition of collateral;

(B) whatever is collected on, or distributed on account of, collateral;

(C) rights arising out of collateral;

(D) to the extent of the value of collateral, claims arising out of the loss, nonconformity, or interference with the use of, defects or infringement of rights in, or damage to, the collateral; or

(E) to the extent of the value of collateral and to the extent payable to the debtor or the secured party, insurance payable by reason of the loss or nonconformity of, defects or infringement of rights in, or damage to, the collateral.

(65) "Promissory note" means an instrument that evidences a promise to pay a monetary obligation, does not evidence an order to pay, and does not contain an acknowledgment by a bank that the bank has received for deposit a sum of money or funds.

(66) "Proposal" means a record authenticated by a secured party which includes the terms on which the secured party is willing to accept collateral in full or partial satisfaction of the obligation it secures pursuant to Sections 9–620, 9–621, and 9–622.

(67) "Public-finance transaction" means a secured transaction in connection with which:

(A) debt securities are issued;

(B) all or a portion of the securities issued have an initial stated maturity of at least 20 years; and

(C) the debtor, obligor, secured party, account debtor or other person obligated on collateral, assignor or assignee of a secured obligation, or assignor or assignee of a security interest is a State or a governmental unit of a State.

(68) "Pursuant to commitment", with respect to an advance made or other value given by a secured party, means pursuant to the secured party's obligation, whether or not a subsequent event of default or other event not within the secured party's control has relieved or may relieve the secured party from its obligation.

(69) "Record", except as used in "for record", "of record", "record or legal title", and "record owner", means information that is inscribed on a tangible medium or which is stored in an electronic or other medium and is retrievable in perceivable form.

(70) "Registered organization" means an organization organized solely under the law of a single State or the United States and as to which the State or the United States must maintain a public record showing the organization to have been organized.

(71) "Secondary obligor" means an obligor to the extent that:

(A) the obligor's obligation is secondary; or

(B) the obligor has a right of recourse with respect to an obligation secured by collateral against the debtor, another obligor, or property of either.

(72) "Secured party" means:

(A) a person in whose favor a security interest is created or provided for under a security agreement, whether or not any obligation to be secured is outstanding;

(B) a person that holds an agricultural lien;

(C) a consignor;

(D) a person to which accounts, chattel paper, payment intangibles, or promissory notes have been sold;

(E) a trustee, indenture trustee, agent, collateral agent, or other representative in whose favor a security interest or agricultural lien is created or provided for; or

(F) a person that holds a security interest arising under Section 2–401, 2–505, 2–711(3), 2A–508(5), 4–210, or 5–118.

(73) "Security agreement" means an agreement that creates or provides for a security interest.

(74) "Send", in connection with a record or notification, means:

(A) to deposit in the mail, deliver for transmission, or transmit by any other usual means of communication, with postage or cost of transmission provided for, addressed to any address reasonable under the circumstances; or

(B) to cause the record or notification to be received within the time that it would have been received if properly sent under subparagraph (A).

(75) "Software" means a computer program and any supporting information provided in connection with a transaction relating to the program. The term does not include a computer program that is included in the definition of goods.

(76) "State" means a State of the United States, the District of Columbia, Puerto Rico, the United States Virgin Islands, or any territory or insular possession subject to the jurisdiction of the United States.

(77) "Supporting obligation" means a letter-of-credit right or secondary obligation that supports the payment or performance of an account, chattel paper, a document, a general intangible, an instrument, or investment property.

(78) "Tangible chattel paper" means chattel paper evidenced by a record or records consisting of information that is inscribed on a tangible medium.

(79) "Termination statement" means an amendment of a financing statement which:

(A) identifies, by its file number, the initial financing statement to which it relates; and

(B) indicates either that it is a termination statement or that the identified financing statement is no longer effective.

(80) "Transmitting utility" means a person primarily engaged in the business of:

(A) operating a railroad, subway, street railway, or trolley bus;

(B) transmitting communications electrically, electromagnetically, or by light;

(C) transmitting goods by pipeline or sewer; or

(D) transmitting or producing and transmitting electricity, steam, gas, or water.

(b) The following definitions in other articles apply to this article:

"Applicant."	Section 5–102
"Beneficiary."	Section 5–102
"Broker."	Section 8–102
"Certificated security."	Section 8–102
"Check."	Section 3–104
"Clearing corporation."	Section 8–102
"Contract for sale."	Section 2–106
"Customer."	Section 4–104
"Entitlement holder."	Section 8–102
"Financial asset."	Section 8–102
"Holder in due course."	Section 3–302

"Issuer" (with respect to a letter of credit or letter-of-credit right).	Section 5–102
"Issuer" (with respect to a security).	Section 8–201
"Lease."	Section 2A–103
"Lease agreement."	Section 2A–103
"Lease contract."	Section 2A–103
"Leasehold interest."	Section 2A–103
"Lessee."	Section 2A–103
"Lessee in ordinary course of business."	Section 2A–103
"Lessor."	Section 2A–103
"Lessor's residual interest."	Section 2A–103
"Letter of credit."	Section 5–102
"Merchant."	Section 2–104
"Negotiable instrument."	Section 3–104
"Nominated person."	Section 5–102
"Note."	Section 3–104
"Proceeds of a letter of credit."	Section 5–114
"Prove."	Section 3–103
"Sale."	Section 2–106
"Securities account."	Section 8–501
"Securities intermediary."	Section 8–102
"Security."	Section 8–102
"Security certificate."	Section 8–102
"Security entitlement."	Section 8–102
"Uncertificated security."	Section 8–102

(c) Article 1 contains general definitions and principles of construction and interpretation applicable throughout this article.

Amended in 1999 and 2000.

§ 9–103. Purchase-Money Security Interest; Application of Payments; Burden of Establishing.

(a) In this section:

(1) "purchase-money collateral" means goods or software that secures a purchase-money obligation incurred with respect to that collateral; and

(2) "purchase-money obligation" means an obligation of an obligor incurred as all or part of the price of the collateral or for value given to enable the debtor to acquire rights in or the use of the collateral if the value is in fact so used.

(b) A security interest in goods is a purchase-money security interest:

(1) to the extent that the goods are purchase-money collateral with respect to that security interest;

(2) if the security interest is in inventory that is or was purchase-money collateral, also to the extent that the security interest secures a purchase-money obligation incurred with respect to other inventory in which the secured party holds or held a purchase-money security interest; and

(3) also to the extent that the security interest secures a purchase-money obligation incurred with respect to software in which the secured party holds or held a purchase-money security interest.

(c) A security interest in software is a purchase-money security interest to the extent that the security interest also secures a purchase-money obligation incurred with respect to goods in which the secured party holds or held a purchase-money security interest if:

(1) the debtor acquired its interest in the software in an integrated transaction in which it acquired an interest in the goods; and

(2) the debtor acquired its interest in the software for the principal purpose of using the software in the goods.

(d) The security interest of a consignor in goods that are the subject of a consignment is a purchase-money security interest in inventory.

(e) In a transaction other than a consumer-goods transaction, if the extent to which a security interest is a purchase-money security interest depends on the application of a payment to a particular obligation, the payment must be applied:

(1) in accordance with any reasonable method of application to which the parties agree;

(2) in the absence of the parties' agreement to a reasonable method, in accordance with any intention of the obligor manifested at or before the time of payment; or

(3) in the absence of an agreement to a reasonable method and a timely manifestation of the obligor's intention, in the following order:

(A) to obligations that are not secured; and

(B) if more than one obligation is secured, to obligations secured by purchase-money security interests in the order in which those obligations were incurred.

(f) In a transaction other than a consumer-goods transaction, a purchase-money security interest does not lose its status as such, even if:

(1) the purchase-money collateral also secures an obligation that is not a purchase-money obligation;

(2) collateral that is not purchase-money collateral also secures the purchase-money obligation; or

(3) the purchase-money obligation has been renewed, refinanced, consolidated, or restructured.

(g) In a transaction other than a consumer-goods transaction, a secured party claiming a purchase-money security interest has the burden of establishing the extent to which the security interest is a purchase-money security interest.

(h) The limitation of the rules in subsections (e), (f), and (g) to transactions other than consumer-goods transactions is intended to leave to the court the determination of the proper rules in consumer-goods transactions. The court may not infer from that limitation the nature of the proper rule in consumer-goods transactions and may continue to apply established approaches.

§ 9–104. Control of Deposit Account.

(a) A secured party has control of a deposit account if:

(1) the secured party is the bank with which the deposit account is maintained;

(2) the debtor, secured party, and bank have agreed in an authenticated record that the bank will comply with instructions originated by the secured party directing disposition of the funds in the deposit account without further consent by the debtor; or

(3) the secured party becomes the bank's customer with respect to the deposit account.

(b) A secured party that has satisfied subsection (a) has control, even if the debtor retains the right to direct the disposition of funds from the deposit account.

§ 9–105. Control of Electronic Chattel Paper.

A secured party has control of electronic chattel paper if the record or records comprising the chattel paper are created, stored, and assigned in such a manner that:

(1) a single authoritative copy of the record or records exists which is unique, identifiable and, except as otherwise provided in paragraphs (4), (5), and (6), unalterable;

(2) the authoritative copy identifies the secured party as the assignee of the record or records;

(3) the authoritative copy is communicated to and maintained by the secured party or its designated custodian;

(4) copies or revisions that add or change an identified assignee of the authoritative copy can be made only with the participation of the secured party;

(5) each copy of the authoritative copy and any copy of a copy is readily identifiable as a copy that is not the authoritative copy; and

(6) any revision of the authoritative copy is readily identifiable as an authorized or unauthorized revision.

§ 9–106. Control of Investment Property.

(a) A person has control of a certificated security, uncertificated security, or security entitlement as provided in Section 8–106.

(b) A secured party has control of a commodity contract if:

(1) the secured party is the commodity intermediary with which the commodity contract is carried; or

(2) the commodity customer, secured party, and commodity intermediary have agreed that the commodity intermediary will apply any value distributed on account of the commodity contract as directed by the secured party without further consent by the commodity customer.

(c) A secured party having control of all security entitlements or commodity contracts carried in a securities account or commodity account has control over the securities account or commodity account.

§ 9–107. Control of Letter-of-Credit Right.

A secured party has control of a letter-of-credit right to the extent of any right to payment or performance by the issuer or any nominated person if the issuer or nominated person has consented to an assignment of proceeds of the letter of credit under Section 5–114(c) or otherwise applicable law or practice.

§ 9–108. Sufficiency of Description.

(a) Except as otherwise provided in subsections (c), (d), and (e), a description of personal or real property is sufficient, whether or not it is specific, if it reasonably identifies what is described.

(b) Except as otherwise provided in subsection (d), a description of collateral reasonably identifies the collateral if it identifies the collateral by:

(1) specific listing;

(2) category;

(3) except as otherwise provided in subsection (e), a type of collateral defined in [the Uniform Commercial Code];

(4) quantity;

(5) computational or allocational formula or procedure; or

(6) except as otherwise provided in subsection (c), any other method, if the identity of the collateral is objectively determinable.

(c) A description of collateral as "all the debtor's assets" or "all the debtor's personal property" or using words of similar import does not reasonably identify the collateral.

(d) Except as otherwise provided in subsection (e), a description of a security entitlement, securities account, or commodity account is sufficient if it describes:

(1) the collateral by those terms or as investment property; or

(2) the underlying financial asset or commodity contract.

(e) A description only by type of collateral defined in [the Uniform Commercial Code] is an insufficient description of:

(1) a commercial tort claim; or

(2) in a consumer transaction, consumer goods, a security entitlement, a securities account, or a commodity account.

[Subpart 2. Applicability of Article]

§ 9–109.   Scope.

(a) Except as otherwise provided in subsections (c) and (d), this article applies to:

(1) a transaction, regardless of its form, that creates a security interest in personal property or fixtures by contract;

(2) an agricultural lien;

(3) a sale of accounts, chattel paper, payment intangibles, or promissory notes;

(4) a consignment;

(5) a security interest arising under Section 2–401, 2–505, 2–711(3), or 2A–508(5), as provided in Section 9–110; and

(6) a security interest arising under Section 4–210 or 5–118.

(b) The application of this article to a security interest in a secured obligation is not affected by the fact that the obligation is itself secured by a transaction or interest to which this article does not apply.

(c) This article does not apply to the extent that:

(1) a statute, regulation, or treaty of the United States preempts this article;

(2) another statute of this State expressly governs the creation, perfection, priority, or enforcement of a security interest created by this State or a governmental unit of this State;

(3) a statute of another State, a foreign country, or a governmental unit of another State or a foreign country, other than a statute generally applicable to security interests, expressly governs creation, perfection, priority, or enforcement of a security interest created by the State, country, or governmental unit; or

(4) the rights of a transferee beneficiary or nominated person under a letter of credit are independent and superior under Section 5–114.

(d) This article does not apply to:

(1) a landlord's lien, other than an agricultural lien;

(2) a lien, other than an agricultural lien, given by statute or other rule of law for services or materials, but Section 9–333 applies with respect to priority of the lien;

(3) an assignment of a claim for wages, salary, or other compensation of an employee;

(4) a sale of accounts, chattel paper, payment intangibles, or promissory notes as part of a sale of the business out of which they arose;

(5) an assignment of accounts, chattel paper, payment intangibles, or promissory notes which is for the purpose of collection only;

(6) an assignment of a right to payment under a contract to an assignee that is also obligated to perform under the contract;

(7) an assignment of a single account, payment intangible, or promissory note to an assignee in full or partial satisfaction of a preexisting indebtedness;

(8) a transfer of an interest in or an assignment of a claim under a policy of insurance, other than an assignment by or to a health-care provider of a health-care-insurance receivable and any subsequent assignment of the right to payment, but Sections 9–315 and 9–322 apply with respect to proceeds and priorities in proceeds;

(9) an assignment of a right represented by a judgment, other than a judgment taken on a right to payment that was collateral;

(10) a right of recoupment or set-off, but:

(A) Section 9–340 applies with respect to the effectiveness of rights of recoupment or set-off against deposit accounts; and

(B) Section 9–404 applies with respect to defenses or claims of an account debtor;

(11) the creation or transfer of an interest in or lien on real property, including a lease or rents thereunder, except to the extent that provision is made for:

(A) liens on real property in Sections 9–203 and 9–308;

(B) fixtures in Section 9–334;

(C) fixture filings in Sections 9–501, 9–502, 9–512, 9–516, and 9–519; and

(D) security agreements covering personal and real property in Section 9–604;

(12) an assignment of a claim arising in tort, other than a commercial tort claim, but Sections 9–315 and 9–322 apply with respect to proceeds and priorities in proceeds; or

(13) an assignment of a deposit account in a consumer transaction, but Sections 9–315 and 9–322 apply with respect to proceeds and priorities in proceeds.

§ 9–110.   Security Interests Arising under Article 2 or 2A.

A security interest arising under Section 2–401, 2–505, 2–711(3), or 2A–508(5) is subject to this article. However, until the debtor obtains possession of the goods:

(1) the security interest is enforceable, even if Section 9–203(b) (3) has not been satisfied;

(2) filing is not required to perfect the security interest;

(3) the rights of the secured party after default by the debtor are governed by Article 2 or 2A; and

(4) the security interest has priority over a conflicting security interest created by the debtor.

Part 2   **Effectiveness of Security Agreement; Attachment of Security Interest; Rights of Parties to Security Agreement**

[Subpart 1. Effectiveness and Attachment]

§ 9–201. General Effectiveness of Security Agreement.

(a) Except as otherwise provided in [the Uniform Commercial Code], a security agreement is effective according to its terms between the parties, against purchasers of the collateral, and against creditors.

(b) A transaction subject to this article is subject to any applicable rule of law which establishes a different rule for consumers and [insert reference to (i) any other statute or regulation that regulates the rates, charges, agreements, and practices for loans, credit sales, or other extensions of credit and (ii) any consumer-protection statute or regulation].

(c) In case of conflict between this article and a rule of law, statute, or regulation described in subsection (b), the rule of law, statute, or regulation controls. Failure to comply with a statute or regulation described in subsection (b) has only the effect the statute or regulation specifies.

(d) This article does not:

(1) validate any rate, charge, agreement, or practice that violates a rule of law, statute, or regulation described in subsection (b); or

(2) extend the application of the rule of law, statute, or regulation to a transaction not otherwise subject to it.

§ 9–202. Title to Collateral Immaterial.

Except as otherwise provided with respect to consignments or sales of accounts, chattel paper, payment intangibles, or promissory notes, the provisions of this article with regard to rights and obligations apply whether title to collateral is in the secured party or the debtor.

§ 9–203. Attachment and Enforceability of Security Interest; Proceeds; Supporting Obligations; Formal Requisites.

(a) A security interest attaches to collateral when it becomes enforceable against the debtor with respect to the collateral, unless an agreement expressly postpones the time of attachment.

(b) Except as otherwise provided in subsections (c) through (i), a security interest is enforceable against the debtor and third parties with respect to the collateral only if:

(1) value has been given;

(2) the debtor has rights in the collateral or the power to transfer rights in the collateral to a secured party; and

(3) one of the following conditions is met:

(A) the debtor has authenticated a security agreement that provides a description of the collateral and, if the security interest covers timber to be cut, a description of the land concerned;

(B) the collateral is not a certificated security and is in the possession of the secured party under Section 9–313 pursuant to the debtor's security agreement;

(C) the collateral is a certificated security in registered form and the security certificate has been delivered to the secured party under Section 8–301 pursuant to the debtor's security agreement; or

(D) the collateral is deposit accounts, electronic chattel paper, investment property, or letter-of-credit rights, and the secured party has control under Section 9–104, 9–105, 9–106, or 9–107 pursuant to the debtor's security agreement.

(c) Subsection (b) is subject to Section 4–210 on the security interest of a collecting bank, Section 5–118 on the security interest of a letter-of-credit issuer or nominated person, Section 9–110 on a security interest arising under Article 2 or 2A, and Section 9–206 on security interests in investment property.

(d) A person becomes bound as debtor by a security agreement entered into by another person if, by operation of law other than this article or by contract:

(1) the security agreement becomes effective to create a security interest in the person's property; or

(2) the person becomes generally obligated for the obligations of the other person, including the obligation secured under the security agreement, and acquires or succeeds to all or substantially all of the assets of the other person.

(e) If a new debtor becomes bound as debtor by a security agreement entered into by another person:

(1) the agreement satisfies subsection (b)(3) with respect to existing or after-acquired property of the new debtor to the extent the property is described in the agreement; and

(2) another agreement is not necessary to make a security interest in the property enforceable.

(f) The attachment of a security interest in collateral gives the secured party the rights to proceeds provided by Section 9–315 and is also attachment of a security interest in a supporting obligation for the collateral.

(g) The attachment of a security interest in a right to payment or performance secured by a security interest or other lien on personal or real property is also attachment of a security interest in the security interest, mortgage, or other lien.

(h) The attachment of a security interest in a securities account is also attachment of a security interest in the security entitlements carried in the securities account.

(i) The attachment of a security interest in a commodity account is also attachment of a security interest in the commodity contracts carried in the commodity account.

§ 9–204. After-Acquired Property; Future Advances.

(a) Except as otherwise provided in subsection (b), a security agreement may create or provide for a security interest in after-acquired collateral.

(b) A security interest does not attach under a term constituting an after-acquired property clause to:

(1) consumer goods, other than an accession when given as additional security, unless the debtor acquires rights in them within 10 days after the secured party gives value; or

(2) a commercial tort claim.

(c) A security agreement may provide that collateral secures, or that accounts, chattel paper, payment intangibles, or promissory notes are sold in connection with, future advances or other value, whether or not the advances or value are given pursuant to commitment.

§ 9–205. Use or Disposition of Collateral Permissible.

(a) A security interest is not invalid or fraudulent against creditors solely because:

(1) the debtor has the right or ability to:

(A) use, commingle, or dispose of all or part of the collateral, including returned or repossessed goods;

(B) collect, compromise, enforce, or otherwise deal with collateral;

(C) accept the return of collateral or make repossessions; or

(D) use, commingle, or dispose of proceeds; or

(2) the secured party fails to require the debtor to account for proceeds or replace collateral.

(b) This section does not relax the requirements of possession if attachment, perfection, or enforcement of a security interest depends upon possession of the collateral by the secured party.

§ 9–206. Security Interest Arising in Purchase or Delivery of Financial Asset.

(a) A security interest in favor of a securities intermediary attaches to a person's security entitlement if:

(1) the person buys a financial asset through the securities intermediary in a transaction in which the person is obligated to pay the purchase price to the securities intermediary at the time of the purchase; and

(2) the securities intermediary credits the financial asset to the buyer's securities account before the buyer pays the securities intermediary.

(b) The security interest described in subsection (a) secures the person's obligation to pay for the financial asset.

(c) A security interest in favor of a person that delivers a certificated security or other financial asset represented by a writing attaches to the security or other financial asset if:

(1) the security or other financial asset:

(A) in the ordinary course of business is transferred by delivery with any necessary indorsement or assignment; and

(B) is delivered under an agreement between persons in the business of dealing with such securities or financial assets; and

(2) the agreement calls for delivery against payment.

(d) The security interest described in subsection (c) secures the obligation to make payment for the delivery.

[Subpart 2. Rights and Duties]

§ 9–207. Rights and Duties of Secured Party Having Possession or Control of Collateral.

(a) Except as otherwise provided in subsection (d), a secured party shall use reasonable care in the custody and preservation of collateral in the secured party's possession. In the case of chattel paper or an instrument, reasonable care includes taking necessary steps to preserve rights against prior parties unless otherwise agreed.

(b) Except as otherwise provided in subsection (d), if a secured party has possession of collateral:

(1) reasonable expenses, including the cost of insurance and payment of taxes or other charges, incurred in the custody, preservation, use, or operation of the collateral are chargeable to the debtor and are secured by the collateral;

(2) the risk of accidental loss or damage is on the debtor to the extent of a deficiency in any effective insurance coverage;

(3) the secured party shall keep the collateral identifiable, but fungible collateral may be commingled; and

(4) the secured party may use or operate the collateral:

(A) for the purpose of preserving the collateral or its value;

(B) as permitted by an order of a court having competent jurisdiction; or

(C) except in the case of consumer goods, in the manner and to the extent agreed by the debtor.

(c) Except as otherwise provided in subsection (d), a secured party having possession of collateral or control of collateral under Section 9–104, 9–105, 9–106, or 9–107:

(1) may hold as additional security any proceeds, except money or funds, received from the collateral;

(2) shall apply money or funds received from the collateral to reduce the secured obligation, unless remitted to the debtor; and

(3) may create a security interest in the collateral.

(d) If the secured party is a buyer of accounts, chattel paper, payment intangibles, or promissory notes or a consignor:

(1) subsection (a) does not apply unless the secured party is entitled under an agreement:

(A) to charge back uncollected collateral; or

(B) otherwise to full or limited recourse against the debtor or a secondary obligor based on the nonpayment or other default of an account debtor or other obligor on the collateral; and

(2) subsections (b) and (c) do not apply.

§ 9–208. Additional Duties of Secured Party Having Control of Collateral.

(a) This section applies to cases in which there is no outstanding secured obligation and the secured party is not committed to make advances, incur obligations, or otherwise give value.

(b) Within 10 days after receiving an authenticated demand by the debtor:

(1) a secured party having control of a deposit account under Section 9–104(a)(2) shall send to the bank with which the deposit account is maintained an authenticated statement that releases the bank from any further obligation to comply with instructions originated by the secured party;

(2) a secured party having control of a deposit account under Section 9–104(a)(3) shall:

(A) pay the debtor the balance on deposit in the deposit account; or

(B) transfer the balance on deposit into a deposit account in the debtor's name;

(3) a secured party, other than a buyer, having control of electronic chattel paper under Section 9–105 shall:

(A) communicate the authoritative copy of the electronic chattel paper to the debtor or its designated custodian;

(B) if the debtor designates a custodian that is the designated custodian with which the authoritative copy of the electronic chattel paper is maintained for the secured party, communicate to the custodian an authenticated record releasing the designated custodian from any further obligation to comply with instructions originated by the secured party and instructing the custodian to comply with instructions originated by the debtor; and

(C) take appropriate action to enable the debtor or its designated custodian to make copies of or revisions to the authoritative copy which add or change an identified assignee of the authoritative copy without the consent of the secured party;

(4) a secured party having control of investment property under Section 8–106(d)(2) or 9–106(b) shall send to the securities inter-

mediary or commodity intermediary with which the security entitlement or commodity contract is maintained an authenticated record that releases the securities intermediary or commodity intermediary from any further obligation to comply with entitlement orders or directions originated by the secured party; and

(5) a secured party having control of a letter-of-credit right under Section 9–107 shall send to each person having an unfulfilled obligation to pay or deliver proceeds of the letter of credit to the secured party an authenticated release from any further obligation to pay or deliver proceeds of the letter of credit to the secured party.

§ 9–209. Duties of Secured Party If Account Debtor Has Been Notified of Assignment.

(a) Except as otherwise provided in subsection (c), this section applies if:

(1) there is no outstanding secured obligation; and

(2) the secured party is not committed to make advances, incur obligations, or otherwise give value.

(b) Within 10 days after receiving an authenticated demand by the debtor, a secured party shall send to an account debtor that has received notification of an assignment to the secured party as assignee under Section 9–406(a) an authenticated record that releases the account debtor from any further obligation to the secured party.

(c) This section does not apply to an assignment constituting the sale of an account, chattel paper, or payment intangible.

§ 9–210. Request for Accounting; Request Regarding List of Collateral or Statement of Account.

(a) In this section:

(1) "Request" means a record of a type described in paragraph (2), (3), or (4).

(2) "Request for an accounting" means a record authenticated by a debtor requesting that the recipient provide an accounting of the unpaid obligations secured by collateral and reasonably identifying the transaction or relationship that is the subject of the request.

(3) "Request regarding a list of collateral" means a record authenticated by a debtor requesting that the recipient approve or correct a list of what the debtor believes to be the collateral securing an obligation and reasonably identifying the transaction or relationship that is the subject of the request.

(4) "Request regarding a statement of account" means a record authenticated by a debtor requesting that the recipient approve or correct a statement indicating what the debtor believes to be the aggregate amount of unpaid obligations secured by collateral as of a specified date and reasonably identifying the transaction or relationship that is the subject of the request.

(b) Subject to subsections (c), (d), (e), and (f), a secured party, other than a buyer of accounts, chattel paper, payment intangibles, or promissory notes or a consignor, shall comply with a request within 14 days after receipt:

(1) in the case of a request for an accounting, by authenticating and sending to the debtor an accounting; and

(2) in the case of a request regarding a list of collateral or a request regarding a statement of account, by authenticating and sending to the debtor an approval or correction.

(c) A secured party that claims a security interest in all of a particular type of collateral owned by the debtor may comply with a request regarding a list of collateral by sending to the debtor an authenticated record including a statement to that effect within 14 days after receipt.

(d) A person that receives a request regarding a list of collateral, claims no interest in the collateral when it receives the request, and claimed an interest in the collateral at an earlier time shall comply with the request within 14 days after receipt by sending to the debtor an authenticated record:

(1) disclaiming any interest in the collateral; and

(2) if known to the recipient, providing the name and mailing address of any assignee of or successor to the recipient's interest in the collateral.

(e) A person that receives a request for an accounting or a request regarding a statement of account, claims no interest in the obligations when it receives the request, and claimed an interest in the obligations at an earlier time shall comply with the request within 14 days after receipt by sending to the debtor an authenticated record:

(1) disclaiming any interest in the obligations; and

(2) if known to the recipient, providing the name and mailing address of any assignee of or successor to the recipient's interest in the obligations.

(f) A debtor is entitled without charge to one response to a request under this section during any six-month period. The secured party may require payment of a charge not exceeding $25 for each additional response.

As amended in 1999.

Part 3   Perfection and Priority

[Subpart 1. Law Governing Perfection and Priority]

§ 9–301. Law Governing Perfection and Priority of Security Interests.

Except as otherwise provided in Sections 9–303 through 9–306, the following rules determine the law governing perfection, the effect of perfection or nonperfection, and the priority of a security interest in collateral:

(1) Except as otherwise provided in this section, while a debtor is located in a jurisdiction, the local law of that jurisdiction governs perfection, the effect of perfection or nonperfection, and the priority of a security interest in collateral.

(2) While collateral is located in a jurisdiction, the local law of that jurisdiction governs perfection, the effect of perfection or nonperfection, and the priority of a possessory security interest in that collateral.

(3) Except as otherwise provided in paragraph (4), while negotiable documents, goods, instruments, money, or tangible chattel paper is located in a jurisdiction, the local law of that jurisdiction governs:

(A) perfection of a security interest in the goods by filing a fixture filing;

(B) perfection of a security interest in timber to be cut; and

(C) the effect of perfection or nonperfection and the priority of a nonpossessory security interest in the collateral.

(4) The local law of the jurisdiction in which the wellhead or minehead is located governs perfection, the effect of perfection or nonperfection, and the priority of a security interest in as-extracted collateral.

§ 9–302. Law Governing Perfection and Priority of Agricultural Liens.

While farm products are located in a jurisdiction, the local law of that jurisdiction governs perfection, the effect of perfection or nonperfection, and the priority of an agricultural lien on the farm products.

§ 9–303. Law Governing Perfection and Priority of Security Interests in Goods Covered by a Certificate of Title.

(a) This section applies to goods covered by a certificate of title, even if there is no other relationship between the jurisdiction under whose certificate of title the goods are covered and the goods or the debtor.

(b) Goods become covered by a certificate of title when a valid application for the certificate of title and the applicable fee are delivered to the appropriate authority. Goods cease to be covered by a certificate of title at the earlier of the time the certificate of title ceases to be effective under the law of the issuing jurisdiction or the time the goods become covered subsequently by a certificate of title issued by another jurisdiction.

(c) The local law of the jurisdiction under whose certificate of title the goods are covered governs perfection, the effect of perfection or nonperfection, and the priority of a security interest in goods covered by a certificate of title from the time the goods become covered by the certificate of title until the goods cease to be covered by the certificate of title.

§ 9–304. Law Governing Perfection and Priority of Security Interests in Deposit Accounts.

(a) The local law of a bank's jurisdiction governs perfection, the effect of perfection or nonperfection, and the priority of a security interest in a deposit account maintained with that bank.

(b) The following rules determine a bank's jurisdiction for purposes of this part:

(1) If an agreement between the bank and the debtor governing the deposit account expressly provides that a particular jurisdiction is the bank's jurisdiction for purposes of this part, this article, or [the Uniform Commercial Code], that jurisdiction is the bank's jurisdiction.

(2) If paragraph (1) does not apply and an agreement between the bank and its customer governing the deposit account expressly provides that the agreement is governed by the law of a particular jurisdiction, that jurisdiction is the bank's jurisdiction.

(3) If neither paragraph (1) nor paragraph (2) applies and an agreement between the bank and its customer governing the deposit account expressly provides that the deposit account is maintained at an office in a particular jurisdiction, that jurisdiction is the bank's jurisdiction.

(4) If none of the preceding paragraphs applies, the bank's jurisdiction is the jurisdiction in which the office identified in an account statement as the office serving the customer's account is located.

(5) If none of the preceding paragraphs applies, the bank's jurisdiction is the jurisdiction in which the chief executive office of the bank is located.

§ 9–305. Law Governing Perfection and Priority of Security Interests in Investment Property.

(a) Except as otherwise provided in subsection (c), the following rules apply:

(1) While a security certificate is located in a jurisdiction, the local law of that jurisdiction governs perfection, the effect of perfection or nonperfection, and the priority of a security interest in the certificated security represented thereby.

(2) The local law of the issuer's jurisdiction as specified in Section 8–110(d) governs perfection, the effect of perfection or nonperfection, and the priority of a security interest in an uncertificated security.

(3) The local law of the securities intermediary's jurisdiction as specified in Section 8–110(e) governs perfection, the effect of perfection or nonperfection, and the priority of a security interest in a security entitlement or securities account.

(4) The local law of the commodity intermediary's jurisdiction governs perfection, the effect of perfection or nonperfection, and the priority of a security interest in a commodity contract or commodity account.

(b) The following rules determine a commodity intermediary's jurisdiction for purposes of this part:

(1) If an agreement between the commodity intermediary and commodity customer governing the commodity account expressly provides that a particular jurisdiction is the commodity intermediary's jurisdiction for purposes of this part, this article, or [the Uniform Commercial Code], that jurisdiction is the commodity intermediary's jurisdiction.

(2) If paragraph (1) does not apply and an agreement between the commodity intermediary and commodity customer governing the commodity account expressly provides that the agreement is governed by the law of a particular jurisdiction, that jurisdiction is the commodity intermediary's jurisdiction.

(3) If neither paragraph (1) nor paragraph (2) applies and an agreement between the commodity intermediary and commodity customer governing the commodity account expressly provides that the commodity account is maintained at an office in a particular jurisdiction, that jurisdiction is the commodity intermediary's jurisdiction.

(4) If none of the preceding paragraphs applies, the commodity intermediary's jurisdiction is the jurisdiction in which the office identified in an account statement as the office serving the commodity customer's account is located.

(5) If none of the preceding paragraphs applies, the commodity intermediary's jurisdiction is the jurisdiction in which the chief executive office of the commodity intermediary is located.

(c) The local law of the jurisdiction in which the debtor is located governs:

(1) perfection of a security interest in investment property by filing;

(2) automatic perfection of a security interest in investment property created by a broker or securities intermediary; and

(3) automatic perfection of a security interest in a commodity contract or commodity account created by a commodity intermediary.

§ 9–306. Law Governing Perfection and Priority of Security Interests in Letter-of-Credit Rights.

(a) Subject to subsection (c), the local law of the issuer's jurisdiction or a nominated person's jurisdiction governs perfection, the effect of perfection or nonperfection, and the priority of a security interest in a letter-of-credit right if the issuer's jurisdiction or nominated person's jurisdiction is a State.

(b) For purposes of this part, an issuer's jurisdiction or nominated person's jurisdiction is the jurisdiction whose law governs the liability of the issuer or nominated person with respect to the letter-of-credit right as provided in Section 5–116.

(c) This section does not apply to a security interest that is perfected only under Section 9–308(d).

§ 9–307. Location of Debtor.

(a) In this section, "place of business" means a place where a debtor conducts its affairs.

(b) Except as otherwise provided in this section, the following rules determine a debtor's location:

(1) A debtor who is an individual is located at the individual's principal residence.

(2) A debtor that is an organization and has only one place of business is located at its place of business.

(3) A debtor that is an organization and has more than one place of business is located at its chief executive office.

(c) Subsection (b) applies only if a debtor's residence, place of business, or chief executive office, as applicable, is located in a jurisdiction whose law generally requires information concerning the existence of a nonpossessory security interest to be made generally available in a filing, recording, or registration system as a condition or result of the security interest's obtaining priority over the rights of a lien creditor with respect to the collateral. If subsection (b) does not apply, the debtor is located in the District of Columbia.

(d) A person that ceases to exist, have a residence, or have a place of business continues to be located in the jurisdiction specified by subsections (b) and (c).

(e) A registered organization that is organized under the law of a State is located in that State.

(f) Except as otherwise provided in subsection (i), a registered organization that is organized under the law of the United States and a branch or agency of a bank that is not organized under the law of the United States or a State are located:

(1) in the State that the law of the United States designates, if the law designates a State of location;

(2) in the State that the registered organization, branch, or agency designates, if the law of the United States authorizes the registered organization, branch, or agency to designate its State of location; or

(3) in the District of Columbia, if neither paragraph (1) nor paragraph (2) applies.

(g) A registered organization continues to be located in the jurisdiction specified by subsection (e) or (f) notwithstanding:

(1) the suspension, revocation, forfeiture, or lapse of the registered organization's status as such in its jurisdiction of organization; or

(2) the dissolution, winding up, or cancellation of the existence of the registered organization.

(h) The United States is located in the District of Columbia.

(i) A branch or agency of a bank that is not organized under the law of the United States or a State is located in the State in which the branch or agency is licensed, if all branches and agencies of the bank are licensed in only one State.

(j) A foreign air carrier under the Federal Aviation Act of 1958, as amended, is located at the designated office of the agent upon which service of process may be made on behalf of the carrier.

(k) This section applies only for purposes of this part.

[Subpart 2. Perfection]

§ 9–308. When Security Interest or Agricultural Lien Is Perfected; Continuity of Perfection.

(a) Except as otherwise provided in this section and Section 9–309, a security interest is perfected if it has attached and all of the applicable requirements for perfection in Sections 9–310 through 9–316 have been satisfied. A security interest is perfected when it attaches if the applicable requirements are satisfied before the security interest attaches.

(b) An agricultural lien is perfected if it has become effective and all of the applicable requirements for perfection in Section 9–310 have been satisfied. An agricultural lien is perfected when it becomes effective if the applicable requirements are satisfied before the agricultural lien becomes effective.

(c) A security interest or agricultural lien is perfected continuously if it is originally perfected by one method under this article and is later perfected by another method under this article, without an intermediate period when it was unperfected.

(d) Perfection of a security interest in collateral also perfects a security interest in a supporting obligation for the collateral.

(e) Perfection of a security interest in a right to payment or performance also perfects a security interest in a security interest, mortgage, or other lien on personal or real property securing the right.

(f) Perfection of a security interest in a securities account also perfects a security interest in the security entitlements carried in the securities account.

(g) Perfection of a security interest in a commodity account also perfects a security interest in the commodity contracts carried in the commodity account.

Legislative Note: Any statute conflicting with subsection (e) must be made expressly subject to that subsection.

§ 9–309. Security Interest Perfected upon Attachment.

The following security interests are perfected when they attach:

(1) a purchase-money security interest in consumer goods, except as otherwise provided in Section 9–311(b) with respect to consumer goods that are subject to a statute or treaty described in Section 9–311(a);

(2) an assignment of accounts or payment intangibles which does not by itself or in conjunction with other assignments to the same assignee transfer a significant part of the assignor's outstanding accounts or payment intangibles;

(3) a sale of a payment intangible;

(4) a sale of a promissory note;

(5) a security interest created by the assignment of a health-care-insurance receivable to the provider of the health-care goods or services;

(6) a security interest arising under Section 2–401, 2–505, 2–711(3), or 2A–508(5), until the debtor obtains possession of the collateral;

(7) a security interest of a collecting bank arising under Section 4–210;

(8) a security interest of an issuer or nominated person arising under Section 5–118;

(9) a security interest arising in the delivery of a financial asset under Section 9–206(c);

(10) a security interest in investment property created by a broker or securities intermediary;

(11) a security interest in a commodity contract or a commodity account created by a commodity intermediary;

(12) an assignment for the benefit of all creditors of the transferor and subsequent transfers by the assignee thereunder; and

(13) a security interest created by an assignment of a beneficial interest in a decedent's estate; and

(14) a sale by an individual of an account that is a right to payment of winnings in a lottery or other game of chance.

§ 9–310. When Filing Required to Perfect Security Interest or Agricultural Lien; Security Interests and Agricultural Liens to Which Filing Provisions Do Not Apply.

(a) Except as otherwise provided in subsection (b) and Section 9–312(b), a financing statement must be filed to perfect all security interests and agricultural liens.

(b) The filing of a financing statement is not necessary to perfect a security interest:

(1) that is perfected under Section 9–308(d), (e), (f), or (g);

(2) that is perfected under Section 9–309 when it attaches;

(3) in property subject to a statute, regulation, or treaty described in Section 9–311(a);

(4) in goods in possession of a bailee which is perfected under Section 9–312(d)(1) or (2);

(5) in certificated securities, documents, goods, or instruments which is perfected without filing or possession under Section 9–312(e), (f), or (g);

(6) in collateral in the secured party's possession under Section 9–313;

(7) in a certificated security which is perfected by delivery of the security certificate to the secured party under Section 9–313;

(8) in deposit accounts, electronic chattel paper, investment property, or letter-of-credit rights which is perfected by control under Section 9–314;

(9) in proceeds which is perfected under Section 9–315; or

(10) that is perfected under Section 9–316.

(c) If a secured party assigns a perfected security interest or agricultural lien, a filing under this article is not required to continue the perfected status of the security interest against creditors of and transferees from the original debtor.

§ 9–311. Perfection of Security Interests in Property Subject to Certain Statutes, Regulations, and Treaties.

(a) Except as otherwise provided in subsection (d), the filing of a financing statement is not necessary or effective to perfect a security interest in property subject to:

(1) a statute, regulation, or treaty of the United States whose requirements for a security interest's obtaining priority over the rights of a lien creditor with respect to the property preempt Section 9–310(a);

(2) [list any certificate-of-title statute covering automobiles, trailers, mobile homes, boats, farm tractors, or the like, which provides for a security interest to be indicated on the certificate as a condition or result of perfection, and any non-Uniform Commercial Code central filing statute]; or

(3) a certificate-of-title statute of another jurisdiction which provides for a security interest to be indicated on the certificate as a condition or result of the security interest's obtaining priority over the rights of a lien creditor with respect to the property.

(b) Compliance with the requirements of a statute, regulation, or treaty described in subsection (a) for obtaining priority over the rights of a lien creditor is equivalent to the filing of a financing statement under this article. Except as otherwise provided in subsection (d) and Sections 9–313 and 9–316(d) and (e) for goods covered by a certificate of title, a security interest in property subject to a statute, regulation, or treaty described in subsection (a) may be perfected only by compliance with those requirements, and a security interest so perfected remains perfected notwithstanding a change in the use or transfer of possession of the collateral.

(c) Except as otherwise provided in subsection (d) and Section 9–316(d) and (e), duration and renewal of perfection of a security interest perfected by compliance with the requirements prescribed by a statute, regulation, or treaty described in subsection (a) are governed by the statute, regulation, or treaty. In other respects, the security interest is subject to this article.

(d) During any period in which collateral subject to a statute specified in subsection (a)(2) is inventory held for sale or lease by a person or leased by that person as lessor and that person is in the business of selling goods of that kind, this section does not apply to a security interest in that collateral created by that person.

Legislative Note: This Article contemplates that perfection of a security interest in goods covered by a certificate of title occurs upon receipt by appropriate State officials of a properly tendered application for a certificate of title on which the security interest is to be indicated, without a relation back to an earlier time. States whose certificate-of-title statutes provide for perfection at a different time or contain a relation-back provision should amend the statutes accordingly.

§ 9–312. Perfection of Security Interests in Chattel Paper, Deposit Accounts, Documents, Goods Covered by Documents, Instruments, Investment Property, Letter-of-Credit Rights, and Money; Perfection by Permissive Filing; Temporary Perfection without Filing or Transfer of Possession.

(a) A security interest in chattel paper, negotiable documents, instruments, or investment property may be perfected by filing.

(b) Except as otherwise provided in Section 9–315(c) and (d) for proceeds:

(1) a security interest in a deposit account may be perfected only by control under Section 9–314;

(2) and except as otherwise provided in Section 9–308(d), a security interest in a letter-of-credit right may be perfected only by control under Section 9–314; and

(3) a security interest in money may be perfected only by the secured party's taking possession under Section 9–313.

(c) While goods are in the possession of a bailee that has issued a negotiable document covering the goods:

(1) a security interest in the goods may be perfected by perfecting a security interest in the document; and

(2) a security interest perfected in the document has priority over any security interest that becomes perfected in the goods by another method during that time.

(d) While goods are in the possession of a bailee that has issued a nonnegotiable document covering the goods, a security interest in the goods may be perfected by:

(1) issuance of a document in the name of the secured party;

(2) the bailee's receipt of notification of the secured party's interest; or

(3) filing as to the goods.

(e) A security interest in certificated securities, negotiable documents, or instruments is perfected without filing or the taking of possession for a period of 20 days from the time it attaches to the extent that it arises for new value given under an authenticated security agreement.

(f) A perfected security interest in a negotiable document or goods in possession of a bailee, other than one that has issued a negotiable document for the goods, remains perfected for 20 days without filing if the secured party makes available to the debtor the goods or documents representing the goods for the purpose of:

(1) ultimate sale or exchange; or

(2) loading, unloading, storing, shipping, transshipping, manufacturing, processing, or otherwise dealing with them in a manner preliminary to their sale or exchange.

(g) A perfected security interest in a certificated security or instrument remains perfected for 20 days without filing if the secured party delivers the security certificate or instrument to the debtor for the purpose of:

(1) ultimate sale or exchange; or

(2) presentation, collection, enforcement, renewal, or registration of transfer.

(h) After the 20-day period specified in subsection (e), (f), or (g) expires, perfection depends upon compliance with this article.

§ 9–313. When Possession by or Delivery to Secured Party Perfects Security Interest without Filing.

(a) Except as otherwise provided in subsection (b), a secured party may perfect a security interest in negotiable documents, goods, instruments, money, or tangible chattel paper by taking possession of the collateral. A secured party may perfect a security interest in certificated securities by taking delivery of the certificated securities under Section 8–301.

(b) With respect to goods covered by a certificate of title issued by this State, a secured party may perfect a security interest in the goods by taking possession of the goods only in the circumstances described in Section 9–316(d).

(c) With respect to collateral other than certificated securities and goods covered by a document, a secured party takes possession of collateral in the possession of a person other than the debtor, the secured party, or a lessee of the collateral from the debtor in the ordinary course of the debtor's business, when:

(1) the person in possession authenticates a record acknowledging that it holds possession of the collateral for the secured party's benefit; or

(2) the person takes possession of the collateral after having authenticated a record acknowledging that it will hold possession of collateral for the secured party's benefit.

(d) If perfection of a security interest depends upon possession of the collateral by a secured party, perfection occurs no earlier than the time the secured party takes possession and continues only while the secured party retains possession.

(e) A security interest in a certificated security in registered form is perfected by delivery when delivery of the certificated security occurs under Section 8–301 and remains perfected by delivery until the debtor obtains possession of the security certificate.

(f) A person in possession of collateral is not required to acknowledge that it holds possession for a secured party's benefit.

(g) If a person acknowledges that it holds possession for the secured party's benefit:

(1) the acknowledgment is effective under subsection (c) or Section 8–301(a), even if the acknowledgment violates the rights of a debtor; and

(2) unless the person otherwise agrees or law other than this article otherwise provides, the person does not owe any duty to the secured party and is not required to confirm the acknowledgment to another person.

(h) A secured party having possession of collateral does not relinquish possession by delivering the collateral to a person other than the debtor or a lessee of the collateral from the debtor in the ordinary course of the debtor's business if the person was instructed before the delivery or is instructed contemporaneously with the delivery:

(1) to hold possession of the collateral for the secured party's benefit; or

(2) to redeliver the collateral to the secured party.

(i) A secured party does not relinquish possession, even if a delivery under subsection (h) violates the rights of a debtor. A person to which collateral is delivered under subsection (h) does not owe any duty to the secured party and is not required to confirm the delivery to another person unless the person otherwise agrees or law other than this article otherwise provides.

§ 9–314. Perfection by Control.

(a) A security interest in investment property, deposit accounts, letter-of-credit rights, or electronic chattel paper may be perfected by control of the collateral under Section 9–104, 9–105, 9–106, or 9–107.

(b) A security interest in deposit accounts, electronic chattel paper, or letter-of-credit rights is perfected by control under Section 9–104, 9–105, or 9–107 when the secured party obtains control and remains perfected by control only while the secured party retains control.

(c) A security interest in investment property is perfected by control under Section 9–106 from the time the secured party obtains control and remains perfected by control until:

(1) the secured party does not have control; and

(2) one of the following occurs:

(A) if the collateral is a certificated security, the debtor has or acquires possession of the security certificate;

(B) if the collateral is an uncertificated security, the issuer has registered or registers the debtor as the registered owner; or

(C) if the collateral is a security entitlement, the debtor is or becomes the entitlement holder.

§ 9–315. Secured Party's Rights on Disposition of Collateral and in Proceeds.

(a) Except as otherwise provided in this article and in Section 2–403(2):

(1) a security interest or agricultural lien continues in collateral notwithstanding sale, lease, license, exchange, or other disposition thereof unless the secured party authorized the disposition free of the security interest or agricultural lien; and

(2) a security interest attaches to any identifiable proceeds of collateral.

(b) Proceeds that are commingled with other property are identifiable proceeds:

(1) if the proceeds are goods, to the extent provided by Section 9–336; and

(2) if the proceeds are not goods, to the extent that the secured party identifies the proceeds by a method of tracing, including application of equitable principles, that is permitted under law other than this article with respect to commingled property of the type involved.

(c) A security interest in proceeds is a perfected security interest if the security interest in the original collateral was perfected.

(d) A perfected security interest in proceeds becomes unperfected on the 21st day after the security interest attaches to the proceeds unless:

(1) the following conditions are satisfied:

(A) a filed financing statement covers the original collateral;

(B) the proceeds are collateral in which a security interest may be perfected by filing in the office in which the financing statement has been filed; and

(C) the proceeds are not acquired with cash proceeds;

(2) the proceeds are identifiable cash proceeds; or

(3) the security interest in the proceeds is perfected other than under subsection (c) when the security interest attaches to the proceeds or within 20 days thereafter.

(e) If a filed financing statement covers the original collateral, a security interest in proceeds which remains perfected under subsection (d)(1) becomes unperfected at the later of:

(1) when the effectiveness of the filed financing statement lapses under Section 9–515 or is terminated under Section 9–513; or

(2) the 21st day after the security interest attaches to the proceeds.

§ 9–316. Continued Perfection of Security Interest Following Change in Governing Law.

(a) A security interest perfected pursuant to the law of the jurisdiction designated in Section 9–301(1) or 9–305(c) remains perfected until the earliest of:

(1) the time perfection would have ceased under the law of that jurisdiction;

(2) the expiration of four months after a change of the debtor's location to another jurisdiction; or

(3) the expiration of one year after a transfer of collateral to a person that thereby becomes a debtor and is located in another jurisdiction.

(b) If a security interest described in subsection (a) becomes perfected under the law of the other jurisdiction before the earliest time or event described in that subsection, it remains perfected thereafter. If the security interest does not become perfected under the law of the other jurisdiction before the earliest time or event, it becomes unperfected and is deemed never to have been perfected as against a purchaser of the collateral for value.

(c) A possessory security interest in collateral, other than goods covered by a certificate of title and as-extracted collateral consisting of goods, remains continuously perfected if:

(1) the collateral is located in one jurisdiction and subject to a security interest perfected under the law of that jurisdiction;

(2) thereafter the collateral is brought into another jurisdiction; and

(3) upon entry into the other jurisdiction, the security interest is perfected under the law of the other jurisdiction.

(d) Except as otherwise provided in subsection (e), a security interest in goods covered by a certificate of title which is perfected by any method under the law of another jurisdiction when the goods become covered by a certificate of title from this State remains perfected until the security interest would have become unperfected under the law of the other jurisdiction had the goods not become so covered.

(e) A security interest described in subsection (d) becomes unperfected as against a purchaser of the goods for value and is deemed never to have been perfected as against a purchaser of the goods for value if the applicable requirements for perfection under Section 9–311(b) or 9–313 are not satisfied before the earlier of:

(1) the time the security interest would have become unperfected under the law of the other jurisdiction had the goods not become covered by a certificate of title from this State; or

(2) the expiration of four months after the goods had become so covered.

(f) A security interest in deposit accounts, letter-of-credit rights, or investment property which is perfected under the law of the bank's jurisdiction, the issuer's jurisdiction, a nominated person's jurisdiction, the securities intermediary's jurisdiction, or the commodity intermediary's jurisdiction, as applicable, remains perfected until the earlier of:

(1) the time the security interest would have become unperfected under the law of that jurisdiction; or

(2) the expiration of four months after a change of the applicable jurisdiction to another jurisdiction.

(g) If a security interest described in subsection (f) becomes perfected under the law of the other jurisdiction before the earlier of the time or the end of the period described in that subsection, it remains perfected thereafter. If the security interest does not become perfected under the law of the other jurisdiction before the earlier of that time or the end of that period, it becomes unperfected and is deemed never to have been perfected as against a purchaser of the collateral for value.

[Subpart 3. Priority]

§ 9–317. Interests That Take Priority over or Take Free of Security Interest or Agricultural Lien.

(a) A security interest or agricultural lien is subordinate to the rights of:

(1) a person entitled to priority under Section 9–322; and

(2) except as otherwise provided in subsection (e), a person that becomes a lien creditor before the earlier of the time:

(A) the security interest or agricultural lien is perfected; or

(B) one of the conditions specified in Section 9–203(b)(3) is met and a financing statement covering the collateral is filed.

(b) Except as otherwise provided in subsection (e), a buyer, other than a secured party, of tangible chattel paper, documents, goods, instruments, or a security certificate takes free of a security interest or agricultural lien if the buyer gives value and receives delivery of the collateral without knowledge of the security interest or agricultural lien and before it is perfected.

(c) Except as otherwise provided in subsection (e), a lessee of goods takes free of a security interest or agricultural lien if the lessee gives value and receives delivery of the collateral without knowledge of the security interest or agricultural lien and before it is perfected.

(d) A licensee of a general intangible or a buyer, other than a secured party, of accounts, electronic chattel paper, general intangibles, or investment property other than a certificated security takes free of a security interest if the licensee or buyer gives value without knowledge of the security interest and before it is perfected.

(e) Except as otherwise provided in Sections 9–320 and 9–321, if a person files a financing statement with respect to a purchase-money security interest before or within 20 days after the debtor receives delivery of the collateral, the security interest takes priority over the rights of a buyer, lessee, or lien creditor which arise between the time the security interest attaches and the time of filing.

As amended in 2000.

§ 9–318. No Interest Retained in Right to Payment That Is Sold; Rights and Title of Seller of Account or Chattel Paper with Respect to Creditors and Purchasers.

(a) A debtor that has sold an account, chattel paper, payment intangible, or promissory note does not retain a legal or equitable interest in the collateral sold.

(b) For purposes of determining the rights of creditors of, and purchasers for value of an account or chattel paper from, a debtor that has sold an account or chattel paper, while the buyer's security interest is unperfected, the debtor is deemed to have rights and title to the account or chattel paper identical to those the debtor sold.

§ 9–319. Rights and Title of Consignee with Respect to Creditors and Purchasers.

(a) Except as otherwise provided in subsection (b), for purposes of determining the rights of creditors of, and purchasers for value of goods from, a consignee, while the goods are in the possession of the consignee, the consignee is deemed to have rights and title to the goods identical to those the consignor had or had power to transfer.

(b) For purposes of determining the rights of a creditor of a consignee, law other than this article determines the rights and title of a consignee while goods are in the consignee's possession if, under this part, a perfected security interest held by the consignor would have priority over the rights of the creditor.

§ 9–320. Buyer of Goods.

(a) Except as otherwise provided in subsection (e), a buyer in ordinary course of business, other than a person buying farm products from a person engaged in farming operations, takes free of a security interest created by the buyer's seller, even if the security interest is perfected and the buyer knows of its existence.

(b) Except as otherwise provided in subsection (e), a buyer of goods from a person who used or bought the goods for use primarily for personal, family, or household purposes takes free of a security interest, even if perfected, if the buyer buys:

(1) without knowledge of the security interest;

(2) for value;

(3) primarily for the buyer's personal, family, or household purposes; and

(4) before the filing of a financing statement covering the goods.

(c) To the extent that it affects the priority of a security interest over a buyer of goods under subsection (b), the period of effectiveness of a filing made in the jurisdiction in which the seller is located is governed by Section 9–316(a) and (b).

(d) A buyer in ordinary course of business buying oil, gas, or other minerals at the wellhead or minehead or after extraction takes free of an interest arising out of an encumbrance.

(e) Subsections (a) and (b) do not affect a security interest in goods in the possession of the secured party under Section 9–313.

§ 9–321. Licensee of General Intangible and Lessee of Goods in Ordinary Course of Business.

(a) In this section, "licensee in ordinary course of business" means a person that becomes a licensee of a general intangible in good faith, without knowledge that the license violates the rights of another person in the general intangible, and in the ordinary course from a person in the business of licensing general intangibles of that kind. A person becomes a licensee in the ordinary course if the license to the person comports with the usual or customary practices in the kind of business in which the licensor is engaged or with the licensor's own usual or customary practices.

(b) A licensee in ordinary course of business takes its rights under a nonexclusive license free of a security interest in the general intangible created by the licensor, even if the security interest is perfected and the licensee knows of its existence.

(c) A lessee in ordinary course of business takes its leasehold interest free of a security interest in the goods created by the lessor, even if the security interest is perfected and the lessee knows of its existence.

§ 9–322. Priorities among Conflicting Security Interests in and Agricultural Liens on Same Collateral.

(a) Except as otherwise provided in this section, priority among conflicting security interests and agricultural liens in the same collateral is determined according to the following rules:

(1) Conflicting perfected security interests and agricultural liens rank according to priority in time of filing or perfection. Priority

dates from the earlier of the time a filing covering the collateral is first made or the security interest or agricultural lien is first perfected, if there is no period thereafter when there is neither filing nor perfection.

(2) A perfected security interest or agricultural lien has priority over a conflicting unperfected security interest or agricultural lien.

(3) The first security interest or agricultural lien to attach or become effective has priority if conflicting security interests and agricultural liens are unperfected.

(b) For the purposes of subsection (a)(1):

(1) the time of filing or perfection as to a security interest in collateral is also the time of filing or perfection as to a security interest in proceeds; and

(2) the time of filing or perfection as to a security interest in collateral supported by a supporting obligation is also the time of filing or perfection as to a security interest in the supporting obligation.

(c) Except as otherwise provided in subsection (f), a security interest in collateral which qualifies for priority over a conflicting security interest under Section 9–327, 9–328, 9–329, 9–330, or 9–331 also has priority over a conflicting security interest in:

(1) any supporting obligation for the collateral; and

(2) proceeds of the collateral if:

(A) the security interest in proceeds is perfected;

(B) the proceeds are cash proceeds or of the same type as the collateral; and

(C) in the case of proceeds that are proceeds of proceeds, all intervening proceeds are cash proceeds, proceeds of the same type as the collateral, or an account relating to the collateral.

(d) Subject to subsection (e) and except as otherwise provided in subsection (f), if a security interest in chattel paper, deposit accounts, negotiable documents, instruments, investment property, or letter-of-credit rights is perfected by a method other than filing, conflicting perfected security interests in proceeds of the collateral rank according to priority in time of filing.

(e) Subsection (d) applies only if the proceeds of the collateral are not cash proceeds, chattel paper, negotiable documents, instruments, investment property, or letter-of-credit rights.

(f) Subsections (a) through (e) are subject to:

(1) subsection (g) and the other provisions of this part;

(2) Section 4–210 with respect to a security interest of a collecting bank;

(3) Section 5–118 with respect to a security interest of an issuer or nominated person; and

(4) Section 9–110 with respect to a security interest arising under Article 2 or 2A.

(g) A perfected agricultural lien on collateral has priority over a conflicting security interest in or agricultural lien on the same collateral if the statute creating the agricultural lien so provides.

§ 9–323.   Future Advances.

(a) Except as otherwise provided in subsection (c), for purposes of determining the priority of a perfected security interest under Section 9–322(a)(1), perfection of the security interest dates from the time an advance is made to the extent that the security interest secures an advance that:

(1) is made while the security interest is perfected only:

(A) under Section 9–309 when it attaches; or

(B) temporarily under Section 9–312(e), (f), or (g); and

(2) is not made pursuant to a commitment entered into before or while the security interest is perfected by a method other than under Section 9–309 or 9–312(e), (f), or (g).

(b) Except as otherwise provided in subsection (c), a security interest is subordinate to the rights of a person that becomes a lien creditor to the extent that the security interest secures an advance made more than 45 days after the person becomes a lien creditor unless the advance is made:

(1) without knowledge of the lien; or

(2) pursuant to a commitment entered into without knowledge of the lien.

(c) Subsections (a) and (b) do not apply to a security interest held by a secured party that is a buyer of accounts, chattel paper, payment intangibles, or promissory notes or a consignor.

(d) Except as otherwise provided in subsection (e), a buyer of goods other than a buyer in ordinary course of business takes free of a security interest to the extent that it secures advances made after the earlier of:

(1) the time the secured party acquires knowledge of the buyer's purchase; or

(2) 45 days after the purchase.

(e) Subsection (d) does not apply if the advance is made pursuant to a commitment entered into without knowledge of the buyer's purchase and before the expiration of the 45-day period.

(f) Except as otherwise provided in subsection (g), a lessee of goods, other than a lessee in ordinary course of business, takes the leasehold interest free of a security interest to the extent that it secures advances made after the earlier of:

(1) the time the secured party acquires knowledge of the lease; or

(2) 45 days after the lease contract becomes enforceable.

(g) Subsection (f) does not apply if the advance is made pursuant to a commitment entered into without knowledge of the lease and before the expiration of the 45-day period.

As amended in 1999.

§ 9–324.   Priority of Purchase-Money Security Interests.

(a) Except as otherwise provided in subsection (g), a perfected purchase-money security interest in goods other than inventory or livestock has priority over a conflicting security interest in the same goods, and, except as otherwise provided in Section 9–327, a perfected security interest in its identifiable proceeds also has priority, if the purchase-money security interest is perfected when the debtor receives possession of the collateral or within 20 days thereafter.

(b) Subject to subsection (c) and except as otherwise provided in subsection (g), a perfected purchase-money security interest in inventory has priority over a conflicting security interest in the same inventory, has priority over a conflicting security interest in chattel paper or an instrument constituting proceeds of the inventory and in proceeds of the chattel paper, if so provided in Section 9–330, and, except as otherwise provided in Section 9–327, also has priority in identifiable cash proceeds of the inventory to the extent the identifiable cash proceeds are received on or before the delivery of the inventory to a buyer, if:

(1) the purchase-money security interest is perfected when the debtor receives possession of the inventory;

(2) the purchase-money secured party sends an authenticated notification to the holder of the conflicting security interest;

(3) the holder of the conflicting security interest receives the notification within five years before the debtor receives possession of the inventory; and

(4) the notification states that the person sending the notification has or expects to acquire a purchase-money security interest in inventory of the debtor and describes the inventory.

(c) Subsections (b)(2) through (4) apply only if the holder of the conflicting security interest had filed a financing statement covering the same types of inventory:

(1) if the purchase-money security interest is perfected by filing, before the date of the filing; or

(2) if the purchase-money security interest is temporarily perfected without filing or possession under Section 9–312(f), before the beginning of the 20-day period thereunder.

(d) Subject to subsection (e) and except as otherwise provided in subsection (g), a perfected purchase-money security interest in livestock that are farm products has priority over a conflicting security interest in the same livestock, and, except as otherwise provided in Section 9–327, a perfected security interest in their identifiable proceeds and identifiable products in their unmanufactured states also has priority, if:

(1) the purchase-money security interest is perfected when the debtor receives possession of the livestock;

(2) the purchase-money secured party sends an authenticated notification to the holder of the conflicting security interest;

(3) the holder of the conflicting security interest receives the notification within six months before the debtor receives possession of the livestock; and

(4) the notification states that the person sending the notification has or expects to acquire a purchase-money security interest in livestock of the debtor and describes the livestock.

(e) Subsections (d)(2) through (4) apply only if the holder of the conflicting security interest had filed a financing statement covering the same types of livestock:

(1) if the purchase-money security interest is perfected by filing, before the date of the filing; or

(2) if the purchase-money security interest is temporarily perfected without filing or possession under Section 9–312(f), before the beginning of the 20-day period thereunder.

(f) Except as otherwise provided in subsection (g), a perfected purchase-money security interest in software has priority over a conflicting security interest in the same collateral, and, except as otherwise provided in Section 9–327, a perfected security interest in its identifiable proceeds also has priority, to the extent that the purchase-money security interest in the goods in which the software was acquired for use has priority in the goods and proceeds of the goods under this section.

(g) If more than one security interest qualifies for priority in the same collateral under subsection (a), (b), (d), or (f):

(1) a security interest securing an obligation incurred as all or part of the price of the collateral has priority over a security interest securing an obligation incurred for value given to enable the debtor to acquire rights in or the use of collateral; and

(2) in all other cases, Section 9–322(a) applies to the qualifying security interests.

§ 9–325.   Priority of Security Interests in Transferred Collateral.

(a) Except as otherwise provided in subsection (b), a security interest created by a debtor is subordinate to a security interest in the same collateral created by another person if:

(1) the debtor acquired the collateral subject to the security interest created by the other person;

(2) the security interest created by the other person was perfected when the debtor acquired the collateral; and

(3) there is no period thereafter when the security interest is unperfected.

(b) Subsection (a) subordinates a security interest only if the security interest:

(1) otherwise would have priority solely under Section 9–322(a) or 9–324; or

(2) arose solely under Section 2–711(3) or 2A–508(5).

§ 9–326.   Priority of Security Interests Created by New Debtor.

(a) Subject to subsection (b), a security interest created by a new debtor which is perfected by a filed financing statement that is effective solely under Section 9–508 in collateral in which a new debtor has or acquires rights is subordinate to a security interest in the same collateral which is perfected other than by a filed financing statement that is effective solely under Section 9–508.

(b) The other provisions of this part determine the priority among conflicting security interests in the same collateral perfected by filed financing statements that are effective solely under Section 9–508. However, if the security agreements to which a new debtor became bound as debtor were not entered into by the same original debtor, the conflicting security interests rank according to priority in time of the new debtor's having become bound.

§ 9–327.   Priority of Security Interests in Deposit Account.

The following rules govern priority among conflicting security interests in the same deposit account:

(1) A security interest held by a secured party having control of the deposit account under Section 9–104 has priority over a conflicting security interest held by a secured party that does not have control.

(2) Except as otherwise provided in paragraphs (3) and (4), security interests perfected by control under Section 9–314 rank according to priority in time of obtaining control.

(3) Except as otherwise provided in paragraph (4), a security interest held by the bank with which the deposit account is maintained has priority over a conflicting security interest held by another secured party.

(4) A security interest perfected by control under Section 9–104(a)(3) has priority over a security interest held by the bank with which the deposit account is maintained.

§ 9–328. Priority of Security Interests in Investment Property.

The following rules govern priority among conflicting security interests in the same investment property:

(1) A security interest held by a secured party having control of investment property under Section 9–106 has priority over a security interest held by a secured party that does not have control of the investment property.

(2) Except as otherwise provided in paragraphs (3) and (4), conflicting security interests held by secured parties each of which has control under Section 9–106 rank according to priority in time of:

(A) if the collateral is a security, obtaining control;

(B) if the collateral is a security entitlement carried in a securities account and:

(i) if the secured party obtained control under Section 8–106(d)(1), the secured party's becoming the person for which the securities account is maintained;

(ii) if the secured party obtained control under Section 8–106(d)(2), the securities intermediary's agreement to comply with the secured party's entitlement orders with respect to security entitlements carried or to be carried in the securities account; or

(iii) if the secured party obtained control through another person under Section 8–106(d)(3), the time on which priority would be based under this paragraph if the other person were the secured party; or

(C) if the collateral is a commodity contract carried with a commodity intermediary, the satisfaction of the requirement for control specified in Section 9–106(b)(2) with respect to commodity contracts carried or to be carried with the commodity intermediary.

(3) A security interest held by a securities intermediary in a security entitlement or a securities account maintained with the securities intermediary has priority over a conflicting security interest held by another secured party.

(4) A security interest held by a commodity intermediary in a commodity contract or a commodity account maintained with the commodity intermediary has priority over a conflicting security interest held by another secured party.

(5) A security interest in a certificated security in registered form which is perfected by taking delivery under Section 9–313(a) and not by control under Section 9–314 has priority over a conflicting security interest perfected by a method other than control.

(6) Conflicting security interests created by a broker, securities intermediary, or commodity intermediary which are perfected without control under Section 9–106 rank equally.

(7) In all other cases, priority among conflicting security interests in investment property is governed by Sections 9–322 and 9–323.

§ 9–329. Priority of Security Interests in Letter-of-Credit Right.

The following rules govern priority among conflicting security interests in the same letter-of-credit right:

(1) A security interest held by a secured party having control of the letter-of-credit right under Section 9–107 has priority to the extent of its control over a conflicting security interest held by a secured party that does not have control.

(2) Security interests perfected by control under Section 9–314 rank according to priority in time of obtaining control.

§ 9–330. Priority of Purchaser of Chattel Paper or Instrument.

(a) A purchaser of chattel paper has priority over a security interest in the chattel paper which is claimed merely as proceeds of inventory subject to a security interest if:

(1) in good faith and in the ordinary course of the purchaser's business, the purchaser gives new value and takes possession of the chattel paper or obtains control of the chattel paper under Section 9–105; and

(2) the chattel paper does not indicate that it has been assigned to an identified assignee other than the purchaser.

(b) A purchaser of chattel paper has priority over a security interest in the chattel paper which is claimed other than merely as proceeds of inventory subject to a security interest if the purchaser gives new value and takes possession of the chattel paper or obtains control of the chattel paper under Section 9–105 in good faith, in the ordinary course of the purchaser's business, and without knowledge that the purchase violates the rights of the secured party.

(c) Except as otherwise provided in Section 9–327, a purchaser having priority in chattel paper under subsection (a) or (b) also has priority in proceeds of the chattel paper to the extent that:

(1) Section 9–322 provides for priority in the proceeds; or

(2) the proceeds consist of the specific goods covered by the chattel paper or cash proceeds of the specific goods, even if the purchaser's security interest in the proceeds is unperfected.

(d) Except as otherwise provided in Section 9–331(a), a purchaser of an instrument has priority over a security interest in the instrument perfected by a method other than possession if the purchaser gives value and takes possession of the instrument in good faith and without knowledge that the purchase violates the rights of the secured party.

(e) For purposes of subsections (a) and (b), the holder of a purchase-money security interest in inventory gives new value for chattel paper constituting proceeds of the inventory.

(f) For purposes of subsections (b) and (d), if chattel paper or an instrument indicates that it has been assigned to an identified secured party other than the purchaser, a purchaser of the chattel paper or instrument has knowledge that the purchase violates the rights of the secured party.

§ 9–331. Priority of Rights of Purchasers of Instruments, Documents, and Securities under Other Articles; Priority of Interests in Financial Assets and Security Entitlements under Article 8.

(a) This article does not limit the rights of a holder in due course of a negotiable instrument, a holder to which a negotiable document of title has been duly negotiated, or a protected purchaser of a security. These holders or purchasers take priority over an earlier security interest, even if perfected, to the extent provided in Articles 3, 7, and 8.

(b) This article does not limit the rights of or impose liability on a person to the extent that the person is protected against the assertion of a claim under Article 8.

(c) Filing under this article does not constitute notice of a claim or defense to the holders, or purchasers, or persons described in subsections (a) and (b).

§ 9–332. Transfer of Money; Transfer of Funds from Deposit Account.

(a) A transferee of money takes the money free of a security interest unless the transferee acts in collusion with the debtor in violating the rights of the secured party.

(b) A transferee of funds from a deposit account takes the funds free of a security interest in the deposit account unless the transferee acts in collusion with the debtor in violating the rights of the secured party.

§ 9–333. Priority of Certain Liens Arising by Operation of Law.

(a) In this section, "possessory lien" means an interest, other than a security interest or an agricultural lien:

(1) which secures payment or performance of an obligation for services or materials furnished with respect to goods by a person in the ordinary course of the person's business;

(2) which is created by statute or rule of law in favor of the person; and

(3) whose effectiveness depends on the person's possession of the goods.

(b) A possessory lien on goods has priority over a security interest in the goods unless the lien is created by a statute that expressly provides otherwise.

§ 9–334. Priority of Security Interests in Fixtures and Crops.

(a) A security interest under this article may be created in goods that are fixtures or may continue in goods that become fixtures. A security interest does not exist under this article in ordinary building materials incorporated into an improvement on land.

(b) This article does not prevent creation of an encumbrance upon fixtures under real property law.

(c) In cases not governed by subsections (d) through (h), a security interest in fixtures is subordinate to a conflicting interest of an encumbrancer or owner of the related real property other than the debtor.

(d) Except as otherwise provided in subsection (h), a perfected security interest in fixtures has priority over a conflicting interest of an encumbrancer or owner of the real property if the debtor has an interest of record in or is in possession of the real property and:

(1) the security interest is a purchase-money security interest;

(2) the interest of the encumbrancer or owner arises before the goods become fixtures; and

(3) the security interest is perfected by a fixture filing before the goods become fixtures or within 20 days thereafter.

(e) A perfected security interest in fixtures has priority over a conflicting interest of an encumbrancer or owner of the real property if:

(1) the debtor has an interest of record in the real property or is in possession of the real property and the security interest:

(A) is perfected by a fixture filing before the interest of the encumbrancer or owner is of record; and

(B) has priority over any conflicting interest of a predecessor in title of the encumbrancer or owner;

(2) before the goods become fixtures, the security interest is perfected by any method permitted by this article and the fixtures are readily removable:

(A) factory or office machines;

(B) equipment that is not primarily used or leased for use in the operation of the real property; or

(C) replacements of domestic appliances that are consumer goods;

(3) the conflicting interest is a lien on the real property obtained by legal or equitable proceedings after the security interest was perfected by any method permitted by this article; or

(4) the security interest is:

(A) created in a manufactured home in a manufactured-home transaction; and

(B) perfected pursuant to a statute described in Section 9–311(a)(2).

(f) A security interest in fixtures, whether or not perfected, has priority over a conflicting interest of an encumbrancer or owner of the real property if:

(1) the encumbrancer or owner has, in an authenticated record, consented to the security interest or disclaimed an interest in the goods as fixtures; or

(2) the debtor has a right to remove the goods as against the encumbrancer or owner.

(g) The priority of the security interest under paragraph (f)(2) continues for a reasonable time if the debtor's right to remove the goods as against the encumbrancer or owner terminates.

(h) A mortgage is a construction mortgage to the extent that it secures an obligation incurred for the construction of an improvement on land, including the acquisition cost of the land, if a recorded record of the mortgage so indicates. Except as otherwise provided in subsections (e) and (f), a security interest in fixtures is subordinate to a construction mortgage if a record of the mortgage is recorded before the goods become fixtures and the goods become fixtures before the completion of the construction. A mortgage has this priority to the same extent as a construction mortgage to the extent that it is given to refinance a construction mortgage.

(i) A perfected security interest in crops growing on real property has priority over a conflicting interest of an encumbrancer or owner of the real property if the debtor has an interest of record in or is in possession of the real property.

(j) Subsection (i) prevails over any inconsistent provisions of the following statutes:

[List here any statutes containing provisions inconsistent with subsection (i).]

Legislative Note: States that amend statutes to remove provisions inconsistent with subsection (i) need not enact subsection (j).

§ 9–335. Accessions.

(a) A security interest may be created in an accession and continues in collateral that becomes an accession.

(b) If a security interest is perfected when the collateral becomes an accession, the security interest remains perfected in the collateral.

(c) Except as otherwise provided in subsection (d), the other provisions of this part determine the priority of a security interest in an accession.

(d) A security interest in an accession is subordinate to a security interest in the whole which is perfected by compliance with the requirements of a certificate-of-title statute under Section 9–311(b).

(e) After default, subject to Part 6, a secured party may remove an accession from other goods if the security interest in the accession has priority over the claims of every person having an interest in the whole.

(f) A secured party that removes an accession from other goods under subsection (e) shall promptly reimburse any holder of a security interest or other lien on, or owner of, the whole or of the other goods, other than the debtor, for the cost of repair of any physical injury to the whole or the other goods. The secured party need not reimburse the holder or owner for any diminution in value of the whole or the other goods caused by the absence of the accession removed or by any necessity for replacing it. A person entitled to reimbursement may refuse permission to remove until the secured party gives adequate assurance for the performance of the obligation to reimburse.

§ 9–336. Commingled Goods.

(a) In this section, "commingled goods" means goods that are physically united with other goods in such a manner that their identity is lost in a product or mass.

(b) A security interest does not exist in commingled goods as such. However, a security interest may attach to a product or mass that results when goods become commingled goods.

(c) If collateral becomes commingled goods, a security interest attaches to the product or mass.

(d) If a security interest in collateral is perfected before the collateral becomes commingled goods, the security interest that attaches to the product or mass under subsection (c) is perfected.

(e) Except as otherwise provided in subsection (f), the other provisions of this part determine the priority of a security interest that attaches to the product or mass under subsection (c).

(f) If more than one security interest attaches to the product or mass under subsection (c), the following rules determine priority:

(1) A security interest that is perfected under subsection (d) has priority over a security interest that is unperfected at the time the collateral becomes commingled goods.

(2) If more than one security interest is perfected under subsection (d), the security interests rank equally in proportion to the value of the collateral at the time it became commingled goods.

§ 9–337. Priority of Security Interests in Goods Covered by Certificate of Title.

If, while a security interest in goods is perfected by any method under the law of another jurisdiction, this State issues a certificate of title that does not show that the goods are subject to the security interest or contain a statement that they may be subject to security interests not shown on the certificate:

(1) a buyer of the goods, other than a person in the business of selling goods of that kind, takes free of the security interest if the buyer gives value and receives delivery of the goods after issuance of the certificate and without knowledge of the security interest; and

(2) the security interest is subordinate to a conflicting security interest in the goods that attaches, and is perfected under Section 9–311(b), after issuance of the certificate and without the conflicting secured party's knowledge of the security interest.

§ 9–338. Priority of Security Interest or Agricultural Lien Perfected by Filed Financing Statement Providing Certain Incorrect Information.

If a security interest or agricultural lien is perfected by a filed financing statement providing information described in Section 9–516(b)(5) which is incorrect at the time the financing statement is filed:

(1) the security interest or agricultural lien is subordinate to a conflicting perfected security interest in the collateral to the extent that the holder of the conflicting security interest gives value in reasonable reliance upon the incorrect information; and

(2) a purchaser, other than a secured party, of the collateral takes free of the security interest or agricultural lien to the extent that, in reasonable reliance upon the incorrect information, the purchaser gives value and, in the case of chattel paper, documents, goods, instruments, or a security certificate, receives delivery of the collateral.

§ 9–339. Priority Subject to Subordination.

This article does not preclude subordination by agreement by a person entitled to priority.

[Subpart 4. Rights of Bank]

§ 9–340. Effectiveness of Right of Recoupment or Set-Off against Deposit Account.

(a) Except as otherwise provided in subsection (c), a bank with which a deposit account is maintained may exercise any right of recoupment or set-off against a secured party that holds a security interest in the deposit account.

(b) Except as otherwise provided in subsection (c), the application of this article to a security interest in a deposit account does not affect a right of recoupment or set-off of the secured party as to a deposit account maintained with the secured party.

(c) The exercise by a bank of a set-off against a deposit account is ineffective against a secured party that holds a security interest in the deposit account which is perfected by control under Section 9–104(a)(3), if the set-off is based on a claim against the debtor.

§ 9–341. Bank's Rights and Duties with Respect to Deposit Account.

Except as otherwise provided in Section 9–340(c), and unless the bank otherwise agrees in an authenticated record, a bank's rights and duties with respect to a deposit account maintained with the bank are not terminated, suspended, or modified by:

(1) the creation, attachment, or perfection of a security interest in the deposit account;

(2) the bank's knowledge of the security interest; or

(3) the bank's receipt of instructions from the secured party.

§ 9–342. Bank's Right to Refuse to Enter into or Disclose Existence of Control Agreement.

This article does not require a bank to enter into an agreement of the kind described in Section 9–104(a)(2), even if its customer so requests or directs. A bank that has entered into such an agreement is not required to confirm the existence of the agreement to another person unless requested to do so by its customer.

Part 4 Rights of Third Parties

§ 9–401. Alienability of Debtor's Rights.

(a) Except as otherwise provided in subsection (b) and Sections 9–406, 9–407, 9–408, and 9–409, whether a debtor's rights in collateral may be voluntarily or involuntarily transferred is governed by law other than this article.

(b) An agreement between the debtor and secured party which prohibits a transfer of the debtor's rights in collateral or makes the transfer a default does not prevent the transfer from taking effect.

§ 9–402. Secured Party Not Obligated on Contract of Debtor or in Tort.

The existence of a security interest, agricultural lien, or authority given to a debtor to dispose of or use collateral, without more, does not subject a secured party to liability in contract or tort for the debtor's acts or omissions.

§ 9–403. Agreement Not to Assert Defenses against Assignee.

(a) In this section, "value" has the meaning provided in Section 3–303(a).

(b) Except as otherwise provided in this section, an agreement between an account debtor and an assignor not to assert against an assignee any claim or defense that the account debtor may have against the assignor is enforceable by an assignee that takes an assignment:

(1) for value;

(2) in good faith;

(3) without notice of a claim of a property or possessory right to the property assigned; and

(4) without notice of a defense or claim in recoupment of the type that may be asserted against a person entitled to enforce a negotiable instrument under Section 3–305(a).

(c) Subsection (b) does not apply to defenses of a type that may be asserted against a holder in due course of a negotiable instrument under Section 3–305(b).

(d) In a consumer transaction, if a record evidences the account debtor's obligation, law other than this article requires that the record include a statement to the effect that the rights of an assignee are subject to claims or defenses that the account debtor could assert against the original obligee, and the record does not include such a statement:

(1) the record has the same effect as if the record included such a statement; and

(2) the account debtor may assert against an assignee those claims and defenses that would have been available if the record included such a statement.

(e) This section is subject to law other than this article which establishes a different rule for an account debtor who is an individual and who incurred the obligation primarily for personal, family, or household purposes.

(f) Except as otherwise provided in subsection (d), this section does not displace law other than this article which gives effect to an agreement by an account debtor not to assert a claim or defense against an assignee.

§ 9–404. Rights Acquired by Assignee; Claims and Defenses against Assignee.

(a) Unless an account debtor has made an enforceable agreement not to assert defenses or claims, and subject to subsections (b) through (e), the rights of an assignee are subject to:

(1) all terms of the agreement between the account debtor and assignor and any defense or claim in recoupment arising from the transaction that gave rise to the contract; and

(2) any other defense or claim of the account debtor against the assignor which accrues before the account debtor receives a notification of the assignment authenticated by the assignor or the assignee.

(b) Subject to subsection (c) and except as otherwise provided in subsection (d), the claim of an account debtor against an assignor may be asserted against an assignee under subsection (a) only to reduce the amount the account debtor owes.

(c) This section is subject to law other than this article which establishes a different rule for an account debtor who is an individual and who incurred the obligation primarily for personal, family, or household purposes.

(d) In a consumer transaction, if a record evidences the account debtor's obligation, law other than this article requires that the record include a statement to the effect that the account debtor's recovery against an assignee with respect to claims and defenses against the assignor may not exceed amounts paid by the account debtor under the record, and the record does not include such a statement, the extent to which a claim of an account debtor against the assignor may be asserted against an assignee is determined as if the record included such a statement.

(e) This section does not apply to an assignment of a health-care-insurance receivable.

§ 9–405. Modification of Assigned Contract.

(a) A modification of or substitution for an assigned contract is effective against an assignee if made in good faith. The assignee acquires corresponding rights under the modified or substituted contract. The assignment may provide that the modification or substitution is a breach of contract by the assignor. This subsection is subject to subsections (b) through (d).

(b) Subsection (a) applies to the extent that:

(1) the right to payment or a part thereof under an assigned contract has not been fully earned by performance; or

(2) the right to payment or a part thereof has been fully earned by performance and the account debtor has not received notification of the assignment under Section 9–406(a).

(c) This section is subject to law other than this article which establishes a different rule for an account debtor who is an individual and who incurred the obligation primarily for personal, family, or household purposes.

(d) This section does not apply to an assignment of a health-care-insurance receivable.

§ 9–406. Discharge of Account Debtor; Notification of Assignment; Identification and Proof of Assignment; Restrictions on Assignment of Accounts, Chattel Paper, Payment Intangibles, and Promissory Notes Ineffective.

(a) Subject to subsections (b) through (i), an account debtor on an account, chattel paper, or a payment intangible may discharge its obligation by paying the assignor until, but not after, the account debtor receives a notification, authenticated by the assignor or the assignee, that the amount due or to become due has been assigned and that payment is to be made to the assignee. After receipt of the notification, the account debtor may discharge its obligation by paying the assignee and may not discharge the obligation by paying the assignor.

(b) Subject to subsection (h), notification is ineffective under subsection (a):

(1) if it does not reasonably identify the rights assigned;

(2) to the extent that an agreement between an account debtor and a seller of a payment intangible limits the account debtor's duty to pay a person other than the seller and the limitation is effective under law other than this article; or

(3) at the option of an account debtor, if the notification notifies the account debtor to make less than the full amount of any installment or other periodic payment to the assignee, even if:

(A) only a portion of the account, chattel paper, or payment intangible has been assigned to that assignee;

(B) a portion has been assigned to another assignee; or

(C) the account debtor knows that the assignment to that assignee is limited.

(c) Subject to subsection (h), if requested by the account debtor, an assignee shall seasonably furnish reasonable proof that the assignment has been made. Unless the assignee complies, the account debtor may discharge its obligation by paying the assignor, even if the account debtor has received a notification under subsection (a).

(d) Except as otherwise provided in subsection (e) and Sections 2A–303 and 9–407, and subject to subsection (h), a term in an agreement between an account debtor and an assignor or in a promissory note is ineffective to the extent that it:

(1) prohibits, restricts, or requires the consent of the account debtor or person obligated on the promissory note to the assignment or transfer of, or the creation, attachment, perfection, or enforcement of a security interest in, the account, chattel paper, payment intangible, or promissory note; or

(2) provides that the assignment or transfer or the creation, attachment, perfection, or enforcement of the security interest may give rise to a default, breach, right of recoupment, claim, defense, termination, right of termination, or remedy under the account, chattel paper, payment intangible, or promissory note.

(e) Subsection (d) does not apply to the sale of a payment intangible or promissory note.

(f) Except as otherwise provided in Sections 2A–303 and 9–407 and subject to subsections (h) and (i), a rule of law, statute, or regulation that prohibits, restricts, or requires the consent of a government, governmental body or official, or account debtor to the assignment or transfer of, or creation of a security interest in, an account or chattel paper is ineffective to the extent that the rule of law, statute, or regulation:

(1) prohibits, restricts, or requires the consent of the government, governmental body or official, or account debtor to the assignment or transfer of, or the creation, attachment, perfection, or enforcement of a security interest in the account or chattel paper; or

(2) provides that the assignment or transfer or the creation, attachment, perfection, or enforcement of the security interest may give rise to a default, breach, right of recoupment, claim, defense, termination, right of termination, or remedy under the account or chattel paper.

(g) Subject to subsection (h), an account debtor may not waive or vary its option under subsection (b)(3).

(h) This section is subject to law other than this article which establishes a different rule for an account debtor who is an individual and who incurred the obligation primarily for personal, family, or household purposes.

(i) This section does not apply to an assignment of a health-care-insurance receivable.

(j) This section prevails over any inconsistent provisions of the following statutes, rules, and regulations:

[List here any statutes, rules, and regulations containing provisions inconsistent with this section.]

Legislative Note: States that amend statutes, rules, and regulations to remove provisions inconsistent with this section need not enact subsection (j).

As amended in 1999 and 2000.

§ 9–407. Restrictions on Creation or Enforcement of Security Interest in Leasehold Interest or in Lessor's Residual Interest.

(a) Except as otherwise provided in subsection (b), a term in a lease agreement is ineffective to the extent that it:

(1) prohibits, restricts, or requires the consent of a party to the lease to the assignment or transfer of, or the creation, attachment, perfection, or enforcement of a security interest in an interest of a party under the lease contract or in the lessor's residual interest in the goods; or

(2) provides that the assignment or transfer or the creation, attachment, perfection, or enforcement of the security interest may give rise to a default, breach, right of recoupment, claim, defense, termination, right of termination, or remedy under the lease.

(b) Except as otherwise provided in Section 2A–303(7), a term described in subsection (a)(2) is effective to the extent that there is:

(1) a transfer by the lessee of the lessee's right of possession or use of the goods in violation of the term; or

(2) a delegation of a material performance of either party to the lease contract in violation of the term.

(c) The creation, attachment, perfection, or enforcement of a security interest in the lessor's interest under the lease contract or the lessor's residual interest in the goods is not a transfer that materially impairs the lessee's prospect of obtaining return performance or materially changes the duty of or materially increases the burden or risk imposed on the lessee within the purview of Section 2A–303(4) unless, and then only to the extent that, enforcement actually results in a delegation of material performance of the lessor.

As amended in 1999.

§ 9–408. Restrictions on Assignment of Promissory Notes, Health-Care-Insurance Receivables, and Certain General Intangibles Ineffective.

(a) Except as otherwise provided in subsection (b), a term in a promissory note or in an agreement between an account debtor and a debtor which relates to a health-care-insurance receivable or a general intangible, including a contract, permit, license, or franchise, and which term prohibits, restricts, or requires the consent of the person obligated on the promissory note or the account debtor to, the assignment or transfer of, or creation, attachment, or perfection of a security interest in, the promissory note, health-care-insurance receivable, or general intangible, is ineffective to the extent that the term:

(1) would impair the creation, attachment, or perfection of a security interest; or

(2) provides that the assignment or transfer or the creation, attachment, or perfection of the security interest may give rise to a default, breach, right of recoupment, claim, defense, termination, right of termination, or remedy under the promissory note, health-care-insurance receivable, or general intangible.

(b) Subsection (a) applies to a security interest in a payment intangible or promissory note only if the security interest arises out of a sale of the payment intangible or promissory note.

(c) A rule of law, statute, or regulation that prohibits, restricts, or requires the consent of a government, governmental body or official, person obligated on a promissory note, or account debtor to the assignment or transfer of, or creation of a security interest in, a promissory note, health-care-insurance receivable, or general intangible, including a contract, permit, license, or franchise between an account debtor and a debtor, is ineffective to the extent that the rule of law, statute, or regulation:

(1) would impair the creation, attachment, or perfection of a security interest; or

(2) provides that the assignment or transfer or the creation, attachment, or perfection of the security interest may give rise to a default, breach, right of recoupment, claim, defense, termination, right of termination, or remedy under the promissory note, health-care-insurance receivable, or general intangible.

(d) To the extent that a term in a promissory note or in an agreement between an account debtor and a debtor which relates to a health-care-insurance receivable or general intangible or a rule of law, statute, or regulation described in subsection (c) would be effective under law other than this article but is ineffective under subsection (a) or (c), the creation, attachment, or perfection of a security interest in the promissory note, health-care-insurance receivable, or general intangible:

(1) is not enforceable against the person obligated on the promissory note or the account debtor;

(2) does not impose a duty or obligation on the person obligated on the promissory note or the account debtor;

(3) does not require the person obligated on the promissory note or the account debtor to recognize the security interest, pay or render performance to the secured party, or accept payment or performance from the secured party;

(4) does not entitle the secured party to use or assign the debtor's rights under the promissory note, health-care-insurance receivable, or general intangible, including any related information or materials furnished to the debtor in the transaction giving rise to the promissory note, health-care-insurance receivable, or general intangible;

(5) does not entitle the secured party to use, assign, possess, or have access to any trade secrets or confidential information of the person obligated on the promissory note or the account debtor; and

(6) does not entitle the secured party to enforce the security interest in the promissory note, health-care-insurance receivable, or general intangible.

(e) This section prevails over any inconsistent provisions of the following statutes, rules, and regulations:

[List here any statutes, rules, and regulations containing provisions inconsistent with this section.]

Legislative Note: States that amend statutes, rules, and regulations to remove provisions inconsistent with this section need not enact subsection (e).

As amended in 1999.

§ 9–409. Restrictions on Assignment of Letter-of-Credit Rights Ineffective.

(a) A term in a letter of credit or a rule of law, statute, regulation, custom, or practice applicable to the letter of credit which prohibits, restricts, or requires the consent of an applicant, issuer, or nominated person to a beneficiary's assignment of or creation of a security interest in a letter-of-credit right is ineffective to the extent that the term or rule of law, statute, regulation, custom, or practice:

(1) would impair the creation, attachment, or perfection of a security interest in the letter-of-credit right; or

(2) provides that the assignment or the creation, attachment, or perfection of the security interest may give rise to a default, breach, right of recoupment, claim, defense, termination, right of termination, or remedy under the letter-of-credit right.

(b) To the extent that a term in a letter of credit is ineffective under subsection (a) but would be effective under law other than this article or a custom or practice applicable to the letter of credit, to the transfer of a right to draw or otherwise demand performance under the letter of credit, or to the assignment of a right to proceeds of the letter of credit, the creation, attachment, or perfection of a security interest in the letter-of-credit right:

(1) is not enforceable against the applicant, issuer, nominated person, or transferee beneficiary;

(2) imposes no duties or obligations on the applicant, issuer, nominated person, or transferee beneficiary; and

(3) does not require the applicant, issuer, nominated person, or transferee beneficiary to recognize the security interest, pay or render performance to the secured party, or accept payment or other performance from the secured party.

As amended in 1999.

Part 5 Filing

[Subpart 1. Filing Office; Contents and Effectiveness of Financing Statement]

§ 9–501. Filing Office.

(a) Except as otherwise provided in subsection (b), if the local law of this State governs perfection of a security interest or agricultural lien, the office in which to file a financing statement to perfect the security interest or agricultural lien is:

(1) the office designated for the filing or recording of a record of a mortgage on the related real property, if:

(A) the collateral is as-extracted collateral or timber to be cut; or

(B) the financing statement is filed as a fixture filing and the collateral is goods that are or are to become fixtures; or

(2) the office of [ ] [or any office duly authorized by [ ]], in all other cases, including a case in which the collateral is goods that

are or are to become fixtures and the financing statement is not filed as a fixture filing.

(b) The office in which to file a financing statement to perfect a security interest in collateral, including fixtures, of a transmitting utility is the office of [ ]. The financing statement also constitutes a fixture filing as to the collateral indicated in the financing statement which is or is to become fixtures.

Legislative Note: The State should designate the filing office where the brackets appear. The filing office may be that of a governmental official (e.g., the Secretary of State) or a private party that maintains the State's filing system.

§ 9–502.   Contents of Financing Statement; Record of Mortgage as Financing Statement; Time of Filing Financing Statement.

(a) Subject to subsection (b), a financing statement is sufficient only if it:

(1) provides the name of the debtor;

(2) provides the name of the secured party or a representative of the secured party; and

(3) indicates the collateral covered by the financing statement.

(b) Except as otherwise provided in Section 9–501(b), to be sufficient, a financing statement that covers as-extracted collateral or timber to be cut, or which is filed as a fixture filing and covers goods that are or are to become fixtures, must satisfy subsection (a) and also:

(1) indicate that it covers this type of collateral;

(2) indicate that it is to be filed [for record] in the real property records;

(3) provide a description of the real property to which the collateral is related [sufficient to give constructive notice of a mortgage under the law of this State if the description were contained in a record of the mortgage of the real property]; and

(4) if the debtor does not have an interest of record in the real property, provide the name of a record owner.

(c) A record of a mortgage is effective, from the date of recording, as a financing statement filed as a fixture filing or as a financing statement covering as-extracted collateral or timber to be cut only if:

(1) the record indicates the goods or accounts that it covers;

(2) the goods are or are to become fixtures related to the real property described in the record or the collateral is related to the real property described in the record and is as-extracted collateral or timber to be cut;

(3) the record satisfies the requirements for a financing statement in this section other than an indication that it is to be filed in the real property records; and

(4) the record is [duly] recorded.

(d) A financing statement may be filed before a security agreement is made or a security interest otherwise attaches.

Legislative Note: Language in brackets is optional. Where the State has any special recording system for real property other than the usual grantor-grantee index (as, for instance, a tract system or a title registration or Torrens system) local adaptations of subsection (b) and Section 9–519(d) and (e) may be necessary. See, e.g., Mass. Gen. Laws Chapter 106, Section 9–410.

§ 9–503.   Name of Debtor and Secured Party.

(a) A financing statement sufficiently provides the name of the debtor:

(1) if the debtor is a registered organization, only if the financing statement provides the name of the debtor indicated on the public record of the debtor's jurisdiction of organization which shows the debtor to have been organized;

(2) if the debtor is a decedent's estate, only if the financing statement provides the name of the decedent and indicates that the debtor is an estate;

(3) if the debtor is a trust or a trustee acting with respect to property held in trust, only if the financing statement:

(A) provides the name specified for the trust in its organic documents or, if no name is specified, provides the name of the settlor and additional information sufficient to distinguish the debtor from other trusts having one or more of the same settlors; and

(B) indicates, in the debtor's name or otherwise, that the debtor is a trust or is a trustee acting with respect to property held in trust; and

(4) in other cases:

(A) if the debtor has a name, only if it provides the individual or organizational name of the debtor; and

(B) if the debtor does not have a name, only if it provides the names of the partners, members, associates, or other persons comprising the debtor.

(b) A financing statement that provides the name of the debtor in accordance with subsection (a) is not rendered ineffective by the absence of:

(1) a trade name or other name of the debtor; or

(2) unless required under subsection (a)(4)(B), names of partners, members, associates, or other persons comprising the debtor.

(c) A financing statement that provides only the debtor's trade name does not sufficiently provide the name of the debtor.

(d) Failure to indicate the representative capacity of a secured party or representative of a secured party does not affect the sufficiency of a financing statement.

(e) A financing statement may provide the name of more than one debtor and the name of more than one secured party.

§ 9–504.   Indication of Collateral.

A financing statement sufficiently indicates the collateral that it covers if the financing statement provides:

(1) a description of the collateral pursuant to Section 9–108; or

(2) an indication that the financing statement covers all assets or all personal property.

As amended in 1999.

§ 9–505.   Filing and Compliance with Other Statutes and Treaties for Consignments, Leases, Other Bailments, and Other Transactions.

(a) A consignor, lessor, or other bailor of goods, a licensor, or a buyer of a payment intangible or promissory note may file a financing statement, or may comply with a statute or treaty described in Section 9–311(a), using the terms "consignor", "consignee", "lessor", "lessee", "bailor", "bailee", "licensor", "licensee", "owner", "registered owner", "buyer", "seller", or words of similar import, instead of the terms "secured party" and "debtor".

(b) This part applies to the filing of a financing statement under subsection (a) and, as appropriate, to compliance that is equivalent to filing a financing statement under Section 9–311(b), but the filing or compliance is not of itself a factor in determining whether the collateral secures an obligation. If it is determined for another reason that the collateral secures an obligation, a security interest held by the consignor, lessor, bailor, licensor, owner, or buyer which attaches to the collateral is perfected by the filing or compliance.

§ 9–506. Effect of Errors or Omissions.

(a) A financing statement substantially satisfying the requirements of this part is effective, even if it has minor errors or omissions, unless the errors or omissions make the financing statement seriously misleading.

(b) Except as otherwise provided in subsection (c), a financing statement that fails sufficiently to provide the name of the debtor in accordance with Section 9–503(a) is seriously misleading.

(c) If a search of the records of the filing office under the debtor's correct name, using the filing office's standard search logic, if any, would disclose a financing statement that fails sufficiently to provide the name of the debtor in accordance with Section 9–503(a), the name provided does not make the financing statement seriously misleading.

(d) For purposes of Section 9–508(b), the "debtor's correct name" in subsection (c) means the correct name of the new debtor.

§ 9–507. Effect of Certain Events on Effectiveness of Financing Statement.

(a) A filed financing statement remains effective with respect to collateral that is sold, exchanged, leased, licensed, or otherwise disposed of and in which a security interest or agricultural lien continues, even if the secured party knows of or consents to the disposition.

(b) Except as otherwise provided in subsection (c) and Section 9–508, a financing statement is not rendered ineffective if, after the financing statement is filed, the information provided in the financing statement becomes seriously misleading under Section 9–506.

(c) If a debtor so changes its name that a filed financing statement becomes seriously misleading under Section 9–506:

(1) the financing statement is effective to perfect a security interest in collateral acquired by the debtor before, or within four months after, the change; and

(2) the financing statement is not effective to perfect a security interest in collateral acquired by the debtor more than four months after the change, unless an amendment to the financing statement which renders the financing statement not seriously misleading is filed within four months after the change.

§ 9–508. Effectiveness of Financing Statement If New Debtor Becomes Bound by Security Agreement.

(a) Except as otherwise provided in this section, a filed financing statement naming an original debtor is effective to perfect a security interest in collateral in which a new debtor has or acquires rights to the extent that the financing statement would have been effective had the original debtor acquired rights in the collateral.

(b) If the difference between the name of the original debtor and that of the new debtor causes a filed financing statement that is effective under subsection (a) to be seriously misleading under Section 9–506:

(1) the financing statement is effective to perfect a security interest in collateral acquired by the new debtor before, and within four months after, the new debtor becomes bound under Section 9B–203(d); and

(2) the financing statement is not effective to perfect a security interest in collateral acquired by the new debtor more than four months after the new debtor becomes bound under Section 9–203(d) unless an initial financing statement providing the name of the new debtor is filed before the expiration of that time.

(c) This section does not apply to collateral as to which a filed financing statement remains effective against the new debtor under Section 9–507(a).

§ 9–509. Persons Entitled to File a Record.

(a) A person may file an initial financing statement, amendment that adds collateral covered by a financing statement, or amendment that adds a debtor to a financing statement only if:

(1) the debtor authorizes the filing in an authenticated record or pursuant to subsection (b) or (c); or

(2) the person holds an agricultural lien that has become effective at the time of filing and the financing statement covers only collateral in which the person holds an agricultural lien.

(b) By authenticating or becoming bound as debtor by a security agreement, a debtor or new debtor authorizes the filing of an initial financing statement, and an amendment, covering:

(1) the collateral described in the security agreement; and

(2) property that becomes collateral under Section 9–315(a)(2), whether or not the security agreement expressly covers proceeds.

(c) By acquiring collateral in which a security interest or agricultural lien continues under Section 9–315(a)(1), a debtor authorizes the filing of an initial financing statement, and an amendment, covering the collateral and property that becomes collateral under Section 9–315(a)(2).

(d) A person may file an amendment other than an amendment that adds collateral covered by a financing statement or an amendment that adds a debtor to a financing statement only if:

(1) the secured party of record authorizes the filing; or

(2) the amendment is a termination statement for a financing statement as to which the secured party of record has failed to file or send a termination statement as required by Section 9–513(a) or (c), the debtor authorizes the filing, and the termination statement indicates that the debtor authorized it to be filed.

(e) If there is more than one secured party of record for a financing statement, each secured party of record may authorize the filing of an amendment under subsection (d).

As amended in 2000.

§ 9–510. Effectiveness of Filed Record.

(a) A filed record is effective only to the extent that it was filed by a person that may file it under Section 9–509.

(b) A record authorized by one secured party of record does not affect the financing statement with respect to another secured party of record.

(c) A continuation statement that is not filed within the six-month period prescribed by Section 9–515(d) is ineffective.

§ 9–511. Secured Party of Record.

(a) A secured party of record with respect to a financing statement is a person whose name is provided as the name of the secured party or a representative of the secured party in an initial financing statement that has been filed. If an initial financing statement is filed under Section 9–514(a), the assignee named in the initial financing statement is the secured party of record with respect to the financing statement.

(b) If an amendment of a financing statement which provides the name of a person as a secured party or a representative of a secured party is filed, the person named in the amendment is a secured party of record. If an amendment is filed under Section 9–514(b), the assignee named in the amendment is a secured party of record.

(c) A person remains a secured party of record until the filing of an amendment of the financing statement which deletes the person.

§ 9–512. Amendment of Financing Statement.

[Alternative A]

(a) Subject to Section 9–509, a person may add or delete collateral covered by, continue or terminate the effectiveness of, or, subject to subsection (e), otherwise amend the information provided in, a financing statement by filing an amendment that:

   (1) identifies, by its file number, the initial financing statement to which the amendment relates; and

   (2) if the amendment relates to an initial financing statement filed [or recorded] in a filing office described in Section 9–501(a)(1), provides the information specified in Section 9–502(b).

[Alternative B]

(a) Subject to Section 9–509, a person may add or delete collateral covered by, continue or terminate the effectiveness of, or, subject to subsection (e), otherwise amend the information provided in, a financing statement by filing an amendment that:

   (1) identifies, by its file number, the initial financing statement to which the amendment relates; and

   (2) if the amendment relates to an initial financing statement filed [or recorded] in a filing office described in Section 9–501(a)(1), provides the date [and time] that the initial financing statement was filed [or recorded] and the information specified in Section 9–502(b).

[End of Alternatives]

(b) Except as otherwise provided in Section 9–515, the filing of an amendment does not extend the period of effectiveness of the financing statement.

(c) A financing statement that is amended by an amendment that adds collateral is effective as to the added collateral only from the date of the filing of the amendment.

(d) A financing statement that is amended by an amendment that adds a debtor is effective as to the added debtor only from the date of the filing of the amendment.

(e) An amendment is ineffective to the extent it:

   (1) purports to delete all debtors and fails to provide the name of a debtor to be covered by the financing statement; or

   (2) purports to delete all secured parties of record and fails to provide the name of a new secured party of record.

Legislative Note: States whose real-estate filing offices require additional information in amendments and cannot search their records by both the name of the debtor and the file number should enact Alternative B to Sections 9–512(a), 9–518(b), 9–519(f), and 9–522(a).

§ 9–513. Termination Statement.

(a) A secured party shall cause the secured party of record for a financing statement to file a termination statement for the financing statement if the financing statement covers consumer goods and:

   (1) there is no obligation secured by the collateral covered by the financing statement and no commitment to make an advance, incur an obligation, or otherwise give value; or

   (2) the debtor did not authorize the filing of the initial financing statement.

(b) To comply with subsection (a), a secured party shall cause the secured party of record to file the termination statement:

   (1) within one month after there is no obligation secured by the collateral covered by the financing statement and no commitment to make an advance, incur an obligation, or otherwise give value; or

   (2) if earlier, within 20 days after the secured party receives an authenticated demand from a debtor.

(c) In cases not governed by subsection (a), within 20 days after a secured party receives an authenticated demand from a debtor, the secured party shall cause the secured party of record for a financing statement to send to the debtor a termination statement for the financing statement or file the termination statement in the filing office if:

   (1) except in the case of a financing statement covering accounts or chattel paper that has been sold or goods that are the subject of a consignment, there is no obligation secured by the collateral covered by the financing statement and no commitment to make an advance, incur an obligation, or otherwise give value;

   (2) the financing statement covers accounts or chattel paper that has been sold but as to which the account debtor or other person obligated has discharged its obligation;

   (3) the financing statement covers goods that were the subject of a consignment to the debtor but are not in the debtor's possession; or

   (4) the debtor did not authorize the filing of the initial financing statement.

(d) Except as otherwise provided in Section 9–510, upon the filing of a termination statement with the filing office, the financing statement to which the termination statement relates ceases to be effective. Except as otherwise provided in Section 9–510, for purposes of Sections 9–519(g), 9–522(a), and 9–523(c), the filing with the filing office of a termination statement relating to a financing statement that indicates that the debtor is a transmitting utility also causes the effectiveness of the financing statement to lapse.

As amended in 2000.

§ 9–514. Assignment of Powers of Secured Party of Record.

(a) Except as otherwise provided in subsection (c), an initial financing statement may reflect an assignment of all of the secured party's power to authorize an amendment to the financing statement by providing the name and mailing address of the assignee as the name and address of the secured party.

(b) Except as otherwise provided in subsection (c), a secured party of record may assign of record all or part of its power to authorize an amendment to a financing statement by filing in the filing office an amendment of the financing statement which:

(1) identifies, by its file number, the initial financing statement to which it relates;

(2) provides the name of the assignor; and

(3) provides the name and mailing address of the assignee.

(c) An assignment of record of a security interest in a fixture covered by a record of a mortgage which is effective as a financing statement filed as a fixture filing under Section 9–502(c) may be made only by an assignment of record of the mortgage in the manner provided by law of this State other than [the Uniform Commercial Code].

§ 9–515. Duration and Effectiveness of Financing Statement; Effect of Lapsed Financing Statement.

(a) Except as otherwise provided in subsections (b), (e), (f), and (g), a filed financing statement is effective for a period of five years after the date of filing.

(b) Except as otherwise provided in subsections (e), (f), and (g), an initial financing statement filed in connection with a public-finance transaction or manufactured-home transaction is effective for a period of 30 years after the date of filing if it indicates that it is filed in connection with a public-finance transaction or manufactured-home transaction.

(c) The effectiveness of a filed financing statement lapses on the expiration of the period of its effectiveness unless before the lapse a continuation statement is filed pursuant to subsection (d). Upon lapse, a financing statement ceases to be effective and any security interest or agricultural lien that was perfected by the financing statement becomes unperfected, unless the security interest is perfected otherwise. If the security interest or agricultural lien becomes unperfected upon lapse, it is deemed never to have been perfected as against a purchaser of the collateral for value.

(d) A continuation statement may be filed only within six months before the expiration of the five-year period specified in subsection (a) or the 30-year period specified in subsection (b), whichever is applicable.

(e) Except as otherwise provided in Section 9–510, upon timely filing of a continuation statement, the effectiveness of the initial financing statement continues for a period of five years commencing on the day on which the financing statement would have become ineffective in the absence of the filing. Upon the expiration of the five-year period, the financing statement lapses in the same manner as provided in subsection (c), unless, before the lapse, another continuation statement is filed pursuant to subsection (d). Succeeding continuation statements may be filed in the same manner to continue the effectiveness of the initial financing statement.

(f) If a debtor is a transmitting utility and a filed financing statement so indicates, the financing statement is effective until a termination statement is filed.

(g) A record of a mortgage that is effective as a financing statement filed as a fixture filing under Section 9–502(c) remains effective as a financing statement filed as a fixture filing until the mortgage is released or satisfied of record or its effectiveness otherwise terminates as to the real property.

§ 9–516. What Constitutes Filing; Effectiveness of Filing.

(a) Except as otherwise provided in subsection (b), communication of a record to a filing office and tender of the filing fee or acceptance of the record by the filing office constitutes filing.

(b) Filing does not occur with respect to a record that a filing office refuses to accept because:

(1) the record is not communicated by a method or medium of communication authorized by the filing office;

(2) an amount equal to or greater than the applicable filing fee is not tendered;

(3) the filing office is unable to index the record because:

(A) in the case of an initial financing statement, the record does not provide a name for the debtor;

(B) in the case of an amendment or correction statement, the record:

(i) does not identify the initial financing statement as required by Section 9–512 or 9–518, as applicable; or

(ii) identifies an initial financing statement whose effectiveness has lapsed under Section 9–515;

(C) in the case of an initial financing statement that provides the name of a debtor identified as an individual or an amendment that provides a name of a debtor identified as an individual which was not previously provided in the financing statement to which the record relates, the record does not identify the debtor's last name; or

(D) in the case of a record filed [or recorded] in the filing office described in Section 9–501(a)(1), the record does not provide a sufficient description of the real property to which it relates;

(4) in the case of an initial financing statement or an amendment that adds a secured party of record, the record does not provide a name and mailing address for the secured party of record;

(5) in the case of an initial financing statement or an amendment that provides a name of a debtor which was not previously provided in the financing statement to which the amendment relates, the record does not:

(A) provide a mailing address for the debtor;

(B) indicate whether the debtor is an individual or an organization; or

(C) if the financing statement indicates that the debtor is an organization, provide:

(i) a type of organization for the debtor;

(ii) a jurisdiction of organization for the debtor; or

(iii) an organizational identification number for the debtor or indicate that the debtor has none;

(6) in the case of an assignment reflected in an initial financing statement under Section 9–514(a) or an amendment filed under Section 9–514(b), the record does not provide a name and mailing address for the assignee; or

(7) in the case of a continuation statement, the record is not filed within the six-month period prescribed by Section 9–515(d).

(c) For purposes of subsection (b):

(1) a record does not provide information if the filing office is unable to read or decipher the information; and

(2) a record that does not indicate that it is an amendment or identify an initial financing statement to which it relates, as required by Section 9–512, 9–514, or 9–518, is an initial financing statement.

(d) A record that is communicated to the filing office with tender of the filing fee, but which the filing office refuses to accept for a reason other than one set forth in subsection (b), is effective as a filed record except as against a purchaser of the collateral which gives value in reasonable reliance upon the absence of the record from the files.

§ 9–517. Effect of Indexing Errors.

The failure of the filing office to index a record correctly does not affect the effectiveness of the filed record.

§ 9–518. Claim Concerning Inaccurate or Wrongfully Filed Record.

(a) A person may file in the filing office a correction statement with respect to a record indexed there under the person's name if the person believes that the record is inaccurate or was wrongfully filed.

[Alternative A]

(b) A correction statement must:

(1) identify the record to which it relates by the file number assigned to the initial financing statement to which the record relates;

(2) indicate that it is a correction statement; and

(3) provide the basis for the person's belief that the record is inaccurate and indicate the manner in which the person believes the record should be amended to cure any inaccuracy or provide the basis for the person's belief that the record was wrongfully filed.

[Alternative B]

(b) A correction statement must:

(1) identify the record to which it relates by:

(A) the file number assigned to the initial financing statement to which the record relates; and

(B) if the correction statement relates to a record filed [or recorded] in a filing office described in Section 9–501(a)(1), the date [and time] that the initial financing statement was filed [or recorded] and the information specified in Section 9–502(b);

(2) indicate that it is a correction statement; and

(3) provide the basis for the person's belief that the record is inaccurate and indicate the manner in which the person believes the record should be amended to cure any inaccuracy or provide the basis for the person's belief that the record was wrongfully filed.

[End of Alternatives]

(c) The filing of a correction statement does not affect the effectiveness of an initial financing statement or other filed record.

Legislative Note: States whose real-estate filing offices require additional information in amendments and cannot search their records by both the name of the debtor and the file number should enact Alternative B to Sections 9–512(a), 9–518(b), 9–519(f), and 9–522(a).

[Subpart 2. Duties and Operation of Filing Office]

§ 9–519. Numbering, Maintaining, and Indexing Records; Communicating Information Provided in Records.

(a) For each record filed in a filing office, the filing office shall:

(1) assign a unique number to the filed record;

(2) create a record that bears the number assigned to the filed record and the date and time of filing;

(3) maintain the filed record for public inspection; and

(4) index the filed record in accordance with subsections (c), (d), and (e).

(b) A file number [assigned after January 1, 2002,] must include a digit that:

(1) is mathematically derived from or related to the other digits of the file number; and

(2) aids the filing office in determining whether a number communicated as the file number includes a single-digit or transpositional error.

(c) Except as otherwise provided in subsections (d) and (e), the filing office shall:

(1) index an initial financing statement according to the name of the debtor and index all filed records relating to the initial financing statement in a manner that associates with one another an initial financing statement and all filed records relating to the initial financing statement; and

(2) index a record that provides a name of a debtor which was not previously provided in the financing statement to which the record relates also according to the name that was not previously provided.

(d) If a financing statement is filed as a fixture filing or covers as-extracted collateral or timber to be cut, [it must be filed for record and] the filing office shall index it:

(1) under the names of the debtor and of each owner of record shown on the financing statement as if they were the mortgagors under a mortgage of the real property described; and

(2) to the extent that the law of this State provides for indexing of records of mortgages under the name of the mortgagee, under the name of the secured party as if the secured party were the mortgagee thereunder, or, if indexing is by description, as if the financing statement were a record of a mortgage of the real property described.

(e) If a financing statement is filed as a fixture filing or covers as-extracted collateral or timber to be cut, the filing office shall index an assignment filed under Section 9–514(a) or an amendment filed under Section 9–514(b):

(1) under the name of the assignor as grantor; and

(2) to the extent that the law of this State provides for indexing a record of the assignment of a mortgage under the name of the assignee, under the name of the assignee.

[Alternative A]

(f) The filing office shall maintain a capability:

(1) to retrieve a record by the name of the debtor and by the file number assigned to the initial financing statement to which the record relates; and

(2) to associate and retrieve with one another an initial financing statement and each filed record relating to the initial financing statement.

[Alternative B]

(f) The filing office shall maintain a capability:

(1) to retrieve a record by the name of the debtor and:

(A) if the filing office is described in Section 9–501(a)(1), by the file number assigned to the initial financing statement to which the record relates and the date [and time] that the record was filed [or recorded]; or

(B) if the filing office is described in Section 9–501(a)(2), by the file number assigned to the initial financing statement to which the record relates; and

(2) to associate and retrieve with one another an initial financing statement and each filed record relating to the initial financing statement.

[End of Alternatives]

(g) The filing office may not remove a debtor's name from the index until one year after the effectiveness of a financing statement naming the debtor lapses under Section 9–515 with respect to all secured parties of record.

(h) The filing office shall perform the acts required by subsections (a) through (e) at the time and in the manner prescribed by filing-office rule, but not later than two business days after the filing office receives the record in question.

[(i) Subsection[s] [(b)] [and] [(h)] do[es] not apply to a filing office described in Section 9–501(a)(1).]

Legislative Notes:

1. States whose filing offices currently assign file numbers that include a verification number, commonly known as a "check digit," or can implement this requirement before the effective date of this Article should omit the bracketed language in subsection (b).

2. In States in which writings will not appear in the real property records and indices unless actually recorded the bracketed language in subsection (d) should be used.

3. States whose real-estate filing offices require additional information in amendments and cannot search their records by both the name of the debtor and the file number should enact Alternative B to Sections 9–512(a), 9–518(b), 9–519(f), and 9–522(a).

4. A State that elects not to require real-estate filing offices to comply with either or both of subsections (b) and (h) may adopt an applicable variation of subsection (i) and add "Except as otherwise provided in subsection (i)," to the appropriate subsection or subsections.

§ 9–520. Acceptance and Refusal to Accept Record.

(a) A filing office shall refuse to accept a record for filing for a reason set forth in Section 9–516(b) and may refuse to accept a record for filing only for a reason set forth in Section 9–516(b).

(b) If a filing office refuses to accept a record for filing, it shall communicate to the person that presented the record the fact of and reason for the refusal and the date and time the record would have been filed had the filing office accepted it. The communication must be made at the time and in the manner prescribed by filing-office rule but [, in the case of a filing office described in Section 9–501(a)(2),] in no event more than two business days after the filing office receives the record.

(c) A filed financing statement satisfying Section 9–502(a) and (b) is effective, even if the filing office is required to refuse to accept it

for filing under subsection (a). However, Section 9–338 applies to a filed financing statement providing information described in Section 9–516(b)(5) which is incorrect at the time the financing statement is filed.

(d) If a record communicated to a filing office provides information that relates to more than one debtor, this part applies as to each debtor separately.

Legislative Note: A State that elects not to require real-property filing offices to comply with subsection (b) should include the bracketed language.

§ 9–521. Uniform Form of Written Financing Statement and Amendment.

(a) A filing office that accepts written records may not refuse to accept a written initial financing statement in the following form and format except for a reason set forth in Section 9–516(b):

[NATIONAL UCC FINANCING STATEMENT (FORM UCC1)(REV. 7/29/98]

[NATIONAL UCC FINANCING STATEMENT ADDENDUM (FORM UCC1Ad)(REV. 07/29/98)]

(b) A filing office that accepts written records may not refuse to accept a written record in the following form and format except for a reason set forth in Section 9–516(b):

[NATIONAL UCC FINANCING STATEMENT AMENDMENT (FORM UCC3)(REV. 07/29/98)]

[NATIONAL UCC FINANCING STATEMENT AMENDMENT ADDENDUM (FORM UCC3Ad)(REV. 07/29/98)]

§ 9–522. Maintenance and Destruction of Records.

[Alternative A]

(a) The filing office shall maintain a record of the information provided in a filed financing statement for at least one year after the effectiveness of the financing statement has lapsed under Section 9–515 with respect to all secured parties of record. The record must be retrievable by using the name of the debtor and by using the file number assigned to the initial financing statement to which the record relates.

[Alternative B]

(a) The filing office shall maintain a record of the information provided in a filed financing statement for at least one year after the effectiveness of the financing statement has lapsed under Section 9–515 with respect to all secured parties of record. The record must be retrievable by using the name of the debtor and:

(1) if the record was filed [or recorded] in the filing office described in Section 9–501(a)(1), by using the file number assigned to the initial financing statement to which the record relates and the date [and time] that the record was filed [or recorded]; or

(2) if the record was filed in the filing office described in Section 9–501(a)(2), by using the file number assigned to the initial financing statement to which the record relates.

[End of Alternatives]

(b) Except to the extent that a statute governing disposition of public records provides otherwise, the filing office immediately may destroy any written record evidencing a financing statement. However, if the filing office destroys a written record, it shall maintain another record of the financing statement which complies with subsection (a).

Legislative Note: States whose real-estate filing offices require additional information in amendments and cannot search their records by both the name of the debtor and the file number should enact Alternative B to Sections 9–512(a), 9–518(b), 9–519(f), and 9–522(a).

§ 9–523. Information from Filing Office; Sale or License of Records.

(a) If a person that files a written record requests an acknowledgment of the filing, the filing office shall send to the person an image of the record showing the number assigned to the record pursuant to Section 9–519(a)(1) and the date and time of the filing of the record. However, if the person furnishes a copy of the record to the filing office, the filing office may instead:

(1) note upon the copy the number assigned to the record pursuant to Section 9–519(a)(1) and the date and time of the filing of the record; and

(2) send the copy to the person.

(b) If a person files a record other than a written record, the filing office shall communicate to the person an acknowledgment that provides:

(1) the information in the record;

(2) the number assigned to the record pursuant to Section 9–519(a)(1); and

(3) the date and time of the filing of the record.

(c) The filing office shall communicate or otherwise make available in a record the following information to any person that requests it:

(1) whether there is on file on a date and time specified by the filing office, but not a date earlier than three business days before the filing office receives the request, any financing statement that:

(A) designates a particular debtor [or, if the request so states, designates a particular debtor at the address specified in the request];

(B) has not lapsed under Section 9–515 with respect to all secured parties of record; and

(C) if the request so states, has lapsed under Section 9–515 and a record of which is maintained by the filing office under Section 9–522(a);

(2) the date and time of filing of each financing statement; and

(3) the information provided in each financing statement.

(d) In complying with its duty under subsection (c), the filing office may communicate information in any medium. However, if requested, the filing office shall communicate information by issuing [its written certificate] [a record that can be admitted into evidence in the courts of this State without extrinsic evidence of its authenticity].

(e) The filing office shall perform the acts required by subsections (a) through (d) at the time and in the manner prescribed by filing-office rule, but not later than two business days after the filing office receives the request.

(f) At least weekly, the [insert appropriate official or governmental agency] [filing office] shall offer to sell or license to the public on a nonexclusive basis, in bulk, copies of all records filed in it under this part, in every medium from time to time available to the filing office.

Legislative Notes:

1. States whose filing office does not offer the additional service of responding to search requests limited to a particular address should omit the bracketed language in subsection (c)(1)(A).

2. A State that elects not to require real-estate filing offices to comply with either or both of subsections (e) and (f) should specify in the appropriate subsection(s) only the filing office described in Section 9–501(a)(2).

§ 9–524. Delay by Filing Office.

Delay by the filing office beyond a time limit prescribed by this part is excused if:

(1) the delay is caused by interruption of communication or computer facilities, war, emergency conditions, failure of equipment, or other circumstances beyond control of the filing office; and

(2) the filing office exercises reasonable diligence under the circumstances.

§ 9–525. Fees.

(a) Except as otherwise provided in subsection (e), the fee for filing and indexing a record under this part, other than an initial financing statement of the kind described in subsection (b), is [the amount specified in subsection (c), if applicable, plus]:

(1) $[X] if the record is communicated in writing and consists of one or two pages;

(2) $[2X] if the record is communicated in writing and consists of more than two pages; and

(3) $[½X] if the record is communicated by another medium authorized by filing-office rule.

(b) Except as otherwise provided in subsection (e), the fee for filing and indexing an initial financing statement of the following kind is [the amount specified in subsection (c), if applicable, plus]:

(1) $_____ if the financing statement indicates that it is filed in connection with a public-finance transaction;

(2) $_____ if the financing statement indicates that it is filed in connection with a manufactured-home transaction.

[Alternative A]

(c) The number of names required to be indexed does not affect the amount of the fee in subsections (a) and (b).

[Alternative B]

(c) Except as otherwise provided in subsection (e), if a record is communicated in writing, the fee for each name more than two required to be indexed is $_____.

[End of Alternatives]

(d) The fee for responding to a request for information from the filing office, including for [issuing a certificate showing] [communicating] whether there is on file any financing statement naming a particular debtor, is:

(1) $_____ if the request is communicated in writing; and

(2) $_____ if the request is communicated by another medium authorized by filing-office rule.

(e) This section does not require a fee with respect to a record of a mortgage which is effective as a financing statement filed as a fixture filing or as a financing statement covering as-extracted collateral or timber to be cut under Section 9–502(c). However, the recording and satisfaction fees that otherwise would be applicable to the record of the mortgage apply.

Legislative Notes:

1. To preserve uniformity, a State that places the provisions of this section together with statutes setting fees for other services should do so without modification.

2. A State should enact subsection (c), Alternative A, and omit the bracketed language in subsections (a) and (b) unless its indexing system entails a substantial additional cost when indexing additional names.

As amended in 2000.

§ 9–526.   Filing-Office Rules.

(a) The [insert appropriate governmental official or agency] shall adopt and publish rules to implement this article. The filing-office rules must be[:

(1)] consistent with this article[; and

(2) adopted and published in accordance with the [insert any applicable state administrative procedure act]].

(b) To keep the filing-office rules and practices of the filing office in harmony with the rules and practices of filing offices in other jurisdictions that enact substantially this part, and to keep the technology used by the filing office compatible with the technology used by filing offices in other jurisdictions that enact substantially this part, the [insert appropriate governmental official or agency], so far as is consistent with the purposes, policies, and provisions of this article, in adopting, amending, and repealing filing-office rules, shall:

(1) consult with filing offices in other jurisdictions that enact substantially this part; and

(2) consult the most recent version of the Model Rules promulgated by the International Association of Corporate Administrators or any successor organization; and

(3) take into consideration the rules and practices of, and the technology used by, filing offices in other jurisdictions that enact substantially this part.

§ 9–527.   Duty to Report.

The [insert appropriate governmental official or agency] shall report [annually on or before _____] to the [Governor and Legislature] on the operation of the filing office. The report must contain a statement of the extent to which:

(1) the filing-office rules are not in harmony with the rules of filing offices in other jurisdictions that enact substantially this part and the reasons for these variations; and

(2) the filing-office rules are not in harmony with the most recent version of the Model Rules promulgated by the International Association of Corporate Administrators, or any successor organization, and the reasons for these variations.

Part 6   Default

[Subpart 1.   Default and Enforcement of Security Interest]

§ 9–601.   Rights after Default; Judicial Enforcement; Consignor or Buyer of Accounts, Chattel Paper, Payment Intangibles, or Promissory Notes.

(a) After default, a secured party has the rights provided in this part and, except as otherwise provided in Section 9–602, those provided by agreement of the parties. A secured party:

(1) may reduce a claim to judgment, foreclose, or otherwise enforce the claim, security interest, or agricultural lien by any available judicial procedure; and

(2) if the collateral is documents, may proceed either as to the documents or as to the goods they cover.

(b) A secured party in possession of collateral or control of collateral under Section 9–104, 9–105, 9–106, or 9–107 has the rights and duties provided in Section 9–207.

(c) The rights under subsections (a) and (b) are cumulative and may be exercised simultaneously.

(d) Except as otherwise provided in subsection (g) and Section 9–605, after default, a debtor and an obligor have the rights provided in this part and by agreement of the parties.

(e) If a secured party has reduced its claim to judgment, the lien of any levy that may be made upon the collateral by virtue of an execution based upon the judgment relates back to the earliest of:

(1) the date of perfection of the security interest or agricultural lien in the collateral;

(2) the date of filing a financing statement covering the collateral; or

(3) any date specified in a statute under which the agricultural lien was created.

(f) A sale pursuant to an execution is a foreclosure of the security interest or agricultural lien by judicial procedure within the meaning of this section. A secured party may purchase at the sale and thereafter hold the collateral free of any other requirements of this article.

(g) Except as otherwise provided in Section 9–607(c), this part imposes no duties upon a secured party that is a consignor or is a buyer of accounts, chattel paper, payment intangibles, or promissory notes.

§ 9–602.   Waiver and Variance of Rights and Duties.

Except as otherwise provided in Section 9–624, to the extent that they give rights to a debtor or obligor and impose duties on a secured party, the debtor or obligor may not waive or vary the rules stated in the following listed sections:

(1) Section 9–207(b)(4)(C), which deals with use and operation of the collateral by the secured party;

(2) Section 9–210, which deals with requests for an accounting and requests concerning a list of collateral and statement of account;

(3) Section 9–607(c), which deals with collection and enforcement of collateral;

(4) Sections 9–608(a) and 9–615(c) to the extent that they deal with application or payment of noncash proceeds of collection, enforcement, or disposition;

(5) Sections 9–608(a) and 9–615(d) to the extent that they require accounting for or payment of surplus proceeds of collateral;

(6) Section 9–609 to the extent that it imposes upon a secured party that takes possession of collateral without judicial process the duty to do so without breach of the peace;

(7) Sections 9–610(b), 9–611, 9–613, and 9–614, which deal with disposition of collateral;

(8) Section 9–615(f), which deals with calculation of a deficiency or surplus when a disposition is made to the secured party, a person related to the secured party, or a secondary obligor;

(9) Section 9–616, which deals with explanation of the calculation of a surplus or deficiency;

(10) Sections 9–620, 9–621, and 9–622, which deal with acceptance of collateral in satisfaction of obligation;

(11) Section 9–623, which deals with redemption of collateral;

(12) Section 9–624, which deals with permissible waivers; and

(13) Sections 9–625 and 9–626, which deal with the secured party's liability for failure to comply with this article.

§ 9–603. Agreement on Standards Concerning Rights and Duties.

(a) The parties may determine by agreement the standards measuring the fulfillment of the rights of a debtor or obligor and the duties of a secured party under a rule stated in Section 9–602 if the standards are not manifestly unreasonable.

(b) Subsection (a) does not apply to the duty under Section 9–609 to refrain from breaching the peace.

§ 9–604. Procedure If Security Agreement Covers Real Property or Fixtures.

(a) If a security agreement covers both personal and real property, a secured party may proceed:

(1) under this part as to the personal property without prejudicing any rights with respect to the real property; or

(2) as to both the personal property and the real property in accordance with the rights with respect to the real property, in which case the other provisions of this part do not apply.

(b) Subject to subsection (c), if a security agreement covers goods that are or become fixtures, a secured party may proceed:

(1) under this part; or

(2) in accordance with the rights with respect to real property, in which case the other provisions of this part do not apply.

(c) Subject to the other provisions of this part, if a secured party holding a security interest in fixtures has priority over all owners and encumbrancers of the real property, the secured party, after default, may remove the collateral from the real property.

(d) A secured party that removes collateral shall promptly reimburse any encumbrancer or owner of the real property, other than the debtor, for the cost of repair of any physical injury caused by the removal. The secured party need not reimburse the encumbrancer or owner for any diminution in value of the real property caused by the absence of the goods removed or by any necessity of replacing them. A person entitled to reimbursement may refuse permission to remove until the secured party gives adequate assurance for the performance of the obligation to reimburse.

§ 9–605. Unknown Debtor or Secondary Obligor.

A secured party does not owe a duty based on its status as secured party:

(1) to a person that is a debtor or obligor, unless the secured party knows:

(A) that the person is a debtor or obligor;

(B) the identity of the person; and

(C) how to communicate with the person; or

(2) to a secured party or lienholder that has filed a financing statement against a person, unless the secured party knows:

(A) that the person is a debtor; and

(B) the identity of the person.

§ 9–606. Time of Default for Agricultural Lien.

For purposes of this part, a default occurs in connection with an agricultural lien at the time the secured party becomes entitled to enforce the lien in accordance with the statute under which it was created.

§ 9–607. Collection and Enforcement by Secured Party.

(a) If so agreed, and in any event after default, a secured party:

(1) may notify an account debtor or other person obligated on collateral to make payment or otherwise render performance to or for the benefit of the secured party;

(2) may take any proceeds to which the secured party is entitled under Section 9–315;

(3) may enforce the obligations of an account debtor or other person obligated on collateral and exercise the rights of the debtor with respect to the obligation of the account debtor or other person obligated on collateral to make payment or otherwise render performance to the debtor, and with respect to any property that secures the obligations of the account debtor or other person obligated on the collateral;

(4) if it holds a security interest in a deposit account perfected by control under Section 9–104(a)(1), may apply the balance of the deposit account to the obligation secured by the deposit account; and

(5) if it holds a security interest in a deposit account perfected by control under Section 9–104(a)(2) or (3), may instruct the bank to pay the balance of the deposit account to or for the benefit of the secured party.

(b) If necessary to enable a secured party to exercise under subsection (a)(3) the right of a debtor to enforce a mortgage nonjudicially, the secured party may record in the office in which a record of the mortgage is recorded:

(1) a copy of the security agreement that creates or provides for a security interest in the obligation secured by the mortgage; and

(2) the secured party's sworn affidavit in recordable form stating that:

(A) a default has occurred; and

(B) the secured party is entitled to enforce the mortgage nonjudicially.

(c) A secured party shall proceed in a commercially reasonable manner if the secured party:

(1) undertakes to collect from or enforce an obligation of an account debtor or other person obligated on collateral; and

(2) is entitled to charge back uncollected collateral or otherwise to full or limited recourse against the debtor or a secondary obligor.

(d) A secured party may deduct from the collections made pursuant to subsection (c) reasonable expenses of collection and enforcement, including reasonable attorney's fees and legal expenses incurred by the secured party.

(e) This section does not determine whether an account debtor, bank, or other person obligated on collateral owes a duty to a secured party.

As amended in 2000.

§ 9–608. Application of Proceeds of Collection or Enforcement; Liability for Deficiency and Right to Surplus.

(a) If a security interest or agricultural lien secures payment or performance of an obligation, the following rules apply:

(1) A secured party shall apply or pay over for application the cash proceeds of collection or enforcement under Section 9–607 in the following order to:

(A) the reasonable expenses of collection and enforcement and, to the extent provided for by agreement and not prohibited by law, reasonable attorney's fees and legal expenses incurred by the secured party;

(B) the satisfaction of obligations secured by the security interest or agricultural lien under which the collection or enforcement is made; and

(C) the satisfaction of obligations secured by any subordinate security interest in or other lien on the collateral subject to the security interest or agricultural lien under which the collection or enforcement is made if the secured party receives an authenticated demand for proceeds before distribution of the proceeds is completed.

(2) If requested by a secured party, a holder of a subordinate security interest or other lien shall furnish reasonable proof of the interest or lien within a reasonable time. Unless the holder complies, the secured party need not comply with the holder's demand under paragraph (1)(C).

(3) A secured party need not apply or pay over for application noncash proceeds of collection and enforcement under Section 9–607 unless the failure to do so would be commercially unreasonable. A secured party that applies or pays over for application noncash proceeds shall do so in a commercially reasonable manner.

(4) A secured party shall account to and pay a debtor for any surplus, and the obligor is liable for any deficiency.

(b) If the underlying transaction is a sale of accounts, chattel paper, payment intangibles, or promissory notes, the debtor is not entitled to any surplus, and the obligor is not liable for any deficiency.
As amended in 2000.

§ 9–609. Secured Party's Right to Take Possession after Default.

(a) After default, a secured party:

(1) may take possession of the collateral; and

(2) without removal, may render equipment unusable and dispose of collateral on a debtor's premises under Section 9–610.

(b) A secured party may proceed under subsection (a):

(1) pursuant to judicial process; or

(2) without judicial process, if it proceeds without breach of the peace.

(c) If so agreed, and in any event after default, a secured party may require the debtor to assemble the collateral and make it available to the secured party at a place to be designated by the secured party which is reasonably convenient to both parties.

§ 9–610. Disposition of Collateral after Default.

(a) After default, a secured party may sell, lease, license, or otherwise dispose of any or all of the collateral in its present condition or following any commercially reasonable preparation or processing.

(b) Every aspect of a disposition of collateral, including the method, manner, time, place, and other terms, must be commercially reasonable. If commercially reasonable, a secured party may dispose of collateral by public or private proceedings, by one or more contracts, as a unit or in parcels, and at any time and place and on any terms.

(c) A secured party may purchase collateral:

(1) at a public disposition; or

(2) at a private disposition only if the collateral is of a kind that is customarily sold on a recognized market or the subject of widely distributed standard price quotations.

(d) A contract for sale, lease, license, or other disposition includes the warranties relating to title, possession, quiet enjoyment, and the like which by operation of law accompany a voluntary disposition of property of the kind subject to the contract.

(e) A secured party may disclaim or modify warranties under subsection (d):

(1) in a manner that would be effective to disclaim or modify the warranties in a voluntary disposition of property of the kind subject to the contract of disposition; or

(2) by communicating to the purchaser a record evidencing the contract for disposition and including an express disclaimer or modification of the warranties.

(f) A record is sufficient to disclaim warranties under subsection (e) if it indicates "There is no warranty relating to title, possession, quiet enjoyment, or the like in this disposition" or uses words of similar import.

§ 9–611. Notification before Disposition of Collateral.

(a) In this section, "notification date" means the earlier of the date on which:

(1) a secured party sends to the debtor and any secondary obligor an authenticated notification of disposition; or

(2) the debtor and any secondary obligor waive the right to notification.

(b) Except as otherwise provided in subsection (d), a secured party that disposes of collateral under Section 9–610 shall send to the persons specified in subsection (c) a reasonable authenticated notification of disposition.

(c) To comply with subsection (b), the secured party shall send an authenticated notification of disposition to:

(1) the debtor;

(2) any secondary obligor; and

(3) if the collateral is other than consumer goods:

(A) any other person from which the secured party has received, before the notification date, an authenticated notification of a claim of an interest in the collateral;

(B) any other secured party or lienholder that, 10 days before the notification date, held a security interest in or other lien on the collateral perfected by the filing of a financing statement that:

(i) identified the collateral;

(ii) was indexed under the debtor's name as of that date; and

(iii) was filed in the office in which to file a financing statement against the debtor covering the collateral as of that date; and

(C) any other secured party that, 10 days before the notification date, held a security interest in the collateral perfected by compliance with a statute, regulation, or treaty described in Section 9–311(a).

(d) Subsection (b) does not apply if the collateral is perishable or threatens to decline speedily in value or is of a type customarily sold on a recognized market.

(e) A secured party complies with the requirement for notification prescribed by subsection (c)(3)(B) if:

(1) not later than 20 days or earlier than 30 days before the notification date, the secured party requests, in a commercially reasonable manner, information concerning financing statements indexed under the debtor's name in the office indicated in subsection (c)(3)(B); and

(2) before the notification date, the secured party:

(A) did not receive a response to the request for information; or

(B) received a response to the request for information and sent an authenticated notification of disposition to each secured party or other lienholder named in that response whose financing statement covered the collateral.

§ 9–612.   Timeliness of Notification before Disposition of Collateral.

(a) Except as otherwise provided in subsection (b), whether a notification is sent within a reasonable time is a question of fact.

(b) In a transaction other than a consumer transaction, a notification of disposition sent after default and 10 days or more before the earliest time of disposition set forth in the notification is sent within a reasonable time before the disposition.

§ 9–613.   Contents and Form of Notification before Disposition of Collateral: General.

Except in a consumer-goods transaction, the following rules apply:

(1) The contents of a notification of disposition are sufficient if the notification:

(A) describes the debtor and the secured party;

(B) describes the collateral that is the subject of the intended disposition;

(C) states the method of intended disposition;

(D) states that the debtor is entitled to an accounting of the unpaid indebtedness and states the charge, if any, for an accounting; and

(E) states the time and place of a public disposition or the time after which any other disposition is to be made.

(2) Whether the contents of a notification that lacks any of the information specified in paragraph (1) are nevertheless sufficient is a question of fact.

(3) The contents of a notification providing substantially the information specified in paragraph (1) are sufficient, even if the notification includes:

(A) information not specified by that paragraph; or

(B) minor errors that are not seriously misleading.

(4) A particular phrasing of the notification is not required.

(5) The following form of notification and the form appearing in Section 9–614(3), when completed, each provides sufficient information:

NOTIFICATION OF DISPOSITION OF COLLATERAL

To: [*Name of debtor, obligor, or other person to which the notification is sent*]

From: [*Name, address, and telephone number of secured party*]

Name of Debtor(s): [*Include only if debtor(s) are not an addressee*]

   [*For a public disposition:*]

We will sell [or lease or license, *as applicable*] the [*describe collateral*] [to the highest qualified bidder] in public as follows:

   Day and Date: _____

   Time: _____

   Place: _____

   [*For a private disposition:*]

We will sell [or lease or license, *as applicable*] the [*describe collateral*] privately sometime after [*day and date*].

You are entitled to an accounting of the unpaid indebtedness secured by the property that we intend to sell [or lease or license, *as applicable*] [for a charge of $_____]. You may request an accounting by calling us at [*telephone number*].

[End of Form]

As amended in 2000.

§ 9–614.   Contents and Form of Notification before Disposition of Collateral: Consumer-Goods Transaction.

In a consumer-goods transaction, the following rules apply:

(1) A notification of disposition must provide the following information:

(A) the information specified in Section 9–613(1);

(B) a description of any liability for a deficiency of the person to which the notification is sent;

(C) a telephone number from which the amount that must be paid to the secured party to redeem the collateral under Section 9–623 is available; and

(D) a telephone number or mailing address from which additional information concerning the disposition and the obligation secured is available.

(2) A particular phrasing of the notification is not required.

(3) The following form of notification, when completed, provides sufficient information:

   [*Name and address of secured party*]

   [*Date*]

NOTICE OF OUR PLAN TO SELL PROPERTY

[*Name and address of any obligor who is also a debtor*]

Subject: [*Identification of Transaction*]

We have your [*describe collateral*], because you broke promises in our agreement.

   [*For a public disposition:*]

We will sell [*describe collateral*] at public sale. A sale could include a lease or license. The sale will be held as follows:

   Date: _____

   Time: _____

   Place: _____

You may attend the sale and bring bidders if you want.

   [*For a private disposition:*]

We will sell [*describe collateral*] at private sale sometime after [*date*]. A sale could include a lease or license.

The money that we get from the sale (after paying our costs) will reduce the amount you owe. If we get less money than you owe, you [*will or will not, as applicable*] still owe us the difference. If we get more money than you owe, you will get the extra money, unless we must pay it to someone else.

You can get the property back at any time before we sell it by paying us the full amount you owe (not just the past due payments), including our expenses. To learn the exact amount you must pay, call us at [*telephone number*].

If you want us to explain to you in writing how we have figured the amount that you owe us, you may call us at [telephone number] [or write us at [*secured party's address*]] and request a written explanation. [We will charge you $_____ for the explanation if we sent you another written explanation of the amount you owe us within the last six months.]

If you need more information about the sale call us at [*telephone number*] [or write us at [secured party's address]].

We are sending this notice to the following other people who have an interest in [*describe collateral*] or who owe money under your agreement:

[*Names of all other debtors and obligors, if any*]

[End of Form]

(4) A notification in the form of paragraph (3) is sufficient, even if additional information appears at the end of the form.

(5) A notification in the form of paragraph (3) is sufficient, even if it includes errors in information not required by paragraph (1), unless the error is misleading with respect to rights arising under this article.

(6) If a notification under this section is not in the form of paragraph (3), law other than this article determines the effect of including information not required by paragraph (1).

§ 9–615. Application of Proceeds of Disposition; Liability for Deficiency and Right to Surplus.

(a) A secured party shall apply or pay over for application the cash proceeds of disposition under Section 9–610 in the following order to:

(1) the reasonable expenses of retaking, holding, preparing for disposition, processing, and disposing, and, to the extent provided for by agreement and not prohibited by law, reasonable attorney's fees and legal expenses incurred by the secured party;

(2) the satisfaction of obligations secured by the security interest or agricultural lien under which the disposition is made;

(3) the satisfaction of obligations secured by any subordinate security interest in or other subordinate lien on the collateral if:

(A) the secured party receives from the holder of the subordinate security interest or other lien an authenticated demand for proceeds before distribution of the proceeds is completed; and

(B) in a case in which a consignor has an interest in the collateral, the subordinate security interest or other lien is senior to the interest of the consignor; and

(4) a secured party that is a consignor of the collateral if the secured party receives from the consignor an authenticated demand for proceeds before distribution of the proceeds is completed.

(b) If requested by a secured party, a holder of a subordinate security interest or other lien shall furnish reasonable proof of the interest or lien within a reasonable time. Unless the holder does so, the secured

party need not comply with the holder's demand under subsection (a)(3).

(c) A secured party need not apply or pay over for application non-cash proceeds of disposition under Section 9–610 unless the failure to do so would be commercially unreasonable. A secured party that applies or pays over for application noncash proceeds shall do so in a commercially reasonable manner.

(d) If the security interest under which a disposition is made secures payment or performance of an obligation, after making the payments and applications required by subsection (a) and permitted by subsection (c):

(1) unless subsection (a)(4) requires the secured party to apply or pay over cash proceeds to a consignor, the secured party shall account to and pay a debtor for any surplus; and

(2) the obligor is liable for any deficiency.

(e) If the underlying transaction is a sale of accounts, chattel paper, payment intangibles, or promissory notes:

(1) the debtor is not entitled to any surplus; and

(2) the obligor is not liable for any deficiency.

(f) The surplus or deficiency following a disposition is calculated based on the amount of proceeds that would have been realized in a disposition complying with this part to a transferee other than the secured party, a person related to the secured party, or a secondary obligor if:

(1) the transferee in the disposition is the secured party, a person related to the secured party, or a secondary obligor; and

(2) the amount of proceeds of the disposition is significantly below the range of proceeds that a complying disposition to a person other than the secured party, a person related to the secured party, or a secondary obligor would have brought.

(g) A secured party that receives cash proceeds of a disposition in good faith and without knowledge that the receipt violates the rights of the holder of a security interest or other lien that is not subordinate to the security interest or agricultural lien under which the disposition is made:

(1) takes the cash proceeds free of the security interest or other lien;

(2) is not obligated to apply the proceeds of the disposition to the satisfaction of obligations secured by the security interest or other lien; and

(3) is not obligated to account to or pay the holder of the security interest or other lien for any surplus.

As amended in 2000.

§ 9–616. Explanation of Calculation of Surplus or Deficiency.

(a) In this section:

(1) "Explanation" means a writing that:

(A) states the amount of the surplus or deficiency;

(B) provides an explanation in accordance with subsection (c) of how the secured party calculated the surplus or deficiency;

(C) states, if applicable, that future debits, credits, charges, including additional credit service charges or interest, rebates, and expenses may affect the amount of the surplus or deficiency; and

(D) provides a telephone number or mailing address from which additional information concerning the transaction is available.

(2) "Request" means a record:

(A) authenticated by a debtor or consumer obligor;

(B) requesting that the recipient provide an explanation; and

(C) sent after disposition of the collateral under Section 9–610.

(b) In a consumer-goods transaction in which the debtor is entitled to a surplus or a consumer obligor is liable for a deficiency under Section 9–615, the secured party shall:

(1) send an explanation to the debtor or consumer obligor, as applicable, after the disposition and:

(A) before or when the secured party accounts to the debtor and pays any surplus or first makes written demand on the consumer obligor after the disposition for payment of the deficiency; and

(B) within 14 days after receipt of a request; or

(2) in the case of a consumer obligor who is liable for a deficiency, within 14 days after receipt of a request, send to the consumer obligor a record waiving the secured party's right to a deficiency.

(c) To comply with subsection (a)(1)(B), a writing must provide the following information in the following order:

(1) the aggregate amount of obligations secured by the security interest under which the disposition was made, and, if the amount reflects a rebate of unearned interest or credit service charge, an indication of that fact, calculated as of a specified date:

(A) if the secured party takes or receives possession of the collateral after default, not more than 35 days before the secured party takes or receives possession; or

(B) if the secured party takes or receives possession of the collateral before default or does not take possession of the collateral, not more than 35 days before the disposition;

(2) the amount of proceeds of the disposition;

(3) the aggregate amount of the obligations after deducting the amount of proceeds;

(4) the amount, in the aggregate or by type, and types of expenses, including expenses of retaking, holding, preparing for disposition, processing, and disposing of the collateral, and attorney's fees secured by the collateral which are known to the secured party and relate to the current disposition;

(5) the amount, in the aggregate or by type, and types of credits, including rebates of interest or credit service charges, to which the obligor is known to be entitled and which are not reflected in the amount in paragraph (1); and

(6) the amount of the surplus or deficiency.

(d) A particular phrasing of the explanation is not required. An explanation complying substantially with the requirements of subsection (a) is sufficient, even if it includes minor errors that are not seriously misleading.

(e) A debtor or consumer obligor is entitled without charge to one response to a request under this section during any six-month period in which the secured party did not send to the debtor or consumer obligor an explanation pursuant to subsection (b)(1). The secured party may require payment of a charge not exceeding $25 for each additional response.

§ 9–617. Rights of Transferee of Collateral.

(a) A secured party's disposition of collateral after default:

(1) transfers to a transferee for value all of the debtor's rights in the collateral;

(2) discharges the security interest under which the disposition is made; and

(3) discharges any subordinate security interest or other subordinate lien [other than liens created under [cite acts or statutes providing for liens, if any, that are not to be discharged]].

(b) A transferee that acts in good faith takes free of the rights and interests described in subsection (a), even if the secured party fails to comply with this article or the requirements of any judicial proceeding.

(c) If a transferee does not take free of the rights and interests described in subsection (a), the transferee takes the collateral subject to:

(1) the debtor's rights in the collateral;

(2) the security interest or agricultural lien under which the disposition is made; and

(3) any other security interest or other lien.

§ 9–618. Rights and Duties of Certain Secondary Obligors.

(a) A secondary obligor acquires the rights and becomes obligated to perform the duties of the secured party after the secondary obligor:

(1) receives an assignment of a secured obligation from the secured party;

(2) receives a transfer of collateral from the secured party and agrees to accept the rights and assume the duties of the secured party; or

(3) is subrogated to the rights of a secured party with respect to collateral.

(b) An assignment, transfer, or subrogation described in subsection (a):

(1) is not a disposition of collateral under Section 9–610; and

(2) relieves the secured party of further duties under this article.

§ 9–619. Transfer of Record or Legal Title.

(a) In this section, "transfer statement" means a record authenticated by a secured party stating:

(1) that the debtor has defaulted in connection with an obligation secured by specified collateral;

(2) that the secured party has exercised its post-default remedies with respect to the collateral;

(3) that, by reason of the exercise, a transferee has acquired the rights of the debtor in the collateral; and

(4) the name and mailing address of the secured party, debtor, and transferee.

(b) A transfer statement entitles the transferee to the transfer of record of all rights of the debtor in the collateral specified in the statement in any official filing, recording, registration, or certificate-of-title system covering the collateral. If a transfer statement is presented with the applicable fee and request form to the official or office responsible for maintaining the system, the official or office shall:

(1) accept the transfer statement;

(2) promptly amend its records to reflect the transfer; and

(3) if applicable, issue a new appropriate certificate of title in the name of the transferee.

(c) A transfer of the record or legal title to collateral to a secured party under subsection (b) or otherwise is not of itself a disposition of collateral under this article and does not of itself relieve the secured party of its duties under this article.

§ 9–620. Acceptance of Collateral in Full or Partial Satisfaction of Obligation; Compulsory Disposition of Collateral.

(a) Except as otherwise provided in subsection (g), a secured party may accept collateral in full or partial satisfaction of the obligation it secures only if:

(1) the debtor consents to the acceptance under subsection (c);

(2) the secured party does not receive, within the time set forth in subsection (d), a notification of objection to the proposal authenticated by:

(A) a person to which the secured party was required to send a proposal under Section 9–621; or

(B) any other person, other than the debtor, holding an interest in the collateral subordinate to the security interest that is the subject of the proposal;

(3) if the collateral is consumer goods, the collateral is not in the possession of the debtor when the debtor consents to the acceptance; and

(4) subsection (e) does not require the secured party to dispose of the collateral or the debtor waives the requirement pursuant to Section 9–624.

(b) A purported or apparent acceptance of collateral under this section is ineffective unless:

(1) the secured party consents to the acceptance in an authenticated record or sends a proposal to the debtor; and

(2) the conditions of subsection (a) are met.

(c) For purposes of this section:

(1) a debtor consents to an acceptance of collateral in partial satisfaction of the obligation it secures only if the debtor agrees to the terms of the acceptance in a record authenticated after default; and

(2) a debtor consents to an acceptance of collateral in full satisfaction of the obligation it secures only if the debtor agrees to the terms of the acceptance in a record authenticated after default or the secured party:

(A) sends to the debtor after default a proposal that is unconditional or subject only to a condition that collateral not in the possession of the secured party be preserved or maintained;

(B) in the proposal, proposes to accept collateral in full satisfaction of the obligation it secures; and

(C) does not receive a notification of objection authenticated by the debtor within 20 days after the proposal is sent.

(d) To be effective under subsection (a)(2), a notification of objection must be received by the secured party:

(1) in the case of a person to which the proposal was sent pursuant to Section 9–621, within 20 days after notification was sent to that person; and

(2) in other cases:

(A) within 20 days after the last notification was sent pursuant to Section 9–621; or

(B) if a notification was not sent, before the debtor consents to the acceptance under subsection (c).

(e) A secured party that has taken possession of collateral shall dispose of the collateral pursuant to Section 9–610 within the time specified in subsection (f) if:

(1) 60 percent of the cash price has been paid in the case of a purchase-money security interest in consumer goods; or

(2) 60 percent of the principal amount of the obligation secured has been paid in the case of a non-purchase-money security interest in consumer goods.

(f) To comply with subsection (e), the secured party shall dispose of the collateral:

(1) within 90 days after taking possession; or

(2) within any longer period to which the debtor and all secondary obligors have agreed in an agreement to that effect entered into and authenticated after default.

(g) In a consumer transaction, a secured party may not accept collateral in partial satisfaction of the obligation it secures.

§ 9–621. Notification of Proposal to Accept Collateral.

(a) A secured party that desires to accept collateral in full or partial satisfaction of the obligation it secures shall send its proposal to:

(1) any person from which the secured party has received, before the debtor consented to the acceptance, an authenticated notification of a claim of an interest in the collateral;

(2) any other secured party or lienholder that, 10 days before the debtor consented to the acceptance, held a security interest in or other lien on the collateral perfected by the filing of a financing statement that:

(A) identified the collateral;

(B) was indexed under the debtor's name as of that date; and

(C) was filed in the office or offices in which to file a financing statement against the debtor covering the collateral as of that date; and

(3) any other secured party that, 10 days before the debtor consented to the acceptance, held a security interest in the collateral perfected by compliance with a statute, regulation, or treaty described in Section 9–311(a).

(b) A secured party that desires to accept collateral in partial satisfaction of the obligation it secures shall send its proposal to any secondary obligor in addition to the persons described in subsection (a).

§ 9–622. Effect of Acceptance of Collateral.

(a) A secured party's acceptance of collateral in full or partial satisfaction of the obligation it secures:

(1) discharges the obligation to the extent consented to by the debtor;

(2) transfers to the secured party all of a debtor's rights in the collateral;

(3) discharges the security interest or agricultural lien that is the subject of the debtor's consent and any subordinate security interest or other subordinate lien; and

(4) terminates any other subordinate interest.

(b) A subordinate interest is discharged or terminated under subsection (a), even if the secured party fails to comply with this article.

§ 9–623. Right to Redeem Collateral.

(a) A debtor, any secondary obligor, or any other secured party or lienholder may redeem collateral.

(b) To redeem collateral, a person shall tender:

(1) fulfillment of all obligations secured by the collateral; and

(2) the reasonable expenses and attorney's fees described in Section 9–615(a)(1).

(c) A redemption may occur at any time before a secured party:

(1) has collected collateral under Section 9–607;

(2) has disposed of collateral or entered into a contract for its disposition under Section 9–610; or

(3) has accepted collateral in full or partial satisfaction of the obligation it secures under Section 9–622.

§ 9–624.   Waiver.

(a) A debtor or secondary obligor may waive the right to notification of disposition of collateral under Section 9–611 only by an agreement to that effect entered into and authenticated after default.

(b) A debtor may waive the right to require disposition of collateral under Section 9–620(e) only by an agreement to that effect entered into and authenticated after default.

(c) Except in a consumer-goods transaction, a debtor or secondary obligor may waive the right to redeem collateral under Section 9–623 only by an agreement to that effect entered into and authenticated after default.

[Subpart 2.   Noncompliance with Article]

§ 9–625.   Remedies for Secured Party's Failure to Comply with Article.

(a) If it is established that a secured party is not proceeding in accordance with this article, a court may order or restrain collection, enforcement, or disposition of collateral on appropriate terms and conditions.

(b) Subject to subsections (c), (d), and (f), a person is liable for damages in the amount of any loss caused by a failure to comply with this article. Loss caused by a failure to comply may include loss resulting from the debtor's inability to obtain, or increased costs of, alternative financing.

(c) Except as otherwise provided in Section 9–628:

(1) a person that, at the time of the failure, was a debtor, was an obligor, or held a security interest in or other lien on the collateral may recover damages under subsection (b) for its loss; and

(2) if the collateral is consumer goods, a person that was a debtor or a secondary obligor at the time a secured party failed to comply with this part may recover for that failure in any event an amount not less than the credit service charge plus 10 percent of the principal amount of the obligation or the time-price differential plus 10 percent of the cash price.

(d) A debtor whose deficiency is eliminated under Section 9–626 may recover damages for the loss of any surplus. However, a debtor or secondary obligor whose deficiency is eliminated or reduced under Section 9–626 may not otherwise recover under subsection (b) for noncompliance with the provisions of this part relating to collection, enforcement, disposition, or acceptance.

(e) In addition to any damages recoverable under subsection (b), the debtor, consumer obligor, or person named as a debtor in a filed record, as applicable, may recover $500 in each case from a person that:

(1) fails to comply with Section 9–208;

(2) fails to comply with Section 9–209;

(3) files a record that the person is not entitled to file under Section 9–509(a);

(4) fails to cause the secured party of record to file or send a termination statement as required by Section 9–513(a) or (c);

(5) fails to comply with Section 9–616(b)(1) and whose failure is part of a pattern, or consistent with a practice, of noncompliance; or

(6) fails to comply with Section 9–616(b)(2).

(f) A debtor or consumer obligor may recover damages under subsection (b) and, in addition, $500 in each case from a person that, without reasonable cause, fails to comply with a request under Section 9–210. A recipient of a request under Section 9–210 which never claimed an interest in the collateral or obligations that are the subject of a request under that section has a reasonable excuse for failure to comply with the request within the meaning of this subsection.

(g) If a secured party fails to comply with a request regarding a list of collateral or a statement of account under Section 9–210, the secured party may claim a security interest only as shown in the list or statement included in the request as against a person that is reasonably misled by the failure.

As amended in 2000.

§ 9–626.   Action in Which Deficiency or Surplus Is in Issue.

(a) In an action arising from a transaction, other than a consumer transaction, in which the amount of a deficiency or surplus is in issue, the following rules apply:

(1) A secured party need not prove compliance with the provisions of this part relating to collection, enforcement, disposition, or acceptance unless the debtor or a secondary obligor places the secured party's compliance in issue.

(2) If the secured party's compliance is placed in issue, the secured party has the burden of establishing that the collection, enforcement, disposition, or acceptance was conducted in accordance with this part.

(3) Except as otherwise provided in Section 9–628, if a secured party fails to prove that the collection, enforcement, disposition, or acceptance was conducted in accordance with the provisions of this part relating to collection, enforcement, disposition, or acceptance, the liability of a debtor or a secondary obligor for a deficiency is limited to an amount by which the sum of the secured obligation, expenses, and attorney's fees exceeds the greater of:

(A) the proceeds of the collection, enforcement, disposition, or acceptance; or

(B) the amount of proceeds that would have been realized had the noncomplying secured party proceeded in accordance with the provisions of this part relating to collection, enforcement, disposition, or acceptance.

(4) For purposes of paragraph (3)(B), the amount of proceeds that would have been realized is equal to the sum of the secured obligation, expenses, and attorney's fees unless the secured party proves that the amount is less than that sum.

(5) If a deficiency or surplus is calculated under Section 9–615(f), the debtor or obligor has the burden of establishing that the

amount of proceeds of the disposition is significantly below the range of prices that a complying disposition to a person other than the secured party, a person related to the secured party, or a secondary obligor would have brought.

(b) The limitation of the rules in subsection (a) to transactions other than consumer transactions is intended to leave to the court the determination of the proper rules in consumer transactions. The court may not infer from that limitation the nature of the proper rule in consumer transactions and may continue to apply established approaches.

§ 9–627. Determination of Whether Conduct Was Commercially Reasonable.

(a) The fact that a greater amount could have been obtained by a collection, enforcement, disposition, or acceptance at a different time or in a different method from that selected by the secured party is not of itself sufficient to preclude the secured party from establishing that the collection, enforcement, disposition, or acceptance was made in a commercially reasonable manner.

(b) A disposition of collateral is made in a commercially reasonable manner if the disposition is made:

(1) in the usual manner on any recognized market;

(2) at the price current in any recognized market at the time of the disposition; or

(3) otherwise in conformity with reasonable commercial practices among dealers in the type of property that was the subject of the disposition.

(c) A collection, enforcement, disposition, or acceptance is commercially reasonable if it has been approved:

(1) in a judicial proceeding;

(2) by a bona fide creditors' committee;

(3) by a representative of creditors; or

(4) by an assignee for the benefit of creditors.

(d) Approval under subsection (c) need not be obtained, and lack of approval does not mean that the collection, enforcement, disposition, or acceptance is not commercially reasonable.

§ 9–628. Nonliability and Limitation on Liability of Secured Party; Liability of Secondary Obligor.

(a) Unless a secured party knows that a person is a debtor or obligor, knows the identity of the person, and knows how to communicate with the person:

(1) the secured party is not liable to the person, or to a secured party or lienholder that has filed a financing statement against the person, for failure to comply with this article; and

(2) the secured party's failure to comply with this article does not affect the liability of the person for a deficiency.

(b) A secured party is not liable because of its status as secured party:

(1) to a person that is a debtor or obligor, unless the secured party knows:

(A) that the person is a debtor or obligor;

(B) the identity of the person; and

(C) how to communicate with the person; or

(2) to a secured party or lienholder that has filed a financing statement against a person, unless the secured party knows:

(A) that the person is a debtor; and

(B) the identity of the person.

(c) A secured party is not liable to any person, and a person's liability for a deficiency is not affected, because of any act or omission arising out of the secured party's reasonable belief that a transaction is not a consumer-goods transaction or a consumer transaction or that goods are not consumer goods, if the secured party's belief is based on its reasonable reliance on:

(1) a debtor's representation concerning the purpose for which collateral was to be used, acquired, or held; or

(2) an obligor's representation concerning the purpose for which a secured obligation was incurred.

(d) A secured party is not liable to any person under Section 9–625(c)(2) for its failure to comply with Section 9–616.

(e) A secured party is not liable under Section 9–625(c)(2) more than once with respect to any one secured obligation.

Part 7 Transition

§ 9–701. Effective Date.

This [Act] takes effect on July 1, 2001.

§ 9–702. Savings Clause.

(a) Except as otherwise provided in this part, this [Act] applies to a transaction or lien within its scope, even if the transaction or lien was entered into or created before this [Act] takes effect.

(b) Except as otherwise provided in subsection (c) and Sections 9–703 through 9–709:

(1) transactions and liens that were not governed by [former Article 9], were validly entered into or created before this [Act] takes effect, and would be subject to this [Act] if they had been entered into or created after this [Act] takes effect, and the rights, duties, and interests flowing from those transactions and liens remain valid after this [Act] takes effect; and

(2) the transactions and liens may be terminated, completed, consummated, and enforced as required or permitted by this [Act] or by the law that otherwise would apply if this [Act] had not taken effect.

(c) This [Act] does not affect an action, case, or proceeding commenced before this [Act] takes effect.

As amended in 2000.

§ 9–703. Security Interest Perfected before Effective Date.

(a) A security interest that is enforceable immediately before this [Act] takes effect and would have priority over the rights of a person that becomes a lien creditor at that time is a perfected security interest under this [Act] if, when this [Act] takes effect, the applicable requirements for enforceability and perfection under this [Act] are satisfied without further action.

(b) Except as otherwise provided in Section 9–705, if, immediately before this [Act] takes effect, a security interest is enforceable and would have priority over the rights of a person that becomes a lien creditor at that time, but the applicable requirements for enforceability or perfection under this [Act] are not satisfied when this [Act] takes effect, the security interest:

(1) is a perfected security interest for one year after this [Act] takes effect;

(2) remains enforceable thereafter only if the security interest becomes enforceable under Section 9–203 before the year expires; and

(3) remains perfected thereafter only if the applicable requirements for perfection under this [Act] are satisfied before the year expires.

§ 9–704.   Security Interest Unperfected before Effective Date.

A security interest that is enforceable immediately before this [Act] takes effect but which would be subordinate to the rights of a person that becomes a lien creditor at that time:

(1) remains an enforceable security interest for one year after this [Act] takes effect;

(2) remains enforceable thereafter if the security interest becomes enforceable under Section 9–203 when this [Act] takes effect or within one year thereafter; and

(3) becomes perfected:

(A) without further action, when this [Act] takes effect if the applicable requirements for perfection under this [Act] are satisfied before or at that time; or

(B) when the applicable requirements for perfection are satisfied if the requirements are satisfied after that time.

§ 9–705.   Effectiveness of Action Taken before Effective Date.

(a) If action, other than the filing of a financing statement, is taken before this [Act] takes effect and the action would have resulted in priority of a security interest over the rights of a person that becomes a lien creditor had the security interest become enforceable before this [Act] takes effect, the action is effective to perfect a security interest that attaches under this [Act] within one year after this [Act] takes effect. An attached security interest becomes unperfected one year after this [Act] takes effect unless the security interest becomes a perfected security interest under this [Act] before the expiration of that period.

(b) The filing of a financing statement before this [Act] takes effect is effective to perfect a security interest to the extent the filing would satisfy the applicable requirements for perfection under this [Act].

(c) This [Act] does not render ineffective an effective financing statement that, before this [Act] takes effect, is filed and satisfies the applicable requirements for perfection under the law of the jurisdiction governing perfection as provided in [former Section 9–103]. However, except as otherwise provided in subsections (d) and (e) and Section 9–706, the financing statement ceases to be effective at the earlier of:

(1) the time the financing statement would have ceased to be effective under the law of the jurisdiction in which it is filed; or

(2) June 30, 2006.

(d) The filing of a continuation statement after this [Act] takes effect does not continue the effectiveness of the financing statement filed before this [Act] takes effect. However, upon the timely filing of a continuation statement after this [Act] takes effect and in accordance with the law of the jurisdiction governing perfection as provided in Part 3, the effectiveness of a financing statement filed in the same office in that jurisdiction before this [Act] takes effect continues for the period provided by the law of that jurisdiction.

(e) Subsection (c)(2) applies to a financing statement that, before this [Act] takes effect, is filed against a transmitting utility and satisfies the applicable requirements for perfection under the law of the jurisdiction governing perfection as provided in [former Section 9–103] only to the extent that Part 3 provides that the law of a jurisdiction other than the jurisdiction in which the financing statement is filed governs perfection of a security interest in collateral covered by the financing statement.

(f) A financing statement that includes a financing statement filed before this [Act] takes effect and a continuation statement filed after this [Act] takes effect is effective only to the extent that it satisfies the requirements of Part 5 for an initial financing statement.

§ 9–706.   When Initial Financing Statement Suffices to Continue Effectiveness of Financing Statement.

(a) The filing of an initial financing statement in the office specified in Section 9–501 continues the effectiveness of a financing statement filed before this [Act] takes effect if:

(1) the filing of an initial financing statement in that office would be effective to perfect a security interest under this [Act];

(2) the pre-effective-date financing statement was filed in an office in another State or another office in this State; and

(3) the initial financing statement satisfies subsection (c).

(b) The filing of an initial financing statement under subsection (a) continues the effectiveness of the pre-effective-date financing statement:

(1) if the initial financing statement is filed before this [Act] takes effect, for the period provided in [former Section 9–403] with respect to a financing statement; and

(2) if the initial financing statement is filed after this [Act] takes effect, for the period provided in Section 9–515 with respect to an initial financing statement.

(c) To be effective for purposes of subsection (a), an initial financing statement must:

(1) satisfy the requirements of Part 5 for an initial financing statement;

(2) identify the pre-effective-date financing statement by indicating the office in which the financing statement was filed and providing the dates of filing and file numbers, if any, of the financing statement and of the most recent continuation statement filed with respect to the financing statement; and

(3) indicate that the pre-effective-date financing statement remains effective.

§ 9–707.   Amendment of Pre-Effective-Date Financing Statement.

(a) In this section, "Pre-effective-date financing statement" means a financing statement filed before this [Act] takes effect.

(b) After this [Act] takes effect, a person may add or delete collateral covered by, continue or terminate the effectiveness of, or otherwise amend the information provided in, a pre-effective-date financing statement only in accordance with the law of the jurisdiction governing perfection as provided in Part 3. However, the effectiveness of a pre-effective-date financing statement also may be terminated in accordance with the law of the jurisdiction in which the financing statement is filed.

(c) Except as otherwise provided in subsection (d), if the law of this State governs perfection of a security interest, the information in a pre-effective-date financing statement may be amended after this [Act] takes effect only if:

   (1) the pre-effective-date financing statement and an amendment are filed in the office specified in Section 9–501;

   (2) an amendment is filed in the office specified in Section 9–501 concurrently with, or after the filing in that office of, an initial financing statement that satisfies Section 9–706(c); or

   (3) an initial financing statement that provides the information as amended and satisfies Section 9–706(c) is filed in the office specified in Section 9–501.

(d) If the law of this State governs perfection of a security interest, the effectiveness of a pre-effective-date financing statement may be continued only under Section 9–705(d) and (f) or 9–706.

(e) Whether or not the law of this State governs perfection of a security interest, the effectiveness of a pre-effective-date financing statement filed in this State may be terminated after this [Act] takes effect by filing a termination statement in the office in which the pre-effective-date financing statement is filed, unless an initial financing statement that satisfies Section 9–706(c) has been filed in the office specified by the law of the jurisdiction governing perfection as provided in Part 3 as the office in which to file a financing statement.

As amended in 2000.

§ 9–708. Persons Entitled to File Initial Financing Statement or Continuation Statement.

A person may file an initial financing statement or a continuation statement under this part if:

   (1) the secured party of record authorizes the filing; and

   (2) the filing is necessary under this part:

      (A) to continue the effectiveness of a financing statement filed before this [Act] takes effect; or

      (B) to perfect or continue the perfection of a security interest.

As amended in 2000.

§ 9–709. Priority.

(a) This [Act] determines the priority of conflicting claims to collateral. However, if the relative priorities of the claims were established before this [Act] takes effect, [former Article 9] determines priority.

(b) For purposes of Section 9–322(a), the priority of a security interest that becomes enforceable under Section 9–203 of this [Act] dates from the time this [Act] takes effect if the security interest is perfected under this [Act] by the filing of a financing statement before this [Act] takes effect which would not have been effective to perfect the security interest under [former Article 9]. This subsection does not apply to conflicting security interests each of which is perfected by the filing of such a financing statement.

As amended in 2000.

The Sarbanes-Oxley Act of 2002 (Excerpts and Explanatory Comments)

Note: The author's explanatory comments appear in italics following the excerpt from each section.

Section 302
Corporate responsibility for financial reports[1]

(a) Regulations required

The Commission shall, by rule, require, for each company filing periodic reports under section 13(a) or 15(d) of the Securities Exchange Act of 1934 (15 U.S.C. 78m, 78o(d)), that the principal executive officer or officers and the principal financial officer or officers, or persons performing similar functions, certify in each annual or quarterly report filed or submitted under either such section of such Act that—

(1) the signing officer has reviewed the report;

(2) based on the officer's knowledge, the report does not contain any untrue statement of a material fact or omit to state a material fact necessary in order to make the statements made, in light of the circumstances under which such statements were made, not misleading;

(3) based on such officer's knowledge, the financial statements, and other financial information included in the report, fairly present in all material respects the financial condition and results of operations of the issuer as of, and for, the periods presented in the report;

(4) the signing officers—

(A) are responsible for establishing and maintaining internal controls;

(B) have designed such internal controls to ensure that material information relating to the issuer and its consolidated subsidiaries is made known to such officers by others within those entities, particularly during the period in which the periodic reports are being prepared;

(C) have evaluated the effectiveness of the issuer's internal controls as of a date within 90 days prior to the report; and

(D) have presented in the report their conclusions about the effectiveness of their internal controls based on their evaluation as of that date;

(5) the signing officers have disclosed to the issuer's auditors and the audit committee of the board of directors (or persons fulfilling the equivalent function)—

---

1. This section of the Sarbanes-Oxley Act is codified at 15 U.S.C. Section 7241.

(A) all significant deficiencies in the design or operation of internal controls which could adversely affect the issuer's ability to record, process, summarize, and report financial data and have identified for the issuer's auditors any material weaknesses in internal controls; and

(B) any fraud, whether or not material, that involves management or other employees who have a significant role in the issuer's internal controls; and

(6) the signing officers have indicated in the report whether or not there were significant changes in internal controls or in other factors that could significantly affect internal controls subsequent to the date of their evaluation, including any corrective actions with regard to significant deficiencies and material weaknesses.

(b) Foreign reincorporations have no effect

Nothing in this section shall be interpreted or applied in any way to allow any issuer to lessen the legal force of the statement required under this section, by an issuer having reincorporated or having engaged in any other transaction that resulted in the transfer of the corporate domicile or offices of the issuer from inside the United States to outside of the United States.

(c) Deadline

The rules required by subsection (a) of this section shall be effective not later than 30 days after July 30, 2002.

* * * *

Explanatory Comments:

Section 302 requires the chief executive officer (CEO) and chief financial officer (CFO) of each public company to certify that they have reviewed the company's quarterly and annual reports to be filed with the Securities and Exchange Commission (SEC). The CEO and CFO must certify that, based on their knowledge, the reports do not contain any untrue statement of a material fact or any half-truth that would make the report misleading, and that the information contained in the reports fairly presents the company's financial condition.

In addition, this section also requires the CEO and CFO to certify that they have created and designed an internal control system for their company and have recently evaluated that system to ensure that it is effectively providing them with relevant and accurate financial information. If the signing officers have found any significant deficiencies or weaknesses in the company's system or have discovered any evidence of fraud, they must have reported the situation, and any corrective actions they have taken, to the auditors and the audit committee.

Section 306
Insider trades during pension fund blackout periods[2]

(a) Prohibition of insider trading during pension fund blackout periods

(1) In general

Except to the extent otherwise provided by rule of the Commission pursuant to paragraph (3), it shall be unlawful for any director or executive officer of an issuer of any equity security (other than an exempted security), directly or indirectly, to purchase, sell, or otherwise acquire or transfer any equity security of the issuer (other than an exempted security) during any blackout period with respect to such equity security if such director or officer acquires such equity security in connection with his or her service or employment as a director or executive officer.

(2) Remedy

(A) In general

Any profit realized by a director or executive officer referred to in paragraph (1) from any purchase, sale, or other acquisition or transfer in violation of this subsection shall inure to and be recoverable by the issuer, irrespective of any intention on the part of such director or executive officer in entering into the transaction.

(B) Actions to recover profits

An action to recover profits in accordance with this subsection may be instituted at law or in equity in any court of competent jurisdiction by the issuer, or by the owner of any security of the issuer in the name and in behalf of the issuer if the issuer fails or refuses to bring such action within 60 days after the date of request, or fails diligently to prosecute the action thereafter, except that no such suit shall be brought more than 2 years after the date on which such profit was realized.

(3) Rulemaking authorized

The Commission shall, in consultation with the Secretary of Labor, issue rules to clarify the application of this subsection and to prevent evasion thereof. Such rules shall provide for the application of the requirements of paragraph (1) with respect to entities treated as a single employer with respect to an issuer under section 414(b), (c), (m), or (o) of Title 26 to the extent necessary to clarify the application of such requirements and to prevent evasion thereof. Such rules may also provide for appropriate exceptions from the requirements of this subsection, including exceptions for purchases pursuant to an automatic dividend reinvestment program or purchases or sales made pursuant to an advance election.

(4) Blackout period

For purposes of this subsection, the term "blackout period", with respect to the equity securities of any issuer—

(A) means any period of more than 3 consecutive business days during which the ability of not fewer than 50 percent of the participants or beneficiaries under all individual account plans maintained by the issuer to purchase, sell, or otherwise acquire or transfer an interest in any equity of such issuer held in such an individual account plan is temporarily suspended by the issuer or by a fiduciary of the plan; and

2. Codified at 15 U.S.C. Section 7244.

(B) does not include, under regulations which shall be prescribed by the Commission—

(i) a regularly scheduled period in which the participants and beneficiaries may not purchase, sell, or otherwise acquire or transfer an interest in any equity of such issuer, if such period is—

(I) incorporated into the individual account plan; and

(II) timely disclosed to employees before becoming participants under the individual account plan or as a subsequent amendment to the plan; or

(ii) any suspension described in subparagraph (A) that is imposed solely in connection with persons becoming participants or beneficiaries, or ceasing to be participants or beneficiaries, in an individual account plan by reason of a corporate merger, acquisition, divestiture, or similar transaction involving the plan or plan sponsor.

(5) Individual account plan

For purposes of this subsection, the term "individual account plan" has the meaning provided in section 1002(34) of Title 29, except that such term shall not include a one-participant retirement plan (within the meaning of section 1021(i)(8)(B) of Title 29).

(6) Notice to directors, executive officers, and the Commission

In any case in which a director or executive officer is subject to the requirements of this subsection in connection with a blackout period (as defined in paragraph (4)) with respect to any equity securities, the issuer of such equity securities shall timely notify such director or officer and the Securities and Exchange Commission of such blackout period.

* * * *

Explanatory Comments:

Corporate pension funds typically prohibit employees from trading shares of the corporation during periods when the pension fund is undergoing significant change. Prior to 2002, however, these blackout periods did not affect the corporation's executives, who frequently received shares of the corporate stock as part of their compensation. During the collapse of Enron, for example, its pension plan was scheduled to change administrators at a time when Enron's stock price was falling. Enron's employees therefore could not sell their shares while the price was dropping, but its executives could and did sell their stock, consequently avoiding some of the losses. Section 306 was Congress's solution to the basic unfairness of this situation. This section of the act required the SEC to issue rules that prohibit any director or executive officer from trading during pension fund blackout periods. (The SEC later issued these rules, entitled Regulation Blackout Trading Restriction, or Reg BTR.) Section 306 also provided shareholders with a right to file a shareholder's derivative suit against officers and directors who have profited from trading during these blackout periods (provided that the corporation has failed to bring a suit). The officer or director can be forced to return to the corporation any profits received, regardless of whether the director or officer acted with bad intent.

Section 402
Periodical and other reports[3]

* * * *

3. This section of the Sarbanes-Oxley Act amended some of the provisions of the 1934 Securities Exchange Act and added the paragraphs reproduced here at 15 U.S.C. Section 78m.

(i) Accuracy of financial reports

Each financial report that contains financial statements, and that is required to be prepared in accordance with (or reconciled to) generally accepted accounting principles under this chapter and filed with the Commission shall reflect all material correcting adjustments that have been identified by a registered public accounting firm in accordance with generally accepted accounting principles and the rules and regulations of the Commission.

(j) Off-balance sheet transactions

Not later than 180 days after July 30, 2002, the Commission shall issue final rules providing that each annual and quarterly financial report required to be filed with the Commission shall disclose all material off-balance sheet transactions, arrangements, obligations (including contingent obligations), and other relationships of the issuer with unconsolidated entities or other persons, that may have a material current or future effect on financial condition, changes in financial condition, results of operations, liquidity, capital expenditures, capital resources, or significant components of revenues or expenses.

(k) Prohibition on personal loans to executives

(1) In general

It shall be unlawful for any issuer (as defined in section 7201 of this title), directly or indirectly, including through any subsidiary, to extend or maintain credit, to arrange for the extension of credit, or to renew an extension of credit, in the form of a personal loan to or for any director or executive officer (or equivalent thereof) of that issuer. An extension of credit maintained by the issuer on July 30, 2002, shall not be subject to the provisions of this subsection, provided that there is no material modification to any term of any such extension of credit or any renewal of any such extension of credit on or after July 30, 2002.

(2) Limitation

Paragraph (1) does not preclude any home improvement and manufactured home loans (as that term is defined in section 1464 of Title 12), consumer credit (as defined in section 1602 of this title), or any extension of credit under an open end credit plan (as defined in section 1602 of this title), or a charge card (as defined in section 1637(c)(4)(e) of this title), or any extension of credit by a broker or dealer registered under section 78o of this title to an employee of that broker or dealer to buy, trade, or carry securities, that is permitted under rules or regulations of the Board of Governors of the Federal Reserve System pursuant to section 78g of this title (other than an extension of credit that would be used to purchase the stock of that issuer), that is—

(A) made or provided in the ordinary course of the consumer credit business of such issuer;

(B) of a type that is generally made available by such issuer to the public; and

(C) made by such issuer on market terms, or terms that are no more favorable than those offered by the issuer to the general public for such extensions of credit.

(3) Rule of construction for certain loans

Paragraph (1) does not apply to any loan made or maintained by an insured depository institution (as defined in section 1813 of Title 12), if the loan is subject to the insider lending restrictions of section 375b of Title 12.

(l) Real time issuer disclosures

Each issuer reporting under subsection (a) of this section or section 78o(d) of this title shall disclose to the public on a rapid and current basis such additional information concerning material changes in the financial condition or operations of the issuer, in plain English, which may include trend and qualitative information and graphic presentations, as the Commission determines, by rule, is necessary or useful for the protection of investors and in the public interest.

Explanatory Comments:

Corporate executives during the Enron era typically received extremely large salaries, significant bonuses, and abundant stock options, even when the companies for which they worked were suffering. Executives were also routinely given personal loans from corporate funds, many of which were never paid back. The average large company during that period loaned almost $1 million a year to top executives, and some companies, including Tyco International and Adelphia Communications Corporation, loaned hundreds of millions of dollars to their executives every year. Section 402 amended the 1934 Securities Exchange Act to prohibit public companies from making personal loans to executive officers and directors. There are a few exceptions to this prohibition, such as home-improvement loans made in the ordinary course of business. Note also that while loans are forbidden, outright gifts are not. A corporation is free to give gifts to its executives, including cash, provided that these gifts are disclosed on its financial reports. The idea is that corporate directors will be deterred from making substantial gifts to their executives by the disclosure requirement—particularly if the corporation's financial condition is questionable—because making such gifts could be perceived as abusing their authority.

Section 403
Directors, officers, and principal stockholders[4]

(a) Disclosures required

(1) Directors, officers, and principal stockholders required to file

Every person who is directly or indirectly the beneficial owner of more than 10 percent of any class of any equity security (other than an exempted security) which is registered pursuant to section 78l of this title, or who is a director or an officer of the issuer of such security, shall file the statements required by this subsection with the Commission (and, if such security is registered on a national securities exchange, also with the exchange).

(2) Time of filing

The statements required by this subsection shall be filed—

(A) at the time of the registration of such security on a national securities exchange or by the effective date of a registration statement filed pursuant to section 78l(g) of this title;

(B) within 10 days after he or she becomes such beneficial owner, director, or officer;

(C) if there has been a change in such ownership, or if such person shall have purchased or sold a security-based swap agreement (as defined in section 206(b) of the Gramm-Leach-Bliley Act (15 U.S.C. 78c note)) involving such equity security, before the end of the second business day following the day on which the subject transaction has been executed, or at such other time as the Commission shall establish, by rule, in any case in which the Commission determines that such 2-day period is not feasible.

---

4. This section of the Sarbanes-Oxley Act amended the disclosure provisions of the 1934 Securities Exchange Act, at 15 U.S.C. Section 78p.

(3) Contents of statements

A statement filed—

(A) under subparagraph (A) or (B) of paragraph (2) shall contain a statement of the amount of all equity securities of such issuer of which the filing person is the beneficial owner; and

(B) under subparagraph (C) of such paragraph shall indicate ownership by the filing person at the date of filing, any such changes in such ownership, and such purchases and sales of the security-based swap agreements as have occurred since the most recent such filing under such subparagraph.

(4) Electronic filing and availability

Beginning not later than 1 year after July 30, 2002—

(A) a statement filed under subparagraph (C) of paragraph (2) shall be filed electronically;

(B) the Commission shall provide each such statement on a publicly accessible Internet site not later than the end of the business day following that filing; and

(C) the issuer (if the issuer maintains a corporate website) shall provide that statement on that corporate website, not later than the end of the business day following that filing.

* * * *

Explanatory Comments:

This section dramatically shortens the time period provided in the Securities Exchange Act of 1934 for disclosing transactions by insiders. The prior law stated that most transactions had to be reported within ten days of the beginning of the following month, although certain transactions did not have to be reported until the following fiscal year (within the first forty-five days). Because some of the insider trading that occurred during the Enron fiasco did not have to be disclosed (and was therefore not discovered) until long after the transactions, Congress added this section to reduce the time period for making disclosures. Under Section 403, most transactions by insiders must be electronically filed with the SEC within two business days. Also, any company that maintains a Web site must post these SEC filings on its site by the end of the next business day. Congress enacted this section in the belief that if insiders are required to file reports of their transactions promptly with the SEC, companies will do more to police themselves and prevent insider trading.

Section 404
Management assessment of internal controls[5]

(a) Rules required

The Commission shall prescribe rules requiring each annual report required by section 78m(a) or 78o(d) of this title to contain an internal control report, which shall—

(1) state the responsibility of management for establishing and maintaining an adequate internal control structure and procedures for financial reporting; and

(2) contain an assessment, as of the end of the most recent fiscal year of the issuer, of the effectiveness of the internal control structure and procedures of the issuer for financial reporting.

(b) Internal control evaluation and reporting

With respect to the internal control assessment required by subsection (a) of this section, each registered public accounting firm that prepares or issues the audit report for the issuer shall attest to, and report on,

the assessment made by the management of the issuer. An attestation made under this subsection shall be made in accordance with standards for attestation engagements issued or adopted by the Board. Any such attestation shall not be the subject of a separate engagement.

* * * *

Explanatory Comments:

This section was enacted to prevent corporate executives from claiming they were ignorant of significant errors in their companies' financial reports. For instance, several CEOs testified before Congress that they simply had no idea that the corporations' financial statements were off by billions of dollars. Congress therefore passed Section 404, which requires each annual report to contain a description and assessment of the company's internal control structure and financial reporting procedures. The section also requires that an audit be conducted of the internal control assessment, as well as the financial statements contained in the report. This section goes hand in hand with Section 302 (which, as discussed previously, requires various certifications attesting to the accuracy of the information in financial reports).

Section 404 has been one of the more controversial and expensive provisions in the Sarbanes-Oxley Act because it requires companies to assess their own internal financial controls to make sure that their financial statements are reliable and accurate. A corporation might need to set up a disclosure committee and a coordinator, establish codes of conduct for accounting and financial personnel, create documentation procedures, provide training, and outline the individuals who are responsible for performing each of the procedures. Companies that were already well managed have not experienced substantial difficulty complying with this section. Other companies, however, have spent millions of dollars setting up, documenting, and evaluating their internal financial control systems. Although initially creating the internal financial control system is a one-time-only expense, the costs of maintaining and evaluating it are ongoing. Some corporations that spent considerable sums complying with Section 404 have been able to offset these costs by discovering and correcting inefficiencies or frauds within their systems. Nevertheless, it is unlikely that any corporation will find compliance with this section to be inexpensive.

Section 802(a)
Destruction, alteration, or falsification of records in Federal investigations and bankruptcy[6]

Whoever knowingly alters, destroys, mutilates, conceals, covers up, falsifies, or makes a false entry in any record, document, or tangible object with the intent to impede, obstruct, or influence the investigation or proper administration of any matter within the jurisdiction of any department or agency of the United States or any case filed under title 11, or in relation to or contemplation of any such matter or case, shall be fined under this title, imprisoned not more than 20 years, or both.

Destruction of corporate audit records[7]

(a) (1) Any accountant who conducts an audit of an issuer of securities to which section 10A(a) of the Securities Exchange Act of 1934 (15 U.S.C. 78j-1(a)) applies, shall maintain all audit or review workpapers for a period of 5 years from the end of the fiscal period in which the audit or review was concluded.

(2) The Securities and Exchange Commission shall promulgate, within 180 days, after adequate notice and an opportunity for comment, such rules and regulations, as are reasonably necessary, relating to the retention of relevant records such as workpapers,

---

5. Codified at 15 U.S.C. Section 7262.

6. Codified at 15 U.S.C. Section 1519.

7. Codified at 15 U.S.C. Section 1520.

documents that form the basis of an audit or review, memoranda, correspondence, communications, other documents, and records (including electronic records) which are created, sent, or received in connection with an audit or review and contain conclusions, opinions, analyses, or financial data relating to such an audit or review, which is conducted by any accountant who conducts an audit of an issuer of securities to which section 10A(a) of the Securities Exchange Act of 1934 (15 U.S.C. 78j-1(a)) applies. The Commission may, from time to time, amend or supplement the rules and regulations that it is required to promulgate under this section, after adequate notice and an opportunity for comment, in order to ensure that such rules and regulations adequately comport with the purposes of this section.

(b) Whoever knowingly and willfully violates subsection (a)(1), or any rule or regulation promulgated by the Securities and Exchange Commission under subsection (a)(2), shall be fined under this title, imprisoned not more than 10 years, or both.

(c) Nothing in this section shall be deemed to diminish or relieve any person of any other duty or obligation imposed by Federal or State law or regulation to maintain, or refrain from destroying, any document.

*   *   *   *

Explanatory Comments:

Section 802(a) enacted two new statutes that punish those who alter or destroy documents. The first statute is not specifically limited to securities fraud cases. It provides that anyone who alters, destroys, or falsifies records in federal investigations or bankruptcy may be criminally prosecuted and sentenced to a fine or to up to twenty years in prison, or both. The second statute requires auditors of public companies to keep all audit or review working papers for five years but expressly allows the SEC to amend or supplement these requirements as it sees fit. The SEC has, in fact, amended this section by issuing a rule that requires auditors who audit reporting companies to retain working papers for seven years from the conclusion of the review. Section 802(a) further provides that anyone who knowingly and willfully violates this statute is subject to criminal prosecution and can be sentenced to a fine, imprisoned for up to ten years, or both if convicted.

This portion of the Sarbanes-Oxley Act implicitly recognizes that persons who are under investigation often are tempted to respond by destroying or falsifying documents that might prove their complicity in wrongdoing. The severity of the punishment should provide a strong incentive for these individuals to resist the temptation.

Section 804
Time limitations on the commencement of civil actions arising under Acts of Congress[8]

(a) Except as otherwise provided by law, a civil action arising under an Act of Congress enacted after the date of the enactment of this section may not be commenced later than 4 years after the cause of action accrues.

(b) Notwithstanding subsection (a), a private right of action that involves a claim of fraud, deceit, manipulation, or contrivance in contravention of a regulatory requirement concerning the securities laws, as defined in section 3(a)(47) of the Securities Exchange Act of 1934 (15 U.S.C. 78c(a)(47)), may be brought not later than the earlier of—

(1) 2 years after the discovery of the facts constituting the violation; or

(2) 5 years after such violation.

*   *   *   *

Explanatory Comments:

Prior to the enactment of this section, Section 10(b) of the Securities Exchange Act of 1934 had no express statute of limitations. The courts generally required plaintiffs to have filed suit within one year from the date that they should (using due diligence) have discovered that a fraud had been committed but no later than three years after the fraud occurred. Section 804 extends this period by specifying that plaintiffs must file a lawsuit within two years after they discover (or should have discovered) a fraud but no later than five years after the fraud's occurrence. This provision has prevented the courts from dismissing numerous securities fraud lawsuits.

Section 806
Civil action to protect against retaliation in fraud cases[9]

(a) Whistleblower protection for employees of publicly traded companies.—

No company with a class of securities registered under section 12 of the Securities Exchange Act of 1934 (15 U.S.C. 78l), or that is required to file reports under section 15(d) of the Securities Exchange Act of 1934 (15 U.S.C. 78o(d)), or any officer, employee, contractor, subcontractor, or agent of such company, may discharge, demote, suspend, threaten, harass, or in any other manner discriminate against an employee in the terms and conditions of employment because of any lawful act done by the employee—

(1) to provide information, cause information to be provided, or otherwise assist in an investigation regarding any conduct which the employee reasonably believes constitutes a violation of section 1341, 1343, 1344, or 1348, any rule or regulation of the Securities and Exchange Commission, or any provision of Federal law relating to fraud against shareholders, when the information or assistance is provided to or the investigation is conducted by—

    (A) a Federal regulatory or law enforcement agency;

    (B) any Member of Congress or any committee of Congress; or

    (C) a person with supervisory authority over the employee (or such other person working for the employer who has the authority to investigate, discover, or terminate misconduct); or

(2) to file, cause to be filed, testify, participate in, or otherwise assist in a proceeding filed or about to be filed (with any knowledge of the employer) relating to an alleged violation of section 1341, 1343, 1344, or 1348, any rule or regulation of the Securities and Exchange Commission, or any provision of Federal law relating to fraud against shareholders.

(b) Enforcement action.—

(1) In general.—A person who alleges discharge or other discrimination by any person in violation of subsection (a) may seek relief under subsection (c), by—

    (A) filing a complaint with the Secretary of Labor; or

    (B) if the Secretary has not issued a final decision within 180 days of the filing of the complaint and there is no showing that such delay is due to the bad faith of the claimant, bringing an action at law or equity for de novo review in the appropriate district court of the United States, which shall have jurisdiction over such an action without regard to the amount in controversy.

---

8. Codified at 28 U.S.C. Section 1658.

9. Codified at 18 U.S.C. Section 1514A.

(2) Procedure.—

(A) In general.—An action under paragraph (1)(A) shall be governed under the rules and procedures set forth in section 42121(b) of title 49, United States Code.

(B) Exception.—Notification made under section 42121(b)(1) of title 49, United States Code, shall be made to the person named in the complaint and to the employer.

(C) Burdens of proof.—An action brought under paragraph (1)(B) shall be governed by the legal burdens of proof set forth in section 42121(b) of title 49, United States Code.

(D) Statute of limitations.—An action under paragraph (1) shall be commenced not later than 90 days after the date on which the violation occurs.

(c) Remedies.—

(1) In general.—An employee prevailing in any action under subsection (b)(1) shall be entitled to all relief necessary to make the employee whole.

(2) Compensatory damages.—Relief for any action under paragraph (1) shall include—

(A) reinstatement with the same seniority status that the employee would have had, but for the discrimination;

(B) the amount of back pay, with interest; and

(C) compensation for any special damages sustained as a result of the discrimination, including litigation costs, expert witness fees, and reasonable attorney fees.

(d) Rights retained by employee.—Nothing in this section shall be deemed to diminish the rights, privileges, or remedies of any employee under any Federal or State law, or under any collective bargaining agreement.

Explanatory Comments:

Section 806 is one of several provisions that were included in the Sarbanes-Oxley Act to encourage and protect whistleblowers—that is, employees who report their employer's alleged violations of securities law to the authorities. This section applies to employees, agents, and independent contractors who work for publicly traded companies or testify about such a company during an investigation. It sets up an administrative procedure at the U.S. Department of Labor for individuals who claim that their employer retaliated against them (fired or demoted them, for example) for blowing the whistle on the employer's wrongful conduct. It also allows the award of civil damages—including back pay, reinstatement, special damages, attorneys' fees, and court costs—to employees who prove that they suffered retaliation. Since this provision was enacted, whistleblowers have filed numerous complaints with the U.S. Department of Labor under this section.

Section 807
Securities fraud[10]

Whoever knowingly executes, or attempts to execute, a scheme or artifice—

(1) to defraud any person in connection with any security of an issuer with a class of securities registered under section 12 of the Securities Exchange Act of 1934 (15 U.S.C. 78l) or that is required to file reports under section 15(d) of the Securities Exchange Act of 1934 (15 U.S.C. 78o(d)); or

(2) to obtain, by means of false or fraudulent pretenses, representations, or promises, any money or property in connection with the purchase or sale of any security of an issuer with a class of

securities registered under section 12 of the Securities Exchange Act of 1934 (15 U.S.C. 78l) or that is required to file reports under section 15(d) of the Securities Exchange Act of 1934 (15 U.S.C. 78o(d)); shall be fined under this title, or imprisoned not more than 25 years, or both.

* * * *

Explanatory Comments:

Section 807 adds a new provision to the federal criminal code that addresses securities fraud. Prior to 2002, federal securities law had already made it a crime—under Section 10(b) of the Securities Exchange Act of 1934 and SEC Rule 10b-5, both of which are discussed in Chapter 31—to intentionally defraud someone in connection with a purchase or sale of securities, but the offense was not listed in the federal criminal code. Also, paragraph 2 of Section 807 goes beyond what is prohibited under securities law by making it a crime to obtain by means of false or fraudulent pretenses any money or property from the purchase or sale of securities. This new provision allows violators to be punished by up to twenty-five years in prison, a fine, or both.

Section 906
Failure of corporate officers to certify financial reports[11]

(a) Certification of periodic financial reports.—Each periodic report containing financial statements filed by an issuer with the Securities Exchange Commission pursuant to section 13(a) or 15(d) of the Securities Exchange Act of 1934 (15 U.S.C. 78m(a) or 78o(d)) shall be accompanied by a written statement by the chief executive officer and chief financial officer (or equivalent thereof) of the issuer.

(b) Content.—The statement required under subsection (a) shall certify that the periodic report containing the financial statements fully complies with the requirements of section 13(a) or 15(d) of the Securities Exchange Act of 1934 (15 U.S.C. 78m or 78o(d)) and that information contained in the periodic report fairly presents, in all material respects, the financial condition and results of operations of the issuer.

(c) Criminal penalties.—Whoever—

(1) certifies any statement as set forth in subsections (a) and (b) of this section knowing that the periodic report accompanying the statement does not comport with all the requirements set forth in this section shall be fined not more than $1,000,000 or imprisoned not more than 10 years, or both; or

(2) willfully certifies any statement as set forth in subsections (a) and (b) of this section knowing that the periodic report accompanying the statement does not comport with all the requirements set forth in this section shall be fined not more than $5,000,000, or imprisoned not more than 20 years, or both.

Explanatory Comments:

As previously discussed, under Section 302 a corporation's CEO and CFO are required to certify that they believe the quarterly and annual reports their company files with the SEC are accurate and fairly present the company's financial condition. Section 906 adds "teeth" to these requirements by authorizing criminal penalties for those officers who intentionally certify inaccurate SEC filings. Knowing violations of the requirements are punishable by a fine of up to $1 million, ten years' imprisonment, or both. Willful violators may be fined up to $5 million, sentenced to up to twenty years' imprisonment, or both. Although the difference between a knowing and a willful violation is not entirely clear, the section is obviously intended to remind corporate officers of the serious consequences of certifying inaccurate reports to the SEC.

10. Codified at 18 U.S.C. Section 1348.
11. Codified at 18 U.S.C. Section 1350.

Sample Answers for End-of-Chapter *Hypothetical Questions* with Sample Answer

1–4A HYPOTHETICAL QUESTION WITH SAMPLE ANSWER

1 The U.S. Constitution—The U.S. Constitution is the supreme law of the land. A law in violation of the Constitution, no matter what its source, will be declared unconstitutional and will not be enforced.

2 The federal statute—Under the U.S. Constitution, when there is a conflict between federal law and state law, federal law prevails.

3 The state statute—State statutes are enacted by state legislatures. Areas not covered by state statutory law are governed by state case law.

4 The U.S. Constitution—State constitutions are supreme within their respective borders unless they conflict with the U.S. Constitution, which is the supreme law of the land.

5 The federal administrative regulation—Under the U.S. Constitution, when there is a conflict between federal law and state law, federal law prevails.

2–2A HYPOTHETICAL QUESTION WITH SAMPLE ANSWER

As the text points out, Thomas has a constitutionally protected right to his religion and the free exercise of it. In denying his unemployment benefits, the state violated these rights. Employers are obligated to make reasonable accommodations for their employees' beliefs, right or wrong, that are openly and sincerely held. Thomas's beliefs were openly and sincerely held. By placing him in a department that made military goods, his employer effectively put him in a position of having to choose between his job and his religious principles. This unilateral decision on the part of the employer was the reason Thomas left his job and why the company was required to compensate Thomas for his resulting unemployment.

3–2A HYPOTHETICAL QUESTION WITH SAMPLE ANSWER

Marya can bring suit in all three courts. The trucking firm did business in Florida, and the accident occurred there. Thus, the state of Florida would have jurisdiction over the defendant. Because the firm was headquartered in Georgia and had its principal place of business in that state, Marya could also sue in a Georgia court. Finally, because the amount in controversy exceeds $75,000, the suit could be brought in federal court on the basis of diversity of citizenship.

4–2A HYPOTHETICAL QUESTION WITH SAMPLE ANSWER

To answer this question, you must first decide if there is a legal theory under which Harley may be able to recover. A possibility is the intentional tort of wrongful interference with a contractual relationship. To recover damages under this theory, Harley would need to show (1) that he and Martha had a valid contract, (2) that Lothar knew of this contractual relationship, and (3) that Lothar intentionally convinced Martha to break her contract with Harley. Even though Lothar hoped that his advertisements would persuade Martha to break her contract with Harley, the question states that Martha's decision to change bakers was based solely on the advertising and not on anything else that Lothar did. Lothar's advertisements did not constitute a tort. Note, though, that while Harley cannot collect from Lothar for Martha's actions, he does have a cause of action against Martha for her breach of their contract.

5–2A HYPOTHETICAL QUESTION WITH SAMPLE ANSWER

1 Making a photocopy of an article in a scholarly journal "for purposes such as . . . scholarship, or research, is not an infringement of copyright" under Section 107 of the Copyright Act (the fair use exception).

2 This is an example of trademark infringement rather than copyright infringement. Whenever a trademark is copied to a substantial degree or used in its entirety by one who is not entitled to its use, the trademark has been infringed.

3 This is the most likely example of copyright infringement. Generally, determining whether the reproduction of copyrighted material constitutes copyright infringement is made on a case-by-case basis under the "fair use" doctrine, as expressed in Section 107 of the Copyright Act. Courts look at such factors as the "purpose and character" of a use, such as whether it is "of a commercial nature"; "the amount and substantiality of the portion used in relation to the copyrighted work as a whole"; and "the effect of the use on the potential market" for the copied work. In this question, the DVD store owner is copying copyright-protected works in their entirety for commercial purposes, thereby affecting the market for the works.

4 Recording a television program "for purposes such as . . . teaching . . . is not an infringement of copyright" under Section 107 of the Copyright Act.

6–2A HYPOTHETICAL QUESTION WITH SAMPLE ANSWER

1 Sarah has wrongfully taken and carried away the personal property of another with the intent to permanently deprive the owner of such property. She has committed the crime of larceny.

2 Sarah has unlawfully and forcibly taken the personal property of another. She has committed the crime of robbery.

3 Sarah has broken and entered a dwelling with the intent to commit a felony. She has committed the crime of burglary. (Most states have dispensed with the requirement that the act take place at night.)

Note the basic differences: Burglary requires breaking and entering into a building without the use of force against a person. Robbery does not involve any breaking and entering, but force is required. Larceny is the taking of personal property without force and without breaking and entering into a building. Generally, because force is used, robbery is considered the most serious of these crimes and carries the most severe penalties. Larceny involves no force or threat to human life; therefore, it carries the least severe penalty of the three. Burglary, because it involves breaking and entering, frequently where people live, carries a lesser penalty than robbery but a greater penalty than larceny.

7-3A HYPOTHETICAL QUESTION WITH SAMPLE ANSWER

The perpetrator in this set of facts is a hacker—someone who uses one computer to break into another. Computers can be hacked, or broken into, in various ways to commit a multitude of crimes. In this problem, the hacker created a *botnet* by appropriating others' computers to forward transmissions to the creditor's system. Here, the crime of altering the figures to show that a debt has been paid is theft (wrongfully taking and carrying away another's property with the intent of depriving the owner permanently of it). "Carrying away" can be done by any act that removes something of value from its owner's possession, and the "property" may be any type of tangible or intangible item. In this problem, the hacker accomplished "carrying away" by altering the figures, and the property taken was the creditor's right to receive payment.

8-2A HYPOTHETICAL QUESTION WITH SAMPLE ANSWER

Ethical and other dilemmas faced by businesspersons are rarely clear-cut choices between good and bad alternatives. This problem is no exception. The questions in the problem indicate some of the issues that businesspersons in such situations should consider. But potentially higher profits and possible negative publicity are not the only considerations—decisions made by businesspersons can have wide-ranging implications. When a firm takes advantage of cheaper overseas labor, it must lay off domestic workers or even close a domestic operation. When workers are laid off, there are repercussions throughout the local economy. Closing an operation reduces the local tax base—property taxes, business taxes, and income taxes—which funds the local infrastructure. Thus, the firm must determine to whom it owes duties (shareholders, employees, or others) and to what degree each group is owed. In addition, all of the factors that exist when business is done internationally must be considered. These include the foreign economic and political situation, and other costs (materials, equipment, foreign taxes, domestic import duties) besides cheap labor. These and other considerations require a balancing known as a trade-off.

9-2A HYPOTHETICAL QUESTION WITH SAMPLE ANSWER

According to the question, Janine was apparently unconscious or otherwise unable to agree to a contract for the nursing services she received while she was in the hospital. As you read in the chapter, however, sometimes the law will create a fictional contract in order to prevent one party from unjustly receiving a benefit at the expense of another. This is known as a quasi contract and provides a basis for Nursing Services to recover the value of the services it provided while Janine was in the hospital. As for the at-home services that were provided to Janine, because Janine was aware that those services were being provided for her, Nursing Services can recover for those services under an implied-in-fact contract. Under this type of contract, the conduct of the parties creates and defines the terms. Janine's acceptance of the services constitutes her agreement to form a contract, and she will probably be required to pay Nursing Services in full.

10-3A HYPOTHETICAL QUESTION WITH SAMPLE ANSWER

1 Death of either the offeror or the offeree prior to acceptance automatically terminates a revocable offer. The basic legal reason is that the offer is personal to the parties and cannot be passed on to others, not even to the estate of the deceased. This rule applies even if the other party is unaware of the death. Thus, Cherneck's offer terminates on Cherneck's death, and Bollow's later acceptance does not constitute a contract.

2 An offer is automatically terminated by the destruction of the specific subject matter of the offer prior to acceptance. Thus, Bollow's acceptance after the fire does not constitute a contract.

3 When the offer is irrevocable, under an option contract, death of the offeror does not terminate the option contract, and the offeree can accept the offer to sell the equipment, binding the offeror's estate to performance. Performance is not personal to Cherneck, as the estate can transfer title to the equipment. Knowledge of the death is immaterial to the offeree's right of acceptance. Thus, Bollow can hold Cherneck's estate to a contract for the purchase of the equipment.

4 When the offer is irrevocable, under an option contract, death of the offeree also does not terminate the offer. Because the option is a separate contract, the contract survives and passes to the offeree's estate, which can exercise the option by acceptance within the option period. Thus, acceptance by Bollow's estate binds Cherneck to a contract for the sale of the equipment.

11-3A HYPOTHETICAL QUESTION WITH SAMPLE ANSWER

Contracts in restraint of trade are usually illegal and unenforceable. An exception to this rule applies to a covenant not to compete that is ancillary to certain types of business contracts in which some fair protection is deemed appropriate (such as in the sale of a business). To be legally enforceable, however, the covenant must be reasonable in terms of time and area. If either term is excessive, the court can declare that the restraint goes beyond what is necessary for reasonable protection. In this event, the court can either declare the covenant illegal, or it can reform the covenant to make the terms of time and area reasonable and then enforce it. Suppose the court declares the covenant illegal and unenforceable. Because the covenant is ancillary and severable from the primary contract, the primary contract is not affected by such a ruling. In the case of Hotel Lux, the primary contract concerns employment; the covenant is ancillary and desirable for the protection of the hotel. The time period of one year may be considered reasonable for a chef with an international reputation. The reasonableness of the three-state area restriction may be questioned, however. If it is found to be reasonable, the covenant probably will be enforced. If it is not found to be reasonable, the court could declare the entire covenant illegal, allowing Perlee to be employed by any restaurant or hotel, including one in direct competition with Hotel Lux. Alternatively, the court could reform the covenant, making its terms reasonable for protecting Hotel Lux's normal customer market area.

12–2A HYPOTHETICAL QUESTION WITH SAMPLE ANSWER

In this situation, Gemma becomes what is known as a *guarantor* on the loan. That is, she guarantees the hardware store that she will pay for the mower if her brother fails to do so. This kind of collateral promise, in which the guarantor states that he or she will become responsible *only* if the primary party does not perform, must be in writing to be enforceable. There is an exception, however. If the main purpose in accepting secondary liability is to secure a personal benefit—for example, if Gemma's brother bought the mower for her—the contract need not be in writing. The assumption is that a court can infer from the circumstances of the case whether the main purpose was to secure a personal benefit and thus, in effect, to answer for the guarantor's own debt.

13–3A HYPOTHETICAL QUESTION WITH SAMPLE ANSWER

As a general rule, any right(s) flowing from a contract can be assigned. There are, however, exceptions, such as when the contract expressly and specifically prohibits or limits the right of assignment. Because of the principle of freedom of contract, this type of prohibition is enforced—unless it is deemed contrary to public policy. Authorities differ on how a case like Aron's should be decided. Some courts would enforce the prohibition completely, holding that Aron's assignment to Erica is completely ineffective without the landlord's consent. Others would permit the assignment to be effective and would limit the landlord's remedies to the normal contract remedies ensuing from Aron's breach.

14–2A HYPOTHETICAL QUESTION WITH SAMPLE ANSWER

Generally, the equitable remedy of specific performance will be granted only if two criteria are met: monetary damages (under the circumstances) must be inadequate as a remedy, and the subject matter of the contract must be unique.

1 In the sale of land, the buyer's contract is for a specific piece of real property. The land under contract is unique because no two pieces of real property have the same legal description. In addition, monetary damages would not compensate a buyer adequately, as the same land cannot be purchased elsewhere. Specific performance is an appropriate remedy.

2 The basic criteria for specific performance do not apply well to personal-service contracts. If the identical service contracted for is readily available from others, the service is not unique and monetary damages for nonperformance are adequate. If, however, the services are so personal that only the contracted party can perform them, the contract meets the test of uniqueness; but the courts will refuse to decree specific performance based on either of two theories. First, the enforcement of specific performance requires involuntary servitude (prohibited by the Thirteenth Amendment to the U. S. Constitution). Second, it is impractical to attempt to force meaningful performance by someone against his or her will. In the case of Marita and Horace, specific performance is not an appropriate remedy.

3 A rare coin is unique, and monetary damages for breach are inadequate, as Juan cannot obtain a substantially identical substitute in the market. This is a typical case where specific performance is an appropriate remedy.

4 The key fact for consideration here is that this is a closely held corporation. Therefore, the stock is not available in the market, and the shares become unique. The uniqueness of these shares is enhanced by the fact that if Cary sells his 4 percent of the shares to De Valle, De Valle will have a controlling voice in the corporation. Because of this, monetary damages for De Valle are totally inadequate as a remedy. Specific performance is an appropriate remedy.

15–3A HYPOTHETICAL QUESTION WITH SAMPLE ANSWER

1 In a destination contract, the risk of loss passes to the buyer when the goods are tendered to the buyer at the specified destination—in this case, San Francisco.

2 In a shipment contract, if the seller is required or authorized to ship goods by carrier, but the contract does not specify a locale, the risk of loss passes to the buyer when the goods are duly delivered to the carrier.

3 If the seller is a merchant, risk of loss to goods held by the seller passes to the buyer when the buyer actually takes physical possession of the goods. If the seller is not a merchant, the risk of loss to goods held by the seller passes to the buyer on tender of delivery.

4 When a bailee is holding goods for a person who has contracted to sell them and the goods are to be delivered without being moved, risk of loss passes to the buyer when (a) the buyer receives a negotiable document of title for the goods, (b) the bailee acknowledges the buyer's right to possess the goods, or (c) the buyer receives a nonnegotiable document of title and has had a reasonable time to present the document to the bailee and demand the goods. (If the bailee refuses to honor the document, the risk of loss remains with the seller.) If the goods are to be delivered by being moved, but the contract does not specify whether it is a destination or a shipment contract, it is presumed to be a shipment contract. If no locale is specified in the contract, risk of loss passes to the buyer when the seller delivers the goods to the carrier.

16–2A HYPOTHETICAL QUESTION WITH SAMPLE ANSWER

No. Cummings had not breached the sales contract because the C.O.D. shipment had deprived him of his absolute right, in the absence of agreement, to inspect the goods before accepting them. Had Cummings requested or agreed to the C.O.D. method of shipment, the result would have been different. Because he had not agreed to the C.O.D. shipment, he was fully within his rights to refuse to accept the goods because he could not inspect them prior to acceptance. In this case, it was the seller who had breached the contract by shipping the goods C.O.D. without Cummings's consent.

17–2A HYPOTHETICAL QUESTION WITH SAMPLE ANSWER

Yes. To disclaim the implied warranty of fitness for a particular purpose, the disclaimer must be in writing and be conspicuous. Although the implied warranty of merchantability can be disclaimed orally, if the disclaimer is in writing it must be conspicuously written. This means that the disclaimer must—either by different color or type size or some other technique—stand out from the context in which it is printed so as to readily alert the reader of the document of the disclaimer. In this case, the disclaimer was printed in the same size and color of type as the rest of the contract and was not conspicuous. If this was the only warranty disclaimer, it is not effective and Tandy can recover.

18–2A HYPOTHETICAL QUESTION WITH SAMPLE ANSWER

For an instrument to be negotiable, it must meet the following requirements:

1 Be in writing.
2 Be signed by the maker or the drawer.
3 Be an unconditional promise or order to pay.
4 State a fixed amount of money.
5 Be payable on demand or at a definite time.
6 Be payable to order or to bearer, unless it is a check.

The instrument in this case meets the writing requirement in that it is handwritten and on something with a degree of permanence that is transferable. The instrument meets the requirement of being signed by the maker, as Muriel Evans's signature (her name in her handwriting) appears in the body of the instrument. The instrument's payment is not conditional and contains Muriel Evans's definite promise to pay. In addition, the sum of $100 is both a fixed amount and payable in money (U.S. currency). Because the instrument is payable on demand and to bearer (Karen Marvin or any holder), the instrument is negotiable.

19–2A HYPOTHETICAL QUESTION WITH SAMPLE ANSWER

Under the Home Mortgage Disclosure Act (HMDA) and the Community Reinvestment Act of 1977, which were passed to prevent discrimination in lending practices, a bank is required to define its market area. This area must be established contiguous to the bank's branch offices. It must be mapped using the existing boundaries of the counties or the standard metropolitan areas (SMAs) in which the offices are located. A bank must delineate the community served, and annually review this delineation. The issue here is how successful iBank, an Internet-only bank, could delineate its community. Does iBank have a physically limited market area or serve a physically distinct community? Will the Federal Reserve Board, the government agency charged with enforcing this law, allow a bank to describe its market area as a "cybercommunity"?

20–2A HYPOTHETICAL QUESTION WITH SAMPLE ANSWER

Mendez has a security interest in Arabian Knight and is a perfected secured party. He has met all the necessary criteria listed under UCC 9–203 to be a secured creditor. Mendez has given value of $5,000 and has taken possession of the collateral, Arabian Knight, owned by Marsh (who has rights in the collateral). Thus, he has a security interest even though Marsh did not sign a security agreement. Once a security interest attaches, a transfer of possession of the collateral to the secured party can perfect the party's security interest without a filing [UCC 9–310(b)(6); 9–313]. Thus, a security interest was created and perfected at the time Marsh transferred Arabian Knight to Mendez as security for the loan.

21–2A HYPOTHETICAL QUESTION WITH SAMPLE ANSWER

The Bankruptcy Code establishes the priority of payment of claims from the debtor's estate. Each class of debt in this priority list must be

fully paid before the next class in priority is entitled to any of the proceeds. If insufficient funds remain to pay an entire class, the proceeds are distributed on a pro rata basis to each creditor within that class. The order of priority for claims listed in this problem is as follows:

1 Administrative bankruptcy costs (Martinez)—$500.
2 Claims for back wages, limited to $4,300 per claimant, provided wages were earned within ninety days of petition (Kohak)—$4,300.
3 Taxes and penalties due and owing (Micanopa County)—$1,000.
4 General creditors, $10,000 (First Bank of Sunny Acres—$5,000; Calvin—$2,500; balance of Kohak wages owed—$2,500).

Because the amount remaining after paying 1, 2, and 3 is only $1,200, the general creditors will share on a pro rata basis. First Bank of Sunny Acres will receive $600 ($5,000/$10,000 × $1,200 = $600), and Calvin and Kohak will each receive $300 ($2,500/$10,000 × $1,200 = $300).

22–2A HYPOTHETICAL QUESTION WITH SAMPLE ANSWER

Yes, it is a reasonable approach to rely on the producers' financial records, which are reasonably reflective of their costs because their normal allocation methodologies were used for a number of years. These records are historically relied on to present important financial information to shareholders, lenders, tax authorities, auditors, and other third parties. Provided that the producers' records and books comply with generally accepted accounting principles and were verified by independent auditors, it is reasonable to use them to determine the production costs and fair market value of canned pineapple in the United States.

23–2A HYPOTHETICAL QUESTION WITH SAMPLE ANSWER

Agency usually is a consensual relationship in that the principal and agent agree that the agent will have the authority to act for the principal, binding the principal to any contract with a third party. If no agency in fact exists, the purported agent's contracts with third parties are not binding on the principal. In this case, no agency by agreement was created. Brown may claim that an agency by estoppel was created; however, this argument will fail. Agency by estoppel is applicable only when a *principal* causes a third person to believe that another person is the principal's agent. Then the third party's actions in dealing with the agent are in reliance upon the principal's words or actions and the third party's reasonable belief that the agent has authority. This is said to estop the principal from claiming that in fact no agency existed. Acts and declarations of the *agent,* however, do not in and of themselves create an agency by estoppel, because such actions should not reasonably lead a third person to believe that the purported agent has authority. In this case, Wade's declarations and allegations alone led Brown to believe that Wade was an agent. Gett's actions were not involved. It is not reasonable to believe that someone is an agent solely because he or she is a friend of the principal. Therefore, Brown cannot hold Gett liable unless Gett ratifies Wade's contract—which is unlikely, as Wade has disappeared with the rare coin.

24–2A HYPOTHETICAL QUESTION WITH SAMPLE ANSWER

The Occupational Safety and Health Act (OSHA) requires employers to provide safe working conditions for employees. The act prohibits employers from discharging or discriminating against any employee who refuses to work when the employee believes in good faith that he or she will risk death or great bodily harm by undertaking the employment activity. Denton and Carlo had sufficient reason to believe that the maintenance job required of them by their employer involved great risk, and therefore, under OSHA, their discharge was wrongful. Denton and Carlo can turn to the Occupational Safety and Health Administration, which is part of the U.S. Department of Labor, for assistance.

25–2A HYPOTHETICAL QUESTION WITH SAMPLE ANSWER

Educational requirements can be legally imposed provided that the educational requirement is directly related to, and necessary for, performance of the job. The requirement of a high school diploma is not a direct, job-related requirement in this case. Chinawa obviously comes under the 1964 Civil Rights Act, Title VII, as amended, and the educational requirement under the circumstances is definitely discriminatory against minorities.

26–2A HYPOTHETICAL QUESTION WITH SAMPLE ANSWER

The court would likely consider the terms of any contracts between the parties and whether the parties were acting in good faith. One way to avoid conflicts such as those described in this problem is to institute a Web site in conjunction with a franchisor's franchisees. When a Web site directs interested parties to a franchisee, for example, all parties would seem to benefit. Because territorial conflicts can occur not only between a franchisor and its franchisees but also between competing franchisees, some companies have instituted specific "no compete" pledges.

27–2A HYPOTHETICAL QUESTION WITH SAMPLE ANSWER

1 A limited partner's interest is assignable. In fact, assignment allows the assignee to become a substituted limited partner with the consent of the remaining partners. The assignment, however, does not dissolve the limited partnership.

2 Bankruptcy of the limited partnership itself causes dissolution, but bankruptcy of one of the limited partners does not dissolve the partnership unless it causes the bankruptcy of the firm.

3 The retirement, death, or insanity of a general partner dissolves the partnership unless the business can be continued by the remaining general partners. Because Dorinda was the only general partner, her death dissolves the limited partnership.

28–2A HYPOTHETICAL QUESTION WITH SAMPLE ANSWER

Although a joint stock company has characteristics of a corporation, it is usually treated as a partnership. Therefore, although the joint stock company issues transferable shares of stock and is managed by directors and officers, the shareholders have personal liability. Unless the shareholders transfer their stock and ownership to a third party, not only are the joint stock company's assets available for damages caused by a breach, but the individual shareholders' estates are also subject to such liability. The business trust resembles and is treated like a corporation in many respects. One is the limited liability of the beneficiaries. Unless by state law the beneficiaries are treated as partners, making them liable to business trust creditors, Faraway Corp. can look to only business trust assets in the event of breach.

29–2A HYPOTHETICAL QUESTION WITH SAMPLE ANSWER

If Artel acquires the stocks and assets of Fox Express, a *merger* will take place. Artel will be the surviving corporation, and Fox Express will disappear as a corporation. If Artel and Fox Express combine so that both corporations cease to exist and a new corporation, A&F Enterprises, is formed, a *consolidation* will take place. In either situation, title to the property of the corporation that ceases to exist will pass automatically to the surviving or new corporation without a formal transfer being necessary. In addition, in a merger, the debt liabilities of Fox Express become the liabilities of Artel. Artel's articles of incorporation are deemed to be amended to include the terms stated in the articles of merger. If a consolidation takes place, A&F Enterprises will automatically acquire title to the properties of both Artel and Fox Express without a formal transfer being necessary. A&F Enterprises also will assume liability for the debts and obligations of Artel and Fox Express. The articles of consolidation take the place of the articles of incorporation of Artel and Fox Express, and they will be regarded thereafter as the articles of incorporation of A&F Enterprises.

30–2A HYPOTHETICAL QUESTION WITH SAMPLE ANSWER

Directors are personally answerable to the corporation and the shareholders for breach of their duty to exercise reasonable care in conducting the affairs of the corporation. Reasonable care is defined as being the degree of care that a reasonably prudent person would use in the conduct of personal business affairs. When directors delegate the running of the corporate affairs to officers, the directors are expected to use reasonable care in the selection and supervision of such officers. Failure to do so will make the directors liable for negligence or mismanagement. A director who dissents from an action by the board is not personally liable for losses resulting from that action. Unless the dissent is entered into the board meeting minutes, however, the director is presumed to have assented. Therefore, the first issue in the case of Starboard, Inc., is whether the board members failed to use reasonable care in the selection of the president, Tyson. If so, and particularly if the board failed to provide a reasonable amount of supervision (and openly embezzled funds indicate that failure), the directors will be personally liable. This liability will include Ellsworth unless she can prove that she dissented and that she tried to reasonably supervise Tyson. Considering the facts in this case, it is questionable that Ellsworth could prove this.

31–2A HYPOTHETICAL QUESTION WITH SAMPLE ANSWER

No. Under federal securities law, a stock split is exempt from registration requirements. This is because no *sale* of stock is involved. The existing shares are merely being split, and no consideration is received by the corporation for the additional shares created.

32–2A HYPOTHETICAL QUESTION WITH SAMPLE ANSWER

Yes. The major antitrust law being violated is the Sherman Act, Section 1. Allitron and Donovan are engaged in interstate commerce, and the agreement to divide marketing territories between them is a contract in restraint of trade. The U.S. Department of Justice could seek fines of up to $1 million from each corporation, and the officers or directors responsible could be imprisoned for up to three years. In addition, the U.S. Department of Justice could institute civil proceedings to restrain this conduct.

33–2A HYPOTHETICAL QUESTION WITH SAMPLE ANSWER

The Truth-in-Lending Act (TILA) deals specifically with lost or stolen credit cards and their unauthorized use. For credit cards *solicited* by the cardholder and then lost or stolen, the act limits the liability of the cardholder to $50 for unauthorized charges made prior to the time the creditor is notified. There is no liability for any unauthorized charges made after the date of notice. In the case of the Midtown Department Store credit card stolen on May 31, the $500 charge made on June 1, which is prior to Ochoa's notice, causes Ochoa to be liable for the $50 limit. For the June 3 charge of $200 made after the notification, Ochoa has no liability. TILA also deals with unsolicited credit cards. Unless a credit cardholder accepts an unsolicited card (such as by using it), the cardholder is not liable for any unauthorized charges. Moreover, the act prohibits the issuance of unsolicited credit cards. No notice by the cardholder of an unsolicited, unaccepted credit card is required to absolve the cardholder from liability for unauthorized charges. Therefore, Ochoa owes $50 to the Midtown Department Store and nothing to High-Flying Airlines.

34-2A HYPOTHETICAL QUESTION WITH SAMPLE ANSWER

Assuming that the circuit court has abandoned the *Ultramares* rule, it is likely that the accounting firm of Goldman, Walters, Johnson & Co. will be held liable to Happydays State Bank for negligent preparation of financial statements. This hypothetical scenario is partially derived from *Citizens State Bank v. Timm, Schmidt & Co.* In *Citizens State Bank,* the Supreme Court of Wisconsin enunciated various policy reasons for holding accountants liable to third parties even in the absence of privity. The court suggested that this potential liability would make accountants more careful in the preparation of financial statements. Moreover, in some situations the accountants may be the only solvent defendants, and hence, unless liability is imposed on accountants, third parties who reasonably rely on financial statements may go unprotected. The court further asserted that accountants, rather than third parties, are in a better position to spread the risks. If third parties such as banks have to absorb the costs of bad loans made as a result of negligently prepared financial statements, then the cost of credit to the public in general will increase. In contrast, the court suggests that accountants are in a better position to spread the risk by purchasing liability insurance.

35-3A HYPOTHETICAL QUESTION WITH SAMPLE ANSWER

For Curtis to recover against the hotel, he must first prove that a bailment relationship was created between himself and the hotel as to the car or the fur coat, or both. For a bailment to exist, there must be a delivery of the personal property that gives the bailee exclusive possession of the property, and the bailee must knowingly accept the bailed property. If either element is lacking, there is no bailment relationship and no liability on the part of the bailee hotel. The facts clearly indicate that the bailee hotel took exclusive possession and control of Curtis's car, and it knowingly accepted the car when the attendant took the car from Curtis and parked it in the underground guarded garage, retaining the keys. Thus, a bailment was created as to the car, and, because a mutual benefit bailment was created, the hotel owes Curtis the duty to exercise reasonable care over the property and to return the bailed car at the end of the bailment. Failure to return the car creates a presumption of negligence (lack of reasonable care), and unless the hotel can rebut this presumption, the hotel is liable to Curtis for the loss of the car. As to the fur coat, the hotel neither knew nor expected that the trunk contained an expensive fur coat. Thus, although the hotel knowingly took exclusive possession of the car, the hotel did not do so with the fur coat. (But the hotel would be liable for a regular coat and other

items likely to be in the car.) Because no bailment of the expensive fur coat was created, the hotel has no liability for its loss.

36-2A HYPOTHETICAL QUESTION WITH SAMPLE ANSWER

Wiley understandably wants a general warranty deed, as this type of deed will give him the most extensive protection against any defects of title claimed against the property transferred. The general warranty would have Gemma warranting the following covenants:

1 Covenant of seisin and right to convey—a warranty that the seller has good title and power to convey.

2 Covenant against encumbrances—a guaranty by the seller that, unless stated, there are no outstanding encumbrances or liens against the property conveyed.

3 Covenant of quiet possession—a warranty that the grantee's possession will not be disturbed by others claiming a prior legal right. Gemma, however, is conveying only ten feet along a property line that may not even be accurately surveyed. Gemma therefore does not wish to make these warranties. Consequently, she is offering a quitclaim deed, which does not convey any warranties but conveys only whatever interest, if any, the grantor owns. Although title is passed by the quitclaim deed, the quality of the title is not warranted. Because Wiley really needs the property, it appears that he has three choices: he can accept the quitclaim deed; he can increase his offer price to obtain the general warranty deed he wants; or he can offer to have a title search made, which should satisfy both parties.

37-2A HYPOTHETICAL QUESTION WITH SAMPLE ANSWER

1 In most states, for a will to be valid, it must be in writing, signed by the testator, and witnessed (attested to) according to the statutes of the state. In some states, the testator is also required to publish (declare) that the document is his or her last will and testament. (This is not required under the Uniform Probate Code.) In the case of Benjamin, the will is unquestionably written (typewritten) and signed by the testator. The only problem is with the witnesses. Some states require three witnesses, and some invalidate a will if a named beneficiary is also a witness. The Uniform Probate Code provides that a will is valid even if attested to by an interested witness. Therefore, whether the will is valid depends on the state laws dealing with witness qualifications.

2 If the will is declared invalid, Benjamin's estate will pass in accordance with the state's intestacy laws. These statutes provide for distribution of an estate when there is no valid will. The intent of the statutes is to distribute the estate in the way that the deceased person would have wished. Generally, the estate is divided between a surviving spouse and all surviving children. Because Benjamin is a widower, if his only surviving child is Edward, the entire estate will go to Edward, and Benjamin's grandchildren, Perry and Paul, will receive nothing from the estate.

3 If the will is valid, the estate will be divided between Benjamin's two children, Patricia and Edward. Should either or both predecease Benjamin, leaving children (Benjamin's grandchildren), the grandchildren take *per stirpes* the share that would have gone to their parent. In this case Edward, as a surviving child of Benjamin, would receive one-half of the estate, and Perry and Paul, as grandchildren, would each receive *per stirpes* one-fourth of the estate (one-half of the share that would have gone to their deceased mother, Patricia).

Case Excerpts for
Case Analysis Questions

CASE NO. 1 (FOR CHAPTER 4)

Lott v. Levitt, United States District Court, 469 F.Supp.2d 575 (E.D.Ill. 2007).

In 2005, well-known economist Steven Levitt ("Levitt") and journalist Stephen J. Dubner ("Dubner") coauthored the best-selling book *Freakonomics*[.] * * * In the book, Levitt and Dubner [discuss] * * * the theory for which fellow economist, * * * John R. Lott, Jr. ("Lott"), is known[:] * * * that laws permitting individuals to carry concealed weapons result in a statistically significant and provable reduction in serious crime rates. Lott filed the instant lawsuit against Levitt and [others] * * * . Lott claims [in part] that an email written by Levitt to another economist * * * constitutes defamation * * * . [Levitt filed a motion to dismiss this claim.]
* * * *

Lott is discussed in the following single paragraph in Chapter 4 of *Freakonomics,* entitled "Where Have All the Criminals Gone?":
* * * There is an * * * argument—that we need more guns on the street, but in the hands of the right people * * * . The economist John R. Lott Jr. is the main champion of this idea. * * * [H]e argues that violent crime has decreased in areas where law abiding citizens are allowed to carry concealed weapons. His theory might be surprising, but it is sensible. If a criminal thinks his potential victim may be armed, he may be deterred from committing the crime. Handgun opponents call Lott a pro-gun ideologue * * * . There was the troubling allegation that Lott actually invented some of the survey data that support his more-guns/less-crime theory. Regardless of whether the data were faked, Lott's admittedly intriguing hypothesis doesn't seem to be true. When other scholars have tried to replicate his results, they found that right-to-carry laws simply don't bring down crime.

On May 24 or May 25, 2005, John McCall ("McCall"), described by Lott as an economist residing in Texas, sent Levitt an email regarding the above passage, stating:
I * * * found the following citations—have not read any of them yet, but it appears they all replicate Lott's research. [McCall referred to a "Special Issue" of *The Journal of Law and Economics* published in October 2001 that contained a collection of articles delivered at an academic conference co-sponsored by the Center for Law, Economics and Public Policy at Yale Law School and the American Enterprise Institute, where Lott had recently been a resident scholar.] *The Journal of Law and Economics* is not chopped liver.

That same day, Levitt responded:

It was not a peer refereed edition of the *Journal.* For $15,000 he was able to buy an issue and put in only work that supported him. My best friend was the editor and was outraged the press let Lott do this.
* * * *

A statement is considered defamatory if it tends to cause such harm to the reputation of another that it lowers that person in the eyes of the community or deters third persons from associating with that person. [Emphasis added.]
* * * *

* * * Lott contends that the statements about him in * * * the email * * * imply that his results were falsified or that his theories lack merit, and thus impute a lack of ability and integrity in his profession as an economist, academic, and researcher. Indeed, a claim that an academic or economist falsified his results and could only publish his theories by buying an issue of a journal and avoiding peer review would surely impute a lack of ability and prejudice that person in his profession.
* * * *

* * * *The First Amendment protects statements that cannot be reasonably interpreted as stating actual facts.* [Emphasis added.]

The test for whether a statement is a factual assertion is whether the statement is precise, readily understood, and susceptible of being verified as true or false. This test * * * is a reasonableness standard; whether a reasonable reader would understand the defendant to be informing him of a fact or opinion. Language that is loose, figurative, or hyperbolic negates the impression that a statement is asserting actual facts. Accordingly, *vague, unprovable statements and statements of opinion do not give rise to a defamation claim.* If it is plain that the speaker is expressing a subjective view, an interpretation, a theory, conjecture, or surmise, rather than claiming to be in possession of objectively verifiable facts, the statement is not actionable. [Emphasis added.]

In this case, however, Levitt's email sounds as if he was in possession of objectively verifiable facts. * * * First, it would be unreasonable to interpret Levitt's unqualified statement that the *Journal* edition was not "peer refereed" as Levitt [argues that he was] merely giving his opinion on the "peers" chosen to review, or referee, the Special Issue. Indeed, the editor of the *Journal* might be able to verify the truth or falsity of whether the Special Issue was reviewed by peers. * * * Second, a reasonable reader would not interpret Levitt's assertion that "For $15,000 [Lott] was able to buy an issue and put in only work that supported him" as simply a statement of Levitt's opinion. Levitt's email appears to state objectively verifiable facts: that Lott paid $15,000 to control the content of the Special Issue. The editor of the *Journal* again might be the source to verify the truth or falsity of this statement. Third, the same editor could verify whether he was "outraged" by the acts described in the foregoing statements. Therefore, the defamatory statements in Levitt's email to McCall are objectively verifiable * * * .

* * * *

* * * In his email to McCall, * * * Levitt made a string of defamatory assertions about Lott's involvement in the publication of the Special Issue of the *Journal* that—no matter how rash or short-sighted Levitt was when he made them—cannot be reasonably interpreted as innocent or mere opinion.

* * * Levitt's motion to dismiss [this part of Lott's] Complaint is denied.

CASE NO. 2 (FOR CHAPTER 10)

Feldman v. Google, Inc., 513 F.Supp.2d 229 (E.D.Pa. 2007).

Before the court is Defendant Google, Inc.'s Motion to * * * Transfer [the case to Santa Clara County].

Also before the court is Plaintiff Lawrence E. Feldman's Cross-Motion for Summary Judgment. The ultimate issues raised by the motions and determined by the court are whether a forum selection clause in an Internet "clickwrap" agreement is enforceable * * *.

Defendant's motion seeks to enforce the forum selection clause in an online "clickwrap" agreement, which provides for venue in Santa Clara County * * *.

On or about January 2003, Plaintiff, a lawyer with his own law firm, Lawrence E. Feldman & Associates, purchased advertising from Defendant Google, Inc.'s "AdWords" Program, to attract potential clients who may have been harmed by drugs under scrutiny by the U.S. Food and Drug Administration.

In the AdWords program, whenever an internet user searched on the internet search engine, Google.com, for keywords or "Adwords" purchased by Plaintiff, such as "Vioxx," "Bextra," and "Celebrex," Plaintiff's ad would appear. If the searcher clicked on Plaintiff's ad, Defendant would charge Plaintiff for each click made on the ad.

This procedure is known as "pay per click" advertising. The price per keyword is determined by a bidding process, wherein the highest bidder for a keyword would have its ad placed at the top of the list of results from a Google.com search by an Internet user.

Plaintiff claims that he was the victim of "click fraud." Click fraud occurs when entities or persons, such as competitors or pranksters, without any interest in Plaintiff's services, click repeatedly on Plaintiff's ad, the result of which drives up his advertising cost and discourages him from advertising. * * * Plaintiff alleges that twenty to thirty percent of all clicks for which he was charged were fraudulent. He claims that Google required him to pay for all clicks on his ads, including those which were fraudulent.

* * * *

The type of contract at issue here is commonly referred to as a "clickwrap" agreement. A clickwrap agreement appears on an Internet web page and requires that a user consent to any terms or conditions by clicking on a dialog box on the screen in order to proceed with the Internet transaction. *Even though they are electronic, clickwrap agreements are considered to be writings because they are printable and storable.* [Emphasis added.]

To determine whether a clickwrap agreement is enforceable, courts * * * apply traditional principles of contract law and focus on whether the plaintiffs had reasonable notice of and manifested assent to the clickwrap agreement. *Absent a showing of fraud, failure to read an enforceable clickwrap agreement, as with any binding contract, will not excuse compliance with its terms.* [Emphasis added.]

* * * *

Plaintiff [Feldman] claims he did not have notice or knowledge of the forum selection clause, and therefore that there was no "meeting of the minds" required for contract formation.

* * * *

* * * In order to activate an AdWords account, the user had to visit a Web page which displayed the Agreement in a scrollable text box. * * * The user did not have to scroll down to a submerged screen or click on a series of hyperlinks to view the Agreement. Instead, text of the AdWords Agreement was immediately visible to the user, as was a prominent admonition in boldface to read the terms and conditions carefully, and with instruction to indicate assent if the user agreed to the terms.

That the user would have to scroll through the text box of the Agreement to read it in its entirety does not defeat notice because there was sufficient notice of the Agreement itself and clicking "Yes" constituted assent to all of the terms. The preamble, which was immediately visible, also made clear that assent to the terms was binding. The Agreement was presented in readable 12-point font. It was only seven paragraphs long—not so long so as to render scrolling down to view all of the terms inconvenient or impossible. A printer-friendly, full-screen version was made readily available. The user had ample time to review the document.

* * * The user * * * had to take affirmative action and click the "Yes, I agree to the above terms and conditions" button in order to proceed to the next step. Clicking "Continue" without clicking the "Yes" button would have returned the user to the same Web page. If the user did not agree to all of the terms, he could not have activated his account, placed ads, or incurred charges.

* * * *

A reasonably prudent Internet user would have known of the existence of terms in the AdWords Agreement. Plaintiff had to have had reasonable notice of the terms. By clicking on "Yes, I agree to the above terms and conditions" button, Plaintiff indicated assent to the terms.

* * * *

For the foregoing reasons, * * * Defendant's motion to transfer is granted and Plaintiff's motion for summary judgment is denied.

CASE NO. 3 (FOR CHAPTER 15)

Spray-Tek, Inc. v. Robbins Motor Transportation, Inc., 426 F.Supp.2d 875 (W.D.Wis. 2006).

* * * *

Plaintiff Spray-Tek, Inc. is engaged in the business of commercial dehydration of food flavor, pharmaceutical and soft chemical products. In 2003 plaintiff entered into a contract with Niro, Inc. (hereinafter Niro) in which Niro was to design and manufacture a fourteen-foot diameter conebottom drying chamber * * * for plaintiff. Pursuant to the terms of the contract Niro was also responsible for shipping the drying chamber from its facility in Hudson, Wisconsin to plaintiff's facility in Bethlehem, Pennsylvania. The contract stated in relevant part:

* * * *

For one (1) Niro-Bowen * * * drying chamber, * * * F.O.B. points of manufacture in the U.S.A. * * * Price * * * $1,161,500.00

* * * *

IX. RISKS OF LOSS. The Purchaser shall bear the risk of loss of or damage to the equipment and parts after delivery of the equipment and parts to the job site or to the shipping point if delivery F.O.B. shipping point is specified.

On October 14, 2004, Niro's representative Mr. David Thoen contacted defendant Robbins Motor Transportation, Inc. to obtain an estimate for transporting the drying chamber to plaintiff. * * * Mr. Robert Kauffman, Jr. who serves as defendant's Southwest Regional Terminal Manager * * * prepared and sent an estimate to Niro. * * *

Mr. Thoen signed the estimate and faxed it back to defendant * * *.

On October 18, 2004, defendant arrived at Niro's facility in Hudson, Wisconsin and the drying chamber was loaded onto its trailer. Niro prepared a Bill of Lading * * *.

* * * *

On or about October 28, 2004 the drying chamber was damaged while it was in transit * * * when it struck an overpass and became dislodged from defendant's vehicle. It was inspected and declared a total loss. Accordingly, Niro manufactured a replacement drying chamber for plaintiff and invoiced it $233,100.00 in replacement costs. * * *

* * * *

[Spray-Tek filed a suit in a federal district court against Robbins under a federal statute known as the Carmack Amendment to recover the replacement cost and other expenses.] The Carmack Amendment * * * states in relevant part:

A carrier providing transportation or service * * * shall issue a receipt or bill of lading for property it receives for transportation under this part. That carrier * * * [is] liable to the person entitled to recover under the receipt or bill of lading. * * *

The purpose of the Carmack Amendment is to establish uniform federal guidelines designed in part to remove the uncertainty surrounding a carrier's liability when damage occurs to a shipper's interstate shipment.

Under the Carmack Amendment plaintiff bears the burden of establishing a *prima facie* [legally sufficient] case which requires it to demonstrate: (1) delivery to the carrier in good condition; (2) arrival in damaged condition; and (3) the amount of damages. * * * The excepted causes [relieving a carrier of liability] are: (1) acts of God; (2) the public enemy; (3) acts of the shipper himself; (4) public authority; or (5) the inherent vice or nature of the goods. * * *

Defendant concedes that it received the drying chamber in good condition. Accordingly, plaintiff's first element of its *prima facie* case is established. * * *

* * * *

It is undisputed that the drying chamber was damaged when it struck an overpass and became dislodged from defendant's vehicle.

Additionally, it is undisputed that after the accident the drying chamber was inspected and declared a total loss. * * *

An * * * argument defendant asserts concerning plaintiff's second element of its *prima facie* case is that plaintiff cannot demonstrate it owned the drying chamber during transport. However, the contract plaintiff entered into with Niro establishes that it was the owner of the drying chamber when it was damaged. The contract provided that the terms of sale were "F.O.B. points of manufacture in the U.S.A." According to * * * plaintiff's vice president and general manager "F.O.B. points of manufacture" means that the drying chamber became plaintiff's property once it was "placed on board the delivery truck at its point of manufacture in Hudson, Wisconsin."

[This] assertion * * * is reinforced by the provision in the contract concerning risks of loss. * * * [T]he "F.O.B. points of manufacture" language * * * demonstrates that plaintiff bore the risk of loss once the drying chamber departed from Niro's Hudson, Wisconsin facility. * * * Accordingly, plaintiff established the second element of its *prima facie* case.

Finally, defendant asserts plaintiff cannot meet its burden of establishing the third element of its *prima facie* case because it failed to demonstrate what "it is obligated to pay for the dryer." However, * * * Niro invoiced plaintiff $233,100.00 for the replacement dryer. Accordingly, plaintiff established the third element of its *prima facie* case because its amount of damages is $233,100.00.

Plaintiff met its burden of establishing a *prima facie* case under the Carmack Amendment. * * * Defendant concedes it failed to produce any evidence establishing that damage to the shipment was due to one of the excepted causes. Accordingly, plaintiff is entitled to summary judgment on the issue of defendant's liability under the Carmack Amendment.

* * * *

[The court allowed the case to go to trial on another issue, however.]

CASE NO. 4 (FOR CHAPTER 19)

NBT Bank, N.A. v. First National Community Bank, 393 F.3d 404 (3d Cir. 2004).

* * * *

* * * [A] small group of Pennsylvania business entities arranged to write checks on one account, drawing on non-existent funds, and then cover these overdrafts with checks drawn on another account that also lacked sufficient funds. * * * The scheme collapsed when three checks initially deposited at [NBT Bank, N.A.,] and subsequently presented for payment to [First National Community Bank (FNCB)] were discovered by FNCB to have been drawn on an FNCB account that lacked sufficient funds. There is no dispute between the parties that two of these three checks were properly returned by FNCB to the [Federal Reserve Bank of Philadelphia] prior to the applicable midnight deadline.

* * * *

[On March 8, 2001, the third check (the "Disputed Check"), which was drawn on an FNCB account in the amount of $706,000, was deposited at NBT by an entity called PA Health.] After the Disputed Check was presented for deposit at NBT, the bank gave provisional credit to the depositor, PA Health, for the amount of the Disputed Check. NBT also transmitted the Disputed Check to the Reserve Bank for presentment to FNCB. * * * The Reserve Bank then forwarded the Disputed Check to FNCB, and FNCB received it on March 12, 2001. * * *

* * * *

On March 13, 2001, FNCB determined it would not pay the Disputed Check because of the absence of sufficient funds in the account on which the check was drawn. That same day, FNCB sought to return the Disputed Check to NBT through the Reserve Bank. * * * [T]he Disputed Check was physically delivered to the Reserve Bank prior to 11:59 P.M. on March 13.* * * FNCB also sent a notice of dishonor to NBT * * * in which FNCB indicated that it did not intend to pay the Disputed Check. NBT received this notice prior to the close of business on March 13. * * *

When FNCB sent the Disputed Check to the Reserve Bank on March 13, 2001, FNCB * * * erroneously encoded [it] with the routing number for PNC Bank instead of the routing number for NBT [Bank].

* * * Because the Disputed Check was improperly encoded, NBT did not receive it back * * * until March 16, 2001. * * * NBT suffered no damages or actual loss as a result of the encoding error * * *

* * * *

NBT instituted this action [in a federal district court] against FNCB on May 25, 2001. * * * NBT claimed that FNCB's encoding error meant FNCB had failed to return the Disputed Check prior to the midnight deadline as required by the UCC, and that FNCB was therefore accountable to NBT for the full amount of the Disputed Check. * * *

The District Court granted FNCB's motion [for summary judgment]. NBT appeals.

* * * *

* * * Federal law forms part of the legal framework within which check-processing activities take place. Of particular relevance to this appeal are the 1988 regulations adopted by the Federal Reserve implementing the Expedited Funds Availability Act. These regulations, referred to collectively as "Regulation CC," complement but do not necessarily replace the requirements of Article 4 of the UCC.

* * * *

* * * Regulation CC indisputably binds the parties, pursuant to both its own terms, as well as [13 Pennsylvania Consolidated Statutes Annotated Section 4103 (Pennsylvania's version of UCC 4–103)], which indicates that "Federal Reserve regulations" are to be treated as agreements that may vary the terms of the UCC.* * *

Because Regulation CC * * * is binding on the parties, and because Regulation CC is the source of the encoding requirement invoked by NBT, the extent of FNCB's liability for its encoding error must be measured by the standards set forth in Regulation CC. *Regulation CC states that a bank that fails to exercise ordinary care in complying with the [encoding] provisions of * * * Regulation CC * * * "may be liable" to the depositary bank.* Then, in broad, unrestricted language, Regulation CC states: [Emphasis added.]

The measure of damages for failure to exercise ordinary care is the amount of the loss incurred, up to the amount of the check, reduced by the amount of the loss that the [plaintiff bank] would have incurred even if the [defendant] bank had exercised ordinary care.

This provision does not provide an exception to this standard for measuring damages in instances where noncompliance with Regulation CC is alleged to have resulted in noncompliance with the UCC's midnight deadline rule. Here, the parties have stipulated that NBT suffered no loss as a result of FNCB's encoding error. Thus, under the plain language of Regulation CC, NBT may not recover from FNCB for the amount of the Disputed Check.

* * * *

Accordingly,* * * we affirm the order of the District Court * * * .

CASE NO. 5 (FOR CHAPTER 25)

Burlington Northern and Santa Fe Railway Co. v. White, 548 U.S. 53, 126 S.Ct. 2405, 165 L.Ed.2d 345 (2006).

* * * *

* * * Sheila White [was] the only woman working in the Maintenance of Way department at [Burlington Northern & Santa Fe Railway Company's] Tennessee Yard. In September 1997, White complained to Burlington officials that her * * * supervisor, Bill Joiner, had repeatedly told her that women should not be working in the Maintenance of Way department. [Joiner was disciplined. White was reassigned from forklift duty to "track laborer" tasks.]

On October 10, White filed a complaint with the Equal Employment Opportunity Commission (EEOC * * *).

[In December, White's supervisor, Percy Sharkey, complained to Burlington officials that White had been insubordinate. She was suspended without pay but reinstated after an investigation and awarded back pay for the period of the suspension. White filed a second charge with the EEOC.]

* * * *

* * * [Later] White filed this Title VII action against Burlington in federal [district] court. * * * [S]he claimed that Burlington's actions—(1) changing her job responsibilities, and (2) suspending her * * * without pay—amounted to unlawful retaliation in violation of Title VII. A jury found in White's favor * * * [and] awarded her $43,500 in * * * damages * * * .

* * * [On appeal, the U.S. Court of Appeals for the Sixth Circuit held that Title VII's antiretaliation ban is limited to acts that adversely affect the terms, conditions, or benefits of employment, and] affirmed the District Court's judgment in White's favor on both retaliation claims. [Burlington appealed to the United States Supreme Court.]

* * * *

* * * The language of the [antidiscrimination] provision differs from that of the antiretaliation provision in important ways.

The * * * words in the [antidiscrimination] provision—"hire," "discharge," "compensation, terms, conditions, or privileges of employment," "employment opportunities," and "status as an employee"—explicitly limit the scope of that provision to actions that affect employment or alter the conditions of the workplace. No such limiting words appear in the antiretaliation provision.

* * * The two provisions differ not only in language but in purpose as well. The antidiscrimination provision seeks a workplace where individuals are not discriminated against because of their racial, ethnic, religious, or gender-based status. *The anti-retaliation provision seeks to secure that primary objective by preventing an employer from interfering (through retaliation) with an employee's efforts to secure*

or advance enforcement of the Act's basic guarantees. The [antidiscrimination] provision seeks to prevent injury to individuals based on who they are, i.e., their status. *The antiretaliation provision seeks to prevent harm to individuals based on what they do, i.e., their conduct.* [Emphasis added.]

To secure the first objective, Congress did not need to prohibit anything other than employment related discrimination.

But one cannot secure the second objective by focusing only upon employer actions and harm that concern employment and the workplace. * * * *An employer can effectively retaliate against an employee by taking actions not directly related to his employment or by causing him harm outside the workplace.* [Emphasis added.]

* * * *

* * * We conclude that * * * the anti-retaliation provision extends beyond workplace related or employment-related retaliatory acts * * *.

* * * *

* * * A plaintiff must show that a reasonable employee would have found the challenged action materially adverse, which in this context means it well might have dissuaded a reasonable worker from making or supporting a charge of discrimination.

* * * *

* * * [In this case] the track labor duties were by all accounts more arduous and dirtier; * * * the forklift operator position required more qualifications, which is an indication of prestige; and * * * the forklift operator position was objectively considered a better job and the male employees resented White for occupying it. Based on this record, a jury could reasonably conclude that the reassignment of responsibilities would have been materially adverse to a reasonable employee.

* * * *

For these reasons, the judgment of the Court of Appeals is affirmed.

CASE NO. 6 (FOR CHAPTER 31)

Merrill Lynch, Pierce, Fenner & Smith, Inc. v. Dabit, 547 U.S. 71, 126 S.Ct. 1503, 164 L.Ed.2d 179 (2006).

* * * *

Petitioner Merrill Lynch, Pierce, Fenner & Smith, Inc. (Merrill Lynch), * * * offers research and brokerage services to investors.

Respondent, Shadi Dabit, is a former Merrill Lynch broker. He filed this class action in the United States District Court for the Western District of Oklahoma on behalf of himself and all other former or current brokers who, while employed by Merrill Lynch, purchased (for themselves and for their clients) certain stocks between December 1, 1999, and December 31, 2000. * * * Dabit * * * advanced his claims under Oklahoma state law.

* * * [Dabit's theory was that Merrill Lynch] research analysts * * * issued overly optimistic appraisals of the stocks' value; the brokers * * * relied on the analysts' reports in advising their investor clients * * * ; and the clients and brokers both continued to hold their stocks long beyond the point when, had the truth been known, they would have sold. * * * [W]hen the truth was actually revealed * * *, the stocks' prices plummeted.

* * * *

* * * [The case was transferred] to the United States District Court for the Southern District of New York * * * [which granted

Merrill Lynch's motion to dismiss. The U.S. Court of Appeals for the Second Circuit reversed this ruling. Merrill Lynch appealed to the United States Supreme Court.]

* * * *

The magnitude of the federal interest in protecting the integrity and efficient operation of the market for nationally traded securities cannot be overstated. In response to the sudden and disastrous collapse in prices of listed stocks in 1929, and the Great Depression that followed, Congress enacted the Securities Act of 1933, and the Securities Exchange Act of 1934. Since their enactment, these two statutes have anchored federal regulation of vital elements of our economy.

* * * *

Policy considerations * * * prompted Congress, in 1995, to adopt [the Private Securities Litigation Reform Act] targeted at perceived abuses of the class-action vehicle in litigation involving nationally traded securities.

* * * *

* * * [P]laintiffs and their representatives began bringing class actions under state law, often in state court. * * * To stem this shift from Federal to State courts * * *, Congress enacted SLUSA.

* * * *

The core provision of SLUSA reads as follows:
* * * No * * * class action based upon the * * * law of any State * * * may be maintained in any * * * court by any private party alleging—* * * a misrepresentation or omission of a material fact in connection with the purchase or sale of a * * * security * * *.

* * * *

* * * Under our precedents, it is enough that the fraud alleged "coincide" with a securities transaction—whether by the plaintiff or by someone else. *The requisite showing, in other words, is deception "in connection with the purchase or sale of any security," not deception of an identifiable purchaser or seller.* Notably, this broader interpretation of the statutory language comports [is consistent] with the long-standing views of the [Securities and Exchange Commission (SEC)]. [Emphasis added.]

Congress can hardly have been unaware of the broad construction adopted by both this Court and the SEC when it imported the key phrase—"in connection with the purchase or sale"—into SLUSA's core provision. *And when judicial interpretations have settled the meaning of an existing statutory provision, repetition of the same language in a new statute indicates * * * the intent to incorporate its * * * judicial interpretations as well.* [Emphasis added.]

* * * A narrow reading of the statute would undercut the effectiveness of the 1995 Reform Act and thus run contrary to SLUSA's stated purpose "to prevent certain State private securities class action lawsuits alleging fraud from being used to frustrate the objectives" of the 1995 Act.

* * * The prospect is raised, then, of parallel class actions proceeding in state and federal court, with different standards governing claims asserted on identical facts. That prospect * * * squarely conflicts with the congressional preference for national standards for securities class action lawsuits involving nationally traded securities.

* * * *

The judgment of the Court of Appeals for the Second Circuit is vacated, and the case is remanded * * *.

CASE NO. 7 (FOR CHAPTER 36)

Kelo v. City of New London, Connecticut, 545 U.S. 469, 125 S.Ct. 2655, 162 L.Ed.2d 439 (2005).

* * * *

The city of New London (hereinafter City) sits at the junction of the Thames River and the Long Island Sound in southeastern Connecticut. Decades of economic decline led a state agency in 1990 to designate the City a "distressed municipality." In 1996, the Federal Government closed the Naval Undersea Warfare Center, which had been located in the Fort Trumbull area of the City and had employed over 1,500 people. In 1998, the City's unemployment rate was nearly double that of the State, and its population of just under 24,000 residents was at its lowest since 1920.

These conditions prompted state and local officials to target New London * * * for economic revitalization. * * * In February [1998] the pharmaceutical company Pfizer Inc. announced that it would build a $300 million research facility on a site immediately adjacent to Fort Trumbull; local planners hoped that Pfizer would draw new business to the area * * *.

* * * *

The city council approved [a] plan in January 2000 [to redevelop the area that once housed the federal facility]. The [City] successfully negotiated the purchase of most of the real estate in the 90-acre area, but its negotiations with [some of the property owners] failed. As a consequence, in November 2000, the [City] initiated * * * condemnation proceedings * * *.

* * * *

* * * Susette Kelo has lived in the Fort Trumbull area since 1997. * * * [S]he prizes [her house] for its water view. * * *

In December 2000 [Kelo and others] brought this action in [a Connecticut state court against the City and others]. They claimed, among other things, that the taking of their properties would violate the "public use" restriction in the [U.S. Constitution's] Fifth Amendment. * * * [The court issued a ruling partly in favor of both sides].

* * * [B]oth sides took appeals to the Supreme Court of Connecticut [which] held * * * that all of the City's proposed takings were valid.* * *

* * * *

We granted *certiorari* to determine whether a city's decision to take property for the purpose of economic development satisfies the "public use" requirement of the Fifth Amendment.

* * * *

* * * [T]his Court long ago rejected any literal requirement that condemned property be put into use for the general public. * * * Not only was the "use by the public" test difficult to administer (e.g., what proportion of the public need have access to the property? at what price?), but it proved to be impractical given the diverse and always evolving needs of society. Accordingly, * * * *this Court* * * * *embraced the broader and more natural interpretation of public use as "public purpose."* * * * [Emphasis added.]

The disposition of this case therefore turns on the question whether the City's development plan serves a "public purpose." * * *

* * * *

Viewed as a whole, our jurisprudence has recognized that the needs of society have varied between different parts of the Nation, just as they have evolved over time in response to changed circumstances. * * * *For more than a century, our public use jurisprudence has wisely eschewed [avoided] rigid formulas and intrusive scrutiny in favor of affording legislatures broad latitude in determining what public needs justify the use of the takings power.* [Emphasis added.]

* * * *

Those who govern the City were not confronted with the need to remove blight in the Fort Trumbull area, but their determination that the area was sufficiently distressed to justify a program of economic rejuvenation is entitled to our deference. The City has carefully formulated an economic development plan that it believes will provide appreciable benefits to the community, including—but by no means limited to—new jobs and increased tax revenue. * * * To effectuate this plan, the City has invoked a state statute that specifically authorizes the use of eminent domain to promote economic development. Given the comprehensive character of the plan, the thorough deliberation that preceded its adoption, and the limited scope of our review, it is appropriate for us * * * to resolve the challenges of the individual owners, not on a piecemeal basis, but rather in light of the entire plan. *Because that plan unquestionably serves a public purpose, the takings challenged here satisfy the public use requirement of the Fifth Amendment.* [Emphasis added.]

* * * *

The judgment of the Supreme Court of Connecticut is affirmed.

Glossary

A

abandoned property • Property that has been discarded by the owner, with no intention of reclaiming it.

acceleration clause • A clause that allows a payee or other holder of a time instrument to demand payment of the entire amount due, with interest, if a certain event occurs, such as a default in the payment of an installment when due.

acceptance • A voluntary act by the offeree that shows assent, or agreement, to the terms of an offer; may consist of words or conduct. In negotiable instruments law, the drawee's signed agreement to pay a draft when it is presented.

acceptor • A drawee that is legally obligated to pay an instrument when it is presented later for payment.

accession • Occurs when an individual adds value to personal property by the use of either labor or materials. In some situations, a person may acquire ownership rights in another's property through accession.

accord and satisfaction • A common means of settling a disputed claim, whereby a debtor offers to pay a lesser amount than the creditor purports to be owed. The creditor's acceptance of the offer creates an accord (agreement), and when the accord is executed, satisfaction occurs.

accredited investors • In the context of securities offerings, "sophisticated" investors, such as banks, insurance companies, investment companies, the issuer's executive officers and directors, and persons whose income or net worth exceeds certain limits.

actionable • Capable of serving as the basis of a lawsuit. An actionable claim can be pursued in a lawsuit or other court action.

act of state doctrine • A doctrine providing that the judicial branch of one country will not examine the validity of public acts committed by a recognized foreign government within its own territory.

actual malice • The deliberate intent to cause harm, which exists when a person makes a statement either knowing that it is false or showing a reckless disregard for whether it is true. In a defamation suit, a statement made about a public figure normally must be made with actual malice for the plaintiff to recover damages.

actus reus • A guilty (prohibited) act. The commission of a prohibited act is one of the two essential elements required for criminal liability, the other element being the intent to commit a crime.

adhesion contract • A "standard-form" contract, such as that between a large retailer and a consumer, in which the stronger party dictates the terms.

adjudicate • To render a judicial decision. In the administrative process, adjudication is the trial-like proceeding in which an administrative law judge hears and decides issues that arise when an administrative agency charges a person or a firm with violating a law or regulation enforced by the agency.

administrative agency • A federal or state government agency established to perform a specific function. Administrative agencies are authorized by legislative acts to make and enforce rules in order to administer and enforce the acts.

administrative law • The body of law created by administrative agencies (in the form of rules, regulations, orders, and decisions) in order to carry out their duties and responsibilities.

administrative law judge (ALJ) • One who presides over an administrative agency hearing and has the power to administer oaths, take testimony, rule on questions of evidence, and make determinations of fact.

administrative process • The procedure used by administrative agencies in administering the law.

administrator • One who is appointed by a court to handle the probate (disposition) of a person's estate if that person dies intestate (without a valid will) or if the executor named in the will cannot serve.

adverse possession • The acquisition of title to real property by occupying it openly, without the consent of the owner, for a period of time specified by a state statute. The occupation must be actual, open, notorious, exclusive, and in opposition to all others, including the owner.

affirmative action • Job-hiring policies that give special consideration to members of protected classes in an effort to overcome present effects of past discrimination.

after-acquired property • Property that is acquired by the debtor after the execution of a security agreement.

agency • A relationship between two parties in which one party (the agent) agrees to represent or act for the other (the principal).

agreement • A meeting of two or more minds in regard to the terms of a contract; usually broken down into two events—an offer by one party to form a contract and an acceptance of the offer by the person to whom the offer is made.

alienation • The process of transferring land out of one's possession (thus "alienating" the land from oneself).

alien corporation • A designation in the United States for a corporation formed in another country but doing business in the United States.

alternative dispute resolution (ADR) • The resolution of disputes in ways other than those involved in the traditional judicial process. Negotiation, mediation, and arbitration are forms of ADR.

answer • Procedurally, a defendant's response to the plaintiff's complaint.

anticipatory repudiation • An assertion or action by a party indicating that he or she will not perform an obligation that the party is contractually obligated to perform at a future time.

antitrust law • Laws protecting commerce from unlawful restraints.

apparent authority • Authority that is only apparent, not real. In agency law, a person may be deemed to have had the power to act as an agent for another party if the other party's manifestations to a third party led the third party to believe that an agency existed when, in fact, it did not.

appraisal right • The right of a dissenting shareholder, who objects to an extraordinary transaction of the corporation (such as a merger or a consolidation), to have his or her shares appraised and to be paid the fair value of those shares by the corporation.

appropriation • In tort law, the use by one person of another person's name, likeness, or other identifying characteristic without permission and for the benefit of the user.

arbitration • The settling of a dispute by submitting it to a disinterested third party (other than a court), who renders a decision that is (most often) legally binding.

arbitration clause • A clause in a contract that provides that, in the event of a dispute, the parties will submit the dispute to arbitration rather than litigate the dispute in court.

arson • The intentional burning of another's building. Some statutes have expanded this to include any real property regardless of ownership and the destruction of property by other means—for example, by explosion.

articles of incorporation • The document filed with the appropriate governmental agency, usually the secretary of state, when a business is incorporated. State statutes usually prescribe what kind of information must be contained in the articles of incorporation.

articles of organization • The document filed with a designated state official by which a limited liability company is formed.

articles of partnership • A written agreement that sets forth each partner's rights and obligations with respect to the partnership.

artisan's lien • A possessory lien given to a person who has made improvements and added value to another person's personal property as security for payment for services performed.

assault • Any word or action intended to make another person fearful of immediate physical harm; a reasonably believable threat.

assignee • A party to whom the rights under a contract are transferred, or assigned.

assignment • The act of transferring to another all or part of one's rights arising under a contract.

assignor • A party who transfers (assigns) his or her rights under a contract to another party (called the assignee).

assumption of risk • A doctrine under which a plaintiff may not recover for injuries or damage suffered from risks he or she knows of and has voluntarily assumed.

attachment • In a secured transaction, the process by which a secured creditor's interest "attaches" to the property of another (collateral) and the creditor's security interest becomes enforceable. In the context of judicial liens, a court-ordered seizure and taking into custody of property prior to the securing of a judgment for a past-due debt.

attempted monopolization • Any actions by a firm to eliminate competition and gain monopoly power.

authorization card • A card signed by an employee that gives a union permission to act on his or her behalf in negotiations with management.

automatic stay • In bankruptcy proceedings, the suspension of almost all litigation and other action by creditors against the debtor or the debtor's property. The stay is effective the moment the debtor files a petition in bankruptcy.

award • In litigation, the amount of monetary compensation awarded to a plaintiff in a civil lawsuit as damages. In the context of alternative dispute resolution, the decision rendered by an arbitrator.

B

bailee • One to whom goods are entrusted by a bailor. Under the UCC, a party who, by a bill of lading, warehouse receipt, or other document of title, acknowledges possession of goods and/or contracts to deliver them.

bailee's lien • A possessory lien, or claim, that a bailee entitled to compensation can place on the bailed property to ensure that he or she will be paid for the services provided. The lien is effective as long as the bailee retains possession of the bailed goods and has not agreed to extend credit to the bailor. Sometimes referred to as an artisan's lien.

bailment • A situation in which the personal property of one person (a bailor) is entrusted to another (a bailee), who is obligated to return the bailed property to the bailor or dispose of it as directed.

bailor • One who entrusts goods to a bailee.

bait-and-switch advertising • Advertising a product at a very attractive price (the bait) and then, once the consumer is in the store, saying that the advertised product either is not available or is of poor quality. The customer is then urged to purchase (switched to) a more expensive item.

bankruptcy court • A federal court of limited jurisdiction that handles only bankruptcy proceedings, which are governed by federal bankruptcy law.

battery • The unexcused, harmful or offensive, intentional touching of another.

bearer • A person in possession of an instrument payable to bearer or indorsed in blank.

bearer instrument • Any instrument that is not payable to a specific person, including instruments payable to the bearer or to "cash."

bequest • A gift of personal property by will (from the verb to bequeath).

beyond a reasonable doubt • The standard of proof used in criminal cases. If there is any reasonable doubt that a criminal defendant committed the crime with which she or he has been charged, then the verdict must be "not guilty."

bilateral contract • A type of contract that arises when a promise is given in exchange for a return promise.

Bill of Rights • The first ten amendments to the U.S. Constitution.

binder • A written, temporary insurance policy.

binding authority • Any source of law that a court must follow when deciding a case. Binding authorities include constitutions, statutes, and regulations that govern the issue being decided, as well as court decisions that are controlling precedents within the jurisdiction.

blank indorsement • An indorsement that specifies no particular indorsee and can consist of a mere signature. An order instrument that is indorsed in blank becomes a bearer instrument.

blue sky laws • State laws that regulate the offering and sale of securities for the protection of the public.

bona fide occupational qualification (BFOQ) • Identifiable characteristics reasonably necessary to the normal operation of a particular business. These characteristics can include gender, national origin, and religion, but not race.

bond • A security that evidences a corporate (or government) debt. It does not represent an ownership interest in the issuing entity.

bond indenture • A contract between the issuer of a bond and the bondholder.

botnet • A network of computers that have been appropriated without the knowledge of their owners and used to spread harmful programs via the Internet; short for robot network.

breach • The failure to perform a legal obligation.

breach of contract • The failure, without legal excuse, of a promisor to perform the obligations of a contract.

brief • A formal legal document prepared by a party's attorney for the appellant or the appellee (in answer to the appellant's brief) and submitted to an appellate court when a case is appealed. The appellant's brief outlines the facts and issues of the case, the judge's rulings or jury's findings that should be reversed or modified, the applicable law, and the arguments on the client's behalf.

browse-wrap term • A term or condition of use that is presented to an Internet user at the time certain products, such as software, are being downloaded but that need not be agreed to (by clicking "I agree," for example) before the user is able to install or use the product.

burglary • The unlawful entry or breaking into a building with the intent to commit a felony. (Some state statutes expand this to include the intent to commit any crime.)

business ethics • Ethics in a business context; a consensus as to what constitutes right or wrong behavior in the world of business and the application of moral principles to situations that arise in a business setting.

business invitee • A person, such as a customer or a client, who is invited onto business premises by the owner of those premises for business purposes.

business judgment rule • A rule that immunizes corporate management from liability for actions that result in corporate losses or damages if the actions are undertaken in good faith and are within both the power of the corporation and the authority of management to make.

business necessity • A defense to allegations of employment discrimination in which the employer demonstrates that an employment practice that discriminates against members of a protected class is related to job performance.

business tort • Wrongful interference with another's business rights.

business trust • A form of business organization in which investors (trust beneficiaries) transfer cash or property to trustees in exchange for trust certificates that represent their investment shares. The certificate holders share in the trust's profits but have limited liability.

buyout price • The amount payable to a partner on his or her dissociation from a partnership, based on the amount distributable to that partner if the firm were wound up on that date, and offset by any damages for wrongful dissociation.

bylaws • A set of governing rules adopted by a corporation or other association.

C

case law • The rules of law announced in court decisions. Case law includes the aggregate of reported cases that interpret judicial precedents, statutes, regulations, and constitutional provisions.

cashier's check • A check drawn by a bank on itself.

categorical imperative • A concept developed by the philosopher Immanuel Kant as an ethical guideline for behavior. In deciding whether an action is right or wrong, or desirable or undesirable, a person should evaluate the action in terms of what would happen if everybody else in the same situation, or category, acted the same way.

causation in fact • An act or omission without which an event would not have occurred.

cease-and-desist order • An administrative or judicial order prohibiting a person or business firm from conducting activities that an agency or court has deemed illegal.

certificate of deposit (CD) • A note issued by a bank in which the bank acknowledges the receipt of funds from a party and promises to repay that amount, with interest, to the party on a certain date.

certificate of limited partnership • The basic document filed with a designated state official by which a limited partnership is formed.

certification mark • A mark used by one or more persons, other than the owner, to certify the region, materials, mode of manufacture, quality, or other characteristic of specific goods or services.

certified check • A check that has been accepted in writing by the bank on which it is drawn. Essentially, the bank, by certifying (accepting) the check, promises to pay the check at the time the check is presented.

charging order • In partnership law, an order granted by a court to a judgment creditor that entitles the creditor to attach profits or assets of a partner on the dissolution of the partnership.

charitable trust • A trust in which the property held by the trustee must be used for a charitable purpose, such as the advancement of health, education, or religion.

chattel • All forms of personal property.

check • A draft drawn by a drawer ordering the drawee bank or financial institution to pay a certain amount of money to the holder on demand.

checks and balances • The principle under which the powers of the national government are divided among three separate branches—the executive, legislative, and judicial branches—each of which exercises a check on the actions of the others.

choice-of-language clause • A clause in a contract designating the official language by which the contract will be interpreted in the event of a future disagreement over the contract's terms.

choice-of-law clause • A clause in a contract designating the law (such as the law of a particular state or nation) that will govern the contract.

citation • A reference to a publication in which a legal authority—such as a statute or a court decision—or other source can be found.

civil law • The branch of law dealing with the definition and enforcement of all private or public rights, as opposed to criminal matters.

civil law system • A system of law derived from that of the Roman Empire and based on a code rather than case law; the predominant system of law in the nations of continental Europe and the nations that were once their colonies. In the United States, Louisiana, because of its historical ties to France, has, in part, a civil law system.

clearinghouse • A system or place where banks exchange checks and drafts drawn on each other and settle daily balances.

click-on agreement • An agreement that arises when a buyer, engaging in a transaction on a computer, indicates assent to be bound by the terms of an offer by clicking on a button that says, for example, "I agree"; sometimes referred to as a click-on license or a click-wrap agreement.

close corporation • A corporation whose shareholders are limited to a small group of persons, often only family members. In a close corporation, the shareholders' rights to transfer shares to others are usually restricted.

closed shop • A firm that requires union membership by its workers as a condition of employment. The closed shop was made illegal by the Labor-Management Relations Act of 1947.

cloud computing • A subscription-based or pay-per-use service that, in real time over the Internet, extends a computer's software or storage capabilities. By using the services of large companies with excess storage and computing capacity, a company can increase its information technology capabilities without investing in new infrastructure, training new personnel, or licensing new software.

codicil • A written supplement or modification to a will. A codicil must be executed with the same formalities as a will.

collateral • Under Article 9 of the UCC, the property subject to a security interest, including accounts and chattel paper that have been sold.

collateral promise • A secondary promise that is ancillary (subsidiary) to a principal transaction or primary contractual relationship, such as a promise made by one person to pay the debts of another if the latter fails to perform. A collateral promise normally must be in writing to be enforceable.

collecting bank • Any bank handling an item for collection, except the payor bank.

collective bargaining • The process by which labor and management negotiate the terms and conditions of employment, including working hours and workplace conditions.

collective mark • A mark used by members of a cooperative, association, union, or other organization to certify the region, materials, mode of manufacture, quality, or other characteristic of specific goods or services.

comity • The principle by which one nation defers to and gives effect to the laws and judicial decrees of another nation. This recognition is based primarily on respect.

commerce clause • The provision in Article I, Section 8, of the U.S. Constitution that gives Congress the power to regulate interstate commerce.

commercial impracticability • A doctrine under which a seller may be excused from performing a contract when (1) a contingency occurs, (2) the contingency's occurrence makes performance impracticable, and (3) the nonoccurrence of the contingency was a basic assumption on which the contract was made. Although UCC Section 2–615 expressly frees only sellers under this doctrine, courts have not distinguished between buyers and sellers in applying it.

commingle • To put funds or goods together into one mass so that they are mixed to such a degree that they no longer have separate identities. In corporate law, if personal and corporate interests are commingled to the extent that the corporation has no separate identity, a court may "pierce the corporate veil" and expose the shareholders to personal liability.

common law • The body of law developed from custom or judicial decisions in English and U.S. courts, not attributable to a legislature.

common stock • Shares of ownership in a corporation that give the owner of the stock a proportionate interest in the corporation with regard to control, earnings, and net assets. Shares of common stock are lowest in priority with respect to payment of dividends and distribution of the corporation's assets on dissolution.

community property • A form of concurrent ownership of property in which each spouse technically owns an undivided one-half interest in property acquired during the marriage. This form of joint ownership occurs in only ten states and Puerto Rico.

comparative negligence • A rule in tort law that reduces the plaintiff's recovery in proportion to the plaintiff's degree of fault, rather than barring recovery completely; used in the majority of states.

compensatory damages • A monetary award equivalent to the actual value of injuries or damage sustained by the aggrieved party.

complaint • The pleading made by a plaintiff alleging wrongdoing on the part of the defendant; the document that, when filed with a court, initiates a lawsuit.

computer crime • Any wrongful act that is directed against computers and computer parts or that involves the wrongful use or abuse of computers or software.

concentrated industry • An industry in which a large percentage of market sales is controlled by either a single firm or a small number of firms.

concurrent conditions • Conditions that must occur or be performed at the same time; they are mutually dependent. No obligations arise until these conditions are simultaneously performed.

concurrent jurisdiction • Jurisdiction that exists when two different courts have the power to hear a case. For example, some cases can be heard in a federal or a state court.

concurrent ownership • Joint ownership.

condemnation • The process of taking private property for public use through the government's power of eminent domain.

condition • A qualification, provision, or clause in a contractual agreement, the occurrence or nonoccurrence of which creates, suspends, or terminates the obligations of the contracting parties.

condition precedent • In a contractual agreement, a condition that must be met before a party's promise becomes absolute.

condition subsequent • A condition in a contract that, if it occurs, operates to terminate a party's absolute promise to perform.

confession of judgment • The act or agreement of a debtor permitting a judgment to be entered against him or her by a creditor, for an agreed sum, without the institution of legal proceedings.

confiscation • A government's taking of a privately owned business or personal property without a proper public purpose or an award of just compensation.

conforming goods • Goods that conform to contract specifications.

confusion • The mixing together of goods belonging to two or more owners to such an extent that the separately owned goods cannot be identified.

consequential damages • Special damages that compensate for a loss that does not directly or immediately result from the breach (for example, lost profits). For the plaintiff to collect consequential damages, they must have been reasonably foreseeable at the time the breach or injury occurred.

consideration • Generally, the value given in return for a promise; involves two elements—the giving of something of legally sufficient value and a bargained-for exchange. The consideration must result in a detriment to the promisee or a benefit to the promisor.

consolidation • A contractual and statutory process in which two or more corporations join to become a completely new corporation. The original corporations cease to exist, and the new corporation acquires all their assets and liabilities.

constitutional law • The body of law derived from the U.S. Constitution and the constitutions of the various states.

constructive delivery • An act equivalent to the actual, physical delivery of property that cannot be physically delivered because of difficulty or impossibility. For example, the transfer of a key to a safe constructively delivers the contents of the safe.

constructive discharge • A termination of employment brought about by making the employee's working conditions so intolerable that the employee reasonably feels compelled to leave.

constructive eviction • A form of eviction that occurs when a landlord fails to perform adequately any of the duties (such as providing heat in the winter) required by the lease, thereby making the tenant's further use and enjoyment of the property exceedingly difficult or impossible.

constructive trust • An equitable trust that is imposed in the interests of fairness and justice when someone wrongfully holds legal title to property. A court may require the owner to hold the property in trust for the person or persons who should rightfully own the property.

consumer-debtor • An individual whose debts are primarily consumer debts (debts for purchases made primarily for personal, family, or household use).

continuation statement • A statement that, if filed within six months prior to the expiration date of the original financing statement, continues the perfection of the original security interest for another five years. The perfection of a security interest can be continued in the same manner indefinitely.

contract • An agreement that can be enforced in court; formed by two or more competent parties who agree, for consideration, to perform or to refrain from performing some legal act now or in the future.

contractual capacity • The threshold mental capacity required by law for a party who enters into a contract to be bound by that contract.

contributory negligence • A rule in tort law that completely bars the plaintiff from recovering any damages if the damage suffered is partly the plaintiff's own fault; used in a minority of states.

conversion • Wrongfully taking or retaining possession of an individual's personal property and placing it in the service of another.

conveyance • The transfer of title to land from one person to another by deed; a document (such as a deed) by which an interest in land is transferred from one person to another.

"cooling-off" laws • Laws that allow buyers a period of time, such as three business days, in which to cancel door-to-door sales contracts.

cooperative • An association, which may or may not be incorporated, that is organized to provide an economic service to its members. Unincorporated cooperatives are often treated like partnerships for tax and other legal purposes. Examples of cooperatives include consumer purchasing cooperatives, credit cooperatives, and farmers' cooperatives.

copyright • The exclusive right of an author or originator of a literary or artistic production to publish, print, or sell that production for a statutory period of time. A copyright has the same monopolistic nature as a patent or trademark, but it differs in that it applies exclusively to works of art, literature, and other works of authorship (including computer programs).

corporate governance • A set of policies or procedures affecting the way a corporation is directed or controlled.

corporate social responsibility • The idea that corporations can and should act ethically and be accountable to society for their actions.

corporation • A legal entity formed in compliance with statutory requirements that is distinct from its shareholder-owners.

correspondent bank • A bank in which another bank has an account (and vice versa) for the purpose of facilitating fund transfers.

cost-benefit analysis • A decision-making technique that involves weighing the costs of a given action against the benefits of that action.

co-surety • A joint surety; a person who assumes liability jointly with another surety for the payment of an obligation.

counteradvertising • New advertising that is undertaken pursuant to a Federal Trade Commission order for the purpose of correcting earlier false claims that were made about a product.

counterclaim • A claim made by a defendant in a civil lawsuit against the plaintiff. In effect, the defendant is suing the plaintiff.

counteroffer • An offeree's response to an offer in which the offeree rejects the original offer and at the same time makes a new offer.

course of dealing • Prior conduct between the parties to a contract that establishes a common basis for their understanding.

course of performance • The conduct that occurs under the terms of a particular agreement. Such conduct indicates what the parties to an agreement intended it to mean.

covenant not to compete • A contractual promise of one party to refrain from conducting business similar to that of another party for a certain period of time and within a specified geographic area. Courts commonly enforce such covenants if they are reasonable in terms of time and geographic area and are part of, or supplemental to, a contract for the sale of a business or an employment contract.

covenant not to sue • An agreement to substitute a contractual obligation for some other type of legal action based on a valid claim.

cover • Under the UCC, a remedy that allows the buyer or lessee, on the seller's or lessor's breach, to purchase the goods, in good faith and within a reasonable time, from another seller or lessor and substitute them for the goods due under the contract. If the cost of cover exceeds the cost of the contract goods, the breaching seller or lessor will be liable to the buyer or lessee for the difference, plus incidental and consequential damages.

cram-down provision • A provision of the Bankruptcy Code that allows a court to confirm a debtor's Chapter 11 reorganization plan even though only one class of creditors has accepted it.

creditors' composition agreement • An agreement formed between a debtor and his or her creditors in which the creditors agree to accept a lesser sum than that owed by the debtor in full satisfaction of the debt.

crime • A wrong against society proclaimed in a statute and, if committed, punishable by society through fines and/or imprisonment—and, in some cases, death.

criminal law • Law that defines and governs actions that constitute crimes. Generally, criminal law has to do with wrongful actions committed against society for which society demands redress.

cross-collateralization • The use of an asset that is not the subject of a loan to collateralize that loan.

cure • The right of a party who tenders nonconforming performance to correct that performance within the contract period [UCC 2–508(1)].

cyber crime • A crime that occurs online, in the virtual community of the Internet, as opposed to in the physical world.

cyber fraud • Any misrepresentation knowingly made over the Internet with the intention of deceiving another and on which a reasonable person would and does rely to his or her detriment.

cyberlaw • An informal term used to refer to all laws governing electronic communications and transactions, particularly those conducted via the Internet.

cyber mark • A trademark in cyberspace.

cybernotary • A legally recognized authority that can certify the validity of digital signatures.

cybersquatting • The act of registering a domain name that is the same as, or confusingly similar to, the trademark of another and then offering to sell that domain name back to the trademark owner.

cyberstalking • The crime of stalking committed in cyberspace though the use of the Internet, e-mail, or another form of electronic communication. Generally, stalking involves harassing a person and putting that person in reasonable fear for his or her safety or the safety of the person's immediate family.

cyberterrorist • A person who uses the Internet to attack or sabotage businesses and government agencies with the purpose of disrupting infrastructure systems.

cyber tort • A tort committed in cyberspace.

D

damages • Money sought as a remedy for a breach of contract or a tortious action.

debtor • Under Article 9 of the UCC, any party who owes payment or performance of a secured obligation, whether or not the party actually owns or has rights in the collateral.

debtor in possession (DIP) • In Chapter 11 bankruptcy proceedings, a debtor who is allowed to continue in possession of the estate in property (the business) and to continue business operations.

deceptive advertising • Advertising that misleads consumers, either by making unjustified claims concerning a product's performance or by omitting a material fact concerning the product's composition or performance.

deed • A document by which title to property (usually real property) is passed.

defalcation • Embezzlement; the misappropriation of funds by a party, such as a corporate officer or public official, in a fiduciary relationship with another.

defamation • Anything published or publicly spoken that causes injury to another's good name, reputation, or character.

default • Failure to observe a promise or discharge an obligation; commonly used to refer to failure to pay a debt when it is due.

default judgment • A judgment entered by a court against a defendant who has failed to appear in court to answer or defend against the plaintiff's claim.

defendant • One against whom a lawsuit is brought; the accused person in a criminal proceeding.

defense • A reason offered and alleged by a defendant in an action or lawsuit as to why the plaintiff should not recover or establish what she or he seeks.

deficiency judgment • A judgment against a debtor for the amount of a debt remaining unpaid after the collateral has been repossessed and sold.

delegatee • A party to whom contractual obligations are transferred, or delegated.

delegation of duties • The act of transferring to another all or part of one's duties arising under a contract.

delegator • A party who transfers (delegates) her or his obligations under a contract to another party (called the delegatee).

depositary bank • The first bank to receive a check for payment.

deposition • The testimony of a party to a lawsuit or a witness taken under oath before a trial.

destination contract • A contract for the sale of goods in which the seller is required or authorized to ship the goods by carrier and tender delivery of the goods at a particular destination. The seller assumes liability for any losses or damage to the goods until they are tendered at the destination specified in the contract.

devise • As a noun, a gift of real property by will; as a verb, to make a gift of real property by will.

devisee • One designated in a will to receive a gift of real property.

digital cash • Funds contained on computer software, in the form of secure programs stored on microchips and on other computer devices.

disaffirmance • The legal avoidance, or setting aside, of a contractual obligation.

discharge • The termination of an obligation. In contract law, discharge occurs when the parties have fully performed their contractual obligations or when events, conduct of the parties, or operation of law releases the parties from performance. In bankruptcy proceedings, the extinction of the debtor's dischargeable debts, thereby relieving the debtor of the obligation to pay the debts.

disclosed principal • A principal whose identity is known to a third party at the time the agent makes a contract with the third party.

discovery • A phase in the litigation process during which the opposing parties may obtain information from each other and from third parties prior to trial.

dishonor • To refuse to pay or accept a negotiable instrument, whichever is required, even though the instrument is presented in a timely and proper manner.

disparagement of property • An economically injurious falsehood made about another's product or property; a general term for torts that are more specifically referred to as slander of quality or slander of title.

disparate-impact discrimination • A form of employment discrimination that results from certain employer practices or procedures that, although not discriminatory on their face, have a discriminatory effect.

disparate-treatment discrimination • A form of employment discrimination that results when an employer intentionally discriminates against employees who are members of protected classes.

dissociation • The severance of the relationship between a partner and a partnership when the partner ceases to be associated with the carrying on of the partnership business.

dissolution • The formal disbanding of a partnership or a corporation. Dissolution of a corporation can take place by (1) an act of the state, (2) agreement of the shareholders and the board of directors, (3) the expiration of a time period stated in the certificate of incorporation, or (4) court order.

dissolution • The formal disbanding of a partnership or a corporation. It can take place by (1) acts of the partners or, in a corporation, acts of the shareholders and board of directors; (2) the subsequent illegality of the firm's business; (3) the expiration of a time period stated in a partnership agreement or a certificate of incorporation; or (4) judicial decree.

distributed network • A network that can be used by persons located (distributed) around the country or the globe to share computer files.

distribution agreement • A contract between a seller and a distributor of the seller's products setting out the terms and conditions of the distributorship.

diversity of citizenship • Under Article III, Section 2, of the U.S. Constitution, a basis for federal district court jurisdiction over a lawsuit between (1) citizens of different states, (2) a foreign country and citizens of a state or of different states, or (3) citizens of a state and citizens or subjects of a foreign country. The amount in controversy must be more than $75,000 before a federal district court can take jurisdiction in such cases.

divestiture • The act of selling one or more of a company's divisions or parts, such as a subsidiary or plant; often mandated by the courts in merger or monopolization cases.

dividend • A distribution to corporate shareholders of corporate profits or income, disbursed in proportion to the number of shares held.

docket • The list of cases entered on a court's calendar and thus scheduled to be heard by the court.

document of title • A paper exchanged in the regular course of business that evidences the right to possession of goods (for example, a bill of lading or a warehouse receipt).

domain name • The last part of an Internet address, such as "westlaw.com." The top level (the part of the name to the right of the period) indicates the type of entity that operates the site (com is an abbreviation for "commercial"). The second level (the part of the name to the left of the period) is chosen by the entity.

domestic corporation • In a given state, a corporation that does business in, and is organized under the law of, that state.

dominion • Ownership rights in property, including the right to possess and control the property.

double jeopardy • A situation occurring when a person is tried twice for the same criminal offense; prohibited by the Fifth Amendment to the U.S. Constitution.

draft • Any instrument drawn on a drawee that orders the drawee to pay a certain sum of money, usually to a third party (the payee), on demand or at a definite future time.

dram shop act • A state statute that imposes liability on the owners of bars and taverns, as well as those who serve alcoholic drinks to the public, for injuries resulting from accidents caused by intoxicated persons when the sellers or servers of alcoholic drinks contributed to the intoxication.

drawee • The party that is ordered to pay a draft or check. With a check, a bank or a financial institution is always the drawee.

drawer • The party that initiates a draft (such as a check), thereby ordering the drawee to pay.

due diligence • A required standard of care that certain professionals, such as accountants, must meet to avoid liability for securities violations.

due process clause • The provisions in the Fifth and Fourteenth Amendments to the U.S. Constitution that guarantee that no person shall be deprived of life, liberty, or property without due process of law. Similar clauses are found in most state constitutions.

dumping • The selling of goods in a foreign country at a price below the price charged for the same goods in the domestic market.

duress • Unlawful pressure brought to bear on a person, causing the person to perform an act that she or he would not otherwise perform.

duty of care • The duty of all persons, as established by tort law, to exercise a reasonable amount of care in their dealings with others. Failure to exercise due care, which is normally determined by the reasonable person standard, constitutes the tort of negligence.

E

e-agent • A computer program that by electronic or other automated means can independently initiate an action or respond to electronic messages or data without review by an individual.

easement • A nonpossessory right to use another's property in a manner established by either express or implied agreement.

e-contract • A contract that is formed electronically.

e-evidence • Evidence that consists of computer-generated or electronically recorded information, including e-mail, voice mail, spreadsheets, word-processing documents, and other data.

electronic fund transfer (EFT) • A transfer of funds through the use of an electronic terminal, a telephone, a computer, or magnetic tape.

emancipation • In regard to minors, the act of being freed from parental control; occurs when a child's parent or legal guardian relinquishes the legal right to exercise control over the child. Normally, a minor who leaves home to support himself or herself is considered emancipated.

embezzlement • The fraudulent appropriation of funds or other property by a person to whom the funds or property has been entrusted.

eminent domain • The power of a government to take land from private citizens for public use on the payment of just compensation.

e-money • Prepaid funds recorded on a computer or a card (such as a smart card or a stored-value card).

employment at will • A common law doctrine under which either party may terminate an employment relationship at any time for any reason, unless a contract specifies otherwise.

employment contract • A contract between an employer and an employee in which the terms and conditions of employment are stated.

employment discrimination • Treating employees or job applicants unequally on the basis of race, color, national origin, religion, gender, age, or disability; prohibited by federal statutes.

enabling legislation • A statute enacted by Congress that authorizes the creation of an administrative agency and specifies the name, composition, purpose, and powers of the agency being created.

encryption • The process by which a message is transmitted into a form or code that the sender and receiver intend not to be understandable by third parties.

entrapment • In criminal law, a defense in which the defendant claims that he or she was induced by a public official—usually an undercover agent or police officer—to commit a crime that he or she would otherwise not have committed.

entrepreneur • One who initiates and assumes the financial risk of a new business enterprise and undertakes to provide or control its management.

environmental impact statement (EIS) • A statement required by the National Environmental Policy Act for any major federal action that will significantly affect the quality of the environment. The statement must analyze the action's impact on the environment and explore alternative actions that might be taken.

equal dignity rule • In most states, a rule stating that express authority given to an agent must be in writing if the contract to be made on behalf of the principal is required to be in writing.

equal protection clause • The provision in the Fourteenth Amendment to the U.S. Constitution that guarantees that no state will "deny to any person within its jurisdiction the equal protection of the laws." This clause mandates that the state governments must treat similarly situated individuals in a similar manner.

equitable principles and maxims • General propositions or principles of law that have to do with fairness (equity).

e-signature • As defined by the Uniform Electronic Transactions Act, "an electronic sound, symbol, or process attached to or logically associated with a record and executed or adopted by a person with the intent to sign the record."

establishment clause • The provision in the First Amendment to the U.S. Constitution that prohibits the government from establishing any state-sponsored religion or enacting any law that promotes religion or favors one religion over another.

estate in property • In bankruptcy proceedings, all of the debtor's interests in property currently held, wherever located, together with certain jointly owned property, property transferred in transactions voidable by the trustee, proceeds and profits from the property of the estate, and certain property interests to which the debtor becomes entitled within 180 days after filing for bankruptcy.

estopped • Barred, impeded, or precluded.

estray statute • A statute defining finders' rights in property when the true owners are unknown.

ethical reasoning • A reasoning process in which an individual links his or her moral convictions or ethical standards to the particular situation at hand.

ethics • Moral principles and values applied to social behavior.

eviction • A landlord's act of depriving a tenant of possession of the leased premises.

exclusionary rule • In criminal procedure, a rule under which any evidence that is obtained in violation of the accused's constitutional rights guaranteed by the Fourth, Fifth, and Sixth Amendments to the U.S. Constitution, as well as any evidence derived from illegally obtained evidence, will not be admissible in court.

exclusive-dealing contract • An agreement under which a seller forbids a buyer to purchase products from the seller's competitors.

exclusive jurisdiction • Jurisdiction that exists when a case can be heard only in a particular court or type of court.

exculpatory clause • A clause that releases a contractual party from liability in the event of monetary or physical injury, no matter who is at fault.

executed contract • A contract that has been completely performed by both parties.

execution • An action to carry into effect the directions in a court decree or judgment.

executor • A person appointed by a testator in a will to see that her or his will is administered appropriately.

executory contract • A contract that has not as yet been fully performed.

export • The sale of goods and services by domestic firms to buyers located in other countries.

express contract • A contract in which the terms of the agreement are stated in words, oral or written.

express warranty • A seller's or lessor's oral or written promise or affirmation of fact ancillary (secondary) to an underlying sales or lease agreement, as to the quality, condition, description, or performance of the goods being sold or leased.

expropriation • The seizure by a government of a privately owned business or personal property for a proper public purpose and with just compensation.

extension clause • A clause in a time instrument that allows the instrument's date of maturity to be extended into the future.

F

family limited liability partnership (FLLP) • A type of limited liability partnership owned by family members or fiduciaries of family members.

federal form of government • A system of government in which the states form a union and the sovereign power is divided between the central government and the member states.

federal question • A question that pertains to the U.S. Constitution, acts of Congress, or treaties. A federal question provides a basis for federal jurisdiction.

Federal Reserve System • A network of twelve district banks and related branches located around the country and headed by the Federal Reserve Board of Governors. Most banks in the United States have Federal Reserve accounts.

fee simple • An absolute form of property ownership entitling the property owner to use, possess, or dispose of the property as he or she chooses during his or her lifetime. On death, the interest in the property descends to the owner's heirs.

fee simple absolute • An ownership interest in land in which the owner has the greatest possible aggregation of rights, privileges, and power. Ownership in fee simple absolute is limited absolutely to a person and her or his heirs.

felony • A crime—such as arson, murder, rape, or robbery—that carries the most severe sanctions, ranging from one year in a state or federal prison to the death penalty.

fictitious payee • A payee on a negotiable instrument whom the maker or drawer does not intend to have an interest in the instrument. Indorsements by fictitious payees are treated as authorized indorsements under Article 3 of the UCC.

fiduciary • As a noun, a person having a duty created by his or her undertaking to act primarily for another's benefit in matters connected with the undertaking. As an adjective, a relationship founded on trust and confidence.

filtering software • A computer program that is designed to block access to certain Web sites, based on their content. The software blocks the retrieval of a site whose URL or key words are on a list within the program.

financing statement • A document prepared by a secured creditor, and filed with the appropriate state or local official, to give notice to the public that the creditor has a security interest in collateral belonging to the debtor named in the statement. The financing statement must contain the names and addresses of both the debtor and the secured party and must describe the collateral by type or item.

firm offer • An offer (by a merchant) that is irrevocable without the necessity of consideration for a stated period of time or, if no definite period is stated, for a reasonable time (neither period to exceed three months). A firm offer by a merchant must be in writing and must be signed by the offeror.

fixed-term tenancy • A type of tenancy under which property is leased for a specified period of time, such as a month, a year, or a period of years; also called a tenancy for years.

fixture • An item thing that was once personal property but has become attached to real property in such a way that it takes on the characteristics of real property and becomes part of that real property.

floating lien • A security interest in proceeds, after-acquired property, or collateral subject to future advances by the secured party (or all three); a security interest in collateral that is retained even when the collateral changes in character, classification, or location.

forbearance • The act of refraining from an action that one has a legal right to undertake.

force majeure clause • A provision in a contract stipulating that certain unforeseen events—such as war, political upheavals, or acts of God—will excuse a party from liability for nonperformance of contractual obligations.

foreign corporation • In a given state, a corporation that does business in the state without being incorporated therein.

foreign exchange market • A worldwide system in which foreign currencies are bought and sold.

forgery • The fraudulent making or altering of any writing in a way that changes the legal rights and liabilities of another.

formal contract • A contract that by law requires a specific form, such as being executed under seal, for its validity.

forum-selection clause • A provision in a contract designating the court, jurisdiction, or tribunal that will decide any disputes arising under the contract.

franchise • Any arrangement in which the owner of a trademark, trade name, or copyright licenses another to use that trademark, trade name, or copyright in the selling of goods or services.

franchisee • One receiving a license to use another's (the franchisor's) trademark, trade name, or copyright in the sale of goods and services.

franchisor • One licensing another (the franchisee) to use the owner's trademark, trade name, or copyright in the selling of goods or services.

fraudulent misrepresentation • Any misrepresentation, either by misstatement or by omission of a material fact, knowingly made with the intention of deceiving another and on which a reasonable person would and does rely to his or her detriment.

free exercise clause • The provision in the First Amendment to the U.S. Constitution that prohibits the government from interfering with people's religious practices or forms of worship.

free-writing prospectus • A free-writing prospectus is any type of written, electronic, or graphic offer that describes the issuing corporation or its securities and includes a legend indicating that the investor may obtain the prospectus at the Securities and Exchange Commission's Web site.

frustration of purpose • A court-created doctrine under which a party to a contract will be relieved of her or his duty to perform when the objective purpose for performance no longer exists (due to reasons beyond that party's control).

fungible goods • Goods that are alike by physical nature, by agreement, or by trade usage (for example, wheat, oil, and wine that are identical in type and quality). When owners hold fungible goods as tenants in common, title and risk can pass without actually separating the goods being sold from the larger mass.

G

garnishment • A legal process used by a creditor to collect a debt by seizing property of the debtor (such as wages) that is being held by a third party (such as the debtor's employer).

generally accepted accounting principles (GAAP) • The conventions, rules, and procedures that define accepted accounting practices at a particular time. The source of the principles is the Financial Accounting Standards Board.

generally accepted auditing standards (GAAS) • Standards concerning an auditor's professional qualities and the judgment exercised by him or her in the performance of an audit and report. The source of the standards is the American Institute of Certified Public Accountants.

general partner • In a limited partnership, a partner who assumes responsibility for the management of the partnership and liability for all partnership debts.

gift • Any voluntary transfer of property made without consideration, past or present.

gift *causa mortis* • A gift made in contemplation of death. If the donor does not die of that ailment, the gift is revoked.

gift *inter vivos* • A gift made during one's lifetime and not in contemplation of imminent death, in contrast to a gift causa mortis.

good faith purchaser • A purchaser who buys without notice of any circumstance that would cause a person of ordinary prudence to inquire as to whether the seller has valid title to the goods being sold.

Good Samaritan Statute • A state statute stipulating that persons who provide emergency services to, or rescue, someone in peril cannot be sued for negligence, unless they act recklessly, thereby causing further harm.

grand jury • A group of citizens called to decide, after hearing the state's evidence, whether a reasonable basis (probable cause) exists for believing that a crime has been committed and that a trial ought to be held.

group boycott • The refusal by a group of competitors to deal with a particular person or firm; prohibited by the Sherman Act.

guarantor • A person who agrees to satisfy the debt of another (the debtor) only after the principal debtor defaults. Thus, a guarantor's liability is secondary.

H

hacker • A person who uses one computer to break into another.

Herfindahl-Hirschman Index (HHI) • An index of market power used to calculate whether a merger of two businesses will result in sufficient monopoly power to violate antitrust laws.

historical school • A school of legal thought that emphasizes the evolutionary process of law and looks to the past to discover what the principles of contemporary law should be.

holder • Any person in possession of an instrument drawn, issued, or indorsed to him or her, to his or her order, to bearer, or in blank.

holder in due course (HDC) • A holder who acquires a negotiable instrument for value; in good faith; and without notice that the instrument is overdue, that it has been dishonored, that any person has a defense against it or a claim to it, or that the instrument contains unauthorized signatures, has been altered, or is so irregular or incomplete as to call into question its authenticity.

holding company • A company whose business activity is holding shares in another company.

holographic will • A will written entirely in the signer's handwriting and usually not witnessed.

homestead exemption • A law permitting a debtor to retain the family home, either in its entirety or up to a specified dollar amount, free from the claims of unsecured creditors or trustees in bankruptcy.

horizontal merger • A merger between two firms that are competing in the same marketplace.

horizontal restraint • Any agreement that in some way restrains competition between rival firms competing in the same market.

hot-cargo agreement • An agreement in which employers voluntarily agree with unions not to handle, use, or deal in other employers' goods that were not produced by union employees; a type of secondary boycott explicitly prohibited by the Labor-Management Reporting and Disclosure Act of 1959.

I

I-9 verification • A process that all employers in the United States must perform within three business days of hiring a new worker to verify the employment eligibility and identity of the worker by completing an I-9 Employment Eligibility Verification form.

I-551 Alien Registration Receipt • A document, commonly known as a green card, that shows that a foreign-born individual has been lawfully admitted for permanent residency in the United States. Persons seeking employment can prove to prospective employers that they are legally within the United States by showing this receipt.

identification • In a sale of goods, the express designation of the goods provided for in the contract.

identity theft • The theft of identity information, such as a person's name, driver's license number, or Social Security number. The information is then usually used to access the victim's financial resources.

implied-in-fact contract • A contract formed in whole or in part from the conduct of the parties (as opposed to an express contract).

implied warranty • A warranty that arises by law because of the circumstances of a sale rather than by the seller's express promise.

implied warranty of fitness for a particular purpose • A warranty that goods sold or leased are fit for a particular purpose. The warranty arises when any seller or lessor knows the particular purpose for which a buyer or lessee will use the goods and knows that the buyer or lessee is relying on the skill and judgment of the seller or lessor to select suitable goods.

implied warranty of habitability • An implied promise by a seller of a new house that the house is fit for human habitation—that is, in a condition that is safe and suitable for people to live there. Also, the implied promise by a landlord that rented residential premises are habitable.

implied warranty of merchantability • A warranty that goods being sold or leased are reasonably fit for the general purpose for which they are sold or leased, are properly packaged and labeled, and are of proper quality. The warranty automatically arises in every sale or lease of goods made by a merchant who deals in goods of the kind sold or leased.

impossibility of performance • A doctrine under which a party to a contract is relieved of his or her duty to perform when performance becomes objectively impossible or totally impracticable (through no fault of either party).

imposter • One who, by use of the mails, Internet, telephone, or personal appearance, induces a maker or drawer to issue an instrument in the name of an impersonated payee. Indorsements by imposters are treated as authorized indorsements under Article 3 of the UCC.

incidental beneficiary • A third party who incidentally benefits from a contract but whose benefit was not the reason the contract was formed. An incidental beneficiary has no rights in a contract and cannot sue to have the contract enforced.

incidental damages • Damages awarded to compensate for expenses that are directly incurred because of a breach of contract—such as those incurred to obtain performance from another source.

incontestability clause • A clause within a life or health insurance policy that states after the policy has been in force for a specified length of time—most often two or three years—the insurer cannot contest statements made in the policyholder's application.

independent contractor • One who works for, and receives payment from, an employer but whose working conditions and methods are not controlled by the employer. An independent contractor is not an employee but may be an agent.

indictment • A charge by a grand jury that a named person has committed a crime.

indorsement • A signature placed on an instrument for the purpose of transferring one's ownership rights in the instrument.

informal contract • A contract that does not require a specified form or formality to be valid.

information • A formal accusation or complaint (without an indictment) issued in certain types of actions (usually criminal actions involving lesser crimes) by a government prosecutor.

information return • A tax return submitted by a partnership that only reports the income and losses earned by the business. The partnership as an entity does not pay taxes on the income received by the partnership.

inside director • A person on the board of directors who is also an officer of the corporation.

insider trading • The purchase or sale of securities on the basis of information that has not been made available to the public.

insolvent • Under the UCC, a term describing a person who ceases to pay "his [or her] debts in the ordinary course of business or cannot pay his [or her] debts as they become due or is insolvent within the meaning of federal bankruptcy law" [UCC 1–201(23)].

installment contract • Under the UCC, a contract that requires or authorizes delivery in two or more separate lots to be accepted and paid for separately.

insurable interest • An interest either in a person's life or well-being or in property that is sufficiently substantial that insuring against injury to (or the death of) the person or against damage to the property does not amount to a mere wagering (betting) contract. In regard to the sale or lease of goods, a property interest in the goods that is sufficiently substantial to permit a party to insure against damage to the goods.

insurance • A contract in which, for a stipulated consideration, one party agrees to compensate the other for loss on a specific subject by a specified peril.

intangible property • Property that cannot be seen or touched but exists only conceptually, such as corporate stocks and bonds, patents and copyrights, and ordinary contract rights. Article 2 of the UCC does not govern intangible property.

integrated contract • A written contract that constitutes the final expression of the parties' agreement. If a contract is integrated, evidence extraneous to the contract that contradicts or alters the meaning of the contract in any way is inadmissible.

intellectual property • Property resulting from intellectual, creative processes.

intended beneficiary • A third party for whose benefit a contract is formed. An intended beneficiary can sue the promisor if such a contract is breached.

intentional tort • A wrongful act knowingly committed.

intermediary bank • Any bank to which an item is transferred in the course of collection, except the depositary or payor bank.

international law • The law that governs relations among nations. International customs, treaties, and organizations are important sources of international law.

international organization • Any member-ship group that operates across national borders. These organizations can be governmental organizations, such as the United Nations, or nongovernmental organizations, such as the Red Cross.

interpretive rule • An administrative agency rule that is simply a statement or opinion issued by the agency explaining how it interprets and intends to apply the statutes it enforces. Such rules are not binding on private individuals or organizations.

interrogatories • A series of written questions for which written answers are prepared by a party to a lawsuit, usually with the assistance of the party's attorney, and then signed under oath.

***inter vivos* trust** • A trust created by the grantor (settlor) and effective during the grantor's lifetime; a trust not established by a will.

intestacy laws • State statutes that specify how property will be distributed when a person dies intestate (without a valid will); also called statutes of descent and distribution.

intestate • As a noun, one who has died without having created a valid will; as an adjective, the state of having died without a will.

investment company • A company that acts on the behalf of many smaller shareholders/owners by buying a large portfolio of securities and professionally managing that portfolio.

investment contract • In securities law, a transaction in which a person invests in a common enterprise reasonably expecting profits that are derived primarily from the efforts of others.

J

joint and several liability • In partnership law, a doctrine under which a plaintiff may sue, and collect a judgment from, all of the partners together (jointly) or one or more of the partners separately (severally, or individually). This is true even if one of the partners sued did not participate in, ratify, or know about whatever it was that gave rise to the cause of action.

joint liability • Shared liability. In partnership law, partners incur joint liability for partnership obligations and debts. For example, if a third party sues a partner on a partnership debt, the partner has the right to insist that the other partners be sued with him or her.

joint stock company • A hybrid form of business organization that combines characteristics of a corporation and a partnership. Usually, a joint stock company is regarded as a partnership for tax and other legal purposes.

joint tenancy • The joint ownership of property by two or more co-owners in which each co-owner owns an undivided portion of the property. On the death of one of the joint tenants, his or her interest automatically passes to the surviving joint tenant(s).

joint venture • A joint undertaking of a specific commercial enterprise by an association of persons. A joint venture normally is not a legal entity and is treated like a partnership for federal income tax purposes.

judicial review • The process by which a court decides on the constitutionality of legislative enactments and actions of the executive branch.

junior lienholder • A party that holds a lien that is subordinate to one or more other liens on the same property.

jurisdiction • The authority of a court to hear and decide a specific case.

jurisprudence • The science or philosophy of law.

justiciable controversy • A controversy that is not hypothetical or academic but real and substantial; a requirement that must be satisfied before a court will hear a case.

L

larceny • The wrongful taking and carrying away of another person's personal property with the intent to permanently deprive the owner of the property. Some states classify larceny as either grand or petit, depending on the property's value.

law • A body of enforceable rules governing relationships among individuals and between individuals and their society.

lease • Under Article 2A of the UCC, a transfer of the right to possess and use goods for a period of time in exchange for payment.

lease agreement • In regard to the lease of goods, an agreement in which one person (the lessor) agrees to transfer the right to the possession and use of property to another person (the lessee) in exchange for rental payments.

leasehold estate • An estate in realty held by a tenant under a lease. In every leasehold estate, the tenant has a qualified right to possess and/or use the land.

legacy • A gift of personal property under a will.

legal positivism • A school of legal thought centered on the assumption that there is no law higher than the laws created by a national government. Laws must be obeyed, even if they are unjust, to prevent anarchy.

legal realism • A school of legal thought of the 1920s and 1930s that generally advocated a less abstract and more realistic approach to the law, an approach that takes into account customary practices and the circumstances in which transactions take place. This school left a lasting imprint on American jurisprudence.

legatee • One designated in a will to receive a gift of personal property.

legislative rule • An administrative agency rule that carries the same weight as a congressionally enacted statute.

lessee • A person who acquires the right to the possession and use of another's goods in exchange for rental payments.

lessor • A person who transfers the right to the possession and use of goods to another in exchange for rental payments.

letter of credit • A written instrument, usually issued by a bank on behalf of a customer or other person, in which the issuer promises to honor drafts or other demands for payment by third parties in accordance with the terms of the instrument.

levy • The obtaining of funds by legal process through the seizure and sale of nonexempt property, usually done after a writ of execution has been issued.

libel • Defamation in writing or other form having the quality of permanence (such as a digital recording).

license • A revocable right or privilege of a person to come onto another person's land. In the context of intellectual property law, an agreement permitting the use of a trademark, copyright, patent, or trade secret for certain limited purposes.

lien • An encumbrance on a property to satisfy a debt or protect a claim for payment of a debt.

life estate • An interest in land that exists only for the duration of the life of some person, usually the holder of the estate.

limited liability company (LLC) • A hybrid form of business enterprise that offers the limited liability of a corporation and the tax advantages of a partnership.

limited liability limited partnership (LLLP) • A type of limited partnership in which the liability of all of the partners, including general partners, is limited to the amount of their investments.

limited liability partnership (LLP) • A hybrid form of business organization that is used mainly by professionals who normally do business in a partnership. An LLP is a pass-through entity for tax purposes, but the personal liability of the partners is limited.

limited partner • In a limited partnership, a partner who contributes capital to the partnership but has no right to participate in the management and operation of the business. The limited partner assumes no liability for partnership debts beyond the capital contributed.

limited partnership • A partnership consisting of one or more general partners (who manage the business and are liable to the full extent of their personal assets for debts of the partnership) and one or more limited partners (who contribute only assets and are liable only up to the extent of their contributions).

liquidated damages • An amount, stipulated in a contract, that the parties to the contract believe to be a reasonable estimation of the damages that will occur in the event of a breach.

liquidated debt • A debt for which the amount has been ascertained, fixed, agreed on, settled, or exactly determined. If the amount of the debt is in dispute, the debt is considered unliquidated.

liquidation • The sale of all of the nonexempt assets of a debtor and the distribution of the proceeds to the debtor's creditors. Chapter 7 of the Bankruptcy Code provides for liquidation bankruptcy proceedings.

litigation • The process of resolving a dispute through the court system.

long arm statute • A state statute that permits a state to obtain personal jurisdiction over nonresident defendants. A defendant must have certain "minimum contacts" with that state for the statute to apply.

lost property • Property with which the owner has involuntarily parted and then cannot find or recover.

M

mailbox rule • A rule providing that an acceptance of an offer becomes effective on dispatch (on being placed in an official mailbox), if mail is, expressly or impliedly, an authorized means of communication of acceptance to the offeror.

maker • One who promises to pay a fixed amount of money to the holder of a promissory note or a certificate of deposit (CD).

malpractice • Professional misconduct or unreasonable lack of skill; the failure of a professional to use the skills and learning common to the average reputable members of the profession or the skills and learning the professional claims to possess, resulting in injury, loss, or damage to those relying on the professional. Negligence—the failure to exercise due care—on the part of a professional, such as a physician, is commonly referred to as malpractice.

malware • Any program that is harmful to a computer or a computer user; for example, worms and viruses.

market concentration • The degree to which a small number of firms control a large percentage share of a relevant market; determined by calculating the percentages held by the largest firms in that market.

market power • The power of a firm to control the market price of its product. A monopoly has the greatest degree of market power.

market-share liability • A theory under which liability is shared among all firms that manufactured and distributed a particular product during a certain period of time. This form of liability sharing is used only when the true source of the harmful product is unidentifiable; it is not recognized in many jurisdictions.

mechanic's lien • A statutory lien on the real property of another to ensure payment for work performed and materials furnished in the repair or improvement of real property, such as a building.

mediation • A method of settling disputes outside the courts by using the services of a neutral third party, who acts as a communicating agent between the parties and assists them in negotiating a settlement.

member • A person who has an ownership interest in a limited liability company.

mens rea • Mental state, or intent. Normally, a wrongful mental state is as necessary as a wrongful act to establish criminal liability. What constitutes such a mental state varies according to the wrongful action. Thus, for murder, the *mens rea* is the intent to take a life.

merchant • A person who is engaged in the purchase and sale of goods. Under the UCC, a person who deals in goods of the kind involved in the sales contract or who holds herself or himself out as having skill or knowledge peculiar to the practices or goods being purchased or sold [UCC 2–104].

merger • A contractual and statutory process in which one corporation (the surviving corporation) acquires all of the assets and liabilities of another corporation (the merged corporation).

meta tag • A key word in a document that can serve as an index reference to the document. On the Web, search engines return results based, in part, on these tags in Web documents.

minimum wage • The lowest wage, either by government regulation or union contract, that an employer may pay an hourly worker.

mirror image rule • A common law rule that requires that the terms of the offeree's acceptance adhere exactly to the terms of the offeror's offer for a valid contract to be formed.

misdemeanor • A lesser crime than a felony, punishable by a fine or incarceration in jail for up to one year.

mislaid property • Property with which the owner has voluntarily parted and then cannot find or recover.

mitigation of damages • A rule requiring a plaintiff to do whatever is reasonable to minimize the damages caused by the defendant.

money laundering • Engaging in financial transactions to conceal the identity, source, or destination of illegally gained funds.

monopolization • The possession of monopoly power in the relevant market and the willful acquisition or maintenance of that power, as distinguished from growth or development as a consequence of a superior product, business acumen, or historic accident.

monopoly • A term generally used to describe a market in which there is a single seller or a very limited number of sellers.

monopoly power • The ability of a monopoly to dictate what takes place in a given market.

moral minimum • The minimum degree of ethical behavior expected of a business firm, which is usually defined as compliance with the law.

mortgage • A written instrument giving a creditor an interest in (lien on) the debtor's real property as security for payment of a debt.

mortgagee • Under a mortgage agreement, the creditor who takes a security interest in the debtor's property.

mortgagor • Under a mortgage agreement, the debtor who gives the creditor a security interest in the debtor's property in return for a mortgage loan.

motion for a directed verdict • In a jury trial, a motion for the judge to take the decision out of the hands of the jury and to direct a verdict for the party who filed the motion on the ground that the other party has not produced sufficient evidence to support her or his claim.

motion for a new trial • A motion asserting that the trial was so fundamentally flawed (because of error, newly discovered evidence, prejudice, or another reason) that a new trial is necessary to prevent a miscarriage of justice.

motion for judgment n.o.v. • A motion requesting the court to grant judgment in favor of the party making the motion on the ground that the jury's verdict against him or her was unreasonable and erroneous.

motion for judgment on the pleadings • A motion by either party to a lawsuit at the close of the pleadings requesting the court to decide the issue solely on the pleadings without proceeding to trial. The motion will be granted only if no facts are in dispute.

motion for summary judgment • A motion requesting the court to enter a judgment without proceeding to trial. The motion can be based on evidence outside the pleadings and will be granted only if no facts are in dispute.

motion to dismiss • A pleading in which a defendant asserts that the plaintiff's claim fails to state a cause of action (that is, has no basis in law) or that there are other grounds on which the suit should be dismissed. Although the defendant normally is the party requesting a dismissal, either the plaintiff or the court can also make a motion to dismiss the case.

multiple product order • An order issued by the Federal Trade Commission to a firm that has engaged in deceptive advertising by which the firm is required to cease and desist from false advertising not only in regard to the product that was the subject of the action but also in regard to all the firm's other products.

mutual fund • A specific type of investment company that continually buys or sells to investors shares of ownership in a portfolio.

N

national law • Law that pertains to a particular nation (as opposed to international law).

natural law • The belief that government and the legal system should reflect universal moral and ethical principles that are inherent in human nature. The natural law school is the oldest and one of the most significant schools of legal thought.

necessaries • Necessities required for life, such as food, shelter, clothing, and medical attention; may include whatever is believed to be necessary to maintain a person's standard of living or financial and social status.

negligence • The failure to exercise the standard of care that a reasonable person would exercise in similar circumstances.

negligence *per se* • An action or failure to act in violation of a statutory requirement.

negotiable instrument • A signed writing (record) that contains an unconditional promise or order to pay an exact sum on demand or at an exact future time to a specific person or order, or to bearer.

negotiation • A process in which parties attempt to settle their dispute informally, with or without attorneys to represent them. In the context of negotiable instruments, the transfer of an instrument in such form that the transferee (the person to whom the instrument is transferred) becomes a holder.

nominal damages • A small monetary award (often one dollar) granted to a plaintiff when no actual damage was suffered.

nonpossessory interest • In the context of real property, an interest in land that does not include any right to possess the property.

normal trade relations (NTR) status • A status granted by each member country of the World Trade Organization to other member countries. Each member is required to treat other members at least as well as it treats the country that receives its most favorable treatment with respect to trade.

notary public • A public official authorized to attest to the authenticity of signatures.

novation • The substitution, by agreement, of a new contract for an old one, with the rights under the old one being terminated. Typically, novation involves the substitution of a new person who is responsible for the contract and the removal of the original party's rights and duties under the contract.

nuisance • A common law doctrine under which persons may be held liable for using their property in a manner that unreasonably interferes with others' rights to use or enjoy their own property.

nuncupative will • An oral will (often called a deathbed will) made before witnesses; usually limited to transfers of personal property.

O

objective theory of contracts • A theory under which the intent to form a contract will be judged by outward, objective facts (what the party said when entering into the contract, how the party acted or appeared, and the circumstances surrounding the transaction) as interpreted by a reasonable person, rather than by the party's own secret, subjective intentions.

obligee • One to whom an obligation is owed.

obligor • One who owes an obligation to another.

offer • A promise or commitment to perform or refrain from performing some specified act in the future.

offeree • A person to whom an offer is made.

offeror • A person who makes an offer.

online dispute resolution (ODR) • The resolution of disputes with the assistance of organizations that offer dispute-resolution services via the Internet.

operating agreement • In a limited liability company, an agreement in which the members set forth the details of how the business will be managed and operated. State statutes typically give the members wide latitude in deciding for themselves the rules that will govern their organization.

option contract • A contract under which the offeror cannot revoke the offer for a stipulated time period. During this period, the offeree can accept or reject the offer without fear that the offer will be made to another person. The offeree must give consideration for the option (the irrevocable offer) to be enforceable.

order for relief • A court's grant of assistance to a complainant. In bankruptcy proceedings, the order relieves the debtor of the immediate obligation to pay the debts listed in the bankruptcy petition.

order instrument • A negotiable instrument that is payable "to the order of an identified person" or "to an identified person or order."

ordinance • A regulation enacted by a city or county legislative body that becomes part of that state's statutory law.

output contract • An agreement in which a seller agrees to sell and a buyer agrees to buy all or up to a stated amount of what the seller produces.

outside director • A person on the board of directors who does not hold a management position at the corporation.

overdraft • A check that is paid by the bank when the checking account on which the check is written contains insufficient funds to cover the check.

P

parol evidence rule • A substantive rule of contracts, as well as a procedural rule of evidence, under which a court will not receive into evidence the parties' prior negotiations, prior agreements, or contemporaneous oral agreements if that evidence contradicts or varies the terms of the parties' written contract.

partially disclosed principal • A principal whose identity is unknown by a third party, but the third party knows that the agent is or may be acting for a principal at the time the agent and the third party form a contract.

partnering agreement • An agreement between a seller and a buyer who frequently do business with each other concerning the terms and conditions that will apply to all subsequently formed electronic contracts.

partnership • An agreement by two or more persons to carry on, as co-owners, a business for profit.

pass-through entity • A business entity that has no tax liability. The entity's income is passed through to the owners, and the owners pay taxes on the income.

past consideration • An act that takes place before the contract is made and that ordinarily, by itself, cannot be consideration for a later promise to pay for the act.

patent • A government grant that gives an inventor the exclusive right or privilege to make, use, or sell his or her invention for a limited time period.

payee • A person to whom an instrument is made payable.

payor bank • The bank on which a check is drawn (the drawee bank).

peer-to-peer (P2P) networking • The sharing of resources (such as files, hard drives, and processing styles) among multiple computers without necessarily requiring a central network server.

penalty • A contractual clause that states that a certain amount of monetary damages will be paid in the event of a future default or breach of contract. The damages are a punishment for a default and not an accurate measure of compensation for the contract's breach. The agreement as to the penalty amount will not be enforced, and recovery will be limited to actual damages.

per capita **•** A Latin term meaning "per person." In the law governing estate distribution, a method of distributing the property of an intestate's estate so that each heir in a certain class (such as grandchildren) receives an equal share.

perfection • The legal process by which secured parties protect themselves against the claims of third parties who may wish to have their debts satisfied out of the same collateral; usually accomplished by filing a financing statement with the appropriate government official.

performance • In contract law, the fulfillment of one's duties arising under a contract with another; the normal way of discharging one's contractual obligations.

periodic tenancy • A lease interest in land for an indefinite period involving payment of rent at fixed intervals, such as week to week, month to month, or year to year.

per se **violation •** A type of anticompetitive agreement that is considered to be so injurious to the public that there is no need to determine whether it actually injures market competition. Rather, it is in itself *(per se)* a violation of the Sherman Act.

personal defense • A defense that can be used to avoid payment to an ordinary holder of a negotiable instrument but not a holder in due course (HDC) or a holder with the rights of an HDC.

personal property • Property that is movable; any property that is not real property.

per stirpes **•** A Latin term meaning "by the roots." In the law governing estate distribution, a method of distributing an intestate's estate so that each heir in a certain class (such as grandchildren) takes the share to which her or his deceased ancestor (such as a mother or father) would have been entitled.

persuasive authority • Any legal authority or source of law that a court may look to for guidance but on which it need not rely in making its decision. Persuasive authorities include cases from other jurisdictions and secondary sources of law.

petition in bankruptcy • The document that is filed with a bankruptcy court to initiate bankruptcy proceedings. The official forms required for a petition in bankruptcy must be completed accurately, sworn to under oath, and signed by the debtor.

petty offense • In criminal law, the least serious kind of criminal offense, such as a traffic or building-code violation.

phishing • The attempt to acquire financial data, passwords, or other personal information from consumers by sending e-mail messages that purport to be from a legitimate business, such as a bank or a credit-card company.

piercing the corporate veil • An action in which a court disregards the corporate entity and holds the shareholders personally liable for corporate debts and obligations.

plaintiff • One who initiates a lawsuit.

plea bargaining • The process by which a criminal defendant and the prosecutor in a criminal case work out a mutually satisfactory disposition of the case, subject to court approval; usually involves the defendant's pleading guilty to a lesser offense in return for a lighter sentence.

pleadings • Statements made by the plaintiff and the defendant in a lawsuit that detail the facts, charges, and defenses involved in the litigation. The complaint and answer are part of the pleadings.

pledge • A common law security device (retained in Article 9 of the UCC) in which personal property is transferred into the possession of the creditor as security for the payment of a debt and retained by the creditor until the debt is paid.

police powers • Powers possessed by the states as part of their inherent sovereignty. These powers may be exercised to protect or promote the public order, health, safety, morals, and general welfare.

policy • In insurance law, a contract between the insurer and the insured in which, for a stipulated consideration, the insurer agrees to compensate the insured for loss on a specific subject by a specified peril.

potentially responsible party (PRP) • A party liable for the costs of cleaning up a hazardous waste-disposal site under the Comprehensive Environmental Response, Compensation, and Liability Act. Any person who generated the hazardous waste, transported it, owned or operated the waste site at the time of disposal, or owns or operates the site at the present time may be responsible for some or all of the clean-up costs.

power of attorney • A written document, which is usually notarized, authorizing another to act as one's agent; can be special (permitting the agent to do specified acts only) or general (permitting the agent to transact all business for the principal).

precedent • A court decision that furnishes an example or authority for deciding subsequent cases involving identical or similar facts.

predatory pricing • The pricing of a product below cost with the intent to drive competitors out of the market.

predominant-factor test • A test courts use to determine whether a contract is primarily for the sale of goods or for the sale of services.

preemption • A doctrine under which certain federal laws preempt, or take precedence over, conflicting state or local laws.

preemptive rights • Rights held by shareholders that entitle them to purchase newly issued shares of a corporation's stock, equal in percentage to shares already held, before the stock is offered to any outside buyers. Preemptive rights enable shareholders to maintain their proportionate ownership and voice in the corporation.

preference • In bankruptcy proceedings, property transfers or payments made by the debtor that favor (give preference to) one creditor over others. The bankruptcy trustee is allowed to recover payments made both voluntarily and involuntarily to one creditor in preference over another.

preferred creditor • In the context of bankruptcy, a creditor who has received a preferential transfer from a debtor.

preferred stock • Classes of stock that have priority over common stock as to both payment of dividends and distribution of assets on the corporation's dissolution.

premium • In insurance law, the price paid by the insured for insurance protection for a specified period of time.

prenuptial agreement • An agreement made before marriage that defines each partner's ownership rights in the other partner's property. Prenuptial agreements must be in writing to be enforceable.

presentment • The act of presenting an instrument to the party liable on the instrument in order to collect payment. Presentment also occurs when a person presents an instrument to a drawee for a required acceptance.

presentment warranties • Implied warranties, made by any person who presents an instrument for payment or acceptance, that (1) the person obtaining payment or acceptance is entitled to enforce the instrument or is authorized to obtain payment or acceptance on behalf of a person who is entitled to enforce the instrument, (2) the instrument has not been altered, and (3) the person obtaining payment or acceptance has no knowledge that the signature of the drawer of the instrument is unauthorized.

price discrimination • Setting prices in such a way that two competing buyers pay two different prices for an identical product or service.

price-fixing agreement • An agreement between competitors to fix the prices of products or services at a certain level.

***prima facie* case** • A case in which the plaintiff has produced sufficient evidence of his or her claim that the case can go to a jury; a case in which the evidence compels a decision for the plaintiff if the defendant produces no affirmative defense or evidence to disprove the plaintiff's assertion.

primary source of law • A document that establishes the law on a particular issue, such as a constitution, a statute, an administrative rule, or a court decision.

principle of rights • The principle that human beings have certain fundamental rights (to life, liberty, and the pursuit of happiness, for example). Those who adhere to this "rights theory" believe that a key factor in determining whether a business decision is ethical is how that decision affects the rights of various groups. These groups include the firm's owners, its employees, the consumers of its products or services, its suppliers, the community in which it does business, and society as a whole.

private equity capital • Private equity capital is a financing method by which a company sells equity in an existing business to a private or institutional investor.

privilege • A legal right, exemption, or immunity granted to a person or a class of persons. In the context of defamation, an absolute privilege immunizes the person making the statements from a lawsuit, regardless of whether the statements were malicious.

privity of contract • The relationship that exists between the promisor and the promisee of a contract.

probable cause • Reasonable grounds for believing that a person should be arrested or searched.

probate • The process of proving and validating a will and settling all matters pertaining to an estate.

probate court • A state court of limited jurisdiction that conducts proceedings relating to the settlement of a deceased person's estate.

procedural law • Law that establishes the methods of enforcing the rights established by substantive law.

proceeds • Under Article 9 of the UCC, whatever is received when collateral is sold or otherwise disposed of, such as by exchange.

product liability • The legal liability of manufacturers, sellers, and lessors of goods to consumers, users, and bystanders for injuries or damage that are caused by the goods.

profit • In real property law, the right to enter onto and remove something of value from the property of another (for example, the right to enter onto another's land and remove sand and gravel).

promise • An assertion that something either will or will not happen in the future.

promisee • A person to whom a promise is made.

promisor • A person who makes a promise.

promissory estoppel • A doctrine that applies when a promisor makes a clear and definite promise on which the promisee justifiably relies. Such a promise is binding if justice will be better served by the enforcement of the promise.

promissory note • A written promise made by one person (the maker) to pay a fixed amount of money to another person (the payee or a subsequent holder) on demand or on a specified date.

property • Legally protected rights and interests in anything with an ascertainable value that is subject to ownership.

prospectus • A written document, required by securities laws, that describes the security being sold, the financial operations of the issuing corporation, and the investment or risk attaching to the security. It is designed to provide sufficient information to enable investors to evaluate the risk involved in purchasing the security.

protected class • A group of persons protected by specific laws because of the group's defining characteristics. Under laws prohibiting employment discrimination, these characteristics include race, color, religion, national origin, gender, age, and disability.

proximate cause • Legal cause; exists when the connection between an act and an injury is strong enough to justify imposing liability.

proxy • In corporate law, a written agreement between a stockholder and another party in which the stockholder authorizes the other party to vote the stockholder's shares in a certain manner.

puffery • A salesperson's often exaggerated claims concerning the quality of property offered for sale. Such claims involve opinions rather than facts and are not considered to be legally binding promises or warranties.

punitive damages • Monetary damages that may be awarded to a plaintiff to punish the defendant and deter similar conduct in the future.

purchase-money security interest (PMSI) • A security interest that arises when a seller or lender extends credit for part or all of the purchase price of goods purchased by a buyer.

Q

qualified indorsement • An indorsement on a negotiable instrument in which the indorser disclaims any contract liability on the instrument. The notation "without recourse" is commonly used to create a qualified indorsement.

quasi contract • A fictional contract imposed on the parties by a court in the interests of fairness and justice; usually imposed to avoid the unjust enrichment of one party at the expense of another.

question of fact • In a lawsuit, an issue that involves only disputed facts, and not what the law is on a given point. Questions of fact are decided by the jury in a jury trial (by the judge if there is no jury).

question of law • In a lawsuit, an issue involving the application or interpretation of a law. Only a judge, not a jury, can rule on questions of law.

quitclaim deed • A deed intended to pass any title, interest, or claim that the grantor may have in the property without warranting that such title is valid. A quitclaim deed offers the least amount of protection against defects in the title.

quorum • The number of members of a decision-making body that must be present before business may be transacted.

quota • A set limit on the amount of goods that can be imported.

R

ratification • The act of accepting and giving legal force to an obligation that previously was not enforceable.

reaffirmation agreement • An agreement between a debtor and a creditor in which the debtor voluntarily agrees to pay, or reaffirm, a debt dischargeable in bankruptcy. To be enforceable, the agreement must be made before the debtor is granted a discharge.

real property • Land and everything attached to it, such as trees and buildings.

reasonable person standard • The standard of behavior expected of a hypothetical "reasonable person"; the standard against which negligence is measured and that must be observed to avoid liability for negligence.

receiver • In a corporate dissolution, a court-appointed person who winds up corporate affairs and liquidates corporate assets.

record • According to the Uniform Electronic Transactions Act, information that is either inscribed on a tangible medium or stored in an electronic or other medium and is retrievable.

recording statutes • Statutes that allow deeds, mortgages, and other real property transactions to be recorded so as to provide notice to future purchasers or creditors of an existing claim on the property.

reformation • A court-ordered correction of a written contract so that it reflects the true intentions of the parties.

Regulation E • A set of rules issued by the Federal Reserve System's Board of Governors to protect users of electronic fund transfer systems.

Regulation Z • A set of rules issued by the Federal Reserve Board of Governors to implement the provisions of the Truth-in-Lending Act.

release • A contract in which one party forfeits the right to pursue a legal claim against the other party.

remedy • The relief given to an innocent party to enforce a right or compensate for the violation of a right.

replevin • An action to recover identified goods in the hands of a party who is wrongfully withholding them from the other party. Under the UCC, this remedy is usually available only if the buyer or lessee is unable to cover.

reply • Procedurally, a plaintiff's response to a defendant's answer.

requirements contract • An agreement in which a buyer agrees to purchase and the seller agrees to sell all or up to a stated amount of what the buyer needs or requires.

resale price maintenance agreement • An agreement between a manufacturer and a retailer in which the manufacturer specifies what the retail prices of its products must be.

rescission • A remedy whereby a contract is canceled and the parties are returned to the positions they occupied before the contract was made; may be effected through the mutual consent of the parties, by the parties' conduct, or by court decree.

res ipsa loquitur • A doctrine under which negligence may be inferred simply because an event occurred, if it is the type of event that would not occur in the absence of negligence. Literally, the term means "the facts speak for themselves."

respondeat superior • Latin for "let the master respond." A doctrine under which a principal or an employer is held liable for the wrongful acts committed by agents or employees while acting within the course and scope of their agency or employment.

restitution • An equitable remedy under which a person is restored to his or her original position prior to loss or injury, or placed in the position he or she would have been in had the breach not occurred.

restrictive indorsement • Any indorsement on a negotiable instrument that requires the indorsee to comply with certain instructions regarding the funds involved. A restrictive indorsement does not prohibit the further negotiation of the instrument.

resulting trust • An implied trust arising from the conduct of the parties. A trust in which a party holds the actual legal title to another's property but only for that person's benefit.

retained earnings • The portion of a corporation's profits that has not been paid out as dividends to shareholders.

revocation • In contract law, the withdrawal of an offer by an offeror. Unless the offer is irrevocable, it can be revoked at any time prior to acceptance without liability.

right of contribution • The right of a co-surety who pays more than her or his proportionate share on a debtor's default to recover the excess paid from other co-sureties.

right of reimbursement • The legal right of a person to be restored, repaid, or indemnified for costs, expenses, or losses incurred or expended on behalf of another.

right of subrogation • The right of a person to stand in the place of (be substituted for) another, giving the substituted party the same legal rights that the original party had.

right-to-work law • A state law providing that employees may not be required to join a union as a condition of retaining employment.

risk • A prediction concerning potential loss based on known and unknown factors.

risk management • Planning that is undertaken to protect one's interest should some event threaten to undermine its security. In the context of insurance, risk management involves transferring certain risks from the insured to the insurance company.

robbery • The act of forcefully and unlawfully taking personal property of any value from another. Force or intimidation is usually necessary for an act of theft to be considered a robbery.

rulemaking • The process undertaken by an administrative agency when formally adopting a new regulation or amending an old one. Rulemaking involves notifying the public of a proposed rule or change and receiving and considering the public's comments.

rule of four • A rule of the United States Supreme Court under which the Court will not issue a writ of certiorari unless at least four justices approve of the decision to issue the writ.

rule of reason • A test by which a court balances the positive effects (such as economic efficiency) of an agreement against its potentially anticompetitive effects. In antitrust litigation, many practices are analyzed under the rule of reason.

S

sale • The passing of title to property from the seller to the buyer for a price.

sales contract • A contract for the sale of goods under which the ownership of goods is transferred from a seller to a buyer for a price.

scienter • Knowledge by the misrepresenting party that material facts have been falsely represented or omitted with an intent to deceive.

S corporation • A close business corporation that has met certain requirements set out in the Internal Revenue Code and thus qualifies for special income tax treatment. Essentially, an S corporation is taxed the same as a partnership, but its owners enjoy the privilege of limited liability.

search warrant • An order granted by a public authority, such as a judge, that authorizes law enforcement personnel to search particular premises or property.

seasonably • Within a specified time period or, if no period is specified, within a reasonable time.

secondary boycott • A union's refusal to work for, purchase from, or handle the products of a secondary employer, with whom the union has no dispute, in order to force that employer to stop doing business with the primary employer, with whom the union has a labor dispute.

secondary source of law • A publication that summarizes or interprets the law, such as a legal encyclopedia, a legal treatise, or an article in a law review.

SEC Rule 10b-5 • A rule of the Securities and Exchange Commission that makes it unlawful, in connection with the purchase or sale of any security, to make any untrue statement of a material fact or to omit a material fact if such omission causes the statement to be misleading.

secured party • A lender, seller, or any other person in whose favor there is a security interest, including a person to whom accounts or chattel paper have been sold.

secured transaction • Any transaction in which the payment of a debt is guaranteed, or secured, by personal property owned by the debtor or in which the debtor has a legal interest.

securities • Generally, stocks, bonds, notes, debentures, warrants, or other items that evidence an ownership interest in a corporation or a promise of repayment by a corporation.

security • Generally, a stock certificate, bond, note, debenture, warrant, or other document or record evidencing an ownership interest in a corporation or a promise of repayment of debt by a corporation.

security agreement • An agreement that creates or provides for a security interest between the debtor and a secured party.

security interest • Any interest in personal property or fixtures that secures payment or performance of an obligation.

self-defense • The legally recognized privilege to protect oneself or one's property against injury by another. The privilege of self-defense usually applies only to acts that are reasonably necessary to protect oneself, one's property, or another person.

self-incrimination • The giving of testimony that may subject the testifier to criminal prosecution. The Fifth Amendment to the U.S. Constitution protects against self-incrimination by providing that no person "shall be compelled in any criminal case to be a witness against himself."

seniority system • In regard to employment relationships, a system in which those who have worked longest for the employer are first in line for promotions, salary increases, and other benefits. They are also the last to be laid off if the workforce must be reduced.

service mark • A mark used in the sale or advertising of services to distinguish the services of one person from those of others. Titles, character names, and other distinctive features of radio and television programs may be registered as service marks.

sexual harassment • In the employment context, the demanding of sexual favors in return for job promotions or other benefits, or language or conduct that is so sexually offensive that it creates a hostile working environment.

share exchange • In a share exchange, some or all of the shares of one corporation are exchanged for some or all of the shares of another corporation, but both corporations continue to exist. Share exchanges are often used to create holding companies (companies that own part or all of other companies' stock).

shareholder's derivative suit • A suit brought by a shareholder to enforce a corporate cause of action against a third person.

shelter principle • The principle that the holder of a negotiable instrument who cannot qualify as a holder in due course (HDC), but who derives his or her title through an HDC, acquires the rights of an HDC.

shipment contract • A contract for the sale of goods in which the seller is required or authorized to ship the goods by carrier. The seller assumes liability for any losses or damage to the goods until they are delivered to the carrier.

short-form (parent-subsidiary) merger • A merger of companies in which one company (the parent corporation) owns at least 90 percent of the outstanding shares of each class of stock of the other corporation (the subsidiary corporation). The merger can be accomplished without the approval of the shareholders of either corporation.

short-swing profits • Profits earned by a purchase and sale, or sale and purchase, of the same security within a six-month period; under Section 16(b) of the 1934 Securities Exchange Act, must be returned to the corporation if earned by company insiders from transactions in the company's stock.

shrink-wrap agreement • An agreement whose terms are expressed in a document located inside a box in which goods (usually software) are packaged; sometimes called a shrink-wrap license.

slander • Defamation in oral form.

slander of quality (trade libel) • The publication of false information about another's product, alleging that it is not what its seller claims.

slander of title • The publication of a statement that denies or casts doubt on another's legal ownership of any property, causing financial loss to that property's owner.

small claims court • A special court in which parties may litigate small claims (such as $5,000 or less). Attorneys are not required in small claims courts and, in some states, are not allowed to represent the parties.

smart card • A card containing a microprocessor that permits storage of funds via security programming, can communicate with other computers, and does not require online authorization for fund transfers.

sociological school • A school of legal thought that views the law as a tool for promoting justice in society.

sole proprietorship • The simplest form of business organization, in which the owner is the business. The owner reports business income on his or her personal income tax return and is legally responsible for all debts and obligations incurred by the business.

sovereign immunity • A doctrine that immunizes foreign nations from the jurisdiction of U.S. courts when certain conditions are satisfied.

spam • Bulk e-mails, particularly of commercial advertising, sent in large quantities without the consent of the recipient.

special indorsement • An indorsement on an instrument that indicates the specific person to whom the indorser intends to make the instrument payable; that is, it names the indorsee.

special warranty deed • A deed in which the grantor warrants only that the grantor or seller held good title during his or her ownership of the property and does not warrant that there were no defects of title when the property was held by previous owners.

specific performance • An equitable remedy requiring exactly the performance that was specified in a contract; usually granted only when monetary damages would be an inadequate remedy and the subject matter of the contract is unique (for example, real property).

spendthrift trust • A trust created to protect the beneficiary from spending all the funds to which she or he is entitled. Only a certain portion of the total amount is given to the beneficiary at any one time, and most states prohibit creditors from attaching assets of the trust.

stale check • A check, other than a certified check, that is presented for payment more than six months after its date.

standing to sue • The requirement that an individual must have a sufficient stake in a controversy before he or she can bring a lawsuit. The plaintiff must demonstrate that he or she has been either injured or threatened with injury.

stare decisis • A common law doctrine under which judges are obligated to follow the precedents established in prior decisions.

Statute of Frauds • A state statute under which certain types of contracts must be in writing to be enforceable.

statute of limitations • A federal or state statute setting the maximum time period during which a certain action can be brought or certain rights enforced.

statutory law • The body of law enacted by legislative bodies (as opposed to constitutional law, administrative law, or case law).

stock • An equity (ownership) interest in a corporation, measured in units of shares.

stock buyback • The purchase of shares of a company's own stock by that company on the open market.

stock certificate • A certificate issued by a corporation evidencing the ownership of a specified number of shares in the corporation.

stock option • An agreement that grants the owner the option to buy a given number of shares of stock, usually within a set time period.

stock warrant • A certificate that grants the owner the option to buy a given number of shares of stock, usually within a set time period.

stop-payment order • An order by a bank customer to his or her bank not to pay or certify a certain check.

stored-value card • A card bearing a magnetic strip that holds magnetically encoded data, providing access to stored funds.

strict liability • Liability regardless of fault. In tort law, strict liability is imposed on those engaged in abnormally dangerous activities, on persons who keep dangerous animals, and on manufacturers or sellers that introduce into commerce goods that are unreasonably dangerous when in a defective condition.

strike • An action undertaken by unionized workers when collective bargaining fails; the workers leave their jobs, refuse to work, and (typically) picket the employer's workplace.

sublease • A lease executed by the lessee of real estate to a third person, conveying the same interest that the lessee enjoys but for a shorter term than that held by the lessee.

substantive law • Law that defines, describes, regulates, and creates legal rights and obligations.

summary jury trial (SJT) • A method of settling disputes, used in many federal courts, in which a trial is held, but the jury's verdict is not binding. The verdict acts only as a guide to both sides in reaching an agreement during the mandatory negotiations that immediately follow the summary jury trial.

summons • A document informing a defendant that a legal action has been commenced against her or him and that the defendant must appear in court on a certain date to answer the plaintiff's complaint.

supremacy clause • The requirement in Article VI of the U.S. Constitution that provides that the Constitution, laws, and treaties of the United States are "the supreme Law of the Land." Under this clause, state and local laws that directly conflict with federal law will be rendered invalid.

surety • A person, such as a cosigner on a note, who agrees to be primarily responsible for the debt of another.

suretyship • An express contract in which a third party to a debtor-creditor relationship (the surety) promises to be primarily responsible for the debtor's obligation.

symbolic speech • Nonverbal expressions of beliefs. Symbolic speech, which includes gestures, movements, and articles of clothing, is given substantial protection by the courts.

syndicate • A group of individuals or firms brought together for the purpose of financing a project that they would not or could not undertake independently; also called an investment group.

T

takeover • The acquisition of control over a corporation through the purchase of a substantial number of the voting shares of the corporation.

taking • The taking of private property by the government for public use. The government may not take private property for public use without "just compensation."

tangible employment action • A significant change in employment status, such as a change brought about by firing or failing to promote an employee; reassigning the employee to a position with significantly different responsibilities; or effecting a significant change in employment benefits.

tangible property • Property that has physical existence and can be distinguished by the senses of touch and sight. A car is tangible property; a patent right is intangible property.

target corporation • The corporation to be acquired in a corporate takeover; a corporation whose shareholders receive a tender offer.

tariff • A tax on imported goods.

tenancy at sufferance • A type of tenancy under which a tenant who, after rightfully being in possession of leased premises, continues (wrongfully) to occupy the property after the lease has terminated. The tenant has no rights to possess the property and occupies it only because the person entitled to evict the tenant has not done so.

tenancy at will • A type of tenancy that either party can terminate without notice; usually arises when a tenant who has been under a tenancy for years retains possession, with the landlord's consent, after the tenancy for years has terminated.

tenancy in common • Co-ownership of property in which each party owns an undivided interest that passes to her or his heirs at death.

tender • An unconditional offer to perform an obligation by a person who is ready, willing, and able to do so.

tender of delivery • Under the Uniform Commercial Code, a seller's or lessor's act of placing conforming goods at the disposal of the buyer or lessee and giving the buyer or lessee whatever notification is reasonably necessary to enable the buyer or lessee to take delivery.

tender offer • An offer made by one company directly to the shareholders of another (target) company to purchase their shares of stock; sometimes referred to as a takeover bid.

testamentary trust • A trust that is created by will and therefore does not take effect until the death of the testator.

testate • Having left a will at death.

testator • One who makes and executes a will.

third party beneficiary • One for whose benefit a promise is made in a contract but who is not a party to the contract.

tippee • A person who receives inside information.

tort • A civil wrong not arising from a breach of contract; a breach of a legal duty that proximately causes harm or injury to another.

tortfeasor • One who commits a tort.

Totten trust • A trust created when a person deposits funds in his or her own name as a trustee for another. It is a tentative trust, revocable at will until the depositor dies or completes the gift in his or her lifetime by some unequivocal act or declaration.

toxic tort • A civil wrong arising from exposure to a toxic substance, such as asbestos, radiation, or hazardous waste.

trade dress • The image and overall appearance of a product—for example, the distinctive decor, menu, layout, and style of service of a particular restaurant. Basically, trade dress is subject to the same protection as trademarks.

trademark • A distinctive mark, motto, device, or emblem that a manufacturer stamps, prints, or otherwise affixes to the goods it produces so that they may be identified on the market and their origins made known. Once a trademark is established (under the common law or through registration), the owner is entitled to its exclusive use.

trade name • A term that is used to indicate part or all of a business's name and that is directly related to the business's reputation and goodwill. Trade names are protected under the common law (and under trademark law, if the name is the same as the firm's trademarked product).

trade secret • Information or process that gives a business an advantage over competitors that do not know the information or process.

transfer warranties • Implied warranties, made by any person who transfers an instrument for consideration to subsequent transferees and holders who take the instrument in good faith, that (1) the transferor is entitled to enforce the instrument; (2) all signatures are authentic and authorized; (3) the instrument has not been altered; (4) the instrument is not subject to a defense or claim of any party that can be asserted against the transferor; and (5) the transferor has no knowledge of any insolvency proceedings against the maker, the acceptor, or the drawer of the instrument.

traveler's check • A check that is payable on demand, drawn on or payable through a financial institution (bank), and designated as a traveler's check.

treaty • In international law, a formal written agreement negotiated between two nations or among several nations. In the United States, all treaties must be approved by the Senate.

treble damages • Damages that, by statute, are three times the amount that the fact finder determines is owed.

trespass to land • The entry onto, above, or below the surface of land owned by another without the owner's permission or legal authorization.

trespass to personal property • The unlawful taking or harming of another's personal property; interference with another's right to the exclusive possession of his or her personal property.

Trojan horse • A computer program that appears to perform a legitimate function but in fact performs a malicious function that allows the sender to gain unauthorized access to the user's computer; named after the wooden horse that enabled the Greek forces to gain access to the city of Troy in the ancient story.

trust • An arrangement in which title to property is held by one person (a trustee) for the benefit of another (a beneficiary).

trust indorsement • An indorsement for the benefit of the indorser or a third person; also known as an agency indorsement. The indorsement results in legal title vesting in the original indorsee.

tying arrangement • An agreement between a buyer and a seller in which the buyer of a specific product or service becomes obligated to purchase additional products or services from the seller.

U

ultra vires • A Latin term meaning "beyond the powers"; in corporate law, acts of a corporation that are beyond its express and implied powers to undertake.

unconscionable (contract or clause) • A contract or clause that is void on the basis of public policy because one party, as a result of disproportionate bargaining power, is forced to accept terms that are unfairly burdensome and that unfairly benefit the dominating party.

underwriter • In insurance law, the insurer, or the one assuming a risk in return for the payment of a premium.

undisclosed principal • A principal whose identity is unknown by a third person, and the third person has no knowledge that the agent is acting for a principal at the time the agent and the third person form a contract.

unenforceable contract • A valid contract rendered unenforceable by some statute or law.

uniform law • A model law created by the National Conference of Commissioners on Uniform State Laws and/or the American Law Institute for the states to consider adopting. Each state has the option of adopting or rejecting all or part of a uniform law. If a state adopts the law, it becomes statutory law in that state.

unilateral contract • A contract that results when an offer can be accepted only by the offeree's performance.

union shop • A firm that requires all workers, once employed, to become union members within a specified period of time as a condition of their continued employment.

universal defense • A defense that is valid against all holders of a negotiable instrument, including holders in due course (HDCs) and holders with the rights of HDCs.

unreasonably dangerous product • In product liability law, a product that is defective to the point of threatening a consumer's health and safety. A product will be considered unreasonably dangerous if it is dangerous beyond the expectation of the ordinary consumer or if a less dangerous alternative was economically feasible for the manufacturer, but the manufacturer failed to produce it.

usage of trade • Any practice or method of dealing having such regularity of observance in a place, vocation, or trade as to justify an expectation that it will be observed with respect to the transaction in question.

U.S. trustee • A government official who performs certain administrative tasks that a bankruptcy judge would otherwise have to perform.

usury • Charging an illegal rate of interest.

utilitarianism • An approach to ethical reasoning that evaluates behavior in light of the consequences of that behavior for those who will be affected by it, rather than on the basis of any absolute ethical or moral values. In utilitarian reasoning, a "good" decision is one that results in the greatest good for the greatest number of people affected by the decision.

V

valid contract • A contract that results when the elements necessary for contract formation (agreement, consideration, legal purpose, and contractual capacity) are present.

venture capital • Capital (funds and other assets) provided by professional, outside investors (venture capitalists, usually groups of wealthy investors and securities firms) to start new business ventures.

venue • The geographic district in which a legal action is tried and from which the jury is selected.

vertically integrated firm • A firm that carries out two or more functional phases (manufacture, distribution, and retailing, for example) of the chain of production.

vertical merger • The acquisition by a company at one level in a marketing chain of a company at a higher or lower level in the chain (such as a company merging with one of its suppliers or retailers).

vertical restraint • Any restraint of trade created by agreements between firms at different levels in the manufacturing and distribution process.

vesting • The creation of an absolute or unconditional right or power.

vicarious liability • Legal responsibility placed on one person for the acts of another; indirect liability imposed on a supervisory party (such as an employer) for the actions of a subordinate (such as an employee) because of the relationship between the two parties.

virus • A computer program that can replicate itself over a network, such as the Internet, and interfere with the normal use of a computer. A virus cannot exist as a separate entity and must attach itself to another program to move through a network.

vishing • A variation of phishing that involves some form of voice communication. The consumer receives either an e-mail or a phone call from someone claiming to be from a legitimate business and asking for personal information; instead of being asked to respond by e-mail as in phishing, the consumer is asked to call a phone number.

void contract • A contract having no legal force or binding effect.

voidable contract • A contract that may be legally avoided (canceled, or annulled) at the option of one or both of the parties.

voir dire • An Old French phrase meaning "to speak the truth." In legal language, the process in which the attorneys question prospective jurors to learn about their backgrounds, attitudes, biases, and other characteristics that may affect their ability to serve as impartial jurors.

W

warranty deed • A deed in which the grantor assures (warrants to) the grantee that the grantor has title to the property conveyed in the deed, that there are no encumbrances on the property other than what the grantor has represented, and that the grantee will enjoy quiet possession of the property; a deed that provides the greatest amount of protection for the grantee.

watered stock • Shares of stock issued by a corporation for which the corporation receives, as payment, less than the stated value of the shares.

wetlands • Water-saturated areas of land that are designated by a government agency (such as the Army Corps of Engineers or the Environmental Protection Agency) as protected areas that support wildlife and therefore cannot be filled in or dredged by private contractors or parties without a permit.

whistleblowing • An employee's disclosure to government authorities, upper-level managers, or the media that the employer is engaged in unsafe or illegal activities.

white-collar crime • Nonviolent crime committed by individuals or corporations to obtain a personal or business advantage.

will • An instrument directing what is to be done with the testator's property on his or her death, made by the testator and revocable during his or her lifetime. No interests in the testator's property pass until the testator dies.

will substitutes • Various documents that attempt to dispose of an estate in the same or similar manner as a will, such as trusts or life insurance plans.

winding up • The second of two stages in the termination of a partnership or corporation. Once the firm is dissolved, it continues to exist legally until the process of winding up all business affairs (collecting and distributing the firm's assets) is complete.

workers' compensation laws • State statutes establishing an administrative procedure for compensating workers for injuries that arise out of—or in the course of—their employment, regardless of fault.

working papers • The various documents used and developed by an accountant during an audit. Working papers include notes, computations, memoranda, copies, and other papers that make up the work product of an accountant's services to a client.

workout • An out-of-court agreement between a debtor and creditors in which the parties work out a payment plan or schedule under which the debtor's debts can be discharged.

worm • A computer program that can automatically replicate itself over a network such as the Internet and interfere with the normal use of a computer. A worm does not need to be attached to an existing file to move from one network to another.

writ of attachment • A court's order, issued prior to a trial to collect a debt, directing the sheriff or other public officer to seize nonexempt property of the debtor. If the creditor prevails at trial, the seized property can be sold to satisfy the judgment.

writ of *certiorari* • A writ from a higher court asking a lower court for the record of a case.

writ of execution • A court's order, issued after a judgment has been entered against a debtor, directing the sheriff to seize and sell any of the debtor's nonexempt real or personal property.

wrongful discharge • An employer's termination of an employee's employment in violation of the law.

Table of Cases

Index

Ethical Issues